THE OFFICIAL® PRICE GUIDE TO

Records

TWELFTH EDITION

JERRY OSBORNE

HOUSE OF COLLECTIBLES • NEW YORK

Important Notice. All of the information, including valuations, in this book has been compiled from the most reliable sources, and every effort has been made to eliminate errors and questionable data. Nevertheless, the possibility of error, in a work of such immense scope, always exists. The publisher will not be held responsible for losses which may occur in the purchase, sale, or other transaction of items because of information contained herein. Readers who feel they have discovered errors are invited to *write* and inform us, so they may be corrected in subsequent editions. Those seeking further information on the topics covered in this book are advised to refer to the complete line of *Official Price Guides* published by the House of Collectibles.

Published by: House of Collectibles
201 East 50th Street
New York, New York 10022

Distributed by Ballantine Books, a division of Random House, Inc., New York, and simultaneously in Canada by Random House of Canada Limited, Toronto.

Cover design by Kristine V. Mills-Noble

Cover photo by George Kerrigan

Manufactured in the United States of America

ISSN: 0747-7392

ISBN: 0-676-60051-4

Twelfth Edition: April 1997

10 9 8 7 6 5 4 3

CONTENTS

ACKNOWLEDGMENTS

The single most important element in updating and revising a price and reference guide is reader input. From dealers and collectors scattered throughout the country we receive suggestions, additions and corrections. Every single piece of data we receive is carefully reviewed, with all appropriate and usable information utilized in the next edition of this guide.

As enthusiastically as we encourage your contribution, let us equally encourage that when you write, you will either type or print your name clearly on both the envelope and contents. It's as frustrating for us to receive a mailing of useful information, and not be able to credit the sender, as it probably is for the sender to not see his or her name in the Acknowledgments section.

In compiling this edition, information supplied by the people whose names appear below was of great importance. To these good folks, our deepest gratitude is extended. The amount of data and investment of time, of course, varied, but without each and every one of them this book would have been something less than it is.

Here then, alphabetically listed, are the contributors to this edition:

William O. Adams
James E. Anderson
Russ Bell
Andy Benyo
Jack Berkus
Jean Blankenship
Margaret Blauvelt
Dale Blount
Chris G. Bowman
Susan K. Bowman
Denise M. Brown
Chris Buccola
Margie Burns
Robert Cassady
Bob Clere
Steve Colbert
John R. Cooper
Kurt Curtis
Nicky D'Andrea
Robert Dalley
Marty Dark
Dave's Record Den
Judy Davis
Charles Dawson
Devon Dawson
William Deibert
Mike De Girolamo
Mark Dillman
James M. Doidge
David Dombroski
Doug Dornbos
Dennis Dow
Kevin Eaton
Judith M. Ebner
Dennis Favreau
Frank Fazio
Sven Forsberg
Emanuel Gambino
Arnie Ganem
Jean-Marc Gargiulo
Rich Gesner
Randy Giroux
James O. Guthrie
Buck Hafeman
Alex Havdouglas
Pauline Hubbard
Terry Mike Jeffrey
Randy Jones
George Kane
Scott Kelley
Don Kirsch
James W. Kolb
Tony Kolodziej
Tracy Kolodziej
Wilhelm Kriegl
Nathan Laney
James D. Leggett
Jacqueline Le Guyader
Joe Lindsay
Dale Little
David C. Lovett
René Lucas
Rick Marshall
Dan Martin
Al MacDonald
Jim Macek
Glenn Major
Jeffrey McIntyre
Dan McKittrick
Wayne Miedema
Don Muller
L. Eddie Muller
Mike Murray
Gary E. Myers
Charles Neu
Gary Noel
Debbie Oberacker
Linda Ann Osborne
Roger Osborne
George Pardo
Victor Pearlin
Alex Peavey
Chester Prudhomme
Fred Preusser
John A. Pyros
Guy Quintino
Andrew Richardson
A.L. Root
Eric Rubin
Bill Sabis
Ron Sataloff
Trish Scarmuzzi
Phil Schwartz
Jerry Sharell
Jeff Starks
Jack Stell
Mike Stewart
Alan Stock
Howard A. Sweet
Bill Taylor
Jim Ulmer
Tom Ulrich
Albert J. Wagner
Steve Wallace
Terry T. Wayland
Thomas J. Whetstone
Joel Whitburn
Danny A. White
Ann Marie Wilson
Morgan Wright
Jerry Zolten
John W. Zurzolo

Records

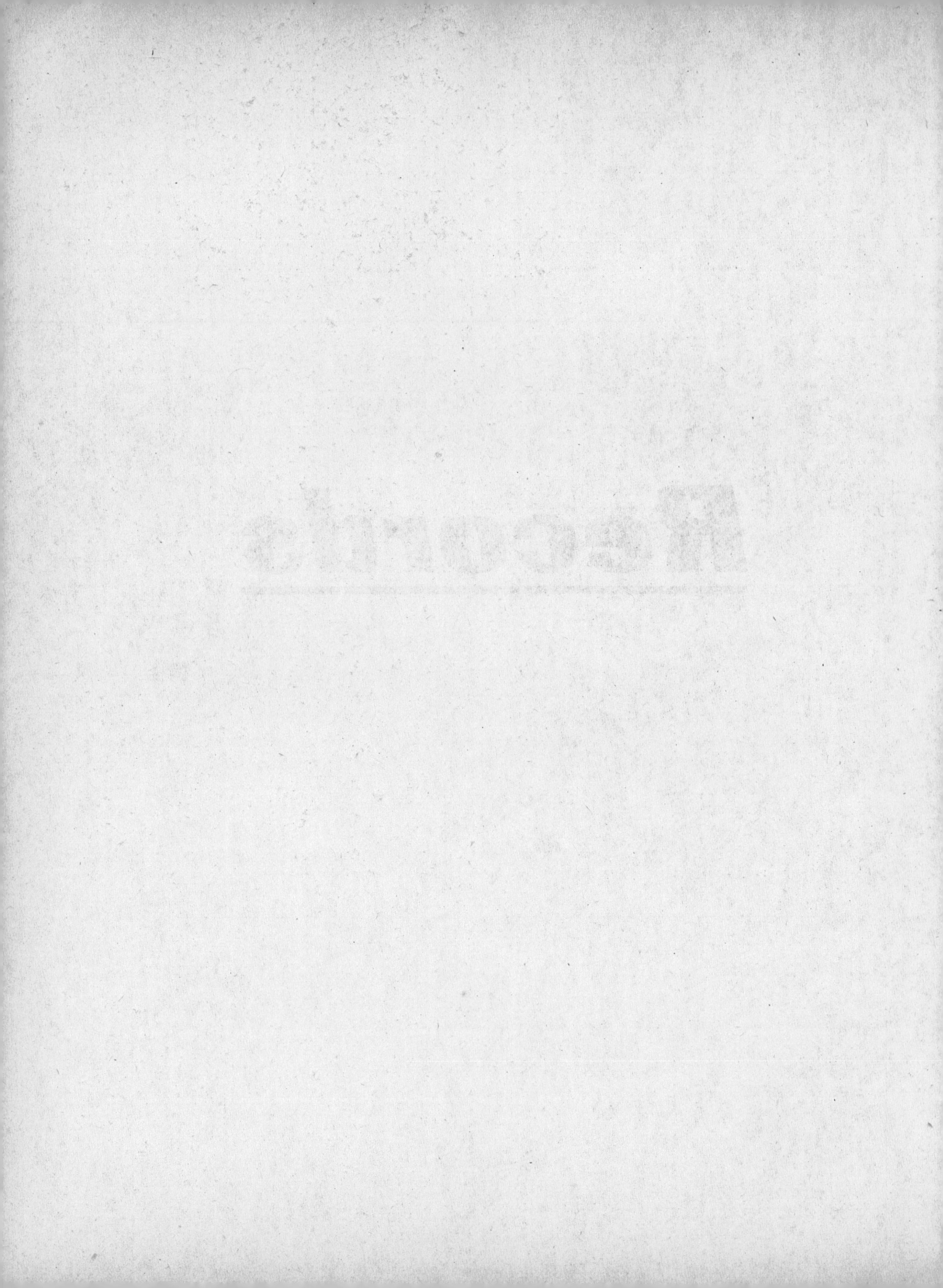

INTRODUCTION

The First Twentysome Years: What a Long Strange Trip It's Been

It is hard to believe it's been 22 years since the world's first *Record Collector's Price Guide* came out. Honestly, though, none of that would matter if, in looking back at that first (1976) book, one failed to see 22 years of improvements within our pages.

We feel certain that this edition, with many thousands of times the number of records priced in our first book, more than adequately represents the payoff for those years of labor.

Nevertheless, it is still a work in progress.

I doubt it would surprise anyone if, come 2006, the 30th Anniversary Edition makes this current edition look tiny and incomplete by comparison. Of course, we can't rule out the possibility that by then all publications containing such voluminous amounts of data are available only on whatever medium is the 2006 equivalent of today's CD ROM technology.

For 22 years you've been there for us. For just as long we've been there for you. A nice arrangement indeed.

We Been Searchin'. . . Yeah Searchin'

Boy, did we ever get dusty this past year. In our never ending quest to make the information in *The Official Price Guide to Records* as accurate as possible, one of our big projects during the past year was to compare the data already in the guide to as many actual record labels as possible.

Made available to us for this undertaking were several private collections that — combined — provided us with hands on access to approximately 10,000 of the world's most valuable 45s, most of which are R&B. Amazingly, close to half of them afforded us some tidbit of new information — from details as critical as correcting errors in an artist's name, label, selection number, or song title, to countless fragments of minutiae that would interest only a few hard-core aficionados — like us. You may refer to this book hundreds of times and not notice even one of these enhancements, but believe us, they are there.

Also, any of these records previously shown and priced only by label are now listed individually, each by selection number and title.

We plan to hit the road again in the months ahead, making comparable improvements in time for the lucky 13th edition.

The Ever-Widening Grading Gap

It will surprise no one to learn that the gulch between GOOD and MINT is gradually becoming a canyon. The drift toward widening the grading gap that began about 10 years ago shows no signs of slowing. To keep pace with this phenomena, changes have been made in the guide to reflect the ever-increasing premiums being paid for mint condition items.

A value spread that a decade ago rated GOOD at about 20% of MINT is now at around 10%. Look for the gap to widen further in years ahead. Most industry observers do not foresee a narrowing trend during this millennium.

Guide to '50s & '60s Canadian Pressings

By Peter S. McCullough

For most record collectors in Canada — as well as U.S. residents who buy from dealers in Canada — the most perplexing issue is usually accurate identification of original and later Canadian issues from the '50s and '60s. This is especially important when trying to use the listings of U.S. releases in *The Official Price Guide to Records* to appraise Canadian pressings that do not yet appear in the guide. It should be noted that an effort has been underway since last year to include as many important Canadian issues as possible in the guide.

To long-time collectors familiar with the Canadian record companies, the label itself, along with the apparent age of the record, can often identify a Canadian original as well as indicate its U.S. counterpart. Sometimes reference is even made to a U.S. label and number making the task simple.

For U.S. collectors — and younger Canadian collectors — being unfamiliar with our labels and with searching for clues on those labels, identification of originals may prove a daunting task. Hopefully, this essay will make accurate identification of Canadian originals easier for collectors on both sides of the border.

Aside from the issue of labels and/or pressings, the value of a '50s or '60s Canadian record traded in the U.S. will sometimes depend on a historical context; one with which U.S. collectors may be unfamiliar.

For example, most collectors of the Band know that their members' early releases were with Ronnie Hawkins and the Hawks, but may *not* know that some recordings were released in Canada with all the individual band members named.

Similarly, Beatles collectors may be unaware that the first single release of *Love Me Do* is a take with a session drummer rather than Ringo Starr. Subsequent album releases in both Canada and the U.S. contain the track with Ringo. This special Canadian alternate release was unavailable in the United States until the 1980 release of *Rarities*. Other striking examples will be outlined here as an aid to evaluating certain Canadian releases in their sometimes unfamiliar historical context.

Some Differences Between Canadian and U.S. Labels

The Canadian recording industry was, to be kind, primitive in the early '50s. The majority of records released were from the large U.S. companies (Columbia, Decca, RCA Victor, Mercury, etc.) marked only as "made in Canada." Canadian labels were few and small. With few exceptions, the established U.S. labels simply reproduced the U.S. "pop" hits for consumption in Canada.

The mid-'50s, however, brought significant changes. With the appearance of many rock and roll recordings by smaller U.S. labels came their need to release their records in Canada. This created a market for a new kind of record company — ones I call "shadow" labels. The term correctly implies a certain unreality, and these labels had virtually no bands nor artists signed. They existed solely to reproduce for the Canadian market the countless independent U.S. issues. Among our shadow labels were: Quality, Reo, Sparton, Regency, Apex and Delta.

Sometimes the shadows used U.S. selection numbers; sometimes Canadian numbers were shown. Occasionally both were used. Often shadow labels would reflect a licensing agreement with text like: "by arrangement with (Whomever) Records." And since these records were usually released simultaneously in Canada and the U.S., both must be considered originals. Overall, there were about 10 shadow labels being manufactured by about five plants, with several being produced by Quality Records Limited — the company as opposed to the record label.

Also, some releases came on a "hybrid" label, where a Canadian shadow company acknowledged the original U.S. label by name, sometimes even showing the U.S. selection number. For example, Quality releases sometimes denoted "King Series" signifying the disc as a Canadian pressing of a U.S.

release from King Records. London records similarly issued some records with "London" at the top and "Liberty" below. These hybrid releases were also simultaneously issued in the U.S. and Canada.

Quite a few Canadian records carried a reproduction of the U.S. label, though some have slightly altered designs and/or different colours. These too are original first pressings. An original '50s and early '60s Warner Bros. release in Canada, for example, was produced by the Compo Company — a fact shown only in fine print — on a deep red label as opposed to the pink label in the U.S. As the pop and rock market grew and production costs dropped, most U.S. labels, majors and independents alike, would "fly their own flag" in Canada, so to speak.

By 1970, virtually all U.S. recordings appeared in Canada simultaneously using a label nearly identical to the U.S. label, but produced by a Canadian manufacturer.

In the early '60s, though, we also saw some discs from truly Canadian independent labels, ones with a stable of Canadian artists. Occasionally one of these releases broke in the U.S. and would be picked up by a U.S. company for distribution. In such cases, the Canadian release usually preceded the U.S. release by a few months, making the Canadian one the true original and potentially more valuable — and probably scarcer — than the U.S. version. More often than not, however, these records failed to realize airplay or sales outside of Canada.

Besides the categories already described, the following minor label variants exist and should be helpful in the area of identification:

British Invasion Oddities

A U.S. subsidiary label, like Capitol Records of Canada, would release a British recording in Canada but the song would only later be released in the U.S. on either an indie or the parent corporation of the Canadian subsidiary, but much later. This particularly applies to the mid-'60s British Invasion years.

Some overseas recordings — primarily British Invasion — came out here exactly as issued in the originating country. Mysteriously, U.S. versions often contained edited or otherwise altered versions of these tracks.

Promotional Issues

Unlike in the States, Canada had very few promotional copies in the '50s and '60s. Dee jays got regular Canadian product shipped slightly in advance of commercial release. Certain regular Canadian issues did, however, strongly resemble promos. Atco, for example, used plain white labels with black lettering, but they are clearly store stock, not promos.

Labels from the Past

Canadian issues often used the correct U.S. label and number, but with an older style label design that was no longer in use in the States.

Identification of Canadian Originals

The detailed description of actual labels falls into basic sections. First, a discussion of the various Canadian labels and Canadian versions of U.S. labels and their identification as true originals and, second, a brief synopsis of certain specific artists and groups, major and minor, whose Canadian original releases pose the greatest problems of identification. This dual approach comes with some risk of duplication, but is necessary in order to avoid even greater confusion overall. In most cases, appearance on a certain Canadian label usually ties it to a corresponding U.S. company — hence its being equivalent to either a first pressing or reissue if that's what the U.S. issue is. In other cases, identification must be determined by facts concerning the recording history of the artists themselves.

It should be noted that the bulk of analysis here pertains to singles — 45 and 78 rpms. This format comprises the vast majority of releases. Furthermore, most LPs can be identified using essentially the same information.

Speaking of 78s, those produced in Canada may also need to be reconsidered. Since the attempted inclusion of all 78 releases in *The Official Price Guide to Records,* it is becoming increasingly apparent that many singles were released only on 45 in the U.S. but on both formats in Canada. Now we can begin to identify a new Canadian source of certain 78 releases which had previously been thought of as unavailable. Understandably, these previously unknown 78s are quite scarce and in high demand among 78 collectors.

Identifying '50s and '60s Canadian Shadow Labels

The colour and design characteristics of most original Canadian shadow labels of the '50s and '60s can be summarized as follows: (Unless otherwise indicated, comments apply to 78s, 45s and LPs.)

Quality: Singles are a pale yellow, with red printing and a prominent Canadian only selection number on the right side. Early releases may have an identifying reference to a U.S. label (e.g. "King Series").

In the very late '60s, the basic colour changed to white with red lettering. LP labels are dark blue in colour with silver lettering. A few exceptions exist that have the yellow and red label.

Other than changing to gold labels with black lettering, reissues are otherwise virtually identical to originals.

Apex: Singles are reddish brown with silver print where relevant (see below). Most of Cadence's U.S. releases were on Apex in Canada. As a label, Apex predates the '50s with 78s on a dark blue label with silver print. These are all pop music releases and normally would be disregarded by rock and R&B aficionados.

Arc: This budget label has almost no releases of merit. Avoiding them is generally recommended.

Barrell: Singles are black with silver print.

Barry: Singles are white with red print — essentially identical to the later Quality releases.

Birchmont: A Quality-owned budget label used for cheapies and reissues.

Delta: Singles are dark reddish brown with silver print. Produced by Quality Records, most Delta issues tend to be blues or rhythm and blues.

London: Effectively a UK label with issues in Canada.

Maple Leaf: With early '50s issues only, they are gray with a red maple leaf. Limited pretty much to country and western material.

Pye: Another UK label with product also issued in Canada. Most singles from the '60s are orange/red, though they changed to blue around 1969.

Regency: Singles have green labels with silver printing. Circa 1960, the label changed to medium blue, black print, and some lime green on each side.

Reo: Singles are dark green with silver print. Reissues are gold with black print. Albums may refer to a U.S. label and number on the sleeve, but the disc itself has the green Reo label.

Reo seems to have been consistently used for Canadian releases of product on smaller, independent U.S. labels.

Sparton: Singles are dark reddish brown with silver print. If an ABC-Paramount release, as most Sparton discs are, there's a silver half moon at the bottom.

Identifying Independent Canadian Labels

As indicated above, "independents" are those labels that had their own talent and were not restricted to merely reproducing U.S. releases. Often these labels were strongly associated with one artist (which we'll try to mention) and differ from the "shadow" labels in the sense that the output was limited to a few select recordings

Attic: Singles, which have light orange labels, include a wide-ranging catalogue of Canadian artists.

Nimbus 9: Singles are a pale light brown with black print and a purple logo: This label had the Guess Who in later years although some singles were on RCA and noted simply as a "Nimbus 9" production.

Roman: Singles are a medium and light blue with black printing. Includes David Clayton-Thomas before his Blood Sweat & Tears years.

Tartan: Singles, which are white and red with a black Scottish kilt design on top, appear restricted to ones by Bobby Curtola — a Canadian star who achieved limited, early '60s attention in the U.S.

Daffodil: Singles have a yellow daffodil with dark green leaves. Canadian bands on Daffodil include Crow Bar and King Biscuit Boy.

Rebel: Singles are white with blue print, and, surprisingly, a Confederate Flag! Primarily associated with Canadian folk singer, Stompin' Tom Connors.

Specifications of U.S. Labels Issued in Canada

The following list highlights the U.S. labels issued in Canada, but only where there are significant variations from the U.S labels with which most collectors are familiar. If a label is *not* listed here, one should not necessarily assume the labels to be identical. Rather, it's that no significant label variation has been noted.

Atco: There is no use of yellow. Early '50s labels are primarily white with black print, changing to black with silver print in the late '50s. Their 78s appear to be only on the black and white labels.

For the record, Atlantic — Atco's parent company — releases pretty much resemble U.S. releases.

RCA Victor: Early and mid-'50s singles, such as most of the Elvis hits, have blue labels. Even the late '50s 45s often do not match up with the "dog on top" type descriptions used in *The Official Price Guide to Records.*

However, Presley album covers do tend to match the detailed descriptions of first and later pressings as provided by *The Official Price Guide to Records.*

Interestingly, RCA sometimes functioned as a shadow label, picking up distribution of U.S. releases on indies or subsidiaries.

Warner Bros.: Labels for 45s are red instead of pink.

U.S. and Canadian Artists As Well As Some Label Aberrations

Sometimes it is impossible to correlate Canadian releases to U.S. ones using label information only. Factors relevant to identification to originals often must be tied to specific artists, and the following list attempts to cover some relevant examples.

Often, a Canadian variant will be identified here that has not yet been noted in *The Official Price Guide to Records*. The greatest variations in U.S. and Canadian releases occurred during the British Invasion. In most cases, Britain's hit singles and albums were released (successfully) in Canada, but many of these same releases never saw U.S. release until much later, if at all.

Barry Allen: This Canadian crooner had one big hit, *Lovedrops*. Both his Capitol single and his LP are now very collectible.

Animals: In the U.S., this group broke in mid-to-late 1964 with *The House of the Rising Sun* 45 and the MGM album, *The Animals*. In Canada, their stuff, including the same LP, was available months earlier on Capitol, though the MGM album was later released in Canada as well. The Capitol release has the unedited version of *The House of the Rising Sun,* with a black and white cover. The MGM album has an edited version of the song, and a colour sleeve. The Canadian Capitol album is much rarer than the MGM issue.

Lavern Baker: Her early singles are on Quality which acknowledges Atlantic.

Hank Ballard: His early releases came out here on Regency.

Band, The: As mentioned, rocker Ronnie Hawkins developed this group. Early Band singles on Capitol credit their individual names only. Beginning with *Music from Big Pink,* U.S. and Canadian releases were identical and credit the Band.

Beatles: All UK singles were released in Canada on the Capitol yellow swirl label. This includes titles like *She Loves You* and *Twist and Shout*, etc. that didn't come out on Capitol at all in the U.S. in the '60s. Those singles eventually released in the U.S. didn't come out there until mid-'64.

The early Canadian albums are significantly different than the U.S. ones. Our first album, *Twist and Shout,* is virtually the same as their first UK album, *The Beatles,* but with some songs shuffled to make room for the then-new *She Loves You.* It is also essentially the same as *The Early Beatles,* the U.S. version.

The second Canadian LP, *Beatlemania,* is identical to the UK's *With the Beatles,* with a similar picture on the front. When finally released in the U.S. as their "first" album, the title became *Meet the Beatles*.

Next in Canada came *Long Tall Sally,* released as *The Beatles' Second Album* in the U.S. Obviously, Capitol wouldn't use "Second" when it was their third LP here. (Capitol's count naturally ignored Vee Jay's 1963 LP *Introducing the Beatles*.)

From *Beatles '65* forward, U.S. and Canadian albums were mostly identical.

There are no known Canadian releases of the material on the oddball labels (MGM, Atco, Tollie, Vee-Jay, etc.) except as further distributions of U.S. releases. (The alternative take of *Love Me Do* is noted in the introduction.)

The Ballad of John and Yoko came out and received air play in an unexpurgated fashion, with "Christ" not edited out, as was common in the U.S.

All the Beatles albums through *Rubber Soul* were originally released in mono only. Stereo collectors should seek out the early UK stereo albums. From the UK's *With The Beatles,* they contain limited true stereo, whereas the compact discs are still only in mono. In addition, the UK albums appear better-produced. Those recordings offer a more authentic harshness in contrast with both the Canadian and American releases, which, overall, seem to have a sweetened sound. Perhaps this was done to make the releases more palatable to the North American audience

Beau-Marks: A Canadian (Montreal) band whose hit *Clap Your Hands* also became big in the States in 1960. Their 45s and LPs, all on Quality, are very collectible.

Bell Notes: Their hits, including the 1959 smash *I've Had It,* came out on Reo.

Pat Boone: Reo issued his earliest singles, though the later ones are on Dot, as in the U.S.

James Brown: Brown's 45s were issued on Regency. King LPs first appear on Regency, then later on King (medium blue label). Regency releases are all originals, though one cannot tell which is which by merely examining the cover. You must look at the disc.

Beau Brummels: All Canadian originals are on Reo.

Johnny Cash: The early Sun releases came out on Quality. By the late '50s, his LPs were being issued in Canada on Sun.

Dave Clark Five: The Canadian releases were on Capitol, whereas Epic handled their U.S. catalog. The albums do have some variations, most notably *Coast to Coast,* a U.S. LP, appeared here appropriately titled *Across Canada*. Otherwise the two albums are identical.

David Clayton-Thomas and the Shays: Circa 1967, a couple of years before joining Blood, Sweat & Tears, David Clayton-Thomas had a monaural R&B album (Roman DRL-101) that contained the hit singles *Boom Boom* and *Take Me Back*. Later on, Roman issued the anti-Vietnam War single *Brainwashed,* aimed at the U.S. market, of course. The original Roman LP was reissued by Decca (DL-75146) in 1969 — when Blood, Sweat & Tears hit it big. Unfortunately, they completely ruined these tracks; first by putting them through that awful rechanneled stereo process, and then by adding a horn section (again trying to jump on the brassy Blood, Sweat & Tears bandwagon). This regurgitated mess is to be avoided; however, the Canadian Roman original is highly prized by collectors.

Dave "Baby" Cortez: Reo issued *The Happy Organ* in Canada.

Crowbar: A very collectible, seminal Canadian blues-rock '70s group. All their releases here are on the Daffodil label.

Fats Domino: Most Domino singles, and all of his albums, were released on Imperial here; however, a few of the early singles did come out on Reo here — both 45s and 78s.

Strangely, *Blueberry Hill* (Reo 8117) was never released on a Imperial 78 in Canada, although the Reo release refers to an Imperial identification number (#1082) on the left side. The earliest Canadian pressings are therefore clearly identifiable as on Reo. After those few early issues, all subsequent Fats Domino releases were on Imperial in Canada.

Esquires: This Canadian group had a few high quality Columbia singles in Canada, which are not scarce. Apparently none other than the 1966 single, *It's a Dirty Shame/Love Hides a Multitude of Sins* (Columbia 43815), got issued in the U.S.

Everly Brothers: All Cadence releases came out in Canada on Apex. The Everly's Warner Bros. records are no different than the U.S. issues.

Five Man Electrical Band: An earlier assemblage of this group performed and released records as the Staccatos. As with the better known Five Man Electrical Band, the Staccatos' material was mostly written by Les Emmerson, the spiritual force behind both bands. Records by the Staccatos are rare and highly collectible.

Foundations: Their Canadian releases are on the Pye (blue label).

Freddie and the Dreamers: The original Canadian Capitol album — identical to their UK release — was never released in the U.S. Most of the singles missing, especially *Just For You*, turned up later in the States on a greatest hits reissue collection.

Bobby Freeman: All U.S. Josie singles appeared in Canada on Jubilee — his U.S. LP label. Jubilee was Josie's parent company. We do not yet know of any Canadian LPs by Freeman, but if any exist they are likely also on Jubilee. Two of his 1958 hits, *Do you Want to Dance* and *Betty Lou Got a New Pair of Shoes*, came out in Canada on 78s. We have yet to verify U.S. issues on 78 of either.

Billy Grammer: In Canada, Monument issued a 78 of *Gotta Travel On.* Don't know yet whether this 1959 hit came on 78 in the U.S.

Guess Who: The nucleus of this famous group first recorded as Chad Allen and The Expressions, though the Canadian group got very little air play. Later, in response to disc jockeys who had refused to play their records, the group's singles were sent to radio stations with the credit simply reading "Guess Who?" The lack of a traditional artist credit was meant to be taken literally since their previous identification as a lowly Canadian group resulted in them being virtually ignored by the Canadian media.

The band wanted to tease dee jays, hoping to make them curious enough to play the record — without identifying the band as Canadian. Ironically, the band eventually adopted this jocular name as their own.

Their early Canadian singles are on Quality, and a collection of the earliest singles are found on *The Guess Who? Super Golden Oldies* (Birchmount BM 568) a must-have LP for this group's fans.

As in the States, RCA had the band's later hit singles and albums in Canada, followed by releases on Nimbus 9.

Herman's Hermits: As with the Animals, the Hermits' early singles in Canada are on Capitol, but, unlike the Animals, their albums turned up on Quality. Both British bands were on M.G.M. in the States.

Honeycombs: All their Canadian releases are on Pye (orange label).

Johnny and the Hurricanes: Canadian releases are on Barry.

King Biscuit Boy: Blues by a very collectible Canadian band. Most of their releases are on Daffodil.

Kingsmen: The original Canadian release of *Kingsmen In Person* is on Reo. Canadian reissues of that album, as well as their other later LPs, are on Wand, as in the U.S.

Kinks: All originals of earlier releases are on Pye (orange label).

Billy J. Kramer and the Dakotas: All their releases are on Capitol.

Larks: All releases appear on Reo in Canada.

Jerry Lee Lewis: All of the Killer's Sun releases were released here by Quality.

Little Richard: His first few Specialty U.S. singles came out in Canada on Regency, with a label acknowledgment to Specialty Records. The early albums have U.S. covers (no reference made to Canada) with the early green/silver Regency label. Later album covers were printed in Canada (and identified as such) with the green/silver labels, then again with the ensuing (blue and black) label design. Subsequent U.S. releases on other labels were virtually identical in Canada.

Manfred Mann: Their first album, on Ascot in the U.S., is on Capitol in Canada. The Canadian pressing, like the UK original, includes *Smokestack Lightning* as the lead song. On the Ascot issue, the tracks are adjusted to feature *Do Wah Diddy Diddy*.

Dutch Mason: A Canadian blues band leader whose releases appear in Canada on Attic.

Monkees: Their albums and singles came out here on RCA rather than Colgems.

Moody Blues: Their early albums are on London.

Mungo Jerry: All Canadian releases are on Pye (blue label).

Music Machine: Surprisingly on Original Sound in the U.S., their label here was Reo.

Paupers: In 1967, this Canadian group released the album *Magic People* on Verve, in both the U.S. and Canada. However, before that there was one or more Canadian-only Verve singles, most notably *If I Called You By Some Name*. The Canadian-only singles are very scarce.

Bill Parsons (Bobby Bare): The 1958 U.S. Fraternity hit, *All American Boy* came out on Reo (#8320) in Canada.

Elvis Presley: His earliest RCA 45s are on a blue label; the 78s on flat black. Our black RCA labels seldom seem to match the detailed descriptions of U.S. originals found in the various Jerry Osborne guides. LP sleeves and discs, however, do match his descriptions of U.S. originals.

As often noted in the Osborne books, certain Elvis releases were unique to Canada. Our 78 of *Blue Suede Shoes* is 20-6492 instead of 20-6636. Interestingly, we know of no U.S. release bearing the number 20-6492. If used, that number would have been something issued about six months before 20-6636.

Lloyd Price: Like most ABC-Paramount acts, his Canadian releases are on Sparton.

Jeannie C. Reiley: Her U.S. releases on Plantation appeared initially in Canada on Reo, with reissues later on Plantation. Only the Reo releases are originals.

Rolling Stones: London had all the Stones' UK singles in Canada: *Time Is on my Side*, *It's All Over Now*, *Route 66* (not a U.S. single), etc. Original 1963 singles labels are blue.

Searchers: All their original releases are on Pye (orange label).

Virtues: Their biggie, *Guitar Boogie Shuffle* came out here on Sparton.

Concluding Comments

This introductory essay, using a few selected artists, will hopefully be revised and expanded in future editions of *The Official Price Guide to Records*. For example, we intend to refresh the list in years to come to include more Canadian '60s psychedelic bands.

Every attempt to ensure accuracy has been made, but the intent here — as with this book itself — is merely to provide guidance. As a rule, Canadian releases of U.S. groups will have about the same value as the U.S. pressings of the same discs.

While quantities originally produced of most Canadian and U.S. recordings is not generally known, we do know that discs by some of the Canadian groups mentioned here are unique, hard-to-find items and would have appropriately higher values.

Now that we have undertaken the task of listing and pricing many of the Canadian records, we welcome corrections, additions and price updates from readers.

I would like to thank Russ Bell, whose essay titled *Canadian Records of Great Quality* inspired my research and contribution. Though Bell's focus was more toward individual records than overall label patterns, I do not disagree with any of his points regarding specific records. I am indebted to him for a useful point of commencement.

Finally, I would like to thank Jerry Osborne for developing this superb format for discussing our mania, er, hobby. Now that some of the variations of Canadian releases are being unearthed, Jerry may suddenly become very busy talking to Canadian dealers. Eh?

Kingston, Ontario, Canada

Using Your PC to Clean the Sound . . . Not the Record

By Jeff Klinedinst

For many years, collectors have cleaned records in much the same way as taking on other forms of domestic cleaning — with soap, water and some elbow grease. However, if you have a PC available, there is a dryer alternative.

Modern software science has finally connected with the world of record restoration and right *now* your IBM personal computer has the capability to be a recording studio, editing suite, and even a noise reduction laboratory.

Noise reduction, or sound cleaning, has existed almost as long as personal computers themselves, but, as with most new technologies, it took awhile for the prices to tumble to reality. Now, owning this system is possible for most of us. As you no doubt know, computers offer incredible power with a wide variety of tools for everyday use — easily justifying their modest price.

For this walk through, we'll be using:

1. Any 486 DX (or faster) computer equipped with: a) Windows 3.1 or Windows 95, b) compatible 16 bit sound card, c) mouse.
2. DART PRO software from Tracer Technologies.
3. Any normal setup for playing records, or other source.

To set up the computer for recording, simply run a line from the amplifier's outputs to the inputs of your sound card. Here your sound card functions exactly like a tape recorder, though it will use your computer's hard drive for storage rather than analog tape.

For recording, any good sound editing program will provide computerized level meters to aid you in finding the appropriate levels for recording. In DART PRO, the controls for recording work exactly like those on an analog tape recorder.

With the levels set, you then begin the recording process. It is a good idea to record several seconds of surface noise before the actual music begins. This noise at the beginning contains important information which is crucial to the noise reduction process. More about that later.

DeClicking

Removing clicks and pops during the restoration process is critical in the restoration of worn vinyl recordings. With DART PRO, this is a fairly straightforward and uncomplicated process. An "Outlier Detector" analyzes the material and automatically searches out disturbances which do not fit within the parameters of the source material. It marks these areas and then replaces them with "good" source material, found immediately before or after the disturbance. The program automatically searches out disturbances that are 100 samples or less — so it won't haphazardly remove cymbal crashes or any other "good" source material.

For dealing with large scratches or cuts in the source material, DART PRO has a manual reparation mode that allows highlighting an area up to 1500 samples, and replacing it with "good" source material. DeClicking is usually the first stage of the noise restoration process and provides amazing results.

DeNoise

Groove noise, distortion, and any other "constant" noise associated with age and poor quality discs are the next targets. You'll recall that when we recorded the source material, it was mentioned that you should leave a bit at the beginning. Now we make use of that noise. Usually, the noise residing at the beginning of the file is the same as found in the rest of the file. DART PRO can analyze that material then remove it from the entire file. This process is called "Noise Printing."

DeHiss

For the record, DeHiss is an intelligent filtering process which provides maximum hiss removal with minimal source material degradation.

The Noise Audition

One major concern of noise reduction is the fear of damaging the source material in the quest to remove the noise. A key feature of DART PRO allows you to actually subtract your "cleaned" file from your original source and hear *only* the noise that you've removed. Then, if you hear what you determine to be too much source material amidst the noise, you can always have DART PRO attack the file less aggressively.

The final step is to use the Play function to record your cleaned material to tape, DAT tape, or even a writable CD. Now you can enjoy your music the way it was meant to be — noise free.

Noise reduction is like any other tool. It takes a bit of playing around to become familiar with all of its features. Once mastered, your PC can be a powerful ally in your pursuit to eliminate noise from your treasured recordings.

Why Certain Records Are Listed and Some Are Not

In determining what to include in *The Official Guide to Records*, many factors have been considered. Our goal is to make the guide helpful, convenient, and applicable; for avid record connoisseurs as well as for those who are casually curious about the value of old records.

As an author-publisher team, we have put together 57 record guides and reference books over the past 22 years. As a result of this considerable experience, we have developed some basic criteria that serve as the foundation for the guide.

First, we had to establish which records most people would own the answer being those records made by charted artists. Thus, we began with the national pop or pop and rock charts published by Billboard, Cash Box, and other trade publications. Then, because there has been so much chart crossover since the development of rock and roll — particularly between the black (rhythm and blues, soul, dance, etc.) music surveys and the top pop hits — we have included those charts as well.

Whether a song charted as a single, an extended play (EP), or a long-playing (LP) record, and regardless of whether it charted as "Race," "Rhythm and Blues," "Soul," "Disco," "Dance music," or "Sepia," you'll find that record priced here.

Performers who regularly appear on other charts — such as "Jazz," "Adult Contemporary," "Country," "Gospel," and "Classical" — do occasionally cross over to the pop/rock and black charts, and all who have are also included in this edition. However, these music forms are intrinsically diverse enough to require separate publications for truly comprehensive coverage.

It is very important to keep in mind the aforementioned guidelines. Much of the mail we receive is from folks who, failing to read the introductory material, cannot comprehend why certain, often obscure, records are not in this edition.

A country music fan, for example, might not understand why Eddy Arnold is listed in this book while Floyd Tillman is not. Similarly the jazz buff might be bewildered when finding Dave Brubeck here but not Art Farmer. While both Tillman and Farmer had numerous hits on their respective charts, they have never appeared on the pop charts. Eddy Arnold and Dave Brubeck, on the other hand, placed both singles and albums on the pop charts.

Surprisingly, of the top 25 artists of each decade of Billboard's country and western charts, from the forties through the eighties, there are only four artists who are not represented in this edition. All of the others managed at least one appearance on the pop charts.

Just because we're listing all of the aforementioned charted artists does not mean we are listing only charted records by those artists. Once an artist is included in the guide, we list and price every known release by that performer. Using country singer Hank Thompson as an example, let's show how comprehensive our coverage really is:

Despite his prominence in country and western music, Hank Thompson had only one song on the Billboard Hot 100; a single that remained on the chart for just one week and only managed to reach #99 (*She's Just a Whole Lot Like You*). Having qualified for this guide with that one charted appearance, every known single (45 and 78 rpm), extended play, and long-playing album by Hank Thompson — from 1946 to present — is documented and priced in this edition. The reason behind the extensiveness of this coverage is if people like a performer well enough to put even one record on the charts, they likely own other records by that artist, without regard to chart success.

In summary, everyone who made the pop/rock charts, from 1950 to present, or black music charts, from 1942 to present, are included here, with not only their charted records, but their entire recorded output. This often includes 78 rpm issues made 20 or 30 years before the '50s and should effectively cover most of the records to be foamed in the library of the average person.

One can price tens of thousands of 78s with this book; records originally issued as far back as the 1920s and as recently as 1962. We provide a separate section and pricing data for simultaneously released 45s and 78s, a common practice for most labels in the '50s.

This is but one of many price and reference books available. If you need information on recordings not found in this edition, please contact the author. Other guides in our series are available for such specialized fields as Country & Western, Movie/TV Soundtracks & Original Casts, Elvis Presley, Beatles, and countless obscure and uncharted recordings. There's even a separate book for collectible compact discs.

How the Prices Are Determined

Record values shown in *The Official Price Guide to Records* are averaged using information derived from a number of reliable, proven sources. Highly influential in arriving at current values is our long-established "marked copy" review program. Dozens of the world's most active dealers and collectors receive a copy of the most recent edition in which, throughout the year, they track and mark changing prices. When it's time to prepare a revised edition, all marked copies are returned to us for analysis and processing.

Besides the annotated copies, we receive hundreds of letters each year, from folks like yourself, suggesting corrections and/or additions to the guide.

Marketplace publications are another extremely important source of pricing information. Through these, hobbyists buy, sell, and trade music collectibles. We painstakingly review those periodicals, as well as other related publications, carefully comparing prices being asked to those shown in our most recent edition. Keep in mind, however, that while *asking* prices are considered, greater weight is given actual *sales* prices.

If active trading indicates prices in the guide need to be increased or decreased, those changes are made. With our annual publishing schedule, it is never long before the corrected data appear in print.

What makes this step in the pricing process so vital is that nothing more verifiably illustrates the out-of-print record marketplace than everyday sales lists placed by dealers from around the country and around the globe.

Also of great assistance to price tracking are the individual sales catalogs and auction results lists we routinely receive from dealers.

Record prices, as with most collectibles, can vary drastically from one area of the country to another. Having reviewers and annotators in every state — as well as in Europe, Asia, and beyond — enables us to present a realistic average of the highest and lowest current trading prices for an identically graded copy of each record.

Other sources of consequential information include: private set sale and auction lists, record convention trading, personal visits with collectors and to retail locations around the country, and hundreds of hours on the telephone with key advisors.

Although the record marketplace information in this edition was believed accurate at press time, it is ever subject to market changes. At any time, major bulk discoveries, quantity dumps, sudden increases brought about by an artist's death, overnight stardom that creates a greater demand for earlier material, and other such events and trends can easily affect scarcity and demand. Through diurnal research, keeping track of the day-to-day changes and discoveries taking place in the fascinating world of record collecting is a relatively simple and ongoing procedure.

To ensure the greatest possible accuracy, *The Official Price Guide to Records* prices are averaged from data culled from all of the aforementioned sources.

When Some Prices Don't Change

Some prices go unchanged year after year because their values simply do not fluctuate beyond the range given. Others, however, should be shifted and are not. This is because *no one* bothers to advise us of those market changes. With the tens of thousands of records priced here, we cannot keep track of all of them without lots of help.

Don't keep such news a secret. And please don't wait for someone else to do it. Let us know of corrections and updates as soon as possible.

A word of caution here, however. Please *do not* submit any information to us merely because it appears in another record guide. Make certain all information can be verified in some other manner.

Artificial Inflation

While on the subject of misleading information in print, one of the hobby's most talked about topics in recent years is artificial inflation.

Sadly for all concerned, a few publications have popped up in recent years, the intent of which seems to be nothing other than to send prices soaring. Why? Two reasons come immediately to mind:

First, of course, to sell each new edition based on its "definitive" new, skyrocketing prices. They might make for interesting reading, but they are not reality based.

Second, it seems, is to allow a handful of unconscionable dealers to justify asking exceptionally high prices. Being able to whip out something called a price guide and support those prices may, to the uninitiated, lend credibility to such gouging.

Though most veterans in the field are quite aware of this problem, there are just enough folks duped that eventually some of those inflated prices get reported back to us — from reliable, well-meaning correspondents — resulting in price hikes in our book.

We may not be able to completely solve this problem, however, we are attempting to verify suggested price increases with more than one source whenever possible.

As to the possibility of getting caught up in a buy-low-with-one-guide, sell-high-with-another scam, one can lessen the chances of being victimized by insisting that the same guide be used for appraising as is used for selling.

About the Format

Our arrangement of listings is the most logical way to present so much information in a single volume — a format with unlimited potential for expansion.

This book's structure allows for inclusion of all of the following formats in one multi-purpose guidebook: 7-inch 45 rpm singles, both 33 rpm and 45 rpm; 78 rpm singles; 12-inch singles, both 33 and 45 rpm; extended play 33 and 45 rpm EPs; 78 rpm albums, long play 10-inch and 12-inch LPs; picture sleeves; promotional issues, picture discs, and more.

Once you locate an artist's section, their records are listed alphabetically by LABEL. Individual listings for each label appear in numerical order. In many instances, listings that are numerical by selection number are also chronological in sequence of release, but there are times when this is not the case. This format is especially helpful when using the guide along with an artist or label discography. Since the year of release is also provided for each listing, the reader knows immediately the pattern being followed by the label at the time.

Once familiar with the format, you'll find it easy and functional. See the "Sample" page for more information. New users should take time to familiarize themselves with the array. Reading all of the introductory pages should answer most reader questions.

The documenting and pricing of so many recordings is made possible by selectively economizing on space; listing individual titles when necessary but not when it's possible to group a number of equally valuable releases together on one line. Again, *any time* it is necessary to have a separate listing on a record in order to clearly and accurately present the information, we will do it. Also, whenever a specific selection number is noted, whether listed as an exception or not, the title will also be given for easy identification.

One facet of our approach of great concern is the artist who had one or more records of a value indicated for a particular label or series, but who also had one release (or more) that is a notable exception. Every effort has been made to separately document such exceptions, however, due to the sheer bulk of information herein, some may be missed. If you know of any, let us know about them.

You will find that the expansion of an artist's section, moving more toward individual rather than grouped listings, will be as commonplace in subsequent volumes of this series as with this edition. There are hundreds of artists with revised sections in this volume, listing many more individual titles and selection numbers than ever before. With some performers, it is, or perhaps soon will be, necessary to list every single record separately.

The ever-increasing number of pages in the guide are but one indication of how many artists' sections are expanded with individual title listings, over previous editions. Again this year, thousands of records are listed and priced individually that previously were not.

The decision to expand a section is partly based on reader input. Many examples of individual pricing in this edition can be directly attributed to a letter or call suggesting the need to do so.

Grading and the Price Range

The pricing shown in this edition represents the price *range* for NEAR-MINT condition copies. The value range allows for the countless variables that affect record pricing. Often, the range will widen as the dollar amount increases, making a $500 to $1,000 range as logical as a $5.00 to $10.00 range.

One standardized system of record grading, used and endorsed by *The Official Price Guide to Records* and buyers and sellers worldwide, is:

MINT: A *mint* item must be absolutely perfect. Nothing less can be honestly described as mint. Even brand new purchases can easily be flawed in some manner and not qualify as mint. To allow for tiny blemishes, the highest grade used in our record guide series is *near-mint.* An absolutely pristine mint, or still sealed, item may carry a slight premium above the near-mint range shown in this guide.

VERY GOOD: Records in *very good* condition should have a minimum of visual or audible imperfections, which should not detract much from your enjoyment of owning them. This grade is halfway between good and near-mint.

GOOD: Practically speaking, the grade of *good* means that the item is good enough to fill a gap in your collection until a better copy becomes available. Good condition merchandise will show definite signs of wear and tear, probably evidencing that no protective care was given the item. Even so, records in good condition should play all the way through without skipping.

Most older records are going to be in something less than near-mint, or "excellent" condition. It is very important to use the near-mint price range in this guide only as a starting point in record appraising. Be honest about actual condition. Apply the same standards to the records you trade or sell as you would want one from whom you were buying to observe. Visual grading may be unreliable. Accurate grading may require playing the record (play-grading).

Use the following formula to determine values on lesser condition copies:

For **VERY GOOD** condition, figure about 40% to 60% of the near-mint price range given in this guide.

With many of the older pieces that cannot be found in near-mint, VG or VG+ may be the highest grade available. This significantly narrows the gap between VG and the near-mint range.

For **GOOD** condition, figure about 10% to 20% of the near-mint price range given in this guide.

The 10 Point Grading System

Another recommended grading system is based on the often-used 10 point scale. Many feel that grading with the 10 point system allows for a more precise description of records that are in less than mint condition. Instead of vague terms, such as VG++ (is this the same as M- -?), assigning a specific number provides a more accurate classification of condition.

Most of the records you are likely to buy or sell will no doubt be graded somewhere between 5 and 10.

After using this system ourselves for a few years, we are inclined to agree that it is more precise. Customers who have purchased records from us have, without exception, been pleased with this way of grading.

The table below shows how the 10 point system equates with the more established terms:

10: MINT
9: NEAR-MINT
8: Better than VG but below NM
7: VERY GOOD
6: Better than G but below VG
5: GOOD
4: Better than POOR but below G
3: POOR
2: Really trashed
1: It hurts to think about it

The Bottom Line

All the price guides and reporting of previous sales in the world won't change the fundamental fact that true value is nothing more than what one person is willing to accept and what another is prepared to pay. Actual value is based on scarcity and demand. It's always been that way and always will.

A recording — or anything for that matter — can be 50 or 100 years old, but if no one wants it, the actual value will certainly be minimal. Just because something is old does not necessarily make it valuable. Someone has to want it!

On the other hand, a recent release, perhaps just weeks old, can have exceptionally high value if it has already become scarce and is by an artist whose following has created a demand. A record does not have to be old to be valuable.

Record Types Defined

With the inconsistent language used by the record companies in describing an EP or an LP, we've determined that a language guideline of some kind is needed in order to compile a useful record guide.

Some labels call a 10-inch album an "EP" if it has something less than the prescribed number of tracks found on their LPs. Others call an EP a "Little LP." A few companies have even created special names, associated only with their own label, for the basic record formats.

Having carefully analyzed all of this, we have adopted the following classifications of record configurations, which consistently categorize all types, sizes, and speeds in one section or another:

Singles: 78 rpm are those that play at 78 rpm. Though 78s are almost always 10-inch discs, a few 7-inch 78 rpm singles have been made.

Singles: 7-Inch can be either 45 rpm or 33 1/3 (always referred to simply as "33") speed singles. If a 7-inch single has more than one track on either side, we consider it an EP.

Singles are priced strictly as a disc, with a separate section devoted to picture sleeves (which are often traded separately). If we know that picture sleeves exist for a given artist, a separate grouping will appear for the label, price, and applicable year of release. Should you know of picture sleeves not documented in this edition, please advise us accordingly.

There have been a few 5- and 6-inch discs manufactured, but for the sake of keeping singles with singles (and since we don't want to establish a "Singles: 5-inch" category), such curios will be tossed in with the 7-inch singles, with an explanatory note.

EPs: 7-Inch are 7-inch discs that have more than one track on one or both sides. They may play at either 33 or 45 rpm. Even if labeled an "EP" by the manufacturer, if it's pressed on a 10-, or 12-inch disc it's an LP in our book. Unless so noted, all EPs are presumed to be accompanied by their original covers, in a condition about equal to the disc. An appropriate adjustment in value should be made to compensate for any differences in this area. Exceptions, such as EPs with paper sleeves or no sleeve at all, are designated as such when known.

LPs: 10/12-Inch is self explanatory. The only possible confusion that might exist here is with 12-inch singles. If it's 10 or 12 inches in diameter, and labeled, priced, and marketed as a 12-inch single (Maxi-Single, etc.), then that's where you'll find it in this guide, regardless of its speed. Often, 12-inch singles will have a 12-inch die-cut cardboard sleeve or jacket; but many have covers that are exactly like LP jackets, with photos of the artist, etc. Unless so noted, all LPs are presumed to be accompanied by their original covers, in a condition about equal to the disc. An appropriate adjustment in value should be made to compensate for any differences in this area.

Other record type headings used such as Picture Sleeves, Promotional Singles, etc., should be clear.

Cross-Referencing and Multiple Artist Recordings

The cross-referencing in *The Official Price Guide to Records* should provide the easiest possible method of discovering other sections of the book where a particular artist is featured or appears in any capacity.

We've tried to hold to a minimum unexplained cross-references, opting to concentrate more on those cross-references for which the reader can effortlessly understand the rationalization. Minimized is the unnecessary duplication of cross-references. For example, it is not necessary to list every group in which Eric Clapton played, under each and every one of those sections. What we've done is simply indicate "Also see Eric Clapton," where you will find a complete cross-referencing to all other sections where he appears.

Some artists have several sections, one right after the other, because they were involved in different duets and/or compilation releases. In such instances, the primary artist (whose section begins first) is not cross-referenced after each and every subsequent section, but only after the last section wherein that artist is involved. This, in effect, blocks the beginning and the end of releases pertaining to that performer. If you don't find the listing you're searching for right away, remember to check the sections that follow, as the artist may have been joined by someone else on that recording causing it to appear in a separate section.

Cross-references in bold typeface are charted artists; those in normal typeface did not chart.

Artist headings and resultant cross-referencing appear in two different formats in this guide. For example:

LEWIS, Jerry Lee, Carl Perkins & Johnny Cash

Listings under this type heading are those wherein the artists perform *together*. Often these releases will also include solo tracks by one or all of the performers in addition to those on which they collaborate.

LEWIS, Jerry Lee / Carl Perkins / Johnny Cash

This heading, with names separated by a slash, indicates there are selections on *separate* tracks by each of the named artists, but they do not perform together.

ISLEY BROTHERS & DAVE "BABY" CORTEZ

This heading, with all names in upper case letters and no slash, indicates the artists perform *together*.

ISLEY BROTHERS / Brooklyn Bridge

This heading, with names after a slash that are in upper and lower case, indicates artists that perform *separately* – usually each being heard on one side of the disc.

The parameter set for these compilation releases in the body of the book is four different performers or less. Compilations containing five or more individual performers are found in the Various Artists Compilations chapter.

Whenever more than one act is featured on a record, cross-references appear under all of the other artists on the disc, who have a section of their own in this edition, directing the reader to the location of the listing in question. If you're looking up a record with a different artist on each side, and you don't find it under one artist, be sure to try looking for the flip-side artist.

Not all releases containing more than one artist are given separate sections. In some cases it makes more sense to include such records in the primary section for the most important artist. We will rarely create separate sections for multiple artist discs when the other performers on the issue do not have a section of their own in this edition.

To illustrate this point, Hank Williams Jr. had several duet issues with Lois Johnson; Gene Ammons shared an LP with Sonny Stitt. Even though Johnson and Stitt do not have individual sections in this book (they didn't make the Billboard pop singles or LPs charts), such recordings may be important to collectors of Williams and Ammons. For that reason, they are included in their respective artist's section.

On the other hand, a duet by Brenda Lee and Willie Nelson requires a separate section, since either or both may be of interest to the researcher. Also, both are individually pop-charted artists. There are a few isolated exceptions to this policy, simply because every section in this edition was separately prepared and customized in whatever manner necessary to provide the user with the most usable information.

Promotional Issues

Separate documenting and pricing of promotional issues is, in most cases, unnecessary. Because most of the records issued during the primary four decades covered in this guide were simultaneously pressed for promotional purposes, a separate listing of them would theoretically double the size of an already large book.

Rather, we've chosen to list promotional copies separately when we have the knowledge that an alternate price (either higher or lower) consistently is asked for them. For the most part, promos of everyday releases will fall into the same range — usually toward the high end — given for store stock copies. Some may stretch the range slightly, but not enough to warrant separate pricing. Premiums may be paid for promos that have different (longer, shorter, differently mixed, etc.) versions of tunes, even though the artist may not be particularly hot in the collecting marketplace.

When identified as a "Promotional issue," we are usually describing a record with a special promotional ("Not For Sale," "Dee Jay Copy," etc.) label or sleeve, and not a *designate* promo. Designate promos are identical to commercial releases, except they have been rubber or mechanically stamped, stickered, written on by hand, or in some way altered to accommodate their use for promotional purposes. There are very few designate promos listed in this edition, and those that are (such as in the Elvis Presley section) are clearly identified as such.

Colored Vinyl Pressings

Records known to exist on both black vinyl and colored vinyl (vinyl is the term used regardless of whether it's polystyrene or vinyl) are listed separately since there is usually a value difference. However, some colored vinyl releases were never pressed on black vinyl, and since there is no way to have the record other than on colored vinyl, it may or may not be specifically noted as being on colored vinyl.

Because the true color of some colored vinyl pressings may be a judgment call (is it red or maroon . . . is it dark blue or is it purple?), we're using "colored vinyl" to indicate most pressings that are not standard black vinyl. Exceptions exist when for the sake of exactness — as when different colors exist and are priced differently — it is necessary to be more specific.

Foreign Releases

Originally, *The Official Price Guide to Records* listed only U.S. releases. Now, there are many exceptions. A handful of records that were widely distributed in the United States or sold via widespread U.S. advertising, even though manufactured outside the country, are included. Such anomalies would appear only in the more sophisticated sections of the guide.

There are also various Canadian releases here, with more being added to each new edition. The collectors' market for out-of-print Canadian records is mostly a U.S. market. The trading of rare Canadian discs between Canadian collectors is not quite as widespread as those instances that involve a U.S. buyer or seller. Yet it is from Canadian collectors that we receive most of our information on those releases, and we expect to have more listed in future editions.

There are millions of overseas releases that have collector value to fans in those countries as well as to stateside collectors. Unfortunately, the tremendous volume of material and the variances in pricing make it impossible to comprehensively document and price imports.

Bootlegs and Counterfeits

Bootleg and counterfeit records are not priced in this guide, though a few are cited, along with information on how to distinguish them from an original.

For the record, a bootleg recording is one illegally manufactured, usually containing material not previously available in a legitimate form. Often, with the serious collector in mind, a boot will package previously issued tracks that have achieved some degree of value or scarcity. If the material is easily available, legally, then there would be no gain for the bootlegger.

The counterfeit record is one manufactured as close as possible in sound and appearance to the source disc from which it was inspired. Not all counterfeits were created to fool an unsuspecting buyer into thinking he or she was buying an authentic issue, but some were. Many were designated in some way, such as a slight marking or variance, so as not to allow them to be confused with originals. Such a fake record primarily exists to fill a gap in the collector's file until the real thing comes along.

With both bootleg and with counterfeit records, the appropriate and deserving recipients of royalties are, of course, denied remuneration for their works.

Since most of the world's valuable records have been counterfeited, it is always a good idea to consult with an expert when there is any doubt. The trained eye can usually spot a fake.

This is not to say *unauthorized* releases are excluded from the book. There are many legitimate releases that are unauthorized by one entity or another; records that are neither bootleg or counterfeit. Unauthorized does not necessarily mean illegal.

Group Names and Personnel

One problem that we'll never completely solve involves the many instances where groups using the exact same name are lumped together with other groups who are completely different. Whenever known to be different, these groups are given separate sections; however, there are times when we simply do not know. If you can shed any light in this area, we'd love to hear from you. Thanks to readers, many such groups have been sorted since our last edition.

The listing sequence for artists using the same name is chronological. Thus, the ABC group, Silk, who had a release in 1969, is listed ahead of the Philadelphia International group, Silk, that first recorded in 1979.

As often as not, there will have been group members that have come and gone over the years. Reflecting this turnover in our listing of members' names may cause some confusion, when the reader sees 12 different members shown for a group named the Five Satins. We've tried, whenever possible, to list the original line-up first, followed by later members. Also, the lead singer is usually listed first. We welcome additional information on group members from readers. One of the most reliable sources of this data is the LP covers, which often list members. If you can fill in the members' names on any groups where we don't list that information, we'll see that it gets into our next edition. Hundreds of group members have been added since the ninth edition of this guide.

When group members' names are given, there is a likelihood that not all of the members named appear on *all* of the releases documented. It is also possible that not all of the members named ever recorded with all of the other members shown at the same time.

When names are given for a solo performer, those named are likely noteworthy sidemen.

As more and more group members are named in future editions, there will be added cross-referencing to reflect the constant shuffle of performers from one group to another.

Parenthetical Notes

Some of the information that may be found in parentheses following the artist heading has already been covered. However, other uses of this space include:

- Complete artist and group or artist and band names. Some artists were shown as being with one group on a few releases, solo on some, and with yet another group on other issues. We've tried to present the information the way, or ways, that it is shown on the actual record label. When encased in quote marks, it means that this particular wording or credit variation is exactly as shown on the label.
- Variations of spelling or names for the same artist. With some artists, it's convenient to have everything in one section; however, when it is illogical to combine listings, perhaps because the performer was popular under more than one name (such as Johnny Cymbal and Derek), you'll find individual sections for each name. Cross-references will be used to help you locate things easily. Having "Kenneth Rogers" in parentheses is not intended to mean that Kenneth is Kenny's real name. Rather, we're letting you know that on at least one of his records he is credited as Kenneth Rogers instead of Kenny Rogers. We may at times provide real names of artists, but only when we feel they need to be given. While we have no desire to give the real names of everyone who has recorded under a pseudonym, there are times when you do need this information. This is especially true when they have also recorded under their real name or when more than one person has recorded under the same pseudonym. To help sort things out, we will, when known, give you the real name of someone who has recorded under a nom de guerre, such as Guitar Slim (a.k.a. Johnny Winter).
- Names of guest performers who may or may not be credited on the actual label, but who we feel you should know were involved in some of the records listed in that section.

Oldies Labels and Reissues

An effort has been made to include many "oldies" or reissue records in the guide. Though many reissues of this type are of no value beyond their current retail cost, some are. Look at some of the early RCA Victor Gold Standard Series Elvis Presley releases, for example. Once in a blue moon a tune will turn up in true stereo on a reissue label that was previously hard to find in stereo. Otherwise, it's just our desire to report comprehensively on all artists that prompted the listing of reissues.

The main reason we've included these reissues is to eliminate confusion, especially among younger collectors. Often, they'll discover a hit tune on a label like Lana or Lost-Nite, and think it's an original release predating the label that had the hit.

If there are reissues numbered as part of a label's standard release series, and not documented in this edition, please tell us about them.

How You Can Help

We can never get too much input or have too many reviewers. We wholeheartedly encourage you to submit anything and everything you feel would be useful in building a better record guide. The quantity of data is not a factor — no amount is too little or too much.

The extensive list of names always found in the Acknowledgments chapter indicates the development of our board of advisors. We want *you* to join the team.

When preparing additions, please try to list records in generally the same format as is used in the guide: artist's name, label, selection number, title, year of release (if known), and price range. Since our data base is stored alphabetically by artist, there's no need to note the current page number.

Please submit information accurately, exactly as it appears on the label. Incomplete copying, especially of artist names, is the reason for embarrassing duplications in the guide. If the credit reads "Winston and the Aardvarks," list it that way. Do not simply tell us it's by the Aardvarks! This oversight can easily create duplicate listings — one under "W" and another under "A." Thank you.

Wax Fax and e-mail

Two frequently used methods of forwarding data to us is by fax and by e-mail. For your convenience, we have a dedicated fax line: (360) 385-6572. Use this service to easily and instantly transmit additions, corrections, price updates, and suggestions. Be sure to include (legibly) your name, address, and phone number so we can acknowledge your contribution and, if necessary, contact you.

Our e-mail address is **jpo@olympus.net.** Again, remember to provide your full name separately since Internet letters normally relay only the sender's e-mail address.

If you help, we want to credit you properly. Just make sure we have — and can read — the information with which to do it.

Send all additions, corrections, comments and suggestions to:

Jerry Osborne
Box 255
Port Townsend, WA 98368
Fax: (360) 385-6572
e-mail: jpo@olympus.net
www.olympus.net/personal/jpo

Using This Guide: Some Additional Points

- A few of the more prolific labels with lengthy names are abbreviated in this guide. They are:

ABC-PAR .... ABC-Paramount
GNP .... GNP/Crescendo
MFSL........... Mobile Fidelity Sound Lab
RCA ....RCA Victor
20TH FOX..................20th Century-Fox
U.A..................................United Artists
W.B. .... Warner Brothers

To avoid confusion, the short-lived Warner records label, active in 1959, is shown as "Warner," never as "W.B." Also, when an artist has records on the old Memphis Sun label, as well as Shelby Singleton's Nashville-based Sun label, the latter is shown as "SSS/Sun."

• The alphabetization in *The Official Price Guide to Records* makes finding any artist or label easy, but a few guidelines may speed the process along for you:

• Names that are simply letters (and are not intended to be pronounced as a word) are found at the beginning of the listings under each letter of the alphabet (i.e., **ABC, AC-DC, GQ, SSQ,** etc.). The same rule applies to acronyms and to initialisms (i.e., **G.T.O, MFSB,** etc.). When known, we'll parenthetically tell you what the abbreviation represents.

• Names are listed in the alphabetical order of the first word. This means you'll find **Rock Squad** before **Rocket.** Hyphenated words are looked upon as whole words (i.e., **Mello-Kings** is treated the same as **Mellokings**). Divided names or names with Spanish articles (i.e., **De Vorzon, Del Satins, El Dorados; Las Vegas, Los Lobos,** etc.) are alphabetically listed as though they were a one-word name.

• Possessive names precede similarly spelled names that are not possessive. For example, **KNIGHT'S** would be found before **KNIGHTS,** regardless of what follows the comma.

• It is flabbergasting to discover how many of the people responsible for crediting bands and groups on record labels have no understanding (or schooling) regarding when to use a possessive apostrophe. This is by far the most frequently found mistake on labels — one which we refuse to blindly copy for our artist headings, lest anyone think that we don't know better. However, for those labels that do credit groups like — to use an actual example — the Capitols (on Gateway) as **CAPITOL'S**, we will indicate that senseless variation under the artist's heading, in parenthesis.

• The articles "A" or "The" have been dropped from group names in this guide even though they may appear on the records as part of the name.

• With record labels in *The Official Price Guide to Records*, the listings appear in alphabetical/numerical/chronological order. Selection prefixes are generally not used (they make it more difficult to scan the numbers) unless they are necessary for identification. With some artists (Beatles, Elvis, etc.) it is essential at times because of constant reissues.

• Some sections make use of the label prefixes to sort things out, but most use a number series. If the numbers are duplicated by the label, or if any of a variety of confusing similarities exist, we may resort to the prefixes for clarity.

• Regarding 78 rpms. As to which late '50s and early '60s tunes came out on 78s, we cannot safely assume much of anything. If you know of 78s from end of the 78 rpm era that we do not list, please advise us accordingly. We would be especially happy to learn of charted hits issued after 1957.

• Whenever possible, records priced in the $25.00 to $35.00 range and up are listed individually with label, selection number, and title.

• Anytime we find that the monaural or the stereo issue of a particular record is in need of a separate listing (because there is a price difference for one that is outside the boundaries of the price range of the other), we will gladly provide same. If there is but one listing, this indicates that we have no reason to believe there is much difference in the two forms. A little application of the known variables will help in this area. For example, if the range is $20.00 to $40.00 for a 1960 LP and you know that the stereo issue is in true stereo, it's safe to place the mono at the low end of the range ($20.00 to $30.00) and the stereo at the high end ($30.00 to $40.00). The calculation may be reversed for late '60s and for most electronically reprocessed issues.

• We believe the year or years of release given in the far-right column to be accurate. If we don't know the correct year, the column is left blank. In some cases the record may have been released in one year and debuted on the nation's music charts the following year. This is common for year-end issues and explains why you may remember a hit as being from 1966, although we list it as a 1965 release.

• When multiple years are indicated, such as "64-66," it means the records described on that line spanned the years 1964 through 1966. They may have had one issue in 1964 and another in 1966, or may have had eight releases during those years. It does *not* mean that we believe the release came out sometime between 1964 and 1966. If the exact year is not known but the decade of release is, then we will provide that ('50s, '60s, '70s, etc.)

• When a selection number series, such as a "4000 series," is shown, it includes numbers 4000 through 4999. If it were meant to indicate only 4000 through 4099, then separate listings would be found for 4100, 4200, etc.

• Goofy as it seems, a few records have been issued with no artist or label given. You will find this on both singles and albums. These items are filed here by title.

• There are hundreds of double albums (two discs in one package) priced in the guide, but they are not necessarily identified as double LPs. They are, nevertheless, included in the price range.

• Mislabeled records are usually no big deal. We constantly hear from folks who think they have struck gold because one of their records has its labels screwed up in some manner. Either they are reversed, with each side bearing the label intended for the other side, or mislabeled altogether with a label from an entirely different record — perhaps even by a completely different artist. Generally, production errors of this kind do not increase value. They may, in some cases, make the disc even less attractive to a collector. For those very, very few exceptions, the necessary information is already noted in *The Official Price Guide to Records*.

• While this guide makes no attempt to fully document gospel recordings per se, the wonderful, soulful harmony of groups like the Swan Silvertones and Soul Stirrers make their records popular among rhythm and blues collectors. For that reason they are included. Others will be added on an as requested basis.

• To conserve space, when the same title is listed as both 45 and 78, we may not list the title in both sections if it requires more than one line. You may therefore find only the label name in the 78 section, whereas the complete number and title will be in the 45 section.

• In most cases, we have no specifics regarding which 78s came on both black and colored plastic. Lacking comments to the contrary, all 78s in *The Official Price Guide to Records* are presumed to be black plastic.

• With all recently added listings, when two (or more) releases came out in the same calendar year, a note reading "First issue" will indicate which came first. Most examples of this occurred with independent labels whose records got picked up by one of the major companies, and issued on their own label. Of course, if the years of release differ from one label to the other there is no need for the note. As we run across them, we will make a similar notation to the older listings in the guide.

• For those who require an even more comprehensive guide for collectibles by either Elvis Presley or the Beatles, we have separate publications available for each that will take you as far into their records and memorabilia as you want to go.

Presley collectors consider Jerry Osborne's *Official Price Guide to Elvis Presley Records & Memorabilia* indispensable, whereas Beatles collectors feel the same about Cox & Lindsay's *Official Price Guide to Beatles Records & Memorabilia.*

Also, those who want to know all there is to know about collecting and appraising vinyl soundtracks and original casts will want the latest edition of Jerry Osborne's *Official Price Guide to Movie/TV Soundtracks & Original Cast Recordings*.

These guides are available at or through most bookstores; however, if you can't find them easily, contact us at: Jellyroll Productions, Box 255, Port Townsend, WA 98368 (360) 385-1200. We'll see that you get the titles you seek.

Guidelines for Pricing Records Not in This Edition

Since it is impossible for us to include *every* record ever produced, a few guidelines may assist you in evaluating records not found in this edition:

♦ Pop Singles on 45 rpm: Most pop (i.e. non-rock) vocal and instrumental 45s from the '50s are available for under $15.00. From many rock-oriented dealers, pop singles can often be bought for less than $10.00. The few exceptions are likely to be folks with charted hits, and those will be found in the guide.

♦ Pop music singles from the '60s to present are seldom going to sell for over $10.00

♦ Pop Singles on 78 rpm: Most pop 78s are available for under $10.00 Albums of 78s — usually in a gatefold binder with individual paper sleeves — will vary, but most are in the $20.00 to $50.00 range.

♦ Pop Long Play Albums: From the '50s, 12-inch pop LPs generally are found for under $40.00. Ten-inch LPs may go for up to $75.00. Exceptions, such as pop stars who made rock or jazz records, should be found in this book.

♦ Most pop LPs from the '60s to present can be found for $5.00 to $15.00.

♦ Pop Extended Play Albums: Pop EPs are scarce, as are all EPs, but many are still very reasonable. Most can be found for $10.00 to $25.00, often for even less.

♦ Easy Listening Music: The average easy listening record will be worth about half of the price ranges shown for Pop Music. Some exceptions, with higher values, are LPs by certain lounge music performers and virtually any with female models pictured in exotic settings and in alluring poses on their covers.

♦ Country Music on 45 rpm: Most country music vocal and instrumental 45s from the '50s are available for under $15.00; many for less than $10.00. Obvious exceptions are any that border on rockabilly or country rock. Don't take any country record for granted! Play both sides of every disc, as it is always possible you'll discover a great country rocker.

♦ Country music singles from the '60s to present are seldom going to sell for more than $10.00.

♦ Country Music on 78 rpm: Most of the country 78s should fall into the $10.00 to $40.00 range. There are, however, many older 78s with prices well into three figures; some even higher.

♦ Country Music Long Play Albums: From the '50s, 12-inch LPs generally are found for under $30.00 to $60.00. Ten-inch LPs may go for $50 to $100. As always, the range will vary widely depending on the following and collectibility of the artist.

♦ Most country LPs from the '60s to present can be found for $15.00 to $25.00. Again, there are exceptions.

♦ Country Music Extended Play Albums: Very, very few country music EPs were big sellers, which means nearly all are rare. You may find they are in the same price range as the '50s LPs above; some will bring even more than LPs from the same time period.

♦ Jazz Singles on 45 rpm: Most jazz 45s from the '50s are available for under $15.00. The few exceptions are likely to be artists with charted hits, which will be found in the guide.

♦ Jazz singles from the '60s to present are seldom going to sell for more than $10.00.

♦ Jazz Singles on 78 rpm: Most jazz 78s are available for under $20.00. Until the late '40s or early '50s, an *album* was a gatefold binder with a number of 78s, usually in individual paper sleeves. Prices on these jazz albums will vary, but most will fall in the $25.00 to $75.00 range.

♦ Jazz Long Play Albums: From the '50s, 12-inch jazz LPs generally are found for under $50 to $100. Ten-inch LPs may go for $75 to $200.

♦ Most jazz LPs from the '60s to present can still be found for $15.00 to $30.00.

♦ Jazz Extended Play Albums: As with country, very few jazz EPs were big sellers. While all are rare, there is not as much demand for them from jazz collectors as for long-play albums. Of course, outside jazz circles there is virtually no demand for them. You may find they are, in general, worth little more than the prices shown above for jazz singles from the same time period.

♦ Comedy and Personality Long Play Albums: From the '50s and '60s, 12-inch comedy and personality (not soundtrack or original cast) LPs generally are found for under $20.00 to $40.00.

♦ Most comedy and personality LPs from the '70s to present can be had for $10.00 to $15.00.

♦ In summary, there is no way these few paragraphs can constitute a complete price guide for the millions of non-rock records that exist. If such generic generalizations were possible, while guaranteeing unerring accuracy, the entire price guide would be about ten pages. It is the exceptions that make record pricing so complicated and difficult to document. Our goal here is simply to provide a rough idea of the value of recordings that are outside the parameters of the guide.

What to Expect When Selling Your Records to a Dealer

As most know, there is a noteworthy difference between the prices reported in this guide and the prices that one can expect a dealer to pay when buying records for resale. Unless a dealer is buying for a personal collection and without thoughts of resale, he or she is simply not in a position to pay full price. Dealers work on a percentage basis, largely determined by the total dollar investment, quality, and quantity of material offered as well as the general financial condition and inventory of the dealer at the time.

Another very important consideration is the length of time it will take the dealer to recover at least the amount of the original investment. The greater the demand for the stock and the better the condition, the quicker the return and therefore the greater the percentage that can be paid. Our experience has shown that, day-in and day-out, most dealers will pay from 25% to 50% of *guide* prices. And that's assuming they are planning to resell at guide prices. If they traditionally sell below guide, that will be reflected in what they can pay for stock.

If you have records to sell, it would be wise to check with several shops. In doing so you'll begin to get a good idea of the value of your collection to a dealer.

Also, consult the Directory of Buyers and Sellers in this guide for the names of many dealers who not only might be interested in buying, but from whom many collectible records are available for purchase.

Whether you wish to sell the records you have, or add out-of-print discs to your collection, check out *DISCoveries* magazine. Each issue is packed with ads, features, discographies, collecting tips and more. If getting into the record marketplace is important to you, *DISCoveries* is not just recommended, it is essential. For more information, contact: Trader Publications, PO Box 1050, Dubuque, Iowa 52003. A sample issue is available upon request.

Concluding Thoughts

The purpose of this guide is to report as accurately as possible the most recent prices asked and paid for records within the area of its coverage. There are two key words here that deserve emphasis: **Guide** and **Report**.

We cannot stress enough that this book is only a guide. There always have been and always will be instances of records selling well above and below the prices shown within these pages. These extremes are recognized in the final averaging process; but it's still important to understand that just because we've reported a 30-year-old record as having a $25.00 to $50.00 near-mint value, doesn't mean that a collector of that material should be hesitant to pay $75.00 for it. How badly he or she wants it and how often it's possible to purchase it *at any price* should be the prime factors considered, not the fact that we last reported it at a lower price. Of course, we'd like to know about sales of this sort so that the next edition can reflect the new pricing information.

One extremely difficult area to keep up with is rare R&B releases. We may report a record for $500 to $1,000, which may have been an accurate appraisal at press time. However, before the new edition hits the streets, the price might be $1,000 to $2,000. One or two transactions and six months later it jumps to $2,000 to $4,000. By the time we're close to the following year's guide, this same disc may be considered a bargain at $5,000.

At that point, people may look at the book and wonder how we could show $500 to $1,000 for a $5,000 record. "Our price is a joke," you'll hear. And, at that point, it is.

If we published monthly, perhaps we could keep pace, but with such a volatile marketplace and an annual schedule — well, just bear with us.

Meanwhile, please keep in mind that any of the world's more valuable records now have the potential to be worth considerably more in the near future than on that day last spring when work ended on this edition. The key is simply this: is it a money record in the first place? If so, remain open to surprising price increases.

Our objective is to report and reflect record marketplace activity; not to *establish* prices. For that reason, and if given the choice, we'd prefer to be a bit behind the times rather than ahead. With this guide being regularly revised, it will never be long before the necessary changes are reported within these pages.

We encourage record companies, artist management organizations, talent agencies, publicists, and performers to make certain that we are on the active mailing list for new release information, press releases, bios, publicity photos, and anything pertaining to recordings.

There is an avalanche of helpful information in this guide to aid the collector in determining what is valuable and what may not be worth fooling with, but the wise fan will also keep abreast of current trends and news through the pages of the fanzines and publications devoted to his or her favorite forms of music.

SAMPLE LISTING

Artist's primary heading.

FLAMINGOS *R&B '56*

(With Red Holloway's Orchestra)

Singles: 78 rpm

CHANCE (1133 " If I Can't Have You") 100-200 53
CHANCE (1145 "Golden Teardrops") 200-300 53
PARROT (808 "Dream of a Lifetime") 100-150 54
PARROT (812 "I'm Yours") 150-200 55

Singles: 7-inch

CHANCE (1133 "If I Can't Have You") 500-750 53
(Black vinyl.)
CHANCE (1133 "If I Can't Have You") 1000-2000 53
(Colored vinyl.)
CHANCE (1145 "Golden Teardrops") 500-750 53
(Black vinyl.)
CHANCE (1145 "Golden Teardrops") 2000-3000 53
(Colored vinyl.)
END (1035 "Please Wait for Me") 30-40 58
(Title later changed to *Lovers Never Say Goodbye*.)
END (1035 "Lovers Never Say Goodbye") 10-20 58
END (1046 "I Only Have Eyes for You"/ "At the Prom") 10-20 59
END (1046 "I Only Have Eyes for You"/ "Goodnight Sweetheart") 15-25 59
(Note different flip.)
END (1046 "I Only Have Eyes for You")................. 40-50 59
(Stereo.)
PARROT (808 "Dream of a Lifetime")...............500-1000 54
(Black vinyl.)
PARROT (808 "Dream of a Lifetime") 2000-3000 54
(Colored vinyl.)
PARROT (811 "I Really Don't Want to Know") 1000-2000 55
(Black vinyl.)
PARROT (811 "I Really Don't Want to Know") 3000-5000 55
(Colored vinyl.)

EPs: 7-inch

END (205 "Goodnight Sweetheart") 40-60 59
(Monaural.)
END (205 "Goodnight Sweetheart") 50-85 59
(Stereo.)

LPs: 10/12-inch

CHECKER (1433 "Flamingos") 75-125 59
(Monaural.)
CHECKER (3005 "Flamingos") 25-50 66
(Stereo.)
END (304 "Flamingo Serenade") 50-100 59
(Monaural.)
END (304 "Flamingo Serenade") 75-125 59
(Stereo.)
END (316 "The Sound of the Flamingos").............. 20-40 62
(Monaural.)
END (316 "The Sound of the Flamingos").............. 25-50 62
(Stereo.)

Members: Sollie McElroy; John Carter; Zeke Carey; Jake Carey; Paul Wilson; Nate Nelson; Tommy Hunt; Terry Johnson.

Also see HUNT, Tommy

Chart or charts and year this artist FIRST appeared on Billboard. For this group, they first hit the R&B chart in 1956.

May also be shown on some releases as ...

Helpful explanatory notes.

Near-mint price range.

Year or years of release.

Label names, selection numbers and titles.

Category or type of items listed in each section.

References to other, related, sections in the guide.

Names of group members and/or recording session participants.

A's LP '81

Singles: 7-inch

ARISTA....3-5 79

LPs: 10/12-inch

ARISTA....5-10 79-81

Members: Richard Bush; Rick DiFonzo; Michael Snyder; Terry Bortman; Rocco Nolte.

A.B. SKHY P&R '69

Singles: 7-inch

MGM....3-5 69-70

Picture Sleeves

MGM....3-5 69-70

LPs: 10/12-inch

MGM....10-12 69-70

Members: Dennis Geyer; Howard Wales; Jim Liban; Jim Marcotte; Terry Anderson; Gary Karp; Curley Cooke; Rick Jaeger.

ABC P&R/LP '82

Singles: 12-inch

MERCURY....4-6 83-87

Singles: 7-inch

MERCURY....3-4 82-87

Picture Sleeves

MERCURY....3-4 82-87

LPs: 10/12-inch

MERCURY....5-10 82-87

Members: Martin Fry; Steve Singleton; Mark White.

AC/DC LP '77

Singles: 12-inch

ATLANTIC....5-10 79

(Promotional issue only.)

Singles: 7-inch

ATCO....3-5 77

ATLANTIC....3-5 77-85

Picture Sleeves

ATLANTIC....3-5 81-83

LPs: 10/12-inch

ATCO....5-15 76-90

ATLANTIC....5-10 77-86

EAST/WEST....5-10 90s

Members: Bonn Scott; Angus Young; Mark Evans; Malcomb Young; Phil Rudd; Cliff Williams; Brian Johnson; Chris Slade; Simon Wright.

Also see DIO, Ronnie

Also see FIRM

ADC BAND R&B/LP '78

Singles: 7-inch

COTILLION....3-5 78-82

LPs: 10/12-inch

COTILLION....5-10 78-82

Members: Michael Judkins; Arwell Mathew Jr; Audrey Mathew; Mark Patterson.

AM-FM R&B '82

Singles: 7-inch

DAKAR....3-5 82

Also see MASON, Vaughn

APB D&D '83

Singles: 12-inch

IMPORT....4-6 83

SLEEPING BAG....4-6 84

Singles: 7-inch

IMPORT....3-4 83

LPs: 10/12-inch

MCA....5-10 83

AWB: see AVERAGE WHITE BAND

AALON R&B '77

Singles: 7-inch

ARISTA....3-5 77

LPs: 10/12-inch

ARISTA....5-10 77

Members: Aalon Butler; Ronnie Hammond.

Also see WAR

ABACO DREAM P&R/R&B '69

Singles: 7-inch

A&M....4-6 69-70

Members: Paul Douglas; Dave Williams; Dennis Williams; Frank Maid; Mike Sassano.

ABBA P&R/LP '74

Singles: 12-inch

ATLANTIC....4-8 77-79

Singles: 7-inch

ATLANTIC....3-6 75-82

Picture Sleeves

ATLANTIC....3-6 77-82

LPs: 10/12-inch

ATLANTIC (Except 300)....10-20 74-84

ATLANTIC (300 "Abba")....15-25 78

(Promotional issue only.)

CBS INT'L....8-12 80

EPIC....5-8 79

K-TEL....8-10 80

NAUTILUS (20 "Arrival")....15-25 82

(Half-speed mastered.)

SILVER EAGLE....8-10 84

Members: Anni-frid Lyngstad; Bjorn Ulvaeus; Benny Andersson; Agnetha Faltskog.

Also see BJORN & BENNY

Also see FALTSKOG, Agnetha

Also see FRIDA

ABBA / Spinners / Firefall / England Dan & John Ford Coley

EPs: 7-inch

W.B. SPECIAL PRODUCTS....5-10 78

(Coca-Cola/Burger King promotional issue. Issued with paper sleeve.)

Also see ABBA

Also see ENGLAND DAN & John Ford Coley

Also see FIREFALL

Also see SPINNERS

ABBEY TAVERN SINGERS P&R '66

Singles: 7-inch

HBR....4-8 66

EPs: 7-inch

V.I.P. (60402 "Off to Dublin in the Green")....15-25 66

LPs: 10/12-inch

V.I.P. (402 "Off to Dublin in the Green")....30-60 66

ABBOTT, Billy, & Jewels P&R '63

Singles: 7-inch

PARKWAY....5-10 63-64

ABBOTT, Gregory P&R/R&B/LP '86

Singles: 12-inch

COLUMBIA....4-6 86-88

Singles: 7-inch

COLUMBIA....3-4 86-88

Picture Sleeves

COLUMBIA....3-4 86-88

LPs: 10/12-inch

COLUMBIA....5-10 87

ABDUL, Paula P&R/R&B/LP '88

(With Wild Pair)

Singles: 7-inch

VIRGIN....3-4 88-91

Picture Sleeves

VIRGIN....3-4 88-89

LPs: 10/12-inch

VIRGIN....5-8 88-89

ABRAMS, Colonel R&B/D&D '84

Singles: 12-inch

MCA....4-6 85-87

STREETWISE....4-6 84

Singles: 7-inch

MCA....3-4 85-87

STREETWISE....3-4 84

Picture Sleeves

MCA....3-4 85-87

LPs: 10/12-inch

MCA....5-8 86

ABRAMS, Miss, & Strawberry Point School Third Grade Class P&R '70

Singles: 7-inch

A&M....3-5 71

REPRISE....3-5 70

Picture Sleeves

REPRISE....3-5 70

LPs: 10/12-inch

REPRISE....8-12 72

ACCENTS P&R '58

(Featuring Robert Draper Jr.)

Singles: 7-inch

BRUNSWICK (55100 "Wiggle Wiggle")....10-15 58

BRUNSWICK (55123 "Ching a Ling")....10-20 59

CORAL....10-15 59

JUBILEE....5-10 59

Members: Robert Draper Jr.; Robert Armstrong; James Jackson; Billy Hood; Arvid Garrett; Israel Goudeau Jr.

ACCENTS (With David Gates): see GATES, David

ACCEPT LP '84

Singles: 7-inch

PORTRAIT....3-4 84-89

Picture Sleeves

PORTRAIT....3-4 84-86

LPs: 10/12-inch

PVC....5-10 83

PASSPORT....5-10 81

PORTRAIT....5-10 84-89

ACE P&R/LP '75

Singles: 7-inch

ABC....3-5 76-78

ANCHOR....3-5 75-77

LPs: 10/12-inch

ANCHOR....8-12 74-77

Members: Paul Carrack; Fran Byrne; Tex Comer; Phil Harris; Alan "Bam" King; Jon Woodhead.

Also see CARRACK, Paul

ACE, Buddy R&B '66

Singles: 78 rpm

DUKE....5-15 56-57

PEACOCK....10-15 55

Singles: 7-inch

DUKE (100 series)....10-20 56-58

DUKE (300 & 400 series)....4-8 60-69

FIDELITY....6-12 59

PAULA....3-5 70-72

PEACOCK (1659 "I Told You So")....15-25 55

SPECIALTY....10-15 59

ACE, Johnny R&B '52

(With the Beale Streeters)

Singles: 78 rpm

DUKE....15-25 52-55

Singles: 7-inch

ABC....3-5 73

DUKE....20-40 52-55

MCA....3-4 84

EPs: 7-inch

DUKE (71 "Johnny Ace")....15-25 63

(Six-track, juke box issue only.)

DUKE (80 "Memorial Album")....150-200 55

DUKE (81 "Tribute Album")....150-200 55

LPs: 10/12-inch

DUKE (70 "Memorial Album")....500-600 55

(10-inch LP.)

DUKE (71 "Memorial Album")....150-250 57

(No playing card shown on cover.)

DUKE (71 "Memorial Album")....60-80 61

(Playing card shown on cover.)

DUKE (X-71 "Memorial Album")....8-10 74

MCA....4-6 83

Also see BLAND, Bobby

Also see OTIS, Johnny

ACE, Johnny / Earl Forrest

Singles: 78 rpm

FLAIR 25-40 53

Singles: 7-inch

FLAIR (1015 "Mid Night Hours Journey") 50-100 53

Also see ACE, Johnny
Also see FORREST, Earl

ACE SPECTRUM — P&R '74

Singles: 7-inch

ATLANTIC 3-5 74-76

LPs: 10/12-inch

ATLANTIC 8-10 74-76

Members: Henry Zant; Troy Johnson; Rudy Gay; Elliot Isaac.

ACKLES, David — LP '72

Singles: 7-inch

ELEKTRA 3-6 68-72

LPs: 10/12-inch

COLUMBIA 5-10 73
ELEKTRA 8-12 69-72

ACKLIN, Barbara — P&R/R&B/LP '68

Singles: 7-inch

BRUNSWICK 4-8 67-73
CAPITOL 3-5 74-75
ERIC 3-4 83
SPECIAL AGENT (203 "I'm Not Mad Anymore") 25-50

Picture Sleeves

BRUNSWICK 5-10 68

LPs: 10/12-inch

BRUNSWICK 10-15 68-71
CAPITOL 5-10 75

Also see CHANDLER, Gene, and Barbara Acklin

ACT I — R&B '73

Singles: 7-inch

SPRING 3-5 73-74

LPs: 10/12-inch

SPRING 5-10 74

ACTUALS: see VOCAL AIRES / Actuals

ACUFF, Roy — P&R '38/C&W '44

(With the Smoky Mountain Boys; with Crazy Tennesseeans)

Singles: 78 rpm

BANNER 10-20
CAPITOL 4-8 53-55
COLUMBIA 5-10 45-49
CONQUEROR 10-20
DECCA 4-8 55
MGM 5-10 51
MELOTONE 10-20
OKEH 5-10 40-45
ORIOLE 10-20
PERFECT 10-20
ROMEO 10-20
VOCALION 8-12 38-40

Singles: 7-inch

CAPITOL (2385 thru 3209) 5-10 53-55
COLUMBIA (20000 series) 10-20 52
DECCA 5-10 55
ELEKTRA 3-5 78
HICKORY (314 thru 362) 3-6 73-75
HICKORY (1073 thru 1664) 4-8 58-72
MGM 10-20 51

EPs: 7-inch

CAPITOL (617 "Songs of the Smokey Mountains") 10-15 55
(Price is for any of three volumes.)
COLUMBIA (Except 2895) 10-20 51-57
COLUMBIA (2895 "Roy Acuff EP") ... 30-50 50s

LPs: 10/12-inch

CAPITOL (617 "Songs of the Smokey Mountains") 20-40 55
CAPITOL (2276 "The Voice of Country Music") 10-20 65
CAPITOL (T-1870 "Country Music Hall of Fame's Roy Acuff") 10-20 63
(Monaural.)
CAPITOL (SM-1870 "Country Music Hall of Fame's Roy Acuff") 5-10 79
(Reprocessed stereo.)
COLUMBIA (9004 "Songs of the Smokey Mountains") 30-50 50
(10-inch LP.)
COLUMBIA (9010 "Old Time Barn Dance") 30-50 50
(10-inch LP.)
COLUMBIA (CS-1034 "Roy Acuff's Greatest Hits") 8-12 70
COLUMBIA (PC-1034 "Roy Acuff's Greatest Hits") 8-12 70
COLUMBIA (39998 "Roy Acuff") 5-8 85
ELEKTRA 5-10 78-82
CAPITOL (2103 "The Great Roy Acuff") 20-30 64
GOLDEN COUNTRY 5-10
HARMONY 8-20 58-70
HICKORY (101 thru 119) 20-35 61-65
HICKORY (125 thru 162) 15-30 65-70
HICKORY/MGM 8-12 74-75
METRO 10-20 65
MGM (3707 "Favorite Hymns") 30-40 58
MGM (4044 "Hymn Time") 15-25 62
PICKWICK 5-10 70s
PICKWICK/HILLTOP 8-15 65-69
ROUNDER 5-8 85
TIME-LIFE 5-10 80s

Session: Jordanaires.
Also see NITTY GRITTY DIRT BAND & ROY ACUFF

ACUFF, Roy, & Kitty Wells

Singles: 78 rpm

DECCA 4-6 56

Singles: 7-inch

DECCA 5-10 56

Also see ACUFF, Roy
Also see WELLS, Kitty
Also see WILLIAMS, Hank / Roy Acuff

AD LIBS — P&R/R&B '65

Singles: 7-inch

A.G.P. (100 "New York in the Dark") 100-150 66
BLUE CAT 5-10 65
CAPITOL 3-6 70
ESKEE ("New York in the Dark") .. 200-300 66
(Number not known.)
KAREN (1527 "Think of Me") 15-20 66
PHILIPS 4-8 67
SHARE 3-6 69

Members: Mary Ann Thomas; Danny Austin; Hugh Harris; J.T. Taylor; Norm Donegan; Dave Watts.

ADAM & ANTS — P&R '82

Singles: 12-inch

EPIC 4-8 81

Singles: 7-inch

EPIC 3-5 81

LPs: 10/12-inch

EDITIONS EG 5-10 82
EPIC 8-10 81-82

Members: Adam Ant; Johnny Bivouac; Andy Watson; Dave Barb.
Also see ANT, Adam
Also see BOW WOW WOW

ADAMS, Bobby — R&B '70

Singles: 7-inch

BATTLE 4-8 63
BIG B. (778 "The Kind of Man") 100-200
COLPIX 5-10 61
HOMETOWN 3-6 70
PET (803 "I Want My Lovin' ") 15-25 58
PURDY (102 "Don't You Feel It") 10-20 64

ADAMS, Bobby, & Norma Jean Carpenter

Singles: 7-inch

KINGSTAR 3-5 71

Also see ADAMS, Bobby

ADAMS, Bryan — P&R/LP '82

(B.G. Adams)

Singles: 12-inch

A&M (Black vinyl) 4-6 82-87
A&M (Colored vinyl) 5-10 84

Singles: 7-inch

A&M (Except 474) 3-6 80-87
A&M (474 "Let Me Take You Dancing") 4-6 79
(Black vinyl.)
A&M (474 "Let Me Take You Dancing") 8-12 79
(Colored vinyl.)

Picture Sleeves

A&M (Except 474) 3-5 80-87
A&M (474 "Let Me Take You Dancing") 10-15 79

LPs: 10/12-inch

A&M 5-10 80-87

Also see DION
Also see SWEENY TODD

ADAMS, Bryan, Sting, & Rod Stewart

Singles: 7-inch

A&M 3-4 93

Picture Sleeves

A&M 3-4 93

Also see STEWART, Rod
Also see STING

ADAMS, Bryan, & Tina Turner

Singles: 7-inch

A&M 3-4 85

Picture Sleeves

A&M 3-4 85

Also see ADAMS, Bryan
Also see TURNER, Tina

ADAMS, Faye — R&B '53

Singles: 78 rpm

ATLANTIC 10-20 52-53
HERALD 10-20 53-57
IMPERIAL 10-20 55-57

Singles: 7-inch

ABC 3-4 73
ATLANTIC 20-40 52-53
COLLECTABLES 3-4 82
HERALD (Black vinyl) 10-20 53-57
HERALD (Colored vinyl) 25-50 53
IMPERIAL 10-20 55-57
LIDO 5-10 59-60
SAVOY 5-10 61
WARWICK 5-10 61

LPs: 10/12-inch

COLLECTABLES 6-8 88
SAVOY 5-10 76
WARWICK (2031 "Shake a Hand") .. 50-75 61

ADAMS, Faye / Little Esther / Maxine Brown

LPs: 10/12-inch

MUSICTONE (7001 "Great Female R&B Package") 20-30 65

Also see BROWN, Maxine

ADAMS, Faye / Little Esther / Shirley & Lee

LPs: 10/12-inch

ALMOR (103 "Golden Souvenirs") 10-20

Also see ADAMS, Faye
Also see LITTLE ESTHER
Also see SHIRLEY & LEE

ADAMS, Gayle — R&B '80

Singles: 7-inch

PRELUDE 3-4 80-81

LPs: 10/12-inch

PRELUDE 5-10 82

ADAMS, Johnny — R&B '62

Singles: 7-inch

ARIOLA AMERICAN 3-5 78
ATLANTIC 3-5 71-72
HELP ME 4-8 74-76
J.B. 3-5 76
MODERN 4-8 67

PACEMAKER (249 "When I'll Stop Loving You")................10-15 65
PACEMAKER (255 "Let Them Talk") 10-15 65
PAID..3-4 84
RIC..6-12 59-62
RON..6-12 64-65
SSS INT'L....................................4-6 68-74
(Black vinyl.)
SSS INT'L (809 "I Won't Cry")............5-10 69
(Colored vinyl.)
TOWNHOUSE..................................3-5
WATCH..4-8 63

LPs: 10/12-inch

ARIOLA AMERICAN..........................5-10 78
CHELSEA....................................10-20 77
HELP ME......................................8-10 74-76
SSS INT'L...................................10-15 70

ADAMS, Johnny, & Gondoliers

Singles: 7-inch

RIC (957 "Knocked Out")..................10-20 59
Also see ADAMS, Johnny

ADAMS, Marie R&B '52

(With Bill Harvey's Band; with Three Tons of Joy)

Singles: 78 rpm

PEACOCK....................................10-15 51-54

Singles: 7-inch

CAPITOL.....................................10-20 58
PEACOCK....................................20-40 51-54
VANTAGE......................................3-5 73
Also see OTIS, Johnny

ADAMS, Oleta LP '90

LPs: 10/12-inch

FONTANA......................................5-8 90

ADDEO, Leo, & His Orchestra LP '61

LPs: 10/12-inch

CAMDEN.......................................5-10 61

ADDERLEY, Julian "Cannonball"

(Cannonball Adderley Orchestra; Quintet; Sextet) P&R/R&B '61

Singles: 7-inch

BLUE NOTE...................................5-10 59
CAPITOL......................................3-8 61-73
RIVERSIDE...................................5-10 61-64

EPs: 7-inch

EMARCY.....................................10-20 55

LPs: 10/12-inch

BLUE NOTE..................................20-30 58
(Label reads "Blue Note Records Inc. - New York, U.S.A.")
BLUE NOTE..................................15-25 66
(Label reads "Blue Note Records - A Division Of Liberty Records Inc.")
CAPITOL (Except 2200 and 2300 series)..8-15 66-80
CAPITOL (2200 and 2300 series).....12-25 64-65
DOBRE...5-8 77
EMARCY (400 series)......................8-12 76
EMARCY (36000 series)...................30-40 55-58
EVEREST......................................8-12 71
FANTASY.....................................8-12 73-75
LIMELIGHT...................................10-20 66
MERCURY (1000 series)...................5-10 81
MERCURY (20000 and 60000 series)......................................15-30 61-62
MILESTONE...................................6-12 73-82
PACIFIC JAZZ...............................15-25 62
RIVERSIDE (032 thru 142)...............5-8 82-85
RIVERSIDE (200 thru 400 series).....15-30 58-63
RIVERSIDE (1100 series)................20-30 59-60
RIVERSIDE (3000 series)................10-15 68
RIVERSIDE (9000 series)................15-25 60-63
SAVOY (2200 series).......................8-12 76
SAVOY (12018 "Presenting Cannonball")................................50-75 55
TRIP..5-10 75
VSP..10-20 65
WING..8-12 68
Also see WILSON, Nancy, & Cannonball Adderley

ADDERLEY, Julian "Cannonball," & John Coltrane

LPs: 10/12-inch

LIMELIGHT..................................10-20 65
MERCURY....................................20-30 61
Also see COLTRANE, John

ADDERLEY, Julian "Cannonball," & Sergio Mendes

LPs: 10/12-inch

CAPITOL.....................................10-15 68-71
EVEREST......................................5-10 73
Also see ADDERLEY, Julian "Cannonball"
Also see MENDES, Sergio

ADDRISI BROTHERS P&R '59

Singles: 7-inch

BELL..3-5 74
BRAD..15-20 58
BUDDAH.......................................3-5 77
COLUMBIA.....................................3-5 72-73
DEL-FI.......................................10-15 59
ELEKTRA......................................3-4 81
IMPERIAL.....................................8-12 60
POM POM.....................................5-10 62
PRIVATE STOCK..............................3-5 75
SCOTTI BROTHERS..........................3-5 79
VALIANT......................................5-10 64-65
W.B. 4-8 62-68

Picture Sleeves

SCOTTI BROTHERS..........................3-5 79

LPs: 10/12-inch

BUDDAH......................................5-10 77
COLUMBIA...................................5-10 72
Members: Dick Addrisi; Don Addrisi.

ADE, King Sunny LP '83

(With His African Beats)

Singles: 12-inch

MANGO..4-6 83

Singles: 7-inch

MANGO..3-4 83

LPs: 10/12-inch

MANGO..5-10 83

ADVANCE D&D '83

Singles: 12-inch

POLYDOR.....................................4-6 83
("American Excello")......................20-25 81
(Label name and selection number not known. Promotional only picture disc.)

Singles: 7-inch

POLYDOR.....................................3-4 83

ADVENTURES P&R/LP '88

Singles: 12-inch

ELEKTRA......................................4-8 88-90

Singles: 7-inch

ELEKTRA......................................3-4 88-90

Picture Sleeves

ELEKTRA......................................3-4 88

LPs: 10/12-inch

ELEKTRA......................................5-8 88
Member: Terry Sharpe.

ADVENTURES OF STEVIE V. P&R '90

Singles: 7-inch

MERCURY.....................................3-4 90
Members: Steve Vincent; Melodie Washington; Mick Walsh.

AEROSMITH P&R/LP '73

Singles: 7-inch

COLUMBIA....................................3-5 73-80
GEFFEN.......................................3-4 85-91

Picture Sleeves

GEFFEN.......................................3-4 85-89

LPs: 10/12-inch

COLUMBIA (Except KC-32005)..........5-15 73-86
COLUMBIA (KC-32005 "Aerosmith")...............................20-25 73
(Orange cover. Incorrectly shows *Walking the Dog* as "Walking the Dig.")
COLUMBIA (KC-32005 "Aerosmith") 10-12 73
(Blue cover. Correctly lists *Walking the Dog*.)
GEFFEN......................................5-10 85-87

Promotional LPs

COLUMBIA (187 "Pure Gold")...........50-55 76
(Boxed set of the group's first three LPs.)
Members: Steve Tyler; Tom Hamilton; Joey Kramer; Joe Perry; Brad Whitford; Rick Dufay; Jimmy Crespo.
Also see PERRY, Joe, Project
Also see RUN-D.M.C.

AFRIKA BAMBAATAA: see BAMBAATAA, Afrika

AFRIQUE P&R/R&B/LP '73

Singles: 7-inch

MAINSTREAM.................................3-5 73

LPs: 10/12-inch

MAINSTREAM.................................8-12 73
Members: David T. Walker; Chuck Rainey.

AFRO CUBAN BAND R&B '78

Singles: 7-inch

ARISTA..3-4 78

LPs: 10/12-inch

ARISTA..5-10 78

AFTER THE FIRE P&R/D&D/LP '83

Singles: 12-inch

EPIC...4-8 83

Singles: 7-inch

EPIC...3-4 83-84

LPs: 10/12-inch

EPIC...5-10 82
Members: Peter Banks; Andy Piercy; Ivor Twidell; Tim Haywell; Nick Battle.
Also see BANKS, Peter

AFTERBACH R&B '81

Singles: 7-inch

COLUMBIA/ARC...............................3-4 81

LPs: 10/12-inch

COLUMBIA/ARC...............................5-10 81
Members: Robert Brooken; Mike Brooken.

AFTERNOON DELIGHTS P&R/R&B '81

Singles: 12-inch

MCA..4-8 81

Singles: 7-inch

MCA..3-4 81

LPs: 10/12-inch

MCA..5-10 81

A-HA P&R/D&D/LP '85

Singles: 7-inch

REPRISE.......................................3-6 85-86
W.B. 3-6 85-87

Picture Sleeves

W.B. (Except 29011)........................3-6 85-87
W.B. (29011 "Take on Me")................5-8 85
(Promotional issue only with booklet.)

LPs: 10/12-inch

REPRISE.......................................5-10 85-86
W.B. 5-10 85-88
Members: Morten Harket; Mags Furuholem; Pal Waaktaar.

AIDA D&D '84

Singles: 12-inch

VANGUARD....................................4-6 84

Singles: 7-inch

VANGUARD....................................3-4 84

LPs: 10/12-inch

VANGUARD....................................5-8 84

AIR SUPPLY P&R/LP '80

Singles: 7-inch

ARISTA..3-4 80-86
FLASHBACK...................................3-4 82

Picture Sleeves

ARISTA..3-4 80-86

LPs: 10/12-inch

ARISTA..5-10 80-86
COLUMBIA...................................10-15 77
MFSL (113 "The One That You Love")..25-30 84
NAUTILUS (31 "Lost in Love")..........15-25 82

Members: Graham Russell; Russell Hitchcock; David Moyse; Criston Barker; Ralph Cooper; David Green; Frank Esler-Smith; Rex Goh.

AIRWAVES P&R '78

Singles: 7-inch

A&M....3-4 78-79

LPs: 10/12-inch

A&M....5-10 78-79

Members: John David; Dave Charles; Ray Martinez.

AKENS, Jewel P&R/R&B '65

Singles: 7-inch

AMERICAN INT'L ARTISTS....3-5 75
CAPEHART....10-15 61
COLGEMS....5-8 67
CREST....5-10 62
ERA....5-8 65
ICEPAC (303 "What Would You Do")....10-15
MINASA....5-10 65
RTV....3-5 72
WEST-ONE....3-5

LPs: 10/12-inch

ERA (110 "The Birds & the Bees")....20-30 65

AKKERMAN, Jan LP '73
(With Kaz Lux)

Singles: 7-inch

ATLANTIC....3-4 77-79

LPs: 10/12-inch

ATCO....10-12 73
ATLANTIC....5-10 76-79
SIRE....10-15 73

AL B. SURE! P&R/R&B/LP '88

Singles: 7-inch

W.B. 3-4 88-90

Picture Sleeves

W.B. 3-4 88-90

LPs: 10/12-inch

W.B. 5-8 88-90

Also see JONES, Quincy, James Ingram, Al B. Sure, El DeBarge & Barry White

ALABAMA C&W '77
(Alabama Band)

Singles: 7-inch

GRT....5-10 77
MDJ....4-6 79-80
RCA....3-5 80-93
RCA GOLD STANDARD....3-4 82
SSS INT'L (Colored vinyl)....5-10 81

Picture Sleeves

GRT....10-20 77
RCA....3-4 80-90

LPs: 10/12-inch

ABC/WATERMARK ("American Country Countdown Presents Alabama")....8-12 88
(No selection number used. Promotional issue only.)
ACCORD....5-10 81
ALABAMA RECORDS (78 9-01 "The Alabama Band")....200-400 78
PLANTATION (44 "Wild Country")....40-60 81
RCA....5-10 80-90
SONNY....30-50 79

Members: Randy Owen; Jeff Cook; Teddy Gentry; R. Scott; Mark Herndon.
Also see RICHIE, Lionel, & Alabama
Also see WILD COUNTRY

ALAIMO, Chuck P&R '57
(Chuck Alaimo Quartet)

Singles: 78 rpm

KEN....5-10 57
MGM....5-10 57

Singles: 7-inch

KEN (311 "Leap Frog")....15-25 57
MGM....10-20 57-58

ALAIMO, Steve P&R '62
(With the Redcoats)

Singles: 7-inch

ABC....5-8 66-67
ABC-PAR....5-10 64-66
ATCO....4-8 67-71
CHECKER....10-15 61-63
DADE (1805 "Love Letters")....15-25 59
DICKSON (6445 "Blue Fire")....10-20 60
ENTRANCE....3-5 71-72
ERIC....3-4 83
IMPERIAL....10-15 60-63
LIFETIME....25-40 58
MARLIN (6064 "I Want You to Love Me")....20-30 59
MARLIN (6067 "She's My Baby")....15-25 59

EPs: 7-inch

ABC-PAR (531 "Where the Action Is")....10-20 65
(Juke box issue only.)

LPs: 10/12-inch

ABC-PAR (501 "Starring Steve Alaimo")....15-20 65
(Monaural.)
ABC-PAR (S-501 "Starring Steve Alaimo")....20-30 65
(Stereo.)
ABC-PAR (531 "Where the Action Is")....15-20 65
(Monaural.)
ABC-PAR (S-531 "Where the Action Is")....20-30 65
(Stereo.)
ABC-PAR (551 "Steve Alaimo Sings & Swings")....15-20 66
(Monaural.)
ABC-PAR (S-551 "Steve Alaimo Sings & Swings")....20-30 66
(Stereo.)
CHECKER (2981 "Twist")....25-40 63
CHECKER (2983 "Mashed Potatoes")....25-40 62
CHECKER (2986 "Everyday I Have to Cry")....25-50 63
CROWN (5382 "Steve Alaimo")....10-20 63

Also see RIVERS, Johnny / Steve Alaimo

ALAIMO, Steve, & Betty Wright

Singles: 7-inch

ATCO....4-8 69

Also see ALAIMO, Steve
Also see WRIGHT, Betty

ALAN, Lee

Singles: 7-inch

LEE ALAN PRESENTS ("A Trip to Miami")....400-500 64
(No selection number used. Includes insert sheet. DJ Lee Alan interviews the Beatles.)
LEE ALAN PRESENTS ("A Trip to Miami")....300-400 64
(Without insert sheet.)

Also see BEATLES

ALARM LP '83

Singles: 7-inch

I.R.S. 3-4 83-90

Picture Sleeves

I.R.S. 3-4 83-89

LPs: 10/12-inch

I.R.S. 5-10 83-91

Members: Mike Peters; Nigel Twist; Dave Sharp; Eddie MacDonald.

ALBERT, Eddie

Singles: 78 rpm

KAPP....4-8 54-56

Singles: 7-inch

COLUMBIA....3-5 68
HICKORY....3-6 64-65
KAPP....5-10 54-56

Picture Sleeves

KAPP (134 "Little Child")....10-15 56

LPs: 10/12-inch

COLUMBIA....8-12 68
HAMILTON....10-15 59

ALBERT, Eddie, & Sondra Lee P&R '56

Singles: 78 rpm

KAPP....4-8 56

Singles: 7-inch

KAPP....5-10 56

Also see ALBERT, Eddie

ALBERT, Morris P&R/LP '75

Singles: 7-inch

RCA....3-5 75-76

LPs: 10/12-inch

RCA....5-10 75-76

ALBERTI, Willy P&R '59

Singles: 7-inch

EPIC....3-6 59
LONDON....3-6 59
PHILIPS....4-6 65

LPs: 10/12-inch

LONDON....5-15 59

ALBRIGHT, Gerald R&B '87

Singles: 7-inch

ATLANTIC....3-4 87-88

LPs: 10/12-inch

ATLANTIC....5-8 88

ALCATRAZZ LP '84

Singles: 7-inch

ROCSHIRE....4-8 83

Picture Sleeves

ROCSHIRE....8-15 83

LPs: 10/12-inch

CAPITOL....15-25 85
ROCSHIRE....15-25 83-84

Members: Graham Bonnet; Steve Vai; Yngwie Malmsteen.
Also see RAINBOW
Also see MALMSTEEN, Yngwie J.
Also see SCHENKER, Michael, Group

ALDO NOVA: see NOVA, Aldo

ALDRICH, Renee R&B '87

Singles: 7-inch

JAM PACKED....3-4 87

ALDRICH, Ronnie LP '61

LPs: 10/12-inch

LONDON PHASE 4....5-15 61-71

ALEEM R&B/D&D '84
(Featuring Leroy Burgess; Aleems)

Singles: 12-inch

ATLANTIC....4-6 87
NIA....5-8 85

Singles: 7-inch

ATLANTIC....3-4 86-87
NIA....3-5 84-85

LPs: 10/12-inch

ATLANTIC....5-10 87

Members: Leroy Burgess; Taharqa Aleem; Tunde-Ra Aleem.
Also see BLACK IVORY

ALEEMS: see ALEEM

ALESSI P&R '82

Singles: 7-inch

A&M....3-4 77-79
QWEST....3-4 82

Picture Sleeves

A&M....3-4 77-79

LPs: 10/12-inch

A&M....5-10 76-79
QWEST....5-10 82

Members: Bill Alessi; Bob Alessi.

ALEXANDER, Arthur P&R/R&B '62

Singles: 7-inch

AT YOU....3-6
BUDDAH....3-6 75-76
DOT....5-10 62-64
GORDA....4-8
MONUMENT....4-8 68
MUSIC MILL....4-8 77
SOUND STAGE 7....4-8 65-71
W.B. 3-6 72-73

EPs: 7-inch

DOT (434 "You Better Move On")....25-35 62
(Stereo. Juke box issue only.)

LPs: 10/12-inch
DOT (3434 "You Better Move On") ... 35-45 62
(Monaural.)
DOT (25434 "You Better Move On") 40-55 62
(Stereo.)
W.B. ... 8-15 72
Also see ALEXANDER, June

ALEXANDER, David R&B '87
Singles: 7-inch
SOUND TOWN ... 3-4 87

ALEXANDER, Goldie R&B '82
Singles: 7-inch
ARISTA ... 3-4 82

ALEXANDER, Joe, & Cubans
Singles: 78 rpm
BALLAD (1008 "Oh Maria") ... 300-500 55
Singles: 7-inch
BALLAD (1008 "Oh Maria") ... 800-1200 55
Members: Joe Alexander; Chuck Berry; Faith Douglas; Freddy Golden.
Also see BERRY, Chuck

ALEXANDER, June
(Arthur Alexander)
Singles: 7-inch
JUDD (1020 "Sally Sue Brown") ... 25-35 60
Also see ALEXANDER, Arthur

ALEXANDER, Margie R&B '74
Singles: 12-inch
CHI-SOUND ... 4-8 77
Singles: 7-inch
ATLANTIC ... 3-5 71
CHI-SOUND ... 3-4 76-77
FUTURE STARS ... 3-5 74

ALFI & HARRY P&R '56
(David Seville)
Singles: 78 rpm
LIBERTY ... 4-8 55-57
Singles: 7-inch
LIBERTY ... 5-10 55-57
Also see SEVILLE, David

ALFIE: see SILAS, Alfie

ALFONZO R&B '82
(Alfonzo Jones)
Singles: 12-inch
JOE-WES ... 4-6 83
Singles: 7-inch
JOE-WES ... 3-4 82
LARC ... 3-4 82
LPs: 10/12-inch
LARC ... 5-10 83

ALI, Muhammad, & Frank Sinatra
LPs: 10/12-inch
ST. JOHN'S (1 "Ali and His Gang Fight Tooth Decay") ... 20-40
(Promotional issue only.)
Also see CLAY, Cassius
Also see SINATRA, Frank

ALIAS LP '90
Singles: 7-inch
MERCURY ... 3-5 79-80
LPs: 10/12-inch
EMI ... 5-8 90
MERCURY ... 5-10 79
Members: Fred Curci; Steve DeMarchi; Dorman Cogburn; Jimmy Dougherty; Jo Jo Billingsley; Leon Wilkeson; Billy Powell; Barry Harwood; Ricky Powell; Artimus Pyle.
Also see COLLINS, Allen, Band
Also see LYNYRD SKYNYRD
Also see SHERIFF

ALICE COOPER: see COOPER, Alice

ALICE IN CHAINS LP '91
LPs: 10/12-inch
COLUMBIA (2192 "Face Lift") ... 50-75 90
(Promotional issue only.)
COLUMBIA (46075 "Face Lift") ... 5-10 91
COLUMBIA (52475 "Face Lift") ... 5-10 92
COLUMBIA (57804 "Jar of Flies") ... 12-18 94
(Promotional issue only.)
COLUMBIA (67248 "Jar of Flies"/"Sap") ... 10-15 94
(Two colored vinyl discs.)

ALICE WONDER LAND P&R '63
Singles: 7-inch
BARDELL (774 "He's Mine") ... 10-20 63
UNITED INTERNATIONAL ... 10-15
Also see SWANS

ALISHA R&B/D&D '84
Singles: 12-inch
VANGUARD ... 4-6 84-86
Singles: 7-inch
MCA ... 3-4 90
RCA ... 3-4 87
VANGUARD ... 3-4 84-86
Picture Sleeves
RCA ... 3-4 87
LPs: 10/12-inch
MCA ... 5-8 90

ALIVE 'N KICKING P&R/LP '70
(Alive 'N Kickin')
Singles: 7-inch
A&M ... 3-4
ROULETTE ... 4-8 70-71
Picture Sleeves
A&M ... 3-4
LPs: 10/12-inch
ROULETTE (42052 "Alive 'N Kickin' ") ... 20-30 70
(Commercial issue.)
ROULETTE (42052 "Alive 'N Kickin' ") ... 40-60 70
(Promotional issue.)

ALL POINTS BULLETIN BAND R&B '76
Singles: 7-inch
LITTLE CITY ... 3-5 75-79

ALL SPORTS BAND P&R '81
Singles: 7-inch
RADIO ... 3-4 81-82
LPs: 10/12-inch
RADIO ... 5-10 81

ALLAN, Davie P&R '65
(With the Arrows)
Singles: 7-inch
A.O.A. ... 3-6 76
CUDE (101 "War Path") ... 30-40 63
MARC (3223 "War Path") ... 20-30 63
MGM ... 3-6 71-73
MRC ... 3-5 84
PRIVATE STOCK ... 3-5 74
SIDEWALK ... 10-15 64
TOWER ... 5-10 65-68
WHAT ... 3-5 82
LPs: 10/12-inch
ALKOR ... 5-10 84
ARROW DYNAMICS ... 8-12 85
TOWER ... 15-25 65-68
WHAT ... 5-10 83
Members: Davie Allan; Steve Pugh; Larry Brown; Paul Johnson; Don Manning; Tony Allwine.
Also see ANNETTE
Also see CURB, Mike
Also see DALE, Dick
Also see HONDELLS
Also see NAYLOR, Jerry
Also see PARIS SISTERS
Also see RONSTADT, Linda
Also see STAFFORD, Terry

ALLAN, Davie / Eternity's Children / Main Attraction / Sunrays
EPs: 7-inch
TOWER (4557 "Selections from April Albums") ... 25-50 68
(Promotional issue only.)
Also see ALLAN, Davie
Also see ETERNITY'S CHILDREN
Also see MAIN ATTRACTION
Also see SUNRAYS

ALLEN, Annisteen R&B '53
(With Her Home Town Boys)
Singles: 78 rpm
CAPITOL ... 10-15 55
DECCA ... 10-15 56-57
FEDERAL ... 10-15 51-52
KING ... 10-15 46-54
Singles: 7-inch
CAPITOL ... 20-30 55
DECCA ... 15-25 56-57
KING ... 20-30 53-54
TODD ... 10-20
TRUE SOUND ... 5-10
WIG ... 5-10 59
Also see ALLEN, Ernestine
Also see GREER, John

ALLEN, Annisteen, & Melvin Moore
Singles: 7-inch
TODD ... 5-10 59
Also see ALLEN, Annisteen

ALLEN, Dayton LP '60
LPs: 10/12-inch
GRAND AWARD ... 10-15 60

ALLEN, Donna R&B '86
Singles: 7-inch
OCEANA ... 3-4 88
TWENTY-ONE ... 3-4 86-87
Picture Sleeves
OCEANA ... 3-4 88
LPs: 10/12-inch
OCEANA ... 5-8 88
TWENTY-ONE ... 5-10 86-87

ALLEN, Ernestine
(Annisteen Allen)
Singles: 7-inch
TRU-SOUND ... 5-10 62
LPs: 10/12-inch
TRU-SOUND ... 20-35 62
Also see ALLEN, Annisteen

ALLEN, Jonelle R&B '78
Singles: 7-inch
ALEXANDER STREET ... 3-4 78

ALLEN, Lee P&R '58
Singles: 78 rpm
ALADDIN ... 10-20 56
EMBER ... 20-40 58
Singles: 7-inch
ALADDIN ... 15-25 56
COLLECTABLES ... 3-4 82
EMBER ... 10-20 58-62
WAND ... 5-10 60s
EPs: 7-inch
EMBER (103 "Walkin' with Mr. Lee") ... 50-75 58
LPs: 10/12-inch
EMBER (200 "Walkin' with Mr. Lee") ... 75-125 58
(Red label.)
EMBER (200 "Walkin' with Mr Lee") ... 60-80 58
("Logs" label. Ember logo is formed with logs.)
EMBER (200 "Walkin' with Mr. Lee") ... 25-40 60
(Black label.)
Also see DOMINO, Fats
Also see BLASTERS
Also see LITTLE RICHARD
Also see SMITH, Huey
Also see STRAY CATS

ALLEN, Peter LP '79
Singles: 12-inch
A&M ... 4-8 79
Singles: 7-inch
A&M ... 3-5 74-82
ARISTA ... 3-4 83-84
METROMEDIA ... 3-5 71-73
LPs: 10/12-inch
A&M ... 5-10 74-82
ARISTA ... 5-10 83-84
METROMEDIA ... 10-15 71-72

Also see ALLEN, Chris & Peter

ALLEN, R. Justice R&B '86

Singles: 7-inch

CATAWBA 3-4 86

ALLEN, Rance, Group R&B '73

Singles: 7-inch

CAPITOL 3-5 77-79
GOSPEL TRUTH 3-5 72-73
STAX 3-4 78-81
TRUTH 3-5 74-75

LPs: 10/12-inch

CAPITOL 5-10 77-79
GOSPEL TRUTH 8-12 72-74
MYRRH 5-10 84
STAX 5-10 78-81
TRUTH 8-10 75
Members: Rance Allen; Thomas Allen; Steven Allen; Esau Allen; Linda Mendez; Annie Mendez; Judy Mendez.

ALLEN, Rex C&W '49
(With the Arizona Wranglers & Jerry Byrd)

Singles: 78 rpm

DECCA (Except 30651) 5-10 52-57
DECCA (30651 "Knock Knock, Rattle") 10-20 56
MERCURY 5-10 49-55

Singles: 7-inch

BUENA VISTA 4-8 59
DECCA (Except 28000 thru 30000 series) 3-8 56-72
DECCA (28000 & 29000 series) 5-10 52-56
DECCA (30000 series except 30651) 5-10 56
DECCA (30651 "Knock Knock, Rattle") 15-20 56
JMI 3-5 73
MCA 3-5 79
MERCURY 5-10 53-62
WILDCAT 4-6

Picture Sleeves

MERCURY 5-10 63

EPs: 7-inch

DECCA 10-20 56
MERCURY 10-20 53-56

LPs: 10/12-inch

BUENA VISTA (3307 "Rex Allen Sings 16 Favorites") 40-50 61
COLLECTOR'S CLASSICS 5-10
CORAL 5-10 73
DECCA (5000 series) 10-15 68-70
(Decca LP numbers in this series preceded by a "7" or a "DL-7" are stereo issues.)
DECCA (8000 series) 20-30 56-58
DESIGN 10-15 62
DISNEYLAND 6-10 70
HACIENDA (101 "Country Songs I Love") 50-60
JMI (4003 "Rex Allen Sings") 20-30
MCA 5-10
MERCURY (20719 "The Faith of a Man") 15-25 62
(Monaural.)
MERCURY (20752 "Rex Allen Sings and Tells Tales") 15-25 62
(Monaural.)
MERCURY (60719 "The Faith of a Man") 20-30 62
(Stereo.)
MERCURY (60752 "Rex Allen Sings and Tells Tales") 20-30 62
(Stereo.)
PICKWICK/HILLTOP 10-15 65
VOCALION 6-10 70
WING 10-15 64-66
Session: Jud Conlon Singers.
Also see PAGE, Patti, & Rex Allen

ALLEN, Richie P&R '60
(With the Pacific Surfers)

Singles: 7-inch

ERA 8-12 61
IMPERIAL 10-20 60-63
TOWER 5-10 66

LPs: 10/12-inch

IMPERIAL 40-60 63
Members: Richie Allen; Ron Lloyd; Jim MacMurdo; Bill Cooper; Ray Pohlman; Sandy Nelson; Les Weiser. Session: Richie Podolor.
Also see NELSON, Sandy
Also see PODOLOR, Richie

ALLEN, Ricky R&B '63

Singles: 7-inch

AGE 5-10 63-64
APOGEE 5-10 64
BRIGHT STAR 4-8 66-67
FOUR BROTHERS (401 "I Can't Stand Signifying") 10-15
U.S.A. 5-10 65

ALLEN, Steve P&R/LP '55

Singles: 78 rpm

BRUNSWICK 4-8 53
CORAL 4-8 55-56

Singles: 7-inch

BRUNSWICK 5-10 53
CORAL 5-10 55-56
DOT 4-8 59-66
DUNHILL (Except 4097) 3-5 67-68
DUNHILL (4097 "Here Comes Sgt. Pepper") 4-8 67
SIGNATURE 3-6 59-60

Picture Sleeves

DOT 5-10 65

EPs: 7-inch

BRUNSWICK 10-20 53
COLUMBIA 10-15 50s
CORAL 10-20 55-56
DECCA 15-20 55
WOODBURY'S 10-20

LPs: 10/12-inch

COLUMBIA (2554 "Steve Allen") 20-30 56
(10-inch LP.)
CORAL (100 "Jazz Story") 25-35 59
(Narration by Steve Allen, music by various artists.)
CORAL (57000 series, except 57099) 15-20 55-56
CORAL (57099 "The James Dean Story") 35-50 56
(With Bill Randle.)
CORAL (57400 series) 10-20 63
(Monaural.)
CORAL (7-57400 series) 10-20 63
(Stereo.)
DECCA 20-25 55
DOT (Except 3472 & 3517) 10-20 59-66
DOT (3472 "Steve Allen's Funny Fone Calls") 15-20 63
DOT (3517 "More Funny Fone Calls) 15-20 63
DUNHILL 8-10 67
EMARCY 15-20 58
HAMILTON 10-15 59-64
MERCURY 10-15 61
PETE 5-10 69
ROULETTE 15-20 59
SIGNATURE (Except 1004) 15-20 59
SIGNATURE (1004 "Man on the Street") 30-40 59
(With Louis Nye, Tom Poston and Don Knotts.)
Also see PRESLEY, Elvis

ALLEN, Steve, & Jayne Meadows

Singles: 78 rpm

CORAL 4-8 55

Singles: 7-inch

CORAL 5-10 55
Also see ALLEN, Steve

ALLEN, Vee R&B '73

Singles: 7-inch

LION 3-5 73
MCA 3-4 83

LPs: 10/12-inch

MCA 5-10 83

ALLEN, Woody LP '64

Singles: 7-inch

U.A. 3-5 72

Picture Sleeves

U.A. 4-6 72

LPs: 10/12-inch

BELL 10-15 67
CAPITOL 8-12 68
CASABLANCA 8-12 79
COLPIX 20-30 64-65
U.A. (800 series) 6-10 77
U.A. (9900 series) 8-12 72

ALLENS, Arvee
(Ritchie Valens)

Singles: 7-inch

DEL-FI (4111 "Fast Freight") 20-30 59
(Reissued as by Ritchie Valens.)
Also see VALENS, Ritchie

ALLEY CATS P&R/R&B '63

Singles: 7-inch

EPIC 5-10 65
PHILLES (108 "Puddin n' Tain") 15-25 62
WHIPPETT (202 "This Thing Called Love") 25-50 56
WHIPPETT (209 "Last Night") 25-50 57
Members: Chester Pipkin; Gary Pipkin; Bobby Sheen; Sheridan Spencer; Brice Coefield; James Barker. Session: Jack Nitzsche.
Also see NITZSCHE, Jack
Also see PIPKINS
Also see SHEEN, Bobby

ALLISON, Gene P&R/R&B '57

Singles: 78 rpm

CALVERT 10-15 56
DECCA 10-15 57
VEE JAY 10-20 57

Singles: 7-inch

CALVERT 15-25 56
CHAMPION 10-15 59
CHEROKEE 10-15 59
DECCA 10-15 57
MONUMENT 5-10 65
REF-O-REE 5-10
VALDOT 5-10 62
VEE JAY 10-20 57-60

LPs: 10/12-inch

VEE JAY (1009 "Gene Allison") 100-125 59
(Maroon label.)
VEE JAY (1009 "Gene Allison") 40-60 59
(Black label.)

ALLISONS P&R '63

Singles: 7-inch

COLUMBIA 4-8 61
SMASH 4-8 62
TIP (1011 "Surfer Street") 15-20 63

ALLMAN, Duane LP '72

LPs: 10/12-inch

CAPRICORN 8-12 72-74
Also see DEREK & DOMINOS

ALLMAN, Duane & Gregg LP '72

Singles: 7-inch

BOLD 5-8 73

LPs: 10/12-inch

BOLD (301 "Duane & Gregg Allman") 20-25 72
(Gatefold cover.)
BOLD (301 "Duane & Gregg Allman") 8-10 73
(Standard cover.)
SPRINGBOARD 8-10 75
Also see ALLMAN, Duane
Also see ALLMAN, Gregg
Also see ALLMAN BROTHERS BAND
Also see ALLMAN JOYS

ALLMAN, Gregg P&R/LP '73
(Gregg Allman Band)

Singles: 7-inch

CAPRICORN 3-5 73-77
EPIC 3-4 87-89

LPs: 10/12-inch

CAPRICORN 8-12 73-77
EPIC 5-10 87-89

ROBERT KLEIN
("Interview") 40-60 81
(Promotional issue only.)
Also see ALLMAN, Duane & Gregg
Also see ALLMAN & WOMAN
Also see ALLMAN BROTHERS BAND
Also see ALLMAN JOYS

ALLMAN & WOMAN

Singles: 7-inch

W.B. 3-5 77

LPs: 10/12-inch

W.B. 8-10 77
Members: Gregg Allman; Cher.
Also see ALLMAN, Gregg
Also see CHER

ALLMAN BROTHERS BAND LP '70

Singles: 7-inch

ARISTA.................................... 3-4 80-81
CAPRICORN (Except 036)................ 3-5 71-79
CAPRICORN (036 "Jessica")........... 30-50 73
EPIC 3-4 90

Picture Sleeves

ARISTA.................................... 3-5 81

EPs: 7-inch

ATLANTIC 10-20 73
(Juke box issue only.)
CAPRICORN.................................... 10-20 73
(Juke box issue only.)

LPs: 10/12-inch

ARISTA.................................... 5-10 80-81
ATCO.................................... 15-20 69-73
CAPRICORN (Except 802)................ 8-15 72-79
CAPRICORN (802 "The Allman Brothers Band at Fillmore East") 15-20 71
EPIC 5-8 90
K-TEL 5-10
MFSL (2-157 "Eat a Peach") 30-45 85
MFSL (213 "Brothers and Sisters") ... 20-25 94
NAUTILUS (30 "Live at the Fillmore") 50-100
(Half-speed mastered.)
POLYDOR (6339 "Best of the Allman Brothers Band") 5-10 89
POLYDOR (839-417 "The Allman Brothers Band") 25-35 89
(Six-LP boxed set, with booklet.)
Members: Duane Allman; Gregg Allman; Dicky Betts; Berry Oakley; Butch Trucks; Johnny Johanson; Les Dudek; Chuck Leavell; David Goldflies; Paul Hornsby; Dan Toler.
Also see ALLMAN, Duane & Gregg
Also see BETTS, Richard
Also see DUDEK, Les
Also see HOUR GLASS
Also see SEA LEVEL
Also see 31ST of FEBRUARY

ALLMAN JOYS

Singles: 7-inch

DIAL (4046 "Spoonful") 25-35 66

LPs: 10/12-inch

DIAL (6005 "Early Allman") 10-15 73
Members: Duane Allman; Gregg Allman; Bob Keller; Maynard Portwood; Ralph Balinger; Ronnie Wilkin; Tommy Amato; Jack Jackson; Bobby Dennis; Bill Connell.
Also see ALLMAN, Duane & Gregg

ALMANAC SINGERS

Singles: 78 rpm

GENERAL 8-12 41-43

Albums: 78 rpm

COMMODORE ("Deep Sea Chanteys & Whaling Ballads") 15-25
(Selection number not known.)
COMMODORE (10 "Sod Buster Ballads") 15-25

LPs: 10/12-inch

COMMODORE (002 "Deep Sea Chanteys & Whaling Ballads" & "Sod Buster Ballads") 20-30 51
FOLKWAYS (85 "Labor Union Songs") 15-25 55
Members: Pete Seeger; Woody Guthrie: Peter Hawes: Millard Lampell
Also see SEEGER, Pete
Also see WEAVERS

ALMEIDA, Laurindo LP '62

(With the Modern Jazz Quartet; with Bossa Nova All Stars)

Singles: 7-inch

ATLANTIC.................................... 4-6 64
CAPITOL.................................... 3-8 55-65
PACIFIC JAZZ 5-8 55

EPs: 7-inch

CAPITOL.................................... 5-15 56-59
CORAL.................................... 5-10 54-56
PACIFIC JAZZ 10-15 54

LPs: 10/12-inch

ATLANTIC.................................... 10-20 64
CAPITOL (Except 8000 series)......... 15-25 59-65
CAPITOL (8000 series).................. 20-35 56-58
CORAL.................................... 25-45 54-56
CRYSTAL CLEAR 5-8 80
DAYBREAK 5-10 73
DOBRE 5-10 76-77
INNER CITY.................................... 5-8 79
PACIFIC JAZZ (7 "Laurindo Almeida Quartet") 50-75 54
(10-inch LP.)
PACIFIC JAZZ (13 "Laurindo Almeida Quartet, Vol. 2") 50-75 54
(10-inch LP.)
SURREY 10-20 65
WORLD PACIFIC 25-40 56-62
Also see BYRD, Charlie
Also see DAVIS, Sammy, Jr., & Laurindo Almeida
Also see GETZ, Stan, & Laurindo Almeida
Also see SOMMERS, Joanie, & Laurindo Almeida

ALMEIDA, Laurindo / Chico Hamilton

LPs: 10/12-inch

JAZZTONE 10-20 64
Also see ALMEIDA, Laurindo
Also see HAMILTON, Chico

ALMOND, Marc P&R/LP '89

Singles: 7-inch

CAPITOL.................................... 3-4 89

Picture Sleeves

CAPITOL.................................... 3-4 89

LPs: 10/12-inch

CAPITOL.................................... 5-8 89
Also see MARK - ALMOND BAND
Also see SOFT CELL

ALPACA PHASE III R&B '74

Singles: 7-inch

ATLANTIC.................................... 3-5 74

ALPERT, Herb P&R/LP '62

(With Tijuana Brass; Herbie Alpert)

Singles: 12-inch

A&M 4-6 79-84
(Black vinyl.)
A&M 5-8 84
(Colored vinyl.)

Singles: 7-inch

A&M (Except 700 series) 3-5 66-87
A&M (700 series) 3-8 62-66
ANDEX.................................... 4-6 59
CAROL.................................... 4-6 59
ROWE/AMI 4-8 66
("Play Me" Sales Stimulator promotional issue.)

Picture Sleeves

A&M (Except 700 series) 3-5 66-87
A&M (700 series) 3-6 65-66

EPs: 7-inch

A&M 4-8 65-66
(Juke box issues only.)

LPs: 10/12-inch

A&M (Except 100 series) 5-10 66-87
A&M (100 series) 8-15 62-66
MFSL (053 "Rise") 25-50 81
Members: Lou Pagani; John Pisano; Bob Edmondson; Tonni Kalash; Nick Ceroli; Pat Senatore.
Also see HALL, Lani, & Herb Alpert

ALPERT, Herb, & Hugh Masekela LP '78

Singles: 7-inch

A&M/HORIZON 3-4 78

Picture Sleeves

A&M/HORIZON 3-5 78

LPs: 10/12-inch

A&M/HORIZON 5-10 78
Also see ALPERT, Herb
Also see MASEKELA, Hugh

ALPHAVILLE P&R/D&D/LP '84

Singles: 12-inch

ATLANTIC 4-6 84-86

Singles: 7-inch

ATLANTIC 3-4 84-88

Picture Sleeves

ATLANTIC 3-4 84-88

LPs: 10/12-inch

ATLANTIC 5-10 84-86
Members: Marian Gold; Bernie Lloyd; Frank Mertens.

ALTON & JOHNNY R&B '80

Singles: 7-inch

POLYDOR.................................... 3-5 80
Members: Johnny Bristol; Alton McClain.
Also see BRISTOL, Johnny
Also see McCLAIN, Alton, & Destiny

ALVIN, Dave LP '87

(With the Red Devils)

Singles: 7-inch

ENIGMA 5-8 87

LPs: 10/12-inch

EPIC 5-10 87
Also see BLASTERS
Also see X

ALVIN LEE: see LEE, Alvin

ALWAYS, Billy R&B '82

Singles: 7-inch

EPIC 3-4 88
WAYLO 3-4 82

AMAZING RHYTHM ACES C&W/P&R/LP '75

Singles: 7-inch

ABC 3-5 75-79
COLUMBIA.................................... 3-4 79
W.B. 3-4 80

LPs: 10/12-inch

ABC 10-20 75-78
COLUMBIA.................................... 10-15 79
W.B. 8-10 80
Members: Russell Smith; James Brown Jr; Byrd Burton; Stick Davis; Billy Earhart III; James Hooker; Butch McDade.

AMAZULU P&R '87

Singles: 7-inch

MANGO 3-4 87
Members: Ann Marie Ruddock; Sharon Bailey; Lesley Beach.

AMBASSADORS R&B '69

Singles: 7-inch

ARCTIC 4-8 68-69
ATLANTIC 5-10 67-68
SOUND STAGE 7 .... 5-10 67-68

LPs: 10/12-inch

ARCTIC 10-20 69
Members: Bobby Todd; Herley Johnson; Orlando Oliphant.
Also see CREME D' COCOA

AMBOY DUKES P&R/LP '68

Singles: 7-inch

MAINSTREAM.................................... 6-12 67-69

LPs: 10/12-inch

AUDIOFIDELITY (1005 "Journey to the Center of the Mind") 20-25 83
(Picture disc.)
DISCREET 10-20
MAINSTREAM (801 "Journeys and Migrations") 15-20 74

MAINSTREAM (6104 "Amboy Dukes")....35-55 68
MAINSTREAM (6112 "Journey to the Center of the Mind")....35-55 68
MAINSTREAM (6118 "Migration")....30-40 68
MAINSTREAM (6125 "Best of the Original Amboy Dukes")....25-35 69
POLYDOR....10-20 70

Members: Ted Nugent; Greg Arama; Rusty Day; John Drake; Steve Farmer; Dave Palmer; Andy Solomon; Rod Grange; K.J. Knight; John Angelos.

Also see NUGENT, Ted

AMBROSIA — P&R/LP '75

Singles: 7-inch

20TH FOX....3-5 74-78
W.B. 3-4 78-82

LPs: 10/12-inch

NAUTILUS....10-15 81
(Half-speed mastered.)
20TH FOX....8-10 74-78
W.B. 5-10 78-82

Members: David Pack; Burleigh Drummond; Joe Puerta; Christopher North.

Also see PACK, David
Also see PARSONS, Alan, Project

AMECHE, Don, & Frances Langford — LP '62

EPs: 7-inch

COLUMBIA....8-15 61
(Promotional only.)

LPs: 10/12-inch

COLUMBIA (1000 & 8000 series)....15-20 61-62
COLUMBIA (30000 series)....8-12 71

AMERICA — P&R/LP '72

Singles: 7-inch

AMERICAN INT'L....3-5 79
CAPITOL....3-4 79-85
W.B. 3-5 72-77

Picture Sleeves

AMERICAN INT'L....3-6 79
CAPITOL....3-4 82-83
W.B. 3-5 72-74

LPs: 10/12-inch

CAPITOL....5-10 79-85
W.B. (Except 2576)....8-12 72-77
W.B. (2576 "America")....15-25 71
(Does NOT include *A Horse with No Name.*)
W.B. (2576 "America")....8-12 72
(Has *A Horse with No Name.*)

Members: Gerry Beckley; Dan Peek; Dewey Bunnell.

Also see PEEK, Dan

AMERICAN BREED — P&R '67

Singles: 7-inch

ABC....3-5 75
ACTA....5-10 67-69
MCA....3-4 84
PARAMOUNT....3-5 70

Picture Sleeves

ACTA....8-10 68

LPs: 10/12-inch

ACTA....15-20 67-68

Members: Gary Loizzo; Al Ciner; Chuck Colbert; Lee Graziano; Kevin Murphy.

Also see RUFUS

AMERICAN COMEDY NETWORK — P&R '84

Singles: 7-inch

CRITIQUE....3-4 84

EPs: 7-inch

CRITIQUE (704 "American Comedy Network")....4-6 84

LPs: 10/12-inch

CRITIQUE....5-10 84

AMERICAN DREAM — LP '70

Singles: 7-inch

AMPEX....3-5 70
DEMIK....4-8 68

Picture Sleeves

AMPEX....3-5 70

LPs: 10/12-inch

AMPEX....15-20 70

Members: Nick Jameson; Dooley Van Winkle; Nicky Indelicato; Don Ferris; Mickey Brook.

AMERICAN FLYER — P&R/LP '76

Singles: 7-inch

U.A. 3-5 76-77

Picture Sleeves

U.A. 3-5 76-77

LPs: 10/12-inch

U.A. 8-10 76-77

Members: Eric Kaz; Steve Katz; Craig Fuller; Doug Yule.

Also see PURE PRAIRIE LEAGUE
Also see VELVET UNDERGROUND

AMES, Ed — P&R '65

Singles: 7-inch

RCA....3-8 63-73

Picture Sleeves

RCA....3-8 67

LPs: 10/12-inch

CAMDEN....4-8 72-73
RCA....5-15 64-77

Also see AMES BROTHERS

AMES, Nancy — P&R '64

Singles: 7-inch

ABC....3-5 68
EPIC (Except 10056)....3-5 66-68
EPIC (10056 "I Don't Want to Talk About It")....8-12 66
LIBERTY....3-6 61-65
SC....3-5 68

Picture Sleeves

EPIC....4-6 66

LPs: 10/12-inch

EPIC....5-12 66-68
LIBERTY....10-20 61-65
SUNSET....5-10 60s

Also see LOPEZ, Trini, with the Ventures & Nancy Ames

AMES BROTHERS — P&R '49

Singles: 78 rpm

CORAL....5-15 50-53
RCA (Except E3-VB-291)....5-10 53-57
RCA (E3-VB-291 "The Man with the Banjo")....10-20 54
(Special "National Banjo Week" issue, "Commemorating the Invention of the Banjo. The First Native American Musical Instrument." Promotional issue only.)

Singles: 7-inch

CORAL....10-20 50-53
EPIC....4-8 62-63
MCA....3-5 73
RCA....10-20 53-62

Picture Sleeves

EPIC....4-8 62
RCA....10-20 60

EPs: 7-inch

CORAL....10-25 50-53
RCA....10-25 53-61

LPs: 10/12-inch

CAMDEN....5-10
CORAL....15-30 53-62
EPIC....10-15 63
RCA (1000 series)....5-10 75
RCA (1200 thru 2200 series)....20-40 55-61
RCA (2800 series)....8-15 64
RCA (6000 series)....5-10 72
VOCALION....5-10 68

Members: Ed Ames; Joe Ames; Gene Ames; Vic Ames.

Also see AMES, Ed
Also see COMO, Perry / Ames Brothers / Harry Belafonte / Radio City Music Hall Orch.
Also see MOONEY, Art, & His Orchestra

AMESBURY, Bill — P&R '74

Singles: 7-inch

CASABLANCA....3-5 74-75

LPs: 10/12-inch

CAPITOL....5-10 76
CASABLANCA....8-10 74

AMMONS, Albert — R&B '47

(With His Rhythm Kings)

Singles: 78 rpm

COMMODORE....10-20 44-47
MERCURY....10-20 45-50

Singles: 7-inch

MERCURY....25-50 51
(We're not yet certain which specific titles are on 45 and which are 78 rpm only.)

EPs: 7-inch

MERCURY (3044 "Boogie Woogie Piano")....50-100 54

LPs: 10/12-inch

BLUES CLASSICS....5-10 83
COMMODORE (20,002 "Boogie Woogie and the Blues")....100-200 52
MERCURY (25012 "Boogie Woogie Piano")....100-200 54
(10-inch LP.)

AMMONS, Albert, & Pete Johnson

(Pete Johnson & Albert Ammons)

Singles: 78 rpm

RCA....5-10 41

EPs: 7-inch

RCA ("EPB" series)....10-20 50s

Also see AMMONS, Albert
Also see JOHNSON, Pete

AMMONS, Gene — R&B '47

Singles: 78 rpm

CHESS....10-15 50
DECCA....5-10 54
MERCURY....5-15 47-53
PRESTIGE....5-10 51-57

Singles: 7-inch

ARGO....4-8 62
DECCA....5-10 54
MERCURY....5-10 50-53
PRESTIGE (100 thru 400 series)....3-8 60-68
PRESTIGE (700 series)....3-5 69-73
(This "700" series can easily be distinguished from the early fifties "700" series that follows. The company address is shown as in New Jersey. In the '50s the company was in New York.)
PRESTIGE (713 thru 921)....5-10 51-57
(Black vinyl.)
PRESTIGE (713 thru 921)....10-20 51-57
(Colored vinyl.)
RAY BRA....4-6
SAVOY....4-8 60
UNITED....5-10 53-54

EPs: 7-inch

EMARCY....20-30 54
PRESTIGE....25-50 51

LPs: 10/12-inch

ARGO....20-30 62
CHESS....30-40 59
EMARCY (400 series)....8-12 76
EMARCY (26000 series)....50-75 54
(10-inch LPs.)
ENJA....5-10 81
MERCURY....20-30 60-63
OLYMPIC....5-10 74
PRESTIGE (014 thru 192)....5-10 82-85
PRESTIGE (7010 thru 7132)....25-50 55-58
(Each of the following LPs in this series was reissued using the original selection number but a different title: Prestige 7050, *All Star Jam Session,* was reissued as *Woofin' & Tweetin;* Prestige 7039, *Hi-Fi Jam Session,* was reissued as *Happy Blues,* and Prestige 7060, *Jammin' with Gene,* was reissued as *Not Really the Blues.* These three 1960 reissues are valued in the $20 to $35 range.)
PRESTIGE (7146 thru 7287)....20-35 58-64
PRESTIGE (7300 & 7400 series)....10-20 65-68
PRESTIGE (7500 thru 7800 series)....8-15 68-70
PRESTIGE (10000 series)....5-10 71-74
PRESTIGE (24000 series)....8-12 73-81
ROOTS....5-10 76
SAVOY....15-25 61
TRIP....5-10 73-75
VEE JAY....15-25 60
WING....10-20 60-63

Also see McDUFF, Brother Jack, & Gene Ammons

AMMONS, Gene, & Richard "Groove" Holmes
LPs: 10/12-inch
PACIFIC JAZZ (32 "Groovin' with Jug") 15-25 61
Also see HOLMES, Richard "Groove"

AMMONS, Gene, & Sonny Stitt
Singles: 78 rpm
PRESTIGE 5-10 50-51
Singles: 7-inch
PRESTIGE (700 series) 5-10 50-51
(Black vinyl.)
PRESTIGE (700 series) 10-20 50-51
(Colored vinyl.)
EPs: 7-inch
PRESTIGE 25-50 51
LPs: 10/12-inch
ARGO 25-35 63
CADET 10-20 67
CHESS 30-40 60
PRESTIGE (107 "Gene Ammons") 75-100 51
(10-inch LP.)
PRESTIGE (112 "Gene Ammons with Sonny Stitt") 75-100 51
(10-inch LP.)
PRESTIGE (127 "The Gene Ammons Band") 75-100 52
(10-inch LP.)
PRESTIGE (149 "The Gene Ammons Quartet") 75-100 51
(10-inch LP.)
PRESTIGE (7600 series) 6-10 69
PRESTIGE (10000 series) 5-10 76
VERVE (8400 series) 15-20 61-62
(Reads "MGM Records - a Division of Metro-Goldwyn-Mayer, Inc." at bottom of label.)
VERVE (8800 series) 8-12 72
(Reads "Manufactured By MGM Record Corp.," or mentions either Polydor or Polygram at bottom of label.)
Also see AMMONS, Gene

AMOS & ANDY P&R '29
Singles: 78 rpm
COLUMBIA 10-15 50s
VICTOR 50-75 29
Singles: 7-inch
COLUMBIA (48002 "The Lord's Prayer") 15-25 50s

AMUZEMENT PARK R&B '82
(Amusement Park Band)
Singles: 7-inch
ATLANTIC 3-4 84-85
OUR GANG 3-4 82-83
LPs: 10/12-inch
ATLANTIC 5-10 84
Members: Paul Richmond; Darryl Ellis; Aaron Jamal; Norval Hodges; Fred Entesari; Reuben Locke Jr.; Rico McFarland.

ANA P&R '87
Singles: 7-inch
PARC 3-4 87-90
Picture Sleeves
PARC 3-4 87

ANACOSTIA R&B '72
Singles: 7-inch
COLUMBIA 3-5 72-75
MCA 3-4 77
ROULETTE 3-4 84
TABU 3-4 78-79
LPs: 10/12-inch
MCA 5-10 77
TABU 5-10 78

ANDERSEN, Eric LP '72
Singles: 7-inch
ARISTA 3-4 75-77
COLUMBIA 3-4 72
W.B. 3-4 68-71
LPs: 10/12-inch
ARISTA 5-10 75-77
COLUMBIA 8-10 72
VANGUARD 15-20 65-70
W.B. 10-15 68-70

ANDERSON, Bill C&W '58
(With the Po' Folks; with Jordanaires; Whispering Bill Anderson)
Singles: 12-inch
MCA 4-8 78
Singles: 7-inch
DECCA (30000 series) 10-15 58-59
DECCA (31000 series) 5-10 60-66
DECCA (32000 & 33000 series) 3-8 67-72
MCA 3-5 73-81
PICKWICK 5-10 70s
SOUTHERN TRACKS 3-4 82-87
SWANEE 3-4 85
TNT (165 "Empty Room") 15-25 59
Picture Sleeves
DECCA 5-10 63-69
EPs: 7-inch
DECCA 5-15 63-65
LPs: 10/12-inch
BILL ANDERSON LABEL (11316 "On the Road") 15-25
(Promotional issue only.)
CORAL 4-6 73
DECCA (4192 thru 4686) 15-20 62-65
DECCA (4771 thru 5344) 10-15 66-72
(Decca LP numbers in this series preceded by a "7" or a "DL-7" are stereo issues.)
DECCA (7100 series) 15-20 69
DECCA (7200 series) 10-12 72
EPIC 5-10 82-85
MCA 5-10 73-80
SOUTHERN TRACKS 5-10 84
VOCALION 8-12 68-71
Session: Jordanaires.
Also see COE, David Allan, & Bill Anderson
Also see KERR, Anita
Also see WELLS, Kitty / Bill Anderson

ANDERSON, Bill, & Jan Howard C&W '66
Singles: 7-inch
DECCA 3-6 66-71
LPs: 10/12-inch
DECCA 6-12 68-72
Also see HOWARD, Jan

ANDERSON, Bill, & Mary Lou Turner C&W '78
Singles: 7-inch
MCA 3-5 78
Also see ANDERSON, Bill

ANDERSON, Carl R&B '84
Singles: 12-inch
EPIC 4-6 82-86
Singles: 7-inch
EPIC 3-4 82-86
LPs: 10/12-inch
EPIC 5-10 82-86
Also see LORING, Gloria, & Carl Anderson

ANDERSON, Elton P&R/R&B '60
Singles: 7-inch
CAPITOL 8-12 62
LANOR (514 "I Love You So") 10-15 63
LANOR (516 "The Crawl") 10-15 63
MERCURY (71542 "Cool Down Baby") 10-15 59
MERCURY (71643 "Walking Alone") 10-15 60
MERCURY (71777 "Please Accept My Love") 10-15 61
TREY 10-15 60
VIN 10-20 58
Session: Mac Rebennack.
Also see REBENNACK, Mac

ANDERSON, Ernestine LP '58
Singles: 7-inch
MERCURY 3-4 60-62
SUE 3-4 63-64
EPs: 7-inch
MERCURY 5-10 59
LPs: 10/12-inch
CONCORD 8-12 76-86
MERCURY 15-25 58-60
OMEGA DISK 10-15 59
SUE 10-15 63
WING 10-15 64

ANDERSON, Jesse P&R/R&B '70
Singles: 7-inch
CADET 4-6 67-68
JEWEL 3-5 72
OUTTA CYTE (100 "Oh Wow Man") ... 8-12
THOMAS 4-8 70

ANDERSON, John C&W '77
Singles: 7-inch
ACE of HEARTS 4-6 74
MCA 3-4 87
W.B. 3-5 77-87
LPs: 10/12-inch
W.B. 5-8 77-87
Session: Waylon Jennings.
Also see HAGGARD, Merle
Also see HARRIS, Emmylou
Also see JENNINGS, Waylon

ANDERSON, Jon LP '76
Singles: 12-inch
ATLANTIC 4-6 82
Singles: 7-inch
ATLANTIC 3-5 76-82
COLUMBIA 3-4 88
ELEKTRA (Except 69580) 3-4 84-85
ELEKTRA (69580 "Save All Your Love") 3-4 85
(Black vinyl.)
ELEKTRA (69580 "Save All Your Love") 4-8 85
(Colored vinyl, special Christmas edition.)
LPs: 10/12-inch
ATLANTIC 5-10 76-82
COLUMBIA 5-10 88
ELEKTRA 5-10 85
Promotional LPs
ATLANTIC ("An Evening with Jon Anderson") 20-30 76
(Jon Anderson interviews, and music from his *Olias of Sunhillow* LP, as well as selections by Yes. Number not known.)
Also see JON & VANGELIS
Also see TANGERINE DREAM / Jon Anderson / Bryan Ferry
Also see YES

ANDERSON, Lale P&R '61
Singles: 7-inch
KING 3-6 61-62
LPs: 10/12-inch
FIESTA 15-25
UNIVERSE 10-20 61

ANDERSON, Laurie LP '82
(With John Giorno & William S. Burroughs)
Singles: 12-inch
W.B. 4-6 81
Singles: 7-inch
W.B. 3-4 81-89
EPs: 7-inch
W.B. 3-5 81
LPs: 10/12-inch
GIORNO POETRY (20 "You're the Guy I Want to Share My Money With") 8-12 84
W.B. (Except 25192) 5-10 82-89
W.B. (25192 "United States Live") 35-45 85
(Five-LP set.)
Also see GLASS, Philip

ANDERSON, Leroy P&R '51
(With His Pops Concert Orchestra)
Singles: 78 rpm
DECCA 3-5 51-57
Singles: 7-inch
DECCA 3-8 51-62
MCA 3-5 73
EPs: 7-inch
DECCA 5-10 51-58
RCA 5-10

LPs: 10/12-inch

DECCA 12-25 51-63
GRAND PRIX 8-12
MGM 10-20 62

ANDERSON, Liz & Lynn C&W '68

Singles: 7-inch

RCA 3-6 68
Also see ANDERSON, Lynn

ANDERSON, Lynn C&W '66

Singles: 7-inch

CBS (165211 "Isn't It Always Love") 30-50 79
(Picture disc. Promotional issue only. 1200 made.)
CHART 3-5 66-71
COLUMBIA 3-4 70-80
MERCURY 3-4 86-89
PERMIAN 3-4 83
RCA 3-5 68

Picture Sleeves

COLUMBIA 3-6 70-72

EPs: 7-inch

COLUMBIA 4-8 72
(Promotional only.)

LPs: 10/12-inch

ALBUM GLOBE 5-10 76
CHART 10-20 67-72
COLUMBIA 5-10 70-80
COLUMBIA HOUSE (6033 "Lynn Anderson Treasury") 30-40 73
(Boxed, five-disc set. Mail order offer.)
COLUMBIA HOUSE (6034 "The Ways to Love a Man") 5-10 73
COLUMBIA SPECIAL PRODUCTS 5-10 83
ERA 5-8 82
51 WEST 5-8 82
HARMONY 5-10 71-73
MOUNTAIN DEW 5-10
PERMIAN 5-10 83
PICKWICK 5-10
TIME-LIFE 5-10 81
Session: Jordanaires.
Also see ANDERSON, Liz, & Lynn

ANDERSON, Lynn, & Jerry Lane C&W '67

Singles: 7-inch

CHART 3-5 67

ANDERSON, Lynn, & Gary Morris C&W '83

Singles: 7-inch

PERMIAN 3-4 83
Also see MORRIS, Gary

ANDERSON, Lynn / Ray Price

LPs: 10/12-inch

COLUMBIA HOUSE (5658 "Heart to Heart") 15-25 72
(Boxed, four-disc set. Mail order offer.)
Also see ANDERSON, Lynn
Also see PRICE, Ray

ANDERSON, Lynn / Charley Pride

LPs: 10/12-inch

TELEHOUSE 5-8
Also see ANDERSON, Lynn
Also see PRIDE, Charley

ANDERSON, Michael LP '88

Singles: 7-inch

A&M 3-4 88

LPs: 10/12-inch

A&M 5-8 88

ANDERSON, Roshell R&B '73

Singles: 7-inch

EXCELLO 3-6 71-73
SUNBURST 3-5 73-74

ANDREA TRUE CONNECTION: see TRUE, Andrea

ANDREWS, Chris P&R '66

Singles: 7-inch

ATCO 5-10 66
RCA 4-6 69

ANDREWS, Inez R&B '73

(With the Andrewettes)

Singles: 7-inch

MCA 3-4 84
SONG BIRD 3-4 64-73

LPs: 10/12-inch

MCA 5-10 84
SAVOY 5-10 80-81

ANDREWS, Julie P&R '62

Singles: 7-inch

BUENA VISTA 3-6 65
COLUMBIA 3-5 67
DECCA 3-5 67
LONDON 3-6 60
RCA 3-4 70

Picture Sleeves

BUENA VISTA 4-8 65

EPs: 7-inch

RCA 10-20 56

LPs: 10/12-inch

ANGEL 15-25 58
COLUMBIA (1700 & 8500 series) 15-25 62
COLUMBIA (31000 series) 8-12 72
HARMONY 8-10 70-72
RCA (1000 series) 8-12 70
RCA (1400 thru 1600 series) 20-30 56-58
RCA (3800 series) 8-15 67
20TH FOX 8-15 68

ANDREWS, Julie, & Carol Burnett LP '62

LPs: 10/12-inch

COLUMBIA (2200 & 5800 series) 15-25 62
COLUMBIA (31000 series) 8-15 72
Also see BURNETT, Carol

ANDREWS, Julie, & Andre Previn

LPs: 10/12-inch

FIRESTONE 8-12 66

ANDREWS, Julie, & Andre Previn / Vic Damone / Jack Jones / Marian Anderson

EPs: 7-inch

RCA (277 "We Wish You a Merry Christmas") 3-5 69
(Radio Shack "Special Collector's Edition.")
Also see ANDREWS, Julie
Also see DAMONE, Vic
Also see JONES, Jack
Also see PREVIN, Andre

ANDREWS, Lee P&R/R&B '57

(With the Hearts; with Frank Slay Orchestra; Pancho Villa Orchestra)

Singles: 78 rpm

ARGO 35-50 57
CHESS 35-50 57
GOTHAM 50-100 56
MAIN LINE 50-100 57
RAINBOW 100-200 54

Singles: 7-inch

ARGO (1000 "Teardrops") 25-50 57
CASINO (110 "Baby, Come Back") .. 25-50 58
CASINO (452 "Try the Impossible") 500-750 58
(Red and white label, with playing cards at top.)
CASINO (452 "Try the Impossible") 100-200 58
(Black label.)
CHESS (1665 "Long Lonely Nights") 20-30 57
(Silver top label with chess pieces.)
CHESS (1665 "Long Lonely Nights") 10-15
(Blue label.)
CHESS (1675 "Teardrops") 20-30 57
(Silver top label with chess pieces.)
CHESS (1675 "Teardrops") 10-15
(Blue label.)
CHESS (9000 series) 4-6
COLLECTABLES 3-4 82
CRIMSON 5-10 67-68
GOTHAM (318 "Bluebird of Happiness") 200-300 56
GOTHAM (320 "Lonely Room") 200-300 56
GOTHAM (321 "Just Suppose") 200-300 56
GOTHAM (323 "Sippin' a Cup of Coffee") 3-5 81
(Colored vinyl. From a 1956 session.)
GOWEN (1403 "Together Again") 20-30 61
GRAND (156 "Teardrops") 10-15 62
GRAND (157 "Long Lonely Nights") .. 10-15 62
JORDAN 15-25 60
LANA 4-8 64
LOST-NITE 4-8 65
MAIN LINE (102 "Long Lonely Nights") 200-300 57
(Green label.)
MAIN LINE (102 "Long Lonely Nights") 150-250 57
(Black label, with Philadelphia address shown.)
MAIN LINE (102 "Long Lonely Nights") 25-50 62
(Black label, no address shown.)
MAIN LINE (105 "Teardrops") 10-15 62
PARKWAY (860 "Gee, But I'm Lonesome") 15-20 62
PARKWAY (866 "Looking Back") 15-20 63
RAINBOW (252 "Maybe You'll Be There") 250-500 54
(Black vinyl.)
RAINBOW (252 "Maybe You'll Be There") 1000-1500 54
(Colored vinyl. Print is small, with the title line being about 1 ½" long.)
RAINBOW (252 "Maybe You'll Be There") 15-25 62
(Colored vinyl. Print is noticeably larger than on 1954 issue.)
RAINBOW (256 "The White Cliffs of Dover") 500-1000 54
(Yellow label.)
RAINBOW (256 "The White Cliffs of Dover") 15-25 62
(Blue label.)
RAINBOW (259 "The Bells of St. Mary's") 500-750 54
(Yellow label.)
RAINBOW (259 "The Bells of St. Mary's") 15-25 62
(Blue label.)
RCA (8929 "Quiet As It's Kept") 10-15 66
SWAN (4065 "I Miss You So") 100-200 60
SWAN (4076 "A Night Like This") 150-250 61
SWAN (4076 "P.S. I Love You") 150-250 61
U.A. (123 "Try the Impossible") 10-20 58
U.A. (136 "Why Do I") 10-20 58
U.A. (151 "Maybe You'll Be There") .. 10-20 58
U.A. (162 "Just Suppose") 10-20 59
U.A. (592 "Try the Impossible") 5-10 63

LPs: 10/12-inch

COLLECTABLES 8-12 81-85
LOST-NITE (1 "Lee Andrews and the Hearts") 10-15 81
(Colored vinyl 10-inch LP.)
LOST-NITE (2 "Lee Andrews and the Hearts") 10-15 81
(Colored vinyl 10-inch LP.)
LOST-NITE (100 series) 15-25 65
POST 10-15 70s
Members: Lee Andrews; Arthur Thompson; Roy Calhoun; Wendell Calhoun; Butch Curry; Ted Weems.
Also see SLAY, Frank, & His Orchestra

ANDREWS, Patty P&R '49

Singles: 78 rpm

CAPITOL 3-5 55-56
DECCA 4-8 50-54

Singles: 7-inch

CAPITOL 4-8 55-56
DECCA 5-10 50-54
Also see ANDREWS SISTERS

ANDREWS, Ruby P&R/R&B '67

Singles: 7-inch

ABC 3-5 76-77

ZODIAC 4-6 67-71

LPs: 10/12-inch

ABC 8-10 77
ZODIAC 10-15 72

Also see STACKHOUSE, Ruby

ANDREWS SISTERS P&R '38

Singles: 78 rpm

CAPITOL 5-10 56-57
DECCA 5-10 38-57

Singles: 7-inch

ABC 3-4 74
CAPITOL 5-15 56
DECCA 10-20 50-57
DOT 3-5 64
KAPP 5-10 59
MCA 3-5 73-78
PARAMOUNT 3-4 73-74

Picture Sleeves

DECCA 10-15 57

EPs: 7-inch

CAPITOL (973 "Dancing '20s") 10-20 56
DECCA 10-20 51-58

LPs: 10/12-inch

ABC 5-10 74
CAPITOL 10-20 64
DECCA (4000 series) 10-15 67
(Decca LP numbers in this series preceded by a "7" or a "DL-7" are stereo issues.)
DECCA (5000 series) 20-50 49-54
(10-inch LPs.)
DECCA (8000 series) 15-25 55-58
DOT 10-20 61-67
HAMILTON 10-20 64-65
MCA 8-12 73
PARAMOUNT 5-10 73-74
VOCALION 5-10

Members: Patty Andrews; Maxene Andrews; Laverne Andrews.
Also see ANDREWS, Patty
Also see CROSBY, Bing
Also see FOLEY, Red, & Andrews Sisters
Also see MIRANDA, Carmen, & Andrews Sisters
Also see PAUL, Les

ANDREWS SISTERS & ERNEST TUBB C&W '49
(With the Texas Troubadors)

Singles: 78 rpm

DECCA 5-8 49

Also see ANDREWS SISTERS
Also see TUBB, Ernest

ANGEL LP '75

Singles: 7-inch

CASABLANCA 3-5 75-80

LPs: 10/12-inch

CASABLANCA 5-10 75-80

Members: Barry Brandt; Frank DiMino; Greg Giuffria; Mickey Jones; Punky Meadows; Felix Robinson.
Also see CHERRY PEOPLE
Also see GIUFFRIA
Also see WILSON, Carl

ANGEL, Johnny T: see JOHNNY T. ANGEL

ANGEL CITY LP '80

Singles: 7-inch

EPIC 3-4 80-82

LPs: 10/12-inch

EPIC 5-10 80-82
MCA 5-10 85

Members: Doc Neeson; Rick Brewster; John Brewster.

ANGELA D&D '85

Singles: 12-inch

SUTRA 4-6 85

ANGELIC GOSPEL SINGERS R&B '49

Singles: 78 rpm

GOTHAM 5-10 49

ANGELS P&R '61

Singles: 7-inch

ASCOT 5-8 63
CAPRICE 5-10 61-62
COLLECTABLES 3-4 82
ERIC 3-4 74
POLYDOR 3-5 74
RCA 5-10 67-68
SMASH 4-8 63-64

Picture Sleeves

SMASH (1854 "I Adore Him") 10-15 63

EPs: 7-inch

CAPRICE 10-15 62

LPs: 10/12-inch

ASCOT (13009 "The Angels Sing 12 of Their Greatest Hits") 20-30 64
(Monaural.)
ASCOT (16009 "The Angels Sing 12 of Their Greatest Hits") 30-40 64
(Stereo.)
CAPRICE (LP-1001 "And the Angels Sing") 40-50 62
(Monaural.)
CAPRICE (SLP-1001 "And the Angels Sing") 50-75 62
(Stereo.)
COLLECTABLES 5-8 80s
SMASH (27039 "My Boyfriend's Back") 30-40 63
(Monaural.)
SMASH (67039 "My Boyfriend's Back") 50-75 63
(Stereo.)
SMASH (27048 "A Halo to You") 30-40 63
(Monaural.)
SMASH (67048 "A Halo to You") 40-60 63
(Stereo.)

Members: Linda Jansen; Barbara Allbut; Phyllis "Jiggs" Allbut; Peggy Santaglia.
Also see DUSK
Also see SEDAKA, Neil, & Tokens / Angels / Jimmy Gilmer & Fireballs
Also see STARLETS

ANIMAL LOGIC LP '89

LPs: 10/12-inch

I.R.S. 5-8 89

ANIMALS P&R '64
(Eric Burdon & the Animals; Original Animals)

Singles: 7-inch

ABKCO 3-5 75
CAPITOL (72171 "The House of the Rising Sun") 25-45 64
(Canadian. Mistakenly pressed with full-length [4:28], LP version. Reissued on Quality using edited [2:58] version, as is on original U.S.A. single on MGM.)
COLLECTABLES 3-4 82
I.R.S. 3-5 83
JET 3-5 77
MGM 5-10 64-71
QUALITY 5-10 60s
(Canadian.)
STARDUST 3-4 94
(U.S. made Canadian reissue label.)

Promotional Singles

ABKCO 4-6 75
I.R.S. 4-6 83
JET 4-6 77
MGM 10-30 64-71
MGM CELEBRITY SCENE ("The Animals") 35-50 66
(Boxed set of five singles with bio insert and title strips.)

Picture Sleeves

MGM (13264 "House of the Rising Sun") 10-20 64
MGM (13274 "I'm Crying") 10-15 64
MGM (13298 "Boom Boom") 10-15 64
MGM (13339 "Bring It on Home to Me") 8-12 65
MGM (13769 "San Franciscan Nights") 5-10 67
MGM (13868 "Monterey") 5-10 67

LPs: 10/12-inch

ABKCO 8-12 73-76
ACCORD 5-10 82
I.R.S. 5-10 83-85
MGM 15-30 64-69
PICKWICK 5-10 71
SCEPTER/CITATION 5-10 76
SPRINGBOARD 5-10 72
U.A. 5-10 77
WAND 8-12 70

Members: Eric Burdon; Alan Price; Hilton Valentine; Chas Chandler; John Steel; John Weider.
Also see BURDON, Eric
Also see PRICE, Alan
Also see WEIDER, John

ANIMOTION D&D '84

Singles: 12-inch

MERCURY 4-6 84-85

Singles: 7-inch

CASABLANCA 3-4 86
MERCURY 3-4 84-85
POLYDOR 3-4 89

Picture Sleeves

CASABLANCA 3-4 86
MERCURY 3-4 84-85
POLYDOR 3-4 89

LPs: 10/12-inch

CASABLANCA 5-10 86
MERCURY 5-10 84-85
POLYDOR 5-8 89

Members: Astrid Plane; Bill Wadhams; Paul Engemann; Cynthia Rhodes; Charles Ottavio.
Also see DEVICE

ANITA & SO-AND-SO'S P&R '62
(Anita Kerr Singers)

Singles: 7-inch

RCA (7975 "Joey Baby") 10-15 62
RCA (8050 "To Each His Own") 8-12 62

Also see KERR, Anita

ANKA, Paul P&R/R&B '57
(With the Don Costa Orchestra)

Singles: 78 rpm

ABC-PAR 15-30 57
RPM 15-20 56
SPARTON/ABC (457 "Diana") 10-20 57
(10-inch LP.)

Singles: 12-inch

COLUMBIA 4-6 83

Singles: 7-inch

ABC-PAR (104 "Share Your Love") .. 15-25 58
(Promotional, fan club issue.)
ABC-PAR (296-1 "My Heart Sings") 25-35 58
(Stereo Compact 33 Single.)
ABC-PAR (9831 thru 9956) 10-20 57-58
ABC-PAR (9987 "My Heart Sings") ... 10-15 58
(Monaural.)
ABC-PAR (9987 "My Heart Sings") ... 25-50 58
(Stereo.)
ABC-PAR (10011 "I Miss You So") ... 10-15 59
(Monaural.)
ABC-PAR (S-10011 "I Miss You So") 25-50 59
(Stereo.)
ABC-PAR (10022 "Lonely Boy") 10-15 59
(Monaural.)
ABC-PAR (S-10022 "Lonely Boy") 25-50 59
(Stereo.)
ABC-PAR (10040 "Put Your Head on My Shoulder") 10-15 59
(Monaural.)
ABC-PAR (S-10040 "Put Your Head on My Shoulder") 25-50 59
(Stereo.)
ABC-PAR (10064 "Time to Cry") 10-15 59
(Monaural.)
ABC-PAR (S-10064 "Time to Cry") ... 25-50 59
(Stereo.)
ABC-PAR (10082 "Puppy Love") 10-15 60
(Monaural.)

ABC-PAR (S-10082 "Puppy Love")... 25-50 60
(Stereo.)
ABC-PAR (10106 "My Home Town") ... 10-15 60
(Monaural.)
ABC-PAR (S-10106 "My Home Town") ... 25-50 60
(Stereo.)
ABC-PAR (10132 "Hello Young Lovers") ... 10-15 60
(Monaural.)
ABC-PAR (10132 "Hello Young Lovers") ... 25-50 60
(Stereo.)
ABC-PAR (10147 "Summer's Gone") ... 10-15 60
(Monaural.)
ABC-PAR (S-10147 "Summer's Gone") ... 25-50 60
(Stereo.)
ABC-PAR (10168 "The Story of My Love") ... 10-15 61
(Monaural.)
ABC-PAR (S-10168 "The Story of My Love") ... 25-50 61
(Stereo.)
ABC-PAR (10194 thru 10338) ... 8-15 61-62
BARNABY ... 3-6 71
BUDDAH ... 3-6 72-78
COLUMBIA ... 3-4 83-85
ERIC ... 3-5 74
FAME ... 3-5 73
RCA (Except 2000, 8000, 9000 and 10000 series) ... 3-8 67-79
RCA (2000 series) ... 10-20 62
(With "VLP" or "VP" prefix. Stereo Compact 33 series.)
RCA (37-7977 "Love Me Warm and Tender") ... 15-25 62
(Compact 33 Single.)
RCA (47-7977 "Love Me Warm and Tender") ... 5-10 62
RCA (8000 series, except 8893) ... 5-10 62-66
RCA (8893 "I Can't Help Lovin' You") ... 15-25 66
RCA (9000 series) ... 5-10 67-69
RCA (10000 series) ... 3-5 78-81
RPM (472 "I Confess") ... 25-50 56
RPM (499 "I Confess") ... 20-40 56
SPARTON/ABC (457 "Diana") ... 10-20 57
(Canadian. Maroon and silver label.)
SPARTON/ABC (457 "Diana") ... 5-10 60s
(Canadian. Pink and black label.)
U.A. ... 3-5 75-77

Picture Sleeves

ABC-PAR (Except 9956) ... 20-30 58-61
ABC-PAR (9956 "Just Young") ... 50-75 58
COLUMBIA ... 3-5 83
ERIC ... 3-5 74
RCA (Except 11000 series) ... 8-15 62-65
RCA (11000 series) ... 3-6 78
U.A. ... 3-6 75

EPs: 7-inch

ABC ... 15-25 60s
(Juke box issue only.)
ABC-PAR ... 25-50 59
SIRE ... 10-12 74
(Juke box issue only.)

LPs: 10/12-inch

ABC-PAR (ABC-240 "Paul Anka") ... 25-35 58
(Monaural.)
ABC-PAR (ABCS-240 "Paul Anka") .. 35-50 58
(Stereo.)
ABC-PAR (ABC-296 "My Heart Sings") ... 25-35 59
(Monaural.)
ABC-PAR (ABCS-296 "My Heart Sings") ... 35-45 59
(Stereo.)
ABC-PAR (ABC-323 "Big 15") ... 25-35 60
(Monaural.)
ABC-PAR (ABCS-323 "Big 15") ... 35-45 60
(Stereo.)
ABC-PAR (ABC-347 "For Young Lovers") ... 25-30 60
(Monaural.)
ABC-PAR (ABCS-347 "For Young Lovers") ... 30-35 60
(Stereo.)
ABC-PAR (ABC-353 "Anka at the Copa") ... 25-30 60
(Monaural.)
ABC-PAR (ABCS-353 "Anka at the Copa") ... 30-35 60
(Stereo.)
ABC-PAR (ABC-360 "It's Christmas Everywhere") ... 25-30 60
(Monaural.)
ABC-PAR (ABCS-360 "It's Christmas Everywhere") ... 30-35 60
(Stereo.)
ABC-PAR (ABC-371 "Strictly Instrumental") ... 20-30 61
(Monaural.)
ABC-PAR (ABCS-371 "Strictly Instrumental") ... 25-35 61
(Stereo.)
ABC-PAR (ABC-390 "His Big 15, Vol. 2") ... 20-30 61
(Monaural.)
ABC-PAR (ABCS-390 "His Big 15, Vol. 2") ... 25-35 61
(Stereo.)
ABC-PAR (ABC-409 "His Big 15, Vol. 3") ... 20-30 62
(Monaural.)
ABC-PAR (ABCS-409 "His Big 15, Vol. 3") ... 25-35 62
(Stereo.)
ABC-PAR (ABC-420 "Diana") ... 20-30 62
(Monaural.)
ABC-PAR (ABCS-420 "Diana") ... 25-30 62
(Stereo.)
ACCORD ... 5-10 81
BARNABY ... 8-12
BUDDAH ... 8-12 71-76
CAMDEN ... 5-10 74
COLUMBIA ... 5-10 83-85
LIBERTY ... 5-10 81-83
PICKWICK ... 5-10 75
RCA (Except "LPM" & "LSP" series)... 5-10 75-81
RCA (2000 thru 4000" series) ... 10-25 62-70
(With "LPM" prefix. Monaural.)
RCA (2000 thru 4000" series) ... 15-30 62-70
(With "LSP" prefix. Stereo.)
RANWOOD ... 5-10 81
RIVERA (0047 "Paul Anka and Others") ... 25-40 63
(Has two tracks by Paul Anka.)
RHINO ... 5-10 86
SIRE ... 10-12 74-78
U.A. ... 5-10 74-78
Also see ANN-MARGRET
Also see COSTA, Don, Orchestra
Also see MARLO, Micki

ANKA, Paul, & Odia Coates P&R '74

Singles: 12-inch

EPIC ... 4-6 77

Singles: 7-inch

EPIC ... 3-4 76
U.A. ... 3-4 74-75
Also see COATES, Odia

ANKA, Paul / Sam Cooke / Neil Sedaka

LPs: 10/12-inch

RCA ... 15-20 64
Also see COOKE, Sam
Also see SEDAKA, Neil

ANKA, Paul, & Karla DeVito

Singles: 12-inch

COLUMBIA ... 4-6 83

Singles: 7-inch

COLUMBIA ... 3-4 83

ANKA, Paul, George Hamilton IV & Johnny Nash P&R '58

Singles: 7-inch

ABC-PAR (9974 "The Teen Commandments") ... 10-15 58
Also see HAMILTON, George
Also see NASH, Johnny

ANKA, Paul / Lloyd Price

EPs: 7-inch

ABC-PAR (14 "Rockin' on 5th Ave.") ... 30-50 61
(Promotional issue made for Luden's, makers of 5th Avenue candy bars.)
Also see ANKA, Paul
Also see PRICE, Lloyd

ANNETTE P&R '59

(Annette Funicello; with the Afterbeats; with Upbeats)

Singles: 78 rpm

DISNEYLAND (102 "How Will I Know") ... 25-50 58

Singles: 7-inch

BUENA VISTA (336, "Jo-Jo the Dog Faced Boy"/"Lonely Guitar") ... 10-15 59
BUENA VISTA (336, "Jo-Jo the Dog Faced Boy"/"Love Me Forever") ... 8-15 59
(Note different flip side.)
BUENA VISTA (339 thru 354) ... 8-15 59-60
BUENA VISTA (359 thru 407) ... 15-25 60-62
BUENA VISTA (414 "Teenage Wedding") ... 20-30 63
BUENA VISTA (427 thru 436) ... 15-25 63-64
BUENA VISTA (337 "The Wah Watusi") ... 10-15 64
BUENA VISTA (438 "Something Borrowed") ... 15-25 65
BUENA VISTA (440 "The Monkey's Uncle") ... 10-20 65
(With the Beach Boys.)
BUENA VISTA (442 thru 475) ... 10-15 65-66
DISNEYLAND ... 8-10 57-58
JUGGY ... 8-10
STARVIEW ... 5-10 83
TOWER (326 "What's a Girl to Do") ... 20-25 67
(Name misspelled, credits: "Annettte.")

Picture Sleeves

BUENA VISTA (339 thru 375) ... 20-30 59-61
BUENA VISTA (384 "Blue Muu Muu") ... 40-60 62
BUENA VISTA (388 thru 407) ... 20-30 62
BUENA VISTA (414 "Teenage Wedding") ... 75-100 63
BUENA VISTA (427 "Promise Me Anything") ... 50-75 63
BUENA VISTA (431 thru 436) ... 20-30 64
BUENA VISTA (437 "The Wah Watusi") ... 15-25 64
BUENA VISTA (438 "Something Borrowed") ... 20-30 65
BUENA VISTA (440 "The Monkey's Uncle") ... 25-35 65
BUENA VISTA (442 thru 475) ... 10-20 65-66
DISNEYLAND (102 "How Will I Know My Love") ... 25-45 58
DISNEYLAND (105 "Meetin' At the Malt Shop") ... 25-45 58

EPs: 7-inch

BUENA VISTA (3301 "Annette") ... 40-60 59
DISNEYLAND (04 "Tall Paul") ... 30-40 58
DISNEYLAND (69 "Mickey Mouse Club Featuring Annette") ... 35-45 58

LPs: 10/12-inch

BUENA VISTA (3301 "Annette") ... 50-75 59
BUENA VISTA (3302 "Annette Sings Anka") ... 50-75 60
(With bonus color photo.)
BUENA VISTA (3302 "Annette Sings Anka") ... 30-50 60
(Without bonus photo.)
BUENA VISTA (3303 thru 3508) ... 25-50 60-64
BUENA VISTA (4037 "Annette Funicello") ... 15-25 72

DISNEYLAND (Except 3906) 15-30 62-75
(Various Mouseketeer cast albums that include or feature Annette.)
DISNEYLAND (3906 "Snow White—As Told By Annette") 20-50
MICKEY MOUSE (12 thru 24) 35-55 57-58
(Various Mouseketeer cast albums that include or feature Annette.)
RHINO (Except 702) 8-10 84
RHINO (702 "Best of Annette") 25-35 84
(Picture disc.)
SILHOUETTE 10-15 81
STARVIEW (4001 "Country Album") ... 8-12 84
(Standard issue.)
STARVIEW (4001 "Country Album") 15-20 84
(Limited Edition series.)
Session: Davie Allan; Phil Baugh; Allan Reuss; Howard Roberts; Tommy Tedesco; Cliff Hils; Ed Hall; Jackie Kelso; Camarata.
Also see ALLAN, Davie
Also see AVALON, Frankie, & Annette
Also see BEACH BOYS

ANNETTE / Jimmy Dodd

Singles: 78 rpm

DISNEYLAND (758 "How Will I Know"/ "Annette") 25-50 58
(10-inch single.)
DISNEYLAND (758 "How Will I Know"/ "Annette") 20-30 58
(Five-inch single.)

Picture Sleeves

DISNEYLAND (758 "How Will I Know"/ "Annette") 25-50 58

ANNETTE / Hayley Mills

LPs: 10/12-inch

BUENA VISTA/DISNEYLAND (3508 "Annette & Hayley Mills") 300-400 64
(Cover reads Buena Vista but label is Disneyland. Issued with paper cover. TV mail order offer. One side by each artist.)
Also see MILLS, Hayley

ANNETTE & TOMMY SANDS

Singles: 7-inch

BUENA VISTA (802 "The Parent Trap") 10-20 61
(45 single.)
BUENA VISTA (802 "The Parent Trap") 25-35 61
(Compact 33 Single.)

Picture Sleeves

BUENA VISTA (802 "The Parent Trap") 20-30 61
Also see ANNETTE
Also see SANDS, Tommy

ANNIE G. — D&D '84

Singles: 12-inch

MCA 4-6 84

Singles: 7-inch

MCA 3-4 84

ANN-MARGRET — P&R '61

Singles: 12-inch

AVCO EMBASSY (4547 "Today") 10-15 70
FIRST AMERICAN (1207 "Everybody Needs Somebody Sometime") 5-10 81
MCA (1867 "Midnight Message") 5-10 80
(Promotional issue only.)
MCA (1867 "What I Do to Men") 5-10 80
OCEAN/ARIOLA AMERICA 4-8 79-80
RAM (1001 "Everybody Needs Somebody Sometime") 5-10 81
RAM 4-8 81

Singles: 7-inch

FIRST AMERICAN 3-5 81
MCA 3-5 79-80
OCEAN/ARIOLA AMERICA 3-5 79-80
RCA (VLP-2251 "Vivacious One") 30-50 62
(Five-disc, juke box set. With title strips.)
RCA (37-7857 "Lost Love") 20-40 61
(Compact 33 Single.)
RCA (47-7857 "Lost Love") 10-15 61
RCA (37-7894 "I Just Don't Understand") 20-30 61
(Compact 33 Single.)
RCA (47-7894 "I Just Don't Understand") 10-15 61
RCA (37-7952 "It Do Me So Good") .. 20-40 61
(Compact 33 Single.)
RCA (47-7952 "It Do Me So Good") .. 10-15 61
RCA (7986 thru 9109) 10-15 61-66

Picture Sleeves

RCA (7894 "I Just Don't Understand") 15-25 61
RCA (7952 "It Do Me So Good") 15-25 61
RCA (7986 "What Am I Supposed to Do") 15-25 61
RCA (8061 "Jim Dandy") 15-25 62
RCA (8168 "Bye Bye Birdie") 15-25 63

EPs: 7-inch

RCA (2251 "The Vivacious One") 15-25 62
RCA (2659 "Mr. Wonderful") 15-25 63
RCA (4358 "On the Way Up") 15-25 62
RCA (9058 "On the Way Up") 15-25 62

LPs: 10/12-inch

LHI 10-20 68-69
LAGNIAPPE 1959 ("Be My Guest") 200-300 59
(Cast LP produced by the Boys Tri-Ship Club of New Trier High School. Includes *Tropical Heat Wave* by Ann-Margret Olson.)
MCA 5-10 80
NORTHWESTERN UNIVERSITY/RCA (5760 "Among Friends") 100-150 60
(Cast LP for the *Waa-Mu Show of 1960* from Northwestern University. Lists Ann-Margret Olson as a dancer.)
RCA (LPM-2399 "And Here She Is") 10-20 61
(Monaural.)
RCA (LSP-2399 "And Here She Is") 15-25 61
(Stereo.)
RCA (LPM-2453 "On the Way Up") .. 10-20 62
(Monaural.)
RCA (LSP-2453 "On the Way Up") ... 15-25 62
(Stereo.)
RCA (LPM-2251 "The Vivacious One") 10-20 62
(Monaural.)
RCA (LSP-2251 "The Vivacious One") 15-25 62
(Stereo. Paradise") 10-20 63
(Monaural.)
RCA (LSP-2659 "Bachelor's Paradise") 15-25 63
(Stereo.)
RCA/NARM ("Tenth Anniversary Convention") 40-60 68
(Has *Bye Bye Birdie* by Ann-Margret, plus tracks by the Limeliters, Al Hirt, Paul Anka, Homer & Jethro, Peter Nero, Eddy Arnold, John Gary, Chet Atkins, Floyd Cramer, Anita Kerr Singers, Boots Randolph, Myron Cohen, Barry Sadler, Henry Mancini, Jack Jones, and Harry Belafonte. Promotional, souvenir issue only.)
Also see ANKA, Paul
Also see ARNOLD, Eddy
Also see ATKINS, Chet
Also see BELAFONTE, Harry
Also see COHEN, Myron
Also see CRAMER, Floyd
Also see HOMER & JETHRO
Also see JONES, Jack
Also see KERR, Anita
Also see LIMELITERS
Also see MANCINI, Henry
Also see NERO, Peter
Also see RANDOLPH, Boots
Also see SADLER, Barry

ANN-MARGRET & JOHN GARY — LP '64

LPs: 10/12-inch

RCA (LPM-2947 "Broadway Hits") 10-20 64
(Monaural.)
RCA (LSP-2947 "Broadway Hits") 15-25 64
(Stereo.)
Also see GARY, John

ANN-MARGRET & LEE HAZLEWOOD

Singles: 7-inch

LHI 5-10 68-69

LPs: 10/12-inch

LHI (12007 "The Cowboy and the Lady") 15-20 69
Also see HAZLEWOOD, Lee

ANN-MARGRET & AL HIRT

Singles: 7-inch

RCA (VLP-2690 "Beauty and the Beard") 25-50 64
(Five-disc, juke box set. With title strips.)
RCA (9524 "Slowly") 5-10 68

EPs: 7-inch

RCA (LSP-2690 "Beauty and the Beard") 15-25 64

LPs: 10/12-inch

RCA (LPM-2690 "Beauty and the Beard") 10-20 64
(Monaural.)
RCA (LSP-2690 "Beauty and the Beard") 15-25 64
(Stereo.)
Also see HIRT, Al

ANN-MARGRET / Kitty Kalen / Della Reese

LPs: 10/12-inch

RCA (2724 "3 Great Girls") 15-20 63
Also see ANN-MARGRET
Also see KALEN, Kitty
Also see REESE, Della

ANOTHER BAD CREATION — LP '91

LPs: 10/12-inch

MOTOWN 5-8 91

ANT, Adam — LP '82

Singles: 12-inch

EPIC 4-6 82-85

Singles: 7-inch

EPIC 3-4 82-85

Picture Sleeves

EPIC 3-4 84

LPs: 10/12-inch

EPIC 5-10 82-85
MCA 5-8 90
Also see ADAM & ANTS

ANTELL, Peter — P&R '62

(Pete Antell)

Singles: 7-inch

BOUNTY (103 "The Times They Are a-Changin' ") 15-25 65
CAMEO 5-10 62-63

ANTHONY, Alan — R&B '82

Singles: 7-inch

CHALET 3-4 82

ANTHONY, Markus — R&B '86

Singles: 7-inch

ROCK & ROLL 3-4 86

ANTHONY, Ray, & His Orch. — P&R '49

Singles: 78 rpm

CAPITOL 3-5 49-57

Singles: 7-inch

CAPITOL 3-6 50-62
RANWOOD 3-5 68

EPs: 7-inch

CAPITOL 5-10 52-59

LPs: 10/12-inch

CAPITOL 5-15 52-62
Also see BEACH BOYS / Ray Anthony
Also see SINATRA, Frank

ANTHONY & CAMP — R&B '86

Singles: 12-inch

W.B. 4-6 86

Singles: 7-inch

W.B. 3-4 86

Picture Sleeves

W.B. 3-4 86

LPs: 10/12-inch

W.B. 5-10 86

Member: Anthony Malloy.
Also see TEMPER

ANTHONY & IMPERIALS: see LITTLE ANTHONY & IMPERIALS

ANTHRAX LP '85

LPs: 10/12-inch

ISLAND....5-10 85-90
MEGAFORCE....5-10 87-91
Members: Joey Belladonna; Greg D'Angelo; Frank Bello.
Also see WHITE LION

AORTA LP '69

Singles: 7-inch

ATLANTIC (2545 "Strange")....10-20 68
COLUMBIA (44870 "Strange")....5-10 69
HAPPY TIGER (567 "Sandcastles")..10-15 70

LPs: 10/12-inch

COLUMBIA (9785 "Aorta")....15-25 69
COLUMBIA (38000 series)....5-10
HAPPY TIGER (1010 "Aorta 2")....35-55 70
Members: Bill Herman; Billy Jones; Jim Donlinger; Jim Nyeholt.

APOLLO 100 P&R/LP '72

Singles: 7-inch

ATCO....3-5 74
EUROGRAM....3-5 77
MEGA....3-5 71-72

LPs: 10/12-inch

MEGA....5-10 72
Member: Tom Parker.

APOLLONIA 6 P&R/R&B/D&D/LP '84

Singles: 12-inch

W.B. 4-6 84-85

Singles: 7-inch

W.B. 3-4 84-85

Picture Sleeves

W.B. 3-4 84-85

LPs: 10/12-inch

W.B. 5-10 84-85
Members: Patty Kotero; Brenda Bennett; Susan Moonsie.
Also see VANITY 6

APPALACHIANS P&R '63

Singles: 7-inch

ABC-PAR....4-8 62-63
GOLDIE....8-10

APPALOOSA LP '69

Singles: 7-inch

CONCORD....3-5 74

LPs: 10/12-inch

COLUMBIA....10-15 69
WHITE GOLD....5-10 82
Members: Robin Batteaux; Al Kooper.
Also see KOOPER, Al

APPLEJACKS P&R '58

Singles: 78 rpm

CAMEO....10-20 57-58
DECCA....5-10 54
PRESIDENT....5-10 56
TONE-CRAFT....5-10 55

Singles: 7-inch

CAMEO (100 series)....10-20 57-60
CAMEO (200 & 300 series)....5-10 61-64
DECCA....10-15 54
PRESIDENT....10-15 56
TONE-CRAFT....10-15 55
Member: Dave Appell.

APRIL
(April Stevens)

Singles: 7-inch

A&M....3-5 74
Also see STEVENS, April

APRIL & NINO: see TEMPO, Nino, & April Stevens

APRIL WINE P&R '72

Singles: 7-inch

BIG TREE....3-5 72-75
CAPITOL....3-4 78-85
LONDON....3-4 76-78

Picture Sleeves

CAPITOL (Except 4975)....3-4 81-84
CAPITOL (4975 "Just Between You and Me")....3-4 81
(Sleeve opens to a 22"x15" poster.)
CAPITOL (4975 "Just Between You and Me")....3-4 81
(Standard sleeve—no poster.)

LPs: 10/12-inch

AQUARIUS....5-10
ATLANTIC....5-10 81
BIG TREE....10-15 72-75
CAPITOL....5-10 78-85
LONDON....10-12 76-77
Members: Steve Lang; Jerry Mercer; Myles Goodwyn; Brian Greenway; Gary Moffet.

AQUARIAN DREAM LP '76

Singles: 7-inch

BUDDAH....3-5 76-77
ELEKTRA....3-4 78

LPs: 10/12-inch

BUDDAH....8-10 76
ELEKTRA....5-10 78-79
Members: Claude Bartee; Pete Bartee; Jacques Burvick; Mike Fowler; Valerie Horn; Gloria Jones; Pat Shannon.
Also see CONNORS, Norman

AQUARIANS LP '69

Singles: 7-inch

UNI....4-6 69

LPs: 10/12-inch

UNI....12-15 69

AQUATONES P&R/R&B '58

Singles: 78 rpm

FARGO (1001 "You")....20-40 58

Singles: 7-inch

FARGO....10-20 58-61

LPs: 10/12-inch

FARGO (3001 "The Aquatones Sing for You")....125-175 64
RELIC/FARGO (5033 "The Aquatones Sing for You")....8-10
Members: Barbara Lee; Larry Vannata; Vic Castro; Russ Nagy; Mike Roma; Tom Vivona.

ARBORS P&R '66

Singles: 7-inch

CARNEY (1011 "A Symphony for Susan")....10-20 66
COLUMBIA....3-5 73
(Black vinyl.)
COLUMBIA....5-10 73
(Colored vinyl. Promotional issue only.)
COLUMBIA HALL of FAME....3-4
DATE....4-6 66-70
(Black vinyl.)
DATE....5-10 66-70
(Colored vinyl. Promotional issues only.)
MERCURY....3-5 65

LPs: 10/12-inch

ARBORS MUSIC....8-10
DATE....12-15 67-68
VANGUARD....15-20 62
Members: Ed Farran; Fred Farran; Scott Herrick; Tom Herrick.

ARCADIA P&R/D&D/LP '85

Singles: 12-inch

CAPITOL....4-6 85-86

Singles: 7-inch

CAPITOL....3-4 85-86

Picture Sleeves

CAPITOL....3-4 85-86

LPs: 10/12-inch

CAPITOL....5-10 85-86
Members: Roger Taylor; Simon LeBon; Nick Rhodes.
Also see DURAN DURAN
Also see TAYLOR, Roger

ARCHIBALD R&B '50
(With Dave Bartholomew's Band)

Singles: 78 rpm

COLONY (105 "Little Miss Muffett")....25-50 51
IMPERIAL....20-40 50-57

Singles: 7-inch

IMPERIAL (Except 5212)....25-75 52-57
IMPERIAL (5212 "Early Morning Blues")....50-100 52

ARCHIES P&R/LP '68

Singles: 7-inch

CALENDAR....5-10 68-69
ERIC....3-4 81
KIRSHNER (Except picture discs)....4-8 69-72
KIRSHNER....6-12 70
(5½" picture discs cut-out from cereal boxes. At least seven different songs are on two different picture styles)
RCA....4-8 72

Picture Sleeves

CALENDAR....8-15 68
KIRSHNER....8-10 69-71

LPs: 10/12-inch

ACCORD (7149 "Straight A's")....8-10 81
BACK-TRAC....5-10 85
BRYLEN (4415 "The Archies")....10-20 82
CALENDAR (101 "The Archies")....50-100 68
(With "Everything's Archie" promotional pack, including: red balloon; blue button; *Archie's Laugh-In Joke Book*; blue sticker; "Letter of Introduction" poster; Don "This Man" Kirshner poster; CBS-TV flyer; "Dealer Imprint" flyer; black and white photo of John Goldwater and Don Kirshner; black and white photo of Filmations animated TV production team; Archies record and 8-track flyer; Archies bio sheet; Don Kirshner bio; September 1968 Calendar LP releases flyer.
CALENDAR (101 "The Archies")....15-25 68
(Album only.)
CALENDAR (103 "Everything's Archie")....15-25 69
CALENDAR (103 "Sugar Sugar")....10-15 70
51 WEST (16002 "The Archies")....5-10 79
KIRSHNER (105 "Jingle Jangle")....15-25 69
KIRSHNER (107 "Sunshine")....15-25 70
KIRSHNER (109 "Greatest Hits")....15-25 70
KIRSHNER (110 "This Is Love")....15-25 71
RCA (0221 "The Archies")....15-25 70
(Promotional issue only.)
Members: Ron Dante, Jeff Barry; Toni Wine, plus assorted guests.
Also see BLOOM, Bobby
Also see GREENWICH, Ellie
Also see KIM, Andy
Also see STEVENS, Ray
Also see TEMPO, Nino

ARCHIES / Johnny Thunder

Singles: 7-inch

COLLECTABLES....3-4 80s
Also see THUNDER, Johnny

ARDEN, Toni P&R '49

Singles: 78 rpm

COLUMBIA....3-6 49-54
DECCA....3-6 57-57
RCA....3-6 55-56

Singles: 7-inch

COLUMBIA....5-10 50-54
DECCA....5-10 57-59
MISHAWAKA....3-5
RCA....5-10 55-56

EPs: 7-inch

DECCA....8-15 58
COLUMBIA....10-15 56

LPs: 10/12-inch

DECCA....12-25 57-59
TIARA....10-15

AREA CODE 615 LP '69

Singles: 7-inch

POLYDOR....3-5 69-70

LPs: 10/12-inch

POLYDOR....8-12 69-70
Members: Charlie McCoy; Norbert Putnam.

Also see McCOY, Charlie

ARENA BRASS LP '63

LPs: 10/12-inch

EPIC 10-15 62

ARGENT P&R/LP '72

Singles: 7-inch

DATE 3-6 70
EPIC 4-8 69-74

LPs: 10/12-inch

EPIC 10-20 69-75
U.A. 5-10 76

Members: Rod Argent; Russ Ballard; Robert Henrit; Jim Rodford; John Verity.
Also see BALLARD, Russ
Also see WINTER, Johnny / Argent / Chambers Brothers / John Hammond
Also see ZOMBIES

ARKADE P&R '70

Singles: 7-inch

DUNHILL 4-6 70-71

Picture Sleeves

DUNHILL 4-6 71

ARLEN, Harold, & "Friend"

LPs: 10/12-inch

COLUMBIA (OL-6520 "Harold Sings Arlen") 25-35 66
(Monaural.)
COLUMBIA (OS-2920 "Harold Sings Arlen") 20-40 66
(Stereo.)
COLUMBIA (CSP-2920 "Harold Sings Arlen") 5-10

Members: Harold Arlen; Barbra Streisand.
Also see STREISAND, Barbra

ARMADA ORCHESTRA LP '76

LPs: 10/12-inch

SCEPTER 4-8 75

ARMAGEDDON LP '75

Singles: 7-inch

CAPITOL 3-6 71-72
CREATIVE SOUND 4-6 71

LPs: 10/12-inch

A&M 8-12 75
AMOS 15-20 70

Members: Keith Relf; Louis Cennamo; Martin Pugh.
Also see RENAISSANCE
Also see YARDBIRDS

ARMATRADING, Joan LP '76

Singles: 12-inch

A&M 4-6 83

Singles: 7-inch

A&M 3-5 74-86
CUBE 4-8 71

Picture Sleeves

A&M 3-5 83

EPs: 7-inch

A&M (2391 "Me, Myself + 6 More") 5-10 83
(Promotional issue only.)

LPs: 10/12-inch

A&M (Except 12) 8-12 73-90
A&M (12 "Talk Under Ladders") 15-25 81
(Promotional issue only.)

ARMEN, Kay P&R '43

Singles: 78 rpm

DECCA 4-8 42-58

Singles: 7-inch

DECCA 5-12 55-59

EPs: 7-inch

MGM 10-20 54-55

LPs: 10/12-inch

DECCA (5000 series) 20-40 54
(10-inch LP)
DECCA (8000 series) 10-20 59
MGM (200 series) 20-40 54
MGM (3000 series) 15-30 55

ARMENTA D&D '83

Singles: 12-inch

SAVOIR FAIRE 4-6 83

ARMORED SAINT LP '84

Singles: 12-inch

CHRYSALIS 4-6 86

Singles: 7-inch

CHRYSALIS 3-4 84-86

LPs: 10/12-inch

CHRYSALIS 5-10 84-87

ARMS, Russell P&R '57

Singles: 78 rpm

EPIC 3-6 54-56
ERA 3-6 56-57

Singles: 7-inch

EPIC 5-10 54-56
ERA 5-10 56-57

LPs: 10/12-inch

ERA 10-20 57

ARMSTRONG, Chuck R&B '76

Singles: 7-inch

R&R 3-5 76

ARMSTRONG, Louis P&R '26
(With His All Stars)

Singles: 78 rpm

CAPITOL 4-8 56
COLUMBIA (2500 thru 2700 series) 15-25 32
COLUMBIA (40000 series) 4-8 56-66
DECCA 5-15 35-58
OKEH 20-30 26-31
RCA 4-8 56
VICTOR 10-20 33
VOCALION 10-20 36

Singles: 7-inch

A&M 3-4 88
ABC 3-5 67-73
AMSTERDAM 3-5 71
AUDIO FIDELITY 3-5 71
AVCO EMBASSY 3-5 71
BRUNSWICK 4-6 67-68
BUENA VISTA 3-6 68
CAPITOL 5-10 56
COLUMBIA 5-10 56-66
CONTINENTAL 3-5 71
DECCA (25000 series) 4-6 61-64
DECCA (27000 thru 29000 series) 8-10 50-56
DECCA (30000 thru 31000 series) 5-10 56-59
DOT 4-8 59
EPIC 3-6 69
KAPP 4-6 64-69
MCA 3-5 73
MGM 4-8 59-60
MERCURY 4-6 64-66
RCA 5-10 56
U.A. 3-6 68-69
VERVE 4-8 59-60

Picture Sleeves

A&M 3-4 88
BUENA VISTA 5-8 68
CONTINENTAL 3-6 71
KAPP 5-10 64
MGM 8-12 59
MERCURY 5-10 64

Note: Multi-disc, 1950s boxed sets are in the $15 to $25 range. At this time we do not have specific numbers and titles.

EPs: 7-inch

COLUMBIA 5-15 55-59
DECCA 8-15 55-57
RCA 10-20 53-59

LPs: 10/12-inch

ABC 5-10 68-76
AMSTERDAM 5-10 70
AUDIO FIDELITY 15-25 60-64
BIOGRAPH 5-10 73
BRUNSWICK (58004 "Jazz Classics") 50-100 50
(10-inch LP.)
BRUNSWICK (75000 series) 8-15 68-71
BUENA VISTA 8-12 68
CHIAROSCURO 5-10 77
COLUMBIA (500 thru 900 series) 25-50 54-57
COLUMBIA (2600 series) 8-15 67
COLUMBIA (9400 series) 8-15 67
COLUMBIA (30000 series) 5-12 71-80
CORAL 5-10 73
DECCA (155 "Satchmo") 50-100 65
(Boxed four-disc set. Includes booklet.)
DECCA (195 "Satchmo at Symphony Hall") 30-50 66
(Boxed two-disc set.)
DECCA (4000 series) 10-20 61-63
DECCA (5000 series) 25-50 51-54
(10-inch LPs.)
DECCA (8000 series) 15-25 55-59
DECCA (9000 series) 8-15 67
(Decca LP numbers in this series preceded by a "7" or a "DL-7" are stereo issues.)
EVEREST 5-10 71-76
GNP 8-12 77
GUEST STAR 5-10 64
HARMONY 5-10 69
JAZZ HERITAGE 5-10 80
JAZZ PANORAMA (1204 "Fireworks") 15-20
JEMI 5-10
KAPP 10-15 64
MCA 6-10 73-82
MERCURY 10-15 66
METRO 10-15 65
MILESTONE 5-10 74-75
MOSAIC (146 "Complete Decca Studio Recordings") 100-120 90s
(Boxed, eight-disc audiophile set. 7500 made.)
OLYMPIC 5-10 74
PAUSA 5-10 83
RCA (1300 & 1400 series) 25-50 53-56
RCA (2300 thru 2900 series) 10-20 61-64
(With "LPM" or "LSP" prefix.)
RCA (2600 series) 5-10 77
(With "CPL1" prefix.)
RCA (5500 series) 8-12 77
RCA (6000 series) 8-12 71
SAGA 5-10 72
STORYVILLE 5-10 80
TRIP 5-10 72
U.A. 8-15 68-69
VANGUARD 8-12 76
VERVE 15-20 60-64
VOCALION 5-10 68-69

Also see BARRY, John
Also see BRUBECK, Dave
Also see CROSBY, Bing, Louis Armstrong, Rosemary Clooney & Hi-Los
Also see FITZGERALD, Ella, & Louis Armstrong
Also see KAYE, Danny, & Louis Armstrong
Also see JENKINS, Gordon
Also see MILLS BROTHERS, & Louis Armstrong

ARMSTRONG, Louis, & Duke Ellington

Singles: 7-inch

ROULETTE 4-6 63

LPs: 10/12-inch

MFSL (155 "Recording for the First Time") 25-35 85
ROULETTE (100 series) 8-12 71
ROULETTE (52000 series) 15-25 63

Also see ELLINGTON, Duke

ARMSTRONG, Louis, & Guy Lombardo

Singles: 7-inch

CAPITOL 3-6 66

Also see LOMBARDO, Guy

ARMSTRONG, Louis, Red Nichols, & Danny Kaye

Singles: 7-inch

DOT 5-10 59

Picture Sleeves

DOT 15-25 59

ARMSTRONG, Louis, & Oscar Peterson

Singles: 7-inch

VERVE 4-6 59

LPs: 10/12-inch

VERVE 15-25 59

Also see ARMSTRONG, Louis
Also see PETERSON, Oscar

ARMSTRONG, Vanessa Bell R&B '87
Singles: 7-inch
JIVE....3-4 87
Picture Sleeves
JIVE....3-4 87

ARNELL, Ginny P&R '63
Singles: 7-inch
DECCA....5-10 60
MGM....4-8 63-65
WARWICK....5-10 61
LPs: 10/12-inch
MGM....15-25 64
Also see JAMIE & JANE

ARNIE'S LOVE R&B '86
Singles: 12-inch
PROFILE....4-6 85-86

ARNO, Audrey P&R '61
(With the Hazy Osterwald Sextet)
Singles: 7-inch
DECCA....4-8 61

ARNOLD, Calvin P&R/R&B '68
Singles: 7-inch
IX CHAINS....3-5 75
VENTURE....4-8 67-69

ARNOLD, Eddy C&W '45
("The Tennessee Plowboy"; with His Tennessee Plowboys)
Singles: 78 rpm
BLUEBIRD (0527 "Each Minute Seems Like a Million Years")....25-50 45
RCA (Except 1800 thru 3100 series)....10-20 46-49
RCA (1800 thru 3100 series)....15-30 46-49
Singles: 7-inch
DIAMOND P (1009 "If the Whole World Stopped Lovin'")....5-10 73
(Promotional issue only.)
MGM....3-5 73-76
RCA (0001 thru 0476)....10-20 50-51
(Black vinyl. Black or turquoise labels.)
RCA (0001 thru 0476)....25-50 50-51
(Colored vinyl. Price for any in this series on colored vinyl.)
RCA (0100 thru 0700 series)....3-5 69-72
(Orange labels.)
RCA (2000 series)....5-10 62
(Compact 33 stereo single.)
RCA (3000 thru 6000 series)....10-20 50-57
RCA (7000 series)....5-12 57-62
RCA (8000 & 9000 series)....3-8 62-71
RCA (10000 thru 13000 series)....3-5 76-83
RCA GOLD STANDARD....3-8 59-70s
(With "447" prefix.)
Picture Sleeves
RCA....8-15 56-66
EPs: 7-inch
RCA (100 series)....10-12 61
(With "LPC" prefix. Compact 33 Double.)
RCA (280 "Best Wishes")....10-20
(Promotional issue only.)
RCA (200 thru 900 series)....10-15 52-56
(With "EPA" prefix.)
RCA (1100 & 1200 series)....15-20 55-56
(With "EPB" prefix.)
RCA (1400 & 1500 series)....8-12 57
(With "EPA" prefix.)
RCA (3000 series)....20-40 52-54
(With "EPB" prefix.)
RCA (4000 & 5000 series)....8-15 57-59
(With "EPA" prefix.)
LPs: 10/12-inch
CAMDEN (Except "ACL1" series)....8-18 60-72
CAMDEN ("ACL1" series)....5-10 72-76
GREEN VALLEY....8-10 76
K-TEL....8-10 74
MGM....8-12 74-76
RCA ("AHL1," "ANL1," "APL1," & "AYL1" series)....5-10 73-81
RCA ("CPL1" series)....8-12 83
RCA (0051 "Greatest Hits")....8-12
(Mail order offer.)
RCA (115 "Eddy Arnold Sings Them Again")....15-25 61
RCA (168 "Welcome to My World")..10-20 75
RCA (209 "Eddy Arnold")....15-20 66
(Promotional issue only.)
RCA (1100 thru 2200 series)....20-30 55-60
(Monaural. with "LPM" prefix.)
RCA (2300 thru 2900 series)....12-20 60-64
(Monaural. with "LPM" prefix.)
RCA (3000 series)....45-55 52-54
(10-inch LPs. with "LPM" prefix.)
RCA (3000 series)....8-12 64-68
(12-inch LPs. with "LPM" prefix.)
RCA (1900 thru 3400 series)....15-25 60-65
(Stereo. with "LSP" prefix. "LSP" numbers below 1900 were reprocessed stereo issues of '50s LPs. They were issued in the '60s and are in the $10-$15 range.)
RCA (3500 thru 4800 series)....10-20 66-73
RCA (6000 series)....8-12 70
RCA SPECIAL PRODUCTS (0051 "Eddy Arnold")....8-12 73
SUNRISE....5-10 79
TIME-LIFE....5-10 81
Also see ANN-MARGRET
Also see PRESLEY, Elvis / Hank Snow / Eddy Arnold / Jim Reeves

ARNOLD, Eddy, & Jaye P. Morgan
Singles: 78 rpm
RCA....5-10
Singles: 7-inch
RCA....5-10

ARNOLD, Eddy, & Jaye P. Morgan / Dorothy Olsen ("The Singing School Teacher")
EPs: 7-inch
RCA (DJ-21 "If 'N")....10-20 56
Also see ARNOLD, Eddy
Also see MORGAN, Jaye P.

ARPEGGIO P&R/R&B/LP '79
Singles: 7-inch
POLYDOR....3-4 78-80
LPs: 10/12-inch
POLYDOR....5-10 78-80

ARRINGTON, Steve R&B '82
(Steve Arrington's Hall of Fame)
Singles: 12-inch
ATLANTIC....4-6 83-86
Singles: 7-inch
ATLANTIC....3-4 83-86
KONGLATHER....3-4 82
MANHATTAN....3-4 87
LPs: 10/12-inch
ATLANTIC....5-10 83-86
Also see SLAVE

ARROWS (With Davie Allan): see ALLAN, Davie

ART ATTACK D&D '83
Singles: 12-inch
B.M.O....4-6 83
Singles: 7-inch
B.M.O....3-4 83
LPs: 10/12-inch
B.M.O....5-10 83

ART IN AMERICA LP '83
Singles: 7-inch
PAVILLION....3-4 83
LPs: 10/12-inch
PAVILLION....5-10 83

ART OF NOISE D&D '83
Singles: 12-inch
CHINA....4-6 86
ISLAND....4-6 83-84
Singles: 7-inch
CHINA....3-4 86-88
ISLAND....3-4 83-84
Picture Sleeves
CHINA....3-4 86-88
LPs: 10/12-inch
CHINA....5-10 86-88
CHRYSALIS....5-10 86-87
ISLAND....5-10 84-85
Members: Anne Dudley; Gary Langan; J.J. Jeczalik.
Also see ELECTRONIC
Also see HORN, Trevor, Paul Morley, & Art of Noise

ART OF NOISE & DUANE EDDY P&R '86
Singles: 7-inch
CHINA....3-4 86
Picture Sleeves
CHINA....3-4 86
Also see EDDY, Duane

ART OF NOISE & MAX HEADROOM P&R '86
Singles: 7-inch
CHINA....3-4 86
Picture Sleeves
CHINA....3-4 86

ART OF NOISE & TOM JONES P&R '88
Singles: 7-inch
CHINA....3-4 88
Picture Sleeves
CHINA....3-4 88
Also see ART of NOISE
Also see JONES, Tom

ARTISTICS R&B '65
Singles: 7-inch
BRUNSWICK....4-8 66-73
OKEH....5-10 63-66
LPs: 10/12-inch
BRUNSWICK....10-20 67-73
OKEH....15-25 67
Members: Marvin Smith; Bernard Reed; Larry Johnson; Tommy Green; Aaron Floyd; Morris Williams.
Also see DUKAYS

ARTISTS UNITED AGAINST APARTHEID P&R/R&B/D&D/LP '85
Singles: 12-inch
MANHATTAN....4-6 85
Singles: 7-inch
MANHATTAN....3-4 85
Picture Sleeves
MANHATTAN....3-4 85
LPs: 10/12-inch
MANHATTAN....5-10 85

ARVON, Bobby P&R '77
Singles: 7-inch
ARIOLA AMERICAN....3-4 76
FIRST ARTISTS....3-4 77-78
LPs: 10/12-inch
FIRST ARTISTS....5-10 78
MTA....5-10
MERCURY....5-10

ASH, Daniel LP '91
LPs: 10/12-inch
BEGGAR'S BANQUET....5-8 91

ASHE, Clarence P&R/R&B '64
Singles: 7-inch
ABC-PAR....5-10 65
CHESS....5-10 64
J&S....5-10 64
MASTER....5-10 65

ASHE, Clarence, & Hartsy Maye
Singles: 7-inch
J&S....5-10 65
Also see ASHE, Clarence

ASHFORD & SIMPSON R&B/LP '73
Singles: 12-inch
CAPITOL....4-6 82-86
W.B....4-6 79
Singles: 7-inch
CAPITOL....3-4 82-89
EMI AMERICA....3-4 84-85
W.B....3-5 73-81

Picture Sleeves
CAPITOL ... 3-4 80-86
W.B. ... 3-5 70s
LPs: 10/12-inch
CAPITOL ... 5-10 82-89
W.B. (Except HS series) ... 5-10 73-81
W.B. ("HS" series) ... 10-20 79-80
(Half-speed mastered.)
Members: Nick Ashford; Valerie Simpson.
Also see JONES, Quincy
Also see SIMPSON, Valerie
Also see VALERIE & NICK

ASHLEY, Del
(David Gates)
Singles: 7-inch
MANCHESTER (101 "There's a Heaven") ... 30-40 60s
PLANETARY (103 "Little Miss Stuck-Up") ... 10-20 65
Also see GATES, David

ASHLEY, Tyrone R&B '70
(With the Funky Music Machine)
Singles: 7-inch
PHIL-L.A. of SOUL ... 3-6 70-71
U.A. ... 3-5 78
LPs: 10/12-inch
U.A. ... 5-10 78

ASHTON, GARDNER & DYKE P&R/LP '71
Singles: 7-inch
CAPITOL ... 3-5 70-72
LPs: 10/12-inch
CAPITOL ... 8-12 70-72
Members: Tony Ashton; Kim Gardner; Roy Dyke.
Also see ASHTON, Tony, & Jon Lord
Also see BADGER

ASIA P&R/LP '82
Singles: 12-inch
GEFFEN ... 4-6 82-85
Singles: 7-inch
GEFFEN ... 3-4 82-85
Picture Sleeves
GEFFEN ... 3-4 81-85
LPs: 10/12-inch
GEFFEN ... 5-10 82-90
Members: Steve Howe; Carl Palmer; John Wetton; Geoff Downes; Mandy Mayer.
Also see BUGGLES
Also see EMERSON, LAKE & PALMER
Also see HOWE, Steve, Band

ASLEEP AT THE WHEEL C&W '74
Singles: 7-inch
ARISTA ... 3-4 90-91
CAPITOL ... 3-4 75-79
EPIC (06671 thru 08087) ... 3-4 87-88
EPIC (50000 series) ... 4-6 74
Picture Sleeves
EPIC ... 3-5 74
LPs: 10/12-inch
CAPITOL ... 10-15 75-79
EPIC (BG-33000 series) ... 15-25 75
EPIC (EG-33000 series) ... 10-15
EPIC (KE-33000 series) ... 10-15 74
EPIC (PE-33000 series) ... 5-10
MCA ... 5-10 80-84
U.A. ... 15-25 73
Members: Ray Benson; Chris O'Connell; Danny Levin; Reuben Gosfield. Session: Texas Playboys.

ASPHALT JUNGLE R&B '80
Singles: 7-inch
TEC ... 3-4 80

ASSEMBLED MULTITUDE P&R '70
Singles: 7-inch
ATLANTIC ... 3-5 70-72
ERIC ... 3-4 81
LPs: 10/12-inch
ATLANTIC ... 8-10 70

ASSOCIATION P&R/LP '66
Singles: 7-inch
COLUMBIA ... 3-5 72
ELEKTRA ... 3-4 81
JUBILEE ... 4-8 65
MUMS ... 3-5 73
RCA ... 3-5 75
VALIANT ... 4-8 66
W.B. ... 3-6 67-71
Picture Sleeves
VALIANT ... 5-10 66
LPs: 10/12-inch
COLUMBIA ... 8-10 72
VALIANT ... 12-20 66
W.B. ... 8-12 67-71
Members: Gary Alexander; Ted Bluechel Jr; Brian Cole; Russ Giguere; Terry Kirkman; Cliff Nivison; Larry Ramos; Richard Thompson; Jim Yester; Larry Ramos.
Also see MAMAS & PAPAS / Association / Fifth Dimension
Also see MIKE & DEAN
Also see NEW CHRISTY MINSTRELS
Also see PEDESTRIANS / Association / Five Americans / Soulblenders

ASSOCIATION / Bobby Vee / Mike Love / Mary MacGregor
LPs: 10/12-inch
HITBOUND (1005 "New Memories") 10-15 83
Also see LOVE, Mike
Also see MacGREGOR, Mary
Also see VEE, Bobby

ASTAIRE, Fred P&R '29
Singles: 78 rpm
BRUNSWICK ... 10-20 35-38
COLUMBIA ... 15-25 29-34
DECCA ... 5-10 43
MGM ... 4-8 51-53
MERCURY ... 3-6 53
RCA ... 3-5 55
VERVE ... 3-5 56
VICTOR ... 15-20 31-33
Singles: 7-inch
AVA ... 4-6 63
CHOREO ... 4-6 62
CLEF ... 5-10 57
KAPP ... 4-8 59
MGM ... 5-10 51-52
MERCURY ... 5-10 53
RCA ... 5-10 55
VERVE ... 5-10 56
EPs: 7-inch
CLEF ... 10-15 57
EPIC ... 10-15 57
MGM ... 10-20 51-53
VERVE ... 10-15 59
LPs: 10/12-inch
CAMDEN ... 10-20 59-60
CHOREO ... 10-20 61
CLEF ... 15-30 57
EPIC (3000 series) ... 15-30 57
EPIC (13000 & 15000 series) ... 8-15 66
KAPP ... 15-25 59
LION ... 10-20 59
MGM (100 series) ... 25-50 52
MGM (3000 series) ... 15-30 52-55
MONMOUTH EVERGREEN ... 10-20 71
VERVE ... 15-30 56-59
VOCALION ... 8-15 64
X ... 20-25 57
Also see CROSBY, Bing, & Fred Astaire

ASTAIRE, Fred, & Jane Powell P&R '51
Singles: 78 rpm
MGM ... 4-8 51
Singles: 7-inch
MGM ... 5-10 51
Also see POWELL, Jane

ASTAIRE, Fred, & Red Skelton / Helen Kane
(With Andre Previn)
EPs: 7-inch
MGM ... 8-10 50
(Not issued with cover, actually a three-track single.)
Also see ASTAIRE, Fred
Also see PREVIN, Andre
Also see SKELTON, Red

ASTLEY, Jon P&R/LP '87
Singles: 7-inch
ATLANTIC ... 3-4 87-88
Picture Sleeves
ATLANTIC ... 3-4 87-88
LPs: 10/12-inch
ATLANTIC ... 5-10 87

ASTLEY, Rick P&R '87
Singles: 7-inch
RCA ... 3-4 87-91
Picture Sleeves
RCA ... 3-4 87-89
LPs: 10/12-inch
RCA ... 5-8 87-89

ASTORS P&R/R&B '65
Singles: 7-inch
STAX (139 "What Can It Be") ... 50-75 63
STAX (170 "Candy") ... 10-15 65
STAX (179 "Mystery Woman") ... 10-15 65
STAX (232 "Daddy Didn't Tell You") ... 8-12 67
Members: Curtis Johnson; Richard Harris; Eddie Stanbeck; Sam Byrnes.

ASTRONAUTS P&R/LP '63
Singles: 7-inch
PALLADIUM (610 "Come Along Baby") ... 75-125 61
RCA ... 10-20 63-65
Picture Sleeves
RCA ... 20-30 63
EPs: 7-inch
RCA ... 25-40 63
RCA WURLITZER DISCOTHEQUE (100 "Discotheque Music") ... 30-40 64
(Promotional issue only.)
LPs: 10/12-inch
RCA ... 20-30 63-67
Members: Rich Fifield; Jon "Stormy" Patterson; Robert Demmon; Dennis Lindsey; James Gallagher.

ASTRONAUTS / Liverpool Five
LPs: 10/12-inch
RCA (251 "Stereo Festival") ... 25-45 67
(Promotional issue only.)
Also see ASTRONAUTS
Also see LIVERPOOL FIVE

ASWAD LP '88
LPs: 10/12-inch
ISLAND ... 5-10 84
MANGO ... 5-10 84-88
Members: Candy McKenzie; Brinsley Forde; Donald Griffiths; Courtney Hemmings; George Oban; Angus Gaye; Bunny McKenzie; Trevor Bow.

ASYLUM CHOIR
Singles: 7-inch
SHELTER ... 3-5 71
SMASH ... 4-6 69
LPs: 10/12-inch
SHELTER (2000 series) ... 8-10 74
SHELTER (8000 series) ... 10-15 71
SHELTER (52000 series) ... 5-10 75
SMASH (67107 "Look Inside") ... 25-30 68
(With toilet tissue cover.)
SMASH (67107 "Look Inside") ... 10-15 68
(With photo cover.)
Members: Leon Russell; Marc Benno.
Also see BENNO, Marc
Also see RUSSELL, Leon

ATKINS R&B '82

Singles: 7-inch

W.B. 3-4 82

LPs: 10/12-inch

W.B. 5-10 82

ATKINS, Chet C&W '55

(With the Anita Kerr Singers)

Singles: 78 rpm

BLUEBIRD (0072 "I Know When I'm Blue") 10-20 50
BULLET (617 "Guitar Blues") 50-100 46
RCA 5-15 47-57

Singles: 7-inch

RCA (0100 thru 0400 series) 12-25 50-51
(Black or turquoise labels.)
RCA (0100 thru 0700 series) 3-5 71-74
(Orange labels.)
RCA (4000 & 5000 series) 10-20 51-55
RCA (6000 & 7000 series) 5-15 55-62
RCA (8000 & 9000 series) 3-8 62-71
RCA (10000 thru 13000 series) 3-5 75-83

Picture Sleeves

RCA 5-10 61-67

EPs: 7-inch

RCA (100 series) 8-12 61
(With "LPC" prefix. Compact 33 Double.)
RCA (500 thru 900 series) 8-15 55-56
(With "EPA" prefix.)
RCA (1100 & 1200 series) 10-20 55-56
(With "EPB" prefix.)
RCA (1300 thru 1500 series) 8-15 56-57
(With "EPA" prefix.)
RCA (3000 series) 15-25 52-54
(With "EPB" prefix.)
RCA (4000 & 5000 series) 5-10 58-60
SESAC (13 "Mr. Atkins, If You Please") 20-30 59
(Promotional issue only.)

LPs: 10/12-inch

CAMDEN 8-12 61-72
CANDLELITE 10-15
COLUMBIA 5-10 83-85
DOLTON 15-20 67
PICKWICK/CAMDEN 8-10 75
RCA (AHL1, ANL1, APL1, & AYL1 series) 5-10 73-83
RCA (CPL1 series) 8-12 77
RCA (1000 series) 25-35 54
(With "LPM" prefix.)
RCA (1100 thru 2200 series, except 1236) 15-25 55-60
(With "LPM" prefix.)
RCA (1236 "Stringin' Along with Chet Atkins") 30-40 55
(With "LPM" prefix.)
RCA (2300 thru 2900 series) 10-15 60-64
(With "LPM" prefix.)
RCA (3000 series) 45-55 53
(10-inch LPs. With "LPM" prefix.)
RCA (3000 series) 8-12 64-68
(12-inch LPs. With "LPM" prefix.)
RCA (2000 & 3000 series) 10-15 66-69
(With "LSC" prefix.)
RCA (1900 thru 3500 series) 10-20 60-66
(Stereo. With "LSP" prefix. LSP numbers below 1900 were reprocessed stereo issues of '50s LPs. They were issued in the '60s are in the $10 to $15 range.)
RCA (3500 thru 4800 series) 8-15 68-73
RCA (6000 series) 8-12 70-72
SESAC ("Chet Atkins") 75-100 59
(Exact title and selection number not known.)
TIME-LIFE 5-10 81

Session: Floyd Cramer; Bob Moore; Jack Shook; Murrey Harman; Anita Kerr Singers.

Also see ANN-MARGRET
Also see ATKINS STRING COMPANY
Also see CHARLES, Ray, George Jones, & Chet Atkins
Also see COUNTRY ALL STARS
Also see COUNTRY HAMS
Also see CRAMER, Floyd
Also see GIBSON, Don
Also see KERR, Anita
Also see MOORE, Bob
Also see NELSON, Willie
Also see PRESLEY, Elvis
Also see PURE PRAIRIE LEAGUE
Also see REED, Jerry, & Chet Atkins
Also see SNOW, Hank, & Chet Atkins
Also see TUBB, Ernest

ATKINS, Chet, & Boston Pops

LPs: 10/12-inch

RCA 10-20 66-69

Also see BOSTON POPS ORCHESTRA

ATKINS, Chet, Floyd Cramer & Danny Davis

(Chet, Floyd & Danny)

Singles: 7-inch

RCA 3-5 77

LPs: 10/12-inch

RCA 5-8 77

Also see DAVIS, Danny

ATKINS, Chet, Floyd Cramer & Boots Randolph

LPs: 10/12-inch

PICKWICK 5-8 71

Also see CRAMER, Floyd
Also see RANDOLPH, Boots

ATKINS, Chet, & Mark Knopfler

LPs: 10/12-inch

COLUMBIA 5-8 90

ATKINS, Chet, & Les Paul

Singles: 7-inch

RCA 3-4 78

LPs: 10/12-inch

RCA 5-10 76-80

Also see PAUL, Les

ATKINS, Chet, Faron Young, & Anita Kerr Singers

EPs: 7-inch

SESAC (48 "No Greater Love") 25-35 59

Also see ATKINS, Chet
Also see KERR, Anita
Also see YOUNG, Faron

ATKINS, Christopher P&R '82

Singles: 7-inch

POLYDOR 3-4 82

Picture Sleeves

POLYDOR 3-4 82

ATKINS STRING COMPANY C&W '75

Singles: 7-inch

RCA 3-4 75

LPs: 10/12-inch

RCA 5-10 75

Members: Chet Atkins; Johnny Gimble; Paul Yandell; Lisa Silver.

Also see ATKINS, Chet

ATLANTA C&W '83

Singles: 7-inch

MCA 3-4 84-85
MDJ 3-5 83
SOUTHERN TRACKS 3-4 87-88

Picture Sleeves

MDJ 3-4 83

LPs: 10/12-inch

MCA 5-10 84

Members: Dick Stevens; Brad Griffis; Tony Ingram; Allen David; John Holder; Jeff Baker; Al Collay; Bill Packard.

Also see VOGUES

ATLANTA DISCO BAND R&B '75

Singles: 7-inch

ARIOLA AMERICA 3-4 76

LPs: 10/12-inch

ARIOLA AMERICA 5-10 76

ATLANTA RHYTHM SECTION P&R/LP '74

Singles: 7-inch

COLUMBIA 3-4 81
DECCA 3-5 72
MCA 3-5 73
POLYDOR 3-5 74-80

LPs: 10/12-inch

COLUMBIA 5-10 81
DECCA 12-20 72
MCA 5-10 77
MFSL (038 "Champagne Jam") 40-60 79
POLYDOR 5-10 74-80

Members: Ronnie Hammond; Rodney Justo; Robert Nix; Barry Bailey; James Cobb; Dean Daughtry; Paul Goddard.

Also see CANDYMEN
Also see CLASSICS IV
Also see MANILOW, Barry / Atlanta Rhythm Section

ATLANTIC STARR R&B '78

Singles: 12-inch

A&M 4-8 79-85
W.B. 4-6 89

Singles: 7-inch

A&M 3-4 78-86
MANHATTAN 3-4 86
W.B. 3-4 87-89

Picture Sleeves

A&M 3-4 78-86
W.B. 3-4 87

LPs: 10/12-inch

A&M 5-10 78-85
W.B. 5-10 87-89

Members: Sharon Bryant; David Lewis; Wayne Lewis; Jonathan Lewis; William Sudderth; Damon Rentie; Clifford Archer; Joe Phillips; Porter Carroll; Koran Daniels; Barbara Weathers.

Also see BRYANT, Sharon

ATOMIC ROOSTER LP '71

Singles: 7-inch

ELEKTRA 3-5 71-72

LPs: 10/12-inch

ELEKTRA 10-20 71-73
PVC 5-10 83

Members: Chris Farlowe; Pete French; Steve Bolton; John Cann; Vincent Crane; Paul Hammond; Carl Palmer; Johnny Mandala; Rick Parnell.

Also see BROWN, Arthur
Also see FARLOWE, Chris

ATTACK, Art: see ART ATTACK

ATTILA

LPs: 10/12-inch

BACK-TRAC 5-10 85
D&J 5-8 80
EPIC (30030 "Attila") 40-50 70

Members: Billy Joel; Jon Small.

Also see JOEL, Billy

ATTITUDE R&B/D&D '83

Singles: 12-inch

ATLANTIC 4-6 83

Singles: 7-inch

ATLANTIC 3-4 83

LPs: 10/12-inch

ATLANTIC 5-10 83

ATTITUDES P&R/R&B '76

Singles: 7-inch

DARK HORSE 3-5 75-76

Picture Sleeves

DARK HORSE 3-5 75

LPs: 10/12-inch

DARK HORSE 5-10 76-77

Members: Danny Kortchmar; David Foster; Jim Keltner; Paul Stallworth.

AU GO-GO SINGERS

Singles: 7-inch

ROULETTE (4577 "Pink Polemoniums") 10-15 64

LPs: 10/12-inch

ROULETTE (R-25280 "They Call Us Au Go-Go Singers") 30-40 64
(Monaural.)
ROULETTE (SR-25280 "They Call Us Au Go-Go Singers") 40-50 64
(Stereo.)

Members: Steven (Stephen) Stills; Richie Furay.

Also see FURAY, Richie
Also see STILLS, Stephen

AUDIENCE P&R '71

Singles: 7-inch

ELEKTRA 3-5 71-72

LPs: 10/12-inch

AUDIENCE 10-15 71-72
ELEKTRA 8-12 72
Members: Trevor Williams; Howard Werth; Pat Neubergh; Nick Judd; Tony Connor; Keith Gemmell.

AUDIO TWO LP '88

LPs: 10/12-inch

FIRST PRIORITY 5-8 88

AUDREY P&R '56

Singles: 78 rpm

PLUS (104 "Dear Elvis") 10-20 56

Singles: 7-inch

PLUS (104 "Dear Elvis") 20-30 56
(Break-in novelty, with excerpts of several Elvis Sun tracks.)
Also see PRESLEY, Elvis

AUGER, Brian P&R/LP '70
(With Trinity; Brian Auger's Oblivion Express)

Singles: 7-inch

ATCO 4-6 68-69
RCA 3-5 70-74

EPs: 7-inch

ATCO (4536 "Red Beans and Rice") 5-8 69
(Labeled an EP by Atco, though only has one track on each side. Not issued with cover.)

LPs: 10/12-inch

ATCO 12-15 69
CAPITOL 10-12 69
POLYDOR 5-10 74
RCA 6-10 70-77
W.B. 5-10 77
Also see DRISCOLL, Julie, & Brian Auger

AUGIE: see MEYERS, Augie

AUGUST, Jan P&R '46

Singles: 78 rpm

MERCURY 3-6 46-57

Singles: 7-inch

MERCURY 4-10 50-62

EPs: 7-inch

MERCURY 5-15 50-56

LPs: 10/12-inch

MERCURY 10-25 50-62
WING 6-12 59
Also see HAYMAN, Richard, Orchestra

AURRA R&B '80

Singles: 12-inch

SALSOUL 4-6 82

Singles: 7-inch

DREAM 3-4 80
SALSOUL 3-4 81-83

LPs: 10/12-inch

DREAM 5-10 80
SALSOUL 5-10 81-83
Members: Curt Jones; Starleana Young; Steve Washington; Tom Lockett Jr.; Phillip Fields.
Also see DEJA
Also see SLAVE

AUSTIN, Gene P&R '25

Singles: 78 rpm

COLUMBIA 3-5 54-56
DECCA 3-5 56
VICTOR 4-8 25-35

Singles: 7-inch

COLUMBIA 4-8 54-56
DECCA 4-8 56
RCA 4-8 57

Picture Sleeves

RCA 5-10 57

EPs: 7-inch

RCA 10-15 53

LPs: 10/12-inch

DECCA 15-25 56
DOT 10-15 60s
RCA 20-40 53-57
"X" 15-25 54

AUSTIN, Patti R&B '69

Singles: 12-inch

QWEST 4-6 84-86

Singles: 7-inch

ABC 5-10 68
CTI 3-5 76-80
COLUMBIA 4-8 71-73
CORAL (62455 "He's Good Enough for Me") 10-20 65
CORAL (62471 "I Wanna Be Loved") 10-20 65
CORAL (62478 "Someone's Gonna Cry") 50-100 66
CORAL (62491 "Take Away the Pain Stain") 10-20 66
CORAL (62500 "Leave a Little Love") 10-20 66
CORAL (62511 "What a Difference a Day Made") 10-20 67
CORAL (62518 "Only All the Time") 10-20 67
CORAL (62541 "You're Too Much a Part of Me") 10-20 67
CORAL (62548 "All My Love") 10-20 68
QWEST 3-4 81-86
U.A. 3-4 69-70

LPs: 10/12-inch

CTI 5-10 77-80
GRP 5-8 90
QWEST 5-10 81-86
Also see JONES, Quincy
Also see WALDEN, Narada Michael, & Patti Austin
Also see YUTAKA

AUSTIN, Patti, & Jerry Butler

Singles: 7-inch

CTI 3-4 83
Also see BUTLER, Jerry

AUSTIN, Patti, & James Ingram P&R '82

Singles: 7-inch

QWEST 3-4 82-84
Also see AUSTIN, Patti
Also see INGRAM, James

AUSTIN, Sil P&R/R&B '56
(With the Allstars)

Singles: 78 rpm

JUBILEE 5-15 54-55
MERCURY 5-15 56-57
WING 5-15 56

Singles: 7-inch

JUBILEE 5-15 54-55
MERCURY 5-15 56-65
SSS INT'L 3-5 70
SEW CITY 4-8 66
WING 5-15 56

EPs: 7-inch

MERCURY 10-15 56-57

LPs: 10/12-inch

MERCURY 10-25 59-67
SSS INT'L 8-10 70-82
WING 10-12 63-68

AUSTIN, Sil, & Red Prysock

Singles: 7-inch

MERCURY 4-6 61

LPs: 10/12-inch

MERCURY (20434 "Battle Royal") 15-25 61
(Monaural.)
MERCURY (60106 "Battle Royal") 20-30 61
(Stereo.)
SSS INT'L 8-10 69
WING 10-12 63-68
Also see AUSTIN, Sil

AUTOGRAPH P&R '84

Singles: 7-inch

RCA 3-4 84-85

Picture Sleeves

RCA 3-4 84-85

LPs: 10/12-inch

RCA 5-10 84-87
Member: Steve Plunkett.

AUTOMATIC MAN LP '76

Singles: 7-inch

ISLAND 3-5 76-77

LPs: 10/12-inch

ISLAND 5-10 76-77
Members: Michael Schrieve; Todd Cochran; Doni Harvey; Pat Thrall.

AUTRY, Gene P&R '33/C&W '44
(With the Cass County Boys & the Pinafores)

Singles: 78 rpm

BRUNSWICK (12936 "There's An Empty Cot in the Bunkhouse Tonight") 100-200 30s
(Flip side, #12899, is credited to "Gene Autry & Jimmy Long.")
CHAMPION (16096 "Cowboy Yodel") 100-150 30s
CHAMPION (16119 "Texas Blues") 100-150 30s
CHAMPION (16141 "In the Jailhouse Now, No. 2") 100-150 30s
CHAMPION (16210 "Mean Mama Blues") 100-150 30s
CHAMPION (16228 "Pistol Packin' Mama") 100-150 30s
CHAMPION (16245 "Blue Days") 100-150 30s
CHAMPION (16275 "T.B. Blues") 100-150 30s
CLARION (5025 "Hobo Yodel") 75-125 30s
CLARION (5026 "No One to Call Me Darling") 75-125 30s
CLARION (5058 "I'll Be Thinking of You Little Girl") 75-125 30s
CLARION (5075 "Cowboy Yodel") 75-125 30s
CLARION (5154 "Dust Pan Blues") 75-125 30s
CLARION (5155 "Waiting for a Train") 75-125 30s
CLARION (5239 "Left My Gal in the Mountains") 75-125 30s
CLARION (5240 "Daddy and Home") 75-125 30s
CLARION (5243 "Lullaby Yodel") 75-125 30s
CLARION (5272 "True Blue Bill") 75-125 30s
CLARION (5308 "A Gangster's Warning") 75-125 30s
CONQUEROR 30-90 30s
COLUMBIA 5-15 45-56
DECCA (5426 "Blue Days") 50-100 30s
DECCA (5464 "In the Shadow of the Pine") 50-100 30s
DECCA (5488 "Bear Cat Papa Blues") 50-100 30s
DECCA (5501 "My Carolina Sunshine Girl") 50-100 30s
DECCA (5426 "Blue Days") 50-100 30s
DECCA (5517 "T.B. Blues") 50-100 30s
DECCA (5527 "Yodeling Hobo") 50-100 30s
DECCA (5544 "Pistol Packin' Mama") 50-100 30s
DIVA (6030 "Hobo Yodel") 50-100 30s
DIVA (6031 "Waiting for a Train") 50-100 30s
DIVA (6032 "Blue Yodel No. 4") 50-100 30s
DIVA (6033 "Lullaby Yodel") 50-100 30s
DIVA (6035 "No One to Call Me Darling") 50-100 30s
DIVA (6037 "Frankie & Johnny") 50-100 30s
DIVA (6049 "My Rough and Rowdy Ways") 50-100 30s
DIVA (6057 "Cowboy Yodel") 50-100 30s
HARMONY (1046 "Blue Yodel No. 5") 25-50 49
MONTGOMERY WARD (4242 "Bear Cat Papa Blues") 100-200 30s
MONTGOMERY WARD (4243 "My Carolina Sunshine Girl") 100-200 30s
MONTGOMERY WARD (4243 "Don't Do Me That Way") 100-200 30s
MONTGOMERY WARD (4244 "High-Steppin' Mama Blues") 100-200 30s

MONTGOMERY WARD (4245 "Rheumatism Blues") 100-200 30s
MONTGOMERY WARD (4275 "Wildcat Mama") 150-250 30s
MONTGOMERY WARD (4326 "That Ramshackle Shack") 100-200 30s
MONTGOMERY WARD (4333 "I'm Always Dreaming of You") 100-200 30s
MONTGOMERY WARD (4767 "Old Woman and the Cow") 200-300 30s
MONTGOMERY WARD (4767 "Left My Gal in the Mountains") 100-200 30s
MONTGOMERY WARD (4768 "She Wouldn't Do It") 100-200 30s
MONTGOMERY WARD (4768 "She's a Low Down Mama") 150-250 30s
MONTGOMERY WARD (4931 "Pictures of My Mother") 100-200 30s
MONTGOMERY WARD (4932 "Yodeling Hobo") 100-200 30s
MONTGOMERY WARD (4933 "In the Shadow of the Pine") 100-200 30s
MONTGOMERY WARD (4975 "In the Jailhouse Now, No. 2") 100-200 30s
MONTGOMERY WARD (4975 "T.B. Blues") 150-250 30s
MONTGOMERY WARD (4976 "True Blue Bill") 100-200 30s
MONTGOMERY WARD (4977 "Jailhouse Blues") 100-200 30s
MONTGOMERY WARD (4977 "Pistol Packin' Mama") 100-200 30s
MONTGOMERY WARD (4978 "Whisper Your Mother's Name") 150-250 30s
MONTGOMERY WARD (4978 "My Carolina Sunshine Girl") 100-200 30s
MONTGOMERY WARD (8016 "Money Ain't No Use Anyway") 100-200 30s
MONTGOMERY WARD (8017 "Cowboy Yodel") 100-200 30s
MONTGOMERY WARD (8017 "Yodeling Hobo") 100-200 30s
MONTGOMERY WARD (8034 "Train Whistle Blues") 150-250 30s
MONTGOMERY WARD (8034 "Texas Blues") 150-250 30s

Note: Some Montgomery Ward numbers appear to have been used twice, with different titles, and often slightly different pricing. Since this information came from the same source, we are assuming it to be accurate until proven otherwise.)

OKEH 10-20 40-45
PERFECT 30-60
QRS (1044 "Living in the Mountains") 3500-4500 29
ROMEO (5109 "Silver Haired Daddy of Mine") 300-500 32
ROMEO (5110 "Jailhouse Blues") 300-500 32
SUPERTONE (9705 "I'll Be Thinking of You Little Gal") 3000-5000 29
VELVET TONE (2338 "True Bill Bill") 50-100 30s
VELVET TONE (2374 "A Gangster's Warning") 50-100 30s
VELVET TONE (7056 "Hobo Yodel") 50-100 30s
VELVET TONE (7057 "Waiting for a Train") 50-100 30s
VELVET TONE (7058 "Blue Yodel No. 4") 50-100 30s
VELVET TONE (7059 "Lullaby Yodel") 50-100 30s
VELVET TONE (7061 "No One to Call Me Darling") 50-100 30s
VELVET TONE (7063 "Frankie & Johnny") 50-100 30s
VELVET TONE (7075 "My Rough and Rowdy Ways") 50-100 30s
VELVET TONE (7083 "Cowboy Yodel") 50-100 30s
VOCALION 25-50 35-40

Singles: 7-inch

COLUMBIA (06189 "Statue in the Bay") 3-4 86
COLUMBIA (20700 thru 21500 series) 5-10 50-56
COLUMBIA (38700 thru 40500 series) 5-10 50-55
COLUMBIA (44000 series) 3-5 68
MISTLETOE 3-5 74
REPUBLIC 3-8 59-76

Picture Sleeves

COLUMBIA HALL of FAME (33165 "Rudolph the Red-Nosed Reindeer") 4-6 69
REPUBLIC (2002 "Santa's Comin' in a Whirlybird") 5-10 59

EPs: 7-inch

COLUMBIA 40-50 51-56

LPs: 10/12-inch

BIRCHMOUNT 8-12
BULLDOG 5-10
CHALLENGE 25-30 58
COLUMBIA (55 thru 154) 80-100 51-55
(10-inch LPs.)
COLUMBIA (600 series) 80-100 55
COLUMBIA (1000 series) 8-10 70-82
COLUMBIA (1500 series) 10-20 61
COLUMBIA (2500 series) 75-100 56
(10-inch LPs.)
COLUMBIA (6020 "Gene Autry Western Classics") 40-60 49
(10-inch LP.)
COLUMBIA (6137 "Merry Christmas") 40-60 50
(10-inch LP.)
COLUMBIA (8000 series) 80-100
COLUMBIA (9001 "Western Classics") 40-60 51
(10-inch LP.)
COLUMBIA (9002 "Western Classics, Vol. 2") 40-60 51
(10-inch LP.)
COLUMBIA (15000 series) 8-10 81
COLUMBIA (37000 series) 5-10 82
DESIGN 8-10
ENCORE 6-10 80
GRT 10-15 77
GOLDEN AGE 5-10 77
GRAND PRIX 8-10
HALLMARK 8-12
HARMONY (7100 thru 7300 series) 20-30 56-65
HARMONY (9500 series) 15-25 59-64
HARMONY (11000 series) 10-15 64-66
HURRAH 5-10
INTERNATIONAL AWARD 5-10
MELODY RANCH (101 "Melody Ranch") 30-50 65
MISTLETOE 8-12 74
MURRAY HILL (61072 "The Gene Autry Collection") 45-55 83
(Boxed, four-disc set.)
MURRAY HILL (897296 "Melody Ranch Radio Show") 45-55 80s
(Boxed, four-disc set.)
RCA (2600 series) 25-30 62
RADIOLA 5-10 75
REPUBLIC (1900 series) 5-10
REPUBLIC (6000 series) 5-15 76-78
STARDAY 6-10 78
TIMELESS TREASURES 5-8 83

Sessions: Johnny Bond; Pat Buttram.
Also see BOND, Johnny
Also see CLAYTON, Bob
Also see CLAYTON and Breen
Also see DODDS, Johnny
Also see HANDY, John
Also see HATFIELD, Overton
Also see HILL, Sam
Also see JOHNSON, Gene
Also see LONG, Tom
Also see PARKER, Fess, & Buddy Ebsen / Gene Autry
Also see SMITH, Jimmy

AVALANCHE '77 — *R&B '77*

Singles: 7-inch

ABC 3-5 77
BOBLO 3-5 77

LPs: 10/12-inch

ABC 5-10 77

AVALON, Frankie — *P&R/R&B '58*

("11 Year Old Frankie Avalon")

Singles: 78 rpm

CHANCELLOR 25-50 57-58
"X" 10-20 54

Singles: 7-inch

ABC 3-5 74
AMOS 4-6 69
BOBCAT 3-5 83
CHANCELLOR (1 "Shy Guy") 20-40
(Acnecare promotional special products issue.)
CHANCELLOR (1004 "Cupid") 20-30 57
CHANCELLOR (1011 thru 1026) 15-25 57-58
CHANCELLOR (1031 "Venus") 10-20 58
(Monaural.)
CHANCELLOR (1031 "Venus") 25-50 58
(Stereo.)
CHANCELLOR (1036 "Bobby Sox to Stockings") 10-20 59
(Monaural.)
CHANCELLOR (1036 "Bobby Sox to Stockings") 25-50 59
(Stereo.)
CHANCELLOR (1040 "Just Ask Your Heart") 10-20 59
(Monaural.)
CHANCELLOR (1040 "Just Ask Your Heart") 25-50 59
(Stereo.)
CHANCELLOR (1045 "Why") 10-20 59
(Monaural.)
CHANCELLOR (1045 "Why") 25-50 59
(Stereo.)
CHANCELLOR (1048 thru 1131) 10-20 60-63
CHANCELLOR (1134 "Come Fly with Me") 15-25 63
CHANCELLOR (1135 "Cleopatra") 10-20 63
CHANCELLOR (1139 "Beach Party") 10-20 64
COLLECTABLES 3-4 81
DE LITE 3-6 76-78
ERIC 3-4 73
MCA 3-4 84
METROMEDIA 3-5 70
REGALIA 3-5 72
REPRISE 4-8 68-69
U.A. 5-10 64-65
"X" "(0006 "Trumpet Sorrento") 20-30 54
"X" "(0026 "Trumpet Tarantella") 20-30 54

Picture Sleeves

CHANCELLOR (1026 thru 1045) 20-30 58-59
CHANCELLOR (1048 thru 1125) 10-20 60-63
DE LITE 4-8 78
U.A. 10-15 64

EPs: 7-inch

CHANCELLOR 20-40 58-60
"X" 20-40 55

Promotional EPs

CHANCELLOR (303 "Ballad of the Alamo") 50-100 60
(With complete publicity kit.)
CHANCELLOR (303 "Ballad of the Alamo") 20-40 60
(Without publicity kit.)
CHANCELLOR (5004 "Swingin' on a Rainbow") 25-50 59
(White label. Includes paper sleeve with note from Frankie, thanking dee jays for their support.)

LPs: 10/12-inch

ABC 5-10 73
CHANCELLOR (5001 "Frankie Avalon") 35-50 58
CHANCELLOR (5002 "Young Frankie Avalon") 35-45 59
(Black vinyl.)
CHANCELLOR (5002 "Young Frankie Avalon") 75-100 59
(Colore vinyl.)
CHANCELLOR (5004 "Swingin' on a Rainbow") 35-45 59
(With bound-in photo page.)

CHANCELLOR (CHL-5011 "Summer Scene") 25-35 60
(Monaural.)
CHANCELLOR (CHLS-5011 "Summer Scene") 30-40 60
(Stereo.)
CHANCELLOR (CHL-5018 "A Whole Lot of Frankie") 25-35 61
CHANCELLOR (CHL-5022 "About Mr. Avalon") 20-30 61
(Monaural.)
CHANCELLOR (CHLS-5022 "About Mr. Avalon") 25-35 61
(Stereo.)
CHANCELLOR (CHL-5025 "Frankie Avalon Italiano") 20-25 62
(Monaural.)
CHANCELLOR (CHLS-5025 "Frankie Avalon Italiano") 20-30 62
(Stereo.)
CHANCELLOR (CHL-5027 "You Are Mine") 20-25 62
(Monaural.)
CHANCELLOR (CHLS-5027 "You Are Mine") 20-30 62
(Stereo.)
CHANCELLOR (CHL-5031 "Christmas Album") 20-25 62
(Monaural.)
CHANCELLOR (CHLS-5031 "Christmas Album") 20-30 62
(Stereo.)
CHANCELLOR (CHL-5032 "Cleopatra") 20-25 62
(Monaural.)
CHANCELLOR (CHLS-5032 "Cleopatra") 20-30 62
(Stereo.)
CHANCELLOR (69801 "Young and in Love") 50-75 60
(LP with felt cover and 3-D portrait, suitable for hanging, in a special box.)
CHANCELLOR (69801 "Young and in Love") 25-40 60
(LP without the box.)
DE-LITE 5-10 76-78
EVEREST 5-10 82
51 WEST 5-10
LIBERTY 5-10 82
MCA 5-10 85
METROMEDIA 5-10 70
SUNSET 8-10 69
TRIP 5-10 77
U.A. 15-20 64
(With "UAL" or "UAS" prefix.)
U.A. 5-10 75
(With "UA-LA" prefix.)
Also see FABIAN / Frankie Avalon

AVALON, Frankie, & Annette

Singles: 12-inch

PACIFIC STAR (5698 "Merry Christmas") 15-25 81
(Picture disc.)

Singles: 7-inch

PACIFIC STAR (569 "Merry Christmas") 3-6 81
(Black vinyl.)
PACIFIC STAR (569 "Merry Christmas") 15-20 81
(Colored vinyl.)

Picture Sleeves

PACIFIC STAR (569 "Merry Christmas") 4-8 81
Also see ANNETTE
Also see AVALON, Frankie

AVANT-GARDE — P&R '68

Singles: 7-inch

COLUMBIA 4-6 67-68

AVERAGE, Johnny, Band: see JOHNNY AVERAGE BAND

AVERAGE WHITE BAND

(AWB) — P&R/R&B/LP '74

Singles: 7-inch

ARISTA 3-4 80
ATLANTIC 3-4 74-80
MCA 3-5 73-74

LPs: 10/12-inch

ARISTA 5-8 80
ATLANTIC (Except 19000 series) 8-12 74-76
ATLANTIC (19000 series) 5-10 77-80
MCA (Except 345) 8-10 73-75
MCA (345 "Show Your Hand") 15-20 73
(With "Jack-in-the-box" cover.)
MCA (345 "Show Your Hand") 8-10 73
(With standard cover.)
Members: Roger Ball; Malcolm Duncan; Steve Ferrone; Alan Gorrie; Robbie McIntosh; Onnie McIntyre; Hamish Stuart.
Also see FOREVER MORE
Also see KING, Ben E., & Average White Band
Also see STONE the CROWS

AXE — P&R/LP '82

Singles: 7-inch

ATCO 3-4 82-84
MCA 3-4 79-80

LPs: 10/12-inch

ATCO 5-10 82-84
MCA 5-10 79-80
Member: Bobby Barth.
Also see BABYFACE

AXTON, Hoyt — C&W/P&R '74

(With the Sherwood Singers)

Singles: 7-inch

A&M 3-5 73-76
BRIAR 5-10 61
CAPITOL 3-5 71-72
COLGEMS 4-6 67
COLUMBIA 4-6 69
ELEKTRA 3-4 81
HORIZON 5-10 62-63
JEREMIAH 3-5 79-83
MCA 3-5 77-78
20TH FOX 4-8 66
VEE JAY 5-10 64-65

Picture Sleeves

A&M 3-5 73-74

LPs: 10/12-inch

A&M 5-10 73-77
ACCORD 5-10 82
ALLEGIANCE 5-10 84
BRYLEN 5-10 82
CAPITOL 8-10 71
COLUMBIA 8-12 69
EXODUS 10-15 66
HORIZON 15-25 62-63
JEREMIAH 8-10 79-82
LAKE SHORE 5-10 81
MCA 5-10 77-78
SURREY 10-20 65
VEE JAY 10-20 64-65
VEE JAY INT'L (Except 1000 series) 5-10 74-77
VEE JAY INT'L (1000 series) 10-12 74
Session: Linda Ronstadt; Tanya Tucker; Ronee Blakley
Also see RONSTADT, Linda
Also see TUCKER, Tanya

AXTON, Hoyt, & Chambers Brothers

Singles: 7-inch

HORIZON 4-8 62

LPs: 10/12-inch

HORIZON 15-20 63
Also see AXTON, Hoyt
Also see CHAMBERS BROTHERS

AYERS, Roy — LP '74

(Roy Ayers' Ubiquity)

Singles: 12-inch

COLUMBIA 4-6 84-85
POLYDOR 4-6 79

Singles: 7-inch

COLUMBIA 3-4 84-86
POLYDOR 3-4 77

LPs: 10/12-inch

ATLANTIC 8-12 68-76
COLUMBIA 5-10 84-86
ELEKTRA 5-10 78
POLYDOR 6-10 70-82
Also see DUNLAP, Gene
Also see MANN, Herbie
Also see UBIQUITY

AYERS, Roy, & Wayne Henderson

Singles: 7-inch

POLYDOR 3-4 79-80

LPs: 10/12-inch

POLYDOR 5-10 80
Also see AYERS, Roy
Also see HENDERSON, Wayne

AZTEC CAMERA — LP '83

Singles: 12-inch

SIRE 5-10 84

Singles: 7-inch

SIRE 3-6 83-88

Picture Sleeves

SIRE 3-6 84-88

LPs: 10/12-inch

SIRE 8-15 83-87

AZTECA — LP '73

Singles: 7-inch

COLUMBIA 3-5 72-73

LPs: 10/12-inch

COLUMBIA 10-12 72-73
Members: Coke Escovedo; Tony Smith.
Also see ESCOVEDO, Coke
Also see MALO
Also see SANTANA

FIRST NAME INITIAL
MY HEART BECAME OF AGE
F-349
Vista
Annette
©WALT DISNEY PRODUCTIONS

Buena Vista Records
presents
ANNETTE and HAYLEY MILLS
Singing 10 of their greatest all time Hits
!
ANNETTE SINGS
1. "Pineapple Princess"
2. "Tall Paul"
3. "Mr. Piano Man"
4. "First Name Initial"
HAYLEY SINGS
1. "Flitterin'"
2. "Castaway"
3. "Let's Get together"
4. "Ding, Ding, Ding"
5. "Cobbler, Cobbler"

THE Archies
FULL FIDELITY
33⅓ RPM
RECORD

a repertory recording
FROM THE SESAC TRANSCRIBED LIBRARY
AD 48
No Greater Love
with
Chet Atkins
Faron Young
and
The Anita Kerr Singers

B ANGIE B *LP '91*

LPs: 10/12-inch

CAPITOL 5-8 91

B.B.C.S. & A. *R&B '82*

Singles: 7-inch

SAM 3-4 82

B.B. & Q. Band *LP '81*
(Brooklyn, Bronx & Queens Band)

Singles: 12-inch

CAPITOL 4-6 81-83

Singles: 7-inch

CAPITOL 3-5 81-83
IN YOUR FACE 3-4 86

LPs: 10/12-inch

CAPITOL 5-10 81-83

B. BEAT GIRLS *D&D '83*

Singles: 12-inch

25 WEST 4-6 83

Singles: 7-inch

25 WEST 3-4 83

B. BUMBLE & STINGERS *P&R '61*

Singles: 7-inch

DYMO 5-10
HIGHLAND 5-10 60s
MERCURY 5-10 66-67
RENDEZVOUS 10-15 61-63
TRIAD 4-6 74
WAX 5-10 64
Members: Billy Brumble; Ron Brady; Fred Richard; Ernie Freeman.
Also see FREEMAN, Ernie

B.C.G.: see CREWE, Bob

B-52s *LP '79*

Singles: 12-inch

W.B. 4-6 86

Singles: 7-inch

B-52s (52 "Rock Lobster") 15-20 78
REPRISE 3-4 89-91
W.B. (Except 927) 3-4 79-86
W.B. (927 "Give Me Back My Man") 3-5 81
(Promotional issue only.)

Picture Sleeves

B-52s (52 "Rock Lobster") 25-50 78
REPRISE 3-4 89
W.B. 3-5 80-83

LPs: 10/12-inch

REPRISE 5-8 89-91
W.B. 5-10 79-86
Members: Cindy Wilson; Keith Strickland; Fred Schneider III; Ricky Wilson; Kate Pierson.

B-H-Y *R&B '79*
(Baker-Harris-Young)

Singles: 7-inch

SALSOUL 3-5 79

LPs: 10/12-inch

SALSOUL 5-10 79
Members: Ron Baker; Norman Harris; Earl Young.
Also see MFSB
Also see TRAMMPS

B.T. EXPRESS *P&R/R&B/LP '74*

Singles: 12-inch

COAST to COAST 4-6 81
COLUMBIA 4-6 81

Singles: 7-inch

COAST to COAST 3-4 82
COLUMBIA 3-5 76-80
EARTHTONE 3-4 84
ROADSHOW 3-5 74-75
SCEPTER 3-6 74

LPs: 10/12-inch

COAST to COAST 5-10 82
COLUMBIA 5-10 76-80
ROADSHOW 10-12 74-76
SCEPTER 8-10 74
Members: Carlos Ward; Bill Risbrook; Richard Thompson; Michael Jones; Dennis Rowe; Leslie Ming; Barbara Joyce Lomas.

BTO: see BACHMAN - TURNER OVERDRIVE

BABE RUTH *LP '73*

Singles: 7-inch

CAPITOL 3-4 76
HARVEST 3-5 73-76

LPs: 10/12-inch

HARVEST 5-10 73-76
Members: Ellie Hope; Steve Gurl; Jenny Haan; Dave Hewitt; Ray Knott; Bernie Marsden; Alan Shacklock; Ed Spevock.

BABY JANE & ROCK-A-BYES
(Baby Jane) *P&R '63*

Singles: 7-inch

SPOKANE (4001 "Hickory Dickory Dock") 10-20 63
(First issue.)
SPOKANE (4004 "Get Me to the Church on Time") 10-20 63
(First issue.)
U.A. (505 "Oh Johnny") 8-12 62
U.A. (560 "Doggie in the Window") 10-15 63
U.A. (593 "Hickory Dickory Dock") 8-12 63

BABY RAY *P&R '66*
(Ray Eddlemon)

Singles: 7-inch

CAPACITY (116 "Dance My Tears Away") 10-15 60s
IMPERIAL 8-15 66-67

LPs: 10/12-inch

IMPERIAL 15-20 67

BABY RAY & FERNS

Singles: 7-inch

DONNA (1378 "How's Your Bird") 25-35 63
Member: Frank Zappa.
Also see ZAPPA, Frank

BABYFACE *P&R '89*

Singles: 7-inch

ASI 3-5 76-77

LPs: 10/12-inch

ASI 10-12 77
Also see AXE

BABYFACE *R&B '87*

Singles: 7-inch

SOLAR 3-4 87-89

LPs: 10/12-inch

SOLAR 5-8 89
EPIC 5-8 90s
Members: Kenny "Babyface" Edmonds; Antonio "L.A." Reid.
Also see DEELE

BABYLON A.D. *LP '89*

LPs: 10/12-inch

ARISTA 5-8 89

BABYS *P&R/LP '77*

Singles: 7-inch

CHRYSALIS 3-5 77-81

Picture Sleeves

CHRYSALIS 3-5 80

LPs: 10/12-inch

CHRYSALIS 5-10 77-81
Members: Mike Corby; John Waite; Tony Brock; Wally Stocker; Johnthan Cain.
Also see BAD ENGLISH
Also see JOURNEY

BACHARACH, Burt *P&R '63*

Singles: 7-inch

A&M 3-5 68-74
CABOT 3-5
KAPP 3-6 63-65
LIBERTY 3-5 66
U.A. 3-5 67

Picture Sleeves

A&M 3-5 71

EPs: 7-inch

A&M 4-8 68-73

LPs: 10/12-inch

A&M (Except 1) 5-10 67-74
A&M (1 "Radio Interview") 8-15 74
(Promotional issue only.)
KAPP 8-15 65
MCA 5-10 73
Also see CAMPBELL, Glen / Dionne Warwick / Burt Bacharach

BACHELORS *P&R/LP '64*

Singles: 7-inch

LONDON 5-10 63-72

Picture Sleeves

LONDON 10-15 64-65

LPs: 10/12-inch

LONDON 10-25 64-72
Members: Con Cluskey; Declan Stokes; John Stokes.

BACHMAN, Randy

Singles: 7-inch

POLYDOR 3-4 78

LPs: 10/12-inch

POLYDOR 5-10 78
RCA (1100 series) 5-10 75
RCA (4300 series) 10-15 70
Also see BACHMAN - TURNER - BACHMAN
Also see BACHMAN - TURNER OVERDRIVE
Also see GUESS WHO
Also see IRONHORSE

BACHMAN-TURNER-BACHMAN

LPs: 10/12-inch

REPRISE (2210 "As Brave Belt") 8-10 74
Members: Randy Bachman; C.F. Turner; Robin Bachman.
Also see BACHMAN-TURNER OVERDRIVE
Also see BRAVE BELT

BACHMAN-TURNER OVERDRIVE *P&R/LP '73*

Singles: 7-inch

COMPLEAT 3-4 84-85
MERCURY 3-5 73-79

Picture Sleeves

MERCURY 3-5 74-75

LPs: 10/12-inch

COMPLEAT 5-10 84-85
CURB 5-8 86
MERCURY 6-12 73-79
Members: Randy Bachman; C.F. Turner; Robin Bachman; Tim Bachman; Jim Clench; Norman Durkee; Blair Thornton.
Also see BACHMAN, Randy

BACK STREET CRAWLER *LP '75*
(Crawler)

Singles: 7-inch

EPIC 3-4 77-78

LPs: 10/12-inch

ATCO 10-12 75-76
EPIC (Except PAL-349001) 5-10 77-78
EPIC (PAL-349001 "Crawler") 25-30 78
(Picture disc.)
Members: Tony Braunagel; John Bundrick; Paul Kossoff; Mike Montgomery; Geoff Whitehorn; Terry Wilson Slesser.
Also see CUMMINGS, Burton / Cheap Trick / Crawler
Also see FREE
Also see KOSSOFF, Paul

BACKUS, Jim *P&R '58*
(With Friend; Mr. McGoo & Dennis Farnon Orchestra; Jim Bakus)

Singles: 7-inch

JUBILEE 10-20 58-59

EPs: 7-inch
RCA (1362 "McGoo in Hi-Fi")........... 25-35 56
LPs: 10/12-inch
DORE 8-10 74
RCA (1362 "McGoo in Hi-Fi")........... 50-75 56
Also see HOPE, Bob

BACKUS, Jim, & Daws Butler
Singles: 7-inch
DICO (101 "I Was a Teenage Reindeer").. 5-10
Also see BACKUS, Jim

BAD BOYS FEATURING K LOVE *R&B/D&D '85*
Singles: 12-inch
STARLITE 4-6 85
Singles: 7-inch
STARLITE 3-4 85

BAD COMPANY *P&R/LP '74*
Singles: 12-inch
ATLANTIC 5-10 88
(Promotional only.)
Singles: 7-inch
ATCO.. 3-6 92
ATLANTIC (80000 series) 3-6 86-89
ATLANTIC (90000 series) 3-5 92
SWAN SONG.................................... 3-6 74-82
Picture Sleeves
ATLANTIC....................................... 3-4 86-89
SWAN SONG.................................... 3-5 79-82
LPs: 10/12-inch
ATCO... 5-8 90-93
ATLANTIC....................................... 5-10 86-88
SWAN SONG.................................... 5-10 74-82
Members: Paul Rodgers; Brian Howe; Boz Burrell; Simon Kirke; Mick Ralphs; Mick Jones.
Also see FIRM
Also see FOREIGNER
Also see FREE
Also see KING CRIMSON
Also see NUGENT, Ted
Also see RODGERS, Paul

BAD ENGLISH *P&R/LP '89*
Singles: 7-inch
EPIC 3-4 90
LPs: 10/12-inch
EPIC 5-8 89
Members: John Waithe; Jonathan Cain; Neal Schon; Ricky Phillips; Dean Castronovo.
Also see BABYS
Also see JOURNEY

BAD GIRLS *R&B '81*
Singles: 7-inch
BC... 3-4 81

BAD HABITS
Singles: 7-inch
PAULA.. 5-10 70-72
Members: Delaney Bramlett; Bonnie Bramlett.
Also see DELANEY & BONNIE

BADAROU, Wally *R&B '86*
Singles: 7-inch
ISLAND... 3-4 86
LPs: 10/12-inch
ISLAND... 5-10 86

BADFINGER *P&R '69*
Singles: 7-inch
AMERICOM (301 "Maybe Tomorrow")................................ 100-200 69
(Plastic "Pocket Disc" soundsheet.)
APPLE (1815 "Come and Get It") 5-15 70
APPLE (1822 "No Matter What")......... 5-15 70
APPLE (1841 "Day After Day")............ 5-15 71
APPLE (1844 "Baby Blue")................. 5-15 72
APPLE (1864 "Apple of My Eye")...... 10-20 73
ATLANTIC 3-4 81
ELEKTRA....................................... 3-5 79
RADIO 3-4 81
W.B. 3-6 74
Promotional Singles
APPLE (1841 "Day After Day")...... 100-125 71
White label.)
APPLE (1844 "Baby Blue").......... 100-125 72
(White label.)
APPLE (1864 "Apple of My Eye") 20-25 73
Picture Sleeves
APPLE (1844 "Baby Blue")............... 10-15 72
LPs: 10/12-inch
APPLE (3364 "Magic Christian Music") 20-30 70
APPLE (3367 "No Dice").................. 15-25 70
APPLE (3387 "Straight Up") 40-60 71
APPLE (3411 "Ass") 15-25 73
ELEKTRA (175 "Airwaves")............. 10-15 79
RADIO (16030 "Say No More").......... 5-10 81
RYKODISC (0189 "Day After Day").. 15-25 90
(Clear vinyl.)
W.B. (2762 "Badfinger").................. 15-20 74
W.B. (2827 "Wish You Were Here") 20-30 74
Members: Tom Evans; Mike Gibbons; Pete Ham; Joey Molland; Peter Clarke; Tony Kaye.
Also see IVEYS

BADGER *LP '73*
LPs: 10/12-inch
ATCO 10-12 73
EPIC.. 8-10 74
Members: Roy Dyke; Kim Gardner; Dave Foster; Tony Kaye; Jackie Lomax; Brian Parrish; Paul Pilnick.
Also see ASHTON, GARDNER & DYKE
Also see LOMAX, Jackie

BADLANDS *LP '89*
LPs: 10/12-inch
ATLANTIC.. 5-8 89-91

BAERWALD, David *LP '90*
LPs: 10/12-inch
A&M 5-8 90

BAEZ, Joan *LP '61*
Singles: 7-inch
A&M 3-5 72-77
DECCA... 3-5 72
PORTRAIT....................................... 3-5 77-79
RCA 3-5 72
VANGUARD (6 "Maria Dolores")........ 5-10
(Stereo. Juke box issue.)
VANGUARD (35000 series)................ 4-8 63-69
VANGUARD (35100 series)................ 3-5 70-71
Picture Sleeves
A&M 4-6 72
PORTRAIT....................................... 3-5 79
RCA 4-6 72
VANGUARD (6 "Deportee")............... 5-10 60s
(Promotional issue only.)
VANGUARD (35031 "There But for Fortune") 15-25 65
LPs: 10/12-inch
A&M (Except 8375)........................... 6-10 72-77
A&M (8375 "Joan Baez - Radio Airplay Album") 10-15 76
(Promotional issue only.)
EMUS... 5-10 79
FANTASY 10-15
MFSL (238 "Diamonds & Rust") 20-25 94
NAUTILUS 25-35 81
(Half-speed mastered.)
PICKWICK....................................... 5-10 73
PORTRAIT....................................... 5-10 77-79
SQUIRE 10-20 63
VANGUARD (41/42 "Ballad Book") .. 10-15 72
VANGUARD (49/50 "Contemporary Ballad Book") 10-15 70s
VANGUARD (105/106 "Country Music Album") 10-20 79
VANGUARD (077 thru 123)............. 20-30 60-63
VANGUARD (160 thru 306).............. 12-25 64-69
VANGUARD (308 thru 332)............... 6-10 69-73
VANGUARD (400 series).................. 5-10
(Vanguard numbers 077 through 446 may be preceded by a "2," indicating stereo, or a "9" or "79" for mono issues.)
VANGUARD (6500 series)................. 8-12 71
VANGUARD (6500 series)............... 10-12 70-71
Also see WILSON, Dennis / Ram Jam / Joan Baez

BAEZ, Joan, Bill Wood & Ted Alevizos
LPs: 10/12-inch
VERITAS (62202 "Folksingers 'Round Harvard Square")............................ 100-200 60
(Does NOT have text in upper right corner reading: "This is the historic album featuring the original first recordings of America's Most Exciting Folk Singer — The Best of Joan Baez." A limited, numbered edition.)
VERITAS (62202 "Folksingers 'Round Harvard Square")......................... 50-100 61
(Cover does read: "This is the historic album featuring the original first recordings of America's Most Exciting Folk Singer — The Best of Joan Baez.")
Also see BAEZ, Joan

BAGBY, Doc *P&R '57*
Singles: 78 rpm
GOTHAM.. 10-20 52
KING 10-20 55
OKEH 10-20 56-57
Singles: 7-inch
END... 8-12 60
GATOR (Pony Walk").......................... 5-10 61
GONE (5087 "Pancake Hop") 8-12 60
GOTHAM "Jumpin' at Smalls")......... 25-40 52
HUNT (323 "Muscle Tough")............ 15-25 59
KAISER 10-15 59
KING (4804 "Grinding") 20-30 55
OKEH 5-10 56-57
PERRI... 5-10 62
RED TOP 15-25 59
TALLY HO 5-10 61
VIM 5-10 63
EPs: 10/12-inch
EPIC (7190 "Dumplins")................... 50-75 57
Also see TERRY, Sonny

BAGBY, Doc / Luis Rivera
LPs: 10/12-inch
KING (631 "Battle of the Organs")..... 25-35 59
Also see BAGBY, Doc

BAGDASARIAN, Ross
Singles: 7-inch
IMPERIAL... 3-5 69
LIBERTY (55000 thru 55200 series) ... 5-10 56-60
LIBERTY (55300 thru 56000 series) 3-8 61-70
MERCURY 5-10 54
LPs: 10/12-inch
LIBERTY.. 20-30 66
Also see SEVILLE, David

BAILEY, Arthur *D&D '84*
Singles: 12-inch
ATLANTIC 4-6 84
Singles: 7-inch
ATLANTIC 3-4 84

BAILEY, J.R. *R&B '68*
Singles: 7-inch
CALLA 5-15 68
MALA... 5-8 60s
MAM 3-5 74
MIDLAND INT'L................................. 3-5 75
RCA 3-5 76
SPRING.. 3-4 84
TOY 3-5 72-73
U.A. 3-4 78
VIRGO 3-5
LPs: 10/12-inch
MAM 8-10 74
U.A. 5-10 78
Also see CADILLACS
Also see CRICKETS
Also see HAWKINS, Sam

BAILEY, Pearl *R&B '46*
Singles: 78 rpm
COLUMBIA....................................... 4-8 46-50
CORAL 3-6 52-55
MERCURY 3-6 56
ROULETTE 3-6 57
SUNSET.. 3-6 56
VERVE 3-6 56

Singles: 7-inch

COLUMBIA (38000 series)...............10-20 50
COLUMBIA (43000 series)...............4-6 66
CORAL...............10-20 52-55
DECCA...............4-6 64
MERCURY...............10-15 56
PROJECT 3...............3-6 68-70
RCA (500 series)...............3-5 71
RCA (9400 series)...............4-6 67
ROULETTE...............5-10 59-68
SUNSET...............10-15 56
VERVE...............10-15 56

EPs: 7-inch

COLUMBIA...............15-25 52-56
CORAL...............15-25 54
ROULETTE...............15-25 57

LPs: 10/12-inch

ACCORD...............5-10 83
COLUMBIA (900 series)...............20-40 57
COLUMBIA (2600 series)...............25-50 56
(10-inch LPs.)
COLUMBIA (6000 series)...............25-50 50
(10-inch LPs.)
CORAL (56000 series)...............25-50 54
(10-inch LPs.)
CORAL (57000 series)...............25-50 57
CO-STAR...............15-25 58
GUEST STAR...............5-10
MERCURY (Except 100 series)...............20-40 56-58
MERCURY (100 series)...............8-12 69
PROJECT 3...............5-10 70
RCA (4500 series)...............5-10 71
ROULETTE (100 series)...............8-12 71
ROULETTE (25000 & 25100 series)...............15-30 57-63
ROULETTE (25200 & 25300 series)...............10-20 64-65
VOCALION...............15-25 58
WING...............15-25 59-63

BAILEY, Pearl, & Margie Anderson

LP: 10/12-inch

CORONET (148 "Singing & Swinging")...............10-20 60s

BAILEY, Pearl, & Mike Douglas

Singles: 7-inch

PROJECT 3...............4-6 68
Also see DOUGLAS, Mike

BAILEY, Pearl / Rose Murphy / Ivie Anderson

LPs: 10/12-inch

GRAND PRIX...............10-15 60s
Also see BAILEY, Pearl
Also see MURPHY, Rose

BAILEY, Philip — R&B/LP '83

Singles: 12-inch

COLUMBIA...............4-6 83-86

Singles: 7-inch

COLUMBIA...............3-4 83-86

Picture Sleeves

COLUMBIA...............3-4 85

LPs: 10/12-inch

COLUMBIA...............5-10 83-86
Also see EARTH, WIND & FIRE

BAILEY, Philip, & Phil Collins — P&R/R&B '84

Singles: 12-inch

COLUMBIA...............4-6 84

Singles: 7-inch

COLUMBIA...............3-4 84

Picture Sleeves

COLUMBIA...............3-4 84
Also see BAILEY, Philip
Also see COLLINS, Phil

BAILEY, Philip, & Little Richard

Singles: 7-inch

WTG (08492 "Twins")...............3-4 88
Also see BAILEY, Phil
Also see LITTLE RICHARD

BAILEY, Razzy — P&R '74/C&W '76

(Razzie Bailey; Razzy)

Singles: 7-inch

ABC-PAR...............5-10 67
B&K (103 "Once We Loved")...............15-25 59
CAPRICORN...............3-5 75
ERASTUS...............3-5 76
MCA...............3-4 84-86
MGM...............3-5 74
1-3-4...............4-6 69
PEACH...............5-10 66
RCA...............3-5 77-84
SOUNDS of AMERICA...............3-4 86-89

Picture Sleeves

RCA...............3-4 80-81

LPs: 10/12-inch

MCA...............5-10 85-86
PLANTATION...............5-8 81
RCA...............5-10 79-84

BAIO, Scott — LP '82

Singles: 7-inch

RCA...............3-4 82-83

LPs: 10/12-inch

RCA...............5-10 82-83

BAJA MARIMBA BAND — P&R '63

Singles: 7-inch

A&M...............3-6 66-67
ALMO...............4-8 63-66
BJ...............3-5
BELL...............3-5 73
SHOUT...............3-4 81

Picture Sleeves

A&M...............4-8 66-68

EPs: 7-inch

A&M...............5-10 68

LPs: 10/12-inch

A&M...............5-15 64-70
BELL...............5-10 73
Member: Julius Wechter.
Also see DENNY, Martin
Also see MONTEZ, Chris

BAKER, Anita — R&B/LP '83

Singles: 7-inch

BEVERLY GLEN...............3-4 83-84
ELEKTRA...............3-4 86-90

Picture Sleeves

ELEKTRA...............3-4 86-89

LPs: 10/12-inch

BEVERLY GLEN...............5-10 83
ELEKTRA...............5-10 86-90
Also see CHAPTER 8
Also see WINANS & Anita Baker

BAKER, Arthur — D&D '84

Singles: 12-inch

ATLANTIC...............4-6 84

BAKER, George — P&R/LP '70

(George Baker Selection)

Singles: 7-inch

COLOSSUS...............4-6 70
W.B. 3-5 75-76

Picture Sleeves

COLOSSUS...............5-8 70

LPs: 10/12-inch

COLOSSUS...............15-20 70
W.B. 10-15 76

BAKER, Ginger — P&R/LP '70

(Ginger Baker's Air Force)

Singles: 7-inch

ATCO...............3-5 70

LPs: 10/12-inch

ATCO...............12-15 70-72
AXIOM...............8-12 90
SIRE...............5-10 77
POLYDOR...............8-10 72-79
Also see BAKER - GURVITZ ARMY
Also see BLIND FAITH
Also see CREAM
Also see WINWOOD, Steve

BAKER, Lavern — R&B '55

(With the Gliders)

Singles: 78 rpm

ATLANTIC...............20-50 53-57

Singles: 7-inch

ATLANTIC (1000 series, except 1004)...............10-25 54-58
ATLANTIC (1004 "Soul on Fire")...............30-40 53
ATLANTIC (2000 series, except 2001)...............10-20 59-65
ATLANTIC (2001 "It's So Fine")...............20-30 58
BRUNSWICK (55291 "Baby")...............10-20 66
BRUNSWICK (55297 "Call Me Darling")...............10-20 66
BRUNSWICK (55311 "Wrapped, Tied and Tangled")...............25-35 67

EPs: 7-inch

ATLANTIC (566 "Lavern Baker - Tweedle Dee")...............50-100 56
ATLANTIC (588 "Lavern Baker - Jim Dandy")...............50-100 57
ATLANTIC (617 "Lavern Baker - I Cried a Tear")...............50-75 58

LPs: 10/12-inch

ATCO...............10-15 71
ATLANTIC (Except 8002, 8007 & 8030)...............25-50 59-63
ATLANTIC (8002 "Lavern")...............150-200 57
(Black label.)
ATLANTIC (8002 "Lavern")...............25-50 59
(Red label.)
ATLANTIC (8007 "Lavern Baker")...............100-150 57
ATLANTIC (8030 "Blues Ballads")...............50-75 59
(Black label.)
ATLANTIC (8030 "Blues Ballads")...............50-75 59
(White label.)
ATLANTIC (8030 "Blues Ballads")...............30-60 59
(Red label.)
BRUNSWICK...............10-15 70
Session: King Curtis.
Also see KING CURTIS
Also see RHODES, Todd
Also see WILSON, Jackie, & LaVern Baker

BAKER, Lavern, & Ben E. King

Singles: 7-inch

ATLANTIC...............10-20 60
Also see KING, Ben E.

BAKER, Lavern, & Jimmy Ricks

Singles: 7-inch

ATLANTIC...............5-10 61
Also see BAKER, Lavern

BAKER - GURVITZ ARMY — LP '75

Singles: 7-inch

ATCO...............3-5 74-76
JANUS...............3-5 75

LPs: 10/12-inch

ATCO...............8-10 75-76
JANUS...............10-12 75
Members: Ginger Baker; Adrian Gurvitz; Paul Gurvitz; Peter Lemer; John Norman; Snips.
Also see BAKER, Ginger
Also see GURVITZ, Adrian

BALAAM & ANGEL — LP '88

LPs: 10/12-inch

VIRGIN...............5-10 87-89
Members: Mark Morris; Jim Morris; Des Morris; Ian McKean.

BALANCE — P&R/LP '81

Singles: 7-inch

PORTRAIT...............3-4 81-82

LPs: 10/12-inch

PORTRAIT...............5-10 81-82
Also see BLUES MAGOOS

BALDRY, Long John — P&R '68

(With the Hootchie Cootchie Men)

Singles: 7-inch

A&M...............4-6 68
ASCOT...............4-8 66-67
EMI AMERICA...............3-4 79
W.B. 3-6 68-72

Picture Sleeves

W.B. 4-8 72

LPs: 10/12-inch
ASCOT 15-25 65
CASABLANCA 5-10 75-76
EMI AMERICA 5-10 79-80
JANUS 10-15
MUSICLINE 5-8 86
U.A. 8-10 71
W.B. 8-10 71-72

BALDRY, Long John, & Kathi McDonald
Singles: 7-inch
EMI AMERICA 3-4 79
Picture Sleeves
EMI AMERICA 3-4 79
Also see BALDRY, Long John
Also see McDONALD, Kathi

BALIN, Marty P&R/LP '81
Singles: 7-inch
CHALLENGE 20-25 62
EMI AMERICA 3-4 81-84
Picture Sleeves
EMI AMERICA 3-4 81
LPs: 10/12-inch
EMI AMERICA 8-10 81-83
Also see JEFFERSON AIRPLANE
Also see JEFFERSON STARSHIP

BALL, Kenny P&R/LP '62
(With His Jazzmen)
Singles: 7-inch
DECCA 3-5 67
GUYDEN 3-5 61
KAPP 3-5 62-64
Picture Sleeves
KAPP 4-8 62
LPs: 10/12-inch
JAZZOLOGY 5-10 79
KAPP 10-25 62-64
Members: Kenny Ball; Johnny Bennett; Dave Jones; Colin Bates; Vic Pitts; Ron Bowden; Diz Disley.

BALLADS P&R/R&B '68
Singles: 7-inch
VENTURE 4-8 68

BALLARD, Hank R&B '68
(With the Midnight Lighters; with Dapps)
Singles: 7-inch
KING 4-8 68
PEOPLE 4-8 72
POLYDOR 3-5 72
SILVER FOX 4-6 70
STANG 3-5 75
LPs: 10/12-inch
KING (1000 series) 10-15 69

BALLARD, Hank, & Midnighters R&B '59
Singles: 7-inch
GUSTO 3-4 78
KING (5171 "The Twist") 10-15 59
KING (5195 "Kansas City") 8-12 59
KING (5215 "Sugaree") 8-12 59
(Monaural.)
KING (S-5215 "Sugaree") 20-25 59
(Stereo.)
KING (5245 thru 6131) 5-15 59-67
LE JOINT 3-5 79
Picture Sleeves
KING (5491 "The Continental Walk") 10-15 61
EPs: 7-inch
FEDERAL (333 "Their Greatest Hits") 200-300 54
KING (333 "Their Greatest Hits") 25-50 58
KING (435 "Singin' & Swingin, Vol. 1") 25-35 59
KING (435 "Singin' & Swingin, Vol. 2") 25-35 59
KING (793 "Jumpin' Hank Ballard") 25-35 62
KING (7815 "1963 Sound of Hank Ballard & Midnighters") 15-25 59
LPs: 10/12-inch
FEDERAL (90 "Their Greatest Hits") 5000-10000 54
(10-inch LP.)
FEDERAL (541 "Their Greatest Hits") 500-750 57
(White cover.)
FEDERAL (541 "Their Greatest Hits") 400-500 57
(Tan or red cover.)
KING (541 "Their Greatest Hits") 50-100 58
KING (581 "Midnighters, Vol. 2") 50-100 58
KING (600 thru 800 series, except KS-740) 25-40 59-64
KING (KS-740 "Spotlight on Hank Ballard") 75-100 61
(Stereo.)
KING (900 series) 15-20 65-68
KING (5000 series) 8-10 77
Also see BALLARD, Hank
Also see MIDNIGHTERS
Also see ROYALS

BALLARD, Hank, & Midnighters / Viceroys
Singles: 7-inch
KING/BETHLEHEM (5719 "That Low Down Move") 10-15 63
(The Viceroys side has a Bethlehem label. Promotional issue only.)
Also see BALLARD, Hank, & Midnighters

BALLARD, Russ P&R/LP '80
Singles: 7-inch
EMI AMERICA 3-4 84-85
EPIC 3-5 74-80
LPs: 10/12-inch
EMI AMERICA 5-8 84-85
EPIC 8-10 74-80
Also see ARGENT
Also see UNIT 4+2

BALLIN' JACK P&R/LP '71
Singles: 7-inch
COLUMBIA 3-5 71
MERCURY 3-5 73
LPs: 10/12-inch
COLUMBIA 10-12 70-72
MERCURY 8-10 73-74

BALLOON FARM P&R '68
Singles: 7-inch
LAURIE 4-8 68

BALTIMORA P&R '85
Singles: 12-inch
MANHATTAN 4-6 86
Singles: 7-inch
MANHATTAN 3-4 85-86
Picture Sleeves
MANHATTAN 3-4 85
LPs: 10/12-inch
MANHATTAN (53026 "Living in the Background") 5-10 85

BALTIMORE & OHIO MARCHING BAND P&R '67
Singles: 7-inch
JUBILEE 3-6 67
LPs: 10/12-inch
JUBILEE 10-15 67

BAMA P&R '79
Singles: 7-inch
FREE FLIGHT (Black vinyl) 3-5 79
FREE FLIGHT (Colored vinyl) 4-6 79
(Promotional issues only.)
LPs: 10/12-inch
FREE FLIGHT 5-10 79

BAMBAATAA, Afrika P&R/R&B '82
(With James Brown; with Soul Sonic Force; with Family)
Singles: 12-inch
TOMMY BOY 4-6 83-86
Singles: 7-inch
EMI 3-4 88
TOMMY BOY 3-5 82-86
Picture Sleeves
EMI 3-4 88
LPs: 10/12-inch
TOMMY BOY 5-10 83-86
Also see BROWN, James
Also see SHANGO

BANANA SPLITS P&R '69
Singles: 7-inch
DECCA 4-8 68-69
Picture Sleeves
DECCA 8-10 69-70
EPs: 7-inch
KELLOGG 8-12 69
LPs: 10/12-inch
DECCA 10-15 69

BANANARAMA P&R/D&D/LP '83
Singles: 12-inch
LONDON 4-6 83-88
Singles: 7-inch
LONDON 3-4 82-88
Picture Sleeves
LONDON 3-4 82-88
LPs: 10/12-inch
LONDON 5-10 83-88
Members: Sarah Dallin; Keren Woodward; Siobhan Fahey.
Also see BAND AID

BAND, The P&R/LP '68
Singles: 7-inch
CAPITOL (Except 2000 series) 3-5 71-77
CAPITOL (2000 series) 4-8 67-70
W.B. 3-4 78
Picture Sleeves
CAPITOL (2705 "Rag Mama Rag") 4-8 70
LPs: 10/12-inch
CAPITOL (Except 2955) 10-15 69-85
CAPITOL (2955 "Music from Big Pink") 15-20 68
MFSL (039 "Music from Big Pink") .. 75-100 80
W.B. (737 "Last Waltz") 20-30 78
(Promotional issue only.)
W.B. (3146 " Last Waltz") 15-20 78
(Three-LP set.)
Members: Levon Helm; Rick Danko; Garth Hudson; Richard Manuel; Robbie Robertson.
Also see DANKO, Rick
Also see DYLAN, Bob
Also see HAWKINS, Ronnie
Also see HELM, Levon
Also see LEVON & HAWKS
Also see MILLER, Steve / Band / Quicksilver Messinger Service
Also see ROBERTSON, Robbie

BAND AID P&R '84
Singles: 7-inch
COLUMBIA (04749 "Do They Know It's Christmas") 3-4 84
Picture Sleeves
COLUMBIA (04749 "Do They Know It's Christmas") 3-5 84
Members: Bananarama; Paul McCartney; Boomtown Rats; Boy George; Phil Collins; Duran Duran; Bob Geldof; Heaven 17; Kool & Gang; George Michael; John Moss; Spandau Ballet; Status Quo; Sting; U2; Ultravox; Paul Weller; Paul Young.
Also see BANANARAMA
Also see BOOMTOWN RATS
Also see COLLINS, Phil
Also see CULTURE CLUB
Also see DURAN DURAN
Also see GELDOF, Bob
Also see HEAVEN 17
Also see KOOL & GANG
Also see SPANDAU BALLET
Also see STATUS QUO
Also see STING
Also see STYLE COUNCIL
Also see U2
Also see ULTRAVOX
Also see WHAM
Also see YOUNG, Paul

BAND OF GOLD P&R/R&B '84
Singles: 7-inch
RCA 3-4 85

BAND OF BLACK WATCH P&R/LP '76

Singles: 7-inch

PRIVATE STOCK................................3-5 75-76

LPs: 10/12-inch

PRIVATE STOCK................................5-10 76

BANDIT P&R '79

Singles: 7-inch

ARIOLA AMERICA................................3-4 79

POLYDOR................................3-4 79

LPs: 10/12-inch

ARIOLA AMERICA................................5-10 78-79

Members: Joey Newman; Kevin Barnhill; Tommy Eaton; Danny Gorman; David Rossa.

BANDOLERO D&D '84

Singles: 12-inch

SIRE................................4-6 84

Singles: 7-inch

SIRE................................3-4 84

LPs: 10/12-inch

ECLIPSE................................8-10 75

BANDWAGON R&B '68

Singles: 7-inch

EPIC................................4-6 68

BANG P&R//LP '72

Singles: 7-inch

CAPITOL................................3-5 72-74

LPs: 10/12-inch

CAPITOL................................8-12 72-73

BANG TANGO LP '89

LPs: 10/12-inch

MECHANIC................................5-8 89-91

BANGLES LP '84

Singles: 12-inch

COLUMBIA................................4-6 85-88

Singles: 7-inch

COLUMBIA................................3-4 84-88

DEF JAM................................3-4 87

DOWNKIDDIE (001 "Getting Out of Hand")................................5-10 81

Picture Sleeves

COLUMBIA................................3-4 84-88

DEF JAM................................3-4 87

DOWNKIDDIE (001 "Getting Out of Hand")................................10-20 81

(Back of sleeve shows Downkiddie Records as being in Los Angeles, California.)

DOWNKIDDIE (001 "Getting Out of Hand")................................8-15 81

(Back of sleeve shows Downkiddie Records as being in Torrance, California.)

LPs: 10/12-inch

COLUMBIA (Except 2270)................................5-10 84-90

COLUMBIA (2270 "Interchords")................................10-20 86

(Promotional issue only.)

I.R.S................................6-10 83

Members: Vicki Peterson; Debbi Peterson; Susanna Hoffs; Annette Zilinskas; Michael Steele.

Also see BANGS

Also see HOFFS, Susanna

BANGLES / Joan Jett

Singles: 7-inch

DEF JAM................................3-4 87

Picture Sleeves

DEF JAM................................3-4 87

Also see BANGLES

Also see JETT, Joan

BANGOR FLYING CIRCUS LP '69

Singles: 7-inch

DUNHILL................................3-5 70

LPs: 10/12-inch

DUNHILL................................12-15 69

Members: Michael Tegza; David Wolinski; Alan DeCarlo.

BANGS

Singles: 7-inch

DOWNKIDDIE (001 "Getting Out of Hand")................................20-30 81

Picture Sleeves

DOWNKIDDIE (001 "Getting Out of Hand")................................30-50 81

Members: Vicki Peterson; Debbi Peterson; Susanna Hoffs.

Also see BANGLES

BANKS, Bunny, Trio R&B '43

Singles: 78 rpm

SAVOY................................10-15 43

Members: Ernie Ransom; Henry Padgett; Clem Moorman.

BANKS, Darrell P&R/R&B '66

Singles: 7-inch

ATCO (6471 "Here Comes the Tears")................................10-20 67

ATCO (6484 "Angel Baby")................................15-25 67

COTILLION................................5-10 68

REVILOT................................10-20 66

SOULTOWN................................5-10 66

VOLT................................4-8 69

LPs: 10/12-inch

ATCO (216 "Darrell Banks Is Here")................................15-25 67

(Monaural.)

ATCO (216 "Darrell Banks Is Here")................................25-30 67

(Stereo.)

VOLT................................10-15 69

BANKS, Peter LP '73

Singles: 7-inch

CAPITOL................................3-5 73

LPs: 10/12-inch

CAPITOL................................10-12 73

Also see AFTER the FIRE

Also see BLODWYN PIG

Also see FLASH

Also see YES

BANKS, Ron R&B '83

Singles: 12-inch

CBS ASSOCIATED................................4-6 83

Singles: 7-inch

ABC................................3-5 75

CBS ASSOCIATED................................3-4 83

LPs: 10/12-inch

CBS ASSOCIATED................................5-10 83

Also see DRAMATICS

BANKS, Rose R&B '76

Singles: 7-inch

MOTOWN................................3-5 76

SOURCE................................3-4 80

LPs: 10/12-inch

MOTOWN................................8-10 76

Also see SLY & Family Stone

BANKS, Tony LP '79

Singles: 7-inch

ATLANTIC................................3-4 83

CHARISMA................................3-4 79

LPs: 10/12-inch

ATLANTIC................................5-10 83

CHARISMA................................5-10 79

Also see GENESIS

BANKS & HAMPTON R&B '77

Singles: 7-inch

W.B.................................3-5 76-77

LPs: 10/12-inch

W.B.................................5-10 77

Members: Homer Banks; Carl Hampton.

BANZAII P&R/R&B '75

Singles: 7-inch

SCEPTER................................3-5 75

BARBARA & BROWNS P&R/R&B '64

Singles: 7-inch

CADET................................4-8 66

SOUND of MEMPHIS................................3-5 72

STAX................................5-10 64

Member: Barbara Brown.

BARBARA & UNIQUES R&B '70

Singles: 7-inch

ABBOTT................................3-6 72

ARDEN................................4-8 70

NEW CHICAGO SOUND................................3-6 70

20TH FOX................................3-5 74

Members: Barbara Livsey; Gwen Livsey; Doris Lindsey.

BARBARA LYNN: see LYNN, Barbara

BARBARIANS P&R '65

Singles: 7-inch

JOY (290 "Hey Little Bird")................................20-30 65

LAURIE (3308 "Are You a Boy or Are You a Girl")................................10-15 65

LAURIE (3321 "What the New Breed Say")................................10-20 65

LAURIE (3326 "Moulty")................................10-20 66

LPs: 10/12-inch

LAURIE (2033 "Barbarians")................................50-70 66

RHINO................................5-10 79

Also see ELEGANTS

BARBER, Chris P&R/R&B '59

(Chris Barber's Jazz Band)

Singles: 7-inch

ATLANTIC................................5-10 59

LAURIE................................5-10 58-63

LONDON................................4-8 62

Picture Sleeves

LAURIE................................10-20 59

LPs: 10/12-inch

ARCHIVE of FOLK MUSIC................................8-12 68

ATLANTIC................................15-25 59

COLPIX................................15-25 59

LAURIE................................20-30 59-62

Also see DR. JOHN & Chris Barber

BARBER, Frank, Orch. P&R/LP '82

Singles: 7-inch

VICTORY................................3-4 82

LPs: 10/12-inch

VICTORY................................5-10 82

BARBIERI, Gato LP '73

Singles: 7-inch

A&M................................3-5 76-79

U.A.................................3-5 73

LPs: 10/12-inch

A&M................................5-10 76-79

ARISTA................................8-10 75

FLYING DUTCHMAN................................5-10 70-80

IMPULSE................................8-10 73-75

U.A.................................5-10 73

BARBOUR, Dave P&R '50

Singles: 78 rpm

CAPITOL................................5-10 50-51

Singles: 7-inch

ARWIN................................4-8 59

CAPITOL................................5-10 50-51

EPs: 7-inch

CAPITOL................................5-15 54

DECCA................................5-15 53

LPs: 10/12-inch

DECCA................................15-25 53

BARBOUR, Keith P&R/LP '69

Singles: 7-inch

BARNABY................................3-5 71

EPIC................................3-6 69-70

LPs: 10/12-inch

EPIC................................15-20 69

BARBUSTERS P&R '87

Singles: 7-inch

CBS ASSOCIATED................................3-4 87

Also see JETT, Joan

BARCLAY, Eddie P&R '55

Singles: 78 rpm

MERCURY................................8-12 57

RAMA................................5-10 55

TICO................................5-10 55

Singles: 7-inch

RAMA................................5-10 55

TICO................................5-10 55

LPs: 10/12-inch

MONUMENT................................10-20 66

BARCLAY JAMES HARVEST LP '77

Singles: 7-inch

HARVEST 3-5 73
MCA 3-5 76-77
POLYDOR 3-5 75-79
SIRE 5-10 68

LPs: 10/12-inch

HARVEST 8-12 73
MCA 8-10 77
POLYDOR 8-10 74-80
SIRE 10-15 70-71

Members: Les Holroyd; John Lees; John Pritchard; Stewart "Wolly" Wolstenholme.

BARD, Annette

Singles: 7-inch

IMPERIAL 20-25 60

Also see CONNORS, Carol

BARDENS, Peter LP '87

(Pete Bardens)

Singles: 7-inch

CAPITOL 3-4 87

Picture Sleeves

CAPITOL 3-4 87

LPs: 10/12-inch

CAPITOL 5-10 87
VERVE/FORECAST 10-12 71

Also see CAMEL
Also see THEM

BARDEUX P&R/LP '88

Singles: 7-inch

ENIGMA 3-4 89
SYNTHICIDE 3-4 88

Picture Sleeves

SYNTHICIDE 3-4 88

LPs: 10/12-inch

ENIGMA 5-8 89
SYNTHICIDE 5-8 88

Members: Stacy Smith; Jazz; Melanie Taylor.

BARE, Bobby C&W/P&R '62

(With the All American Boys; with Hillsiders; with Bobby Bare Jr; with Family; with Jeannie Bare)

Singles: 78 rpm

CAPITOL 5-10 57

Singles: 7-inch

CAPITOL 10-15 57
COLUMBIA 3-5 78-85
EMI AMERICA 3-4 85-86
FRATERNITY 10-20 58-61
MERCURY 3-5 70-72
RCA (Except 8000 & 9000 series) 3-6 69-77
RCA (8000 & 9000 series) 4-8 62-68
RICE 3-5 73-75

Picture Sleeves

RCA 5-15 62-65

LPs: 10/12-inch

CAMDEN 8-12 68-73
COLUMBIA 5-10 78-85
MERCURY 10-15 70-72
OVATION 5-10 80
PHONORAMA 5-8 82
PICKWICK 5-10 75-80
PICKWICK/HILLTOP 10-15 65
RCA (ANL1 & APL1 series) 8-12 73-77
RCA (AYL1 series) 5-10 81
RCA (0079 "Singin' in the Kitchen") .. 15-25 74
(Promotional issue only.)
RCA (LPM-2776 thru LPM-3994) 10-20 63-68
(Monaural.)
RCA (LSP-2776 thru LSP-3994) 15-25 63-68
(Stereo.)
RCA (4000 series) 10-15 69-71
RCA (6000 series) 8-15 73
SEARS 10-15
SUN (136 "Bobby Bare's Greatest Hits") 15-25 74
U.A. 8-12 75-76

Session: Anita Kerr Singers; Floyd Cramer; Lacy J. Dalton; Charlie Daniels; Waylon Jennings.
Also see BOWMAN, Don
Also see CASH, Rosanne, & Bobby Bare
Also see CRAMER, Floyd
Also see DANIELS, Charlie
Also see JENNINGS, Waylon
Also see KERR, Anita
Also see ORBISON, Roy / Bobby Bare / Joey Powers
Also see PARSONS, Bill

BARE, Bobby, Liz Anderson & Norma Jean C&W '66

Singles: 7-inch

RCA 4-6 66

LPs: 10/12-inch

BARE TRACKS 8-12
RCA 12-20 66

BARE, Bobby, & Skeeter Davis C&W '65

(Skeeter Davis & Bobby Bare)

Singles: 7-inch

RCA (8000 & 9000 series) 3-6 65-70

LPs: 10/12-inch

RCA 15-20 65-70

Also see DAVIS, Skeeter

BARE, Bobby, / Donna Fargo / Jerry Wallace

LPs: 10/12-inch

OUT of TOWN DIST 5-10 82

Also see BARE, Bobby
Also see FARGO, Donna
Also see WALLACE, Jerry

BAR-KAYS P&R/R&B '67

Singles: 12-inch

MERCURY 4-6 79-85

Singles: 7-inch

MERCURY 3-5 76-89
STAX 3-5 78-81
VOLT 4-8 67-74

Picture Sleeves

MERCURY 3-4 88-89

LPs: 10/12-inch

MERCURY 5-10 76-87
STAX 5-10 78-81
VOLT 10-15 67-74

Members: Jimmy King; Phalon Jones; Carl Cunningham; Ron Caldwell; Larry Dodson; James Alexander; Charles Allen; Vernon Burch; Ben Cauley; Donnelle Hagan; Harvey Henderson; Winston Stewart.
Also see REDDING, Otis
Also see NEWCOMERS

BARKER, Blue Lu R&B '48

Singles: 78 rpm

APOLLO 5-10 46-48
CAPITOL 10-15 48-50
DECCA 10-20 39-40

Singles: 7-inch

CAPITOL 20-30 50

BARKLEY, Tyrone R&B '79

Singles: 7-inch

MIDSONG INT'L 3-4 79

BARLOW, Dean

(With the Crickets)

Singles: 78 rpm

JAY-DEE 50-75 54

Singles: 7-inch

BEACON (463 "True Love") 10-20 59
JAY-DEE (785 "Your Love") 100-200 54
JAY-DEE (786 "Just You") 100-200 54
JAY-DEE (789 "Are You Looking for a Sweetheart") 100-200 54
JAY-DEE (795 "I'm Going to Live My Life Alone") 100-200 54
LESCAY (3004 "Baby Doll") 10-20 61
LESCAY (3010 "The Night Before Last") 10-20 61
RUST (5068 "Don't Let Him Take My Baby") 8-10 63
7 ARTS (704 "Little Sister") 10-15 61
TCF (12 "Glory of Love") 10-15 64
UT (4001 "You're Mine") 100-200 59
WARWICK (618 "It's All in Your Mind") 15-25 61

Also see CRICKETS

BARLOW, Dean, & Crickets / Deep River Boys

Singles: 78 rpm

BEACON 20-40 54

Singles: 7-inch

BEACON (104 "Be Faithful"/"Sleepy Little Cowboy") 40-60 54

Also see BARLOW, Dean
Also see DEEP RIVER BOYS

BARNES, Cheryl P&R '79

Singles: 7-inch

MILLENNIUM 3-4 77
POLYDOR 3-4 80
RCA 3-4 79

BARNES, J.J. P&R/R&B '66

(With the Dell Fi's)

Singles: 7-inch

BUDDAH 4-8 69
GROOVESVILLE 10-15 67
INVASION 4-6 70
KABLE (437 "Won't You Let Me Know") 75-125 60
MAGIC TOUCH 4-6 70
MICKAY'S (3004 "Just One More Time") 50-75 62
MICKAY'S (4472 "Get a Hold of Yourself") 50-75 62
PERCEPTION 4-6 74
REVILOT (Except 222) 10-15 68
REVILOT (222 "Out Love Is in the Pocket") 50-75 68
RICH (1005 "Won't You Let Me Know") 50-100 60
RIC-TIC 10-15 65-66
RING (101 "She Ain't Ready") 20-30 64
SCEPTER (1266 "Just One More Time") 20-30 64
VOLT 10-15 69

LPs: 10/12-inch

PERCEPTION 10-15 74

BARNES, J.J., & Steve Mancha

LPs: 10/12-inch

VOLT (6001 "Rare Stamps") 10-15 69

Also see BARNES, J.J.
Also see HOLIDAYS
Also see MANCHA, Steve

BARNES, Jimmy P&R/LP '86

Singles: 7-inch

GEFFEN 3-4 86-88

Picture Sleeves

GEFFEN 3-4 88

LPs: 10/12-inch

GEFFEN 5-10 86

Also see COLD CHISEL
Also see INXS & Jimmy Barnes

BARNET, Charlie, & Orch. R&B '42

Singles: 78 rpm

APOLLO 4-8 48
BANNER 4-8 34
BLUEBIRD 5-10 35-41
CONQUEROR 4-8 34
DECCA 4-8 42-43
MELOTONE 4-8 34
ORIOLE 4-8 34
PERFECT 4-8 33
ROMEO 4-8 33

LPs: 10/12-inch

FM VERI SONICS 5-10

BARNUM, H.B. P&R '61

Singles: 7-inch

CAPITOL (Except 5932) 5-10 65-68
CAPITOL (5932 "Heartbreaker") 20-40 67
DECCA 3-5 71
ELDO 5-10 60-61
FIDELITY 5-10
IMPERIAL 8-12 58-64
MUN RAB 8-12 59
RCA (Except 8112) 8-12 61-63
RCA (8112 "It Hurts Too Much to Cry") 40-60 62
ULTRA SONIC 8-12 60

U.A. 3-5 73
Picture Sleeves
RCA (8112 "It Hurts Too Much to Cry") 50-75 62
LPs: 10/12-inch
CAPITOL 12-20 65
RCA 15-20 62
TROPIC ISLE 15-25 59
Also see BARNUM, H.B.
Also see ROBINS

BARONS — R&B '56
Singles: 78 rpm
IMPERIAL 25-50 55-56
Singles: 7-inch
IMPERIAL (5343 "Eternally Yours"). 50-100 55
(Black vinyl.)
IMPERIAL (5343 "Eternally Yours") 200-300 55
(Colored vinyl. Promotional issue.)
IMPERIAL (5359 "My Dream My Love") 50-100 55
IMPERIAL (5370 "Cold Kisses") 50-100 55
IMPERIAL (5383 "So Long My Darling") 50-100 56
IMPERIAL (5397 "Don't Walk Out") .. 50-75 56
IMPERIAL (66000 series) 8-12 64

BARRABAS — LP '75
Singles: 7-inch
ATCO 3-5 75-76
LPs: 10/12-inch
ATCO 5-10 75-76
RCA 8-10 72-73
Members: Jo Tejada; Ricky Morales; Miquel Morales; Juan Videl; Daniel Louis; Ernest Duarte.

BARRACUDA — D&D '83
Singles: 12-inch
EPIC 4-6 83
Singles: 7-inch
EPIC 3-4 83

BARRETT, Richard — P&R '58
(With the Chantels; with Sevilles)
Singles: 7-inch
ATLANTIC 5-10 62
CRACKERJACK 10-15 63
GONE 15-25 59
MGM 15-25 58
METRO 10-15 58
SEVILLE 10-15 60
20TH FOX 8-12 59
Also see CHANTELS

BARRETT, Syd — LP '74
Singles: 12-inch
CAPITOL 8-12 88
(Promotional only. With special cover.)
LPs: 10/12-inch
CAPITOL 5-10 74-88
HARVEST (Except 11314) 10-20 70-74
HARVEST (11314 "Madcap Laughs") 20-30 70
Members: Syd Barrett; Dave Gilmour; Roger Waters; Vic Seywell; Mike Ratledge.
Also see PINK FLOYD

BARRETTO, Ray — P&R/R&B '63
Singles: 7-inch
ASCOT 5-10 66
ATLANTIC 3-6 77-78
FANIA 5-15 68-72
RIVERSIDE 5-10 61
ROULETTE 3-4
TICO 5-10 63
U.A. 5-10 65-67
LPs: 10/12-inch
ATLANTIC 5-10 76-78
CTI 5-10 81
FANIA 5-10 68-73
FANTASY 8-10 73
RIVERSIDE 10-15 61-66
TICO 10-15 62-63
U.A. 8-15 65-67
Also see LYTLE, Johnny, & Ray Barretto

BARRON KNIGHTS — P&R '79
Singles: 7-inch
DECCA 5-10 67
EPIC (Except 9835) 3-4 79
EPIC (9835 "Pop Go the Workers") 5-10 65
MERCURY 3-5 72
Members: Barron Anthony; Peanut Langford; Butch Baker; Dave Ballinger; Duke D'mond.

BARROW, Keith — R&B '78
Singles: 12-inch
COLUMBIA 4-6 79
Singles: 7-inch
CAPITOL 3-4 80
COLUMBIA 3-4 76-79
JEWEL 3-5 73
LPs: 10/12-inch
CAPITOL 5-10 80
UMBIA 5-10 77
JEWEL 8-10 73

BARRY, Claudja — P&R/LP '78
Singles: 12-inch
CHRYSALIS 4-6 79
EPIC 4-6 86-87
PERSONAL 4-6 83
TSR 4-6 85
Singles: 7-inch
CHRYSALIS 3-4 79-84
EPIC 3-4 86-87
MIRAGE 3-4 82
PERSONAL 3-4 83
SALSOUL 3-4 77-78
LPs: 10/12-inch
CHRYSALIS 5-10 79-84
HANDSHAKE 5-10 82
SALSOUL 5-10 77-78

BARRY, Claudja, & Ronnie Jones
LPs: 10/12-inch
HANDSHAKE 5-10 82
Also see BARRY, Claudja

BARRY, Jan: see BERRY, Jan

BARRY, Joe — P&R/R&B '61
Singles: 7-inch
ABC/DOT 3-4 77
JIN 10-15 60-62
NUGGET 4-8
SHOW-BIZ (2001 "I Can't Do Without You") 15-25 59
SMASH 4-8 61-62
Picture Sleeves
SMASH 10-15 61
LPs: 10/12-inch
ABC/DOT 5-10 77

BARRY, John, Orchestra — P&R '65
Singles: 12-inch
CASABLANCA (20146 "The Chase") 10-12 78
Singles: 7-inch
A&M 3-4 83
CAPITOL (4200 series) 4-6 59
CAPITOL (5400 series) 3-4 86
COLUMBIA 3-5 65-70
EPIC 3-4 72
KING 3-6 61
MCA 3-4 85
MGM 3-5 66
MERCURY 3-6 64
20TH FOX 3-5 64
U.A. 3-6 63-65
W.B. 3-5 68
Picture Sleeves
U.A. 5-10 65
LPs: 10/12-inch
CAPITOL (2500 series) 10-15 66
COLUMBIA (1003 "Ready When You Are Mr. J.B.") 8-12 70
COLUMBIA (2493 "Great Movie Themes") 10-15 66
COLUMBIA (2708 "You Only Live Twice") 8-12 67
(Stereo.)
COLUMBIA (9293 "Great Movie Themes") 10-15 66
COLUMBIA (9508 "You Only Live Twice") 8-12 67
(Monaural.)
U.A. (91 "James Bond Tenth Anniversary") 8-12 72
U.A. (3424 "Goldfinger and Other Favorites") 8-12 65
U.A. (6424 "Goldfinger and Other Favorites") 10-12 65
You'll find many more listings by this artist in *The Official Price Guide to Movie/TV Soundtracks and Original Cast Albums,* containing over 8,000 listings.
Also see ARMSTRONG, Louis
Also see BASIE, Count
Also see BASSEY, Shirley
Also see JONES, Tom
Also see MONRO, Matt
Also see SINATRA, Nancy

BARRY, Len — P&R/R&B/LP '65
Singles: 7-inch
AMY 4-6 68-69
BUDDAH 3-5 72
CAMEO 5-10 64
DECCA 5-10 65-66
MCA 3-4 73-83
MERCURY 5-10 64
PARAMOUNT 3-5 73
PARKWAY 5-10 65
RCA 5-10 67-68
SCEPTER 4-6 69-70
EPs: 7-inch
DECCA (74720 "1-2-3") 8-15 65
(Juke box issue only.)
LPs: 10/12-inch
BUDDAH 10-15 72
CAMEO 20-25 64
DECCA 20-25 65
RCA 15-20 67
Also see DOVELLS

BARRY & TAMERLANES — P&R/R&B '63
Singles: 7-inch
VALIANT 8-12 63-65
LPs: 10/12-inch
A&M 10-15
VALIANT (406 "I Wonder What She's Doing Tonight") 50-75 63
Members: Barry DeVorzon; Terry Smith; Bodie Chandler.
Also see DE VORZON, Barry

BARTHOLOMEW, Dave — R&B '50
Singles: 78 rpm
BAYOU 10-20 53
DECCA 10-20 51
DELUXE 10-20 47-50
IMPERIAL 10-20 50-57
JAX 10-20 50
KING 20-40 51-52
Singles: 7-inch
DECCA (48216 "Tra-La-La") 75-100 51
IMPERIAL (5210 "Who Drank the Beer While I Was in the Rear") 75-100 52
IMPERIAL (5249 "No More Black Nights") 75-100 51
IMPERIAL (5273 "Texas Hop") 75-125 53
IMPERIAL (5322 "Another Mule") 20-40 54
IMPERIAL (5350 "Every Night Every Day") 20-40 55
IMPERIAL (5373 "Shrimp and Gumbo") 20-30 56
IMPERIAL (5390 "Would You") 20-30 56
IMPERIAL (5408 "Lovin' You") 15-25 56
IMPERIAL (5500 thru 5800 series) 10-20 56-61
KING (4482 "Sweet Home Blues") 100-150 51
KING (4508 "In the Alley") 100-200 52
KING (4523 "Lawdy, Lawdy Lard") 100-150 52
(Black vinyl.)
KING (4523 "Lawdy, Lawdy Lard") 200-300 52
(Colored vinyl.)
KING (4544 "My Ding-A-Ling") 100-200 52

KING (4559 "The Golden Rule")...... 50-100 52
KING (4585 "High Flying Woman")...... 50-100 53

LPs: 10/12-inch

IMPERIAL (9162/12076 "Fats Domino Presents Dave Bartholomew & His Great Big Band")...... 40-50 61
IMPERIAL (9217/12217 "New Orleans House Party")...... 40-50 63
Imperial 9000 numbers are mono, 12000 are stereo.
Also see ARCHIBALD
Also see DOMINO, Fats
Also see KING, Jewel
Also see RHODES, Todd
Also see LEWIS, Smiley

BARTLEY, Chris
P&R/R&B '67

Singles: 7-inch

BUDDAH...... 3-5 71
MUSICOR...... 3-5 72
VANDO...... 4-8 67-68

LPs: 10/12-inch

VANDO...... 15-20 67

BARTON, Eileen
P&R '50

Singles: 78 rpm

CORAL...... 4-8 51-56
MERCURY...... 4-8 53
NATIONAL...... 5-10 50

Singles: 7-inch

CORAL...... 5-10 51-56
CREST...... 4-8 62
MGM...... 5-8 59
MERCURY...... 5-10 53
20TH FOX...... 3-6 63
U.A. (Except 206)...... 4-8 59
U.A. (206 "The Joke")...... 15-25 60

EPs: 7-inch

CORAL...... 5-10 54

LPs: 10/12-inch

CORAL...... 15-25 54
Also see BREWER, Teresa / Eileen Barton
Also see DESMOND, Johnny, Eileen Barton & McGuire Sisters

BARTON, Lou Ann
LP '82

Singles: 7-inch

ASYLUM...... 3-4 82

LPs: 10/12-inch

ANTONE'S...... 5-10 89
ASYLUM...... 8-12 82

BARTZ, Gary
R&B '77

(Gary Bartz Nu Troop)

Singles: 7-inch

ARISTA...... 3-4 80
CAPITOL...... 3-4 77-78

LPs: 10/12-inch

ARISTA...... 5-10 80
CAPITOL...... 5-10 77-78
CATALYST...... 5-10 76
MILESTONE...... 10-15 68-69
PRESTIGE...... 6-10 73-75
VEE JAY...... 5-10 78

BASIA
P&R/LP '88

(Basia Trzetrzelewska)

Singles: 7-inch

EPIC...... 3-4 88-90

LPs: 10/12-inch

EPIC...... 5-8 88-90

BASIC BLACK
LP '90

LPs: 10/12-inch

MOTOWN...... 5-8 90

BASIE, Count
P&R '37

Singles: 78 rpm

COLUMBIA...... 5-10 43-51
CLEF...... 4-8 52-56
DECCA (Except 1300 thru 3000 series)...... 5-10 41-53
DECCA (1300 thru 3000 series)...... 8-15 37-40
MERCURY...... 4-8 52-53
OKEH...... 4-8 52

Singles: 7-inch

ABC-PAR...... 3-5 66
BRUNSWICK...... 3-5 67
CLEF...... 5-10 52-56
COLUMBIA (33000 series)...... 3-4 76
COLUMBIA (38000 & 39000 series)...... 5-10 50-51
COMMAND...... 3-5 67
DECCA...... 5-10 53
HAPPY TIGER...... 3-5 70
MERCURY...... 5-10 52-53
OKEH...... 5-10 52
REPRISE...... 3-6 63
ROULETTE (Except "SSR" series)...... 4-8 58-63
ROULETTE ("SSR" series)...... 8-15 59
(Stereo.)
U.A....... 3-5 66
VERVE...... 3-5 60-67

EPs: 7-inch

BRUNSWICK...... 10-15 54
CAMDEN...... 8-15 58
CLEF...... 10-20 52-55
COLUMBIA...... 10-20 50
CORAL...... 10-20
DECCA...... 10-20 53
EPIC...... 10-20 55
RCA (Except 5000 series)...... 10-20 54
RCA (5000 series)...... 8-12 59
ROULETTE...... 8-12 58-60
VERVE...... 10-15 56

LPs: 10/12-inch

ABC...... 5-10 76
ABC-PAR...... 10-15 66
ACCORD...... 5-10 82-83
AMERICAN...... 15-25 57
BRIGHT ORANGE...... 5-10 73
BRUNSWICK (54000 series)...... 10-20 63-67
BRUNSWICK (58000 series)...... 25-35 54
(10-inch LPs.)
CAMDEN...... 10-20 58-60
CIRCLE...... 40-50 54
CLEF (120 "Count Basie & His Orchestra")...... 100-200 52
(10-inch LP.)
CLEF (148 "The Count Basie Big Band")...... 100-200 52
(10-inch LP.)
CLEF (164 "The Count Basie Sextet")...... 100-200 52
(10-inch LP.)
CLEF (626 "Dance Session")...... 50-100 53
CLEF (647 "Dance Session, Volume 2")...... 50-100 53
CLEF (633 "Basieana")...... 50-100 53
CLEF (666 "Basie")...... 50-100 54
CLEF (678 "Basie Swings - Joe Williams Sings")...... 50-100 55
CLEF (685 "Count Basie")...... 50-80 56
CLEF (700 series)...... 20-30 56
COLISEUM...... 8-12 67
COLUMBIA (700 & 900 series)...... 20-30 56-57
COLUMBIA (6079 "Dance Parade")...... 25-35 49
(10-inch LPs)
COLUMBIA (31000 series)...... 10-12 72
COMMAND...... 10-15 66-71
CORAL...... 10-20
CROWN ("Music Composed By Count Basie")...... 10-15 60s
(Selection number not known. Credits: "Members of the Count Basie Orchestra—B.B. King Guest Vocalist.")
DAYBREAK...... 6-10 71
DECCA (100 series)...... 15-25 64
DECCA (5000 series)...... 25-35 50-53
(10-inch LPs.)
DECCA (8000 series)...... 10-15 65
DOCTOR JAZZ...... 5-10 85-86
DOT...... 8-12 68
EMARCY (26000 series)...... 30-45 54
(10-inch LPs.)
EMUS...... 5-10 79
EPIC (1000 & 1100 series)...... 25-35 54
(10-inch LPs.)
EPIC...... 25-35 55
FLYING DUTCHMAN...... 6-10 71
HAPPY TIGER...... 8-12 70
HARMONY (7000 series)...... 10-20 60
HARMONY (11000 series)...... 5-10 67-69
IMPULSE...... 10-20 62
JAZZ PANORAMA...... 50-75 52
MCA...... 8-12 77-82
MGM...... 6-10 70
MFSL (129 "Basie Plays Hefti")...... 25-30 85
MFSL (237 "April in Paris")...... 20-25 94
MPS...... 10-12 72
MERCURY (25000 series)...... 25-35 50-51
(10-inch LPs.)
METRO...... 6-10 65-66
MOSAIC (135 "Complete Roulette Live Recordings of Count Basie")...... 100-125 90s
(12 LP boxed set. 7500 made.)
MOSAIC (149 "Complete Roulette Studio Recordings of Count Basie")...... 200-225 90s
(15 audiophile LP boxed set. 3500 made.)
OLYMPIC...... 5-10 74
PABLO...... 5-10 74-83
PAUSA...... 5-10 83
PRESTIGE...... 5-10 82
RCA (500 series)...... 10-15 65
RCA (1100 series)...... 25-35 54
REPRISE...... 10-15 63-65
ROULETTE (100 series)...... 12-18 71
ROULETTE (52003 thru 52106)...... 15-20 58-64
ROULETTE (52111/12/13 "The World of Count Basie")...... 30-40 64
(Three-LP set.)
SCEPTER...... 5-10 74
SOLID STATE...... 8-12 68
TRIP...... 5-10 75
U.A....... 10-15 66
VSP...... 10-15 66
VANGUARD...... 15-25 57
VERVE...... 5-10 73-84
(Reads "Manufactured By MGM Record Corp.," or mentions either Polydor or Polygram at bottom of label.)
VERVE (2000 series)...... 20-30 56
(Reads "Verve Records, Inc." at bottom of label.)
VERVE (2500 series)...... 8-12 77-82
VERVE (2600 series)...... 5-10 82
VERVE (6000 series)...... 20-30 56
(Reads "Verve Records, Inc." at bottom of label.)
VERVE (8000 & 8100 series)...... 15-25 56-57
(Reads "Verve Records, Inc." at bottom of label.)
VERVE (8200 thru 8400)...... 15-20 58-61
(Reads "Verve Records, Inc." at bottom of label.)
VERVE (8500 thru 8600 series)...... 10-15 62-67
(Reads "MGM Records - a Division of Metro-Goldwyn-Mayer, Inc." at bottom of label.)
VERVE (8700 series)...... 6-10 69
(Reads "MGM Records - a Division of Metro-Goldwyn-Mayer, Inc." at bottom of label.)
VERVE (68000 series)...... 10-20 63-65
(Reads "MGM Records - a Division of Metro-Goldwyn-Mayer, Inc." at bottom of label.)
Also see BARRY, John
Also see BENNETT, Tony, & Count Basie
Also see BREWER, Teresa, & Count Basie
Also see CROSBY, Bing, & Count Basie
Also see DAVIS, Sammy, Jr., & Count Basie
Also see FITZGERALD, Ella, & Count Basie
Also see JACQUET, Illinois, & Count Basie
Also see KING, B.B.
Also see MILLS BROTHERS, & Count Basie
Also see PRYSOCK, Arthur, & Count Basie
Also see SINATRA, Frank, & Count Basie
Also see STARR, Kay, & Count Basie
Also see WILLIAMS, Joe
Also see WILSON, Jackie, & Count Basie

BASIE, Count, & Tony Bennett

EPs: 7-inch

ROULETTE...... 6-10 59

LPs: 10/12-inch

ROULETTE...... 10-20 59-63
Also see BENNETT, Tony

BASIE, Count, & Billy Eckstine

Singles: 7-inch

ROULETTE (Except "SSR" series)...... 4-8 59
ROULETTE ("SSR" series)...... 8-15 59

LPs: 10/12-inch

ROULETTE...... 15-20 59
Also see ECKSTINE, Billy

BASIE, Count, & Duke Ellington

Singles: 7-inch

COLUMBIA....4-6 62

LPs: 10/12-inch

ACCORD....5-10 82
COLUMBIA....15-20 62
Also see ELINGTON, Duke

BASIE, Count, & Maynard Ferguson

LPs: 10/12-inch

ROULETTE....10-20 65
Also see FERGUSON, Maynard

BASIE, Count, & Benny Goodman

LPs: 10/12-inch

ABC....8-12 73
VANGUARD....15-25 59
Also see GOODMAN, Benny

BASIE, Count, & Oscar Peterson

LPs: 10/12-inch

PABLO....5-10 75-83
VERVE....15-20 59
Also see PETERSON, Oscar

BASIE, Count, & Sarah Vaughan

LPs: 10/12-inch

ROULETTE....15-20 61

BASIE, Count, Sarah Vaughan & Joe Williams

Singles: 7-inch

ROULETTE....4-8 60

LPs: 10/12-inch

ROULETTE....15-20 60
Joe Williams is also a featured vocalist on many of the recordings included in the section of listings for Count Basie.
Also see BASIE, Count
Also see VAUGHAN, Sarah

BASIL, Toni *P&R/LP '82*

Singles: 12-inch

CHRYSALIS....4-6 82-85

Singles: 7-inch

A&M (791 "Breakaway")....100-200 66
CHRYSALIS....3-4 82-85
CHRYSALIS/VIRGIN (2638 Mickey")....4-6 81
(With Radialchoice logo.)

Picture Sleeves

CHRYSALIS....3-4 82-84

LPs: 10/12-inch

CHRYSALIS....5-10 82-84

BASKERVILLE HOUNDS *P&R '69*

Singles: 7-inch

AVCO EMBASSY (4504 "Hold Me")....4-6 69
BUDDAH....5-10 67
DOT....5-10 67
TEMA ("Hold Me")....5-10 68
(No selection number used.)
TEMA (125 "Debbie")....8-12 66
TEMA (128 "Space Rock")....5-10 67
TEMA (131 "Christmas Is Here")....5-10 67

LPs: 10/12-inch

DOT....15-20 67

BASS, Fontella *P&R/R&B '65*

Singles: 7-inch

ABC....3-4 74
BOBBIN....5-10 61
CHECKER....5-10 65-66
CHESS....3-8 75-85
ERIC....3-5 73
GUSTO....3-4
MCA....3-4 83
PAULA....3-5 74
PRANN (5005 "My Good Lovin'")....5-10
SONJA (2006 "Poor Little Fool")....10-15 62

LPs: 10/12-inch

CHECKER....15-20 66
CHESS....5-10
PAULA....5-10 71

BASS, Fontella, & Bobby McClure *P&R/R&B '65*

Singles: 7-inch

CHECKER....3-5 65-66
Also see McCLURE, Bobby

BASS, Fontella, & Tina Turner

Singles: 7-inch

VESUVIUS (1002 "Poor Little Fool")....10-15 60s
(Also issued crediting only Fontella Bass.)
Also see BASS, Fontella
Also see TURNER, Tina

BASSEY, Shirley *P&R/LP '65*

Singles: 78 rpm

COLUMBIA....5-10 57

Singles: 12-inch

U.A. 4-6 79

Singles: 7-inch

COLUMBIA....5-10 57
EPIC....4-8 59
MGM....3-6 60
U.A. 3-5 61-79

LPs: 10/12-inch

EPIC....10-20 62
LIBERTY....4-6 81-82
MGM....12-20 60
PHILIPS....10-15 65
SPRINGBORAD....5-10 75
U.A. 4-6 80
(With "LM" prefix.)
U.A. 10-15 62-72
(With "UAL" or "UAS" prefix.)
U.A. 5-10 73-79
(With "UA-LA" prefix.)
Also see BARRY, John
Also see NELSON, Willie / Nat "King" Cole / Johnny Mathis / Shirley Bassey

BATAAN, Joe *R&B '69*
(With the Mestizo Band)

Singles: 7-inch

FANIA....5-15
SALSOUL....3-4 80
UPTITE....3-5 69

LPs: 10/12-inch

SALSOUL....5-10 80-81

BATDORF & RODNEY *LP '72*

Singles: 7-inch

ARISTA....3-5 75
ASYLUM....3-5 72
ATLANTIC....3-5 71-72

LPs: 10/12-inch

ATLANTIC....8-12 71
ARISTA....6-10 75
ASYLUM....8-10 72
Members: John Batdorf: Mark Rodney.

BAUHAUS *LP '89*

Singles: 7-inch

A&M....3-4 83

LPs: 10/12-inch

A&M....5-10 83
BEGGARS BANQUET....8-12 89
Members: Daniel Ash; David Jor; Kevin Haskins.
Also see LOVE & ROCKETS

BAUMANN, Peter *D&D '83*

Singles: 12-inch

PORTRAIT....4-6 82-83

Singles: 7-inch

PORTRAIT....3-4 83

LPs: 10/12-inch

PORTRAIT....5-10 82-83
VIRGIN....8-10 77
Also see TANGERINE DREAM

BAXTER, Duke *P&R '69*

Singles: 7-inch

MERCURY....3-5 70
VMC....5-10 69

LPs: 10/12-inch

VMC....15-20 69

BAXTER, Les *P&R '51*
(With His Orchestra & Chorus; Les Baxter Balladeers)

Singles: 78 rpm

CAPITOL....3-6 50-57

Singles: 7-inch

A/S....3-4 70
CAPITOL....4-8 50-61
GNP....3-5 64-69
LINK....3-5 64
REPRISE....3-5 62-63

Picture Sleeves

REPRISE (20120 "Theme from *The Manchurian Candidate*"....40-60 62
(Primarily a Frank Sinatra collectible, as his name is shown on this cover.)

EPs: 7-inch

CAPITOL....5-10 51-56
GNP....5-10 67-69
RCA....5-10 52
REPRISE....4-8 64

LPs: 10/12-inch

ALSHIRE....5-10 70-85
AMERICAN INT'L (1028 "Dunwich Horror")....20-25 70
(Soundtrack.)
CAPITOL (200 thru 900 series)....10-20 51-58
CAPITOL (1000 thru 1800 series)....5-15 58-63
CAPITOL (11000 series)....4-6 77-79
GNP....5-10 69
RCA....15-25 52
REPRISE....10-15 62-63
VARESE SARABANDE (81103 "Dunwich Horror")....8-10 79
Also see CHEERS
Also see CROSBY, Bing, & Bob Hope
Also see WAKELY, Jimmy

BAY CITY ROLLERS *P&R/LP '75*

Singles: 7-inch

ARISTA....3-4 75-78
BELL....3-5 72-76
FLASHBACK....3-4 80

Picture Sleeves

ARISTA....3-4 75-77

LPs: 10/12-inch

ARISTA....5-10 75-79
BELL....6-12 74
Members: Les McKeowen; Eric Faulkner; Stuart Wood; Alan Longmuir; Derek Longmuir; Billy Lyall; Pat McGlynn; Ian Mitchell.
Also see ROLLERS

BAYER, Carole: see SAGER, Carole Bayer

BAZUKA *P&R/R&B '75*
(Tony Camillo's Bazuka)

Singles: 7-inch

A&M....3-5 75
VENTURE....3-4 79

LPs: 10/12-inch

A&M....5-10 75

BEACH BOYS *P&R/LP '62*

Singles: 12-inch

CAPITOL (9711 "Rock & Roll to the Rescue")....10-15 86
(Promotional issue only.)
CAPITOL (9796 "California Dreamin'")....10-15 86
(Promotional issue only.)
CAPITOL (15234 "Rock & Roll to the Rescue")....5-10 86
CARIBOU (2080 "Getcha Back")....10-15 86
(Promotional issue only.)
CARIBOU (9028 "Here Comes the Night")....5-10 79
CARIBOU (9028 "Here Comes the Night")....20-25 79
(Promotional issue only.)

Singles: 7-inch

BROTHER....5-10 67
CANDIX (301 "Surfin'")....150-250 61
(Label reads "Distributed by Era Record Sales Inc.")
CANDIX (301 "Surfin'")....200-250 61
(Label does NOT say "Distributed by Era Record Sales Inc.")
CANDIX (331 "Surfin'")....125-175 62
CAPITOL (2000 series except 2765)....5-10 67-69

CAPITOL (2765 "Cottonfields") 15-20 70
CAPITOL (3924 "Surfin' USA") 3-5 74
(Some copies indicate "Stereo" but play mono; others indicate "Mono" but play stereo.)
CAPITOL (4000 series except 4880) ... 8-12 62-63
CAPITOL (4880 "Ten Little Indians") 15-20 62
CAPITOL (5000 series, except 5096 & 5312) 5-10 63-66
(Orange/yellow labels.)
CAPITOL (5096 "Little Saint Nick") ... 12-18 63
CAPITOL (5312 "The Man with All the Toys") 12-18 63
CAPITOL (5000 series) 3-4 81-86
(Black labels.)
CAPITOL (6000 series) 5-10 67-68
CAPITOL (44000 series) 3-4 89
CARIBOU 3-5 79-86
ODE '70 .... 12-15 71
REPRISE (0101 thru 0107) 4-6 73
("Back to Back" reissue series.)
REPRISE (0894 "Add Some Music to Your Day") 5-10 70
REPRISE (0929 "Slip On Through") ... 5-10 70
REPRISE (0957 "Tears in the Morning") 12-15 70
REPRISE (0998 "Cool, Cool Water") 60-75 71
REPRISE (1015 "Long Promised Road") 20-25 71
REPRISE (1047 "Long Promised Road") 20-25 71
REPRISE (1058 "Surf's Up") 45-50 71
REPRISE (1091 "Cuddle Up") 25-30 72
REPRISE (1101 "Marcella") 25-30 72
REPRISE (1138 "Sail On Sailor") 8-12 73
REPRISE (1156 "California Saga") ... 10-15 73
REPRISE (1310 "I Can Hear Music") 3-5 74
REPRISE (1321 "Child of Winter") 20-30 74
REPRISE (1325 "Sail On Sailor") 5-10 75
REPRISE (1336 "Wouldn't It Be Nice") 5-10 75
REPRISE (1354 thru 1394) 3-5 76-78
X (301 "Surfin' ") 300-400 61

Promotional Singles

CAPITOL (2360 "Bluebirds Over the Mountain") 15-20 69
CAPITOL (2936/7 "Salt Lake City") 175-200 65
CAPITOL (4093 "Little Honda") 15-20 75
CAPITOL CUSTOM ("Spirit of America") 125-150 63
CARIBOU (557 "Here Comes the Night") 10-12 79
(Blue vinyl.)
CARIBOU (557 "Here Comes the Night") 50-60 79
(Special Edition autographed copies. Blue vinyl.)
CARIBOU (9026 "Here Comes the Night") 10-15 79
EVA-TONE (0300 "Living Doll") 3-4 87
(Barbie Doll promotional issue.)
ODE '70 (66016 "Wouldn't It Be Nice-Live Version") 35-40 71
REPRISE (557-2 "Sail On Sailor") .. 75-100 73
REPRISE (0998 "Cool, Cool Water") 45-50 71
REPRISE (1310 "I Can Hear Music") 30-50 74
WHAT'S IT ALL ABOUT (449/450 & 507/508) 20-25
(Public service radio station issues. Program disc 449/450 has the Beach Boys on one side and Dr. Hook on the flip. 507/508 features the Beach Boys on one side and the Rolling Stones on the other.)
Note: Promo singles not listed separately are presumed to fall into the same price range as commercial issues.

Picture Sleeves

BROTHER (1001 "Heroes and Villains") 50-100 67
CAPITOL (2068 "Darlin' ") 10-20 67
CAPITOL (4777 "Surfin' Safari") 20-30 62
CAPITOL (4880 "Ten Little Indians") 75-100 62
CAPITOL (5118 "Fun, Fun, Fun") 10-20 63
CAPITOL (5174 "I Get Around") 10-20 64
CAPITOL (5245 "When I Grow Up") 10-20 64
CAPITOL (5306 "Dance, Dance, Dance") 10-20 64
CAPITOL (5372 "Do You Wanna Dance") 10-20 65
CAPITOL (5395 "Help Me Rhonda") 10-20 65
CAPITOL (5464 "California Girls") 10-20 65
CAPITOL (5540 "The Little Girl I Once Knew") 10-20 65
CAPITOL (5561 "Barbara Ann") 100-125 65
CAPITOL (5595 "Rock 'N' Roll to the Rescue") 3-5 86
CAPITOL (5602 "Sloop John B.") 10-20 66
CAPITOL (5676 "Good Vibrations") .. 10-20 66
CARIBOU 3-6 79-86

EPs: 7-inch

BROTHER (1 "Radio Spot Backing Tracks") 225-250 73
(Promotional issue only.)
CAPITOL (189 "Best of the Beach Boys") 15-20 66
(With "LLP" prefix. Juke box issue only.)
CAPITOL (1981 "Surfer Girl") 45-55 63
CAPITOL (2027 "Shut Down, Vol. 2") 45-55 64
CAPITOL (2269 "The Beach Boys Today") 50-75 65
(Juke box issue only.)
CAPITOL (2293/94 "Beach Boys' Party") 125-150 65
(Juke box issue only.)
CAPITOL (2545 "Best of the Beach Boys") 50-75 66
(With "DU" prefix. Juke box issue only.)
CAPITOL (2545 "Best of the Beach Boys") 15-20 66
CAPITOL (2754/55 "Brian Wilson Introduces Selections") 350-375 64
(Promotional issue only. Includes selections from *Beach Boys Concert* and *Beach Boys Songbook*.)
CAPITOL (5267 "4 by the Beach Boys") 35-45 66
REPRISE (2118 "Mount Vernon and Fairway") 8-10 73
(Originally packaged with Reprise LP 2118, "Holland.")
ROCK SHOPPE ("The Beach Years") 75-100 75
(Demo disc for "A Six Hour Radio Special." Also contains excerpts by Jan & Dean, Dick Dale, and the Surfaris. Narrated by Roger Christian. Promotional issue, pressed in a quantity of 200 copies.)
SUB-POP ("I Just Wasn't Made for These Times") 5-8 96
(Three track disc.)
W.B. (422 "Sunflower Promotional Spots") 100-125 70
W.B. (534 "Vote '72") 35-45 72
(Promotional issue only.)
WHAT'S IT ALL ABOUT 20-25 70s
(Promotional issue only.)

LPs: 10/12-inch

ACCORD 5-10 83
AUDIO FIDELITY (335 "Beach Boys") 8-12 84
(Picture disc.)
AXIS/CAPITOL (8 "Their 22 Greatest Hits") 6-12 73
BROTHER (9001 "Smiley Smile") 15-20 67
BROTHER/SUNKIST (9431 "25 Years of Good Vibrations") 10-20 86
(Includes tour booklet. Sold at Beach Boys concerts.)
CAPITOL (133 "20/20") 10-20 69
CAPITOL (133 "20/20") 30-35 69
(With "SKAO-8" prefix. Capitol Record Club issue.)
CAPITOL (253 "Close Up") 35-40 69
CAPITOL (442 "Good Vibrations") 20-25 70
CAPITOL (500 "All Summer Long"/"California Girls") 8-12 70
CAPITOL (701 "Dance, Dance, Dance"/"Fun, Fun, Fun") 8-12 71
CAPITOL (1808 thru 1998) 15-25 63-67
(With "DT" prefix.)
CAPITOL (1808 thru 1998) 5-10 75-78
(With "SM" prefix.)
CAPITOL (1808 thru 1998) 20-35 62-63
(With "T" or "ST" prefix.)
CAPITOL (2027 "Shut Down, Vol. 2") 8-15 63
(With "DT" prefix.)
CAPITOL (2027 "Shut Down, Vol. 2") 5-10 75
(With "SM" prefix.)
CAPITOL (2027 "Shut Down, Vol. 2") 15-20 63
(With "T" or "ST" prefix.)
CAPITOL (2110 "All Summer Long") 25-30 64
(With "Don't Break Down." On this pressing, *Don't Back Down* is incorrectly shown as "Don't Break Down.")
CAPITOL (2110 "All Summer Long") 15-20 64
(With "Don't Back Down" shown correctly.)
CAPITOL (2164 "Beach Boys' Christmas Album") 5-10 75
(With "SM" prefix.)
CAPITOL (2164 "Beach Boys' Christmas Album") 20-35 64
(With "T" or "ST" prefix.)
CAPITOL (2198 "Beach Boys Concert") 10-15 64
(With "T" or "ST" prefix.)
CAPITOL (2198 "Beach Boys Concert") 5-10
(With "SM" prefix.)
CAPITOL (2269 "The Beach Boys Today") 15-20 65
(With "T" or "DT" prefix.)
CAPITOL (2354 "Summer Days and Summer Nights") 20-35 65
(With "T" or DT" prefix.)
CAPITOL (2398 "Beach Boys Party") 30-35 65
(With "SMAS" prefix. Price includes 15 bonus photos. Deduct $8-12 if these photos are missing.)
CAPITOL (2398 "Beach Boys Party") 20-30 65
(With "MAS" prefix. Price includes 15 bonus photos. Deduct $8 to $12 if these photos are missing.)
CAPITOL (2458 "Pet Sounds") 15-20 66
(With "T" or DT" prefix.)
CAPITOL (2545 "Best of the Beach Boys") 10-15 66
(With "T" or DT" prefix.)
CAPITOL (2706 "Best of the Beach Boys, Vol. 2") 10-15 67
(With "T" or "DT" prefix.)
CAPITOL (2813 "Beach Boys Deluxe Set") 100-125 67
(With "TCL" prefix.)
CAPITOL (2813 "Beach Boys Deluxe Set") 35-40 67
(With "DTCL" prefix.)
CAPITOL (2859 "Wild Honey") 10-15 67
(With "T" or "ST" prefix.)
CAPITOL (ST-8-2891 "Smiley Smile") 60-75 69
(With "ST-8" prefix. Capitol Record Club issue.)
CAPITOL (2893 "Stack-o-Tracks") 100-150 68
(With music-lyrics booklet.)
CAPITOL (2893 "Stack-o-Tracks") 50-75 68
(Without music-lyrics booklet.)
CAPITOL (2893 "Stack-o-Tracks") 100-125 69
(With "ST-8" prefix. Capitol Record Club issue.)
CAPITOL (2895 "Friends") 10-15 68

CAPITOL (2945 "Best of the Beach Boys, Vol. 3") 35-40 68
CAPITOL (3352 "Sunflower") 30-35 70
(With "SKAO-9" prefix. Capitol Record Club issue.)
CAPITOL (8300 series) 5-8 83
CAPITOL (6994 "Golden Years of the Beach Boys") 25-30 75
(TV mail-order offer.)
CAPITOL (48421 "Pet Sounds") 5-8 90
CAPITOL (11000 thru 16000, except 11384) 5-15 74-86
CAPITOL (11384 Spirit of America") 15-20 75
CAPITOL (29600 series) 10-15 96
(Digitally remastered.)
CAPITOL (90427 "Beach Boys Concert") 10-15 96
CAPITOL (92639 "Still Cruisin' ") 5-10 89
CAPITOL (123946 "Best of the Beach Boys, Vol. 1") 20-25 74
(RCA Record Club issue.)
CAPITOL (153477 "Rarities") 20-25 75
(RCA Record Club issue.)
CAPITOL (233559 "Endless Summer") 20-25 74
(RCA Record Club issue.)
CAPITOL (233593 "American Summer") 20-25 75
(RCA Record Club issue.)
CAPITOL STARLINE 10-15 60s
CARIBOU 5-10 78-85
ERA 12-18 69
EVEREST 5-10 81
HIGHLIGHT (9926 "Beach Boys") 5-8 80s
MFSL (116 "Surfer Girl") 20-35 84
PAIR 10-12 84
PICKWICK 8-12 72-75
REPRISE (2118 "Holland") 15-20 73
(With *Mount Vernon & Fairway* EP.)
REPRISE (2118 "Holland") 8-12 73
(Without *Mount Vernon & Fairway* EP.)
REPRISE (2166 "Wild Honey"/"20-20") 8-10 74
REPRISE (2166 "Friends/Smiley Smile") 8-10 74
REPRISE (2223 "Good Vibrations"/"Best of the Beach Boys") 8-10 75
REPRISE (2251 "15 Big Ones") 8-10 76
REPRISE (2258 "Love You") 8-10 77
REPRISE (2268 "M.I.U. Album") 8-10 78
REPRISE (6382 "Sunflower") 8-12 70
REPRISE (6453 "Surf's Up") 20-25 71
(Capitol Record Club issue.)
REPRISE (6484 "The Beach Boys in Concert") 8-10 73
RONCO 8-10 78
SCEPTER 8-12
SEARS (608 "Summertime Blues") 100-125 70
(Sold only at Sears retail stores.)
SESSIONS 15-20 80
SPRINGBOARD (4021 "Greatest Hits: 1961-1963") 8-12 72
SUNDAZED (5005 "Lost & Found") .. 10-15
(Colored vinyl.)
WAND (688 "Greatest Hits") 10-15 72

Promotional LPs

BROTHER (9431 "Good Vibrations from the Beach Boys") 10-15 86
(Sunkist promotional issue.)
CAPITOL (1 "Open House") 175-200 78
CAPITOL (2754/5 "Beach Boys' Concert") 300-350 64
CAPITOL (3123 "Silver Platter Service") 75-100 64
(With selections by the Hollyridge Strings.)
CAPITOL (3133 "Silver Platter Service") 125-150 64
("Beach Boys Christmas Special.")
CAPITOL (3266 "Silver Platter Service") 75-100 67
CARIBOU (1024 "Keepin' the Summer Alive") 45-50 80
CRAWDADDY ("Brian Wilson Interview") 90-100 77
(Issued to radio stations only.)
MORE MUSIC (03-179-72 "Good Vibrations from London") 50-60
MUTUAL RADIO ("Dick Clark Presents the Beach Boys") 150-175 81
(Three-LP boxed set.)
REPRISE ("Radio Spot Backing Tracks for Beach Boys in Concert") 225-250 73
TIME-LIFE 10-15 86

Members: Brian Wilson; Carl Wilson; Dennis Wilson; Mike Love; Al Jardine; David Marks; Bruce Johnston; Ricky Fataar; Blondie Chaplin.

Note: Promos NOT listed separately are priced in the same range as commercial issues.

Also see ANNETTE
Also see BEATLES / Beach Boys / Buddy Holly
Also see CAMPBELL, Glen
Also see CAPTAIN & TENNILLE
Also see CHICAGO
Also see CLAYTON, Merry
Also see DALE, Dick / Surfaris / Surf Kings
Also see DR. HOOK
Also see EVERLY BROTHERS & Beach Boys
Also see FAT BOYS & Beach Boys
Also see JAN & DEAN / Beach Boys
Also see JETT, Joan
Also see KENNY & CADETS
Also see PETERSEN, Paul
Also see ROLLING STONES
Also see ROTH, David Lee
Also see SURVIVORS
Also see WILSON, Brian
Also see WILSON, Brian, and Mike Love
Also see WILSON, Carl
Also see WILSON, Dennis

BEACH BOYS / Ray Anthony

EPs: 7-inch

CAPITOL (2186 "10 Little Indians") 500-750 64
(Promotional issue only.)
Also see ANTHONY, Ray

BEACH BOYS / Jan & Dean

LPs: 10/12-inch

CAPITOL (8149 "The Beach Boys/Jan & Dean") 10-20 81
(Sold only at Radio Shack stores. Realistic #S1-7010.)
EXACT 5-8 81
Also see JAN & DEAN

BEACH BOYS / Little Richard (Beach Boys & Little Richard / Beach Boys) P&R '88

Singles: 7-inch

CRITIQUE (99392 "Happy Endings").... 3-5 87
ELEKTRA (69385 "Kokomo") 3-4 88

Picture Sleeves

CRITIQUE (99392 "Happy Endings").... 3-5 87
Also see LITTLE RICHARD

BEACH BOYS / Tony & Joe

Singles: 7-inch

ERA 3-5 70
Also see TONY & JOE

BEACH BOYS & FRANKIE VALLI & 4 SEASONS

Singles: 7-inch

FBI 3-5 84
Also see 4 SEASONS

BEACH BOYS / Carl Wilson

LPs: 10/12-inch

BROTHER (2083 "Pet Sounds"/"So Tough") 10-20 72
Also see BEACH BOYS

BEACH BUMS

Singles: 7-inch

ARE YOU KIDDING ME? (1010 "Ballad of the Yellow Baret") 25-35 66
Member: Bob Seger.
Also see SEGER, Bob

BEACON STREET UNION LP '68

Singles: 7-inch

MGM 5-10 67-69
RTP 5-10 69

LPs: 10/12-inch

MGM (4517 "The Eyes of the Beacon Street Union") 15-25 68
MGM (4568 "The Clown Died in Marvin Gardens") 15-25 68
Members: John Lincoln Wright; Robert Rhodes; Paul Tartachny; Wayne Ulaky; Richard Weisberg.

BEAR, Edward: see EDWARD BEAR

BEAR ESSENCE STARRING MARIANNA D&D '84

Singles: 12-inch

MOBY DICK 4-6 84

BEARS LP '88

LPs: 10/12-inch

I.R.S. 8-10 87-88

BEASLEY, Walter R&B '87

Singles: 12-inch

POLYDOR 4-6 88

Singles: 7-inch

POLYDOR 3-4 87-88

LPs: 10/12-inch

POLYDOR 5-10 87-88

BEAST LP '69

LPs: 10/12-inch

COTILLION 10-12 69
EVOLUTION 8-10 70

BEASTIE BOYS P&R/R&B/LP '86

Singles: 12-inch

DEF JAM 4-6 86-87

Singles: 7-inch

DEF JAM 3-4 86-87

LPs: 10/12-inch

CAPITOL (Except 79461) 5-8 89
CAPITOL (79461 "Hip Hop Sampler") 35-45 89
(Promotional issue only.)
DEF JAM 5-10 86-87
Members: Adam Horovitz; Adam Yaunch; Michael Diamond.

BEASTMASTER R&B '84

Singles: 12-inch

TOMMY BOY 4-6 84

BEAT, B: see B. BEAT GIRLS

BEAT FARMERS LP '85

Singles: 7-inch

RHINO 3-4 85

LPs: 10/12-inch

MCA/CURB 5-10 86-87
RHINO 5-10 85

BEATLES P&R '64

Singles: 12-inch

CAPITOL (SPRO-9758 "Movie Medley") 40-50 81
(Promotional issue only.)
ULTIMIX (120 "Twist & Shout") 100-125 88
(Promotional issue only.)

Singles: 7-inch

APPLE 8-15 69-75
APPLE 25-35 71
(With black star on label.)
ATCO (6302 "Sweet Georgia Brown") 175-200 64
(Shown as by "The Beatles with Tony Sheridan.")
ATCO (6308 "Ain't She Sweet") 50-60 64
(Yellow and white label. Without cut-out hole.)
ATCO (6308 "Ain't She Sweet") 20-30 64
(Yellow and white label. With cut-out hole.)
ATCO (6308 "Ain't She Sweet") 30-40 69
(Yellow and white label with "Mfg by Atlantic.." print.)
ATLANTIC 10-20 83-85
APPLE (2056 "Hello Goodbye") 25-35 71
(With black star on label.)

APPLE (2056 "Hello Goodbye") 10-20 71
(No black star on label.)
APPLE (2138 "Lady Madonna") 25-35 71
(With black star on label.)
APPLE (2138 "Lady Madonna") 10-20 71
(No black star on label.)
APPLE (2276 "Hey Jude") 10-15 68
(Apple label with Capitol logo.)
APPLE (2276 "Hey Jude") 5-10 71
(Apple label with "Mfd by Apple, etc." perimeter print.)
APPLE (2276 "Hey Jude") 15-20 75
(Apple label with "All Rights Reserved, etc." perimeter print.)
APPLE (2654 "Something") 75-100 69
(Apple label with Capitol logo.)
APPLE (2654 "Something") 8-12 71
(Apple label with "Mfd by Apple, etc." perimeter print.)
APPLE (2654 "Something") 15-20 75
(Apple label with "All Rights Reserved, etc." perimeter print.)
APPLE (2764 "Let It Be") 8-12 69
(Apple label with Capitol logo, or with "Mfd by Apple, etc." perimeter print.)
APPLE (2764 "Let It Be") 15-20 75
(Apple label with "All Rights Reserved, etc." perimeter print.)
APPLE (2832 "Long and Winding Road") 15-20 69
(Apple label with Capitol logo.)
APPLE (2832 "Long and Winding Road") 6-10 71
(Apple label with "Mfd by Apple, etc." perimeter print.)
APPLE (2832 "Long and Winding Road") 15-20 75
(Apple label with "All Rights Reserved, etc." perimeter print.)
APPLE (2490 "Get Back") 6-10 69
(Apple label with Capitol logo, or with "Mfd by Apple, etc." perimeter print.)
APPLE (2490 "Get Back") 15-20 75
(Apple label with "All Rights Reserved, etc." perimeter print.)
APPLE (2531 "Ballad of John and Yoko") 10-15 69
APPLE (5112 "I Want to Hold Your Hand") 30-40 71
(Has black star on label.)
APPLE (5112 "I Want to Hold Your Hand") 10-15 71
(No black star on label.)
APPLE (5150 "Can't Buy Me Love") 25-35 71
(Has black star on label.)
APPLE (5150 "Can't Buy Me Love") 10-15 71
(No black star on label.)
APPLE (5222 "A Hard Day's Night") 25-35 71
(With black star on label.)
APPLE (5222 "A Hard Day's Night") 10-15 71
(No black star on label.)
APPLE (5327 "I Feel Fine") 25-35 71
(With black star on label.)
APPLE (5327 "I Feel Fine") 10-15 71
(No black star on label.)
APPLE (5234 "I'll Cry Instead") 25-35 71
(With black star on label.)
APPLE (5234 "I'll Cry Instead") 10-15 71
(No black star on label.)
APPLE (5235 "And I Love Her") 25-35 71
(With black star on label.)
APPLE (5235 "And I Love Her") 10-15 71
(No black star on label.)
APPLE (5255 "Matchbox") 25-35 71
(With black star on label.)
APPLE (5255 "Matchbox") 10-15 71
(No black star on label.)
APPLE (5371 "Eight Days a Week") 25-35 71
(Has black star on label.)
APPLE (5371 "Eight Days a Week") 10-15 71
(No black star on label.)
APPLE (5407 "Ticket to Ride") 25-35 71
(With black star on label.)
APPLE (5407 "Ticket to Ride") 10-15 71
(No black star on label.)
APPLE (5476 "Help") 25-35 71
(With black star on label.)
APPLE (5476 "Help") 10-15 71
(No black star on label.)
APPLE (5498 "Yesterday") 25-35 71
(With black star on label.)
APPLE (5498 "Yesterday") 10-15 71
(No black star on label.)
APPLE (5555 "We Can Work It Out") 25-35 71
(With black star on label.)
APPLE (5555 "We Can Work It Out") 10-15 71
(No black star on label.)
APPLE (5587 "Nowhere Man") 25-35 71
(With black star on label.)
APPLE (5587 "Nowhere Man") 10-15 71
(No black star on label.)
APPLE (5651 "Paperback Writer") ... 25-35 71
(With black star on label.)
APPLE (5651 "Paperback Writer") ... 10-15 71
(No black star on label.)
APPLE (5715 "Yellow Submarine") .. 25-35 71
(With black star on label.)
APPLE (5715 "Yellow Submarine") .. 10-15 71
(No black star on label.)
APPLE (5810 "Penny Lane") 25-35 71
(With black star on label.)
APPLE (5810 "Penny Lane") 10-15 71
(No black star on label.)
APPLE (5964 "All You Need Is Love") 25-35 71
(With black star on label.)
APPLE (5964 "All You Need Is Love") 10-15 71
(No black star on label.)
BRS (1/2 "Murray the 'K' and the Beatles As It Happened") 30-40 64
CAPITOL (2056 "Hello Goodbye") 20-30 67
(Yellow/orange swirl label without "Subsidiary of Capitol, etc." perimeter print.)
CAPITOL (2056 "Hello Goodbye") 40-50 68
(Yellow/orange swirl label with "Subsidiary of Capitol, etc." perimeter print.)
CAPITOL (2056 "Hello Goodbye") 55-65 69
(Red/orange label with dome logo.)
CAPITOL (2056 "Hello Goodbye") 15-20 69
(Red/orange label with round logo.)
CAPITOL (2056 "Hello Goodbye") 5-8 76
(Orange label.)
CAPITOL (2056 "Hello Goodbye") 10-15 78
(Purple or black label.)
CAPITOL (2138 "Lady Madonna") 20-30 68
(Yellow/orange swirl label without "Subsidiary of Capitol, etc." perimeter print.)
CAPITOL (2138 "Lady Madonna") 40-50 68
(Yellow/orange swirl label with "Subsidiary of Capitol, etc." perimeter print.)
CAPITOL (2138 "Lady Madonna") 55-65 69
(Red/orange label with dome logo.)
CAPITOL (2138 "Lady Madonna") 15-20 69
(Red/orange label with round logo.)
CAPITOL (2138 "Lady Madonna") 5-8 76
(Orange or purple or black label.)
CAPITOL (2276 "Hey Jude") 5-8 76
(Orange or purple or black label.)
CAPITOL (2490 "Get Back") 5-8 76
(Orange or purple or black label.)
CAPITOL (2531 "Ballad of John and Yoko") 5-8 78
(Purple or black label.)
CAPITOL (2654 "Something") 5-8 76
(Orange or purple or black label.)
CAPITOL (2764 "Let It Be") 5-8 76
(Orange or purple or black label.)
CAPITOL (2832 "Long and Winding Road") 5-8 76
(Orange or purple or black label.)
CAPITOL (4274 "Got to Get You into My Life") 5-10 76
(Orange or purple or black label.)
CAPITOL (4347 "Ob-La-Di, Ob-La-Da") 5-10 76
(Orange or purple or black label.)
CAPITOL (4612 "Sgt. Pepper's Lonely Hearts Club Band" & "With A Little Help From My Friends") 5-8 78
(Purple or black label.)
CAPITOL (B-5100 "Movie Medley"/"Fab Four on Film") 40-50 82
(First issued with *Movie Medley* backed with *Fab Four on Film,* the Beatles talking about the film *A Hard Day's Night.*)
CAPITOL (B-5107 "Movie Medley"/"I'm Happy Just to Dance with You") 3-4 82
CAPITOL (5112 "I Want to Hold Your Hand") 35-45 64
(Yellow/orange swirl label without "Subsidiary of Capitol, etc." perimeter print. Perimeter has *white* print. Reissue in 1984 has *black* perimeter print.)
CAPITOL (5112 "I Want to Hold Your Hand") 60-70 68
(Yellow/orange swirl label with "Subsidiary of Capitol, etc." perimeter print.)
CAPITOL (5112 "I Want to Hold Your Hand") 65-75 69
(Red/orange label with dome logo.)
CAPITOL (5112 "I Want to Hold Your Hand") 15-25 69
(Red/orange label with round logo.)
CAPITOL (5112 "I Want to Hold Your Hand") 5-10 76
(Orange label.)
CAPITOL (5112 "I Want to Hold Your Hand") 10-15 78
(Purple label "Mfd. by Capitol, etc." perimeter print.)
CAPITOL (5112 "I Want to Hold Your Hand") 3-5 84
(Yellow/orange swirl label with *black* perimeter print. Original 1964 issue has *white* perimeter print.)
CAPITOL (5112 "I Want to Hold Your Hand") 5-8 86
(Black label.)
CAPITOL (5112 "I Want to Hold Your Hand") 4-6 88
(Purple label with "Manufactured by Capitol, etc." perimeter print.)
CAPITOL (5112 "I Want to Hold Your Hand") 3-5 94
(Yellow/orange swirl label. Has "NR-58123" in trail-off area.)
CAPITOL (5150 "Can't Buy Me Love") 25-35 64
(Yellow/orange swirl label without "Subsidiary of Capitol, etc." perimeter print.)
CAPITOL (5150 "Can't Buy Me Love") 40-50 68
(Yellow/orange swirl label with "Subsidiary of Capitol, etc." perimeter print.)
CAPITOL (5150 "Can't Buy Me Love") 60-70 69
(Red/orange label with dome logo.)
CAPITOL (5150 "Can't Buy Me Love") 15-20 69
(Red/orange label with round logo.)
CAPITOL (5150 "Can't Buy Me Love") .. 5-8 76
(Orange label.)
CAPITOL (5150 "Can't Buy Me Love") 10-15 78
(Purple label.)
CAPITOL (B-5189 "Love Me Do") 4-6 82
(Yellow/orange or black or purple label.)
CAPITOL (5222 "A Hard Day's Night") 25-35 64
(Yellow/orange swirl label without "Subsidiary of Capitol, etc." perimeter print.)
CAPITOL (5222 "A Hard Day's Night") 40-50 64
(Yellow/orange swirl label with "Subsidiary of Capitol, etc." in *white* perimeter print.)

CAPITOL (5222 "A Hard Day's Night")....75-100 64
(Yellow/orange swirl label with "Subsidiary of Capitol, etc." in *black* perimeter print.)
CAPITOL (5222 "A Hard Day's Night")....60-70 69
(Red/orange label with dome logo.)
CAPITOL (5222 "A Hard Day's Night")....15-20 69
(Red/orange label with round logo.)
CAPITOL (5222 "A Hard Day's Night")....5-8 76
(Orange label.)
CAPITOL (5222 "A Hard Day's Night")....10-15 78
(Purple label.)
CAPITOL (5234 "I'll Cry Instead")......25-35 64
(Yellow/orange swirl label without "Subsidiary of Capitol, etc." perimeter print.)
CAPITOL (5234 "I'll Cry Instead")....50-70 64
(Yellow/orange swirl label with "Subsidiary of Capitol, etc." perimeter print.)
CAPITOL (5234 "I'll Cry Instead")......60-75 69
(Red/orange label with dome logo.)
CAPITOL (5234 "I'll Cry Instead")......15-20 69
(Red/orange label with round logo.)
CAPITOL (5234 "I'll Cry Instead")........5-8 76
(Orange label.)
CAPITOL (5234 "I'll Cry Instead")......10-15 78
(Purple label.)
CAPITOL (5235 "And I Love Her")....25-35 64
(Yellow/orange swirl label without "Subsidiary of Capitol, etc." perimeter print.)
CAPITOL (5235 "And I Love Her")....40-50 64
(Yellow/orange swirl label with "Subsidiary of Capitol, etc." in *white* perimeter print.)
CAPITOL (5235 "And I Love Her")....60-70 64
(Yellow/orange swirl label with "Subsidiary of Capitol, etc." in *black* perimeter print.)
CAPITOL (5235 "And I Love Her")....60-70 69
(Red/orange label with dome logo.)
CAPITOL (5235 "And I Love Her")....15-20 69
(Red/orange label with round logo.)
CAPITOL (5235 "And I Love Her")........5-8 76
(Orange label.)
CAPITOL (5235 "And I Love Her")....10-15 78
(Purple label.)
CAPITOL (5255 "Matchbox")............25-35 64
(Yellow/orange swirl label without "Subsidiary of Capitol, etc." perimeter print.)
CAPITOL (5255 "Matchbox")............40-50 64
(Yellow/orange swirl label with "Subsidiary of Capitol, etc." perimeter print.)
CAPITOL (5255 "Matchbox")............60-70 69
(Red/orange label with dome logo.)
CAPITOL (5255 "Matchbox")............15-20 69
(Red/orange label with round logo.)
CAPITOL (5255 "Matchbox")................5-8 76
(Orange label.)
CAPITOL (5255 "Matchbox")............10-15 78
(Purple label.)
CAPITOL (5327 "I Feel Fine")..........25-35 64
(Yellow/orange swirl label without "Subsidiary of Capitol, etc." perimeter print.)
CAPITOL (5327 "I Feel Fine")..........40-50 64
(Yellow/orange swirl label with "Subsidiary of Capitol, etc." perimeter print.)
CAPITOL (5327 "I Feel Fine")..........60-70 69
(Red/orange label with dome logo.)
CAPITOL (5327 "I Feel Fine")..........15-20 69
(Red/orange label with round logo.)
CAPITOL (5327 "I Feel Fine")..............5-8 76
(Orange label.)
CAPITOL (5327 "I Feel Fine")..........10-15 78
(Purple label.)
CAPITOL (5371 "Eight Days a Week")....25-35 65
(Yellow/orange swirl label without "Subsidiary of Capitol, etc." perimeter print.)
CAPITOL (5371 "Eight Days a Week")....40-50 68
(Yellow/orange swirl label with "Subsidiary of Capitol, etc." perimeter print.)
CAPITOL (5371 "Eight Days a Week")....60-70 69
(Red/orange label with dome logo.)
CAPITOL (5371 "Eight Days a Week")....15-20 69
(Red/orange label with round logo.)
CAPITOL (5371 "Eight Days a Week")....5-8 76
(Orange label.)
CAPITOL (5371 "Eight Days a Week")....10-15 78
(Purple label.)
CAPITOL (5407 "Ticket to Ride")..... 25-35 64
(Yellow/orange swirl label without "Subsidiary of Capitol, etc." perimeter print.)
CAPITOL (5407 "Ticket to Ride")..... 40-50 64
(Yellow/orange swirl label with "Subsidiary of Capitol, etc." in *white* perimeter print.)
CAPITOL (5407 "Ticket to Ride")... 75-100 64
(Yellow/orange swirl label with "Subsidiary of Capitol, etc." in *black* perimeter print.)
CAPITOL (5407 "Ticket to Ride")..... 60-70 69
(Red/orange label with dome logo.)
CAPITOL (5407 "Ticket to Ride")..... 15-20 69
(Red/orange label with round logo.)
CAPITOL (5407 "Ticket to Ride")........ 5-8 76
(Orange label.)
CAPITOL (5407 "Ticket to Ride")..... 10-15 78
(Purple label.)
CAPITOL (5476 "Help")................... 25-35 65
(Yellow/orange swirl label without "Subsidiary of Capitol, etc." perimeter print.)
CAPITOL (5476 "Help")................... 40-50 68
(Yellow/orange swirl label with "Subsidiary of Capitol, etc." in *white* perimeter print.)
CAPITOL (5476 "Help")................. 75-100 68
(Yellow/orange swirl label with "Subsidiary of Capitol, etc." in *black* perimeter print.)
CAPITOL (5476 "Help")................... 60-70 69
(Red/orange label with dome logo.)
CAPITOL (5476 "Help")................... 15-20 69
(Red/orange label with round logo.)
CAPITOL (5476 "Help")....................... 5-8 76
(Orange label.)
CAPITOL (5476 "Help")................... 10-15 78
(Purple label.)
CAPITOL (5498 "Yesterday")........... 20-30 64
(Yellow/orange swirl label without "Subsidiary of Capitol, etc." perimeter print.)
CAPITOL (5498 "Yesterday")........... 40-50 68
(Yellow/orange swirl label with "Subsidiary of Capitol, etc." in *white* perimeter print.)
CAPITOL (5498 "Yesterday")......... 75-100 68
(Yellow/orange swirl label with "Subsidiary of Capitol, etc." in *black* perimeter print.)
CAPITOL (5498 "Yesterday")........... 60-70 69
(Red/orange label with dome logo.)
CAPITOL (5498 "Yesterday")........... 15-20 69
(Red/orange label with round logo.)
CAPITOL (5498 "Yesterday")............... 5-8 76
(Orange label.)
CAPITOL (5498 "Yesterday")........... 10-15 78
(Purple label.)
CAPITOL (5555 "We Can Work It Out")....20-30 66
(Yellow/orange swirl label without "Subsidiary of Capitol, etc." perimeter print.)
CAPITOL (5555 "We Can Work It Out")....40-50 68
(Yellow/orange swirl label with "Subsidiary of Capitol, etc." perimeter print.)
CAPITOL (5555 "We Can Work It Out")....1200-1500 69
(Red and white label. "Starline" series.)
CAPITOL (5555 "We Can Work It Out")....60-75 69
(Red/orange label with dome logo.)
CAPITOL (5555 "We Can Work It Out")....15-20 69
(Red/orange label with round logo.)
CAPITOL (5555 "We Can Work It Out")....5-8 76
(Orange label.)
CAPITOL (5555 "We Can Work It Out")....10-15 78
(Purple label.)
CAPITOL (5587 "Nowhere Man")......25-50 66
(Yellow/orange swirl label without "Subsidiary of Capitol, etc." perimeter print.)
CAPITOL (5587 "Nowhere Man")......40-50 68
(Yellow/orange swirl label with "Subsidiary of Capitol, etc." perimeter print.)
CAPITOL (5587 "Nowhere Man")......60-75 69
(Red/orange label with dome logo.)
CAPITOL (5587 "Nowhere Man")......15-20 69
(Red/orange label with round logo.)
CAPITOL (5587 "Nowhere Man")..........5-8 76
(Orange label.)
CAPITOL (5587 "Nowhere Man")......10-15 78
(Purple label.)
CAPITOL (B-5624 "Twist & Shout")......4-6 86
(Black or purple label.)
CAPITOL (5651 "Paperback Writer")....25-50 66
(Yellow/orange swirl label without "Subsidiary of Capitol, etc." perimeter print.)
CAPITOL (5651 "Paperback Writer")....40-50 68
(Yellow/orange swirl label with "Subsidiary of Capitol, etc." in *white* perimeter print.)
CAPITOL (5651 "Paperback Writer")....75-100 68
(Yellow/orange swirl label with "Subsidiary of Capitol, etc." in *black* perimeter print.)
CAPITOL (5651 "Paperback Writer")....60-75 69
(Red/orange label with dome logo.)
CAPITOL (5651 "Paperback Writer")....15-20 69
(Red/orange label with round logo.)
CAPITOL (5651 "Paperback Writer")....5-8 76
(Orange label.)
CAPITOL (5651 "Paperback Writer")....10-15 78
(Purple label.)
CAPITOL (5715 "Yellow Submarine")....20-30 66
(Yellow/orange swirl label without "Subsidiary of Capitol, etc." perimeter print.)
CAPITOL (5715 "Yellow Submarine")....40-50 68
(Yellow/orange swirl label with "Subsidiary of Capitol, etc." perimeter print.)
CAPITOL (5715 "Yellow Submarine")....60-70 69
(Red/orange label with dome logo.)
CAPITOL (5715 "Yellow Submarine")....15-20 69
(Red/orange label with round logo.)
CAPITOL (5715 "Yellow Submarine")....5-8 76
(Orange label.)
CAPITOL (5715 "Yellow Submarine")....10-15 78
(Purple label.)
CAPITOL (5810 "Penny Lane").........25-35 66
(Yellow/orange swirl label without "Subsidiary of Capitol, etc." perimeter print.)
CAPITOL (5810 "Penny Lane").........40-50 68
(Yellow/orange swirl label with "Subsidiary of Capitol, etc." perimeter print.)
CAPITOL (5810 "Penny Lane").........60-70 69
(Red/orange label with dome logo.)
CAPITOL (5810 "Penny Lane").........15-20 69
(Red/orange label with round logo.)
CAPITOL (5810 "Penny Lane")............5-8 76
(Orange label.)
CAPITOL (5810 "Penny Lane").........10-15 78
(Purple label.)
CAPITOL (5964 "All You Need Is Love")....20-30 67
(Yellow/orange swirl label without "Subsidiary of Capitol, etc." perimeter print.)
CAPITOL (5964 "All You Need Is Love")....40-50 68
(Yellow/orange swirl label with "Subsidiary of Capitol, etc." perimeter print.)

CAPITOL (5964 "All You Need Is Love") 60-75 69
(Red/orange label with dome logo.)
CAPITOL (5964 "All You Need Is Love") 15-20 69
(Red/orange label with round logo.)
CAPITOL (5964 "All You Need Is Love") 5-8 76
(Orange label.)
CAPITOL (5964 "All You Need Is Love") 10-15 78
(Purple label.)
CAPITOL (6061 "Twist & Shout") 100-125 65
(Green label. "Starline" series.)
CAPITOL (6062 "Love Me Do") 100-125 65
(Green label. "Starline" series.)
CAPITOL (6063 "Please Please Me") 100-125 65
(Green label. "Starline" series.)
CAPITOL (6064 "Do You Want to Know a Secret") 100-125 65
(Green label. "Starline" series.)
CAPITOL (6065 "Misery") 100-125 65
(Green label. "Starline" series.)
CAPITOL (6065 "Misery") 20-30 71
(Red/orange label. "Starline" series.)
CAPITOL (6066 "Kansas City") 70-90 65
(Green label. "Starline" series.)
CAPITOL (6066 "Kansas City") 20-30 71
(Red/orange label. "Starline" series.)
CAPITOL (A-6278 "I Want to Hold Your Hand") 15-25 81
(Blue label reads "stereo" but plays mono. "Starline" series.)
CAPITOL (A-6278 "I Want to Hold Your Hand") 20-30 81
(Blue label reads "mono." "Starline" series.)
CAPITOL (X-6278 "I Want to Hold Your Hand") 10-15 81
(Blue label reads "mono." "Starline" series.)
CAPITOL (A-6279 "Can't Buy Me Love") 5-8 81
(Blue label reads "stereo" but plays mono. "Starline" series.)
CAPITOL (A-6279 "Can't Buy Me Love") 15-25 81
(Blue label reads "mono." "Starline" series.)
CAPITOL (X-6279 "Can't Buy Me Love") 4-6 81
(Blue label reads "mono." "Starline" series.)
CAPITOL (6279 "Can't Buy Me Love") 4-6 86
(Black or purple label. "Starline" series.)
CAPITOL (A-6281 "A Hard Day's Night") 5-8 81
(Blue label reads "stereo" but plays mono. "Starline" series.)
CAPITOL (A-6281 "A Hard Day's Night") 15-25 81
(Blue label reads "mono." "Starline" series.)
CAPITOL (X-6281 "A Hard Day's Night") 4-6 81
(Blue label reads "mono." "Starline" series.)
CAPITOL (6281 "A Hard Day's Night") 4-6 86
(Black or purple label "Starline" series.)
CAPITOL (A-6282 "I'll Cry Instead") 5-8 81
(Blue label reads "stereo" but plays mono. "Starline" series.)
CAPITOL (A-6282 "I'll Cry Instead") 15-25 81
(Blue label reads "mono." "Starline" series.)
CAPITOL (X-6282 "I'll Cry Instead") 4-6 81
(Blue label reads "mono." "Starline" series.)
CAPITOL (6282 "I'll Cry Instead") 4-6 86
(Black or purple label "Starline" series.)
CAPITOL (A-6283 "And I Love Her") 5-8 81
(Blue label reads "stereo" but plays mono. "Starline" series.)
CAPITOL (A-6283 "And I Love Her") 15-25 81
(Blue label reads "mono." "Starline" series.)
CAPITOL (X-6283 "And I Love Her") 4-6 81
(Blue label reads "mono." "Starline" series.)
CAPITOL (6283 "And I Love Her") 4-6 86
(Black or purple label. "Starline" series.)
CAPITOL (A-6284 "Matchbox") 5-8 81
(Blue label reads "stereo" but plays mono. "Starline" series.)
CAPITOL (A-6284 "Matchbox") 15-25 81
(Blue label reads "mono." "Starline" series.)
CAPITOL (X-6284 "Matchbox") 4-6 81
(Blue label reads "mono." "Starline" series.)
CAPITOL (6284 "Matchbox") 4-6 86
(Black or purple label. "Starline" series.)
CAPITOL (A-6286 "I Feel Fine") 5-8 81
(Blue label reads "stereo" but plays mono. "Starline" series.)
CAPITOL (A-6286 "I Feel Fine") 15-25 81
(Blue label reads "mono." "Starline" series.)
CAPITOL (X-6286 "I Feel Fine") 4-6 81
(Blue label reads "mono." "Starline" series.)
CAPITOL (6286 "I Feel Fine") 4-6 86
(Black or purple label. "Starline" series.)
CAPITOL (A-6287 "Eight Days a Week") 5-8 81
(Blue label reads "stereo" but plays mono. "Starline" series.)
CAPITOL (A-6287 "Eight Days a Week") 15-25 81
(Blue label reads "mono." "Starline" series.)
CAPITOL (X-6287 "Eight Days a Week") 4-6 81
(Blue label reads "mono." "Starline" series.)
CAPITOL (6287 "Eight Days a Week") 4-6 86
(Black or purple label. "Starline" series.)
CAPITOL (A-6288 "Ticket to Ride") 5-8 81
(Blue label reads "stereo" but plays mono. "Starline" series.)
CAPITOL (A-6288 "Ticket to Ride") 15-25 81
(Blue label reads "mono." "Starline" series.)
CAPITOL (X-6288 "Ticket to Ride") 4-6 81
(Blue label reads "mono." "Starline" series.)
CAPITOL (6288 "Ticket to Ride") 4-6 86
(Black or purple label. "Starline" series.)
CAPITOL (A-6290 "Help") 5-8 81
(Blue label reads "stereo" but plays mono. "Starline" series.)
CAPITOL (A-6290 "Help") 15-25 81
(Blue label reads "mono." "Starline" series.)
CAPITOL (X-6290 "Help") 4-6 81
(Blue label reads "mono." "Starline" series.)
CAPITOL (6290 "Help") 4-6 86
(Black or purple label "Starline" series.)
CAPITOL (A-6291 "Yesterday") 5-8 81
(Blue label reads "stereo" but plays mono. "Starline" series.)
CAPITOL (A-6291 "Yesterday") 15-25 81
(Blue label reads "mono." "Starline" series.)
CAPITOL (X-6291 "Yesterday") 4-6 81
(Blue label reads "mono." "Starline" series.)
CAPITOL (6291 "Yesterday") 4-6 86
(Black or purple label "Starline" series.)
CAPITOL (A-6293 "We Can Work It Out") 5-8 81
(Blue label reads "stereo" but plays mono. "Starline" series.)
CAPITOL (A-6293 "We Can Work It Out") 15-25 81
(Blue label reads "mono." "Starline" series.)
CAPITOL (X-6293 "We Can Work It Out") 4-6 81
(Blue label reads "mono." "Starline" series.)
CAPITOL (6293 "We Can Work It Out") 4-6 86
(Black or purple label "Starline" series.)
CAPITOL (A-6294 "Nowhere Man") 5-8 81
(Blue label reads "stereo" but plays mono. "Starline" series.)
CAPITOL (A-6294 "Nowhere Man") 15-25 81
(Blue label reads "mono." "Starline" series.)
CAPITOL (X-6294 "Nowhere Man") 4-6 81
(Blue label reads "mono." "Starline" series.)
CAPITOL (6294 "Nowhere Man") 4-6 86
(Black or purple label "Starline" series.)
CAPITOL (A-6296 "Paperback Writer") 5-8 81
(Blue label reads "stereo" but plays mono. "Starline" series.)
CAPITOL (A-6296 "Paperback Writer") 15-25 81
(Blue label reads "mono." "Starline" series.)
CAPITOL (X-6296 "Paperback Writer") 4-6 81
(Blue label reads "mono." "Starline" series.)
CAPITOL (6296 "Paperback Writer") 4-6 86
(Black or purple label "Starline" series.)
CAPITOL (A-6297 "Yellow Submarine") 5-8 81
(Blue label reads "stereo" but plays mono. "Starline" series.)
CAPITOL (A-6297 "Yellow Submarine") 15-25 81
(Blue label reads "mono." "Starline" series.)
CAPITOL (X-6297 "Yellow Submarine") 4-6 81
(Blue label reads "mono." "Starline" series.)
CAPITOL (6297 "Yellow Submarine") 4-6 86
(Black or purple label "Starline" series.)
CAPITOL (A-6299 "Penny Lane") 5-8 81
(Blue label reads "stereo" but plays mono. "Starline" series.)
CAPITOL (A-6299 "Penny Lane") 15-25 81
(Blue label reads "mono." "Starline" series.)
CAPITOL (X-6299 "Penny Lane") 4-6 81
(Blue label reads "mono." "Starline" series.)
CAPITOL (6299 "Penny Lane") 4-6 86
(Black or purple label "Starline" series.)
CAPITOL (A-6300 "All You Need Is Love") 5-8 81
(Blue label reads "stereo" but plays mono. "Starline" series.)
CAPITOL (A-6300 "All You Need Is Love") 15-25 81
(Blue label reads "mono." "Starline" series.)
CAPITOL (X-6300 "All You Need Is Love") 4-6 81
(Blue label reads "mono." "Starline" series.)
CAPITOL (6300 "All You Need Is Love") 15-20 86
(Black label. "Starline" series.)
CAPITOL (17488 "Birthday") 40-50 94
(Black vinyl, 30th Anniversary juke box issue.)
CAPITOL (17488 "Birthday") 3-4 94
(Colored vinyl, 30th Anniversary juke box issue.)
CAPITOL (17488 "Birthday") 3-4 94
(Colored vinyl, 30th Anniversary juke box issue.)
CAPITOL (17688 "She Loves You") 3-4 94
(Colored vinyl, 30th Anniversary juke box issue.)
CAPITOL (17689 "I Want to Hold Your Hand") 3-4 94
(Colored vinyl, 30th Anniversary juke box issue.)
CAPITOL (17690 "Can't Buy Me Love") 3-4 94
(Colored vinyl, 30th Anniversary juke box issue.)
CAPITOL (17691 "Help") 3-4 94
(Colored vinyl, 30th Anniversary juke box issue.)
CAPITOL (17692 "A Hard Day's Night") 3-4 94
(Colored vinyl, 30th Anniversary juke box issue.)
CAPITOL (17693 "All You Need Is Love") 3-4 94
(Colored vinyl, 30th Anniversary juke box issue.)
CAPITOL (17694 "Hey Jude") 3-4 94
(Colored vinyl, 30th Anniversary juke box issue.)
CAPITOL (17695 "Let It Be") 3-4 94
(Colored vinyl, 30th Anniversary juke box issue.)
CAPITOL (17696 "Eleanor Rigby") 3-4 94
(Colored vinyl, 30th Anniversary juke box issue.)
CAPITOL (17697 "Penny Lane") 3-4 94
(Colored vinyl, 30th Anniversary juke box issue.)
CAPITOL (17698 "Something") 3-4 94
(Colored vinyl, 30th Anniversary juke box issue.)
CAPITOL (17699 "Twist & Shout") 3-4 94
(Colored vinyl, 30th Anniversary juke box issue.)
CAPITOL (17700 "Here Comes the Sun") 3-4 94
(Colored vinyl, 30th Anniversary juke box issue.)
CAPITOL (17701 "Sgt. Pepper's Lonely Hearts Club Band") 3-4 94
(Colored vinyl, 30th Anniversary juke box issue.)
CAPITOL (18889 "You've Got to Hide Your Love Away") 3-4 96

(Colored vinyl.)
CAPITOL (18890 "Magical Mystery Tour")....3-4 96
(Colored vinyl.)
CAPITOL (18891 "Across the Universe")....3-4 96
(Colored vinyl.)
CAPITOL (18892 "While My Guitar Gently Sleeps")....3-4 96
(Colored vinyl.)
CAPITOL (18893 "It's All Too Much")....3-4 96
(Colored vinyl.)
CAPITOL (18894 "Nowhere Man")....3-4 96
(Colored vinyl.)
CAPITOL (18895 "Can't Buy Me Love")....3-4 96
(Colored vinyl.)
CAPITOL (18896 "Lucy in the Sky with Diamonds")....3-4 96
(Colored vinyl.)
CAPITOL (18897 "Here, There and Everywhere")....3-4 96
(Colored vinyl.)
CAPITOL (18898 "Long and Winding Road")....3-4 96
(Colored vinyl.)
CAPITOL (18899 "Got to Get You into My Life")....3-4 96
(Colored vinyl.)
CAPITOL (18900 "Ob-La-Di, Ob-La-Da")....3-4 96
(Colored vinyl.)
CAPITOL (18901 "Yesterday")....3-4 96
(Colored vinyl.)
CAPITOL (18902 "Paperback Writer")....3-4 96
(Colored vinyl.)
CAPITOL (56785 "Love Me Do")....25-30 92
(Intended to be black vinyl but issued on red vinyl by mistake. Reportedly 1,500 made. 30th Anniversary juke box issue.)
CAPITOL (56785 "Love Me Do")....3-4 92
(Black vinyl. 30th Anniversary juke box issue.)
CAPITOL (58123 "I Want to Hold Your Hand")....3-4 96
CAPITOL (58497 "Free As a Bird")....3-4 96
CAPITOL (58544 "Real Love")....3-4 96
CAPITOL (72144 "All My Loving")....80-100 71
(An error in production created a U.S. pressing of the Canadian release, *All My Loving/This Boy*.)
CAPITOL (79551 "Love Me Do")....20-25 92
(Mail-order only.)
CARROLL JAMES (3301 "Carroll James Interview with the Beatles")....4-8 84
CICADELIC/BIODISC (001 "A Hard Day's Night")....15-20 90
(Open-end interview picture disc. With script.)
CICADELIC/BIODISC (001 "A Hard Day's Night")....25-35 90
(Open-end interview picture disc. With script. Promotional only issue made for "Records, Etc. of Payson, Az." 55 made.)
CICADELIC/BIODISC (002 "Help: Open-end Interview")....5-8 90
(With script.)
COLLECTABLES....3-4 82
CREATIVE RADIO (B-1 "The Beatle Invasion")....10-20 80s
(Radio show demo. Flip side is "Inside Paul McCartney.")
DECCA (31382 "My Bonnie")....8000-12000 62
(Shown as by Tony Sheridan & Beat Brothers. Note: Price is for a *COMMERCIAL*, not promotional, issue. Commercial copies are on Decca's black label with silver print and a multi-color stripe across the center of the label. Black and silver Decca labels without the other colors are bootlegs.)
IBC (0082 "Murray the 'K' and the Beatles As It Happened")....8-10 76
MGM (13213 "My Bonnie")....40-50 64
(Shown as by the Beatles with Tony Sheridan.)
MGM (13227 "Why")....100-125 64
(Shown as by the Beatles with Tony Sheridan.)
MURRAY the "K" & the BEATLES....20-25 64
(33 Single. Reissued in 1976 as IBC 0082.)
OLDIES 45....8-15 65
SILHOUETTE (1451 "Timeless 2 ½")....10-15 83
(Picture disc.)
SWAN (4152 "She Loves You")....600-650 63
(White label, with red or blue print.)
SWAN (4152 "She Loves You")....25-50 64
(Black label.)
SWAN (4182 "Sie Liebt Dich")....125-150 64
(White label with red print.)
SWAN (4182 "Sie Liebt Dich")....150-175 64
(White label with orange print.)
TOLLIE (9001 "Twist & Shout")....60-70 64
(Black label.)
TOLLIE (9001 "Twist & Shout")....60-80 64
(Yellow label with purple print.)
TOLLIE (9001 "Twist & Shout")....50-60 64
(Yellow label with blue print.)
TOLLIE (9001 "Twist & Shout")....50-75 64
(Yellow label with black print.)
TOLLIE (9001 "Twist & Shout")....60-80 64
(Yellow label with green print has logo in box.)
TOLLIE (9001 "Twist & Shout")....40-50 64
(Yellow label with green print has logo without box.)
TOLLIE (9008 "Love Me Do")....50-60 64
(Black label.)
TOLLIE (9008 "Love Me Do")....40-50 64
(Yellow label.)
TOPAZ (1353 "Seattle Press Conference")....4-6 89
VEE JAY (498 "Please Please Me")....1400-1600 63
(Credits "BEATTLES." Black label with rainbow circle. Has thin lettering and oval logo.)
VEE JAY (498 "Please Please Me")....800-1000 63
(Credits "BEATTLES." Black label with rainbow circle. Has bold lettering and oval logo.)
VEE JAY (498 "Please Please Me")....1500-1800 63
(Credits "BEATLES." Black label with rainbow circle. Has thin lettering and oval label logo.)
VEE JAY (498 "Please Please Me")....700-900 63
(Credits "BEATLES." Black label with rainbow circle. Has bold lettering and oval label logo.)
VEE JAY (498 "Please Please Me")....1800-2000 63
(Credits "BEATLES." Black label with rainbow circle. Has brackets label logo.)
VEE JAY (522 "From Me to You")....700-800 63
(Black label with horizontal silver lines.)
VEE JAY (522 "From Me to You") 800-900 63
(Black label with rainbow circle and brackets logo.)
VEE JAY (522 "From Me to You")....500-700 63
(Black label with rainbow circle and oval logo.)
VEE JAY (581 "Please Please Me")....200-250 64
(Purple label.)
VEE JAY (581 "Please Please Me")....140-160 64
(White label. Not a promotional issue.)
VEE JAY (581 "Please Please Me")....60-75 64
(Yellow label.)
VEE JAY (581 "Please Please Me")....35-45 64
(Black label with horizontal silver lines.)
VEE JAY (581 "Please Please Me")....50-75 64
(Black label. No rainbow circle.)
VEE JAY (581 "Please Please Me")....50-60 64
(Black label with rainbow circle.)
VEE JAY (587 "Do You Want to Know a Secret")....35-45 64
(Solid black label with horizontal silver lines.)
VEE JAY (587 "Do You Want to Know a Secret")....50-65 64
(Solid black label or yellow label.)
VEE JAY (587 "Do You Want to Know a Secret")....40-50 64
(Black label with rainbow circle.)

Picture Sleeves

APPLE (2531 "Ballad of John & Yoko")....60-80 69
APPLE (2764 "Let It Be")....60-80 70
APPLE (2832 "Long and Winding Road")....60-80 70
ATCO (6308 "Ain't She Sweet")....350-500 64
BRS (1/2 "Murray the 'K' and the Beatles As It Happened")....150-200 64
CAPITOL/HOLIDAY INN....800-1000 64
(Promotional sleeve, pictures the four Beatles on front and their first three Capitol LPs on the back. Not known to have been issued containing any particular single.)
CAPITOL (2056 "Hello Goodbye")....60-80 67
CAPITOL (2138 "Lady Madonna")....70-90 68
CAPITOL (2138 "Lady Madonna")....15-20 68
(Fan Club flyer insert.)
CAPITOL (4274 "Got to Get You into My Life")....3-6 88
CAPITOL (4347 "Ob-La-Di, Ob-La-Da")....5-8 76
CAPITOL (4506 "Girl")....10-15 78
CAPITOL (4612 "Sgt. Pepper's Lonely Hearts Club Band" & "With A Little Help From My Friends")....15-20 78
CAPITOL (B-5100 "Movie Medley"/ "Fab Four on Film")....15-20 82
CAPITOL (B-5107 "Movie Medley"/"I'm Happy Just to Dance with You")....3-4 82
CAPITOL (B-5189 "Love Me Do")....3-4 82
CAPITOL (5112 "I Want to Hold Your Hand")....50-75 64
(This original sleeve has no periods placed at end of the small print in "Reg. U.S. Pat. Off." in Capitol logo. Reissue in 1994 has periods.)
CAPITOL (5112 WMCA Radio Promotional Sleeve)....2000-2200 64
(Back side of this sleeve pictures WMCA dee jays. Front side is identical to standard commercial issue.)
CAPITOL (5112 "I Want to Hold Your Hand")....4-6 84
(This reissue sleeve is clearly dated "1984" in lower left corner.)
CAPITOL (5112 "I Want to Hold Your Hand")....4-6 94
(This reissue sleeve has periods placed at end of the small print in "Reg. U.S. Pat. Off." in Capitol logo. Original in 1964 has no periods.)
CAPITOL (5150 "Can't Buy Me Love")....500-600 64
CAPITOL CUSTOM (2637 "Music City KFWBeatles")....800-1000 64
(Promotional sleeve for the "Souvenir Record" from KFWB and Wallichs Music City.)
CAPITOL (5222 "A Hard Day's Night")....50-75 64
CAPITOL (5234 "I'll Cry Instead")....140-160 64
CAPITOL (5235 "And I Love Her")....125-150 64
CAPITOL (5255 "Slow Down")....50-75 64
CAPITOL (5327 "I Feel Fine")....50-70 64
CAPITOL (5371 "Eight Days a Week")....25-50 65
CAPITOL (5407 "Ticket to Ride")....75-100 65
CAPITOL (5439 "Leave My Kitten Alone")....35-45 85
CAPITOL (5476 "Help")....50-75 65
CAPITOL (5498 "Yesterday")....50-75 65
CAPITOL (5555 "We Can Work It Out")....50-75 65
CAPITOL (5587 "Nowhere Man")....40-50 66
CAPITOL (5651 "Paperback Writer")....50-75 66
CAPITOL (5715 "Yellow Submarine")....75-100 66
CAPITOL (5810 "Penny Lane")....75-100 67

CAPITOL (5964 "All You Need Is Love") 40-50 67
CAPITOL (58123 "I Want to Hold Your Hand") 3-4 96
CAPITOL (58497 "Free As a Bird") 3-4 96
CAPITOL (58544 "Real Love") 3-4 96
CAPITOL (79551 "Love Me Do") 15-20 92
CARROLL JAMES (3301 "Carroll James Interview with the Beatles") 4-8 84
CICADELIC/BIODISC (002 "Help: Open-end Interview") 5-8 90
COLLECTABLES 3-4 82
IBC (0082 "Murray the 'K' and the Beatles As It Happened") 6-10 76
MGM (13213 "My Bonnie") 75-100 64
MGM (13227 "Why") 300-400 64
SWAN (4152 "She Loves You") 100-125 63
TOLLIE (9008 "Love Me Do") 100-125 64
TOPAZ 4-6 89
U.A. (42370 "Let It Be") 100-150 70
(Custom mailer envelope for promo radio spots single.)
VEE JAY SPECIAL CHRISTMAS SLEEVE 70-90 64
(Standard center-cut paper sleeve printed with the Beatles' faces and "We Wish You a Merry Christmas and a Happy New Year." Issued with assorted Vee Jay singles during the holiday season.)
VEE JAY (581 "Please Please Me") 400-500 64
(Pictures the four Beatles.)
VEE JAY (581 "Please Please Me") 2000-3000 64
(Promotional only sleeve. Reads "The Record That Started Beatlemania" across the top. Does not picture the group.)
VEE JAY (587 "Do You Want to Know a Secret") 100-125 64

Promotional Singles

APPLE ("Let It Be") 50-60 70
(Identified as "Beatles Promo 1970." Single-sided promo issue.)
ATCO (6302 "Sweet Georgia Brown" 175-200 64
ATCO (6308 "Ain't She Sweet") 250-300 64
BACKSTAGE (1112 "Oui Presents the Silver Beatles") 20-25 82
(*Oui* magazine promotional giveaway. Features a *Like Dreamers Do/Love of the Loved* montage. Mailing also included *Oui* News Release and subscription form. This is not a picture disc single, as the other Backstage 1100 series singles are.)
BACKSTAGE (1122 "Love of the Loved") 20-25 83
(Promotional only picture disc.)
BACKSTAGE (1133 "Like Dreamers Do") 20-25 83
(Promotional only picture disc.)
BACKSTAGE (1133 "Like Dreamers Do") 40-50 83
(Picture disc, with photo of *Penthouse* "Pet.")
CAPITOL (2056 "Hello Goodbye") 200-250 67
CAPITOL (2138 "Lady Madonna") 150-200 68
CAPITOL (4274 "Got to Get You Into My Life") 30-40 76
CAPITOL (4274 "Helter Skelter") 30-40 76
CAPITOL (4347 "Ob-La-Di, Ob-La-Da") 30-40 76
CAPITOL (4506 "Girl") 175-200 78
CAPITOL (4612 "Sgt. Pepper's Lonely Hearts Club Band" & "With a Little Help From My Friends") 30-40 78
CAPITOL (PB-5100 "Movie Medley"/"Fab Four on Film") 20-25 82
CAPITOL (P-5112/PRO-9076 "I Want to Hold Your Hand") 10-15 84
CAPITOL (PB-5150 "Can't Buy Me Love") 5000-10000
(Yellow vinyl. Experimental pressing only.)
CAPITOL (PB-5150 "Can't Buy Me Love") 4000-6000
(Black and yellow vinyl. Experimental pressing only.)
CAPITOL (PB-5189 "Love Me Do") .. 10-15 82
CAPITOL (PB-5624 "Twist & Shout") 10-15 86
CAPITOL (5810 "Penny Lane") 250-300 67
(With trumpet solo at end of song.)
CAPITOL (5810 "Penny Lane") 550-600 67
(No trumpet solo at end of song.)
CAPITOL (5964 "All You Need Is Love") 200-250 67
(This promo, as well as many Capitol issues by other artists, was shipped in a "Rush" paper sleeve. It's possible a slight premium may be placed on these sleeves, although they were NOT identified in any way as a Beatles item.)
CAPITOL CUSTOM (2637 "Music City KFWBeatles") 800-1000 64
(Radio KFWB and Wallichs Music City promo disc, "The Beatles Talking"/ "You Can't Do That.")
CARROLL JAMES (3301 "Carroll James Interview with the Beatles") 6-8 84
DECCA (31382 "My Bonnie") 1500-2000 62
(Shown as by Tony Sheridan & Beat Brothers. Pink label with black lettering.)
MBRF (55551 "Decade") 150-250 74
(Contains radio spots for the "Beatles 1962-1966" and "Beatles 1967-1970." May be bootleg, and not an authorized record.)
MGM (13213 "My Bonnie") 200-250 64
(Shown as by the Beatles with Tony Sheridan.)
MGM (13227 "Why") 200-250 64
(Shown as by the Beatles with Tony Sheridan.)
SWAN (4152 "She Loves You") 450-500 63
SWAN (4152 "I'll Get You") 550-650 64
(Single-sided pressing. Flip side has blank grooves.)
SWAN (4182 "Sie Liebt Dich") 400-450 64
TOLLIE (9001 "Twist & Shout") 100-125 64
TOLLIE (9008 "Love Me Do") 400-450 64
TOPAZ (1353 "Seattle Press Conference") 4-8 89
U.A. (2357 "A Hard Day's Night") 1200-1500 64
(Theater lobby advertisements. Orange label.)
U.A. (10029 "A Hard Day's Night") 2000-3000 64
(Open-end interview. Has small play hole.)
U.A. (42370 "Let It Be") 1000-1200 70
(Has three radio advertisements for the film.)
VEE JAY (8 "Anna"/"Ask Me Why") 10000-12000 64
VEE JAY (498 "Please Please Me") 1000-1200 63
VEE JAY (522 "From Me to You") 400-500 63
VEE JAY (581 "Please Please Me") 500-600 64
(Blue and white label.)
VEE JAY (587 "Do You Want to Know a Secret") 550-650 64
WHAT'S IT ALL ABOUT 15-20

Plastic Soundsheets/Flexi-Discs

AMERICOM ("Yellow Submarine") 1500-1800 69
(Plastic "Pocket Disc" soundsheet. Number not known.)
AMERICOM (221 "Hey Jude") 250-300 69
(Plastic "Pocket Disc" soundsheet.)
AMERICOM (335 "Get Back") 800-1000 69
(Plastic "Pocket Disc" soundsheet.)
AMERICOM (382 "Ballad of John & Yoko") 600-800 69
(Plastic "Pocket Disc" soundsheet.)
EVA-TONE (830771 "Till There Was You") 4-6 83
EVA-TONE (420826 "All My Loving") 5-10 82
(Back side reads either "Compliments of Musicland.")
EVA-TONE (420826 "All My Loving") 15-25 82
(Back side reads "Compliments of Sam Goody" or "Compliments of Discount.")
EVA-TONE (420827 "Magical Mystery Tour") 5-10 82
(Back side reads either "Compliments of Musicland")
EVA-TONE (420827 "Magical Mystery Tour") 15-25 82
(Back side reads "Compliments of Sam Goody" or "Compliments of Discount.")
EVA-TONE (420828 "Rocky Raccoon") 5-10 82
(Back side reads either "Compliments of Musicland".)
EVA-TONE (420828 "Rocky Raccoon") 15-25 82
(Back side reads "Compliments of Sam Goody" or "Compliments of Discount.")
EVA-TONE (1214825 "The Beatles German Medley) 50-60 83
OFFICIAL BEATLES FAN CLUB ("1964 Season's Greetings from the Beatles") 250-300 64
OFFICIAL BEATLES FAN CLUB ("1965 Beatles Christmas Record") 150-175 65
(Includes picture sleeve.)
OFFICIAL BEATLES FAN CLUB ("1966 Season's Greetings from the Beatles") 125-150 66
OFFICIAL BEATLES FAN CLUB ("1967 Christmas Time Is Here Again") .. 125-150 67
OFFICIAL BEATLES FAN CLUB ("1968 Beatles Christmas Record") 100-125 68
(Includes picture sleeve.)
OFFICIAL BEATLES FAN CLUB ("1969 Happy Christmas") 75-100 69
(Includes picture sleeve.)

EPs: 7-inch

CAPITOL (EAP 1-2121 "Four by the Beatles") 30-400 64
CAPITOL (R-5365 "4-by the Beatles") 200-250 65
CAPITOL (59348 "Baby It's You") 4-6 95
CAPITOL COMPACT 33 (2047 "Meet the Beatles") 500-700 64
(Juke box issue only. Add $15 to 25 for each insert.)
CAPITOL COMPACT 33 (2080 "The Beatles' Second Album") 500-700 64
(Juke box issue only. Add $15 to 25 for each insert.)
CAPITOL COMPACT 33 (2108 "Something New") 700-900 64
(Juke box issue only. Add $10 to 30 for each insert.)
VEE JAY (VJEP 1-903 "Souvenir of Their Visit to America") 200-225 64
(Solid black label with either oval or brackets or block style Vee Jay logo.)
VEE JAY (VJEP 1-903 "Souvenir of Their Visit to America") 80-100 64
(Black label with rainbow color-band with oval logo.)
VEE JAY (VJEP 1-903 "Souvenir of Their Visit to America") 200-225 64
(Black label with rainbow color-band with brackets logo.)

Promotional EPs

CAPITOL COMPACT 33 (2548/49 "Open-End Interview") 1200-1500 64
(Issued with a paper sleeve/script, which represents about $700-$800 of the value.)
CAPITOL COMPACT 33 (2598/99 "Second Open-End Interview") 1200-1400 64
(Issued with a paper sleeve/script, which represents about $600-$700 of the value.)
CAPITOL (2720/21 "The Beatles Introduce New Songs") 1500-2000 64
(45 rpm EP with John Lennon about Cilla Black's *It's for You,* and Paul talking about Peter & Gordon's *I Don't Want to See You Again.*)
CAPITOL 33 COMPACT (2905/06 "The Capitol Souvenir Record") 400-500 64
(Issued with a paper sleeve and script, which represents about $200-$250 of the value. Contains excerpts of 15 different songs by 15 artists, including the Beatles.)

POLYGRAM (PRO-1113 "Backbeat")....................................40-50 94
(Soundtrack.)
VEE JAY (903 "Souvenir of Their Visit to America")...................................300-350 64
(White label with blue print. Price is for disc only.)
VEE JAY (VJEP 1-903 "Ask Me Why")......................................7500-8500 64
(The high price is for the paper, EP sleeve promoting *Ask Me Why* but still with the same Vee Jay EP number as *Souvenir of Their Visit to America*.)

LPs: 10/12-inch

ADIRONDACK (8146 "Happy Michaelmas")...................................15-20 81
APPLE ("Beatles Special Limited Edition")................................1000-1200 74
(10 LP boxed set.)
APPLE (101 "The Beatles")...........100-150 68
(With Capitol logo at bottom of label. Limited numbered edition. Includes photos and poster.)
APPLE (101 "The Beatles")..............40-50 71
(Without Capitol logo at bottom of label. Includes photos and poster.)
APPLE (101 "The Beatles")..............15-25 76-83
(Orange labels, or purple labels, or black labels. Includes photos and poster.)
APPLE (153 "Yellow Submarine")...20-30 69
(With Capitol logo at bottom of label.)
APPLE (153 "Yellow Submarine").....15-25 71
(Without Capitol logo at bottom of label.)
APPLE (383 "Abbey Road")..............50-75 69
(With Capitol logo at bottom of label.)
APPLE (383 "Abbey Road")..............15-25 71
(Without Capitol logo at bottom of label.)
APPLE (385 "Hey Jude")..................30-35 70
(Has title, *The Beatles Again* on label.)
APPLE (385 "Hey Jude")..................60-80 70
(With Capitol logo at bottom of label.)
APPLE (385 "Hey Jude")..................15-25 71
(Without Capitol logo at bottom of label.)
APPLE (ST-2047 "Meet the Beatles")..25-35 68
(With Capitol logo at bottom of label.)
APPLE (ST-2047 "Meet the Beatles")..15-25 71
(Without Capitol logo at bottom of label.)
APPLE (ST-2080 "The Beatles' Second Album")...25-35 68
(With Capitol logo at bottom of label.)
APPLE (ST-2080 "The Beatles' Second Album")...15-25 71
(Without Capitol logo at bottom of label.)
APPLE (ST-2108 "Something New")..25-35 68
(With Capitol logo at bottom of label.)
APPLE (ST-2108 "Something New")..15-25 71
(Without Capitol logo at bottom of label.)
APPLE (ST-2222 "The Beatles' Story")..40-50 68
(With Capitol logo at bottom of label.)
APPLE (ST-2222 "The Beatles' Story")..30-40 71
(Without Capitol logo at bottom of label.)
APPLE (ST-2228 "Beatles '65")........25-35 68
(With Capitol logo at bottom of label.)
APPLE (ST-2228 "Beatles '65")........15-25 71
(Without Capitol logo at bottom of label.)
APPLE (ST-2309 "Early Beatles").....25-35 68
(With Capitol logo at bottom of label.)
APPLE (ST-2309 "Early Beatles").....15-25 71
(Without Capitol logo at bottom of label.)
APPLE (ST-2358 "Beatles VI")..........25-35 68
(With Capitol logo at bottom of label.)
APPLE (ST-2358 "Beatles VI")..........15-25 71
(Without Capitol logo at bottom of label.)
APPLE (ST-2386 "Help")..................25-35 68
(With Capitol logo at bottom of label.)
APPLE (ST-2386 "Help")..................15-25 71
(Without Capitol logo at bottom of label.)
APPLE (ST-2442 "Rubber Soul")......25-35 68
(With Capitol logo at bottom of label.)
APPLE (ST-2442 "Rubber Soul")......15-25 71
(Without Capitol logo at bottom of label.)
APPLE (2553 "Yesterday and Today")..25-35 68
(With Capitol logo at bottom of label.)
APPLE (2553 "Yesterday and Today")..15-25 71
(Without Capitol logo at bottom of label.)
APPLE (ST-2576 "Revolver")..........25-35 68
(With Capitol logo at bottom of label.)
APPLE (ST-2576 "Revolver")..........15-25 71
(Without Capitol logo at bottom of label.)
APPLE (SMAS-2653 "Sgt. Pepper's Lonely Hearts Club Band")................................30-40 68
(With Capitol logo at bottom of label.)
APPLE (SMAS-2653 "Sgt. Pepper's Lonely Hearts Club Band")................................15-25 71
(Without Capitol logo at bottom of label.)
APPLE (SMAL-2835 "Magical Mystery Tour")...30-40 68
(With Capitol logo at bottom of label.)
APPLE (SMAL-2835 "Magical Mystery Tour")...15-25 71
(Without Capitol logo at bottom of label.)
APPLE (3403 "1962-1966").............30-40 73
APPLE (3404 "1967-1970").............30-40 73
APPLE (34001 "Let It Be")..............20-30 70
ATCO (169 "Ain't She Sweet")......250-300 64
(Monaural. Also contains selections by the Swallows.)
ATCO (169 "Ain't She Sweet")......300-400 64-69
(Stereo. Also contains selections by the Swallows.)
AUDIO FIDELITY (339 "First Movement")..8-12 82
AUDIO FIDELITY (339 "First Movement")......................................15-20 82
(Picture disc.)
AUDIO RARITIES (2452 "The Complete Silver Beatles")..10-15 82
AUDIO RARITIES (30003 "The Silver Beatles")..20-25 82
(Picture disc.)
BACKSTAGE (201 "Like Dreamers Do")..40-60 82
(Two-LP set. One picture disc and one colored vinyl.)
BACKSTAGE (1111 "Like Dreamers Do")..30-40 82
(Three-LP set. Contains two picture discs and a white vinyl LP.)
BACKSTAGE (1111 "Like Dreamers Do")..70-90 82
(Three-LP set. Contains two picture discs and a GRAY vinyl LP.)
BACKSTAGE (1111 "Like Dreamers Do")..50-60 82
(Three-LP set. Includes any of the custom issues, which had various logos printed on the reverse side of the picture discs.)
BACKSTAGE (1111 "Like Dreamers Do")..30-40 82
(Three-LP set. No custom artwork on picture disc. With gatefold cover.)
BACKSTAGE (1165 "Beatles Talk with Jerry G. Volume 1")...................................15-20 82
(Picture disc.)
BACKSTAGE (1175 "Beatles Talk with Jerry G. Volume 2")...................................15-20 82
(Picture disc.)
CAPITOL (101 "The Beatles")..........20-25 76
(Orange label.)
CAPITOL (101 "The Beatles")..........15-20 78
(Purple label.)
CAPITOL (101 "The Beatles")..........25-30 83
(Black label.)
CAPITOL (153 "Yellow Submarine")... 8-12 76
(Orange label.)
CAPITOL (153 "Yellow Submarine")... 6-10 78
(Purple label.)
CAPITOL (153 "Yellow Submarine"). 10-15 84
(Black label.)
CAPITOL (383 "Abbey Road")........... 8-12 76
(Orange label.)
CAPITOL (383 "Abbey Road")........... 6-10 78
(Purple label.)
CAPITOL (383 "Abbey Road")..........20-30 83
(Black label.)
CAPITOL (385 "Hey Jude")................8-12 76
(Orange label.)
CAPITOL (385 "Hey Jude")................6-10 78
(Purple label.)
CAPITOL (385 "Hey Jude")..............30-50 83
(Black label.)
CAPITOL (T-2047 "Meet the Beatles")..125-150 64
(Monaural.)
CAPITOL (ST-2047 "Meet the Beatles")..80-100 64
(Stereo. Black label with white print around border. Does not have "Subsidiary of Capitol, etc." perimeter print.)
CAPITOL (ST-2047 "Meet the Beatles")..40-50 64
(Stereo. Black label with white print around border. Has "Subsidiary of Capitol, etc." print.)
CAPITOL (ST-2047 "Meet the Beatles")..30-40 69
(Green label.)
CAPITOL (ST-2047 "Meet the Beatles")..8-12 76
(Orange label.)
CAPITOL (ST-2047 "Meet the Beatles")..6-10 78
(Purple label.)
CAPITOL (ST-2047 "Meet the Beatles")..10-15 83
(Black label with black print around border.)
CAPITOL (ST-8-2047 "Meet the Beatles")..200-250 64
(Capitol Record Club issue, black label.)
CAPITOL (ST-8-2047 "Meet the Beatles")..80-100 69
(Capitol Record Club issue, green label.)
CAPITOL (T-2080 "The Beatles' Second Album")..120-140 64
(Monaural.)
CAPITOL (ST-2080 "The Beatles' Second Album")..90-100 64
(Stereo. Black label with white print around border. Does not have "Subsidiary of Capitol, etc." perimeter print.)
CAPITOL (ST-2080 "The Beatles' Second Album")..40-50 64
(Stereo. Black label with white print around border. Has "Subsidiary of Capitol, etc." print.)
CAPITOL (ST-2080 "The Beatles' Second Album")..40-50 69
(Green label.)
CAPITOL (ST-2080 "The Beatles' Second Album")..8-12 76
(Orange label.)
CAPITOL (ST-2080 "The Beatles' Second Album")..6-10 78
(Purple label.)
CAPITOL (ST-2080 "The Beatles' Second Album")..10-15 83
(Black label with black print around border.)
CAPITOL (ST-8-2080 "The Beatles' Second Album")..400-450 64
(Capitol Record Club issue, black label.)
CAPITOL (ST-8-2080 "The Beatles' Second Album")..300-350 69
(Capitol Record Club issue, green label.)
CAPITOL (T-2108 "Something New")..100-125 64
(Monaural.)
CAPITOL (ST-2108 "Something New")..80-90 64
(Stereo. Black label with white print around border. Does not have "Subsidiary of Capitol, etc." perimeter print.)
CAPITOL (ST-2108 "Something New")..40-50 64
(Stereo. Black label with white print around border. Has "Subsidiary of Capitol, etc." print.)
CAPITOL (ST-2108 "Something New")..30-40 69
(Green label.)

CAPITOL (ST-2108 "Something New") 8-12 76
(Orange label.)
CAPITOL (ST-2108 "Something New") 6-10 78
(Purple label.)
CAPITOL (ST-2108 "Something New") 10-15 83
(Black label with black print around border.)
CAPITOL (ST-8-2108 "Something New") 200-250 64
(Record Club issue, black label.)
CAPITOL (ST-8-2108 "Something New") 90-120 69
(Record Club issue, green label.)
CAPITOL (TBO-2222 "The Beatles' Story") 200-250 64
(Monaural.)
CAPITOL (STBO-2222 "The Beatles' Story") 125-175 64
(Stereo. Black label with white print around border. Does not have "Subsidiary of Capitol, etc." perimeter print.)
CAPITOL (STBO-2222 "The Beatles' Story") 50-60 69
(Stereo. Black label with white print around border. Has "Subsidiary of Capitol, etc." print.)
CAPITOL (STBO-2222 "The Beatles' Story") 40-50 69
(Green label.)
CAPITOL (STBO-2222 "The Beatles' Story") 15-20 76
(Orange labels, or purple labels.)
CAPITOL (STBO-2222 "The Beatles' Story") 40-50 83
(Black label with black print around border.)
CAPITOL (T-2228 "Beatles '65") 90-120 65
(Monaural.)
CAPITOL (ST-2228 "Beatles '65") 70-90 65
(Stereo. Black label with white print around border.)
CAPITOL (ST-2228 "Beatles '65") 30-40 69
(Green label.)
CAPITOL (ST-2228 "Beatles '65") 8-12 76
(Orange label.)
CAPITOL (ST-2228 "Beatles '65") 6-10 78
(Purple label.)
CAPITOL (ST-2228 "Beatles '65") 10-15 83
(Black label with black print around border.)
CAPITOL (T-2309 "The Early Beatles") 125-150 65
(Monaural.)
CAPITOL (ST-2309 "The Early Beatles") 90-120 65
(Stereo. Black label with white print around border. Does not have "Subsidiary of Capitol, etc." perimeter print.)
CAPITOL (ST-2309 "The Early Beatles") 40-50 69
(Stereo. Black label with white print around border. Has "Subsidiary of Capitol, etc." print.)
CAPITOL (ST-2309 "The Early Beatles") 30-40 69
(Green label.)
CAPITOL (ST-2309 "The Early Beatles") 8-12 76
(Orange label.)
CAPITOL (ST-2309 "The Early Beatles") 6-10 78
(Purple label.)
CAPITOL (ST-2309 "The Early Beatles") 15-25 83
(Black label with black print around border.)
CAPITOL (T-2358 "Beatles VI") 100-125 65
(Monaural.)
CAPITOL (ST-2358 "Beatles VI") 70-90 65
(Stereo. Black label with white print around border.)
CAPITOL (ST-2358 "Beatles VI") 30-40 69
(Green label.)
CAPITOL (ST-2358 "Beatles VI") 8-12 76
(Orange label.)
CAPITOL (ST-2358 "Beatles VI") 6-10 78
(Purple label with "Mfd.." perimeter print.)
CAPITOL (ST-2358 "Beatles VI") 10-15 83
(Black label with black print around border.)
CAPITOL (ST-2358 "Beatles VI") 60-80 88
(Purple label with "Manufactured by Capitol, etc." perimeter print.)
CAPITOL (ST-8-2358 "Beatles VI") 250-300 69
(Green label. Capitol Record Club issue.)
CAPITOL (MAS-2386 "Help") 100-125 65
(Monaural.)
CAPITOL (SMAS-2386 "Help") 60-80 65
(Stereo. Black label with white print around border. Does not have "Subsidiary of Capitol, etc." perimeter print.)
CAPITOL (SMAS-2386 "Help") 40-50 69
(Stereo. Black label with white print around border. Has "Subsidiary of Capitol, etc." print.)
CAPITOL (SMAS-2386 "Help") 30-40 69
(Green label.)
CAPITOL (SMAS-2386 "Help") 8-12 76
(Orange label.)
CAPITOL (SMAS-2386 "Help") 6-10 78
(Purple label.)
CAPITOL (SMAS-2386 "Help") 10-15 83
(Black label with black print around border.)
CAPITOL (SMAS-8-2386 "Help").. 300-500 65
(Capitol Record Club, or Longines Symphonette Record Club issue, black label.)
CAPITOL (SMAS-8-2386 "Help").. 200-300 69
(Capitol Record Club issue, green label.)
CAPITOL (T-2442 "Rubber Soul") 100-120 65
(Monaural.)
CAPITOL (ST-2442 "Rubber Soul").. 70-90 65
(Stereo. Black label with white print around border. Does not have "Subsidiary of Capitol, etc." perimeter print.)
CAPITOL (ST-2442 "Rubber Soul").. 40-50 65
(Stereo. Black label with white print around border. Has "Subsidiary of Capitol, etc." print.)
CAPITOL (ST-2442 "Rubber Soul").. 30-40 69
(Green label.)
CAPITOL (ST-2442 "Rubber Soul") 8-12 76
(Orange label.)
CAPITOL (SW-2442 "Rubber Soul") .. 6-10 78
(Purple label.)
CAPITOL (SW-2442 "Rubber Soul") 10-15 83
(Black label with black print around border.)
CAPITOL (ST-8-2442 "Rubber Soul") 200-250 65
(Capitol Record Club issue, black label.)
CAPITOL (ST-8-2442 "Rubber Soul") 80-100 69
(Capitol Record Club issue, green label.)
CAPITOL (T-2553 "Yesterday and Today") 2000-3000 66
(Monaural. FIRST STATE "Butcher cover" issues.)
CAPITOL (ST-2553 "Yesterday and Today") 5000-7000 66
(Stereo. FIRST STATE "Butcher Cover" issues.)
CAPITOL (T-2553 "Yesterday and Today") 500-700 66
(Monaural. PASTE OVER or PEELED "Butcher cover" copies.)
CAPITOL (ST-2553 "Yesterday and Today") 1000-1200 66
(Stereo. PASTE OVER or PEELED "Butcher cover" copies.)
Note: the wide range of values exists here due to varied opinions on the practice of peeling the "Trunk cover" from the "Butcher cover." The expertise used in the peeling is also a major factor affecting the value of these LPs.
CAPITOL (T-2553 "Yesterday and Today") 120-140 66
(Monaural. "Trunk cover.")
CAPITOL (ST-2553 "Yesterday and Today") 80-100 66
(Stereo. Black label with white print around border. Does not have "Subsidiary of Capitol, etc." perimeter print.)
CAPITOL (ST-2553 "Yesterday and Today") 40-50 69
(Stereo. Black label with white print around border. Has "Subsidiary of Capitol, etc." print. "Trunk cover.")
CAPITOL (ST-2553 "Yesterday and Today") 30-40 69
(Green label.)
CAPITOL (ST-2553 "Yesterday and Today") 8-12 76
(Orange label.)
CAPITOL (ST-2553 "Yesterday and Today") 6-10 78
(Purple label.)
CAPITOL (ST-2553 "Yesterday and Today") 10-15 83
(Black label with black print around border.)
CAPITOL (ST-8-2553 "Yesterday and Today") 200-250 66
(Capitol Record Club issue, black label.)
CAPITOL (ST-8-2553 "Yesterday and Today") 80-100 69
(Capitol Record Club issue, green label.)
CAPITOL (T-2576 "Revolver") 100-120 66
(Monaural.)
CAPITOL (ST-2576 "Revolver") 70-90 66
(Stereo. Black label with white print around border. Does not have "Subsidiary of Capitol, etc." perimeter print.)
CAPITOL (ST-2576 "Revolver") 40-50 66
(Stereo. Black label with white print around border. Has "Subsidiary of Capitol, etc." print.)
CAPITOL (ST-2576 "Revolver") 30-40 69
(Green label.)
CAPITOL (ST-2576 "Revolver") 250-300 71
(Red label.)
CAPITOL (ST-2576 "Revolver") 8-12 76
(Orange label.)
CAPITOL (ST-2576 "Revolver") 6-10 78
(Purple label.)
CAPITOL (ST-2576 "Revolver") 10-15 83
(Black label with black print around border.)
CAPITOL (ST-8-2576 "Revolver"). 175-200 66
(Capitol Record Club issue, black label.)
CAPITOL (ST-8-2576 "Revolver") 70-90 69
(Capitol Record Club issue, green label.)
CAPITOL (ST-8-2576 "Revolver"). 175-200 76
(Capitol Record Club issue, orange label.)
CAPITOL (MAS-2653 "Sgt. Pepper's Lonely Hearts Club Band") 200-250 67
(Monaural.)
CAPITOL (SMAS-2653 "Sgt. Pepper's Lonely Hearts Club Band") 125-150 67
(Stereo. Black label with white print around border. Does not have "Subsidiary of Capitol, etc." perimeter print.)
CAPITOL (SMAS-2653 "Sgt. Pepper's Lonely Hearts Club Band") 50-60 69
(Stereo. Black label with white print around border. Has "Subsidiary of Capitol, etc." print.)
CAPITOL (SMAS-2653 "Sgt. Pepper's Lonely Hearts Club Band") 40-50 69
(Green label.)
CAPITOL (SMAS-2653 "Sgt. Pepper's Lonely Hearts Club Band") 8-12 76
(Orange label.)
CAPITOL (SMAS-2653 "Sgt. Pepper's Lonely Hearts Club Band") 6-10 78
(Purple label.)
CAPITOL (SMAS-2653 "Sgt. Pepper's Lonely Hearts Club Band") 10-15 83
(Black label with black print around border.)
CAPITOL (MAL-2835 "Magical Mystery Tour") 200-250 67
(Monaural.)
CAPITOL (SMAL-2835 "Magical Mystery Tour") 70-90 67
(Stereo. Black label with white print around border. Does not have "Subsidiary of Capitol, etc." perimeter print.)
CAPITOL (SMAL-2835 "Magical Mystery Tour") 40-50 68
(Stereo. Black label with white print around border. Has "Subsidiary of Capitol, etc." print.)
CAPITOL (SMAL-2835 "Magical Mystery Tour") 40-50 69
(Green label.)

CAPITOL (SMAL-2835 "Magical Mystery Tour")........8-12 76
(Orange label.)
CAPITOL (SMAL-2835 "Magical Mystery Tour")........6-10 78
(Purple label.)
CAPITOL (SMAL-2835 "Magical Mystery Tour")........10-15 83
(Black label with black print around border.)
CAPITOL (3403 "The Beatles/ 1962-1966")........15-20 78
CAPITOL (3404 "The Beatles/ 1967-1970")........15-20 78
CAPITOL (SPRO-8969 "Rarities")....40-50 78
(Bonus LP in *Beatles Collection* boxed set.)
CAPITOL (11537 "Rock 'n' Roll Music")........30-40 76
CAPITOL (11638 "Beatles at the Hollywood Bowl")........8-10 77
CAPITOL (11711 "Love Songs")........30-40 77
CAPITOL (11840 "Sgt. Pepper's Lonely Hearts Club Band")........20-30 78
(Picture disc.)
CAPITOL (11840 "Sgt. Pepper")........30-45 78
(Picture disc. Has drum photo on both sides.)
CAPITOL (11841 "The Beatles")...100-200 78
(Gray splash-colored vinyl. Experimental item only.)
CAPITOL (11841 "The Beatles")........30-40 78
(White vinyl.)
CAPITOL (11842 "The Beatles/ 1962-1966")........30-40 78
(Colored vinyl.)
CAPITOL (11843 "The Beatles/ 1967-1970")........30-40 78
(Colored vinyl.)
CAPITOL (11900 "Abbey Road")......50-60 78
(Picture disc.)
CAPITOL (11921 "A Hard Day's Night")........8-10 80
(Purple label with "Mfd..." perimeter print.)
CAPITOL (11921 "A Hard Day's Night")........10-15 84
(Black label with black print around border.)
CAPITOL (11921 "A Hard Day's Night")........15-25 88
(Purple label with "Manufactured..." perimeter print.)
CAPITOL (11922 "Let It Be")........8-12 79
(Purple label.)
CAPITOL (11922 "Let It Be")........10-15 83
(Black label with black print around border.)
CAPITOL (12009 "Rarities")........200-250 78
CAPITOL (12080 "Rarities")........15-20 80
CAPITOL (12199 "Reel Music")........8-12 82
CAPITOL (12245 "The Beatles 20 Greatest Hits")........15-25 82-88
(Purple or black label.)
CAPITOL (16020 "Rock 'N' Roll Music, Volume I")........5-10 80
CAPITOL (16021 "Rock 'N' Roll Music, Volume II")........5-10 80
CAPITOL (31796 "Live at the BBC")........30-40 94
CAPITOL (34448 "Anthology II")........30-35 96
(Three LP set.)
CAPITOL (46435 thru 46447, except 46443)........15-25 87-90
CAPITOL (46443 "The Beatles")........30-40 88
CAPITOL (48062 "Magical Mystery Tour")........15-25 87
CAPITOL (90043 "Past Masters, Vol. 1")........6-10 88
CAPITOL (90044 "Past Masters, Vol. 2")........6-10 88
CAPITOL (90435 thru 90454)........20-30 88
CAPITOL (91302 "Beatles Deluxe Box Set")........200-250 88
(14 LP boxed set.)
CICADELIC........6-12 85-87
CLARION (601 "The Amazing Beatles & Other Great English Sounds")........150-200 66
(Stereo. Back cover lists song titles. Also contains selections by the Swallows.)
CLARION (601 "The Amazing Beatles & Other Great English Sounds")........175-200 66
(Stereo. Back cover does NOT list song titles. Also contains selections by the Swallows.)
CLARION (601 "The Amazing Beatles & Other Great English Sounds")........100-125 66
(Monaural. Also contains selections by the Swallows.)
CREATIVE RADIO ("The Beatle Invasion")........35-45 80s
(Three-LP set, includes 12x19 poster.)
DESERT VIBRATIONS........20-25 82
GREAT NORTHWEST MUSIC CO. (4007 Beatle Talk")........5-10 78
GREAT NORTHWEST MUSIC CO. (4007 "Beatle Talk")........25-50 78
(Columbia Record Club issue.)
HALL of MUSIC........30-40 81
HERITAGE SOUND........30-40 82
I-N-S RADIO NEWS ("American Tour with Ed Rudy #2")........15-25 80
LINGASONG (7001 "Live at the Starclub in Hamburg Germany, 1962")........15-20 77
(Black vinyl.)
LLOYDS (AG-8146 "The Great American Tour 1965 Live Beatlemania Concert")........500-700 65
(With selections by the Liverpool Lads.)
METRO (M-563 "This Is Where It Started")........80-100 66
(Also contains selections by Tony Sheridan and by the Titans.)
METRO (MS-563 "This Is Where It Started")........175-225 66
(Also contains selections by Tony Sheridan and by the Titans.)
MFSL (1 "The Beatles, the Collection")........400-500 82
(Boxed, 14-disc set. Includes booklet and alignment tool.)
MFSL (023 "Abbey Road")........40-50 79
MFSL (047 "Magical Mystery Tour").55-65 81
MFSL (2-072 "The Beatles")........40-50 82
MFSL (UHQR 100 "Sgt. Pepper's Lonely Hearts Club Band")........250-300 82
(Boxed set. Silver label.)
MFSL (100 "Sgt. Pepper's Lonely Hearts Club Band")........30-40 85
(White label.)
MFSL (101 "Please Please Me")........25-35 86
MFSL (102 "With the Beatles")........150-200 86
MFSL (103 "A Hard Day's Night")........30-40 87
MFSL (104 "Beatles for Sale")........30-40 87
MFSL (105 "Help")........30-40 85
MFSL (106 "Rubber Soul")........30-40 84
MFSL (107 "Revolver")........30-40 86
MFSL (108 "Yellow Submarine")........50-60 87
MFSL (109 "Let It Be")........30-40 87
(Gatefold cover.)
MFSL (109 "Let It Be")........150-200 87
(Single pocket cover.)
MGM (E-4215 "The Beatles with Tony Sheridan and Guests")........200-225 64
(Monaural. With selections by Tony Sheridan and by the Titans.)
MGM (SE-4215 "The Beatles with Tony Sheridan and Guests")........600-800 64
(Stereo. With selections by Tony Sheridan and by the Titans.)
MUSIC INTERNATIONAL........40-50 85
PAC........30-50 81
PBR INT'L........70-90 78
(Colored vinyl.)
PBR INT'L........50-60 78
(Black vinyl.)
PHOENIX 10........8-12 82
PHOENIX 20........15-20 82-83
PICKWICK (Except 90071)........20-30 78-79
PICKWICK (90071 "Recorded Live in Hamburg, 1962, Volume 3")........30-40 78
POLYDOR (4504 "In the Beginning, Circa 1960")........20-30 70
(With gatefold cover.)
POLYDOR (4504 "In the Beginning, Circa 1960")........6-12 81-84
(With standard cover.)
POLYDOR (93199 "In the Beginning, Circa 1960")........20-30 70
(Capitol Record Club issue.)
POLYDOR (422-825-073 "In the Beginning, Circa 1960")........15-20 88
RAVEN (8911 "Talk Down Under")......5-10 81
RAVEN (8911 "Talk Down Under")...60-80 81
(Promotional issue.)
RPN (RADIO PULSEBEAT NEWS) ("American Tour with Ed Rudy #2")........40-50 64
(This LP was occasionally issued with a "Teen Talk" booklet. The value of the booklet is approximately the same as for the LP. This edition has NO pictures of the Beatles on the LP cover.)
RPN (RADIO PULSEBEAT NEWS) ("1965 Talk Album, Ed Rudy / New US Tour")........100-150 65
SAVAGE (69 "The Savage Young Beatles")........1200-1500 68
(Label is yellow. Cover is glossy orange.)
SAVAGE (69 "The Savage Young Beatles")........100-125 68
(Label is orange. Cover is orange.)
SILHOUETTE........25-35 81-84
(Picture discs.)
SILHOUETTE........10-15 84-85
(Black vinyl.)
SILHOUETTE........60-80 84-85
(Colored vinyl.)
STERLING PRODUCTIONS (6481 "I Apologize")........300-350 66
(Price includes bonus 8x10 photo, which represents $15-$25 of the value.)
U.A. (UAL-3366 "A Hard Day's Night")........150-225 64
(Monaural.)
U.A. (UAS-6366 "A Hard Day's Night")........200-250 64
(Stereo. Black label. Black vinyl.)
U.A. (UAS-6366 "A Hard Day's Night")........50-60 68-70
(Stereo. Pink and orange or black and orange label.)
U.A. (UAS-6366 "A Hard Day's Night")........15-25 71
(Stereo. Tan label.)
U.A. (UAS-6366 "A Hard Day's Night")........15-20 77
(Stereo. Orange and yellow label.)
U.A. (T-90828 "A Hard Day's Night")........800-900 65
(Monaural. Capitol Record Club issue.)
U.A. (ST-90828 "A Hard Day's Night")........400-500 65
(Stereo. Capitol Record Club issue.)
VEE JAY (202 "Hear the Beatles Tell All")........250-350 64
(Monaural. Black label with rainbow color-band.)
VEE JAY (202 "Hear the Beatles Tell All")........7000-8000 64
(Promotional issue.)
VEE JAY (202 "Hear the Beatles Tell All")........5-10 79
(Stereo.)
VEE JAY (202 "Hear the Beatles Tell All")........20-30 87
(Shaped picture disc.)
VEE JAY (1062 "Introducing the Beatles")........1800-2000 63
(Monaural. With *Love Me Do* and *P.S. I Love You.* Back cover pictures 25 other Vee Jay albums.)
VEE JAY (1062 "Introducing the Beatles")........6000-7000 63
(Stereo. With *Love Me Do* and *P.S. I Love You.* Back cover pictures 25 other Vee Jay albums.)
VEE JAY (1062 "Introducing the Beatles")........900-1100 63-64
(Monaural. With *Love Me Do* and *P.S. I Love You.* Back cover is blank.)

VEE JAY (1062 "Introducing the Beatles") 3000-4000 63-64
(Stereo. With *Love Me Do* and *P.S. I Love You*. Back cover is blank.)
VEE JAY (1062 "Introducing the Beatles") 800-900 64
(Monaural. With *Love Me Do* and *P.S. I Love You*. Back cover lists contents. Has brackets style label logo.)
VEE JAY (1062 "Introducing the Beatles") 2000-3000 64
(Stereo. With *Love Me Do* and *P.S. I Love You*. Back cover lists contents. Has brackets style label logo.)
VEE JAY (1062 "Introducing the Beatles") 700-800 64
(Monaural. With *Love Me Do* and *P.S. I Love You*. Back cover lists contents. Oval style label logo.)
VEE JAY (1062 "Introducing the Beatles") 2000-3000 64
(Stereo. With *Love Me Do* and *P.S. I Love You* listed on cover and disc, but actually plays *Ask Me Why* and *Please Please Me*.)
VEE JAY (1062 "Introducing the Beatles") 1800-2200 64
(Stereo. With *Ask Me Why* and *Please Please Me*. For any of the label styles or logo designs.)
VEE JAY (1062 "Introducing the Beatles") 250-350 64
(Monaural, rainbow color-band label. With *Ask Me Why* and *Please Please Me*. Add $50 to $75 if accompanied by "Featuring Twist and Shout" and "Please Please Me" sticker.)
VEE JAY (1062 "Introducing the Beatles") 250-350 64
(Monaural, black label, no color-band. With *Ask Me Why* and *Please Please Me*. With "Vee Jay Records" printed under "VJ" logo, or oval style logo. Add $50 to $75 if accompanied by "Featuring Twist and Shout" and "Please Please Me" sticker.)
VEE JAY (1062 "Introducing the Beatles") 1000-1200 64
(Monaural, black label, no color-band. With *Ask Me Why* and *Please Please Me*. With brackets logo. Add $50 to $75 if accompanied by "Featuring Twist and Shout" and "Please Please Me" sticker.)
VEE JAY (1092 "Songs, Pictures and Stories") 300-400 64
(Monaural.)
VEE JAY (1092 "Songs, Pictures and Stories") 2000-2200 64
(Stereo. Promotional issue only.)
VEE JAY (1092 "Songs and Pictures") 8-10
(Reissue.)

Promotional LPs

APPLE (SBC-100 "The Beatles' Christmas Album") 200-250 70
(Special issue for Beatles fan club members.)
APPLE (SPRO 11206/207 "College Radio Sampler") 125-175 96
APPLE FILMS (KAL 1004 "The Yellow Submarine") 900-1200 69
(Contains the advertisements used on radio stations to promote the film.)
ATCO (169 "Ain't She Sweet") 700-900 64
(Also contains selections by the Swallows.)
BACKSTAGE (1111 "Like Dreamers Do") 30-40 82
(Colored vinyl)
CAPITOL ("The Platinum Beatles Collection") 500-600 84
(Boxed, 18-disc set.)
CAPITOL (SMAS-11638 "Beatles at the Hollywood Bowl") 300-400 77
(Promotional issue.)
CAPITOL (SMAS-11638 "Beatles at the Hollywood Bowl") 15-25 77
(Without bar code [UPC] symbol.)
CAPITOL (SMAS-11638 "Beatles at the Hollywood Bowl") 30-40 89
(With bar code [UPC] symbol.)
CAPITOL (12199 "Reel Music") 30-40 82
(Promotional issue. Colored vinyl. White cover.)
CAPITOL (12199 "Reel Music") 15-20 82
(Promotional issue. Colored vinyl. Regular cover.)
CAPITOL/EMI (BC-13 "The Beatles Collection") 400-450 78
(Boxed, 14-disc set.)
I-N-S RADIO NEWS (DOC-1 "Beatlemania Tour Coverage") 900-1200 64
(Promotional only issue. An open-end interview. Includes a script.)
LINGASONG (7001 "Live at the Starclub in Hamburg Germany, 1962") 30-40 77
(Promotional issue. Black vinyl.)
LINGASONG (7001 "Live at the Starclub in Hamburg Germany, 1962") 250-350 77
(Promotional issue. Colored vinyl.)
ORANGE (12880 "Silver Beatles") 250-350 85
RAVEN 15-20 81
SILHOUETTE 30-40 84
U.A. (UA-HELP "United Artists Presents *Help!*") 800-900 65
(Contains the advertisements used on radio stations to promote the film.)
U.A. (UA-HELP INT "Special Open-End Interview") 1000-1200 65
(Price includes script and programming information, which represents about $75-100 of the value.)
U.A. (UA-HELP-SHOW "United Artists Presents *Help!*") 2000-2200 65
(Single-sided open-end interview. Price includes script which represents about $75 to $100 of the value.)
U.A. (2359/60 "Special Beatles Half Hour Open End Interview") 1000-1200 64
(Price includes 12-pages of script and programming information, which represents about $75 to $100 of the value.)
U.A. (2362/63 "United Artists Presents *A Hard Day's Night*") 700-800 64
(Contains the advertisements used on radio stations to promote the film.)
U.A. (UAL-3366 "A Hard Day's Night") 2000-2500 64
(Monaural. White label.)
U.A. (UAL-6366 "A Hard Day's Night") 10000-12000 64
(Pink vinyl. Likely an experimental pressing.)
Members: John Lennon; Paul McCartney; George Harrison; Pete Best; Ringo Starr.
Also see ALAN, Lee
Also see BEST, Pete
Also see CLAY, Tom
Also see HARRISON, George
Also see LENNON, John
Also see MARTIN, George
Also see McCARTNEY, Paul
Also see PRESLEY, Elvis / Beatles
Also see PRESTON, Billy
Also see SHANKAR, Ravi
Also see SILKIE
Also see STARR, Ringo

BEATLES / Beach Boys / Buddy Holly

LPs: 10/12-inch

CREATIVE RADIO SHOWS (Demo of "Specials") 75-100 79
(Promotional issue only.)
Also see HOLLY, Buddy

BEATLES / Beach Boys / Kingston Trio

Plastic Soundsheets/Flexi-Discs:

EVA-TONE (8464 "Surprise Gift from the Beatles, Beach Boys & Kingston Trio") 450-550 64
(Seven-inch tri-fold card.)
EVA-TONE (8464 "Surprise Gift from the Beatles, Beach Boys & Kingston Trio") 300-350 64
(Five-inch round plastic soundsheet.)
EVA-TONE (8464 "Surprise Gift from the Beatles, Beach Boys & Kingston Trio") 2000-2500 64
(Mailer envelope for five-inch round plastic soundsheet.)
Also see BEACH BOYS
Also see KINGSTON TRIO

BEATLES / Jerry Blabber

Singles: 7-inch

QUEST 5-10 65

BEATLES / 4 Seasons — LP '64

LPs: 10/12-inch

VEE JAY (DX-30 "Beatles Vs. the Four Seasons") 600-800 64
(Monaural.)
VEE JAY (DXS-30 "Beatles Vs. the Four Seasons") 1800-2000 64
(Stereo.)
Price includes a bonus Beatles poster, which represents $150 to $200 of the value.
Also see 4 SEASONS

BEATLES / Frank Ifield — LP '64

LPs: 10/12-inch

VEE JAY (1085 "The Beatles & Frank Ifield") 2500-3000 64
(Monaural. Pictures the Beatles on cover.)
VEE JAY (1085 "The Beatles & Frank Ifield") 8000-9000 64
(Stereo. Pictures the Beatles on cover.)
VEE JAY (1085 "Jolly What! the Beatles & Frank Ifield") 200-250 64
(Monaural. Pictures an Englishman on cover.)
VEE JAY (1085 "Jolly What! the Beatles & Frank Ifield") 500-600 64
(Stereo. Pictures an Englishman on cover.)
Also see IFIELD, Frank

BEATLES / Loretta Lynn

Singles: 7-inch

VEE JAY (581 "Please Please Me"/ "Before I'm Over You") 50-100 64
(This pairing is the result of a production error.)
Also see BEATLES
Also see LYNN, Loretta

BEATLES BLAST at STADIUM (Described by Erupting Fans)

LPs: 10/12-inch

AUDIO JOURNAL 10-20 66
(*Beatles Blast at Stadium* is the title of the LP. Featuring only noise, made by fans at a Shea Stadium concert. No artists are credited.

BEATS INTERNATIONAL — P&R/LP '90

LPs: 10/12-inch

ELEKTRA 5-8 90
Members: Norman Cook; Lester Noel; Lindy Layton; Andy Boucher; Luke Cresswell.
Also see HOUSEMARTINS

BEATTY, E.C. — P&R '59

Singles: 7-inch

CAMPBELL 5-10 64
COLONIAL 8-15 59-61

BEAU, Toby: see TOBY BEAU

BEAU BRUMMELS — P&R/LP '65

Singles: 7-inch

AUTUMN (8 "Laugh Laugh") 8-12 64
(White label.)
AUTUMN (8 "Laugh Laugh") 5-10 64
(Orange label. Different edit than on white label.)
AUTUMN (10 thru 24) 5-10 65
PEP 3-4
RHINO 3-4 82
VAULT 4-6 67
W.B. 4-8 66-75

Picture Sleeves

PEP 3-4
RHINO 3-4 82

LPs: 10/12-inch

ACCORD 5-10 82
AUTUMN (103 "Introducing the Beau Brummels") 40-50 65
AUTUMN (104 "Beau Brummels, Vol. 2") 40-50 65
JAS 8-10
POST 8-10
RHINO 5-10 81-82

VAULT (114 "Best of the Beau Brummels")....................25-30 67
VAULT (121 "Beau Brummels, Vol. 44")....................15-20 68
W.B. (Except 1644)....................20-25 67-75
W.B. (1644 "Beau Brummels '66")....30-35 66
Members: Sal Valentino; Ron Elliott; Ron Meagher; Declan Mulligan; John Petersen.

BEAU COUP — P&R '87

Singles: 7-inch

AGORA (82734 "Still in My Heart").....5-10
AMHERST....................3-4 87
ROCK & ROLL....................3-4 84-85

BEAU-MARKS — P&R '60

Singles: 7-inch

MAINSTREAM (688 "Clap Your Hands")....................5-10 68
PORT (70029 "Lovely Little Lady")....15-25 62
QUALITY ("Clap Your Hands")..........20-40 60
(Canadian. Selection number not known.)
QUALITY ("Cause We're in Love")...20-40 60
(Canadian. Selection number not known.)
QUALITY (1404 "Tender Years").....20-30 61
(Canadian.)
QUALITY (1423 "Tender Years")......15-25 62
(Canadian.)
RUST (5035 "School Is Out")...........20-30 61
RUST (5050 "Tender Years")...........15-25 61
SHAD (5017 "Clap Your Hands").........10-15 60
SHAD (5021 "Cause We're in Love")....................10-15 60
TIME (1032 "Rockin' Blues")............20-30 61

BEAUMONT, Jimmy — P&R '61

(With the Skyliners; Jimmie Beaumont)

Singles: 7-inch

BANG (525 "You Got Too Much Going for You")....................15-20 66
CAPITOL....................3-5 74
COLPIX....................5-10 61
DRIVE....................3-5 76
GALLANT (3012 "Love Is a Dangerous Game")....................5-10 60s
MAY....................8-10 61-63
Also see SKYLINERS

BEAUVOIR, Jean — P&R/LP '86

Singles: 12-inch

COLUMBIA....................4-6 86

Singles: 7-inch

COLUMBIA....................3-4 86

Picture Sleeves

COLUMBIA....................3-4 86

LPs: 10/12-inch

COLUMBIA....................5-10 86
Also see LITTLE STEVEN & Disciples of Soul
Also see PLASMATICS

BE-BOP DELUXE — LP '76

Singles: 7-inch

HARVEST....................3-5 75-78

LPs: 10/12-inch

HARVEST (Black vinyl)....................5-10 76-78
HARVEST (Colored vinyl)..............15-20 77-78

Promotional LPs

HARVEST (8531 "Be Bop's Biggest")....................25-35 75
Members: Richard Brown; Robert Bryan; Nicholas Chatterton-Dew; Andrew Clarke; Simon Fox; Paul Jeffreys; Milton R. James; Bill Nelson; Ian Parkin; Charles Tumahai.

BECK, Jeff — P&R/LP '68

(Jeff Beck Group; with Terry Bozzio & Tony Hymas)

Singles: 7-inch

EPIC (10000 series)....................4-8 67-69
EPIC (50000 series)....................3-6 75-76

LPs: 10/12-inch

ACCORD....................5-10 81
EPIC (Except 43000 series)..............8-12 68-89
EPIC (43000 series)....................15-20 80-82
(Half-speed mastered.)
MFP....................8-10
SPRINGBOARD....................5-10 75

Promotional LPs

EPIC (151 "Everything You Always Wanted to Hear")....................15-25 76
EPIC (850 "Then and Now")..........25-30 80
Also see BECK, BOGERT & APPICE
Also see CLAPTON, Eric, Jeff Beck & Jimmy Page
Also see DONOVAN & Jeff Beck Group
Also see HALL, Jimmy
Also see HAMMER, Jan
Also see HARRISON, George / Jeff Beck / Dave Edmunds
Also see HONEYDRIPPERS
Also see LORD SUTCH
Also see POWELL, Cozy
Also see YARDBIRDS

BECK, Jeff, & Rod Stewart — P&R '85

Singles: 7-inch

EPIC....................3-4 85

Picture Sleeves

EPIC....................3-4 85

BECK, Jeff, Ronnie Wood & Rod Stewart

LPs: 10/12-inch

EPIC (33779 "Truth")....................10-15 75
Also see BECK, Jeff
Also see STEWART, Rod
Also see WOOD, Ron

BECK, Jimmy — P&R '59

Singles: 7-inch

ASTRA....................5-10
CHAMPION....................10-20 59

BECK, Joe — LP '75

Singles: 7-inch

CHARLES (577 "Daddy Cool").........10-15
POLYDOR....................3-5 77
RADAR (1010 "Cool Moose")...........10-20 62

LPs: 10/12-inch

KUDU....................8-10 75
POLYDOR....................5-10 77
VERVE/FORECAST....................10-15 69
Also see PHILLIPS, Esther, & Joe Beck

BECK, BOGERT & APPICE

Singles: 7-inch

EPIC....................3-5 73

LPs: 10/12-inch

EPIC....................10-12 73
Members: Jeff Beck; Tim Bogert; Carmine Appice.
Also see BECK, Jeff
Also see CACTUS
Also see SCOTT, Neal
Also see VANILLA FUDGE

BECK FAMILY — R&B '79

Singles: 7-inch

LE JOINT....................3-5 79
Members: Tony Beck; Tyrone Beck; Mendy Beck; Joanna Beck; Donnie Wilson; Nick Mundy.

BECKHAM, Bob — P&R '59

Singles: 7-inch

DECCA....................4-8 59-63
MONUMENT....................3-5 67
SMASH....................3-6 65

Picture Sleeves

DECCA....................5-10 59

LPs: 10/12-inch

DECCA....................15-20 59

BECKMEIER BROTHERS — P&R '79

Singles: 7-inch

CASABLANCA....................3-4 79

LPs: 10/12-inch

CASABLANCA....................5-10 79
Members: Fred Beckmeier; Steve Beckmeier.

BEE, Celi: *see* CELI BEE

BEE, Jimmy — R&B '76

(With Ernie Fields Jr.'s Orchestra)

Singles: 7-inch

ALA....................3-5 73
CALLA....................3-5 76
KENT....................3-5 70
KIMBERLY....................5-10
HAMILTON....................5-10 59
20TH FOX....................5-8 66-67
U.A....................3-5 71

LPs: 10/12-inch

ALA (1975 "Live")....................10-15 73

BEE, Molly — P&R '53

Singles: 78 rpm

CAPITOL....................3-8 53-58
CORAL....................3-6 55
DOT....................3-6 56

Singles: 7-inch

CAPITOL....................5-10 53-58
CORAL....................5-10 55
DOT....................5-10 56
GRANITE....................3-5 74-75
LIBERTY....................4-8 63-64
MGM....................3-6 65-67

Picture Sleeves

MGM....................5-10 65

EPs: 7-inch

CAPITOL....................5-10 58

LPs: 10/12-inch

ACCORD....................5-10 82
ALBUM GLOBE....................5-10
CAPITOL....................15-25 58
GRANITE....................5-10 74
MGM....................10-15 65-67

BEE GEES — P&R/LP '67

Singles: 12-inch

W.B....................5-10 80s

Singles: 7-inch

ATCO....................4-10 67-72
ATLANTIC....................3-5
RSO....................3-5 73-84
W.B....................3-4 87-89

Picture Sleeves

RSO....................3-5 83
W.B....................3-4 87-89

EPs: 7-inch

ATCO (4523 Horizontal")...............15-25 68
(Promotional issue only. Tracks are from *Horizontal,* though shown only as "Atco LP 33-233" on this label.)
ATCO (4535 Odessa")....................10-20 69
(Promotional issue only.)
ATCO (37264 "Rare, Precious and Beautiful")....................8-15 69
(Promotional issue only.)
RSO (200 "Greatest Hits")...............5-10 79
(Promotional issue only.)

LPs: 10/12-inch

ATCO (Except TL-ST-142)..............12-25 67-72
ATCO (TL-ST-142 "Odessa")...........30-50 69
(Promotional issue only.)
NAUTILUS....................15-25
(Half-speed mastered.)
RSO (Except 1 & 3042)....................5-10 73-84
RSO (1 "Words & Music")...............40-60
(Promotional issue only.)
RSO (3042 "Spirits Having Flown")...10-15 79
(Picture disc.)
W.B....................5-10 87-89
Members: Barry Gibb; Maurice Gibb; Robin Gibb; Vince Melouney; Colin Petersen.
Session: Alan Kendall; Blue Weaver; Dennis Bryon.
Also see GIBB, Andy
Also see GIBB, Barry
Also see GIBB, Maurice
Also see GIBB, Robin
Also see SANG, Samantha

BEECHER, Johnny, & His Buckingham Road Quintet — P&R '63

Singles: 7-inch

ASTRA....................4-6
CHARTER....................10-20 63
OMEGA....................5-10 58
W.B....................5-10 63

LPs: 10/12-inch

CHARTER (102 "Sax 5th Avenue")...20-40 63
CHARTER (104 "On the Scene")......20-30 63

BEEFEATERS

Singles: 7-inch

ELEKTRA (45013 "Please Let Me Love You")....50-75 64

Members: David Crosby; Gene Clark; Jim McGuinn.

Also see BYRDS

BEEFHEART, Captain: see CAPTAIN BEEFHEART

BEGINNING OF THE END P&R/R&B '71

Singles: 7-inch

ALSTON....3-5 71-72

LPs: 10/12-inch

ALSTON....10-12 71-76

BELAFONTE, Harry P&R '52

Singles: 78 rpm

JUBILEE....8-12 54
RCA....5-10 57
ROOST (501 "Lean on Me")....10-15 49

Singles: 7-inch

COLUMBIA....3-4 81
JUBILEE....10-20 54
RCA (0300 series)....5-10 57
RCA (0400 thru 0600 series)....3-5 71-72
RCA (4000 & 5000 series)....10-20 52-55
RCA (6000 & 7000 series)....5-10 55-62
RCA (8000 & 9000 series)....4-6 62-67

Picture Sleeves

RCA (Except 9200 series)....10-15 55-59
RCA (9200 series)....4-8 69

EPs: 7-inch

CAPITOL (619 "Close You Eyes")....15-20 55
JUBILEE....20-30 54
RCA (Except 24)....10-20 54-61
RCA (SPD-24 "Best of Belafonte")....40-60 56
(Ten-EP boxed set, with inserts.)

LPs: 10/12-inch

BOOK of the MONTH....15-20 83
CAMDEN....5-10 73-74
COLUMBIA....5-10 81
CORONET....8-15
RCA (0000 thru 0900 series)....5-10 73
RCA (1000 thru 1900 series)....15-25 54-59
(With "LOP," "LPM" or "LSP" prefix.)
RCA (2400 series)....5-10 78-81
(With "AYL1 or "CPL1" prefix.)
RCA (2000 & 3000 series, except 2449)....10-20 60-67
(With "LPM" or "LSP" prefix.)
RCA (2449 "The Midnight Special")..20-40 62
(Has Bob Dylan playing harmonica on the title track—his first appearance on record.)
RCA (1000 series)....5-10
RCA (3800 series)....5-10 75
RCA (4000 series)....10-15 68-71
RCA (6000 series)....15-25 59-72

Also see ANN-MARGRET
Also see COMO, Perry / Ames Brothers / Harry Belafonte / Radio City Music Hall Orch.
Also see DYLAN, Bob
Also see ROBINSON, Sugar "Chile" / Harry Belafonte

BELAFONTE, Harry, & Lena Horne LP '59

LPs: 10/12-inch

RCA....15-25 59

Also see HORNE, Lena

BELAFONTE, Harry / Islanders

LPs: 10/12-inch

CELEBRITY....10-20

Also see ISLANDERS

BELAFONTE, Harry, & Miriam Makeba LP '65

LPs: 10/12-inch

RCA....10-15 65

Also see MAKEBA, Miriam

BELAFONTE, Harry, & Nana Mouskouri LP '66

LPs: 10/12-inch

RCA....10-15 66

Also see BELAFONTE, Harry
Also see MOUSKOURI, Nana

BELEW, Adrian LP '82

Singles: 7-inch

ATLANTIC....3-4 89-90

Picture Sleeves

ATLANTIC....3-4 89

LPs: 10/12-inch

ATLANTIC....5-8 89-90
ISLAND....5-10 82-83

Also see KING CRIMSON

BELL, Archie P&R/R&B/LP '68

(With the Drells)

Singles: 12-inch

PHILADELPHIA INT'L....4-6 79
PLAYHOUSE....4-6 84

Singles: 7-inch

ATLANTIC....4-8 68-72
BECKETT....3-4 81-84
EAST-WEST....3-4
GLADES....3-5 73
OVIDE (228 "Tighten Up")....15-25 67
PHILADELPHIA INT'L....3-6 76-79
TSOP....3-6 75-76

LPs: 10/12-inch

ATLANTIC....10-15 68-69
BECKETT....5-10 81-84
PHILADELPHIA INT'L....8-10 75-79
TSOP....5-8 75

Members: Archie Bell; Huey Butler; James Wise; Joe Cross; Lee Bell; Willie Parnell.

Also see PHILADELPHIA INTERNATIONAL ALL STARS

BELL, Benny P&R '75

(Featuring Paul Wynn)

Singles: 78 rpm

COCKTAIL PARTY SONGS (202 "Shaving Cream")....15-25 46

Singles: 7-inch

ENTERPRISE....4-8 62
VANGUARD....3-5 75

LPs: 10/12-inch

BELL ENTERPRISES....10-20
VANGUARD....10-15 75
ZION....10-20

BELL, Biv DeVoe LP '90

LPs: 10/12-inch

MCA....5-8 90

BELL, Jerry R&B '81

Singles: 7-inch

MCA....3-4 80-81

BELL, Madeline P&R/R&B '68

Singles: 7-inch

ASCOT....5-8 64-65
BRUT....3-5 73
MOD....4-6 67
PHILIPS....4-6 67-68
PYE....3-5 76

LPs: 10/12-inch

PHILIPS....15-20 68
PYE....8-10 76

Also see BLUE MINK
Also see MANN, Manfred
Also see SPACE
Also see WATERS, Roger

BELL, Maggie P&R/LP '74

Singles: 7-inch

ATLANTIC....3-5 73-74
SWAN SONG....3-5 76

LPs: 10/12-inch

ATLANTIC....10-12 74
SWAN SONG....8-10 75

Also see STONE the CROWS

BELL, Maggie, & B.A. Robertson

Singles: 7-inch

SWAN SONG....3-4

Picture Sleeves

SWAN SONG....3-4

BELL, Maggie, & Bobby Whitlock

Singles: 7-inch

SWAN SONG....3-4 83-84

Also see BELL, Maggie
Also see WHITLOCK, Bobby

BELL, Randy P&R '84

Singles: 7-inch

EPIC....3-4 84

Picture Sleeves

EPIC....3-4 84

BELL, Rueben R&B '72

Singles: 7-inch

ALARM....3-5 75-77
DELUXE....3-5 72-73
MURCO (1035 "It's Not That Easy")....5-10 68
MURCO (1046 "You're Gonna Miss Me")....25-50 68
SILVER FOX....4-6 69

BELL, Vincent P&R/LP '70

(With the Bell Men)

Singles: 7-inch

DECCA....4-8 67-70
INDEPENDENT (102 "Quicksand")..20-30 60
INDEPENDENT (1214 "Caravan")....20-30 60
MUSICOR....5-10 64
VERVE (10308 "Shindig")....8-12 63

LPs: 10/12-inch

DECCA....10-15 67-70
INDEPENDENT....20-30 60
MUSICOR....10-20 64
VERVE....10-20 64

Also see FERRENTE & TEICHER
Also see RAMRODS

BELL, William P&R '62

Singles: 7-inch

ANDEE....5-8
KAT FAMILY....3-4 83-84
MERCURY....3-5 76-77
STAX (Except 100 series)....3-8 67-74
STAX (100 series)....10-15 61-67
WILBE....3-4 86

LPs: 10/12-inch

KAT FAMILY....5-10 83-84
MERCURY....8-10 77
STAX....10-15 67-74

Also see CLAY, Judy, & William Bell

BELL, William, & Janice Bullock R&B '86

Singles: 7-inch

WILBE....3-4 86

Also see BULLOCK, Janice

BELL, William, & Mavis Staples

Singles: 7-inch

STAX....4-6 69

Also see STAPLES, Mavis

BELL, William, & Carla Thomas

Singles: 7-inch

STAX....4-6 69-70

Also see BELL, William
Also see THOMAS, Carla

BELL & JAMES R&B '78

Singles: 12-inch

A&M....4-6 79
LORIMAR....4-6 80

Singles: 7-inch

A&M....3-4 78-84
LORIMAR....3-4 80

Picture Sleeves

A&M....3-5 78-81

LPs: 10/12-inch

A&M....5-10 79-84

Members: Leroy Bell; Casey James.

BELL BIV DeVOE P&R '90

Singles: 7-inch

MCA....3-4 90

LPs: 10/12-inch

MCA....5-8 90

Members: Ricky Bell; Michael Bivins; Ronnie DeVoe.

Also see NEW EDITION

BELL NOTES P&R/R&B '59

Singles: 7-inch

AUTOGRAPH....10-20 60
ERIC....3-5 73
MADISON....5-10 60
TIME (Blue label)....15-20 59
TIME (Red label)....5-10 59-60

EPs: 7-inch

TIME (100 "I've Had It")....60-100 59
Members: Carl Bonura; Ray Ceroni; Lenny Giambalvo; Pete Kane; John Casey.

BELL SISTERS P&R '52

(With Phil Harris)

Singles: 78 rpm

BERMUDA....4-8 53
RCA....4-8 50-53

Singles: 7-inch

BERMUDA....5-10 53
BRAD (2210 "Honey Baby")....8-12
RCA....5-10 50-53
Members: Kay Bell; Cynthia Bell.
Also see HARRIS, Phil
Also see RENE, Henri, & His Orchestra

BELLAMY, David P&R '75

Singles: 7-inch

W.B. 3-5 75
Also see BELLAMY BROTHERS

BELLAMY BROTHERS C&W/P&R/LP '76

Singles: 7-inch

CURB....3-4 84-87
CURB/MCA....3-4 88-89
ELEKTRA/CURB....3-4 82
MCA....3-4 87
W.B./CURB....3-4 76-83

LPs: 10/12-inch

ELEKTRA....5-10 83
MCA/CURB....5-10 84-90
W.B. 8-10 76-83
Members: David Bellamy; Howard Bellamy.
Also see BELLAMY, David

BELLAMY BROTHERS & FORESTER SISTERS C&W '86

Singles: 7-inch

CURB....3-4 86
W.B. 3-4 90
Also see BELLAMY BROTHERS
Also see FORESTER SISTERS

BELLE, Regina P&R/R&B/LP '87

Singles: 7-inch

COLUMBIA....3-4 87-89
ELEKTRA....3-4 87-88

LPs: 10/12-inch

COLUMBIA....5-10 87-88
Also see BRYSON, Peabo, & Regina Belle

BELLE EPOQUE P&R/R&B '78

Singles: 7-inch

BIG TREE....3-4 78

BELLE STARS P&R/D&D/LP '83

Singles: 12-inch

W.B. 4-6 83-84

Singles: 7-inch

CAPITOL....3-4 89
W.B. 3-4 83-84

Picture Sleeves

W.B. 3-4 83

LPs: 10/12-inch

W.B. 5-10 83-84

BELLS P&R/LP '71

Singles: 7-inch

MGM....3-5 73
POLYDOR....3-5 70-73

LPs: 10/12-inch

POLYDOR....10-15 71-72
Members: Jacki Ralph; Cliff Edwards; Frank Mills.
Also see MILLS, Frank

BELLUS, Tony P&R '59

Singles: 7-inch

ABC....3-4 73
COLLECTABLES....3-4 81
KING....4-8 65
NRC....10-20 59-60

Picture Sleeves

NRC (035 "Hey Little Darlin' ")....25-40 59
NRC (051 "The Echo of an Old Song")....20-30 60

LPs: 10/12-inch

NRC (8 "Robbin' the Cradle with Tony Bellus")....50-100 60
SHI-FI (11 "Gems of Tony Bellus")....20-40

BELMONTS P&R '61

(Belmonts with Dion)

Singles: 12-inch

STRAWBERRY (1107 "I'll Never Fall in Love Again")....5-10 76

Singles: 7-inch

COLLECTABLES....3-4 81
CRYSTAL BALL....4-8 79
DOT....10-15 68-69
LAURIE (Except 3080)....3-5 75-78
LAURIE (3080 "Such a Long Way")..10-15 61
MOHAWK (106 "Teenage Clementine")....25-50 57
ROULETTE....3-5
SABINA (Except 521)....10-20 61-64
SABINA (521 "Nothing in Return")....20-30 64
SABRINA (500 "Tell Me Why")....15-25 61
SABRINA (501 "Don't Get Around Much Anymore")....15-25 61
(In 1961, after #502, Sabrina changed its name, slightly, to Sabina.)
STRAWBERRY....3-5 76-77
SURPRISE (1000 "Tell Me Why")..75-125 61
U.A. (809 thru 966)....10-15 65
U.A. (50007 "Come with Me")....15-20 66

LPs: 10/12-inch

BUDDAH (5123 "Cigars, Acappella, Candy")....25-50 72
CRYSTAL BALL....8-12 80
DOT (25949 "Summer Love")....25-30 69
SABINA (5001 "Carnival of Hits")...75-125 62
STRAWBERRY....10-15 78
UPTOWN....5-10 88
Members: Carlo Mastrangelo; Fred Milano; Angelo D'Aleo; Frank Lyndon.
Also see DION & BELMONTS
Also see SOUL, Jimmy / Belmonts

BELMONTS, Freddy Cannon & Bo Diddley

Singles: 12-inch

ROCK & ROLL TRAVELLING SHOW..4-6

LPs: 10/12-inch

DOWNTOWN....5-10
Also see BELMONTS
Also see CANNON, Freddy
Also see DIDDLEY, Bo

BELOUIS SOME P&R/D&D '85

Singles: 12-inch

CAPITOL....4-6 85

Singles: 7-inch

CAPITOL....3-4 85

LPs: 10/12-inch

CAPITOL....5-8 85

BELOVED, The LP '90

LPs: 10/12-inch

ATLANTIC....5-8 90

BELOYD R&B '77

Singles: 7-inch

20TH FOX....3-4 77

BELUSHI, John P&R '78

Singles: 7-inch

MCA....3-4 78
Also see BLUES BROTHERS
Also see NATIONAL LAMPOON

BELVIN, Jesse R&B '56

(With the Sharptones)

Singles: 78 rpm

CASH....25-50 56
HOLLYWOOD....50-75 53-56
MODERN....15-25 56-57
SPECIALTY (435 "Confusin' Blues")....40-60 52
SPECIALTY (550 "Gone")....25-50 55

Singles: 7-inch

ALADDIN (3431 "Let Me Dream")....25-40 58
CASH (1056 "Beware")....150-200 56
(Reissued in 1959 as by the Capris.)
CLASS (267 "Deep in My Heart")....10-20 60
COLLECTABLES....3-4 81
CUSTOM....4-8
ERIC....3-5 73
HOLLYWOOD (412 "Love Comes Tumbling Down"....150-250 53
HOLLYWOOD (1059 "Betty My Darling"....100-200 56
IMPACT (23 "Tonight My Love")....10-15 62
JAMIE (1145 "Goodnight My Love")..10-20 59
KENT (236 "Sentimental Reasons")....10-20 59
KNIGHT (2012 "Little Darling")....10-20 59
MODERN (1005 "Goodnight My Love")....25-50 56
MODERN (1025 "You Send Me")....20-30 57
MODERN (1027 "Just to Say Hello").20-40 57
RCA (7310 "Volare")....15-25 58
RCA (7387 "Funny")....15-25 58
RCA (47-7469 "Guess Who")....15-25 59
(Monaural.)
RCA (61-7469 "Guess Who")....25-45 59
(Stereo.)
RCA (7543 "Here's a Heart")....15-25 59
RCA (7596 "Give Me Love")....15-25 59
RCA (7675 "Something Happens to Me")....10-20 60
RCA (8040 "Guess Who")....5-10 62
SPECIALTY (435 "Confusin' Blues")....75-100 52
SPECIALTY (550 "Gone")....25-50 55
TENDER (518 "Beware")....25-50 59

EPs: 7-inch

RCA (2089 "Just Jesse Belvin")....25-50 59
RCA (2105 "Mr. Easy")....25-50 60

LPs: 10/12-inch

CAMDEN....15-20 66
CORONET....8-12 60s
CROWN....20-25 60-63
RCA (0900 series)....8-10 75
RCA (LPM-2089 "Just Jesse Belvin")....30-50 59
(Monaural.)
RCA (LSP-2089 "Just Jesse Belvin")....30-60 59
(Stereo.)
RCA (LPM-2105 "Mr. Easy")....30-50 60
(Monaural.)
RCA (LSP-2105 "Mr. Easy")....30-60 60
(Stereo.)
UNITED....10-15
Also see BENTON, Brook / Jesse Belvin
Also see CAPRIS
Also see CHARGERS
Also see CLIQUES
Also see JESSE & MARVIN
Also see SHIELDS

BELVIN, Jesse, & Five Keys / Feathers

Singles: 7-inch

CANDLELITE (427 "Love Song")....10-15 63
Also see FIVE KEYS

BELVIN, Jesse, & Three Dots & a Dash

Singles: 78 rpm

IMPERIAL (5115 "All That Wine Is Gone")....75-125 51
IMPERIAL (5164 "I'll Never Love Again")....75-125 51

Singles: 7-inch

IMPERIAL (5115 "All That Wine Is Gone")....400-500 51
IMPERIAL (5164 "I'll Never Love Again")....400-500 51
Also see BELVIN, Jesse

BENATAR, Pat *P&R/LP '79*

Singles: 12-inch

CHRYSALIS ... 4-8 79-86
COLUMBIA ("Le Bel Age") ... 10-15
(No selection number used. Promotional issue only.)

Singles: 7-inch

CHRYSALIS ... 3-5 79-89
SUNSHINE ... 8-12 78
TRACE (5293 "Day Gig") ... 20-30 74

Picture Sleeves

CHRYSALIS ... 3-5 79-89

LPs: 10/12-inch

CHRYSALIS ... 5-10 79-91
MFSL (057 "In the Heat of the Night") ... 20-40 81
Also see COXON'S ARMY

BENNETT, Boyd *P&R/R&B '55*
(With the Rockets; with Southlanders)

Singles: 78 rpm

KING ... 15-25 54-57

Singles: 7-inch

KING (1400 series) ... 25-50 54-55
(Maroon labels.)
KING (1400 series) ... 20-30 56
(Blue labels.)
KING (4000 series) ... 20-40 56-58
KING (5000 series) ... 10-15 58-63
MERCURY ... 10-20 59-61

EPs: 7-inch

KING (377 "Boyd Bennett") ... 100-200 56
KING (383 "Rock & Roll with Boyd Bennett & His Rockets") ... 100-200 56

LPs: 10/12-inch

KING (594 "Boyd Bennett") ... 1500-2000 58
(Counterfeits exist.)

BENNETT, Joe, & Sparkletones *P&R/R&B '57*

Singles: 78 rpm

ABC-PAR ... 25-50 57-58

Singles: 7-inch

ABC ... 3-4 73
ABC-PAR ... 15-25 57-58
PARIS ... 10-15 59-60

LPs: 10/12-inch

MCA ... 5-10 83

BENNETT, Tony *P&R '51*

Singles: 78 rpm

COLUMBIA ... 4-8 50-57

Singles: 7-inch

BRUT ... 3-5 74
COLUMBIA (1600 series) ... 5-10
(Colored vinyl. Promotional issue only.)
COLUMBIA (06000 series) ... 3-4 86
COLUMBIA (38000 thru 41000 series) ... 8-15 50-61
COLUMBIA (42000 thru 45000 series) ... 4-10 61-70
COLUMBIA/AUROVISION ("Ca C'est L'Amour") ... 5-10 60s
(Square cardboard picture disc. Promo issue made for Waterman Pens.)
IMPROV ... 3-4 75-77
MGM ... 3-5 73
VERVE ... 3-5 72-73

Picture Sleeves

COLUMBIA (1600 series) ... 5-10
(Promotional issue only.)
COLUMBIA (40000 & 41000 series) ... 5-10 53-61
COLUMBIA (42000 thru 44000 series) ... 3-6 61-67
IMPROV ... 3-4 75

EPs: 7-inch

COLUMBIA ... 5-15 55-59

LPs: 10/12-inch

COLUMBIA (Except 600 thru 1200 series) ... 6-12 59-86
COLUMBIA (600 thru 1200 series) ... 10-25 55-59
FANTASY ... 8-12
GUEST STAR ... 5-10
HARMONY ... 5-10 69-73
IMPROV ... 5-10 75-78
MGM ... 6-10 73
MGM/VERVE ... 6-10 72
MFSL ... 20-30 84
Also see GETZ, Stan

BENNETT, Tony, & Count Basie

EPs: 7-inch

COLUMBIA ... 6-10 59

LPs: 10/12-inch

COLUMBIA ... 10-20 59
Also see BASIE, Count

BENNETT, Tony / Al Tornello

LPs: 10/12-inch

GUEST STAR ... 5-10 64
Also see BENNETT, Tony

BENNO, Marc *LP '72*

Singles: 7-inch

A&M ... 3-5 71-79

LPs: 10/12-inch

A&M ... 8-12 70-79
MCA ... 5-10

BENSON, George *LP '69*
(George "Bad" Benson)

Singles: 78 rpm

GROOVE ... 10-15 54

Singles: 12-inch

W.B. ... 4-6 80-83

Singles: 7-inch

A&M ... 3-6 68-70
ARISTA ... 3-5 77
CTI ... 3-5 75-78
COLUMBIA ... 4-8 66-67
GROOVE (0024 "It Should Have Been Me #2") ... 20-40 54
PRESTIGE ... 4-8 64
W.B. ... 3-4 76-89

Picture Sleeves

ARISTA ... 3-5 77
W.B. ... 3-4 78-86

LPs: 10/12-inch

A&M ... 8-12 68-76
CTI ... 8-10 71-78
COLUMBIA ... 8-10 66-67
(With "CL" or "CS" prefix.)
COLUMBIA ... 5-10 76
(With "CG" or "PC" prefix.)
MFSL (011 "Breezin'") ... 25-50 78
POLYDOR ... 5-10 76
VERVE ... 10-12 69
W.B. ... 5-10 75-89
Also see FRANKLIN, Aretha, & George Benson
Also see McDUFF, Brother Jack

BENSON, George, & Earl Klugh *LP '87*

LPs: 10/12-inch

W.B. ... 5-8 87
Also see BENSON, George
Also see KLUGH, Earl

BENT FABRIC: see FABRIC, Bent

BENTLEY, Erlene *D&D '83*

Singles: 12-inch

MEGATONE ... 4-6 83
TVI ... 4-6 84

Singles: 7-inch

MEGATONE ... 3-4 83

BENTON, Brook *P&R '58*
(With the Dixie Flyers)

Singles: 78 rpm

EPIC ... 8-15 56
OKEH ... 8-15 55

Singles: 7-inch

ALL PLATINUM ... 3-5 76
BRUT ... 3-5 73
COTILLION ... 5-10 68-72
EPIC ... 10-20 56
MGM ... 3-5 72
MERCURY (10000 series) ... 8-15 59-65
(Monaural.)
MERCURY (70000 series) ... 10-15 60
(Monaural.)
MERCURY (70000 series) ... 15-25 60-61
(Stereo.)
MUSICOR ... 3-5 77
OKEH ... 15-25 55
OLDE WORLD ... 3-5 77-78
POLYDOR ... 3-5 79
RCA ... 6-12 65-67
REPRISE ... 4-8 67-68
STAX ... 3-5 74
VIK ... 10-20 57-58

Picture Sleeves

MERCURY ... 10-20 60-64
RCA ... 10-15 65

EPs: 7-inch

MERCURY ... 10-20 59-61

LPs: 10/12-inch

ALL PLATINUM ... 8-10 76
CAMDEN (Except 564) ... 8-10 70
CAMDEN (564 "Brook Benton") ... 15-20 60
COTILLION ... 8-10 69-72
EPIC (3573 "Brook Benton at His Best") ... 15-25 59
HARMONY ... 8-12 65
MGM ... 8-10 73
MERCURY (20000 series) ... 15-30 59-65
(Monaural.)
MERCURY (60000 series) ... 20-35 59-65
(Stereo.)
MERCURY (822321 "Greatest Hits") ... 5-8 84
MUSICOR ... 8-10 77
OLDE WORLD ... 5-10 77
RCA (APL1 series) ... 8-10 75
(With "APL1" prefix.)
RCA (LPM/LSP series) ... 10-12 66
(With "LPM" or "LSP" prefix.)
REPRISE ... 8-12 67-68
TEE VEE ... 5-10
WING ... 8-10 66
Session: King Curtis.
Also see KING CURTIS
Also see TROGGS / Brook Benton

BENTON, Brook / Jesse Belvin

LPs: 10/12-inch

CROWN ... 12-15 63
Also see BELVIN, Jesse

BENTON, Brook, & Damita Jo

Singles: 7-inch

MERCURY ... 5-10 63
Also see DAMITA JO

BENTON, Brook / Chuck Jackson / Jimmy Soul

LPs: 10/12-inch

ALMOR (106 "Stargazing") ... 10-20 60s
Also see JACKSON, Chuck
Also see SOUL, Jimmy

BENTON, Brook / Jackie Jocko

LPs: 10/12-inch

STRAND (1121 "The Dynamic Brook Benton Sings") ... 15-25 63

BENTON, Brook, & Dinah Washington *P&R '60*

Singles: 7-inch

MERCURY (10032 "A Rockin' Good Way") ... 10-20 60
(Stereo.)
MERCURY (71565 "Baby") ... 5-10 60
MERCURY (71629 "A Rockin' Good Way") ... 5-10 60
(Monaural.)

Picture Sleeves

MERCURY ... 5-10 60

EPs: 7-inch

MERCURY ... 10-15 60

LPs: 10/12-inch

MERCURY ... 15-25 60
Also see BENTON, Brook
Also see WASHINGTON, Dinah

BERG, Gertrude *LP '65*

LPs: 10/12-inch

AMY ... 8-15 65

BERGEN, Polly LP '57

Singles: 78 rpm

COLUMBIA 3-6 57
JUBILEE 4-6 56
RCA 4-8 50-51
RKO UNIQUE 4-6 57

Singles: 7-inch

COLUMBIA 5-10 57-61
JUBILEE 5-10 56
RCA 5-10 50-51
RKO UNIQUE 5-10 57

EPs: 7-inch

COLUMBIA 5-15 57
JUBILEE 5-15 56

LPs: 10/12-inch

CAMDEN 15-20 56
COLUMBIA 15-25 57-61
HARMONY 10-20 60
JUBILEE 15-25 56
PHILIPS 10-20 63

BERGEN, Polly / Fran Warren / Lynn Roberts

LPs: 10/12-inch

RKO 10-20 59
Also see BERGEN, Polly

BERLIN P&R/D&D/LP '83

Singles: 12-inch

GEFFEN 4-6 83-84

Singles: 7-inch

COLUMBIA 3-4 86
GEFFEN 3-4 82-86
I.R.S. 3-4 80

Picture Sleeves

COLUMBIA 3-4 86
GEFFEN 3-4 83-86

LPs: 10/12-inch

ENIGMA ("Pleasure Victim") 50-100 82
GEFFEN 5-10 82-86
Members: Terri Nunn; John Crawford; Rob Brill.

BERLIN / Madonna

Singles: 7-inch

GEFFEN 3-5 85

Picture Sleeves

GEFFEN 3-5 85
Also see BERLIN
Also see MADONNA

BERLIN PHILHARMONIC P&R '70

(Conducted by Karl Böhm)

Singles: 7-inch

POLYDOR 4-6 69

BERMAN, Shelley LP '59

LPs: 10/12-inch

METRO 8-12 65
VERVE (15000 series) 10-20 59-64

BERMUDAS P&R '64

Singles: 7-inch

ERA 5-10 64
Member: Rickie Page.

BERNARD, Chuck R&B '66

(Chuck Benard)

Singles: 7-inch

MAVERICK (1009 "Indian Giver") 5-10 67
(Different recording than issued on Satellite.)
MI BOUTE 8-12 60s
ST. LAWRENCE 5-10 67
SATELLITE 5-10 65-66
ZODIAC 3-6 70-71

BERNARD, Rod P&R/R&B '59

(With the Twisters)

Singles: 7-inch

ABC 3-4 74
ARBEE 4-8 65-66
ARGO 8-10 59
CARL 10-20 57
COLLECTABLES 3-4 81
COPYRIGHT 4-6 68
CRAZY CAJUN 3-4 78
HALL 5-10 61-64
HALLWAY 5-10 61-64
JIN (105 "This Should Go On Forever") 25-40 59
JIN (200 series) 3-5 74-76
MERCURY 5-10 59-61
TEARDROP 5-10 64-65

LPs: 10/12-inch

JIN (4007 "Rod Bernard") 50-75 60s
Also see SHONDELLS / Rod Bernard / Warren Storm / Skip Stewart

BERNARD, Rod / Clifton Chenier

Singles: 7-inch

JIN (9014 "Boogie in Black") 10-15
Also see BERNARD, Rod

BERNSTEIN, Elmer, & Orch. P&R '56

Singles: 78 rpm

DECCA 3-6 56

Singles: 7-inch

AVA 3-8 62-65
CAPITOL 4-8 59-60
CHOREO 3-5 62
COLUMBIA 3-5 65
DECCA 4-8 56
DOT 3-5 66
U.A. 3-5 65-68

EPs: 7-inch

CAPITOL 3-8 59

LPs: 10/12-inch

CAPITOL 4-8 59-60
COLUMBIA 5-15 60
DOT 10-15 59
HAMILTON 4-8 59
Also see CARR, Vikki
You'll find many more listings by this artist in *The Official Price Guide to Movie/TV Soundtracks and Original Cast Albums,* containing over 8,000 listings.

BERNSTEIN, Leonard, & Orch. LP '60

LPs: 10/12-inch

CAMDEN 8-15 55-56
COLUMBIA (919 "What Is Jazz") 20-40 56
COLUMBIA (31000 series) 5-10 71
COLUMBIA MASTERWORKS 10-20
You'll find many more listings by this artist in *The Official Price Guide to Movie/TV Soundtracks and Original Cast Albums,* containing over 8,000 listings.

BERNSTEIN, Leonard, & Dave Brubeck

LPs: 10/12-inch

COLUMBIA 12-25 60
Also see BERNSTEIN, Leonard, & His Orchestra
Also see BRUBECK, Dave

BERRY, Chuck P&R/R&B '55

Singles: 78 rpm

CHESS (1600 series) 30-60 55-58
CHESS (1700 thru 1729) 50-100 58-59
CHESS (1737 "My Childhood Sweetheart") 75-125 59
CHESS (1747 "Too Pooped to Pop") 100-200 60

Singles: 7-inch

ATCO 3-4 79
CHESS (1604 thru 1615) 15-25 55-56
CHESS (1626 thru 1645) 10-20 56
CHESS (1653 thru 1729) 10-15 57-59
CHESS (1737 thru 1963) 5-10 59-69
CHESS (2000 & 9000 series) 3-5 70-73
ERIC 3-4 73
MERCURY 4-8 66-72
PHILO 8-15 66
("Hip Pocket" Record.)

Picture Sleeves

CHESS (1898 "No Particular Place to Go") 10-20 64
CHESS (1906 "You Never Can Tell") 10-20 64
CHESS (1912 "Little Marie") 10-20 64
CHESS (1916 "Promised Land") 10-20 64

EPs: 7-inch

CHESS (5118 "After School Session") 40-60 57
CHESS (5118 "Head Over Heels") 75-100 57
CHESS (5119 "Rock & Roll Music") 40-60 58
CHESS (5121 "Sweet Little 16") 40-60 58
CHESS (5124 "Pickin' Berries") 40-60 58
CHESS (5126 "Sweet Little Rock & Roller") 40-60 58

LPs: 10/12-inch

ACCORD 5-10 82
ATCO 5-10 79
AUDIO FIDELITY 8-10 84
(Picture disc.)
BROOKVILLE 12-15 73
CHESS (Except 1400 & 9000 series) 10-20 66-76
CHESS (1426 "After School Session") 50-75 57
CHESS (1432 "One Dozen Berrys") 50-75 58
CHESS (1435 "Chuck Berry's on Top") 50-75 59
CHESS (1448 "Rockin' at the Hops") 50-75 59
CHESS (1456 "Chuck Berry's New Juke box Hits") 25-40 61
CHESS (1465 "More Chuck Berry") 30-40 62
CHESS (1465 "Chuck Berry Twist") 20-25 62
(Reissue with title change.)
CHESS (1480 "Chuck Berry on Stage") 20-25 63
CHESS (1485 "Chuck Berry's Greatest Hits") 25-30 64
CHESS (1488 "St. Louis to Liverpool") 20-25 64
CHESS (1495 "Chuck Berry in London") 25-30 65
CHESS (1498 "Fresh Berrys") 20-25 65
CHESS (9000 series) 5-10 85
CHESS/MCA 5-8 89
EVEREST 8-10 76
GUSTO 5-10 78
MCA 8-12 86-87
MAGNUM 10-12 69
MERCURY 15-25 67-72
PICKWICK 8-10 72
TRIP 8-10 78
UPFRONT 5-10 79
Also see ALEXANDER, Joe, & Cubans
Also see DIDDLEY, Bo, & Chuck Berry
Also see MILLER, Steve

BERRY, Chuck, & Howlin' Wolf

LPs: 10/12-inch

CHESS 15-20 69
Also see BERRY, Chuck
Also see HOWLIN' WOLF

BERRY, Jan

(Jan; Jan Barry)

Singles: 7-inch

A&M 5-10 77-78
LIBERTY (55845 "The Universal Coward") 10-15 66
ODE '70 (Except 66023 & 66034) 15-20 72-77
ODE '70 (66023 "Mother Earth") 20-40 72
(With insert note from Jan. Promotional issue only.)
ODE '70 (66023 "Mother Earth") 20-30 72
(Without insert note from Jan.)
ODE '70 (66034 "Don't You Just Know It") 30-40 73
(With Brian Wilson.)
RIPPLE (6101 "Tomorrow's Teardrops") 30-45 61

Picture Sleeves

LIBERTY (55845 "The Universal Coward") ... 100-125 66

Also see JAN & ARNIE
Also see JAN & DEAN
Also see WILSON, Brian

BERTEI, Adele — D&D '83

Singles: 12-inch

GEFFEN ... 4-6 83

Singles: 7-inch

GEFFEN ... 3-4 83

BERTRAND, Plastic — P&R '78

Singles: 7-inch

SIRE ... 4-6 78

Picture Sleeves

SIRE ... 5-10 78

BEST, Peter

Singles: 7-inch

CAMEO (391 "Boys") ... 20-35 66
(Shown as by "Peter Best, formerly of the Beatles.")
CAPITOL (2092 "Carousel of Love") ... 20-35 67
HAPPENING (117 "If You Can't Get Her") ... 40-50 66
HAPPENING (405 "Don't Play with Me Little Girl") ... 40-50 66
MR. MAESTRO (711 "I Can't Do Without You Now") ... 40-50 65
(Shown as by "Best of the Beatles, Peter Best.")
MR. MAESTRO (712 "Casting My Spell") ... 40-50 65
(Shown as by "Best of the Beatles, Peter Best.")
ORIGINAL BEATLES DRUMMER (800 "I'll Try Anyway") ... 40-50 64

Picture Sleeves

CAMEO (391 "Boys") ... 50-75 66

LPs: 10/12-inch

BEST FAN CLUB ... 25-30 66
PHOENIX 10 ... 10-15 82
SAVAGE (71 "Best of the Beatles") ... 100-125 65

Also see BEATLES

BETHEA, Harmon — R&B '73

(Bethea; with Maskman & the Agents)

Singles: 7-inch

BBC ... 3-5
CAP CITY ... 3-5
DYNAMO ... 4-8 69-71
INTERSTATE ... 3-5 74
JAN JAN ... 3-5 74
LEBBY ... 3-5 72
MUSICOR ... 3-5 70-74
ROADHOUSE ... 3-5
RUJAC ... 3-5
SMITHS ... 3-5 76

Also see MASKMAN & AGENTS

BETTERS, Harold — P&R/R&B '64

Singles: 7-inch

GATEWAY ... 4-6 63-65
REPRISE ... 4-6 66-67

LPs: 10/12-inch

GATEWAY ... 10-20 64-66
REPRISE ... 10-20 65-67

BETTS, Dickey: see BETTS, Richard

BETTS, Richard — LP '74

(Dickey Betts & Great Southern; Dickey Betts Band)

Singles: 7-inch

ARISTA ... 3-5 77-78
CAPRICORN ... 3-5 74-76

LPs: 10/12-inch

ARISTA ... 5-10 77-78
CAPRICORN ... 8-10 74
EPIC ... 5-8 88

Also see ALLMAN BROTHERS BAND

BEVEL, Charles — R&B '74

(Charles "Mississippi" Bevel)

Singles: 7-inch

A&M ... 3-5 73-74

LPs: 10/12-inch

A&M ... 8-10 73-74

BEVERLY & DUANE — R&B '78

Singles: 7-inch

ARIOLA AMERICA ... 3-5 78-79

Members: Beverly Wheeler; Duane Williams.

BEVERLY SISTERS — P&R '56

(Beverley Sisters)

Singles: 78 rpm

LONDON ... 4-6 56

Singles: 7-inch

LONDON ... 5-10 56
MERCURY ... 5-10 60

LPs: 10/12-inch

CAPITOL ... 10-20 61

BICKERSONS: see AMECHE, Don, & Frances Langford

BIDDU — P&R/R&B '75

(Biddu Orchestra)

Singles: 7-inch

COLOSSUS ... 3-5 70
EPIC ... 3-5 75-77

LPs: 10/12-inch

EPIC ... 5-10 76-77

BIG AUDIO DYNAMITE — LP '85

Singles: 12-inch

COLUMBIA (1739 "James Brown") ... 6-10 89
(Promotional issue only.)
COLUMBIA (1899 "Contact") ... 5-8 89
(Promotional issue only.)
COLUMBIA (2302 "Medicine Show") ... 5-8 86
(Promotional issue only.)
COLUMBIA (2520 "C'mon Every Beatbox") ... 5-8 86
(Promotional issue only.)
COLUMBIA (2697 "Hollywood Boulevard") ... 5-8 86
(Promotional issue only.)
COLUMBIA (07955 "Just Play Music") ... 4-6
COLUMBIA (8133 "Other 99") ... 5-8 88
(Promotional issue only.)
COLUMBIA (5000 thru 8000 series) ... 4-6 85-90

Singles: 7-inch

COLUMBIA (5000 series except 5841) ... 3-5 85
COLUMBIA (5841 "Medicine Show") ... 4-6 85
(White label. Promotional issue only.)
COLUMBIA (6000 series, except 6053) ... 3-5 86
COLUMBIA (6053 "E = MC^2 ") ... 4-6 85
(White label. Promotional issue only.)
COLUMBIA (6364 "C'mon Every Beatbox") ... 4-6 86
(White label. Promotional issue only.)
COLUMBIA (6708 "Badrock City") ... 4-6 86
(White label. Promotional issue only.)
COLUMBIA (8000 series) ... 3-5 88

Picture Sleeves

COLUMBIA (5841 "Medicine Show") ... 5-8 85
(Promotional issue only.)
COLUMBIA (6053 "E = MC^2 ") ... 5-8 85
(Promotional issue only.)
COLUMBIA (8094 "Other 99") ... 4-6 88

LPs: 10/12-inch

COLUMBIA ... 5-10 85-89
MCA ... 5-10

Members: Mick Jones; Don Letts; Leo Williams; Greg Roberts; Dan Donovan; Flea.

Also see BIG AUDIO DYNAMITE II
Also see CLASH

BIG AUDIO DYNAMITE II

Singles: 12-inch

COLUMBIA (4044 "Rush Dance") ... 5-8 91
COLUMBIA (657640 "Rush") ... 5-10 91
(Promotional issue only.)

LPs: 10/12-inch

COLUMBIA ... 8-10 91

Members: Mick Jones; Gary Stonadge; Chris Kavanagh; Nick Hawkins.

Also see BIG AUDIO DYNAMITE

BIG BOPPER — P&R/R&B '58

(Jape Richardson; Jiles Perry Richardson Jr.)

Singles: 7-inch

D (1008 "Chantilly Lace") 100-200 ... 58
MERCURY (71343 "Chantilly Lace") ... 10-15 58
MERCURY (71375 "Big Bopper's Wedding") ... 10-15 58
MERCURY (71416 "Walking Through My Dreams") ... 10-15 59
(Black label.)
MERCURY (71416 "Walking Through My Dreams") ... 20-30 59
(White label. Has alternate take of A-side. Promotional issue only.)
MERCURY (71451 "It's the Truth Ruth") ... 10-15 59
MERCURY (71482 "Pink Petticoats") ... 10-15 59
MERCURY CELEBRITY SERIES (30072 "Chantilly Lace") ... 5-10 60

LPs: 10/12-inch

MERCURY (20402 "Chantilly Lace") ... 250-300 59
(Black label.)
MERCURY (20402 "Chantilly Lace") ... 250-300 59
(Pink label. Promotional issue only.)
MERCURY (20402 "Chantilly Lace") ... 75-100 64
(Red label.)
MERCURY (20402 "Chantilly Lace"). 10-15 81
(Chicago "skyline" label.)
PICKWICK ... 20-30 73
RHINO ... 5-8 89

Also see DEL-VIKINGS / Diamonds / Big Bopper / Gaylords
Also see RICHARDSON, Jape

BIG BROTHER & HOLDING CO. — LP '67

(Big Brother)

Singles: 7-inch

COLUMBIA ... 5-10 68-71
MAINSTREAM ... 5-10 67-68

Picture Sleeves

COLUMBIA (44626 "Piece of My Heart") ... 10-20 68

LPs: 10/12-inch

COLUMBIA ... 15-25 68-71
MADE to LAST ... 5-10 84
MAINSTREAM (6099 "Big Brother and the Holding Company") ... 20-35 67

Members: Janis Joplin; David Getz; Sam Andrew; Peter Albin; Jim Gurley; David Schallock; Nick Gravenites; Kathi McDonald.

Also see JOPLIN, Janis
Also see McDONALD, Kathi

BIG COUNTRY — P&R/D&D/LP '83

Singles: 12-inch

MERCURY ... 4-6 83-86

Singles: 7-inch

MERCURY ... 3-4 83-86
REPRISE ... 3-4 88-89

Picture Sleeves

MERCURY (Except 811450) ... 3-4 83-84
MERCURY (811450 "Fields of Fire") ... 4-8 84
(Poster sleeve.)
REPRISE ... 3-4 89

LPs: 10/12-inch

MERCURY ... 5-10 83-86
REPRISE ... 5-8 88

Members: Stuart Adamson; Bruce Watson; Mark Brzezicki; Tony Butler.

BIG MACEO — R&B '45

(Major Merriweather)

Singles: 78 rpm

BLUEBIRD ... 15-30 42-45
FORTUNE (137 "Leavin' Blues") ... 25-50 52

FORTUNE (805 "Worried Life Blues, No. 2") ... 20-40 52
GROOVE ... 10-20 54
RCA ... 15-25 47-48
SPECIALTY (320 "Do You Remember") ... 10-20 49
SPECIALTY (346 "One Sunday Morning") ... 10-20 49

Singles: 7-inch

GROOVE (5001 "Chicago Breakdown") ... 30-40 54
RCA (50-0002 "Chicago Breakdown") ... 50-100 49

LPs: 10/12-inch

BLUEBIRD ... 10-12 75
Also see TAMPA RED

BIG MAYBELLE *R&B '53*
(Mable Smith)

Singles: 78 rpm

KING ... 10-20 48-49
OKEH ... 10-20 53-56
SAVOY ... 10-20 56-58

Singles: 7-inch

BRUNSWICK ... 5-10 63
CHESS ... 4-8 66
OKEH ... 20-40 53-56
PARAMOUNT ... 3-5 73
PORT ... 5-10 65
ROJAC ... 10-15 64-69
SAVOY ... 10-20 56-61
SCEPTER ... 10-15 64

EPs: 7-inch

EPIC (7071 "Big Maybelle Sings the Blues") ... 40-60 57

LPs: 10/12-inch

BRUNSWICK ... 15-25 62-68
ENCORE ... 10-15 67
EPIC ... 8-10 83
PARAMOUNT ... 8-10 73
ROJAC ... 10-12 67-69
SAVOY (14005 "Big Maybelle Sings") ... 40-50 57
SAVOY (14011 "Blues, Candy and Big Maybelle") ... 40-50 57
SCEPTER ... 15-20 64
UPFRONT ... 8-10 73

BIG PIG *P&R/LP '88*

Singles: 7-inch

A&M ... 3-4 88

Picture Sleeves

A&M ... 3-4 88

BIG RIC *P&R '83*

Singles: 7-inch

ROCK & ROLL ... 3-4 83
SCOTTI BROTHERS ... 3-4 83

LPs: 10/12-inch

SCOTTI BROTHERS ... 5-10 83-84
Member: Joel Porter.

BIG SAMBO *P&R '62*
(With the House Wreckers)

Singles: 7-inch

ERIC ... 4-8 62

BIG THREE

Singles: 7-inch

FM ... 5-10 63
ROULETTE ... 4-8 66
TOLLIE ... 4-8 64

LPs: 10/12-inch

ACCORD ... 5-10 82
FM ... 15-25 63-64
ROULETTE ... 15-20 68
Members: Cass Elliott; Tim Rose; Denny Dougherty.
Also see ELLIOTT, Cass
Also see MAMAS & PAPAS

BIG THREE TRIO *R&B '48*

Singles: 78 rpm

BULLET ... 15-25 47
COLUMBIA ... 15-30 47-51
DELTA ... 15-25 49
DOT ... 10-20 52
OKEH ... 15-25 51-53

Singles: 7-inch

COLUMBIA (30239 "Blip Blip") ... 50-75 51
OKEH ... 25-50 51-53
Members: Willie Dixon; Leonard "Baby Doo" Caston; Bernard Dennis.
Also see DIXON, Willie
Also see HOWARD, Rosetta

BILK, Mr. Acker *P&R/R&B/LP '62*
(With His Paramount Jazz Band; with Leon Young String Chorale)

Singles: 7-inch

ATCO ... 4-6 61-66
REPRISE ... 3-5 62

LPs: 10/12-inch

ASCOT ... 8-15 62
ATCO ... 10-20 62-66

BILK, Mr. Acker, & Bent Fabric

LPs: 10/12-inch

ATCO ... 8-12 65
Also see BILK, Mr. Acker
Also see FABRIC, Bent

BILL BLACK'S COMBO: see BLACK, Bill

BILLION DOLLAR BABIES *LP '77*

Singles: 7-inch

POLYDOR (Except 14406) ... 4-6 77
POLYDOR (14406 "Too Young") ... 8-12 77
(Promotional issue only.)

LPs: 10/12-inch

POLYDOR (Except 022) ... 12-15 77
POLYDOR (022 "Battle Axe") ... 20-25 77
(Promotional issue only.)
Also see COOPER, Alice

BILLY ALWAYS: see ALWAYS, Billy

BILLY & BABY GAP *R&B '85*

Singles: 7-inch

TOTAL EXPERIENCE ... 3-4 85
Members: Billy Young; Anthony Walker
Also see GAP BAND

BILLY & BEATERS *LP '81*

Singles: 7-inch

ALFA ... 3-4 81

Picture Sleeves

ALFA ... 3-4 81

LPs: 10/12-inch

ALFA ... 5-10 81
Member: Billy Vera.
Also see VERA, Bill

BILLY & LILLIE *P&R/R&B '58*
(Billy Ford & the Thunderbirds; vocal by Freddie Pinkard)

Singles: 78 rpm

SWAN ... 25-50 57

Singles: 7-inch

ABC ... 3-5 73
ABC-PAR (10421 "Love Me Sincerely") ... 15-25 63
CAMEO ... 4-8 66
COLLECTABLES ... 3-4 81
SWAN ... 10-20 57-61
Members: Billy Ford; Lillie Bryant.

BILLY & SUE

Singles: 7-inch

CREW ... 3-5 70
Members: William Oliver Swofford; Lesley Gore.
Also see GORE, Lesley
Also see OLIVER

BILLY JOE & CHECKMATES
(Billy Joe Hunter) *P&R '62*

Singles: 7-inch

DORE ... 5-15 61-66

BILLY SATELLITE *P&R/LP '84*

Singles: 7-inch

CAPITOL ... 3-4 84

Picture Sleeves

CAPITOL ... 3-4 84

LPs: 10/12-inch

CAPITOL ... 5-10 84
Member: Monty Bryom.

BIMBO JET *P&R '75*

Singles: 7-inch

SCEPTER ... 3-5 75

BIONIC BOOGIE *R&B/LP '78*

Singles: 12-inch

RP ... 4-8

Singles: 7-inch

POLYDOR ... 3-4 77-78

LPs: 10/12-inch

POLYDOR ... 5-10 78
Member: Gregg Diamond.

BIRD, J. *D&D '84*

Singles: 12-inch

WARRIOR ... 4-6 84

BIRDLEGS & PAULINE & THEIR VERSATILITY BIRDS *P&R/R&B '63*

Singles: 7-inch

CUCA (1125 "Spring") ... 20-35 63
(Credits "Birdlegs & His Versatility Birds.")
VEE JAY (510 "Spring") ... 5-10 63

LPs: 10/12-inch

CUCA (4000 "Birdlegs & Pauline") ... 50-100 64
Members: Sidney Banks; Pauline Shivers Banks.
Also see LITTLE BEAVER

BIRDSONG, Edwin *R&B '81*

Singles: 12-inch

PHILADELPHIA INT'L ... 4-6 78-79
SALSOUL ... 4-6 81-84

Singles: 7-inch

BAMBOO ... 3-6 75
PHILADELPHIA INT'L ... 3-5 78
POLYDOR ... 3-5 71-72
SALSOUL ... 3-4 81-84

LPs: 10/12-inch

PHILADELPHIA INT'L ... 5-10 78
POLYDOR ... 8-10 71-73

BIRDSONG, Larry *R&B '56*

Singles: 78 rpm

CALVERT ... 10-20 56
DECCA ... 10-15 56
EXCELLO ... 10-15 55-56

Singles: 7-inch

ACE ... 10-15 60
CALVERT ... 15-25 56
CHAMPION ... 10-20 59
CHEROKEE ... 15-25 59
DECCA ... 10-20 56
EXCELLO ... 10-20 55-56
HOME of the BLUES ... 5-10 61
REF-O-REE ... 5-10
VEE JAY ... 10-15 57-58

BIRKIN, Jane, & Serge Gainsbourg *P&R '69*

Singles: 7-inch

FONTANA ... 3-6 69

LPs: 10/12-inch

FONTANA ... 6-12 70

BISHOP, Elvin *P&R/LP '74*
(Elvin Bishop Group; with Crabshaw Rising)

Singles: 7-inch

CAPRICORN ... 3-5 74-79
EPIC ... 3-5 72-75
FILLMORE ... 3-5 70-71
W.B. ... 3-5 72

LPs: 10/12-inch

ALLIGATOR ... 5-8 91
CAPRICORN ... 8-12 74-78
EPIC ... 8-12 72-75
FILLMORE ... 10-15 69-72
Also see BUTTERFIELD, Paul
Also see GRATEFUL DEAD / Elvin Bishop Group

BISHOP, Stephen *P&R '76*

Singles: 7-inch

ABC ... 3-5 76-78
W.B. ... 3-4 80-83

Picture Sleeves

ABC (12435 "Animal House")................4-8 78

LPs: 10/12-inch

ABC 6-12 76-78
MCA..5-10 80
W.B. 5-10 80

Also see GRUSIN, Dave
Also see NEWMAN, Randy

BISHOP, Stephen, & Yvonne Elliman

Singles: 7-inch

W.B. 3-4 80

Also see BISHOP, Stephen
Also see ELLIMAN, Yvonne

BITS & PIECES R&B '81

(Bits 'N' Pieces)

Singles: 7-inch

MANGO..3-4 81
NASCO..3-5 73-74
PARAMOUNT 3-5 74

BIZ MARKIE R&B '86

(Marcel Hall)

Singles: 7-inch

COLD CHILL 3-4 88-90
PRISM 3-4 86

Picture Sleeves

COLD CHILL 3-4 90

LPs: 10/12-inch

COLD CHILL 5-8 88-90

BJORN & BENNY

Singles: 7-inch

PLAYBOY.......................................8-10 72-74
(With Anna and Frieda.)
Members: Bjorn Ulvaeus; Benny Anderson.

Also see ABBA

BLACK, Bill P&R/R&B '59

(Bill Black's Combo)

Singles: 7-inch

COLUMBIA.......................................3-5 70
ECHO 3-5 72
GUSTO...3-4 83
HI (Except 2000 series) 3-6 67-78
HI (2000 series) 5-15 59-66
LONDON 3-4 84
MEGA...3-5 71-74
MOTOWN..3-4 83

Picture Sleeves

HI 5-10 60-62

EPs: 7-inch

HI (52 "King of the Road") 8-12 64
HI (22001 "Dee J. Special")...............10-20 60s
(Promotional only issue.)
MEGA (192 "Juke box Favorites").......5-10 72
(Juke box issue.)

LPs: 10/12-inch

COLUMBIA.......................................8-10 69-70
51 WEST...5-10 84
HI (6000 & 8000 series)....................5-10 77-78
HI (12001 "Smokie")........................30-60 60
HI (12002 thru 12005)......................20-40 60-62
HI (12006 thru 12041)......................10-20 62-68
(Monaural.)
HI (32000 thru 32010)......................15-30 61-63
(Stereo.)
HI (32011 thru 32110)......................10-20 63-77
(Stereo.)
MEGA...5-10 71-74
ZODIAC..8-12 77

Also see CANNON, Ace
Also see PRESLEY, Elvis

BLACK, Cilla P&R '64

Singles: 7-inch

BELL..3-4 68
CAPITOL 5-10 64-66
DJM 3-6 68-70
EMI AMERICA..................................3-5 74
PRIVATE STOCK..............................3-5 75-76

LPs: 10/12-inch

CAPITOL (T-2308 "Is It Love") 20-30 65
(Monaural.)
CAPITOL (ST-2308 "Is It Love") 25-35 65
(Stereo.)

BLACK, Clint C&W/LP '89

Singles: 7-inch

RCA 3-4 89-92

LPs: 10/12-inch

RCA 5-8 89-90

Also see ROGERS, Roy, & Clint Black

BLACK, Jay P&R '80

Singles: 12-inch

MILLENIUM (20614 "Love Is in the Air") 15-20 78
(Single-sided disc. Promotional issue only.)
MILLENIUM (20614 "Love Is in the Air"/"Please Stay")... 8-12 78

Singles: 7-inch

ATLANTIC/MIGRATION 3-5 75
K-TEL (562 "This Magic Moment") ... 30-40 82
(Canadian. Credited to "Jay Black of Jay and the Americans.")
MIDSONG 3-4 80
MILLENNIUM.................................... 3-5 78
PRIVATE STOCK.............................. 3-5 76
ROULETTE (7198 "One Night Affair") 10-15 76
(Same track on both sides. Promotional issue only.)
U.A. 4-8 67

Picture Sleeves

U.A. 5-10 67

Also see JAY & AMERICANS

BLACK, Jay / Caress

Singles: 12-inch

ROULETTE (2005 "One Night Affair") 10-15 76
(For the promotional issue, with Jay Black on both sides, see his section above.)

Also see BLACK, Jay

BLACK, Jeanne C&W/P&R/R&B '60

Singles: 7-inch

CAPITOL.. 4-8 60-62

LPs: 10/12-inch

CAPITOL.. 15-20 60

BLACK, Marion R&B '71

Singles: 7-inch

AVCO EMBASSY 3-5 71
SHAKAT.. 3-5 74

BLACK, Oscar P&R '61

Singles: 78 rpm

ATLANTIC.. 25-50 51
GROOVE 15-25 54-55

Singles: 7-inch

ATLANTIC (956 "Troubled Mind Blues").. 50-100 51
GROOVE 25-50 54-55
SAVOY.. 5-10 61

BLACK, Oscar, & Sue Allen

Singles: 78 rpm

GROOVE 15-25 54-55

Singles: 7-inch

GROOVE 25-50 54-55

Also see BLACK, Oscar

BLACK, Shelly R&B '76

Singles: 7-inch

VIGOR.. 3-5 76-77

BLACK, Stanley, & His Orch. LP '62

LPs: 10/12-inch

LONDON PHASE 4 .... 5-15 62-65

BLACK, Terry P&R '64

Singles: 7-inch

DUNHILL... 4-8 65-66
TOLLIE.. 5-10 64-65

Picture Sleeves

TOLLIE.. 5-10 65

BLACK, Terry, & Laurel Ward P&R '72

Singles: 7-inch

KAMA SUTRA.................................. 3-5 72

Also see BLACK, Terry

BLACK BLOOD R&B '75

Singles: 7-inch

CHRYSALIS 3-5 77
MAINSTREAM.................................. 3-5 75

LPs: 10/12-inch

CHRYSALIS 5-10 77
MAINSTREAM.................................. 8-10 75

BLACK BOX P&R/LP '90

Singles: 7-inch

RCA 3-4 90

LPs: 10/12-inch

RCA 5-8 90

Member: Martha Wash.

Also see WEATHER GIRLS

BLACK CROWES P&R/LP '90

Singles: 7-inch

DEF AMERICAN 3-4 91

LPs: 10/12-inch

DEF AMERICAN 5-8 90
W.B. 5-8 90s

Members: Chris Robinson; Rich Robinson; Steve Cease; Johnny Colt; Steve Gorman.

BLACK FLAMES R&B '87

Singles: 7-inch

DEF JAM 3-4 87

BLACK HEAT R&B '73

Singles: 7-inch

ATLANTIC 3-5 72-74

LPs: 10/12-inch

ATLANTIC 8-10 72-75

BLACK ICE R&B '77

Singles: 7-inch

AMHERST 3-5 76
HDM 3-5 77
MONTAGE 3-4 81-84

LPs: 10/12-inch

AMHERST 8-10 76
MONTAGE 5-10 82

BLACK IVORY R&B '71

Singles: 7-inch

BUDDAH 3-5 75-84
KWANZA.. 3-5 74
PANORAMIC.................................... 3-4 85
PERCEPTION 3-5 72
TODAY.. 4-6 71-73

LPs: 10/12-inch

BUDDAH 5-10 75-84
TODAY.. 10-12 72-73

Member: Leroy Burgess.

Also see ALEEM

BLACK MAMBA D&D '84

Singles: 12-inch

GARAGE 4-6 84

BLACK 'N BLUE LP '84

Singles: 7-inch

GEFFEN.. 3-4 84-88

LPs: 10/12-inch

GEFFEN.. 5-10 84-88

BLACK OAK ARKANSAS LP '71

(Black Oak)

Singles: 7-inch

ATCO.. 3-5 71-75
CAPRICORN 3-5 77-78
ENTERPRISE 3-5 70
MCA... 3-5 75-77

LPs: 10/12-inch

ATCO.. 8-15 71-84
CAPRICORN 8-10 77-78
MCA... 8-12 75-77
STAX.. 10-15 74

Members: Jim Mangrum; Ruby Starr; Rickie Reynolds; Stanley Knight; Harvey Jett; Jimmy Henderson; Pat Daugherty; Tom Aldridge.

BLACK OAK ARKANSAS / Cooper Brothers

LPs: 10/12-inch

CAPRICORN (0005 "I'd Rather Be Sailing") 10-15 78
(Promotional issue only.)
Also see BLACK OAK ARKANSAS
Also see COOPER BROTHERS

BLACK PEARL LP '69

Singles: 7-inch

ATLANTIC 3-6 69
PROPHESY 3-6 70

LPs: 10/12-inch

ATLANTIC 12-15 69
PROPHESY 15-20 70

BLACK SABBATH P&R/LP '70

Singles: 7-inch

I.R.S. 3-4 89
W.B. 3-5 70-76

EPs: 7-inch

W.B. (241 "Sabbath Bloody Sabbath") 15-25 74
(Juke box EP.)

LPs: 10/12-inch

I.R.S. 5-8 89
W.B. (PRO-417 "Radio Spots") 150-200 69
W.B. (Except 1000 & 2000 series) 5-10 76-84
W.B. (1000 & 2000 series) 8-15 70-76
W.B. 5-10 87
Members: Ozzy Osbourne; Tony Iommi; Kip Treavor; Bill Ward; Ronnie Dio; Terry "Geezer" Butler.
Also see DIO, Ronnie
Also see OSBOURNE, Ozzy

BLACK SATIN R&B '75
(Featuring Fred Parris)

Singles: 7-inch

BUDDAH 3-5 75

LPs: 10/12-inch

BUDDAH (5654 "Black Satin") 8-10 76
BUDDAH (5654 "Black Satin") 25-35 76
(Promotional issue.)
Members: Fred Parris; Rich Freeman; Jimmy Curtis; Nate Marshall.
Also see FIVE SATINS

BLACK UHURU LP '82

Singles: 7-inch

ISLAND 3-4 84

LPs: 10/12-inch

ISLAND 5-10 84
MANGO 5-10 80-85
MESA 5-8 90

BLACKBYRDS P&R/R&B/LP '74

Singles: 7-inch

FANTASY 3-5 74-84

LPs: 10/12-inch

FPM 10-12 75
FANTASY 10-15 74-84
Members: Gary Hart; Joe Hall III; Stephe Johnson; Keith Killgo; Orville Saunders; Kevin Toney.
Also see BYRD, Donald

BLACKFOOT P&R/LP '79

Singles: 7-inch

ATCO 3-4 79-84

LPs: 10/12-inch

ANTILLES 5-10 78
ATCO 5-10 79-84
EPIC 8-10 76
ISLAND 10-12 75
Members: Rick Medlocke; Jackson Spires; Charlie Hargrett; Greg Walker.
Also see LYNYRD SKYNYRD

BLACKFOOT, J.D. R&B '83
(With Ann Hines; J. Blackfoot)

Singles: 7-inch

EDGE 3-4 86-87
FANTASY 4-8 74
PHILIPS 8-12 69-70
SOUND TOWN 3-5 83-86

LPs: 10/12-inch

FANTASY (9468 "Song of Crazy Horse") 15-25 74
FANTASY (9487 "Southbound & Gone") 15-25 75
MERCURY (61288 "The Ultimate Prophecy") 40-60 70
SOUND TOWN 5-10 84-85
Also see SOUL CHILDREN

BLACKJACK P&R/LP '79

Singles: 7-inch

POLYDOR 3-5 79-84
20TH FOX 4-8 76

LPs: 10/12-inch

POLYDOR 5-10 79-80
Members: Michael Bolotin; Tony Battaglia; Bruce Kulick; Chuck Kirkpatrick; Jan Mullaney.
Also see BOLTON, Michael

BLACKMORE, Ritchie
(Ritchie Blackmore's Rainbow)

Singles: 7-inch

POLYDOR 3-5 75

LPs: 10/12-inch

POLYDOR (6049 "Ritchie Blackmore's Rainbow") 8-10 75
Also see BLACKMORE'S RAINBOW
Also see LORD SUTCH

BLACKMORE'S RAINBOW LP '75

Singles: 7-inch

OYSTER 3-5 76
POLYDOR 3-5 75-79

LPs: 10/12-inch

OYSTER 8-12 75-76
Members: Ritchie Blackmore; Roger Glover; Ronnie Dio.
Also see BLACKMORE, Ritchie
Also see DEEP PURPLE
Also see DIO, Ronnie
Also see RAINBOW

BLACKSMOKE R&B '76

Singles: 7-inch

CHOCOLATE CITY 3-5 76

BLACKWELL P&R '69

Singles: 7-inch

ASTRO 3-6 69-70
BUTTERFLY 3-4 78

LPs: 10/12-inch

ASTRO 8-10 69
BUTTERFLY 5-10 78

BLACKWELL, Charlie P&R '59

Singles: 7-inch

W.B. 4-8 59

BLADES, Ruben LP '88

Singles: 7-inch

ATLANTIC 3-5
ELEKTRA 3-4 88

BLADES OF GRASS P&R '67

Singles: 7-inch

FINE (57027 "It Isn't Easy") 20-30 67
JUBILEE 4-8 67-68

LPs: 10/12-inch

JUBILEE 12-20 67
Members: Bruce Ames; Marc Black; Frank DiChiara; Dave Gordon.

BLAKE & HINES R&B '87

Singles: 7-inch

MOTOWN 3-4 87
Members: Cory Blake; Andra Hines.

BLANC, Mel P&R '48
(With the Sportsmen & Billy May)

Singles: 78 rpm

CAPITOL (5221 "Seasons Greetings from Capitol") 10-20 49
(Promotional issue only. Also contains greetings from other Capitol artists.)
CAPITOL 10-20 48-54

Singles: 7-inch

CAPITOL (Except PRO-15) 15-30 50-54
CAPITOL (PRO-15 "I Taut I Taw a Record Dealer") 30-50 51
(Mel Blanc provides the voice of assorted cartoon characters, though he is not credited on label. Promotional issue only.)
PETER PAN 3-5 72
W.B. 5-10 60

EPs: 7-inch

CAPITOL (436 "Party Panic") 35-50 53

LPs: 10/12-inch

CAPITOL (436 "Party Panic") 50-75 53
(10-inch LP.)
CAPITOL (3200 series) 15-30 61-63
GOLDEN 10-20 61
Also see HUNT, Pee Wee

BLANCHARD, Jack, & Misty Morgan C&W '69

Singles: 7-inch

EPIC 3-4 73-75
MEGA 3-5 71-73
WAYSIDE 3-5 69-70

LPs: 10/12-inch

MEGA 8-12 72
WAYSIDE 10-15 70

BLANCMANGE D&D '83

Singles: 12-inch

ISLAND 4-6 83-84
SIRE 4-6 84-85

Singles: 7-inch

ISLAND 3-4 83-84
SIRE 3-4 84-85

LPs: 10/12-inch

ISLAND 5-10 82-84
SIRE 5-10 84-85

BLAND, Billy P&R/R&B '60

Singles: 78 rpm

OLD TOWN 10-20 55-57

Singles: 7-inch

ATLANTIC 3-4 84
COLLECTABLES 3-4 81
TIP TOP 10-15 58
OLD TOWN (1016 thru 1035) 10-20 55-57
OLD TOWN (1076 thru 1143) 6-12 60-63
ST. LAWRENCE 4-8

BLAND, Bobby R&B '57
(Bobby "Blue" Bland)

Singles: 78 rpm

CHESS (1489 "Crying") 20-40 54
DUKE (105 "I.O.U. Blues") 40-60 54
DUKE (115 "No Blow No Show") 25-50 54
DUKE (141 "It's My Life, Baby") 20-40 56
DUKE (146 thru 196) 15-30 57-58
MODERN (848 "Crying All Night Long") 15-25 52
MODERN (868 "Good Lovin'") 15-25 52

Singles: 7-inch

ABC 3-4 73-78
DUKE (105 "I.O.U. Blues") 75-100 54
DUKE (115 "No Blow, No Show") 50-100 54
DUKE (141 "It's My Life, Baby") 30-60 56
DUKE (146 thru 196) 15-30 57-58
DUKE (300 series) 5-10 60-66
DUKE (400 series) 4-8 66-72
DUNHILL 3-4 74
FAIRWAY 8-10 79
KENT 5-10
MCA 3-4 79-84
MALACO 3-4
ST. LAWRENCE 4-8

LPs: 10/12-inch

ABC 5-10 75-78
ABC/DUKE 5-10 73
BLUESWAY 5-10 73
DUKE (74 "Two Steps from the Blues") 50-75 61
DUKE (75 "Here's the Man") 45-55 62
DUKE (77 "Call On Me") 35-50 63
DUKE (78 "Ain't Nothing You Can Do") 35-50 64
DUKE (79 "Soul of the Man") 25-45 66
DUKE (84 "Best of Bobby Bland") 25-40 67

DUKE (86 "Best of Bobby Bland, Vol. 2") 25-40 68
DUKE (88 "Touch of the Blues") 25-40 68
DUKE (89 "Spotlighting the Man") 20-40 69
DUKE (90 "If Loving You Is Wrong") 15-25 70
DUKE (92 "Introspective") 20-25 74
DUNHILL 8-15 73-74
MCA 5-10 79-84
Also see ACE, Johnny

BLAND, Bobby, & B.B. King R&B '76

Singles: 7-inch

ABC 3-4 78
IMPULSE 3-5 76

LPs: 10/12-inch

DUNHILL 10-12 74
IMPULSE 8-10 76
MCA 5-10 82
Also see KING, B.B.

BLAND, Bobby / Little Junior Parker

LPs: 10/12-inch

DUKE (DLP-72 "Barefoot Rock") ..100-150 58
DUKE (X-72 "Barefoot Rock") 10-12 74
Also see PARKER, Little Junior

BLAND, Bobby, & Ike Turner

Singles: 7-inch

KENT 5-10 62
Also see TURNER, Ike

BLAND, Bobby / Johnny Guitar Watson

LPs: 10/12-inch

CROWN (5358 "2 in Blues") 20-30 63
Also see BLAND, Bobby
Also see WATSON, Johnny

BLANE, Marcie P&R/R&B '62

Singles: 7-inch

LONDON 3-4 84
SEVILLE 5-10 62-65

BLAST, C.L. R&B '80

Singles: 7-inch

ATLANTIC 4-8 69
CLIMTONE (9 "Leftover Love") 10-20 60s
COTILLION 3-5 80
PARK PLACE 3-4 85
STAX 5-10 67
UNITED 5-10 70-71

LPs: 10/12-inch

COTILLION 5-10 80

BLASTERS LP '82

Singles: 7-inch

MCA 3-4 84
SLASH 3-5 81-85

Picture Sleeves

SLASH 3-4 81-85

LPs: 10/12-inch

ROLLIN' ROCK (021 "American Music") 50-75 80
SLASH 8-12 81-85
Members: David Alvin; Phil Alvin; John Bazz; Gene Taylor; Bill Bateman; Steve Berlin; Lee Allen.
Also see ALLEN, Lee
Also see ALVIN, Dave
Also see HARTMAN, Dan / Blasters
Also see X

BLAZE P&R '76

Singles: 7-inch

EPIC 3-5 76-77
FRATERNITY 3-5 76

BLEND P&R '78

Singles: 7-inch

MCA 3-4 78-79

LPs: 10/12-inch

MCA 5-10 78-79
Member: Jim Drown.

BLENDELLS P&R '64

Singles: 7-inch

COLLECTABLES 3-4 81
COTILLION 4-8 68
ERA 3-5 73
RAMPART 8-10 64
REPRISE 4-8 64-65
Also see SONNY & CHER / Bill Medley / Lettermen / Blendells

BLENDERS P&R '63

Singles: 7-inch

CORTLAND 5-10 62
MAR-V-LUS ("Your Love Has Got Me Down") 100-200 66
(No selection number used.)
VISION (1000 "I Asked for Your Hand") 40-50 57
WITCH (114 "Daughter") 10-20 62
WITCH (117 "Boys Think") 10-20 63
WITCH (122 "One Time") 10-20 63

BLEYER, Archie P&R '54

(With Maria Alba)

Singles: 78 rpm

ARC 8-15 35
CADENCE 5-10 54-57
VOCALION 8-15 34

Singles: 7-inch

CADENCE 8-15 54-57
SCHOLASTIC (2701 "Bedtime for Francis") 3-5 74
(Compact 33 single.)

LPs: 10/12-inch

CADENCE (3044 "Moonlight Serenade") 15-25 62
(Monaural.)
CADENCE (25044 "Moonlight Serenade") 20-30 62
(Stereo.)
Also see CHORDETTES
Also see GODFREY, Arthur, with Archie Bleyer
Also see HAYES, Bill

BLIND FAITH LP '69

Singles: 7-inch

RSO 3-6 77

LPs: 10/12-inch

ATCO (304A "Blind Faith") 20-30 69
(Front cover pictures a nude girl.)
ATCO (304B "Blind Faith") 10-12 69
(Front cover pictures the group.)
MFSL (186 "Blind Faith") 25-35 69
(Half-speed mastered.)
RSO 5-10 76
(Reissue. Pictures nude girl.)
Members: Eric Clapton; Ginger Baker; Steve Winwood; Rick Grech.
Also see BAKER, Ginger
Also see CLAPTON, Eric
Also see FAMILY
Also see WINWOOD, Steve

BLOCH, Ray, & Orchestra P&R '46

Singles: 78 rpm

CORAL 4-8 52-57
SIGNATURE 4-8 47

Singles: 7-inch

CORAL 5-12 53

Picture Sleeves

CORAL (9-1327 "From Here to Eternity") 300-500 53
(Pictures Frank Sinatra, Burt Lancaster, Montgomery Clift, Donna Reed, and Deborah Kerr.)

LPs: 10/12-inch

AMBASSADOR 8-12
CORAL 10-25 52-57
Also see SINATRA, Frank

BLODWYN PIG LP '69

Singles: 7-inch

A&M 3-6 69-70

LPs: 10/12-inch

A&M (3000 series) 5-10 82
A&M (4000 series) 10-15 69-70
Members: Blodwyn; Mick Abrahams; Peter Banks; Ron Berg; Clive Bunker; Jack Lancaster; Andy Pyle.
Also see ABRAHAMS, Mick, Band
Also see BANKS, Peter

BLONDIE LP '78

Singles: 12-inch

CHRYSALIS 5-10 78-84

Singles: 7-inch

CHRYSALIS 3-5 77-84
PRIVATE STOCK 6-10 76-77

Picture Sleeves

CHRYSALIS 3-8 79-82

LPs: 10/12-inch

CAPITOL (32748 "Remix Project") 10-15 90s
CHRYSALIS (Except 5001) 5-10 76-84
CHRYSALIS (5001 "Parallel Lines") 15-25 78
(Picture disc.)
MFSL (050 "Parallel Lines") 20-40 81
PRIVATE STOCK 15-20 75
Members: Deborah Harry; Clem Burke; Jimmy Destri; Chris Stein; Gary Valentine; Fred Smith; Nigel Harrison.
Also see HARRY, Debbie

BLOOD, SWEAT & TEARS LP '68

Singles: 7-inch

ABC 3-4 78
COLUMBIA 3-5 69-77

Picture Sleeves

COLUMBIA 3-5 70-72

LPs: 10/12-inch

ABC 5-10 77
COLUMBIA (Except 9619 & 49619) 10-15 69-76
COLUMBIA (9619 "Child Is Father to the Man") 20-30 68
COLUMBIA (49619 "Child Is Father to the Man") 25-35 68
(Half-speed mastered.)
LAX (1865 "Nuclear Blues") 5-10 80
(Black vinyl.)
LAX (1865 "Nuclear Blues") 10-12 80
(Colored vinyl. Promotional issue only.)
MFSL (251 "Blood, Sweat & Tears") 15-25
Members: David Clayton-Thomas; Al Kooper; Jerry Hyman; Fred Lipsius; Dick Halligan; Bobby Colomby; Lew Soloff; Chuck Winfield; Steve Katz; James Thomas Fielder; Dave Bargeron; Georg Wadenius; Lou Matini Jr.; Bobby Doyle; Jerry Fisher.
Also see CLAYTON-THOMAS, David
Also see FRANKLIN, Aretha / Union Gap / Blood, Sweat & Tears / Moby Grape
Also see KOOPER, Al
Also see STREISAND, Barbra

BLOODROCK P&R '71

Singles: 7-inch

CAPITOL 3-6 69-75

Promotional Singles

CAPITOL (3451 "Bloodrock Interview By Sol Smaizys") 4-8 72

LPs: 10/12-inch

CAPITOL 15-35 69-75
Members: Jim Rutledge; Eddie Grundy; Steve Hill; Lee Pickens; Nick Taylor; Warren Ham.

BLOODSTONE P&R/R&B/LP '73

Singles: 12-inch

MOTOWN 4-6 79
T-NECK 4-6 82-85

Singles: 7-inch

EPIC 3-4 82
LONDON 3-5 73-76
MOTOWN 3-4 79
T-NECK 3-4 82-85

Picture Sleeves

LONDON 3-5 74-76

LPs: 10/12-inch

LONDON 8-10 73-74
MOTOWN 5-10 78
T-NECK 5-10 82
Members: Harry Williams; Charles McCormick; Charles Love; Steve Ferrone; Roger Lee Durham; Willis Draffen.

BLOOM, Bobby P&R/LP '70

Singles: 7-inch

EARTH 4-8 69

KAMA SUTRA....................5-10 67
L&R....................4-8 70
MGM....................5-10 70-73
ROULETTE....................3-5 70
WHITE WHALE....................4-8 69

LPs: 10/12-inch

BUDDAH....................8-12 71
L&R....................10-15 70

Also see ARCHIES
Also see MUSIC EXPLOSION

BLOOMFIELD, Mike — LP '69

LPs: 10/12-inch

CLOUDS....................5-10 78
COLUMBIA (9000 series)....................12-15 69
COLUMBIA (37000 series)....................6-10 81-83
GUITAR PLAYER....................8-10 77
HARMONY....................8-10 71
TAKOMA....................5-10 77-81
W.B. (7674 "Steelyard Blues")....................4-8 73
WATERHOUSE....................5-10 81

Also see DYLAN, Bob
Also see KGB

BLOOMFIELD, Mike, Dr. John & John Paul Hammond — LP '73

LPs: 10/12-inch

COLUMBIA....................8-10 73

Also see DR. JOHN
Also see HAMMOND, John

BLOOMFIELD, Mike, & Nick Graventes

LPs: 10/12-inch

COLUMBIA....................10-12 69

Also see ELECTRIC FLAG

BLOOMFIELD, Mike, & Al Kooper — LP '69

LPs: 10/12-inch

COLUMBIA....................12-20 68
MFSL (178 "Super Session")....................15-25 85

Also see KOOPER, Al
Also see MOBY GRAPE

BLOOMFIELD, Mike, Al Kooper & Steve Stills — LP '68

Singles: 7-inch

COLUMBIA....................3-6 68

LPs: 10/12-inch

COLUMBIA....................10-15 68
MFSL....................15-20 85

Also see BLOOMFIELD, Mike
Also see STILLS, Stephen

BLOSSOMS — P&R '61

Singles: 7-inch

BELL....................4-8 69-70
CAPITOL....................10-15 57-58
CHALLENGE (9138 "Big Talking Jim")....................10-15 62
CHALLENGE (59122 "Write Me a Letter")....................20-30 62
CLASSIC ARTISTS....................3-5 89
EEOC (8172 "Things Are Changing")....................75-100 65
(Equal Employment Opportunity Center promotional issue.)
EPIC....................3-5 77
LION....................3-5 72
MGM....................8-12 68
ODE....................5-10 67-69
OKEH....................5-10 62-63
REPRISE....................4-8 65-67

Picture Sleeves

EEOC (8172 "Things Are Changing")....................75-100 65
(Promotional issue only.)

LPs: 10/12-inch

LION....................8-12 72

Members: Darlene "Love" Wright; Gloria Jones; Fanita James-Barrett; Annette Williams; Nanette Williams-Jackson; Grazia Nitzsche; Jean King.
Also see BOB B. SOXX & BLUE JEANS
Also see EDDY, Duane
Also see EVERETT, Betty
Also see FABARES, Shelley
Also see LOVE, Darlene
Also see PRESLEY, Elvis
Also see WILSON, Brian

BLOSSOMS / Coeds

Singles: 7-inch

CHALLENGE (9109 "Son-in-Law")....................10-15 61

Also see BLOSSOMS

BLOW, Kurtis — P&R/R&B/LP '80

Singles: 12-inch

MERCURY....................4-6 80-86

Singles: 7-inch

MERCURY....................3-4 80-86
POLYDOR....................3-4 85

LPs: 10/12-inch

MERCURY....................5-10 80-86

Also see KING DREAM CHORUS & Holiday Crew
Also see KRUSH GROVE ALL STARS

BLOW MONKEYS — P&R/LP '86

Singles: 12-inch

RCA....................4-6 85-87

Singles: 7-inch

RCA....................3-4 85-87

LPs: 10/12-inch

RCA....................5-10 85-87

Members: Robert Howard; Tony Kiley; Neville Henry; Mick Anker.

BLOWFLY — LP '80

Singles: 7-inch

WEIRD WORLD....................3-4 80

LPs: 10/12-inch

WEIRD WORLD....................8-10 80

BLU, Peggi — R&B '87

Singles: 7-inch

CAPITOL....................3-4 87

BLU, Peggi, & Bert Robinson — R&B '87

Singles: 7-inch

CAPITOL....................3-4 87

Also see BLU, Peggi
Also see ROBINSON, Bert

BLUE — P&R '77

Singles: 7-inch

IRIS....................3-4
MCA/PIG (Colored vinyl)....................4-6 77
(Promotional issue only.)
RSO....................3-5 73-75
ROCKET....................3-5 77

LPs: 10/12-inch

RSO....................8-10 73
ROCKET....................5-10 77

Members: Tim Donald; Ian MacMillan; Jimmy McCullough; Hugh Nicholson.
Also see MARMALADE

BLUE, David — P&R '73

(David Cohen)

Singles: 7-inch

ASYLUM....................3-5 73
REPRISE....................3-6 69

LPs: 10/12-inch

ASYLUM....................8-10 73-76
ELEKTRA....................12-15 66
REPRISE....................12-15 68

Also see COUNTRY JOE & FISH

BLUE BARRON & HIS ORCH. — P&R '38

Singles: 78 rpm

BLUEBIRD....................4-6 38-41
MGM....................3-6 47-55

Singles: 7-inch

MGM....................4-6 50-55

EPs: 7-inch

MGM....................4-8 54-55

LPs: 10/12-inch

MGM....................10-20 54

BLUE BELLES — R&B '62

(Starlets)

Singles: 7-inch

NEWTOWN....................8-10 62
PEAK....................5-10 62

Picture Sleeves

PEAK....................15-25 62

Also see LABELLE, Patti

BLUE CHEER — P&R/LP '68

Singles: 7-inch

MERCURY....................3-5 76
PHILIPS....................8-12 68-70

Picture Sleeves

PHILIPS (40516 "Summertime Blues")....................10-15 68

LPs: 10/12-inch

MEGAFORCE....................5-10 85
PHILIPS (9001 "Vincebus Eruption")....................5-10 80
PHILIPS (200264 "Vincebus Eruption")....................40-60 68
(Monaural.)
PHILIPS (600264 "Vincebus Eruption")....................30-50 68
(Stereo.)
PHILIPS (600278 "Outside Inside")....................40-60 68
PHILIPS (600305 "New! Improved!")....................30-50 69
PHILIPS (600333 "Blue Cheer")....................30-50 70
PHILIPS (600347 "Original Human Being")....................30-50 70
PHILIPS (600350 "Oh Pleasant Hope")....................40-60 71

Members: Leigh Stephens; Paul Whaley; Dick Peterson; Randy Holden; Tony Rainer; Bruce Stephens; Ralph Kellogg; Gary Yoder.

BLUE DIAMONDS — P&R '60

Singles: 7-inch

LONDON....................5-10 62-63

LP: 10/12-inch

LONDON....................10-20 63

Members: Riem de Wolf; Rudy de Wolf.

BLUE HAZE — P&R '72

Singles: 7-inch

A&M....................3-5 72-74

BLUE JAYS — P&R '61

("Lead Vocal - Leon Peels")

Singles: 7-inch

CLASSIC ARTISTS....................3-5 89
COLLECTABLES....................3-4 81
ERA....................3-4 72
MILESTONE (2008 "Lover's Island")....................15-30 61
(Blue label. Opinions differ as to which came first—the dark blue, or light blue and white label.)
MILESTONE (2008 "Lover's Island")....................10-15 61
(Green label.)
MILESTONE (2009 "Tears Are Falling")....................25-35 61
MILESTONE (2010 "Let's Make Love")....................15-25 61
MILESTONE (2012 "The Right to Love")....................15-25 62
MILESTONE (2014 "Venus My Love")....................50-75 62

Member: Leon Peels.

BLUE JAYS / Little Caesar & Romans

LPs: 10/12-inch

MILESTONE (1001 "Blue Jays Meet Little Caesar & the Romans")....................50-100 62
(Black vinyl.)
MILESTONE (1001 "Blue Jays Meet Little Caesar & the Romans")....................150-200 62
(Colored vinyl.)

Also see BLUE JAYS
Also see LITTLE CAESAR & ROMANS

BLUE MAGIC — R&B '73

Singles: 12-inch

MIRAGE....................4-6 83

Singles: 7-inch

ATCO....................3-5 73-76
CAPITOL....................3-4 81
LIBERTY....................3-6 69
MIRAGE....................3-4 83
WMOT....................3-5 76

LPs: 10/12-inch

ATCO....................8-10 74-77
ATLANTIC....................5-10 83

CAPITOL 5-10 81
COLLECTABLES 6-8 86
MIRAGE 5-10 83
Members: Ted Mills; Margie Joseph; Vernon Sawyer; Wendell Sawyer; Richard Pratt; Keath Beaton.
Also see JOSEPH, Margie

BLUE MERCEDES — P&R/LP '88

Singles: 7-inch
MCA 3-4 88
Picture Sleeves
MCA 3-4 88
LPs: 10/12-inch
MCA 5-8 88
Members: David Titlow; Duncan Millar.

BLUE MINK — P&R '70

Singles: 7-inch
BELL 3-5 71-72
MCA 3-5 73-74
PHILIPS 3-6 69-70
Picture Sleeves
PHILIPS 4-8 70
LPs: 10/12-inch
MCA 8-10 73
PHILIPS 12-15 69-70
Members: Madeline Bell; Roger Cook; Barry Morgan; Herbie Flowers; Alan Parker; Ann Odell; Roger Coulan; Ray Cooper.
Also see BELL, Madeline

BLUE MURDER — LP '89

Singles: 7-inch
GEFFEN 3-4 89
LPs: 10/12-inch
GEFFEN 5-8 89
Member: Tony Franklin.
Also see FIRM

BLUE NILE — LP '90

LPs: 10/12-inch
A&M 5-8 90

BLUE NOTES — P&R '60

Singles: 78 rpm
JOSIE 35-75 56-57
Singles: 7-inch
COLLECTABLES 3-4 81
GAMUT (1000 "My Heart Cries for You") 15-25 61
JALYNNE 20-40 60
(Title and number not known.)
JOSIE (800 "If You Love Me") 100-200 56
JOSIE (814 "Letters") 75-125 57
JOSIE (823 "Retribution Blues") 75-125 57
LOST NITE 4-8
RED TOP (135 "My Hero") 20-40 63
3 SONS (103 "W-P-L-J") 50-100 62
UNI 5-10 69
VAL-UE (213 "My Hero") 50-100 60
VAL-UE (215 "O Holy Night") 50-100 60
LPs: 10/12-inch
COLLECTABLES 5-10 82
Members: Harold Melvin; Jesse Gillis Jr.; Roosevelt Brodie; Frank Peaker; Bernard Williams; John Atkins; Lawrence Brown.
Members: Harold Melvin; Jesse Gillis Jr.; Roosevelt Brodie; Frank Peaker; Bernard Williams; John Atkins; Lawrence Brown.
Also see BLUENOTES
Also see MELVIN, Harold, & Blue Notes

BLUE OYSTER CULT — LP '72

Singles: 12-inch
COLUMBIA 4-6 80
Singles: 7-inch
COLUMBIA 3-4 72-84
WHAT'S IT ALL ABOUT 8-12
(Promotional issue only.)
Picture Sleeves
COLUMBIA (02000 & 04000 series) 3-4 81-84
COLUMBIA (45000 series) 4-8 72
EPs: 7-inch
COLUMBIA (40 "Bootleg EP") 20-25 72
LPs: 10/12-inch
ABC RADIO ("A Night on the Road") 35-50 81
(Promotional issue only.)
COLUMBIA (Except 31000 thru 33000 series) 5-10 76-84
COLUMBIA (31000 thru 33000 series) 6-12 72-75
Members: Al Bouchard; Joe Bouchard; Eric Bloom; Alan Lanier; Donald "Buck Dharma" Roeser.

BLUE PRINT — D&D '83

Singles: 12-inch
FANTASY 4-6 83

BLUE RIDGE RANGERS (John Fogerty) — C&W/P&R '73

Singles: 7-inch
FANTASY 3-5 72-73
Picture Sleeves
FANTASY 4-8 72
LPs: 10/12-inch
FANTASY 10-12 73
Also see FOGERTY, John

BLUE STARS — P&R '55

Singles: 78 rpm
MERCURY 3-6 55-56
Singles: 7-inch
MERCURY 5-10 55-56
Member: Blossom Dearie.

BLUE SWEDE — P&R/LP '74

Singles: 7-inch
EMI AMERICA 3-5 73-75
Picture Sleeves
EMI AMERICA 3-5 73-74
LPs: 10/12-inch
EMI AMERICA 8-10 74-75
Members: Bjorn Skifs; Jan Guldback; Bosse Liljedahl; Michael Areklew; Ladislau Balaz; Tommy Berglund; Hinke Ekestubble.

BLUE ZONE U.K. — P&R '88

Singles: 7-inch
ARISTA 3-4 88
Picture Sleeves
ARISTA 3-4 88
Members: Lisa Stansfield; Andy Morris; Ian Devaney.

BLUENOTES — P&R '59

Singles: 7-inch
BROOKE (111 "I Don't Know What It Is") 10-20 59
BROOKE (116 "Forever on My Mind") 10-20 60
BROOKE (119 "Summer Love") 10-20 60
Picture Sleeves
BROOKE 25-45 60
Members: Tom Underwood; Joe Tanner; Pat Patterson; Ralph Harrington.
Also see BLUE NOTES
Also see FRANKLIN, Doug
Also see HAMILTON, George, IV

BLUENOTES / Five Echoes / Five Chances

LPs: 10/12-inch
CONSTELLATION (5 "Collectors Showcase, Groups Three") 20-25 64
Also see BLUENOTES

BLUES BROTHERS — P&R/LP '78

Singles: 7-inch
ATLANTIC 3-5 78-81
(Black vinyl.)
ATLANTIC 5-10
(Colored vinyl. Promotional issue only.)
Picture Sleeves
ATLANTIC 3-6 78-80
LPs: 10/12-inch
ATLANTIC 10-15 78-81
Members: Dan Aykroyd; John Belushi.
Also see BELUSHI, John

BLUES IMAGE — LP '69

Singles: 7-inch
ATCO 4-8 69-71
LPs: 10/12-inch
ATCO 10-20 69-70
Members: Mike Pinera; Joe Lala; Frank Konte; Malcolm Jones; Manuel Bertematti.
Also see PINERA, Mike

BLUES MAGOOS — P&R/LP '66

Singles: 7-inch
ABC 4-8 68-70
GANIM (1000 "Who Do You Love") 20-40 69
MERCURY (30000 series) 3-5 76
MERCURY (70000 series) 8-12 66-68
VERVE/FOLKWAYS (5006 "So I'm Wrong") 20-30 66
VERVE/FOLKWAYS (5044 "So I'm Wrong") 15-25 67
Picture Sleeves
MERCURY (72660 "Pipe Dream") 10-20 67
MERCURY (72692 "One By One") 10-20 67
LPs: 10/12-inch
ABC 8-10 69-70
MERCURY (21096 "Psychedelic Lollipop") 40-50 66
(Monaural.)
MERCURY (21104 "Electric Comic Book") 30-40 67
(Monaural. Add $5 to $10 if accompanied by comic book insert.)
MERCURY (61096 "Psychedelic Lollipop") 25-40 66
(Red label. Stereo.)
MERCURY (61096 "Psychedelic Lollipop") 8-10
(Chicago "skyline" label.)
MERCURY (61104 "Electric Comic Book") 30-45 67
(Stereo. Add $5 to $10 if accompanied by comic book insert.)
MERCURY (61167 "Basic Blues Magoos") 20-30 68
Members: Geoff Daking; Mike Esposito; Ron Gilbert; Ralph Scala; Emil Thielhelm.
Also see BALANCE

BLUES PROJECT — LP '66

Singles: 7-inch
CAPITOL 5-8 72
MCA 3-5 73
VERVE/FOLKWAYS 10-15 66-67
LPs: 10/12-inch
CAPITOL 10-15 72
ELEKTRA 5-10 80
MCA 8-10 73
MGM 8-12 70-74
VERVE/FOLKWAYS 15-25 66
VERVE/FORECAST 12-20 66-70
Members: Al Kooper; Roy Blumenfeld; David Cohen; Tommy Flanders; Richard Green; John Gregory; Don Gretmar; Danny Kalb; Steve Katz; Andy Kulbert; Bill Lussenden; Chicken Hirsch.
Also see KOOPER, Al
Also see SEATRAIN

BLUES TRAVELER — LP '91

LPs: 10/12-inch
A&M 5-8 91

BLUES WOMAN (Marion Abernathy) — R&B '46

Singles: 78 rpm
JUKE BOX 10-15 46

BO, Eddie — P&R/R&B '69

Singles: 78 rpm
ACE 10-20 56-57
APOLLO (Except 509) 10-20 55-56
APOLLO (509 "Dearest One") 30-60 57
Singles: 7-inch
ACE 10-20 56-59
APOLLO (Except 509) 15-25 55-56
APOLLO (509 "Dearest One") 30-60 57
AT LAST 8-12 63

BLUE JAY....4-8 64
BO-SOUND....3-5 71
CAPITOL....5-10 61
CHECKER....10-15 58
CHESS (Except 1600 series)....4-8 62
CHESS (1600 series)....10-15 58
CINDERELLA....4-8 63
RIC....5-10 59-62
RIP....10-20
SEVEN B....4-8 66-68
SCRAM....4-6 69
SWAN....5-10 62

LPs: 10/12-inch

ROUNDER....5-8
Also see BO, Little
Also see PARKER, Robert

BO, Eddie, & Inez Cheatham

Singles: 7-inch

SEVEN B....4-8 68
Also see BO, Eddie

BO, Little
(Eddie Bo)

Singles: 78 rpm

ACE (501 "Baby")....25-50 55

Singles: 7-inch

ACE (501 "Baby")....50-75 55
Also see BO, Eddie

BO DIDDLEY: see DIDDLEY, Bo

BO PETE
(Harry Nilsson)

Singles: 7-inch

CRUSADER (103 "Baa Baa Black Sheep")....20-30 64
TRY (501 "Groovy Little Suzy")....20-40 64
Also see NILSSON

BOB & EARL — P&R '62
(With René Hall Orchestra)

Singles: 7-inch

ABC....3-4 73
CHENE....5-10 64
COLLECTABLES....3-4 81
CRESTVIEW....4-8 69
ISLAND....3-5
LOMA....5-10 64
MARC....8-15 63-64
MIRWOOD....5-8 66
TEMPE (102 "Don't Ever Leave Me")....15-25 62
TEMPE (104 "Oh Baby Doll")....15-25 62
TIP (1013 "As We Dance")....8-12 64
UNI....4-8 70
WHITE WHALE....10-15 69

LPs: 10/12-inch

CRESTVIEW....15-20 69
TIP (9011 "Harlem Shuffle")....20-30 64
UPFRONT....10-15
Members: Earl Nelson; Bobby Relf.
Also see WHITE, Barry

BOB B. SOXX & BLUE JEANS — P&R/R&B '62

Singles: 7-inch

PHILLES (107 "Zip-a-Dee Doo-Dah")....10-15 62
PHILLES (110 "Why Do Lovers Break Each Other's Heart")....10-15 63
PHILLES (113 "Not Too Young to Get Married")....10-15 63

LPs: 10/12-inch

PHILLES (4002 "Zip-a-Dee Doo-Dah")....75-125 63
Members: Bobby Sheen; Darlene Love; Carolyn Willis; Fanita James-Barrett.
Also see BLOSSOMS
Also see HONEY CONE
Also see LOVE, Darlene
Also see RONETTES / Crystals / Darlene Love / Bob B. Soxx & Blue Jeans
Also see SHEEN, Bobby

BOBBETTES — P&R/R&B '57

Singles: 78 rpm

ATLANTIC....20-40 57

Singles: 7-inch

ATLANTIC....10-20 57-60
DIAMOND....5-10 62-65
END....5-10 61
GALLIANT....10-15 60
GONE....10-15 61
JUBILEE....5-10 62
KING....5-10 61-62
MAYHEW....3-5 72-74
RCA....10-20 66
TRIPLE-X....10-20 60
Members: Emma Pought; Jannie Pought; Heather Dixon; Laura Webb; Helen Gathers. Session: King Curtis.
Also see KING, Ben E.
Also see KING CURTIS

BOBBY & MIDNITES — LP '81

Singles: 7-inch

ARISTA....3-4 81
COLUMBIA....3-4 84

LPs: 10/12-inch

ARISTA....5-10 81
COLUMBIA....5-10 84
Members: Bob Weir; David Garland.
Also see WEIR, Bob

BOBBY LEE: see LEE, Bobby

BOBO, Willie — LP '66
(With the Bo-Gents)

Singles: 7-inch

BLUE NOTE....3-5 77
CAPITOL....3-5 76
JUPITER JAZZ....3-5 75
TICO....8-12 59
VERVE....4-8 65-69

LPs: 10/12-inch

BLUE NOTE....5-10 77
COLUMBIA....8-10 78-79
MGM....5-10
ROULETTE....15-25 63-64
SUSSEX....8-10
TICO....10-20
TRIP....5-10
VERVE....10-20 65-69
Also see DIXIE HUMMINGBIRDS
Also see HANCOCK, Herbie, & Willie Bobo

BOCEPHUS
(Hank Williams Jr.)

Singles: 7-inch

VERVE (10540 "Meter Reader Maid")....20-30 67
VERVE (10572 "Splish Splash")....20-30 67
(May have been issued only as a promo.)
Also see WILLIAMS, Hank, Jr.

BoDEANS — LP '86

Singles: 7-inch

SLASH....3-4 86-89

LPs: 10/12-inch

SLASH....5-10 86-89
SLASH/REPRISE....5-8 91
Members: Sammy Llanas; Kurt Neumann; Guy Hoffman; Bob Griffin.

BOFILL, Angela — R&B/LP '79

Singles: 12-inch

ARISTA....4-6 81-85

Singles: 7-inch

ARISTA....3-4 81-85
GRP....3-5 79

LPs: 10/12-inch

ARISTA....5-10 81-85
GRP....8-10 78-79

BOHANNON — R&B '74
(Hamilton Bohannon)

Singles: 12-inch

COMPLEAT....4-6 84-85
MERCURY....5-8 77-80
MCA....4-6 84
PHASE II....4-6 80-83

Singles: 7-inch

DAKAR....3-5 73-75
MERCURY....3-4 77-80
PHASE 2....3-4 80-83

LPs: 10/12-inch

DAKAR....10-12 73-75
MERCURY....8-10 77-80
PHASE 2....5-10 80-83

BOHANNON, Hamilton, & Dr. Perri Johnson — R&B '81

Singles: 12-inch

PHASE 2....4-6 81

Singles: 7-inch

PHASE 2....3-4 81
Also see BOHANNON

BOHN, Rudi, & His Band — LP '61

LPs: 10/12-inch

LONDON PHASE 4....5-12 61

BOILING POINT — R&B '78

Singles: 7-inch

BULLET....3-5 78

BOLIN, Tommy — LP '75

Singles: 7-inch

NEMPEROR....3-5 76

LPs: 10/12-inch

COLUMBIA....8-10 76
NEMPEROR (400 series)....10-12 75
NEMPEROR (37000 series)....5-10 81
Also see DEEP PURPLE
Also see JAMES GANG
Also see ZEPHYR

BOLTON, Michael — P&R/LP '83
(Michael Boloton)

Singles: 12-inch

COLUMBIA....4-8 85
(Promotional issue only.)

Singles: 7-inch

COLUMBIA....3-4 83-91
RCA....3-5 75-76

Picture Sleeves

COLUMBIA....3-4 88

LPs: 10/12-inch

COLUMBIA....5-10 83-91
RCA....8-10 75-76
Also see BLACKJACK

BOMBERS — R&B '79

Singles: 7-inch

WEST END....3-5 79

LPs: 10/12-inch

WEST END....8-12 79

BON JOVI, Jon — P&R/LP '84
(Bon Jovi)

Singles: 7-inch

MERCURY....3-4 84-90

Picture Sleeves

MERCURY....3-4 84-89

LPs: 10/12-inch

MERCURY....5-10 84-90
POLYGRAM (830 822 "Slippery When Wet")....15-20 87
(Picture disc.)
POLYGRAM (422-863 499 "New Jersey")....15-20 88
(Picture disc.)
Members: Jon Bon Jovi; Richie Sambora; David Bryan; Alec John Such; Tico Torres.
Members: Jon Bon Jovi; Richie Sambora; David Bryan; Alec John Such; Tico Torres.

BON ROCK — D&D '84

Singles: 12-inch

EARTHTONE....4-6 84

LPs: 10/12-inch

EARTHTONE....5-10 84
Member: Keith Rogers.

BOND, Angelo — R&B/LP '75

Singles: 7-inch

ABC....3-5 75-76

LPs: 10/12-inch

ABC....8-10 75-77

BOND, Bobby — C&W '72

Singles: 7-inch

DANCELAND....5-10 61
HICKORY....3-5 72

MGM....3-5 68
PARROT....4-8 66
WAND....4-8 65
W.B....3-5 69

BOND, Johnny C&W '47
(With the Red River Valley Boys)
Singles: 78 rpm
COLUMBIA (Except 21521)....5-15 45-56
(Columbia 20545 through 20787 were also issued on 7-inch 33 singles, any of which may be in the $15 to $25 range.)
COLUMBIA (21521 "The Little Rock Roll")....8-12 56
Singles: 7-inch
COLUMBIA (Except 21521)....10-20 51-56
COLUMBIA (21521 "The Little Rock Roll")....30-45 56
CONQUEROR....10-25
DITTO....5-10 59
GILLETTE....3-4
KING....3-4
LAMB & LION....3-5 74
LONDON....3-5
MGM....3-5 73
OKEH....8-15 41-45
REPUBLIC (2000 series)....5-10 60
SMASH....4-6 62
STARDAY (618 thru 951)....4-8 63-72
STARDAY (7021 thru 9292)....3-4 72-74
20TH FOX....4-8 60
EPs: 7-inch
COLUMBIA....10-20 58
REPUBLIC....10-20 60
STARDAY....10-15 63
LPs: 10/12-inch
CMH....5-10 77
CAPITOL....8-12 69
CATTLE....5-10
DANNY....5-10
HARMONY....10-20 64-65
LAMB & LION....5-10 74
NASHVILLE....5-10 71
SHASTA....10-15
STARDAY (147 thru 298)....20-30 61-64
STARDAY (333 "Ten Little Bottles")....15-20 65-66
STARDAY (354 "Famous Hot Rodders I Have Known")....25-30 65
STARDAY (368 thru 472)....10-20 66-71
STARDAY (900 series)....6-10 74
Also see HANK & FRANK
Also see TRAVIS, Merle, & Johnny Bond

BOND, Johnny, & Lefty Frizzell
Singles: 78 rpm
COLUMBIA....5-10 56-57
Singles: 7-inch
COLUMBIA....10-15 56-57
Also see BOND, Johnny
Also see FRIZZELL, Lefty

BONDS, Gary "U.S." P&R/R&B '60
(U.S. Bonds)
Singles: 12-inch
EMI (9666 "Gary U.S. Bonds")....25-30 81
(Promotional issue only.)
Singles: 7-inch
ABC....3-4 73
ATCO....3-6 69
BLUFF CITY....3-5 74
BOTANIC....4-6 68
COLLECTABLES....3-4 81
EMI AMERICA....3-4 81-82
LEGRAND (1003 thru 1012)....10-15 60-61
(Purple label.)
LEGRAND (1003 thru 1012)....5-10 62-63
(Multi-color label.)
LEGRAND (1015 thru 1020)....8-12 62
LEGRAND (1022 thru 1041)....10-20 62-66
LEGRAND (1043 thru 1046)....10-15 66-67
MCA....3-4 84
PRODIGAL....3-5 75
SUE....3-6 70
Picture Sleeves
EMI AMERICA....4-8 81-82
LEGRAND (1008 "Quarter to Three")....10-15 61
LEGRAND (1009 "School Is Out")....10-15 61
LPs: 10/12-inch
EMI AMERICA....5-10 81-82
LEGRAND (1000 series)....5-10 79-86
LEGRAND (3001 "Dance 'Till Quarter to Three")....40-60 61
LEGRAND (3002 "Twist Up Calypso")....40-60 62
LEGRAND (3003 "Greatest Hits")....40-60 62
MCA....5-10 84
PHOENIX....5-10 84
RHINO....5-10 84
Session: Bruce Springsteen.
Also see CHECKER, Chubby / Gary U.S. Bonds
Also see GREENWICH, Ellie
Also see JACKSON, Chuck
Also see KING, Ben E.
Also see SPRINGSTEEN, Bruce

BONE SYMPHONY D&D '83
Singles: 12-inch
CAPITOL....4-6 83
Singles: 7-inch
CAPITOL....3-4 83
LPs: 10/12-inch
CAPITOL....5-10 83

BONES P&R '72
Singles: 7-inch
MCA....3-5 73
SIGNPOST....4-6 72
LPs: 10/12-inch
MCA....8-10 73
SIGNPOST....10-12 72
Members: Dan Faragher; Jimmy Faragher.
Also see FARAGHER BROTHERS

BONES, Elbow: see ELBOW BONES

BONES, Mr. Goon, & Mr. Ford: see MR. GOON BONES & MR. FORD

BONEY M P&R '77
Singles: 12-inch
CARRERE....4-6 85
SIRE....4-6 79
Singles: 7-inch
ATCO....3-5 76-77
ATLANTIC....3-5 77
SIRE....3-4 78-79
Picture Sleeves
SIRE....3-4 79
LPs: 10/12-inch
ATCO....10-12 76
ATLANTIC....8-10 77
SIRE....5-10 77-79
Members: Marcia Barrett; Bobby Farrell; Liz Mitchell; Maizie Williams.

BONHAM P&R/LP '89
Singles: 7-inch
WTG....3-4 89
LPs: 10/12-inch
WTG....5-8 89
Members: Daniel MacMaster; Jason Bonham; Ian Hatton; John Smithson.

BONNIE & TREASURES P&R '65
(Featuring Charlott O'Hara)
Singles: 7-inch
PHI DAN (5505 "Home of the Brave")....20-30 65
Also see MID AMERICANS / Bonnie & Treasures

BONNIE LOU C&W '53
(Bonnie Lou Kath)
Singles: 78 rpm
KING....4-8 53-55
Singles: 7-inch
FRATERNITY....5-10 58
KING....5-10 53-55

BONNIE SISTERS P&R '56
(With Mickey "Guitar" Baker Orch; with Randy Carlos Cha Cha Rhythms)
Singles: 78 rpm
RAINBOW....10-15 56
Singles: 7-inch
RAINBOW....15-20 56
Members: Jean Bonnie; Pat Bonnie; Sylvia Bonnie. Session: Mickey Baker.
Also see BAKER, Mickey

BONO, Sonny: see SONNY

BONOFF, Karla LP '77
Singles: 7-inch
COLUMBIA....3-4 77-84
Picture Sleeves
COLUMBIA....3-4 77-84
LPs: 10/12-inch
COLUMBIA....5-10 77-82

BONZO DOG BAND LP '72
(Bonzo Dog Doo-Dah Band)
Singles: 7-inch
IMPERIAL....3-6 69
LIBERTY....4-8 68
U.A.....3-5 71-72
LPs: 10/12-inch
IMPERIAL....15-20 68-70
LIBERTY....5-10 83
U.A.....10-15 71-74
Members: Vivian Stanshall; Neil Innes; Roger Ruskin Spear; Hughie Flint; Tony Kaye; Dave Richards; Andy Roberts.
Also see RUTLES

BONZO GOES TO WASHINGTON D&D '84
Singles: 12-inch
SLEEPING BAG....4-6 84

BOOGALOO R&B '56
(With the Gallant Crew; Kent Harris)
Singles: 78 rpm
CREST....10-20 56
Singles: 7-inch
CREST (1030 "Cops & Robbers")....15-25 56
(Black vinyl.)
CREST (1030 "Cops & Robbers")....35-55 56
(Colored vinyl.)

BOOGIE BOYS R&B/D&D/LP '85
Singles: 12-inch
CAPITOL....4-6 84-88
Singles: 7-inch
CAPITOL....3-4 84-88
Picture Sleeves
CAPITOL....3-4 86
LPs: 10/12-inch
CAPITOL....5-10 85-88
Member: William Stroman.

BOOGIE DOWN PRODUCTIONS LP '88
LPs: 10/12-inch
JIVE....5-8 88-91

BOOGIE MAN
(John Lee Hooker)
Singles: 78 rpm
ACORN (308 "Morning Blues")....30-50 50
Also see HOOKER, John Lee

BOOGIE MAN ORCHESTRA R&B '75
Singles: 7-inch
BOOGIE MAN....3-5 75

BOOK OF LOVE D&D '85
Singles: 12-inch
SIRE....4-6 84-85
Singles: 7-inch
SIRE....3-4 84-90
Picture Sleeves
SIRE....3-4 88
LPs: 10/12-inch
SIRE....5-10 86-91

BOOKER, Chuckii P&R/LP '89
Singles: 7-inch
ATLANTIC....3-4 89
LPs: 10/12-inch
ATLANTIC....5-8 89

BOOKER, James *P&R/R&B '60*

Singles: 7-inch

PEACOCK....6-12 60-64

LPs: 10/12-inch

ROUNDER....5-10 84

Also see LITTLE BOOKER

BOOKER, John Lee

(John L. Booker; John Lee Hooker)

Singles: 78 rpm

CHANCE....25-75 51
CHESS....20-40 51
DELUXE....15-25 53
GONE (60 "Mad Man Blues")....100-200 51
MODERN....10-20 51
ROCKIN'....15-25 53

Singles: 7-inch

CHANCE (1108 "Miss Lorraine")...300-500 51
CHANCE (1110 "Graveyard Blues")....300-500 51
CHANCE (1122 "609 Boogie")....300-500 51
DELUXE (6004 "Blue Monday")....75-100 53
DELUXE (6032 "Pouring Down Rain")....50-100 53
DELUXE (6004 "Blue Monday")....50-100 53
DELUXE (6046 "My Baby Don't Love Me")....50-100 53
MODERN (852 "Ground Hog Blues")....50-75 51
ROCKIN' (525 "Stuttering Blues")...75-100 53

Also see HOOKER, John Lee

BOOKER T. & PRISCILLA *LP '71*

Singles: 7-inch

A&M....3-5 71-73

LPs: 10/12-inch

A&M....8-10 71-73

Members: Booker T. Jones; Priscilla Coolidge-Jones.

Also see COOLIDGE-JONES, Priscilla

BOOKER T. & MGs *P&R/R&B/LP '62*

Singles: 12-inch

A&M....4-8 82-84

Singles: 7-inch

A&M....3-4 81-82
ASYLUM....3-5 77
EPIC....3-5 75
STAX (Except 100 series)....4-8 67-71
STAX (100 series)....5-10 62-66
VOLT (102 "Green Onions")....20-30 62

LPs: 10/12-inch

A&M....8-10 72-81
ASYLUM....5-10 77
ATLANTIC....10-12 68
ATLANTIC/ATCO (133 "Excerpts from *In the Christmas Spirit*)....15-20 66
(Promotional issue only. One side is excerpts from *Soul Christmas*, a various artists LP.)
EPIC....8-10 74
PICKWICK....5-10
STAX (700 series, except 701 & 713)....20-30 65-68
STAX (701 "Green Onions")....25-40 62
STAX (713 "In the Spirit of Chirstmas")....25-35 66
(Hands and keyboard drawing on front cover. Back has 1966 copyright date.)
STAX (713 "In the Spirit of Christmas")....15-25 67
(Christmas ornament cover. Back has 1967 copyright date.)
STAX (2000 series)....10-20 68-71
STAX (8000 series)....5-10 81-84

Members: Booker T. Jones; Steve Cropper; Al Jackson Jr.; Louis Steinberg; Willie Hall.

Also see BOOKER T. & PRISCILLA
Also see CROPPER, Steve
Also see MGs
Also see MAR-KEYS / Booker T. & MGs
Also see RANDLE, Del
Also see REDDING, Otis
Also see SANTANA
Also see SIMON, PAUL

BOOM, Taka *P&R/R&B/LP '79*

Singles: 7-inch

ARIOLA....3-4 79
MIRAGE....3-4 85

LPs: 10/12-inch

ARIOLA....5-10 79

Also see UNDISPUTED TRUTH

BOOMTOWN RATS *LP '79*

Singles: 7-inch

COLUMBIA....3-4 79-80

LPs: 10/12-inch

COLUMBIA....5-10 79-85
MERCURY....8-12 77

Members: Bob Geldof; Pete Briquette; Gerry Cott; Simon Crowe; Johnny Fingers; Garry Roberts.

Also see BAND AID
Also see GELDOF, Bob

BOONE, Daniel *P&R/LP '72*

Singles: 7-inch

EPIC....3-5 72
MERCURY....3-5 72-74
PYE....3-4 75

LPs: 10/12-inch

MERCURY....10-12 72

BOONE, Debby *P&R/C&W/LP '77*

Singles: 7-inch

LAMB & LION....3-4 80-84
W.B./CURB....3-4 77-81

Picture Sleeves

W.B./CURB....3-4 78

LPs: 10/12-inch

LAMB & LION....5-10 80-84
W.B./CURB....5-10 77-80

Also see BOONE, Pat, & Boone Girls
Also see BOONE GIRLS

BOONE, Pat *P&R/R&B '55*

Singles: 78 rpm

DOT....10-25 55-58
REPUBLIC....5-10 54

Singles: 7-inch

ABC....3-4 74-75
BUENA VISTA....3-5 73
CAPITOL....3-5 70
CHEVROLET/RCA (4988 "June Is Bustin' Out All Over")....10-15 58
(Promotional issue for Chevrolet dealers. Narration by Bob Lund.)
DOT (200 series)....8-12 59-60
(Stereo.)
DOT (15000 series)....5-10 55-57
(Maroon label.)
DOT (15000 & 16000 series, except 16658)....4-8 57-66
(Black label.)
DOT (16658 "Beach Girl")....5-10 64
(With Bruce Johnston and Terry Melcher.)
DOT (17000 series)....3-6 66-75
HITSVILLE....3-5 76-77
LION....3-4 72
MC....3-4 77
MCA....3-4 84
MGM....3-5 71-73
MELODYLAND....3-5 74-76
ORCHID....3-4 89
REPUBLIC....10-15 54
SRG....3-4 88
TETRAGRAMMATON....3-5 69
W.B.....3-4 80-81

Picture Sleeves

DOT....8-15 57-62

EPs: 7-inch

DOT....8-12 57-60

LPs: 10/12-inch

ABC....5-10 74
BIBLE VOICE....5-10 70
CANDLELITE....6-10
(Mail-order offer.)
DOT (3000 series)....20-35 55-56
(Maroon label.)
DOT (3000 series, except 3501)....10-20 57-67
(Black label. Monaural series.)
DOT (3501 "Pat Boone Sings Guess Who")....25-35 63
DOT (9000 "April Love")....30-40 57
(Soundtrack.)
DOT (25000 series, except 25270 & 25501)....10-20 58-68
(Stereo series.)
DOT (25270 "Moonglow")....10-20 60
(Black vinyl.)
DOT (25270 "Moonglow")....30-50 60
(Colored vinyl.)
DOT (25501 "Pat Boone Sings Guess Who")....25-40 63
FAMOUS TWINSET....5-8 74
HAMILTON....10-12 65
HITSVILLE....8-10 76
LAMB & LION....5-10 73-81
MC....5-10 77
MCA....5-10 82
MGM....5-10 73
PARAMOUNT....5-10 74
PICKWICK....5-10 79
SUPREME....6-10 70
TETRAGRAMMATON....10-12 69
WORD....5-10 75-84

Also see BRUCE & TERRY
Also see FONTANE SISTERS
Also see HUSKY, Ferlin / Pat Boone
Also see JENKINS, Gordon, & His Orchestra
Also see WARD, Robin

BOONE, Pat & Shirley

(Pat Boone Family)

Singles: 7-inch

DOT....4-6 62-64
MGM....3-5 72
MELODYLAND....3-5 75
MOTOWN....3-5 74
W.B.....3-4 79

EPs: 7-inch

DOT....5-10 59

LPs: 10/12-inch

DOT....10-20 62
LION....5-10 72
WORD....5-10 71

BOONE, Pat, & Boone Girls

Singles: 7-inch

LION....3-4 72

Also see BOONE, Pat & Shirley
Also see BOONE GIRLS

BOONE FAMILY: see BOONE, Pat & Shirley

BOONE GIRLS

(Boones)

Singles: 7-inch

LAMB & LION....3-4 77
LION....3-4 72
MGM....3-5 71-73
MOTOWN....3-5 75
W.B.....3-4 77

LPs: 10/12-inch

LAMB & LION....5-10 77-83

Also see BOONE, Debbie
Also see BOONE, Pat, & Boone Girls

BOONE'S JUMPIN' JACKS *R&B '43*

Singles: 78 rpm

DECCA (8644 "Please Be Careful")....25-50 43

Members: Chester Boone; George Johnson; Chauncey Graham; Vernon King; Lloyd Phillips; Buster Smith.

BOOTEE, Duke *R&B '82*

Singles: 7-inch

MERCURY....3-4 84

Also see MELLE MEL & Duke Bootee

BOOTSY'S RUBBER BAND

(William "Bootsy" Collins; Bootsy) *R&B/LP '76*

Singles: 12-inch

W.B.....5-10 79-82

Singles: 7-inch

W.B.....3-4 75-82

Picture Sleeves
W.B. 3-4 75-82
LPs: 10/12-inch
W.B. 5-15 76-82
Members: William "Bootsy" Collins; Phelp Collins; Frankie Waddy; Gary Cooper; Fred Wesley; Rick Gardner; Robert Johnson; Maceo Parker; Gary Shider; Mike Hampton; Bennie Worrell.
Also see PARLIAMENT
Also see SWEAT BAND
Also see ZAPP

BOOTY PEOPLE R&B '76
Singles: 7-inch
CALLA 3-5 76
LPs: 10/12-inch
ABC 5-10 77

BOO-YAA T.R.I.B.E. LP '90
LPs: 10/12-inch
4TH & BROADWAY 5-8 90

BOOZE, Bea R&B '42
(Muriel Nichols)
Singles: 78 rpm
APOLLO 15-25 50
DECCA 20-35 42-44

BOPPERS R&B '79
Singles: 7-inch
FANTASY 3-4 78

BOSTIC, Earl R&B '48
Singles: 78 rpm
GOTHAM 5-15 46-51
KING 5-15 47-58
MAJESTIC 5-10 46
Singles: 7-inch
GOTHAM (7154 "845 Stomp") 15-25 51
KING (500 series) 3-5 77
KING (4000 series, except 4491) 10-15 50-57
(Black vinyl.)
KING (4491 "I Got Loaded") 25-35 52
KING (4000 series) 20-30 52-56
(Colored vinyl.)
KING (5000 series) 5-10 57-65
KING (6000 series) 4-8 65-69
KING (15000 series) 3-5 72
20TH FOX (5017 "Hot Sauce! Boss") 10-20
EPs: 7-inch
KING 10-25 52-62
LPs: 10/12-inch
KING (64 "Earl Bostic & His Alto Sax") 50-100 51
(Black vinyl. 10-inch LP.)
KING (64 "Earl Bostic & His Alto Sax") 100-200 51
(Colored vinyl. 10-inch LP.)
KING (72 "Earl Bostic & His Alto Sax") 50-100 52
(10-inch LP.)
KING (76 "Earl Bostic & His Alto Sax") 50-100 52
(10-inch LP.)
KING (77 "Earl Bostic & His Alto Sax") 50-100 52
(10-inch LP.)
KING (78 "Earl Bostic & His Alto Sax") 50-100 52
(10-inch LP.)
KING (79 "Earl Bostic & His Alto Sax") 50-100 52
(10-inch LP.)
KING (95 "Earl Bostic Plays Old Standards") 50-100 54
(10-inch LP.)
KING (103 "Earl Bostic & His Alto Sax") 50-100 54
(10-inch LP.)
KING (119 "Earl Bostic & His Alto Sax") 50-100 54
(10-inch LP.)
KING (500 series) 20-50 55-58
KING (600 thru 1000 series) 8-18 59-70
KING (5000 series) 10-15 77
Also see HAMPTON, Lionel
Also see PAGE, Hot Lips

BOSTIC, Earl, & Bill Doggett
Singles: 78 rpm
KING 6-12 56
Singles: 7-inch
KING 10-15 56
Also see BOSTIC, Earl

BOSTIC, Earl / Jimmie Lunceford
LP: 10/12-inch
ALLEGRO 8-12
Also see DOGGETT, Bill

BOSTIC, Sam R&B '85
Singles: 7-inch
ATLANTIC 3-4 85

BOSTON P&R/LP '76
Singles: 12-inch
EPIC (491 "Don't Look Back") 5-8 78
(Promotional issue only.)
Singles: 7-inch
EPIC 3-5 76-79
MCA 3-4 85-87
Picture Sleeves
MCA 3-4 85-87
LPs: 10/12-inch
EPIC (E99-34188 "Boston") 15-25 78
(Picture disc. Without cover.)
EPIC (E99-34188 "Boston") 30-40 78
(Picture disc. With cover.)
EPIC (HE-34188 "Boston") 12-15 80
(Half-speed mastered.)
EPIC (34188 "Boston") 15-25 76
(With "JE" or "PE" prefix.)
EPIC (35000 series, except 35050) .. 10-12 78
EPIC (35050 "Don't Look Back") 10-20 78
(Promotional black vinyl issue.)
EPIC (35050 "Don't Look Back") 50-60 80
(Picture disc.)
EPIC (35050 "Don't Look Back") 65-75 80
(Promotional picture disc.)
EPIC (HE-45000 series) 12-15 81
(Half-speed mastered.)
MCA 5-10 85-87
MFSL (249 "Boston") 15-25
Members: Brad Delp; Tom Scholz; Barry Goudreau; Sib Hashian; Fran Sheehan.
Also see GOUDREAU, Barry
Also see ORION the HUNTER

BOSTON POPS ORCHESTRA P&R '38
(Conducted by Arthur Fiedler)
Singles: 78 rpm
RCA 3-5 49-57
VICTOR 3-6 38
Singles: 7-inch
POLYDOR 3-4 70
RCA 3-8 50-65
RCA RED SEAL (Colored vinyl) 5-10 50s
Picture Sleeves
RCA (8378 "I Want to Hold Your Hand") 10-15 64
EPs: 7-inch
RCA 4-8 50-61
RCA RED SEAL (Colored vinyl) 8-12 50s
LPs: 10/12-inch
CAMDEN 4-8
DEUTSCHE GRAMMOPHON 4-8 78
FLEETWOOD 4-8 72
MIDSONG INT'L 4-8 79
PICKWICK/CAMDEN 4-8
POLYDOR 5-10 71-72
RCA 5-20 50-69
RCA/READER'S DIGEST (48 "Boston Pops Orchestra") 25-50 67
(Boxed 10-disc set.)
Also see ATKINS, Chet, & Boston Pops
Also see ELLINGTON, Duke, & Boston Pops
Also see HIRT, Al, & Boston Pops
Also see NERO, Peter
Also see SHERMAN, Allan

BOSTON POPS ORCH. LP '80
(Conducted by John Williams)
LPs: 10/12-inch
PHILIPS 5-10 80-86
Also see WILLIAMS, John

BOSWELL, Connee P&R '32
Singles: 78 rpm
BRUNSWICK 5-10 32-44
DECCA 5-10 35-56
Singles: 7-inch
CHARLES 4-8 62
DECCA 5-10 50-56
EPs: 7-inch
DECCA 5-15 56
RCA 5-10 57
LPs: 10/12-inch
DECCA 15-25 56
RCA 10-20 57
Also see BOSWELL SISTERS
Also see CROSBY, Bing, & Connee Boswell

BOSWELL SISTERS P&R '31
Singles: 78 rpm
BRUNSWICK 5-15 31-35
DECCA 5-10 35-37
Members: Connie Boswell; Martha Boswell; Vet Boswell.
Also see BOSWELL, Connie

BOTTOM & COMPANY R&B '74
Singles: 7-inch
MOTOWN 3-5 74-75
LPs: 10/12-inch
GORDY 8-10 76

BOTTOM LINE R&B '76
Singles: 7-inch
GREEDY 3-5 76
LPs: 10/12-inch
GREEDY 8-10 76

BOURGEOIS - TAGG P&R/LP '86
Singles: 7-inch
ISLAND 3-4 86-87
LPs: 10/12-inch
ISLAND 5-10 86-87
Members: Brent Bourgeois; Larry Tagg.

BOW WOW WOW LP '81
Singles: 12-inch
RCA 4-6 83
Singles: 7-inch
RCA 3-4 81-84
Picture Sleeves
RCA 3-4 82
LPs: 10/12-inch
HARVEST 5-10 82
RCA 5-10 81-84
Promotional LPs
RCA ("Special Radio Series") 10-15 81
Members: Annabella Lu Win; Matt Ashman; Dave Barbarossa; Leroy Gorman.
Also see ADAM & ANTS

BOWEN, Jimmy P&R/R&B '57
Singles: 78 rpm
ROULETTE 25-50 57
Singles: 7-inch
CAPEHART 5-10 61-62
CREST 5-10 61
REPRISE 5-10 64-66
ROULETTE (Except 4002) 10-20 57-60
ROULETTE (4002 "Party Doll") 30-40 57
(Credited to "Jimmy Bowen with the Rhythm Orchids" though actually by Buddy Knox.)
Picture Sleeves
CAPEHART (5005 "Teenage Dreamworld") 30-40 61
EPs: 7-inch
ROULETTE (302 "Jimmy Bowen") 50-75 57
LPs: 10/12-inch
REPRISE (6210 "Sunday Morning with the Comics") 20-25 66
ROULETTE (25004 "Jimmy Bowen") 75-100 57
(Black label.)

ROULETTE (25004 "Jimmy Bowen")....................100-150 57
(White label. Promotional issue only.)
ROULETTE (25004 "Jimmy Bowen")........................5-10
(Reissue for the Outlet Book Co. and Publishers Central Bureau, and labeled as such.)
Members (Rhythm Orchids): Buddy Knox; Jimmy Bowen; Dave Alldred; Don Lanier.
Also see KNOX, Buddy / Jimmy Bowen

BOWIE, David P&R/LP '72

Singles: 12-inch

EMI AMERICA........................5-10 82-87
RCA........................10-15 79-80

Promotional 12-inch Singles

EMI AMERICA........................8-15 82-87
RCA........................15-25 79-80

Singles: 7-inch

BACKSTREET........................3-5 82
DERAM (85009 "Rubber Band").......20-40 67
EMI AMERICA........................3-5 83-87
(Black vinyl.)
EMI AMERICA (8231 "Blue Jean").......5-8 84
(Colored vinyl.)
LONDON (20079 "The Laughing Gnome")........................15-25 73
MCA/BACKSTREET ("Cat People")........................50-65 82
(Promotional only picture disc. No selection number used.)
MCA/BACKSTREET ("Cat People")........................75-90 82
(Promotional only picture disc. No selection number used. B-side says: "Filmex" promo.)
MERCURY (72949 "Space Oddity")........................30-50 69
MERCURY (73075 "Memory of a Free Festival")........................35-50 70
MERCURY (73173 "All the Madmen")........................40-60 71
RCA........................3-6 71-84
W.B. (5815 "Can't Help Thinking About Me")........................50-75 66

Picture Sleeves

BACKSTREET (1767 "Cat People").....4-8 82
EMI AMERICA........................3-5 83-87
RCA (0001 "Time")........................200-400 73
RCA (0719 "Starman")........................15-20 72
RCA (0876 "Space Oddity")..........10-15 73
RCA (12078 "Ashes to Ashes")..........10-15 80
RCA (12134 "Fashion")........................5-10 80
RCA (13660 "White Light White Heat")........................3-5 83
RCA (13769 "1984")........................3-5 80

Promotional Singles

BACKSTREET........................5-10 82
DERAM (85009 "Rubber Band")........30-40 67
EMI AMERICA (8158 thru 8190)..........4-8 83-84
EMI AMERICA (8231 "Blue Jean").......4-8 84
EMI AMERICA (8246 thru 8308)..........4-8 83-86
EMI AMERICA (8380 "Day In, Day Out")........................4-8 87
EMI AMERICA (8380 "Day In, Day Out")........................15-20 87
(Colored vinyl. Boxed edition.)
EMI AMERICA (43000 series)..........4-8 87
LONDON (20079 "The Laughing Gnome")........................15-25 73
MERCURY (311 "All the Madmen")..40-60 70
MERCURY (72949 "Space Oddity")........................30-50 69
MERCURY (73075 "Memory of a Free Festival")........................40-60 70
RCA........................5-12 71-84
W.B. (5815 "Can't Help Thinking About Me")........................50-75 66
WHAT'S IT ALL ABOUT..........10-20 70s

EPs: 7-inch

RCA........................20-25 70s
(Promotional issues only.)

LPs: 10/12-inch

DERAM (16003 "David Bowie").....100-125 67
(Monaural.)
DERAM (18003 "David Bowie")....100-150 67
(Stereo.)
EMI AMERICA........................5-10 83-87
LONDON........................10-20 73-85
MFSL (064 "Rise and Fall of Ziggy Stardust")........................40-60 82
MFSL (083 "Let's Dance")..........25-35 82
MERCURY (61246 "Man of Words/Man of Music")........................75-100 69
MERCURY (61246 "Space Oddity")........................10-15 72
MERCURY (61325 "The Man Who Sold the World")........................25-40 71
PRECISION (1 "Don't Be Fooled By the Name")........................20-25 81
(10-inch LP.)
RCA (0291 "Bowie Pin Ups")..........10-15 73
RCA (0576 "Diamond Dogs")........................1500-2000 74
(With "Dog Genitals" cover.)
RCA (0576 "Diamond Dogs")........................10-15 74
(With dog's genitals covered.)
RCA (0700 thru 1300 series)..........10-15 74-76
RCA (1732 "Changesone Bowie")........................100-125 76
(With alternate take of *John, I'm Only Dancing.*)
RCA (1732 "Changesone Bowie")....10-20 76
(With the commonly issued take of *John, I'm Only Dancing.*)
RCA (2000 thru 2500)........................10-15 77
RCA (2743 "Peter and the Wolf").....10-15 78
(Black vinyl. With Eugene Ormandy & the Philadelphia Orchestra.)
RCA (2743 "Peter and the Wolf").....35-55 78
(Colored vinyl. With Eugene Ormandy & the Philadelphia Orchestra.)
RCA (2900 thru 4200 series)..........5-10 79-82
RCA (4600 thru 4800 series)..........10-15 71-73
(With "LSP" prefix.)
RCA (4700 thru 4900 series, except 4862)........................5-10 83-84
(With "AFL," "AYL" or "CPL" prefix.)
RCA 4862 "Ziggy Stardust")..........5-10 83
(Black vinyl.)
RCA 4862 "Ziggy Stardust")..........40-80 83
(Clear vinyl.)
RYKODISC (Except 0120/2)..........8-12 87-90
RYKODISC (0120/2 "Sound and Vision")........................50-75 89
(Boxed, six-disc set.)

Promotional LPs

DERAM (18003 "David Bowie")........................200-300 67
EMI AMERICA (9960 "Let's Talk")........................40-70 83
MERCURY (61246 "Man of Words/Man of Music")........................75-125 69
MERCURY (61325 "The Man Who Sold the World")........................75-125 71
RCA (0200 thru 4800 series)..........20-40 71-73
(With programmer's strip on front cover.)
RCA (2697 "Bowie Now")..........30-50 78
RCA (3016 "An Evening with David Bowie")........................100-200 78
RCA (3545 "Bowie 1980")..........50-75 80
RCA (3829 "RCA Special Radio Series")........................30-50 80
RCA (3840 "Interview")..........35-50 80
RCA (11306 "Peter and the Wolf")...30-40 78
Also see HOUSTON, Cissy
Also see KHAN, Chaka
Also see QUEEN & David Bowie
Also see SPIDERS from MARS
Also see TURNER, Tina
Also see VANDROSS, Luther

BOWIE, David / Joe Cocker / Youngbloods

LPs: 10/12-inch

MERCURY (SRD-2-29 "Zig Zag Festival")........................40-60 70
(Promotional issue only.)
Also see COCKER, Joe
Also see YOUNGBLOODS

BOWIE, David, & Bing Crosby

Singles: 7-inch

RCA (13400 "Peace on Earth")..........8-12 77
(Promotional issue only.)
RCA........................3-6 83

Picture Sleeves

RCA (13400 "Peace on Earth")..........8-12 77
(Promotional issue only.)
RCA........................4-8 83
Also see CROSBY, Bing

BOWIE, David, & Mick Jagger P&R/D&D '85

Singles: 12-inch

EMI AMERICA (19200 "Dancing in the Streets")........................8-12 85

Singles: 7-inch

EMI AMERICA (8288 "Dancing in the Streets")........................3-4 85

Picture Sleeves

EMI AMERICA (8288 "Dancing in the Streets")........................3-5 85
Also see JAGGER, Mick

BOWIE, David, & Pat Metheny Group P&R/D&D '85

Singles: 12-inch

EMI AMERICA........................4-8 85

Singles: 7-inch

EMI AMERICA........................3-4 85

Picture Sleeves

EMI AMERICA........................3-4 85

LPs: 10/12-inch

EMI AMERICA........................5-10 85
Also see METHENY, Pat

BOWIE, David / Iggy Pop

Singles: 12-inch

RCA (10956 "Sound & Vision")..........30-50 77
(Promotional issue only.)
Also see BOWIE, David
Also see POP, Iggy

BOWLES, Rick P&R '82

Singles: 7-inch

POLYDOR........................3-4 82

LPs: 10/12-inch

POLYDOR........................5-10 82

BOX OF FROGS LP '84

Singles: 7-inch

EPIC........................3-4 84-86

LPs: 10/12-inch

EPIC........................5-10 84-86
Members: Chris Dreja; Jim McCarty; Jeff Beck.
Also see YARDBIRDS

BOX TOPS P&R/R&B/LP '67

Singles: 7-inch

BELL........................3-5 70-71
GUSTO........................3-4 84
HI........................3-5 72-73
MALA........................4-8 67-69
SPHERE SOUND........................4-8 67
STAX........................3-5 74

LPs: 10/12-inch

BELL........................10-20 67-69
COTILLION........................10-15 71
KORY........................5-10 76
RHINO........................5-10 82
Members: Alex Chilton; Rick Allen; Tom Boggs; Harold Cloud; Bill Cunningham; John Evans; Swain Scharfar; Gary Talley; Danny Smythe; Rick Stevens.

BOY GEORGE P&R/R&B/LP '87

(George O'Dowd)

Singles: 7-inch

VIRGIN........................3-4 87-89

Picture Sleeves

VIRGIN........................3-4 87

LPs: 10/12-inch

VIRGIN........................5-10 87-89
Also see CULTURE CLUB

BOY MEETS GIRL P&R/LP '85

Singles: 7-inch

A&M....3-4 85
RCA....3-4 88-89

Picture Sleeves

A&M....3-4 85
RCA....3-4 88-89

LPs: 10/12-inch

A&M....5-10 85
RCA....5-8 88

Members: George Merrill; Shannon Rubicam.

BOYCE, Tommy P&R '62

Singles: 7-inch

A&M (Except 826)....4-8 66
A&M (826 "In Case the Wind Should Blow")....10-12 66
CAPITOL....3-5 71
COLPIX....8-10 66
DOT....10-15 60
MGM....8-10 65
RCA (7000 series)....15-25 61
RCA (8000 series)....8-12 62-63
R-DELL....15-25 58
WOW....8-12 61

LPs: 10/12-inch

CAMDEN....15-20 68

Also see CLOUD, Christopher

BOYCE, Tommy, & Bobby Hart
(Boyce & Hart) P&R/LP '67

Singles: 7-inch

A&M....4-8 67-69
AQUARIAN....3-6 68

Picture Sleeves

A&M....5-10 67-69
AQUARIAN....5-8 68

LPs: 10/12-inch

A&M....10-20 67-69

Also see ATTORNEYS
Also see BOYCE, Tommy
Also see DOLENZ, JONES, BOYCE & HART

BOYD, Eddie R&B '52
(With His Chess Men; Eddie Boyd Blues Combo; Little Eddie Boyd & His Boogie Band)

Singles: 78 rpm

CHESS....15-25 50-56
HERALD....50-75 52
J.O.B....15-45 52-57
RCA....15-25 47-50

Singles: 7-inch

ART TONE....5-10 62
BEA & BABY (101 "I'm Comin' Home")....10-20 59
CHESS (1523 "Cool Kind Treatment")....25-50 52
CHESS (1533 "24 Hours")....25-50 53
CHESS (1541 "Third Degree")....25-50 53
CHESS (1552 "That's When I Miss You")....25-50 53
CHESS (1561 "Picture in the Frame")....20-40 54
CHESS (1573 "Hush Baby, Don't You Cry")....20-40 54
CHESS (1576 "Driftin'")....20-40 54
CHESS (1582 "The Story of Bill")....15-30 55
CHESS (1595 "Real Good Feeling")....15-30 55
CHESS (1606 "I'm a Prisoner")....15-30 55
CHESS (1634 "Just a Fool")....15-25 56
CHESS (1660 "I Got a Woman")....15-25 56
CHESS (1674 "I Got the Blues")....15-25 57
CHESS (Colored vinyl)....100-200 54
(We are unable at this time to specify exactly which Chess numbers were pressed on colored vinyl.)
HERALD (406 "I'm Goin' Downtown")....75-125 52
J.O.B. (1007 "Five Long Years")....75-125 52
(Black vinyl.)
J.O.B. (1007 "Five Long Years")....200-300 52
(Colored vinyl.)
J.O.B. (1009 "It's Miserable to Be Alone")....40-60 53
J.O.B. (1114 "I Love You")....30-50 57
LA SALLE....5-10 61
MOJO....5-10
ORIOLE (1316 "Five Long Years")....20-30 58
PALOS....4-8 63-64
PUSH....5-10 62
RCA (50-0006 "What Makes These Things Happen to Me")....35-50 50
(Colored vinyl.)

EPs: 7-inch

ESQUIRE....15-25 60

LPs: 10/12-inch

EPIC....15-25 69
LONDON....15-20 69

Also see DIXON, Willie
Also see GREEN, Peter

BOYD, Jimmy P&R/C&W '52
(Little Jimmy Boyd)

Singles: 78 rpm

COLUMBIA (Except 21571)....4-8 52-56
COLUMBIA (21571 "Rockin' Down the Mississippi")....10-15 56

Singles: 7-inch

CAPITOL....4-8 63
COLUMBIA (152 "I Saw Mommy Kissing Santa Claus")....10-20 52
COLUMBIA (21571 "Rockin' Down the Mississippi")....30-40 56
COLUMBIA (39000 & 40000 series)....10-20 52-56
IMPERIAL....3-6 66-67
MGM (12788 "Cream Puff")....40-50 59
TAKE TEN....4-8 63
VEE JAY....4-8 65

Picture Sleeves

COLUMBIA (152 "I Saw Mommy Kissing Santa Claus")....15-25 52
(With die-cut center hole.)

EPs: 7-inch

COLUMBIA (1913 "Jimmy Boyd")....10-15 50s

Also see LAINE, Frankie, & Jimmy Boyd

BOYD, Jimmy, & Rosemary Clooney P&R '53

Singles: 78 rpm

COLUMBIA....4-8 53

Singles: 7-inch

COLUMBIA (39000 series)....8-12 53
COLUMBIA (41000 series)....4-8 60

Also see BOYD, Jimmy
Also see CLOONEY, Rosemary

BOYD, Robert

Singles: 78 rpm

WASCO (201 "East St. Louis Baby")....75-125 50

Also see PROFESSOR LONGHAIR

BOYD, Little Eddie: see BOYD, Eddie

BOYER, Bonnie P&R '79

Singles: 12-inch

COLUMBIA....4-6 79

Singles: 7-inch

COLUMBIA....3-4 79

LPs: 10/12-inch

COLUMBIA....5-10 79

BOYER, Charles LP '66

Singles: 7-inch

VALIANT....3-6 65

LPs: 10/12-inch

VALIANT....10-20 65

BOYLAN, Terence LP '77

Singles: 7-inch

ASYLUM....3-4 77-80

LPs: 10/12-inch

ASYLUM....5-10 77-80
VERVE/FORECAST....12-15 69

Session: Darius Davenport.

BOYS P&R/LP '88

Singles: 7-inch

MOTOWN....3-4 88-90

Picture Sleeves

MOTOWN....3-4 88

LPs: 10/12-inch

MOTOWN....5-8 88-90

BOYS BAND P&R '82

Singles: 7-inch

ELEKTRA....3-4 82

Picture Sleeves

ELEKTRA....3-4 82

LPs: 10/12-inch

ASYLUM....5-10 82

Members: Rusty Golden; Chris Golden; Greg Gordon; B.J. Lowry.

BOYS CLUB P&R/LP '88

Singles: 7-inch

MCA....3-4 88

Picture Sleeves

MCA....3-4 88

LPs: 10/12-inch

MCA....5-8 88

Members: Joe Pasquale; Gene Hunt.
Also see JETS

BOYS DON'T CRY P&R/LP '86

Singles: 12-inch

PROFILE....4-6 86

Singles: 7-inch

ATLANTIC....3-4 88
PROFILE....3-4 86

Picture Sleeves

ATLANTIC....3-4 88
PROFILE....3-4 86

LPs: 10/12-inch

PROFILE....5-10 86

Member: Nick Richards.

BOYS IN THE BAND P&R/R&B '70

Singles: 7-inch

SPRING....3-5 70

BOYS ON THE BLOCK R&B '87

Singles: 7-inch

FANTASY....3-4 87

BOYZ II MEN P&R/R&B/LP '91

Singles: 7-inch

MOTOWN....3-4 91

LPs: 10/12-inch

MOTOWN....5-8 91

BOZE, Calvin R&B '50

Singles: 78 rpm

ALADDIN....20-50 50-52
G&G (1029 "Safronia B.")....30-60 46
SCORE (4003 "Satisfied")....15-25 48

Singles: 7-inch

ALADDIN (3045 "Waitin' and Drinkin'")....100-150 50
ALADDIN (3055 "Safronia B.")....100-150 50
ALADDIN (3065 "Lizzie Lou")....50-100 50
ALADDIN (3072 "Stinkin' from Drinkin'")....50-100 50
ALADDIN (3079 "Beale Street on Saturday Night")....50-100 51
ALADDIN (3086 "Slippin' and Slidin'")....50-100 51
ALADDIN (3100 "I've Got News for You")....50-100 51
ALADDIN (3110 "I'm Gonna Steam Off the Stamp")....50-100 52
ALADDIN (3160 "Shamrock")....50-100 52
ALADDIN (3122 "My Friend Told Me")....50-100 52
ALADDIN (3132 "Good Time Sue")....50-100 52
ALADDIN (3147 "Looped")....50-100 52
ASTRA....5-10
IMPERIAL....10-15 62

Also see JOHNSON, Marvin

BRADLEY, James R&B '79
(With the Bill Smith Combo)

Singles: 7-inch

CHESS....5-10 60
MALACO....3-4 79-84
MANCO....5-10 61

LPs: 10/12-inch

MALACO....5-10 84

BRADLEY, Jan *P&R/R&B '63*

Singles: 7–inch

ADANTI....4-8 65
CHESS....4-8 62-68
DOYLEN....4-8 70
ERIC....3-4 73
FORMAL (Except 1044)....5-10 62-63
FORMAL (1044 "Mama Didn't Lie")...15-25 62
HOOTENANNY....5-8 62
NIGHT OWL....5-8 63
SOUND SPECTRUM....4-8 65

BRADLEY, Owen *C&W/P&R '49*
(Owen Bradley Quintet)

Singles: 78 rpm

CORAL....4-8 49-50
DECCA....5-10 54-57

Singles: 7–inch

CORAL....5-10 50
DECCA....5-15 54-61

EPs: 7–inch

CORAL....10-20 54
DECCA....10-20 58

LPs: 10/12–inch

CORAL....20-30 53-55
DECCA....15-25 58-60
VOCALION....5-15 60s
Also see PLEIS, Jack, & Owen Bradley

BRADSHAW, Terry *C&W/P&R '76*

Singles: 7–inch

BENSON....3-4 80
MERCURY....3-5 76

Picture Sleeves

BENSON....3-4 80

LPs: 10/12–inch

BENSON....5-10 80
HEARTWARMING....5-10 82
MERCURY....6-12 76

BRADSHAW, Tiny *R&B '50*

Singles: 78 rpm

KING (4357 "I Hate You")....15-25 50
KING (4397 "Butterfly")....15-25 50
KING (4457 "Bradshaw Boogie")....15-25 50
KING (4487 "T-99")....25-50 52
KING (4497 "The Train Kept A-Rollin'")....25-50 52
KING (4547 "Rippin' & Runnin' ")....25-50 52
KING (4577 thru 4787)....10-20 52-55

Singles: 7–inch

GUSTO....3-4 80-83
KING (4357 "I Hate You")....25-50 50
KING (4397 "Butterfly")....25-50 50
KING (4457 "Bradshaw Boogie")....25-50 50
KING (4487 "T-99")....75-150 52
KING (4497 "The Train Kept A-Rollin'")....75-150 52
KING (4547 "Rippin' & Runnin'")....75-150 52
KING (4577 thru 4787)....20-40 52-55
(For King 4000 series colored vinyl singles, the price range will double or triple.)

EPs: 7–inch

KING (208 thru 360)....25-50 52-56

LPs: 10/12–inch

KING (74 "Off and On")....100-200 52
(10–inch LP.)
KING (501 "Tiny Bradshaw")....75-125 55
KING (653 "Great Composer")....30-50 59
KING (953 "24 Great Songs")....20-30 66

BRAGG, Billy *LP '88*

Singles: 7–inch

ELEKTRA....3-4 88

LPs: 10/12–inch

ELEKTRA....5-8 88

BRAINSTORM *P&R/R&B/LP '77*

Singles: 12–inch

TABU....4-6 77-79

Singles: 7–inch

RCA....3-4 82
TABU....3-4 76-79

LPs: 10/12–inch

RCA....5-10 82
TABU....5-10 77-79
Members: Belita Woods; Charles Overton; Jeryl Bright; Larry Sims; Jerry Kent; Renell Gousalves; Willie Wooten; Lamont Johnson; Trenita Womack.

BRAM TCHAIKOVSKY: see TCHAIKOVSKY, Bram

BRAMLETT, Bonnie *LP '75*

Singles: 7–inch

CAPRICORN....3-5 75-78
COLUMBIA....3-5 72-73
REFUGE....3-4 81

LPs: 10/12–inch

CAPRICORN....8-10 75-78
COLUMBIA....10-12 72-73
Also see DELANEY & BONNIE
Also see LITTLE FEAT

BRAMLETT, Delaney
(With Bekka Bramlett; with Blue Diamond)

Singles: 7–inch

COLUMBIA (45950 "Are You a Beatle Or a Rolling Stone")....5-10 73
CREAM....3-4 81
GNP....4-8 64-66
INDEPENDENCE....4-8 67

LPs: 10/12–inch

COLUMBIA....8-10 72-73
MGM....8-10 75
PRODIGAL....8-10 77
Also see DELANEY & BONNIE
Also see RIO, Chuck, & Delaney

BRAND X *LP '76*

Singles: 7–inch

PASSPORT....3-4 78

LPs: 10/12–inch

PASSPORT....5-10 76-84
Members: Phil Collins; John Goodsall; Percy Jones; Robin Lumley; Morris Pert.
Also see COLLINS, Phil

BRAND NUBIAN *LP '91*

LPs: 10/12–inch

ATLANTIC....4-8 91

BRANDON, Bill *R&B '72*

Singles: 7–inch

BELL (733 "Rainbow Road")....5-10 68
MOONSONG....10-20 72-73
PIEDMONT....3-6 76
PRELUDE....3-5 77-78
QUINVY (7007 "Strange Feeling")....50-75
SOUTH CAMP....5-10 67
TOWER (430 "Rainbow Road")....20-30 68

BRANDOS *LP '87*

LPs: 10/12–inch

RELATIVITY....5-10 87

BRANIGAN, Laura *P&R/LP '82*

Singles: 12–inch

ATLANTIC....4-8 82-87

Singles: 7–inch

ATLANTIC....3-4 80-90
EMI AMERICA....3-4 84

Picture Sleeves

ATLANTIC....3-4 80-87

LPs: 10/12–inch

ATLANTIC....5-10 82-90
EMI AMERICA....5-10 84
Also see COHEN, Leonard
Also see MEADOW

BRANIGAN, Laura, & Joe Esposito

Singles: 7–inch

ATCO....3-5

Picture Sleeves

ATCO....5-8
Also see BRANIGAN, Laura
Also see ESPOSITO, Joe "Bean"

BRANNEN, John *LP '88*

LPs: 10/12–inch

APACHE....5-8 88

BRASS CONSTRUCTION *P&R/R&B/LP '76*

Singles: 12–inch

CAPITOL....4-6 83
LIBERTY....4-6 82

Singles: 7–inch

CAPITOL....3-4 83
DOCC....3-5
LIBERTY....3-4 82
U.A....3-5 75-80

Picture Sleeves

U.A....3-5

LPs: 10/12–inch

CAPITOL....5-10 83
U.A....5-10 75-80
LIBERTY....5-10 82
Members: Randy Muller; Wade Williamston; Joe Wong; Wayne Parris; Mickey Grudge; Morris Price; Jesse Ward; Sandy Billups; Larry Payton.

BRASS FEVER *R&B '77*

Singles: 7–inch

IMPULSE....3-5 76-77

LPs: 10/12–inch

IMPULSE....8-10 76

BRASS RING *P&R/LP '66*

Singles: 7–inch

ABC....3-5 70
DUNHILL (Except 4090)....4-6 66-69
DUNHILL (4090 "Love in the Open Air")....10-20 67
ITCO....3-5 69

Picture Sleeves

DUNHILL (4090 "Love in the Open Air")....15-25 67
(Billed on sleeve as "Paul McCartney's First NON Beatle Song.")

LPs: 10/12–inch

DUNHILL....8-12 66-73
ITCO....6-10 70
PROJECT 3....6-10 72
Members: Phil Bodner.
Also see BODNER, Phil, Sextet
Also see McCARTNEY, Paul

BRAT PACK *P&R '90*

Singles: 7–inch

VENDETTA....3-4 90

BRAUN, Bob *P&R/LP '62*
(With the Fun Bunch)

Singles: 7–inch

AUDIO FIDELITY....3-6 65
APPLEGATE....4-6
CANDEE....4-8
DECCA....4-8 62
FRATERNITY....3-6 64-66
KING....4-8 59
QCA....3-5 73
U.A....3-5 67
WRAYCO....3-5 71

Picture Sleeves

DECCA....5-8 62
QCA....3-5 73

EPs: 7–inch

DECCA....5-10 63

LPs: 10/12–inch

AUDIO FIDELITY....8-12 65
DECCA....10-20 62
U.A....8-12 67
WRAYCO....5-10 71

BRAVOS, Los: see LOS BRAVOS

BRAVE BELT

Singles: 7–inch

REPRISE....3-5 71-72

LPs: 10/12–inch

REPRISE (2057 "Brave Belt II")....15-20 72
REPRISE (6447 "Brave Belt")....15-20 71
Members: Chad Allan; Randy Bachman; Robert Bachman; C.F. Turner.
Also see BACHMAN - TURNER - BACHMAN

BRAXTON, Dhar *R&B '86*
(With Chocolette)

Singles: 12–inch

SLEEPING BAG....4-6 86

Singles: 7-inch
SLEEPING BAG....3-4 86

BREAD LP '69
(David Gates & Bread)
Singles: 7-inch
ASYLUM (45054 "Make It with You")....4-6 70s
(Label misprint; Asylum should be Elektra.)
ELEKTRA (Except 45666 & 45668)......3-5 70-77
ELEKTRA (45666 "Dismal Day")..........5-8 69
ELEKTRA (45668 "Could I")..................4-6 69
Picture Sleeves
ELEKTRA....4-8 70-72
LPs: 10/12-inch
ELEKTRA (100 & 1000 series)...........8-12 73-77
ELEKTRA (5000 series)...................15-25 72-73
(Quadrophonic series.)
ELEKTRA (74000 & 75000 series, except 75015 & 75056)....10-15 69-73
ELEKTRA (75015 "Baby I'm a Want You")....15-25 72
(With die-cut cover.)
ELEKTRA (75015 "Baby I'm a Want You")....10-15 72
(Standard cover.)
ELEKTRA (75056 "Best of Bread")...25-35 73
K-TEL....5-10 82
Members: David Gates; James Griffin; Mike Botts; Larry Knechtel; Robb Royer.
Also see GATES, David
Also see GRIFFIN, James

BREAK MACHINE R&B/D&D '84
Singles: 12-inch
SIRE....4-6 84
Singles: 7-inch
BLACK SCORPIO....3-5
SIRE....3-4 84
Members: Lindell Blake; Lindsay Blake; Cortez Jordan.

BREAKFAST CLUB P&R/R&B/LP '87
Singles: 7-inch
MCA....3-4 87
Picture Sleeves
MCA....3-4 87
LPs: 10/12-inch
MCA....5-10 87

BREAKWATER R&B/LP '79
Singles: 7-inch
ARISTA....3-5 79-80
LPs: 10/12-inch
ARISTA....5-10 79-80
Members: Kae Williams; Lincoln Gilmore; James Jones; Gene Robinson Jr.; Vince Garnell; Greg Scott; John Braddock; Steve Green.
Also see BLACK MAGIC

BREATHE P&R/LP '88
Singles: 12-inch
A&M....4-8 87
Singles: 7-inch
A&M....3-4 87-90
Picture Sleeves
A&M....3-8 88-89
LPs: 10/12-inch
A&M....5-10 87-90
Members: David Glasper; Ian Spice; Michael Delahunty; Marcus Lillington.

BREATHLESS P&R '80
Singles: 7-inch
EMI AMERICA....3-4 79
LPs: 10/12-inch
EMI AMERICA....5-10 79-80

BRECKER BROS. P&R/R&B/LP '75
Singles: 7-inch
ARISTA....3-5 75-80
LPs: 10/12-inch
ARISTA....5-10 75-81
Members: Mike Brecker; Randy Brecker; Dave Sanborn.
Also see DREAMS

BREMERS, Beverly P&R '71
Singles: 7-inch
COLUMBIA....3-5 75-77
ERIC....3-4 83
SCEPTER....3-5 71-75
Picture Sleeves
SCEPTER....4-6 72
LPs: 10/12-inch
SCEPTER....8-10 72

BRENDA & HERB R&B '78
Singles: 7-inch
H&L....3-5 78
Members: Brenda Reid; Herb Rooney.
Also see EXCITERS

BRENDA & PETE: see LEE, Brenda, & Pete Fountain

BRENDA & BIG DUDES R&B '86
Singles: 12-inch
CAPITOL....4-6 86
Singles: 7-inch
CAPITOL....3-4 86
LPs: 10/12-inch
CAPITOL....5-10 86

BRENDA & TABULATIONS P&R/R&B/LP '67
Singles: 12-inch
CHOCOLATE CITY....4-6 77
Singles: 7-inch
CHOCOLATE CITY....3-5 76-77
DIONN....5-10 67-69
EPIC....3-5 72-75
TOP & BOTTOM....4-6 69-71
LPs: 10/12-inch
CHOCOLATE CITY....5-10 77
DIONN (2000 "Dry Your Eyes")........20-30 67
TOP & BOTTOM....15-20 70
Members: Brenda Payton; Jerry Joures; Eddie Jackson; Maurice Coates; Dennis Dozier; Donald Ford; Deborah Martin; Lee Smith; Kenneth Wright; Pat Mercer.
Also see SIX TEENS / Brenda & Tabulations

BRENDA LEE: see LEE, Brenda

BRENNAN, Walter P&R '60
(With Billy Vaughn's Orchestra & Chorus; with Patriots)
Singles: 7-inch
DOT....5-10 60
KAPP....3-5 71
LIBERTY....4-8 62-64
RPC....8-10 61
Picture Sleeves
DOT....10-15 60
LIBERTY....8-12 62-63
LPs: 10/12-inch
DOT....20-30 60
EVEREST....20-30 60
HAMILTON....15-25 65
LIBERTY....20-30 62
LONDON....15-20 70
RPC....20-30 62
SUNSET....8-10 66
U.A....5-10 75
Also see VAUGHN, Billy

BRENSTON, Jackie R&B '51
(With His Delta Cats)
Singles: 78 rpm
CHESS (Except 1458)....15-30 51-53
CHESS (1458 "Rocket 88")....50-100 51
(See note below regarding 45 rpms.)
FEDERAL....10-40 56-57
Singles: 7-inch
CHESS (1458 "Rocket 88")....300-500 51
(With Ike Turner on guitar. Original 45s from 1951 are not known to exist. There are legit reissue 45s, made circa 1954. These have a delta symbol [Δ] and the number stamped in the trail-off. Fakes, without the delta mark, also exist.)
CHESS (1469 "In My Real Gone Rocket")....150-250 51
CHESS (1472 "Juiced")....150-250 52
CHESS (1496 "Leo the Louse")....100-150 52
CHESS (1532 "The Blues Got Me Again")....50-100 53
FEDERAL....20-35 56-57
SUE....5-10 61
Also see TURNER, Ike

BRENSTON, Jackie / Muddy Waters
Singles: 7-inch
CHESS (113 "Rocket 88")....3-5
Also see BRENSTON, Jackie
Also see WATERS, Muddy

BREWER, Teresa P&R '50
(With the Lancers; with Dixieland Band; with Mickey Mantle; with Bobby Wayne)
Singles: 78 rpm
CORAL....5-15 52-57
LONDON....5-15 50-52
Singles: 7-inch
ABC....3-5 67
AMSTERDAM....3-5 72-73
CORAL (60000 & 61000 series)........10-20 52-58
CORAL (62000 & 65000 series)..........5-10 58-64
DOCTOR JAZZ....3-4 83
FLYING DUTCHMAN....3-5 72
LONDON....8-12 50-52
PHILIPS....4-8 63-67
PROJECT 3....3-4 82
RCA (11882 "Merry Christmas")............4-6 79
(With picture label. Special products issue.)
SSS INT'L....3-5 68
SIGNATURE....3-4 74-83
Picture Sleeves
CORAL....10-15 58-60
SIGNATURE....3-5 80
EPs: 7-inch
CORAL....10-20 55-60
LONDON (6039 "Teresa Brewer")....20-30 51
LONDON (6041 "Teresa Brewer")....20-30 51
LPs: 10/12-inch
AMSTERDAM....6-10 73-74
COLUMBIA....5-10 81
CORAL (7 "Best of Teresa Brewer")....15-25 65
CORAL (56072 "A Bouquet of Hits from Teresa Brewer")....50-75 52
(10-inch LP.)
CORAL (56093 "Till I Waltz Again with You")....50-75 53
(10-inch LP.)
CORAL (57027 thru 57297)..............25-50 55-59
(Monaural. Stereo numbers in the 57000 series are preceded by a "7.")
CORAL (57315 thru 57414)..............15-30 60-65
(Monaural. Stereo numbers in the 57000 series are preceded by a "7.")
DOCTOR JAZZ....5-10 79-83
FLYING DUTCHMAN....6-10 73-74
IMAGE....5-10 78
LONDON (1006 "Teresa Brewer")...50-100 51
(10-inch LP.)
MCA....5-10 83
PHILIPS....10-20 63-67
PROJECT 3....5-10 82
RCA....5-10 75
SIGNATURE....5-10 74-75
VOCALION....8-15 69
WING....8-10 66
Also see McGUIRE SISTERS / Lancers / Dorothy Collins / Teresa Brewer

BREWER, Teresa / Eileen Barton
Singles: 78 rpm
CORAL....5-10 50s
Also see BARTON, Eileen

BREWER, Teresa, & Count Basie
LPs: 10/12-inch
DOCTOR JAZZ....5-10 84
Also see BASIE, Count

BREWER, Teresa, & Duke Ellington
LPs: 10/12-inch
COLUMBIA....5-10 81
FLYING DUTCHMAN....6-10 74
Also see BREWER, Teresa
Also see ELLINGTON, Duke

BREWER & SHIPLEY *P&R/LP '71*

Singles: 7-inch

A&M....4-8 68-69
BUDDAH....3-5 70
CAPITOL....3-5 74-75
KAMA SUTRA....3-5 70-73

Picture Sleeves

KAMA SUTRA....3-6 72

LPs: 10/12-inch

A&M....12-15 68
ACCORD....5-10 83
CAPITOL....8-10 74-75
KAMA SUTRA....10-12 70-76

Members: Mike Brewer; Tom Shipley.

BRIAN & BRENDA *R&B '78*

Singles: 7-inch

ROCKET....3-5 76-78

Members: Brian Russell; Brenda Russell.

BRICK *P&R/R&B/LP '76*

Singles: 12-inch

BANG....4-6 79-82

Singles: 7-inch

BANG....3-5 76-82
MAINSTREET....4-8 76
STREET....3-5 76

LPs: 10/12-inch

BANG....5-10 76-82

Members: Jimmy Brown; Regi Hargis; Eddie Irons; Ray Ransom; Don Nevins.

BRICKELL, Edie *P&R/LP '88*
(With the New Bohemians)

Singles: 7-inch

GEFFEN....3-4 88-90

Picture Sleeves

GEFFEN....3-4 88-89

LPs: 10/12-inch

GEFFEN....5-8 88-90

BRIDES OF FUNKENSTEIN *R&B/LP '78*

Singles: 7-inch

ATLANTIC....3-4 78-80

LPs: 10/12-inch

ATLANTIC....5-10 78-80

Members: Lynn Mabry; Dawn Silva.
Also see PARLIAMENT

BRIDGES, Alicia *P&R/R&B/LP '78*

Singles: 12-inch

SECOND WAVE....4-6 84
POLYDOR....4-6 78-79

Singles: 7-inch

A.V.I....3-4 82
MEGA....3-5 72
POLYDOR....3-4 78-79
SECOND WAVE....3-4 84
ZODIAC....3-5 73

LPs: 10/12-inch

POLYDOR....5-10 78-79

BRIDGEWATER, Dee Dee *R&B/LP '78*

Singles: 12-inch

ELEKTRA....4-6 79-80

Singles: 7-inch

ELEKTRA....3-5 78-79

LPs: 10/12-inch

ATLANTIC....8-10 76
ELEKTRA....5-10 78-80

BRIEF ENCOUNTER *R&B '76*

Singles: 7-inch

CAPITOL....3-5 76-77
SEVENTY SEVEN....3-5 72-73

Members: Maurice Whittington; Gary Bailey; Larry Bailey; Belmont Bailey; Monte Bailey.

BRIGGS, Lillian *P&R '55*

Singles: 78 rpm

EPIC....5-10 56

Singles: 7-inch

ABC-PAR....4-8 61
CORAL....5-10 59-60
EPIC....10-20 56
SUNBEAM....5-10 58

EPs: 7-inch

EPIC (7163 "High Priestess of Rock 'N' Roll")....20-30 56

BRIGHT, Larry *P&R '60*
(Pete Roberts)

Singles: 7-inch

BRIGHT....4-8 65
DEL-FI (Except 4204)....5-10 63-64
DEL-FI (4204 "Surfin' Queen")....10-20 63
DONNA....4-8 64
DOT....4-8 66
EDIT....8-12 62
HIGHLAND....8-12 61
JOJO....3-5 76
ORIGINAL SOUND....3-5 71
RENDEZVOUS (124 "Hold Me")....8-10 60
(Reissued as by Pete Roberts.)
TIDE (006 thru 1083)....10-20 60-62

Also see ROBERTS, Pete

BRIGHT, Larry / Humdingers

Singles: 7-inch

JAYE JOSEPH....4-8 64

Also see BRIGHT, Larry

BRIGHTER SIDE OF DARKNESS *P&R/R&B '72*

Singles: 7-inch

STAR VUE....5-10
20TH FOX....3-5 72-75

LPs: 10/12-inch

20TH FOX....8-10 73

Members: Darryl Lamont; Ralph Eskridge; Larry Washington; Randolph Murph.

BRILEY, Martin *P&R '83*

Singles: 7-inch

EMI AMERICA....3-4 84
MERCURY....3-4 81-84

LPs: 10/12-inch

MERCURY....5-10 81-85

Also see GREENSLADE

BRIMMER, Charles *R&B '75*

Singles: 7-inch

CHELSEA....4-8 75-76

LPs: 10/12-inch

CHELSEA....8-10 76-77

BRINKLEY & PARKER *R&B '74*

Singles: 7-inch

DARNEL....3-5 74

BRISCOE, Jimmy, & Little Beavers *R&B '73*

Singles: 7-inch

ATLANTIC....3-5 71
J-CITY....3-5 72
PHI-KAPPA....3-5 73-75
SALSOUL....3-4 79
WANDERICK....3-5 77

LPs: 10/12-inch

PHI-KAPPA....10-12 74
WANDERICK....8-10 77

Members: Jimmy Briscoel; Stanford Stansbury; Robert Makins; Kevin Brown; Maurice Pully.

BRISTOL, Johnny *P&R/R&B/LP '74*

Singles: 7-inch

ATLANTIC....3-5 76-78
HANDSHAKE....3-4 80-81
MGM....3-5 74-75

LPs: 10/12-inch

ATLANTIC....5-10 76-78
HANDSHAKE....5-10 81
MGM....8-12 74-75

Also see ALTON & JOHNNY
Also see STEWART, Amii, & Johnny Bristol

BRISTOL, Johnny, & Spyder Turner

Singles: 7-inch

POLYDOR....3-4 83

Also see BRISTOL, Johnny
Also see TURNER, Spyder

BRITISH LIONS *P&R/LP '78*

Singles: 7-inch

RSO....3-5 78

LPs: 10/12-inch

RSO....5-10 78

Members: John Fiddler; Dale Griffin; Overend Watts; Ray Major; Morgan Fisher.
Also see MOTT the HOOPLE

BRITNY FOX *P&R/LP '88*

Singles: 7-inch

COLUMBIA....3-4 88-89

LPs: 10/12-inch

COLUMBIA....5-8 88-89

Member: Dean Davidson.

BRITT, Tina *R&B '65*

Singles: 7-inch

EASTERN (604 "The Real Thing")....50-100 65
MINIT....5-10 69
VEEP....5-10 68-69

BRITTEN, Benjamin *LP '63*

LPs: 10/12-inch

LONDON....10-20 63

BROADWAY *P&R/R&B '76*

Singles: 7-inch

GRANITE....3-5 76
HILLTAK....3-4 78

LPs: 10/12-inch

HILLTAK....8-10 79

BROMBERG, David *LP '72*

Singles: 7-inch

COLUMBIA....3-5 72-73
FANTASY....3-4 77-79

LPs: 10/12-inch

ATLANTIC....5-10 80
COLUMBIA....8-12 72-77
FANTASY....8-12 76-80

Also see GRATEFUL DEAD
Also see HARRISON, George
Also see LOGGINS & MESSINA / David Bromberg
Also see SAHM, Doug

BRONNER BROTHERS *R&B '84*

Singles: 7-inch

NEIGHBOR....3-4 84

Picture Sleeves

NEIGHBOR....3-4 84

BRONSKI BEAT *P&R/D&D '84*

Singles: 12-inch

MCA....4-6 84-86

Singles: 7-inch

MCA....3-4 84-86

Picture Sleeves

MCA....3-4 84

LPs: 10/12-inch

MCA....5-10 85-86

Members: Jimmy Somerville; Steve Bronski; Larry Steinbachek.
Also see COMMUNARDS
Also see SOMERVILLE, Jimmy

BROOD, Herman *P&R/LP '79*
(With Wild Romance)

Singles: 7-inch

ARIOLA AMERICA....3-4 79

LPs: 10/12-inch

ARIOLA AMERICA....8-10 79-80
TOWNHOUSE....5-10 82

BROOKINS, Robert *R&B '86*

Singles: 12-inch

MCA....4-6 86

Singles: 7-inch

MCA....3-4 86

Picture Sleeves

MCA....3-4 87

BROOKLYN BRIDGE *P&R '68*
(Johnny Maestro & Brooklyn Bridge)

Singles: 7-inch

BROOKLYN BRIDGE (881 "Christmas Is")....10-15 88
BUDDAH....4-8 68-72

COLLECTABLES 3-4 84
ERIC 3-5 78
FLASHBACK 3-5 70s
HARVEY (500 "Worst That Could Happen") 5-10 81
(Colored vinyl.)
RADIO ACTIVE GOLD 3-5

LPs: 10/12-inch

BUDDAH (5000 series) 20-25 69-72
BUDDAH (69000 series) 5-10 84
COLLECTABLES 5-10 82

Members: Johnny Maestro; Fred Ferrara; Les Cauchi; Mike Gregorio; Tom Sullivan; Carolyn Wood; Jimmy Rosica; Richie Macioce; Artie Cantanzarita; Shelly Davis; Joe Ruvio.
Also see ISLEY BROTHERS / Brooklyn Bridge
Also see MAESTRO, Johnny

BROOKLYN DREAMS — P&R '77

Singles: 12-inch

CASABLANCA 4-6 79
MILLENNIUM 4-6 78

Singles: 7-inch

CASABLANCA 3-4 79-80
MILLENNIUM 3-5 77-78

LPs: 10/12-inch

CASABLANCA 5-10 79-80
MILLENNIUM 8-10 77

Members: Joe Esposito; Eddie Hokenson; Bruce Sudano.
Also see ESPOSITO, Joe "Bean"
Also see SUMMER, Donna

BROOKS, Donnie — P&R '60

Singles: 7-inch

CHALLENGE 4-8 66
COLLECTABLES 3-4 81
DJ 4-8 65
ERA (3000 series) 8-15 59-62
ERA (3100 series) 4-6 68
HAPPY TIGER 3-5 70-71
MIDSONG 3-5 79
OAK 3-5 71
REPRISE 3-5 64-65
USA 10-15 60s
YARDBIRD 4-6 68-69

Picture Sleeves

ERA 10-20 60-61

Promotional Singles

ERA ("Mission Bell"/"Doll House") 50-75 60
(Distributed during a personal appearance.)

LPs: 10/12-inch

ERA (105 "The Happiest") 30-40 61
OAK 8-10 71
WISHBONE 5-10 75

Also see BUSH, Dick
Also see FAIRE, Johnny
Also see JORDAN, Johnny

BROOKS, Ella — R&B '87

Singles: 7-inch

QMI 3-4 87

Picture Sleeves

QMI 3-4 87

BROOKS, Eloise, & Dreamers

Singles: 78 rpm

ALADDIN (3303 "My Plea") 20-30 55

Singles: 7-inch

ALADDIN (3303 "My Plea") 100-150 55

BROOKS, Garth — C&W '89

Singles: 7-inch

CAPITOL 3-4 89-92

LPs: 10/12-inch

CAPITOL 5-8 90-92

BROOKS, Hadda — R&B '47

(Hadda Brooks Trio)

Singles: 78 rpm

LONDON 15-25 50
MODERN 15-30 45-56
MODERN MUSIC 15-25 47
OKEH 10-20 54

Singles: 7-inch

ALWIN 4-6 69
ARWIN 5-10 59
LONDON (684 "I Hadn't Anyone Till You") 25-50 50
MODERN (100 series) 15-25 52
MODERN (804 "Let's Be Sweethearts Again") 50-100 51
MODERN (825 "When a Woman Cries") 50-100 51
MODERN (841 "I Feel So Good") ... 50-100 51
MODERN (861 "Romance in the Dark") 50-100 52
MODERN (1008 "Close Your Eyes") 25-50 56
MODERN MUSIC (Colored vinyl) 4-6 86
OKEH 20-40 54

EPs: 7-inch

LONDON (6149 "Presenting Hadda Brooks") 50-75 54
MODERN (114 "Boogie") 50-100 52

LPs: 10/12-inch

CROWN (5010 "Femme Fatale") 35-50 57
CROWN (5374 "Hadda Brooks Sings and Swings") 15-25 63
MODERN (1210 "Femme Fatale") 100-200 56

Members: Hadda Brooks; Basie Day; Al Wichard; Jim Black.

BROOKS, Hadda / Pete Johnson

LPs: 10/12-inch

CROWN (5058 "Boogie") 20-35 58

Also see BROOKS, Hadda
Also see JOHNSON, Pete

BROOKS, Louis — R&B '55

(With His Hi-Toppers)

Singles: 78 rpm

EXCELLO 15-25 52-57

Singles: 7-inch

EXCELLO (2000 series) 25-50 52-53
EXCELLO (2100 series) 15-25 57-59

BROOKS, Mel — R&B '82

Singles: 7-inch

WMOT 3-4 82

Also see REINER, Carl, & Mel Brooks

BROOKS, Nancy — P&R '79

Singles: 7-inch

ARISTA 3-4 79

BROOKS, Ramona — R&B '77

Singles: 7-inch

MANHATTAN 3-5 77
U.A. 3-5 77

LPs: 10/12-inch

MANHATTAN 8-10 78

BROOM, Bobby — R&B '81

Singles: 7-inch

ARISTA 3-4 81-84
GRP 3-4 81

LPs: 10/12-inch

GRP 5-10 81

BROS — P&R/LP '88

Singles: 7-inch

EPIC 3-4 88

Picture Sleeves

EPIC 3-4 88

LPs: 10/12-inch

EPIC 5-8 88

BROTHER BLUES & BACK ROOM BOYS

(Champion Jack Dupree)

Singles: 78 rpm

ABBEY 20-30 50

Also see DUPREE, Champion Jack

BROTHER BONES — R&B '49

(With His Shadows)

Singles: 78 rpm

TEMPO (652 "Sweet Georgia Brown") 15-25 48
TEMPO (4566 "Bubber's Boogie") 10-15 54

Singles: 7-inch

HARLEM GLOBETROTTER (300 "Sweet Georgia Brown") 8-12
TEMPO (4566 "Bubber's Boogie") 15-25 54

Member: Joe Darensbourg.
Also see DARENSBOURG, Joe

BROTHER TO BROTHER — P&R/R&B '74

Singles: 7-inch

SUGAR HILL 3-4 81
TURBO 3-5 74-77
WIN OR LOSE 3-5

LPs: 10/12-inch

SUGAR HILL 5-10 81
TURBO 10-12 74-77

Members: Michael Burton; Bill Jones; Frankie Prescott; Yogi Horton.

BROTHERHOOD — R&B '76

Singles: 7-inch

COLUMBIA 3-5 70
DIAL 3-6 69
MCA 3-4 78
RCA 3-6 69

Picture Sleeves

RCA 4-8 69

LPs: 10/12-inch

MCA 5-10 78
RCA 12-15 69

Members: Drake Levin; Michael Smith; Phil Volk; Ron Collins.
Also see REVERE, Paul, & Raiders
Also see WOMACK, Bobby

BROTHERHOOD OF MAN — P&R/LP '70

Singles: 7-inch

BELL 3-5 74
DERAM 3-6 70-72
LONDON 5-8
PRELUDE 3-5 78
PRIVATE STOCK 3-5 77
PYE 3-5 75-76

LPs: 10/12-inch

DERAM 10-12 70
PYE 8-10 76

Members: Tony Burrows; Sunny; Johnny Goddison; Hal Atkinson; Nicky Stevens; Sandra Stevens; Martin Lee; Lee Sheridan.
Also see BURROWS, Tony

BROTHERLY LOVE — R&B '72

Singles: 7-inch

MUSIC MERCHANT 5-10 72

LPs: 10/12-inch

MUSIC MERCHANT (104 "Brotherly Love") 25-50 72

BROTHERS BY CHOICE — R&B '78

Singles: 7-inch

ALA 3-4 78-80
FRETONE 3-5 75

BROTHERS FOUR — P&R/LP '60

Singles: 7-inch

AURAVISION (6725 "San Francisco Bay Blues") 10-15 64
(Cardboard flexi-disc, one of six by six different artists. Columbia Record Club "Enrollment Premium." Set came in a special paper sleeve.)
COLUMBIA (Except 43547) 5-10 59-69
COLUMBIA (43547 "Ratman & Bobbin in the Clipper Caper") 8-12 69
FANTASY 3-5 70

Picture Sleeves

COLUMBIA 10-15 60-63

LPs: 10/12-inch

COLUMBIA 10-20 59-69
FANTASY 8-12 70
FIRST AMERICAN 5-10 81
GRT 10-12 77
HARMONY 6-10 69-72

Members: Bob Flick; Dick Foley; John Paine; Mike Kirkland.

BROTHERS GUIDING LIGHT — R&B '73

(Featuring David)

Singles: 7-inch

MERCURY 3-5 73

BROTHERS JOHNSON — P&R '75

Singles: 12-inch

A&M (Black vinyl) 4-6 78-85

A&M (Colored vinyl)............................5-10 78-85

Singles: 7-inch

A&M...3-4 76-88

Picture Sleeves

A&M...3-5 76-85

LPs: 10/12-inch

A&M (Except PR-4714)......................5-10 76-85
A&M (PR-4714 "Blam")......................6-12 79
(Picture disc. No tour info on B-side.)
A&M (PR-4714 "Blam")......................20-30 79
(Picture disc. Has tour information on B-side. 250 made.)

Members: Louis Johnson; George Johnson.

BROTHERS OF SOUL R&B '68

Singles: 7-inch

BOO (112 "Love Is Fever")................15-25 70
BOO (1004 "Hurry Don't Linger").......15-25 68
BOO (1005 "Come On Back")...........15-25 68
BOO (1006 "I'd Be Grateful")...........50-100 69
CRISS-CROSS (1001 "Can't Get You Out of My Mind")..25-50 60s
SHOCK (1314 "Candy").....................15-25 60s

Members: Richard Knight; Robert Eaton; Fred Bridges.

BROWN, Al, & His Tunetoppers

(Featuring Cookie Brown) P&R/R&B '60

Singles: 7-inch

AMY...5-10 60-61

EPs: 7-inch

AMY (1 "Madison Dance Party")........35-45 60

LPs: 10/12-inch

AMY (1 "Madison Dance Party")........45-50 60

BROWN, Alex P&R/D&D '85

Singles: 12-inch

MERCURY...4-6 85

Singles: 7-inch

MERCURY...3-4 85
ROXBURY...3-5 76

BROWN, Arthur P&R/LP '68

(Crazy World of Arthur Brown; Arthur Brown's Kingdom Come)

Singles: 7-inch

ATLANTIC...4-8 68
TRACK...4-6 68-69

LPs: 10/12-inch

ATLANTIC...15-20 68
GULL...8-10 75
PASSPORT..10-12 74
RECKLESS...5-10 88
REPUBLIC (001 "Speak No Tech")...10-20 82
(Picture disc.)
TRACK...10-15 68

Also see ATOMIC ROOSTER
Also see PARSONS, Alan, Project

BROWN, Bobby P&R/R&B/LP '86

Singles: 12-inch

MCA..4-6 86

Singles: 7-inch

MCA..3-4 86-89

Picture Sleeves

MCA..3-4 86-89

LPs: 10/12-inch

MCA..5-10 86-89

Also see MEDEIROS, Glenn, & Bobby Brown
Also see NEW EDITION

BROWN, Boots P&R '58

(With Blockbusters; with Dan Drew; with Pelugelpipers; with Shorty Rogers)

Singles: 78 rpm

RCA..5-15 53-57

Singles: 7-inch

DOT..4-6 67-68
RCA..8-15 53-60

EPs: 7-inch

GROOVE (1000 "Rock That Beat")...25-50 55

LPs: 10/12-inch

GROOVE (1000 "Rock That Beat").50-100 55

BROWN, Buster P&R/R&B '60

(With Chas. Lucas & Thrillers)

Singles: 78 rpm

FIRE (1008 "Fannie Mae")............300-400 59

Singles: 7-inch

ABC...3-4 73
CHECKER..10-15 63
FIRE...15-25 59-62
GWENN..10-15 62
NOCTURN (1000 "I Love You for Sentimental Reasons").......................................25-50 64
OLDIES 45..4-6
RCA...4-6 74
ROULETTE..3-5 72
SEROCK..10-15 63

LPs: 10/12-inch

COLLECTABLES.................................6-8 88
FIRE (101/102 "The New King of the Blues")..300-400 60
(Blue cover. Track listing includes *Blueberry Hill* and *When Things Go Wrong.* Disc number is 101 though cover indicates 102.)
FIRE (101/102 "The New King of the Blues")..150-300 60
(White cover. With *Blueberry Hill* and *When Things Go Wrong* replaced by *Going on a Picnic* and *Corena.* Disc number is 101 though cover indicates 102.)
SOUFFLE..10-20 73

BROWN, Charles R&B '49

(With Johnny Moore's Three Blazers)

Singles: 78 rpm

ALADDIN...15-25 49-57
CASH..15-25 57
HOLLYWOOD.....................................15-25 54
SWING TIME......................................25-50 52

Singles: 7-inch

ACE (561 "Educated Fool")...............5-10 59
ALADDIN (3076 "Black Night").......50-100 51
ALADDIN (3091 "I'll Always Be in Love with You")..50-75 51
ALADDIN (3092 "Seven Long Days")...50-75 52
ALADDIN (3116 "Hard Times").........50-75 52
ALADDIN (3120 "My Last Affair")......50-75 52
ALADDIN (3138 "Without Your Love")..50-75 52
ALADDIN (3157 "Rollin' Like a Pebble in the Sand")..50-100 52
ALADDIN (3163 "Evening Shadows").......................................25-50 53
ALADDIN (3176 "Take Me")..............25-50 53
ALADDIN (3191 "Lonesome Feeling")..25-50 53
ALADDIN (3200 & 3300 series)........15-30 53-58
EAST-WEST.......................................10-20 58
GALAXY..5-8 66
HOLLYWOOD (1006 "Pleading for Your Love")..20-40 54
IMPERIAL..5-10 62-63
JEWEL...3-5 71-74
KING...5-10 60-64
LIBERTY..3-4 84
LILLY...5-10 62
MAINSTREAM....................................4-8 65
NOLA...5-10 63
STARDAY...3-6 69
SWING TIME (253 "I'll Miss You")..50-100 52
SWING TIME (259 "Be Fair with Me")..50-100 52

LPs: 10/12-inch

ALADDIN (702 "Mood Music")......400-600 52
(10-inch LP. Black vinyl.)
ALADDIN (702 "Mood Music")..1500-3000 52
(10-inch LP. Colored vinyl.)
ALADDIN (809 "Mood Music")......100-200 57
BIG TOWN...8-10 77-78
BLUES SPECTRUM............................4-6
BLUESWAY..8-10 70
IMPERIAL (9178 "Million Sellers")....50-75 62
JEWEL...8-15 72
KING (775 "Christmas Songs")..........30-50 61
KING (878 "The Great Charles Brown")..30-50 63
KING (5000 series)............................5-10
MAINSTREAM (300 series)................8-12 72
MAINSTREAM (6000/56000 series)..10-20 65
SCORE (4011 "Driftin' Blues").......100-150 57

Also see BROWN, Floyd
Also see CHARLES, Ray / Charles Brown
Also see McCRACKLIN, Jimmy / T-Bone Walker / Charles Brown
Also see MOORE, Johnny
Also see SCOTT, Mabel

BROWN, Charles / Basin Street Boys

Singles: 78 rpm

CASH..15-25 57

Singles: 7-inch

CASH (1052 "Lost in the Night").......20-30 57

Also see BASIN STREET BOYS

BROWN, Charles / Lloyd Glenn

(With Johnny Moore's 3 Blazers)

Singles: 78 rpm

HOLLYWOOD......................................10-20 54

Singles: 7-inch

HOLLYWOOD (1021 "Merry Christmas Baby")..20-30 54

Also see GLENN, Lloyd

BROWN, Charles, & Jimmy McCracklin

LPs: 10/12-inch

IMPERIAL (9257 "Best of the Blues")...25-50 64

Also see McCRACKLIN, Jimmy

BROWN, Charles, & Amos Milburn

(Charles Brown / Amos Milburn)

Singles: 7-inch

ACE..5-10 59
KING (5000 series)............................5-10 61
KING (6000 series)............................3-5 75

LPs: 10/12-inch

GRAND PRIX (421 "Original Blues Sound")..10-15 64
(With Jackie Shane and Bob Marshall & Crystals.)

Also see BROWN, Charles
Also see MILBURN, Amos

BROWN, Chuck, & Soul Searchers R&B '78

Singles: 12-inch

SOURCE...4-8 78-79

Singles: 7-inch

MCA..3-5 79
SOUL SEARCHERS.............................3-4 84
SOURCE...3-5 78-80
T.T.E.D..3-4 84

LPs: 10/12-inch

SOURCE...5-10 79

BROWN, Clarence "Gatemouth" R&B '49

Singles: 78 rpm

ALADDIN...15-25 47
PEACOCK..10-20 49-54

Singles: 7-inch

CINDERELLA (1021 "Okie Dokie")...10-20 65
CINDERELLA (1022 "Chicken Shake")..10-20 65
CUE..5-10 64
PEACOCK (1600 "Baby Take It Easy")..50-100 52
PEACOCK (1607 "You Got Money")..20-40 52
PEACOCK (1617 "Boogie Uproar")...20-40 53
PEACOCK (1619 "Please Tell Me Baby")..20-40 53
PEACOCK (1633 "Midnight Hour")...20-40 54
PEACOCK (1637 "Okie Dokie Stomp")..20-40 54
PEACOCK (1692 "Just Before Dawn")..10-25 60
PEACOCK (1696 "Slop Time").........10-25 60

LPs: 10/12-inch

BLUE STAR.......................................30-40
MUSIC IS MEDICINE..........................8-12 78
ROUNDER..5-10 82

Also see McVEA, Jack

BROWN, Clarence "Gatemouth"/ Camille Howard / Bill Johnson Quartet / Van "Piano Man' Walls
EPs: 7–inch
BIG TOWN (150 "Without Me Baby") ... 25-50 50s
(Probably not issued with cover. For easy reference, title shown is of the Clarence Brown track, not the EP overall.)
Also see BROWN, Clarence "Gatemouth"
Also see HOWARD, Camille

BROWN, Cleo R&B '49
Singles: 78 rpm
BLUE ... 5-10 51
CAPITOL ... 5-10 49

BROWN, Clyde R&B '73
Singles: 7–inch
ATLANTIC ... 3-5 73-74

BROWN, Danny Joe, & Danny Joe Brown Band LP '81
Singles: 7–inch
EPIC ... 3-4 81
LPs: 10/12–inch
EPIC ... 5-10 81
Also see MOLLY HATCHET

BROWN, Dee, & Lola Grant R&B '66
Singles: 7–inch
SHURFINE ... 4-8 66

BROWN, Dennis R&B '82
Singles: 12–inch
A&M ... 4-6 82
Singles: 7–inch
A&M ... 3-4 81-82
STUDIO ONE ... 3-5 72
LPs: 10/12–inch
A&M ... 5-10 81-82

BROWN, Don P&R '78
Singles: 7–inch
FIRST AMERICAN ... 3-5 77-78

BROWN, Gloria D. R&B '86
Singles: 7–inch
KRYSTAL ... 3-4 86

BROWN, James R&B '56
(With His Famous Flames; with the J.B.s)
Singles: 12–inch
CHURCHILL ... 4-6 83
POLYDOR ... 4-6 78
Singles: 78 rpm
FEDERAL (Except 12348) ... 20-40 56-58
FEDERAL (12348 "I Want You So Bad") ... 50-100 59
Singles: 7–inch
AUGUSTA ... 3-4 83
BACKSTREET ... 3-4 83
BETHLEHEM ... 8-15 69
CHURCHILL ... 3-4 83
FEDERAL (12258 "Please Please Please") ... 50-100 56
FEDERAL (12311 "Baby Cries Over the Ocean") ... 50-75 57
FEDERAL (12337 "Try Me") ... 40-60 58
FEDERAL (12348 "I Want You So Bad") ... 30-50 59
FEDERAL (S-12352 "I've Got to Change") ... 25-35 59
(Monaural.)
FEDERAL (S-12352 "I've Got to Change") ... 50-75 59
(Stereo.)
FEDERAL (S-12361 "Good, Good Lovin'") ... 25-35 59
(Monaural.)
FEDERAL (S-12361 "Good, Good Lovin'") ... 50-75 59
(Stereo.)
FEDERAL (12378 "This Old Heart") ... 20-30 60
KING (5000 series) ... 15-25 60-65
KING (6000 series) ... 5-15 65-71
PEOPLE ... 3-6 71-76
POLYDOR (Except 14304) ... 3-6 71-84
POLYDOR (14304 "For Sentimental Reasons") ... 5-10 70s
RIPETE ... 3-4 80s
SCOTTI BROTHERS ... 3-4 85-88
SMASH ... 8-15 64-66
T.K. ... 3-5 80-81
Picture Sleeves
KING (5842 "Oh Baby Don't You Weep") ... 10-20 64
POLYDOR ... 3-5 72-84
SCOTTI BROTHERS ... 3-4 85-86
SMASH ... 10-15 64
EPs: 7–inch
KING ... 20-40 59-63
SMASH ... 15-25 65-66
(Juke box issues only.)
LPs: 10/12–inch
AGUSTA SOUND ... 5-8
AUDIO FIDELITY (326 "James Brown") ... 10-15 83
(Picture disc.)
CHURCHILL ... 5-10 83
HRB ... 8-10 73
KING (610 "Please, Please, Please") ... 100-150 59
(Cover pictures a woman's legs.)
KING (635 "Try Me") ... 100-150 59
(Cover pictures a woman with a smoking gun.)
KING (683 "James Brown & His Famous Flames *Think*") ... 100-150 60
(Cover pictures a baby.)
KING (683 "James Brown & His Famous Flames *Think*") ... 25-40 61
(Cover has pictures of James Brown.)
KING (743 "The Always Amazing James Brown and the Famous Flames") ... 50-75 61
(Cover is pink and blue.)
KING (771 "Jump Around") ... 50-75 62
KING (780 "The Exciting James Brown") ... 50-75 62
KING (804 "James Brown and the Famous Flames Tour the U.S.A.") ... 50-75 62
KING (826 "Apollo Theatre Presents the James Brown Show") ... 40-60 63
KING (851 "Prisoner of Love") ... 30-50 63
KING (883 "Pure Dynamite") ... 25-50 64
KING (900 series) ... 15-25 65-66
KING (1000 & 1100 series, except 1024 and 1038) ... 10-15 67-71
KING (1024 "Show of Tomorrow") 100-150 67
KING (1038 "Thinking About Little Willie John") ... 30-35 68
POLYDOR ... 5-10 71-84
SCOTTI BROTHERS ... 5-8 86-88
SMASH ... 10-20 64-68
SOLID SMOKE ... 5-10 80-81
T.K. ... 5-10 80
Also see BAMBAATAA, Afrika, James Brown
Also see BYRD, Bobby, & James Brown
Also see J.B.s
Also see POETS

BROWN, James, & Vicki Anderson P&R '67
Singles: 7–inch
KING ... 4-6 67-70

BROWN, James, Band
Singles: 7–inch
KING ... 4-8 61
Also see WESLEY, Fred, & Horny Horns

BROWN, James, & Lyn Collins P&R/R&B '72
Singles: 7–inch
POLYDOR ... 3-5 72
Also see COLLINS, Lyn

BROWN, James / Martha & Vandellas
Singles: 7–inch
A&M (3022 "I Got You") ... 3-4 88
Picture Sleeves
A&M (3022 "I Got You") ... 3-4 88
Also see MARTHA & VANDELLAS

BROWN, James, & Marva Whitney
Singles: 7–inch
KING ... 3-6 69
Also see BROWN, James
Also see WHITNEY, Marva

BROWN, Jim Ed C&W '65
(Jim Edward Brown)
Singles: 7–inch
RCA (Except 8000 & 9000 series) ... 3-5 69-81
RCA (8000 & 9000 series) ... 3-8 65-68
LPs: 10/12–inch
PICKWICK ... 5-8 80
RCA (Except 3000 & 4000 series) ... 5-10 73-81
RCA (3000 & 4000 series) ... 8-15 66-72
(With "LPM" or "LSP" prefix.)
Session: Mary Cates; Margie Cates.
Also see BROWNS
Also see CATES SISTERS
Also see SOME of CHET'S FRIENDS

BROWN, Jim Ed, & Helen Cornelius C&W '76
Singles: 7–inch
RCA ... 3-5 76-81
LPs: 10/12–inch
RCA ... 5-10 77-82
Also see BROWN, Jim Edward
Also see CORNELIUS, Helen

BROWN, Jim Edward & Maxine: see BROWNS

BROWN, Jim Edward, Maxine & Bonnie: see BROWNS

BROWN, Jocelyn P&R/R&B/D&D '84
Singles: 12–inch
JELLYBEAN ... 4-6 86
VINYL DREAMS ... 4-6 84
Singles: 7–inch
JELLYBEAN ... 3-4 86
VINYL DREAMS ... 3-4 84
W.B. ... 3-4 86-87
LPs: 10/12–inch
JELLYBEAN ... 5-10 86
VINYL DREAMS ... 5-10 84
Also see INNER LIFE
Also see SALSOUL ORCHESTRA

BROWN, Julie LP '85
Singles: 7–inch
BULLETZ ... 3-5 83
RHINO ... 3-4 84
SIRE ... 3-4 87
Picture Sleeves
BULLETZ ... 3-5 83
LPs: 10/12–inch
RHINO ... 5-10 85

BROWN, Julius D&D '83
Singles: 12–inch
WEST END ... 4-6 83-84

BROWN, Les, & His Orch. P&R '39
(With His Band of Renown; with His Duke University Blue Devils)
Singles: 78 rpm
BLUEBIRD ... 5-10 38-40
CAPITOL ... 3-5 56-57
COLUMBIA ... 5-10 42-57
CONQUEROR ... 5-10 41
CORAL ... 3-6 53-57
DECCA ... 5-10 36-40
OKEH ... 5-10 41-42
Singles: 7–inch
CAPITOL ... 3-8 56-59
COLUMBIA ... 5-10 50-60
CORAL ... 3-6 53-59
SIGNATURE ... 3-6 60
EPs: 7–inch
CAPITOL ... 5-10 56-58
COLUMBIA ... 5-10 54-56
CORAL ... 5-10 53-56
LPs: 10/12–inch
CAPITOL ... 10-20 56-59
COLUMBIA ... 10-25 50-61

CORAL 15-30 55-60
HARMONY 8-15 59
KAPP 8-15 59
MEDALLION 8-15 61
Also see DAY, Doris

BROWN, Louise *P&R '61*

Singles: 7-inch
WITCH (101 "Son-in-Law") 25-45 61

BROWN, Maxine *P&R '60*

Singles: 7-inch
ABC 3-4 75
ABC-PAR 5-10 61-62
AVCO EMBASSY 3-5 71
COLLECTABLES 3-4 81
COMMONWEALTH UNITED 4-6 69-70
ERIC 3-4 83
NOMAR 5-10 61
WAND 5-10 63-67
WHAM 4-8
Picture Sleeves
WAND (135 "Ask Me") 10-15 63
WHAM (7036 "All in My Mind") 10-15
EPs: 7-inch
COMMONWEALTH UNITED (1001 "Maxine Brown") 5-10 69
(Promotional issue only.)
LPs: 10/12-inch
COLLECTABLES 6-8 88
COMMONWEALTH UNITED 10-12 69
GUEST STAR 10-12 64
WAND 15-25 63-67
Also see ADAMS, Faye / Little Esther / Maxine Brown
Also see JACKSON, Chuck, & Maxine Brown

BROWN, Maxine / Irma Thomas

LPs: 10/12-inch
GRAND PRIX 12-15 64
Also see BROWN, Maxine
Also see THOMAS, Irma

BROWN, Maxine *C&W '68*

Singles: 7-inch
CHART 4-6 68
LPs: 10/12-inch
CHART 10-20 69
Also see BROWNS

BROWN, Miquel *D&D '83*

Singles: 12-inch
TSR 4-6 83
Singles: 7-inch
POLYDOR 3-4 79
TSR 3-4 83
Picture Sleeves
TSR 3-4 83
LPs: 10/12-inch
POLYDOR 5-10 78
TSR 5-10 85

BROWN, Nappy *P&R/R&B '55*
(With the Gibralters; with Southern Sisters)

Singles: 78 rpm
SAVOY 10-20 55-57
Singles: 7-inch
SAVOY (1100 series) 15-25 55
SAVOY (1500 series) 10-20 57-60
SAVOY (1600 series) 8-15 61-63
LPs: 10/12-inch
LANDSLIDE 5-8
SAVOY (14002 "Nappy Brown Sings") 50-100 57
SAVOY (14025 "The Right Time") 40-60 60
SAVOY (14427 "Nappy Brown") 8-15 77

BROWN, O'chi *R&B '86*

Singles: 12-inch
MERCURY 4-6 86
Singles: 7-inch
MERCURY 3-4 86
LPs: 10/12-inch
MERCURY 5-10 86

BROWN, Odell *LP '67*
(With the Organ-izers)

Singles: 7-inch
CADET 3-6 67-68
LPs: 10/12-inch
CADET 10-15 67-69
PAULA 8-10 74

BROWN, Oscar, Jr. *P&R/R&B '74*

Singles: 7-inch
ATLANTIC 3-5 74
COLUMBIA 5-10 60-62
FONTANA 4-8 65-66
MAD 8-12 59
LPs: 10/12-inch
ATLANTIC 5-10
COLUMBIA 15-25 61-63
FONTANA 10-15 66

BROWN, Peter *P&R/R&B '77*

Singles: 12-inch
COLUMBIA 4-6 84
RCA 4-6 83
Singles: 7-inch
COLUMBIA 3-4 84
DRIVE 3-5 77-80
RCA 3-4 83
Picture Sleeves
COLUMBIA 3-4 84
LPs: 10/12-inch
COLUMBIA 5-10 84
DRIVE 5-10 78
RCA 5-10 82-83

BROWN, Peter, & Betty Wright *P&R/R&B '78*

Singles: 7-inch
DRIVE 3-5 78
Also see BROWN, Peter
Also see WRIGHT, Betty

BROWN, Polly *P&R/R&B '75*

Singles: 7-inch
ARIOLA AMERICA 3-5 75-76
BEL 3-5 73
GTO 3-5 74
Also see PICKETTYWITCH
Also see SWEET DREAMS

BROWN, Randy *R&B '78*
(Randy Brown & Company)

Singles: 12-inch
MILLENNIUM 4-6 78
Singles: 7-inch
CHOCOLATE CITY 3-4 80-81
IX CHAINS 3-5 75
PARACHUTE 3-5 78-79
STAX 3-4 80
TRUTH 3-5 74-75
LPs: 10/12-inch
CHOCOLATE CITY 5-10 80-81
PARACHUTE 5-10 78-79
STAX 5-10 80-81

BROWN, Roy *R&B/C&W '48*
(With His Mighty-Mighty Men)

Singles: 78 rpm
DELUXE 20-50 47-51
GOLD STAR 15-25 48
IMPERIAL 15-25 57
KING 15-25 52-57
Singles: 7-inch
BLUESWAY 4-8 67
DELUXE (3319 "Bar Room Blues") 150-200 51
(Black vinyl.)
DELUXE (3319 "Bar Room Blues") 200-400 51
(Colored vinyl.)
DELUXE (3323 "I've Got the Last Laugh Now") 75-100 51
(Black vinyl.)
DELUXE (3323 "I've Got the Last Laugh Now") 150-250 51
(Colored vinyl.)
FRIENDSHIP 5-10
GUSTO 3-4 83
HOME of the BLUES (107 "Man with the Blues") 15-25 60
HOME of the BLUES (110 "Rockin' All the Time") 15-25 60
HOME of the BLUES (115 "Sugar Baby") 15-25 60
HOME of the BLUES (122 "Rock & Roll Jamboree") 15-25 61
IMPERIAL (5422 "Saturday Night") 20-30 57
IMPERIAL (5427 "Party Doll") 20-30 57
IMPERIAL (5439 "Let the Four Winds Blow") 20-30 57
IMPERIAL (5510 "Hip Shakin' Baby") 20-30 57
KING (4602 "Travelin' Man") 25-50 53
(Black vinyl.)
KING (4602 "Travelin' Man") 100-150 53
(Colored vinyl.)
KING (4609 "Money Can't Buy Love") 25-50 53
KING (4627 "Gamblin' Man") 25-50 53
KING (4637 "Old Age Boogie") 25-50 53
KING (4654 "Laughing But Crying") 25-50 53
KING (4669 "A Fool in Love") 25-50 53
KING (4684 "Midnight Lover Man") 25-50 53
KING (4704 "Bootleggin' Baby") 25-50 54
KING (4715 "This Is My Last Goodbye") 25-50 54
KING (4722 "Don't Let It Rain") 25-50 54
KING (4731 "Ain't It a Shame") 25-50 54
KING (4743 "Worried Life Blues") 25-50 54
KING (4761 "Fanny Brown Got Married") 25-50 54
KING (4816 "Letter to Baby") 25-50 55
KING (4834 "She's Gone Too Long") 25-50 55
KING (5000 series) 10-20 56-60
MERCURY 3-5 71
MOBILE FIDELITY 3-5 72
TRU-LOVE 4-6
EPs: 7-inch
KING (254 "Roy Brown") 50-100 53
LPs: 10/12-inch
BLUESWAY 10-20 68-73
EPIC 10-15 71
GUSTO 8-12
INTERMEDIA 5-10 84
KING (956 "24 Hits") 35-45 66
KING (1100 series) 10-15 71
KING (5000 series) 8-10 79
Also see HARRIS, Wynonie / Roy Brown
Also see VINSON, Eddie / Roy Brown / Wynonie Harris

BROWN, Ruth *R&B '49*
(With the Rhythmakers)

Singles: 78 rpm
ATLANTIC 15-30 49-57
Singles: 7-inch
ATLANTIC (919 "Teardrops from My Eyes") 200-250 50
ATLANTIC (948 "Shine On") 25-50 51
ATLANTIC (962 thru 993) 20-30 52-53
ATLANTIC (1005 thru 1091) 10-20 53-56
ATLANTIC (1100 series) 10-15 57-58
ATLANTIC (2000 series) 5-10 59-60
DECCA 4-8 64
MAINSTREAM 5-8
NOSLEN 4-8 64
PHILIPS 5-10 62
SYKE 4-8 69
EPs: 7-inch
ATLANTIC (505 "Ruth Brown Sings") 50-75 53
ATLANTIC (535 "Ruth Brown Sings") 50-75 53
ATLANTIC (585 "Ruth Brown") 35-60 57
PHILIPS 10-15 62
LPs: 10/12-inch
ATLANTIC (1308 "Last Date with Ruth Brown") 50-70 59
ATLANTIC (SD-1308 "Last Date with Ruth Brown") 75-100 59
(Stereo.)
ATLANTIC (8004 "Ruth Brown") 50-75 57
(Black label.)
ATLANTIC (8004 "Ruth Brown") 30-40 60
(Red label.)
ATLANTIC (8026 "Miss Rhythm") 35-50 59
(Black label.)

ATLANTIC (8026 "Miss Rhythm") 35-50 59
(White label.)
ATLANTIC (8026 "Miss Rhythm") 15-25 60
(Red label.)
ATLANTIC (8080 "Best of Ruth Brown") 15-25 63
COBBLESTONE 8-10 72
DOBRE 5-10 78
MAINSTREAM (300 series) 8-10 72
MAINSTREAM (6000 series) 12-15 65
PHILIPS 12-15 62
SKYE 10-12 70
Also see BRADLEY, Will, & Ray McKinley
Also see JACKSON, Willis
Also see JOHNSON, Buddy

BROWN, Ruth, & Clyde McPhatter — R&B '55

Singles: 78 rpm

ATLANTIC 10-20 55

Singles: 7-inch

ATLANTIC 10-20 55
Also see BROWN, Ruth
Also see McPHATTER, Clyde

BROWN, Sam — P&R '89

Singles: 7-inch

A&M 3-4 89

Picture Sleeves

A&M 3-4 89

BROWN, Savoy: see SAVOY BROWN

BROWN, Sawyer: see SAWYER BROWN

BROWN, Sharon — R&B '82

Singles: 12-inch

PROFILE 4-6 83

Singles: 7-inch

PROFILE 3-4 82-83

BROWN, Shawn — R&B/D&D '85

Singles: 12-inch

JWP 4-6 85

Singles: 7-inch

JWP 3-4 85

BROWN, Sheree — R&B '81

Singles: 12-inch

CAPITOL 4-6 81

Singles: 7-inch

CAPITOL 3-4 81-82

LPs: 10/12-inch

CAPITOL 5-10 81-82

BROWN, Shirley — P&R/R&B '74

Singles: 12-inch

MERCURY 4-6 83

Singles: 7-inch

ABET 4-6 71
ARISTA 3-5 77-78
CHELSEA AVE. 4-6
SOUND TOWN 3-4 84-85
STAX 3-5 79
TRUTH 3-5 74-76
20TH FOX 3-4 80

LPs: 10/12-inch

ARISTA 5-10 77
COLUMBIA 10-15 68-72
SOUND TRACK 5-10 85
STAX 5-10 77-79
TRUTH 8-10 75

BROWN, Veda — R&B '73

Singles: 7-inch

RAKEN 3-5 75
STAX 3-5 73-74

BROWN, Wini — R&B '52

(With the Boyfriends)

Singles: 78 rpm

COLUMBIA 10-20 51
MERCURY 25-50 52

Singles: 7-inch

COLUMBIA (872 "A Good Man Is Hard to Find") 15-25 51
JARO (77018 "Gone Again") 10-15 60
MERCURY (5870 "Here in My Heart") 75-125 52
MERCURY (8270 "Be Anything") 75-125 52
Members: Wini Brown; Joe Van Loan; Percy Green; Fred Francis; Warren Suttles.
Also see DOGGETT, Bill
Also see HAMPTON, Lionel

BROWN SUGAR — P&R '76

Singles: 7-inch

ABKCO 3-5 72
CAPITOL 3-5 76
CHELSEA 3-5 73-74
Member: Clydie King.
Also see KING, Clydie

BROWNE, Duncan — LP '79

Singles: 7-inch

IMMEDIATE 3-6 69
RAK 3-5 72
SIRE 3-4 79

Picture Sleeves

IMMEDIATE 5-10 68

LPs: 10/12-inch

IMMEDIATE 10-15 68
SIRE 5-10 79

BROWNE, Jackson — P&R/LP '72

Singles: 12-inch

ASYLUM 4-6 81-82
ELEKTRA 4-8 89
(Promotional only.)

Singles: 7-inch

ASYLUM 3-4 72-86
COLUMBIA 3-4 86
ELEKTRA 3-4 80-89

Picture Sleeves

ASYLUM 3-5 80-86
ELEKTRA 4-8 80

LPs: 10/12-inch

ASYLUM (Except 5051) 8-10 72-86
ASYLUM (5051 "Jackson Browne") .. 10-15 72
(With burlap cover.)
ASYLUM (5051 "Jackson Browne") 8-10 72
(Without burlap.)
ELEKTRA ("Jackson Browne's First Album") 25-35 67
(Promotional issue only.)
ELEKTRA (60830 "World in Motion") ... 5-8 89
MFSL (055 "Pretender") 25-50 81
Also see CLEMONS, Clarence, & Jackson Browne
Also see LINDLEY, David
Also see SPRINGSTEEN, Bruce / Jackson Browne

BROWNE, Reno, & Her Buckaroos: see HALEY, Bill

BROWNE, Tom — LP '79

Singles: 12-inch

ARISTA 4-6 83

Singles: 7-inch

ARISTA 3-4 83-84
GRP 3-4 79-82

LPs: 10/12-inch

ARISTA 5-10 83-84
GRP 5-10 79-82

BROWNMARK — R&B '88

Singles: 7-inch

MOTOWN 3-4 88
Also see MAZARATI
Also see PRINCE

BROWNS — C&W '54

(Jim Edward & Maxine Brown; Jim Edward, Maxine & Bonnie Brown; with the Louisiana Hayride Band; Browns featuring Jim Edward Brown)

Singles: 78 rpm

FABOR 5-15 54-55
RCA 5-15 56-57

Singles: 7-inch

COLUMBIA 4-8 62
FABOR 10-20 54-55
RCA (6480 thru 7427) 10-15 56-58
RCA (47-7555 "The Three Bells") 5-10 59
(Monaural.)
RCA (61-7555 "The Three Bells") 10-15 59
(Stereo.)
RCA (47-7614 "Scarlet Ribbons") 5-10 59
(Monaural.)
RCA (61-7614 "Scarlet Ribbons") 10-15 59
(Stereo.)
RCA (47-7700 "Old Lamplighter") 5-10 60
(Monaural.)
RCA (61-7700 "Old Lamplighter") 10-15 60
(Stereo.)
RCA (47-7755 "Lonely Little Robin") ... 5-10 60
(Monaural.)
RCA (61-7755 "Lonely Little Robin") 10-15 60
(Stereo.)
RCA (47-7780 "Wiffenpoof Song") 5-10 60
(Monaural.)
RCA (61-7780 "Wiffenpoof Song") 10-15 60
(Stereo.)
RCA (47-7820 "Send Me the Pillow You Dream On") 5-10 60
(Monaural.)
RCA (61-7820 "Send Me the Pillow You Dream On") 10-15 60
(Monaural.)
RCA (7820 "Blue Christmas") 5-10 60
RCA (37-7866 "Angel's Dolly") 10-15 61
(Compact 33 single.)
RCA (47-7866 "Angel's Dolly") 4-8 61
RCA (37-7917 "My Baby's Gone") 10-15 61
(Compact 33 single.)
RCA (47-7917 "My Baby's Gone") 4-8 61
RCA (37-7969 "Foolish Pride") 10-15 61
(Compact 33 single.)
RCA (47-7969 "Foolish Pride") 4-8 61
RCA (37-7997 "Remember Me") 10-15 62
(Compact 33 single.)
RCA (47-7997 "Remember Me") 4-8 62
RCA (8066 thru 9364) 4-8 62-67

Picture Sleeves

RCA (7700 "The Old Lamplighter") 10-15 60
RCA (7755 "Lonely Little Robin") 10-15 60
RCA (7780 "Wiffenpoof Song") 10-15 60

EPs: 7-inch

RCA 10-20 57-60

LPs: 10/12-inch

CAMDEN 8-12 65-68
CANDLELITE (0422 "Beautiful Country Music of the Browns") 5-10 80
(Mail order offer.)
MCA/DOT 5-8 86
RCA (524 "20 of the Best") 5-8 85
RCA (1000 thru 3000 series) 5-10 75-81
(With "ANL1" or "AYL1" prefix.)
RCA (1438 Jim Edward, Maxine and Bonnie Brown") 35-55 57
(With "LPM" prefix.)
RCA (2000 series) 15-30 59-65
(With "LPM" or "LSP" prefix.)
RCA (3000 series) 12-20 65-67
(With "LPM" or "LSP" prefix.)
Members: Jim Edward Brown; Maxine Brown; Bonnie Brown.
Also see BROWN, Jim Ed
Also see BROWN, Maxine
Also see COOKE, Sam / Rod Lauren / Neil Sedaka / Browns

BROWNSVILLE

Singles: 7-inch

EPIC 3-4 79

LPs: 10/12-inch

EPIC (Black vinyl) 8-10 79
EPIC (Colored vinyl) 12-15 79
Also see BROWNSVILLE STATION

BROWNSVILLE STATION — P&R/LP '72

Singles: 7-inch

BIG TREE 3-5 72-74
EPIC 3-5 79
HIDEOUT (1957 "Rock & Roll Holiday") 8-12 69
PALLADIUM (1075 "Be-Bop Confidential") 5-10 70
POLYDOR 3-5 70
PRIVATE STOCK 3-5 77
W.B. (7501 "That's Fine") 4-8 71

LPs: 10/12-inch

BIG TREE..10-12 72-75
EPIC (Black vinyl)..............................8-10 78
EPIC (Colored vinyl)..........................10-20 78
(Promotional issue only.)
PALLADIUM (1004 "Brownsville Station")..20-25 70
PRIVATE STOCK...............................8-10 77
W.B. 12-15 70

Members: Tony Driggins; Cub Koda; Michael Lutz; Henry Weck; Bruce Nazarian.

Also see BROWNSVILLE
Also see SEGER, Bob

BRUBECK, Dave, Quartet LP '55

(Dave Brubeck Trio; Octet; with Paul Desmond)

Singles: 78 rpm

COLUMBIA...4-8 55-57
FANTASY..4-8 52-55

Singles: 7-inch

COLUMBIA (Except 40000 & 41000 series) 3-6 62-65
COLUMBIA (40000 & 41000 series) ... 5-10 55-61
FANTASY (500 series).......................5-10 52-55

Picture Sleeves

COLUMBIA...5-10 61-63

EPs: 7-inch

COLUMBIA...10-25 55-59
FANTASY...15-30 51-57

LPs: 10/12-inch

ATLANTIC (79 "Fantasy Years").........8-12 74
COLUMBIA (566 "Jazz Goes to College")..50-75 54
COLUMBIA (590 "Dave Brubeck at Storyville").......................................50-75 54
COLUMBIA (622 "Brubeck Time") 40-60 55
COLUMBIA (699 "Jazz: Red Hot and Cool")..40-60 55
COLUMBIA (826 "Dave Brubeck Quintet at Carnegie Hall.................................20-30 63
COLUMBIA (878 "Brubeck Plays Brubeck")..30-50 56
COLUMBIA (932 "Brubeck, Jay & Kai at Newport")...30-50 57
COLUMBIA (984 "Jazz Impressions of the U.S.A.")..30-50 57
COLUMBIA (1000 thru 1200 series)..20-35 57-59
(Monaural.)
COLUMBIA (1300 thru 2300 series)..12-25 59-65
(Monaural.)
COLUMBIA (6321 "Jazz Goes to College")....................................50-100 54
(10-inch LP.)
COLUMBIA (6322 "Jazz Goes to College")...50-75 54
(10-inch LP.)
COLUMBIA (6330 "Dave Brubeck at Storyville").......................................50-75 54
(10-inch LP.)
COLUMBIA (6331 "Dave Brubeck at Storyville").......................................50-75 54
(10-inch LP.)
COLUMBIA (8000 series).................20-45 57-59
(Stereo.)
COLUMBIA (8100 thru 9300 series)..15-30 59-66
(Stereo.)
CROWN 10-15 62-64
FANTASY (1 "Dave Brubeck Trio")..100-150 51
(10-inch LP. Colored vinyl.)
FANTASY (2 "Dave Brubeck Trio")..100-150 51
(10-inch LP. Colored vinyl.)
FANTASY (3 "Dave Brubeck Octet")..100-150 52
(10-inch LP. Colored vinyl.)
FANTASY (5 "Dave Brubeck Quartet with Paul Desmond")..................................100-150 52
(10-inch LP. Colored vinyl.)
FANTASY (7 "Dave Brubeck Quartet with Paul Desmond") 100-150 53
(10-inch LP. Colored vinyl.)
FANTASY (8 "At Storyville") 100-150 53
(10-inch LP. Colored vinyl.)
FANTASY (10 "Jazz at the Black Hawk")...100-150 53
(10-inch LP. Colored vinyl.)
FANTASY (11 "Jazz at Oberlin") 100-150 53
(10-inch LP. Colored vinyl.)
FANTASY (13 "Jazz at the College of the Pacific") 100-150 54
(10-inch LP. Colored vinyl.)
FANTASY (16 "Old Sounds from San Francisco") 100-150 55
(10-inch LP. Colored vinyl.)
FANTASY (204 "Dave Brubeck Trio")...75-125 56
(Colored vinyl.)
FANTASY (205 "Dave Brubeck Trio")...50-100 56
FANTASY (210 "Jazz at the Black Hawk")...50-100 56
FANTASY (223 "Jazz at the College of the Pacific") 50-100 56
FANTASY (229 "Dave Brubeck Quartet with Paul Desmond") 50-100 56
FANTASY (230 "Dave Brubeck Quartet with Paul Desmond") 50-100 56
FANTASY (239 "Dave Brubeck Octet") 50-100 56
FANTASY (240 "Dave Brubeck at Storyville") 50-100 57
FANTASY (245 "Jazz at Oberlin") 50-100 57
FANTASY (3300 series) 15-25 62
HORIZON... 5-10 76
JAZZTONE (1272 "Dave Brubeck").. 25-50 57

Members: Dave Brubeck; Paul Desmond; Cal Tjader; Dick Collins; David Van Kriedt; Joe Morello; Eugene Wright.

Also see ARMSTRONG, Louis
Also see BERNSTEIN, Leonard, & Dave Brubeck
Also see RUSHING, Jimmy
Also see TJADER, Cal

BRUBECK, Dave, & Paul Desmond LP '76

Singles: 7-inch

A&M... 3-5 76
HORIZON... 3-5 75

LPs: 10/12-inch

HORIZON... 6-10 74-75

As a member of Dave Brubeck's group, Paul Desmond was often credited prominently on releases which, for consistency, appear in the Brubeck section.

Also see DESMOND, Paul

BRUBECK, Dave, & Gerry Mulligan

Singles: 7-inch

COLUMBIA 4-6 68

LPs: 10/12-inch

COLUMBIA 8-15 68-73
VERVE.. 8-12 73

Also see BRUBECK, Dave
Also see MULLIGAN, Gerry

BRUCE, Jack LP '69

(Jack Bruce Band; with Friends)

Singles: 7-inch

RSO 3-5 74-75

LPs: 10/12-inch

ATCO.. 10-15 69-71
EPIC.. 5-10 80
POLYDOR 8-12 72
RSO 5-10 74-77

Also see CREAM
Also see MAYALL, John
Also see ROCKET 88
Also see WEST, BRUCE & LAING

BRUCE, Jack, & Robin Trower LP '82

LPs: 10/12-inch

CHRYSALIS (1352 "Truce")...............5-10 82

BRUCE, Jack, Bill Lordan & Robin Trower LP '81

LPs: 10/12-inch

CHRYSALIS (1324 "B.L.T.") 5-10 81

Also see BRUCE, Jack
Also see TROWER, Robin

BRUCE, Lenny LP '75

Singles: 7-inch

FANTASY (Black vinyl) 5-10
FANTASY (Colored vinyl)..................10-15

Picture Sleeves

W.B. (598 "The Law, Language and Lenny Bruce")...20-30 74

EPs: 7-inch

FANTASY (2 "Curran Theater Concert")...10-20
(Promotional issue only.)

LPs: 10/12-inch

CAPITOL (2630 "Why Did Lenny Bruce Die")..15-20 66
DOUGLAS.......................................15-25 68-71
FANTASY (1 "Lenny Bruce")............50-75
(Promotional issue only.)
FANTASY (7001 "Lenny Bruce's Interviews of Our Times") 30-40 58
(THICK red vinyl.)
FANTASY (7001 "Lenny Bruce's Interviews of Our Times") 15-25
(Black vinyl.)
FANTASY (7001 "Lenny Bruce's Interviews of Our Times") 8-12
(THIN red vinyl.)
FANTASY (7003 "The Sick Humor of Lenny Bruce")..30-40 58
(THICK red vinyl.)
FANTASY (7003 "The Sick Humor of Lenny Bruce")..15-20
(Black vinyl.)
FANTASY (7003 "The Sick Humor of Lenny Bruce")..8-12
(THIN red vinyl.)
FANTASY (7007 "I Am Not a Nut, Elect Me") 30-40 59
(THICK red vinyl.)
FANTASY (7007 "I Am Not a Nut, Elect Me") 15-20
(Black vinyl.)
FANTASY (7007 "I Am Not a Nut, Elect Me") 8-12
(THIN red vinyl.)
FANTASY (7011 "Lenny Bruce, American")..30-40 62
(THICK red vinyl.)
FANTASY (7011 "Lenny Bruce, American")..15-20
(Black vinyl.)
FANTASY (7011 "Lenny Bruce, American")..8-12
(THIN red vinyl.)
FANTASY (7012 "The Best of Lenny Bruce")..25-30 63
(THICK red vinyl.)
FANTASY (7012 "The Best of Lenny Bruce")..15-20
(Black vinyl.)
FANTASY (7012 "The Best of Lenny Bruce")..8-12
(THIN red vinyl.)
FANTASY (7017 "Thank You Masked Man") 10-15 72
FANTASY (34201 "Lenny Bruce Live at the Curran Theatre")......................................10-15 72
FANTASY (79003 "The Real Lenny Bruce")..8-12 75
LENNY BRUCE RECORDS ("Recordings Submitted As Evidence in the San Francisco Obscenity Trial, in March 1962")....75-100 62
PHILLES (4010 "Lenny Bruce Is Out Again")...50-75 66

REPRISE (6329 "The Berkeley Concert") ... 15-20 69
U.A. (3580 "Midnight Concert") ... 15-20 67
U.A. (9800 "At Carnegie Hall") ... 15-25 71
(Three LPs.)
W.B. (9101 "The Law, Language and Lenny Bruce") ... 10-20 74
(Promotional issue only.)

BRUCE & TERRY — P&R '64

Singles: 7-inch

COLUMBIA ... 5-10 64-66
Members: Bruce Johnston; Terry Melcher.
Also see BOONE, Pat
Also see HONDELLS
Also see JOHNSTON, Bruce
Also see MELCHER, Terry, & Bruce Johnston
Also see NEWTON, Wayne
Also see RIP CHORDS
Also see SAGITTARIUS

BRUFORD, Bill — LP '79

Singles: 7-inch

POLYDOR ... 3-5 78-80

LPs: 10/12-inch

POLYDOR ... 5-10 79-80
Also see YES

BRUNSON, Tyrone "Tystick" — R&B '82

Singles: 12-inch

BELIEVE in a DREAM ... 4-6 82-84

Singles: 7-inch

BELIEVE in a DREAM ... 3-4 82-84

LPs: 10/12-inch

BELIEVE in a DREAM ... 5-10 82-84
Also see SPECIAL DELIVERY

BRYANT, Anita — P&R '59

Singles: 7-inch

CARLTON ... 4-8 58-61
COLUMBIA ... 4-8 61-67
DISNEYLAND ... 3-4
TRIP ... 3-5

Picture Sleeves

COLUMBIA ... 4-8 61-67
DISNEYLAND ... 3-5

EPs: 7-inch

ACSP (1779 "See America with AC") ... 5-10
(Promotional issue for AC Spark Plugs.)

LPs: 10/12-inch

CARLTON ... 10-20 59-61
COLUMBIA ... 8-15 62-67
HARMONY ... 6-12

BRYANT, Anita / Jo Stafford & Gordon MacRae

Singles: 7-inch

COLUMBIA ... 5-10 60
Also see MacRAE, Gordon, & Jo Stafford

BRYANT, Leon — R&B '81

Singles: 7-inch

DE-LITE ... 3-4 81-84

LPs: 10/12-inch

DE-LITE ... 5-10 84

BRYANT, Ray — P&R/R&B '60
(Ray Bryant Combo)

Singles: 7-inch

ATLANTIC ... 5-10
CADET ... 4-8 66-67
COLUMBIA ... 5-10 60-64
SIGNATURE ... 5-10 60
SUE ... 5-10 61

Picture Sleeves

CADET ... 5-10 67
COLUMBIA ... 10-15 60

LPs: 10/12-inch

CADET ... 10-20 66-67
COLUMBIA ... 15-30 60-62
EPIC (3279 "Ray Bryant Trio") ... 40-60 56
PRESTIGE/NEW JAZZ ... 15-25 62
SIGNATURE ... 15-25 60
SUE ... 15-30 60-64
Also see CARTER, Betty, & Ray Bryant

BRYANT, Sharon — P&R/LP '89

Singles: 7-inch

WING ... 3-4 89

Picture Sleeves

WING ... 3-4 89

LPs: 10/12-inch

WING ... 5-8 89
Also see ATLANTIC STARR

BRYSON, Peabo — R&B '76

Singles: 7-inch

BULLET ... 3-5 76-77
CAPITOL ... 3-4 77-83
COLUMBIA ... 3-4 91
ELEKTRA ... 3-4 84-88
MCA ... 3-4 84
SHOUT ... 3-5 75

Picture Sleeves

CAPITOL ... 3-4 81-83
ELEKTRA ... 3-4 85-88

LPs: 10/12-inch

BULLET ... 8-10 76
CAPITOL ... 5-10 78-84
COLUMBIA ... 5-8 91
ELEKTRA ... 5-10 84-86
Also see COLE, Natalie, & Peabo Bryson
Also see MANCHESTER, Melissa, & Peabo Bryson
Also see ZAGER, Michael, Moon Band, & Peabo Bryson

BRYSON, Peabo, & Regina Belle — R&B '87

Singles: 7-inch

ELEKTRA ... 3-4 88

Picture Sleeves

ELEKTRA ... 3-4 88
Also see BELLE, Regina
Also see COLE, Natalie, & Peabo Bryson
Also see FLACK, Roberta, & Peabo Bryson

BUBBLE PUPPY — P&R/LP '69

Singles: 7-inch

INT'L ARTISTS (128 "Hot Smoke and Sasafrass") ... 15-20 69
INT'L ARTISTS (133 "Beginning") ... 15-25 69
INT'L ARTISTS (136 "Days of Our Time") ... 15-25 70
INT'L ARTISTS (138 "Hurry Sundown") ... 15-25 69

Promotional Singles

INT'L ARTISTS (Black vinyl) ... 20-30 69-70
INT'L ARTISTS (Colored vinyl) ... 25-50 70

LPs: 10/12-inch

INT'L ARTISTS (10 "A Gathering of Promises") ... 100-125 69
(Green label)
INT'L ARTISTS (10 "A Gathering of Promises") ... 150-200 69
(White label. Promotional issue only.)
Members: Rod Prince; Todd Potter; Roy Cox; M. Taylor; Dave Fore.
Also see MUSIC MACHINE / Bubble Puppy

BUCHANAN, Bill

Singles: 7-inch

GONE (5032 "The Thing") ... 15-25 58
U.A. ... 8-12 62
Also see BUCHANAN & ANCELL
Also see BUCHANAN & CELLA
Also see BUCHANAN & GOODMAN
Also see BUCHANAN & GREENFIELD

BUCHANAN, Roy — LP '72

Singles: 7-inch

ALLIGATOR ... 3-4 85-86
ATLANTIC ... 3-4 76-78
BOMARC ... 10-15 61
POLYDOR ... 3-5 72-75
SWAN ... 4-8 61

LPs: 10/12-inch

ALLIGATOR ... 5-10 85
ATLANTIC ... 5-10 76-77
BIOYA ... 30-40 71
POLYDOR ... 8-15 72-75
WATERHOUSE ... 10-15 81
Also see CANNON, Freddy
Also see GREGG, Bobby
Also see HAWKINS, Dale

BUCHANAN & ANCELL — P&R '57

Singles: 78 rpm

FLYING SAUCER ... 20-30 57

Singles: 7-inch

FLYING SAUCER (501 "The Creature") ... 20-30 57
Members: Bill Buchanan; Bob Ancell.
Also see BUCHANAN, Bill

BUCHANAN & CELLA

Singles: 7-inch

ABC-PAR (10033 "String Along with Pal-O-Mine") ... 10-20 59
Member: Bill Buchanan.
Also see BUCHANAN, Bill

BUCHANAN & GOODMAN — P&R/R&B '56

Singles: 78 rpm

LUNIVERSE (Except 101) ... 15-25 56-58
LUNIVERSE (101 "Flying Saucer") ... 25-35 56
(Label is printed "Universe," with a handwritten "L," making "Luniverse.")
LUNIVERSE (101 "Flying Saucer") ... 15-25 56
(Label is "Luniverse.")
LUNIVERSE (101X "Back to Earth") ... 25-50 56
RADIO-ACTIVE ... 10-15

Singles: 7-inch

COMIC ... 10-15 59
LUNIVERSE (Except 101) ... 15-30 56-58
LUNIVERSE (101 "Flying Saucer") ... 30-40 56
(Label is printed "Universe," with a handwritten "L," making "Luniverse.")
LUNIVERSE (101 "Flying Saucer") ... 15-25 56
(Label is "Luniverse.")
LUNIVERSE (101X "Back to Earth") ... 100-125 56
NOVELTY ... 10-15 59
RADIO-ACTIVE (101 "Flying Saucer") ... 50-75 56
(No artist credit shown. Unauthorized issue.)
Members: Bill Buchanan; Dickie Goodman.
Also see BUCHANAN, Bill
Also see GOODMAN, Dickie

BUCHANAN & GREENFIELD

Singles: 7-inch

NOVEL (711 "The Invasion") ... 15-20 64
(Red label.)
NOVEL (711 "The Invasion") ... 3-5 72
(Red and white label.)
Members: Bill Buchanan; Howard Greenfield.
Also see BUCHANAN, Bill

BUCHANAN BROTHERS — C&W '46

Singles: 78 rpm

VICTOR ... 5-10 46

BUCHANAN BROTHERS — P&R '69

Singles: 7-inch

EVENT ... 3-6 69-71

LPs: 10/12-inch

EVENT (101 "Medicine Man") ... 20-25 69
Members: Terry Cashman; Gene Pistilli; Tommy West.
Also see CASHMAN, PISTILLI & WEST

BUCK — R&B '75

Singles: 7-inch

PLAYBOY ... 3-5 75

BUCKEYE — P&R '79

Singles: 7-inch

POLYDOR ... 3-4 79

LPs: 10/12-inch

POLYDOR ... 5-10 79
Member: Ronn Price.

BUCKINGHAM, Lindsey — P&R/LP '81

Singles: 7-inch

ASYLUM ... 3-4 81
ELEKTRA ... 3-4 84
W.B. ... 3-4 83

Picture Sleeves

ASYLUM ... 3-4 81
ELEKTRA ... 3-4 84

LPs: 10/12-inch

ASYLUM............5-10 81
ELEKTRA............5-10 84
Also see BUCKINGHAM NICKS
Also see EGAN, Walter
Also see FLEETWOOD MAC
Also see STEWART, John

BUCKINGHAM NICKS

Singles: 7-inch

POLYDOR (14335 "Down Let Me Down Again")............20-30 76
POLYDOR (14428 "Crying in the Night")............20-30 77

Picture Sleeves

POLYDOR (14428 "Crying in the Night")............40-60 77
Members: Lindsey Buckingham; Stevie Nicks.
Also see BUCKINGHAM, Lindsey
Also see NICKS, Stevie

BUCKINGHAMS — P&R '66

Singles: 7-inch

COLUMBIA............4-8 67-70
RED LABEL............3-4 85
ROWE/AMI............10-20 66
("Play Me" Sales Stimulator promotional issue.)
SPECTRA-SOUND............10-20 67
U.S.A. 10-15 66-67

Picture Sleeves

COLUMBIA............8-15 67-68

LPs: 10/12-inch

COLUMBIA............15-25 67-75
RED LABEL............5-10 85
U.S.A. (107 "Kind of a Drag")............50-75 67
(With 13 tracks.)
U.S.A. (107 "Kind of a Drag")............30-40 67
(With 12 tracks.)
Members: Dennis Tufano; Carl Giammarese; Nick Fortune; Marty Grebb; Dennis Miccoli; Jon-Jon Poulos.
Also see TUFANO & GIAMMARESE

BUCKLEY, Tim — LP '67

Singles: 7-inch

DISC REET............3-5 73-74
ELEKTRA............4-8 66-67

LPs: 10/12-inch

DISC REET............8-10 73-74
ELEKTRA (Except 74004)............15-20 67-70
ELEKTRA (74004 "Tim Buckley")............25-35 66
RHINO............5-10 83
STRAIGHT (Except 1060)............15-25 70
STRAIGHT (1060 "Blue Afternoon")............25-35 69
W.B. 10-15 70-72

BUCKNER & GARCIA — P&R '80

Singles: 12-inch

COLUMBIA............4-6 82

Singles: 7-inch

BGO (1001 "Pac-Man Fever")............5-8 81
(First issue.)
COLUMBIA (Except 02945)............3-4 81
COLUMBIA (02945 "Pac-Man Fever")............8-12 82
(Square picture disc.)

Picture Sleeves

COLUMBIA............3-4 81

LPs: 10/12-inch

COLUMBIA............5-10 82
Members: Jerry Buckner; Gary Garcia.
Also see WILLIS "The Guard" & Vigorish

BUCKWHEAT — P&R/LP '72

Singles: 7-inch

LONDON............3-5 71-73

LPs: 10/12-inch

LONDON............10-12 71-73

BUCKWHEAT ZYDECO — LP '87

LPs: 10/12-inch

ISLAND............5-10 87-90

BUD & TRAVIS — P&R '60

Singles: 7-inch

LIBERTY............5-10 59-65
WORLD PACIFIC............5-10 59

LPs: 10/12-inch

LIBERTY............10-20 59-65
SUNSET............8-15 67
Members: Bud Dashiel; Travis Edmonson.
Also see DASHIEL, Bud, & Kinsmen
Also see EDMONSON, Travis

BUDD, Julie

(Julie)

Singles: 7-inch

A&M............3-4 81
ALSTON............3-4 77
BELL............3-5 70
MGM............3-6 68
RCA............3-5 72-73
TOM CAT............3-5 76-77

LPs: 10/12-inch

MGM............12-20 68
RCA............10-15 71
Also see JULIE

BUDDY & CLAUDIA — R&B '55

Singles: 78 rpm

CHESS............8-10 55

Singles: 7-inch

CHESS............10-15 55
Members: Buddy Griffin; Claudia Swann.

BUENA VISTAS — P&R '66

Singles: 7-inch

BB............4-6
MARQUEE............5-10 68
SWAN............10-15 66

BUFFALO SPRINGFIELD — P&R/LP '67

Singles: 7-inch

ATCO............5-10 67-68

LPs: 10/12-inch

ATCO (105 "Retrospective")............8-10 75
ATCO (200 "Buffalo Springfield")............30-50 66
(Contains *Baby Don't Scold Me.*)
ATCO (200 "Buffalo Springfield")............15-25 67
(*Baby Don't Scold Me* replaced by *For What It's Worth.*)
ATCO (226 thru 283)............20-30 67-69
ATCO (806 "Buffalo Springfield")............15-20 73
Members: Stephen Stills; Neil Young; Jim Messina; Richie Furay; Jim Fielder; Doug Hastings; Dewey Martin; Bruce Palmer.
Also see FURAY, Richie
Also see MARTIN, Dewey, & Medicine Ball
Also see MESSINA, Jim
Also see PALMER, Bruce
Also see POCO
Also see STILLS, Stephen
Also see YOUNG, Neil

BUFFETT, Jimmy — C&W '73

Singles: 7-inch

ABC............3-5 75-78
ASYLUM............3-4 80
BARNABY............3-5 70-72
DUNHILL............3-5 73-75
FULL MOON............3-4 80
MCA (Black vinyl)............3-4 79-86
MCA (Colored vinyl)............3-6 85

Picture Sleeves

ABC............3-5
MCA............3-4

LPs: 10/12-inch

ABC............8-10 76-78
BARNABY (6014 "High Cumberland Jubilee")............50-100 76
BARNABY (30093 "Down to Earth")............150-250 70
DUNHILL............10-15 73-74
MCA............5-10 79-90
U.A. 8-10 75

BUFFETT, Mary — D&D '84

Singles: 12-inch

MOBY DICK............4-6 84

Singles: 7-inch

MOBY DICK............3-4 84

BUGGLES — P&R/LP 79

Singles: 7-inch

CARRERE............3-4 82
ISLAND............3-4 79-83

Promotional Singles

CARRERE ("Fade Away")............3-4 82
(Soundsheet. Originally included in a magazine.)

LPs: 10/12-inch

CARRERE............5-10 82
ISLAND............5-10 80
Members: Trevor Horn; Geoff Downes.
Also see ASIA
Also see YES

BUGNON, Alex — LP '89

LPs: 10/12-inch

ORPHEUS............5-8 89-90

BULL & MATADORS — P&R/R&B '68

Singles: 7-inch

TODDLIN' TOWN............5-10 68-69

BULLDOG — P&R/LP '72

Singles: 7-inch

BUDDAH............3-5 72-74
DECCA............3-5 72
GUYDEN............3-5 71
MCA............3-5 73

LPs: 10/12-inch

BUDDAH............8-12 74
DECCA............12-20 72
Members: Gene Cornish; Dino Danelli; Billy Hocher; Eric Thorngren; John Turi.
Also see RASCALS

BULLENS, Cindy — P&R '79

Singles: 7-inch

CASABLANCA............3-4 79-80
U.A. 3-4 78-79

LPs: 10/12-inch

CASABLANCA............5-10 79
U.A. 5-10 78
Also see ALPHA BAND

BULLET — P&R '71

Singles: 7-inch

BIG TREE............3-5 71-72

BULLETBOYS — LP '88

Singles: 7-inch

W.B. 3-4 89

Picture Sleeves

W.B. 3-4 89

LPs: 10/12-inch

W.B. 5-8 89

BULLOCK, Janice — R&B '87

Singles: 7-inch

WRC............3-4 87
Also see BELL, William, & Janice Bullock

BUMBLE, B: see B. BUMBLE & STINGERS

BUMBLE BEE UNLIMITED — P&R/R&B '76

Singles: 12-inch

RED GREG............4-8 70s

Singles: 7-inch

MERCURY............3-5 76-77
RCA............3-4 79

LPs: 10/12-inch

RCA............5-10 79

BUONO, Victor — LP '71

Singles: 7-inch

DORE............3-5 71
FAMILY............3-5 71

LPs: 10/12-inch

DORE............5-10 71

BUOYS — P&R '71

Singles: 7-inch

POLYDOR............3-5 73
RANSOM............5-10
SCEPTER............3-6 69-71

Picture Sleeves

SCEPTER............4-6 70

LPs: 10/12-inch

SCEPTER............10-15 71
Members: Jerry Hludzik; Bill Kelly; Chris Hanlon; Fran Brozena; Carl Siracuse.

Also see DAKOTA
Also see JERRY KELLY

BURBANK, Gary, & Band McNally / Tennessee Valley Authority — C&W/P&R '80

Singles: 7-inch

OVATION 3-5 80

BURCH, Vernon — R&B '75

Singles: 12-inch

CHOCOLATE CITY 4-6 79-80
SPECTOR 4-6 81

Singles: 7-inch

CHOCOLATE CITY 3-4 78-80
COLUMBIA 3-4 77-78
SPECTOR 3-4 81-84
U.A. 3-5 75

LPs: 10/12-inch

CHOCOLATE CITY 5-10 79-80
COLUMBIA 8-10 77-78
SPECTOR 5-10 81-84
U.A. 8-10 74-76

BURDON, Eric — LP '74

(Eric Burdon Band)

Singles: 7-inch

CAPITOL 3-5 74

LPs: 10/12-inch

CAPITOL 8-10 74-75
LAX 5-10 81-84
VERVE 10-12 72
Also see ANIMALS

BURDON, Eric, & War — P&R/LP '70

(With Sharon Scott)

Singles: 7-inch

ABC 3-5 76
CAPITOL 5-10 74-75
LIBERTY 3-5
MGM 5-10 70

Picture Sleeves

MGM 4-6 70

LPs: 10/12-inch

ABC 8-10 77
MGM (Except 4710) 10-15 70
MGM (4710 "Black Man's Burdon") ... 20-30 70
(Promotional issue only.)
Also see WAR

BURDON, Eric, & Jimmy Witherspoon

Singles: 7-inch

MGM 3-5 71

LPs: 10/12-inch

MGM 10-15 71
Also see BURDON, Eric
Also see WITHERSPOON, Jimmy

BURGESS, Richard James — D&D '84

Singles: 12-inch

CAPITOL 4-6 84

Singles: 7-inch

CAPITOL 3-4 84

LPs: 10/12-inch

CAPITOL 5-10 84

BURKE, Ceele — R&B '43

Singles: 78 rpm

CAPITOL 10-15

BURKE, Keni — R&B '81

Singles: 7-inch

DARK HORSE 3-5 77-78
RCA 3-4 81-82

LPs: 10/12-inch

DARK HORSE 8-10 77
RCA 5-10 81-82
Also see FIVE STAIRSTEPS

BURKE, Solomon — P&R/R&B '61

Singles: 12-inch

SAVOY 4-6 84

Singles: 78 rpm

APOLLO 15-25 56-57

Singles: 7-inch

ABC/DUNHILL 3-5 74
AMHERST 3-5 78
APOLLO 15-25 56-58
ATLANTIC 4-8 61-68
BELL 3-6 69-70
CHESS 3-5 75-77
DUNHILL 3-5 74
INFINITY 3-5 79
MGM 3-5 70-73
ODEON 4-6
PRIDE 3-5 72-73
SINGULAR 5-10 60

EPs: 7-inch

ATLANTIC (SD-8109 "The Best of Solomon Burke") 10-20 65
(Stereo. Juke box issue only.)

LPs: 10/12-inch

ABC/DUNHILL 10-12 74
APOLLO (498 "Solomon Burke") 60-100 62
ATLANTIC (8000 series) 25-45 62-64
ATLANTIC (8100 series) 15-30 65-68
(No W.B. logo on label.)
ATLANTIC (8100 series) 5-10 80s
(Has Warner Bros. logo on label.)
BELL 15-20 69
CHESS 8-10 75-76
CLARION 12-20 64
INFINITY 5-10 79
KENWOOD 12-20 64
MGM 10-15 71-72
PRIDE 8-12 73
ROUNDER 5-10 84
SAVOY 5-10 81-83
Also see CHARLES, Ray / Somomon Burke
Also see SOUL CLAN

BURKE, Solomon, & Lady Lee

Singles: 7-inch

PRIDE 3-5 73
Also see BURKE, Solomon

BURNETT, Carol — LP '72

Singles: 7-inch

RCA 4-6 67

LPs: 10/12-inch

DECCA 15-25 61-64
COLUMBIA 8-12 71
RCA 10-15 67
TETRAGRAMMATON 8-12 69
VOCALION 8-12 68
Also see ANDREWS, Julie, & Carol Burnett

BURNETT, J. Henry

Singles: 7-inch

UNI 4-6 72

LPs: 10/12-inch

UNI 10-15 72
Also see BURNETT, T-Bone

BURNETT, T-Bone — LP '83

(J. Henry Burnett)

Singles: 7-inch

W.B. 3-4 83

LPs: 10/12-inch

TAKOMA 5-10 80
W.B. 5-10 82-83
Also see BLACK TIE
Also see BURNETT, J. Henry
Also see LEGENDARY STARDUST COWBOY

BURNETTE, Billy — C&W '79

(With Jawbone)

Singles: 7-inch

A&M 3-5 76
COLUMBIA 3-4 80-81
CURB 3-4 86
POLYDOR 3-5 79
W.B. (7300 series) 4-6 69

LPs: 10/12-inch

COLUMBIA 5-10 80-81
ENTRANCE 10-12 72
MCA/CURB 5-10 86
POLYDOR 5-10 79
Also see FLEETWOOD MAC

BURNETTE, Billy, & Christine McVie

Singles: 12-inch

MCA/CURB (17040 "It Ain't Over") 5-8 85
(Promotional issue only.)
Also see BURNETTE, Billy
Also see McVIE, Christine

BURNETTE, Billy Joe — C&W '90

(Billy Burnette)

Singles: 7-inch

BADGER 3-4 90
DEVILLE (134 "Blue Misery") 8-12 65
GOLD STANDARD 3-5
GUSTO-STARDAY (167 "Welcome Home Elvis") 4-8 77
GUSTO-STARDAY (9009 "The Colonel and the King") 8-12 78
(Promotional issue only.)
K-ARK 3-5 70
MAGIC LAMP (613 "Miss Ping Pong") 10-15 65
PD 3-5
PALOMINO 3-5
TEDDY BEAR 4-6 77
TELEMEDIA 3-4 81
W.B. 4-8 69

LPs: 10/12-inch

GUSTO 10-20 77
Also see BARNETT, Billy
Also see LEGENDS

BURNETTE, Dorsey — P&R '60

Singles: 78 rpm

ABBOTT 15-25 56

Singles: 7-inch

ABBOTT (188 "Devil's Queen") 25-50 56
ABBOTT (190 "At a Distance") 25-50 56
CALLIOPE 3-5 77
CAPITOL 3-5 71-74
CEE-JAM (16 "Bertha-Lou") 50-100 57
COLLECTABLES 3-4 81
CONDOR 4-6 70
DOT (16230 "Raining in My Heart") . 10-15 61
DOT (16265 "Sad Boy") 10-15 61
ELEKTRA 3-5 79-80
ERA 8-15 60-69
HAPPY TIGER 4-6 70
HICKORY 4-8 67
IMPERIAL (5561 "Try") 15-25 59
IMPERIAL (5597 "Misery") 15-25 59
IMPERIAL (5668 "Your Love") 15-25 60
IMPERIAL (5987 "Circle Rock") 10-15 63
LIBERTY (56087 "The Greatest Love") 5-10 69
MC 3-5 77
MEL-O-DY (113 "Little Acorn") 10-15 64
MEL-O-DY (116 "Jimmy Brown") 10-15 64
MEL-O-DY (118 "Ever Since the World Began") 10-15 64
MELODYLAND 3-5 75-76
MERRI (206 "Lucy Darling") 8-12 60
MOVIE STAR 4-8
MUSIC FACTORY 4-8 68
REPRISE 10-20 62-63
SMASH 5-10 66
SURF (5019 "Bertha Lou") 150-200 57
U.S. NAVY ("Be a Navy Man") 10-20 60s
(U.S. Navy recruiting promotional issue.)

Picture Sleeves

ERA (3033 "The River and the Mountain") 15-25 61
REPRISE (246 "Four for Texas") 20-30 63
U.S. NAVY ("Be a Navy Man") 15-25 60s
(U.S. Navy recruiting promotional issue.)

LPs: 10/12-inch

BUCKBOARD (1024 "Dorsey") 8-10
CALLIOPE 8-10 77
CAPITOL 10-12 72-73
DOT (3456 "Dorsey Burnette Sings") 20-40 63
(Monaural.)
DOT (25456 "Dorsey Burnette Sings") 25-50 63
(Stereo.)
ERA (EL-102 "Tall Oak Tree") 40-80 60
(Monaural.)
ERA (ES-102 "Tall Oak Tree") 100-150 60
(Stereo.)
ERA (800 series) 15-20 69
GUSTO 5-10 79
TRIP 8-12 74

Also see BURNETTE, Johnny & Dorsey

BURNETTE, Johnny *P&R '60*
(With the Rock'n Roll Trio)
Singles: 78 rpm
CORAL.........25-50 56-57
VON (106 "Go Mule Go")..........100-150 54
Singles: 7-inch
CAPITOL..........8-12 63-64
CHANCELLOR (1116 "I Wanna Thank You Folks")..........10-15 62
CHANCELLOR (1129 "Remember Me")..........10-15 62
CORAL (61651 "Tear It Up")..........60-80 56
CORAL (61651 "Tear It Up")..........75-100 56
(Promotional issue only.)
CORAL (61675 "Midnight Train")..........60-80 56
CORAL (61675 "Midnight Train")..........75-100 56
(Promotional issue only.)
CORAL (61719 "Honey Hush")..........60-80 56
CORAL (61719 "Honey Hush")..........75-100 56
(Promotional issue only.)
CORAL (61758 "Lonesome Train")..........60-80 56
CORAL (61758 "Lonesome Train")..........75-100 56
(Promotional issue only.)
CORAL (61829 "Eager Beaver Baby")..........40-60 57
CORAL (61829 "Eager Beaver Baby")..........60-80 57
(Promotional issue only.)
CORAL (61869 "Drinkin' Wine Spo-Dee-O-Dee")..........40-60 57
CORAL (61869 "Drinkin' Wine Spo-Dee-O-Dee")..........60-80 57
(Promotional issue only.)
CORAL (61918 "Rock Billy Boogie")..........40-60 57
CORAL (61918 "Rock Billy Boogie")..........60-80 57
(Promotional issue only.)
FREEDOM (44001 "I'm Restless")..........30-40 58
FREEDOM (44011 "Gumbo")..........30-40 59
FREEDOM (44017 "Sweet Baby Doll")..........20-40 59
LIBERTY..........10-20 60
(Green and silver label.)
LIBERTY..........8-15 60-62
(Multi-color label.)
LIBERTY ALL-TIME HITS..........3-5
MAGIC LAMP (515 "Bigger Man")..........20-30 64
SAHARA..........5-10 64
U.A...........3-4 84
VON (106 "Go Mule Go")..........300-600 54
Picture Sleeves
LIBERTY (55285 "You're Sixteen")..........15-20 60
LIBERTY (55298 "Little Boy Sad")..........15-20 61
LIBERTY (55318 "Big, Big World")..........15-20 61
MAGIC LAMP (515 "Bigger Man")..........75-100 64
EPs: 7-inch
LIBERTY (1004 "Dreamin'")..........40-60 60
LIBERTY (1011 "Johnny Burnette's Hits")..........50-75 61
LPs: 10/12-inch
CORAL (57080 "Johnny Burnette and the Rock'n Roll Trio")..........3000-4000 56
(Counterfeits can be identified by their lack of printing on the spine and hand-etched identification numbers in the trail-off. Originals have the numbers mechanically stamped. Canadian issues are worth at least as much as U.S. issues.)
LIBERTY (3179 "Dreamin'")..........30-40 60
(Monaural.)
LIBERTY (3183 "Johnny Burnette")..........30-40 61
(Monaural.)
LIBERTY (3190 "Johnny Burnette Sings")..........30-40 61
(Monaural.)
LIBERTY (3206 "Johnny Burnette's Hits and Other Favorites")..........30-40 62
(Monaural.)
LIBERTY (3255 "Roses Are Red")..........30-40 62
(Monaural.)
LIBERTY (3389 "The Johnny Burnette Story")..........40-50 64
(Monaural.)
LIBERTY (7179 "Dreamin'")..........40-60 60
(Stereo.)
LIBERTY (7183 "Johnny Burnette")..........40-50 61
(Stereo.)
LIBERTY (7190 "Johnny Burnette Sings")..........40-50 61
(Stereo.)
LIBERTY (7206 "Johnny Burnette's Hits and Other Favorites")..........40-50 62
(Stereo. Black & rainbow colored label with gold & white logo.)
LIBERTY (7206 "Johnny Burnette's Hits and Other Favorites")..........15-25 66
(Stereo. Black & rainbow label with box style logo.)
LIBERTY (7206 "Johnny Burnette's Hits and Other Favorites")..........5-10 91
(Stereo. Peach and coral colored label.)
LIBERTY (7255 "Roses Are Red")..........40-50 62
(Stereo.)
LIBERTY (7389 "The Johnny Burnette Story")..........50-60 64
(Stereo.)
LIBERTY (7300 series)..........25-30 63
LIBERTY (10000 series)..........5-10 81
MCA..........5-10 82
SOLID SMOKE (Black vinyl)..........5-10 78-80
SOLID SMOKE (Colored vinyl)..........10-15 78
SUNSET..........15-25 67
U.A...........10-15 75
Members (Trio): Johnny Burnette; Dorsey Burnette; Paul Burlison.
Also see BURLISON, Paul
Also see BURNETTE, Dorsey
Also see BURNETTE, Johnny
Also see VEE, Bobby / Johnny Burnette / Ventures / Fleetwoods

BURNETTE, Johnny & Dorsey
(Burnette Brothers)
Singles: 7-inch
CORAL (62190 "Blues Stay Away from Me")..........25-35 60
IMPERIAL..........15-20 58
REPRISE..........5-10 63
Also see BURNETTE, Dorsey
Also see BURNETTE, Johnny
Also see TEXANS

BURNETTE, Rocky *P&R/LP '80*
(With the Rock 'N Roll Trio)
Singles: 7-inch
EMI AMERICA..........3-5 80
LPs: 10/12-inch
EMI AMERICA..........5-10 80-82
GOODS..........5-10 82
KYD..........5-10 83
Also see BURNETTE, Randy, & Rocky Burnette

BURNING SENSATIONS *LP '83*
Singles: 7-inch
CAPITOL..........3-4 83
LPs: 10/12-inch
CAPITOL..........5-10 83

BURNS, George *P&R/C&W/LP '80*
Singles: 7-inch
MERCURY..........3-4 80-81
Picture Sleeves
MERCURY..........3-4 80
EPs: 7-inch
COLPIX..........5-10 60s
LPs: 10/12-inch
BUDDAH..........6-10 72
MERCURY..........5-10 80
PRIDE..........5-10
Also see MARTIN, Dean

BURNS, George, & Gracie Allen *P&R '33*
Singles: 78 rpm
COLUMBIA..........10-20 33
LPs: 10/12-inch
MARK '56..........8-15
Also see BURNS, George

BURRAGE, Harold *R&B '65*
(Harold Barrage)
Singles: 78 rpm
ALADDIN..........15-25 52
COBRA..........15-25 56-57
DECCA..........15-25 50
STATES..........25-50 54
Singles: 7-inch
ALADDIN (3194 "Sweet Brown Gal")..........25-50 52
COBRA..........20-40 56-58
DECCA (48175 "Hi-Yo")..........30-60 50
FOXY..........8-12 62
M-PAC..........5-10 62-65
PASO..........8-12 61
STATES (144 "Feel So Fine")..........50-100 54
(Black vinyl.)
STATES (144 "Feel So Fine")..........100-200 50
(Colored vinyl.)
VEE JAY..........10-20 60
VIVID..........4-8 64

BURRELL *R&B '88*
Singles: 7-inch
VIRGIN..........3-4 88

BURRELL, Kenny *LP '63*
Singles: 7-inch
CADET..........4-8 66
LPs: 10/12-inch
CADET..........10-20 66
VERVE..........10-15 68

BURRELL, Kenny, & Jimmy Smith *LP '63*
LPs: 10/12-inch
VERVE..........10-20 66-68
Also see BURRELL, Kenny
Also see SMITH, Jimmy

BURRITO BROTHERS *C&W '81*
Singles: 7-inch
CURB..........3-4 81-84
EPIC..........3-4 81
LPs: 10/12-inch
A&M..........8-10 80
CURB..........5-10 81-82
Members: Pete Battin; Pete Kleinow; Greg Harris; Ed Ponder; Gib Guilbeau; John Beland.
Also see BATTIN, Pete
Also see FLYING BURRITO BROTHERS
Also see SWAMPWATER

BURROWS, Tony *P&R '70*
Singles: 7-inch
BELL..........3-5 70-72
Also see BROTHERHOOD of MAN
Also see EDISON LIGHTHOUSE
Also see FIRST CLASS
Also see PIPKINS
Also see WHITE PLAINS

BURTNICK, Glen *P&R/LP '87*
Singles: 7-inch
A&M..........3-4 87
Picture Sleeves
A&M..........3-4 87
LPs: 10/12-inch
A&M..........5-10 87

BURTON, Jenny *R&B/D&D '83*
Singles: 12-inch
ATLANTIC..........4-6 83-85
Singles: 7-inch
ATLANTIC..........3-4 83-86
LPs: 10/12-inch
ATLANTIC..........5-10 83-85
Also see C-BANK

BURTON, Jenny, & Patrick Jude — P&R '84

Singles: 7-inch

ATLANTIC 3-4 84

Picture Sleeves

ATLANTIC 3-4 84

Also see BURTON, Jenny

BURTON, Richard — P&R '65

Singles: 7-inch

MGM 4-6 65

BUS BOYS — LP '80

Singles: 7-inch

ARISTA 3-4 80-84

LPs: 10/12-inch

ARISTA 5-10 80-82

Members: Gus Loundermon; Brian O'Neal; Kevin O'Neal; Michael Jones; Victor Johnson; Steve Felix.

BUSCH, Lou, Orchestra — P&R '55

Singles: 78 rpm

CAPITOL 3-5 55-56

Singles: 7-inch

CAPITOL 4-8 55-56

Also see CARR, Joe "Fingers"

BUSH, Kate — P&R '79

Singles: 12-inch

EMI AMERICA 4-6 85-86

Singles: 7-inch

COLUMBIA 3-4 89
EMI AMERICA (8000 series) 3-8 78-86
EMI AMERICA (9605 "Hounds of Love") 8-10 85
(Long version/Short version. Promotional issue only.)
EMI AMERICA (EMR-20490 "Them Heavy People") 25-50
(Promotional issue only.)
GEFFEN 3-4 87
HARVEST 5-8 78-79

Picture Sleeves

EMI AMERICA (8285 "Running Up That Hill") 4-6 85
EMI AMERICA (8302 "Hounds of Love") 4-6 85
EMI AMERICA (EMR-20490 "Them Heavy People") 25-50
(Promotional issue only.)
GEFFEN 3-4 87
HARVEST 10-15 78

LPs: 10/12-inch

COLUMBIA 5-10 89
EMI AMERICA 6-12 78-86
HARVEST 10-15 78

Also see GABRIEL, Peter, & Kate Bush

BUSH, Little David — (David Ruffin)

Singles: 7-inch

VEGA (1002 "You and I") 150-200 59

Also see RUFFIN, David

BUSHKIN, Joe — LP '56

LPs: 10/12-inch

CAPITOL 15-25 56

Singles: 7-inch

ARLEN 10-20 63-64

Members: Jack Baker; Fran Parda; Rick LaFrenier; Richard Eriksen; Tink Hermanson.

Also see BOLD
Also see COLE, Fred E.
Also see TROPHIES

BUSTERS — P&R '63

Singles: 7-inch

ARLEN (735 "Bust Out") 10-20 63
ARLEN (740 "All American Surfer") .. 10-20 63
ARLEN (745 "Heartaches") 10-20 64

Members: Jack Baker; Fran Parda; Rick LaFrenier; Richard Eriksen; Tink Hermanson.

BUTANES — P&R '61

Singles: 7-inch

ENRICA 10-20 61

BUTCHER, Jon — P&R '83

(John Butcher Axis)

Singles: 7-inch

CAPITOL 3-4 85-89
POLYDOR 3-4 83-84

Picture Sleeves

CAPITOL 3-4 85-87

LPs: 10/12-inch

CAPITOL 5-10 85-89
POLYDOR 5-10 83-84

Members: Jon Butcher; Thom Gimbell; Derek Blevins; Bob Jefferies.

BUTLER, Billy — P&R/R&B '65

(With the Chanters; with Infinity; with Enchanters)

Singles: 7-inch

BRUNSWICK 6-12 66-68
CURTOM 3-5 76
OKEH 4-8 63-66
MEMPHIS 3-5 71
OKEH (Except 7207) 6-12 63-66
OKEH (7207 "My Sweet Woman") 10-20
PRIDE 3-5 72-73

LPs: 10/12-inch

EDSEL 5-10 86
OKEH 15-20 66
PRESTIGE 10-15 69-70
PRIDE 10-12 73

Members: Billy Butler; Earl Batts; Jess Tillman; Larry Wade; Phyllis Know.

Also see CHANTERS
Also see INFINITY

BUTLER, Carl — C&W '61

Singles: 78 rpm

CAPITOL 5-10 51-52
OKEH 4-8 54-55

Singles: 7-inch

CAPITOL 8-12 51-52
COLUMBIA 4-8 59-63
OKEH 6-10 54-55

LPs: 10/12-inch

COLUMBIA 10-20 63
HARMONY 8-15 66-71

BUTLER, Carl & Pearl — C&W '62

Singles: 7-inch

COLUMBIA 4-8 62-69

LPs: 10/12-inch

CMH 5-10 80
CHART 3-5 71
COLUMBIA 10-20 64-70
HARMONY 8-12 72
PEDACA 5-10

Also see BUTLER, Carl
Also see BUTLER, Pearl

BUTLER, Champ — P&R '51

Singles: 78 rpm

COLUMBIA 3-8 50-54
CORAL 3-8 55-56

Singles: 7-inch

COLUMBIA 5-10 50-54
CORAL 5-10 55-56
GILLETTE 4-6 62
VISCOUNT 5-10 59

EPs: 7-inch

COLUMBIA 8-15 53

LPs: 10/12-inch

GILLETTE 10-20 62

BUTLER, Champ, & George Cates

Singles: 78 rpm

CORAL 3-5 55

Singles: 7-inch

CORAL 4-8 55

Also see BUTLER, Champ
Also see CATES, George

BUTLER, Jerry — P&R/R&B '58

(With the Impressions; with Riley Hampton's Orchestra)

Singles: 78 rpm

ABNER (1013 "For Your Precious Love") 50-100 58
ABNER (1024 "Lost") 75-125 59
FALCON (1013 "For Your Precious Love") 50-100 58

Singles: 7-inch

ABNER (1013 "For Your Precious Love") 20-30 58
ABNER (1024 "Lost") 15-25 59
ABNER (1028 "Hold Me Darling") 15-25 59
ABNER (1030 "I Was Wrong") 15-25 59
ABNER (1035 "I Found a Love") 15-25 60
COLLECTABLES 3-4 81
ERIC 3-4 73
FALCON (1013 "For Your Precious Love") 25-35 58
FOUNTAIN 3-4 82
ICHIBAN 3-4 92-93
MCA 3-4 83
MERCURY 3-8 67-74
MISTLETOE 3-5 75
MOTOWN 3-5 76-77
OLDIES 45 3-5
PHILADELPHIA INT'L 3-4 78-81
TRIP 3-5
VEE JAY (280 "For Your Precious Love") 3000-4000 58
VEE JAY (354 thru 715) 5-10 60-66
VEE JAY (1971 "Aware of Love") 15-25 63
(Stereo compact 33 single.)

Picture Sleeves

VEE JAY 8-12 61-64

LPs: 10/12-inch

ABNER (2001 "Jerry Butler Esquire") 75-125 59
BUDDAH 12-20 69
EXODUS 5-10
FOUNTAIN 5-10 82
DYNASTY 12-18
KENT 10-15 68
LOST-NITE 8-12 81
MERCURY 8-15 67-84
MOTOWN 5-10 76-77
PHILADELPHIA INT'L 5-10 78-81
POST 5-10
PRIDE 8-10 72
UPFRONT 8-10
SCEPTER 8-10
SIRE 8-12 77
SUNSET 10-12 68
TRIP 10-12 71-78
U.A. 8-10 75
VEE JAY (1000 series, except 1038) 25-45 60-64
VEE JAY (1038 "Aware of Love") 40-60
VEE JAY (1100 series) 20-30 64-65

Members (Impressions): Jerry Butler; Sam Gooden; Richard Brooks; Arthur Brooks; Curtis Mayfield.

Also see AUSTIN, Patti, & Jerry Butler
Also see CHANDLER, Gene, & Jerry Butler
Also see IMPRESSIONS
Also see McPHATTER, Clyde / Little Richard / Jerry Butler
Also see RIVERS, Johnny / 4 Seasons / Jerry Butler / Jimmy Soul

BUTLER, Jerry, & Brenda Lee Eager — P&R/R&B '72

Singles: 7-inch

MERCURY 3-4 71-73

LPs: 10/12-inch

MERCURY 8-10 73

Also see EAGER, Brenda Lee

BUTLER, Jerry, & Betty Everett — LP '64

Singles: 7-inch

ABC 3-4 73
VEE JAY 3-5 64

LPs: 10/12-inch

BUDDAH 10-15 69
TRADITION 5-10 82
VEE JAY 20-30 64

Also see DELLS
Also see EVERETT, Betty

BUTLER, Jerry, & Debra Henry R&B '82

Singles: 7-inch

PHILADELPHIA INT'L 3-4 80

Also see SILK

BUTLER, Jerry, & Stix Hooper

Singles: 7-inch

MCA 3-4 83

Also see HOOPER, Stix

BUTLER, Jerry, & Thelma Houston LP '77

Singles: 7-inch

MOTOWN 3-5 77

LPs: 10/12-inch

MOTOWN 5-10 77

Also see BUTLER, Jerry
Also see HOUSTON, Thelma

BUTLER, Jonathan LP '86

Singles: 7-inch

JIVE 3-4 86-88

Picture Sleeves

JIVE 3-4 87

LPs: 10/12-inch

JIVE 5-10 86-88

Also see TURNER, Ruby

BUTLER, Larry, & Friends

LPs: 10/12-inch

PICKWICK (3726 "Larry Butler & Friends, Featuring Crystal Gayle & Billy Jo Spears") 5-10 77

Also see GAYLE, Crystal
Also see SPEARS, Billy Jo

BUTTERFIELD, Paul LP '65

(Butterfield Blues Band; Paul Butterfield's Better Days)

Singles: 7-inch

BEARSVILLE 3-5 73-81
ELEKTRA 4-8 67-69

Picture Sleeves

ELEKTRA 4-8 67

LPs: 10/12-inch

AMHERST 5-8 86
BEARSVILLE 8-10 73-81
ELEKTRA 10-20 65-76
RED LIGHTNIN' ("An Offer You Can't Refuse") 30-40 72
(Single-sided promotional LP.)

Also see BISHOP, Elvin

BUTTERFLYS P&R '64

(Ellie Greenwich)

Singles: 7-inch

RED BIRD 10-20 64

Also see GREENWICH, Ellie

BUZZCOCKS LP '80

Singles: 7-inch

I.R.S. 3-5 79-80

Picture Sleeves

I.R.S. 3-5 79

LPs: 10/12-inch

I.R.S. 5-10 79

Members: Pete Shelley; Steve Diggle; Howard Devoto; Steve Garvey; John Maher.
Also see SHELLEY, Pete

BY ALL MEANS R&B '88

Singles: 7-inch

ATCO/VIRGIN 3-4 89-90
ISLAND 3-4 88-89

LPs: 10/12-inch

ISLAND 5-8 89

Members: James Vorner; Lynn Roderick; Billy Sheppard.

BYAS, Don R&B '48

Singles: 78 rpm

SAVOY 10-20 48

BYRD, Bobby R&B '65

(With the Byrds; with James Brown Band)

Singles: 7-inch

BROWNSTONE 3-5 71-72
FEDERAL 5-10 63
INTERNATIONAL BROS. 3-5 75
KING 3-6 67-71
KWANZA 3-5 73
SMASH 8-15 64-65
ZEPHYR 15-20 57

LPs: 10/12-inch

KING 10-15 70

Also see KING, Anna, & Bobby Byrd

BYRD, Bobby, & James Brown R&B '68

Singles: 7-inch

KING 4-6 68

Also see BROWN, James
Also see BYRD, Bobby

BYRD, Charlie P&R '62

Singles: 7-inch

COLUMBIA 3-6 69
RIVERSIDE 3-6 62-63

LPs: 10/12-inch

COLUMBIA 15-25 65-69
FANTASY (9429 "Chrystal Silence") 10-15 73
MFSL (515 "At the Village Gate") 25-30 80s
OFFBEAT 25-35 59-60
RIVERSIDE 15-25 62-82
SAVOY 30-50 58

Also see ALMEIDA, Laurindo
Also see GETZ, Stan, & Charlie Byrd

BYRD, Charlie, & Woody Herman

LPs: 10/12-inch

EVEREST 10-20 63
PICKWICK 6-12 66

Also see BYRD, Charlie
Also see HERMAN, Woody

BYRD, Donald LP '64

Singles: 7-inch

BLUE NOTE 3-5 75-77
ELEKTRA 3-4 78-82

LPs: 10/12-inch

BETHLEHEM 15-25 60
BLUE NOTE 15-25 59-65
(Label reads "Blue Note Records Inc. - New York, U.S.A.")
BLUE NOTE 10-20 66-77
(Label reads "Blue Note Records - a Division of Liberty Records Inc.")
COLUMBIA (998 "Jazz Lab") 40-60 57
(With Gigi Gryce.)
COLUMBIA (1058 "Jazz Lab, Vol. 2, Modern Jazz Perspective") 40-60 57
(With Gigi Gryce.)
ELEKTRA 5-10 78-82
JAZZLAND (6 "Hard Bop") 30-40
JUBILEE (1059 "Jazz Lab") 40-60 57
(With Gigi Gryce.)
PRESTIGE (7062 "Two Trumpets") 75-100 56
(Yellow label. With Art Farmer.)
PRESTIGE (7080 "Youngbloods") 60-80 57
(Yellow label. With Phil Woods.)
PRESTIGE (7092 "Three Trumpets") 60-80 57
(Yellow label. With Art Farmer & Idrees Sulieman.)
REGENT (6056 "Jazz Eyes") 40-60 57
SAVOY (12032 "Byrd's Word") 40-60 56
(With Frank Foster.)
TRANSITION (4 "Byrd's Eye View") . 50-80 55
(With Hank Mobley.)
TRANSITION (5 "Byrd Jazz") 50-80 55
(With Yusef Lateef.)
TRANSITION (17 "Byrd Blows on Beacon Hill") 50-80 56
VERVE 20-30 58

Also see BLACKBYRDS

BYRD, Gary R&B '83

(With G.B. Experience)

Singles: 12-inch

WONDIRECTION 4-6 83

Singles: 7-inch

RCA 3-5 73
REAL THING 3-5

BYRD, Jerry P&R '50

Singles: 78 rpm

MERCURY 4-6 53-55

Singles: 7-inch

MERCURY 4-8 53-55
MONUMENT 4-6 60-67

EPs: 7-inch

DECCA 8-12 58
MERCURY 10-20 53-55
RCA 8-12 58

LPs: 10/12-inch

DECCA 20-35 58
LEHUA 8-10
MERCURY (Except 25000 series) 10-20 58-64
MERCURY (25000 series) 20-40 53-54
(10-inch LPs.)
MONUMENT 12-25 61-63
RCA 30-40 58
SESAC 40-60 59
WING 10-15 60-66

Also see ALLEN, Rex
Also see KIRK, Red

BYRD, Roy R&B '50

(With His Blues Jumpers; Roy "Bald Head" Byrd; with His New Orleans Rhythm; Roland Byrd)

Singles: 78 rpm

ATLANTIC (947 "Hey Little Girl") 50-100 50
FEDERAL (12061 "K.C. Blues") 50-100 52
(All Federal 45s known to exist are bootlegs.)
FEDERAL (12073 "Rockin' with Fess") 50-100 52
MERCURY (8175 "Bald Head") 50-75 50
MERCURY (8184 "Her Mind Is Gone") 50-75 50

Also see PROFESSOR LONGHAIR

BYRD, Russell P&R '61

Singles: 7-inch

SYMBOL 5-10 62
WAND 5-10 61

BYRDS P&R/LP '65

Singles: 7-inch

ASYLUM 3-5 73
COLUMBIA (1600 series) 4-6 73
COLUMBIA (43271 "Mr. Tambourine Man") 5-10 65
(Black vinyl.)
COLUMBIA (43271 "Mr. Tambourine Man") 50-75 65
(Colored vinyl. Promotional issue only.)
COLUMBIA (43332 "I'll Feel a Whole Lot Better") 5-10 65
(Black vinyl.)
COLUMBIA (43332 "I'll Feel a Whole Lot Better") 50-75 65
(Colored vinyl. Promotional issue only.)
COLUMBIA (43332 "All I Really Want to Do") 5-10 65
(Black vinyl.)
COLUMBIA (43332 "All I Really Want to Do") 50-75 65
(Colored vinyl. Promotional issue only.)
COLUMBIA (43424 "Turn Turn Turn") 5-10 65
(Black vinyl.)
COLUMBIA (43424 "Turn Turn Turn") 50-75 65
(Colored vinyl. Promotional issue only.)
COLUMBIA (43501 thru 45761) 4-8 66-72

Picture Sleeves

COLUMBIA (43271 "Mr. Tambourine Man") 100-150 65
(Promotional issue only.)
COLUMBIA (43578 "Eight Miles High") 15-25 65
COLUMBIA (44157 "Have You Seen Her Face") 15-25 65

EPs: 7-inch

COLUMBIA (10287 "The Byrds") 40-60 66
(Columbia Special Products issue for the

Scholastic Book Services. Issued with paper cover.)
COLUMBIA (116003/4 "Fifth Dimension Open-End Interview")..50-75 66
(Promotional issue only.)

LPs: 10/12-inch

ASYLUM..8-10 73
COLUMBIA (2000 series).................20-25 65-67
COLUMBIA (9000 series).................15-25 65-69
COLUMBIA (30000 thru 33000 series)..8-12 70-75
COLUMBIA (34000 thru 37000 series)..5-10 75-81
COLUMBIA (46773 "The Byrds") 30-40 90
(Four-LP set. Includes booklet.)
TOGETHER 15-20 69

Promotional LPs

BROADCAST ("Byrds Live") 35-45 81
COLUMBIA (2000 series).................40-50 65-67
(White label.)
COLUMBIA (9000 series).................35-45 65-69
(White label.)
COLUMBIA (116003/4 "Fifth Dimension" Interview Album) 100-125 66
MURRAY HILL 5-10 87
PAIR 10-12 83
REALM 8-12 76
RHINO...5-10 88

Members: Jim (Roger) McGuinn; Gene Clark; David Crosby; Chris Hillman; Michael Clarke; Gram Parsons; Clarence White; Gene Parsons; John York; Skip Battin. Session: Jay Dee Maness; Bayard Jones; Jim Wessely; Frank Laurie; John Jamnick; Frank Inman; Robert Stanley.

Also see BEEFEATERS
Also see CLARK, Gene
Also see CROSBY, David
Also see HILLMAN, Chris
Also see McGUINN, Roger
Also see PACIFIC STEEL CO.
Also see PARSONS, Gram

BYRNE, David — LP '81

Singles: 12-inch

SIRE 4-6 82

LPs: 10/12-inch

ECM...5-8 85
LUAKA BOP 5-8 89
SIRE 5-10 81

Also see ENO, Brian
Also see GLASS, Philip
Also see TALKING HEADS

BYRNES, Edd "Kookie," & Joanie Sommers & Mary Kaye Trio

Singles: 7-inch

W.B. 5-10 59

Picture Sleeves

W.B. 8-12 59

Also see KAYE, Mary
Also see SOMMERS, Joanie

BYRNES, Edward — P&R '59

(Edd "Kookie" Byrnes; with Connie Stevens & Don Ralke's Orchestra; with Friend; with Mary Kaye Trio.)

Singles: 7-inch

W.B. (5047 "Kookie Kookie") 5-10 59
(Monaural.)
W.B. (S-5047 "Kookie Kookie").........10-20 59
(Stereo.)
W.B. (5087 thru 5121) 5-10 59

Picture Sleeves

W.B. 15-20 59

EPs: 7-inch

W.B. (1309 "Edd "Kookie" Byrnes") ..15-25 59

LPs: 10/12-inch

W.B. (1309 "Kookie") 25-35 59

Also see BYRNES, Edd "Kookie," with Joanie Sommers & Mary Kaye Trio
Also see RALKE, Don
Also see STEVENS, Connie

BYRON, D.L. — LP '80

Singles: 7-inch

ARISTA...3-4 80

Picture Sleeves

ARISTA...3-5 80

LPs: 10/12-inch

ARISTA...5-10 80

BYRON, Junior — D&D '83

Singles: 12-inch

VANGUARD.......................................4-6 83

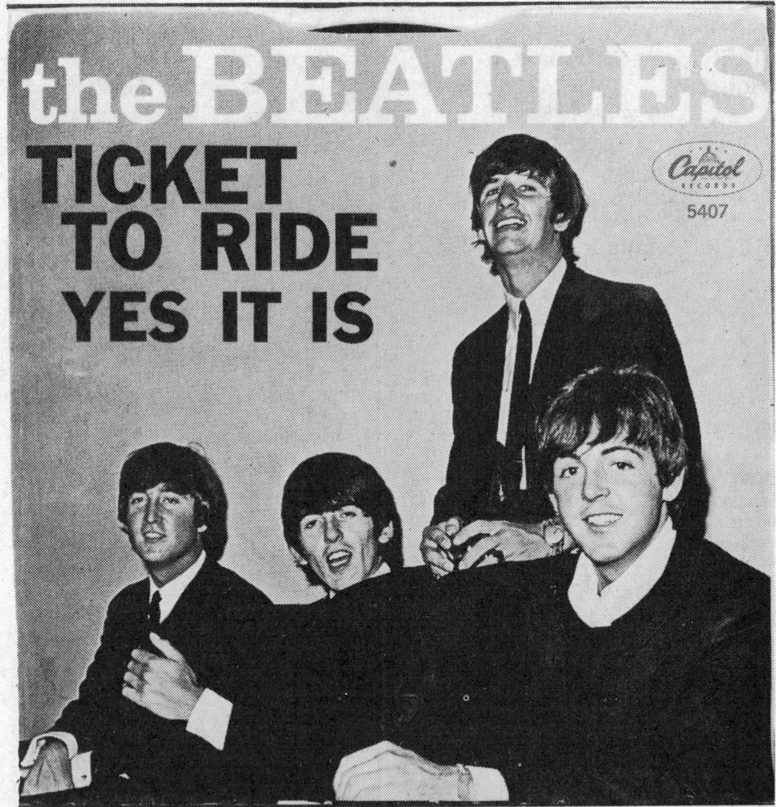

C & C MUSIC FACTORY — LP '91
(Clivilles & Cole)

Singles: 7-inch

COLUMBIA 3-4 90-91

LPs: 10/12-inch

COLUMBIA 5-8 91

C & SHELLS — R&B '69

Singles: 7-inch

COTILLION 4-6 69
ZANZEE 3-6 72

Members: Calvin White; Andrea Bolden; Lonzine Wright.
Also see SANDPEBBLES

C-BANK — R&B/D&D '83
(Featuring Jenny Burton)

Singles: 7-inch

NEXT PLATEAU 3-4 83

Also see BURTON, Jenny

C.C. & COMPANY — P&R '76

Singles: 7-inch

SUSSEX 3-5 75
20TH CENTURY/WESTBOUND 3-5 75

Also see C.J. & CO.

C.C.S. — P&R/LP '71
(Collective Consciousness Society)

Singles: 7-inch

BELL 3-5 73
RAK 4-8 71

LPs: 10/12-inch

RAK 15-20 71-72

Member: Alexis Korner.

C.J. & CO. — P&R '77
(C.C. & COMPANY)

Singles: 7-inch

WESTBOUND 3-5 77-78

LPs: 10/12-inch

WESTBOUND 5-10 77-78

Members: Dennis Coffey; Cornelius Brown; Joni Tolbert; Charles Clark; Connie Durden; Curtis Durden.
Also see C.C. & COMPANY
Also see COFFEY, Dennis

C.L. BLAST: see BLAST, C.L.

C.O.D.s — P&R '65

Singles: 7-inch

KELLMAC (1003 "Michael") 5-10 65
KELLMAC (1005 "Pretty Baby") 8-12 66
KELLMAC (1012 "Coming Back Girl") 50-100 66

Members: Larry Brownlee; Robert Lewis; Carl Washington.
Also see LOST GENERATION
Also see MYSTIQUE

C.Q.D. — D&D '83

Singles: 12-inch

EMERGENCY 4-6 83

CABOOSE — P&R '70

Singles: 7-inch

ENTERPRISE 3-5 70

LPs: 10/12-inch

ENTERPRISE 10-15 71

CACTUS — LP '70

Singles: 7-inch

ATCO 5-8 70-72

LPs: 10/12-inch

ATCO 20-25 70-72

Members: Carmine Appice; Tim Bogert; Pete French; Werner Fritzschings; Duane Hitchings; Jerry Norris; Mike Pinera; Roland Robinson; Rusty Day; Jim McCarty.
Also see BECK, BOGERT & APPICE
Also see DAY, Rusty
Also see NEW CACTUS BAND
Also see PINERA, Mike
Also see THEE IMAGE

CACTUS WORLD NEWS — LP '86

Singles: 7-inch

MCA 3-4 86

LPs: 10/12-inch

MCA 5-10 86

CADETS — P&R/R&B '56

Singles: 78 rpm

MODERN (Except 971) 20-50 55-57
MODERN (971 "If It Is Wrong") 50-75 55

Singles: 7-inch

COLLECTABLES 3-4 81
MODERN (Except 971) 25-50 55-57
MODERN (971 "If It Is Wrong") 75-125 55

LPs: 10/12-inch

CROWN (370 "The Cadets") 25-50 63
CROWN (5015 "Rockin' 'n Reelin'") 75-100 57
RELIC 10-15

Members: Ted Taylor; Aaron Collins; Will "Dub" Jones; Willie Davis; Lloyd McGraw; Prentice Moreland; Tom Fox; Randolph Jones.
Also see FLARES
Also see JACKS
Also see TAYLOR, Ted

CADILLAC, Flash: see FLASH CADILLAC

CADILLACS — P&R '55
(With the Jesse Powell Orchestra)

Singles: 78 rpm

JOSIE (765 "Gloria") 75-125 54
JOSIE (769 "Wishing Well") 50-75 54
JOSIE (773 thru 820) 25-50 55-57
REO 25-50 55
(Canadian.)

Singles: 7-inch

ABC 3-4 73
ARCTIC (101 "Fool") 50-100 64
CAPITOL 8-12 62
JOSIE (765 "Gloria") 300-400 54
JOSIE (769 "Wishing Well") 350-450 54
JOSIE (773 "No Chance") 50-75 55
JOSIE (778 "Down the Road") 75-100 55
JOSIE (785 "Speedoo") 50-75 55
JOSIE (792 "Zoom") 40-60 56
JOSIE (798 "Betty My Love") 40-60 56
JOSIE (800 series, except 820) 15-30 56-60
JOSIE (820 "My Girl Friend") 40-60 57
JOSIE (900 series) 10-15 63
JUBILEE (9010 "Romeo") 40-60 62
(Stereo.)
LANA 4-6 64
MERCURY 15-25 61
REO (8002 "No Chance") 50-80 55
(Canadian.)
REO (8139 "Rudolph, the Red-Nosed Reindeer") 50-80 55
(Canadian.)
REO (8163 "Broken Heart") 50-80 55
(Canadian.)
REO (8071 "Speedoo") 50-80 55
(Canadian.)
SMASH 5-10 61
VIRGO 3-5 72-73

LPs: 10/12-inch

CADAVER 5-10
HARLEM HITPARADE 10-15 70s
JUBILEE (1045 "The Fabulous Cadillacs") 300-400 57
(Blue label.)
JUBILEE (1045 "The Fabulous Cadillacs") 200-250 59
(Flat black label.)
JUBILEE (1045 "The Fabulous Cadillacs") 50-100 60
(Glossy black label.)
JUBILEE (1089 "The Crazy Cadillacs") 150-250 58
(Flat black label.)
JUBILEE (1089 "The Crazy Cadillacs") 75-125 60
(Glossy black label.)
JUBILEE (5009 "Twistin' with the Cadillacs") 50-75 62
(Monaural.)
JUBILEE (5009 "Twistin' with the Cadillacs") 75-125 62
(Stereo.)
MURRAY HILL (1195 "The Very Best of the Cadillacs") 5-10 88
MURRAY HILL (1285 "The Cadillacs") 30-35
(Five-LP boxed set.)

Members: Earl "Speedoo" Carroll; Jim "Papa" Clark; Gus Willingham; Bobby Phillips; Laverne Drake; Charles Brooks; James Bailey; Earl Wade.
Also see BAILEY, J.R.
Also see BREWSTER, Ray, & Cadillacs
Also see CARROL, Earl, & Original Cadillacs
Also see CRICKETS
Also see CRYSTALS
Also see FIVE CROWNS
Also see HOWARD, Gregory
Also see MISSLES
Also see NEW YORK CITY
Also see OPALS
Also see ORIGINAL CADILLACS
Also see PEARLS
Also see POWELL, Jesse
Also see RAY, Bobby, & Cadillacs
Also see SCHOOLBOYS
Also see SOLITAIRES
Also see SPEEDO & CADILLACS

CADILLACS / Orioles

LPs: 10/12-inch

JUBILEE (1117 "The Cadillacs Meet the Orioles") 75-100 61

Also see CADILLACS
Also see ORIOLES

CAESAR, Shirley — P&R/R&B '75
(With the Caesar Singers)

Singles: 7-inch

HOB/SCEPTER 3-5 73-75
ROADSHOW 3-5 77-78

LPs: 10/12-inch

HOB 8-12 70-75
ROADSHOW 5-10 77
TRIP 5-10 77

CAESAR & CLEO — P&R '65

Singles: 7-inch

REPRISE 10-15 64-65
VAULT 15-25 63

Picture Sleeves

REPRISE (0419 "Let the Good Times Roll") 25-50 65

Members: Salvatore "Sonny" Bono; Cher LaPiere.
Also see SONNY & CHER

CAESAR & ROMANS: see LITTLE CAESAR & ROMANS

CAESARS — R&B '67

Singles: 7-inch

LANIE (2001 "Lala I Love You") 75-125 67
LANIE (2002 "Girl I Miss You") 25-35 67

CAFÉ — D&D '84
(With the Hearns Sisters)

Singles: 12-inch

MONTAGE 4-6 84

CAFFERTY, John — LP '83
(With the Beaver Brown Band)

Singles: 7-inch

SCOTTI BROTHERS 3-4 84-86

Picture Sleeves

SCOTTI BROTHERS 3-4 84-86

LPs: 10/12-inch

SCOTTI BROTHERS 5-10 84-89

Also see EDDIE & CRUISERS

CAIN, Joe, & Red Parrot Orchestra — R&B '83

Singles: 7-inch

ZOO YORK 3-4 83

CAIN, Jonathan — P&R '76

(Jonathan Cain Band)

Singles: 7-inch

BEARSVILLE 3-5 76
OCTOBER 3-5 75-76

LPs: 10/12-inch

BEARSVILLE 5-10 77

Also see BABYS
Also see CAIN, Tane
Also see JOURNEY

CAIN, Tane — P&R/LP '82

Singles: 7-inch

RCA 3-4 82-83

LPs: 10/12-inch

RCA 5-10 82

Also see CAIN, Jonathan

CAIN, Tasso: see TASSO-CAIN

CAINE, General — R&B '82

Singles: 12-inch

CAPITOL 4-6 84
TABU 4-6 82-84

Singles: 7-inch

CAPITOL 3-4 84
TABU 3-4 82-84

LPs: 10/12-inch

TABU 5-10 82-84

CAIOLA, Al — P&R '60

(Al Caiola & His Orchestra)

Singles: 78 rpm

CORAL 5-10 57
RCA 4-8 53-55
REGENCY 4-8 56

Singles: 7-inch

AVLANCHE 3-4 73
CORAL (61855 "Honky Tonk Parade") 5-10 57
CORAL (61890 "Blue Angel Blues") 5-10 58
PREFERRED 5-10 59-60
RCA 5-10 53-55
REGENCY 5-10 56
U.A. 4-8 60-68

EPs: 7-inch

RCA (551 "Latin Beat") 10-15 53
RCA (555 "Guitar Sketches") 10-15 53
SESAC (85 "Boffola Caiola") 10-15 60

LPs: 10/12-inch

ATCO 10-15 60
BAINBRIDGE 5-8 80
CAMDEN 8-12 62
CHANCELLOR 10-15 60
RCA 10-15 59
ROULETTE 10-15 60
SAVOY 15-25 56
TIME 10-20 60-61
TWO WORLDS 8-10 72
UNART 8-12 67
U.A. 10-15 60-69

Also see TONES

CALDERA — R&B/LP '77

Singles: 7-inch

CAPITOL 3-5 76

LPs: 10/12-inch

CAPITOL 8-10 76-79

CALDWELL, Bobby — P&R/R&B/LP '78

Singles: 12-inch

MCA 4-6 84-85

Singles: 7-inch

CLOUDS 3-4 78-80
PBR INT'L 3-4 76
POLYDOR 3-4 82-83
MCA 3-4 84-85

LPs: 10/12-inch

CLOUDS 5-10 78-80
MCA 5-10 84
POLYDOR 5-10 82

Also see CAPTAIN BEYOND

CALDWELL, Rue — R&B/D&D '83

Singles: 12-inch

CRITIQUE 4-6 83

Singles: 7-inch

CRITIQUE 3-4 83

CALE, J.J. — P&R/LP '72

Singles: 7-inch

LIBERTY (55840 "Dick Tracy") 5-10 66
MERCURY 3-4 83-84
SHELTER 3-5 71-81

LPs: 10/12-inch

MCA 5-10 81
MERCURY 5-10 82-85
SHELTER 10-15 71-79
SILVERTONE 5-8 80

Also see LEATHERCOATED MINDS

CALE, John — LP '81

Singles: 7-inch

A&M 3-4 81
COLUMBIA 3-5 70
I.R.S. 3-4 79-80
REPRISE 3-5 72

Picture Sleeves

I.R.S. 3-4 79-80

LPs: 10/12-inch

A&M 5-10 81
COLUMBIA 12-15 70-71
I.R.S. 5-10 79
ISLAND 8-10 75-77
PASSPORT 5-10 84
REPRISE 10-12 72-73
ZE 5-10 83

Also see AYERS, Kevin
Also see EARTH OPERA
Also see PRIMATIVES
Also see REED, Lou, & John Cale
Also see VELVET UNDERGROUND

CALEN, Frankie — P&R '61

Singles: 7-inch

BEAR 4-8 62
EPIC 4-8 63-64
KIP (1517 "Pretty Dimple") 8-12
NRC (029 "Angel Face") 5-10 59
NRC (5008 "Angel Face") 5-10 59
SPARK 15-20 61
U.A. 4-8 62

CALHOON — R&B '75

Singles: 12-inch

W.B./SPECTOR 4-8 75

Singles: 7-inch

W.B./SPECTOR 3-5 75-76

CALIFORNIA RAISINS — LP '87

Singles: 7-inch

ATLANTIC 3-4 88
PRIORITY (Black vinyl) 3-4 87-88
PRIORITY (7915 "What Does It Take to Win Your Love") 4-6 88
(Colored vinyl.)

Picture Sleeves

ATLANTIC 3-5 88
PRIORITY 3-5 87-88

LPs: 10/12-inch

PRIORITY 5-10 87-88

Member: Buddy Miles.
Also see MILES, Buddy

CALL, The — P&R/LP '83

Singles: 12-inch

ELEKTRA 4-6 86

Singles: 7-inch

ELEKTRA 3-4 86
MCA 3-4 89
MERCURY 3-4 83

Picture Sleeves

ELEKTRA 3-4 86
MCA 3-4 89
MERCURY 3-4 83

LPs: 10/12-inch

ELEKTRA 5-10 86-87
MCA 5-8 89
MERCURY 5-10 82-83

CALLENDER, Bobby — P&R '63

(Bob Callender)

Singles: 7-inch

CORAL 10-15 67
GOLD (102 "Baby, I'm Ready") 50-100 61
ROULETTE (4471 "Little Star") 15-25 63

LPs: 10/12-inch

MGM (4557 "Rainbow") 75-125 68
(Includes lyrics insert.)

CALLIER, Terry — R&B '79

Singles: 12-inch

ERECT 4-6 82

Singles: 7-inch

CADET (Except 5623) 50-75 68
CADET (5623 "Look at Me Now") 5-10 69-73
ELEKTRA 3-5 78-79

LPs: 10/12-inch

CADET 10-12 72-73
CHESS 10-15 71
ELEKTRA 8-10 78-79

CALLOWAY — P&R/LP '90

Singles: 7-inch

SOLAR 3-4 89-90

Picture Sleeves

SOLAR 3-4 90

LPs: 10/12-inch

SOLAR 5-8 90

Members: Cino-Vincent Calloway; Reggie Calloway.
Also see MIDNIGHT STAR

CALLOWAY, Cab — P&R '30

(With Cab Jivers; with Caballiers)

Singles: 78 rpm

ABC-PAR 5-10 56
BANNER 8-12 31-32
BELL 4-8 53-55
BLUEBIRD 5-10 49
BRUNSWICK 5-15 30-36
CAMEO 6-12
COLUMBIA 5-10 42-49
CONQUEROR 6-12 38-41
DOMINO 10-15 30
FILMOPHONE 8-12
HI-TONE 5-10 49
JEWEL 8-12 31
MEL-O-DEE 10-15 31
MELOTONE 8-12 32-33
OKEH 5-10 40-42
ORIOLE 8-12 32-33
PERFECT 8-12 32
RCA 4-8 49
REGAL 6-12 31-51
ROMEO 8-12 32-33
SIGNATURE 5-8 49
VARIETY 8-12 33-37
VICTOR 5-15 33-34
VOCALION 5-10 38-40

Singles: 7-inch

ABC-PAR 5-10 56
BOOM 4-6 65
CORAL 4-8 61-62
GONE 8-15 58
OKEH (6896 "Willow Weep for Me") 20-30 52
RCA (007 "Rooming House Boogie") 50-75 49
RCA (8000 series) 4-6 62
RCA (11000 series) 3-5 78

EPs: 7-inch

EPIC (7000 series) 10-20 53

LPs: 10/12-inch

BRUNSWICK (58010 "Cab Calloway") 40-60 52
COLUMBIA 10-20 73
CORAL (57408 "Blues Make Me Happy") 15-20 62
(Monaural.)
CORAL (757408 "Blues Make Me Happy") 20-30 62
(Stereo.)

EPIC (3265 "Cab Calloway") 30-50 57
GONE (101 "Cotton Club Revue") 30-50 58
GUEST STAR 10-15 60s
MARK '56.......................................15-25 60s
RCA (LPM-2021 "Hi De Hi De Ho")...15-25 60
(Monaural.)
RCA (LSP-2021 "Hi De Hi De Ho") ...25-35 60
(Stereo.)

CALVERT, Eddie P&R '53

Singles: 78 rpm

CAPITOL 3-5 56
ESSEX...3-5 53-54

Singles: 7-inch

ABC-PAR 4-6 60-61
CAPITOL 4-8 56
ESSEX...4-8 53-54

LPs: 10/12-inch

ABC-PAR 10-15 60-62

CAMBRIDGE, Godfrey LP '64

LPs: 10/12-inch

EPIC 10-20 64-68

CAMBRIDGE STRINGS & SINGERS P&R '61

Singles: 7-inch

LONDON 3-5 61
Also see KNIGHTSBRIDGE STRINGS

CAMEL LP '74

Singles: 7-inch

JANUS...3-5 74-77

LPs: 10/12-inch

ARISTA...5-10 79
JANUS...8-10 74-77
PASSPORT.......................................5-10 81
Members: Peter Bardens; Doug Ferguson; Andy Latimer; Andy Ward.
Also see BARDENS, Peter
Also see STRANGE BREW

CAMEO R&B/LP '77

Singles: 12-inch

ATLANTA ARTISTS............................4-6 83-86
CHOCOLATE CITY.............................4-6 78-80

Singles: 7-inch

ATLANTA ARTISTS............................3-4 83-88
CHOCOLATE CITY.............................3-5 75-82

Picture Sleeves

ATLANTA ARTISTS............................3-4 86-88

LPs: 10/12-inch

ATLANTA ARTISTS...........................5-10 83-90
CHOCOLATE CITY............................5-10 77-82
Members: Tomi Jenkins; Larry Blackmon; Nathan Leftenant.
Also see EAST COAST
Also see SINGLETON, Charlie

CAMERON R&B/LP '80

(Rafael Cameron)

Singles: 7-inch

SALSOUL..3-4 80-82

LPs: 10/12-inch

SALSOUL...5-10 80-82

CAMERON, G.C. R&B '71

Singles: 7-inch

MALACO 3-4 83
MOTOWN..3-5 73-77
MOWEST 3-5 71-73

LPs: 10/12-inch

MOTOWN...5-10 74-77
Also see SPINNERS

CAMERON, Rafael: see CAMERON

CAMOUFLAGE P&R '88

Singles: 12-inch

ROULETTE 4-6 79

Singles: 7-inch

ATLANTIC...3-4 88
ROULETTE 3-5 76

Picture Sleeves

ATLANTIC...3-4 88

LPs: 10/12-inch

ATLANTIC...5-8 88

CAMP, Hamilton P&R '68

(Hamid Hamilton Camp & Skymonters; Bob Camp)

Singles: 7-inch

AMERICAN INT'L..................................3-5 71
W.B. 4-8 68

LPs: 10/12-inch

ELEKTRA (200 series).....................12-15 64
ELEKTRA (75000 series)..................8-10 73
MOUNTAIN RAILROAD 5-10
W.B. 10-15 67-69
Also see GIBSON, Bob, & Bob Camp

CAMPBELL, Debbie P&R '75

Singles: 7-inch

PLAYBOY 3-5 75

CAMPBELL, Glen P&R '61

(With the Glen-Aires; with Green River Boys; with Bandits)

Singles: 7-inch

ATLANTIC AMERICA 3-4 82-86
CAPEHART 10-20 61
CAPITOL (2000 & 3000 series) 3-6 68-74
CAPITOL (4000 series)........................3-5 75-81
(Orange or purple labels.)
CAPITOL (4783 thru 5360)...............5-10 61-65
(Orange/yellow swirl labels.)
CAPITOL (5441 "Guess I'm Dumb") 30-40 65
(With Brian Wilson.)
CAPITOL (5504 thru 5939, except 5927)...4-8 65-67
CAPITOL (5927 "My Baby's Gone/Kelli Hoedown"..6-12 67
(Has alternate takes. Promotional issue only.)
CAPITOL STARLINE...........................3-5
CENECO (1324 "Dreams for Sale") . 10-25 59
CENECO (1356 "You, You, You") 10-15 60s
CREST..10-15 61-62
(Mistakenly credits "Glen Cambpbell" on some Crest labels.)
EVEREST 3-6 69
STARDAY 3-6 68
MCA 3-4 84-89
MIRAGE..3-4 81
UNIVERSAL...3-4 89
W.B. 3-4 80

Picture Sleeves

ATLANTIC AMERICA............................3-4
CAPITOL (Except 4856 & 5279)...........3-6 68-74
CAPITOL (4856 "Long Black Limousine") 10-15 62
CAPITOL (5279 "Summer, Winter, Spring and Fall")..8-12 64

EPs: 7-inch

CAPITOL...5-10 68-69
(Juke box issues.)
CAPITOL/CHEVROLET (55 "The Glen Campbell Good Time Hour") 5-10 60s
CAPITOL CREATIVE PRODUCTS..5-10 60s

LPs: 10/12-inch

ATLANTIC AMERICA 5-10 82-86
BUCKBOARD 8-10
CAPITOL (103 thru 752)....................8-15 68-71
CAPITOL (1810 "Big Bluegrass Special")...25-75 62
(Credits the "Green River Boys Featuring Glen Campbell.")
CAPITOL (1881 thru 2392).............. 10-20 63-65
(With "T" or "ST" prefix.)
CAPITOL (2809 thru 2978)................8-15 67-69
(With "T" or "ST" prefix.)
CAPITOL (SM-300 series).................5-10 82
CAPITOL (SM-2000 series)...............5-10 78
CAPITOL (4000 series).....................5-10 73
CAPITOL (11000 thru 16000 series) .. 5-10 72-85
CAPITOL (11722 "Basic")..............50-100 78
(Picture disc. Promotional issue only. One of a four-artist, four-LP set. 250 made.)
CAPITOL (80000 series)....................5-10
CAPITOL (94000 series)....................8-15 72
(Capitol Record Club issues.)
CAPITOL (120000 series) 5-10
(Capitol Record Club issues.)
CAPITOL CREATIVE PRODUCTS.....8-12
CAPITOL SPECIAL PRODUCTS 5-8 84
CUSTOM TONE..................................15-20
LONGINES (5408 "Gentle on My Mind")...5-10 69
LONGINES ("Glen Campbell's Golden Favorites") 20-30 72
(Boxed, six-disc set.)
PAIR 5-8 84
PICKWICK..8-10 64-79
SEARS 8-12
STARDAY 15-20 68-69
Session: Jerry Puckett.
Also see BACHARACH, Burt / Glen Campbell / Dionne Warwick
Also see BEACH BOYS
Also see CAPEHART, Jerry
Also see CHAMPS
Also see FABARES, Shelley
Also see FANN BAND
Also see FLEAS
Also see FOLKSWINGERS
Also see FORD, Tennessee Ernie, & Glen Campbell
Also see GEE CEES
Also see HONDELLS
Also see IN-GROUP
Also see JAN & DEAN
Also see LEGENDARY MASKED SURFERS
Also see MARTIN, Dean / Glen Campbell
Also see NELSON, Willie
Also see PUCKETT, Jerry
Also see RIP CHORDS
Also see ROGERS, Weldon
Also see SAGITTARIUS
Also see SWEET SOULS
Also see TILLIS, Mel, & Glen Campbell
Also see TUCKER, Tanya, & Glen Campbell
Also see WILSON, Brian
Also see YORK, Dave, & Beachcombers

CAMPBELL, Glen, & Rita Coolidge C&W/P&R '80

Singles: 7-inch

CAPITOL 3-4 80
Also see COOLIDGE, Rita

CAMPBELL, Glen, & Bobbie Gentry C&W/LP '68

Singles: 7-inch

CAPITOL 3-5 68-70

EPs: 7-inch

CAPITOL 8-10 68
(Juke box issue only.)

LPs: 10/12-inch

CAPITOL 8-10 68
Also see GENTRY, Bobbie

CAMPBELL, Glen / Lettermen / Ella Fitzgerald / Sandler & Young

LPs: 10/12-inch

CAPITOL (56 "B.F. Goodrich Presents Christmas 1969") 10-15 69
(Promotional, special products issue.)
Also see FITZGERALD, Ella
Also see LETTERMEN
Also see SANDLER & YOUNG

CAMPBELL, Glen, & Anne Murray C&W/P&R/LP '71

Singles: 7-inch

CAPITOL 3-5 71-72

LPs: 10/12-inch

CAPITOL 5-10 71-80

CAMPBELL, Glen / Anne Murray / Kenny Rogers / Crystal Gayle

LPs: 10/12-inch

CAPITOL/U.A. (11743-F-19 "Glen/Anne/ Kenny/ Crystal") 300-500 78
(Four framed picture disc set. Promotional issue only. 250 made)
Also see GAYLE, Crystal
Also see MURRAY, Anne
Also see ROGERS, Kenny

CAMPBELL, Glen, & Billy Strange

LPs: 10/12-inch

SURREY..12-20 65

Also see STRANGE, Billy

CAMPBELL, Glen / Texas Opera Company

Singles: 7-inch

W.B./VIVA 3-5 80

CAMPBELL, Glen, & Steve Wariner C&W '87

Singles: 7-inch

MCA 3-4 87

Also see WARINER, Steve

CAMPBELL, Glen / Dionne Warwick / Burt Bacharach

LPs: 10/12-inch

CHEVROLET (6658 "On the Move") ... 5-10 70
(Chevrolet promotional issue.)

Also see CAMPBELL, Glen

CAMPBELL, Jim P&R '70

Singles: 7-inch

LAURIE 3-6 69-70

CAMPBELL, Jo Ann P&R '60

Singles: 78 rpm

ELDORADO 25-50 57
POINT 10-20 56

Singles: 7-inch

ABC-PAR 10-20 60-62
(Monaural.)
ABC-PAR (10134 "Kookie Little Paradise") 20-40 60
(Stereo.)
CAMEO 5-10 62-63
ELDORADO (504 "Forever Young") 15-25 57
GONE 10-20 59
POINT 15-25 56
RORI 5-10 62

LPs: 10/12-inch

ABC-PAR (393 "Twistin' and Listenin'") 40-50 62
(Monaural.)
ABC-PAR (393 "Twistin' and Listenin'") 50-60 62
(Stereo.)
CAMEO (1026 "All the Hits of Jo Ann Campbell") 25-30 62
CORONET (199 "Starring Jo Ann Campbell") 10-20 62
END (306 "I'm Nobody's Baby") 40-60 59

Also see JO ANN & TROY

CAMPER VAN BEETHOVEN LP '88

LPs: 10/12-inch

VIRGIN 5-8 88-89

CANDELA R&B '82

Singles: 12-inch

ARISTA 4-6 83

Singles: 7-inch

ARISTA 3-4 82-83

CANDI P&R '88

Singles: 7-inch

I.R.S. 3-4 88

Picture Sleeves

I.R.S. 3-5 88

CANDLEMASS LP '89

LPs: 10/12-inch

METAL BLADE 5-8 89

CANDY & KISSES P&R/R&B '64

Singles: 7-inch

CAMEO 10-15 64
COLLECTABLES 3-4 81
DECCA 4-8 68
R&L 10-15 63
SCEPTER 8-12 65-66

Members: Candy Nelson; Suzanne Nelson; Jeanette Johnson.

CANDYMAN P&R/LP '90

Singles: 7-inch

EPIC 3-4 90

LPs: 10/12-inch

EPIC 5-8 90

CANDYMEN P&R/LP '67

Singles: 7-inch

ABC 4-8 67-69
LIBERTY 3-6 70

LPs: 10/12-inch

ABC 15-25 67-68

Members: Rodney Justo; Barry Bailey; Dean Daughtry; Billy Gilmore; Paul Goddard; John Adkins; Bob Nix.

Also see ATLANTA RHYTHM SECTION
Also see BEAVERTEETH
Also see CLASSICS IV
Also see ORBISON, Roy

CANE, Gary P&R '60
(With His Friends)

Singles: 7-inch

SHELL 8-12 60-61

CANNED HEAT LP '67
(Heat Brothers)

Singles: 7-inch

ALA 3-4 84
ATLANTIC 3-5 74
LIBERTY 4-8 68-71
U.A. 3-5 71-73

Picture Sleeves

LIBERTY 5-10 67-69

LPs: 10/12-inch

ACCORD 5-10 81
ALA 8-10 84
ATLANTIC 10-12 73-74
HAPPY BIRD (90135 "Dog House Blues") 10-20 83
(Picture disc.)
JANUS (3009 "Vintage") 10-15 69
LIBERTY (1000 series) 5-10 80
LIBERTY (3526 "Canned Heat") 25-40 67
(Monaural.)
LIBERTY (7526 "Canned Heat") 15-25 67
(Stereo.)
LIBERTY (7541 "Boogie") 15-25 68
LIBERTY (7618 "Hallelujah") 15-20 69
LIBERTY (10000 series) 5-10 81
LIBERTY (11000 "Cook Book") 10-15 69
LIBERTY (11002 "Future Blues") 10-15 70
LIBERTY (27200 "Living the Blues") 10-20 68
PICKWICK 5-10 70s
SCEPTER 10-15
SPRINGBOARD 5-10
SUNSET 10-15 71
U.A. 10-15 71-75
WAND 15-20 70

Members: Bob Hite; Joel Scott Hill; Harvey Mandel; Mark Andes; Ed Bayer; Frank Cook; Richard Hite; Chris Morgan; James Shane; Gene Taylor; Larry Taylor; Henry Vestine; Alan Wilson; Adolfo "Fito" de la Parra.

Also see GAMBLERS
Also see HILL, Joel
Also see HOOKER, John Lee, & Canned Heat
Also see LITTLE RICHARD
Also see MANDEL, Harvey
Also see SMOKE

CANNED HEAT & CHIPMUNKS

Singles: 7-inch

LIBERTY 15-25 68-70

Also see CANNED HEAT
Also see CHIPMUNKS

CANNIBAL & HEADHUNTERS P&R/LP '65

Singles: 7-inch

AIRES 5-10 68
CAPITOL 4-8 69
COLLECTABLES 3-4 81
DATE 5-10 66
ERA 3-5 73
RAMPART 10-15 65-66

LPs: 10/12-inch

DATE (3001 "Land of 1000 Dances") 20-30 66
RAMPART (3302 "Land of 1000 Dances") 40-60 65

Members: Frankie "Cannibal" Garcia; Robert Jaramillo; Joe Jaramillo; Richard Lopez.

CANNON, Ace P&R '61
(Johnny "Ace" Cannon)

Singles: 7-inch

FERNWOOD (135 "Hoe Down Rock") 5-10 63
FERNWOOD (137 "Big Shot") 5-10 64
(First issued as by Johnny Cannon.)
HI (2000 series) 5-10 61-66
HI (2100 thru 2300 series) 3-8 66-76
LOUIS (2001 "Tuff") 20-30 61
MOTOWN 3-4 82
SANTO 5-10 62

Picture Sleeves

HI 5-10 62-63

EPs: 7-inch

HI (1133 "In the Spotlight") 5-10 68
(Juke box issue.)

LPs: 10/12-inch

ALLEGIANCE 5-10 84
GUSTO 5-10 80
HI (007 thru 040) 10-20 62-67
(Numbers in this series are preceeded by a "12" for mono or a "32" for stereo issues.)
HI (043 thru 090) 8-15 68-75
(Numbers in this series are preceded by a "32," indicating stereo.)
HI (6000 & 8000 series) 8-10 77-79
MOTOWN 5-10 83

Also see BLACK, Bill
Also see CANNON, Johnny

CANNON, Freddy P&R/R&B '59
(Freddie Cannon)

Singles: 7-inch

AMHERST 3-5 88
BUDDAH 3-5 71
CLARIDGE 3-5 74-76
ERIC 3-4 78
HQ ("Kennywood Park") 4-6 87
(KDKA promotional issue only. No selection number used.)
MCA 3-5 74
METROMEDIA 3-5 72
ROYAL AMERICAN 3-6 69-70
SIRE 4-6 69
SWAN 5-10 59-64
W.B. 4-8 64-67
WE MAKE ROCK & ROLL RECORDS 4-6 68

Picture Sleeves

HQ ("Kennywood Park") 5-8 87
(KDKA promotional issue only. No selection number used.)
SWAN 15-25 59-62
W.B. 10-20 64-65

LPs: 10/12-inch

RHINO 5-10 82
SWAN (502 "The Explosive Freddy Cannon" 50-100 60
(Monaural.)
SWAN (502 "The Explosive Freddy Cannon" 75-125 60
(Stereo.)
SWAN (504 "Happy Shades of Blue") 50-75 62
SWAN (505 "Solid Gold Hits") 100-200 61
SWAN (507 "Palisades Park") 50-75 62
SWAN (511 "Freddy Cannon Steps Out") 50-75 62
W.B. (1544 "Freddie Cannon") 30-40 64
W.B. (1612 "Action") 30-40 64
W.B. (1628 "Greatest Hits") 30-40 64

Also see BUCHANAN, Roy
Also see DANNY & JUNIORS
Also see G-CLEFS
Also see SLAY, Frank
Also see SPINDRIFTS

CANNON, Freddy, & Belmonts

Singles: 7-inch

MIA SOUND 4-6 81

Also see BELMONTS, Freddy Cannon & Bo Diddley

Also see CANNON, Freddy

CANO, Eddie *LP '62*

Singles: 7-inch

DUNHILL........................3-6 66-67
GNP........................4-6 62
REPRISE........................4-8 62-65

LPs: 10/12-inch

DUNHILL........................10-15 67
GNP........................8-15 61-62
RCA........................8-15 62
REPRISE........................8-15 62-65

CANTINA BAND *P&R '81*

Singles: 7-inch

MILLENNIUM........................5-8 81
Member: Lou Christie.
Also see CHRISTIE, Lou

CANTRELL, Lana *LP '68*

Singles: 7-inch

EAST COAST........................3-4 74
POLYDOR........................3-4 74-75
RCA........................3-6 66-69

LPs: 10/12-inch

RCA........................8-15 67-69

CANYON *P&R '75*

Singles: 7-inch

MAGNA-GLIDE........................3-5 75

CAPALDI, Jim *P&R/LP '72*

Singles: 12-inch

ISLAND........................4-8 88
(Promotional only.)
RSO........................4-6 79

Singles: 7-inch

ATLANTIC........................3-4 83
ISLAND........................3-5 72-88
RSO........................3-4 78

Picture Sleeves

ATLANTIC........................3-4 83

LPs: 10/12-inch

ATLANTIC........................5-10 83
CAPITOL........................8-10 72
ISLAND........................6-12 73-88
RSO........................5-10 78-79
Also see TRAFFIC

CAPITOL'S MYSTERY ARTIST
(Nancy Wilson)

Singles: 7-inch

CAPITOL (1667 "Something Wonderful Happens")........................5-10 60
(Promotional issue only. Nancy's name is not shown on label.)
Also see WILSON, Nancy

CAPITOLS *P&R/R&B/LP '66*

Singles: 7-inch

COLLECTABLES........................3-4 81
KAREN........................4-8 66-68

LPs: 10/12-inch

ATCO........................15-20 66
COLLECTABLES........................6-8 88
SOLID SMOKE........................5-10 85
Members: Sam George; Don Storball; Richard McDougall.

CAPRELLS *R&B '77*

Singles: 7-inch

ARIOLA AMERICA........................3-5 76
BANO (100 "Walk On By")........................8-10
CRS (008 "Which One Will It Be")........5-8

CAPRIS

Singles: 7-inch

TENDER (518 "Endless Love"/ "Beware")........................75-125 59
(*Beware* is by Jesse Belvin, and was issued in 1956 on Cash by him.)
Member: Jesse Belvin.
Also see BELVIN, Jesse

CAPRIS *P&R '60*
("With Rhythm Accompaniment")

Singles: 7-inch

AMBIENT SOUND........................3-6 82
JANUS (714 "Why Did I Cry")........................4-6 77
COLLECTABLES........................3-4 81
DELTA (3118 "There's a Moon Out Tonight")........................10-20 61
(Canadian.)
LOST-NITE (101 "There's a Moon Out Tonight")........................40-60 60
(Pink label. Black vinyl.)
LOST-NITE (101 "There's a Moon Out Tonight")........................75-125 60
(Pink label. Colored vinyl.)
LOST NITE (101 "There's a Moon Out Tonight")........................5-10 60s
(Yellow label.)
MR. PEEKE (118 "Limbo")........................10-20 63
OLD TOWN (1094 "There's a Moon Out Tonight")........................10-20 60
OLD TOWN (1099 "Where I Fell in Love")........................25-35 60
OLD TOWN (1103 "Why Do I Cry")........................20-30 60
OLD TOWN (1107 "Girl in My Dreams")........................30-50 61
PLANET (1010 "There's a Moon Out Tonight")........................250-350 60
TROMMERS (101 "There's a Moon Out Tonight")........................30-40 60

LPs: 10/12-inch

AMBIENT SOUND........................5-10 82
COLLECTABLES........................5-10 84
Members: Nick "Santos" Santamaria; Mike Mitchell; Vince Narcardo; John Apostol; Frank Reina.

CAPTAIN & TENNILLE *P&R/LP '75*

Singles: 7-inch

A&M........................3-5 75-78
BUTTERSCOTCH CASTLE (001 "The Way I Want to Touch You")........................50-75 73
JOYCE (101 "The Way I Want to Touch You")........................20-40 74
CASABLANCA........................3-5 79-80

Picture Sleeves

A&M........................4-6 75-78

LPs: 10/12-inch

A&M........................8-10 75-79
CASABLANCA........................5-10 79
Members: Daryl Dragon; Toni Tennille.
Also see BEACH BOYS
Also see DRAGONS
Also see TENNILLE, Toni
Also see YELLOW BALLOON

CAPTAIN BEEFHEART *LP '72*
(With His Magic Band)

Singles: 7-inch

A&M (794 "Diddy Wah Diddy")........50-75 66
A&M (818 "Moonchild")........................40-60 66
BUDDAH........................4-8 67-69
EPIC........................3-5 82
MERCURY........................3-5 74
REPRISE........................3-6 72
VIRGIN........................3-5 82

Promotional Singles

REPRISE (434 "Lick My Decals Off, Baby")........................40-50 70
REPRISE (447 "Talking About")........40-50 71
REPRISE (514 "Click Clack")........25-40 71
REPRISE (547 "Low Yo Yo Stuff")...40-50 72
(Issued with gatefold, EP-like, cover.)

LPs: 10/12-inch

A&M........................5-10 84
ACCORD........................5-10 83
BIZARRE........................10-12 72
BLUE THUMB (1 "Strictly Personal") 20-30 68
(Black label.)
BLUE THUMB (1 "Strictly Personal") 10-15 69
(Tan label.)
BUDDAH (1001 "Safe As Milk")........25-35 67
(Monaural. Add $10 to $15 if accompanied by 4" x 15" *Safe As Milk* bumper sticker.)
BUDDAH (5001 "Safe As Milk")........25-30 67
(Stereo. Add $10 to $15 if accompanied by 4" x 15" *Safe As Milk* bumper sticker.)
BUDDAH (5077 "Mirror Man")........10-15 71
BUDDAH (5063 "Safe As Milk")........8-12 70
D.I.R. (57 "Direct News, Week of 12-18-78")........................35-45 78
(Five, 5-minute radio programs, one of which has an interview with Don Van Vliet. Promotional issue only.)
EPIC........................5-10 82
MERCURY (709 "Unconditionally Guaranteed")........................8-12 74
MERCURY (1018 "Bluejeans and Moonbeams")........................8-12 74
REPRISE (2027 "Trout Mask Replica")........................8-12 77
REPRISE (2050 "Spotlight Kid")........10-15 72
REPRISE (2115 "Clear Spot")........10-20 72
(With embossed "Clear Spot" plastic bag.)
REPRISE (2115 "Clear Spot")........15-20 72
(White label. Has printed inserts instead of standard cover. Promotional issue only.)
STRAIGHT (1053 "Trout Mask Replica")........................30-40 68
(With lyrics sleeve.)
STRAIGHT (1053 "Trout Mask Replica")........................20-25 68
(Without lyrics sleeve.)
STRAIGHT (6420 "Lick My Decals Off, Baby")........................10-15 70
VIRGIN........................5-10 80-82
W.B........................5-10 78
Members: Don "Captain Beefheart" Van Vliet; Doug Moon; Paul Blakely; Alex St. Claire; Jerry Handley; Ry Cooder; Jeff Cotton; John French; Bill "Zoot Horn Rollo" Harkleroad; Rockette Morton; Jimmy Semens; Jerry Handsley; Ty Grimes.
Also see COODER, Ry
Also see MALLARD
Also see MOTHERS of INVENTION
Also see MU
Also see TRIANGLE

CAPTAIN BEYOND *LP '72*

Singles: 7-inch

CAPRICORN........................3-5 73

LPs: 10/12-inch

CAPRICORN (Except 0105)........8-12 72-73
CAPRICORN (0105 "Captain Beyond")........................45-55 72
(With 3-D cover.)
CAPRICORN (0105 "Captain Beyond")........................15-25 72
(With standard cover.)
W.B........................8-10 77
Members: Bobby Caldwell; Rod Evans; Willie Daffern; Lee Dorman; Larry Reinhardt.
Also see CALDWELL, Bobby
Also see DEEP PURPLE
Also see IRON BUTTERFLY

CAPTAIN RAPP *D&D '83*

Singles: 12-inch

BECKET........................4-6 83

Singles: 7-inch

BECKET........................3-4 83

CAPTAIN SKY *R&B '78*
(Daryl Cameron)

Singles: 12-inch

WMOT........................4-6 81

Singles: 7-inch

A.V.I........................3-5 79-82
TEC........................3-4 80
TRIPLE........................3-4 86
WMOT........................3-4 81

LPs: 10/12-inch

A.V.I........................5-10 78-82
TEC........................5-10 80

CARA, Irene *P&R '80*
(Irene Cara / Helen St. John; Irene Cara / Contemporary Gospel Chorus)

Singles: 12-inch

CASABLANCA........................4-6 83
GEFFEN........................4-6 83

Singles: 7-inch

CASABLANCA........................3-4 83
GEFFEN........................3-4 83-85
RSO........................3-4 80

NETWORK 3-4 81

Picture Sleeves

GEFFEN 3-4 83

LPs: 10/12-inch

GEFFEN 5-10 83-85
NETWORK 5-10 82
RSO 5-10 80

CARAVAN LP '75

Singles: 7-inch

BTM 3-5 75
DK 3-4 83
LONDON 3-5 71

LPs: 10/12-inch

ARISTA 5-10 76
BTM 5-10 75
LONDON 12-15 71-75
VERVE/FORECAST 15-20 69
Members: Steve Miller; Richard Coughlan; Pye Hastings; John Perry; Geoff Richards; Jan Schelhaas; Dave Sinclair; Richard Sinclair; Mike Wedgewood.
Also see HATFIELD & NORTH

CARAVELLES P&R '63

Singles: 7-inch

SMASH 4-8 63-65

LPs: 10/12-inch

SMASH (27044 "You Don't Have to Be a Baby to Cry") 20-40 63
(Monaural.)
SMASH (67044 "You Don't Have to Be a Baby to Cry") 20-40 63
(Stereo.)
Members: Lois Wilkinson; Andrea Simpson.

CARDENAS, Luis P&R '86

Singles: 7-inch

ALLIED ARTISTS 3-4 86

Picture Sleeves

ALLIED ARTISTS 3-4 86

LPs: 10/12-inch

ALLIED ARTISTS 5-10 86
Also see RENEGADE

CARDINALS R&B '51

Singles: 78 rpm

ATLANTIC (938 "Shouldn't I Know") 50-100 51
ATLANTIC (958 thru 1126) 25-75 51-57

Singles: 7-inch

ATLANTIC (952 "I'll Always Love You") 150-250 51
ATLANTIC (958 "Wheel of Fortune") 150-250 52
ATLANTIC (972 "The Bump") 50-100 52
ATLANTIC (995 "You Are My Only Love") 100-200 53
ATLANTIC (1025 "Under a Blanket of Blue") 100-200 54
ATLANTIC (1054 "The Door Is Still Open") 50-75 55
ATLANTIC (1067 "Two Things I Love") 50-75 55
ATLANTIC (1079 "There Goes My Heart to You") 50-75 55
ATLANTIC (1090 "Off Shore") 25-50 56
ATLANTIC (1103 "The End of the Story") 15-25 56
ATLANTIC (1126 "Near You") 15-25 57

EPs: 7-inch

BIM BAM BOOM (1000 "The Cardinals") 6-12 70s
Members: Ernie Warren; Meredith Brothers; Leon Hardy; Donald Johnson; Jack "Sam" Aydelotte; Luther MacArthur; James Brown; Lee Tarver.

CAREFREES P&R '64

Singles: 7-inch

LONDON INT'L (10614 "We Love You Beatles") 8-12 64
LONDON INT'L (10615 "Paddy Wack") 5-8 64

Picture Sleeves

LONDON INT'L (10614 "We Love You Beatles") 10-20 64

LPs: 10/12-inch

LONDON (379 "We Love You All") ... 35-45 64
Members: Lyn Cornell; Betty Prescott; Barbara Kay.
Also see BREAKAWAYS
Also see VERNON'S GIRLS

CAREY, Mariah P&R/LP '90

Singles: 7-inch

COLUMBIA 3-4 90-93

LPs: 10/12-inch

COLUMBIA 5-8 90

CAREY, Tony P&R/LP '83

Singles: 7-inch

MCA 3-4 84
ROCSHIRE 3-4 83

Picture Sleeves

MCA 3-4 84
ROCSHIRE 3-4 83

LPs: 10/12-inch

MCA 5-10 84
ROCSHIRE 5-10 83
Also see PLANET P PROJECT
Also see RAINBOW

CARGILL, Henson P&R/C&W '67

Singles: 7-inch

ARCO 4-6 67
ATLANTIC 3-5 73-74
COPPER MOUNTAIN 3-4 79-80
ELEKTRA 3-5 75
MEGA 3-5 71-73
MONUMENT 4-6 67-70
RUFF 4-6
TOWER 3-6 68

LPs: 10/12-inch

ATLANTIC 6-10 73
BUCKBOARD 5-10
HARMONY 6-10 72
MEGA 6-10 72
MONUMENT 8-12 68-70

CARLA & RUFUS: see RUFUS & CARLA

CARLIN, George LP '72

Singles: 7-inch

LITTLE DAVID 3-5 72-75
RCA 4-8 67

Picture Sleeves

LITTLE DAVID 5-10 72

LPs: 10/12-inch

ATLANTIC 5-10 81
CAMDEN 8-10 72
EARDRUM 5-10 84
ERA 8-12 72
LITTLE DAVID 5-10 72-85
RCA 10-15 67

CARLISLE, Belinda P&R/LP '86

Singles: 12-inch

I.R.S. 4-6 86

Singles: 7-inch

I.R.S. 3-4 86-87
MCA 3-4 87-90

Picture Sleeves

I.R.S. 3-4 86-87
MCA 3-4 87-88

LPs: 10/12-inch

I.R.S. 5-10 86-87
MCA 5-10 87-90
Also see GO-GOs

CARLISLE, Steve P&R '81

Singles: 7-inch

MCA 3-4 81-82

LPs: 10/12-inch

MCA 5-10 82

CARLOS, Walter LP '69

LPs: 10/12-inch

COLUMBIA 8-12 69-72

CARLTON, Carl P&R/R&B '68
(Little Carl Carlton)

Singles: 12-inch

20TH FOX 4-6 80

Singles: 7-inch

ABC 3-5 73-76
BACK BEAT 3-6 68-75
CASABLANCA 3-4 86
GOLDEN WORLD (23 "Nothin' No Sweeter Than Love") 10-20 65
LANDO (8527 "So What") 30-40 65
MCA 3-4 84
MERCURY 3-5 77
RCA 3-4 82
20TH FOX 3-4 81-82

LPs: 10/12-inch

ABC 10-12 74
BACK BEAT 10-15 73
CASABLANCA 5-10 86
RCA 5-10 82
20TH FOX 5-10 81

CARLTON, Larry LP '78

Singles: 7-inch

GRP 3-4 90
MCA 3-4 85-86
UNI 4-6 68-69
W.B. 3-5 78-83

LPs: 10/12-inch

ATLANTIC 5-10 84
BLUE THUMB 10-12 73
GRP 5-8 90
MCA 5-10 85-87
UNI 12-18 68
W.B. 5-10 78-83
Also see CRUSADERS
Also see POST, Mike

CARMAN, Pauli R&B '86

Singles: 12-inch

COLUMBIA 4-6 86

Singles: 7-inch

COLUMBIA 3-4 86-87

LPs: 10/12-inch

COLUMBIA 5-10 86

CARMEN, Eric P&R/LP '75

Singles: 12-inch

GEFFEN 4-6 85

Singles: 7-inch

ARISTA (Except 9000 series) 3-5 75-80
ARISTA (9000 series) 3-4 88
COOL 3-4 86
EPIC 3-6 70
GEFFEN 3-4 84-85
RCA 3-4 87

Picture Sleeves

ARISTA (0266 "She Did It") 3-5 77
ARISTA (0295 "Boats Against the Current") 4-6 77
(Promotional issue only.)
ARISTA (9000 series) 3-4 88
GEFFEN 3-4 85

LPs: 10/12-inch

ARISTA (Except 4057) 5-10 77-88
ARISTA (AL-4057 "Eric Carmen") 8-10 75
ARISTA (AQ-4057 "Eric Carmen") 15-20 75
(Quadraphonic.)
GEFFEN 5-10 85
Also see CYRUS ERIE
Also see MANDRELL, Louise, & Eric Carmen
Also see QUICK
Also see RASPBERRIES

CARMEN, Eric / Tom Johnston

Singles: 7-inch

RCA 3-4 87
Also see CARMEN, Eric
Also see JOHNSTON, Tom

CARN, Jean: see CARNE, Jean

CARNE, Jean R&B/LP '77
(Jean Carn)

Singles: 7-inch

ATLANTIC 3-4 88
MOTOWN 3-4 82
OMNI 3-4 86
PHILADELPHIA INT'L 3-4 77-80
TSOP 3-4 81

LPs: 10/12-inch

OMNI 5-10 86
PHILADELPHIA INT'L 5-10 76-80
MOTOWN 5-10 82

TSOP.............................5-10 81
Also see JOHNSON, Al, & Jean Carn
Also see MILITELLO, Bobby, & Jean Carn

CARNES, Kim P&R '79

Singles: 12-inch

EMI AMERICA.............................4-6 80-85

Singles: 7-inch

A&M.............................3-5 75-82
AMOS.............................3-6 71-72
EMI AMERICA.............................3-4 79-86
ELEKTRA.............................3-4 84

Picture Sleeves

EMI AMERICA.............................3-4 80-86

LPs: 10/12-inch

A&M (3000 series).............................5-10 82
A&M (4000 series).............................8-10 75-77
AMOS.............................12-18 71
EMI AMERICA.............................5-10 79-86
MCA.............................5-10 84
MFSL (073 "Mistaken Identity").............................25-35 82
Session: Lyle Lovett.
Also see COTTON, Gene, & Kim Carnes
Also see LOVETT, Lyle
Also see ROGERS, Kenny, & Kim Carnes
Also see STREISAND, Barbra, & Kim Carnes
Also see SUGAR BEARS
Also see U.S.A. for AFRICA

CARNES, Kim, & Dave Ellington

Singles: 7-inch

AMOS.............................3-5 72
Also see CARNES, Kim

CARNIVAL LP '69

Singles: 7-inch

U.A.............................3-5 71
WORLD PACIFIC.............................3-6 69

LPs: 10/12-inch

WORLD PACIFIC.............................10-15 69
Member: Terry Fisher.
Also see FISHER, Terry

CAROSONE, Renato P&R '58

Singles: 7-inch

CAPITOL.............................4-8 58

CARPENTER, Carleton, & Debbie Reynolds P&R '51

Singles: 78 rpm

MGM.............................5-10 51

Singles: 7-inch

MGM.............................8-12 51

EPs: 7-inch

MGM (1008 "Debbie Reynolds & Carleton Carpenter Sing").............................10-15 51
Also see REYNOLDS, Debbie

CARPENTER, Mary Chapin C&W/LP '89

Singles: 7-inch

COLUMBIA.............................3-4 89-92

LPs: 10/12-inch

COLUMBIA.............................5-8 89-90

CARPENTER, Thelma P&R '60

Singles: 78 rpm

COLUMBIA.............................5-10 50
MAJESTIC.............................5-10 45-46

Singles: 7-inch

COLUMBIA.............................10-15 50
CORAL (Except 62272).............................5-10 60-62
CORAL (62272 "Heartaches").............................20-30 61

LPs: 10/12-inch

CORAL (57433 "Thinking of You Tonight").............................15-25 63
(Monaural.)
CORAL (7-57433 "Thinking of You Tonight").............................25-35 63
(Stereo.)

CARPENTERS P&R/LP '70

Singles: 7-inch

A&M (Except 2735).............................3-6 69-85
A&M (2735 "Yesterday Once More").............................10-15 85
(Promotional issue only.)

Picture Sleeves

A&M (Except 2735).............................5-12 70-81
A&M (2735 "Yesterday Once More").............................10-15 85
(Promotional issue only. With paper sleeve.)

EPs: 7-inch

A&M.............................10-15 72-85

LPs: 10/12-inch

A&M (3000 series).............................8-15 71-85
A&M (4000 series, except 4205).............................8-15 70-83
A&M (4205 "Offering").............................20-35 69
A&M (4205 "Ticket to Ride").............................10-15 71
A&M (5100 series").............................5-8 90
A&M (50000 series).............................15-25 74-75
(Quadraphonic series.)
A&M (6000 series).............................8-12 85
MFP (50431 "Ticket to Ride").............................10-15 70
Members: Karen Carpenter; Richard Carpenter; Tony Peluso.
Also see CARPENTER, Karen
Also see CARPENTER, Richard

CARR, Cathy P&R '56

Singles: 78 rpm

CORAL.............................5-10 53-56
FRATERNITY.............................5-15 55-56

Singles: 7-inch

ABC.............................3-4 73
COLLECTABLES.............................3-4 81
CORAL.............................8-10 53-56
FRATERNITY.............................10-20 55-56
LAURIE.............................5-10 62-63
ROULETTE (Except 4152).............................5-10 59-61
ROULETTE (4152 "I'm Gonna Change Him").............................5-10 59
(Monaural.)
ROULETTE (SSR-4152 "I'm Gonna Change Him").............................15-25 59
(Stereo.)
SMASH.............................4-8 61

EPs: 7-inch

BRUNSWICK.............................10-20 57

LPs: 10/12-inch

DOT.............................15-25 66
FRATERNITY (1005 "Ivory Tower").............................50-100 57
RCA.............................15-25 64
ROULETTE (R-25077 "Shy").............................30-40 59
(Monaural.)
ROULETTE (SR-25077 "Shy").............................40-60 59
(Stereo.)

CARR, James P&R/R&B '66

Singles: 7-inch

ATLANTIC.............................3-5 71
GOLDWAX.............................4-8 65-69

LPs: 10/12-inch

GOLDWAX.............................12-20 67-68
Also see SOUL STIRRERS

CARR, Jerry R&B '81

Singles: 7-inch

CHERIE.............................3-4 81

CARR, Joe "Fingers" P&R '50
(Lou Busch)

Singles: 78 rpm

CAPITOL.............................3-6 50-57

Singles: 7-inch

CAPITOL.............................5-10 50-59
CORAL.............................4-6 63
DOT.............................3-6 66
W.B.............................4-8 60-62

EPs: 7-inch

CAPITOL.............................5-15 51-57

LPs: 10/12-inch

CAPITOL (Except 2000 series).............................15-30 51-61
CAPITOL (2000 series).............................10-15 64
CORAL.............................10-15 63
DOT.............................10-15 66
W.B.............................10-20 60-62
Also see BUSCH, Lou
Also see FORD, Tennessee Ernie, & Joe "Fingers" Carr
Also see FRAZIER, Dallas, & Joe "Fingers" Carr
Also see PROVINE, Dorothy, & Joe "Fingers" Carr
Also see YOUNG, Vicki, & Joe Carr

CARR, Valerie P&R '58

Singles: 7-inch

ATLAS.............................4-8 64
ROULETTE.............................5-10 58-61

LPs: 10/12-inch

ROULETTE (25094 "Ev'ry Hour, Ev'ry Day").............................25-35 59

CARR, Vikki LP '64

Singles: 7-inch

COLUMBIA.............................3-5 71-75
LIBERTY.............................4-8 62-69

Picture Sleeves

COLUMBIA.............................3-5 74
LIBERTY.............................4-8 67

LPs: 10/12-inch

COLUMBIA.............................8-10 71-75
LIBERTY (Except 10000 series).............................10-20 63-70
LIBERTY (10000 series).............................5-10 81
SUNSET.............................8-12
U.A.............................5-10 71-80
Also see BERNSTEIN, Elmer

CARR, Wynona R&B '57
(Sister Wynona Carr)

Singles: 78 rpm

SPECIALTY.............................5-15 56-58

Singles: 7-inch

REPRISE.............................5-10 61-63
SPECIALTY.............................10-20 56-60

LPs: 10/12-inch

REPRISE.............................15-25 62
SPECIALTY.............................8-10 88

CARRACK, Paul P&R/LP '82

Singles: 12-inch

CHRYSALIS.............................4-8 87
(Promotional only.)

Singles: 7-inch

CHRYSALIS.............................3-4 87
EPIC.............................3-4 82

Picture Sleeves

CHRYSALIS.............................3-4 87-88

LPs: 10/12-inch

CHRYSALIS.............................5-10 87-89
EPIC.............................5-10 82
Also see ACE
Also see MIKE + the MECHANICS
Also see ROXY MUSIC
Also see SQUEEZE

CARRADINE, Keith P&R/LP '76

Singles: 7-inch

ABC.............................3-5 75
ASYLUM.............................3-5 78
VALA.............................3-4 83

LPs: 10/12-inch

ASYLUM.............................8-10 76

CARRINGTON, Terri Lyne LP '89

LPs: 10/12-inch

FORECAST.............................5-8 89

CARROLL, Andrea P&R '63

Singles: 7-inch

BIG TOP (515 "The Doolang").............................30-40 64
BIG TOP (3156 "It Hurts to Be Sixteen").............................8-12 63
EPIC (9438 "Young and Lonely").............................50-100 61
(Yellow label.)
EPIC (9438 "Young and Lonely").............................50-75 61
(White label. Promotional issue.)
EPIC (9450 "Please Don't Talk to the Lifeguard").............................10-15 61
EPIC (9471 "Gee Dad").............................15-20 61
EPIC (9523 "Fifteen Shades of Pink").............................15-20 62

Picture Sleeves

EPIC (9471 "Gee Dad").............................25-35 61
RCA (8618 "Sally Fool").............................8-12 65
U.A. (982 "The World Isn't Big Enough").............................8-15 66
U.A. (50039 "Hey Beach Boy").............................8-15 66

LPs: 10/12-inch

B.T. PUPPY (1017 "Side by Side").............................20-30 60s
(With Beverly Warren.)

CARROLL, Andrea / Beverly Warren

LPs: 10/12-inch

B.T. PUPPY (1017 "Andrea Carroll and Beverly Warren") 50-75 69

Also see CARROLL, Andrea
Also see WARREN, Beverly

CARROLL, Bernadette P&R '64

Singles: 7-inch

COLLECTABLES 3-4 81
JULIA 4-8 62
LAURIE 5-10 63-64

CARROLL, Bob P&R '53

Singles: 78 rpm

BALLY 5-10 56-57
DERBY 4-8 53
MGM 4-8 55

Singles: 7-inch

BALLY 5-10 56-57
DERBY 5-10 53
DOT 3-6 66
MGM 5-10 55
MURBO 3-6 67
UNART 4-8 59
U.A. 4-8 59-59

Picture Sleeves

U.A. 5-10 58

Also see JENKINS, Gordon, & His Orchestra

CARROLL, Cathy P&R '62

Singles: 7-inch

CHEER 10-15 63-64
DOT 4-8 66
MUSICOR 4-8 65
PHILIPS 4-8 63
TRIODEX 10-15 61
W.B. 5-10 62-63

CARROLL, David, Orchestra P&R '54

Singles: 78 rpm

MERCURY 3-5 53-57

Singles: 7-inch

MERCURY 4-8 53-62

EPs: 7-inch

MERCURY 5-10 54-59

LPs: 10/12-inch

MERCURY 8-18 53-62
WING 5-10 59

Also see CONTINO, Dick

CARROLL, Delores, & Four Tops

(With Maurice King & His Wolverines)

Singles: 78 rpm

CHATEAU (2002 "Everybody Knows") 50-100 56

Singles: 7-inch

CHATEAU (2002 "Everybody Knows") 150-250 56

Also see FOUR TOPS
Also see HAYES, Carolyn, & Four Tops

CARROLL, Earl, & Original Cadillacs

Singles: 7-inch

JOSIE (829 "Buzz-Buzz-Buzz") 20-30 57
REO (8195 "Buzz-Buzz-Buzz") 20-30 57
(Canadian.)

Also see CADILLACS
Also see COASTERS
Also see ORIGINAL CADILLACS
Also see SPEEDO & CADILLACS

CARROLL, Jim LP '80

(Jim Carroll Band)

Singles: 12-inch

ATLANTIC 4-8 83
(Promotional only.)

Singles: 7-inch

A&M 3-5 72
ATCO 3-4 80-81
ATLANTIC 3-4 83

LPs: 10/12-inch

A&M 10-15 71
ATCO 5-10 80-82
ATLANTIC 5-10 83

CARROLL, Ronnie P&R '63

Singles: 7-inch

PHILIPS 4-8 63-66

CARROLL BROTHERS P&R '62

Singles: 7-inch

CAMEO (140 "Red Hot") 50-75 58
CAMEO (200 series) 5-10 62
FELSTED 5-10 59

LPs: 10/12-inch

CAMEO (1015 "College Twist Party") 25-35 62

Members: Pete Carroll; Dick Noble; Bill McGraw; Jimmy Chick; Kenneth Dorn.

CARS P&R/LP '78

Singles: 12-inch

ELEKTRA 5-10 86
(Promotional issues only.)

Singles: 7-inch

ELEKTRA 3-5 78-88

Picture Sleeves

ELEKTRA 3-5 78-88

LPs: 10/12-inch

ELEKTRA (Except 5E-567) 5-10 78-87
ELEKTRA (5E-567 "Shake It Up") 120-140 81
(Picture disc with blank B-side. Promotional issue only. 500 made.)
ELEKTRA (5E-567 "Shake It Up") 150-175 81
(Picture disc with KMET radio logo on B-side. Promotional issue only. 50 made.)
NAUTILUS (49 "Candy-O") 20-30 82
(Half-speed mastered.)

Members: Ric Ocasek; Elliot Easton; Benjamin Orr; Greg Hawkes; Dave Robinson.
Also see EASTON, Elliot
Also see MILKWOOD
Also see OCASEK, Ric
Also see ORR, Benjamin

CARSON, Kit P&R '55

Singles: 78 rpm

CAPITOL 4-8 55

Singles: 7-inch

CAPITOL 8-10 55

CARSON, Mindy P&R '46

Singles: 78 rpm

COLUMBIA 5-10 52-56

Singles: 7-inch

COLUMBIA 8-12 52-56
JOY 4-8 60
RCA 8-12 50-52

Also see MITCHELL, Guy, & Mindy Carson

CARTER, Benny, & His Orchestra R&B/C&W '44

(Featuring Savannah Churchill)

Singles: 78 rpm

BLUEBIRD 4-8 41
BRUNSWICK 4-8 46
CAPITOL 4-8 42-44
COLUMBIA (2898 "Devil's Holiday") 10-20 33
(Colored plastic.)
DECCA 4-8 40
OKEH 4-8 40
VOCALION 4-8 35-40

Also see CHURCHILL, Savannah

CARTER, Carlene C&W '79

(With Rockpile)

Singles: 7-inch

EPIC 3-4 83
REPRISE 3-4 90-91
W.B. 3-4 78-82

LPs: 10/12-inch

EPIC 5-10 83
W.B. 5-10 78-82

Also see CARTER FAMILY
Also see EDMUNDS, Dave, & Carlene Carter
Also see ORRALL, Robert Ellis
Also see ROCKPILE
Also see SOUTHERN PACIFIC & Carlene Carter

CARTER, Carlene, & Dave Edmunds C&W '80

Singles: 7-inch

W.B. 3-4 80

Also see CARTER, Carlene
Also see EDMUNDS, Dave

CARTER, Clarence P&R/R&B '67

Singles: 12-inch

ICHIBAN 4-6 88

Singles: 7-inch

ABC 3-5 75-76
ATLANTIC (2000 series) 4-8 68-72
ATLANTIC (13000 series) 3-4
FAME (Except 1000 series) 3-5 72-73
FAME (1000 series) 4-8 67
FUTURE STARS 3-5
ICHIBAN 3-4 88-92
RONN 3-5 77
VENTURE 3-4 80-81

LPs: 10/12-inch

ABC 8-10 74-76
ATLANTIC 10-20 68-71
BIG C 5-10 83
BRYLEN 5-10 84
FAME 10-12 73
ICHIBAN 5-10 86-88
VENTURE 5-10 80-81

CARTER, Clarence & Candi

Singles: 7-inch

ATLANTIC 3-5 72

Also see CARTER, Clarence

CARTER, Mel P&R/R&B '63

Singles: 7-inch

ABKCO 3-4 84
AMOS 3-5 69-70
ARWIN 5-10 60
BELL 3-6 68-69
CREAM 3-4 81
DERBY 8-12 63
IMPERIAL 4-8 64-66
LIBERTY 4-6 67-68
MERCURY 4-8 62
PHILIPS 4-8 62
ROMAR 3-5 73-74
TRI-STATE 10-15 59

LPs: 10/12-inch

AMOS 10-12 70
DERBY (702 "When a Boy Falls in Love") 50-100 63
IMPERIAL 15-20 65-66
LIBERTY 12-20 67
SUNSET 10-12 68-70

CARTER, Mel / Vic Dana

EPs: 7-inch

ROWE/AMI 5-10 60s
(Colored vinyl. Juke box issue.)

Also see DANA, Vic

CARTER, Mel, & Clydie King

Singles: 7-inch

PHILIPS 4-8 62

Also see CARTER, Mel
Also see KING, Clydie, & Sweet Things

CARTER, Ralph P&R/R&B '75

Singles: 7-inch

MERCURY 3-5 75-76

CARTER, Ron LP '77

LPs: 10/12-inch

MILESTONE 5-10 77-78
MOTOWN 5-8 84

CARTER, Valerie LP '77

Singles: 7-inch

COLUMBIA 3-4 77-79

LPs: 10/12-inch

COLUMBIA 8-10 77-78

Also see LITTLE FEAT
Also see MONEY, Eddie, & Valerie Carter

CARTER, Valerie, & Henry Paul

Singles: 7-inch

ATLANTIC 3-4 82

Also see CARTER, Valerie

CARTER BROTHERS *R&B '65*

Singles: 7-inch

COLEMAN.......8-10 64
JEWEL.......4-8 65-67
MISTY.......5-10 60s
TALENT SCOUT.......5-10 60s
Members: Jerry Carter; Al Carter; Roman Carter.

CARTER FAMILY *P&R '28*

Singles: 78 rpm

BANNER.......15-25 35
BLUEBIRD.......15-25 30s
DECCA.......10-20 30s
MONTEGOMERY WARD.......15-25 30s
VICTOR (20000 series).......50-150 28
VICTOR (40000 series).......25-75 28
VOCALION.......25-35

EPs: 7-inch

ACME.......25-50 50s
DECCA.......10-20 65

LPs: 10/12-inch

ACME (1 "All Time Favorites").......100-200 50s
ACME (2 "In Memory of A.P. Carter: Keep on the Sunny Side").......100-200 50s
ANTHOLOGY of COUNTRY MUSIC.......10-15
COLUMBIA ("CL" & "CS" series).......10-20 64-67
DECCA (4404 "The Carter Family").......20-30 63
DECCA (4557 "More Favorites").......20-30 65
LIBERTY.......15-25 62
CAMDEN (Except 586)....... 71-74
CAMDEN (586 "Original and Great Carter Family").......15-20 62
COLUMBIA ("KC" & "PC" series).......5-10 72-80s
HARMONY (7280 "Famous Carter Family").......15-25 61
HARMONY (7300 "Carter Family").......15-25 63
HARMONY (7344 "Home Among the Hills").......15-25 65
HARMONY (7396 "Sacred Songs").......10-15 66
HARMONY (7422 "Country Sounds").......10-20 67
HARMONY (11000 series).......10-15 69-70
J.E.M.F.......10-15
OLD HOMESTEAD.......5-8
OLD TIME CLASSICS.......5-10
PICKWICK.......5-10 75
PINE MOUNTAIN.......8-10
RCA (Except 2772).......5-15 75-78
RCA (2772 "Mid the Green Fields of Virginia").......15-25 63
SUNSET.......10-15 67
Members: A.P. Carter; Sara Carter; Maybelle Carter; Anita Carter; June Carter; Helen Carter; Joe Carter; Janette Carter; Carlene Carter.
Also see CARTER, Anita
Also see CARTER, June
Also see CARTER SISTERS
Also see CASH, Johnny, & Carter Family
Also see HAGGARD, Merle

CARTRELL, Delia *R&B '71*

Singles: 7-inch

RIGHT ON.......3-5 71-72

CARTRIDGE, Flip *P&R '66*

Singles: 7-inch

PARROT.......4-8 66-67

CASCADES *P&R/R&B/LP '63*

Singles: 7-inch

ABC.......3-4 73
ARWIN.......4-8 66
CANBASE.......3-5 72
CHARTER.......10-15 64
COLLECTABLES.......3-4 81
GOLDIES.......3-5 73
LIBERTY.......4-8 65
PROBE.......3-6 68
RCA.......5-10 63-64
RENEE.......10-20
SMASH.......4-8 67
UNI.......3-6 69-70
VALIANT.......5-10 62-63
W.B. 3-4

Picture Sleeves

PROBE.......4-8 68
RCA.......8-12 63

LPs: 10/12-inch

BLOSSOM.......10-15
CASCADES (6820 "What Goes on Inside the Cascades").......20-35
UNI.......15-20 69
VALIANT (W-405 "Rhythm of the Rain").......40-60 63
(Monaural.)
VALIANT (WS-405 "Rhythm of the Rain").......50-100 63
(Stereo.)
Members: Bill Preston; Dick Snyder; Danny Mark; Tommy Larson; Dave Zaibel; Larry Prater; John Gummoe; David Stevens; David Wilson.

CASCADES / Sir Douglas Quintet

Singles: 7-inch

TRIP.......3-5 70s
Also see CASCADES
Also see SIR DOUGLAS QUINTET

CASEY, Al *P&R/R&B '62*

(Al Casey Combo; with the K-C Ettes)

Singles: 78 rpm

DOT.......20-30 56-57
MCI.......10-20 55

Singles: 7-inch

BLUE HORIZON (925 "Cookin'").......15-25 62
CHALLENGE.......5-10 60
DOT (15524 "Fool's Blues").......10-20 56
DOT (15563 "Guitar Man").......15-25 57
GREGMARK (5 "Caravan").......5-10 61
(Shown as by Duane Eddy, but actually by Al Casey.)
HIGHLAND (1002 "Got the Teenage Blues").......25-40 59
HIGHLAND (1004 "Night Beat").......15-25 60
LIBERTY.......10-20 58
MCI.......15-25 55
RAMCO.......8-10 61
STACY (Except 962).......10-20 62-64
STACY (962 "Surfin' Hootenany").......10-20 63
(Black vinyl.)
STACY (962 "Surfin' Hootenany").......25-50 63
(Colored vinyl.)
U.A. (158 "Stinger").......10-20 59

LPs: 10/12-inch

STACY (100 "Surfin' Hootenany").......30-50 63
(Black vinyl.)
STACY (100 "Surfin' Hootenany") 100-125 63
(Colored vinyl.)
Also see CLARK, Sanford
Also see EDDY, Duane
Also see EXOTIC GUITARS
Also see HONEYS
Also see JONES, Art
Also see RAINTREE COUNTY SINGERS
Also see REYNOLDS, Jody
Also see ROGERS, Frantic Johnny
Also see SHARPE, Ray
Also see STORMS

CASH, Alvin *P&R '65*

(With Crawlers; with Registers)

Singles: 7-inch

CHESS.......3-5 70
COLLECTABLES.......3-4 81
DAKAR.......3-5 76
ERIC.......3-4 73
MAR-V-LUS.......5-10 65-67
SEVENTY SEVEN.......3-5 72
SOUND STAGE 7.......8-12
TODDLIN' TOWN.......5-10 68-69
TRIP.......4-6
WESTBOUND.......3-6
XL ("Twine Time").......20-30 65
(Selection number not known.)

LPs: 10/12-inch

MAR-V-LUS.......15-20 65
SOUND STAGE "7".......10-15 73

CASH, Johnny *C&W '55*

(With the Tennessee Two; with Tennessee Three)

Singles: 78 rpm

SUN.......20-40 55-57

Singles: 7-inch

CACHET.......3-5 80
COLUMBIA (Except 41000 thru 43000 series).......3-8 67-85
COLUMBIA (41000 & 42000 series).......10-20 60-62
(With "3" prefix. Compact 33 singles)
COLUMBIA (41000 & 42000 series).......6-12 58-64
(With "4" prefix.)
COLUMBIA (43000 series).......4-8 64-66
COLUMBIA BOOK/RECORD LIBRARY ("The Bug That Tried to Crawl Around the World").......4-8 60s
SSS/SUN (Black vinyl).......3-5 69-70
SSS/SUN (Colored vinyl).......5-10 69-70
(Promotional issues only.)
SCOTTI BROS.......3-4 82
SUN (200 series).......10-20 55-58
SUN (300 series).......8-12 58-62

EPs: 7-inch

COLUMBIA.......15-30 58-69
SUN.......15-30 58

Picture Sleeves

COLUMBIA (Except 41000 & 42000 series).......3-5 67-85
COLUMBIA (41000 series).......10-15 58-61
COLUMBIA (42000 series).......5-10 61-64
COLUMBIA (44000 series).......4-6 68
SUN (295 "Guess Things Happen That Way").......10-15 58

LPs: 10/12-inch

AMERICAN.......8-10 90s
BLAINE HOUSE.......6-12
(Mail order offer.)
BUCKBOARD.......5-10
CBS.......5-10 82
CACHET.......5-10
COLUMBIA (29 "The World of Johnny Cash").......8-12 70
COLUMBIA (363 "Legends and Love Songs").......10-15 68
(Columbia Record Club issue.)
COLUMBIA (1200 thru 1799).......15-30 58-61
(With "CL" prefix. Monaural.)
COLUMBIA (8100 thru 8599).......20-40 58-61
(With "CS" prefix. Stereo.)
COLUMBIA (1800 thru 2650).......10-20 62-68
(With "CL" prefix. Monaural.)
COLUMBIA (2004 "The Heart of Johnny Cash").......15-25 60s
(Columbia Star Series.)
COLUMBIA (8600 thru 9478).......10-20 62-68
(With "CS" prefix. Stereo.)
COLUMBIA (9600 thru 9943).......8-12 69-70
(With "CS" prefix.)
COLUMBIA (10000 series).......5-10 73
COLUMBIA (30000 thru 38000 series).......5-15 70-82
COLUMBIA SPECIAL PRODUCTS.......5-10 75
COLUMBIA/SUFFOLK.......8-10 79
DESIGN.......5-8
DORAL.......20-40
(Promotional mail-order LP from Doral cigarettes.)
HARMONY.......8-12 69
IMPERIAL HOUSE.......5-10
(Mail order offer.)
LONGINES.......5-8
(Mail order offer.)
MERCURY.......5-10 87
OUT of TOWN DIST.......5-10 82
PICKWICK.......5-10 70s
POWER PAK.......5-10
PRIORITY.......5-10 81-82
SSS/SUN.......5-15 69-84
(Some may be colored vinyl.)
SHARE.......5-10
STACK-O-HITS.......5-8
SUN (1220 "Johnny Cash and His Hot and Blue Guitar").......20-40 56

SUN (1235 "Songs That Made Him Famous") 20-40 58
SUN (1240 "Greatest") 20-30 59
SUN (1245 "Johnny Cash Sings Hank Williams and Other Favorties") 15-25 60
SUN (1255 "Now Here's Johnny Cash") 15-25 61
SUN (1270 "All Aboard the Blue Train") 15-25 63
SUN (1275 "Original Sun Sound of Johnny Cash") 15-25 64
SUN/CAPITOL (90000 series) 15-20 60s
(Record club issues.)
SUNRISE MEDIA 5-10 81
SUNNYVALE 5-8
TIME-LIFE ("Johnny Cash") 10-15 82
(Three-disc set.)
TRIP 8-10 74
U.A. 10-12 68

Session: George Jones; Marty Robbins; Waylon Jennings.
Also see BROOKS, Karen, & Johnny Cash
Also see DEL RAY, Martin
Also see HARRIS, Emmylou
Also see JONES, George
Also see KILGORE, Merle
Also see RICH, Charlie
Also see ROBBINS, Marty / Johnny Cash / Ray Price
Also see STATLER BROTHERS
Also see TUBB, Ernest

CASH, Johnny, & June Carter

(Johnny Cash & June Carter Cash) C&W '64

Singles: 7-inch

COLUMBIA 3-5 67-83

LPs: 10/12-inch

COLUMBIA (9500 series) 10-20 64-67
COLUMBIA (32000 series) 5-10 73
HARMONY 6-10 72

Also see CARTER, June
Also see JENNINGS, Waylon, Willie Nelson, Johnny Cash, & Kris Kristofferson

CASH, Johnny, & Carter Family

(Carter Family with Johnny Cash) C&W '63

Singles: 7-inch

COLUMBIA 3-8 63-72

CASH, Johnny, Carter Family & Oak Ridge Boys C&W '73

Singles: 7-inch

COLUMBIA 3-5 73

Also see CARTER FAMILY
Also see OAK RIDGE BOYS

CASH, Johnny, & Mother Maybelle Carter C&W '73

Singles: 7-inch

COLUMBIA 3-5 73

Also see CARTER FAMILY

CASH, Johnny, Rosanne Cash & Everly Brothers C&W '89

Singles: 7-inch

MERCURY (872 420-7 "Ballad of a Teenage Queen") 3-5 89

Also see CASH, Rosanne
Also see EVERLY BROTHERS

CASH, Johnny / Roy Clark / Linda Ronstadt

LPs: 10/12-inch

POINTED STAR (10178 "Concert Behind Prison Walls") 10-15 78
(NAPA special products TV soundtrack.)

Also see CASH, Rosanne
Also see CLARK, Roy
Also see RONSTADT, Linda

CASH, Johnny / Billy Grammer / Wilburn Brothers

LPs: 10/12-inch

PICKWICK/HILLTOP 10-15 65

Also see GRAMMER, Billy

CASH, Johnny, & Levon Helm

Singles: 7-inch

A&M 3-4 80

Also see HELM, Levon

CASH, Johnny, & Waylon Jennings C&W '86

Singles: 7-inch

COLUMBIA 3-4 78-86
EPIC 3-4 80

Also see JENNINGS, Waylon

CASH, Johnny / Jerry Lee Lewis / Jeanie C. Riley

LPs: 10/12-inch

PICKWICK 5-10 70s

Also see RILEY, Jeanie C.

CASH, Johnny, Carl Perkins & Jerry Lee Lewis

LPs: 10/12-inch

COLUMBIA 5-10 82

Also see PERKINS, Carl, Jerry Lee Lewis, Roy Orbison & Johnny Cash

CASH, Johnny / Jeanie C. Riley

LPs: 10/12-inch

LONGINES (5288 "Rock Island Line") 5-8
(Mail order offer.)

Also see RILEY, Jeanie C.

CASH, Johnny, & Hank Williams Jr. C&W '88

Singles: 7-inch

MERCURY 3-4 88

Also see WILLIAMS, Hank, Jr.

CASH, Johnny / Tammy Wynette

LPs: 10/12-inch

COLUMBIA (5418 "King & Queen") .. 10-15
(Columbia Musical Treasury issue.)

Also see CASH, Johnny
Also see WYNETTE, Tammy

CASH, Rosanne C&W '80

Singles: 7-inch

COLUMBIA 3-4 80-90

Picture Sleeves

COLUMBIA 3-4 81

EPs: 7-inch

COLUMBIA 4-8 85

LPs: 10/12-inch

COLUMBIA 5-10 79-90

Session: Bobby Bare; Rodney Crowell; Emmylou Harris; Ricky Skaggs.
Also see CASH, Johnny, Rosanne Cash & Everly Brothers
Also see CROWELL, Rodney, & Rosanne Cash
Also see HARRIS, Emmylou
Also see NITTY GRITTY DIRT BAND, Rosanne Cash & John Hiatt
Also see SKAGGS, Ricky

CASH, Rosanne, & Bobby Bare C&W '79

Singles: 7-inch

COLUMBIA 3-4 79

Also see BARE, Bobby
Also see CASH, Rosanne

CASH, Tommy C&W '68

Singles: 7-inch

AUDIOGRAPH 3-4 83
ELEKTRA 3-5 75
EPIC 3-6 68-73
MONUMENT 3-4 77-79
MUSICOR 4-8 65
20TH FOX 3-4 76
U.A. 4-6 66-68

LPs: 10/12-inch

ELEKTRA 5-10 75
EPIC 8-12 69-72
MONUMENT 5-10 78
U.A. 10-12 68

CA$HFLOW R&B/LP '86

Singles: 12-inch

ATLANTA ARTISTS 4-6 86

Singles: 7-inch

ATLANTA ARTISTS 3-4 86
MERCURY 3-4 86

LPs: 10/12-inch

ATLANTA ARTISTS 5-10 86

CASHMAN, Terry P&R '76

(With The Men)

Singles: 7-inch

BOOM (005 "Try Me") 8-10 66
LIFESONG (Except 45096 thru 45115) 3-5 76-82
LIFESONG (45096 thru 45115 "Talkin' Baseball") 3-5 76
(Price is for any individual disc. Full set of 20 versions may be valued at $50 to $125.)

Picture Sleeves

LIFESONG (45096 thru 45115 "Talkin' Baseball") 3-8 76
(Price is for any individual sleeve. Complete set of 20 may be valued at $50 to $125.)

LPs: 10/12-inch

LIFESONG 5-10 76-77

CASHMAN & WEST P&R/LP '72

Singles: 7-inch

ABC 3-4 74
DUNHILL 3-5 72-74
LIFESONG 3-5 75

Picture Sleeves

DUNHILL 3-5 72

LPs: 10/12-inch

ABC 8-10 74
DUNHILL 8-12 72-74

Members: Terry Cashman; Tommy West.
Also see CROCE, Jim
Also see GENE & TOMMY
Also see MORNING MIST

CASHMAN & WEST / Gordon Jenkins & His Orchestra

LPs: 10/12-inch

DUNHILL (SPDJ-17 "Manhattan Tower") 10-15 72
(10-inch LP.)

Also see CASHMAN & WEST
Also see JENKINS, Gordon, & His Orchestra

CASHMAN, PISTILLI & WEST

Singles: 7-inch

ABC 4-6 68
CAPITOL 3-5 69-71

LPs: 10/12-inch

ABC 12-15 68
CAPITOL 10-15 69-71

Members: Terry Cashman; Gene Pistilli; Tommy West.
Also see BUCHANAN BROTHERS
Also see CASHMAN, Terry
Also see PISTILLI, Gene
Also see WEST, Tommy

CASHMAN, PISTILLI & WEST / Steve Karmen

Singles: 7-inch

PONTIAC ("GTO Rock") 10-15 70
(Promotional issue of "1970 Pontiac Theme Music.")

Also see CASHMAN, PISTILLI & WEST

CASHMERE R&B/D&D '83

Singles: 12-inch

PHILLY WORLD 4-6 83
TNT 4-6 84

Singles: 7-inch

PHILLY WORLD 3-4 83-85

LPs: 10/12-inch

PHILLY WORLD 5-10 83-85

CASINOS P&R/LP '67

(Gene Hughes & Casinos; with Saturns)

Singles: 7-inch

ABC 3-5 73
AIRTOWN (002 "That's the Way") 10-15 67
CERTRON 5-8 70
COLLECTABLES 3-4 81
FRATERNITY 6-12 65-71
MILLION 5-8 72

TERRY (115 "Gee Whiz") 50-75 64
TERRY (116 "That's the Way") 25-50 64
TRIP 3-5
U.A. 4-6 68

LPs: 10/12-inch

FRATERNITY (1019 "Then You Can Tell Me Goodbye") 20-30 67
Member: Gene Hughes.

CASINOS / Fireflies

Singles: 7-inch

ERA 3-5 70s
Also see CASINOS
Also see FIREFLIES

CASLONS P&R '61

Singles: 7-inch

AMY 10-20 61-62
SEECO 10-20 61

CASON, Rich, & Galactic Orchestra R&B '83

Singles: 12-inch

PRIVATE I 4-6 84

Singles: 7-inch

LARC 3-4 83
PRIVATE I 3-4 84

CASPER R&B '80

Singles: 7-inch

A.V.I. 3-4 84
ATLANTIC 3-4 83-84

LPs: 10/12-inch

A.V.I. 5-10 84
ATLANTIC 5-10 83

CASS, Mama: see ELLIOTT, Cass

CASSIDY, David P&R '71

Singles: 7-inch

BELL 3-5 71-73
FLASHBACK 3-4 73
MCA 3-4 79
RCA 3-5 75-77

Picture Sleeves

BELL 3-5 71-73

LPs: 10/12-inch

BELL 10-15 72-74
RCA 8-12 74-76
Also see PARTRIDGE FAMILY
Also see WILSON, Carl

CASSIDY, Shaun P&R/LP '77

Singles: 7-inch

W.B. 3-4 77-80

Picture Sleeves

W.B. 3-4 77-78

LPs: 10/12-inch

W.B. 8-10 77-80

CASSIDY, Shaun, and Todd Rundgren's Utopia

Singles: 7-inch

W.B. 3-4 80
Also see CASSIDY, Shaun
Also see UTOPIA

CASTAWAYS P&R '65

Singles: 7-inch

APEX 12-18 65
BEAR (2000 "Feel So Fine") 25-35 67
COLLECTABLES 3-4 81
ERA 3-5 72
ERIC 3-4 78
FONTANA 12-18 68
LANA 4-6 64
SOMA (Except 1461) 8-12 65
SOMA (1461 "Girl in Love") 15-25 67
TAUNAH (7745 "I Feel So Fine") 15-25 67
TERRIFIC 4-8

EPs: 7-inch

SOMA (03 "Liar Liar") 10-20
(Reportedly 500 made.)
Members: Merlin Dean; Richard Robey; Robert Folschon; Ron Hensley; James Donna; Dennis Craswell.
Also see CROW

CASTAWAYS / Gestures

Singles: 7-inch

TERRIFIC 4-6 60s
Also see CASTAWAYS
Also see GESTURES

CASTELLS P&R '61

Singles: 7-inch

COLLECTABLES 3-4 80
DECCA 5-10 65-66
ERA 10-20 61-63
LAURIE 15-20 68
U.A. 5-10 68
W.B. (Except 5421) 5-10 64
W.B. (5421 "I Do") 50-60 64
(With Brian Wilson.)

LPs: 10/12-inch

ERA (EL-109 "So This Is Love") 50-100 62
(Monaural.)
ERA (ES-109 "So This Is Love")... 100-150 62
(Stereo.)
Members: Chuck Girard; Bob Ussery; Tom Hicks; Joe Kelly.
Also see GIRARD, Chuck
Also see WILSON, Brian

CASTER, Jimmy: see CASTOR, Jimmy

CASTLE, David P&R '77

Singles: 7-inch

PARACHUTE 3-5 77-79

LPs: 10/12-inch

PARACHUTE 8-10 77-79

CASTLE SISTERS P&R '62

Singles: 7-inch

ROULETTE 5-10 59-60
TERRACE 5-10 62-63
TRIODEX 5-10 61

Picture Sleeves

TERRACE 10-15 62

CASTLEMAN, Boomer P&R '75

(Boomer Clarke)

Singles: 7-inch

CREME 3-4 86
MUMS 3-5 75
SRO (218 "Summertime Blues") 4-6 86
(Promotional issue only.)
Also see LEWIS & CLARKE

CASTOR, Jimmy P&R/R&B '66

(Jimmy Castor Bunch; Jimmy Caster Quintet)

Singles: 12-inch

SALSOUL 4-6 83

Singles: 7-inch

ATLANTIC 3-5 74-77
CAPITOL 4-6 68-69
CLOWN 5-10 62
COMPASS 4-6 68
COTILLION 3-4 79
DECCA 4-8 66
DREAM 3-4 84-85
DRIVE 3-4 78
JET SET 4-8 65
KINETIC 3-6 70
LM 5-8
LONG DISTANCE 3-4 81
RCA 3-5 71-73
SALSOUL 3-4 82
SLEEPING BAG 3-4 88
SMASH 4-8 66-67

LPs: 10/12-inch

ATLANTIC 8-10 74-77
COTILLION 5-10 79
CRYSTAL BALL 8-10 81
DREAM 5-10 83
DRIVE 5-10 78
LONG DISTANCE 5-10 80
PAUL WINLEY 5-15
RCA 10-15 72-75
SMASH 15-20 67
Members: Jimmy Castor; Gerry Thomas; Doug Gibson; Lenny Fridie Jr.; Harry Jensen; Bobby Manigault.
Also see CLINTONIAN CUBS
Also see JOEY & TEENAGERS
Also see LYMON, Lewis

CASTOR, Jimmy, & Juniors

Singles: 78 rpm

ATOMIC (100 "This Girl of Mine") ... 75-150 57
WING (90078 "I Promise") 50-75 56

Singles: 7-inch

ATOMIC (100 "This Girl of Mine") 100-200 57
WING (90078 "I Promise") 75-125 56
Also see CASTOR, Jimmy

CASWELL, Johnny P&R '63

Singles: 7-inch

DECCA (32017 "I.O.U.") 50-75 66
LUV (250 "Faces") 8-12 67
SMASH 5-10 63-64
Also see CRYSTAL MANSION

CAT MOTHER P&R/LP '69

(With the All Night News Boys)

Singles: 7-inch

POLYDOR 3-6 69-72

LPs: 10/12-inch

POLYDOR 20-30 69-73

CATCH R&B '84

Singles: 12-inch

COLUMBIA 4-6 84-85

Singles: 7-inch

COLUMBIA 3-4 84-85

CATE BROTHERS P&R/R&B/LP '76

(Cates Gang)

Singles: 7-inch

ASYLUM 3-5 76-78
ELEKTRA 3-4 77
METROMEDIA 3-5 70

LPs: 10/12-inch

ASYLUM 5-10 75-77
ATLANTIC 5-10 79
METROMEDIA 10-12 70-73
Members: Earl Cate; Ernie Cate.

CATES, George P&R '55

Singles: 78 rpm

CORAL 3-6 51-57

Singles: 7-inch

CORAL 5-10 51-57
DOT 3-6 62
SIGNATURE 3-6 59-60

EPs: 7-inch

CORAL 5-10 54-57

LPs: 10/12-inch

CORAL 10-20 54-57
Also see BUTLER, Champ, & George Cates

CATHY & JOE P&R '64

Singles: 7-inch

SMASH 4-8 64-65
Members: Cathy Bunn; Joe Wegman.

CATHY JEAN P&R '61

(With the Roomates)

Singles: 7-inch

ERIC 3-4 73
PHILIPS (Except 40014) 8-12 63
PHILIPS (40014 "Believe Me") 10-20 62
QUALITY (1251 "Please Love Me Forever") 10-15 61
(Canadian.)
VALMOR 10-15 61-62

LPs: 10/12-inch

VALMOR (78 "At the Hop") 400-500 62
(Reissue. Has titles printed on cover. Does not picture the group.)
VALMOR (789 "At the Hop") 350-450 61
(Pictures Cathy Jean & Roomates. Note different number.)
Also see ROOMATES

CAVALIERE, Felix P&R '80

Singles: 7-inch

BEARSVILLE 3-5 74-75
EPIC 3-4 80

LPs: 10/12-inch

BEARSVILLE 10-12 74-75
EPIC (705 "Castles in the Air") 15-20 79
(Interview and music. Promotional issue only.)
EPIC (35990 "Castles in the Air") 5-10 79

Also see RASCALS

CAVALLARO, Carmen P&R '45

Singles: 78 rpm

DECCA....3-6 45-57

Singles: 7-inch

DECCA....4-8 50-61

EPs: 7-inch

DECCA (Except 844)....5-10 50-59

DECCA (844 "The Eddy Duchin Story")....20-30 56

(Boxed three-EP set.)

LPs: 10/12-inch

DECCA (Except "The Eddy Duchin Story")....10-20 50-61

DECCA (DL-8289 "Eddy Duchin Story")....25-35 56

(Soundtrack. Monaural.)

DECCA (DL7-8289 "The Eddy Duchin Story")....25-30 59

(Soundtrack. Stereo.)

DECCA (8396 "The Eddy Duchin Story")....60-75 56

(Soundtrack. Also has music from three other shows.)

DECCA (DL-9121 "The Eddy Duchin Story")....10-15 65

(Soundtrack. Monaural.)

DECCA (DL7-9121 "The Eddy Duchin Story")....10-15 65

(Soundtrack. Stereo.)

VOCALION....10-15 59

CAVALLARO, Carmen, Featuring Al Cernick

Singles: 78 rpm

DECCA (24330 "Dream Girl")....15-25 48

DECCA (24410 "Evelyn")....15-25 48

DECCA (24488 "Ah, But It Happens")....15-25 48

Also see CAVALLARO, Carmen

Also see MITCHELL, Guy

CAZZ P&R '78

(Robert Lewis)

Singles: 7-inch

NUMBER....3-4 78

CELEBRATION P&R '78

(Featuring Mike Love)

Singles: 7-inch

MCA....3-4 78

PACIFIC ARTS....5-10 79

Promotional Singles

MCA (1982 "Almost Summer, KRTH 101 Version")....10-12 78

(Made for radio station KRTH.)

LPs: 10/12-inch

MCA (3037 "Almost Summer")....8-10 78

(Soundtrack.)

PACIFIC ARTS....8-12 79

Members: Mike Love; Charles Lloyd; Steve Leach; Ron Altbach; Linda Mallah; Suzanne Wallach; Irene Cathaway; Al Perkins; Tim Weston.

Also see LOVE, Mike

CELI BEE & BUZZY BUNCH P&R/R&B/LP '77

Singles: 7-inch

APA....3-5 77-78

LPs: 10/12-inch

APA....5-10 77-79

CELLARFUL OF NOISE P&R '88

Singles: 7-inch

CBS....3-4 88

CELLOS P&R '57

Singles: 78 rpm

APOLLO (Except 510)....25-50 57

APOLLO (510 "Rang Tang Ding Dong")....50-75 57

(No subtitle used.)

APOLLO (510 "Rang Tang Ding Dong [I Am the Japanese Sandman]")....15-25 57

(With subtitle.)

Singles: 7-inch

APOLLO (510 "Rang Tang Ding Dong")....50-100 57

(No subtitle used.)

APOLLO (510 "Rang Tang Ding Dong [I Am the Japanese Sandman]")....15-25 57

(With subtitle.)

APOLLO (515 "Under Your Spell")...25-50 57

APOLLO (516 "The Be-Bop Mouse")....25-50 57

APOLLO (524 "I Beg for Your Love")....40-60 58

Members: Cliff Williams; Ken Levinson; Alvin Campbell; Bill Montgomery; Alton Thomas.

CENTERFOLD R&B '88

Singles: 7-inch

COLUMBIA....3-4 88

CENTRAL LINE P&R/R&B '81

Singles: 12-inch

MERCURY....4-6 84-85

Singles: 7-inch

MERCURY....3-4 81-85

LPs: 10/12-inch

MERCURY....5-10 82-85

Members: Linton Beckles; Lipson Francis; Henry Defoe; Camelle Hinds.

CERRONE P&R/R&B/LP '77

(Jean-Marc Cerrone)

Singles: 12-inch

PAVILLION....4-6 82

PERSONAL....4-6 84

Singles: 7-inch

ATLANTIC....3-4 79

COTILLION....3-5 77-78

PAVILLION....3-4 82

PERSONAL....3-4 84

LPs: 10/12-inch

ATLANTIC....5-10 79

COTILLION....5-10 77-79

PAVILLION....5-10 82

CERRONE & LA TOYA JACKSON R&B '86

Singles: 12-inch

PALASS....4-6 86

Also see CERRONE

Also see JACKSON, La Toya

CETERA, Peter LP '82

Singles: 7-inch

FULL MOON....3-4 82-88

Picture Sleeves

FULL MOON....3-4 82-88

LPs: 10/12-inch

FULL MOON....5-10 81-88

W.B. 5-8 86

Also see CHER & Peter Cetera

Also see CHICAGO

Also see FALTSKOG, Agnetha, & Peter Cetera

CETERA, Peter, & Amy Grant P&R '87

Singles: 7-inch

FULL MOON....3-4 86

Picture Sleeves

FULL MOON....3-4 86

Also see CETERA, Peter

Also see GRANT, Amy

CHABUKOS R&B '73

Singles: 7-inch

MAINSTREAM....3-5 73

CHACKSFIELD, Frank, Orchestra P&R '53

Singles: 78 rpm

LONDON....3-6 53-57

Singles: 7-inch

LONDON....4-8 53-61

EPs: 7-inch

LONDON....5-10 53-61

LPs: 10/12-inch

LONDON....5-15 53-61

RICHMOND....5-12 59-62

CHAD R&B '87

Singles: 7-inch

RCA....3-4 87-88

CHAD & JEREMY P&R/LP '64

Singles: 7-inch

COLLECTABLES....3-4 81

COLUMBIA (Except 43277)....4-8 65-68

COLUMBIA (43277 "Before and After")....4-8 65

(Black vinyl.)

COLUMBIA (43277 "Before and After")....10-15 65

(Colored vinyl. Promotional issues only.)

ERIC....3-4 73

LANA....3-6 60s

ROCSHIRE....3-4 84

TEEN SCOOP ("Interview")....20-30 60s

(Square cardboard picture disc still bound in *Teen Scoop* magazine.)

TEEN SCOOP ("Interview")....15-20 60s

(Square cardboard picture disc by itself)

TRIP....3-5 70s

WORLD ARTISTS....5-10 64-65

Picture Sleeves

COLUMBIA....5-10 65-66

WORLD ARTISTS....8-12 64-65

LPs: 10/12-inch

CAPITOL (2000 series)....15-20 66

CAPITOL (12000 & 16000 series)....5-10 80

COLUMBIA....20-25 65-68

FIDU....10-12

HARMONY....12-15 69

MDA (6000 "Olde English Gold")....10-20

ROCSHIRE....5-10 84

SIDEWALK....12-20 69

TRADITION REST....10-12

WORLD ARTISTS (2002 "Yesterday's Gone")....20-40 64

(Monaural.)

WORLD ARTISTS (2005 "Chad & Jeremy Sing for You")....20-40 65

(Monaural.)

WORLD ARTISTS (3002 "Yesterday's Gone")....30-50 64

(Stereo.)

WORLD ARTISTS (3005 "Chad & Jeremy Sing for You")....30-50 65

(Stereo.)

Members: Chad Stuart; Jeremy Clyde.

Also see STUART, Chad

CHAIN REACTION R&B '77

Singles: 7-inch

ARIOLA AMERICA....3-5 76

DELICKS....5-10 69

DIAL....5-10 68

GRT....4-6 70

OSHOWLEO (1 "Lady in Red")....10-15

VERVE....10-20 68

Member: Norris Harris.

Also see CHOCOLATE SYRUP

Also see MOMENT of TRUTH

CHAIRMEN OF THE BOARD P&R/R&B/LP '70

(Chairmen; Chairman of the Board)

Singles: 7-inch

INVICTUS....3-6 70-76

SURFSIDE....4-8 82

Picture Sleeves

INVICTUS....3-5 70-72

LPs: 10/12-inch

INVICTUS....12-20 70-74

Members: General Norman Johnson; Eddie Curtis; Harrison Kennedy; Danny Woods.

Also see JOHNSON, General

CHAKA KHAN: see KHAN, Chaka

CHAKACHAS P&R/R&B/LP '72

Singles: 7-inch

AVCO EMBASSY....3-5 72

JANUS....3-5 74

POLYDOR....3-5 71-75

LPs: 10/12-inch

AVCO EMBASSY....8-10 72

POLYDOR 8-12 72

CHAKIRIS, George LP '62

Singles: 7-inch

CAPITOL 3-6 62-65
HORIZON 4-6 62

Picture Sleeves

CAPITOL 5-10 63

LPs: 10/12-inch

CAPITOL 10-20 62-65
HORIZON 15-20 62

CHAMBERLAIN, Richard P&R '62

Singles: 7-inch

MCA 3-4 77
MGM 4-6 62-65

Picture Sleeves

MGM 5-10 62-65

LPs: 10/12-inch

MGM 15-20 63-65
METRO 8-12 66

CHAMBERS BROTHERS P&R/LP '68

Singles: 7-inch

AVCO 3-6 74-75
COLUMBIA 6-15 66-73
PROVERB (1021 "I Trust in God") ... 10-20 60s
ROXBURY 3-6 76
TEAR DROP 3-6 74
VAULT 8-15 65-69

Picture Sleeves

COLUMBIA 6-12 68-69

LPs: 10/12-inch

AVCO 8-12 74-75
CHELSEA 8-10 77
COLUMBIA (20 "Love, Peace and Happiness") 20-30 69
(Two LPs, the second being *The Chambers Brothers Live at Bill Graham's Fillmor East.*)
COLUMBIA (2000 & 9000 series) 15-20 67-68
COLUMBIA (30000 series, except 31158) 10-20 71-75
COLUMBIA (31158 "Oh My God") 40-60 72
FANTASY 10-15 74
RIVERSIDE 10-15 68
ROXBURY 8-10 76
VAULT (100 series) 15-20 67-70
VAULT (9003 "People Get Ready") ... 20-30 65

Members: Joe Chambers; Willie Chambers; Lester Chambers; George Chambers; Brian Keenan.

Also see AXTON, Hoyt, & Chambers Brothers
Also see DANE, Barbara, & Chambers Brothers
Also see PEANUT BUTTER CONSPIRACY / Ashes / Chambers Brothers
Also see WINTER, Johnny / Argent / Chambers Brothers / John Hammond

CHAMBLEE, Eddie R&B '49

Singles: 78 rpm

CORAL 10-20 52
FEDERAL 15-25 52
MERCURY 15-25 57
UNITED 15-25 54
MIRACLE 10-20 47-51
UNITED 10-15 53

Singles: 7-inch

CORAL 20-35 52
FEDERAL 20-35 52
MERCURY 10-20 57
UNITED 15-25 54

LPs: 10/12-inch

EMARCY (36124 "Chamblee Music") 30-60 58
EMARCY (36131 "Doodin'") 30-60 58
MERCURY (60127 "Chamblee Music") 30-40 59
MERCURY (80007 "Doodin'") 30-40 58
PRESTIGE (7321 "Eddie Chamblee") 25-35 64
(Yellow label.)
PRESTIGE (7321 "Eddie Chamblee") 20-30 64
(Blue label.)

Also see WASHINGTON, Dinah

CHAMPAGNE P&R '77

Singles: 7-inch

ARIOLA AMERICA 3-5 77-78

Picture Sleeves

ARIOLA AMERICA 3-5 77

CHAMPAIGN P&R/R&B/LP '81

Singles: 12-inch

COLUMBIA 4-6 83

Singles: 7-inch

COLUMBIA 3-4 81-85

LPs: 10/12-inch

COLUMBIA 5-10 81-85

Members: Rena Jones; Pauli Carman; Michael Day; Dana Walden; Michael Reed; Howard Reeder; Rocky Maffit.

CHAMPLIN, Bill P&R '81

Singles: 7-inch

ELEKTRA 3-4 81-82
EPIC 3-5 78

LPs: 10/12-inch

ELEKTRA 5-10 82
EPIC 5-10 78

Also see CHICAGO
Also see SONS of CHAMPLIN

CHAMPS P&R/R&B '58

Singles: 78 rpm

CHALLENGE 35-55 58

Singles: 7-inch

CHALLENGE 8-18 58-65
ERIC 3-4 78
HI OLDIES 3-5 77
LANA 3-6 64
REPUBLIC (246 "Tequila '76") 3-5 76

Picture Sleeves

REPUBLIC (246 "Tequila '76") 4-6 76

EPs: 7-inch

CHALLENGE (7100 "Tequila") 25-50 58
CHALLENGE (7101 "Caramba") 25-50 58

LPs: 10/12-inch

CHALLENGE (601 "Go Champs Go!") 50-100 58
(Black vinyl.)
CHALLENGE (601 "Go Champs Go!") 250-350 58
(Colored vinyl.)
CHALLENGE (605 "Everybody's Rockin' with the Champs") 50-75 58
CHALLENGE (613 "Go Champs Go!") 40-60 62
CHALLENGE (614 "The Champs Play *All American*") 40-60 62
(Monaural.)
CHALLENGE (2514 "The Champs Play *All American*") 50-75 62
(Stereo.)
DESIGN SPOTLIGHT 10-20 60s
INTERNATIONAL AWARD 10-20 60s
POINT 10-20 60s
SPECTRUM 10-20 60s

Members: Dave Burgess; Danny "Chuck Rio" Flores; Gene Alden; Dale Norris; Joe Burness; Van Norman; Jim Seals; Dash Crofts; Dean Beard; Bob Morris; Glen Campbell; Jerry Cole; Keith MacKendrick; Chuch Downs; Rich Grissom; Keith MacKendrick; Mo Marshall; Dean McDaniel; Johnny Meeks; Gary Nieland; Curtis Paul; Jerry Puckett; Leon Sanders; Dave Smith; John Trombatore.

Also see APOLLOS
Also see BEARD, Dean
Also see BURGESS, Dave
Also see CAMPBELL, Glen
Also see COLE, Jerry
Also see DEMONS
Also see RIO, Chuck
Also see ROXSTERS
Also see SEALS & CROFTS
Also see SHADOWS FIVE
Also see THINK
Also see VINCENT, Gene

CHAMPS / Cyclones

LPs: 10/12-inch

DESIGN SPOTLIGHT 10-20 60s

Also see CHAMPS

CHAMPS' BOYS ORCH. P&R/R&B '76

Singles: 7-inch

JANUS 3-5 76

CHANDLER, Gene P&R/R&B/LP '62
(Eugene Dixon)

Singles: 12-inch

20TH FOX 4-8 79

Singles: 7-inch

BRUNSWICK 4-8 67-68
CHECKER 5-10 66-69
CHI-SOUND 3-5 79-82
COLLECTABLES 3-4 81
CONSTELLATION 6-12 63-66
CURTOM 3-6 72-73
ERIC 3-4 73
FASTFIRE 3-4 86
MCA 3-4 84
MARSEL 3-5 76
MERCURY 4-6 70
SOLID SMOKE 3-4 84
20TH FOX 3-4 78-79
VEE JAY (Black label) 5-10 61-63
VEE JAY (White labes) 10-20 61
(Promotional issues only.)
U.A. 3-5 78

LPs: 10/12-inch

BRUNSWICK 12-15 67-69
CHECKER 15-20 67
CHI-SOUND/20TH-FOX 5-10 78-79
CONSTELLATION 15-25 64-66
KENT 5-10 86
MERCURY 10-15 70
SOLID SMOKE 5-10 84
20TH FOX 5-10 78-81
UPFRONT 8-10
VEE JAY (1040 "The Duke of Earl") 50-100 62
(Monaural.)
VEE JAY (1040 "The Duke of Earl") 100-150 62
(Stereo.)

At least six early Vee Jay tracks, including *Duke of Earl*, are actually by the Dukays, not just Gene Chandler.

Also see CARTER, Calvin
Also see DUKAYS
Also see DUKE of EARL

CHANDLER, Gene, & Barbara Acklin P&R/R&B '68

Singles: 7-inch

BRUNSWICK 4-8 68-69

Also see ACKLIN, Barbara

CHANDLER, Gene, & Jerry Butler P&R/R&B/LP '71
(Gene & Jerry)

Singles: 7-inch

MERCURY 3-6 70

Also see BUTLER, Jerry

CHANDLER, Gene, & Jamie Lynn R&B '83

Singles: 7-inch

SALSOUL 3-4 83

Also see CHANDLER, Gene

CHANDLER, Karen P&R '52
(Eve Young)

Singles: 78 rpm

CORAL 4-8 52-55
DECCA 4-8 56

Singles: 7-inch

CARLTON 5-10 60
CORAL 5-10 52-58
DECCA 8-15 56
DOT 3-5 67-68
MOHAWK 4-8 62
STRAND 5-10 61
SUNBEAM 5-10 59
TIVOLI 4-6 65

EPs: 7-inch

CORAL 8-15 52

LPs: 10/12-inch

STRAND.. 10-20 61
Also see FONTAINE, Eddie, & Karen Chandler

CHANDLER, Karen, & Jimmy Wakely

Singles: 78 rpm

DECCA.. 4-8 56

Singles: 7-inch

DECCA.. 5-10 56
Also see CHANDLER, Karen
Also see WAKELY, Jimmy

CHANDLER, Kenny P&R '63

Singles: 7-inch

AMY.. 4-8 63
COLLECTABLES.. 3-4 81
CORAL.. 4-8 62
EPIC.. 4-8 65-66
LAURIE.. 5-10 62-63
TOWER.. 4-8 67-68
U.A. 8-10 61

CHANELS

Singles: 7-inch

DEB (500 "The Reason") 25-50 58
(Reissued as by the 5 Chanels.)
Also see 5 CHANELS

CHANGE P&R/R&B/LP '80

Singles: 12-inch

ATLANTIC.. 4-6 84
RFC.. 4-6 83

Singles: 7-inch

ATLANTIC.. 3-4 81-85
RFC.. 3-4 80
W.B. 3-4 80

LPs: 10/12-inch

ATLANTIC.. 5-10 81-85
RFC.. 5-10 80
W.B. 5-10 80
Members: Paolo Granolio; David Romani; James Robinson; Deborah Cooper.
Also see VANDROSS, Luther

CHANGIN' TIMES P&R '65

Singles: 7-inch

PHILIPS 10-20 65-66

CHANNEL, Bruce P&R/R&B/LP '62
(With the Straitjackets)

Singles: 7-inch

BROWNFIELD (29 "Don't Let Go") 8-12 65
CHARAY.. 4-6 68
COLLECTABLES.. 3-4 81
ELEKTRA.. 3-5 80
KING.. 10-20 59-60
JADE.. 5-10 60s
LE CAM (122 "Going Back to Louisiana").. 4-8
LE CAM (125 "Blue Monday") 8-12 64
LE CAM (953 "Hey Baby").................. 15-25 61
LE CAM (963 "Number One Man").... 10-20 62
LE CAM (1100 series) 3-5 77
LE CAM (7277 "The King Is Free")........ 5-8 77
MALA.. 5-10 67-68
MANCO (1035 "Run Romance, Run").. 10-20 62
MEL-O-DY (112 "Satisfied Mind") 10-15 64
MEL-O-DY (114 "You Never Looked Better").. 10-15 64
NAP.. 3-5
SHAH (304 "Court of Love").............. 8-12 64
SMASH.. 5-10 62-63
SOFT.. 5-10 60s
TEEN AGER (601 "Run Romance, Run").. 20-30 59
SHALIMAR.. 5-10
ZUMA 3-5 77

Picture Sleeves

SMASH.. 10-15 62-63

LPs: 10/12-inch

SMASH (27008 "Hey! Baby") 30-50 62
(Monaural.)
SMASH (67008 "Hey! Baby") 25-40 62
(Stereo.)
Session: Delbert McClinton.
Also see McCLINTON, Delbert

CHANNEL, Bruce / Paul & Paula

Singles: 7-inch

ERA.. 3-4
Also see CHANNEL, Bruce
Also see PAUL & PAULA

CHANSON P&R/LP '78

Singles: 7-inch

ARIOLA AMERICA.. 3-4 78-79

LPs: 10/12-inch

ARIOLA AMERICA 5-10 78
Also see EVANS, Linda

CHANTAYS P&R/R&B/LP '63

Singles: 7-inch

ABC.. 3-4 74
COLLECTABLES.. 3-4 81
DOT.. 4-8 63
DOWNEY (104 "Pipeline")................ 20-30 63
DOWNEY (108 "Monsoon").............. 15-25 63
DOWNEY (116 thru 130) 10-20 63-65
MCA.. 3-4 84

LPs: 10/12-inch

DOT (3516 "Pipeline").......................... 25-30 63
(Monaural.)
DOT (25516 "Pipeline").......................... 30-40 63
(Stereo.)
DOT (3771 "Two Sides of the Chantays").. 25-30 63
(Monaural.)
DOT (25771 "Two Sides of the Chantays").. 30-40 63
(Stereo.)
DOWNEY (1002 "Pipeline").......... 150-200 63
Members: Bob Marshall; Bob Welch; Bob Spickard; Brian Carman; Steve Cahn; Warren Waters

CHANTELS P&R '57

Singles: 78 rpm

END 25-50 57-58

Singles: 7-inch

ABC.. 3-5 73
CARLTON (555 "Look in My Eyes").. 10-20 61
CARLTON (564 "Well I Told You") ... 10-20 61
CARLTON (569 "Here It Comes Again").. 10-20 61
END (1001 "He's Gone")................... 40-60 57
(Black label.)
END (1005 "Maybe").......................... 30-50 57
(Black label.)
END (1005 "Maybe").......................... 15-25 50s
(White label.)
END (1005 "Maybe").......................... 10-15 60s
(Multi-color label.)
END (1015 "Every Night").................. 25-50 59
(White label.)
END (1015 "Every Night").................. 10-15 60s
(Multi-color label.)
END (1020 "I Love You So").............. 20-40 58
END (1026 "Sure of Love")............... 20-40 58
END (1030 "Congratulations") 20-40 58
END (1037 "I Can't Take It") 20-40 58
END (1048 "I'm Confessin'") 20-30 59
END (1069 "Whoever You Are")....... 15-25 60
END (1103 "Believe Me")................... 15-25 61
END (1105 "There's Our Song") 15-25 61
END (1120 "To Live My Life Again").. 15-25 63
ERIC.. 3-4 73
LANA.. 4-8 64
LUDIX (101 "Eternally")...................... 25-50 63
LUDIX (106 "That's Why You're Happy") 15-25 63
RCA.. 3-6 70
ROULETTE.. 3-6 69-71
TCF.. 5-10 65
VERVE.. 5-10 66

EPs: 7-inch

END (201 "I Love You So").......... 100-150 58
END (202 "I Love You So").......... 100-150 58

LPs: 10/12-inch

CARLTON (LP-144 "The Chantels on Tour – Look in My Eyes") 50-100 62
(Monaural.)
CARLTON (STLP-144 "The Chantels on Tour – Look in My Eyes") 75-150 62
(Stereo.)
END (301 "We're the Chantels") 1000-2000 58
(Pictures the group on front cover.)
END (301 "The Chantels") 150-300 59
(Pictures a juke box on front cover.)
END (312 "There's Our Song Again") 50-100 62
FORUM (9104 "The Chantels Sing Their Favorites") 25-50 64
ROULETTE 5-10
Members: Arlene Smith; Lois Harris; Rene Minus; Sonia Gorring; Jackie Landry; Annette Smith; Sandra Dawn. Session: Richard Barrett; Buddy Lucas Orchestra.
Also see BARRETT, Richard

CHANTERS P&R/R&B '61

Singles: 7-inch

DE LUXE (6162 "My My Darling")...... 30-40 58
DE LUXE (6166 "Row Your Boat").... 25-35 58
(Black label.)
DE LUXE (6166 "Row Your Boat").... 10-15
(Yellow label.)
DE LUXE (6172 "Five Little Kisses").. 30-40 58
DE LUXE (6191 "No, No, No") 20-30 61
DE LUXE (6194 "My My Darling")...... 20-30 61
DE LUXE (6200 "Row Your Boat").... 10-15 63
GUSTO.. 3-4 77
SSP (1001 "Heavenly You") 15-20
Members: Bud Johnson Jr; Larry Pendegrass; Fred Paige; Bobby Thompson; Elliot Green.
Also see JOHNSON, Bud, Orchestra
Also see VOICES FIVE

CHAPIN, Harry P&R/LP '72

Singles: 7-inch

BOARDWALK.. 3-4 80-81
DUNHILL 3-4 88
ELEKTRA.. 3-5 72-79

LPs: 10/12-inch

BOARDWALK.. 5-10 80
DUNHILL.. 5-10 88
ELEKTRA.. 8-12 72-79

CHAPLAIN, Paul P&R '60
(With His Emeralds; Paul Chaplin)

Singles: 7-inch

ELGIN.. 5-10
HARPER 10-20 60-61
PAT (101 "Caledonia") 60-80

CHAPLIN, Angelica R&B '87

Singles: 7-inch

MERCURY 3-4 87

CHAPLIN, Paul: see CHAPLAIN, Paul

CHAPMAN, Tracy P&R/LP '88

Singles: 7-inch

ELEKTRA.. 3-4 88-89

Picture Sleeves

ELEKTRA.. 3-4 88-89

LPs: 10/12-inch

ELEKTRA.. 5-8 88-89

CHAPTER 8 R&B '79

Singles: 12-inch

ARIOLA AMERICA.. 4-8 79
BEVERLY GLEN.. 4-6 85

Singles: 7-inch

ARIOLA AMERICA.. 3-5 79-80
BEVERLY GLEN.. 3-4 85
Members: Anita Baker; Michael Powell; David Washington; Carolyn Crawford; Valerie Pinkston.

LPs: 10/12-inch

ARIOLA AMERICA.. 5-10 79
Also see BAKER, Anita
Also see DETROIT EMERALDS

CHARADE D&D '83
(Featuring Jessica)

Singles: 12-inch

PROFILE 4-6 83

CHARGERS P&R '58

Singles: 7–inch

RCA (7301 "Old MacDonald") 15-25 58
RCA (7417 "Here in My Heart") 15-25 58
Members: Jesse Belvin; James Scott; Ben Easley; Dunbar White; Johnny White; Mitchell Alexander; Jimmy Norman.
Also see BELVIN, Jesse
Also see NORMAN, Jimmy

CHARIOTEERS P&R '40

Singles: 78 rpm

BRUNSWICK 25-50 38-39
COLUMBIA 25-50 39-49
DECCA 20-30 35
JOSIE 15-25 55
KEYSTONE 10-20 52
LANG-WORTH 10-20 40s
(16–inch transcriptions.)
MGM 20-30 57
OKEH 15-25 40-42
TUXEDO 15-25 55
VOCALION 15-25 38-39

Singles: 7–inch

COLUMBIA (168 "A Kiss and a Rose") 400-600 50
(Microgroove 33 single.)
COLUMBIA (363 "This Side of Heaven") 400-600 50
(Microgroove 33 single.)
JOSIE (787 "I've Got My Heart on My Sleeve") 50-75 55
MGM (12569 "The Candles") 50-75 57
TUXEDO (891 "Thanks for Yesterday") 50-75 55

LPs: 10/12–inch

COLUMBIA (6014 "Sweet and Low") 150-200 49
(10–inch LP.)
HARMONY (7089 "The Charioteers & Billy Williams") 50-100 57
Members: Billy Williams; Eddie Jackson; Ira Williams; Howard Daniel; James Sherman.
Also see SINATRA, Frank, & Charioteers
Also see WILLIAMS, Billy

CHARLENE P&R '77

(Charlene Duncan)

Singles: 7–inch

MOTOWN 3-5 76-85
PRODIGAL 3-5 76-77

Picture Sleeves

PRODIGAL 3-5 77

LPs: 10/12–inch

MOTOWN 5-10 82-85
PRODIGAL 8-10 76

CHARLENE & STEVIE WONDER P&R '82

Singles: 7–inch

MOTOWN 3-4 82

Picture Sleeves

MOTOWN 3-4 82
Also see CHARLENE
Also see WONDER, Stevie

CHARLES, Bobby R&B '56

Singles: 78 rpm

CHESS (1609 thru 1638) 15-30 55-56
CHESS (1647 thru 1670) 25-50 57

Singles: 7–inch

BEARSVILLE 3-5 73
CHESS (1609 "On Bended Knee") ... 20-40 55
CHESS (1617 "Why Did You Leave") 20-40 56
CHESS (1628 "Time Will Tell") 20-40 56
CHESS (1638 "Laura Lee") 20-40 56
CHESS (1647 "Put Your Arms Around Me Honey") 20-40 57
CHESS (1658 "No More") 20-30 57
CHESS (1670 "One-Eyed Jack") 20-30 57
HUB CITY 5-10 63
IMPERIAL 8-15 58-60
JEWEL 5-10 64
PAULA 4-8 65
RICE & GRAVY 3-4 86-90

LPs: 10/12–inch

BEARSVILLE 10-15 72
CHESS 8-12 76

CHARLES, Jimmy P&R/R&B '60

(With the Revelletts)

Singles: 7–inch

ABC 3-5 73
COLLECTABLES 3-4 81
ERIC 3-4 79
MCA 3-4 84
PROMO (1002 "A Million to One") 10-20 60
PROMO (1003 "The Age for Love") .. 10-15 60
PROMO (1004 "I Saw Mommy Kissing Santa Claus") 10-15 60
PROMO (1005 "Christmasville U.S.A.") 10-15 61
ROULETTE 3-5 71

Picture Sleeves

PROMO (1003 "The Age for Love") .. 15-25 60
PROMO (1004 "I Saw Mommy Kissing Santa Claus") 15-25 60
PROMO (1005 "Christmasville U.S.A.") 15-25 61

CHARLES, Lee R&B '68

Singles: 7–inch

BAMBOO 4-6 70-71
BRUNSWICK 5-10 69
HOT WAX 3-5 73
INVICTUS 3-5 74
REVUE 10-15 68

CHARLES, Ray R&B '51

(With the Raelettes)

Singles: 78 rpm

ATLANTIC 10-30 52-58
JAX 15-25 52
ROCKIN' 15-25 53
SWING BEAT 20-30 49
SWING TIME 15-30 50-53

Singles: 7–inch

ABC 3-8 66-73
ABC-PAR (Monaural) 5-10 60-66
ABC-PAR (Stereo) 10-20 61-62
ABC/TRC 3-6
ATLANTIC (976 "Roll with Me Baby") 50-75 52
ATLANTIC (984 "The Sun's Gonna Shine Again") 30-60 53
ATLANTIC (999 "Mess Around") 30-60 53
ATLANTIC (1000 series) 12-25 53-57
ATLANTIC (2000 series) 5-10 58-68
ATLANTIC (3000 series) 3-5 77-79
BARONET 4-8 62
COLUMBIA 3-4 82-87
CROSSOVER 3-5 73-78
DUNHILL GOLDIES 3-4 73
HURRAH 8-12
IMPULSE 5-10 61
MAYFAIR (121 "Pony Boy") 4-8
(With "Uncle Stu.")
RCA 3-5 76
ROCKIN' (504 "Walkin' and Talkin'") 100-200 53
SITTIN' in WITH (641 "Baby Let Me Hear You Call My Name") 75-150 52
SWING TIME (250 "Baby Let Me Hold Your Hand") 75-100 51
SWING TIME (274 "Kiss Me Baby") 75-100 52
SWING TIME (300 "Baby Let Me Hear You Call My Name") 75-100 52
SWING TIME (326 "The Snow Is Falling") 50-100 53
TANGERINE 3-4 71
TIME 3-5 62

Picture Sleeves

ABC 3-6 68-70

EPs: 7–inch

ABC-PAR (335 "Basin St. Blues") 15-25 60
(Stereo. Juke box issue only.)
ABC-PAR (415 "Greatest Hits") 15-25 62
(Stereo. Juke box issue only.)
ABC-PAR (465 "Ingredients in a Recipe for Soul") 15-25 63
(Stereo. Juke box issue only.)
ATLANTIC (567 "Ray Charles") 25-45 56
ATLANTIC (587 "Ray Charles") 25-45 57
ATLANTIC (597 "The Great Ray Charles") 25-45 57
ATLANTIC (607 "Rock with Ray Charles") 25-45 58
ATLANTIC (614 "Soul Brothers") 25-45 58
(With Milt Jackson.)
ATLANTIC (619 "The Genius of Ray Charles") 25-45 59
ATLANTIC (8029 "What'd I Say") 25-45 59
U.A. (1004 "In the Heat of the Night") 10-20 67
(Promotional issue only.)

LPs: 10/12–inch

ABC (Except 590) 10-12 66-73
ABC (590 "A Man and His Soul") 20-25 67
ABC-PAR (300 series) 15-25 60-61
ABC-PAR (400 & 500 series) 10-20 62-66
AHED 8-12
(TV mail-order offer.)
ARCHIVES 8-12
ATLANTIC (500 series) 10-15 73
ATLANTIC (900 "The Ray Charles Story, Vols. 1 & 2") 30-40 62
(Combines Atlantic 8063 and 8064.)
ATLANTIC (1259 "The Great Ray Charles") 50-75 57
ATLANTIC (1279 "Soul Brothers") 40-60 58
(With Milt Jackson.)
ATLANTIC (1289 "Ray Charles at Newport") 40-60 58
ATLANTIC (1312 "The Genius of Ray Charles") 30-50 59
ATLANTIC (1360 "Soul Meeting") 25-35 62
(With Milt Jackson. Number indicates a '61 release, but not actually issued until 1962.)
ATLANTIC (1369 "Genius After Hours") 25-35 61
ATLANTIC (1500 series) 10-20 70
ATLANTIC (3700 series) 20-25 82
ATLANTIC (7000 series) 15-20 64
ATLANTIC (8006 "Ray Charles") 50-100 57
(Black label.)
ATLANTIC (8006 "Ray Charles") 25-45 59
(Red label.)
ATLANTIC (8025 "Yes Indeed") 40-60 59
(Black label.)
ATLANTIC (8025 "Yes Indeed") 25-45 60
(Red label.)
ATLANTIC (8029 "What'd I Say") 40-50 59
(Black label.)
ATLANTIC (8029 "What'd I Say") 25-45 60
(Red label.)
ATLANTIC (8039 "Ray Charles in Person") 30-50 60
(Black label.)
ATLANTIC (8039 "Ray Charles in Person") 25-35 60
(Red label.)
ATLANTIC (8052 "The Genius Sings the Blues") 20-30 61
ATLANTIC (8054 "Dot the Twist") 20-30 61
ATLANTIC (8063 "The Ray Charles Story, Vol. 1") 20-25 62
ATLANTIC (8064 "The Ray Charles Story, Vol. 2") 20-25 62
ATLANTIC (8083 "The Ray Charles Story, Vol. 3") 20-25 63
ATLANTIC (8094 "The Ray Charles Story, Vol. 4") 20-25 64
ATLANTIC (19000 series) 5-12 77-80
BARONET 15-20 62
BLUESWAY 8-10 73
BULLDOG 5-10 84
COLUMBIA 5-10 83-86
CORONET 8-12 60s
CROSSOVER 8-15 73-76
DESIGN 10-20 62
EVEREST 8-10 70-82
GRAND PRIX 10-20 60s
GUEST STAR 10-20 64

HOLLYWOOD (504 "The Original Ray Charles")100-150 59
HOLLYWOOD 505: see CHARLES, Ray / Charles Brown)
HURRAH 8-15
IMPULSE 20-30 61
INTERMEDIA 5-10 84
JAZZ INT'L....................15-25
KING....................8-10 77
PALACE 5-10
PREMIER 8-10
SCEPTER 8-12
SPIN-O-RAMA....................10-15 60s
STRAND....................10-15 60s
TANGERINE 10-12 70-73
UPFRONT....................8-10 70s
Also see COOKIES
Also see GUITAR SLIM
Also see FULSON, Lowell
Also see JOEL, Billy, & Ray Charles
Also see JONES, Quincy, Ray Charles & Chaka Khan
Also see MAXIM TRIO
Also see RAELETTES
Also see U.S.A. for AFRICA

CHARLES, Ray / Charles Brown

LPs: 10/12-inch

HOLLYWOOD (505 "Fabulous Artistry of Ray Charles")....................100-150 59
(Brown, barely credited, provides four tracks.)

CHARLES, Ray / Solomon Burke

LPs: 10/12-inch

GRAND PRIX....................10-20 64
Also see BURKE, Solomon

CHARLES, Ray, & Betty Carter LP '61

Singles: 7-inch

ABC-PAR 5-10 61-62

LPs: 10/12-inch

ABC-PAR (ABC-385 "Ray Charles & Betty Carter") 50-75 61
(Monaural.)
ABC-PAR (ABCS-385 "Ray Charles & Betty Carter")....................75-100 61
(Stereo.)
DCC (2005 "Ray Charles & Betty Carter") 8-12 95
Also see CARTER, Betty

CHARLES, Ray, & Clint Eastwood C&W '80

Singles: 7-inch

W.B. 3-4 80

CHARLES, Ray, & Mickey Gilley C&W '85

Singles: 7-inch

COLUMBIA....................3-4 85
Also see GILLEY, Mickey

CHARLES, Ray / Ivory Joe Hunter / Jimmy Rushing

LPs: 10/12-inch

DESIGN (909 "Three of a Kind") 15-20 60s
(Black label, silver print.)
DESIGN (909 "Three of a Kind") 10-15 60s
(Black, red, blue and yellow label.)
Also see HUNTER, Ivory Joe

CHARLES, Ray, George Jones & Chet Atkins C&W '83

Singles: 7-inch

COLUMBIA....................3-4 83
Also see ATKINS, Chet
Also see JONES, George

CHARLES, Ray, & Cleo Laine LP '76

LPs: 10/12-inch

RCA....................10-12 76
Also see LAINE, Cleo

CHARLES, Ray & Jimmy Lewis P&R/R&B '69

Singles: 7-inch

ABC 3-4 69
TANGERINE 3-6 68

CHARLES, Ray / Little Richard / Sam Cooke

LPs: 10/12-inch

ALMOR (102 "Soul Blues").............. 10-20
Also see COOKE, Sam
Also see LITTLE RICHARD

CHARLES, Ray, & Willie Nelson C&W '84

Singles: 7-inch

COLUMBIA 3-4 84
Also see NELSON, Willie

CHARLES, Ray / Arbee Stidham / Li'l Son Jackson / James Wayne.

LPs: 10/12-inch

MAINSTREAM.................... 8-12 71
Also see JACKSON, Li'l Son
Also see WAYNE, James

CHARLES, Ray, & B.J. Thomas C&W '84

Singles: 7-inch

COLUMBIA 3-4 85
Also see THOMAS, B.J.

CHARLES, Ray, & Hank Williams Jr. C&W '85

Singles: 7-inch

COLUMBIA 3-4 85
Also see WILLIAMS, Hank, Jr.

CHARLES, Ray, & Jimmy Witherspoon

LPs: 10/12-inch

CROWN.................... 15-25 60s
Also see CHARLES, Ray
Also see WITHERSPOON, Jimmy

CHARLES, Ray, Singers P&R '55

Singles: 78 rpm

JUBILEE 3-5 54
MGM 3-6 51-56

Singles: 7-inch

COMMAND 3-5 64-70
DECCA 3-6 58-59
JUBILEE 4-8 54
MGM 4-8 51-56

EPs: 7-inch

CADENCE.................... 5-10 50s
DECCA 5-10 59
ESSEX.................... 5-10 50s
JAMESTOWN.................... 8-15 57
MGM 5-15 55-57

LPs: 10/12-inch

ABC.................... 5-10 73
ALSHIRE.................... 5-10 70
ATCO 8-12 68
CAMDEN 6-10 67
COMMAND.................... 8-12 62-71
DECCA 10-15 58-60
MCA 4-6 82
MGM (100 series) 5-10 71
MGM (3000 series) 10-20 55-60
MGM (4000 series) 8-15 63-66
METRO 6-10 65
SOMERSET.................... 5-10 64
VOCALION 8-10 66
Also see COMO, Perry

CHARLES, Sonny P&R/R&B '69

(With Checkmates Ltd.)

Singles: 7-inch

A&M 4-8 68-73
CAPITOL.................... 4-8 66-67
FRATERNITY 4-8 64
HIGHRISE.................... 3-4 82
RCA 3-5 72

LPs: 10/12-inch

HIGHRISE.................... 5-10 82
A&M 15-25 69
Also see CHECKMATES LTD.

CHARLES, Tommy P&R '56

Singles: 78 rpm

DECCA 10-20 56
WILLETT (111 "Hey There Baby").. 50-100 57

Singles: 7-inch

DECCA....................10-20 56
WILLETT (111 "Hey There Baby") 40-60 57
Session: Anita Kerr Singers.
Also see KERR, Anita

CHARLESTON CITY ALL STARS LP '57

LPs: 10/12-inch

GRAND AWARD....................5-15 57-59

CHARLESTON EXPRESS & JESSE WALES C&W '84

Singles: 7-inch

SOUNDWAVES 3-4 84-85

CHARLIE P&R/LP '77

Singles: 7-inch

ARISTA....................3-5 79
JANUS....................3-4 77-78
MIRAGE 3-4 83
RCA....................3-4 81

Picture Sleeves

ARISTA....................3-5 79
MIRAGE 3-4 83

LPs: 10/12-inch

ARISTA....................5-10 79
COLUMBIA....................8-10 76
JANUS....................8-10 77-78
MIRAGE 5-10 83
RCA....................5-10 81
Member: Terry Thomas.

CHARME R&B '84

Singles: 7-inch

ATLANTIC 3-4 84
RCA....................3-4 79-85

LPs: 10/12-inch

RCA....................5-10 79-85

CHARMETTES P&R/R&B '63

(Charmetts)

Singles: 7-inch

FEDERAL (12345 "Johnny Johnny")....................25-35 59
HI....................10-15 59
KAPP (547 "Please Don't Kiss Me Again")....................15-25 63
KAPP (570 "He's a Wise Guy") 10-20 64
MALA....................5-10 64
MARKAY (101 "Donnie")....................25-35 62
MARLIN (16001 "One More Time")...20-30 62
MELOMEGA....................5-10 62
MONA (553 "The Deeds to My Heart")....................25-35 60
TRI DISC (103 "Why Oh Why").........10-20 62
WORLD ARTISTS (1053 "Sugar Boy") 10-20 65

CHARMS P&R/R&B '54

(Otis Williams & the Charms; Otis Williams & His New Group; Otis Williams)

Singles: 78 rpm

CHART....................20-35 55-56
DELUXE....................25-75 54-57
QUALITY/KING 40-60 54
(Canadian.)
ROCKIN'....................50-75 53

Singles: 7-inch

CHART (608 "Love's Our Inspiration")....................30-50 55
(Has "Vocal Group The Charms" between the horizontal line patterns.)
CHART (608 "Love's Our Inspiration")....................25-35 55
(Has "Vocal Group The Charms" below horizontal rope-like lines.)
CHART (613 "Heart of a Rose")........30-50 56
CHART (623 "I'll Be True") 50-100 56
DELUXE (6000 "Heaven Only Knows") 100-200 53
DELUXE (6014 "Happy Are We")....................100-200 53
DELUXE (6034 "Bye-Bye Baby")...100-200 54
DELUXE (6050 "Quiet Please").....100-200 54

DELUXE (6056 "My Baby Dearest Darling")....100-200 54
DELUXE (6062 "Who Knows")....50-100 54
DELUXE (6065 "Two Hearts")....25-50 54
DELUXE (6072 "Crazy Crazy Crazy")....25-50 54
DELUXE (6076 "Ling Ting Tong")....25-50 54
DELUXE (6080 "Ko Ko Mo")....25-50 55
DELUXE (6082 "Whadya Want")....15-25 55
DELUXE (6087 "When We Get Together")....20-40 55
DELUXE (6088 "Tell Me Now")....20-40 55
DELUXE (6089 "One Fine Day")....20-40 55
DELUXE (6091 "That's Your Mistake")....15-25 55
DELUXE (6092 "Rolling Home")....15-25 55
DELUXE (6093 "Ivory Tower")....15-25 56
DELUXE (6095 "It's All Over")....15-25 56
DELUXE (6097 "I'd Like to Thank You Mr. Dee Jay")....20-40 56
DELUXE (6098 "I'll Remember You")....15-25 56
DELUXE (6105 "Blues Stay Away from Me")....15-25 56
DELUXE (6115 "Walking After Midnight")....15-25 57
DELUXE (6130 "Nowhere on Earth")....20-40 57
DELUXE (6137 "Talking to Myself")....25-35 57
DELUXE (6138 "United")....25-35 57
DELUXE (6149 "Dynamite Darling")....15-25 57
DELUXE (6158 "Could This Be Magic")....15-25 57
DELUXE (6160 "Baby-O")....20-40 57
DELUXE (6165 "Burning Lips")....15-25 58
DELUXE (6174 "Don't Wake Up the Kids")....15-25 58
DELUXE (6178 "My Friends")....15-25 58
DELUXE (6181 "Welcome Home")....15-25 59
DELUXE (6183 "My Prayer Tonight")....15-25 59
DELUXE (6185 "Tears of Happiness")....15-25 59
(Monaural.)
DELUXE (6185 "Tears of Happiness")....50-75 59
(Stereo.)
DELUXE (6186 "Who Knows")....15-25 59
DELUXE (6187 "Blues Stay Away from Me")....15-25 59
GUSTO....3-5 77
KING (5323 "It's a Treat")....15-25 60
KING (5332 "Rickety Rickshaw Man")....15-25 60
KING (5372 "Image of a Girl")....25-50 60
KING (5389 "So Be It")....10-20 60
KING (5421 "Wait")....10-20 60
KING (5455 "Little Turtle Dove")....10-20 61
KING (5497 "Just Forget About Me")....10-20 61
KING (5527 "Pardon Me")....10-20 61
KING (5558 "Two Hearts")....10-20 61
KING (5682 "When We Get Together")....10-20 62
KING (5816 "It Just Ain't Right")....10-20 63
KING (5880 "Unchain My Heart")....10-20 63
OKEH....5-10 65-66
QUALITY/KING (4302 "Hearts of Stone")....50-100 54
(Canadian.)
ROCKIN' (516 "Heaven Only Knows")....200-350 53
STOP....5-8

EPs: 7-inch

DELUXE (357 "Hits By the Charms")....200-300 55
DELUXE (364 "Hits By the Charms")....200-300 55
DELUXE (385 "Otis Williams & the Charms")....200-300 56
KING (357 "Hits By the Charms")....50-100 58
KING (364 "Hits By the Charms, Vol. 2")....50-100 58
KING (385 "Otis Williams & His Charms")....50-100 58

LPs: 10/12-inch

DELUXE (570 "All Their Hits")....300-500 58
(With color photo of the group on cover.)
KING (614 "This Is Otis Williams and the Charms")....100-200 59
KING/GUSTO....8-10 78
POWER PAK....8-10 74

Members: Otis Williams; Ron Bradley; Don Peark; Joe Renn; Richard Parker.

Also see WILLIAMS, Otis

CHARO — LP '77

(With the Salsoul Orchestra)

Singles: 7-inch

CAPITOL....3-5 76
SALSOUL....3-5 77-78

Picture Sleeves

SALSOUL....3-5 78

LPs: 10/12-inch

SALSOUL....5-10 77-78

Also see SALSOUL ORCHESTRA

CHARTBUSTERS — P&R '64

Singles: 7-inch

BELL....4-8 67
CRUSADER....8-12 65
MUTUAL....5-10 64-65

CHARTS — P&R '57

Singles: 7-inch

EVERLAST (5001 "Deserie")....100-150 57

Singles: 7-inch

ABC....3-4 73
COLLECTABLES....3-4 80s
ENJOY (1002 "Deserie")....20-30 62
EVERLAST (5001 "Deserie")....50-100 57
EVERLAST (5002 "Dance Girl")....50-100 57
EVERLAST (5006 "You're the Reason")....50-75 58
EVERLAST (5008 "All Because of Love")....50-75 58
EVERLAST (5010 "My Diane")....60-80 58
EVERLAST (5026 "Deserie")....10-20 63
GUYDEN (2021 "For the Birds")....10-15 59
LOST-NITE....4-8
VEL-V-TONE (102 "Keep Dancing with Me")....50-100
WAND (1112 "Deserie")....15-25 66
WAND (1124 "Livin' the Nightlife")....25-50 66

LPs: 10/12-inch

COLLECTABLES....8-10 86
LOST-NITE....8-12 81

Members: Joe Grier; Steve Brown; Ross Buford; Glen Jackson; Leroy Binns.

Also see COOPER, Les

CHARTS / Bop-Chords / Ladders / Harmonaires

LPs: 10/12-inch

EVERLAST (201 "Our Best to You")....100-200

Also see CHARTS

CHASE — P&R/LP '71

Singles: 7-inch

EPIC....3-5 71-76

LPs: 10/12-inch

EPIC....10-12 71-76

Members: Bill Chase; Jerry Van Blair; Jay Burrid; Dennis Johnson; Ted Piercefield: Phil Porter; Terry Richards; Angel South; Alan Ware.

CHASE, Ellison — P&R '76

Singles: 7-inch

BIG TREE....3-5 76-77
COLUMBIA....3-4 82
MAGNA-GLIDE....3-5 75

LPs: 10/12-inch

COLUMBIA/ARC....5-10 82

CHATER, Kerry — P&R '77

Singles: 7-inch

W.B.....3-5 76-78

LPs: 10/12-inch

W.B.....5-10 77-78

Also see PUCKETT, Gary

CHAZ — R&B '82

Singles: 7-inch

PROMISE....3-4 82

CHEAP TRICK — LP '77

Singles: 12-inch

EPIC....5-15 83

Singles: 7-inch

ASYLUM....3-4 81
COLUMBIA....3-4 86
EPIC....3-5 77-91
PASHA....3-4 84
W.B.....3-4 83

Picture Sleeves

EPIC (Except 50814)....3-5 79-88
EPIC (50814 "Voices")....5-10 79
(Promotional issue only.)

EPs: 7-inch

CSP....5-10 81
(Promotional issue only. Made for Nestle's.)

LPs: 10/12-inch

EPIC (Except 35773)....5-10 76-90
EPIC (35773 "Dream Police")....35-40 80
(Picture disc. Promotional issue only.)
EPIC/NU-DISC....10-15 80
(Includes bonus single.)
PASHA....5-10 84

Members: Robin Zander; Tom Petersson; Rick Nielson; Bun E. Carlos; Jon Briant.

Also see CUMMINGS, Burton / Cheap Trick / Crawler
Also see FUSE
Also see NAZZ

CHEAP TRICK / Aldo Nova / Saxon

Singles

CBS ("Southwest Tour")....8-12 82
(Square cardboard picture disc. Selection number not known.)

Also see CHEAP TRICK
Also see NOVA, Aldo
Also see SAXON

CHEATHAM, Oliver — R&B '83

Singles: 7-inch

CRITIQUE....3-4 86-87
MCA....3-4 83

LPs: 10/12-inch

MCA....5-10 83

CHECKER, Chubby — P&R '59

(With Dee Dee Sharp)

Singles: 7-inch

ABKCO....3-4 72
AMHERST....3-5 76
BUDDAH....4-6 69
MCA....3-4 82
PARKWAY (006 "The Jet")....10-15 62
PARKWAY (100 series)....5-10 66
PARKWAY (706 "Twist to Blueberry Hill")....10-20 60s
(Promotional issue only.)
PARKWAY (804 thru 810)....10-20 59-60
PARKWAY (811 "The Twist"/"Toot")....15-25 60
(White label.)
PARKWAY (811 "The Twist"/"Toot")....10-15 60
(Orange label.)
PARKWAY (811 "The Twist"/"Twistin' U.S.A.")....5-10 61
(Yellow/orange or orange label.)
PARKWAY (811 "The Twist")....20-30 61
(Colored vinyl.)
PARKWAY (813 thru 959, except 824)....5-10 60-66
PARKWAY (824 "Let's Twist Again")..5-10 61
(Black vinyl.)
PARKWAY (824 "Let's Twist Again")....20-30 61
(Colored vinyl.)
PARKWAY (965 "You Just Don't Know")....100-200 66

PARKWAY (989 "Hey You! Little Boo-Ga-Loo")....................................5-10 66
20TH FOX 4-6 73-74

Picture Sleeves

PARKWAY 8-15 61-65

EPs: 7-inch

PARKWAY 15-20 61
(Includes Compact 33 Doubles.)

LPs: 10/12-inch

ABKCO..8-12 72
D.C.M. 5-10
EVEREST..5-10 81
51 WEST 5-10 84
MCA..8-10 82
PARKWAY (5001 "Chubby Checker")...............................20-30 62
PARKWAY (7001 "Twist with Chubby Checker")...............................20-30 60
PARKWAY (7002 "For Twisters Only")..20-30 60
PARKWAY (7002 "For Teen Twisters Only")..20-30 61
(Monaural.)
PARKWAY (SP-7002 "For Teen Twisters Only")..30-40 61
(Stereo.)
PARKWAY (7003 "It's Pony Time")...20-30 61
PARKWAY (7004 "Let's Twist Again")..20-30 61
PARKWAY (7007 "Your Twist Party with the King of the Twist")...........................20-30 61
PARKWAY (7008 "Twistin' 'Round the World")..20-30 62
(Monaural.)
PARKWAY (SP-7008 "Twistin' 'Round the World")..30-40 62
(Stereo.)
PARKWAY (7009 "For Teen Twisters Only")..25-35 62
PARKWAY (SP-7009 "For Teen Twisters Only")..30-40 62
PARKWAY (7014 "All the Hits").......20-30 62
(Monaural.)
PARKWAY (SP-7014 "All the Hits")..25-35 62
(Stereo.)
PARKWAY (7020 "Limbo Party")......20-30 62
(Monaural.)
PARKWAY (SP-7020 "Limbo Party")..25-35 62
(Stereo.)
PARKWAY (7022 "Biggest Hits")......20-30 62
(Monaural.)
PARKWAY (SP-7022 "Biggest Hits")..25-35 62
(Stereo.)
PARKWAY (7026 "In Person").........20-30 63
(Monaural.)
PARKWAY (SP-7026 "In Person")....25-35 63
(Stereo.)
PARKWAY (7027 "Let's Limbo Some More")..20-30 63
(Monaural.)
PARKWAY (SP-7027 "Let's Limbo Some More")..25-35 63
(Stereo.)
PARKWAY (7030 "Beach Party")......20-30 63
(Monaural.)
PARKWAY (SP-7030 "Beach Party")..25-35 63
(Stereo.)
PARKWAY (7036 "Chubby Checker")..20-30 63
(Monaural.)
PARKWAY (SP-7036 "Chubby Checker")..25-35 63
(Stereo.)
PARKWAY (7040 "Folk Album").......20-30 63
(Monaural.)
PARKWAY (SP-7040 "Folk Album")..25-35 63
(Stereo.)
PARKWAY (7045 "Discoteque").......15-25 65
(Monaural.)
PARKWAY (SP-7045 "Discoteque")...............................20-30 65
(Stereo.)
PARKWAY (7048 "18 Golden Hits")..15-25 66
(Monaural.)
PARKWAY (SP-7048 "18 Golden Hits")..20-30 66
(Stereo.)
Also see DREAMLOVERS
Also see FAT BOYS & Chubby Checker

CHECKER, Chubby / Gary U.S. Bonds

LPs: 10/12-inch

EXACT 5-10 80
Also see BONDS, Gary "U.S."

CHECKER, Chubby, & Bobby Rydell — LP '61

Singles: 7-inch

CAMEO (12 "Your Hits and Mine")... 10-20 61
(Promotional issue only.)
CAMEO (200 series)......................8-15 61-62

Picture Sleeves

CAMEO...5-10 61

LPs: 10/12-inch

CAMEO (1013 "Chubby Checker & Bobby Rydell")..20-30 61
CAMEO (1063 "Chubby Checker & Bobby Rydell")..20-30 63
Also see RYDELL, Bobby

CHECKER, Chubby, & Dee Dee Sharp — LP '62

Singles: 7-inch

PARKWAY (835 "Slow Twistin' ")....... 5-10 62
PARKWAY (7041 "The Twist")......... 10-15 63
(Promotional issue only.)

LPs: 10/12-inch

CAMEO (1029 "Down to Earth")....... 20-30 62
Also see CHECKER, Chubby
Also see SHARP, Dee Dee

CHECKMATES LTD. — P&R/LP '69

(Featuring Sonny Charles)

Singles: 7-inch

A&M 4-6 69
CAMEO (5603 "Do the Walk")........ 10-20 66
CAPITOL (5753 "Kissin' Her and Cryin' for You")..20-30 66
CAPITOL (5814 "Please Don't Take My World Away")..10-20 67
CAPITOL (5922 "A&I")..................... 10-20 67
FANTASY 3-5 77-78
GREEDY..3-5 77
RUSTIC..3-5 74

LPs: 10/12-inch

A&M (4183 "Love Is All We Have to Give")..15-25 69
CAPITOL (2840 "Live")................... 25-35 67
FANTASY 8-10 77
IKON 5-10
POLYDOR 8-10 76
RUSTIC..8-10 74
Members: Sonny Charles; Bill Van Buskirk; Marvin Smith; Bobby Stevens; Harvey Trees.
Also see CHARLES, Sonny

CHEECH & CHONG — LP '71

Singles: 7-inch

A&M 3-4
EPIC/ODE 3-5 77
MCA 3-4 85
ODE 3-5 71-77
W.B. 3-4 78

Picture Sleeves

A&M 3-4
MCA 3-4 85
ODE 8-12 73-77
W.B. 3-4 78

EPs: 7-inch

ODE (8 "Cheech & Chong")..................5-8 71

LPs: 10/12-inch

("Cheech & Chong")........................ 40-50 83
(No label name or selection number used. Promotional only, unplayable picture disc.)
EPIC/ODE 8-10 77
MCA..5-8 85
ODE..8-12 71-76
W.B. 8-10 78-80
Members: Richard Marin; Thomas Chong.
Also see TAYLOR, Bobby

CHEE-CHEE & PEPPY — P&R/R&B '71

Singles: 7-inch

BUDDAH 3-5 71

LPs: 10/12-inch

BUDDAH 10-15 72
Members: Dorothy Moore; Keith Bolling.
Also see MOORE, Dorothy

CHEEKS, Judy — P&R/R&B '78

Singles: 7-inch

DREAM..3-4 80
SALSOUL..3-4 78
U.A. 3-5 73

LPs: 10/12-inch

SALSOUL..5-10 78
U.A. 8-10 73

CHEERS — P&R '54

(With Les Baxter's Orchestra & Chorus)

Singles: 78 rpm

CAPITOL..10-20 54-56
MERCURY 10-15 57

Singles: 7-inch

CAPITOL..20-30 54-56
MERCURY 15-25 57

EPs: 7-inch

CAPITOL (584 "Bazoom")................50-100 55
Members: Bert Convy; Gil Garfield; Susan Allen.
Also see BAXTER, Les

CHEMAY, Joe — P&R '81

(Joe Chemay Band)

Singles: 7-inch

UNICORN..3-4 81

LPs: 10/12-inch

UNICORN..5-10 81

CHEQUERED PAST — LP '84

Singles: 7-inch

EMI AMERICA..3-4 84

LPs: 10/12-inch

EMI AMERICA..5-10 84
Members: Clem Burke; Nigel Harrison.

CHER — P&R/LP '65

(Cher Bono; Cher Allman)

Singles: 12-inch

CASABLANCA..8-10 79-82

Singles: 7-inch

ATCO..3-6 69-72
ATLANTIC 4-6 69
CASABLANCA 3-5 79
COLUMBIA..3-5 82
GEFFEN..3-4 87-91
IMPERIAL..5-10 64-68
KAPP..3-5 71-72
LIBERTY..3-4 82
MCA..3-5 73-75
U.A. 3-5 71-72
W.B. 3-5 75-77
W.B./SPECTOR 3-5 74

Picture Sleeves

COLUMBIA..3-5 82
GEFFEN..3-4 87-89

LPs: 10/12-inch

ATCO..15-20 69
CASABLANCA (Except NBPIX-7133)..8-12 79
CASABLANCA (NBPIX-7133 "Take Me Home")..50-75 79
(Picture disc.)
COLUMBIA..5-10 82
GEFFEN..5-12 87-91
IMPERIAL..15-25 65-68
KAPP..12-15 71-72
LIBERTY..5-10 81
MCA..10-15 73-74

SPRINGBOARD........ 8-10 72
SUNSET........ 8-10 70
U.A. 8-10 71-75
W.B. 8-15 75-77
Also see ALLMAN & WOMAN
Also see CHERILYN / Cherilyn's Group
Also see MASON, Bonnie Jo
Also see SONNY & CHER

CHER & PETER CETERA — P&R '89

Singles: 7-inch

GEFFEN........ 3-4 89

Picture Sleeves

GEFFEN........ 3-4 89
Also see CETERA, Peter

CHER & NILSSON

Singles: 7-inch

SPECTOR........ 3-5 75
Members: Cher; Harry Nilsson.
Also see CHER
Also see NILSSON, Harry

CHERI — P&R/R&B '82

Singles: 12-inch

21........ 4-6 83

Singles: 7-inch

21........ 3-4 83
VENTURE........ 3-4 82
Members: Rosalind Hunt; Amy Roslyn.

CHERILYN / Cherilyn's Group

(Cher Bono)

Singles: 7-inch

IMPERIAL (66081 "Dream Baby")..... 20-30 64
Also see CHER

CHERRELLE — P&R/R&B/D&D/LP '84

Singles: 12-inch

TABU........ 4-6 84-86

Singles: 7-inch

TABU........ 3-4 84-88

Picture Sleeves

TABU........ 3-4 88

LPs: 10/12-inch

TABU........ 5-10 84-88
Also see O'NEAL, Alexander, & Cherrelle

CHERRY, Ava — R&B '80

Singles: 12-inch

CAPITOL........ 4-6 82

Singles: 7-inch

CAPITOL........ 3-4 82
CURTOM........ 3-4 80
RSO........ 3-4 80

LPs: 10/12-inch

RSO........ 5-10 80

CHERRY, Don — P&R '54

Singles: 78 rpm

COLUMBIA........ 5-10 55-57
DECCA........ 5-10 50-56

Singles: 7-inch

COLUMBIA........ 5-10 55-59
DECCA........ 8-12 50-56
MONUMENT........ 3-5 65-78
STRAND........ 4-8 59
VERVE........ 4-8 62
WARWICK........ 4-8 60

EPs: 7-inch

COLUMBIA........ 8-15 56

LPs: 10/12-inch

COLUMBIA........ 15-25 56
HARMONY........ 10-15 59
MONUMENT........ 8-12 66-73
Also see DAY, Doris, & Don Cherry

CHERRY, Neneh — P&R/LP '89

Singles: 7-inch

VIRGIN........ 3-4 89

Picture Sleeves

VIRGIN........ 3-4 89

LPs: 10/12-inch

VIRGIN........ 5-8 89

CHERRY PEOPLE — P&R '68

Singles: 7-inch

HERITAGE........ 4-8 68-69

Picture Sleeves

HERITAGE........ 6-10 68

LPs: 10/12-inch

HERITAGE........ 15-20 68
Members: Punky Meadows; Doug Grimes; Chris Grimes; Rocky Isaac.
Also see ANGEL

CHERYL LYNN: see LYNN, Cheryl

CHESNUTT, Mark — C&W/LP '90

Singles: 7-inch

MCA........ 3-4 90-91

LPs: 10/12-inch

MCA........ 5-8 90-91

CHET, FLOYD & DANNY: see ATKINS, Chet, Floyd Cramer & Danny Davis

CHEYNE — R&B/D&D '85

Singles: 12-inch

MCA........ 4-6 85

CHIC — P&R/R&B/LP '77

Singles: 12-inch 33/45

ATLANTIC (Except 131)........ 4-8 78-83
ATLANTIC (131 "Le Freak")........ 20-25 78
(Picture disc. Promotional issue only.)

Singles: 7-inch

ATLANTIC........ 3-5 77-83
MIRAGE........ 3-4 82

Picture Sleeves

ATLANTIC........ 3-5 78-80

LPs: 10/12-inch

ATLANTIC........ 5-10 77-82
Also see HONEYDRIPPERS
Also see NORMA JEAN
Also see RODGERS, Nile
Also see ROUNDTREE

CHIC / Leif Garrett / Roberta Flack / Genesis

EPs: 7-inch

W.B. SPECIAL PRODUCTS........ 8-12 78
(Coca-Cola/Burger King promotional issue. Issued with paper sleeve.)
Also see CHIC
Also see FLACK, Roberta
Also see GARRETT, Leif
Also see GENESIS

CHICAGO — P&R/LP '69

Singles: 12-inch

COLUMBIA........ 4-8 80

Singles: 7-inch

COLUMBIA........ 3-6 69-80
FULL MOON........ 3-4 82-86
REPRISE........ 3-4 88-91
W.B. 3-4 87

Picture Sleeves

COLUMBIA........ 3-6 69-77
FULL MOON........ 3-4 84-86
REPRISE........ 3-4 88-89
W.B. 3-4 87

EPs: 7-inch

COLUMBIA........ 10-15 70-73
(Juke box issues only.)

LPs: 10/12-inch

ACCORD........ 5-10 81
COLUMBIA ("Chicago")........ 200-250 76
(No selection number used. Boxed set of first 10 LPs [17 discs]. Promotional issue only.)
COLUMBIA (8 "Chicago Transit Authority")........ 25-35 69
COLUMBIA (24 "Chicago II")........ 20-30 70
COLUMBIA (C2-30110 "Chicago III") 10-20 70
COLUMBIA (C2Q-30110 "Chicago III")........ 20-25 74
(Quadrophonic.)
COLUMBIA (30863 "Chicago IV")..... 15-20 71
COLUMBIA (CAX-30865 "Chicago IV")........ 20-30 71
(Boxed, four-disc set. Includes three posters, booklet and card.)
COLUMBIA (CQ-30865 "Chicago IV")........ 20-30 74
(Quadrophonic.)
COLUMBIA (31102 thru 38590)........ 8-15 72-82
(With "C2," "FC," "HC," "KC," "JC," or "PC" prefix.)
COLUMBIA (31102 thru 34200)........ 15-25 74-76
(Quadrophonic. With "CQ," "C2Q," "GQ," or "PCQ" prefix.)
COLUMBIA (43000 & 44000 series)........ 15-25 82
(Half-speed mastered.)
FULL MOON........ 5-10 82-86
MFSL (2-128 "Chicago Transit Authority")........ 30-40 85
REPRISE........ 5-8 88-89
SHOWCASE (121 "Chicago Live")..... 8-10 85
MAGNUM........ 10-12 78
W.B. 5-8 86
Members: Peter Cetera; Terry Kath; Robert Lamm; James Pankow; Lee Loughnane; Daniel Seraphine; Walter Parazaider; Bill Champlin; Donnie Dacus; Jason Scheff.
Also see BEACH BOYS
Also see CETERA, Peter
Also see CHAMPLIN, Bill
Also see LAMM, Robert

CHICAGO BEARS SHUFFLIN' CREW — P&R/R&B '86

Singles: 12-inch

RED LABEL........ 4-8 85

Singles: 7-inch

RED LABEL........ 3-4 85

Picture Sleeves

RED LABEL........ 3-4 85
Members: Walter Payton; Willie Gault; Mike Singletary; Jim McMahon; Otis Wilson; Steve Fuller; Mike Richardson; Richard Dent; Gary Fencik; William Perry.

CHICAGO GANGSTERS — R&B '75

Singles: 7-inch

GOLD PLATE........ 3-5 75-76
RCA........ 3-5 78
RED COACH........ 3-5 74-75

LPs: 10/12-inch

GOLD PLATE........ 10-12 75-76
Members: Sam McCant; James McCant; Larry McCant; Chris McCant.

CHICAGO LOOP — P&R '66

Singles: 7-inch

DYNO VOICE........ 4-8 66-67
MERCURY........ 4-8 67-68

CHICAGO TRANSIT AUTHORITY: see CHICAGO

CHICANO, El: see EL CHICANO

CHICORY — P&R '72

(Chicory Tip)

Singles: 7-inch

EPIC........ 3-5 72-73

LPs: 10/12-inch

EPIC........ 10-12 72

CHIEFTAINS — LP '76

Singles: 7-inch

ISLAND........ 3-5 76

LPs: 10/12-inch

COLUMBIA........ 5-10 78-80
ISLAND........ 5-10 75-78
Also see MORRISON, Van, & Chieftains

CHIFFONS — P&R '60

Singles: 7-inch

B.T. PUPPY (558 "My Secret Love")..... 4-8 70
BIG DEAL (6003 "Tonight's the Night")........ 50-75 60
BUDDAH (171 "So Much in Love")....... 4-8 71
LAURIE........ 5-10 63-76
REPRISE (20103 "Doctor of Hearts")........ 20-30 62
WILDCAT (601 "Never Never")........ 20-30 61

LPs: 10/12-inch

B.T. PUPPY (1011 "My Secret Love")........ 35-45 70
COLLECTABLES........ 5-10 87
LAURIE (2018 "He's So Fine")........ 35-50 63

LAURIE (2020 "One Fine Day") 35-50 63
LAURIE (LLP-2036 "Sweet Talkin' Guy") 35-45 66
(Monaural.)
LAURIE (SLP-2036 "Sweet Talkin' Guy") 40-50 66
(Stereo.)
LAURIE (4001 "Everything You Always Wanted to Hear") 10-20 74
Members: Judy Craig; Barbara Lee; Patricia Bennett; Sylvia Peterson.
Also see CHRISTIE, Lou, & Classics / Isley Brothers / Chiffons
Also see COASTERS / Crew-Cuts / Chiffons
Also see FOUR PENNIES

CHILD, Desmond, & Rouge — P&R/R&B/LP '79

Singles: 12-inch

CAPITOL 4-8 79

Singles: 7-inch

CAPITOL (Black vinyl) 3-4 79-82
CAPITOL (Colored vinyl) 4-6 79

LPs: 10/12-inch

CAPITOL (Black vinyl) 5-10 79
CAPITOL (Colored vinyl) 15-20 79
Also see VIDAL, Maria

CHILD, Jane — P&R/LP '90

Singles: 7-inch

W.B. 3-4 90

LPs: 10/12-inch

W.B. 3-4 90

CHILDS, Toni — P&R/LP '88

Singles: 7-inch

A&M 3-4 88-90

Picture Sleeves

A&M 3-4 88

LPs: 10/12-inch

A&M 5-8 88-91

CHI-LITES — P&R/R&B/LP '69

Singles: 12-inch

LARC 4-8 83
PRIVATE 1 ....4-6 84

Singles: 7-inch

BLUE ROCK (4007 "I'm So Jealous") 15-25 65
BLUE ROCK (4020 "The Monkey") ...15-25 65
BLUE ROCK (4037 "She's Mine") 25-50 65
BRUNSWICK 3-8 69-78
CHI-SOUND 3-4 80-82
EPIC 3-4 83
INPHASION 3-5 79
LARC 3-4 83
MERCURY 3-5 76-77
O'RETTA 4-8 70
PRIVATE I 3-4 84
REVUE 5-10 67-68
20TH FOX 3-4 81

LPs: 10/12-inch

BRUNSWICK 10-15 69-74
CHI-SOUND 5-8 80-82
EPIC 5-10 83-84
LARC 5-10 83
MERCURY 5-10 77
PICKWICK 5-10 70s
20TH FOX 5-10 80-81
Members: Eugene Record; Creadel Jones; Robert Lester; Marshall Thompson; Danny Johnson.
Also see HI-LITES
Also see JOHNSON, Danny
Also see PITMAN, Donnell
Also see RECORD, Eugene
Also see WILSON, Jackie, & Chi-Lites

CHILL FACTOR — R&B '87

Singles: 7-inch

W.B. 3-4 87

CHILL TOWN — D&D '83

Singles: 12-inch

A&M 4-6 83

CHILLIWACK — P&R '72

Singles: 12-inch

MUSHROOM (0611 "Dreams, Dreams, Dreams") 10-15 78
(Clear vinyl. Promotional issue only.)

Singles: 7-inch

A&M 3-5 72
MILLENNIUM 3-4 81-83
MUSHROOM 3-5 76-80
PARROT 3-5 71
SIRE 3-5 74-76

LPs: 10/12-inch

A&M 10-15 71-73
MILLENNIUM 5-10 81-82
MUSHROOM 8-12 77-80
PARROT 15-20 70
SIRE 10-15 75
Members: Bill Henderson; Howard Froese; Claire Lawrence; Glen Miller; Ross Turney.

CHIMES — P&R '60

Singles: 7-inch

ABC 3-4 75
COLLECTABLES 3-4 81
ERIC 3-4 70s
LAURIE (3211 "Who's Heart Are You Breaking Now") 10-15 63
LOST-NITE 4-8 70s
METRO (1 "Who's Heart Are You Breaking Now") 25-35 63
MUSIC NOTE (1101 "Once in Awhile") 15-25 61
RESERVE (120 "When School Starts Again") 30-50 57
TAG (444 "Once in Awhile"/"Summer Night") 50-75 60
(Maroon label. "Tag" in normal letters.)
TAG (444 "Once in Awhile"/"Summer Night") 100-150 60
(Blue label. "Tag" in normal letters.)
TAG (444 "Once in Awhile"/"Summer Night") 15-25 60
(Green label. Has "Tag" in a triangle.)
TAG (444 "Once in Awhile"/"Oh How I Love You So") 15-25 60
(Though shown as by the Chimes, *Oh How I Love You So* is by the BiTones.)
TAG (445 "I'm in the Mood for Love") 15-25 61
TAG (447 "Let's Fall in Love") 15-25 61
TAG (450 "My Love") 15-25 62
TRIP 3-5 70s

LPs: 10/12-inch

CHIMES 10-15 83
Member: Lenny Cocco.

CHIMES / Huey "Piano" Smith

Singles: 7-inch

OLDIES 45 3-5
Also see CHIMES
Also see SMITH, Huey

CHIMES — P&R/LP '90

LPs: 10/12-inch

COLUMBIA 5-8 90
Member: Pauline Henry.

CHINA CRISIS — D&D '84

Singles: 12-inch

VIRGIN 4-6 82
W.B. 4-6 83-84

Singles: 7-inch

VIRGIN 3-4 82
W.B. 3-4 84

LPs: 10/12-inch

A&M 5-10 87
W.B. 5-10 84-85

CHIP E. INC. Featuring K. Joy — D&D '85

Singles: 12-inch

D.J. INT'L 4-6 85

CHIPMUNKS — P&R/R&B '58

(Starring Alvin, Theodore, & Simon; Featuring David Seville)

Singles: 7-inch

AMERICAN TELECARD 10-15 64
(Cardboard flexi-disc.)
DOT 4-6 67
LIBERTY (Except 77000 series) 5-10 58-74
LIBERTY (77000 series) 10-20 59
(Stereo.)
MISTLETOE 3-5 75
SUNSET 3-6 68
U.A. 3-5 74

Picture Sleeves

LIBERTY 5-10 59-65

EPs: 7-inch

LIBERTY 10-20 59-64

LPs: 10/12-inch

LIBERTY (3132 "Let's All Sing with the Chipmunks") 20-30 59
(Monaural. Black vinyl. Cover shows Chipmunks as animals. If Chipmunks are drawn as cartoon characters, deduct 50%.)
LIBERTY (3132 "Let's All Sing with the Chipmunks") 25-40 59
(Monaural. Colored vinyl. Cover shows Chipmunks as animals. If Chipmunks are drawn as cartoon characters, deduct 50%.)
LIBERTY (3159 "Sing Again with the Chipmunks") 20-30 60
(Monaural. Cover shows Chipmunks as animals. If Chipmunks are drawn as cartoon characters, deduct 50%.)
LIBERTY (3170 "Around the World with the Chipmunks") 20-30 60
(Monaural. Cover shows Chipmunks as animals. If Chipmunks are drawn as cartoon characters, deduct 50%.)
LIBERTY (3200 thru 3400 series) 10-20 61-65
(Monaural.)
LIBERTY (7132 "Let's All Sing with the Chipmunks") 20-35 59
(Stereo. Black vinyl. Cover shows Chipmunks as animals. If Chipmunks are drawn as cartoon characters, deduct 50%.)
LIBERTY (7132 "Let's All Sing with the Chipmunks") 25-45 59
(Stereo. Colored vinyl. Cover shows Chipmunks as animals. If Chipmunks are drawn as cartoon characters, deduct 50%.)
LIBERTY (7159 "Sing Again with the Chipmunks") 20-35 60
(Stereo. Cover shows Chipmunks as animals. If Chipmunks are drawn as cartoon characters, deduct 50%.)
LIBERTY (7170 "Around the World with the Chipmunks") 20-35 60
(Stereo. Cover shows Chipmunks as animals. If Chipmunks are drawn as cartoon characters, deduct 50%.)
LIBERTY (7200 thru 7400 series) 10-20 61-65
(Stereo.)
LIBERTY (10000 series) 5-10 82
PICKWICK 5-10 80
SUNSET 8-15 68-69
U.A. 5-10 74-76
Also see CANNED HEAT & CHIPMUNKS
Also see SEVILLE, David

CHIPMUNKS — LP '80

(Starring Alvin, Theodore, & Simon; Featuring David Seville Jr.)

Singles: 7-inch

EXCELSIOR 3-4 80
RCA 3-4 81-82

Picture Sleeves

EXCELSIOR 3-4 80
RCA 3-4 81

LPs: 10/12-inch

EXCELSIOR 5-10 80
PICKWICK INT'L 5-10 80
RCA 5-10 81-82

CHIYO & CRESCENTS: see CRESCENTS

CHOCOLATE MILK *R&B/LP '75*

Singles: 12-inch

RCA....4-6 83

Singles: 7-inch

RCA....3-5 75-83

LPs: 10/12-inch

RCA....5-10 77-82

Members: Frank Richard; Amadee Castanell; Robert Doban; Joe Foxx; Mario Tio; Dwight Richards.

CHOCOLATE SYRUP *R&B '71*

Singles: 7-inch

AVCO EMBASSY....3-5 71
BROWN DOG....3-5 74
LAW TON....3-5

Members: L.J. Reynolds; Lenny Wolfe; Jimmy Holiday; Norris Harris.
Also see CHAIN REACTION
Also see MOMENT of TRUTH
Also see REYNOLDS, L.J.

CHOCOLETE *D&D '85*

Singles: 12-inch

SUPERTRONICS....4-6 85

CHOICE FOUR *R&B '74*

Singles: 7-inch

RCA....3-5 74-76

LPs: 10/12-inch

RCA....8-10 74-75

Members: Bobby Hamilton; Pete Marshall; Ted Maduro; Charles Blagmore.

CHOICE MCs Featuring Fresh Gordon *R&B/D&D '85*

Singles: 12-inch

TOMMY BOY....4-6 85

Singles: 7-inch

TOMMY BOY....3-4 85

CHOIR *P&R '67*

Singles: 7-inch

CANADIAN AMERICAN (203 "It's Cold Outside")....25-35 67
INTREPID....4-6 70
ROULETTE....10-15 67-68

EPs: 7-inch

BOMP....8-10 76

Members: Wally Bryson; David Smalley; Jim Bonfanti.
Also see RASPBERRIES

CHOIRBOYS *P&R '89*

Singles: 7-inch

WTG....3-4 89

Member: Mark Gable.

CHOPS *R&B '84*

Singles: 12-inch

ATLANTIC....4-6 84

Singles: 7-inch

ATLANTIC....3-4 84

LPs: 10/12-inch

ATLANTIC....5-10 84

CHORDCATS

Singles: 78 rpm

CAT (109 "Zippety Zum")....15-20 54
CAT (112 "Hold Me, Baby")....20-25 54

Singles: 7-inch

CAT (109 "Zippety Zum")....20-30 54
CAT (112 "Hold Me, Baby")....30-50 54

Members: Carl Feaster; Claude Feaster; Jimmy Keys; Floyd McRae; William Edwards.
Also see CHORDS

CHORDETTES *P&R '54*
(With Archie Bleyer; with Jeff Kron & Jackie Ertel)

Singles: 78 rpm

CADENCE....5-10 54-57
COLUMBIA....5-10 50-54

Singles: 7-inch

BARNABY....3-5 70-76
CADENCE....8-15 54-63
COLUMBIA....10-15 50-54
ERIC....3-4 78

Picture Sleeves

CADENCE (Except 1366)....10-20 58-61
CADENCE (1366 "No Wheels")....15-25 59
(Promotional issue only. Pictures Jeff and Jackie. Sleeve and disc has *No Wheels* on both sides.)
CADENCE (1366 "A Girl's Work Is Never Done")....10-15 59
(Pictures only Jackie.)

EPs: 7-inch

CADENCE....10-20 57-61
COLUMBIA (Except 201 thru 401)....10-25 54-57
COLUMBIA (201 "Harmony Time")....30-40 50
(Boxed, four-disc set.)
COLUMBIA (241 "Harmony Time, Vol. 2")....30-40 51
(Boxed, four-disc set.)
COLUMBIA (309 "Harmony Encores")....30-40 52
(Boxed, four-disc set.)
COLUMBIA (401 "Your Requests")....30-40 53
(Boxed, four-disc set.)

LPs: 10/12-inch

BACK-TRAC....5-10
BARNABY....8-10 76
CADENCE (1002 "Close Harmony")....20-30 55
CADENCE (3001 "Chordettes")....20-35 57
CADENCE (3020 "Barbershop Harmonies")....20-30 58
CADENCE (3062 "Never on Sunday")....20-30 62
CADENCE (25062 "Never on Sunday")....25-35 62
COLUMBIA (956 "Listen")....20-35 57
COLUMBIA (2519 "Chordettes")....25-35 56
(10-inch LP.)
COLUMBIA (6111 "Harmony Time")....30-40 50
(10-inch LP.)
COLUMBIA (6170 "Harmony Time, Vol. 2")....30-40 51
(10-inch LP.)
COLUMBIA (6218 "Harmony Encores")....30-40 52
(10-inch LP.)
COLUMBIA (6285 "Your Requests")..30-40 53
(10-inch LP.)
EVEREST....5-10 82
HARMONY....12-15 59

Members: Margie Needham; Janet Ertel; Carol Bushman; Lynn Evans.
Also see BLEYER, Archie

CHORDS *P&R/R&B '54*

Singles: 78 rpm

CAT (104 "Sh-Boom"/"Cross Over the Bridge")....20-40 54
CAT (104 "Sh-Boom"/"Little Maiden")....15-25 54
CAT (109 "Zippety Zum")....10-20 54
REO (1268 "Sh-Boom")....35-50 54
(Canadian.)
REO (1293 "Zippety Zum")....10-20 54
(Canadian.)

Singles: 7-inch

CAT (104 "Sh-Boom"/"Cross Over the Bridge")....50-100 54
CAT (104 "Sh-Boom"/"Little Maiden")....25-50 54
CAT (109 "Zippety Zum")....25-50 54
LOST-NITE....4-8
REO (1268 "Sh-Boom")....150-200 54
(Canadian.)
REO (1293 "Zippety Zum")....15-25 54
(Canadian.)

Members: Carl Feaster; Claude Feaster; Jimmy Keys; Floyd McRae; William Edwards.
Also see CHORDCATS
Also see SH-BOOMS

CHRIS & KATHY
(Chris Montez & Kathy Young)

Singles: 7-inch

MONOGRAM (517 "All You Had to Do")....10-15 64
MONOGRAM (520 "Shoot That Curl")....10-15 64

Members: Chris Montez; Kathy Young.
Also see MONTEZ, Chris
Also see YOUNG, Kathy

CHRISTIAN, Chris *P&R '81*
(With Amy Holland)

Singles: 7-inch

BOARDWALK....3-4 81-82

Picture Sleeves

BOARDWALK....3-4 81

LPs: 10/12-inch

BORADWALK....5-10 81
HOME SWEET HOME....5-10 81
MYRRH....5-10 83-84

Also see COTTON, LLOYD & CHRISTIAN
Also see HOLLAND, Amy

CHRISTIANS *LP '88*

LPs: 10/12-inch

ISLAND....5-8 88

CHRISTIE *P&R/LP '70*

Singles: 7-inch

EPIC....3-5 70-71

LPs: 10/12-inch

EPIC....10-15 70

Members: Jeff Christie; Mike Blakely; Vic Elmes.

CHRISTIE, Dean *P&R '62*
(Dean Christy)

Singles: 7-inch

MERCURY....4-8 63-64
SWL....5-10 62
SELECT (715 "Heart Breaker")....10-15 62
SELECT (718 "Teenage Jezebel")....15-25 62
TOP FLIGHT (113 "So Much")....20-30 60s

CHRISTIE, Janice *D&D '85*

Singles: 12-inch

SUPERTRONICS....4-6 85-86

Singles: 7-inch

SUPERTRONICS....3-4 85-86

Also see FATBACK

CHRISTIE, Lou *P&R/R&B/LP '63*
(With the Classics; Lou Christy)

Singles: 12-inch

PLATEAU (101 "Guardian Angels")....40-50 81
(Promotional issue only.)
PLATEAU (4551 "Guardian Angels")....40-50 81

Singles: 7-inch

ABC....3-5 73
ALCAR (207 "Close Your Eyes")....25-35 63
ALCAR (208 "You're with It")....30-50 63
AMERICAN MUSIC MAKERS (006 "The Jury")....25-30
BUDDAH....5-15 68-72
C&C (102 "The Gypsy Cried")....75-100 62
CO & CE (235 "Outside the Gates of Heaven")....5-10 66
COLPIX....10-15 64-66
COLUMBIA....10-15 67
EPIC....10-15 76
MGM (Except 13473)....5-10 65-66
MGM (13473 "Rhapsody in the Rain")....10-15 66
(With "making out in the rain" lyrics.)
MGM (13473 "Rhapsody in the Rain")....5-10 66
(With "fell in love in the rain" lyrics.)
MIDLAND INT'L....10-15 76-77
MIDSONG....10-12 77
PLATEAU (4551 "Guardian Angels")....40-50 81
RHINO....3-5 90s
ROULETTE (4457 "The Gypsy Cried")....15-20 62
(White label with color spokes.)
ROULETTE (4457 "The Gypsy Cried")....5-10 63
(Pink label.)

ROULETTE (4481 "Two Faces Have I") 15-25 63
(White label with color spokes.)
ROULETTE (4481 "Two Faces Have I") 5-10 63
(Pink label.)
ROULETTE (4457 thru 4527) 5-10 62-63
ROULETTE (4545 "Stay") 10-15 64
ROULETTE (4554 "When You Dance") 20-25 64
SLIPPED DISC 10-15 75
THREE BROTHERS 5-15 73-75
WORLD (1002 "The Jury") 25-30

Picture Sleeves

COLPIX (799 "Big Time") 10-20 66
MGM (13473 "Rhapsody in the Rain") 8-12 66
MGM (13533 "Painter") 8-12 66
MGM (13576 "If My Car Could Only Talk") 20-25 66

LPs: 10/12-inch

BUDDAH (5052 "I'm Gonna Make You Mine") 10-15 69
BUDDAH (5073 "Paint America Love") 15-20 71
CO & CE (1231 "Lou Christie Strikes Back") 30-50 66
COLPIX (4001 "Lou Christie Strikes Again") 20-25 66
(Gold label.)
COLPIX (4001 "Lou Christie Strikes Again") 10-20 66
(Blue label.)
CSP (18260 "Lou Christie Does Detroit") 5-8
51 WEST ("Lou Christie Does Detroit") 10-15 83
MGM (4360 "Lightnin' Strikes") 12-18 66
MGM (4394 "Painter of Hits") 15-20 66
RHINO 5-8 88
ROULETTE (25208 "Lou Christie") ... 50-60 63
(Cover has a blue background.)
ROULETTE (25208 "Lou Christie") ... 30-40 63
(Cover has white wall background.)
ROULETTE (25332 "Lou Christie Strikes Again") 20-30 63
(Repackage of Co & Ce 1231, *Lou Christie Strikes Back*.)
UNDERGROUND (50002 "Self Expression") 8-10 83
(Canadian.)
THREE BROTHERS (2000 "Lou Christie") 15-20 74
Also see CHRISTY, Chic
Also see CLASSICS
Also see CRITTERS / Young Rascals / Lou Christie
Also see GORE, Leslie, & Lou Christie
Also see LUGEE & LIONS
Also see MARCY JOE
Also see SACCO
Also see ZADORA, Pia, & Lou Christie

CHRISTIE, Lou / Len Barry & Dovells / Bobby Rydell / Tokens

LPs: 10/12-inch

WYNCOTE 10-20 60s
Also see DOVELLS
Also see RYDELL, Bobby
Also see TOKENS

CHRISTIE, Lou, & Classics / Isley Brothers / Chiffons

LPs: 10/12-inch

SPIN-O-RAMA (173 "Lou Christie and the Classics") 20-30 66
Also see CHIFFONS
Also see ISLEY BROTHERS

CHRISTIE, Susan — P&R '66

Singles: 7-inch

COLUMBIA 4-8 66-67

CHRISTMAS SPIRIT

Singles: 7-inch

WHITE WHALE (290 "Christmas Is My Time of Year") 50-75 69
Members: Mark Volman; Howard Kaylan; Linda Ronstadt.
Also see RONSTADT, Linda
Also see TURTLES

CHRISTOPHER, Gavin — R&B '79

Singles: 7-inch

E.M.I. 3-4 88
ISLAND 3-5 76
MANHATTAN 3-4 86
RSO 3-4 79

Picture Sleeves

MANHATTAN 3-4 86

LPs: 10/12-inch

ISLAND 8-10 76
MANHATTAN 5-10 86
RSO 5-10 79

CHRISTOPHER, Paul & Shawn — P&R '75

Singles: 7-inch

CASABLANCA 3-5 75
Also see CHRISTOPHER, Shawn

CHRISTY, Chic

Singles: 7-inch

HAC 15-25 62
Members: Lou Christie; Kay Chick; Susan Christie.
Also see CHRISTIE, Lou

CHRISTY, Dean: see CHRISTIE, Dean

CHRISTY, Don
(Sonny Bono)

Singles: 7-inch

FIDELITY 10-15 60
GO 10-15 60
NAME 10-15 60
SPECIALTY 10-15 59
Also see SONNY

CHRISTY, June — P&R '53

Singles: 78 rpm

CAPITOL 3-8 51-57

Singles: 7-inch

CAPITOL (1800 thru 3900 series) 5-10 51-58
CAPITOL (4000 thru 4800 series) 3-8 59-62

EPs: 7-inch 33/4rpm

CAPITOL 5-15 53-55

LPs: 10/12-inch

CAPITOL (516 "Something Cool") 25-40 54
(With "H" prefix. 10-inch LP.)
CAPITOL (516 "Something Cool") 15-25 55
(Green label. With "T" prefix.)
CAPITOL (516 "Something Cool") 10-20 60
(Black label. With "T" or "ST" prefix.)
CAPITOL (516 "Something Cool") 5-10 75
(With "SM" prefix.)
CAPITOL (600 thru 900 series) 15-25 55-57
(Green label.)
CAPITOL (600 thru 900 series) 10-15 60
(Black label.)
CAPITOL (1000 thru 2400 series) 10-20 60-65
CAPITOL (11000 series) 5-10 79
DISCOVERY 5-10 82
SEABREEZE 5-10 80

CHRISTY, June, & Stan Kenton

EPs: 7-inch

CAPITOL 5-10 56

LPs: 10/12-inch

CAPITOL (656 "Duet") 20-35 56
(10-inch LP.)
Also see JONES, Jonah
Also see KENTON, Stan, & His Orchestra

CHRISTY, June / Fran Warren

LP: 10/12-inch

CAMAY 8-12
Also see CHRISTY, June

CHRISTY, Lou: see CHRISTIE, Lou

CHUBB ROCK — LP '91

LPs: 10/12-inch

SELECT 5-8 91

CHUCKLES
(Featuring Teddy Randazzo)

Singles: 7-inch

ABC-PAR (10276 "Runaround") 8-12 61
Also see RANDAZZO, Teddy
Also see THREE CHUCKLES

CHUNG, Wang: see WANG CHUNG

CHUNKY A — P&R/LP '89
(Arsenio Hall)

Singles: 7-inch

MCA 3-4 89

Picture Sleeves

MCA 3-4 89

LPs: 10/12-inch

MCA 5-8 89

CHURCH, Eugene — P&R/R&B '58
(With the Fellows)

Singles: 7-inch

CLASS 5-10 58-60
COLLECTABLES 3-4 81
KING 5-10 61-63
RENDEZVOUS 5-10 60
SPECIALTY 10-20 57
WORLD PACIFIC (77866 "Dollar Bill") 10-15 67
Also see CLIQUES

CHURCHILL, Savannah — R&B '45
(With the Five Kings; with Striders; with Four Tunes)

Singles: 78 rpm

ARGO 5-10 56
DECCA 5-10 53-55
KAY-RON 5-10 56
MANOR 5-10 45-48
RCA 5-10 51-52
REGAL (3309 "Once There Lived a Fool") 25-50 50
REGAL (3313 "Wedding Bells") 5-10 50

Singles: 7-inch

ARGO 10-20 56
DECCA 8-15 53-55
JAMIE 8-15 60
KAY-RON 10-15 56
RCA 10-20 51-52
REGAL (468 "Once There Lived a Fool") 100-200 50
(Differs from 78 rpm number series.)

EPs: 7-inch

CAMDEN (270 "Love and Sin") 35-50 55
CAMDEN (282 "Savannah Churchill Sings") 35-50 55
Also see CARTER, Benny, & Orchestra
Also see FOUR TUNES

CI CI — R&B '85

Singles: 7-inch

CREATIVE FUNK 3-4 85

CINDERELLA — P&R/LP '86

Singles: 12-inch

MERCURY 4-8 88
(Promotional only.)

Singles: 7-inch

MERCURY 3-4 86-90

Picture Sleeves

MERCURY 3-4 86-89

LPs: 10/12-inch

MERCURY 5-10 86-90
Members: Tom Keifer; Fred Coury; Eric Brittingham; Jeff LaBar.

CINDY & ROY — R&B '79

Singles: 12-inch

CASABLANCA 4-8 79

Singles: 7-inch

CASABLANCA 3-4 79

LPs: 10/12-inch

CASABLANCA 5-10 79
Member: Cynthia Biggs.

CINEMA — D&D '84

Singles: 12-inch

PROFILE 4-6 84

CIRCUS P&R '73

Singles: 7-inch

METROMEDIA....3-6 72-73

LPs: 10/12-inch

HEMISPHERE....10-15 74
METROMEDIA....15-25 73

Members: Tom Dobeck; Frank Salle; Craig Balzer; Phil Alexander; Mick Sabol; Bruce Balzer.

Also see STANLEY, Michael, Band

CIRCUT D&D '84

Singles: 12-inch

4TH & BROADWAY....4-6 84-85

CISSEL, Chuck R&B '79

Singles: 7-inch

ARISTA....3-5 79-80

LPs: 10/12-inch

ARISTA....5-10 80

CISSEL, Chuck, & Marva King R&B '82

Singles: 7-inch

ARISTA....3-4 82

Also see CISSEL, Chuck

CISYK, Kacey P&R '77

("Original Cast of You Light Up My Life")

Singles: 7-inch

ABC....3-5 78
ARISTA....3-5 78

CITISPEAK R&B/D&D/ '84

Singles: 7-inch

STREETWISE....3-4 84

CITY BOY LP '76

Singles: 7-inch

AIRBOY....3-5 77
ATLANTIC....3-4 79-81
MERCURY....3-5 76-78

Picture Sleeves

MERCURY....3-5 78

LPs: 10/12-inch

ATLANTIC....5-10 80
MERCURY....8-10 76-78

Members: Steve Broughton; Lol Mason; Mike Slamer; Max Thomas; Roy Ward; Chris Dunn; Roger Kent.

CLANCY BROTHERS

(With Lou Killen; with Robbie O'Connell)

LPs: 10/12-inch

AUDIO FIDELITY....8-12 71-73
COLUMBIA....8-15 70
VANGUARD....5-12 74-83

CLANCY BROTHERS & TOMMY MAKEM LP '63

Singles: 7-inch

COLUMBIA....4-6 62-69

LPs: 10/12-inch

COLUMBIA....10-20 62-69
GWP....10-15
HARMONY....6-10 71-72
SHANACHIE....5-10
TRADITION....10-15 67-69

Also see CLANCY BROTHERS

CLANDESTINE D&D '84

Singles: 12-inch

SLEEPING BAG....4-6 84

CLANNAD LP '86

LPs: 10/12-inch

RCA....5-10 84-88

CLANTON, Ike P&R '60

Singles: 7-inch

ACE....5-10 59-60
MERCURY....5-10 62-63

Also see DEL-VIKINGS / Ike Clanton
Also see EDDY, Duane

CLANTON, Jimmy P&R/R&B '58

(With His Rockets; Jimmie Clanton)

Singles: 78 rpm

ACE....25-50 57

Singles: 7-inch

ABC....3-4 73
ACE (Except 567)....8-15 57-63
ACE (567 "My Own True Love")....10-15 59
(Monaural.)
ACE (567 "My Own True Love")....25-50 59
(Stereo.)
COLLECTABLES....3-4 81
ERIC....3-4 73
IMPERIAL....4-8 67-68
LAURIE....4-8 69
MALA....4-8 65
OLDIES 45....3-5
PHILIPS....4-8 63-64
SPIRAL....3-5 71
STARCREST....3-5 76
STARFIRE (Except picture discs)....3-5 78
STARFIRE ("I Wanna Go Home")....10-15 81
(Picture disc. Selection number not known.)
VIN....4-8 62

Promotional Singles

ACE (664 "Venus in Blue Jeans")....15-25 62
ACE (51860 "The Slave")....10-20 60
(Promotional, bonus disc with the *Jimmy's Happy/Jimmy's Blue* LP.)
U.A. ("Teenage Millionaire")....10-20 62
(Cardboard 6-inch flexi-disc.)

Picture Sleeves

ACE (Except 51860)....8-15 59-63
ACE (51860 "The Slave")....15-25 60
(Promotional only, mail-order bonus offer to buyers of the *Jimmy's Happy/Jimmy's Blue* LP. All copies of this sleeve were autographed by Clanton.)
PHILIPS....5-10 64
STARCREST....4-6 76

EPs: 7-inch

ACE ("Jimmy's Happy/Jimmy's Blue")....25-50 60
(Colored vinyl. Exact title and selection number not known.)
ACE (101 "Just a Dream")....20-40 59
ACE (102 "Thinking of You")....20-40 59
ACE (103 "I'm Always Chasing Rainbows")....20-30 59
ACE (642 "Teenage Millionaire")....15-25 61

LPs: 10/12-inch

ACE (100 "Jimmy's Happy/Jimmy's Blue")....50-75 60
(Black vinyl.)
ACE (100 "Jimmy's Happy/Jimmy's Blue")....75-125 60
(Colored vinyl.)
ACE (1001 "Just a Dream")....50-75 59
ACE (1007 "Jimmy's Happy")....40-50 60
ACE (1008 "Jimmy's Blue")....40-50 60
ACE (1011 "My Best to You")....50-75 61
ACE (1014 "Teenage Millionaire")....50-75 61
ACE (1026 "Venus in Blue Jeans")....40-60 61
MONTAGNE....10-15 81
PHILIPS....15-25 64

Also see DALE, Jimmy

CLANTON, Jimmy / Frankie Ford / Jerry Lee Lewis / Patsy Cline

EPs: 7-inch

MEMORY LANE....3-5 92
(Promotional issue only.)

Also see CLINE, Patsy
Also see FORD, Frankie
Also see LEWIS, Jerry Lee

CLANTON, Jimmy / Bristow Hopper

LPs: 10/12-inch

DESIGN....15-20

CLANTON, Jimmy, & Mary Ann Mobley

Singles: 7-inch

ACE....5-10 61

Picture Sleeves

ACE....10-15 61

Also see CLANTON, Jimmy

CLAPTON, Eric P&R/LP '70

Singles: 12-inch

W.B. (2248 "Forever Man")....5-10 85
(Promotional issue only.)
W.B. (2683 "Miss You")....5-10 85
(Promotional issue only.)

Singles: 7-inch

ATCO....4-6 70-71
DUCK....3-4 83-86
POLYDOR....3-5 72-73
RSO....3-5 74-82
W.B.....3-4 86

Picture Sleeves

DUCK....3-4 85-89
POLYDOR....3-6
RSO....3-5 80-81
W.B.....3-4 86

LPs: 10/12-inch

ATCO (329 "Eric Clapton")....20-30 70
ATCO (803 "History of Eric Clapton")....20-30 72
DUCK....5-10 83-89
MFSL (030 "Slowhand")....75-100 79
MFSL (183 "Bluesbreakers")....25-35 87
MFSL (220 "Eric Clapton")....20-25 94
NAUTILUS (32 "Just One Night")....75-100 80
(Half-speed mastered.)
POLYDOR (Except 835261)....8-15 72-73
POLYDOR (835261 "Crossroads")....30-40 88
(Boxed six-disc set.)
RSO (Except 035, 1009 & 4801)....8-20 73-82
RSO (035 "Slowhand")....20-25 77
(Colored vinyl. Promotional issue only.)
RSO (1009 "Limited Backless)....40-50 78
(Colored vinyl. Promotional issue only.)
RSO (4801 "461 Ocean Blvd.")....8-12 74
(With *Give Me Strength*.)
RSO (4801 "461 Ocean Blvd.")....5-10 74
(*Give Me Strength* is replaced with *Better Make It Through the Day*.)

Also see BLIND FAITH
Also see COOLIDGE, Rita
Also see CREAM
Also see CURTIS, Sonny
Also see DELANEY & BONNIE
Also see DEREK & DOMINOES
Also see GUY, Buddy, with Dr. John & Eric Clapton / Buddy Guy & J. Geils Band
Also see HARRISON, George
Also see LEVY, Marcy
Also see LOMAX, Jackie
Also see MAYALL, John
Also see RUSSELL, Leon
Also see SPANN, Otis
Also see STARR, Ringo
Also see TOWNSHEND, Pete, & Ronnie Lane
Also see WATERS, Roger
Also see YARDBIRDS

CLAPTON, Eric, Jeff Beck & Jimmy Page

LPs: 10/12-inch

RCA (4624 "Guitar Boogie")....10-15 71

Also see BECK, Jeff
Also see PAGE, Jimmy

CLAPTON, Eric, & Tina Turner

Singles: 7-inch

DUCK....3-4 87

Picture Sleeves

DUCK....3-4 87

Also see CLAPTON, Eric
Also see TURNER, Tina

CLARK, Chris R&B '66

Singles: 7-inch

MOTOWN....10-15 67-68
V.I.P. (25031 "Do Right Baby Do Right")....10-15 65
V.I.P. (25038 "Love's Gone Mad")....50-60 66
(Title incorrect on label.)
V.I.P. (25038 "Love's Gone Bad")....10-20 66
(Title corrected.)
V.I.P. (25041 " I Love You")....10-15 67

LPs: 10/12-inch

MOTOWN (664 "Soul Sounds")........40-60 67
WEED (801 "CC Rides Again")........50-75

CLARK, Claudine P&R/R&B '62

(With the Spinners)

Singles: 7-inch

CHANCELLOR..........5-10 62-63
COLLECTABLES..........3-4 81
ERIC..........3-4 73
HERALD (521 "Teenage Blues")........20-30 58
JAMIE..........4-8 64
TCF..........4-8 64

LPs: 10/12-inch

CHANCELLOR (5029 "Party Lights")..........40-60 62

CLARK, Dave, Five P&R/LP '64

(With Friends)

Singles: 7-inch

CONGRESS (212 "I Knew It All the Time")..........10-15 64
EPIC (2000 series)..........4-6 72
EPIC (9656 thru 10894)..........5-15 64-72
EPIC MEMORY LANE..........3-5
HOLLYWOOD..........3-4 93
JUBILEE (5476 "Chaquita")..........10-20 64
LAURIE (3188 "I Walk the Line")..........25-35 63
RUST (5078 "I Walk the Line")..........20-30 64

Promotional Singles

EPIC (9656 thru 9833)..........10-20 64-65
EPIC (9863 "Over & Over")..........10-20 65
(Black vinyl.)
EPIC (9863 "Over & Over")..........25-35 65
(Colored vinyl.)
EPIC (9882 thru 10894)..........10-20 65-72

Picture Sleeves

CONGRESS (212 "I Knew It All the Time")..........15-25 64
EPIC (2000 series)..........5-8 72
EPIC (9656 thru 10265)..........10-20 64-67
EPIC (10375 thru 10684)..........15-25 68-72
HOLLYWOOD (65909 "Over and Over")..........4-6 93
HOLLYWOOD (65912 "Do You Love Me")..........4-6 93

EPs: 7-inch

COLUMBIA/AURAVISION ("Catch Us If You Can")..........20-40 65
(Promotional issue made for Ponds. Single-sided, square, cardboard picture disc.)
EPIC..........15-25 66
(Juke box issues only.)

LPs: 10/12-inch

EPIC (24093 "Glad All Over")..........75-125 64
(Instruments are not pictured on cover.)
EPIC (24093 "Glad All Over")..........20-30 64
(Instruments are pictured on cover.)
EPIC (24104 "The Dave Clark Five Return")..........20-30 64
EPIC (24117 "American Tour")..........20-30 64
EPIC (24128 "Coast to Coast")..........20-30 64
EPIC (24139 "A Weekend in London")..........20-30 65
EPIC (24162 "Having a Wild Weekend")..........20-30 65
EPIC (24178 "I Like It Like That")..........20-30 65
EPIC (24185 "Greatest Hits")..........20-30 66
EPIC (24198 "Try Too Hard")..........20-30 66
EPIC (24212 "Satisfied with You")..........20-30 66
EPIC (24221 "More Greatest Hits")..........20-30 66
EPIC (24236 "5 by 5")..........20-30 67
EPIC (24312 "You Got What It Takes")..........20-30 67
EPIC (24354 "Everybody Knows")..........20-30 68
EPIC (26000 series)..........15-25 64-68
(Reprocessed stereo issues.)
EPIC (30434 "Dave Clark Five")..........35-50 71
EPIC (33459 "Glad All Over Again")..........20-25 75

Promotional LPs

EPIC (77238 "The Dave Clark Interviews")..........40-45 65
I-N-S RADIO NEWS (1006 "It's Here Luv")..........75-100 64

Members: Dave Clark; Mike Smith; Lenny Davidson; Denny Payton; Rick Huxley.

CLARK, Dave, Five / Rick Astor & Switchers

LPs: 10/12-inch

CORTLEIGH (1073 "Dave Clark Five")..........15-25 66
(Has only two Dave Clark Five tracks.)

CLARK, Dave, Five / Lulu

Singles: 7-inch

EPIC (10260/65 "Everybody Knows"/"Best of Both Worlds")..........10-20 67
(Promotional issue only.)
Also see LULU

CLARK, Dave, Five / New Christy Minstrels / Bobby Vinton / Jerry Vale

EPs: 7-inch

COLUMBIA SPECIAL PRODUCTS (223 "Limited Edition")..........10-15 65
Also see NEW CHRISTY MINSTRELS
Also see VALE, Jerry
Also see VINTON, Bobby

CLARK, Dave, Five / Playbacks

LPs: 10/12-inch

CROWN (400 "Playbacks")..........20-25 64
(Stereo.)
CROWN (5400 "Playbacks")..........20-25 64
(Monaural.)
CROWN (473 "Chaquita – In Your Heart")..........20-25 65
(Stereo.)
CROWN (5473 "Chaquita – In Your Heart")..........20-25 65
(Monaural.)
CUSTOM (1098 "It's Happening")..........15-20 65
(Each Crown and Custom LP has only two Dave Clark Five tracks.)
Also see CLARK, Dave, Five

CLARK, Dee P&R/R&B '58

(With the Riley Hampton Orchestra)

Singles: 78 rpm

ABNER (1019 "Nobody But You")..........50-75 59
ABNER (1029 "Hey Little Girl")..........50-100 59
FALCON (1002 "Gloria")..........15-25 57

Singles: 7-inch

ABC..........3-4 73
ABNER (Monaural)..........10-20 58-60
ABNER (Stereo)..........25-50 59-60
CHELSEA..........3-5 75
COLLECTABLES..........3-4 83
ERIC..........3-4 73
COLUMBIA..........5-10 67
CONSTELLATION..........8-15 63-65
FALCON (1002 "Gloria")..........15-25 57
LIBERTY..........8-15 70
MCA..........3-4 84
ROCKY..........3-5 73
VEE JAY (Monaural)..........5-10 60-63
VEE JAY (Stereo)..........20-30 60-63
U.A...........3-5 71
WAND..........4-8 68
W.B...........3-5 73

Picture Sleeves

ABNER (1029 "Hey Little Girl")..........15-25 59

EPs: 7-inch

ABNER (900 "Dee Clark")..........40-60 61
VEE JAY (900 "Dee Clark")..........25-50 61

LPs: 10/12-inch

ABNER (LP-2000 "Dee Clark")..........40-60 59
(Monaural.)
ABNER (SR-2000 "Dee Clark")..........50-75 59
(Stereo.)
ABNER (LP-2002 "How About That")..........40-60 59
(Monaural.)
ABNER (SR-2002 "How About That")..........50-75 59
(Stereo.)
SOLID SMOKE..........5-10 84
SUNSET (5217 "Wondering")..........10-15 68
VEE JAY (1019 "You're Looking Good")..........20-30 60
VEE JAY (1028 "Dee Clark")..........20-30 61
VEE JAY (1037 "Hold On, It's Dee Clark")..........20-30 61
VEE JAY (1047 "The Best of Dee Clark")..........20-30 64
Also see DELLS
Also see UPCHURCH, Phil

CLARK, Gene LP '74

(With the Gosdin Brothers)

Singles: 7-inch

ASYLUM..........3-5 74
COLUMBIA (43000 series)..........5-8 66
RSO..........3-4 77

LPs: 10/12-inch

A&M..........10-15 71
ASYLUM..........8-10 74
COLUMBIA (2618 "Gene Clark")..........20-30 67
(Monaural.)
COLUMBIA (9418 "Gene Clark")..........25-35 67
(Stereo.)
COLUMBIA (31123 "Early L.A. Sessions")..........10-15 72
RSO..........5-10 77
TAKOMA..........5-10 84
Also see BYRDS
Also see DILLARD & CLARK
Also see NEW CHRISTY MINSTRELS

CLARK, Petula P&R '64

(Pet Clark)

Singles: 78 rpm

CORAL..........5-15 53-54
KING..........5-15 54
MGM..........5-15 55

Singles: 7-inch

CORAL..........10-20 53-54
DUNHILL..........3-5 74
ERIC..........3-4 83
IMPERIAL..........5-10 59-60
JANUS..........3-5 76
KING..........10-20 54
LAURIE..........4-8 62-63
LONDON..........4-8 62
MGM (12000 series)..........10-20 55
MGM (14000 series, except 14392)..........3-6 72-74
MGM (14392 "Little Bit of Lovin' ")..........15-25
ROWE/AMI..........5-10 66
("Play Me" Sales Stimulator promotional issue.)
SCOTTI BROTHERS..........3-4 82
W.B...........3-8 64-69
WARWICK..........5-10 61

EPs: 7-inch

W.B...........5-10 65-66
(Juke box issues only.)

LPs: 10/12-inch

GNP..........5-8 73
IMPERIAL (9079 "Pet Clark")..........20-40 59
(Monaural.)
IMPERIAL (9281 "Uptown")..........15-25 65
IMPERIAL (12027 "Pet Clark")..........20-30 65
(Stereo.)
LAURIE (2032 "In Love")..........20-25 65
(Monaural.)
LAURIE (S-2032 "In Love")..........25-35 65
(Stereo.)
LAURIE (2043 "Petula Clark Sings for Everybody")..........15-20 65
(Monaural.)
LAURIE (2043 "Petula Clark Sings for Everybody")..........20-25 65
(Stereo.)
MGM..........8-12 72
PREMIER..........15-25 64
SUNSET..........10-20 66
W.B...........10-20 65-71
Also see FELICIANO, Jose / Petula Clark

CLARK, Roy C&W/P&R '63

Singles: 78 rpm

4 STAR..........15-25 54

Singles: 7-inch

ABC..........3-5 74-79
ABC/DOT..........3-5 75-77
CAPITOL..........4-8 61-66

CHURCHILL....3-4 82-84
DOT....3-6 68-74
4 STAR (1659 "Mysteries of Life")....25-50 54
HALLMARK....3-4 89
MCA....3-4 79-84
SILVER DOLLAR....3-4 86
SONGBIRD....3-4 81
TOWER....3-6 67

LPs: 10/12-inch

ABC....5-10 77-79
ABC/DOT....6-10 74-77
ABC SPECIAL PRODUCTS (1002 "Roy Clark")....10-15 78
(Promotional issue, made for Pringles.)
CAPITOL (300 series)....10-12 69
CAPITOL (1700 thru 2500 series)....10-25 62-66
(With "T" or "ST" prefix.)
CAPITOL (2400 series)....5-10 81
(With "SM" prefix.)
CAPITOL (11000 series)....8-12 74-75
CAPITOL (12000 thru 16000 series)....5-10 80-81
CHURCHILL....5-10 82
DOT....8-12 68-74
GUEST STAR....8-12 60s
MCA....5-8 79-84
PICKWICK....5-10 70s
PICKWICK/HILLTOP....8-15 66
SONGBIRD....5-10 81
TOWER....10-15 67-68
WORD....5-10 75
Also see CASH, Johnny / Roy Clark / Linda Ronstadt

CLARK, Sanford — *P&R/R&B/C&W '56*

Singles: 78 rpm

DOT....15-25 56
MCI (1003 "The Fool")....25-50 55

Singles: 7-inch

ABC....3-5 74
DOT (15000 series)....20-30 56
(Maroon label.)
DOT (15000 series, except 15738)....10-20 56-58
(Black label.)
DOT (15738 "Modern Romance")....75-100 58
JAMIE....10-15 58-60
LHI (9 "Footprints in Her Yard")....4-8 68
LHI (9 "Farm Labor Camp #9")....4-8 69
LHI (1203 "Son of Hickory Holler's Tramp")....4-8 68
LHI (12003 "Return of the Fool")....8-15 68
MCI (1003 "The Fool")....50-75 55
RAMCO....4-8 66
REO (8143 "9 Lb. Hammer")....20-30 57
(Canadian.)
TREY....8-12 61
W.B....6-12 64-65
Also see CASEY, Al
Also see REYNOLDS, Jody

CLARK, Sanford, & Duane Eddy

Singles: 7-inch

JAMIE (1107 "Sing 'Em Some Blues")....15-25 58
Also see CLARK, Sanford
Also see EDDY, Duane

CLARK, Steve — *C&W '84*

Singles: 7-inch

MERCURY....3-4 84

CLARK SISTERS — *R&B/D&D '83*

Singles: 12-inch

ELEKTRA....4-6 83

Singles: 7-inch

ELEKTRA....3-4 83

CLARKE, Allan — *P&R '78*

Singles: 7-inch

ASYLUM....3-5 76
ATLANTIC....3-5 78
ELEKTRA....3-4 80
EPIC....3-5 72

LPs: 10/12-inch

ASYLUM....8-10 76
ATLANTIC....5-10 78
ELEKTRA....5-10 80
EPIC....10-15 72
Also see HOLLIES
Also see PARSONS, Alan, Project

CLARKE, Stanley — *LP '75*
(Stan Clarke)

Singles: 12-inch

EPIC....4-6 83-85
NEMPEROR....4-8 79

Singles: 7-inch

EPIC....3-4 80-85
NEMPEROR....3-5 75-79

LPs: 10/12-inch

EPIC....5-10 80-85
NEMPEROR....8-12 74-79
POLYDOR....10-12 73
Also see RETURN to FOREVER

CLARKE, Stanley, & George Duke — *P&R/R&B '81*

Singles: 12-inch

EPIC....4-6 83

Singles: 7-inch

EPIC....3-4 81-84

LPs: 10/12-inch

EPIC....5-10 81-83
Also see CLARKE, Stanley
Also see DUKE, George

CLARKE, Tony — *P&R/R&B '64*

Singles: 7-inch

CHESS....6-12 64-65
CHICKORY....4-6 70
ERIC....3-5 78
M-S (206 "A Wrong Man")....50-100 68

CLASH — *LP '79*

Singles: 12-inch

EPIC (617 "Gates of the West")....15-20 79
(Promotional issue only.)
EPIC (723 "Clampdown")....15-20 79
(Promotional issue only.)
EPIC (905 "Magnificent Seven")....15-20 80
(Promotional issue only.)
EPIC (2036 "Call Up")....8-12 81
(Blue label. Promotional issue only.)
EPIC (2036 "Call Up")....8-12 81
(Roulette wheel label. Promotional issue only.)
EPIC (2230 "This Is England")....8-12 85
(Promotional issue only.)
EPIC (2277 "Fingerpoppin'")....8-12 85
(Blue label. Promotional issue only.)
EPIC (2662 "This Is Radio Clash")....15-20 81
(Promotional issue only.)
EPIC (3144 "Rock the Casbah")....8-12 82
EPIC (6899 "Radio Clash")....5-10 87
EPIC (7829 "Rock the Casbah")....5-10 89
(Mixed masters issue.)

Singles: 7-inch

EPIC (1178 "Gates of the West")....4-6 79
(Promotional issue only. Issued with promo edition of *The Clash*.)
EPIC (3006 "Should I Stay")....8-10 82
(Promotional issue only.)
EPIC (3088 "London Calling")....5-8 80
(Hall of Fame series.)
EPIC (3245 "Rock the Casbah")....8-10 82
(Promotional issue only.)
EPIC (3547 "Should I Stay")....3-5 82
EPIC (3571 "Should I Stay")....15-20 82
(Single-sided disc. Promotional issue only.)
EPIC (5749 "Train in Vain")....15-20 79
(10-inch single. Promotional issue only.)
EPIC (5788 "Clampdown")....15-20 79
(10-inch single. Promotional issue only.)
EPIC (8470 "Should I Stay")....5-8 82
(Hall of Fame series.)
EPIC (20000 series)....3-5 82
EPIC (30000 series)....3-5 82
EPIC (50000 series, except 50738, 50851 & 51013)....3-5 79-81
EPIC (50738 "White Man in Hammersmith Palais")....5-10 79
EPIC (50851 "Train in Vain")....10-15 79
(Promotional issue only.)
EPIC (51013 "Hitsville UK")....10-15 80
(Promotional issue only.)

Picture Sleeves

EPIC (3061 "Should I Stay")....10-15 82
(Shown as "Special Limited Edition.")
EPIC (3547 "Should I Stay")....5-10 82
(Lists B-side, *Cool Confusion*.)
EPIC (3547 "Should I Stay")....10-15 82
(No B-side shown. Promotional issue only.)

LPs: 10/12-inch

EPIC (913 "Sandinista Now")....15-20 80
(Promotional issue only.)
EPIC (952 "If Music Could Talk")....15-20 81
(Promotional issue only.)
EPIC (1574 "World According to Clash")....30-35 82
(Black cover, with printing.)
EPIC (1574 "World According to Clash")....25-30 82
(Black cover, with no printing.)
EPIC (1592 "Combat Rock")....40-50 82
(Logo picture disc, with "Face the Future" sticker. Promotional issue only.)
EPIC (35543 "Give 'Em Enough Rope")....5-10 78
(Blue label.)
EPIC (35543 "Give 'Em Enough Rope")....10-15 78
(White label. Promotional issue only. With insert.)
EPIC (36060 "The Clash")....5-10 79
EPIC (36060 "The Clash")....15-20 79
(White label. Promotional issue only. With lyric insert and bonus single, #1178 *Gates of the West*)
EPIC (36328 "London Calling")....10-15 79
EPIC (36328 "London Calling")....15-20 79
(White label. Promotional issue only. With lyric sleeve.)
EPIC (37037 "Sandinista")....15-20 80
(Promotional issue only. With *Armagideon Times #3*)
EPIC (37037 "Sandinista")....10-15 80
(With *Armagideon Times #3*.)
EPIC (37689 "Combat Rock")....8-10 82
(Black label.)
EPIC (37689 "Combat Rock")....5-8 82
(Blue label.)
EPIC (37689 "Combat Rock")....10-15 82
(Promotional issue only. With lyric sleeve.)
EPIC (37689 "Combat Rock")....40-50 82
(Limited edition, camouflage vinyl. Promotional issue only. With "Face the Future" sticker.)
EPIC (38540 "Black Market Clash")....5-10 80
EPIC (40017 "Cut the Crap")....5-10 85
EPIC (40017 "Cut the Crap")....10-15 85
(Promotional issue only.)
EPIC (44035 "Story of the Clash")....10-15 88
EPIC (53191 "Super Black Market Clash")....30-40 93
(Limited edition, three 10-inch LPs.)
EPIC/NU-DISC (36846 "Black Market Clash")....10-15 80
(10-inch LP.)
Members: Joe Strummer; Mick Jones; Nick Sheppard; Pete Howard; Paul Simonon; Topper Headon; Terry Chimes; Vince White.
Also see BIG AUDIO DYNAMITE

CLASS ACTION — *D&D '83*

Singles: 12-inch

SLEEPING BAG....4-6 83

CLASSIC IV: see CLASSICS IV

CLASSIC SULLIVANS — *R&B '73*

Singles: 7-inch

KWANZA....4-6 73
MASTER KEY (03 "Shame, Shame, Shame")....15-25
Members: Eddie Sullivan; Lorraine; Barbara Sullivan.

CLASSICS

Singles: 7-inch

STARR (508 "Close Your Eyes")....100-200 60
(Reissued on Alcar 207, credited to Lou Christie & Classics.)

Members: Lou Christie; Kay Chick; Shirley Herbert; Ken Krease.
Also see CHRISTIE, Lou
Also see LUGEE & LIONS

CLASSICS R&B '61

Singles: 7-inch

BED-STUY (222 "Again") ... 15-25
COLLECTABLES (1275 "P.S. I Love You") ... 3-4 83
(Colored vinyl.)
DART (1015 "Cinderella") ... 20-30 60
DART (1024 "Life Is But a Dream") ... 100-200 61
DART (1032 "Angel Angela") ... 30-50 61
ERIC ... 3-4 82
MERCURY (71829 "Life Is But a Dream Sweetheart") ... 20-30 61
MUSICNOTE (118 "P.S. I Love You") ... 20-30 63
(White label.)
MUSICNOTE (118 "P.S. I Love You") ... 10-20 63
(Blue label.)
MUSICNOTE (1116 "Till Then") ... 10-20 63
(Black vinyl.)
MUSICNOTE (1116 "Till Then") ... 100-200 63
(Colored vinyl.)
PICCOLO (500 "I Apologize") ... 15-25 65
STORK (2 "You'll Never Know") ... 15-25 64
STREAMLINE (1028 "Life's But a Dream") ... 15-25 61
TRIP ... 3-5

LPs: 10/12-inch

CRYSTAL BALL ... 8-10 84
Members: Emil Stuccio; Tony Victor; John Gamble; Jamie Troy.

CLASSICS IV P&R '67
(Dennis Yost & Classics IV; Classics)

Singles: 7-inch

AMERICAN PIE ... 3-4 90s
CAPITOL ... 10-15 66-67
GUSTO ... 3-4
IMPERIAL (Except 66328) ... 4-8 67-70
IMPERIAL (66328 "Stormy"/"Ladies Man") ... 10-20 68
IMPERIAL (66328 "Stormy"/"24 Hours of Loneliness") ... 4-8 68
(Note different flip.)
LIBERTY (Except SP-36) ... 3-5 70
LIBERTY (SP-36 "Song") ... 15-25 70
(Radio spots. Promotional issue only.)
MGM ... 3-5 75
MGM/SOUTH ... 3-5 72-73
PLAYBACK ... 3-4 90
SILVER SPOTLIGHT ... 3-5
U.A. ... 3-5 71

LPs: 10/12-inch

IMPERIAL ... 12-20 68-69
KOALA (14258 "Greatest Hits of the Classic IV") ... 8-10 79
(Mistakenly credits group as the "Classic IV.")
LIBERTY (10000 series) ... 5-10 81-85
LIBERTY (11000 series) ... 10-12 70
MGM/SOUNDS of the SOUTH ... 8-10 73
SUNSET ... 10-12 70
U.A. ... 8-10 75
Members: Dennis Yost; James Cobb; Dean Daughtry; Wally Eaton; Auburn Burrell; Kim Venable; Joe Wilson; Mike Sharpe.
Also see ATLANTA RHYTHM SECTION
Also see CANDYMEN
Also see YOST, Dennis

CLASSICS IV / Mac Davis

LPs: 10/12-inch

VINTAGE ... 10-15
Also see CLASSICS IV
Also see DAVIS, Mac

CLAY, Andrew Dice LP '89

LPs: 10/12-inch

DEF AMERICAN ... 5-8 89-91

CLAY, Cassius LP '63
(Cassius Marcellus Clay Jr; Muhammed Ali)

Singles: 7-inch

COLUMBIA (43007 "Stand by Me") .. 10-20 64
COLUMBIA (75717 "Will the Real Sonny Liston Please Fall Down") ... 25-40 64
(Promotional issue only.)

Picture Sleeves

COLUMBIA (43007 "Stand by Me") .. 25-35 64

LPs: 10/12-inch

COLUMBIA (2093 "I Am the Greatest") ... 30-40 63
(Monaural.)
COLUMBIA (8893 "I Am the Greatest") ... 35-45 63
(Stereo.)
Also see ALI, Muhammad, & Frank Sinatra

CLAY, Judy R&B '70

Singles: 7-inch

ATLANTIC ... 3-5 69-70
EMBER ... 5-10 61-62
LA VETTE (1004 "Let It Be Me") ... 5-10
SCEPTER ... 4-8 64-66
STAX ... 4-6 68-69
Also see VERA, Billy, & Judy Clay

CLAY, Judy, & William Bell P&R/R&B '68

Singles: 7-inch

STAX ... 4-6 68
Also see BELL, William
Also see CLAY, Judy

CLAY, Otis R&B '67

Singles: 12-inch

PAULA ... 4-8 85

Singles: 7-inch

COTILLION ... 3-6 68-71
DAKAR ... 3-6 69
ECHO (2002 "Check It Out") ... 8-12
ELKA ... 4-6 75
GLADES (1736 "All I Need Is You") ... 5-10
HI ... 3-6 72-73
KAYVETTE ... 3-5 77
ONE-DERFUL ... 4-8 65-67

LPs: 10/12-inch

HI ... 8-12 73-77

CLAY, Tom P&R/R&B/LP '71
(With the Blackberries; with Raybor Voices)

Singles: 7-inch

BIG TOP (3055 "That's All") ... 10-15 60
CHANT (103 "Marry Me") ... 50-100 59
MOTOWN ... 3-4 81
MOWEST ... 3-5 71
OFFICIAL IBBB INTERVIEW (97436 "Remember, We Don't Like Them, We Love Them") ... 50-75 64
(Tom Clay interviews the Beatles. Promotional issue only.)
OFFICIAL IBBB INTERVIEW (45629 "We Don't Like Them, We Love Them") ... 125-150 65
(Tom Clay interviews the Beatles. Promotional issue only.)

Picture Sleeves

OFFICIAL IBBB INTERVIEW (97436 "Remember, We Don't Like Them, We Love Them") ... 100-150 64

LPs: 10/12-inch

MOWEST ... 10-15 71
Also see BEATLES

CLAYDERMAN, Richard LP '84

LPs: 10/12-inch

COLUMBIA ... 5-8 84

CLAYTON, BOB
(Gene Autry)

Singles: 78 rpm

BROADWAY (4004 "Dallas County Jail Blues") ... 25-75
BROADWAY (4062 "In the Jailhouse Now, No. 2") ... 25-75
BROADWAY (4067 "Jailhouse Blues") ... 25-75
BROADWAY (4073 "Silver Haired Daddy of Mine") ... 25-75
BROADWAY (4093 "Crimes I Didn't Do") ... 25-75
BROADWAY (4094 "Back to Old Smokey Mountain") ... 25-75
BROADWAY (4095 "My Carolina Mountain Home") ... 25-75
Also see AUTRY, Gene
Also see CLAYTON & BREEN

CLAYTON, Merry P&R '70

Singles: 7-inch

CAPITOL ... 4-8 63-65
MCA ... 3-4 80-88
ODE '70 ... 3-5 70-76

LPs: 10/12-inch

MCA ... 5-10 80
ODE (34000 series) ... 5-10 77
ODE (77000 series) ... 10-12 71-75
Also see BEACH BOYS
Also see FIVE SATINS / Merry Clayton
Also see SCOTT, Tom
Also see WYCOFF, Michael

CLAYTON, Willie R&B '84

Singles: 7-inch

COMPLEAT ... 3-4 85

CLAYTON & BREEN

Singles: 78 rpm

BROADWAY (4095 "Alone with My Sorrows") ... 25-75
Member: Gene Autry.
Also see AUTRY, Gene

CLAYTON-THOMAS, David LP '69

Singles: 7-inch

ATCO (6347 "Hey Hey Hey") ... 8-12 65
COLUMBIA ... 3-6 71
DECCA ... 4-8 69
EPIC ... 3-4 83
ROMAN ("Boom Boom") ... 10-15 68
(Selection number not known. Canadian.)
ROMAN ("Brainwashed") ... 10-15 68
(Selection number not known. Canadian.)
ROULETTE ... 4-8 69
TOWER ... 5-10 66

LPs: 10/12-inch

ABC ... 5-10 78
COLUMBIA ... 10-15 72
DECCA (75146 "David Clayton-Thomas") ... 10-20 69
(Remixed rechanneled reissue of the Roman LP.)
RCA ... 8-12 73-74
ROMAN (101 "David Clayton-Thomas & the Shays") ... 50-100 67
(Canadian.)
Also see BLOOD, SWEAT & TEARS

CLEAN LIVING P&R '72

Singles: 7-inch

VANGUARD ... 3-5 72

LPs: 10/12-inch

VANGUARD ... 8-10 72-73

CLEAR LIGHT LP '67

Singles: 7-inch

ELEKTRA ... 5-10 67

LPs: 10/12-inch

ELEKTRA (4011 "Clear Light") ... 15-25 67
Members: Cliff DeYoung; Douglas Lubahn; Michael Ney; Ralph Schuckett; Bob Seal; Dallas Taylor.

CLEFS OF LAVENDER HILL P&R '66

Singles: 7-inch

DATE (1510 "Stop! Get a Ticket") ... 10-20 66
DATE (1530 "One More Time") ... 10-20 66
DATE (1533 "Play with Fire") ... 10-20 66
DATE (1567 "Gimme One Good Reason") ... 10-20 67
THAMES (100 "Stop! Get a Ticket") ... 25-35 66
Members: Travis Fairchild; Coventry; Bill Moss; Fred Moss.

CLEFTONES — P&R/R&B '56
(Herb Cox & Cleftones)

Singles: 78 rpm

GEE 20-30 56-57
ROULETTE 30-40 58

Singles: 7-inch

ABC 3-5 73
CLASSIC ARTISTS 3-5 90
GEE (1000 "You Baby, You") 50-75 56
GEE (1011 "Little Girl of Mine") 40-60 56
GEE (1016 "Can't We Be Sweethearts") 25-50 56
(Red and black label.)
GEE (1016 "Can't We Be Sweethearts") 15-25 60
(Gary label.)
GEE (1025 "String Around My Heart") 25-50 56
GEE (1031 "Why Do You Do Me Like You Do") 20-40 56
GEE (1038 "See You Next Year") 20-40 57
GEE (1041 "Hey Babe") 20-40 57
GEE (1048 "Lover Boy") 20-40 57
(Red and black label.)
GEE (1048 "Lover Boy") 15-25 60
(Gray label.)
GEE (1064 "Heart & Soul") 20-30 61
GEE (1067 "For Sentimental Reasons") 20-30 61
GEE (1074 "Earth Angel") 20-30 62
GEE (1077 "Again") 20-30 62
GEE (1079 "There She Goes") 20-30 62
GEE (1080 "How Deep Is the Ocean") 20-30 62
ROULETTE (4094 "She's So Fine") 15-25 58
ROULETTE (4161 "Mish-Mash Baby") 15-25 59
ROULETTE (4302 "She's Gone") 15-25 59
ROULETTE GOLDEN GOODIES 3-5 70s
WARE (6001 "He's Forgotten You") 10-20 64

LPs: 10/12-inch

EMUS 5-10 79
GEE (GLP-705 "Heart and Soul") 100-200 61
(Monaural.)
GEE (SGLP-705 "Heart and Soul") 150-250 61
(Stereo.)
GEE (GLP-707 "For Sentimental Reasons") 150-250 62
(Monaural.)
GEE (SGLP-707 "For Sentimental Reasons") 200-300 62
(Stereo.)

Members: Herbie Cox; Berman Patterson; Bill McClain; Charles James; Warren Corbin; Pat Span; Eugene Pearson.

Also see DRIFTERS
Also see HARPTONES / Cleftones

CLEGG, Johnny, & Savuka — LP '88

Singles: 7-inch

CAPITOL 3-4 88-89

LPs: 10/12-inch

CAPITOL 5-8 88-90

CLEMMONS, Angela — R&B '80

Singles: 12-inch

PORTRAIT 4-6 82

Singles: 7-inch

EPIC 3-4 80
PORTRAIT 3-4 82-87

LPs: 10/12-inch

PORTRAIT 5-10 82

CLEMONS, Clarence — LP '83
(With the Red Bank Rockers)

Singles: 7-inch

COLUMBIA 3-4 83-85

LPs: 10/12-inch

COLUMBIA 5-10 83-85

Also see FRANKLIN, Aretha
Also see SPRINGSTEEN, Bruce

CLEMONS, Clarence, & Jackson Browne — P&R '85

Singles: 7-inch

COLUMBIA 3-4 85

Also see BROWNE, Jackson

CLIFF, Jimmy — P&R '69

Singles: 12-inch

COLUMBIA 4-6 83-84

Singles: 7-inch

A&M 3-6 69-70
COLUMBIA 3-4 82-84
MANGO 3-5 73-75
MCA 3-5 81
REPRISE 3-5 73-77
VEEP 4-8 67-68

Picture Sleeves

A&M 3-6 69

LPs: 10/12-inch

A&M 10-20 70
COLUMBIA 5-10 82
ISLAND 8-10 74
MCA 5-10 80-81
MANGO 8-10 75
REPRISE 8-10 73-76
VEEP 15-20 69
W.B. 5-10 78

CLIFF, Jimmy, Elvis Costello & Attractions

Singles: 12-inch

COLUMBIA 5-10 86
(Promotional issue only.)

Singles: 7-inch

COLUMBIA 3-4 86

Picture Sleeves

COLUMBIA 3-4 86

Also see CLIFF, Jimmy
Also see COSTELLO, Elvis

CLIFFORD, Buzz — P&R/C&W/R&B '61

Singles: 7-inch

BOW ("14 Karet") 20-30 59
(Selection number not known.)
CAPITOL 4-8 67
COLUMBIA (41774 "Hello Mr. Moonlight") 10-15 60
COLUMBIA (41876 "Baby Sittin' Boogie") 30-50 60
(With "3" prefix. Compact 33 Single.)
COLUMBIA (41979 "Simply Because") 30-50 61
(With "3" prefix. Compact 33 Single.)
COLUMBIA (42019 "I'll Never Forget") 30-50 61
(With "3" prefix. Compact 33 Single.)
COLUMBIA (42290 "Forever") 30-50 62
(With "3" prefix. Compact 33 Single.)
COLUMBIA (41876 "Baby Sitter Boogie") 20-30 60
(Note slightly different title. With "4" prefix.)
COLUMBIA (41876 "Baby Sittin' Boogie") 5-10 61
(With "4" prefix.)
COLUMBIA (41979 "Simply Because") 15-25 61
(With "4" prefix.)
COLUMBIA (42019 "I'll Never Forget") 15-25 61
(With "4" prefix.)
COLUMBIA (42177 "Moving Day") 5-10 61
(With "4" prefix.)
COLUMBIA (42290 "Forever") 15-25 62
(With "4" prefix.)
DOT 4-6 69-70
ERIC 3-4 83
RCA 4-8 66
ROULETTE 5-10 62-63

Picture Sleeves

COLUMBIA (41774 "Hello Mr. Moonlight") 15-25 60
COLUMBIA (41876 "Baby Sittin' Boogie") 15-25 60
COLUMBIA (41979 "Simply Because") 15-25 61
COLUMBIA (42019 "I'll Never Forget") 15-25 61
COLUMBIA (42177 "Moving Day") 15-25 61
COLUMBIA (42290 "Forever") 15-25 62

LPs: 10/12-inch

COLUMBIA (1616 "Baby Sittin' Boogie") 50-75 61
(Monaural.)
COLUMBIA (8416 "Baby Sittin' Boogie") 50-100 61
(Monaural.)
DOT 15-20 69

CLIFFORD, Linda — R&B '74

Singles: 12-inch

CAPITOL 4-6 82
RSO 4-8 79
RED LABEL 4-6 85

Singles: 7-inch

CAPITOL 3-4 80-82
CURTOM 3-4 77-78
GEMIGO 3-5 75
PARAMOUNT 3-5 74
POLYDOR 3-5 73
RSO 3-4 79-80
RED LABEL 3-4 84-85

LPs: 10/12-inch

CAPITOL 5-10 80-82
CURTOM 8-10 77-80
RSO 5-10 79-80

Also see MAYFIELD, Curtis, & Linda Clifford

CLIFFORD, Mike — P&R '62

Singles: 7-inch

AIR 3-5 71
AMERICAN INT'L 3-5 70
CAMEO 4-8 65-66
COLUMBIA 4-8 61-62
LIBERTY 5-10 59
SIDEWALK 4-8 67-68
U.A. 4-8 62-65

Picture Sleeves

COLUMBIA 5-10 61

LPs: 10/12-inch

U.A. 15-25 65

CLIFFORD, Mike, & Patience & Prudence

Singles: 7-inch

LIBERTY 8-12 59

Also see CLIFFORD, Mike
Also see PATIENCE & PRUDENCE

CLIFTON, Johnny, & His String Band
(Bill Haley)

Singles: 78 rpm

CENTER (102 "Stand Up and Be Counted") 1000-1500 50

Also see HALEY, Bill

CLIMAX — P&R/LP '72
(Sonny Geraci & Climax)

Singles: 7-inch

ARISTA 3-4 81
BELL 3-5 71
CAROUSEL 3-5 70-71
FLASHBACK 3-4 73
PARAMOUNT 3-5 70
PATTI PLATTERS 4-8 67
ROCKY ROAD 3-5 72-73

LPs: 10/12-inch

ROCKY ROAD 12-15 72

Members: Sonny Geraci; John Bahler; Tom Bahler; Jon Jon Gultman; Walt Nims.

Also see LOVE GENERATION
Also see OUTSIDERS

CLIMAX BLUES BAND — LP '70

Singles: 7-inch

SIRE 3-5 71-79
W.B. 3-4 79-82

LPs: 10/12-inch

SIRE (Except 6000 series) 10-15 69-76
SIRE (6000 series) 8-10 77-79
VIRGIN 5-10 83
W.B. 5-10 79-81

Members: Climax Chicago Blues Band; Colin Cooper; John Cuffley; Peter Haycock; Derek Holt; Richard Jones; Arthur Wood.

CLIMIE FISHER *P&R/LP '88*

Singles: 7-inch

CAPITOL....3-4 88

Picture Sleeves

CAPITOL....3-4 88

LPs: 10/12-inch

CAPITOL....5-8 88

Members: Simon Clime; Rob Fisher.
Also see NAKED EYES

CLINE, Patsy *C&W/P&R '57*

Singles: 78 rpm

CORAL....20-30 55-56
DECCA (30221 "Walking After Midnight")....50-80 57

Singles: 7-inch

CORAL (61464 "Honky Tonk Merry Go Round")....25-50 55
CORAL (61523 "Turn the Cards Slowly")....25-50 55
CORAL (61583 "I Love You Honey")....25-50 56
(First issue.)
DECCA (25000 series)....4-8 65-69
DECCA (29963 thru 30846)....10-25 57-59
DECCA (30929 "Gotta Lot of Rhythm in My Soul")....10-20 59
DECCA (31000 series)....5-10 59-64
EVEREST (2000 series)....5-10 62-64
EVEREST (20005 "I Can't Forget")...10-15 62
4 STAR (11 "I Love You Honey")....20-30 56
4 STAR (1033 "Life's Railway to Heaven")....3-5 78
KAPP....4-8 65
MCA....3-5 73-80
STARDAY (7000 series)....4-8 65
STARDAY (8000 series)....3-5 71

Picture Sleeves

DECCA (Except 30221)....10-20 62-63
DECCA (30221 "Walkin After Midnight")....20-30 57

EPs: 7-inch

CORAL (81159 "Songs By Patsy Cline")....50-75 58
DECCA (Except 2542)....15-25 61-65
DECCA (2542 "Patsy Cline")....35-50 57
4 STAR ("Patsy Cline")....25-35 57
(Reissue of *Patsy Cline* [Decca 2542]. Issued with paper sleeve. Number not known. Promotional issue only.)
PATSY CLINE....25-35 57

LPs: 10/12-inch

ACCORD....5-10 81
ALBUM GLOBE....5-10
ALLEGIANCE....5-10 84
AUDIO FIDELITY (204 "Patsy Cline")....10-15 84
(Picture disc.)
AUDIO FIDELITY (205 "Crazy Dreams")....25-50 84
(Picture disc.)
BREAKAWAY....5-10
BULLDOG....5-10
COLUMBIA....12-15 69
(Columbia Musical Treasury issue.)
COUNTRY FIDELITY....5-10 82
DECCA (176 "Patsy Cline Story")....25-40 63
(Monaural. Includes booklet.)
DECCA (7-176 "Patsy Cline Story")..30-50 63
(Stereo. Includes booklet.)
DECCA (4202 "Showcase")....20-30 61
(Monaural.)
DECCA (7-4202 "Showcase")....25-35 61
(Stereo.)
DECCA (4282 "Sentimentally Yours")....15-25 62
(Monaural.)
DECCA (4282 "Sentimentally Yours")....20-30 61
(Stereo.)
DECCA (4508 "Portrait")....15-25 64
(Monaural.)
DECCA (7-4508 "Portrait")....20-30 64
(Stereo.)
DECCA (4586 "That's How a Heartache Begins")....30-50 64
(Monaural.)
DECCA (7-4586 "That's How a Heartache Begins")....40-60 64
(Stereo.)
DECCA (4854 "Greatest Hits")....10-15 67
(Monaural.)
DECCA (7-4854 "Greatest Hits")....10-15 67
(Stereo.)
DECCA (8611 "Patsy Cline")....30-50 57
EVEREST (300 series)....5-10 75
EVEREST (1200 series)....15-20 62-64
EVEREST (90000 series)....8-12
51 WEST....5-10 82
H.S.R.D.....8-10 84
LONGINES....8-12
MCA....5-10 80-89
METRO....10-20 65
MUSIC MASTERS....5-10
PICCADILLY....5-10 80
PICKWICK....5-12 70s
PICKWICK/HILLTOP....10-12 65-68
ROLLER SKATE....5-10 82
SEARS....10-15
VOCALION....10-15 65-69

Session: Jordanaires; Anita Kerr Singers.
Also see HAGGARD, Merle / Patsy Cline
Also see KERR, Anita
Also see PIERCE, Webb / Patsy Cline / T. Texas Tyler
Also see REEVES, Jim, & Patsy Cline
Also see TUBB, Ernest

CLINE, Patsy / Cowboy Copas / Hawkshaw Hawkins

LPs: 10/12-inch

STARDAY....15-20 65

Also see HAWKINS, Hawkshaw

CLINE, Patsy / Cowboy Copas / Johnny Horton

LPs: 10/12-inch

HILLTOP....10-15 60s

Also see COPAS, Cowboy
Also see HORTON, Johnny

CLINE, Patsy / Hank Locklin / Miller Brothers / Eddie Marvin

EPs: 7-inch

4 STAR (136 "Hidin' Out")....25-50 56
(Promotional 10-inch, 45rpm. Not issued with cover.)

Also see LOCKLIN, Hank

CLINE, Patsy / Pete Pike / Jack Bradshaw / Miller Brothers

EPs: 7-inch

4 STAR (137 "Come On In")....25-50 56
(Promotional 10-inch, 45rpm. Not issued with cover.)

CLINE, Patsy / T. Texas Tyler / Bill Taylor / Eddie Marvin

EPs: 7-inch

4 STAR (139 "Dear God")....25-50 56
(Promotional 10-inch, 45 rpm. Not issued with cover.)

Also see CLINE, Patsy

CLINTON, George *R&B/LP '82*
(George Clinton Band)

Singles: 12-inch

CAPITOL....4-8 82-86

Singles: 7-inch

ABC....3-5 74
CAPITOL....3-4 83-86
PAISLEY PARK....3-4 89

Picture Sleeves

CAPITOL....3-4 83

LPs: 10/12-inch

ABC....8-10 74
CAPITOL....5-10 82-86
INVICTUS....10-12 73
PAISLEY PARK....5-8 89

Also see PARLIAMENTS

CLINTON, Mac, & Straitjackets

Singles: 7-inch

LE CAM (714 "Wake Up Baby")....35-50 60

Members: Delbert McClinton; Robert Harwell; Ralph Dixon; Billy Cox; Ray Clark.
Also see McCLINTON, Delbert

CLIQUE *P&R '69*

Singles: 7-inch

ABC....3-5 73
CINEMA (001 "Splash")....25-35 67
SCEPTER....10-20 67
WHITE WHALE....8-15 69-71

LPs: 10/12-inch

WHITE WHALE (7126 "The Clique")....10-20 69

CLIQUES *P&R '56*

Singles: 78 rpm

MODERN....10-20 56

Singles: 7-inch

MODERN (987 "The Girl in My Dreams")....20-30 56

Members: Jesse Belvin; Eugene Church.
Also see BELVIN, Jesse
Also see CHURCH, Eugene

CLOCKS *P&R '82*

Singles: 7-inch

BOULEVARD....3-4 82

LPs: 10/12-inch

BOULEVARD....5-10 82

CLOCKWORK *R&B/D&D '84*

Singles: 12-inch

PRIVATE I....4-6 84

Singles: 7-inch

PRIVATE I....3-4 84

CLOONEY, Rosemary *P&R '51*
(Clooney Sisters)

Singles: 78 rpm

COLUMBIA....4-8 50-57

Singles: 7-inch

APCO....3-5 75
COLUMBIA....10-20 50-57
CORAL....5-10 59
DOT....4-6 68
GIBSON/COLUMBIA....10-20 55
("Musicards," with fold-out covers.)
MGM....5-15 59-65
RCA....5-10 60-61
REPRISE....5-10 63-64
SATURDAY EVENING POST (1055 "Hollywood's Favorite Songbird")....15-25 54
(Promotional issue only. Includes interview script.)

Picture Sleeves

RCA....10-15 60

EPs: 7-inch

COLUMBIA....15-25 51-56
EPIC (7139/7140/7141 "Clooney Sisters")....10-20 56
(Price is for any of three volumes.)
MGM....8-15 58-60

LPs: 10/12-inch

COLUMBIA (500 thru 1200 series, except 6297)....15-25 54-58
COLUMBIA (2500 series)....20-30 50s
(10-inch LPs.)
COLUMBIA (6297 "While We're Young")....25-35 51
(10-inch LP.)
CONCORD JAZZ....5-10 78-83
CORAL....15-25 59
EPIC (3160 "The Clooney Sisters")...20-30 56
HARMONY....8-15 59-68
MGM (Except 1000 series)....10-15 59-62
MGM (1000 series)....8-12 67
RCA....15-25 60-63
REPRISE....10-25 63-64

Also see BOYD, Jimmy, & Rosemary Clooney
Also see CROSBY, Bing, Louis Armstrong, Rosemary Clooney & Hi-Los
Also see GOODMAN, Benny, Trio, & Rosemary Clooney
Also see HERMAN, Woody
Also see HOPE, Bob, & Rosemary Clooney

CLOONEY, Rosemary, & Bing Crosby

Singles: 7-inch

RCA....4-8 59

LPs: 10/12-inch

CAMDEN....6-10 69
CAPITOL (2300 series)....8-12 65
CAPITOL (11000 series)....5-10 77
Also see CROSBY, Bing

CLOONEY, Rosemary, & Marlene Dietrich

Singles: 78 rpm

COLUMBIA....4-8 52

Singles: 7-inch

COLUMBIA....5-10 52

EPs: 7-inch

COLUMBIA (1699 "Rosie & Marlene")....15-20 52
Also see DIETRICH, Marlene

CLOONEY, Rosemary, & Jose Ferrer

Singles: 78 rpm

COLUMBIA....4-8 54

EPs: 7-inch

MGM....10-20 58
Also see FERRER Jose

CLOONEY, Rosemary, & Hi-Los LP '57

EPs: 7-inch

COLUMBIA....5-10 57

LPs: 10/12-inch

COLUMBIA (1006 "Ring Around Rosie")....20-25 57
Also see HI-LOs

CLOONEY, Rosemary, & Dick Haymes

LPs: 10/12-inch

EXACT....5-10 80
Also see HAYMES, Dick

CLOONEY, Rosemary, & Guy Mitchell P&R '51

(With Joanne Gilbert)

EPs: 7-inch

COLUMBIA (377 "Red Garters")....15-20 54
(Soundtrack.)

LPs: 10/12-inch

COLUMBIA (6282 "Red Garters")....40-50 54
(10-inch LP. Soundtrack.)
Also see MITCHELL, Guy

CLOONEY, Rosemary, & Perez Prado

Singles: 7-inch

RCA....4-8 60

LPs: 10/12-inch

RCA....10-12 60
Also see CLOONEY, Rosemary
Also see PRADO, Perez

CLOUD, Christopher

(Tommy Boyce)

Singles: 7-inch

CHELSEA....3-5 72-73

LPs: 10/12-inch

CHELSEA....10-15 73
Also see BOYCE, Tommy

CLOUT P&R '78

Singles: 7-inch

EPIC....3-4 78-79

LPs: 10/12-inch

EPIC....5-10 79-80

CLOVERS R&B '51

("Featuring Buddy Bailey")

Singles: 78 rpm

ATLANTIC....20-50 51-57
RAINBOW (122 "Yes Sir, That's My Baby")....200-300 51

Singles: 7-inch

ATLANTIC (934 "Don't You Know I Love You")....100-200 51
ATLANTIC (944 "Fool, Fool, Fool")....100-150 51
ATLANTIC (963 "One Mint Julep")....50-100 52
ATLANTIC (969 "Ting-A-Ling")....50-100 52
ATLANTIC (977 "I Played the Fool")....50-100 52
ATLANTIC (989 "Yes It's You")....50-100 53
ATLANTIC (1000 "Good Lovin' ")....50-100 53
ATLANTIC (1010 "Comin' On")....50-100 53
ATLANTIC (1022 "Lovey Dovey")....50-100 54
ATLANTIC (1035 "Your Cash Ain't Nothin' But Trash")....50-100 54
ATLANTIC (1046 "I Confess")....50-100 54
ATLANTIC (1052 "Blue Velvet")....50-100 54
ATLANTIC (1060 "Love Bug")....50-100 55
ATLANTIC (1073 "Nip Sip")....50-100 55
ATLANTIC (1083 "Devil Or Angel")....50-100 56
ATLANTIC (1094 "Your Tender Lips")....50-100 56
ATLANTIC (1107 "From the Bottom of My Heart")....25-50 56
ATLANTIC (1118 "A Lonely Fool")....25-50 56
ATLANTIC (1129 "You Good Looking Woman")....25-50 57
ATLANTIC (1139 "So Young")....25-50 57
ATLANTIC (1152 "Down in the Alley")....25-50 57
ATLANTIC (1175 "Wishing for Your Love")....25-50 58
ATLANTIC (2129 "Drive It Home")....10-20 61
BRUNSWICK (55249 "Love Love Love")....10-20 63
JOSIE....5-10 68
POPLAR (110 "The Gossip Wheel")....15-25 58
POPLAR (111 "The Good Old Summertime")....15-25 58
PORT (3004 "Poor Baby")....10-20 65
PORWIN (1001 "Stop Pretending")....15-25 63
(Has sans-serif logo and straight horizontal lines.)
PORWIN (1002 "Stop Pretending")....10-20 63
(Has serif logo and wavy horizontal lines.)
RIPETE....3-5 88
U.A....10-15 59-61
WINLEY (255 "Wrapped Up in a Dream")....20-30 61
WINLEY (655 "I Need You Now")....20-30 62

EPs: 7-inch

ATLANTIC (504 "The Clovers Sing")....100-200 56
ATLANTIC (537 "The Clovers Sing")....100-200 56
ATLANTIC (590 "The Clovers")....100-150 57

LPs: 10/12-inch

ATCO....10-15 71
ATLANTIC (1248 "The Clovers")....300-400 56
ATLANTIC (8009 "The Clovers")....200-300 57
(Black label.)
ATLANTIC (8009 "The Clovers")....50-100 59
(Red label.)
ATLANTIC (8034 "The Clovers' Dance Party")....50-100 59
GRAND PRIX....10-20 64
POPLAR (1001 "The Clovers in Clover")....100-150 58
TRIP....8-10 72
U.A. (3033 "Clovers in Clover")....50-100 59
(Monaural.)
U.A. (6033 "Clovers in Clover")....100-125 59
(Stereo.)
U.A. (3099 "Love Potion Number Nine")....50-100 60
(Monaural.)
U.A. (6099 "Love Potion Number Nine")....100-125 60
(Stereo.)

Members: John "Buddy" Bailey; Harold Winley; Hal Lucas; Bill Harris; Matthew McQuater; Charlie White; Billy Mitchell. Session: King Curtis.
Also see HARPTONES / Paragons / Jesters / Clovers
Also see JACKSON, Willis
Also see KING CURTIS
Also see MITCHELL, Billy

CLOWNEY, David, Band

(David Cortez Clowney)

Singles: 78 rpm

EMBER (1010 "Soft Lights") 15-25....56

Singles: 7-inch

EMBER (1010 "Soft Lights") 20-40....56
PARIS (513 "Shakin'")....15-25 58
Also see CORTEZ, Dave "Baby"
Also see JESTERS

CLUB HOUSE P&R/R&B '83

Singles: 12-inch

ATLANTIC....4-6 83

Singles: 7-inch

ATLANTIC....3-4 83

CLUB NOUVEAU R&B/LP '86

Singles: 12-inch

W.B. 4-6 86

Singles: 7-inch

TOMMY BOY....3-4 88
W.B. 3-4 86-88

LPs: 10/12-inch

W.B. 5-10 86-88

COASTERS P&R/R&B '56

Singles: 78 rpm

ATCO....20-50 56-57

Singles: 7-inch

ATCO (6064 "Down in Mexico")....50-75 56
(Maroon label.)
ATCO (6073 "One Kiss Led to Another")....35-50 56
(Maroon label.)
ATCO (6087 "Searchin' ")....20-40 57
(Maroon label.)
ATCO (6087 "Searchin' ")....15-25 57
(Yellow and white label.)
ATCO (6098 thru 6178)....10-20 57-60
ATCO (6186 thru 6356)....8-15 61-65
ATCO (6379 "Crazy Baby")....20-30 65
ATCO (6407 "She's a Yum Yum")....8-10 66
DATE....5-10 67-68
KING....3-6 71-73
KING/GUSTO....3-5 79
TURNTABLE....4-8 69

EPs: 7-inch

ATCO (4501 "Rock & Roll with the Coasters")....50-70 58
ATCO (4503 "Keep Rockin' ")....50-70 58
ATCO (4506 "The Coasters")....30-50 59
ATCO (4507 "Top Hits")....30-50 59

LPs: 10/12-inch

ARCHIVES....8-12
ATCO (101 "The Coasters")....75-100 58
(Yellow label.)
ATCO (101 "The Coasters")....25-50 59
(Yellow and white label.)
ATCO (111 "Greatest Hits")....50-75 59
ATCO (123 "One by One")....40-50 60
(Monaural.)
ATCO (SD-123 "One By One")....50-60 60
(Stereo.)
ATCO (135 "Coast Along")....30-40 59
(Monaural.)
ATCO (SD-135 "Coast Along")....40-50 59
(Stereo.)
ATCO (371 "Their Greatest Recordings")....10-20 71
ATLANTIC....10-12 82
CLARION....10-15 64
GUSTO....5-8
KING....10-15 71
PHOENIX 20....5-8
POWER PAK....5-10 83
TRIP....8-10 72-76
WEST-ONE....8-15

Members: Bobby Nunn; Leon Hughes; Carl Gardner; Billy Guy; Adolph Jacobs; Cornel Gunter; Will Jones; Earl Carroll; Ronnie Bright; Jimmy Norman. Session: King Curtis.
Also see CARROLL, Earl, & Original Cadillacs
Also see HENDRICKS, Bobby
Also see KING, Ben E.
Also see KING CURTIS
Also see NORMAN, Jimmy
Also see ROBINS

COASTERS / Crew-Cuts / Chiffons

LPs: 10/12-inch

EXACT....5-10 80
Also see CHIFFONS
Also see CREW-CUTS

COASTERS / Drifters

LPs: 10/12-inch

TVP....10-15
(TV mail-order offer.)
Also see DRIFTERS

COATES, Odia — P&R '75

Singles: 12-inch

EPIC....4-6 77

Singles: 7-inch

BUDDAH....3-5 73
EPIC....3-4 78
U.A. 3-4 74-75

LPs: 10/12-inch

U.A. 8-10 75
Also see ANKA, Paul, & Odia Coates

COBB, Joyce — P&R '79

Singles: 7-inch

CREAM....3-4 79-80
TRUTH....3-5 75

COBHAM, Billy — LP '73

(Billy Cobham's Glass Menagerie; with George Duke Band)

Singles: 12-inch

COLUMBIA....4-6 80

Singles: 7-inch

ATLANTIC....3-5 75-77
COLUMBIA....3-4 78-80

Picture Sleeves

ATLANTIC....3-5 70s

LPs: 10/12-inch

ATLANTIC....5-10 73-79
COLUMBIA....5-10 77-80
ELEKTRA....5-10 82-83
Also see DUKE, George

COCCIANTE, Richard — P&R '76

Singles: 7-inch

20TH FOX....3-5 76

LPs: 10/12-inch

20TH FOX....5-10 76

COCHISE — P&R '71

Singles: 7-inch

U.A. 3-5 71

EPs: 7-inch

U.A. 10-12 71

LPs: 10/12-inch

U.A. 10-12 71
Member: Mick Grabham.

COCHRAN, Eddie — P&R/R&B '57

Singles: 78 rpm

CREST (1026 "Skinny Jim")....75-125 56
LIBERTY....50-100 57-58

Singles: 7-inch

CAPEHART (5003 "Rough Stuff")....10-20 60
CREST (1026 "Skinny Jim")....200-300 56
LIBERTY (54000 series)....5-10 62
LIBERTY (55056 "Sittin' in the Balcony")....15-25 57
LIBERTY (55070 "Mean When I'm Mad")....15-25 58
LIBERTY (55087 "Drive in Show")....15-25 57
LIBERTY (55112 "Twenty Flight Rock")....20-30 58
LIBERTY (55123 "Jeannie Jeannie Jeannie")....20-30 58
LIBERTY (55138 "Pretty Girl")....15-25 58
LIBERTY (55144 "Summertime Blues")....15-25 58
LIBERTY (55166 "C'mon Everybody")....15-25 58
(Green label.)
LIBERTY (55166 "C'mon Everybody")....10-20 58
(Black label.)
LIBERTY (55177 "Teenage Heaven")....15-25 59
LIBERTY (55203 "Somethin' Else")..15-25 59
(With horizontal silver lines.)
LIBERTY (55203 "Somethin' Else")..10-20 59
(Without horizontal silver lines.)
LIBERTY (55217 "Hallelujah, I Love Her So")....10-20 59
LIBERTY (55242 "Cut Across Shorty")....15-25 60
(Green label.)
LIBERTY (55242 "Cut Across Shorty")....10-20 61
(Black label.)
LIBERTY (55278 "Sweetie Pie")....10-20 60
LIBERTY (55389 "Weekend")....20-30 61

Picture Sleeves

CAPEHART (5003 "Rough Stuff")....35-50 60
LIBERTY (55070 "Mean When I'm Mad")....750-1000 58

EPs: 7-inch

LIBERTY (3061-1/2/3 "Singin' to My Baby")....100-150 58
(Price is for any of three volumes.)

LPs: 10/12-inch

LIBERTY (3061 "Singin' to My Baby")....200-300 58
(Green label.)
LIBERTY (3061 "Singin' to My Baby")....40-60 60
(Black label.)
LIBERTY (3172 "Memorial Album")....50-100 60
LIBERTY (3220 "Never to Be Forgotten")....50-100 62
(Black label.)
LIBERTY (3220 "Never to Be Forgotten")....75-90 62
(Yellow label. Promotional issue only.)
LIBERTY (10000 series)....5-10 81-83
SUNSET (1123 "Summertime Blues")....30-40 66
U.A. (428 "Very Best of Eddie Cochran")....10-15 75
U.A. (9959 "Legendary Masters")....15-20 71
Also see COCHRAN BROTHERS

COCHRAN, Hank — C&W '62

Singles: 7-inch

CAPITOL....3-4 78
DOT....3-5 70
ELEKTRA....3-4 80
GAYLORD....4-8 62-63
LIBERTY....4-8 62-63
MONUMENT....3-6 67-68
RCA....4-8 64-66

LPs: 10/12-inch

CAPITOL....5-10 78
ELEKTRA....5-10 80
MONUMENT....10-15 68
RCA....10-20 65
Session: Merle Haggard; Willie Nelson.
Also see COCHRAN BROTHERS
Also see HAGGARD, Merle

COCHRAN, Hank, & Willie Nelson

Singles: 7-inch

CAPITOL....3-5 78
Also see COCHRAN, Hank
Also see NELSON, Willie

COCHRAN, Wayne — LP '68

(With the C.C. Riders; with Fabulous C.C. Riders; with Rockin' Capris)

Singles: 7-inch

BETHLEHEM (3097 "Hey Jude")....4-8 69
BOBLO (101 "Hey Baby")....5-10 68
CHESS....5-10 67-68
CONFEDERATE (155 "Linda Lu")....10-20 63
DECK (151 "Monkey Monkey")....10-20 63
DRIVE (6249 "Sea Cruise")....4-6 76
EPIC....3-5 72
ERA (18 "Last Kiss")....3-5 78
(Credits Cochran but track is by J. Frank Wilson.)
GALA (117 "Last Kiss")....10-20 62
GALICO (105 "Last Kiss")....15-25 61
KING (5000 series)....5-15 63-65
KING (6000 series)....4-8 69-71
KING GOLD....3-5 72
MERCURY....4-8 65-67
SCOTTIE (1303 "The Coo")....25-50 59
SOFT (779 "Harlem Shuffle")....8-12 65
SOFT (1009 "Hang on Sloopy")....5-10 68
SOFT (1010 "Hey Baby")....5-10 68

Picture Sleeves

CHESS (2020 "Some-A Your Sweet Love")....5-10 67
MERCURY (72507 "Harlem Shuffle")....8-12 65

EPs: 7-inch

PLAYBACK (32 "Long Long Day")....8-12 72
(Also has tracks by other artists.)

LPs: 10/12-inch

BETHLEHEM (10002 "High & Ridin'")....10-20 70
CHESS (1519 "Wayne Cochran")....20-30 68
EPIC (30989 "Cochran")....8-12 72
KING (1116 "Alive & Well")....15-25 70
KING (16001 "Old King Gold")....5-10 75
Also see GREAT SEBASTIAN
Also see REDDING, Otis

COCHRAN BROTHERS

Singles: 78 rpm

EKKO (1003 "Two Blue Singing Stars")....50-100 56
EKKO (1005 "Guilty Conscience")...50-100 56
EKKO (3001 "Tired and Sleepy")....75-125 56

Singles: 7-inch

EKKO (1003 "Two Blue Singing Stars")....75-125 56
EKKO (1005 "Guilty Conscience")...75-125 56
EKKO (3001 "Tired and Sleepy")..100-150 56
Members: Eddie Cochran; Hank Cochran. (Eddie and Hank were not really brothers).
Also see COCHRAN, Eddie
Also see COCHRAN, Hank

COCHRANE, Tom — LP '86

(With Red Rider)

Singles: 7-inch

CAPITOL....3-4 86
RCA....3-4 88

Picture Sleeves

RCA....3-5 88

LPs: 10/12-inch

CAPITOL....5-10 86
RCA....5-8 88
Also see RED RIDER

COCK ROBIN — P&R/D&D '85

Singles: 12-inch

COLUMBIA....4-6 85

Singles: 7-inch

COLUMBIA....3-4 85

Picture Sleeves

COLUMBIA....3-5 85

LPs: 10/12-inch

COLUMBIA....5-10 85-87
Members: Peter Kingsbery: Anna LaCazio.

COCKBURN, Bruce — P&R/LP '80

Singles: 7-inch

GOLD MOUNTAIN....3-4 84
MCA....3-4 86
MILLENNIUM....3-4 80

LPs: 10/12-inch

EPIC....10-15 71-72
GOLD CASTLE....5-8 89
GOLD MOUNTAIN....5-10 '84
ISLAND....8-10 77-78
MCA....5-10 86
MILLENNIUM....5-10 80-81
TRUE NORTH....8-10 77-78

COCKER, Joe P&R '68
(With the Chris Stainton Band)

Singles: 7-inch

A&M 3-6 68-78
ASYLUM 3-4 78-79
CAPITOL 3-4 84-88
ISLAND 3-4 82-83
PHILIPS 10-15 65

Picture Sleeves

A&M 3-5 69-74
CAPITOL 3-4 84
ISLAND 3-4

LPs: 10/12-inch

A&M (Except 3100 series) 8-15 69-77
A&M (3100 series) 5-10 82
ASYLUM (Except 145) 5-10 78-79
ASYLUM (145 "Luxury You Can Afford") 5-10 79
ASYLUM (145 "Luxury You Can Afford") 15-25 79
(Picture disc. Promotional issue only.)
CAPITOL 5-10 84-90
ISLAND 5-8 82
MFSL (223 "Sheffield Steel") 20-25 94
Also see ARNOLD, Vance, & Avengers
Also see BOWIE, David / Joe Cocker / Youngbloods
Also see CRUSADERS
Also see GREASE BAND
Also see RUSSELL, Leon

COCKER, Joe, & Jennifer Warnes P&R '82

Singles: 7-inch

ISLAND 3-4 82

Picture Sleeves

ISLAND 3-4 82
Also see COCKER, Joe
Also see WARNES, Jennifer

COCO, El: see EL COCO

COCTEAU TWINS LP '88

LPs: 10/12-inch

CAPITOL 5-8 88
4AD 5-8 90

CODAY, Bill R&B '71

Singles: 7-inch

CRAJON (48202 "Sixty Minute Teaser") 10-15 69
CRAJON (48203 "Right On Baby") 50-75 70
CRAJON (48204 "Get Your Lie Straight") 4-8 71
(At least one source shows this label as "Crayon." We're not yet sure who's right.)
EPIC 4-8 73-75
GALAXY (777 "Get Your Lie Straight") 4-6 71
GALAXY (779 "When You Find a Fool, Bump His Head") 4-8 71
GALAXY (781 "I Got a Thing") 4-8 71

CODY, Commander: see COMMANDER CODY

COE, David Allan C&W '74

Singles: 7-inch

COLUMBIA 3-5 74-87
PLANTATION 3-5 73
SSS INT'L (Black vinyl) 3-5 71-72
SSS INT'L (Colored vinyl) 5-10 71-72
(Promotional issues only.)

Picture Sleeves

COLUMBIA 3-5

LPs: 10/12-inch

COLUMBIA 5-10 72-86
SSS INT'L (9 "Penitentiary Blues") 25-40 70
Session: Lacy J. Dalton; Dianne Sherrill; Eve Shaprio; Bill Anderson; George Jones; Dickey Betts; Kris Kristofferson; Guy Clark; Larry Jon Wilson; Waylon Jennings.
Also see JONES, George, & David Allan Coe

COE, David Allan, & Bill Anderson

Singles: 7-inch

COLUMBIA 3-5 80
Also see ANDERSON, Bill

COE, David Allan, & Willie Nelson C&W '86

Singles: 7-inch

COLUMBIA 3-4 86
Also see COE, David Allan
Also see NELSON, Willie
Also see NELSON, Willie / Jerry Lee Lewis / Carl Perkins / David Allan Coe

COFFEE R&B '82

Singles: 7-inch

DELITE 3-4 80-82

COFFEY, Dennis P&R/LP '71
(With the Detroit Guitar Band; with Lyman Woodward Trio)

Singles: 7-inch

SUSSEX 3-5 70-74
W.B. 3-5 74
20TH CENTURY/WESTBOUND 3-5 75-76
WESTBOUND 3-4 77-78

LPs: 10/12-inch

SUSSEX 10-12 70-75
20TH CENTURY/WESTBOUND 8-10 75-76
WESTBOUND 5-10 77
Also see C.C. & COMPANY
Also see C.J. & CO.

COHEN, Leonard LP '68

Singles: 7-inch

COLUMBIA 3-6 68-73

LPs: 10/12-inch

COLUMBIA 10-12 68-85
W.B. 8-12 77
Also see BRANIGAN, Laura

COHEN, Myron LP '66

LPs: 10/12-inch

RCA 10-15 66
Also see ANN-MARGRET

COHN, Marc C&W/LP '91

Singles: 7-inch

ATLANTIC 3-4 91

LPs: 10/12-inch

ATLANTIC 5-8 91

COLD BLOOD LP '69
(Lydia Pense & Cold Blood)

Singles: 7-inch

ABC 3-5 75
REPRISE 3-5 72-73
SAN FRANCISCO 3-6 70

EPs: 7-inch

SAN FRANCISCO (3309 "Cold Blood") 5-10 70
(Promotional issue only.)

LPs: 10/12-inch

ABC 8-10 76
REPRISE 10-12 72-73
SAN FRANCISCO 12-15 69-70
W.B. 8-10 74
Members: Lydia Pense; Michael Andreas; Rod Ellicott; Frank Davis; Jerry Jonutz; Danny Hull; Larry Field; Raul Matute; Larry Jonutz; David Padron.
Also see PENSE, Lydia, & New Invaders

COLD CHISEL LP '81

Singles: 7-inch

ELEKTRA 3-4 81

LPs: 10/12-inch

ELEKTRA 5-10 80-82
Members: Jimmy Barnes; Don Walker; Steve Prestwich; Phil Small; Ian Moss.
Also see BARNES, Jimmy

COLDER, Ben C&W/P&R '62
(Sheb Wooley)

Singles: 7-inch

MGM 4-8 62-73
PORTLAND 3-6 78
SCORPION 3-5 79-80
SUNBIRD 3-4 80
TPL 3-5 87

LPs: 10/12-inch

LAKESHORE (621 "Ben Colder & Sheb Wooley") 10-20
(Mail order offer.)
LAKESHORE/GUSTO (110 "Greatest Hits of Sheb Wooley & Ben Colder") 8-12 79
(Mail order offer.)
MGM (139 "Ben Colder") 8-12 70
MGM (4421 thru 4876) 10-20 66-73
MGM (4173 "Spoofing the Big Ones") 15-25 63
Also see WOOLEY, Sheb

COLE, Ann R&B '56
(With the Suburbans)

Singles: 78 rpm

BATON 10-20 56-57
TIMELY 5-10 54

Singles: 7-inch

BATON 10-20 56-57
MGM 5-10 60
ROULETTE 10-20 62
SIR 5-10 59-60
TIMELY 10-20 54

COLE, Bobby P&R '68

Singles: 7-inch

DATE 3-6 68-69

COLE, Cozy R&B '44
(With His All Stars; with Gary Chester; with Pete Johnson; with Red Norvo; Cozy Cole Septet)

Singles: 78 rpm

KEYNOTE 10-15 44
MGM 5-10 54

Singles: 7-inch

ARTISTIQUE 4-8 61
BETHLEHEM 4-8 63
CHARLIE PARKER 4-8 62
COLUMBIA 4-8 66
CORAL 4-8 62-67
FELSTED 5-10 58
GRAND AWARD 5-8 58
KING 4-8 59-60
LOVE 10-15 58-59
MGM 5-10 54
MERCURY 5-8 58
RANDOM 4-8 60

Picture Sleeves

RANDOM 5-10 60

EPs: 7-inch

AFTER HOURS 15-20 55
MGM 15-20 54
WALDORF 5-8

LPs: 10/12-inch

AFTER HOURS 25-30 55
CHARLIE PARKER 15-20 62
COLUMBIA 10-15 66
CORAL 15-20 62-64
EVEREST 8-10 74
FELSTED 15-20 59
KING 20-25 59-60
LOVE 20-25 59
PARIS 20-25 58
SAVOY 8-12 72-77
TRIP 8-10 74
Also see HAMPTON, Lionel
Also see SHEARING, George, Quintet

COLE, Cozy, & Illnois Jacquet

LPs: 10/12-inch

AUDITION 25-35 55
Also see COLE, Cozy
Also see JACQUET, Illnois

COLE, Gardner P&R '88

Singles: 7-inch

W.B. 3-4 88

Picture Sleeves

W.B. 3-4 88

COLE, Jude P&R/LP '90

Singles: 7-inch

REPRISE 3-4 90

LPs: 10/12-inch

REPRISE 5-8 90
Also see MARTIN, Moon

COLE, King, Trio: see COLE, Nat King

COLE, Nat "King" — R&B '42
(King Cole Trio; Quintet; Quartet)

Singles: 78 rpm

AMMOR....15-25 42
ATLAS....10-20 43-45
CAPITOL (100 thru 700 series)....5-10 43-49
CAPITOL (800 thru 4600 series)....4-8 50-58
CAPITOL (15000 series)....3-8 47-49
DAVIS & SCHWEGLER....20-40 39-40
DECCA....10-20 42-47
DISC....15-25 42
EXCELSIOR....10-20 42-45
PREMIER....10-20 44
SAVOY....10-15 46
VARSITY....15-25 40

Singles: 7-inch

CAPITOL (Except 800 thru 4200 series)....4-8 61-69
CAPITOL (889 thru 4623)....5-15 50-61
(Purple label.)
TAMPA (134 "Vom-Vim-Veedle")....8-12 57

Picture Sleeves

CAPITOL....5-10 59-66
TAMPA (134 "Vom-Vim-Veedle")....10-20 57

EPs: 7-inch

CAPITOL....10-20 50-60
DECCA....10-20 56

LPs: 10/12-inch

CAMAY....8-12
CAPITOL (Except 100 thru 2900 series)....5-15 61-82
CAPITOL (H-156 "Nat King Cole at the Piano")....50-100 49
(10-inch LP.)
CAPITOL (H-177 "Nat King Cole Trio")....50-75 49
(10-inch LP.)
CAPITOL (H-220 "Nat King Cole Trio")....50-75 50
(10-inch LP.)
CAPITOL (H-332 "Penthouse Serenade")....50-75 52
(10-inch LP.)
CAPITOL (H-357 "Unforgetable")....50-75 52
(10-inch LP.)
CAPITOL (100 thru 900 series)....20-35 55-58
(With "T" or "W" prefix.)
CAPITOL (1000 thru 2900 series)....10-20 58-68
(With "T," "ST" or "W" prefix.)
CAPITOL....5-10
(With "SM" prefix.)
CROWN....8-12 64
DECCA (8260 "In the Beginning")....35-50 56
DYNAMIC HOUSE....5-10 72
MCA....5-10 73
MARK '56....5-10 76
MONARCH ("Nat King Cole")....75-100 53
(Colored vinyl.)
PICKWICK....5-10 70s
SCORE (4019 "King Cole Trio")....20-40 58
SPINORAMA....10-15 60s
VSP....10-15 66
WYNCOTE....10-15 63

Members: (King Cole Trio): Harry Edison; Willie Smith; Juan Tizol.
Also see FOUR KNIGHTS
Also see KENTON, Stan
Also see LUTCHER, Nellie, & Nat "King" Cole
Also see MARTIN, Dean, & Nat "King" Cole
Also see NELSON, Willie / Nat "King" Cole / Johnny Mathis / Shirley Bassey
Also see PRESLEY, Elvis
Also see PRESLEY, Elvis / Frank Sinatra / Nat "King" Cole
Also see SINATRA, Frank / Nat King Cole

COLE, Nat "King" / Phil Flowers

LPs: 10/12-inch

EXCELSIOR....5-10

COLE, Nat "King," & Stubby Kaye

Singles: 7-inch

CAPITOL....3-6 65

Picture Sleeves

CAPITOL....4-8 65

COLE, Nat "King," & His Trio / George Kingston

LPs: 10/12-inch

WYNCOTE....10-15 60s
Also see COLE, Nat "King"

COLE, Nat "King," & George Shearing

LPs: 10/12-inch

CAPITOL....20-30 61
Also see SHEARING, George, Quintet

COLE, Natalie — P&R/R&B/LP '75
(With George Shearing)

Singles: 12-inch

EPIC....4-6 83
MODERN....4-6 85

Singles: 7-inch

CAPITOL....3-4 75-80
EMI....3-4 88-89
EPIC....3-4 83
MANHATTAN....3-4 87
MODERN....3-4 85

Picture Sleeves

EMI....3-4 88-89
MANHATTAN....3-4 87
MODERN....3-4 85

LPs: 10/12-inch

CAPITOL....8-12 75-82
EMI....5-8 89
ELEKTRA....5-8 91
EPIC....5-10 83
MANHATTAN....5-10 87
MFSL (032 "Thankful")....25-50 79
MFSL (081 "Natalie Cole Sings, George Shearing Plays")....20-30 82
MODERN....5-10 85
Also see PARKER, Ray, Jr., & Natalie Cole
Also see SHEARING, George, Quintet

COLE, Natalie, & Peabo Bryson — R&B/LP '79

Singles: 7-inch

CAPITOL....3-4 79

LPs: 10/12-inch

CAPITOL....5-10 79
Also see BRYSON, Peabo
Also see COLE, Natalie

COLE, Sami Jo — C&W/P&R '74
(Sami Jo & Friends; Sami Jo Cole)

Singles: 7-inch

ELEKTRA....3-4 81
FAME....3-5 71-72
MGM....3-5 74-75
POLYDOR....3-5 76

LPs: 10/12-inch

MGM....5-10 74-75

COLE, Tony — P&R '72

Singles: 7-inch

20TH FOX....3-4 73-74

LPs: 10/12-inch

20TH FOX....8-10 73

COLEMAN, Durell — R&B/LP '85

Singles: 7-inch

ISLAND....3-4 85

LPs: 10/12-inch

ISLAND....5-10 85

COLLAGE — R&B '83

Singles: 12-inch

CONSTELLATION....4-6 86
MCA....4-6 85
SOLAR....4-6 83

Singles: 7-inch

CONSTELLATION....3-4 86
MCA....3-4 85
SOLAR....3-4 82-83

LPs: 10/12-inch

CONSTELLATION....5-10 86
SOLAR....5-10 81-83

COLLAY & SATELLITES — P&R '60

Singles: 7-inch

SHO-BIZ (1002 "Last Chance")....15-25 60

COLLEY, Keith — P&R '63

Singles: 7-inch

CHALLENGE....4-6 66-70
COLUMBIA....4-6 68
ERA....5-10 61-62
JAF....5-10
UNICAL....5-10 63-64
VEE JAY....4-8 65

COLLIER, Mitty — R&B '63

Singles: 7-inch

CHESS....5-10 61-68
ENTRANCE....3-5 72
ERIC....3-4 78
PEACHTREE....3-6 69-70

LPs: 10/12-inch

CHESS....15-25 65-66
GOSPEL ROOTS....5-10 79

COLLINS, Al — P&R '53
(Al "Jazzbo" Collins)

Singles: 78 rpm

BRUNSWICK....10-15 53

Singles: 7-inch

BRUNSWICK (86001 "Little Red Riding Hood")....10-20 53
IDONGOTOSHOWYOUNOSTINKINBADGES (1225 "Hip Nite B-4 Xmas")....10-15
(Label name is correct—as in "I Don't Got to Show You No Stinkin' Badges" and is not the result of a typist gone berserk.)
SINCERELY YOURS (3491 "Lullaby")....5-10

Picture Sleeves

BRUNSWICK (86001 "Little Red Riding Hood")....20-30 53

LPs: 10/12-inch

CORAL (57035 "East Coast Jazz Scene")....50-100 56

COLLINS, Al "Jazzbo," & Lou Stein

Singles: 78 rpm

BRUNSWICK (80226 "Three Little Pigs")....5-10 53
CAPITOL....5-10 53

Singles: 7-inch

BRUNSWICK (80226 "Three Little Pigs")....10-15 53
CAPITOL (2580 "Snow White and the Seven Dwarfs")....10-20 53
Also see COLLINS, Al
Also see STEIN, Lou

COLLINS, Albert — R&B/LP '72
(With the Ice Breakers; with His Rhythm Rockers)

Singles: 12-inch

ALLIGATOR (5 "Cold Snap")....5-10 86
(Promotional issue only.)

Singles: 7-inch

GREAT SCOTT (007 "Albert's Alley")....15-25 59
HALL....8-12 64
HALL WAY....8-12 63
IMPERIAL....4-6 69
KANGAROO (103 "Freeze")....25-50 58
LIBERTY....3-5 70
TCF HALL....4-8 65-66
TRACIE (2003 "I Don't Know")....10-20 62
TUMBLEWEED....3-5 72-73
20TH FOX....5-10 68

LPs: 10/12-inch

ALLIGATOR....6-10 79-87
BLUE THUMB....10-15 69
BRYLEN....5-10 84
IMPERIAL....12-25 69-70
MFSL (226 "Cold Snap")....15-25
TCF HALL (8002 "Cool Sound of Albert Collins")....30-35 65
TUMBLEWEED....10-15 71

COLLINS, Albert, Robert Cray & Johnny Copeland — LP '86

Singles: 12-inch

ALLIGATOR (5 "T-Bone Shuffle")....5-10 86
(Promotional issue only.)

LPs: 10/12-inch

ALLIGATOR 5-10 86
MFSL (217 "Showdown") 20-25 90s

Also see COLLINS, Albert
Also see CRAY, Robert

COLLINS, Dave & Ansell *P&R '71*

Singles: 7-inch

BIG TREE 3-5 71-72

LPs: 10/12-inch

BIG TREE 10-12 71

COLLINS, Dorothy *P&R '55*

Singles: 78 rpm

AUDIOVOX 4-8 54-55
CORAL 4-8 55-56
DECCA 4-8 52
MGM 4-8 50-51

Singles: 7-inch

AUDIOVOX 5-10 54-55
CORAL 5-10 55-56
DECCA 5-10 52
GOLD EAGLE 4-8 61
MGM 5-10 50-51
ROULETTE 4-6 63
TOP RANK 5-10 59-60

EPs: 7-inch

CORAL 5-10 55-56
MGM 5-10 55

LPs: 10/12-inch

CORAL 15-25 55-57
MOTIVATION 10-15 62
TOP RANK 10-15 60
VOCALION 5-10 65

Also see McGUIRE SISTERS / Lancers / Dorothy Collins / Teresa Brewer

COLLINS, Judy *LP '64*

Singles: 7-inch

ELEKTRA (Except 45253 & 45008 thru 45680) 3-5 70-84
ELEKTRA (45253 "Send in the Clowns") 3-5 75
ELEKTRA (45008 thru 45680) 4-8 64-69

Picture Sleeves

ELEKTRA (Except "The Hostage") 3-5 69-84
ELEKTRA ("The Hostage") 4-8 73
(Promotional issue only.)

LPs: 10/12-inch

ELEKTRA (Except 200 & 300 series) 10-15 67-84
ELEKTRA (209 "Maid of Constant Sorrow") 30-40 61
ELEKTRA (222 "Golden Apples of the Sun") 25-35 62
ELEKTRA (243 "Judy Collins No. 3") 20-30 63
(Monaural.)
ELEKTRA (7-243 "Judy Collins No. 3") 25-35 63
(Stereo.)
ELEKTRA (253 "Running for My Life") 5-8 80
ELEKTRA (300 series) 15-20 65-68
(Monaural.)
ELEKTRA (7-300 series) 15-20 65-72
(Stereo.)
ELEKTRA (60001 "Times of Our Lives") 5-8 82

COLLINS, Judy, & T.G. Sheppard *C&W '84*

Singles: 7-inch

ELEKTRA 3-4 84

Also see COLLINS, Judy
Also see SHEPPARD, T.G.

COLLINS, Keanya *R&B '69*
(Kenya Collins)

R&B '69

Singles: 7-inch

BLUE ROCK 3-6 69
ITCO 3-6 69
KEANYA (1 "Love Bandit") 15-25
PM 3-5

COLLINS, Lyn *P&R/R&B '72*
(With the Famous Flames)

Singles: 7-inch

PEOPLE 3-5 72-76

LPs: 10/12-inch

PEOPLE 10-12 72-75

Also see BROWN, James & Lyn Collins

COLLINS, Phil *P&R/LP '81*

Singles: 12-inch

ATLANTIC 4-6 84-86

Singles: 7-inch

ATLANTIC 3-4 81-90

Picture Sleeves

ATLANTIC 3-4 81-90

LPs: 10/12-inch

ATLANTIC 5-10 81-90

Also see BAILEY, Philip, & Phil Collins
Also see BAND AID
Also see BRAND X
Also see FLAMING YOUTH
Also see GENESIS

COLLINS, Phil, & Marilyn Martin *P&R '85*

Singles: 7-inch

ATLANTIC 3-4 85

Picture Sleeves

ATLANTIC 3-4 85

Also see COLLINS, Phil
Also see MARTIN, Marilyn

COLLINS, Rodger *R&B '67*
(Roger Collins)

Singles: 7-inch

FANTASY 3-5 73
GALAXY 3-8 66-73
POMPEII 3-6 69

COLLINS, William: see BOOTSY'S RUBBER BAND

COLLINS, Willie *R&B '86*

Singles: 7-inch

CAPITOL 3-4 86

COLLINS & COLLINS *R&B '80*

Singles: 7-inch

A&M 3-4 80

LPs: 10/12-inch

A&M 5-10 80

Members: Bill Collins; Tonee Collins.

COLOMBO, Chris: see COLUMBO, Chris

COLONEL ABRAMS: see ABRAMS, Colonel

COLORS *D&D '83*

Singles: 12-inch

FIRST TAKE 4-6 83

Singles: 7-inch

BECKET 3-4 82
INFINITE 3-4 80s

Picture Sleeves

INFINITE 3-5 80s

COLOSSEUM *LP '71*

Singles: 7-inch

DUNHILL 3-6 69-71

LPs: 10/12-inch

DUNHILL 10-15 69-70
W.B. 10-15 71

Members: Jon Heisman; Dick Heckstall-Smith; David Greenslade; Dave Clempson; Mark Clarke; Chris Farlowe; Barbara Thompson; Louis Gennamo.
Also see FARLOWE, Chris

COLTER, Jessi *C&W/P&R '75*
(Mirriam Johnson; Mirriam Eddy)

Singles: 7-inch

CAPITOL 3-5 75-82
RCA 3-6 69-72

LPs: 10/12-inch

CAPITOL 5-10 75-81
RCA (4333 "A Country Star Is Born") 10-20 70

Session: Waylon Jennings; Gary Scruggs.
Also see EDDY, Duane & Mirriam
Also see JENNINGS, Waylon, & Jessi Colter

COLTRANE, Alice *LP '71*

LPs: 10/12-inch

IMPULSE 8-10 71-74
W.B. 5-10 77-78

COLTRANE, Alice, & Carlos Santana *LP '74*

LPs: 10/12-inch

COLUMBIA 6-10 74

Also see SANTANA

COLTRANE, Alice, & Pharoah Sanders

LP: 10/12-inch

ARISTA 6-10 70s

Also see COLTRANE, Alice
Also see SANDERS, Pharoah

COLTRANE, Chi *P&R/LP '72*

Singles: 7-inch

CLOUDS 3-5 78
COLUMBIA 3-5 72-73

LPs: 10/12-inch

CLOUDS 5-10 77
COLUMBIA 8-12 72-73

COLTRANE, John *LP '67*

Singles: 78 rpm

PRESTIGE 10-20 57

Singles: 7-inch

ATLANTIC 4-8 60-61
PRESTIGE 5-10 57-64

LPs: 10/12-inch

ATLANTIC (1300 & 1400 series) 20-40 59-66
BLUE NOTE (1577 "Blue Train") ... 100-150 51
(Label gives New York street address for Blue Note Records.)
BLUE NOTE (1577 "Blue Train") 35-55 59
(Label reads "Blue Note Records Inc. - New York, U.S.A.")
COLTRANE (4950 "Cosmic Music") 150-200 66
COLTRANE (5000 "Cosmic Music") 150-200 66
IMPULSE (Except 6 thru 77) 10-25 66-71
IMPULSE (6 thru 77) 25-45 61-65
JAZZLAND 20-40 61
PRESTIGE (7043 "Two Tenors") 50-100 56
(Yellow label.)
PRESTIGE (7043 "Two Tenors") 25-35 64
(Blue label.)
PRESTIGE (7105 "Coltrane") 50-100 57
(Yellow label.)
PRESTIGE (7105 "Coltrane") 25-35 57
(Blue label.)
PRESTIGE (7123 "John Coltrane & Red Garland Trio") 50-75 57
(Yellow label.)
PRESTIGE (7123 "Traneing In") 25-35 64
(Blue label, logo on right. Reissue of *John Coltrane & Red Garland Trio.*)
PRESTIGE (7123 "Traneing In") 15-25 69
(Blue label, logo at top.)
PRESTIGE (7142 "Soultrane") 40-70 58
(Yellow label.)
PRESTIGE (7158 "Cattin'") 40-70 59
(Yellow label.)
PRESTIGE (7158 "Cattin'") 25-35 64
(Blue label.)
PRESTIGE (7131 "Wheelin' and Dealin'") 40-70 59
(Yellow label.)
PRESTIGE (7188 "Lush Life") 40-70 60
(Yellow label.)
PRESTIGE (7188 "Lush Life") 25-35 64
(Blue label.)
PRESTIGE (7200 series) 20-40 61-64
(Yellow label.)
PRESTIGE (7200 series) 15-25 64
(Blue label.)
PRESTIGE (7300 series) 15-25 65
U.A. 25-35 62

Also see ADDERLEY, Julian "Cannonball," & John

Coltrane
Also see ELLINGTON, Duke, & John Coltrane

COLTRANE, John, & Miles Davis

LPs: 10/12-inch

PRESTIGE 10-20 64
Also see DAVIS, Miles

COLTRANE, John, & Thelonious Monk

LPs: 10/12-inch

JAZZLAND 20-30 61
MILESTONE 8-12 73
RIVERSIDE (Except 039) 10-20 65-68
RIVERSIDE (039 "Thelonious Monk & John Coltrane") 5-10 82
Also see COLTRANE, John
Also see MONK, Thelonious

COLTS R&B '55

Singles: 78 rpm

ANTLER (4003 "Never No More") 50-75 57
ANTLER (4007 "Guiding Angel") 50-75 57
MAMBO (112 "Adorable") 100-150 55
VITA (112 "Adorable") 35-55 55
VITA (121 "Sweet Sixteen") 25-50 56
VITA (130 "Never No More") 25-50 56

Singles: 7-inch

ANTLER (4003 "Never No More") ... 75-100 57
ANTLER (4007 "Guiding Angel") 75-100 57
MAMBO (112 "Adorable") 200-500 55
PLAZA (505 "Sweet Sixteen") 15-25 62
VITA (112 "Adorable") 100-200 55
VITA (121 "Sweet Sixteen") 75-100 56
VITA (130 "Never No More") 75-100 56
Members: Eddie Williams; Joe Crunby; Rubin Grunby; Leroy Smith; Carl Moland; Don Wyatt.

COLUMBO, Chris P&R '63

(Chris Colombo Quintet)

Singles: 7-inch

BATTLE 4-8 62
MAXX 3-6 64
STRAND 4-8 63

LPs: 10/12-inch

MERCURY 5-10 75
STRAND 10-15 63

COLVIN, Shawn LP '89

LPs: 10/12-inch

COLUMBIA 5-8 89

COMATEENS D&D '83

Singles: 12-inch

MERCURY 4-6 83-84

Singles: 7-inch

MERCURY 3-4 83-84

LPs: 10/12-inch

CACHALOT 5-10 81
MERCURY 5-10 83

COMER, Tony & Crosswinds R&B '84

Singles: 7-inch

VIDCOM 3-4 84

COMMANDER CODY LP '71

(With His Lost Planet Airmen)

Singles: 7-inch

ABC 3-5 75
ARISTA 3-5 77
DOT 3-5 73-74
MCA 3-4 83
PARAMOUNT 3-5 71-74
W.B. 3-5 75

Picture Sleeves

PARAMOUNT 3-5 72-73

LPs: 10/12-inch

ARISTA 5-10 77
PARAMOUNT 10-12 71-74
W.B. 8-10 75-76

COMMODORES P&R/R&B/LP '74

Singles: 12-inch

MOTOWN 4-8 79-85
POLYDOR 4-6 86

Singles: 7-inch

ATLANTIC 5-10 69
MOTOWN 3-5 74-85
(Black vinyl.)
MOTOWN (1307 "Machine Gun") 4-6 74
(Colored vinyl. Promotional issue only.)
MOWEST 3-5 72
POLYDOR 3-4 86

Picture Sleeves

MOTOWN 3-5 85
POLYDOR 3-4 86

LPs: 10/12-inch

MOTOWN (Except 39) 8-10 74-87
MOTOWN (39 "1978 Platinum Tour") 15-20 78
(Promotional issue only.)
POLYDOR 5-10 86
Members: Lionel Ritchie; William King; Ronald LaPread; Tommy McClary; Walter Orange; Milan Williams.
Also see McCLARY, Thomas
Also see RICHIE, Lionel

COMMON SENSE R&B '81

Singles: 7-inch

BC 3-4 81

COMMUNARDS P&R/LP '86

Singles: 12-inch

MCA 4-6 86

Singles: 7-inch

MCA 3-4 86-88

LPs: 10/12-inch

MCA 5-10 86-88
Members: Jimmy Sommerville; Sara Jane Morris; Richard Coles.
Also see BRONSKI BEAT
Also see SOMERVILLE, Jimmy

COMO, Perry P&R '43

(With Hugo Winterhalter's Orchestra; with Ramblers; with Ray Charles Singers)

Singles: 78 rpm

BLUEBIRD 5-10 50
RCA 5-10 43-58

Singles: 7-inch

BLUEBIRD 10-20 50
(May also be shown as RCA Victor "Bluebird Children's Records.")
RCA (237 "Supper Club Favorites") .. 15-25 49
(Three disc set.)
RCA (0071 "Ave Maria") 10-15 49
(Black vinyl.)
RCA (0071 "Ave Maria") 15-25 49
(Colored vinyl.)
RCA (0100 thru 0900 series) 3-6 69-73
RCA (VP-2000 series) 8-12 59
(Stereo.)
RCA (2700 thru 7400 series) 8-20 48-59
RCA (61-7000 series) 8-12 58-60
(Stereo.)
RCA (7500 thru 9700 series) 4-10 59-69
RCA (10000 thru 13000 series) 3-5 74-83

Picture Sleeves

RCA (3800 thru 7100 series) 10-20 53-58
RCA (7200 thru 9700 series) 5-15 58-69

EPs: 7-inch

CAMDEN 5-10 50s
RCA (Except SPD series) 10-25 52-70
RCA (SPD-27 "Perry Como") 40-60 56
(Boxed 10-EP set. Includes inserts and biography booklet.)
RCA (SPD-28 "Perry Como Highlighter") 20-30 56
(Sampler from Kleenex Tissue. Includes picture cover.)

LPs: 10/12-inch

CAMDEN 5-15 57-74
RCA (0100 thru 4000 series) 5-15 73-83
(With "AFL1," "ANL1," "APL1," "AQL1," "AYL1," "CPL1," or "DVL2" prefix.)
RCA (1004 "Saturday Night with Mr. C") 20-30 58
RCA (1007 "Golden Records") 20-30 58
RCA (LPM-1085 "So Smooth") 20-40 55
RCA (LPM-1172 "I Believe") 20-40 56
RCA (LPM-1176 "Relaxing with Perry Como") 20-40 56
RCA (LPM-1177 "Sentimental Date with Perry Como") 20-40 56
RCA (LPM-1191 "Perry Como Sings Hits from Broadway Shows") 20-40 56
RCA (LPM-1243 Perry Sings Christmas Music") 20-40 56
RCA (LPM-1463 We Get Letters") 20-30 57
RCA (LPM-1800 thru LPM-2900 series) 15-25 58-63
RCA (LSP-1085 thru LSP-1463) 10-20 62-68
(Electronic stereo reissues.)
RCA (LSP-1800 thru LSP-2900 series) 15-30 58-63
(Stereo.)
RCA (3013 "TV Favorites") 25-50 52
(10-inch LP.)
RCA (3044 "Supper Club Favorites") 25-50 52
(10-inch LP.)
RCA (3124 "Broadway") 25-50 53
(10-inch LP.)
RCA (3133 "Christmas") 25-50 53
(10-inch LP.)
RCA (3188 "I Believe") 25-50 53
(10-inch LP.)
RCA (3224 "Golden Records") 25-50 54
(10-inch LP.)
RCA (3300 thru 4500 series) 8-15 64-71
(With "LPM" or "LSP" prefix.)
READER'S DIGEST 8-15 75
Also see CHARLES, Ray, Singers

COMO, Perry / Ames Brothers / Harry Belafonte / Radio City Music Hall Orchestra

EPs: 7-inch

RCA (SP-35 "Merry Christmas") 10-20 56
(Record dealer giveaway. Issued with paper sleeve.)
Also see AMES BROTHERS
Also see BELAFONTE, Harry
Also see WINTERHALTER, Hugo, & His Orchestra

COMO, Perry, & Eddie Fisher P&R '52

Singles: 78 rpm

RCA 4-8 52

Singles: 7-inch

RCA 5-10 52
Also see FISHER, Eddie

COMO, Perry, & Fontane Sisters P&R '50

Singles: 78 rpm

RCA 4-8 50-51

Singles: 7-inch

RCA 8-15 50-51
Also see FONTANE SISTERS

COMO, Perry, & Betty Hutton P&R '50

Singles: 78 rpm

RCA 4-8 50

Singles: 7-inch

RCA 8-15 50
Also see HUTTON, Betty

COMO, Perry, & Jaye P. Morgan

Singles: 78 rpm

RCA 4-8 55

Singles: 7-inch

RCA 5-10 55
Also see COMO, Perry
Also see MORGAN, Jaye P.

COMPAGNONS DE LA CHANSON: see LES COMPAGNONS DE LA CHANSON

COMPANY B P&R/LP '87

Singles: 7-inch

ATLANTIC 3-4 87-89

LPs: 10/12-inch

ATLANTIC 5-10 87-89
Members: Donna Huntley; Julie Marie; Susan Johnson; Lori L.

COMPANY OF WOLVES LP '90

LPs: 10/12-inch

MERCURY 5-8 90

COMPTON'S MOST WANTED LP '90

LPs: 10/12-inch

ORPHEUS 5-8 90-91

COMSTOCK, Bobby P&R '59

(With the Counts)

Singles: 7-inch

ASCOT 8-15 64-66
ATLANTIC 10-15 60
BLAZE (349 "Tennessee Waltz") 10-20 59
ERIC 3-4 73
FESTIVAL 10-15 61
JUBILEE 5-10 60-63
LAWN 8-12 62-64
MOHAWK 10-15 61
TRIUMPH 10-15 59

LPs: 10/12-inch

ASCOT (16026 "Out of Sight") 30-45 66
BLAZE ("Tennessee Waltz") 100-150
Session: King Curtis.
Also see KING CURTIS

CON FUNK SHUN P&R/R&B/LP '77

Singles: 12-inch

MERCURY 4-6 83-86

Singles: 7-inch

FRETONE 3-5 74
MERCURY 3-4 77-86

LPs: 10/12-inch

51 WEST 5-10 83
MERCURY (Except 3754) 5-10 76-86
MERCURY (3754 "Candy") 10-20 79
(Picture disc. Has die-cut cover.)
MERCURY (3754 "Candy") 15-25 79
(Picture disc. Has plastic cover. Promotional issue only.)
Members: Michael Cooper; Louis McCall; Karl Fuller; Paul Harrell; Danny Thomas; Felton Pilate II.
Also see COOPER, Michael

CONCEPT R&B '85

Singles: 7-inch

TUCKWOOD 3-4 85

CONCRETE BLONDE LP '87

Singles: 7-inch

I.R.S. 3-4 87-90

LPs: 10/12-inch

I.R.S. 5-10 87-90
Members: Johnette Napolitano; James Mankey.

CONDUCTOR P&R '82

Singles: 7-inch

JAMIE 5-10 61
MONTAGE 3-4 82

LPs: 10/12-inch

MONTAGE 5-10 82

CONEY HATCH LP '83

LPs: 10/12-inch

MERCURY 5-10 83-85

CONLEE, John C&W '78

Singles: 7-inch

ABC 3-4 78
ABC/DOT 3-4 76-77
COLUMBIA 3-4 86-87
MCA 3-4 79-85
16TH AVE. 3-4 89-90

LPs: 10/12-inch

ABC 8-10 78
COLUMBIA 5-10 86-87
MCA 5-10 79-86

CONLEY, Arthur P&R/R&B/LP '67

Singles: 7-inch

ATCO 3-5 67-70
CAPRICORN 3-4 71-74
FAME (1007 "In The Same Old Way") 8-12 66
JOTIS 3-5 66

LPs: 10/12-inch

ATCO 15-25 67-69
Also see ARTHUR & CORVETS
Also see SOUL CLAN

CONNICK, Harry, Jr. LP '89

(Harry Connick Jr. Trio)

LPs: 10/12-inch

COLUMBIA 5-8 90-91

CONNIE R&B/D&D '85

Singles: 12-inch

SUNNYVIEW 4-6 85-86

Singles: 7-inch

SUNNYVIEW 3-4 85-86

CONNIFF, Ray P&R/LP '57

(With the Rockin' Rhythm Boys; Ray Conniff Orchestra & Chorus)

Singles: 78 rpm

BRUNSWICK 4-8 57
COLUMBIA 3-5 56-57
CORAL 4-8 55

Singles: 7-inch

BRUNSWICK 5-10 57
COLUMBIA 3-8 56-82
CORAL 5-10 55

Picture Sleeves

COLUMBIA 3-8 60-64

EPs: 7-inch

COLUMBIA (Except 10041/2/3) 5-10 56-59
COLUMBIA (10041/2/3 "Dance the Bop") 8-12 57
(Price is for either volume.)

LPs: 10/12-inch

COLUMBIA (Except 925 & 1004) 5-15 58-82
COLUMBIA (925 "S' Wonderful") 10-20 56
COLUMBIA (1004 "Dance the Bop") 15-25 57
HARMONY 4-8 69
Also see MATHIS, Johnny
Also see ROBBINS, Marty

CONNOR, Chris P&R '56

Singles: 78 rpm

ATLANTIC 5-15 56-57
BETHLEHEM 5-10 54-55

Singles: 7-inch

ATLANTIC 8-15 56-62
BETHLEHEM (1200 & 1300 series) . 10-20 54-55
BETHLEHEM (3000 series) 4-8 64
FM 4-8 63

EPs: 7-inch

ATLANTIC (593/4/5/6 "Chris Connor Sings the George Gershwin Almanac") 30-40 57
(Price is for any of four volumes.)
ATLANTIC (580 "I Miss You So") 30-40 57
ATLANTIC (615 "Jazz Date") 30-40 58
BETHLEHEM 20-40 54-56

LPs: 10/12-inch

ABC-PAR 10-20 65-66
ATLANTIC (601 "Chris Connor Sings the George Gershwin Almanac") 50-100 57
ATLANTIC (1240 "He Loves Me He Loves Me Not") 50-100 57
ATLANTIC (1228 "Chris Connor") .. 50-100 57
ATLANTIC (1286 "Jazz Date") 50-75 58
ATLANTIC (1290 "Chris Craft") 50-75 58
ATLANTIC (1307 "Sad Cafe") 50-75 59
(Monaural.)
ATLANTIC (SD-1307 "Sad Cafe") 60-80 59
(Stereo.)
ATLANTIC (8014 "I Miss You So") ... 50-75 58
ATLANTIC (8032 "Witchcraft") 50-75 59
(Monaural.)
ATLANTIC (SD-8032 "Witchcraft") ... 60-80 59
(Stereo.)
ATLANTIC (8040 "In Person") 40-60 59
(Monaural.)
ATLANTIC (SD-8040 "In Person") 50-75 59
(Stereo.)
ATLANTIC (8046 "A Portrait") 30-50 60
(Monaural.)
ATLANTIC (SD-8046 "A Portrait") 40-60 60
(Stereo.)
ATLANTIC (8061 "Free Spirits") 25-50 62
(Monaural.)
ATLANTIC (SD-8061 "Free Spirits") 30-60 62
(Stereo.)
BETHLEHEM (20 "This Is Chris") 50-100 55
(Maroon label.)
BETHLEHEM (56 "Chris") 50-100 56
(Maroon label.)
BETHLEHEM (1001 Lullabys of Birdland") 75-125 54
(10-inch LP.)
BETHLEHEM (1002 Lullabys for Lovers, Vol. 2") 75-125 54
(10-inch LP.)
BETHLEHEM (6000 series) 10-12 78
(Gray label.)
BETHLEHEM (6004 "Lullabys of Birdland") 50-100 56
(Maroon label.)
BETHLEHEM (6005 "Lullabys for Lovers") 50-100 56
(Maroon label.)
FM 10-15 63
Also see BON BONS
Also see FERGUSON, Maynard, & Chris Connor
Also see SIMONE, Nina, Chris Connor & Carmen McRae

CONNOR, Chris / Julie London / Carmen McRae

LPs: 10/12-inch

BETHLEHEM (6006 "Bethlehem Girlfriends") 50-100 56
(Maroon label.)
Also see CONNOR, Chris
Also see LONDON, Julie
Also see McRAE, Carmen

CONNORS, Norman R&B/LP '75

Singles: 7-inch

ARISTA 3-4 78-81
BUDDAH 3-5 74-77
CAPITOL 3-4 88

LPs: 10/12-inch

ARISTA 5-10 78-81
BUDDAH 10-12 75-78
NOVUS 5-10 81
Session: Michael Henderson; Pharoah Sanders; Jean Cain; Phyllis Hyman; Prince Phillip Mitchell.
Also see AQUARIAN DREAM
Also see HENDERSON, Michael
Also see HYMAN, Phyllis

CONSUMER RAPPORT P&R/R&B '75

Singles: 7-inch

WING and a PRAYER 3-5 75-76
Member: Frank Floyd.

CONTI, Bill P&R '77

Singles: 7-inch

ARISTA 3-4 82
U.A. 3-5 77-78

LPs: 10/12-inch

MCA 5-10 79
U.A. 8-12 78-79

CONTINENTAL 4 P&R/R&B '71

(Continental Four)

Singles: 7-inch

JAY WALKING 4-8 71-72

LPs: 10/12-inch

JAY WALKING 10-15 71
Members: Fred Kelly; Anthony Burke; Ronnie McGregor; Larry McGregor.

CONTINENTAL MINIATURES P&R '78

Singles: 7-inch

LONDON 3-5 78

Picture Sleeves

LONDON 3-5 78

CONTINO, Dick P&R '54

Singles: 78 rpm

MERCURY 3-5 54-57

Singles: 7-inch

DOT 3-6 66-67
MERCURY 4-8 54-64

EPs: 7-inch

MERCURY 5-10 55-59

LPs: 10/12-inch

DOT 5-15 64-66
HAMILTON 5-10 64-66
MERCURY 8-15 56-63
WING 5-10 63
Also see CARROLL, David

CONTOURS *P&R/R&B '62*
(With Jack Surrell)

Singles: 12-inch

MOTOWN 4-8 88

Singles: 7-inch

GORDY 8-15 62-67
HOB (116 "I'm So Glad") 75-100 61
MOTOWN (400 series) 3-4 82-88
MOTOWN (1008 "Whole Lotta Woman") 350-450 61
MOTOWN (1012 "Funny") 450-650 61
TAMLA (7012 "Shake Sherry") 75-125 62
(Tamla label with Gordy selection number.)
ROCKET 3-4 80

Picture Sleeves

MOTOWN 3-4 88

EPs: 7-inch

MOTOWN (2002 "The Contours") 15-25 60s

LPs: 10/12-inch

GORDY (901 "Do You Love Me") 50-100 62
MOTOWN 5-10 82
Members: Dennis Edwards; Bill Gordon; Sylvester Potts; Billy Hoggs; Joe Billingslea; Joe Stubbs; Hubert Johnson; Huey Davis.
Also see EDWARDS, Dennis

CONTRABAND *LP '91*

LPs: 10/12-inch

IMPACT 5-8 91

CONTROLLERS *R&B '76*
(With Valerie DeMece)

Singles: 12-inch

MCA 4-6 85-86

Singles: 7-inch

JUANA 3-4 76-82
MCA 3-4 85-88

LPs: 10/12-inch

JUANA 8-10 77-79
MCA 5-10 86
WINDHAM HILL 5-10 85
Members: Larry McArthur; Regie McArthur; Ricky Lewis; Leonard Brown.

CONVERTION *R&B '81*

Singles: 7-inch

SAM 3-4 81
VANGUARD 3-4 83

LPs: 10/12-inch

VANGUARD 5-10 83

CONWAY BROTHERS *R&B '85*

Singles: 7-inch

ICHIBAN 3-4 87
PBT 3-4 86
PAULA 3-4 85
Members: Huston Conway; Jim Conway; Fredrick Conway; Hiawatha Conway.

CONWELL, Tommy, & Young Rumblers *P&R/LP '88*

Singles: 12-inch

COLUMBIA 4-8 88
(Promotional only.)

Singles: 7-inch

COLUMBIA 3-4 88

Picture Sleeves

COLUMBIA 3-4 88

LPs: 10/12-inch

ANTENNA 10-15 86
COLUMBIA 5-8 88
Members: Tommy Conwell; Rob Miller; Paul Slivka; Jim Hannum; Chris Day.
Also see HOOTERS

COODER, Ry *LP '72*

Singles: 7-inch

MUSICOR 4-8 66
REPRISE 3-6 69-72
W.B. 3-5 77-82

LPs: 10/12-inch

MFSL (085 "Jazz") 25-50 82
REPRISE 8-12 72-76
W.B. 5-10 77-87
Also see CAPTAIN BEEFHEART
Also see HOPKINS, Nicky
Also see LITTLE FEAT

COOK, Tony *D&D '84*

Singles: 12-inch

HALFMOON 4-6 84

COOKE, Dale
(Sam Cooke)

Singles: 78 rpm

SPECIALTY (596 "Forever") 15-25 57

Singles: 7-inch

SPECIALTY (596 "Forever") 15-25 57
Also see COOKE, Sam

COOKE, SAM *P&R/R&B '57*
(With the Soul Stirrers)

Singles: 78 rpm

KEEN 50-75 57
SPECIALTY 20-40 57

Singles: 7-inch

CHERIE 3-5 71
COLLECTABLES 3-4 81
KEEN (Black & silver label) 20-35 57
KEEN (Multi-color label) 15-25 57-60
(Monaural.)
KEEN (Multi-color label) 25-50 58-60
(Stereo.)
KEEN (Black & multi-color label) 15-25 59-61
(Monaural.)
KEEN (Black & multi-color label) 25-50 60
(Stereo.)
RCA (7000 series) 25-50 61-62
(With "37" prefix. Compact 33 Singles.)
RCA (7000 & 8000 series) 10-20 60-66
(With "47" prefix.)
RCA (7000 series) 25-50 60-61
(Stereo. With "61" prefix.)
SPECIALTY (SPBX series) 12-18 87
(Boxed set of six colored vinyl singles.)
SPECIALTY (500 & 600 series) 15-25 57-59
SPECIALTY (900 series) 3-5 70-72

Picture Sleeves

RCA 10-20 60-65

EPs: 7-inch

KEEN (2001/2002/2003 "Songs by Sam Cooke") 30-40 57
(Price is for any of three volumes.)
KEEN (2012/2013/2014 "Tribute to the Lady") 20-30 59
(Price is for any of three volumes.)
KEEN (2006 "Encore") 20-40 58
KEEN (2008 "Encore, Vol. 2") 20-40 58
RCA (126 "Sam Cooke Sings") 25-50 61
(Compact 33.)
RCA (3373 "Sam Cooke") 15-20 64
(Juke box issue.)
RCA (4375 "Another Saturday Night") 15-25 63

LPs: 10/12-inch

CAMDEN 8-10 68-74
CANDLELITE 15-20 74
(Mail-order offer.)
CHERIE 8-10 71
FAMOUS 10-20 69
KEEN (2001 "Sam Cooke") 40-60 58
KEEN (2003 "Encore") 35-45 58
KEEN (2004 "Tribute to the Lady") 30-40 59
KEEN (86101 "Hit Kit") 35-50 59
KEEN (86103 "I Thank God") 30-40 60
KEEN (86106 "Wonderful World") 30-40 60
PHOENIX 10 ....5-10 81
PICKWICK 5-10 76
RCA (2000 & 3000 series) 15-35 60-68
(With "LPM" or "LSP" prefix.)
RCA (2000 thru 5000 series) 5-10 78-85
(With "AFL1," "ANL1" or "AYL1" prefix.)
RCA (7000 series) 8-12 86
SAR 3-5 61
SOUFFLE 5-10
SPECIALTY 8-12 69-89
TRIP 8-10 72-76
UPFRONT 8-10 73
Also see ANKA, Paul / Sam Cooke / Neil Sedaka
Also see CHARLES, Ray / Little Richard / Sam Cooke
Also see COOKE, Dale
Also see RAWLS, Lou
Also see SOUL STIRRERS

COOKE, Sam / Rod Lauren / Neil Sedaka / Browns

EPs: 7-inch

RCA (33-99 "Compact 33 Double") ... 15-20 60
(Has the same four songs on each side, mono on one side, stereo on the reverse.)
Also see BROWNS
Also see LAUREN, Rod
Also see SEDAKA, Neil

COOKE, Sam / Lloyd Price / Larry Williams / Little Richard

LPs: 10/12-inch

SPECIALTY (2112 "Our Significant Hits") 25-35 60
(Black and gold label.)
Also see COOKE, Sam
Also see LITTLE RICHARD
Also see PRICE, Lloyd
Also see WILLIAMS, Larry

COOKER *P&R '74*
(Norman Des Rosiers)

Singles: 7-inch

SCEPTER 3-5 73-74

LPs: 10/12-inch

SCEPTER 8-10 74

COOKER, John Lee
(John Lee Hooker)

Singles: 7-inch

KING (4504 "Stomp Boogie") 50-100 52
Also see HOOKER, John Lee

COOKIE & HIS CUPCAKES *P&R '59*
(Cookie & His Berry Cups)

Singles: 7-inch

CHESS 5-10 63
JUDD 10-20 59
KHOURY'S (703 "Matilda") 20-30 59
LYRIC 10-15 63-64
MERCURY 5-10 61
PAULA 4-8 65-68
Members: Terry "Cookie" Clinton; Shelton Dunaway; Lil' Alfred.

COOKIE & HIS CUPCAKES / Little Alfred

Singles: 7-inch

LYRIC 8-12 64
Also see COOKIE & His Cupcakes

COOKIES *R&B '56*

Singles: 78 rpm

ATLANTIC 10-25 55-57
JOSIE (822 "King of Hearts") 15-25 57
LAMP (8008 "Don't Let Go") 10-20 54

Singles: 7-inch

ATLANTIC (1061 "Precious Love") ... 15-25 55
ATLANTIC (1084 "Passing Time") 15-25 56
ATLANTIC (1110 "My Lover") 10-20 56
ATLANTIC (2079 "Passing Time") 10-15 60
JOSIE (822 "King of Hearts") 15-25 57
LAMP (8008 "Don't Let Go") 20-30 54
Members: Earl-Jean McCree; Margie Hendrix; Pat Lyles.
Also see CHARLES, Ray
Also see COOKIES (Group that follows)
Also see DILLARD, Varetta
Also see WILLIS, Chuck

COOKIES *P&R/R&B '62*

Singles: 7-inch

ABC 3-5 74
DIMENSION (1002 "Chains") 10-20 62
DIMENSION (1008 "Don't Say Nothin' Bad About My Baby") 10-20 63
DIMENSION (1012 "Will Power") 10-20 63

DIMENSION (1020 "Girls Grow Up Faster Than Boys") 10-20 63
DIMENSION (1032 "The Old Crowd") 15-25 63
ERIC 3-5 73
MCA 3-5 83
Members: Earl-Jean McCree; Margaret Ross; Dorothy Jones.
Also see EARL-JEAN

COOKIES / Little Eva / Carole King

LPs: 10/12-inch

DIMENSION (6001 "The Dimension Dolls, Vol. 1") 50-75 63
Also see COOKIES
Also see KING, Carole
Also see LITTLE EVA

COOL HEAT — P&R '70

Singles: 7-inch

FORWARD (152 "Are You Nuts") 5-10 70
Also see WIND

COOLEY, Eddie — P&R '56

(With the Dimples)

Singles: 78 rpm

ROYAL ROOST 20-40 56-57

Singles: 7-inch

ABC 3-4 73
ROULETTE 5-10 60
ROYAL ROOST 10-20 56-57
TRIUMPH 8-12 59

COOLIDGE, Rita — P&R '69

Singles: 7-inch

A&M 3-5 71-83
PEPPER 4-8 68-69

Picture Sleeves

A&M 3-6 72-83

LPs: 10/12-inch

A&M 5-10 71-83

Promotional LPs

A&M ("In-Store Sampler - Rita Coolidge") 10-15
Also see CAMPBELL, Glen, & Rita Coolidge
Also see CLAPTON, Eric
Also see KRISTOFFERSON, Kris, & Rita Coolidge

COOPER, Alice — LP '69

(Alice Cooper Group)

Promotional Singles: 12-inch

EPIC (1347 "I Got a Line on You") 5-8
EPIC (1663 "Poison") 5-8 89
EPIC (1686 "Trash") 5-8 89
EPIC (1890 "I'm Your Gun") 5-8 89
MCA (17177 "He's Back") 5-8 86
MCA (17205 "Give It Up") 5-8 86
W.B. (864 "Clones") 10-15 80
W.B. (1059 "I Like Girls") 5-8

Singles: 7-inch

ATLANTIC 3-5 75
EPIC 3-4 89-90
MCA 3-4 86-87
STRAIGHT (101 "Reflected") 15-25 69
STRAIGHT (7398 "Shoe Salesman") 15-20 70
W.B. 3-5 70-82

Promotional Singles

ATLANTIC 5-10 75
MCA 3-6 86-87
W.B. 8-12 70-80

Picture Sleeves

MCA 3-4 87
W.B. 4-8 72-80

EPs: 7-inch

W.B. 15-25 73
(Juke box issues only.)

LPs: 10/12-inch

ATLANTIC 5-10 75-78
EPIC 5-8 89
MFSL (063 "Welcome to My Nightmare") 40-60 82
MCA 5-10 86-87
STRAIGHT (1051 "Pretties for You") 30-40 69
(Cover has a drawing of a woman raising her dress, with a yellow sticker covering her crotch area. Price is for cover with sticker still intact.)
STRAIGHT (1051 "Pretties for You") 20-30 69
(Cover shows the woman with the sticker removed and panties showing.)
W.B. (Except 1883, 2567 & 2623) 8-12 73-84
W.B. (1883 "Love It to Death") 25-30 71
(Black cover has Cooper's right thumb showing through his wrap. Does NOT have white block reading "Including Their Hit *I'm Eighteen.*")
W.B. (1883 "Love It to Death") 15-20 71
(Black cover has Cooper's right thumb showing through his wrap. Has white block reading "Including Their Hit *I'm Eighteen.*" Also includes issue with huge white stripes at top and bottom of cover.)
W.B. (1883 "Love It to Death") 5-10 71
(Black cover does NOT have Cooper's right thumb showing through his wrap. Has the white block reading "Including Their Hit *I'm Eighteen.*")
W.B. (2567 "Killer") 15-18 71
(With poster and 1972 calendar.)
W.B. (2567 "Killer") 5-10 72
(Without poster and calendar.)
W.B. (2623 "School's Out") 30-40 72
(With panties attached. Panties came in four different colors: pink, white, yellow, and blue. Back cover does not list titles.)
W.B. (2623 "School's Out") 15-20 72
(With panties attached. Back cover lists titles.)
W.B. (2623 "School's Out") 5-10 72
(With no paper panties. Back cover lists titles.)
W.B. (2685 "Billion Dollar Babies") 5-10 73
W.B. (BS4-2685 "Billion Dollar Babies") 20-25 73
(Quad issue.)
W.B. (2748 "Muscle of Love") 5-10 73
W.B. (BBS4-2748 "Muscle of Love") 20-25 73
(Quad issue.)
W.B. (2803 thru 3581) 5-10 74-81
W.B./STRAIGHT (1051 "Pretties for You") 15-18 69
W.B./STRAIGHT (1845 "Easy Action") 30-35 70
(With the name "Alice Cooper" in black letters on front cover.)
W.B./STRAIGHT (1845 "Easy Action") 5-10 70
(With "Alice Cooper" in white letters on front.)

Promotional LPs

CHELSEA PROD ("Allison's Tea House") 25-30 74
STRAIGHT (1051 "Pretties for You") 45-55 69
(Cover has drawing of a woman raising her dress, with a yellow sticker covering her crotch area. Price is for cover with sticker still intact.)
STRAIGHT (1051 "Pretties for You") 30-40 69
(Cover shows the woman with the sticker removed and panties showing.)
STRAIGHT (1845 "Easy Action") 25-30 70
STRAIGHT (1883 "Love It to Death") 20-25 71
W.B. 20-40 71-78
(Includes all white label promo labels.)
W.B./STRAIGHT ("Pretties for You") 25-30 69
Members: Alice Cooper; Dennis Dunaway; Glen Buxton; Michael Bruce; Neal Smith; Kane Roberts; Ken K. Mary.
Also see BILLION DOLLAR BABIES
Also see FROST
Also see NAZZ
Also see SPIDERS

COOPER, Les, & Soul Rockers — P&R/R&B '62

Singles: 7-inch

ABC 3-4 73
ARRAWAK 4-8 65
ATCO 3-6 69
DIMENSION (1023 "Motor City") 10-15 64
ENJOY 4-8 65
EVERLAST 5-10 62
SAMAR 4-8 66

LPs: 10/12-inch

EVERLAST (202 "Wiggle Wobble") 40-60 63
Members: Les Cooper; Joe Grier.
Also see CHARTS

COOPER, Michael — R&B '87

Singles: 7-inch

W.B. 3-4 87-88

LPs: 10/12-inch

W.B. 5-8 88
Also see CON FUNK SHUN

COOPER, Pat — LP '66

LPs: 10/12-inch

U.A. 10-15 66-69

COOPER BROTHERS — P&R '78

Singles: 7-inch

CAPRICORN 3-4 78-79

LPs: 10/12-inch

CAPRICORN 5-10 78-79
Members: Richard Cooper; Brian Cooper.
Also see BLACK OAK ARKANSAS / Cooper Brothers

COPAS, Cowboy — C&W '46

(Cowboy "Poppy" Copas; Lloyd Copas; with Kathy Copas)

Singles: 78 rpm

KING 5-15 44-57

Singles: 7-inch

DOT 10-20 57-58
KING (951 thru 1507) 10-20 50-55
KING (4865 thru 5270) 5-10 55-59
KING (5392 thru 5734) 4-8 60-63
STARDAY (476 thru 750) 4-8 60-66
STARDAY (7000 series) 3-6 64
STARDAY (8000 series) 3-4 71

EPs: 7-inch

KING 15-25 52-53
STARDAY 10-20 60

LPs: 10/12-inch

BUCKBOARD 5-10
GUEST STAR 10-15
KING (553 "All-Time Hits") 45-55 57
KING (556 "Favorite Sacred Songs") 40-50 57
KING (619 thru 835) 25-35 59-64
KING (894 thru 1049) 8-12 64-69
NASHVILLE 8-12 68-70
PICKWICK/HILLTOP 10-12 66
STARDAY (113 "All Time Country Music Great") 20-30 60
STARDAY (133 "Inspirational Songs") 20-30 61
STARDAY (144 "Songs That Made Him Famous") 20-30 62
STARDAY (157 "Opry Star Spotlight") 20-30 63
STARDAY (175 "Mr. Country Music") 20-30 64
STARDAY (200 series) 12-25 64-67
STARDAY (300 series) 10-20 65-67
STARDAY (400 series) 8-12 68-70
Also see COPAS, Lloyd
Also see MULLICAN, Moon / Cowboy Copas / Red Sovine

COPAS, Cowboy / Hawkshaw Hawkins

LPs: 10/12-inch

KING 12-25 63-66
Also see CLINE, Patsy / Cowboy Copas / Hawkshaw Hawkins
Also see COPAS, Cowboy
Also see HAWKINS, Hawkshaw

COPAS, Lloyd

Singles: 7-inch

DOT (15735 "Circle Rock") 60-80 58
Also see COPAS, Cowboy

COPE, Julian — P&R/LP '87

Singles: 7-inch

ISLAND 3-4 87-88

Picture Sleeves

ISLAND 3-4 87

LPs: 10/12-inch

ISLAND....5-10 87-88

Also see TEARDROP EXPLODES

COPELAND, Ken

Singles: 78 rpm

IMPERIAL....10-20 57
LIN....10-20 58

Singles: 7-inch

DOT....8-12 58
IMPERIAL....10-15 57
LIN (5007 "Fanny Brown")....20-30 58

COPELAND, Ken / Mints P&R '57

Singles: 78 rpm

IMPERIAL....10-20 57
LIN....10-20 56-57

Singles: 7-inch

IMPERIAL....10-15 57
LIN (5007 "Pledge of Love")....15-25 56
LIN (5017 "Fanny Brown")....20-30 57

Also see COPELAND, Ken

COPELAND, Stewart LP '83

(Stuart Copeland)

LPs: 10/12-inch

A&M....5-10 83-85

Also see POLICE

COPELAND, Stewart, & Adam Ant

Singles: 7-inch

MCA/I.R.S. 3-4 86

Also see ANT, Adam

COPELAND, Stewart, & Stan Ridgway

Singles: 7-inch

A&M....3-4 83

Also see COPELAND, Stewart
Also see WALL of VOODOO

COPELAND, Vivian R&B '69

Singles: 7-inch

D'ORO....3-6 69
MALA....4-8 67

CORDEL, Pat

(With the Crescents "Later Known As the Elegants"; with Cherokee & Band; with Elegants)

Singles: 7-inch

CLUB (1011 "Darling Come Back")....250-500 56
MICHELE (503 "Darling Come Back")....100-200 59
VICTORY (1001 "Darling Come Back")....50-75 63

Also see ELEGANTS

COREA, Chick LP '76

Singles: 7-inch

POLYDOR....3-4 79

LPs: 10/12-inch

BLUE NOTE....8-12 75-78
ECM....5-10 75-80
ELEKTRA....5-8 83
PACIFIC JAZZ....5-8 81
POLYDOR....6-12 76-78
VERVE....8-10 76
W.B. 5-8 80-81

Also see HANCOCK, Herbie, & Chick Corea
Also see RETURN to FOREVER

COREY, Jill P&R '54

Singles: 78 rpm

COLUMBIA....3-6 54-57

Singles: 7-inch

COLUMBIA....5-10 54-60
MERCURY....4-8 62

EPs: 7-inch

COLUMBIA....8-12 55-57

LPs: 10/12-inch

COLUMBIA....15-25 56-57

CORLEY, Al P&R '85

Singles: 7-inch

MERCURY....3-4 85

Picture Sleeves

MERCURY....3-4 85

CORLEY, Bob P&R '55

Singles: 78 rpm

RCA....3-5 56
STARS....10-20 55

Singles: 7-inch

RCA....5-10 56
STARS....20-25 55

CORNBREAD & BISCUITS P&R/R&B '60

(With Lea Lendon & Orchestra)

Singles: 7-inch

ANNA (102 "The Big Time Spender")....25-50 59
(This is the Maske disc with an Anna label sticker applied to each side, covering "Maske.")
MASKE (102 "The Big Time Spender")....15-25 60

CORNELIUS BROTHERS & SISTER ROSE P&R/R&B '71

Singles: 7-inch

PLATINUM....8-12 70
U.A. 3-5 70-74

LPs: 10/12-inch

PICKWICK....5-10 76
U.A. 10-15 72-76

Members: Ed Cornelius; Carter Cornelius; Rose Cornelius.

CORNELL, Don P&R '50

Singles: 78 rpm

CORAL....4-10 52-57

Singles: 7-inch

ABC-PAR....3-6 65
CORAL....5-15 52-57
DOT....4-8 59-60
JAYBEE....3-5 69
JUBILEE....3-6 62
SIGNATURE....4-8 59-60
20TH FOX....3-6 64

EPs: 7-inch

CORAL....5-10 54-56

LPs: 10/12-inch

ABC-PAR....8-12 66
CORAL....15-25 54-57
DOT....10-15 59
MOVIETONE....5-10 66
SIGNATURE....10-15 59
VOCALION....8-15 59

Also see KAYE, Sammy

CORNELL, Don, Johnny Desmond & Alan Dale P&R '53

Singles: 78 rpm

CORAL....3-6 53

Singles: 7-inch

CORAL....5-10 53

EPs: 7-inch

CORAL....5-10 54

Also see CORNELL, Don
Also see DALE, Alan
Also see DESMOND, Johnny

CORNER BOYS R&B '69

Singles: 7-inch

NEPTUNE....4-6 69

Members: Victor Drayton; Jerry Akines; Reginald Turner; Ernie Brooks; Johnny Bellman.

CORONETS R&B '53

(With Sax Mallard & Combo)

Singles: 78 rpm

CHESS....25-50 53
GROOVE....25-50 55

Singles: 7-inch

CHESS (1549 "Nadine")....150-250 53
(Silver top label with chess pieces.)
CHESS (1549 "Nadine")....10-20
(Blue label.)
CHESS (1553 "It Would Be Heavenly")....250-350 53
(Black vinyl. Silver top label with chess pieces.)
CHESS (1553 "It Would Be Heavenly")....10-20 53
(Black vinyl. Blue label.)
CHESS (1553 "It Would Be Heavenly")....750-1000 53
(Colored vinyl.)
GROOVE (0114 "I Love You More")....200-300 55
GROOVE (0116 "Hush")....200-300 55

Members: Charles Carothers; Lester Russaw; George Lewis; William Griggs; Sam Griggs; Babby Ward.

CORPORATION LP '69

Singles: 7-inch

ABC-PAR....10-15 68
AGE OF AQUARIUS (1496 "You Make Me Feel So Good")....10-20 69
CAPITOL (2467 "Highway")....10-15 69
CUCA (1496 "You Make Me Feel Good")....10-15 68
MUSICOR (1418 "Candida")....5-10 68

LPs: 10/12-inch

AGE of AQUARIUS (4150 "The Corporation")....30-50 70
AGE of AQUARIUS (4250 "Hassels in My Mind")....20-30 69
CAPITOL (175 "The Corporation")....20-30 69

Members: Danny Peil; Ken Berdoll; John Kondos; Nicholas Kondos; Pat McCarthy; Gerald Smith.

CORSAIRS P&R '61

(Featuring Jay "Bird" Uzzell)

Singles: 7-inch

CHESS (1808 "Smokey Places")....6-12 61
CHESS (1818 "I'll Take You Home")....6-12 62
ERIC....3-4 78
SMASH (1715 "Time Waits")....6-12 61
TUFF (1 "The Ring")....15-25 61
TUFF (375 "Save a Little Monkey")....5-10 64
TUFF (1808 "Smokey Places")....10-15 61
TUFF (1818 "I'll Take You Home")....10-15 62
(First issue.)
TUFF (1830 "While")....15-25 62
TUFF (1840 "At the Stroke of Midnight")....10-15 62
TUFF (1847 "Stormy")....10-15 63

CORTEZ, Dave "Baby" P&R/R&B '59

(With the Moon People; Baby Cortez)

Singles: 78 rpm

CLOCK (1009 "The Happy Organ")....50-75 59

Singles: 7-inch

ABC....3-4 74
ALL PLATINUM....3-5 72
ARGO....4-8 64
CHESS....4-8 63
CLOCK....10-20 59-62
COLLECTABLES....3-4 81
EMIT....5-10 62
ERIC....3-4 73
FIRE....5-10 60
HI OLDIES....4-6 77
JULIA....15-25 62
OKEH (7100 series)....15-25 58
OKEH (7200 series)....10-15 64
ROULETTE....4-8 65-68
SOUND....3-5 71
SPEED....3-5
T-NECK....3-6 69
WINLEY....4-8 62

EPs: 7-inch

CLOCK (4039 " Dave 'Baby' Cortez & His Happy Organ")....20-30 61
RCA (EPA-4342 "Dave 'Baby' Cortez & His Happy Organ")....20-30 59
(Monaural.)
RCA (ESP-4342 "Dave 'Baby' Cortez & His Happy Organ")....35-50 59
(Stereo.)

LPs: 10/12-inch

CHESS....25-30 62
CLOCK....25-35 60-63
CORONET....10-15 60s
CROWN....15-20 63
DESIGN....10-15 60s
METRO....10-20 65

RCA (LPM-2099 "Dave 'Baby' Cortez & His Happy Organ") 25-35 59
(Monaural.)
RCA (LSP-2099 "Dave `Baby' Cortez & His Happy Organ") 35-50 59
(Stereo.)
ROULETTE 15-20 65-66
Also see CLOWNEY, David, Band
Also see ISLEY BROTHERS & Dave "Baby" Cortez
Also see JESTERS
Also see PARAGONS
Also see VALENTINES

CORTEZ, Dave "Baby" / Jerry's House Rockers

LPs: 10/12-inch

CROWN 10-20 63
Also see CORTEZ, Dave "Baby"

CORYELL, Larry LP '69

LPs: 10/12-inch

ARISTA 5-10 76
VANGUARD 10-15 69
Also see ELEVENTH HOUR / ELEVENTH HOUSE
Also see MOUZON, Alphonse, & Larry Croyell

COSBY, Bill LP '64

Singles: 12-inch

MOTOWN (110 "Super Special for Radio") 5-10 82
(Promotional issue only.)

Singles: 7-inch

CAPITOL 3-5 76-78
UNI 3-6 69-70
W.B. 3-5 65-67

EPs: 7-inch

W.B. (274 "A Taste of Cosby") 5-10
(Promotional issue only.)

LPs: 10/12-inch

CAPITOL 5-10 76-78
COLUMBIA (40270 "Music from the Bill Cosby Show") 5-10 86
(Featuring Grover Washington Jr.)
GEFFEN 5-10 86
MCA 5-10 73
MOTOWN 5-10 82
PARTEE 5-10
TETRAGRAMMATON 6-10 69
UNI 5-10 69-72
W.B. (Except 249) 10-15 64-70
W.B. (249 "Best of Bill Cosby") 15-20 69
(Promotional issue only.)
Also see ROSS, Diana, & Bill Cosby / Diana Ross & Jackson Five
Also see WASHINGTON, Grover, Jr.

COSBY, Bill, & Ozzie Davis

LPs: 10/12-inch

BLACK FORUM 8-12 72
Also see COSBY, Bill

COSTA, Don, Orchestra P&R '59

Singles: 78 rpm

ABC-PAR 4-8 56-57
ESSEX 4-8 55

Singles: 7-inch

ABC-PAR 5-10 56-57
COLUMBIA 3-5 62-63
DCP 3-5 64-65
ESSEX 5-10 55
JAMIE 4-8 59
MGM 3-5 66-72
MERCURY 3-5 68
U.A. 4-8 59-62
VERVE 3-5 67

Picture Sleeves

U.A. 5-10 60
VERVE 4-8 67

LPs: 10/12-inch

ABC-PAR 15-30 56-61
COLUMBIA 10-20 62-63
DCP 5-10 64-65
HARMONY 5-10 65
MERCURY 5-10 68-69
U.A. 10-20 59-62
VERVE 5-10 67
Also see ANKA, Paul
Also see DE CASTRO SISTERS
Also see GALLOP, Frank
Also see MANN, Gloria

COSTANDINOS, Alec R. LP '78

(With the Syncophonic Orchestra)

Singles: 7-inch

CASABLANCA 3-4 79

LPs: 10/12-inch

CASABLANCA 5-10 78-79

COSTELLO, Elvis LP '77

(With the Attractions; Costello Show)

Singles: 12-inch

COLUMBIA 5-15 83-85

Singles: 7-inch

CBS (Black vinyl) 3-5 79
CBS (Colored vinyl) 10-20 79
COLUMBIA 3-5 77-86
W.B. 3-4 89

Promotional Singles

COLUMBIA 5-10 77-86

Picture Sleeves

COLUMBIA (Except 10919) 3-6 81-85
COLUMBIA (10919 "Accidents Will Happen") 15-20 78
(Promotional issue only.)
W.B. 3-4 89

EPs: 7-inch

COLUMBIA (529 "Live at Hollywood High") 10-20 78
(Bonus EP. Included with the LP *Armed Forces*.)
COLUMBIA (11251 "I Can't Stand Up for Falling Down") 10-20 80
COLUMBIA (11251 "I Can't Stand Up for Falling Down") 20-30 80
(White label. Promotional issue only.)

LPs: 10/12-inch

COLUMBIA (30000 series, except 35709) 8-12 77-86
COLUMBIA (35709 "Armed Forces") 15-25 79
(Includes the bonus EP *Live at Hollywood High*.)
COLUMBIA (35709 "Armed Forces") 8-12 79
(Without *Live at Hollywood High* EP.)
COLUMBIA (35709 "Armed Forces") 30-40 79
(Colored vinyl.)
COLUMBIA/COSTELLO (35331 "This Year's Model") 20-30 78
COLUMBIA (40000 series, except 48157) 5-8 85-86
COLUMBIA (48157 "Imperial Bedroom") 30-40 82
(Half-speed mastered.)
W.B. 5-10 89-91

Promotional LPs

COLUMBIA ("My Aim Is True"/"This Year's Model") 125-150 79
(Picture disc. No number given.)
COLUMBIA (529 "Live at Hollywood High") 30-45 79
COLUMBIA (958 "Tom Snyder Interview") 25-35 81
COLUMBIA (1318 "Almost Blue") 25-35 81
COLUMBIA (35709 "Armed Forces") 20-25 79
(With programming sticker on cover.)
COLUMBIA/COSTELLO (847 "Taking Liberties") 30-35 80
KING BISCUIT FLOWER HOUR (For July 13, 1980) 75-125
WESTWOOD ONE ("Off the Record") 40-60
Also see CLIFF, Jimmy, Elvis Costello & Attractions
Also see HIATT, John
Also see NICK & ELVIS
Also see WHEELER, Caron

COTTON, Gene P&R '74

Singles: 7-inch

ABC 3-5 75-77
ARIOLA AMERICA 3-5 77-79
GENE COTTON ("Child of Peace") 4-6 81
(No actual label name or number. A gift to radio stations. With explanatory insert.)
KNOLL 3-4 81-82
MYRRH 3-5 74

LPs: 10/12-inch

ABC 8-10 76-77
ACCORD 5-10 83
ARIOLA AMERICA 5-10 78-79
BUDDAH 8-10 74-75
CAPITOL 8-10 71
IMPACT 15-20
KNOLL 5-10 81-82
MYRRH 8-10 73

COTTON, Gene, & Kim Carnes P&R '78

Singles: 7-inch

ARIOLA AMERICA 3-4 78
Also see CARNES, Kim
Also see COTTON, Gene

COTTON, James LP '67

(James Cotton Blues Band; with Matt "Guitar" Murphy & Luther Tucker)

Singles: 12-inch

ERECT 4-6 82

Singles: 78 rpm

SUN (199 "My Baby") 200-300 54
SUN (206 "Cotton Crop Blues") 200-300 54

Singles: 7-inch

BACKROOM 4-6
BUDDAH 3-5 75
LOMA 10-15 66
SUN (199 "My Baby") 400-500 54
SUN (206 "Cotton Crop Blues") 500-600 54
VERVE/FOLKWAYS 4-8 67
VERVE/FORECAST 4-8 67-69

LPs: 10/12-inch

ACCORD 5-10 83
ALLIGATOR 5-10 84
ANTONE'S 5-10 88
BUDDAH (Except 5661) 10-15 74-76
BUDDAH (5661 "Live and on the Move") 20-25 76
CAPITOL 10-12 71
ERECT 5-10 82
INTERMEDIA 5-10 84
VANGUARD 10-15 68
VERVE/FOLKWAYS 10-20 67
VERVE/FORECAST 10-15 66-69
Also see WATERS, Muddy

COTTON, James, Carey Bell, Junior Wells, & Billy Branch

LPs: 10/12-inch

ALLIGATOR (4790 "Harp Attack") 5-10 90
Also see BELL, Carey
Also see WELLS, Junior

COTTON, Josie P&R/LP '82

Singles: 12-inch

BOMP 5-10 80
ELEKTRA (11538 "Johnny Are You Queer") 5-10 82

Singles: 7-inch

ELEKTRA (Black vinyl) 3-4 82-84
ELEKTRA (Colored vinyl) 5-10 82
WEA (79292 "Johnny Are You Queer") 3-5 82

Picture Sleeves

ELEKTRA 3-4 82-84
WEA (79292 "Johnny Are You Queer") 3-5 82

LPs: 10/12-inch

ELEKTRA 5-10 82

COTTON, LLOYD & CHRISTIAN P&R '75

Singles: 7-inch

20TH FOX 3-5 75-76

LPs: 10/12-inch

20TH FOX 8-12 75-76
Members: Darryl Cotton; Michael Lloyd; Chris Christian.
Also see CHRISTIAN, Chris

COUCHOIS LP '79

Singles: 7-inch

W.B. 3-4 79-80

LPs: 10/12-inch

W.B. 5-10 79-80

COUGAR, John: see MELLENCAMP, John Cougar

COULTER, Clifford R&B '80

Singles: 7-inch

COLUMBIA....3-4 80

LPs: 10/12-inch

COLUMBIA....5-10 80

COUNT BASIE: see BASIE, Count

COUNT FIVE P&R/LP '66

Singles: 7-inch

DOUBLE-SHOT (104 "Psychotic Reaction")....8-12 66
(Label name at top.)
DOUBLE-SHOT (104 "Psychotic Reaction")....4-6 66
(Label name on left side.)
DOUBLE-SHOT (106 thru 141)....5-10 66-69

LPs: 10/12-inch

DOUBLE-SHOT (1001 "Psychotic Reaction")....25-35 66
(Monaural.)
DOUBLE-SHOT (5001 "Psychotic Reaction")....30-40 66
(Stereo.)
PERFORMANCE (398 "Psychotic Reaction")....8-10

COUNTRY BOYS & CITY GIRLS R&B '76

Singles: 7-inch

HAPPY FOX....3-5 76
Member: Lee Maye.

COUNTRY COALITION P&R '70

Singles: 7-inch

ABC....3-5 70-73
ABC/BLUESWAY....3-5 70

LPs: 10/12-inch

ABC/BLUESWAY....10-12 70

COUNTRY ALL STARS

Singles: 78 rpm

RCA....5-10 52-56

Singles: 7-inch

RCA....10-20 52-56
Members: Chet Atkins; Homer & Jethro.
Also see ATKINS, Chet
Also see HOMER & JETHRO

COUNTRY HAMS

Singles: 7-inch

EMI (3977 "Walking in the Park with Eloise")....10-20 74

Picture Sleeves

EMI (3977 "Walking in the Park with Eloise")....50-60 74

Promotional Singles

EMI (3977 "Walking in the Park with Eloise")....25-35 74
Members: Paul McCartney & Wings; Chet Atkins; Floyd Cramer.
Also see ATKINS, Chet
Also see CRAMER, Floyd
Also see McCARTNEY, Paul

COUNTRY JOE & FISH P&R/LP '67

Singles: 7-inch

VANGUARD....5-10 67-69

Picture Sleeves

VANGUARD....8-15 68

EPs: 7-inch

RAG BABY (1001 "Rag Baby")....30-40 66
RAG BABY (1002 "Rag Baby")....30-40 66
RAG BABY (1003 "Rag Baby")....30-40 66

LPs: 10/12-inch

FANTASY....8-10 75-77
VANGUARD (Except 9266)....10-20 67-71
VANGUARD (9266 "I Feel Like I'm Fixin' to Die")....20-30 67
(With cut-out pictures and poster game.)
VANGUARD (9266 "I Feel Like I'm Fixin' to Die")....10-20 67
(Without pictures and poster.)
Members: Country Joe McDonald; David Cohen; Mark Kapner; Barry Melton; Bob Steele; Richard Saunders; Mark Ryan.
Also see BLUE, David
Also see McDONALD, Country Joe

COUNTS R&B '54

Singles: 78 rpm

DOT....15-25 53-56
NOTE (20000 "Sweet Names")....50-75 56

Singles: 7-inch

DOT (1199 "Hot Tamales")....25-50 54
DOT (1188 "Darling Dear")....25-50 53
DOT (1210 "My Dear My Darling")....40-60 54
DOT (1226 "Baby, I Want You")....40-60 54
DOT (1235 "Let Me Go Lover")....25-50 54
DOT (1243 "From This Day On")....25-50 55
DOT (1265 "Sally Walker")....20-30 55
DOT (1275 "Heartbreaker")....20-30 56
DOT (16105 "Darling Dear")....15-25 60
NOTE (20000 "Sweet Names")....100-200 56

COUNTS LP '72

Singles: 7-inch

AWARE....3-5 74
WESTBOUND....3-5 72
YES (103 "Ask the Lonely")....8-10

LPs: 10/12-inch

AWARE....8-10 75
AWARE/GRC....8-10 73
GRC....8-10 73
TCB....4-8
WESTBOUND....8-10 72

COURTNEY, David LP '75

LPs: 10/12-inch

U.A.....8-10 75

COURTNEY, Lou P&R/R&B '67
(Lew Courtney)

Singles: 7-inch

BUDDAH....10-15 69
EPIC....3-5 73-75
HURDY GURDY....3-5
IMPERIAL....5-10 63-64
PHILIPS (40287 "I Watched You Slowly Slip Away")....50-100 65
POP SIDE....5-10 67
RAGS....4-8 73
RIVERSIDE....5-10 66-67
VERVE....5-10 68

LPs: 10/12-inch

EPIC....8-10 74
RCA....8-10 76
RIVERSIDE....15-20 67

COURTSHIP P&R '72

Singles: 7-inch

CAPITOL....3-5 70
GLADES....3-5 72
TAMLA....3-5 72

COUSIN ICE D&D '85

Singles: 12-inch

URBAN ROCK....4-6 85

COVAY, Don P&R '62
(With the Goodtimers; with Jefferson Lemon Blues Band; Don "Pretty Boy" Covay)

Singles: 7-inch

ARNOLD (1002 "Pony Time")....10-15 61
ATLANTIC....5-10 65-70
BIG TOP....8-12 60
BLAZE (350 "Standing in the Doorway")....20-30 58
CAMEO....8-15 62-63
COLUMBIA (42197 "Now That I Need You")....75-100 61
LANDA....5-10 64
MERCURY....3-6 72-75
NEWMAN....3-4 80
PARKWAY....10-20 63-64
PHILADELPHIA INT'L....3-6 76
ROSEMART....5-10 64
SUE (709 "Believe It Or Not")....20-30 58
U-VON....5-10 77

LPs: 10/12-inch

ATLANTIC....15-25 65-69
JANUS....8-12 72
MERCURY....8-10 74
PHILADELPHIA INT'L....8-10 76
VERSATILE....8-10 78
Also see GOODTIMERS
Also see PRETTY BOY
Also see SOUL CLAN

COVEN P&R '71

Singles: 7-inch

BUDDAH....3-5 74
LION....3-5 71
MGM....3-5 71-73
MERCURY....3-6 69
SGC....5-8 68
W.B.....3-5 71-73

LPs: 10/12-inch

BUDDAH....8-10 74
MGM....10-12 71-72
MERCURY....12-15 69
Members: Jinx Dawson; Teresa Kelly.

COVER GIRLS P&R/R&B/LP '87

Singles: 7-inch

FEVER....3-4 87-88

Picture Sleeves

FEVER....3-4 87-88

LPs: 10/12-inch

CAPITOL....5-8 89-90
FEVER....5-10 87

COWARD, Noel LP '56
(With Leo Reisman Orchestra)

EPs: 7-inch

COLUMBIA....5-10 55

LPs: 12-inch 78 rpm

COLUMBIA (5063 "Noel Coward at Las Vegas")....20-30 55
RCA VICTOR (39002 "RCA Presents Noel Coward")....300-400 30s
(Picture disc.)

COWBOY COPAS: see COPAS, Cowboy

COWBOY CHURCH SUNDAY SCHOOL P&R '55

Singles: 78 rpm

DECCA....3-5 54-55
VOSS....3-5 54

Singles: 7-inch

DECCA....5-10 54-55
VOSS....5-10 54

Picture Sleeves

DECCA....10-20 54

EPs: 7-inch

DECCA....8-12 55

COWBOY JUNKIES LP '89

Singles: 7-inch

RCA....3-4 89

Picture Sleeves

RCA....3-4 89

LPs: 10/12-inch

RCA....5-8 89-90

COWSILLS P&R/LP '67

Singles: 7-inch

JODA (103 "All I Really Want to Be Is Me")....10-20 65
LONDON....3-4 71-72
MGM....3-5 67-71
PHILIPS....4-8 66-67

Picture Sleeves

MGM....4-8 67-69
PHILIPS....5-10 66

EPs: 7-inch

MGM (1 "The Cowsills")....15-25 68
(Promotional issue from the American Dairy Assocaition.)

LPs: 10/12-inch

LONDON....8-10 71
MGM....10-12 67-71
WING....10-12 68

Members: Bill Cowsill; Barry Cowsill; John Cowsill; Susan Cowsill; Bob Cowsill; Paul Cowsill; Barbara Cowsill.
Also see COWSILL, Bill
Also see COWSILL, John
Also see COWSILL, Susan

COX, Wally P&R '53

Singles: 78 rpm
RCA 3-5 53
Singles: 7-inch
ARVEE 4-8 60
GEORGE 4-8 61
RCA (5278 "What a Crazy Guy") 5-10 53
WAND 3-5 70
Picture Sleeves
RCA (5278 "What a Crazy Guy") 10-20 53

COXON'S ARMY

LPs: 10/12-inch
TRACE ("Coxson's Army") 300-500 75
(No selection number used.)
Members: Phil Coxson; Pat Benatar.
Also see BENATAR, Pat

COYOTE SISTERS P&R '84

Singles: 7-inch
MOROCCO 3-4 84
Picture Sleeves
MOROCCO 3-4 84
LPs: 10/12-inch
MOROCCO 5-10 84
Members: Leah Kunkel; Marty Gwinn; Renee Armand.

CRABBY APPLETON P&R/LP '70

Singles: 7-inch
ELEKTRA 3-5 70-72
LPs: 10/12-inch
ELEKTRA 8-10 70-71
Member: Michael Fennelly.

CRACK THE SKY LP '76

Singles: 12-inch
GRUDGE 4-8 88
(Promotional only.)
Singles: 7-inch
GRUDGE 3-4 88-90
LIFESONG 3-5 76-79
LPs: 10/12-inch
GRUDGE 5-8 88-90
LIFESONG (Except 8000 series) 10-15 75-78
LIFESONG (8000 series) 5-10 81
Members: Rick Withowski; Joe Macre; Joe D'Amico.

CRADDOCK, Billy "Crash P&R '59
(Billy Craddock "Crash" Craddock; Billy Graddock)

Singles: 7-inch
ABC 3-5 72-78
ABC/DOT 3-5 75-77
ATLANTIC 3-4 89
CAPITOL 3-5 78-82
CARTWHEEL 3-5 71-72
CEE CEE 3-4 83
CHART 3-6 67-73
COLONIAL 10-15 58
COLUMBIA 5-10 59-60
DATE 8-12 58
KING (Except 5912) 5-10 64-65
KING (5912 "Betty Betty") 15-25 64
MERCURY 5-10 61-62
SKY CASTLE ("Smacky Mouth") 20-30
(No selection number used. Shows Columbia identification numbers, 26671/26672.)
Picture Sleeves
COLUMBIA (41470 "Don't Destroy Me") 15-25 59
COLUMBIA (41619 "All I Want Is You") 15-25 60
EPs: 7-inch
ABC 5-10 74
(Juke box issue only.)
LPs: 10/12-inch
ABC 6-10 72-78
ABC/AT EASE 10-12 78
(Special issue for the Armed Forces.)
ABC/DOT 8-10 76-77
CAPITOL 5-10 78-83
CARTWHEEL 10-12 71-72
CHART 8-12 73
HARMONY 10-12 73
KING (912 "I'm Tore Up") 45-55 64
PICKWICK 5-10 79
POWER PAK 5-10 75
STARDAY 8-10
MCA 5-10 82

CRAMER, Floyd P&R '54
(With the Louisiana Hayride Band; with Keyboard Kick Band)

Singles: 78 rpm
ABBOTT 3-5 53-54
MGM 3-5 55-57
Singles: 7-inch
ABBOTT 5-10 53-54
MGM 5-8 55-57
RCA (Except 7000 & 8000 series) 3-5 67-81
RCA (7000 & 8000 series) 4-8 61-66
Picture Sleeves
RCA 6-12 61-63
EPs: 7-inch
MGM 8-12 57
RCA 5-10 61-63
LPs: 10/12-inch
ALSHIRE 8-12 68
CAMDEN 6-12 65-74
MGM (3500 series) 15-20 57
MGM (4200 series) 10-15 64
MGM (4600 series) 8-12 70
RCA (0100 thru 4000 series) 5-10 73-81
(With "AHL1," ANL1," "APD1," "APL1," or "AYL1" prefix.)
RCA (2000 thru 4000 series) 10-20 60-73
(With "LPM" or "LSP" prefix.)
Also see ANN-MARGRET
Also see ATKINS, Chet, Floyd Cramer & Danny Davis
Also see ATKINS, Chet, Floyd Cramer & Boots Randolph
Also see BARE, Bobby
Also see COUNTRY HAMS
Also see FRANCIS, Connie
Also see KERR, Anita
Also see PRESLEY, Elvis
Also see REEVES, Jim
Also see SOME of CHET'S FRIENDS

CRAMER, Floyd / Peter Nero / Frankie Carle

LPs: 10/12-inch
RCA 10-15 63
Also see CRAMER, Floyd
Also see NERO, Peter

CRAMPTON SISTERS P&R '64

Singles: 7-inch
ABC 4-8 66
DCP 5-10 64

CRANE, Les P&R/LP '71

Singles: 7-inch
W.B. 3-5 71
Picture Sleeves
W.B. 4-8 71
LPs: 10/12-inch
W.B. 5-10 71

CRAWFORD, Caroline: see CRAWFORD, Carolyn

CRAWFORD, Carolyn R&B '65
(Caroline Crawford)

Singles: 7-inch
MERCURY 3-4 78-79
MOTOWN (1050 "Forget About Me") 20-40 63
MOTOWN (1064 "My Smile Is Just a Frown Turned Upside Down") 25-50 64
MOTOWN (1064 "My Smile Is Just a Frown [Turned Upside Down]") 15-25 64
(Repressing—note slight title variation.)
MOTOWN (1070 "My Heart") 30-40 64
PHILADELPHIA INT'L 3-5 74-75
LPs: 10/12-inch
MERCURY 6-12 78-79
Also see CHAPTER 8

CRAWFORD, Hank LP '64

Singles: 7-inch
ATLANTIC 3-8 61-70
KUDU 3-5 72
LPs: 10/12-inchs
ATLANTIC 10-20 61-73
KUDU 10-12 72-76
MFSL (224 "Soul of the Ballad") 20-25 94

CRAWFORD, Johnny P&R '61

Singles: 7-inch
ABC 3-4 73
CINDY 4-6
COLLECTABLES 3-4 81
DEL-FI 5-10 61-64
SIDEWALK 4-8 67-68
WYNNE (124 "Ask") 10-15 60
Picture Sleeves
DEL-FI 10-15 61-63
SIDEWALK 5-8 68
EPs: 7-inch
GRASON (6515 "The Restless Ones") 10-15 66
LPs: 10/12-inch
DEL-FI (1220 "The Captivating Johnny Crawford") 20-30 62
DEL-FI (1223 "A Young Man's Fancy") 20-30 62
DEL-FI (1224 "Rumors") 20-30 63
DEL-FI (1229 "Greatest Hits") 20-30 63
DEL-FI (1248 "Greatest Hits, Vol. 2") 20-30 63
GUEST STAR 15-20 63
RHINO 5-10 82
SUPREME (110 "Songs from *The Restless Ones*) 15-20 66
(Soundtrack. Monaural.)
SUPREME (210 "Songs from *The Restless Ones*) 20-30 66
(Soundtrack. Stereo.)

CRAWFORD, Michael LP '88

LPs: 10/12-inch
COLUMBIA 5-8 88

CRAWFORD, Randy R&B '79

Singles: 12-inch
W.B. 4-6 83
Singles: 7-inch
COLUMBIA 3-5 72-73
MCA 3-4 81
W.B. 3-5 77-86
Picture Sleeves
COLUMBIA 3-5 72
LPs: 10/12-inch
RCA 5-10 84
W.B. 8-10 76-89
Also see CRUSADERS
Also see JARREAU, Al, & Randy Crawford
Also see SPRINGFIELD, Rick, & Randy Crawford

CRAWLER: see BACK STREET CRAWLER

CRAY, Robert LP '86
(Robert Cray Band)

Singles: 12-inch
MERCURY 4-8 88
(Promotional only.)
Singles: 7-inch
MERCURY 3-4 87-88
Picture Sleeves
MERCURY 3-4 87-88
LPs: 10/12-inch
HIGHTONE 5-10 83-87
MERCURY 5-10 86
TOMATO 10-20 80
Also see COLLINS, Albert, Robert Cray & Johnny Copeland

CRAY, Robert, Band, & Memphis Horns LP '90

LPs: 10/12-inch
MERCURY 5-8 90

Also see CRAY, Robert
Also see MEMPHIS HORNS

CRAYTON, Pee Wee *R&B '48*

Singles: 78 rpm

ALADDIN.......................................40-60 51
FLAIR...15-25 55
4 STAR (1304 "After Hours Boogie")..25-50 47
IMPERIAL.....................................25-50 54-55
MODERN......................................25-50 49-51
POST...25-50 55
RECORDED in HOLLYWOOD.........40-60 54
VEE JAY......................................20-30 56-57

Singles: 7-inch

ALADDIN (3112 "When It Rains It Pours")...................................100-200 51
BLACK DIAMOND..........................15-25
BLUES SPECTRUM (15 "Texas Bop")...10-20
EDCO (1009 "Ev'ry Night 'Bout This Time")......................................20-30
EDCO (1010 "Money Tree")............25-50
FLAIR (1061 "Central Avenue Blues")..25-50 55
(Actually by Pee Wee Crayton though shown as by the Carroll County Boys. The flip, *Dizzy,* is by the Carroll County Boys.)
FOX (10069 "Give Me One More Chance")....................................15-25
GUYDEN (2048 "I'm Still in Love with You")...10-20 61
IMPERIAL (5288 "Do Unto Others")..50-75 54
IMPERIAL (5297 "Win-o")................50-75 54
IMPERIAL (5321 "I Need Your Love")...50-75 54
IMPERIAL (5338 "My Idea About You")...50-75 55
IMPERIAL (5345 "Eyes Full of Tears")...50-75 55
IMPERIAL (5353 "Yours Truly").........50-75 55
JAMIE (1190 "Little Bitty Things")......10-15 61
MODERN (892 "Cool Evening").......50-75 51
MODERN (892 "Cool Evening").......50-75 51
POST (2007 "I Must Go On")...........50-75 55
RECORDED in HOLLYWOOD (408 "Crying & Walking")..................................75-125 54
RECORDED in HOLLYWOOD (426 "Baby Pat the Floor")....................................75-125 54
SMASH (1774 "Hillbilly Blues")..........10-15 62
VEE JAY (214 "Frosty Night")...........40-60 56
VEE JAY (252 "I Found Peace of Mind")..40-60 57
VEE JAY (266 "Fiddle De Dee")........40-60 57

LPs: 10/12-inch

CROWN (5175 "Pee Wee Crayton")......................................50-100 59
MURRAY BROTHERS......................5-10 83
VANGUARD...................................8-12 71

CRAZY ELEPHANT *P&R '69*

Singles: 7-inch

BELL..4-8 69-70
SPHERE SOUND..............................4-6 69

LPs: 10/12-inch

BELL..15-20 69
Member: Robert Spencer.

CRAZY HORSE *LP '71*

Singles: 7-inch

EPIC..3-5 72
M.O.C. 4-8
REPRISE.......................................3-5 71-72

LPs: 10/12-inch

EPIC..8-12 72-76
RCA...5-10 78
REPRISE......................................10-15 71-72
Members: Ralph Molina; Billy Talbot; Leon Whitsell; George Whitsell; Ry Cooder; Mike Curtis; Greg Leroy; Bob Notkoff; Neil Young.
Also see YOUNG, Neil

CRAZY OTTO *P&R/LP '55*

Singles: 78 rpm

DECCA...3-5 55-57

Singles: 7-inch

DECCA 4-8 55-61
MGM 3-5 62

EPs: 7-inch

DECCA 5-10 55-58

LPs: 10/12-inch

DECCA 8-18 55-61
MGM 6-12 63
VOCALION 8-10 59

CRAZY WORLD of ARTHUR BROWN: see BROWN, Arthur

CREACH, Papa John *LP '72*

Singles: 7-inch

BUDDAH...3-5 76
DJM...3-4 79
GRUNT 3-5 71-72

LPs: 10/12-inch

BUDDAH...8-12 75-77
DJM...6-10 77-78
GRUNT 10-15 71-74
Also see HOT TUNA
Also see JEFFERSON STARSHIP

CREAM *LP '67*

Singles: 7-inch

ATCO 4-8 67-70

EPs: 7-inch

ATCO ("Goodbye Cream")................ 10-15 69
(Promotional issue only.)

LPs: 10/12-inch

ATCO (206 "Fresh Cream")............ 25-35 67
(With *I Feel Free.* On RSO reissues, this track is replaced with *Spoonful.*)
ATCO (206 "Fresh Cream")............. 10-20 67
(Without *I Feel Free.*)
ATCO (232 "Disraeli Gears")............ 20-30 67
ATCO (291 "The Best of Cream")..... 20-30 69
ATCO (328 "Live Cream")................ 20-30 70
ATCO (700 "Wheels of Fire")........... 20-30 68
ATCO (7001 "Goodbye")................. 20-30 69
ATCO (7005 "Live Cream, Vol. 2") ... 20-30 72
MFSL (066 "Wheels of Fire")........... 40-60 82
POLYDOR 10-12 72-73
RSO (Except 015)............................ 5-10 72-83
RSO (015 "Classic Cuts")................ 35-45 75
(Promotional issue only.)
SPRINGBOARD 10-12
Members: Eric Clapton; Jack Bruce; Ginger Baker.
Also see BAKER, Ginger
Also see BRUCE, Jack
Also see CLAPTON, Eric

CREATIVE SOURCE *R&B '73*

Singles: 7-inch

POLYDOR 3-5 75
SUSSEX 3-5 73-74

LPs: 10/12-inch

POLYDOR 8-10 75-76
SUSSEX 10-12 74
Members: Don Wyatt; Celeste Rhodes; Steve Flanagan; Barbara Berryman; Barbara Lewis.
Also see COLTS

CREATURES *LP '90*

LPs: 10/12-inch

GEFFEN 5-8 90

CREEDENCE CLEARWATER REVIVAL *P&R/LP '68*

Singles: 12-inch

FANTASY (238 "Creedence Medley")....................................... 10-15 85
FANTASY (759 "I Heard It Through the Grapevine").................................... 15-20 76
(Promotional issue only.)

Singles: 7-inch

FANTASY (Except 2832).................... 3-6 69-85
FANTASY (2832 "45 Revolutions Per Minute")... 40-60 70
LIBERTY 3-5
SCORPIO (412 "Porterville") 15-25 68

Picture Sleeves

FANTASY (Except 2832).................. 5-10 69-76

LPs: 10/12-inch

FANTASY (2832 "45 Revolutions Per Minute")......................................20-25 70

LPs: 10/12-inch

BEVERLY ("Willie and the Poor Boys") 75-100
(Half-speed mastered. Number not known.)
FANTASY (1 thru 70).......................8-15 73-78
FANTASY (4500 series)....................5-10 80-85
(Includes reissues of 8382 through 9404.)
FANTASY (8382 thru 9404) 8-15 68-72
FANTASY (9418 thru 9621) 5-10 72-82
K-TEL 8-12 78
MFSL (037 "Cosmo's Factory") 75-125 79
SWEET THUNDER (13 "Green River")...75-100 75
(Half-speed mastered.)
W.B. SPECIAL PRODUCTS (3514 "Greatest Hits") 10-15 85
(TV mail-order offer.)
Members: John Fogerty; Tom Fogerty; Doug Clifford; Stuart Cook.
Also see FOGERTY, John
Also see FOGERTY, Tom
Also see GOLLIWOGS
Also see HARRISON, Don, Band

CREME, Lol, & Kevin Godley: see GODLEY, Kevin, & Lol Creme

CREME D'COCOA *R&B '78*

Singles: 7-inch

VENTURE 3-5 78-80

LPs: 10/12-inch

VENTURE 8-10 79
Also see AMBASSADORS
Also see EBONYS

CRENSHAW, Marshall *P&R/LP '82*

Singles: 12-inch

SHAKE (104 "Marshall Crenshaw")...20-25 81
W.B. 5-10 82

Singles: 7-inch

W.B. 3-4 82-85

LPs: 10/12-inch

W.B. 5-10 82-85

CREOLE, Kid: see KID CREOLE

CRESCENDOS *P&R/R&B '58*

Singles: 78 rpm

NASCO (6005 "Oh Julie") 50-75 57

Singles: 7-inch

ABC...3-4 73
MCA...3-4 84
NASCO (6005 "Oh Julie") 10-20 57
NASCO (6009 "School Girl")..............10-20 58
NASCO (6021 "Young and in Love"). 10-20 58
SCARLET...10-15 60-61
TAP (7027 "Oh Julie") 10-15 57

Picture Sleeves

NASCO (6009 "School Girl")..............20-30 58
NASCO (6021 "Young and in Love"). 20-30 58
TAP (7027 "Oh Julie") 15-25 57

LPs: 10/12-inch

GUEST STAR (1453 "Oh Julie").......20-30 62
Members: George Lanuis; Ken Brigham; James Hall; Tommy Fortner.
Also see 4 SEASONS

CRESCENTS *P&R '63*

(Chiyo & Crescents)

Singles: 7-inch

BREAK OUT (4 "Pink Dominos") 15-25 63
(With straight horizontal lines.)
BREAK OUT (4 "Pink Dominos") 15-20 63
(With jagged horizontal lines.)
ERA (3116 "Pink Dominos")..............5-10 63

CRESTS *P&R '57*

(With Johnny Maestro; Original Crests; with Al Browne & His Orchestra; "Crest's")

Singles: 78 rpm

JOYCE 103 ("Sweetest One").........75-125 57
JOYCE 105 ("No One to Love") 75-125 57

Singles: 7-inch

ABC...3-4 73
APT (25075 "She's All Mine Alone")...10-20 65

CAMEO (256 "I'll Be True") 25-35 64
CAMEO (305 "Lean on Me") 10-20 64
COED (501 "Pretty Little Angel")... 100-200 58
COED (506 "16 Candles") 25-50 58
(Red label.)
COED (506 "16 Candles") 15-25 61
(Black label.)
COED (509 "Six Nights a Week") 25-50 59
COED (511 "Molly Mae") 25-50 59
COED (515 "The Angels Listened In") 25-50 59
COED (521 "A Year Ago Tonight").... 20-40 59
COED (525 "Step By Step") 20-40 60
COED (531 "Trouble in Paradise").... 20-40 60
COED (535 "Journey of Love") 20-40 60
COED (537 "Isn't It Amazing") 20-40 60
COED (543 "In the Still of the Night") 20-40 60
COED (561 "Little Miracles") 15-25 61
COLLECTABLES 3-4 81-83
CORAL (62403 "You Blew Out the Candles") 15-25 64
ERIC 3-4 73
GOLDIES 45 3-4
HARVEY (501 "16 Candles") 5-10 81
(Colored vinyl.)
JOYCE 103 ("Sweetest One") 100-200 57
(With the oversize letter "Y" in the Joyce logo.)
JOYCE 103"(Sweetest One") 15-25
(With all of the letters the same size in the Joyce logo.)
JOYCE 105"(No One to Love") 100-200 57
KING TUT 4-8
LANA 4-8 64
LOST-NITE 4-8
MCA 3-5 73
MUSICTONE (1106 "Sweetest One") 20-30 62
ORIGINAL SOUND 3-5 87
QUALITY 15-30
(Canadian.)
SELMA (311 "Guilty") 20-40 62
SELMA (4000 "Did I Remember") 30-50 63
TIMES SQUARE (2 "No One to Love") 20-40 62
(Colored vinyl.)
TIMES SQUARE (6 "Baby") 15-25 64
(Selection number on both sides is 6.)
TIMES SQUARE (97 "Baby") 20-30 64
(Selection number on B-side is 6.)
TRANS ATLAS (696 "The Actor") 25-50 62
TRIP 3-5 70s

EPs: 7-inch

COED (101 "The Angels Listened In") 300-400 59

LPs: 10/12-inch

COED (901 "The Crests Sing All Biggies") 250-500 60
COED (904 "Best of the Crests") .. 200-350 60
COLLECTABLES (5009 "Greatest Hits") 8-10 82
COLLECTABLES (P-5009 "Greatest Hits") 10-15 82
(Picture disc.)
POST 8-12 70s
RHINO 5-10 90

Members: Johnny Maestro; Tom Gough; Harold Torres; Jay Carter; James Ancrum.
Also see MAESTRO, Johnny

CRESTS / Skyliners

Singles: 7-inch

ORIGINAL SOUND 3-4 84
Also see SKYLINERS

CRESTS / Cal York & Roamers

Singles: 7-inch

HIT 5-15 60s
Also see CRESTS

CRETONES — P&R/LP '80

Singles: 7-inch

PLANET 3-4 80-81

Picture Sleeves

PLANET 3-4 80

LPs: 10/12-inch

PLANET 5-10 80-81

CREW-CUTS — P&R '54

Singles: 78 rpm

MERCURY 5-15 54-57

Singles: 7-inch

ABC-PAR 4-6 63
CHESS 4-6 64
FIREBIRD 3-5 70
MERCURY 5-15 54-57
RCA 4-8 58-60
VEE JAY 4-6 63
WARWICK 4-8 60-61
WHALE 4-6 62

EPs: 7-inch

MERCURY 10-20 54-57

LPs: 10/12-inch

CAMAY 10-15
MERCURY 25-50 55-56
PICCADILLY 8-10 80
RCA 20-30 59-60
WING 15-25 59-60

Members: Ray Perkins; John Perkins; Rudi Maugeri; Pat Barrett.
Also see COASTERS / Crew-Cuts / Chiffons

CREW-CUTS / Junior Powell & Charlotte Grubic

LPs: 10/12-inch

RCA CUSTOM ("The Crew-Cuts Have a Ball") 20-30 59
(Special products issue for Ebonite Co. One side has "Bowling Tips By Top Stars")
Also see CREW-CUTS

CREWE, Bob — P&R '60

(Bob Crewe Generation; B.C.G.; with Rays)

Singles: 78 rpm

CORAL 5-10 56

Singles: 7-inch

ABC-PAR 10-15 61
DYNO VOICE 5-10 66-68
CORAL 10-20 56
CREWE 3-5 71
ELEKTRA 3-5 76-77
ERIC 3-4 73
GAMBLE 3-5 69
JUBILEE 10-20 54
MELBA 10-20 57
METROMEDIA 3-5 72
SPOTLIGHT 15-25 56
20TH FOX 3-5 76
U.T. 10-15 59
VIK (0337 "Charm Bracelet") 20-30 57
WARWICK 10-15 59-61

Picture Sleeves

DYNO VOICE 4-8 67

LPs: 10/12-inch

CGC 10-12 70
CREWE 10-15
DYNO VOICE 10-12 67-68
ELEKTRA 8-10 76-77
GAMBLE 3-4 69
PHILIPS (200150 "All the Song Hits of the 4 Seasons") 15-20 64
(Monaural. Includes lyrics sheet.)
PHILIPS (200238 "The 4 Seasons Hits") 10-15 67
(Monaural.)
PHILIPS (600150 "All the Song Hits of the 4 Seasons") 15-20 64
(Stereo. Includes lyrics sheet.)
PHILIPS (600238 "The 4 Seasons Hits") 10-15 67
(Stereo.)
WARWICK (2009 "Kicks") 25-35 60
WARWICK (2034 "Crazy in the Heart") 25-35 61
Also see LA ROSA, Julius, & Bob Crew Generation

CRICKETS — R&B '53

(Crickets Featuring Dean Barlow)

Singles: 78 rpm

BEACON 40-60 54
JAY-DEE 50-75 53
MGM 50-75 53

Singles: 7-inch

BEACON (104 "Be Faithful"/"I'm Not the One You Love") 75-100 54
BEACON (555 "Be Faithful"/"I'm Not the One You Love") 20-30 63
DAVIS (459 "I'm Going to Live My Life Alone") 50-100 58
JAY-DEE (777 "Dreams and Wishes") 150-250 53
JAY-DEE (781 "I'm Not the One You Love") 150-250 53
MGM (11428 "You're Mine") 150-250 53
MGM (11507 "For You I Have Eyes") 150-250 53

LPs: 10/12-inch

RELIC 8-12

Members: Harold Johnson; Leon Carter; Eugene Stapleton; Rodney Jackson; Grover "Dean" Barlow; J.R. Bailey; Robert Spencer; Freddy Barksdale; Robert Bynum; William Lindsay; Joe Dias.
Also see BARLOW, Dean
Also see BARLOW, Dean, & Crickets / Deep River Boys
Also see CADILLACS

CRICKETS

Singles: 7-inch

BARNABY 15-25 72
BRUNSWICK (55124 "Love's Made a Fool of You") 15-25 59
BRUNSWICK (55153 "When You Ask About Love") 15-25 59
CORAL (62198 "More Than I Can Say") 15-25 60
EPIC (08028 "T-Shirt") 3-4 88
LIBERTY 10-20 61-65
(Black labels.)
LIBERTY 15-25 61-65
(Promotional issues. With cream color or white labels.)
MGM 10-15 73
MUSIC FACTORY 15-20 68
Note: Records by Buddy Holly & Crickets, even if credited only to the Crickets, are listed in the BUDDY HOLLY section.

Promotional Singles

BRUNSWICK (55124 "Love's Made a Fool of You") 20-30 59
BRUNSWICK (55153 "When You Ask About Love") 20-30 59
CORAL (62198 "More Than I Can Say") 20-30 60
EPIC (08028 "T-Shirt") 3-4 88

EPs: 7-inch

B.H.M.S. 3-6 78
CORAL (81192 "Crickets") 75-100 63
(With Buddy Holly on one track, *It's Too Late*.)

LPs: 10/12-inch

BARNABY (30268 "Rockin' '50s Rock & Roll") 15-25 70
CORAL (57320 "In Style") 40-60 60
KOALA 8-10
LIBERTY (3272 "Something Old, Something New, Something Blue, Somethin' Else")... 30-40 64
(Monaural.)
LIBERTY (3351 "California Sun") 30-40 64
(Monaural.)
LIBERTY (7272 "Something Old, Something New, Something Blue, Somethin' Else")... 40-50 64
(Stereo.)
LIBERTY (7351 "California Sun") 40-50 64
(Stereo.)
VERTIGO 10-20 73
Note: Records by Buddy Holly & Crickets, even if credited only to the Crickets, are listed in the BUDDY HOLLY section.

Members: Sonny Curtis; Jerry Naylor; Glen D. Hardin; Jerry Allison; Joe Mauldin; Earl Sinks; David Box.
Also see HOLLY, Buddy
Also see IVAN
Also see JENNINGS, Waylon
Also see NAYLOR, Jerry
Also see PRESLEY, Elvis
Also see VEE, Bobby, & Crickets

CRIMSON, King: see KING CRIMSON

CRISS, Peter LP '78

Singles: 7-inch

CASABLANCA 3-5 79-80

LPs: 10/12-inch

CASABLANCA (7122 "Peter Criss") 12-20 78
(With poster order form.)
CASABLANCA (7122 "Peter Criss") ... 8-12 78
(Without poster order form.)
CASABLANCA (7240 "Out of Control") 25-50 80
Also see KISS

CRITTERS P&R/LP '66

Singles: 7-inch

KAPP 5-10 65-69
MCA 3-5 73-84
MUSICOR (1044 "Georgianna") 10-20 65
PRANCER 4-8 68
PROJECT 3 .... 4-8 67-69

Picture Sleeves

KAPP (769 "Mr. Dieingly Sad") 8-12 66
PROJECT 3 .... 4-8 67-69

LPs: 10/12-inch

BACK-TRAC 5-10 85
KAPP (1485 "Younger Girl") 20-30 66
(Monaural.)
KAPP (3485 "Younger Girl") 25-35 66
(Stereo.)
PROJECT 3 .... 15-20 68

CRITTERS / Young Rascals / Lou Christie

LPs: 10/12-inch

BOTIQUE 10-20 66
(Tracks shown as by the Young Rascals are actually by Felix & Escorts.)
Also see CHRISTIE, Lou
Also see CRITTERS

CROCE, Jim P&R/LP '72

Singles: 7-inch

ABC 3-5 72-74
LIFESONG 3-5 75-76

Picture Sleeves

ABC 4-6 73

EPs: 7-inch

ABC 10-12 73
(Juke box issue only.)

LPs: 10/12-inch

ABC (Except 100) 10-12 72-74
ABC (100 "A Jim Croce Christmas Programming Sampler) 15-20 73
(Promotional issue only.)
BURNS MEDIA (1-2 "The Faces I've Been") 40-60 75
(Two-LP set. Promotional issue only.)
CASHWEST 8-10 77
COMMAND 12-15 74-75
LIFESONG 10-15 75-78
MFSL (079 "You Don't Mess Around with Jim") 25-50 82
Session: Maury Muehleisen; Tommy West; Gary Chester; Marty Nelson; Joe Macho; Terry Cashman; Ellie Greenwich; David Spinozza.
Also see CASHMAN & WEST
Also see GREENWICH, Ellie

CROCE, Jim & Ingrid

(Jim & Ingrid)

Singles: 7-inch

CAPITOL 10-15 69

LPs: 10/12-inch

CAPITOL (315 "Croce") 30-35 69
PICKWICK 5-10 70s
Also see CROCE, Jim

CROCHET, Cleveland P&R '60

(With the Sugar Bees; with His Hillbilly Ramblers)

Singles: 7-inch

GOLDBAND 5-10 60-61
LYRIC 5-10

LPs: 10/12-inch

GOLDBAND (7749 "Cleveland Crochet and All the Sugar Bees") 50-75 61

CROCKETT, G.L. P&R/R&B '65

(G. Davy Crockett)

Singles: 78 rpm

CHIEF (7010 "Look Out Mabel") 50-75 57

Singles: 7-inch

CHECKER (1121 "Look Out Mabel") 20-30 65
CHIEF (7010 "Look Out Mabel") 50-75 57
4 BROTHERS 5-10 65

CROOK, General R&B '70

Singles: 7-inch

CAPITOL 3-6 69
DOWN to EARTH 3-6 70-71
WAND 3-5 74

LPs: 10/12-inch

CAPITOL 10-15 70
WAND 10-12 74

CROSBY, Beverly R&B '77

Singles: 7-inch

BAREBACK 3-5 77

CROSBY, Bing P&R '31

(With the Andrews Sisters; with Gary Crosby; with Victor Young Orchestra; with Grady Martin & His Slew Foot Five)

Singles: 78 rpm

BRUNSWICK 10-20 32-34
DECCA 5-15 34-57
KAPP 3-5 57
VICTOR 10-20 31

Singles: 7-inch

AMOS 3-5 69
CAPITOL 4-6 63
COLUMBIA 4-6 59
CROWLEY'S/CROSBY ("How Lovely Is Christmas") 10-20
(Promotional issue made for Crowley's Milk Co.)
DAYBREAK 3-5 71
DECCA (23281 thru 30828) 5-10 51-59
DECCA (31000 series) 4-8 61-65
KAPP 4-6 57
LONDON 3-4 77
MGM 4-6 60
POLYDOR 3-4 78
RCA 4-6 60
REPRISE 4-6 64-67
U.A. 3-5 75
VERVE 4-6

Picture Sleeves

DECCA 5-10 53-63
DAYBREAK 3-5 71
KAPP 4-8 57

EPs: 7-inch

BRUNSWICK 5-15 50-55
COLUMBIA 8-12 50-57
DECCA ("Old Masters") 20-30
(Boxed EP set. No number shown.)
DECCA (Except 1700) 6-15 50-59
DECCA (1700 "Deluxe Box Set") 75-100 54
(Boxed, 17-disc set.)
RCA 5-10 57
THREE on ONE (407 "Bing Crosby Sings 2 New Christmas Songs") 5-10 50s
(Though labeled "45 Extended Play," actually has only one song on each side. May not have been issued with cover.)
VERVE (5022 "Bing Sings While Bregman Swings") 10-15 59
(With envelope/sleeve.)

LPs: 10/12-inch

AMOS 8-10 69
ARGO 10-15 76
BIOGRAPH 5-10 73
BRUNSWICK (54000 series) 15-25 55
BRUNSWICK (58000 series) 25-40 52
(10-inch LPs.)
CAPITOL (2300 series) 8-12 65
CAPITOL (11000 series) 5-10 77-78
CITADEL 5-10 78
COLUMBIA (43 "Bing in Hollywood") 10-15 67
COLUMBIA (2502 "Der Bingle") 20-30 56
(10-inch LP.)
COLUMBIA (6027 "Classics") 20-40 49
(10-inch LP.)
COLUMBIA (6105 "Classics, Vol. 2") 20-40 50
(10-inch LP.)
COLUMBIA (35000 series) 5-10 78-79
COLUMBIA SPECIAL PRODUCTS 5-8 77
DECCA (154 "Bing") 50-100 54
(Boxed five-disc set. Includes booklet.)
DECCA (184 "Best of Bing Crosby") 10-15 65
DECCA (4000 series) 20-50 61-64
DECCA (5000 series) 15-25 49-55
(10-inch LPs.)
DECCA (6000 series) 25-50 55-56
(10-inch LPs.)
DECCA (8000 series) 15-25 54-59
(Black label with silver print.)
DECCA (8000 series) 8-15 60-72
(Black label with horizontal rainbow stripe.)
DECCA (8700 series) 8-12 64
DECCA (9000 series) 10-20 61-62
(Decca LP numbers in this series preceded by a "7" or a "DL-7" are stereo issues.)
DECCA CUSTOM (34461 "Bing Crosby") 10-20
(Promotional issue, made for La-Z-Boy.)
ENCORE 8-10 68
GOLDEN 10-15 57-59
HARMONY (7000 series) 10-15 57
HARMONY (11000 series) 5-10 69
LONDON 5-10 77
MCA 5-10 73-82
MGM 10-15 61-64
METRO 5-10 65
P.I.P. 5-10 71
POLYDOR 5-10 77
RCA (500 series) 6-10 72
RCA (1400 thru 2000 series) 10-20 57-59
(With "LPM" or "LSP" prefix.)
RCA (2000 series) 5-10 77
(With "CPL1" prefix.)
REPRISE 8-12 64
20TH FOX 5-10 79
U.A. 5-10 76
VERVE/MGM (2030 "Bing Sings While Bregman Swings") 25-50 56
VOCALION (3600 series) 10-15 57
VOCALION (3700 series) 5-10 66
W.B. 10-15 60-62
"X" 15-25 54
Also see ANDREWS SISTERS
Also see BOWIE, David, & Bing Crosby
Also see CROSBY, Gary, & Friend
Also see CROSBY, Gary, Phillip, Dennis, Lindsay & Bing
Also see DORSEY, Jimmy
Also see MARTIN, Grady, & His Slew Foot Five
Also see SINATRA, Frank, Bing Crosby & Dean Martin
Also see YOUNG, Victor

CROSBY, Bing & Gary P&R '50

Singles: 78 rpm

DECCA 3-5 50-51

Singles: 7-inch

DECCA 4-8 50-51

CROSBY, Bing, & Louis Armstrong P&R '51

Singles: 78 rpm

CAPITOL 3-5 56
DECCA 3-5 51

Singles: 7-inch

CAPITOL 4-8 56
DECCA 4-8 51
MGM 3-5 60

LPs: 10/12-inch

MGM (100 series) 5-10 70
MGM (3800 series) 10-20 60
SOUNDS RARE 5-10 83

CROSBY, Bing, Louis Armstrong, Rosemary Clooney & Hi-Los

Singles: 7-inch

COLUMBIA (6277 "Music to Shave By") 5-10 50s
(Special products flexi-disc from Remington.)
Also see ARMSTRONG, Louis
Also see CLOONEY, Rosemary
Also see CROSBY, Bing, & Louis Armstrong

CROSBY, Bing, & Fred Astaire

LPs: 10/12-inch

U.A. 5-8 77
Also see ASTAIRE, Fred

CROSBY, Bing, & Count Basie

LPs: 10/12-inch

DAYBREAK.......... 8-12 72
Also see BASIE, Count

CROSBY, Bing, & Connee Boswell P&R '37

Singles: 78 rpm

DECCA.......... 4-8 37-40

LPs: 10/12-inch

DECCA.......... 15-25 52
Also see BOSWELL, Connee

CROSBY, Bing, & Judy Garland P&R '45

Singles: 78 rpm

DECCA.......... 5-10 45
Also see GARLAND, Judy

CROSBY, Bing, Dick Haymes & Andrews Sisters P&R '47

Singles: 78 rpm

DECCA.......... 5-10 47
Also see HAYMES, Dick

CROSBY, Bing, & Bob Hope P&R '45

Singles: 78 rpm

DECCA.......... 5-10 45

EPs: 7-inch

CAPITOL CUSTOM (2263 "Vacation Road to Minnesota").......... 5-10
(Issued to promote Minnesota tourism.)
Also see BAXTER, Les
Also see HOPE, Bob

CROSBY, Bing, & Louis Jordan P&R '45

Singles: 78 rpm

DECCA.......... 5-10 45
Also see JORDAN, Louis

CROSBY, Bing, & Grace Kelly / Bing Crosby & Frank Sinatra P&R '56
(With Johnny Green's Orchestra)

Singles: 78 rpm

CAPITOL.......... 3-5 56

Singles: 7-inch

CAPITOL.......... 5-10 56
Also see SINATRA, Frank

CROSBY, Bing / Grace Kelly / Frank Sinatra / Celeste Holm

Singles: 7-inch

CAPITOL (281 "Interviews for use with Capitol Soundtrack LP, *High Society*").......... 50-100 56
(Promotional issue only.)

CROSBY, Bing, & Peggy Lee

Singles: 78 rpm

DECCA.......... 3-5 52

Singles: 7-inch

DECCA.......... 5-10 52
Also see LEE, Peggy

CROSBY, Bing, & Johnny Mercer P&R '38

Singles: 78 rpm

DECCA.......... 5-8 38-40
Also see MERCER, Johnny

CROSBY, Bing, & Mills Brothers P&R '31
(With Connee Boswell)

Singles: 78 rpm

BRUNSWICK.......... 5-10 31-32
Also see MILLS BROTHERS

CROSBY, Bing, & Frank Sinatra

Singles: 78 rpm

CAPITOL.......... 3-5 56

Singles: 7-inch

CAPITOL.......... 5-10 56
Also see SINATRA, Frank

CROSBY, Bing, & Mel Torme P&R '46
(With the Mel-Tones)

Singles: 78 rpm

DECCA.......... 4-8 46
Also see TORME, Mel

CROSBY, Bing, & Orson Welles

LPs: 10/12-inch

DECCA (6000 "The Small One, the Happy Prince").......... 10-25 50
(10-inch LP.)
Also see CROSBY, Bing
Also see WELLES, Orson

CROSBY, Chris P&R '64

Singles: 7-inch

ATLANTIC.......... 4-8 67
CHALLENGE.......... 4-8 64-65
COLUMBIA.......... 3-6 69
DORE.......... 4-8 61
MGM.......... 4-8 64
W.B. 3-5 63

Picture Sleeves

MGM.......... 5-10 64

LPs: 10/12-inch

MGM.......... 15-20 64

CROSBY, David LP '71

Singles: 7-inch

ATLANTIC.......... 3-5 71

LPs: 10/12-inch

A&M.......... 5-8 89
ATLANTIC.......... 10-15 71
Also see BYRDS
Also see GRATEFUL DEAD
Also see JEFFERSON AIRPLANE
Also see SLICK, Grace

CROSBY, David, & Graham Nash P&R '71

Singles: 7-inch

ABC.......... 3-5 75-77
ATLANTIC.......... 3-5 72

LPs: 10/12-inch

ABC.......... 8-10 75-78
ATLANTIC.......... 10-15 72
MCA.......... 5-10 75
Also see CROSBY, David
Also see NASH, Graham

CROSBY, Eddie C&W '49

Singles: 78 rpm

DECCA.......... 4-8 49

CROSBY, Gary

Singles: 7-inch

DECCA.......... 5-10 55
GREGMARK (11 "That's Alright Baby").......... 10-15 62
HICKORY (1448 "Town Girl").......... 5-10 66

CROSBY, Gary, & Friend (Bing Crosby)

EPs: 7-inch

DECCA (2001 "Gary Crosby & Friend").......... 10-15 54

CROSBY, Gary, Phillip, Dennis, Lindsay & Bing P&R '50

Singles: 78 rpm

DECCA.......... 5-8 50

Singles: 7-inch

DECCA (40181 "A Crosby Christmas").......... 10-15 50

Picture Sleeves

DECCA (1-134 "A Crosby Christmas").......... 20-40 50
(Sleeve for 45)
DECCA (796 "A Crosby Christmas").......... 10-20 50
(Sleeve for 78.)
Also see CROSBY, Bing
Also see CROSBY, Gary

CROSBY, STILLS & NASH P&R/LP '69

Singles: 7-inch

ATLANTIC.......... 3-6 69-89

Picture Sleeves

ATLANTIC.......... 3-8 70-89

LPs: 10/12-inch

ATLANTIC (Except 8229).......... 8-10 77-83
ATLANTIC (8229 "Crosby, Stills & Nash").......... 15-20 69
Members: David Crosby; Stephen Stills; Graham Nash.

CROSBY, STILLS, NASH & YOUNG P&R/LP '70

Singles: 7-inch

ATLANTIC.......... 3-5 70

Picture Sleeves

ATLANTIC.......... 3-6 70

EPs: 7-inch

ATLANTIC.......... 10-15 70
(Juke box issue only.)

LPs: 10/12-inch

ATLANTIC (165 "Celebration Copy").......... 25-35 70s
(Promotional issue only.)
ATLANTIC (902 "4-Way Street").......... 12-20 71
(With photo applied to cover.)
ATLANTIC (7200 "Deja Vu").......... 15-20 70
(With photo applied to cover.)
ATLANTIC (7200 "Deja Vu").......... 8-12
(With photo *printed* on cover.)
ATLANTIC (16000 thru 19000 series).......... 5-10 74-82
ATLANTIC (8000 series).......... 5-10 83
MFSL (088 "Deja Vu").......... 40-60 82

Promotional LPs

Members: David Crosby; Stephen Stills; Graham Nash; Neil Young.
Also see CROSBY, David
Also see CROSBY, STILLS & NASH
Also see NASH, Graham
Also see STILLS, Stephen
Also see YOUNG, Neil

CROSS, Christopher P&R/LP '80

Singles: 7-inch

COLUMBIA.......... 3-4 85
REPRISE.......... 3-4 88
W.B. 3-4 79-85

Picture Sleeves

REPRISE.......... 3-4 88
W.B. 3-4 80-85

LPs: 10/12-inch

COLUMBIA.......... 5-10 85
REPRISE.......... 5-8 88
W.B. (Except 1172).......... 3-4 79-85
W.B. (1172 "Theme from *Arthur*").......... 20-25 81
(Picture disc. Promotional issue only.)
Also see McDONALD, Michael

CROSS, Jimmy P&R '65

Singles: 7-inch

CHICKEN.......... 4-8 65
RECORDO.......... 5-10 61
RED BIRD.......... 5-10 65
REO.......... 8-12 64
(Canadian.)
TOLLIE.......... 5-10 64

CROSS COUNTRY P&R/LP '73
(Tokens)

Singles: 7-inch

ATCO.......... 3-6 73-74

LPs: 10/12-inch

ATCO.......... 10-15 73
Members: Jay Siegel; Phil Margo; Mitch Margo.
Also see TOKENS

CROUCH, Andrae R&B '80
(With His Disciples)
Singles: 7-inch
LIGHT ... 3-4 76-80
W.B. ... 3-4 81
LPs: 10/12-inch
ACCORD ... 82 5-8
LIGHT ... 5-8 68-82
W.B. ... 5-8 81
Also see JACKSON, Michael

CROW P&R/LP '69
(David Wagner)
Singles: 7-inch
AMARET ... 3-6 69-72
INNER EAR (427 "Autumn of Tomorrow") ... 25-50
PEAK ... 8-12 83
(Colored vinyl)
LPs: 10/12-inch
AMARET ... 10-15 69-73
PEAK ... 4-8 83
Members: David Waggoner; Dennis Craswell; Kink Middleliest.
Also see CASTAWAYS

CROWD PLEASERS R&B '79
Singles: 7-inch
WESTBOUND ... 3-4 79
LPs: 10/12-inch
WESTBOUND ... 5-10 79

CROWDED HOUSE LP '86
Singles: 12-inch
CAPITOL ... 4-6 86
Singles: 7-inch
CAPITOL ... 3-4 86-88
Picture Sleeves
CAPITOL ... 3-4 87-88
LPs: 10/12-inch
CAPITOL ... 5-10 86-88
Members: Neil Finn; Paul Hester; Nick Seymour; Tim Finn.
Also see SPLIT ENZ

CROWELL, Rodney C&W '78
Singles: 7-inch
COLUMBIA ... 3-4 86-90
W.B. ... 3-4 78-82
LPs: 10/12-inch
COLUMBIA ... 5-8 86-90
W.B. ... 5-10 78-81
Session: Karen Brooks.
Also see HARRIS, Emmylou
Also see STEWART, Gary

CROWELL, Rodney, & Rosanne Cash C&W '88
Singles: 7-inch
COLUMBIA ... 3-4 88
Also see CASH, Rosanne
Also see CROWELL, Rodney

CROWN HEIGHTS AFFAIR R&B '74
Singles: 12-inch
SBK ... 4-6 89
Singles: 7-inch
DELITE ... 3-5 75-82
RCA ... 3-5 73-74
LPs: 10/12-inch
DELITE ... 5-10 75-82
RCA ... 10-12 74-78
Members: Phil Thomas; Ray Rock; Bert Reid; James Baynard; Ray Reid; William Anderson; Howard Young; Muki Wilson.

CROWS P&R/R&B '54
(With Melino & His Orchestra)
Singles: 78 rpm
QUALITY (1236 "Gee") ... 50-75 53
(Canadian.)
RAMA (3 "Seven Lonely Days") ... 100-200 53
RAMA (5 "Gee") ... 50-100 53
RAMA (10 "Heartbreaker") ... 50-100 53
RAMA (29 "Baby") ... 75-125 54
RAMA (30 "Miss You") ... 100-200 54
RAMA (50 "Baby Doll") ... 50-100 54
TICO (1082 "Mambo Shevitz") ... 50-100 51
Singles: 7-inch
QUALITY (1236 "Gee") ... 100-150 53
(Canadian.)
RAMA (3 "Seven Lonely Days") ... 500-750 53
RAMA (5 "Gee") ... 50-100 53
(Black vinyl. Blue label. No clouds or lines around "Rama" logo.)
RAMA (5 "Gee") ... 40-60 53
(Black vinyl. Blue label. With clouds and lines around "Rama" logo.)
RAMA (5 "Gee") ... 300-500 53
(Colored vinyl.)
RAMA (5 "Gee") ... 20-40 56
(Red label.)
RAMA (10 "Heartbreaker") ... 300-500 53
(Black vinyl.)
RAMA (10 "Heartbreaker") ... 1000-2000 53
(Colored vinyl.)
RAMA (29 "Baby") ... 200-300 54
RAMA (30 "Miss You") ... 250-350 54
(Black vinyl.)
RAMA (30 "Miss You") ... 1000-2000 54
(Colored vinyl.)
RAMA (50 "Baby Doll") ... 250-350 54
TICO (1082 "Mambo Shevitz") ... 200-300 51
(Black vinyl.)
TICO (1082 "Mambo Shevitz") ... 500-750 51
(Colored vinyl.)
LPs: 10/12-inch
MURRAY HILL ... 5-8 88
Members: Daniel "Sonny" Norton; Harold Major; Jerry Hamilton; Mark Jackson; Bill Davis.
Also see HARPTONES / Crows

CRUDUP, Big Boy R&B '45
(Arthur "Big Boy" Crudup)
Singles: 78 rpm
ACE (503 "I Wonder") ... 200-300 53
BLUEBIRD ... 10-30 41-46
CHAMPION (108 "I Wonder") ... 200-300 52
GROOVE ... 20-30 53-54
RCA ... 10-25 47-53
Singles: 7-inch
FIRE (1501 "Mean Ol' Frisco") ... 10-15 62
FIRE (1502 "Katie Mae") ... 10-15 62
GROOVE (0011 "I Love My Baby") ... 30-40 53
GROOVE (0026 "She's Got No Hair") ... 30-40 54
GROOVE (5005 "Mean Ol' Frisco") .. 30-40 54
RCA (0000 "That's All Right") ... 200-225 49
(Colored vinyl.)
RCA (0001 "Boy Friend Blues") ... 50-100 49
(Colored vinyl.)
RCA (0013 "Shout Sister, Shout") .. 50-100 49
(Colored vinyl.)
RCA (0032 "Hoodoo Lady Blues") .. 50-100 50
(Colored vinyl.)
RCA (0046 "Come Back Baby") ... 50-100 49
(Colored vinyl.)
RCA (0074 "Dust My Broom") ... 50-100 50
(Colored vinyl.)
RCA (0092 "Mean Old Santa Fe") ... 50-100 50
(Colored vinyl.)
RCA (0100 "Lonesome World to Me") ... 50-100 50
(Colored vinyl.)
RCA (0105 "She's Just Like Caldonia") ... 50-100 50
(Colored vinyl.)
RCA (0117 "Nobody Wants Me") ... 50-100 50
(Colored vinyl.)
RCA (0126 "Roberta Blues") ... 50-100 50
(Colored vinyl.)
RCA (0141 "Too Much Competition") ... 50-100 50
(Colored vinyl.)
RCA (4367 "Love Me Mama") ... 50-100 51
RCA (4572 "Goin' Back to Georgia") ... 50-75 52
RCA (4753 "Worried About You Baby") ... 50-75 52
RCA (4933 "Second Man Blues") ... 50-75 52
RCA (5070 "Pearly Lee") ... 50-75 52
RCA (5167 "Keep on Drinkin'") ... 50-75 53
RCA (5563 "My Wife and Women") .. 50-75 53
EPs: 7-inch
CAMDEN (415 "Arthur 'Big Boy' Crudup") ... 100-125 57
LPs: 10/12-inch
COLLECTABLES ... 6-8 88
DELMARK ... 15-25 69
FIRE (103 "Mean Ol' Frisco") ... 150-200 62
RCA ... 10-20 71
TRIP (7501 "Mean Ol' Frisco") ... 8-12 75
Also see CRUDUP, Percy Lee
Also see CRUMP, Arthur
Also see JAMES, Elmore
Also see LITTLE RICHARD / Arthur Crudup / Red Callendar Sextet

CRUDUP, Percy Lee
(Arthur Crudup)
Singles: 78 rpm
CHECKER (754 "Open Your Book") ... 25-50 52
Also see CRUDUP, Big Boy

CRUISE, Pablo: see PABLO CRUISE

CRUM, Simon C&W '55
(Ferlin Husky)
Singles: 78 rpm
CAPITOL ... 5-15 55-57
Singles: 7-inch
ABC ... 3-5 74
CAPITOL ... 5-15 55-63
LPs: 10/12-inch
CAPITOL (1880 "The Unpredictable Simon Crum") ... 75-100 63
Also see HUSKY, Ferlin

CRUMP, Arthur
(Arthur Crudup)
Singles: 78 rpm
CHAMPION ("I Wonder") ... 75-100
Also see CRUDUP, Big Boy

CRUSADERS LP '71
Singles: 7-inch
ABC ... 3-4 78
BLUE THUMB ... 3-5 72-77
CHISA ... 3-5 71
MCA (8783 "Street Life") ... 20-30 79
(Picture disc. Promotional issue only. Reportedly 125 made.)
MOWEST ... 3-5
LPs: 10/12-inch
BLUE THUMB ... 10-12 73-77
GRP ... 5-8 91
MCA ... 8-10 79-86
MFSL (010 "Chain Reaction") ... 25-50 78
(Half-speed mastered.)
MOTOWN ... 10-12 73
MOWEST ... 10-12 72
Members: Larry Carlton; Pops Popwell.
Also see CARLTON, Larry
Also see COCKER, Joe
Also see CRAWFORD, Randy
Also see HOOPER, Stix
Also see JAZZ CRUSADERS
Also see SAMPLE, Joe

CRUSADERS & B.B. KING
Singles: 7-inch
MCA ... 3-4 82
LPs: 10/12-inch
MCA ... 8-10 82
Also see CRUSADERS
Also see KING, B.B.

CRUZADOS LP '85
Singles: 7-inch
ARISTA ... 3-4 85
LPs: 10/12-inch
ARISTA ... 5-10 85-87
Members: Tito Larriva; Chalo Quintana; Steve Hufsteter; Tony Marsico; Marshall Rohner.

CRYAN' SHAMES P&R '66
Singles: 7-inch
COLUMBIA ... 4-8 66-70
DESTINATION ... 5-10 66

Picture Sleeves
COLUMBIA..8-12 67
LPs: 10/12-inch
BACK-TRAC.......................................5-10 85
COLUMBIA (2589 "Sugar and Spice")...20-25 66
(Monaural.)
COLUMBIA (2786 "A Scratch in the Sky")...20-25 67
(Monaural.)
COLUMBIA (9389 "Sugar and Spice")...15-20 66
(Stereo.)
COLUMBIA (9586 "A Scratch in the Sky")...15-20 67
(Stereo.)
COLUMBIA (9719 "Synthesis")........15-20 69

CRYSTAL, Billy *P&R/D&D/LP '85*
Singles: 12-inch
A&M..4-6 85
Singles: 7-inch
A&M..3-4 85
Picture Sleeves
A&M..3-5 85
LPs: 10/12-inch
A&M..5-10 85

CRYSTAL GAYLE: see GAYLE, Crystal

CRYSTAL GRASS *R&B '75*
Singles: 7-inch
POLYDOR...3-5 75
PRIVATE STOCK..................................3-5 76
LPs: 10/12-inch
MERCURY..5-10 78
POLYDOR...8-10 75

CRYSTAL MANSION *P&R '68*
Singles: 7-inch
CAPITOL..3-6 68-70
COLOSSUS..3-5 70-71
RARE EARTH......................................3-5 72
20TH FOX...3-4 79
LPs: 10/12-inch
CAPITOL..12-15 69
RARE EARTH......................................10-12 72
20TH FOX...5-10 79
Also see CASWELL, Johnny

CRYSTALS *P&R/R&B '61*
Singles: 7-inch
GUSTO...3-5 '80s
MICHELLE (4113 "Ring-a-Ting-a-Ling")...5-10 67
PAVILLION..4-6 82
PHILLES (100 "There's No Other")...10-20 61
PHILLES (102 "Uptown")..................10-20 62
PHILLES (105 "He Hit Me")...............20-30 62
PHILLES (106 "He's a Rebel")...........10-20 62
PHILLES (109 "He's Sure the Boy I Love")...10-20 62
PHILLES (111 "Let's Dance the Screw")...................................300-500 63
(White label. Promotional Issue Only.)
PHILLES (111 "Let's Dance the Screw")...................................500-750 63
(Blue label. Has "Let's Dance" in smaller print and in parenthesis. Also has identification numbers *stamped* in vinyl. Blue label copies with "Let's Dance" in the same size print as "The Screw - Part 1" and with identification numbers hand etched are counterfeits.)
PHILLES (112 "Da Do Ron Ron").....10-20 63
PHILLES (115 "Then He Kissed Me")...10-20 63
PHILLES (119 "Little Boy")...............15-25 63
PHILLES (119X "Little Boy").........200-300 63
(Single-sided disc.)
PHILLES (122 "All Grown Up").........10-20 64
U.A. (927 "My Place")......................5-10 65
U.A. (994 "I Got a Man")...................5-10 66
LPs: 10/12-inch
PHILLES (4000 "The Crystals Twist Uptown")...................................200-300 62
(Monaural. Blue label.)
PHILLES (4000 "The Crystals Twist Uptown")...................................500-750 62
(Monaural. White label. Promotional issue only.)
PHILLES (4000 "The Crystals Twist Uptown")...................................400-600 62
(Stereo.)
PHILLES (4001 "He's a Rebel")....200-300 63
(Monaural. Blue label.)
PHILLES (4001 "He's a Rebel")....500-750 63
(White label. Promotional issue only.)
PHILLES (4003 "The Crystals")....150-250 63
(Monaural. Blue label.)
PHILLES (4003 "The Crystals")....500-750 63
(White label. Promotional issue only.)
PHILLES (90722 "The Crystals Twist Uptown")...................................750-1000 62
(Capitol Record Club issue.)
Members: Barbara Alston; Lala Brooks; Dee Dee Kennibrew; Patricia Wright; Mary Thomas.
Also see LOVE, Darlene
Also see RONETTES / Crystals / Darlene Love / Bob B. Soxx & Blue Jeans

CUBA, Joe *P&R/R&B/LP '66*
(Joe Cuba Sextet)
Singles: 7-inch
ROULETTE..3-5 71
TICO..4-6 66
LPs: 10/12-inch
SEECO..10-15
TICO..10-15 66-67
Session: Jose Feliciano.
Also see FELICIANO, Jose

CUCA *R&B '88*
Singles: 7-inch
ALPHA INT.......................................3-4 88

CUES *P&R '55*
Singles: 78 rpm
CAPITOL..10-15 55-56
JUBILEE..10-15 55
LAMP...10-15 54
PREP...10-20 57
Singles: 7-inch
CAPITOL..15-25 55-56
JUBILEE..15-20 55
LAMP...10-20 54
PREP...10-15 57
Members: Ollie Jones; Jimmy Breedlove; Abe DeCosta; Robey Kirk; Eddie Barnes.
Also see RAVENS

CUFF LINKS *P&R/LP '69*
Singles: 7-inch
ATCO..3-5 72
DECCA..3-6 69-71
MCA...3-4 84
Picture Sleeves
DECCA (32533 "Tracy").....................5-10 69
(Gatefold sleeve. Promotional issue only.)
LPs: 10/12-inch
DECCA..15-25 69-70
Members: Ron Dante; Rupert Holmes.
Also see HOLMES, Rupert

CUGAT, Xavier *P&R '35*
Singles: 78 rpm
COLUMBIA..4-8 41-55
RCA...3-6 50-57
VICTOR...4-8 35-41
Singles: 7-inch
COLUMBIA..5-10 50-55
DECCA..3-5 65
MERCURY..4-6 62-64
RCA...5-10 50-62
EPs: 7-inch
COLUMBIA..5-15 55-59
MERCURY..5-15 53-54
LPs: 10/12-inch
CAMDEN..10-15 59
COLUMBIA..10-20 62
DECCA..10-20 65-69
HARMONY...10-15 60
MERCURY..10-30 53-67
RCA (Except 3021)...........................15-25 58-60
RCA (3021 "Siboney").......................25-40 53
(10-inch LP.)

CUGAT, Xavier, & Dinah Shore
LPs: 10/12-inch
RCA (3022 "Tangos")........................25-40 53

CUGINI *P&R '79*
(Donald Cugini)
Singles: 7-inch
SCOTTI BROTHERS............................3-5 79

CULLEY, Frank *R&B '49*
(Frank "Floorshow" Culley; with the Buddy Tate Orchestra)
Singles: 78 rpm
ATLANTIC...20-40 49-51
BATON..10-20 56
LENOX..15-25 49
Singles: 7-inch
BATON..15-25 56
EPs: 7-inch
BATON (7001/2 "Rock & Roll").......50-100 56
(Price is for either volume.)
LPs: 10/12-inch
BATON (1201 "Rock & Roll")........150-250 56

CULT *LP '85*
(Southern Death Cult; Death Cult)
Singles: 12-inch
BEGGARS BANQUET (260T "Heart of Soul")...5-10 86
(Limited numbered edition.)
BEGGARS BANQUET (2691 "Love Removal Machine")......................................5-10 87
(Promotional issue only.)
SIRE...4-6 85-86
Singles: 7-inch
SIRE...3-4 85-89
Picture Sleeves
SIRE...3-4 85-89
LPs: 10/12-inch
BEGGARS BANQUET (98 "Sonic Temple")..10-15 89
(Colored vinyl.)
SIRE...5-10 85-89
Members: Ian Astbury; Billy Duffy; Jamie Stewart; Les Warner; Matt Sorum.
Also see GUNS 'N' ROSES

CULTURE CLUB *P&R '82*
(Featuring Boy George)
Singles: 12-inch
EPIC/VIRGIN.....................................4-6 82-86
Singles: 7-inch
EPIC/VIRGIN.....................................3-4 82-86
Picture Sleeves
EPIC/VIRGIN.....................................3-4 83-86
LPs: 10/12-inch
EPIC/VIRGIN (Except 39237).............5-10 82-86
EPIC/VIRGIN (39237 "Colour by Numbers")..8-10 84
(Picture disc.)
VIRGIN (2330 "Waking Up with the House on Fire")...8-10 84
(Picture disc.)
Members: Boy George; Jon Moss; Roy Hay; Michael Craig.
Also see BAND AID
Also see BOY GEORGE
Also see STEWART, Jermaine

CUMMINGS, Burton *P&R/LP '76*
Singles: 7-inch
ALFA..3-4 81
PORTRAIT..3-6 76-78
Picture Sleeves
ALFA..3-4 81
PORTRAIT..3-6 78
EPs: 7-inch
PORTRAIT..4-8 77
(Issued with a paper sleeve.)
LPs: 10/12-inch
ALFA..5-10 81
PORTRAIT..8-10 76-78
Also see GUESS WHO
Also see ROGERS, Dann

CUMMINGS, Burton / Cheap Trick / Crawler

EPs: 7-inch

COLUMBIA (1129 "Music for Every Ear") 15-25 77
(Promotional issue only.)
Also see CHEAP TRICK
Also see CUMMINGS, Burton
Also see BACK STREET CRAWLER
Also see WILSON, Dennis / Ram Jam / Joan Baez

CUNHA, Rick P&R/C&W '74

Singles: 7-inch

COLUMBIA 3-5 75
GRC 3-5 74

LPs: 10/12-inch

COLUMBIA 8-10 75
GRC 10-12 74
SIERRA BRIAR 5-10
Also see JENNINGS, Waylon

CUPIDS P&R '63

Singles: 7-inch

AANKO (1002 "Brenda") 50-100 63
(First issue.)
KC (115 "Brenda") 25-50 63

CURB, Mike P&R/LP '70
(Mike Curb Congregation; with Sidewalk Sounds; with Curbstones; with Rebalairs; with Waterfall)

Singles: 7-inch

BUENA VISTA 3-5 75
FORWARD 3-6 69
MGM 3-4 70
REPRISE (0287 "Hot Dawg") 10-20 64
SMASH (1938 "The Rebel") 10-15 64
TOWER 10-15 66
W.B. 3-5 77

Picture Sleeves

BUENA VISTA 5-10 75
FORWARD 4-8 69

LPs: 10/12-inch

BUENA VISTA 8-12
COBURT 8-12 70
FORWARD 5-10
MGM 5-10 71
Also see ALLAN, Davie
Also see DAVIS, Sammy, Jr.
Also see OSMONDS
Also see WILLIAMS, Hank, Jr.

CURE D&D/LP '83

Singles: 12-inch

ELEKTRA 4-6 85-86
SIRE 4-6 83-85

Singles: 7-inch

ELEKTRA 3-4 85-89
SIRE 3-4 83-85

Picture Sleeves

ELEKTRA 3-4 86-89

LPs: 10/12-inch

A&M 8-10 81
ELEKTRA 5-10 85-89
PVC 8-10 80
SIRE 5-10 83-85
Members: Robert Smith; Laurence Tolhurst.

CURIOSITY KILLED THE CAT P&R/LP '87

Singles: 7-inch

MERCURY 3-4 87

Picture Sleeves

MERCURY 3-4 87

LPs: 10/12-inch

MERCURY 5-8 87

CURRENT P&R '77

Singles: 7-inch

PLAYBOY 3-4 77

CURRIE, Cherie & Marie P&R '79

Singles: 7-inch

CAPITOL 3-5 79-80

Picture Sleeves

CAPITOL 3-5 79

LPs: 10/12-inch

CAPITOL 5-10 79-81
Also see RUNAWAYS

CURRY, Clifford P&R/R&B '67
(Cliff Curry)

Singles: 7-inch

ABBOTT 3-6 72
C.C. 4-8
CAPRICE 3-6 72
ELF 10-20 67-69
RIDGECREST (1202 "Kiss Kiss Kiss") 15-25 59
SSS INT'L (812 "I Don't Need You") 10-15 70

LP: 10/12-inch

WOODSHED 8-12
Also see NOTATIONS

CURRY, Louis R&B '68

Singles: 7-inch

M-S 5-10 68
REEL 10-20

CURRY, Mini R&B '87

Singles: 7-inch

TOTAL EMP 3-4 87

CURRY, Tim P&R/LP '79
(With Original Roxy Cast)

Singles: 7-inch

A&M 3-4 78-81
ODE 3-5 76
ODE '70 .... 3-4 74

Picture Sleeves

A&M 3-4 79

LPs: 10/12-inch

A&M 5-10 78-89
Also see WILSON, Brian

CURTIE & BOOMBOX P&R/D&D '85

Singles: 12-inch

RCA 4-6 85

Singles: 7-inch

RCA 3-4 85
Member: Curtie Fortune.

CURTIS, Chantal R&B '79

Singles: 7-inch

KEYLOCK 3-5 79

CURTIS, T.C. D&D '85

Singles: 12-inch

SIRE 4-6 85

CURTOLA, Bobby P&R '62
(With the Martells)

Singles: 7-inch

DEL-FI 8-12 61-63
KING 4-8 67
TARTAN 5-10 63-66

Picture Sleeves

DEL-FI 10-15 61-62

CUT R&B '86

Singles: 7-inch

SUPERTRONICS 3-4 86

CUTTING CREW P&R/LP '87

Singles: 12-inch

VIRGIN (1003 "I Just Died in Your Arms") 10-15 87
(Saw blade-shaped disc. Promotional issue only.)

Singles: 7-inch

VIRGIN 3-4 87-89

Picture Sleeves

VIRGIN 3-4 87-89

LPs: 10/12-inch

VIRGIN 5-10 87-89

CYBOTRON R&B '83

Singles: 12-inch

FANTASY 4-6 82-84

Singles: 7-inch

FANTASY 3-4 83-84

LPs: 10/12-inch

FANTASY 5-10 83-84

CYCLONES P&R '58

Singles: 7-inch

TROPHY (500 "Bullwhip Rock") 15-25 58
TROPHY (503 "Aftermath") 15-25 58
Member: Bill Taylor.

CYMANDE P&R/R&B/LP '73

Singles: 7-inch

JANUS 3-5 72-73

LPs: 10/12-inch

JANUS 10-12 72-74

CYMARRON P&R/LP '71

Singles: 7-inch

ENTRANCE 3-5 71-72

LPs: 10/12-inch

ENTRANCE 10-12 71
Members: Rick Yancey; Richard Mainegra; Sherrill Parks.

CYMBAL, Johnny P&R '63

Singles: 7-inch

AMARET 3-6 69
COLUMBIA 4-8 66
DCP (1135 "Go VW, Go") 10-15 65
KAPP 8-15 63-64
KEDLEN 10-15 63
MCA 3-4 84
MGM 8-15 60-61
MUSICOR 4-8 67
VEE JAY 4-8 63

Picture Sleeves

DCP (1135 "Go VW, Go") 15-25 65

LPs: 10/12-inch

KAPP (1324 "Mr. Bass Man") 25-40 63
(Monaural.)
KAPP (3324 "Mr. Bass Man") 35-50 63
(Stereo.)
Also see DEREK

CYMONE, Andre R&B '82

Singles: 12-inch

COLUMBIA 4-6 82-86

Singles: 7-inch

COLUMBIA 3-4 82-86

LPs: 10/12-inch

COLUMBIA 5-10 82-86
Also see PRINCE
Also see WATLEY, Jody

CYNTHIA & JOHNNY O P&R '90

LPs: 10/12-inch

MICMAC 5-8 90

CYRÉ R&B '87

Singles: 7-inch

FRESH 3-4 87

CYRKLE P&R/LP '66

Singles: 7-inch

COLUMBIA (Except 43589) 5-10 65-68
COLUMBIA (43589 "Red Rubber Ball") 5-10 65
(Black vinyl.)
COLUMBIA (43589 "Red Rubber Ball") 10-15 65
(Colored vinyl. Promotional issue only.)

Picture Sleeves

COLUMBIA 20-30 66-68

LPs: 10/12-inch

COLUMBIA (2544 "Red Rubber Ball") 20-25 66
COLUMBIA (9344 "Red Rubber Ball") 25-30 66
COLUMBIA (2632 "Neon") 20-25 67
(Monaural.)
COLUMBIA (9432 "Neon") 20-30 67
(Stereo.)
FLYING DUTCHMAN/AMSTERDAM (12007 "The Minx") 20-25 70
(Soundtrack.)

CYRKLE / Paul Revere & Raiders

Singles: 7-inch

COLUMBIA (466 "Camaro") 10-15 66
(Special Products Chevrolet promotional issue only.)

Picture Sleeves

COLUMBIA (466 "Camaro").............. 15-25 66
(Special Products Chevrolet promotional issue only.)
COLUMBIA (43000 series).................. 5-10 66-67
Members: Don Danneman; Marty Fried; Tom Dawes; John Simon; Michael Losekamp.
Also see CYRKLE
Also see REVERE, Paul, & Raiders
Also see SIMON, Paul

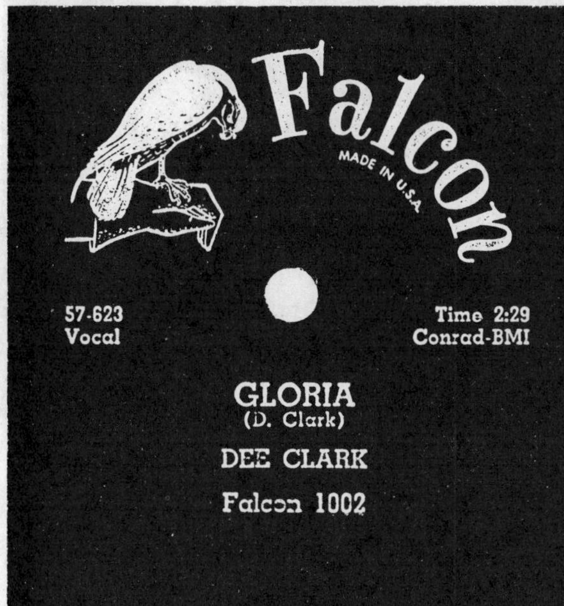

GALICO
LAST KISS
(Wayne Cochran)
Record No.
G-45-105-A
Macon Music
Time 2:10
Prod. by:
Bobby Smith
DJ COPY
WAYNE COCHRAN
Bobby Smith Production, Southern United Bldg., Macon, Ga.

Specialty
Pub: Venice-BMI
Time: 2:11
TOUCH AND GO
(S. Bono)
WYNONA CARR
628
(5111)

CLOCK
DISTRIBUTED BY EMBER DISTRIBUTORS, INC.
(CL 106)
Lowell Music
BMI
Instrumental
Time 2:01
C. 1009
THE HAPPY ORGAN
(Wood-Clowney-Kriegsmann)
Featuring at the Organ
DAVE 'BABY' CORTEZ
CLOCK RECORD CO., NEW YORK, N. Y.

RINKY DINK
(D. Clowney)
Dist. by
JULIA
CHESS
U 452 A
ARC-Cortez
Ninny
BMI
BABY CORTEZ
1829
MANUFACTURED BY CHESS PRODUCING CORP., CHICAGO, ILLINOIS, U.S.A.

D MOB *P&R '89*
(Featuring Cathy Dennis)
Singles: 7-inch
FFRR 3-4 89-90
LPs: 10/12-inch
FFRR 3-4 89

D - NICE *LP '90*
LPs: 10/12-inch
JIVE 5-8 90

"D" TRAIN *LP '82*
Singles: 12-inch
PRELUDE 4-6 81-85
Singles: 7-inch
PRELUDE 3-4 81-85
LPs: 10/12-inch
PRELUDE 5-10 82-85
Members: James "D Train" Williams; Hubert Eaves III.
Also see WILLIAMS, James "D Train"

D., Eddie: see EDDIE D.

DB's *LP '87*
LPs: 10/12-inch
I.R.S. 5-10 87

DFX2 *LP '83*
Singles: 7-inch
MCA 3-4 83
LPs: 10/12-inch
MCA 5-10 83

D.J. JAZZY JEFF & FRESH PRINCE *R&B '86*
Singles: 7-inch
JIVE 3-4 87-89
WORD-UP 3-4 86
Picture Sleeves
JIVE 3-4 88-89
LPs: 10/12-inch
JIVE 5-10 87-89
Also see SIMPSONS

D.J. MAGIC MIKE *LP '90*
LPs: 10/12-inch
CHEETAH 5-8 90
Also see VICIOUS BASE Featuring D.J. Magic Mike

DMX, Davy: see DAVY DMX

DNA Featuring Suzanne Vega *P&R '90*
Singles: 7-inch
A&M 3-4 90
Also see VEGA, Suzanne

D.O.A. *LP '90*
LPs: 10/12-inch
RESTLESS 5-8 90

D.O.C. *LP '89*
LPs: 10/12-inch
RUTHLESS 5-8 89

D.R.I. *LP '88*
LPs: 10/12-inch
METAL BLADE 5-8 88-89

DADDY DEWDROP *P&R '71*
Singles: 7-inch
CAPITOL 3-5 75
INPHASION 3-4 78-79
SUNFLOWER 3-6 70-72
SUNFLOWER/MGM 3-5 73
LPs: 10/12-inch
SUNFLOWER 12-15 71

DADDY O's *P&R '58*
Singles: 7-inch
CABOT 8-10 58

DAFFAN, Ted *P&R '43*
(With His Texans)
Singles: 78 rpm
COLUMBIA 4-8 46-55
OKEH 4-8 43-45
Singles: 7-inch
COLUMBIA 5-10 55
Members: George Strange; Chuck Keeshan; Leon Seago.

DAHL, Steve, & Teenage Radiation *P&R '79*
Singles: 7-inch
COHO 3-5 79
OVATION 3-5 79
Picture Sleeves
OVATION 3-5 79

DAILY, E.G. *P&R/R&B '86*
(Elizabeth G. Daily)
Singles: 12-inch
A&M 4-6 86
Singles: 7-inch
A&M 3-4 86
Picture Sleeves
A&M 3-4 86
LPs: 10/12-inch
A&M 5-10 86

DAISY DILLMAN BAND: see DILLMAN BAND

DA'KRASH *R&B/LP '88*
Singles: 7-inch
CAPITOL 3-4 88
LPs: 10/12-inch
CAPITOL 5-8 88

DALBELLO *D&D '84*
Singles: 12-inch
CAPITOL 4-6 84
Singles: 7-inch
CAPITOL 3-4 84

DALE, Alan *P&R '48*
(With Connie Haines)
Singles: 78 rpm
COLUMBIA 4-6 50-51
CORAL 3-6 52-56
DECCA 3-5 52
Singles: 7-inch
ABC-PAR 3-6 64
ADVANCE 3-6
COLUMBIA 5-10 50-51
CORAL (60000 & 61000 series) 5-10 52-56
CORAL (62000 series) 3-6 63
DECCA 4-8 52
EMKAY 3-6 62
FTP 3-6 61
MGM 4-8 59
SINCLAIR (1003 "A Teenage Girl") 15-25 61
EPs: 7-inch
CORAL 5-15 52-56
LPs: 10/12-inch
CORAL 15-25 55-56
FORD 10-15 63
U.A. 10-15 60
Also see CORNELL, Don, Johnny Desmond & Alan Dale

DALE, Dick *P&R '61*
(With His Del-tones)
Singles: 7-inch
CAPITOL 8-12 63-64
COLUMBIA 3-5 87
CONCERT ROOM 4-8 63
COUGAR 4-8 67
CUPID 10-20 60
DELTONE (4939 "Misirlou") 40-60 58
DELTONE (4940 "Peppermint Man") 40-60 58
DELTONE (5012 "Oh Wee Marie") 35-50 58
DELTONE (5013 "Stop Teasing") 25-35 59
DELTONE (5014 "Jessie Pearl") 35-50 60
DELTONE (5017 "Let's Go Trippin' ") 10-15 61
(No mention of Rendezvous Records.)
DELTONE (5017 "Let's Go Trippin' ") 8-10 61
(Reads "Distributed by Rendezvous Records.")
DELTONE (5018 "Shake and Stomp") 10-15 62
DELTONE (5019 "Miserlou") 10-15 62
(Reissue of 4939. Note slight spelling change.)
DELTONE (5020 "Peppermint Man") 10-15 62
DELTONE (5028 "Run for Life") 10-15 63
GNP 4-8 75
RENDEZVOUS (204 "Reincarnation Parts 1 & 2") 8-12 62
SATURN 10-15 63
YES 10-20
Promotional Singles
CAPITOL ("Thunder Wave"/"Spanish Kiss") 8-10 64
(Bonus single, packaged with the *Surf Age* LP by Jerry Cole and His Spacemen.)
CAPITOL (2320 "Peppermint Man") 25-35 63
(Compact 33 Single)
Picture Sleeves
CAPITOL (Except 2320) 12-25 63
CAPITOL (2320 "Peppermint Man") 35-45 63
(Promotional Compact 33 Single sleeve.)
COLUMBIA 4-6 87
YES 4-8
LPs: 10/12-inch
BALBOA 5-10 83
CAPITOL (T-1930 "King of the Surf Guitar") 30-40 63
(Monaural.)
CAPITOL (ST-1930 "King of the Surf Guitar") 40-50 63
(Stereo.)
CAPITOL (T-2002 "Checkered Flag") 25-35 63
(Monaural.)
CAPITOL (ST-2002 "Checkered Flag") 30-40 63
(Stereo.)
CAPITOL (T-2053 "Mr. Eliminator") 30-35 64
(Monaural.)
CAPITOL (ST-2053 "Mr. Eliminator") 35-40 64
CAPITOL (T-2111 "Summer Surf") 50-75 64
(Monaural. With *Movin' Surf*, a bonus single by Jerry Cole & His Spacemen.)
CAPITOL (T-2111 "Summer Surf") 35-45 64
(Monaural. Without bonus single.)
CAPITOL (ST-2111 "Summer Surf") 45-55 64
(Stereo. With *Movin' Surf*, a bonus single by Jerry Cole & His Spacemen.)
CAPITOL (ST-2111 "Summer Surf") 40-50 64
(Stereo. Without bonus single.)
CAPITOL (T-2293 "Rock Out with Dick Dale Live at Ciro's") 30-35 65
(Monaural.)
CAPITOL (2293 "Rock Out with Dick Dale Live at Ciro's") 35-40 65
(Stereo.)
DELTONE (1001 "Surfer's Choice") 30-40 61
DELTONE (1886 "Surfer's Choice") 40-60 63
(Distributed by Capitol.)
DUBTONE 15-20 63
GNP 8-12 75
Also see ALLAN, Davie
Also see BEACH BOYS / Dick Dale / Surfaris / Surf Kings
Also see VAUGHAN, Stevie Ray, & Dick Dale

DALE, Dick / Jerry Cole / Super Stocks / Mr. Gasser & Weirdos
EPs: 7-inch
CAPITOL (2663 "The Big Surfing Sounds") 35-50 64
(Promotional issue only.)

DALE, Dick / Surfaris / Fireballs

LPs: 10/12-inch

ALMOR (108 "World of Surfin'") 10-20 60s
ALMOR (109 "Hot Rod Drag Races") 10-20 60s
Also see FIREBALLS

DALE, Dick / Surfaris / Surf Kings (Beach Boys)

LPs: 10/12-inch

GUEST STAR (1433 "Surf Kings") 20-30 63
(Credits the Beach Boys, though there are no tracks by the Beach Boys. Also, tracks credited to the Surfaris are by the Original Surfaris.)
GUEST STAR (1433 "Surf Kings") 15-20 63
(Does not credit the Beach Boys.)
Also see ORIGINAL SURFARIS

DALE, Dick, His Del-Tones, & Francine York / Craig Adams & His Country Cousins

(With the Overland Swingin' Top Brass)

Singles: 7-inch

UNITED STATES ARMY (1301 "Enlistment Twist") 10-20 62
(Colored vinyl. Promotional issue only.)

Picture Sleeves

UNITED STATES ARMY (1301 "Enlistment Twist") 10-20 62
Also see DALE, Dick

DALE, Jimmy

(Jimmy Clanton)

Singles: 7-inch

DREW-BLAN (1003 "My Pride and Joy") 15-25 61
Also see CLANTON, Jimmy

DALE & GRACE — P&R/R&B '63

Singles: 7-inch

COLLECTABLES 3-4 70s
ERIC 3-4 70s
GUYDEN 3-5 72
HBR 4-8 66
MICHELLE 5-10 63-64
MONTEL 4-8 63-67
MONTEL MICHELLE (942 "What Am I Living For") 4-8 64
(Shows both label names.)
TRIP 3-4 70s

LPs: 10/12-inch

MONTEL (100 "I'm Leaving It Up to You") 35-50 64
Members: Dale Houston; Grace Broussard.

DALHART, Vernon — P&R '17

(With Gladys Rice; with Al Bernard)

Singles: 78 rpm

BANNER 15-25 20s
BLACK PATTI 75-125
BRUNSWICK 10-20 20s
BUDDY 50-100
CAMEO 15-25 20s
CHAMPION 15-25 20s
CLARION 10-20
COLUMBIA 5-15 22-30s
DOMINO 15-25 20s
EDISON 20-50 17-20s
EDISON AMBEROL 15-25 20s
GENNETT 15-25 20s
HARMONY 15-25 20s
HERSCHEL 25-50
HERWIN 25-50
OKEH 10-20 24
PATH 15-25 20s
PERFECT 15-25 20s
RCA 5-10 49
REGAL 15-25 20s
SILVERTONE 15-25
VICTOR 10-20 21-30s
VOCALION 15-25 20s

Singles: 7-inch

RCA (0016 "The Prisoner's Song") ... 15-25 49

LPs: 10/12-inch

DAVIS UNLIMITED 10-20
GOLDEN OLDEN COUNTRY 8-10
MARK 56 8-10
OLD HOMESTEAD 8-10

DALHART, Vernon, & Carson Robison — P&R '28

Singles: 78 rpm

VICTOR 10-20 27-28
Also see DALHART, Vernon

DALLARA, Tony — P&R '58

Singles: 7-inch

MERCURY 5-10 58-60
VESUVIUS 4-8 61-62

LPs: 10/12-inch

VESUVIUS 8-10 62

DALTON, Kathy — P&R/LP '74

Singles: 7-inch

DISC REET 3-5 74

LPs: 10/12-inch

DISC REET 8-12 73-74

DALTON & DUBARRI — R&B '79

Singles: 7-inch

ABC 3-5 76
COLUMBIA 3-5 73-74
HILLTAK 3-4 79

LPs: 10/12-inch

ABC 8-10 76
COLUMBIA 10-12 73-74
HILLTAK 5-10 79
Members: Gary Dalton; Kent Dubarri.

DALTREY, Roger — P&R/LP '73

Singles: 7-inch

A&M 3-5 75-76
ATLANTIC 3-4 84-87
MCA 3-5 73-82
MCA/GOLDHAWKE 3-5 75-77
ODE 3-5 72-73
POLYDOR 3-4 80-81
TRACK 3-5 73

Picture Sleeves

ATLANTIC 3-4 84-85
POLYDOR 3-5 80

LPs: 10/12-inch

ATLANTIC 5-10 84-87
MCA 10-15 71-82
POLYDOR 5-8 80
TRACK 10-12 73
Also see WHO

DALTREY, Roger, & Steve Gibbons

Singles: 12-inch

MCA 5-10
(Promotional issue only.)
Also see GIBBONS, Steve, Band

DALTREY, Roger, & Rick Wakeman

Singles: 7-inch

A&M 3-5 75

LPs: 10/12-inch

A&M 8-10 75
Also see DALTREY, Roger
Also see WAKEMAN, Rick

DAMARIS — R&B '84

Singles: 7-inch

COLUMBIA 3-4 84

DAMIAN, Michael — P&R '81

Singles: 7-inch

CYPRESS 3-4 89
LEG 3-4 81

Picture Sleeves

CYPRESS 3-4 89
LEG 3-4 81

LPs: 10/12-inch

CYPRESS 5-8 89

DAMIANO, Joe — P&R '59

(Josef Damiano)

Singles: 7-inch

CHANCELLOR 5-10 59-60

DAMITA JO — P&R '53

(Damita Joe)

Singles: 78 rpm

RCA 4-6 53

Singles: 7-inch

BANG BANG 4-8
EPIC (Black vinyl) 3-5 65-67
EPIC (Colored vinyl) 4-8 66
MELIC 3-6 64
MERCURY 4-8 60-64
RCA 5-10 53
RANWOOD 3-5 68-71
VEE JAY 3-6 65

Picture Sleeves

EPIC 4-8 65
MERCURY 5-10 61-63

EPs: 7-inch

MERCURY 5-10 60-61

LPs: 10/12-inch

CAMDEN 6-10 65
EPIC 8-15 65-67
MERCURY 12-25 61-63
RANWOOD 5-10 68
VEE JAY 10-15 65
Also see BENTON, Brook, & Damita Jo

DAMITA JO & BILLY ECKSTINE

Singles: 7-inch

MERCURY 3-6 63
Also see ECKSTINE, Billy

DAMITA JO & STEVE GIBSON & RED CAPS

Singles: 78 rpm

RCA (6281 "Always") 8-15 55

Singles: 7-inch

ABC-PAR 5-10 61
RCA (6281 "Always") 10-20 55

LPs: 10/12-inch

ABC-PAR (378 "Big 15") 40-60 61
Also see DAMITA JO
Also see GIBSON, Steve

DAMN YANKEES — P&R/LP '90

Singles: 7-inch

W.B. 3-4 90

LPs: 10/12-inch

W.B. 5-8 90
Members: Ted Nugent; Jack Blades; Tommy Shaw; Michael Cartellone.
Also see NIGHT RANGER
Also see NUGENT, Ted
Also see STYX

DAMNATION — LP '70

(Featuring Adam Blessing)

Singles: 7-inch

U.A. 3-5 71-72

LPs: 10/12-inch

U.A. 10-15 69-71

DAMON, Liz — P&R '70

(Liz Damon's Orient Express)

Singles: 7-inch

ABC 3-5 73
ANTHEM 5-10 71-72
DONCY 5-8 78
MAKAHA 5-10 70
WHITE WHALE 3-5 70

LPs: 10/12-inch

ANTHEM ("Liz Damon and the Orient Express") 15-25 71
DELILAH 8-12
MAKAHA 10-20 70
WHITE WHALE 8-12 71

DAMONE, Vic — P&R '47

Singles: 78 rpm

COLUMBIA 3-6 56-57
MERCURY 3-6 48-55
MERCURY/SAV-WAY (5053 "Ivy") 100-150 47
(Picture disc. Promotional issue only.)

Singles: 7-inch

CAPITOL 4-6 61-64
COLUMBIA 5-10 56-61
DOLTON 4-6 62
MGM 3-5 72-73
MERCURY 5-10 50-55
RCA 3-6 66-69
REBECCA 3-5 77

UNITED TALENT....................3-5 70
W.B. 4-6 65-66

EPs: 7-inch

CAPITOL CUSTOM ("Vic Damone Swings with A&W)...............................10-15 62
(Special products issue for A&W Root Beer.)
COLUMBIA.............................5-10 56-58
MERCURY 8-12 50-56

LPs: 10/12-inch

CAPITOL..............................10-20 61-64
COLUMBIA (900 thru 1500 series)....15-25 56-61
COLUMBIA (1900 series)..............10-20 62
COLUMBIA (8000 thru 8300 series).................................20-30 58-61
COLUMBIA (8700 series)..............10-15 62
DOLTON..............................10-15 64
HARMONY.............................5-10 66-67
HOLLYWOOD...........................5-10
MERCURY (Except 25000 series) 8-12 69
MERCURY (25000 series) 15-30 50-56
RCA..................................8-12 66-68
UNITED TALENT 5-10
W.B. 10-15 65
WING.................................10-15 59-63
Also see ANDREWS, Julie & Andre Previn / Vic Damone / Jack Jones / Marian Anderson
Also see FISHER, Eddie / Vic Damone / Dick Haymes
Also see PAGE, Patti, & Vic Damone

Singles: 7-inch

KIRSHNER.............................4-8
Also see TOKENS

DANA, Bill — LP '60

(Jose Jimenez; Bill Dana & Friends)

Singles: 7-inch

A&M...................................4-8 65-66
KAPP..................................5-15 61-63
SIGNATURE 5-10 60

Picture Sleeves

KAPP..................................10-20 61-62

EPs: 7-inch

KAPP..................................10-20 61

LPs: 10/12-inch

A&M...................................8-12 68
CAPITOL...............................6-10 70
HBR...................................8-10 66
KAPP..................................12-25 60-64
ROULETTE 12-25 61
SIGNATURE 20-25 60

DANA, Vic — P&R '61

Singles: 7-inch

CASINO................................3-5 76
COLUMBIA..............................3-5 71
DOLTON................................4-8 61-65
LIBERTY...............................3-6 68-70
MGM...................................3-5 75

Picture Sleeves

DOLTON................................5-10 62-66

LPs: 10/12-inch

DOLTON (Except 2013/8013) 15-25 62-65
DOLTON (2013 "This Is Vic Dana")..15-25 61
(Monaural.)
DOLTON (8013 "This Is Vic Dana")..20-30 61
(Stereo.)
LIBERTY...............................8-15 67-70
SUNSET................................8-10 67
Also see CARTER, Mel / Vic Dana

DANCER, Terri — R&B '86

Singles: 7-inch

REFLECTION............................3-4 86

DANCER, PRANCER & NERVOUS — P&R '59

Singles: 7-inch

CAPITOL...............................5-10 59

Picture Sleeves

CAPITOL...............................8-10 59
Member: Russ Regan.

DANDERLIERS — R&B '55

("James Campbell & Dallas Taylor Vocalists")

Singles: 78 rpm

STATES (147 "Chop Chop Boom")..................................75-125 55
STATES (150 "Shu-Wop")..............50-75 55
STATES (152 "May God Be with You")..................................50-75 56
STATES (160 "My Love") 75-125 56

Singles: 7-inch

B&F (150 "Shu-Wop")..................12-20 60
B&F (160 "My Love")..................12-20 60
B&F (1344 "Shu-Wop")................10-15 61
MIDAS (9004 "All the Way") 10-20 67
STATES (147 "Chop Chop Boom") 150-250 55
(Black vinyl.)
STATES (147 "Chop Chop Boom") 600-800 55
(Colored vinyl.)
STATES (150 "Shu-Wop")...............75-100 55
STATES (152 "May God Be with You") 100-150 56
STATES (160 "My Love") 100-150 56
Members: Dallas Taylor; James Campbell; Richard Thomas; Walter Stephenson; Bernard Dixon; Louis Johnson.

DANDLEERS: see DANLEERS

DANE, Dana — R&B '85

Singles: 12-inch

PROFILE...............................4-6 85

Singles: 7-inch

PROFILE...............................3-4 85-90

LPs: 10/12-inch

PROFILE...............................5-10 86-90

DANGERFIELD, Rodney — LP '80

Singles: 12-inch

RCA...................................4-6 83

Singles: 7-inch

RCA...................................3-4 83

Picture Sleeves

RCA...................................3-4 83

LPs: 10/12-inch

DECCA.................................15-20 66
CASABLANCA...........................5-10 80
RCA...................................5-10 83
RHINO.................................5-10 80

DANGEROUS TOYS — LP '89

Singles: 7-inch

COLUMBIA 5-8 89-90

LPs: 10/12-inch

COLUMBIA 5-8 89-91

DANIELS, Charlie — C&W/P&R/LP '73

(Charlie Daniels Band; with the Jaguars)

Singles: 7-inch

EPIC..................................3-5 76-86
HANOVER (4541 "Robot Romp")..... 10-20 59
KAMA SUTRA............................3-6 73-76
PAULA (200 series) 5-10 66
PAULA (400 series) 3-5 76

EPs: 7-inch

KAMA SUTRA (10 "Volunteer Jam") 5-8 74
(Bonus EP packaged with *Fire on the Mountain* LP.)

LPs: 10/12-inch

CAPITOL (11000 series)...............8-10 75
CAPITOL (16000 series)...............5-10 80
EPIC (Except 273) 5-10 76-91
EPIC (273 "Everything You Always Wanted to Hear")...............................10-15 77
(Promotional issue only.)
KAMA SUTRA............................10-15 73-76
MFSL (176 "Million Mile Reflections")........................15-20 85
Also see BARE, Bobby
Also see HELM, Levon, Johnny Cash, Emmylou Harris & Charlie Daniels
Also see LEE, Johnny, Michael Martin Murphey, & Charlie Daniels
Also see TUBB, Ernest

DANKO, Rick — LP '77

Singles: 7-inch

ARISTA................................3-4 78

LPs: 10/12-inch

ARISTA................................8-10 77
Also see BAND

DANKWORTH, Johnny — P&R '56

(Johnnie Dankworth)

Singles: 78 rpm

CAPITOL...............................3-8 55-56

Singles: 7-inch

CAPITOL...............................4-8 55-56
FONTANA 3-5 63-66
20TH FOX 3-5 66

LPs: 10/12-inch

FONTANA (Except 7559).................6-12 64-69
FONTANA (27559 "The Idol") 15-20 66
(Soundtrack. Monaural.)
FONTANA (67559 "The Idol") 20-25 66
(Soundtrack. Stereo.)
ROULETTE..............................10-15 60-61
TOP RANK..............................10-15 60

DANLEERS — P&R/R&B '58

(Dandleers)

Singles: 7-inch

ABC...................................3-4 75
AMP 3 (1005 " One Summer Night")...............................20-30
(Credits Danleers.)
AMP 3 (2115 " One Summer Night")...............................50-100 58
(Credits "Dandleers.")
COLLECTABLES..........................3-4 80s
EPIC (9367 "Half a Block from an Angel")..............................25-50 60
EPIC (9421 "Little Lover")............50-75 60
EVEREST (19412 "Foolish")............20-30 61
LE MANS (005 "The Truth Hurts") 15-25 64
LE MANS (008 "I'm Sorry")............15-25 64
MERCURY (71322 "One Summer Night")...............................15-25 58
MERCURY (71356 "I Really Love You")................................15-25 58
(Blue label.)
MERCURY (71356 "I Really Love You")................................25-50 58
(Black label.)
MERCURY (71356 "I Really Love You")................................15-25 58
MERCURY (71401 "Picture of You")................................25-35 58
MERCURY (71441 "Your Love")......40-60 59
SMASH (1872 "If")....................15-25 64
SMASH (1895 "Where Is My Love") 15-25 64
Members: Jimmy Weston; Johnny Lee; Nat McCune; Willie Ephriam; Roosevelt Mays; Doug Ebron; Louis Williams; Terry Wilson; Frank Clemens; Bill Carey.
Also see FOUR FELLOWS

DANNY & JUNIORS — P&R/R&B '57

(With Joe Terry)

Singles: 78 rpm

ABC-PAR 25-75 57-58

Singles: 7-inch

ABC...................................3-5 73
ABC-PAR (9871 "At the Hop")..........20-30 57
ABC-PAR (9888 "Rock & Roll Is Here to Stay")...............................20-30 58
ABC-PAR (9926 "Dottie")..............20-30 58
ABC-PAR (9953 "Crazy Cave").........15-25 58
ABC-PAR (9978 "I Feel So Lonely")..............................15-25 58
ABC-PAR (10004 "Do You Love Me")................................15-25 59
ABC-PAR (10052 "Playing Hard to Get") 15-25 59
CRUNCH................................4-6 73
DOWNTOWN..............................3-4 93
GOLDIES 45............................3-5 73
GUSTO.................................3-5 79
GUYDEN (2076 "Now and Then").....15-25 62
LUV...................................5-10 68
MCA...................................3-4 70s
MERCURY (72240 "Sad Girl") 10-20 64
ROULETTE..............................3-5 70s
SINGULAR (711 "At the Hop")......200-400 57
(Blue label.)

SINGULAR (711 "At the Hop") 10-15
(Black label.)
SWAN (4060 "Twistin' USA") 10-20 60
SWAN (4064 "Candy Cane Sugar Plum") 15-25 60
SWAN (4068 "Pony Express") 10-20 61
SWAN (4072 "Cha Cha Go Go") 10-20 61
SWAN (4082 "Back to the Hop") 15-20 61
SWAN (4084 "Just Because") 10-20 61
SWAN (4100 "Mashed Potatoes") 10-20 62
SWAN (4113 "Funnny") 10-20 62
TOPAZ 3-6 87

Picture Sleeves

SWAN (4064 "Candy Cane Sugar Plum") 50-75 60

EPs: 7-inch

ABC-PAR (11 "At the Hop") 250-350 58
SWAN (4084 "Just Because") 75-125 62
(Not issued with cover. Promotional issue only.)

LPs: 10/12-inch

MCA (1555 "Rockin' with Danny and the Juniors") 5-10 83
Members: Danny Rapp; Frank Maffei; Joe Terry; Dave White.
Also see CANNON, Freddy

DANNY WILSON — *P&R/LP '87*

Singles: 7-inch

VIRGIN 3-4 87

Picture Sleeves

VIRGIN 3-4 87

LPs: 10/12-inch

VIRGIN 5-10 87
Members: Gary Clark; Kit Clark; Ged Grimes.

DANSE SOCIETY — *D&D '84*

Singles: 12-inch

ARISTA 4-6 84

Singles: 7-inch

ARISTA 3-4 84

DANTE — *P&R '60*

(With the Evergreens; with His Friends)

Singles: 7-inch

A&M 5-10 66
IMPERIAL 15-25 61-62
MADISON 8-12 60-61

LPs: 10/12-inch

MADISON (1002 "Dante and the Evergreens") 150-200 61
Members: Don "Dante" Drowty; Bill Young; Frank Rosenthal; Tony Moon.

DANTE & His Friends: see DANTE

DANTE & EVERGREENS: see DANTE

DANZIG — *LP '88*

Singles: 7-inch

DEF AMERICAN 3-4 88-90

LPs: 10/12-inch

DEF AMERICAN 5-8 88-90

D'ARBY, Terence Trent — *P&R/R&B/LP '87*

Singles: 7-inch

COLUMBIA 3-4 87-89

Picture Sleeves

COLUMBIA 3-4 87-89

LPs: 10/12-inch

COLUMBIA 5-10 87-89

DARENSBOURG, Joe, & His Dixie Flyers — *P&R '58*

Singles: 7-inch

LARK 4-8 58-59

LPs: 10/12-inch

DIXIELAND JUBILEE 5-10 75
GHB 5-10 77

DARIAN, Fred — *P&R '61*

(Freddy Darian)

Singles: 7-inch

DEL-FI 5-10 60
GARDENA 5-10 61
JAF 4-8 61-63
MAHALO 4-8 63
OKEH 5-10 59
RCA 5-10 59
U.A. 4-8 63

DARIN, Bobby — *P&R/R&B/C&W '58*

(With the Jaybirds; with Rinky Dinks; Bob Darin)

Singles: 78 rpm

ATCO 30-50 57-58
DECCA 20-30 56-57

Singles: 7-inch

ATCO ("She's Tanfastic") 25-35
(Promotional issue only. No selection number used.)
ATCO (6092 "So Mean") 15-25 57
ATCO (6103 "Pretty Betty") 25-35 57
ATCO (6109 "Just in Case You Change Your Mind") 25-35 58
ATCO (6121 "Early in the Morning") 20-30 58
(This same track was previously issued as by "The Rinky Dinks on Atco and by the Ding Dongs, on Brunswick.")
ATCO (6127 "Queen of the Hop") 10-20 58
ATCO (6128 "Mighty Mighty Man") ... 25-35 58
ATCO (6133 "Plain Jane") 10-20 59
(Monaural.)
ATCO (SD-45-6133 "Plain Jane") 25-50 59
(Stereo.)
ATCO (6140 thru 6334) 8-15 59-65
ATLANTIC 4-8 65-67
CAPITOL (2263 "18 Yellow Roses") 20-30 63
(Promotional issue only.)
CAPITOL 5-8 62-65
DECCA (29883 "Rock Island Line") 20-30 56
DECCA (29922 "Blue Eyed Mermaid") 30-50 56
DECCA (30031 "The Greatest Builder") 20-30 56
DECCA (30225 "Dealer in Dreams") 25-40 57
DECCA (30737 "Dealer in Dreams") 10-20 59
DIMENSION 3-6 70
DIRECTION 3-6 68-70
MOTOWN 3-5 71-72

Picture Sleeves

ATCO (6133 thru 6206) 20-40 59-61
ATCO (6211 "Ave Maria") 75-100 61
ATCO (6214 thru 6221) 10-25 62
CAPITOL (2263 "18 Yellow Roses") 25-50 63
(Promotional issue only.)
CAPITOL (4837 thru 5443) 10-20 62-65

EPs: 7-inch

ATCO (115 "This Is Darin") 50-100 59
(Promotional issue only. Issued with paper sleeve.)
ATCO (1001 "For Teenagers Only") 50-100 60
(Promotional issue only. Issued with paper sleeve.)
ATCO (4502 "Bobby Darin") 35-50 58
ATCO (4504 "That's All") 25-40 59
ATCO (4505 "Queen of the Hop") 30-50 59
ATCO (4508 "This Is Darin") 20-40 59
ATCO (4512 "Darin at the Copa") 20-40 60
ATCO (4513 "For Teenagers Only") 30-50 60
CAPITOL (1791 "Look at Me Now") .. 25-50 62
(Juke box issue only.)
CAPITOL CUSTOM ("Scripto Presents Bobby Darin") 25-50 63
(Promotional issue only. Made with two different color paper sleeves, each offered in conjunction with a different pen: One with light blue sleeve came with Scripto Wordmaster ball point pen; one with yellow sleeve came with ink cartridge fountain pen. Picture of Bobby Darin is the same on both sleeves.)
CAPITOL CUSTOM/ARTISTIC ("Bobby Darin") 25-50 63
(Promotional issue only. Issued with paper sleeve.)
DECCA (2676 "Here Them Bells") ... 50-75 60

LPs: 10/12-inch

ATCO (102 "Bobby Darin") 50-75 58
ATCO (104 "That's All") 25-45 58
(Monaural.)
ATCO (SD-104 "That's All") 35-55 58
(Stereo.)
ATCO (115 "This Is Darin") 15-25 60
(Monaural.)
ATCO (SD-115 "This Is Darin") 20-30 60
(Stereo.)
ATCO (122 "Darin at the Copa") 15-25 60
(Monaural.)
ATCO (SD-122 "Darin at the Copa") 20-30 60
(Stereo.)
ATCO (124 "It's You Or No One") 15-25 63
(Monaural.)
ATCO (SD-124 "It's You Or No One") 20-30 63
(Stereo.)
ATCO (125 "The 25th Day of December") 25-35 60
(Monaural.)
ATCO (SD-125 "The 25th Day of December") 35-50 60
(Stereo.)
ATCO (131 "The Bobby Darin Story") 35-45 61
(Monaural. White cover.)
ATCO (SD-131 "The Bobby Darin Story") 45-55 61
(Stereo. White cover.)
ATCO (131 "The Bobby Darin Story") 10-15 72
(Black cover.)
ATCO (134 "Love Swings") 15-25 61
(Monaural.)
ATCO (SD-134 "Love Swings") 20-30 61
(Stereo.)
ATCO (138 "Twist") 15-25 61
(Monaural.)
ATCO (SD-138 "Twist") 20-30 61
(Stereo.)
ATCO (140 "Bobby Darin Sings Ray Charles") 15-25 62
(Monaural.)
ATCO (SD-140 "Bobby Darin Sings Ray Charles") 20-30 62
ATCO (146 "Things") 15-25 61
(Monaural.)
ATCO (SD-146 "Things") 20-30 61
(Stereo.)
ATCO (167 "Winners") 15-25 64
(Monaural)
ATCO (SD-167 "Winners") 20-30 64
(Stereo.)
ATCO (1001 "Bobby Darin for Teenagers Only") 100-150 60
(With color foldout photo.)
ATLANTIC 15-25 66-67
BAINBRIDGE 5-10 81
CANDLELITE 15-20 76
CAPITOL 20-25 62-66
CLARION 15-20 64
DIRECTION 12-20 68-70
IMPERIAL HOUSE 12-15 76
MOTOWN (100 series) 5-10 82
MOTOWN (738 "Finally") 150-250 72
(Promotional issue only.)
MOTOWN (753 "Bobby Darin") 10-20 72
MOTOWN (813 "Darin: 1936-1973"). 10-20 74
W.B. (3501 "Original Bobby Darin") .. 20-30 76
(Three-LP mail-order offer.)
Session: King Curtis.
Also see DING DONGS
Also see KING CURTIS
Also see RINKY DINKS

DARIN, Bobby, & Johnny Mercer

LPs: 10/12-inch

ATCO (126 "Two of a Kind") 15-25 61
(Monaural.)
ATCO (SD-126 "Two of a Kind") 20-30 61
(Stereo.)
Also see DARIN, Bobby
Also see MERCER, Johnny

DARK ANGEL LP '89

Singles: 7-inch

COMBAT 3-4 89
METAL STORM (8602 "Merciless Death") 15-25 87
(Saw blade-shaped picture disc. 25 made.)
METAL STORM (8602 "Merciless Death") 10-20 87
(Rectangular picture disc. 50 made.)
METAL STORM (8602 "Merciless Death") 5-8 87
(Skull or torture wheel shape picture disc. 500 made of each.)
METAL STORM (8817 "We Have Arrived") 10-20 88
(Cross shaped picture disc. 25 made. Promotional issue only.)
METAL STORM (8817 "We Have Arrived") 5-8 88
(Square picture disc. 500 made.)

LPs: 10/12-inch

COMBAT 5-8 89
METALSTORM (8501 "We Have Arrived") 10-15 87
(Picture disc. 500 made for USA. 500 made for Europe.)

DARLIN, Florraine P&R '62

Singles: 7-inch

EPIC 8-10 62-63
RIC 4-8 64

DARLING CRUEL LP '89

LPs: 10/12-inch

MIKA 5-8 89

DARNELL, Larry R&B '49

(With the Fortunes)

Singles: 78 rpm

DELUXE 15-25 57
OKEH 10-20 51-53
REGAL 10-20 49-51
SAVOY 10-20 55

Singles: 7-inch

ANNA (1109 (With Tears in My Eyes") 200-300 60
ARGO (5364 "Look at Me") 20-30 60
ARGO (5372 "With Tears in My Eyes") 15-25 60
DELUXE 15-25 57
MISTY 4-6
OKEH 10-20 51-53
REGAL 10-20 51
SAVOY (1151 "That's All I Want from You") 15-25 55
WARWICK 8-12 59

EPs: 7-inch

EPIC (7072 "For You My Love") 30-40 61
Session: Mickey Baker.

DARRELL, Johnny C&W '65

Singles: 7-inch

CAPRICORN 3-5 74-75
CARTWHEEL 3-5 71-72
GUSTO 3-4 78
MONUMENT 3-5 73
U.A. 4-6 65-70

Picture Sleeves

U.A. 3-6 67

LPs: 10/12-inch

CAPRICORN 6-10 75
GUSTO 5-10 78
SUNSET 6-10 68-70
U.A. 8-12 66-70

DARRELL, Johnny / George Jones / Willie Nelson

LPs: 10/12-inch

SUNSET 8-12 69
Also see DARRELL, Johnny
Also see JONES, George
Also see NELSON, Willie

DARREN, James P&R '59

(Jimmy Darren)

Singles: 7-inch

ABC 3-4 74
BUDDAH 3-5 70
COLPIX (102 "There's No Such Thing") 5-10 58
COLPIX (113 "Gidget") 5-10 59
COLPIX (119 "Angel Face") 5-10 59
(Monaural.)
COLPIX (SCP-119 "Angel Face") 10-20 59
(Stereo.)
COLPIX (128 thru 708) 5-10 59-63
COLPIX (758 "Punch and Judy") 10-20 64
COLPIX (765 "Married Man") 5-10 64
ERIC 3-4
KIRSHNER 3-5 71-72
MCA 3-4
MGM 3-5 73
PRIVATE STOCK 3-5 75-77
RCA 3-5 78
W.B. 4-8 65-68

Picture Sleeves

COLPIX 8-15 58-61

EPs: 7-inch

RMR JUNIORS ("James Darren") 10-15
(Promotional issue, with fashion spots.)

LPs: 10/12-inch

COLPIX (406 "Album No. 1") 20-30 60
COLPIX (418 "Gidget Goes Hawaiian") 20-30 61
COLPIX (424 "For All Sizes") 20-30 62
COLPIX (428 "Love Among the Young") 20-30 62
(Monaural.)
COLPIX (SCP-428 "Love Among the Young") 30-40 62
(Stereo.)
KIRSHNER 10-20 71-72
W.B. 15-20 67

DARREN, James / Shelley Fabares / Paul Petersen LP '63

LPs: 10/12-inch

COLPIX (444 "Teenage Triangle") 25-35 63
COLPIX (468 "More Teenage Triangle") 25-35 63
Also see DARREN, James
Also see FABARES, Shelley
Also see PETERSEN, Paul

DARTELLS P&R/R&B/LP '63

Singles: 7-inch

ARLEN (509 "Hot Pastrami") 8-12 63
(Black vinyl.)
ARLEN (509 "Hot Pastrami") 20-30 63
(Colored vinyl.)
ARLEN (513 "Dance Everybody, Dance") 10-15 63
DOT 4-8 63-64
HBR 4-8 66

LPs: 10/12-inch

DOT (3522 "Hot Pastrami") 25-30 63
(Monaural.)
DOT (25522 "Hot Pastrami") 25-30 63
(Stereo.)
Member: Doug Phillips.

DASH, Sarah P&R/R&B/LP '79

Singles: 12-inch

MEGATONE 4-6 83

Singles: 7-inch

KIRSHNER 3-4 79-81

LPs: 10/12-inch

KIRSHNER 5-10 78-81
Also see LABELLE, Patti

DATE WITH SOUL

Singles: 7-inch

YORK (408 "Yes Sir That's My Baby") 15-25 67
(Previously issued as by Hale and the Hushabyes. See that listing for members.)
Also see HALE & HUSHABYES

DAVE & SUGAR C&W '75

(Dave Rowland & Sugar)

Singles: 7-inch

ELEKTRA 3-4 81
RCA 3-5 75-82

LPs: 10/12-inch

ELEKTRA 5-10 81
RCA 5-10 76-82
Members: Dave Rowland; Vicki Hackeman-Baker; Jackie Frantz; Sue Powell; Melissa Dean; Jamie Kaye.
Also see PRIDE, Charley

DAVID, F.R. P&R '83

Singles: 7-inch

CARRERE AMERICA 3-4 83

LPs: 10/12-inch

CARRERE AMERICA 5-10 83

DAVID & DAVID P&R/LP '86

Singles: 7-inch

A&M 3-4 86-87

Picture Sleeves

A&M 3-4 86-87

LPs: 10/12-inch

A&M 5-10 86
Members: David Baerwald; David Rickets.

DAVID & JONATHAN P&R '66

Singles: 7-inch

AMY 4-8 68
CAPITOL 4-8 66-67
20TH FOX 4-6 66

Picture Sleeves

CAPITOL 5-10 66

LPs: 10/12-inch

CAPITOL (2473 "Michelle") 20-30 66
Members: Roger Greenaway; Roger Cook.

DAVID & LEE

Singles: 7-inch

G.S.P. (1 "Sad September") 20-30 62
Members: David Gates; Leon Russell.
Also see GATES, David
Also see RUSSELL, Leon

DAVIDSON, John LP '66

Singles: 7-inch

COLUMBIA 3-6 66-71
MERCURY 3-5 73
20TH FOX 3-5 73-77

Picture Sleeves

COLUMBIA 4-6 66-69

LPs: 10/12-inch

COLPIX 10-15 65
COLUMBIA 5-10 66-80
HARMONY 4-6 72
MERCURY 5-10 73
20TH FOX 5-10 74-76

DAVIE, Hutch P&R '58

(With His Honky-Tonkers)

Singles: 7-inch

ATCO 10-15 58-59
CANADIAN AMERICAN 5-10 61
CLARIDGE 4-8 66
CONGRESS 5-10 62
DYNO VOICE 4-6 68
NEW VOICE 4-8 67

LPs: 10/12-inch

ATCO (105 "Much Hutch") 30-40 59
CONGRESS (3004 "Piano Memories") 25-35 62
Also see RAY, James

DAVIES, Dave LP '80

Singles: 7-inch

RCA 3-5 80
REPRISE 15-20 67-68
W.B. 3-4 83

Picture Sleeves

RCA (12089 "Wild Man") 10-15 80

LPs: 10/12-inch

RCA 8-12 80-81
W.B. 5-10 83
Also see KINKS

DAVIS, Betty R&B '73

Singles: 7-inch

ISLAND 3-5 75-76
JUST SUNSHINE 3-5 73-74

LPs: 10/12-inch

ISLAND 5-10 75

JUST SUNSHINE.................................6-10 73-74

DAVIS, Billy, Jr. — R&B '75

(Billy Davis)

Singles: 7-inch

ABC..................................3-5 75
COBBLESTONE..................................4-6 69
EPSOM..................................4-8 61
HI..................................4-8 68

LPs: 10/12-inch

SAVOY..................................5-10 82
Also see FIFTH DIMENSION

DAVIS, Carl, & Chi-Sound Orchestra — R&B '77

Singles: 7-inch

CHI-SOUND..................................3-5 77

DAVIS, Danny — LP '69

(With the Nashville Brass; with Arlene Baird; with Titans; with Nashville Strings; Danny Davis Orchestra;)

Singles: 78 rpm

BLUE JAY..................................3-5 54
HICKORY..................................3-5 54
MGM..................................3-6 51-53

Singles: 7-inch

BLUE JAY..................................4-8 54
CABOT..................................3-6 59
HICKORY..................................4-8 54
LIBERTY (55213 "Glory Bugle")........10-15 59
MGM (11000 series)..................................5-10 51-53
MGM (13000 series)..................................3-5 62-65
RCA..................................3-4 69-84
THUNDER (102 "Glory Bugle")........15-25 59
VERVE..................................3-5 61

LPs: 10/12-inch

MGM..................................8-18 61-65
RCA SPECIAL PROD. (0176 "America, 200 Years Young")..................................10-15 76
(Special Products issue for the Amana Corp.)
RCA..................................5-10 69-84
Also see ATKINS, Chet, Floyd Cramer & Danny Davis
Also see LOCKLIN, Hank, with Danny Davis & Nashville Brass

DAVIS, Danny, & Byron Lee

Singles: 7-inch

MGM..................................4-6 64

DAVIS, Danny, Nashville Brass & Dona Mason — C&W '87

Singles: 7-inch

JAROCO..................................3-4 87

DAVIS, Danny, Willie Nelson, & Nashville Brass — LP '80

Singles: 7-inch

RCA..................................3-4 80

LPs: 10/12-inch

RCA..................................5-10 80
Also see DAVIS, Danny
Also see LOCKLIN, Hank
Also see NEWMAN, Jimmy C., Danny Davis & Nashville Brass

DAVIS, Geater — R&B '70

Singles: 7-inch

HOUSE of ORANGE..................................6-12 70
SEVENTY-SEVEN..................................3-5 73

DAVIS, Jimmy & Junction — P&R/LP '87

Singles: 7-inch

QMI MUSIC..................................3-4 87

Picture Sleeves

QMI MUSIC..................................3-4 87

LPs: 10/12-inch

MCA..................................5-10 87

DAVIS, John, & Monster Orchestra — R&B '76

Singles: 12-inch

COLUMBIA..................................4-8 79

Singles: 7-inch

COLUMBIA..................................3-5 78-79
SAM..................................3-5 76-78

LPs: 10/12-inch

COLUMBIA..................................5-10 79

DAVIS, Krystal — D&D '85

Singles: 12-inch

URBAN ROCK..................................4-6 85

DAVIS, Mac — C&W/P&R '70

Singles: 7-inch

CAPITOL..................................4-8 65
COLUMBIA..................................3-5 70-78
CASABLANCA..................................3-4 80-84
JAMIE (1227 "I'm a Poor Loser")......10-20 62
MCA..................................3-4 85-86
VEE JAY (492 "Lookin' at Linda").......8-12 63
VEE JAY (565 "Honey Love")............8-12 63

Picture Sleeves

COLUMBIA..................................3-5 70-75

LPs: 10/12-inch

ACCORD..................................5-10 82
BUCKBOARD..................................5-10
CASABLANCA..................................5-10 81-85
COLUMBIA..................................8-10 70-83
MCA..................................5-10 86
SPRINGBOARD..................................6-10
TRIP..................................8-10 73
Also see CLASSICS IV / Mac Davis

DAVIS, Martha — R&B '48

Singles: 78 rpm

CORAL..................................5-10 51-52
DECCA..................................5-10 48
JEWEL..................................5-15 48
URBAN..................................5-15 46

Singles: 7-inch

CORAL..................................10-20 51-52

LPs: 10/12-inch

ABC-PAR (213 "Tribute to Fats Waller")..................................40-50 57
Also see JORDAN, Louis

DAVIS, Martha — P&R/LP '87

Singles: 7-inch

CAPITOL..................................3-4 87

Picture Sleeves

CAPITOL..................................3-4 87

LPs: 10/12-inch

CAPITOL..................................5-10 87
Also see MOTELS

DAVIS, Mary — R&B '87

Singles: 7-inch

FAT BACK..................................5-8
TABU..................................3-4 87

DAVIS, Miles — LP '61

(Miles Davis Sextet)

Singles: 78 rpm

BLUE NOTE..................................10-20 54-56
PRESTIGE..................................10-20 52-57

Singles: 7-inch

BLUE NOTE (1600 series)..................5-10 54-56
COLUMBIA (02000 thru 03000 series)..................................3-4 81-83
COLUMBIA (10000 series)..................3-6 75
COLUMBIA (41000 thru 46000 series)..................................3-8 61-74
PRESTIGE (100 thru 400 series)........5-10 57-66
PRESTIGE (700 thru 900 series)......15-25 52-55

EPs: 7-inch

BLUE NOTE..................................15-25 52
CAPITOL (459 "Jeru")..................50-100 53
COLUMBIA..................................6-10 59
PRESTIGE..................................12-20 52-53

LPs: 10/12-inch

BLUE NOTE (100 series)..................8-12 73
BLUE NOTE (1500 series)..................25-50 56-58
(Label gives New York street address for Blue Note Records.)
BLUE NOTE (1500 series)..................15-25 58
(Label reads "Blue Note Records Inc. - New York, U.S.A.")
BLUE NOTE (1500 series)..................10-20 66
(Label shows Blue Note Records as a division of either Liberty or United Artists.)
BLUE NOTE (5013 "Miles Davis")..................................100-150 52
(10-inch LP.)
BLUE NOTE (5022 "Tempus Fugit")..................................100-150 53
(10-inch LP.)
BLUE NOTE (5044 "Miles Davis")..................................100-150 54
(10-inch LP.)
CAPITOL (H-459 "Jeru")..................100-150 53
(10-inch LP.)
CAPITOL (T-459 "Jeru")..................35-50 53
CAPITOL (762 "Birth of Cool")..........50-75 56
CAPITOL (1900 series)..................10-20 63
CAPITOL (11000 series)..................8-12 72
CAPITOL (16000 series)..................5-10 81
COLUMBIA (20 "Friday and Saturday Nights in Person")..................................25-30 61
(Monaural.)
COLUMBIA (26 "Bitches Brew")..........8-12 70
COLUMBIA (820 "Friday and Saturday Nights in Person")..................................30-40 61
(Stereo.)
COLUMBIA (900 thru 1600 series)....20-35 57-61
(With six black Columbia "eye" logos on red label.)
COLUMBIA (1800 thru 2300 series)..................................15-25 61-65
COLUMBIA (8000 thru 8400 series)..................................20-35 58-62
(With six black Columbia "eye" logos on red label.)
COLUMBIA (8600 thru 9800 series)..................................10-20 61-69
COLUMBIA (10000 series)..................6-10 73
COLUMBIA (30000 series, except 36976)..................................6-12 70-85
COLUMBIA (36976 "The Miles Davis Collection")..................................30-40 80
(Boxed, six-disc set.)
COLUMBIA (40000 series)..................8-12 81-85
DEBUT (043 "Blue Moods")..................5-8 83
DEBUT (120 "Blue Moods")..........50-100 55
FANTASY..................................15-20 62
FONTANA..................................10-15 65
MFSL (177 "Someday My Prince Will Come")..................................20-30 85
MOODSVILLE..................................15-20 63
MOSAIC (158 "Complete Plugged Nickel Sessions")..................................125-150 90s
(10 audiophile LP boxed set. 5000 made.)
MOSAIC (164 "Complete Columbia Studio Recordings")..................................135-160 90s
(11 audiophile LP boxed set. 5000 made. With Gil Evans.)
NEW JAZZ..................................10-15 64
PRESTIGE (004 thru 093)..................5-8 80-85
PRESTIGE (100 series)..................50-100 52-54
(10-inch LPs.)
PRESTIGE (7007 thru 7166)..............40-60 55-59
(Yellow label.)
PRESTIGE (7168 thru 7281)..............20-30 60-64
(Yellow label.)
PRESTIGE (7000 thru 7600 series)......6-12 64-69
(Blue label.)
PRESTIGE (7700 thru 7800 series)....6-12 70-71
PRESTIGE (24000 series)..................8-12 72-78
SAVOY..................................12-20 61
TRIP..................................5-10 73
U.A...................................8-10 71
W.B...................................5-10 86-90
Also see COLTRANE, John, & Miles Davis
Also see FORREST, Jimmy

DAVIS, Miles, & Thelonious Monk

LPs: 10/12-inch

COLUMBIA..................................10-20 64
Also see DAVIS, Miles
Also see JACQUET, Illinois, & Miles Davis
Also see MONK, Thelonious

DAVIS, Miz — R&B '76

Singles: 7-inch

NEW..................................3-5 76

DAVIS, Paul — P&R '70

(With Susan Collins)

Singles: 7-inch

ARISTA..................................3-4 81-82

BANG (Except 500 series) 3-5 73-80
BANG (500 series) 4-6 68-72
CAPITOL/CURB 3-4 86
FLASHBACK 3-4 82
SOLID GOLD 3-5 73

LPs: 10/12-inch

ARISTA 5-10 81
BANG 10-12 72-82
Also see OSMOND, Marie, & Paul Davis
Also see TUCKER, Tanya, Paul Davis & Paul Overstreet

DAVIS, Rainy R&B '86

Singles: 12-inch

SUPERTRONICS 4-6 86

Singles: 7-inch

COLUMBIA 3-4 87-88
SUPERTRONICS 3-4 86

DAVIS, Ruth R&B '78

Singles: 7-inch

CLARIDGE 3-4 78
Also see KIRKLAND, Bo, & Ruth Davis

DAVIS, Sammy, Jr. P&R '54
(Sammy Davis)

Singles: 7-inch

A.L.B.B. (38032 "The House I Live In") 3-5
(Promotional issue only.)
APPLAUSE 3-4 82
DECCA (25500 series) 3-6 62
DECCA (29000 thru 31000 series) 5-10 54-60
DECCA (32000 series) 3-5 69
ECOLOGY 3-4 71
MGM 3-5 71-79
VERVE 4-6 60
REPRISE 3-6 61-71
20TH FOX 3-5 75-76
W.B. 3-4 77

Picture Sleeves

A.L.B.B. (38032 "The House I Live In") 5-10
(Promotional issue only.)

EPs: 7-inch

CAPITOL (555 "Sammy Davis Jr.") 10-20 54
DECCA 10-20 54-55

LPs: 10/12-inch

DECCA (100 series) 10-20 66
DECCA (4000 series) 10-20 61-65
DECCA (8100 thru 8700 series) 20-30 54-58
DECCA (8900 series) 10-20 59
DECCA (9032 "Mr. Wonderful") 60-70 56
(Soundtrack.)
HARMONY 5-10 69-71
MCA 5-10 77
MGM 5-10 72-73
MOTOWN 6-10 70
RCA (1086 "Three Penny Opera") 15-25 64
REPRISE 10-20 61-69
20TH FOX (Except 5014) 5-10 76
20TH FOX (FXG-5014 "Of Love and Desire") 25-30 64
(Soundtrack. Monaural.)
20TH FOX (SXG-5014 "Of Love and Desire") 35-40 64
(Soundtrack. Stereo.)
W.B. 5-10 77
U.A. (5187 "Salt and Pepper") 15-20 68
(Soundtrack.)
VOCALION 5-10 68
Also see CURB, Mike
Also see SINATRA, Frank, Sammy Davis Jr. & Dean Martin

DAVIS, Sammy, Jr., & Laurindo Almeida

LPs: 10/12-inch

REPRISE 10-15 67
Also see ALMEIDA, Laurindo

DAVIS, Sammy, Jr., & Count Basie LP '65

Singles: 7-inch

VERVE 3-5 65

LPs: 10/12-inch

MGM 6-10 73
VERVE 10-15 65
Also see BASIE, Count

DAVIS, Sammy, Jr., & Carmen McRae

Singles: 7-inch

DECCA 5-10 55

EPs: 7-inch

DECCA 5-10 59

LPs: 10/12-inch

DECCA 10-20 59
Also see McRAE, Carmen

DAVIS, Sammy, Jr., & Buddy Rich

LPs: 10/12-inch

REPRISE 10-20 66
Also see RICH, Buddy

DAVIS, Sammy, Jr. / Joya Sherril

LPs: 10/12-inch

DESIGN 5-10 60s
Also see DAVIS, Sammy, Jr.

DAVIS, Sherry
(With Buddy Holly)

Singles: 7-inch

FASHION (1001 "Humble Heart") 50-75 57
Also see HOLLY, Buddy

DAVIS, Skeeter C&W '58

Singles: 7-inch

MERCURY 3-5 76-77
PART TWO 3-5 80
RCA (Except 7000 thru 9600 series) 3-6 69-74
RCA (7000 thru 8300 series) 6-15 58-64
RCA (8400 thru 9600 series) 5-10 64-68

Picture Sleeves

RCA 5-10 63

EPs: 7-inch

RCA 5-10 63

LPs: 10/12-inch

CAMDEN 5-10 65-74
GUSTO 5-10 78
RCA (2179 thru 4818, except 3790) 10-20 60-73
RCA (3790 "Skeeter Davis Sings Buddy Holly") 20-30 67
TUDOR 5-10 84
Also see BARE, Bobby, & Skeeter Davis
Also see DAVIS SISTERS
Also see HAMILTON, George, IV, & Skeeter Davis
Also see JENNINGS, Waylon
Also see POSEY, Sandy / Skeeter Davis
Also see WAGONER, Porter, & Skeeter Davis

DAVIS, Skeeter, & Don Bowman C&W '68

Singles: 7-inch

RCA 4-8 68

LPs: 10/12-inch

RCA 10-15 68

DAVIS, Skeeter, & George Hamilton IV C&W '70

Singles: 7-inch

RCA 3-5 70

LPs: 10/12-inch

RCA 10-12 70
Also see HAMILTON, George, IV

DAVIS, Skeeter, & NRBQ

Singles: 7-inch

ROUNDER 3-5 85
Also see DAVIS, Skeeter
Also see NRBQ

DAVIS, Spencer P&R '66
(Spencer Davis Group; with Peter Jameson)

Singles: 7-inch

ALLEGIANCE 3-4 84
ATCO 5-10 66
FONTANA 8-12 64
U.A. 4-8 66-72
VERTIGO 3-4 73-74

Picture Sleeves

U.A. 8-12 66-67

LPs: 10/12-inch

ALLEGIANCE 5-10 84
DATE 10-12 70
FONTANA 20-30 66
ISLAND 5-10 83
MEDIARTS 10-12 71
RHINO 5-10 84
U.A. 15-30 67-75
VERTIGO 10-12 73-74
WING 10-15
Members: Spencer Davis; Steve Winwood; Pete York; Brian Dexter; Ray Fenwick; Ken Salmon; Muff Winwood.
Also see WINWOOD, Steve

DAVIS, Tim P&R '72
(With the Chordairs)

Singles: 7-inch

LEAF (6467 "Wine Wine Wine") 10-20 64
METROMEDIA 3-5 72-73

LPs: 10/12-inch

METROMEDIA 8-10 72-73
Members: Jim Marcotte; David Chaffee; Curley Cooke; Jim Peterman; Dick Personett; Denny Geyer.
Also see MILLER, Steve

DAVIS, Tyrone P&R/R&B '68
(Tyrone "Wonder Boy" Davis)

Singles: 7-inch

ABC 4-6 68
COLUMBIA 3-5 76-81
DAKAR 3-6 68-77
EPIC 3-4 83
FUTURE 3-4 87-88
HIGHRISE 3-5 82-83
HIT SOUND 10-20
ICHIBAN 3-4 91-94
OCEAN FRONT 3-4 83-84
SACK 10-20

LPs: 10/12-inch

COLUMBIA 8-10 76-81
DAKAR 10-15 69-76
EPIC 5-10 83
HIGHRISE 5-10 82

DAVIS SISTERS C&W '53

Singles: 78 rpm

FORTUNE 10-20 52
RCA 10-15 53-56

Singles: 7-inch

FORTUNE (174 "Kaw-Liga") 15-25 52
FORTUNE (3000 series) 4-8
RCA (5000 & 6000 series) 10-15 53-56
Members: Skeeter Davis; Betty J. "Bee Jay" Davis.
Also see DAVIS, Skeeter

DAVIS SISTERS / Chuck Hatfield & Treble-Aires

Singles: 7-inch

FORTUNE 10-15 52

Singles: 7-inch

FORTUNE (175 "Heartbreak Ahead") 15-25 52

DAVIS SISTERS / Roy Hall & His Cahutta Mountain Boys

Singles: 78 rpm

FORTUNE 10-20 53

Singles: 7-inch

FORTUNE (170 "Jealous Love") 20-40 53
Also see DAVIS SISTERS
Also see HALL, Roy

DAVY DMX R&B/D&D '84
(Davy D; David Reeves)

Singles: 12-inch

CBS ASSOCIATED 4-6 84

Singles: 7-inch

CBS ASSOCIATED 3-4 84
DEF JAM 3-4 87

DAWN P&R/LP '70
(With Tony Orlando)

Singles: 7-inch

BELL 3-5 70-72
FLASHBACK 3-5 70s

LPs: 10/12-inch

BELL 10-12 70-71

Members: Tony Orlando; Joyce Wilson; Telma Hopkins.
Also see ORLANDO, Tony, & Dawn

DAWN

Singles: 7-inch

ARISTA......3-5 75
ELEKTRA......3-5 76-77
Members: Joyce Wilson; Telma Hopkins.
Also see DAWN (With Tony Orlando)

DAWSON, Cliff R&B '82

Singles: 7-inch

BOARDWALK......3-4 82

DAWSON, Cliff, & Renee Diggs R&B '83

Singles: 7-inch

BOARDWALK......3-4 83
Also see DAWSON, Cliff
Also see STARPOINT

DAY, Arlan P&R '81

Singles: 7-inch

PASHA......3-4 81

DAY, Bobby P&R '57

(With the Satellites; with Blossoms; Bobby Byrd)

Singles: 78 rpm

CLASS......20-40 57

Singles: 7-inch

CLASS......10-20 57-59
RCA (8133 "Another Country, Another World")......15-25 63
RCA (8196 "Buzz Buzz Buzz")......8-12 63
RCA (8230 "Down on My Knees")......8-12 63
RCA (8316 "When I See My Baby Smile")......8-12 64
RENDEZVOUS......5-10 60-62
SURE SHOT......4-8 67

LPs: 10/12-inch

CLASS (5002 "Rockin' with Robin")......75-125 59
RHINO......5-10 84

DAY, Dennis P&R '47

(With Jack Benny)

Singles: 78 rpm

CAPITOL......3-5 56
RCA......3-5 47-54

Singles: 7-inch

CAPITOL......4-8 56
RCA......4-8 50-54
REPRISE......3-6 62
SHAMROCK......3-6 59

EPs: 7-inch

CAPITOL......5-10 56
RCA......5-10 50-59

LPs: 10/12-inch

BLUEBIRD......5-10 60
CAMDEN......5-10 64-66
CAPITOL......10-20 56
DESIGN......5-10
MASTERSEAL......10-20
RCA (3036 "My Wild Irish Rose")......15-25 52
REPRISE......5-10 63
ROULETTE......10-15 63

DAY, Doris P&R '47

(With the Mellomen; with Norman Luboff Choir; with Buddy Clark)

Singles: 78 rpm

COLUMBIA......5-15 47-57

Singles: 7-inch

ARWIN (250 "Everlasting Arms")......5-15 50s
COLUMBIA (38000 & 39000 series)......5-15 50-53
COLUMBIA (40000 thru 44000 series)......4-8 54-67

Picture Sleeves

COLUMBIA......10-20 57-61

EPs: 7-inch

COLUMBIA......10-30 50-59

LPs: 10/12-inch

COLUMBIA (1 "Listen to Day")......20-30 60
COLUMBIA (600 thru 1300 series)......15-30 55-59
COLUMBIA (1400 thru 2100 series)......10-20 60-64
COLUMBIA (2500 series)......20-35 56
(10-inch LPs.)
COLUMBIA (6000 series)......25-50 49-55
(10-inch LPs.)
COLUMBIA (8000 thru 8900 series)......15-30 58-64
COLUMBIA (2200 thru 2300 series)......10-25 64-65
(Monaural.)
COLUMBIA (9000 thru 9100 series)......15-35 64-65
(Stereo.)
HARMONY......8-12 66-72
Also see BROWN, Les, & His Orchestra
Also see STREISAND, Barbra / Doris Day / Jim Nabors / Andre Kostelanetz

DAY, Doris, & Don Cherry

EPs: 7-inch

COLUMBIA......10-20 56
Also see CHERRY, Don

DAY, Doris, & Frankie Laine P&R '52

Singles: 78 rpm

COLUMBIA......5-10 52

Singles: 7-inch

COLUMBIA......5-15 52
Also see LAINE, Frankie

DAY, Doris, & Andre Previn

LPs: 10/12-inch

COLUMBIA......10-20 62
Also see PREVIN, Andre

DAY, Doris, & Johnnie Ray P&R '53

Singles: 78 rpm

COLUMBIA......5-10 52-53

Singles: 7-inch

COLUMBIA......5-15 52-53
Also see RAY, Johnnie

DAY, Doris, & Frank Sinatra P&R '49

Singles: 78 rpm

COLUMBIA......5-10 49

Singles: 7-inch

COLUMBIA......5-15 49

DAY, Doris / Frank Sinatra LP '55

EPs: 7-inch

COLUMBIA (571 "Young at Heart")......10-15 55
COLUMBIA (34178 "Young at Heart")......30-50 54
(Promotional issue only.)

LPs: 10/12-inch

COLUMBIA (6339 "Young at Heart")......40-60 55
(Soundtrack. 10-inch LP.)
Also see DAY, Doris, & Frank Sinatra
Also see SINATRA, Frank

DAY, Doris, & Danny Thomas

EPs: 7-inch

COLUMBIA (289 "I'll See You in My Dreams")......10-15
Also see DAY, Doris

DAY, Margie R&B '50

Singles: 78 rpm

CAT (118 "Ho-Ho")......10-20 55
DECCA......5-10 54
DOT......5-10 54

Singles: 7-inch

CAT (118 "Ho-Ho")......20-30 55
COED......4-8 61
DECCA......15-25 54
DOT......15-20 54
LEGRAND......10-20 62
MARTHAY......10-20 60s
Also see GRIFFIN BROTHERS

DAY, Morris P&R/R&B/D&D/LP '85

Singles: 12-inch

W.B.......4-6 85-86

Singles: 7-inch

W.B.......3-4 85-88

Picture Sleeves

W.B.......3-4 85-88

LPs: 10/12-inch

W.B.......5-10 85-88
Also see TIME

DAYBREAK P&R '70

Singles: 7-inch

PRELUDE......3-4 80
UNI......3-4 70

DAYE, Cory P&R/LP '79

Singles: 7-inch

N.Y.I.......3-5 79

Picture Sleeves

N.Y.I.......3-5 79

LPs: 10/12-inch

N.Y.I.......5-10 79
Also see DR. BUZZARD'S ORIGINAL SAVANNAH BAND

DAYE, Johnny R&B '65

Singles: 7-inch

JOMADA......4-8 65-66
PARKWAY......4-8 66
STAX......4-6 68

DAYNE, Taylor P&R '87

Singles: 7-inch

ARISTA......3-4 87-90

Picture Sleeves

ARISTA......3-4 87-89

LPs: 10/12-inch

ARISTA......5-8 87-90

DAYTON R&B '81

Singles: 7-inch

CAPITOL......3-4 82-85
LIBERTY......3-4 81-82
U.A. 3-4 80

LPs: 10/12-inch

CAPITOL......5-10 83
LIBERTY......5-10 81-82
U.A. 5-10 80

DAZZ BAND R&B '80

Singles: 12-inch

GEFFEN......4-6 86
MOTOWN......4-8 80-85

Singles: 7-inch

GEFFEN......3-4 86
MOTOWN......3-4 80-85
RCA......3-4 88

LPs: 10/12-inch

GEFFEN......5-10 86
MOTOWN......5-10 80-85
Members: Rob Harris; Michael Calhoun; Kenny Pettus; Ike Wiley; Mike Wiley; Ed Meyers; Skip Martin; Pierre De Mudd; Eric Fearman; Kevin Kendrick; Marlon McClain.
Also see KINSMAN DAZZ

DE LA SOUL LP '89

Singles: 12-inch

TOMMY B......4-6 89

Singles: 7-inch

TOMMY B......3-4 89

D'COCOA, Creme: see CREME D'COCOA

DEACONS R&B '68

Singles: 7-inch

CAMELOT......8-10
SHAMA......10-20 68

DEAD BOYS LP '77

Singles: 7-inch

SIRE......3-5 77-78
SIRE......5-10 77-78
(Promotional issues only.)

LPs: 10/12-inch

BOMP......8-10 80
SIRE......15-25 77-78
Members: Stiv Bators; Jimmy Zero, John Blitz; Cheetah Chrome; Jeff Jizz.
Also see BATORS, Stiv

DEAD MILKMEN LP '87

Singles: 7-inch

ENIGMA......3-4 87-90

LPs: 10/12-inch
ENIGMA 5-10 87-90

DEAD OR ALIVE D&D '84
Singles: 12-inch
EPIC 4-6 84-86
Singles: 7-inch
EPIC 3-4 84-89
Picture Sleeves
EPIC 3-4 84-89
LPs: 10/12-inch
EPIC 5-10 84-89
Members: Pete Burns; Wayne Hussey.
Also see MISSION
Also see SISTERS of MERCY

DEADLY NIGHTSHADE P&R '76
Singles: 7-inch
PHANTOM 3-5 76
LPs: 10/12-inch
PHANTOM 8-10 76

DEAL, Bill P&R '69
(With the Rhondels)
Singles: 7-inch
BEACH (1601 "May I") 20-30 60s
BUDDAH 3-5 71-72
CHESLICK 4-6
COLLECTABLES 3-4 80s
ERIC 3-4 70s
HERITAGE 4-8 68-70
POLYDOR 3-5 70-73
RED LION 3-4 79
Picture Sleeves
HERITAGE 8-10 69
LPs: 10/12-inch
HERITAGE 15-20 69
RHINO 5-10 86

DEAN, Alan P&R '52
Singles: 78 rpm
LONDON 3-5 51
MGM 3-5 51-56
RAMA 4-6 56-57
Singles: 7-inch
LONDON 5-10 51
MGM 4-8 51-56
RAMA 5-10 56-57

DEAN, Debbie P&R '61
(With the Petites; with Paulette Singers)
Singles: 7-inch
MOTOWN (1007 "Don't Let Him Shop Around") 25-35 61
MOTOWN (1014 "Itsy Bity Pity Love") 15-25 62
MOTOWN (1025 "Everybody's Talking About My Baby") 20-30 62
TREVA (223 "Take My Hand") 10-15 66
V.I.P. (25044 "Why Am I Lovin' You") 100-200 68
Picture Sleeves
MOTOWN (1025 "Everybody's Talking About My Baby") 50-100 62

DEAN, Hazell D&D '83
(Hazel Dean)
Singles: 12-inch
QUALITY 4-6 84
TSR 4-6 83
Singles: 7-inch
LONDON 3-5 76

DEAN, Jimmy P&R '57
(Jimmie Dean)
Singles: 78 rpm
COLUMBIA 5-10 57
4 STAR 5-10 54
MERCURY 4-8 56
Singles: 7-inch
CASINO 3-5 76
CHURCHILL 3-4 83
COLUMBIA (40000 thru 43000 series, except 42175) 5-10 57-66
COLUMBIA (42175 "Big John") 10-12 61
(Dean says: "At the bottom of this mine lies one hell of a man.")
COLUMBIA (42175 "Big Bad John") 4-8 61
(Dean says: "At the bottom of this mine lies a big, big man." Note slight title change.)
COLUMBIA (45000 & 46000 series) 3-5 74
4 STAR (1600 series) 10-15 54
4 STAR (1700 series) 5-8 59
KING 4-6 64
MERCURY 5-10 56
RCA 3-6 66-71
Picture Sleeves
COLUMBIA (Except 41025) 5-10 59-66
COLUMBIA (41025 "Little Sandy Sleighfoot") 10-20 57
EPs: 7-inch
COLUMBIA 8-12 57
LPs: 10/12-inch
ACCORD 5-10 82
BRYLEN 5-10
CASINO 5-10 76
COLUMBIA (1025 thru 2500 series) 10-25 57-66
(Monaural.)
COLUMBIA (8000 & 9000 series) 10-25 61-68
(Stereo. With "CS" prefix.)
COLUMBIA (9200 series) 5-10
(With "PC" prefix.)
COLUMBIA (10000 series) 6-10 73
COLUMBIA SPECIAL PRODUCTS 5-10
CROWN 10-15 60s
CUSTOM 5-10
GRT 5-10 77
GUEST STAR 8-10 60s
HARMONY 8-12 60-69
KING (686 "Favorites of Jimmy Dean") 25-35 60
LA BREA (8014 "Bummin' Around with Jimmy Dean") 20-30
MERCURY (20319 "Jimmy Dean Sings His Television Favorites") 15-25 57
PICKWICK 5-10 70s
PICKWICK/HILLTOP 10-12 65
PREMIER 5-10
RCA 8-12 67-71
SPIN-O-RAMA 8-10 60s
WING 8-12 64

DEAN, Jimmy / Luke Gordon
LPs: 10/12-inch
PREMIER 10-15 60s
SPIN-O-RAMA 10-15 60s

DEAN, Jimmy / Johnny Horton
LPs: 10/12-inch
STARDAY 15-20 65
Also see HORTON, Johnny

DEAN, Jimmy / David Houston / Warner Mack / Autry Inman
LPs: 10/12-inch
DIPLOMAT 10-15 60s
Also see HOUSTON, David
Also see INMAN, Autry
Also see MACK, Warner

DEAN, Jimmy / Marvin Rainwater
LPs: 10/12-inch
MOUNT VERNON 5-10
PREMIER (9054 "Nashville Showtime") 5-10

DEAN, Jimmy / Marvin Rainwater / Rusty Evans
LPs: 10/12-inch
ALMOR 5-10 60s
Also see RAINWATER, Marvin

DEAN, Jimmy / Stoneman Family
LPs: 10/12-inch
WYNCOTE 5-10 62

DEAN, Jimmy, & Dottie West
Singles: 7-inch
RCA 3-5 71
LPs: 10/12-inch
RCA 10-20 70
Also see DEAN, Jimmy
Also see WEST, Dottie

DEAN, Paul LP '89
LPs: 10/12-inch
COLUMBIA 5-8 89

DEAN & JEAN P&R '63
Singles: 78 rpm
EMBER (1048 "We're Gonna Get Married") 25-50 58
Singles: 7-inch
EMBER 5-10 58-62
RUST 5-8 63-65
Members: Welton Young; Brenda Lee Jones.
Also see JONES, Brenda

DEAN & MARC P&R '59
Singles: 7-inch
BULLSEYE (1025 "Tell Him No") 10-20 59
BULLSEYE (1026 "Beginning of Love") 10-20 59
CHECK MATE (1008 "Boogie-Woogie Twist") 15-25 61
HICKORY 4-8 63-65
MAY 5-10 63
Members: Dean Mathis; Marc Mathis.
Also see NEWBEATS

DEANE, Debbie: see DEAN, Debbie

DEANE, Shelbra R&B '76
Singles: 7-inch
CASINO 3-5 76-77

DEAUVILLE, Ronnie LP '57
Singles: 7-inch
ERA (1056 "Laura") 10-15 58
IMPERIAL (5559 "King of Fools") 8-12 59
Picture Sleeves
ERA (1056 "Laura") 20-40 58
LPs: 10/12-inch
ERA (20002 "Smoke Dreams") 20-40 57

DE BARGE R&B/LP '82
(DeBarges)
Singles: 12-inch
GORDY 4-6 85-86
Singles: 7-inch
GORDY 3-4 85-86
STRIPED HORSE 3-4 87
Picture Sleeves
GORDY 3-4 85-86
STRIPED HORSE 3-4 87
LPs: 10/12-inch
GORDY 5-10 81-86
MOTOWN 5-8 80s
Members: Eldra BeBarge; Marty DeBarge; James DeBarge; Bunny De Barge.
Also see DE BARGE, Bunny
Also see DE BARGE, EL
Also see JONES, Quincy, James Ingram, Al B. Sure, El DeBarge & Barry White
Also see KING DREAM CHORUS & Holiday Crew
Also see SWITCH

DE BARGE, Bunny R&B/LP '87
Singles: 12-inch
GORDY 4-6 87
Singles: 7-inch
GORDY 3-4 87
LPs: 10/12-inch
MOTOWN 5-8 87
Also see DE BARGE

DE BARGE, Chico P&R/R&B/LP '86
Singles: 12-inch
MOTOWN 4-6 86-87
Singles: 7-inch
MOTOWN 3-4 86-88
Picture Sleeves
MOTOWN 3-4 86
LPs: 10/12-inch
MOTOWN 5-10 86-87

DE BARGE, El R&B/D&D '85
(With DeBarge)
Singles: 12-inch
GORDY 4-6 86-87
Singles: 7-inch
GORDY 3-4 81-87

LPs: 10/12-inch
GORDY 5-10 81-87
Also see DE BARGE

DEBBIE DEB R&B/D&D '84

Singles: 12-inch
JAMPACKED 4-6 85
SUNNYVIEW 4-6 84
Singles: 7-inch
JAMPACKED 3-4 84-87
Also see TRINERE / Freestyle / Debbie Deb

DEBLANC R&B '76

Singles: 7-inch
ARISTA 3-5 75-76
Members: Ralph DeBlanc; Linda Carriere.
Also see DYNASTY
Also see STARFIRE

DE BURGH, Chris P&R '83

Singles: 7-inch
A&M 3-5 75-87
Picture Sleeves
A&M 3-4 86-87
LPs: 10/12-inch
A&M 8-10 76-86

DE CARO, Nick P&R/LP '69

Singles: 7-inch
A&M 3-5 67-69
LPs: 10/12-inch
A&M 5-10 69
BLUE THUMB 5-10 77

DE CASTRO SISTERS P&R '54

(With Don Costa's Orchestra; with Joe Reisman's Orchestra & Chorus)
Singles: 78 rpm
ABBOTT 4-8 54-56
RCA 4-8 56
TICO 4-8 52
Singles: 7-inch
ABC-PAR 5-10 58
ABBOTT 10-20 54-56
CAPITOL 5-10 60-61
RCA 8-12 56
TICO 10-15 52
ZODIAC 3-5 77
LPs: 10/12-inch
ABBOTT (5002 "DeCastro Sisters") 40-60 56
CAPITOL 15-25 60-61
20TH FOX 8-15 65
Members: Peggy DeCastro; Babette DeCastro; Cherie DeCastro.
Also see COSTA, Don, Orchestra
Also see DE CASTRO, Peggy

DE CASTRO SISTERS / Hugo Winterhalter & His Orchestra

EPs: 7-inch
RCA (DJ-51 "I Never Meant to Hurt You") 10-20 56
(Promotional issue only. Not issued with cover.)
Also see DE CASTRO SISTERS
Also see WINTERHALTER, Hugo, & His Orchestra

DECO R&B '83

Singles: 12-inch
QWEST 4-6 84-85
Singles: 7-inch
QWEST 3-4 84-85
LPs: 10/12-inch
QWEST 5-10 84
Members: Philip Ingram; Zane Giles.
Also see PAYNE, Scherrie
Also see SWITCH

DEE, Dave, Dozy, Beaky, Mick & Tich LP '67

Singles: 7-inc
ATLANTIC 3-4 83
FONTANA 5-10 66-67
IMPERIAL 4-8 67-68
LPs: 10/12-inch
FONTANA (27567 "Greatest Hits") ... 20-30 67
(Monaural.)
FONTANA (67567 "Greatest Hits") ... 25-30 67
(Stereo.)
IMPERIAL (12402 "Time to Take Off") 20-25 68
Also see DOZY, BEAKY, MICK & TICH

DEE, Jackie

(Jackie DeShannon)
Singles: 78 rpm
GONE (5008 "I'll Be True") 50-100 57
Singles: 7-inch
GONE (5008 "I'll Be True") 30-50 57
LIBERTY (55148 "Buddy") 25-45 58
Also see DE SHANNON, Jackie

DEE, Jay R&B '74

(Earl Nelson)
Singles: 7-inch
W.B. 3-5 74

DEE, Jimmy P&R '58

(With the Offbeats)
Singles: 78 rpm
DOT (15664 "Henrietta") 50-75 57
TNT (148 "Henrietta") 75-125 57
Singles: 7-inch
CUTIE 4-8 63
DOT (15664 "Henrietta") 15-25 57
DOT (15721 "You're Late Miss Kate") 20-30 58
HEAR ME 5-10
INNER-GLO (105 "Guitar Pickin' Man") 75-100 57
SCOPE (103 "I Ain't Givin' Up Nothin' ") 15-25 59
TNT (148 "Henrietta") 25-50 57
TNT (152 "You're Late Miss Kate") ... 50-75 58
TNT (161 "I Feel Like Rockin' ") 40-60 59
TAPER (101 "I Ain't Givin' Up Nothin' ") 30-50 59
V-TONE 15-25 62

DEE, Joey P&R/R&B/LP '61

(With the Starliters; with Starlites; with New Starliters; with the Hawk)
Singles: 7-inch
ABC 3-4 73
BONUS (7009 "Lorraine") 25-50 63
CANEIL 4-6
JANUS 4-8 70s
JUBILEE 5-10 66-67
LITTLE (813 "Lorraine") 1000-2000 60
ROULETTE 10-20 61-65
ROULETTE GOLDEN GOODIES 3-4
SCEPTER (1210 "Face of an Angel") 15-25 60
SUNBURST 3-5 73
TONSIL RECORDS 4-8 70
VASELINE HAIR TONIC (12 "Learn to Dance the Peppermint Twist") 15-25 62
(Special products issue from Chesebrough-Ponds.)
Picture Sleeves
BONUS (7009 "Lorraine") 50-75 63
ROULETTE 15-25 62
LPs: 10/12-inch
ACCORD 5-10 82
JUBILEE (8000 "Hitsville") 15-25 66
ROULETTE 15-25 61-63
SCEPTER (503 "The Peppermint Twisters") 15-25 62
Members: Joey Dee; Tony Scuito; John Yanic; Vinnie Correo; Ralph Fazio; Roger Freeman; David Brigati; Willie Davis; Carlton Latimore; Joe Pesci. Session: Ronettes.
Also see RASCALS
Also see RONETTES

DEE, Joey, & Starliters / Dion

Singles: 7-inch
MONUMENT 5-10 61
Also see DION

DEE, Joey, & Starliters / Randy Andy & Candymen

EPs: 7-inch
DIPLOMAT (66-2 "Come Twist with Me") 15-20 62

DEE, Joey, & Lois Lee

Singles: 7-inch
STEADY (37004 "Storybook Children") 3-6 70s
Also see DEE, Joey

DEE, Johnny P&R '57

(John D. Loudermilk; "Featuring Joe Tanner on Guitar")
Singles: 78 rpm
COLONIAL (430 "Sittin' in the Balcony") 25-50 57
Singles: 7-inch
COLONIAL (430 "Sittin' in the Balcony") 15-20 57
(Has "45 RPM" on left side of label.)
COLONIAL (430 "Sittin' in the Balcony") 10-15 57
(Has "45 RPM" on right side of label.)
COLONIAL (430 "Sittin' in the Balcony") 8-12 57
(No "45 RPM" on label. Reads "Dist. by AM-PAR Record Corp.")
COLONIAL (435 "1000 Concrete Blocks") 15-20 57
DOT 5-10 58
Picture Sleeves
COLONIAL (430 "Sittin in the Balcony") 30-40 57
Also see LOUDERMILK, John D.

DEE, Kiki P&R '71

(Kiki Dee Band)
Singles: 7-inch
LIBERTY 4-6 68
MCA 3-5 73-77
POSSE 3-4 81
RCA 3-4 81
RARE EARTH 3-5 71
ROCKET 3-5 73-79
TAMLA 3-6 70
WORLD PACIFIC 4-8 66
Picture Sleeves
TAMLA 3-6 70
LPs: 10/12-inch
LIBERTY (7600 series) 15-20 69
LIBERTY (10000 series) 5-10 81
MCA/ROCKET 8-12 73-74
RCA 5-10 81
ROCKET 8-10 77-78
TAMLA 15-20 70
Also see JOHN, Elton, & Kiki Dee

DEE, Lenny P&R/LP '55

Singles: 78 rpm
DECCA 3-4 56-61
Singles: 7-inch
DECCA 3-5 56-61
EPs: 7-inch
DECCA 4-8 59
LPs: 10/12-inch
DECCA 5-15 55-70

DEE, Lola P&R '54

(With Stubby & the Buccaneers)
Singles: 78 rpm
BALLY 3-6 57
MERCURY 3-5 54-56
WING 5-10 55-56
Singles: 7-inch
BALLY 5-10 57
MERCURY 5-10 54-56
WING 10-20 55-56

DEE, Lola, & Rusty Draper

Singles: 78 rpm
MERCURY 3-6 56
Singles: 7-inch
MERCURY 5-10 56
Also see DEE, Lola
Also see DRAPER,Rusty

DEE, Neecy
D&D '85

Singles: 12-inch

TNT...4-6 85

DEE, Tommy
P&R '59

(With the Mellotones)

Singles: 7-inch

A&M...3-4 80
CHALLENGE...8-10 60
CREST (1067 "Angel of Love")...8-12 59
K-ARK...3-5 70
PIKE...5-10 61
SIMS...10-15 66

DEE, Tommy, & Teen Tones & Orchestra / Teen Tones
P&R '59

Singles: 7-inch

CREST (1057 "Three Stars")...15-25 59
(Flip, *I'll Never Change,* is also credited to Teen Tones here and to Carol Kay and the Teen-Aires on copies below. The track is exactly the same on both discs.)

DEE, Tommy, & Carol Kay & Teen-Aires / Carol Kay & Teen-Aires
P&R '59

Singles: 7-inch

CREST (1057 "Three Stars")...15-25 59
(Monaural.)
CREST (1057 "Three Stars")...35-50 59
(Stereo.)
Also see DEE, Tommy

DEE JAY & RUNAWAYS
P&R '66

Singles: 7-inch

COULEE (109 "Love Bug Crawl")...25-35 64
DEE JAY...3-6 82
IGL (100 "Jenny Jenny")...100-150 65
IGL (103 "Peter Rabbit")...20-40 66
SMASH...5-10 66
SONIC (132 "Don't You Ever")...25-50 66
STONE (45 "Don't You Ever")...25-50 66

Picture Sleeves

DEE JAY...4-8 82
(With insert)
Members: Denny Storey; John Senn; Gary Lind; Terry Klein; Bob; Tom.

DEEE-LITE
P&R/LP '90

LPs: 10/12-inch

ELEKTRA...5-8 90

DEELE
R&B '83

Singles: 7-inch

SOLAR...3-4 83-88

LPs: 10/12-inch

SOLAR...5-10 84-88
Members: Kenny "Babyface" Edmonds; Antonio "L.A." Reid; Darnell Bristol; Kevin Roberson; Carlos Green.
Also see BABYFACE
Also see MANCHILD

DEEP PURPLE
P&R/LP '68

Singles: 12-inch

MERCURY...4-8 87

Singles: 7-inch

GRP...3-5 73
MERCURY...3-4 84-87
TETRAGRAMMATON...5-10 68-69
W.B. ...3-6 70-73
W.B./PURPLE...3-4 74-75

Picture Sleeves

MERCURY...3-5 85
TETRAGRAMMATON...8-15 68
W.B./PURPLE...3-5 74-75

EPs: 7-inch

W.B./PURPLE...10-20 74
(Juke box issue.)

LPs: 10/12-inch

MERCURY...6-12 84-88
PASSPORT...5-10 88
PORTRAIT...5-10 82
RCA...5-8 90
SCEPTER/CITATION...8-10 72
TETRAGRAMMATON (102 "Shades of Deep Purple")...20-30 68
TETRAGRAMMATON (107 "Book of Taliesyn")...20-30 69
TETRAGRAMMATON (119 "Deep Purple")...20-30 69
W.B. (Except 3000 series)...15-25 70-74
W.B. (3000 series)...5-10 77
W.B./PURPLE...10-15 74-80
Members: Ritchie Blackmore; Jon Lord; Ian Paice; Rod Evans; Nick Simper; Roger Glover; Ian Gillan; David Coverdale.
Also see BLACKMORE'S RAINBOW
Also see BOLIN, Tommy
Also see CAPTAIN BEYOND
Also see COVERDALE, David
Also see GILLAN, Ian
Also see GLOVER, Roger
Also see LORD, Jon
Also see PAICE, ASHTON & LORD
Also see TRAPEZE
Also see WHITESNAKE

DEEP RIVER BOYS
P&R '48

Singles: 78 rpm

BEACON...20-30 52-54
BLUEBIRD (10676 "I Was a Fool to Let You Go")...20-40 40
BLUEBIRD (10847 "Bird in the Hand")...20-40 40
BLUEBIRD (11178 "My Heart at Thy Sweet Voice")...20-40 41
BLUEBIRD (11217 "I Wish I Had Died in My Cradle")...20-40 41
JAY-DEE...15-25 54
LANG-WORTH...10-25
(16-inch transcriptions, made in the '40s.)
PILOTONE...10-25 46
RCA...10-25 40-53
VICTOR...15-25 40
VIK...10-15 56

Singles: 7-inch

BEACON (104 "Sleepy Little Cowboy")...40-60 54
BEACON (9143 "Truthfully")...40-60 52
BEACON (9146 "All I Need Is You")...40-60 52
GALLANT...10-15 59
JAY-DEE (788 "No One Else Will Do")...25-35 54
MICHELLE...4-8 65
RCA (0078 "Free Grace")...30-50 50
(Colored vinyl.)
RCA (5268 "Biggest Fool")...20-30 53
SEECO...10-15 60
VIK (0205 "All My Love Belongs to You")...15-20 56
VIK (0224 "You're Not to Old")...15-20 56
WAND...5-10 61

Picture Sleeves

GALLANT (2001 "I Don't Know Why")...15-25 59

EPs: 7-inch

CAMDEN (341 "Presenting the Deep River Boys")...20-30 56
WALDORF MUSIC HALL (113 "Songs of Jubilee")...50-75 56
(May also be shown as *Spirituals and Jubilees.*)
WALDORF MUSIC HALL (114 "Songs of Jubilee")...50-75 56
(Black vinyl. Has picture of group on cover.
WALDORF MUSIC HALL (114 "Spirituals & Jubilees")...75-100 56
(Colored vinyl. No picture of group on cover.)

LPs: 10/12-inch

CAMDEN (303 "Presenting the Deep River Boys")...40-60 56
CAPITOL (6050 "Presenting Harry Douglas and the Deep River Boys")...20-40
(Canadian.)
QUE (104 "Midnight Magic")...50-75 57
WALDORF MUSIC HALL (108" Songs of Jubilee")...75-125 56
(10-inch LP. Label gives title as *Spirtuals and Jubilees.*)
"X" (1019 "Deep River Boys")...60-80 56
Members: Harry Douglas; Vernon Gardner; George Lawson; Ed Ware; Carter Wilson.
Also see BARLOW, Dean, & Crickets / Deep River Boys

DEEP VELVET
R&B '73

Singles: 7-inch

AWARE...3-5 73

DEES, Rick
P&R/R&B '76

(With His Cast of Idiots; Rick & Cast of Idiots)

Singles: 12-inch

RSO...4-8 78
STAX...4-8 78

Singles: 7-inch

ATLANTIC (89481 "I Wanna Be Elvis")...4-8 85
FRETONE (040 "Disco Duck")...5-10 76
RSO (Except 860)...3-5 76-77
RSO (860 "He Ate Too Many Jelly Donuts")...8-10 77
RSO/POLYDOR...3-5 76-77
STAX...3-5 78

Picture Sleeves

ATLANTIC...3-4 86
STAX...3-5 78

LPs: 10/12-inch

ATLANTIC...5-10 85
RSO...8-10 77

DEES, Sam
R&B '73

Singles: 7-inch

ATLANTIC...3-5 73-75
CHESS...3-5 71
LOLO...4-6 69
POLYDOR...3-4 78
SSS INT'L (732 "I Need You Girl")...15-25 68

LPs: 10/12-inch

ATLANTIC...5-10 75

DEES, Sam, & Bettye Swann

Singles: 7-inch

BIG TREE...3-5 76
Also see DEES, Sam
Also see SWANN, Bettye

DEF LEPPARD
LP '80

Singles: 12-inch

MERCURY...4-8 80-87
(Promotional only.)

Singles: 7-inch

MERCURY...3-4 80-89

EPs: 7-inch

BLUDGEON RIFFOLA...10-15 78

Picture Sleeves

MERCURY (Except 811-215-7)...3-4 80-89
MERCURY (811-215-7 "Photograph")...4-6 83

LPs: 10/12-inch

MERCURY (Except 832-962)...5-10 80-88
MERCURY (832-962 "Hysteria")...25-35 87
(Picture disc.)
Members: Joe Elliott; Pete Willis; Rick Allen; Steve Clark; Phil Collen; Rick Savage; Vivian Campbell
Also see DIO, Ronnie

DE FRANCO FAMILY
P&R/LP '73

(Featuring Tony DeFranco)

Singles: 7-inch

20TH FOX (Except 2214)...3-5 73-74
20TH FOX (2214 "We Belong Together")...4-8 75

Picture Sleeves

20TH FOX...3-5 73-74

LPs: 10/12-inch

20TH FOX...8-12 73-74
Members: Tony DeFranco; Benny DeFranco; Merlina DeFranco; Marisa DeFranco; Nino DeFranco.

DEJA
P&R/R&B/LP '87

Singles: 7-inch

VIRGIN...3-4 87-88

Picture Sleeves

VIRGIN...3-4 87-88

LPs: 10/12-inch

VIRGIN...5-10 87-88
Members: Curt Jones; Starleana Young.

Also see AURRA
Also see SLAVE

DE JOHN SISTERS P&R '54

Singles: 78 rpm

COLUMBIA........8-12 57
EPIC........4-8 54-56
OKEH........4-8 53

Singles: 7-inch

COLUMBIA........10-15 57
EPIC........8-12 54-56
OKEH........10-15 53
SUNBEAM........8-12 59
U.A. 4-8 60

LPs: 10/12-inch

U.A. 15-25 60
Members: Julie DeGiovanni; Dux DeGiovanni.

DEJONAY, Zena D&D '84

Singles: 12-inch

TVI........4-6 84

DEKKER, Desmond, & Aces P&R/LP '69

Singles: 7-inch

UNI........3-6 69-70

LPs: 10/12-inch

UNI........20-25 69

DEL AMITRI LP '90

LPs: 10/12-inch

A&M........5-8 90

DELACARDOS P&R '61

Singles: 7-inch

ELGEY (1001 "Letter to a School Girl")........30-40 59
IMPERIAL........5-10 63
SHELL (308 "Dream Girl")........15-25 61
SHELL (311 "Love Is the Greatest Thing")........15-25 62
U.A. 10-15 61

DELANEY & BONNIE LP '69
(Delaney & Bonnie and Friends)

Singles: 7-inch

ATCO........3-6 70-72
COLUMBIA........3-5 72-73
ELEKTRA........3-5 69
INDEPENDENCE........4-8 67
STAX........4-8 68-69

LPs: 10/12-inch

ATCO........15-25 70-72
COLUMBIA........15-25 72
ELEKTRA........15-25 69
GNP........15-25 70
STAX........15-25 69
Members: Delaney Bramlett; Bonnie Bramlett.
Also see BAD HABITS
Also see BRAMLETT, Bonnie
Also see BRAMLETT, Delaney
Also see CLAPTON, Eric
Also see ROGERS, Dann
Also see SHINDOGS
Also see WHITLOCK, Bobby

DELBERT & GLEN P&R '72

Singles: 7-inch

CLEAN........3-5 72-73

LPs: 10/12-inch

CLEAN (601 "Subject to Change")........15-20 72
Members: Delbert McClinton; Glen Clark.
Also see McCLINTON, Delbert
Also see PRINE, John / Daryl Hall & John Oates / Barnaby Bye / Delbert & Glen

DELEGATES P&R '72

Singles: 7-inch

MAINSTREAM........5-10 72

LPs: 10/12-inch

MAINSTREAM........10-15 73

DELEGATION P&R/R&B/LP '79

Singles: 12-inch

SHADYBROOK........4-8 77

Singles: 7-inch

MCA........3-5 76
MERCURY........3-4 80-81
SHADYBROOK........3-4 77-79

LPs: 10/12-inch

MERCURY........5-10 80-81
SHADYBROOK........5-10 79
Members: Ray Patterson; Ricky Bailey; Bruce Dunbar.

DELFONICS P&R/R&B '68

Singles: 7-inch

CAMEO........4-8 67
COLLECTABLES........3-4 80s
FLASHBACK........3-5 70s
MOON SHOT........4-8 68
PHILLY GROOVE........3-6 68-73
ROULETTE........3-5 73

LPs: 10/12-inch

KORY........8-10 77
PHILLY GROOVE........10-20 68-74
POOGIE........5-10 81
COLLECTABLES........6-8 88
Members: Major Harris; William Hart; Wilbert Hart; Randy Cain; Richie Daniels.
Also see HARRIS, Major

DEL FUEGOS LP '85

Singles: 7-inch

CZECH........4-8 82
SLASH........3-4 85-87

Picture Sleeves

CZECH........5-10 82
SLASH........3-4 86

LPs: 10/12-inch

RCA........5-8 89
SLASH........5-10 85-87

DELIVERANCE P&R '80

Singles: 7-inch

COLUMBIA........3-4 80

DELLS R&B '56

Singles: 78 rpm

VEE JAY (166 "Dreams of Contentment")........50-75 55
VEE JAY (200 series)........20-50 56-57

Singles: 12-inch

ABC........4-6 79

Singles: 7-inch

ABC........3-5 73-78
ARGO (5415 "God Bless the Child")........8-12 62
ARGO (5428 "Eternally")........8-12 62
ARGO (5442 "If It Ain't One Thing It's Another")........5-10 63
CADET........4-8 67-75
CHESS........3-5 73
COLLECTABLES........3-4 80s
MCA........3-4 79
MERCURY........3-5 75-77
OLDIES 45........4-8 60s
PRIVATE I........3-4 84
20TH FOX........3-5 80-82
VEE JAY (166 "Dreams of Contentment")........100-150 55
Note: Vee Jay 134, *Tell the World*, is listed in the following section for DELLS / Count Morris.
VEE JAY (204 "Oh, What a Night")........50-75 56
VEE JAY (230 "Movin' On")........20-40 56
VEE JAY (236 "Why Do You Have to Go")........20-40 57
VEE JAY (251 "Distant Love")........20-40 57
VEE JAY (258 "Pain in My Heart")........20-40 57
VEE JAY (274 "The Springer")........15-25 58
VEE JAY (292 "I'm Calling")........15-25 58
VEE JAY (300 "Wedding Day")........50-75 58
VEE JAY (324 "Dry Your Eyes")........20-40 58
VEE JAY (338 thru 712)........5-15 59-65

LPs: 10/12-inch

ABC........8-10 78
BUDDAH........10-15 69
CADET........10-20 68-75
LOST-NITE........8-12 81
MERCURY........10-15 75-77
PRIVATE I........5-10 84
TRIP........10-12 73
20TH FOX........5-10 80-81
UPFRONT........10-15 68
VEE JAY (1010 "Oh What a Night")........400-500 59
(Maroon label, with thin circular ring.)
VEE JAY (1010 "Oh What a Night")........300-400 59
(Maroon label, with thick circular ring.)
VEE JAY (1010 "Oh What a Night")........100-200 61
(Black label. Monaural.)
VEE JAY (1010 "Oh What a Night")........100-200 61
(Black label. Stereo.)
VEE JAY (1141 "It's Not Unusual")........100-200 65
Members: Johnny Funches; Mike McGill; Marvin Junior; Vern Allison; Johnny Carter.

Also see BUTLER, Jerry, & Betty Everett
Also see CLARK, Dee
Also see LEWIS, Barbara
Also see SOUTH, Joe / Dells

DELLS / Count Morris

Singles: 78 rpm

VEE JAY (134 "Tell the World")........100-200 55

Singles: 7-inch

VEE JAY (134 "Tell the World")........400-500 55
(Black vinyl.)
VEE JAY (134 "Tell the World")........700-900 55
(Colored vinyl.)
Also see DELLS

DELLS & DRAMATICS R&B '75

Singles: 7-inch

CADET........3-5 75
Also see DELLS
Also see DRAMATICS

DE LORY, Al P&R '70

Singles: 7-inch

CAPITOL........3-6 68-71
CHAAT (1001 "Hot Saki")........5-10
EUREKA........4-8 61
PHI DAN........4-8 65

LPs: 10/12-inch

CAPITOL........5-15 69-70

DEL-PHIS
(Martha & the Vandellas)

Singles: 7-inch

CHECK MATE (1005 "It Takes Two")........100-200 61
Members: Gloria Williamson; Martha Reeves; Annette Beard; Rosalind Ashford.
Also see MARTHA & VANDELLAS
Also see VELLS

DELPHS, Jimmy P&R/R&B '68

Singles: 7-inch

CARLA (1904 "Dancing a Hold in the World")........100-200 68
CARLA (2535 "Almost")........10-20 67
KAREN........5-10 68

DELTA JOHN
(John Lee Hooker)

Singles: 78 rpm

REGENT (1001 "Helpless Blues")........40-60 49
Also see HOOKER, John Lee

DELTA RHYTHM BOYS P&R/R&B '46

Singles: 78 rpm

ATLANTIC (889 "The Laugh's on Me")........50-75 49
ATLANTIC (900 "Nobody Knows")........40-60 50
DECCA........20-30 42-55
MUSICRAFT........15-25 49
RCA........15-25 47-48

Singles: 7-inch

DECCA (29000 series)........20-35 54-55
DECCA (48140 "You Are Closer to My Heart")........50-75 50
DECCA (48148 "It's All in Your Mind")........50-75 50
LONDON (1145 "Blow Out the Candle")........15-25 52

MERCURY (1407 "I've Got You Under My Skin") 20-30 52
MERCURY (1408 "They Didn't Believe Me") 20-30 52
MERCURY (1409 "All the Things You Are") 10-20 52
PHILIPS 5-10 62
RCA (5094 "I'll Never Get Out of This World Alive") 25-35 53
RCA (5217 "Long Gone Baby") 20-25 53

EPs: 7-inch

RCA (3085 "Dry Bones") 75-100 50
(Double EP.)

LPs: 10/12-inch

CAMDEN (313 "The Delta Rhythm Boys") 40-50 56
CORAL (57358 "Swingin' Spirituals") 20-30 60
(Monaural.)
CORAL (757358 "Swingin' Spirituals") 25-40 60
(Stereo.)
ELEKTRA (138 "The Delta Rhythm Boys") 25-35 57
JUBILEE (1022 "Delta Rhythm Boys in Sweden") 25-50 57
(Black vinyl.)
JUBILEE (1022 "Delta Rhythm Boys in Sweden") 75-100 57
(Colored vinyl.)
MERCURY (25153 "The Delta Rhythm Boys") 75-100 53
(10-inch LP.)
RCA (3085 "Dry Bones") 100-150 50
(10-inch LP.)
Members: Traverse Crawford; Karl Jones; Kell Pharr; Lee Gaines.
Also see LUNCEFORD, Jimmie, & Orchestra

DEL-VIKINGS *P&R/R&B '57*

(Featuring Krips Johnson; with Joey Biscoe; Del Vikings; Dell-Vikings)

Singles: 78 rpm

DOT 25-50 57
FEE BEE 20-40 56-57
MERCURY 20-40 57

Singles: 7-inch

ABC 3-5 75
ABC-PAR (10208 "I'll Never Stop Crying") 15-25 61
ABC-PAR (10248 "I Hear Bells") 50-75 61
ABC-PAR (10278 "Kiss Me") 15-25 62
ABC-PAR (10304 "One More River to Cross") 15-25 62
ABC-PAR (10341 "Confession of Love") 15-25 62
ABC-PAR (10385 "An Angel Up in Heaven") 75-100 63
(Vinyl pressing.)
ABC-PAR (10385 "An Angel Up in Heaven") 50-75 63
(Polystyrene pressing.)
ABC-PAR (10425 "Too Many Miles") 15-25 63
ALPINE (66 "Pistol Packin' Mama") 50-100 60
BVM 3-5 90
BIM BAM BOOM 4-8 72
BLUE SKY 3-5
BROADCAST 3-5
COLLECTABLES 3-4 80
CRUISIN' 3-5
DRC (101 "Can't You See") 30-50 57
DOT (15538 "Come Go with Me") 15-25 57
DOT (15571 "What Made Maggie Run") 15-25 57
DOT (15592 "Whispering Bells") 15-25 57
DOT (16092 "Come Go with Me") 10-15 60
DOT (16236 "Come Go with Me") 10-15 61
FEE BEE (173 "Welfare Blues") 5-8 77
FEE BEE (205 "Come Go with Me") 100-150 56
(Has "45 RPM" on each side at top of label. With two sets of thin, horizontal, double parallel lines.)
FEE BEE (205 "Come Go with Me") 20-30 61
(Does not have "45 RPM." With one set of lines, one thick, one thin.)
FEE BEE (206 "Down in Bermuda") 50-100 57
FEE BEE (210 "What Made Maggie Run"/"Down by the Stream") 50-100 57
FEE BEE (210 "What Made Maggie Run"/"Uh Uh Baby") 50-100 57
FEE BEE (210 "What Made Maggie Run"/"When I Come Home") 75-125 57
FEE BEE (214 "Whispering Bells") 100-150 57
FEE BEE (218 "I'm Spinning") 50-75 58
(First issued, on 218-A, as by the "Del Viking Kripp Johnson." See his section for that listing.)
FEE BEE (221 "Willette") 50-75 58
(First issued as by the "Dell Viking Kripp Johnson and Charles Jackson." See their section for that listing.)
FEE BEE (227 "Tell Me") 20-30 59
FEE BEE (902 "True Love") 20-30 61
GATEWAY (743 "We Three") 15-25 64
GOLDIES 3-4
JOJO 3-6 76
LIGHTNING 3-4
LUNIVERSE (106 "Somewhere Over the Rainbow") 50-100 57
LUNIVERSE (110 "Heaven in Paradise") 50-100 58
LUNIVERSE (113 "White Cliffs of Dover") 50-100 58
LUNIVERSE (114 "There I Go") 50-100 58
MCA 3-4 70s
MERCURY (30112 "Come Along with Me") 10-15 61
MERCURY (71132 "Cool Shake") 15-25 57
MERCURY (71180 "Come Along with Me") 15-25 57
MERCURY (71198 "I'm Spinning") 15-25 59
MERCURY (71241 "Your Book of Life") 15-25 57
MERCURY (71266 "Voodoo Man") 15-25 58
MERCURY (71345 "You Cheated") 25-35 58
(Blue label.)
MERCURY (71345 "You Cheated") 15-25 58
(Black label.)
MERCURY (71390 "How Could You") 20-30 58
SCEPTER (12367 "Come Go with Me") 4-6 72
SHIP 3-4
SPARTON/ABC-PAR (1104 "Confession of Love") 15-25 62
(Canadian.)

Picture Sleeves

ALPINE (66 "The Sun") 100-150 60

EPs: 7-inch

DOT (1058 "Come Go with Us") 200-300 57
MERCURY (3359 "They Sing, They Swing") 50-100 57
MERCURY (3362 "They Sing, They Swing") 75-100 57
MERCURY (3363 "They Sing, They Swing") 75-100 57

LPs: 10/12-inch

BVM 5-10 91
COLLECTABLES 6-8 80-83
DOT (3695 "Come Go with Me") 200-400 66
JANGO (778 "Greatest Hits") 15-20
LUNIVERSE (1000 "Come Go with the Del Vikings") 500-750 57
MERCURY (20314 "They Sing, They Swing") 100-200 57
MERCURY (20353 "Del Vikings' Record Session") 100-200 58
Members: Kripp Johnson; Norman Wright; Clarence Quick; Don Jackson; Gus Backus; Joey Briscoe; David Lerchey; Bill Blakely; Ritzi Lee; Billy Woodruff.
Also see KING, Ben E.

DEL-VIKINGS / Ike Clanton

Singles: 7-inch

ERA 3-5
Also see CLANTON, Ike

DEL-VIKINGS / Diamonds / Big Bopper / Gaylords

Singles: 7-inch

MERCURY (53 "60 Second Spots") 20-40 58
(Promotional issue only.)
Also see BIG BOPPER
Also see DIAMONDS
Also see GAYLORDS

DEL-VIKINGS / Sonnets

LPs: 10/12-inch

CROWN (5368 "The Del-Vikings and the Sonnets") 20-30 63
(Tracks shown by the Sonnets are actually by either the Meadowlarks or the Sounds.)
Also see DEL-VIKINGS

DE MARCO, Ralph *P&R '59*

(With Billy Mure & Orchestra)

Singles: 7-inch

GUARANTEED (202 "Old Shep") 10-15 59
SHELLEY (1011 "Donna") 50-100 60
20TH FOX (309 "Lonely for a Girl") 5-10 62

Picture Sleeves

GUARANTEED (202 "Old Shep") 20-30 59
Also see MURE, Billy

DE MATTEO, Nicky *P&R '60*

(With the Sorrows)

Singles: 7-inch

ABC-PAR 5-10 61
ACE (110 "Please Don't Go Away") 20-30 57
CAMEO 5-10 65-66
DIAMOND 5-15 63
END (1021 "School House Rock") 15-25 58
GUYDEN 5-10 60
PARIS 8-12 59
TORE 8-12 59

DEMENSIONS *P&R '60*

(Dimensions)

Singles: 7-inch

COLLECTABLES 3-4 80s
CORAL (Except 65611) 10-20 61-63
CORAL (65611 "As Time Goes By") 5-8 67
MOHAWK (116 "Over the Rainbow") 20-30 60
(Maroon label.)
MOHAWK (116 "Over the Rainbow") 15-20 60
(Brown label.)
MOHAWK (116 "Over the Rainbow") 10-15 61
(Red label.)
MOHAWK (120 "Zing Went the Strings of My Heart") 10-15 60
MOHAWK (121 "God's Christmas") 20-30 60
MOHAWK (123 "A Tear Fell") 40-60 60
OLD HIT 3-5

Picture Sleeves

CORAL (62344 "My Foolish Heart") 15-25 63

LPs: 10/12-inch

CORAL (57430 "My Foolish Heart") 75-125 63
(Monaural.)
CORAL (7-57430 "My Foolish Heart") 85-125 63
(Stereo.)
CRYSTAL BALL 8-10 82
MCA 5-10
Members: Lenny Dell; Phil Del Giudice; Howard Margolin; Marisa Martelli.

DEMIAN, Max *LP '79*

(Max Demian Band)

Singles: 7-inch

RCA 3-4 79

LPs: 10/12-inch

RCA 8-10 79-80

DENNIS, Cathy LP '90

LPs: 10/12-inch

POLYDOR 5-8 90

DENNY, Martin P&R/R&B/LP '59

(Exotic Sounds of Martin Denny)

Singles: 7-inch

LIBERTY (55000 series) 3-8 59-67
LIBERTY (56000 series) 3-5 69
LIBERTY (77000 series) 5-15 59-60
(Stereo.)

Picture Sleeves

LIBERTY 5-15 59-63

EPs: 7-inch

LIBERTY 5-15 59

LPs: 10/12-inch

FIRST AMERICAN 5-10 81
LIBERTY 20-30 59-60s
(With bird calls and animal sounds and covers picturing model Sandy Warner. Perhaps a Martin Denny fan will provide us with a list of which specific LPs are included in this group.)
LIBERTY 5-10 60s
(Without bird calls and covers picturing model Sandy Warner.)
SUNSET 5-10 66-68
U.A. 5-10 74-80
Also see BAJA MARIMBA BAND
Also see ZENTER, Si

DENNY, Sandy LP '74

Singles: 7-inch

A&M 3-5 72-73

LPs: 10/12-inch

A&M 8-12 71-72
ISLAND 8-10 74-76
Also see FAIRPORT CONVENTION
Also see LED ZEPPELIN

DENNY, Sandy, & Strawbs

LPs: 10/12-inch

PICKWICK 10-15 73
Also see DENNY, Sandy
Also see STRAWBS

DENVER, John LP '69

Singles: 12-inch

RCA (11189 "Bet on the Blues") 5-10 77
(Promotional issue only.)

Singles: 7-inch

ALLEGIANCE 3-4
CBS 3-4 90s
CHERRY MOUNTAIN (02 "Flying Or Me") 3-5 86
RCA (Except 0067 thru 0955) 3-5 74-86
RCA (0067 thru 0955) 4-8 70-74

Promotional Singles

EVA-TONE (106026 "Trees for America") 3-5 86
RCA (2008 "Rocky Mountain High") 5-10 72

Picture Sleeves

ALLEGIANCE 3-4
CBS 3-4 90s
CHERRY MOUNTAIN (02 "Flying Or Me") 3-5 86
RCA (Except 2008) 3-5 74-86
RCA (2008 "Rocky Mountain High") 5-10 72
(Promotional issue only.)

LPs: 10/12-inch

HJD (66 "John Denver Sings") 200-300 66
(Promotional issue only. Less than 300 copies made as Christmas gifts for friends.)
MOS ("Something to Sing About") .. 50-100 66
(Promotional issue only. No actual label name is used. Various artists LP with three Denver tracks not available elsewhere.)
MERCURY (704 "Beginnings") 10-15 72
(Pictures John Denver on cover.)
MERCURY (704 "Beginnings") 8-10 74
(With mountain scene photo on cover.)
RCA (0101 thru 3449) 5-10 73-80
RCA (0075 "The John Denver Radio Show") 20-30 74
(Single-sided LP. Promotional issue only.)
RCA (0683 "The Second John Denver Radio Show") 20-30 74
RCA (4000 series) 10-15 69-72
(Orange labels.)
RCA (4000 & 5000 series) 5-10 81-85
(Black labels.)
RCA (5398 "The John Denver Holiday Radio Show") 10-20 84
(Promotional issue only.)
WINDSTAR 5-8 90
Session: Hal Blaine; John Sommers; Steve Weisberg; Dick Kniss; Lee Holdridge; James Burton.
Also see BURTON, James
Also see DENVER, BOISE & JOHNSON
Also see MITCHELL, Chad, Trio
Also see MURPHEY, Michael
Also see TRAVERS, Mary
Also see WONDER, Stevie / John Denver

DENVER, John, & Placido Domingo P&R '82

Singles: 7-inch

COLUMBIA 3-4 82
Also see DOMINGO, Placido

DENVER, John, & Emmylou Harris C&W '83

Singles: 7-inch

RCA 3-4 83
Also see HARRIS, Emmylou

DENVER, John, & Muppets LP '79

Singles: 7-inch

RCA 3-4 79

LPs: 10/12-inch

RCA 5-10 79-83

DENVER, John, & Olivia Newton-John P&R '75

Singles: 7-inch

RCA 3-5 75
Also see NEWTON-JOHN, Olivia

DENVER, John, & Nitty Gritty Dirt Band C&W '89

Singles: 7-inch

UNIVERSAL 3-4 89
Also see NITTY GRITTY DIRT BAND

DENVER, John / Diana Ross

Singles: 7-inch

WHAT'S IT ALL ABOUT 4-8 81
(Public service, radio station issue.)
Also see ROSS, Diana

DENVER, John, & Sylvie Vartan

Singles: 7-inch

RCA 3-4 84

DENVER, BOISE & JOHNSON

Singles: 7-inch

REPRISE (0695 "Take Me to Tomorrow") 5-10 68
Member: John Denver; Michael Johnson.
Also see DENVER, John
Also see JOHNSON, Michael

DEODATO P&R/R&B/LP '73

(Eumir Deodato)

Singles: 12-inch

W.B. 4-6 84

Singles: 7-inch

CTI 3-4 73-77
MCA 3-4 74-76
W.B. 3-4 78-84

Picture Sleeves

CTI 3-4 73

LPs: 10/12-inch

CTI 8-10 73-74
MCA 6-10 76
MUSE 8-10 73-76
W.B. 5-10 78-82
Also see TROPEA

DEPECHE MODE LP '81

Singles: 12-inch

SIRE (Except 2271 & 2952) 4-6 81-87
SIRE (2271 "Blasphemous Rumors") 40-50
(Promotional issue only.)
SIRE (2952 "Behind the Wheel") 20-30 87
(Promotional issue only.)

Singles: 7-inch

SIRE 3-4 81-90

Picture Sleeves

SIRE 3-4 85-88

LPs: 10/12-inch

SIRE 5-10 81-90

DEREK P&R '68

(Johnny Cymbal)

Singles: 7-inch

BANG 4-8 68-69
SOLID GOLD 3-5 73
Also see CYMBAL, Johnny

DEREK B R&B '88

Singles: 7-inch

PROFILE 3-4 88

DEREK & CYNDI R&B '74

Singles: 7-inch

THUNDER 3-5 74

Picture Sleeves

THUNDER 3-5 74

DEREK & DOMINOS LP '70

Singles: 7-inch

ATCO 3-5 70-72
RSO 3-4 73

LPs: 10/12-inch

ATCO (704 "Layla") 20-30 70
MFSL (2-239 "In Concert") 25-35 90s
POLYDOR 8-10 74
RSO 5-10 77
Members: Eric Clapton; Jim Gordon; Carl Radle; Bobby Whitlock; Duane Allman.
Also see ALLMAN, Duane
Also see CLAPTON, Eric
Also see WHITLOCK, Bobby

DERRINGER, Rick LP '73

(With the McCoys; Derringer)

Singles: 7-inch

BLUE SKY 3-5 74-80
EPIC 3-4 83

LPs: 10/12-inch

BLUE SKY 8-18 73-81
MERCURY 10-20 74
PASSPORT 5-10 83
Also see McCOYS

DERRINGER, Rick, & Edgar Winter Group

LPs: 10/12-inch

BLUE SKY 8-10 75
Also see DERRINGER, Rick
Also see WINTER, Edgar

DESANTO, Sugar Pie R&B '60

("Sugar Pie" De Santo; Umpeylia Balinton)

Singles: 7-inch

BRUNSWICK 5-10 67-68
CADET 5-10 66
CHECK 10-20 60
CHECKER 5-10 63-66
GEDINSON 5-10 62
JASMAN 4-6 74
SOUL CLOCK 4-6 69
VELTONE 10-20 60
WAX 8-12 64

EPs: 7-inch

CHECKER (2979 "Sugar Pie") 30-50 61
(Stereo. Juke box issue only.)

LPs: 10/12-inch

CHECKER (2979 "Sugar Pie") 50-100 61
Also see HANK & Sugar Pie
Also see JAMES, Etta, & Sugar Pie DeSanto

DE SARIO, Teri P&R '78

Singles: 7-inch

CASABLANCA 3-5 78

LPs: 10/12-inch

CASABLANCA 5-10 80
DAYSPRING 5-8 85

DE SARIO, Teri, & K.C. R&B '80

Singles: 7-inch

CASABLANCA 3-5 79-80

Also see DE SARIO, Teri
Also see K.C. & Sunshine Band

DE SHANNON, Jackie — P&R '63

Singles: 7-inch

AMHERST 6-12 78
ATLANTIC 5-10 72-74
CAPITOL 5-10 71
COLUMBIA (Except 10221) 5-10 75
COLUMBIA (10221 "Boat to Sail") 10-15 76
(With Brian Wilson.)
EDISON INT'L (416 "I Wanna Go Home") 50-100 60
EDISON INT'L (418 "Put My Baby Down") 50-100 60
IMPERIAL 5-10 65-70
LIBERTY (55000 series, except 55602) 15-25 60-64
LIBERTY (55602 "Little Yellow Roses") 8-10 63
(Black vinyl.)
LIBERTY (55602 "Little Yellow Roses") 15-25 63
(Colored vinyl. Promotional issue only.)
LIBERTY (56000 series) 5-10 70
MGM 4-8 65
RCA 3-4 80

Picture Sleeves

LIBERTY (55526 "Faded Love") 75-100 63

LPs: 10/12-inch

AMHERST (1010 "You're the Only Dancer") 15-25 77
ATLANTIC 10-15 72-74
CAPITOL 15-20 71
COLUMBIA 10-15 75
IMPERIAL (9286 "This Is Jackie De Shannon") 25-50 65
(Monaural.)
IMPERIAL (9294 "You Won't Forget Me") 25-50 65
(Monaural.)
IMPERIAL (9296 "In the Wind") 25-50 65
(Monaural.)
IMPERIAL (9328 "Are You Ready for This") 25-50 66
(Monaural.)
IMPERIAL (9344 "New Image") 25-50 67
(Monaural.)
IMPERIAL (9352 "For You") 25-50 67
(Monaural.)
IMPERIAL (12286 "This Is Jackie De Shannon") 25-50 65
(Stereo.)
IMPERIAL (12294 "You Won't Forget Me") 25-50 65
(Stereo.)
IMPERIAL (12296 "In the Wind") 25-50 65
(Stereo.)
IMPERIAL (12328 "Are You Ready for This") 25-50 66
(Stereo.)
IMPERIAL (12344 "New Image") 25-50 67
(Stereo.)
IMPERIAL (12352 "For You") 25-50 67
(Stereo.)
IMPERIAL (12386 "Me About You") 25-50 68
IMPERIAL (12404 "What the World Needs Now Is Love") 25-50 68
IMPERIAL (12415 "Laurel Canyon") 25-50 68
IMPERIAL (12442 "Put a Little Love in Your Heart") 25-50 69
IMPERIAL (12453 "To Be Free") 25-50 70
LIBERTY (3320 "Jackie De Shannon") 50-100 63
(Monaural.)
LIBERTY (3390 "Breakin' It Up On the Beatles Tour") 50-100 64
(Monaural.)
LIBERTY (7320 "Jackie De Shannon") 75-100 63
(Stereo.)
LIBERTY (7390 "Breakin' It Up on the Beatles Tour") 75-100 64
(Stereo.)
LIBERTY (10000 series) 5-10 82
SUNSET 10-15 68-71
U.A. 8-10 75

Also see DEE, Jackie
Also see HALE & HUSHABYES
Also see SHANNON, Jackie
Also see WILSON, Brian

DE SHANNON, Jackie / Bobby Vee / Eddie Hodges

LPs: 10/12-inch

LIBERTY (3430 "C'mon Let's Live a Little") 15-20 66
(Monaural. Soundtrack)
LIBERTY (7430 "C'mon Let's Live a Little") 20-25 66
(Stereo. Soundtrack)

Also see DE SHANNON, Jackie
Also see HODGES, Eddie
Also see VEE, Bobby

DESHAWN, Tony — R&B '87

Singles: 7-inch

AMAZON 3-4 87

DESMOND, Johnny — P&R '46

Singles: 78 rpm

CORAL 3-5 52-56
MGM 3-6 50-51

Singles: 7-inch

COLUMBIA 4-8 59-60
CORAL 5-10 52-56
DIAMOND 3-6 62
EDGEWOOD 3-6 62
MGM 5-10 50-51
MUSICANZA 3-4
RCA 3-6 63
RED LITE 5-8
20TH FOX 3-6 64
VIGOR 3-4 73

Picture Sleeves

CORAL 5-10 55

EPs: 7-inch

CORAL 8-15 54-56
MGM 10-20 52
P.R.I. (11 "So Nice") 5-10

LPs: 10/12-inch

CAMDEN 10-20 53-54
COLUMBIA 5-10 59-60
CORAL 15-25 55-56
LION 10-15 56
MGM 10-20 55
MAYFAIR 10-15 58
MOVIETONE 5-10 66
P.R.I. (98 "90th Anniversary Album") 10-20
(Colored vinyl. Promotional issue for Montgomery Ward stores.)
VOCALION 5-10 66

Also see CORNELL, Don, Johnny Desmond & Alan Dale

DESMOND, Johnny, Eileen Barton & McGuire Sisters — P&R '54

Singles: 78 rpm

CORAL 4-8 54

Also see BARTON, Eileen
Also see McGUIRE SISTERS

DESMOND, Johnny / John Gary / Gordon MacRae

LPs: 10/12-inch

INT'L AWARD 8-15 60s

Also see DESMOND, Johnny
Also see GARY, John
Also see MacRAE, Gordon

DESMOND, Paul — LP '63

(Paul Desmond Quartet)

Singles: 7-inch

A&M 3-5 69-70
RCA VICTOR 3-8 62-63

LPs: 10/12-inch

A&M 5-15 69-76
CTI 8-12 75
CAMDEN 8-12 73
DISCOVERY 5-8 81
FANTASY (21 "Paul Desmond") 50-100 54
(10-inch LP.)
FANTASY (220 "Paul Desmond") 40-60 56
RCA (2400 & 2500 series) 15-25 62-63
RCA (2800 series) 5-10 78
RCA (3300 & 3400 series) 10-20 65-66
W.B. 20-30 60

Also see BRUBECK, Dave, & Paul Desmond
Also see MULLIGAN, Gerry, & Paul Desmond

DESTINATION — R&B '77

Singles: 12-inch

BUTTERFLY 4-6 79

Singles: 7-inch

A.V.I. 3-5 77
BUTTERFLY 3-4 79

LPs: 10/12-inch

A.V.I. 8-10 77
BUTTERFLY 5-10 79

DET REIRRUC & CLUB RAPPERS — D&D '85

Singles: 12-inch

CLUB 4-6 85

DETECTIVE — LP '77

Singles: 7-inch

SWAN SONG 3-5 77-78

LPs: 10/12-inch

SWAN SONG 10-12 77-78

Member: Michael Des Barres.

DETERGENTS — P&R '64

Singles: 7-inch

KAPP 5-10 66
ROULETTE 5-10 64-65

Picture Sleeves

ROULETTE (4590 "Leader of the Laundromat") 15-25 64

LPs: 10/12-inch

ROULETTE (25308 "The Many Faces of the Detergents") 25-35 65

Members: Ron Dante; Tommy Wynn; Danny Jordan.

DETROIT — LP '72

Singles: 7-inch

PARAMOUNT 3-5 70-71

LPs: 10/12-inch

PARAMOUNT 10-15 71-72

Also see DETROIT WHEELS
Also see ROCKETS
Also see RYDER, Mitch, & Detroit Wheels

DETROIT EMERALDS — P&R/R&B '68

Singles: 7-inch

RIC-TIC 10-15 68
WESTBOUND 3-6 70-78

LPs: 10/12-inch

WESTBOUND 10-15 71-78

Members: Abrim Tilmon; Ivory Tilmon; Cleophus Tilmon; Raymond Tilmon; James Mitchell; Paul Riser; Maurice King; Johnny Allen.

Also see CHAPTER 8

DETROIT WHEELS

Singles: 7-inch

INFERNO (5002 "Tally Ho") 10-20 68

Also see DETROIT

DETROYT — R&B '84

Singles: 7-inch

TABU 3-4 84

DE VAUGHN, William — P&R/R&B/LP '74

Singles: 7-inch

ROXBURY 3-5 74
TEC 3-4 80

LPs: 10/12-inch

ROXBURY 8-10 74
TEC 5-10 80

Also see MFSB

DEVICE — P&R/LP '86

Singles: 12-inch

CHRYSALIS 4-8 86
(Promotional issue only.)

Singles: 7-inch

CHRYSALIS 3-4 86

Picture Sleeves

CHRYSALIS 3-4 86

LPs: 10/12-inch

CHRYSALIS 5-8 86

Members: Paul Engemann; Holly Knight; Gene Black.

Also see ANIMOTION

Also see KNIGHT, Holly

DEVO LP '78

Singles: 12-inch

ENIGMA 4-6 88
W.B (Except 2006)....... 4-8 80-85
W.B. (2006 "That's Good") 15-20 83
(Picture disc. Promotional issue only.)

Singles: 7-inch

ASYLUM 3-4 81
BOOJI BOY 4-8 78
ENIGMA 3-4 88
FULL MOON 3-4 81
W.B. (Except 49826) 3-6 78-85
W.B. (49826 "Beautiful World") 10-15 81
(Space helmet shaped picture disc.)
W.B. (49826 Beautiful World") 40-80 81
(Space helmet shaped colored vinyl. Experimental pressing only. 20 made.)

Picture Sleeves

FULL MOON 3-4 81
W.B. 3-5 79-85

LPs: 10/12-inch

ENIGMA 5-10 88
W.B. 5-10 78-88

Members: Mark Mothersbaugh; Bob Mothersbaugh; David Kendrick; Bob Casale; Gerald Casale.

Also see JACKSON, Jermaine

DE VOL, Frank, Orchestra P&R '50

(With the Rainbow Strings)

Singles: 78 rpm

CAPITOL 3-5 50-56
KEM 3-5 55

Singles: 7-inch

ABC-PAR 3-5 64-65
CAPITOL 3-6 50-56
COLGEMS 3-5 68
COLUMBIA 3-5 59-62
KEM 3-6 55

Picture Sleeves

COLGEMS 3-5 68

LPs: 10/12-inch

ABC-PAR 5-10 65-66
COLGEMS (COM-108 "Guess Who's Coming to Dinner") 20-25 68
(Soundtrack. Monaural.)
COLGEMS (COS-108 "Guess Who's Coming to Dinner") 25-30 68
(Soundtrack. Stereo.)
COLGEMS (COMO-5006 "The Happening") 15-20 67
(Soundtrack. Monaural.)
COLGEMS (COSO-5006 "The Happening") 20-25 67
(Soundtrack. Stereo.)
COLUMBIA 8-10 59-63
HARMONY 5-10 65

DEVONS R&B '69

Singles: 7-inch

KING 3-6 69

DE VORZON, Barry LP '76

Singles: 7-inch

COLUMBIA 8-12 59-61
RCA 10-20 57-59
W.B. 3-4 81

LPs: 10/12-inch

A&M 5-10 76
ARISTA 5-10 76

Also see BARRY & TAMERLANES

DE VORZON, Barry, & Perry Botkin Jr. P&R '76

Singles: 7-inch

A&M 3-5 76-77

Picture Sleeves

A&M 3-5 76

LPs: 10/12-inch

A&M 5-10 76

Also see DE VORZON, Barry

DEVOTIONS P&R '64

Singles: 7-inch

DELTA (1001 "Rip Van Winkle") 50-100 61
KAPE 5-10
ROULETTE (4406 "Rip Van Winkle") 25-50 61
(White label.)
ROULETTE (4541 "Rip Van Winkle") 10-15 64
(Orange label.)
ROULETTE (4556 "Sunday Kind of Love") 25-35 64
ROULETTE (4580 "Snow White") 10-20 64

Members: Joe Pardo; Frank Pardo; Bob Weisbrod; Ray Sanchez; Bob Havorka; Louis DeCarlo; Larry Frank

DEVOTIONS R&B '70

Singles: 7-inch

COLOSSUS 3-6 70

DEXTER, Al, & Troopers P&R/R&B '43

Singles: 7-inch

COLUMBIA 4-8 46
EKKO 4-6 55
OKEH 5-10 43-44
VOCALION 10-20

Singles: 7-inch

EKKO 5-10 55

LPs: 10/12-inch

AUDIO LAB 8-12
CAPITOL (1701 "Greatest Hits") 20-30 62
COLUMBIA (9005 "Songs of the Southwest") 30-40
(10-inch LP.)
HARMONY 8-10
HILLTOP 8-10

DEXY'S MIDNIGHT RUNNERS P&R/LP '83

Singles: 7-inch

EMI AMERICA 3-4 81
MERCURY 3-4 82-83

Picture Sleeves

MERCURY 5-10 82-83

LPs: 10/12-inch

EMI AMERICA 5-10 81
MERCURY 5-10 82-83

DEY, Tracey P&R '63

Singles: 7-inch

AMY 8-12 63-65
COLUMBIA 5-10 66
LIBERTY 10-20 63
VEE JAY 10-20 62

DE YOUNG, Cliff P&R '74

Singles: 7-inch

MCA 3-5 73-75

Picture Sleeves

MCA 3-5 74

LPs: 10/12-inch

MCA 10-12 73-75

DE YOUNG, Dennis P&R/LP '84

Singles: 12-inch

MCA 4-8 88
(Promotional only.)

Singles: 7-inch

A&M 3-4 83-86

Picture Sleeves

A&M 3-4 84-86

LPs: 10/12-inch

A&M 5-10 84-86
MCA 5-8 88

Also see STYX

DIABLOS R&B '56

(Featuring Nolan Strong; with Maurice King Orchestra)

Singles: 78 rpm

FORTUNE 10-25 54-57

Singles: 7-inch

FORTUNE (509 thru 522) 15-25 54-56
FORTUNE (525 thru 563) 10-20 57-64
FORTUNE (574 "The Way You Dog Me Around") 10-15 80
(Colored vinyl.)

Picture Sleeves

FORTUNE 15-25 64

LPs: 10/12-inch

FORTUNE (8010 "Fortune of Hits") 50-75 61
FORTUNE (8012 "Fortune of Hits, Vol. 2") 40-60 62
FORTUNE (8015 "Mind Over Matter") 40-60 63
FORTUNE (80810 "Fortune of Hits") 10-15

Members: Nolan Strong; Bob "Chico" Edwards; Juan Guiterriec; Willie Hunter, Quentin Eubanks; Jim Strong; George Scott; J.W. Johnson.

DIAMOND, Gregg R&B '78

(Gregg Diamond's Starcruiser; Gregg Diamond's Bionic Boogie)

Singles: 12-inch

POLYDOR 4-6 79

Singles: 7-inch

MARLIN 3-5 78
POLYDOR 3-4 79-80

LPs: 10/12-inch

MARLIN 5-10 78
MERCURY 5-10 79
POLYDOR 5-10 77-78

DIAMOND, Joel P&R '81

(Joel Diamond Experience)

Singles: 12-inch

CASABLANCA 4-6 79

Singles: 7-inch

ATLANTIC 3-4 82
CASABLANCA 3-4 79-84
MOTOWN 3-4 81

LPs: 10/12-inch

CASABLANCA 8-10 79

DIAMOND, Leo P&R '53

Singles: 78 rpm

AMBASSADOR 3-5 51-53
RCA 3-5 55
ROULETTE 4-8 57

Singles: 7-inch

AMBASSADOR 4-8 53
RCA 3-6 55
ROULETTE 5-10 57

DIAMOND, Neil P&R/LP '66

Singles: 12-inch

COLUMBIA (1586 "Heartlight") 6-10 82
COLUMBIA (99-1586 "Heartlight") 25-35 83
(Picture disc. Promotional issue only.)

Singles: 7-inch

BANG (100 series) 3-4
("Best Hits" reissue series.)
BANG (500 & 700 series) 5-10 66-73
CAPITOL 3-4 80-81
COLUMBIA (02600 thru 06100 series) 3-4 81-86
COLUMBIA (10000 & 11000 series) 3-5 74-80
COLUMBIA (33000 series) 3-4
("Hall of Fame" series.)
COLUMBIA (42809 "Clown Town") 300-500 63
COLUMBIA (45000 series) 3-5 73-74
MCA (40000 series) 3-5 73
MCA (60000 series) 3-4 73
PHILCO 15-25 66-67
("Hip-Pocket" flexi-disc.)
SOLID ROCK 3-4
UNI 4-8 68-72

Promotional Singles

BANG (Except 55075) 6-12 66-73
UNI (55075 "Two-Bit Manchild") 20-30 68
(Colored vinyl.)
CAPITOL 3-5 80-81
COLUMBIA (1115 "Song Sung Blue") 3-6 77
COLUMBIA (1193 "September Morn") 3-6 79
(Alternate version.)
COLUMBIA (02600 thru 11000) 3-5 74-86
COLUMBIA (42809 "Clown Town") 300-500 63
COLUMBIA (45000 series) 4-8 73-74
MCA 3-5 73
UNI 5-10 68-72
WHAT'S IT ALL ABOUT 8-15 70s

Picture Sleeves

CAPITOL 3-5 80-81
COLUMBIA 3-6 73-86
UNI 5-10 68-70

EPs: 7-inch

COLUMBIA (32919 "Serenade") 15-25 74
MCA (34989 "12 Greatest Hits") 15-25 74
UNI (34818 "Neil Diamond Gold") 15-25 71
UNI (34871 "Stones") 15-25 71
Note: all EPs listed were made for juke box use.

LPs: 10/12-inch

BANG (214 "The Feel of Neil Diamond") 75-125 66
BANG (217 "Just For You") 25-50 67
BANG (219 "Greatest Hits") 25-50 68
BANG (221 "Shilo") 50-75 70
BANG (224 "Do It") 40-60 71
BANG (227 "Double Gold") 25-35 73
CAPITOL 5-10 80
COLUMBIA (30000 series, except 39915) 8-12 73-86
COLUMBIA (39915 "Primitive") 20-25 84
(Picture disc.)
COLUMBIA (40000 series) 5-10 86-89
COLUMBIA (42550 "Jonathan Livingston Seagull") 15-25 81
(Half-speed mastered.)
COLUMBIA (45025 "Best Years of Our Lives") 5-8 89
COLUMBIA (46525 "You Don't Bring Me Flowers") 15-25 80
(Half-speed mastered.)
COLUMBIA (47628 "On the Way to the Sky") 15-25 82
(Half-speed mastered.)
DIRECT-to-DISK 10-20
FROG KING (1 "Early Classics") 40-60 78
(Includes music and lyrics songbook. Columbia Record Club issue.)
HARMONY (30023 "Chartbusters") 20-30 70
(Various artists LP, containing the 1963 Columbia tracks, and the otherwise unavailable *I've Never Been the Same.*)
MCA 6-15 72-81
MFSL (2-024 "Hot August Night") 40-60 79
MFSL (071 "Jazz Singer") 30-40 82
UNI (11 Neil Diamond D.J. Sampler") 35-50 71
(Promotional souvenir issue only.)
UNI (1913 "Open-End Interview with Neil Diamond") 35-50 72
(Promotional issue only.)
UNI (73030 "Velvet Gloves and Spit") 25-35 68
(Does not contain *Shilo*)
UNI (73030 "Velvet Gloves and Spit") 15-25 70
(With *Shilo*.)
UNI (73047 "Brother Love's Traveling Salvation Show") 25-35 69
UNI (73047 "Sweet Caroline – Brother Love's Traveling Salvation Show") 15-25 69
UNI (73071 "Touching You, Touching Me") 15-25 69
UNI (73084 "Gold") 15-25 70
UNI (73092 "Tap Root Manuscript") 15-25 70
(Some 70000 series LPs were reissued in the 90000 series, with the only change being the first digit.)
UNI (93106 "Stones") 15-25 71
UNI (93136 "Moods") 15-25 72
UNI (93501 "Tap Root Manuscript") 15-25 70
(Capitol Record Club issue.)
Also see NEIL & JACK
Also see STREISAND, Barbra, & Neil Diamond
Also see TEN BROKEN HEARTS

DIAMOND, Neil / Diana Ross & Supremes

LPs: 10/12-inch

MCA (734727 "It's Happening") 30-40 72
(One side of LP devoted to each artist.)
Also see DIAMOND, Neil
Also see SUPREMES

DIAMOND REO — P&R '75

Singles: 7-inch

BIG TREE 3-5 75
BUDDAH 3-5 77

LPs: 10/12-inch

BIG TREE 8-10 75
KAMA SUTRA 8-10 76
PICCADILLY 5-10 79
Members: Frank Czuri; Bob McKeag.
Also see SILENCERS

DIAMOND RIO — C&W/LP '91

Singles: 7-inch

ARISTA 3-4 91

LPs: 10/12-inch

ARISTA 5-8 91
Members: Marty Roe; Dan Truman; Brian Prout; Jim Olander; Dana Williams; Gene Johnson.

DIAMONDS — P&R/R&B '56

Singles: 78 rpm

CORAL 5-10 55-56
MERCURY (Except 71060) 5-15 56-57
MERCURY (71060 "Little Darlin'") 25-50 57

Singles: 7-inch

CHURCHILL 3-4 87
CORAL 10-15 55-56
MERCURY (Maroon label) 15-25 56
MERCURY (Black label) 10-15 56-62

Picture Sleeves

MERCURY (71291 "High Sign") 10-20 58

EPs: 7-inch

BRUNSWICK 15-20 57
MERCURY 10-20 56-61

LPs: 10/12-inch

MERCURY 20-40 57-60
WING 15-25 59
Members: David Somerville; Phil Leavitt; Bill Reed; Ted Kowalski; Bob Duncan.
Also see DEL-VIKINGS / Diamonds / Big Bopper / Gaylords
Also see VEE, Bobby / Diamonds / Drifters

DIAMONDS / Georgia Gibbs / Sarah Vaughan / Florian Zabach

EPs: 7-inch

MERCURY (4026 "Tops in Pops") 15-20 50s
Also see GIBBS, Georgia
Also see VAUGHAN, Sarah
Also see ZABACH, Florian

DIAMONDS & PETE RUGOLO

LPs: 10/12-inch

MERCURY (60076 "The Diamonds Meet Pete Rugolo") 45-55 59
Also see DIAMONDS

DIANE RAY: see RAY, Diane

DIBANGO, Manu — P&R/R&B/LP '73

Singles: 7-inch

ATLANTIC 3-5 73

LPs: 10/12-inch

ATLANTIC 8-10 73

DICK & DEEDEE — P&R '61

Singles: 7-inch

DOT 4-8 68-69
LAMA (7778 "The Mountain's High") 15-25 61
LAMA (7780 "Goodbye to Love") 15-25 61
LAMA (7783 "Tell Me") 15-25 61
LIBERTY 5-10 61-62
U.A. 3-4
W.B. 4-8 62-69

Picture Sleeves

W.B. 12-25 63-64

LPs: 10/12-inch

LIBERTY (3236 "Tell Me"/"The Mountain's High") 40-50 62
(Monaural.)
LIBERTY (7236 "Tell Me"/"The Mountain's High") 40-50 62
W.B. (1500 "Young and in Love") 20-30 63
W.B. (1538 "Turn Around") 20-30 64
W.B. (1586 "Thou Shalt Not Steal") 25-35 65
W.B. (1623 "Songs We've Sung on Shindig") 20-30 65
Members: Dick St. John; Dee Dee Sperling.

DICK & DON: see ADDRISI BROTHERS

DICK LEE: see LEE, Dick

DICKENS, Jimmy — C&W '49

(Little Jimmy Dickens; Jimmie Dickens)

Singles: 78 rpm

COLUMBIA 5-10 49-57

Singles: 7-inch

COLUMBIA (10000 series) 3-5 76
COLUMBIA (20000 & 21000 series) 10-20 50-56
COLUMBIA (40000 series) 8-12 56
COLUMBIA (41000 series, except 41173) 8-12 57-60
COLUMBIA (41173 "I Got a Hole in My Pocket") 30-45 57
COLUMBIA (42000 thru 44000 series) 4-8 60-67
DECCA 3-6 67-69
LITTLE GEM 3-5 75
PARTRIDGE 3-4 80
STARDAY 3-5 73
U.A. 3-5 70-72

EPs: 7-inch

COLUMBIA (Except 2800 series) 15-20 52-57
COLUMBIA (2800 series) 10-15 57-58

LPs: 10/12-inch

COLUMBIA (1047 "Raisin' the Dickens") 40-50 57
COLUMBIA (1500 thru 2500 series) 10-20 60-66
(Monaural.)
COLUMBIA (8300 thru 9600 series, except 9025) 15-25 60-68
(Stereo.)
COLUMBIA (9025 "The Old Country Church") 50-100 54
(10-inch LP.)
COLUMBIA (10000 & 11000 series) 6-10 70-73
COLUMBIA (38000 series) 5-10 84
DECCA 10-15 68-69
GUSTO 5-10
HARMONY (7000 series) 15-25 64-65
HARMONY (11000 series) 8-12 67
QCA 5-10 75

DICKY DOO & DONT'S — P&R/R&B '58

Singles: 7-inch

ASCOT 4-8 65
CASINO 3-5
COLLECTABLES 3-4 80s
DANNA 4-8 67
ITZY 4-8
SWAN 8-12 58-59
U.A. 8-10 60-61

LPs: 10/12-inch

DANNA (1566 "Live at Eagle Rock") 40-60 60s
U.A. (3094 "The Madison and Other Dances") 25-30 60
(Monaural.)
U.A. (3097 "Teen Scene") 25-30 60
U.A. (6094 "The Madison and Other Dances") 30-40 60
(Stereo.)
U.A. (6097 "Teen Scene") 30-40 60
(Stereo.)

Members: Gerry Granahan; Harvey Davis; Jerry Grant; Ray Gangi; Joey Paige.
Also see GRANAHAN, Gerry

DICKIE LEE: see LEE, Dickie

DICKINSON, Bruce LP '90
LPs: 10/12-inch
COLUMBIA............5-8 90

DICTATORS LP '77
Singles: 7-inch
ASYLUM............3-4 77
LPs: 10/12-inch
ASYLUM............8-12 77-78
EPIC............10-12 75

DIDDLEY, Bo R&B '55
Singles: 78 rpm
CHECKER............25-75 55-57
Singles: 7-inch
ABC............3-5 74
CHECKER (814 thru 850)............20-50 55-56
CHECKER (860 thru 896)............15-30 57-58
CHECKER (907 "Bo Meets the Monster")............20-40 58
CHECKER (914 thru 997)............10-20 59-62
CHECKER (1019 thru 1200)............5-10 62-69
CHESS............3-5 71-72
GOLDEN GOODIES............4-6
RCA............3-5 76
EPs: 7-inch
CHESS (5125 "Bo Diddley")............40-60 58
(With cardboard cover.)
CHESS (5125 "Bo Diddley")............30-40 58
(With paper cover.)
LPs: 10/12-inch
ACCORD............5-10 82
CHECKER (1436 "Go Bo Diddley")............75-100 57
CHECKER (2974 "Have Guitar Will Travel")............50-75 59
CHECKER (2976 "Bo Diddley in the Spotlight")............50-75 60
CHECKER (2977 "Bo Diddley Is a Gunslinger")............65-75 61
CHECKER (2980 "Bo Diddley in a Lover")............40-60 61
CHECKER (2982 "Bo Diddley's a Twister")............40-50 62
CHECKER (2984 "Bo Diddley")............35-45 62
CHECKER (2985 "Bo Diddley and Company")............40-60 63
CHECKER (2987 "Surfin' with Bo Diddley")............35-45 63
(Most of the tracks on this LP are by the Megatons.)
CHECKER (2988 "Bo Diddley's Beach Party")............35-45 63
CHECKER (2989 "Bo Diddley's 16 All-Time Greatest Hits")............25-35 63
CHECKER (2992 "Hey Good Lookin'")............25-35 64
CHECKER (2996 "500% More Man")............25-35 64
CHECKER (3001 "The Originator")............25-35 66
CHECKER (3006 "Go Bo Diddley")............25-35 67
CHECKER (3007 "Boss Man")............40-60 67
CHECKER (3013 "The Black Gladiator")............25-35 69
CHESS (1431 "Bo Diddley")............75-100 58
CHESS (8000 series)............5-10 83
CHESS (60000 series)............15-25 74
MCA/CHESS............5-8 88
RCA (1229 "20th Anniversary of Rock 'N Roll")............10-20 76
(With numerous guest stars.)
Members: Jody Williams; Cliff James; Frank Kirkland; Jerome Green. Session: Willie Dixon; Otis Spann; Moonglows.
Also see BELMONTS, Freddy Cannon & Bo Diddley
Also see DIXON, Willie
Also see MOONGLOWS
Also see SPANN, Otis

DIDDLEY, Bo, & Chuck Berry
Singles: 7-inch
CHECKER (13370 "Bo's Beat")............4-8 64
LPs: 10/12-inch
CHECKER (2991 "Two Great Guitars")............20-25 64
Also see BERRY, Chuck

DIDDLEY, Bo, Howlin' Wolf & Muddy Waters
LPs: 10/12-inch
CHECKER (3010 "Super Super Blues Band")............15-20 68
Also see DIDDLEY, Bo
Also see HOWLIN' WOLF
Also see WATERS, Muddy

DIESEL P&R/LP '81
Singles: 7-inch
REGENCY............3-4 81
LPs: 10/12-inch
REGENCY............8-10 81

DIETRICH, Marlene P&R '52
Singles: 78 rpm
COLUMBIA............4-8 55
Singles: 7-inch
COLUMBIA............5-10 55
LPs: 10/12-inch
COLUMBIA (105 "Marlena Dietrich Overseas")............40-60 52
(10-inch LP.)
COLUMBIA (316 "Dietrich in Rio")............25-35 59
COLUMBIA (2615 "Marlena Dietrich Overseas")............30-50 56
(10-inch LP.)
COLUMBIA (4975 "At the Cafe de Paris")............30-50 55
DECCA (5100 "Souvenir Album")............40-60 49
(10-inch LP.)
DECCA (7021 "Curtain Call")............30-40 51
DECCA (8465 "Marlene Dietrich")............25-35 57
MCA (1501 "Her Complete Recordings")............5-10 70s
VOX (3040 "Dietrich Sings")............50-75
Also see CLOONEY, Rosemary, & Marlene Dietrich

DIFFORD & TILBROOK LP '84
Singles: 7-inch
A&M............3-4 84
LPs: 10/12-inch
A&M............5-10 84
Members: Chris Difford; Glenn Tilbrook.
Also see SQUEEZE

DIFOSCO R&B '76
(Difosco Erwin)
Singles: 7-inch
EARTHQUAKE............3-5 71
ROXBURY............3-5 76
20TH FOX............3-5 78
Also see IRWIN, Big D.

DIGITAL UNDERGROUND P&R/LP '90
LPs: 10/12-inch
TOMMY BOY............5-8 90-91

DILLARD, Varetta R&B '52
(With the Roamers; with Four Students)
Singles: 78 rpm
GROOVE............10-20 55-56
RCA............10-15 57
SAVOY............10-15 53-55
Singles: 7-inch
CUB............4-8 60-61
GROOVE (0139 "Darling, Listen to the Words of This Song")............20-30 56
GROOVE (0152 thru 0177)............12-25 56-57
RCA............10-15 57
SAVOY............10-20 53-55
TRIUMPH............8-12 59
Also see COOKIES

DILLARD & CLARK
LPs: 10/12-inch
A&M............10-15 68-69
Members: Doug Dillard; Gene Clark.
Also see CLARK, Gene
Also see DILLARDS

DILLARDS P&R '71
Singles: 7-inch
ANTHEM............3-5 71-72
CAPITOL............4-6 65
ELEKTRA............4-8 63-69
POPPY............3-5 74
U.A. 3-5 75
WHITE WHALE............3-5 70
LPs: 10/12-inch
ANTHEM............6-10 72
ELEKTRA (200 series)............20-30 63-65
(Gold label.)
ELEKTRA (7-200 series)............20-30 63-65
(Gold label.)
ELEKTRA (7-200 series)............10-15
(Brown label.)
ELEKTRA (74000 series)............8-12 68
FLYING FISH............5-10 77-81
POPPY............8-12 73
20TH FOX............8-12 73
Members: Doug Dillard; Rodney Dillard; Dean Webb; Mitch Jayne; Joe Osborn.
Also see DILLARD & CLARK
Also see NELSON, Rick

DILLARDS & JOHN HARTFORD
LPs: 10/12-inch
FLYING FISH............5-10 77-80s
Also see DILLARDS
Also see HARTFORD, John

DILLMAN BAND LP '78
(Daisy Dillman Band)
Singles: 7-inch
RCA............3-4 81
U.A. 3-5 77-78
LPs: 10/12-inch
RCA............5-10 81
U.A. 5-10 78
Members: Steve Seamans; Steve Solmonson; Tom Eckhoff.

DI MEOLA, Al LP '76
(Al Di Meola Project)
Singles: 12-inch
COLUMBIA............4-6 84
Singles: 7-inch
COLUMBIA............3-4 76-84
LPs: 10/12-inch
COLUMBIA............5-10 76-83
EMI............5-10 88
Also see RETURN to FOREVER

DING DONGS
(Bobby Darin)
Singles: 7-inch
BRUNSWICK (55073 "Early in the Morning")............100-150 58
(This same track was reissued as by "The Rinky Dinks" and later by "Bobby Darin & the Rinky Dinks.")
Also see DARIN, Bobby
Also see RINKY DINKS

DINNING, Mark P&R '59
Singles: 78 rpm
MGM............10-20 57
Singles: 7-inch
CAMEO............4-8 64
HICKORY............4-8 65-66
MGM (Except 12775 & 12980)............5-10 57-63
MGM (12775 "Cutie Cutie")............10-15 59
MGM (12980 "Top 40, News, Weather and Sports")............15-20 61
(With mention of Patrice Lumumba in lyrics.)
MGM (12980 "Top 40, News, Weather and Sports")............5-10 61
(With no mention of Patrice Lumumba in lyrics.)
MGM GOLDEN CIRCLE............3-5
U.A. 3-5 67-68
Picture Sleeves
MGM............10-15 60
LPs: 10/12-inch
MGM (E-3828 "Teen Angel")............40-60 60
(Monaural.)

MGM (SE-3828 "Teen Angel") 50-75 60
(Stereo.)
MGM (E-3855 "Wanderin' ") 40-60 60
(Monaural.)
MGM (SE-3855 "Wanderin' ") 50-75 60
(Stereo.)

DINO — P&R '88

Singles: 7-inch

4TH & BROADWAY 3-4 88-89
ISLAND 3-4 90

Picture Sleeves

4TH & BROADWAY 3-4 89

LPs: 10/12-inch

4TH & BROADWAY 5-8 89
ISLAND 5-8 90

DINO, Kenny — P&R '61

Singles: 12-inch

KDK PRODUCTIONS ("Love Songs for Seka") 15-25 80
(Picture disc. Has photo of adult film star, Seka.)

Singles: 7-inch

COLUMBIA (43062 "Betty Jean") 5-10 64
DOT 4-8 61
MUSICOR 5-10 61-62
RADNOR 4-6 60s
SMASH 4-8 63-64

DINO, Paul — P&R '61

Singles: 7-inch

ENTRE 4-8 63
PROMO 5-10 60-61

DINO, DESI & BILLY — P&R/LP '65

Singles: 7-inch

COLUMBIA 3-6 69
UNI 3-6 69
REPRISE (Except 0965) 4-8 64-69
REPRISE (0965 "Lady Love") 10-15 70

Picture Sleeves

REPRISE 5-10 65-68

LPs: 10/12-inch

REPRISE 15-25 65-66
UNI 12-20 69
Members: Dino Martin; Desi Arnaz Jr; Billy Hinsche.

DIO: see DIO, Ronnie

DIO, Ronnie — LP '83

(With the Redcaps; with Prophets; Dio)

Singles: 7-inch

ATLANTIC (2145 "Love Pains") 20-40 62
JOVE 15-25 63
KAPP 5-10 65
LAWN (218 "Gonna Make It Alone") 15-25 63
PARKWAY 4-8 67
SENCA 25-50 61
SWAN (4165 "Mr. Misery") 10-20 63
W.B. 3-4 83-86

LPs: 10/12-inch

JOVE ("Dio At Domino's") 50-100 63
W.B. 5-10 83-87
Members: Ronnie James Dio; Vinny Appice; Jimmy Bain; Vivian Campbell; Claude Schell; Craig Goldie;Rowan Robertson; Jen Johansson; Simon Wright; Terry Cook.
Also see AC/DC
Also see BLACKMORE'S RAINBOW
Also see HEAR 'N AID
Also see MALMSTEEN, Yngwie J.

DION — P&R '60

(Dion DiMucci)

Singles: 7-inch

ARISTA 3-4 89
BIG TREE/SPECTOR 3-5 76
COLUMBIA (3-42662 "Ruby Baby") .. 25-35 62
(Compact 33 single.)
COLUMBIA (4-42662 "Ruby Baby") 5-10 62
COLUMBIA (42776 "This Little Girl") 5-10 63
COLUMBIA (42810 "Be Careful of Stones You Throw") 5-10 63
(Black vinyl.)
COLUMBIA (42810 "Be Careful of Stones You Throw") 25-50 63
(Colored vinyl. Promotional issue only.)
COLUMBIA (42852 "Donna the Prima Donna") 5-10 63
(Black vinyl.)
COLUMBIA (42852 "Donna the Prima Donna") 25-50 63
(Colored vinyl. Promotional issue only.)
COLUMBIA (42917 thru 44719) 5-10 63-68
DAY SPRING (642 "Hearts Made of Stone") 3-5 81
LAURIE (100 series) 3-5
LAURIE (3000 & 3100 series) 8-15 60-63
LAURIE (3400 series) 5-10 68-69
LIFESONG 3-5 78-79
MYRRH 3-5 85
SPECTOR 3-5 75
W.B. (Except 814) 3-6 69-79
W.B. (814 "The Wanderer") 5-10 79
(Promotional issue only.)
W.B./SPECTOR 3-5 75

Picture Sleeves

ARISTA 3-4 89
COLUMBIA (Except 42662) 10-20 64-66
COLUMBIA (42662 "Ruby Baby") 30-50 62
(Promotional sleeve for *Ruby Baby,* but does not show title or selection number. Simply reads, "Dion Is Now on Columbia Records.")
COLUMBIA (42662 "Ruby Baby") 10-15 62
(Commercially issued sleeve.)
LAURIE 10-20 60-62

LPs: 10/12-inch

ARISTA 6-12 77-89
COLLECTABLES 6-8 83-87
COLUMBIA 15-25 63-73
DAY SPRING 5-10 80-86
LAURIE (2004 "Alone with Dion") 20-30 61
LAURIE (2009 "Runaround Sue") 20-30 61
(Black vinyl.)
LAURIE (2009 "Runaround Sue") ... 75-100 61
(Colored vinyl.)
LAURIE (2012 "Lovers Who Wander") 20-30 62
LAURIE (2015 "Love Came to Me") 20-30 63
LAURIE (2017 "Dion Sings to Sandy and All Other Girls") 20-30 63
LAURIE (2019 "15 Million Sellers") ... 20-30 63
LAURIE (2022 "More of Dion's Greatest Hits") 20-30 63
LAURIE (2047 "Dion") 15-20 68
LAURIE (4000 series) 8-15 70s
LIFESONG 5-10 78
PAIR 10-12 86
REALM 5-10
W.B. 10-15 69-76
Also see ADAMS, Bryan
Also see DEE, Joey, & Starliters / Dion
Also see EDMUNDS, Dave
Also see LANG, K.D.
Also see REED, Lou
Also see SIMON, Paul
Also see SMYTH, Patty

DION / Glen Stuart Chorus

LPs: 10/12-inch

ABEL 8-10 60s

DION & BELMONTS

(Featuring Dion DiMucci)

P&R/R&B '58

Singles: 7-inch

ABC (10868 "My Girl the Month of May") 5-10 66
ABC (10896 "For Bobbie") 5-10 67
COLLECTABLES 3-4 80s
LAURIE (3013 "I Wonder Why") 25-50 58
(Gary label.)
LAURIE (3013 "I Wonder Why") 15-25 58
(Blue label.)
LAURIE (3013 "I Wonder Why") 10-15 59
(Red and white label.)
LAURIE (3015 "No One Knows") 20-30 58
(Blue label.)
LAURIE (3015 "No One Knows") 10-15 58
(Red and white label.)
LAURIE (3021 "Don't Pity Me") 15-25 58
LAURIE (3027 "A Teenager in Love") 10-20 59
(Monaural.)
LAURIE (S-3027 "A Teenager in Love") 25-50 59
(Stereo.)
LAURIE (3035 "Every Little Thing I Do") 10-20 59
LAURIE (3044 "Where Or When") 10-20 59
LAURIE (3052 "Wonderful Girl") 10-20 60
LAURIE (3059 "In the Still of the Night") 10-20 60
LAURIE DOUBLE GOLD 3-5 78
MOHAWK (107 "Tag Along") 30-40 57
REO (8363 "A Teenager in Love") 15-25 59
(Canadian.)
ROCK'N MANIA 3-5

Picture Sleeves

LAURIE (3035 "Every Little Thing I Do") 20-30 59
LAURIE (3044 "Where Or When") 20-30 59
LAURIE (3052 "Wonderful Girl") 20-30 60
LAURIE (3059 "In the Still of the Night") 20-30 60

EPs: 7-inch

LAURIE (301 "Their Hits") 50-100 59
LAURIE (302 "Where Or When") 50-75 59

LPs: 10/12-inch

ABC (599 "Together Again") 15-25 67
ARISTA 8-12 84
COLLECTABLES 5-10 83
GRT 8-10 75
JUKE BOX (95140 "A Teenager in Love") 20-30 70s
(Boxed, four-disc set. Also includes Dion solo tracks.)
LAURIE (1002 "Presenting Dion and the Belmonts") 100-150 59
LAURIE (2002 "Presenting Dion and the Belmonts") 50-100 60
LAURIE (2006 "Wish Upon a Star") .. 30-50 60
LAURIE (2013 "Dion Sings His Greatest Hits - with the Belmonts") 40-60 62
LAURIE (2016 "By Special Request") 30-50 62
LAURIE (4002 "Everything You Always Wanted to Hear") 10-15 76
LAURIE (6000 "60 Greatest") 15-20
(Standard cover.)
LAURIE (6000 "60 Greatest") 20-30
(Boxed edition.)
PICKWICK 8-10 75
RHINO 5-10 87
W.B. 10-15 73
Also see BELMONTS

DION & BELMONTS / Belmonts

LPs: 10/12-inch

MIASOUND (001 "Half & Half") 15-20 81
(One side by Dion & the Belmonts, the other by just the Belmonts.)

DION & TIMBERLANES

(Featuring Dion DiMuci)

Singles: 7-inch

JUBILEE (5294 "Chosen Few") 15-25 57
MOHAWK (105 "Chosen Few") 30-35 57
VIRGO 3-5 73
Also see DION

DION, Celine — LP '91

Singles: 7-inch

EPIC 3-4 91

LPs: 10/12-inch

EPIC 5-8 88

DIONNE & FRIENDS — P&R/R&B '85

Singles: 7-inch

ARISTA 3-4 85

Picture Sleeves

ARISTA 3-4 85
Members: Dionne Warwick; Elton John; Stevie Wonder; Gladys Knight.
Also see JOHN, Elton

Also see KNIGHT, Gladys
Also see WONDER, Stevie

DIONNE & KASHIF P&R/R&B '87

Singles: 7-inch

ARISTA....3-4 87

Members: Dionne Warwick; Kashif.
Also see KASHIF
Also see WARWICK, Dionne

DIPLOMATS P&R/R&B '64

Singles: 7-inch

AROCK (1004 "Here's a Heart")....10-20 64
AROCK (1008 "Help Me")....10-20 64
DYNAMO (Except 122)....5-10 68-69
DYNAMO (122 "I Can Give You Love")....15-20
HOLIDAY (106 "Point of No Return")....10-20 61
MAY (105 "Let's Be in Love")....20-30 61
MINIT....8-12 66
WAND....8-12 65

DIRECT CURRENT R&B '79

Singles: 7-inch

T.E.C....3-5 79

DIRE STRAITS P&R/LP '79

Singles: 12-inch

W.B....4-6 83

Singles: 7-inch

W.B....3-4 79-88

Picture Sleeves

W.B....3-4 79-86

LPs: 10/12-inch

W.B....5-10 78-88

Member: Mark Knopfler.

DIRKSEN, Senator Everett McKinley P&R '66

Singles: 7-inch

CAPITOL....3-6 66

Picture Sleeves

CAPITOL....4-8 66

LPs: 10/12-inch

BELL....5-10 70
CAPITOL....10-15 66-67

DIRT BAND: see NITTY GRITTY DIRT BAND

DIRTY LOOKS LP '88

LPs: 10/12-inch

ATLANTIC....5-8 88-89
STIFF....5-10 80

DISCO FOUR R&B '82

Singles: 12-inch

PROFILE....4-6 83

Singles: 7-inch

PROFILE....3-4 82-83

DISCO 3 R&B '84

Singles: 12-inch

SUTRA....4-6 83

Singles: 7-inch

SUTRA....3-4 84

Members: Darren Robinson; Mark Morales; Damon Wimbley.
Also see FAT BOYS

DISCOTAYS / Guess Who: see GUESS WHO / Discotays

DISCO-TEX & HIS SEX-O-LETTES P&R/R&B '74

Singles: 7-inch

CHELSEA....3-5 74-76

LPs: 10/12-inch

CHELSEA....8-10 75-76
MUSICOR....5-10 79

DIVINE D&D '83

LPs: 10/12-inch

O....5-10 83

DIVINE SOUNDS R&B/D&D '84

Singles: 7-inch

SPECIFIC....3-4 84

DIVING for PEARLS P&R '89

Singles: 7-inch

EPIC....3-4 89

DIVINYLS LP '85

Singles: 12-inch

CHRYSALIS....4-6 85

Singles: 7-inch

CHRYSALIS....3-4 83-86
VIRGIN....3-4 91

Picture Sleeves

CHRYSALIS....3-4 85

LPs: 10/12-inch

CHRYSALIS....5-10 83-86
VIRGIN....5-8 91

Members: Christina Amphlett; Mark McEntee; Rick Grossman.
Also see HOODOO GURUS

DIXIE CUPS P&R/R&B/LP '64

Singles: 7-inch

ABC-PAR....8-12 65-66
ANTILLES....3-4 87
LANA....3-6 60s
RED BIRD (001 "Chapel of Love")....8-12 64
RED BIRD (006 "People Say")....8-12 64
RED BIRD (012 "You Should Have Seen the Way He Looked at Me")....8-12 64
RED BIRD (017 "Little Bell")....10-20 65
TRIP....3-5 70s

Picture Sleeves

ANTILLES....3-5 87

EPs: 7-inch

ABC-PAR....15-25 65

LPs: 10/12-inch

ABC-PAR (ABC-525 "Riding High")..25-30 65
(Monaural.)
ABC-PAR (ABCS-525 "Riding High")....30-40 65
(Stereo.)
BACK-TRAC....8-12
(Colored vinyl.)
RED BIRD (RB-100 "Chapel of Love")....35-45 64
(Monaural.)
RED BIRD (RBS-100 "Chapel of Love")....50-75 64
(Stereo.)
RED BIRD (RB-103 "Iko Iko")....35-45 64
(Monaural.)
RED BIRD (RBS-103 "Iko Iko")....40-60 64
(Stereo.)

Members: Barbara Hawkins; Rosa Hawkins; Joan Johnson.

DIXIE DREGS LP '78
(Dregs)

Singles: 12-inch

CAPRICORN....4-6 79

Singles: 7-inch

ARISTA....3-4 80-82
CAPRICORN....3-4 77-79

LPs: 10/12-inch

ARISTA....5-10 80-82
CAPRICORN....5-10 78-79

Members: Steve Morse; Rog Morganstein; T. Lavitz; Andy West; Alan Sloan.
Also see MORSE, Steve, Band

DIXIE DRIFTER P&R/R&B '65
(Enoch Gregory)

Singles: 7-inch

AMY....4-6 68
IX CHAINS....3-5 74
ROULETTE....4-8 65

DIXIE HUMMINGBIRDS R&B '73

Singles: 78 rpm

OKEH....4-8 53

Singles: 7-inch

ABC....3-5 73-74
OKEH....5-10 53
PEACOCK....3-6 59-74

LPs: 10/12-inch

CONSTELLATION....5-10 64
GOSPEL ROOTS....5-10 80
PEACOCK....5-10 59-78

Members: Ira Tucker; James Walker; James Davis; Willie Bobo; Beechie Thompson; Howard Carroll.
Also see BOBO, Willie
Also see SIMON, Paul

DIXIEAIRES R&B '48
(Dixie-Aires)

Singles: 78 rpm

EXCLUSIVE....15-25 48-49
GOTHAM....15-25 48
HARLEM....25-50 55
LENOX....15-25 49
SITTIN' in WITH....15-25 50

Singles: 7-inch

HARLEM (2326 "Traveling All Alone")....100-150 55

Members: Joe Van Loan; Clyde Reddick; Henry Owens; Conrad Frederick; Arlandus Wilson; Willie Ray; Joe Floyd; John Hines; Bob Kornegay; J.C. Giuyard.
Also see DU DROPPERS

DIXIEBELLES P&R/R&B '63

Singles: 7-inch

MONUMENT....3-5 72
SOUND STAGE 7....4-8 63-64

EPs: 7-inch

SOUND STAGE 7....15-20 63

LPs: 10/12-inch

SOUND STAGE 7....20-30 63
MONUMENT....15-20 65

Also see SMITH, Jerry

DIXON, Don LP '87

LPs: 10/12-inch

ENIGMA....5-10 87

DIXON, Floyd R&B '49

Singles: 78 rpm

ALADDIN....15-35 50-52
CASH....15-25 54
CAT....15-25 54
EBB....10-15 57
MODERN....15-25 49-50
PEACOCK....15-25 50
SPECIALTY....15-25 53-54
SUPREME....15-25 47
SWING TIME....15-25 47

Singles: 7-inch

ALADDIN (3135 "Wine Wine Wine")....75-150 52
ALADDIN (3144 "Red Cherries")....75-100 52
(Black vinyl.)
ALADDIN (3144 "Red Cherries")...150-250 52
(Colored vinyl.)
ALADDIN (3151 "Tired, Broke and Busted")....75-100 52
CASH (1057 "Oh Baby")....25-50 54
CAT (106 "Moonshine")....25-50 54
CAT (114 "Hey Bartender")....20-40 54
CHATTAHOOCHEE....4-8 64
CHECKER....10-20 58
DODGE....8-12 61
EBB....15-20 57
JELLO....10-15 60
KENT....8-12 58
REVA (7 "Late Freight")....8-12 62
SPECIALTY (468 "Hard Living Alone")....25-50 53
(Black vinyl.)
SPECIALTY (468 "Hard Living Alone")....75-125 53
(Colored vinyl.)
SPECIALTY (477 "Hole in the Wall")....25-50 53
(Black vinyl.)
SPECIALTY (477 "Hole in the Wall")....75-125 53
(Colored vinyl.)
SPECIALTY (486 "Ooh-Eee Ooh-Eee")....25-50 54
(Black vinyl.)
SPECIALTY (486 "Ooh-Eee Ooh-Eee")....75-125 54
(Colored vinyl.)

SWINGIN' 8-10 60

LPs: 10/12-inch

INCULCATION 8-10

DIXON, Floyd, & Johnny Moore's Three Blazers

Singles: 78 rpm

ALADDIN 20-30 50

Singles: 7-inch

ALADDIN (3101 "Do I Love You") 40-60 50
ALADDIN (3166 "Broken Hearted Traveller") 40-60 50
ALADDIN (3196 "Married Woman") .. 40-60 50
ALADDIN (3221 "Bad Neighborhood") 40-60 50
ALADDIN (3230 "You Need Me Now") 40-60 50

Also see MOORE, Johnny

DIXON, Willie R&B '55
(With the Big Wheels)

Singles: 78 rpm

CHECKER 15-25 55-56

Singles: 7-inch

CHECKER (822 "Walkin the Blues"). 25-40 55
CHECKER (828 "Crazy for My Baby") 25-40 55
CHECKER (851 "Twenty-Nine Ways") 25-40 56
CHECKER (1100 series) 5-10 67
CHY-TOWNS 4-8 65
CONDUC 4-8 65
FEDERAL 5-10 64
JERMA 4-8 65
TODDLIN' TOWN 4-8 67

LPs: 10/12-inch

BLUE HORIZON 10-12 70
COLUMBIA 10-15 70
OVATION 8-10 74-76
ROOTS N' BLUES 5-8 90
SPIVEY 8-10
YAMBO 8-10

Also see BOYD, Eddie
Also see DIDDLEY, Bo
Also see REED, Jimmy
Also see TAYLOR, Koko
Also see WELLS, Junior
Also see WILLIAMSON, Sonny Boy
Also see WITHERSPOON, Jimmy

DIXON, Willie, & Memphis Slim

Singles: 7-inch

PRESTIGE BLUESVILLE 4-8 62

LPs: 10/12-inch

BATTLE 20-40 63
FOLKWAYS 8-12
PRESTIGE BLUESVILLE (1003 "Willie's Blues") 25-35 60
VERVE (3007 "Blues Every Which Way") 25-35 61

Also see BIG THREE TRIO
Also see DIXON, Willie
Also see MEMPHIS SLIM

DOBKINS, Carl, Jr. P&R/R&B '59

Singles: 7-inch

ATCO 4-8 64
CHALET 3-6 69
COLPIX 4-8 65
DECCA 5-10 59-62
FRATERNITY 5-10 58
MCA 3-4 73

Picture Sleeves

DECCA 5-10 59-60

EPs: 7-inch

DECCA (2664 "My Heart Is an Open Book") 50-75 59

LPs: 10/12-inch

DECCA (8938 "Carl Dobkins Jr.") 40-50 59
(Monaural.)
DECCA (7-8938 "Carl Dobkins Jr.") .. 50-65 59
(Stereo.)

Also see LEE, Brenda / Carl Dobkins Jr.

DOC BOX & B. FRESH P&R '90

Singles: 7-inch

MOTOWN 3-4 90

DOC SAUSAGE & HIS MAD LADS R&B '50

Singles: 78 rpm

REGAL 5-10 50

DOCKETT, Jimmy R&B '73

Singles: 7-inch

FLO FEEL 3-5 73
HULL 4-8 64-65

DR. AMERICA R&B '82

Singles: 7-inch

ELEKTRA 3-4 82

DOCTOR & MEDICS P&R/LP '86

Singles: 7-inch

I.R.S. 3-4 86

Picture Sleeves

I.R.S. 3-4 86

LPs: 10/12-inch

I.R.S. 5-8 86

DR. BUZZARD'S ORIGINAL SAVANNAH BAND P&R/R&B/LP '76

Singles: 7-inch

RCA 3-5 76-80

LPs: 10/12-inch

ELEKTRA 5-10 79
PASSPORT 5-10
RCA 8-10 76-80

Members: August Darnell; Stony Browder Jr.; Cora Daye; Mickey Sezilla; Andy Hernandez.

Also see DAYE, Cory
Also see KID CREOLE & COCONUTS

DOCTOR FEELGOOD P&R '62
(Doctor Feelgood & Interns)

Singles: 7-inch

COLUMBIA 4-8 65-66
EPIC 3-5 70s
MASTER SOUND 4-8 67
OKEH 5-10 62-63
1-3-4 .... 4-8 68

LPs: 10/12-inch

OKEH (12101 "Doctor Feelgood") 25-35 62
(Monaural.)
OKEH (14101 "Doctor Feelgood") 35-45 62
(Stereo.)
NUMBER ONE 15-20

Also see PIANO RED

DR. HOOK P&R/LP '72
(With the Medicine Show)

Singles: 7-inch

CAPITOL (4000 series) 3-5 75-80
CAPITOL (8220 "The Stimu") 4-8 75
(Promotional issue only.)
CASABLANCA 3-4 80-82
COLUMBIA 3-5 71-74

Picture Sleeves

CAPITOL (4000 series) 3-5 75-80
CAPITOL (8220 "The Stimu") 8-10 75
(Promotional issue only.)
CASABLANCA 3-4 82
COLUMBIA 3-5 71-72

LPs: 10/12-inch

CAPITOL 8-10 75-81
CASABLANCA 5-10 80-82
COLUMBIA (Except 34147) 15-20 72-74
COLUMBIA (34147 "Best of Dr. Hook") 5-10 76

Also see BEACH BOYS
Also see SAWYER, Ray

DOCTOR J.R. KOOL & OTHER ROXANNES LP '85

Singles: 12-inch

COMPLEAT 4-6 85

Singles: 7-inch

COMPLEAT 3-4 85

LPs: 10/12-inch

COMPLEAT 5-10 85

DR. JECKYLL & MR. HYDE R&B '82

Singles: 12-inch

PROFILE 4-6 83-86

Singles: 7-inch

PROFILE 3-4 83-86

LPs: 10/12-inch

PROFILE 5-10 84-86

DR. JOHN LP '71
(Mac Rebennack)

Singles: 7-inch

ATCO 3-5 72-74
COLUMBIA 3-4 82
HORIZON 3-4 79
RCA 3-4 78
STREETWISE 3-4 84
W.B. 3-4 81

EPs: 7-inch

ATCO (4521 "Dr. John") 5-10 72
(Promotional issue only.)

LPs: 10/12-inch

A&M 8-10 79
ACCORD 5-10 81
ACE 10-12
ALLIGATOR 5-8 80s
ATCO (Except 200 & 300 series) 8-12 72-74
ATCO (200 & 300 series) 12-15 68-71
BAROMETER 10-12 74
CLEANCUTS 5-10 82-84
HORIZON 5-10 79
KARATE 8-10 78
SPRINGBOARD 10-12 72
TRIP 8-10 75-76
U.A. 8-10 75
W.B. 5-10 89

Also see BLOOMFIELD, Mike, Dr. John & John Paul Hammond
Also see GUY, Buddy, Dr. John & Eric Clapton / Buddy Guy & J. Geils Band
Also see REBENNACK, Mac
Also see SAHM, Doug
Also see SIMPSONS

DR. JOHN & CHRIS BARBER'S JAZZ & BLUES BAND

LPs: 10/12-inch

GREAT SOUTHERN 8-10 90

Also see BARBER, Chris

DR. JOHN & LIBBY TITUS

Singles: 7-inch

W.B. 3-4 81

Also see DR. JOHN

DR. WEST'S MEDICINE SHOW & JUNK BAND P&R '66

Singles: 7-inch

GO GO (100 "The Eggplant That Ate Chicago") 5-10 66
GO GO (102 "Playboys and Bums") 5-10 67
GO GO (104 "You Can Fly") 5-10 67
GREGAR 4-8 68
ROWE/AMI 4-8 66
("Play Me" Sales Stimulator promotional issue.)

Picture Sleeves

GO GO (102 "Playboys and Bums") 10-20 67

LPs: 10/12-inch

GO GO (002 "The Eggplant That Ate Chicago") 20-30 67
GREGAR 15-20 60s

Also see GREENBAUM, Norman

DODDS, Johnny
(Gene Autry)

Singles: 78 rpm

OKEH (45317 "Railroad Boomer") 25-75 30s
OKEH (45417 "Frankie & Johnny") ... 25-75 30s
OKEH (45462 "No One to Call Me Darling") 25-75 30s
OKEH (45472 "Slu Foot Lou") 25-75 30s
OKEH (45560 "Cowboy Yodel") 25-75 30s

Also see AUTRY, Gene

DODDS, Nella P&R/R&B '64

Singles: 7-inch

WAND (167 "Come See About Me") ... 8-12 64
WAND (171 thru 187) 5-10 64
WAND (1111 "Gee Whiz") 10-15 65
WAND (1136 "Honey Boy") 50-75 65

DOE, John
LP '90

LPs: 10/12-inch

DGC.......5-8 90

Also see X

DOGGETT, Bill
P&R/R&B '56

Singles: 78 rpm

KING.......5-10 53-57

Singles: 7-inch

ABC-PAR.......3-6 64
CHUMLEY.......3-4 74
COLUMBIA.......4-8 62-63
GUSTO.......3-4 80s
KING (4000 series).......10-20 53-56
(Black vinyl.)
KING (4000 series).......20-40 50s
(Colored vinyl. We're not yet sure how many different releases came on colored plastic.)
KING (5000 series).......6-15 56-65
KING (6000 series).......3-8 66-71
ROULETTE.......3-6 67
SUE.......4-6 64
W.B.......4-8 60-61

Picture Sleeves

COLUMBIA.......5-10 62

EPs: 7-inch 33/45

KING.......8-15 53-59

LPs: 10/12-inch

ABC-PAR.......10-15 65
COLUMBIA.......10-20 62-63
HARMONY.......10-15 67
KING (82 thru 118).......20-40 52-55
(10-inch LPs.)
KING (500 thru 900 series).......12-25 56-66
ROULETTE.......10-15 66
STARDAY.......5-10
W.B.......12-20 61-62

Session: Howard Tate; Bill Butler; Clifford Scott.

Also see BOSTIC, Earl, & Bill Doggett
Also see BROWN, Wini
Also see FITZGERALD, Ella, & Bill Doggett
Also see HUMES, Helen
Also see JACQUET, Illinois
Also see TATE, Howard

DOKKEN
LP '83

(Don Dokken)

Singles: 7-inch

ELEKTRA.......3-4 83-88

Picture Sleeves

ELEKTRA.......3-4 87

LPs: 10/12-inch

ELEKTRA.......5-10 83-88
GEFFEN.......5-8 90

Also see HEAR 'N AID

DOLBY, Thomas
P&R/R&B/D&D/LP '83

Singles: 12-inch

CAPITOL.......4-6 83-84

Singles: 7-inch

CAPITOL.......3-4 83-84
HARVEST.......3-4 82

Picture Sleeves

CAPITOL.......3-4 83-84

LPs: 10/12-inch

CAPITOL.......5-10 83-84
EMI.......5-8 88
HARVEST.......5-10 83

Also see DOLBY'S CUBE

DOLBY'S CUBE

(Thomas Dolby)

Singles: 12-inch

CAPITOL.......4-6 84

Singles: 7-inch

CAPITOL.......3-4 84

Also see DOLBY, Thomas

DOLCE, Joe
P&R/LP '81

Singles: 7-inch

MCA.......3-5 81
METROMEDIA.......3-4 81

LPs: 10/12-inch

MCA.......5-8 81

DOLENZ, Micky
P&R '67

(Mickey Dolenz)

Singles: 7-inch

CHALLENGE (59353 "Don't Do It").. 10-20 66
CHALLENGE (59372 "Huff Puff")..... 10-20 67
MGM.......8-12 71-72
ROMAR.......8-10 73-74

Picture Sleeves

CHALLENGE (59353 "Don't Do It").. 10-20 66
CHALLENGE (59372 "Huff Puff")..... 20-30 67

LPs: 10/12-inch

CHRYSALIS.......8-10 79

Also see MONKEES
Also see NILSSON

DOLENZ, Micky, Davy Jones & Peter Tork

Singles: 7-inch

CHRISTMAS RECORDS.......8-12 76
(Fan club, mail-order issue. Issued with special poster.)

Members: Micky Dolenz; David Jones; Peter Tork.

Also see MONKEES

DOLENZ, JONES, BOYCE & HART

Singles: 7-inch

CAPITOL (4180 "I Remember the Feeling").......10-15 75
CAPITOL (4271 "I Love You").......10-15 75

LPs: 10/12-inch

CAPITOL.......10-15 76

Members: Micky Dolenz; David Jones; Tommy Boyce; Bobby Hart.

Also see BOYCE, Tommy, & Bobby Hart
Also see DOLENZ, Micky
Also see JONES, Davy, & Micky Dolenz

DOLLAR
P&R '79

Singles: 7-inch

CARRERE.......3-5 79

DOLPHINS
P&R '64

Singles: 7-inch

EMPRESS (102 "Rainbow's End") ... 10-20 61
FRATERNITY.......5-10 64-65
GEMINI.......5-10 62
LAURIE.......5-10 63
SHAD (5020 "Tell-Tale Kisses")....... 20-30 60

DOMINGO, Placido
P&R/LP '81

Singles: 7-inch

CBS.......3-4 81-84

LPs: 10/12-inch

CBS.......5-10 81-84
EMI.......5-8 91
RCA.......5-10 82

Also see DENVER, John, & Placido Domingo

DOMINO, Fats
R&B '50

Singles: 78 rpm

IMPERIAL (5058 thru 5477).......30-60 50-57
IMPERIAL (5492 "Yes My Darling").. 50-75 58
IMPERIAL (5515 "Sick & Tired")....... 50-75 58
IMPERIAL (5526 "Little Mary")....... 50-75 58

Singles: 7-inch

ABC.......3-5 73
ABC-PAR (455 "I Got a Right to Cry").......10-20 63
(Stereo Compact 33.)
ABC-PAR (10000 series).......5-10 63-64
BROADMOOR.......4-8 67
IMPERIAL (5099 "Korea Blues")... 400-500 52
IMPERIAL (5167 "You Know I Miss You").......150-200 52
IMPERIAL (5180 "Goin' Home") ... 100-150 52
IMPERIAL (5197 "Poor Poor Me") .. 50-100 52
IMPERIAL (5209 "How Long").......50-100 52
(Black vinyl.)
IMPERIAL (5209 "How Long")....... 150-250 52
(Colored vinyl.)
IMPERIAL (5220 "Nobody Loves Me").......50-100 53
(Black vinyl.)
IMPERIAL (5220 "Nobody Loves Me").......150-250 53
(Colored vinyl.)
IMPERIAL (5231 "Going to the River").......50-100 53
(Black vinyl.)
IMPERIAL (5231 "Going to the River").......150-250 53
(Colored vinyl.)
IMPERIAL (5240 "Please Don't Leave Me").......40-80 53
(Black vinyl.)
IMPERIAL (5240 "Please Don't Leave Me").......150-250 53
(Colored vinyl.)
IMPERIAL (5251 "You Said You Love Me").......40-80 53
IMPERIAL (5262 "Something's Wrong").......25-50 53
(Black vinyl.)
IMPERIAL (5262 "Something's Wrong").......100-200 53
(Colored vinyl.)
IMPERIAL (5272 "Little School Girl").......20-50 54
IMPERIAL (5283 "Baby, Please")..... 20-50 54
IMPERIAL (5301 "You Can Pack Your Suitcase").......20-50 54
IMPERIAL (5313 "Love Me").......20-50 54
IMPERIAL (5323 "I Know").......20-50 54
IMPERIAL (5340 "Don't You Know").......20-40 55
IMPERIAL (5348 thru 5396).......15-25 55-56
IMPERIAL (5407 "Blueberry Hill")...... 10-20 56
(Black vinyl.)
IMPERIAL (5407 "Blueberry Hill").......100-200 56
(Colored vinyl.)
IMPERIAL (5417 thru 5477).......10-20 56-57
IMPERIAL (5492 "Yes, My Darling").......10-15 58
(Black vinyl.)
IMPERIAL (5492 "Yes, My Darling").......100-150 58
(Colored vinyl.)
IMPERIAL (5515 thru 5980).......8-15 58-63
IMPERIAL (66000 series).......4-6 64
IMPERIAL GOLDEN SERIES.......3-5 70s
MERCURY.......5-10 65
REPRISE.......4-6 68-70
TOOT TOOT (001 "My Toot Toot").......3-5 85
(With Doug Kershaw.)
U.A.......3-5 74
W.B.......3-5 80

Picture Sleeves

IMPERIAL (5428 "I'm Walkin'").......15-25 57
IMPERIAL (5477 "The Big Beat")...... 15-20 57
IMPERIAL (5606 "I Want to Walk You Home").......10-20 59
IMPERIAL (5629 "Be My Guest")...... 10-20 59
MERCURY (72485 "It's Never Too Late").......20-30 65

EPs: 7-inch

ABC-PAR.......15-25 64-65
IMPERIAL (Except 127).......25-50 56-57
IMPERIAL (127 "Fats Domino—America's Outstanding Piano Stylist").......50-100 53
(Red, script logo label.)
IMPERIAL (127 "Fats Domino—America's Outstanding Piano Stylist").......25-50 56
(Maroon label.)
MERCURY.......15-25 65
(Juke box issues only.)

LPs: 10/12-inch

ABC-PAR.......15-20 63-65
AUDIO FIDELITY.......10-15 84
(Picture disc.)
CANDLELITE.......12-15 76
EVEREST.......8-10 74-77
GRAND AWARD.......10-15 60s
HARLEM HITPARADE.......8-10 75
HARMONY.......10-15 69
IMPERIAL (Except 9004 thru 9040) .. 25-50 58-63
IMPERIAL (9004 "Rock 'n Rollin'").......100-200 56
IMPERIAL (9009 "Fats Domino Rock 'n Rollin'").......100-150 56

IMPERIAL (9028 "This Is Fats Domino")....100-150 57
IMPERIAL (9038 "Here Stands Fats Domino")....75-125 57
IMPERIAL (9040 "This Is Fats")....75-125 57
LIBERTY....5-10 80-81
MERCURY (21039 "Fats Domino '65")....15-20 65
(Monaural.)
MERCURY (61039 "Fats Domino '65")....15-20 65
(Stereo.)
PICKWICK....8-12 70s
REPRISE (6304 "Fats Is Back")....20-30 68
REPRISE (6439 "Fats")....300-400 71
SILVER EAGLE....5-8 86
SUNSET....12-15 66-71
TOMATO....10-20 89
U.A....8-10 71-80
Members (Band): Dave Bartholomew; Ernest McLean; Herbert Hardesty; Clarence Hall; Alvin "Red" Tyler; Joe Harris; Salvador Doucette; Lee Allen.
Also see ALLEN, Lee
Also see BARTHOLOMEW, Dave
Also see PRICE, Lloyd

DOMINATRIX *D&D '84*

Singles: 12-inch

STREETWISE....4-6 84

DOMINOES *R&B/P&R '51*

Singles: 78 rpm

DELUXE (309 "Sixty Minute Man"/ "Chicken Blues")....300-500 51
(Canadian. Note different flip than U.S. issue.)
FEDERAL (12001 "Do Something for Me")....75-125 50
FEDERAL (12010 "Harbor Lights")....200-300 50
(Original 45s of #12010 are not known to exist.)
FEDERAL (12022 "Sixty Minute Man")....100-150 51
FEDERAL (12039 "I Am with You")....50-100 51
FEDERAL (12059 "That's What You're Doing to Me")....50-100 52
FEDERAL (12068 "Have Mercy Baby")....50-100 52
FEDERAL (12072 "Love, Love, Love")....50-100 52

Singles: 7-inch

FEDERAL (12001 "Do Something for Me")....750-1000 50
FEDERAL (12022 "Sixty Minute Man")....400-600 51
FEDERAL (12039 "I Am with You")....500-750 51
FEDERAL (12059 "That's What You're Doing to Me")....500-750 52
FEDERAL (12068 "Have Mercy Baby")....300-400 52
FEDERAL (12072 "Love, Love, Love")....300-400 52
For later Federal singles — as well all EPs and LPs — see the Billy Ward & Dominoes section.
GUSTO....3-5 80s
Members: Billy Ward; Clyde McPhatter; Charlie White; William Lamont; Bill Brown.
Also see GREENWOOD, Lil, & Dominoes
Also see LITTLE ESTHER & DOMINOES
Also see McPHATTER, Clyde
Also see WARD, Billy, & Dominoes

DON & GOODTIMES *P&R/LP '67*

(Don Gallucci)

Singles: 7-inch

BURDETTE (3 "Colors of Life")....10-20 66
DUNHILL....5-10 65
EPIC....5-10 67-68
JERDEN....8-12 66
PICCADILLY....5-10 60s
WAND....5-10 64

Picture Sleeves

EPIC (10199 "Happy & Me")....10-20 67

LPs: 10/12-inch

BURDETTE (300 "Greatest Hits")....40-50 66
EPIC (24311 "So Good")....15-20 67
(Monaural.)
EPIC (26311 "So Good")....15-20 67
(Stereo.)
PANORAMA (104 "Harpo")....30-40
PICCADILLY (3394 "Goodtime Music")....5-10 82
WAND (679 "Where the Action Is")..25-35 67
Members: Don Gallucci; Jeff Hawks; Joe Newman.
Also see KINGSMEN
Also see TOUCH

DON & JUAN *P&R '62*

Singles: 7-inch

BIG TOP (3079 "What's Your Name")....8-12 62
BIG TOP (3106 "Two Fools Are We")....10-15 62
BIG TOP (3121 "Magic Wand")....20-30 62
BIG TOP (3145 "True Love Never Runs Smooth")....10-20 63
ERIC....3-4 70s
MALA (469 "Lonely Man")....8-12 63
MALA (484 "Sincerely")....8-12 63
MALA (509 "Heartbreaking Truth")...15-25 65
TERRIFIC....3-5 70s
TWIRL (2021 "Because I Love You")....15-25 66
Members: Roland Trone: Claude Johnson.

DON, DICK N' JIMMY *P&R '54*

Singles: 78 rpm

CROWN....5-10 54-55
DOT....5-10 54

Singles: 7-inch

CROWN....8-15 54-55
DOT....8-15 54

LPs: 10/12-inch

CROWN (5005 "Spring Fever")....25-35 57
DOT....15-25 59
MODERN (1205 "Spring Fever")....35-50 56
VERVE....15-25 59
Members: Don Sutton; Dick Rock; Jimmy Cook.

DONALDSON, Bo, & Heywoods *P&R '72*

(Heywoods)

Singles: 7-inch

ABC....3-5 73-75
CAPITOL....3-5 76
FAMILY....3-5 72-74
PLAYBOY....3-5 77

Picture Sleeves

ABC....3-5 74

LPs: 10/12-inch

ABC....5-10 74
CAPITOL....5-8 76
FAMILY....8-12 72

DONALDSON, Lou *LP '63*

(Lou Donaldson Quintet)

Singles: 78 rpm

BLUE NOTE....3-8 52-57

Singles: 7-inch

ARGO....4-6 63-65
BLUE NOTE (100 thru 300 series)....3-5 73-74
BLUE NOTE (1500 & 1600 series)....5-10 52-58
BLUE NOTE (1700 thru 1900 series)...4-8 58-72

LPs: 10/12-inch

ARGO....15-25 63-65
BLUE NOTE....8-15 64-80
(Label shows Blue Note Records as a division of either Liberty or United Artists.)
BLUE NOTE (1500 series)....50-75 57-58
(Label gives New York street address for Blue Note Records.)
BLUE NOTE (1500 series)....30-40 58
(Label reads "Blue Note Records Inc. - New York, USA.")
BLUE NOTE (1500 series)....15-20 66
(Label shows Blue Note Records as a division of either Liberty or United Artists.)
BLUE NOTE (4000 & 84000 series)....15-25 58-63
(Label reads "Blue Note Records Inc. - New York, U.S.A.")
BLUE NOTE (5000 series)....50-100 52-54
(10-inch LPs.)
BLUE NOTE (5000 series)....50-100 52-54
(10-inch LPs.)
CADET....8-12 65-71
COTILLION....5-10 76-77
SUNSET....5-10 69-71
TRIP....5-10 79

DONEGAN, Lonnie *P&R '56*

(With His Skiffle Group)

Singles: 78 rpm

LONDON....5-10 56
MERCURY....5-10 56

Singles: 7-inch

ABC....3-5 76
APT....4-8 62
ATLANTIC....5-10 60-61
DOT....5-10 61
FELSTED....5-10 61
HICKORY....4-6 64-65
LONDON....10-15 56
MCA....3-4
MERCURY....10-15 56

LPs: 10/12-inch

ABC-PAR....15-20 63
ATLANTIC....20-30 60
DOT (3159 "Lonnie Donegan")....25-35 59
DOT (3394 "Lonnie Donegan")....20-30 61
MERCURY....25-40 57
U.A....10-12 77

DONNA LYNN: see LYNN, Donna

DONNER, Ral *P&R '61*

(With the Starfires; with Scotty Moore, D.J. Fontana & Jordanaires)

Singles: 7-inch

ABC....3-5 73
CHICAGO FIRE....8-10 74
END (19 "You Don't Know What You've Got")....10-20 63
FONTANA (1502 "Poison Ivy League")....10-20 64
FONTANA (1515 "Good Lovin' ")....10-20 65
GONE (5102 "Girl of My Best Friend")....30-40 60
(Black label.)
GONE (5100 series, except 5108 & 5119)....10-15 61-62
(Multi-color labels.)
GONE (5108 "To Love"/"And Then")....15-25 61
(Shortly after this release, *You Don't Know What You've Got* was issued using the same selection number.)
GONE (5108 "You Don't Know What You've Got")....10-15 61
GONE (5114 "Please Don't Go")....8-12 61
GONE (5119 "School of Heartbreakers")....30-40 61
GONE (5121 "She's Everything"/ "Because We're Young")....10-20 61
GONE (5121 "She's Everything"/"Will You Love Me in Heaven")....15-25 61
(Though credited to "Ral Donner," *Will You Love Me in Heaven* is by a thus far unidentified girl group.)
GONE (5125 "To Love Someone"/"Will You Love Me in Heaven")....10-15 61
(*Will You Love Me in Heaven* is credited to and sung by Ral Donner.)
GONE (5129 "Loveless Life")....10-15 62
GONE (5133 "To Love")....10-15 61
MJ (222 "My Heart Sings")....4-8 70
MID-EAGLE....4-8 68-76
RED BIRD (057 "Love Isn't Like That")....100-150 66
REPRISE (20135 "Christmas Day")..20-30 62
REPRISE (20141 "I Got Burned")....20-30 63
REPRISE (20192 "Run Little Linda").20-30 63
RISING SONS....5-10 68

ROULETTE ... 3-5 71
SCOTTIE (1310 "Tell Me Why") ... 200-300 59
SMASH (34774 "Good Lovin'") ... 25-35 65
(Promotional issue only.)
STARFIRE (100 "Wait a Minute Now") ... 5-10 78
STARFIRE (103 "Christmas Day") ... 5-10 78
STARFIRE (114 "Rip It Up") ... 5-10 79
(Black vinyl.)
STARFIRE (114 "Rip It Up") ... 10-25 79
(Picture disc.)
SUNLIGHT ... 8-10 72
TAU (105 "Lonliness of a Star") ... 35-50 63
(Blue label. First issue. 1,000 made.)
TAU (105 "Lonliness of a Star") ... 20-30 63
(Yellow label. 2,000 made.)
THUNDER (7801 "The Day the Beat Stopped") ... 4-6 78
(Clear vinyl.)

Picture Sleeves

MJ (222 "My Heart Sings") ... 5-10 70
REPRISE (20141 "I Got Burned") ... 50-75 63
STARFIRE ... 5-10 78-79

LPs: 10/12-inch

AUDIO RESEARCH ... 12-15 80
GONE (5012 "Takin' Care of Business") ... 100-200 61
GONE (5033 "Elvis Scrapbook") ... 10-15 61
GYPSY ... 8-12 79
MIDEAGLE (7902 "1935-1977 - Been Away for a While Now") ... 40-60 79
MURRAY HILL ... 5-10 88
STARFIRE (1004 "An Evening with Ral Donner") ... 10-15 82
(Multi-color vinyl.)
STARFIRE (1004 "An Evening with Ral Donner") ... 10-20 82
(Picture disc.)
Session: Scotty Moore; Jordanaires.
Also see PRESLEY, Elvis

DONNER, Ral / Ray Smith / Bobby Dale

LPs: 10/12-inch

CROWN ... 15-20 63
Also see SMITH, Ray

DONNER, Ral / Zantees

Singles: 7-inch

EVA-TONE/GOLDMINE ... 3-4 79
(Soundsheet.)
Also see DONNER, Ral

DONNIE & DREAMERS — P&R '61

Singles: 7-inch

DECCA (31312 "Carole") ... 30-40 61
WHALE (500 "Count Every Star") ... 15-25 61
WHALE (505 "My Memories of You") ... 25-35 61

DONOVAN — P&R/LP '65

(Donovan P. Leitch)

Singles: 12-inch

ALLEGIANCE (1437 "Donovan") ... 5-10 83

Singles: 7-inch

ALLEGIANCE ... 3-4 83
ARISTA ... 3-5 77
EPIC ... 4-8 66-76
(Black vinyl.)
EPIC (10045 "Sunshine Superman") 10-15 66
(Colored vinyl. Promotional issue only.)
EPIC MEMORY LANE ... 3-5
HICKORY ... 8-15 65-68

Picture Sleeves

EPIC ... 5-10 66-71

LPs: 10/12-inch

ALLEGIANCE ... 5-10 83
ARISTA ... 8-10 77
BELL ... 10-12 73
COLUMBIA ... 5-10 73
EPIC (Except 26439) ... 10-20 66-76
EPIC (BXN-26439 "Greatest Hits") ... 15-20 69
(Gatefold cover. Includes booklet.)
EPIC (PE-26439 "Greatest Hits") ... 5-10 77
HICKORY (123 "Catch the Wind") ... 20-40 65
HICKORY (127 "Fairy Tale") ... 20-40 65
HICKORY (135 "The Real Donovan") ... 20-40 66
HICKORY (143 "Like It Is") ... 20-40 68
HICKORY (149 "The Best of Donovan") ... 20-40 69
JANUS ... 10-12 70-71
KORY ... 5-10 77
PYE ... 8-10 76

DONOVAN & JEFF BECK GROUP — P&R '69

Singles: 7-inch

EPIC ... 4-8 69
Also see BECK, Jeff
Also see DONOVAN

DOO, Dickey: see DICKEY DOO & DON'TS

DOOBIE BROTHERS — P&R/LP '72

Singles: 12-inch

W.B. ... 4-8 79

Singles: 7-inch

ASYLUM ... 3-4 80
CAPITOL ... 3-4 89
SESAME STREET ... 3-4 81
W.B. ... 3-6 71-83

Picture Sleeves

CAPITOL ... 3-4 89
SESAME STREET ... 3-4 81
W.B. ... 3-5 79-83

EPs: 7-inch

W.B. ... 10-20 74
(Juke box issue.)

LPs: 10/12-inch

CAPITOL ... 5-8 89-91
MFSL (122 "Takin' It to the Streets") ... 20-30 84
NAUTILUS (5 "Captain and Me") ... 25-35 80
(Half-speed mastered.)
NAUTILUS (18 "Minute By Minute") .. 15-20 81
(Half-speed mastered.)
PICKWICK ... 6-10 80
W.B. ... 6-12 71-83
Members: Tom Johnston; Patrick Simmons; John Hartman; Tiran Porter; Jeff "Skunk" Baxter; Michael McDonald; John McFee; Chet McCracken;
Also see McDONALD, Michael
Also see SIMMONS, Patrick

DOOBIE BROTHERS, JAMES HALL & JAMES TAYLOR

Singles: 7-inch

ASYLUM ... 3-4 80
Also see TAYLOR, James

DOOBIE BROTHERS & NICOLETTE LARSON

Singles: 7-inch

W.B. ... 3-5 79
Also see LARSON, Nicolette

DOOBIE BROTHERS / Kate Taylor & Simon-Taylor Family

Singles: 7-inch

W.B. ... 3-4 80

Picture Sleeves

W.B. ... 3-4 80
Also see DOOBIE BROTHERS
Also see SIMON SISTERS
Also see TAYLOR, James
Also see TAYLOR, Kate
Also see TAYLOR, Livingston

DOOLITTLE BAND — P&R '80

(Dandy & Doolittle Band)

Singles: 7-inch

COLUMBIA ... 3-4 80

DOORS — P&R/LP '67

Singles: 7-inch

ELEKTRA (Except 45000 series) ... 3-4 79-83
ELEKTRA (45000 series) ... 4-8 67-72

Promotional Singles

ELEKTRA (45000 series) ... 8-15 67-72

Picture Sleeves

ELEKTRA (45000 series) ... 10-15 67-69

LPs: 10/12-inch

ELEKTRA (500 series) ... 5-10 78-80
ELEKTRA (4007 "The Doors") ... 20-35 67
(Monaural.)
ELEKTRA (4014 "Strange Days") ... 15-25 67
(Monaural.)
ELEKTRA (5035 "Best of the Doors") ... 15-20 73
ELEKTRA (EKS-6001 "Weird Scenes Inside the Gold Mine") ... 12-15 72
ELEKTRA (8E-6001 "Weird Scenes Inside the Gold Mine") ... 8-12 73
ELEKTRA (9002 "Absolutely Live") ... 15-20 70
(Red label.)
ELEKTRA (60000 series) ... 5-10 83-91
ELEKTRA (60269 "Alive, She Cried") ... 10-15 83
(Promotional issue.)
ELEKTRA (74007 "The Doors") ... 20-25 67
(Gold label.)
ELEKTRA (74014 "Strange Days") ... 15-25 67
(Gold label.)
ELEKTRA (74024 "Waiting for the Sun") ... 15-20 68
(Gold label.)
ELEKTRA (75005 "The Soft Parade") ... 10-20 69
(Red label.)
ELEKTRA (75007 "Morrison Hotel/Hard Rock Cafe") ... 12-15 70
(Red label.)
ELEKTRA (74079 "Doors 13") ... 12-15 70
ELEKTRA (75011 "L.A. Woman") ... 25-35 71
(With die-cut cover.)
ELEKTRA (75011 "L.A. Woman") ... 5-10 Re
(With standard cover.)
ELEKTRA (75017 "Other Voices") ... 8-12 71
ELEKTRA (75038 "Full Circle") ... 8-12 72
MFSL (051 "The Doors") ... 50-70 81
Members: Jim Morrison; Robbie Krieger; Ray Manzarek; John Densmore.
Also see MANZAREK, Ray

DORADOS, El: see EL DORADOS

DO-RAY-ME TRIO — R&B '48

(Do-Re-Mi-Trio Featuring Buddy Hawkins; Do Ray & Me)

Singles: 78 rpm

BRUNSWICK ... 5-15 53
COMMODORE ... 10-20 47-48
CORAL ... 5-15 54
IVORY ... 10-15 49-50
RAINBOW ... 5-15 52
VARIETY ... 5-15 57

Singles: 7-inch

BRUNSWICK ... 15-25 53
CORAL ... 15-25 54
IVORY (001 "Let's Go Down Town") ... 20-30 50
RAINBOW (181 "She Would Not Yield") ... 20-30 52
REET ... 5-10 50s
STEREO CRAFT (112 "Saturday Night Fish Fry") ... 30-50 59
VARIETY ... 8-10 57

LPs: 10/12-inch

STEREO CRAFT (508 "That Wonderfully Musically Do Ray Mi Trio") ... 30-45 59

DORE, Charlie — P&R/LP '80

Singles: 7-inch

CHRYSALIS ... 3-4 81
ISLAND ... 3-4 80-81

LPs: 10/12-inch

ISLAND ... 5-10 80-81

DORMAN, Harold — P&R/R&B '60

Singles: 7-inch

ABC ... 3-5 73
COLLECTABLES ... 3-4
RITA ... 8-12 60
SANTO ... 4-8 62
SUN ... 5-10 61-62
TINCE ... 5-10 60

DORSEY, Gerry

Singles: 7-inch

HICKORY (1337 "Baby, Turn Around") ... 8-12 65

Also see HUMPERDINCK, Engelbert

DORSEY, Jimmy, Orchestra & Chorus P&R '35

(With Bob Eberly)

P&R '35

Singles: 78 rpm

BELL ... 3-5 54
COLUMBIA ... 3-5 50-52
DECCA ... 2-6 35-57
FRATERNITY ... 3-5 57
MGM ... 3-5 54
OKEH ... 10-15 29

Singles: 7-inch

ABC ... 3-4 73
BELL ... 3-5 54
COLUMBIA ... 3-6 50-52
CORAL ("60M" Series) ... 10-15 50
(Boxed, four-disc sets.)
DECCA ... 3-6 51-67
DOT ... 3-4 63
EPIC ... 3-4 59
FRATERNITY ... 3-5 57-60
MGM ... 3-4 54

EPs: 7-inch

COLUMBIA ... 4-8 52-56

LPs: 10/12-inch

COLUMBIA ... 10-20 55-56
CORAL ... 10-20 54
DECCA ... 10-20 57-66
EPIC ... 8-12 59
FRATERNITY ... 10-20 57
HINDSIGHT ... 5-10 81
LION ... 10-20 56
MCA ... 5-10 75

Also see CROSBY, Bing, & Jimmy Dorsey
Also see MARTIN, Dean / Bob Eberly / Gordon MacRae

DORSEY, Lee P&R/R&B '61

Singles: 7-inch

ABC ... 3-4 78
ABC-PAR (10192 "Lotti Mo") ... 8-12 61
ACE ... 10-20 61
AMY ... 4-8 65-69
BELL ... 5-8
CONSTELLATION ... 10-20 64
FLASHBACK ... 3-5 65
FURY ... 8-15 61-63
GUSTO ... 3-4 80s
POLYDOR ... 3-5 70-72
REX (1005 "Rock") ... 15-25 58
ROULETTE ... 3-5 70s
SANSU ... 5-10 67
SMASH ... 4-8 63
SPRING ... 3-5 71
VALIANT (1001 "Lotti Mo") ... 20-30 58

LPs: 10/12-inch

ABC (1048 "Night People") ... 8-12 78
AMY (8010 "Ride Your Pony") ... 20-30 66
AMY (8011 "New Lee Dorsey") ... 20-30 66
ARISTA ... 5-10 85
FURY (1002 "Ya Ya") ... 100-200 62
POLYDOR ... 10-12 70
SPHERE SOUND (7003 "Ya Ya") ... 15-25 67

Also see JAMES, Tommy & Shondells / Lee Dorsey

DORSEY, Lee, & Betty Harris

Singles: 7-inch

SANSU (474 "Love Lots of Lovin'") ... 8-12 67

Also see DORSEY, Lee
Also see HARRIS, Betty

DORSEY, Tommy, Orch. P&R '35

(Starring Warren Covington)

Singles: 78 rpm

BELL ... 4-8 54
(7-inch disc.)
BLUEBIRD ... 3-6 40
DECCA ... 3-5 52-64
OKEH ... 10-15 29
RCA ... 3-5 41-57
VICTOR ... 3-6 35-48

Singles: 7-inch

DECCA ... 5-10 52-64
MCA ... 3-4 73
RCA ... 5-10 50-57

EPs: 7-inch

COLUMBIA ... 5-10 52-56
DECCA ... 5-10 52-63
RCA ... 5-10 51-61
WALDORF ... 5-10 50s

LPs: 10/12-inch

ACCORD ... 5-10 82
BRIGHT ORANGE ... 5-10 73
CAMDEN (Except 200 series) ... 5-10 61-73
CAMDEN (200 series) ... 10-20 53-55
COLPIX ... 10-20 58-63
COLUMBIA ... 10-20 58
CORAL ... 5-10 73
CORONET ... 5-10 60s
DECCA ... 10-20 52-60
GOLDEN MUSIC SOCIETY ... 15-20 56
HARMONY ... 5-10 65-72
MCA ... 5-10 75-81
MOVIETOWN ... 8-10 67
RCA ... 10-20 51-82
SPIN-O-RAMA ... 5-10 60s
SPRINGBORAD ... 5-10 77
20TH FOX ... 10-15 59-73

Also see GARLAND, Judy / Tommy Dorsey
Also see SINATRA, Frank

DOSS, Kenny R&B '80

Singles: 7-inch

BEARSVILLE ... 3-5 80

LPs: 10/12-inch

BEARSVILLE ... 5-10 80

DOTTIE & RAY R&B '65

Singles: 7-inch

LE SAGE ... 4-8 65

DOUBLE P&R/LP '86

Singles: 12-inch

A&M ... 4-8 86

Singles: 7-inch

A&M ... 3-4 86

Picture Sleeves

A&M ... 3-4 86

LPs: 10/12-inch

A&M ... 5-10 86

Members: Kurt Maloo; Felix Haug.

DOUBLE ENTENTE D&D '84

Singles: 12-inch

COLUMBIA ... 4-6 84

Singles: 7-inch

COLUMBIA ... 3-4 84

DOUBLE EXPOSURE P&R/R&B/LP '76

Singles: 12-inch

GOLD COAST ... 4-6 81

Singles: 7-inch

SALSOUL ... 3-4 76-79

LPs: 10/12-inch

SALSOUL ... 8-10 76-79

Members: James Williams; Joseph Harris; Leonard Davis; Charles Whittington.

DOUBLE IMAGE P&R '83

Singles: 7-inch

CBS ASSOCIATED ... 3-4 83
CURB ... 3-4 83

LPs: 10/12-inch

ECM ... 5-10 79

DOUBLE VISION D&D '84

Singles: 12-inch

PROFILE ... 4-6 84

DOUCETTE P&R/LP '78

(Jerry Doucette)

Singles: 7-inch

MUSHROOM ... 3-4 77-79

LPs: 10/12-inch

MUSHROOM ... 5-10 78-79

DOUG E. FRESH & GET FRESH CREW R&B/D&D '85

Singles: 12-inch

REALITY ... 4-6 85

Singles: 7-inch

REALITY ... 3-4 85-88

LPs: 10/12-inch

REALITY ... 5-8 88

DOUGLAS, Carl P&R/R&B/LP '74

(With the Big Stampede)

Singles: 7-inch

ERIC ... 3-4 70s
OKEH ... 5-10 66-67
20TH FOX ... 4-6 74-75

LPs: 10/12-inch

20TH FOX ... 10-15 74

DOUGLAS, Carol P&R/R&B '74

Singles: 12-inch

MIDSONG INT'L ... 4-6 78

Singles: 7-inch

MIDLAND INT'L ... 3-5 74-79
RCA ... 3-5 76
20TH FOX ... 3-4 81

Picture Sleeves

MIDLAND INT'L ... 3-5 77-88

LPs: 10/12-inch

MIDLAND INT'L ... 8-10 75-80

DOUGLAS, Mike P&R '65

Singles: 7-inch

BANANA ... 5-10
BLUE RIVER ... 4-6 66
DECCA ... 3-6 69
EPIC ... 4-6 65-67
IMAGE ... 3-5 77
MGM ... 3-4 71-73
PROJECT 3 ... 3-5 68
STAX ... 3-5 74

Picture Sleeves

EPIC ... 4-8 65-66

LPs: 10/12-inch

ATLANTIC ... 5-10 76
EPIC ... 10-15 65-67
HARMONY ... 8-12 68

Also see BAILEY, Pearl, & Mike Douglas

DOUGLAS, Ronny P&R '61

Singles: 7-inch

DECCA ... 4-8 63
EPIC ... 4-8 65
EVEREST ... 5-10 61

DOVALE, Debbie P&R '63

Singles: 7-inch

ROULETTE ... 10-15 63-64

DOVE, Ronnie P&R '64

(With the Beltones)

Singles: 7-inch

ABC ... 3-4 74
DECCA (31288 "Party Doll") ... 10-15 61
DECCA (32000 & 33000 series) ... 3-5 71-73
DIAMOND (100 & 200 series) ... 4-8 64-70
DIAMOND (300 series) ... 3-4 87
ERIC ... 3-4 70s
HITSVILLE ... 3-5 76
JALO (1406 "Saddest Song") ... 25-50 62
MC ... 3-4 78
MCA ... 3-4 73
MELODYLAND ... 3-5 75-76
MOTION ... 3-4 81
MOON SHINE ... 3-4 83
SWAN (4231 "Happy") ... 5-10 63
WRAYCO ... 3-5 71

Picture Sleeves

DIAMOND ... 5-10 66

LPs: 10/12-inch

CERTRON ... 10-12 70
DIAMOND ... 15-25 65-70
DESIGN (186 "Swingin' Teen Sounds") ... 10-15 64
(Has four tracks by Dove; six by Terry Phillips.)
MCA ... 8-10 72-73
POWER PAK ... 8-12 75

DOVELLS P&R/R&B '61

Singles: 7-inch

ABKCO ... 3-4 83
COLLECTABLES ... 3-4 80s
DECCA ... 3-6 70
EVENT ... 3-6 70-74
MGM ... 4-6 66-73
PARKWAY (Except 819 & 827) ... 5-10 62-63
PARKWAY (819 "No No No") ... 10-15 61
PARKWAY (827 "Bristol Stomp"/"Out in the Cold") ... 10-15 61
PARKWAY (827 "Bristol Stomp"/"Letters of Love") ... 5-8 61
(Note different flip.)
SWAN ... 4-8 65
VERVE ... 3-5 73

Picture Sleeves

PARKWAY ... 5-10 62-63

LPs: 10/12-inch

DOVCO ... 5-10 76
PARKWAY (7006 "The Bristol Stomp") ... 30-50 61
PARKWAY (7010 "All the Hits of the Teen Groups") ... 40-60 62
PARKWAY (7021 "For Your Hully Gully Party") ... 50-75 63
PARKWAY (7025 "You Can't Sit Down") ... 30-50 63
WYNCOTE ... 10-20 65
Members: Len Barry; Arnie Satin; Jerry Summers; Danny Brooks; Mike Dennis.
Also see BARRY, Len
Also see CHRISTIE, Lou / Len Barry & Dovells / Bobby Rydell / Tokens
Also see ORLONS / Dovells

DOWELL, Joe P&R '61

Singles: 7-inch

JOURNEY ... 3-5 73
MONUMENT ... 4-6 66
SMASH ... 4-8 61-63

Picture Sleeves

JOURNEY ... 3-5 73
SMASH ... 5-10 61-62

LPs: 10/12-inch

SMASH ... 15-25 61-62
WING ... 10-15 66

DOWN HOMERS C&W '49
(Kenny Roberts & the Downhomers; Wowo Down Homers)

Singles: 78 rpm

CORAL ... 4-8 49-50
VOGUE (736 "Who's Gonna Kiss You When I'm Gone") ... 200-300 46
(Picture disc.)
VOGUE (786 "Boogie Woogie Yodel") ... 300-500 47
(Picture disc.)

LPs: 10/12-inch

SOMERSET (22400 "The Downhomers") ... 15-20 60s
Members: Bob Mason; Bill Haley; Shorty Cook; Guy Campbell; Lloyd Cornell.

DOWNING, Al P&R '63
(Big Al Downing)

Singles: 7-inch

CARLTON (489 "Miss Lucy") ... 30-50 58
CHALLENGE (59006 "Down on the Farm") ... 20-40 58
CHESS (1000 series) ... 5-10 62
CHESS (2000 series) ... 3-5 75
COLUMBIA ... 4-8 64
DOOR KNOB ... 3-4 89
HOUSE of the FOX ... 3-5 71
JANUS ... 3-5 74
KANSOMA ... 5-10 62
LENOX ... 4-8 63
POLYDOR ... 3-5 76
SILVER FOX ... 4-8 69
TEAM ... 3-4 82-84
V-TONE ... 5-10 61
VINE ST. ... 3-4 87
W.B. ... 3-5 78-80
WHITE ROCK (1111 "Down on the Farm") ... 50-100 58
WHITE ROCK (1113 "Miss Lucy") ... 50-100 58

LPs: 10/12-inch

TEAM ... 5-10 83-85
Also see LITTLE ESTHER & Big Al Downing

DOWNING, Don R&B '73

Singles: 7-inch

ABNER ... 4-8 62
CHAN ... 4-8 62
ROADSHOW ... 3-5 73
SCEPTER ... 3-5 74

LPs: 10/12-inch

ROADSHOW ... 5-10 79

DOWNING, Will R&B '88

Singles: 7-inch

ISLAND ... 3-4 88

DOZIER, Gene, & Brotherhood R&B '67

Singles: 7-inch

MINIT ... 4-8 67-68

LPs: 10/12-inch

MINIT ... 10-15 67

DOZIER, Lamont P&R/R&B '72

Singles: 12-inch

M&M ... 4-6 82
W.B. ... 4-8 79

Singles: 7-inch

ABC ... 3-5 73-76
COLUMBIA ... 3-4 81
INVICTUS ... 3-5 72-73
M&M ... 3-4 82
MEL-O-DY (102 "Dearest One") ... 75-100 62

LPs: 10/12-inch

ABC ... 8-10 73-74
COLUMBIA ... 5-10 81
INVICTUS ... 8-12 74
M&M ... 5-10 82
W.B. ... 8-10 76-79
Also see ANTHONY, Lamont
Also see HOLLAND, Eddie, & Lamont Dozier
Also see VOICE MASTERS

DRAFI P&R '66
(Drafi Deutscher)

Singles: 7-inch

LONDON ... 4-8 66-67

DRAGON P&R/D&D '84

Singles: 12-inch

POLYDOR ... 4-6 84

Singles: 7-inch

POLYDOR ... 3-4 83-84
PORTRAIT ... 3-5 78-79

LPs: 10/12-inch

POLYDOR ... 5-10 83
PORTRAIT ... 5-10 78

DRAGON, Carmen LP '62

LPs: 10/12-inch

CAPITOL ... 10-20 62

DRAKE, Charlie P&R '62

Singles: 7-inch

CAPITOL (72015 "My Boomerang Won't Come Back") ... 15-25 61
(Canadian. Longer version than on U.A. With "Practiced till I was BLACK in the face" lyrics.)
U.A. (Except 398) ... 5-10 61-62
U.A. (398 "My Boomerang Won't Come Back") ... 15-25 61
(With "Practiced till I was BLACK in the face" lyrics.)
U.A. (398 "My Boomerang Won't Come Back") ... 5-10 61
(With "Practiced till I was BLUE in the face" lyrics.)

DRAKE, Guy C&W/P&R '70

Singles: 7-inch

MALLARD ... 3-5 71
ROYAL AMERICAN ... 3-5 70
TRIP UNIVERSAL ... 3-5 70s

LPs: 10/12-inch

OVATION ... 5-10 74
ROYAL AMERICAN ... 15-20 70
TRIP UNIVERSAL ... 8-12 70s

DRAKE, Pete P&R/LP '64
(With His Talking Steel Guitar)

Singles: 7-inch

SMASH ... 4-8 62-65
STARDAY ... 3-6 66
STOP ... 3-5 68-70

LPs: 10/12-inch

CANAAN ... 8-12 68
CUMBERLAND ... 12-20 63
PICKWICK/HILLTOP ... 8-12 67
MOUNTAIN DEW ... 8-10
SMASH ... 10-15 64-65
STARDAY ... 15-25 62-65
STOP ... 6-10 70
Also see TUBB, Ernest

DRAMATICS R&B '67
(Ron Banks & Dramatics)

Singles: 7-inch

ABC ... 3-6 75-77
BELL (5 "Toy Soldier") ... 20-30 60s
CADET ... 3-6 74
CAPITOL ... 3-4 82
CRACKERJACK (4015 "Toy Soldier") ... 50-75 63
FANTASY ... 3-4 86
MAINSTREAM ... 3-6 75
MCA ... 3-4 79-80
SPORT (101 "All Because of You") ... 40-60 67
VOLT ... 4-8 71-73
WINGATE (22 "Baby I Need You") ... 25-35 67

LPs: 10/12-inch

ABC ... 8-10 75-78
CADET ... 8-12 74
CAPITOL ... 5-10 82
FANTASY ... 5-10 86
MCA ... 5-10 80
STAX ... 8-10 77-78
VOLT ... 10-15 72-74
Members: Ron Banks; Elbert Wilkins; L.J. Reynolds; William Howard; Larry Demps; Lenny Mayes; Carl Smalls; Willie Ford.
Also see BANKS, Ron
Also see DELLS & DRAMATICS
Also see DYNAMICS
Also see REYNOLDS, L.J.
Also see UNDISPUTED TRUTH

DRAPER, Rusty C&W/P&R '53

Singles: 78 rpm

MERCURY (Except 70921) ... 5-10 52-57
MERCURY (70921 "Pink Cadillac") ... 10-15 56

Singles: 7-inch

KL ... 3-5 80
MERCURY (Except 70921) ... 5-15 52-62
MERCURY (70921 "Pink Cadillac") ... 15-25 56
MONUMENT ... 4-8 63-70

EPs: 7-inch

MERCURY ... 10-15 54-56

LPs: 10/12-inch

GOLDEN CREST ... 5-10 73
HARMONY ... 5-10 72
MERCURY ... 15-30 54-62
MONUMENT ... 8-12 65-75
WING ... 8-12 63-64
Also see DEE, Lola, & Rusty Draper

DREAD ZEPPELIN LP '90

LPs: 10/12-inch

I.R.S. ... 5-8 90

DREAM ACADEMY P&R/LP '85

Singles: 7-inch

W.B. ... 3-4 85-86

Picture Sleeves

W.B. ... 3-4 85-86

LPs: 10/12-inch

REPRISE ... 5-10 87
W.B. ... 5-10 85

DREAM SYNDICATE LP '84

LPs: 10/12-inch

A&M ... 5-10 84

SLASH....5-10
Also see TEXTONES

DREAM WEAVERS P&R '55
(Featuring Wade Buff)
Singles: 78 rpm
DECCA....10-15 55-56
Singles: 7-inch
DECCA....15-25 55-56
EPs: 7-inch
DECCA....20-40 56
Member: Wade Buff.

DREAMBOY R&B/LP '84
Singles: 7-inch
QWEST....3-4 83-84
LPs: 10/12-inch
QWEST....5-10 83-84

DREAMLOVERS P&R '61
Singles: 7-inch
CAMEO (326 "Oh Baby Mine")....10-15 64
CASINO (1308 "Amazons and Coyotes")....10-20 64
COLLECTABLES....3-4 82
COLUMBIA (42698 "Sad Sad Boy")....15-20 63
COLUMBIA (42752 "Sad Sad Boy")....10-15 63
COLUMBIA (42842 "Pretty Little Girl")....30-40 63
DOWN (2004 "If I Should Lose You")....250-500 61
END (1114 "If I Should Lose You")....15-25 62
HERITAGE (102 "When We Get Married")....15-25 61
HERITAGE (104 "Welcome Home")....15-25 61
HERITAGE (107 "Zoom Zoom Zoom")....25-50 62
LEN (1006 "For the First Time")....400-600 60
LOST NITE....4-8
MERCURY (72595 "Bless Your Soul")....10-15 66
MERCURY (72630 "Calling Jo Ann")....20-30 66
SWAN (4167 "Amazons and Coyotes")....20-30 63
(White label.)
SWAN (4167 "Amazons and Coyotes")....10-20 63
(Black label.)
V-TONE (211 "Anabelle Lee")....10-20 60
V-TONE (229 "May I Kiss the Bride")....10-20 61
W.B. (5619 "You Gave Me Somebody to Love")....10-20 65
LPs: 10/12-inch
COLLECTABLES ("Dreamlovers")....5-10 82
(Selection number not known.)
COLLECTABLES (5005 "Volume Two")....10-15 82
(Picture disc.)
COLUMBIA (2020 "The Bird")....20-40 63
(Monaural.)
COLUMBIA (8820 "The Bird")....25-50 63
(Stereo.)
HERITAGE....8-12 79
Members: Tommy Ricks; Cleveland Hammock; Cliff Dunn; Morris Gardner; Ray Dunn.
Also see CHECKER, Chubby

DREAMS LP '70
Singles: 7-inch
COLUMBIA....3-5 71-72
D.C....4-6 69
LPs: 10/12-inch
COLUMBIA....10-15 70-71
Also see BRECKER BROTHERS

DREAMS SO REAL LP '88
LPs: 10/12-inch
ARISTA....5-8 88
FATHER'S HOUSE....8-10 86
I.R.S....5-10 87

Members: Barry Marler; Drew Worsham; Trent Allen.

DRENNON, Eddie, & B.B.S. Unlimited R&B '75
Singles: 7-inch
FRIENDS & CO....3-5 75

DRESSLAR, Len P&R '56
(Len Dresslar Singers)
Singles: 78 rpm
MERCURY....4-8 56
Singles: 7-inch
CAPITOL....3-6 63
MERCURY....5-15 56
UNIVERSAL (76936 "Cubs' Song")....5-10

DREW, Patti P&R/R&B '67
(With the Drew-Vels)
Singles: 7-inch
CAPITOL....4-8 67-69
INNOVATION....3-5 75
QUILL....4-8 65
LPs: 10/12-inch
CAPITOL (Except 408)....10-20 69-70
CAPITOL (408 "Wild Is Love")....60-90 79
(Picture disc. Promotional issue only. With plastic cover.)
CAPITOL (408 "Wild Is Love")....80-100 79
(Picture disc. Promotional issue only. With cardboard album jacket.)

DREW-VELS P&R '63
("Featuring Patti Drew")
Singles: 7-inch
CAPITOL....8-12 63-64
LPs: 10/12-inch
CAPITOL (2804 "Tell Him")....20-30 67
Members: Patti Drew; Erma Drew; Lorraine Drew; Carlton Black.
Also see DREW, Patti

DREWS, J.D. P&R '80
Singles: 7-inch
UNICORN....3-4 80

DRIFTER, Dixie: see DIXIE DRIFTER,

DRIFTERS R&B '53
(Clyde McPhatter & the Drifters)
Singles: 78 rpm
ATLANTIC....15-35 53-57
CROWN....50-75 54
Singles: 7-inch
ANDEE (0014 "Black Silk")....10-15 60s
ATLANTIC (1006 "Money Honey")....50-75 53
ATLANTIC (1019 "Such a Night")....30-60 54
ATLANTIC (1029 "Honey Love")....30-60 54
ATLANTIC (1043 "Bip Bam")....25-50 54
ATLANTIC (1048 "White Christmas")....25-50 54
ATLANTIC (1055 "Whatcha Gonna Do")....10-20 55
ATLANTIC (1078 "Adorable")....10-20 55
ATLANTIC (1089 thru 2127)....10-20 56-62
ATLANTIC (2134 thru 2786)....5-15 62-71
ATLANTIC OLDIES SERIES....3-5 70s
BELL....3-5 73-74
CROWN (108 "The World Is Changing")....100-150 54
Picture Sleeves
ATLANTIC (2260 "Saturday Night at the Movies")....10-15 64
ATLANTIC (2261 "The Christmas Song")....15-25 64
EPs: 7-inch
ATLANTIC (534 "The Drifters Featuring Clyde McPhatter")....75-100 55
ATLANTIC (592 "The Drifters")....40-60 58
LPs: 10/12-inch
ARISTA....8-12 76
ATCO....10-12 71
ATLANTIC (8003 "Clyde McPhatter and the Drifters")....100-200 57
(Black label.)
ATLANTIC (8003 "Clyde McPhatter and the Drifters")....30-40 59
(Red label.)
ATLANTIC (8022 "Rockin' and Driftin'")....100-150 59
(Black label.)
ATLANTIC (8022 "Rockin' and Driftin'")....100-150 59
(White label.)
ATLANTIC (8022 "Rockin' and Driftin'")....25-35 59
(Red label.)
ATLANTIC (8041 "The Drifters' Greatest Hits")....40-60 60
ATLANTIC (8059 "Save the Last Dance for Me")....40-60 62
(Monaural.)
ATLANTIC (SD-8059 "Save the Last Dance for Me")....50-70 62
(Stereo.)
ATLANTIC (8073 "Up on the Roof")....30-40 63
(Monaural.)
ATLANTIC (SD-8073 "Up on the Roof")....40-50 63
(Stereo.)
ATLANTIC (8093 "Biggest Hits")....30-40 64
(Monaural.)
ATLANTIC (SD-8093 "Biggest Hits")....40-50 64
(Stereo.)
ATLANTIC (8099 "Under the Boardwalk")....40-60 64
(Monaural. With black and white group photo.)
ATLANTIC (8099 "Under the Boardwalk")....20-30 64
(Monaural. With color group photo.)
ATLANTIC (SD-8099 "Under the Boardwalk")....50-70 64
(Stereo. With black and white group photo.)
ATLANTIC (SD-8099 "Under the Boardwalk")....25-35 64
(Stereo. With color group photo.)
ATLANTIC (8100 series)....20-30 65-68
CANDLELITE....10-15 70s
CLARION....15-20 64
51 WEST....5-10
GUSTO....5-10 80
MUSICOR....5-10 74
TRIP....5-10 76
Members: Clyde McPhatter; Johnny Moore; Ben E. King; Rudy Lewis; Bobby Hendricks; Johnny Williams; Elsbeary Hobbs; William Anderson; David Baldwin; James Johnson; Charlie Hughes; Charlie Thomas; Bill Pinckney; Andrew Thrasher; Gerhart Thrasher; Willie Ferbie; Walter Adams; Jimmy Milner; Reggie Kimber; Jimmy Oliver; David Baughn; Tommy Evans; Eugene Pearson; Billy Davis (Abdul Samad); Tommy Evans; Dock Green; Johnny Terry; Butch Leak; Grant Kitchings; Bill Fredericks; Butch Mann.
Also see CLEFTONES
Also see COASTERS / Drifters
Also see HENDRICKS, Bobby
Also see JOHN, Little Willie / Drifters
Also see KING, Ben E.
Also see McPHATTER, Clyde
Also see MOONGLOWS
Also see VEE, Bobby / Diamonds / Drifters

DRIFTERS / Lesley Gore / Roy Orbison / Los Bravos
EPs: 7-inch
SWINGERS for COKE....50-75 66
(Promotional issue only. Each artist sings a song about Coca Cola. Has paper cover.)
Also see GORE, Lesley
Also see LOS BRAVOS
Also see ORBISON, Roy

DRIFTERS / Little Joey & Flips
Singles: 7-inch
GRAY'S FERRY....3-5
Also see DRIFTERS
Also see LITTLE JOEY & FLIPS

DRIVIN' 'N' CRYIN' LP '88

LPs: 10/12-inch

ISLAND....5-8 88-91
688 RECORDS....5-10 86
Members: Kevin Kinney; Tim Nielsen; Paul Lenz.

DRUPI P&R '73

Singles: 7-inch

A&M....3-5 73

DRUSKY, Roy C&W '60

Singles: 78 rpm

COLUMBIA....5-10 55-56
STARDAY....5-10 55

Singles: 7-inch

CAPITOL....3-5 74-76
COLUMBIA....8-12 55-56
DECCA....5-10 60-64
MERCURY....3-8 63-73
PLANTATION....3-4 79-80
SCORPION....3-5 77
STARDAY (185 "Such a Fool")....10-15 55

EPs: 7-inch

DECCA....4-8 61-63

LPs: 10/12-inch

CAPITOL....5-10 76
DECCA....12-20 61-62
HARMONY....10-12 65
MCA....5-8 80s
MERCURY....10-20 64-72
PICKWICK/HILLTOP....8-12 70s
PLANTATION....5-10 79-80
SCORPION....5-10 76
VOCALION....8-12 70
WING....10-15 64-66
Also see WELLS, Kitty, & Roy Drusky

DRUSKY, Roy, & Priscilla Mitchell C&W '67

Singles: 7-inch

MERCURY....4-6 67
Also see DRUSKY, Roy

DUALS P&R '61

Singles: 7-inch

COLLECTABLES....3-4 80s
INFINITY (032 "Big Race")....20-30 64
STAR REVUE (1031 "Stick Shift")....50-75 61
SUE (745 "Stick Shift")....10-15 61

LPs: 10/12-inch

SUE (2002 "Stick Shift")....50-80 61
Members: John Lagemann; Henry Bellinger.

DUBS P&R '57

(Richard Blandon & Dubs)

Singles: 78 rpm

GONE (5002 "Don't Ask Me")....50-100 57

Singles: 7-inch

ABC-PAR (10056 "Early in the Morning")....20-30 59
ABC-PAR (10100 "Don't Laugh at Me")....40-60 60
ABC-PAR (10150 "For the First Time")....20-30 60
ABC-PAR (10198 "If I Only Had Magic")....25-50 61
ABC-PAR (10269 "Lullaby")....25-50 61
CLASSIC ARTISTS....3-5 90
CLIFTON....4-8 73
END (1108 "This to Me Is Love")....50-75 62
GONE (5002 "Don't Ask Me")....50-100 57
(With double image, shadow-like lettering.)
GONE (5002 "Don't Ask Me")....40-60 57
(With normal lettering.)
GONE (5011 "Could This Be Magic")....50-100 57
GONE (5020 "Beside My Love")....50-100 58
GONE (5034 "Be Sure My Love")....50-100 58
GONE (5046 "Chapel of Dreams")....50-100 58
(Black label.)
GONE (5046 "Chapel of Dreams")....25-50 60
(Multi-color label.)
GONE (5138 "Is There a Love for Me")....50-100 62
(Black label.)
JOHNSON (97 "Connie")....4-8 73
JOHNSON (98 "Somebody Goofed")....4-8 73
JOHNSON (102 "Don't Ask Me")....1000-2000 57
JOSIE (911 "This I Swear")....30-50 63
LANA....4-8 64
MARK-X (8008 "Be Sure My Love")....15-25 60
OLDIES 45....4-8 64
REO (8186 "Could This Be Magic")....50-75 57
(Canadian.)
ROULETTE....3-5 70s
VICKI (229 "Lost in the Wilderness")....10-20 62
WILSHIRE (201 "Just You")....25-40 63
ZIRKON (5002 "Chapel of Dreams")....5-10

LPs: 10/12-inch

CANDLELITE....10-15 73
MURRAY HILL....5-10 88
Members: Richard Blandon; Billy Carlisle; Cleveland Still; James Miller; Tom Gardner; Tom Grate; Cordell Brown; Dave Shelley.

DUBS / Actuals

Singles: 78 rpm

CANDLELITE (438 "We Three")....5-10 72

DUBS / Shells

LPs: 10/12-inch

CANDLELITE....8-10 70s
JOSIE (4001 "The Dubs Meet the Shells")....75-150 62
Also see DUBS
Also see SHELLS

DUBSET D&D '84

Singles: 12-inch

ELEKTRA....4-6 84

DUCES OF RHYTHM & TEMPO TOPPERS

(Featuring Little Richard)

Singles: 78 rpm

PEACOCK....25-50 53-54

Singles: 7-inch

PEACOCK (1616 "Fool at the Wheel")....50-75 53
PEACOCK (1628 "Always")....50-75 54
Also see LITTLE RICHARD
Also see TEMPO TOPPERS

DUCHIEN, Armand D&D '84

Singles: 12-inch

A&M....4-6 84

DUDEK, Les LP '77

Singles: 7-inch

COLUMBIA....3-5 77-78

LPs: 10/12-inch

COLUMBIA....8-12 75-81
Also see ALLMAN BROTHERS BAND

DUDLEY, Dave P&R '63

Singles: 78 rpm

KING....5-10 55-56

Singles: 7-inch

CIRCLE DOT....5-10 60
COLUMBIA....3-4 78
CURIO....4-8
GOLDEN RING....4-8 63
GOLDEN WING (3020 "Six Days on the Road")....5-8 63
(Black vinyl.)
GOLDEN WING (3020 "Six Days on the Road")....10-20 63
(Colored vinyl.)
JUBILEE....5-10 62
KING (4000 series, except 4933)....8-12 55-56
KING (4933 "Rock & Roll Nursery Rhyme")....15-25 56
KING (5000 series)....4-8 63
MERCURY....3-8 63-73
NRC....8-12 59
NEW STAR....4-8 62
PELHAM....5-10 63
RICE....3-5 73-78
STARDAY....5-10 58-60
SUN (Black vinyl)....3-4 79-80
SUN (Colored vinyl)....4-6 79-80
U.A.....3-5 75-76
VEE (7003 "Maybe I Do")....10-15 61

LPs: 10/12-inch

CORONET/PREMIER....8-12 60s
CROWN....8-12 60s
DESIGN....8-12 60s
GOLDEN RING (110 "Six Days on the Road")....25-30 63
GUEST STAR....8-12
HILLTOP....8-12
MERCURY....10-15 64-73
MOUNTAIN DEW....8-12 69
NASHVILLE....8-12 68
PICKWICK....5-10 70s
PLANTATION....5-10 81
RICE....3-4 78
SPIN-O-RAMA....5-10 60s
SUN....5-10 80
U.A.....8-12 75-76
WING....8-12 68
Also see JAMES, Sonny / Dave Dudley / Sunny Williams

DUDLEY, Dave, & Tom T. Hall C&W '70

Singles: 7-inch

MERCURY....3-5 70
Also see HALL, Tom T.

DUDLEY, Dave, & Karen O'Donnal C&W '72

Singles: 7-inch

MERCURY....3-5 72

DUDLEY, Dave / Link Wray

LPs: 10/12-inch

GUEST STAR....15-25 63
Also see DUDLEY, Dave
Also see WRAY, Link

DU DROPPERS R&B '53

Singles: 78 rpm

GROOVE....25-50 53-55
RCA....20-30 53
RED ROBIN....50-100 52-53

Singles: 7-inch

GROOVE (0001 "Dead Broke")....40-60 54
GROOVE (0013 "Just Whisper")....50-75 54
GROOVE (0036 "Let Nature Take It's Course")....30-40 54
GROOVE (0104 "Talk That Talk")....20-40 55
GROOVE (0120 "You're Mine Already")....20-40 55
RCA (5229 "I Wanna Know")....25-35 53
RCA (5321 "I Found Out")....25-30 53
RCA (5425 "Whatever You're Doin' ")....25-30 53
RCA (5504 "Don't Pass Me By")....25-30 53
RCA (5543 "The Note in the Bottle")....25-30 53
RED ROBIN (108 "Can't Do Sixty No More")....100-125 52
(Black vinyl.)
RED ROBIN (108 "Can't Do Sixty No More")....200-300 52
(Colored vinyl.)
RED ROBIN (116 "Come On and Love Me Baby")....100-125 53

EPs: 7-inch

GROOVE (2 "Talk That Talk")....100-200 55
GROOVE (5 "Tops in Rhythm & Blues")....100-200 55
Members: Julius Ginyard; Willie Ray; Eddie Hashaw; Harvey Ray; Bob Kornegay; Prentice Moreland; Joe Van Loan; Charlie Hughes.
Also see DIXIEAIRES
Also see GALE, Sunny, & Du Droppers

DUKAYS P&R '61

Singles: 7-inch

JERRY-O (105 "Jerk")....10-15 64
NAT (4001 "The Girl's a Devil")....15-20 61
NAT (4002 "Nite Owl")....15-20 61
OLDIES 45....4-6 60s

VEE JAY (430 "Nite Owl") 10-20 62
VEE JAY (442 "Please Help") 10-20 62
VEE JAY (460 "I Never Knew") 10-20 62
Members: Eugene "Gene Chandler" Dixon; James Lowe; Earl Edwards; Ben Broyles; Shirley Jones; Charles Davis; Claude McRae.
Also see ARTISTICS
Also see CHANDLER, Gene

DUKE, Doris P&R/R&B '70
Singles: 7-inch
CANYON 4-8 70
MANKIND 3-5 72
RRG.. 3-5
SAM.. 3-5

DUKE, George LP '75
Singles: 12-inch
ELEKTRA 4-6 85-86
EPIC 4-6 83
Singles: 7-inch
ELEKTRA 3-4 85-86
EPIC 3-4 77-83
LPs: 10/12-inch
ELEKTRA 5-10 85-86
EPIC 5-10 77-83
MPS/BASF 8-10 74-76
Also see CLARKE, Stanley, & George Duke
Also see COBHAM, Billy
Also see MOTHERS of INVENTION

DUKE, Patty P&R/LP '65
Singles: 7-inch
U.A. 4-8 65-68
Picture Sleeves
U.A. 8-10 65
LPs: 10/12-inch
U.A. 15-20 65-68

DUKE & DRIVERS P&R '75
Singles: 7-inch
ABC 3-5 75
LPs: 10/12-inch
ABC 8-10 76

DUKE BAYOU
(Champion Jack Dupree)
Singles: 78 rpm
APOLLO 25-50 50
Also see DUPREE, Champion Jack

DUKE JUPITER P&R '82
Singles: 7-inch
COAST to COAST.................................. 3-4 82
MOROCCO 3-4 84-85
(Black vinyl.)
MOROCCO 4-6 84
(Colored vinyl. Promotional issue only.)
LPs: 10/12-inch
COAST TO COAST 5-10 82-83
MERCURY 5-10 80
MOROCCO 5-10 84
Members: Marshall James Styler; Greg Walker; Rickey Ellis; David Corcoran.

DUKE OF EARL P&R '62
(Gene Chandler)
Singles: 7-inch
VEE JAY... 5-10 62
Also see CHANDLER, Gene

DUKES OF DIXIELAND LP '57
LPs: 10/12-inch
AUDIO FIDELITY 5-15 55-61
COLUMBIA.. 5-10 62
EPIC 5-15 56
RCA VICTOR 5-10 59

DULFER, Candy LP '91
LPs: 10/12-inch
ARISTA.. 5-8 91

DUNCAN, Darryl R&B '88
Singles: 7-inch
MOTOWN.. 3-4 88

DUNCAN SISTERS R&B '79
Singles: 12-inch
EAR MARC.. 4-6 79
Singles: 7-inch
EAR MARC.. 3-5 79-80
HI... 4-8 75

DUNDAS, David P&R '76
Singles: 7-inch
CHRYSALIS.. 3-5 76-77
LPs: 10/12-inch
CHRYSALIS.. 8-10 77

DUNLAP, Gene R&B '81
(With the Ridgeways)
Singles: 12-inch
CAPITOL... 4-6 82
Singles: 7-inch
CAPITOL... 3-4 81-83
LPs: 10/12-inch
CAPITOL... 5-10 81-83
Also see AYERS, Roy
Also see WYNNE, Philippe

DUNN & BRUCE STREET R&B '82
Singles: 7-inch
DEVAKI.. 3-4 81-82
Members: Dunn Pearson; Bruce Gray

DUNN & McCASHEN P&R '70
Singles: 7-inch
CAPITOL... 3-6 69-70
LPs: 10/12-inch
CAPITOL... 10-12 69-70
COLUMBIA 12-15 71
Members: Don Dunn; Tony McCashen.

DUPREE, Champion Jack R&B '55
Singles: 78 rpm
ALERT 15-25 46
APOLLO... 15-25 49-50
CELEBRITY.. 15-25 46
CONTINENTAL.. 15-25 45
JOE DAVIS 15-25 46
KING 10-20 53-56
RED ROBIN 25-75 53-54
VIK 15-25 57
Singles: 7-inch
ATLANTIC... 5-10 61
EVERLAST 4-8 64
FEDERAL 5-10 61
GUSTO 3-4 80s
KING (4695 "Walkin' Upside Your Head") 15-25 53
KING (4706 "Rub a Little Boogie").... 15-25 53
KING (4812 "Walking the Blues") 15-25
KING (4938 "Big Leg Emma's") 15-25 56
RED ROBIN (109 "Stumblin' Block Blues")... 150-200 53
RED ROBIN (112 "Highway Blues")... 150-200 53
RED ROBIN (130 "Drunk Again")... 150-200 54
VIK (260 "Dirty Woman") 20-30 57
VIK (279 "Old Time Rock & Roll")..... 20-30 57
LPs: 10/12-inch
ARCHIVE of FOLK MUSIC 10-15 68
ATLANTIC (8019 "Blues from the Gutter")... 75-100 59
(Green label.)
ATLANTIC (8019 "Blues from the Gutter")... 40-60 59
(Black label.)
ATLANTIC (8019 "Blues from the Gutter")... 40-60 59
(White label.)
ATLANTIC (8019 "Blues from the Gutter")... 20-30 59
(Red label.)
ATLANTIC (8045 "Natural and Soulful Blues")... 30-40 61
(Monaural.)
ATLANTIC (SD-8045 "Natural and Soulful Blues")... 40-50 61
(Stereo.)
ATLANTIC (8056 "Champion of the Blues")... 30-40 61
(Monaural.)
ATLANTIC (SD-8056 "Champion of the Blues")... 40-50 61
(Stereo.)
ATLANTIC (8255 "Blues from the Gutter")... 8-10 70
BLUE HORIZON.................................. 10-15 69
EVEREST.. 8-12
FOLKWAYS (3825 "Women Blues of Champion Jack Dupree")................................. 20-30 61
GNP.. 8-12 74
JAZZMAN 5-10 82
KING (735 "Champion Jack Dupree Sings the Blues")... 50-60 61
KING (1084 "Walking the Blues")...... 10-15 70
LONDON.. 10-15 69
OKEH (12103 "Cabbage Greens").... 50-75 63
STORYVILLE 5-10 82
Members: Jack Dupree; Larry Dale; Al Lucas; Gene Moore; Stick McGhee; Willie Jones; Pete Brown.
Also see McGHEE, Brownie
Also see McGHEE, Stick

DUPREE, Champion Jack, & Mickey Baker
LPs: 10/12-inch
SIRE 10-15 69

DUPREE, Jack, & Mr. Bear
Singles: 78 rpm
GROOVE.. 10-15 56
KING 10-20 55
Singles: 7-inch
GROOVE (0171 "Lonely Road Blues")... 15-25 56
KING (4812 "Walking the Blues")...... 15-25 55
Members: Jack Dupree; Teddy "Mr. Bear" McRae; Larry Dale; Al Lucas; Gene Moore.
Also see DUPREE, Champion Jack

DUPREE, Robbie P&R/R&B/LP '80
Singles: 7-inch
ELEKTRA 3-4 80-81
Picture Sleeves
ELEKTRA 3-4 80
LPs: 10/12-inch
ELEKTRA 5-10 80-81

DUPREES P&R/LP '62
Singles: 7-inch
COED (569 thru 580).......................... 10-20 62-63
COED (584 "Why Don't You Believe Me"/"The Things I Love")................................. 25-35 63
COED (584 "Why Don't You Believe Me"/"My Dearest One")................................... 10-15 63
(Note different flip.)
COED (585 thru 596).......................... 10-15 63-65
COLLECTABLES 3-4 80
COLUMBIA... 8-12 65-67
ERIC 3-4 70s
1ST CHOICE.. 3-5 89
HERITAGE 4-8 68-70
LOST-NITE.. 4-6 70s
(Black vinyl.)
LOST-NITE.. 10-15
(Colored vinyl.)
RCA... 3-6 75
Picture Sleeves
COLUMBIA... 10-20 66
HERITAGE 4-8 68
LPs: 10/12-inch
COED (905 "You Belong to Me")..... 50-100 62
COED (906 "Have You Heard")....... 50-100 63
COLLECTABLES 5-10 80
(Black vinyl.)
COLLECTABLES 10-15 82
(Picture disc.)
1ST CHOICE.. 10-15 87
HERITAGE (35002 "Total Recall").... 20-30 68
PICCADILLY.. 8-12 80
POST (1000 "The Duprees Sing")..... 15-25
POST (11000 "The Duprees Sing, Vol. 2") 15-20
Members: Joey "Vann" Canzano; Mike Arnone; Tom Bialaglow; John Salvato; Joe Santollo; Richie Rosato.

Also see ITALIAN ASPHALT & Pavement Company

DUPREES / RIVIERAS

LPs: 10/12-inch

LOST NITE (122 Jerry Blavat Presents Drive-In Sounds")..10-15 70s
Also see DUPREES
Also see RIVIERAS

DURAN DURAN P&R/LP '82

(Duranduran)

Singles: 12-inch

CAPITOL..4-8 82-87

Singles: 7-inch

CAPITOL (Except 12352)......................4-8 82-87
CAPITOL (12352 "The Reflex").........10-20 84
(Picture disc.)

Singles: 7-inch

CAPITOL (Black vinyl)..........................3-4 82-90
CAPITOL (Colored vinyl)....................5-10 86-87
(Promotional issues only.)
HARVEST 3-4 81-82

Picture Sleeves

CAPITOL (Except 5345)........................3-4 83-89
CAPITOL (5345 "The Reflex")...............3-4 84
(Poster sleeve.)
CAPITOL (5438 "Save a Prayer") 5-10 82
(Promotional issue only.)
HARVEST 3-4 82

EPs: 7-inch

HARVEST 15-20 82

LPs: 10/12-inch

CAPITOL..5-10 82-90
HARVEST (12158 "Duran Duran")......8-12 82
MFSL (110 "Rio")...............................25-35 84
MFSL (182 "Seven and the Ragged Tiger")..25-35 87
Members: Nick Rhodes; Roger Taylor; John Taylor, Andy Taylor; Simon LeBon; Warren Cuccurullo.
Also see ARCADIA
Also see BAND AID
Also see MISSING PERSONS
Also see POWER STATION
Also see TAYLOR, Andy
Also see TAYLOR, John

DURANTE, Jimmy P&R '34

Singles: 78 rpm

BRUNSWICK 5-10 34
DECCA..4-8 44-57

Singles: 7-inch

DECCA..4-8 51-59
W.B. 3-4 63-70

EPs: 7-inch

DECCA..5-10 54-56
MGM...5-10 53-55
VARSITY 5-10 55

LPs: 10/12-inch

DECCA (9000 series).........................15-25 54-56
DECCA (78000 series).........................8-12 70
HARMONY 8-12 68
LIGHT..5-10 71
LION 15-20 56
MGM (3200 series).............................15-25 55
MGM (4200 series).............................10-15 64
ROULETTE 15-20 61
W.B. 10-15 63-67
Also see GOLDSBORO, Bobby / Jimmy Durante
Also see KAYE, Danny, Jimmy Durante, Jane Wyman & Groucho Marx
Also see MARTIN, Dean
Also see PRESLEY, Elvis

DURY, Ian, & Blockheads LP '78

Singles: 7-inch

STIFF (Except 23 & 1179)....................3-5 79-81
STIFF/COLUMBIA (23 "Sweet Gene Vincent")..5-10 78
(Yellow vinyl. Promotional issue only.)
STIFF (1179 "Hit Me with Your Rhythm Stick") 4-8 79
(Bonus issued with the *Do It Yourself* LP. Promotional issue only.)

Picture Sleeves

STIFF/EPIC (Except 1179)...................3-5 79-81
STIFF/COLUMBIA (23 "Sweet Gene Vincent")..4-8
(Yellow vinyl.)
STIFF/EPIC (1179 "Hit Me with Your Rhythm Stick")..4-8 78
(Bonus issue with the *Do It Yourself* LP. Promotional issue only.)

LPs: 10/12-inch

POLYDOR 5-10 81
STIFF/EPIC (Except 36104) 5-10 78-82
STIFF/EPIC (36104 "Do It Yourself") 10-15 79
(Includes bonus single *Hit Me with Your Rhythm Stick.*)
Also see JANKEL, Chas

DUSK P&R '71

Singles: 7-inch

BELL 4-6 71-72
Member: Peggy Santiglia.
Also see ANGELS

DUVALL, Huelyn P&R '59

Singles: 78 rpm

CHALLENGE 25-50 58

Singles: 7-inch

CHALLENGE (1012 "Comin' Or Goin' ") 25-35 58
(Blue label.)
CHALLENGE (1012 "Comin' Or Goin' ") 10-20 58
(Maroon label.)
CHALLENGE (59002 "Humdinger") . 10-20 58
CHALLENGE (59014 "Little Boy Blue")..15-25 58
CHALLENGE (59025 "Juliette")........10-20 58
CHALLENGE (59069 "Pucker Paint")...15-25 59
STARFIRE (600 "It's No Wonder") ... 30-35 59
TWINKLE (506 "Beautiful Dreamer")...40-60 50s

DYER, Ada R&B '88

Singles: 7-inch

MOTOWN 3-4 88

DYKE & BLAZERS P&R/R&B/LP '67

Singles: 7-inch

ARTCO 8-10 67
ORIGINAL SOUND.............................4-8 67-70

LPs: 10/12-inch

ORIGINAL SOUND (8876 "Funky Broadway")......................................30-35 67
ORIGINAL SOUND (8877 "Dyke's Greatest Hits")..20-30 67
Member: Arlester "Dyke" Christian.

DYLAN, Bob LP '63

(With the Band)

Singles: 7-inch

ASYLUM 3-6 74
COLUMBIA (10106 "Tangled Up in Blue")..8-12 75
COLUMBIA (10217 "Million Dollar Bash")..8-12 75
COLUMBIA (10245 "Hurricane")...........3-5 75
COLUMBIA (10298 "Mozambique")...... 3-5 75
COLUMBIA (10454 "Rita Mae") 8-12 77
COLUMBIA (10805 "Baby Stop Crying") 4-8 78
COLUMBIA (10851 "Changing of the Guards")...8-12 78
COLUMBIA (11000 series) 3-5 79-80
COLUMBIA (13-0000 series) 3-4
COLUMBIA (18-0000 series) 3-4 81
COLUMBIA (38-0000 thru 0400)...........3-4 84-86
COLUMBIA (42656 "Mixed Up Confusion")...............................500-1000 63
COLUMBIA (42856 "Blowin' in the Wind") 150-200 63
COLUMBIA (43242 "Subterranean Homesick Blues")..10-20 65
(Gray label.)
COLUMBIA (43242 "Subterranean Homesick Blues")..4-8 65
(Red label.)
COLUMBIA (43346 "Like a Rolling Stone") 4-8 65
COLUMBIA (43389 "Positively 4th Street")..10-20 65
(Gray label.)
COLUMBIA (43389 "Positively 4th Street")..4-8 65
(Red label.)
COLUMBIA (43477 "Can You Please Crawl Out Your Window")................................10-12 65
COLUMBIA (43683 "I Want You").........4-8 66
COLUMBIA (43541 "One of Us Must Know") 8-12 66
COLUMBIA (43592 "Rainy Day Women #12 and 35")...4-8 66
COLUMBIA (43792 "Just Like a Woman")..4-8 66
COLUMBIA (44069 "Leopard-Skin Pill-Box Hat")..8-12 67
COLUMBIA (44826 "I Threw It All Away")..8-10 69
COLUMBIA (44926 "Lay Lady Lay").....4-8 69
COLUMBIA (45004 "Tonight I'll Be Staying Here with You)..8-10 69
COLUMBIA (45199 "Wigwam")...........5-10 69
COLUMBIA (45409 "Watching the River Flow")..5-10 71
COLUMBIA (45516 "George Jackson")..8-10 71
COLUMBIA (45913 "Knockin' on Heaven's Door") 3-5 73
COLUMBIA (45982 "A Fool Such As I") 3-5 73
MCA (52811 "Band of the Hand")..........4-6 86

Picture Sleeves

COLUMBIA (02510 "Heart of Mine") 4-8 81
COLUMBIA (04301 "Sweetheart Like You")..4-6 84
COLUMBIA (04933 "Tight Connection to My Heart")..4-6 85
COLUMBIA (10245 "Hurricane").......25-50 75
COLUMBIA (11235 "Slow Train").........5-10 80
COLUMBIA (43242 "Subterranean Homesick Blues") 300-500 65
(Promotional issue only.)
COLUMBIA (43242 "Subterranean Homesick Blues")..40-60 65
(Columbia "Hit Pack" picture sleeve.)
COLUMBIA (43389 "Positively 4th Street")...25-35 65
COLUMBIA (43683 "I Want You").....20-25 66
MCA (52811 "Band of the Hand").......4-6 86

Promotional Singles

ASYLUM..8-12 74
COLUMBIA (25 "All the Tired Horses")...30-40 70
COLUMBIA (1039 "If Not for You")....30-40 71
COLUMBIA (10106 "Tangled Up in Blue")..10-20 75
COLUMBIA (10245 "Hurricane").........15-20 75
COLUMBIA (10245 "Hurricane").......20-30 75
(Compact 33 Single.)
COLUMBIA (10298 "Mozambique") 8-10 75
COLUMBIA (10454 "Rita Mae") 10-20 77
COLUMBIA (10805 "Baby Stop Crying")..10-20 78
COLUMBIA (11000 series)....................4-8 79-80
COLUMBIA (18-0000 series)................3-6 81
COLUMBIA (38-0000 thru 0400) 3-5 84-86
COLUMBIA (42656 "Mixed Up Confusion")...................................500-750 63
COLUMBIA (42856 "Blowin' in the Wind")..200-300 63
(Add $100 to $200 if accompanied by "Rebel with a Cause" letter-insert, which introduces Bob Dylan.)
COLUMBIA (43242 "Subterranean Homesick Blues") 40-60 65
(Black vinyl.)
COLUMBIA (43242 "Subterranean Homesick Blues")..50-100 65
(Colored vinyl.)
COLUMBIA (43346 "Like a Rolling Stone")...40-60 65
(Black vinyl. Labels may show identification numbers "JZSP-110939/110940," but not selection number, 43346.)

COLUMBIA (43346 "Like a Rolling Stone")....................50-100 65
(Colored vinyl.)
COLUMBIA (43389 "Positively 4th Street")....................30-40 65
(Black vinyl.)
COLUMBIA (43389 "Positively 4th Street")....................50-100 65
(Colored vinyl.)
COLUMBIA (43389 "Positively 4th Street")....................75-100 65
(Outtake promo. Has an alternate take of *Can You Please Crawl Out Your Window.*)
COLUMBIA (43477 "Can You Please Crawl Out Your Window")....................40-60 65
COLUMBIA (43683 "I Want You")..... 30-45 66
(Black vinyl.)
COLUMBIA (43683 "I Want You")... 50-100 66
(Colored vinyl.)
COLUMBIA (43541 "One of Us Must Know")....................40-55 66
COLUMBIA (43592 "Rainy Day Women #12 and 35")....................30-40 66
COLUMBIA (43792 "Just Like a Woman")....................30-40 66
(Black vinyl.)
COLUMBIA (43792 "Just Like a Woman")....................50-100 66
(Colored vinyl.)
COLUMBIA (44069 "Leopard-Skin Pill-Box Hat")....................30-40 67
COLUMBIA (44826 "I Threw It All Away")....................15-25 69
COLUMBIA (44926 "Lay Lady Lay")....................15-25 69
COLUMBIA (45004 "Tonight I'll Be Staying Here with You")....................15-25 69
COLUMBIA (45199 "Wigwam")........ 15-25 69
COLUMBIA (45409 "Watching the River Flow")....................15-25 71
COLUMBIA (45516 "George Jackson")....................15-25 71
COLUMBIA (45913 "Knockin' on Heaven's Door")....................10-20 73
COLUMBIA (45982 "A Fool Such As I")....................10-20 73
COLUMBIA (75606 "Blowin' in the Wind")....................250-400 63
("Special Album Excerpt.")

EPs: 7–inch

COLUMBIA (319 "Step Lively")..... 100-150 65
COLUMBIA (9128 "Bringing It All Back Home")....................125-175 65
(Juke box issue only.)
COLUMBIA/PLAYBACK....................75-100 73
(Promotional issue only. Contains four tracks by four different artists.)

LPs: 10/12–inch

ASYLUM (201 "Before the Flood").... 10-15 74
ASYLUM (1003 "Planet Waves")...... 15-20 74
(Without cut corner.)
ASYLUM (1003 "Planet Waves")........ 8-10 74
(With cut corner.)
ASYLUM (EQ-1003 "Planet Waves")....................15-20 74
(Quadrophonic.)
COLUMBIA (C2L-41 "Blonde on Blonde")....................40-60 66
(Monaural. With "female photos" on inside of jacket.)
COLUMBIA (C2L-41 "Blonde on Blonde")....................15-25 66
(Monaural. With Dylan photo replacing female photos.)
COLUMBIA (C2S-841 "Blonde on Blonde")....................40-60 66
(Stereo. With "female photos" on inside of jacket.)
COLUMBIA (C2S-841 "Blonde on Blonde")....................15-25 66
(Stereo. With Dylan photo replacing female photos.)
COLUMBIA (CL-1779 "Bob Dylan")....................125-175 62
(Monaural. Red and black label with six Columbia "eye" boxes.)
COLUMBIA (CL-1779 "Bob Dylan")....................20-30 62
(Monaural. Red label, without six Columbia "eye" boxes.)
COLUMBIA (CL-1986 "The Freewheelin' Bob Dylan")....................10000-15000 63
(Monaural. With *Let Me Die in My Footsteps, Talkin' John Birch Society Blues, Gamblin' Willie's Dead Man's Hand,* and *Rocks and Gravel,* which may also be shown as *Solid Gravel.* We suggest verification of the above tracks by listening to the LP, rather than accepting the information printed on the label. In fact, some copies of the rare pressing have reissue labels. Identification numbers of this press are XLP-58717-1A and XLP-58718-1A.)
COLUMBIA (CL-1986 "The Freewheelin' Bob Dylan")....................20-30 63
(Monaural. With the above tracks replaced by four others.)
COLUMBIA (CL-2105 "The Times They Are A-Changin'")....................20-30 64
(Monaural.)
COLUMBIA (CL-2193 "Another Side of Bob Dylan")....................15-20 64
(Monaural.)
COLUMBIA (CL-2328 "Bringin' It All Back Home")....................15-25 65
(Monaural.)
COLUMBIA (CL-2389 "Highway 61 Revisited")....................150-200 65
(Monaural. With alternate take of *From a Buick 6.* The alternate take begins with a harmonica riff. This pressing has a "-1" at the end of the identification number, stamped in the vinyl trailoff.)
COLUMBIA (CL-2389 "Highway 61 Revisited")....................10-15 65
(Monaural.)
COLUMBIA (KCL-2663 "Bob Dylan's Greatest Hits")....................15-25 67
(Monaural.)
COLUMBIA (CL-2804 "John Wesley Harding")....................60-100 68
(Monaural.)
COLUMBIA (CS-8579 "Bob Dylan")....................150-200 62
(Stereo. Red and black label with six Columbia "eye" boxes.)
COLUMBIA (CS-8579 "Bob Dylan")....................25-40 62
(Stereo. Red label, without six Columbia "eye" boxes. Some—perhaps all—Canadian pressings fail to list *Don't Think Twice, It's Alright* on the back cover, though the song is on the disc—Side 2, Track 1.)
COLUMBIA (PC-8579 "Bob Dylan").... 5-10
COLUMBIA (CS-8786 "The Freewheelin' Bob Dylan")....................20-30 63
(Stereo.)
COLUMBIA (PC-8786 "The Freewheelin' Bob Dylan")....................5-10
COLUMBIA (CS-8905 "The Times They Are A-Changin'")....................20-30 64
(Stereo.)
COLUMBIA (CS-8993 "Another Side of Bob Dylan")....................15-25 64
(Stereo.)
COLUMBIA (CS-9128 "Bringin' It All Back Home")....................15-25 65
(Stereo.)
COLUMBIA (PC-9128 "Bringin' It All Back Home")....................5-10 70s
COLUMBIA (CS-9189 "Highway 61 Revisited")....................100-150 65
(Stereo. With alternate take of *From a Buick 6.* The alternate take begins with a harmonica riff. This pressing has a "-1" at the end of the identification number, stamped in the vinyl trailoff.)
COLUMBIA (CS-9189 "Highway 61 Revisited")....................10-20 65
(Stereo.)
COLUMBIA (KCS-9463 "Bob Dylan's Greatest Hits")....................15-25 67
(Stereo.)
COLUMBIA (CS-9604 "John Wesley Harding")....................20-30 68
(Stereo.)
COLUMBIA (KCS-9825 "Nashville Skyline")....................8-12 69
COLUMBIA (C2X-30050 "Self Portrait")....................50-60 70
(With "360-Degree Stereo" at bottom of label.)
COLUMBIA (C2X-30050 "Self Portrait")....................10-15 70
(Without "360-Degree Stereo" at bottom of label.)
COLUMBIA (KC-30290 "New Morning")....................8-10 70
COLUMBIA (KC-31120 "Greatest Hits, Vol. 2")....................10-12 71
COLUMBIA (KC-32460 "Pat Garrett and Billy the Kid")....................8-10 73
(Soundtrack.)
COLUMBIA (KC-32747 "Dylan")........ 8-10 73
COLUMBIA (CQ-32872 "Nashville Skyline")....................40-60 74
(Quadrophonic.)
COLUMBIA (PC-33235 "Blood on the Tracks")....................25-35 75
(With mural pictured on the back cover.)
COLUMBIA (PC-33235 "Blood on the Tracks")....................8-12 75
(With liner notes on the back cover.)
COLUMBIA (PC2-33682 "The Basement Tapes")....................10-12 75
COLUMBIA (PC-33893 "Desire")........ 8-10 76
COLUMBIA (PCQ-33893 "Desire")... 25-35 76
(Quadrophonic.)
COLUMBIA (PC-34349 "Hard Rain").. 8-10 76
COLUMBIA (JC-35453 "Street Legal")....................8-10 78
COLUMBIA (PC2-36067 "Bob Dylan at Budokan")....................8-10 79
COLUMBIA (FC-36120 "Slow Train Comin'")....................8-10 79
COLUMBIA (FC-36553 "Saved")......... 8-10 80
COLUMBIA (FC-37496 "Shot of Love")....................8-10 81
COLUMBIA (PC-38819 "Infidels")...... 8-10 83
COLUMBIA (C5X-38830 "Biograph")....................20-30 85
(Boxed, five-disc set. includes 36-page booklet.)
COLUMBIA (FC-39944 "Real Live")....................5-10 84
COLUMBIA (FC-40110 "Empire Burlesque")....................5-10 85
COLUMBIA (OC-40439 "Knocked Out Loaded")....................5-10 86
COLUMBIA (OC-40957 "Down in the Groove")....................5-10 88
COLUMBIA (HC-43235 "Blood on the Tracks")....................20-30 83
(Half-speed mastered.)
COLUMBIA (45281 "Oh Mercy")......... 5-10 89
COLUMBIA (46794 "Under the Red Sky")....................5-10 90
COLUMBIA (47382 "The Bootleg Series Volumes 1 - 3")....................15-20 89
COLUMBIA (HC-49825 "Nashville Skyline")....................20-30 81
(Half-speed mastered.)
FOLKWAYS (5322 "Bob Dylan Vs. A.J. Weberman")....................100-175
ISLAND (1 "Before the Flood")......... 25-30 74
MFSL (114 "The Times They Are A-Changing")....................10-15

Promotional LPs

ASYLUM (201 "Before the Flood")..... 25-40 74
ASYLUM (1003 "Planet Waves")...... 25-40 74
COLUMBIA (422 "Renaldo and Clara")....................25-35 76
(Soundtrack.)
COLUMBIA (798 "Saved")....................25-35 80
COLUMBIA (1259 "Dylan London Interview")....................25-35 80
COLUMBIA (1263 "Shot of Love")..... 25-35 81
COLUMBIA (1471 "Electric Lunch").. 15-25 83

COLUMBIA (1770 "Infidels") 10-20 83
COLUMBIA (C2L-41 "Blonde on Blonde") 60-75 66
(Monaural. With "female photos" on inside of jacket.)
COLUMBIA (C2S-841 "Blonde on Blonde") 60-75 66
(Stereo. With "female photos" on inside of jacket.)
COLUMBIA (CL-1779 "Bob Dylan") 200-300 62
(Monaural.)
COLUMBIA (CL-1986 "The Freewheelin' Bob Dylan") 10000-15000 63
(Monaural. With *Let Me Die in My Footsteps, Talkin' John Birch Society Blues, Gamblin' Willie's Dead Man's Hand,* and *Rocks and Gravel,* which may also be shown as *Solid Gravel.* We suggest verification of the above tracks by listening to the LP, rather than accepting the information printed on the label. In fact, some copies of the rare pressing have reissue labels. Identification numbers of this press are XLP-58717-1A and XLP-58718-1A.)
COLUMBIA (CL-1986 "The Freewheelin' Bob Dylan") 75-100 63
(Monaural. With the above tracks replaced by four others.)
COLUMBIA (CL-2105 "The Times They Are A-Changin' ") 75-100 64
COLUMBIA (CL-2193 "Another Side of Bob Dylan") 60-75 64
(Monaural.)
COLUMBIA (CL-2328 "Bringin' It All Back Home") 60-75 65
(Monaural.)
COLUMBIA (CL-2389 "Highway 61 Revisited") 60-75 65
(Monaural.)
COLUMBIA (KCL-2663 "Bob Dylan's Greatest Hits") 60-75 67
(Monaural.)
COLUMBIA (CL-2804 "John Wesley Harding") 50-60 68
(Monaural.)
COLUMBIA (CS-8579 "Bob Dylan") 200-300 62
(Stereo.)
COLUMBIA (CS-8786 "The Freewheelin' Bob Dylan") 75-100 63
(Stereo.)
COLUMBIA (CS-8905 "The Times They Are A-Changin' ") 75-100 64
(Stereo.)
COLUMBIA (CS-8993 "Another Side of Bob Dylan") 60-75 64
(Stereo.)
COLUMBIA (CS-9128 "Bringin' It All Back Home") 60-75 65
(Stereo.)
COLUMBIA (CS-9189 "Highway 61 Revisited") 60-75 65
(Stereo.)
COLUMBIA (KCS-9463 "Bob Dylan's Greatest Hits") 60-75 67
(Stereo.)
COLUMBIA (KCS-9825 "Nashville Skyline") 50-60 69
COLUMBIA (30050 "Self Portrait") 50-60 70
COLUMBIA (31120 "Greatest Hits Vol. 2") 10-20 71
COLUMBIA (32460 "Pat Garrett and Billy the Kid") 15-25 73
(Soundtrack.)
COLUMBIA (32747 "Dylan") 10-15 73
COLUMBIA (33235 "Blood on the Tracks") 20-25 75
COLUMBIA (33682 "The Basement Tapes") 10-15 75
COLUMBIA (33893 "Desire") 10-15 76
COLUMBIA (34349 "Hard Rain") 10-15 76
COLUMBIA (35453 "Street Legal") ... 10-15 78
(With programmer's timing strip.)
COLUMBIA (36067 "Bob Dylan at Budokan") 10-20 79
COLUMBIA (36120 "Slow Train Comin' ") 10-15 79
COLUMBIA (36553 "Saved") 10-15 80
COLUMBIA (37496 "Shot of Love") .. 10-15 81
COLUMBIA (38819 "Infidels") 10-15 83
COLUMBIA (39944 "Real Live") 10-15 84
COLUMBIA (40110 "Empire Burlesque") 10-15 85
COLUMBIA (40439 "Knocked Out Loaded") 10-15 86
COLUMBIA (43235 "Blood on the Tracks") 25-50 83
(Half-speed mastered.)
COLUMBIA (49825 "Nashville Skyline") 25-35 81
(Half-speed mastered.)
COLUMBIA (67000 "Unplugged") 10-15 90s
FOLKWAYS (5322 "Bob Dylan Vs. A.J. Weberman") 75-100
ISLAND (1 "Before the Flood") 25-35 74
MFSL (114 "The Times They Are A-Changin' ") 20-30 80s
WESTWOOD ONE ("Dylan on Dylan") 150-200 84
(Five-LP set. Issued for radio broadcast only.)
WESTWOOD ONE ("Dylan on Dylan") 100-150 84
(Three-LP set. Shorter version of the above show.)
Session: Michael Bloomfield; Al Kooper; Paul Griffin; Bobby Gregg; Charlie McCoy; Frank Owens; Russ Savakus; Harvey Goldstein.
Also see BAND
Also see BELAFONTE, Harry
Also see BLOOMFIELD, Mike
Also see GREGG, Bobby
Also see HARRISON, George
Also see KOOPER, Al
Also see McCOY, Charlie
Also see SAHM, Doug
Also see TRAVELING WILBURYS
Also see U.S.A. for AFRICA

DYLAN, Bob, & Grateful Dead — *LP '89*

LPs: 10/12-inch

COLUMBIA (45056 "Dylan and the Dead") 5-10 89
Also see GRATEFUL DEAD

DYLAN, Bob, & Heartbreakers / Michael Rubini

Singles: 7-inch

MCA 3-4 86
Also see DYLAN, Bob
Also see PETTY, Tom, & Heartbreakers

DYNAMIC BREAKERS — *R&B '85*

Singles: 12-inch

SUNNYVIEW 4-6 85

Singles: 7-inch

SUNNYVIEW 3-4 85

DYNAMIC CORVETTES — *R&B '75*

Singles: 7-inch

ABET 5-10 75
RU JAC 3-5

DYNAMIC SUPERIORS — *P&R/R&B '74*

Singles: 12-inch

MOTOWN 4-6 77

Singles: 7-inch

MOTOWN 3-5 74-77

LPs: 10/12-inch

MOTOWN 8-10 74-77
Members: Tony Washington; Maurice Washington; Michael McCalpin; George Spann; George Peterback.

DYNAMICS — *P&R/R&B '63*

Singles: 7-inch

BIG TOP 5-10 63-64
BLACK GOLD 4-8 73-74
COTILLION 5-10 68-69

LPs: 10/12-inch

BLACK GOLD 8-10 73
COTILLION 12-15 69
Members: Sam Stevenson; Zeke Harris; Fred Baker; George White.

DYNA-SORES — *P&R '60*

Singles: 7-inch

RENDEZVOUS 8-12 60
Member: Jimmy Norman.
Also see NORMAN, Jimmy

DYNASTY — *R&B '79*

Singles: 7-inch

SOLAR 3-4 79-88

LPs: 10/12-inch

SOLAR 5-10 79-82
Members: Kevin Spencer; Nidra Beard; Linda Carriere; Leon Sylvers.
Also see DE BLANK
Also see STARFIRE
Also see SYLVERS

DYNATONES — *P&R/R&B '66*

Singles: 7-inch

HBR 4-8 66
ST. CLAIR 8-10 66

LPs: 10/12-inch

HBR 20-25 66

DYNELL, Johnny, & New York 88 — *D&D '83*

Singles: 12-inch

ACME 4-6 83-84

DYSON, Clifton — *R&B '82*

Singles: 12-inch

MOTOWN 4-8 79

Singles: 7-inch

MOTOWN 3-4 79
NETWORK 3-4 82

LPs: 10/12-inch

AFTER HOURS 5-10 82
NETWORK 5-10 82

DYSON, Ronnie — *P&R/R&B/LP '70*

Singles: 12-inch

COTILLION 4-6 83

Singles: 7-inch

COLUMBIA 3-5 69-78
COTILLION 3-4 82-83

Picture Sleeves

COLUMBIA 3-5 73-75

LPs: 10/12-inch

COLUMBIA 8-10 70-79
COTILLION 5-10 82-83

E., Sheila: see SHEILA E.

EBN/OZN *D&D '83*
(EBN-OZN)
Singles: 12-inch
ELEKTRA 4-6 83-84
Singles: 7-inch
ELEKTRA 3-4 84
LPs: 10/12-inch
ELEKTRA 5-10 84
Members: Ebn; Ozn.

EBO *R&B '85*
Singles: 12-inch
DOMINO 4-6 85
Singles: 7-inch
DOMINO 3-4 85

ELO: see ELECTRIC LIGHT ORCHESTRA

EMF *LP '91*
LPs: 10/12-inch
EMI 5-8 91

EPMD *R&B/LP '88*
LPs: 10/12-inch
FRESH 5-8 88-89
RAL/COLUMBIA 5-8 91
Members: Erick Sermon; Parrish Smith.

EQ *D&D '86*
Singles: 12-inch
ATLANTIC 4-6 86

E.U. *R&B '88*
(Experience Unlimited)
Singles: 7-inch
ISLAND 3-4 86
MANHATTAN 3-4 88
Picture Sleeves
MANHATTAN 3-4 88
LPs: 10/12-inch
ISLAND 5-10 86
VIRGIN 5-8 89

EAGER, Brenda Lee *R&B '73*
(With the Peaches)
Singles: 12-inch
PRIVATE I 4-6 84
Singles: 7-inch
MERCURY 3-5 72-74
PLAYBOY 3-5 75
PRIVATE I 3-4 84
Also see BUTLER, Jerry, & Brenda Lee Eager

EAGLES *P&R/LP '72*
Singles: 12-inch
ASYLUM (11402 "Please Come Home for Christmas & Funky New Year") 5-10 78
(Promotional issue only.)
Singles: 7-inch
ASYLUM 3-5 72-80
FULL MOON 3-4 81
Picture Sleeves
ASYLUM 3-5 78
LPs: 10/12-inch
ASYLUM 8-12 72-82
MFSL (126 "Hotel California") 25-35 84
Members: Don Felder; Glenn Frey; Don Henley; Randy Meisner; Timothy B. Schmit; Joe Walsh; Bernie Leadon.
Also see FELDER, Don
Also see FREY, Glenn
Also see HENLEY, Don
Also see LEADON, Bernie
Also see LEE, Johnny / Eagles
Also see MEISNER, Randy
Also see NEWMAN, Randy
Also see POCO
Also see RONSTADT, Linda
Also see SCHMIT, Timothy B.
Also see SIMMONS, Patrick
Also see VITALE, Joe
Also see WALSH, Joe

EARLAND, Charles *LP '70*
(Charles Earland's Odyssey; Charlie Earland Jr.)
Singles: 7-inch
COLUMBIA 3-4 81-82
MERCURY 3-5 76
PRESTIGE 3-5 70-74
QUAKER TOWN 4-8 64
LPs: 10/12-inch
COLUMBIA 5-10 80
MERCURY 5-10 76-78
MUSE 5-10 80
PRESTIGE 5-10 70-75
RARE BIRD 5-10 71
TRIP 5-10 73

EARLE, Steve *C&W '83*
(With the Dukes)
Singles: 12-inch
MCA 4-6 86
Singles: 7-inch
EPIC 3-4 83-85
MCA 3-4 86-90
UNI 3-4 88
Picture Sleeves
EPIC 3-4 84
EPs: 7-inch
LSI 5-10 82
LPs: 10/12-inch
MCA 5-10 86-90
UNI 5-8 88

EARL-JEAN *P&R '64*
(Earl Jean McCree)
Singles: 7-inch
COLPIX 4-8 64
Also see COOKIES
Also see KING, Ben E.
Also see RAELETTES

EARLS *P&R '62*
(Larry Chance & the Earls)
Singles: 12-inch
WOODBURY 6-10 76-77
Singles: 7-inch
ABC 5-10 68
ATLANTIC 3-5
BARRY 4-8 63
CLIFTON 4-8 74
COLLECTABLES 3-4 80s
COLUMBIA 3-5 75
HARVEY 4-8 75
MEMORIES 3-5
MR. "G" 5-10 67
OLD TOWN (1130 "Remember Then") 25-50 62
(Blue label. Publisher credit is "January Music." Artist credit in serif style typeface.)
OLD TOWN (1130 "Remember Then") 20-40 62
(Blue label. Publisher credit is "Maureen Music." Artist credit in sans-serif style.)
OLD TOWN (1130 "Remember Then") 10-20 63
(Multi-color label.)
OLD TOWN (1133 "Never") 20-40 63
(Blue label.)
OLD TOWN (1133 "Never") 10-20 63
(Multi-color label.)
OLD TOWN (1141 "Look My Way") 10-20 63
OLD TOWN (1145 "Kissin' ") 10-20 63
OLD TOWN (1149 "I Believe") 20-30 63
(Blue label.)
OLD TOWN (1149 "I Believe") 10-20 63
(Multi-color label.)
OLD TOWN (1169 "Ask Anybody") .. 10-20 64
OLD TOWN (1181 "Remember Me Baby") 30-40 65
(Promotional issue only.)
OLD TOWN (1182 "Remember Me Baby") 10-20 65
ROADHOUSE (1021 "I'm All Alone") 4-6
(Colored vinyl.)
ROME (101 "Life Is But a Dream"/"It's You") 100-150 61
ROME (101 "Life Is But a Dream"/"Without You") 30-50 61
(Note different flip side title.)
ROME (102 "Lookin' for My Baby") 30-50 61
ROME (112 "Little Boy and Girl") 3-5 76
ROME (114 "All Through Our Teens") 5-10 76
(Black vinyl.)
ROME (114 "All Through Our Teens") 10-15 76
(Colored vinyl.)
ROME (5117 "My Heart's Desire") 20-40 62
(Black vinyl.)
WOODBURY 3-5 77
EPs: 7-inch
CRYSTAL BALL 5-10
LPs: 10/12-inch
CHANCE (1001 "Today") 8-12 83
CRYSTAL BALL 8-10 82
OLD TOWN (104 "Remember Me Baby") 200-400 63
(Counterfeits exist but can be identified by their 1/2-inch vinyl trail-off and poor fidelity. Originals have a 3/4-inch trail-off and excellent fidelity.)
RAINBOW (1001 "Live") 8-12 87
WOODBURY (104 "Remember Me Baby") 10-15 76
(Red label.)
WOODBURY (104 "Remember Me Baby") 8-12 77
(Green & brown label.)
Members: Larry Chance; Robert Del Din; Jack Wray; Ed Harder; Larry Polumbo.

EARLS / Pretenders
Singles: 7-inch
ROME/POWER MARTIN 3-5 76
Also see EARLS

EARONS *R&B '83*
Singles: 12-inch
ISLAND 4-6 84
Singles: 7-inch
BOARDWALK 3-4 83
ISLAND 3-4 84
Members: Earon .28; Earon .18; Earon .22; Earon .33; Earon .69.

EARTH OPERA *P&R/LP '69*
Singles: 7-inch
ELEKTRA 4-8 67-69
LPs: 10/12-inch
ELEKTRA 10-15 68-69
Members: Peter Rowan; Paul Dillon; Dave Grishman; Bill Stevenson; John Nagy; Billy Mundi; John Cale.
Also see CALE, John
Also see RHINOCEROS

EARTH QUAKE: see EARTHQUAKE

EARTH, WIND & FIRE *P&R/R&B/LP '71*
Singles: 12-inch
COLUMBIA 4-8 75-83
Singles: 7-inch
ARC 3-4 78-82
COLUMBIA 3-5 73-90
W.B. 3-5 71
Picture Sleeves
ARC 3-4 80
COLUMBIA 3-5 74-88
LPs: 10/12-inch
COLUMBIA (Except 47000 series) 8-15 72-90
COLUMBIA (47000 series) 15-20 81-82
(Half-speed mastered.)
COLUMBIA/ARC (Except 35647) 8-15 75-81

COLUMBIA/ARC (35647 "Best of Earth, Wind & Fire")........8-10 79
COLUMBIA/ARC (35647 "Best of Earth, Wind & Fire")........15-20 79
(Picture disc. Promotional issue only.)
MFSL (159 "That's the Way of the World")........20-30 85
W.B. 10-15 71-74
Members: Philip Bailey; Maurice White; Verdine White; Ronnie Laws; Fred White; Andy Woolfolk; Larry Dunn; Ralph Johnson; Al McKay; Johnny Graham; Wade Flemons.
Also see BAILEY, Philip
Also see FLEMONS, Wade
Also see LAWS, Ronnie
Also see LEWIS, Ramsey

EARTH, WIND & FIRE & EMOTIONS P&R/R&B '79

Singles: 12-inch

ARC........4-8 79

Singles: 7-inch

ARC........3-4 79-80

LPs: 10/12-inch

ARC........5-10 79
Also see EMOTIONS

EARTH, WIND & FIRE & RAMSEY LEWIS R&B '74

Singles: 7-inch

COLUMBIA........3-5 74-75
Also see EARTH, WIND & FIRE
Also see LEWIS, Ramsey

EARTHQUAKE LP '69

(Earth Quake)

Singles: 7-inch

A&M........3-5 72
BESERKLEY........3-5 76-77

LPs: 10/12-inch

A&M........10-12 71-78
BESERKLEY........8-10 76-80
Also see KIHN, Greg, Band / Earthquake / Modern Lovers / Rubinoos
Also see KIHN, Greg, Band / Earthquake / Rubinoos / Jonathan Richman

EAST, Thomas R&B '69

(With the Fabulous Playboys)

Singles: 7-inch

LION........3-5 73
MGM........3-5 73
TODDLIN' TOWN........4-8 68-69

EAST COAST R&B "79

Singles: 7-inch

RSO........3-5 79
Members: Gregory Johnson; Larry Blackmon; Gary Dow; Eric Rurham; Anthony Lockett; Arnett Leftenant; Nathan Leftenant.
Also see CAMEO

EAST L.A. CAR POOL P&R '75

Singles: 7-inch

GRC........3-5 75

EASTBOUND EXPRESSWAY R&B "79

Singles: 7-inch

AVI........3-5 78-79

EASTERHOUSE P&R '89

Singles: 7-inch

COLUMBIA........3-4 89
Members: Andy Perry; Ivor Perry.

EASTON, Elliot LP '85

Singles: 7-inch

ELEKTRA........3-4 85

LPs: 10/12-inch

ELEKTRA........5-10 85
Also see CARS

EASTON, Sheena P&R/LP '81

Singles: 12-inch

EMI AMERICA........4-6 81-86

Singles: 7-inch

EMI AMERICA........3-4 81-86
LIBERTY........3-4 81
MCA........3-4 88-91
RCA........3-4 89

Picture Sleeves

EMI AMERICA........3-6 81-86
RCA........3-4 89

LPs: 10/12-inch

EMI AMERICA........5-10 81-86
MCA........5-8 88-91
Also see PRINCE & Sheena Easton
Also see ROGERS, Kenny, & Sheena Easton

EASTWOOD, Clint

Singles: 7-inch

CAMEO (240 "Rowdy")........10-20 63
CERTRON........4-6 70
GNP (177 "Get Yourself Another Fool")........15-25 65
GOTHIC (005 "Unknown Girl")........10-20 61
PARAMOUNT........4-8 69
W.B. 3-4 81

Picture Sleeves

CAMEO (240 "Rowdy")........30-50 63
CERTRON........5-8 70
GNP (177 "Get Yourself Another Fool")........50-75 65
GOTHIC (005 "Unknown Girl")........10-20 61

LPs: 10/12-inch

CAMEO (1056 "Cowboy Favorites")........75-125 63
Also see CHARLES, Ray, & Clint Eastwood
Also see HAGGARD, Merle, & Clint Eastwood
Also see SHEPPARD, T.G., & Clint Eastwood

EASY RIDERS

(With Terry Gilkyson)

Singles: 78 rpm

COLUMBIA........4-8 57

Singles: 7-inch

COLUMBIA........5-10 57

LPs: 10/12-inch

EPIC........10-15 63
Also see GILKYSON, Terry

EASY STREET P&R '76

Singles: 7-inch

CAPRICORN........3-5 76

LPs: 10/12-inch

CAPRICORN........8-10 76-77

EASYBEATS P&R/LP '67

Singles: 7-inch

ASCOT........8-12 66
RARE EARTH........4-8 69
U.A. 5-8 67-69

Picture Sleeves

ASCOT........10-20 66

LPs: 10/12-inch

RARE EARTH (517 "Easy Ridin' ")........10-20 70
RHINO........5-10 85
U.A. (3588 "Friday on My Mind")........30-40 67
(Monaural.)
U.A. (6588 "Friday on My Mind")........30-40 67
(Stereo.)
U.A. (6667 "Falling off the Edge of the World")........30-40 68
Members: Steve Wright; Harry Vanda; George Young; Dick Diamonde.
Also see FLASH & PAN

EAZY-E LP '88

LPs: 10/12-inch

RUTHLESS........5-8 88

EBB TIDE R&B '75

(Ebb K. Harrison, Sr.)

Singles: 7-inch

SOUND GEMS........3-5 75-76

EBONEE WEBB R&B/LP '81

(Ebony Web)

Singles: 7-inch

CAPITOL........3-4 81-84
HI........3-5 70-73

LPs: 10/12-inch

CAPITOL........5-10 81-84

EBONY D&D '83

Singles: 12-inch

QUALITY/RFC........4-6 83-84

EBONY, IVORY & JADE R&B '75

Singles: 7-inch

COLUMBIA........3-5 75

EBONY RHYTHM FUNK CAMPAIGN R&B '75

Singles: 7-inch

INNOVATION........3-5 75
MCA........3-5 72

LPs: 10/12-inch

UNI........5-10 72

EBONY WEB: see EBONEE WEBB

EBONYS P&R/R&B '71

Singles: 7-inch

BUDDAH........3-5 76
PHILADELPHIA INT'L........3-5 71-74
SOUL CLOCK........3-5 70s

LPs: 10/12-inch

PHILADELPHIA INT'L........8-10 73
Members: Jenny Holmes; David Beasley; James Tuten; Clarence Vaughn.
Also see CREME D'COCOA

ECHO & BUNNYMEN LP '81

Singles: 12-inch

SIRE........5-10 81-86

Singles: 7-inch

SIRE........3-4 81-87

Picture Sleeves

SIRE........3-4 87

LPs: 10/12-inch

SIRE........5-10 81-87

ECHOES P&R '61

Singles: 7-inch

ASCOT (2188 "I Love Candy")........15-20 65
COLUMBIA (41549 "Do I Love You")........10-15 59
COLUMBIA (41709 "Ecstasy")........10-15 60
FELSTED (8614 "Angel of Love")........30-40 61
SRG (101 "Baby Blue")........150-200 60
SEG-WAY (103 "Baby Blue")........15-25 61
SEG-WAY (106 "Sad Eyes")........15-25 61
SEG-WAY (1002 "Angel of My Heart")........20-30 62
ZIRCON (1044 "Baby Blue")........30-40 60
(Canadian.)

EPs: 7-inch

CRYSTAL BALL........4-8

LPs: 10/12-inch

CRYSTAL BALL........5-10
Members: Harry Doyle; Tom Morrissey; Tom Duffy.

ECHOES / Four Esquires

Singles: 7-inch

ROULETTE GOLDEN GOODIES........3-5 70s
Also see ECHOES
Also see FOUR ESQUIRES

ECKSTINE, Billy R&B '44

Singles: 78 rpm

DELUXE........10-15 45
EMARCY........5-10 54
MGM........5-10 47-56
NATIONAL........5-10 45-48
RCA........4-8 56

Singles: 7-inch

A&M........3-5 76
EMARCY........5-10 54
ENTERPRISE........3-5 70-74
MGM........8-15 50-56
MGM GOLDEN CIRCLE (100 series)........3-6 60s
MERCURY........4-8 59-64
MOTOWN........8-15 65-68
RCA........8-12 56
ROULETTE........5-10 59-60

Picture Sleeves

MERCURY........5-10 62

EPs: 7-inch

EMARCY........10-20 54-55
KING........10-20 53
MGM........10-20 50-56
MOTOWN (60632 "Prime of My Life")........15-25 65

RENDITION 15-25 50
LPs: 10/12-inch
AUDIO LAB (1549 "Mr. B") 30-40 60
EMARCY (26025 "Blues for Sale") 50-100 54
(10-inch LP.)
EMARCY (26027 "Love Songs of Mr. B") 50-100 54
EMARCY (36010 "I Surrender Dear") 30-60 55
EMARCY (36029 "Blues for Sale") 25-50 55
EMARCY (36030 "Love Songs of Mr. B") 50-100 55
EMARCY (36129 "Eckstine's Imagination") 25-50 55
ENTERPRISE 5-10 71-74
KING (12 "The Great Mr. B") 75-125 52
(10-inch LP.)
MGM (219 "Tenderly") 30-50 53
(10 Inch LP.)
MGM (257 "I Let a Song Go Out of My Heart") 40-60 55
(10-inch LP.)
MGM (3176 "Mr. B with a Beat") 15-25 55
MGM (3209 "Rendezvous") 15-25 55
MGM (3275 "That Old Feeling") 15-25 55
MERCURY 15-25 57-64
METRO 10-15 65
MOTOWN (632 "Prime of My Life") ... 15-25 65
MOTOWN (646 "My Way") 15-25 66
MOTOWN (677 "For Love of Ivy") 10-20 69
NATIONAL (2001 "Billy Eckstine Sings") 75-125 50
(10-inch LP.)
REGENT 20-40 56-57
ROULETTE 15-25 60
SAVOY 8-10 76-79
TRIP 5-10 75
WING 8-12 67
Also see BASIE, Count, & Billy Eckstine
Also see DAMITA JO & Billy Eckstine

ECKSTINE, Billy, & Woody Herman

Singles: 78 rpm
MGM 4-8 51
Singles: 7-inch
MGM 5-10 51
Also see HERMAN, Woody, & Orch.

ECKSTINE, Billy, & Quincy Jones

Singles: 7-inch
MERCURY 3-6 62
LPs: 10/12-inch
MERCURY 15-25 62
Also see JONES, Quincy

ECKSTINE, Billy /Arthur Prysock

LPs: 10/12-inch
GUEST STAR 5-10 64
Also see PRYSOCK, Arthur

ECKSTINE, Billy, & Sarah Vaughan

Singles: 78 rpm
MGM 4-8 52
Singles: 7-inch
MGM 5-10 52
MERCURY 5-10 57-59
LPs: 10/12-inch
GUEST STAR 5-10 64
LION 15-25 59
MERCURY (20316 "Best of Irving Berlin") 20-30 57
Also see ECKSTINE, Billy
Also see VAUGHAN, Sarah

ECSTASY, PASSION & PAIN — P&R/R&B '74

Singles: 12-inch
ROULETTE 4-6 84
Singles: 7-inch
ROULETTE 3-4 74-76
LPs: 10/12-inch
ROULETTE 8-10 74
Members: Barbara Roy; Bill Gardner; Joseph Williams Jr.; Althea Smith; Alan Tizer.
Also see ROY, Barbara

EDDIE, John — P&R/LP '86

Singles: 7-inch
COLUMBIA 3-4 86
Picture Sleeves
COLUMBIA 3-4 86
LPs: 10/12-inch
COLUMBIA 5-10 86

EDDIE & BETTY — P&R '59

Singles: 7-inch
LARK 5-10 59
SIX THOUSAND 10-15 57
W.B. 5-10 59
LPs: 10/12-inch
W.B. 20-30 59
Members: Eddie Cole; Betty Cole.

EDDIE & CRUISERS — P&R '83

(John Cafferty & Beaver Brown Band)
Singles: 7-inch
SCOTTI BROTHERS 3-4 83
Also see CAFFERTY, John

EDDIE & DUTCH — P&R '70

Singles: 7-inch
IVANHOE 3-5 70
Members: Eddie Mascari; Dutch Wenzloff.

EDDIE & ERNIE — R&B '65

Singles: 7-inch
CHECKER 5-10 63
CHESS 4-8 66
EASTERN 4-8 65-66
REVUE 3-5 69
Members: Eddie Campbell; Ernie Johnson.

EDDIE & FREDDIE — R&B '77

Singles: 7-inch
OCTOBER 3-5 77

EDDIE & TIDE — P&R '85

(Eddie Rice)
Singles: 12-inch
SPIN 4-8 88
(Promotional only.)
Singles: 7-inch
ATCO 3-4 85
Picture Sleeves
ATCO 3-4 87

EDDIE D. — R&B '85

(Eddie Drummond)
Singles: 12-inch
PHILLY WORLD 4-6 85
Singles: 7-inch
PHILLY WORLD 3-4 85

EDDY, Duane — P&R/C&W/R&B '58

(With the Rebels; with Rebelettes; with His Rock-a-billies; with His Twangy Guitar)
Singles: 78 rpm
FORD (500 "Ramrod") 75-125 57
JAMIE (1101 "Moovin' N' Groovin' ") 50-75 58
(Pink label.)
JAMIE (1101 "Moovin' N' Groovin' ") 25-50 58
(Yellow label.)
JAMIE (1104 "Rebel-'Rouser") 25-50 58
JAMIE (1109 "Ramrod") 25-50 58
JAMIE (1111 "Cannonball") 25-50 58
JAMIE (1117 "The Lonely One") 50-75 59
JAMIE (1122 "Yep!") 50-100 59
Singles: 7-inch
BIG TREE 5-10 72
CAPITOL 3-4 87
COLPIX 5-10 65-66
CONGRESS 3-5 70
ELEKTRA 3-5 77
FORD (500 "Ramrod") 75-125 57
(Credits Duane Eddy, but is by Al Casey.)
GREGMARK (5 "Caravan") 5-10 61
(Credits Duane Eddy, but is by Al Casey.)
JAMIE (73 "Peter Gunn") 25-50 61
(Compact 33 single.)
JAMIE (1100 series) 10-20 58-61
(Monaural.)
JAMIE (1100 series) 20-40 59-60
(Stereo.)
JAMIE (1200 series) 8-15 61-62
RCA (Except 8507) 8-15 61-65
RCA (8507 "Moon Shot") 25-35 65
REPRISE 5-15 66-68
UNI 4-6 70
Picture Sleeves
CAPITOL 3-4 87
COLPIX (788 "House of the Rising Sun") 25-40 66
JAMIE 15-25 59-61
RCA 10-15 62-64
EPs: 7-inch
JAMIE 20-40 59-60
RCA/WURLITZER DISCOTHEQUE MUSIC 15-25 64
LPs: 10/12-inch
CAMDEN 8-15
CAPITOL 8-10 87
COLPIX (490 "Duane A-Go-Go") 25-30 65
COLPIX (494 "Duane Eddy Does Bob Dylan") 25-30 65
JAMIE (Except 3000, 3011 & 3026) .. 15-30 59-63
JAMIE (3000 "Have Twangy Guitar Will Travel") 20-40 58
(White cover.)
JAMIE (3000 "Have Twangy Guitar Will Travel") 15-30 58
(Red cover.)
JAMIE (3011 "Songs of Our Heritage") 50-75 60
(Colored vinyl.)
JAMIE (3011 "Songs of Our Heritage") 20-30 60
(Gatefold cover. Black vinyl.)
JAMIE (3011 "Songs of Our Heritage") 15-20 61
(Standard cover. Black vinyl.)
JAMIE (3026 "16 Greatest Hits") 15-20 64
RCA ("LPM"/"LSP" series) 20-30 62-66
RCA ("ANL1" series) 5-10 78
REPRISE 15-20 66-67
SIRE 10-15 75
Session: Duane Eddy; Al Casey; Corki Casey; Donnie Owens; Plas Johnson; Steve Douglas; Ike Clanton; Mike Bermani; Waylon Jennings; Willie Nelson; Kin Vassy.
Also see ART of NOISE
Also see BLOSSOMS
Also see CASEY, Al
Also see CLANTON, Ike
Also see CLARK, Sanford, & Duane Eddy
Also see DOUGLAS, Steve
Also see FOGERTY, John
Also see JENNINGS, Waylon
Also see JIMMY & DUANE
Also see JOHNSON, Plas
Also see NELSON, Willie
Also see OWENS, Donnie
Also see SHARPE, Ray
Also see THOMAS, B.J.

EDDY, Duane & Mirriam

Singles: 7-inch
REPRISE (0622 "Guitar on My Mind") 10-15 67
Also see EDDY, Duane

EDELMAN, Randy — P&R '75

Singles: 7-inch
ARISTA 3-5 77-79
LION 3-5 73
MGM 3-5 73
SUNFLOWER 3-5 71-72
20TH FOX 3-5 74-76
LPs: 10/12-inch
ARISTA 5-10 77-79
LION 8-10 72
SUNFLOWER 8-12 71
20TH FOX 8-10 74-78

EDEN'S CHILDREN — LP '68

Singles: 7-inch
ABC 11053 "Goodbye Girl") 5-10 68
LPs: 10/12-inch
ABC (624 "Eden's Children") 20-30 68
ABC (652 "Sure Looks Real") 15-25 68

EDGE, Graeme — LP '75

(Graeme Edge Band; with Adrian Gurvitz)

Singles: 7-inch

LONDON ... 3-5 77
THRESHOLD ... 3-5 74

LPs: 10/12-inch

LONDON (686 "Paradise Ballroom") ... 8-12 77
THRESHOLD (15 "Kick off Your Muddy Boots") ... 10-15 75

Also see GURVITZ, Adrian
Also see MOODY BLUES

EDISON LIGHTHOUSE — P&R '70

Singles: 7-inch

BELL ... 3-6 70-71
FLASHBACK ... 3-5 70s

Member: Tony Burrows.
Also see BURROWS, Tony

EDMUNDS, Dave — P&R '70

Singles: 12-inch

COLUMBIA (Except 1725) ... 4-8 85-87
(Promotional issue only.)
COLUMBIA (1725 "Information") ... 15-20 84
(Picture disc. Promotional issue only.)

Singles: 7-inch

ARISTA (522 "Slipping Away") ... 3-5 83
(Clear vinyl.)
COLUMBIA ... 3-5 80-85
MAM (3601 "I Hear You Knocking") ... 5-8 70
(Black label.)
MAM (3601 "I Hear You Knocking") ... 3-6 70
(Blue label.)
MAM (3608 "I'm Coming Home") ... 3-6 71
RCA ... 3-6 73-74
SWAN SONG ... 3-5 77-81

Promotional Singles

COLUMBIA (1576 "Run Rudolph Run") ... 4-6 82
(Compact 33 single.)
COLUMBIA (03428 "Run Rudolph Run") ... 3-5 82

Picture Sleeves

COLUMBIA ... 3-4 85
SWAN SONG ... 3-5 81

LPs: 10/12-inch

ATLANTIC (320 "College Network") ... 35-45
(Promotional issue only.)
CAPITOL ... 5-8 90
COLUMBIA (Except 1725) ... 5-10 80-87
COLUMBIA (1725 "Information") ... 15-25 83
(Picture disc. Promotional issue only.)
MAM (3 "Rockpile") ... 30-40 72
RCA (4238 "Subtle As a Flying Mallet") ... 5-10 82
RCA (5003 "Subtle As a Flying Mallet") ... 10-12
SWAN SONG ... 8-10 77-81

Also see CARTER, Carlene, & Dave Edmunds
Also see DION
Also see EDMUNDS, Dave
Also see HARRISON, George / Jeff Beck / Dave Edmunds
Also see LEWIS, Huey, & News
Also see LOVE SCULPTURE
Also see LOWE, Nick, & Dave Edmunds

EDSELS — P&R '61

Singles: 7-inch

ABC ... 3-5 75
CAPITOL ... 10-20 61-62
DOT (16311 "My Whispering Heart") 15-20 62
DUB (2843 "Lama Rama Ding Dong") ... 40-60 58
(Black and gold label. Copies with black and silver labels are counterfeits. Humorously, fakes have the 1961 Twin label track, which is noticeably different than the Dub one.)
DUB (2843 "Rama Lama Ding Dong") ... 10-20 58
(Note title correction.)
EMBER (1078 "Three Precious Words") ... 10-20 61
LOST-NITE ... 4-6 70s
MUSICTONE ... 5-10 64
REGENCY ("Rama Lama Ding Dong") ... 10-20 61
(Canadian. Has the Twin track.)
ROULETTE (4151 "Do You Love Me") ... 15-20 59
TAMMY (1010 "What Brought Us Together") ... 30-40 60
TAMMY (1014 "Three Precious Words") ... 30-40 61
TAMMY (1023 "The Girl I Love") ... 25-35 61
TAMMY (1027 "Count the Tears") ... 25-35 61
TWIN (700 "Rama Lama Ding Dong") ... 10-20 61
(This track is noticeably different than the one previously issued on Dub.)

Members: George Jones Jr; Larry Green; James Reynolds; Marshall Sewell; Harry Green.

EDWARD BEAR — P&R '70

Singles: 7-inch

CAPITOL ... 3-6 70-74
CAPITOL STARLINE (22007 "You, Me and Mexico") ... 4-8 72
(Canadian.)

Picture Sleeves

CAPITOL ... 3-6 72-73

LPs: 10/12-inch

CAPITOL ... 8-10 70-73

EDWARDS, Alton — R&B '82

Singles: 12-inch

COLUMBIA ... 4-6 82

Singles: 7-inch

COLUMBIA ... 3-4 82

EDWARDS, Bobby — P&R/C&W '61

Singles: 7-inch

BLUEBONNET ... 5-10 59
CAPITOL ... 4-8 61-63
CHART ... 4-6 68
CREST ... 5-10 61
MANCO ... 4-8 62
MUSICOR ... 4-8 65
POLARIS ... 3-5

EDWARDS, Dee — R&B '79

Singles: 12-inch

COTILLION ... 4-6 79

Singles: 7-inch

COTILLION ... 3-6 78-80
D TOWN (1024 "He Told Me Lies") .. 20-40 65
D TOWN (1031 "What a Party") ... 10-20 66
D TOWN (1048 "His Majesty My Love") ... 15-25 66
D TOWN (1063 "All the Way Home") ... 20-40 66
RCA ... 5-10 72
TUBA ... 10-20 62

LPs: 10/12-inch

COTILLION ... 5-10 80

EDWARDS, Dennis — P&R/R&B/LP '84

Singles: 12-inch

GORDY ... 4-6 84

Singles: 7-inch

GORDY ... 3-4 84-85
INT'L SOULVILLE (100 "I Didn't Have to But I Did") ... 400-600
MOTOWN ... 3-4

LPs: 10/12-inch

GORDY ... 5-10 84-85

Also see CONTOURS
Also see TEMPTATIONS

EDWARDS, Jayne — D&D '83

Singles: 12-inch

PROFILE ... 4-6 83-84

Singles: 7-inch

PROFILE ... 3-4 83-84

LPs: 10/12-inch

PROFILE ... 5-10 84

EDWARDS, Jimmy — C&W '57

(Jimmie Edwards)

Singles: 78 rpm

MERCURY ... 10-15 57

Singles: 7-inch

MERCURY ... 15-25 57-58
RCA ... 10-20 59-60

EDWARDS, John — R&B '73

Singles: 7-inch

AWARE ... 4-8 73-74
BELL (45205 "Look on Your Face") .. 25-50 72
COTILLION ... 3-6 76-77

LPs: 10/12-inch

AWARE ... 5-10 74
CREED ... 5-10 75
GENERAL/GRC ... 5-10 74

EDWARDS, Jonathan — P&R/LP '71

Singles: 7-inch

ATCO ... 3-5 72-73
CAPRICORN ... 3-5 71
W.B. ... 3-4 77

LPs: 10/12-inch

AMERICAN MELODY ... 5-8
ATCO ... 8-10 72-74
CAPRICORN ... 10-12 71
REPRISE ... 8-10 74
W.B. ... 8-10 77

EDWARDS, Jonathan & Darlene

(Paul Weston & Jo Stafford)

LPs: 10/12-inch

COLUMBIA (1024 "Piano Artistry") ... 25-40 57
CORINTHIAN ... 5-10

Also see STAFFORD, Jo
Also see WESTON, Paul, Orchestra

EDWARDS, Tom — P&R '57

Singles: 78 rpm

CORAL ... 5-10 57

Singles: 7-inch

CORAL ... 5-10 57

EDWARDS, Tommy — P&R/R&B '51

Singles: 78 rpm

MGM (10000 & 11000 series) ... 5-15 51-55
MGM (12000 series) ... 15-25 58
TOP ... 10-20 49-50

Singles: 7-inch

MGM (10000 & 11000 series) ... 10-20 51-55
MGM (12000 & 13000 series) ... 5-15 55-65
MGM (50000 series) ... 20-30 59
(Stereo.)

Picture Sleeves

MGM ... 8-12 60

EPs: 7-inch

MGM (1003 "It's All In the Game") ... 20-30 52
MGM (1614 "It's All In the Game") ... 10-20 58
MGM (1666/1667/1668 "For Young Lovers") ... 10-15 59
(Monaural. Price is for any of three volumes.)
MGM (SX-1666/1667/1668 "For Young Lovers") ... 10-20 59
(Stereo. Price is for any of three volumes.)

LPs: 10/12-inch

LION ... 15-25 59
MGM ... 20-40 58-63
METRO ... 8-12 65
REGENT (6096 "Tommy Edwards Sings") ... 20-30 58

EDWARDS, Vincent — P&R/LP '62

(Vince Edwards)

Singles: 7-inch

CAPITOL ... 4-8 62
COLPIX ... 4-8 65
DECCA (31000 series) ... 4-8 62-63
DECCA (34039 "Open End Interview") ... 8-12 62
(Promotional issue only.)
DECCA (34074 "Unchained Melody") ... 5-10 62
(Stereo 33.)
KAMA SUTRA ... 4-6 67
RUSS-FI (1 "Oh Babe") ... 5-10 59
RUSS-FI (7001 "Why Did You Leave Me") ... 4-8 62

Picture Sleeves

COLPIX ... 4-8 65

DECCA (4311 "Vincent Edwards Sings") 10-20 62
(Monaural.)
DECCA (7-4311 "Vincent Edwards Sings") 15-25 62
(Stereo.)
KAMA SUTRA 4-8 67

EPs: 7-inch

DECCA 8-10 62

LPs: 10/12-inch

DECCA 10-20 62-63

EGAN, Walter
P&R/LP '77

Singles: 7-inch

BACKSTREET 3-4 83
COLUMBIA 3-4 77-79

Picture Sleeves

BACKSTREET 3-4 83

LPs: 10/12-inch

BACKSTREET 5-8 83
COLUMBIA 5-10 77-80
Also see BUCKINGHAM, Lindsey
Also see NICKS, Stevie

EGG CREAM Featuring Andy Adams
LP '77

Singles: 7-inch

PYRAMID 3-5 77

LPs: 10/12-inch

PYRAMID 5-10 77
Member: Andy Adams.

EGYPTIAN LOVER
R&B '84

Singles: 12-inch

EGYPTIAN 4-6 84-86

Singles: 7-inch

EGYPTIAN 3-4 84-86
FREAK BEAT 3-4 84

LPs: 10/12-inch

EGYPTIAN 5-10 85

EIGHT SECONDS
P&R '87

Singles: 7-inch

POLYDOR 3-4 87

Picture Sleeves

POLYDOR 3-4 87

8TH DAY
P&R/R&B/LP '71

(Eighth Day)

Singles: 7-inch

A&M 3-4 83
INVICTUS 3-5 71-72
KAPP 4-8 67-69

Picture Sleeves

KAPP 5-8 68

LPs: 10/12-inch

A&M 5-10 83
INVICTUS 8-10 71-73
KAPP 10-15 68
Members: Melvin Davis; Tony Newton; Bruce Nazarion; Michael Anthony; Anita Sherman; Carole Stallings; Lynn Harter.

EIGHTH WONDER
P&R '88

Singles: 7-inch

WTG 3-4 88-89

Picture Sleeves

WTG 3-4 88
Members: Patsy Kensit; Jamie Kensit.

ELAINE & ELLEN
R&B '80

Singles: 7-inch

OVATION 3-4 80

ELBERT, Donnie
P&R/R&B '57

Singles: 78 rpm

DELUXE 15-25 57

Singles: 7-inch

A-O 3-5 75
ALL PLATINUM 3-5 72
AVCO 3-5 72
CHECKER (1062 "Everything to Me") 10-15 63
COMMAND PERFORMANCE 3-5
CUB (9125 "Don't Cry My Love") 10-15 63
DELUXE (6143 "Believe It Or Not") 20-30 57
DELUXE (6161 "My Confession of Love") 30-40 58
DELUXE (6164 "Someone Made You for Me") 20-30 58
DELUXE (6168 "I Want to Be Near You") 20-30 58
ELBERT 4-6
GATEWAY 4-8 64-65
GUSTO 3-4 80s
JALYNNE (107 "Mommies' [sic] Gone") 15-25 60
JALYNNE (110 "Lucille") 5-10 62
PARKWAY 5-10 62
RARE BULLET 3-5 70
RED TOP (122 "Hey Baby") 15-25
RED TOP (130 "Someday") 15-25
TRIP 3-5
UP STATE 5-8
VEE JAY (336 "Hey Baby") 10-15 60
VEE JAY (353 "Half As Old") 10-15 60
VEE JAY (370 "I Beg of You") 10-15 60

LPs: 10/12-inch

ALL PLATINUM 10-15 71
DELUXE 10-15 71
KING (629 "The Sensational Donnie Elbert Sings") 100-200 59
SUGARHILL 5-10 81
TRIP 8-10 72

ELBOW BONES & RACKETEERS
D&D '83

Singles: 12-inch

EMI AMERICA 4-6 83

Singles: 7-inch

EMI AMERICA 3-4 84
Members: Ginchy Dan; Stephanie Fuller.

EL CHICANO
P&R/R&B/LP '70

Singles: 7-inch

GORDO 3-6 70
KAPP/GORDO 3-6 70-72
MCA 3-5 73-75
RFR 3-4 82
SHADYBROOK 3-5 77-78

LPs: 10/12-inch

KAPP 10-12 70-72
MCA 8-10 73-74
Members: Jerry Salas; Mickey Lespron; Fred Sanchez; Bob Espinosa; Andre Baeza.
Also see TIERRA

EL COCO
P&R/R&B '76

(Coco)

Singles: 12-inch

A.V.I. 4-8 76-85

Singles: 7-inch

A.V.I. 3-5 75-85

LPs: 10/12-inch

A.V.I. 5-10 75-85

EL DEBARGE: see DE BARGE, El

EL DORADOS
P&R/R&B '55

Singles: 78 rpm

VEE JAY (115 "Baby I Need You") 25-50 54
VEE JAY (118 "Annie's Answer") 25-50 54
(With Hazel McCollum.)
VEE JAY (127 "One More Chance") 50-100 54
VEE JAY (147 thru 302) 20-50 56-57

Singles: 7-inch

COLLECTABLES 3-4
VEE JAY (115 "Baby I Need You") 50-100 54
(Black vinyl.)
VEE JAY (115 "Baby I Need You") 400-600 54
(Colored vinyl.)
VEE JAY (118 "Annie's Answer") 50-100 54
(Black vinyl. With Hazel McCollum.)
VEE JAY (118 "Annie's Answer") 250-500 54
(Colored vinyl.)
VEE JAY (127 "One More Chance") 150-250 54
VEE JAY (147 "At My Front Door") 25-50 55
VEE JAY (165 "I'll Be Forever Lovin' You") 25-50 55
VEE JAY (180 "Now That You've Gone") 25-50 56
VEE JAY (197 "A Fallen Tear") 25-50 56
VEE JAY (211 "Bim Bam Boom") 25-50 56
VEE JAY (250 "Tears on My Pillow") 20-30 57
VEE JAY (263 "Three Reasons Why") 75-125 58
VEE JAY (302 "Lights Are Low") 75-125 58

LPs: 10/12-inch

COLLECTABLES (20 "Best of the El Dorados") 8-10 80s
(10-inch LP.)
LOST-NITE 8-12 81
SOLID SMOKE 5-10 82
VEE JAY (1001 "Crazy Little Mama") 300-500 58
(Maroon label.)
VEE JAY (1001 "Crazy Little Mama") 200-300 58
(Black label.)
Note: Vee Jay 1001 also contains two tracks by the Magnificants.
Members: Pirkle Lee Moses Jr; Arthur Bassett; Louis Bradley; James Maddox; Jewel Jones; Richard Nickens; Johnny Carter; Ted Long; John McCall; Douglas Brown.
Also see MAGNIFICENTS
Also see THOSE FOUR ELDORADOS

ELECTRIC BOYS
P&R/LP '90

Singles: 7-inch

ATCO 3-4 90

LPs: 10/12-inch

ATCO 5-8 90

ELECTRIC EXPRESS
P&R/R&B '71

Singles: 7-inch

AVCO 4-8
KEY-VAC (2930 "Hearsay") 40-60
LINCO 4-8 71

ELECTRIC FLAG
LP '68

(Electric Flag Music Band)

Singles: 7-inch

ATLANTIC 3-5 74-75
COLUMBIA 4-8 67
SIDEWALK 8-12 67

Picture Sleeves

COLUMBIA 5-10 67

LPs: 10/12-inch

ATLANTIC 8-10 74
COLUMBIA 10-15 68-71
Also see BLOOMFIELD, Mike, & Nick Gravenites
Also see GRAVENTES, Nick
Also see MILES, Buddy, Express

ELECTRIC INDIAN
P&R/R&B/LP '69

Singles: 7-inch

MARMADUKE 5-10 69
U.A. 3-6 69

LPs: 10/12-inch

U.A. 10-15 69
Also see MFSB

ELECTRIC LIGHT ORCHESTRA
LP '72

(ELO)

Singles: 12-inch

JET (Black vinyl) 10-15 76-78
JET (137 "Livin' Thing") 15-20 76
(Colored vinyl. Promotional issue only.)

Singles: 7-inch

JET/CBS 3-5 77-86
JET/U.A. (Except 1000) 3-5 77
JET/U.A. (1000 "Telephone Line") 4-8 77
(Colored vinyl. Promotional issue only.)
JET/U.A. (1145 "Sweet Talkin' Woman") 4-8 77
(Colored vinyl. Promotional issue only.)
MCA 3-4 80
U.A. 3-4 72-77

Picture Sleeves

JET 3-5 78-79
JET/CBS 3-4 86
JET/U.A. 3-5 77

MCA....3-4 80
U.A. 3-6 74-77

LPs: 10/12–inch

CBS....8-10 86
JET/CBS (Except 36966 & 40000 series)....5-10 78-86
JET/CBS (36966 "Box of Their Best")....20-25 80
(Boxed set of two LPs, *Out of the Blue* and *Discovery*, and the bonus single, *Doin' That Crazy Thing*.)
JET/CBS (40000 series)....20-25 80-83
(Half-speed mastered.)
U.A. (Except 546)....10-15 72-76
U.A. (546 "Face the Music")....25-30 75
(Banded for airplay.Promotional issue only.)
U.A./JET (Black vinyl)....8-12 76-77
U.A./JET (123 "Olé ELO")....25-35 76
(Colored vinyl. Promotional issue only.)
U.A./JET (679 "A New World Record")....10-20 76
(Colored vinyl.)
U.A./JET (823 "Out of the Blue")....30-40 76
(Colored vinyl. Promotional issue only.)
Also see LYNNE, Jeff
Also see NEWTON-JOHN, Olivia, & Electric Light Orchestra
Also see WOOD, Roy

ELECTRIC MIND — D&D '83

Singles: 12–inch

EMERGENCY....4-6 83

ELECTRIC PRUNES — P&R '66

Singles: 7–inch

REPRISE (PRO-277 "Sanctus")....35-45 67
(Promotional issue only.)
REPRISE (PRO-0305 "Help Us")....25-35 68
(Promotional issue only.)
REPRISE (0473 "Little Olive")....25-35 66
REPRISE (0532 "I Had Too Much to Dream")....10-15 66
REPRISE (0564 "Get Me to the World on Time")....10-20 67
REPRISE (0594 "Dr. Do Good")....10-20 67
REPRISE (0607 "The Great Banana Hoax")....10-20 67
REPRISE (0652 "You Never Had It Better")....20-30 68
REPRISE (0805 "Hey Mr. President")....10-20 69
REPRISE (0833 "Violet Rose")....25-35 69
REPRISE (0858 "Love Grows")....15-20 69

LPs: 10/12–inch

REPRISE (6248 "I Had Too Much to Dream")....20-30 67
REPRISE (6262 "Underground")....30-40 67
REPRISE (6257 "Mass in F Minor")....20-30 67
REPRISE (6262 "Release of an Oath")....15-25 68
REPRISE (6342 "Just Good Rock 'N' Roll")....15-25 69

ELECTRONIC — P&R '90

Singles: 7–inch

W.B. 3-4 90

LPs: 10/12–inch

W.B. 5-8 91
Members: Bernard Sumner; John Marr; Neil Tennant; David Palmer; Anne Dudley.
Also see ART of NOISE
Also see NEW ORDER
Also see PET SHOP BOYS

ELECTRONIC CONCEPT ORCHESTRA — LP '69

LPs: 10/12–inch

LIMELIGHT....5-10 69
MERCURY....5-10 70
Member: Eddie Higgins.

ELEGANTS — P&R/R&B '58

(Vito & Elegants)

Singles: 7–inch

ABC (2404 "Little Star")....3-5 73
ABC-PAR (10219 "Tiny Cloud")....20-30 61
APT (25005 "Little Star")....35-50 58
(Silver print on black label. No mention of ABC-Paramount on label.)
APT (25005 "Little Star")....25-35 58
(Silver print on black label. Reads: "A Product of AM-PAR Record Corp." at bottom of label.)
APT (25005 "Little Star")....15-25 58
(White or multi-color label.)
APT (25017 "Goodnight")....25-35 58
APT (25029 "Payday")....15-25 59
BIM BAM BOOM....8-12 74
(Black vinyl.)
BIM BAM BOOM....5-10 74
(Colored vinyl.)
CRYSTAL BALL....4-8 81
HULL (732 "Little Boy Blue")....35-45 60
LAURIE (3283 "Barbara Beware")....15-25 65
LAURIE (3298 "Wake Up")....20-30 65
LAURIE (3324 "Belinda")....10-15 65
MCA....3-4
PHOTO (2662 "A Dream Can Come True")....15-25 63
PLANET (2727 "Human Angel")....3-5
(Colored vinyl.)
ROULETTE....3-4 71
SPARTON/ABC-PAR (620 "Little Star")....15-25 58
(Canadian.)
U.A. 10-15 60-61

Picture Sleeves

CRYSTAL BALL....4-8
PHOTO (2662 "A Dream Can Come True")....25-35 63
(Add $10 to $20 if accompanied by printed insert.)

LPs: 10/12–inch

CRYSTAL BALL....8-10 82
MURRAY HILL (210 "Little Star")....8-10 86
Members: Vito Picone; Frank Tardagno; Carman Romano; Jimmy Moschella; Artie Venosa.
Also see BARBARIANS
Also see CORDEL, Pat

ELEGANTS / Poni-Tails

Singles: 7–inch

ROULETTE....3-5 73
Also see ELEGANTS
Also see PONI-TAILS

ELEKTRIK DRED — R&B '83

Singles: 7–inch

SOUNDS of FLORIDA....3-4 83

ELEKTRO, Eve — D&D '84

Singles: 12–inch

BLACK SUIT....4-6 84

ELEPHANTS MEMORY — LP '69

Singles: 7–inch

APPLE (1854 "Liberation Special"/"Madness")....5-10 72
APPLE (1854 "Liberation Special"/"Power Boogie")....300-400 72
(Note different flip side.)
BUDDAH....4-8 69
METROMEDIA....3-6 70-71
RCA....3-5 74

Promotional Singles

APPLE (1854 "Liberation Special")....20-25 72

Picture Sleeves

APPLE (1854 "Liberation Special")....8-10 72
METROMEDIA....4-8 70

LPs: 10/12–inch

APPLE (3389 "Elephants Memory") . 10-15 72
BUDDAH....10-15 69-74
METROMEDIA....10-12 70
MUSE....8-10 70s
RCA....8-10 74
Also see LENNON, John

ELEVENTH HOUR — P&R '74

Singles: 7–inch

BELL....3-5 71
20TH FOX....3-5 74-76

LPs: 10/12–inch

ARISTA....6-10 75
20TH FOX....8-10 74-76

ELEVENTH HOUSE — LP '74

(With Larry Coryell)

Singles: 7–inch

VANGUARD....3-5 74

LPs: 10/12–inch

ARISTA....5-10 75
VANGUARD (40036 "Introducing the Eleventh House with Larry Coryell")....10-20 74
(Quadrophonic.)
VANGUARD (79342 "Introducing the Eleventh House with Larry Coryell")....8-12 74
Members: Larry Coryell; Kenny Nolan.
Also see CORYELL, Larry
Also see MOUZON, Alphonse, & Larry Croyell

ELGART, Larry — P&R/LP '82

(With His Manhattan Swing Orchestra)

Singles: 78 rpm

DECCA....3-5 54-55

Singles: 7–inch

DECCA....3-8 54-55
MGM....3-5 61-62
RCA....3-6 59-83

EPs: 7–inch

BRUNSWICK....5-10 54
DECCA....5-10 54-55

LPs: 10/12–inch

BRUNSWICK....15-25 54
(10–inch LPs.)
CAMDEN....5-10 60-73
DECCA....10-20 54-55
MGM....8-12 60-62
RCA....5-10 59-83

ELGART, Les, Orchestra — P&R/LP '56

Singles: 78 rpm

COLUMBIA....3-5 53-57

Singles: 7–inch

COLUMBIA (40000 series, except 40180)....3-8 53-62
COLUMBIA (40180 "Bandstand Boogie")....15-20 54
COLUMBIA (56767 "Bandstand Twist")....5-10 62
(Promotional issue only.)
GOLD-MOR....3-4 73

EPs: 7–inch

COLUMBIA....5-10 53-59

LPs: 10/12–inch

COLUMBIA....10-20 53-62
HARMONY....5-10 66

ELGART, Les & Larry — LP '64

Singles: 7–inch

COLUMBIA....3-4 64-68
SWAMPFIRE....3-4 69

Picture Sleeves

COLUMBIA....3-5 65

LPs: 10/12–inch

COLUMBIA (Except 38000 series)....8-15 57-68
COLUMBIA (38000 series)....5-10 82
HARMONY....5-10 68-73
SWAMPFIRE....5-10 70
Also see ELGART, Larry
Also see ELGART, Les

ELGINS — P&R/R&B '66

Singles: 7–inch

V.I.P. 10-20 66-71

LPs: 10/12–inch

V.I.P. (400 "Darling Baby")....50-100 66
Members: Saundra Mallet; Cleo Miller; Robert Flemming; John Dawson; Norbert McClean.

ELI'S SECOND COMING — R&B '76

Singles: 7–inch

SILVER BLUE....3-5 76-78
Members: Bobby Eli.
Also see MFSB

ELLEDGE, Jimmy — P&R '61

Singles: 7–inch

4 STAR....3-5 75
HICKORY....4-8 65-67
LITTLE DARLIN'....4-6 68
RCA (Except 7910 & 8012)....6-12 61-64

RCA (7910 "Swanee River Rocket")....25-35 61
RCA (8012 "Can't You See It in My Eyes")....10-20 62
SIMS....4-8 64

Picture Sleeves

RCA....10-15 62-63

LPs: 10/12-inch

LITTLE DARLIN'....8-12 68

ELLIMAN, Yvonne P&R '71

Singles: 7-inch

DECCA....3-5 71-72
MCA....3-4
RSO....3-5 74-79

Picture Sleeves

RSO....3-5 78

LPs: 10/12-inch

DECCA....10-15 72
MCA....8-12 73
RSO....6-10 77-79

Also see BISHOP, Stephen, & Yvonne Elliman

ELLIMAN, Yvonne / Carl Anderson

Singles: 7-inch

MCA....3-5 73

Also see ANDERSON, Carl
Also see ELLIMAN, Yvonne

ELLINGTON, Duke P&R '27

Singles: 78 rpm

CAPITOL....3-8 53-56
COLUMBIA....3-8 50-53
RCA....3-8 51-55

Singles: 7-inch

BELL....3-4 73
BETHLEHEM....5-10 58-60
CAPITOL (2000 series)....5-15 53-56
COLUMBIA (33000 series)....3-4 76
COLUMBIA (39000 series)....8-15 50-53
COLUMBIA (40000 thru 42000 series)....4-8 58-61
COLUMBIA PRICELESS EDITION....5-10
RCA (0300 series)....3-5 74
RCA (4000 thru 6000 series)....8-15 51-55
REPRISE....4-8 67

EPs: 7-inch

BRUNSWICK....10-20 54
CAPITOL....10-20 53-56
COLUMBIA....10-20 50-56
RCA....10-20 52-60
ROYALE....10-20 50s

LPs: 10/12-inch

ALLEGIANCE....5-8 84
ALLEGRO....25-50 54
(10-inch LPs.)
ATLANTIC....5-10 71-82
BASF....5-10 73
BETHLEHEM....15-30 56-57
BRIGHT ORANGE....5-10 73
BRUNSWICK (54000 series)....15-30 56
BRUNSWICK (58000 series)....30-50 54
(10-inch LPs.)
CAMDEN (400 series)....15-25 58
CAPITOL (400 series)....25-50 53
(With "H" prefix. 10-inch LPs.)
CAPITOL (400 thru 600 series)....25-40 55-57
CAPITOL (1600 series)....10-20 61
(With "T" prefix.)
CAPITOL (11000 series)....5-10 72-77
CAPITOL (16000 series)....4-6 81
COLUMBIA (27 "The Ellington Era, Volume 1)....25-40 63
COLUMBIA (39 "The Ellington Era, Volume 2, 1927-1940)....25-40 66
COLUMBIA (500 thru 900 series)....20-30 54-57
COLUMBIA (1085 thru 2029 except 1360)....15-30 57-63
(Monaural.)
COLUMBIA (1360 "Anatomy of a Murder")....35-50 59
(Soundtrack. Monaural.)
COLUMBIA (4000 series)....25-50 55
COLUMBIA (6000 series)....30-60 50
(10-inch LPs.)
COLUMBIA (8053 thru 9600, except 8166)....10-20 57-68
(Stereo.)
COLUMBIA (8166 "Anatomy of a Murder")....45-60 59
(Soundtrack. Stereo.)
COLUMBIA (14000 series)....5-10 79
(Columbia Special Products series.)
COLUMBIA (32000 thru 38000 series)....5-10 73-82
COLUMBIA SPECIAL PRODUCTS....8-10 82
DECCA....8-15 67-70
DOCTOR JAZZ....5-8 84
EVEREST....5-10 70-73
FANTASY....6-12 71-75
FLYING DUTCHMAN....5-10 69
HARMONY....5-10 67-71
IMPULSE (Except 9200 series)....15-20 62
IMPULSE (9200 series)....8-12 73
MOSAIC (160 "Complete Capitol Recordings of Duke Ellington")....100-120 90s
(Boxed, eight-disc set. 5000 made.)
ODYSSEY....8-12 68
PABLO....5-10 76-80
PRESTIGE....6-12 73-77
RCA (500 series)....10-20 64-69
RCA (0700 thru 2000 series)....5-8 75-78
(With "ANL1" or "APL1" prefix.)
RCA (1000 series)....25-40 54
(With "LJM" or "LPT" prefix.)
RCA (1300 thru 2800 series)....10-30 57-66
(With "LPM" or "LSP" prefix.)
RCA (3000 series)....25-50 52-53
(10-inch LPs.)
RCA (3500 thru 3900 series)....8-15 66-68
RCA (4000 series)....8-10 81
RCA (6009 "The Indispensible Duke Ellington")....20-30 61
RCA (6042 "This Is Duke Ellington")....10-15 71
REPRISE....10-20 63-68
RIVERSIDE (Except 100 series)....10-20 62-64
RIVERSIDE (100 series)....15-30 56-59
RON-LETTE....15-30 58
SOLID STATE....5-10 70
SUNSET....5-10 69
TRIP....5-10 75-76
U.A. (Except 14000 & 15000 series)....5-10 72
U.A. (14000 & 15000 series)....15-25 62
VERVE....10-15 67
"X" (3037 "Duke Ellington")....25-50 55
(10-inch LP.)

Also see ARMSTRONG, Louis, & Duke Ellington
Also see BASIE, Count, & Duke Ellington
Also see BREWER, Teresa, & Duke Ellington
Also see CARROLL, Diahann, & Duke Ellington Orchestra
Also see FITZGERALD, Ella, & Duke Ellington
Also see HIBBLER, Al, & Duke Ellington
Also see JACKSON, Mahalia, & Duke Ellington
Also see SINATRA, Frank, & Duke Ellington

ELLINGTON, Duke, & Boston Pops Orchestra LP '66

LPs: 10/12-inch

RCA....10-15 66

Also see BOSTON POPS ORCHESTRA

ELLINGTON, Duke, & John Coltrane

LPs: 10/12-inch

IMPULSE....15-25 63

Also see COLTRANE, John

ELLINGTON, Duke, & Johnny Hodges

LPs: 10/12-inch

PRESTIGE....8-10 81
VERVE (Except 8800 series)....15-30 59-60
VERVE (8800 series)....8-12 73

Also see ELLINGTON, Duke
Also see HODGES, Johnny

ELLIOT, Cass P&R/LP '68

(Mama Cass)

Singles: 7-inch

DUNHILL....3-6 68-70
RCA....3-5 71-73

LPs: 10/12-inch

DUNHILL....10-20 68-72
PICKWICK....8-12
RCA....10-15 72-73

Also see BIG THREE
Also see MAMAS & PAPAS
Also see MASON, Dave, & Mama Cass
Also see MUGWUMPS

ELLIS, Ray, Orchestra P&R '60

Singles: 78 rpm

COLUMBIA....3-8 57

Singles: 7-inch

COLUMBIA....3-8 57
MGM....3-5 59-60
RCA....3-5 61

EPs: 7-inch

COLUMBIA....5-10 57

LPs: 10/12-inch

COLUMBIA....10-20 57
HARMONY....10-15 59
MGM....10-15 59-60
RCA....10-15 61

ELLIS, Shirley P&R/R&B '63

Singles: 7-inch

COLUMBIA....4-8 67
CONGRESS....5-10 63-65
MCA....3-5 73

Picture Sleeves

CONGRESS....5-10 64-65

LPs: 10/12-inch

COLUMBIA....15-20 67
CONGRESS....20-25 64-65

Also see SHIRLEE MAY

ELLISON, Lorraine R&B '65

Singles: 7-inch

LOMA....3-5 67-68
MERCURY....4-8 65-66
SHARP....4-8 63
W.B.....3-6 66-69

LPs: 10/12-inch

W.B. (1000 series)....15-20 67-69
W.B. (2000 series)....8-10 74

ELMO & ALMO P&R '67

Singles: 7-inch

DADDY BEST....4-6 67

ELMO 'N' PATSY C&W '84

Singles: 7-inch

ELMO 'N' PATSY....3-5 79
EPIC....3-4 84
OINK....3-4 80
SOUNDWAVES....3-4 81

Picture Sleeves

EPIC....3-4 84

LPs: 10/12-inch

OINK....5-10 80

Members: Elmo Shropshire; Patsy Trigg.

ELUSION R&B '81

Singles: 7-inch

COTILLION....3-4 81

LPs: 10/12-inch

COTILLION....5-10 81

ELY, Joe C&W '77

Singles: 7-inch

MCA....3-4 77-81
SOUTHCOAST....3-4 81

LPs: 10/12-inch

MCA....5-10 77-81
SOUTHCOAST....5-10 81

EMERSON, Keith LP '81

LPs: 10/12-inch

BACKSTREET....5-10 81

EMERSON, Keith, & Nice

Singles: 7-inch

MERCURY....3-5 72

LPs: 10/12-inch

MERCURY....12-15 72

Also see EMERSON, Keith
Also see EMERSON, LAKE & PALMER
Also see NICE

EMERSON, LAKE & PALMER *P&R/LP '71*

Singles: 7-inch

ATLANTIC 3-5 77-80
COTILLION 3-5 71-72
MANTICORE 3-5 74
POLYDOR 3-4 86

Promotional Singles

ATLANTIC ("Brain Salad Surgery") 4-6 78
(Selection number not known.)

LPs: 10/12-inch

ATLANTIC (Except 281) 8-10 77-80
ATLANTIC (281 "Emerson, Lake & Palmer") 12-15 77
(With the London Philharmonic Orchestra. Also contains interviews with the three members. Promotional issue only.)
COTILLION 12-15 71-72
MFSL (031 "Pictures at an Exhibition") 25-40 79
MFSL (203 "Tarkus") 20-25 94
MFSL (218 "Trilogy") 20-25 94
MANTICORE 10-12 73-74
Members: Keith Emerson; Greg Lake; Carl Palmer.
Also see ASIA
Also see EMERSON, LAKE & POWELL
Also see 3

EMERSON, LAKE & POWELL *P&R/LP '86*

Singles: 7-inch

POLYDOR 3-4 86

Picture Sleeves

POLYDOR 3-4 86

LPs: 10/12-inch

POLYDOR 5-10 86
Members: Keith Emerson; Greg Lake; Cozy Powell.
Also see EMERSON, Keith
Also see EMERSON, LAKE & PALMER
Also see LAKE, Greg
Also see POWELL, Cozy

EMMERSON, Les *P&R '73*

Singles: 7-inch

LION 3-5 73
Also see FIVE MAN ELECTRICAL BAND

EMOTIONS *P&R '62*
(With the Billy Mure Orchestra)

Singles: 7-inch

BRAINSTORM 4-8 68
CALLA 5-10 65
CRYSTAL BALL 4-8 90
JASON SCOTT 4-8
KAPP (490 "Echo") 15-25 62
KAPP (513 "L-o-v-e") 20-30 63
KARATE 5-10 64
LAURIE (3167 "Starlit Night") 10-15 63
20TH FOX (430 "Story Untold") 10-20 63
20TH FOX (452 "Rainbow") 10-20 63
20TH FOX (478 "I Love You Madly") 10-20 64
VARDAN (201 "Love of a Girl") 20-40 65

LPs: 10/12-inch

CRYSTAL BALL 5-10 90
MAGIC CARPET 5-10 82
Members: Joe Favale; Tony Maltese; Don Colluri; Larry Cusamanno; Joe Nigro; Sal Covais.
Also see MURE, Billy

EMOTIONS *P&R/R&B '69*

Singles: 12-inch

RED LABEL 4-6 84

Singles: 7-inch

ARC 3-4 80-81
COLUMBIA 3-5 76-81
STAX 3-4 77-79
MOTOWN 3-4 85
RED LABEL 3-4 84
TWIN STACKS 4-8 68
VOLT 3-6 69-74

LPs: 10/12-inch

ARC 5-8 79-81
COLUMBIA 5-10 76-81
MOTOWN 5-10 85
RED LABEL 5-10 84
STAX 5-10 77-79
VOLT 10-20 69-74
Members: Sheila Hutchinson; Wanda Hutchinson; Jeanette Hutchinson.
Also see EARTH, WIND & FIRE with the EMOTIONS

EMPERORS *P&R/R&B '66*

Singles: 7-inch

BRUNSWICK 4-8 67
MALA 5-10 66-67

ENCHANTERS *P&R '61*
(With the Dave McRae Orchestra)

Singles: 7-inch

BALD EAGLE (3001 "Come on Baby, Let's Do the Stroll") 15-25 58
BAMBOO (513 "Touch of Love") 10-20 61
CANDELITE (432 "Oh Rose Marie") 10-15 64
EP-SOM (103 "I Need Your Love") 200-300 62
J.J.&M. (1562 "Oh Rose Marie") 100-200 62
MUSITRON (1072 "I Lied to My Heart") 30-40 61
ORBIT (532 "Touch of Love") 25-50 59
SHARP (105 "We Make Mistakes") 10-20 60
STARDUST (102 "Spellbound By the Moon") 1000-2000 58
TOM TOM (301 "Surf Blast") 25-35 63

ENCHANTERS *P&R/R&B '64*

Singles: 7-inch

LOMA 4-8 65-66
W.B. 5-10 64
Members: Samuel Bell; Charles Boyer; Zola Pearnell.
Also see MIMMS, Garnet, & Enchanters

ENCHANTMENT *R&B '76*

Singles: 7-inch

COLUMBIA 3-4 82-84
DESERT MOON 3-5 76
RCA 3-4 80
ROADSHOW 3-5 77-78
U.A. 3-5 76-77

LPs: 10/12-inch

COLUMBIA 5-10 82
RCA 5-10 80
ROADSHOW 8-10 77-79
U.A. 8-10 77
Members: Bobby Green; Mickey Clanton; Joe Thomas; Davis Banks; Emanuel Johnson.

ENDGAMES *D&D '83*

Singles: 12-inch

FLIP 4-6 83
MCA 4-6 83

Singles: 7-inch

MCA 3-4 84

LPs: 10/12-inch

MCA 5-10 84

ENERGETICS *R&B '79*

Singles: 7-inch

ATLANTIC 3-5 79
TIP TOP 4-6

LPs: 10/12-inch

ATLANTIC 5-10 79

ENGLAND DAN & JOHN FORD COLEY *P&R/LP '76*

Singles: 7-inch

A&M 3-5 71-77
BIG TREE 3-5 76-80
MCA 3-4 80

LPs: 10/12-inch

A&M 10-12 71-73
BIG TREE 8-10 76-79
MCA 5-10 80
Members: Dan Seals; John Ford Coley.
Also see ABBA / Spinners / Firefall / England Dan & John Ford Coley
Also see COLEY, John Ford
Also see SEALS, Dan
Also see SOUTHWEST F.O.B.

ENGLISH, Barbara *R&B '73*
(Barbara Jean English)

Singles: 7-inch

ALITHIA 4-6 73-74
AURORA (155 "Sittin' in the Corner") 50-75 65
MALA (488 "Easy Come Easy Go") 10-20 64
REPRISE (290 "I've Got a Date") 10-20 65
REPRISE (349 "Small Town Girl") 10-20 65
ROULETTE (4428 "We Need Them") 20-30 62
W.B. (5685 "All Because I Love Somebody") 10-15 65

LPs: 10/12-inch

ALITHIA 8-10 73

ENGLISH, Jackie *P&R '80*

Singles: 7-inch

VENTURE 3-4 80

ENGLISH, Scott *P&R '64*
(With the Accents; with Dedications)

Singles: 7-inch

DOT (16099 "White Cliffs of Dover") 15-25 60
JANUS (171 "Brandy") 8-12 71
JANUS (192 "Woman in My Life") 3-6 72
JOKER (777 "Ugly Pills") 15-25 62
SPOKANE (4003 "High on a Hill") 15-25 64
SPOKANE (4007 "Here Comes the Pain") 15-25 64
SULTAN (4003 "High on a Hill") 30-50 63

ENGLISH BEAT *LP '80*

Singles: 12-inch

I.R.S. 4-6 83-85

Singles: 7-inch

I.R.S. 3-4 83-85

LPs: 10/12-inch

I.R.S. 5-10 82-85
SIRE 5-10 80-81
Members: Andy Cox; David Steele; Roger Charley; Dave Wakeling.
Also see FINE YOUNG CANNIBALS
Also see GENERAL PUBLIC

ENGLISH CONGREGATION *P&R '72*

Singles: 7-inch

ATCO 3-5 72
SIGNPOST 3-5 73

LPs: 10/12-inch

SIGNPOST 8-10 73

ENIGMA *LP '91*

LPs: 10/12-inch

CHARISMA 5-8 91

ENNIS, Ethel *LP '64*

Singles: 78 rpm

JUBILEE 4-8 56

Singles: 7-inch

JUBILEE 5-10 56
RCA 5-10 64

EPs: 7-inch

CAPITOL 5-10 57

LPs: 10/12-inch

CAPITOL 15-25 58
JUBILEE 20-40 56-63
RCA 15-25 64

ENO, Brian *LP '74*
(Eno)

Singles: 7-inch

ISLAND 3-5 72

LPs: 10/12-inch

ANTILLES 8-10 73-78
EDITIONS E.G. 5-10 81-82
ISLAND 8-10 73-78
PVC 5-10 79
SIRE 5-10 81
Also see BYRNE, David
Also see ROXY MUSIC

ENTERTAINERS IV *R&B '66*

Singles: 7-inch

DORE 4-8 66

ENTOUCH P&R/LP '90
(Featuring Keith Sweat)
Singles: 7-inch
VINTERTAINMENT....3-4 90
LPs: 10/12-inch
VINTERTAINMENT....5-8 90
Members: Eric McCaine; Free.
Also see SWEAT, Keith
Also see TOUCH

ENUFF Z'NUFF P&R '89
Singles: 7-inch
ATCO....3-4 89-90
Picture Sleeves
ATCO....3-4 89

ENTWISTLE, John LP '71
(John Entwistle's Rigor Mortis; John Entwistle's Ox)
Singles: 7-inch
DECCA....3-5 72
TRACK....3-5 73
LPs: 10/12-inch
ATCO....5-10 81
DECCA....10-15 71-72
MCA/TRACK....8-10 72-75
Also see TOWNSHEND, Pete, & Ronnie Lane
Also see WHO

ENUFF Z'NUFF LP '89
LPs: 10/12-inch
ATCO....5-8 89-91

EN VOGUE P&R/LP '90
LPs: 10/12-inch
ATLANTIC....5-8 90

ENYA P&R/LP '89
Singles: 7-inch
GEFFEN....3-4 89
Picture Sleeves
GEFFEN....3-4 89
LPs: 10/12-inch
GEFFEN....5-8 89

EON R&B '78
Singles: 7-inch
ARIOLA AMERICA....3-4 78
LPs: 10/12-inch
ARIOLA AMERICA....5-10 78
SCEPTER....8-10 73

EPIC SPLENDOR P&R '67
Singles: 7-inch
HOT BISCUIT....4-8 67-68
Picture Sleeves
HOT BISCUIT (1452 "It Could Be Wonderful")....8-10 68

EPOQUE, Belle: see BELLE EPOQUE

EPPS, Preston P&R '59
Singles: 7-inch
ADMIRAL....4-8 65
EMBASSY....5-10 62
JO JO....4-6 69
MAJESTY (1300 "Bongo Boogie")....5-10 60
ORIGINAL SOUND (4 "Bongo Rock")....10-20 60
(Monaural.)
ORIGINAL SOUND (4 "Bongo Rock")....25-40 60
(Stereo.)
ORIGINAL SOUND (9 thru 17)....8-15 60-61
POLO (218 "Bongo Rock 1965")....5-10 65
TOP RANK (2067 "Blue Bongo")....10-15 60
TOP RANK (2091 "Bongo Hop")....10-15 60
EPs: 7-inch
ORIGINAL SOUND (1001 "Bongo Rock")....15-25 60
LPs: 10/12-inch
CROWN....10-15
ORIGINAL SOUND (5002 "Bongo Bongo Bongo")....30-40 60
(Monaural.)
ORIGINAL SOUND (8851 "Bongo Bongo Bongo")....30-50 60
(Stereo.)
ORIGINAL SOUND (5009 "Surfin' Bongos")....25-40 63
(Monaural.)
ORIGINAL SOUND (8872 "Surfin' Bongos")....25-50 63
(Stereo.)
TOP RANK (349 "Bongola")....30-50 61
Also see SKYLINERS / Preston Epps

EQUALS P&R '68
Singles: 7-inch
BANG....5-10 70
PRESIDENT....5-10 67-68
RCA....4-8 68
LPs: 10/12-inch
LAURIE (2045 "Unequalled")....20-25 67
PRESIDENT....15-25 68-69
RCA....10-15 68
Members: Eddy Grant; Derv Gordon.
Also see GRANT, Eddy

ERAMUS HALL R&B '84
Singles: 12-inch
CAPITOL....4-6 84
Singles: 7-inch
CAPITOL....3-4 84
LPs: 10/12-inch
CAPITOL....5-10 84

ERASURE LP '87
Singles: 7-inch
SIRE....3-4 82-89
Picture Sleeves
SIRE....3-4 88
LPs: 10/12-inch
SIRE....5-10 82-89

ERIC D&D '84
Singles: 12-inch
MEMO....4-6 84

ERIC B. & RAKIM R&B '86
Singles: 7-inch
4TH & BROADWAY....3-4 87-88
ZAKIA....3-4 86
LPs: 10/12-inch
4TH & BROADWAY....5-10 87
MCA....5-8 90
UNI....5-8 88

ERNIE / Sesame Street Kids
(Jim Henson as "Ernie") P&R '79
Singles: 7-inch
COLUMBIA....3-5 70
Also see HENSON, Jim

ERUPTION P&R/R&B/LP '78
Singles: 12-inch
ARIOLA AMERICA....4-8 78
HANSA....4-8 70s
Singles: 7-inch
ARIOLA AMERICA....3-4 78
LPs: 10/12-inch
ARIOLA AMERICA....5-10 78
Member: Precious Wilson.
Also see WILSON, Precious

ESCAPE CLUB P&R/LP '88
Singles: 7-inch
ATLANTIC....3-4 88-91
Picture Sleeves
ATLANTIC....3-4 88-89
LPs: 10/12-inch
ATLANTIC....5-8 88-91

ESCORTS R&B '73
Singles: 7-inch
ALITHIA....3-5 73-74
LPs: 10/12-inch
ALITHIA....8-10 73-74
Members: Reginald Hayes; Robert Arrington; Laurence Franklin; Stephen Carter; William Dugger; Frank Heard; Marion Murphy.

ESCOVEDO, Coke P&R/LP '76
Singles: 7-inch
MERCURY....3-5 76-77
LPs: 10/12-inch
MERCURY....5-10 76-77
Also see AZTECA
Also see SANTANA

ESMERALDA, Santa: see SANTA ESMERALDA

ESPOSITO, Joe "Bean" P&R '83
Singles: 7-inch
CASABLANCA....3-4 83
Also see BRANIGAN, Laura, & Joe Esposito
Also see BROOKS, Pattie, & Joe Esposito
Also see BROOKLYN DREAMS
Also see RUSSELL, Brenda

ESQUIRE LP '87
LPs: 10/12-inch
GEFFEN....5-10 87

ESQUIRE BOYS P&R '53
Singles: 78 rpm
DOT....8-10 55
GUYDEN....8-10 54
MEDIA....8-12 55
NICKELODEON....8-10 53
RAINBOW....10-15 52-53
Singles: 7-inch
DOT....10-15 55
FRANSIL....5-10 61
GUYDEN....10-15 54
MEDIA (1004 "Play Me Boogie")....10-20 55
NICKELODEON (102 "Guitar Boogie Shuffle")....10-15 53
RAINBOW (100 & 200 series)....10-20 52-53
(Black vinyl.)
RAINBOW (100 & 200 series)....20-35 52-53
(Colored vinyl.)
20TH FOX (110 "Taboo")....8-10 58

ESQUIRES P&R/R&B '67
Singles: 7-inch
B&G....4-8 69
BUNKY....4-8 67-68
CAPITOL....3-6 69
FEATURE....4-8 67
HOT LINE....3-5 72
JU-PAR....3-5 76
LAMAR....3-5 71
LASCO....4-8 79
ROCKY RIDGE....3-5 71
SALEM....5-10 65
TOWER....5-10 65
WAND....4-8 68-69
LPs: 10/12-inch
BUNKY (300 "Get on Up and Get Away")....20-25 68
Members: Millard Evans; Gilbert Alvis; Betty Moorer; Sam Pace; Harvey Scales; Sean Taylor; Gilbert Moorer; Alvis Moorer; .Sam Davidson; John Bursey; Danny Reed; Ortez Guzman; Clint Mosley.
Also see SCALES, Harvey

ESSENCE R&B '75
Singles: 7-inch
EPIC....3-5 75-77
LPs: 10/12-inch
SAVOY....5-10 78
Members: Marzette Griffith; Anthony Redmond.

ESSEX P&R/R&B/LP '63
Singles: 7-inch
BANG....4-8 66
ROULETTE....5-8 63-64
LPs: 10/12-inch
ROULETTE (25234 "Easier Said Than Done")....25-35 63
ROULETTE (25235 "A Walkin' Miracle")....20-35 63
ROULETTE (25246 "Young and Lively")....20-30 64
Members: Anita Humes; Walter Vickers; Rodney Taylor; Billie Hill; Rudolph Johnson.

ESSEX, David P&R '73
Singles: 7-inch
COLUMBIA....3-5 73-76
RSO....3-4 79

UNI 4-8 67

Picture Sleeves

COLUMBIA 3-5 73-75
UNI 5-10 67

LPs: 10/12-inch

COLUMBIA (CQ-32560 "Rock On") .. 15-25 74
(Quadrophonic)
COLUMBIA (KC-32560 "Rock On") .. 15-20 73
COLUMBIA (33289 "David Essex") 8-15 74
COLUMBIA (33813 "All the Fun of the Fair") 8-15 75
MERCURY 5-10 83

ESTEFAN, Gloria P&R/LP '89

Singles: 7-inch

EPIC 3-4 89-91

LPs: 10/12-inch

EPIC 5-8 89-91
Also see MIAMI SOUND MACHINE

ESTUS, Deon LP '89

Singles: 7-inch

MIKA 3-4 89

LPs: 10/12-inch

MIKA 5-8 89

ESTUS, Deon, & George Michael P&R '89

Singles: 7-inch

MIKA 3-4 89

Picture Sleeves

MIKA (871538 "Heaven Help Me") 5-8 89
(With George Michael's name.)
MIKA (871538 "Heaven Help Me") 3-4 89
(Without George Michael's name.)
Also see ESTUS, Deon
Also see MICHAEL, George

ETERNALS P&R '59

Singles: 7-inch

COLLECTABLES 3-4
HOLLYWOOD (68 "Rockin' in the Jungle") 40-60 59
(White label.)
HOLLYWOOD (68 "Rockin' in the Jungle") 30-50 59
(Blue label. Has label name at bottom.)
HOLLYWOOD (68 "Rockin' in the Jungle") 20-40 60s
(Blue label. Has label name at top.)
HOLLYWOOD (68 "Rockin' in the Jungle") 10-20 60s
(Yellow label. Label name is changed slightly to "Transphonic Hollywood Productions.")
HOLLYWOOD (70 "Babalu's Wedding Day") 25-50 59
(Red label.)
HOLLYWOOD (70 "Babalu's Wedding Day") 15-25 59
(Blue label.)
LOST NITE 3-5
MUSICTONE (1110 "Babalu's Wedding Day") 8-12 62
MUSICTONE (1111 "Rockin' in the Jungle") 8-12 62
WARWICK (611 "Blind Date") 15-25 60
Members: Charles Girona; Alex Miranda; Fred Hodge; Ernie Sierra; Arnold Torres; George Villanueva.

ETERNITY'S CHILDREN P&R '68

Singles: 7-inch

A&M 5-8 67
LIBERTY 4-6 70
TOWER 4-6 68-69

Picture Sleeves

TOWER 5-10 68

LPs: 10/12-inch

TOWER (5123 "Eternity's Children") . 20-25 68
TOWER (5144 "Timeless") 20-25 68
Member: Bruce Blackman.
Also see ALLAN, Davie / Eternity's Children / Main Attraction / Sunrays
Also see KORONA
Also see STARBUCK

ETHERIDGE, Melissa LP '88

Singles: 7-inch

ISLAND 3-4 89

Picture Sleeves

ISLAND 3-4 89

LPs: 10/12-inch

ISLAND 5-8 89

ETHICS R&B '69

Singles: 7-inch

GOLDEN FLEECE 4-8 74
PHALANX 10-20
VENT 8-12 68-69
Member: Ronald Tyson.
Also see LOVE COMMITTEE

ETTA & HARVEY P&R/R&B '60

Singles: 7-inch

CHESS (1760 "If I Can't Have You") 10-20 60
CHESS (1771 "Spoonful") 10-20 60
Members: Etta James; Harvey Fuqua.
Also see HARVEY
Also see JAMES, Etta

ETZEL, Roy LP '65
(With the Jupiter Serenaders)

Singles: 7-inch

HICKORY 4-8 63
MGM 4-6 65-67
PRESIDENT 4-8 61
TIME 4-8 61

LPs: 10/12-inch

MGM 8-12 65

EUBANKS, Jack P&R '61

Singles: 7-inch

MONUMENT 4-8 61-64

LPs: 10/12-inch

MONUMENT 10-20 66

EUCLID BEACH BAND P&R '79

Singles: 7-inch

EPIC/CLEVELAND INT'L 3-4 78-79
SCENE 4-6 78

LPs: 10/12-inch

EPIC 5-10 79

EUROGLIDERS P&R/LP '84

Singles: 7-inch

COLUMBIA 3-4 84-86

Picture Sleeves

COLUMBIA 3-4 86

LPs: 10/12-inch

COLUMBIA 5-10 84
Member: Grace Knight.

EUROPE LP '86

Singles: 12-inch

EPIC 4-8 86
(Promotional only.)

Singles: 7-inch

EPIC 3-4 86-88

Picture Sleeves

EPIC 3-4 87-88

LPs: 10/12-inch

EPIC 5-10 86-88
Members: Joey Tempest; John Leven; Mic Michaeli; Kee Marcello; Ian Haughland.

EURYTHMICS P&R/D&D/LP '83

Singles: 12-inch

RCA 4-6 83-86

Singles: 7-inch

ARISTA 3-4 89-91
RCA 3-6 83-88

Picture Sleeves

ARISTA 3-4 89
RCA 3-6 83-88

LPs: 10/12-inch

ARISTA 5-8 89-91
RCA 5-10 83-88
Members: Annie Lennox; Dave Stewart.
Also see LENNOX, Annie, & Al Green
Also see TOURISTS

EURYTHMICS & ARETHA FRANKLIN P&R/D&D '85

Singles: 12-inch

RCA 4-6 85

Singles: 7-inch

RCA 3-4 85
Also see EURYTHMICS
Also see FRANKLIN, Aretha

EVANS, Linda R&B '79

Singles: 7-inch

ARIOLA 3-5 79
WATTSOUND 3-5 73
Also see CHANSON

EVANS, Margie R&B '73

Singles: 7-inch

ICA 3-5 77
U.A. 3-5 73

EVANS, Paul P&R '59
(With the Curls)

Singles: 7-inch

ATCO 8-12 59-60
BIG TREE 3-5 75
CARLTON 8-15 61-62
CINNAMON INT'L 3-4 80
COLLECTABLES 3-4 80s
COLUMBIA 3-6 68
DECCA 5-10 58
DOT 3-5 73
EPIC 4-8 64-65
GUARANTEED 10-20 59-60
KAPP 5-10 62-63
LAURIE 3-5 71
MERCURY 3-5 74-75
MUSICOR 3-5 77
RCA 10-20 57
RANWOOD 3-5 72
SPRING 3-5 78-79

LPs: 10/12-inch

CARLTON (129 "Hear Paul Evans in Your Home Tonight") 20-30 61
(Monaural.)
CARLTON (129 "Hear Paul Evans in Your Home Tonight") 25-35 61
(Stereo.)
CARLTON (130 "Folk Songs of Many Lands") 15-25 61
(Monaural.)
CARLTON (130 "Folk Songs of Many Lands") 20-30 61
(Stereo.)
GUARANTEED (1000 "Fabulous Teens") 20-40 60
(Monaural.)
GUARANTEED (1000 "Fabulous Teens") 30-40 60
(Stereo.)
KAPP (1346 "21 Years in a Tennessee Jail") 15-25 64
(Monaural.)
KAPP (1475 "Another Town, Another Jail") 15-25 66
(Monaural.)
KAPP (3346 "21 Years in a Tennessee Jail") 20-30 64
(Stereo.)
KAPP (3475 "Another Town, Another Jail") 20-30 66

EVANS, Paul & Mimi

Singles: 7-inch

EPIC 4-8 64
Also see EVANS, Paul

EVANS, Warren R&B '45

Singles: 78 rpm

NATIONAL 10-15 45
Also see JOHNSON, Buddy

EVASIONS R&B '81

Singles: 7-inch

SAM 3-5 81
SOIF (1000 "Son of Surf") 10-15 82
(Picture disc. 500 made.)

EVE ELEKTRO: see ELEKTRO, Eve

EVERETT, Betty *P&R/R&B '63*
(With the Daylighters)

Singles: 7-inch

ABC....4-6 66-67
C.J....10-20 61-64
COBRA....15-25 57-58
COLLECTABLES....3-4 80s
DOTTIE (1126 "Tell Me Darling")....15-25
ERIC....3-4 70s
FANTASY....3-5 70-74
OLDIES 45....3-5 60s
ONE-DERFUL....5-10 62
UNI....4-6 68-69
VEE JAY....5-10 63-65

LPs: 10/12-inch

FANTASY....8-10 75
SUNSET....10-15 68
UNI....10-15 69
VEE JAY (1077 "It's in His Kiss")....25-50 64
VEE JAY (1122 "The Very Best of Betty Everett")....25-35 65
Session: Blossoms.
Also see BLOSSOMS
Also see BUTLER, Jerry, & Betty Everett

EVERETT, Betty / Ketty Lester

LPs: 10/12-inch

GRAND PRIX....10-15 64
Also see LESTER, Ketty

EVERETT, Betty / Impressions

LPs: 10/12-inch

CUSTOM....10-15 64
Also see EVERETT, Betty
Also see IMPRESSIONS

EVERLY, Don *C&W '76*

Singles: 7-inch

ABC/HICKORY....4-8 75-77
HICKORY/MGM....4-8 76
ODE....4-8 70-74

LPs: 10/12-inch

ABC/HICKORY....8-12 76-77
ODE....8-12 70-74
Also see HARRIS, Emmylou
Also see KIMBERLY, Adrian

EVERLY, Phil *C&W '80*

Singles: 7-inch

CAPITOL....3-4 83
CURB....3-4 80-81
ELEKTRA....3-4 79
PYE....3-5 73-76
RCA....3-5 73

LPs: 10/12-inch

ELECTRA....5-10 79
PYE....8-10 75-76
RCA....8-10 73

EVERLY BROTHERS *P&R/R&B '57*

Singles: 78 rpm

CADENCE....50-100 57-58
COLUMBIA (21496 "The Sun Keeps Shining")....50-75 56

Singles: 7-inch

BARNABY....3-4 70-76
CADENCE....10-15 57-61
(Silver and maroon, or blue labels)
CADENCE....5-10 61-62
(Red label.)
COLUMBIA (21496 "The Sun Keeps Shining")....75-100 56
ERIC....3-4 70s
MERCURY....3-4 84-86
RCA....3-6 72-73
W.B. (5151 "Cathy's Clown")....8-10 60
(Monaural.)
W.B. (S-5151 "Cathy's Clown")....20-30 60
(Stereo.)
W.B. (5163 thru 5833)....5-10 60-69
W.B. (5857 "Fifi the Flea")....15-25 67
(Credits "Don Everly Brother" on one side, and "Phil Everly Brother" on the flip.)
W.B. (5901 thru 7425)....4-8 67-70

Promotional Singles

BARNABY....3-6 70-76
CADENCE....15-25 57-62
(Black vinyl.)
CADENCE (1348 "All I Have to Do Is Dream")....25-50
(Colored vinyl.)
COLUMBIA (21496 "The Sun Keeps Shining")....150-250 56
MERCURY....3-5 84-86
RCA....4-8 72-73
W.B. (5151 "Cathy's Clown")....40-60 60
(Colored vinyl.)
W.B. (5163 "So Sad")....40-60 60
(Colored vinyl.)
W.B. (5199 "Ebony Eyes")....40-60 61
(Colored vinyl.)

Picture Sleeves

CADENCE (1337 "Wake Up Little Susie")....50-100 57
CADENCE (1355 "Problems")....20-40 58
CADENCE (1369 "Till I Kissed You")....20-40 59
CADENCE (1376 "Let It Be Me")....20-40 60
W.B. (5151 "Cathy's Clown")....40-60 60
W.B. (5163 "So Sad")....40-60 60
W.B. (5199 "Ebony Eyes")....40-60 61
W.B. (5220 "Temptation")....15-25 61
W.B. (5250 "Crying in the Rain")....15-25 62
W.B. (5273 "That's Old Fashioned")....15-25 62
W.B. (5297 "Don't Ask Me to Be Friends")....15-25 62
MERCURY....3-6 84

EPs: 7-inch

CADENCE (3 "Rockin' with the Everly Brothers")....25-35 61
(Has single sheet cardboard insert/cover. Compact 33.)
CADENCE (4 "Dream with the Everly Brothers")....25-35 61
(Has single sheet cardboard insert/cover. Compact 33.)
CADENCE (104 "The Everly Brothers")....30-50 57
CADENCE (105 "The Everly Brothers")....30-50 57
CADENCE (107 "The Everly Brothers")....30-50 58
CADENCE ("Songs Our Daddy Taught Us")....100-150 58
(White, typewritten label. No selection number shown, only identification numbers "K80H-1718/20." Labeled "Cadence Disc Jockey Pressing." Promotional issue only.)
CADENCE (108/109/110 "Songs Our Daddy Taught Us")....25-50 58
(Price is for any of three volumes.)
CADENCE (111 "The Everly Brothers")....25-50 59
CADENCE (118 "The Everly Brothers")....25-35 59
CADENCE (121 "Very Best of The Everly Brothers")....25-35 60
W.B. (120 "Everly Brothers' Show")....15-25 70
(Juke box EP.)
W.B. (1381-1 "Foreverly Yours")....15-25 60
(Black vinyl.)
W.B. (1381-1 "Foreverly Yours")....25-50 60
(Colored vinyl. Promotional issue only.)
W.B. (1381-2 "Especially for You")....15-25 60
W.B. (5501 "The Everly Brothers Plus Two Oldies")....15-25 61

LPs: 10/12-inch

ARISTA....8-12 84
BARNABY (350 "Original Greatest Hits")....10-15 70
BARNABY (30260 "End of an Era")....10-15 71
BARNABY (4000 series)....6-10 77
BARNABY (6006 "Greatest Hits")....8-12
CADENCE (3003 "The Everly Brothers")....75-125 58
CADENCE (3016 "Songs Our Daddy Taught Us")....50-75 58
CADENCE (3025 "The Everly Brothers' Best")....75-100 59
(Blue cover.)
CADENCE (3040 "The Fabulous Style of the Everly Brothers")....50-75 60
CADENCE (3059 "Folk Songs")....35-40 63
CADENCE (3062 "15 Everly Hits")....45-65 63
CADENCE (25040 "The Fabulous Style of the Everly Brothers")....75-100 60
(Stereo.)
CADENCE (25059 "Folk Songs")....35-40 63
(Stereo.)
CADENCE (25062 "15 Everly Hits")....45-65 63
(Stereo.)
CANDLELITE....10-15 76
EXCELSIOR....5-10
HARMONY....10-12 68-70
HAPPY DAYS....5-10
MERCURY....5-10 84-86
PAIR....8-12 84
PASSPORT....5-12 84-86
RCA....8-12 72
RHINO (214 "All They Had to Do Was Dream")....5-10 85
RHINO (258 "Heartache and Memories")....8-10 85
(Picture disc.)
RONCO....8-10
TIME-LIFE....10-15 86
W.B. (1381 "It's Everly Time")....25-40 60
W.B. (1395 "A Date with the Everly Brothers")....30-40 60
(With gatefold cover and eight "wallet pix" cut-out photos.)
W.B. (1395 "A Date with the Everly Brothers")....15-20 61
(With standard cover.)
W.B. (1418 "Songs for Both Sides of an Evening")....25-30 61
W.B. (1430 "Instant Party")....20-30 62
W.B. (1471 "Golden Hits")....20-30 62
W.B. (1483 "Christmas with the Everly Brothers")....20-25 61
W.B. (1513 "Great Country Hits")....20-25 63
W.B. (1554 "Very Best of the Everly Brothers")....15-20 64
(Yellow cover. Gray label.)
W.B. (1554 "Very Best of the Everly Brothers")....10-15 70
(Blue cover. Gray label.)
W.B. (1554 "Very Best of the Everly Brothers")....8-12 72
(Blue cover. "Skyline" label.)
W.B. (1578 "Rock 'N Soul")....20-25 65
W.B. (1585 "Gone Gone Gone")....20-25 65
W.B. (1605 "Beat & Soul")....15-25 65
W.B. (1620 "In Our Image")....30-45 66
W.B. (1646 "Two Yanks in London")....15-25 66
(With the Hollies.)
W.B. (1676 "The Hit Sound of the Everly Brothers")....15-20 67
W.B. (1708 "Everly Brothers Sing")....15-25 67
W.B. (1752 "Roots")....15-25 68
W.B. (1858 "The Everly Brothers Show")....12-15 70

Promotional LPs

W.B. (134 "The Everly Brothers")....75-100 61
(One sided, 10-inch LP with five tracks from *The Everly Brothers - Both Sides of an Evening* [WB 1418]. Promotional issue only.)
W.B. (135 "Souvenir Sampler")....50-80 61
(Don and Phil discussing *The Everly Brothers - Both Sides of an Evening.* Has an LP discount coupon on sleeve. Promotional issue only.)
W.B. (1381 "It's Everly Time")....50-100 60
W.B. (1395 "A Date with the Everly Brothers")....75-100 60
(With gatefold cover and eight "wallet pix" cut-out photos.)
W.B. (1418 "Both Sides of an Evening")....50-75 61
W.B. (1430 "Instant Party")....50-75 62
W.B. (1471 "Golden Hits")....50-75 62
W.B. (1483 "Christmas with the Everly Brothers")....50-75 61
W.B. (1513 "Great Country Hits")....30-60 63

W.B. (1554 "Very Best of the Everly Brothers")..30-60 64
(Yellow cover.)
W.B. (1578 "Rock 'N Soul")..............30-60 65
W.B. (1585 "Gone Gone Gone").......30-60 65
W.B. (1605 "Beat 'N Soul")...............25-50 65
W.B. (1620 "In Our Image")...............25-50 66
W.B. (1646 "Two Yanks in London")...25-50 66
W.B. (1676 "The Hit Sound of the Everly Brothers")...................................25-50 67
W.B. (1708 "The Everly Brothers Sing")..25-50 67
W.B. (1752 "Roots").........................20-40 68
W.B. (1858 "The Everly Brothers Show")...20-30 70
Members: Don Everly; Phil Everly.
Also see CASH, Johnny, Rosanne Cash & Everly Brothers
Also see EVERLY, Don
Also see EVERLY, Phil
Also see HOLLIES

EVERLY BROTHERS & BEACH BOYS

Singles: 7-inch
CAPITOL (44297 "Don't Worry Baby")..3-5 88
Picture Sleeves
CAPITOL (44297 "Don't Worry Baby")..3-5 88
Also see BEACH BOYS

EVERY FATHER'S TEENAGE SON — P&R '67

Singles: 7-inch
BUDDAH 4-8 67

EVERY MOTHER'S NIGHTMARE — LP '70

LPs: 10/12-inch
ARISTA...5-8 90

EVERY MOTHER'S SON — P&R/LP '67

Singles: 7-inch
MGM 4-8 67-68
POLYDOR..3-4
Picture Sleeves
MGM 4-8 67
LPs: 10/12-inch
MGM 10-20 67

EVERYTHING BUT THE GIRL — LP '90

LPs: 10/12-inch
ATLANTIC 5-8 90

EVERYTHING IS EVERYTHING — P&R '69

Singles: 7-inch
VANGUARD APOSTOLIC 4-6 69
LPs: 10/12-inch
VANGUARD 15-20 69

EXCELLENTS — P&R '62

Singles: 7-inch
BLAST (205 "Coney Island Baby")....20-30 62
(Red label.)
BLAST (205 "Coney Island Baby")....10-20 62
(Red and white label.)
BLAST (205 "Coney Island Baby")....50-75 62
(White label.)
(Promotional issue only.)
BLAST (205 "Coney Island Baby")....15-25 65
(Purple label.)
COLLECTABLES 3-4
MERMAID (106 "Love No One But You")..75-125 61
(Label pictures a mermaid.)
MERMAID (106 "Love No One But You")..25-50 64
(Mermaid not pictured.)
OLD TIMER 4-8 64
LPs: 10/12-inch
ON the CORNER (135 "Excellents Go Bob, Bob, Bobbin' Along")..............................10-15 90

EXCELLENTS (Ultimates)

Singles: 7-inch
BLAST (207 "I Hear a Rhapsody").... 35-55 63
(Not the same artist as on the preceding Blast issues. This group is really the Ultimates.)

EXCELS — P&R '61

Singles: 7-inch
GONE (5094 "My Foolish Heart")..... 15-25 60
RSVP (111 "Can't Help Lovin' That Girl of Mine")... 20-30 61

EXCITERS — P&R/R&B '62

Singles: 7-inch
BANG (515 "A Little Bit of Soap")....... 5-10 66
BANG (518 "Weddings Make Me Cry")... 15-25 66
LIBERTY 3-4
ROULETTE... 5-10 64
RCA (9633 "If You Want My Love").. 15-25 68
RCA (9723 "Blowing Up My Mind")... 15-25 68
SHOUT 5-10 66-67
TODAY.. 4-8 70
U.A. 5-10 62-63
Picture Sleeves
ROULETTE.. 10-20 64
LPs: 10/12-inch
RCA (4211 "Caviar and Chitlins")..... 20-30 69
ROULETTE.. 15-20 66
SUNSET 10-12 70
TODAY... 8-10 71
U.A. (3264 "Tell Him")..................... 30-40 63
(Monaural.)
U.A. (6264 "Tell Him")...................... 40-50 63
(Stereo.)
Members: Brenda Reid; Herb Rooney; Carol Johnson; Lillian Walker.
Also see BRENDA & HERB

EXECUTIVE — R&B '81

Singles: 7-inch
20TH FOX.. 3-4 81

EXECUTIVE SUITE — R&B '73

Singles: 7-inch
BABYLON (1109 "I'm a Winner Now")... 8-15 73
BABYLON (1111 "When the Fuel Runs Out").. 5-10 74
BABYLON (1113 "Your Love Is Paradise")... 8-15 74
JUBILEE 5-10 69
NORTH BAY... 3-5
U.A. 3-5 75

EXILE — P&R '77

Singles: 7-inch
ARISTA.. 3-4 89-91
ATCO 3-5 77
COLUMBIA 3-6 69-70
EPIC.. 3-4 83-88
MCA/CURB.. 3-4 85-86
W.B./CURB.. 3-4 78-81
WOODEN NICKEL................................ 3-5 72-73
LPs: 10/12-inch
EPIC... 5-10 83-88
MCA/CURB... 5-8 85-86
RCA 5-10 78
W.B. 5-10 78-81
WOODEN NICKEL................................ 8-10 73
Members: J.P. Pennington; Les Taylor; Sonny LeMaire; Marlon Hargis; Steve Goetzman.

EXITS — R&B '67

Singles: 7-inch
GEMINI 5-10 67
KAPP (2028 "Another Sundown in Watts")... 15-25 69

EXODUS — LP '87

LPs: 10/12-inch
ARISTA... 5-10 87
CAPITOL... 5-8 90
COMBAT... 5-8 87-89

EXOTIC GUITARS — LP '68

Singles: 7-inch
RANWOOD 3-5 68-70
LPs: 10/12-inch
RANWOOD 5-10 68-70
Member: Al Casey.
Also see CASEY, Al
Also see PLATTERS / Exotic Guitars

EXPOSE — D&D '85

Singles: 12-inch
ARISTA... 4-6 85-89
Singles: 7-inch
ARISTA... 3-4 85-90
Picture Sleeves
ARISTA... 3-4 87-89
LPs: 10/12-inch
ARISTA... 5-10 86-89
Members: Jeanette Jurado; Gioia Bruno; Ann Curless.

EXPRESS, B.T: see B.T. EXPRESS

EXTRA Ts — R&B '82

Singles: 7-inch
SUNNYVIEW... 3-4 82

EXTREME — LP '89

LPs: 10/12-inch
A&M.. 5-8 89-90

EYE TO EYE — P&R/LP '82

Singles: 7-inch
W.B. 3-4 82-83
LPs: 10/12-inch
W.B. 5-10 82-83
Also see MARSHALL-HAIN

EZO — LP '87

LPs: 10/12-inch
GEFFEN 5-10 87

F., Simon — P&R '87
(Simon Fellowes)

Singles: 7-inch

CHRYSALIS 3-4 86-87
REPRISE 3-4 87

Picture Sleeves

CHRYSALIS 3-4 86-87

FCC — P&R/LP '79
(Funky Communication Committee)

Singles: 7-inch

FREE FLIGHT (Black vinyl) 3-4 79
FREE FLIGHT (Colored vinyl) 3-5 79
(Promotional issue only.)

LPs: 10/12-inch

FREE FLIGHT 5-8 79
RCA 5-10 80

FLB: see FAT LARRY'S BAND

FABARES, Shelley — P&R/LP '62

Singles: 7-inch

COLPIX (Except 721) 5-10 62-64
COLPIX (721 "Football Season's Over") 50-100 64
DUNHILL (4001 "My Prayer") 15-25 65
DUNHILL (4041 "See Ya 'Round on the Rebound") 15-25 65
ERIC 3-4
VEE JAY (632 "Lost Summer Love") 15-25 64

Picture Sleeves

COLPIX (621 "Johnny Angel") 50-100 62
COLPIX (636 "Johnny Loves Me") 40-60 62

LPs: 10/12-inch

COLPIX (426 "Shelley") 35-45 62
(Monaural.)
COLPIX (426 "Shelley") 45-55 62
(Stereo.)
COLPIX (431 "The Things We Did Last Summer") 35-45 62
(Monaural.)
COLPIX (431 "The Things We Did Last Summer") 45-55 62
(Stereo.)
Session: Sally Stevens.
Also see BLOSSOMS
Also see DARREN, James / Shelley Fabares / Paul Petersen
Also see PETERSEN, Paul, & Shelley Fabares

FABIAN — P&R/R&B/LP '59
(With the Fabulous Four)

Singles: 7-inch

ABC 3-5 74
CHANCELLOR (1020 "I'm in Love") 15-25 58
CHANCELLOR (1024 "Be My Steady Date") 15-25 58
CHANCELLOR (1029 "I'm a Man") 15-25 58
(Monaural.)
CHANCELLOR (1029 "I'm a Man") 25-50 58
(Stereo.)
CHANCELLOR (1033 "Turn Me Loose") 15-25 59
(Monaural.)
CHANCELLOR (1033 "Turn Me Loose") 25-50 59
(Stereo.)
CHANCELLOR (1037 "Tiger") 15-20 59
(Monaural.)
CHANCELLOR (1037 "Tiger") 25-50 59
(Stereo.)
CHANCELLOR (1041 "Come on and Get Me") 10-20 59
(Monaural.)
CHANCELLOR (1041 "Come on and Get Me") 25-50 59
(Stereo.)
CHANCELLOR (1044 "Hound Dog Man") 10-20 59
(Monaural.)
CHANCELLOR (1044 "Hound Dog Man") 25-50 59
(Stereo.)
CHANCELLOR (1047 "String Along") 10-20 60
(Monaural.)
CHANCELLOR (1047 "String Along") 25-50 60
(Stereo.)
CHANCELLOR (1051 "I'm Gonna Sit Right Down and Write Myself a Letter") 10-15 60
CHANCELLOR (1055 "King of Love") 10-20 60
CHANCELLOR (1061 "Kissin' & Twistin'") 10-20 60
CHANCELLOR (1067 "Hold On") 10-20 60
CHANCELLOR (1072 "David & Goliath") 10-15 61
CHANCELLOR (1079 "You're Only Young Once") 10-15 61
CHANCELLOR (1084 "Dream Factory") 10-15 61
CHANCELLOR (1086 "Kansas City") 10-15 61
CHANCELLOR (1092 "Wild Party") 10-15 61
COLLECTABLES 3-4 80s
CREAM 3-5 77
DOT (16413 "Break Down and Cry") 8-12 62
ERIC 3-4 70s

Picture Sleeves

CHANCELLOR (1029 "I'm a Man") 20-30 58
CHANCELLOR (1033 "Turn Me Loose") 20-30 59
CHANCELLOR (1037 "Tiger") 20-30 59
CHANCELLOR (1041 "Come on and Get Me") 15-25 59
CHANCELLOR (1044 "Hound Dog Man") 15-25 59
CHANCELLOR (1047 "String Along") 15-25 60
CHANCELLOR (1051 "Strollin' in the Springtime") 15-25 60
CHANCELLOR (1055 "King of Love") 15-25 60
CHANCELLOR (1061 "Kissin' and Twistin'") 15-25 60
CHANCELLOR (1067 "Hold On") 15-25 61
CHANCELLOR (1079 "You're Only Young Once") 15-25 61
CHANCELLOR (1084 "A Girl Like You") 15-25 61
CHANCELLOR (1092 "Wild Party") 15-25 61
CREAM 4-6 77

EPs: 7-inch

CHANCELLOR (301 "Hound Dog Man") 20-40 60
CHANCELLOR (5003 "Hold That Tiger!") 20-40 59
(Black label. Price for any of three volumes.)
CHANCELLOR (5003 "Excerpts from *Hold That Tiger!*") 30-50 59
(With paper sleeve. White label. Promotional issue only.)
CHANCELLOR (5005 "The Fabulous Fabian") 20-40 60
CHANCELLOR (5012 "The Good Old Summertime") 20-40 60
(Black label. Price is for any of three volumes.)
CHANCELLOR (9802 "Young and Wonderful") 20-40 60

LPs: 10/12-inch

ABC 10-12 73
CHANCELLOR (5003 "Hold That Tiger") 50-75 59
(Monaural.)
CHANCELLOR (5003 "Hold That Tiger") 50-100 59
(Stereo.)
CHANCELLOR (5005 "The Fabulous Fabian") 40-60 59
(Monaural.)
CHANCELLOR (5005 "The Fabulous Fabian") 50-75 59
(Stereo.)
CHANCELLOR (5012 "The Good Old Summertime") 40-60 60
(Monaural.)
CHANCELLOR (5012 "The Good Old Summertime") 50-75 60
(Stereo.)
CHANCELLOR (5019 "Rockin' Hot") 50-75 61
CHANCELLOR (5024 "16 Fabulous Hits") 50-75 62
CHANCELLOR (69802 "Young and Wonderful") 40-60 60
EVEREST 5-10 83
MCA 5-10 85
TRIP 8-10 77
U.A. 10-15 75
Also see FABULOUS FOUR

FABIAN / Frankie Avalon

Singles: 7-inch

CHANCELLOR/WIBG 99 ("When the Saints Go Marchin' In") 25-50 61
(Colored vinyl. Radio station special products issue. No selection number used. Flip is by the Live Five, who were the WIBG dee jays.)

LPs: 10/12-inch

CHANCELLOR (5009 "The Hit Makers") 75-100 60
MCA 5-10 85
Also see AVALON, Frankie
Also see FABIAN

FABRIC, Bent — P&R/LP '62

Singles: 7-inch

ATCO 4-6 62-65

Picture Sleeves

ATCO (6226 "Alley Cat") 10-15 62

LPs: 10/12-inch

ATCO 8-15 62-63
Also see BILK, Mr. Acker, & Bent Fabric

FABRIQUE, Tina — D&D '84

Singles: 12-inch

PRISM 4-6 84

FABULOUS COUNTS — R&B '69

Singles: 7-inch

HIGHLAND (1171 "So Far Away") 25-50 60s
KIM (811 "Money") 5-10 60s
MOIRA 3-6 68-70

LPs: 10/12-inch

COTILLION 10-12 69

FABULOUS FARQUAHR — LP '70
(Farquahr)

Singles: 7-inch

ELEKTRA 3-5 71
VERVE/FORECAST 4-8 68-69
W.B. 3-6 70

LPs: 10/12-inch

ELEKTRA 8-10 70
VERVE/FORECAST 10-15 69

FABULOUS POODLES — P&R/LP '79

Singles: 7-inch

EPIC 3-5 79

LPs: 10/12-inch

EPIC 5-10 76-79

FABULOUS RHINESTONES — P&R/LP '72

Singles: 7-inch

JUST SUNSHINE 3-5 72

Picture Sleeves

JUST SUNSHINE 3-5 72

LPs: 10/12-inch

JUST SUNSHINE 8-10 72-73

FABULOUS THUNDERBIRDS — LP '81

Singles: 7-inch

CBS ASSOCIATED 3-4 86-89
CHRYSALIS 3-5 79-81

ELEKTRA 3-4 88

Picture Sleeves

CBS ASSOCIATED.............................. 3-4 86-87

LPs: 10/12-inch

CBS ASSOCIATED.............................. 5-10 86-89
CHRYSALIS 5-10 79-81
TAKOMA 10-15 79
Members: Kim Wilson; Jimmie Vaughan; Preston Hubbard; Fran Christina.
Also see SANTANA
Also see VAUGHAN BROTHERS

FACE TO FACE — P&R/D&D/LP '84

Singles: 12-inch

EPIC 4-6 84
PORTRAIT 4-6 84

Singles: 7-inch

EPIC 3-4 84
MERCURY 3-4 88
PORTRAIT 3-4 84

Picture Sleeves

EPIC 3-4 84

LPs: 10/12-inch

EPIC 5-10 84
MERCURY 5-8 88

FACENDA, Tommy — P&R/R&B '59

Singles: 7-inch

ATLANTIC (2051 "High School U.S.A. [Virginia]") 15-25 59
ATLANTIC (2052 "High School U.S.A. [New York City Area]") 15-25 59
ATLANTIC (2053 "High School U.S.A. [North Carolina – South Carolina]") 15-25 59
ATLANTIC (2054 "High School U.S.A. [Washington D.C. Area]") 15-25 59
ATLANTIC (2055 "High School U.S.A. [Philadelphia Area]") 15-25 59
ATLANTIC (2056 "High School U.S.A. [Detroit Area]") 15-25 59
ATLANTIC (2057 "High School U.S.A. [Pittsburgh Area]") 15-25 59
ATLANTIC (2058 "High School U.S.A. [Minneapolis – St. Paul Area]") 15-25 59
ATLANTIC (2059 "High School U.S.A. [Florida]") 15-25 59
ATLANTIC (2060 "High School U.S.A. [Newark Area]") 15-25 59
ATLANTIC (2061 "High School U.S.A. [Boston Area]") 15-25 59
ATLANTIC (2062 "High School U.S.A. [Cleveland Area]") 15-25 59
ATLANTIC (2063 "High School U.S.A. [Buffalo Area]") 15-25 59
ATLANTIC (2064 "High School U.S.A. [Hartford Area]") 15-25 59
ATLANTIC (2065 "High School U.S.A. [Nashville Area]") 15-25 59
ATLANTIC (2066 "High School U.S.A. [Indiana]") 15-25 59
ATLANTIC (2067 "High School U.S.A. [Chicago Area]") 15-25 59
ATLANTIC (2068 "High School U.S.A. [New Orleans Area]") 15-25 59
ATLANTIC (2069 "High School U.S.A. [St. Louis – Kansas City Area]") 15-25 59
ATLANTIC (2070 "High School U.S.A. [Alabama -- Georgia]") 15-25 59
ATLANTIC (2071 "High School U.S.A. [Cincinnati Area]") 15-25 59
ATLANTIC (2072 "High School U.S.A. [Memphis Area]") 15-25 59
ATLANTIC (2073 "High School U.S.A. [Los Angeles Area]") 15-25 59
ATLANTIC (2074 "High School U.S.A. [San Francisco Area]") 15-25 59
ATLANTIC (2075 "High School U.S.A. [Texas]") 15-25 59
ATLANTIC (2076 "High School U.S.A. [Seattle – Portland Area]") 15-25 59
ATLANTIC (2077 "High School U.S.A. [Denver Area]") 15-25 59
ATLANTIC (2078 "High School U.S.A. [Oklahoma]") 15-25 59
LEGRANDE (1001 "High School U.S.A.") 10-20 59
(We've yet to learn how to positively identify original pressings, as many reissues exist.)
NASCO 10-20 58
Session: King Curtis.
Also see KING CURTIS
Also see VINCENT, Gene

FACES — LP '70

Singles: 7-inch

W.B. 3-6 71-75

Picture Sleeves

W.B. 3-6 73

LPs: 10/12-inch

MERCURY 8-12 73
W.B. 10-20 70-76
Members: Rod Stewart; Ron Wood; Ronnie Lane.
Also see McLAGAN, Ian
Also see SMALL FACES
Also see STEWART, Rod
Also see WOOD, Ron

FACHIN, Eria — P&R '88

Singles: 7-inch

CRITIQUE 3-4 88

Picture Sleeves

CRITIQUE 3-4 88

FACTS OF LIFE — R&B '76

Singles: 7-inch

KAYVETTE 3-5 76-77

LPs: 10/12-inch

KAYVETTE 8-10 77
Members: Jean Davis; Keith William; Chuck Carter.

FAGEN, Donald — P&R/R&B/LP '82

Singles: 7-inch

W.B. 3-4 82-88

Picture Sleeves

W.B. 3-4 82-88

LPs: 10/12-inch

MFSL (120 "Nightfly") 20-30 84
W.B. 5-10 82-88
Also see JAY & AMERICANS
Also see STEELY DAN

FAGEN, Donald, & Walter Becker

LPs: 10/12-inch

PVC 5-10 85
Also see FAGEN, Donald

FAGIN, Joe — P&R '82

Singles: 7-inch

MILLENNIUM 3-4 82

FAIR, Yvonne — R&B '74

Singles: 7-inch

DADE 5-10 63
KING 5-10 62
MOTOWN 3-5 74-76
SMASH 5-10 66
SOUL (Black vinyl) 3-6 70
SOUL (Colored vinyl) 5-10 70
(Promotional issue only.)

LPs: 10/12-inch

MOTOWN 5-10 76

FAIRCHILD, Barbara — C&W '69

Singles: 7-inch

CAPITOL 3-4 86
COLUMBIA 3-4 69-78
DOWN HOME 3-4 80
KAPP 3-5 68

LPs: 10/12-inch

AUDIOGRAPH 5-10 82
COLUMBIA 8-12 70-78
PAID 5-10 81
Session: Jordanaires.
Also see WALKER, Billy, & Barbara Fairchild

FAIRE, Johnny
(Donnie Brooks)

Singles: 7-inch

FABLE (601 "If I'm a Fool"/"You Gotta Walk That Line") 40-50 57
FABLE (601 "If I'm a Fool"/"Make Up Your Mind Baby") 40-50 57
(Note different flip.)
SURF (5019 "Bertha Lou") 40-50 58
SURF (5024 "Betcha I Getcha") 20-30 58
Also see BROOKS, Donnie

FAIRGROUND ATTRACTION — P&R '88

Singles: 7-inch

RCA 3-4 88-89

Picture Sleeves

RCA 3-4 88

LPs: 10/12-inch

RCA 5-8 88
Members: Eddi Reader; Mark Nevin.

FAIRPORT CONVENTION — LP '71

Singles: 7-inch

A&M 3-5 71-72

LPs: 10/12-inch

A&M 10-12 69-74
COTILLION 10-15 70
VARRICK/ROUNDER 5-10 86
ISLAND 8-10 74-75
Also see DENNY, Sandy
Also see MATTHEWS, Ian
Also see THOMPSON, Richard

FAIRWEATHER
(Andy Fairweather-Low)

LPs: 10/12-inch

NEON 8-10 71
Also see FAIRWEATHER-LOW, Andy

FAIRWEATHER-LOW, Andy — P&R '75

Singles: 7-inch

A&M 3-5 75-77

LPs: 10/12-inch

A&M 8-10 74-76
W.B. 5-10 80
Also see FAIRWEATHER
Also see WILLIE & Poor Boys

FAITH, Adam — P&R '65

Singles: 7-inch

AMY 4-8 64-65
CAPITOL 4-8 65-66
CUB 5-10 59
DOT 4-8 62

LPs: 10/12-inch

AMY (8005 "Adam Faith") 20-30 65
MGM (3951 "England's Top Singer") 25-30 61
W.B. 8-12 74

FAITH, Gene — R&B '70

Singles: 7-inch

VIRTUE 3-6 69-70

FAITH, Percy, Orchestra — P&R '50

Singles: 78 rpm

COLUMBIA 3-4 50-57

Singles: 7-inch

COLUMBIA 3-10 50-76

Picture Sleeves

COLUMBIA 5-10 60

EPs: 7-inch

COLUMBIA 5-10 50-59
ROYALE 5-10 50s

LPs: 10/12-inch

COLUMBIA 5-15 51-82
HARMONY 5-10 68-72
Also see SANDERS, Felicia

FAITH, Percy, Orchestra / Johnny Mathis

Singles: 7-inch

COLUMBIA 5-10
Also see FAITH, Percy, Orchestra
Also see MATHIS, Johnny

FAITH BAND — P&R '78

Singles: 7-inch

AZRA ("Can't Say Goodbye") 6-12 88
(Mickey Mouse-shaped picture disc. No selection number used.)
MERCURY 3-5 78-79
VILLAGE 3-6 78

LPs: 10/12-inch

BROWN BAG 10-12 73
MERCURY 5-10 78-79
VILLAGE 6-12 77

FAITH, HOPE & CHARITY *P&R/R&B '70*

Singles: 7-inch

MAXWELL....3-5 70
RCA....3-5 75-77
SUSSEX....3-5 72
20TH FOX....3-4 78-80

LPs: 10/12-inch

RCA....8-10 75
SUSSEX....8-10 72
20TH FOX....5-10 80

Members: Brenda Hilliard; Albert Bailey; Zulema Crusseaux; Daine Destry.
Also see ZULEMA

FAITH NO MORE *P&R/LP '90*

Singles: 7-inch

SLASH....3-4 90

LPs: 10/12-inch

SLASH....5-8 90

Members: Chuck Moseley; Roddy Bottum; Bill Gould; Mike Bordin; Jim Martin; Mike Patton.

FAITHFULL, Marianne *P&R '64*

Singles: 12-inch

ISLAND....4-6 83

Singles: 7-inch

ISLAND (49121 "Broken English"/"Brain Drain")....3-5 79
ISLAND (94997 "Why D'Ya Do It"/ "Broken English")....8-12 79
LONDON (Except 1022)....4-8 64-72
LONDON (1022 "Sister Morphine")....75-100 69
(With the Rolling Stones.)

Picture Sleeves

LONDON....5-10 65

LPs: 10/12-inch

ISLAND....5-10 79-90
LONDON....15-25 65-69
Also see ROLLING STONES

FALANA, Lola *R&B '75*

Singles: 7-inch

AMOS....3-5
RCA....3-4 75
REPRISE....5-10 67

FALCO *D&D/LP '83*

Singles: 12-inch

A&M....4-6 82-86

Singles: 7-inch

A&M....3-4 82-86
SIRE....3-4 87

Picture Sleeves

A&M....3-4 86
SIRE....3-4 87

LPs: 10/12-inch

A&M....5-10 83-86

FALCONS *P&R/R&B '59*

(With Al Smith's Orchestra; "Musical Direction Sax Kari")

Singles: 78 rpm

SILHOUETTE....200-300 57

Singles: 7-inch

ANNA (1110 "Just for Your Love") 100-150 60
ATLANTIC (2153 "Darling")....10-20 62
ATLANTIC (2175 "Take This Love")....10-20 63
ATLANTIC (2207 "Oh Baby")....10-20 63
BIG WHEEL....5-10 66
CHESS (1743 "Just for Your Love")....20-3 59
FALCON (1006 "Now That It's Over")....150-250 57
FLICK (001 "You're So Fine")....150-250 59
FLICK (008 "You Must Know I Love You")....100-150 60
KUDO (661 "This Heart of Mine")....300-400 58
LIBERTY....3-4
LU PINE (103 "I Found a Love")....30-50 62
LU PINE (124 "Lonely Nights")....50-100 62
LU PINE (1003 "I Found a Love")....10-20 62
LU PINE (1024 "Lonely Nights")....20-40 62
MERCURY (70940 "Baby That's It")....50-75 56
SILHOUETTE (522 "Can This Be Christmas")....250-350 57
(Flip, *Sent Up*, is Silhouette 521, a number also used for a Charmers release.)
UNART (2013 "You're So Fine")....20-30 59
UNART (2013-S "You're So Fine")....50-100 59
(Stereo—albeit reprocessed.)
UNART (2022 "Country Shack")....15-25 59
U.A. (229 "The Teacher")....15-25 60
U.A. (255 "Wonderful Love")....15-25 60
U.A. (289 "Working Man's Song")....15-25 60
U.A. (420 "You're So Fine")....10-15 62

EPs: 7-inch

U.A. (10010 "The Falcons")....250-350 59

Members: Wilson Pickett; Joe Stubbs; Eddie Floyd; Arnet Robinson; Ben Rice; Lance Finnie; Sonny Monroe.
Also see FLOYD, Eddie
Also see PICKETT, Wilson

FALTERMEYER, Harold *P&R/R&B '85*

Singles: 7-inch

MCA....3-4 85

Picture Sleeves

MCA....3-4 85

LPs: 10/12-inch

MCA....5-10 85
Also see LABELLE, Patti, & Harold Faltermeyer

FALTERMEYER, Harold / Glenn Frey

Singles: 7-inch

MCA....3-4 84
Also see FREY, Glenn

FALTERMEYER, Harold, & Steve Stevens

Singles: 12-inch

COLUMBIA....4-8 86
(Promotional issue only.)

Singles: 7-inch

COLUMBIA....3-4 86
Also see FALTERMEYER, Harold

FALTSKOG, Agnetha *P&R/LP '83*

Singles: 7-inch

POLYDOR....3-4 83

Picture Sleeves

POLYDOR....3-5 83

LPs: 10/12-inch

POLYDOR....5-10 83
Also see ABBA

FALTSKOG, Agnetha, & Peter Cetera *P&R '88*

Singles: 7-inch

ATLANTIC....3-4 88

Picture Sleeves

ATLANTIC....3-4 88
Also see CETERA, Peter
Also see FALTSKOG, Agnetha

FAME: see KIDS from "FAME"

FAME, Georgie *P&R/LP '65*

(With the Blue Flames)

Singles: 7-inch

EPIC....3-6 68-70
IMPERIAL....4-8 65-67
ISLAND....3-5 75

EPs: 7-inch

EPIC....5-10 68
(Juke box issues only.)

LPs: 10/12-inch

EPIC....10-20 68-70
IMPERIAL....15-20 65-66
ISLAND....8-10 75
Also see FAME & PRICE – Price & Fame Together

FAME & PRICE – PRICE & FAME TOGETHER

Singles: 7-inch

REPRISE....3-5 71

Members: Georgie Fame; Alan Price.
Also see FAME, Georgie
Also see PRICE, Alan

FAMILY *LP '72*

Singles: 7-inch

LITTLE CITY....3-5 77
U.A....3-5 71-73

LPs: 10/12-inch

REPRISE....15-20 68-70
U.A....10-12 71-73

Members; Rick Grech; John Weider.
Also see BLIND FAITH
Also see WEIDER, John

FAMILY *P&R/R&B/D&D/LP '85*

Singles: 12-inch

PAISLEY PARK....4-6 85

Singles: 7-inch

PAISLEY PARK....3-4 85

Picture Sleeves

PAISLEY PARK....3-4 85

LPs: 10/12-inch

PAISLEY PARK....5-10 85

Members: Paul Peterson; Jerome Benton; Susannah Melvoin; Jellybean Johnson.
Also see TIME

FAMILY DREAM *R&B '87*

Singles: 7-inch

MOTOWN....3-4 87

FAMILY PLANN *R&B '75*

Singles: 7-inch

DRIVE....3-5 75

FANCY *P&R '74*

Singles: 7-inch

BIG TREE....3-5 74
POISON RING....3-6 71

LPs: 10/12-inch

BIG TREE....8-10 74
POISON RING....12-20 71
RCA....5-10 79

Members: Al Ranaudo; Billy Durso.

FANCY *D&D '85*

Singles: 12-inch

PERSONAL....4-6 85

FANNY *P&R/LP '71*

Singles: 7-inch

CASABLANCA....3-5 74-75
REPRISE....3-5 70-73

LPs: 10/12-inch

CASABLANCA....8-10 74
REPRISE....10-12 70-73

Members: Jean Millington; June Millington; Alice de Buhr; Nickey Barclay; Patti Quatro; Wendy Haas; Brie Howard.

FANTASTIC FIVE KEYS

Singles: 7-inch

CAPITOL....5-10 62
Also see FIVE KEYS

FANTASTIC FOUR *P&R/R&B '67*

Singles: 7-inch

EASTBOUND....3-5 73-74
RIC-TIC (Except 113 & 121)....10-20 66-68
RIC-TIC (113 "Can't Stop Looking for My Baby")....100-200 66
RIC-TIC (121 "Can't Stop Looking for My Baby")....50-75 66
SOUL....8-15 68-70
WESTBOUND....3-5 75-79

LPs: 10/12-inch

SOUL (717 "Best of the Fantastic Four")....25-40 69
20TH FOX/WESTBOUND....8-10 76
WESTBOUND....8-10 75-78

Members: Joe Pruitt; James Epps; Robert Pruitt; Toby Childs; Ernest Newsome; Cleveland Horn.

FANTASTIC JOHNNY C.

(Johnny Corley) *P&R/R&B '67*

Singles: 7-inch

BRANDING IRON (170 "Let's Do It Together")....10-20
KAMA SUTRA....3-5 70
PHIL L.A. of SOUL....4-8 67-73

LPs: 10/12-inch

PHIL L.A. of SOUL 15-20 68

FANTASTICS P&R '72

Singles: 7-inch

BELL........ 10-20 71-72
DERAM........ 5-10 69
Members: Jerome Ramos; Don Haywoode; John Cheatdom; Rich Pitts.
Also see VELOURS

FANTASY P&R/LP '70

Singles: 7-inch

IMPERIAL........ 3-6 69
LIBERTY........ 3-5 70

LPs: 10/12-inch

LIBERTY........ 10-15 70

FANTASY R&B '81

Singles: 12-inch

QUALITY........ 4-6 83

Singles: 7-inch

PAVILLION 3-4 81

LPs: 10/12-inch

PAVILLION 5-10 81-82

FANTAYZEE, Haysi: see HAYSI FANTAYZEE

FAR CORPORATION P&R '86

Singles: 7-inch

ATCO........ 3-4 86

Picture Sleeves

ATCO........ 3-4 86

LPs: 10/12-inch

ATCO........ 5-10 86
Members: Robin McAuley; Bobby Kimball; Steve Lukather; Dave Paich.
Also see TOTO

FARAGHER BROTHERS P&R '79

Singles: 7-inch

ABC 3-5 76-77
POLYDOR........ 3-4 79

LPs: 10/12-inch

ABC 5-10 79
POLYDOR........ 5-10 78-79
Members: Jimmy Faragher; Dan Faragher; Tom Faragher; Dave Faragher.
Also see BONES

FARDON, Don P&R '68

Singles: 7-inch

CHELSEA........ 3-5 73
GNP........ 4-8 68

LPs: 10/12-inch

DECCA........ 10-12 70
GNP........ 15-20 68

FARGO, Donna C&W/P&R/LP '72

Singles: 7-inch

ABC 3-4 78
ABC/DOT 3-5 74-77
CHALLENGE (59387 "Daddy") 5-10 68
CHALLENGE (59391 "Wishful Thinking")........ 5-10 68
CLEVELAND INT'L........ 3-4 84-91
COLUMBIA........ 3-4 83
DECCA (33001 "Daddy")........ 4-6 72
DOT 3-5 72-74
MCA........ 3-4 81
MERCURY 3-4 86-87
RCA 3-4 82
RAMCO (1982 "You Make Me Feel Like a Woman")........ 8-12 67
RAMCO (1988 "Whose Been Playing House")........ 8-12 67
RAMCO (1988 "Whose Been Sleeping on My Bed")........ 8-12 67
(Note change in title.)
RAMCO (1991 "Kinda Glad I'm Me")... 8-12 67
SONGBIRD 3-4 81
W.B. 3-5 76-81

Picture Sleeves

DOT 3-6 72-74
W.B. 3-5 76-80

LPs: 10/12-inch

ABC/DOT 5-10 74-77
DOT 8-12 72-73
MCA 5-8 80s
MERCURY........ 5-10 86
PICKWICK/HILLTOP........ 5-10 70s
RCA 5-10 83
SONGBIRD........ 4-8 81
W.B. 5-10 76-80
Session: Jordanaires.
Also see BARE, Bobby / Donna Fargo / Jerry Wallace

FARGO, Donna, & Billy Joe Royal C&W '87

Singles: 7-inch

MERCURY........ 3-4 87
Also see FARGO, Donna
Also see ROYAL, Billy Joe

FARNHAM, John P&R '90

(Johnny Farnham)

Singles: 7-inch

CAPITOL........ 4-6 67
RCA 3-4 90
Also see LITTLE RIVER BAND

FARQUAHR: see FABULOUS FARQUAHR

FARRELL, Billy R&B '49

(Bill Farrell)

Singles: 78 rpm

EPIC........ 15-25 57
IMPERIAL 8-12 54
MGM 10-15 49
MERCURY........ 8-12 56

Singles: 7-inch

CUB 5-10 59
DATE 10-20 58
EPIC........ 10-20 57
IMPERIAL 15-25 54
MERCURY........ 10-20 56
TEL (1000 "You Were Only Fooling")........ 15-25 58

FARRELL, Eileen LP '61

Singles: 7-inch

LONDON........ 3-5 65

LPs: 10/12-inch

COLUMBIA 10-20 60-63
HARMONY........ 5-10 68

FARRENHEIT LP '87

Singles: 12-inch

W.B. 4-8 87
(Promotional only.)

Singles: 7-inch

W.B. 3-4 87

LPs: 10/12-inch

W.B. 5-10 87

FARROW, Cee P&R/R&B '83

Singles: 7-inch

ROCSHIRE........ 3-4 83

Picture Sleeves

ROCSHIRE........ 3-4 83

FASCINATIONS R&B '66

Singles: 7-inch

A&G (101 "Since You Went Away").. 25-40 65
MAYFIELD 5-10 66-67
Members: Bernadine Boswell Smith; Shirley Walker; Fern Bledsoe; Joanne Levell.
Also see FASINATIONS

FASINATIONS

Singles: 7-inch

ABC-PAR........ 5-10 62-63
Also see FASCINATIONS

FAST RADIO D&D '83

Singles: 12-inch

RADAR 4-6 83

FASTER PUSSYCAT LP '87

Singles: 7-inch

ELEKTRA........ 3-4 87-90

Picture Sleeves

ELEKTRA........ 3-4 88

LPs: 10/12-inch

ELEKTRA........ 5-10 87-90
Members: Taime Downe; Brent Muscat; Greg Steele; Mark Michals; Eric Stacy; Brett Bradshaw.

FASTWAY LP '83

Singles: 12-inch

COLUMBIA (1727 "Easy Living") 10-12 83
(Picture disc. Promotional issue only.)

Singles: 7-inch

COLUMBIA........ 3-4 83-86

LPs: 10/12-inch

COLUMBIA........ 5-10 83-86
GWR........ 5-8 89

FAT BOYS R&B '84

Singles: 12-inch

EMPEROR 4-6 92
SUTRA 4-6 84-86

Singles: 7-inch

SUTRA 3-4 84-86
TIN PAN APPLE........ 3-4 87-89

Picture Sleeves

TIN PAN APPLE........ 3-5 88

LPs: 10/12-inch

SUTRA........ 5-10 84-87
TIN PAN APPLE........ 5-10 87-89
Members: Darren Robinson; Mark Morales; Damon Wimbley.
Also see DISCO 3
Also see KING DREAM CHORUS & Holiday Crew
Also see KRUSH GROVE ALL STARS

FAT BOYS & BEACH BOYS P&R/R&B '87

Singles: 7-inch

TIN PAN APPLE (885960 "Wipeout") ... 4-6 87
(Credits only "Fat Boys.")
TIN PAN APPLE (885960 "Wipeout") ... 3-4 87
(Credits "Fat Boys and the Beach Boys.")

Picture Sleeves

TIN PAN APPLE (885960 "Wipeout") ... 3-5 87
Also see BEACH BOYS

FAT BOYS & CHUBBY CHECKER P&R/R&B '88

Singles: 7-inch

TIN PAN APPLE........ 3-4 88

Picture Sleeves

TIN PAN APPLE........ 3-4 88
Also see CHECKER, Chubby
Also see FAT BOYS

FAT LARRY'S BAND R&B '78

(FLB)

Singles: 12-inch

WMOT 4-6 78-79

Singles: 7-inch

FANTASY........ 3-4 79-82
OMMI........ 3-4 86
STAX........ 3-5 77
WMOT 3-4 78-82

LPs: 10/12-inch

FANTASY........ 5-10 80
OMMI........ 5-10 86
STAX........ 8-10 77
WMOT 5-10 78-82
Members: Larry James; Art Capehart; Doug Jones; Jimmy Lee; Erskine Williams; Ted Cohen; Darryl Grant; Larry Labes.

FAT MATTRESS LP '69

LPs: 10/12-inch

ATCO........ 10-20 69-70

FATBACK R&B '73

(Fatback Band)

Singles: 12-inch

SPRING........ 4-6 83-84

Singles: 7-inch

COTILLION........ 3-4 83-85
EVENT 3-5 74-76
PERCEPTION 3-5 72-74
POLYDOR 3-4 79
SPRING........ 3-5 76-85

LPs: 10/12-inch

COTILLION 5-10 83-85
EVENT 8-10 74-76

PERCEPTION....8-10 72
POLYDOR....5-10 79
SPRING....5-10 76-84
Members: Bill Curtis; Johnny King; George Williams; Johnny Flippin; Earl Shelton; George Adam; Fred Demerey; George Victory; Gerry Thomas.
Also see CHRISTIE, Janice

FATES WARNING LP '87
Soundsheet
EVATONE (103504 "Anarchy Devine")....4-6 88
LPs: 10/12-inch
ENIGMA....5-10 87
METAL BLADE (Except 73330)....5-8 88-89
METAL BLADE (73330 "No Exit")....10-12 88
(Picture disc. Promotional issue only.)

FAX, Tony R&B '68
Singles: 7-inch
CALLA (151 "Lean on Me")....10-15 68

FAYE, Alma R&B '79
Singles: 12-inch
CASABLANCA....4-6 79
Singles: 7-inch
CASABLANCA....3-4 79

FAZE-O R&B/LP '78
Singles: 7-inch
SHE....3-5 77-79
LPs: 10/12-inch
SHE....5-10 77-79
Members: Keith Harrison; Ralph Aikens; Roger Parker; Tyrone Crum; Robert Neal Jr.

FEARON, Phil R&B '86
Singles: 7-inch
COOLTEMPO....3-4 86
ISLAND....3-4 86

FEATHER P&R '70
Singles: 7-inch
WHITE WHALE....3-5 70
LPs: 10/12-inch
COLUMBIA....10-12 70

FEATHERBED
(Barry Manilow)
Singles: 7-inch
BELL (133 "Could It Be Magic")....15-25 71
BELL (971 "Amy")....15-25 71
Also see MANILOW, Barry

FEE WAYBILL: see WAYBILL, Fee

FEEL R&B '82
Singles: 12-inch
SUTRA....4-6 82-83
Singles: 7-inch
SUTRA....3-4 82-83

FEELGOOD, DR: see DR. FEELGOOD

FEELIES LP '88
LPs: 10/12-inch
A&M....5-8 88

FELDER, Don P&R '81
Singles: 7-inch
ASYLUM....3-4 83
FULL MOON/ASYLUM....3-4 81
MCA....3-4
Picture Sleeves
FULL MOON/ASYLUM....3-4 81
LPs: 10/12-inch
ASYLUM....5-10 83
ELEKTRA....5-8 83
Also see EAGLES
Also see PURE PRAIRIE LEAGUE

FELDER, Wilton R&B/LP '78
Singles: 7-inch
ABC....3-4 78
MCA....3-4 79-85
LPs: 10/12-inch
ABC....5-10 78
MCA....5-10 80-85
PACIFIC JAZZ....8-12 69
Also see JAZZ CRUSADERS
Also see TASTE of HONEY

FELDER, Wilton, & Bobby Womack R&B '85
Singles: 7-inch
MCA....3-4 80-85
Picture Sleeves
MCA....3-4 80-85
Also see FELDER, Wilton
Also see WOMACK, Bobby

FELDMAN, Victor P&R '62
(Victor Feldman All Stars; Trio; Quartet; Vic Feldman)
Singles: 7-inch
AVA....3-5 63
INFINITY....3-5 62
PACIFIC JAZZ....3-5 66
VEE JAY....3-5 64
LPs: 10/12-inch
AVA....10-20 63
CONTEMPORARY....15-25 58-60
INTERLUDE....15-20 59
MODE....20-30 58
NAUTILUS....10-20 82
(Half-speed mastered.)
PACIFIC JAZZ....10-15 67-68
PALTO ALTO....5-10 83-84
RIVERSIDE....15-20 61
VEE JAY....15-25 59-65
WORLD PACIFIC....15-25 62

FELICIANO, Jose P&R/R&B/LP '68
Singles: 7-inch
ALA....3-4 80
MOTOWN....3-4 81-83
PRIVATE STOCK....3-5 76-77
RCA....3-6 64-75
LPs: 10/12-inch
CAMDEN....8-10 72
MOTOWN....5-10 81
PRIVATE STOCK....6-10 76-77
RCA....8-15 65-76
Also see SCHUUR, Diane

FELICIANO, Jose / Petula Clark
EPs: 7-inch
TK (334 "Mackenna's Gold")....10-20 69
Also see CLARK, Petula

FELICIANO, Jose, & Quincy Jones
LPs: 10/12-inch
RCA (4096 "Mackenna's Gold")....15-25 69
(Soundtrack.)
Also see FELICIANO, Jose
Also see JONES, Quincy

FELIX & JARVIS R&B '82
Singles: 7-inch
RFC/QUALITY....3-4 82-83

FELLINI, Suzanne P&R '80
Singles: 7-inch
CASABLANCA....3-4 80
LPs: 10/12-inch
CASABLANCA....5-10 80

FELONY P&R/LP '83
Singles: 7-inch
ROCK & ROLL....3-4 83-84
LPs: 10/12-inch
ROCK & ROLL....5-10 83

FELTS, Narvel P&R '60
Singles: 78 rpm
MERCURY....10-20 57
Singles: 7-inch
ABC....3-5 78
ABC/DOT....3-5 75-77
ACTION....4-8 70
ARA....5-10 64-65
CELEBRITY CIRCLE....4-8 65
CINNAMON....3-5 73-74
COLLAGE....3-5 79
COMPLEAT....3-4 82-83
CONE....3-4 92
DOT....3-5 75-77
EVERGREEN....3-4 82-91
GMC....3-4 81
GROOVE....5-10 63
HI (2100 series)....4-8 67
HI (2300 series)....3-5 76
HI COUNTRY (8000 series)....4-6 72-73
KARI....3-4 80
LOBO....3-4 82
MCA....3-4 79
MERCURY (71140 "Kiss a Me Baby")....20-30 57
MERCURY (71249 "Dream World")....20-30 57
MERCURY (77190 "Cry Baby Cry")....20-30 57
PINK....10-20 59-60
RENAY....5-10 62-65
RENEGADE....2-4 91
STARLINE....8-12 62
Picture Sleeves
CONE....3-4 92
LPs: 10/12-inch
ABC....5-10 78-79
ABC/DOT....8-10 75-77
ACTION....30-40 70
CINNAMON....8-10 73-74
MCA....5-8 80s
HI....8-10 76

FELTS, Narvel / Red Sovine / Mel Tillis
LPs: 10/12-inch
POWER PAK....5-10 80s
Also see SOVINE, Red

FELTS, Narvel, & Sharon Vaughn C&W '74
Singles: 7-inch
CINNAMON....3-5 74
Also see FELTS, Narvel

FEMME FATALE LP '89
LPs: 10/12-inch
MCA....5-8 89

FENDER, Freddy C&W/P&R/LP '75
(Baldemar Huerta)
Singles: 7-inch
ABC....3-4 76-79
ABC/DOT....4-6 75-77
ARV INT'L....4-8 75
ARGO....10-15 60
DISCOS DOMINANTE....5-10
DUNCAN....10-20 59
FALCON....5-10
GRT....4-8 75-76
GOLDBAND....5-10 60s
GOLDIES 45....3-5 74
IDEAL....10-20 60s
IMPERIAL....8-12 60
MCA....3-4 82
NORCO....5-10 63-65
STARFLITE....3-4 79-80
W.B.....3-4 83
LPs: 10/12-inch
ABC....5-10 78-79
ABC/DOT....8-10 75-77
ACCORD....5-10 81
BIRCHMONT....5-10 80s
BRYLEN....5-10 82
51 WEST....5-10 79
GRT....8-10 75
PICCADILLY....5-10 81
PICKWICK....5-10 70s
POWER PAK....5-10 75-80s
STARFLITE....5-10 80
SUFFOLK MARKETING....5-10 76
Also see HUERTA, Baldemar
Also see WAYNE, Scotty

FENDER, Freddy, & Tommy McLain
LPs: 10/12-inch
CRAZY CAJUN....5-10 78
Also see McLAIN, Tommy

FENDER, Freddy, & Sir Douglas
LPs: 10/12-inch
CRAZY CAJUN....5-10 78
Also see SAHM, Doug

FENDER, Freddy, & Noel Vill

Singles: 7-inch

NORCO (107 "Magic of Love") 4-8 65
SOCK-O (101 "Magic of Love") 10-15 65
Also see FENDER, Freddy

FENDERMEN — P&R/C&W '60

Singles: 7-inch

APEX (21802 "Mule Skinner Blues") 10-15 60s
(Canadian. Reissue)
APEX (76683 "Mule Skinner Blues") 20-30 60
(Canadian.)
COLLECTABLES 3-4 80s
CUCA (1003 "Mule Skinner Blues") 50-100 60
ERA 3-5 72
ERIC 3-4 70s
KOALA 3-4
SOMA 10-15 60-61

LPs: 10/12-inch

POINT (213 "Mule Skinner Blues") 200-300 61
SOMA (1240 "Mule Skinner Blues") 800-1200 60
(Solid black vinyl.)
SOMA (1240 "Mule Skinner Blues") 1000-1500 60
(Vinyl is clearer and appears colored when held to a light.)
Members: Phil Humphrey; Jimmy Sundquist; John Hauer; Denny Dale Gudin.

FERGUSON, Helena — P&R/R&B '67

Singles: 7-inch

COMPASS 4-8 67-68

FERGUSON, Jay — P&R '77

Singles: 7-inch

ASYLUM 3-5 77-79
CAPITOL 3-4 82

LPs: 10/12-inch

ASYLUM 8-10 76-79
CAPITOL 5-10 80-82
Also see JO JO GUNNE
Also see SPIRIT

FERGUSON, Johnny — P&R '60

Singles: 7-inch

DECCA (30731 "Last Date") 10-20 58
MGM (12789 "Afterglow") 10-20 59
MGM (12855 "Angela Jones") 10-20 60
MGM (12905 "I Understand") 10-20 60
MGM (12960 "Valley of Love") 10-20 60

FERGUSON, Maynard — LP '73

(Maynard Ferguson Sextet)

Singles: 78 rpm

CAPITOL 3-8 50-51
EMARCY 3-8 54
MERCURY 3-8 55

Singles: 12-inch

COLUMBIA 4-6 79

Singles: 7-inch

CAMEO 3-5 63
CAPITOL 5-10 50-51
COLUMBIA 3-4 71-82
EMARCY 5-10 54
MAINSTREAM 3-5 71-72
MERCURY 5-10 55
ROULETTE 4-8 59-62

EPs: 7-inch

EMARCY 5-15 54-57

LPs: 10/12-inch

BETHLEHEM 5-10 78
CAMEO 15-20 63
COLUMBIA 5-10 71-82
EMARCY (400 series) 5-10 76
EMARCY (1000 series) 5-10 81
EMARCY (26017 "Hollywood Party") 50-100 54
(10-inch LP.)
EMARCY (26024 "Dimensions") 50-100 54
(10-inch LP.)
EMARCY (36000 series) 20-40 55-57
ENTERPRISE 8-12 68
MAINSTREAM (300 series) 6-10 71-72
MAINSTREAM (6000 series) 15-20 64
(Stereo.)
MAINSTREAM (56000 series) 10-20 64
(Monaural.)
MERCURY 12-20 60
MOSAIC (156 "Complete Roulette Recordings of Maynard Ferguson") 200-225 90s
(Boxed 14 audiophile LP set. 5000 made.)
PALTO ALTO 5-10 83
PRESTIGE 8-12 69
ROULETTE 12-25 58-72
SKYLARK (17 "Great Jazz Solos") ... 25-50 53
TRIP 5-10 74
WYNCOTE 5-10 60s
Also see BASIE, Count, & Maynard Ferguson
Also see KENTON, Stan
Also see MANN, Herbie / Maynard Ferguson

FERGUSON, Maynard, & Chris Connor

Singles: 7-inch

ATLANTIC 4-6 61

LPs: 10/12-inch

ATLANTIC (8049 "Double Exposure") 25-35 61
(Monaural.)
ATLANTIC (SD-8049 "Double Exposure") 35-45 61
(Stereo.)
ROULETTE (52068 "Two's Company") 40-60 58
Also see CONNOR, Chris
Also see FERGUSON, Maynard

FERKO STRING BAND — P&R '48

Singles: 78 rpm

MEDIA 3-5 55
PALDA 4-6 48
SAVOY 3-5 55

Singles: 7-inch

ARGO 3-5 63
FERKO 4-8 50s
MEDIA 4-8 55
SAVOY 4-8 55

LPs: 10/12-inch

ABC-PAR 10-15 63
ALSHIRE 4-6 76
REGENT 12-20 56-59
SURE 6-12 65-73

FERRANTE & TEICHER — P&R/R&B '60

Singles: 78 rpm

COLUMBIA 3-5 53
ENTRE 3-6 53

Singles: 7-inch

ABC-PAR 3-6 58-62
COLUMBIA 4-8 53
ENTRE 5-10 53
U.A. 3-5 59-79

Picture Sleeves

U.A. (Except 231 to 300) 4-8 63-69
U.A. (231 to 300) 5-10 60-61

EPs: 7-inch

ABC-PAR 4-8 58-60
MGM 10-20 54
U.A. 4-8 69

LPs: 10/12-inch

ABC 5-10 73-76
ABC-PAR 8-15 58-66
AVANT GARDE 5-10
COLUMBIA 8-15 55-73
DORAL 10-20
(Promotional mail-order issue, from Doral cigarettes.)
GUEST STAR 4-8 64
HARMONY 5-10 64-70
LIBERTY 5-10 81-84
MGM 20-40 54
METRO 5-10 66
MISTLETOE 4-6 75
SUNSET 5-10 70-71
WESTMINSTER 12-20 55-58
UNART 5-10 67
U.A. 5-15 60-80
URANIA 4-8
Members: Arthur Ferrante; Louis Teicher.
Also see BELL, Vincent

FERRARI — R&B '82

Singles: 12-inch

SUGAR HILL 4-6 82

Singles: 7-inch

SUGAR HILL 3-4 82

FERRER, Jose — P&R '54

(With the Ferrers)

Singles: 78 rpm

COLUMBIA 3-5 54-55

Singles: 7-inch

COLUMBIA 4-8 54-55
EPIC 3-5 68
RCA 4-6 60

Picture Sleeves

RCA 4-6 60

LPs: 10/12-inch

MGM 8-12 62-65
Also see CLOONEY, Rosemary, & Jose Ferrer

FERRY, Bryan — P&R/LP '76

Singles: 12-inch

W.B. 4-6 85

Singles: 7-inch

ATLANTIC 3-4 74-79
REPRISE 3-4 88
W.B. 3-4 85

Picture Sleeves

REPRISE 3-4 88

LPs: 10/12-inch

ATLANTIC 10-12 72-78
REPRISE 5-10 87
W.B. 5-10 85
Also see TANGERINE DREAM / Jon Anderson / Bryan Ferry

FERRY, Bryan, & Roxy Music — LP '89

LPs: 10/12-inch

REPRISE 5-10 89
Also see FERRY, Bryan
Also see ROXY MUSIC

FESTIVAL — P&R/LP '80

Singles: 7-inch

RSO 3-4 79

LPs: 10/12-inch

RSO 5-10 79

FESTIVALS — R&B '70

Singles: 7-inch

BLUE ROCK 3-6 69
COLOSSUS 3-5 70-71
GORDY 3-5 72
SMASH 4-8 66-68

FETCHIN' BONES — LP '89

LPs: 10/12-inch

CAPITOL 5-8 89

FEVA, Sandra — R&B '79

Singles: 7-inch

CATAWBA 3-4 87
KRISMA 3-4 86
VENTURE 3-5 79-81

LPs: 10/12-inch

VENTURE 5-10 81

FEVER — R&B '79

Singles: 12-inch

FANTASY 4-6 79-82
JDC 4-6 85

Singles: 7-inch

FANTASY 3-4 79-82

LPs: 10/12-inch

FANTASY 5-10 79-80
Member: Clydene Jackson.

FEVER TREE — P&R/LP '68

Singles: 7-inch

AMPEX 10-20 70
MAINSTREAM 5-10 67
UNI (Except 55060) 10-20 68-69
UNI (55060 "San Francisco Girls") 8-12 68
(Black vinyl.)
UNI (55060 "San Francisco Girls") 20-40 68
(Colored vinyl. Promotional issue only.)

LPs: 10/12-inch
AMPEX....12-20 70
MCA....8-10 76
UNI (73024 "Fever Tree")....20-30 68
UNI (73040 "Another Time, Another Place")....15-25 68
UNI (73067 "Creation")....15-25 70
Members: Dennis Keller; Rob Landes; E.E. Wolfe; John Tuttle. Session: Frank Davis.

FIDELITYS P&R '58
(With Sammy Lowe & Orchestra)
Singles: 7-inch
BATON (252 "The Things I Love")....10-15 58
BATON (256 "Memories of You")....10-15 58
BATON (261 "My Greatest Thrill")....10-15 58
SIR (271 "Marie")....10-20 59
SIR (274 "Only to You")....10-20 59
SIR (276 "Where in the World")....10-20 60
SIR (277 "Wishing Star")....20-30 60
Member: Buddy Miles.
Also see MILES, Buddy

FIEDLER, Arthur: see BOSTON POPS ORCHESTRA

FIELD, Sally P&R/LP '67
Singles: 7-inch
COLGEMS....4-6 67-68
Picture Sleeves
COLGEMS....4-8 67
LPs: 10/12-inch
COLGEMS....10-20 67

FIELDS, Ernie P&R/R&B '59
(With His Orchestra)
Singles: 7-inch
FRISCO (3 "Thursday Evening Blues")....15-20 47
GOTHAM (273 "Butch's Blues")....10-20 52
Singles: 7-inch
CAPITOL....5-10 64
GOTHAM (273 "Butch's Blues")....20-30 52
HIGHLAND....8-12
JAMIE (1102 "Annie's Rock")....10-15 58
RENDEZVOUS....10-15 59-62
LPs: 10/12-inch
RENDEZVOUS (1309 "In the Mood")....40-60 60

FIELDS, Kim R&B '84
Singles: 12-inch
CRITIQUE....4-6 84
Singles: 7-inch
CRITIQUE....3-4 84

FIELDS, Lee R&B '86
Singles: 7-inch
ANGLE 3....3-5 79
BDA....3-4 86
NORFOLK....3-5
SOUND PLUS....3-5

FIELDS, Richard "Dimples"
(Dimples) R&B/LP '81
Singles: 12-inch
RCA....4-6 84-85
Singles: 7-inch
BOARDWALK....3-4 81-83
COLUMBIA....3-4 87
RCA....3-4 84-85
LPs: 10/12-inch
BOARDWALK....5-10 81-82
RCA....5-10 84

FIELDS, W.C. LP '69
LPs: 10/12-inch
AMERICAN....5-10 75
BLUE THUMB....8-12
COLUMBIA....6-10 69-77
DECCA....8-12 68
HARMONY....6-10 70
HUDSON....15-25 60
JAY (2001 "Temperance Lecture")....15-25 50s
(10-inch LP.)
MARK '56 (571 "Original Radio Broadcasts")....10-15 73
MARK '56 (571 "Nostalgia")....70-90 78
(Picture disc. Two variations made, one with full photo of Fields standing, other shows only his upper body. Original Radio Broadcasts.)

FIELDS, W.C., & Mae West
LPs: 10/12-inch
HARMONY....6-10 70
PROSCENIUM....15-20 60
Also see FIELDS, W.C.
Also see WEST, Mae

FIESTA R&B '78
Singles: 7-inch
ARISTA....3-5 78

FIESTAS P&R/R&B '59
Singles: 7-inch
CHIMNEYVILLE (10221 "Is That Long Enough for You")....10-15 70s
COLLECTABLES....3-4 80s
OLD TOWN (1062 "So Fine")....25-35 59
(With piano intro. Identification number is "ZTSP 29364.")
OLD TOWN (1062 "So Fine")....10-20 59
(No piano intro. Identification number is "920.")
OLD TOWN (1069 thru 1104)....10-20 59-60
OLD TOWN (1111 "Hobo's Prayer")..25-35 59-60
OLD TOWN (1122 thru 1166)....10-20 62-64
OLD TOWN (1178 "Think Smart")....50-75 65
OLD TOWN (1189 "Ain't She Sweet")....10-15 65
RESPECT....3-5 75
STRAND (25046 "Julie")....20-30 61
VIGOR....3-5 74
Members: Tom Bullock; Eddie Morris; Sam Ingalls; Preston Lane.
Also see ROBERT & JOHNNY / Fiestas

FIFTH ANGEL LP '88
Soundsheet
EVATONE (103537)....4-6 88
(No song titles used.)
LPs: 10/12-inch
EPIC....5-8 88

FIFTH AVE. R&B '87
Singles: 7-inch
PARADISE....3-4 87

FIFTH DIMENSION P&R/LP '67
(5th Dimension)
Singles: 7-inch
ABC....3-5 75-76
ARISTA....3-5 75
BELL....3-5 70-74
MOTOWN....3-4 78-79
SOUL CITY....4-8 66-70
SUTRA....3-4 83
Picture Sleeves
SOUL CITY....4-8 67-69
LPs: 10/12-inch
ABC....8-10 75
ARISTA....8-10 75
BELL....8-12 70-74
KORY....8-10 77
MOTOWN....5-10 78-79
RHINO....5-10 86
SOUL CITY....10-15 67-70
Members: Marilyn McCoo; Billy Davis Jr; Lamonte McLemore; Florence LaRue; Ron Townson; Danny Miller Beard; Terri Bryant; Michel Bell.
Also see DAVIS, Billy, Jr.
Also see MAMAS & PAPAS / Association / Fifth Dimension
Also see McCOO, Marilyn, & Billy Davis Jr.

FIFTH ESTATE P&R '67
Singles: 7-inch
JUBILEE....5-10 67-69
RED BIRD (064 "Love Is All a Game")....10-15 66
LPs: 10/12-inch
JUBILEE (JGM-8005 "Ding Dong the Witch Is Dead")....20-30 67
(Monaural.)
JUBILEE (JGS-8005 "Ding Dong the Witch Is Dead")....25-35 67
(Stereo.)
Members: Wayne Wadhams; Rick Engler; Doug Ferrara; Bill Shute; Ken Evans.

50 GUITARS OF TOMMY GARRETT LP '61
Singles: 7-inch
LIBERTY....3-5 66-68
LPs: 10/12-inch
LIBERTY....5-15 61-71
MUSICOR....5-10 76-78
U.A.....5-8 73
Also see GARRETT, Tommy

52ND STREET D&D '83
Singles: 12-inch
A&M....4-6 83
MCA....4-6 85-87
PROFILE....4-6 84
Singles: 7-inch
MCA....3-4 85-86
LPs: 10/12-inch
MCA....5-10 86

FIGURES ON THE BEACH D&D '84
Singles: 12-inch
METRO AMERICAN....4-6 84
Singles: 7-inch
SIRE....3-4 89
Picture Sleeves
SIRE....3-4 89

FILE 13 D&D '84
Singles: 12-inch
PROFILE....4-6 84

FINE YOUNG CANNIBALS P&R/LP '86
Singles: 12-inch
I.R.S.....4-6 86-89
Singles: 7-inch
I.R.S.....3-4 86-90
Picture Sleeves
I.R.S.....3-4 86-89
LPs: 10/12-inch
I.R.S.....5-10 86-90
Members: Roland Gift; Danny Cox; David Steele.
Also see ENGLISH BEAT

FINISHED TOUCH R&B '78
Singles: 7-inch
MOTOWN....3-5 78
LPs: 10/12-inch
MOTOWN....5-10 78
Members: Harold Johnson; Kenny Stover; Mike Sutton; Brenda Sutton; Michael McGloiry.

FINN, Tim LP '83
Singles: 7-inch
A&M....3-4 83
LPs: 10/12-inch
A&M....5-10 83
Also see SPLIT ENZ

FINNEGAN, Larry P&R '62
Singles: 7-inch
CORAL....4-8 62
OLD TOWN....5-10 62-63
RIC....8-10 64

FINNEY, Albert LP '77
Singles: 7-inch
MOTOWN....3-4 77
LPs: 10/12-inch
MOTOWN....5-10 77

FIONA P&R/LP '85
(Fiona Flanagan; with Kip Winger)
Singles: 7-inch
ATLANTIC....3-4 84-89
Picture Sleeves
ATLANTIC....3-4 84-89
LPs: 10/12-inch
ATLANTIC....5-10 84-89

FIORILLO, Elisa — P&R/LP '88

Singles: 7-inch

CHRYSALIS 3-4 88-90

Picture Sleeves

CHRYSALIS 3-4 88

LPs: 10/12-inch

CHRYSALIS 5-8 88

Also see JELLYBEAN & Elisa Fiorillo

FIRE & RAIN — P&R '73

Singles: 7-inch

MERCURY 3-5 73

LPs: 10/12-inch

MERCURY 8-10 73

FIRE INC. — P&R '84

Singles: 7-inch

MCA 3-4 84

Picture Sleeves

MCA 3-4 84

FIREBALLET — LP '75

Singles: 7-inch

PASSPORT 3-5 75-76

LPs: 10/12-inch

PASSPORT 8-10 75-76

FIREBALLS — P&R '59

Singles: 7-inch

ASTRA (1021 "Sweet Talk") 4-8 66
ATCO 4-8 67-70
DOT 4-8 63-67
HAMILTON (5036 "Tuff-A-Nuff") 10-20 63
KAPP (248 "Fireball") 75-100 59
QUALITY 8-15 61
(Canadian.)
TOP RANK (2008 "Torquay") 8-12 59
TOP RANK (2026 "Bulldog") 8-12 59
(Monaural.)
TOP RANK (2026-ST "Bulldog") 15-25 59
(Stereo.)
TOP RANK (2038 "Foot Patter") 8-12 60
(Monaural.)
TOP RANK (2038-ST "Foot Patter") 15-25 60
(Stereo.)
TOP RANK (2054 "Vaquero") 8-12 61
TOP RANK (2081 "Sweet Talk") 8-12 61
TOP RANK (3003 "Rik-A-Tik") 8-12 61
WARWICK 5-10 61

EPs: 7-inch

TOP RANK (1000 "The Fireballs") 50-75 60

LPs: 10/12-inch

ATCO 10-20 68-69
TOP RANK (324 "The Fireballs") 45-65 60
TOP RANK (343 "Vaquero") 50-75 60
(Monaural.)
TOP RANK (643 "Vaquero") 75-100 60
(Stereo.)
WARWICK (2042 "Here Are the Fireballs") 45-65 61

Members: Chuck Tharp; George Tomsco; Dan Trammell; Eric Budd; Stan Lark; Doug Roberts; Jimmy Gilmer; Keith McCormick.
Also see DALE, Dick / Surfaris / Fireballs
Also see GILMER, Jimmy
Also see STRING-A-LONGS

FIREFALL — P&R/LP '76

Singles: 7-inch

ATLANTIC 3-5 76-82

Picture Sleeves

ATLANTIC 3-5 78-79

LPs: 10/12-inch

ATLANTIC 5-10 76-83

Members: Rick Roberts; Jack Bartley; Larry Burnette; Mike Clarke; Scott Kirkpatrick; Dave Muse; Mark Andes; Peter Graves.
Also see ABBA / Spinners / Firefall / England Dan & John Ford Coley
Also see FLYING BURRITO BROTHERS
Also see MANILOW, Barry / Firefall
Also see ROBERTS, Rick
Also see SPIRIT

FIREFLIES — P&R '59

Singles: 7-inch

CANADIAN AMERICAN (117 "Give All Your Love to Me") 15-25 60
ERIC 3-5 70s
HAMILTON 4-8 63
RIBBON (6901 "You Were Mine") 15-25 59
RIBBON (6904 "I Can't Say Goodbye") 15-25 59
RIBBON (6906 "My Girl") 15-25 60
TAURUS (355 "You Were Mine") 10-20 62
TAURUS (366 "My Prayer for You") 10-20 62
TAURAUS (376 "Could You Mean More") 10-20 62

LPs: 10/12-inch

TAURUS (1002 "You Were Mine") 75-125 61
(Monaural.)
TAURUS (1002 "You Were Mine") 250-350 61
(Stereo.)

Members: Ritchie Adams; Lee Reynolds; John Viscelli; Paul Giacolone.
Also see CASINOS / Fireflies

FIREFLY — P&R/R&B '75

Singles: 7-inch

A&M 3-5 75

FIREFLY — R&B '81

Singles: 7-inch

EMERGENCY 3-5 81

FIREHOUSE — LP '91

LPs: 10/12-inch

EPIC 5-8 91

FIRESIGN THEATRE — LP '69

Singles: 7-inch

COLUMBIA (Except 34) 3-6 69
COLUMBIA (34 "This Side") 4-8 70
(Single-sided, promotional disc.)
RHINO (904 "Fighting Clowns") 6-12 80
(Picture disc.)
RHINO (904 "Fighting Clowns") 10-15 80
(Picture disc with 12-inch card.)

Picture Sleeves

COLUMBIA (34 "This Side") 5-10 70

LPs: 10/12-inch

BUTTERFLY 5-10 77
COLUMBIA 8-15 69-74
EPIC 5-10 74
MORWAY 5-8 85
RHINO 5-10 79-82

Members: Philip Proctor; Phil Austin; David Ossman; Peter Bergman.

FIRM, The — P&R/LP '85

Singles: 7-inch

ATLANTIC 3-4 85-86

Picture Sleeves

ATLANTIC 3-4 85-86

LPs: 10/12-inch

ATLANTIC 5-10 85-86

Members: Jimmy Page; Paul Rodgers; Tony Franklin; Chris Slade.
Also see AC/DC
Also see BAD COMPANY
Also see BLUE MURDER
Also see MANN, Manfred
Also see PAGE, Jimmy
Also see RODGERS, Paul

FIRST CHOICE — P&R/R&B/LP '73

Singles: 12-inch

FIRST CHOICE 4-6 83
SALSOUL 4-6 84

Singles: 7-inch

GOLD MINE 3-5 77-79
PHILLY GROOVE 3-5 73-74
WAND 3-5 72
W.B. 3-5 76

LPs: 10/12-inch

GOLD MINE 5-10 77-80
KORY 8-10 77
PHILLY GROOVE 8-10 73-74

Members: Rochelle Fleming; Annette Guest; Joyce Jones; Wardell Piper.
Also see PIPER, Wardell

FIRST CIRCLE — R&B '87

Singles: 7-inch

EMI AMERICA 3-4 87

FIRST CLASS — R&B '74

Singles: 7-inch

ALL PLATINUM 3-5 76-77
EBONY SOUNDS 3-5 75
TODAY 3-5 74

LPs: 10/12-inch

ALL PLATINUM 5-10 76
PARK-WAY 5-10 80
SUGARHILL 5-10 81

Members: Harold Bell; Fred Marshall; Sylvester Redditt.

FIRST CLASS — P&R '74

Singles: 7-inch

PRIVATE STOCK/UK 3-5 76
UK 3-5 74-75

LPs: 10/12-inch

UK 8-10 74

Members: Tony Burrows; John Carter; Charles Mills; Del John; Spencer James; Eddie Richards; Robin Shaw; Clive Barrett.
Also see BROTHERHOOD of MAN
Also see BURROWS, Tony
Also see EDISON LIGHTHOUSE
Also see PIPKINS

FIRST EDITION — P&R/LP '68

Singles: 7-inch

REPRISE 4-8 67-68

LPs: 10/12-inch

INTERMEDIA/QUICKSILVER (5056 "The First Edition") 10-15 84
(Picture disc.)
REPRISE 12-25 67-68

Members: Kenny Rogers; Mike Settle; Thelma Lou Camacho; Terry Williams; Mickey Jones.
Also see CAMACHO, Thelma
Also see NEW CHRISTY MINSTRELS
Also see ROGERS, Kenny, & First Edition

FIRST FAMILY — R&B '74

Singles: 7-inch

POLYDOR 3-5 74

FIRST LOVE — R&B '80

Singles: 12-inch

CHYCAGO INT'L 4-6 82

Singles: 7-inch

CHYCAGO INT'L 3-4 82
CIM 3-4 83
DAKAR 3-4 80

LPs: 10/12-inch

CHYCAGO INT'L 5-10 82

Members: Yvonne Gage.
Also see GAGE, Yvonne

FISCHER, Lisa — LP '91

LPs: 10/12-inch

ELEKTRA 5-8 91

FISCHER, Wild Man

LPs: 10/12-inch

BIZARRE (6332 "An Evening with Wild Man Fischer") 20-30 69
(With Frank Zappa & Mothers of Invention.)
RHINO 5-10 81

Also see MOTHERS of INVENTION

FISCHOFF, George — P&R '74

(George Fischoff Keyboard Komplex; with the Peppers; with Luv Ens)

Singles: 7-inch

COLUMBIA 3-5 77
DRIVE 3-5 79
HERITAGE 3-4 81
P.I.P. 3-5 75
RANWOOD 3-5 76
REWARD 3-4 84
U.A. 3-5 72-74

FISHBONE LP '88

Singles: 7-inch

COLUMBIA....3-4 85

LPs: 10/12-inch

COLUMBIA....5-8 88-91

FISHER, Eddie P&R '50

Singles: 78 rpm

RCA....5-10 50-57

Singles: 7-inch

ABC-PAR....5-10 61
DOT....4-8 65-66
MUSICOR....3-6 69
RCA (3000 thru 6000 series)....10-20 50-57
RCA (7000 thru 9000 series)....5-10 57-68
RAMROD....5-10 60-63
7 ARTS....5-10 61
TRANS ATLAS....4-8 62

Picture Sleeves

RCA (5000 series)....15-25 53-55
RCA (6000 series)....10-15 55-57
RAMROD....8-12 60

EPs: 7-inch

RCA....10-20 51-58
RCA/COCA-COLA....10-20 50s

LPs: 10/12-inch

CAMDEN....6-10 63
CROWN....8-12
DOT....10-15 65-67
FAMOUS TWINSETS....8-12 74
HAMILTON....6-10 66
RCA (1024 thru 2504)....15-30 55-62
RCA (3025 thru 3231)....20-35 52-54
(10-inch LPs.)
RCA (3375 "Best of Eddie Fisher")...10-15 65
RCA (3700 & 3800 series)....10-20 66-67
RAMROD (1 "At the Winter Garden")....10-20 63
RAMROD (6001 "Scent of Mystery")....50-60 60
(Soundtrack. Monaural.)
RAMROD (6001 "Scent of Mystery")....75-85 60
(Soundtrack Stereo.)
Also see COMO, Perry, & Eddie Fisher

FISHER, Eddie / Vic Damone / Dick Haymes

LPs: 10/12-inch

ALMOR....10-15
Also see DAMONE, Vic
Also see HAYMES, Dick

FISHER, Eddie, & Debbie Reynolds

EPs: 7-inch

RCA (4018 "Bundle of Joy")....15-25 56
(Soundtrack.)

LPs: 10/12-inch

RCA (1399 "Bundle of Joy")....40-50 56
(Soundtrack.)
Also see FISHER, Eddie
Also see REYNOLDS, Debbie

FISHER, Herb, Trio R&B '50

Singles: 78 rpm

MODERN....5-15 50

FISHER, Mary Ann P&R '61

Singles: 7-inch

FIRE....5-10 59-60
IMPERIAL....4-8 62
SEG-WAY....4-8 61

FISHER, Miss Toni: see FISHER, Toni

FISHER, Toni P&R '59
(Miss Toni Fisher)

Singles: 7-inch

BIG TOP....5-10 62
CAPITOL....4-8 67
COLLECTABLES....3-4 80s
COLUMBIA....5-10 61
ERA....3-5 72
SIGNET....5-10 59-64
SMASH....4-8 63

LPs: 10/12-inch

SIGNET (509 "The Big Hurt")....30-50 60

FISHER, Tricia Leigh P&R '90

Singles: 7-inch

ATCO....3-4 90

FISHER, Willie R&B '77

Singles: 7-inch

TIGRESS....3-5 77

FIT R&B '88

Singles: 7-inch

A&M....3-4 88
Members: Vince Ebo; Chuck Gentry.
Also see SWEET INSPIRATIONS

FITZGERALD, Ella P&R '36

Singles: 78 rpm

DECCA (800 thru 3000 series)....10-15 36-41
DECCA (18000 thru 29000 series)....5-10 42-54
VERVE....3-5 54-57

Singles: 7-inch

CAPITOL....3-5 67-68
DECCA (27000 & 28000 series)....10-20 50-53
DECCA (29000 series)....8-15 54-56
DECCA (30000 series except 30405)....5-10 56-67
DECCA (30405 "Goody Goody")....15-25 57
PABLO....3-4 75
PRESTIGE....3-5 69
REPRISE....3-5 69-71
SALLE....4-6 68
VERVE (10000 series)....5-10 56-59
VERVE (10100 thru 10300 series, except 10340)....4-6 60-65
VERVE (10340 "Ringo Beat")....8-12 64

Picture Sleeves

VERVE....5-10 59-60

EPs: 7-inch

DECCA....15-30 50-58
VERVE....10-25 56-61

LPs: 10/12-inch

ATLANTIC....5-10 72
BAINBRIDGE....5-10 81
CAPITOL (2000 series)....8-15 67-68
CAPITOL (11000 series)....5-10 78
CAPITOL (16000 series)....4-6 82
COLUMBIA....5-12 73
CORAL....4-8 73
DECCA (156 "The Best of Ella Fitzgerald")....25-45 58
(Black label with silver print.)
DECCA (156 "The Best of Ella Fitzgerald")....15-20 65
(Black label with horizontal rainbow band.)
DECCA (4000 series)....10-20 61-67
DECCA (5084 "Souvenir Album")...75-125 49
(10-inch LP.)
DECCA (5300 "Gershwin Songs")..75-125 51
(10-inch LP.)
DECCA (8000 series)....20-40 55-59
EVEREST....5-10 73
MCA....5-10 76-82
MGM....5-10 70
MPS....5-10 72
METRO....10-15 65-66
OLYMPIC....5-10 74
PABLO....5-10 75-83
REPRISE....8-12 69-71
VERVE (29 "Ella Fitzgerald Sings the George & Ira Gershwin Songbook")....30-50 64
(Boxed, five-disc reissue of Verve 4029.)
VERVE (2500 & 2600 series)....5-10 76-82
(Reads "Manufactured By MGM Record Corp.," or mentions either Polydor or Polygram at bottom of label.)
VERVE (4001 thru 4009)....50-75 56
(Reads "Verve Records, Inc." at bottom of label.)
VERVE (4010 "Ella Fitzgerald Sings the Duke Ellington Song Book")....100-125 56
(Boxed, four-disc set.)
VERVE (4013 thru 4015)....30-50 57
(Reads "Verve Records, Inc." at bottom of label.)
VERVE (4019 "Ella Fitzgerald Sings the Irving Berlin Songbook")....30-50 58
VERVE (4020 thru 4028)....25-50 58-59
(Reads "Verve Records, Inc." at bottom of label.)
VERVE (4029 "Ella Fitzgerald Sings the George & Ira Gershwin Songbook")....50-100 59
(Boxed, five-disc set, containing individual LPs 4024 thru 4028.)
VERVE (4036 thru 4071)....10-20 59-66
VERVE (6000 series)....25-50 57-59
(Reads "Verve Records, Inc." at bottom of label.)
VERVE (6100 series)....15-25 60
(Reads "Verve Records, Inc." at bottom of label.)
VERVE (8200 series)....20-40 58
(Reads "Verve Records, Inc." at bottom of label.)
VERVE (64036 thru 64071)....15-30 59-66
VERVE (67000 & 68000 series)....8-15 67-73
VERVE (2610000 series)....20-30 83
VOCALION....6-10 67
Also see CAMPBELL, Glen / Lettermen / Ella Fitzgerald / Sandler & Young
Also see RIDDLE, Nelson

FITZGERALD, Ella, & Louis Armstrong R&B '46

Singles: 78 rpm

DECCA....3-6 53

EPs: 7-inch

VERVE....15-30 56

LPs: 10/12-inch

MFSL (248 "Ella & Louie Again")....25-30
METRO....5-10 67
VERVE (4003 "Ella & Louis")....50-100 56
VERVE (4006 "Ella & Louis Again")....50-100 56
VERVE (4011 "Porgy & Bess")....40-60 57
(Monaural.)
VERVE (6040 "Porgy & Bess")....50-100 57
(Stereo.)
VERVE (8811 "Ella & Louis")....5-10 72
Also see ARMSTRONG, Louis

FITZGERALD, Ella, & Count Basie LP '63

LPs: 10/12-inch

PABLO....5-10 79
VERVE....15-20 63
Also see BASIE, Count

FITZGERALD, Ella / Bill Doggett

Singles: 78 rpm

DECCA....3-5 53

Singles: 7-inch

DECCA....5-10 53

LPs: 10/12-inch

VERVE....10-20 62
Also see DOGGETT, Bill

FITZGERALD, Ella, & Duke Ellington

Singles: 7-inch

VERVE....4-6 66

LPs: 10/12-inch

VERVE....10-20 65-67
Also see ELLINGTON, Duke

FITZGERALD, Ella / Billie Holiday

LPs: 10/12-inch

MCA....5-10 76
VERVE (6022 "At Newport")....40-60 58
(Stereo.)
VERVE (8234 "At Newport")....30-50 58
(Monaural.)

FITZGERALD, Ella / Billie Holiday / Lena Horne

EPs: 7-inch

COLUMBIA (2531 "Ella, Lena & Billie")....25-45 56

LPs: 10/12-inch

COLUMBIA (2531 "Ella, Lena & Billie")....75-100 56
(10-inch LP.)
Also see HOLIDAY, Billie
Also see HORNE, Lena

FITZGERALD, Ella, & Ink Spots

Singles: 78 rpm

DECCA (18000 series)....4-8 44-45

EPs: 7-inch

DECCA....5-10 53
Also see INK SPOTS

FITZGERALD, Ella, & Antonio Carlos Jobim

LPs: 10/12-inch

PABLO 5-10 81

Also see JOBIM, Antonio Carlos

FITZGERALD, Ella, & Louis Jordan R&B '46

Singles: 78 rpm

DECCA (23000 series) 4-8 46

Also see JORDAN, Louis

FITZGERALD, Ella, & Peggy Lee LP '55

LPs: 10/12-inch

DECCA (8166 "Pete Kelly's Blues") 40-60 55

Also see LEE, Peggy

FITZGERALD, Ella, & Mills Brothers P&R '37

Singles: 78 rpm

DECCA 4-8 37

Also see MILLS BROTHERS

FITZGERALD, Ella, & Oscar Peterson

LPs: 10/12-inch

PABLO 5-10 76

Also see FITZGERALD, Ella
Also see PETERSON, Oscar

FIVE AMERICANS P&R/LP '66

Singles: 7-inch

ABC-PAR (10686 "Love Love Love") .. 5-10 65
ABNAK (Except 109) 10-15 67-69
(Black vinyl.)
ABNAK (Except 109) 15-25 67-69
(Colored vinyl.)
ABNAK (109 "I See the Light") 15-25 65
(Black vinyl.)
ABNAK (109 "I See the Light") 15-25 65
(Colored vinyl.)
HBR 5-10 65-66
JETSTAR (104 "It's You Girl") 10-15 65
JETSTAR (105 "Slippin' & Slidin' ") ... 15-20 65
PHILCO/FORD (10 "Western Union") 10-20 67
("Hip-Pocket" flexi-disc.)

Picture Sleeves

ABNAK (125 "Stop Light") 10-15 67
ABNAK (126 "Guided Tour") 10-15 68
HBR (468 "Evol-Not Love") 10-20 66

LPs: 10/12-inch

ABNAK 20-30 67-68
HBR (8503 "I See the Light") 30-35 66
(Monaural.)
HBR (9503 "I See the Light") 35-40 66
(Stereo.)

Members: Michael Rabon; Jimmy Wright; John Durrill.
Also see PEDESTRIANS / Association / Five Americans / Soulblenders

FIVE BLOBS P&R '58

Singles: 7-inch

COLUMBIA (41250 "The Blob") 15-20 58
JOY 10-15 59

Member: Bernie Nee (only member).

FIVE BY FIVE P&R '68

Singles: 7-inch

PAULA 5-15 67-70

LPs: 10/12-inch

PAULA 15-20 69

5 CHANELS P&R '58

(Chanels)

Singles: 7-inch

DEB (500 "The Reason") 15-25 58

Also see CHANELS

FIVE DU-TONES P&R/R&B '63

Singles: 7-inch

LOST NITE 4-8
ONE-DERFUL 5-10 63-65

Members: Andrew Butler; Frank McCurrey; Willie Guest; LeRoy Joyce; Andy Butler.

FIVE EMPREES P&R '65

(Five Empressions)

Singles: 7-inch

FREEPORT 5-10 65-66
GOLD STANDARD (262 "Little Miss Sad") 10-20 60s
(Colored vinyl.)
SMASH 4-8 66

LPs: 10/12-inch

FREEPORT (3001 "The Five Emprees [Little Miss Sad]") 35-45 65
(Monaural.)
FREEPORT (3001 "Little Miss Sad") 20-30 66
(Reissue.)
FREEPORT (4001 "The Five Emprees [Little Miss Sad]") 30-40 65
(Stereo.)
FREEPORT (4001 "Little Miss Sad") 25-35 66
(Reissue.)

Also see FIVE EMPRESSIONS

FIVE EMPRESSIONS

(Five Emprees)

Singles: 7-inch

FREEPORT (1001 "Little Miss Sad") 10-20 65

Also see FIVE EMPREES

FIVE FLIGHTS UP P&R '70

Singles: 7-inch

T.A. 3-5 70-71

FIVE KEYS R&B '51

(Rudy West & the Five Keys; "Featuring Rudy West"; 5 Keys)

Singles: 78 rpm

ALADDIN (3085 "With a Broken Heart") 200-400 51
ALADDIN (3099 "The Glory of Love") 200-400 51
ALADDIN (3113 "It's Christmas Time") 200-400 51
ALADDIN (3118 "Yes Sir, That's My Baby") 200-400 52
ALADDIN (3119 "Darlin' ") 200-400 52
ALADDIN (3127 "Red Sails in the Sunset") 200-400 52
ALADDIN (3131 "Mistakes") 200-400 52
ALADDIN (3136 "I Hadn't Anyone 'Til You") 200-400 52
ALADDIN (3158 "I Cried for You") 200-400 52
ALADDIN (3167 "Can't Keep from Crying") 200-400 53
ALADDIN (3175 "There Ought to Be a Law") 200-400 53
ALADDIN (3190 "These Foolish Things") 300-400 53
ALADDIN (3204 "Teardrops in Your Eyes") 200-400 53
ALADDIN (3214 "My Saddest Hour") 200-400 53
ALADDIN (3228 "Someday Sweetheart") 200-400 54
ALADDIN (3245 "Deep in My Heart") 200-400 54
ALADDIN (3263 "My Love") 100-200 55
ALADDIN (3312 "Story of Love") .. 100-200 56
CAPITOL 15-25 54-57
GROOVE (0031 "I'll Follow You") 500-1000 51

Singles: 7-inch

ALADDIN (3099 "The Glory of Love") 800-1200 51
ALADDIN (3113 "It's Christmas Time") 800-1200 51
ALADDIN (3118 "Yes Sir, That's My Baby") 800-1200 52
ALADDIN (3119 "Darlin'") 800-1200 52
ALADDIN (3127 "Red Sails in the Sunset") 800-1200 52
ALADDIN (3131 "Mistakes") 800-1200 52
ALADDIN (3136 "I Hadn't Anyone 'Til You") 800-1200 52
ALADDIN (3158 "I Cried for You") 800-1200 52
ALADDIN (3167 "Can't Keep from Crying") 500-1000 53
ALADDIN (3175 "There Ought to Be a Law") 500-1000 53
ALADDIN (3190 "These Foolish Things") 800-1200 53
ALADDIN (3204 "Teardrops in Your Eyes") 500-1000 53
ALADDIN (3214 "My Saddest Hour") 700-1000 53
(Flat blue label.)
ALADDIN (3214 "My Saddest Hour") 500-750 53
(Glossy blue label.)
ALADDIN (3228 "Someday Sweetheart") 500-1000 54
ALADDIN (3245 "Deep in My Heart") 500-1000 54
ALADDIN (3263 "My Love") 400-800 55
ALADDIN (3312 "Story of Love") ... 400-800 56
CAPITOL (828 "Just for a Thrill") 50-75 57
(Promotional issue only.)
CAPITOL (2945 "Ling Ting Tong") 25-50 54
CAPITOL (3032 "Close Your Eyes") 25-50 55
CAPITOL (3127 "The Verdict") 25-50 55
CAPITOL (3185 "I Wish I'd Never Learned to Read") 25-50 55
CAPITOL (3267 "Gee Whittakers") ... 25-50 55
CAPITOL (3318 "What Goes On") ... 25-50 56
CAPITOL (3392 "I Dreamt I Dwelt in Heaven") 25-50 56
(Standard 45rpm hole.)
CAPITOL (3392 "I Dreamt I Dwelt in Heaven") 50-75 56
(LP-size, ¼-inch hole. Purple label.)
CAPITOL (3392 "I Dreamt I Dwelt in Heaven") 50-75 56
(LP-size, ¼-inch hole. White label. Promotional issue only.)
CAPITOL (3455 "Peace and Love") .. 25-50 56
CAPITOL (3502 "Out of Sight, Out of Mind") 25-50 56
CAPITOL (3597 "Wisdom of a Fool") 25-50 56
CAPITOL (3660 "Let There Be You") 25-50 57
CAPITOL (3710 "Four Walls") 25-50 57
CAPITOL (3738 "This I Promise You") 25-50 57
CAPITOL (3786 "Face of an Angel") 20-40 57
CAPITOL (3830 "Do Anything") 20-40 57
CAPITOL (3861 "From Me to You") .. 20-40 58
CAPITOL (3948 "With All My Heart") 20-40 58
CAPITOL (4009 "Handy Andy") 20-40 58
CAPITOL (4092 "Our Great Love") ... 20-40 58
CAPITOL (6000 series) 10-15 64
CLASSIC ARTISTS 3-5 89
GUSTO 3-5
IMPERIAL (016 "The Glory of Love") 5-10 62
INFERNO (4500 "No Matter") 10-20 67
KEY (62 "Wisdom of a Fool") 5-10
KEY (63 "The Verdict") 5-10
KING (5221 "I Took Your Love for a Toy") 25-50 59
KING (5273 "Dream On") 15-25 59
KING (5302 "How Can I Forget You") 15-25 59
KING (5330 "Rosetta") 15-25 60
KING (5358 "I Didn't Know") 15-25 60
KING (5398 "Valley of Love") 15-25 60
KING (5446 "You Broke the Only Heart") 15-25 61
KING (5496 "Stop Your Crying") 15-25 61

KING (5877 "I Can't Escape from You")....10-20 64
LANDMARK (101 "Goddess of Love")....5-8 73
OWL....3-5 73
SEG-WAY (1008 "Out of Sight Out of Mind")....10-20 62

EPs: 7-inch

CAPITOL (572 "The Five Keys")...100-200 55
CAPITOL (828 "The Five Keys on Stage")....250-400 57
(Pictures one group member's thumb in a phallic-like position.)
CAPITOL (828 "The Five Keys on Stage")....100-200 57
(Reworked cover, with offending thumb removed from picture.)
CRYSTAL (101 "Five Keys")....10-15

LPs: 10/12-inch

ALADDIN (806 "Best of the 5 Keys")....2000-4000 56
(Maroon label. Bootlegs have the Score reissue cover art but using the Aladdin name and number. There is no original Aladdin LPs titled *On the Town.*)
CAPITOL (828 "The Five Keys on Stage")....500-750 57
(In cover photo, group member on left is holding his right hand in in a phallic-like position.)
CAPITOL (828 "The Five Keys on Stage")....100-200 57
(Reworked cover, with offending hand removed from the picture.)
CAPITOL (1769 "The Fantastic Five Keys")....100-200 62
(With "T" prefix.)
CAPITOL (1769 "The Fantastic Five Keys")....8-12 77
(With "M" prefix.)
GREAT GROUP CLASSICS....8-12 70s
HARLEM HITPARADE....10-15 72
KING (688 "The Five Keys")....200-400 60
KING (692 "Rhythm & Blues Hits: Past and Present")....200-300 60
SCORE (4003 "On the Town")....500-750 57
(Repackage of *Best of the 5 Keys,* Aladdin 806. See that listing for bootleg information.)

Members: Rudy West; Ripley Ingram; Maryland Pierce; Dickie Smith; Ray Loper; Bernie West; Ulysses Hicks; Thomas Threat.
Also see BELVIN, Jesse, & Five Keys / Feathers
Also see FANTASTIC FIVE KEYS
Also see TEAGARDEN, Jack

FIVE KEYS / Ferlin Husky

EPs: 7-inch

CAPITOL (503 "Five Keys/Ferlin Husky")....60-80 57
Also see FIVE KEYS
Also see HUSKY, Ferlin

FIVE MAN ELECTRICAL BAND — P&R/LP '71

Singles: 7-inch

CAPITOL....4-8 68-69
LION....3-5 72-73
LIONEL....3-5 71
MGM....4-8 70
POLYDOR....3-5 74

LPs: 10/12-inch

CAPITOL....15-20 69
LION....10-12 73
LIONEL....10-15 70-71
MGM....10-15 70
PICKWICK....5-10 70s

Member: Les Emmerson.
Also see EMMERSON, Les

FIVE RED CAPS — P&R/R&B/C&W '44

(5 Red Caps)

Singles: 78 rpm

BEACON....10-20 43-45
GANNETT....10-20 43-45
JOE DAVIS....10-20 43-45
DAVIS....10-15 46
MGM....10-15 48

Members: Steve Gibson; Jim Springs; Romaine Brown; Dave Patillo; Emmett Matthews.
Also see GIBSON, Steve

FIVE ROYALES — R&B '53

(5 Royales)

Singles: 78 rpm

APOLLO....50-75 51-55
KING....25-75 54-57

Singles: 7-inch

ABC-PAR (10348 "Catch That Teardrop")....10-15 62
ABC-PAR (10368 "I Want It Like That")....10-15 62
APOLLO (441 "Courage to Love")..75-125 52
(Black vinyl.)
APOLLO (441 "Courage to Love")....300-500 52
(Colored vinyl.)
APOLLO (443 "Baby Don't Do It")...75-125 52
(Black vinyl.)
APOLLO (443 "Baby Don't Do It")....300-500 52
(Colored vinyl.)
APOLLO (446 "Help Me, Somebody")....75-125 53
APOLLO (448 "Laundromat Blues")....100-150 53
APOLLO (449 "I Want to Thank You")....75-125 53
APOLLO (452 "I Do")....50-100 54
APOLLO (454 "Cry Some More")....50-100 54
APOLLO (458 "What's That")....50-100 54
APOLLO (467 "With All Your Heart")....50-100 55
GUSTO....3-5 80s
HOME of the BLUES (112 "Please, Please, Please")....10-20 60
HOME of the BLUES (218 "If You Need Me")....10-20 61
HOME of the BLUES (232 "Not Going to Cry")....10-20 61
HOME of the BLUES (234 "They Don't Know")....10-20 61
HOME of the BLUES (257 "Catch That Teardrop")....10-20 62
KING (4740 "I'm Gonna Run It Down")....50-75 54
KING (4744 "Monkey Hips and Rice")....50-75 54
KING (4762 "One Mistake")....50-75 54
KING (4785 "Mohawk Squaw")....50-75 55
KING (4806 "When I Get Like This")....40-60 55
KING (4819 "Do Unto You")....40-60 55
KING (4830 "Someone Made You for Me")....40-60 55
KING (4869 "Right Around the Corner")....40-60 56
KING (4901 "I Could Love You")....40-60 56
KING (4952 "Come on and Save Me")....40-60 56
KING (4973 "Just As I Am")....40-60 56
KING (5032 "Tears of Joy")....25-50 57
KING (5053 "Think")....25-50 57
KING (5082 "Messin' Up")....25-50 57
KING (5098 "Dedicated to the One I Love")....25-50 57
KING (5131 "The Feeling Is Real")...20-30 58
KING (5141 "Double Or Nothing")....20-30 58
KING (5153 "Don't Let It Be in Vain")....20-30 58
KING (5162 "The Real Thing")....20-30 59
KING (5191 "Miracle of Love")....20-30 59
KING (5237 "Tell Me You Care")....20-30 59
KING (5266 "It Hurts Inside")....20-30 59
KING (5329 "I'm with You")....15-25 60
KING (5357 "Why")....15-25 60
KING (5453 "Dedicated to the One I Love")....15-25 61
KING (5756 "Dedicated to the One I Love")....10-20 63
KING (5892 "I Need You Lovin' Baby")....10-20 64
SMASH (1936 "I Like It Like That")...10-20 64
SMASH (1963 "Faith")....10-20 65
TODD (1086 "Doin' Everything")....10-20 63
TODD (1088 "Baby Don't Do It")....10-20 63
VEE JAY (412 "Much in Need")....10-20 61
VEE JAY (431 "Talk About My Woman")....10-20 61
WHITE CLIFFS (224 "I'm on the Right Road Now")....10-15 60s

LPs: 10/12-inch

APOLLO (488 "The Rockin' 5 Royales")....1500-2000 59
(Green cover.)
APOLLO (488 "The Rockin' 5 Royales")....800-1200 59
(Yellow cover.)
KING (580 "Dedicated to You")....350-500 58
KING (616 "The 5 Royales Sing for You")....200-300 59
KING (678 "The 5 Royales")....200-300 60
KING (955 "24 All Time Hits")....50-75 66

Members: Johnny Tanner; Eugene Tanner; Lowman Pauling; Clarence Pauling; Jim Moore; Otto Jeffries; Obadiah "Scoop" Carter; Eudell Graham; Bobby Burris; .
Also see JOHN, Little Willie / 5 Royales / Earl (Connelly) King / Midnighters
Also see ROYAL SONS QUINTET

FIVE SATINS — P&R/R&B '56

(5 Satins; Featuring Fred Parris; "Featuring Dick Arnold")

Singles: 78 rpm

EMBER....50-100 56-57
REO....10-20 56
(Canadian.)
STANDORD (100 "All Mine")....200-400 57
STANDORD (200 "In the Still of the Nite")....300-500 56

Singles: 7-inch

ABC....3-5 73
ANOTHER FIRST (104 "When Your Love Comes Along")....30-50 59
(First issue. Reissued on "First" label.)
FIRST (104 "When Your Love Comes Along")....20-30 59
(First issued on "Another First.")
CANDLELITE (411 "She's Gone")....15-25 63
CHANCELLOR (1110 "The Masquerade Is Over")....20-30 62
CHANCELLOR (1121 "Do You Remember")....20-30 62
COLLECTABLES....3-4 80s
CUB (9071 "Your Memory")....15-25 60
CUB (9077 "These Foolish Things")....15-25 60
CUB (9090 "Can I Come Over Tonight")....15-25 60
EMBER (1005 "In the Still of the Nite")....200-300 56
(Has Ember label pasted over Standord label. Can be identified by the identification number 6106 in the vinyl trail-off.)
EMBER (1005 "In the Still of the Nite")....25-50 56
EMBER (1005 "[I'll Remember] in the Still of the Nite")....100-200 56
(White label. Promotional issue.)
EMBER (1005 "[I'll Remember] in the Still of the Nite")....50-75 59
(Red label. Reads "Special Demand Release.")
EMBER (1005 "[I'll Remember] in the Still of the Nite")....25-35 60
(Multi-color "logs" label.)
EMBER (1005 "[I'll Remember] in the Still of the Nite")....15-25 60s
(Black label. Some pressings read *In the Still of the Night,* instead of "Nite.")
EMBER (1008 "Wonderful Girl")....25-50 56
EMBER (1014 "Oh, Happy Day")....25-50 57
EMBER (1019 "To the Aisle")....25-50 57
EMBER (1025 "Our Anniversary")....25-50 57
(Red label.)
EMBER (1025 "Our Anniversary")....20-25 57
(Black label.)
EMBER (1028 "Million to One")....25-50 58

EMBER (1038 "A Night to Remember") 25-35 58
EMBER (1056 "Shadows") 25-35 58
EMBER (1061 "I'll Be Seeing You") .. 25-35 60
EMBER (1066 "Candlelight") 25-35 60
EMBER (1070 "Wishing Ring") 25-35 61
ELEKTRA (47411 "Memories of Days Gone By") 15-25 82
FLASHBACK 5-8 65
KIRSHNER 4-6 73-74
KLIK 5-10 73
LANA 5-8 64
LOST NITE 4-8
MUSICTONE (1108 "To the Aisle") ... 10-15 61
NIGHTRAIN 4-8 70
RCA 3-6 71-87
REO (8463 "In the Still of the Nite") ... 15-25 56
(Canadian.)
ROULETTE 5-8 64
SAMMY (103 "No One Knows") 50-75
S.G. 3-5 90
STANDORD (100 "All Mine") 500-1000 56
(Red label. Copies on a maroon-brown label are unauthorized reissues.)
STANDORD (200 "In the Still of the Nite") 1000-2000 56
(Red label. Reads "Produced By Martin Kuegull.")
STANDORD (200 "In the Still of the Nite") 500-1000 56
(Red label.)
STANDORD (5051 "All Mine") 250-500 57
STANDORD (7107 "The Time") 4-6 90s
(Colored vinyl.)
TIME MACHINE 4-8 62
TIMES SQUARE 10-15 63
(Colored vinyl.)
U.A. 10-20 61
W.B. 5-10 63

EPs: 7-inch

EMBER (100 "The Five Satins Sing") 50-100 60
(Red label.)
EMBER (100 "The Five Satins Sing") 25-50 61
(Black or multi-color label.)
EMBER (101 "The Five Satins Sing, Vol. 2") 50-100 60
(Red label.)
EMBER (101 "The Five Satins Sing, Vol. 2") 25-50 61
(Black or multi-color label.)
EMBER (102 "The Five Satins Sing, Vol. 3") 50-100 60
(Red label.)
EMBER (102 "The Five Satins Sing, Vol. 3") 25-50 61
(Black or multi-color label.)
EMBER (104 "In the Still of the Night") 250-350 61

LPs: 10/12-inch

CELEBRITY SHOWCASE 10-12 70
COLLECTABLES 5-10 83
EMBER (100 "The Five Satins Sing") 250-500 57
(Red label. Group is pictured on front cover.)
EMBER (100 "The Five Satins Sing") 100-200 58
(Multi-color label. Black vinyl.)
EMBER (100 "The Five Satins Sing") 500-1000 58
(Multi-color label. Colored vinyl.)
EMBER (100 "The Five Satins Sing") 50-100 60
(Black label.)
EMBER (401 "The Five Satins Encore") 50-100 60
(Black label.)
EMBER (401 "The Five Satins Encore") 40-60 61
(Multi-color label.)
LOST-NITE 8-12 81
MT. VERNON (108 "The Five Satins Sing") 20-30
RELIC 8-10

Members: Fred Parris; Louis Peebles; Stan Dortch; Jim Freeman; Nate Moseley; Bill Baker; Jimmy Curtis; Nate Marshall; Ed Martin; John Brown; Tom Killebrew; Al Denby; Jess Murphy; Wes Forbes; Richard Freeman; Dick Arnold.
Freeman; Dick Arnold.
Also see BLACK SATIN
Also see CARYL, Naomi
Also see GRANAHAN, Gerry
Also see NEW YORK CITY
Also see NEW YORKERS
Also see PARRIS, Fred
Also see SOUTHSIDE JOHNNY & Asbury Dukes

FIVE SATINS / Merry Clayton

Singles: 7-inch

RCA (6986 "In the Still of the Night") 3-5
Also see CLAYTON, Merry

FIVE SATINS / Gerry Granahan & Five Satins

Singles: 7-inch

X-BAT (1000 "When the Swallows Come Back to Capistrano") 3-4 95
(Colored vinyl. 500 made.)

Picture Sleeves

X-BAT (1000 "When the Swallows Come Back to Capistrano") 3-4 95
(500 made.)
Also see GRANAHAN, Gerry
Also see WILDWOODS

FIVE SATINS / Pharotones

Singles: 7-inch

TIMES SQUARE 5-10 63

FIVE SATINS / Youngtones / Youngsters / Shells

EPs: 7-inch

NEW YORK CITY (1002 "Gus Gossert Presents") 10-15 71
Also see FIVE SATINS
Also see SHELLS

FIVE SPECIAL — P&R/R&B/LP '79

Singles: 7-inch

ELEKTRA 3-4 79-80

LPs: 10/12-inch

ELEKTRA 5-10 79
Member: Byran Banks.

FIVE STAIRSTEPS — P&R/R&B '66

(Stairsteps; with Cubie)

Singles: 7-inch

BUDDAH 4-6 67-68
COLLECTABLES 3-4 80s
CURTOM 4-6 68-69
GOLD 4-6
WINDY C 4-8 66-67

Picture Sleeves

BUDDAH 4-8 67-68

LPs: 10/12-inch

BUDDAH 10-12 68-70
COLLECTABLES 6-8 85
CURTOM 8-10 69
WINDY C 10-15 67
Members: Clarence Burke Jr.; James Burke; Keni Burke; Dennis Burke; Cubie Burke; Aloha Burke.
Also see BURKE, Keni
Also see INVISIBLE MAN'S BAND
Also see ISLEY BROTHERS / Brooklyn Bridge
Also see STAIRSTEPS

FIVE STAR — P&R/R&B/D&D/LP '85

Singles: 12-inch

RCA 4-6 85-86

Singles: 7-inch

RCA 3-4 85-87

Picture Sleeves

RCA 3-4 86

LPs: 10/12-inch

RCA 5-10 85-86

5000 VOLTS — P&R '75

Singles: 7-inch

PHILIPS 3-5 75
PRIVATE STOCK 3-5 76

FIXX — P&R/LP '82

Singles: 12-inch

MCA 4-6 82-86

Singles: 7-inch

MCA 3-5 82-90
RCA 3-4 89

Picture Sleeves

MCA 3-5 83-84
RCA 3-4 89

LPs: 10/12-inch

MCA (Except 8642) 5-10 82-91
MCA (8642 "Talkabout") 8-12 80s
(Interviews with Fixx. Promotional issue only.)
RCA 5-8 89
Members: Cy Curnin; Adam Woods; Danny Brown; Alfi Agies; Jamie West; Rupert Greenall.

FIZZY QWICK — R&B '86

Singles: 7-inch

MOTOWN 3-4 86

FLACK, Roberta — LP '70

Singles: 7-inch

ATLANTIC 3-5 69-88
MCA 3-4 81
VIVA 3-4 83

Picture Sleeves

ATLANTIC 3-4 78-82

LPs: 10/12-inch

ATLANTIC 5-10 69-88
VIVA 5-10 83
Also see CHIC / Leif Garrett / Roberta Flack / Genesis
Also see McCANN, Les
Also see WATANABE, Sadao, & Roberta Flack

FLACK, Roberta, & Peabo Bryson — R&B/LP '80

Singles: 7-inch

ATLANTIC 3-4 80
CAPITOL 3-4 83

Picture Sleeves

CAPITOL 3-4 83

LPs: 10/12-inch

ATLANTIC 5-10 80
CAPITOL 5-10 83
Also see BRYSON, Peabo
Also see FLACK, Roberta

FLACK, Roberta, & Donny Hathaway — R&B/LP '72

Singles: 7-inch

ATLANTIC 3-5 71-80

LPs: 10/12-inch

ATLANTIC 5-10 72-80
Also see HATHAWAY, Donny

FLACK, Roberta, & Eric Mercury — R&B '83

Singles: 7-inch

ATLANTIC 3-4 83
Also see FLACK, Roberta

FLAGG, Fannie — LP '67

LPs: 10/12-inch

RCA 10-15 66

FLAIRS

Singles: 7-inch

PALMS (726 "Roll Over Beethoven") 25-50 61
(Reissued as by the Velaires.)
Also see VELAIRES

FLAME — P&R '70

Singles: 7-inch

BROTHER 10-15 70-71

LPs: 10/12-inch

BROTHER (2500 "The Flame") 20-30 70
(Includes bonus poster.)
Members: Rick Fataar; Terry "Blondie" Chaplin; Steve Fataar; Brother Fataar.
Also see RUTLES

FLAME LP '77

Singles: 7-inch

RCA....3-4 78

LPs: 10/12-inch

RCA....5-10 77-78

Members: Marge Raymond; Jim Crespo; Frank Ruby.

FLAMIN' GROOVIES LP '76

Singles: 7-inch

BOMP....3-5 74
EPIC....4-6 69-70
KAMA SUTRA....3-5 71
SIRE....4-6 76-79

Picture Sleeves

BOMP....4-8 74

EPs: 7-inch

SKYDOG....5-10

LPs: 10/12-inch

BUDDAH....10-12 77
EPIC (26487 "Supernazz")....35-45 69
KAMA SUTRA (2021 "Flamingo")....15-25 70
(Pink label.)
KAMA SUTRA (2021 "Flamingo")....10-15 70s
(Blue label.)
KAMA SUTRA (2031 "Teenage Head")....15-25 71
(Pink label.)
KAMA SUTRA (2031 "Teenage Head")....10-15 70s
(Blue label.)
SIRE....10-12 76-79
SNAZZ (2371 "Sneakers")....60-80 68
(10-inch LP.)
VOXX....5-10

Members: Roy Loney; Cyril Jordan; George Alexander; Tim Lynch; Danny Mihm; Chris Wilson; James Farrell; David Wright.

FLAMING EMBER P&R '69

Singles: 7-inch

HOT WAX....3-6 69-70

LPs: 10/12-inch

HOT WAX....10-15 70-71

Members: Joe Sladich; Jerry Plunk; Bill Ellis; Jim Bugnel.
Also see FLAMING EMBERS

FLAMINGOS R&B '56
(With Red Holloway's Orchestra)

Singles: 78 rpm

CHANCE (1133 " If I Can't Have You")....100-200 53
CHANCE (1140 "That's My Desire")....100-200 53
CHANCE (1145 "Golden Teardrops")....200-300 53
CHANCE (1149 "Plan for Love")....100-200 53
CHANCE (1154 "Cross Over the Bridge")....100-200 54
CHANCE (1162 "Blues in the Letter")....100-150 54
CHECKER....15-30 55-57
DECCA....15-25 57
PARROT (808 "Dream of a Lifetime")....100-150 54
PARROT (812 "I'm Yours")....150-200 55

Singles: 7-inch

ABC....3-5 73
CHANCE (1133 "If I Can't Have You")....500-750 53
(Black vinyl.)
CHANCE (1133 "If I Can't Have You")....1000-2000 53
(Colored vinyl.)
CHANCE (1140 "That's My Desire")....500-750 53
(Black vinyl.)
CHANCE (1140 "That's My Desire")....1000-2000 53
(Colored vinyl.)
CHANCE (1145 "Golden Teardrops")....500-750 53
(Black vinyl.)
CHANCE (1145 "Golden Teardrops")....2000-3000 53
(Colored vinyl.)
CHANCE (1149 "Plan for Love")....500-750 53
(Yellow and black label.)
CHANCE (1149 "Plan for Love")....300-500 53
(Blue and silver label.)
CHANCE (1154 "Cross Over the Bridge")....500-750 54
CHANCE (1162 "Blues in the Letter")....250-500 54
CHECKER (815 "When")....25-50 55
CHECKER (821 "Please Come Back Home")....25-50 55
CHECKER (830 "I'll Be Home")....25-50 56
CHECKER (837 "A Kiss from Your Lips")....20-30 56
CHECKER (846 "The Vow")....20-30 56
CHECKER (853 "Would I Be Crying")....20-30 56
CHECKER (915 "Dream of a Lifetime")....15-25 59
CHECKER (1084 "Lover Come Back to Me")....10-15 64
CHECKER (1091 "Goodnight Sweetheart")....5-10 64
CHESS....3-4 73
COLLECTABLES....3-4 80s
DECCA (30335 "Ladder of Love")....15-25 57
DECCA (30454 "Helpless")....15-25 57
DECCA (30687 "Rock & Roll March")....15-25 58
DECCA (30880 "Kiss-A-Me")....15-25 58
DECCA (30948 "Hey Now")....15-25 59
END (1035 "Please Wait for Me")....30-40 58
(Title later changed to *Lovers Never Say Goodbye.*)
END (1035 "Lovers Never Say Goodbye")....10-20 58
END (1040 "I Shed a Tear at Your Wedding")....10-20 58
END (1044 "At the Prom")....10-20 58
END (1046 "I Only Have Eyes for You"/ "At the Prom")....10-20 59
END (1046 "I Only Have Eyes for You"/ "Goodnight Sweetheart")....15-25 59
(Note different flip.)
END (1046 "I Only Have Eyes for You")....40-50 59
(Stereo.)
END (1055 "Love Walked In")....8-12 59
(Monaural.)
END (1055 "Love Walked In")....35-45 59
(Stereo.)
END (1062 thru 1124)....8-12 59-62
JULMAR....4-6 69
LOST NITE....4-8
OLDIES 45....4-8 64
PARROT (808 "Dream of a Lifetime")....500-1000 54
(Black vinyl.)
PARROT (808 "Dream of a Lifetime")....2000-3000 54
(Colored vinyl.)
PARROT (811 "I Really Don't Want to Know")....1000-2000 55
(Black vinyl.)
PARROT (811 "I Really Don't Want to Know")....3000-5000 55
(Colored vinyl.)
PARROT (812 "I'm Yours")....250-300 55
(Black vinyl.)
PARROT (812 "I'm Yours")....750-1000 55
(Colored vinyl.)
PHILIPS....10-15 66
POLYDOR....3-5 70
RONZE....3-5 71-76
ROULETTE....5-8 63
TIMES SQUARE....8-12 64
VEE JAY....5-10 61
WORLDS....3-5 75

EPs: 7-inch

END (205 "Goodnight Sweetheart")..40-60 59
(Monaural.)
END (205 "Goodnight Sweetheart")..50-85 59
(Stereo.)

LPs: 10/12-inch

CHECKER (1433 "Flamingos")....75-125 59
(Monaural.)
CHECKER (3005 "Flamingos")....25-50 66
(Stereo.)
CHESS....6-12 76-84
CONSTELLATION....15-20 64
EMUS....5-10 79
END (304 "Flamingo Serenade")....50-100 59
(Monaural.)
END (304 "Flamingo Serenade")....75-125 59
(Stereo.)
END (307 "Flamingo Favorites")....25-50 60
(Monaural.)
END (307 "Flamingo Favorites")....40-60 60
(Stereo.)
END (308 "Requestfully Yours")....25-50 60
(Monaural.)
END (308 "Requestfully Yours")....40-60 60
(Stereo.)
END (316 "The Sound of the Flamingos")....20-40 62
(Monaural.)
END (316 "The Sound of the Flamingos")....25-50 62
(Stereo.)
LOST-NITE....8-12 81
MEKA....10-15
PHILIPS....15-25 66
RONZE....10-15 72-73
ROULETTE....8-10 81-84
SOLID SMOKE....5-10 82

Members: Sollie McElroy; John Carter; Zeke Carey; Jake Carey; Paul Wilson; Nate Nelson; Tommy Hunt; Terry Johnson.
Also see HUNT, Tommy

FLAMINGOS / Moonglows

Singles: 7-inch

TRIP....3-5

LPs: 10/12-inch

VEE JAY (1052 "The Flamingos Meet the Moonglows")....30-40 62

Also see FLAMINGOS
Also see MOONGLOWS

FLANAGAN, Ralph P&R '49

Singles: 78 rpm

BLUEBIRD....3-6 49
RCA....3-5 50-57

Singles: 7-inch

CORAL....3-6 61
IMPERIAL....3-8 59
RCA....4-8 50-57

EPs: 7-inch

CAMDEN....4-8 54
RCA....5-10 51-57

LPs: 10/12-inch

CAMDEN....10-20 54
GOLDEN ERA....4-8 76
IMPERIAL....8-15 58-59
RCA....10-20 51-57

FLARES P&R/R&B '61
(Flairs)

Singles: 7-inch

COLLECTABLES....3-4 80s
FELSTED (8604 "Loving You")....8-12 60
FELSTED (8607 "Jump & Bump")....8-12 60
PRESS....4-8 62-63

Picture Sleeves

FELSTED (8607 "Jump & Bump")....20-30 60

LPs: 10/12-inch

PRESS (73001 "Encore of Foot Stompin' Hits")....30-50 61
(Monaural.)
PRESS (83001 "Encore of Foot Stompin' Hits")....50-75 61
(Stereo.)

Members: Aaron Collins; Willie Davis; Tom Miller; Randy Jones.
Also see CADETS
Also see PEPPERS

FLARES / Ramrocks

Singles: 7-inch

FELSTED (8624 "Foot Stompin' ")......6-10 61
Also see FLARES

FLASH P&R/LP '72

Singles: 7-inch

CAPITOL..........3-5 72

LPs: 10/12-inch

CAPITOL (11000 series)..........5-10 77
(With "SM" prefix.)
CAPITOL (11000 series)..........8-10 72-73
(With "SMAS" or "ST" prefix.)
Also see BANKS, Peter

FLASH & PAN P&R/LP '79

Singles: 12-inch

EPIC..........4-6 81-83

Singles: 7-inch

EPIC..........3-4 79-83

LPs: 10/12-inch

EPIC..........5-10 79-82
Members: Harry Vanda; George Young.
Also see EASYBEATS

FLASH CADILLAC & CONTINENTAL KIDS P&R '74

Singles: 7-inch

EPIC..........4-8 72-74
PRIVATE STOCK..........4-6 74-77

LPs: 10/12-inch

EPIC..........10-12 72-74
PRIVATE STOCK..........8-10 75
Also see WOLFMAN JACK

FLATT, Lester, & Bill Monroe

LPs: 10/12-inch

RCA..........5-10 74-81

FLATT, Lester, & Earl Scruggs

(With the Foggy Mountain Boys; Flatt & Scruggs) C&W '52

Singles: 78 rpm

COLUMBIA..........5-15 51-57
MERCURY..........5-10 49-53

Singles: 7-inch

COLUMBIA (20000 & 21000 series)...8-15 51-56
COLUMBIA (40000 thru 42000 series)..........5-10 56-63
COLUMBIA (43000 thru 45000 series)..........4-8 64-67
MERCURY..........10-15 50-53

Picture Sleeves

COLUMBIA..........4-8 62-68
MERCURY..........4-6 68

EPs: 7-inch

COLUMBIA..........10-20 57-60

LPs: 10/12-inch

CBS..........5-10
COLUMBIA (30 "Flatt & Scruggs")......8-12 75
COLUMBIA (400 series)..........10-15 69
COLUMBIA (1000 & 2000 series, except 1019)..........10-25 60-68
COLUMBIA (1019 "Foggy Mountain Jamboree")..........30-50 57
COLUMBIA (8000 & 9000 series).....10-25 60-70
(With "CS" prefix.)
COLUMBIA (8000 & 9000 series).......5-10
(With "PC" prefix.)
COLUMBIA (10000 series)..........6-12 73
COLUMBIA (30000 thru 37000 series)..........5-12 70-82
COPPER CREEK..........5-10
COUNTY..........5-10
EVEREST..........5-10 71-82
51 WEST..........5-10 80s
HARMONY..........8-15 60-71
MERCURY (20000 series)..........20-40 58-63
(Monaural.)
MERCURY (60000 series)..........20-30 63
(Stereo.)
MERCURY (61000 series)..........10-15 68
NASHVILLE..........8-10 70
PICKWICK/HILLTOP..........8-12 68
POWER PAK..........5-10
ROUNDER..........5-8
WING..........8-12 68
Members: Lester Flatt; Earl Scruggs; Mac Wiseman; Jim Shoemate; Cedric Rainwater.
Also see SCRUGGS, Earl

FLATT, Lester, Earl Scruggs & Jim & Jesse

LPs: 10/12-inch

STARDAY..........15-20 66

FLATT, Lester, Earl Scruggs & Bill Monroe

LPs: 10/12-inch

ROUNDER..........5-8 80s

FLATT, Lester, Earl Scruggs, & Doc Watson

LPs: 10/12-inch

COLUMBIA..........10-15 67
Also see FLATT, Lester, & Earl Scruggs
Also see WATSON, Doc

FLAVOR P&R '68

Singles: 7-inch

COLUMBIA..........4-6 68

Picture Sleeves

COLUMBIA..........4-6 68

LPs: 10/12-inch

JU-PAR..........8-10 77

FLAVOUR, La: see LA FLAVOUR

FLEAS

Singles: 7-inch

CHALLENGE (9115 "Scratchin' ")....20-30 61
Members: Dave Burgess; Glen Campbell; Jerry Fuller; Ricky Nelson.
Also see CLAMPBELL, Glen
Also see FULLER, Jerry
Also see NELSON, Rick

FLEETWOOD, Mick LP '81

LPs: 10/12-inch

RCA (4080 "The Visitor")..........5-10 81
Also see FLEETWOOD MAC

FLEETWOOD MAC LP '68

Singles: 12-inch

W.B. (652 "Go Your Own Way")......15-25 76
(Promotional issue only.)
W.B. (2688 "Big Love")..........15-25 87
(Promotional issue only.)
W.B. (2728 "Tango in the Night")......15-25 87
(Promotional issue only.)
W.B. (20842 "Family Man")..........8-12 87

Singles: 7-inch

BLUE HORIZON..........4-8 70
DJM..........4-8 73
EPIC (10351 "Black Magic Woman")..5-10 68
EPIC (10368 "Stop Messin' Around")..........5-10 68
EPIC (10436 "Albatross")..........4-6 69
EPIC (11029 "Albatross")..........3-5 73
EPIC (139609 "Albatross")..........5-8
(Promotional issue only.)
REPRISE..........3-6 69-76
W.B. (Except 8304)..........3-4 77-90
W.B. (8304 "Go Your Own Way").......8-12 76

Picture Sleeves

EPIC (139609 "Albatross")..........8-10 69
(Promotional issue only.)
W.B...........3-6 77-88

LPs: 10/12-inch

BLUE HORIZON (3801 "Fleetwood Mac in Chicago")..........20-25 70
BLUE HORIZON (4803 "Blues Jam in Chicago, Vol. 1")..........20-25 70
BLUE HORIZON (4805 "Blues Jam in Chicago, Vol. 2")..........20-25 70
BLUE HORIZON (66227 "Blues Jam at Chess")..........20-25 69
BLUE HORIZON (83110 "Mr. Wonderful")..........20-25
COLUMBIA SPECIAL PROD..........8-12 73
EPIC (26402 "Peter Green's Fleetwood Mac")..........20-30 68
EPIC (26446 "English Rose")..........20-25 69
EPIC (30632 "Black Magic Woman")..........15-25 71
(Repackage of *Fleetwood Mac* and *English Rose.*)
EPIC (33740 "English Rose")..........10-15 73
EPIC (33740 "Fleetwood Mac/English Rose")..........10-15 74
(Repackage of *Black Magic Woman.*)
MFSL (012 "Fleetwood Mac")..........60-80 78
MFSL (119 "Mirage")..........25-35 84
NAUTILUS (8 "Rumours")..........25-35 80
(Half-speed mastered.)
REPRISE (Except 6368)..........8-15 70-77
REPRISE (6368 "Then Play On")......15-25 69
(Without *Oh Well.*)
REPRISE (6368 "Then Play On")......10-15 69
(With *Oh Well.*)
SIRE..........8-10 75-77
VARRICK..........5-10 85
W.B...........8-12 77-90
Members: Mick Fleetwood; John McVie; Peter Green; Jeremy Spencer; Danny Kirwin; Christine McVie; Bob Welch; Bob Weston; Dave Walker; Lindsay Buckingham; Stevie Nicks; Rick Vito; Billy Burnette.
Also see BUCKINGHAM, Lindsay
Also see BURNETTE, Billy
Also see FLEETWOOD, Mick
Also see GREEN, Peter
Also see MAYALL, John
Also see McVIE, Christine
Also see NICKS, Stevie
Also see WELCH, Bob

FLEETWOOD MAC / Danny Kirwan

Singles: 7-inch

DJM..........4-8 73
Also see FLEETWOOD MAC

FLEETWOODS P&R/R&B '59

Singles: 7-inch

DOLPHIN (1 "Come Softly to Me")....15-25 59
(No mention of distribution by Liberty.)
DOLPHIN (1 "Come Softly to Me")....10-20 59
(Reads: "Distributed by Liberty Record Sales Co.")
DOLTON (3 "Graduation's Here").......5-10 59
(Monaural.)
DOLTON (S3 "Graduation's Here")...15-25 59
(Stereo.)
DOLTON (5 thru 315)..........5-15 59-66
LIBERTY (55188 "Come Softly to Me")..........8-12 59
(Monaural.)
LIBERTY (77188 "Come Softly to Me")..........10-20 59
(Stereo.)
QUALITY..........10-20
(Canadian.)
U.A...........3-5 74

Picture Sleeves

DOLTON (22 "Runaround")..........10-15 60

EPs: 7-inch

DOLTON (502 "The Fleetwoods")......20-30 60

LPs: 10/12-inch

DOLTON (2001 "Mr. Blue")..........25-35 59
(Monaural.)
DOLTON (8001 "Mr. Blue")..........30-40 59
(Stereo.)
DOLTON (2002 thru 2039)..........20-30 60-65
(Monaural.)
DOLTON (8002 thru 8039)..........20-35 60-65
(Stereo.)
LIBERTY..........5-10 82-83
SUNSET..........10-15 66
U.A...........8-10 75
Members: Gary Troxel; Barbara Ellis; Gretchen Christopher.
Also see VEE, Bobby / Johnny Burnette / Ventures / Fleetwoods

FLEMONS, Wade P&R/R&B '58

(With the Newcomers; Wade Flemmons)

Singles: 7-inch

RAMSEL (1001 "Jeannette")..........10-20
VEE JAY (Maroon label)..........15-25 58-59
VEE JAY (Black label, except 368)...10-20 60-63

VEE JAY (368 "I'll Come Running") .. 20-30 60

LPs: 10/12-inch

VEE JAY (1011 "Wade Flemons") .. 50-100 59
(Maroon label.)

VEE JAY (1011 "Wade Flemons") 25-50 61
(Black label.)

Also see EARTH, WIND & FIRE
Also see SKYLINERS / Wade Flemons

FLENOY, Julian R&B '86

Singles: 7-inch

KMA 3-4 86

FLESH for LULU LP '87

Singles: 12-inch

MCA 4-6 85

Singles: 7-inch

MCA 3-4 85

LPs: 10/12-inch

CAPITOL 5-10 87
MCA 5-10 85

Members: Nick Marsh; James Mitchell; Rocco Barker; Kevin Mills; Derek Grenning.

FLESHTONES LP '82

Singles: 7-inch

I.R.S. 3-4 81-82

LPs: 10/12-inch

I.R.S. 5-10 81-82

Members: Jonithan Weiss; Marek Pakulski; Keith Streng; Bill Milhiser; Peter Zaremba.

FLETCHER, Darrow P&R/R&B '66

Singles: 7-inch

ATLANTIC 3-5 81
CONGRESS 3-5 70
CROSSOVER 3-4 75-79
GROOVY 5-10 66
REVUE 5-10 68
UNI 3-5 70-71

FLETCHER, Dusty R&B '47

Singles: 78 rpm

NATIONAL 10-15 47

Singles: 7-inch

SAVOY 5-10 60

FLETCHER, Lois P&R '74

Singles: 7-inch

PLAYBOY 3-5 74

FLEX, M.C., & FBI Crew D&D '84

Singles: 12-inch

POSSE 3-4 84

FLINT, Shelby P&R '60

Singles: 7-inch

CADENCE 5-10 58
QUANTUM 4-6 62
VALIANT 4-8 60-66

LPs: 10/12-inch

VALIANT (401 "Shelby Flint") 25-40 61
VALIANT (403 "Shelby Flint Sings Folk") 25-35 61
(Monaural.)

VALIANT (WS-403 "Shelby Flint Sings Folk") 35-50 61
(Stereo.)

VALIANT (5003 "Cast Your Fate to the Wind") 15-25 66
(Monaural.)

VALIANT (25003 "Cast Your Fate to the Wind") 20-30 66
(Stereo.)

FLIP CARTRIDGE: see CARTRIDGE, Flip

FLIRTATIONS P&R '69

Singles: 7-inch

DERAM 4-6 69
PARROT 4-8 68

LPs: 10/12-inch

DERAM 15-20 69

Members: Ernestine Pearce; Shirley Pearce; Viola Billups.

Also see GYPSIES

FLIRTATIONS D&D '83

Singles: 12-inch

D&D 4-6 83

FLIRTS D&D '84

Singles: 12-inch

CBS ASSOCIATES 4-6 86
TELEFON 4-6 84

Singles: 7-inch

CBS ASSOCIATES 3-4 86
O RECORDS 3-4 82

LPs: 10/12-inch

CBS ASSOCIATES 5-10 86
O RECORDS 5-10 82

FLOATERS P&R/R&B/LP '77

Singles: 7-inch

ABC 3-4 77-79

Picture Sleeves

ABC 3-4 77

LPs: 10/12-inch

ABC 5-10 77-79

Members: Charles Clark; Paul Mitchell; Ralph Mitchell; Larry Cunningham; Jonathan Murray.

FLOCK, The LP '69

Singles: 7-inch

COLUMBIA 4-6 69-70
DESTINATION 5-10 66-67
U.S.A. 4-8 68

LPs: 10/12-inch

COLUMBIA 10-15 69-71
MERCURY 8-10 75

Members: Jerry Goodman; John Billings.

FLOCK OF SEAGULLS P&R/LP '82

Singles: 12-inch

JIVE 4-6 82-83

Singles: 7-inch

ARISTA 3-4
JIVE 3-4 82-86

Picture Sleeves

ARISTA 3-4
JIVE 3-4 82-84

LPs: 10/12-inch

JIVE 5-10 82-86

FLOOD, Dick P&R '59
(With the Pathfinders)

Singles: 7-inch

EPIC 4-8 61-62
KAPP 3-6 65
MONUMENT 5-10 59-60
NASCO 3-5 71-72
NUGGET 4-6 68
TOTEM 4-6 67

FLOS R&B '87

Singles: 7-inch

SUPERSTAR I 3-4 87

FLOTSAM & JETSAM LP '88

Singles: 12-inch

ELEKTRA 4-8 88
(Promotional only.)

Singles: 7-inch

ELEKTRA 3-4 88

LPs: 10/12-inch

ELEKTRA 5-8 88
MCA 5-8 90
METAL BLADE (72208 "Doomsday for the Deceiver") 10-15 87
(Picture disc.)

FLOYD, Eddie P&R/R&B '66

Singles: 7-inch

ATLANTIC 8-12 65
LU-PINE (115 "Set My Soul on Fire") 15-25 63
LU-PINE (122 "I'll Be Home") 15-25 63
MALACO 3-6 77
MERCURY 3-6 78
SAFICE (334 "Never Get Enough of Your Love") 10-15 64
STAX 4-8 66-75

LPs: 10/12-inch

ATCO 8-10 74
MALACO 5-10 77
STAX 10-20 67-79

Also see FALCONS
Also see MOORE, Dorothy, & Eddie Floyd
Also see REDDING, Otis / Carla Thomas / Sam & Dave / Eddie Floyd

FLOYD, Eddie, & Mavis Staples

Singles: 7-inch

STAX 3-6 69

Also see FLOYD, Eddie
Also see STAPLES, Mavis

FLOYD, King: see KING FLOYD

FLYING BURRITO BROTHERS LP '69

Singles: 7-inch

A&M 3-6 69-70
COLUMBIA 3-5 76
REGENCY 3-4 80

LPs: 10/12-inch

A&M 10-15 69-76
COLUMBIA 8-10 75-76
REGENCY 5-10 80

Members: Gram Parsons; Chris Hillman; Bernie Leadon; Al Perkins; Rick Roberts; Mike Clarke; Pete Battin; "Sneaky" Pete Kleinow; Greg Harris; Ed Ponder; Floyd "Gib" Guilbeau; John Beland

Also see BURRITO BROTHERS
Also see FIREFALL
Also see HILLMAN, Chris
Also see PARSONS, Gram

FLYING LIZARDS P&R '79

Singles: 7-inch

VIRGIN 3-4 79

Picture Sleeves

VIRGIN 3-4 79

LPs: 10/12-inch

VIRGIN 5-10 80

FLYING MACHINE P&R/LP '69

Singles: 7-inch

CONGRESS 4-8 69-70
JANUS 4-8 69

LPs: 10/12-inch

JANUS 10-15 69

Members: Tony Newman; Stuart Coleman; Steve Jones; Paul Wilkinson.

Also see TAYLOR, James

FOCUS P&R/LP '73

Singles: 7-inch

ATCO 3-5 75
SIRE 3-5 73

LPs: 10/12-inch

ATCO 8-10 74-75
SIRE 8-10 72-77

Also see AKKERMAN, Jan

FOCUS R&B '87

Singles: 7-inch

EMI AMERICA 3-4 87

FOCUS & P.J. PROBY

LPs: 10/12-inch

HARVEST 5-10 78

Also see FOCUS
Also see PROBY, P.J.

FOGELBERG, Dan LP '74

Singles: 7-inch

COLUMBIA 4-6 73
EPIC 3-5 74-75
FULL MOON/EPIC 3-5 75-82
FULL MOON 3-4 82-87

Picture Sleeves

FULL MOON/EPIC 3-4 80-87

LPs: 10/12-inch

COLUMBIA 10-15 72
EPIC 8-10 74-78
EPIC/FULL MOON 8-10 75-82
FULL MOON 5-10 82-90

Also see FOOLS GOLD

FOGELBERG, Dan, & Tim Weisberg LP '78

Singles: 7–inch

FULL MOON/EPIC 3-4 78-80

LPs: 10/12–inch

FULL MOON/EPIC 5-10 78

Also see FOGELBERG, Dan
Also see WEISBERG, Tim

FOGERTY, John P&R '72

Promotional Singles: 12–inch

W.B. (2234 "Old Man Down the Road")................................5-10 84
W.B. (2267 "Rock & Roll Girls")..........5-10 85
W.B. (2337 "I Can't Help Myself")........5-10 85
W.B. (2362 "Vanz Kant Danz)...............5-10 85
W.B. (2363 "Vanz Kant Danz-Edit")....5-10 85
W.B. (2514 "Eye of the Zombie") 5-10 86

Singles: 7–inch

ASYLUM................................3-5 75-76
FANTASY................................3-6 73
W.B. 3-4 84-86

Picture Sleeves

W.B. (Except 291007)................................3-5 84-87
W.B. (29100 "The Old Man Down the Road")................................3-5 84
(With blue pictures.)
W.B. (29100 "The Old Man Down the Road")................................5-8 84
(With black pictures.)

LPs: 10/12–inch

ASYLUM (1046 "John Fogerty")..........5-10 75
W.B. (25203 "Centerfield")..................10-15 84
(Last track is mistitled, *Zanz Kant Danz.*)
W.B. (25203 "Centerfield")...................5-8 85
(Last track is *Vanz Kant Danz.*)
W.B. (25449 "Eye of the Zombie") 5-8 85

Also see BLUE RIDGE RANGERS
Also see CREEDENCE CLEARWATER REVIVAL
Also see EDDY, Duane

FOGERTY, Tom LP '72

(With the Blue Velvets)

Singles: 7–inch

FANTASY................................3-5 71-82
ORCHESTRA ("Now You're Not Mine")................................35-50 62
(Selection number not known.)
ORCHESTRA (1010 "Have You Ever Been Lonely")................................35-50 61
ORCHESTRA (6177 "Come on Baby")................................35-50 61
(Despite the higher number, this is the first Orchestra single.)

Picture Sleeves

FANTASY................................3-5 71

LPs: 10/12–inch

FANTASY................................8-10 72-81

Members: Tom Fogerty; John Fogerty; Doug Clifford; Stuart Cook.
Also see CREEDENCE CLEARWATER REVIVAL
Also see SAUNDERS, Merl

FOGHAT P&R/LP '72

Singles: 7–inch

BEARSVILLE (725 "Stone Blue")........5-10 78
(Promotional issue only, colored vinyl.)

Singles: 7–inch

BEARSVILLE 3-5 72-80
MARK-O HILDENEN ("Goin' Home for Christmas '86")................................3-4 86

Picture Sleeves

BEARSVILLE 3-5 79
MARK-O HILDENEN ("Goin' Home for Christmas '86")................................3-4 86

LPs: 10/12–inch

BEARSVILLE 5-10 72-83

Members: Dave Peverett; Roger Earl; Rod Price; Tony Stevens; Erik Cartwright; Nick Jameson.
Also see JAMESON, Nick
Also see SAVOY BROWN
Also see WISHBONE ASH

FOLEY, Ellen P&R/LP '79

Singles: 7–inch

EPIC/CLEVELAND INT'L................................3-4 79-83

Picture Sleeves

EPIC/CLEVELAND INT'L................................3-5 80

LPs: 10/12–inch

EPIC/CLEVELAND INT'L................................5-10 79-83

Also see MEAT LOAF

FOLEY, Red C&W '44

(With the Cumberland Valley Boys; with His Log Cabin Quartet; with Betty Foley; with Anita Kerr Singers; with Grady Martin & His Slew Foot Five)

Singles: 78 rpm

BANNER................................10-15
DECCA (Except 30067 & 30674)........4-10 42-57
DECCA (30067 "Rock 'N Reelin' ") ... 10-20 56
DECCA (30674 "Crazy Little Guitar Man")................................10-20 58
MELOTONE................................10-15
ORIOLE................................10-15

Singles: 7–inch

DECCA (25000 series)................................4-8 61-67
DECCA (27000 thru 29000 series) ... 10-20 50-56
DECCA (30000 series, except 30067 & 30674)................................10-20 56-59
DECCA (30067 "Rock 'N Reelin' ") ... 25-35 56
DECCA (30674 "Crazy Little Guitar Man")................................25-35 58
DECCA (31000 thru 32000 series) 4-8 60-67
DECCA (46411 "Lonely Mile")................................4-6 68
MCA 3-5 73

EPs: 7–inch

DECCA 10-20 53-59

LPs: 10/12–inch

CORAL................................5-8 73
COUNTRY MUSIC................................6-10 76
DECCA (100 series)................................15-25 64
DECCA (4000 series, except 4140).. 10-25 61-67
DECCA (4140 "Company's Comin' ") 10-20 61
DECCA (5303 "The Red Foley Souvenir Album")................................40-60 51
(10–inch LP.)
DECCA (5338 "Lift Up Your Voice")................................40-60 51
(10–inch LP.)
DECCA (7100 series)................................15-25 64
DECCA (8294 "The Red Foley Souvenir Album")................................20-30 56
DECCA (8296 "Beyond the Sunset") 15-25 56
DECCA (8767 "He Walks with Thee")................................10-20 58
DECCA (8806 "My Keepsake Album")................................20-30 58
DECCA (8847 "Let's All Sing with Red Foley")................................15-25 59
DECCA (8903 "Let's All Sing to Him")................................10-20 59
DECCA (74000 & 75000 series)........ 8-12 68-69
DECCA/DICKIES ("Red Foley's Dickies Souvenir Album")................................50-100 58
(Special Products issue for the Dickies company.)
MCA 5-8 80s
PICKWICK/HILLTOP................................8-12 66
VOCALION 6-12 65-71

Also see KERR, Anita
Also see WELK, Lawrence, & His Orchestra
Also see WELLS, Kitty, & Red Foley

FOLEY, Red, & Andrews Sisters

Singles: 78 rpm

DECCA 4-8 54

Also see ANDREWS SISTERS

FOLEY, Red, & Little Foleys

Singles: 78 rpm

DECCA 4-8 50

Singles: 7–inch

DECCA 10-15 50

Picture Sleeves

DECCA 20-30 50

Members: Red Foley; Shirley Foley, Julie Foley; Jenny Foley.
Also see FOLEY, Red

FOLKSWINGERS LP '63

Singles: 7–inch

WORLD PACIFIC 4-6 66

LPs: 10/12–inch

WORLD PACIFIC................................10-20 63-66

Members: Glen Campbell; Tut Taylor; Harihar Rao.
Also see CAMPBELL, Glen
Also see SHANK, Bud

FONTAINE, Eddie P&R '58

(With the Excels; Eddie Reardon)

Singles: 78 rpm

DECCA................................10-20 56-57
JALO................................25-50 56
VIK................................10-15 56
"X"................................10-20 54-56

Singles: 7–inch

ARGO 10-15 58-59
CHANCELLOR................................15-25 58
DECCA................................10-20 56-57
JALO (102 "Where Is Da Woman")... 50-75 56
LIBERTY................................5-10 65
SUNBEAM (105 "Nothing Shakin' ").. 30-50 58
VIK................................10-20 56
W.B................................8-12 62-63
"X" (0096 "Rock Love")................................25-50 54
"X" (0108 "On Bended Knee")..........25-50 54

Also see REARDON, Eddie

FONTAINE, Eddie, & Karen Chandler

Singles: 78 rpm

DECCA................................5-10 57

Singles: 7–inch

DECCA................................5-10 57

Also see CHANDLER, Karen

FONTAINE, Eddie, & Gerry Granahan

Singles: 7–inch

SUNBEAM................................10-15 58

Also see FONTAINE, Eddie
Also see GRANAHAN, Gerry

FONTAINE, Frankie LP '63

(Frank Fontaine)

Singles: 7–inch

ABC-PAR 3-6 62-65
CAPITOL 3-6 63

Picture Sleeves

ABC-PAR 5-8 62
CAPITOL 5-8 63

LPs: 10/12–inch

ABC-PAR 10-20 62-66
MGM................................6-10 67

FONTANA, Wayne

Singles: 7–inch

BRUT................................3-5 73
MGM................................4-8 66-67
METROMEDIA................................4-6 69

LPs: 10/12–inch

MGM (4459 "Wayne Fontana") 15-25 67

FONTANA, Wayne, & Mindbenders P&R/LP '65

Singles: 7–inch

FONTANA 5-10 65

LPs: 10/12–inch

FONTANA (27542 "The Game of Love")................................30-35 65
(Monaural.)
FONTANA (67542 "The Game of Love")................................35-40 65
(Stereo.)

Members: Wayne Fontana; Graham Gouldman; Bob Land; Paul Hancox; Eric Stewart; Rick Rothwell; James O'Neil.
Also see FONTANA, Wayne
Also see MINDBENDERS

FONTANE SISTERS P&R '51

Singles: 78 rpm

DOT................................5-15 54-57
RCA................................5-10 51-54

Singles: 7–inch

DOT................................5-15 54-60
RCA................................10-20 51-54

Picture Sleeves
RCA (5524 "Kissing Bridge")............15-25 54
EPs: 7-inch
DOT 10-20 56-57
LPs: 10/12-inch
DOT (Except 108).........................20-40 56-63
DOT (108 "Fontane Sisters")............25-50 55
(10-inch LP.)
Members: Bea Fontane; Marge Fontane; Geri Fontane.
Also see BOONE, Pat
Also see COMO, Perry, & Fontane Sisters

FOOLS, The P&R/LP '80
Singles: 12-inch
PVC 4-6
Singles: 7-inch
EMI AMERICA (Except 9324)................3-5 80-81
EMI AMERICA (9324 "It's a Night for Beautiful Girls")..................................5-10 80
(Picture disc. Promotional issue only.)
Picture Sleeves
EMI AMERICA 3-5 80
LPs: 10/12-inch
EMI AMERICA (Except 9393).............5-10 80-81
EMI AMERICA (9393 "April Fools Day")...................................10-15 80
(Promotional issue only.)

FOOLS GOLD P&R/LP '76
Singles: 7-inch
COLUMBIA................................3-5 77
MORNING SKY.............................3-5 76
LPs: 10/12-inch
COLUMBIA................................8-10 77
MORNING SKY.............................8-10 76
Also see FOGELBERG, Dan

FORBERT, Steve P&R/LP '79
Singles: 7-inch
GEFFEN..................................3-4 88
NEMPEROR................................3-5 79-82
Picture Sleeves
GEFFEN..................................3-4 88
LPs: 10/12-inch
NEMPEROR................................5-10 79-82

FORCE M.D.s R&B/LP '84
Singles: 12-inch
TOMMY BOY...............................4-6 84-86
Singles: 7-inch
TOMMY BOY...............................3-4 84-88
W.B. 3-4 86
Picture Sleeves
TOMMY BOY...............................3-4 86-88
W.B. 3-4 86
LPs: 10/12-inch
TOMMY BOY...............................5-10 84-87

FORD, Ernie: see FORD, Tennessee Ernie

FORD, Frankie P&R/R&B '59
Singles: 78 rpm
ACE (549 "Cheatin' Woman")...........25-50 58
ACE (554 "Sea Cruise") 200-300 59
Singles: 7-inch
ABC 3-4 73-74
ACE.....................................8-15 58-60
BRIARMEADE..............................3-5
CINNAMON................................3-5
COLLECTABLES 3-4 81
CONSTELLATION 4-8 63
DOUBLOON................................4-8 67
IMPERIAL................................5-10 60-62
PAULA...................................3-5 71
SYC 3-4 82
20TH FOX 4-8 60s
Picture Sleeves
ACE (592 "Chinatown")..................15-25 60
EPs: 7-inch
ACE (105 "Best of Frankie Ford") 50-75 59
LPs: 10/12-inch
ACE (1005 "Let's Take a Sea Crusie")...............................75-125 59
BRIARMEADE..............................8-10 76
Also see CLANTON, Jimmy / Frankie Ford / Jerry Lee Lewis / Patsy Cline

Also see SMITH, Huey

FORD, Lita LP '84
Singles: 7-inch
MERCURY.................................3-5 84
RCA 3-4 88-90
Picture Sleeves
RCA 3-4 88-90
LPs: 10/12-inch
MERCURY.................................5-10 84
RCA 5-8 88-90
Also see RUNAWAYS

FORD, Lita, & Ozzy Osbourne
Singles: 7-inch
RCA 3-4 89
Picture Sleeves
RCA 3-4 89
Also see FORD, Lita
Also see OSBOURNE, Ozzy

FORD, Mary: see PAUL, Les, & Mary Ford

FORD, Pennye R&B '84
Singles: 12-inch
TOTAL EXPERIENCE........................4-6 84-85
Singles: 7-inch
TOTAL EXPERIENCE........................3-4 84-85
LPs: 10/12-inch
TOTAL EXPERIENCE........................5-10 85

FORD, Robben LP '88
LPs: 10/12-inch
W.B. 5-8 88

FORD, Tennessee Ernie
(With the Green Valley Singers & Orchestra; Tennessee Ernie) C&W/P&R '49
Singles: 78 rpm
CAPITOL (1 "Sixteen Tons")............5-10 69
(Promotional "Special Commemorative Pressing" for Ford's 20th year on Capitol.)
CAPITOL (1200 thru 2900 series) 5-15 50-57
CAPITOL (40000 series)..................5-10 49-50
Singles: 7-inch
CAPITOL (1275 thru 2900 series) 10-30 50-54
(Purple labels. Ford's many "Boogie" titles represent the higher end of this price range.)
CAPITOL (2000 thru 4100 series) 3-5 70-75
(Orange labels.)
CAPITOL (3000 thru 4400 series, except 3343)...................................5-15 54-60
CAPITOL (3343 "Bright Lights & Blond-Haired Women")...............................15-25 56
CAPITOL (4500 thru 5700 series) 3-6 61-67
Picture Sleeves
CAPITOL.................................10-20 55-60
EPs: 7-inch
CAPITOL (Except 413) 5-10 55-61
CAPITOL (413 "Backwoods Boogie and Blues")................................20-30 53
GREEN GIANT (2566 "When Pea-Pickers Get Together") 10-15
(Mail order offer. Add $3 to $5 if accompanied by special mailer/sleeve. Promotional issue made for the Green Giant Co.)
LPs: 10/12-inch
CAPITOL (Except 888) 5-15 56-80
CAPITOL (888 "Ol' Rockin' Ern")......25-50 57
EVEREST.................................5-10 70s
LONGINES 5-10
PICKWICK................................5-10 70s
READER'S DIGEST (241 "Tennessee Ernie Ford") 20-40
(Boxed, eight-disc set. With booklet.)
Session: Jordanaires.
Also see HUTTON, Betty, & Tennessee Ernie Ford
Also see LAWRENCE, Steve / Tennessee Ernie Ford
Also see LEE, Brenda / Tennessee Ernie Ford
Also see OWENS, Buck / Tennessee Ernie Ford
Also see STARR, Kay, & Tennessee Ernie Ford

FORD, Tennessee Ernie, & Glen Campbell
LPs: 10/12-inch
CAPITOL.................................10-12 75
Also see CAMPBELL, Glen

FORD, Tennessee Ernie, & Joe "Fingers" Carr C&W '51
Singles: 78 rpm
CAPITOL 4-8 51
Singles: 7-inch
CAPITOL 5-10 51
Also see CARR, Joe "Fingers"

FORD, Tennessee Ernie, & Dinning Sisters
Singles: 78 rpm
CAPITOL 4-8 50s
Singles: 7-inch
CAPITOL 5-10 50s

FORD, Tennessee Ernie, & Andra Willis C&W '75
Singles: 7-inch
CAPITOL.................................3-5 75
Also see FORD, Tennessee Ernie

FORDHAM, Julia LP '88
Singles: 7-inch
VIRGIN 3-4 88-89
Picture Sleeves
VIRGIN 3-4 88-89
LPs: 10/12-inch
VIRGIN 5-8 88-90

FORECAST R&B '80
Singles: 12-inch
RCA.....................................4-6 83
Singles: 7-inch
ARIOLA 3-4 80
RCA.....................................3-4 83
LPs: 10/12-inch
RCA.....................................5-10 83

FOREIGNER P&R/LP '77
Singles: 7-inch
ATLANTIC (Black vinyl)..................3-5 77-90
ATLANTIC (3543 "Blue Morning, Blue Day")..................................4-8 78
(Colored vinyl. Promotional issue only.)
ATLANTIC/W.B. 3-5 79
Picture Sleeves
ATLANTIC................................3-5 78-88
LPs: 10/12-inch
ATLANTIC................................5-10 77-91
GEFFEN..................................5-10 85
MFSL (052 "Double Vision")............25-50 81
Members: Lou Gramm; Rick Wills; Mick Jones; Dennis Elliott; Ian McDonald; Al Greenwood.
Also see BAD COMPANY
Also see FRASER, Andy
Also see NEW JERSEY MASS CHOIR
Also see SPYS
Also see WALKER, Junior

FOREST, Earl: see FORREST, Earl

FOREST, Jimmy R&B '52
(Jimmy Forrest)
Singles: 78 rpm
UNITED 5-15 52-55
Singles: 7-inch
PRESTIGE................................4-8 61-62
TRIUMPH.................................5-10 59
UNITED (Except 113).....................5-15 52-55
UNITED (110 "Night Train") 15-25 52
(Black vinyl.)
UNITED (110 "Night Train") 25-50 52
(Colored vinyl.)
LPs: 10/12-inch
NEW JAZZ (8250 "Forrest Fire").......25-50 60
NEW JAZZ (8293 "Soul Street") 25-50 62
PRESTIGE................................20-30 61-62
(Yellow label.)
PRESTIGE 10-20 64
(Blue label.)
UNITED 002 "Night Train").............75-100 57
(10-inch LP.)
Also see DAVIS, Miles

FORESTER SISTERS C&W '85

Singles: 7–inch

W.B. 3-4 84-91

LPs: 10/12–inch

W.B. 5-8 85-91

Members: Kathy Forester; Kim Forester; June Forester; Christy Forester.

Also see BELLAMY BROTHERS & Forester Sisters

FOREVER MORE LP '70

Singles: 7–inch

RCA 3-5 69-70

LPs: 10/12–inch

RCA 10-15 69-70

Also see AVERAGE WHITE BAND

FORMATIONS P&R '68

Singles: 7–inch

BANK (1007 "At the Top of the Stairs") 20-30 67

MGM (13899 "At the Top of the Stairs") 5-8 68

MGM (13963 "Love's Not Only for the Heart") 10-20 68

MGM (14009 "Don't Get Close") 8-12 68

Members: Victor Drayton; Jerry Akines; Reginald Turner; Ernie Brooks; Johnny Bellman.

Also see CORNER BOYS

FORREST D&D '83

Singles: 12–inch

PROFILE 4-6 83

FORREST, Earl R&B '53

(Earl Forest)

Singles: 78 rpm

DUKE (Except 103) 15-25 52

DUKE (103 "Rock the Bottle") 25-50 52

METEOR 50-75 53

Singles: 7–inch

DUKE (108 "Whoopin' and Hollerin' ") 25-35 52

DUKE (113 "Last Night's Dream") 20-30 53

DUKE (121 "Out on a Party") 20-30 54

DUKE (130 "Your Kind of Love") 20-30 54

DUKE (300 series) 10-20 62-63

METEOR (5005 "I Wronged a Woman") 50-100 53

Also see ACE, Johnny / Earl Forrest

FORREST, Jimmy: see FOREST, Jimmy

FORTUNE P&R '85

Singles: 7–inch

MCA/CAMEL 3-4 85

Picture Sleeves

MCA/CAMEL 3-4 85

LPs: 10/12–inch

MCA/CAMEL 5-10 86

FORTUNES P&R '65

Singles: 7–inch

CAPITOL 3-5 71-74

COLLECTABLES 3-4 80s

LONDON 3-4

PRESS (9773 "You've Got Your Troubles") 10-15 65
(White label, commercial issue.)

PRESS (9773 "You've Got Your Troubles") 5-10 65
(Color label.)

PRESS (9798 "Here It Comes Again") 10-15 65
(White label, commercial issue.)

PRESS (9798 "Here It Comes Again") 10-15 65
(Red or orange labels.)

PRESS (9811 "This Golden Ring") 5-10 66

U.A. 4-8 67-68

WORLD PACIFIC 3-5 70

LPs: 10/12–inch

CAPITOL 8-10 71-73

COCA-COLA (21904 "It's the Real Thing") 30-40 60s
(Special products issue.)

PRESS (73002 "The Fortunes") 20-25 65
(Monaural.)

PRESS (83002 "The Fortunes") 25-30 65
(Stereo.)

WORLD PACIFIC 8-10 70

Members: Glen Dale; Barry Pritchard; Shel MacRae.

FORUM P&R '67

Singles: 7–inch

MIRA 10-15 67

PENTHOUSE 10-20 66

LPs: 10/12–inch

MIRA 15-20 67

Members: Phil Campos; Rene Nole; Riselle Vaine.

FOSTER, Bruce P&R '77

Singles: 7–inch

MILLENIUM 3-5 77

Picture Sleeves

MILLENIUM 5-10 77

LPs: 10/12–inch

MILLENIUM 8-15 77

FOSTER, David P&R '85

Singles: 7–inch

ATLANTIC 3-4 85-88

Picture Sleeves

ATLANTIC 3-4 85-88

LPs: 10/12–inch

ATLANTIC 5-10 86-88

MFSL (123 "The Best of Me") 15-25 84

FOSTER, David, & Olivia Newton-John P&R '86

Singles: 7–inch

ATLANTIC 3-4 86

Also see FOSTER, David

Also see NEWTON-JOHN, Olivia

FOSTER, Ian R&B '87

Singles: 7–inch

MCA 3-4 87

FOSTER & LLOYD C&W '87

Singles: 7–inch

RCA 3-4 87-90

LPs: 10/12–inch

RCA 5-10 86-90

Members: Radney Foster; Bill Lloyd.

FOTOMAKER P&R/LP '78

Singles: 7–inch

ATLANTIC 3-5 78-79

LPs: 10/12–inch

ATLANTIC 5-10 78-79

Members: Gene Cornish; Dino Dannelli; Wally Bryson.

Also see RASCALS

Also see RASPBERRIES

FOUNDATIONS P&R '67

Singles: 7–inch

ERIC (912 "Build Me Up Buttercup") 3-4 70s
(True stereo.)

UNI 3-6 67-71

LPs: 10/12–inch

UNI 15-20 68-69

Members: Clem Curtis; Colin Young.

FOUNTAIN, Pete P&R/LP '60

Singles: 7–inch

CORAL 3-5 58-62

LPs: 10/12–inch

CORAL 5-15 59-69

FIRST AMERICAN 4-8 78

GUEST STAR 5-10 64

SOUTHLAND (215 "New Orleans to L.A.") 15-25 56

Also see HIRT, Al, & Pete Fountain

Also see LEE, Brenda, & Pete Fountain

FOUNTAIN, Roosevelt, & Pens of Rhythm P&R '63

Singles: 7–inch

PRINCE-ADAMS 10-20 62-63

FOUR ACES P&R '51

Singles: 78 rpm

DECCA 5-15 51-57

FLASH (103 "Who's to Blame") 15-25 50

MERION (104 "Wanted") 15-25 52

VICTORIA (Black vinyl) 10-15 51

VICTORIA (101 "Sin") 20-30 51
(Colored vinyl.)

Singles: 7–inch

ABC-PAR 5-10 60

DECCA (25000 series) 4-8 61-64

DECCA (27000 & 28000 series) 10-20 51-53

DECCA (29000 thru 31000 series) 5-15 54-60

FLASH (103 "Who's to Blame") 15-25 50

MERION (104 "Wanted") 10-20 52

VICTORIA (101 "Sin") 15-25 51
(Black vinyl.)

VICTORIA (101 "Sin") 40-60 51
(Colored vinyl.)

VICTORIA (102 "There's a Christmas Tree in Heaven") 15-25 51

Picture Sleeves

ABC-PAR 5-10 60

EPs: 7–inch

DECCA 10-20 52-59

LPs: 10/12–inch

ACCORD 5-10 81-82

CRANE NOTTIS 8-10 77

DECCA (4013 "Golden Hits") 15-25 60

DECCA (5429 "Four Aces") 20-40 52
(10–inch LP.)

DECCA (8122 thru 8693) 15-30 55-58

DECCA (8766 "Swingin' Aces") 15-25 58
(Monaural.)

DECCA (8766 "Swingin' Aces") 20-30 58
(Stereo. With "DL-7" prefix.)

DECCA (8855 "Hits from Broadway") 15-25 59
(Monaural.)

DECCA (8855 "Hits from Broadway") 20-30 59
(Stereo. With "DL-7" prefix.)

DECCA (8944 "Beyond the Blue Horizon") 10-20 59
(Monaural.)

DECCA (8944 "Beyond the Blue Horizon") 15-25 59
(Stereo.)

MCA 5-10 74

U.A. 10-15 61

VOCALION 5-10 69

WESTOWN 5-8

Members: Al Alberts; Louis Silvestri; Dave Mahoney; Sol Vocarro.

Also see LEE, Brenda / Bill Haley & Comets / Kalin Twins / Four Aces

FOUR ACES / Four Lads / Four Preps

LPs: 10/12–inch

EXACT 5-10 80

Also see FOUR ACES

Also see FOUR LADS

Also see FOUR PREPS

FOUR BLAZES R&B '52

Singles: 78 rpm

UNITED 10-20 52-55

Singles: 7–inch

UNITED (114 "Mary Jo") 30-50 52
(Black vinyl.)

UNITED (114 "Mary Jo") 75-100 52
(Colored vinyl.)

UNITED (125 "Night Train") 15-25 52

UNITED (127 "Stop Boogie Woogie") 15-25 52

UNITED (146 "Not Any More Tears") 15-25 53

UNITED (158 "Ella Louise") 15-25 53

UNITED (168 "My Great Love Affair") 15-25 54

UNITED (177 "Do the Do") 15-25 54

UNITED (191 "She Needs to Be Loved") 15-25 55
(Reissued as by the Blasers.)

Member: Tommy Braden.

FOUR BUDDIES
R&B '51

(With Lefty Bates Orchestra)

Singles: 78 rpm

SAVOY 50-75 50-53

Singles: 7-inch

CORAL (62217 "Hurt") 15-25 60
CORAL (62325 "The Light") 15-25 62
IMPERIAL (66018 "I Want to Be the Boy You Love") 50-75 64
PHILIPS (40122 "Lonely Summer") 10-20 63
SAVOY (769 "I Will Wait") 300-500 50
SAVOY (779 "Don't Leave Me Now") 300-500 51
SAVOY (789 "My Summer's Gone") 200-400 51
SAVOY (817 "Heart and Soul") 200-400 51
SAVOY (845 "You're Part of Me") 200-400 52
SAVOY (866 "What's the Matter with Me") 200-400 52
SAVOY (888 "My Mother's Eyes") 200-400 53
SAVOY (891 "I'd Climb the Highest Mountain") 200-400 53

Members: Leon Harrison; Greg Carroll; Bert Palmer; Tommy Smith.
Also see FOUR BUDS

FOUR BUDS

Singles: 78 rpm

SAVOY 100-200 50

Singles: 7-inch

SAVOY (769 "I Will Wait") 250-350 50
(Second pressings shown as by the Four Buddies.)
Also see FOUR BUDDIES

4 BY FOUR
P&R/R&B/LP '87

Singles: 7-inch

CAPITOL 3-4 87

Picture Sleeves

CAPITOL 3-4 87

LPs: 10/12-inch

CAPITOL 5-10 87

FOUR COINS
P&R '54

Singles: 78 rpm

EPIC 3-6 54-59

Singles: 7-inch

COLUMBIA 3-6 67
EPIC 5-10 54-59
JOY 3-6 64
JUBILEE 3-6 61-62
MGM 4-8 60-61
VEE JAY 4-8 62-63

Picture Sleeves

EPIC 5-10 57

EPs: 7-inch

EPIC 8-12 55-58

LPs: 10/12-inch

EPIC 15-25 55-58
MGM 10-15 61
ROULETTE 10-15 65

FOUR DATES
P&R '58

Singles: 7-inch

CHANCELLOR 8-12 58
Also see FABIAN

FOUR ELDORADOS: see THOSE FOUR ELDORADOS

FOUR ESQUIRES
P&R '56

Singles: 78 rpm

CADENCE 5-10 55
PARIS 10-20 57
PILGRIM 5-10 56

Singles: 7-inch

CADENCE 5-10 55
PARIS 10-15 57
PILGRIM 5-10 56
TERRACE 4-8 63
Also see ECHOES / Four Esquires

FOUR FELLOWS
R&B '55

(With the Abie Baker Orchestra)

Singles: 78 rpm

DERBY 100-200 54
GLORY 20-40 55-57

Singles: 7-inch

DERBY (862 "I Tried") 200-300 54
GLORY (231 "I Wish I Didn't Know You") 50-100 55
GLORY (234 "Soldier Boy") 50-75 55
GLORY (236 "Angels Say") 50-75 55
GLORY (238 "Fallen Angel") 50-75 56
GLORY (241 "Petticoat Baby") 50-100 56
GLORY (242 "Darling You") 50-100 56
GLORY (244 "I Sit in My Window") 50-75 56
GLORY (248 "You Don't Know Me") 50-75 56
GLORY (250 "Give Me Back My Broken Heart") 50-75 57
GLORY (263 "You're Still in My Heart") 50-75 57
NESTOR (27 "Remember") 150-250 58

Members: David Jones; Ted Williams; Larry Banks; Jim McGowan.
Also see McLAURIN, Bette

450 SL
R&B '85

Singles: 7-inch

GOLDEN BOY 3-4 85

FOUR FRESHMEN
P&R '52

Singles: 78 rpm

CAPITOL 5-10 50-57

Singles: 7-inch

CAPITOL 5-15 50-65
DECCA 4-6 67
LIBERTY 4-6 68

Picture Sleeves

CAPITOL 5-10 63

EPs: 7-inch

CAPITOL 10-20 54-59

LPs: 10/12-inch

CAPITOL (With "SM" prefix) 5-10 75-79
CAPITOL (522 thru 992) 20-40 54-58
(With "T" prefix.)
CAPITOL (1000 & 2000 series) 10-25 58-64
(With "T" or "ST" prefix.)
CREATIVE WORLD 5-10 72
LIBERTY 5-10 68-82
PHONORAMA 5-8 82
SUNSET 5-10 70

Members: Don Barbour; Ross Barbour; Ken Errair; Bob Flanagan; Hal Kratzsch; Bill Comstock; Ken Albers.

FOUR FRESHMEN / Kirby Stone Four / University Four

LPs: 10/12-inch

CORONET 5-10 60s
Also see FOUR FRESHMEN
Also see STONE, Kirby, Four

FOUR JACKS
R&B '49

Singles: 78 rpm

ALADDIN 50-75 55
ALLEN (21000 "I Challenge Your Kiss") 25-50 49
FEDERAL (12075 "You Met a Fool") 50-100 52
FEDERAL (12087 "The Last of the Good Rockin' Men") 20-40 52
GOTHAM (219 "Take Me") 25-50 50

Singles: 7-inch

ALADDIN (3274 "Tired of Your Sexy Ways") 200-300 55
FEDERAL (12075 "You Met a Fool") 500-1000 52
FEDERAL (12087 "The Last of the Good Rockin' Men") 300-500 52

FOUR JACKS / Allen Trio

Singles: 78 rpm

ALLEN (21001 "Carless Love") 25-50 49
Also see FOUR JACKS

FOUR JACKS & A JILL
P&R/LP '68

Singles: 7-inch

RCA 4-8 68

LPs: 10/12-inch

RCA 10-15 68

FOUR KNIGHTS
P&R '51

Singles: 78 rpm

CAPITOL 10-30 51-57
CORAL 10-20 49
DECCA 15-25 46-47
LANG-WORTH 10-20 40s
(16-inch transcriptions.)

Singles: 7-inch

CAPITOL (346 "Spotlight Songs") 30-50 52
(Boxed set of three singles.)
CAPITOL (1587 thru 1914) 15-30 51-52
CAPITOL (1930 thru 2517) 10-20 52-53
CAPITOL (2654 "Oh Baby Mine") 20-30 53
CAPITOL (2654 "I Get So Lonely") 8-12 53
(Note title change.)
CAPITOL (2782 thru 3730) 8-12 54-57
CORAL (61936 thru 62110) 5-10 58-59
DECCA (48018 "He'll Understand and Say Well Done") 50-75 52
SOUVENIR 4-8 62

EPs: 7-inch

CAPITOL (346 "Spotlight Songs") 50-75 52
(Two-EP set.)
CAPITOL (414 "The Four Knights Sing") 40-60 53
CAPITOL (506 "I Get So Lonely") 40-60 54

LPs: 10/12-inch

CAPITOL (H-346 "Spotlight Songs") 100-200 52
(10-inch LP.)
CAPITOL (T-346 "Spotlight Songs") 100-200 55
CORAL (57221 "Four Knights") 50-100 58
CORAL (57309 "Million Dollar Baby") 30-60 60
(Monaural.)
CORAL (757309 "Million Dollar Baby") 50-75 60
(Stereo.)

Members: Gene Alford; John Wallace; Clarence Dixon; Oscar Broadway.
Also see COLE, Nat "King"
Also see HUNT, Pee Wee

FOUR LADS
P&R '52

Singles: 78 rpm

COLUMBIA 4-8 52-58
OKEH 4-8 52

Singles: 7-inch

COLUMBIA 10-20 52-60
DOT 4-8 62
FONA 3-5 77-78
KAPP 5-10 60-61
OKEH 5-10 52
U.A. 4-6 63-69

Picture Sleeves

COLUMBIA 10-15 56-59
KAPP 5-10 60

EPs: 7-inch

COLUMBIA 5-15 55-59

LPs: 10/12-inch

AC 8-10
COLUMBIA (912 "On the Sunny Side") 20-30 56
COLUMBIA (1045 "The Four Lads Sing Frank Loesser") 20-30 57
COLUMBIA (1111 "Four on the Aisle") 15-25 58
(Monaural.)
COLUMBIA (1223 "Breezin' Along") 15-25 58
(Monaural.)
COLUMBIA (1235 "Greatest Hits") 15-25 58
COLUMBIA (1299 thru 1550) 10-20 59-60
(Monaural.)
COLUMBIA (2576 "Stage Show") 20-30 56
(10-inch LP.)
COLUMBIA (6329 "Stage Show") 25-40 54
(10-inch LP.)

COLUMBIA (8035 "Breezin' Along")....20-30 58
(Stereo.)
COLUMBIA (8047 "Four on the Aisle")....20-30 58
(Stereo.)
COLUMBIA (8106 thru 8350)....15-25 59-60
(Stereo.)
DOT....10-15 62-63
ENCORE....5-8 86
FONA....8-12 76-77
KAPP....10-15 61
HARMONY....5-10 69
U.A. 8-12 64
VIKING....5-10
Members: Frankie Busseri; Jimmy Arnold; Connie Coderini; Bernie Toorish.
Also see FOUR ACES / Four Lads / Four Preps
Also see LAINE, Frankie, & Four Lads
Also see RAY, Johnnie

FOUR LOVERS *P&R '56*

Singles: 78 rpm

EPIC (9255 "My Life for Your Love")....250-300 57
RCA....15-30 56-57

Singles: 7-inch

EPIC (9255 "My Life for Your Love")....250-300 57
MAGIC CARPET....3-5
RCA (6518 "You're the Apple of My Eye")....25-35 56
RCA (6519 "Honey Love")....25-35 56
RCA (6646 "Jambalaya")....15-25 56
RCA (6768 "Happy Am I")....15-25 57
RCA (6812 "Shake a Hand")....20-30 57
RCA (6819 "Night Train")....15-25 57

EPs: 7-inch

RCA (869 "Four Lovers")....150-200 56
RCA (871 "Joyride")....400-500 56

LPs: 10/12-inch

RCA (1317 "Joyride")....500-750 56
Members: Frankie Valli; Tom Devito; Nick Devito; Hank Majewski.
Also see 4 SEASONS
Also see VALLI, Frankie

FOUR LOVERS / Homer & Jethro

EPs: 7-inch

RCA (47 "The Four Lovers / Homer & Jethro")....30-50 56
(Promotional only. Not issued with cover.)
Also see HOMER & JETHRO

FOUR LOVERS / Teddi King

EPs: 7-inch

RCA (64 "The Four Lovers / Teddi King")....30-50 56
(Promotional only. Not issued with cover.)

FOUR MINTS *R&B '73*

Singles: 7-inch

CAPSOUL....8-15 73
HOLIDAY....10-20 73

LPs: 10/12-inch

CAPSOUL....10-20 73

FOUR PENNIES *P&R '63*

Singles: 7-inch

LAURIE....3-5
RUST (5070 "When the Boy's Happy")....15-25 63
RUST (5071 "My Block")....15-25 63
Members: Judy Craig; Barbara Lee; Patricia Bennett; Sylvia Peterson.
Also see CHIFFONS

FOUR PREPS *P&R '56*

Singles: 78 rpm

CAPITOL....5-10 56-57

Singles: 7-inch

CAPITOL (3576 thru 5074, except 4568)....5-10 56-63
CAPITOL (4568 "Dream Boy, Dream")....20-30 61
CAPITOL (5143 "A Letter to the Beatles")....15-25 64
CAPITOL (5178 thru 5921)....4-8 64-67

Picture Sleeves

CAPITOL....8-12 61-62

EPs: 7-inch

CAPITOL (862 "Dreamy Eyes")....10-20 56
CAPITOL (994 "Four Preps")....10-20 57
CAPITOL (1015 "26 Miles")....10-20 58

LPs: 10/12-inch

CAPITOL....15-30 58-67
Members: Bruce Belland; Glen Larson; Marv Ingraham; Ed Cobb; Don Clarke.
Also see FOUR ACES / Four Lads / Four Preps
Also see KINGSTON TRIO / Four Preps

4 SEASONS *P&R/R&B/LP '62*

(Four Seasons; Frankie Valli & 4 Seasons)

Singles: 7-inch

AURAVISION (6724 "Big Man's World")....20-30 64
(Cardboard flexi-disc, one of six by six different artists. Columbia Record Club "Enrollment Premium." Set came in a special paper sleeve.)
BOB CREWE PRESENTS....10-15 70
(Promotional issue only.)
COLLECTABLES (Except 9)....3-4 81
COLLECTABLES (9 "Greatest Hits")....30-40 81
(Boxed, six-disc set. Colored vinyl.)
CREWE (333 "And That Reminds Me")....4-8 69
GONE (5122 "Bermuda")....35-55 61
MCA/CURB....3-5 85-86
MOTOWN....5-10 73
MOWEST....5-10 72
OLDIES 45....5-10 62-63
PHILIPS (40166 thru 40662)....5-10 64-69
PHILIPS (40688 "Lay Me Down")....15-25 70
PHILIPS (40694 "Where Are My Dreams")....20-25 70
PHILIPS DOUBLE-HIT....4-8
RAINBOW....5-10 62
SEASONS....3-5 75
SEASONS 4-EVER (Black vinyl)....4-6 71
SEASONS 4-EVER (Colored vinyl)....10-15 71
VEE JAY (456 thru 562)....10-15 62-63
VEE JAY (576 "Stay"/"Peanuts")....40-50 63
VEE JAY (582 "Stay"/"Goodnight My Love")....10-15 64
VEE JAY (597 "Alone")....10-20 64
(Yellow label.)
VEE JAY (597 "Alone")....8-12 64
(Black label.)
VEE JAY (597 "Alone")....5-10 64
(Multi-color label.)
VEE JAY (608 thru 719)....10-15 64-66
VEE JAY (901 "Peanuts")....100-150 63
(Single-sided. Promotional issue only.)
WABC RADIO (77 "Cousin Brucie Go Go")....75-125 64
(Special products custom pressing. Colored vinyl.)
WXYZ-DETROIT (121003 "Jody Reynolds' Theme")....50-75 65
(Special products custom pressing.)
W.B. 3-5 75-80
WIBBAGE (WIBG "Jody Reynolds' Theme")....50-75 65
(Special products custom pressing.)

Picture Sleeves

CREWE (333 "And That Reminds Me")....10-15 69
PHILIPS (Except 40542)....10-20 64-70
PHILIPS (40542 "Saturday's Father")....20-30 68
(Fold-out sleeve.)
PHILIPS (40542 "Saturday's Father")....5-10 68
(Standard sleeve.)
PHILIPS DOUBLE-HIT....4-8
VEE JAY (539 "Candy Girl")....40-60 64
VEE JAY (597 "Alone")....40-60 64
VEE JAY (626 "I Saw Mommy Kissing Santa Claus")....25-35 64

EPs: 7-inch

MAGIC CARPET....4-8
PHILIPS (2705 "Edizone D'Oro")....20-30 68
(Juke box issue.)
VEE JAY (901 "Peanuts + 3")....20-35 64
VEE JAY (902 "Alone + 3")....20-35 64

LPs: 10/12-inch

ARISTA....8-12 84
CANDLELITE (151 "Complete Musical Treasury")....35-45 82
(Boxed, five-disc set.)
CANDLELITE (151B "Souvenirs in Gold")....10-15 82
(Bonus LP, offered to buyers of the above set.)
ERA....5-10 82
FBI....10-15 84
GUEST STAR (1481 "Bermuda & Spanish Lace")....15-20 64
(Also has tracks by the Barrons, a.k.a. the Crescendos.)
KOALA....5-10 80
K-TEL....15-20 77
LONGINES (95833 "Greatest Hits of Frankie Valli & the 4 Seasons")....25-35
(Boxed, four-disc set. TV mail-order offer.)
LONGINES (95833 "Greatest Hits of Frankie Valli & the 4 Seasons")....20-30
(Gatefold, four-disc set. TV mail-order offer.)
MCA....5-10 85
MCA/CURB....5-10 88
MOTOWN....5-10 80
MOWEST....10-12 72
PHILIPS (2-6501 "Edizone D'Oro")....20-25 68
(With either red or blue cover.)
PHILIPS (200124 "Dawn and 11 Other Great Hits")....15-20 64
(Monaural.)
PHILIPS (200129 "Born to Wander") 15-20 64
(Monaural.)
PHILIPS (200146 "Rag Doll")....15-20 64
(Monaural.)
PHILIPS (200164 "The 4 Seasons Entertain You")....15-20 65
(Monaural.)
PHILIPS (200193 "Big Hits by Burt Bacharach, Hal David & Bob Dylan")....50-65 65
(Photos of group on front and back cover. Monaural.)
PHILIPS (200193 "Big Hits by Burt Bacharach, Hal David & Bob Dylan")....15-20 65
(No group photos on cover. Monaural.)
PHILIPS (200196 "Gold Vault of Hits")....15-20 65
(Monaural.)
PHILIPS (200201 "Working My Way Back to You")....15-20 66
(Monaural.)
PHILIPS (200221 "2nd Gold Vault of Hits")....15-20 66
(Monaural.)
PHILIPS (200222 "Lookin' Back")....15-20 66
(Monaural.)
PHILIPS (200223 "Christmas Album")....15-25 66
(Stereo.)
PHILIPS (200243 "New Gold Hits")....15-20 67
(Monaural.)
PHILIPS (600124 "Dawn and 11 Other Great Hits")....15-20 64
(Stereo.)
PHILIPS (600129 "Born to Wander") 15-20 64
(Stereo.)
PHILIPS (600146 "Rag Doll")....15-20 64
(Stereo.)
PHILIPS (600164 "The 4 Seasons Entertain You")....15-20 65
(Stereo.)
PHILIPS (600193 "Big Hits by Burt Bacharach, Hal David & Bob Dylan")....50-65 65
(Photos of group on front and back cover. Stereo.)
PHILIPS (600193 "Big Hits by Burt Bacharach, Hal David & Bob Dylan")....15-20 65
(No group photos on cover. Stereo.)

PHILIPS (600196 "Gold Vault of Hits")....15-20 65
(Stereo.)
PHILIPS (600201 "Working My Way Back to You")....15-20 66
(Stereo.)
PHILIPS (600221 "2nd Gold Vault of Hits")....15-20 66
(Stereo.)
PHILIPS (600222 "Lookin' Back")....15-20 66
(Stereo.)
PHILIPS (600223 "Christmas Album")....15-25 66
(Stereo.)
PHILIPS (600243 "New Gold Hits")....15-20 67
(Stereo.)
PHILIPS (600290 "Genuine Imitation Life Gazette")....35-45 69
(Yellow cover.)
PHILIPS (600290 "Genuine Imitation Life Gazette")....10-15 69
(White cover.)
PHILIPS (600341 "Half and Half")....10-15 70
PICKWICK....8-10 70
PRIORITY....8-10 86
PRIVATE STOCK....10-12 75
RHINO (Except 72998)....6-12
RHINO (72998 "25th Anniversary")....15-25 87
(Four-disc set.)
SEARS (609 "Brotherhood of Man")....20-30 70
TIME-LIFE (15 "Rock & Roll Era")....15-20 87
VEE JAY (1053 "Sherry")....30-40 62
(Monaural.)
VEE JAY (1053 "Sherry")....50-75 62
(Stereo.)
VEE JAY (1055 "Four Seasons Greetings")....30-40 62
VEE JAY (1056 "Big Girls Don't Cry")....30-40 63
VEE JAY (1059 "Ain't That a Shame")....30-40 63
VEE JAY (1065 "Golden Hits")....30-40 63
VEE JAY (1082 "Folk-Nanny")....40-50 64
VEE JAY (1082 "Stay and Other Great Hits")....20-30 64
(Repackage of *Folk-Nanny*.)
VEE JAY (1088 "More Golden Hits")....25-35 64
VEE JAY (1121 "We Love Girls")....25-35 64
VEE JAY (1154 "Recorded Live on Stage")....25-35 65
WCI (502 "Silver Anniversary")....15-25 85
(Three-disc set.)
W.B.....8-12 75-81
Members: Frankie Valli; Tom Devito; Nick Devito; Hank Majewski; Bob Gaudio; Charlie Calello; Nick Massi; Joe Long; Don Ciccione; Bill Deloach; Paul Wilson; Jerry Corbetta.
Also see BEACH BOYS with Frankie Valli & 4 Seasons
Also see BEATLES / 4 Seasons
Also see CRESCENDOS
Also see CREWE, Bob
Also see FOUR LOVERS
Also see JAN & DEAN / Roy Orbison / 4 Seasons / Shirelles
Also see RASCALS / Buggs / Four Seasons / Johnny Rivers
Also see RIVERS, Johnny / 4 Seasons / Jerry Butler / Jimmy Soul
Also see ROYAL TEENS
Also see SANTOS, Larry
Also see SIMON, Paul
Also see VALLI, Frankie
Also see WONDER WHO

4 SEASONS / Connie Francis / Barbara Brown & Buggs

LPs: 10/12-inch

CORONET (244 "At the Hop")....15-25 64
PREMIER (9052 "At the Hop")....15-25
Also see FRANCIS, Connie

4 SEASONS / Little Royal

Singles: 7-inch

GORDA....4-8 65

4 SEASONS / Scarlets

Singles: 7-inch

OLDIES 45....5-10 63

4 SEASONS / Neil Sedaka / J Brothers / Johnny Rivers

LP: 10/12-inch

DESIGN....10-20 60s

4 SEASONS / Ray Stevens

Singles: 7-inch

OLDIES 45....5-10 63
Also see 4 SEASONS
Also see STEVENS, Ray

FOUR SONICS *P&R/R&B '68*

Singles: 7-inch

SPORT (110 "You Don't Have to Say You Love Me")....6-12 68
SPORT (111 "Easier Said Than Done")....10-15 68
Members: Eddy Daniels; James Johnson; Steve Gaston; Willie Frazier.

FOUR SPORTSMEN *P&R '61*

Singles: 7-inch

SUNNYBROOK (1 "Surrender")....30-50 60
SUNNYBROOK (2 "Lucille")....15-25 61
SUNNYBROOK (4 "Pitter Patter")....15-25 61
SUNNYBROOK (5 "Sixty Minute Man")....15-25 61
SUNNYBROOK (6 "If Your Heart Can Take It")....20-30 61

FOUR TOPS *P&R/R&B '64*

Singles: 12-inch

ABC....4-8 77-78
MOTOWN....4-8 80

Singles: 78 rpm

CHESS (1623 "Could It be You")....75-125 56

Singles: 7-inch

ABC/DUNHILL....3-5 75-79
ARISTA....3-4 88
CASABLANCA....3-4 81-82
CHESS (1623 "Could It be You")....100-200 56
COLUMBIA (41755 "Lonely Summer")....50-75 60
COLUMBIA (43356 "Lonely Summer")....15-25 65
DUNHILL....3-5 72-74
MOTOWN (Colored vinyl)....8-12 70
(Promotional issue only.)
MOTOWN (400 series)....3-4
MOTOWN (1062 thru 1254)....5-10 64-72
MOTOWN (1706 thru 1854)....3-4 83-86
MOTOWN/TOPPS (5 "I Can't Help Myself")....50-75 67
(Topps Chewing Gum promotional item. Single-sided, cardboard flexi, six-inch picture disc. Issued with generic paper sleeve.)
MOTOWN/TOPPS (9 "Baby I Need Your Loving")....50-75 67
(Topps Chewing Gum promotional item. Single-sided, cardboard flexi, six-inch picture disc. Issued with generic paper sleeve.)
RSO....3-4 82
RELIANT....3-4 88
RIVERSIDE (4534 "Pennies from Heaven")....50-75 62

Picture Sleeves

ARISTA....3-4 88
MOTOWN (1073 "Ask the Lonely")....50-75 64
MOTOWN (1098 "Reach Out I'll Be There")....20-40 66
MOTOWN (1164 "It's All in the Game")....8-10 70
MOTOWN (1175 "Just Seven Numbers")....8-10 71
RSO....3-5 82

EPs: 7-inch

MOTOWN (60647 "On Top")....25-50 66

LPs: 10/12-inch

ABC....8-10 75-78
ARISTA....5-8 88
CASABLANCA....5-10 81-82
COMMAND....10-12 74
DUNHILL....8-10 72-74
GORDY....5-10 85
MOTOWN (100 & 200 series)....5-10 82-84
MOTOWN (622 "Four Tops")....20-30 64
MOTOWN (634 "Second Album")....15-25 65
MOTOWN (647 "On Top")....15-20 66
MOTOWN (654 "Live")....15-25 66
MOTOWN (662 "Greatest Hits")....12-20 67
MOTOWN (669 "Yesterday's Dream")....12-20 68
MOTOWN (675 thru 748)....10-20 69-72
MOTOWN (764 "Best of the Four Tops")....10-15 73
MOTOWN (6000 series)....5-8 83-86
MOTOWN (9809 "Anthology")....15-20 74
MOTOWN (M9809 "Anthology")....10-15 86
PICKWICK....5-8 74
NATURAL RESOURCES....8-10 78
WORKSHOP (217 "Breaking Through")....1000-1500 62
WORKSHOP (217 "Jazz Impressions by the Four Tops")....500-1000 62
(Retitled reissue.)
Members: Levi Stubbs; Lawrence Payton; Abdul "Duke" Fakir; Obie Benson.
Also see CARROLL, Delores, & Four Tops
Also see FOUR AIMS
Also see HAYES, Carolyn, & Four Tops
Also see HOLLAND - DOZIER
Also see PAYTON, Lawrence
Also see SUPREMES & Four Tops

FOUR TOPS / Temptations

LPs: 10/12-inch

SILVER EAGLE....6-10 87
Also see FOUR TOPS
Also see TEMPTATIONS

FOUR TUNES *P&R/R&B '53*

("Featuring Jimmie Nabbie")

Singles: 78 rpm

ARCO....5-15 50
COLUMBIA....5-15 48
JUBILEE....10-20 53-57
MANOR....10-20 46-49
RCA....10-20 49-53

Singles: 7-inch

CROSBY (3 "Never Look Down")....15-20 60
CROSBY (4 "Twinkle Eyes")....25-35 60
(Colored vinyl.)
JUBILEE (5128 "Marie")....25-50 53
JUBILEE (5132 "I Understand")....20-30 54
JUBILEE (5135 "My Wild Irish Rose")....10-20 54
JUBILEE (5152 "Lonesome")....10-20 54
JUBILEE (5165 "Don't Cry Darling")....20-30 54
JUBILEE (5174 "Let Me Go Lover")....20-30 54
JUBILEE (5183 "I Close My Eyes")....20-30 55
JUBILEE (5200 "Time Out for Tears")....20-30 55
JUBILEE (5212 "Brooklyn Bridge")....10-20 55
JUBILEE (5218 "You Are My Love")....10-20 55
JUBILEE (5232 "Our Love")....10-20 56
JUBILEE (5239 "I Gotta Go")....10-20 56
JUBILEE (5245 "Far Away Places")....10-20 56
JUBILEE (5255 "The Ballad of James Dean")....20-30 56
JUBILEE (5276 "Cool Water")....10-20 57
JUBILEE (6000 "Marie")....5-10 59
KAY-RON (1000 "I Want to Be Loved")....25-50 54
KAY-RON (1005 "I Understand")....25-50 54
RCA (0008 "You're Heartless")....150-250 49
(Colored vinyl.)
RCA (0016 "My Last Affair")....150-250 49
(Colored vinyl.)
RCA (0042 "I'm Just a Fool in Love")....150-250 49
(Colored vinyl.)
RCA (0072 "Am I Blue")....100-200 50
(Colored vinyl.)

RCA (0085 "Old Fashioned Love") 100-200 50
(Colored vinyl.)
RCA (0131 "May That Day Never Come") 100-150 51
RCA (3881 "Do I Worry") 50-75 50
RCA (3967 "Cool Water") 50-75 50
RCA (4102 "Wishing You Were Here Tonight") 40-60 51
RCA (4241 "I Married an Angel") 40-60 51
RCA (4280 "It's No Sin") 40-60 51
RCA (4305 "Early in the Morning") 40-60 51
RCA (4427 "I'll See You in My Dreams") 40-60 51
RCA (4489 "Come What May") 20-40 52
RCA (4663 "I Wonder") 20-40 52
RCA (4828 "They Don't Understand") 20-40 52
RCA (4968 "I Don't Want to Set the World on Fire") 25-50 52
RCA (5532 "Don't Get Around Much Anymore") 25-50 53
VIRGO 3-5 72

EPs: 7-inch

RCA (586 "Four Tunes") 100-150 54

LPs: 10/12-inch

JUBILEE (1039 "12 x 4") 100-200 57
Members: Jim Nabbie; Danny Owens; William "Pat" Best; Jimmy Gordon; Deek Watson.
Also see CHURCHILL, Savannah

FOUR TUNES / Shadows

LPs: 10/12-inch

CHICAGO 8-10 88
Also see FOUR TUNES

FOUR VAGABONDS — P&R/R&B '43

Singles: 78 rpm

APOLLO 15-25 46-47
ATLAS 15-25 46
BLUEBIRD 20-30 42-43
LLOYDS (102 "PS I Love You") 50-100 53
MERCURY 15-25 46
MIRACLE 15-25 49

Singles: 7-inch

LLOYDS (102 "PS I Love You") 250-350 53

EPs: 7-inch

LLOYDS (706 "Four Vagabonds") 300-500 54
Members: Johnny Jordan; Robert O'Neal; Ray Grant; Norval Taborn.
Also see VAGABONDS

FOUR VOICES — P&R '56

Singles: 78 rpm

COLUMBIA 5-10 55-57

Singles: 7-inch

ABC-PAR 5-10 61
COLUMBIA 8-15 55-60
PEACOCK 5-10 62
VOICE (1112 "Your Love Is Getting Stronger") 10-20
VOICE (1113 "Summer Kind of Love") 10-20

FOUR WINDS

(4 Winds; Tokens)

Singles: 7-inch

B.T. PUPPY 5-10 69
CRYSTAL BALL 4-8 77
SWING 10-20 64
Also see TOKENS

FOUR-EVERS — P&R '64

(Four Evers)

Singles: 7-inch

CHATTAHOOCHEE 4-8 64
COLUMBIA (42303 "You Belong to Me") 30-50 62
COLUMBIA (42303 "You Belong to Me") 75-100 62
(With "3" prefix. Compact 33 Single.)
COLUMBIA (43886 "A Lovely Way to Spend an Evening") 5-10 66
CONSTELLATION 10-15 65
CRYSTAL BALL 4-8
JAMIE 5-10 63
JASON SCOTT 4-8
RED BIRD 10-15 66
SMASH (1853 "It's Love") 10-15 63
SMASH (1887 "Please Be Mine") 10-20 63
SMASH (1887 "Be My Girl") 10-20 64
(Same selection number used on both issues above.)
SMASH (1921 "Doo Be Dum") 10-15 63

LPs: 10/12-inch

MAGIC CARPET 8-10

FOURPLAY — LP '91

LPs: 10/12-inch

W.B. 5-8 91
Members: Bob James; Lee Ritenour; Harvey Mason; Nathan East.
Also see JAMES, Bob
Also see RITENOUR, Lee

FOWLEY, Kim — LP '69

Singles: 7-inch

CAPITOL 4-6 72-73
CREATIVE FAMILY 15-25
IMPERIAL 5-10 68-69
LIVING LEGEND 10-15 65-66
LOMA 5-10 66
ORIGINAL SOUND 4-8 60s
REPRISE 5-10 67
TOWER 5-10 67

LPs: 10/12-inch

CAPITOL (11075 "I'm Bad") 15-25 72
CAPITOL (11159 "International Heroes") 10-20 73
CAPITOL (11248 "Automatic") 10-20 74
IMPERIAL (12413 "Born to Be Wild") 15-25 68
IMPERIAL (12423 "Outrageous") 15-25 69
IMPERIAL (12443 "Good Clean Fun") 15-20 69
PVC (7906 "Sunset Boulevard") 8-12 79
TOWER (5080 "Love Is Alive and Well") 25-30 67
Also see KING LIZARD
Also see PAUL & VICTORS / Kim Fowley

FOX — P&R '75

(Noosha Fox)

Singles: 7-inch

ARIOLA/GTO 3-5 75
GTO 3-5 74

LPs: 10/12-inch

ARIOLA AMERICA 8-10 75

FOX, Charles — P&R '81

Singles: 7-inch

HANDSHAKE 3-4 81

FOX, Samantha — P&R/LP '86

Singles: 12-inch

JIVE 4-6 86

Singles: 7-inch

JIVE 3-4 86-89

Picture Sleeves

JIVE 3-4 86-89

LPs: 10/12-inch

JIVE 5-10 86-88

FOX, Virgil — LP '71

LPs: 10/12-inch

DECCA 10-12 71

FOXX, Inez — P&R/R&B '63

(With Charlie Foxx)

Singles: 7-inch

DYNAMO 4-6 67-70
LANA 3-6 60s
MUSICOR 4-8 66-68
SUE 4-8 65
SYMBOL 5-10 63-64
VOLT 3-5 72-73
U.A. 3-5 74

LPs: 10/12-inch

DYNAMO 10-15 67
SUE (1037 "Inez & Charlie Foxx") 20-40 65
(Monaural.)
SUE (1037 "Inez & Charlie Foxx") 25-50 65
(Stereo.)
SYMBOL (4400 "Mockingbird") 100-150 63
VOLT 8-10 73
Also see PLATTERS / Inez & Charlie Foxx / Jive Five / Tommy Hunt

FOXX, Redd — LP '72

(With Hattie Noel)

Singles: 78 rpm

DOOTO (Except 416) 5-10 57
DOOTO (416 "Real Pretty Mama") 10-15 57
DOOTONE 3-5 56-57
SAVOY 5-10 46

Singles: 7-inch

DOOTO (Except 416) 5-10 57-61
DOOTO (416 "Real Pretty Mama") 15-25 57
DOOTONE 8-12 56-57

EPs: 7-inch

DOOTO 5-10 57-61
DOOTONE 5-10 56-57

LPs: 10/12-inch

ATLANTIC 5-10 75
AUTHENTIC 15-25 55-56
DOOTO 5-15 60-74
DOOTONE 10-20 57
KING 5-10 69-71
LAFF 5-10 79
LOMA 8-12 66-68
MF 5-8
RCA 5-10 72
W.B. 8-10 69

FOZZIE BEAR: see KERMIT / Fozzie Bear

FRAMPTON, Peter — LP '72

Singles: 7-inch

A&M (Except 1988) 3-5 74-81
A&M (1988 "Tried to Love") 3-6 77
(With Mick Jagger.)
A&M (1988 "Tried to Love") 10-15 77
(White label, promotional issue.)
ATLANTIC 3-4 86

Picture Sleeves

A&M (Except 1988) 3-5 74-81
A&M (1988 "Tried to Love") 4-6 77
ATLANTIC 3-4 86

LPs: 10/12-inch

A&M (3000 & 4000 series) 6-12 72-82
ATLANTIC 5-10 86-89

Promotional LPs

A&M (3703 "Frampton Comes Alive") 10-15 79
(Picture disc.)
A&M (4704 "I'm in You") 15-25 77
(Picture disc. Promotional issue only.)
ATLANTIC (848 "Frampton Is Alive") 8-15 86
Also see FRAMPTON'S CAMEL
Also see JAGGER, Mick
Also see STARR, Ringo

FRAMPTON'S CAMEL

(Peter Frampton)

Singles: 7-inch

A&M 5-10 72-73

LPs: 10/12-inch

A&M 10-20 73
Also see FRAMPTON, Peter
Also see HUMBLE PIE

FRANCE JOLI: see JOLI, France

FRANCHI, Sergio — LP '62

(With Anna Moffo)

Singles: 7-inch

LAX 3-4 79
METROMEDIA 3-4 71-72
RCA 3-6 62-67
U.A. 3-5 69-70

LPs: 10/12-inch

FOUR CORNERS 6-10 66
RCA 5-15 62-77
U.A. 5-10 70

FRANCIS, Connie — P&R/R&B '58

Singles: 78 rpm

MGM 10-30 55-58

Singles: 7-inch

GSF 3-5 73
IVANHOE 3-5 70s

MGM CELEBRITY SCENE (CS6-5 "Connie Francis") 30-40 66
(Boxed, five-disc set with bio insert and title strips.)
MGM (9 "Rock-a-Bye Your Baby with a Dixie Melody") 20-30 60
(Stereo.)
MGM (10 "I Almost Lost My Mind") 20-30 60
(Stereo.)
MGM (3000 series) 3-5 71
MGM (12015 "Freddy") 25-50 55
MGM (12056 "Oh, Please Make Him Jealous") 25-50 55
MGM (12122 thru 12555) 15-25 55-57
MGM (12588 thru 13116) 5-15 58-63
MGM (13127 thru 14091 except 13550) 5-10 64-69
MGM (13550 "A Nurse in the U.S. Army Corp") 20-25 66
(Promotional issue only.)
MGM (14500 series) 3-5 81
MGM (50117 "My Happiness") 20-30 58
(Stereo.)
MGM (50129 "You're Gonna Miss Me") 20-30 59
(Stereo.)
MGM (50133 "Among My Souvenirs") 20-30 59
(Stereo.)
POLYDOR 3-4 83

Picture Sleeves

MGM (12000 series except 12738) 5-15 58-61
MGM (12738 "My Happiness") 10-15 58
(Pink sleeve.)
MGM (12738 "My Happiness") 15-25 58
(Black and white sleeve.)
MGM (13000 series, except 13505 & 13773) 5-10 61-68
MGM (13505 "Empty Chapel") 10-20 66
MGM (13773 "My Heart Cries for You") 10-20 67
MGM (14000 series, except 14058 & 14091) 3-6 68-69
MGM (14058 "Gone Like the Wind") 10-20 69
MGM (14091 "Mr. Love") 10-20 69

EPs: 7-inch 33/45

MGM 10-20 58-62

LPs: 10/12-inch

LEO 12-15 60s
LION/METRO ("Fun Songs for Children") 40-50 60s
(This reissue of MGM 4023 may be on either Lion or Metro. Selection number not known.)
MGM (100 series) 10-15 70
MGM (E-3686 "Who's Sorry Now") 30-40 58
(Yellow label. Monaural.)
MGM (SE-3686 "Who's Sorry Now") 15-25 60
(Reprocessed stereo.)
MGM (E-3761 "Exciting Connie Francis") 25-35 58
(Yellow label. Monaural.)
MGM (SE-3761 "Exciting Connie Francis") 30-40 58
(Yellow label. Stereo.)
MGM (E-3776 thru E-3969) 20-30 60-61
(Monaural.)
MGM (SE-3776 thru SE-3969) 20-35 60-61
(Monaural.)
MGM (E-4000 series, except E-4023) 15-25 62-68
(Monaural.)
MGM (SE-4000 series) 15-30 62-69
(Stereo.)
MGM (E-4023 "Fun Songs for Children") 50-70 61
MGM (5400 series) 5-10
MGM (10000 series) 8-12 71
MGM (90000 series) 10-15 60s
(Capitol Record Club series.)
MATI-MOR (8002 "Brylcreem Presents Sing Along with Connie Francis") 10-20 61
(Promotional issue, made for Brylcreem.)
METRO 10-15 65-66
MGM/SESSIONS 10-12 75
POLYDOR 5-10 83
SUFFOLK 8-12
Session: Jordanaires; Boots Randolph.
Also see CRAMER, Floyd
Also see 4 SEASONS / Connie Francis / Barbara Brown & Buggs
Also see RANDOLPH, Boots

FRANCIS, Connie, & Marvin Rainwater

Singles: 78 rpm

MGM (12555 "Majesty of Love") 10-20 57

Singles: 7-inch

MGM (12555 "Majesty of Love") 15-25 57
Also see FRANCIS, Connie
Also see RAINWATER, Marvin

FRANCIS, Connie, & Hank Williams Jr.

LPs: 10/12-inch

MGM (4251 "Great Country Favorites") 15-25 64
Also see FRANCIS, Connie
Also see WILLIAMS, Hank, Jr.

FRANKE & KNOCKOUTS *P&R/LP '81*

Singles: 7-inch

MCA 3-4 84
MILLENNIUM 3-4 81-82

LPs: 10/12-inch

MCA 5-10 84
MILLENNIUM 5-10 81-82

FRANKIE & SPINDELS *R&B '68*

(Franky & Spindles)

Singles: 7-inch

CANYON 3-5
FUNNY 4-8
ROC-KER 4-8 68

FRANKIE GOES TO HOLLYWOOD *P&R/D&D/LP '84*

Singles: 12-inch

ISLAND 4-6 84-86

Singles: 7-inch

ISLAND 3-4 84-86

Picture Sleeves

ISLAND 3-4 84-85

LPs: 10/12-inch

ISLAND 5-10 84-86
Members: Holly Johnson; Paul Rutherford.
Also see JOHNSON, Holly

FRANKLIN, Aretha *R&B '60*

(With Rev. C.L. Franklin.)

Singles: 78 rpm

CHECKER 10-20 57

Singles: 12-inch

ARISTA 4-8 84-86

Singles: 7-inch

ARISTA 3-5 80-91
ATLANTIC (2000 series) 3-6 67-74
ATLANTIC (3000 series) 3-4 74-79
ATLANTIC (13000 series) 3-4
BATTLE (45000 series) 4-6 62
CHECKER (800 series) 10-20 57
CHECKER (900 series) 8-12 60
COLUMBIA (Except 44000 series) 5-10 60-67
COLUMBIA (44000 series) 3-6 67-68
CHESS 3-5 73

Picture Sleeves

ARISTA 3-4 85-87
COLUMBIA 5-10 62-63

EPs: 7-inch

ATLANTIC (8176 "Lady Soul") 10-20 68
(Stereo. Juke box issue only.)
ATLANTIC (33093 "Let It Be") 10-15 70
(Promotional issue only.)
COLUMBIA 10-15 64
(Juke box issues.)

LPs: 10/12-inch

ARISTA 5-10 80-89
ATLANTIC (Except "QD" series) 8-15 67-79
ATLANTIC ("QD" series) 15-20 73
(Quadrophonic.)
BATTLE 5-15
CANDLELITE 8-10 77
CHECKER 15-20 65
COLUMBIA (12 "Aretha Franklin") 10-15 68
COLUMBIA (1612 thru 2281) 12-25 61-64
(Monaural.)
COLUMBIA (2300 thru 2700 series) 10-20 65-67
(Monaural.)
COLUMBIA (8402 thru 9081) 15-30 61-64
(With "CS" prefix. Stereo.)
COLUMBIA (9100 thru 9700 series) 10-15 65-69
(With "CS" prefix. Stereo.)
COLUMBIA (10000 series) 5-10 73
COLUMBIA (30000 series) 5-10 72-82
HARMONY 10-12 68-71
UPFRONT 5-10 79
Also see CLEMONS, Clarence
Also see EURYTHMICS & Aretha Franklin
Also see SANTANA
Also see SIMON, Paul
Also see SWEET INSPIRATIONS
Also see WOLF, Peter

FRANKLIN, Aretha, & George Benson *P&R/R&B '81*

Singles: 7-inch

ARISTA 3-4 81

Picture Sleeves

ARISTA 3-4 81
Also see BENSON, George

FRANKLIN, Aretha, & James Cleveland & Southern California Community Choir

EPs: 7-inch

ATLANTIC (1025 "Amazing Grace") 4-8 72
(Promotional issue only.)

LPs: 10/12-inch

ATLANTIC 6-10 72

FRANKLIN, Aretha, & Larry Graham

Singles: 7-inch

ARISTA 3-4 87
Also see GRAHAM, Larry

FRANKLIN, Aretha, & Whitney Houston *P&R '89*

Singles: 7-inch

ARISTA 3-4 89

Picture Sleeves

ARISTA 3-4 89
Also see HOUSTON, Whitney

FRANKLIN, Aretha, & Elton John *P&R '89*

Singles: 7-inch

ARISTA 3-4 89

Picture Sleeves

ARISTA 3-4 89
Also see JOHN, Elton

FRANKLIN, Aretha, & George Michael *P&R/R&B '87*

Singles: 7-inch

ARISTA 3-4 87

Picture Sleeves

ARISTA 3-4 87
Also see MICHAEL, George

FRANKLIN, Aretha / Union Gap / Blood, Sweat & Tears / Moby Grape

EPs: 7-inch

COLUMBIA (791 "The Tipalet Experience") 15-25 68
(Columbia Special Products issue for Tipalet cigars.)
Also see BLOOD, SWEAT & TEARS
Also see FRANKLIN, Aretha
Also see MOBY GRAPE
Also see PUCKETT, Gary

FRANKLIN, Bobby *R&B '75*

(With Insanity; with Friends)

Singles: 7-inch

BABYLON 3-5 75

COLUMBIA....3-5 76
FEE....3-5
LAKESIDE....3-5 72
THOMAS....4-8 69

FRANKLIN, Carolyn R&B '69

Singles: 7-inch

RCA....3-5 69-73

LPs: 10/12-inch

RCA....10-12 69-73

FRANKLIN, Doug P&R '58

(With the Bluenotes)

Singles: 7-inch

COLONIAL....10-20 58-59

Also see BLUENOTES

FRANKLIN, Erma P&R/R&B '67

Singles: 7-inch

BRUNSWICK....4-8 69
EPIC....10-20 61-63
SHOUT....5-10 67-68

LPs: 10/12-inch

BRUNSWICK....10-15 69
EPIC (619 "Her Name Is Erma")....30-40 62
(Stereo.)
EPIC (3824 "Her Name Is Erma")....20-30 62
(Monaural.)

FRANKLIN, Rev. C.L.: see FRANKLIN, Aretha

FRANKLIN, Rodney R&B/LP '80

Singles: 7-inch

COLUMBIA....3-4 80-86

LPs: 10/12-inch

COLUMBIA....5-10 80-86

FRANKS, Michael P&R/LP '76

Singles: 7-inch

JOHN HAMMOND....3-5 83
REPRISE....3-5 76
W.B. 3-4 77-83

Picture Sleeves

JOHN HAMMOND....3-5

LPs: 10/12-inch

JOHN HAMMOND....5-10 83
REPRISE....5-10 76-90
W.B. 5-10 77-87

FRANTICS P&R '59

Singles: 7-inch

BOLO....15-20 62
DOLTON....10-15 59-61
SEAFAIR....5-10 64
VIBRA-SONIC....5-10 60s

Members: Ron Petersen; Dick Goodman; Jim Manolides; Chuck Schoning; Bob Hosko.

Also see MOBY GRAPE

FRASER, Andy P&R '84

Singles: 7-inch

ISLAND....3-4 84

Picture Sleeves

ISLAND....3-4 84

Also see FREE

FRAZIER, Dallas P&R '66

Singles: 78 rpm

CAPITOL....5-10 54

Singles: 7-inch

AUDAN....4-8 60s
CAPITOL (2000 thru 2400 series)....4-8 67-69
CAPITOL (2800 & 2900 series)....10-15 54
CAPITOL (5500 series)....4-8 65
JAMIE....8-12 59
MERCURY....4-8 64
MUSIKON....5-10 61
RCA....3-5 71-73
20TH FOX....3-5 75

LPs: 10/12-inch

CAPITOL....10-20 66-67
RCA....8-12 70-71

FRAZIER, Dallas, & Joe "Fingers" Carr

Singles: 78 rpm

CAPITOL....3-5 54

Singles: 7-inch

CAPITOL....5-10 54

EPs: 7-inch

CAPITOL....8-12 54

Also see CARR, Joe "Fingers"
Also see FRAZIER, Dallas

FREBERG, Stan P&R '51

(Stan Freberg Show; with Billy May's Orchestra)

Singles: 78 rpm

CAPITOL....10-30 50-57

Singles: 7-inch

BELFAST SPARKLING WATER (1515 "Invisible Bubbles")....50-75
(Product commercials for radio use.)
BIG SOUND (2 "Jockey's Little Helper")....35-50
(Product commercials for radio use.)
BUBBLE UP (2227 "Music to Bubble Up By")....20-30 60s
(Product commercials for radio use.
BUTTERNUT COFFEE (2000 "Instant Sales for Instant Butternut by Instant Freberg")....40-50 60s
(Product commercials for radio use.
BUTTERNUT COFFEE (2237 "Amazing Butternut Coffee")....25-35 60s
(Product commercials for radio use.)
CAPITOL (303 "The Do-It-Yourself Dragnet")....50-100 53
(Capitol in-house, record sales promotional issue only.)
CAPITOL (1200 thru 3100 series, except 2125)....15-25 50-54
CAPITOL (2125 "Abe Snake for President")....30-40 52
CAPITOL (3200 thru 5700 series)....10-20 54-66
COCA COLA BOTTLING CO. (2227 Music to Bubble-Up By")....30-50 60s
(Product commercials for radio use.)
CONTADINA (4476 "The Whole Peeled Bounce")....35-50
(Product commercials for radio use. With the Hi Lo's.)
MILKY WAY (23300 "Tom Sweet and His Electric Milky Way Machine")....35-50
PITTSBURGH PAINT (1/2 "Four Pittsburgh Paint Commercials")....20-30
(Product commercials for radio use.)
RADIO (2225 "Who Listens to Radio")....25-40
(Promotional spots for advertising with radio.)
SOUTHERN BAPTIST CHURCH (101578 "Southern Baptist Radio and TV Commission")....15-20
(Product commercials for radio use.)
STAINLESS STEEL (1369 "Stainless Steel")....35-50
(Product commercials for radio use.)
STAN FREBERG on COMMERCIALS ("Rubblemeyer Farms")....40-60 70s
(Promotional issue only. Commercial parodies, comparing right and wrong production of radio spots.)
TERMINIX (3540 "Floor Show, Now Going on at Your House")....30-40
(Product commercials for radio use.)
UNITED PRESBYTERIAN CHURCH (101578 "The Presbyterian Church")....15-20
(Product commercials for radio use.)
ZEE (2020 "Zee with Freberg - Hey You Up There")....35-50
(Product commercials for radio use.)
ZEE (24005 "Zee Spot Commercials")....35-50
(Product commercials for radio use.)

Picture Sleeves

BUBBLE UP (2227 "Music to Bubble Up By")....85-100 60s
(Gatefold sleeve.)
CAPITOL (415 "Wun'erful Wun'erful")....15-20 57
(Promotional issue only.)
CAPITOL (4097 "Green Christmas")..8-12 58
CAPITOL (4329 "The Old Payola Roll Blues")....15-20 60
CAPITOL (5726 "Flackman and Reagan")....10-15 66
H.I.S. (122667 "Funny Record by Stan Freberg for H.I.S.")....35-50
(Product commercials for radio use.)
PITTSBURGH PAINT (1/2 "Four Pittsburgh Paint Commercials")....20-30
(Reads: "The Stations Representatives Assn. presents: Some Exciting new commercials for Radio!")
RADIO (2225 "Who Listens to Radio")....25-40
(Promotional spots for using radio advertising.)
SOUTHERN BAPTIST CHURCH (101578 "Southern Baptist Radio & TV Commission")....15-20
(Product commercials for radio use.)
TERMINIX (3540 "Floor Show")....10-20
(Product commercials for radio use.)
ZEE (2020 "Zee Here, Mr. Freberg")....35-50
(Product commercials for radio use.)

EPs: 7-inch

CAPITOL (415 "Wun'erful Wun'erful")....15-25 57
(Single-sided, two track promotional issue. Add $10 to $20 if accompanied by "Two Sides of Bubbling Hilarity" insert. Issued with generic Capitol paper sleeve.)
CAPITOL (496 "Any Requests")....20-30 54
CAPITOL (628 "Real St. George")....15-25 55
CAPITOL (731 "Elderly Man River")....40-50 58
(Promotional issue only.)
CAPITOL (1101 "Omaha")....15-25 59
CAPITOL (1589 "Stan Freberg")....25-40 61
(Compact 33.)
CAPITOL (3192 "Ugly Duckling")....15-25
SWIMSUITSMANSHIP (2080 "Swimsuitsmanship")....100-125
(Promotional issue only. Cover reads: "Fit Facts and Figures, You and Rose Marie Reid.")
UNITED PRESBYTERIAN CHURCH (1400 "Is God Dead?")....30-45
(Product commercials for radio use.)

LPs: 10/12-inch

BEKINS (27713 "Bekins Presents the Sound of Moving")....35-50
(Product commercials for radio use.)
BUTTERNUT COFFEE (2000 "Instant Butternut Coffee")....40-60 60s
(Product commercials for radio use.)
CAPITOL (777 "A Child's Garden of Freberg")....20-40 57
CAPITOL (1035 "The Best of the Stan Freberg Shows")....40-60 58
CAPITOL (1242 "Stan Freberg with the Original Cast")....20-35 59
(With "T" prefix.)
CAPITOL (1242 "Stan Freberg with the Original Cast")....12-20 69
(With "DT" prefix.)
CAPITOL (1242 "Stan Freberg with the Original Cast")....5-10 75
(With "SM" prefix.)
CAPITOL (1573 "Stan Freberg Presents the United States of America, Volume 1 - the Early Years")....25-25 61
(With "W" or "SW" prefix.)
CAPITOL (1694 "Face the Funnies") 25-35 62
CAPITOL (1816 "Madison Avenue Werewolf")....25-35 62
CAPITOL (2020 "Best of Stan Freberg")....15-25 64
CAPITOL (2551 "Freberg Underground")....15-25 66
(With "T" or "ST" prefix.)
CAPITOL (2551 "Freberg Underground")....5-10 75
(With "SM" prefix.)
CAPITOL (3264 "Mickey Mouse's Birthday Party")....15-25 63
CAPITOL (11000 series)....5-10 78

CAPITOL (80700 "Uncle Stan Wants You")....60-80 61
(Promotional issue for the LP series, *Stan Freberg Presents the United States of America.*)
COCA COLA (2468 "The Freedle Family Singers")....175-200
COLUMBIA (105948 "Hey, Look Us Over")....60-75
(Promotional issue only. With booklet.)
ESSKAY (59-2 "Esskay Commericals")....60-75
(Four one-minute spots.)
FREBERG LTD. (2343 "Woburn-Salada Tea")....35-50
(Product commercials for radio use.)
KAISER FOIL ("Message to Grocers")....35-50
(10-inch LP. Single-sided.)
KAISER FOIL (22077 "A Kaiser Foil Salesman Faces Life")....125-175
(10-inch LP. Product commercials for radio use.)
MEADOWGOLD (2152 "Meadowgold Dairies")....85-100
(Product commercials for radio use.)
OREGON (2039 "Oregon Soundtrack")....125-150
(Product commercials for radio use. Includes press kit.)
RAB ("More Here Than Meets The Ear")....75-125
(Promotional issue only.)
RADIO (3 "Radio Briefings")....35-50
(Promotional spots for using radio advertising.)
RADIO (1499 "More Here Than Meets the Ear")....30-45
(Promotional spots for using radio advertising.)
RADIO (2226 "Who Listens to Radio")....35-50
(Promotional spots for using radio advertising.)
TV GUIDE (2889 "TV Guide Spots")....60-75
(Product commercials for radio use.)
Note: Advertising agency discs containing commercials for radio station use are listed by product name, since there are no other label names used.
Members: Stan Freberg; Daws Butler; June Foray; George Burns; Jesse White; Peter Leeds; Paul Frees; Billy May.

FRED, John — P&R '59
(With His Playboy Band)

Singles: 7-inch

BELL....3-5 73
JEWEL....5-10 64-65
MONTEL....10-15 59-62
N-JOY....8-12
PAULA....4-8 65-69
UNI....3-6 69-70

LPs: 10/12-inch

PAULA....15-25 66-68
UNI....10-15 70

FRED & NEW J.B.s
(Fred Wesley)

Singles: 7-inch

PEOPLE....3-5 75

LPs: 10/12-inch

PEOPLE....5-10 75
Also see WESLEY, Fred

FREDDIE & DREAMERS — P&R/LP '65

Singles: 7-inch

CAPITOL (5053 "I'm Telling You Now")....15-20 63
CAPITOL (5137 "You Were Made for Me")....15-20 63
ERIC....3-4 70s
MERCURY....4-8 64-65
SUPER K....3-6 70
TOWER (125 "I'm Telling You Now")..5-10 65

Picture Sleeves

MERCURY....5-10 65

EPs: 7-inch

MERCURY (74 "Interview with the Dreamers")....20-30 65
(Promotional issue only.)
MERCURY (661 "Fun Loving Freddie and the Dreamers")....20-30 65
(Juke box issue only.)

LPs: 10/12-inch

CAPITOL....8-10 76-79
MERCURY....20-30 65-66
Members: Derek Quinn; Roy Crewdson; Pete Birrell; Bernie Dwyer; Freddie Garrity.
Also see JONES, Tom / Freddie & Dreamers / Johnny Rivers

FREDDIE & DREAMERS / Beat Merchants — P&R '65

Singles: 7-inch

TOWER (127 "You Were Made for Me")....5-10 65
Also see FREDDIE & DREAMERS

FREDDIE & DREAMERS / Just Four Men

Singles: 7-inch

TOWER (163 "Send a Letter to Me")..5-10 65
Also see FREDDIE & DREAMERS

FREDERICK — R&B/D&D '85

Singles: 12-inch

HEAT....4-6 85

Singles: 7-inch

HEAT....3-4 85

FREDERICK II — R&B '71

Singles: 7-inch

VULTURE....3-5 71

FREE — LP '69

Singles: 7-inch

A&M....3-6 70-71
ISLAND....3-5 72

Picture Sleeves

A&M....4-6 70

LPs: 10/12-inch

A&M....8-15 69-75
ISLAND (Except 7)....8-10 73
ISLAND (7 "The Free Story")....25-30 73
(Includes booklet. Promotional issue only.)
Members: Andy Fraser; Paul Rodgers; Simon Kirke; Paul Kossoff.
Also see BACK STREET CRAWLER
Also see BAD COMPANY
Also see FRASER, Andy
Also see KOSSOFF, Paul
Also see RODGERS, Paul
Also see WILLIE & Poor Boys

FREE EXPRESSION — R&B '81

Singles: 7-inch

VANGUARD....3-4 81

FREE LIFE — R&B '79

Singles: 7-inch

EPIC....3-5 78

LPs: 10/12-inch

EPIC....5-10 78

FREE MOVEMENT — P&R/R&B '71

Singles: 7-inch

COLUMBIA....3-5 71
DECCA....3-5 71

LPs: 10/12-inch

COLUMBIA....8-10 72

FREE MOVEMENT / Love Unlimited

Singles: 7-inch

MCA....3-5 73
Also see FREE MOVEMENT
Also see LOVE UNLIMITED

FREED, Alan
(With His Rock 'N Roll Band)

Singles: 78 rpm

CORAL....10-30 56-58

Singles: 7-inch

CORAL....10-20 56-58

EPs: 7-inch

CORAL (81136 "Rock 'N Roll Dance Party")....30-50 56

LPs: 10/12-inch

BRUNSWICK (54043 "The Alan Freed Rock 'N Roll Show")....75-100 59
(With "Guests" Buddy Holly & Crickets, Jackie Wilson & Terry Noland.)
CORAL (57063 "Rock 'N Roll Dance Party, Vol. 1")....40-60 56
(With the Modernaires.)
CORAL (57115 "Rock 'N Roll Dance Party, Vol. 2")....40-60 56
(With Jimmy Cavello & His House Rockers.)
CORAL (57177 "TV Record Hop")....40-60 57
CORAL (57213 "Rock Around the Block")....40-60 58
CORAL (57216 "Alan Freed Presents the King's Henchmen")....40-60 58
(With King Curtis, Sam "The Man" Taylor, Count Hastings, Kenny Burrell, Everett Barksdale, Ernie Hayes.)
Also see KING CURTIS
Also see HOLLY, Buddy
Also see WILSON, Jackie

FREED, Alan, Steve Allen, Al "Jazzbo" Collins & Modernaires

Singles: 78 rpm

CORAL....5-10 56

Singles: 7-inch

CORAL....10-15 56
Also see COLLINS, Al
Also see FREED, Alan

FREEDOM — R&B '79

Singles: 7-inch

ABC....3-5 70
BUDDAH....3-5 75
FREEDOM....15-25
MALACO....3-4 79

LPs: 10/12-inch

ABC....10-12 70
COTILLION....10-12 71

FREEEZ — R&B/D&D '83

Singles: 12-inch

STREETWISE....4-6 83

Singles: 7-inch

STREETWISE....3-4 83

LPs: 10/12-inch

STREETWISE....5-10 83
Also see ROCCA, John

FREEMAN, Bobby — P&R/R&B '58

Singles: 7-inch

JOSIE (835 "Do You Want to Dance")....50-100 58
JOSIE (841 "Betty Lou Got a New Pair of Shoes")....50-100 58
(We know that both of these 78s came out in Canada. U.S. 78s have not yet been verified.)

Singles: 7-inch

ABC....3-5 73
AUTUMN....5-10 63-64
DOUBLE SHOT....4-8 69-70
GUSTO....3-5 80s
JOSIE....15-30 58-62
KING....10-20 60-65
LOMA....5-10 67
RNOR....3-4
VIRGO....3-5 72

Picture Sleeves

RNOR....5-10

LPs: 10/12-inch

AUTUMN (102 "C'mon & Swim")....20-30 64
JOSIE (4007 "Get in the Swim")....15-25 65
JUBILEE (1086 "Do You Wanna Dance")....35-50 59
(Monaural.)
JUBILEE (1086 "Do You Wanna Dance")....50-75 59
(Stereo.)
JUBILEE (5010 "Twist with Bobby Freeman")....20-30 62
KING (930 "The Lovable Style of Bobby Freeman")....30-35 65

FREEMAN, Bobby, & Chuck Jackson

LPs: 10/12-inch

GRAND PRIX 15-20 64
Also see FREEMAN, Bobby
Also see JACKSON, Chuck

FREEMAN, Ernie R&B '56
(Ernie Freeman Combo)

Singles: 78 rpm

CASH 5-10 56
IMPERIAL 8-12 57
MAMBO 8-12 55

Singles: 7-inch

AVA 4-8 64
CASH 8-12 56
IMPERIAL (Except 5752) 8-15 57-62
IMPERIAL (5752 "Theme from Igor") 10-20 61
KING 5-10 60
LIBERTY 4-8 62
MAMBO (107 "Poor Fool") 10-20 55

EPs: 7-inch

DOOTONE (209 "Jazz Organ") 10-15 56

LPs: 10/12-inch

DUNHILL 10-15 67
IMPERIAL 20-30 57-62
LIBERTY 10-20 62-63
Members: Ernie Freeman; Irvin Ashby; Joe Comfort; R. Martinez.
Also see B. BUMBLE & STINGERS
Also see JOINER, ARKANSAS JUNIOR HIGH SCHOOL BAND
Also see NELSON, Willie
Also see OTIS, Johnny
Also see SIR CHAUNCEY
Also see WITHERSPOON, Jimmy

FREEMAN, John R&B '77

Singles: 7-inch

DAKAR 3-5 77

FREESTYLE R&B '84
(Freestyle Express)

Singles: 7-inch

MUSIC SPECIALISTS 3-4 84-86
Member: Tony Butler.
Also see TRINERE / Freestyle / Debbie Deb

FREHLEY, Ace P&R/LP '78

Singles: 7-inch

MEGAFORCE 3-5 87
CASABLANCA 3-5 78

Picture Sleeves

MEGAFORCE 3-5 87

LPs: 10/12-inch

CASABLANCA (7121 "Ace Frehley") 12-20 78
(With poster order form.)
CASABLANCA (7121 "Ace Frehley") .. 8-12 78
(Without poster order form.)
CASABLANCA (PIX-7121 "Ace Frehley") 50-60 79
(Picture disc.)
MEGAFORCE 5-10 87-89
Also see FREHLEY'S COMET
Also see KISS

FREHLEY'S COMET LP '88

LPs: 10/12-inch

MEGAFORCE 5-8 88
Also see FREHLEY, Ace

FRENCH, Don P&R '59

Singles: 7-inch

LANCER 5-10 59

FRESH, Doug, E.: see DOUG E. FRESH & Get Fresh Crew

FRESH BAND D&D '84

Singles: 12-inch

ARE 'N BE 4-6 84

FRESH 3 MCs R&B '84

Singles: 12-inch

PROFILE 4-6 84

Singles: 7-inch

PROFILE 3-4 84

LPs: 10/12-inch

PROFILE 5-10 84
Also see PUMPKIN & Profile All-Stars

FREY, Glenn P&R/LP '82

Singles: 12-inch

MCA 4-6 84-85

Singles: 7-inch

ASYLUM 3-4 82
MCA 3-4 84-89

Picture Sleeves

ASYLUM 3-4 82
MCA 3-4 84-88

LPs: 10/12-inch

ASYLUM 5-10 82
MCA 5-10 84-89
Also see EAGLES
Also see FALTERMEYER, Harold / Glenn Frey

FRIDA P&R/LP '82
(Anni-Frid Lyngstad)

Singles: 7-inch

ATLANTIC 3-5 82

LPs: 10/12-inch

ATLANTIC 5-10 82
Also see ABBA

FRIEDMAN, Dean P&R/LP '77

Singles: 7-inch

LIFESONG 3-4 77-78

LPs: 10/12-inch

LIFESONG 5-10 77-78
RECORD CO-OP 5-10 82

FRIEDMAN, Kinky C&W '73

Singles: 7-inch

ABC 3-5 75
EPIC 3-4 76-85
SOUND FACTORY 3-4 81
SUNRISE 3-4 83

LPs: 10/12-inch

ABC 5-10 74
EPIC 5-10 76
VANGUARD 5-10 73

FRIEND & LOVER P&R '68

Singles: 7-inch

ABC 4-8 67
CADET CONCEPT 3-5
VERVE/FORECAST 4-8 68

LPs: 10/12-inch

VERVE/FORECAST 12-15 68
Members: James Post; Cathy Post.

FRIENDS OF DISTINCTION P&R/R&B/LP '69

Singles: 7-inch

RCA 3-5 69-73

LPs: 10/12-inch

COLLECTABLES 5-10 88
RCA 10-15 69-73
Members: Floyd Butler; Jessica Cleaves; Harry Elston; Charlene Gibson; Barbara Jean Love.

FRIJID PINK P&R/LP '70

Singles: 7-inch

LION 4-8 72
LONDON 3-5
PARROT 5-10 69-71

LPs: 10/12-inch

FANTASY (9464 "All Pink Inside") 10-15 74
LIONEL (1004 "Earth Omen") 10-20 72
PARROT (71033 "Frijid Pink") 15-25 70
PARROT (71041 "Defrosted") 15-25 70

FRIPP, Robert LP '79

LPs: 10/12-inch

EDITIONS E.G. 5-10 79-81
POLYDOR 5-10 79-81
Also see KING CRIMSON

FRIPP, Robert, & Andy Summers LP '82

LPs: 10/12-inch

A&M 5-10 82-84
Also see FRIPP, Robert
Also see POLICE

FRIPP & ENO

LPs: 10/12-inch

ANTILLES 8-10 73
Members: Robert Fripp; Brian Eno.
Also see ENO, Brian
Also see FRIPP, Robert

FRITZ, Joe R&B '50
(Joe "Papoose" Fritz)

Singles: 78 rpm

MODERN 5-15 50
PEACOCK 10-20 51-54
SITTIN' in WITH 15-25 50-51

Singles: 7-inch

JET STREAM 4-8 66
PEACOCK (1606 "Real Fine Girl") 20-40 52
PEACOCK (1627 "Honey Honey") 20-40 53
PEACOCK (1640 "Cerelle") 20-40 55
SITTIN' in WITH (559 "Please Get Off My Mind") 50-75 50

FRIZZELL, David C&W '70

Singles: 7-inch

CAPITOL 3-5 73-74
CARTWHEEL 3-5 71
COLUMBIA 3-5 70
COMPLEAT 3-4 87
NASHVILLE AMERICA 3-4 86
MCA 3-4 83
RSO 3-5 76
VIVA 3-4 83-85
W.B. 3-4 81-82

LPs: 10/12-inch

MCA 5-8 83
VIVA 5-8 81-84
W.B. 5-10 82-83
Also see HAGGARD, Merle

FRIZZELL, David, & Shelly West C&W '81
(Frizzell & West)

Singles: 7-inch

VIVA 3-4 83-85
W.B. 3-4 81-83

LPs: 10/12-inch

VIVA 5-8 81-84
W.B. 5-10 81-83

FRIZZELL, Lefty C&W '50

Singles: 78 rpm

COLUMBIA 5-15 50-57

Singles: 7-inch

ABC 3-5 73-76
COLUMBIA (20000 & 21000 series) 10-20 50-56
COLUMBIA (40000 & 41000 series) ... 5-15 56-61
COLUMBIA (42000 thru 45000 series, except 42924) 3-8 61-72
COLUMBIA (42924 "Saginaw, Michigan") 4-6 64
(Black vinyl.)
COLUMBIA (42924 "Saginaw, Michigan") 10-15 64
(Colored vinyl. Promotional issue only.)

EPs: 7-inch

COLUMBIA 15-35 51-59

LPs: 10/12-inch

ABC 8-12 73-77
COLUMBIA (1342 "The One and Only Lefty Frizzell") 15-25 59
COLUMBIA (2169 "Saginaw, Michigan") 15-25 64
COLUMBIA (2386 "The Sad Side of Life") 15-25 65
COLUMBIA (2488 "Lefty Frizzell's Greatest Hits") 15-25 66
(Monaural.)
COLUMBIA (2772 "Puttin' On") 15-25 67
COLUMBIA (8969 "Saginaw, Michigan") 15-25 64
COLUMBIA (9019 "Songs of Jimmie Rodgers") 75-100 51
(10-inch LP.)
COLUMBIA (9021 "Listen to Lefty") 75-100 52
(10-inch LP.)

COLUMBIA (9186 "The Sad Side of Life") 20-25 65
COLUMBIA (9288 "Lefty Frizzell's Greatest Hits") 20-25 66
(Stereo. With "CS" prefix.)
COLUMBIA (9288 "Lefty Frizzell's Greatest Hits") 5-10
(With "PC" prefix.)
COLUMBIA (9572 "Puttin' On") 20-25 67
COLUMBIA (10000 series) 5-12 73-83
COLUMBIA (30000 series) 5-12 75-82
HARMONY (7241 "Songs of Jimmie Rodgers") 15-25 60
HARMONY (11000 series) 8-15 66-68
MCA 8-12 82
ROUNDER 5-10 80-83
2 X 4 (111 "Lefty Frizzell Story") 5-10 80
Also see BOND, Johnny, & Lefty Frizzell
Also see PRICE, Ray / Lefty Frizzell / Carl Smith
Also see SMITH, Carl / Lefty Frizzell / Marty Robbins

FROGMEN *P&R '61*

Singles: 7-inch

ASTRA (1009 "Underwater") 25-35 61
ASTRA (1010 "Beware Below") 25-35 61
CANDIX (314 "Underwater") 15-25 61
CANDIX (326 "Beware Below") 15-25 61
SCOTT (101 "Tioga") 10-20 64
SCOTT (102 "Underwater") 10-20 64
TEE JAY (131 "Sea Haunt") 15-25 64
(Black vinyl.)
TEE JAY (131 "Sea Haunt") 25-50 64
(Colored vinyl.)

FROMAN, Jane *P&R '34*

Singles: 78 rpm

CAPITOL 3-8 52-56
DECCA 5-10 34

Singles: 7-inch

CAPITOL 5-10 52-56

EPs: 7-inch

CAPITOL 5-15 52-56

LPs: 10/12-inch

CAPITOL 15-25 52-56
STAR-TONE 10-15
Also see MARTIN, Dean / Jane Froman

FRONT, The *LP '90*

LPs: 10/12-inch

COLUMBIA 5-8 90

FROST *LP '69*

(Dick Wagner & Frost)

Singles: 7-inch

DATE 5-10 68
VANGUARD 4-8 69-70

LPs: 10/12-inch

VANGUARD 10-20 69-70
Also see COOPER, Alice

FROST, Frank *R&B '66*

(With the Night Hawks)

Singles: 7-inch

JEWEL 4-8 66-67
PHILLIPS INT'L 8-12 61

LPs: 10/12-inch

JEWEL 10-20 74
PHILLIPS INT'L. (1975 "Hey Boss Man!") 800-1200 61

FROST, Max, & Troopers *P&R '68*

Singles: 7-inch

SIDEWALK 8-12 68
TOWER 8-12 68-69

Picture Sleeves

TOWER (419 "Shapes of Things to Come") 10-15 68
TOWER (478 "Paxton Quigley's Had the Course") 10-15 68

LPs: 10/12-inch

TOWER (5147 "Shape of Things to Come") 25-35 68
Member: Davie Allan.
Also see ALLAN, Davie

FROST, Thomas & Richard *P&R '69*

Singles: 7-inch

IMPERIAL 3-6 69
UNI 3-6 72

LPs: 10/12-inch

UNI 8-10 72

FROZEN GHOST *P&R/LP '87*

Singles: 7-inch

ATLANTIC 3-4 87

LPs: 10/12-inch

ATLANTIC 5-10 87
Members: Wolf Hassel; Arnold Lanni.
Also see SHERIFF

FRYE, David *LP '69*

LPs: 10/12-inch

BUDDAH 5-10 71-72
ELEKTRA 8-12 69-71

FUGS *LP '66*

(Village Fugs)

Singles: 7-inch

ESP 5-10 66

LPs: 10/12-inch

BROADSIDE (304 "Ballads of Contemporary Protest, Point of Views, and General Dissatisfaction") 300-400 65
(Double slot cover; one for disc and one for quarter-folded insert.
ESP (1018 "Fugs First Album") 30-50 65
(Reissue of Broadside 304.)
ESP (1028 "The Fugs") 25-40 66
ESP (1038 "Virgin Fugs") 25-40 67
ESP (2018 "Fugs Four") 20-25 67
PVC 5-10 82
REPRISE (6280 "Tenderness Junction") 15-25 67
REPRISE (6305 "It Crawled Into My Hand, Honest") 15-25 67
REPRISE (6359 "A Belle of Avenue") 10-20 69
REPRISE (6396 "Golden Filth") 10-20 70
Members: Ed Saunders; John Anderson; Lee Crabtree; Pete Kearney; Tuli Kupferberg; Vinny Leary; Ken Weaver; Pete Stampfel; Steve Weber.
Also see HOLY MODAL ROUNDERS

FULL FORCE *R&B/D&D '85*

Singles: 12-inch

COLUMBIA 4-6 85-86

Singles: 7-inch

COLUMBIA 3-4 85-87

Picture Sleeves

COLUMBIA 3-4 87-88

LPs: 10/12-inch

COLUMBIA 5-10 85-87
Also see LISA LISA

FULLER, Bobby *P&R/LP '66*

(Bobby Fuller Four; with Jim Reese & Embers; with Fanatics)

Singles: 7-inch

ABC 3-4 73
HI-TONE 4-8
DONNA (1403 "Those Memories of You") 25-35 65
EASTWOOD (0345 "Not Fade Away") 15-25 62
ERIC 3-4 70s
EXETER (122 "Wine, Wine, Wine") 50-100 64
EXETER (124 "I Fought the Law") 75-125 64
EXETER (126 "Fool of Love") 50-100 64
LIBERTY (55812 "Let Her Dance") 10-20 65
MUSTANG (3004 "Take My Word") 10-20 66
MUSTANG (3006 "Let Her Dance") 10-20 65
MUSTANG (3011 "Never to Be Forgotten") 10-20 65
MUSTANG (3012 "Let Her Dance") 10-20 65
MUSTANG (3014 "I Fought the Law") 8-12 65
MUSTANG (3016 "Love's Made a Fool of You") 10-20 66
MUSTANG (3018 "My True Love") 10-20 66
REGENCY (965 "I Fought the Law") 10-15 65
(Canadian.)
TODD (1090 "Saturday Night") 15-25 60s
YUCCA (140 "Guess We'll Fall in Love") 25-35 62
YUCCA (141 "You're in Love") 25-35 62
YUCCA (144 "My Heart Jumped") 25-35 62

LPs: 10/12-inch

MUSTANG (900 "KRLA King of the Wheels") 60-75 66
(Monaural.)
MUSTANG (900 "KRLA King of the Wheels") 75-100 66
(Stereo.)
MUSTANG (901 "I Fought the Law") 35-45 66
(Monaural.)
MUSTANG (901 "I Fought the Law") 45-55 66
(Stereo.)
RHINO 5-10 81
VOXX 5-10 84
Members: Bobby Fuller; Randy Fuller; Duane Quirico; Jim Reese; Dalton Powell; Johnny Barbata.
Also see SHINDIGS

FULLER, Bobby / Seeds

Singles: 7-inch

TRIP 3-6 70s
Also see FULLER, Bobby
Also see SEEDS

FULLER, Jerry *P&R '59*

Singles: 7-inch

ABC 3-5 78
BELL 4-6 72
CHALLENGE (59052 "Betty My Angel") 20-25 59
CHALLENGE (59085 thru 59269) 10-20 60-65
CHALLENGE (59279 "I Got Carried Away") 20-30 65
CHALLENGE (59307 "Don't Look at Me Like That") 5-10 65
CHALLENGE (59329 "Double Life") 15-25 66
COLUMBIA 3-5 70
LIN (5011 "Blue Memories") 15-25 58
LIN (5012 "Teenage Love") 15-25 58
LIN (5015 "Angel from Above") 15-25 58
LIN (5016 "The Door Is Open") 15-25 58
LIN (5019 "Lipstick & Rouge") 15-25 59
MCA 3-5 79

LPs: 10/12-inch

LIN (100 "Teenage Love") 25-35 60
MCA 5-10 79
Also see FLEAS
Also see FULLER BROTHERS

FULLER, Jerry, & Diane Maxwell

Singles: 7-inch

CHALLENGE (59074 "Above and Beyond") 10-15 60
Also see MAXWELL, Diane

FULLER BROTHERS

Singles: 7-inch

CHALLENGE 5-10 61-62
Members: Jerry Fuller; Bill Fuller.
Also see FULLER, Jerry

FULSON, Lowell *R&B '48*

(Lowell Folsom; Lowel Fulsom)

Singles: 78 rpm

ALADDIN 25-45 51
BIG TOWN 15-25 46-47
CASH (1051 "Blue Shadows") 15-25 57
CHECKER (804 thru 865) 10-25 54-57
CHECKER (882 "I Want to Make Love to You") 20-30 57
CHECKER (937 "It Took a Long Time") 25-50 59
Note: Checker 937 may be the last 78 with the checkerboard design at top, as opposed to 45s which switched designs beginning with #876. Also, 78s as early as #900 have Checker name vertically on left side.
CHECKER (952 "Have You Changed Your Mind") 150-250 60
DOWN TOWN 10-20 49

GILT EDGE 10-20 51
HOLLYWOOD 10-20 55
PARROT 25-50 53
RPM 10-20 50
SCOTTY'S RADIO 10-20 46
SWING TIME 10-20 46-53
TRILON 10-20 47-48

Singles: 7-inch

ALADDIN (3088 "Double Trouble Blues") 50-100 53
ALADDIN (3104 "Night and Day") ... 50-100 51
ALADDIN (3104 "Stormin' and Rainin'") 50-100 53
(Black vinyl.)
ALADDIN (3104 "Stormin' and Rainin'") 100-200 53
(Colored vinyl.)
ALADDIN (3217 "Don't Leave Me, Baby") 35-50 53
ALADDIN (3233 "Blues Never Fail") 35-50 53
CASH (1051 "Blue Shadows") 20-30 57
CHECKER (804 "Reconsider Baby") 40-60 54
CHECKER (812 "Loving You") 25-40 55
CHECKER (820 "Lonely Hours") 25-40 55
CHECKER (829 "Trouble Trouble") .. 25-40 55
CHECKER (841 "It's All Your Fault Baby") 25-40 56
CHECKER (854 "Baby Please Don't Go") 25-40 56
CHECKER (865 "You're Gonna Miss Me") 20-30 57
CHECKER (882 "I Want to Make Love to You") 20-30 57
CHECKER (937 "It Took a Long Time") 15-25 59
CHECKER (952 "Have You Changed Your Mind") 15-25 60
CHECKER (959 "I'm Glad You Reconsidered") 10-20 60
CHECKER (972 "I Want to Know") ... 10-20 60
CHECKER (992 "So Many Tears") 10-20 61
CHECKER (1027 "Shed No Tears") . 10-20 62
CHECKER (1046 "Trouble with the Blues") 10-20 62
GRANITE 3-4 76
HOLLYWOOD (1029 "Rocking After Midnight") 20-40 55
HOLLYWOOD (1103 "Guitar Shuffle") 10-15 62
JEWEL 3-6 69-73
KENT 3-8 64-70
MOVIN' 8-12 64
PARROT (787 "I've Been Mistreated") 75-100 53
(Black vinyl.)
PARROT (787 "I've Been Mistreated") 150-250 53
(Colored vinyl.)
SWING TIME (289 "Let's Live Right") 25-50 51
SWING TIME (295 "Guitar Shuffle") 25-50 51
SWING TIME (301 "The Highway Is My Home") 25-50 51
SWING TIME (308 "Black Widow Spider") 25-50 51
SWING TIME (315 "Raggedy Daddy Blues") 25-50 52
SWING TIME (320 "Ride Until the Sun Goes Down") 25-50 52
SWING TIME (325 "Upstairs") 25-50 52
SWING TIME (330 "I Love My Baby") 25-50 52
SWING TIME (335 "Cash Box Boogie") 25-50 53
SWING TIME (338 "I've Been Mistreated") 25-50 52

Picture Sleeves

KENT 5-10 67

LPs: 10/12-inch

ARHOOLIE 10-12 62
BIG TOWN 5-10 78
CHESS (205 "Blues Masters Series") 15-20
CHESS (408 "Hung Down Head") 15-20
JEWEL 8-10 70-73
KENT 10-15 65-71
UNITED 8-12

Session: Lloyd Glenn; Earl Brown; Bob Harvey; Bill Hadnott.
Also see CHARLES, Ray
Also see GLENN, Lloyd
Also see JAMES, Ulysses / Lowell Fulson
Also see MEMPHIS SLIM & Lowell Fulson
Also see TURRENTINE, Stanley

FUN & GAMES — *P&R '69*

Singles: 7-inch

UNI 5-10 68

LPs: 10/12-inch

UNI (73042 "Elephant Candy") 15-25 68

Members: Paul Guille; Joe Romano; Rick Romano; Sam Irwin; Joe Dugan; Carson Graham.

FUN BOY THREE — *LP '83*

Singles: 7-inch

CHRYSALIS 3-4 82-83

LPs: 10/12-inch

CHRYSALIS 5-10 82-83

Also see SPECIALS

FUN FUN — *D&D '84*

Singles: 12-inch

TSR 4-6 84-85

FUNICELLO, Annette: see ANNETTE

FUNK, Professor: see PROFESSOR FUNK

FUNK DELUXE — *R&B/D&D '84*

Singles: 7-inch

SALSOUL 3-4 83-84

LPs: 10/12-inch

SALSOUL 5-10 83

FUNKADELIC — *P&R/R&B '69*

(Featuring George Clinton)

Singles: 7-inch

W.B. 3-6 78-79
WESTBOUND 3-8 69-76

Picture Sleeves

W.B. 3-6 78-81

EPs: 7-inch

W.B. (3209 "One Nation Under a Groove") 10-15 78

LPs: 10/12-inch

20TH CENTURY/WESTBOUND 8-15 75
W.B. 5-10 76-81
WESTBOUND (215 "Let's Take It to the Stage") 30-50 75
WESTBOUND (227 "Tales of Kidd Funkadelic") 30-50 76
WESTBOUND (1001 "Standing on the Verge") 30-50 74
WESTBOUND (1004 "Greatest Hits") 25-35 75
WESTBOUND (2000 "Funkadelic") .. 40-50 70
WESTBOUND (2001 "Free Your Mind") 30-50 70
WESTBOUND (2007 "Maggot Brain") 40-60 71
WESTBOUND (2020 "America Eats Its Young") 30-50 72
WESTBOUND (2022 "Cosmic Slop") 30-50 73

Also see PARLIAMENTS

FUNKADELIC — *R&B/LP '81*

Singles: 7-inch

LAX 3-4 81

LPs: 10/12-inch

LAX 5-10 81

Note: This group was formed by three former members of the preceding Westbound/Warner Bros. band.
Also see FUNKADELIC (Featuring George Clinton)
Also see JUNIE

FUNKY COMMUNICATION COMMITTEE: see FCC

FUNKY KINGS — *P&R '76*

Singles: 7-inch

ARISTA 3-5 76

LPs: 10/12-inch

ARISTA 5-10 76

FUNN — *R&B '81*

Singles: 7-inch

MAGIC 3-5 81

FURAY, Richie — *LP '76*

Singles: 7-inch

ASYLUM 3-4 77-79

LPs: 10/12-inch

ASYLUM 5-10 76-82

Also see BUFFALO SPRINGFIELD
Also see POCO
Also see SOUTHER-HILLMAN-FURAY

FURIOUS FIVE — *R&B '84*

Singles: 12-inch

SUGAR HILL 4-6 84-85

Singles: 7-inch

ATLANTIC 3-4
SUGAR HILL 3-4 84-85

Picture Sleeves

ATLANTIC 3-4

FURIOUS FIVE & SUGARHILL GANG — *R&B '81*

Singles: 12-inch

SUGAR HILL 4-6 81

Singles: 7-inch

SUGAR HILL 3-4 81

Also see FURIOUS FIVE
Also see SUGARHILL GANG

FURYS — *P&R '63*

Singles: 7-inch

MACK IV (112 "Zing! Went the Strings of My Heart") 20-30 62

Member: Jerome Evans.

FUSE

Singles: 7-inch

EPIC (10514 "Hound Dog") 8-12 69

LPs: 10/12-inch

EPIC (26502 "Fuse") 30-35 70

Members: Rick Neilsen; Joe Sunberg; Craig Myers; Tom Peterson.
Also see CHEAP TRICK

FUSE ONE — *LP '82*

LPs: 10/12-inch

CTI 5-10 82

FUTURE — *R&B '88*

Singles: 7-inch

HOUSTON INT'L 3-4 87

FUTURES — *R&B '73*

Singles: 7-inch

AVALANCHE 3-4
GAMBLE 3-5 73
PHILADELPHIA INT'L 3-4 81

LPs: 10/12-inch

PHILADELPHIA INT'L 5-10 81

Members: James King; Kenny Crew; Harry McGilkerry; Frank Washington; John King.
Also see MASON, Barbara

FUZZ — *P&R/R&B/LP '71*

Singles: 7-inch

CALLA 3-5 71
ROULETTE 3-5 70s

LPs: 10/12-inch

CALLA 10-12 71

Members: Sheila Young; Barbara Gilliam; Val Williams.

G., Kenny: see KENNY G.

G - CLEFS *P&R/R&B '56*
(With Jay Raye & Orchestra)
Singles: 78 rpm
PARIS ... 10-20 57
PILGRIM ... 10-20 56
Singles: 7–inch
DITTO (503 "I'll Remember") ... 15-25 62
LOMA ... 5-10 66
PARIS (502 "Symbol of Love") ... 15-25 57
PARIS (502 "Symbol of Love") ... 10-20 57
PILGRIM (715 "Ka Ding Dong") ... 15-25 56
(Purple label – no pilgrims shown.)
PILGRIM (715 "Ka Ding Dong") ... 8-12 56
(Red label – pilgrims shown.)
PILGRIM (720 "Cause You're Mine") ... 10-20 56
REGINA (1314 "I Believe in All I Feel") ... 10-20 64
REGINA (1319 "Angel, Listen to Me") ... 15-25 64
ROULETTE ... 3-5 70s
TERRACE ... 5-10 61-63
VEEP ... 5-10 65-66
Also see CANNON, Freddy

G.L.O.B.E. & WHIZ KID *R&B '83*
Singles: 12–inch
TOMMY BOY ... 4-6 83
Singles: 7–inch
TOMMY BOY ... 3-4 83

GQ *P&R/R&B/LP '79*
Singles: 7–inch
ARISTA ... 3-5 79-82
LPs: 10/12–inch
ARISTA ... 5-10 79-81

G.T. *R&B '83*
(Gary Taylor)
Singles: 12–inch
A&M ... 4-6 83
Singles: 7–inch
A&M ... 3-4 83
LPs: 10/12–inch
A&M ... 5-8 83

GABOR SZABO: see SZABO, Gabor

GABRIEL *P&R '78*
Singles: 7–inch
ABC ... 3-5 76-77
EPIC ... 3-4 78-79
LPs: 10/12–inch
ABC ... 8-10 75-76
EPIC ... 5-10 78
Members: Terry Lauber; Frank Butorac.

GABRIEL, Peter *P&R/LP '77*
Singles: 12–inch
GEFFEN ... 4-6 82-86
Singles: 7–inch
ATCO ... 3-5 77
ATLANTIC ... 3-5 78
GEFFEN ... 3-4 82-90
MERCURY ... 3-4 80
WTG ... 3-4 89
W.B. ... 3-4 86
Picture Sleeves
GEFFEN ... 3-4 86
MERCURY ... 3-4 80
LPs: 10/12–inch
ATCO ... 10-12 77
ATLANTIC ... 8-10 78
GEFFEN ... 5-10 82-90
MERCURY ... 5-10 80
Also see GENESIS

GABRIEL, Peter, & Kate Bush *P&R '87*
Singles: 7–inch
GEFFEN ... 3-4 87
Picture Sleeves
GEFFEN ... 3-4 87
Also see BUSH, Kate

GABRIEL & ANGELS *P&R '62*
Singles: 7–inch
AMY (802 "Chumba") ... 15-25 60
AMY (823 "Zing Went the Strings of My Heart") ... 25-35 61
AMY (35802 "Chumba") ... 10-20 60
NORMAN ... 8-12 61-62
SWAN ... 8-12 62-63

GADABOUTS *P&R '56*
Singles: 78 rpm
MERCURY ... 5-10 54-56
WING ... 5-10 55
Singles: 7–inch
JARO ... 5-10 60
MERCURY ... 10-15 54-56
WING ... 5-15 55

GADSON, James *R&B '72*
Singles: 7–inch
CREAM ... 3-5 72
Also see SOUL RUNNERS

GADSON, Mel *P&R '60*
Singles: 7–inch
BIG TOP (3034 "Comin' Down with Love") ... 10-20 60

GAGE, Yvonne *R&B '84*
Singles: 7–inch
ATLANTIC ... 3-5 81
CIM ... 3-4 84
Also see FIRST LOVE

GAGNON, Andre *P&R '76*
Singles: 7–inch
LONDON ... 3-5 76

GAIL, Sunny: see GALE, Sunny

GAILLARD, Slim *P&R/R&B '46*
(Slim Gaillard Trio)
Singles: 78 rpm
ATOMIC ... 10-15 46
BEL-TONE ... 10-15 45
CADET ... 10-15 46
CLEF ... 5-10 53-54
COLUMBIA ... 5-10 40s
4 STAR ... 5-10 46
MAJESTIC ... 10-15 46
OKEH ... 5-15 40-42
20TH CENTURY ... 10-15 46
VOCALION ... 10-20 38-40
Singles: 7–inch
CLEF ... 10-20 53-54
DOT (15919 "Down by the Station") ... 10-15 59
ELGO (3001 "Angel") ... 25-50 62
EPIC ... 5-10 68
EPs: 7–inch
CLEF ... 10-20 53
KING ... 10-20 54
NORGRAN ... 10-20 54
ROYALE ... 10-20 50s
LPs: 10/12–inch
CLEF (126 "Mish Mash") ... 25-50 53
CLEF (138 "Slim Cavorts") ... 25-50 53
DOT (3190 "Slim Gaillard Rides Again") ... 20-30 59
(Monaural.)
DOT (25190 "Slim Gaillard Rides Again") ... 25-40 59
(Stereo.)
KING (80 "Boogie") ... 50-75 50s
(10–inch LP.)
NORGRAN (13 "Slim Gaillard") ... 25-40 54
VERVE (2013 "Smorgasbord") ... 20-40 56
Also see GILLESPIE, Dizzy, & Slim Gaillard

GAINES, Earl *R&B '66*
(Earl Gains)
Singles: 7–inch
ACE ... 8-10
CHAMPION ... 10-20 58-60
DELUXE ... 5-8 68-69
EXCELLO (2217 "Baby, Baby, What's Wrong") ... 10-20 62
HBR ... 5-10 66
HOLLYWOOD ... 4-8 67
SEVENTY SEVEN ... 3-6 73
LPs: 10/12–inch
DELUXE ... 10-15 69
HBR ... 10-15 66

GAINES, Rosie *R&B '85*
Singles: 7–inch
EPIC ... 3-4 85

GALE, Eric *LP '77*
Singles: 7–inch
COLUMBIA ... 3-5 78-80
LPs: 10/12–inch
COLUMBIA ... 5-10 77-80
ELEKTRA ... 5-10 83
KUDU ... 8-10 73
Also see GRUSIN, Dave

GALE, Sunny *P&R '52*
(With the Saints & Sinners Dixieland Band; with Ralph Burns Orchestra; Sunny Gail)
Singles: 78 rpm
DECCA ... 3-8 56-57
DERBY ... 3-6 52
RCA ... 3-6 52-56
Singles: 7–inch
BLAINE ... 3-5 65
CANADIAN AMERICAN ... 3-6 63-64
DECCA ... 5-10 56-59
DERBY (700 series) ... 10-20 52
(Colored vinyl.)
RCA (4000 thru 6000 series) ... 6-12 52-56
RCA (9000 series) ... 3-5 68
RIVERSIDE ... 3-5 63
STAGE ... 4-8 62
TERRACE ... 3-6 62
THIMBLE ... 3-4 74
WARWICK ... 4-8 60-61
EPs: 7–inch
KING ... 5-10
RCA ... 5-10 56
LPs: 10/12–inch
CANADIAN AMERICAN ... 10-20 64
RCA (1277 "Sunny & Blue") ... 20-30 56
WARWICK (2018 "Sunny") ... 15-25 60
Also see WILCOX, Eddie, Orchestra

GALE, Sunny, & Du Droppers
Singles: 78 rpm
RCA ... 10-15 53
Singles: 7–inch
RCA (5543 "The Note in the Bottle") ... 15-25 53
Also see DU DROPPERS
Also see GALE, Sunny

GALENS *P&R '63*
Singles: 7–inch
CHALLENGE ... 5-8 63-65

GALLAGHER, Rory *LP '72*
LPs: 10/12–inch
ATCO ... 10-12 71-72
CHRYSALIS ... 5-10 75-80
MERCURY ... 5-10 82
POLYDOR ... 8-10 72-75
SPRINGBOARD ... 8-12 76
Also see TASTE

GALLAGHER & LYLE *P&R '76*
Singles: 7–inch
A&M ... 3-4 73-78
LPs: 10/12–inch
A&M ... 8-10 73-78
CAPITOL (SM-10000 series) ... 5-10 77

CAPITOL (ST-11000 series) 8-12 72
Members: Ben Gallagher; Graham Lyle.
Also see McGUINNESS FLINT

GALLAHADS P&R '56

Singles: 78 rpm

CAPITOL 5-10 55
JUBILEE 5-10 56
VIK 5-10 57

Singles: 7-inch

CAPITOL 10-20 55
JUBILEE 10-20 56
VIK 10-20 57

GALLERY P&R/LP '72

Singles: 7-inch

SUSSEX 3-5 72

Picture Sleeves

SUSSEX (239 "I Believe in Music") 4-6 72

LPs: 10/12-inch

SUSSEX 10-12 72-73
Member: Jim Gold.

GALLOP, Frank P&R '58
(With Don Costa & His Orchestra)

Singles: 7-inch

ABC-PAR 5-10 58
KAPP 4-6 66
MUSICOR 4-6 66

Picture Sleeves

MUSICOR 4-8 66

LPs: 10/12-inch

MUSICOR 10-15 66
Also see COSTA, Don, Orchestra

GALLOWAY, Leata R&B '88

Singles: 7-inch

COLUMBIA 3-4 88

GALWAY, James LP '79

Singles: 7-inch

RCA 3-4 81

LPs: 10/12-inch

RCA 5-8 79-80
Also see LAINE, Cleo, & James Galway

GALWAY, James, & Sylvia C&W '83

Singles: 7-inch

RCA 3-4 83
Also see GALWAY, James
Also see SYLVIA

GAMBLE, Dee Dee Sharp: see SHARP, Dee Dee

GAMMA LP '79

Singles: 7-inch

ELEKTRA 3-4 79-82

LPs: 10/12-inch

ELEKTRA 5-10 79-82
Members: Dave Pattison; Ronnie Montrose; Denny Carmassi.
Also see HEART
Also see MONTROSE

GANG OF FOUR LP '81

Singles: 12-inch

W.B. 4-6 80-84

Singles: 7-inch

W.B. 3-4 80-84

LPs: 10/12-inch

W.B. 5-10 80-83
Also see SHRIEKBACK

GANG STARR LP '91

LPs: 10/12-inch

CHRYSALIS 5-8 91

GANG'S BACK R&B '82

Singles: 7-inch

HANDSHAKE 3-4 82

GANGSTERS R&B '79

Singles: 7-inch

HEAT 3-4 79-81
MONTAGE 3-4 82

LPs: 10/12-inch

MONTAGE 5-10 82

GANT, Cecil R&B '44
(Pvt. Cecil Gant "The G.I. Sing-Sation"; with His Trio)

Singles: 78 rpm

BOP 15-20
BRONZE 10-20 44
BULLET 10-20 46
DOT (1000 series) 5-15 50-51
DOWN BEAT 5-15 49
4 STAR 5-15 47-52
GILT-EDGE (500 "I Wonder") 75-100 45
(Cardboard picture disc. Add $10 to $15 for mailer.)
IMPERIAL 5-15 50-51
IMPERIAL 5-15 50-51
KING 10-15 47
NATIONAL 5-15 44
SWING TIME 5-10 49

Singles: 7-inch

DECCA (30320 "I Wonder") 10-20 57
DECCA (48171 "Someday You'll Be Sorry") 20-30 50
DECCA (48185 "It's Christmas Time Again") 20-30 50
DECCA (48191 "Train Time Blues, No. 2") 20-30 50
DECCA (48200 "Shot Gun Boogie") 25-40 51
DECCA (48212 "My Little Baby") 20-30 51
DECCA (48231 "Owl Stew") 20-30 50
DECCA (48249 "God Bless My Daddy") 20-30 50
DOT (1121 "Train Time Blues") 20-30 52
GILT-EDGE (5090 "I Wonder") 20-30 55

LPs: 10/12-inch

KING (671 "The Incomprable Cecil Gant") 40-50 60
RED MILL ("Piano and Voice") 50-100
(No selection number used. Colored vinyl.)
SOUND (601 "The Incomprable Cecil Gant") 75-100 57

GANTS P&R '65

Singles: 7-inch

LIBERTY 10-15 65-67
STATUE (605 "Road Runner") 30-40 65

LPs: 10/12-inch

LIBERTY 15-25 65-66

GAP, Billy & Baby: see BILLY & Baby Gap

GAP BAND R&B '77

Singles: 12-inch

PASSPORT 4-6 83
TOTAL EXPERIENCE 4-6 82-86

Singles: 7-inch

A&M 3-5 75
ARISTA 3-4 89
CAPITOL 3-4 89
MEGA 3-4 84
MERCURY 3-4 79-84
PASSPORT 3-4 83
RCA 3-4 87
SHELTER 3-5 74
TATTOO 3-5 77
TOTAL EXPERIENCE 3-4 82-87

Picture Sleeves

ARISTA 3-4 89
TOTAL EXPERIENCE 3-4 82

LPs: 10/12-inch

CAPITOL 5-8 89
MERCURY 5-10 79-80
PASSPORT 5-10 83
SHELTER 8-10 74
TATTOO 8-10 77
TOTAL EXPERIENCE 5-10 82-86
Members: Charles Wilson; Ronnie Wilson; Robert Wilson.
Also see BILLY & Baby Gap

GARCIA, Jerry P&R/LP '72
(Jerry Garcia Band)

Singles: 7-inch

DOUGLAS 4-8 73
ROUND 4-8 72-74
W.B. 4-8 72

LPs: 10/12-inch

ARISTA 5-10 78-82
ROUND 8-10 74-75
U.A. 8-10 76
W.B. (2582 "Garcia") 35-45 72
Also see DYLAN, Bob, & Grateful Dean
Also see GRATEFUL DEAD
Also see HART, Mickey
Also see IT'S a BEAUTIFUL DAY
Also see JAMES & Good Brothers
Also see JEFFERSON AIRPLANE
Also see LAMB
Also see OLD and in the WAY
Also see ROWANS
Also see WALES, Howard, & Jerry Garcia

GARCIA, Jerry, & Robert Hunter

Singles: 7-inch

ROUND (102 "Sampler for Dead Heads") 50-75 74
(Includes letter about the Grateful Dead LP, *The Mars Hotel,* and some miniature LP covers. Promotional fan club issue.)
ROUND (102 "Sampler for Dead Heads") 25-35 74
(Price for disc without inserts.)
Also see GARCIA, Jerry
Also see GRATEFUL DEAD

GARDNER, Dave P&R '57
(Brother Dave Gardner)

Singles: 7-inch

DECCA (30627 "Slick Slacks") 15-30 58
OJ 5-10 57
RCA 3-8 59-61

LPs: 10/12-inch

CAMDEN 5-10 73
CAPITOL 15-25 63
RCA 15-25 60-64
TOWER 10-20 67

GARDNER, Don, & Dee Dee Ford P&R/R&B '62

Singles: 7-inch

FIRE 8-15 62
FLASHBACK 3-5 65
KC 5-10 62
LUDIX 4-8 63
RED TOP 4-8 63
TRU-GLO-TOWN 4-8 66

LPs: 10/12-inch

FIRE (105 "Need Your Lovin' ") 50-100 62
SUE (1044 "Don Gardner & Dee Dee Ford in Sweden") 20-30 66
Also see WASHINGTON, Baby, & Don Gardner

GARDNER, Joanna R&B '85

Singles: 7-inch

PHILLY WORLD 3-4 85

GARDNER, Reggie R&B '71

Singles: 7-inch

CAPITOL 3-5 71

GARDNER, Taana R&B '81

Singles: 7-inch

WEST END 3-4 81

GARFUNKEL, Art P&R/LP '73

Singles: 7-inch

COLUMBIA (Except SQ-45926) 3-4 73-88
COLUMBIA (SQ-45926 "All I Know") ..5-10 73
(Quadraphonic. Promotional issue only.)

Picture Sleeves

COLUMBIA 3-4 81

LPs: 10/12-inch

COLUMBIA (30000 series) 8-12 73-81
(With "FC," "JC," "KC" or "PC" prefix.
COLUMBIA (30000 series) 10-20 73-75
(With "CQ" or "PCQ" prefix. Quad issues.)
COLUMBIA (40000 series) 5-8 88
COLUMBIA (47000 series) 10-20 78
(Half-speed mastered.)
Also see GARR, Artie
Also see SIMON & GARFUNKEL

GARFUNKEL, Art / Amy Grant

LPs: 10/12–inch

COLUMBIA (40212 "Animals' Christmas") 8-10 86
(Includes booklet.)
Also see GRANT, Amy

GARFUNKEL, Art, James Taylor & Paul Simon P&R '78

Singles: 7–inch

COLUMBIA 3-5 78
Also see GARFUNKEL, Art
Also see SIMON, Paul
Also see TAYLOR, James

GARI, Frank P&R '60

Singles: 7–inch

ATLANTIC 5-8 62
CAPITOL 4-6 68
CRUSADE 6-12 60-62
RIBBON 6-12 59

Picture Sleeves

CRUSADE 10-20 61-62

GARLAND, Judy P&R '39

Singles: 78 rpm

CAPITOL 3-8 56-57
COLUMBIA 3-8 53-54
DECCA (Except 2000 through 4000 series) 5-15 42-55
DECCA (2000 thru 4000 series) 10-20 39-42

Singles: 7–inch

ABC 3-5 67
CAPITOL 5-10 56-63
COLUMBIA (40000 series) 8-15 53-54
DECCA (25000 series) 4-8 65
DECCA (29000 series) 8-10 55
MCA 3-5 73-78
MGM GOLDEN CIRCLE 3-5 69
W.B. 3-5 63

Promotional Singles

CAPITOL ("After You've Gone"/"When You're Smiling") 10-20 59

Picture Sleeves

CAPITOL ("After You've Gone"/"When You're Smiling") 15-25 59
(Sleeve reads "Two of the Top Tunes from *Garland at the Grove.*")

EPs: 7–inch

CAPITOL (676 "Miss Show Business") 10-20 55
CAPITOL (734 "Judy") 10-20 56
CAPITOL (835 "Alone") 10-20 57
CAPITOL (1569 "Judy at Carnegie Hall") 10-15 62
COLUMBIA (1201 "A Star Is Born") .. 15-20 54
(Soundtrack.)
COLUMBIA (2598 "Judy Garland") 20-30 57
COLUMBIA (7621 "Born in a Trunk") 25-50 56
DECCA (620 "Judy Garland at the Palace/ Greatest Performances") 10-20 55
DECCA (661 "The Wizard of Oz") 15-25 51
DECCA (2050 "Judy Garland, Volume 2") 12-20 53
MGM (40 "Easter Parade") 30-50 50
(Gatefold cover.)
MGM (268 "If You Feel Like Singing, Sing") 10-20 54
MGM (1038 "Get Happy") 10-20 55
MGM (1116 "Look for the Silver Lining") 10-20 55
MGM (1122 "Judy Garland") 10-20 55

LPs: 10/12–inch

ABC (620 Judy Garland at Home at the Palace") 10-15 67
ABC (30007 "Judy Garland the ABC Collection") 5-10 76
AEI (3101 "Meet Me in St. Louis"/"The Harvey Girls") 10-15
(Soundtrack. Reissue.)
ACCESSOR 8-15
AUDIOFIDELITY (311 "Judy Garland") 15-20 83
(Picture disc.)
C.I.T. 8-12
CAPITOL (676 "Miss Show Business") 30-40 55
(With "W" prefix.)
CAPITOL (676 "Miss Show Business") 10-20 63
(With "SW" prefix.)
CAPITOL (734 "Judy") 25-35 56
(With "T" prefix.)
CAPITOL (734 "Judy") 10-20 63
(With "DT" prefix.)
CAPITOL (835 "Alone") 25-35 57
(With "T" prefix.)
CAPITOL (835 "Alone") 10-20 63
(With "DT" prefix.)
CAPITOL (1036 "Judy in Love") 20-35 58
CAPITOL (1118 "Garland at the Grove") 40-60 59
CAPITOL (1188 "The Letter") 25-35 59
(With John Ireland.)
CAPITOL (1467 "Judy – That's Entertainment") 20-35 60
CAPITOL (1569 "Judy at Carnegie Hall") 20-35 61
CAPITOL (1710 "The Garland Touch") 20-30 62
CAPITOL (1861 "I Could Go On Singing") 25-30 63
(Soundtrack. With "W" prefix.)
CAPITOL (1861 "I Could Go On Singing") 35-40 63
(Soundtrack. With "SW" prefix.)
CAPITOL (1941 "Our Love Letter") ... 15-20 63
(With John Ireland.)
CAPITOL (1999 "The Hits of Judy Garland") 20-30 64
(With "T" or "ST" prefix.)
CAPITOL (1999 "The Hits of Judy Garland") 5-10 75
(With "SM" prefix.)
CAPITOL (2062 "Just for Openers") 15-25 64
CAPITOL (2988 "Judy Garland Deluxe Set") 20-35 68
CAPITOL (11763 "Alone") 5-10 78
CAPITOL (11876 "Judy – That's Entertainment") 5-10 79
CAPITOL (12034 "Just for Openers") 5-10 80
CAPITOL (16175 "The Hits of Judy Garland") 4-6 81
COLUMBIA (762 "Born in a Trunk") 50-100 56
(10–inch LP.)
COLUMBIA (1101 "A Star Is Born") .. 20-25 58
(Soundtrack.)
COLUMBIA (1201 "A Star Is Born") .. 35-45 54
(Soundtrack. Deluxe boxed edition.)
COLUMBIA (8740 "A Star Is Born") .. 20-30 63
(Soundtrack.)
COLUMBIA (10011 "A Star Is Born") .. 6-12 73
(Soundtrack.)
COLUMBIA/CSP (8740 "A Star Is Born") 5-10
(Soundtrack.)
COMPUNSONIC 8-12
DRG 10-20
DECCA (5 "Collector's Items: 1936-1945") 15-25 70
DECCA (172 "The Best of Judy Garland") 15-20 63
(Monaural.)
DECCA (7-172 "The Best of Judy Garland") 15-20 63
(Stereo.)
DECCA (4199 "The Magic of Judy Garland") 15-20 61
DECCA (5152 "Wizard of Oz") 25-50 52
(Soundtrack. 10–inch LP.)
DECCA (6020 "Judy Garland at the Palace") 35-45 55
DECCA (8190 "Judy Garland – Greatest Performances") 35-45 55
DECCA (8387 "The Wizard of Oz") .. 20-35 56
(Soundtrack. One side, *The Song Hits from Pinocchio,* does not feature Judy Garland.)
DECCA (8498 "Meet Me in St. Louis"/ "The Harvey Girls") 60-70 57
(Soundtrack. Different show on each side.)
DECCA (75150 "Judy Garland's Greatest Hits") 8-12 69
DECCA (78387 "Wizard of Oz") 10-15 67
(Soundtrack.)
51 WEST 5-10
HARMONY (11366 "A Star Is Born"). 10-15 69
(Soundtrack.)
JUNO (1000 "Judy: London 1969") 6-12 69
MCA (4003 "The Best of Judy Garland") 10-15 73
MFSL (048 "Live at London Palladium") 30-40 80
MGM (1 "Golden Years at MGM") 15-25 69
MGM (21 "The Pirate") 50-75 51
(Soundtrack. With Gene Kelly. 10–inch LP.)
MGM (82 "Judy Garland Sings") 50-100 51
MGM (113 "Judy Garland") 8-12 70
MGM (3149 "Judy Garland") 35-45 54
MGM (3234 "The Pirate") 25-30 55
(Soundtrack. With Gene Kelly.)
MGM (3464 "The Wizard of Oz") 35-45 61
(Soundtrack.)
MGM (3771 "Words and Music") 15-25 60
MGM (3989 "The Judy Garland Story, Vol. 1") 15-20 61
MGM (3996 "The Wizard of Oz") 15-20 61
(Soundtrack.)
MGM (4005 "The Judy Garland Story, Vol. 2") 15-20 61
MGM (4204 "The Very Best of Judy Garland") 12-20 64
MARK 56 (632 "Live In San Francisco") 125-150 79
(Picture disc.)
METRO (505 "Judy Garland") 10-15 65
METRO (581 "Judy Garland in Song") 10-15 66
PARAGON 5-10
PHOENIX 10 8-12
PICKWICK 5-10 70s
RADIANT 6-12
RADIOLA 5-10
SPRINGBOARD 5-10
STANYAN 5-10 74
STAR TONE 5-10
TRIP (9 "16 Greatest Hits") 5-10 76
TROPHY 5-10
Also see CROSBY, Bing, & Judy Garland
Also see HAYMES, Dick, & Judy Garland
Also see MARTIN, Dean
Also see YOUNG, Victor

GARLAND, Judy / Tommy Dorsey

Singles: 78 rpm

VOGUE ("The Trolley Song") 750-1000 46
(Picture disc.)
Also see DORSEY, Tommy

GARLAND, Judy, & Liza Minnelli LP '65

Singles: 7–inch

CAPITOL 4-8 65

LPs: 10/12–inch

CAPITOL (2295 "Live at the London Palladium") 15-20 65
CAPITOL (11191 "Live at the London Palladium") 5-10 73
MFSL (048 "Live at the London Palladium") 20-35 81
TROLLEY CAR 5-10
Also see GARLAND, Judy
Also see MINNELLI, Liza

GARLOW, Clarence R&B '50

Singles: 78 rpm

ALADDIN 25-50 52
FEATURE 20-30 51-54
FLAIR 25-50 54
FOLK STAR 15-25 54
GOLDBAND 10-20 56-57
LYRIC 10-20 51
MACY'S 10-15 49

Singles: 7–inch

ALADDIN (3179 "New Bon Ton Roula") 50-75 52
ALADDIN (3225 "You Got Me Crying") 50-75 52
FEATURE (3005 "If I Keep on Worrying") 40-60 54
FLAIR (1021 "Crawfishin' ") 50-75 54
FOLK STAR (1130 "Za Belle") 25-40 54
FOLK STAR (1199 "No No Baby") 25-40 54
GOLDBAND 20-25 56-57

GARNER, Erroll R&B '49

(Erroll Garner Trio)

Singles: 78 rpm

BLACK & WHITE (16 "Movin' Around") 6-12 45
COLUMBIA 3-8 50-57
MERCURY 4-8 54
SAVOY 4-8 45-49

Singles: 7–inch

ABC-PAR 3-6 61-62
COLUMBIA 3-8 50-70
MGM 3-5 66-69
MERCURY (70000 series) 4-8 54
MERCURY (72000 & 73000 series) 3-6 63-71
REPRISE 3-6 63
SAVOY 4-8 50s

EPs: 7–inch

ATLANTIC 10-15 56
BRUNSWICK 10-15 53
COLUMBIA 10-15 50-59
EMARCY 10-15 56
KING 10-15 54
MERCURY 10-15 54-56
SAVOY 10-15 51-55

LPs: 10/12–inch

ABC-PAR 15-25 61
ATLANTIC (109 "Rhapsody") 50-100 49
(10–inch LP.)
ATLANTIC (112 "Piano Solos") 50-100 50
(10–inch LP.)
ATLANTIC (128 "Passport to Fame") 50-100 51
(10–inch LP.)
ATLANTIC (138 "Piano Solos") 50-100 52
(10–inch LP.)
ATLANTIC (1227 "Greatest Garner") 30-40 56
BARONET 15-25 61
BLUE NOTE (5000 series) 20-40 52-53
(10–inch LP.)
COLUMBIA (535 "At the Piano") 45-65 53
(Red and gold label.)
COLUMBIA (535 "At the Piano") 30-50 56
(Red and black label.)
COLUMBIA (583 "Gems") 40-60 54
(Red and gold label.)
COLUMBIA (583 "Gems") 30-50 56
(Red and black label.)
COLUMBIA (617 "Gonest") 40-60 55
(Red and gold label.)
COLUMBIA (617 "Gonest") 30-50 56
(Red and black label.)
COLUMBIA (651 "Music for Tired Lovers") 25-50 55
(Red and gold label.)
COLUMBIA (883 "Concert by the Sea") 25-50 56
COLUMBIA (939 thru 1587) 15-35 57-61
COLUMBIA (2540 "Garnerland") 30-50 56
(10–inch LP.)
COLUMBIA (6139 "Piano Moods") 50-75 50
COLUMBIA (6173 "Gems") 50-75 51
COLUMBIA (8000 series) 15-25 60
COLUMBIA (9000 series) 6-12 70
COLUMBIA SPECIAL PRODUCTS 5-8 79
DIAL (205 "Garner Trio") 75-100 50
(10–inch LP.)
DIAL (902 "Gaslight Session") 60-80 50
(10–inch LP.)
EMARCY (26000 series) 20-40 54
(10–inch LP.)
EMARCY (36000 series) 20-30 55-56
ENRICA 15-25 59
EVEREST 5-10 70
GRAND AWARD 20-35 56
HARMONY 8-12 68
JAZZTONE 20-35 57
KING (265-17 "Erroll Garner") 50-75 54
(10–inch LP.)
KING (540 "Erroll Garner") 25-35 58
LONDON 8-12 72-73
MGM 10-20 65-68
MERCURY (20009 "At the Piano") ... 50-75 50
MERCURY (20055 "Mambo") 40-60 54
MERCURY (20063 "Solitaire") 40-60 54
MERCURY (20090 "Afternoon of an Elf") 40-60 55
MERCURY (20662 thru 20859) 15-25 62-63
(Monaural.)
MERCURY (25117 "At the Piano") ... 50-75 51
(10–inch LP.)
MERCURY (25157 "Gone with Garner") 50-75 51
(10–inch LP.)
MERCURY (60662 thru 60859) 20-30 62-63
(Stereo.)
MERCURY (61000 series) 8-12 70
REPRISE 12-25 63
RONDO-LETTE 15-25 58
ROOST (10 "Piano Magic") 40-60 52
(10–inch LP.)
ROOST (2213 "Giants") 25-40 56
SAVOY (1100 series) 5-10 78
SAVOY (2000 series) 5-10 76
SAVOY (12002 "Erroll Garner") 30-50 55
SAVOY (12003 "Erroll Garner, Vol. 2") 30-50 55
SAVOY (12008 "Erroll Garner") 30-50 55
SAVOY (15000 "At the Piano") 75-125 49
(10–inch LP.)
SAVOY (15001 "At the Piano, Vol. 2") 75-125 50
(10–inch LP.)
SAVOY (15002 "At the Piano, Vol. 3") 75-125 50
(10–inch LP.)
SAVOY (15004 "At the Piano, Vol. 4") 75-125 50
(10–inch LP.)
SAVOY (15026 "At the Piano, Vol. 5") 75-125 50
(10–inch LP.)
TRIP 5-10 74
WING 10-20 62
Also see STARR, Kay / Erroll Garner

GARNETT, Gale P&R/C&W/LP '64

Singles: 7–inch

RCA 5-10 64-67

Picture Sleeves

RCA 8-12 64

LPs: 10/12–inch

RCA 10-20 64-66

GARNETT, Gale, & Gentle Reign

Singles: 7–inch

COLUMBIA 4-6 68

LPs: 10/12–inch

COLUMBIA 8-12 68-69
Also see GARNETT, Gale

GARR, Artie

(Art Garfunkel)

Singles: 7–inch

OCTAVIA (8002 "Private Love") 20-30 61
WARWICK (515 "Beat Love") 20-30 59
Also see GARFUNKEL, Art

GARRAFFA, Donna D&D '85

Singles: 12–inch

ARTIST INT'L 4-6 85

GARRETT, Lee P&R/R&B '76

Singles: 7–inch

CHRYSALIS 3-5 76

GARRETT, Leif P&R/LP '77

Singles: 7–inch

ATLANTIC 3-5 77-78
SCOTTI BROS 3-4 78-81

Picture Sleeves

ATLANTIC 3-5 77-78
SCOTTI BROS 3-4 78-81

LPs: 10/12–inch

ATLANTIC 5-10 77
SCOTTI BROS 5-10 78-81
Also see CHIC / Roberta Flack / Leif Garrett / Genesis

GARRETT, Scott P&R '59

(Scott Garret)

Singles: 7–inch

LAURIE (3023 "House of Love") 10-15 59
LAURIE (3029 "Love Story") 20-30 59
(With the Mystics.)
LAURIE (3034 "Where Are You") 10-15 59
OKEH 8-10 60
Session: Mystics.
Also see MYSTICS

GARRETT, Siedah R&B/D&D '85

Singles: 12–inch

QWEST 4-6 85

Singles: 7–inch

QWEST 3-4 85-88

Picture Sleeves

QWEST 3-4 85-88
Also see JACKSON, Michael

GARRETT, Tommy

(Tommy Garrett & 25 Pianos)

LPs: 10/12–inch

LIBERTY 8-15 62
Also see 50 GUITARS of TOMMY GARRETT

GARRETT, Vernon R&B '69

Singles: 78 rpm

MODERN 10-20 57

Singles: 7–inch

ICA 3-5 77
KAPP 4-6 70
KENT (459 "Shine It On") 10-15 64
KENT (476 "Running Out") 10-15 65
MODERN 10-20 57
VENTURE 5-10 69

GARRETT, Vernon, & Marie Franklin

Singles: 7–inch

VENTURE 3-5 76

GARRETT'S CREW R&B '83

Singles: 7–inch

CLOCKWORK 3-4 83

GARY, John LP '63

Singles: 7–inch

ACE 3-5 62
BIG B 3-5 64
FRATERNITY 3-6 59-66
RCA 3-5 63-71
ST. JAMES 3-5 63

EPs: 7–inch

RCA (2804 "John Gary") 4-8 63
(Stereo Compact 33.)

LPs: 10/12–inch

CAMDEN 5-10 68
CHURCHILL 4-8 77
METRO 5-10 65
RCA 5-15 63-78
SPIN-O-RAMA 5-10 60s
WYNCOTE 5-10 60s
Also see ANN-MARGRET & John Gary
Also see DESMOND, Johnny / John Gary / Gordon MacRae

GARY & CLYDE

Singles: 7–inch

REV (3523 "Why Not Confess") 20-30 59
SHAD (5016 "Tami's Dance") 10-20 60
Members: Gary Paxton; Clyde Batton.
Also see SKIP & FLIP

GARY & DAVE P&R '73

Singles: 7–inch

LONDON 3-5 73
Members: Gary Weeks; Dave Beckett.

GARY O' P&R '81
(Gary O'Connor)
Singles: 7-inch
RCA 3-4 85
Picture Sleeves
RCA 3-4 85
LPs: 10/12-inch
CAPITOL 5-10 81

GARY'S GANG P&R/R&B/LP '79
Singles: 12-inch
COLUMBIA 4-8 79
RADAR 4-6 83
Singles: 7-inch
COLUMBIA 3-5 79
RADAR 3-4 83
LPs: 10/12-inch
COLUMBIA 5-10 79
Members: Gary Turnier; Eric Matthew.

GASCA, Luis LP '72
LPs: 10/12-inch
BLUE THUMB 8-10 72

GATES, David P&R/LP '73
(With the Accents)
Singles: 7-inch
ARISTA 3-4 81
DEL-FI (4206 "No One Really Loves a Clown") 10-20 63
EAST WEST (123 "Walkin' and Talkin' ") 75-100 59
ELEKTRA 3-5 73-80
MALA (413 "You'll Be My Baby") 60-80 60
MALA (418 "Happiest Man Alive") 40-50 61
MALA (427 "Jo-Baby") 40-50 61
PERSPECTIVE ("Jo-Baby") 50-100 58
(No selection number used. 1200 made.)
PLANETARY (108 "Once Upon a Time") 10-15 65
ROBBINS (1008 "Jo-Baby") 35-45 61
Picture Sleeves
ELEKTRA 3-5 77
LPs: 10/12-inch
ARISTA 5-10 81
ELEKTRA 8-15 73-80
Also see ASHLEY, Del
Also see BREAD
Also see JENNIE & JAY
Also see PETERSEN, Paul
Also see VIBES

GATES, Ed "Great" R&B '49
(Great Gates; Ed [The Great] Gates; Edward White)
Singles: 78 rpm
ALADDIN 8-12 55
RECORDED in HOLLYWOOD 15-25 52
SELECTIVE 10-20 49
Singles: 7-inch
ALADDIN 15-25 55
4 STAR (1712 "You Are My Love") ... 10-20 57
ROBINS NEXT (103 "Can You Feel It") 10-20 62
SPECIALTY 10-15 59

GATLIN, Larry P&R '74
(With the Gatlin Brothers Band; with Family & Friends; Gatlin Quartet)
Singles: 7-inch
CAPITOL 3-4 90
COLUMBIA 3-5 79-88
MONUMENT 3-5 73-78
UNIVERSAL 3-4 89
LPs: 10/12-inch
COLUMBIA 5-10 79-86
HITSVILLE 5-10 76
MONUMENT 5-10 74-78
SWORD & SHIELD (9009 "The Old Country Church") 25-50 61
(By the Gatlin Quartet, which included sister Donna.)
Members: Larry Gatlin; Steve Gatlin; Rudy Gatlin.

GATLIN, Larry, & Janie Frickie
(With the Gatlin Brothers) C&W '87
Singles: 7-inch
COLUMBIA 3-4 87

GATTON, Danny LP '91
(Danny Gatton Band; with Billy Windsor)
Singles: 7-inch
NRG 3-4 87-90
Picture Sleeves
NRG 3-4 90
LPs: 10/12-inch
ELEKTRA 5-8 91
NRG 5-10 87
Members: Danny Gatton; Billy Windsor; John Previti; Dave Elliot; Jim Cavanaugh; Randy Hart.

GAYE, Ellie
(Ellie Greenwich)
Singles: 7-inch
RCA ("Silly Isn't It") 15-25 50s
(Selection number not known.)
Also see GREENWICH, Ellie

GAYE, Marvin P&R/R&B '62
(With the Love Tones)
Singles: 12-inch
COLUMBIA (Except 40133) 4-6 83-85
COLUMBIA (40133 "Sanctified Lady") 10-15 85
(Picture disc.)
MOTOWN 4-8 78
Singles: 7-inch
COLUMBIA 3-4 82-85
DETROIT FREE PRESS ("The Teen Beat Song") 50-100 66
(Promotional issue only.)
JOBETE (1 "Save the Children") 20-30
MOTOWN 3-4
MOTOWN/TOPPS (6 "How Sweet It Is to Be Loved by You") 50-75 67
(Topps Chewing Gum promotional item. Single-sided, cardboard flexi, picture disc. Issued with generic paper sleeve.)
TAMLA ("Witchcraft") 300-500 61
(Promotional issue only. No selection number used. Credited to "Marvin Gay.")
TAMLA ("My Way") 30-50 65
(Promotional issue only. No selection number used.)
TAMLA (1800 series) 3-4 86
TAMLA (54041 "Let Your Conscience Be Your Guide") 50-75 61
TAMLA (54055 "Sandman") 45-55 62
TAMLA (54063 "Soldier's Plea") 25-30 62
(Credits only Marvin Gaye.)
TAMLA (54063 "Soldier's Plea") 15-25 62
(Credits Marvin Gaye and "Love Tones.")
TAMLA (54068 "Stubborn Kind of Fellow") 15-25 62
TAMLA (54075 thru 54185) 5-15 63-69
TAMLA (54190 "Gonna Give Her All the Love I've Got") 4-8 69
(Black vinyl.)
TAMLA (54190 "Gonna Give Her All the Love I've Got") 10-15 69
(Colored vinyl. Promotional issue only.)
TAMLA (54195 thru 54280) 3-6 70-77
(Black vinyl.)
TAMLA (54000 series) 5-10 72-76
(Colored vinyl. Promotional issues only.)
Picture Sleeves
TAMLA (1800 series) 3-4 86
TAMLA (54095 "Try It Baby") 20-40 64
TAMLA (54101 "Baby, Don't You Do It") 20-40 64
TAMLA (54138 "Little Darlin I Need You") 30-50 66
TAMLA (54280 "Got to Give It Up") 4-8 77
EPs: 7-inch
MOTOWN (2016 "Marvin Gaye") 15-25 60s
TAMLA (60252 "Greatest Hits") 20-30 66
LPs: 10/12-inch
COLUMBIA 5-10 82-85
KORY 8-10 76-77
MOTOWN 8-12 64-83
NATURAL RESOURCES 5-10 78
TAMLA (221 "Soulful Moods") 400-600 61
TAMLA (239 "That Stubborn Kind of Fella") 75-125 63
TAMLA (242 "On Stage") 25-50 63
TAMLA (251 "When I'm Alone I Cry") 25-50 64
TAMLA (252 "Greatest Hits") 15-25 64
TAMLA (258 "How Sweet It Is") 15-25 65
TAMLA (266 "Moods") 40-60 66
TAMLA (278 thru 299) 10-20 67-69
TAMLA (300 series) 8-15 70-81
TAMLA (6100 series) 5-10 86
Also see MARTHA & VANDELLAS
Also see MARVELETTES / Mary Wells / Miracles / Marvin Gaye
Also see MOONGLOWS

GAYE, Marvin / Gladys Knight & Pips
Singles: 7-inch
MOTOWN 4-8 68
Also see KNIGHT, Gladys

GAYE, Marvin, & Diana Ross LP '73
Singles: 7-inch
MOTOWN 3-5 73-74
LPs: 10/12-inch
MOTOWN 8-12 73
Also see ROSS, Diana

GAYE, Marvin, & Tammi Terrell P&R '67
Singles: 7-inch
TAMLA (Black vinyl) 4-8 67-70
TAMLA (54192 "Onion Song") 8-12 69
(Colored vinyl. Promotional issue only.)
LPs: 10/12-inch
MOTOWN 5-10 80-82
TAMLA 10-15 67-70
Also see TERRELL, Tammi

GAYE, Marvin, & Mary Wells P&R/R&B/LP '64
Singles: 7-inch
MOTOWN 5-10 64
Picture Sleeves
MOTOWN (1057 "What's the Matter with You Baby") 20-40 64
LPs: 10/12-inch
MOTOWN (613 "Together") 40-50 64
Also see WELLS, Mary

GAYE, Marvin, & Kim Weston P&R/R&B '64
Singles: 7-inch
TAMLA 5-10 64-67
LPs: 10/12-inch
TAMLA (270 "Marvin Gaye & Kim Weston") 20-25 66
Also see GAYE, Marvin
Also see WESTON, Kim

GAYLE, Crystal C&W '70
Singles: 7-inch
COLUMBIA 3-5 79-82
DECCA 4-6 70-72
ELEKTRA 3-4 82
MCA 3-4 77
U.A. 3-5 74-80
W.B. 3-4 83-90
Picture Sleeves
COLUMBIA 3-5 79-82
U.A. 4-8 77
LPs: 10/12-inch
COLUMBIA 5-10 79-83
ELEKTRA 5-10 82
LIBERTY 5-10 80-82
MCA 5-10 78
MFSL (043 "We Must Believe in Magic") 20-40 80
U.A. (Except "Somebody Loves You" picture disc) 5-10 75-80

U.A. ("Somebody Loves You") 50-100 78
(Picture disc. Promotional issue only. One of a four-artist, four-disc set. 250 made.)
W.B. 5-10 83-90
Also see BUTLER, Larry, & Friends
Also see CAMPBELL, Glen / Anne Murray / Kenny Rogers / Crystal Gayle
Also see RABBITT, Eddie, & Crystal Gayle

GAYLE, Crystal, & Gary Morris C&W '88

Singles: 7-inch

W.B. 3-4 85-88
Also see MORRIS, Gary

GAYLE, Crystal, & Tom Waits

LPs: 10/12-inch

COLUMBIA....................................5-10 82
Also see GAYLE, Crystal
Also see WAITS, Tom

GAYLORD, Ronnie P&R '54

Singles: 78 rpm

MERCURY 4-8 54-55
WING...4-8 55-56

Singles: 7-inch

MERCURY 5-10 54-55
WING...5-10 55-56

EPs: 7-inch

MERCURY 5-10 55
Also see GAYLORD & HOLIDAY

GAYLORD & HOLIDAY LP '76

Singles: 7-inch

NATURAL RESOURCES.................3-4 77
PALMER...3-6 67
PRODIGAL.....................................3-4 76
VERVE...4-8 66

LPs: 10/12-inch

NATURAL RESOURCES.................5-10 76
PRODIGAL.....................................5-10 75
VMI 5-10 72
Members: Ronnie Gaylord; Burt Holiday.
Also see GAYLORD, Ronnie
Also see GAYLORDS

GAYLORDS P&R '52

Singles: 78 rpm

MERCURY 5-15 52-57

Singles: 7-inch

MERCURY 10-20 52-62
TIME 5-10 64

EPs: 7-inch

MERCURY 15-25 54-56

LPs: 10/12-inch

MERCURY (Except 25198) 15-35 55-63
MERCURY (25198 "By Request").....25-50 55
(10-inch LP.)
TIME 10-15 64
WING...10-20 59-64
Members: Ronnie Gaylord; Don Rea; Burt (Holiday) Bonaldi; Billy Christ.
Also see GAYLORD & HOLIDAY
Also see DEL-VIKINGS / Diamonds / Big Bopper / Gaylords

GAYNOR, Gloria P&R '74

Singles: 12-inch

POLYDOR.......................................4-6 78
SILVER BLUE 4-6 83

Singles: 7-inch

COLUMBIA.....................................3-5 73
JOCIDA 4-8 65
MGM...3-5 74-75
POLYDOR.......................................3-5 76-81
SILVER BLUE 3-4 83

LPs: 10/12-inch

ATLANTIC 5-10 82
MGM...8-10 75
POLYDOR.......................................5-10 76-80

GAYNOR, Mel R&B '55

Singles: 78 rpm

MODERN...5-10 55

Singles: 7-inch

MODERN...10-15 55

GAYTEN, Paul R&B '47

Singles: 78 rpm

ARGO 15-25 57
CHECKER 10-15 55-56
DELUXE..10-15 47-49
OKEH..10-15 52-55
REGAL...10-15 49-51

Singles: 7-inch

ANNA..10-20 59-60
ARGO 15-25 57-58
CHECKER (801 thru 836)...............10-20 55-58
OKEH..15-25 52-55
Also see HENRY, Clarence
Also see NEWSOM, Chubby, & Her Hip Shakers

GEDDES, David P&R '75

Singles: 7-inch

ATCO..3-5 75
BIG TREE 3-5 75
H&L 3-5 77
ZODIAC...3-5 77

LPs: 10/12-inch

BIG TREE 8-10 75

GEE, Ellie
(Ellie Greenwich)

Singles: 7-inch

MADISON (160 "Red Corvette")....... 15-25 61
Also see GREENWICH, Ellie

GEE, Spoonie: see SPOONIE GEE

GEILS, J., Band P&R/LP '71
(Geils)

Singles: 12-inch

EMI AMERICA (Except 9133)......... 4-8 82-84
EMI/AMERICA (9133 "Wildman")..... 10-20 78
(Colored vinyl. Promotional issue only.)

Singles: 7-inch

ATLANTIC..3-5 71-78
EMI AMERICA (Black vinyl)..............3-4 78-84
EMI AMERICA (Colored vinyl) 5-8 78
(Promotional issue only.)
EMI AMERICA (8119 "Centerfold").... 10-15 81
(Potato head-shaped picture disc.)
PRIVATE I...3-4 85

Picture Sleeves

ATLANTIC..3-5 73-78
EMI AMERICA 3-4 78-84
PRIVATE I...3-4 85

EPs: 7-inch

EMI AMERICA (9801 "Angel In Blue")..10-15 81
(Potato head-shaped picture disc. Promotional issue only.)

LPs: 10/12-inch

ATLANTIC (Black vinyl) 8-12 70-82
ATLANTIC (Colored vinyl) 15-20 73
EMI AMERICA 5-10 78-84
NAUTILUS (25 "Love Stinks") 15-20 82
(Half-speed mastered.)
Also see GUY, Buddy, with Dr. John & Eric Clapton / Buddy Guy with the J. Geils Band
Also see WOLF, Peter

GELDOF, Bob P&R '86

Singles: 7-inch

ATLANTIC..3-4 86

Picture Sleeves

ATLANTIC..3-4 86

LPs: 10/12-inch

ATLANTIC..5-10 86
Also see BAND AID
Also see BOOMTOWN RATS

GEM D&D '84

Singles: 12-inch

STREETKING....................................4-6 84

Singles: 7-inch

STREETKING....................................3-4 84

GENE & DEBBE P&R '67

Singles: 7-inch

HICKORY..3-5 70
TRX..4-6 67-69

LPs: 10/12-inch

TRX (1001 "Here and Now")............ 15-25 68
Members: Gene Thomas; Debbe Nevills.
Also see THOMAS, Gene

GENE & EUNICE R&B '55

Singles: 78 rpm

ALADDIN..10-15 55
COMBO 10-15 55

Singles: 7-inch

ALADDIN..15-25 55
CASE...10-15 59
COLLECTABLES 3-4
COMBO 15-25 55
ERA 3-5 72
LILLY 5-10 62
U.A. 3-4

EPs: 7-inch

CASE (100 "Gene & Eunice") 25-50 59
(Issued with paper sleeve.)
Members: Gene Forrest; Eunice Levy.

GENE (Chandler) & JERRY (Butler): see CHANDLER, Gene, & Jerry Butler

GENE & TOMMY

Singles: 7-inch

ABC 4-8 67
Members: Terry Cashman; Tommy West.
Also see CASHMAN & WEST

GENE & WENDELL R&B '61
(With the Sweethearts)

Singles: 78 rpm

SPECIALTY (613 "Lula Baby")..........20-30 57

Singles: 7-inch

PHILIPS...5-10 62-63
RAY STARR.......................................8-12 61-62
SPECIALTY (613 "Lula Baby")..........10-20 57

GENE LOVES JEZEBEL LP '86

Singles: 12-inch

GEFFEN 4-6 86

Singles: 7-inch

GEFFEN...3-4 86-90

Picture Sleeves

GEFFEN 3-4 88

LPs: 10/12-inch

GEFFEN...5-10 86-90
Members: Michael Aston; Jay Aston; James Stevenson; Chris Bell; Peter Rizzo.
Also see THOMPSON TWINS

GENERAL CAINE: see CAINE, General

GENERAL KANE R&B '86

Singles: 12-inch

MOTOWN..5-10 86

Singles: 7-inch

MOTOWN..3-4 86-87

LPs: 10/12-inch

MOTOWN..5-10 86

GENERAL PUBLIC P&R/D&D/LP '84

Singles: 12-inch

I.R.S. 4-6 84-86

Singles: 7-inch

I.R.S. 3-4 84-86

Picture Sleeves

I.R.S. 3-4 84

LPs: 10/12-inch

I.R.S. 5-10 84-86
Members: Roger Charley; Dave Wakeling.
Also see ENGLISH BEAT

GENESIS

Singles: 7-inch

MERCURY (72806 "Angeline") 5-10 68
MERCURY (72869 "Gloomy Sunday")..5-10 68

LPs: 10/12-inch

MERCURY (61175 "In the Beginning") 15-25 68
Members: Sue Richman; Jack Tanna; Bob Metke; Kent Henry; Fred Rivera.

GENESIS LP '73

Singles: 12-inch

ATLANTIC 4-6 86

Singles: 7-inch

ATCO...3-5 76-77
ATLANTIC 3-4 78-91

CHARISMA....4-6 73
PARROT (3018 "Silent Sun")....10-15 68
(Promotional issue only.)

Promotional Singles

ATCO....3-5 76-77
ATLANTIC....3-4 78-86
CHARISMA....4-8 73
PARROT....10-15 68

Picture Sleeves

ATLANTIC....3-5 80-87

EPs: 7-inch

ATLANTIC (1800 "Spot the Pigeon")....5-10 77
(Promotional issue only.)

LPs: 10/12-inch

ABC....8-10 74
ATCO....8-15 74-77
ATLANTIC....5-10 78-86
BUDDAH (5659 "Best of Genesis")...10-15 76
CHARISMA....8-12 72-79
IMPULSE....15-25 70
LONDON (600 series)....10-15 74
LONDON (50000 series)....5-10 77
MCA....5-10 78
MFSL (062 "Trick of the Tail")....40-60 82

Members: Phil Collins; Peter Gabriel; Tony Banks; Steve Hackett; Anthony Phillips; Mike Rutherford.

Also see BANKS, Tony
Also see CHIC / Roberta Flack / Leif Garrett / Genesis
Also see COLLINS, Phil
Also see GABRIEL, Peter
Also see HACKETT, Steve
Also see PHILLIPS, Anthony
Also see RUTHERFORD, Mike

GENTLE GIANT LP '72

Singles: 7-inch

CAPITOL....3-5 74-78
COLUMBIA....3-5 72-73

LPs: 10/12-inch

CAPITOL....5-10 74-80
COLUMBIA....8-10 72-73
VERTIGO....10-15 71

Members: Derek Shulman; Ray Shulman; Phil Shulman; Gary Green; Kerry Minnear; Tony Visconti; John Weathers; Martin Smith.

GENTLE PERSUASION P&R '83

Singles: 7-inch

CAPITOL....3-4 83
W.B.....5-10 78

GENTRY, Bobbie P&R/C&W/R&B/LP '67

Singles: 7-inch

BRUNSWICK....3-5 75
CAPITOL....3-6 67-76
W.B.....3-5 76-78

Picture Sleeves

CAPITOL....3-6 67-72
W.B.....3-5 76

LPs: 10/12-inch

CAPITOL (Except "SM" series)....8-15 67-71
CAPITOL ("SM" series)....5-10 81
W.B. ("*Ode to Billie Joe:* Radio Salute to Bobbie Gentry")....15-20 76
(Promotional issue only.)

Also see CAMPBELL, Glen, & Bobbie Gentry
Also see REYNOLDS, Jody, & Bobbie Gentry

GENTRYS P&R/LP '65

Singles: 7-inch

BELL....4-8 68
CAPITOL....3-5 72
MGM (Except 13690)....4-8 65-67
MGM (13690 "There's a Love")....8-10 67
STAX....3-5 74
SUN (1108 thru 1122)....4-6 70-71
(Black vinyl, whether commercial or promo.)
SUN (1108 thru 1122)....10-15 70-71
(Colored vinyl. Promotional issues only.)
SUN (1126 "God Save Our Country")....10-20 71
YOUNGSTOWN (600 "Little Drops of Water")....15-25 65
YOUNGSTOWN (601 "Keep on Dancing")....15-25 65

Picture Sleeves

MGM....5-10 65

LPs: 10/12-inch

MGM....20-30 65-70
SUN....20-30 70

Members: Larry Raspberry; Jimmy Johnson; Bruce Bowles; Pat Neal; Jimmy Hart.

GENTY R&B '80

Singles: 7-inch

VENTURE....3-5 80

GEORGE, Barbara P&R/R&B '61

Singles: 7-inch

AFO....8-15 61-62
HEP'ME....5-10
SUE....5-10 62-63
U.A.....3-5 74

LPs: 10/12-inch

AFO (5001 "I Know")....50-75 62

GEORGE, Lowell LP '79

Singles: 7-inch

W.B.....3-5 78-79

LPs: 10/12-inch

W.B.....5-10 78-79

Also see LITTLE FEAT
Also see MOTHERS of INVENTION

GEORGE, Robin P&R '85

Singles: 7-inch

BRONZE....3-4 85

Picture Sleeves

BRONZE....3-4 85

GEORGE & GENE (Jones & Pitney): see JONES, George, & Gene Pitney

GEORGIA SATELLITES P&R/LP '86

Singles: 12-inch

ELEKTRA....4-8 89
(Promotional only.)

Singles: 7-inch

ELEKTRA....3-4 86-89

Picture Sleeves

ELEKTRA....3-4 86-87

LPs: 10/12-inch

ELEKTRA....5-10 86-89

Members: Dan Baird; Rick Richards; Rich Price.

GEORGIO P&R/R&B/LP '87

Singles: 7-inch

MACOLO....3-4 87
MOTOWN....3-4 87

Picture Sleeves

MOTOWN....3-4 87

LPs: 10/12-inch

MOTOWN....5-10 87

GERARD, Danyel P&R '72

Singles: 7-inch

COLUMBIA....4-6 72
MGM/VERVE....3-5 72

LPs: 10/12-inch

VERVE....8-12 71

GERARDO LP '91

LPs: 10/12-inch

INTERSCOPE....5-8 91

GERRARD, Donny P&R '76

Singles: 7-inch

GREEDY....3-5 76-77
ROCKET....3-5 76

LPs: 10/12-inch

GREEDY....8-10

Also see SKYLARK

GERRY & PACEMAKERS P&R/LP '64

Singles: 7-inch

ERIC....3-4 70s
LAURIE (3196 "I Like It")....10-15 63
LAURIE (3233 "How Do You Do It")...8-12 64
LAURIE (3251 thru 3370)....5-10 64-67

LPs: 10/12-inch

ACCORD....5-10 81
CAPITOL....5-10 79
LAURIE....15-25 64-66
LAURIE/CAPITOL....8-10 81
(Label reads "Mfd. by Capitol Records." Record club issue.)
U.A.....20-25 65

Member: Gerry Marsden.

Also see MARTIN, George, & His Orchestra

GESTURES P&R '64

Singles: 7-inch

APEX....10-15 60s
SOMA (Black vinyl)....8-12 64-65
SOMA (1417 "Run Run Run")....25-35 64
(Colored vinyl.)

Member: Dale Menton.

Also see CASTAWAYS / Gestures

GET WET P&R '81

Singles: 7-inch

BOARDWALK....3-4 81

Picture Sleeves

BOARDWALK....3-4 81

LPs: 10/12-inch

BOARDWALK....5-10 81

GETO BOYS LP '90

(Ghetto Boys)

LPs: 10/12-inch

DEF AMERICAN....5-8 90
RAP-A-LOT....5-8 90

GETZ, Stan LP '92

(Stan Getz Quintet)

Singles: 78 rpm

CLEF....3-8 53-54
DAWN....3-8 54
MERCURY....3-8 53
NORGRAN....3-8 54-55
PRESTIGE....3-8 50-53
ROOST....3-8 50-53

Singles: 7-inch

CLEF....5-10 53-54
COLUMBIA....3-4 75-80
DAWN....5-10 54
MGM....3-5 65
MERCURY....5-10 53
NORGRAN....5-10 54-55
PRESTIGE....5-10 50-53
ROOST....5-10 50-53
VERVE....3-8 60-72

EPs: 7-inch

CLEF....10-20 53
DALE....15-25 51
NORGRAN (11 thru 155)....20-30 53-55
NORGRAN (2000-6 "At the Shrine")....50-100 55
(Boxed, six-disc set.)
PRESTIGE (1309 "Stan Getz")....20-40 52
ROOST....15-25 50-53

LPs: 10/12-inch

A&M....5-8 90
AMERICAN RECORDING SOCIETY....20-30 57
BARONET....10-20 62
BLUE RIBBON....10-20 61
CLEF (137 "Stan Getz Plays")....75-100 53
(10-inch LP.)
CLEF (143 "Artistry of Stan Getz")..75-100 53
(10-inch LP.)
COLUMBIA....5-10 74-82
CONCORD JAZZ....5-10 81
CROWN (5002 "Groovin' High")....20-35 57
DALE (21 "Retrospect")....100-150 51
(10-inch LP.)
INNER CITY....5-10 78
JAZZ MAN....5-10 82
JAZZTONE....20-30 57
MGM (Except 4312)....5-10 70
MGM (4312 "Mickey One")....12-20 65
(Soundtrack.)
METRO....10-15 65
MODERN (1202 "Groovin' High")....35-50 56
NEW JAZZ....15-25 59
NORGRAN (4 "Stan Getz")....100-150 53
(10-inch LP.)
NORGRAN (1000 "Interpretations") 50-100 54

NORGRAN (1008 "Interpretations, Vol. 2") 50-100 54
NORGRAN (1029 "Interpretations, Vol. 3") 50-100 55
NORGRAN (1032 "West Coast Jazz") 40-60 55
NORGRAN (1087 "Stan Getz '57") ... 40-60 57
NORGRAN (2000-2 "At the Shrine") 100-200 55
(With booklet.)
PRESTIGE (102 "Stan Getz") 100-200 52
(10–inch LPs)
PRESTIGE (7002 thru 7022) 25-50 56
(Yellow label.)
PRESTIGE (7252 thru 7256) 25-50 56
(Yellow label.)
PRESTIGE (7000 series) 8-18 64-68
(Blue label.)
PRESTIGE (24000 series) 8-12 72-79
ROOST (103 "Stan Getz Years") 30-40 64
ROOST (402 "Stan Getz") 100-150 50
(10–inch LPs)
ROOST (404 "Stan Getz and the Swedish All Stars") 100-125 51
(10–inch LPs)
ROOST (407 "Jazz at Storyville") 75-100 53
(10–inch LPs)
ROOST (411 "Jazz at Storyville, Vol. 2") 75-100 54
(10–inch LP.)
ROOST (420 "Jazz at Storyville, Vol. 3") 75-100 54
(10–inch LP.)
ROOST (417 "Chamber Music") 75-100 54
(10–inch LP.)
ROOST (2207 "Sounds of Stan Getz") 25-40 56
ROOST (2249 thru 2258) 20-30 63
ROULETTE 8-12 71-72
SAVOY (1100 series) 5-10 77
SAVOY (9004 "All Star Series") 100-150 51
(10–inch LPs)
SEECO (7 "Highlights in Modern Jazz") 75-125 54
(10–inch LP.)
VSP 8-12 66-67
VERVE 25-50 57-60
(Reads "Verve Records, Inc." at bottom of label.)
VERVE 15-30 61-72
(Reads "MGM Records - a Division of Metro-Goldwyn-Mayer, Inc." at bottom of label.)
VERVE 5-10 73-84
(Reads "Manufactured By MGM Record Corp.," or mentions either Polydor or Polygram at bottom of label.)
Also see BENNETT, Tony
Also see GILLESPIE, Dizzy, & Stan Getz
Also see HAMPTON, Lionel, & Stan Getz
Also see HOLIDAY, Billie, & Stan Getz
Also see TJADER, Cal, & Stan Getz

GETZ, Stan, & Laurindo Almeida

Singles: 7–inch

VERVE 4-6 66

LPs: 10/12–inch

VERVE 10-15 66
Also see ALMEIDA, Laurindo

GETZ, Stan, & Boston Pops Orchestra

LPs: 10/12–inch

RCA 10-20 67
Also see BOSTON POPS ORCHESTRA

GETZ, Stan, & Charlie Byrd — *P&R/LP '62*

Singles: 7–inch

MGM 3-4 78
VERVE 3-5 62

LPs: 10/12–inch

VERVE 15-25 62
Also see BYRD, Charlie

GETZ, Stan, & Oscar Peterson

LPs: 10/12–inch

VERVE 20-40 57-60
(Reads "Verve Records, Inc." at bottom of label.)
VERVE 10-25 61-72
(Reads "MGM Records - a Division of Metro-Goldwyn-Mayer, Inc." at bottom of label.)
Also see PETERSON, Oscar

GETZ & GILBERTO — *P&R/LP '64*

(With Joao & Astrud Gilberto)

Singles: 7–inch

MGM 3-4 78
VERVE 4-6 64-65

LPs: 10/12–inch

MFSL (208 "Getz & Gilberto") 20-25 94
VERVE (8545 "Getz & Gilberto") 20-30 64
Also see GETZ, Stan
Also see GILBERTO, Astrud

GIANT — *P&R/LP '89*

Singles: 7–inch

A&M 3-4 89-90

LPs: 10/12–inch

A&M 5-8 89
MERCURY 8-10 70
Members: Dann Huff; David Huff.

GIANT STEPS — *P&R/LP '88*

Singles: 7–inch

A&M 3-4 88-89

LPs: 10/12–inch

A&M 5-8 88

GIBB, Andy — *P&R/R&B/LP '77*

Singles: 7–inch

RSO 3-4 77-81

Picture Sleeves

RSO 3-4 77-78

LPs: 10/12–inch

RSO 5-10 77-80
Also see BEE GEES
Also see NEWTON-JOHN, Olivia, & Andy Gibb

GIBB, Andy, & Victoria Principal — *P&R '81*

Singles: 7–inch

RSO 3-5 81

Picture Sleeves

RSO 5-10 81
Also see GIBB, Andy

GIBB, Barry — *P&R '80*

Singles: 12–inch

MCA 4-6 84

Singles: 7–inch

ATCO (6786 "One Bad Thing") 100-150 69
MCA 3-4 84

Picture Sleeves

MCA 3-4 84

LPs: 10/12–inch

MCA 5-10 84
Also see BEE GEES
Also see STREISAND, Barbra, & Barry Gibb
Also see WARWICK, Dionne

GIBB, Maurice

Singles: 7–inch

ATCO 3-5 70
Also see BEE GEES

GIBB, Robin — *P&R '78*

Singles: 12–inch

MIRAGE 4-6 84

Singles: 7–inch

ATCO 3-5 69-71
EMI AMERICA 3-4 85
MIRAGE 3-4 84
POLYDOR 3-4 83
RSO 3-5 78
SESAME STREET 3-5 78

Picture Sleeves

EMI AMERICA 3-4 85
MIRAGE 3-4 84
POLYDOR 3-4 83
SESAME STREET 3-5 78

LPs: 10/12–inch

ATCO 8-10 70
MIRAGE 5-10 84
POLYDOR 5-10 83
Also see BEE GEES
Also see LEVY, Marcy, & Robin Gibb

GIBBONS, Steve, Band — *P&R '76*

Singles: 7–inch

MCA/GOLD HAWKE 3-5 76-78
POLYDOR 3-5 78

LPs: 10/12–inch

MCA 8-10 76-77
POLYDOR 5-10 78-80
Also see DALTREY, Roger, & Steve Gibbons

GIBBS, Doug — *R&B '72*

Singles: 7–inch

OAK 3-5 72

GIBBS, Georgia — *P&R '50*

Singles: 78 rpm

CORAL 5-10 50-51
MERCURY 5-10 51-57

Singles: 7–inch

BELL 4-8 64-66
CORAL 10-20 50-51
EPIC (Except 9606) 4-8 63-64
EPIC (9606 "Tater Poon") 10-15 63
IMPERIAL 5-10 60
KAPP 5-10 59
MERCURY 10-20 51-57
RCA (Except 6922 & 7047) 5-15 57-67
RCA (6922 "I'm Walking the Floor Over You") 15-25 57
RCA (7047 "Fun Lovin' Baby") 15-25 57
ROULETTE 5-10 58-59

EPs: 7–inch

MERCURY 10-20 54-56
ROYALE (239 "Georgia Gibbs Sings") 10-20 50s
(Colored vinyl.)

LPs: 10/12–inch

BELL 10-15 66
CORAL (56037 "Ballin' the Jack") 30-50 51
(10–inch LP.)
CORAL (57183 "Her Nibs") 20-40 57
EMARCY (36103 "Swingin' with Gibbs") 20-40 57
EPIC 10-20 63
IMPERIAL 10-20 60
MERCURY (20071 "Music and Memories") 20-40 55
MERCURY (20114 "Song Favorites of Georgia Gibbs") 20-40 56
MERCURY (20170 "Swingin' with Her Nibs") 20-40 56
MERCURY (25175 "Georgia Gibbs Sings Oldies") 40-60 53
(10–inch LP.)
MERCURY (25199 "The Man That Got Away") 40-60 54
(10–inch LP.)
RONDO 8-12
SUNSET 8-12 66
TOPPS 10-20
Also see DIAMONDS / Georgia Gibbs / Sarah Vaughan

GIBBS, Terri — *C&W '80*

Singles: 7–inch

HORIZON 3-4 87
MCA 3-4 80-83
TEM 3-4 82
W.B. 3-4 85

LPs: 10/12–inch

HORIZON 5-8 87
MCA 5-10 81-83
PHONORAMA 5-10 84
W.B. 5-8 85
Also see MATTEA, Kathy

GIBSON, Beverly Ann — *R&B '59*

Singles: 7–inch

DEB 5-10 59
JUBILEE 4-8 63
LANDA 4-8 61

GIBSON, Debbie P&R/LP '87
Singles: 7-inch
ATLANTIC ... 3-4 87-90
Picture Sleeves
ATLANTIC ... 3-4 87-90
LPs: 10/12-inch
ATLANTIC ... 5-10 87-89

GIBSON, Don C&W '56
Singles: 78 rpm
COLUMBIA ... 5-10 52-54
MGM ... 15-35 55-56
RCA ... 8-12 51
Singles: 7-inch
ABC/HICKORY ... 3-5 75-78
COLUMBIA (20000 series) ... 8-15 52-54
HICKORY ... 3-5 70-72
MCA ... 3-5 79
MGM (12109 "Run Boy") ... 15-25 55
MGM (12194 "Sweet Dreams") ... 15-25 56
MGM (12290 "I Ain't Gonna Waste My Time") ... 20-30 56
MGM (12331 "I Believed in You") ... 15-25 56
MGM (12393 "I'm Gonna Fool Everybody") ... 20-30 57
MGM (12494 "I Ain't A-Studying You Baby") ... 25-35 57
RCA (0400 series) ... 10-20 51
RCA (4300 & 4400 series) ... 10-20 51-52
RCA (7000 series, except 7762) ... 8-15 58-61
RCA (47-7762 "Legend in My Time") .. 6-10 60
(Monaural.)
RCA (61-7762 "Legend in My Time") ... 15-20 60
(Stereo.)
RCA (8000 & 9000 series) ... 4-8 62-70
W.B./CURB ... 3-4 80
Picture Sleeves
RCA ... 5-10 63
EPs: 7-inch
COLUMBIA ... 15-20 57
RCA ... 10-20 58-59
LPs: 10/12-inch
ABC/HICKORY ... 6-10 75-78
CAMDEN ... 10-15 65-74
HARMONY (7300 series) ... 15-20 65
HARMONY (31000 series) ... 5-10 72
HICKORY ... 8-12 70-72
HICKORY/MGM ... 6-10 73-75
LION (70069 "Songs by Don Gibson") ... 25-50 58
MGM ... 8-12 70
METRO ... 12-18 65
RCA (1743 thru 2878) ... 15-30 58-63
(With "LPM" prefix. Monaural.)
RCA (1743 thru 2878) ... 20-40 58-63
(With "LSP" prefix. Stereo.)
RCA (3376 thru 4378) ... 10-20 63-70
(With "LPM" or "LSP" prefix.)
Session: Jordanaires.
Also see WEST, Dottie, & Don Gibson

GIBSON, Don, & Sue Thompson C&W '71
Singles: 7-inch
HICKORY ... 3-5 71-76
LPs: 10/12-inch
HICKORY ... 8-12 73
HICKORY/MGM ... 5-10 75
Also see GIBSON, Don
Also see THOMPSON, Sue

GIBSON, Ginny P&R '53
Singles: 78 rpm
ABC-PAR ... 3-8 56
DERBY ... 3-8 52
MGM ... 3-8 51-55
Singles: 7-inch
ABC-PAR ... 5-10 56
DERBY ... 5-10 52
MGM ... 5-10 51-55
EPs: 7-inch
JD ... 8-12

GIBSON, Johnny P&R '62
(Johnny Gibson Trio)
Singles: 7-inch
BIG TOP (3088 "Midnight") ... 10-20 62
BIG TOP (3118 "After Midnight") ... 10-20 62
BIG TOP (3149 "Ooh Poo Pah") ... 10-20 63
LAURIE (3256 "Beachcomber") ... 8-12 64
TWIRL (2012 "Beachcomber") ... 10-20 64
(First issue.)
Also see JOHNNY & HURRICANES

GIBSON, Steve P&R '48
(With the Red Caps; with Original Red Caps; Red Caps; "Vocal Solo By George Tinley")
Singles: 78 rpm
ABC-PAR ... 10-25 56-57
BEACON ... 15-25 44
MERCURY ... 25-50 47-54
RCA ... 20-30 51-55
Singles: 7-inch
ABC-PAR (9702 "Love Me Tender") ... 15-25 56
ABC-PAR (9750 "Write to Me") ... 15-25 56
ABC-PAR (9796 "You May Not Love Me") ... 15-25 57
ABC-PAR (9856 "Silhouettes") ... 15-25 57
BAND BOX (325 "No More") ... 10-15 62
CASA BLANCA (5505 "Where Are You") ... 100-200 59
(First issue.)
HI LO (101 "I Want to Be Loved") ... 25-50 58
HI LO (103 "It's Love") ... 25-50 58
HUNT (326 "Cheryl Lee") ... 25-35 59
HUNT (330 "Where Are You") ... 20-30 59
JAY DEE (796 "It Hurts Me But I Like It") ... 50-100 54
MERCURY (1253 "I Don't Want to Set the World on Fire") ... 100-200 49
MERCURY (1255 "Blueberry Hill") ... 100-200 49
MERCURY (5380 "I'll Never Love Anyone Else") ... 100-200 50
MERCURY (8038 "San Antonio Rose") ... 50-100 51
MERCURY (8069 "Wedding Bells") ... 50-100 51
MERCURY (8146 "Blueberry Hill") ... 50-100 51
MERCURY (70389 "Wedding Bells") ... 40-60 54
RCA (0127 "I'm to Blame") ... 50-100 51
RCA (0138 "Would I Mind") ... 50-100 51
RCA (3986 "The Thing") ... 75-125 50
RCA (4076 "Three Dollars and Ninety-Eight Cents") ... 30-60 51
RCA (4294 "Shame") ... 30-60 51
RCA (4670 "Two Little Kisses") ... 30-60 52
RCA (4835 "I Went to Your Wedding") ... 30-60 52
RCA (5103 "Truthfully") ... 30-60 52
RCA (5130 "Big Game Hunter") ... 30-60 53
RCA (6096 "Feelin' Kinda Happy") ... 25-50 55
RCA (6345 "How I Cry") ... 25-50 55
ROSE (555 "My Heart Belongs to Only You") ... 15-25 59
ROSE (5534 "Bless You") ... 15-25 60
STAGE (3001 "Blueberry Hill") ... 15-25
EPs: 7-inch
MERCURY (3215 "Blueberry Hill") ... 200-300 52
LPs: 10/12-inch
MERCURY (25115 "You're Driving Me Crazy") ... 300-400 52
(10-inch LP. Title on label is *Harmony Time.*)
MERCURY (25116 "Blueberry Hill") ... 300-400 52
(10-inch LP. Title on label is *Singing & Swinging.*)
Member: George Tinley.
Also see DAMITA JO with Steve Gibson & Red Caps
Also see FIVE RED CAPS
Also see GIBSON, Steve
Also see GREGG, Bobby

GIBSON, Steve, & His Red Caps / Damita Jo with Steve Gibson & Red Caps
Singles: 78 rpm
RCA (5987 "My Tzatskele") ... 15-25 55
Singles: 7-inch
RCA (5987 "My Tzatskele") ... 30-40 55
Also see DAMITA JO with Steve Gibson & Red Caps
Also see GIBSON, Steve

GIBSON BROTHERS P&R/R&B/LP '79
Singles: 12-inch
ISLAND ... 4-6 79
Singles: 7-inch
ISLAND ... 3-4 79
LPs: 10/12-inch
HOMESTEAD ... 5-8 90
ISLAND ... 5-8 79

GIDEA PARK P&R '82
(Featuring Adrian Baker)
Singles: 7-inch
PROFILE ... 3-4 82

GILBERTO, Astrud LP '64
Singles: 7-inch
CTI ... 3-5 71
VERVE ... 3-5 67-70
LPs: 10/12-inch
IMAGE ... 5-10 78
PERCEPTION ... 5-10 72
VERVE ... 8-15 65-70
Also see GETZ & GILBERTO
Also see JOBIM, Antonio Carlos
Also see JONES, Quincy
Also see WANDERLEY, Walter

GILBERTO, Astrud, & Stanley Turrentine
LPs: 10/12-inch
CTI ... 5-10 71
Also see GILBERTO, Astrud
Also see TURRENTINE, Stanley

GILDER, Nick P&R/LP '78
Singles: 7-inch
CHRYSALIS ... 3-5 76-79
RCA ... 3-4 85
Picture Sleeves
CHRYSALIS ... 3-5 78
RCA ... 3-4 85
LPs: 10/12-inch
CASABLANCA ... 5-10 80
CHRYSALIS ... 5-10 77-79
Also see SWEENY TODD

GILKYSON, Terry P&R '57
(With the Easy Riders; with South Coasters)
Singles: 78 rpm
COLUMBIA ... 4-8 54-57
DECCA ... 4-8 51-52
Singles: 7-inch
COLUMBIA ... 5-10 54-57
DECCA ... 5-10 51-52
Picture Sleeves
COLUMBIA (40817 "Marianne") ... 10-15 57
EPs: 7-inch
COLUMBIA ... 5-15 57
DECCA ... 5-15 53
LPs: 10/12-inch
DECCA (5263 "Folk Songs by a Solitary Singer") ... 20-40 50
DECCA (5305 "Solitary Singer") ... 25-50 51
(10-inch LP.)
DECCA (5457 "Golden Minutes of Folk Music") ... 25-50 53
(10-inch LP.)
KAPP ... 10-20 60-63
Members: Terry Gilkyson; Rich Dehr.
Also see EASY RIDERS
Also see LAINE, Frankie, & Easy Riders
Also see MARTIN, Dean
Also see WEAVERS & Terry Gilkyson

GILL, Johnny R&B '83
Singles: 7-inch
COTILLION ... 3-4 83-85
MOTOWN ... 3-4 90

Picture Sleeves

MOTOWN....3-4 90

LPs: 10/12-inch

COTILLION....5-10 83-85
MOTOWN....5-8 90
Also see LATTISAW, Stacy, & Johnny Gill
Also see NEW EDITION

GILL, Vince — C&W '84

Singles: 7-inch

MCA....3-4 89-91
RCA....3-4 84-89

LPs: 10/12-inch

MCA....5-8 90-91
RCA....5-8 84-89
Also see PURE PRAIRIE LEAGUE

GILLAN, Ian — LP '80

(Gillan)

Singles: 7-inch

OYSTER....3-5 76

LPs: 10/12-inch

ISLAND....5-10 77-78
OYSTER....8-10 76
VIRGIN....5-10 80
Also see DEEP PURPLE

GILLESPIE, Dizzy — P&R '45

(With His All Star Quintet)

Singles: 7-inch

ATLANTIC....5-10 52-53
CONTEMPORARY....5-10 53
GUILD....5-10 45
NORGRAN....5-10 54-56
PRESTIGE....5-10 51
RCA....5-10 48-52

Singles: 7-inch

ATLANTIC....10-20 52-53
CONTEMPORARY....10-20 53
LIMELIGHT....4-8 65-67
NORGRAN....10-20 54-56
PERCEPTION....4-8 69
PHILIPS....4-6 64
SOLID STATE....3-6 69
VERVE....5-10 57-62

EPs: 7-inch

ATLANTIC (514/521 "Dizzy Gillespie")....25-50 52
CLEF (153 "Dizzy with Strings")....25-50 53
CLEF (291/292/293/294 "Roy and Diz")....20-40 55
(Price is for any volume.)
DEE GEE (4000/4003/4004 "Dizzy Gillespie")....40-60 51
(Price is for any volume.)
DISCOVERY (13 "Dizzy Plays")....25-50 50
GNP (1/2/3 "Dizzy Gillespie")....25-50 50
(Price is for any volume.)
NORGRAN (114/115 "Big Band")....25-50 55
(Price is for either volume.)
RCA (432 "Dizzier and Dizzier")....20-40 54

LPs: 10/12-inch

ALLEGRO (3017 "Dizzy Gillespie Plays")....50-100 52
(10-inch LP.)
ALLEGRO (3083 "Dizzy Gillespie")....50-100 52
(10-inch LP.)
ALLEGRO (4023 "Dizzy Gillespie")....50-100 53
(10-inch LP.)
AMERICAN RECORDING SOCIETY (405 "Jazz Creations")....75-125 55
AMERICAN RECORDING SOCIETY (423 "Big Band Jazz")....75-125 55
ATLANTIC (138 "Dizzy Gillespie")....200-300 52
(10-inch LP.)
ATLANTIC (142 "Dizzy Gillespie, Vol. 2")....200-300 52
ATLANTIC (1257 "Dizzy at Home and Abroad")....75-100 57
(Black label, silver print.)
BARONET (105 "A Handful of Modern Jazz")....20-40 61
BLUE NOTE (5017 "Horn of Plenty")....150-200 52
(10-inch LP.)
CLEF (136 "Dizzy with Strings")....125-150 53
(10-inch LP.)
CLEF (641 "Roy & Diz")....75-100 55
(With Roy Eldridge.)
CLEF (671 "Roy & Diz, Vol. 2")....75-100 55
CLEF (730 "Trumpet Kings")....75-100 56
CLEF (731 "Trumpet Battle")....75-100 56
CONTEMPORARY (2504 "Dizzy in Paris")....100-150 53
(10-inch LP.)
DEE GEE (1000 "Dizzy Gillespie")....200-250 51
(10-inch LP.)
DIAL (212 "Modern Trumpets")....75-125 52
(10-inch LP.)
DISCOVERY (3013 "Dizzy Plays")....150-200 50
(10-inch LP.)
GNP (4 "Dizzy Gillespie")....100-200 50
(10-inch LP.)
GNP (23 "Dizzy Gillespie")....50-75 57
IMPULSE....10-20 67
LIMELIGHT....15-25 64-67
MERCURY....15-25 66
NORGRAN (1003 "Afro Dizzy")....75-100 54
NORGRAN (1023 "Big Band")....75-100 55
NORGRAN (1083 "Jazz Recital")....75-100 56
NORGRAN (1084 "World Statesman")....75-100 56
NORGRAN (1090 "Big Band")....60-80 56
PHILIPS....20-30 62-65
RCA (530 "Dizzy Gillespie")....15-25 66
RCA (1009 "Dizzier and Dizzier")....50-75 54
RCA (2398 "The Greatest")....30-50 61
REGENT (6043 "School Days")....50-75 57
RON-LETTE (11 "Dizzy Gillespie")....25-50 58
ROOST (106 "Diz & Bird")....75-100 59
(Boxed two-disc set.)
ROOST (414 "Dizzy over Paris")....150-200 53
ROOST (2214 "Concert in Paris")....50-75 57
ROOST (2234 "Diz and Bird in Concert")....50-75 59
SAVOY (12000 series)....25-50 55-57
SOLID STATE....10-20 68-69
TRIBUTE....10-15 69
VSP....15-25 66
VERVE (6047 "Have Trumpet, Will Excite")....50-75 59
(Stereo.)
VERVE (6068 "Ebullient")....50-75 59
(Stereo.)
VERVE (6117 "Greatest Trumpet")....50-75 60
(Stereo.)
VERVE (8000 series)....15-30 62-67
(With "MGM Records - a Division of Metro-Goldwyn-Mayer, Inc." at bottom of label.)
VERVE (8015 "Jazz from Paris")....50-75 57
(Reads "Verve Records, Inc." at bottom of label.)
VERVE (8017 "Dizzy in Greece")....50-75 57
(Reads "Verve Records, Inc." at bottom of label.)
VERVE (8109 "Trumpet Kings")....50-75 57
(Reads "Verve Records, Inc." at bottom of label.)
VERVE (8110 "Trumpet Battle")....50-75 57
(Reads "Verve Records, Inc." at bottom of label.)
VERVE (8173 "Jazz Recital")....50-75 57
(Reads "Verve Records, Inc." at bottom of label.)
VERVE (8174 "World Statesman")....50-75 57
(Reads "Verve Records, Inc." at bottom of label.)
VERVE (8178 "Big Band")....50-75 57
(Reads "Verve Records, Inc." at bottom of label.)
VERVE (8191 "Afro Dizzy")....50-75 57
(Reads "Verve Records, Inc." at bottom of label.)
VERVE (8198 "For Musicians Only")....50-75 58
(Reads "Verve Records, Inc." at bottom of label.)
VERVE (8208 "Mantecia")....50-75 58
(Reads "Verve Records, Inc." at bottom of label.)
VERVE (8214 "Dizzy & Stuff")....40-60 58
(Reads "Verve Records, Inc." at bottom of label.)
VERVE (8260 "Duets")....50-75 58
(Reads "Verve Records, Inc." at bottom of label.)
VERVE (8262 "Sunny Side Up")....50-75 58
(Reads "Verve Records, Inc." at bottom of label.)
VERVE (8313 "Have Trumpet, Will Excite")....50-75 59
(Monaural. Reads "Verve Records, Inc." at bottom of label.)
VERVE (8328 "Ebullient")....50-75 59
(Monaural. Reads "Verve Records, Inc." at bottom of label.)
VERVE (8352 "Greatest Trumpet")....50-75 60
(Monaural. Reads "Verve Records, Inc." at bottom of label.)
VERVE (8386 "Portrait")....50-75 60
(Monaural. Reads "Verve Records, Inc." at bottom of label.)
VERVE (8394 "Gillespiana")....50-75 61
(Monaural. Reads "Verve Records, Inc." at bottom of label.)
VERVE (68386 "Portrait")....50-75 60
(Stereo. Reads "Verve Records, Inc." at bottom of label.)
VERVE (68394 "Gillespiana")....50-75 61
(Stereo. Reads "Verve Records, Inc." at bottom of label.)

GILLESPIE, Dizzy, & Slim Gaillard

LPs: 10/12-inch

ULTRAPHONIC (50273 "Gaillard & Gillespie")....30-50 58
Also see GAILLARD, Slim

GILLESPIE, Dizzy, & Stan Getz

EPs: 7-inch

NORGRAN (3/4 "Dizzy Gillespie & Stan Getz Sextet")....40-60 53
(Price is for either volume.)
NORGRAN (32 "Dizzy Gillespie & Stan Getz Sextet [Vol. 2]")....40-60 53

LPs: 10/12-inch

NORGRAN (2 "Dizzy Gillespie & Stan Getz Sextet")....150-250 53
(10-inch LP.)
NORGRAN (18 "Dizzy Gillespie & Stan Getz Sextet [Vol. 2]")....150-250 53
NORGRAN (1050 "Dizzy Gillespie & Stan Getz Sextet")....75-125 56
VERVE (8141 "Dizzy Gillespie & Stan Getz Sextet")....50-75 57
VERVE (68141 "Diz & Getz")....15-25 66
Also see GETZ, Stan
Also see GILLESPIE, Dizzy

GILLEY, Mickey — P&R '74

(With the Urban Cowboy Band)

Singles: 7-inch

ACT 1....4-8 66
ASYLUM....3-4 80
ASTRO (Except 100 series)....3-5 71-73
ASTRO (100 series)....10-20 63-65
DARYL....4-8 63
DOT (15706 "Call Me Shorty")....50-75 58
EPIC....3-4 78-86
ERIC....4-6 64
GOLDBAND....4-8 64
GRT....3-5 70
KHOURY'S (712 "Drive-In Movie")....15-20 59
LYNN....10-20 60-61
MINOR (106 "Ooh Wee")....60-80 57
PAULA (Except 400 series)....6-12 66-68
PAULA (400 series)....3-5 74-84
PLAYBOY....3-5 74-77
POTOMAC....10-15 60
PRINCESS....8-12 62
RESCO....3-5 74
REX (1007 "Grapevine")....20-25 58
SABRA....10-15 61
SAN....10-15 63
SUPREME....8-12 62
TCF HALL....4-8 65

LPs: 10/12-inch

ASTRO (Except 101)....8-10 73-78
ASTRO (101 "Lonely Wine")....75-150 64
EPIC....5-10 79-86
51 WEST....5-10 79
PAULA (Except 2000 series)....5-10 81

PAULA (2195 "Down the Line")........20-25 67
PAULA (2224 "Mickey Gilley at His Best")........10-12 74
PAULA (2234 "Mickey Gilley")........8-10 78
PLAYBOY........8-12 74-78
Also see CHARLES, Ray, & Mickey Gilley
Also see HAGGARD, Merle / Mickey Gilley / Willie Knight

GILLEY, Mickey, & Barbi Benton C&W '75
Singles: 7-inch
PLAYBOY........3-5 75
Picture Sleeves
PLAYBOY........3-5 75

GILLEY, Mickey, & Johnny Lee
Singles: 7-inch
EPIC........3-4 81
Also see LEE, Johnny
Also see NELSON, Willie / Johnny Lee / Mickey Gilley

GILLEY, Mickey, & Charly McClain C&W '84
(Charly McClain & Mickey Gilley)
Singles: 7-inch
EPIC........3-4 83-84
Also see GILLEY, Mickey

GILMER, Jimmy P&R/R&B/LP '63
(With the Fireballs)
Singles: 7-inch
ABC........3-5 74
ATCO........5-10 68
DECCA........10-15 59
DOT........5-10 63-66
HAMILTON (55037 "It Won't Be Long")........10-15 63
WARWICK (547 "True Love Ways")........10-20 60
LPs: 10/12-inch
ATCO........10-15 68-69
CROWN........15-20 63
DOT (3512 "Torquay")........15-25 63
(Monaural.)
DOT (3545 "Sugar Shack")........15-25 63
(Monaural.)
DOT (3577 "Buddy's Buddy")........40-50 64
(Monaural.)
DOT (3643 "Lucky 'Leven")........15-25 63
(Monaural.)
DOT (3668 "Folkbeat")........15-25 63
(Monaural.)
DOT (3709 "Campusology")........15-25 63
(Monaural.)
DOT (25512 "Torquay")........20-30 63
(Stereo.)
DOT (25545 "Sugar Shack")........20-30 63
(Stereo.)
DOT (25577 "Buddy's Buddy")........75-100 64
(Stereo.)
DOT (25643 "Lucky 'Leven")........20-30 63
(Stereo.)
DOT (25668 "Folkbeat")........20-30 63
(Stereo.)
DOT (25709 "Campusology")........20-30 63
(Stereo.)
DOT (25856 "Firewater")........20-30 63
Also see FIREBALLS
Also see JIM & MONICA
Also see SEDAKA, Neil, & Tokens / Angels / Jimmy Gilmer and the Fireballs

GILMOUR, David LP '78
Singles: 12-inch
COLUMBIA........4-6 84-86
Singles: 7-inch
COLUMBIA........3-4 84-86
Picture Sleeves
COLUMBIA........3-4 84
LPs: 10/12-inch
COLUMBIA........5-10 78-85
Also see PINK FLOYD

GILREATH, James P&R/R&B '63
Singles: 7-inch
JOY........4-8 63-64

GILSTRAP, Jim P&R/R&B/LP '75
Singles: 7-inch
BELL........3-5 74
ROXBURY........3-5 75-76
LPs: 10/12-inch
ROXBURY........5-10 75-76

GINA GO-GO P&R '89
Singles: 7-inch
CAPITOL........3-4 89

GINIE LYNN: see LYNN, Ginie

GINO & GINA P&R/R&B '58
Singles: 7-inch
BRUNSWICK........4-8 61
MERCURY........10-15 58
WARWICK........5-10 60
Members: "Gino" Giosasi; Irene Giosasi.

GIORGIO: see MORODER, Giorgio

GIOVANNI, Nikki, & New York Community Choir LP '71
LPs: 10/12-inch
RIGHT-ON........4-8 71

GIPSY KINGS LP '88
LPs: 10/12-inch
MUSICIAN........5-8 88-89

GIRLFRIENDS P&R '63
Singles: 7-inch
COLPIX........10-15 63-64
MELIC........5-10 63
PIONEER........10-15 60
Members: Carolyn Willis; Gloria Goodson; Nannette Jackson.
Also see HONEY CONE

GIRLS CAN'T HELP IT D&D '83
LPs: 10/12-inch
SIRE........5-10 83-84

GIRLSCHOOL LP '82
Singles: 7-inch
MERCURY........3-4 82
LPs: 10/12-inch
MERCURY........5-10 82
STIFF AMERICA........5-10 82

GIRLTALK D&D '84
Singles: 7-inch
GEFFEN........3-4 84

GIUFFRIA P&R/LP '84
Singles: 12-inch
MCA........4-8 84
(Promotional only.)
Singles: 7-inch
MCA........3-4 84-85
MCA/CAMEL........3-4 85-86
Picture Sleeves
MCA........3-4 84-85
LPs: 10/12-inch
MCA........5-10 84-85
MCA/CAMEL........5-10 85-86
Members: Gregg Giuffria; David Glen Eisley; Craig Goldy; Chuck Wright; Lanny Cordola; David Sikes; Alan Krigger.
Also see ANGEL
Also see HEAR 'N AID
Also see HOUSE of LORDS

GIVENS FAMILY R&B '85
Singles: 7-inch
PJ........3-4 86
SUGAR HILL........3-4 85

GLADIOLAS P&R/R&B '57
Singles: 78 rpm
EXCELLO........15-25 57
Singles: 7-inch
EXCELLO (2101 "Little Darlin' ")........25-50 57
EXCELLO (2110 "Run, Run Little Joe")........25-50 57
EXCELLO (2120 "I Wanta Know")........25-50 57
EXCELLO (2136 "Say You'll Be Mine")........20-40 58
Members: Maurice Williams; Norman Wade; Bill Massey; Willie Jones; Earl Gainey; Bobby Robinson.
Also see WILLIAMS, Maurice, & Zodiacs

GLADSTONE P&R '72
Singles: 7-inch
ABC........3-5 72
LPs: 10/12-inch
ABC........8-10 72-73
Members: H.L. Voelker; Michael Rabon; Doug Rhone.

GLAHE, Will, & His Orchestra P&R '39
Singles: 78 rpm
LONDON........3-5 55-57
RCA........3-5 48
VICTOR........3-5 39-40
Singles: 7-inch
LONDON........4-8 55-60
LPs: 10/12-inch
LONDON........10-15 55-60

GLASS, Philip LP '82
LPs: 10/12-inch
ANTILLES........8-12 83
CBS........5-20 82-86
(Prices at the high end of range are multi-disc sets.)
VIRGIN........5-10 77
Also see ANDERSON, Laurie
Also see BYRNE, David
Also see RONSTADT, Linda
Also see SIMON, Paul
Also see VEGA, Suzanne

GLASS BOTTLE P&R '71
Singles: 7-inch
AVCO........3-5 71
AVCO EMBASSY........3-5 70
LPs: 10/12-inch
AVCO........8-12 71
Member: Gary Criss.

GLASS FAMILY R&B '78
Singles: 7-inch
SIDEWALK (920 "Teenage Rebellion")........10-20 67
W.B. (309 "Guess I'll Let You Go")........10-15 69
(Promotional issue only.)
W.B. (7262 "Guess I'll Let You Go")........5-10 69
LPs: 10/12-inch
W.B. (1776 "Electric Band")........15-25 69
Members: Ralph Parrett; Gary Green.

GLASS HARP LP '71
Singles: 7-inch
DECCA........4-8 71-72
UNITED AUDIO........8-12
LPs: 10/12-inch
DECCA........10-20 71-72
MCA........5-10
Members: Phil Keaggy; Dan Pecchio; John Ferra.

GLASS HOUSE P&R/R&B '69
Singles: 7-inch
INVICTUS........3-6 69-72
LPs: 10/12-inch
INVICTUS........8-10 71-72
KIRSHNER........8-10 71
Members: Scherrie Payne; Ty Hunter; Larry Mitchell; Pearl Jones; Eric Dunham.
Also see HUNTER, Ty
Also see PAYNE, Scherrie

GLASS MOON LP '80
Singles: 7-inch
RADIO........3-4 82
LPs: 10/12-inch
RADIO........5-10 80-82

GLASS TIGER P&R/LP '86
Singles: 12-inch
MANHATTAN........4-6 86
Singles: 7-inch
EMI/MANHATTAN........3-4 88
MANHATTAN........3-4 86-87

Picture Sleeves
EMI/MANHATTAN....3-4 88
MANHATTAN....3-4 86-87
LPs: 10/12-inch
EMI/MANHATTAN....5-8 88
MANHATTAN....5-10 86

GLAZER, Tom P&R/LP '63
(With the Children's Do-Re-Mi Chorus; with Dotty Evans & Robin Morgan)
Singles: 78 rpm
COLUMBIA....5-10 53-55
CORAL....5-10 56
Singles: 7-inch
COLUMBIA....5-10 53-55
CORAL....5-10 56
KAPP....4-8 63-64
U.A. 4-8 66-67
Picture Sleeves
KAPP....5-10 63
LPs: 10/12-inch
CAMDEN....5-10 64-65
KAPP....10-20 63-64
COLUMBIA....20-30 55
HARMONY....10-20 59
MERCURY....15-25 55
MOTIVATION....5-10 62
RIVERSIDE....10-20 61
U.A.....10-20 66
WASHINGTON....10-20 59
WONDERLAND....10-20 63

GLEASON, Jackie P&R '53
(Jackie Gleason's Orchestra)
Singles: 78 rpm
CAPITOL....3-5 52-57
DECCA (27000 series)....3-5 51
Singles: 7-inch
CAPITOL....5-10 52-62
DECCA (27000 series)....4-8 51
EPs: 7-inch
CAPITOL (Except 511)....5-15 53-60
CAPITOL (511 "And Awa-a-ay We Go")....50-75 54
(Double EP set.)
CAPITOL (511 "And Awa-a-ay We Go")....75-100 54
(With "EBF" prefix. Boxed, two-disc set.)
LPs: 10/12-inch
CAPITOL (Except 511)....5-15 53-69
CAPITOL (511 "And Awa-a-y We Go")....75-100 54
(10-inch LP. Has songs by Jackie, sung in character by: Joe the Bartender; The Loud Mouth; Ralph Kramden; Fenwick Babbitt; Reggie Van Gleason III, & the Poor Soul.)
Also see MARTIN, Dean / Jackie Gleason

GLENCOVES P&R '63
Singles: 7-inch
SELECT....5-8 63-64

GLENN, Darrell C&W/P&R '53
Singles: 78 rpm
DOT....3-6 56
RCA....3-6 54
VALLEY....4-8 53
Singles: 7-inch
ARLEN....8-10 60s
COLUMBIA....3-6 66-67
DOT....10-20 56
FASHION....5-10 60
LONGHORN....4-8 65
NRC....10-15 58
POMPEII....3-6 68-69
RCA....10-20 54
ROBBIE....4-6 64
TWINKLE (505 "That's Right")....30-50 58
VALLEY....10-20 53
LPs: 10/12-inch
NRC (5 "Crying in the Chapel")....20-35 59

GLENN, Garry R&B '87
(With Soul Set)
Singles: 7-inch
CO & CE....5-8 60s

MOTOWN....3-4 87
PPL....3-4

GLENN, Lloyd R&B '50
Singles: 78 rpm
ALADDIN....5-10 56-57
HOLLYWOOD....5-10 54
SWING TIME....5-15 52-54
Singles: 7-inch
ALADDIN....8-12 56-59
HOLLYWOOD....10-15 54
IMPERIAL....4-8 62
SWING TIME....20-30 52-54
LPs: 10/12-inch
ALADDIN (808 "Chica-Boo")....50-75 56
(Black vinyl.)
ALADDIN (808 "Chica-Boo")....150-200 56
(Colored vinyl.)
BLACK & BLUE....8-10 77
IMPERIAL (9174 "Chica-Boo")....30-40 62
(Monaural.)
IMPERIAL (12174 "Chica-Boo")....30-40 62
(Stereo.)
SCORE (4006 "Piano Stylings")....50-100 56
SCORE (4020 "After Hours")....50-100 57
SWING TIME (1901 "Lloyd Glenn")....125-150 54
(10-inch LP.)
Also see BROWN, Charles / Lloyd Glenn
Also see FULSON, Lowell
Also see MILLER, Red, Trio
Also see WALKER, T-Bone

GLITTER, Gary P&R/LP '72
(With the Glitter Band)
Singles: 7-inch
ARISTA....3-5 75
BELL....3-5 72-74
LPs: 10/12-inch
BELL....8-10 72
EPIC....6-10 81
Also see GLITTER BAND

GLITTER BAND P&R/R&B '76
Singles: 7-inch
ARISTA....3-5 75-76
LPs: 10/12-inch
ARISTA....8-10 76
Member: Pete Gill.
Also see GLITTER, Gary
Also see MOTORHEAD

GLORIES P&R/R&B '67
Singles: 7-inch
DATE (1553 "I Stand Accused")....5-10 67
DATE (1559 "Sing Me a Love Song")....10-20 67
DATE (1593 "Stand By")....10-20 68
DATE (1615 "I Worship You Baby")..20-40 67
DATE (1622 "No News")....10-20 67
Members: Yvonne Gearing; Betty Stokes; Mildred Vaney.
Also see QUIET ELEGANCE

GLOVER, Roger LP '76
Singles: 7-inch
21....3-4 84
UK....8-10 75
LPs: 10/12-inch
POLYDOR....5-10 78
21....5-10 84
U.K.....8-10 75
Also see DEEP PURPLE
Also see RAINBOW

GO WEST P&R/R&B/D&D/LP '85
Singles: 12-inch
CHRYSALIS....4-6 85
Singles: 7-inch
CHRYSALIS....3-4 85-87
Picture Sleeves
CHRYSALIS....3-4 85-87
LPs: 10/12-inch
CHRYSALIS....5-10 85-87
Members: Peter Cox; Richard Drummie.

GOANNA P&R/LP '83
Singles: 7-inch
ATCO....3-4 83
Picture Sleeves
ATCO....3-4 83
LPs; 10/12-inch
ATCO....5-10 83

GODFATHERS LP '88
LPs: 10/12-inch
EPIC....5-8 88-89

GODFREY, Arthur P&R '47
Singles: 78 rpm
COLUMBIA....3-5 50-56
DECCA (29000 series)....3-5 55
Singles: 7-inch
COLUMBIA....5-10 50-56
CONTEMPO....3-6 63-64
DECCA (29000 series)....5-8 55
MGM....3-6 66
MTA....3-5 69
PILGRIM....4-8
SIGNATURE....4-8 60
VEE JAY....3-6 65
Picture Sleeves
MGM....5-10 66
EPs: 7-inch
COLUMBIA....8-15 52-56
LPs: 10/12-inch
ADMIRAL....8-12 67
CAMDEN....8-12 66-67
CAPITOL....8-15 62
COLUMBIA....10-20 53-61
CONTEMPO....8-15
HARMONY....10-15 59
RCA....5-10 73
SIGNATURE....8-15 60
Also see MARINERS

GODFREY, Arthur, & Archie Bleyer
EPs: 7-inch
CADENCE....10-20 54
LPs: 10/12-inch
CADENCE (540 "Christmas with Godfrey and the Little Godfreys")....30-40 54
(10-inch LP.)
Also see BLEYER, Archie

GODFREY, Arthur /Carmel Quinn / Frank Parker / Janette Davis
(With Will Rowland & His Orchestra)
EPs: 7-inch
COLUMBIA ("Arthur Godfrey & His Friends")....8-10 50s
(No selection number used.)
Also see GODFREY, Arthur
Also see QUINN, Carmel

GODFREY, John, Trio R&B '51
Singles: 78 rpm
CHESS....5-10 51
HILLTOP....5-10 51

GODLEY, Kevin, & Lol Creme
(Godley & Creme) P&R/D&D/LP '85
Singles: 12-inch
POLYDOR....4-8 85
Singles: 7-inch
MERCURY....3-5 77
MIRAGE....3-4 82
POLYDOR....3-4 85
Picture Sleeves
POLYDOR....3-4 85
LPs: 10/12-inch
MERCURY....10-15 77
MIRAGE....5-10 82
POLYDOR....5-10 85
Also see SCAFFOLD
Also see 10CC

GODSPELL P&R '72
(Robin Lamont & Original "Godspell" Cast)
Singles: 7-inch
BELL....3-5 72

GODWIN, Peter
D&D '83

Singles: 12-inch

POLYDOR ... 4-6 83

GODZ
LP '78

Singles: 7-inch

MILLENIUM ... 3-5 78

LPs: 10/12-inch

CASABLANCA ... 5-10 78
MILLENIUM/CASABLANCA ... 5-10 78

GOFFIN, Louise
P&R/LP '79

Singles: 7-inch

ASYLUM ... 3-5 79
ELEKTRA ... 3-5 79

LPs: 10/12-inch

ASYLUM ... 5-10 79-81

GO-GOs
P&R/LP '81

Singles: 12-inch 33/45

I.R.S. ... 4-8 82-84

Singles: 7-inch

I.R.S. (Except 8001) ... 3-5 81-85
I.R.S. (8001 "We Got the Beat") ... 4-8 82
(Picture disc.)

Picture Sleeves

I.R.S. ... 3-5 81-85

LPs: 10/12-inch

I.R.S. ... 5-10 81-90
Members: Belinda Carlisle; Charlotte Caffey; Jane Wiedlin; Margot Olaverria; Elissa Bello; Gina Schook; Kathy Valentine.
Also see CARLISLE, Belinda
Also see GRACES
Also see TEXTONES
Also see VENTURES
Also see WIEDLIN, Jane

GOLD, Angie
D&D '85

Singles: 12-inch

PASSION ... 4-6 85

GOLD, Marty, & His Orchestra
LP '63

Singles: 7-inch

KAPP ... 3-5 58-59
RCA ... 3-5 60-61
RCA/BLUEBIRD ... 3-5

EPs: 7-inch

KAPP ... 4-8 59
VIK ... 5-10 56-57

LPs: 10/12-inch

KAPP ... 8-12 59
RCA ... 8-12 59-63
VIK ... 10-20 56-57

GOLDDIGGERS
LP '69

Singles: 7-inch

METROMEDIA ... 3-5 69
RCA ... 3-5 72

LPs: 10/12-inch

METROMEDIA ... 8-12 69
RCA ... 5-10 71
Member: Jimmi Cannon.
Also see MARTIN, Dean

GOLDE, Frannie
P&R '79

Singles: 7-inch

ATLANTIC ... 3-5 76-77
BIG TREE ... 3-5 76
PORTRAIT ... 3-5 79

LPs: 10/12-inch

ATLANTIC ... 8-10 76-79
PORTRAIT ... 5-10 79

GOLDEN EARRING
P&R/LP '74

Singles: 7-inch

ATLANTIC ... 3-5 70
DWARF (2000 "Back Home") ... 10-20 69
MCA ... 3-5 76-78
POLYDOR (2000 series) ... 3-4 79
POLYDOR (14000 series) ... 3-6 69
TRACK ... 3-5 74-75
21 ... 3-4 82-86

Picture Sleeves

DWARF (2000 "Back Home") ... 15-25 69
21 ... 3-5 84

LPs: 10/12-inch

ATLANTIC ... 15-20 69
CAPITOL (164 "Miracle Mirror") ... 30-35 69
CAPITOL (2823 "Winter Harvest") ... 30-35 67
CAPITOL (11315 "Golden Earring") ... 10-12 74
DWARF ... 10-20
MCA ... 6-10 75-81
POLYDOR ... 5-10 79-80
TRACK (396 "Moontan") ... 20-25 73
(With nude showgirl on cover.)
TRACK (396 "Moontan") ... 10-12 73
(Showgirl not nude on cover.)
TRACK (2139 "Switch") ... 8-12 75
21 ... 5-10 82-86

GOLDEN GATE STRINGS
(With Stu Phillips)
LP '67

LPs: 10/12-inch

Singles: 7-inch

EPIC ... 3-5 67

EPs: 7-inch

EPIC (26158 "Bob Dylan Song Book") ... 10-15 67
Also see HOLLYRIDGE STRINGS

GOLDSBORO, Bobby
P&R '62

Singles: 7-inch

CURB ... 3-4 80-82
EPIC ... 3-5 77
LAURIE ... 5-8 62-63
U.A. (Except 672 thru 980) ... 4-6 66-73
U.A. (672 thru 980) ... 5-8 63-66
VISTA ... 3-5 74

Picture Sleeves

U.A. (Except 710) ... 4-8 66-74
U.A. (710 "Whenever He Holds You") ... 8-12 64

LPs: 10/12-inch

CURB ... 5-10 80-82
DORAL ... 15-25
(Promotional mail-order issue, from Doral cigarettes.)
EPIC ... 8-10 77
K-TEL ... 5-10
LIBERTY ... 5-10 81
SUNSET ... 8-12 60s
U.A. ... 10-20 64-76
Also see ORBISON, Roy
Also see REEVES, Del, & Bobby Goldsboro

GOLDSBORO, Bobby / Jimmy Durante

Singles: 7-inch

LIGHT (608 "We Gotta Start Lovin' ") ... 4-8 71
Also see GOLDSBORO, Bobby
Also see DURANTE, Jimmy

GOLLIWOGS

Singles: 7-inch

FANTASY (590 "Don't Tell Me No Lies") ... 40-60 64
FANTASY (597 "You Came Walking") ... 40-60 65
FANTASY (599 "You got Nothing on Me") ... 30-50 65
SCORPIO (404 "Brown Eyed Girl") ... 30-50 65
SCORPIO (405 "Fragile Child") ... 30-50 66
SCORPIO (408 "Walking on the Water") ... 30-50 66
SCORPIO (412 "Porterville") ... 40-60 67

LPs: 10/12-inch

FANTASY (9474 "Pre-Creedence") ... 10-15 75
Members: John Fogerty; Tom Fogerty; Doug Clifford; Stuart Cook.
Also see CREEDENCE CLEARWATER REVIVAL

GOMM, Ian
P&R/LP '79

Singles: 7-inch

STIFF ... 3-5 79

LPs: 10/12-inch

STIFF ... 5-10 79-80

GONE ALL STARS
P&R '58

Singles: 7-inch

GONE ... 10-15 58
ROULETTE ... 3-5 71

EPs: 7-inch

GONE (101 "Dancin' Bandstand") ... 35-55 58
Member: Buddy Lucas.
Also see LUCAS, Buddy

GONZALES, Terri
R&B '82

Singles: 7-inch

BECKET ... 3-4 82

GONZALEZ
P&R/R&B/LP '79

Singles: 12-inch

CAPITOL ... 4-6 79

Singles: 7-inch

CAPITOL ... 3-5 78-79

LPs: 10/12-inch

CAPITOL ... 5-10 78-80

GOOD QUESTION
P&R '88

Singles: 7-inch

PAISLEY PARK ... 3-4 88

Picture Sleeves

PAISLEY PARK ... 3-4 88

GOODIE
R&B '82

Singles: 12-inch

TOTAL EXPERIENCE ... 4-6 82-84

Singles: 7-inch

TOTAL EXPERIENCE ... 3-4 82-84

LPs: 10/12-inch

TOTAL EXPERIENCE ... 5-10 83

GOODIES
P&R '75

Singles: 7-inch

20TH FOX ... 3-5 75

GOODING, Cuba
R&B/D&D '83

Singles: 12-inch

STREETWISE ... 4-6 83

Singles: 7-inch

MOTOWN ... 3-5 78-79
STREETWISE ... 3-4 83

LPs: 10/12-inch

MOTOWN ... 5-10 78-79
Also see MAIN INGREDIENT

GOODMAN, Benny, Orchestra
(Benny Goodman Sextet)
P&R '31

Singles: 78 rpm

CAPITOL ... 3-6 40s
COLUMBIA (Except 2856) ... 5-15 33-56
COLUMBIA (2856 "Your Mother's Son-In-Law") ... 30-50 34
(Colored plastic. Vocal by Billie Holiday.)
MELOTONE ... 10-20 31
VICTOR (Except 25808) ... 5-15 36-58
VICTOR (25808 "Popcorn Man") ... 750-1000 39

Singles: 7-inch

CAPITOL ... 4-8 50s
CHESS ... 4-6 59
COLUMBIA (Except 250) ... 4-8 50-56
COLUMBIA (250 "1938 Carnegie Hall Concert") ... 25-45 50s
(Boxed, two-disc set.)
COMMAND ... 3-5 67
DECCA ... 3-5 62
RCA ... 4-8 50-59

EPs: 7-inch

BRUNSWICK ... 5-10 54
CAPITOL ... 5-10 55-56
COLUMBIA ... 5-10 50-58
DECCA (798 "The Benny Goodman Story") ... 10-15 56
MGM ... 4-8 59
RCA ... 5-10 50-59

LPs: 10/12-inch

ABC ... 5-10 76
BRIGHT ORANGE ... 5-10 73
BRUNSWICK ... 10-20 54
CAMDEN ... 5-10 63-65
CAPITOL ... 5-15 55-78
CENTURY ... 5-10 79
CHESS ... 5-15 59
COLPIX ... 8-12 62
COLUMBIA (Except 160) ... 5-15 50-82
COLUMBIA (160 "The Famous 1938 Carnegie Hall Concert") ... 25-40
(Boxed, two-disc set. Includes cardboard inner sleeves.)
COMMAND ... 5-10 67

DECCA (188 "The Benny Goodman Story, Volumes 1 & 2") 25-35
DECCA (8252 "The Benny Goodman Story, Volume 1") 20-30 56
DECCA (8253 "The Benny Goodman Story, Volume 2") 20-30 56
DECCA (7-8252 "The Benny Goodman Story, Volume 1") 15-20 59
(Reprocessed stereo.)
DECCA (7-8253 "The Benny Goodman Story, Volume 2") 15-20 59
(Reprocessed stereo.)
EVEREST 5-10 73
HARMONY 5-10 59-60
LONDON 5-10 72-78
LONDON/PHASE 4 .... 5-10 71-72
MCA 5-10 80
MGM 5-15 59
MARK '56 .... 5-10 77
MEGA 5-10 72-74
MUSICMASTERS 5-10
PAUSA 5-10 83
PRESTIGE 5-10 69
QUINTESSENCE 4-8 79
RCA (Except 6703) 5-15 50-78
(Includes 10- & 12-inch LPs.)
RCA (6703 "Golden Age of Swing") .. 15-20 55
SUNBEAM 5-10 73
TIME-LIFE (354 "Into the '70s" 10-20 72
(Boxed, three-disc set. Includes booklet.)
WESTINGHOUSE ("World Favorites") 20-30 58
((No selection number used.)
"X" 10-15 54
Also see BASIE, Count, & Benny Goodman
Also see HOLIDAY, Billie
Also see LEE, Peggy

GOODMAN, Benny, Trio, & Rosemary Clooney

Singles: 78 rpm

COLUMBIA 3-5 50-56

Singles: 7-inch

COLUMBIA 5-10 56

LPs: 10/12-inch

COLUMBIA 15-25 56
Also see CLOONEY, Rosemary
Also see GOODMAN, Benny, Orchestra

GOODMAN, Dickie — *P&R '61*

Singles: 7-inch

AUDIO SPECTRUM 10-20 64
CASH 4-6 75
COTIQUE 4-8 69
DIAMOND 10-15 62
EXTRAN 5-8 82
GOODNAME 3-5 88
HOTLINE 4-6 79
J.M.D 15-20 62
JANUS 3-6 77
M.D 10-20 61
MARK-X 10-20 61
MONTAGE 3-5 82
PRELUDE 3-5 80
RAINY WEDNESDAY 4-8 73-75
RAMGO 8-12 70
RED BIRD 10-15 66
RHINO 3-5 84
RORI 10-15 61
SHARK 4-6 79
SHELL 3-5 84
SHOCK 4-6 77
20TH FOX 10-15 63
TWIRL 10-15 66
WACKO 3-5 81
Z-100 .... 3-5 84

LPs: 10/12-inch

CASH (6000 "Mr. Jaws") 25-30 75
COMET (69 "My Son the Joke") 20-30 64
IX CHAINS 12-15 73
RHINO 5-10 83
RORI (3301 "The Many Heads of Dickie Goodman") 50-75 62
Also see BUCHANAN & GOODMAN

GOODMAN, Steve — *LP '75*

Singles: 7-inch

ASYLUM 3-5 75-81
BUDDAH 3-5 72-73

LPs: 10/12-inch

ASYLUM 5-10 75-80
BUDDAH 8-12 71-76
RED PAJAMAS 5-10 83-87

GOODMAN, Steve, & Phoebe Snow

Singles: 7-inch

ASYLUM 3-4 80
Also see GOODMAN, Steve
Also see SNOW, Phoebe

GOODTIMERS — *P&R '61*

Singles: 7-inch

ARNOLD (1002 "Pony Time") 8-12 61
EPIC (9484 "It's Twistin' Time") 5-10 61
Member: Don Covay.
Also see COVAY, Don

GOODWIN, Don — *P&R '73*

Singles: 7-inch

SILVER BLUE 3-5 73

GOODWIN, Ron — *P&R '57*

Singles: 78 rpm

CAPITOL 3-5 56-57

Singles: 7-inch

CAPITOL 5-10 56-59
KING 4-6 61

LPs: 10/12-inch

CAPITOL 8-15 57-60
Also see VINCENT, Gene / Frank Sinatra / Sonny James / Ron Goodwin

GOODY GOODY — *P&R/R&B '78*

Singles: 7-inch

ATLANTIC 3-5 78

LPs: 10/12-inch

ATLANTIC 5-10 78

GOON SQUAD — *R&B/D&D '85*

Singles: 12-inch

EPIC 4-6 85

Singles: 7-inch

EPIC 3-4 85

GOOSE CREEK SYMPHONY (Goose Creek) — *P&R/LP '72*

Singles: 7-inch

CAPITOL 3-6 70-72

LPs: 10/12-inch

CAPITOL (444 "Est. 1970") 10-15 70
CAPITOL (690 "Welcome to Goose Creek") 10-15 72
CAPITOL (11044 "Words of Earnest") 10-15 73
COLUMBIA (32918 "Do Your Thing, But Don't Touch Mine") 8-12 74
Members: Charles R. Gearheart; Mike McFadden; Ed Black Paul Spradlin

GORDON, Barry (With Art Mooney & His Orchestra) — *P&R '55*

Singles: 78 rpm

MGM 4-8 55-56

Singles: 7-inch

ABC 4-6 68
CAPITOL 3-8 65-71
CADENCE 5-10 62
DUNHILL 4-6 68
ERA 5-10 59
MGM 8-15 55-56
MERCURY 5-10 61
U.A. 4-8 64-66

Picture Sleeves

MGM (12092 "Nuttin' for Christmas") 10-20 56
MGM (12367 "I Like Christmas") 10-20 56

LPs: 10/12-inch

U.A. 8-15 66
Also see MOONEY, Art, & His Orchestra

GORDON, Robert (With Link Wray) — *P&R/LP '77*

Singles: 12-inch

PRIVATE STOCK 10-15 78
RCA 8-12 81
(Promotional issue only.)

Singles: 7-inch

PRIVATE STOCK 4-6 77-78
RCA (Black vinyl) 3-5 79-81
RCA (Colored vinyl) 8-12 79-81
(Promotional issue only.)

Picture Sleeves

PRIVATE STOCK (45203 "Fire") 5-10 79
RCA (11471 "It's Only Make Believe") 5-10 79

LPs: 10/12-inch

PRIVATE STOCK 8-10 77-78
RCA (Black vinyl) 5-10 79-82
RCA (Colored vinyl) 20-30 79

Promotional LPs

RCA (3411 "Robert Gordon"/"Live From Paradise in Boston") 35-45 79
Also see WRAY, Link

GORDON, Roscoe — *R&B '51*

Singles: 78 rpm

CHESS (1487 "Booted") 50-100 52
DUKE (101 "Tell Daddy") 50-75 52
DUKE (106 thru 129) 20-50 53-54
FLIP (227 "Just Love Me Baby") 50-100 55
FLIP (237 "The Chicken") 20-40 56
RPM 20-50 50-53
SUN (Except 227 & 237) 50-75 56-58
SUN (227 "Just Love Me Baby") ... 100-200 55
SUN (237 "The Chicken") 75-125 56

Singles: 7-inch

ABC-PAR 5-10 62-63
CHESS (1487 "Booted") 200-300 52
COLLECTABLES 3-4 81
DUKE (106 "T-Model Boogie") 40-60 53
DUKE (109 "Too Many Women") 25-50 53
DUKE (114 "Ain't No Use") 25-50 53
DUKE (129 "Three Cent Love") 25-50 54
DUKE (300 series) 5-10 60
FLIP (227 "Just Love Me Baby") 200-300 55
FLIP (237 "The Chicken") 20-30 56
OLD TOWN 4-6 64
RPM (324 "Saddle the Cow") 250-350 50
RPM (336 "Dime a Dozen") 100-200 50
RPM (344 "Booted") 50-100 51
RPM (350 "No More Doggin' ") 50-75 51
RPM (358 "New Orleans Wimmen") 50-75 51
RPM (365 "What You Got on Your Mind") 50-75 51
RPM (369 "Trying") 40-60 52
RPM (373 "Lucille") 40-60 52
RPM (379 "Just in from Texas") 40-60 52
RPM (384 "We're All Loaded") 40-60 52
SUN (Except 227 & 237) 25-50 56-58
SUN (227 "Just Love Me Baby") ... 400-500 55
SUN (237 "The Chicken") 100-200 56
VEE JAY 5-10 59-61
Also see ROSCOE & BARBARA

GORE, Lesley — *P&R/R&B/LP '63*

Singles: 7-inch

A&M 3-6 75-76
CREWE 3-6 70-71
MERCURY (72119 thru 72206) 5-10 63
MERCURY (72245 "Je Ne Sais Plus") 10-20 64
MERCURY (72259 thru 72726) 6-12 64-67
MERCURY (72842 thru 72969) 10-15 68-69
MOWEST 4-6 72

Picture Sleeves

A&M 5-10 75-76
MERCURY 10-15 63-67

LPs: 10/12-inch

A&M 8-10 75
MERCURY (8000 series) 5-10 80
MERCURY (20000 & 60000 series) .. 20-30 63-68
MOWEST 8-12 72
POLYDOR 5-10 85
WING 10-20 67-69
Also see BILLY & SUE
Also see DRIFTERS / Leslie Gore / Roy Orbison / Los Bravos

GORE, Leslie, & Lou Christie

Singles: 7–inch

MANHATTAN (50039 "Since I Don't Have You") 5-8 86

Also see CHRISTIE, Lou

Also see GORE, Leslie

GORE, Martin L. LP '89

LPs: 10/12–inch

SIRE 5-8 89

GORE, Michael P&R '84

Singles: 7–inch

CAPITOL 3-4 84

GORKY PARK LP '89

Singles: 7–inch

MERCURY 3-4 90

LPs: 10/12–inch

MERCURY 5-8 89

GORL, Robert D&D '84

Singles: 12–inch

ELEKTRA 4-6 84

Singles: 7–inch

ELEKTRA 3-4 84

GORME, Eydie P&R '54

Singles: 78 rpm

ABC-PAR 3-5 55-62

Singles: 7–inch

ABC-PAR 4-8 55-62
CALENDAR 3-6 67
COLUMBIA 3-8 62-68
(Black vinyl.)
COLUMBIA (43082 "I Want You to Be My Baby") 5-10 64
(Colored vinyl.)
CORAL 5-10 53-55
GALA 3-5 76
MGM 3-5 71-73
RCA 3-5 69-70
U.A. 3-6 60-76

Picture Sleeves

COLUMBIA 4-8 62-63

LPs: 10/12–inch

ABC-PAR 15-25 57-65
APPLAUSE 4-6 81
COLUMBIA 10-20 63-73
GALA 5-8 76
HARMONY 5-10 68-71
MGM 5-10 71
RCA 5-10 68-70
U.A. 10-20 61-62
VOCALION 8-15 63

Also see LAWRENCE, Steve, & Eydie Gorme

GOUDREAU, Barry LP '80

Singles: 7–inch

PORTRAIT 3-4 79

LPs: 10/12–inch

PORTRAIT 5-10 79

Also see BOSTON

GOULET, Robert P&R/LP '62

Singles: 7–inch

ABC 3-5 74
ARTISTS of AMERICA 3-5 75
COLUMBIA (Black vinyl) 3-6 61-70
COLUMBIA (Colored vinyl) 5-10 63
MGM 3-5 73
MERLIN 3-5 71
PARAMOUNT 3-5 74

Picture Sleeves

ABC 3-6 74
COLUMBIA (Except 59227) 3-6 62-65
COLUMBIA (59227 "The Moon Was Yellow") 5-10 63
(Promotional issue only.)

EPs: 7–inch

COLUMBIA 4-8 65
(Juke box issues.)

LPs: 10/12–inch

ARTISTS of AMERICA 5-10 76
COLUMBIA 5-15 61-73
HARMONY 5-10 71-72
MERLIN 5-10 71
ORINDA 5-10 78

GRACE, Fredi, & Rhinestone R&B '82

Singles: 7–inch

RCA 3-4 82

GRACE, Leda R&B '81

Singles: 7–inch

POLYDOR 3-4 81

GRACES P&R/LP '89

LPs: 10/12–inch

A&M 5-8 89

Members: Charlotte Caffey; Meredith Brooks; Gia Ciambotti.

Also see GO-GOs

GRACIE, Charlie P&R/R&B '57

Singles: 78 rpm

CADILLAC 25-50 53-54
CAMEO 15-30 57
20TH CENTURY 15-25 55

Singles: 7–inch

ABKCO 3-5 75
CADILLAC (141 "Boogie Woogie Blues") 75-125 53
CADILLAC (144 "Rockin' and Rollin'") 75-125 54
CAMEO 12-25 57-59
CORAL 10-15 59
DIAMOND 10-20 65
FELSTED 5-10 61
PRESIDENT 5-10 62
SOCK & SOUL 4-6 70
ROULETTE 5-10 59-61
20TH CENTURY (5035 "Honey Honey") 40-60 55

LPs: 10/12–inch

REVIVAL (0001 "Early Recordings") 10-20

GRADDOCK, Billy: see CRADDOCK, Billy

GRADUATES P&R '59

Singles: 7–inch

CORSICAN (0058 "What Good Is Graduation") 20-30 59
SHAN-TODD (0055 "Ballad of a Girl and Boy") 15-25 59

Picture Sleeves

CORSICAN (0058 "What Good Is Graduation") 30-50 59

GRAHAM, Jaki R&B '85

Singles: 12–inch

CAPITOL 4-6 86

Singles: 7–inch

CAPITOL 3-4 86

LPs: 10/12–inch

CAPITOL 5-10 86

GRAHAM, Jaki, & David Grant R&B '86

Singles: 12–inch

CAPITOL 4-6 86

Singles: 7–inch

CAPITOL 3-4 86

Also see GRAHAM, Jaki

Also see GRANT, David

GRAHAM, Larry P&R/LP '74

(Graham Central Station; with Graham Central Station)

Singles: 7–inch

ARISTA 3-4 87
W.B. 3-5 74-83

Picture Sleeves

W.B. 3-5 80

LPs: 10/12–inch

W.B. 5-10 73-83

Also see FRANKLIN, Aretha, & Larry Graham

Also see SLY & Family Stone

GRAINGERS R&B '81

Singles: 7–inch

BC 3-4 81

GRAMM, Lou P&R/LP '87

Singles: 7–inch

ATLANTIC 3-4 87-90

Picture Sleeves

ATLANTIC 3-4 87

LPs: 10/12–inch

ATLANTIC 5-10 87-89

Also see FOREIGNER

GRAMMER, Billy P&R/R&B '58

Singles: 7–inch

MONUMENT (400 "Gotta Travel On") 40-60 59

Singles: 7–inch

DECCA 4-8 61-66
EPIC 4-6 66-67
EVEREST 5-8 60
MERCURY 3-6 68-69
MONUMENT (Except 400 series) 3-5 75-76
MONUMENT (400 series) 5-15 59-63
RICE (5025 "Mabel") 5-10 67
STOP 3-6 69

EPs: 7–inch

DECCA 5-10 64

LPs: 10/12–inch

CLASSIC CHRISTMAS 5-10 77
DECCA 10-15 62-64
EPIC 8-12 67
MONUMENT (4000 "Travelin' On") ... 20-30 59
(With *Lost in a Small Cafe.*)
MONUMENT (8039 "Travelin' On") ... 10-15 66
(*Lost in a Small Cafe* is replaced with *Gotta Travel On.*)
SKYLITE 5-8
STONEWAY 5-10 75
VOCALION 6-12 68

Also see CASH, Johnny / Billy Grammer / Wilburn Brothers

Also see TUBB, Ernest

GRAMMER, Billy / Judy Lynn / Link Wray

LPs: 10/12–inch

GUEST STAR 10-15 60s

Also see GRAMMER, Billy

Also see WRAY, Link

GRANAHAN, Gerry P&R '58

(With the Hutch Davie Orchestra; Granahan-Quintal Band)

Singles: 12–inch

DOWNTOWN 5-8 87

Singles: 7–inch

ATCO (6122 "Sweet Affection") 15-25 58
CANADIAN AMERICAN (116 "In My Heart") 5-10 60
CANADIAN AMERICAN (119 "Where's the Girl") 5-10 60
CAPRICE (106 "Dancing Man") 5-10 61
CAPRICE (108 "Dance Girl Dance") 50-75 61
(With the Wildwoods, a.k.a. the Five Satins.)
COLLECTABLES 3-4
GONE 8-12 59-60
SUNBEAM (102 "No Chemise, Please") 15-25 58
SUNBEAM (108 "Baby Wait") 15-25 58
SUNBEAM (122 "King Size") 15-25 59
SUNBEAM (127 "A Ring, a Bracelet, a Heart") 15-25 59
20TH FOX 5-10 63
VEEP 4-8 65

Picture Sleeves

GONE (5081 "Look for Me") 25-50 60

Also see DICKY DOO & DON'TS

Also see FIVE SATINS

Also see FIVE SATINS / Gerry Granahan & Five Satins

Also see FONTAINE, Eddie, & Gerry Granahan

Also see GRANT, Jerry, & Rockabilly Bandits

GRANATA, Rocca, & International Quintet P&R '59

Singles: 7–inch

LAURIE 3-6 59

Picture Sleeves

LAURIE 5-8 59

GRAND CANYON
P&R '74

Singles: 7-inch

BANG 4-6 74
FAITHFUL VIRTUE 3-5 70

GRAND FUNK RAILROAD
(Grand Funk) P&R/LP '69

Singles: 7-inch

CAPITOL (Black vinyl) 3-6 69-76
CAPITOL (Colored vinyl) 5-8 73
(Promotional issue only.)
FULL MOON 3-4 81
MCA 3-5 76-77

Picture Sleeves

CAPITOL 3-6 71-76
FULL MOON 3-4 81
MCA 3-5 76

LPs: 10/12-inch

CAPITOL (307 thru 853) 8-15 69-71
CAPITOL (11000 series, except 11207) 6-12 72-76
CAPITOL (11207 "We're an American Band") 6-10 73
(Black vinyl.)
CAPITOL (11207 "We're an American Band") 20-30 73
(Colored vinyl. Promotional issue only.)
CAPITOL (12000 & 16000 series) 5-10 80-81
FULL MOON 5-10 81-83
MCA 8-10 76
Members: Mark Farner; Don Brewer; Mel Schacher; Craig Frost.
Also see FARNER, Mark, & Don Brewer
Also see KNIGHT, Terry, & Pack

GRANDMASTER FLASH & FURIOUS FIVE
R&B '80

(With the Furious Five; with Melle Mel; Grandmaster Flash)

Singles: 12-inch 33/45

ATLANTIC 4-6 84
ELEKTRA 4-6 85-86
SUGAR HILL 4-6 80-85

Singles: 7-inch

ATLANTIC 3-4 84
ELEKTRA 3-4 85-87
MCA 3-4 85
SUGAR HILL 3-5 80-85

Picture Sleeves

ATLANTIC 3-4 84

LPs: 10/12-inch

ELEKTRA 5-10 86-88
SUGAR HILL 5-10 82-85
Also see JACKSON, Rebbie
Also see KHAN, Chaka
Also see KING DREAM CHORUS & Holiday Crew
Also see MELLE MEL & Duke Bootee

GRANDMIXER D. ST.
R&B/D&D '83

Singles: 12-inch

ISLAND 4-6 83

Singles: 7-inch

ISLAND 3-4 83

GRANT, Al
(Al Cernick)

Singles: 78 rpm

KING (15004 thru 15045) 10-20 49-50
Also see MITCHELL, Guy

GRANT, Amy
P&R/LP '85

Promotional 12-inch Singles

A&M (75161 "Heart in Motion") 5-10 91
A&M (23821 "Good for Me") 6-12 91
A&M (83311 "Lucky One") 5-10 94

Promotional Singles

A&M 4-8 85-91

Singles: 7-inch

A&M 3-4 85-91
COLLECTABLES 3-4 90s
MYRRH 3-5 80-85

Picture Sleeves

A&M 3-4 85-88

EPs: 7-inch

MYRRH (001 "Ageless Medley") 4-8 83

LPs: 10/12-inch

A&M (Black vinyl) 5-10 85-92
A&M ("Home for Christmas") 40-80 92
(Picture disc. Promotional issue only. Selection number not known.)
MYRRH (Except 901644158) 5-10 80-85
MYRRH (901644158 "Collection") 20-30 86
(Picture disc. Promotional issue only.)
Also see CETERA, Peter, & Amy Grant
Also see GARFUNKEL, Art / Amy Grant

GRANT, Amy, & Vince Gill

Singles: 7-inch

A&M 3-5 94
Also see GILL, Vince
Also see GRANT, Amy

GRANT, David
R&B/D&D '83

Singles: 12-inch

CHRYSALIS 4-6 83

Singles: 7-inch

CAPITOL 3-4 86
CHRYSALIS 3-4 83
Also see GRAHAM, Jaki, & David Grant
Also see LINX

GRANT, Earl
P&R/R&B '58

Singles: 78 rpm

PRINCE 4-8 56

Singles: 7-inch

DECCA 3-8 58-70
PRINCE (1201 "One-Way Street") 5-10 56
(Black vinyl.)
PRINCE (1201 "One-Way Street") 10-20 56
(Colored vinyl.)

EPs: 7-inch

DECCA 5-10 59-62

LPs: 10/12-inch

DECCA 8-18 59-70
MCA 5-10 76
VOCALION 5-10 69-70

GRANT, Eddy
R&B '79

Singles: 12-inch

EPIC 4-6 80-82
PORTRAIT 4-6 83-85

Singles: 7-inch

EPIC 3-4 79-80
PORTRAIT 3-4 83-85

Picture Sleeves

PORTRAIT 3-4 84

LPs: 10/12-inch

EPIC 5-10 79-80
PORTRAIT 5-10 83-85
Also see EQUALS

GRANT, Eleanor
R&B '76

Singles: 7-inch

CBS ASSOCIATED 3-4 84-85
CATAWBA 3-4 83
COLUMBIA 3-4 76

GRANT, Gogi
P&R '55

Singles: 78 rpm

ERA 8-15 55-56
RCA 5-10 52-57

Singles: 7-inch

CHARTER 4-8 63
ERA 10-20 55-56
LIBERTY 5-10 60-61
MONUMENT 4-6 66-67
PETE 4-6 68-69
RCA 10-20 52-58
20TH FOX 4-6 61-62

Picture Sleeves

20TH FOX 5-10 61

EPs: 7-inch

ERA 10-20 56
RCA (Except 1030) 5-10 57-58
RCA (4112 "Helen Morgan Story") 15-25 57
(Soundtrack.)

LPs: 10/12-inch

CHARTER 8-12 64
ERA (106 "The Wayward Wind") 10-20 60s
ERA (20001 "Suddenly There's Gogi Grant") 25-40 56
(Black vinyl.)
ERA (20001 "Suddenly There's Gogi Grant") 50-100 56
(Colored vinyl.)
LIBERTY 10-20 60
PETE 6-10 68-70
RCA (Except 1030) 15-25 57-59
RCA (1030 "Helen Morgan Story") 60-70 57
(Soundtrack.)
Also see PRESLEY, Elvis / Vaughn Monroe / Gogi Grant / Robert Shaw

GRANT, Janie
P&R '61

Singles: 7-inch

CAPRICE 10-15 61-62
DOT 10-15 57
PARKWAY (982 "My Heart, Your Heart") 15-25 66
STEPHANY (1821 "Pinball Machine") 15-25 58
U.A. 5-10 63-65
Session: James Ray.
Also see RAY, James

GRANT, Jerry, & Rockabilly Bandits
(Gerry Granahan)

Singles: 7-inch

ATCO (6100 "Talkin' About Love") 20-30 57
Also see GRANAHAN, Gerry

GRANT, Tom
R&B '81

Singles: 7-inch

WMOT 3-5 81

GRAPEFRUIT
P&R '68

Singles: 7-inch

EQUINOX 4-8 68

LPs: 10/12-inch

DUNHILL 10-12 68
RCA 10-12 69

GRASS ROOTS
P&R '66

(Rob Grill & the Grass Roots)

Singles: 7-inch

ABC 3-5 70
DUNHILL (Except 4013) 4-8 66-74
DUNHILL (4013 "Mr. Jones") 8-12 65
DUNHILL OLDIES 3-5 70s
HAVEN 3-5 75-76
MCA 3-4 82
OAK 4-6
ROULETTE 3-5 70s

Picture Sleeves

DUNHILL 5-8 67-70

EPs: 7-inch

DUNHILL (165 "Grass Roots") 8-12 71
(Promotional issue only.)

LPs: 10/12-inch

ABC 8-10 76
COMMAND 8-10 74
DUNHILL 10-20 66-73
GUSTO 5-8 78
HAVEN 8-10 75
MCA 5-10 81-82
PICKWICK 5-8 78
Members: Rob Grill; Warren Entner; Creed Bratton; Erik Coonce. Session: Denny Provisor; Joel Larson; Joe Osborn; P.F. Sloan; Reid Kailing.
Also see MERRY-GO-ROUND
Also see SLOAN, P.F.

GRATEFUL DEAD
LP '67

Singles: 12-inch

ARISTA 5-10 88

Singles: 7-inch

ARISTA (Black vinyl) 3-5 77-88
ARISTA (Colored vinyl) 4-6 87
FLASHBACK 3-4 80
GRATEFUL DEAD 8-15 73-76
SCORPIO (201 "Don't Ease Me In") 75-150 66
W.B. 10-15 67-73

Promotional Singles

ARISTA 4-6 77-87
GRATEFUL DEAD 12-20 73-76
W.B. 10-20 67-73

Picture Sleeves

ARISTA (0519 "Alabama Getaway") 4-6 80
ARISTA (9606 "Touch of Grey") 3-5 87
GRATEFUL DEAD (03 "U.S. Blues") 15-20 74
W.B. (7186 "Dark Star") 35-55 68

EPs: 7-inch

W.B. (226 "American Beauty") 20-30 70
(Juke box issue only.)
W.B. (438 "American Beauty") 100-200 70
(Radio Spots.)
W.B. (544 "Europe 72") 20-30 72
(Juke box issue only.)

LPs: 10/12-inch

ARISTA 5-10 77-90
DIRECT-DISK 10-15 79
GRATEFUL DEAD (01 "Wake of the Flood") 20-25 73
(No mention on cover of distribution by United Artists.)
GRATEFUL DEAD (01 "Wake of the Flood") 15-20 70s
(Reads "Distribution by United Artists" on cover.)
GRATEFUL DEAD (102 "Mars Hotel") 20-25 74
(No mention on cover of distribution by United Artists.)
GRATEFUL DEAD (102 "Mars Hotel") 10-15 70s
(Reads "Distribution by United Artists" on cover.)
GRATEFUL DEAD (494 "Blues for Allah") 20-25 75
GRATEFUL DEAD (620 "Steal Your Face") 25-30 76
GRATEFUL DEAD (40132 "One from the Vault") 5-10 91
MFSL (014 "American Beauty") 60-80 78
MFSL (172 "From the Mars Hotel") ... 40-60 85
PAIR 6-12 84
PRIDE 12-20 73
SUNFLOWER (5001 "Vintage Dead") 25-35 70
SUNFLOWER (5004 "Historic Dead") 25-35 71
W.B. (W-1689 "Grateful Dead") 40-60 67
(Monaural. Gold label.)
W.B. (WS-1689 "Grateful Dead") 25-35 67
(Stereo. Gold label.)
W.B. (1689 "Grateful Dead") 20-30 67
(With Warner Bros. - Seven Arts "W7" label.)
W.B. (1689 "The Grateful Dead") 10-20 71
(With Warner Bros. "Arrowhead" label. Cover has copyright date on back.)
W.B. (1749 "Anthem of the Sun") 20-30 68
(Background cover color is purple. With Warner Bros. - Seven Arts "W7" label.)
W.B. (1749 "Anthem of the Sun") 10-20 71
(Background cover color is white. With Warner Bros. "Arrowhead" logo on label.)
W.B. (1790 "Aoxomoxoa") 20-30 69
(With Warner Bros. - Seven Arts "W7" label.)
W.B. (1790 "Aoxomoxoa") 10-20 71
(With Warner Bros. "Arrowhead" label. Cover has copyright date on back.)
W.B. (1830 "Live Dead") 25-35 69
(With Warner Bros. - Seven Arts "W7" label. Issued with bonus pamphlet.)
W.B. (1830 "Live Dead") 15-20 71
(With Warner Bros. "Arrowhead" label. Cover has copyright date on back.)
W.B. (1869 "Workingman's Dead") ... 20-30 70
(With Warner Bros. - Seven Arts "W7" label.)
W.B. (1869 "Workingman's Dead") ... 10-15 71
(With Warner Bros. "Arrowhead" label. Cover has copyright date on back.)
W.B. (1893 "American Beauty") 15-25 70
(With Warner Bros. - Seven Arts "W7" label.)
W.B. (1893 "American Beauty") 10-15 71
(With Warner Bros. "Arrowhead" label. Cover has copyright date on back.)
W.B. (1893 "American Beauty") 5-10 75
(With Warner Blvd./street and trees label.)
W.B. (1935 "Skull & Roses") 15-25 71
(Title shown is commonly used to describe what is actually an untitled LP. Includes bonus sticker picturing cover art.)
W.B. (2668 "Europe '72") 15-25 72
W.B. (2721 "History of the Grateful Dead, Vol. 1") 10-15 73
W.B. (2764 "Skeletons from the Closet") 8-12 74
W.B. (3091 "What a Strange Trip It's Been") 8-10 77

Promotional LPs

ARISTA (35 "Grateful Dead Sampler") 40-50 78
ARISTA (7001 "Terrapin Station") 20-25 77
(The lengthy *Terrapin Station* track is banded for radio station airplay.)
U.A. (SP-114 "For Dead Heads") 25-50 75
Members: Jerry Garcia; Ron McKernan; Bob Weir; Bill Kreutzman; Phil Lesh; Mickey Hart; Tom Constanten; Ned Lagin; Robert Hunter; Keith Godchaux; Donna Godchaux; Brent Mydland.
Also see CROSBY, David
Also see GARCIA, Jerry
Also see GARCIA, Jerry, & Robert Hunter
Also see HART, Mickey
Also see KANTER, Paul, & Grace Slick
Also see NEW RIDERS of the Purple Sage
Also see SILVER
Also see WEIR, Bob

GRATEFUL DEAD / Elvin Bishop Group

Singles: 7-inch

W.B. (7627 "Johnny B. Goode") 10-20 72
Also see BISHOP, Elvin
Also see GRATEFUL DEAD

GRAVES, Billy — P&R '59

Singles: 7-inch

MONUMENT (Except 401) 4-8 59-66
MONUMENT (401 "The Shag") 8-12 59

GRAVES, Carl — P&R/R&B '74

Singles: 7-inch

A&M 3-5 74
ARIOLA AMERICA 3-5 75-77
Also see SKYLARK

GRAY, Claude — C&W '60

Singles: 7-inch

COLUMBIA 4-6 64-66
COUNTRY INT'L 3-4 81-86
D 5-10 59-60
DECCA 3-6 66-71
GRANNY 3-5 76-82
MERCURY 4-8 60-64
MILLION 3-5 72-73
MINOR 8-12

LPs: 10/12-inch

DECCA 8-12 67-68
MERCURY 15-25 62
MILLION 5-10 72
PICKWICK/HILLTOP 8-12 67

GRAY, Claude, & Norma Jean — C&W '82

Singles: 7-inch

GRANNY WHITE 3-4 82
Also see GRAY, Claude

GRAY, Diva, & Oyster — R&B '80

Singles: 7-inch

COLUMBIA 3-4 79-80

LPs: 10/12-inch

COLUMBIA 5-10 79
Also see ROUNDTREE

GRAY, Dobie — P&R '63

Singles: 12-inch

INFINITY 5-8 79

Singles: 7-inch

ARISTA 3-4 83
CAPITOL (Except 5853) 3-4 86
CAPITOL (5853 "River Deep, Mountain High") 5-8 67
CAPRICORN 3-5 76-77
CHARGER 4-8 64-66
COLLECTABLES 3-4 81
CORDAK 5-10 62-64
DECCA 3-5 73
ERIC 3-4 70s
GUSTO 3-4 85
INFINITY 3-5 78-79
JAF 4-8 63
MCA 3-4 73-75
REAL FINE 8-12 62
ROBOX 3-4 81
STRIPE 8-12 60-61
WHITE WHALE (300 "Rose Garden") .. 4-8 69
WHITE WHALE (330 "What a Way to Go") 100-200 69
WHITE WHALE (342 "Honey, You Can't Take It Back") 25-50 70

LPs: 10/12-inch

CAPITOL 5-10 86
CAPRICORN 8-10 76
CHARGER 15-20 65
DECCA 8-10 73
INFINITY 6-10 79
MCA 8-10 73-74
ROBOX 5-10 81
STRIPE 10-12

GRAY, Glen, & Casa Loma Orchestra — P&R '31

Singles: 78 rpm

CAPITOL 3-5 56-57
DECCA 3-5 55
MERCURY 3-5 47

Singles: 7-inch

CAPITOL 4-8 56-58
DECCA 4-8 55

EPs: 7-inch

CAPITOL 5-10 56-58

LPs: 10/12-inch

CAPITOL 5-15 56-63

GRAY, Maureen — P&R '62

Singles: 7-inch

CHANCELLOR (1082 "Crazy Over You") 10-20 61
CHANCELLOR (1091 "I Don't Want to Cry") 10-20 61
CHANCELLOR (1100 "There Is a Boy") 25-45 62
LANDA (689 "Dancin' the Strand") 10-20 62
MERCURY 6-12 63-64

GREAN, Charles — P&R/LP '69

(Charles Randolph Grean Sounde)

Singles: 7-inch

DOT 3-6 67
RANWOOD 3-5 69-79

LPs: 10/12-inch

RANWOOD 6-12 69-70

GREASE BAND — LP '71

Singles: 7-inch

SHELTER 3-5 71

LPs: 10/12-inch

SHELTER 8-10 71
Member: Henry McCullough.
Also see COCKER, Joe
Also see McCARTNEY, Paul

GREAT!! SOCIETY!!

Singles: 7-inch

COLUMBIA (44583 "Sally Go 'Round the Roses") 10-15 68
NORTHBEACH (1001 "Someone to Love") 75-150 66
Member: Grace Slick.
Also see JEFFERSON AIRPLANE
Also see SLICK, Grace

GREAT SEBASTIAN

(Wayne Cochran)

Singles: 7-inch

REBEL (1333 "The Naughty Coo") 50-100 57
Also see COCHRAN, Wayne

GREAT WHITE — LP '84

Singles: 7-inch

CAPITOL 3-4 86-90
EMI AMERICA 3-4 84

Picture Sleeves

CAPITOL 3-4 86-89

LPs: 10/12-inch

CAPITOL 5-10 86-91
EMI AMERICA 5-10 84
ENIGMA 5-8 88

GREENWORLD 5-10 85
Members: Jack Russell; Mark Kendall; Michael Ardie; Audie Desbrow; Tony Montana.

GREAVES, R.B. *P&R/R&B '69*

Singles: 7-inch

ATCO................................3-5 69-70
BAREBACK................................3-5 77
MGM................................3-5 73
MIDSONG................................3-4 80
SUNFLOWER................................3-5 72
20TH FOX................................3-5 74

LPs: 10/12-inch

ATCO................................15-20 69

GREBENSHIKOV, Boris *LP '89*

LPs: 10/12-inch

COLUMBIA................................5-8 89

GRECCO, Cyndi *P&R '76*

Singles: 7-inch

PRIVATE STOCK................................3-5 76-77

LPs: 10/12-inch

PRIVATE STOCK................................5-8 76

GRECH, Rick *LP '73*

Singles: 7-inch

RSO................................3-5 73

LPs: 10/12-inch

RSO................................5-10 73

GRECO, Buddy *P&R '47*
(Buddy Greco Trio)

Singles: 78 rpm

CORAL................................3-8 51-55
KAPP................................3-8 56

Singles: 7-inch

CORAL................................5-15 51-55
EPIC................................5-15 58-67
HERALD................................5-10 59
KAPP................................5-10 56
MGM................................3-5 71-72
REPRISE................................4-8 66-68
SCEPTER................................4-6 69

Picture Sleeves

EPIC................................5-10 64-65

EPs: 7-inch

CORAL................................5-15 55

LPs: 10/12-inch

CORAL................................15-25 55
EPIC................................10-15 60-66
HARMONY................................8-12 68
KAPP................................10-15 61
MVM................................10-15 60s
SCEPTER................................5-10 69-73
VOCALION................................8-12 64

GREELEY, George *LP '61*

Singles: 7-inch

W.B.................................3-5 59-62

Picture Sleeves

W.B.................................3-5 62

EPs: 7-inch

CAPITOL................................5-10 56

LPs: 10/12-inch

CAPITOL................................5-15 56
RAVE................................10-20 56
W.B.................................5-10 59-61

GREEN, Al *P&R/R&B '67*
(With the Soul Mates)

Singles: 7-inch

A&M................................3-4 87-89
BELL................................3-5 72-73
FLASHBACK................................3-5 70s
HI................................3-5 70-78
HOT LINE................................8-12 67
MOTOWN................................3-4 82-85

Picture Sleeves

HI................................3-5 77

LPs: 10/12-inch

A&M................................5-10 87
BELL................................8-10 72
CAPITOL (Black vinyl)................................5-8 90s
CAPITOL (Colored vinyl)................................10-12 90s
HI................................5-15 69-78
(Black vinyl.)
HI (27121 "Let's Stay Together")................................8-10 95
(Colored vinyl.)
HI (27127 "I'm Still in Love with You")................................8-10 95
(Colored vinyl.)
HOT LINE (1500 "Back Up Train") ... 20-40 67
KORY................................8-10 77
MELODY................................5-10
MOTOWN................................5-10 82-85
MYRRH................................5-10 80-83
RIGHT STUFF (27121 "Let's Stay Together")................................10-12 95
(Colored vinyl.)
RIGHT STUFF (27627 "I'm Still in Love with You")................................10-12 95
(Colored vinyl.)
Also see LENNOX, Annie, & Al Green

GREEN, Darren *R&B '73*

Singles: 7-inch

RCA................................3-5 73-74

GREEN, Garland *P&R/R&B '69*

Singles: 7-inch

CASINO................................3-5 76
COTILLION................................3-6 71
GAMMA................................20-40 67
OCEAN FRONT................................3-4 83
RCA................................3-6 77
REVUE................................5-10 67-68
SPRING................................5-10 74-75
UNI................................4-8 69

LPs: 10/12-inch

OCEAN FRONT................................5-10 83
RCA................................8-10 74-78
UNI................................10-12 70

GREEN, Grant *LP '71*

LPs: 10/12-inch

BLUE NOTE................................15-25 61-65
(Label reads "Blue Note Records Inc. - New York, U.S.A.")
BLUE NOTE................................10-15 66-71
(Label reads "Blue Note Records - a Division of Liberty Records Inc.")
VERVE................................10-18 65
VERSATILE................................5-10 78

GREEN, Jack *LP '80*

Singles: 7-inch

RCA................................3-4 80

LPs: 10/12-inch

RCA................................5-10 80
Also see PRETTY THINGS
Also see T. REX

GREEN, Lil: see GREENE, Lil

GREEN, Lorne: see GREENE, Lorne

GREEN, Peter *LP '80*

Singles: 7-inch

SAIL................................3-5 79

LPs: 10/12-inch

REPRISE................................8-10 71
SAIL................................5-10 79-80
Also see BOYD, Eddie
Also see FLEETWOOD MAC

GREEN, Sonny *R&B '73*

Singles: 7-inch

HILL................................3-5 73
MRH................................5-8
UNITED ARTISTS................................3-5

GREEN BERETS *R&B '70*

Singles: 7-inch

UNI................................3-5 70

GREEN ON RED *LP '86*

LPs: 10/12-inch

ENIGMA................................5-10 85
MERCURY................................5-10 86

GREEN RIVER BOYS: see CAMPBELL, Glen

GREENBAUM, Norman *P&R/LP '70*

Singles: 7-inch

GREGAR................................4-6 69-70
REPRISE................................3-5 70-71

Picture Sleeves

REPRISE................................5-8 69

LPs: 10/12-inch

GREGAR................................15-20 70
REPRISE................................12-15 69-72
Also see DR. WEST'S MEDICINE SHOW & Junk Band

GREENBERG, Steve *P&R '69*

Singles: 7-inch

TRIP................................4-6 69

GREENE, Al: see GREEN, Al

GREENE, Barbara *P&R/R&B '68*

Singles: 7-inch

ATCO (6250 "Long Tall Sally")................................25-30 62
RENEE................................8-10 68
VIVID................................4-8 64
Also see DELLS

GREENE, Jack *C&W '65*
(With the Jolly Green Giants)

Singles: 7-inch

DECCA................................3-8 65-72
EMH................................3-4 83-84
FRONTLINE................................3-5 80
MCA................................3-5 73-74

LPs: 10/12-inch

CORAL................................4-8 73
DECCA................................8-18 66-71
51 WEST................................5-10 84
FRONTLINE................................5-10 80
MCA................................5-10 73
PICKWICK................................5-10 70s
VOCALION................................8-12 60s

GREENE, Jack, & Jeannie Seely *C&W '72*

Singles: 7-inch

DECCA................................3-5 69-72

LPs: 10/12-inch

DECCA................................8-12 70-72
GUSTO................................5-8
MCA................................4-6 73
PINNACLE................................5-10 78
RDS................................5-10 79
Also see GREENE, Jack
Also see SEELY, Jeannie

GREENE, Laura *R&B '80*
(With Johnny McKinnis)

Singles: 7-inch

RCA................................10-20 67
SILVER FOX................................3-5
SOUND TREK................................3-5 80

GREENE, Lil *P&R '40*

Singles: 78 rpm

ALADDIN................................25-50 50
ATLANTIC (951 "Every Time")................................25-50 51
BLUEBIRD................................12-25 39-46
GROOVE................................8-15 56
RCA................................10-20 46-48

Singles: 7-inch

ATLANTIC (951 "Every Time")................................50-100 51
GROOVE (5004 "Why Don't You Do Right")................................10-20 56

LPs: 10/12-inch

ROSETTA................................5-10 86

GREENE, Lorne *P&R/C&W/LP '64*

Singles: 7-inch

COLUMBIA................................3-6 69
GRT................................3-5 70-71
RCA................................5-10 62-66

Picture Sleeves

RCA................................5-10 63-65

LPs: 10/12-inch

CAMDEN................................5-10 70
MGM................................5-10 71
RCA................................10-20 63-66

GREENWICH, Ellie P&R '67

Singles: 7-inch

BELL.....5-10 69
RED BIRD (034 "Baby").....20-30 65
U.A......8-12 67
VERVE.....4-6 70-73

LPs: 10/12-inch

U.A. (6648 "Ellie Greenwich Composes, Produces and Sings").....30-40 68
VERVE.....10-15 73

Also see ARCHIES
Also see BONDS, Gary "U.S."
Also see BUTTERFLYS
Also see CROCE, Jim
Also see GAYE, Ellie
Also see GEE, Ellie
Also see RAINDROPS

GREENWOOD, Lee C&W '81
(Lee Greenwood Affair)

Singles: 7-inch

DOT.....3-6 69
MCA.....3-4 81-88
PARAMOUNT.....3-5 71

Picture Sleeves

MCA.....3-4 83

LPs: 10/12-inch

MCA (Except 5305).....5-10 83-88
MCA (5305 "Inside and Out").....10-15 82
(Slightly incorrect title used.)
MCA (5305 "Inside Out").....5-10 82
(Title corrected.)

Also see MANDRELL, Barbara, & Lee Greenwood

GREENWOOD COUNTY SINGERS
(Greenwoods) P&R '64

Singles: 7-inch

DECCA.....4-6 64-66
KAPP.....4-6 64-66

Picture Sleeves

KAPP.....4-6 64

LPs: 10/12-inch

DECCA.....10-15 64
KAPP.....10-15 64-66
RCA.....8-12 70

GREENWOODS: see GREENWOOD COUNTY SINGERS

GREER, Big John, & Four Students

Singles: 78 rpm

GROOVE.....10-20 55

Singles: 7-inch

GROOVE (0131 "A Man and a Woman").....20-30 55

Also see GREER, John

GREER, John R&B '52
(Big John Greer; with Rhythm Rockers)

Singles: 78 rpm

GROOVE.....15-25 54
RCA.....20-30 49-53

Singles: 7-inch

MINARET (148 "Take This Hurt Off Me").....10-20
GROOVE (002 "Bottle It Up and Go").....20-30 54
RCA (0007 "Drinkin' Wine Spoo-Dee-O-Dee").....35-50 49
(Colored vinyl.)
RCA (0029 "If I Told You Once").....35-50 49
(Colored vinyl)
RCA (0051 "Rocking Jenny Jones").....35-50 50
(Colored vinyl)
RCA (0076 "I'll Never Do That Again").....35-50 50
(Colored vinyl.)
RCA (0096 "Cheatin' ").....35-50 50
(Colored vinyl.)
RCA (0104 "Red Juice").....35-50 50
(Colored vinyl.)
RCA (0108 "Once There Lived a Fool").....15-25 51
RCA (0113 "Why Did You Go").....15-25 51
RCA (0125 "Clambake Boogie").....15-25 51
RCA (0137 "Rockin' with Big John").....15-25 51
RCA (4293 "Have Another Drink").....15-25 51
RCA (4348 "Got You on My Mind").....15-25 51
RCA (4484 "Strong Red Whiskey").....15-25 52
RCA (5037 "I'm the Fat Man").....15-25 52
RCA (5170 "You Played on My Piano").....15-25 53
RCA (5259 "Ride Pretty Baby").....15-25 53
RCA (5531 "Drinkin' Fool").....15-25 53

Also see ALLEN, Annisteen
Also see GREER, Big John, & Four Students

GREGG, Bobby P&R/R&B '62
(With His Friends; Bobby Grego)

Singles: 7-inch

COTTON.....10-15 62
EPIC.....8-12 62-66

LPs: 10/12-inch

EPIC (24051 "Let's Stomp and Wild Weekend").....20-25 63
(Monaural.)
EPIC (26051 "Let's Stomp and Wild Weekend").....25-30 63
(Stereo.)

Also see BUCHANAN, Roy
Also see DYLAN, Bob
Also see GIBSON, Steve

GREGORY, Dick LP '61

Singles: 7-inch

VEE JAY.....4-8 62

LPs: 10/12-inch

COLPIX.....10-20 61-64
POPPY.....8-15 69-73
VEE JAY.....10-20 62-64

GREY & HANKS R&B '78

Singles: 7-inch

RCA.....3-5 78-80

LPs: 10/12-inch

RCA.....5-10 79-80

Members: Zane Grey; Len Hanks

GRIFFIN, Billy R&B '83

Singles: 7-inch

ATLANTIC.....3-4 86
COLUMBIA.....3-4 83-86

LPs: 10/12-inch

COLUMBIA.....5-10 84-86

Also see MIRACLES

GRIFFIN, Merv P&R '51
(With the Griffin Family Singers; with Percy Faith Orchestra)

Singles: 78 rpm

COLUMBIA.....3-5 53
RCA.....3-5 51-52

Singles: 7-inch

CAMEO.....3-5 63-64
CARLTON.....4-8 61
COLUMBIA.....5-10 53-56
CORAL.....3-6 66
DECCA.....10-20 50s
DOT.....3-5 68
GRIFFIN.....3-5 73
MGM.....4-6 65-67
MERCURY.....4-6 62
METROMEDIA.....3-5 70
RCA.....5-10 51-52

EPs: 7-inch

RCA (3000 series).....5-10 52

LPs: 10/12-inch

CAMEO.....8-15 64
CARLTON.....10-20 61
MGM.....8-15 65-66
METROMEDIA.....5-10 69
RCA (3000 series).....15-25 52
(10-inch LPs.)

Also see MARTIN, Freddy, & His Orchestra

GRIFFIN, Reggie, & Technofunk R&B '82

Singles: 7-inch

SWEET MOUNTAIN.....3-4 82

Also see MANCHILD
Also see WEST STREET MOB

GRIFFIN BROTHERS R&B '50
(Featuring Tommy Brown; featuring Margie Day)

Singles: 78 rpm

DOT.....10-20 50-52

Singles: 7-inch

DOT (1070 "Stubborn As a Mule").....25-50 51
DOT (1071 "Weeping and Crying").....25-50 51
DOT (1094 "It'd Surprise You").....20-40 51
DOT (1095 "The Teaser").....20-40 51
DOT (1104 "I'm Gonna Jump in the River").....20-40 52
DOT (1105 "Coming Home").....20-40 52
DOT (1108 "Ace in the Hole").....25-50 52
DOT (1114 "My Story").....20-30 53
DOT (1117 "I Wanna Go Back").....20-30 53
DOT (1144 "My Story").....20-30 53
DOT (1145 "Black Bread").....20-30 53
DOT (16000 series).....10-15 60

Members: Jimmy Griffin; Edward "Buddy" Griffin.

Also see DAY, Margie

GRIFFITH, Andy P&R '54
(Deacon Andy Griffith)

Singles: 78 rpm

CAPITOL.....5-15 53-57

Singles: 7-inch

CAPITOL (2500 series).....4-6 69
CAPITOL (2600 thru 3600 series).....10-20 53-57
CAPITOL (4000 & 5000 series).....4-8 59-63
(Purple or orange/yellow swirl labels.)
CAPITOL (4000 series).....3-5 76
(Orange labels.)
COLONIAL ("What It Was—Was Football").....15-25 53
(Number not known.)
COLUMBIA.....5-10 72

EPs: 7-inch

CAPITOL.....20-30 54-61

LPs: 10/12-inch

CAPITOL (872 "A Face in the Crowd").....35-50 57
(Soundtrack.)
CAPITOL (962 "Just for Laughs").....35-45 58
CAPITOL (1100 thru 1600 series).....30-40 59-61
CAPITOL (2000 series).....15-25 64-67
COLUMBIA.....5-10 72

GRIFFITH, Johnny, Inc. R&B '73

Singles: 7-inch

RCA.....3-5 73

GRIFFITHS, Marcia P&R '89

Singles: 7-inch

MANGO.....3-4 89

GRIM REAPER LP '84

Singles: 7-inch

RCA/EBONY.....3-4 80s
RCA/EBONY/EVA-TONE.....5-10 85
(Soundsheet. Promotional issue only.)
RCA (Except 715001).....3-4 85
RCA (715001 "Rock You to Hell").....4-6 87
(Square cardboard picture disc.)

Picture Sleeves

RCA/EBONY.....3-4

LPs: 10/12-inch

RCA.....5-10 84-87

GRIMES, Tiny R&B '48
(Tiny Grimes Quintet; Swingtet)

Singles: 78 rpm

APOLLO.....5-10 53
ATLANTIC.....10-25 48-52
BLUE NOTE.....5-15 47
GOTHAM.....5-10 49-56
RED ROBIN.....10-20 52
SAVOY.....5-15 46-48

Singles: 7-inch

APOLLO.....10-15 53
ATLANTIC (990 "Begin the Beguine").....20-30 52
B&F.....4-8 59
GOTHAM.....10-20 50-56
PRESTIGE.....8-12 59

RED ROBIN (123 "Juicy Fruit")........15-25 52
UNITED..........10-20 55

LPs: 10/12-inch

PRESTIGE SWINGSVILLE..........15-25 60
U.A. 10-20 62

GRIN
LP '71

Singles: 7-inch

A&M..........3-5 74
SPINDIZZY..........3-5 71-72
THUNDER..........3-5

LPs: 10/12-inch

A&M..........8-10 73
COLUMBIA..........5-10
SPINDIZZY..........8-10 71-73
Member: Nils Lofgren.
Also see LOFGREN, Nils

GRINDERSWITCH
LP '77

Singles: 7-inch

ATCO..........3-5 77-78

LPs: 10/12-inch

ATCO..........8-10 77
CAPRICORN..........8-10 74-76

GRISMAN, David
LP '80

LPs: 10/12-inch

HORIZON..........5-10 79
ROUNDER..........5-8 83
W.B. 5-10 80-81

GRISSOM, Jimmy
R&B '51

(With the Red Callender Sextet)

Singles: 78 rpm

HOLLYWOOD..........5-10 51

Singles: 7-inch

ARGO..........4-8 64

LPs: 10/12-inch

ARGO..........10-15 64

GROCE, Larry
P&R/C&W/LP '76

Singles: 7-inch

PEACEABLE..........3-5 75
W.B. 3-5 75

LPs: 10/12-inch

DAYBREAK..........8-10 71-72
W.B. 8-10 76

GROSS, Felix
R&B '49

Singles: 78 rpm

DOWN BEAT..........15-25 54-49
SAVOY..........15-25 49

GROSS, Henry
P&R/LP '75

Singles: 7-inch

A&M..........3-5 74-75
LIFESONG..........3-5 76-78

LPs: 10/12-inch

ABC-PAR..........8-10 71
A&M..........8-10 73-75
CAPITOL..........5-10 81
LIFESONG..........8-10 76-78
Also see SHA NA NA

GROUND HOG
R&B '74

(Joe Richardson)

Singles: 7-inch

GEMIGO..........3-5 74
Also see TENDER SLIM

GRUSIN, Dave
LP '80

(Dave Grusin Quintet; Dave Grusin & NY/LA Dream Band)

Singles: 7-inch

DECCA..........3-6 68-69
EPIC..........4-8 63
W.B. 3-4 83

LPs: 10/12-inch

COLUMBIA..........10-20 65
EPIC..........15-25 62
GRP..........5-10 80-89
POLYDOR..........5-10 77
SHEFFIELD LAB..........8-15 77-82
VERSATILE..........5-10 78
Also see BISHOP, Stephen
Also see GALE, Eric

GRUSIN, Dave, & Lee Ritenour
LP '85

LPs: 10/12-inch

GRP..........5-10 85
Also see GRUSIN, Dave
Also see RITENOUR, Lee

GUADALCANAL DIARY
LP '88

LPs: 10/12-inch

ELEKTRA..........5-10 86-89
Members: Rhett Crowe; Murray Attaway; John Poe; Jeff Walls.

GUARALDI, Vince
P&R '62

(Vince Guaraldi Trio)

Singles: 7-inch

FANTASY..........4-6 62-66

LPs: 10/12-inch

FANTASY (3200 series)..........20-30 56-58
FANTASY (3300 series)..........15-25 62-66
FANTASY (8000 series)..........15-25 62
FANTASY (8300 series)..........10-20 63-66
MFSL (112 "Jazz Impressions of Black Orpheus")..........20-40 84
W.B. 8-12 68-69

GUARD, Dave, & Whiskeyhill Singers

Singles: 7-inch

CAPITOL..........4-8 62

LPs: 10/12-inch

CAPITOL..........15-20 62
Members: Dave Guard; Cyrus Faryar; Judy Hensky; David "Buck" Wheat.
Also see KINGSTON TRIO

GUCCI CREW II
LP '89

LPs: 10/12-inch

GUCCI..........5-8 89

GUESS WHO
P&R '65

Singles: 7-inch

AMY..........10-20 67
FONTANA..........10-15 69
HILLTAK..........3-5 78-79
QUALITY..........10-20 65-68
(Canadian.)
RCA..........3-6 69-76
RCA RECORDING SERVICES (55829 "Two Wheel Freedom")..........4-8
SCEPTER (1295 "Shakin' All Over")..8-12 65
SCEPTER (12000 series)..........10-20 65-66

Picture Sleeves

RCA..........8-12 70

LPs: 10/12-inch

HILLTAK..........5-10 79
MGM..........12-15 69
PICKWICK..........8-10 72
PIP..........8-10 71
PRIDE..........8-10 73
RCA (Except "AYL1" & LSP-4000 series)..........8-12 73-80
RCA ("AYL1" series)..........5-10 80
RCA (LSP-4141 thru LSP-4830).......12-25 69-72
RCA (1004 "Best of the Guess Who")..........10-20 71
(With bonus, black light poster.)
RCA (1004 "Best of the Guess Who")..........8-12 71
(Without poster.)
SCEPTER..........8-10 73
SPRINGBOARD..........8-10 72
WAND..........12-15 69
Members: Chad Allen; Burton Cummings; Randy Bachman; Domenic Troiano.
Also see BACHMAN, Randy
Also see CUMMINGS, Burton
Also see TROIANO, Domenic
Also see WOLFMAN JACK

GUESS WHO / Discotays

Singles: 7-inch

SCEPTER (1295 "Shakin' All Over") 15-20 65
Also see GUESS WHO

GUIDRY, Greg
P&R/LP '82

Singles: 7-inch

COLUMBIA..........3-4 82

LPs: 10/12-inch

COLUMBIA/BADLAND..........5-10 82

GUITAR, Bonnie
C&W/P&R '57

Singles: 78 rpm

DOT..........10-15 57
FABOR (Except 4018)..........5-10 55-56
FABOR (4018 "Dark Moon")..........15-25 57
4 STAR..........5-10 56

Singles: 7-inch

ABC..........3-5 74
CHARTER..........4-6
COLUMBIA..........3-5 72
DOLTON..........5-10 59
DOT (15000 series)..........8-15 57-59
DOT (16000 & 17000 series)..........4-6 66-69
FABOR (138 "Ra Ta Ta Ta")..........4-8 64
FABOR (4013 "If You See My Love Dancing")..........10-20 55
FABOR (4017 "Clinging Vine")..........10-20 56
FABOR (4018 "Dark Moon")..........20-30 57
4 STAR (1003 "Honey on the Moon")....3-5 80
4 STAR (1006 "I Want to Spend My Life with You")..........10-20 56
JERDEN..........5-10 63
MCA..........3-5 74
PARAMOUNT..........3-5 70
PLAYBACK..........3-4 89
RCA..........10-20 61-62
RADIO..........5-10 58

LPs: 10/12-inch

CAMDEN..........6-12 69
DOT (Except 3069 & 3385)..........10-15 59-68
DOT (3069 "Moonlight and Shadows")..........15-25 57
DOT (3385 "Dark Moon")..........15-20 63
HAMILTON..........8-12 65
PARAMOUNT..........8-12 70
PICKWICK..........6-12 70

GUITAR SLIM
P&R/R&B '54

(Eddie Jones)

Singles: 78 rpm

ATCO..........10-15 56
IMPERIAL..........15-25 54
SPECIALTY..........10-15 55

Singles: 7-inch

ATCO (6072 "Oh Yeah")..........20-30 56
ATCO (6097 "It Hurts to Love Someone")..........15-25 57
ATCO (6108 "I Don't Mind At All").....15-25 58
IMPERIAL (5278 "Woman Troubles")..........40-50 54
IMPERIAL (5310 "New Arrival")..........40-50 54
SPECIALTY (482 "The Things That I Used to Do")..........20-30 55
SPECIALTY (490 "The Story of My Life")..........20-30 54
SPECIALTY (527 "Later for You, Baby")..........15-25 56
SPECIALTY (536 "Sufferin' Mind")....15-25 55
SPECIALTY (542 "Our Only Child")..15-25 55
SPECIALTY (551 "I Got Sumpin' for You")..........15-25 55
SPECIALTY (557 "Quicksand")..........15-25 56
SPECIALTY (569 "Sum'thin' to Remember You By")..........15-25 56

LPs: 10/12-inch

SPECIALTY..........8-10 70-88
Also see CHARLES, Ray

GUITAR SLIM

(Johnny Winter)

Singles: 7-inch

DIAMOND JIM (204 "Crying in My Heart")..........100-150 62
(Reissued as by Texas "Guitar" Slim.)
Also see TEXAS "GUITAR" SLIM
Also see WINTER, Johnny

GUN
LP '90

LPs: 10/12-inch

A&M..........5-8 90

Members: Mark Rankin; Giuliano Gizzi; Dante Gizzi; Scott Shields; Baby Stafford.

GUNHILL ROAD P&R '73

Singles: 7-inch

KAMA SUTRA ... 3-5 73
MERCURY ... 3-5 72

LPs: 10/12-inch

KAMA SUTRA ... 8-10 72
MERCURY ... 8-10 71

GUNS 'N' ROSES LP '87

Singles: 12-inch

GEFFEN ... 4-8 89

Singles: 7-inch

GEFFEN ... 3-4 88-92

Picture Sleeves

GEFFEN ... 3-4 88-89

EPs: 7-inch

UZI SUICIDE ("Live Like a Suicide") ... 150-200 86

LPs: 10/12-inch

GEFFEN (Except 24148 & 24617) ... 5-10 88-89
GEFFEN (24148 "Appetite for Destruction") ... 50-75 87
(With robot/rape painting on cover.)
GEFFEN (24148 "Appetite for Destruction") ... 5-8 87
(With skulls and cross cover.)
GEFFEN (24617 "Spaghetti Incident") ... 10-15 93
(Colored vinyl.)

Members: Axl Rose; Slash; Duff McKagan; Saul Hudson; Steve Adler; Izzy Stradlin; Matt Sorum; Dizzy Reed; Gilby Clarke.
Also see CULT

GUNTER, Arthur R&B '55

Singles: 78 rpm

EXCELLO ... 15-30 54-57

Singles: 7-inch

EXCELLO (2047 "Baby Let's Play House") ... 30-50 54
EXCELLO (2053 "She's Mine, All Mine") ... 25-40 55
EXCELLO (2058 "Honey Babe") ... 25-40 55
EXCELLO (2073 thru 2204) ... 12-25 56-61

LPs: 10/12-inch

EXCELLO ... 10-15 71

GUNTER, Shirley R&B '54
(With the Flairs; with Queens)

Singles: 78 rpm

FLAIR (Except 1076) ... 8-15 54-55
FLAIR (1076 "How Can I Tell You") .. 20-30 55
MODERN ... 8-12 56

Singles: 7-inch

FLAIR (Except 1076) ... 15-25
FLAIR (1076 "How Can I Tell You") .. 30-60 55
MODERN ... 10-20 56
TANGERINE ... 4-8 65

Members: Shirley Gunter; Lula Bea Kinney; Lula Mae Suggs; Zola Taylor.

GUTHRIE, Arlo LP '67

Singles: 7-inch

REPRISE ... 3-6 67-77

LPs: 10/12-inch

REPRISE ... 8-10 67-76
U.A. ... 10-15 69
W.B. ... 5-10 77-81

Also see SEEGER, Pete, & Arlo Guthrie

GUTHRIE, Gwen R&B '82

Singles: 12-inch

GARAGE ... 4-6 85
ISLAND ... 4-6 83-85

Singles: 7-inch

GARAGE ... 3-4 85
ISLAND ... 3-4 82-85
POLYDOR ... 3-4 86-87
W.B. ... 3-4 88

Picture Sleeves

POLYDOR ... 3-4 86

LPs: 10/12-inch

GARAGE ... 5-10 85
ISLAND ... 5-10 85

POLYDOR ... 5-8 86

Also see HOWARD, George
Also see LIMIT

GUY R&B/LP '88

LPs: 10/12-inch

MCA ... 5-8 90
UPTOWN ... 5-8 88

GUY, Bob
(Frank Zappa)

Singles: 7-inch

DONNA (1380 "Letter from Jeepers") ... 50-75 61

Also see ZAPPA, Frank

GUY, Buddy R&B '62

Singles: 7-inch

ARTISTIC ... 20-30 58-59
CHESS ... 10-20 60-65

LPs: 10/12-inch

BLUE THUMB ... 8-10 70
BLUES BALL ... 15-25
CHESS ... 10-12 69
VANGUARD ... 12-18 68

Also see WELLS, Junior, & Buddy Guy

GUY, Buddy, & Dr. John & Eric Clapton / Buddy Guy & J. Geils Band

Singles: 7-inch

ATCO (6890 "Man of Many Words") 4-8 72

Also see CLAPTON, Eric
Also see DR. JOHN
Also see GEILS, J., Band

GYPSIES R&B '65

Singles: 7-inch

CAPRICE ... 5-10 66
OLD TOWN (1168 "Blue Bird") ... 10-20 64
OLD TOWN (1180 "Jerk It") ... 10-20 65
OLD TOWN (1184 "It's a Woman's World") ... 40-60 65
OLD TOWN (1193 "Oh I Wonder Why") ... 10-20 66

Members: Betty Pearce; Ernestine Pearce; Shirley Pearce; Lestine Johnson.
Also see FLIRTATIONS

GYPSY P&R/LP '70

Singles: 7-inch

COGNITO ... 3-5
DORE (907 "Don't Stop for Nothin' ") 20-30
METROMEDIA ... 3-5 70
RCA ... 3-5 71-72

LPs: 10/12-inch

METROMEDIA ... 8-12 70-71
RCA ... 8-12 72-73

Checker
RECORD CO.
7762
ARC
Voca
B.M.I
D.J.
COPY
NOT FOR
SALE
LONELY HOURS
(L. Fulson)
LOWELL FULSON
820
MANUFACTURED BY CHECKER RECORD CO. CHICAGO,

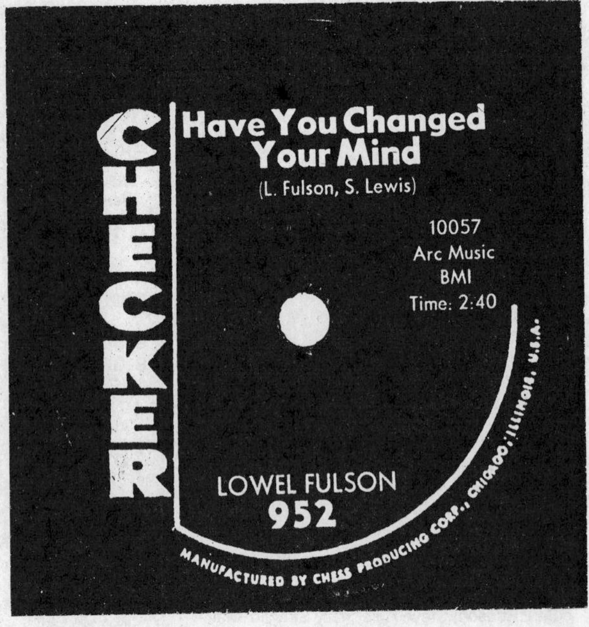
CHECKER
Have You Changed
Your Mind
(L. Fulson, S. Lewis)
10057
Arc Music
BMI
Time: 2:40
LOWEL FULSON
952
MANUFACTURED BY CHESS PRODUCING CORP., CHICAGO, ILLINOIS, U.S.A.

Frisco
(F-107)
Vocal By
Mel Moore
THURSDAY EVENING BLUES
(Fields-West-Moore)
ERNIE FIELDS
and His Orchestra
3A
LICENSED BY MANUFACTURER ONLY FOR NON COMMERCIAL USE FOR PHONOGRAPHS IN HOMES. MANUFACTURER AND ORIGINAL PURCHASER AGREE THIS RECORD SHALL NOT BE RESOLD FOR ANY OTHER PURPOSE

COLUMBIA
®"Columbia," Marcas Reg.
SQ*/QUAD
Intro. :25
3:48
Strings
arranged &
conducted by
E. Freeman
Produced by:
Art Garfunkel
& Roy Halee
45 RPM
Radio
Station Copy
4-45926
QJZSS 157755
℗ 1973 CBS, Inc.
Publisher:
Canopy Mus.,
Inc. (ASCAP)
Engineer:
Roy Halee
NOT
FOR SALE
ART GARFUNKEL
ALL I KNOW
- J. Webb -
This SQ* Quadraphonic disc is fully
compatible and may be played on
conventional stereo equipment.
*TM CBS, Inc.

HACKETT, Buddy P&R '53

Singles: 78 rpm

CORAL 3-5 53-56

Singles: 7-inch

CORAL 5-10 53-56
LAUREL 4-8 60

LPs: 10/12-inch

CORAL 8-15 65
DOT 10-15 59

HACKETT, Steve LP '76

Singles: 7-inch

CHARISMA 3-4 80
CHRYSALIS 3-5 76-79
EPIC 3-4 81

LPs: 10/12-inch

CHARISMA 5-10 80
CHRYSALIS 5-10 76-79
EPIC 5-10 81
Also see GTR
Also see GENESIS

HAGAR, Sammy P&R/LP '77

Singles: 7-inch

CAPITOL 3-5 76-79
COLUMBIA 3-4 87
GEFFEN (Except 29246) 3-4 82-87
GEFFEN (29246 "Two Sides of Love") 3-4 84
(Black vinyl.)
GEFFEN (29246 "Two Sides of Love") 4-8 84
(Colored vinyl.)

Picture Sleeves

CAPITOL 3-5 79
COLUMBIA 3-4 87
GEFFEN 3-4 82-87

LPs: 10/12-inch

CAPITOL 5-10 77-82
GEFFEN 5-10 82-87
Also see HAGAR, SCHON, AARONSON, SHRIEVE
Also see MONTROSE
Also see VAN HALEN

HAGAR, SCHON, AARONSON, SHRIEVE P&R/LP '84

Singles: 7-inch

GEFFEN 3-4 84

Picture Sleeves

GEFFEN 3-4 84

LPs: 10/12-inch

GEFFEN 5-10 84
Members: Sammy Hagar; Neal Schon; Ken Aaronson; Michael Shrieve.
Also see HAGAR, Sammy
Also see SCHON, Neal, & Jan Hammer
Also see SANTANA

HAGEN, Nina LP '82
(Nina Hagen Band)

Singles: 12-inch

COLUMBIA 4-6 84-85

Singles: 7-inch

COLUMBIA 3-4 80-85

LPs: 10/12-inch

COLUMBIA 5-10 80-83

HAGGARD, Merle C&W '63
(With the Strangers)

Singles: 7-inch

CAPITOL 3-8 65-77
COLUMBIA 3-4 83
CURB 3-4 90
EPIC 3-4 81-89
MCA 3-5 77-85
MERCURY 3-4 83
TALLY 10-20 63-65

Picture Sleeves

CAPITOL 4-8 67-71
MCA 3-5 77-80

EPs: 7-inch

CAPITOL 8-15 71
(Juke box issues only.)

LPs: 10/12-inch

ALBUM GLOBE (9005 "Melody Ranch Featuring Merle Haggard & Friends") 40-50 80s
CAPITOL (168 thru 735) 8-15 69-71
(With "T," "ST," "STBB" or "SWBB" prefix.)
CAPITOL (168 thru 735) 4-8 69-71
(With "SKAO" or SM" prefix.)
CAPITOL (796 "Merle Haggard's Strangers and Friends Honky Tonkin' ") 20-30 71
CAPITOL (803 "Land of Many Churches") 30-50 71
(With "SWBO" prefix.)
CAPITOL (835 "Someday We'll Look Back") 8-12 71
CAPITOL (882 "Let Me Tell You About a Song") 8-12 72
CAPITOL (2373 thru 2972) 15-25 65-68
(With "T," "ST" or, in the case of 2951, an "SKAO" prefix.)
CAPITOL (2702 thru 2972) 5-10 80s
(With "SM" prefix.)
CAPITOL (11000 thru 16000 series) .. 5-10 72-82
EPIC 5-10 81-86
MCA 4-8 77-84
MERCURY 5-10 83
PICKWICK/HILLTOP 8-12 60s
RADIANT 5-10 81
RONCO 5-8
SONGBIRD 5-10 81
SPARTON 30-60
(Canadian.)
TEE VEE 5-10 77
Session: Biff Adam; Norm Hamlet; Dennis Hromek; Roy Nichols; Bobby Wayne; Johnny Gimble; Jordanaires; James Burton; Marty Haggard; Ronnie Reno; Bonnie Owens; Carter Family.
Also see ANDERSON, John
Also see COCHRAN, Hank
Also see HAGGARD, Marty
Also see PAYCHECK & HAGGARD
Also see TUBB, Ernest

HAGGARD, Merle / Patsy Cline

LPs: 10/12-inch

OUT of TOWN DIST 5-10 82
Also see CLINE, Patsy

HAGGARD, Merle, & Clint Eastwood C&W '80

Singles: 7-inch

ELEKTRA 3-4 80

Picture Sleeves

ELEKTRA 3-4 80

HAGGARD, Merle, & Janie Fricke C&W '84

Singles: 7-inch

EPIC 3-4 84

HAGGARD, Merle / Mickey Gilley / Willie Knight

LPs: 10/12-inch

OUT of TOWN DIST 5-10 82
Also see GILLEY, Mickey

HAGGARD, Merle / Sonny James

LPs: 10/12-inch

CAPITOL 10-15 60s
Also see JAMES, Sonny

HAGGARD, Merle, & George Jones C&W/LP '82
(George Jones & Merle Haggard)

Singles: 7-inch

EPIC (03405 "C.C. Waterback") 3-4 82
EPIC (03405 "C.C. Waterback") 40-50 82
(Picture disc. Autographed.)
EPIC (03405 "C.C. Waterback") 10-15 82
(Picture disc. Not signed.)

LPs: 10/12-inch

EPIC 5-10 82
Also see JONES, George

HAGGARD, Merle, & Willie Nelson
(Willie Nelson & Merle Haggard) C&W/LP '83

Singles: 7-inch

EPIC 3-4 83-87

LPs: 10/12-inch

EPIC 5-10 83
Also see NELSON, Willie

HAGGARD, Merle, & Bonnie Owens C&W '64

TALLY (181 "Just Between the Two of Us") 10-20 64

LPs: 10/12-inch

CAPITOL (2453 "Just Between the Two of Us") 20-30 66

HAGGARD, Merle, & Leona Williams C&W '78

Singles: 7-inch

CAPITOL 3-5 78
MERCURY 3-4 83

LPs: 10/12-inch

MERCURY 5-10 83

HAHN, Carol D&D '83

Singles: 12-inch

NICKLE 4-6 83

HAHN, Joyce P&R '57

Singles: 78 rpm

CADENCE 4-8 57

Singles: 7-inch

CADENCE 4-8 57

HAIRCUT ONE HUNDRED P&R/LP '82

Singles: 7-inch

ARISTA 3-4 82

LPs: 10/12-inch

ARISTA 5-10 82
Member: Nick Heyward.
Also see HEYWARD, Nick

HAIRSTON, Curtis D&D '83

Singles: 12-inch

PRETTY PEARL 4-6 83

Singles: 7-inch

ATLANTIC 3-4 87
PRETTY PEARL 3-4 84-85

HALE & HUSHABYES

Singles: 7-inch

APOGEE (104 "Yes Sir, That's My Baby") 50-100 65
REPRISE (0299 "Yes Sir, That's My Baby") 20-40 64
(Reissued in 1967 as by a Date with Soul.)
Members: Brian Wilson; Sonny & Cher; Blossoms; Jack Nitzsche; Jackie DeShannon; Darlene Love; Edna Wright; Albert Stone.
Also see BLOSSOMS
Also see DATE with SOUL
Also see DE SHANNON, Jackie
Also see HONEY CONE
Also see LOVE, Darlene
Also see NITZSCHE, Jack
Also see SONNY & CHER
Also see WILSON, Brian

HALEY, Bill P&R '53
(With His Comets; with Saddlemen; with Saddle Men; with Four Aces of Western Swing; with Reno Browne & Her Buckaroos)

Singles: 78 rpm

ATLANTIC (727 "I'm Gonna Dry Ev'ry Tear with a Kiss") 250-350 50
COWBOY (1201 "Too Many Parties Too Many Pals") 300-500 48
COWBOY (1202 "Candy Kisses") 300-500 49
COWBOY (1203 "The Covered Wagon Rolled Right Along") 250-300 49
COWBOY (1204 "Behind the Eight Ball") 250-300 50
COWBOY (1205 "Candy Kisses") 250-350 50
COWBOY (1701 "Candy Kisses") 250-350 49

COWBOY (1701 "My Palomino and I") 250-350 49
(By "Reno Browne & Her Buckaroos featuring Bill Haley." The Cowboy 1701 number is used twice.)
DECCA (29124 "Rock Around the Clock")............................50-100 54
(Black label with gold print.)
DECCA (29124 "Rock Around the Clock") 25-50 54
(Black label with silver print. Decca multi-color labels are $4 to $8 reissues.)
DECCA (29204 "Shake, Rattle & Roll") 50-80 54
(Black label with gold print.)
DECCA (29204 "Shake, Rattle & Roll")...................................25-50 54
(Black label with silver print.)
DECCA (29317 thru 30530)..............20-50 54-57
DECCA (30592 thru 30781) 20-40 58
DECCA (30844 "I Got a Woman") 25-50 59
DECCA (30873 "A Fool Such As I")..40-60 59
DECCA (30926 "Caldonia")...............50-75 59
DECCA (30956 "Ooh, Look-a-There Ain't She Pretty")..50-100 59
ESSEX...20-40 52-55
HOLIDAY (105 "Rocket 88")..........100-150 51
HOLIDAY (108 "Green Tree Boogie")..100-150 51
HOLIDAY (111 "A Year Ago This Christmas")...................................100-150 51
HOLIDAY (113 "Juke box Cannonball")...............................100-150 51
KEYSTONE (5101 "Deal Me a Hand")..500-750 50
KEYSTONE (5102 "Susan Van Dusan")....................................500-1000 50
QUALITY (1120 "Crazy Man, Crazy") 100-150 53
(Canadian.)
QUALITY (1399 "Rock the Joint") ... 50-100 55
(Canadian.)

Singles: 7-inch

APT (25081 "Burn That Candle") 15-20 65
APT (25087 "Haley A-Go-Go").......... 15-20 65
ARZEE..8-12 77
DECCA (29000 series)..................... 20-35 54-56
(With silver lines on both sides of the name Decca.)
DECCA (29000 series)......................10-20 54-56
(With a star and silver lines under the name Decca.)
DECCA (30000 series)......................10-20 56-59
DECCA (31000 series)........................5-10 60-64
DECCA (72000 series)............................4-6 69
ESSEX (102 "Rock Around the Clock") 10-20 60s
(Though once considered by many to be a bootleg, this 45 was reportedly made by Essex owner, Dave Miller. We are therefore treating it as a reissue.)
ESSEX (303 "Rock the Joint").......500-750 52
(Colored vinyl.)
ESSEX (303 "Rock the Joint")...........65-75 52
(Black vinyl. Block style logo.)
ESSEX (303 "Rock the Joint")...........55-65 52
(Black vinyl. Script style logo.)
ESSEX (305 "Rocking Chair on the Moon") 50-100 52
ESSEX (310 "Real Rock Drive") 50-100 52
ESSEX (321 "Crazy Man Crazy").......50-75 53
ESSEX (327 "Fractured")..................30-40 53
ESSEX (332 "Live It Up")..................25-35 53
ESSEX (340 "Ten Little Indians")......25-35 53
ESSEX (348 "Chattanooga Choo-Choo")......................................20-30 54
ESSEX (374 "Juke box Cannonball")....................................50-75 54
ESSEX (381 "Rocket 88") 100-125 55
ESSEX (399 "Rock the Joint")...........50-75 55
GONE (5111 "Spanish Twist") 15-25 61
GONE (5116 "Riviera").......................15-25 61
HOLIDAY (113 "Juke box Cannonball") 300-400 51
JANUS..8-12 71
JUKE BOX...3-4 90
KAMA SUTRA.....................................5-10 70
MCA 3-5 73-80
NEWTOWN (5013 "Tenor Man")...... 10-15 63
NEWTOWN (5014 "Midnight in Washington").................................. 10-15 63
NEWTOWN (5024 "Dance Around the Clock")... 10-15 63
NEWTOWN (5025 "Tandy") 10-15 63
OLD GOLD 3-5 82
QUALITY (1120 "Crazy Man, Crazy")... 50-75 53
(Canadian.)
QUALITY (1399 "Rock the Joint")..... 25-50 55
(Canadian.)
RADIO ACTIVE..4-8 70
TRANSWORLD (200 & 300 series).. 60-75 54
TRANSWORLD (718 "Real Rock Drive") 50-75 53
U.A. 5-10 69
W.B. (5145 "Candy Kisses")............. 15-25 60
W.B. (5154 "Chick Safari").............. 15-25 60
W.B. (5171 "So Right Tonight") 15-25 60
W.B. (5228 "Flip, Flop & Fly") 15-25 60
W.B. (7124 "Rock Around the Clock").. 10-15 68

Picture Sleeves

ARZEE 8-12 77
DECCA (30314 "Billy Goat") 40-60 57
DECCA (30530 "Mary Mary Lou")..... 25-35 58

EPs: 7-inch

ARZEE (137 "Bill Haley Sings")........ 20-30 77
CLAIRE (4779 "Bill Haley and the Comets") 15-20 78
DECCA (2168 "Shake, Rattle & Roll").. 40-60 54
DECCA (2209 "Dim, Dim the Lights").. 40-60 55
DECCA (2322 "Razzle Dazzle")........ 40-60 56
DECCA (2398/2399/2400 "He Digs Rock & Roll").. 40-60 56
(Price is for any of three volumes.)
DECCA (2416/2417/2418 "Rock'n Roll Stage Show").. 40-50 56
(Price is for any of three volumes.)
DECCA (2532 "Rockin' the Oldies").. 30-40 57
DECCA (2533 "Rock 'N' Roll Party") 30-40 57
DECCA (2534 "Rockin' & Rollin' ").... 30-40 57
DECCA (2564 "Rockin' Around the World").. 30-40 57
DECCA (2576 "Rockin' Around Europe").. 30-40 57
DECCA (2577 "Rockin' Around the Americas")....................................... 30-40 57
DECCA (2615/2616 "Rockin' the Joint").. 30-40 58
(Price is for either of two volumes.)
DECCA (2638 "Bill Haley's Chicks").. 30-40 58
DECCA (2670 "Bill Haley and His Comets") 30-40 59
DECCA (2671 "Strictly Instrumental") 30-40 59
DECCA (72638 "Bill Haley's Chicks")... 50-75 59
(Stereo.)
DECCA (72670 "Bill Haley and His Comets") 50-75 59
(Stereo.)
DECCA (72671 "Strictly Instrumental")................................... 50-75 59
(Stereo.)
ESSEX (102 "Dance Party") 50-100 54
ESSEX (117/118/119 "Rock with Bill Haley & the Comets") 50-100 54
(Price is for any of three volumes.)
SOMERSET (460 "Rock with Bill Haley & the Comets") 40-60 55
TRANSWORLD (117/118/119 "Rock with Bill Haley & the Comets")........................ 50-100 54
(Price is for any of three volumes. May be titled *For Your Dance Party.*)

LPs: 10/12-inch

AEI (3106 "Rock Around the Clock")..8-12 82
ACCORD..5-10 81-82
ALSHIRE 8-10 79
AMBASSADOR 8-15 70-87
BUDDAH 5-10 84
CORAL...8-10 73
DECCA (5560 "Shake, Rattle & Roll")....................................250-350 54
(10–inch LP.)
DECCA (7211 "Golden Hits") 12-18 72
DECCA (8225 "Rock Around the Clock")......................................75-125 55
(All black label with silver print.)
DECCA (8225 "Rock Around the Clock") 20-40 60
(Black label with rainbow color stripe. Reads "M'F'D by Decca Records Inc. New York, U.S.A.")
DECCA (8225 "Rock Around the Clock") 15-20 68
(Black label with rainbow color stripe. Reads "Mfr'd by Decca Records, a Div. of MCA Inc. New York, U.S.A.")
DECCA (8315 "He Digs Rock & Roll")...100-200 56
DECCA (8345 "Rock'n Roll Stage Show")..100-200 56
DECCA (8569 "Rockin' the Oldies")......................................100-200 57
DECCA (8692 "Rockin' Around the World")...50-100 58
DECCA (8775 "Rockin' the Joint") .. 50-100 58
DECCA (8821 "Bill Haley's Chicks") 50-75 58
DECCA (8964 "Strictly Instrumental") 40-60 60
DECCA (75027 "Greatest Hits")........ 15-20 68
DECCA (78225 "Rock Around the Clock")..50-100 59
(All black label with silver print.)
DECCA (78225 "Rock Around the Clock") 50-100 59
(Black label with rainbow color stripe.)
DECCA (78692 "Rockin' Around the World")...20-40 62
DECCA (78821 "Bill Haley's Chicks") 50-100 58
DECCA (78964 "Strictly Instrumental") 50-75 60
ESSEX (202 "Rock with Bill Haley and the Comets")...................................300-500 54
EXACT...5-10 80
51 WEST..5-10 83
GNP...8-12 74-76
GREAT NORTHWEST 8-12 81
GUEST STAR 12-20 65
JANUS...15-25 72
JOKER...5-10 81
KAMA SUTRA (2014 "Bill Haley's Scrapbook") 20-30 70
KOALA...8-10 79
MCA...6-10 73-88
PAIR 5-8 86
PHOENIX 5-10 81
PICKWICK..8-10 71-74
ROULETTE 15-20 62
SILHOUETTE...5-10 81
SOMERSET (4600 "Rock with Bill Haley & Comets")..75-125 58
SPRINGBOARD..8-10 77
SUN...10-15 80
TRANSWORLD (202 "Rock with Bill Haley & the Comets")...................................200-300 56
VOCALION 15-25 63
W.B. (W-1378 "Bill Haley & His Comets")...25-35 60
(Monaural.)
W.B. (WS-1378 "Bill Haley & His Comets")...35-45 60
(Stereo.)
W.B. (W-1391 "Haley's Juke box").... 25-35 60
(Monaural.)

WARNER (WS-1391 "Haley's Juke box")....35-45 60
(Stereo.)
W.B. (1831 "Rock & Roll Revival")......8-12 70
Members: Bill Haley; Rudy Pompilli; Bill Miller; Ray Crawley; Buddy Dee.
Also see BROWNE, Reno, & Her Buckaroos
Also see CLIFTON, Johnny, & His String Band
Also see DOWN HOMERS
Also see KINGSMEN
Also see LEE, Brenda / Bill Haley & Comets / Kalin Twins / Four Aces
Also see LOPEZ, Trini / Scott Gregory

HALEY, Bill / Phil Flowers

Singles: 7-inch

KASEY (7006 "ABC Boogie")....10-15 61

Picture Sleeves

KASEY (7006 "ABC Boogie")....25-35 61

HALEY, Bill / Bunny Paul / Dinning Sisters

EPs: 7-inch

SOMERSET (460 "Rock and Roll Dance Party")....30-40 55
Also see PAUL, Bunny, & Harptones

HALEY, Bill / Boots Randolph

Singles: 7-inch

LOGO (7005 "Yakety Sax")....8-12 61
Also see HALEY, Bill
Also see RANDOLPH, Boots

HALL, Daryl LP '80
(With Gulliver)

Singles: 7-inch

AMY....4-8 69
CHELSEA....3-6 76
RCA....3-4 80-87

Picture Sleeves

RCA....3-4 80-87

LPs: 10/12-inch

RCA....5-10 80-86
Also see KNIGHT, Holly
Also see U.S.A. for AFRICA

HALL, Daryl, & Ruth Copeland

Singles: 7-inch

RCA....3-4 76
Also see HALL, Daryl

HALL, Daryl, & John Oates
(Hall & Oates) P&R/LP '74

Singles: 12-inch

RCA (Except 13705)....4-8 78-85
RCA (13705 "Jingle Bell Rock")....30-40 83
(Picture disc. Promotional issue only.)

Singles: 7-inch

ARISTA....3-4 88-90
ATLANTIC....3-5 72-77
CHELSEA....3-5 76
RCA....3-5 76-84
SIRE....3-4
RCA GOLD STANDARD....3-4 83-84

Picture Sleeves

ARISTA....3-4 88
RCA....3-5 77-85
SIRE....3-4

Picture Sleeves

ARISTA....3-4 88
RCA....3-5 77-85

Promotional Singles

RCA (Colored vinyl)....5-8 85
(One side by Daryl Hall and one side by John Oates.)

EPs: 7-inch

ATLANTIC (265 "She's Gone")....8-12 73
(Promotional issue only.)

LPs: 10/12-inch

ARISTA....5-8 88-90
ATLANTIC....8-12 72-77
CHELSEA....10-12 76
MFSL (069 "Abandoned Luncheonette")....25-35 82
RCA (Black vinyl)....5-10 75-84
RCA (Colored vinyl)....10-15 78

Promotional LPs

RCA ("Special Radio Series")....15-25 81

Also see PRINE, John / Daryl Hall & John Oates / Barnaby Bye / Delbert & Glen

HALL, Daryl, John Oates, David Ruffin & Eddie Kendrick P&R/R&B/LP '85

Singles: 7-inch

RCA....3-4 85

Picture Sleeves

RCA....3-4 85

LPs: 10/12-inch

RCA....5-8 85
Also see KENDRICK, David
Also see RUFFIN, David

HALL, Ellis, Jr. R&B '83

Singles: 7-inch

H.C.R.C....3-4 83

HALL, Jimmy P&R/LP '80

Singles: 7-inch

EPIC....3-5 80-82

LPs: 10/12-inch

EPIC....5-10 80
Also see BECK, Jeff
Also see WET WILLIE

HALL, John P&R/LP '81
(John Hall Band)

Singles: 7-inch

ASYLUM....3-5 78
COLUMBIA....3-5 79
EMI AMERICA....3-4 81-83

LPs: 10/12-inch

ASYLUM....5-10 78
COLUMBIA....8-10 70
EMI AMERICA....5-10 81-82
Also see ORLEANS

HALL, Lani P&R '81

Singles: 7-inch

A&M....3-5 71-85

Picture Sleeves

A&M....3-5 72-85

LPs: 10/12-inch

A&M....5-10 72-85
Also see MENDES, Sergio

HALL, Lani, & Herb Alpert

Singles: 7-inch

A&M....3-4 81
Also see ALPERT, Herb
Also see HALL, Lani

HALL, Larry P&R '59

Singles: 7-inch

BARREL (621 "Sandy")....8-12 59
(Canadian.)
EVER GREEN (1001 "Sandy")....25-35 59
GOLD LEAF....5-10 62
HOT (1 "Sandy")....15-25 59
STRAND....5-10 59-62

LPs: 10/12-inch

STRAND (1005 "Sandy")....40-50 60

HALL, Randy R&B '84

Singles: 7-inch

MCA....3-4 84-88

LPs: 10/12-inch

MCA....5-10 84

HALL, Tom T. C&W '67
(With the Storytellers)

Singles: 7-inch

MERCURY (Except 70000 series)....3-5 77-86
MERCURY (70000 series)....3-8 67-77
RCA....3-5 77-81

LPs: 10/12-inch

K-TEL....5-10 77
MERCURY (500 thru 1100 series)....5-10 73-77
MERCURY (5000 thru 8000 series)....5-10 78-84
MERCURY (61000 series)....8-15 69-71
MERCURY (80000 series)....5-10 83-86
OUT of TOWN DIST....5-10 82
RCA....5-10 78-81
Session: Johnny Rodriguez; Gary Sargeants.
Also see DUDLEY, Dave, & Tom T. Hall
Also see PAGE, Patti, & Tom T. Hall

Also see RODRIGUEZ, Johnny

HALL, Tom T., & Earl Scruggs C&W '82

Singles: 7-inch

COLUMBIA....3-4 82

LPs: 10/12-inch

COLUMBIA....5-10 82
Also see FLATT, Lester, & Earl Scruggs
Also see HALL, Tom T.

HALL & OATES: see HALL, Daryl, & John Oates

HALLORAN, Jack, Singers P&R '62

Singles: 7-inch

DOT....3-5 63

HALLYDAY, David P&R '87

Singles: 7-inch

SCOTTI BROS....3-4 87

Picture Sleeves

SCOTTI BROS....3-4 87

HALOS P&R '61

Singles: 7-inch

7 ARTS (709 "Nag")....10-20 61
7 ARTS (720 "Come On")....10-20 62
TRANS ATLAS (690 "Village of Love")....8-12 62

LPs: 10/12-inch

WARWICK (2046 "The Halos")....100-150 62
Member: Arthur Crier.
Also see KING, Ben E.
Also see LEE, Curtis
Also see MANN, Barry

HAMBLEN, Stuart C&W '49

Singles: 78 rpm

COLUMBIA....4-8 49-57

Singles: 7-inch

BLUEBIRD....5-10 59
COLUMBIA....5-10 50-62
CORAL....4-8 59
KAPP....4-8 66
LAMB & LION....3-5 74
RCA (0500 series)....3-5 71
RCA (5000 & 6000 series)....5-15 54-56

EPs: 7-inch

COLUMBIA....5-10 58-59
RCA....5-15 54-60

LPs: 10/12-inch

CAMDEN....5-15 59-66
COLUMBIA....5-15 61-62
CORAL....10-20 60
KAPP....5-10 66
LAMB & LION....5-8 74
RCA....15-30 54-57
SACRED....5-8
WORD....5-8

HAMILTON, Bobby P&R '58

Singles: 7-inch

APT....8-12 58-59
DECCA....5-10 59
DIANA....5-10 59

HAMILTON, Chico LP '64
(Chico Hamilton Trio; Quartet; Quintet; with Players)

Singles: 7-inch

COLUMBIA....4-6 61
CORAL....4-6 62
ENTERPRISE....3-5 74
IMPULSE....5-8 64-67
PACIFIC JAZZ (600 series)....8-15 54-55
PACIFIC JAZZ (88000 series)....4-6 66

EPs: 7-inch

DECCA....15-25 57
PACIFIC JAZZ....20-40 55-56

LPs: 10/12-inch

BLUE NOTE....5-10 75
COLUMBIA....15-25 60-62
CROWN....10-20 63
DECCA (8614 "Jazz from Sweet Smell of Success")....25-40 57
DISCOVERY....5-8 81
ELEKTRA....5-8 80

EVEREST....5-8 79
FLYING DUTCHMAN....8-10 71
IMPULSE....10-20 63-71
INSTANT....10-20 64
MERCURY....5-10 77
ODYSSEY....10-20 68
PACIFIC JAZZ (17 "The Chico Hamilton Trio")....75-100 55
(10–inch LP.)
PACIFIC JAZZ (39 "Spectacular Chico Hamilton")....15-25 62
PACIFIC JAZZ (1209 "Chico Hamilton Quintet")....50-75 55
PACIFIC JAZZ (1216 "In Hi Fi")....50-75 56
PACIFIC JAZZ (1220 "Chico Hamilton Trio")....50-75 57
PACIFIC JAZZ (1225 "Chico Hamilton Quintet")....50-75 57
PACIFIC JAZZ (20000 series)....10-20 68
REPRISE....15-25 63
SESAC....35-55 59
SOLID STATE....10-15 68-69
SUNSET....8-15 68
W.B. (1245 "With Strings Attached")....50-75 58
W.B. (1271 "Goings East")....50-75 58
W.B. (1344 "Three Faces of Chico")....40-60 59
WORLD PACIFIC (1000 & 1200 series)....25-40 58-60
Also see ALMEIDA, Laurindo / Chico Hamilton

HAMILTON, Chico, & Charles Lloyd

LPs: 10/12–inch

COLUMBIA....10-15 68
Also see HAMILTON, Chico
Also see LLOYD, Charles, Quartet

HAMILTON, George, IV *P&R '56*

(With the Country Gentlemen; with Arthur Smith)

Singles: 78 rpm

ABC-PAR....10-20 56-57
COLONIAL (420 "A Rose and a Baby Ruth")....30-40 56
COLONIAL (451 "Sam")....10-20 56

Singles: 7–inch

ABC....3-5 78
ABC/DOT....3-5 77
ABC-PAR (9000 series)....10-20 56-59
ABC-PAR (10000 series)....5-15 59-65
COLONIAL (420 "A Rose and a Baby Ruth")....25-40 56
COLONIAL (451 "Sam")....20-30 56
GRT....3-5 76
MCA....3-5 79-80
RCA....3-8 61-74

EPs: 7–inch

ABC-PAR (220 "On Campus")....15-25 58

LPs: 10/12–inch

ABC....8-10 72-77
ABC-PAR (ABC-220 "George Hamilton IV on Campus")....20-40 58
(Monaural.)
ABC-PAR (ABCS-220 "George Hamilton IV on Campus")....25-50 58
(Stereo.)
ABC-PAR (ABC-251 "Sing Me a Sad Song")....20-40 58
(Monaural.)
ABC-PAR (ABCS-251 "Sing Me a Sad Song")....25-50 58
(Stereo.)
ABC-PAR (ABC-461 "George Hamilton IV - Big 15")....20-30 63
(Monaural.)
ABC-PAR (ABCS-461 "George Hamilton IV - Big 15")....25-35 63
(Stereo.)
CAMDEN....8-10 68-73
GRAND AWARD....5-10
HARMONY....8-10 70
MCA....5-10 80
RCA ("APL1" series)....8-10 74-76
RCA ("LPM" & "LSP" series)....10-20 61-73
Also see ANKA, Paul, George Hamilton IV & Johnny Nash
Also see BLUENOTES
Also see DAVIS, Skeeter, & George Hamilton IV

HAMILTON, George, IV / Arthur Smith

LPs: 10/12–inch

LAMB & LION....5-8 74
Also see HAMILTON, George, IV
Also see SMITH, Arthur

HAMILTON, Roy *P&R/R&B '54*

Singles: 78 rpm

EPIC....5-10 54-57

Singles: 7–inch

AGP....8-12 69
CAPITOL....4-8 67
EPIC....5-15 54-67
MGM (13138 thru 13175)....5-10 63
MGM (13217 "The Panic Is On")....25-35 64
MGM (13247 "Unchained Melody")....5-10 64
MGM (13291 "You Can Count on Me")....25-35 64
MGM (13315 "Sweet Violet")....5-10 65
RCA (8641 thru 8841)....5-10 65-66
RCA (8960 "Crackin' Up Over You")....15-25 66
RCA (9061 "I Taught Her Everything She Knows")....8-12 67
RCA (9171 "So High My Love")....25-45 67

Picture Sleeves

EPIC....10-20 60-62

EPs: 7–inch

EPIC....10-20 54-59

LPs: 10/12–inch

CBS....5-8
EPIC (518 "With All My Love")....25-35 58
(Stereo.)
EPIC (525 "Why Fight the Feeling")....20-30 59
(Stereo.)
EPIC (530 "Come Out Swingin' ")....20-30 59
(Stereo.)
EPIC (535 "Have Blues Must Travel")....20-30 59
(Stereo.)
EPIC (551 "Spirituals")....20-25 60
(Stereo.)
EPIC (578 "Soft 'N Warm")....20-25 60
(Stereo.)
EPIC (595 "You Can Have Her")....20-25 61
(Stereo.)
EPIC (610 "Only You")....20-25 61
(Stereo.)
EPIC (632 "You'll Never Walk Alone")....10-20 65
(Stereo.)
EPIC (1023 "You'll Never Walk Alone")....50-100 54
(10–inch LP.)
EPIC (1103 "The Voice of Roy Hamilton")....50-100 55
(10–inch LP.)
EPIC (3176 "Roy Hamilton")....25-50 57
EPIC (3294 "You'll Never Walk Alone")....50-75 54
EPIC (3364 "Golden Boy")....30-40 57
EPIC (3519 "With All My Love")....15-25 58
(Monaural.)
EPIC (3545 "Why Fight the Feeling") 15-25 59
(Monaural.)
EPIC (3561 "Come Out Swingin' ")....15-25 59
(Monaural.)
EPIC (3580 "Have Blues Must Travel")....15-25 59
(Monaural.)
EPIC (3628 "At His Best")....15-25 60
(Monaural.)
EPIC (3654 "Spirituals")....15-25 60
(Monaural.)
EPIC (3717 "Soft 'N Warm")....15-25 60
(Monaural.)
EPIC (3775 "You Can Have Her")....15-25 61
(Monaural.)
EPIC (3807 "Only You")....15-25 61
(Monaural.)
EPIC (24000 "Mr. Rock & Soul")....15-25 62
(Monaural.)
EPIC (24009 "Greatest Hits")....15-25 63
(Monaural.)
EPIC (24316 "Greatest Hits, Vol. 2")....10-20 67
(Monaural.)
EPIC (26000 "Mr. Rock & Soul")....20-25 62
(Stereo.)
EPIC (26009 "Greatest Hits")....15-25 63
(Stereo.)
EPIC (26316 "Greatest Hits, Vol. 2")....10-20 67
(Stereo.)
MGM (4139 "Warm Soul")....15-25 63
MGM (4233 "Sentimental, Lonely and Blue")....15-25 64
RCA (3532 "Impossible Dream")....15-25 66
SEAGULL....8-12

HAMILTON, Russ *P&R/R&B '57*

Singles: 78 rpm

KAPP....5-10 57

Singles: 7–inch

KAPP....5-10 57-64
MGM....4-8 60

LPs: 10/12–inch

KAPP (1076 "Rainbow")....45-55 57

HAMILTON, JOE FRANK & DENNISON *P&R '76*

Singles: 7–inch

PLAYBOY....3-5 76-77

Picture Sleeves

PLAYBOY....3-5 76

LPs: 10/12–inch

PLAYBOY....8-10 76-77
Members: Dan Hamilton; Joe Frank Carollo; Alan Dennison.

HAMILTON, JOE FRANK & REYNOLDS *P&R/LP '71*

Singles: 7–inch

ABC....3-5 72
DUNHILL....3-5 71
PLAYBOY....3-5 75-76

Picture Sleeves

PLAYBOY....3-5 76

LPs: 10/12–inch

DUNHILL....8-10 71-72
PICKWICK....5-8 70s
PLAYBOY....8-10 75-77
Members: Dan Hamilton; Joe Frank Carollo; Tom Reynolds.
Also see HAMILTON, JOE FRANK & DENNISON
Also see T-BONES

HAMLISCH, Marvin *P&R/LP '74*

Singles: 12–inch

U.A....4-6 77

Singles: 7–inch

A&M....3-5 74-76
ARISTA....3-4 79
MCA....3-5 74-83
PLANET....3-4 80
U.A....3-4 71-77

LPs: 10/12–inch

MCA....5-10 74
SOUTHERN CROSS....5-10 83

HAMMEL, Karl, Jr. *P&R '61*

(Carl Hammel)

Singles: 7–inch

ARLISS (1007 "Summer Souvenirs") 10-20 61
ARLISS (1011 "Sittin' Alphabetically")....30-40 61
GONE (5059 "My Broken Heart")....10-15 59
LAURIE....5-10 63
20TH FOX....4-8 66

HAMMER, Jan *P&R/R&B/D&D '85*

(Jan Hammer Group)

Singles: 12–inch

MCA....4-6 85

Singles: 7–inch

ASYLUM....3-4 79

MCA....3-4 85
NEMPEROR....3-5 76-78

Picture Sleeves

MCA....3-4 85

LPs: 10/12-inch

ECM....5-10
MPS....5-10 76
NEMPEROR....5-10 74-86
VANGAURD....5-10 77

Also see BECK, Jeff
Also see GOODMAN, Jerry, & Jan Hammer
Also see SCHON, Neal, & Jan Hammer

HAMMER, M.C. LP '88
(Hammer; Stanley Burrell)

Singles: 7-inch

CAPITOL....3-4 88-90

LPs: 10/12-inch

CAPITOL....5-8 88-90

Also see OAKTOWN'S 3-5-7

HAMMOND, Albert P&R/LP '72

Singles: 7-inch

EPIC....3-5 76
MUMS....3-5 72-75

LPs: 10/12-inch

COLUMBIA....5-10 81-82
EPIC....8-10 77
MUMS....8-10 72-74

Also see MAGIC LANTERNS
Also see SPRINGSTEEN, Bruce / Albert Hammond / Loudon Wainwright, III / Taj Mahal

HAMMOND, Johnny LP '71
(John Hammond)

Singles: 7-inch

MILESTONE....4-8 75

LPs: 10/12-inch

KUDU....8-12 71-72

HAMPSHIRE, Keith P&R '72
(With the Ladys)

Singles: 7-inch

A&M....3-5 72-74
RCA....3-5 71

HAMPTON, Lionel P&R '37
(With the Hamptones)

Singles: 78 rpm

CLEF....4-8 55
DECCA....5-10 42-53
MGM....4-8 51-56
NORGREN....4-8 56
VICTOR....5-15 37-41

Singles: 7-inch

CLEF....5-10 55
BRUNSWICK....3-5 74
COLUMBIA....3-4 76
DECCA (Except 140 & 154)....5-10 50-53
DECCA (140 "Moonglow")....15-25 51
(Boxed, four-disc set)
DECCA (154 "Just Jazz")....15-25 53
(Boxed, four-disc set)
GLAD HAMP....4-6 60-67
IMPULSE....4-6 65
MGM....5-10 51-61
NORGREN....5-10 56

EPs: 7-inch

CAMDEN....10-15 50s
CLEF....15-30 53-56
COLUMBIA....10-20 56
DECCA....10-20 51-53
EMARCY....10-20 56
EPIC....10-20 56
GLAD HAMP....5-10 62
MGM....10-20 56
MERCURY....10-20 55
NORGREN....10-30 55
RCA....10-20 54-57

LPs: 10/12-inch

AMERICAN RECORDING SOCIETY (403 "Swinging Jazz")....100-150 56
(Includes booklet.)
AUDIO FIDELITY....20-40 57-59
BLUENOTE (5046 "Rockin' and Groovin'")....100-150 53
(10-inch LP.)
BRUNSWICK....5-10 74
CAMDEN (400 & 500 series)....20-30 58-59
CLEF (142 "Lionel Hampton Quartet")....75-125 53
(10-inch LP.)
CLEF (611 "Lionel Hampton Quartet")....50-100 53
CLEF (628 "Lionel Hampton Quintet")....50-100 54
CLEF (642 "Lionel Hampton Quintet")....50-100 54
CLEF (667 "Quartet/Quintet")....50-100 55
CLEF (670 "Big Band")....50-100 55
CLEF (673 "Big Band")....50-100 55
CLEF (735 "Flying Home")....50-100 56
CLEF (736 "Swingin' with Hamp")....50-100 56
CLEF (744 "Hamp's Big Four")....50-100 56
CLEF (709 "Lionel Hampton Trio")....50-100 56
COLUMBIA (711 "Wailin' at the Trianon")....50-100 56
COLUMBIA (1304 thru 1661)....20-40 59-61
(Monaural.)
COLUMBIA (8110 thru 8461)....25-50 59-61
(Stereo.)
CONTEMPORARY (3502 "Lionel Hampton Swings in Paris")....50-100 55
CORAL....15-25 63
DECCA (4000 series)....20-40 61-63
(Monaural.)
DECCA (7-4000 series)....25-50 61-63
(Stereo.)
DECCA (5230 "Boogie Woogie")....50-100 51
(10-inch LP.)
DECCA (7013 "Just Jazz")....50-100 53
(10-inch LP.)
DECCA (8200 series)....40-60 56
DECCA (9000 series)....25-50 58
DECCA (79000 series)....10-15 69
EMARCY (26037 "In Paris")....50-100 53
(10-inch LP.)
EMARCY (26038 "Crazy Hamp")....50-100 53
(10-inch LP.)
EMARCY (36032 "In Paris")....50-75 53
EMARCY (36034 "Crazy Hamp")....50-75 56
EPIC (3190 "Lionel Hampton Apollo Hall Concert 1954")....50-75 56
EPIC (16027 "Many Splendored Vibes")....20-40 62
(Monaural.)
EPIC (17027 "Many Splendored Vibes")....25-50 62
(Stereo.)
GNP (15 "Lionel Hampton with the Jazz All Stars")....50-100 57
GLAD HAMP (1001 thru 1009)....15-25 61-65
GLAD HAMP (1020 & 1021)....5-10 80
GLAD HAMP (3000 series)....15-25 62
HARMONY (7000 series)....20-35 58-61
HARMONY (32000 series)....5-10 73
IMPULSE....15-25 65
LAURIE....5-10 78
MCA....5-8 75-82
MGM (285 "Oh Rock")....75-125 51
(10-inch LP.)
MGM (3386 "Oh Rock")....50-75 56
MUSE....5-8 79
NORGREN (1080 "Lionel Hampton and His Giants")....50-100 55
PERFECT (12002 "Hampton Swings")....40-60 59
RCA (1000 "Hot Mallets")....50-100 54
RCA (1422 "Jazz Flamenco")....50-75 57
RCA (LPM-2318 "Swing Classics")....25-40 61
(Monaural.)
RCA (LSP-2318 "Swing Classics")....35-55 61
(Stereo.)
RCA (3900 series)....10-15 68
RCA (5536 "The Complete Lionel Hampton")....50-75 76
(Boxed, six-disc set.)
SUTRA....5-10 81
VERVE (2018 "Lionel Hampton Plays Love Songs")....50-100 56
VERVE (2500 series)....5-10 82
VERVE (8019 thru 8228)....40-60 57-58
WHO'S WHO in JAZZ....5-10 78-81

Also see BOSTIC, Earl
Also see BROWN, Wini
Also see CARTER, Betty
Also see COLE, Cozy
Also see JACQUET, Illinois

HAMPTON, Lionel & Stan Getz

LPs: 10/12-inch

NORGREN (1037 "Hamp and Getz")....75-100 55
VERVE (8128 "Hamp and Getz")....40-60 57

Also see GETZ, Stan

HAMPTON, Lionel & Dinah Washington R&B '44

Singles: 78 rpm

DECCA....5-15 44-47

LPs: 10/12-inch

DECCA (8088 "All American Award Concert")....40-60 54

Also see HAMPTON, Lionel
Also see WASHINGTON, Dinah

HANCOCK, Herbie LP '67

Singles: 12-inch

COLUMBIA (Except 39913)....4-6 79-85
COLUMBIA (39913 "Rock It")....10-15 84
(Picture disc.)

Singles: 7-inch

BLUE NOTE....3-6 62-65
COLUMBIA....3-5 74-88
W.B.....3-5 69-72

LPs: 10/12-inch

BLUE NOTE....15-25 62-65
(Label reads "Blue Note Records Inc. - New York, U.S.A.")
BLUE NOTE....8-15 66-71
(Label shows Blue Note Records as a division of either Liberty or United Artists.)
COLUMBIA....6-12 67-85
W.B.....8-15 70-74

Also see SANTANA
Also see SUMMERS, Bill

HANCOCK, Herbie, & Willie Bobo

LPs: 10/12-inch

BLUE NOTE....5-10 73

Also see BOBO, Willie
Also see HANCOCK, Herbie

HANCOCK, Herbie, & Chick Corea LP '79

LPs: 10/12-inch

COLUMBIA....5-10 79
POLYDOR....8-10 79

Also see COREA, Chick
Also see HANCOCK, Herbie

HANDY, John
(Gene Autry)

Singles: 78 rpm

BENNETT (7290 "Hobo Bill's Last Ride")....25-75
BENNETT (7310 "Dust Pan Blues")....25-75
RADIEX....25-75

Also see AUTRY, Gene

HANDY, John P&R/R&B/LP '76
(John Handy Quartet; Quintet)

Singles: 7-inch

IMPULSE....3-5 76-77
COLUMBIA....4-6 66-69

LPs: 10/12-inch

IMPULSE....5-10 76-77
COLUMBIA....10-15 66-68
RCA....10-15 67
ROULETTE (52000 series)....15-25 60
ROULETTE (52100 series)....10-15 66-67
W.B.....5-10 78

HANK & SUGAR PIE

Singles: 78 rpm

FEDERAL....10-15 55

Singles: 7-inch

FEDERAL (12217 "I'm So Lonely")....20-25 55

Member: Hank Huston; Umpeylia Balinton.

Also see DESANTO, Sugar Pie

HANSON & DAVIS D&D '85

Singles: 12-inch

FRESH 4-6 85-86

Singles: 7-inch

FRESH 3-4 86

HANSSON, Bo LP '73

Singles: 7-inch

CHARISMA 3-5 73
SIRE 3-5 76-77

LPs: 10/12-inch

FAMOUS CHARISMA 8-10 72-73
PVC 5-10 79
SIRE 8-10 76-77

HAPPENINGS P&R/LP '66

Singles: 7-inch

ABC 3-4 73
B.T. PUPPY (Except 181) 4-8 66-69
B.T. PUPPY (181 "Have Yourself a Merry Little Christmas") 20-30 67
(Promotional issue only.)
BIG TREE 3-5 72
ERIC 3-4
JUBILEE 3-6 69-71
MIDLAND INT'L 3-5 77
MUSICORE 3-5 72
TRIP 3-5
VIRGO 3-4 72

Picture Sleeves

B.T. PUPPY 5-15 67-69

LPs: 10/12-inch

B.T. PUPPY (1001 "The Happenings") 15-25 66
B.T. PUPPY (1003 "Psycle") 15-25 67
B.T. PUPPY (1004 "Golden Hits") 25-35 68
JUBILEE (8028 "Piece of Mind") 15-20 69
JUBILEE (8030 "Greatest Hits") 15-20 69
POST 8-12 70s
Member: Bob Miranda; Tom Guliano; Ralph DeVito; Dave Libert; Bernie Laporte; Mike LaNeue.
Also see TOKENS / Happenings

HAPPY MONDAYS LP '91

LPs: 10/12-inch

ELEKTRA (60854 "Bummed") 10-12 89
(With "nude" inner sleeve.)
ELEKTRA (60854 "Bummed") 5-10 89
(Without "nude" inner sleeve.)
ELEKTRA (60986 "Pills & Thrills and Bellyaches") 5-10 91

HARBOR, Pearl: see PEARL HARBOR

HARDCASTLE, Paul R&B/D&D '84

Singles: 12-inch

CHRYSALIS 4-6 85-86
PROFILE 4-6 84

Singles: 7-inch

CHRYSALIS 3-4 85-86
PROFILE 3-4 84-85

Picture Sleeves

CHRYSALIS 3-4 85

LPs: 10/12-inch

CHRYSALIS 5-10 86
PROFILE 5-10 85

HARDEN TRIO P&R/LP '66

Singles: 7-inch

COLUMBIA 3-4 65-68
PAPA JOE 3-4 72

LPs: 10/12-inch

COLUMBIA 10-15 66-68
HARMONY 8-12 70
Members: Arlene Harden; Bobby Harden; Robbie Harden. Session: Karen Wheeler.

HARDIN, Tim P&R/LP '69

Singles: 7-inch

COLUMBIA 3-5 69-72
VERVE/FOLKWAYS 3-5 66-70
VERVE/FORECAST 3-5 67-71

LPs: 10/12-inch

ANTILLES 5-10 73
ATCO 8-15 67
COLUMBIA (9787 "Suite for Susan Moore and Damian") 20-30 69
COLUMBIA (30551 "Bird on a Wire") 15-20 70
COLUMBIA (37164 "Shock of Grace") 5-10 81
MGM 6-10 70-74
POLYDOR 5-10 81
VERVE/FORECAST 10-20 66-69
(May show "Verve/Folkways" on spine. Some have a silver sticker covering that name with "Verve/Folkways.")

HARDLY WORTHIT PLAYERS
(Featuring Senator Bobby & Senator McKinley) P&R '67

Singles: 7-inch

PARKWAY 4-8 66-67

LPs: 10/12-inch

PARKWAY 10-20 66-67
Also see SENATOR BOBBY

HARDTIMES P&R '66

Singles: 7-inch

WORLD PACIFIC 5-10 66-68

LPs: 10/12-inch

WORLD PACIFIC 15-25 66-68
Members: Lee Kiefer; Rudy Romero; Bob Morris; Bill Richardson.
Also see STEPPENWOLF
Also see T.I.M.E.

HARDY, Hagood P&R '75

Singles: 7-inch

CAPITOL 3-5 75-78
HERITAGE 3-5 71

LPs: 10/12-inch

CAPITOL 4-8 75-76

HARDY BOYS LP '69

Singles: 7-inch

RCA 4-6 69-70

LPs: 10/12-inch

RCA 10-15 69-70

HARLEM RIVER DRIVE R&B '75
(Featuring Eddie Palmieri)

Singles: 7-inch

ARISTA 3-5 75
ROULETTE 3-5 70-72

LPs: 10/12-inch

ROULETTE 8-10 71
TICO 5-10 72
Members: Eddie Palmieri; Jimmy Norman.
Also see NORMAN, Jimmy

HARLEY, Steve P&R '76
(With Cockney Rebel)

Singles: 7-inch

CAPITOL 3-5 78
EMI 3-5 75-77

LPs: 10/12-inch

CAPITOL 5-10 78
EMI 5-10 75-77

HARMONICATS P&R '47
(Jerry Murad's Harmonicats)

Singles: 78 rpm

MERCURY 3-5 50-57
UNIVERSAL 3-6 48
VITACOUSTIC 4-8 47

Singles: 7-inch

COLUMBIA 3-6 61-67
MERCURY 5-10 50-60

Picture Sleeves

COLUMBIA 5-10 60

EPs: 7-inch

MERCURY 5-10 50-61

LPs: 10/12-inch

COLUMBIA 8-15 61-67
HARMONY 5-10 66
MERCURY 5-15 50-69
WING 5-10 59-64
Members: Jerry Murad; Al Fiore; Don Les.

HARNELL, Joe, His Orchestra
(With His Trio) P&R '62

Singles: 7-inch

COLUMBIA 3-6 66-68
EPIC 5-10 59-60
KAPP 4-8 61-65
MCA 3-4 78
MEDALLION 4-8 61-62
MOTOWN 4-8 69-70

Picture Sleeves

KAPP 5-10 63

LPs: 10/12-inch

CAPITOL 5-8 77
COLUMBIA 5-10 66
EPIC 5-15 59-63
KAPP 5-15 63-66
MEDALLION 5-15 61
MOTOWN (698 "Moving On") 25-45 70

HARNEY, Ben, & Sheryl Lee Ralph R&B '83

Singles: 7-inch

GEFFEN 3-4 83
Also see RALPH, Sheryl Lee

HAROLD, Prince: see PRINCE HAROLD

HARPER, Janice P&R '57

Singles: 7-inch

CAPITOL 5-10 58-60
PREP 5-10 57
RCA 4-6 66

LPs: 10/12-inch

CAPITOL 15-20 58-60

HARPER, Toni R&B '48
(With the Eddie Beale Sextet)

Singles: 78 rpm

COLUMBIA 5-10 48

Singles: 7-inch

RCA 5-10 60-61

LPs: 10/12-inch

RCA 15-20 60
Also see LIMELITERS

HARPERS BIZARRE P&R/LP '67

Singles: 7-inch

FOREST BAY CO 3-5 76
W.B. 3-6 67-72

EPs: 7-inch

W.B. 4-8 68
(Juke box issues only.)

LPs: 10/12-inch

FOREST BAY CO 8-10 76
W.B. 10-20 67-68
Members: Ted Templeman; John Petersen; Dick Yount; Dick Scoppettone; John Peterson.

HARPO, Slim P&R/R&B '61

Singles: 78 rpm

EXCELLO 15-25 57

Singles: 7-inch

ABC 3-5 73
EXCELLO (2113 "I'm a King Bee") 35-55 57
(Orange label.)
EXCELLO (2113 "I'm a King Bee") 40-60 57
(White label. Promotional issue only.)
EXCELLO (2138 "Wondering and Worrying") 15-25 58
(Orange label.)
EXCELLO (2138 "Wondering and Worrying") 15-25 58
(White label. Promotional issue only.)
EXCELLO (2162 "One More Day") 15-25 59
(Orange label.)
EXCELLO (2162 "One More Day") 15-25 59
(White label. Promotional issue only.)
EXCELLO (2184 "Blues Hang Over") 15-25 60
EXCELLO (2194 "Rainin' in My Heart") 10-15 61
EXCELLO (2200 series) 5-15 62-68
EXCELLO (2300 series) 4-8 69-71

LPs: 10/12-inch

EXCELLO (Except 8003 & 8005) 10-20 68-70

EXCELLO (8003 "Raining in My Heart") 30-50 61
(Orange and blue label.)
EXCELLO (8003 "Raining in My Heart") 5-10 95
(Blue label. Reprocessed stereo.)
EXCELLO (8005 "Baby, Scratch My Back") 20-30 66

HARPTONES *P&R '61*

(Harp-Tones; "Featuring Willie Winfield")

Singles: 78 rpm

ANDREA 20-40 56
BRUCE 25-50 53-55
GEE 25-50 57
PARADISE 25-50 56
RAMA 20-40 56-57
TIP TOP 25-50 56

Singles: 7-inch

AMBIENT SOUND 4-6 82
ANDREA (100 "What Is Your Decision") 40-60 56
(White label. Has rope-like horizontal lines.)
ANDREA (100 "What Is Your Decision") 20-30 56
(Pink label. Has straight horizontal lines.)
BRUCE (101 "A Sunday Kind of Love") 300-500 53
(Has "Bruce" in script lettering.)
BRUCE (101 "A Sunday Kind of Love") 50-75 56
(Has "Bruce" in block lettering. With straight horizontal lines.)
BRUCE (101 "A Sunday Kind of Love") 25-50 61
(Has "Bruce" in block lettering. With jagged horizontal lines.)
BRUCE (102 "My Memories of You"/"It Was Just for Laughs") 100-200 54
(With straight horizontal lines.)
BRUCE (102 "My Memories of You"/"The Laughs [sic] on You") 50-100 56
(Note different title on flip label. Actual track is identical to *It Was Just for Laughs*)
BRUCE (102 "My Memories of You") 20-30 61
(With jagged horizontal lines.)
BRUCE (102 "My Memories of You"/"It Was Just for Laughs") 60-80 54
(Has straight horizontal lines on A-side, but jagged lines on B-side.)
BRUCE (104 "I Depended on You") 100-125 54
BRUCE (109 "Forever Mine") 75-100 54
(With the Shytans. Has "Mfg. By Nu-Way Enterprises, Inc." at top.)
BRUCE (109 "Forever Mine") 75-100 54
(With the Shytans. Has "Mfg. By Nu-Way Enterprises, Inc." on side.)
BRUCE (113 "Since I Fell for You") 100-125 54
(Reads "Mfg. By Nu-Way Enterprises, Inc.")
BRUCE (113 "Since I Fell for You") 20-40
(No mention of "Mfg. By Nu-Way.")
BRUCE (123 "Loving a Girl Like You") 25-45 61
(Colored vinyl. "Collectors Series" issue.)
BRUCE (128 "I Almost Lost My Mind") 50-100 55
(Reads "Mfg. By Nu-Way Enterprises, Inc.")
BRUCE (128 "I Almost Lost My Mind") 20-40 55
(No mention of "Mfg. By Nu-Way.")
COED (540 "Answer Me My Love") ... 15-25 60
COMPANION (102 "All in Your Mind") 40-60 61
COMPANION (103 "What Will I Tell My Heart") 75-100 61
CUB (9097 "Devil in Velvet") 25-35 61
GEE (1045 "Cry Like I Cried") 50-75 57
(Red label.)
GEE (1045 "Cry Like I Cried") 15-25 61
(Gray label.)
KT (201 "Sunset") 40-50 63
OLDIES 45 .... 4-8 60s
PARADISE (101 "Life Is But a Dream") 100-200 56
(Maroon label.)
PARADISE (101 "Life Is But a Dream") 50-75 56
(Purple label.)
PARADISE (103 "My Success [It All Depends on You]") 200-400 56
PARADISE (103 "It All Depends on You") 100-200 56
(Maroon label. Note slight title change.)
PARADISE (103 "It All Depends on You") 50-75 56
(Purple label.)
RAMA (203 "Three Wishes") 50-100 56
RAMA (214 "The Masquerade Is Over") 50-100 56
RAMA (221 "The Shrine of Saint Cecilia") 50-100 57
RAVEN (8001 "Sunday Kind of Love") 20-30 62
(Has bird at the top of label, over logo.)
RAVEN (8001 "Sunday Kind of Love") 15-25 62
(No bird on label.)
ROULETTE GOLDEN GOODIES 4-6 71
TIP TOP (401 "My Memories of You") 50-100 56
WARWICK (500 "Laughing on the Outside") 35-45 59
("Warwick" is in sans-serif, or block style type.)
WARWICK (500 "Laughing on the Outside") 25-35 59
("Warwick" is in serif style type.)
WARWICK (512 "Love Me Completely") 25-35 59
WARWICK (551 "No Greater Miracle") 25-35 59

EPs: 7-inch

BRUCE (201 "The Sensational Harptones") 8000-12000 54

LPs: 10/12-inch

AMBIENT SOUND (37718 "Love Needs") 8-12 82
HARLEM HITPARADE (5006 "The Harptones") 10-15 70s
MURRAY HILL 5-8 88
RARE BIRD 8-10
RELIC 8-10 70s
Members: Willie Winfield; Nicky Clark; Bill Brown; Bill Dempsey; Bill "Dicey" Galloway; Raoul Cita; Jimmy Beckum; Lynn Daniels; Vicki Burgess; Margaret Moore; Fred Taylor.
Also see PAUL, Bunny, & Harptones

HARPTONES / Cleftones

Singles: 7-inch

ROULETTE 3-5 71
Also see CLEFTONES

HARPTONES / Crows

LPs: 10/12-inch

ROULETTE 15-20 72
Also see CROWS

HARPTONES / Paragons

LPs: 10/12-inch

MUSICNOTE 20-30 64

HARPTONES / Paragons / Jesters / Clovers

LPs: 10/12-inch

GRAND PRIX 10-20 60s
Also see CLOVERS
Also see HARPTONES
Also see JESTERS
Also see PARAGONS

HARRELL, Grady *R&B '85*

Singles: 7-inch

MCA 3-5 85

HARRIS, Betty *P&R/R&B '63*

Singles: 7-inch

JUBILEE 8-12 63-69
PROM 3-4
SSS INT'L 4-8 69
SANSU 5-10 66-68
Also see DORSEY, Lee, & Betty Harris

HARRIS, Bobby *R&B '65*

Singles: 7-inch

ATLANTIC 4-8 65
Also see LUNDY, Pat, & Bobby Harris

HARRIS, Brenda Jo *R&B '68*

Singles: 7-inch

BETTER 5-10 60s
ROULETTE 4-6 68

HARRIS, Damon *R&B '79*

Singles: 12-inch

WMOT 4-6 78-79

Singles: 7-inch

WMOT 3-5 78-79

LPs: 10/12-inch

WMOT 5-10 78
Also see IMPACT
Also see TEMPTATIONS

HARRIS, David *R&B '74*

Singles: 7-inch

PLEASURE 3-5 74

HARRIS, Eddie *P&R/R&B/LP '61*

Singles: 7-inch

ABC 3-5 73
ATLANTIC 3-6 65-77
COLUMBIA 4-6 64
VEE JAY 5-8 61-63
W.B. 3-4 81

LPs: 10/12-inch

ANGELACO 5-10 81
ATLANTIC 6-12 65-81
BUDDAH 8-12 69
COLUMBIA 10-20 64-68
CRUSADERS 5-10 82
GNP 5-10 73
HARMONY 5-10 72
RCA 5-10 78
SUNSET 5-10 69
TRIP 5-10 73
VEE JAY (3016 thru 3028) 20-35 61-62
VEE JAY (3031 thru 3034) 15-25 63
Also see McCANN, Les, & Eddie Harris
Also see MOORE, Shelly, & Eddie Harris

HARRIS, Eddie, & John Klemmer

LPs: 10/12-inch

CRUSADERS 5-8 82
Also see HARRIS, Eddie
Also see KLEMMER, John

HARRIS, Emmylou *C&W/P&R '75*

(With Her Hot Band; with Cheryl White & Sharon White)

Singles: 7-inch

JUBILEE 5-10 69-70
REPRISE (Except 1341) 3-5 75-77
REPRISE (1341 "Light of the Stable") ... 4-6 75
W.B. 3-5 77-86

Picture Sleeves

REPRISE 3-5 75-77
WARNER 3-4 80-86

LPs: 10/12-inch

EMUS 10-20 79
JUBILEE (8031 "Gliding Bird") 60-80 69
MFSL (015 "Quarter Moon in a Ten-Cent Town") 30-40 78
REPRISE 8-10 75
W.B. 5-10 77-87
Members: James Burton; Glen D. Hardin; Emory Gordy; Ronnie Tutt.
Also see ANDERSON, John
Also see CASH, Johnny
Also see CASH, Rosanne
Also see CONLEY, Earl Thomas, & Emmylou Harris
Also see CRICKETS
Also see CROWELL, Rodney
Also see DENVER, John, & Emmylou Harris
Also see EVERLY, Don
Also see JENNINGS, Waylon
Also see KENDALLS
Also see LITTLE FEAT
Also see NELSON, Willie
Also see ORBISON, Roy, & Emmylou Harris / Craig

Hundley
Also see OWENS, Buck, & Emmylou Harris
Also see PARSONS, Gram
Also see PARTON, Dolly
Also see PARTON, Dolly, Linda Ronstadt, & Emmylou Harris
Also see PRESLEY, Elvis
Also see RONSTADT, Linda, & Emmylou Harris
Also see STEWART, Gary
Also see TUCKER, Tanya
Also see WINCHESTER, Jesse
Also see YOUNG, Neil

HARRIS, Emmylou, & Don Williams — C&W '81

Singles: 7-inch

W.B. 3-4 81
Also see WILLIAMS, Don

HARRIS, Gene — R&B '74

(With the Three Sounds)

Singles: 7-inch

BLUE NOTE 3-5 71-77

LPs: 10/12-inch

BLUE NOTE 5-10 71-77

HARRIS, Huey "Baby" — R&B '85

Singles: 7-inch

PROFILE 3-4 85

HARRIS, Major — P&R/R&B/LP '75

(Major Harris Boogie Blues Band)

Singles: 7-inch

ATLANTIC 4-6 75-76
OKEH (7314 "Just Love Me") 15-25 68
OKEH (7327 "Like a Rolling Stone") 30-60 69
POP ART 3-4 83
WMOT 3-5 76-81

LPs: 10/12-inch

ATLANTIC 8-10 75
RCA 5-10 78
WMOT 8-10 76
Also see DELFONICS

HARRIS, Peppermint: see PEPPERMINT HARRIS

HARRIS, Phil — P&R '33

Singles: 78 rpm

ARA 4-8 46
COLUMBIA 4-8 33
DECCA 4-6 35
RCA 5-10 47-54

Singles: 7-inch

COLISEUM 3-5 68
MEGA 3-4 73
MONTCLARE 3-4 76
RCA 10-20 50-54
REPRISE 3-5 62
VISTA 3-5 67-70

Picture Sleeves

MONTCLARE 3-5 76

EPs: 7-inch

RCA 5-10 53-60

LPs: 10/12-inch

CAMDEN 8-12 63
MEGA 5-10 72-74
RCA (1900 series) 10-20 59
RCA (3000 series) 20-30 53-54
ZODIAC 5-10 77
Also see BELL SISTERS
Also see SHORE, Dinah, Tony Martin, Betty Hutton & Phil Harris

HARRIS, Richard — P&R/LP '68

Singles: 7-inch

ATLANTIC 3-5 74-75
DUNHILL 3-6 68-75

Picture Sleeves

DUNHILL (Except 4134) 4-8 70-72
DUNHILL (4134 "MacArthur Park") 3-6 68
DUNHILL (4134 "MacArthur Park") 8-12 68
(Special promotional sleeve, labeled as such.)

EPs: 7-inch

DUNHILL 4-6 68
(Juke box issues only.)

LPs: 10/12-inch

ATLANTIC 6-10 74-75
DUNHILL 8-15 68-74
PICKWICK 5-8 78

HARRIS, Rolf — P&R/R&B/LP '63

Singles: 7-inch

EPIC (Except 9721) 4-8 63-66
EPIC (9721 "Ringo for President") 10-15 64
MGM 3-5 70
20TH FOX 8-12 60-61

Picture Sleeves

EPIC 8-12 63-64

LPs: 10/12-inch

EPIC 20-30 63-64

HARRIS, Sam — P&R/D&D/LP '84

Singles: 12-inh 33/45rpm

MOTOWN 4-6 84-86

Singles: 7-inch

MOTOWN 3-4 84-86

Picture Sleeves

MOTOWN 3-4 84-86

LPs: 10/12-inch

MOTOWN 5-10 84-86

HARRIS, Thurston — P&R/R&B '57

(With the Sharps)

Singles: 78 rpm

ALADDIN 10-15 57

Singles: 7-inch

ALADDIN 15-25 57-61
CUB 4-8 62
DOT 4-8 62-63
IMPERIAL 4-8 63
REPRISE 4-8 64

HARRIS, Tony — P&R '57

Singles: 78 rpm

EBB 5-10 56-57

Singles: 7-inch

EBB 10-15 56-57

HARRIS, Wynonie — R&B '46

(With Lucky Millinder)

Singles: 78 rpm

ALADDIN 20-30 47
APOLLO 20-30 45-46
ATCO 10-20 56
BULLET 15-25 46
HAMP-TONE 15-25 45
KING 20-40 47-57
PHILO 15-25 45

Singles: 7-inch

ATCO (6081 "Destination Love") 15-25 56
KING (4210 "Good Rockin' Tonight") 50-100 52
KING (4461 "Bloodshot Eyes") 50-100 51
KING (4468 "I'll Never Give Up") 50-100 51
KING (4485 "Lovin' Machine") 50-100 51
(Black vinyl.)
KING (4485 "Lovin' Machine") 200-300 51
(Colored vinyl.)
KING (4507 "My Playful Baby's Gone") 50-100 51
KING (4526 "Keep on Churnin' ") 50-100 52
KING (4555 "Night Train") 50-100 52
KING (4565 "Adam, Come and Get Your Rib") 50-100 52
KING (4592 "Greyhound") 50-100 52
KING (4593 "Bad News, Baby") 50-100 52
KING (4620 "Wasn't That Good") 50-100 53
KING (4635 "The Deacon Don't Like It") 50-100 53
KING (4662 "Tremblin' ") 50-75 53
KING (4668 "Please, Louise") 50-75 53
KING (4685 "Quiet Whiskey") 50-75 53
KING (4716 "Shake That Thing") 50-75 54
KING (4724 "Don't Take My Whiskey Away from Me") 50-75 54
KING (4763 "Christina") 25-50 54
KING (4774 "Good Mambo Tonight") 25-50 54
KING (4789 "Mr. Dollar") 25-50 54
KING (4814 "Drinkin' Sherry Wine") 25-50 54
KING (4826 "Wine, Wine, Sweet Wine") 25-40 54
KING (4839 "Shotgun Wedding") 25-40 54
KING (4900 & 5000 series) 15-25 56-57
KING (5050 "Big Old Country Fool") 10-20 57
KING (5073 "There's No Substitute for Love") 10-20 57
KING (5100 thru 5400 series) 5-10 58-60
KING (6011 "Bloodshot Eyes") 10-15
ROULETTE 4-8 60

EPs: 7-inch

KING (260 "Wynonie Harris") 300-400 54

LPs: 10/12-inch

KING (1086 "Good Rockin' Blues") 10-15 72
Also see MILBURN, Amos / Wynonie Harris / Crown Prince Waterford
Also see MILLINDER, Lucky, & His Orchestra

HARRIS, Wynonie / Roy Brown

LPs: 10/12-inch

KING (607 "Battle of the Blues") 100-200 58
KING (627 "Battle of the Blues, Vol. 2") 100-200 58

HARRIS, Wynonie / Roy Brown / Eddie Vinson

LPs: 10/12-inch

KING (668 "Battle of the Blues, Vol. 4") 200-300 60
Also see BROWN, Roy
Also see HARRIS, Wynonie
Also see VINSON, Eddie

HARRISON, Don, Band — P&R/LP '76

Singles: 7-inch

ATLANTIC 4-8 76
MERCURY 4-8 77

LPs: 10/12-inch

ATLANTIC 8-10 76
MERCURY 8-10 77
Members: Don Harrison; Doug Clifford; Stu Cook.
Also see CREEDENCE CLEARWATER REVIVAL

HARRISON, George — LP '69

Singles: 12-inch

DARK HORSE (949 "All Those Years Ago") 25-30 81
(Promotional issue only. Includes title sleeve.)
DARK HORSE (1075 "Wake Up My Love") 20-30 82
(Promotional issue only. Includes title sleeve.)
DARK HORSE (2845 "Got My Mind Set on You") 20-30 87
(Promotional issue only. Includes picture cover.)
DARK HORSE (2885 "When We Was Fab") 20-30 88
(Promotional issue only.)
DARK HORSE (2889 "Devil's Radio") 20-30 87
(Promotional issue only. Includes picture cover.)

Singles: 7-inch

APPLE (1828 "What Is Life") 10-15 71
(With black star on label.)
APPLE (1828 "What Is Life") 5-8 71
(No black star on label.)
APPLE (1836 "Bangla Desh") 15-25 71
(With black star on label.)
APPLE (1836 "Bangla Desh") 5-8 71
(No black star on label.)
APPLE (1862 "Give Me Love") 5-8 73
APPLE (1877 "Dark Horse") 8-10 74
APPLE (1879 "Ding Dong Ding Dong") 5-8 74
(Black with *white* tint photo label.)
APPLE (1879 "Ding Dong Ding Dong") 200-250 74
(Black with *blue* tint photo label.)
APPLE (1884 "You") 5-8 75
APPLE (1885 "This Guitar") 20-25 75
APPLE (2995 "My Sweet Lord") 30-40 70
(With black star on label.)
APPLE (2995 "My Sweet Lord") 5-8 70
(No black star on label. Does not have "All Rights Reserved, etc." print on label.)
APPLE (2995 "My Sweet Lord") 15-25 70
(With "All Rights Reserved, etc." on label.)
CAPITOL (Orange label) 25-35 76
CAPITOL (Tan "Starline" label) 5-8 77
CAPITOL (Purple label) 5-8 78

CAPITOL (Black label, except 6245)....10-15 83
CAPITOL (Tan or purple label)....4-6 88
CAPITOL (6245 "Dark Horse")....30-40 87
DARK HORSE (0410 "All Those Years Ago")....4-6 81
(Tan label.)
DARK HORSE (0410 "All Those Years Ago")....4-6 91
(White or cream label.)
DARK HORSE (8294 "This Song")....5-10 76
DARK HORSE (8313 "Crackerbox Palace")....4-6 77
DARK HORSE (8763 "Blow Away")....4-6 79
(Tan label with "Loka Productions" print on label.)
DARK HORSE (8763 "Blow Away")..15-20 79
(Tan label without "Loka Productions" print on label.)
DARK HORSE (8844 "Love Comes to Everyone")....5-10 79
DARK HORSE (27913 "This Is Love")....3-5 88
DARK HORSE (28131 "When We Was Fab")....3-5 88
DARK HORSE (28178 "Got My Mind Set on You")....3-5 87
DARK HORSE (29744 "I Really Love You")....20-25 83
DARK HORSE (29864 "Wake Up My Love")....5-10 82
DARK HORSE (49725 "All Those Years Ago")....3-5 81
DARK HORSE (49785 "Teardrops")....5-10 81
W.B. (22807 "Cheer Down") 10-15....89

Picture Sleeves

APPLE (1828 "What Is Life")....30-40 71
APPLE (1836 "Bangla Desh")....15-20 71
APPLE (1877 "Dark Horse")....50-75 74
APPLE (1879 "Ding Dong Ding Dong")....10-15 74
APPLE (1884 "You")....10-15 75
APPLE (2995 "My Sweet Lord")....30-40 70
DARK HORSE (8294 "This Song")....20-30 76
DARK HORSE (8294 "This Song")....60-80 76
(Special promotional sleeve issued with promo single. Price includes insert flyer with "The Story Behind *This Song,*" which represents about $30-$40 of the value.)
DARK HORSE (8763 "Blow Away")....4-6 79
DARK HORSE (8844 "Love Comes to Everyone")....700-800 79
DARK HORSE (27913; "This Is Love")....3-5 88
DARK HORSE (28131 "When We Was Fab")....3-5 88
DARK HORSE (28178 "Got My Mind Set on You")....3-5 87
DARK HORSE (49725 "All Those Years Ago")....3-4 81
W.B. (22807 "Cheer Down")....10-15 89

Promotional Singles

APPLE (1862 "Give Me Love")....35-45 73
APPLE (1879 "Ding Dong Ding Dong")....25-30 74
APPLE (1877 "Dark Horse")....40-60 74
APPLE (1879 "Ding Dong Ding Dong")....25-35 74
APPLE (1884 "You")....25-35 75
APPLE (1885 "This Guitar")....35-45 75
APPLE/20TH FOX (791 "Concert for Bangla Desh")....700-750 71
(Four radio spots. Issued only to radio stations.)
DARK HORSE (8294 "This Song")....15-25 76
DARK HORSE (8313 "Crackerbox Palace")....10-15 77
DARK HORSE (8763 "Blow Away")..10-15 79
DARK HORSE (8844 "Love Comes to Everyone")....10-15 79
DARK HORSE (27913 "This Is Love")....10-15 88
DARK HORSE (28131 "When We Was Fab")....10-15 88
DARK HORSE (28178 "Got My Mind Set on You")....10-15 87
DARK HORSE (29744 "I Really Love You")....10-15 83
DARK HORSE (29864 "Wake Up My Love")....10-15 82
DARK HORSE (49725 "All Those Years Ago")....10-15 81
DARK HORSE (49785 "Teardrops")..10-15 81
W.B. (22807 "Cheer Down")....150-200 89

LPs: 10/12-inch

APPLE (639 "All Things Must Pass")....30-40 70
(Boxed, three-disc set. Includes bonus poster. Disc does not have "S" in trail-off area.)
APPLE (639 "All Things Must Pass")....50-75 88
(Boxed, three-disc set. Includes bonus poster. Disc has "S" in trail-off area.)
APPLE (3350 "Wonderwall Music")..20-30 68
(Apple label without Capitol logo.)
APPLE (3350 "Wonderwall Music")....100-125 68
(Apple lable with Capitol logo.)
APPLE (3385 "Concert for Bangla Desh")....40-50 71
(Boxed, three-disc set. Includes 64-page booklet. Also has Eric Clapton, Bob Dylan, Ringo Starr, Leon Russell, Ravi Shankar, and others.)
APPLE (3410 "Living in the Material World")....10-15 73
APPLE (3418 "Dark Horse")....15-20 73
APPLE (3420 "Extra Texture")....10-15 75
CAPITOL (639 "All Things Must Pass")....20-30 76-78
(Boxed, three-disc set. Orange or purple labels. Includes bonus poster.)
CAPITOL (639 "All Things Must Pass")....70-90 83
(Black label. Boxed, three-disc set. Includes bonus poster.)
CAPITOL (3410 "Living in the Material World")....10-15 80
CAPITOL (3420 "Extra Texture")....15-25 80
CAPITOL (11578 "The Best of George Harrison")....10-15 76
(Custom label with six photos of Harrison. Also contains tracks by the Beatles that feature George.)
CAPITOL (11578 "The Best of George Harrison")....125-150 77
(Orange label.)
CAPITOL (11578 "The Best of George Harrison")....8-10 78
(Purple label with "Mfd. by Capitol, etc." on perimeter print.)
CAPITOL (11578 "The Best of George Harrison")....15-25 83
(Black label or apple label.)
CAPITOL (11578 "The Best of George Harrison")....50-75 89
(Purple label with "Manufactured by Capitol, etc." on perimeter print.)
CAPITOL (12248 "Concert For Bangla Desh")....300-350 82
(Two-disc set.)
CAPITOL (16000 series)....10-20 81
DARK HORSE (3005 "Thirty-Three and 1/3")....8-10 76
DARK HORSE (3255 "George Harrison")....8-10 79
DARK HORSE (3255 "George Harrison")....30-40 79
(Columbia Record Club issue.)
DARK HORSE (3492 "Somewhere in England")....5-10 81
DARK HORSE (23734 "Gone Troppo")....8-12 82
DARK HORSE (25643 "Cloud Nine")....10-15 87
DARK HORSE (25726 "Best of Dark Horse")....15-25 89
ZAPPLE (3358 "Electronic Music")....20-30 69

Promotional LPs

DARK HORSE ("Dark Horse Radio Special")....250-300 74
DARK HORSE (649 "A Personal Music Dialogue with George Harrison at 331/3")....30-40 76
DARK HORSE (23734 "Gone Troppo")....20-25 82
(Audiophile Quiex II vinyl pressing.)

Also see BEATLES
Also see BROMBERG, David
Also see CLAPTON, Eric
Also see DYLAN, Bob
Also see HODGE, Chris
Also see RUSSELL, Leon
Also see SCOTT, Tom
Also see SHANKAR, Ravi
Also see SPLINTER
Also see TRAVELING WILBURYS

HARRISON, George / Jeff Beck / Dave Edmunds

Singles: 12-inch

COLUMBIA (2034 "I Don't Want to Do It")....10-20 85
(Has one song by each artist. Promotional issue only.)
COLUMBIA (2085 "I Don't Want to Do It")....10-20 85
(Promotional issue only. Has the Harrison song on both sides.)

Singles: 7-inch

COLUMBIA (04887 "I Don't Want to Do It")....3-4 85

Promotional Singles

COLUMBIA (04887 "I Don't Want to Do It")....8-12 85
(Has the Harrison song on both sides.)

Also see BECK, Jeff
Also see EDMUNDS, Dave
Also see HARRISON, George

HARRISON, Jerry — LP '88

(With the Casual Gods)

LPs: 10/12-inch

FLY/SIRE....5-8 90
SIRE....5-8 88

HARRISON, Reggie: see HIPPIES / Reggie Harrison

HARRISON, Wes — LP '63

Singles: 78 rpm

LIN (5002 "There Y'Are")....10-15 56

Singles: 7-inch

LIN (5002 "There Y'Are")....15-25 56

LPs: 10/12-inch

PHILIPS....15-25 63

HARRISON, Wilbert — P&R/R&B '59

(With the Roamers; with His Kansas City Playboys; Wilbert Harrison One Man Band; Wilburt Harrison; Wilbur Harrison)

Singles: 78 rpm

DELUXE....20-30 52-53
SAVOY....10-20 54

Singles: 7-inch

ABC....3-4 73
BARREL....5-10
BRUNSWICK....3-5 74
CONSTELLATION....4-8 64
DELUXE (6002 "This Woman of Mine")....40-50 52
DELUXE (6031 "Gin and Coconut Milk")....40-50 53
DOC....5-10 62
FURY....5-10 59-62
GLADES....8-12 59
HOUSE of SOUND....4-6
NEPTUNE....4-8 61
PORT....4-8 65
ROCKIN' (526 "This Woman of Mine")....75-100 52
ROULETTE....3-5 67
SSS INT'L (830 "My Heart Is")....8-12 71
SAVOY (Except 1138)....8-12
SAVOY (1138 "Don't Drop It")....20-30 54
SEA HORN....4-8 63
SUE (11 "Let's Work Together")....10-20 69
(No company address shown.)
SUE (11 "Let's Work Together")....5-10 69
(Company address at bottom of label.)

SUE (11 "Let's Work Together")............4-8 69
(Company address at top.)
SUE (11 "Let's Work Together")............3-6 69
(Company address on left side.)

LPs: 10/12-inch

BUDDAH..10-18 71
CHELSEA..8-10 77
FURY..5-8
JUGGERNAUT.................................15-25 71
RELIC..5-10 90
RES IPSA..10-15
SPHERE SOUND...............................25-40 65
SUE..15-25 70
WET SOUL..10-15 70

HARRY, Debbie *P&R/R&B/LP '81*
(Deborah Harry)

Singles: 12-inch

CHRYSALIS..4-6 81-83
GEFFEN..4-6 85-86

Singles: 7-inch

CHRYSALIS..3-5 81-88
GEFFEN..3-4 85-87

Picture Sleeves

CHRYSALIS..3-5 81-88
GEFFEN..3-4 86-87

LPs: 10/12-inch

CHRYSALIS......................................5-10 81
GEFFEN..5-10 86
SIRE..5-8 89
Also see BLONDIE
Also see WIND in the WILLOWS

HART, Corey *P&R/D&D/LP '84*

Singles: 7-inch

EMI AMERICA.....................................3-4 84-87
EMI MANHATTAN................................3-4 88

Picture Sleeves

EMI AMERICA (Except 8268)..............3-4 84-86
EMI AMERICA (8268 "Never Surrender")..4-6 85
(Poster sleeve.)
EMI MANHATTAN................................3-4 88

LPs: 10/12-inch

EMI AMERICA...................................5-10 84-86
EMI MANHATTAN................................5-8 89

HART, Freddie *C&W '59*
(With the Heartbeats)

Singles: 78 rpm

CAPITOL...5-10 53-55
COLUMBIA (Except 21512)...............5-15 56-57
COLUMBIA (21512 "Dig Boy Dig").....15-25 56

Singles: 7-inch

CAPITOL (2500 thru 3000 series).......5-15 53-55
(Purple labels.)
CAPITOL (2600 thru 4600 series).........3-5 70-79
(Orange labels.)
COLUMBIA (Except 21512)................5-15 56-63
COLUMBIA (21512 "Dig Boy, Dig")...25-35 56
KAPP..3-8 65-72
MCA...3-5 73
MONUMENT..4-6 63-64
SUNBIRD..3-4 80-81

Picture Sleeves

KAPP..4-6 68
SUNBIRD..3-5 80

LPs: 10/12-inch

BRYLEN..5-10 84
CAPITOL...5-10 70-79
COLUMBIA (1700 series)..................20-25 62
COLUMBIA (13000 series)................10-12 72
CORAL..5-8 73
HARMONY..8-12 67-73
KAPP..8-15 65-69
MCA...8-12 75
PICKWICK..5-10 70s
PICKWICK/HILLTOP...........................8-12 70s
SUNBIRD..5-10 80
VOCALION...8-10 72

HART, Freddie / Sammi Smith / Jerry Reed

LPs: 10/12-inch

HARMONY..6-10 72
Also see HART, Freddie
Also see REED, Jerry
Also see SMITH, Sammi

HART, Mickey *LP '72*

Singles: 7-inch

W.B. 4-8 71-72

LPs: 10/12-inch

RELIX (Except 2026)........................5-10 85
RELIX (2026 "Rolling Thunder").......25-30 87
(Picture disc.)
W.B. 10-20 72
Also see GRATEFUL DEAD

HART, Mickey, Airto & Flora Purim

LPs: 10/12-inch

REFERENCE......................................8-10 83
Also see HART, Mickey
Also see MOREIRA, Airto
Also see PURIM, Flora

HART, Rita *D&D '84*

Singles: 12-inch

ENVELOPE...4-6 84

HART, Rod *C&W/P&R '76*

Singles: 7-inch

IBC...3-4 80
PHOENIX SUN......................................3-6 68
PLANTATION...3-5 76-77

LPs: 10/12-inch

PLANTATION.......................................5-10 76

HARTFORD, John *C&W '67*

Singles: 7-inch

AMPEX..3-5 71
FLYING FISH.......................................3-4 84
RCA..4-8 66-70

LPs: 10/12-inch

FLYING FISH.....................................5-10 76-84
RCA...8-12 67-70
W.B. 8-10 71-72
Also see DILLARDS & John Hartford

HARTLEY, Keef, Band *LP '70*

Singles: 7-inch

DERAM..3-5 70-73

LPs: 10/12-inch

DERAM...10-12 69-73
Also see MAYALL, John

HARTMAN, Dan *P&R/R&B/LP '78*

Singles: 12-inch

BLUE SKY..4-6 78-81
MCA..4-6 84-85

Singles: 7-inch

BLUE SKY..3-5 76-81
MCA..3-4 84-85
PORTRAIT..3-4 81

Picture Sleeves

MCA..3-4 84-85

LPs: 10/12-inch

BLUE SKY (Except 246)......................5-10 76-81
BLUE SKY (246 "Who Is Dan Hartman")..8-15 75
(Promotional issue only.)
MCA..5-10 84-85
Also see WINTER, Edgar

HARTMAN, Dan / Blasters

Singles: 7-inch

MCA..3-4 84

Picture Sleeves

MCA..3-4 84
Also see BLASTERS
Also see HARTMAN, Dan

HARVEST, Barclay James: see BARCLAY JAMES HARVEST

HARVEST, King: see KING HARVEST

HARVEY
("Former Lead of the Moonglows"; Harvey Fuqua)

Singles: 7-inch

CHESS (1713 "I Want Somebody").. 20-30 59
CHESS (1725 "Twelve Months of the Year")..20-30 59
CHESS (1749 "Blue Skies")..............10-20 60
TRI-PHI (1010 "She Loves Me So").. 20-30 62
TRI-PHI (1017 "She Loves Me So")..20-30 62
TRI-PHI (1024 "Come On and Answer Me")..25-40 63
Also see ETTA & HARVEY
Also see HARVEY & ANN
Also see HARVEY & MOONGLOWS
Also see HARVEY & SPINNERS
Also see NEW BIRTH

HARVEY, Alex *LP '75*
(Sensational Alex Harvey Band)

Singles: 7-inch

ATLANTIC..3-5 75
CAPITOL...3-5 72
VERTIGO...3-5 73-75

LPs: 10/12-inch

CAPITOL...8-12 72
ATLANTIC...8-10 75
VERTIGO..8-10 73-75

HARVEY, Phil
(Phil Spector)

Singles: 7-inch

IMPERIAL (5583 "Bumbershoot").....50-75 59
Also see HARVEY & DOC & DWELLERS
Also see RONETTES / Crystals / Darlene Love / Bob B. Soxx & Blue Jeans
Also see TEDDY BEARS

HARVEY, Steve *D&D '84*

Singles: 12-inch

LONDON...4-6 84

Singles: 7-inch

LONDON...3-4 84

HARVEY & ANN

Singles: 7-inch

HARVEY (121 "What Can You Do")...20-30 63
Members: Harvey Fuqua; Ann Bogan.
Also see HARVEY
Also see LOVE, PEACE & HAPPINESS

HARVEY & DOC & DWELLERS
(Phil Spector)

Singles: 7-inch

ANNETTE (1002 "Oh Baby")............10-20
Also see HARVEY, Phil

HARVEY & MOONGLOWS
(Harvey Fuqua)

Singles: 7-inch

CHESS (1705 "Ten Commandments of Love")..15-25 58
CHESS (1738 "Mama Loocie").........10-20 59
Also see HARVEY
Also see MOONGLOWS

HARVEY & SEVEN SOUNDS
(Harvey Scales)

Singles: 7-inch

CUCA (1155 "New York City")...............4-8 63
Also see SCALES, Harvey

HARVEY & SPINNERS
("Harvey [Former Lead of the Moonglows] & the Spinners")

TRI-PHI (1010 "She Loves Me So")..30-50 62
(Reissued sans credit to the Spinners.)
Also see HARVEY
Also see SPINNERS

HARVEY BOYS *P&R '57*

Singles: 78 rpm

CADENCE...5-10 57

Singles: 7-inch

CADENCE...5-10 57

HASHIM *D&D '84*

Singles: 12-inch

CUTTING EDGE...................................4-6 84

HASLAM, Annie *LP '77*

Singles: 7-inch

SIRE..3-5 78

LPs: 10/12-inch

SIRE..8-12 77
Also see RENAISSANCE

HASSAN & 7-11 *R&B/D&D '84*

Singles: 7-inch

EASY STREET....3-4 84

HASSLES

Singles: 7-inch

U.A. 8-12 67-69

Picture Sleeves

U.A. 10-12 67-69

LPs: 10/12-inch

LIBERTY....8-10 81
U.A. (6631 "The Hassles") 20-30 68
U.A. (6699 "Hour of the Wolf") 20-30 68

Members: William (Billy) Joel; Howard Blauvelt; Johathan Small; Richard McKenner; John Dizek.
Also see JOEL, Billy

HATCHER, Roger *R&B '76*
(Little Roger Hatcher)

Singles: 7-inch

BROWN DOG 3-5 76
DOTTY'S....5-10 64
EXCELLO (2297 "Sweetest Girl in the World")....15-25 68

HATFIELD, Bobby *P&R '69*

Singles: 7-inch

MOONGLOW....5-10 63
VERVE 4-8 68-69
W.B. 3-5 72

LPs: 10/12-inch

MGM....10-12 71
Also see RIGHTEOUS BROTHERS

HATFIELD, Overton
(Gene Autry)

Singles: 78 rpm

Columbia (15987 "A Gangster's Warning")....50-75 30s
Also see AUTRY, Gene

HATHAWAY, Donny *P&R/R&B '70*

Singles: 7-inch

ATCO....3-6 69-78

LPs: 10/12-inch

ATCO....8-10 70-78
ATLANTIC....5-10 80
Also see FLACK, Roberta, & Donny Hathaway

HATHAWAY, Donny, & June Conquest *P&R '72*

Singles: 7-inch

CURTOM (1971 "I Thank You") 3-5 72
(Previously issued as by June & Donnie.)
Members: Donny Hathaway; June Conquest.
Also see CONQUEST, June
Also see JUNE & DONNIE

HATHAWAY, Donny, & Margie Joseph

Singles: 7-inch

ATCO....3-5 72
Also see HATHAWAY, Donny
Also see JOSEPH, Margie

HATHAWAY, Lalah *LP '90*

LPs: 10/12-inch

VIRGIN 5-8 90

HAVENS, Richie *LP '68*

Singles: 7-inch

A&M....3-5 77
DOUGLAS....4-8 68
ELEKTRA....3-4 80
MGM....3-5 70
ODE '70....3-5 72
STORMY FOREST 3-5 70-74
VERVE/FOLKWAYS 4-8 66-68
VERVE/FORECAST 4-8 68-69

LPs: 10/12-inch

A&M....8-10 76
DOUGLAS....12-15 68
ELEKTRA....5-10 80
MGM....8-10 70
ODE '70 ....8-10 73
RBI....5-10 87
STORMY FOREST 10-12 69-74
VERVE/FOLKWAYS 12-15 67-68
VERVE/FORECAST 12-15 67-69

HAWK, The
(Jerry Lee Lewis)

Singles: 7-inch

PHILLIPS INT'L (3559 "In the Mood")....15-25 60
Also see LEWIS, Jerry Lee

HAWKINS, Dale *P&R/R&B '57*
(With the Escapades)

Singles: 78 rpm

CHECKER (843 "See You Soon Baboon") 20-30 56
CHECKER (863 "Suzi-Q") 20-30 57
CHECKER (876 "Baby, Baby") 20-30 57
CHECKER (892 "Little Pig") 25-50 58
CHECKER (900 "La-Do-Dada")....25-50 58
CHECKER (906 "A House, a Car, and a Wedding Ring") 40-60 58
CHECKER (913 "Someday One Day") 50-75 58
CHECKER (923 "Ain't That Lovin' You Baby")....50-100 59

Note: Checker 78s as late as #937 exist with the checkerboard design at top, as opposed to 45s which switched designs beginning with #876. Also, 78s as early as #900 have Checker name vertically on left side.

Singles: 7-inch

ABC-PAR (10668 "La La Song")....8-12 65
ATLANTIC (1022 "Peaches")....10-20 61
ATLANTIC (2126 "Stay at Home Lulu") 10-20 61
ATLANTIC (2150 "What a Feeling") 10-20 62
BELL (807 "Little Rain Cloud")....5-10 69
CHECKER (843 "See You Soon Baboon") 30-40 56
(Maroon label with checkerboard design at top. Deduct 50% for maroon reissues with Checker name vertically on left side.)
CHECKER (863 "Suzi-Q") 20-30 57
(Maroon label with checkerboard design at top. Deduct 50% for maroon reissues with Checker name vertically on left side.)
CHECKER (876 "Baby, Baby") 25-35 57
(Maroon label with checkerboard design at top. Deduct 50% for maroon reissues with Checker name vertically on left side.)
CHECKER (892 "Little Pig") 20-30 58
(Maroon label.)
CHECKER (900 "La-Do-Dada")....20-30 58
(Maroon label.)
CHECKER (906 "A House, a Car, and a Wedding Ring") 20-30 58
(Maroon label.)
CHECKER (913 "Someday One Day") 20-30 58
(Maroon label.)
CHECKER (914 "Take My Heart")....15-25 59
(Maroon label.)
CHECKER (916 "Class Cutter") 20-25 59
(Maroon label.)
CHECKER (916 "Yea-Yea [Class Cutter]") 15-20 59
(Maroon label. Note title variation.)
CHECKER (923 "Ain't That Lovin' You Baby")....15-25 59
(Maroon label.)
CHECKER (929 "Our Turn")....10-20 59
(Maroon label.)
CHECKER (934 "Back to School Blues")....10-20 59
(Maroon label.)
CHECKER (940 "Hot Dog")....10-20 60
(Maroon label.)
CHECKER (944 "Poor Little Rhode Island") 10-20 60
(Maroon label.)
CHECKER (962 "Linda")....10-20 61
(Maroon label.)
CHECKER (970 "I Want to Love You") 10-20 61
(Maroon label.)
CHECKER (Blue label)....5-10 60s
(Reissues.)
LINCOLN (002 "Baby We Had It")....8-12
TILT (781 "Money Honey")....10-20 61
TILT (783 "Wish I Hadn't Called Home")....10-20 61
ZONK (1002 "Gotta Dance") 10-20 62

Picture Sleeves

CHECKER (944 "Poor Little Rhode Island")....100-150 60

LPs: 10/12-inch

BELL (6036 "L.A., Memphis and Tyler, Texas") 20-30 69
CHESS (1429 "Suzy-Q") 250-350 58
ROULETTE (R-25175 "Let's All Twist at Miami Beach Peppermint Lounge")....50-75 62
(Monaural.)
ROULETTE (SR-25175 "Let's All Twist at Miami Beach Peppermint Lounge")....50-100 62
(Stereo.)
Also see BUCHANAN, Roy

HAWKINS, Edwin, Singers *P&R/R&B/LP '69*

Singles: 7-inch

BUDDAH 3-5 71-72
PAVILION....3-6 69

LPs: 10/12-inch

BUDDAH 8-12 71-72
PAVILION....10-12 69

Members: Edwin Hawkins; Walter Hawkins; Tramaine Hawkins; Daniel Hawkins; Elaine Kelley; Norma King; Dorothy Morrison; Barbara Gill; Shirley Miller; Edwin Miller; Donald Henderson.
Also see ISLEY BROTHERS / Brooklyn Bridge
Also see MELANIE
Also see MORRISON, Dorothy

HAWKINS, Erskine *P&R '36*

Singles: 78 rpm

BLUEBIRD....5-15 39-44
BRUNSWICK 5-10 53
DECCA....5-10 56
CORAL 5-10 50-54
KING....5-10 51-52
VICTOR/RCA 5-10 45-52
VOCALION 5-15 36-37

Singles: 7-inch

BRUNSWICK 5-10 53
DECCA....5-10 56
CORAL....5-10 52-54
KING (4514 "Steel Guitar Rag")....15-20 52
(Black vinyl.)
KING (4514 "Steel Guitar Rag")....30-40 52
(Colored vinyl.)
KING (4522 "Down Home Jump")....15-20 52
(Black vinyl.)
KING (4522 "Down Home Jump")....30-40 52
(Colored vinyl.)
KING (4574 "New Gin Mill Special") 15-20 52
KING (4597 "The Way You Look Tonight")....15-20 52
KING (4686 "Double Shot")....15-20 53

EPs: 7-inch

RCA....10-20 59

LPs: 10/12-inch

CORAL....30-50 54
DECCA....20-30 61
IMPERIAL....20-30 62
RCA....25-40 60

HAWKINS, Erskine, & Four Hawks

Singles: 78 rpm

KING (4671 "My Baby, Please")....25-50 53
KING (4686 "Double Shot")....15-25 53

Singles: 7-inch

KING (4671 "My Baby, Please")....50-75 53
KING (4686 "Double Shot")....25-50 53
Also see HAWKINS, Erskine

HAWKSHAW, Hawkshaw *C&W '48*

Singles: 78 rpm

KING....4-8 46-53
RCA....4-8 55-57

Singles: 7-inch

COLUMBIA 4-8 59-62
KING (900 thru 1100 series) 5-10 50-53
KING (5000 series) 4-8 60-64
RCA 5-10 55-59
STARDAY 3-5 71

EPs: 7-inch

KING 8-12 53

LPs: 10/12-inch

CAMDEN 10-15 64-66
HARMONY 10-15 63
KING (587 "Hawkshaw Hawkins, Vol. 1") 40-60 58
KING (592 "Hawkshaw Hawkins Sings Grand Ole Opry Favorites, Vol. 2") 40-60 58
KING (599 "Hawkshaw Hawkins") 40-60 59
KING (808 "All New Hawkshaw Hawkins") 20-40 63
KING (858 "Taken From Our Vaults, Vol. 1") 15-20 63
KING (858 "Taken From Our Vaults, Vol. 2") 15-20 63
KING (858 "Taken From Our Vaults, Vol. 3") 15-20 64
KING (1043 "Lonesome 7-7203") 8-12 69
LA BREA (8020 "Hawkshaw Hawkins") 25-50 60s
NASHVILLE 8-12 69
STARDAY 5-10 77

Also see CLINE, Patsy / Cowboy Copas / Hawkshaw Hawkins
Also see COPAS, Cowboy / Hawkshaw Hawkins

HAWKINS, Jennell — *R&B '61*

Singles: 7-inch

AMAZON 8-12 61-63
DYNAMIC 8-12 61
DYNAMITE 8-12 61
OLDIES 45 4-6

LPs: 10/12-inch

AMAZON (AM-1001 "Many Moods of Jenny") 25-50 61
(Monaural.)
AMAZON (AS-1001 "Many Moods of Jenny") 40-60 61
(Stereo.)
AMAZON (AM-1002 "Moments to Remember") 25-50 62
(Monaural.)
AMAZON (AS-1002 "Moments to Remember") 40-60 62

HAWKINS, Ronnie — *P&R/R&B '59*

(With the Hawks)

Singles: 7-inch

COTILLION 3-5 70-71
HAWK 5-10
MONUMENT 3-5 72-73
QUALITY 10-20
(Canadian.)
ROULETTE (4154 "Forty Days") 10-15 59
ROULETTE (SSR-4154 "Forty Days") 25-50 59
(Stereo.)
ROULETTE (4177 "Mary Lou") 10-15 59
ROULETTE (SSR-4177 "Mary Lou") 25-50 59
(Stereo.)
ROULETTE (4209 thru 4502) 5-10 59-63
YORKVILLE 8-12

LPs: 10/12-inch

ACCORD 5-10 83
COTILLION 10-15 70-71
MONUMENT 8-12 72-75
ROULETTE (25078 "Ronnie Hawkins") 50-100 59
(Black vinyl. Monaural.)
ROULETTE (SR-25078 "Ronnie Hawkins") 100-200 59
(Black vinyl. Stereo.)
ROULETTE (25078 "Ronnie Hawkins") 200-300 59
(Colored vinyl.)
ROULETTE (25102 "Mr. Dynamo") 50-100 60
(Black vinyl. Monaural.)
ROULETTE (SR-25102 "Mr. Dynamo") 100-200 60
(Black vinyl. Stereo.)
ROULETTE (25102 "Mr. Dynamo") 200-300 60
(Colored vinyl.)
ROULETTE (25120 "Folk Ballads") 50-100 60
(Monaural.)
ROULETTE (SR-25120 "Folk Ballads") 100-200 60
(Stereo.)
ROULETTE (25137 "Songs of Hank Williams") 50-100 60
(Monaural.)
ROULETTE (SR-25137 "Songs of Hank Williams") 100-200 60
(Stereo.)
ROULETTE (25255 "Ronnie Hawkins") 75-125
(Canadian.)
ROULETTE (25390 "Mojo Man") 50-100
(Canadian.)
ROULETTE (42045 "Best of Ronnie Hawkins") 25-35 70
U.A. 5-10 79

Also see BAND
Also see LENNON, John
Also see LEVON & HAWKS

HAWKINS, Roy — *R&B '50*

Singles: 78 rpm

DOWN TOWN (2018 "Christmas Blues") 15-25 48
DOWN TOWN (2020 "It's Too Late to Change") 15-25 48
DOWN TOWN (2024 "Forty Jim") 15-25 48
DOWN TOWN (2025 "Quarter to One") 15-25 48
MODERN 10-20 48-54
RPM 10-20 54

Singles: 7-inch

KENT 5-10 62
MODERN (826 "The Thrill Is Gone") 40-60 51
MODERN (852 "Gloom and Misery All Around") 40-60 51
MODERN (853 "I Don't Know Just What to Do") 40-60 51
MODERN (859 "Highway 59") 25-40 52
MODERN (869 "Doin' All Right") 25-40 52
MODERN (898 "Bad Luck Is Falling") 25-40 54
RPM (440 "Is It Too Late") 25-30 54
RHYTHM (120 "I Hate to Be Alone") 30-50 58

HAWKINS, Sam — *R&B '65*

(With the Crystals)

Singles: 7-inch

ARNOLD 4-8 63
BLUE CAT (112 "Hold On Baby") 5-10 65
DECCA 8-12 59-61
EPIC (10520 "Dream Lover") 4-8 69
GONE (5042 "King of Fools") 15-25 58
GONE (5054 "When Nobody Loves You") 15-25 59
SHELL 4-8

Session: Ronnie Bright; J.R. Bailey; Freddie Barksdale.
Also see BAILEY, J.R.

HAWKS — *P&R '81*

Singles: 7-inch

COLUMBIA 3-4 81

LPs: 10/12-inch

COLUMBIA 5-10 81

HAWKWIND — *LP '73*

Singles: 7-inch

ATCO 3-5 75
U.A. 3-5 71-73

LPs: 10/12-inch

ATCO 8-10 75
SIRE 5-10 78
U.A. 10-15 71-74

Also see MOTORHEAD

HAWLEY, Deane — *P&R '60*

(With the Crystals)

Singles: 7-inch

DORE 8-12 59-61
LIBERTY 8-12 61-62
SUNDOWN 4-8
VALOR (2003 "Don't Keep Me Guessin'") 25-35 59
W.B. 4-8 64

HAY, Colin James — *P&R/LP '87*

(Colin Hay Band)

Singles: 7-inch

COLUMBIA 3-4 87

Picture Sleeves

COLUMBIA 3-4 87

LPs: 10/12-inch

COLUMBIA 5-10 87
MCA 5-10 90

Also see MEN AT WORK

HAYES, Bill — *P&R '55*

(With the Archie Bleyer's Orchestra)

Singles: 78 rpm

ABC-PAR 8-12 57
CADENCE 8-12 55-56
MGM 3-6 55

Singles: 7-inch

ABC-PAR (Except 9895) 10-15 57
ABC-PAR (9895 "Bop Boy") 40-60 58
ABLE 4-8
BARNABY 3-5 76
CADENCE 10-20 55-56
DAYBREAK 3-5 74
KAPP 5-10 59
MGM 5-10 55
SHAW 4-6 65

Picture Sleeves

ABC-PAR 8-12 57
CADENCE (1/1256 "Ballad of Davy Crockett") 20-30 55
(Sleeve is numbered CCS-1 ["Cadence Children's Series], disc is 1256.)

EPs: 7-inch

MGM (312 "Bill Hayes") 10-20 55

LPs: 10/12-inch

ABC-PAR (194 "Bill Hayes Sings the Best of Walt Disney") 25-50 57
DAYBREAK 5-10 74
KAPP 10-20 60

Also see BLEYER, Archie

HAYES, Carolyn, & Four Tops

Singles: 78 rpm

CHATEAU 25-50 55

Singles: 7-inch

CHATEAU (2001 "Baby Say You Love Me") 50-100 55

Also see CARROLL, Delores, & Four Tops
Also see FOUR TOPS

HAYES, Isaac — *P&R/R&B/LP '69*

(Isaac Hayes Movement)

Singles: 12-inch

COLUMBIA 4-6 85-86

Singles: 7-inch

ABC 3-5 77
BRUNSWICK 4-8 64
COLUMBIA 3-4 85-87
ENTERPRISE 3-6 69-74
HBS 3-5 75-76
POLYDOR 3-4 78-80
SAN AMERICAN 3-5 70
STAX 3-6 78

LPs: 10/12-inch

ABC-PAR 8-10 75-77
ATLANTIC 8-10 72
COLUMBIA 5-10 86
ENTERPRISE 10-12 68-75
HBS 8-12 75-77
POLYDOR 5-10 77-81
STAX 5-10 77-82

Also see REDDING, Otis

HAYES, Isaac, & Millie Jackson R&B/LP '79

Singles: 7-inch

POLYDOR....3-4 79-80

LPs: 10/12-inch

POLYDOR....5-10 79

Also see JACKSON, Millie

HAYES, Isaac, & David Porter R&B '72

Singles: 7-inch

ENTERPRISE....3-5 72

Also see PORTER, David

HAYES, Isaac, & Dionne Warwick R&B/LP '77

Singles: 7-inch

ABC....3-5 77

LPs: 10/12-inch

ABC....10-15 77

Also see HAYES, Isaac
Also see WARWICK, Dionne

HAYES, Linda R&B '53

(With the Platters; with Tony Williams; with Flairs)

Singles: 78 rpm

ANTLER....10-20 56
DECCA....10-20 55
HOLLYWOOD (Except 1032)....10-15 53-55
HOLLYWOOD (1032 "Our Love Is Forever Blessed")....20-30 55
KING....10-20 55
RECORDED in HOLLYWOOD....10-20 53

Singles: 7-inch

ANTLER (4000 "I Had a Dream")....30-40 56
DECCA (29644 "Our Love's Forever Blessed")....20-30 55
HOLLYWOOD (Except 1032)....20-40 53-55
HOLLYWOOD (1032 "Our Love Is Forever Blessed")....40-60 55
KING (4752 "My Name Ain't Annie")....50-100 54
KING (4773 "Please Have Mercy")....35-50 55
RECORDED in HOLLYWOOD....30-40 53

Also see MOORE, Johnny, & Linda Hayes
Also see PLATTERS

HAYES, Peter Lind P&R '49

Singles: 78 rpm

DECCA....4-6 49

Singles: 7-inch

DOT....4-8 59

HAYES, Peter Lind, & Mary Healy

Singles: 7-inch

COLUMBIA....4-8 55
ESSEX....4-8 53
KAPP....4-8 56

Also see HAYES, Peter Lind

HAYES, Richard P&R '49

Singles: 78 rpm

MERCURY....5-10 49-55

Singles: 7-inch

ABC-PAR....15-25 56
COLUMBIA....10-20 60-61
CONTEMPO....4-6 64
DECCA....4-6 61
MERCURY....10-20 50-55

EPs: 7-inch

MERCURY....15-25 54

LPs: 10/12-inch

MERCURY....20-30 55

HAYES, Richard, & Kitty Kallen P&R '51

Singles: 78 rpm

MERCURY....4-8 50-51

Singles: 7-inch

MERCURY....5-10 50-51

Also see HAYES, Richard
Also see KALLEN, Kitty

HAYMAN, Richard, Orchestra

(With Jan August) P&R '53

Singles: 78 rpm

MERCURY....3-6 50-57

Singles: 7-inch

COMMAND....3-5 69
MGM....3-6 65
MERCURY....3-8 50-62
MUSICOR....3-5 73

EPs: 7-inch

MERCURY....4-8 51-59

LPs: 10/12-inch

ASCOT....5-10 64
COMMAND....5-10 69
MAINSTREAM....5-10 67
MERCURY....10-20 51-64
TIME....5-10 63-64
WING....5-10 62-64

Also see AUGUST, Jan

HAYMES, Dick P&R/R&B '43

Singles: 78 rpm

CAPITOL....3-5 56
DECCA....4-8 43-54

Singles: 7-inch

CAPITOL....5-10 56
GNP....3-5 75
DECCA....5-10 50-54
WARWICK....3-6 60

EPs: 7-inch

CAPITOL....5-10 56
DECCA....5-10 50-54

LPs: 10/12-inch

AUDIOPHILE....5-10 78
CAPITOL....10-20 56
CORAL....4-6 73
DAYBREAK....5-10 74
DECCA....10-20 50-54
GLENDALE....5-10 84
MCA....5-10 76-83
WARWICK....8-15 60

Also see CLOONEY, Rosemary, & Dick Haymes
Also see CROSBY, Bing, Dick Haymes & Andrews Sisters
Also see FISHER, Eddie / Vic Damone / Dick Haymes
Also see JAMES, Harry, & Dick Haymes
Also see MERMAN, Ethel, Dick Haymes

HAYMES, Dick, & Andrews Sisters P&R '48

Singles: 78 rpm

DECCA....4-6 48

Also see ANDREWS SISTERS

HAYMES, Dick, & Judy Garland P&R '47

Singles: 78 rpm

DECCA....4-6 47

Also see GARLAND, Judy
Also see HAYMES, Dick

HAYWARD, Justin P&R '75

Singles: 7-inch

COLUMBIA....3-5 78
DERAM....3-5 77

LPs: 10/12-inch

DERAM (4801 "Night Flight")....8-12 80
DERAM (18073 "Songwriter")....10-20 77

HAYWARD, Justin, & John Lodge P&R/LP '75

Singles: 7-inch

THRESHOLD....3-5 75

Picture Sleeves

THRESHOLD....3-5 75

LPs: 10/12-inch

THRESHOLD (14 "Blue Jays")....10-15 75
THRESHOLD (101 "Blue Jays")....15-25 75
(Promotional issue only. Interview with script.)

Also see HAYWARD, Justin
Also see LODGE, John
Also see MOODY BLUES

HAYWARD, Leon: see HAYWOOD, Leon

HAYWOOD, Leon P&R/R&B '65

(Leon Hayward)

Singles: 12-inch

CASABLANCA....4-6 83
MCA....4-8 79
20TH FOX....4-6 80

Singles: 7-inch

ATLANTIC....3-5 71-72
CAPITOL....10-15 69-70
CASABLANCA....3-4 83
COLUMBIA....3-5 76-77
DECCA....4-6 67-68
EPIC....3-4 80-81
EVEJIM....4-8
FANTASY (581 "The Truth About Money")....10-20 64
FAT FISH (8005 "Soul Cargo")....15-25 66
GALAXY....4-6 67
IMPERIAL....5-15 65-66
MCA....3-5 77-79
MODERN....3-4 84
20TH FOX....3-5 74-80

LPs: 10/12-inch

CASABLANCA....5-10 83
DECCA....8-12 67
GALAXY....8-12 67
MCA....5-10 78-79
20TH FOX....5-10 73-80

HAZARD, Robert P&R/LP '83

Singles: 7-inch

RCA....3-4 83

LPs: 10/12-inch

RCA....5-10 83

HAZE R&B '75

Singles: 7-inch

ASI....3-5 75
MOONSPELL....5-8 78

LPs: 10/12-inch

ASI....8-10 74

HAZLEWOOD, Lee

Singles: 7-inch

CAPITOL....3-5 72
JAMIE....5-10 60
LHI....4-6 68
MCA....3-4 79-80
MGM....4-6 66-67
REPRISE....4-6 65-68
SMASH....5-8 61

LPs: 10/12-inch

CAPITOL....8-10 72
HARMONY....8-12 67
MGM....10-15 66-67
MERCURY....10-20 63
REPRISE....10-15 64-65

Also see ANN-MARGRET & Lee Hazlewood
Also see SHACKLEFORDS
Also see SINATRA, Nancy, & Lee Hazlewood

HEAD, Murray P&R '70

(With the Trinidad Singers; Murry Head)

Singles: 12-inch

CHESS....4-6 85

Singles: 7-inch

A&M....3-5 76
CAPITOL....4-6 67
CHESS....3-4 84-85
DECCA....3-6 69-71
RCA....3-4 85

Picture Sleeves

CHESS....3-4 85
DECCA....3-6 70-71
RCA....3-4 85

LPs: 10/12-inch

A&M....8-10 76
COLUMBIA....5-10 72

HEAD, Roy P&R/R&B/LP '65

(With the Traits)

Singles: 7-inch

ABC....3-5 73-79
ABC/DOT....3-5 76-77
AVION....3-4 83
BACK BEAT....5-10 65-67
CHURCHILL....3-4 81

DUNHILL 3-5 70
ELEKTRA 3-4 79-80
MEGA 3-5 74
MERCURY 4-6 68
NSD 3-4 82
SCEPTER 4-8 65-66
SHANNON 3-5 75
SUAVE 10-20
TMI 3-5 71-73
TNT 8-12 65
TEXAS CRUDE 3-4 85

LPs: 10/12-inch

ABC 5-10 73-78
CRAZY CAJUN 5-10 77
DUNHILL 8-12 70
ELEKTRA 5-10 79-80
SCEPTER (532 "Treat Me Right") 15-25 65
(Monaural.)
SCEPTER (532 "Treat Me Right") 20-30 65
(Stereo. With an "SS" prefix.)
TMI (1000 "Dismal Prisoner") 8-10 72
TNT (101 "Roy Head and the Traits") 100-150 65
(Counterfeits can be identified by their content. They include *Treat Her Right,* as well as other later Head tracks on side two. Originals do not have these.)
TEXAS CRUDE 5-10 85

Also see ROY - SARAH & TRAITS

HEAD EAST
P&R/LP '75

Singles: 7-inch

A&M 3-5 75-79

Picture Sleeves

A&M 3-5 78

LPs: 10/12-inch

A&M 5-10 75-80
ALLEGIANCE 5-10 83

Members: John Schlitt; Mike Sommerville; Roger Boyd; Steve Huston.

HEADBOYS
P&R/LP '79

Singles: 7-inch

RSO 3-5 79

LPs: 10/12-inch

RSO 5-10 79

HEADHUNTERS
LP '75

LPs: 10/12-inch

ARISTA 5-10 75-78

HEADPINS
P&R '83

Singles: 7-inch

ATCO 3-5 82
SOLID GOLD 3-5 83

Picture Sleeves

SOLID GOLD 3-5 83

LPs: 10/12-inch

ATCO 5-10 82
SOLID GOLD 5-8 83

Member: Darby Mills.

HEALEY, Jeff
LP '88

(Jeff Healey Band)

Singles: 7-inch

ARISTA 3-4 89-90
FORTE (001 "Adrianna") 8-10 86

Picture Sleeves

ARISTA 3-4 89
FORTE (001 "Adrianna") 10-15 86

LPs: 10/12-inch

ARISTA 5-8 89-90

Members: Jeff Healey; Joe Rockman; Tom Stephen.

HEAP, Jimmy
P&R/C&W '56

(With the Melody Masters & Perk Williams)

Singles: 78 rpm

CAPITOL 5-15 53-55
IMPERIAL 8-12 50-52

Singles: 7-inch

CAPITOL 10-20 53-55
D 8-10 59
DART 5-10 60
FAME (502 "Little Jewel") 200-250 58
FAME (509 "Night Cap") 8-15 61
FAME (510 "Go Get Em") 8-15 61
FAME (511 "Flint Rock") 8-15 61
IMPERIAL (8325 "When They Operated on Papa They Opened Mama's Male") 5-10 60

HEAR 'N AID
LP '86

Singles: 7-inch

MERCURY 3-4 85

LPs: 10/12-inch

MERCURY/POLYGRAM 5-10 85

Members: Tommy Aldridge; Dave Alford; Carmine Appice; Vinny Appice; Jimmy Bain; Frankie Banali; Eric Bloom; Mick Brown; Vivian Campbell; Carlos Cavazo; Amir Derakh; Ronnie James Dio; Don Dokken; Kevin Dubrow; Brad Gillis; Craig Goldy; Chris Hager; Rob Halford; Chris Holmes; Blackie Lawless; Geroge Lynch; Yngwie Malmsteed; Mick Mars; Dave Meniketti; Dave Murray; Vince Neil; Ted Nugent; Eddie Ojeda; Jeff Pilson; Donald Roeser; Rudy Sarzo; Chaude Schnell; Neal Schon; Paul Shortino; Adrian Smith; Spinal Tap; Mark Stein; Geoff Tate Matt Thor.

Also see DIO, Ronnie
Also see DOKKEN
Also see GIUFFRIA
Also see MALMSTEEN, Yngwie J.
Also see NUGENT, Ted
Also see QUIET RIOT
Also see SPINAL TAP

HEART
P&R/LP '76

Singles: 12-inch

CAPITOL 4-6 85
MUSHROOM 4-8 76
PORTRAIT 4-8 77-79

Promotional 12-inch Singles

MUSHROOM (7023 "Dreamboat Annie) 8-10 76
PORTRAIT (16445 "Straight On") 8-10 78

Singles: 7-inch

CAPITOL 3-4 85-90
EPIC 3-5 81-83
MUSHROOM 3-6 76-79
PORTRAIT 3-5 77-79

Picture Sleeves

CAPITOL 3-4 85-90
EPIC (Except 04047) 3-5 82-83
EPIC (04047 "How Can I Refuse") 3-5 83
EPIC (04047 "How Can I Refuse") 8-10 83
(Promotional sleeve. Labeled: "Demonstration Only—Not for Sale.)

LPs: 10/12-inch

CAPITOL 5-10 85-90
CAPITOL RADIO STAR ("Audio Cue Card") 10-15 87
(Radio interview. Promotional issue only.)
EPIC 5-10 80-83
MUSHROOM (MRS-5005 "Dreamboat Annie") 8-12 76
MUSHROOM (MRS-5008 "Magazine") 50-75 77
(First issue. Last track on Side One is *Magazine.*)
MUSHROOM (MRS-5008 "Magazine") 5-10 77
(Second issue. First track on Side Two is *Magazine.* There are also other differences in song order.)
MUSHROOM (MRS-5008 Magazine") 50-75 78
(Promotional only picture disc.)
MUSHROOM (MRS-1-SP "Magazine") 15-25 78
(Picture Disc.)
MUSHROOM (MRS-2-SP "Dreamboat Annie") 20-30 79
(Picture Disc.)
NAUTILUS 20-25 80
(Half-speed mastered.)
PORTRAIT (30000 series) 5-10 77-81
PORTRAIT (40000 series) 12-15 81
(Half-speed mastered.)

Members: Nancy Wilson; Ann Wilson; Howard Leese; Steve Fossen; Roger Fisher; Mike Derosier; Mark Andes; Denny Carmassi.

Also see BORDERSONG
Also see GAMMA
Also see SPIRIT
Also see WILSON, Ann & Daybreaks
Also see WILSON, Nancy

HEART & SOUL
P&R/R&B '77

(Heart & Soul Orchestra)

Singles: 7-inch

CASABLANCA 3-5 77

HEART BEATS QUINTET

("Russell Jacquet & His Orch. - The Heart Beats Quintet")

Singles: 10-inch

CANDLELITE (437 "Tormented") 20-30 72
(Colored vinyl 45 rpm.)
CANDLELITE (437 "Tormented") 10-20 72
(Black vinyl 45 rpm.)

Singles: 7-inch

CANDLELITE (1135 "Tormented") 3-5 76
NETWORK (71200 "Tormented") 100-150 55
(Black vinyl. Pastel yellow label.)
NETWORK (71200 "Tormented") ... 50-100 55
(Black vinyl. Bright yellow label.)
NETWORK (71200 "Tormented") 15-25 55
(Colored vinyl.)

Members: James Sheppard; Albert Crump; Vernon Walker; Wally Roker; Rob Adams.

Also see HEARTBEATS
Also see JACQUET, Russell

HEARTBEATS
P&R/R&B '56

Singles: 78 rpm

GEE 25-50 57
HULL 25-50 55-56
RAMA 25-50 56-57

Singles: 7-inch

COLLECTABLES 3-4
GEE (1043 "When I Found You") 25-50 57
GEE (1047 "After New Year's Eve") 25-50 57
(Red label.)
GEE (1047 "After New Year's Eve") 15-25 57
(Gray label.)
GEE (1061 "People Are Talking") 15-25 60
GEE (1062 "Darling, How Long") 15-25 60
GUYDEN (2011 "One Million Years") 20-40 59
(Yellow label.)
GUYDEN (2011 "One Million Years") 15-25 59
(Purple label.)
HULL (711 "Crazy for You") 300-400 55
(White label. Promotional issue only.)
HULL (711 "Crazy for You") 250-350 55
(Pink label.)
HULL (711 "Crazy for You") 100-125 55
(Black label.)
HULL (713 "Darling How Long") 150-250 56
HULL (716 "People Are Talking") 150-250 56
HULL (720 "A Thousand Miles Away") 200-300 56
(Black label.)
HULL (720 "A Thousand Miles Away") 75-100 56
(Red label.)
RAMA (216 "A Thousand Miles Away") 75-100 56
RAMA (222 "I Won't Be the Fool Anymore") 50-100 57
RAMA (231 "Everybody's Somebody's Fool") 50-100 57
ROULETTE (4054 "Down on My Knees") 15-25 58
ROULETTE (4091 "One Day Next Year") 15-25 58
ROULETTE (4194 "Crazy for You") .. 15-25 58

LPs: 10/12-inch

EMUS 5-10 79
ROULETTE (25107 "A Thousand Miles Away") 100-200 60
ROULETTE (59019 "A Thousand Miles Away") 5-10 81

LPs: 10/12-inch

EMUS 8-10 79

- ROULETTE (25107 "A Thousand Miles Away") ... 75-125 60
- ROULETTE (59019 "A Thousand Miles Away") ... 8-10 81

Members: James Sheppard; Albert Crump; Vernon Walker; Wally Roker; Rob Adams.
Also see HEART BEATS QUINTET

HEARTBEATS / Shep & Limelights

LPs: 10/12-inch

- ROULETTE (115 "Echoes of a Rock Era") ... 40-60 72

Also see HEARTBEATS
Also see SHEP & LIMELIGHTS

HEARTS — R&B '55

Singles: 78 rpm

- BATON ... 10-20 55-56

Singles: 7-inch

- BATON (208 "Lonely Nights") ... 25-50 55
- BATON (211 "All My Love Belongs to You") ... 25-50 55
- BATON (215 "Gone Gone Gone") ... 25-50 55
- BATON (222 "Going Home to Stay") ... 15-25 56
- BATON (228 "I Had a Guy") ... 15-25 56
- J&S (1002 "If I Had Known") ... 15-25 57
- J&S (1180 "You Weren't Home") ... 25-50 57
- J&S (1626 "I Want Your Love Tonight") ... 25-50 58
- J&S (1657 "Dancin' in a Dream World") ... 25-50 57
- J&S (1660 "So Long Baby") ... 25-50 57
- J&S (4571 "Goodbye Baby") ... 20-30
- LAVENDER ... 5-10 62
- TUFF ... 5-10 63
- ZELLS ... 5-10 63

LPs: 10/12-inch

- ZELLS (337 "I Feel Good") ... 200-300 63

Members: Justine "Baby" Washington; Rex Garvin; Pat Ford; Joyce Peterson; Zell Sanders.
Also see JAYNETTS
Also see WASHINGTON, Baby

HEARTSFIELD — P&R '74

Singles: 7-inch

- MERCURY ... 3-5 74

LPs: 10/12-inch

- COLUMBIA ... 5-10 77
- MERCURY ... 8-10 73-75

HEARTSMAN, Johnny — R&B '57

(With the Gaylarks)

- MUSIC CITY ... 10-15 57
- RHYTHM ... 10-15 53

Singles: 7-inch

- BIG J (101 "Syrup Sopping") ... 10-15
- MUSIC CITY (807 "Johnny's House Party") ... 10-20 57
- MUSIC CITY (811 "Johnny's Thunderbird") ... 10-20 57
- WORLD PACIFIC (372 "Sizzlin") ... 10-20 63

LPs: 10/12-inch

- CAT 'N HAT ... 10-15

HEAT — R&B '80

Singles: 7-inch

- MCA ... 3-5 79-81

LPs: 10/12-inch

- MCA ... 5-10 79-81

HEATH, Ted — P&R '56

Singles: 78 rpm

- LONDON ... 3-4 50-61

Singles: 7-inch

- LONDON ... 3-6 50-61

EPs: 7-inch

- LONDON ... 4-8 51-56

LPs: 10/12-inch

- LONDON ... 5-15 50-62
- RICHMOND ... 5-10 62

HEATH, Walter — R&B '74

Singles: 7-inch

- BUDDAH ... 3-5 74

HEATH BROTHERS — R&B '81

Singles: 7-inch

- COLUMBIA ... 3-5 79-81

LPs: 10/12-inch

- COLUMBIA ... 5-10 79-81

HEATHERTON, Joey — P&R/LP '72

Singles: 7-inch

- CORAL (62422 "That's How It Goes") ... 10-20 64
- CORAL (62451 "Hullabaloo") ... 10-20 65
- CORAL (62459 "But He's Not Mine") ... 10-20 65
- DECCA (31962 "When You Call Me Baby") ... 25-50 66
- MGM ... 5-10 72-73

Picture Sleeves

- CORAL (62422 "That's How It Goes") ... 15-25 64
- MGM ... 5-10 72

LPs: 10/12-inch

- MGM ... 10-15 72

HEATWAVE — P&R/R&B/LP '77

(Heat Wave)

Singles: 12-inch

- EPIC ... 4-8 77-82

Singles: 7-inch

- EPIC ... 3-5 77-82

LPs: 10/12-inch

- EPIC ... 5-10 77-82

Member: Keith Wilder; Rod Temperton; Ernie Berger; John Wilder; Eric Johns.

HEAVEN & EARTH — R&B '76

Singles: 7-inch

- OVATION ... 3-5 72-73

LPs: 10/12-inch

- OVATION ... 8-10 73

HEAVEN BOUND — P&R '71

(With Tony Scotti)

Singles: 7-inch

- MGM ... 3-5 71

LPs: 10/12-inch

- MGM ... 8-12 72

Members: Joan Medora; Eddie Medora; Michael Lloyd; Tom Oliver.

HEAVEN'S EDGE — LP '90

LPs: 10/12-inch

- COLUMBIA ... 5-8 90

HEAVEN 17 — P&R/D&D/LP '83

Singles: 12-inch

- ARISTA ... 4-6 83-84

Singles: 7-inch

- ARISTA ... 3-4 83-84

LPs: 10/12-inch

- ARISTA ... 8-10 83
- VIRGIN ... 5-10 87

Members: Glenn Gregory; Craig Marsh; Martyn Ware.
Also see BAND AID
Also see HUMAN LEAGUE

HEAVENER, David — C&W '81

Singles: 7-inch

- BRENT ... 3-4 81-82

HEAVY D. & BOYZ — R&B '86

Singles: 12-inch

- MCA ... 4-6 86

Singles: 7-inch

- MCA ... 3-4 86-88

LPs: 10/12-inch

- MCA ... 5-10 86-87
- UPTOWN ... 5-8 89

HEBB, Bobby — P&R/R&B/LP '66

Singles: 7-inch

- BOOM ... 4-8 66
- CADET ... 3-6 72
- FM ... 5-10 61
- LAURIE ... 3-5 75
- PHILIPS ... 5-10 66-67
- RICH ... 10-20 60
- SCEPTER ... 4-8 66

Picture Sleeves

- PHILIPS ... 5-10 66

LPs: 10/12-inch

- EPIC ... 10-12 70
- PHILIPS ... 15-20 66

HEBB, Bobby / Billy Sha-Rae

Singles: 7-inch

- LAURIE ... 3-4

Also see HEBB, Bobby

HEDGEHOPPERS ANONYMOUS — P&R '65

Singles: 7-inch

- PARROT ... 5-8 65-66

Also see KING, Jonathan

HEFTI, Neal — LP '55

(With His Orchestra; Neal Hefti Quintet; with Mello-Larks)

Singles: 78 rpm

- CORAL ... 3-5 51-57
- EPIC ... 3-5 55-56

Singles: 7-inch

- COLUMBIA ... 3-5 65
- CORAL ... 4-6 51-59
- DOT ... 3-5 67-68
- EPIC ... 4-6 55-56
- RCA ... 3-5 66
- REPRISE ... 3-5 62
- U.A. ... 3-5 65-66

Picture Sleeves

- RCA ... 4-8 66-67
- RCA GOLD STANDARD ... 3-4 89

EPs: 7-inch

- CORAL ... 5-10 52-56
- EPIC ... 5-10 56
- "X" ... 5-10 55

LPs: 10/12-inch

- COLUMBIA ... 8-15 60
- CORAL ... 10-20 52-60
- EPIC ... 10-15 56
- RCA (3621 "Hefti in Gotham City") ... 10-20 66
- REPRISE ... 8-15 62
- 20TH FOX ... 8-12 64
- U.A. (573 "Definitely Hefti") ... 8-15 67
- "X" ... 10-20 55

You'll find many more listings by this artist in *The Official Price Guide to Movie/TV Soundtracks and Original Cast Albums*, containing over 8,000 listings.

HEIGHT, Donald — R&B '66

Singles: 7-inch

- DAKAR ... 3-5 76
- JUBILEE ... 5-10 63-69
- KING ... 10-20 60
- OLD TOWN ... 10-20 64-65
- RCA ... 5-10 65
- ROULETTE ... 5-10 65
- SHOUT ... 5-10 66-68
- SOOZEE ... 8-12 62

Also see HOLLYWOOD FLAMES

HEIGHT, Ronnie — P&R '59

Singles: 7-inch

- BAMBOO ... 5-10 61
- DORE ... 8-12 59
- ERA ... 5-10 59-61

HEINTJE — LP '70

Singles: 7-inch

- MGM ... 3-6 70

LPs: 10/12-inch

- MGM ... 8-10 70

HELIX — LP '83

LPs: 10/12-inch

- CAPITOL ... 5-10 83-87
- GRUDGE ... 5-8 90

HELLO PEOPLE — LP '74

Singles: 7-inch

- ABC/DUNHILL ... 3-5 75-76
- PHILIPS ... 4-6 68

Picture Sleeves

- PHILIPS ... 5-8 68

LPs: 10/12-inch

ABC/DUNHILL ... 8-10 74
ABC-PAR ... 8-10 75
MEDIARTS ... 12-15 70
PHILIPS ... 15-20 68

HELLOWEEN LP '87

LPs: 10/12-inch

MX ... 10-15 86
RCA ... 5-10 87-89

HELM, Levon LP '77

(With the RCO All-Stars)

Singles: 7-inch

A&M ... 3-4 80
ABC ... 3-5 78
CAPITOL ... 3-4 82
MCA ... 3-4 80

LPs: 10/12-inch

ABC-PAR (Except 4-5) ... 5-10 77-78
ABC-PAR (4-5 "Levon Helm") ... 15-20 78
(Picture disc. Promotional issue only.)
A&M ... 5-10 80
CAPITOL ... 5-10 82
MCA ... 5-10 80
Also see BAND
Also see HAMMOND, John
Also see LEVON & HAWKS

HELM, Levon, Johnny Cash, Emmylou Harris & Charlie Daniels

LPs: 10/12-inch

A&M ... 5-10 80
Also see CASH, Johnny
Also see DANIELS, Charlie
Also see HARRIS, Emmylou
Also see HELM, Levon

HELMS, Bobby C&W/P&R/R&B '57

Singles: 78 rpm

DECCA ... 5-15 56-57

Singles: 7-inch

BLACK ROSE ... 3-4 83-84
CAPITOL ... 3-5 70
CERTRON ... 3-5 70
COLUMBIA ... 4-8 64
DECCA (Except 29947) ... 8-15 57-62
DECCA (29947 "Tennessee Rock and Roll") ... 20-30 56
GUSTO ... 3-5 74
KAPP ... 4-6 65-67
LARRICK ... 3-5 75
LITTLE DARLIN' ... 3-6 67-79
MCA ... 3-4
MILLION ... 3-5 72
MISTLETOE ... 3-5 74
PLAYBACK ... 3-4

Picture Sleeves

CERTRON ... 4-6 70
DECCA ("New Singing Sensation") ... 10-20 57
(Pictures Helms, but no number or title shown. With die-cut center hole.)
DECCA (30194 "Fraulein") ... 15-20 57
DECCA (30513 "Jingle Bell Rock") ... 8-15 57

EPs: 7-inch

DECCA ... 10-20 57-59

LPs: 10/12-inch

CERTRON ... 8-10 70
COLUMBIA ... 12-15 63
DECCA (8638 "Bobby Helms Sings to My Special Angel") ... 30-40 57
HARMONY ... 10-12 67
HOLIDAY ... 5-10 80
KAPP ... 10-15 66
LITTLE DARLIN' ... 10-12 68
MCA ... 5-10 83
MISTLETOE ... 5-10 74
VOCALION ... 10-12 65
Also see KERR, Anita

HELMS, Jimmy R&B '73

Singles: 78 rpm

CAPITOL ... 5-10 55

Singles: 7-inch

CAPITOL ... 10-15 55
DATE ... 4-8 67
MGM ... 3-5 73

HENDERSON, Finis R&B '83

Singles: 7-inch

MOTOWN ... 3-4 83

LPs: 10/12-inch

MOTOWN ... 5-10 83
Also see WEAPONS of PEACE

HENDERSON, Joe P&R/R&B/LP '62

Singles: 7-inch

ABC ... 3-5 73
FONTANA ... 5-10 67
KAPP ... 5-10 64
RIC ... 5-10 64
TODD ... 5-10 62-63
VIRGO ... 3-5 72

LPs: 10/12-inch

FONTANA (27590 "Hits Hits Hits") ... 20-30 67
(Monaural.)
FONTANA (67590 "Hits Hits Hits") ... 25-35 67
(Stereo.)
TODD (2701 "Snap Your Fingers") ... 30-40 62

HENDERSON, Michael R&B/LP '76

Singles: 12-inch

EMI AMERICA ... 4-6 86

Singles: 7-inch

BUDDAH ... 3-5 76-83
EMI AMERICA ... 3-4 86

LPs: 10/12-inch

ACCORD ... 5-10
BUDDAH ... 8-12 76-83
EMI AMERICA ... 5-10 86
Also see CONNORS, Norman
Also see HYMAN, Phyllis, & Michael Henderson

HENDERSON, Ron, & Choice of Colour R&B '77

Singles: 7-inch

CHELSEA ... 3-5 77

HENDERSON, Skitch LP '65

Singles: 7-inch

COLUMBIA ... 3-6 65-66

EPs: 7-inch

CAPITOL ... 10-20 50-54
DECCA ... 5-15 56
RCA ... 5-10 57-58

LPs: 10/12-inch

CAPITOL (H-110 "Keyboard Sketches") ... 25-45 50
(10-inch LP.)
CAPITOL (502 "A Man and His Music") ... 15-25 54
COLUMBIA ... 5-15 65-66
DECCA (8000 series) ... 15-25 56
RCA ... 15-25 57-58
SEECO (62 "Skitch Henderson") ... 25-45 50s
SEECO (401 "Latin Favorites") ... 20-35 56

HENDERSON, Wayne R&B '78

(With the Freedom Sounds)

Singles: 7-inch

POLYDOR ... 3-5 78-79

LPs: 10/12-inch

ABC ... 5-10 77
ATLANTIC ... 8-12 67-68
POLYDOR ... 5-10 78-79
Also see AYERS, Roy, & Wayne Henderson

HENDERSON, Willie P&R/R&B '70

(With the Soul Explosions)

Singles: 7-inch

BRUNSWICK ... 3-6 70
PLAYBOY ... 3-5 74

LPs: 10/12-inch

BRUNSWICK ... 10-12 69-74

HENDRICKS, Bobby P&R/R&B '58

Singles: 7-inch

MGM ... 10-20 63
MERCURY ... 5-10 61
SUE ... 10-20 58-60
Also see COASTERS
Also see DRIFTERS

HENDRIX, Jimi P&R/LP '67

Singles: 7-inch

AUDIO FIDELITY (167 "No Such Animal") ... 10-20
REPRISE (Except 0572, 0665 & 0905) ... 5-10 67-72
REPRISE (0572 "Hey Joe") ... 20-40 67
REPRISE (0665 "Up from the Skies") ... 10-20 68
REPRISE (0905 "Stepping Stone") ... 25-50 70
TRIP ... 3-5 72

Promotional Singles

REPRISE (Except 0572, 0665 & 0905) ... 5-15 67-72
REPRISE (0572 "Hey Joe") ... 25-50 67
REPRISE (0665 "Up from the Skies") ... 15-25 68
REPRISE (0905 "Stepping Stone") ... 25-50 70

Picture Sleeves

AUDIO FIDELITY (167 "No Such Animal") ... 15-25
REPRISE (0572 "Hey Joe") ... 60-80 67

EPs: 7-inch

REPRISE (595 "And a Happy New Year") ... 75-100 74
(Promotional issue only. Issued with paper sleeve.)

LPs: 10/12-inch

ACCORD ... 5-10 81
AUDIO FIDELITY (320 "Jimi Hendrix") ... 10-20 84
(Picture disc.)
CAPITOL (12000 series) ... 5-10 86
CAPITOL (15000 series) ... 4-8 86
(Mini LP.)
CAPITOL (96414 "Band of Gypsies") ... 8-10 95
(Limited numbered edition.)
CRAWDADDY ... 200-250 75
PHOENIX 10 (320 "Rare Hendrix") ... 8-10 80s
PICKWICK ... 8-10 75
NUTMEG (1001 "High, Live 'N Dirty") ... 15-20 78
(Colored vinyl.)
RCA (68233 "Storm") ... 10-12 90s
(Picture disc.)
REPRISE (840 "Jimi Hendrix – Christmas Medley") ... 50-100 79
(Promotional issue only.)
REPRISE (2025 "Smash Hits") ... 25-35 69
(Orange and brown label. Price includes bonus poster, which represents about $15 to $20 of the value.)
REPRISE (2025 "Smash Hits") ... 8-10 71
(Brown label.)
REPRISE (2029 "Historic Performances") ... 8-10 70
REPRISE (2034 "The Cry of Love") ... 8-10 70
REPRISE (2040 "Rainbow Bridge") .. 10-15 71
REPRISE (2049 "In the West") ... 10-15 72
REPRISE (2103 "War Heroes") ... 10-15 72
REPRISE (2204 "Crash Landing") ... 10-15 75
REPRISE (2229 "Midnight Lightning") ... 10-15 75
REPRISE (2245 "Essential Jimi Hendrix") ... 8-12 78
REPRISE (2276 "Smash Hits") ... 5-10 77
REPRISE (2293 "Essential Jimi Hendrix, Vol. 2") ... 20-50 79
(Includes the bonus single, *Gloria*, extended version. Prices vary even more widely than the range shown here – from less than $10 to nearly $100. Egad!)
REPRISE (2293 "Essential Jimi Hendrix, Vol. 2") ... 8-15 79
(Without the bonus single.)
REPRISE (2299 "Nine to the Universe") ... 5-10 80
REPRISE (R-6261 "Are You Experienced") ... 45-65 67
(Monaural. Green, pink and yellow label.)
REPRISE (RS-6261 "Are You Experienced") ... 45-65 67
(Stereo. Green, pink and yellow label.)

REPRISE (6261 "Are You Experienced") 12-20 68
(Orange and brown label.)
REPRISE (6261 "Are You Experienced") 5-10 71
(Brown label.)
REPRISE (R-6281 "Axis: Bold As Love") 175-225 68
(Monaural. Orange and brown label.)
REPRISE (RS-6281 "Axis: Bold As Love") 15-20 68
(Stereo. Green, pink and yellow label.)
REPRISE (RS-6281 "Axis: Bold As Love") 5-10 71
(Brown label.)
REPRISE (6307 "Electric Ladyland") 12-15 68
(Orange and brown label.)
REPRISE (6307 "Electric Ladyland") .. 8-10 71
(Brown label.)
REPRISE (6481 "From the film *Jimi Hendrix*") 15-20 73
(Soundtrack.)
REPRISE (22306 "Jimi Hendrix Concerts") 8-10 82
REPRISE (25119 "Kiss the Sky") 5-10 84
REPRISE (25358 "Jimi Plays Monterey") 5-10 86
RHINO (254 "Interview") 15-20 82
(Picture disc.)
RYKO 10-15 87-88
SHOUT 10-15 72
(White label with red and blue printing.)
SHOUT 8-10
(Yellow label.)
SPRINGBOARD 8-10 72
TRIP (3505 "Superpak") 15-25 74
TRIP (3509 "Superpak") 15-25 74
(Same title but different tracks than Trip 3505.)
TRIP (9500 "Rare Hendrix") 15-25 72
(Gatefold cover with Hendrix poster inside.)
TRIP (9500 "Rare Hendrix") 10-15 72
(Standard cover.)
TRIP (9501 "Roots of Hendrix") 10-15 72
TRIP (9523 "Genius of Jimi Hendrix") 10-15 74
U.A. 8-10 75
Also see REDDING, Otis / Jimi Hendrix

HENDRIX, Jimi, & Isley Brothers

LPs: 10/12-inch

T-NECK 10-15 71
Also see ISLEY BROTHERS

HENDRIX, Jimi, & Curtis Knight

LPs: 10/12-inch

CAPITOL (659 "Flashing") 8-10 70
CAPITOL (2856 "Get That Feeling") 10-15 67
CAPITOL (2894 "Flashing") 10-15 68
51 WEST 5-10 82

HENDRIX, Jimi, & Lightnin' Rod

Singles: 12-inch

CELLULOID (166 "Doriella Du Fontaine") 5-10 84

HENDRIX, Jimi, & Little Richard

Singles: 7-inch

ALANNA 3-6 72

LPs: 10/12-inch

ALANNA 10-12 72
EVEREST 6-10 74
PICKWICK 6-10 73
Also see LITTLE RICHARD

HENDRIX, Jimi, & Buddy Miles

LPs: 10/12-inch

CAPITOL (472 "Band of Gypsies") 10-12 70
Also see MILES, Buddy

HENDRIX, Jimi, & Lonnie Youngblood — LP '71

Singles: 7-inch

FAIRMOUNT 10-15 65

LPs: 10/12-inch

MAPLE (6004 "Two Great Experiences Together") 20-25 71
Also see HENDRIX, Jimi
Also see YOUNGBLOOD, Lonnie

HENDRIX, Patti — R&B '78

Singles: 7-inch

HILLTAK 3-5 78
20TH FOX 3-5 74

HENDRYX, Nona — P&R/R&B/D&D/LP '83

Singles: 12-inch

RCA 4-6 83-86

Singles: 7-inch

EMI AMERICA 3-4 87
EPIC 3-5 77
RCA 3-4 83-87

Picture Sleeves

EMI AMERICA 3-4 87

LPs: 10/12-inch

EMI AMERICA 5-8 87
EPIC 5-10 77
RCA 5-10 83-87
Also see LABELLE, Patti

HENHOUSE FIVE PLUS TOO — P&R '77

Singles: 7-inch

W.B./AHAB 3-5 76-77
Member: Ray Stevens.
Also see STEVENS, Ray

HENLEY, Don — P&R/LP '82

Singles: 12-inch

GEFFEN 4-6 85

Singles: 7-inch

ASYLUM 3-4 82-83
GEFFEN 3-4 84-90

Picture Sleeves

ASYLUM 3-4 82
GEFFEN 3-4 84-89

LPs: 10/12-inch

ASYLUM 5-10 82-83
GEFFEN 5-10 84-89
Also see EAGLES
Also see HORNSBY, Bruce
Also see NICKS, Stevie, & Don Henley

HENRY, Clarence — P&R/R&B '56

(Clarence "Frogman" Henry)

Singles: 78 rpm

ARGO 10-20 56-57

Singles: 7-inch

ARGO (5200 series) 15-20 56-58
ARGO (5300 & 5400 series) 8-15 59-63
CADET 4-8 66
DIAL 4-8 67
PARROT 4-8 64-66
CHESS 3-5 73
ERIC 3-5 73
MAISON DE SOUL 3-5 77

LPs: 10/12-inch

ARGO (4009 "You Always Hurt the One You Love") 75-125 61
CFH (101 "Bourbon St. New Orleans") 15-20
CADET (4009 "You Always Hurt the One You Love") 20-30 65
(Cadet 4009 LPs can be found in Argo 4009 covers.)
ROULETTE (42039 "Clarence 'Frogman' Henry Is Alive & Well") 15-25 69
Also see GAYTEN, Paul

HENSLEY, Ken — LP '73

Singles: 7-inch

MERCURY 3-5 73

LPs: 10/12-inch

MERCURY 8-10 73
W.B. 8-10 75
Also see URIAH HEEP

HENSON, Jim — P&R '70

(Jim Henson's Muppets)

Singles: 7-inch

COLUMBIA 3-5 72
SIGNATURE 5-8 60

Singles: 12-inch

COLUMBIA 5-10 71
Also see ERNIE
Also see KERMIT / Fozzie Bear

HERB THE "K" — R&B '85

Singles: 7-inch

PRIVATE I 3-4 85

HERMAN, Keith — P&R '79

Singles: 7-inch

RADIO 3-5 79

HERMAN, Woody, & Orch. — P&R '37

Singles: 78 rpm

CAPITOL 3-5 54-56
COLUMBIA 3-6 45-48
DECCA 4-6 37-45
MARS 3-5 52-53

Singles: 7-inch

CADET 3-5 69
CAPITOL 4-8 54-56
CENTURY 3-4 79
CHURCHILL 3-4 79
COLUMBIA 3-5 65-76
FANTASY 3-5 73-74
MCA 3-5 73
MARS 4-8 52-53
PHILIPS 3-5 62

EPs: 7-inch

CAPITOL 5-10 55-56
COLUMBIA 8-12 52-54
DECCA 5-10 56
MGM 5-10 52-55

LPs: 10/12-inch

ACCORD 5-10 82
ATLANTIC (1300 series) 10-20 60
ATLANTIC (90000 series) 5-10 82
BRIGHT ORANGE 5-10 73
CADET 8-12 69-71
CAPITOL 5-10 72-75
(With "M" or "SM" prefix.)
CAPITOL 10-25 55-62
(With "T" or "ST" prefix.)
CENTURY 5-10 78
CHESS 5-10 76
COLUMBIA (500 series) 15-25 55
COLUMBIA (2300 & 2400 series) 5-15 65-66
COLUMBIA (2500 series) 15-25 52-54
(10-inch LPs.)
COLUMBIA (6000 series) 15-25 49-55
COLUMBIA (9000 series) 5-15 65-67
COLUMBIA (32000 series) 5-10 74
CONCORD JAZZ 5-10 81-83
CROWN 10-15 59
DECCA (4000 series) 8-15 64
DECCA (8000 series) 10-25 56
EVEREST (Except 200 & 300 series) 10-20 59-63
EVEREST (200 & 300 series) 5-10 74-78
FPM 5-10 75
FANTASY 5-10 71-81
HARMONY 5-10 72
JAZZLAND 10-20 60
MGM 10-25 55
METRO 5-12 65
PHILIPS 10-15 62-65
ROULETTE 10-20 59
SURREY 8-12 66
TREND 5-10 81
TRIP 5-10 75
VSP 8-12 66-67
VERVE 8-15 63-68
WHO'S WHO in JAZZ 5-10 78
WING 5-10
Also see BYRD, Charlie, & Woody Herman
Also see CLOONEY, Rosemary
Also see ECKSTINE, Billy, & Woody Herman

HERMAN'S HERMITS — P&R '64

Singles: 7-inch

ABKCO 3-4
BUDDAH 3-5 74-76
MGM 4-6 64-69
PRIVATE STOCK 3-5 75

Picture Sleeves

MGM 5-12 65-67

LPs: 10/12-inch

ABKCO ... 5-10 73-76

MGM (E-4000 series, except 4478) ... 10-20 65-67
(Monaural.)

MGM (SE-4000 series, except 4478) ... 8-15 65-68

MGM (E-4478 "Blaze") ... 35-45 67
(Monaural.)

MGM (SE-4478 "Blaze") ... 8-15 67
(Stereo.)

Members: Peter Noone; Derek Leckenby; Karl Green; Keith Hopwood; Barry Whitwham.

Also see PAGE, Jimmy

HERNANDEZ, Patrick — P&R/LP '79

Singles: 12-inch

COLUMBIA ... 4-6 79

Singles: 7-inch

COLUMBIA ... 3-4 79

LPs: 10/12-inch

COLUMBIA ... 5-10 79

HESITATIONS — R&B '67

Singles: 7-inch

B.T. PUPPY ... 4-8 68

GWP ... 4-8 69

KAPP ... 8-15 66-68

LPs: 10/12-inch

KAPP ... 10-15 67-68

Members: George Scott; Fred Deal; Leonard Veal.

HEWETT, Howard — R&B '85

Singles: 7-inch

ARISTA ... 3-4 88

ELEKTRA ... 3-4 85-90

Picture Sleeves

ELEKTRA ... 3-4 86

LPs: 10/12-inch

ELEKTRA ... 5-8 85-90

Also see SHALAMAR

Also see WARWICK, Dionne, & Howard Hewett

HEYETTES — P&R '76

Singles: 7-inch

LONDON ... 3-5 76

Picture Sleeves

LONDON ... 5-10 76

LPs: 10/12-inch

LONDON ... 5-10 76

HEYWARD, Nick — LP '84

Singles: 7-inch

ARISTA ... 3-4 83-84

LPs: 10/12-inch

ARISTA ... 5-10 83

Also see HAIRCUT ONE HUNDRED

HEYWOOD, Eddie — P&R '45

Singles: 78 rpm

DECCA ... 3-5 45-53

MERCURY ... 3-5 55-57

Singles: 7-inch

DECCA ... 4-6 51-53

LIBERTY ... 3-5 61-63

MERCURY ... 3-6 55-61

20TH FOX ... 3-5 63

EPs: 7-inch

COLUMBIA ... 4-8 52

DECCA ... 4-8 56

MERCURY ... 4-8 55-56

LPs: 10/12-inch

BRUNSWICK ... 10-15 55

CAPITOL ... 5-10 67-69

COLUMBIA ... 10-20 52

CORAL ... 10-15 55

DECCA ... 10-15 56

EPIC ... 10-15 56

LIBERTY ... 8-12 62-63

MERCURY ... 10-15 55-60

RCA ... 10-12 59

SUNSET ... 5-10 66

VOCALION ... 5-10 66

WING ... 8-12 59-64

Also see HOLIDAY, Billie, & Eddie Heywood

Also see WINTERHALTER, Hugo, & His Orchestra

HEYWOODS: see DONALDSON, Bo, & Heywoods

HI TEX 3 Featuring Ya Kid K — P&R '90

Singles: 7-inch

SBK ... 3-4 90

HIATT, John — LP '87

Singles: 12-inch

A&M ... 4-8 87
(Promotional only.)

GEFFEN ... 4-8 85
(Promotional only.)

Singles: 7-inch

A&M ... 3-4 87-90

ATLANTIC ... 3-4 85

GEFFEN ... 3-4 85

MCA ... 3-4 79-90

Picture Sleeves

A&M ... 3-4 87

LPs: 10/12-inch

A&M ... 5-10 87-90

GEFFEN ("Riot with Hiatt") ... 25-35
(Promotional issue only.)

MFSL (210 "Bring the Family") ... 20-25 94

Also see COSTELLO, Elvis

HIBBLER, Al — R&B '48

Singles: 78 rpm

ALADDIN ... 4-8 56

ATLANTIC ... 5-10 50

CHESS ... 5-10 51

CLEF ... 4-6 54

COLUMBIA ... 4-6 50

DECCA ... 4-8 55-57

MERCURY ... 4-6 52-56

MIRACLE ... 5-10 48

NORGRAN ... 4-6 54-55

ORIGINAL ... 4-8 55

Singles: 7-inch

ALADDIN ... 5-10 56

ATLANTIC (925 "The Blues Came Tumbling Down") ... 30-40 51

ATLANTIC (932 "Travelin' Light") ... 30-40 51

ATLANTIC (945 "This Is Always") ... 30-40 51

ATLANTIC (1071 "Danny Boy") ... 15-25 55

CLEF ... 4-8 54

COLUMBIA ... 5-10 50

DECCA ... 4-8 55-59

MCA ... 3-4 74

MERCURY ... 4-8 52-56

NORGRAN ... 4-8 54-55

ORIGINAL ... 5-10 55

REPRISE ... 4-6 61-62

SATIN ... 3-6 66

TOP RANK ... 4-6 60

VEGAS ... 3-6 67

EPs: 7-inch

CLEF ... 10-20 51

DECCA ... 10-20 55-57

NORGRAN ... 10-20 53

RCA ... 10-15 55

LPs: 10/12-inch

ATLANTIC ... 25-50 56

CLEF ... 25-50 54

DECCA (8000 series) ... 20-40 56-59

DECCA (75000 series) ... 5-10 69

LMI ... 8-12 65

MCA ... 5-10 76

NORGRAN (4 "Favorites") ... 25-50 53

REPRISE ... 10-15 61

TRIP ... 4-8 77

VERVE ... 10-20 55

Also see HOLIDAY, Billie, & Al Hibbler

Also see McSHANN, Jay

HIBBLER, Al, & Duke Ellington

Singles: 7-inch

COLUMBIA (33000 series) ... 3-4 76

LPs: 10/12-inch

COLUMBIA ... 15-25 56

Also see ELLINGTON, Duke

Also see HIBBLER, Al

HICKEY, Ersel — P&R '58

Singles: 7-inch

APOLLO (761 "Upside Down Love") ... 15-25 62

BLACK CIRCLE ... 3-5 72

EPIC ... 10-15 58-60

JANUS ... 3-5 71

KAPP ... 8-12 61

LAURIE ... 8-12 63

MAGNUM ... 3-4 84

RAMESES ... 3-5 76

TOOT ... 8-12

UNIFAX ... 3-5 74

EPs: 7-inch

EPIC (7206 "Ersel Hickey in Lover's Land") ... 75-100 58

HICKS, Clair, & Love Exchange — D&D '84

Singles: 12-inch

KN ... 4-6 84

HICKS, Dan, & His Hot Licks — LP '71

Singles: 7-inch

BLUE THUMB ... 3-5 73-74

LPs: 10/12-inch

BLUE THUMB ... 8-10 71-73

EPIC ... 10-12 69

W.B. ... 5-10 78

HIDDEN STRENGTH — R&B '76

Singles: 7-inch

U.A. ... 3-5 76

HI-FI FOUR — P&R '56

Singles: 78 rpm

KING ... 5-10 56

Singles: 7-inch

KING ... 10-15 56

HI-FIVE — LP '90

LPs: 10/12-inch

JIVE ... 5-8 90

HIGGINS, Bertie — P&R '81

Singles: 7-inch

CBS ASSOCIATED ... 3-4 85

KAT FAMILY ... 3-4 81-82

SOUTHERN TRACKS ... 3-4 87-89

LPs: 10/12-inch

KAT FAMILY ... 5-10 82

HIGGINS, Bertie, & Roy Orbison

Singles: 7-inch

SOUTHERN TRACKS (2010 "Leah") ... 3-5 89

Also see HIGGINS, Bertie

Also see ORBISON, Roy

HIGGINS, Monk — R&B '66
(With the Specialties)

Singles: 7-inch

BUDDAH ... 3-5 74

CHESS ... 3-6 67

SOLID STATE ... 3-6 68

ST. LAWRENCE ... 4-6 66

U.A. ... 3-5 72-73

LPs: 10/12-inch

BUDDAH ... 5-10 74

SOLID STATE ... 8-12 69

U.A. ... 8-10 72

Also see MASON, Barbara

HIGH INERGY — P&R/R&B/LP '77

Singles: 12-inch

GORDY ... 4-6 83

Singles: 7-inch

GORDY (Black vinyl) ... 3-5 77-83

GORDY (Colored vinyl) ... 3-6
(Promotional only.)

LPs: 10/12-inch

GORDY ... 5-10 77-83

Members: Barbara Mitchell; Vernessa Mitchell; Linda Howard; Michelle Rumph.

Also see ROBINSON, Smokey, & Barbara Mitchell

HIGH KEYES — P&R '63

Singles: 7-inch

ATCO ... 10-20 63-64

Members: Troy Keyes; Jim Williams; Bob Haggard; Cliff Rice.

HIGHLIGHTS P&R '56
(Featuring Frank Pizani)
Singles: 78 rpm
BALLY 10-20 56-57
Singles: 7-inch
BALLY (1016 "City of Angels") 15-25 56
BALLY (1027 "Will I Ever Know") 15-25 57

HIGHTOWER, Willie R&B '69
Singles: 7-inch
CAPITOL 4-6 69
FAME........ 3-5 70

HIGHWAYMEN P&R/LP '61
Singles: 7-inch
ABC-PAR 5-10 65-66
LIBERTY........ 3-5 81
U.A. 5-15 61-64
LPs: 10/12-inch
ABC-PAR 10-15 66
LIBERTY........ 5-8 82
U.A. 15-30 61-65
Members: Steve Butts; Chan Daniels; Gil Robbins; Dave Fisher.

HI-LITES
(Chi-Lites)
Singles: 7-inch
DARAN (011 "You Did That to Me").. 25-50
(Reportedly, there are two or three other Daran releases made by the Chi-Lites, recording as the Hi-Lites. For now, we lack their titles and selection numbers.)
Also see CHI-LITES

HILL, Bobby R&B '69
Singles: 7-inch
LOLO (2305 "The Children") 5-8 69
LOLO (2307 "To the Bitter End") 25-50 70

HILL, Bunker P&R/R&B '62
Singles: 7-inch
MALA (Except 464) 5-8 62
MALA (464 "The Girl Can't Dance") 8-12 63
Also see MIGHTY CLOUDS of JOY

HILL, Dan LP '75
Singles: 7-inch
COLUMBIA........ 3-4 87
EPIC 3-4 80-81
20TH FOX 3-5 75-79
Picture Sleeves
20TH FOX 3-5 78
LPs: 10/12-inch
EPIC 5-10 80-81
20TH FOX 5-10 75-80

HILL, Dan, & Vonda Sheppard P&R '87
Singles: 7-inch
COLUMBIA........ 3-4 87
LPs: 10/12-inch
COLUMBIA........ 5-10 87
Also see HILL, Dan

HILL, David P&R '59
Singles: 78 rpm
ALADDIN........ 5-10 57
RCA........ 5-10 57
Singles: 7-inch
ALADDIN 10-15 57
KAPP........ 10-15 59
RCA........ 10-15 57-58

HILL, Jessie P&R/R&B '60
Singles: 7-inch
BLUE THUMB 5-10
CHESS........ 8-12
DOWNEY 5-10 64
KERWOOD 10-15
MINIT........ 8-12 60-62
YOGI-MAN (607 "Hey Now Mama").. 10-15
LPs: 10/12-inch
BLUE THUMB 10-20 72

HILL, Lonnie R&B '84
Singles: 7-inch
URBAN SOUND 3-4 84-85
LPs: 10/12-inch
URBAN SOUND 5-10 85

HILL, Sam
(Gene Autry)
Singles: 78 rpm
GREYBULL (4281 "My Oklahoma Home") 25-50
GREYBULL (4310 "No One to Call Me Darling") 25-50
GREYBULL (4314 "Stay Away from My Chicken House") 25-50
VAN DYKE (5001 "Why Don't You Come Back Home") 25-50
VAN DYKE (7481 "My Oklahoma Home") 25-50
VAN DYKE (84310 "No One to Call Me Darling") 25-50
Also see AUTRY, Gene

HILL, Z.Z. P&R/R&B '64
Singles: 7-inch
ATLANTIC........ 4-8 69-70
AUDREY 4-8 71-72
COLUMBIA 3-5 77-78
HILL........ 3-6 71-73
KENT 5-15 64-71
M.H. 5-10 63
M.H.R 4-8 75
MALACO 3-4 82-84
MAILBU 3-4
MESA........ 8-12 64
MANKIND........ 4-6 71-72
QUINCY 4-6 70
RARE BULLET 3-4 84
U.A. 3-6 73-75
LPs: 10/12-inch
COLUMBIA 5-10 78-79
KENT 10-20 69-71
MALACO 5-10 82-84
MANKIND........ 8-12 71
U.A. 8-10 72-75

HILLAGE, Steve LP '77
Singles: 7-inch
ATLANTIC........ 3-5 76-77
LPs: 10/12-inch
ATLANTIC........ 8-10 76-77
VIRGIN........ 8-10 75

HILLMAN, Chris LP '76
Singles: 7-inch
ASYLUM 3-5 76-77
LPs: 10/12-inch
ASYLUM 5-10 76-77
SUGAR HILL........ 5-10 82-84
Also see BYRDS
Also see DESERT ROSE BAND
Also see FLYING BURRITO BROTHERS
Also see McGUINN, CLARK & HILLMAN
Also see SOUTHER - HILLMAN - FURAY BAND

HILLMAN, Chris, & Roger McGuinn C&W '89
Singles: 7-inch
UNIVERSAL........ 3-4 89
Members: Roger McGuinn; Chris Hillman.
Also see HILLMAN, Chris
Also see McGUINN, Roger

HILLSIDE SINGERS P&R '71
Singles: 7-inch
METROMEDIA........ 3-5 71-72
LPs: 10/12-inch
METROMEDIA........ 8-12 71

HILLTOPPERS P&R '52
(Hill Toppers)
Singles: 78 rpm
DOT 5-10 52-57
Singles: 7-inch
ABC........ 3-4 74
DOT (15000 series) 5-15 52-60
DOT (16000 series) 4-6 63
3-J 3-6 66
EPs: 7-inch
DOT........ 10-15 54-56
LPs: 10/12-inch
DOT (105 "The Hilltoppers")........ 30-40 54
(10-inch LP.)
DOT (106 "The Hilltoppers")........ 30-40 54
(10-inch LP.)
DOT (3003 "Tops in Pops")........ 20-30 55
DOT (3029 "Towering Hilltoppers") ... 20-30 56
DOT (3073 "The Hilltoppers")........ 20-30 57
SOUVENIR........ 8-15 73
Members: Jimmy Sacca; Billy Vaughn; Don McGuire; Seymour Spiegelman.
Also see VAUGHN, Billy

HI-LOs P&R '54
Singles: 78 rpm
COLUMBIA........ 5-10 57
STARLITE 3-8 55-56
TREND 3-8 54
Singles: 7-inch
COLUMBIA........ 5-10 57-60
REPRISE........ 4-8 62
STARLITE 5-12 55-56
TREND........ 8-15 54
EPs: 7-inch
COLUMBIA........ 5-15 57-58
KAPP........ 5-15 56
STARLITE........ 10-20 56
TREND (514 "The Hi-Los") 10-20 54
LPs: 10/12-inch
COLUMBIA........ 15-25 57-60
KAPP........ 15-25 56-60
STARLITE (6004 "The Hi-Los")........ 20-30 55
STARLITE (6005 "The Hi-Los I Presume")........ 20-30 56
STARLITE (7005 "Under Glass") 20-30 56
Members: Clark Burroughs; Don Shelton; Bob Morse; Gene Puerling.
Also see CLOONEY, Rosemary, & Hi-Los

HINDSIGHT R&B '88
Singles: 7-inch
VIRGIN 3-4 88
Picture Sleeves
VIRGIN 3-4 88

HINDU LOVE GODS LP '90
Singles: 7-inch
I.R.S. 3-4 86
Picture Sleeves
I.R.S. 3-4 86
LPs: 10/12-inch
GIANT........ 5-8 90
Members: Bill Berry Peter Buck; Mike Mills; Warren Zevon.
Also see R.E.M.
Also see ZEVON, Warren

HINES, Gregory R&B '88
Singles: 7-inch
EPIC 3-4 87-88
Also see VANDROSS, Luther, & Gregory Hines

HINES, J., & Fellows R&B '73
(With the Boys)
Singles: 7-inch
DELUXE 4-8 73
NATION-WIDE (105 "Going Down for the Last Time") 15-20

HINTON, Joe P&R/R&B '63
(Little Joe Hinton)
Singles: 78 rpm
BACK BEAT (519 "I Know") 40-60 58
Singles: 7-inch
ARVEE (5028 "My Love Is Real")...... 10-15 61
ARVEE (5029 "Let's Start a Romance") 10-15 61
BACK BEAT (519 "I Know") 15-25 58
BACK BEAT (526 "Pretty Little Mama") 10-20 59
BACK BEAT (532 "If You Love Me") 10-20 60
BACK BEAT (537 "Lovesick Blues") ... 8-12 63
BACK BEAT (539 "Better to Give Than to Receive") 8-12 64
BACK BEAT (540 "You're My Girl")..... 8-12 64
BACK BEAT (541 thru 594)........ 5-10 64-68

HOTLANTA 8-10 74
SOUL (35080 "You Are Blue") 5-10 71
(Black vinyl.)
SOUL (35080 "You Are Blue") 15-20 71
(Colored vinyl. Promotional issue only.)

Picture Sleeves

BACK BEAT (526 "Pretty Little Mama") 15-25 59

LPs: 10/12-inch

BACKBEAT (60 "Funny") 20-30 65
DUKE 8-10 73

HIPPIES / Reggie Harrison P&R '63

Singles: 7-inch

PARKWAY (863 "Memory Lane") 8-10 63
Also see STEREOS
Also see TAMS

HIPSWAY P&R/LP '87

Singles: 7-inch

COLUMBIA 3-4 87

Picture Sleeves

COLUMBIA 3-4 87

LPs: 10/12-inch

COLUMBIA 5-10 87
Member: John McElhone.
Also see TEXAS

HIROSHIMA LP '79

Singles: 12-inch

EPIC 4-6 85

Singles: 7-inch

ARISTA 3-4 80-84
EPIC 3-4 85

LPs: 10/12-inch

ARISTA 5-10 79-84
EPIC 5-10 83-89
MFSL (525 "Hiroshima") 15-25 79

HIRT, Al LP '61

Singles: 7-inch

CORAL 3-5 65
GWP 3-5 69-70
MONUMENT 3-4 74
RCA 3-6 61-68

Picture Sleeves

RCA 4-8 61-66

EPs: 7-inch

RCA 4-8 62

LPs: 10/12-inch

ACCORD 4-8 82
AUDIO FIDELITY 10-15 59-61
CAMDEN 5-10 67-71
CORAL 8-15 65
GWP 5-10 70-71
LONGINES 5-10
METRO 5-10 65
MONUMENT 5-8 74
RCA (Except 3309) 5-15 61-78
RCA (LPM-3309 "Best of Al Hirt") 10-15 65
(Monaural. Has Ann-Margret on one track.)
RCA (LSP-3309 "Best of Al Hirt") 15-20 65
(Stereo. Has Ann-Margret on one track.)
VOCALION 5-10 70
Also see ANN-MARGRET & Al Hirt

HIRT, Al, & Boston Pops Orchestra

LPs: 10/12-inch

RCA 10-15 64
Also see BOSTON POPS ORCHESTRA

HIRT, Al, & Pete Fountain LP '62

Singles: 7-inch

CORAL 3-6 61

EPs: 7-inch

CORAL 4-8 62

LPs: 10/12-inch

CORAL 8-15 61-62
MGM 8-15 64
MONUMENT 5-10 75
VERVE 10-20 61
Also see FOUNTAIN, Pete

HIRT, Al / Henry Mancini / Perez Prado

LPs: 10/12-inch

RCA 8-15 63
Also see MANCINI, Henry
Also see PRADO, Perez

HIRT, Al, & Hugo Montenegro

LPs: 10/12-inch

RCA (4275 "Viva Max") 15-20 70
(Soundtrack.)
Also see MONTENEGRO, Hugo

HIRT, Al, & Boots Randolph

Singles: 7-inch

MONUMENT 3-5 75
Also see HIRT, Al
Also see RANDOLPH, Boots

HITCHCOCK, Robyn LP '88

(With the Egyptians)

Singles: 7-inch

A&M 3-4 88-90

LPs: 10/12-inch

A&M 5-8 88-90
RELATIVITY 5-10 86

HO, Don P&R/LP '66

(With the Aliis)

Singles: 7-inch

HEL 3-5 77
MEGA 3-5 74-75
REPRISE 3-6 65-71

Picture Sleeves

HEL 3-5 77

LPs: 10/12-inch

MEGA 4-8 74
REPRISE 5-15 65-70

HODGE, Chris P&R '72

(With George Harrison)

Singles: 7-inch

APPLE (1850 "We're on Our Way") 5-10 72
APPLE (1858 "Goodbye Sweet Lorraine") 5-10 73
RCA 3-5 73-75

Picture Sleeves

APPLE (1850 "We're on Our Way") 5-10 72
Also see HARRISON, George

HODGES, Charles R&B '70

Singles: 7-inch

ALTO (2016 "There Is Love") 10-15 65
ALTO (2022 "Who's Crying Now") 10-15 65
CALLA 4-6 70

HODGES, Eddie P&R '61

Singles: 7-inch

AURORA 4-6 65-66
BARNABY 3-5 76
CADENCE 8-15 61-62
COLUMBIA 4-8 62-63
DECCA 5-10 59
MGM 4-8 64

Picture Sleeves

CADENCE 10-15 61
COLUMBIA 5-10 63

EPs: 7-inch

CADENCE (33-6 "Eddie Hodges") ... 15-25 61
("Cadence Little LP." With cardboard insert in clear cover.)
Also see DE SHANNON, Jackie / Bobby Vee / Eddie Hodges
Also see MILLS, Hayley, & Eddie Hodges

HODGES, Johnny P&R '37

(J. Hodges)

Singles: 78 rpm

BLUEBIRD 5-8 40-44
CLEF 4-6 53-56
COLUMBIA 4-6 51
GROOVE 4-6 56
MERCURY 4-6 51-53
NORGRAN 4-6 54-56
VARIETY 5-10 33
VOCALION 5-10 37

Singles: 7-inch

CLEF 5-15 53-56
COLUMBIA 5-15 51
GROOVE 5-15 56
MERCURY 5-15 51-53
NORGRAN 5-15 54-56
VMC 3-6 68
VARIETY 5-15 33
VERVE 4-8 57-67

EPs: 7-inch

ATLANTIC 20-30 54
EPIC 15-25 55
NORGRAN 25-50 54
RCA (3000 "Alto Sax") 50-75 52

LPs: 10/12-inch

AMERICAN RECORDING (421 "Johnny Hodges & Ellington All Stars") 40-60 57
CLEF (111 "Johnny Hodges Collates") 100-200 52
(10-inch LP.)
CLEF (128 "Johnny Hodges Collates, Vol. 2") 100-200 52
(10-inch LP.)
ENCORE 10-15 68
EPIC (3105 "Hodge Podge") 50-75 55
EPIC (22000 series) 8-12 74
IMPULSE 10-20 65
INSTANT 15-20 64
MCA 5-10 82
NORGRAN (1 "Swing with Johnny Hodges") 150-250 53
(10-inch LP.)
NORGRAN (1004 "Memories of Ellington") 100-200 54
NORGRAN (1009 "More Johnny Hodges") 100-200 54
NORGRAN (1024 "Dance Bash") 100-200 55
NORGRAN (1045 "Creamy") 100-200 56
NORGRAN (1048 "Castle Rock") 100-200 56
NORGRAN (1055 "Ellingtonia") 75-150 56
NORGRAN (1059 "In a Tender Mood") 75-150 56
NORGRAN (1060 "Used to Be Duke") 75-150 56
NORGRAN (1061 "The Blues") 75-150 56
PABLO 5-10 78
RCA (500 series) 10-20 66
RCA (3000 "Alto Sax") 200-300 52
(10-inch LP.)
RCA (3800 series) 10-20 67
VSP 10-20 66-67
VERVE (8179 "Perdido") 50-100 57
VERVE (8180 "In a Mellow Tone") .. 50-100 57
VERVE (8203 "Duke's in Bed") 50-100 57
VERVE (8271 "Big Sound") 50-100 58
(Reads "Verve Records, Inc." at bottom of label.)
VERVE (8271 "Big Sound") 15-25
(Reads "MGM Records - A Division Of Metro-Goldwyn-Mayer, Inc." at bottom of label.)
VERVE (8314 thru 8358) 25-45 59-60
(Reads "Verve Records, Inc." at bottom of label.)
VERVE (8314 thru 8358) 15-25 61-69
(Reads "MGM Records - A Division Of Metro-Goldwyn-Mayer, Inc." at bottom of label.)
VERVE 8-15 74-79
(Reads "Manufactured By MGM Record Corp.," or mentions either Polydor or Polygram at bottom of label.)
Also see ELLINGTON, Duke, & Johnny Hodges
Also see MULLIGAN, Gerry, & Johnny Hodges

HODGES, Johnny, & Lawrence Welk

LPs: 10/12-inch

DOT 10-20 66
Also see WELK, Lawrence

HODGES, Johnny, & Wild Bill Davis LP '65

LPs: 10/12-inch

RCA 10-20 65-67
VERVE 15-30 61-66
Also see HODGES, Johnny

HODGES, JAMES & SMITH P&R/R&B '77

Singles: 12-inch

LONDON 4-8 79

Singles: 7-inch

LONDON 3-5 76-79
PEOPLE 3-5 70s

20TH FOX 3-5 75

LPs: 10/12-inch

LONDON 5-10 78

Members: Pat Hodges; Denita James; Jessica Smith.

HODGSON, Roger P&R/LP '84

Singles: 7-inch

A&M 3-4 84

LPs: 10/12-inch

A&M 5-10 84-87

Also see SUPERTRAMP

HOFFS, Susanna LP '91

LPs: 10/12-inch

COLUMBIA 5-8 91

Also see BANGLES

HOG HEAVEN P&R '71

Singles: 7-inch

ROULETTE 3-5 71

LPs: 10/12-inch

ROULETTE 10-12 71

Members: Ron Rosman; Mike Vale; Peter Lucia; Eddie Gray.

Also see JAMES, Tommy, & Shondells

HOGG, Andrew

Singles: 78 rpm

EXCLUSIVE (89 "He Knows How Much We Can Bear") 30-40 47

Also see HOGG, Smokey

HOGG, Smokey R&B '48

(Andrew Hogg)

Singles: 78 rpm

BULLET 20-40 48
COLONY 25-50 50
COMBO 25-50 52
CROWN 10-20 54
DECCA 30-50 37
EXCLUSIVE 25-50 47
FEDERAL 15-25 53
FIDELITY 10-20 52
IMPERIAL 20-30 50-53
INDEPENDENT 15-25 49
JADE 25-35 51
MACY'S 20-30 49
MERCURY 20-30 51
METEOR 30-50 54
MODERN 20-30 48-52
RAY'S RECORD 30-50 52
RECORDED in HOLLYWOOD 10-20 52
SHOW TIME 20-30 54
SITTIN' in WITH 10-20 51-52
SPECIALTY (300 series) 10-15 49
TOP HAT 15-25 52

Singles: 7-inch

COMBO (11 "Believe I'll Change Towns") 75-125 52
CROWN (122 "I Declare") 50-100 54
EBB 10-20 58
FEDERAL (12109 "Keep A-Walking") 50-75 53
FEDERAL (12117 "Your Little Wagon") 50-75 53
FEDERAL (12127 "Gone, Gone, Gone") 50-75 53
IMPERIAL (5269 "When I've Been Drinkin'") 50-75 53
IMPERIAL (5290 "My Baby's Gone)" 50-75 53
MERCURY (8235 "Miss Georgia") 50-75 51
MERCURY (8228 "She's Always on My Mind") 50-75 51
METEOR (5021 "I Declare") 50-75 54
MODERN (884 "Baby Don't You Tear My Clothes") 50-75 51
MODERN (896 "Too Late, Old Man") 50-75 51
MODERN (924 "Can't Do Nothin'") 50-75 52
RAY'S RECORD (33 "Penitentiary Blues") 75-100 52
RAY'S RECORD (35 "I've Been Happy") 75-100 52
SHOW TIME (1101 "Ain't Gonna Play Second No Mo'") 50-75 54

LPs: 10/12-inch

CROWN (5526 "Smokey Hogg Sings the Blues") 20-30 62
KENT 10-15
TIME (6 "Smokey Hogg") 40-50 62
UNITED 5-10

Also see HOGG, Andrew

HOLDEN, Ron P&R/R&B '60

(With the Thunderbirds; with Twiliters)

Singles: 7-inch

ABC 3-5 73
APEX (76645 "Love You So") 15-25 59
(Canadian.)
BARONET (3 "Things Don't Happen That Way") 150-250 62
CHALLENGE (59360 "I Tried") 20-30 67
COLLECTABLES 3-4
DONNA (1315 "Love You So") 15-25 59
(Blue or Green label.)
DONNA (1315 "Love You So") 10-20 60
(Black label.)
DONNA (1324 thru 1335) 10-20 60-62
ELDO 10-20 61
LANA 3-6 60s
LOST NITE 4-8
NITE OWL (10 "Love You So") 50-75 60
NOW 3-6 74
RAMPART 5-10 65

LPs: 10/12-inch

DONNA (DLP-2111 "Love You So") 40-60 60
(Monaural.)
DONNA (DLPS-2111 "Love You So") 50-75 60
(Stereo.)

Session: Bruce Johnston.

Also see LITTLE CAESAR & ROMANS / Ron Holden

HOLIDAY, Billie P&R '35

Singles: 78 rpm

BRUNSWICK 10-20 35-38
CAPITOL 5-10 42
CLEF 5-10 53-55
COLUMBIA 5-10 51-52
COMMODORE 10-15 39
DECCA 10-20 45-52
MERCURY 5-10 52-53
OKEH 10-10 41
VOCALION 10-15 36-38

Singles: 7-inch

CLEF 10-20 53-55
COLUMBIA (30000 series) 10-20 51-52
DECCA (250 "Lover Man") 30-50 52
(Boxed set of four singles.)
DECCA (27000 series) 10-20 50-52
DECCA (48000 series) 10-20 51-52
KENT 3-5 73
MCA 3-5 73
MGM 8-12 59
MERCURY (89000 series) 10-20 52-53
U.A. 3-5 72
VERVE 8-12 59-62

Picture Sleeves

MGM (12813 "Just One More Chance") 15-25 59

EPs: 7-inch

CLEF 20-30 53-54
COLUMBIA 15-25 54-58
DECCA 5-15 56

LPs: 10/12-inch

AJ 10-20
ALADDIN 50-75 56
(Title and selection number not known.)
AMERICAN RECORDING SOCIETY (409 "Billie Holiday Sings") 50-100 56
AMERICAN RECORDING SOCIETY (431 "Lady Sings the Blues") 50-100 56
ATLANTIC 5-10 72
AUDIO FIDELITY (312 "Billie Holiday") 10-20 84
(Picture disc.)
CLEF (118 "Favorites") 150-250 53
(10-inch LP.)
CLEF (144 "Evening with Billie") 150-250 54
(10-inch LP.)
CLEF (161 "Favorites") 150-250 54
(10-inch LP.)
CLEF (169 "Jazz at the Philharmonic") 100-250 55
CLEF (669 "Music for Torching") 30-50 55
CLEF (686 "A Recital") 100-150 56
CLEF (690 "Solitude") 100-150 56
CLEF (713 "Velvet Moods") 100-150 56
CLEF (718 "Jazz Recital") 100-150 56
CLEF (721 "Lady Sings the Blues") 100-150 56
COLUMBIA (21 "The Golden Years") 50-75 62
(Boxed, three-disc set.)
COLUMBIA (40 "The Golden Years, Vol. 2") 25-35 66
(Boxed, three-disc set.)
COLUMBIA (637 "Lady Day") 100-150 54
(Red label with gold printing.)
COLUMBIA (637 "Lady Day") 50-75 56
(Red label with black and white printing.)
COLUMBIA (2600 series) 8-15 67
COLUMBIA (6129 "Billie Holiday Sings") 150-200 50
(10-inch LP.)
COLUMBIA (6163 "Billie Holiday Favorites") 150-200 51
(10-inch LP.)
COLUMBIA (1157 "Lady in Satin") 30-50 58
COLUMBIA (30000 series, except 32134) 8-15 72-73
COLUMBIA (32134 "Billie Holiday Story, Vol. 2") 50-100 73
(Two discs.)
DECCA (100 series) 10-20 65-72
DECCA (5345 "Lover Man") 150-250 52
(10-inch LP.)
DECCA (8215 "The Lady Sings") 50-100 56
DECCA (8701 "Blues Are Brewin'") 50-100 58
DECCA (75000 series) 8-15 68
ESP 8-12 71-73
EVEREST 5-10 73-75
HARMONY 5-10 73
JAZZTONE (1209 "Billie Holiday Sings") 30-40 56
JOLLY ROGER (5020 "Billie Holiday") 75-100 54
KENT 5-10 73
MCA 5-10 73
MFSL (201 "In Rehearsal") 25-35 87
MFSL (247 "Body & Soul") 20-25 95
MGM (100 series) 6-10 70
MGM (3700 series) 25-50 59
MGM (4900 series) 5-10 74
MAINSTREAM 10-20 65
METRO 10-20 65
MONMOUTH-EVERGREEN 5-10 72
PARAMOUNT 5-10 73
PICKWICK 5-10
RIC 10-20 64
SCORE 25-50 57
SOLID STATE 8-12 69
TRIP 5-10 73
U.A. (5600 series) 5-10 72
U.A. (14000 & 15000 series) 20-30 62
VSP 8-15 66
VERVE 25-50 57-60
(Reads "Verve Records, Inc." at bottom of label.)
VERVE 10-25 61-72
(Reads "MGM Records - a Division of Metro-Goldwyn-Mayer, Inc." at bottom of label.)
VERVE 5-10 73-84
(Reads "Manufactured By MGM Record Corp.," or mentions either Polydor or Polygram at bottom of label.)

Also see FITZGERALD, Ella / Billie Holiday / Lena Horne

HOLIDAY, Billie, & Stan Getz

LPs: 10/12-inch

DALE (25 "Billie & Stan") 150-250 51
(10-inch LP.)

Also see GETZ, Stan

Also see GOODMAN, Benny, Orchestra

Also see LYNNE, Gloria / Nina Simone / Billie Holiday

HOLIDAY, Billie, & Eddie Heywood

LPs: 10/12-inch

COMMODORE (20005 "Billie Holiday, Vol. 1") 100-200 50
(10-inch LP.)
COMMODORE (20006 "Billie Holiday, Vol. 2") 100-200 50
(10-inch LP.)
COMMODORE (30008 "Billie Holiday, Vol. 1") 50-75 59
COMMODORE (30011 "Billie Holiday, Vol. 2") 50-75 59
Also see HEYWOOD, Eddie

HOLIDAY, Billie, & Al Hibbler

LPs: 10/12-inch

IMPERIAL 20-30 62
SUNSET 8-15 67
Also see HIBBLER, Al
Also see HOLIDAY, Billie

HOLIDAY, Chico — P&R '59

(Chico)

Singles: 7-inch

CORAL 5-10 61-63
KARATE 5-10 65
NEW PHOENIX 8-12 61
RCA 5-10 59
SHAMLEY 4-8 69

EPs: 7-inch

RAYNARD (10065 "What Did I Do") 15-25 58

LP: 10/12-inch

ASEPH 5-8 89
EAGLE WING 5-8 89
MELODYLAND 10-20 75-78
SONGSPIRATION 5-10 73

HOLIDAY, Jimmy — P&R/R&B '63

Singles: 7-inch

DIPLOMACY 4-8 65
EVEREST 4-8 63-65
KT 5-10
KENT 4-6 68
MINIT 4-8 66-68

LPs: 10/12-inch

MINIT (24005 "Turning Point") 15-25 66

HOLIDAY, Jimmy, & Clydie King

Singles: 7-inch

MINIT 4-8 67
Also see HOLIDAY, Jimmy
Also see KING, Clydie

HOLIDAYS — P&R/R&B '66

Singles: 7-inch

GOLDEN WORLD (36 "I Love You Forever") 10-20 66
GOLDEN WORLD (47 "No Greater Love") 10-20 66
GROOVE CITY (206 "Easy Living") .. 50-75 60s
REVILOT (210 "I Know She Cares") 15-25 67
Members: Edwin Starr; Steve Mancha; J.J. Barnes.
Also see BARNES, J.J., & Steve Mancha
Also see STARR, Edwin

HOLIEN, Danny — P&R '72

Singles: 7-inch

MOUNTAIN 3-5 71
TUMBLEWEED 3-5 72

HOLLAND, Amy — P&R/LP '80

Singles: 7-inch

CAPITOL 3-4 80-83

Picture Sleeves

CAPITOL 3-4 80

LPs: 10/12-inch

CAPITOL 5-10 80-83
Also see CHRISTIAN, Chris
Also see McDONALD, Michael

HOLLAND, Brian — R&B '72

(Briant Holland with the Band)

Singles: 7-inch

INVICTUS 4-6 72-73
KUDO (667 "In Nature Boy") 300-500 58
Also see HOLLAND, Eddie
Also see HOLLAND - DOZIER

HOLLAND, Eddie — P&R/R&B '62

(With the Rayber Voices)

Singles: 7-inch

MERCURY (71290 "You") 75-100 58
MOTOWN (Except 1049) 15-25 61-64
MOTOWN (1049 "I'm on the Outside Looking In") 50-100 64
TAMLA (102 "Merry-Go-Round") .. 100-200 59
U.A. (172 "Merry-Go-Round") 15-25 59
U.A. (191 "Because I Love Her") 15-25 59
U.A. (207 "Magic Mirror") 15-25 60
U.A. (280 "Last Laugh") 15-25 61

Picture Sleeves

MOTOWN (1030 "If Cleopatra Took a Chance") 30-50 62

LPs: 10/12-inch

MOTOWN (604 "Eddie Holland") 50-75 63
Members (Rayber Voices): Brian Holland; Raynoma Gordy; Robert Bateman; Sonny Sanders; Gwen Murray.
Also see HOLLAND, Brian
Also see JOHNSON, Marv
Also see STRONG, Barrett

HOLLAND, Eddie, & Lamont Dozier

Singles: 7-inch

MOTOWN 8-12 63
Also see DOZIER, Lamont
Also see HOLLAND, Eddie
Also see HOLLAND - DOZIER

HOLLAND – DOZIER — P&R '72

(With the Andantes & Four Tops; featuring Lamont Dozier)

Singles: 7-inch

INVICTUS 3-5 72-73
MOTOWN 15-20 63
Members: Brian Holland; Lamont Dozier
Also see FOUR TOPS
Also see HOLLAND, Brian
Also see HOLLAND, Eddie, & Lamont Dozier

HOLLIDAY, Jennifer — P&R/R&B '82

Singles: 12-inch

GEFFEN 4-6 83-86

Singles: 7-inch

GEFFEN 3-4 82-87

Picture Sleeves

GEFFEN 3-4 85-86

LPs: 10/12-inch

GEFFEN 5-10 82-86

HOLLIES — P&R '64

Singles: 12-inch

ATLANTIC (502 "Stop in the Name of Love") 6-12 83
(Promotional issue only.)
EPIC (08157 "Draggin' My Heels") 8-10 77

Singles: 7-inch

ATLANTIC (89819 "Stop in the Name of Love") 3-4 83
EPIC (2000 series) 3-5 71
(Reissue series.)
EPIC (10180 thru 10613) 4-8 67-70
EPIC (10677 "Dandelion Wine") 5-10 70
EPIC (10716 "Survival of the Fittest") 8-12 71
EPIC (10754 "Row the Boat Together") 5-10 71
EPIC (10842 "The Baby") 5-10 72
EPIC (10871 thru 11100) 3-8 72-74
EPIC (50000 series) 3-5 75-78
IMPERIAL (66026 thru 66070) 10-20 64-65
IMPERIAL (66099 "Yes I Will") 20-40 65
IMPERIAL (66119 thru 66258) 5-10 66-68
IMPERIAL (66271 "If I Needed Someone") 20-40 65
LIBERTY (55674 "Stay") 25-40 64

Picture Sleeves

ATLANTIC (89819 "Stop in the Name of Love") 3-4 83
EPIC (10234 "King Midas in Reverse") 5-10 67
EPIC (10251 "Dear Eloise") 5-10 67
IMPERIAL (66231 "On a Carousel") 5-10 67

LPs: 10/12-inch

ATLANTIC (81905 "Buster") 5-10 83
CAPITOL (16056 "Greatest") 6-10 80
EMI (92882 "Best of the Hollies") 5-10 80s
EPIC (24315 "Evolution") 25-35 67
(Monaural.)
EPIC (26315 "Evolution") 15-25 67
(Stereo.)
EPIC (26538 "He Ain't Heavy He's My Brother") 10-20 70
EPIC (30255 "Moving Finger") 10-20 71
EPIC (KE-30958 "Distant Light") 10-20 72
EPIC (AL-30958 "Distant Light") 5-10 77
EPIC (31000 thru 35000 series) 6-12 73-78
IMPERIAL (9265 "Here I Go Again") 125-175 64
(Monaural. Black label with five stars under "Imperial" and straight lines from "10" to "2" [if label were a clock face].)
IMPERIAL (9265 "Here I Go Again") 50-75 64
(Monaural. Multi-color label.)
IMPERIAL (9299 "Hear! Here!") 40-60 65
(Monaural.)
IMPERIAL (9312 "The Hollies [Beat Group]") 35-50 66
(Monaural.)
IMPERIAL (9330 "Bus Stop") 35-50 66
(Monaural.)
IMPERIAL (9339 "Stop! Stop! Stop!") 35-50 67
(Monaural.)
IMPERIAL (9350 "Greatest Hits") 40-60 67
(Monaural.)
IMPERIAL (12265 "Here I Go Again") 75-125 64
(Stereo. Black "Imperial Stereo" label.)
IMPERIAL (12299 "Hear! Here!") 30-50 65
(Stereo.)
IMPERIAL (12312 "The Hollies [Beat Group]") 25-50 66
(Stereo.)
IMPERIAL (12330 "Bus Stop") 25-50 66
(Stereo.)
IMPERIAL (12339 "Stop! Stop! Stop!") 25-50 67
(Stereo.)
IMPERIAL (12350 "Greatest Hits") 25-50 67
(Stereo.)
LIBERTY 5-10 84
U.A. (329 "Very Best") 8-12 75
Members: Allan Clarke; Graham Nash; Bobby Elliott; Tony Hicks; Terry Sylvester.
Also see BAMBOO
Also see CLARKE, Allan
Also see EVERLY BROTHERS
Also see NASH, Graham
Also see PARSONS, Alan, Project
Also see SPRINGSTEEN, Bruce / Johnny Winter / Hollies
Also see TREMELOES / Hollies

HOLLIES / Peter Sellers

Singles: 7-inch

U.A. (50079 "After the Fox") 10-20 66

LPs: 10/12-inch

U.A. (286 "After the Fox") 8-10 74
(Soundtrack.)
U.A. (4148 "After the Fox") 15-25 66
(Soundtrack. Monaural.)
U.A. (5148 "After the Fox") 25-35 66
(Soundtrack. Stereo.)
Also see HOLLIES

HOLLOWAY, Brenda — P&R/R&B '64

(With the Carrolls)

Singles: 7-inch

BREVIT 5-10 63
CATCH (109 You're My Only Love") 15-25 64
DONNA (1358 "Echo") 20-40 62
TAMLA ("Play It Cool, Stay in School") 300-500 60s
(No selection number used. Promotional issue only.)

TAMLA (54094 "Every Little Bit Hurts")....................5-10 64
TAMLA (54099 "I'll Always Love You")....................10-15 65
TAMLA (54099 "I'll Always Love You")....................50-100 65
(Single-sided. Promotional issue only.)
TAMLA (54111 "When I'm Gone") 5-10 65
TAMLA (54115 thru 54137)..............10-20 65-66
TAMLA (54144 "Til Johnny Comes")....................100-200 67
TAMLA (54148 "Just Look What You've Done")....................10-20 67
TAMLA (54155 "I Got to Find It").......10-20 67

Picture Sleeves

TAMLA (54111 "When I'm Gone") 20-40 65

LPs: 10/12-inch

MOTOWN (5242 "Every Little Bit Hurts")....................5-10 80s
(Stereo.)
TAMLA (257 "Every Little Bit Hurts")....................100-200 65

HOLLOWAY, Brenda, & Jess Harris

Singles: 7-inch

BREVIT ("Never Knew You Looked") 25-35 63
(Number not known.)
Also see HOLLOWAY, Brenda

HOLLOWAY, Loleatta R&B '73

(With the Salsoul Orchestra)

Singles: 12-inch

SALSOUL....................4-8 83
STREETWISE....................4-8 84

Singles: 7-inch

AWARE....................3-5 73-75
GRC....................3-5 73
GALAXY....................3-5 71
GOLD MINE....................3-5 76-77
SALSOUL....................3-4 77-83

LPs: 10/12-inch

GOLD MINE....................5-10 77
Also see SALSOUL ORCHESTRA

HOLLOWAY, Loleatta, & Bunny Sigler P&R/R&B '78

Singles: 7-inch

GOLD MINE....................3-5 78
Also see HOLLOWAY, Loleatta
Also see SIGLER, Bunny

HOLLY, Buddy P&R/R&B '57

(With the Crickets; with Three Tunes; with Picks)

Singles: 12-inch

SOLID SMOKE....................10-20 79
(Picture disc.)

Singles: 78 rpm

BRUNSWICK (55009 "That'll Be the Day")....................100-150 57
BRUNSWICK (55035 "Oh Boy") ... 100-150 58
BRUNSWICK (55053 "Maybe Baby")....................100-150 58
BRUNSWICK (55072 "Think It Over")....................100-150 58
BRUNSWICK (55094 "It's So Easy")....................100-150 58
CORAL (61852 "Words of Love")....................150-250 57
CORAL (61885 "Peggy Sue")........100-150 57
CORAL (61947 "Listen to Me")......100-150 58
CORAL (61985 "Rave On")..........100-150 58
CORAL (62006 "Early in the Morning")....................100-150 58
CORAL (62051 "Heartbeat") 100-150 58
DECCA (29854 "Blue Days - Black Nights")....................100-150 56
DECCA (30166 "Modern Don Juan")....................100-150 56
DECCA (30434 "That'll Be the Day")....................100-150 57
DECCA (30543 "Love Me") 100-150 58
DECCA (30650 "Ting-A-Ling") 100-150 58

Singles: 7-inch

BRUNSWICK (55009 "That'll Be the Day")....................25-35 57
BRUNSWICK (55035 "Oh Boy")....... 25-35 58
BRUNSWICK (55053 "Maybe Baby")....................20-30 58
BRUNSWICK (55072 "Think It Over")....................20-30 58
BRUNSWICK (55094 "It's So Easy")....................20-30 58
CORAL (61852 "Words of Love")....................150-200 57
CORAL (61885 "Peggy Sue")........... 20-30 57
CORAL (61947 "Listen to Me")......... 20-30 58
CORAL (61985 "Rave On") 20-30 58
CORAL (62006 "Early in the Morning")....................20-30 58
CORAL (62051 "Heartbeat")............ 20-30 58
CORAL (62074 "It Doesn't Matter Anymore")....................20-30 59
CORAL (62134 "Peggy Sue Got Married")....................30-40 59
(Orange label.)
CORAL (62134 "Peggy Sue Got Married")....................10-20 62
(Yellow label.)
CORAL (62210 "True Love Ways") .. 30-40 60
CORAL (62329 "Reminiscing")......... 20-30 62
CORAL (62352 "Bo Diddley") 25-35 63
CORAL (62369 "Brown Eyed Handsome Man")....................25-35 63
CORAL (62390 "Rock Around with Ollie Vee")....................30-40 64
CORAL (62407 "Maybe Baby")......... 30-40 64
CORAL (62448 "Slippin' & Slidin' ") .. 50-75 65
CORAL (62554 "Rave On") 25-35 68
CORAL (62558 "Love Is Strange") ... 15-25 69
CORAL (65618 "That'll Be the Day") 15-25 69
DECCA (29854 "Blue Days - Black Nights")....................100-150 56
(With silver lines on both sides of the name Decca.)
DECCA (29854 "Blue Days - Black Nights")....................75-100 56
(With a star and silver lines under the name Decca.)
DECCA (30166 "Modern Don Juan")....................100-150 56
(With silver lines on both sides of the name Decca.)
DECCA (30166 "Modern Don Juan")....................75-100 56
(With a star and silver lines under the name Decca.)
DECCA (30434 "That'll Be the Day")....................100-150 57
(With silver lines on both sides of the name Decca.)
DECCA (30434 "That'll Be the Day")....................75-100 57
(With a star and silver lines under the name Decca.)
DECCA (30543 "Love Me")........... 100-150 58
(With silver lines on both sides of the name Decca.)
DECCA (30543 "Love Me")............ 75-100 58
(With a star and silver lines under the name Decca.)
DECCA (30650 "Ting-A-Ling")...... 100-150 58
(With silver lines on both sides of the name Decca.)
DECCA (30650 "Ting-A-Ling")....... 75-100 58
(With a star and silver lines under the name Decca.)
MCA....................3-6 73-78
MEMORY LANE....................3-5

Promotional Singles

BRUNSWICK (55009 "That'll Be the Day")....................50-100 57
BRUNSWICK (55035 "Oh Boy")..... 50-100 58
BRUNSWICK (55053 "Maybe Baby")....................50-100 58
BRUNSWICK (55072 "Think It Over")....................50-100 58
BRUNSWICK (55094 "It's So Easy")....................50-100 58
CORAL (61852 "Words of Love")....................150-200 57
CORAL (61885 "Peggy Sue")........100-150 57
CORAL (61947 "Listen to Me")........50-100 58
CORAL (61985 "Rave On")............50-100 58
CORAL (62006 "Early in the Morning")....................50-75 58
CORAL (62051 "Heartbeat") 50-75 58
CORAL (62074 "It Doesn't Matter Anymore")....................50-75 59
CORAL (62134 "Peggy Sue Got Married")....................50-75 59
CORAL (62210 "True Love Ways")... 50-75 60
CORAL (62329 "Reminiscing") 50-75 62
CORAL (62352 "Bo Diddley")............50-75 63
CORAL (62369 "Brown Eyed Handsome Man")....................50-75 63
CORAL (62390 "Rock Around with Ollie Vee")....................50-75 64
CORAL (62407 "Maybe Baby") 50-75 64
CORAL (62448 "Slippin' & Slidin' ")... 50-75 65
CORAL (62554 "Rave On")..............40-60 68
CORAL (62558 "Love Is Strange")....40-60 69
(Price doubles if accompanied by dee jay insert sheet.)
CORAL (65618 "That'll Be the Day")....................40-60 69
DECCA (29854 "Blue Days - Black Nights")....................100-150 56
DECCA (30166 "Modern Don Juan")....................100-150 56
DECCA (30434 "That'll Be the Day")....................100-150 57
DECCA (30543 "Love Me").......... 100-150 58
DECCA (30650 "Ting-A-Ling") 100-150 58

Picture Sleeves

CORAL (62558 "Love Is Strange").... 10-15 69
MCA....................3-5 78

EPs: 7-inch

BRUNSWICK (71036 "The Chirping Crickets")....................300-350 57
(With printed back cover.)
BRUNSWICK (71036 "The Chirping Crickets")....................350-450 57
(With blank back cover.)
BRUNSWICK (71038 "The Sound of the Crickets")....................100-200 58
CORAL (81169 "Listen to Me")...... 200-300 58
CORAL (81182 "The Buddy Holly Story")....................150-250 59
CORAL (81191 "Buddy Holly")...... 150-250 62
CORAL (81193 "Brown Eyed Handsome Man")....................100-200 63
DECCA (2575 "That'll Be the Day")....................500-750 58
(With liner notes on the back cover.)
DECCA (2575 "That'll Be the Day")....................400-600 58
(With EP ads on the back cover.)

LPs: 10/12-inch

BRUNSWICK (54038 "The Chirping Crickets")....................200-300 57
CORAL (8 "Best of Buddy Holly").... 75-125 66
CORAL (57210 "Buddy Holly") 100-150 58
(Maroon label.)
CORAL (57210 "Buddy Holly") 25-50 63
(Black label.)
CORAL (57279 "The Buddy Holly Story")....................75-100 59
(Maroon label. Red and black print on the back cover.)
CORAL (57279 "The Buddy Holly Story")....................50-75 59
(Maroon label. Black print on the back cover.)
CORAL (57279 "The Buddy Holly Story")....................30-40 63
(Black label. Has either pictures of other LPs, or black print, on the back cover.)
CORAL (57326 "The Buddy Holly Story, Vol. II")....................100-125 60
(Maroon label.)
CORAL (57326 "The Buddy Holly Story, Vol. II")....................25-50 63
(Black label.)
CORAL (57405 "Buddy Holly and the Crickets")....................50-75 62
(Maroon label.)

CORAL (57405 "Buddy Holly and the Crickets") 25-45 63
(Black label.)
CORAL (57426 "Reminiscing") 50-75 63
(Maroon label.)
CORAL (57426 "Reminiscing") 20-40 63
(Black label.)
CORAL (57450 "Showcase")....40-50 64
CORAL (57463 "Holly in the Hills") 75-100 65
CORAL (57492 "Buddy Holly's Greatest Hits") 75-100 67
CORAL (757279 "The Buddy Holly Story") 25-35 63
(Stereo.)
CORAL (757405 "Buddy Holly and the Crickets") 50-75 62
(Maroon label. Stereo.)
CORAL (757405 "Buddy Holly and the Crickets") 25-45 63
(Black label. Stereo.)
CORAL (757463 "Holly in the Hills") 40-60 65
(Stereo.)
CORAL (757504 "Giant")....40-80 69
(Stereo.)
CREATIVE RADIO ("The Day the Music Died") 25-30
(Two-LP set, includes poster.)
DECCA (207 "A Rock & Roll Collection") 15-20 72
DECCA (8707 "That'll Be the Day") 250-350 58
(Black label.)
DECCA (8707 "That'll Be the Day") 150-250 61
(Multi-color label.)
LIFE (8707 "That'll Be the Day")....150-250 61
(Multi-color Decca label, but with "Life" on label instead of Decca. Cover shows Decca, not Life.)
MCA (Except 6-80000)....8-15 75-85
MCA (6-80000 "The Complete Buddy Holly") 30-40 81
(Boxed six-disc set.)
VOCALION (3811 "The Great Buddy Holly") 90-110 67
(Monaural.)
VOCALION (73811 "The Great Buddy Holly") 20-30 67
(Reprocessed stereo.)
VOCALION (73923 "Good Rockin' Buddy Holly") 100-125 71
(Reprocessed stereo.)

Promotional LPs

BRUNSWICK (54038 "The Chirping Crickets") 300-400 57
CORAL (Except 757504)....50-75 58-65
CORAL (757504 "Giant")....35-45 69
DECCA (8707 "That'll Be the Day") 400-500 58
(Pink label.)
PICK (1111 "Buddy Holly and the Picks")....10-12 86

Also see BEATLES / Beach Boys / Buddy Holly
Also see CRICKETS
Also see FREED, Alan
Also see JENNINGS, Waylon
Also see KING, Ben E.
Also see PETTY, Norman, Trio
Also see PRESLEY, Elvis / Buddy Holly

HOLLY & ITALIANS LP '81

(Featuring Holly Beth Vincent)

Singles: 7-inch

OVAL....3-5
VIRGIN 3-4 82

Picture Sleeves

OVAL....3-5

LPs: 10/12-inch

VIRGIN 5-10 81-82

HOLLYRIDGE STRINGS P&R/LP '64

(Stu Phillips & Hollyridge Strings)

Singles: 7-inch

CAPITOL....3-6 61-68

EPs: 7-inch

CAPITOL (2626 "Selections from *Beatles Songbook*")....5-10 64
(Promotional issue only.)

LPs: 10/12-inch

CAPITOL....5-15 64-78

Also see GOLDEN GATE STRINGS

HOLLYWOOD ARGYLES P&R/R&B '60

Singles: 7-inch

ABC....3-4 74
CHATTAHOOCHEE 4-8 65
ERA....3-5 72
FELSTED....4-8 63
FINER ARTS....4-8 61
LUTE....5-10 60
PAXLEY 5-10 61

LPs: 10/12-inch

LUTE (9001 "Alley Oop") 250-350 60
Members: Gary Paxton; Gary Webb; Bobby Rey. Session: Gaynel Hodge.

HOLLYWOOD FLAMES

(Dave Ford & Hollywood Flames; "with Orchestra Acc.") P&R/R&B '57

Singles: 78 rpm

DECCA 20-30 54-55
EBB....10-20 57-58
LUCKY (001 "One Night with a Fool")....100-150 54
LUCKY (006 "Peggy") 100-150 54
LUCKY (009 "Let's Talk It Over")....50-100 54
MONEY (202 "I'm Leaving")....100-150 54
SWING TIME (345 "Let's Talk It Over") 100-200 53
SWING TIME (346 "Go and Get Some More")....100-200 54

Singles: 7-inch

ATCO (6155 "If I Thought You Needed Me")....15-20 59
ATCO (6164 "Ball and Chain")....10-20 60
ATCO (6171 "Devil Or Angel")....15-20 60
ATCO (6180 "Money Honey") 15-20 60
CHESS (1787 "Gee")....15-20 61
DECCA (29285 "Peggy") 50-100 54
DECCA (48331 "Let's Talk It Over")....50-100 55
EBB (119 "Buzz, Buzz, Buzz")....15-25 57
EBB (131 "Give Me Back My Heart")....15-25 58
EBB (144 "Strollin' on the Beach")....15-25 58
EBB (146 "Chains of Love")....15-25 58
EBB (149 "A Star Fell")....15-25 58
EBB (153 "Just for You")....15-25 58
EBB (158 "So Good")....15-25 58
EBB (162 "Now That You've Gone")....15-25 59
EBB (163 "In the Dark") 15-25 59
GOLDIE (1101 "Believe in Me")....10-15 62
LUCKY (001 "One Night with a Fool")....500-750 54
LUCKY (006 "Peggy")....500-750 54
LUCKY (009 "Let's Talk It Over")..300-500 54
MONA-LEE (135 "Buzz, Buzz, Buzz")....15-25 59
MONEY (202 "I'm Leaving")....500-750 54
SWING TIME (345 "Let's Talk It Over")....500-750 53
SWING TIME (346 "Go and Get Some More")....500-750 54
SYMBOL (211 "Dance Senorita") 10-20 65
SYMBOL (215 "I'm Coming Home")....10-20 66
VEE JAY (515 "Letter to My Love")...10-20 63

LPs: 10/12-inch

SPECIALTY 8-10 88
Members: David Ford; Bobby Byrd; Gaynel Hodge; Clyde Tillis; Earl Nelson; Curtis Williams; Donald Height; Ray Brewster; John Berry; George Home.

HOLLYWOOD STARS P&R '77

Singles: 7-inch

ARISTA....3-5 77

LPs: 10/12-inch

ARISTA....8-10 77

Also see KINKS / Hollywood Stars

HOLLYWOOD STUDIO ORCH. LP '61

Singles: 7-inch

U.A. 4-8 59

LPs: 10/12-inch

U.A. 10-15 61

HOLM, Michael P&R '74

Singles: 7-inch

MERCURY 3-5 74

HOLMAN, Eddie R&B '65

Singles: 7-inch

ABC 5-10 69-71
AGAPE 3-4 82
ASCOT (2142 "Laughing at Me") 10-20 63
BELL....10-20 68
CAMEO (253 "Crossroads")....15-25 63
DON-EL (124 "She's Beautiful")....15-25 60s
GSF 3-6 73
PARKWAY 10-20 65-67
SALSOUL....3-5 77
SILVER BLUE 3-6 74

LPs: 10/12-inch

ABC-PAR 10-12 70
SALSOUL....5-10 77

HOLMAN, Eddie / Lamplighters

Singles: 7-inch

SCRIPT (12212 "Never Let Go")....10-20
(Colored vinyl. Promotional issue only.)

Also see HOLMAN, Eddie

HOLMES, Clint P&R/LP '73

Singles: 7-inch

ATCO....3-5 74
EPIC 3-5 73
PRIVATE STOCK....3-5 76-79

LPs: 10/12-inch

EPIC 10-12 73

HOLMES, Jake P&R/LP '70

Singles: 7-inch

COLUMBIA....3-5 71-72
POLYDOR....3-5 70
TOWER....4-6 67

Picture Sleeves

TOWER....4-6 67

LPs: 10/12-inch

POLYDOR....8-12 70
TOWER....10-15 67

HOLMES, Jan R&B '85

Singles: 7-inch

JAY JAY 3-4 85

HOLMES, Leroy, Orchestra P&R '54

Singles: 78 rpm

MGM....3-5 51-57

Singles: 7-inch

MGM....4-8 51-61
METRO....3-6 59
U.A. 3-5 67-68

Picture Sleeves

U.A. 4-8 67

EPs: 7-inch

MGM....4-8 52-56
U.A. (10041 "Leroy Holmes & His Orchestra") 4-8 67
(Promotional issue only.)

LPs: 10/12-inch

LION 5-10 59-60
MGM....5-15 52-62
U.A. 4-8 67-68

HOLMES, Richard "Groove"

P&R/R&B/LP '66

Singles: 7-inch

BLUE NOTE 3-5 71
FLYING DUTCHMAN....3-5 76
PACIFIC JAZZ....4-8 61-69
PRESTIGE 3-6 66-69

LPs: 10/12-inch

BLUE NOTE 5-10 71
FLYING DUTCHMAN....5-10 75-76
GROOVE MERCHANT 5-10 72-75
LOMA 10-15 66

MUSE 5-10 78-80
PACIFIC JAZZ (Except 20000 series) 15-25 61-62
PACIFIC JAZZ (20000 series) 8-15 68-69
PRESTIGE 8-15 66-70
VERSATILE 5-10 78
W.B. 10-20 64
WORLD PACIFIC JAZZ 8-12 70
Also see AMMONS, Gene, & Richard "Groove" Holmes
Also see JONES, Brenda, & "Groove" Holmes
Also see McGRIFF, Jimmy
Also see WITHERSPOON, Jimmy

HOLMES, Richard "Groove," & Les McCann

LPs: 10/12-inch

PACIFIC JAZZ 15-25 62
Also see HOLMES, Richard "Groove"
Also see McCANN, Les

HOLMES, Rupert P&R '78

Singles: 7-inch

EPIC 3-6 74-76
INFINITY (50035 "Escape") 3-5 79
(May also be found on exact same label, but with MCA instead of Infinity.)
MCA 3-5 80-81
PRIVATE STOCK 3-5 78

Picture Sleeves

EPIC 3-4 75

LPs: 10/12-inch

ELEKTRA 5-10 81
EPIC 8-12 74-75
EXCELSIOR 5-8 80-81
INFINITY 5-10 79
MCA 5-10 80
PRIVATE STOCK 5-10 78
Also see CUFF LINKS
Also see STREET PEOPLE

HOMBRES P&R/LP '67

Singles: 7-inch

SUN 4-8 69
VERVE/FORECAST (Except 5058) 4-8 67-68
VERVE/FORECAST (5058 "Let It All Hang Out") 5-10 67
VERVE/FORECAST (5058 "Let It Out") 4-8 67
(Note shortened title.)

LPs: 10/12-inch

VERVE/FORECAST 15-20 67

HOMER & JETHRO C&W/P&R '49

Singles: 78 rpm

KING 5-15 46-53
FEDERAL 8-15 51
RCA 5-15 50-58

Singles: 7-inch

BLUEBIRD 4-8 59
KING 3-6 63
RCA (0100 series) 30-50 50
(Colored vinyl.)
RCA (0100 thru 0468) 15-30 50-51
(Black vinyl.)
RCA (0500 series) 3-5 71
RCA (4290 thru 7704) 10-20 51-59
RCA (47-7744 "Sink the Bismarck") 8-12 60
(Monaural.)
RCA (61-7744 "Sink the Bismarck") .. 15-25 60
(Stereo.)
RCA (7790 thru 9922) 4-8 60-70

Picture Sleeves

RCA (5000 series) 8-12 53
RCA (8000 series) 3-6 64

EPs: 7-inch

AUDIO LAB 10-20 59
KING 15-25 53-54
RCA 15-25 53-57

LPs: 10/12-inch

AUDIO LAB (1513 "Musical Madness") 25-50 58
CAMDEN 10-20 62-71
DIPLOMAT 8-12
GUEST STAR 10-15 63
KING (639 "They Sure Are Corny") ... 20-30 59
KING (800 series) 10-20 63
KING (1000 series) 8-12 67
NASHVILLE 8-12 69
RCA (1412 "Barefoot Ballads") 20-40 57
RCA (1516 "Worst of Homer & Jethro") 20-40 57
RCA (LPM-1880 "Life Can Be Miserable") 20-30 58
(Monaural.)
RCA (LSP-1880 "Life Can Be Miserable") 25-35 58
(Stereo.)
RCA (2100 thru 2900 series) 15-25 60-64
(Monaural. With "LPM" prefix.)
RCA (2100 thru 2900 series) 20-30 60-64
(Stereo. With "LSP" prefix.)
RCA (3112 "Homer & Jethro Fracture Frank Loesser") 30-60 53
(10-inch LP.)
RCA (3300 thru 4600 series) 15-30 65-72
Members: Henry "Homer" Haynes; Kenneth "Jethro" Burns.
Also see ANN-MARGRET
Also see COUNTRY ALL STARS
Also see FOUR LOVERS / Homer & Jethro
Also see JONES, Spike

HOMER & JETHRO & JUNE CARTER C&W '49

Singles: 78 rpm

RCA 5-10 49
Also see HOMER & JETHRO

HONDELLS P&R/LP '64

Singles: 7-inch

AMOS 4-8 69-70
COLUMBIA 5-10 67-68
MERCURY (72324 "Little Honda") 10-15 64
MERCURY (72366 "My Buddy Seat") 10-15 64
MERCURY (72405 "Little Sidewalk Surfer Girl") 8-12 65
MERCURY (72443 "Sea of Love") 8-12 65
MERCURY (72479 "Sea Cruise") 5-10 65
MERCURY (72523 "Follow Your Heart") 5-10 66
MERCURY (72563 "Younger Girl") 5-10 67
MERCURY (72605 "Kissin' My Life Away") 5-10 67

Promotional Singles

MERCURY (72324 "Hot Rod High") 20-25 64
(Shows *Hot Rod High* as the "A" side.)
MERCURY (72324 "Little Honda") 15-20 64
(Shows *Little Honda* as the "A" side.)
MERCURY (72366 "My Buddy Seat") 15-20 64
MERCURY (72405 thru 72605) 8-12 65-67

Picture Sleeves

MERCURY (72366 "My Buddy Seat") 10-20 64
MERCURY (72479 "Sea Cruise") 10-20 65

LPs: 10/12-inch

MERCURY (20940 "Go, Little Honda") 20-25 64
(Monaural.)
MERCURY (60940 "Go, Little Honda") 25-30 64
(Stereo.)
MERCURY (20982 "The Hondells") .. 20-25 64
(Monaural.)
MERCURY (20982 "The Hondells") .. 25-30 65
(Stereo.)
Members: Chuck Girard; Richard Burns; Brian Wilson; Wayne Edwards; Glen Campbell; Joe Kelly; Bruce Johnston; Terry Melcher; Jerry Naylor; Gary Usher. Session: Davie Allan.
Also see ALLEN, Davie
Also see BRUCE & TERRY
Also see CAMPBELL, Glen
Also see NAYLOR, Jerry
Also see WILSON, Brian

HONDELLS / Del Shannon / Martha & Vandellas

EPs: 7-inch

PEPSI-COLA (8256 "Pepsi-Cola Ad Radio Youth Market, 1966") 15-20 66
(Promotional issue only.)
Also see MARTHA & VANDELLAS
Also see SHANNON, Del

HONDELLS / Dusty Springfield

Singles: 7-inch

COLLECTABLES 3-4 86
Also see HONDELLS
Also see SPRINGFIELD, Dusty

HONEY CONE P&R/R&B '69

Singles: 7-inch

HOT WAX 3-6 69-76

LPs: 10/12-inch

HOT WAX 8-10 70-72
Members: Edna Wright; Carolyn Willis; Shellie Clark; Sharon Cash.
Also see BOB B. SOXX & Blue Jeans
Also see GIRLFRIENDS

HONEYCOMBS P&R '64

Singles: 7-inch

INTERPHON 5-10 64-65
W.B. 5-10 65-66

Picture Sleeves

INTERPHON (7713 "I Can't Stop") 10-20 64

LPs: 10/12-inch

INTERPHON (88001 "Here Are the Honeycombs") 20-30 64
VEE JAY (88001 "Here Are the Honeycombs") 35-45 64
Members: Honey Lantree; John Lantree; Martin Murray; Denis D'Ell; Alan Ward.

HONEYCONES P&R '58

Singles: 7-inch

EMBER 8-12 58-59

HONEYCUTT, Miki R&B '77

Singles: 7-inch

PAULA 3-5 77

HONEYDRIPPERS P&R/LP '84

Singles: 7-inch

ESPARANZA 3-4 84-85

Picture Sleeves

ESPARANZA 3-4 84-85

LPs: 10/12-inch

ESPARANZA 5-10 84
Members: Jeff Beck; Jimmy Page; Robert Plant; Nile Rodgers.
Also see BECK, Jeff
Also see CHIC
Also see PAGE, Jimmy
Also see PLANT, Robert
Also see RODGERS, Nile

HONEYMOON SUITE P&R/LP '84

Singles: 7-inch

W.B. 3-4 84-88

Picture Sleeves

W.B. 3-4 84-88

LPs: 10/12-inch

W.B. 5-10 84-88

HOODOO GURUS LP '86

Singles: 7-inch

A&M 3-4 85
RCA 3-4 89-90

LPs: 10/12-inch

A&M 5-10 85
ELEKTRA 5-10 86-87
RCA 5-8 89-91
Members: David Faulkner; Rick Grossman.
Also see DIVINYLS

HOOK, Dr: see DR. HOOK

HOOKER, Frank, & Positive People R&B '79

Singles: 7-inch

PANORAMA 3-4 79-80

HOOKER, John Lee — R&B '49

Singles: 78 rpm

CHART....10-20 53
CHESS (1505 "High Priced Woman")....50-75 52
CHESS (1513 "Walkin' the Boogie")....25-50 52
CHESS (1562 "It's My Own Fault")....20-30 54
JVB....20-30 53
MODERN....20-30 48-56
REGAL....15-25 50-51
SENSATION....20-30 49-50
SPECIALTY....10-20 54
VEE JAY....10-20 55-60

Singles: 7-inch

ABC....3-5 71-73
BATTLE....4-8 62
BLUESWAY....4-6 67-69
CHART....10-15 53
CHESS (1505 "High Priced Woman")....200-300 52
CHESS (1513 "Walkin' the Boogie")....100-150 52
CHESS (1562 "It's My Own Fault")....50-100 54
CHESS (1900 series)....4-8 66
ELMOR (303 "Blues for Christmas")....10-20
FEDERAL....10-15 60
FORTUNE....5-10 60
GALAXY....4-8 63
HI-Q (5018 "609 Boogie")....10-20 61
JVB (30 "Boogie Rambler")....100-150 53
JEWEL....3-5 70-77
KING....3-5 70
LAUREN....4-8 61
MODERN (835 "How Can You Do It")....30-60 51
MODERN (862 "Cold Chills All Over Me")....30-60 52
MODERN (886 "Bluebird Blues")....30-60 52
MODERN (893 "New Boogie Chillen")....30-60 52
MODERN (897 "Rock House Boogie")....30-60 53
MODERN (901 "It's a Stormin' and Rainin' ")....25-50 53
MODERN (908 "Love Money Can't Buy")....25-50 53
MODERN (916 "Too Much Boogie")....25-50 53
MODERN (923 "Down Child")....25-50 54
MODERN (931 "I Wonder Little Darling")....25-50 54
MODERN (935 "I Tried Hard")....20-40 54
MODERN (942 "Cool Little Car")....20-40 54
MODERN (948 "Half a Stranger")....20-40 55
MODERN (958 "You Receive Me")....20-40 55
MODERN (966 "Hug & Squeeze")....20-40 55
MODERN (978 "Lookin' for a Woman")....20-40 56
SPECIALTY (528 "Everybody's Blues")....20-40 54
STARDAY....3-5 70
STAX....4-6 69
VEE JAY (164 "Mambo Chillen")....20-30 55
VEE JAY (188 "Every Night")....20-30 56
VEE JAY (205 "Baby Lee")....20-30 56
VEE JAY (233 "I'm So Worried, Baby")....15-25 57
VEE JAY (245 "I'm So Excited")....15-25 57
VEE JAY (255 "Little Wheel")....15-25 57
VEE JAY (265 "You Can Lead Me, Baby")....15-25 58
VEE JAY (293 "I Love You Honey")....15-25 58
VEE JAY (308 "Maudie")....15-25 59
VEE JAY (319 "Tennessee Blues")....15-25 59
VEE JAY (331 "Hobo Blues")....15-25 59
VEE JAY (349 "No Shoes")....15-25 60
VEE JAY (366 "Dusty Road")....15-25 60
VEE JAY (397 "Want Ad Blues")....15-25 60
VEE JAY (438 "Boom Boom")....10-15 62
VEE JAY (453 "She's Mine")....10-15 62
VEE JAY (493 "I Love Her")....25-50 63
VEE JAY (538 thru 708)....8-15 63-65

EPs: 7-inch

IMPULSE....8-10 66
(Juke box issues only.)

LPs: 10/12-inch

ABC....10-20 71-74
ARCHIVE of FOLK MUSIC....10-12 68
ATCO (151 "Don't Turn Me from Your Door")....20-25 63
(Monaural.)
ATCO (SD-151 "Don't Turn Me from Your Door")....25-30 63
(Stereo.)
ATLANTIC....8-10 72
BATTLE (6113 "John Lee Hooker")....30-50 60
BLUESWAY....15-30 66-73
BRYLEN....5-10 84
BUDDAH....12-15 69
CHAMELEON....5-8 89
CHESS (1438 "House of the Blues")....25-35 61
CHESS (1454 "John Lee Hooker Plays and Sings the Blues")....25-35 61
CHESS (1500 series)....15-20 66
CHESS (9000 series)....8-10
CHESS (60011 "Mad Man Blues")....10-15
CROWN....10-20 62-63
CUSTOM....10-15
EVEREST....5-10 79-83
EXODUS....8-10
FANTASY....8-10 72-77
FORTUNE....20-30 69
GNP....8-10 74
GALAXY (201 "John Lee Hooker")....20-30 63
GREEN BOTTLE....10-12 72
IMPULSE....12-15 66
JEWEL....10-12 71
KENT....10-12 71
KING (727 "John Lee Hooker Sings Blues")....50-75 61
KING (1000 series)....10-12 70
MCA....5-10 83
MUSE....5-10 80
SPECIALTY....10-15 70
(Black and gold label.)
SPECIALTY....5-10 88
(Black and white label.)
STAX (2000 series)....10-12 69
STAX (4000 series)....8-10 77
TOMATO....5-10 78
TRADITION....10-12 69
TRIP....8-10 73-78
UNITED....10-12
U.A.....12-15 71-73
VEE JAY (1007 "I'm John Lee Hooker")....40-60 59
(Maroon label.)
VEE JAY (1007 "I'm John Lee Hooker")....20-30 61
(Black label.)
VEE JAY (1023 thru 1043)....25-40 60-62
VEE JAY (1049 thru 1078)....15-25 62-64
VEE JAY (8502 "Is He the World's Greatest Blues Singer?")....25-35
VERVE/FOLKWAYS....10-15 66
WAND....10-12 70

Also see BIRMINGHAM SAM & His Magic Guitar
Also see BOOGIE MAN
Also see BOOKER, John Lee
Also see COOKER, John Lee
Also see DELTA JOHN
Also see JOHN LEE
Also see JOHNNY LEE
Also see LITTLE PORK CHOPS
Also see MARTHA & VANDELLAS
Also see McGHEE, Sticks / John Lee Hooker
Also see MEMPHIS SLIM
Also see TEXAS SLIM
Also see WILLIAMS, Johnny

HOOKER, John Lee, & Canned Heat — LP '71

Singles: 7-inch

U.A. 3-5 71

LPs: 10/12-inch

LIBERTY....10-15 71
TRIP....5-10 74

Also see CANNED HEAT

HOOKER, John Lee / Lightnin' Hopkins / J. Carroll

LPs: 10/12-inch

GUEST STAR....15-20 64

Also see HOPKINS, Lightnin'

HOOKER, John Lee, & Little Eddie Kirkland

Singles: 78 rpm

MODERN (876 "It's Hurts Me So ")....15-25 52

Singles: 7-inch

MODERN (876 "It's Hurts Me So ")....30-60 52

HOOKER, John Lee / Eddie Kirkland / Eddie Burns / Sylvester Cotton

LPs: 10/12-inch

UNITED (7783 "Detroit Blues")....10-20

Also see HOOKER, John Lee

HOOPER, Stix — LP '79

Singles: 7-inch

MCA....3-4 79-82

LPs: 10/12-inch

MCA....5-10 79-82

Also see BUTLER, Jerry, & Stix Hooper
Also see CRUSADERS

HOOTERS — P&R/LP '85

Singles: 7-inch

ANTENNA (84 "Hanging on to a Heartbeat")....4-6 84
COLUMBIA....3-4 85-89
88 PERCENT (80 "Fightin' on the Same Side")....5-10 81
88 PERCENT (82 "All You Zombies")....5-10 82
MONTAGE....3-4 83

Picture Sleeves

ANTENNA (84 "Hanging on to a Heartbeat")....4-8 84
COLUMBIA....3-4 85-87
88 PERCENT ("Fightin' on the Same Side")....5-10 81
88 PERCENT (82 "All You Zombies")....5-10 82

LPs: 10/12-inch

COLUMBIA....5-10 85-89

Members: Rob Hyman; Eric Bazillian.

Also see CONWELL, Tommy, & Young Rumblers
Also see LAUPER, Cyndi

HOPE, Bob — LP '76

Singles: 78 rpm

CAPITOL....3-5 52
RCA....3-5 56
("The Paleface")....75-100 44
(Label name and selection number not known. Santa Claus-shaped cardboard. Promotional issue only for the film *The Paleface*.)

Singles: 7-inch

CAPITOL....5-10 52
RCA....5-10 56

LPs: 10/12-inch

CAPITOL....5-10 76
DECCA....10-20 63
RCA....15-25 60

Also see BACKUS, Jim
Also see CROSBY, Bing, & Bob Hope
Also see MARTIN, Dean

HOPE, Bob, & Eydie Adams

Singles: 7-inch

U.A.....4-6 63

Picture Sleeves

U.A.....4-8 63

HOPE, Bob, & Rosemary Clooney

Singles: 7-inch

RCA....4-8 59

Also see HOPE, Bob
Also see CLOONEY, Rosemary

HOPE, Ellie — D&D '83

Singles: 12-inch

QUALITY....4-6 83

HOPE, Lynn — R&B '50
(Lynn Hope Quintet)

Singles: 78 rpm

ALADDIN ... 15-25 54-56
PREMIUM ... 5-10 50

Singles: 7-inch

ALADDIN ... 10-20 54-56
CHESS ... 5-10
KING ... 5-10 60

LPs: 10/12-inch

ALADDIN (707 "Lynn Hope & His Tenor Sax") ... 100-200 55
(10-inch LP.)
ALADDIN (850 "Lynn Hope") ... 100-150 56
IMPERIAL ... 15-25 62
KING ... 15-25 61
SCORE (4015 "Tenderly") ... 50-75 57

HOPKIN, Mary — P&R '68
(Mary Hopkins)

Singles: 7-inch

APPLE/AMERICOM (238 "Those Were the Days") ... 250-350 69
(Four-inch flexi, "pocket disc.")
APPLE ... 5-10 68-72
ESKEE ... 4-8 66
RCA ... 3-5 76

Promotional Singles

ESKEE ... 4-8 66
RCA ... 3-5 76

Picture Sleeves

APPLE ... 5-10 68-70

LPs: 10/12-inch

AIR ... 8-10 72
APPLE ... 15-25 69-72
APPLE/CAPITOL RECORD CLUB (5-3351 "Postcard") ... 30-40 69

HOPKINS, Lightnin' — R&B '49
(Lightning Hopkins)

Singles: 78 rpm

ACE ... 10-20 56
ALADDIN (3063 thru 3262) ... 25-50 50
CHART ... 10-15 55
DECCA ... 10-15 53
GOLD STAR (Except 671) ... 20-40 47-50
GOLD STAR (671 "Henny Penny Blues") ... 25-50 50
HARLEM ... 20-30 54-55
HERALD ... 25-35 54-55
JAX ... 25-50 53-54
LIGHTNING ... 100-150 55
MERCURY ... 15-25 52
MODERN ... 20-40 47-49
RPM ... 20-40 52-54
SITTIN' in WITH ... 25-50 51-53
TNT ... 50-75 53-54

Singles: 7-inch

ACE (516 "My Little Kewpie Doll") ... 20-30 56
ALADDIN (3063 "Shotgun") ... 75-100 50
ALADDIN (3077 "Moonrise Blues") ... 75-100 50
ALADDIN (3096 "Abilene") ... 75-100 51
ALADDIN (3117 "You Are Not Going to Worry My Life Anymore") ... 75-100 52
ALADDIN (3262 "My California") ... 50-75 54
ARHOOLIE ... 4-8 65
BLUESVILLE ... 8-15 60-63
CANDID ... 4-8 60-62
CHART ... 10-20 55
DART ... 5-10 60
DECCA (28841 "The War Is Over") ... 15-25 53
DECCA (48306 "Merry Christmas") ... 15-25 53
DECCA (48312 "Highway Blues") ... 15-25 53
DECCA (48321 "I'm Wild About You, Baby") ... 15-25 53
FIRE ... 4-8 61
FLASHBACK ... 3-6 65
HARLEM (2321 "Contrary Mary") ... 100-150 54
HARLEM (2324 "Lightnin's Boogie") ... 100-150 54
HARLEM (2331 "Fast Life") ... 100-150 55
HARLEM (2336 "Old Woman Blues") ... 100-150 55
HERALD (425 "Lightnin's Boogie") ... 20-30 54
HERALD (428 "Lightnin's Special") ... 20-30 54
HERALD (436 "Sick Feeling Blues") ... 20-30 54
HERALD (443 "Nothin' But the Blues") ... 20-30 54
HERALD (449 "They Wonder Who I Am") ... 20-30 55
HERALD (471 "Hopkins' Sky Hop") ... 20-30 55
HERALD (476 "Grandma's Boogie") ... 20-30 56
HERALD (500 series) ... 15-25 59-60
IMPERIAL ... 10-15 62
IVORY ... 8-12 61
JAX (315 "No Good Woman") ... 150-250 53
(Colored vinyl.)
JAX (318 "Automobile") ... 150-250 53
(Colored vinyl.)
JAX (321 "Contrary Mary") ... 150-250 54
(Colored vinyl.)
JAX (635 "Coffee Blues") ... 100-200 54
(Colored vinyl.)
JAX (642 "You Caused My Heart to Weep") ... 100-200 54
(Colored vinyl.)
JEWEL ... 3-6 68-72
KENT ... 3-5
KIMBERLEY ... 5-10 60
LIGHTNING (104 "Unsuccessful Blues") ... 250-350 55
MERCURY (70081 "Ain't It a Shame") ... 50-75 52
MERCURY (70191 "My Mama Told Me") ... 50-75 52
MERCURY (8274 "Sad News from Korea") ... 50-75 52
MERCURY (8293 "Gone with the Wind") ... 50-75 52
PRESTIGE ... 4-8 60-67
RPM (337 "Beggin' You to Stay") ... 25-40 51
RPM (346 "Jake Head") ... 50-75 52
RPM (351 "Don't Keep My Baby Long") ... 50-75 52
RPM (359 "Needed Time") ... 50-75 52
RPM (378 "Another Fool in Town") ... 50-75 53
RPM (388 "Black Cat") ... 50-75 53
RPM (398 "Sante Fe") ... 50-75 54
SHAD ... 5-10 59
SITTIN' in WITH (621 "New York Boogie") ... 150-250 51
(Colored vinyl.)
SITTIN' in WITH (635 "Coffee Blues") ... 150-250 52
(Colored vinyl.)
SITTIN' in WITH (642 "You Caused My Heart to Weep") ... 150-250 52
(Colored vinyl.)
SITTIN' in WITH (644 "Jailhouse Blues") ... 150-250 52
(Colored vinyl.)
SITTIN' in WITH (647 "Dirty House") ... 150-250 52
(Colored vinyl.)
SITTIN' in WITH (652 "Papa Bones Boogie") ... 150-250 52
(Colored vinyl.)
SITTIN' in WITH (658 "Broken Hearted Blues") ... 150-250 53
(Colored vinyl.)
SITTIN' in WITH (660 "I've Been a Bad Man") ... 150-250 53
(Colored vinyl.)
SITTIN' in WITH (661 "Down to the River") ... 150-250 53
(Colored vinyl.)
TNT (8002 "Late in the Evening") ... 200-300 54
TNT (8003 "Leavin' Blues") ... 200-300 54
TNT (8010 "Moanin' Blues") ... 200-300 55
VAULT ... 3-5 70

There is confusion as to which Jax and Sittin' in With singles are on colored plastic, which are black, and which came both ways. Any additional information will appear in the first available edition of the guide.

LPs: 10/12-inch

ARHOOLIE ... 10-15 68
BARNABY ... 8-10 71
BULLDOG ... 12-15 65
CANDID ... 20-30 61
COLLECTABLES ... 6-8 88
CROWN ... 20-25 61
DART ... 10-15
EVEREST (241 "Lightnin' Hopkins") ... 10-15 69
EVEREST (342 "Autobiography in Blues") ... 5-10 79
FANTASY ... 8-10 72-81
FIRE (104 "Mojo Hand") ... 75-100 62
GUEST STAR ... 15-20 64
HARLEM HITPARADE ... 5-10
HERALD (1012 "Lightnin' and the Blues") ... 150-250 60
IMPERIAL ... 20-30 62
INT'L ARTISTS (6 "Free Form Patterns") ... 50-100 68
JAZZ MAN ... 5-10 82
JEWEL ... 10-12 67-70
MAINSTREAM ... 8-10 71-74
MOUNT VERNON ... 15-20
OLYMPIC ... 8-10 73
PICKWICK ... 8-10
POPPY ... 12-15 69
PRESTIGE (Except 7370) ... 10-15 65-70
PRESTIGE (7370 "Interview") ... 20-25
PRESTIGE/BLUESVILLE ... 20-25 61-64
RHINO ... 5-10 82
SCORE (4022 "Lightnin' Hopkins Strums the Blues") ... 50-75 59
SOUL PARADE ... 8-10
TIME ... 25-30 60-62
TOMATO ... 5-10 77
TRADITION (1035 thru 1040) ... 20-30 60
TRADITION (1056 thru 2000) ... 10-15 67-72
TRIP ... 5-10 71-78
UNITED ... 8-10
UPFRONT ... 8-12
VAULT ... 10-12 69
VEE JAY ... 20-30 62
VERVE ... 15-20 62
VERVE/FOLKWAYS ... 12-15 65-67
WORLD PACIFIC (1817 "First Meeting") ... 30-35

Also see HOOKER, John Lee / Lightnin' Hopkins / Johnny Carroll

HOPKINS, Lightnin,' & Sonny Terry

Singles: 7-inch

PRESTIGE BLUESVILLE ... 4-8 61

LPs: 10/12-inch

PRESTIGE BLUESVILLE ... 15-20 61-63
Also see TERRY, Sonny

HOPKINS, Lightnin' / Brownie McGhee & Sonny Terry

LPs: 10/12-inch

HORIZON (WP-1617 "Blues Hoot") ... 20-25 63
(Monaural.)
HORIZON (ST-1617 "Blues Hoot") ... 25-30 63
(Stereo.)
Also see McGHEE, Brownie, & Sonny Terry

HOPKINS, Lightnin,' & Thunder Smith

Singles: 78 rpm

ALADDIN (165 "West Coast Blues") ... 75-100 47
ALADDIN (167 "Katie Mae Blues") ... 75-100 47
ALADDIN (168 "Feel So Bad") ... 75-100 47
Also see HOPKINS, Lightnin'

HOPKINS, Nicky — LP '72

Singles: 7-inch

COLUMBIA ... 3-5 72
DECCA (32139 "Mr. Pleasant") ... 5-10 67

LPs: 10/12-inch

COLUMBIA ... 8-10 73
ROLLING STONE ... 10-15 72
Session: Mick Jagger; Bill Wyman; Charlie Watts; Ry Cooder.
Also see COODER, Ry

Also see JEFFERSON AIRPLANE
Also see LORD SUTCH
Also see NIGHT
Also see QUICKSILVER
Also see ROLLING STONES

HORAN, Eddie — R&B '78

Singles: 7-inch

HDM 3-5 78
MGM 3-5 74

HORN, Paul — R&B '78

Singles: 7-inch

MUSHROOM 3-5 78

HORN, Paul — R&B '78

Singles: 7-inch

MUSHROOM 3-5 78

LPs: 10/12-inch

COLUMBIA (36803 "Jingle Bell Jazz") .. 5-8 85
COLUMBIA (1677 thru 2050) 20-30 61-63
(Monaural.)
COLUMBIA (8477 thru 8850) 25-35 61-63
(Stereo.)
DOT (3091 "House of Horn") 40-60 57
DOT (9002 "Plenty of Horn") 40-60 58
EPIC 6-12 69-76
EVEREST 5-10 75
GPB 5-8 87
HI-FI JAZZ (615 "Something Blue") ... 30-50 60
IMPULSE 5-10 78
KUCKUCK 5-10 80-88
MUSHROOM 5-10 77-78
OVATION 8-12 70
RCA (3414 thru 3613) 15-25 65-66
(With "LPM" prefix. Monaural.)
RCA (3414 thru 3613) 15-30 65-66
(With "LSP" prefix. Stereo.)
SHELTER 8-12 71
WHO'S WHO in JAZZ 5-8 86-88
WORLD PACIFIC (Except 1266) 10-20 67-68
WORLD PACIFIC (1266 "Impressions") 30-50 59

HORNE, Jimmy "Bo" — R&B '75

Singles: 12-inch

SUNSHINE SOUND 4-8 79

Singles: 7-inch

ALSTON 3-5 75-77
DADE (2031 "I Can't Speak") 35-55
SUNSHINE SOUND 3-5 77-80

LPs: 10/12-inch

SUNSHINE SOUND 5-10 78-80

HORNE, Lena — P&R '43

Singles: 78 rpm

RCA 3-5 52-57

Singles: 7-inch

BUDDAH 3-5 71
CHARTER 4-6 63
DRG 3-4 86
GRYPHON 3-5 76
MCA 3-4 78
RCA (4000 thru 7000 series) 5-10 52-61
20TH FOX 4-6 63-64
U.A. 3-6 65-66

Picture Sleeves

RCA 4-8 62

EPs: 7-inch

MGM 5-10 54-55
RCA 5-10 56-59

LPs: 10/12-inch

BUDDAH 5-10 71
CAMDEN 10-20 56
CHARTER 10-15 63
CORONET 5-10
DRG 5-10 86
GOLDEN TONE 5-10
GRYPHON 5-10 75-76
LIBERTY 5-8 81
MFSL (094 "Lady and Her Music") 25-40 82
MGM 15-30 54-55
POLYDOR 4-8
QWEST 5-10 81
RCA (Except 4300 series) 10-30 52-63
RCA (4300 series) 4-8 81
RADIO CRAFTSMEN 10-20
SPRINGBOARD 4-8 77
TOPS 15-30 56
20TH FOX 8-15 64
U.A. 8-15 65-66
Also see BELAFONTE, Harry, & Lena Horne
Also see FITZGERALD, Ella / Billie Holiday / Lena Horne

HORNE, Lena, & Michel Legrand

LPs: 10/12-inch

GRYPHON 5-10 75
Also see LEGRAND, Michel

HORNE, Lena, & Gabor Szabo — LP '70

(Lena & Gabor)

Singles: 7-inch

SKYE (4523 "Rocky Raccoon") 4-6 70

LPs: 10/12-inch

SKYE (15 "Lena & Gabor") 8-15 70
Also see HORNE, Lena
Also see SZABO, Gabor

HORNSBY, Bruce, & Range — P&R/LP '86

Singles: 7-inch

RCA 3-4 86-90

Picture Sleeves

RCA 3-4 87-88

LPs: 10/12-inch

RCA 5-10 86-90
Also see HENLEY, Don

HORSLIPS — LP '78

Singles: 7-inch

DJM (Except 1036) 3-5 77-79
DJM (1036 "Sure the Boy Was Green") 4-8 77
(Colored vinyl.)
MERCURY 3-5 79
RCA 3-5 75

LPs: 10/12-inch

ATCO 10-12 73-74
DJM 5-10 77-79
MERCURY 5-10 79-80
RCA 8-10 74
Members: Eamon Carr; John Fean; Jim Lockhart; Barry Devlin; Charles O'Connor.

HORTON, Jamie — P&R '60

Singles: 7-inch

ERIC 3-5 68
JOY 8-12 59-61

HORTON, Johnny — C&W '56

Singles: 78 rpm

ABBOTT 15-25 51-52
COLUMBIA 10-25 56-57
CORMAC 25-50 51
MERCURY 10-20 54-55

Singles: 7-inch

ABBOTT (100 "Candy Jones") 20-30 51
ABBOTT (101 "Happy Millionaire") ... 20-30 51
ABBOTT (102 "Plaid and Calico") 20-30 51
ABBOTT (103 "Birds and Butterflies") 20-30 51
ABBOTT (104 "Go and Wash") 20-30 51
ABBOTT (105 "Shadows on the Old Bayou") 20-30 51
ABBOTT (106 "Words") 20-30 51
ABBOTT (107 "Long Rocky Road") .. 20-30 52
ABBOTT (108 "Somebody's Rockin' My Broken Heart") 20-30 52
ABBOTT (109 "Rhythm in My Baby's Walk") 20-30 52
ABBOTT (135 "Plaid and Calico") 15-20 53
CORMAC (1193 "Plaid and Calico") 75-100 51
CORMAC (1197 "Birds and Butterflies") 75-100 51
COLUMBIA (21504 "Honky Tonk Man") 15-25 56
COLUMBIA (21538 "I'm a One-Woman Man") 10-20 56
COLUMBIA (40813 "I'm Coming Home") 15-25 57
COLUMBIA (40919 "She Knows Why") 10-15 57
COLUMBIA (40986 "I'll Do It Every Time") 10-15 57
COLUMBIA (41043 "Lover's Rock") .. 15-25 57
COLUMBIA (41110 "Honky Tonk Hardwood Floor") 30-50 58
COLUMBIA (41210 "All Grown Up") 10-15 58
COLUMBIA (41308 thru 44156) 5-10 58-67
DOT (15996 "Plaid and Calico") 8-12 59
MERCURY (6412 "The Devil Sent Me You") 15-25 52
MERCURY (6418 "The Rest of Your Life") 15-25 52
MERCURY (70014 "I Won't Forget") 15-25 52
MERCURY (70100 "Tennessee Jive") 15-25 53
MERCURY (70156 "S.S. Lureline") ... 15-25 53
MERCURY (70198 "You You You") .. 15-25 53
MERCURY (70227 "All for the Love of a Girl") 15-25 53
MERCURY (70325 "Move Down the Line") 15-25 54
MERCURY (70399 "The Door of Your Mansion") 15-25 54
MERCURY (70462 "No True Love") 15-25 54
MERCURY (70636 "Ridin' the Sunshine Special") 15-25 55
MERCURY (70707 "Big Wheels Rollin' ") 15-25 55

Picture Sleeves

COLUMBIA (Except 41308) 10-15 59-64
COLUMBIA (41308 "When It's Springtime in Alaska") 15-20 59
(Blue and white sleeve. Promotional only.)
DOT 10-15 59

EPs: 7-inch

COLUMBIA (2130 "Honky Tonk Man") 25-50 57
COLUMBIA (13621/22/23 "The Spectactular Johnny Horton ") 20-40 60
(Price is for either volume.)
COLUMBIA (14781/82/83 "Johnny Horton Makes History") 20-40 60
(Price is for either volume.)
MERCURY (3091 "Requestfully Yours") 25-50 55
SESAC (1201 "Free and Easy Songs") 30-50 59

LPs: 10/12-inch

BRIAR INT'L (104 "Done Rovin' "). 100-150 60s
COLUMBIA (CL-1362 "The Spectactular Johnny Horton ") 20-30 60
(Monaural.)
COLUMBIA (CL-1478 "Johnny Horton Makes History") 20-30 60
(Monaural.)
COLUMBIA (CL-1596 "Johnny Horton's Greatest Hits") 20-30 61
(Monaural. Add $15 to $25 if accompanied by bonus photo.)
COLUMBIA (CL-1721 "Honky Tonk Man") 20-30 62
(Monaural.)
COLUMBIA (CL-2566 "Johnny Horton on the Louisiana Hayride") 20-25 66
(Monaural.)
COLUMBIA (CL-2566 "Johnny Horton on Stage") 10-20 66
(Monaural. Repackage of *Johnny Horton on the Louisiana Hayride*.)
COLUMBIA (CS-8167 "The Spectactular Johnny Horton ") 25-35 60
(Stereo.)
COLUMBIA (CS-8269 "Johnny Horton Makes History") 25-35 60
(Stereo.)
COLUMBIA (CS-8396 "Johnny Horton's Greatest Hits") 25-35 61
(Stereo. Add $15 to $25 if accompanied by bonus photo.)
COLUMBIA (PC-8396 "Johnny Horton's Greatest Hits") 5-10
COLUMBIA (CS-8779 "Honky Tonk Man") 25-35 62
(Stereo.)

COLUMBIA (CS-9099 "I Can't Forget You")....15-20 65
(Stereo.)
COLUMBIA (CS-9366 "Johnny Horton on the Louisiana Hayride")....20-25 66
(Stereo.)
COLUMBIA (CS-9366 "Johnny Horton on Stage")....10-15 66
(Stereo. Repackage of *Johnny Horton on the Louisiana Hayride.*)
COLUMBIA (CS-9940 "Johnny Horton on the Road")....10-15 69
COLUMBIA (KG-30884 "The World of Johnny Horton")....15-20 71
COLUMBIA (CG-30884 "The World of Johnny Horton")....10-15
COLUMBIA HOUSE (6418/19 "Johnny Horton, the Legend")....10-15 75
CROWN....10-20 63
CUSTOM....10-15 60s
DOT (3221 "Johnny Horton")....30-50 59
(Monaural.)
DOT (25221 "Johnny Horton")....20-30 66
(Stereo.)
HARMONY (11291 "The Unforgettable Johnny Horton")....10-15 70
HARMONY (11384 "The Legendary Johnny Horton")....10-15 70
HARMONY (30394 "The Battle of New Orleans")....10-15 71
JUKE BOX....5-10
MERCURY (20478 "The Fantastic Johnny Horton")....35-50 59
PICKWICK/HILLTOP (6060 "All for the Love of a Girl")....10-15 65
PICKWICK/HILLTOP (6012 "The Voice of Johnny Horton")....10-15 68
SEARS (110 "Legend of Johnny Horton")....10-15 60s
SESAC (1201 "Free and Easy Songs")....75-125 59
Also see CLINE, Patsy / Cowboy Copas / Johnny Horton
Also see DEAN, Jimmy / Johnny Horton
Also see PRICE, Ray / Johnny Horton / Carl Smith / George Morgan

HORTON, Johnny / Sonny James

LPs: 10/12-inch

CUSTOM....6-12
Also see JAMES, Sonny

HORTON, Johnny / Texas Slim

LPs: 10/12-inch

CROWN....6-12 60s
Also see HORTON, Johnny

HOSANNA R&B '76

Singles: 7-inch

CALLA....3-5 76

HOT P&R/R&B/LP '77

Singles: 7-inch

BIG TREE....3-5 77-79

LPs: 10/12-inch

BIG TREE....5-10 77-79
Members: Gwen Owens; Cathy Carson; Juanita Curiel.

HOT BUTTER P&R/LP '72

Singles: 7-inch

MUSICOR....3-5 72

LPs: 10/12-inch

MUSICOR....8-10 72-74
Members: Steve Jerome; Bill Jerome; Johnny Abbott; Stan Free; Dave Mullaney.

HOT CHOCOLATE P&R/R&B '75

(Hot Chocolate Band)

Singles: 7-inch

APPLE....5-10 69
BELL....3-5 74
BIG TREE....3-5 75-77
EMI AMERICA....3-4 82
INFINITY....3-5 78-79
RAK....3-5 72-73

LPs: 10/12-inch

BIG TREE....8-10 74-77
EMI AMERICA....5-10 82
INFINITY....5-10 78-79
Members: Errol Brown; Tony Wilson; Harvey Hinsley; Larry Ferguson; Tony Conner; Patrick Olive.

HOT CUISINE R&B '81

Singles: 7-inch

PRELUDE....3-4 81

HOT LINE R&B '74

Singles: 12-inch

MEMO....4-6 84

Singles: 7-inch

RED COACH....3-5 74

HOT SAUCE P&R/R&B '72

Singles: 7-inch

VOLT....5-10 72-74

HOT STREAK D&D '83

Singles: 12-inch

EASY STREET....4-6 83

HOT TODDYS P&R '59

(Featuring Bill Pernell; Hot-Toddys)

Singles: 7-inch

BARREL (602 "Rockin' Crickets")....15-20 59
(Canadian.)
CORSICAN (0056 "Rockin' Crickets")....15-25 59
SHAN-TODD (0056 "Rockin' Crickets")....15-25 59
STRAND (25001 "Hoe-Down")....10-15 60
(Issued with two different flip sides.)
SWAN (4140 "Rockin' Crickets")....10-20 63

HOT TUNA LP '70

Singles: 7-inch

GRUNT....3-6 71-76

Picture Sleeves

GRUNT....4-8 72

LPs: 10/12-inch

GRUNT....10-20 72-78
RCA (3000 series)....5-10 81
RCA (4000 series)....10-15 70-71
RELIX ("Acoustic Hot Tuna Splashdown")....10-15 84
(No selection number used.)
RELIX (2004 "Tuna Splashed")....25-30 84
(Picture disc.)
Members: Jack Casady; Jorma Kaukonen; Papa John Creach; Sammy Piazza.
Also see CREACH, Papa John
Also see JOPLIN, Janis / Hot Tuna
Also see KAUKONEN, Jorma

HOTBOX R&B/D&D '84

Singles: 12-inch

POLYDOR....4-6 84

Singles: 7-inch

POLYDOR....3-4 84

HOTEL P&R '78

Singles: 7-inch

MCA....3-4 79-80
MERCURY....3-5 78

LPs: 10/12-inch

MCA....5-10 79-80

HOTHOUSE FLOWERS LP '88

Singles: 7-inch

LONDON....3-4 88-90

LPs: 10/12-inch

LONDON....5-10 88-90
Members: Liam O'Maonlai; Fiachna O'Braonain; Peter O'Toole; Leo Barnes.

HOTLEGS P&R '70

Singles: 7-inch

CAPITOL (Except 3043)....3-5 70-71
CAPITOL (3043 "Run, Baby, Run")..10-15 71

LPs: 10/12-inch

CAPITOL....15-20 71
Members: Eric Stewart; Kevin Godley; Lol Cream.
Also see 10CC

HOT-TODDYS: see HOT TODDYS

HOUR GLASS

(Greg Allman & Hour Glass)

Singles: 7-inch

LIBERTY (56002 "Nothing But Tears")....10-15 68
LIBERTY (56029 "Power of Love")....10-15 68
LIBERTY (56091 "I've Been Trying")..10-15 69

Picture Sleeves

LIBERTY (56002 "Nothing But Tears")....40-60 68

LPs: 10/12-inch

LIBERTY....15-20 67-68
U.A....10-15 73
Members: Duane Allman; Gregg Allman.
Also see ALLMAN BROTHERS BAND

HOUSE OF FREAKS LP '89

LPs: 10/12-inch

RHINO....5-8 89

HOUSE OF LORDS LP '88

Singles: 7-inch

RCA/SIMMONS....3-4 89

Picture Sleeves

RCA/SIMMONS....3-4 89

LPs: 10/12-inch

RCA/SIMMONS....5-8 88
SIMMONS....5-8 90
Members: James Christian; Gregg Giuffria; Chuck Wright; Lanny Cordola; Ken Mary.
Also see GIUFFRIA

HOUSE OF LOVE LP '88

LPs: 10/12-inch

FONTANA....5-8 90
RELATIVITY....5-8 88

HOUSEMARTINS LP '87

LPs: 10/12-inch

ELEKTRA....5-10 87-88
Member: Norman Cook.
Also see BEATS INTERNATIONAL

HOUSTON, Cissy R&B '70

(Sissie Houston; Cissie Houston)

Singles: 7-inch

COLUMBIA....3-4 79-80
COMMONWEALTH UNITED....3-5 70
CONGRESS (268 "Bring Him Back")....30-50 66
JANUS....3-5 71
KAPP (814 "Don't Come Running to Me")....15-25 67
PRIVATE STOCK....3-5 77-78

LPs: 10/12-inch

COLUMBIA....5-10 79-80
JANUS....8-10 70
PRIVATE STOCK....5-10 77-78
Also see BOWIE, David
Also see MANN, Herbie, & Cissy Houston
Also see SWEET INSPIRATIONS

HOUSTON, David C&W '63

(With Calvin Crawford)

Singles: 78 rpm

IMPERIAL....8-12 55
RCA (6611 "Sugar Sweet")....8-12 56
RCA (6696 "Blue Prelude")....8-12 56
RCA (6927 "One and Only")....15-25 57
RCA (7001 "Teenage Frankie and Johnny")....15-25 57

Singles: 7-inch

BLACK ROSE....3-4 82
COLONIAL....3-5 78
COUNTRY INT'L....3-4 80
DERRICK....3-4 79
ELEKTRA....3-5 78-79
EXCELSIOR....3-4 81
EPIC....3-8 63-76
IMPERIAL....10-20 55
NRC (005 "Waited So Long")....25-35 59
PHILLIPS INT'L....5-10 61
RCA (6611 "Sugar Sweet")....10-20 56
RCA (6696 "Blue Prelude")....10-20 56
RCA (6927 "One and Only")....30-40 57
RCA (7001 "Teenage Frankie and Johnny")....15-25 57

SOUNDWAVES 3-4 83
STARDAY 3-5 77
SUN (400 series) 5-10 66
SUN (1100 series) 3-5 72

Picture Sleeves

EPIC 5-8 66-69

LPs: 10/12-inch

CAMDEN 8-12 66
COLUMBIA 6-10 73
DELTA 5-10 82
EPIC 5-15 64-76
EXACT 5-10 80
EXCELSIOR 5-10 81
51 WEST 5-10 84
GUEST STAR 6-12 64
GUSTO 5-10 78
HARMONY 8-12 70-72
STARDAY 6-10 77

Also see DEAN, Jimmy / David Houston / Warner Mack / Autry Inman
Also see JAMES, Sonny / David Houston
Also see JONES, George / Buck Owens / David Houston / Tommy Hill.

HOUSTON, David, & Barbara Mandrell C&W '70

Singles: 7-inch

EPIC 3-5 70-74

LPs: 10/12-inch

EPIC 8-15 72-75

Also see MANDRELL, Barbara

HOUSTON, David, & Tammy Wynette C&W '68

Singles: 7-inch

EPIC 4-6 67

LPs: 10/12-inch

EPIC 8-12 67
51 WEST 5-10 82

Also see HOUSTON, David
Also see WYNETTE, Tammy

HOUSTON, Joe R&B '52

(With His Rockets; Mighty Joe Houston; Fabulous Joe Houston; Joe Houston Orchestra)

Singles: 78 rpm

BAYOU 8-12 53
CASH 8-12 55
COMBO 8-12 54-57
CROWN 8-12 56
FREEDOM 20-30 49-50
IMPERIAL 10-20 52
LUCKY 10-20 54
MACY'S 10-20 51
MERCURY 10-20 51
MODERN 10-15 52
MONEY 8-12 55
RPM 8-12 55
RECORDED in HOLLYWOOD 10-20 54
SPHINX 10-20 51

Singles: 7-inch

BAYOU (004 "Moody") 15-25 53
BAYOU (012 "Chittlin") 15-25 53
BAYOU (015 "Blues Jump the Rabbit") 15-25 53
BAYOU (017 "Scramble") 15-25 53
BIG TOWN 3-6 79
CASH (1013 "Flying Home") 15-25 55
COMBO 10-15 54-65
CROWN 10-15 56
DOOTO 8-12 58
IMPERIAL (5183 "Ace of Clubs") 20-30 52
IMPERIAL (5196 "Hurricane") 20-30 52
IMPERIAL (5201 "Earthquake") 20-30 52
IMPERIAL (5213 "Atom Bomb") 20-30 53
IMPERIAL (5334 "Tough Enough") 20-30 55
KEM 5-10 61
KENT 10-20 61
LUCKY 15-25 54
MAGNUM 10-20 64-65
MERCURY (8248 "Hard Time Baby") 15-25 51
MODERN (830 "Blow Joe, Blow") 30-50 51
MODERN (850 "Have a Ball") 20-30 52
MODERN (863 "Doin' the Lindy Hop") 20-30 52
MODERN (879 "Dig It") 20-30 52
MODERN (917 "Blowin' Crazy") 20-30 52
MONEY 10-20 55
RONNEX (1103 "All Night Long") 15-25 55
RPM 10-20 55
RECORDED in HOLLYWOOD (423 "Jay's Boogie") 20-30 54

EPs: 7-inch

COMBO (3 "Joe Houston") 40-60 54
COMBO (10 "Joe Houston") 40-60 55
MODERN/RPM (200 "The Fabulous Joe Houston") 50-75
(Cover shows Modern, but label shows RPM.)
TOPS (607 "Rock & Roll Party") 40-60 58

LPs: 10/12-inch

BIG TOWN 5-10 78
COMBO (100 "Joe Houston") 150-200 55
(Cover has titles and color photo of Houston)
COMBO (100 "Joe Houston") 50-100
(No photo or titles on cover. Has a saxophone as the "J" in Joe. No artist or title shown on label.)
COMBO (400 "Rockin' at the Drive-In") 50-100 55
CROWN 15-30 62-63
GOLD AWARD (8033 "Rock & Roll") 30-40
(Colored vinyl.)
MODERN (1206 "Joe Houston Blows All Night Long") 75-125 56
TOPS (1518 "Rock & Roll with Joe Houston") 50-80 58

HOUSTON, Thelma P&R '70

(With Pressure Cooker)

Singles: 12-inch

MCA 4-6 83

Singles: 7-inch

CAPITOL (5767 "Baby Mine") 25-50 66
DUNHILL (Except 11) 4-8 70
DUNHILL (11 "Everybody Gets to Go to the Moon") 10-15 69
(Special Apollo 11 Mission promotional issue.)
MCA 3-4 83
MOTOWN 3-4 74-78
MOWEST 3-6 71-73
RCA 3-4 80-81
TAMLA 3-4 76-79

Picture Sleeves

DUNHILL (11 "Everybody Gets to Go to the Moon") 10-15 69
(Special Apollo 11 Mission promotional issue.)

LPs: 10/12-inch

DUNHILL 10-15 69
MCA 5-10 83
MOTOWN 5-10 81-82
MOWEST 8-12 72
RCA 5-10 80-81
SHEFFIELD (2 "I've Got the Music in Me") 25-30 74
SHEFFIELD (200 "I've Got the Music in Me") 5-10 82
TAMLA 5-10 76-79
MYRRH 8-10 74

Also see BUTLER, Jerry, & Thelma Houston

HOUSTON, Whitney P&R/R&B/LP '85

Singles: 12-inch

ARISTA 4-6 85-89

Singles: 7-inch

ARISTA 3-4 85-91

Picture Sleeves

ARISTA 3-4 85-88

LPs: 10/12-inch

ARISTA 5-10 85-91

Also see FRANKLIN, Aretha, & Whitney Houston
Also see KING DREAM CHORUS & Holiday Crew
Also see PENDERGRASS, Teddy, & Whitney Houston

HOWARD, Camille R&B '48

(With Her Boy Friends; Camille Howard Trio)

Singles: 78 rpm

FEDERAL 10-15 53
IMPERIAL 10-15 53
SPECIALTY 10-15 48-53
VEE JAY 8-12 56

Singles: 7-inch

FEDERAL (12125 "Excite Me, Daddy") 20-30 53
FEDERAL (12134 "Hurry Back, Baby") 20-30 53
FEDERAL (12147 "You're Lower Than a Mole") 20-30 53
IMPERIAL 15-25 53
SPECIALTY (359 "Ferocious Boogie") 30-40 50
SPECIALTY (370 "Fire Ball Boogie") 30-40 51
SPECIALTY (443 "Old Baldy Boogie") 20-30 53
SPECIALTY (449 "Bacarolle Boogie") 20-30 53
VEE JAY 10-20 56

Members: Camille Howard; Roy Milton; Dallas Bartley.
Also see BROWN, Clarence "Gatemouth"/ Camille Howard / Bill Johnson Quartet / Van "Piano Man" Walls
Also see MILTON, Roy

HOWARD, Don P&R '52

Singles: 78 rpm

ESSEX 4-8 52
MERCURY 3-5 56
TRIPLE A 10-15 52

Singles: 7-inch

ESSEX (311 "Oh Happy Day") 8-15 52
(Black vinyl.)
ESSEX (311 "Oh Happy Day") 15-25 52
(Colored vinyl.)
MERCURY 5-10 56
TRIPLE A (2503 "Oh Happy Day") 20-30 52

HOWARD, Eddy P&R '40

Singles: 78 rpm

MAJESTIC 4-8 46
MERCURY 3-5 50-57

Singles: 7-inch

MERCURY 5-10 50-61
MISHAWAKA 3-5 72

EPs: 7-inch

MERCURY 5-10 50-59

LPs: 10/12-inch

IMPERIAL 8-15 61
MERCURY 10-20 50-65
WING 5-10 60-63

HOWARD, George R&B '83

(With Gwen Guthrie)

Singles: 12-inch

MCA 4-6 86

Singles: 7-inch

MCA 3-4 86-90
PALO ALTO 3-4 83
TBA 3-4 84-86

LPs: 10/12-inch

GRP 5-8 91
MCA 5-10 86-90
PALO ALTO 5-10 83
TBA 5-10 84-86

Also see GUTHRIE, Gwen

HOWARD, Gregory

Singles: 7-inch

KAPP (536 "When in Love") 100-200 63
(Black label.)
KAPP (536 "When in Love") 50-100 63
(White label. Promotional issue only.)
Copies of *When in Love* on Gee, credited to the Gee-Tones, are boots from the mid-'70s.
Session: Cadillacs.
Also see CADILLACS

HOWARD, Miki R&B '86

Singles: 7-inch

ATLANTIC 3-4 86-90

LPs: 10/12-inch

ATLANTIC 5-10 86-90

Also see SIDE EFFECT

HOWARD, Miki, & Gerald Levert
R&B '88

Singles: 7-inch

ATLANTIC ... 3-4 88

Also see HOWARD, Miki

HOWARD, Rosetta
R&B '48

(With the Big Three Trio)

Singles: 78 rpm

COLUMBIA ... 8-15 48-55

Singles: 7-inch

COLUMBIA ... 15-25 51-55

Also see BIG THREE TRIO

HOWE, Steve, Band
LP '75

Singles: 7-inch

ATLANTIC ... 3-5 75-79

LPs: 10/12-inch

ATLANTIC ... 5-10 75-79

Also see ASIA
Also see GTR
Also see YES

HOWLIN' WOLF
R&B '51

(Chester Burnett)

Singles: 78 rpm

CHESS (1479 thru 1695) ... 20-40 51-58
CHESS (1712 "I'm Leaving You") ... 50-75 58
CHESS (1726 "Howlin' Blues") ... 50-100 59
CHESS (1735 "I've Been Abused") ... 75-125 59
RPM (333 "Riding in the Moonlight") ... 50-75 51
RPM (340 "Passing By Blues") ... 50-75 51
RPM (347 "My Baby Stole Off") ... 50-75 51

Singles: 7-inch

CADET CONCEPT ... 4-8 69
CHESS (1528 "My Last Affair") ... 75-100 53
CHESS (1557 "All Night Boogie") ... 50-75 53
CHESS (1566 "No Place to Go") ... 40-60 54
CHESS (1575 "Baby, How Long") ... 40-60 54
CHESS (1584 "I'll Be Around") ... 25-50 55
CHESS (1593 "Who Will Be Next") ... 25-50 55
CHESS (1607 "Come to Me Baby") .. 15-25 55
CHESS (1618 "Smokestack Lightning") ... 15-25 56
CHESS (1632 "I Asked for Water") ... 15-25 56
CHESS (1648 "Going Back Home") . 15-25 57
CHESS (1668 "Somebody in My Home") ... 15-25 57
CHESS (1679 "Poor Boy") ... 15-25 57
CHESS (1695 "I Didn't Know") ... 15-25 58
CHESS (1712 thru 1793) ... 10-20 58-61
CHESS (1804 thru 1968) ... 8-15 61-66
CHESS (2000 series) ... 4-8 67-71

LPs: 10/12-inch

CADET ... 10-12 69
CHESS (Except 1400 and 1500 series) ... 8-10 71-77
CHESS (1434 "Moaning in the Moonlight") ... 50-100 58
(Black label.)
CHESS (1469 "Howlin' Wolf") ... 50-100 62
(Black label.)
CHESS (1469 "Howlin' Wolf") ... 200-300 62
(White label. Promotional issue only.)
CHESS (1500 series, except 1502) ... 15-20 67-69
CHESS (1502 "Real Folk Blues") ... 25-35 66
CHESS/MCA (Except 9332) ... 5-8 89
CHESS/MCA (9332 "Howlin' Wolf") .. 35-45 91
(Five LP boxed set, with 32-page booklet.)
CROWN ... 15-20 62
CUSTOM ... 10-12
KENT ... 10-15 67
RPM (340 "Passing By Blues") . 1000-2000 51
RPM (347 "My Baby Stole Off") ... 100-200 51
UNITED ... 8-10

Also see BERRY, Chuck, & Howlin' Wolf
Also see DIDDLEY, Bo, Howlin' Wolf & Muddy Waters
Also see ROBINSON, Freddy
Also see WATERS, Muddy, & Howlin' Wolf

HUANG CHUNG: see WANG CHUNG

HUBBARD, Freddie
LP '73

Singles: 12-inch

FANTASY ... 4-8 81

Singles: 7-inch

ATLANTIC ... 3-5 69
BLUE NOTE ... 4-8 61-64
COLUMBIA ... 3-7 74-76

LPs: 10/12-inch

ATLANTIC ... 8-15 67-76
BLUE NOTE ... 15-25 60-65
(Label reads "Blue Note Records Inc. - New York, U.S.A.")
BLUE NOTE ... 8-15 66-76
(Label shows Blue Note Records as a division of either Liberty or United Artists.)
CTI ... 6-12 70-75
COLUMBIA ... 5-10 74-83
ELEKTRA ... 5-8 82
ENJA ... 5-8 81
FANTASY ... 5-8 81-83
IMPULSE ... 10-20 63-73
LIBERTY ... 5-8 81
PABLO ... 5-8 82-83
PAUSA ... 5-8 82

HUBBARD, Freddie, & Oscar Peterson

LPs: 10/12-inch

PABLO ... 5-10 80

Also see PETERSON, Oscar

HUBBARD, Freddie, & Stanley Turrentine

LPs: 10/12-inch

CTI ... 6-12 74

Also see HUBBARD, Freddie
Also see TURRENTINE, Stanley

HUDMON, R.B., Jr.
R&B '76

Singles: 7-inch

ATLANTIC ... 3-5 76-77
CAPITOL ... 3-5 71
COTILLION ... 3-5 78
1-2-3 ... 3-6 68-70

LPs: 10/12-inch

COTILLION ... 5-10 78

HUDSON

Singles: 7-inch

ELEKTRA ... 3-4 80
LIONEL ... 3-5 71
PLAYBOY ... 3-5 73
ROCKET ... 3-5 73

LPs: 10/12-inch

ELEKTRA ... 5-10 80

Members: Bill Hudson; Brett Hudson; Mark Hudson.
Also see HUDSON BROTHERS

HUDSON, Al
R&B '76

(With the Soul Partners)

Singles: 12-inch

ABC ... 4-8 77

Singles: 7-inch

ABC ... 3-5 76-79
ATCO ... 3-5 75-76

LPs: 10/12-inch

ABC ... 8-10 77

Also see ONE WAY

HUDSON, David
P&R/R&B/LP '80

Singles: 7-inch

ALSTON ... 3-4 80

LPs: 10/12-inch

ALSTON ... 5-10 80

HUDSON, Pookie
P&R '63

(With the Spaniels)

Singles: 7-inch

CHESS ... 5-10 66
DOUBLE-L (711 "I Know, I Know") ... 10-20 63
DOUBLE-L (720 "Miracles") ... 10-20 63
JAMIE (1319 "This Gets to Me") ... 25-50 66
NEPTUNE (124 "For Sentimental Reasons") ... 10-15 61
PARKWAY (839 "Turn Out the Lights") ... 10-15 62

Also see SPANIELS

HUDSON & LANDRY
P&R/LP '71

Singles: 7-inch

DORE ... 3-5 71-74

LPs: 10/12-inch

DORE (Except 326) ... 10-20 71-77
DORE (326 "Losing Their Heads") ... 8-12 77
(Picture disc.)

Members: Bob Hudson; Ron Landry.
Also see HUDSON, "Emperor" Bob, & Lawrence Welk

HUDSON BROTHERS
P&R/LP '74

Singles: 7-inch

ARISTA ... 3-5 76-78
CASABLANCA ... 3-5 74
MCA/ROCKET ... 3-5 74-76

Picture Sleeves

MCA/ROCKET ... 3-5 75

LPs: 10/12-inch

CASABLANCA ... 8-10 74
PLAYBOY ... 8-10 72
MCA/ROCKET ... 8-10 74-75

Members: Bill Hudson; Brett Hudson; Mark Hudson.
Also see HUDSON

HUERTA, Baldemar

(El Bebop Kid)

Singles: 7-inch

FALCON (838 "Encaje De Chantilly [Chantilly Lace]") ... 15-25 58

Also see FENDER, Freddy

HUES CORPORATION
P&R '73

Singles: 7-inch

RCA ... 3-5 73-75
W.B. ... 3-5 77

LPs: 10/12-inch

RCA ... 8-10 73-77
W.B. ... 5-10 77-78

Members: St. Clair Lee; H. Ann Kelly; Tommy Brown; Karl Russell; Fleming Williams.

HUFF, Leon
R&B '80

(Leon "Fingers" Huff)

Singles: 7-inch

JAMIE (1254 "Soul City") ... 10-20 62
PHILLY INT'L ... 3-5 80-81

Also see MFSB
Also see ROMEOS

HUFF, Terry
R&B '76

(With Special Delivery)

Singles: 7-inch

MAINSTREAM ... 3-5 76
PHILADELPHIA INT'L ... 3-4 80

LPs: 10/12-inch

MAINSTREAM ... 5-10 76

Also see SPECIAL DELIVERY

HUGH, Grayson
LP '88

Singles: 7-inch

RCA ... 3-4 89-90

Picture Sleeves

RCA ... 3-4 89

LPs: 10/12-inch

RCA ... 5-8 88

HUGH, Grayson, & Betty Wright

Singles: 7-inch

RCA ... 3-4 89

Also see HUGH, Grayson
Also see WRIGHT, Betty

HUGHES, Fred
P&R/R&B '65

(Freddie Hughes)

Singles: 7-inch

BRUNSWICK ... 3-8 69-71
CADET ... 5-10 68
COLLECTABLES ... 3-4 81
EXODUS ... 5-10 66
MINASA (709 "One Step Too Far") ... 15-25 65
VEE JAY ... 8-10 65
WAND ... 6-12 68-69
WEE ... 4-8

LPs: 10/12-inch

BRUNSWICK ... 8-12 70
WAND ... 10-15 68

HUGHES, Jimmy *P&R/R&B '64*

Singles: 7-inch

ATLANTIC 4-8 68
COLLECTABLES 3-5 81
FAME 5-10 64-67
GUYDEN 4-8 62
JAMIE (1280 "My Loving Time") 8-12 64
VOA (4002 "I Like Everything About Him") 5-8
VOLT 3-6 69-71

LPs: 10/12-inch

ATCO 10-15 67
STAX 5-10 85
VEE JAY 15-20 64
VOLT 10-12 69

HUGHES, Rhetta *R&B '69*

Singles: 12-inch

ARIA 4-6 83

Singles: 7-inch

ARIA 3-4 83
COLUMBIA 4-6 67-68
SUTRA 3-4 80
TETRAGRAMMATON 4-6 68-69

LPs: 10/12-inch

SUTRA 5-10 80
TETRAGRAMMATON 10-12 69

HUGHES, Rhetta, & Tennyson Stephens

LPs: 10/12-inch

COLUMBIA 12-18 65
Also see HUGHES, Rhetta
Also see STEPHENS, Tennyson

HUGHES - THRALL *P&R '82*

Singles: 7-inch

BOULEVARD 3-4 82
Members: Glenn Hughes; Pat Thrall.

HUGO & LUIGI *P&R '55*
(Hugo & Luigi Chorus)

Singles: 78 rpm

MERCURY 3-5 55-56

Singles: 7-inch

MERCURY 5-10 55-56
RCA 4-8 59-60
ROULETTE 4-8 58

Picture Sleeves

ROULETTE 5-10 58

LPs: 10/12-inch

FORUM 5-10 60
MERCURY 5-15 56
RCA 5-10 60-63
ROULETTE 5-12 59
WING 5-10 60
Members: Hugo Peretti; Luigi Creatore.

HULIN, T.K. *P&R '63*

Singles: 7-inch

SMASH (1830 "I'm Not a Fool Anymore") 4-8 63
L.K. (1001 "Little Bitty Boy") 100-200 60
L.K. (1116 "On Lonely Street") 15-25 62
L.K. (1118 "As You Pass Me By") 15-25 62
L.K. (1119 "Baby, Be My Steady") 15-25 63

LPs: 10/12-inch

STARFLITE 20-30

HULLABALOOS *P&R '64*

Singles: 7-inch

ROULETTE 5-10 64-65

Picture Sleeves

ROULETTE 10-20 64-65

LPs: 10/12-inch

ROULETTE (25297 "England's Newest Singing Sensations") 25-30 65
ROULETTE (25310 "The Hullabaloos on Hullabaloo") 25-30 65

HUMAN BEINZ *P&R '67*
(Human Beingz; with the Mammals)

Singles: 7-inch

CAPITOL 5-8 67-69
ELYSIAN (3376 "Hey Joe") 15-25 67
ELYSIAN (8687 "My Generation") 15-25 66
GATEWAY (828 "Gloria") 5-10 68
GATEWAY (838 "My Generation") 5-10 68

Picture Sleeves

CAPITOL (2119 "Turn on Your Lovelight") 10-15 68

LPs: 10/12-inch

CAPITOL (2906 "Nobody But Me") 15-25 68
CAPITOL (2926 "Evolutions") 25-35 68
GATEWAY (3012 "Nobody But Me") 25-35 68
Members: Richard Belley; Mel Pachuta; Mike Tatman; Ting Markulin.

HUMAN BODY *R&B '84*

Singles: 7-inch

BEARSVILLE 3-4 84

HUMAN LEAGUE *P&R/LP '82*

Singles: 12-inch

A&M 4-6 82-86

Singles: 7-inch

A&M 3-4 82-86

Picture Sleeves

A&M 3-4 82-85

LPs: 10/12-inch

A&M 5-10 82-86
Members: Phil Oakey; Craig Marsh; Martyn Ware; Colin Thurston.
Also see HEAVEN 17
Also see LEAGUE UNLIMITED ORCHESTRA
Also see MORODER, Giorgio, & Phil Oakey

HUMBLE PIE *P&R/LP '71*

Singles: 7-inch

A&M 3-5 71-75
ATCO 3-4 80
IMMEDIATE 4-8 69

Picture Sleeves

A&M 4-8 71-72

LPs: 10/12-inch

A&M 8-12 70-82
ACCORD 5-10 82
ATCO 5-10 80-81
IMMEDIATE 10-15 68-72
Members: Steve Marriott; Peter Frampton; Greg Ridley; B.J. Cole; Jerry Shirley; Lyn Dobson; Dave Clempson.
Also see FRAMPTON, Peter
Also see SMALL FACES

HUMES, Helen *R&B '45*
(With the Bill Doggett Octet)

Singles: 78 rpm

ALADDIN 5-10 45
DECCA 4-8 52
MODERN (779 "I'm Gonna Let Him Ride") 20-30 50

Singles: 7-inch

DECCA (28113 "They Raided the Joint") 15-25 52

LPs: 10/12-inch

COLUMBIA 8-10
Members (Octet): Bill Doggett; Johnny Brown; Bill Moore; Ernest Thompson; Ross Butler; Alfred Moore; Charles Harris; Elmer Warner.
Also see DOGGETT, Bill
Also see MILTON, Roy

HUMPERDINCK, Engelbert *P&R/LP '67*
(Gerry Dorsey)

Singles: 7-inch

EPIC/CBS (35020 "Last of the Romantics") 50-70 76
(Picture disc. Promotional issue only.)

Singles: 7-inch

EH (1 "For My Friends") 10-15
(Promotional issue only.)
EPIC 3-5 76-83
PARROT 3-6 67-73

Picture Sleeves

PARROT 3-6 67-71

EPs: 7-inch

PARROT 5-10 67-69
(Juke box issues.)

LPs: 10/12-inch

EPIC 5-10 76-83
LONDON 5-10 77
PARROT 5-15 67-77
TEE VEE 5-10
(TV mail order offer.)
Also see DORSEY, Gerry

HUMPHREY, Bobbi *R&B/LP '74*

Singles: 12-inch

EPIC 4-8 78-79

Singles: 7-inch

BLUE NOTE 3-5 71-76
EPIC 3-5 77-79

LPs: 10/12-inch

BLUE NOTE 5-10 71-76
EPIC 5-10 78-79

HUMPHREY, Della *P&R/R&B '68*

Singles: 7-inch

ARCTIC 4-6 68

HUMPHREY, Paul, & His Cool Aid Chemists *P&R/R&B/LP '71*

Singles: 7-inch

LIZARD 3-6 70-71

LPs: 10/12-inch

LIZARD 8-12 71

HUMPHRIES, Teddy *R&B '59*

Singles: 7-inch

KING (5000 series) 10-15 59-61
(Monaural.)
KING (S-5205 "What a Night") 20-30 59
(Stereo.)
Session: Mickey Baker.

HUNT, Geraldine *R&B '70*

Singles: 7-inch

ABC (10859 "Winner Take All") 15-25 67
BOMBAY (4501 "He's for Real") 50-75 64
CHECKER (1028 "I Let Myself Go") 10-20 62
PRISM 3-4 80
ROULETTE 4-6 70-73
U.S.A. (732 "Sneak Around") 15-25 62
U.S.A. (737 "Sneak Around") 10-20 63

HUNT, Geraldine, & Charlie Hodges

Singles: 7-inch

CALLA 4-6 70
Also see HODGES, Charles
Also see HUNT, Geraldine

HUNT, Pee Wee *P&R '48*

Singles: 78 rpm

CAPITOL 3-5 48-57

Singles: 7-inch

CAPITOL 5-10 50-62
SAVOY 5-10 51

EPs: 7-inch

CAPITOL 5-10 50-56
SAVOY 5-10 51

LPs: 10/12-inch

CAPITOL 4-8 78
(With "SM" prefix.)
CAPITOL 15-30 50-63
(With "T" or "ST" prefix.)
GLENDALE 4-8 78
SAVOY (15042 "Dixieland") 25-35 54
(10-inch LP.)
TOPS 15-25 57
Also see BLANC, Mel
Also see FOUR KNIGHTS

HUNT, Tommy *P&R/R&B '61*

Singles: 7-inch

ATLANTIC 4-8 65
CAPITOL 4-8 66
DYNAMO 4-8 67
SCEPTER 4-8 61-63

LPs: 10/12-inch

DYNAMO (8001 "Greatest Hits") 15-25 67
SCEPTER (506 "I Just Don't Know What to Do with Myself") 25-35 62
Also see FLAMINGOS
Also see PLATTERS / Inez & Charlie Foxx / Jive Five / Tommy Hunt

HUNTER, Ian *LP '75*

Singles: 7-inch

CHRYSALIS 3-4 79
COLUMBIA 3-5 75-83

LPs: 10/12–inch
CHRYSALIS 5-10 79-81
COLUMBIA 8-10 75-79
Also see MOTT the HOOPLE

HUNTER, Ian, & Mick Ronson — LP '89
LPs: 10/12–inch
MERCURY 5-8 89
Also see HUNTER, Ian
Also see RONSON, Mick

HUNTER, Ivory Joe — R&B '45
(With the Ivorytones)
Singles: 78 rpm
ATLANTIC 20-30 55-58
EXCLUSIVE 15-25 45
4 STAR 25-50 48-51
KING 10-20 47-57
MGM 10-15 49-54
PACIFIC 15-25 45-47
Singles: 7–inch
ATLANTIC 15-30 55-58
CAPITOL 5-10 61-62
DOT 15-25 58-59
GOLDISC 10-15 60
GOLDWAX (307 "Every Little Bit Helps") 15-25
JOIE 8-12
KING (4424 "False Friend Blues") 25-50 51
KING (4443 "She's Gone Blues") 25-50 51
KING (4455 "Old Gal and New Gal Blues") 25-50 51
KING (5280 "Guess Who") 10-15 59
MGM (500 series) 3-5 78
MGM (8011 "I Almost Lost My Mind") 25-50 49
MGM (10000 & 11000 series) 20-30 49-54
MGM (10578 "I Almost Lost My Mind") 25-50 49
PARAMOUNT 4-6 73
SMASH 5-10 63
SOUND STAGE 7 .... 4-8 68
STAX 5-10 64
VEE JAY 8-12 62
VEEP 5-10 67
EPs: 7–inch
ATLANTIC (589 "Ivory Joe Hunter") 50-75 58
ATLANTIC (608 "Rock with Ivory Joe Hunter") 50-75 58
DOT (34010 "Ivory Joe Hunter") 30-50 59
(French import. Listed because it is, by mistake, pictured in the color section of this edition.)
KING (265 "Ivory Joe Hunter") 50-75 54
MGM (1376/1377/1378 "I Get That Lonesome Feeling") 20-40 57
(Price is for any of three volumes.)
LPs: 10/12–inch
ATLANTIC (8008 "Ivory Joe Hunter") 50-100 58
(Black Label.)
ATLANTIC (8008 "Ivory Joe Hunter") 40-60 59
(Red Label.)
ATLANTIC (8015 "Ivory Joe Hunter Sings the Old & New") 50-100 58
(Black Label.)
ATLANTIC (8015 "Ivory Joe Hunter Sings the Old & New") 40-60 59
(Red Label.)
DOT 15-25 64
EPIC 8-10 71
EVEREST 8-10 74
GOLDISC (403 "Fabulous Ivory Joe Hunter") 25-35 61
GRAND PRIX 10-15
HOME COOKING 5-10 89
KING (605 "16 Greatest Hits") 50-80 58
LION 15-20
MGM (3488 "I Get That Lonesome Feeling") 50-100 57
PARAMOUNT 8-10 74
SAGE (603 "Ivory Joe Hunter") 35-50 59
SMASH 15-20 63
SOUND (603 "Ivory Joe Hunter") 50-100 57
Also see CHARLES, Ray / Ivory Joe Hunter / Jimmy Rushing
Also see TURNER, Sammy / Ivory Joe Hunter

HUNTER, Ivory Joe / Memphis Slim
LPs: 10/12–inch
STRAND (1123 "The Artistry of Ivory Joe Hunter") 15-25
Also see HUNTER, Ivory Joe
Also see MEMPHIS SLIM

HUNTER, John — P&R '84
Singles: 7–inch
PRIVATE I 3-4 84-85
LPs: 10/12–inch
PRIVATE I 5-10 85

HUNTER, Tab — P&R/R&B '57
Singles: 78 rpm
DOT 5-15 56-57
HEAR ("Tab Hunter") 20-30 56
(Seven–inch, cardboard disc, originally attached to front cover of *Hear* magazine. Double this price for magazine with record intact. Back cover has a similar disc by Jayne Mansfield.)
Singles: 7–inch
DOT 10-20 56-62
W.B. (Monaural) 8-15 58-59
W.B. (S-5032 "I'll Be with You in Apple Blossom Time") 15-25 59
(Stereo.)
W.B. (S-5051 "There's No Fool Like a Young Fool") 15-25 59
(Stereo.)
Picture Sleeves
W.B. (5008 "Jealous Heart" 10-20 58
W.B. (5093 "Waitin' for Fall" 10-20 60
W.B. (5160 "Again") 10-20 61
EPs: 7–inch
W.B. (EA-1221 "Tab Hunter") 15-25 58
(Monaural. Has one track not found on stereo version.)
W.B. (ESB-1221 "Tab Hunter") 20-35 58
(Stereo. Has one track not found on mono version.)
LPs: 10/12–inch
DOT (3370 "Young Love") 25-45 61
(Monaural.)
DOT (25370 "Young Love") 30-40 61
(Stereo.)
W.B. (1221 "Tab Hunter") 30-40 58
(Monaural.)
W.B. (1221 "Tab Hunter") 30-50 58
(Stereo.)
W.B. (1292 "When I Fall in Love") 30-40 58
(Monaural.)
W.B. (1292 "When I Fall in Love") 30-50 58
(Stereo.)
W.B. (1367 "R.F.D.") 30-40 60
(Monaural.)
W.B. (1367 "R.F.D.") 30-50 60
(Stereo.)

HUNTER, Ty — R&B '60
(With the Voice Masters)
Singles: 7–inch
ANNA (1114 "Everything About You") 20-30 60
ANNA (1123 "Everytime") 20-30 60
CHECK MATE (1002 "Memories") 15-25 61
CHECK MATE (1015 "Lonely Baby") 15-25 61
CHESS 10-20 62-64
INVICTUS 10-15 72
Also see GLASS HOUSE
Also see ORIGINALS
Also see VOICE MASTERS

HUNTLEY, Chet, & David Brinkley — LP '64
LPs: 10/12–inch
RCA 8-15 64-66

HURD, Debra — R&B '83
Singles: 7–inch
GEFFEN 3-4 83

HURRICANE — LP '88
Singles: 7–inch
MCA 3-4 87
Picture Sleeves
MCA 3-4 87
LPs: 10/12–inch
ENIGMA 5-10 85-90
Members: Robert Sarzo; Kelly Hansen; Jay Schellen; Tony Cavazo; Doug Aldrich.

HURT, Jim — P&R '80
Singles: 7–inch
SCOTTI BROTHERS 3-4 80

HURT 'EM BAD & S.C. BAND — R&B '82
Singles: 7–inch
PROFILE 3-4 82

HUSKER DU — LP '86
Singles: 12–inch
W.B. 4-6 86
Singles: 7–inch
SST 3-4 85
W.B. 3-4 86
Picture Sleeves
SST 3-4 85
LPs: 10/12–inch
SST 5-10 85
W.B. 5-10 86-87
Members: Bob Mould; Grant Hart; Greg Norton.

HUSKEY, Ferlin: see HUSKY, Ferlin

HUSKY, Ferlin — C&W '55
(With the Hush Puppies; with Hushpuppies; with Coon Creek Girls; with Bettie Husky; Ferlin Huskey)
Singles: 78 rpm
CAPITOL 5-15 52-57
Singles: 7–inch
ABC 3-5 73-75
ABC/DOT 3-5 75
CAPITOL (2000 thru 3400) 3-6 67-72
(Orange labels.)
CAPITOL (2300 thru 4300) 8-15 52-60
(Purple labels.)
CAPITOL (4400 thru 5900) 4-8 60-67
CACHET 3-4 80
FIRST GENERATION 3-5 78
KING 4-8 60-61
EPs: 7–inch
CAPITOL (609 "Ferlin Husky") 25-35 55
CAPITOL (1-2-3 718 "Songs of the Home and Heart") 20-40 56
(Price is for any of three volumes.)
CAPITOL (837 "Husky Hits") 15-25 57
CAPITOL (1-2-3 880 "Boulevard of Broken Dreams") 15-25 57
(Price is for any of three volumes.)
CAPITOL (921 "Songs from Country Music Holiday") 15-25 57
CAPITOL (1-2-3 1280 "Ferlin Favorites") 10-20 60
(Price is for any of three volumes.)
CAPITOL (1516 "Wings of a Dove") 15-25 60
Picture Sleeves
CAPITOL 5-10 62-68
LPs: 10/12–inch
ABC 5-10 73-75
AUDIOGRAPH ALIVE 5-10 82
CAPITOL (718 "Songs of the Home and Heart") 30-50 56
CAPITOL (880 "Boulevard of Broken Dreams") 25-45 57
CAPITOL (1200 thru 2800 series) 10-20 60-68
(With "T" or "ST" prefix.)
CAPITOL (1200 thru 2800 series) 5-10 68-75
(With "DT" or "SM" prefix.)
FIRST GENERATION 5-10 81
KING (647 "Country Tunes Sung from the Heart") 25-35 59
KING (728 "Easy Livin'") 25-35 60
PHONORAMA 5-8 83
PICKWICK 5-10 70s
PICKWICK/HILLTOP 8-12 65
STARDAY 5-10 77
Also see FIVE KEYS / Ferlin Husky

Also see OWENS, Buck / Faron Young / Ferlin Husky
Also see SHEPARD, Jean, & Ferlin Husky
Also see TUBB, Ernest
Also see VINCENT, Gene / Tommy Sands / Sonny James / Ferlin Husky

HUSKY, Ferlin / Pat Boone

Singles: 7–inch

U.S.A.F. 5-10 60
(Promotional issue only.)

Also see BOONE, Pat
Also see HUSKY, Ferlin

HUTCH, Willie — *P&R/R&B/LP '73*

Singles: 78 rpm

MODERN 8-12 57

Singles: 7–inch

DUNHILL (4012 "The Duck") 25-50 65
MAVERICK 5-10 68
MODERN (1021 "I Can't Get Enough") 20-30 57
MOTOWN 3-5 73-82
RCA 4-8 69
SOUL CITY 4-8
WHITFIELD 3-5 78-79

Picture Sleeves

MOTOWN 3-5 75

LPs: 10/12–inch

MOTOWN 5-10 73-82
RCA 10-12 69
WHITFIELD 5-10 78-79

HUTSON, Leroy — *R&B '73*

(With the Free Spirit Symphony)

Singles: 7–inch

CURTOM 3-5 73-78
RSO 3-5 79

LPs: 10/12–inch

CURTOM 8-10 73-78

Also see IMPRESSIONS

HUTTON, Betty — *P&R '44*

Singles: 78 rpm

CAPITOL 4-8 44-56
RCA 4-6 50
VICTOR 4-8 46

Singles: 7–inch

CAPITOL 5-10 50-56

EPs: 7–inch

CAPITOL 10-20 50-54

LPs: 10/12–inch

CAPITOL (256 "Square in a Social Circle") 30-50 50
(10–inch LP.)
CAPITOL (547 "Satins & Spurs") 20-40 54
W.B. 15-25 59

Also see COMO, Perry, & Betty Hutton
Also see SHORE, Dinah, Tony Martin, Betty Hutton & Phil Harris

HUTTON, Betty, & Tennessee Ernie Ford

Singles: 78 rpm

CAPITOL 4-8 54

Singles: 7–inch

CAPITOL 5-10 54

Also see FORD, Tennessee Ernie
Also see HUTTON, Betty

HUTTON, Danny — *P&R '65*

Singles: 7–inch

HBR 4-8 65
MGM 4-8 66

Picture Sleeves

HBR 10-15 65
MGM 8-12 66

LPs: 10/12–inch

MGM 8-10 70

Also see THREE DOG NIGHT

HYDE, Paul, & Payolas — *P&R/LP '85*

Singles: 7–inch

A&M 3-4 85
I.R.S. 3-4

Picture Sleeves

A&M 3-4 85
I.R.S. 3-4

LPs: 10/12–inch

A&M 5-10 85

HYLAND, Brian — *P&R/R&B '60*

Singles: 7–inch

ABC 3-5 73
ABC-PAR (Except 10400) 5-10 61-64
ABC-PAR (10400 "If Mary's There") 5-10 63
(Black vinyl.)
ABC-PAR (10400 "If Mary's There") 15-20 63
(Colored vinyl. Promotional issue only.)
DOT 4-6 67-69
KAPP 4-8 60-61
LEADER 10-15 60
MCA 3-4 73
PHILIPS 4-8 64-67
ROWE/AMI 5-10 66
("Play Me" Sales Stimulator promotional issue.)
ROULETTE 3-4
UNI 3-5 70-72

Picture Sleeves

ABC-PAR 8-15 61-63
KAPP (342 "Itsy Bitsy Teenie Weenie Yellow Polkadot Bikini") 15-20 60
KAPP (352 "Four Little Heels") 20-30 60
(Black and white sleeve. Promotional issue only.)
KAPP (352 "Four Little Heels") 10-20 60
(Color sleeve.)
KAPP (363 "I Gotta Go") 15-25 60
PHILIPS 4-8 64-67

LPs: 10/12–inch

ABC-PAR 20-25 61-64
DOT 10-12 69
KAPP (1202 "Bashful Blonde") 25-30 60
(Monaural.)
KAPP (3202 "Bashful Blonde") 30-40 60
PHILIPS 15-20 64-66
PICKWICK 5-10
PRIVATE STOCK 5-10 77
RHINO 5-8
UNI 8-10 71
WING 10-12 67

HYMAN, Dick — *P&R '54*

(Dick Hyman Trio; with His Electric Eclectics)

Singles: 78 rpm

MGM 3-5 54-57

Singles: 7–inch

COLUMBIA 3-5 74-75
COMMAND 3-8 61-70
EVEREST 4-8 60
MGM 5-10 54-62
RCA 4-8 62

Picture Sleeves

MGM (12149 "Mack the Knife") 10-15 55

LPs: 10/12–inch

ATLANTIC 5-10 75
COLUMBIA 5-10 74
COMMAND 5-15 60-73
EVEREST 5-10 60
FAMOUS DOOR 5-10 73
MCA 5-10 77
MGM 10-20 54-63
PROJECT 3 5-10 71
RCA 4-8 80-83
SUNSET 5-10 66

HYMAN, Phyllis — *R&B '76*

Singles: 12–inch

ARISTA 4-6 83

Singles: 7–inch

ARISTA 3-5 78-83
BUDDAH 3-5 77
DESERT MOON 3-5 76
PHILADELPHIA INT'L 3-4 86

LPs: 10/12–inch

ARISTA 5-10 79-83
BUDDAH 5-10 77
PHILADELPHIA INT'L 5-10 86

HYMAN, Phyllis, & Michael Henderson

Singles: 7–inch

ARISTA 3-4 81

Also see CONNORS, Norman
Also see HENDERSON, Michael
Also see HYMAN, Phyllis

I LEVEL — *D&D '83*

Singles: 12–inch

VIRGIN 4-6 82-84

Singles: 7–inch

VIRGIN 3-4 82-84

LPs: 10/12–inch

VIRGIN 5-10 83

I.A.& P. CO: see ITALIAN ASPHALT & Pavement Co.

I.R.T. — *D&D '84*

(Interboro Rhythm Team)

Singles: 12–inch

RCA 4-6 84

Singles: 7–inch

RCA 3-4 84

IAN, Janis — *P&R/LP '67*

Singles: 7–inch

CAPITOL 3-5 71
CASABLANCA 3-4 80
COLUMBIA 3-5 74-81
POLYDOR 3-5 78
VERVE 3-5
VERVE/FOLKWAYS 4-8 66-67
VERVE/FORECAST 4-6 68-69

Picture Sleeves

COLUMBIA 3-6 75

LPs: 10/12–inch

CAPITOL 8-12 71-75
COLUMBIA 8-10 74-81
MGM 8-10 70
POLYDOR 8-10 75
VERVE/FOLKWAYS 10-15 67
VERVE/FORECAST 10-15 68-69

IAN & SYLVIA — *LP '63*

Singles: 7–inch

COLUMBIA 3-5 71-72
MGM 4-6 67-69
VANGUARD 4-8 63-68
VERVE/FOLKWAYS 3-6 67

Picture Sleeves

COLUMBIA 3-5 71

LPs: 10/12–inch

AMPEX 8-10 70
COLUMBIA 6-10 71-73
MGM 8-12 67-70
VANGUARD 10-20 63-71
VERVE/FOLKWAYS 8-15 67

Members: Ian Tyson; Sylvia Fricker.

ICE CUBE — *LP '90*

LPs: 10/12–inch

PRIORITY 5-8 90-91

ICE-T — *LP '87*

Singles: 7–inch

SIRE 3-4 88-90

Picture Sleeves

SIRE 3-4 88

LPs: 10/12–inch

SIRE 5-10 87-91

ICEHOUSE — *P&R/LP '81*

Singles: 12–inch

CHRYSALIS 4-6 81-86

Singles: 7–inch

CHRYSALIS 3-4 81-88

Picture Sleeves

CHRYSALIS 3-4 81-88

LPs: 10/12–inch

CHRYSALIS 5-10 81-88

ICICLE WORKS P&R/D&D/LP '84

Singles: 12-inch

ARISTA....4-6 84

Singles: 7-inch

ARISTA....3-4 84

LPs: 10/12-inch

ARISTA....5-10 84

ICON LP '84

LPs: 10/12-inch

CAPITOL....5-10 84

Members: Steve Clifford; Dan Wexler; Pat Dixon; John Aquilino; Tracy Wallach; Jerry Harrison.

IDEALS R&B '66

Singles: 7-inch

CHECKER (920 "Knee Socks")....15-25 59
CHECKER (979 "Knee Socks")....10-15 61
PASO (6401 "Together")....30-50 61
PASO (6402 "Magic")....30-50 61
SATELLITE (2007 "Kissin' ")....5-10 65
SATELLITE (2009 "You Hurt Me")....10-15 66
SATELLITE (2011 "Kissing Won't Go Out of Style")....15-25 66

Members: Major Lance; Sam Stewart; Reggie Jackson; Leonard Mitchell.

Also see LANCE, Major

IDES OF MARCH P&R '66

Singles: 7-inch

KAPP....4-6 69
PARROT....5-10 66-67
RCA....3-5 72-73
W.B.....3-6 69-71

LPs: 10/12-inch

RCA....8-12 72-73
W.B.....10-15 70-71

Members: Jim Peterik; Mike Borch; Ray Herr; Bob Bergland; Chuck Soumar; John Larson; Larry Millas.

IDLE RACE

Singles: 7-inch

LIBERTY (55997 "Here We Go Round the Lemon Tree")....10-15 67

LPs: 10/12-inch

LIBERTY (7603 "Birthday Party")....25-30 69
SUNSET....8-12 72

Members: Jeff Lynne; Greg Masters; Roger Spencer; Dave Pritchard.

Also see LYNNE, Jeff

IDOL, Billy LP '81

Singles: 12-inch

CHRYSALIS (Black vinyl)....4-8 81-86
CHRYSALIS (8V8-42719 "Eyes Without a Face")....10-15 84
(Picture disc.)

Singles: 7-inch

CHRYSALIS....3-4 81-90

Picture Sleeves

CHRYSALIS....3-5 82-90

LPs: 10/12-inch

CHRYSALIS (1377 "Billy Idol")....10-20 82
(Promotional issue only.)
CHRYSALIS (4000 "Don't Stop")....8-10 81
CHRYSALIS (20000 series)....5-8 90
CHRYSALIS (40000 series)....5-10 82-87

IFIELD, Frank P&R '62

Singles: 7-inch

CAPITOL....5-10 63-65
HICKORY....4-8 66-71
MAM....3-5 71
VEE JAY....5-10 62-63
W.B.....3-5 79

LPs: 10/12-inch

CAPITOL....10-20 63
COLUMBIA....10-20
HICKORY....10-20 66-68
VEE JAY....10-20 62

Also see BEATLES / Frank Ifield

IGLESIAS, Julio LP '83

Singles: 7-inch

ALAHAMBRA....3-6 72-75
COLUMBIA....3-4 83-89

LPs: 10/12-inch

COLUMBIA (Except 39928)....5-10 83-90
COLUMBIA (39928 "1100 Bel Air Place")....10-15 84
(Picture disc.)

IGLESIAS, Julio, & Willie Nelson
(Willie Nelson & Julio Iglesias) C&W/P&R '84

Singles: 7-inch

COLUMBIA (Except 04495)....3-4 84
COLUMBIA (04495 "As Time Goes By")....8-12 84

Picture Sleeves

COLUMBIA (Except 04495)....3-4 84
COLUMBIA (04495 "As Time Goes By")....10-15 84

Also see NELSON, Willie

IGLESIAS, Julio, & Diana Ross P&R '84

Singles: 7-inch

COLUMBIA....3-4 84

Picture Sleeves

COLUMBIA....3-4 84

Also see ROSS, Diana

IGLESIAS, Julio, & Stevie Wonder P&R '88

Singles: 7-inch

COLUMBIA....3-4 88

Picture Sleeves

COLUMBIA....3-4 88

Also see IGLESIAS, Julio
Also see WONDER, Stevie

IGGY & STOOGES: see POP, Iggy

IKETTES P&R/R&B '62

Singles: 7-inch

ATCO....5-10 61-62
INNIS....4-8 64
MODERN....4-8 64-66
PHI-DAN....4-8
POMPEII....4-8 68
TEENA....4-8 63
U.A.....3-6 71-72

LPs: 10/12-inch

MODERN....15-20 65
U.A.....8-10 73-75

Members: Delores Johnson; Eloise Hester; Joshie Jo Armstead; Vanetta Fields; Jessie Smith; Robbie Montgomery. Session: Tina Turner.

Also see MAXAYN
Also see MIRETTES
Also see TURNER, Ike & Tina

ILLINOIS SPEED PRESS LP '69

Singles: 7-inch

COLUMBIA....4-8 68-70

LPs: 10/12-inch

COLUMBIA....10-15 69-70

Members: Paul Cotton; Rob Lewine; Fred Page; Kal David; Mike Anthony; Frank Bartoli.

Also see POCO

ILLUSION P&R/LP '69
(The Illusion)

Singles: 7-inch

DYNO VOICE....4-8 68
STEED....4-6 69-71

LPs: 10/12-inch

STEED....10-20 69-70

ILLUSION LP '77

Singles: 7-inch

ISLAND....3-5 77-78

LPs: 10/12-inch

ISLAND....5-10 77-78

ILLUSION R&B '82

Singles: 7-inch

SUGAR HILL....3-4 82

ILLUSTRATED MAN D&D '84

Singles: 7-inch

CAPITOL....3-4 84

IMAGINATION R&B '82

Singles: 12-inch

ELEKTRA....4-6 84
MCA....4-6 83

Singles: 7-inch

ELEKTRA....3-4 83
MCA....3-4 82-83
RCA....3-4 87

LPs: 10/12-inch

MCA....5-10 82

IMPACT P&R/R&B '76

Singles: 7-inch

ATCO....3-5 76
FANTASY....3-5 77-78

LPs: 10/12-inch

ATCO....8-10 75
FANTASY....5-10 77

Members: Damon Harris; John Simms; Donald Tilghman; Charles Timmons.

Also see HARRIS, Damon

IMPALAS P&R/R&B '59
("Featuring Joe 'Speedo' Frazier")

Singles: 7-inch

CUB (9022 "I Ran All the Way Home")....50-75 59
CUB (9022 "Sorry I Ran All the Way Home")....15-25 59
(Note slightly different title.)
CUB (9033 "Oh What a Fool")....15-25 59
CUB (9053 "Peggy Darling")....15-25 60
HAMILTON (50026 "I Was a Fool")....15-25 59
MGM....3-6 64-78
U.G.H.A. (17 "My Hero")....3-5 82

Picture Sleeves

U.G.H.A. (17 "My Hero")....3-5 82

EPs: 7-inch

CUB (5000 "Sorry, I Ran All the Way Home")....100-150 59

LPs: 10/12-inch

CUB (CUB-8003 "Sorry, I Ran All the Way Home")....100-150 59
(Monaural.)
CUB (CUBS-8003 "Sorry, I Ran All the Way Home")....150-250 59
(Stereo.)

Also see SPEEDO & IMPALAS

IMPALAS / Horst Jankowski & His Orchestra

Singles: 7-inch

COLLECTABLES....3-4 85

Also see IMPALAS
Also see JANKOWSKI, Horst, & His Orchestra

IMPELLITTERI LP '88

LPs: 10/12-inch

RELATIVITY....5-8 88

IMPERIALS R&B/P&R '58

Singles: 7-inch

CAPITOL....8-12 63
CARLTON....10-15 61
END (1027 "Tears on My Pillow")....25-50 58
(First pressing. Quickly repressed, crediting "Little Anthony & Imperials.")
LIBERTY....8-12 58

Also see LITTLE ANTHONY & IMPERIALS

IMPRESSIONS R&B '58
("Featuring Jerry Butler"; with Riley Hampton's Orchestra)

Singles: 12-inch

20TH FOX....4-8 79

Singles: 78 rpm

ABNER (1017 "Come Back My Love")....50-75 58

Singles: 7-inch

ABC....4-8 66-68
ABC-PAR (Except 10328)....5-15 61-66
ABC-PAR (10328 "Never Let Me Go")....20-30 62
ABNER (1017 "Come Back My Love")....20-30 58
ABNER (1023 "The Gift of Love")....20-30 58
ABNER (1025 "Lonely One")....20-30 59

ABNER (1034 "Say That You Love Me") 25-50 59
ADORE (901 "Popcorn Willie") 50-75 64
BANDERA (2504 "Listen") 35-50 59
CHI-SOUND 3-5 81
COTILLION 3-5 76-77
CURTOM 3-6 68-76
ICHIBAN 3-4 94
MCA 3-4 87
PORT 5-10 62
SWIRL (107 "I Need Your Love") 20-40 62
20TH FOX 3-5 81
VEE JAY (424 thru 574) 10-15 61-63
(Vee Jay 280, *For Your Precious Love*, appears in the Jerry Butler section.)
VEE JAY (621 "Say That You Love Me") 20-30 64

Picture Sleeves

CURTOM 4-8 68

EPs: 7-inch

CURTOM (20 "Do You Want to Win") 5-10 70
(Promotional issue only.)

LPs: 10/12-inch

ABC 10-15 66-76
ABC-PAR 15-20 63-66
COTILLION 8-10 76
CURTOM 8-10 68-76
MCA 5-10 82
PICKWICK 8-10 75
SCEPTER/CITATION 8-10
SIRE 8-12 76
20TH FOX 5-10 79-81
UPFRONT 8-10

Members: Curtis Mayfield; Sam Gooden; Richard Brooks; Fred Cash; Leroy Hutson; Reggie Torlan; Ralph Johnson; Nate Evans.
Also see EVERETT, Betty / Impressions
Also see HUTSON, Leroy
Also see MAYFIELD, Curtis
Also see MYSTIQUE

IMPRESSIONS / Jerry Butler

LPs: 10/12-inch

SIRE 5-10 77

Also see BUTLER, Jerry
Also see IMPRESSIONS

IMPRESSORS

Singles: 7-inch

CUB (9010 "Do You Love Her") 10-20 58
ONYX (514 "Is It Too Late") 30-40 57

IN CROWD — *P&R '66*

Singles: 7-inch

BRENT 5-10 65
HICKORY 10-15 65
MUSICOR (1111 "Do the Surfer Jerk") 10-20 65
RONN 10-20
SWAN 4-8 65
TOWER 5-8 65-66
VIVA 4-8 66-67

INCREDIBLE BONGO BAND — *P&R/R&B '73*

Singles: 7-inch

MGM 3-5 73
PRIDE 3-5 72-74

LPs: 10/12-inch

PRIDE 8-10 73-74

INCREDIBLE STRING BAND — *LP '68*

LPs: 10/12-inch

ELEKTRA 8-12 67-72
REPRISE 8-12 72-74

INCREDIBLES — *R&B '66*

Singles: 7-inch

AUDIO ARTS 4-8 66-68
CLASS 4-8 66
TETRAGRAMMATON 3-6 69

LPs: 10/12-inch

AUDIO ARTS 10-12 70

INDECENT OBSESSION — *P&R/LP '90*

Singles: 7-inch

MCA 3-4 90

LPs: 10/12-inch

MCA 5-8 90

INDEEP — *R&B/D&D '83*

Singles: 12-inch

SOUND of NEW YORK 4-6 83-85

Singles: 7-inch

SOUND of NEW YORK 3-4 83-85

LPs: 10/12-inch

SOUND of NEW YORK 5-10 83

INDEPENDENTS — *P&R/R&B '72*

Singles: 7-inch

WAND 3-6 72-74

LPs: 10/12-inch

WAND 8-12 72-74

Members: Chuck Jackson; Maurice Jackson; Eric Thomas; Helen Curry.

INDIA — *D&D '83*

Singles: 12-inch

WEST END 4-6 83

INDIGO GIRLS — *P&R/LP '89*

Singles: 7-inch

EPIC 3-4 89-90

LPs: 10/12-inch

EPIC 5-8 89-90

INDIGOS — *R&B '66*

Singles: 7-inch

DATE 4-8 66
VERVE/FOLKWAYS 5-10 65

INDIOS TABAJARAS, Los: see LOS INDIOS TABAJARAS

INDIVIDUALS — *R&B '75*

Singles: 7-inch

P.I.P. 3-5 75
21 3-5

INDUSTRY — *P&R '83*

Singles: 7-inch

CAPITOL 3-4 83

INFINITY — *R&B '69*

(Featuring Billy Butler)

Singles: 7-inch

FOUNTAIN 4-6 69
MERCURY 3-5 70
UNI 3-5 72

Members: Billy Butler; Earl Batts; Jess Tillman; Larry Wade; Phyllis Know.
Also see BUTLER, Billy

INFORMATION SOCIETY — *P&R/LP '88*

Singles: 7-inch

TOMMY BOY 3-4 88-90

Picture Sleeves

TOMMY BOY 3-4 88

LPs: 10/12-inch

TOMMY BOY 5-8 88-90

INGMANN, Jørgen — *P&R/R&B '61*

Singles: 78 rpm

MERCURY 4-8 56

Singles: 7-inch

ATCO 5-10 60-66
MERCURY 8-12 56
PARROT 4-8 64
U.A. INT'L 4-6 68

LPs: 10/12-inch

ATCO 25-35 62
MERCURY 25-35 56
U.A. INT'L 8-12 68

INGRAM — *R&B '77*

Singles: 7-inch

H&L 3-5 77

LPs: 10/12-inch

H&L 8-10 77

INGRAM, James — *R&B/D&D/LP '83*

Singles: 12-inch

QWEST 4-6 83

Singles: 7-inch

MCA 3-4 87
QWEST 3-4 83-86
W.B. 3-4 90

Picture Sleeves

QWEST 3-4 83-86

LPs: 10/12-inch

QWEST 5-10 83-86
W.B. 5-8 90

Also see AUSTIN, Patti, & James Ingram
Also see JONES, Quincy, & James Ingram
Also see ROGERS, Kenny, Kim Carnes & James Ingram
Also see RONSTADT, Linda, & James Ingram
Also see U.S.A. for AFRICA

INGRAM, James, & Michael McDonald — *P&R/R&B '83*

Singles: 7-inch

QWEST 3-4 83

Also see INGRAM, James
Also see McDONALD, Michael

INGRAM, Luther — *R&B '69*

(With the G-Men)

Singles: 7-inch

DECCA (31794 "Ain't That Nice") 4-8 65
ERIC 3-4 70s
HIB (698 "If It's All the Same to You Babe") 50-75 67
KO KO 5-10 67-78
PROFILE 3-4 86-87
SMASH (2019 "Foxy Devil") 10-15 66

LPs: 10/12-inch

KO KO 8-10 71-76
(May also be shown as Koko – one word.)

INK SPOTS — *P&R '39*

(Charlie Fuqua's Ink Spots; Charlie Owens & Sensational Ink Spots)

Singles: 78 rpm

BLUEBIRD (6530 "Swingin' on the Strings") 15-25 36
DECCA (800 series) 10-15 36
DECCA (1000 thru 4000 series) 5-15 36-42
DECCA (18000 thru 30000 series) 4-10 42-57

Singles: 7-inch

DECCA 5-15 50-61
GRAND AWARD 5-10 56
VERVE 4-8 60
X-TRA 4-8 60

EPs: 7-inch

DECCA 5-15 54-56
GRAND AWARD 5-15 56
TOPS (606 "Ink Spots") 10-15 59
(Two-EP set.)
WALDORF MUSIC HALL 5-15 55

LPs: 10/12-inch

AUDITION 10-20 56
COLORTONE 15-20 58
CORAL 4-6 73
CORONET 10-15 60s
CROWN (144 "Greatest Hits") 10-15 59
(Black vinyl.)
CROWN (144 "Greatest Hits") 20-40 59
(Colored vinyl.)
CROWN (217 "Sensational Ink Spots") 10-15 60s
CROWN (448 "If I Didn't Care") 10-15 60s
CROWN (5197 "Sensational Ink Spots") 10-15 60s
DECCA (182 "Best of the Ink Spots") 10-20 65
(Monaural.)
DECCA (7-182 "Best of the Ink Spots") 10-20 65
(Stereo.)
DECCA (4297 "Our Golden Favorites") 10-20 63
(Monaural.)
DECCA (7-4297 "Our Golden Favorites") 10-20 63
(Stereo.)
DECCA (5000 series) 20-40 51-53
(10-inch LPs.)
DECCA (7000 & 8000 series) 15-30 54-59
DESIGN 5-10 60s
DIPLOMAT 5-10 64
EVEREST 5-10 82
EXACT 5-10 80

FORD (115 "Hawaiian Wedding Song") 15-25 62
GOLDEN TONE 5-10
GRAND AWARD 10-20 56-59
HURRAH 10-15 60s
MCA 5-10 73
MAYFAIR 8-15
MODERN (7023 "Fabulous Ink Spots") 75-125
PAULA 5-10 72
PIROUETTE 10-20
SPIN-O-RAMA 5-10 60s
TOPS (1561 "The Ink Spots") 20-30 57
TOPS (1668 "The Ink Spots, Vol. 2") 15-20 59
VERVE 15-25 56-60
VOCALION 8-15 59-65
WALDORF MUSIC HALL (144 Spirituals and Jubilees") 30-40 55
WALDORF MUSIC HALL (152 Spirituals and Jubilees, Vol. 2") 30-40 55
WESCO ("Hawaiian Wedding Song") 25-35 62
(Number not known.)

Members: Bill Kenny; Orville Jones; Herb Kenny; Charlie Fuqua; Ivory "Deek" Watson; Bernie Mackey; Cliff Givens; Billy Bowen; Charlie Owens.

Also see FITZGERALD, Ella, & Ink Spots

INMAN, Autry — C&W '53

Singles: 78 rpm

DECCA (Except 28629 & 29936) 4-8 53-56
DECCA (28629 "That's All Right") 5-10 56
DECCA (29936 "Be Bop Baby") 5-10 56

Singles: 7-inch

DECCA (Except 28629 & 29936) 5-10 53-56
DECCA (28629 "That's All Right") 15-25 56
DECCA (29936 "Be Bop Baby") 25-50 56
EPIC 4-8 67-69
GLAD 5-10 60
JUBILEE 4-8 65-69
MERCURY 4-8 62
MILLION 3-5 72
RCA 5-10 58
RISQUE (103 "Niteclubbin' ") 5-10 67
RISQUE (105 "The Golf Game") 5-10 67
SIMS 4-8 63-64
U.A. 5-8 60

LPs: 10/12-inch

ALSHIRE 8-12 69
EPIC 10-15 68
GUEST STAR 8-12
JUBILEE 10-20 64-69
MOUNTAIN DEW 15-25 63
SIMS 15-20 64

Also see DEAN, Jimmy / David Houston / Warner Mack / Autry Inman

INMATES — P&R/LP '79

Singles: 7-inch

POLYDOR/RADAR 3-5 79

LPs: 10/12-inch

POLYDOR 5-10 79-80

INNER CITY — P&R/LP '89

Singles: 7-inch

VIRGIN 3-4 89-90

Picture Sleeves

VIRGIN 3-4 89

LPs: 10/12-inch

VIRGIN 5-8 89

INNER CITY JAM BAND — R&B '77

Singles: 7-inch

BAREBACK 3-5 77

INNER LIFE — R&B '79

Singles: 12-inch

SALSOUL 4-6 83

Singles: 7-inch

PERSONAL 3-4 84
PRELUDE 3-5 79-80
SALSOUL 3-4 83

Member: Jocelyn Brown.

Also see BROWN, Jocelyn

INNERVISION — R&B '75

Singles: 7-inch

ARIOLA AMERICA 3-5 77
PRIVATE STOCK 3-5 75

INNOCENCE — P&R '66

Singles: 7-inch

KAMA SUTRA 4-8 66-67

LPs: 10/12-inch

KAMA SUTRA 15-20 67

Members: Pete Anders; Vinnie Poncia.

INNOCENCE IN DANGER — D&D '84

Singles: 12-inch

EPIC 4-6 84

Singles: 7-inch

EPIC 3-4 84

INNOCENCE MISSION — LP '90

LPs: 10/12-inch

A&M 5-8 90

INNOCENTS — P&R '60

Singles: 7-inch

DECCA (31519 "Don't Cry") 15-25 63
ERA 3-5 72
INDIGO (105 "Honest I Do") 15-25 60
INDIGO (111 "Gee Whiz") 15-25 60
INDIGO (116 "Kathy") 15-25 61
INDIGO (124 "Beware") 15-25 61
INDIGO (128 "Donna") 15-25 61
INDIGO (132 "Pains in My Heart") 15-25 61
INDIGO (141 "Time") 10-20 62
PORT (3026 "Gee Whiz") 5-10 60s
REPRISE (20112 "Oh How I Miss My Baby"/"Be Mine") 15-25 62
REPRISE (20125 "Oh How I Miss My Baby"/" You're Never Satisfied") 10-20 62
TRANS WORLD (7001 "Tick Tock") 15-25 60
W.B. (5450 "My Heart Stood Still") ... 20-30 64

LPs: 10/12-inch

INDIGO (503 "Innocently Yours") 50-100 61

Members: Darron Stankey; Al Candaleria; Jim West.

Also see YOUNG, Kathy

INSIDERS — LP '87

Singles: 12-inch

EPIC ("Ghost on the Beach") 4-8 87
(Promotional issue only.)

Singles: 7-inch

EPIC (07352 "Ghost on the Beach") 3-4 87
(Black vinyl.)
EPIC (07352 "Ghost on the Beach") 4-8 87
(Colored vinyl. Promotional issue only.)

Picture Sleeves

EPIC (07352 "Ghost on the Beach") 3-4 87

LPs: 10/12-inch

EPIC (40630 "Ghost on the Beach") ... 5-10 87

INSTANT FUNK — P&R/R&B/LP '79

Singles: 12-inch

SALSOUL 4-8 79-83

Singles: 7-inch

SALSOUL 3-5 78-83
TSOP 3-5 75-77

LPs: 10/12-inch

SALSOUL 5-10 79-83
TSOP 5-10 76

INTERLUDE — R&B '80

Singles: 7-inch

STAR VISION INT'L 3-4 80

INTERNATIONAL ALL STARS — LP '61

LPs: 10/12-inch

LONDON 5-10 61

INTRIGUES — P&R/R&B '69

Singles: 7-inch

TOOT 4-8 68
YEW 3-6 69-71

LPs: 10/12-inch

YEW 10-15 70

INTRIQUE — R&B '87

Singles: 7-inch

COOLTEMPO 3-4 87

INTRUDERS — P&R '59

(Intruders Trio)

Singles: 7-inch

BELTONE (1009 "Camptown Rock") .. 5-10 61
FAME (101 "Jeffries Rock") 10-20 59
FAME (313 "Creepin") 10-20 59
FAME (616 "Rock-A-Ma-Roll") 10-20 59
VALTONE (409 "Rockamaroll") 15-25 59

INTRUDERS — P&R/R&B '66

Singles: 7-inch

EXCEL 10-15
GAMBLE 5-10 66-73
GOWEN (1401 "Come Home Soon") 20-40 62
PHILADELPHIA INT'L 3-5 72
RIPETE 3-5 85
TSOP 3-5 74-75

Picture Sleeves

GAMBLE 4-8 66

LPs: 10/12-inch

GAMBLE 10-15 67-73
TSOP 8-10 75

Members: Sam Brown; Eugene Doughtry; Phil Terry; Robert Edwards; Bobby Starr.

INVINCIBLES — R&B '65

Singles: 7-inch

DOUBLE SHOT 5-10 66
INVINCIBLE 5-10 66
LOMA 5-10 66
RAMPART 5-10 69
W.B. 5-10 64-67

INVISIBLE MAN'S BAND — P&R/R&B/LP '80

Singles: 7-inch

BOARDWALK 3-4 81-82
MANGO 3-4 80
MOVE'N GROOVE 3-4 83

LPs: 10/12-inch

BOARDWALK 10-20 81
MANGO 5-8 80

Members: Clarence Burke; Ken Burke; James Burke; Dennis Burke.

Also see FIVE STAIRSTEPS

INVITATIONS — R&B '73

Singles: 7-inch

SILVER BLUE 5-10 73

Members: Herman Colefield; Gary Grant; Bill Morris; Bobby Rivers.

INXS — P&R/LP '83

Singles: 12-inch

ATCO 4-6 84
ATLANTIC (Except 86563) 4-6 85-86
ATLANTIC (86563 "New Sensation") 10-15 88
(Picture disc.)
ATLANTIC (86563 "New Sensation") 15-20 88
(Picture disc. Promotional issue only.)

Singles: 7-inch

ATCO 3-4 83-85
ATLANTIC 3-4 85-90

Picture Sleeves

ATCO 3-4 83-84
ATLANTIC 3-4 85-90

LPs: 10/12-inch

ATCO 5-10 83-85
ATLANTIC 5-10 85-90

Members: Micheal Hutchence; Tim Farriss; Andrew Farriss; Jon Farriss; Gary Beers; Kirk Pengilly.

INXS & JIMMY BARNES — P&R '87

Singles: 7-inch

ATLANTIC 3-4 87

Also see BARNES, Jimmy
Also see INXS

IRBY, Joyce "Fenderella" P&R '90

Singles: 12-inch

MOTOWN....4-8 90

Singles: 7-inch

MOTOWN....3-4 90

LPs: 10/12-inch

MOTOWN....5-8 90

Also see KLYMAXX

IRIS, Donnie P&R/LP '80

Singles: 7-inch

HME....3-4 85
MCA....3-4 80-83

Picture Sleeves

HME....3-4 85
MCA....3-4 82-83

LPs: 10/12-inch

HME....5-10 85
MCA....5-10 80-83
MIDWEST....5-10 80

Also see JAGGERZ

IRISH ROVERS P&R/LP '68

Singles: 7-inch

DECCA....3-6 68-70

LPs: 10/12-inch

CLEVELAND INT'L....5-8 81
DECCA....8-15 68-72
MCA....5-10 73-77
SANDCASTLE....5-10 76

IRON BUTTERFLY P&R/LP '68

Singles: 7-inch

ATCO....3-8 68-71
MCA....3-4 75

EPs: 7-inch

ATCO (4524 "Iron Butterfly")....20-30 68
(Promotional issue only. Issued with paper sleeve.)

LPs: 10/12-inch

ATCO (Except 227)....10-15 68-71
ATCO (227 "Heavy")....15-20 68
MCA....8-10 75

Members: Doug Ingle; Mike Pinera; Larry Reinhardt; Ron Bushy; Lee Dorman; Erik Brann.
Also see CAPTAIN BEYOND
Also see PINERA, Mike

IRON MAIDEN LP '81

Singles: 7-inch

CAPITOL (Except V-15375)....3-4 88
CAPITOL (V-15375 "Can I Play with Madness")....10-20 88
(Shaped picture disc.)

LPs: 10/12-inch

CAPITOL (Except "SEAX" & "SJ" series)....5-10 82-88
CAPITOL (SEAX-12215 "Number of the Beast")....35-45 82
(Picture disc.)
CAPITOL (SEAX-12306 "Piece of Mind")....40-60 83
(Picture disc.)
CAPITOL (SJ-12321 "Powerslave")....8-12
("Special Limited Edition, Virgin Maiden Vinyl Pressing.")
EPIC....5-8 90
HARVEST....5-10 80-82

Members: Bruce Dickinson; Dave Murray; Adrian Smith; Niko Mc Brian; Steve Harris.

IRONHORSE P&R/LP '79

Singles: 7-inch

SCOTTI BROS....3-4 79-80

LPs: 10/12-inch

SCOTTI BROS....5-10 79-80

Member: Randy Bachman.
Also see BACHMAN, Randy

IRWIN, Big Dee P&R '63

(Difosco Erwin; Dee Irwin; with Little Eva)

Singles: 7-inch

BLISS....5-10
DIMENSION....5-10 63-64
FAIRMOUNT....8-12 66
IMPERIAL....5-10 68
ROTATE....10-20 65
20TH FOX....5-10

Also see DIFOSCO
Also see ERWIN, Dee
Also see IRWIN, Dee, & Mamie Galore
Also see LITTLE EVA
Also see PASTELLS

IRWIN, Dee

Singles: 7-inch

REDD COACH....5-10

IRWIN, Dee, & Mamie Galore

Singles: 7-inch

IMPERIAL....4-8 68-69

Also see IRWIN, Big Dee

ISAAK, Chris LP '87

Singles: 12-inch

W.B. (2265 "Dancin' ")....8-12 80s
(Promotional issue.)

Singles: 7-inch

REPRISE....3-4 91
W.B....3-4 85

LPs: 10/12-inch

REPRISE....5-8 89
W.B....5-10 87

ISLANDERS P&R '59

(Featuring Randy Starr)

Singles: 7-inch

MAYFLOWER....5-10 59-60

LPs: 10/12-inch

MAYFLOWER....20-30 60

Members: Randy Starr; Frank Metis.
Also see BELAFONTE, Harry / Islanders
Also see STARR, Randy

ISLE OF MAN P&R/LP '86

Singles: 7-inch

PASHA....3-4 86

Picture Sleeves

PASHA....3-4 86

LPs: 10/12-inch

PASHA....5-10 86

ISLEY, Ernie LP '90

Singles: 7-inch

ELEKTRA....3-4 90

LPs: 10/12-inch

ELEKTRA....5-8 90

Also see ISLEY BROTHERS

ISLEY, Ron

Singles: 7-inch

W.B....3-4 89

LPs: 10/12-inch

W.B....5-8 89

Also see ISLEY BROTHERS
Also see STEWART, Rod, & Ronald Isley

ISLEY BROTHERS P&R '59

("Featuring Ronald Isley")

Singles: 78 rpm

TEENAGE (1004 "Angels Cried")....200-400 57

Singles: 12-inch

T-NECK....4-8 79-83
W.B....4-6 87

Singles: 7-inch

ATLANTIC....5-10 61-65
CINDY (3009 "Don't Be Jealous")....50-100 58
EARLY BIRD (1007 "Don't Be Jealous")....4-6 96
(Colored vinyl.)
GONE (5022 "Everybody's Gonna Rock & Roll")....25-50 58
GONE (5048 "My Love")....25-50 59
MARK-X (7003 "Rockin' MacDonald)....25-50 57
MARK-X (8000 "Rockin' MacDonald)....15-25 58
RCA (447-0500 series)....4-6 61
(Black label, RCA dog on top. Gold Standard.)
RCA (447-0500 series)....3-5 65
(Black label, RCA dog on left side. Gold Standard.)
RCA (47-7000 series)....10-20 59-60
RCA (61-7588 "Shout")....25-35 59
(Stereo.)
T-NECK (Except 501)....3-6 69-84
T-NECK (501 "Testify")....4-8 64
TAMLA....5-15 66-69
TEENAGE (1004 "Angels Cried")....200-400 57
U.A....10-20 63-64
V.I.P. (25020 "I Hear a Symphony")....300-500 65
VEEP....4-8 66
WAND....8-12 62-63
W.B....3-4 85-88

Picture Sleeves

W.B....3-4 87-89

LPs: 10/12-inch

BUDDAH....10-12 76
CAMDEN....8-10 73-75
COLLECTABLES....6-8 88
MOTOWN....5-10 80-82
PHILADELPHIA INT'L....5-10 78
PICKWICK....5-10 77
RCA (LPM-2156 "Shout!")....35-45 59
(Monaural.)
RCA (LSP-2156 "Shout!")....45-55 59
(Stereo.)
SCEPTER....10-20 66
SUNSET....8-10 69
T-NECK (Except 137)....8-10 69-84
T-NECK (137 "Everything You Always Wanted to Hear")....10-15 76
(Promotional issue only.)
TAMLA (269 "This Old Heart of Mine")....25-50 66
TAMLA (275 "Soul on the Rocks")....15-25 67
TAMLA (287 "Doin' Their Thing")....15-20 69
TRIP....8-10 76
U.A. (500 series)....8-10 75
U.A. (6000 series)....20-25 63
WAND (WD-653 "Twist & Shout")....20-30 62
(Monaural.)
WAND (WDS-653 "Twist & Shout")..30-40 62
(Stereo.)
W.B....5-10 85-87

Members: Ron Isley; Rudy Isley; O'Kelly Isley; Ernie Isley; Marvin Isley.
Also see CHRISTIE, Lou, & Classics / Isley Brothers / Chiffons
Also see HENDRIX, Jimi, & Isley Brothers
Also see ISLEY, Ernie
Also see ISLEY, Ron
Also see ISLEY - JASPER - ISLEY
Also see RASCALS / Isley Brothers

ISLEY BROTHERS & DAVE "BABY" CORTEZ

LPs: 10/12-inch

T-NECK....8-10 69

Also see CORTEZ, Dave "Baby"

ISLEY BROTHERS / Brooklyn Bridge

LPs: 10/12-inch

T-NECK (3004 "Live at Yankee Stadium")....20-30 69
(With guests, Edwin Hawkins Singers; Five Stairsteps, Sweet Cherries, and Judy White.)

Also see BROOKLYN BRIDGE
Also see FIVE STAIRSTEPS
Also see HAWKINS, Edwin, Singers

ISLEY BROTHERS / Go-Go's

EPs: 7-inch

RCA/WURLITZER....10-15 64
(Promotional issue only.)

ISLEY BROTHERS / Marvin & Johnny

LPs: 10/12-inch

CROWN....10-20 63

Also see MARVIN & JOHNNY

ISLEY - JASPER - ISLEY R&B '84

Singles: 12-inch

CBS ASSOCIATED....4-6 85-86

Singles: 7-inch

CBS ASSOCIATED....3-4 85-87

LPs: 10/12-inch

CBS ASSOCIATED............................5-10 85-86

Members: Marvin Isley; Chris Jasper; Ernie Isley.

Also see ISLEY BROTHERS

Also see JASPER, Chris

IT'S A BEAUTIFUL DAY LP '69

(Featuring David LaFlamme)

Singles: 7-inch

COLUMBIA............................4-8 69-73
SAN FRANCISCO SOUND................8-12 70

LPs: 10/12-inch

COLUMBIA (1058 "Marrying Maiden")..........................15-20 70
COLUMBIA (9768 "It's a Beautiful Day")..........................20-30 69
COLUMBIA (30734 "Choice Quality Stuff/Anytime")..........................10-15 71
COLUMBIA (31338 "Live at Carnegie Hall")..........................10-15 72
COLUMBIA (32181 "It's a Beautiful Day . . . Today")..........................10-15 73
COLUMBIA (32660 "1001 "Nights") .. 30-40 73
(Promotional issue only.)
SAN FRANCISCO SOUNDS (11790 "It's a Beautiful Day")..........................25-35 70

Also see GARCIA, Jerry
Also see LA FLAMME, David
Also see PABLO CRUISE

ITALIAN ASPHALT & PAVEMENT COMPANY P&R '70

(Duprees)

Singles: 7-inch

COLOSSUS..........................3-5 70

Picture Sleeves

COLOSSUS..........................4-6 70

LPs: 10/12-inch

COLOSSUS..........................8-10 70

Also see DUPREES

IVAN P&R '58

(Jerry Ivan Allison)

Singles: 7-inch

CORAL (62017 "Real Wild Child") 35-50 58
CORAL (62081 "Frankie Frankenstein")..........................50-75 59
CORAL (65607 "Real Wild Child") 20-25 67

Also see CRICKETS

IVAN / Johnny Tillotson

Singles: 7-inch

OLDIES 45..........................5-8 64

Also see IVAN
Also see TILLOTSON, Johnny

IVES, Burl P&R '48

(With the Trinidaddies)

Singles: 78 rpm

COLUMBIA..........................5-10 50-51
DECCA..........................5-10 47-57

Singles: 7-inch

BELL..........................3-5 70
BIG TREE..........................3-5 71
BUENA VISTA..........................4-8 63
COLUMBIA (39000 series)..............10-15 50-51
COLUMBIA (44000 series)..............4-8 68-69
COLUMBIA (70000 series)..............4-6 69
CYCLONE..........................3-5 70
DECCA (25000 series)..............4-8 66-69
DECCA (27000 thru 30000 series)......8-15 50-59
DECCA (31000 thru 33000 series)........3-8 60-73
DISNEYLAND..........................4-8 64
MCA..........................3-5 73-74
MONKEY JOE..........................3-5 78

Picture Sleeves

BUENA VISTA..........................5-10 63
DECCA..........................5-10 62
U.A...........................5-10 62

EPs: 7-inch

COLUMBIA..........................10-20 51-55
DECCA..........................10-20 49-65

LPs: 10/12-inch

BELL..........................5-10 71
CAEDMON..........................4-8 72
COLUMBIA (628 "Wayfaring Stranger")..........................15-25 55
COLUMBIA (1459 "Return of the Wayfaring Stranger")..........................10-20 60
COLUMBIA (2570 "Children's Favorites")..........................25-50 55
(10-inch LP.)
COLUMBIA (6058 "Wayfaring Stranger")..........................25-50 50
(10-inch LP.)
COLUMBIA (6109 "Wayfaring Stranger, Vol. 2")..........................25-50 51
(10-inch LP.)
COLUMBIA (6144 "Wayfaring Stranger, Vol. 3")..........................25-50 51
(10-inch LP.)
COLUMBIA (9000 series)..............8-12 68-69
CORAL..........................4-8 73
DECCA (100 series)..............15-25 61
DECCA (4000 series)..............10-20 62-68
(Decca LP numbers in this series preceded by a "7" or a "DL-7" are stereo issues.)
DECCA (5013 "Ballads and Folk Songs")..........................25-50 49
(10-inch LP.)
DECCA (5080 "Ballads and Folk Songs, Vol. 2")..........................25-50 49
(10-inch LP.)
DECCA (5490 "Women – Songs of the Fair Sex")..........................25-50 53
(10-inch LP.)
DECCA (8000 series)..............10-20 55-59
DISNEYLAND..........................8-12 63-64
EVEREST..........................5-10 78
HARMONY..........................8-15 59-70
MCA..........................5-10 73-75
PICKWICK..........................5-10
SUNSET..........................5-10 70
UNART..........................6-12 67
U.A...........................10-20 59-62
WORD..........................5-10 63-66

Session: Anita Kerr Singers.

Also see KERR, Anita
Also see MILLS, Hayley, & Burl Ives

IVES, Burl, with Grady Martin & His Slew Foot Five C&W '52

Singles: 78 rpm

DECCA..........................4-8 52

Singles: 7-inch

DECCA..........................8-12 49

IVES, Burl, with Captain Stubby & Buccaneers C&W '49

Singles: 78 rpm

DECCA..........................4-8 49

Also see IVES, Burl

IVEYS P&R '69

(Badfinger)

Singles: 7-inch

APPLE (1803 "Maybe Tomorrow").... 10-15 69
APPLE/AMERICOM (301 "Maybe Tomorrow")..........................150-250 69
(Four-inch flexi, "pocket disc.")

Also see BADFINGER

IVY R&B '86

Singles: 7-inch

HEAT..........................3-4 86

IVY LEAGUE P&R '65

Singles: 7-inch

CAMEO..........................8-12 65-66

LPs: 10/12-inch

CAMEO (2000 "Tossing and Turning")..........................20-30 65

Members: John Carter; Ken Lewis; Perry Ford.

IVY THREE P&R/R&B '60

Singles: 7-inch

SHELL (302 "I Cried Enough for Two")..........................50-100 61
SHELL (302 "I Cried Enough for Two")..........................20-30 61
SHELL (719 "I'll Walk the Earth") 10-20 60
SHELL (720 "Yogi")..........................15-20 60
(Blue label.)
SHELL (720 "Yogi")..........................10-15 60
(Multi-color label.)
SHELL (723 "Alone in the Chapel")... 15-25 60

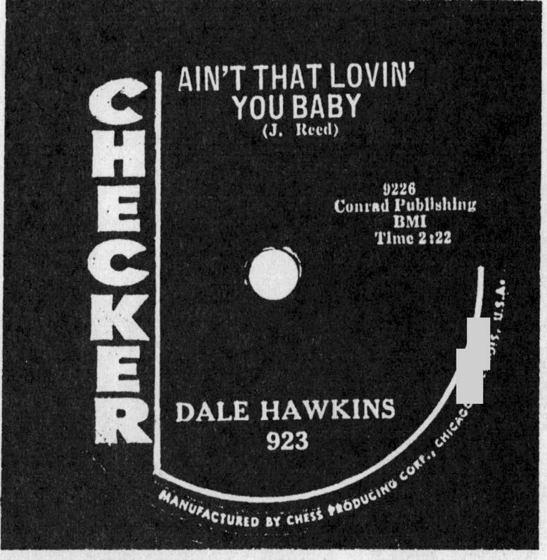

reprise:
PROMOTION
NOT FOR SALE
JIMI HENDRIX EXPERIENCE
Produced by Chas. Chandler
0665
(KA6360)
From The Reprise Album RS-6281 "Axis: Bold as Love"
UP FROM THE SKIES
(Jimi Hendrix)
Sea-Lark Enterprises, Inc.
BMI - 2:55
A YAMETA PRODUCTION
MADE IN U.S.A. • WARNER BROS. RECORDS, INC.

BACK BEAT
RECORDS
BACKBEAT • 2809 ERASTUS STREET • HOUSTON 26, TEXAS
FR 5042
Lion Publishing Co.
Mellin
BMI - 2:51
I KNOW
(Johnston-Smith-Johnston)
JOE HINTON
519

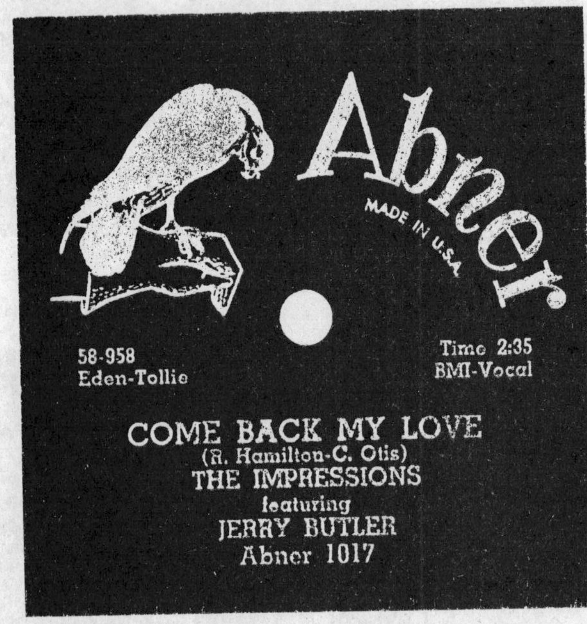
Abner
MADE IN U.S.A.
58-958
Eden-Tollie
Time 2:35
BMI-Vocal
COME BACK MY LOVE
(R. Hamilton-C. Otis)
THE IMPRESSIONS
featuring
JERRY BUTLER
Abner 1017

K-434
KAPP RECORDS
SING ALONG WITH JOSE
as sung by BILL DANA & FRIENDS
SHINE ON
HARVEST MOON
(CHINE ON
ARBESS MOON)
JINGLE
BELLS
(HINGLE
BELLS)

J.B.s P&R '72
(J.B.'s Internationals)
Singles: 7-inch
PEOPLE ... 3-5 72-76
POLYDOR ... 3-5 77-78
LPs: 10/12-inch
PEOPLE ... 5-8 72-75

J.E. THE P.C. FROM D.C. R&B '87
Singles: 7-inch
PROFILE ... 3-4 87

J.J. FAD P&R/R&B/LP '88
Singles: 7-inch
RUTHLESS ... 3-4 88
Picture Sleeves
RUTHLESS ... 3-4 88
LPs: 10/12-inch
RUTHLESS ... 5-8 88
Members: Juana Burns; Dania Birks; Michelle Franklin.

JACK, Ballin': see BALLIN' JACK

JACKIE & STARLITES R&B '62
Singles: 78 rpm
FIRE & FURY (1000 "They Laughed at Me") ... 75-125 57
Singles: 7-inch
FIRE & FURY (1000 "They Laughed at Me") ... 1000-2000 57
FURY (1057 "I'm Coming Home") ... 20-30 62
HULL (760 "I Cried My Heart Out") ... 25-50 63
MASCOT (128 "For All We Know") ... 35-50 62
(No horseshoe on label.)
MASCOT (128 "For All We Know") ... 25-45 62
(Has horseshoe around hole.)
MASCOT (130 "You Keep Telling Me") ... 50-75 63
MASCOT (131 "Walking from School") ... 50-75 63
LPs: 10/12-inch
LOST-NITE ... 8-12 81
Member: Jackie Rue.
Also see STARLITES

JACKIE LEE: see LEE, Jackie

JACKS P&R/R&B '55
Singles: 78 rpm
RPM (Except 428) ... 15-25 55-56
RPM (428 "Why Don't You Write Me"/ "Smack Dab in the Middle") ... 50-75 55
RPM (428 "Why Don't You Write Me"/ "My Darling") ... 25-35 55
(Note different flip side.)
Singles: 7-inch
KENT (344 "Why Don't You Write Me") ... 10-20 60
RPM (428 "Why Don't You Write Me"/ "Smack Dab in the Middle") ... 100-200 55
RPM (428 "Why Don't You Write Me"/ "My Darling") ... 50-100 55
(Note different flip side.)
RPM (433 "I'm Confessin'") ... 50-100 55
RPM (444 "This Empty Heart") ... 50-75 55
RPM (454 "How Soon") ... 50-75 56
RPM (458 "Why Did I Fall in Love") ... 50-75 56
RPM (467 "Let's Make Up") ... 50-75 56
LPs: 10/12-inch
BEST ... 15-25
CROWN (372 "The Jacks") ... 50-75 62
(Stereo.)
CROWN (5021 "Jumpin' with the Jacks") ... 100-200 56
CROWN (5372 "The Jacks") ... 50-75 62
(Monaural.)
RPM (3006 "Jumpin' with the Jacks") ... 250-500 56
RELIC ... 10-15
UNITED ... 8-10 70s
Members: Willie Davis; Ted Taylor; Aaron Collins; Will Jones; Lloyd McCraw; Prentice Moreland.
Also see CADETS

JACKS, Susan P&R '75
Singles: 7-inch
EPIC ... 3-4 80
MERCURY ... 3-5 75-76
LPs: 10/12-inch
EPIC ... 5-8 80
Also see POPPY FAMILY

JACKS, Terry P&R/LP '74
Singles: 7-inch
BELL ... 3-5 74
FLASHBACK ... 3-5 75
LONDON ... 3-5 73
PRIVATE STOCK ... 3-5 75-76
LPs: 10/12-inch
BELL ... 8-10 74
Also see POPPY FAMILY

JACKSON, Bull Moose R&B '46
(With His Buffalo Bearcats; with Flashcats; Moose Jackson)
Singles: 78 rpm
ENCINO ... 25-50 57
KING ... 20-40 45-55
MGM ... 10-20 47
QUEEN ... 10-20 45-46
Singles: 7-inch
BOGUS ... 4-6 85
ENCINO (1004 "Understanding") ... 25-50 57
GUSTO ... 3-5
KING (4181 "I Love You, Yes I Do") . 25-50 51
KING (4189 "I Want a Bowlegged Woman") ... 50-100 51
KING (4451 "Trust in Me") ... 25-50 51
KING (4462 "Unless") ... 25-50 51
KING (4472 "Cherokee Boogie") ... 25-50 51
KING (4493 "I'll Be Home for Xmas") ... 25-50 51
KING (4524 "Nosey Joe") ... 50-75 52
KING (4535 "Let Me Love You All Night") ... 25-50 52
KING (4551 "Bearcat Blues") ... 25-50 52
KING (4580 "Big Ten-inch Record") ... 100-200 52
KING (4600 thru 4800 series) ... 15-25 53-55
SEVEN ARTS ... 5-10 61
WARWICK ... 5-10 60
Picture Sleeves
BOGUS ... 3-4 85
EPs: 7-inch
KING (211 "Bull Moose Jackson Sings His All-Time Hits") ... 50-100 52
KING (261 "Bull Moose Jackson Sings His All-Time Hits, Vol. 2") ... 50-100 54
LPs: 10/12-inch
AUDIO LAB (1524 "Bullmoose Jackson") ... 100-200 59
BOGUS ... 5-8 85

JACKSON, Chuck P&R/R&B '61
(With the Vikings)
Singles: 7-inch
ABC ... 3-5 73-74
ALL PLATINUM ... 3-5 75-77
AMY ... 8-12 62
ATCO ... 5-8 61
BELTONE ... 5-10 61
DAKAR ... 3-5 72
EMI AMERICA ... 3-4 80
FEE BEE ... 10-20 60
MOTOWN (1118 thru 1152) ... 10-15 68-69
MOTOWN (1160 "The Day the World Stood Still") ... 150-250 70
SCEPTER ... 3-5 73
SUGAR HILL ... 3-4 81
VIBRATION ... 3-5 77
V.I.P. (25052 thru 25059) ... 10-15 69-71
V.I.P. (25067 "Who You Gonna Run To") ... 100-200 71
WAND ... 6-12 61-67
Picture Sleeves
WAND ... 5-10 63
LPs: 10/12-inch
ABC ... 8-10 73
ALL PLATINUM ... 8-10 76
EMI-AMERICA ... 5-8 80
MOTOWN (667 "Chuck Jackson Arrives") ... 25-40 67
MOTOWN (687 "Goin' Back") ... 20-30 69
SCEPTER ... 8-10 72
SPINORAMA ... 10-15 60s
U.A. ... 8-10 75
V.I.P. (403 "Teardrops Keep Fallin'") ... 20-40 70
WAND (Except 654 & 680) ... 15-30 61-67
WAND (654 "Any Day Now") ... 40-60 62
WAND (680 "Dedicated to the King") ... 20-40 66
Also see BENTON, Brook / Chuck Jackson / Jimmy Soul
Also see BONDS, Gary "U.S."
Also see FREEMAN, Bobby, & Chuck Jackson
Also see JOHNSON, Kripp, & Chuck Jackson

JACKSON, Chuck, & Maxine Brown P&R/R&B '65
Singles: 7-inch
WAND ... 4-8 65-67
LPs: 10/12-inch
COLLECTABLES ... 6-8 88
WAND ... 15-25 65-66
Also see BROWN, Maxine

JACKSON, Chuck / Percy Sledge
Singles: 7-inch
TRIP ... 3-5
Also see SLEDGE, Percy

JACKSON, Chuck, & Tammi Terrell
LPs: 10/12-inch
WAND ... 15-25 67
Also see TERRELL, Tammi

JACKSON, Chuck / Young Jesse
LPs: 10/12-inch
GUEST STAR ... 8-12 64
Also see JACKSON, Chuck

JACKSON, Clarence R&B '85
Singles: 7-inch
R&R ... 3-4 85

JACKSON, Deon P&R/R&B '66
Singles: 7-inch
ABC ... 3-5 75
ATLANTIC ... 5-10 63-64
CARLA ... 4-8 66-69
LPs: 10/12-inch
ATCO ... 15-20 66
COLLECTABLES ... 6-8 88

JACKSON, Earnest P&R/R&B '73
Singles: 7-inch
STONE ... 3-5 73

JACKSON, Freddie P&R/R&B/D&D/LP '85
Singles: 12-inch
CAPITOL ... 4-6 85-86
Singles: 7-inch
CAPITOL ... 3-4 85-90
Picture Sleeves
CAPITOL ... 3-4 85-88
LPs: 10/12-inch
CAPITOL ... 5-8 85-90
Also see LAURENCE, Paul
Also see MOORE, Melba, & Freddie Jackson
Also see MYSTIC MERLIN

JACKSON, George R&B '70
Singles: 7-inch
CHESS ... 3-6 75
CAMEO ... 5-10 66
DOT ... 5-10 65

DOUBLE R 5-10
ER MUSIC 3-5 76
FAME 4-8 69
HAPPY HOOKERS 3-4 85
HI (2100 series) 5-10 67
HI (2200 series) 3-6 72-73
MGM 3-6 73-74
MERCURY 10-20 67-68
MUSCLE SHOALS SOUNDS 3-6 79
PRANN 10-20 63
PUBLIC 10-15 68
VERVE (10658 "Love Highjacker") ... 15-25 70
WASHATAU 3-4 84
Also see OVATIONS

JACKSON, J.J. *P&R/R&B '66*

(With the Jackels; with Jackals)

Singles: 7–inch

ABC 3-5 73
CALLA 4-8 66-67
CANDIX 12-18
EVEREST 4-8 62
LOMA 4-8 67-68
MAGNA GLIDE 3-5 75
PRELUDE 10-20 59
STORM 10-15 59
W.B. 4-6 69

LPs: 10/12–inch

CALLA 15-25 67
CONGRESS 15-20 68
PERCEPTION 10-15 69-70
W.B. 10-20 69

JACKSON, Janet *P&R/R&B/LP '82*

Singles: 12–inch

A&M 4-6 82-90

Singles: 7–inch

A&M 3-4 82-90

Picture Sleeves

A&M 3-4 83-87

LPs: 10/12–inch

A&M 5-8 82-90

JACKSON, Jenny *R&B '76*

Singles: 7–inch

FARR 3-5 76

JACKSON, Jermaine *P&R/R&B/LP '72*

Singles: 12–inch

ARISTA 4-6 84-89
MOTOWN 4-8 80-83

Singles: 7–inch

ARISTA (Black vinyl) 3-4 84-89
ARISTA (9190 "Dynamite") 3-4 84
(Colored vinyl.)
MOTOWN 3-5 72-83

Picture Sleeves

ARISTA 4-6 84-89
MOTOWN 3-5 81

LPs: 10/12–inch

ARISTA 5-8 84-89
MOTOWN 5-8 72-82
Also see DEVO
Also see JACKSONS
Also see ORIGINALS & Jermaine Jackson

JACKSON, Jermaine, & Michael Jackson

Singles: 12–inch

ARISTA 4-6 84
Also see JACKSON, Michael

JACKSON, Jermaine, & Pia Zadora *P&R/R&B '85*

Singles: 7–inch

CURB 3-4 85
Also see JACKSON, Jermaine
Also see ZADORA, Pia

JACKSON, Joe *P&R/LP '79*

Singles: 12–inch

A&M 4-6 82-86

Singles: 7–inch

A&M (Except 18000) 3-5 79-86
A&M (18000 "I'm the Man") 10-15 79
(Boxed set of five 45s with sleeves and poster. Labeled "The 7–inch Album.")

Picture Sleeves

A&M 3-5 79-86

LPs: 10/12–inch

A&M (3666 "Look Sharp") 10-20 79
(Double 10–inch LP set. Add $4 to $6 if "Look Sharp" button is included.)
A&M (3900 series) 5-8 87
A&M (4000 & 5000 series) 5-10 79-89
A&M (6000 series) 8-12 86-88
MFSL (080 "Night and Day") 25-35 82
VIRGIN 5-8 91

JACKSON, LaToya *R&B/LP '80*

Singles: 12–inch

LARC 4-6 83
PRIVATE I 4-6 84

Singles: 7–inch

LARC 3-4 83
POLYDOR 3-4 80-81
PRIVATE I 3-4 84-86

Picture Sleeves

PRIVATE I 3-4 84

LPs: 10/12–inch

POLYDOR 5-8 80-81
PRIVATE I 5-8 84
Also see CERRONE & LaToya Jackson

JACKSON, Lil' Son *R&B '48*

(With His Rockin' Rollers; Little Son Jackson)

Singles: 78 rpm

GOLD STAR 10-20 48-50
IMPERIAL 20-40 51-57
MODERN 10-20 49
POST 10-20 53

Singles: 7–inch

IMPERIAL (5204 "Journey Back Home") 50-100 52
IMPERIAL (5218 "Black and Brown") 50-100 52
IMPERIAL (5229 "Lonely Blues") 50-100 53
IMPERIAL (5237 "Spending Money Blues") 50-100 53
IMPERIAL (5248 "Movin' to the Country") 50-100 53
IMPERIAL (5259 "Dirty Work") 50-100 53
IMPERIAL (5267 "Thrill Me, Baby") 50-75 53
IMPERIAL (5276 "Big Rat") 50-75 53
IMPERIAL (5286 "Trouble Don't Last Always") 50-75 53
IMPERIAL (5300 "Get High Everybody") 50-75 53
IMPERIAL (5312 "How Long") 50-75 53
IMPERIAL (5319 "My Younger Days") 50-75 54
IMPERIAL (5339 "Sugar Mama") 50-75 54
IMPERIAL (5400 thru 5900 series) ... 15-25 56-63
POST (2014 "No Money") 25-35 53

EPs: 7–inch

BLACK DIAMOND (450 "Everybody Blues") 20-30

LPs: 10/12–inch

ARHOOLIE (1004 "Lil' Son Jackson") 15-30 60
IMPERIAL (9142 "Rockin' and Rollin' ") 75-100 61
Also see CHARLES, Ray / Arbee Stidham / Li'l Son Jackson / James Wayne.

JACKSON, Mahalia *P&R '48*

Singles: 78 rpm

APOLLO 3-5 50-57
COLUMBIA 3-5 55-57

Singles: 7–inch

APOLLO (200 thru 500 series) 5-10 50-59
APOLLO (600 thru 700 series) 4-6 .. 59-62
COLUMBIA 4-8 55-70
GRAND AWARD 4-8 58-59
KENWOOD 3-6 64-69

Picture Sleeves

APOLLO 4-8 62

EPs: 7–inch

APOLLO 5-10 54-59
COLUMBIA 5-10 55-60

LPs: 10/12–inch

APOLLO (201/2 "Spirituals") 15-20 54
APOLLO (482 "No Matter How You Pray") 10-15 59
APOLLO (499 "Mahalia Jackson") 10-15 62
APOLLO (1001 "Command Performance") 10-15 61
AUDIOFIDELITY 4-8
(Reissue of Apollo 499.)
CAEDMON 4-8 73
COLORTONE 5-8
(Reissue of Grand Award 265.)
COLUMBIA (CL-600 thru CL-2100 series) 10-20 55-64
COLUMBIA (CL-2400 thru CL-2600 series) 5-15 66-67
COLUMBIA (CS-8000 thru CS-8900 series) 10-20 59-64
(Stereo.)
COLUMBIA (CS-9200 thru CS-9900 series) 5-15 66-69
(Stereo. Reissues, with a "CSP," "JCS" or "PC" prefix, are in the $5 to $10 range.)
COLUMBIA (10000 series) 4-8 73
COLUMBIA (30000 series) 5-10 71-72
GRAND AWARD (265 "Spirituals") 5-10 66
(Reissue of Grand Award 326.)
GRAND AWARD (326 "Spirituals") 15-25 55
HARMONY 5-10 68-72
KENWOOD 5-10 64-73
PRIORITY 4-6 82

JACKSON, Mahalia, & Duke Ellington

LPs: 10/12–inch

COLUMBIA (CL-1162 "Black, Brown and Beige") 25-35 58
(Monaural.)
COLUMBIA (CS-8015 "Black, Brown and Beige") 35-40 58
(Stereo.)
COLUMBIA (JCS-1162 "Black, Brown and Beige") 5-10
Also see ELLINGTON, Duke
Also see JACKSON, Mahalia

JACKSON, Marlon *R&B/LP '87*

Singles: 7–inch

CAPITOL 3-4 87

LPs: 10/12–inch

CAPITOL 5-8 87

JACKSON, Michael *P&R/R&B '71*

Singles: 12–inch

EPIC 4-8 79-87

Singles: 7–inch

EPIC (Except 07253) 3-5 79-88
EPIC (07253 "I Just Can't Stop Loving You") 3-5 87
(Black vinyl.)
EPIC (07253 "I Just Can't Stop Loving You") 5-8 87
(Colored vinyl. Promotional issue only.)
MCA (1786 "Someone in the Dark") 25-50 83
(Promotional issue only.)
MOTOWN (Except 1914) 3-5 71-88
MOTOWN (1914 "Twenty Five Miles") 4-8 84
(Colored vinyl. Promotional issue only.)

Picture Sleeves

EPIC 3-5 83-88
MCA (1786 "Someone in the Dark") 25-50 83
(Promotional issue only.)
MOTOWN (1202 "I Wanna Be Where You Are") 3-5 72
MOTOWN (1914 "Twenty Five Miles") .. 4-8 84
(Promotional issue only.)

LPs: 10/12–inch

EPIC (35000 thru 40000) 5-8 79-87
(Black vinyl.)
EPIC (8E8-38867 "Thriller") 10-15 82
(Picture disc.)
EPIC (45000 series) 10-15 80
(Half-speed mastered.)
EPIC (9E9-44043 "Bad") 8-12 87
(Picture disc.)

MOTOWN.. 5-10 72-85
Also see CROUCH, Andrae
Also see GARRETT, Siedah
Also see JACKSON, Jermaine, & Michael Jackson
Also see JACKSONS
Also see JONES, Quincy
Also see McCARTNEY, Paul, & Michael Jackson
Also see ROCKWELL
Also see ROSS, Diana, & Michael Jackson
Also see U.S.A. for AFRICA
Also see VAN HALEN, Edward
Also see WINANS
Also see WONDER, Stevie, & Michael Jackson

JACKSON, Michael, & Mick Jagger / Jacksons P&R '84

Singles: 12-inch

EPIC (5022 "State of Shock")............. 8-12 84
(With special cover.)
EPIC (05022 "State of Shock")......... 15-20 84
(Promotional issue with cover.)

Singles: 7-inch

EPIC (4503 "State of Shock")............... 3-5 84

Picture Sleeves

EPIC (4503 "State of Shock")............... 3-5 84
Also see JACKSON, Michael
Also see JACKSONS
Also see JAGGER, Mick

JACKSON, Mick P&R '78

Singles: 7-inch

ATCO.. 3-5 78

JACKSON, Millie R&B '71

Singles: 7-inch

GEFFEN.. 3-4 87
JIVE.. 3-4 86-88
MGM.. 3-6 69
SPRING... 3-5 71-83

LPs: 10/12-inch

JIVE.. 5-8 86
SPRING... 5-8 73-83
POLYDOR.. 5-8 79
Also see HAYES, Isaac, & Millie Jackson
Also see JOHN, Elton, & Millie Jackson
Also see WHODINI & Millie Jackson

JACKSON, Moose: see JACKSON, Bull Moose

JACKSON, Paul, Jr. R&B '88

Singles: 7-inch

ATLANTIC.. 3-4 88

JACKSON, Python Lee: see PYTHON LEE JACKSON

JACKSON, Randy R&B '78

Singles: 7-inch

EPIC 3-5 78
Also see JACKSONS

JACKSON, Rebbie P&R/R&B/D&D/LP '84

Singles: 12-inch

COLUMBIA.. 4-6 84-86

Singles: 7-inch

COLUMBIA.. 3-4 84-86

Picture Sleeves

COLUMBIA.. 3-4 84

LPs: 10/12-inch

COLUMBIA.. 5-8 84-86
Also see GRANDMASTER FLASH & Furious Five
Also see JACKSONS

JACKSON, Rebbie, & Robin Zander R&B '86

Singles: 7-inch

COLUMBIA.. 3-4 86
Also see JACKSON, Rebbie

JACKSON, Shawne R&B '74

Singles: 7-inch

PLAYBOY.. 3-5 74

JACKSON, Stonewall C&W '58

Singles: 7-inch

COLUMBIA (Except 41000 series)....... 3-8 61-73
COLUMBIA (41000 series)................. 4-8 58-61
FIRST GENERATION.......................... 3-4 81
GRT.. 3-5 74
LITTLE DARLIN'.................................. 3-5 78-79
MGM.. 3-5 73
PHONORAMA....................................... 3-4 83

Picture Sleeves

COLUMBIA (41393 "Waterloo")......... 8-10 59

EPs: 7-inch

COLUMBIA 5-10 59

LPs: 10/12-inch

AUDIOGRAPH ALIVE.......................... 5-8 82
COLUMBIA (1391 "The Dynamic Stonewall Jackson") 20-30 59
(Monaural.)
COLUMBIA (1700 thru 2700 series) ... 8-15 62-67
(Monaural.)
COLUMBIA (8186 "The Dynamic Stonewall Jackson") 25-40 59
(Stereo.)
COLUMBIA (8500 thru 9900 series) ... 8-15 62-70
(Stereo.)
COLUMBIA (10000 series) 5-8 73
COLUMBIA (30000 series) 5-10 70-72
FIRST GENERATION.......................... 5-8 78
GRT.. 5-10 75-76
HARMONY.. 8-12 66-74
LITTLE DARLIN'.................................. 5-8 79
MYRRH... 5-8 76
PHONORAMA 5-8
SUNBIRD.. 5-8 80
Session: Jordanaires.

JACKSON, Walter P&R/R&B '64

Singles: 7-inch

BRUNSWICK....................................... 3-6 73
CHI-SOUND.. 3-5 76-78
COLUMBIA (02000 series) 3-4 81
COLUMBIA (42000 series) 10-20 62-63
COTILLION.. 4-8 69
EPIC.. 5-10 66-68
KELLI-ARTS 3-6 83
OKEH (Except 7204) 5-10 64-67
OKEH (7204 "It's All Over").............. 5-10 64
(Black vinyl.)
OKEH (7204 "It's All Over").............. 15-25 64
(Colored vinyl.)
20TH FOX... 3-6 79
U.A. 3-6 78
USA.. 6-12 60s
WAND... 3-5 72

Picture Sleeves

OKEH.. 8-12 66-67

LPs: 10/12-inch

CHI-SOUND.. 8-10 76-78
COLUMBIA 5-8 81
EPIC.. 8-10 77
OKEH.. 10-20 65-69
20TH FOX... 5-8 79

JACKSON, Wanda P&R '60

(With the Party Timers)

Singles: 78 rpm

CAPITOL... 15-40 56-57
DECCA 10-20 54-55

Singles: 7-inch

ABC... 3-5 75
CAPITOL (2000 thru 3000 series) 3-8 67-72
(Orange or orange/yellow labels.)
CAPITOL (3400 thru 4600 series) 10-25 56-61
(Purple labels.)
CAPITOL (4700 thru 5900 series) 5-10 61-67
DECCA (29253 "Right to Love") 20-40 54
DECCA (29514 "Tears at the Grand Ole Op'ry") 20-40 55
DECCA (29677 "It's the Same World") 10-20 55
DECCA (29803 "Wasted") 20-40 55
JIN... 3-6
MYRRH... 3-4 73-75

Picture Sleeves

CAPITOL... 5-10 62-66

EPs: 7-inch

CAPITOL (1041 "Wanda Jackson").. 25-50 58

LPs: 10/12-inch

CAPITOL (100 thru 600 series) 15-20 69-71
CAPITOL (1041 "Wanda Jackson") 75-150 58
CAPITOL (1384 "Rockin' with Wanda").. 50-100 60
CAPITOL (1511 "There's a Party Goin' On").. 40-80 61
(With "T" prefix. Monaural.)
CAPITOL (1511 "There's a Party Goin' On").. 50-100 61
(With "ST" prefix. Stereo.)
CAPITOL (1596 "Right Or Wrong")... 25-50 61
(With "T" prefix. Monaural.)
CAPITOL (1596 "Right Or Wrong")... 30-55 61
(With "ST" prefix. Stereo.)
CAPITOL (1776 "Wonderful Wanda").. 20-30 62
(With "T" prefix. Monaural.)
CAPITOL (1776 "Wonderful Wanda").. 25-35 62
(With "ST" prefix. Stereo.)
CAPITOL (1911 "Love Me Forever").. 20-30 63
(With "T" prefix. Monaural.)
CAPITOL (1911 "Love Me Forever").. 25-35 63
(With "ST" prefix. Stereo.)
CAPITOL (2030 "Two Sides of Wanda Jackson").. 25-35 64
(With "T" prefix. Monaural.)
CAPITOL (2030 "Two Sides of Wanda Jackson").. 30-40 64
(With "ST" prefix. Stereo.)
CAPITOL (2300 thru 2900 series).. 10-20 65-68
CAPITOL (11000 series) 5-8 72-73
DECCA (4224 "Lovin' Country Style").. 40-50 62
GUSTO.. 5-8 80
MYRRH 5-8 73-76
PICKWICK/HILLTOP.......................... 8-12 65-68
VARRICK/ROUNDER 5-8 87
VOCALION... 8-12 69
WORD 4-8 77

JACKSON, Wanda, & Billy Gray C&W '54

Singles: 7-inch

DECCA (29140 "You Can't Have My Love") 20-40 54
DECCA (29267 "If You Don't Somebody Else Will") 20-40 54
Also see JACKSON, Wanda

JACKSON, Willis LP '66

(Willis "Gator Tail" Jackson & His Orch.; vocal By the 4'Gaters; with Jack McDuff)

Singles: 78 rpm

APOLLO 10-20 50
ATLANTIC... 20-50 51-53
DELUXE.. 4-8 53
MODERN.. 10-15 52

Singles: 7-inch

ATCO (6089 "Later 'Gator")............... 15-25 57
ATLANTIC (946 "Harlem Nocturne").. 75-125 51
ATLANTIC (957 "Wine-O-Wine").... 75-125 52
ATLANTIC (967 "Rock, Rock, Rock") 50-75 52
ATLANTIC (975 "Gator's Groove").... 40-60 52
ATLANTIC (998 "Shake Dance") 40-60 53
CADET 4-8 66
COTILLION.. 3-5 76
DELUXE 10-15 53
FIRE 5-10 59
MODERN (906 "Let's Jump") 15-25 52
PAUL WINLEY (1101 "Bow Legged Daddy").. 10-20 64
PRESTIGE 5-10 59-69
TRU-SOUND (410 "Backtrack")........ 10-15 62
TRU-SOUND (410 "That Twistin' Train") 8-12 62
(Retitled reissue.)
VERVE 4-8 64

LPs: 10/12-inch

ATLANTIC 5-8 75
AUDIO-LAB... 15-25 59
BIG CHANCE 5-10 75

CADET 10-20 66
COTILLION 5-8 76
MGM 10-20 64
MOODSVILLE 15-20 62
MUSE 5-8 76-81
PRESTIGE (2500 series) 5-8 82
PRESTIGE (7100 & 7200 series) 15-25 59-64
(Yellow label.)
PRESTIGE (7100 & 7200 series) 10-20 65
(Blue label.)
PRESTIGE (7300 thru 7800 series) 8-15 65-71
TRIP 5-10 73
VERVE 10-20 64-69
Also see BROWN, Ruth
Also see CLOVERS
Also see McDUFF, Brother Jack, & Willis Jackson

JACKSON SISTERS *R&B '73*

Singles: 7-inch

PROPHESY 3-5 73

JACKSONS *P&R/R&B '69*

(Jackson 5; Michael Jackson & Jackson 5)

Singles: 12-inch

EPIC 4-8 79-84
MOTOWN 5-10 83

Singles: 7-inch

DYNAMO (Except 146) 3-5
DYNAMO (146 "You Don't Have to Be Over 21") 15-25 71
EPIC 3-5 76-81
MCA 3-4 87
MOTOWN ("ABC") 20-30 70
(Six-inch, cardboard cutout picture disc. No selection number used.)
MOTOWN ("Sugar Daddy") 10-20 70
(Six-inch, cardboard cutout picture disc. No selection number used. Artists neither pictured nor credited.)
MOTOWN (1157 "I Want You Back") 4-8 69
MOTOWN (1157 "I Want You Back") 15-20 69
(Colored vinyl. Promotional issue only.)
MOTOWN (1163 "ABC") 4-8 70
MOTOWN (1166 "The Love You Save") 4-6 70
(Black vinyl.)
MOTOWN (1166 "I Found That Girl") 15-20 70
(Colored vinyl. Same song on both sides. Promotional issue only.)
MOTOWN (1166 "Love You Save") .. 15-20 70
(Colored vinyl. Same song on both sides. Promotional issue only.)
MOTOWN (1171 thru 1310) 3-6 70-75
MOTOWN (1177 "Mama's Pearl") 12-18 71
(Colored vinyl. Promotional issue only.)
MOTOWN (1277 "Get It Together") 10-15 73
(Colored vinyl. Promotional issue only.)
MOTOWN (1356 "Forever Came Today") 3-5 75
(Black vinyl.)
MOTOWN (1356 "Forever Came Today") 10-15 75
(Colored vinyl. Promotional issue only.)
STEEL-TOWN (681 "Big Boy") 30-40 68
STEEL-TOWN (682 "We Don't Have to Be Over 21") 25-35 71

Picture Sleeves

EPIC 3-5 76-84
MCA 3-4 87
MOTOWN 4-6 71-75

EPs: 7-inch

MOTOWN ("Jackson Five") 25-50 70
(Five track flexi-disc.)
MOTOWN ("Sugar Daddy") 20-40 70s
(Three track, cardboard flexi-disc.)
MOTOWN (60718 "Jackson Five, Third Album") 15-25 70

LPs: 10/12-inch

EPIC (30000 series, except picture discs) 5-8 76-84
EPIC (PAL 34835 "Goin' Places") 20-25 78
(Picture disc. Promotional issue only. Has same picture on both sides.)
EPIC (PAL 34835 "Goin' Places") 200-250 78
(Picture disc. Promotional issue only. Has "Radio Ten Q" logo on one side.)
EPIC (8E8-39576 "Victory") 15-25 84
(Picture disc.)
EPIC (40000 series) 5-8 89
EPIC (46000 series) 10-15 81
(Half-speed mastered.)
MCA 5-8 87
MOTOWN (100 series) 5-10 80
MOTOWN (700 series, except 713) 8-15 69-74
MOTOWN (713 "The Jackson 5 Christmas Album") 10-20 70
MOTOWN (800 series) 8-15 75-76
MOTOWN (5000 series) 5-8
MOTOWN (6000 series) 5-8 84
NATURAL RESOURCES 8-12 79
(Promotional issues only.)
PHILLY INTL (34229 "The Jacksons") 125-150 78
(Picture disc. Promotional issue only.)
PICKWICK 5-10 70s
Members: Michael Jackson; Jermaine Jackson; Jackie Jackson; Marlon Jackson; Tito Jackson; Randy Jackson; Rebbie Jackson.
Also see JACKSON, Jermaine
Also see JACKSON, Michael
Also see JACKSON, Randy
Also see JACKSON, Rebbie
Also see RIPPLES & WAVES Plus Michael
Also see ROSS, Diana, & Bill Cosby / Diana Ross & Jackson Five
Also see WONDER, Stevie

JACOBI, Lou *LP '66*

LPs: 10/12-inch

CAPITOL 6-12 66
VERVE 5-10 67

JACOBS, Debbie *R&B/LP '79*

Singles: 12-inch

PERSONAL 4-6 84

Singles: 7-inch

MCA 3-4 79-80

LPs: 10/12-inch

MCA 5-10 79-80

JACOBS, Dick, & His Orch. *P&R '56*

Singles: 7-inch

CORAL 3-5 54-62

EPs: 7-inch

CORAL 5-15 56

LPs: 10/12-inch

CORAL 10-20 56-60
VOCALION 5-10 60

JACOBS, Hank *P&R/R&B '64*

Singles: 7-inch

CALL ME 4-6
IMPERIAL (5894 "Sting Ray") 10-15 62
SUE 5-10 63-64

LPs: 10/12-inch

SUE (1023 "So Far Away") 20-30 64

JACQUET, Illinois *R&B '52*

(With His All-Stars; Jacque Rabbit; with Russell Jacquet)

Singles: 78 rpm

ARA 5-10 46
ALADDIN 5-15 45-54
APOLLO 5-10 46-47
MERCURY 5-10 52
PHILO 5-10 45
RCA 5-15 48-51
SAVOY 5-10 46

Singles: 7-inch

ALADDIN 10-20 53-54
ARGO 4-8 63-65
MGM (89001 "One-Nighter Boogie") 15-25
MERCURY 10-15 52
PRESTIGE 3-6 68-69
RCA (0011 "Black Velvet") 10-20 49
(Black vinyl.)
RCA (0011 "Black Velvet") 20-30 49
(Colored vinyl.)
RCA (0021 "Big Foot") 20-30 49
(Colored vinyl.)
RCA (0047 "Blue Satin") 20-30 49
(Colored vinyl.)
RCA (0087 "My Old Gal") 20-30 49
(Colored vinyl.)
RCA (0097 "Slow Down, Baby") 15-20 49
(Colored vinyl.)
VERVE 4-8 62

EPs: 7-inch

APOLLO (602 "Jam Session") 50-75 50
CLEF (126 "Illinois Jacquet Collates") 25-40 51
CLEF (143 "Illinois Jacquet Collates") 25-40 51
CLEF (166 "Illinois Jacquet Collates, No. 2") 20-40 52
CLEF (167 "Illinois Jacquet Collates, No. 2") 20-40 52
CLEF (207 "Jazz Moods") 20-40 54
CLEF (374 "Illinois Jacquet & His Orchestra") 20-40 55
RCA (3236 "Black Velvet") 40-60 53
SAVOY 20-30 50-53

LPs: 10/12-inch

ACCORD 5-8 82
ALADDIN (800 series) 50-60 56
APOLLO (104 "Jam Session") 150-250 50
ARGO 15-25 63-65
CLEF (112 "Illinois Jacquet Collates") 100-125 51
(10-inch LP. Has Mercury label with Clef logo and number.)
CLEF (129 "Illinois Jacquet Collates, No. 2") 100-125 52
(10-inch LP. Has Mercury label with Clef logo and number.)
CLEF (622 "Jazz Moods") 50-100 54
CLEF (676 "Illinois Jacquet & His Orchestra") 50-75 55
CLEF (680 "The Kid & Brute") 50-75 55
CLEF (700 "Jazz Moods") 40-60 56
CLEF (702 "Groovin' ") 40-60 56
CLEF (750 "Swing's the Thing") 40-60 56
EPIC 15-25 63
GRAND AWARD (315 "Uptown Jazz") 20-35 56
IMPERIAL 15-25 62
JRC 5-8 79
MOSAIC (165 "Complete Illinois Jacquet Sessions 1945-50") 70-90 90s
(Boxed, six-disc audiophile set. 5000 made.)
PRESTIGE 8-12 69-75
RCA (3236 "Black Velvet") 50-75 53
(10-inch LP.)
ROULETTE 20-30 60
SAVOY (15024 "Tenor Sax") 50-100 53
(10-inch LP.)
TRIP 5-8 79
VERVE (2500 series) 5-10 82-87
VERVE (8000 series) 25-50 57-58
(Reads "Verve Records, Inc." at bottom of label.)
VERVE (8000 series) 10-20 61-65
(Reads "MGM Records - a Division of Metro-Goldwyn-Mayer, Inc." at bottom of label.)
Members: Illinois Jacquet; Johnny Otis; Russell Jacquet; Arthur Dennis; Henry Coker; Sir Charles; Ulysses Livingston; William Hadnott.
Also see COLE, Cozy, & Illinois Jacquet
Also see DOGGETT, Bill
Also see HAMPTON, Lionel
Also see HEART BEATS QUINTET
Also see JAZZ at the Philharmonic
Also see OTIS, Johnny
Also see X-RAYS

JACQUET, Illinois, & Count Basie

LPs: 10/12-inch

CLEF (701 "Port of Rico") 40-60 56
Also see BASIE, Count

JACQUET, Illinois, & Miles Davis

EPs: 7-inch

ALADDIN (504 "Illinois Jacquet & His Tenor Sax") 50-65 54
ALADDIN (511 "Illinois Jacquet & His Tenor Sax") 50-65 54

LPs: 10/12-inch

ALADDIN (708 "Illinois Jacquet & His Tenor Sax") 100-150 54
(10-inch LP.)
Also see DAVIS, Miles

JACQUET, Illinois / Lester Young

EPs: 7-inch

ALADDIN (501 "Battle of the Saxes") 50-100 54

LPs: 10/12-inch

ALADDIN (701 "Battle of the Saxes") 150-250 54
(10-inch LP. Black vinyl.)
ALADDIN (701 "Battle of the Saxes") 500-1000 54
(10-inch LP. Colored vinyl.)
ALADDIN (803 "Illinois Jacquet & His Tenor Sax") 75-100 56
(Has the eight tracks from *Battle of the Saxes*, plus four others.)

JADE WARRIOR — LP '72

Singles: 7-inch

VERTIGO 3-4 71-72

LPs: 10/12-inch

ANTILLES 5-8 78
ISLAND 8-10 74-76
VERTIGO 10-12 71-72

JAGGER, Chris — LP '73

LPs: 10/12-inch

ASYLUM 8-10 73-74

JAGGER, Mick — P&R/R&B/D&D/LP '85

Singles: 12-inch

ATLANTIC ("Sweet Thing") 20-30 93
(Colored vinyl. Promotional issue only. Includes six versions.)
COLUMBIA (2060 "Lucky in Love") 4-8 85
(With special cover.)
COLUMBIA (2060 "Lucky in Love") 15-20 85
(Promotional issue with special cover.)
COLUMBIA (5181 "Just Another Night") 4-8 85
(With special cover.)
COLUMBIA (5181 "Just Another Night") 15-20 85
(Promotional issue with special cover.)
COLUMBIA (6926 "Let's Work") 5-10 87
COLUMBIA (7492 "Throwaway") 5-10 87
EPIC (5931 "Ruthless People") 10-15 86
(With special cover.)

Singles: 7-inch

COLUMBIA (04743 "Just Another Night") 3-5 85
COLUMBIA (04893 "Lucky in Love") 3-5 85
COLUMBIA (07306 "Let's Work") 3-5 87
COLUMBIA (07653 "Throwaway") 3-5 87
EPIC (06211 "Ruthless People") 3-5 86

Picture Sleeves

COLUMBIA (04743 "Just Another Night") 3-5 85
COLUMBIA (04893 "Lucky in Love") 3-5 85
COLUMBIA (07306 "Let's Work") 3-5 87
COLUMBIA (07653 "Throwaway") 3-5 87
EPIC (06211 "Ruthless People") 3-5 86

Promotional Singles

COLUMBIA (04743 "Just Another Night") 8-10 85
COLUMBIA (04893 "Lucky in Love") 8-10 85
COLUMBIA (07306 "Let's Work") 8-10 87
COLUMBIA (07653 "Throwaway") 8-10 87
EPIC (06211 "Ruthless People") 5-10 86

LPs: 10/12-inch

COLUMBIA (39940 "She's the Boss") 8-10 85
COLUMBIA (40919 "Primitive Cool") 8-10 87
EPIC 8-12 86
LONDON WAVELENGTH (006 "The Mick Jagger Special") 75-100 81
(Promotional issue only.)
ROLLING STONES (164 "Interview with Mick Jagger") 75-100 71
(Promotional issue only.)
U.A. (300 "Ned Kelly") 10-15 74
(Soundtrack.)
U.A. (5213 "Ned Kelly") 15-20 70
(Soundtrack.)
Also see BOWIE, David, & Mick Jagger
Also see FRAMPTON, Peter
Also see JACKSON, Michael, & Mick Jagger
Also see ROLLING STONES
Also see SIMON, Carly
Also see TOSH, Peter, & Mick Jagger
Also see WEST, Leslie
Also see WOLF, Peter, & Mick Jagger

JAGGERZ — P&R/LP '70

Singles: 7-inch

GAMBLE 4-8 68
JAGGERZ 3-5 74
KAMA SUTRA 3-6 70
WOODEN NICKEL 3-5 75

LPs: 10/12-inch

GAMBLE (5006 "Introducing the Jaggerz") 15-20 69
KAMA SUTRA 10-15 70
WOODEN NICKEL 8-10 75
Members: Dominic Ierace (a.k.a. Donnie Iris); Jim Pugliano; Jim Ross; Bill Maybray; Ben Faiella.
Also see IRIS, Donnie
Also see Q

JAGS — P&R '80

Singles: 7-inch

ISLAND 3-5 79-80

Picture Sleeves

ISLAND 3-5 79-80

LPs: 10/12-inch

ISLAND 5-8 80-81

JAISUN — R&B '78

Singles: 7-inch

JETT SETT 3-5 78

JAK — R&B '85

Singles: 7-inch

EPIC 3-4 84-86

LPs: 10/12-inch

EPIC 5-8 85

JA-KKI — P&R '76

Singles: 7-inch

PYRAMID 3-5 76
WEST END 3-5

JAM — LP '80

Singles: 7-inch

POLYDOR 3-5 78-83

Picture Sleeves

POLYDOR 3-5 80-83

LPs: 10/12-inch

POLYDOR 5-8 77-83
Also see STYLE COUNCIL

JAMAICA BOYS — R&B '87

Singles: 7-inch

W.B. 3-4 87-88

JAMAICA GIRLS — D&D '83

Singles: 12-inch

SLEEPING BAG 4-6 83

JAMAL, Ahmad — R&B/LP '58

(Ahmad Jamal Trio; Quintet)

Singles: 7-inch

ARGO 4-8 57-65
CADET 3-6 66-68
CHESS 3-5 73
PARROTT 5-10 55
20TH FOX 3-5 73-80

EPs: 7-inch

ARGO 8-15 59-61

LPs: 10/12-inch

ABC 8-12 68
ARGO (610 thru 662) 20-40 56-60
ARGO (667 thru 758) 15-25 61-65
CADET 10-25 65-73
CATALYST 5-10 76
EPIC (600 series) 15-30 63-65
EPIC (3212 "Ahmad Jamal Trio") 30-50 56
EPIC (3600 series) 20-30 59
IMPULSE 10-20 69-73
MOTOWN 5-10 80
PERSONAL CHOICE 5-8 82
SHUBRA 5-8 83
20TH FOX 5-10 73-80
WHO'S WHO in JAZZ 5-10 81

JAMES, Bob — P&R '74

(Bob James Trio)

Singles: 7-inch

CTI 3-5 74-77
COLUMBIA 3-5 79-83
TAPPAN ZEE/COLUMBIA 3-5 77-85

Picture Sleeves

COLUMBIA 3-5 79-80

LPs: 10/12-inch

CTI 5-10 74-77
COLUMBIA 5-8 83
ESP 10-15 65
MERCURY 15-25 63
TAPPAN ZEE/COLUMBIA 5-10 77-85
Also see FOURPLAY

JAMES, Bob, & Earl Klugh — LP '79

Singles: 7-inch

CAPITOL 3-4 82
TAPPAN ZEE/COLUMBIA 3-5 79

LPs: 10/12-inch

CAPITOL 5-8 82
MFSL (124 "2 of a Kind") 20-30 84
TAPPAN ZEE/COLUMBIA 5-10 79
Also see KLUGH, Earl

JAMES, Bob, & David Sanborn — LP '86

LPs: 10/12-inch

W.B. 5-8 86-88
Also see JAMES, Bob
Also see SANBORN, David

JAMES, Elmore — R&B '52

(With His Broomdusters; Elmo James)

Singles: 78 rpm

ACE 50-75 53
CHECKER 100-150 53
CHIEF 25-50 57
FLAIR 50-100 54-56
METEOR (5000 "I Believe") 50-100 53
METEOR (5003 "Sinful Woman") 50-100 53
MODERN (983 "Wild About You") 25-50 56
TRUMPET (146 "I Believe My Time Ain't Long") 25-50 52
VEE JAY 10-20 57

Singles: 7-inch

ACE (508 "My Time Ain't Long") 100-200 53
CHECKER (777 "Country Boogie") 200-400 53
CHESS 5-10 60
CHIEF (7001 "The Twelve Year Old Boy") 25-50 57
CHIEF (7004 "It Hurts Me Too") 25-50 57
CHIEF (7006 "Cry for Me Baby") 25-50 57
CHIEF (7020 "Knocking at Your Door") 15-25 58
ENJOY (2015 "It Hurts Me Too") 10-20 65
FIRE 10-20 60-62
FLAIR (1011 "Early in the Morning") 150-200 54
FLAIR (1014 "Can't Stop Lovin'") 150-200 54
FLAIR (1022 "Strange Kinda Feeling") 100-150 55
FLAIR (1031 "Make My Dreams Come True") 100-200 55
FLAIR (1039 "Sho'nuff, I Do") 100-200 55
FLAIR (1048 "Dark and Dreary") 100-200 56
FLAIR (1057 "Standing at the Crossroads") 100-200 55
FLAIR (1062 "Late Hours at Midnight") 75-125 56
FLAIR (1069 "Happy Home") 75-125 56
FLAIR (1074 "Dust My Blues") 100-150 56

FLAIR (1079 "Blues Before Sunrise") 75-100 56
FLASHBACK 3-6 65
JEWEL (764 "Dust My Broom") 4-8 66
JEWEL (783 "Catfish Blues") 4-8 66
(Though credited to Elmo James, the flip sides of Jewel 764 and 783 are actually by Big Boy Crudup.)
KENT 5-15 60-67
METEOR (5000 "I Believe") 200-300 53
METEOR (5003 "Sinful Woman") 200-300 53
MODERN (983 "Wild About You") 150-250 56
M-PAC 4-8
S&M 4-8
SOUND 4-8
PHERE SOUND 4-8 65
VEE JAY 10-20 57

LPs: 10/12-inch

BELL 10-12 68-69
BLUE HORIZON 10-12
CHESS 10-12 69
COLLECTABLES 6-8 88
CROWN (5168 "Blues After Hours") 40-50 61
CUSTOM 8-12
INTERMEDIA 5-8 84
KENT (5022 "Original Folk Blues") 20-30 64
KENT (9000 series) 10-20 67-69
KENT TREASURE SERIES 5-8 86
RELIC 5-10 88
SPHERE SOUND (7002 "The Sky Is Crying") 25-35 60s
SPHERE SOUND (7008 "I Need You") 25-35 60s
TRIP 8-10 71-78
UNITED 10-12 60s
UPFRONT 8-10 70s
Also see CRUDUP, Big Boy

JAMES, Elmore, & John Brim

LPs: 10/12-inch

CHESS 10-15 69
Also see JAMES, Elmore

JAMES, Etta — R&B '55

(Etta "Miss Peaches" James)

Singles: 78 rpm

MODERN 10-20 55-56

Singles: 7-inch

ABC 3-5 74
ARGO 5-10 60-64
CADET 4-8 67-72
CHESS 3-5 73-76
KENT 10-15 58-60
MODERN (900 series) 15-25 55-56
MODERN (1000 series) 10-15 57-58
REGENCY 10-20
T-ELECTRIC 3-5 80
W.B. 3-5 78

LPs: 10/12-inch

ARGO 20-30 61-65
ARRIVAL 5-10 83
CADET 10-15 67-71
CHESS 10-12 71-76
CROWN 20-30 61-63
INTERMEDIA 5-8 84
KENT (3002 "Miss Etta James") 15-25 61
(Black vinyl.)
KENT (3002 "Miss Etta James") 30-40 61
(Colored vinyl.)
T-ELECTRIC 5-8 80
UNITED 10-12
W.B. 5-8 78
WESTBOUND 8-10
Session: Richard Berry.
Also see ETTA & HARVEY

JAMES, Etta, & Sugar Pie DeSanto — P&R '65

Singles: 7-inch

CADET 4-8 65-66
Also see DESANTO, Sugar Pie
Also see JAMES, Etta

JAMES, Harry, & His Orch. — P&R '38

Singles: 78 rpm

BRUNSWICK 3-6 38
COLUMBIA 3-6 40-57
VARIETY 4-8 40

Singles: 7-inch

COLUMBIA (33000 series) 3-5 76
COLUMBIA (38000 thru 40000 series) 5-8 50-56
DOT 3-6 65-66
GOLD-MOR 3-5 73
MGM 4-6 59-63

EPs: 7-inch

COLUMBIA 5-15 50-56

LPs: 10/12-inch

BAINBRIDGE 5-8 83
BRIGHT ORANGE 5-8 73
CAPITOL (600 thru 1500 series) 15-30 55-61
(With "T" or "ST" prefix.)
CAPITOL (1500 series) 10-20 62
(With "DT" prefix.)
CAPITOL (1500 series) 5-8 77
(With "M" prefix.)
COLUMBIA 10-30 50-67
COLUMBIA SPECIAL PRODUCTS 5-8 79
DOT 8-15 66-67
HARMONY 10-20 59-72
LONDON 5-10 68
MGM 10-20 59-65
METRO 8-15 65-67
PICKWICK 5-10 70s
SHEFFIELD LAB 5-8 77-79
Also see KALLEN, Kitty
Also see SINATRA, Frank

JAMES, Harry, & Dick Haymes

LPs: 10/12-inch

CIRCLE 5-8 81
Also see HAYMES, Dick
Also see JAMES, Harry, & His Orchestra

JAMES, Jesse — P&R/R&B '67

Singles: 7-inch

BUDDAH 5-10
T.T.E.D. 3-4 87
20TH FOX 3-8 67-75
UNI 5-8 69
ZEA (ZAY) 3-5 70-71

LPs: 10/12-inch

20TH FOX 8-10 67

JAMES, Jimmy, & Vagabonds — P&R/R&B '68

Singles: 7-inch

ATCO 4-8 67-68
PYE 3-5 75-76

LPs: 10/12-inch

ATCO 10-15 67
PYE 5-8 75

JAMES, Joni — P&R '52

Singles: 78 rpm

MGM (222 "Let There Be Love") 100-200 53
(Four-disc boxed set.)
MGM (234 "Award Winning Album") 100-200 54
(Four disc boxed set.)
MGM (272 "Little Girl Blue") 100-200 54
(Four-disc boxed set.)
MGM (11000 & 12000 series) 10-20 52-58
MGM (30000 series) 5-10 54
SHARP (46 "Let There Be Love") 25-50 52
SHARP (50 "You Belong to Me") 25-50 52

Singles: 7-inch

MGM (16 thru 19) 20-40 59-60
(Stereo compact 33 singles.)
MGM (11223 thru 12660) 15-25 52-58
MGM (12706 "There Goes My Heart") 10-15 58
(Monaural.)
MGM (12706 "There Goes My Heart") 20-30 58
(Stereo. Unusual numbering—most MGM stereo 45s are in the 50000 series. Billed as the industry's "First Single Stereo Disc.")
MGM (12746 thru 13304) 10-20 59-64
MGM (13288 "Sentimental Me") 50-75 64
(Promotional issue only.)
MGM (30000 series) 10-20 54
MGM (50111 "There Must be a Way") 15-25 59
(Stereo.)
MGM/GOLDEN CIRCLE (101 thru 104) 5-10 61
SHARP (46 "Let There Be Love") 150-250 52
SHARP (50 "You Belong to Me") 100-200 52

Picture Sleeves

MGM (12565 "Never Till Now") 10-20 57
MGM (12706 "There Goes My Heart") 25-50 58
MGM (12779 "I Still Get a Thrill") 10-20 59
MGM (12895 "We Know") 10-20 60
MGM (12933 "My Last Date") 10-20 60
MGM (12948 "Be My Love") 10-20 61
MGM (13037 "You Were Wrong") 10-20 62

EPs: 7-inch

MGM (222 "Let There Be Love") 50-75 53
MGM (234 "Award Winning Album") 50-75 54
MGM (272 "Little Girl Blue") 50-75 54
MGM (326 "When I Fall in Love") 20-40 55
(EPs 222 through 326 are two-disc sets.)
MGM (1160 "When I Fall in Love") 10-20 55
MGM (1172 "Have Yourself a Merry Little Christmas") 25-50 55
MGM (1211 thru 1617) 10-20 56-58
MGM (1652/3/4 "Songs of Hank Williams") 10-15 59
(Monaural. Price is for any of three volumes.)
MGM (1652/3/4 "Songs of Hank Williams") 30-40 59
(Stereo. Price is for any of three volumes.)
MGM (1656/7/8 "100 Strings and Joni") 10-15 59
(Monaural. Price is for any of three volumes.)
MGM (1656/7/8 "100 Strings and Joni") 30-40 59
(Stereo. Price is for any of three volumes.)
MGM (1672/3/4 "Joni Swings Sweet") 10-15 59
(Monaural. Price is for any of three volumes.)
MGM (1672/3/4 "Joni Swings Sweet") 30-40 59
(Stereo. Price is for any of three volumes.)
MGM (3328 "In the Still of the Night") 20-35 56
MGM (3533 "Songs By Jerome Kern & Harry Warren") 20-35 57

LPs: 10/12-inch

MGM (222 "Let There Be Love") 75-125 53
(10-inch LP.)
MGM (234 "Award Winning Album") 75-125 54
(10-inch LP.)
MGM (272 "Little Girl Blue") 75-125 54
(10-inch LP.)
MGM (3240 "When I Fall in Love") 30-50 55
MGM (3328 "In the Still of the Night") 30-50 56
MGM (3346 "Award Winning Album, Vol. 1") 30-50 56
MGM (3347 "Little Girl Blue") 30-50 56
MGM (3348 "Let There Be Love") 30-50 56
MGM (3449 "Songs By Victor Young & Frank Losser") 30-50 56
MGM (3468 "Merry Christmas") 30-50 56
MGM (3528 "Give Us This Day") 25-45 57
MGM (3533 "Songs By Jerome Kern & Harry Warren") 25-45 57
MGM (3602 "Among My Souvenirs") 25-45 58
MGM (3623 "Ti Voglio Bene") 25-45 58
MGM (3706 "Award Winning Album, Vol. 1") 25-45 58
MGM (E-3718 "Je T'Aime") 25-45 58
(Monaural.)
MGM (SE-3718 "Je T'Aime") 35-55 58
(Stereo.)

MGM (E-3729 "Songs By Hank Williams") 25-45 59
(Monaural.)
MGM (SE-3729 "Songs By Hank Williams") 35-55 59
(Stereo.)
MGM (E-3749 thru E-4286) 20-30 59-65
(Monaural.)
MGM (SE-3749 thru SE-4286) 20-35 59-65
(Stereo.)

JAMES, Melvin LP '87

LPs: 10/12-inch

MCA 5-8 87

JAMES, Rick P&R/R&B/LP '78

(With the Stone City Band)

Singles: 12-inch

GORDY 4-6 79-85
MOTOWN 4-6 78-85

Singles: 7-inch

GORDY 3-5 78-85
MOTOWN 3-4 86
REPRISE 3-4 88

Picture Sleeves

GORDY 3-5 79-85

LPs: 10/12-inch

GORDY 5-8 78-86
REPRISE 5-8 88
Also see TEMPTATIONS & Rick James

JAMES, Rick, & Friend R&B '83

(With Smokey Robinson)

Singles: 7-inch

GORDY 3-5 83

JAMES, Rick, & Smokey Robinson P&R '83

Singles: 7-inch

GORDY 3-5 83
Also see JAMES, Rick
Also see JAMES, Rick, & Friend
Also see ROBINSON, Smokey

JAMES, Rick, & Roxanne Shante R&B '88

Singles: 7-inch

REPRISE 3-4 88
Also see SHANTE, Roxanne

JAMES, Sonny C&W '53

(With the Southern Gentlemen; with Silver; with Tennessee State Prison Band; the Southern Gentleman)

Singles: 78 rpm

CAPITOL 5-15 52-57

Singles: 7-inch

CAPITOL (2000 thru 3900) 3-6 67-74
(Orange labels.)
CAPITOL (2200 thru 3800) 10-20 52-57
(Purple labels.)
CAPITOL (3900 thru 5900) 5-10 58-67
(Purple or orange/yellow swirl labels.)
CAPITOL (6000 series) 4-6 60s
CAPITOL CUSTOM ("Salute to KRAK") 15-25 67
(Promotional issue for a Sacramento radio station.)
COLUMBIA 3-5 72-78
DIMENSION 3-4 81-83
DOT 4-6 62
GROOVE 4-8 61
MONUMENT 3-5 79
NRC 5-8 60
RCA 4-8 61-62

Picture Sleeves

CAPITOL (Except 4268) 4-10 65-71
CAPITOL (4268 "Who's Next in Line") 6-10 59
COLUMBIA 3-5 72-75
DIMENSION 3-5 80s
NRC (050 "Jenny Lou") 10-15 60

EPs: 7-inch

CAPITOL 8-15 57-58
CAPITOL CREATIVE PRODUCTS 5-10 68

LPs: 10/12-inch

ABC 5-8 77
BROOKVILLE 8-12 75
CAMDEN 8-12 60s
CAPITOL (100 thru 800 series) 8-12 68-71
CAPITOL (779 "The Southern Gentleman") 25-35 57
CAPITOL (867 "Sonny") 20-30 57
CAPITOL (988 "Honey") 20-30 58
CAPITOL (1100 series) 15-25 59
CAPITOL (2000 thru 2800 series) 8-15 64-68
CAPITOL (11000 series) 5-8 72-75
COLUMBIA 5-10 72-78
CROWN 8-12 60s
DIMENSION 5-8 82
DOT 15-20 62
GUEST STAR 10-15 64
HAMILTON 8-12 65
MONUMENT 5-8 79
PICKWICK 5-8 76-78
PICKWICK/HILLTOP 8-12 69
SUNRISE MEDIA 5-10
TEE VEE 8-12 79
TVP 8-12 75
WYNCOTE 8-12 60s
Also see HAGGARD, Merle / Sonny James
Also see HORTON, Johnny / Sonny James
Also see VINCENT, Gene / Tommy Sands / Sonny James / Ferlin Husky
Also see VINCENT, Gene / Frank Sinatra / Sonny James / Ron Goodwin

JAMES, Sonny / Dave Dudley / Sunny Williams

LPs: 10/12-inch

DIPLOMAT 5-10 60s
Also see DUDLEY, Dave

JAMES, Sonny / David Houston

LPs: 10/12-inch

PICKWICK/HILLTOP 8-12 67
Also see HOUSTON, David

JAMES, Sonny / Seekers

Singles: 7-inch

CAPITOL (5375 "I'll Keep Holding On"/"I'll Never Find Another You") 4-8 65
(These two tracks were unintentionally pressed back-to-back.)
Also see JAMES, Sonny
Also see SEEKERS

JAMES, Tommy P&R/R&B/LP '66

(With the Shondells)

Singles: 7-inch

ABC 3-5 73
FANTASY 3-4 75-80
MCA 3-5 74
MILLENNIUM 3-5 79-81
PHILCO 10-20 67
("Hip-Pocket" flexi-disc.)
ROULETTE 4-8 66-73
TWENTY-ONE 3-4 83

Picture Sleeves

FANTASY 3-5 76
MILLENNIUM 3-5 71
ROULETTE 5-10 66-67
TWENTY-ONE 3-4 83

LPs: 10/12-inch

FANTASY 8-10 76-80
MILLENNIUM 5-8 80
RHINO 8-12 89
ROULETTE 10-20 66-72
SCEPTER 8-10 73
SCEPTER/CITATION 5-8 82
TWENTY-ONE 5-8 83
Members: Tommy James; Mike Vale; Ed Gray; Ron Rosman; Pete Lucia.
Also see HOG HEAVEN
Also see SHONDELLS

JAMES, Tommy & Shondells / Lee Dorsey

Singles: 7-inch

ROULETTE (4710 "It's Only Love"/"Ya Ya") 5-10 66
(Credits Tommy James & Shondells, but plays Lee Dorsey.)
Also see DORSEY, Lee
Also see JAMES, Tommy

JAMES BOYS P&R/R&B '68

Singles: 7-inch

PHIL L.A. of SOUL 4-6 68
Also see MFSB

JAMES GANG LP '69

Singles: 7-inch

ABC 3-5 70-72
ATCO 3-5 74-75
BLUESWAY 4-6 69

LPs: 10/12-inch

ABC 10-12 70-73
ATCO 8-10 74-76
BLUESWAY 10-15 69
COMMAND 8-10 74
MCA 5-8
Members: Joe Walsh; Tommy Bolin; Dominic Troiano Dale Peters; Jim Fox..
Also see BOLIN, Tommy
Also see WALSH, Joe

JAMESON, Cody C&W/P&R '77

Singles: 7-inch

ATCO 3-5 77

JAMESON, Nick P&R '86

Singles: 7-inch

MOTOWN 3-4 86

LPs: 10/12-inch

BEARSVILLE (6972 "Already Free") 8-12 77
MOTOWN 5-8 86
Also see FOGHAT

JAMESTOWN MASSACRE P&R '72

Singles: 7-inch

W.B. 3-5 72

JAMIE & JANE

Singles: 7-inch

DECCA (30862 "Strolling") 15-20 59
DECCA (30934 "Faithful Our Love") 15-20 59
Members: Gene Pitney; Ginny Arnell.
Also see ARNELL, Ginny
Also see PITNEY, Gene

JAMIES P&R '58

Singles: 7-inch

EPIC 5-10 58-63
EPIC (11000 series) 3-4 74
U.A. 4-6 59

Picture Sleeves

EPIC (9281 "Summertime Summertime") 15-20 58-63
Members: Tom Jamison; Serena Jamison.

JAMMERS R&B '82

Singles: 7-inch

JUBILEE 4-8 66
LOMA 4-8 67

JAMUL P&R '70

Singles: 7-inch

LIZARD 3-5 70

LPs: 10/12-inch

LIZARD 10-12 70

JAN & ARNIE P&R '58

(With Don Ralke's Orchestra; with Adam Ross Orchestra)

Singles: 78 rpm

ARWIN (108 "Jennie Lee") 150-250 58

Singles: 7-inch

ARWIN (108 "Jennie Lee") 15-25 58
ARWIN (111 "Gas Money") 15-25 58
ARWIN (113 "I Love Linda") 15-25 58
DOT (16116 "Gas Money") 10-20 58
DORE (522 "Baby Talk") 300-400 59
(By Jan & Dean though shown on first pressings as by Jan & Arnie.)
QUALITY (1761 "Gas Money") 15-25 58
(Canadian.)

EPs: 7-inch

DOT (1097 "Jan & Arnie") 350-450 60
Members: Jan Berry; Arnie Ginsburg.
Also see BERRY, Jan
Also see JAN & DEAN
Also see RALKE, Don

JAN & DEAN
P&R/R&B '59

Singles: 7–inch

AURAVISION (6723 "Linda")............40-60 64
(Cardboard flexi-disc, one of six by six different artists. Columbia Record Club "Enrollment Premium." Set came in a special paper sleeve.)
CAPITOL (89 "Jennie Lee")..................3-5 89
(By Jan & Dean instead of Jan & Arnie.)
CHALLENGE (9120 "Wanted: One Girl")..10-20 61
CHALLENGE (9111 "Heart and Soul"/ "Those Words")..25-35 61
CHALLENGE (9111 "Heart and Soul"/"Midsummer Night's Dream") 10-20 61
(Note different flip side.)
CHALLENGE (59111 "Heart and Soul")...10-20 61
COLUMBIA (44036 "Yellow Balloon") 15-25 67
DORE 15-25 59-61
J&D (1 "Oh What a Beautiful Morning") 150-200 87
(Private, limited, promotional, red vinyl pressing by Dean Torrence which he used as Christmas gifts. With Chris Farmer and Phil Bardowell.)
J&D (001 "California Lullabye") 20-30 66
J&D (402 "Like a Summer Rain")......20-30 66
JAN & DEAN (10 "Hawaii") 45-60 66
JAN & DEAN (11 "Fan Tan")..............50-75 66
LIBERTY (55397 "A Sunday Kind of Love") 10-20 61
LIBERTY (55454 "Tennessee").........10-20 62
LIBERTY (55496 "Who Put the Bomp")..20-30 62
LIBERTY (55522 "She's Still Talkin' Baby Talk") 50-75 62
LIBERTY (55531 "Linda")...................8-12 63
LIBERTY (55580 thru 55727).............5-10 63-64
LIBERTY (55766 thru 55923).............8-12 63-66
MAGIC LAMP (401 "California Lullabye")..15-25 66
ODE (66111 "Fun City") 15-25 75
U.A. 10-20 72-76
W.B. (7151 "Only a Boy") 25-35 67
W.B. (7219 "I Know My Mind") 25-35 68

Picture Sleeves

DORE (555 "We Go Together") 35-50 60
DORE (576 "Gee") 75-100 60
LIBERTY (Except 55766 & 55849)....15-25 63-65
LIBERTY (55766 "From All Over the World")..80-125 65
LIBERTY (55849 "Folk City")............20-30 65
U.A. (50859 "Jenny Lee") 15-25 71

LPs: 10/12-inch

AUDIO ENCORE...............................5-8 89
AXIS (45 "Very Best")........................5-10
COLUMBIA (9461 "Save for a Rainy Day")...............................1500-2000 67
(At least one sale of this LP has been confirmed. It DOES exist but is probably not a U.S. issue. Tracks are remixed from what is heard on the J&D LP of the same title. Does have one track, *Lullaby in the Rain,* which is not on the J&D LP.)
DEADMAN'S CURVE ("Live at Keystone Berkeley") 15-25 78
(With Papa Doo Ron Ron.)
DESIGN/STEREO SPECTRUM 10-20 63
DORE (101 "Jan & Dean") 200-300 60
(Price includes a 12" x 12" Jan & Dean color photo, which represents $50 to $100 of the value.)
EMI 10-15 86
EMI/LIBERTY 10-20 90
EXACT..5-8 80
EXCELSIOR 10-15 80
IMPERIAL HOUSE 5-8 80
INTERNATIONAL AWARD................8-10
J&D (101 "Save for a Rainy Day")...200-300 67
K-TEL 5-10 70-89
LIBERTY (3248 thru 3403)................20-25 62-65
(Monaural.)
LIBERTY (3414 "Pop Symphony Number 1")....................................40-45 65
(Monaural.)
LIBERTY (3417 thru 3460)...............20-25 65-66
(Monaural.)
LIBERTY (7248 thru 7403)...............20-30 62-65
(Stereo.)
LIBERTY (7414 "Pop Symphony Number 1")....................................40-50 65
(Stereo.)
LIBERTY (7417 thru 7460)...............20-30 65-66
(Stereo.)
LIBERTY (10000 series)....................8-12 81-82
MAGIC CARPET.................................10-12
NEON (333006 "Greatest Hits").........8-10 83
PAIR (1071 "California Gold")..........10-15
RHINO (1498 "One Summer Night Live") 25-45 82
SILVER EAGLE (1039 "Silver Summer")..25-35 86
(Mail-order offer.)
SUNDAZED (5022 "Save for a Rainy Day") 15-18 96
(Colored vinyl. Two-discs.)
SUNDAZED (5040 "Jan & Dean") 8-10 96
(Colored vinyl. Includes poster.)
SUNSET 10-15 67
U.A. 10-12 71-79

Members: Jan Berry; Dean Torrence.
Session: Glen Campbell; Leon Russell; Hal Blaine; Sally Stevens; Carol Kaye; Ray Pholman; Don Randi; Chris Farmer: Phil Bardowell.
Also see BEACH BOYS
Also see BEACH BOYS / Jan & Dean
Also see BERRY, Jan
Also see CAMPBELL, Glen
Also see JAN & ARNIE
Also see LEGENDARY MASKED SURFERS
Also see RUSSELL, Leon

JAN & DEAN / Roy Orbison / Shirelles / 4 Seasons

EPs: 7-inch

COKE ("Let's Swing the Jingle for Coca-Cola")...................................40-60 65
(Coca-Cola radio spots. Issued to radio stations only.)
Also see 4 SEASONS
Also see ORBISON, Roy
Also see SHIRELLES

JAN & DEAN & RANDELL KIRSCH

Singles: 7-inch

JAN & DEAN (1 "Wa Ichi Nichi Shiow")...5-10 87
Members: Jan Berry; Dean Torrence; Randell Kirsch; Gary Griffin; Chris Farmer; John Cowsil; Phil Bardowell; Mark Ward; Kevin Leonard; Bill Hollingshead; Dave Hoffman; Sue Nelson; Members of Shangahi audience.

JAN & DEAN / Soul Surfers

LPs: 10/12-inch

L-J (101 "Jan & Dean with the Soul Surfers") 35-45 63

JAN & DEAN / Bobby Vinton / Andy Williams

Singles

AURAVISION (2 "Special Teen Preview Record #2")..12-20 64
(Square cardboard picture disc. Columbia Record Club bonus. Has song excerpts by each artist, plus *Pipeline* by an unknown band.)
Also see JAN & DEAN
Also see VINTON, Bobby
Also see WILLIAMS, Andy

JAN & KJELD
P&R '60

Singles: 7-inch

ALONCA 4-6 66
IMPERIAL 5-10 59
JARO INT'L..5-10 60
KAPP 5-10 60-61

Picture Sleeves

JARO INT'L..5-10 60
KAPP 5-10 60

LPs: 10/12-inch

KAPP (1190 "Banjo Boy")..................20-30 60

JANE, Baby: see BABY JANE

JANE'S ADDICTION
LP '88

LPs: 10/12-inch

TRIPLE X..10-20
(Clear vinyl.)
W.B. 5-8 88-90

JANICE
R&B '86

Singles: 7-inch

BORN AGAIN 3-4 80
COTILLION..3-5 76
FANTASY..3-5 75-76
ROULETTE (7083 "I Thank You Kindly")..10-20 70

LPs: 10/12-inch

FANTASY..6-10 75

JANIS, Johnny
P&R '57

Singles: 78 rpm

ABC-PAR 5-10 57

Singles: 7-inch

ABC-PAR 5-10 57
BOMARC...5-10 59-60
COLUMBIA..5-10 60
CORAL 5-10 55
MONUMENT 4-6 66-68

LPs: 10/12-inch

ABC-PAR (140 "For the First Time")..35-50 57
COLUMBIA...15-20 61
MONUMENT 10-15 65

JANKEL, Chas
R&B/LP '82

Singles: 12-inch

A&M...4-6 83

Singles: 7-inch

A&M...3-4 82

LPs: 10/12-inch

A&M...5-8 82
Also see DURY, Ian, & Blockheads

JANKOWSKI, Horst, Orchestra
P&R/LP '65

Singles: 7-inch

MERCURY 3-6 65-68

Picture Sleeves

MERCURY 4-6 65

LPs: 10/12-inch

MERCURY 5-15 65-69
Also see IMPALAS / Horst Jankowski & His Orchestra

JARMELS
P&R/R&B '61

Singles: 7-inch

LAURIE..10-15 61-63

LPs: 10/12-inch

COLLECTABLES 6-8 87
Members: Nate Ruff; Ray Smith; Tom Eldridge; Paul Burnett; Earl Christian; Major Harris.

JARRE, Jean-Michael
LP '77

Singles: 12-inch

POLYDOR 4-6 86

Singles: 7-inch

POLYDOR 3-5 78-87

LPs: 10/12-inch

DREYFUS 5-8 85-86
MFSL (212 "Oxygene")......................20-25 94
MFSL (227 "Equinoxe")....................20-25 95
POLYDOR 5-8 77-87
Also see ANDERSON, Laurie
Also see U.S.A. for AFRICA

JARREAU, Al
R&B/LP '76

(Jarreau)

Singles: 7-inch

MCA...3-4 87
RAYNARD (10022 "I'm Not Afraid")..50-100 65
RAYNARD (10024 "Shake Up")......50-100 65
REPRISE..3-5 76-88
W.B. 3-5 77-86

Picture Sleeves

MCA...3-4 87

W.B. 3-5 83-84

LPs: 10/12-inch

MFSL (019 "All Fly Home") 40-60 78
REPRISE 5-10 75-88
W.B. 5-10 77-86
Also see U.S.A. for AFRICA

JARREAU, Al, & Randy Crawford R&B '82

Singles: 7-inch

W.B. 3-4 82
Also see CRAWFORD, Randy
Also see JARREAU, Al

JARRETT, Keith LP '75

LPs: 10/12-inch

ATLANTIC 8-10 75
ECM 8-12 76-80
IMPULSE 8-10 75-77

JARVIS, Carol P&R '57

Singles: 78 rpm

BALLY 4-6 57
DOT 4-6 57

Singles: 7-inch

BALLY 5-10 57
DOT 5-10 57-59
ERA 5-10 60-61

JARVIS, Marion R&B '74

Singles: 7-inch

ROXBURY 3-5 74

JASMIN D&D '84

Singles: 12-inch

TVI 4-6 84

JASON & SCORCHERS LP '84
(Jason & Nashville Scorchers)

Singles: 7-inch

EMI AMERICA 3-4 84-86
PRAXIS 10-15 83-84

LPs: 10/12-inch

EMI AMERICA 5-8 84-86
Member: Jason Ringenberg.

JASPER, Chris R&B '87

Singles: 7-inch

CBS ASSOCIATED 3-4 87-88

LPs: 10/12-inch

CBS ASSOCIATED 3-4 87
Also see ISLEY - JASPER - ISLEY

JAY, Dee: see DEE JAY

JAY, Jazzy: see JAZZY JAY

JAY, Morty P&R '63
(With the Surfin' Cats)

Singles: 7-inch

KAYDEN 5-10 60s
LEGEND 10-15 63
20TH FOX 5-10 63

Picture Sleeves

LEGEND 15-25 63

JAY & AMERICANS P&R '62

Singles: 7-inch

COLLECTABLES 3-5 92-93
EEOC (1140 "Things Are Changing") 50-100 65
(Equal Employment Opportunity Center promotional issue.)
FUTURA 3-5 72
U.A. (353 thru 992) 4-8 61-66
U.A. (50000 series) 3-6 66-71
U.A. (1600 series) 3-4
U.A. SILVER SPOTLIGHT 3-5

Picture Sleeves

EEOC (1140 "Things Are Changing") 50-100 65
(Equal Employment Opportunity Center promotional issue.)
U.A. 5-10 65-66

LPs: 10/12-inch

PAIR 8-10 88
RHINO 5-8 86
SUNSET 10-12 69-70
UNART 8-12 67
U.A. (300 series) 5-8 75
U.A. (1000 series) 5-8 80
U.A. (3222 "She Cried") 20-25 62
(Monaural.)
U.A. (3300 "At the Café Wha") 20-25 63
(Monaural.)
U.A. (3407 "Come a Little Bit Closer") 15-25 64
(Monaural.)
U.A. (3417 thru 3562) 15-20 64-67
(Monaural.)
U.A. (6222 "She Cried") 20-30 62
(Stereo.)
U.A. (6300 "At the Café Wha") 20-30 63
(Stereo.)
U.A. (6407 "Come a Little Bit Closer") 20-25 64
(Stereo.)
U.A. (6417 thru 6762, except 6671) .. 10-20 64-70
U.A. (6671 "Sands of Time") 20-30 69
U.A. (90814 "Greatest Hits") 15-20 60s
(Record club issue.)
Members: Jay Traynor; Kenny Vance; Howard Kane; Jay Black; Marty Sanders; Sandy Yaguda.
Also see BLACK, Jay
Also see FAGEN, Donald

JAY & TECHNIQUES P&R/R&B/LP '67

Singles: 7-inch

EVENT 4-6 75-76
GORDY 4-6 72
SILVER BLUE 4-8 74
SMASH 5-8 67-69

Picture Sleeves

SMASH 5-10 67-68

LPs: 10/12-inch

EVENT 8-12 75
SMASH 15-20 67-68
Members: Jay Proctor; John Walsh; Ron Goosly; Chuck Crowl; Dante Dancho; Karl Landis.

JAYA P&R '89

Singles: 7-inch

LMR 3-4 89
Also see STEVIE B

JAYE, Jerry P&R/LP '67

Singles: 7-inch

COLUMBIA 3-5 75
CONNIE (101) 10-15 67
(Title not known.)
HI (2100 series) 4-8 67-68
HI (2300 series) 3-5 76-77
MEGA 3-5 71-74
RAINTREE 3-5 72

LPs: 10/12-inch

HI (32000 series) 15-20 67
HI (32100 series) 5-8 76

JAYE, Miles R&B/LP '87

Singles: 7-inch

ISLAND 3-4 87-89

LPs: 10/12-inch

BEJAY (1370) 20-25 70
BEJAY (300 series) 8-10 84
ISLAND 5-8 87-89
MCA 5-8 87

JAYHAWKS P&R/R&B '56

Singles: 78 rpm

ALADDIN (3393 "Everyone Should Know") 50-75 57
FLASH (Except 105) 10-20 56
FLASH (105 "Counting My Teardrops") 50-75 56

Singles: 7-inch

ALADDIN (3393 "Everyone Should Know") 50-100 57
EASTMAN (792 "I Wish the World Owed Me a Living") 100-200 59
EASTMAN (798 "New Love") 100-200 59
FLASH (105 "Counting My Teardrops") 200-300 56
FLASH (109 "Stranded in the Jungle") 25-50 56
FLASH (111 "Love Train") 25-50 56
OLDIES 45 .... 4-8 60s
Members: James Johnson; Carl Fisher; Dave Govan; Carver Bunkern; Richard Owens.
Also see MARATHONS
Also see VIBRATIONS

JAYNETTS P&R/R&B '63
(Jaynetts / Art Butler)

Singles: 7-inch

GOLDIE 3-5
J&S 5-10 65
TUFF (369 "Sally Go 'Round the Roses") 5-10 63
TUFF (370 "Keep an Eye on Her") 5-10 63
TUFF (370 "Dear Abby") 5-10 63
TUFF (374 "Snowman Snowman, Sweet Potato Nose") 5-10 63
TUFF (377 "Johnny Don't Cry") 5-10 64

LPs: 10/12-inch

TUFF (13 "Sally, Go 'Round the Roses") 150-250 63
(Includes *Dear Abby* by the Hearts.)
Members: Ethel Davis; Johnnie Louise; Mary Sue Wells; Ada Ray; Yvonne Bushnell.
Also see HEARTS
Also see JOHNNIE & JOE

JAZZ at PHILHARMONIC R&B '49

Singles: 78 rpm

MERCURY 4-6 49
Also see JACQUET, Illonis

JAZZ CRUSADERS P&R '66

Singles: 7-inch

CHISA 3-5 70-71
PACIFIC JAZZ 4-8 62-68
WORLD PACIFIC 4-8 64-65

LPs: 10/12-inch

BLUE NOTE 5-10 75-80
CHISA 8-12 70
LIBERTY 8-12 70
PACIFIC JAZZ (27 thru 87) 20-35 61-64
PACIFIC JAZZ (10000 & 20000 series) 10-20 65-69
PAUSA 5-8 82
WORLD PACIFIC 8-15 65
Members: Wilton Felder; Stix Hooper; Wayne Henderson; Joe Sample.
Also see CRUSADERS
Also see FELDER, Wilton

JAZZY JAY R&B '84

Singles: 7-inch

ATLANTIC 3-4 84

JEAN, Cathy: see CATHY JEAN

JEAN, Earl: see EARL-JEAN

JEAN, Norma: see NORMA JEAN

JEAN & DARLINGS P&R '67

Singles: 7-inch

VOLT 4-8 67-69

JECKYLL, Dr: see DR. JECKYLL

JEFF & ALETA R&B '80

Singles: 7-inch

SRI 3-5 80

JEFFERSON P&R '69
(Geoff Turton)

Singles: 7-inch

DECCA 4-6 69
JANUS 4-6 69

LPs: 10/12-inch

JANUS 10-15 69

JEFFERSON, Morris R&B '77

Singles: 7-inch

PARACHUTE 3-5 78

LPs: 10/12-inch

PARACHUTE 5-8 78

JEFFERSON AIRPLANE LP '66

Singles: 7-inch

ELEKTRA 3-4 88
GRUNT (0500 thru 0511) 3-5 71-72

GRUNT (10988 "White Rabbit")........10-20 77
(Colored vinyl. Promotional issue only.)
RCA (0150 thru 0343)....................4-6 69-70
RCA (5156 "White Rabbit")..................4-8 87
(Colored vinyl. Promotional issue only.)
RCA (8769 thru 9644)........................5-10 66-68
(Dog on side of label.)
RCA (9000 series)................................3-4 89
(Dog near top of label.)

Picture Sleeves

GRUNT (0500 "Pretty As You Feel")...5-10 71
GRUNT (0506 "Long John Silver")....10-15 72
RCA (Except 5156)...........................8-12 68-70
RCA (5156 "White Rabbit")..................4-8 87
(Promotional issue only.)

EPs: 7-inch

RCA (SP33-564 "Jefferson Airplane")...20-30 69
(Promotional issue only.)

LPs: 10/12-inch

EPIC...5-8 89
GRUNT (0147 "Thirty Seconds Over Winterland")....................................10-15 73
GRUNT (1001 "Bark")........................30-60 71
GRUNT (1007 "Long John Silver")....30-60 72
GRUNT (0437 "Early Flight")............10-15 74
GRUNT (4386 "Bark")........................10-15 82
PAIR..8-10 84
RCA (0320 ("Volunteers")..................15-20 73
(Quadrophonic.)
RCA (1511 "After Bathing at Baxter's")......................................20-30 67
(Black label. With "LPM" or "LSP" prefix.)
RCA (1511 "After Bathing at Baxter's")......................................10-12 70s
(Orange or tan label.)
RCA (3584 "Jefferson Airplane Takes Off")...75-125 66
(Has 12 tracks. With "LPM" or "LSP" prefix.)
RCA (3584 "Jefferson Airplane Takes Off")...15-25 66
(Has 11 tracks. With "LPM" or "LSP" prefix.)
RCA (3584 "Jefferson Airplane Takes Off")...10-15 69
(Orange label.)
RCA (3661 "Worst of Jefferson Airplane").....................................5-10 80
RCA (3739 "Jefferson Airplane Takes Off")......................................5-10 80
RCA (3766 "Surrealistic Pillow")........20-30 67
(Black label. With "LPM" or "LSP" prefix.)
RCA (3766 "Surrealistic Pillow")........10-12 69
(Orange label.)
RCA (3766 "Surrealistic Pillow")............5-8 80s
(With "AYL" prefix.)
RCA (3797 "Crown of Creation").........5-10 80
RCA (3798 "Bless Its Pointed Little Head")...5-10 80
RCA (3867 "Volunteers")....................5-10 81
RCA (4058 "Crown of Creation").......10-15 68
RCA (4133 "Bless Its Pointed Little Head")...10-20 69
(Includes artwork insert.)
RCA (4238 "Volunteers")..................10-15 69
RCA (4448 "Blows Against the Empire")..10-15 70
(Black vinyl. Add $4 to $6 if accompanied by booklet.)
RCA (4448 "Blows Against the Empire")..75-100 70
(Clear vinyl. Promotional issue only.)
RCA (LSP-4459 "Worst of Jefferson Airplane")....................................10-15 70
RCA (AFL1-4459 "Worst of Jefferson Airplane")......................................5-10 80s
RCA (5724 "2400 Fulton Street") 8-12 87

Members: Signe Anderson; Marty Balin; Paul Kantner; Jack Casady; Jorma Kaukonen; Skip Spence; Grace Slick; Craig Chaquico; Joey Covington; Papa John Creach; Spencer Dryden; Dave Freiberg.

Also see BALIN, Marty
Also see CREACH, Papa John
Also see CROSBY, David
Also see GARCIA, Jerry
Also see GREAT!! SOCIETY!!
Also see HAMMOND, John Paul
Also see HOPKINS, Nicky
Also see JEFFERSON STARSHIP
Also see KBC BAND
Also see KANTNER, Paul, & Grace Slick
Also see KAUKONEN, Jorma
Also see QUICKSILVER
Also see SLICK, Grace
Also see STILLS, Stephen

JEFFERSON STARSHIP *LP '74*

Singles: 7-inch

GRUNT 3-5 74-84

Picture Sleeves

GRUNT 3-5 78-87
RCA 3-4 87-89

LPs: 10/12-inch

GRUNT (0717 thru 1557)..................10-15 74-76
GRUNT (1255 "Flight Log, 1966-1976")..15-20 77
(With simulated leather cover. Also has Jefferson Airplane, Hot Tuna, Grace Slick and Paul Kanter tracks.)
GRUNT (1255 "Flight Log, 1966-1976")..10-20 81
(With standard cover.)
GRUNT (2515 thru 3247)..................10-15 78-79
GRUNT (3363 "Gold").........................15-20 79
(Picture disc.)
GRUNT (3452 thru 6413)....................6-12 79-87
RCA 5-8 81-89

Members: Grace Slick; Marty Balin; Paul Kantner; Aynsley Dunbar; Pete Sears; Mickey Thomas; John Barbata.

Note: Cross references that already appear under Jefferson Airplane are not duplicated below.

Also see HART, Mickey
Also see HOT TUNA
Also see JEFFERSON AIRPLANE
Also see KANTNER, Paul, & Jefferson Starship
Also see STARSHIP

JEFFREE *R&B '78*

Singles: 7-inch

MCA 3-5 78-79

LPs: 10/12-inch

MCA 5-8 79

JEFFREY, Joe *P&R '69*

(Joe Jeffrey Group)

Singles: 7-inch

WAND..4-6 69

LPs: 10/12-inch

WAND..10-15 69

JEFFREYS, Garland *LP '77*

Singles: 7-inch

A&M 3-5 77-79
ARISTA...3-5 75
ATLANTIC...3-5 73
EPIC...3-4 81-83

EPs: 7-inch

EPIC (1223 "Escape Artist") 4-8 81
(Promotional issue only.)

LPs: 10/12-inch

A&M 5-8 77-79
ATLANTIC...8-10 73
EPIC...5-8 81-83

JEFFREYS, Garland, & Phoebe Snow

Singles: 7-inch

A&M 3-5 78

Picture Sleeves

A&M 3-5 78

Also see JEFFREYS, Garland
Also see SNOW, Phoebe

JELLY BEANS *P&R/R&B '64*

Singles: 7-inch

ESKEE (001 "I'm Hip to You") 15-25 65
RED BIRD (003 "I Wanna Love Him So Bad")..8-12 64
RED BIRD (011 "Baby, Be Mine").......8-12 64

Members: Diane Taylor; Maxine Herbert; Elyse Herbert; Alma Brewer.

JELLYBEAN *D&D '84*

("Jellybean" Benitez; Featuring Steven Dante)

Singles: 12-inch

EMI AMERICA.....................................4-6 84-86

Singles: 7-inch

CHRYSALIS 3-4 87
EMI AMERICA.....................................3-4 84-86

Picture Sleeves

CHRYSALIS 3-4 87
EMI AMERICA.....................................3-4 85

LPs: 10/12-inch

CHRYSALIS 5-8 87
EMI AMERICA.....................................5-8 84-86

JELLYBEAN & ELISA FIORILLO *P&R '87*

Singles: 7-inch

CHRYSALIS 3-4 87

Picture Sleeves

CHRYSALIS 3-4 87

Also see FIORILLO, Elisa
Also see JELLYBEAN

JENKINS, Donald *P&R '63*

(With the Delighters)

Singles: 7-inch

BLACK BEAUTY (302 "Elephant Walk")..5-10 60s
CORTLAND (109 "Elephant Walk")..10-15 63
CORTLAND (112 "Somebody Help Me")...15-25 63
CORTLAND (116 "I've Settled Down")..15-25 64
DUCHESS (104 "Happy Days") 10-20 65

JENKINS, Gordon, & Orchestra *P&R '42*

Singles: 78 rpm

DECCA..3-6 50-56

Singles: 7-inch

COLUMBIA..4-6 64
DECCA..5-10 50-56
KAPP...4-8 60-64
TIME..4-6 62
"X"..4-8 55

EPs: 7-inch

DECCA..5-15 51-56

LPs: 10/12-inch

CAPITOL (700 series)........................15-25 56
(With "T" prefix.)
CAPITOL (700 series) 10-15 61
(With "DT" prefix.)
CAPITOL (700 series) 4-8 75
(With "SM" prefix.)
COLUMBIA..10-20 62-63
CORAL 5-8 73
CUSTOM...5-10
DECCA..15-30 51-63
(Decca LP numbers in this series preceded by a "7" or a "DL-7" are stereo issues.)
DOT 5-10 66
GWP...5-10 71
MCA..5-8 73-75
SUNSET..5-10 67
TIME 10-15 62-64

Also see ARMSTRONG, Louis
Also see BOONE, Pat
Also see CARROLL, Bob
Also see CASHMAN & WEST / Gordon Jenkins & His Orchestra
Also see LEE, Peggy
Also see WEAVERS

JENKINS, Gus *P&R/R&B '56*

(Gus Jinkins)

Singles: 78 rpm

COMBO 10-20 54
FLASH...10-20 56-57

Singles: 7-inch

CATALINA..5-10 63
COMBO (87 "I Been Working") 30-50 54
FLASH...15-25 56-57
GENERAL ARTIST 8-15 64-69
PIONEER INT'L....................................5-10 59-62
SAR 5-10 64

TOWER 5-10 64-65

JENKINS, Kechia R&B '88

Singles: 7-inch

PROFILE 3-4 88

JENKINS, Norma R&B '76

Singles: 7-inch

CARNIVAL (528 "Need Someone to Love") 15-25 67
DESERT MOON 3-5 76
JEAN 5-8
Also see KEYES, Troy, & Norma Jenkins

JENNIE & JAY

Singles: 7-inch

RESCUE (102 "Jo Baby") 20-40
(Reissue of David Gates & Accents' 1958 Perspective release.)
Member: David Gates.
Also see GATES, David

JENNIFER

(Jennifer Warnes)

Singles: 7-inch

PARROT 4-6 67-70

LPs: 10/12-inch

PARROT 10-20 68-70
Also see WARNES, Jennifer

JENNINGS, Waylon C&W '65

(With the Waylors; with Kimberlys; with Crickets; Waylon)

Singles: 7-inch

A&M (739 "Four Strong Winds") 10-15 64
A&M (722 "Rave On") 10-20 63
A&M (753 "The Race Is On") 10-20 64
A&M (762 "The Real House of the Rising Sun") 10-20 65
BAT (121636 "White Lightning") 30-50 62
BAT (121639 "Dream Baby") 25-35 62
BRUNSWICK (55130 "Jole Blon") 100-150 59
(Maroon label. With Buddy Holly & King Curtis.)
BRUNSWICK (55130 "Jole Blon") .. 75-100 59
(Yellow label. Promotional issue only.)
COLUMBIA 3-4 83
EPIC 3-4 91
RCA (Except 8572 thru 9642) 3-6 69-82
RCA (8572 thru 9642) 5-10 65-68
RAMCO 8-12 67
TREND '61 (102 "Another Blue Day") 20-30 61
TREND '63 (106 "The Stage") 50-75 63

Picture Sleeves

RCA 3-5 79-80

LPs: 10/12-inch

A&M (4238 "Don't Think Twice") 25-30 69
BAT (1001 "Waylon Jennings at JD's") 200-300 64
(500 copies were made on Bat, then another 500 were done on Sounds Ltd.)
CAMDEN 8-15 67-76
EPIC 5-8 90
MCA 5-8
PICKWICK 5-10 75
RCA (AFL-1 series) 5-10 78
RCA (0240 thru 3378) 5-10 73-79
RCA (3406 "Greatest Hits") 30-40 79
(Picture disc.)
RCA (3493 "What Goes Around Comes Around") 5-10 79
RCA (3523 "Folk Country") 15-25 66
RCA (3602 "Music Man") 5-10 80
RCA (3620 "Leavin' Town") 20-30 66
RCA (3660 "Waylon Sings Ol' Harlan") 15-20 67
RCA (3663 "Are You Ready for the Country") 5-8 80
RCA (3736 "Nashville Rebel") 15-25 66
(Soundtrack.)
RCA (3737 "Good Hearted Woman") 5-8 80
RCA (3825 "Love of the Common People") 15-25 67
RCA (3897 "Honky Tonk Heroes") 5-8 81
RCA (3918 "Hangin' On") 15-20 68
RCA (3942 "This Time") 5-8 81
RCA (4023 "Only the Greatest") 15-20 68
RCA (4072 "Dreaming My Dreams") 5-8 81
RCA (4073 "The Ramblin' Man") 5-8 81
RCA (4085 "Jewels") 15-20 68
RCA (4137 "Just to Satisfy You") 15-20 69
RCA (4163 "Waylon Live") 5-8 81
RCA (4164 "I've Always Been Crazy") .. 5-8 81
RCA (4180 "Country Folk") 15-25 69
RCA (4247 "Black on Black") 5-8 82
RCA (4250 "Music Man") 5-8 82
RCA (4260 "Waylon") 10-15 70
RCA (4341 "Best of Waylon Jennings") 8-10 77
RCA (4418 "Singer of Sad Songs") .. 10-15 70
RCA (4487 "The Taker/Tulsa") 10-15 71
RCA (4567 "Cedartown, Georgia") ... 10-15 71
RCA (4647 "Good Hearted Woman") 10-15 72
RCA (4673 "It's Only Rock & Roll") 5-8 83
RCA (4751 "Ladies Love Outlaws") .. 10-15 72
RCA (4826 "Waylon & Co.") 5-8 83
RCA (4828 "Best of Waylon Jennings") 5-8 83
RCA (4854 "Lonesome, On'ry and Mean") 10-15 73
RCA (5473 "Collector's Series") 5-10 85
SEAGULL 5-8 83
SOUNDS (1001 "Waylon Jennings at JD's") 200-250 64
(First issued on Bat.)
TIME-LIFE 5-8 81
VOCALION 15-20 69
Session: Buddy Holly; King Curtis; James Burton.
Also see ANDERSON, John
Also see BARE, Bobby
Also see BOWMAN, Don
Also see CRICKETS
Also see CUNHA, Rick
Also see DAVIS, Skeeter
Also see EDDY, Duane
Also see HARRIS, Emmylou
Also see HOLLY, Buddy
Also see JONES, George
Also see KIMBERLYS
Also see KING CURTIS
Also see MANDRELL, Barbara
Also see NELSON, Willie
Also see RODRIGUEZ, Johnny
Also see SCHNEIDER, John
Also see TUBB, Ernest
Also see U.S.A. for AFRICA
Also see WHITE, Tony Joe
Also see YOUNG, Neil

JENNINGS, Waylon, & Anita Carter C&W '68

Singles: 7-inch

RCA 4-8 68

JENNINGS, Waylon, & Jesse Colter

(Waylon & Jessi) LP '81

Singles: 7-inch

RCA 3-5 69-71

LPs: 10/12-inch

RCA (3931 "Leather & Lace") 5-10 81
Also see COLTER, Jesse

JENNINGS, Waylon, & Willie Nelson

(Waylon & Willie) P&R '77

Singles: 7-inch

COLUMBIA 3-4 83
MCA 3-4 86
RCA 3-5 76-86

LPs: 10/12-inch

AURA 5-8 83
COLUMBIA 5-8 83
OUT of TOWN DIST 5-8 80s
RCA (2686 "Waylon & Willie") 5-10 78
RCA (2686 "Waylon & Willie") 20-25 78
(Colored vinyl. Promotional issue only.)
RCA (4455 "Waylon & Willie II") 5-8 82

JENNINGS, Waylon, Willie Nelson, Jessi Colter, & Tompall Glaser LP '76

LPs: 10/12-inch

RCA (1321 "The Outlaws") 5-10 76

JENNINGS, Waylon, Willie Nelson, Johnny Cash, & Kris Kristofferson LP '85

Singles: 7-inch

COLUMBIA 3-4 85-90

LPs: 10/12-inch

COLUMBIA 5-8 85-90
Also see CASH, Johnny
Also see KRISTOFFERSON, Kris
Also see NELSON, Willie

JENNINGS, Waylon / Johnny Paycheck

LPs: 10/12-inch

OUT of TOWN DIST 5-8 82
Also see PAYCHECK, Johnny

JENNINGS, Waylon, & Jerry Reed

Singles: 7-inch

RCA 3-4 83
Also see REED, Jerry

JENNINGS, Waylon / White Water

Singles: 7-inch

RCA 3-4 81

JENNINGS, Waylon, & Hank Williams Jr.

Singles: 7-inch

RCA 3-4 83
Also see JENNINGS, Waylon
Also see WILLIAMS, Hank, Jr.

JENSEN, Kris P&R '62

Singles: 7-inch

A&M 3-5 70
COLPIX 5-10 59
HICKORY 5-10 62-65
KAPP 5-10 61
LEADER 10-15 60-61

Picture Sleeves

HICKORY 10-15 62-64

LPs: 10/12-inch

HICKORY (110 "Torture") 40-50 62

JEROME, Henry, & His Orch. LP '61

Singles: 7-inch

DECCA 3-5 60-64

EPs: 7-inch

DECCA 4-6 61

LPs: 10/12-inch

DECCA 5-12 60-64
ROULETTE 5-15 59

JERRY, Mungo: see MUNGO JERRY

JERRYO P&R/R&B '67

(Jerry Murray)

Singles: 7-inch

SHOUT 4-8 67
WHITE WHALE 3-6 69
Also see TOM & JERRIO

JESSE & MARVIN R&B '53

Singles: 78 rpm

SPECIALTY (447 "Dream Girl") 20-30 52

Singles: 7-inch

SPECIALTY (447 "Dream Girl") 50-75 52
(Black vinyl.)
SPECIALTY (447 "Dream Girl") 100-200 52
(Colored vinyl.)
Members: Jesse Belvin; Marvin Phillips.
Also see BELVIN, Jesse
Also see MARVIN & JOHNNY

JESTERS P&R '57

Singles: 78 rpm

WINLEY 25-35 57

Singles: 7-inch

ABC 3-4 73
AMY 3-5 62
COLLECTABLES 3-4 80s
CYCLONE (5011 "I Laughed") 50-75 58
(Title and artist in normal bold print. Songwriting credit is *directly* under title.)
CYCLONE (5011 "I Laughed") 25-50
(Title and artist in narrow, extra bold print.

Songwriting credit is approximately centered between title and artist.)
LOST-NITE....................................4-8 63
WINLEY (218 "So Strange")............ 50-75 57
(Has "Winley" in 3/8–inch letters.)
WINLEY (218 "So Strange")............ 20-30 61
(Has "Winley" in 1/4–inch letters.)
WINLEY (221 "I'm Fallin in Love")..... 50-75 57
WINLEY (221 "I'm Falling in Love")... 20-30 61
(Note slight title change.)
WINLEY (225 "The Plea")................ 40-60 58
(Has "Winley" in 3/8–inch letters.)
WINLEY (225 "The Plea")................ 20-30 61
(Has "Winley" in 1/4–inch letters.)
WINLEY (242 "The Wind")............... 40-60 60
WINLEY (248 "That's How It Goes")....................................... 100-200 61
(Colored vinyl.)
WINLEY (248 "That's How It Goes").. 20-30 61
(Black vinyl.)
WINLEY (252 "Come Let Me Show You").. 20-30 61

LPs: 10/12–inch

COLLECTABLES.............................6-8 86
LOST-NITE....................................8-12 81
Members: Len McKay; Adam Jackson; Jimmy Smith; Noel Grant; Leo Vincent; Melvin Lewis; Don Lewis.
Also see HARPTONES / Paragons / Jesters / Clovers

JESTERS / Paragons

LPs: 10/12–inch

JOSIE ("Jesters Meet the Paragons").................................. 50-75 60s
(Selection number not known.)
JUBILEE (1098 "Jesters Meet the Paragons")................................ 100-200 59
PAUL WINLEY PROD. (102 "Jesters Meet the Paragons")..................................... 20-40 65
WINLEY (6003 "War: Jesters Meet the Paragons")................................... 50-100 60
Also see JESTERS
Also see PARAGONS

JESUS & MARY CHAIN LP '86

Singles: 7–inch

W.B. 3-4 87-89

LPs: 10/12–inch

REPRISE.......................................5-8 86
W.B. 5-8 87-89

JESUS JONES LP '91

LPs: 10/12–inch

SBK 5-8 91

JETBOY LP '88

LPs: 10/12–inch

MCA...5-8 88

JETE, Le: see LE JETE

JETER, Genobia R&B '86

Singles: 12–inch

RCA...4-6 86

Singles: 7–inch

RCA...3-4 86-87

LPs: 10/12–inch

RCA...5-8 86

JETER, Genobia, & Glenn Jones R&B '87

Singles: 7–inch

RCA...3-4 87
Also see JONES, Glenn

JETHRO TULL LP '69

Singles: 12–inch

CHRYSALIS....................................4-8 88-89
(Promotional only.)

Singles: 7–inch

CHRYSALIS....................................3-5 72-88
CHRYSALIS/REPRISE.....................4-8 69-72

Picture Sleeves

CHRYSALIS....................................3-5 74

EPs: 7–inch

CHRYSALIS....................................8-12 71

LPs: 10/12–inch

CHRYSALIS (Except CH4 & V5X series) 6-12 73-89
CHRYSALIS (CH4 series) 10-12 73-74
(Quadrophonic issues.)
CHRYSALIS (V5X-41653 "Twenty Years of Jethro Tull").. 50-75 88
(Boxed, five-disc set.)
MFSL (061 "Aqualung") 25-50 82
MFSL (092 "Broadsword and the Beast").. 20-30 82
MFSL (187 "Thick As a Brick") 15-25 80s
REPRISE 10-15 69-72
REPRISE/CHRYSALIS (2106 "Living in the Past").. 15-20 72
(Price includes bonus, color booklet.)
Members: Ian Anderson; Clive Bunker; Glen Cormick; John Evan; Barry Barlow; David Palmer; John Glascock; Jeff Hammond; Mick Abrahams.
Also see ABRAHAMS, Mick, Band
Also see WILD TURKEY

JETS R&B/D&D '85

Singles: 12–inch

MCA 4-6 85-88

Singles: 7–inch

MCA 3-4 85-89

Picture Sleeves

MCA 3-4 86-88

LPs: 10/12–inch

MCA 5-8 85-89
Members: Elizabeth Wolfgram; Eugene Wolfgram (a.k.a. Gene Hunt).
Also see BOYS CLUB

JETT, Joan LP '81

(With the Blackhearts)

Singles: 12–inch

BLACKHEART/CBS 4-8 88
(Promotional only.)
MCA 4-8 83

Singles: 7–inch

BLACKHEART/CBS 3-4 83-90
BOARDWALK.................................... 3-5 81-82
MCA 3-5 83

Picture Sleeves

BLACKHEART/CBS 3-4 83-88
BOARDWALK.................................... 3-5 81-82
MCA 3-5 83

LPs: 10/12–inch

BLACKHEART.............................. 50-75 80
(Red label with black heart. No mention of CBS. Number not known.)
BLACKHEART/CBS 5-8 83-90
BOARDWALK.................................... 5-8 81-82
MCA 5-8 83-84
RHINO (250 "Little Lost Girls").......... 15-20 82
(Picture disc.)
W.B. 8-10 90s
Also see BANGLES / Joan Jett
Also see BARBUSTERS
Also see BEACH BOYS
Also see RUNAWAYS

JEWELS

(Crows)

Singles: 78 rpm

RAMA (10 "Heartbreaker")........... 200-250 53

Singles: 7–inch

RAMA (10 "Heartbreaker"/"Call a Doctor") 500-750 53
(Black vinyl. May show *Heartbreaker* by the Crows and *Call a Doctor* by the Jewels on some labels.)
RAMA (10 "Heartbreaker")........ 1000-2000 53
(Colored vinyl.)
Also see CROWS

JEWELS P&R/R&B '64

Singles: 7–inch

DIMENSION.................................... 10-15 64-65
Members: Sandra Bears; Margie Clark; Martha Harvin; Grace Ruffin.

JIGSAW P&R/LP '75

Singles: 7–inch

CHELSEA 3-5 75-76
20TH FOX 3-5 77-78

LPs: 10/12–inch

CHELSEA..8-10 75
ELEKTRA...5-8 82
20TH FOX 5-8 77

JILL & RAY

Singles: 7–inch

LE CAM (979 "Hey Paula")............... 25-35 62
Members: Jill Jackson; Ray Hildebrand.
Also see PAUL & PAULA

JIM & INGRID: see CROCE, Jim & Ingrid

JIM & JEAN P&R '68

Singles: 7–inch

VERVE/FOLKWAYS 5-10 68

LPs: 10/12–inch

VERVE/FOLKWAYS 10-20 68
Members: Jim Glover; Jean Glover

JIM & MONICA P&R '64

Singles: 7–inch

BETTY...8-12 64
Member: Jimmy Gilmer.
Also see GILMER, Jimmy

JIMENEZ, Jose: see DANA, Bill

JIMMY, Bobby, & Critters R&B/LP '86

Singles: 12–inch

MACOLA 4-6 86

LPs: 10/12–inch

MACOLA 5-8 86
Member: Russ Parr.

JIMMY & DUANE

Singles: 7–inch

EB X. PRESTON (212 "Soda Fountain Girl").......................................200-300 55
Members: Jimmy Delbridge; Duane Eddy.
Also see EDDY, Duane

JIMMY G. & TACKHEADS R&B '86

Singles: 7–inch

CAPITOL 3-4 85-86

LPs: 10/12–inch

CAPITOL...5-8 86

JIMMY LEE & ARTIS: see LEE, Jimmy, & Artis

JINKINS, Gus: see JENKINS, Gus

JIVE BOMBERS P&R/R&B '57

(Featuring Clarence "Bad Boy" Palmer; Clarence Palmer & Jive Bombers)

Single: 78 rpm

CITATION.................................25-40 52
SAVOY 10-20 57

Singles: 7–inch

CITATION (1160 "It's Spring Again") 50-80 52
CITATION (1161 "Brown Boy") 50-80 52
COLLECTABLES..................................3-4 85
MIDDLE TONE (20 "Anytime")..........15-25 64
SAVOY 10-20 57-59

LPs: 10/12–inch

SAVOY 5-8 86
Members: Clarence Palmer; Earl Johnson; Allen Tinney; William Tinney.

JIVE BUNNY & MASTERMIXERS P&R '89

Singles: 7–inch

MUSIC FACTORY...............................3-4 89-90

LPs: 10/12–inch

MUSIC FACTORY...............................5-8 89

JIVE FIVE P&R/R&B '61

("Featuring Eugene Pitt"; Jive Fyve; with Horace & Orchestra)

Singles: 7–inch

AMBIENT SOUND 3-5 82
BELTONE (1006 "My True Story") 10-20 61
BELTONE (1014 "Never Never") 15-25 61
BELTONE (2019 "No Not Again") 10-20 62
BELTONE (2024 "What Time Is It") .. 30-40 62
(White label. Vinyl is more brown than black.)

1. 2. 3.

4. 5. 6.

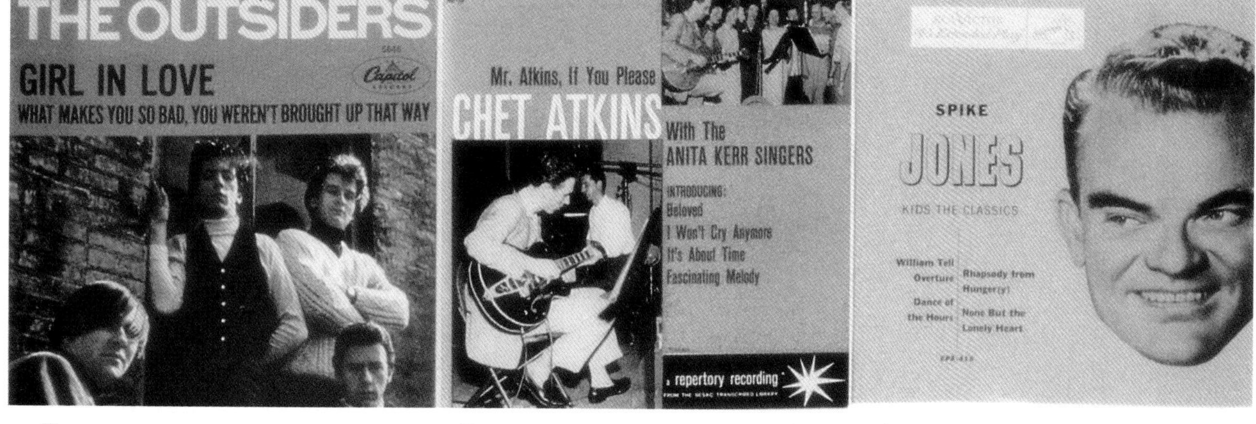

7. 8. 9.

1. Roy Hamilton *Don't Let Go* (EP $10–$20). 2. Jimi Hendrix *Hey Joe* (PS $80–$120). 3. Arthur Smith *Original Guitar Boogie* (EP $8–$12). 4. Sheena Easton *Morning Train* (PS $6–$10). 5. Dick Dalc & Francine York *Enlistment Twist* (PS $20–$40). 6. Ivory Joe Hunter *Rock with Ivory Joe Hunter* (EP $50–$75). 7. Outsiders *Girl in Love* (PS $12–$22). 8. Chet Atkins & Anita Kerr Singers *Mr. Atkins, If You Please* (EP $10–$15). 9. Spike Jones *Spike Jones Kids the Classics* (EP $20–$30).

1. 2. 3.

4.

5.

6.

7.

8.

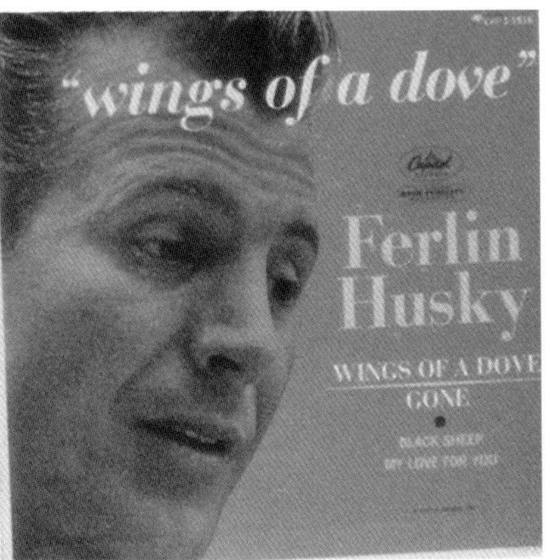

9.

1. Arthur Alexander *You Better Move On* (EP $25–$35). 2. Byrds *Eight Miles High* (PS $20–$30). 3. Bell Notes *I've Had It* (EP $60–$100). 4. Wilson Pickett *Right On* (EP $10–$15). 5. King Curtis *The Best of King Curtis* (EP $5–$10). 6. Willie Mitchell *It's Dance Time* (EP $10–$15). 7. Duane Eddy & the Rebels *Yep!* (EP $20–$40). 8. Ventures *Slaughter on 10th Avenue* (PS $10–$20). 9. Ferlin *Husky Wings of a Dove* (EP $15–$25).

1.

2.

3.

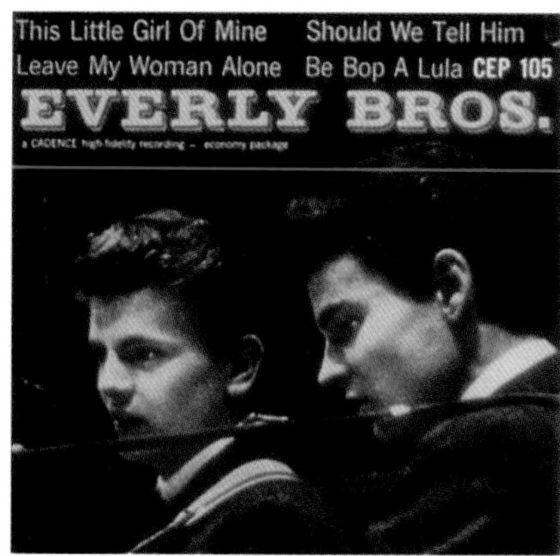

4.

5.

6.

7. 8. 9.

1. Frankie Ford *The Best of Frankie Ford* (EP $50–$75). 2. Aretha Franklin *Lady Soul* (EP $10–$20). 3. Little Richard *Little Richard* (EP $150–$200). 4. Everly Brothers *Everly Bros.* (EP $30–$50). 5. Ike & Tina Turner *A Fool for a Fool* (PS $15–$25). 6. "Deacon" Andy Griffith *What It Was Was Football* (EP $20–$30). 7. Fleetwood Mac *Fireflies* (PS $6–$12). 8. Marvin Gaye *Try It Baby* (PS $25–$50). 9. Pat Benatar *Promises in the Dark* (PS $8–$15).

1. 2. 3.

4. 5. 6.

7. 8. 9.

1. Jimmy Bowen *Jimmy Bowen* (EP $50–$75). 2. Nat King Cole & His Trio *After Midnight* (EP $15–$20). 3. Oscar Peterson *Oscar Peterson Plays Jimmy McHugh* (EP $25–$50). 4. Ed Townsend *Ed Townsend — What Shall I Do* (EP $20–$40). 5. David Seville *Witch Doctor* (EP $35–$50). 6. George Burns *I Wish I Was Eighteen Again* (PS $6–$8). 7. Chuck Berry *Sweet Little 16* (EP $40–$60). 8. Captain Beefheart & the Magic Band *Low Yo Yo Stuff* (PS $40–$50). 9. Les Paul & Mary Ford *Bye Bye Blues* (EP $15–$20).

1. 2. 3.

4. 5. 6.

7. 8. 9.

1. Ral Donner *Rip It Up* (PS $10–$20). 2. Pearl Jam *Angel* (PS $10–$15). 3. Larry Williams *Slow Down* (PS $35–$55). 4. Frankie Lymon *Frankie Lymon at the London Palladium* (EP $50–$75). 5. Elvis Presley *Elvis Presley* (EP $300–$500). 6. Dean Martin *Sunny Italy* (EP $25–$50). 7. Byrds *The Byrds* (EP $40–$60). 8. Lee Allen & His Band *Walkin' with Mr. Lee* (EP $50–$75). 9. Al Caiola *Boffola Caiola* (EP $10–$15).

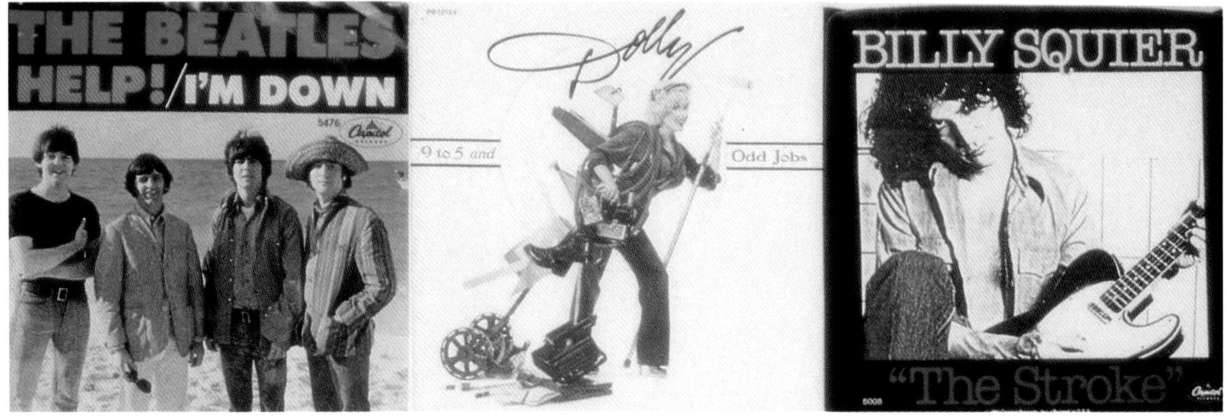

1. 2. 3.

4. 5. 6.

7. 8. 9.

1. Beatles *Help!* (PS $50–$100). 2. Dolly Parton *9 to 5* (PS $6–$12). 3. Billy Squier *The Stroke* (PS $6–$10). 4. Solomon Burke *The Best of Solomon Burke* (EP $10–$20). 5. Wink Martindale *Deck of Cards* (PS $15–$25). 6. Teresa Brewer *Teresa Brewer – Music! Music! Music!* (EP $20–$30). 7. Little Willie John *Come On and Join Little Willie John at a Recording Session* (EP $15–$25). 8. Ray Charles *The Genius of Ray Charles* (EP $25–$50). 9. Jerry Lee Lewis *Jerry Lee Lewis* (EP $50–$100).

1.

2.

3.

4.

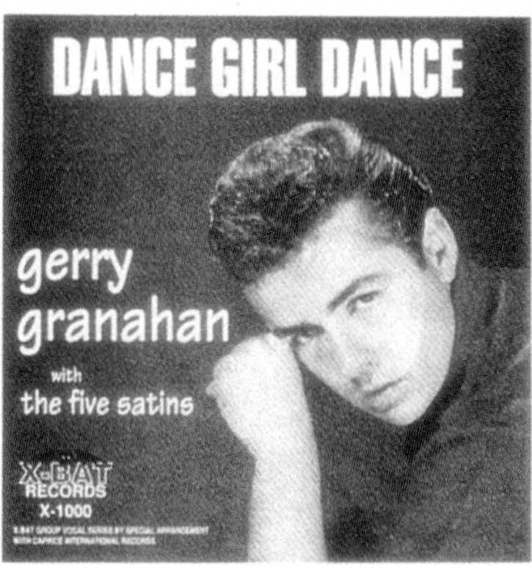

5.

6.

7.

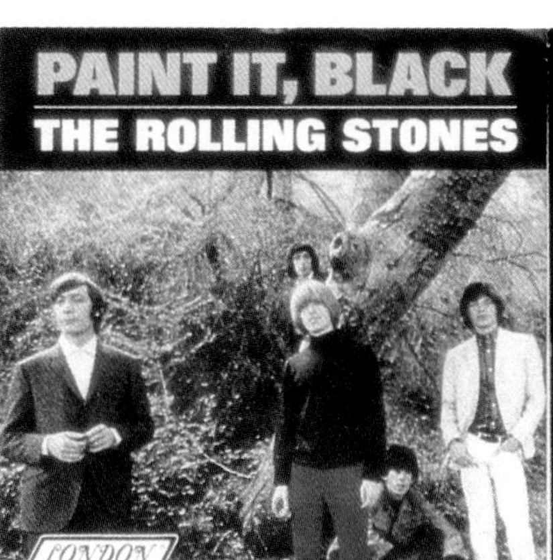

8.

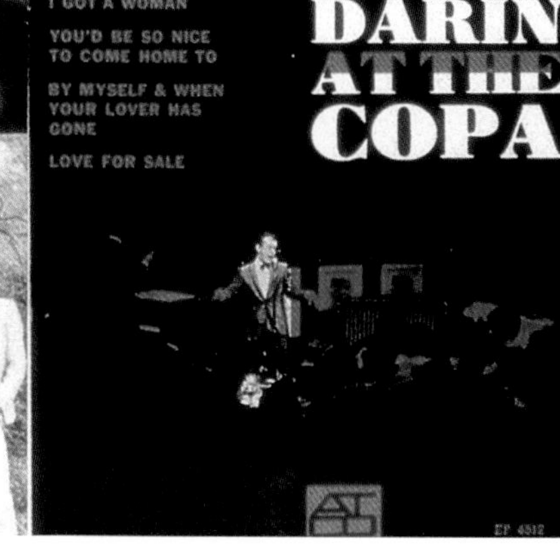

9.

1. Jack Scott *Jack Scott* (EP \$50–\$100). 2. Ernest Tubb *Walking the Floor Over You* (PS \$12–\$20). 3. Al Hibbler *Starring Al Hibbler* (EP \$10–\$20). 4. Heart *If Looks Could Kill* (PS \$6–\$8). 5. Gerry Granahan & the Five Satins *Dance Girl Dance* (PS \$6–\$8). 6. Julie London *Make Love to Me* (EP \$10–\$20). 7. "Sugar Pie" DeSanto *Sugar Pie* (EP \$30–\$50). 8. Rolling Stones *Paint It Black* (PS \$20–\$30). 9. Bobby Darin *Darin at the Copa* (EP \$20–\$40).

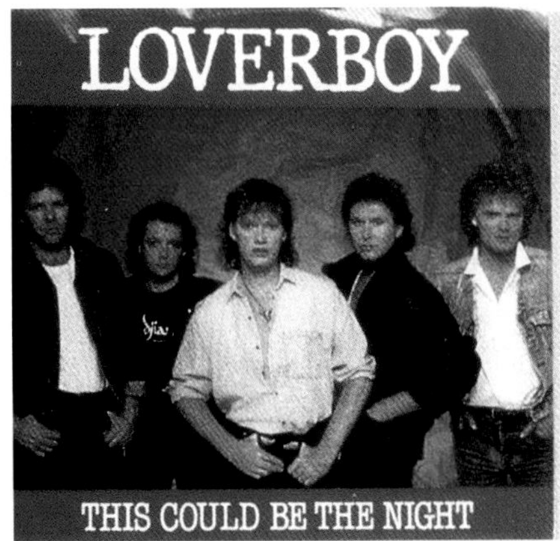

1.

2.

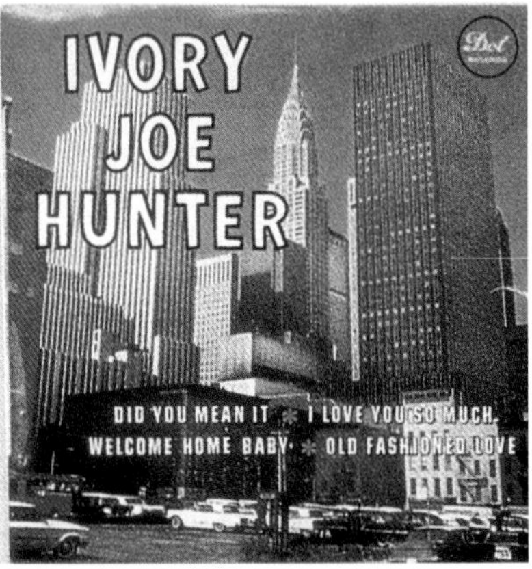

3.

4.

5.

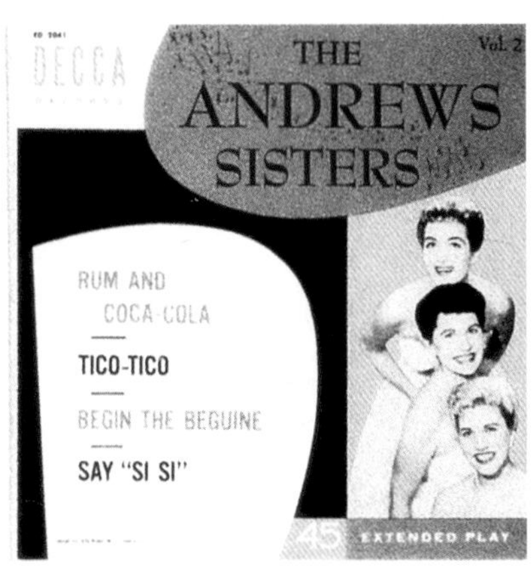

6.

7.

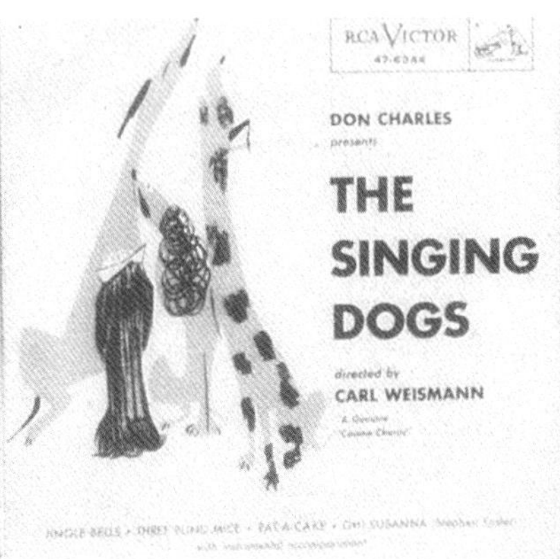

8.

9.

1. Loverboy *This Could Be the Night* (PS $6–$10). 2. Teresa Brewer *Some Songs* (PS $5–$8). 3. Ivory Joe Hunter *Ivory Joe Hunter* (EP $30–$50). 4. Little Willie John *The Sweet, the Hot, the Teen-Age Beat* (EP $15–$25). 5. Ral Donner *Rip It Up* (Picture disc $12–$25). 6. Andrews Sisters *The Andrews Sisters* (EP $10–$20). 7. Split Enz *One Step Ahead* (PS $6–$10). 8. Singing Dogs *Oh! Susanna* (PS $15–$25). 9. Homer & Jethro *Seasoned Greetings* (EP $15–$25).

MCA (40993 "Song for Guy")................4-8 78
(Promotional issue only.)
MCA (41042 thru 41293)......................3-6 79-80
MCA (53196 thru 53000 series) 3-6 87-88
MCA/ROCKET 3-6 76-77
ROCKET 3-6 76-77

EPs: 7-inch

MCA (Except 40105) 8-10 73
(Juke box issues.)
MCA (40105 "Saturday Night's Alright for Fighting") 3-5 73
(Single with two tracks on side two. Not issued with EP cover.)
UNI 10-12 70
(Juke box issue only.)

LPs: 10/12-inch

COLUMBIA SPECIAL PRODUCTS......5-8 81
DCC (2004 "Madman Across the Water") 10-15 95
(Analog audiophile pressing.)
D.D.L. (16614 "Goodbye Yellow Brick Road")..50-75 73
(Half-speed mastered.)
DJLP (403 "Empty Sky")...................20-25 69
(U.K. issue, distributed in the U.S.A.)
GEFFEN...5-8 81-87
MCA (2015 thru 2130)......................6-10 73-75
(Includes MCA reissues of UNI albums.)
MCA (2142 "Captain Fantastic and the Brown Dirt Cowboy") 10-12 75
(Includes poster, lyrics booklet, bio scrapbook and comic insert. Deduct $3 to $5 if these items are missing.)
MCA (2142 "Captain Fantastic")......50-100 79
(Colored vinyl. Promotional issue only.)
MCA (2163 thru 5121) 5-10 75-80
MCA (6000 series)................................5-8 88-89
MCA (8000 series).............................10-12 87
MCA (10003 "Goodbye Yellow Brick Road") 10-12 73
MCA (13921 "Thom Bell Sessions")....5-10 79
MCA (14591 "A Single Man") 15-20 79
(Picture disc. Both sides have front view of Elton.)
MCA (14591 "A Single Man") 50-60 79
(Promotional picture disc. B-side has back view of Elton.)
MCA (37000 series)...............................4-8 79
MCA/ROCKET (Except 1953 & 11004)..10-12 76-77
MCA/ROCKET (1953 "Get Up and Dance")..20-25 77
(Promotional issue only.)
MCA/ROCKET (11004 "Blue Moves")...8-12 70s
MFSL (160 "Goodbye Yellow Brick Road")..30-40 73
(Half-speed mastered.)
NAUTILUS (10003 "Goodbye Yellow Brick Road")...30-40 82
(Half-speed mastered.)
PARAMOUNT (6004 "Friends") 10-15 71
(Soundtrack.)
PICKWICK (3598 "Friends")...............8-10 70s
(Soundtrack.)
SASSON/GEFFEN (2176 "Sasson Presents Elton John") 20-30 81
(Single-sided, four-track LP. Promotional issue only.)
UNI (73090 "Elton John") 15-20 70
(Includes booklet.)
UNI (73096 "Tumbleweed Connection") 15-20 71
(Includes booklet.)
UNI (93105 "11-17-70")....................15-20 71
UNI (93120 "Madman Across the Water") 15-20 71
(Includes booklet.)
UNI (93135 "Honky Chateau")...........15-20 72
VIKING (105 "The Games")...........150-175 70
(Soundtrack. With Francis Lai & Barbara Moore Singers.)
Also see DIONNE & FRIENDS
Also see FRANKLIN, Aretha, & Elton John
Also see LAI, Francis, & His Orchestra
Also see MICHAEL, George
Also see OLSSON, Nigel
Also see RUSH, Jennifer, & Elton John
Also see SEDAKA, Neil
Also see STARR, Ringo
Also see WONDER, Stevie

JOHN, Elton, & Kiki Dee — P&R '76

Singles: 7-inch

ROCKET... 3-5 76

Picture Sleeves

ROCKET... 3-5 76
Also see DEE, Kiki

JOHN, Elton, & Lesley Duncan

Singles: 7-inch

MCA (1938 "Love Song").................. 15-20 76
(Promotional issue only.)

JOHN, Elton, & Millie Jackson

Singles: 7-inch

GEFFEN 3-4 85

Picture Sleeves

GEFFEN 3-4 85
Also see JACKSON, Millie

JOHN, Elton / John Lennon — P&R '76

Singles: 7-inch

MCA (40364 "Philadelphia Freedom").. 3-5 75

Picture Sleeves

MCA (40364 "Philadelphia Freedom").. 3-5 75
MCA (40364 WFIL radio "Philadelphia Freedom") 30-40 75
(Promotional issue only.)
Also see LENNON, John

JOHN, Elton / Tina Turner

Singles: 7-inch

POLYDOR (002 "Pinball Wizard") 25-35 75
(Promotional issue only.)
Also see JOHN, Elton
Also see TURNER, Tina

JOHN, Little Willie — R&B '55

Singles: 78 rpm

KING 10-20 56-57

Singles: 7-inch

GUSTO ("Fever").................................. 3-4 87
KING (500 series) 3-5
KING (4818 thru 5394)..................... 10-20 56-60
KING (5428 thru 5949)....................... 5-10 61-64

Picture Sleeves

GUSTO ("Fever")................................. 3-4 87

EPs: 7-inch

KING (423 "Talk to Me") 25-50 58
KING (767 "The Sweet, the Hot, the Teen-Age Beat") 15-25 61
(Stereo. Juke box issue only.)
KING (802 "At a Recording Session") 15-25 62
(Stereo. Juke box issue only.)

LPs: 10/12-inch

BLUESWAY....................................... 10-15 73
KING (564 "Fever") 70-90 56
(With brown cover.)
KING (564 "Fever") 20-40 59
(With blue cover.)
KING (596 "Talk to Me") 40-60 58
KING (603 "Mr. Little Willie John").... 40-60 58
KING (691 "In Action") 100-125 60
KING (739 "Sure Things").................. 20-40 61
KING (767 "The Sweet, the Hot, the Teenage Beat") 20-40 61
KING (802 "At a Recording Session").. 20-30 62
KING (895 "These Are My Favorite Songs")... 20-30 64
KING (949 "All Originals")................ 20-30 66
KING (1081 "Free at Last") 20-30 70
Also see WILLIAMS, Paul

JOHN, Little Willie / Hank Ballard & Midnighters

Singles: 7-inch

KING (5428 "Walk Slow"/"Hoochi Coochi Coo") 10-20 60

JOHN, Little Willie / Drifters

Singles: 7-inch

ATLANTIC (89189 "Fever") 3-4 89

Picture Sleeves

ATLANTIC (89189 "Fever")..................3-4 89
Also see DRIFTERS

JOHN, Little Willie / 5 Royales / Earl King / Midnighters

EPs: 7-inch

KING (387 "Rock & Roll Hit Parade").......................................75-100 56
Also see 5 ROYALES
Also see JOHN, Little Willie
Also see MIDNIGHTERS

JOHN, Mable — P&R/R&B '66

Singles: 7-inch

MOTOWN (54081 "Who Wouldn't Love a Man Like That") 300-400 63
(May have been promotional only. Should have been on Tamla, as selection number indicates.)
STAX...5-15 66-68
TAMLA (54031 "Who Wouldn't Love a Man Like That")...75-100 60
TAMLA (54040 "No Love")...............50-100 61
TAMLA (54050 "Take Me")...............30-60 61
TAMLA (54081 "Who Wouldn't Love a Man Like That")...50-100 63
Also see RAELETTES

JOHN, Pope: see POPE JOHN

JOHN, Robert — P&R '68

(Bobby Pedrick Jr.)

Singles: 12-inch 33/45

CBS ASSOCIATED..............................4-6 84

Singles: 7-inch

A&M...3-5 70-72
ARIOLA 3-5 78
ATLANTIC 3-5 71-73
COLUMBIA (Except 44697) 4-8 68-69
COLUMBIA (44697 "Can't Stop Loving You")..8-12 68
EMI AMERICA.......................................3-4 79-80
MOTOWN...3-4 83

LPs: 10/12-inch

COLUMBIA.......................................10-20 68
EMI AMERICA.......................................5-8 79-82
HARMONY..8-10 72
Also see PEDRICK, Bobby

JOHN & ERNEST — P&R/R&B '73

Singles: 7-inch

RAINY WEDNESDAY.............................4-8 73
Members: John Free; Ernest Smith.

JOHN DAVID & CINDERS

Singles: 7-inch

W.B. (5825 "No, Not My Heart")..........8-12 66
Member: John David Souther.
Also see SOUTHER, J.D.

JOHN LEE

(John Lee Hooker; John Lee's Groundhogs)

Singles: 78 rpm

GOTHAM (515 "Mean Old Train")..... 15-25 53

Singles: 7-inch

PLANET 5-8 67
Also see HOOKER, John Lee

JOHNNIE & JOE — P&R/R&B '57

(Johnny & Joe; with Rex Garvin & His Orchestra; with Shytone 5 Orchestra)

Singles: 78 rpm

CHESS (1654 "Over the Mountain")...25-50 57

Singles: 7-inch

ABC-PAR 8-15 60
AMBIENT SOUND 3-5 82
CHESS (1641 "I'll Be Spinning") 10-20 57
CHESS (1654 "Over the Mountain")...10-20 57
(Silver and blue label.)
CHESS (1654 "Over the Mountain").... 8-10 60
(Blue or multi-color label.)
CHESS (1769 "Across the Sea")....... 15-25 60
GONE (5024 "Who Do You Love").... 15-25 61
J&S (Except 1664 & 4000 series)...... 15-25 57-59

BELTONE (2024 "What Time Is It") .. 10-20 62
(Orange label.)
BELTONE (2029 "These Golden Rings") 30-40 62
(White label.)
BELTONE (2029 "These Golden Rings") 10-20 62
(Orange label.)
BELTONE (2030 "Lily Marlene") 10-20 62
BELTONE (2034 "Rain") 10-15 63
(Black vinyl.)
BELTONE (2034 "Rain") 20-30 63
(Vinyl color is more brown than black.)
BELTONE (3000 series) 10-15 62
DECCA (32671 "You Showed Me the Light of Love") 5-10 70
DECCA (32736 "I Want You to Be My Baby") 5-10 70
LANA 4-6
LOST-NITE 4-6 70s
MUSICOR (1250 "Crying Like a Baby") 6-12 67
MUSICOR (1270 "No More Tears") 6-12 67
MUSICOR (1305 "Sugar") 6-12 68
OLDIES 45 .... 4-8 60s
RELIC 4-8 75-78
SIR RENDER (007 "Falling Tears") 5-8
(Colored vinyl.)
SKETCH (219 "United") 20-30 64
STOOP SOUNDS (101 "Where Do We Go from Here") 100-150 96
(Limited edition of only a few dozen made.)
U.A. (807 "United") 10-20 64
U.A. (853 "I'm a Happy Man") 10-20 65
U.A. (936 "A Bench in the Park") 10-20 65
U.A. (50004 "Main Street") 10-20 66
U.A. (50033 "In My Neighborhood") .. 10-20 66
U.A. (50069 "Ha Ha") 10-20 66
U.A. (50107 "You") 10-20 66

LPs: 10/12-inch

AMBIENT SOUND 5-8 82
AMBIENT SOUND/ROUNDER 5-8 84
COLLECTABLES 6-8 85
RELIC 8-10
U.A. (3455 "The Jive Five") 25-50 65
(Monaural.)
U.A. (6455 "The Jive Five") 30-60 65
(Stereo.)
Members: Eugene Pitt; Norm Johnson; Richard Harris; Jerry Hannah; Billy Prophet; Johnny Watson; Casey Spencer; Webster Harris.
Also see GENIES
Also see JYVE FYVE
Also see PLATTERS / Inez & Charlie Foxx / Jive Five / Tommy Hunt

JIVIN' GENE — P&R '59

(With the Jokers)

Singles: 7-inch

ABC 3-5 73
CHESS 5-10 64
HALL WAY 5-10 64
JIN (109 "Going Out with the Tide") .. 20-30 59
JIN (116 "Breakin' Up Is Hard to Do") 20-40 59
JIN (7331 "Going Out with the Tide") 15-25 59
MERCURY (71485 "Breakin' Up Is Hard to Do") 10-20 59
MERCURY (71561 "Go On, Go On") 10-20 60
MERCURY (71680 "Going Out with the Tide") 10-20 60
MERCURY (71751 "Poor Me") 10-20 61
MERCURY (71802 "Don't Pretend") . 10-20 61
MERCURY (71863 "I Cried") 10-20 61
MERCURY (72403 "Memory of You") 10-20 62
TFC/HALL 4-8 65
Member: Gene Bourgeois.

JO, Damita: see DAMITA Jo

JO, Marcy: see MARCY JOE

JO, Sami: see SAMI JO

JO ANN & TROY — P&R '64

Singles: 7-inch

ATLANTIC 8-12 64
Members: Jo Ann Campbell; Troy Seals.
Also see CAMPBELL, Jo Ann

JO JO GUNNE — P&R/LP '72

Singles: 7-inch

ASYLUM 3-5 72

LPs: 10/12-inch

ASYLUM (Except 5071) 8-10 72-74
ASYLUM (5071 "Jumpin' the Gunne") 10-15 73
(With gatefold cover.)
ASYLUM (5071 "Jumpin' the Gunne") 8-10 73
(With standard cover.)
Member: Jay Ferguson.
Also see FERGUSON, Jay

JOBIM, Antonio Carlos — LP '65

Singles: 7-inch

A&M 4-6 67
CTI 3-5 70
MCA 3-5 74
VERVE 4-6 63-64

LPs: 10/12-inch

A&M 8-12 67-70
CTI 8-12 70-71
CAPITOL 10-20 64
DISCOVERY 5-8 82
MCA 5-8 73
VERSATILE 5-8 78
VERVE (Except 3000 series) 10-20 63
VERVE (3000 series) 5-8 82
W.B. 8-15 65-80
Also see FITZGERALD, Ella, & Antonio Carlos Jobim
Also see GILBERTO, Astrud
Also see SINATRA, Frank, & Antonio Carlos Jobim

JOBOXERS — P&R/LP '83

Singles: 7-inch

RCA 3-4 83

LPs: 10/12-inch

RCA 5-8 83

JOE, Billy: see BILLY JOE

JOE, Marcy: see MARCY JOE

JOE & ANN — R&B '60

Singles: 7-inch

ACE 5-10 60-62

JOE & EDDIE — LP '64

Singles: 7-inch

CAPITOL 5-10 59
FLIP (348 "Debbie Jill") 10-15 59
GNP 4-8 62-65

LPs: 10/12-inch

GNP 10-20 63-66
Members: Joe Gilbert; Eddie Brown.

JOEL, Billy — P&R/LP '74

Singles: 12-inch

COLUMBIA 4-8 83

Singles: 7-inch

COLUMBIA (2628 "She's Got a Way") . 4-6 81
(Promotional issue only.)
COLUMBIA (02518 thru 06526) 3-4 81-86
COLUMBIA (10000 & 11000 series) 3-5 74-80
COLUMBIA (40000 series) 3-5 73-74
COLUMBIA (70000 series) 3-4 89-94
EPIC 3-4 86
FAMILY (0900 "She's Got a Way") ... 10-20 73
FAMILY (0906 "Tomorrow Is Today") 10-20 73

Picture Sleeves

COLUMBIA (Except 02628) 3-5 79-87
COLUMBIA (02628 "She's Got a Way") 4-6 81
(Promotional issue only.)

LPs: 10/12-inch

COLUMBIA (30000 & 40000 series) ... 5-10 73-89
(With "FC," "JC," "KC," "OC," "PC," "QC," or "TC" prefix.)
COLUMBIA (30000 series) 10-15 74-76
(With "CQ" or "PCQ" prefix. Quadraphonic.)
COLUMBIA (40000 series) 8-12
(With "C2X" prefix.)
COLUMBIA (HC-40000 series) 10-15 80-87
(Half-speed mastered.)
FAMILY PRODUCTIONS (2700 "Cold Spring Harbor") 35-45 71

Promotional LPs

COLUMBIA (326 "Souvenir") 25-35 77
COLUMBIA (402 "Interchords") 25-35 77
COLUMBIA (452 "Now Playing") 20-30 78
COLUMBIA (1343 "Interview Album") 15-25 81
SKYCLAD (102 "A Tribute to Billy Joel") 6-8 91
(Clear vinyl. Intentionally has no music—by Billy Joel or anyone. Limited edition of 666 copies.)
Also see ATTILA
Also see HASSLES
Also see KHAN, Steve
Also see U.S.A. for AFRICA

JOEL, Billy, & Ray Charles — P&R '87

Singles: 7-inch

COLUMBIA 3-4 87

Picture Sleeves

COLUMBIA 3-4 87
Also see CHARLES, Ray

JOEL, Billy / Ricky Van Shelton

Singles: 7-inch

EPIC (74422 "All Shook Up") 3-4 92
Also see JOEL, Billy
Also see SHELTON, Ricky Van

JOESKI LOVE — R&B '86

Singles: 7-inch

VINTERTAINMENT 3-4 86

JOHANSEN, David — LP '79

Singles: 7-inch

BLUE SKY 3-5 78-82

Picture Sleeves

BLUE SKY 4-6

LPs: 10/12-inch

BLUE SKY 5-8 78-82
Also see NEW YORK DOLLS
Also see POINDEXTER, Buster, & His Banshees of Blue

JOHN, Dr: see DR. JOHN

JOHN, Elton — P&R/LP '70

Singles: 12-inch

GEFFEN 4-8 83-85
(Promotional only.)
MCA 4-8 78-88
(Promotional only.)

Singles: 7-inch

COLLECTABLES (4900 series) 3-5 92
(Colored vinyl.)
CONGRESS (6017 "Lady Samatha") 20-30 69
CONGRESS (6022 "Border Song") ... 20-30 70
DJM (70008 "Lady Samatha") 40-60 69
EPIC 3-4 87
GEFFEN (Except 2176) 3-5 81-86
GEFFEN (2176 "Sasson") 5-10 84
(Single-sided. Promotional issue only.)
MCA (40000 thru 40505) 3-6 72-76
MCA (40892 thru 40973) 3-5 78
MCA (40993 "Song for Guy") 4-6 78
(Promotional issue only.)
MCA (41042 thru 41293) 3-5 79-80
MCA (53196 thru 53953) 3-4 87-90
MCA/ROCKET 3-5 76-77
ROCKET 3-5 76-77
UNI (55246 "Border Song") 5-10 70
UNI (55265 thru 55343) 4-8 70-72
UNI (55351 "Crocodile Rock") 25-50 72
(Canadian. In error, first issues were on UNI, instead of MCA.)
VIKING (1010 "From Denver to L.A.") 30-60 69
(Flip is by the Barbara Moore Singers.)

Picture Sleeves

GEFFEN 3-5 81-86
MCA (40344 thru 40505) 3-6 74-75
MCA (40892 thru 40973) 3-6 78

JOHNSON, Meat Head
(Champion Jack Dupree)
Singles: 78 rpm
APEX....15-25 50
GOTHAM....10-12 50
Also see DUPREE, Champion Jack

JOHNSON, Michael P&R/R&B/LP '78
Singles: 7-inch
ATCO....3-5 73
EMI AMERICA....3-5 78-80
RCA....3-4 86-88
Picture Sleeves
EMI AMERICA....3-5 78
LPs: 10/12-inch
ATCO....8-10 73
EMI AMERICA....5-8 78-82
Session: Michael Young; Russ Pahl; Denny Dadmum-Bixby.
Also see BACK PORCH MAJORITY
Also see DENVER, BOISE & JOHNSON
Also see GREAT PLAINS
Also see MITCHELL TRIO
Also see SYLVIA & Michael Johnson

JOHNSON, Orlando, & Trance D&D '83
Singles: 12-inch
EASYSTREET....4-6 83

JOHNSON, Paul R&B '88
Singles: 7-inch
EPIC....3-4 88

JOHNSON, Pete R&B '45
(Pete Johnson All-Star Orchestra)
Singles: 78 rpm
APOLLO....4-8 46-49
BRUNSWICK....4-8 44
DOWN BEAT....4-6 49
MODERN....4-6 47
NATIONAL....4-6 45-46
Singles: 7-inch
APOLLO....5-10 50s
EPs: 7-inch
APOLLO (608 "Pete Johnson")....15-25 50s
BRUNSWICK....10-20 55
LPs: 10/12-inch
SAVOY (14018 "Pete's Blues")....30-40 58
Also see AMMONS, Albert, & Pete Johnson
Also see BROOKS, Hadda / Pete Johnson
Also see TURNER, Joe

JOHNSON, Robert LP '90
Singles: 78 rpm
ORIOLE (7-04-60 "32-20 Blues")....1500-2500 37
VOCALION ("Love in Vain")....2000-3000 38
(Selection number not known.)
VOCALION (03416 "Kind Hearted Woman Blues")....300-400
VOCALION (03475 "I Believe I'll Dust My Broom")....1000-2000 37
VOCALION (03445 "32/20 Blues")....1000-1500 37
VOCALION (03519 "Cross Road Blues")....1500-2500 37
VOCALION (03563 "Come On in My Kitchen")....1000-2000 37
VOCALION (03601 "Sweet Home Chicago")....1000-1500 37
VOCALION (03623 "Hell Hound on My Trail")....1000-2000 37
VOCALION (03665 "Milkcow's Calf Blues")....1000-2000 37
VOCALION (03723 "Stones in My Passway")....1000-2000 38
VOCALION (04002 "Stop Breakin' Down Blues")....1000-2000 38
VOCALION (04108 "Me and the Devil Blues")....1000-2000 38
LPs: 10/12-inch
COLUMBIA (1654 "King of the Delta Blues Singers")....35-50 61
COLUMBIA (30034 "Robert Johnson, Vol. 2")....10-15 70
COLUMBIA (46222 "The Complete Recordings")....8-12 90
ROOTS 'N' BLUES....5-8 90

JOHNSON, Robert LP '79
Singles: 7-inch
INFINITY....3-5 78
LPs: 10/12-inch
INFINITY....5-8 78

JOHNSON, Rozetta P&R/R&B '70
Singles: 7-inch
CLINTONE....3-5 70

JOHNSON, Ruby R&B '66
Singles: 7-inch
NEBS....10-15 65
VOLT....10-20 66
V-TONE....10-20 60

JOHNSON, Sweetpea
(Billy Strange)
Singles: 7-inch
LIBERTY (55315 "The Crawdad Scene")....15-25 61
Also see STRANGE, Billy

JOHNSON, Syl P&R/R&B '67
Singles: 12-inch
BOARDWALK....4-6 82
Singles: 7-inch
CHA CHA....10-20
EPIC....8-10
FEDERAL....8-15 59-62
HI....3-5 73-79
SHAMA....3-6 77
SPECIAL AGENT (20079 "Do You Know What Love Is")....15-25
TAG LTD. (1 "Surround")....15-25
TMP-TING....5-10 65
TWILIGHT....5-10 67-68
TWINIGHT....5-10 69
LPs: 10/12-inch
HI....8-10 73-75
TWINIGHT....10-15 68

JOHNSON, Troy R&B '86
Singles: 7-inch
KALLISTA....3-4 86

JOHNSTON, Tom P&R/LP '79
Singles: 7-inch
W.B.....3-5 79-81
LPs: 10/12-inch
W.B.....5-8 79-81
Also see CHARADES
Also see DOOBIE BROTHERS

JOINER, ARKANSAS JUNIOR HIGH SCHOOL BAND P&R '60
(Ernie Freeman)
Singles: 7-inch
LIBERTY....8-12 60-61
Also see FREEMAN, Ernie

JOLI, France P&R/R&B/LP '79
Singles: 12-inch
EPIC....4-6 83-85
Singles: 7-inch
EPIC....3-4 83-85
PRELUDE....3-5 79-82
LPs: 10/12-inch
EPIC....5-8 83-85
PRELUDE....5-8 79-80

JOLLY, Pete LP '63
(Pete Jolly Trio & Friends)
Singles: 7-inch
A&M....3-5 68-69
AVA....4-8 63-64
COLUMBIA....3-6 66
MAINSTREAM....3-6 69
LPs: 10/12-inch
A&M....8-12 68-71
AVA....10-20 63-64
CHARLIE PARKER....15-20 62
COLUMBIA....10-20 65
MGM....8-15 63
METROJAZZ....15-25 60
RCA (1100 thru 1300 series)....20-30 55-57
TRIP....5-8 75
Also see MONTEZ, Chris

JOLO D&D '84
Singles: 12-inch
MEGATONE....4-6 84

JON & ROBIN P&R '67
(With the In Crowd)
Singles: 7-inch
ABNAK....4-8 67-68
LPs: 10/12-inch
ABNAK....15-20 67-68
Members: Jon Abnor; Robin Abnor.

JON & VANGELIS P&R/LP '80
Singles: 7-inch
POLYDOR....3-5 77-83
LPs: 10/12-inch
POLYDOR....5-8 80-83
Members: Jon Anderson; Vangelis.
Also see ANDERSON, Jon
Also see VANGELIS

JONAE, Gwen D&D '83
Singles: 12-inch
ARIAL....4-6 83
C&M....4-6 83

JONES, Brenda R&B '82
(Brenda Lee Jones)
Singles: 7-inch
FLYING DUTCHMAN....3-5 76
MERCURY....3-5 74
RUST....4-8 66
WAVE....3-4 82
Also see DEAN & JEAN
Also see LEE, Brenda

JONES, Brenda, & "Groove" Holmes
Singles: 7-inch
FLYING DUTCHMAN....3-5 76
Also see HOLMES, Richard "Groove"
Also see JONES, Brenda

JONES, Brian
LPs: 10/12-inch
ROLLING STONES (49100 "Pipes of Pan")....10-15 71
Promotional LPs
ROLLING STONES (49100 "Pipes of Pan")....30-35 71
(Includes poster and cue sheets.)
Also see ROLLING STONES

JONES, Corky
(Buck Owens)
Singles: 78 rpm
DIXIE....15-25 56
PEP....20-40 56
Singles: 7-inch
DIXIE (505 "Rhythm and Booze")....75-100 56
PEP (107 "Hot Dog")....100-150 56
Also see OWENS, Buck

JONES, Davy P&R '65
(David Jones)
Singles: 7-inch
BELL....8-10 71-72
COLPIX....10-20 65
MGM....10-15 72-73
MY FAVORITE MONKEE – DAVY JONES SINGS ("A Little Bit Me, a Little Bit You")..50-100 67
(Promotional issue only. No selection number used.)
Picture Sleeves
COLPIX (764 "Dream Girl")....20-30 65
COLPIX (784 "What Are We Going to Do")....20-30 65
COLPIX (789 "Girl from Chelsea")....20-30 65
LPs: 10/12-inch
BELL (6067 "Davy Jones")....15-25 71
COLPIX (CP-493 "David Jones")....20-25 65
(Monaural.)
COLPIX (SCP-493 "David Jones")....25-30 65
(Stereo.)
Also see NILSSON, Harry

JONES, Davy, & Mickey Dolenz

Singles: 7-inch

BELL....8-10 71
MCA....3-5 78

Picture Sleeves

MCA....3-5 78

JONES, Davy, Mickey Dolenz, & Peter Tork

LPs: 10/12-inch

RHINO/FOSHOFF (71110 "20th Anniversary Tour")....20-30 87
Also see JONES, Davy
Also see DOLENZ, Micky
Also see MONKEES

JONES, Etta *P&R/R&B '60*

Singles: 7-inch

KING....4-8 61-62
PRESTIGE....4-8 60-65
20TH FOX/WESTBOUND....3-5 75

LPs: 10/12-inch

GRAND PRIX....8-12 60s
KING (544 "Etta Jones Sings")....40-60 58
KING (707 "Etta Jones Sings")....35-50 61
MUSE....5-8 77-81
PRESTIGE (7100 & 7200 series)....25-50 60-63
(Yellow labels.)
PRESTIGE (7100 & 7200 series)....15-25 65
(Blue labels.)
PRESTIGE (7400 thru 7700 series)..10-20 67-70
ROULETTE....10-20 66
20TH FOX/WESTBOUND....5-10 75

JONES, George *C&W '55*

(With the Jones Boys; with Sonny Burns; Tina & Daddy)

Singles: 78 rpm

DIXIE (#534)....25-50 56
(With Sleepy La Beef. Title not known. 78 rpm EP. Not issued with cover.)
DIXIE (#535)....25-50 56
(78 rpm EP. Not issued with cover.)
MERCURY....10-25 57
STARDAY....10-25 54-57

Singles: 7-inch

D....4-8 65-66
EPIC....3-5 72-82
MERCURY (71000 & 72000 series)....5-15 57-64
MUSICOR....3-8 65-71
PROMOTIONAL COPIES ("The Race Is On")....20-25 64
(No actual label name, other than "Promotional Copies," is shown.)
RCA....3-5 72-74
STARDAY (Except 100 & 200 series)...4-8 64-71
STARDAY (100 & 200 series)....10-20 54-57
(Black vinyl.)
STARDAY (264 "Just One More")....30-40 56
(Colored vinyl.)
U.A....4-8 62-67

Picture Sleeves

MERCURY....8-12 62-64
MUSICOR....5-10 65
U.A....5-10 62-63

EPs: 7-inch

DIXIE (501 "Why Baby Why")....25-50 56
(Not issued with cover.)
DIXIE (505 "Heartbreak Hotel")....25-50 56
(Not issued with cover.)
DIXIE (516 "Poor Old Me")....25-50 56
(Not issued with cover.)
DIXIE (518 "Stolen Moments")....25-50 56
(Not issued with cover.)
DIXIE (525 "Don't Do This to Me")....15-25 59
(Has one George Jones track. Not issued with cover.)
MERCURY....10-20 61
RECORD of the MONTH (280 "Heartbreak Hotel")....30-40 56
(Colored vinyl.)
STARDAY....8-15 65
(Juke box issues. May include title strips.)

LPs: 10/12-inch

ACCORD....4-6 82
ALBUM GLOBE....5-8 81
ALLEGIANCE....4-8 84
AMBASSADOR....5-8
AURA....5-8 82
BUCKBOARD....5-8 76
BULLDOG....8-10
CAMDEN....5-8 72-74
COLUMBIA....5-8 80-83
EPIC....10-30 72-82
EVEREST....5-8 79
51 WEST....5-8 79-82
GRASS COUNTRY....8-10 80s
GUEST STAR....8-12 63
GUSTO....5-8 78-81
I&M....5-8 82
KOALA....5-8
K-TEL....5-8
LIBERTY....5-8 82
MCA....3-4 91-92
MERCURY (8000 series)....5-10 72
MERCURY (20306 "14 Country Favorites")....40-60 58
MERCURY (20462 "Country Church Time")....40-60 59
MERCURY (20477 "White Lightning")....40-60 59
MERCURY (20621 thru 20836)....20-30 60-63
(Monaural.)
MERCURY (20906 thru 21048)....20-30 64-65
(Monaural.)
MERCURY (60257 thru 60836)....25-35 60-63
(Stereo.)
MERCURY (60906 thru 61048)....15-25 64-65
(Stereo.)
MOUNTAIN DEW....5-8
MUSIC DISC....6-10 69
MUSICOR....10-20 65-77
MUSICOR/RCA....10-20 74-75
NASHVILLE....10-20 70-71
PAIR....6-10 70s
PHOENIX 10....5-8 81
PHOENIX 20....5-8 81
PICADILLY....5-8 81
PICKWICK....4-8 80
PICKWICK/HILLTOP....8-12 69
POWER PAK....5-8 75
RCA....10-20 72-75
ROUNDER....5-8 82-84
RUBY....5-8
SEARS....8-12
STARDAY (101 "The Grand Ole Opry's New Star")....100-150 58
STARDAY (102 "George Jones")....50-75 59
STARDAY (125 "George Jones: Crown Prince of Country Music")....50-75 60
STARDAY (150 "George Jones Sings His Greatest Hits")....40-60 62
STARDAY (151 "Fabulous Country Music Sound of George Jones")....40-60 62
STARDAY (335 "George Jones")....25-35 65
STARDAY (344 "Long Live King George")....25-35 65
STARDAY (366 "The George Jones Story")....25-35 66
(With bonus 8" x 10" color photo.)
STARDAY (366 "The George Jones Story")....15-25 66
(Without bonus photo.)
STARDAY (400 series, except 401)....15-20 69
STARDAY (401 "George Jones Song Book & Picture Album")....35-45 67
(With 32-page song booklet.)
STARDAY (401 "George Jones Song Book & Picture Album")....15-25 68
(Without song booklet.)
STARDAY (3000 series)....5-8 77
STARDAY (90000 series)....8-12
SUNRISE....5-8 81
TIME-LIFE....5-15 81-82
TRIP....5-8 76
TROLLY CAR....5-8
UNART....8-12 67-68
U.A. (85 "Superpak")....10-15 71
U.A. (100 series)....5-8 73
U.A. (3000 series)....10-20 62-67
(Monaural.)
U.A. (6000 series)....12-25 62-69
(Stereo.)
WHITE LIGHTNING....12-18
WING....8-12 64-68
WING/PICKWICK....4-6
Session: Jordanaires; Oak Ridge Boys; Waylon Jennings.
Also see CHARLES, Ray, George Jones & Chet Atkins
Also see DARRELL, Johnny / George Jones / Willie Nelson
Also see HAGGARD, Merle, & George Jones
Also see JENNINGS, Waylon
Also see JONES, Thumper
Also see OAK RIDGE BOYS
Also see PARTON, Dolly / George Jones
Also see SMITH, Hank
Also see TRAVIS, Randy, & George Jones
Also see TUBB, Ernest
Also see WILLIAMS, Hank, Jr.

JONES, George / Benny Barnes

EPs: 7-inch

DIXIE (518 "Stolen Moments")....25-50 56
(Not issued with cover.)

JONES, George, & Brenda Lee *C&W '84*

Singles: 7-inch

EPIC....3-4 84
Also see LEE, Brenda

JONES, George, & Brenda Carter *C&W '68*

Singles: 7-inch

MUSICOR....4-6 68

JONES, George, & David Allan Coe

Singles: 7-inch

COLUMBIA....3-4 81
Also see COE, David Allan

JONES, George, & Lacy J. Dalton *C&W '85*

Singles: 7-inch

EPIC....3-4 85

JONES, George, & Jeanette Hicks *C&W '57*

Singles: 7-inch

STARDAY....5-8 57

Singles: 7-inch

STARDAY....10-20 57

JONES, George, & Alan Jackson

Singles: 7-inch

MCA....3-5 90s
Also see JACKSON, Alan

JONES, George, & Shelby Lynne *C&W '88*

Singles: 7-inch

EPIC....3-4 88

JONES, George, & Melba Montgomery *C&W '63*

Singles: 7-inch

CURIO....4-8 60s
MUSICOR....4-8 66-67
U.A....4-8 63-66

Picture Sleeves

CURIO (7020 "You're in My Heart")....8-10 60s

LPs: 10/12-inch

BUCKBOARD....5-8 76
GUEST STAR....20-30 60s
LIBERTY....4-6 82
MUSIC DISC....6-10 69
MUSICOR....8-12 66-74
MUSICOR/RCA....8-10 74
U.A. (200 series)....5-8 73
U.A. (3000 series)....10-20 63-66
(Monaural.)
U.A. (6000 series)....12-25 63-66
(Stereo.)
Also see MONTGOMERY, Melba

JONES, George / Buck Owens / David Houston / Tommy Hill

LPs: 10/12-inch

NASHVILLE 10-15 60s
Also see HOUSTON, David
Also see OWENS, Buck

JONES, George, & Johnny Paycheck C&W '80

Singles: 7-inch

EPIC 3-5 78-80

LPs: 10/12-inch

EPIC 5-8 80
Also see PAYCHECK, Johnny

JONES, George, & Gene Pitney C&W/LP '65

(George & Gene, with the Jordanaires)

Singles: 7-inch

MUSICOR 4-8 65-66

Picture Sleeves

MUSICOR 5-10 65

LPs: 10/12-inch

DESIGN 6-10
INTERNATIONAL AWARD 8-10
MUSIC DISC 10-12 69
MUSICOR (3044 "George Jones & Gene Pitney") 15-25 65
(Front cover shows title as "For the First Time! Two Great Stars, George Jones & Gene Pitney.")
MUSICOR (3044 "George Jones & Gene Pitney") 15-20 65
(Front cover shows title as "Recorded in Nashville, Tennessee, George Jones & Gene Pitney.")
MUSICOR (3065 "It's Country Time Again") 10-20 65
TS (439 "Country Cousins") 5-10
Session: Jordanaires.
Also see PITNEY, Gene

JONES, George, Gene Pitney, & Melba Montgomery

LPs: 10/12-inch

MUSICOR 10-20 66
(Contains duets by these artists, but there are no tracks where all three perform together.)
Also see MONTGOMERY, Melba

JONES, George, & Margie Singleton C&W '61

Singles: 7-inch

MERCURY 4-8 61-62

LPs: 10/12-inch

MERCURY (20747 "Duets") 15-25 62
(Monaural.)
MERCURY (60747 "Duets") 20-30 62
(Stereo.)
WING 10-15 66

JONES, George, & Ernest Tubb

Singles: 7-inch

FIRST GENERATION 3-4 81

JONES, George, & Tammy Wynette C&W/LP '71

(George, Tammy & Tina)

Singles: 7-inch

EPIC 3-5 71-80

LPs: 10/12-inch

COLUMBIA 5-8 81
EPIC 8-12 71-81
TEE VEE/CBS 5-8 79
Also see JONES, George
Also see WYNETTE, Tammy

JONES, Glenn R&B/D&D '83

Singles: 12-inch

RCA 4-6 83-85

Singles: 7-inch

JIVE 3-4 87-88
RCA 3-4 83-87

Picture Sleeves

JIVE 3-4 87

LPs: 10/12-inch

JIVE 5-8 87
RCA 5-8 83-84
Also see JETER, Genobia, & Glenn Jones
Also see WARWICK, Dionne, & Glenn Jones

JONES, Grace P&R/LP '77

Singles: 12-inch

ISLAND 4-6 83
MANHATTAN 4-6 85

Singles: 7-inch

BEAM JUNCTION 3-5 76-77
ISLAND 3-5 78-83
MANHATTAN 3-4 85-86

Picture Sleeves

MANHATTAN 3-4 86

LPs: 10/12-inch

ISLAND 5-8 77-82
MANHATTAN 5-8 85-86

JONES, Grant R&B '51

(Grant "Mr. Blues" Jones & Brown's Blues Blowers)

Singles: 78 rpm

DECCA 15-25 50
STATES 15-25 52
UNITED 15-25 52

Singles: 7-inch

DECCA (48129 "For You, My Love") 50-75 50
DECCA (48133 "Crying Good Morning Blues") 50-75 50
DECCA (48163 "Hospitality Blues") .. 50-75 50
DECCA (48169 "It's Been a Long Time, Baby") 50-75 50
DECCA (48179 "Night Time Is the Right Time") 50-75 50
STATES (114 "Stormy Monday") 30-50 52
STEPHENY (1821 "Pinball Machine") 15-20 58
UNITED (112 "Strange Man") 30-40 52
UNITED (133 "Hello Stranger") 30-50 52

JONES, Howard P&R/D&D/LP '84

Singles: 12-inch

ELEKTRA 4-6 83-85

Singles: 7-inch

ELEKTRA 3-4 83-89

Picture Sleeves

ELEKTRA 3-4 84-89

LPs: 10/12-inch

ELEKTRA 5-8 83-89

JONES, Ignatius D&D '83

Singles: 12-inch

W.B. 4-6 83

Singles: 7-inch

W.B. 3-4 83

JONES, Jack P&R '62

Singles: 7-inch

CAPITOL 4-8 59-60
KAPP 4-6 60-67
POLYDOR 3-4 83
RCA 3-6 67-77

Picture Sleeves

CAPITOL 5-10 59
KAPP 4-8 63-69

LPs: 10/12-inch

CAMDEN 5-8 73
CAPITOL 10-20 59-64
KAPP 10-20 61-69
MCA 5-8 77
MGM 5-8 79
RCA 5-10 67-77
SEARS 5-10
Also see ANDREWS, Julie & Andre Previn / Vic Damone / Jack Jones / Marian Anderson
Also see ANN-MARGRET

JONES, Jimmy P&R '59

(With the Jones Boys; with Savoys)

Singles: 7-inch

ARROW (717 "Heaven in Your Eyes") 100-200 57
BELL 4-8 67
CUB 8-15 59-62
EPIC (9339 "Whenever You Need Me") 75-125 59
MGM 3-5 78
PARKWAY 4-8 66
ROULETTE (4232 "Lover") 15-25 60
ROULETTE (4608 "Walkin'") 5-10 64
SAVOY (1586 "Say You're Mine") 10-20 60
SAVOY (1586 " Please Say You're Mine") 10-15 61
(Rerecorded. Has slightly different title.)
VEE JAY 4-8 63

Picture Sleeves

CUB (9072 "That's When I Cried") 15-20 60

LPs: 10/12-inch

JEN JILLUS 5-10 77
MGM (E-3847 "Good Timin'") 35-45 60
(Monaural.)
MGM (SE-3847 "Good Timin'") 45-60 60
(Stereo.)
Also see JONES, Jimmy, & Pretenders

JONES, Jimmy, & Pretenders

Singles: 78 rpm

RAMA (207 "Lover") 50-75 56
RAMA (210 "Lover") 30-50 56

Singles: 7-inch

ABC-PAR (10094 "Blue & Lonely") ... 10-15 60
RAMA (207 "Lover") 200-300 56
RAMA (210 "Lover") 100-200 56
Also see JONES, Jimmy

JONES, Jimmy R&B '76

Singles: 7-inch

CONCHILLO 3-5 76

JONES, Joe P&R/R&B '60

Singles: 78 rpm

CAPITOL 8-15 54

Singles: 7-inch

ABC 3-5 73
CAPITOL 10-20 54
RIC 10-15 60
ROULETTE 5-10 60-61

LPs: 10/12-inch

PRESTIGE 10-15 69
ROULETTE (R-25143 "You Talk Too Much") 25-30 61
(Monaural.)
ROULETTE (SR-25143 "You Talk Too Much") 30-40 61
(Stereo.)

JONES, Johnny R&B '68

Singles: 7-inch

BRUNSWICK 3-5 70
HERMITAGE 4-8
FURY 5-10 68

LPs: 10/12-inch

ALLIGATOR 10-12

JONES, Jonah LP '58

(Jonah Jones Quartet)

Singles: 78 rpm

GROOVE 3-8 56

Singles: 7-inch

BETHLEHEM 4-6 59
CAPITOL 4-6 58-63
DECCA 3-6 65
GROOVE 5-10 56
MOTOWN (1144 "For Better Or Worse") 50-100 69

EPs: 7-inch

BETHLEHEM 5-15 55
CAMDEN 5-8 69
CAPITOL 5-10 58-59
GROOVE 5-15 56
RCA 5-10 59

LPs: 10/12-inch

ANGEL 20-30 56
BETHLEHEM 20-40 55-60
CAPITOL (1000 thru 2800 series) 10-25 58-67
(With "T" or "ST" prefix.)
CAPITOL (1600 series) 5-8 77
(With "SM" prefix.)
CAPITOL (11000 series) 5-8 75
DECCA 10-20 65-67
GROOVE 30-40 56
INNER CITY 5-8 81
MOTOWN (683 "Along Came Jonah") 30-50 69
MOTOWN (690 "Dis & Dat") 30-50 69
RCA 15-25 59-63

Also see CHRISTY, June
Also see SINATRA, Frank / Jonah Jones

JONES, Kay Cee P&R '55

Singles: 78 rpm

AMERICAN....5-10 56
DECCA....5-10 57
MARQUEE....5-10 55

Singles: 7-inch

AMERICAN....8-12 56
CHANCELLOR....5-10 59
DECCA....5-10 57
MARQUEE....5-10 55

JONES, Klinte D&D '84

Singles: 12-inch

OH MY....4-6 84

JONES, Linda P&R/R&B '67
(With the Whatnauts)

Singles: 7-inch

ATCO (6344 "I'm Taking Back My Love")....15-25 65
BLUE CAT (128 "Hit Me Like TNT")....15-25 65
COTIQUE....8-12 69
LOMA....5-10 67-68
NEPTUNE....4-8 69
STANG....4-8 72
TURBO....3-6 71-72
W.B. (7278 "My Heart")....15-25 69

LPs: 10/12-inch

LOMA (5907 "Hyptomized")....20-30 67
TURBO....10-15 72

JONES, Mick LP '89

LPs: 10/12-inch

ATLANTIC....5-8 89

JONES, Oran "Juice" P&R/R&B/LP '86
(Juice)

Singles: 7-inch

DEF JAM....3-4 86-87

LPs: 10/12-inch

DEF JAM....5-8 86

JONES, Quincy LP '62

Singles: 7-inch

A&M (Except 9288)....3-5 69-81
A&M (9288 "Quincy Jones")....50-75 78
(Octagon picture disc. Promotional issue only.)
ABC....3-6 68
BELL....3-6 69
COLGEMS....3-6 68
IMPULSE....4-8 62
MERCURY....5-12 59-66
RCA....3-6 69
REPRISE....3-5 72
UNI....3-6 69
U.A.....3-5 70

Picture Sleeves

A&M....3-5 77-81
COLGEMS....4-8 68

LPs: 10/12-inch

A&M....5-10 69-82
ABC (700 series)....8-12 73
ABC-PAR (149 "How I Feel About Jazz")....75-100 56
ABC-PAR (186 "Go West, Man")....75-100 57
ALLEGIANCE....5-8 84
COLGEMS....20-30 68
EMARCY (36083 "Jazz Abroad")....75-100 56
IMPULSE (11 "Quintessence")....15-25 62
IMPULSE (9300 series)....8-12 78
LIBERTY....10-20 67
MFSL (078 "You've Got It Bad")....25-35 82
MERCURY (623 "Ndeda")....15-20 72
MERCURY (2014 "Around the World")....20-30 61
(Monaural.)
MERCURY (20444 "Birth of a Band")....40-50 59
(Monaural.)
MERCURY (20561 "Great, Wide World")....40-50 60
(Monaural.)
MERCURY (20612 "I Dig Dancers")....40-50 60
(Monaural.)
MERCURY (20653 "Quincy Jones at Newport '61")....20-30 61
(Monaural.)
MERCURY (20751 "Big Band Bossa Nova")....20-30 62
(Monaural.)
MERCURY (20799 "Hip Hits")....20-30 63
(Monaural.)
MERCURY (20863 thru 21070)....10-20 64-66
(Monaural.)
MERCURY (6014 "Around the World")....25-35 61
(Stereo.)
MERCURY (60444 "Birth of a Band")....45-60 59
(Stereo.)
MERCURY (60561 "Great, Wide World")....45-55 60
(Stereo.)
MERCURY (60612 "I Dig Dancers")....45-55 60
(Stereo.)
MERCURY (60653 "Quincy Jones at Newport '61")....25-35 61
(Stereo.)
MERCURY (60751 "Big Band Bossa Nova")....25-35 62
(Stereo.)
MERCURY (60799 "Hip Hits")....25-35 63
(Stereo.)
MERCURY (60863 thru 61070)....15-25 64-66
NAUTILUS (52 "The Dude")....15-25 82
PRESTIGE (172 "Sweden-American All Stars")....200-250 53
(10-inch LP.)
QWEST....5-8 89
TRIP....5-8 74-76
U.A.....10-15 70
VERVE....15-20 67
WING....6-12 69

Also see ASHFORD & SIMPSON
Also see AUSTIN, Patti
Also see ECKSTINE, Billy, & Quincy Jones
Also see FELICIANO, Jose, & Quincy Jones
Also see GILBERTO, Astrud
Also see JACKSON, Michael
Also see RIPERTON, Minnie
Also see SINATRA, Frank, with Quincy Jones & His Orchestra
Also see U.S.A. for AFRICA
Also see VAUGHAN, Sarah, & Quincy Jones
Also see WASHINGTON, Dinah

JONES, Quincy, & Brothers Johnson P&R '75

Singles: 7-inch

A&M....3-5 75

Picture Sleeves

A&M....3-5 75

Also see BROTHERS JOHNSON

JONES, Quincy, & Tevin Campbell P&R '90

Singles: 7-inch

QWEST....3-4 90

JONES, Quincy, Ray Charles & Chaka Khan P&R '89

Singles: 7-inch

QWEST....3-4 89

Picture Sleeves

QWEST....3-4 89

Also see CHARLES, Ray
Also see KHAN, Chaka

JONES, Quincy, & James Ingram P&R/R&B '81

Singles: 7-inch

A&M....3-5 81

Also see JONES, Quincy

JONES, Quincy, James Ingram, Al B. Sure, El DeBarge & Barry White P&R '90

Singles: 7-inch

QWEST....3-4 90

Picture Sleeves

QWEST....3-4 90

Also see AL B. SURE!
Also see DE BARGE
Also see INGRAM, James
Also see JONES, Quincy, & James Ingram
Also see WHITE, Barry

JONES, Rickie Lee P&R/R&B/LP '79

Singles: 7-inch

W.B.....3-5 79-84

Picture Sleeves

W.B.....3-5 84

EPs: 10-inch

W.B. (23805 "Girl at Her Volcano")....10-15 83

LPs: 10/12-inch

GEFFEN....5-8 89
MFSL (089 "Rickie Lee Jones")....30-50 82
W.B.....5-8 79-84

JONES, Shirley R&B/LP '86

Singles: 7-inch

PHILADELPHIA INT'L....3-4 86-87

LPs: 10/12-inch

PHILADELPHIA INT'L....5-8 86

Also see JONES GIRLS

JONES, Spencer D&D '83

Singles: 12-inch

NEXT PLATINUM....4-6 83

Singles: 7-inch

NEXT PLATINUM....3-4 83
PROFILE....3-4 86

JONES, Spike P&R '42
(With the City Slickers)

Singles: 78 rpm

BLUEBIRD....10-20 42-43
RCA....5-15 46-55
VICTOR....8-12 44-45

Singles: 7-inch

LIBERTY....5-10 59-65
MUSICAL POSTCARD....15-25 50s
(Cardboard picture disc series.)
RCA (0500 series)....3-5 71
RCA (3287-89 "Spike Jones Favorites")....40-60 49
(Boxed, three-disc set.)
RCA (2900 thru 6000 series)....10-20 49-55
(Black vinyl.)
RCA (Colored vinyl)....20-40 50s
W.B.....5-10 59

Picture Sleeves

RCA (5067 "I Saw Mommy Kissing Santa Claus")....20-30 53
RCA (5742 "I'm in the Mood for Love")....20-30 54

EPs: 7-inch

RCA....20-30 51-59
VERVE....15-25 56-57

LPs: 10/12-inch

GLENDALE....5-8 78
LIBERTY....15-25 60-65
MGM....8-12 70
PICKWICK....8-12
RCA (18 "Spike Jones Plays the Charleston")....50-100 51
RCA (1000 series)....5-10 75
RCA (2200 series)....20-25 60
RCA (2300 series)....5-10 77
RCA (3054 "Bottoms Up")....40-60 52
RCA (3128 "Spike Jones Kids the Classics")....40-60 53
RCA (3200 series)....8-12 71
RCA (3700 series)....4-8 80
RCA (3800 series)....10-15 67
(With "LPM" or "LSP" prefix.)
RCA (3800 series)....5-8 81
(With "AYL1" prefix.)
TIARA....8-12
U.A.....5-10 75

VERVE (Except 8500 series) 20-40 56-59
VERVE (8500 series) 12-20 63
W.B. 15-25 59-60
Session: Homer & Jethro.
Also see HOMER & JETHRO
Also see INGLE, Red, & Natural Seven
Also see KATZ, Mickey, & His Orchestra

JONES, Steve — LP '89

LPs: 10/12-inch

MCA 5-8 89

JONES, Tamiko — P&R/R&B '75

Singles: 12-inch

T.K. (6 "Let It Flow") 10-15 76

Singles: 7-inch

A&M 4-6 68-69
ARISTA 3-5 75
ATLANTIC 4-8 66
ATLANTIS 3-5 77
CONTEMPO 3-5 76
DECEMBER 4-8 67-68
GOLDEN WORLD (40 "I'm Spellbound") 15-25 66
POLYDOR 3-5 79
SUTRA 3-4 86
T.K. 3-5 76
20TH FOX 3-5 74

LPs: 10/12-inch

A&M 10-12 68
DECEMBER 10-12 68
Also see TAMIKO

JONES, Tamiko, & Herbie Mann — P&R '66

Singles: 7-inch

ATLANTIC 4-6 66

LPs: 10/12-inch

ATLANTIC 8-15 67
Also see JONES, Tamiko
Also see MANN, Herbie

JONES, Thelma — R&B '67

Singles: 7-inch

BARRY 4-8 66-68
COLUMBIA 3-5 78

JONES, Thumper

(George Jones)

Singles: 78 rpm

STARDAY (240 "Rock-It") 50-75 56

Singles: 7-inch

STARDAY (240 "Rock-It") 75-100 56

EPs: 7-inch

DIXIE (502 "Thumper Jones") 20-30 58
(Contains three Jones tracks. Not issued with cover.)

LPs: 10/12-inch

TEENAGE HEAVEN 8-12
Also see JONES, George

JONES, Tom — P&R/R&B/LP '65

Singles: 7-inch

EPIC 3-5 76-80
LONDON 3-5 77
MCA 3-5 79
MERCURY 3-4 81-85
PARROT 3-8 65-75
SYMBOL 4-8 65
TOWER 4-8 65

Picture Sleeves

PARROT (9737 thru 9801) 4-8 65
PARROT (40000 series) 3-6 69-71

LPs: 10/12-inch

EPIC 8-12 70-77
LONDON 5-8 77
MERCURY 5-8 81-85
PARROT 10-20 65-74
Also see ART of NOISE & Tom Jones
Also see BARRY, John

JONES, Tom / Freddie & Dreamers / Johnny Rivers

LPs: 10/12-inch

TOWER (5007 "Three at the Top") ... 15-20 65
Also see FREDDIE & DREAMERS
Also see JONES, Tom
Also see RIVERS, Johnny

JONES GIRLS — P&R/R&B/LP '79

Singles: 7-inch

CURTOM 3-5 75
EPIC 3-4 81
PARAMOUNT 3-5 74
PHILADELPHIA INT'L 3-5 79-82
RCA 3-4 83

LPs: 10/12-inch

PHILADELPHIA INT'L 5-8 79-81
RCA 5-8 83
Members: Shirley Jones; Brenda Jones; Valorie Jones.
Also see JONES, Shirley

JONESES — P&R/R&B '74

Singles: 7-inch

MERCURY 3-5 74-83
VMP (00005 "Pretty Pretty") 8-15 72

Picture Sleeves

MERCURY 3-5 75

LPs: 10/12-inch

EPIC 5-8 77
MERCURY 5-8 74-83
Members: Glenn Dorsey; Harold Taylor; Cy Brooks; Ernest Holt; Wendell Noble; Reginald Noble; Larry Noble; Sam White.

JONZUN, Michael — R&B '86

Singles: 12-inch

A&M 4-6 85
(Black vinyl.)
A&M 5-8 85
(Colored vinyl.)

Singles: 7-inch

A&M 3-4 85
Also see JONZUN CREW

JONZUN CREW — R&B '82

Singles: 12-inch

A&M 4-6 84-85
TOMMY BOY 4-6 82-85

Singles: 7-inch

A&M 3-4 84-85
TOMMY BOY 3-4 82-85

LPs: 10/12-inch

A&M 5-8 84-85
TOMMY BOY 5-8 83-85
Members: Michael Jonzun; Soni Jonzun; Steve Thorpe; Gordy Worthy.
Also see JONZUN, Michael

JOPLIN, Janis — P&R/LP '69

(With Big Brother & Full Tilt)

Singles: 7-inch

COLUMBIA 4-8 69-72
SIMON & SHUSTER ("Janis") 3-5
(Soundsheet. Included with the book *Janis*.)

LPs: 10/12-inch

COLUMBIA (KCS-9913 "I Got Dem 'Ol Kozmic Blues Again, Mama") 20-25 69
COLUMBIA (PC-9913 "I Got Dem 'Ol Kozmic Blues Again, Mama") 5-8
COLUMBIA (30000 series) 10-15 71-75
(With "C2," "KC" or "PG" prefix.)
COLUMBIA (30000 series) 12-20 74
(With "CQ" prefix. Quad.)
COLUMBIA (30000 series) 5-8 82-84
(With "PC" prefix.)
MEMORY 5-10
Also see BIG BROTHER & Holding Company

JOPLIN, Janis / Hot Tuna

LPs: 10/12-inch

GRUNT ("Last Interview") 25-35 72
(Promotional issue only. Includes bonus Joplin home recording.)
Also see HOT TUNA
Also see JOPLIN, Janis

JORDAN, Jerry — LP '75

(Jordans)

Singles: 7-inch

MCA 3-5 75-76

LPs: 10/12-inch

MCA 5-8 75-76

JORDAN, Lonnie — R&B '76

Singles: 7-inch

BOARDWALK 3-4 82
MCA 3-5 78
U.A. 3-5 76-77

LPs: 10/12-inch

MCA 5-8 78
Also see WAR

JORDAN, Louis — R&B '42

(Louis Jordan's Elk Rendezvous Band; with His Tympani 5)

Singles: 78 rpm

DECCA (7500 thru 8600 series) 5-15 38-43
DECCA (18000 thru 30000 series) 5-10 44-50
VIK 5-10 56

Singles: 7-inch

ALADDIN (3223 "Whiskey Do Your Stuff") 20-30 54
ALADDIN (3227 "Ooo-Wee") 20-30 54
ALADDIN (3242 "A Dollar Down") 25-35 54
ALADDIN (3246 "Messy Bessie") 20-30 54
ALADDIN (3249 "Louis' Blues") 20-30 54
ALADDIN (3264 "Put Some Money in the Pot") 20-30 54
ALADDIN (3270 "Fat Back and Corn Liquor") 20-30 54
ALADDIN (3279 "Gal, You Need a Whippin' ") 20-30 54
DECCA (20000 thru 30000 series) 15-25 50-54
LOU-WA 5-10 60
MERCURY 10-20 56-58
PZAZZ 4-6 68
TANGERINE 4-8 62-66
VIK 8-12 56
WARWICK 5-10 60-61
"X" 8-12 55

EPs: 7-inch

DECCA 15-25 56
MERCURY 15-25 57

LPs: 10/12-inch

CLASSICAL JAZZ 5-8 82
DECCA (5035 "Greatest Hits") 10-20 68
DECCA (8551 "Let the Good Times Roll") 30-40 56
MCA 5-8 75-80
MERCURY (20242 "Somebody Up There Digs Me") 25-30 57
MERCURY (20331 "Man, We're Wailin' ") 25-30 58
SCORE (4007 "Go Blow Your Horn") 75-125 57
TANGERINE 12-15 64
TRIP 8-10 75
WING 15-20 63
Also see CROSBY, Bing, & Louis Jordan
Also see DAVIS, Martha
Also see FITZGERALD, Ella, & Louis Jordan

JORDAN, Stanley — LP '85

LPs: 10/12-inch

BLUE NOTE 5-8 85-87
EMI 5-8 88

JORDAN, Tenita — R&B '85

Singles: 7-inch

CBS ASSOCIATED 3-4 85

JORDANS: see JORDAN, Jerry

JOSEPH, David — R&B/D&D '83

Singles: 12-inch

MANGO 4-6 83

Singles: 7-inch

MANGO 3-4 83

JOSEPH, Margie — R&B '70

(With Blue Magic)

Singles: 12-inch

H.C.R.C. 4-6 83

Singles: 7-inch

ATCO 3-5 75
ATLANTIC 3-5 72-78
COTILLION 3-5 76-84
H.C.R.C. 3-4 82-83
OKEH 4-8 68
VOLT 3-5 68-71

LPs: 10/12–inch

ATLANTIC 8-10 73-74
H.C.R.C. 5-8 83
VOLT 10-12 71

Also see BLUE MAGIC
Also see HATHAWAY, Donny, & Margie Joseph

JOSIAS, Cory D&D '83

Singles: 12–inch

SIRE 4-6 83

JOURNEY LP '75

Singles: 12–inch

COLUMBIA 5-10 82

Singles: 7–inch

COLUMBIA 3-5 74-87
GEFFEN 3-4 85

Picture Sleeves

COLUMBIA 3-5 81-87
GEFFEN 3-4 85

EPs: 7–inch

CSP 4-6 81
(Nestle's candy promotional issue.)

LPs: 10/12–inch

COLUMBIA ("Captured") 100-120 81
(10-inch picture disc. No selection number used. Promotional issue only.)
COLUMBIA (662 "Live Sampler") 12-15 75
(Promotional issue only.)
COLUMBIA (914 "Journey") 12-15 75
(Promotional issue only.)
COLUMBIA (30000 series) 5-10 75-82
COLUMBIA (KC2-37016 "Captured") 80-100 81
(Picture disc made for promotional use, but, due to a production error, the actual recordings are by unidentified artists.)
COLUMBIA (46000 & 47000 series) 20-40 81-82
(Half-speed mastered.)
MFSL (144 "Escape") 100-200 85

Members: Steve Perry; Neal Schon; Aynsley Dunbar; Gregg Rolie; Ross Valory; Jonathan Cain; Robert Fleishman.
Also see BABYS
Also see BAD ENGLISH
Also see CAIN, Jonathan
Also see PERRY, Steve
Also see SCHON, Neal, & Jan Hammer

JOVI, Bon: see BON JOVI

JOY, Roddie P&R/R&B '65

Singles: 7–inch

PARKWAY 5-10 66-67
RED BIRD (021 "Come Back Baby") .. 8-12 65
RED BIRD (031 "He's So Easy to Love") 10-20 65
RED BIRD (037 "If There's Anything You Want") 20-30 66

JOY DIVISION LP '88

LPs: 10/12–inch

FACTORY 5-8 81
QWEST 5-8 88

Members: Bernard Sumner; Peter Hook; Gillian Gilbert; Stephen Morris.
Also see NEW ORDER

JOY OF COOKING P&R/LP '71
(The Joy)

Singles: 7–inch

BROWNSVILLE 3-5 71
CAPITOL 3-5 71-73
FANTASY 3-5 77-78

LPs: 10/12–inch

CAPITOL 8-10 71-72
FANTASY 5-10 77-78

Members: Terry Garthwaite; Toni Brown; Fritz Kasten; David Garthwaite; Ron Wilson.

JUBALAIRES R&B '46
(With Andy Kirk's Orchestra)

Singles: 78 rpm

CORAL 10-20 49
DECCA 10-20 46
KING 10-20 49-50
QUEEN (4163 "A Sunday Kind of Love") 15-25 47
QUEEN (4166 "Jubes' Blues") 15-25 47
QUEEN (4167 "God Almighty's Gonna Cut You Down") 15-25 47
QUEEN (4168 "My God Called Me This Morning") 15-25 47
QUEEN (4172 "Icky, Yacky") 15-25 47

Also see KIRK, Andy, & His Clouds of Joy

JUDAS PRIEST LP '78

Singles: 7–inch

ATLANTIC 3-4 88
COLUMBIA 3-5 79-84

Picture Sleeves

COLUMBIA 3-5 81

LPs: 10/12–inch

COLUMBIA (Except picture discs) 5-8 77-90
COLUMBIA (99-1543 "Screaming for Vengeance") 15-20 84
(World Tour picture disc.)
COLUMBIA (99-1543 "Screaming for Vengeance") 20-30 84
(Picture disc that, due to a production error, plays Neil Diamond's *Primitive* album.)
COLUMBIA (99-1851 "Love Bites") .. 60-70 84
(Picture disc with bite mark on outer edge.)
COLUMBIA (99-1851 "Love Bites") .. 15-25 84
(Picture disc.)
COLUMBIA (39926 "Great Vinyl and Concert Hits") 25-30 84
(Picture disc.)
JANUS 6-10 76
OVATION 5-8 80
RCA 5-8 83-84
VISA 5-8 78-81

Members: Rob Halford; K.K. Downing; Glenn Tipton; Ian Hill; Dave Holland; Scott Travis.

JUDDS C&W '83

Singles: 7–inch

CURB/RCA 3-4 90-91
RCA 3-5 83-88
RCA/CURB 3-4 89-89

Promotional Singles

RCA 5-10 83-88
(Black vinyl.)
RCA (13673 "Had a Dream") 15-20 83
(Colored vinyl.)
RCA (13923 "Why Not Me") 10-20 84
(Colored vinyl.)
RCA (13673 "Had a Dream") 15-20 83
(Colored vinyl.)

LPs: 10/12–inch

RCA 5-8 83-88
RCA/CURB 5-8 89-89

Members: Naomi Judd; Wynonna Judd.

JUICY R&B '83

Singles: 12–inch

ATLANTIC 4-8 83-84
PRIVATE I 4-6 85

Singles: 7–inch

ARISTA 3-4 83
ATLANTIC 3-4 83-84
CBS ASSOC 3-4 86
PRIVATE I 3-4 85-86

LPs: 10/12–inch

ARISTA 5-8 83
ATLANTIC 5-8 84

Members: Jerry Barnes; Katreese Barnes

JUKES: see SOUTHSIDE JOHNNY

JULIE P&R '76
(Julie Budd)

Singles: 7–inch

A&M 3-4 84-85
TOM CAT 3-5 76

Also see BUDD, Julie

JULUKA LP '83

Singles: 7–inch

W.B. 3-4 83-84

LPs: 10/12–inch

W.B. 5-8 83-84

JUMBO R&B '77

Singles: 7–inch

PRELUDE 3-5 77

LPs: 10/12–inch

PYE 5-8 77

JUMP 'N THE SADDLE BAND P&R '83

Singles: 7–inch

ACME 4-6 82
ATLANTIC 3-4 83

Picture Sleeves

ATLANTIC 3-4 83

JUNE & DONNIE R&B '69

Singles: 7–inch

CURTOM (1935 "I Thank You Baby") ... 4-8 68

Members: June Conquest; Donny Hathaway.
Also see HATHAWAY, Donny, & June Conquest

JUNGKLAS, Rob LP '86

Singles: 7–inch

MANHATTAN 3-4 87

Picture Sleeves

MANHATTAN 3-4 87

LPs: 10/12–inch

MANHATTAN 5-8 86

JUNIE R&B '74
(Walter Morrison; Junie Morrison)

Singles: 7–inch

COLUMBIA 3-4 81
EASTBOUND 3-5 74
20TH FOX/WESTBOUND 3-5 75-76

LPs: 10/12–inch

20TH FOX/WESTBOUND 5-8 76

Also see FUNKADELIC
Also see MORRISON, Junie
Also see OHIO PLAYERS

JUNIOR P&R/R&B/LP '82
(Junior Giscombe)

Singles: 12–inch

LONDON 4-6 84
MERCURY 4-6 83

Singles: 7–inch

CASABLANCA 3-4 83
LONDON 3-4 84-88
MERCURY 3-4 82-86

LPs: 10/12–inch

MERCURY 5-8 82-83

JUNKYARD LP '89

LPs: 10/12–inch

GEFFEN 5-8 89

JU-PAR UNIVERSAL ORCH. R&B '77

Singles: 7–inch

JU-PAR 3-5 77

JUPITER, Duke: see DUKE JUPITER

JUST US P&R '66

Singles: 7–inch

ATLANTIC 3-5 71
COLPIX 4-8 66
KAPP 4-8 66-67
MINUTEMAN 4-8 66

Picture Sleeves

KAPP 4-8 66

LPs: 10/12–inch

KAPP 10-15 66

Members: Chip Taylor; Al Gorgoni.

JUSTIS, Bill P&R/R&B/C&W '57
(With the Jury; Bill Justis Orchestra; with Roger Fakes & Spinners)

Singles: 78 rpm

PHILLIPS INT'L 15-30 57

Singles: 7–inch

BELL 3-5 70
MONUMENT 3-5 76
PHILLIPS INT'L 8-15 57-59
PLAY ME 8-12 59
MCA 3-5 77
MONUMENT 4-8 66
NRC 4-8 60
SMASH 4-8 63-65

Picture Sleeves

SMASH........5-10 63

LPs: 10/12-inch

HARMONY........8-10 72
PHILLIPS INT'L (1950 "Cloud 9")......50-75 57
SMASH........15-20 62-66
SUN........8-10 69
WING........10-20 65

JUSTIS, Bill / Jerry Reed

EPs: 7-inch

MCA (1961 "Music from *Smokey and the Bandit*")........10-15 77
(Promotional issue only.)
Also see JUSTIS, Bill
Also see REED, Jerry

JUVET, Patrick LP '78

Singles: 12-inch

CASABLANCA........4-6 78-79

Singles: 7-inch

CASABLANCA........3-5 78-79

LPs: 10/12-inch

CASABLANCA........5-8 78-79

JYVE FYVE

Singles: 7-inch

BRUT........3-5 74
Also see JIVE FIVE

KBC BAND P&R/LP '86

Singles: 7-inch

ARISTA........3-4 86

Picture Sleeves

ARISTA........3-4 86

LPs: 10/12-inch

ARISTA........5-8 86
Members: Paul Kantner; Marty Balin; Jack Casady.
Also see JEFFERSON AIRPLANE

KC & SUNSHINE BAND R&B '73

(KC; Sunshine Band)

Singles: 12-inch

EPIC........4-6 82
MECA........4-6 83-85
SUNSHINE SOUND........4-6 81

Singles: 7-inch

CASABLANCA........3-4 80-83
EPIC........3-4 81-83
MECA........3-4 83-85
SUNSHINE SOUND........3-4 81
TK........3-5 73-81

Picture Sleeves

TK........3-5 77-78

LPs: 10/12-inch

CASABLANCA........5-8 81
EPIC........5-8 81-82
MECA........5-8 84
SUNSHINE SOUND........5-8 81
TK........8-10 74-80
Also see DE SARIO, Teri, & K.C.
Also see WRIGHT, Betty

KGB LP '76

Singles: 7-inch

MCA........3-5 76

LPs: 10/12-inch

MCA........8-10 76
Members: Ray Kennedy; Rick Grech; Mike Bloomfield; Barry Goldberg; Carmine Appice.
Also see BLOOMFIELD, Mike
Also see KENNEDY, Ray

K.I.D. R&B '81

Singles: 12-inch

SAM........4-6 81

Singles: 7-inch

SAM........3-5 81

K-9 POSSE LP '89

LPs: 10/12-inch

ARISTA........5-8 89

KTP: see KISSING the PINK

KADO, Ernie: see K-DOE, Ernie

KADOR, Ernest: see K-DOE, Ernie

KAEMPFERT, Bert, & His Orchestra P&R/R&B/LP '60

Singles: 7-inch

DECCA........3-8 60-71

Picture Sleeves

DECCA........4-8 66

EPs: 7-inch

DECCA........5-8 61

LPs: 10/12-inch

CADENCE........10-15 61
DECCA........10-15 59-72
MCA........5-10 73-76

KAJAGOOGOO P&R/D&D/LP '83

(Kaja)

Singles: 12-inch

EMI AMERICA........4-6 83-85

Singles: 7-inch

EMI AMERICA........3-4 83-85

Picture Sleeves

EMI AMERICA........3-4 83

LPs: 10/12-inch

EMI AMERICA........5-8 83-85
Also see LIMAHL

KALEIDOSCOPE LP '69

Singles: 7-inch

A&M........3-5 73
EPIC (10117 "Elevator Man")........15-25 67
EPIC (10219 "Little Orphan Nannie") 15-25 67
EPIC (10239 "I Found Out")........15-25 67
EPIC (10332 "Just a Taste")........15-25 68
EPIC (10481 "Lie to Me")........15-25 69
EPIC (10500 "Tempe, Arizona")........15-25 69
TSOP........4-8 75

LPs: 10/12-inch

BACK-TRAC........5-8 85
EPIC (24304 "Side Trips")........50-100 67
(Monaural.)
EPIC (24333 "Beacon from Mars")...40-60 67
(Monaural.)
EPIC (26304 "Side Trips")........50-75 67
(Stereo.)
EPIC (26333 "Beacon from Mars")...50-75 67
(Stereo.)
EPIC (26467 "Incredible Kaleidoscope")........20-40 69
EPIC (26508 "Bernice")........15-20 70
PACIFIC ARTS........5-10 78
Members: David Lindley; Solomon Feldthouse; John Vidican; John Welsh; Rick O'Neil; Brian Monsour; Chris Darrow.
Also see WILLIAMS, Larry, & Johnny Guitar Watson

KALIN TWINS P&R/C&W/R&B '58

Singles: 78 rpm

DECCA........20-40 58

Singles: 7-inch

AMY........4-8 66
DECCA (Except 30642)........8-15 58-62
DECCA (30642 "When")........15-25 58
(With silver lines on both sides of the name "Decca.")
DECCA (30642 "When")........8-15 58
(With a star and silver lines under the name "Decca.")
MCA........3-5 73

Picture Sleeves

DECCA (30977 "Why Don't You Believe Me")........10-20 59

EPs: 7-inch

DECCA (2623 "Kalin Twins")........25-50 58
DECCA (2641 "Forget Me Not")........25-50 59

LPs: 10/12-inch

DECCA (8812 "Kalin Twins")........50-75 58
VOCALION (73771 "Kalin Twins")....30-40 66
Members: Hal Kalin; Herb Kalin.
Also see LEE, Brenda / Bill Haley & Comets / Kalin Twins / Four Aces

KALLEN, Kitty P&R '49

Singles: 78 rpm

DECCA........4-8 54-57
COLUMBIA........4-8 54
MERCURY........4-8 51-54

Singles: 7-inch

BELL........4-6 67
DECCA........5-10 54-59
COLUMBIA (40000 series)........5-10 54
COLUMBIA (41000 series)........4-8 59-61
MGM........4-6 65
MERCURY........5-10 51-54
PHILIPS........4-6 66
RCA........4-8 63
20TH-CENTURY-FOX........4-8 64
U.A.........4-8 65

Promotional Singles

DECCA (78094 "Personal Introduction by Kitty Kallen to '54 Christmas Seal Song")........8-12 54
(Single-sided promotional pressing.)

Picture Sleeves

DECCA (290 "It's Not the Whistle")...10-15 55

EPs: 7-inch

DECCA........10-15 54-56
COLUMBIA........10-15 54
MERCURY........10-15 55

LPs: 10/12-inch

COLUMBIA........10-20 60-61
DECCA (8397 "It's a Lonesome Old Town")........20-30 56
MCA........4-8 83
MERCURY (25206 "Pretty Kitty Kallen Sings")........30-50 55
(10-inch LP.)
MOVIETONE........8-12 67
RCA........10-20 63
20TH-CENTURY-FOX........10-15 64
VOCALION........10-20 59
WING........10-15 63
Also see ANN-MARGRET / Kitty Kallen / Della Reese
Also see HAYES, Richard, & Kitty Kallen
Also see JAMES, Harry, & His Orchestra

KALLEN, Kitty, & Georgie Shaw

Singles: 78 rpm

DECCA........4-8 55

Singles: 7-inch

DECCA........5-10 55
Also see KALLEN, Kitty
Also see SHAW, Georgie

KALLMANN, Gunter, Chorus LP '65

Singles: 7-inch

4 CORNERS........4-6 65-68

LPs: 10/12-inch

4 CORNERS........8-12 65-68
POLYDOR........5-10 70

KALYAN R&B/LP '77

Singles: 7-inch

MCA........3-5 77

LPs: 10/12-inch

MCA........8-10 77

KAMIKAZE D&D '84

Singles: 12-inch

A&M........4-6 84

Singles: 7-inch

A&M........3-4 84

KAMON, Karen P&R '84

Singles: 7-inch

COLUMBIA........3-4 84

Picture Sleeves

COLUMBIA........3-4 84

KANE, Big Daddy LP '88

Singles: 7-inch

REPRISE........3-4 89

Picture Sleeves

REPRISE........3-4 89

LPs: 10/12-inch

COLD CHILL 5-8 88-90

KANE, Madleen P&R '82

Singles: 12-inch

CHALET 4-6 82
TSR 4-6 85

Singles: 7-inch

CHALET 3-4 82
W.B. 3-5 78-79

Picture Sleeves

W.B. 3-5 78-79

LPs: 10/12-inch

CHALET 5-8 82
W.B. 5-8 78-79

KANE, Paul

(Paul Simon)

Singles: 7-inch

TRIBUTE (128 "Carlos Dominguez") 50-75 63
(Copies crediting "Paul Simon" as the singer are bootlegs.)
Also see SIMON, Paul

KANE GANG P&R/LP '87

Singles: 12-inch

LONDON 4-6 86

Singles: 7-inch

CAPITOL 3-4 87
LONDON 3-4 86

Picture Sleeves

CAPITOL 3-4 87

LPs: 10/12-inch

CAPITOL 5-8 87
LONDON 5-8 86
POLYGRAM 5-8 85

KANO R&B '80

Singles: 7-inch

EMERGENCY 3-5 80
MIRAGE 3-4 81

LPs: 10/12-inch

EMERGENCY 5-8 81
MIRAGE 5-8 81

KANSAS LP '74

Singles: 12-inch

CBS ASSOCIATED 5-10 83
(Promotional only.)
MCA 5-8 88
(Promotional only.)

Singles: 7-inch

CBS ASSOCIATED 3-4 83
KIRSHNER 3-5 74-82
MCA (17290 "Power") 3-6 87
(CD mix on vinyl. Promotional issue only.)
MCA (50000 series) 3-4 86-87

Picture Sleeves

CBS ASSOCIATED 3-4 83
KIRSHNER 3-5 82
MCA 3-4 86-87

LPs: 10/12-inch

CBS ASSOCIATED 5-8 83-84
KIRSHNER (30000 series) 8-12 74-82
KIRSHNER (40000 series) 15-25 81-82
(Half-speed mastered.)
MCA 5-8 86-88

Promotional LPs

BURNS MEDIA ("Two for the Show") 15-25 78
KIRSHNER (34929 "Point of Know Return") 50-75 79
(Picture disc.)
KIRSHNER (555 "Two for the Show") 10-15 78
Members: Dave Hope; Rich Williams; Phil Ehart; Kerry Livgren; Robbie Shakespeare; Steve Walsh; Terry Brock.
Also see MORSE, Steve, Band
Also see STREETS
Also see WALSH, Steve

KANTNER, Paul R&B '79

Singles: 7-inch

MALACO 3-5 79
RCA 5-10 83

KANTNER, Paul, & Grace Slick

(With David Freiberg) LP '71

Singles: 7-inch

GRUNT 3-5 72

Picture Sleeves

GRUNT 3-6 72

LPs: 10/12-inch

GRUNT (0100 series) 8-10 71-73
GRUNT (2002 "Sunfighter") 10-15 71
(Includes booklet.)
GRUNT (4000 series) 5-8 82
Also see GRATEFUL DEAD
Also see JEFFERSON AIRPLANE
Also see SLICK, Grace

KANTNER, Paul, & Jefferson Starship LP '70

Singles: 7-inch

RCA 3-6 71
Also see KANTNER, Paul
Also see JEFFERSON STARSHIP

KAOMA LP '90

Singles: 7-inch

EPIC 3-4 90

LPs: 10/12-inch

EPIC 5-8 89

KAPLAN, Gabriel P&R '77

Singles: 7-inch

ABC 3-5 74
ELEKTRA 3-5 76-77

Picture Sleeves

ELEKTRA 3-5 77

LPs: 10/12-inch

ABC 8-10 74

KARAS, Anton P&R '50

Singles: 78 rpm

LONDON 4-6 50

Singles: 7-inch

LONDON 5-10 50

EPs: 7-inch

LONDON (6035 "Anton Karas") 15-25 50

KAREN, Kenny P&R '73

(Ken Karen)

Singles: 7-inch

BIG TREE 3-5 73
COLUMBIA (3-42264 "Oh Susie, Forgive Me") 15-25 62
(Compact 33 Single.)
COLUMBIA (3-42452 "To Sandy, with Love") 15-25 62
(Compact 33 Single.)
COLUMBIA (3-42638 "16 Years Ago Tonight") 15-25 62
(Compact 33 Single.)
COLUMBIA (4-42264 "Oh Susie, Forgive Me") 5-10 62
COLUMBIA (4-42452 "To Sandy, with Love") 5-10 62
COLUMBIA (4-42638 "16 Years Ago Tonight") 5-10 62
STRAND 5-10 59-60

Picture Sleeves

COLUMBIA (42264 "Oh Susie, Forgive Me") 10-15 62
COLUMBIA (42452 "To Sandy, with Love") 10-15 62

KARI, Harry, & His Six Saki Sippers

(Harry Stewart) P&R '53

Singles: 78 rpm

CAPITOL 4-8 53-55

Singles: 7-inch

CAPITOL 8-15 53-55
Also see YORGESSON, Yogi

KARL, Frankie P&R/R&B '68

(With the Dreams)

Singles: 7-inch

D.C. 5-10 68
LIBERTY (56164 "Don't Sleep Too Long") 10-20 70
PHILTOWN (105 "You Should O' Held On") 5-10

KARMA R&B '77

Singles: 7-inch

HORIZON 3-5 79

LPs: 10/12-inch

A&M 8-10 77

KARTOON KREW R&B '85

Singles: 7-inch

PROFILE 3-4 86

KASANDRA P&R/R&B/LP '68

(With the Midnight Riders; John Anderson)

Singles: 7-inch

CAPITOL 4-8 68
IMPERIAL 5-10 60

LPs: 10/12-inch

CAPITOL 10-15 68

KASENETZ - KATZ SINGING ORCHESTRAL CIRCUS P&R '68

(Kasenetz - Katz Super Cirkus; Kasenetz-Katz Fighter Squadron)

Singles: 7-inch

BELL (966 "When He Comes") 5-10 71
(With 10CC.)
BUDDAH 4-8 68
EPIC 3-5 77
MAGNA-GLIDE 3-5 75
SUPER K 3-5 69-71

LPs: 10/12-inch

BUDDAH 10-15 68
Also see MUSIC EXPLOSION
Also see 1910 FRUITGUM COMPANY
Also see OHIO EXPRESS
Also see 10CC

KASHIF R&B/D&D/LP '83

Singles: 12-inch

ARISTA 4-6 83-86

Singles: 7-inch

ARISTA 3-4 83-88

LPs: 10/12-inch

ARISTA 5-8 83-87
Also see KENNY G. & Kashif
Also see MOORE, Melba, & Kashif
Also see WARWICK, Dionne, & Kashif

KASHIF & MELI'SA MORGAN R&B '87

Singles: 7-inch

ARISTA 3-4 87
Also see MORGAN, Meli'sa

KATFISH P&R '75

Singles: 7-inch

BIG TREE 3-5 75

KATRINA & WAVES P&R/LP '85

Singles: 7-inch

CAPITOL 3-4 85-86
SBK 3-4 89

Picture Sleeves

CAPITOL 3-4 85-86
SBK 3-4 89

LPs: 10/12-inch

CAPITOL 5-8 85-86
SBK 5-8 89
Members: Katrina Leskanich; Kimberley Rew; Alex Cooper; Vince de La Cruz.

KATZ, Mickey, & His Orch. P&R '50

Singles: 78 rpm

CAPITOL 4-8 51-57

Singles: 7-inch

CAPITOL 5-12 51-62

EPs: 7-inch

CAPITOL 10-20 53-56

LPs: 10/12-inch

CAPITOL (Except SM-298) 15-35 53-65
CAPITOL (SM-298 "Mickey Katz") 5-8 78
Also see JONES, Spike

KAUKONEN, Jorma LP '81

(With Vital Parts)

Singles: 7-inch

GRUNT 3-5 73

LPs: 10/12-inch

GRUNT 8-12 73
RCA 5-10 79-81

RELIX (2027 "Quah")........................10-20 87
(Picture disc.)
Also see HOT TUNA
Also see JEFFERSON AIRPLANE

KAY, John P&R/LP '72
(With Steppenwolf; with Sparrows)
Singles: 7-inch
DUNHILL..............................3-5 72-73
MERCURY..............................3-5 78
LPs: 10/12-inch
COLUMBIA..............................10-20 69
DUNHILL..............................8-10 72-73
MERCURY..............................5-8 78
QWIL..............................5-8 87
Also see STEPPENWOLF

KAY GEES: see KAY-GEES

KAYAK LP '76
Singles: 7-inch
JANUS..............................3-5 78
MERCURY..............................3-4 80
LPs: 10/12-inch
HARVEST..............................8-10 74
JANUS..............................5-10 75-79
MERCURY..............................5-8 80
Also see WERNER, Max

KAYE, Danny P&R '47
(Danny Kaye & Co.)
Singles: 78 rpm
COLUMBIA..............................4-8 49-54
DECCA..............................4-8 50-56
RCA..............................4-8 47-48
Singles: 7-inch
COLUMBIA..............................3-10 49-70
DECCA..............................5-10 50-56
REPRISE..............................5-10 62
Picture Sleeves
DECCA (151 "Little White Duck")......10-15 50s
REPRISE (20105 "D-o-d-g-e-r-s
Song")..............................8-12 62
EPs: 7-inch
CAPITOL..............................5-10 58
COLUMBIA..............................10-20 49-54
DECCA..............................8-15 54-57
LPs: 10/12-inch
CAMDEN..............................15-25 57
CAPITOL..............................15-25 58
COLUMBIA (6000 series)..............25-50 49-54
(10-inch LPs.)
DECCA (100 series)..............................10-20 63
DECCA (5000 series)..............................20-40 54
(10-inch LPs.)
DECCA (8000 series)..............................20-40 54-59
DECCA (78000 series)..............................10-15 67
GOLDEN..............................5-10 62
HARMONY (7000 series)..............................15-25 57
HARMONY (7300 series)..............................8-15 64

KAYE, Danny, & Louis Armstrong
Singles: 7-inch
DOT..............................4-8 59-64
Picture Sleeves
DOT..............................5-10 59
Also see ARMSTRONG, Louis

KAYE, Danny, Jimmy Durante, Jane Wyman & Groucho Marx P&R '51
Singles: 78 rpm
DECCA..............................3-8 51
Singles: 7-inch
DECCA..............................5-10 51
Also see DURANTE, Jimmy
Also see KAYE, Danny
Also see MARX, Groucho

KAYE, Mary P&R '52
(Mary Kaye Trio)
Singles: 78 rpm
CAPITOL..............................3-6 52
DECCA..............................3-6 55-56
RCA..............................3-6 54
Singles: 7-inch
BLUE-J..............................4-8
CAMELOT..............................4-6 67
CAPITOL..............................5-10 52
DECCA..............................5-10 55-56
LECTRON..............................4-6 65
RCA..............................5-10 54
VERVE..............................4-8 60
W.B...............................4-8 59
EPs: 7-inch
DECCA..............................5-10 56
LPs: 10/12-inch
COLUMBIA..............................8-15 62
DECCA..............................10-25 56
MOVIETONE..............................8-12 67
20TH FOX..............................8-15 64
VERVE..............................10-15 60-62
W.B...............................10-20 59
Also see BYRNES, Edd "Kookie," with Joanie Sommers & Mary Kaye Trio

KAYE, Sammy, & His Orch. P&R '37
Singles: 78 rpm
COLUMBIA..............................3-6 50-57
RCA..............................3-6 52-53
Singles: 7-inch
COLUMBIA..............................5-10 50-60
DECCA..............................4-6 60-70
PROJECT 3..............................3-5 72
RCA..............................5-10 52-53
EPs: 7-inch
COLUMBIA..............................5-15 50-60
DECCA..............................4-6 64
RCA..............................5-15 52-53
LPs: 10/12-inch
CAMDEN..............................10-25 53-56
COLUMBIA..............................10-25 50-62
DECCA..............................8-15 60-70
HARMONY..............................5-10 59-68
MCA..............................5-10 74
PROJECT 3..............................5-8 72
RCA..............................5-10 68-72
VOCALION..............................5-10 71
Also see CORNELL, Don

KAY-GEES R&B '74
Singles: 7-inch
DE-LITE..............................3-5 78-79
GANG..............................3-5 74-76
LPs: 10/12-inch
DELITE..............................5-8 78-79
GANG..............................5-10 75

KAYLI, Bob P&R '58
(With the Berry Gordy Orchestra; Robert Gordy)
Singles: 7-inch
ANNA (1104 "Never More")..............25-35 59
CARLTON (482 "Everyone Was
There")..............................20-30 58
GORDY (7004 "Toodle Loo"/"Hold On
Pearl")..............................30-50 62
GORDY (7008 "Toodle Loo"/"Hold On
Pearl")..............................20-30 62
TAMLA (54051 "Small Sad Sam")......20-30 61

K-DOE: see K-DOE, Ernie

K-DOE, Ernie P&R/R&B '61
(Ernest Kador; Ernie Kado; K-Doe)
Singles: 78 rpm
SPECIALTY (563 "Eternity")..............10-20 55
Singles: 7-inch
DUKE..............................5-10 64-69
EMBER (1050 "My Love for You")......25-35 59
EMBER (1075 "My Love for You")......10-20 61
INSTANT..............................5-10 63-64
MINIT..............................10-20 59-63
SANSU (1016 "She Gave It All to
Me")..............................10-20
SPECIALTY (563 "Eternity")..............20-30 55
SYLA..............................4-8
LPs: 10/12-inch
JANUS..............................8-10 71
MINIT (0002 "Mother-in-Law")..............60-80 61
Also see SPELLMAN, Benny
Also see THOMAS, Irma / Ernie K-Doe / Showmen / Benny Spellman.

K-DOE, Ernie / Phil Phillips
Singles: 7-inch
RIPETE..............................3-4
Also see K-DOE, Ernie
Also see PHILLIPS, Phil

KEANE BROTHERS P&R '76
Singles: 12-inch
ABC..............................4-8 79
Singles: 7-inch
ABC..............................3-5 79
20TH FOX..............................3-4 76
LPs: 10/12-inch
ABC...............................5-8 79

KEEL LP '85
Singles: 7-inch
GOLD MOUNTAIN..............................3-4 84-85
LPs: 10/12-inch
GOLD MOUNTAIN..............................5-8 85
MCA..............................5-8 86-87

KEENE, Tommy LP '86
Singles: 7-inch
GEFFEN..............................3-4 86
LPs: 10/12-inch
GEFFEN..............................5-8 86

KEITH P&R '66
(James Keefer)
Singles: 7-inch
DISCREET..............................3-5 71-74
MERCURY..............................4-8 66-68
RCA..............................4-6 69
Picture Sleeves
MERCURY..............................4-8 66-68
LPs: 10/12-inch
MERCURY..............................15-20 67
RCA..............................15-25 69
Also see TOKENS

KELLEM, Manny, & Orch. P&R/LP '68
Singles: 7-inch
EPIC..............................4-6 68
METROMEDIA..............................4-6 69
LPs: 10/12-inch
EPIC..............................5-10 68

KELLER, Jerry P&R '59
Singles: 7-inch
CAPITOL..............................5-10 61
CORAL..............................5-10 63-64
JUBILEE..............................5-10 58
KAPP (K-277 "Here Comes
Summer")..............................8-12 59
(Monaural.)
KAPP (KS-277 "Here Comes
Summer")..............................20-30 59
(Stereo.)
KAPP (310 thru 353)..............................5-10 59-60
RCA..............................5-10 67
REPRISE..............................5-10 65
WEB..............................5-10 58
Picture Sleeves
KAPP (277 "Here Comes
Summer")..............................10-15 59
KAPP (295 "If I Had a Girl")..............10-15 59
LPs: 10/12-inch
KAPP (1178 "Here Comes Jerry
Keller")..............................20-30 59
(Monaural.)
KAPP (3178 "Here Comes Jerry
Keller")..............................25-35 59
(Stereo.)

KELLUM, Murry P&R '63
Singles: 7-inch
CINNAMON..............................3-5 74
EPIC..............................3-5 71-72
MUSIC MILL..............................3-5 76
PLANTATION..............................3-5 78
RANWOOD..............................3-5 76
LPs: 10/12-inch
PLANTATION..............................5-8 78

KELLUM, Murry, & Alton Lott
Singles: 7-inch
K&M..............................3-5 61

KELLUM, Murry / Glenn Sutton

Singles: 7-inch

ABC ... 3-5 73
M.O.C. (Except 658) ... 10-15 63-64
M.O.C. (658 "I Dreamed I Was a Beatle") ... 15-20 64
Also see KELLUM, Murry
Also see SUTTON, Glenn

KELLY, Casey P&R '72

Singles: 7-inch

ELEKTRA ... 3-5 72-73
PRIVATE STOCK ... 3-5 77

LPs: 10/12-inch

ELEKTRA ... 8-10 72

KELLY, Grace: see CROSBY, Bing, & Grace Kelly

KELLY, Herman, & Life R&B '78

Singles: 7-inch

ALSTON ... 3-5 78

KELLY, J., & Premiers R&B '74
(J. Kely & Premiers)

Singles: 7-inch

ROADSHOW ... 3-5 74

KELLY, Monty, & His Orch. P&R '53

Singles: 78 rpm

ESSEX ... 3-5 53-54

Singles: 7-inch

CARLTON ... 4-8 59-60
ESSEX ... 5-10 53-54

LPs: 10/12-inch

ALSHIRE ... 4-8 72
CARLTON ... 10-20 59

KELLY, Paul P&R/R&B '70

Singles: 7-inch

DIAL ... 5-10 65-68
HAPPY TIGER ... 3-6 70
PHILIPS ... 10-20 66-68
TK ... 10-20 60
W.B. ... 3-6 73-76

Picture Sleeves

PHILIPS ... 10-20 66

LPs: 10/12-inch

HAPPY TIGER ... 8-10 70
W.B. ... 8-10 72-76
Also see TEX, Joe
Also see VALADIERS

KELLY BROTHERS R&B '66

Singles: 7-inch

EXCELLO (2286 "You Put Your Touch on Me") ... 8-12 67
EXCELLO (2290 "That's What You Mean to Me") ... 8-12 67
EXCELLO (2295 "Haven't I Been Good to You") ... 8-12 68
EXCELLO (2300 "It Takes Two") ... 8-12 68
EXCELLO (2308 "My Baby Loves Me") ... 8-12 69
FEDERAL (12373 "I've Been Striving for So Long") ... 25-50 60
FEDERAL (12404 "He's All Right") ... 25-50 60
SIMS (210 "Counting on You") ... 10-20 65
SIMS (239 "Got the Feeling") ... 10-20 65
SIMS (247 "Love Time") ... 10-20 65
SIMS (265 "Falling in Love Again") ... 10-20 66
SIMS (281 "Make Me Glad") ... 10-20 66
SIMS (287 "My Love Grows Stronger") ... 10-20 66
SIMS (293 "Can't Stand It No Longer") ... 10-20 66
SIMS (310 "If That Will Hold You") ... 10-20 66
SIMS (313 "Ouch! Oh Baby") ... 10-20 67
SIMS (317 "You Put Your Touch on Me") ... 10-20 67
(First issue.)

LPs: 10/12-inch

EXCELLO (8007 "Sweet Soul") ... 15-25 68
Members: Andrew Kelly; Robert Kelly; Curtis Kelly. Session: Charles Lee; Offe Reese.
Also see KING PINS

KELSEY, Rev. R&B '48
(Rev. Kelsey's Congregation)

Singles: 78 rpm

SUPER DISC ... 8-12 48

KEMP, Johnny R&B '86

Singles: 7-inch

COLUMBIA ... 3-4 86-89

Picture Sleeves

COLUMBIA ... 3-4 86-89

LPs: 10/12-inch

COLUMBIA ... 5-8 86-89

KEMP, Tara LP '91

LPs: 10/12-inch

GIANT ... 5-8 91

KENDALL SISTERS P&R/R&B '58

Singles: 7-inch

ARGO ... 5-10 57-58
CHECKER ... 5-10 58

KENDALLS C&W '70
(Featuring Jeannie Kendall)

Singles: 7-inch

DOT ... 3-5 72-73
EPIC ... 3-4 89
MCA/CURB ... 3-4 86
MERCURY ... 3-4 81-85
OVATION ... 3-5 77-80
STEP ONE ... 3-4 87-88
STOP ... 3-6 70
U.A. ... 3-5 75-76
VARSITY ... 10-15 69

LPs: 10/12-inch

DOT ... 8-12 72
GUSTO ... 5-8 78
MCA/CURB ... 5-8 86
MERCURY ... 5-8 81-85
OVATION ... 5-10 76-80
STOP ... 10-15 70
PICKWICK ... 5-8 79
POWER PAK ... 5-8 74
Members: Jeannie Kendall; Royce Kendall.
Also see HARRIS, Emmylou

KENDRICK, Nat, & Swans P&R/R&B '60

Singles: 7-inch

DADE (1000 series) ... 5-10 59-60
DADE (5000 series) ... 4-8 63
Members: Nat Kendrick; J.C. Adams; Bobby Roach; Fats Gonder; Bernard Odum.
Also see WESLEY, Fred, & J.B.s

KENDRICKS, Eddie P&R/R&B/LP '71
(Eddie Kendrick)

Singles: 7-inch

ARISTA ... 3-5 78-80
ATLANTIC ... 3-4 80-81
CORNER STREET ... 3-4 84
MOTOWN ... 3-5 76
RCA ... 3-4 85-88
TAMLA ... 3-5 71-77

LPs: 10/12-inch

ARISTA ... 5-8 78
ATLANTIC ... 5-8 81
MOTOWN ... 5-8 75-82
MS. DIXIE ... 5-8 83
TAMLA ... 8-10 71-78
Also see HALL, Daryl, John Oates, David Ruffin & Eddie Kendrick
Also see RUFFIN, David, & Eddie Kendricks
Also see TEMPTATIONS

KENDRICKS, Linda D&D '84

Singles: 12-inch

AIRWAVE ... 4-6 84

Singles: 7-inch

AIRWAVE ... 3-4 84

KENNEDY, John Fitzgerald LP '63

LPs: 10/12-inch

CAEDMON ... 5-10 64
CHALLENGE ... 8-15 64
COLPIX ... 10-20 64
COLUMBIA ... 10-20 65
DECCA ... 10-20 63
DIPLOMAT ... 5-15 63
DOCUMENTARIES ... 10-20 63
GATEWAY ... 8-15 64
HARMONIA ... 8-15 64
LEGACY ... 10-20 65
PALACE ... 8-15 64
PHILIPS ... 8-15 64
PICKWICK ... 8-12 63
PREMIER ... 10-20 63
RCA ... 8-15 64
REGINA ... 5-15 64
SOMERSET ... 5-15 63
20TH FOX ... 10-20 63
Most of the albums listed above are a tribute of some type to President Kennedy after his assassination on November 22, 1963. Most contain excerpts of his speeches.

KENNEDY, John Fitzgerald / Richard M. Nixon

LPs: 10/12-inch

COLUMBIA ... 10-15 68
Also see KENNEDY, John Fitzgerald

KENNEDY, Joyce R&B/LP '84

Singles: 7-inch

A&M ... 3-4 84-85
BLUE ROCK (4016 "I'm a Good Girl") ... 20-25 65
BLUE ROCK (4023 "Hi-Fi, Albums and I") ... 15-20 65
FONTANA (1924 "Could This Be Love") ... 10-15 64
RAN DEE (110 "I Still Love You") ... 10-20 63
RAN DEE (118 "How Old Is Old") ... 10-20 63

LPs: 10/12-inch

A&M ... 5-8 84
Also see MOTHER'S FINEST

KENNEDY, Joyce, & Jeffrey Osborne R&B '84

Singles: 7-inch

A&M ... 3-4 84
Also see KENNEDY, Joyce
Also see OSBORNE, Jeffrey

KENNEDY, Mike P&R '72

Singles: 7-inch

ABC ... 3-5 72

LPs: 10/12-inch

ABC ... 8-10 72
Also see LOS BRAVOS

KENNEDY, Ray P&R '80

Singles: 7-inch

ARC ... 3-5 80

Picture Sleeves

ARC ... 3-5 80

LPs: 10/12-inch

CREAM ... 10-12 72
Also see KGB

KENNEDY, Robert Francis LP '69

LPs: 10/12-inch

COLUMBIA ... 8-15 68

KENNER, Chris R&B '57

Singles: 78 rpm

BATON ... 10-20 55
IMPERIAL ... 10-20 57

Singles: 7-inch

BATON (220 "Don't Let Her Pin That Charge") ... 30-40 55
IMPERIAL ... 20-30 57-58
INSTANT ... 8-15 61-64
PRIGAN ... 10-20 61
RON ... 10-15 61
UPTOWN ... 5-10 65
VALIANT (3229 "I Like It Like That") ... 25-50 61

LPs: 10/12-inch

ATLANTIC (8117 "Land of 1,000 Dances") ... 20-30 66

KENNY & CADETS

Singles: 7-inch

RANDY (422 "Barbie") ... 400-600 62
(Black vinyl.)

RANDY (422 "Barbie")................750-1000 62
(Colored vinyl.)
Members: Brian Wilson; Carl Wilson; Al Jardine; Audree Wilson.
Also see BEACH BOYS

KENNY & JOHNNY R&B '86

Singles: 7-inch

PHILADELPHIA INT'L.........................3-4 86
Members: Kenny Whitehead; Johnny Whitehead.
Also see WHITEHEAD, Kenny & Johnny

KENNY G. R&B/LP '84

(With G Force; Kenny Gorelick)

Singles: 7-inch

ARISTA...3-4 83-89

Picture Sleeves

ARISTA...3-4 87-89

LPs: 10/12-inch

ARISTA...5-10 83-89
Also see LORBER, Jeff
Also see LOVE UNLIMITED

KENNY G. & KASHIF

Singles: 7-inch

ARISTA...3-4 85
Also see KASHIF

KENNY G. & SMOKEY ROBINSON

Singles: 7-inch

ARISTA...3-4 89
Also see ROBINSON, Smokey

KENNY G. & LENNY WILLIAMS

Singles: 7-inch

ARISTA...3-4 83-86
Also see KENNY G.
Also see WILLIAMS, Lenny

KENT, Al P&R/R&B '67

Singles: 78 rpm

CHECKER (881 "Dat's Why")..........25-50 57

Singles: 7-inch

BARITONE (942 "Hold Me")..........50-100 60
CHECKER (881 "Dat's Why")..........25-50 57
RIC-TIC (127 "You've Got to Pay the Price")..........10-20 67
RIC-TIC (133 "Ooh! Pretty Lady").....10-20 68
WINGATE (4 "You Know I Love You")..........15-25 65
WIZARD (100 "Hold Me")..............75-100 59
Also see FLAMING EMBERS / Al Kent

KENTON, Stan, & His Orch. P&R '44

Singles: 78 rpm

CAPITOL...3-6 45-57

Singles: 7-inch

CAPITOL (Purple label)......................5-15 50-61
CAPITOL (Orange & Yellow label)........4-6 61-68
CAPITOL STARLINE..........................3-5 60s

Picture Sleeves

CAPITOL ("Stan Kenton Prologue: This Is an Orchestra")..........10-20 50s
(Number not known.)

EPs: 7-inch

CAPITOL...5-15 50-59

LPs: 10/12-inch

BRIGHT ORANGE...............................5-8 73
CAPITOL (H-155 "Encores")............50-75 49
(10-inch LP.)
CAPITOL (T-155 "Encores")............25-50 55
CAPITOL (H-167 "Artistry in Rhythm")..........50-75 49
(10-inch LP.)
CAPITOL (T-167 "Artistry in Rhythm")..........25-50 55
(With "T" prefix.)
CAPITOL (DT-167 "Artistry in Rhythm")..........5-10 69
(Stereo.)
CAPITOL (SM-167 "Artistry in Rhythm")..........5-8 75
CAPITOL (H-172 "Progressive Jazz")..........50-75 50
(10-inch LP.)
CAPITOL (T-172 "Progressive Jazz")..........25-50 55
CAPITOL (H-190 "Milestones").........50-75 50
(10-inch LP.)
CAPITOL (T-190 "Milestones")........25-50 55
CAPITOL (H-248 "Stan Kenton Presents")..........50-75 50
(10-inch LP.)
CAPITOL (T-248 "Stan Kenton Presents")..........25-50 55
CAPITOL (H-353 "City of Glass").....50-75 52
(10-inch LP.)
CAPITOL (T-353 "City of Glass")......25-50 55
CAPITOL (H-358 "Classics")...........50-75 52
(10-inch LP.)
CAPITOL (T-358 "Classics")............25-50 55
CAPITOL (H-386 "This Is an Orchestra")..........50-75 53
(10-inch LP.)
CAPITOL (T-421 "Popular Favorites By Stan Kenton")..........25-50 54
CAPITOL (H-462 "Standards").........50-75 53
(10-inch LP.)
CAPITOL (T-462 "Standards")..........25-50 55
CAPITOL (H-525 "Showcase")..........50-75 54
(10-inch LP.)
CAPITOL (W-525 "Showcase")..........25-75 55
CAPITOL (H-526 "Showcase")..........50-75 54
(10-inch LP.)
CAPITOL (W-526 "Showcase")..........25-50 55
CAPITOL (305 "Hair")........................5-10 69
CAPITOL (600 thru 1200 series).....15-25 56-59
CAPITOL (1300 thru 2900 series)....10-20 60-68
CAPITOL (11000 & 12000 series)........5-8 72-80
CAPITOL (16000 series)......................4-6 81
CREATIVE WORLD..............................5-8 71-80
HINDSIGHT...4-8 84
LONDON...5-8 72-77
MARK '56..5-8 77
MFSL (091 "Stan Kenton Plays Wagner")..........15-25 82
Also see CHRISTY, June, & Stan Kenton
Also see COLE, Nat "King"
Also see FERGUSON, Maynard

KENTON, Stan, & Tex Ritter

LPs: 10/12-inch

CAPITOL (T-1757 "Stan Kenton & Tex Ritter")..........40-60 62
(Monaural.)
CAPITOL (ST-1757 "Stan Kenton & Tex Ritter")..........50-75 62
(Stereo.)
Also see KENTON, Stan
Also see RITTER, Tex

KENTUCKY HEADHUNTERS

C&W/LP '89

Singles: 7-inch

MERCURY..3-4 89-91

LPs: 10/12-inch

MERCURY..5-8 89-91
Members: Fred Young; Richard Young; Greg Martin; Ricky Lee Phelps; Doug Phelps; Mark Orr; Anthony Kenny.

KERMIT P&R '79

(Jim Henson)

Singles: 7-inch

ATLANTIC..3-5 79

KERMIT / Fozzie Bear

(Jim Henson)

Singles: 7-inch

ATLANTIC..3-5 80
Also see KERMIT
Also see HENSON, Jim

KERR, Anita LP '69

(Anita Kerr Singers; Quartette)

Singles: 78 rpm

DECCA..3-6 51-57

Singles: 7-inch

AMPEX..3-5 71
DECCA (27000 thru 30000 series).....5-10 51-60
DECCA (31000 thru 33000 series).......3-6 60-72
DOT..3-5 69-70
RCA..3-8 63-75
W.B. 3-6 66-68

Picture Sleeves

DECCA..4-8

EPs: 7-inch

SESAC..10-15 59
(Also has tracks by Buddy Hacket, Elliot Lawrence, and Bill Snyder.)

LPs: 10/12-inch

AMPEX..5-8 71
BAINBRIDGE.......................................4-6 81
CAMDEN..5-10 68
CENTURY..4-8 79
DECCA..8-15 60-69
DOT..5-10 69-70
RCA..8-15 62-77
VOCALION...5-10 70
W.B. 8-12 66
WORD...4-8 75-77
Also see ANDERSON, Bill
Also see ANITA & So-And-So's
Also see ANN-MARGRET
Also see ATKINS, Chet
Also see ATKINS, Chet, Faron Young, & Anita Kerr Singers
Also see BARE, Bobby
Also see CHARLES, Tommy
Also see CLINE, Patsy
Also see CRAMER, Floyd
Also see FOLEY, Red
Also see FOWLER, Wally
Also see HELMS, Bobby
Also see IVES, Burl
Also see LEE, Brenda
Also see LITTLE DIPPERS
Also see MULLICAN, Moon
Also see NELSON, Willie
Also see PRESLEY, Elvis
Also see REEVES, Jim
Also see RICH, Charlie
Also see SNOW, Hank
Also see WILBURN BROTHERS
Also see YOUNG, Faron

KERR, George R&B '70

Singles: 7-inch

ALL PLATINUM....................................3-5 70

KERSHAW, Nik P&R/LP '84

Singles: 7-inch

MCA..3-4 84-85

Picture Sleeves

MCA..3-5 84

LPs: 10/12-inch

MCA..5-8 84-85

KEYES, Troy P&R/R&B '68

Singles: 7-inch

ABC (11027 "Love Explosion")............4-8 67
ABC (11060 "No Sad Songs")............8-12 68
CHUMLEY..3-5 74
Also see HIGH KEYES

KEYES, Troy, & Norma Jenkins

Singles: 7-inch

ABC (11116 "A Good Love Gone Bad")..........10-20 68
Also see JENKINS, Norma
Also see KEYES, Troy

KHAN, Chaka P&R/R&B/LP '78

Singles: 12-inch

W.B. 4-6 79-87

Singles: 7-inch

ATLANTIC..3-4 78-87
MCA..3-4 80-86
W.B. 3-5 78-88

Picture Sleeves

MCA..3-4 85
W.B. 3-5 78-86

LPs: 10/12-inch

ELEKTRA...5-10 70s
W.B. 5-8 78-88
Also see BOWIE, David
Also see GRANDMASTER FLASH & Furious Five
Also see JONES, Quincy, with Ray Charles & Chaka Khan
Also see RUFUS
Also see WONDER, Stevie

KHAN, Steve LP '78

Singles: 7-inch

TAPPAN ZEE.......................................3-5 78

LPs: 10/12-inch

COLUMBIA....5-8 79
NOVAS....5-8 80
TAPPAN ZEE....5-8 78
Also see JOEL, Billy

KHEMISTRY R&B '82

Singles: 7-inch

COLUMBIA....3-4 82

LPs: 10/12-inch

COLUMBIA....5-8 82

KIARA R&B '85

Singles: 7-inch

ARISTA....3-4 87
WARLOCK....3-4 85

Picture Sleeves

ARISTA....3-4 87

LPs: 10/12-inch

ARISTA....5-8 88

KIARA & SHANICE WILSON P&R '89

Singles: 7-inch

ARISTA....3-4 89

Picture Sleeves

ARISTA....3-4 89
Also see KIARA
Also see WILSON, Shanice

KICK AXE LP '84

LPs: 10/12-inch

PASHA....5-8 84

KID, Joey P&R '90

Singles: 7-inch

ATLANTIC....3-4 90
BASSMENT....3-5 90

KID CREOLE & COCONUTS LP '81

Singles: 12-inch

ATLANTIC....4-6 84-85

Singles: 7-inch

ANTILLES....3-5 80
ATLANTIC....3-4 84-85
SIRE....3-4 81-82
ZE....3-4 81

LPs: 10/12-inch

ANTILLES....8-10 80
SIRE....5-8 81-82
Also see DR. BUZZARD'S ORIGINAL SAVANNAH BAND
Also see MANILOW, Barry / Kid Creole & Coconuts

KID FROST LP '90

LPs: 10/12-inch

VIRGIN....5-8 90

KID 'N' PLAY LP '88

LPs: 10/12-inch

SELECT....5-8 88-90

KID SENSATION LP '90

LPs: 10/12-inch

NASTYMIX....5-8 90

KIDDO R&B '83

Singles: 12-inch

A&M....4-6 83

Singles: 7-inch

A&M....3-4 83-84

LPs: 10/12-inch

A&M....5-8 83

KIDS at WORK R&B '84

Singles: 7-inch

CBS ASSOCIATED....3-4 84
Member: Teddy Riley.

KIDS FROM "FAME" LP '82

Singles: 7-inch

RCA....3-4 82-83

Picture Sleeves

RCA....3-4 82-83

LPs: 10/12-inch

RCA....5-8 82-83

KIDS NEXT DOOR P&R '65

Singles: 7-inch

DECCA....4-8 67
4 CORNERS of the WORLD....4-8 65

Picture Sleeves

4 CORNERS of the WORLD....5-10 65

KIHN, Greg, Band LP '78
(Greg Kihn)

Singles: 12-inch

BESERKLEY....4-8 78-83

Singles: 7-inch

BESERKLEY....3-5 78-83
EMI AMERICA....3-4 85-86

Picture Sleeves

BESERKLEY....3-4 81-82
EMI AMERICA....3-4 85-86

LPs: 10/12-inch

BESERKLEY....8-10 76-84
EMI AMERICA....5-8 85-86

KIHN, Greg, Band / Earthquake / Modern Lovers / Rubinoos

EPs: 7-inch

BESERKLEY (1120 "Great Ideas")....5-8 77
Also see MODERN LOVERS

KIHN, Greg, Band / Earthquake / Rubinoos / Jonathan Richman

LPs: 10/12-inch

BESERKLEY (0044 "Beserkley Chartbusters, Vol. 1")....8-12 77
(Promotional issue only.)
Also see EARTHQUAKE
Also see KIHN, Greg, Band
Also see RUBINOOS

KILGORE, Theola P&R/R&B '63

Singles: 7-inch

CANDIX....10-20 60
KT....5-10 64
SEROCK....5-10 63

KILLER DWARFS LP '88

LPs: 10/12-inch

EPIC....5-8 88

KILLING JOKE LP '87

LPs: 10/12-inch

EDITIONS....5-8 81-82
VIRGIN....5-8 87

KILZER, John LP '88

LPs: 10/12-inch

GEFFEN....5-8 88

KIM, Andy P&R '68

Singles: 7-inch

ABC....3-5 74
CAPITOL....3-5 74-76
RED BIRD....4-8 65
STEED....3-6 68-71
TCF....4-8 64
20TH FOX....4-8 68
UNI....3-5 72-73
U.A.....4-8 63

Picture Sleeves

CAPITOL....3-5 74
STEED....4-6 69-71

LPs: 10/12-inch

CAPITOL....8-12 74-75
DUNHILL....8-12 74
STEED....10-15 68-71
UNI....8-12 72-73
Also see ARCHIES

KIMBERLY, Adrian P&R '61
(Don Everly)

Singles: 7-inch

CALLIOPE (6501 "Pomp and Circumstance")....10-20 61
CALLIOPE (6503 "Greensleeves")....25-35 61
CALLIOPE (6504 "Draggin' Dragon")....25-35 61
Also see EVERLY, Don

KIMBERLYS P&R '71

Singles: 7-inch

CANADIAN AMERICAN....4-8 62-63
COLUMBIA....4-8 65-66
HAPPY TIGER....3-5 70-71
RCA....3-5 69

LPs: 10/12-inch

HAPPY TIGER....8-12 70
Also see JENNINGS, Waylon

KIMBLE, Neal R&B '68

Singles: 7-inch

TRC....4-6 71
VENTURE....4-8 68

KIME, Warren, & His Brass Impact Orchestra LP '67

LPs: 10/12-inch

COMMAND....5-10 67

KIMMEL, Tom P&R/LP '87

Singles: 7-inch

MERCURY....3-4 87

Picture Sleeves

MERCURY....3-4 87

LPs: 10/12-inch

MERCURY....5-8 87

KING P&R/D&D/LP '85

Singles: 12-inch

EPIC....4-6 85

Singles: 7-inch

EPIC....3-4 85

Picture Sleeves

EPIC....3-4 85

LPs: 10/12-inch

ELEKTRA....5-8 80-81
EPIC....5-8 85
Member: Paul King.

KING, Al R&B '66

Singles: 7-inch

KENT....4-8
MODERN....4-8 68
RONN....5-10
SAHARA....5-10 66
SHIRLEY....5-10 64

KING, Albert R&B '61

Singles: 78 rpm

PARROT (798 "Bad Luck Blues")....25-50 53

Singles: 7-inch

BOBBIN....5-10 59-62
COUN-TREE....8-12 65
KING....8-12 61-63
PARROT (798 "Bad Luck Blues") 100-200 53
STAX....3-8 66-74
TOMATO....3-6 78-79
UTOPIA....3-6 76-77

LPs: 10/12-inch

ATLANTIC....8-12 69-82
FANTASY....5-8
KING (852 "Big Blues")....50-75 63
KING (1000 series)....10-12 69
STAX (Except 723 & 2000 series)....8-12 72-81
STAX (723 "Born Under a Bad Sign")....15-25 67
STAX (2000 series)....10-15 68-71
STAX (8000 series)....5-10 90
TOMATO....8-12 77-79
UTOPIA....10-15 76-77
Also see LITTLE MILTON & Albert King
Also see STAPLES, Roebuck

KING, Albert, & Otis Rush

LPs: 10/12-inch

CHESS....10-15 69
Also see KING, Albert
Also see RUSH, Otis

KING, Anna P&R/R&B '64

Singles: 7-inch

END (1126 "Mama's Got a Bag of Her Own")....15-25 63
LUDIX (103 "Big Change")....20-30 63
MALIBU (1020 "In Between Tears")..10-20 61
RUST....8-12 64
SMASH....5-10 63-65

LPs: 10/12-inch

SMASH (27059 "Back to Soul")....15-20 64
(Monaural.)
SMASH (67059 "Back to Soul")....20-25 64
(Stereo.)

KING, Anna, & Bobby Byrd *P&R '64*

Singles: 7-inch

SMASH....4-8 64
Also see BYRD, Bobby
Also see KING, Anna

KING, B.B. *R&B '51*

Singles: 78 rpm

BULLET (309 "Miss Martha King")..50-100 49
BULLET (315 "Got the Blues")....50-100 49
RPM....10-20 50-57

Singles: 7-inch

ABC....3-8 66-78
ABC-PAR....4-8 62-66
BLUESWAY....4-6 67-70
KENT (300 series)....5-10 58-64
KENT (400 series)....4-8 64-68
KENT (4000 & 5000 series)....3-5
MCA....3-4 80-85
PAULA....3-4 81
RPM (339 "3 O'Clock Blues")....25-50 52
RPM (348 "Fine Looking Woman")...25-50 52
RPM (355 "Shake It Up and Go")....25-50 52
RPM (363 "You Didn't Want Me")....25-50 52
RPM (360 "Someday, Somewhere") 20-40 52
RPM (380 "Woke Up This Morning"). 20-40 53
RPM (374 "Story from My Heart and Soul")....20-40 53
RPM (386 "Please Love Me")....20-40 53
RPM (391 "Neighbourhood Affair")....20-40 53
RPM (395 "Why Did You Love Me") .20-40 53
RPM (403 thru 501)....10-20 54-57

Picture Sleeves

BLUESWAY....4-6 69
MCA....3-4 85

EPs: 7-inch

ABC-PAR....8-10 63
(Juke box issue only.)
RPM (459 "Disc Jockey Special EP - Dark Is the Night")....75-125 56
(Not issued with cover. Promotional issue only.)

LPs: 10/12-inch

ABC....8-10 70-78
ABC-PAR....15-25 63-65
ACCORD....5-8 82
BLUESWAY....10-20 67-73
COMMAND....10-12 74
CROWN (Except 147)....15-25 59-63
CROWN (147 "B.B. King Wails")....15-25 60
(Black vinyl.)
CROWN (147 "B.B. King Wails")....75-125 60
(Colored vinyl.)
CRUSADERS....5-8 82
CUSTOM....8-10
FANTASY....5-8 81
GALAXY....15-20 63
KENT....10-15 64-73
("B.B. King Live")....250-500
(Picture disc. No label name or selection number used. Promotional issue only.)
MCA....5-8 79-85
MFSL (235 "Lucille")....20-25 94
PICKWICK....5-10
UNITED....10-12
Also see BASIE, Count
Also see BLAND, Bobby, & B.B. King
Also see CRUSADERS, & B.B. King
Also see KING, Carole
Also see SIMPSONS
Also see U2 & B.B. King

KING, B.B., Jr., & Blues Messengers

Singles: 7-inch

L. BROWN (101 "I'm So Glad It's All Over")....10-15 64

KING, Ben E. *P&R '60*

Singles: 7-inch

ATLANTIC (Except 89361)....3-5 75-81
ATLANTIC (89361 "Stand By Me Medley")....4-8 86
(Promotional issue only. Has excerpts of nine songs from the film soundtrack, by: Ben E. King, Buddy Holly, Shirley & Lee, Bobbettes, Chordettes, Del Vikings, Coasters, Silhouettes, and Jerry Lee Lewis.)
ATCO (Except 6100 & 6200 series)....4-6 64-69
ATCO (6100 & 6200 series)....4-8 60-64
ELEKTRA....3-5 76
MANDALA....3-5 72-73
MAXWELL....3-6 69

Picture Sleeves

ATLANTIC....3-5 86

LPs: 10/12-inch

ATCO (133 "Spanish Harlem")....20-30 61
(Monaural.)
ATCO (SD-133 "Spanish Harlem")...30-40 61
(Monaural.)
ATCO (137 "For Soulful Lovers")....20-30 62
(Monaural.)
ATCO (SD-137 "For Soulful Lovers")....25-35 62
(Stereo.)
ATCO (142 "Don't Play That Song") 20-30 62
(Monaural.)
ATCO (SD-142 "Don't Play That Song")....25-35 62
(Stereo.)
ATCO (165 "Greatest Hits")....20-30 64
(Monaural.)
ATCO (SD-165 "Greatest Hits")....25-35 64
(Stereo.)
ATCO (174 "Seven Letters")....20-30 65
(Monaural.)
ATCO (SD-174 "Seven Letters")....25-35 65
(Stereo.)
ATLANTIC....8-12 75-81
KING (3008 "Audio Biography")....10-15
MANDALA....8-12 72
MAXWELL....10-15 70
Also see BAKER, Lavern, & Ben E. King
Also see BOBBETTES
Also see BONDS, Gary "U.S."
Also see CHORDETTES
Also see COASTERS
Also see DEL-VIKINGS
Also see DRIFTERS
Also see EARL-JEAN
Also see HALOS
Also see HOLLY, Buddy
Also see LEWIS, Jerry Lee
Also see LITTLE EVA
Also see SHIRLEY & LEE
Also see SILHOUETTES
Also see SOUL CLAN

KING, Ben E., & Average White Band *R&B/LP '77*

Singles: 7-inch

ATLANTIC....3-5 77

LPs: 10/12-inch

ATLANTIC....8-10 77
Also see AVERAGE WHITE BAND

KING, Ben E., & Dee Dee Sharp

Singles: 7-inch

ATCO....4-8 68
Also see KING, Ben E.
Also see SHARP, Dee Dee

KING, Bobby *R&B '84*
(Featuring Alfie Silas)

Singles: 7-inch

MOTOWN....3-4 84
RODEO....10-15
Also see SILAS, Alfie

KING, Carole *P&R '62*

Singles: 7-inch

ABC....3-5 74
ABC-PAR (9921 "Goin' Wild")....30-40 58
ABC-PAR (9986 "Baby Sittin' ")....30-40 59
ALPINE (57 "Oh, Neil")....50-75 60
ATLANTIC....3-5 82-83
AVATAR....3-5 77-78
CAPITOL....3-5 77-80
COMPANION (2000 "It Might As Well Rain Until September")....40-60 62
DIMENSION (1009 "He's a Bad Boy")....10-20 63
DIMENSION (1004 "School Bells Are Ringing")....10-20 63
DIMENSION (2000 "It Might As Well Rain Until September")....5-10 62
ODE (Except 66112)....3-5 71-76
ODE (66112 "Pierre")....5-10 75
(Compact 33.)
RCA (7560 "Short Mort")....35-45 59
TOMORROW (7502 "A Road to Nowhere")....10-15 66

Picture Sleeves

ATLANTIC....3-5 82
AVATAR....3-5 77
CAPITOL....3-5 77-80
ODE....3-5 71-75

LPs: 10/12-inch

ATLANTIC....5-8 82-83
AVATAR....8-12 78
CAPITOL (Except 11000 series)....5-8 80
CAPITOL (11000 series)....8-10 77-79
EPIC/ODE (30000 series)....5-8 78-80
EPIC/ODE (40000 series)....12-15 80
(Half-speed mastered.)
ODE....10-12 70-78
Also see COOKIES / Little Eva / Carole King
Also see KING, B.B.
Also see SHIRELLES

KING, Claude *C&W/P&R '61*

Singles: 7-inch

CINNAMON....3-5 74
COLUMBIA....3-8 61-71
DEE JAY (1248 "Run Baby, Run")....30-50 57
TRUE....3-5 77-80

Picture Sleeves

COLUMBIA....4-8 61-69

LPs: 10/12-inch

COLUMBIA....10-20 62-70
GUSTO....5-8 80
HARMONY....8-12 68
TRUE....8-10 77
Also see YOUNG, Faron / Carl Perkins / Claude King

KING, Clydie *R&B '71*
(With the Sweet Things)

Singles: 78 rpm

SPECIALTY....8-12 57

Singles: 7-inch

IMPERIAL....10-20 65-66
LIZARD....3-5 71
MINIT....5-10 67-69
PHILIPS....8-12 62-63
SPECIALTY....10-20 57

LPs: 10/12-inch

LIZARD....8-12 71
Also see BROWN SUGAR
Also see CARTER, Mel, & Clydie
Also see HOLIDAY, Jimmy, & Clydie King
Also see RAELETTS

KING, Earl *R&B '55*

Singles: 78 rpm

ACE....10-25 55-57
SPECIALTY....10-20 54-55

Singles: 7-inch

ACE (509 "Those Lonely, Lonely Nights")....40-60 55
ACE (514 "My Love Is Strong")....35-55 56
ACE (517 "It Must Have Been Love")....35-55 56
ACE (520 "Is Everything Alright")....35-55 56
ACE (529 "Those Lonely, Lonely Feelings")....25-50 57
ACE (543 "I'll Never Get Tired")....25-50 58
ACE (598 "Buddy It's Time to Go")....15-25 60
IMPERIAL (5713 "Come On")....15-25 60
IMPERIAL (5730 "Love Me Now")....15-25 61
IMPERIAL (5750 "Come Along with Me")....15-25 61
IMPERIAL (5774 "You Better Know")....10-15 61
IMPERIAL (5811 "Always a First Time")....10-15 62
IMPERIAL (5858 "We Are Just Friends")....10-15 62
IMPERIAL (5891 "Come Along with Me")....10-15 62
REX (1015 "I Can't Help Myself")....15-25 61
SPECIALTY (495 "I'm Your Best Bet, Baby")....50-75 54
SPECIALTY (531 "Eating and Sleeping")....50-75 54

SPECIALTY (558 "Funny Face")....... 50-75 55
Also see SMITH, Huey

KING, Earl, & Roomful of Blues

LPs: 10/12-inch

BLACK TOP (1035 "Glazed")............ 5-10 87
Also see KING, Earl

KING, Evelyn P&R/R&B/LP '78

(Evelyn "Champagne" King)

Singles: 12-inch

PRIVATE I........................ 4-6 85
RCA........................ 4-8 78-86

Singles: 7-inch

EMI........................ 3-4 90
EMI MANHATTAN........................ 3-4 88-86
RCA........................ 3-4 78-86

Picture Sleeves

RCA........................ 3-6 78-86

LPs: 10/12-inch

EMI........................ 5-8 90
EMI MANHATTAN........................ 5-8 88
RCA........................ 5-8 77-86

KING, Freddie P&R/R&B '61

(Freddy King)

Singles: 78 rpm

EL-BEE (157 "Country Boy")............ 20-30 56

Singles: 7-inch

COTILLION........................ 3-6 68-70
EL-BEE (157 "Country Boy")............ 50-75 56
FEDERAL........................ 10-20 60-65
GUSTO........................ 3-5 78
KING........................ 3-5 69

LPs: 10/12-inch

COTILLION........................ 10-15 69-70
GUSTO (5033 "Hide Away")............ 10-12 78
KING (762 "Freddy King Sings the Blues")........................ 30-40 61
KING (773 "Let's Hide Away and Dance Away")........................ 35-50 61
KING (821 "Bossa Nova & Blues").... 20-30 62
KING (856 "Freddy King Goes Surfin' ")........................ 20-30 63
KING (900 series)........................ 15-20 65-66
KING (1000 series)........................ 10-15 69
MCA........................ 5-8 80s
RSO........................ 8-10 74-77
SHELTER........................ 8-10 71-75
Also see ROGERS, Jimmy, and Freddie King

KING, Freddie, & Lulu Reed

Singles: 7-inch

FEDERAL (12477 "Say Hey, Pretty Baby")........................ 15-25 62

KING, Freddie / Lulu Reed / Sonny Thompson

LPs: 10/12-inch

KING (777 "Boy-Girl-Boy")............ 20-30 62
Also see KING, Freddie
Also see RUSSELL, Leon
Also see THOMPSON, Sonny

KING, Jewel R&B '50

(With Dave Bartholomew's Orchestra)

Singles: 78 rpm

IMPERIAL........................ 15-25 49
Also see BARTHOLOMEW, Dave

KING, Jonathan P&R '65

Singles: 7-inch

PARROT........................ 4-8 65-72
UK........................ 3-5 73-74
UK/BIG TREE........................ 3-5 75

LPs: 10/12-inch

PARROT (71013 "Jonathan King, Or Then Again")........................ 25-30 67
UK........................ 10-20 72-73
Also see HEDGEHOPPERS ANONYMOUS

KING, Kid R&B '53

(Kid King's Combo)

Singles: 78 rpm

EXCELLO........................ 8-15 53-57

Singles: 7-inch

EXCELLO........................ 10-20 53-60

KING, Marcel D&D '84

Singles: 12-inch

A&M........................ 4-6 84

Singles: 7-inch

A&M........................ 3-4 84

KING, Martin Luther: see KING, Rev. Martin Luther, Jr.

KING, Morgana LP '64

Singles: 78 rpm

MERCURY........................ 4-6 56

Singles: 7-inch

MAINSTREAM........................ 4-8 64
MERCURY........................ 5-10 56
PARAMOUNT........................ 3-5 73-74
REPRISE........................ 4-6 66-67
20TH FOX........................ 4-8 59
VERVE........................ 4-6 68
WING........................ 5-10 56

Picture Sleeves

PARAMOUNT........................ 3-5 73

LPs: 10/12-inch

ASCOT........................ 15-25 65-66
CAMDEN........................ 15-25 60
EMARCY (36079 "For You, for Me, Forever More")........................ 30-50 56
MAINSTREAM (300 series)............... 5-10 72
MAINSTREAM (6000 series)........... 15-25 64-65
MERCURY (20231 "Morganna King Sings the Blues")........................ 30-40 57
MUSE........................ 5-8 79-82
PARAMOUNT........................ 5-10 73
REPRISE........................ 15-25 65-67
TRIP........................ 5-8 74
U.A. (3028 "Folk Songs ala King").... 30-40 59
(Monaural.)
U.A. (3028 "Folk Songs ala King").... 40-50 59
(Stereo.)
U.A. (30020 "Let Me Love You")....... 30-40 60
VERVE........................ 10-15 68
WING........................ 10-20 65

KING, Pee Wee C&W/P&R '48

(With Redd Stewart; with His Golden West Cowboys)

Singles: 78 rpm

BLUEBIRD........................ 5-10 49
RCA........................ 4-8 50-55

Singles: 7-inch

BRIAR........................ 4-8 61
JARO........................ 5-10 60
CUCA........................ 5-10 64-68
LANDA........................ 4-8 61
RCA........................ 10-20 50-55
STARDAY........................ 4-6 64-71
TODD........................ 8-12 59

EPs: 7-inch

RCA (797 "Swing West")................ 15-30 56
RCA (3028 "Country Classics")........ 15-30 53
RCA (3071 "Western Hits")............ 15-30 53
RCA (3109 "Country Classics, Vol. 2")........................ 15-30 53
RCA (3280 "Swing West")............... 15-30 56

LPs: 10/12-inch

BRIAR (102 "Golden Olde-Tyme Dances")........................ 50-70 62
CAMDEN........................ 8-15 65-71
CUCA........................ 20-40 64
DETOUR........................ 5-10
LONGHORN........................ 5-10
RCA (1237 "Swing West")............... 40-60 56
RCA (2464 "Swing West")............... 5-8 77
RCA (3071 "Western Hits")............ 25-50 53
(10-inch LP.)
RCA (3109 "Country Classics")........ 50-75 53
(10-inch LP.)
STARDAY (200 series)................. 10-20 64
STARDAY (900 series)................. 8-10 75-76

KING, Peggy P&R '55

Singles: 78 rpm

COLUMBIA........................ 3-5 54-56
MGM........................ 3-5 52

Singles: 7-inch

BUENA VISTA........................ 4-8 62
BULLET........................ 3-5 71
COLUMBIA........................ 5-10 54-56
MGM........................ 5-10 52
ROULETTE........................ 4-8 61

Picture Sleeves

BUENA VISTA........................ 4-8 62

EPs: 7-inch

COLUMBIA........................ 8-12 55

LPs: 10/12-inch

COLUMBIA........................ 15-25 55
IMPERIAL........................ 10-20 59
Also see VALE, Jerry, Peggy King & Felicia Sanders

KING, Rev. Martin Luther, Jr.

(Rev. Martin Luther King) LP '63

Singles: 7-inch

DOOTO........................ 4-6 68
MERCURY........................ 4-6 68

EPs: 7-inch

GORDY (906 "Speech Excerpts")..... 15-25 63

LPs: 10/12-inch

AUDIO FIDELITY (343 "Martin Luther King")........................ 15-20 84
(Picture disc.)
BLACK FORUM........................ 5-10 70
BUDDAH........................ 8-15 69
CREED........................ 8-12 68-71
DOTTO........................ 8-15 62-68
EXCELLO........................ 8-15 68
GORDY (906 "The Great March")..... 25-50 63
GORDY (929 "Free at Last")........... 15-25 68
MERCURY........................ 8-15 68
MR. MAESTRO........................ 10-15 63
NASHBORO........................ 5-8 72
20TH FOX........................ 8-15 63-68
UNART........................ 8-12 68
These recordings contain speeches or excerpts of speeches by King.
Also see LANDS, Liz / Martin Luther King

KING, Saunders R&B '49

Singles: 78 rpm

ALADDIN........................ 10-20 49
FLAIR........................ 15-20 54
MODERN........................ 10-20 48
RHYTHM........................ 10-20 42-47

Singles: 7-inch

FLAIR (1035 "My Close Friend")....... 30-40 54
FLAIR (1045 "Quit Hangin' 'Round Me")........................ 30-40 54
GALAXY (712 "S.K. Blues")............ 10-20 62
RPM (341 "Lazy Woman")............... 25-35 51
RPM (375 "New S.K. Blues")........... 25-35 52
RPM (497 "S.K. Blues")................ 15-25 56

KING, Sleepy P&R '61

Singles: 7-inch

AWAKE........................ 10-15
JOY........................ 5-10 61

KING, Teddi P&R '56

Singles: 78 rpm

RCA........................ 3-5 56-57

Singles: 7-inch

CHAMPION........................ 5-10
RCA........................ 5-10 56-57

LPs: 10/12-inch

CORAL (57278 "All the King's Songs")........................ 40-60 59
(Monaural.)
CORAL (757278 "All the King's Songs")........................ 50-75 59
(Stereo.)
RCA (1147 "Bidin' My Time")........... 50-75 56
RCA (1313 "From Teddi King")......... 50-75 57
RCA (1454 "A Girl and Her Songs") . 50-75 57
STORYVILLE (302 "'Round Midnight")........................ 100-200 54
(10-inch LP.)
STORYVILLE (314 "Storyville Presents Teddi King")........................ 100-200 54
(10-inch LP.)
STORYVILLE (903 "Now in Vogue")........................ 75-125 56

KING, Will — R&B '85
(Willard King)

Singles: 7-inch

CAPITOL 3-5 73
TOTAL EXPERIENCE 3-4 85

KING BISCUIT BOY — LP '70
(With Crowbar)

Singles: 7-inch

EPIC 3-5 75
PARAMOUNT 3-5 70-73

LPs: 10/12-inch

EPIC 8-10 74
PARAMOUNT 10-15 70-73

KING COLE TRIO: see COLE, Nat "King"

KING CRIMSON — LP '69

Singles: 12-inch

W.B. 4-6 84

Singles: 7-inch

ATLANTIC 3-5 70-74
W.B. 3-4 81-84

LPs: 10/12-inch

ATLANTIC (Except 18000 & 19000 series) 10-20 69-74
ATLANTIC (18000 & 19000 series) 8-10 74-75
EDITIONS 5-10
MFSL (075 "In the Court of the Crimson King") 35-50 82
W.B. 5-8 81-84
WIZARDO 10-12
WORLD RECORD CLUB 12-15

Members: Greg Lake; Robert Fripp; Boz Burrell; Bill Bruford; Adrian Belew; Ian MacDonald; Michael Giles; Peter Sinfield.
Also see BAD COMPANY
Also see BELEW, Adrian
Also see FRIPP, Robert
Also see LAKE, Greg
Also see YES

KING CURTIS — P&R/R&B '62
(With the Kingpins; with Nobel Knights; King Curtis Combo)

Singles: 78 rpm

APOLLO (507 "King's Rock") 10-20 57
GEM (208 "Tenor in the Sky") 10-20 54
GROOVE (0160 "Movin' On'") 10-15 56
MONARCH (702 "Wine Head") 20-30 53
RPM (383 "Boogie in the Moonlight") 15-25 53

Singles: 7-inch

ABC-PAR 5-10 60
ALCOR 5-10 62
APOLLO (507 "King's Rock") 15-25 57
ATCO 5-10 59-71
CAPITOL 5-10 62-65
DELUXE (6142 "Steel Guitar Rag") 10-20 57
DELUXE (6157 "Wicky Wacky") 10-20 57
ENJOY 8-12 62
EVEREST 8-12 61
GEM (208 "Tenor in the Sky") 40-60 54
GROOVE (0160 "Movin' On'") 10-20 56
KING 8-12 62
MONARCH (702 "Wine Head") 50-75 53
NEW JAZZ 5-10 61
RPM (383 "Boogie in the Moonlight") 40-60 53
SEG-WAY 10-15 61
TRU-SOUND 8-12 61-63

Picture Sleeves

CAPITOL (5377 "Bill Bailey") 5-10 65

EPs: 7-inch

ATCO (33-266 "Best of King Curtis") 5-10 68
(Stereo. Juke box issue only.)
CAPITOL 8-15 63

LPs: 10/12-inch

ATCO (113 "Have Tenor Sax Will Blow") 75-100 59
(Monaural.)
ATCO (SD-113 "Have Tenor Sax Will Blow") 100-125 59
(Stereo.)
ATCO (189 thru 385) 10-20 66-72
CAMDEN 10-15 68
CAPITOL (2000 series) 10-20 64-68
CAPITOL (11000 series) 5-8 78-79
CLARION 8-10 60s
COLLECTABLES 6-8 88
ENJOY (2001 "Soul Twist") 30-50 62
EVEREST (1121 "Azure") 20-30 61
HARLEM HIT PARADE 8-10 70s
MOUNT VERNON 10-12
NEW JAZZ (8237 "New Scene") 20-30 60
PRESTIGE (7200 series) 15-20 62
PRESTIGE (7700 series) 8-12 69-70
RCA 15-25 60s
TRU-SOUND 15-20 62

Also see BAKER, Lavern
Also see BENTON, Brook
Also see BOBBETTES
Also see CLOVERS
Also see COASTERS
Also see COMSTOCK, Bobby
Also see DARIN, Bobby
Also see FACENDA, Tommy
Also see FREED, Alan
Also see JENNINGS, Waylon
Also see KING PINS
Also see LED ZEPPELIN / King Curtis
Also see MANN, Herbie
Also see McPHATTER, Clyde
Also see MITCHELL, Freddie
Also see PAT & SATELLITES
Also see RAMRODS
Also see RESTIVO, Johnny
Also see SEDAKA, Neil
Also see SHARPE, Ray
Also see SHIRELLES & King Curtis
Also see SUNNYLAND SLIM
Also see TURNER, Joe
Also see TURNER, Sammy

KING DIAMOND — LP '87

LPs: 10/12-inch

ROADRACER 5-8 87-90

KING DREAM CHORUS & HOLIDAY CREW — R&B '86

Singles: 12-inch

MERCURY 4-6 86

Singles: 7-inch

MERCURY 3-4 86

Picture Sleeves

MERCURY 3-4 86

Members: Kurtis Blow; El De Barge; Fat Boys; Grandmaster Melle Mel; Whitney Houston; Stacy Lattisaw; Lisa Lisa & Full Force; Teena Marie; Menudo; Stephanie Mills; New Edition; Run-DMC; James Taylor; Whodini; Greg Phillinganes.
Also see BLOW, Kurtis
Also see DE BARGE
Also see FAT BOYS
Also see GRANDMASTER FLASH & Furious Five
Also see HOUSTON, Whitney
Also see LATTISAW, Stacy
Also see LISA LISA & Cult Jam with Full Force
Also see MARIE, Teena
Also see MENUDO
Also see MILLS, Stephanie
Also see NEW EDITION
Also see PHILLINGANES, Greg
Also see RUN-D.M.C.
Also see TAYLOR, James
Also see WHODINI

KING FAMILY — LP '65

Singles: 7-inch

W.B. 3-5 65-66

LPs: 10/12-inch

CAPITOL 5-15 65
W.B. 5-15 65

KING FLOYD — P&R/R&B '70
(With the Three Queens)

Singles: 7-inch

CHIMNEYVILLE 3-5 70-76
ORIGINAL SOUND 4-8 64
PULSAR 4-8
UPTOWN 4-8 66

Picture Sleeves

CHIMNEYVILLE 3-5 71

LPs: 10/12-inch

ATCO 8-10 73
CHIMNEYVILLE 8-10 72
COTILLION 8-12 71
PULSAR 10-15 69
V.I.P. (407 "Heart of the Matter") 20-25 70

KING HANNIBAL — R&B '73
(James T. Shaw)

Singles: 7-inch

AWARE 3-5 73

LPs: 10/12-inch

AWARE 8-10 73

KING HARVEST — P&R '72

Singles: 7-inch

A&M 3-5 75-76
PERCEPTION 3-5 72-73

LPs: 10/12-inch

A&M 10-15 75
PERCEPTION 8-12 73

Also see LOVE, Mike
Also see WILSON, Carl

KING LIZARD
(Kim Fowley)

Singles: 7-inch

ORIGINAL SOUND 8-12 75

Also see FOWLEY, Kim

KING PINS — P&R/R&B '63
(King-Pins; Kingpins)

Singles: 7-inch

ATCO 5-10 67
FEDERAL (12480 "Believe in Me") 15-25 62
FEDERAL (12484 "How Long Will It Last") 15-25 63
FEDERAL (12505 "With the Other Guy") 15-25 63
FEDERAL (12512 "Wonderful One") 15-25 63
FEDERAL (12517 "Two Hearts") 15-25 64
FEDERAL (12519 "I Won't Have It") 15-25 64
FEDERAL (12525 "Just Keep on Smiling") 15-25 64
VEE JAY (494 "A Lucky Guy") 15-25 62

LPs: 10/12-inch

KING (865 "It Won't Be This Way Always") 35-50 63

Members: Andrew Kelly; Robert Kelly; Curtis Kelly. Session: Charles Lee; Offe Reese.
Also see KELLY BROTHERS
Also see KING CURTIS

KING PLEASURE — R&B '52
(Clarence Beeks)

Singles: 78 rpm

ALADDIN 10-15 57
JUBILEE 8-15 55
PRESTIGE 8-15 52-55

Singles: 7-inch

ALADDIN 10-15 57
HI-FI 5-10 60
JUBILEE 10-15 55
PRESTIGE (100 series) 5-10 60
PRESTIGE (800 & 900 series) 10-20 52-55
U.A. 5-10 62

LPs: 10/12-inch

HI-FI (425 "Golden Days") 35-55 60
PRESTIGE (208 "King Pleasure Sings") 75-125 55
(10-inch LP.)
PRESTIGE (7128 "King Pleasure Sings") 50-75 57
U.A. (14031 "Mr. Jazz") 30-40 62
(Monaural.)
U.A. (15031 "Mr. Jazz") 35-50 62
(Stereo.)

KING RICHARD'S FLUEGEL KNIGHTS — LP '68

Singles: 7-inch

MTA 3-6 66-68

LPs: 10/12-inch

MTA 5-10 67-70

KING SUN-D MOET — R&B '87

Singles: 7-inch

ZAKIA 3-4 87

KING SWAMP LP '89

Singles: 7-inch

VIRGIN ... 3-4 89

Picture Sleeves

VIRGIN ... 3-4 89

LPs: 10/12-inch

VIRGIN ... 5-8 89

KING TEE LP '89

LPs: 10/12-inch

CAPITOL ... 5-8 89-90

KINGBEES P&R/LP '80

(Nino Tempo & Kingbees)

Singles: 7-inch

RSO ... 3-5 80-81

Picture Sleeves

RSO ... 4-6 80-81

LPs: 10/12-inch

RSO ... 5-10 80-81

Members: Jamie James; Michael; Rex.

Also see TEMPO, Nino

KINGDOM COME P&R/LP '88

Singles: 7-inch

POLYDOR ... 3-4 88

Picture Sleeves

POLYDOR ... 3-4 88

LPs: 10/12-inch

POLYDOR ... 5-8 88-89

KINGFISH LP '76

Singles: 7-inch

JET ... 3-5 78
ROUND ... 3-5 76

LPs: 10/12-inch

ACCORD ... 5-8 81
JET ... 8-10 77
ROUND ... 10-20 76

Members: Bob Weir; David Torbert; Matt Kelly.

Also see NEW RIDERS of the Purple Sage
Also see WEIR, Bob

KINGS P&R/LP '80

Singles: 7-inch

ELEKTRA ... 3-5 80-81

LPs: 10/12-inch

ELEKTRA ... 5-8 80-81

KINGS OF SUN P&R/LP '88

Singles: 12-inch

RCA ... 4-8 88-89

Singles: 7-inch

RCA ... 3-4 88-90

Picture Sleeves

RCA ... 3-4 88

LPs: 10/12-inch

RCA ... 5-8 88-90

KING'S X LP '88

Singles: 12-inch

MEGAFORCE ... 4-8 88
(Promotional only.)

LPs: 10/12-inch

MEGAFORCE ... 5-8 88-90

KINGSMEN P&R '58

Singles: 7-inch

EAST WEST ... 10-20 58

Also see HALEY, Bill

KINGSMEN P&R '63

Singles: 7-inch

CAPITOL ... 3-5 72
EARTH ... 4-6 69
ERIC ... 3-5 70s
JERDEN (712 "Louie Louie") ... 40-60 63
REO (028 "Louie Louie") ... 5-8 66
(Canadian.)
REO (8745 "Louie Louie") ... 25-50 63
(Canadian.)
WAND (Except 1107 & 1115) ... 5-10 63-68
WAND (1107 "It's Only the Dog") ... 10-15 65
WAND (1115 "Killer Joe") ... 8-12 65

Picture Sleeves

WAND (1118 "The Krunch") ... 10-20 66

LPs: 10/12-inch

ARISTA ... 8-10 81
HEAVY WEIGHT ... 20-25 67
PICADILLY ... 5-8 80
RHINO ... 5-8 80s
SCEPTER/CITATION ... 8-12 72
WAND (657 "The Kingsmen in Person") ... 30-35 64
WAND (659 "The Kingsmen, Vol. 2") ... 50-100 64
(Without *Death of an Angel*.)
WAND (659 "The Kingsmen, Vol. 2") ... 25-35 64
(With *Death of an Angel*.)
WAND (662 "The Kingsmen, Vol. 3") ... 25-30 65
WAND (670 thru 681) ... 20-25 65-67

Members: Lynn Easton; Mike Mitchell; Don Gallucci; Norm Sundholm; Gary Abbot; Jack Eley; Barry Curtis; Dick Peterson.

Also see DON & GOODTIMES

KINGSTON TRIO P&R/R&B/LP '58

Singles: 7-inch

CAPITOL (856 "Merry Minuet") ... 20-30 59
(Promotional issue only.)
CAPITOL (1400 & 1800 series) ... 10-20 60-63
(Compact 33 Singles.)
CAPITOL (2006 "Farewell Adelita") .. 15-25 60
(Special products giveaway for Welgrume Sportswear.)
CAPITOL (2782 "Molly Dee") ... 15-25 59
(Promotional issue only.)
CAPITOL (3970 thru 4114) ... 10-15 58-59
CAPITOL (4167 "Tijuana Jail") ... 10-15 59
CAPITOL (S-4167 "Tijuana Jail") ... 20-30 59
(Stereo.)
CAPITOL (4221 "M.T.A.") ... 10-15 59
CAPITOL (4221 "M.T.A.") ... 25-35 59
(Promotional "Special Preview Record." Label pictures the Trio.)
CAPITOL (4271 "A Worried Man") ... 10-15 59
CAPITOL (4303 "Coo Coo-U") ... 8-12 59
CAPITOL (S-4303 "Coo Coo-U") ... 15-25 59
(Stereo.)
CAPITOL (4338 thru 5166) ... 5-10 59-64
CAPITOL (6000 series) ... 4-6 62-65
CAPITOL/LION OF TROY (2006 "Farewell Adelita") ... 10-20 60
(Capitol Special Products issue for Lion of Troy shirt buyers.)
DECCA ... 5-10 64-66
TETRAGRAMMATON ... 4-6 69
NAUTILUS ... 4-6 79
XERES ... 3-5 82

Picture Sleeves

CAPITOL (2006 "Farewell Adelita") .. 20-30 60
(Special products issue for Welgrume Sportswear.)
CAPITOL (2782 "Molly Dee") ... 20-30 59
(Promotional issue only.)
CAPITOL (4338 "El Matador") ... 15-25 60
CAPITOL (4740 "Scotch & Soda") ... 10-20 62
CAPITOL (4842 "One More Town") .. 10-20 62
CAPITOL/LION OF TROY (2006 "Farewell Adelita") ... 15-25 60
(Capitol Special Products issue for Lion of Troy shirts.)
DECCA (31702 "Hope You Understand") ... 15-25 65
DECCA (31790 "Yes, I Can Feel It") ... 15-25 65
DECCA (31860 "Runaway Song") ... 15-25 65
XERES ... 3-5 82

EPs: 7-inch

CAPITOL ... 15-30 58-61
CAPITOL CUSTOM (2670 "Cool Cargo") ... 30-40 60
(Special products issue for 7 Up.)

LPs: 10/12-inch

CANDLELITE (6971 "Historic Recordings") ... 15-25 70s
CAPITOL (500 series) ... 8-15 70
CAPITOL (T-996 "The Kingston Trio") ... 50-75 58
(Green label. Monaural.)
CAPITOL (T-996 "The Kingston Trio") ... 25-40 58
(Black label. Monaural.)
CAPITOL (DT-996 "The Kingston Trio") ... 10-15 69
(Reprocessed stereo.)
CAPITOL (T-1107 "From the Hungry i") ... 30-40 59
(Monaural.)
CAPITOL (ST-1183 "Stereo Concert") ... 25-35 59
(Stereo.)
CAPITOL (T-1199 "Kingston Trio at Large") ... 25-35 59
(Monaural.)
CAPITOL (ST-1199 "Kingston Trio at Large") ... 30-40 59
(Stereo.)
CAPITOL (T-1258 "Here We Go Again") ... 25-35 59
(Monaural.)
CAPITOL (ST-1258 "Here We Go Again") ... 30-40 59
(Stereo.)
CAPITOL (T-1352 "Sold Out") ... 20-30 60
(Monaural.)
CAPITOL (ST-1352 "Sold Out") ... 25-35 60
(Stereo.)
CAPITOL (T-1407 "String Along ... 20-30 60
(Monaural.)
CAPITOL (ST-1407 "String Along ... 25-35 60
(Stereo.)
CAPITOL (T-1446 thru T-2081) ... 20-30 60-64
(Monaural.)
CAPITOL (ST-1446 thru ST-2081) ... 25-35 60-64
(Stereo.)
CAPITOL (T-2180 "Folk Era") ... 30-40 64
(Monaural. Three-disc set with bound-in booklet.)
CAPITOL (ST-2180 "Folk Era") ... 35-45 64
(Stereo. Three-disc set with bound-in booklet.)
CAPITOL (T-2280 thru T-2614) ... 15-25 65-66
(Monaural.)
CAPITOL (ST-2280 thru ST-2614) ... 15-30 65-66
(Stereo.)
CAPITOL (11000 series) ... 5-8 79
CAPITOL (16000 series) ... 4-6 81
DECCA (4000 series) ... 15-25 64-65
(Monaural.)
DECCA (7-4000 series) ... 15-30 64-65
(Stereo.)
INTERMEDIA ... 5-8 85
NAUTILUS ... 20-25 79
PICKWICK ... 5-10 70s
TETRAGRAMMATON ... 10-15 69
XERES ... 5-10 82

Members: John Stewart; Dave Guard; Nick Reynolds; Bob Shane.

Also see BEATLES / Beach Boys / Kingston Trio
Also see NEW KINGSTON TRIO
Also see STEWART, John
Also see STEWART, John, & Nick Reynolds

KINGSTON TRIO / Four Preps

Singles: 7-inch

U.S.A.F. (103 "El Matador") ... 20-25 60
(Promotional, radio station issue only.)

Also see FOUR PREPS

KINGSTON TRIO / Dinah Shore

Singles: 7-inch

U.S.A.F. (129 "Everglades") ... 20-25 60
(Promotional, radio station issue only.)

Also see SHORE, Dinah

KINGSTON TRIO / Frank Sinatra

EPs: 7-inch

CAPITOL (2229 "Excerpts from Great New Releases") ... 40-60 62
(Promotional issue only.)

Also see KINGSTON TRIO
Also see SINATRA, Frank

KINISON, Sam LP '86

LPs: 10/12-inch

W.B. 5-8 86-90

KINKS P&R/LP '64

Singles: 12-inch

ARISTA 4-8 79-83

Singles: 7-inch

ARISTA 3-6 77-85
CAMEO (308 "Long Tall Sally") 75-100 64
CAMEO (345 "Long Tall Sally") 40-60 65
CAMEO (348 "You Still Want Me") 100-200 65
ERIC 3-5
MCA 3-5 86
RCA 4-6 72-76
REPRISE (0306 thru 0647) 5-8 65-67
REPRISE (0691 thru 0863) 8-12 68-69
REPRISE (0930 thru 1094) 4-8 70-72

Promotional Singles

ARISTA (Except 5) 3-6 77-85
ARISTA (5 "Sleepwalker") 10-15 77
(Colored vinyl.)
CAMEO (308 "Long Tall Sally") 50-75 64
CAMEO (345 "Long Tall Sally") 35-45 65
CAMEO (348 "You Still Want Me") 100-150 65
REPRISE (0306 thru 0647) 10-20 65-67
REPRISE (0691 thru 0863) 10-15 68-69
REPRISE (0930 thru 1094) 6-12 70-72

Picture Sleeves

ARISTA 3-5 80-84

EPs: 7-inch

ARISTA (22 "The Kinks Misfit Record") 20-25 78
(Promotional issue only.)
CAMEO 4-6 78
REPRISE (352 "Arthur") 10-20 69
(Promotional issue only.)

LPs: 10/12-inch

ARISTA 6-12 77-86
COMPLEAT 5-8
MCA 5-8 86-89
MFSL (070 "Misfits") 20-30 82
PICKWICK 5-10 72-79
PYE 8-10 75-76
RCA (Except "AYL1" series) 10-15 71-76
RCA VICTOR ("AYL1" series) 5-8 80-82
REPRISE (2127 "The Great Lost Kinks Album") 20-30 73
REPRISE (R-6143 "You Really Got Me") 50-100 64
(Monaural.)
REPRISE (RS-6143 "You Really Got Me") 20-30 64
(Stereo.)
REPRISE (R-6158 "Kinks Size") 50-75 65
(Monaural.)
REPRISE (RS-6158 "Kinks Size") 20-30 65
(Stereo.)
REPRISE (R-6173 "Kinda Kinks") 50-75 65
(Monaural.)
REPRISE (RS-6173 "Kinda Kinks") 20-30 65
(Stereo.)
REPRISE (R-6184 "Kinks Kinkdom") 50-75 65
(Monaural.)
REPRISE (RS-6184 "Kinks Kinkdom") 20-30 65
(Stereo.)
REPRISE (R-6197 "The Kink Kontroversy") 50-75 66
(Monaural.)
REPRISE (RS-6197 "The Kink Kontroversy") 20-30 66
(Stereo.)
REPRISE (R-6217 "The Kinks' Greatest Hits") 50-75 66
(Monaural.)
REPRISE (RS-6217 "The Kinks' Greatest Hits") 20-30 66
(Stereo.)
REPRISE (R-6228 "Face to Face") 50-75 66
(Monaural.)
REPRISE (RS-6228 "Face to Face") 20-30 66
(Stereo.)
REPRISE (R-6260 "Live Kinks") 50-75 67
(Monaural.)
REPRISE (RS-6260 "Live Kinks") 20-30 67
(Stereo.)
REPRISE (R-6279 "Something Else") 50-75 67
(Monaural.)
REPRISE (RS-6279 "Something Else") 20-30 67
(Stereo.)
REPRISE (6327 "Village Green Preservation Society") 25-35 69
REPRISE (6366 "Arthur") 15-20 69
(Price includes lyrics insert.)
REPRISE (6423 "Lola Vs. the Powerman") 12-15 69
(Blue and white cover.)
REPRISE (6423 "Lola Vs. the Powerman") 6-10 69
(Black, blue and white cover.)
REPRISE (6454 "The Kink Kronikles") 8-12 69
(Original Reprise Kinks LPs from the '60s are on a multi-colored label. All 11 of these LPs have been reissused on the brown Reprise label and are valued at $10 to $15.)

Promotional LPs

ARISTA (Except 69) 10-15 77-84
ARISTA (69 "Low Budget Radio Interview") 40-50 79
REPRISE (2127 "The Great Lost Kinks Album") 50-75 73
REPRISE (R-6143 "You Really Got Me") 50-100 64
(White label, monaural.)
REPRISE (R-6158 "Kinks Size") 100-200 65
(White label, monaural.)
REPRISE (R-6173 "Kinda Kinks") 100-200 65
(White label, monaural.)
REPRISE (R-6184 "Kinks Kingdom") 100-200 65
(White label, monaural.)
REPRISE (R-6197 "The Kink Kontroversy") 100-200 66
(White label, monaural.)
REPRISE (R-6217 "The Kinks' Greatest Hits") 100-200 66
(White label, monaural.)
REPRISE (R-6228 "Face to Face") 75-150 66
(White label, monaural.)
REPRISE (R-6260 "Live Kinks") 75-150 67
(White label, monaural.)
REPRISE (R-6279 "Something Else") 75-150 67
REPRISE (RS-6000 series) 30-60 64-72
(White label, stereo.)
W.B. (328 Complete "Kinks Kit"/"Then Now and In-Between") 325-375 69
(Boxed set, includes Then Now and In-Between LP, button, pin, postcard, letter, decal, and other promotional materials.)
W.B. (328 "Then Now and In-Between") 75-100 69
(Price for LP only.)
Members: Ray Davies; Dave Davies; Mick Avory; Peter Quaife; John Dalton; John Gosling; Ian Gibbons; Jim Rodford; Bob Henrit; John Beecham; Mike Cotton.
Also see DAVIES, Dave

KINKS / Hollywood Stars

Singles: 7-inch

ARISTA (5 "Sleepwalker") 8-10 77

Picture Sleeves

ARISTA (5 "Sleepwalker") 10-15 77
Also see HOLLYWOOD STARS
Also see KINKS

KINNEY, Fern P&R/R&B '79

Singles: 7-inch

ATLANTIC 4-6 68
MALACO 3-5 79-80

KINSMAN DAZZ R&B '78

Singles: 7-inch

20TH FOX 3-5 78-79

LPs: 10/12-inch

20TH FOX 5-8 79
Members: Rob Harris; Michael Calhoun; Kenny Pettus; Ike Wiley; Mike Wiley; Ed Meyers; Skip Martin; Pierre De Mudd; Eric Fearman; Kevin Kendrick.
Also see DAZZ BAND

KIRBY, Kathy P&R '65

Singles: 7-inch

ASCOT 4-6 67
LONDON 4-8 62-65
PARROT 4-8 65-66

KIRBY STONE FOUR: see STONE, Kirby, Four

KIRK, Andy, & His 12 Clouds of Joy
(With the Jubalaires; Andy Kirk & His Orchestra; with 12 Clouds; with June Richmond) R&B '42

Singles: 78 rpm

CORAL 10-20 49
DECCA 10-20 42-46
Also see JUBALAIRES

KIRK, Jim, & TM Singers P&R '80

Singles: 7-inch

CAPITOL 3-5 80

Picture Sleeves

CAPITOL 3-5 80

KIRKLAND, Bo R&B '75

Singles: 7-inch

CLARIDGE 3-5 75

KIRKLAND, Bo, & Ruth Davis
(Bo & Ruth) R&B '76

Singles: 7-inch

CLARIDGE 3-5 75-78

LPs: 10/12-inch

CLARIDGE 5-10 76
Also see DAVIS, Ruth
Also see KIRKLAND, Bo

KIRTON, Lew R&B '77

Singles: 7-inch

BELIEVE 3-4 83
MARLIN 3-5 77

KISS P&R/LP '74

Singles: 12-inch

CASABLANCA 10-20 78-82
MERCURY 10-20 83-88

Singles: 7-inch

CASABLANCA 4-8 74-82
MERCURY (Except 0002) 3-6 85-88
MERCURY (0002 "World Without Heroes") 15-25 81
(Picture disc.)

Picture Sleeves

CASABLANCA (858 "Flaming Youth") 8-10 75
CASABLANCA (2365 "I Love It Loud") 8-10 81
MERCURY 4-8 85-87

LPs: 10/12-inch

CASABLANCA (7001 "Kiss") 10-20 70s
(Reissue of 9001.)
CASABLANCA (7006 "Hotter Than Hell") 10-15 74
CASABLANCA (7016 "Dressed to Kill") 10-15 75
CASABLANCA (7020 "Alive") 15-20 75
(With 8-page color booklet.)
CASABLANCA (7020 "Alive") 10-15 75
(Without booklet.)
CASABLANCA (7025 "Destroyer") 10-15 75
CASABLANCA (7032 "The Originals") 50-75 76
(With inserts: Army sticker; 16-page booklet; six trading cards.)
CASABLANCA (7032 "The Originals") 10-15 76
(Without inserts.)

CASABLANCA (7037 "Rock & Roll Over") 20-25 76
(With sticker-sheet order form.)
CASABLANCA (7037 "Rock & Roll Over") 10-15 76
(Without sticker-sheet.)
CASABLANCA (7057 "Love Gun").... 25-75 77
(With cardboard gun. Apart from the LP unused cardboard gun is valued at $35 to $50. Labels on some pressings have tracks listed in the wrong sequence.)
CASABLANCA (7057 "Love Gun").... 10-15 77
(Without cardboard gun.)
CASABLANCA (7076 "Alive II") 250-300 77
(Has three tracks not found on later issues: *Take Me, Hooligan,* and *Do You Love Me.* Reportedly 50 copies made.)
CASABLANCA (7076 "Alive II") 40-50 77
(With 8-page tatoo booklet. Add $20-30 if cover lists the three tracks, *Take Me, Hooligan,* and *Do You Love Me,* that are not on LP.)
CASABLANCA (7076 "Alive II") 10-15 77
(Without tatoo booklet. Add $20-30 if cover lists the three tracks, *Take Me, Hooligan,* and *Do You Love Me,* that are not on LP.)
CASABLANCA (7100 "Double Platinum") 30-40 78
(With platinum award order form.)
CASABLANCA (7100 "Double Platinum") 15-20 78
(Without platinum award order form.)
CASABLANCA (7152 "Dynasty") 8-12 79
CASABLANCA (7225 "Kiss Unmasked") 8-10 80
CASABLANCA (7261 "Music from the Elder") 25-35 81
(With lyric sheet.)
CASABLANCA (7261 "Music from the Elder") 8-12 81
(Without lyric sheet.)
CASABLANCA (7270 "Creatures of the Night") 30-45 82
(With make up.)
CASABLANCA (7270 "Creatures of the Night") 8-10 82
(Without make up.)
DYNASTY (7152 "Dynasty") 15-20 79
(With poster order form.)
DYNASTY (7152 "Dynasty") 8-12 79
(Without poster order form.)
CASABLANCA (9001 "Kiss") 25-50 74
MERCURY (814297 "Lick It Up") 5-8 83
MERCURY (822495 "Animalize") 5-8 84
MERCURY (826099 "Asylum") 5-8 85
MERCURY (832626 "Crazy Nights") 5-8 86
MERCURY (836887 "Smashes, Thrashes and Hits") 20-30 88
(Picture disc. Gatefold cover.)
MERCURY (836913 "Hot in the Shade") 5-8 89
MERCURY (522123 "Kiss My Ass") 25-30 94
(Colored vinyl, limited edition.)
POLYGRAM ("Kiss Alive III") 20-25 94
(Colored vinyl. Limited edition.)
POLYGRAM (832-903 "Crazy Nights") 20-25 87
(Picture disc.)
UNMASKED (7225 "Kiss Unmasked") 15-20 80
(With poster order form.)
UNMASKED (7225 "Kiss Unmasked") 8-10 80
(Without poster order form.)

Promotional LPs

BURNS MEDIA ("Rock & Roll Over with Kiss") 50-75 76
CASABLANCA ("A Taste of Platinum") 30-50 78
CASABLANCA ("Rock & Roll Over") 30-50 76
CASABLANCA (76 "Kiss Tour Album") 30-50 76
CASABLANCA (7001 "Kiss") 40-60 74
(Without *Kissin' Time.*)
CASABLANCA (7001 "Kiss") 20-30 74
(With *Kissin' Time.*)
CASABLANCA (7032 "The Originals") 100-125 76
(With inserts.)
CASABLANCA (9001 "Kiss") 75-125 74
CASABLANCA (20137 "Criss, Frehley, Simmons, Stanley") 20-30 78
MERCURY (792-1 "First Kiss, Last Licks") 75-100 90

Members: Gene Simmons; Ace Frehley; Paul Stanley; Peter Criss; Bruce Kulick; Eric Carr; Vinnie Vincent.
Also see CRISS, Peter
Also see FREHLEY, Ace
Also see SIMMONS, Gene
Also see STANLEY, Paul
Also see VINCENT, Vinnie, Invasion

KISS / Mighty Bosstones

Singles: 7-inch

MERCURY (858894 "Detroit Rock City") 3-6
(Colored vinyl.)
Also see KISS

KISSING THE PINK — P&R '83
(KTP)

Singles: 7-inch

ATLANTIC 3-5 83
MERCURY 3-4 87

Picture Sleeves

MERCURY 3-4 87

LPs: 10/12-inch

ATLANTIC 5-8 83
MERCURY 5-8 87

KISSOON, Katie — D&D '84

Singles: 12-inch

JIVE 4-6 84

KISSOON, Mac & Katie — P&R '71

Singles: 7-inch

ABC 3-5 71
BELL 3-5 72
MCA/STATE 3-5 75-76

LPs: 10/12-inch

MCA/STATE 8-12 76
Also see KISSOON, Katie
Also see WATERS, Roger

KITARO — LP '85
(Mansanori Takahashi)

Singles: 12-inch

GEFFEN 4-8 86
(Promotional only.)

Singles: 7-inch

GEFFEN 3-4 86

LPs: 10/12-inch

GEFFEN 5-8 85-90
GRAMAVISION 5-8 85-86

KITT, Eartha — P&R '53

Singles: 12-inch

STREETWISE 4-6 83

Singles: 78 rpm

RCA 4-8 53-57

Singles: 7-inch

DECCA 4-8 65
KAPP 5-10 59-66
RCA 10-20 53-57
STREETWISE 3-4 83

Picture Sleeves

RCA 15-25 54-55

EPs: 7-inch

RCA 20-30 53-57

LPs: 10/12-inch

CAEDMON 5-10 69
DECCA 10-15 65
GNP 10-15 65
KAPP 10-20 59-60
MGM 10-20 62
PHILIPS 8-15 68
RCA 25-50 53-57
STANYAN 5-10 72
SUNNYVIEW 5-8 84

KITT, Eartha, & Perez Prado

Singles: 78 rpm

RCA 4-8 50s

Singles: 7-inch

RCA 10-15 50s
Also see KITT, Eartha
Also see PRADO, Perez

KITTY & HAYWOODS — R&B '77

Singles: 7-inch

MERCURY 3-5 77

LPs: 10/12-inch

MERCURY 8-10 77

KIX — LP '83

Singles: 7-inch

ATLANTIC 3-4 81-89

Picture Sleeves

ATLANTIC 3-4 89

LPs: 10/12-inch

ATLANTIC 5-8 81-89

KLAATU — P&R/LP '77

Singles: 12-inch

CAPITOL 3-4 80
(Promotional only.)

Singles: 7-inch

CAPITOL 3-5 77-80
ISLAND 4-6 75

Picture Sleeves

CAPITOL 3-5 77

LPs: 10/12-inch

CAPITOL 8-12 76-80
Members: John Woloschuk; Cary Draper; David Long;; Dino Tome.

KLEEER — R&B '79

Singles: 7-inch

ATLANTIC 3-5 79-85

LPs: 10/12-inch

ATLANTIC 5-8 79-85
Members: Paul Crutchfield; Richard Lee; Norm Durham.
Also see UNIVERSAL ROBOT BAND

KLEIN, Robert — LP '73

Singles: 7-inch

BRUT 4-8 73
CASABLANCA 3-5 79

LPs: 10/12-inch

BRUT 8-12 73

KLEIN & MBO — D&D '83

Singles: 12-inch

ATLANTIC 4-6 83

Singles: 7-inch

ATLANTIC 3-4 83

KLEMMER, John — LP '69

Singles: 7-inch

ABC 3-5 76
CADET CONCEPT 4-6 69

LPs: 10/12-inch

ABC 5-10 75-79
CADET CONCEPT 8-12 69
CHESS 8-12 76
ELEKTRA 5-8 80-83
MCA 5-10 79-82
NAUTILUS 5-8 80-81
NOVUS 5-8 79
Also see HARRIS, Eddie, & John Klemmer

KLINT, Pete, Quintet — P&R '67

Singles: 7-inch

ATLANTIC 8-12 68
IGL (127 "Very Last Day") 15-25 64
MERCURY 8-12 67
P.K.Q. 8-12 60s
TWIN SPIN 12-18 60s

KLIQUE — R&B '81

Singles: 12-inch

MCA 4-6 81-85

Singles: 7-inch

MCA 3-4 81-85

LPs: 10/12-inch

MCA 5-8 81-85

Members: Howard Huntsberry; Deborah Hunter; Isaac Suthers.

KLOCKWISE
R&B '84

Singles: 7-inch

SINBAN ... 3-4 84-85

KLOWNS
P&R/LP '70

Singles: 7-inch

RCA ... 3-5 70

Picture Sleeves

RCA ... 3-5 70

LPs: 10/12-inch

RCA ... 8-10 70

KLUGH, Earl
R&B/LP '77

Singles: 7-inch

BLUE NOTE ... 3-5 76-77
LIBERTY ... 3-4 81
U.A. ... 3-4 78-79
W.B. ... 3-4 85

LPs: 10/12-inch

BLUE NOTE ... 5-8 76-77
CAPITOL ... 5-8 83-84
LIBERTY ... 5-8 80-81
MFSL (025 "Finger Paintings") ... 30-40 79
MFSL (UHQR 025 "Finger Paintings") ... 50-75 79
(Boxed set.)
MFSL (076 "Late Night") ... 25-35 82
U.A. ... 5-10 78-80
W.B. ... 5-8 84-91

Also see BENSON, George, & Earl Klugh
Also see JAMES, Bob, & Earl Klugh
Also see LAWS, Hubert, & Earl Klugh

KLYMAXX
R&B '81

Singles: 12-inch

CONSTELLATION ... 4-6 84-87
MCA ... 4-6 84-86

Singles: 7-inch

CONSTELLATION ... 3-4 84-87
MCA ... 3-4 84-86
SOLAR ... 3-5 81-83

Picture Sleeves

CONSTELLATION ... 3-4 85-87
MCA ... 4-6 84-86

LPs: 10/12-inch

CONSTELLATION ... 5-8 85-87
MCA ... 5-8 90
SOLAR ... 5-8 81-83

Members: Lorena Hardiman; Ann Williams; Cheryl Coolen; Robbin Grider; Lynn Malsby; Joyce Irby; Bernadette Cooper; Judy Takeuchi.
Also see IRBY, Joyce "Fenderella"

KNACK
P&R/LP '79

Singles: 7-inch

ATCO (7051 "Pick It Up") ... 3-5 77
CAPITOL (4000 series) ... 3-5 79-81
RCA (62800 "My Sharona") ... 3-4 94

Picture Sleeves

CAPITOL (4731 "My Sharona") ... 4-8 79
CAPITOL (4771 "Good Girls Don't") ... 3-5 79
CAPITOL (4822 "Baby Talks Dirty") ... 8-10 80
CAPITOL (5054 "Pay the Devil") ... 8-10 80
RCA (62800 "My Sharona") ... 3-4 94

LPs: 10/12-inch

CAPITOL ... 8-10 79-81
CHARISMA ... 5-8 91

Members: Doug Fieger; Bruce Gary; Berton Averre; Prescott Niles.
Also see SKY

KNICKERBOCKERS
P&R '65

Singles: 7-inch

CHALLENGE (59268 "All I Need Is You") ... 10-20 65
CHALLENGE (59293 thru 59384) ... 5-10 65-67
ERIC ... 3-5 70s
LANA ... 3-6 60s

LPs: 10/12-inch

CHALLENGE (621 "Jerk and Twine Time") ... 45-55 66
CHALLENGE (622 "Lies") ... 50-75 66
CHALLENGE (12664 "Lloyd Thaxton Presents the Knickerbockers") ... 50-75 65

SUNDAZED ... 5-10 89

Members: Buddy Randell; Beau Charles; Jimmy Walker; John Charles.

KNIGHT, Evelyn, & Red Foley
C&W '51

Singles: 78 rpm

DECCA ... 4-8 51

Singles: 7-inch

DECCA ... 5-10 51

Also see FOLEY, Red

KNIGHT, Frederick
P&R/R&B '72

Singles: 7-inch

JUANA ... 3-4 81
MAXINE ... 4-6 69
1-2-3 ... 10-15
STAX ... 3-5 72
TRUTH ... 3-5 75

LPs: 10/12-inch

STAX ... 8-10 73

KNIGHT, Gladys
P&R/R&B '61

(Pips; with the Pips)

Singles: 12-inch

COLUMBIA ... 4-8 79-85
MCA ... 4-6 86

Singles: 7-inch

ABC ... 3-5 73
BRUNSWICK (55048 "Whistle, My Love") ... 75-100 58
BUDDAH ... 3-5 73-79
CASABLANCA ... 3-5 77-78
COLUMBIA ... 3-5 79-85
ENJOY ... 10-20 64
ERIC ... 3-5 78
EVERLAST (5025 "Happiness") ... 15-20 63
FLASHBACK ... 3-5 67
FURY (1050 thru 1067) ... 10-20 61-62
FURY (1073 "Come See About Me") ... 20-30 63
HUNTOM (2510 "Every Beat of My Heart") ... 300-500 61
MCA ... 3-4 86-88
MAXX ... 10-20 64-65
SOUL ... 6-12 67-74
VEE JAY (386 "Every Beat of My Heart") ... 10-15 61
VEE JAY (545 "Queen of Tears") ... 10-20 63

Picture Sleeves

BUDDAH ... 3-5 73-75
COLUMBIA ... 3-5 81
MCA ... 3-4 87

LPs: 10/12-inch

ACCORD ... 5-8 81-82
ALLEGIANCE ... 5-8 84
BELL ... 10-15 68-75
BUDDAH ... 8-12 73-78
CASABLANCA ... 5-10 77-78
COLUMBIA ... 5-8 79-85
51 WEST ... 5-8 80s
FURY (1003 "Letter Full of Tears") 75-100 62
LOST-NITE ... 8-12 81
MCA ... 5-8 87
MCP ... 8-10 76
MAXX (3000 "Gladys Knight and the Pips") ... 20-30 64
MOTOWN (Except 792) ... 5-8 80-82
MOTOWN (792 "Anthology") ... 8-12 74
NATURAL RESOURCES ... 5-8 78
PICKWICK ... 8-10 73
RELIC ... 5-10 90
SOUL (706 "Everybody Needs Love") ... 20-30 67
SOUL (707 "Feelin' Bluesy") ... 15-25 67
SOUL (711 "Silk 'N' Soul") ... 15-25 69
SOUL (713 "Nitty Gritty") ... 15-25 69
SOUL (723 thru 744) ... 8-15 70-75
SPHERE SOUND (7006 "Gladys Knight and the Pips") ... 20-30 65
SPRINGBOARD ... 8-10 75
TRIP ... 8-10 73
U.A. ... 10-15 75
UPFRONT ... 10-12
VEE JAY ... 10-15 75

Members: Gladys Knight; Merald Knight; William Guest; Edward Guest.
Also see DIONNE & Friends
Also see GAYE, Marvin / Gladys Knight & Pips
Also see PIPS

KNIGHT, Gladys, & Johnny Mathis

Singles: 7-inch

COLUMBIA ... 3-5 80

Also see MATHIS, Johnny

KNIGHT, Gladys, & Bill Medley

Singles: 7-inch

SCOTTI BROS. ... 3-4 86

Also see KNIGHT, Gladys
Also see MEDLEY, Bill

KNIGHT, Holly
P&R '88

Singles: 7-inch

COLUMBIA ... 3-4 88

Picture Sleeves

COLUMBIA ... 3-4 88

LPs: 10/12-inch

COLUMBIA (44243 "Holly Knight") ... 5-10 88

Session: Nancy Wilson; Daryl Hall.
Also see DEVICE
Also see HALL, Daryl
Also see SPIDER
Also see WILSON, Nancy

KNIGHT, Jean
P&R/R&B/LP '71

(With Premium)

Singles: 7-inch

CHELSEA ... 3-5 75
COTILLION ... 3-5 81-82
DIAL ... 3-5 74
JETSTREAM ... 4-8 65
MIRAGE ... 3-4 85
OLA ... 3-5 77
OPEN ... 3-5 76
SOULIN ... 4-8 81-85
STAFF ... 5-10 72
STAX ... 3-5 71-73
TRIBE ... 5-10 65

Picture Sleeves

MIRAGE ... 3-4 85

LPs: 10/12-inch

COTILLION ... 5-8 81
MIRAGE ... 5-8 85
STAX ... 10-15 71

KNIGHT, Jerry
R&B/LP '80

Singles: 7-inch

A&M ... 3-4 80-83

Picture Sleeves

A&M ... 3-4 80

LPs: 10/12-inch

A&M ... 5-8 80-81

Also see OLLIE & JERRY
Also see RAYDIO

KNIGHT, Marie
R&B '49

Singles: 78 rpm

DECCA (Except 48315) ... 5-15 49-54
DECCA (48315 "You Got a Way of Making Love") ... 10-20 54
MERCURY ... 10-15 56
WING ... 5-10 56

Singles: 7-inch

ADDIT ... 8-10
DECCA (Except 48315) ... 10-20 51-54
DECCA (48315 "You Got a Way of Making Love") ... 25-35 54
DIAMOND ... 8-12 63
MERCURY ... 15-20 56
MUSICOR (1076 "Cry Me a River") ... 10-20 65
MUSICOR (1106 "Say It Again") ... 25-50 65
MUSICOR (1128 "You Lie So Well") 10-20 65
OKEH ... 5-10 61-65
WING ... 10-15 56

Picture Sleeves

OKEH (7141 "Come Tomorrow") ... 10-15 61

LPs: 10/12-inch

BLUE LABOR ... 15-25
CARLTON (119 "Lift Every Voice and Sing") ... 25-50 60

Session: Louisiana Red.
Also see MARIE & REX

KNIGHT, Robert *P&R/R&B/LP '67*

Singles: 7-inch

DOT....4-8 61
ELF....4-8 68-69
MONUMENT....3-5 74
PRIVATE STOCK....3-5 75
RISING SONS....4-8 67-68

LPs: 10/12-inch

RISING SONS/MONUMENT (17000 "Everlasting Love")....15-25 67

KNIGHT, Sonny *P&R '56*

(With the Cleeshays)

Singles: 78 rpm

ALADDIN....15-25 53
DOT....10-20 56
SPECIALTY....15-25 57
VITA....15-25 56

Singles: 7-inch

A&M....5-10 63-64
ALADDIN (3195 "Dear Wonderful")...25-50 53
ALADDIN (3207 "But Officer")....25-50 53
AURA (403 "If You Want This Love")..5-10 64
AURA (4505 "Love Me")....5-10 65
DOT (15507 "Confidential")....30-40 56
(Maroon label.)
DOT (15507 "Confidential")....10-20 57
(Black label.)
EASTMAN (787 "Lipstick Kisses")....20-40 59
FIFO (105 "Small Girl, Big World")....50-75 61
MERCURY (72033 "Just One More Chance")....10-15 62
ORIGINAL SOUND (2 "Once in Awhile")....25-35 58
ORIGINAL SOUND (18 "Those Oldies But Goodies Are Dedicated to You")....10-15 62
SPECIALTY (547 "Keep a Walkin' ")....25-50 55
STARLA (Except 1)....15-25 58-59
STARLA (1 "Dedicated to You")....25-50 57
VITA (137 "Confidential")....40-60 56
WORLD PACIFIC (403 "If You Want This Love")....10-20 64
(Reissued a few months later on Aura 403.)
WORLD PACIFIC (77811 "If I May")...5-10 66

Picture Sleeves

AURA (4505 "Love Me")....10-20 64

LPs: 10/12-inch

AURA (A-3001 "If You Want This Love")....15-25 64
(Monaural.)
AURA (AS-3001 "If You Want This Love")....25-35 64
(Stereo.)

KNIGHT, Terry *P&R/LP '66*

(With the Pack; with Fabulous Pack)

Singles: 7-inch

A&M....5-10 65
ABKCO....3-5 75
CAMEO (482 "Lizbeth Peach")....5-10 67
CAMEO (495 "Come Home Baby")....5-10 67
CAPITOL (2506 "Saint Paul")....8-12 69
FRATERNITY....5-10 67
LUCKY ELEVEN (225 "How Much More")....15-25 66
LUCKY ELEVEN (226 "Better Man Than I")....15-25 66
LUCKY ELEVEN (229 "A Change on the Way")....10-15 66
LUCKY ELEVEN (230 "I")....10-15 66
LUCKY ELEVEN (235 "This Precious Time")....10-15 67
LUCKY ELEVEN (236 "One Monkey Don't Stop No Show")....10-15 67
Note: Label may be shown as either "Lucky 11" or "Lucky Eleven.
SPICE....5-10 60s

LPs: 10/12-inch

ABKCO....10-15 72
CAMEO (2007 "Reflections")....20-30 67
LUCKY ELEVEN (8000 "Terry Knight and the Pack")....25-35 66
LUCKY ELEVEN (8001 "Reflections")....25-35 67
Members: Terry Knapp (a.k.a. Knight); Mark Farner; Don Brewer; Bob Caldwell; Curt Johnson.
Also see GRAND FUNK RAILROAD

KNIGHT BROTHERS *P&R/R&B '65*

Singles: 7-inch

CHECKER....5-8 63-66
MERCURY....4-6 67-68
Members: Richard Dunbar; Jerry Diggs.

KNIGHTSBRIDGE STRINGS *P&R '59*

Singles: 7-inch

MONUMENT....3-6 66
TOP RANK....4-8 59-60

LPs: 10/12-inch

MONUMENT....5-10 66-69
PURIST....5-10 64
RIVERSIDE....5-12 62-64
SESAC....8-15 59
TOP RANK....5-15 59-60
Also see CAMBRIDGE STRINGS & SINGERS
Also see RANDOLPH, Boots

KNOBLOCK, Fred *C&W/P&R/LP '80*

Singles: 7-inch

SCOTTI BROS....3-4 80-82

LPs: 10/12-inch

SCOTTI BROS....5-8 80-82

KNOBLOCK, Fred, & Susan Anton *C&W/P&R '80*

Singles: 7-inch

SCOTTI BROS....3-5 80
Also see KNOBLOCK, Fred

KNOCKOUTS *P&R '59*

Singles: 7-inch

SHAD (5013 "Darling Lorraine")....10-20 59
SHAD (5018 "Rich Boy, Poor Boy")..10-20 60
TRIBUTE (199 "Got My Mojo Working")....8-10 64
TRIBUTE (201 "What's on Your Mind")....10-15 64
TRIBUTE (1039 "Don't Say Goodbye")....8-10 65

LPs: 10/12-inch

TRIBUTE (1202 "Go Ape")....50-60 64
Member: Robert D'Andrea.

KNOX, Buddy *P&R/R&B '57*

("Lieutenant Buddy Knox"; with the Rhythm Orchids)

Singles: 78 rpm

ROULETTE....15-40 57

Singles: 7-inch

ABC....3-5 73
LIBERTY....5-10 60-64
REPRISE....4-8 65-66
ROULETTE (4002 "Party Doll")....20-30 57
(With roulette wheel circling label.)
ROULETTE (4002 "Party Doll")....15-20 57
(With roulette wheel on top half of label.)
ROULETTE (4002 "Party Doll")....10-15 58
(No roulette wheel on label.)
ROULETTE (4009 "Rock Your Little Baby to Sleep")....20-30 57
(With roulette wheel circling label.)
ROULETTE (4009 "Rock Your Little Baby to Sleep")....25-20 57
(With roulette wheel on top half of label.)
ROULETTE (4009 "Rock Your Little Baby to Sleep")....10-15 58
(No roulette wheel on label.)
ROULETTE (4018 thru 4262)....8-15 57-60
RUFF....4-8 65
U.A.....4-8 68-71

Picture Sleeves

LIBERTY (55305 "Ling Ting Tong")..10-20 61

EPs: 7-inch

ROULETTE (301 "Buddy Knox")....50-75 57

LPs: 10/12-inch

ACCORD....5-8 82-83
LIBERTY (3251 "Golden Hits")....20-30 62
(Monaural.)
LIBERTY (7251 "Golden Hits")....25-35 62
(Stereo.)
ROULETTE (25003 "Budd Knox")....75-100 57
U.A.....10-15 69
Members (Rhythm Orchids): Buddy Knox; Jimmy Bowen; Dave Alldred; Don Lanier.

KNOX, Buddy / Jimmy Bowen

(With the Rhythm Orchids) *P&R/R&B '57*

Singles: 78 rpm

ROULETTE....20-40 57
TRIPLE-D (797 "Party Doll"/"I'm Stickin' with You")....50-100 57

Singles: 7-inch

ROULETTE (4001 "My Baby's Gone"/ "I'm Stickin' with You")....30-50 57
TRIPLE-D (797 "Party Doll"/"I'm Stickin' with You")....300-400 57

LPs: 10/12-inch

MURRAY HILL....5-8 80s
ROULETTE (25048 "Buddy Knox & Jimmy Bowen")....75-125 58
Members (Rhythm Orchids): Buddy Knox; Jimmy Bowen; Dave Alldred; Don Lanier.
Also see BOWEN, Jimmy
Also see KNOX, Buddy

KOFFIE *D&D '83*

Singles: 12-inch

PAN DISC....4-6 83

KOFFMAN, Moe *P&R '58*

(Moe Koffman Quartette; Quintet; Septette)

Singles: 7-inch

ABC....3-5 73
ASCOT....4-6 62
ATCO....4-6 65
GOLD EAGLE....4-8 61
JUBILEE....3-8 58-68
PALETTE....4-6 60-63
VIRGO....3-5 72

LPs: 10/12-inch

ASCOT....10-15 62
JANUS....5-8 78
JUBILEE (1000 series)....15-25 57-58
JUBILEE (8000 series)....8-12 68
U.A.....15-25 62-63

KOKOMO *P&R '61*

(James Wisner)

Singles: 7-inch

FELSTED....5-10 61-62
FUTURE (1023 "Asia Minor")....10-20 61

Picture Sleeves

FELSTED....8-12 61

LPs: 10/12-inch

FELSTED....15-20 61

KOKOMO *LP '75*

Singles: 7-inch

COLUMBIA....3-5 75-76

LPs: 10/12-inch

COLUMBIA....8-10 75-76
Member: Tony O'Malley.
Also see 10CC

KOKO-POP *R&B '84*

Singles: 7-inch

MOTOWN....3-4 84-85

LPs: 10/12-inch

MOTOWN....5-8 84
Members: Eric O'Neal; Matt Seward; Chris Powell; Recco Philmore; Alexandro.

KOLBY, Diane *P&R '70*

Singles: 7-inch

COLUMBIA....3-5 70-71

KOMIKO *R&B '82*

Singles: 7-inch

SAM....3-4 82

KON KAN *P&R '88*

Singles: 7-inch

ATLANTIC....3-4 88-89

Picture Sleeves

ATLANTIC....3-4 88-89

KONGAS P&R/LP '78

Singles: 7-inch

POLYDOR 3-5 78

LPs: 10/12-inch

POLYDOR 5-8 78
SALSOUL 5-8 78

KONGOS, John P&R '71
(John T. Kongos; Johnny Kongos)

Singles: 7-inch

ELEKTRA 3-5 71-72
GROOVE 8-12 61
KAPP 4-8 67
RCA 6-12 63

Picture Sleeves

ELEKTRA 3-5 71

LPs: 10/12-inch

ELEKTRA 8-10 72
JANUS 8-10 71

KONK D&D '84

Singles: 12-inch

SLEEPING BAG 4-6 84

KOOL, Dr. J.R: see DR. J.R. KOOL

KOOL & GANG P&R/R&B '69

Singles: 12-inch

DE-LITE 4-8 79-85
MERCURY 4-6 86-87

Singles: 7-inch

DE-LITE 3-5 69-85
MERCURY 3-4 86-87

Picture Sleeves

DE-LITE 3-5 85
MERCURY 3-4 86-87

LPs: 10/12-inch

DE-LITE (Except 8502) 8-10 69-87
DE-LITE (8502 "Something Special") 8-10 81
DE-LITE (8502 "History of Kool and the Gang") 15-20 81
(Promotional issue only. With interviews.)
MERCURY 5-8 86-88
Members: Robert "Kool" Bell; Ronald Bell; George Brown; Curtis Williams; Charles Smith; James Taylor.
Also see BAND AID

KOOL MOE DEE P&R/R&B/LP '87

Singles: 7-inch

JIVE 3-4 87-88

LPs: 10/12-inch

JIVE 5-8 87-91

KOOPER, Al LP '69

Singles: 7-inch

AURORA 4-8 67
COLUMBIA 3-6 69-71
VERVE/FOLKWAYS 4-8 66

Picture Sleeves

COLUMBIA 3-5 69

LPs: 10/12-inch

COLUMBIA 10-15 69-82
U.A. 8-10 76
Also see APPALOOSA
Also see BLOOD, SWEAT & TEARS
Also see BLOOMFIELD, Mike, & Al Kooper
Also see BLUES PROJECT
Also see DYLAN, Bob
Also see ROYAL TEENS

KOOPER, Al / Blood, Sweat & Tears

Singles

AURAVISION ("You've Got It First") 6-12 79
(Square cardboard picture disc from a teen magazine.)
Also see BLOOD, SWEAT & TEARS

KOOPER, Al, & Steve Mills

Singles: 7-inch

COLUMBIA 4-8 68

KOOPER, Al, & Shuggie Otis LP '70

LPs: 10/12-inch

COLUMBIA 10-15 69
Also see KOOPER, Al
Also see OTIS, Shuggie

KOPPER R&B '86

Singles: 7-inch

KMA 3-4 86-87

KORGIS P&R/LP '80

Singles: 7-inch

ASYLUM 3-5 80
W.B. 3-6 79

LPs: 10/12-inch

ASYLUM 5-8 80
W.B. 5-10 79
Members: Andrew Davis; Jim Warren.
Also see STACKRIDGE

KORONA P&R '80

Singles: 7-inch

U.A. 3-5 79-80

LPs: 10/12-inch

U.A. 5-8 80
Members: Bruce Blackman; Bob Gauthler.
Also see ETERNITY'S CHILDREN
Also see STARBUCK

KOSSOFF, Paul LP '75

LPs: 10/12-inch

DJM 10-12 77
ISLAND 8-10 73-75
Also see BACK STREET CRAWLER
Also see FREE

KOSSOFF / Kirke / Tetsu / Rabbit

LPs: 10/12-inch

ISLAND 8-10 72
Members: Paul Kossoff; Simon Kirke.
Also see FREE
Also see KOSSOFF, Paul

KOSTELANETZ, Andre, & His Orchestra LP '55

Singles: 78 rpm

COLUMBIA 3-5 50-57

Singles: 7-inch

COLUMBIA 4-8 50-61

EPs: 7-inch

COLUMBIA 5-10 50-59

LPs: 10/12-inch

COLUMBIA 5-15 50-71
HARMONY 5-10
Also see STREISAND, Barbra / Doris Day / Jim Nabors / Andre Kostelanetz

KOTTKE, Leo LP '71

Singles: 7-inch

CAPITOL 3-5 75

LPs: 10/12-inch

CAPITOL (Except 16000 series) 8-12 71-76
CAPITOL (16000 series) 5-8 81
CHRYSALIS 5-10 76-81
OBLIVION 15-20
SYMPOSIUM 10-12 70
TAKOMA 8-12 71-74

KOTTKE, Leo, John Fahey & Peter Lang

LPs: 10/12-inch

TAKOMA 8-10 74
Also see FAHEY, John
Also see KOTTKE, Leo

KOZ, Dave LP '91

LPs: 10/12-inch

CAPITOL 5-8 91

KRAFTWERK P&R/LP '75

Singles: 12-inch

W.B. 4-6 83

Singles: 7-inch

CAPITOL 3-5 76-78
VERTIGO 3-5 75
W.B. 3-4 81-83

Picture Sleeves

W.B. 3-4 81-83

LPs: 10/12-inch

CAPITOL 8-10 75-78
MERCURY 5-8 77
VERTIGO 8-10 73-75
W.B. 5-8 80-86

KRAMER, Billy J., & Dakotas P&R/LP '64

Singles: 7-inch

EPIC 4-8 68
ERIC 3-5
IMPERIAL 4-8 64-66
LIBERTY (55586 "Do You Want to Know a Secret"/"I'll Be on My Way") 8-12 63
LIBERTY (55626 "Bad to Me") 8-10 64
LIBERTY (55643 "I'll Keep You Satisfied") 8-10 64
LIBERTY (55667 "Do You Want to Know a Secret"/"Bad to Me") 5-8 64

Picture Sleeves

IMPERIAL (66051 "From a Window") 10-15 64

LPs: 10/12-inch

CAPITOL 8-10 78-79
IMPERIAL (9267 "Little Children") 25-35 64
(Monaural.)
IMPERIAL (9273 "I'll Keep You Satisfied") 25-35 64
(Monaural.)
IMPERIAL (9291 "Trains and Boats and Planes") 25-35 65
(Monaural.)
IMPERIAL (12267 "Little Children") 25-40 64
(Stereo.)
IMPERIAL (12273 "I'll Keep You Satisfied") 25-40 64
(Stereo.)
IMPERIAL (12291 "Trains and Boats and Planes") 25-40 65
(Stereo.)

KRANZ, George D&D '83

Singles: 12-inch

PERSONAL 4-6 83

Singles: 7-inch

PERSONAL 3-4 83-84

KRAVITZ, Lenny LP '89

Singles: 7-inch

VIRGIN 3-4 89-90

LPs: 10/12-inch

VIRGIN 5-8 89-91

KRISTOFFERSON, Kris P&R/LP '71

Singles: 7-inch

A&M 3-4 73
COLUMBIA 3-5 77-81
EPIC 4-8 67
MONUMENT 3-5 70-81

Picture Sleeves

A&M 3-4 73

EPs: 7-inch

MONUMENT (532 "Kristofferson") 5-10 71
(Promotional issue only.)

LPs: 10/12-inch

COLUMBIA 5-8 77-81
MONUMENT 8-12 70-76
Session: Larry Gatlin; Rita Coolidge.
Also see JENNINGS, Waylon, Willie Nelson, Johnny Cash, & Kris Kristofferson
Also see NELSON, Willie, & Kris Kristofferson

KRISTOFFERSON, Kris, & Rita Coolidge C&W '73

Singles: 7-inch

A&M 3-5 73-74
MONUMENT 3-5 74-75

Picture Sleeves

A&M 3-5 73

LPs: 10/12-inch

A&M (Except PR-4690) 8-12 73-79
A&M (PR-4690 "Natural Act") 10-15 79
(Picture disc, numbered edition. Promotional issue only.)
MONUMENT 8-10 74
Also see COOLIDGE, Rita

KRISTOFFERSON, Kris, Willie Nelson, Dolly Parton, & Brenda Lee

LPs: 10/12-inch

Monument....8-12 82

Also see KRISTOFFERSON, Kris
Also see NELSON, Willie
Also see PARTON, Dolly

KROKUS LP '81

Singles: 7-inch

ARIOLA AMERICA....3-4 81
ARISTA....3-4 82-86

Picture Sleeves

ARISTA....3-4 84-86

LPs: 10/12-inch

ARIOLA AMERICA....5-8 81
ARISTA....5-8 82-86
MCA....5-8 88

Members: Dani Crivelli; Chris Von Rohr; Marc Storace; Fernando Von Arb; Mark Kohler.

KRUSH GROOVE ALL STARS R&B '85

Singles: 12-inch

W.B. 4-6 85

Also see BLOW, Kurtis
Also see SHEILA E.
Also see FAT BOYS
Also see RUN D.M.C.

KRYSTAL GENERATION R&B '71

Singles: 7-inch

BUDDAH 4-6 69
MR. CHAND 3-5 71

Members: Joyce Smith; Darlene Arnold; Mary Shelley; Mary Lead; Wylie Dixon; Walter "Simtec" Simmons.
Also see SIMTEC & WYLIE

KRYSTOL R&B/D&D '84

Singles: 12-inch

EPIC 4-6 84-86

Singles: 7-inch

EPIC 3-4 84-86

LPs: 10/12-inch

EPIC 5-8 86

KUBAN, Bob P&R/LP '66
(With the In-Men; Bob Kuban Band)

Singles: 7-inch

ERIC....3-5 70s
MUSICLAND USA (Except 20001)......5-10 66-67
MUSICLAND USA. (20001 "The Cheater") 10-20 66
("Vocal by Walter Scott" shown on both sides.)
MUSICLAND USA (20001 The Cheater") 5-10 66
("Vocal by Walter Scott" shown only on flip, *Try Me Baby.*)
MUSICLAND USA (20001 "The Cheater") 4-8 66
("Vocal by Walter Scott" not on either side.)
NORMAN....5-15 65-66
(Walter Scott may be shown as "Little Walter.")
REPRISE....4-8 70

LPs: 10/12-inch

MUSICLAND USA (3500 "Look Out for the Cheater") 25-35 66

Members: Walter Scott; Bob Kuban; John Krenski; Greg Hoeltzel.
Also see CASH, J.D., & Bob Kuban Brass

KUF-LINX P&R '58
("Featuring John Jennings"; Kuff-Linx)

Singles: 78 rpm

CHALLENGE....25-50 57-58

Singles: 7-inch

CHALLENGE (1013 "So Tough")......25-50 57
(Blue or white label.)
CHALLENGE (1013 "So Tough")......15-25 58
(Maroon label.)
CHALLENGE (59004 "Service with a Smile") 15-25 58
CHALLENGE (59015 "Climb Love's Mountain")....25-50 58

Member: John Jennings.

KULIS, Charlie P&R '75

Singles: 7-inch

PLAYBOY 3-5 75

KWAME LP '89
(With a New Beginning)

LPs: 10/12-inch

ATLANTIC....5-8 89-90
POLYDOR 5-8 80

KWICK R&B '80

Singles: 12-inch

CAPITOL....4-6 83

Singles: 7-inch

CAPITOL....3-4 83
EMI AMERICA 3-4 80-82

LPs: 10/12-inch

CAPITOL....5-8 83
EMI AMERICA 5-8 80-81

Members: Terry Bartlett; Bert Brown; William Sumlin; Vince Williams.
Also see NEWCOMERS

KYM R&B '84

Singles: 12-inch

AWARD....4-6 84

Singles: 7-inch

AWARD 3-4 84

KYPER P&R/LP '90

Singles: 7-inch

ATLANTIC....3-4 90

LPs: 10/12-inch

ATLANTIC....5-8 90

L.A. BOPPERS — R&B/LP '80
Singles: 7-inch
MCA 3-4 82
MERCURY 3-5 80-81
LPs: 10/12-inch
MCA 5-8 82
MERCURY 5-10 80-81
Also see SIDE EFFECT

L.A. DREAM TEAM — R&B/LP '86
Singles: 12-inch
MCA 4-6 86
Singles: 7-inch
MCA 3-4 86
LPs: 10/12-inch
MCA 5-8 86-87
Members: Rudy Pardee; Chris Wilson.

L.A. EXPRESS — LP '76
Singles: 7-inch
CARIBOU 3-5 75-78
LPs: 10/12-inch
CARIBOU 8-10 75-76
Also see MITCHELL, Joni, & L.A. Express
Also see SCOTT, Tom

L.A. GUNS — LP '88
LPs: 10/12-inch
VERTIGO 5-8 88-89
Members: Philip Lewis; Tracii Guns; Kelly Nickels; Mick Cripps; Steve Riley.
Also see W.A.S.P.

L.A. JETS — P&R '76
Singles: 7-inch
RCA 3-5 76
LPs: 10/12-inch
RCA 8-10 76

L.L. COOL J — R&B '85
(Ladies Love Cool James; James Todd Smith)
Singles: 12-inch
COLUMBIA 4-6 85-86
Singles: 7-inch
COLUMBIA 3-4 85-86
DEF JAM 3-4 87-90
MOTOWN 3-4 90
Picture Sleeves
DEF JAM 3-4 88
LPs: 10/12-inch
CAPITOL 5-10 90s
COLUMBIA 5-8 85
DEF JAM 5-10 87-90

L7 — LP '92
LPs: 10/12-inch
EPITAPH (86401 "L7") 5-8 88
(With lyrics insert.)
W.B. (45624 "Hungry for Stink") 5-8 90s
W.B. (86401 "L7") 5-8 90s
Members: Suzi Gardner; Jennifer Finch; Donita Sparks; Roy Koutsky; René Lucas.

L.T.D. — P&R/R&B/LP '76
(Love, Togetherness & Devotion)
Singles: 7-inch
A&M 3-5 76-80
MONTAGE 3-4 83
Picture Sleeves
A&M 3-5 76-78
LPs: 10/12-inch
A&M 8-10 74-81
MONTAGE 5-8 83
SPRINGBOARD 8-10 77
Members: Jeffrey Osborne; Leslie Ray; Andre Ray.
Also see OSBORNE, Jeffrey

LTG EXCHANGE — R&B '74
Singles: 7-inch
FANIA 3-5 74
WAND 3-5 74

LABAN — P&R '86
Singles: 7-inch
CRITIQUE 3-4 86

LABELLE, Patti — P&R '63
(With the Blue Belles; Pattie La Belle; Labelle)
Singles: 12-inch
EPIC 4-8 78-79
MCA 4-6 85
PHILADELPHIA INT'L 4-6 83-85
Singles: 7-inch
ATLANTIC 5-10 65-70
EPIC 3-6 74-80
KING 8-12 63
MISTLETOE 3-5 73
PHILADELPHIA INT'L 3-5 81-85
MCA 3-4 85-87
NEWTIME (510 "Love Me Just a Little") 10-15 62
NEWTOWN (5777 "Down the Aisle") 10-15 63
(Reads "Pressed by King Records.")
NEWTOWN (5777 "Down the Aisle") 5-10 63
(No mention of King Records.")
NICETOWN 5-10 64
PARKWAY 5-10 64
RCA 3-6 73
TRIP 3-6 71
W.B. 3-6 71-72
Picture Sleeves
MCA 3-4 85-86
LPs: 10/12-inch
ATLANTIC 15-25 65-67
EPIC 8-10 74-82
MCA 5-8 85-89
MISTLETOE 10-20 60s
NEWTOWN (631 "Sweethearts of the Apollo") 50-75 63
NEWTOWN (632 "Sleigh Bells, Jingle Bells and Blue Bells") 50-75 63
PARKWAY (7043 "On Stage") 30-40 64
PHILADELPHIA INT'L 5-8 81-85
RCA (0200 series) 8-10 73
RCA (4100 series) 5-8 82
TRIP 8-10 71-75
U.A. 8-10 74-75
UPFRONT 10-15
W.B. 8-10 71-72
Also see BLUE BELLES
Also see DASH, Sarah
Also see HENDRIX, Nona
Also see NYRO, Laura
Also see WOMACK, Bobby, & Patti Labelle

LABELLE, Patti, & Bill Champlin
Singles: 7-inch
MCA 3-4 87
Picture Sleeves
MCA 3-4 87
Also see CHAMPLIN, Harold

LABELLE, Patti / Harold Faltermeyer
Singles: 7-inch
MCA 3-4 85
Also see FALTERMEYER, Harold

LABELLE, Patti, & Michael McDonald — P&R/R&B '86
Singles: 7-inch
MCA 3-4 86
Picture Sleeves
MCA 3-4 86
Also see McDONALD, Michael

LABELLE, Patti, & Grover Washington Jr. — R&B '82
Singles: 7-inch
ELEKTRA 3-4 82
Also see LABELLE, Patti
Also see WASHINGTON, Grover, Jr.

LA BOUNTY, Bill — P&R '78
Singles: 7-inch
20TH FOX 3-5 75-76
W.B. 3-5 78

LABYRINTH — R&B '85
Singles: 7-inch
21 3-4 85
Member: Julie Loco.

LACE — R&B '87
Singles: 7-inch
WING 3-4 87
LPs: 10/12-inch
WING 5-8 87

LADD, Cheryl — P&R/LP '78
Singles: 12-inch
CAPITOL (8894 "Skinnydippin' ") 10-15 78
(Promotional issue only.)
Singles: 7-inch
CAPITOL 3-5 76-79
Picture Sleeves
CAPITOL 3-5 78-79
W.B. 4-6 74
LPs: 10/12-inch
CAPITOL 8-10 78-79
Also see JOSIE & PUSSYCATS
Also see VALLI, Frankie, & Cheryl Ladd

LADIES' CHOICE — R&B '83
Singles: 7-inch
STREETWISE 3-4 83

LADY — R&B '82
Singles: 7-inch
MEGA 3-4 82

LADY FLASH — P&R '76
Singles: 7-inch
RSO 3-5 76
LPs: 10/12-inch
RSO 8-12 76
Members: Monica Burruss; Debra Byrd; Reparata.
Also see MANILOW, Barry
Also see REPARATA

LAFAYETTES — P&R '62
(With Frank James)
Singles: 7-inch
BONA (1741 "I Lost My Way") 25-50
RCA (8044 "Life's Too Short") 20-30 62
RCA (8082 "Caravan of Lonely Men") 15-25 62
Member: Frank Bonarrigo.

LA FLAMME, David — P&R/LP '76
Singles: 7-inch
AMHERST 3-5 76-77
Picture Sleeves
AMHERST 3-5 76
LPs: 10/12-inch
AMHERST 8-10 76-78
Also see IT'S a BEAUTIFUL DAY

LA FLAVOUR — R&B '79
Singles: 12-inch
SWEET CITY 8-10 80
Singles: 7-inch
MERCURY 3-5 79
SWEET CITY 3-5 80
LPs: 10/12-inch
SWEET CITY 5-8 80

LA FORGE, Jack — P&R '65
("With His Piano & Orchestra")
Singles: 7-inch
REGINA (Except 284) 4-8 63-66
REGINA (284 "Cleopatra Kick") 8-15 63
RIO 4-6 62
LPs: 10/12-inch
AUDIO FIDELITY 6-12 66
PURPLETONE 8-15 62
REGINA 8-15 63-65

LAI, Francis, & His Orchestra — P&R '71
Singles: 7-inch
PARAMOUNT 3-5 70

Picture Sleeves
PARAMOUNT 3-5 70
Also see JOHN, Elton
You'll find many more listings by this artist in *The Official Price Guide to Movie/TV Soundtracks and Original Cast Albums,* containing over 8,000 listings.

LAID BACK D&D '83
Singles: 12-inch
SIRE 4-6 84-85
W.B. 4-6 83
Singles: 7-inch
SIRE 3-4 84-85
W.B. 3-4 83-84
LPs: 10/12-inch
SIRE 5-8 84
Members: Timothy Stahl; John Guldberg.

LAINE, Cleo LP '74
Singles: 7-inch
RCA 3-5 74-80
LPs: 10/12-inch
BUDDAH 8-10 74
FONTANA 10-15 66
GNP 5-10 74
QUINTESSENCE 5-8 80
RCA 5-10 73-80
Also see CHARLES, Ray, & Cleo Laine

LAINE, Cleo, & James Galway LP '80
LPs: 10/12-inch
RCA 5-8 80
Also see GALWAY, James
Also see LAINE, Cleo

LAINE, Frankie P&R/R&B '47
(With Paul Weston & the Mellomen)
Singles: 78 rpm
MERCURY 5-15 47-51
MERCURY/SAV-WAY (1027 "On the Sunny Side of the Street") 150-200 47
(Picture disc. Promotional issue only.)
MERCURY/SAV-WAY (1028 "West End Blues") 150-200 47
(Picture disc. Promotional issue only.)
MERCURY/SAV-WAY (5059 "Kiss Me Again") 100-200 47
(Picture disc. Promotional issue only.)
COLUMBIA 5-15 51-57
Singles: 7-inch
ABC 3-5 67-69
AMOS 3-5 70-71
CAPITOL 4-8 64-66
COLUMBIA (39367 thru 41486) 10-20 51-59
COLUMBIA (41613 thru 42966) 5-10 60-64
MAINSTREAM 3-5 75
MERCURY (5000 series) 10-20 50-51
SUNFLOWER 3-5 72
W.B. 3-5 74
Picture Sleeves
COLUMBIA 15-25 56-57
EPs: 7-inch
COLUMBIA 10-20 52-59
MERCURY 10-20 51-54
LPs: 10/12-inch
ABC (600 series) 8-15 67-69
ABC (30000 series) 5-8 76
AMOS 8-12 70-71
CAPITOL 10-15 65
COLUMBIA (600 thru 1200 series) 15-30 54-58
COLUMBIA (1300 thru 1900 series) 10-20 59-63
(Monaural.)
COLUMBIA (2500 series) 20-30 56
(10-inch LPs.)
COLUMBIA (6000 series) 20-40 53-54
(10-inch LPs.)
COLUMBIA (8100 thru 8700 series) 10-20 59-63
(Stereo.)
HARMONY 8-15 65-71
HINDSIGHT 4-8 84
MERCURY (20000 series) 20-40 54-61
MERCURY (25000 series) 50-75 51-52
(10-inch LPs.)
MERCURY (60000 series) 15-25 61
PICKWICK 5-10 78
TOWER 8-15 67
TRIP 5-8 75
WING 8-15 60-67
Also see DAY, Doris, & Frankie Laine
Also see MILLER, Mitch

LAINE, Frankie, & Jimmy Boyd P&R '53
Singles: 78 rpm
COLUMBIA 4-8 53
Singles: 7-inch
COLUMBIA 10-20 53
Also see BOYD, Jimmy

LAINE, Frankie, & Easy Riders P&R '57
Singles: 78 rpm
COLUMBIA 4-8 57
Singles: 7-inch
COLUMBIA 10-20 57
Also see GILKYSON, Terry

LAINE, Frankie, & Four Lads P&R '54
Singles: 78 rpm
COLUMBIA 4-8 54
Singles: 7-inch
COLUMBIA 10-20 54
EPs: 7-inch
COLUMBIA 10-20 56
LPs: 10/12-inch
COLUMBIA 20-30 56
Also see FOUR LADS

LAINE, Frankie, & Andre Previn
LP: 10/12-inch
RONDO 8-12
Also see PREVIN, Andre

LAINE, Frankie, & Jo Stafford P&R '51
Singles: 78 rpm
COLUMBIA 4-8 51-53
Singles: 7-inch
COLUMBIA 10-20 51-53
EPs: 7-inch
COLUMBIA 10-20 54
LPs: 10/12-inch
COLUMBIA 20-40 54
Also see LAINE, Frankie
Also see STAFFORD, Jo

LAKE P&R/LP '77
Singles: 7-inch
CARIBOU 3-5 81
COLUMBIA 3-5 77-79
LPs: 10/12-inch
CARIBOU 5-8 81
COLUMBIA 5-10 77-79

LAKE, Greg P&R '75
Singles: 7-inch
ATLANTIC 3-5 75-77
CHRYSALIS 3-5 81
Picture Sleeves
ATLANTIC 3-5 75
LPs: 10/12-inch
CHRYSALIS 5-10 81
Also see EMERSON, LAKE & PALMER
Also see KING CRIMSON

LAKESIDE R&B '78
Singles: 7-inch
ABC-PAR 3-5 77
ELEKTRA 3-4
SOLAR 3-5 78-87
Picture Sleeves
SOLAR 3-5
LPs: 10/12-inch
ABC-PAR 8-10 77
SOLAR 5-8 77-84
Members: Tiemeyer McCain; Thomas Shelby; Mark Woods; Otis Stokes; Steve Shockley; Marvin Craig; Norman Beavers; Fred Alexander; Fred Lewis.

LA LA R&B '87
(La Forest Cope)
Singles: 7-inch
ARISTA 3-4 87

LA LA, Prince: see PRINCE LA LA

LAMAS, Lorenzo P&R '84
Singles: 7-inch
SCOTTI BROTHERS 3-4 84-85
Picture Sleeves
SCOTTI BROTHERS 3-4 84

LAMB, Kevin P&R '78
Singles: 7-inch
ARISTA 3-5 78

LAMBERT, Guy: see PRESLEY, Elvis

LAMOND, George P&R/LP '90
Singles: 7-inch
COLUMBIA 3-4 90
LPs: 10/12-inch
COLUMBIA 5-8 90

LAMONT, Lee R&B '65
Singles: 7-inch
BACK BEAT 5-10 64-66

L'AMOUR D&D '84
Singles: 12-inch
BROCCOLLI 4-6 84

LAMP SISTERS R&B '68
Singles: 7-inch
DUKE 4-8 68-69

LANCE, Herb R&B '49
(With the Classics; with Roger Sherman & Orchestra)
Singles: 78 rpm
DELUXE 15-25 57
SITTIN' in WITH (514 "Close Your Eyes") 20-40 49
SITTIN' in WITH (519 "Because") 20-40 49
Singles: 7-inch
DELUXE (6150 "You Can't Be Sure") 25-35 57
MALA (404 "Like a Baby") 10-20 59
MALA (405 "Some Love") 10-20 59
MALA (420 "Deep in My Heart") 10-20 60
PROMO (1010 "Blue Moon") 20-30 61
LPs: 10/12-inch
CHESS (1506 "Comeback") 20-30 66

LANCE, Major P&R/R&B/LP '63
Singles: 12-inch
KAT FAMILY 4-6 82
Singles: 7-inch
COLUMBIA 3-5 77
CURTOM 4-6 70
DAKAR 5-10 69
EPIC 4-8 66
KAT FAMILY 3-4 82
MERCURY (71582 "I've Got a Girl") 20-30 60
OKEH (7168 thru 7197) 5-10 63-64
OKEH (7200 "Think Nothing About It") 25-50 64
OKEH (7203 thru 7266) 8-15 64-66
OKEH (7284 "You Don't Want Me No More") 25-50 67
OKEH (7298 "Forever") 5-10 67
OSIRIS 3-5 75
PLAYBOY 3-5 74-75
SOUL 3-5 78
VOLT 3-5 72
Picture Sleeves
OKEH 5-10 63-65
EPs: 7-inch
OKEH 10-15 64
(Juke box issue only.)
LPs: 10/12-inch
BACK-TRAC 5-8 85
CONTEMPO 10-12
KAT FAMILY 5-8 83
OKEH 15-20 63-64
SOUL 5-8 78

LANCERS P&R '53
Singles: 78 rpm
CORAL 4-6 54-56
Singles: 7-inch
CORAL 5-10 54-56
IMPERIAL 5-8 59

LANCELOT 4-8
SWF 4-8 62
TREND 5-10 54

Picture Sleeves

SWF 4-8 62

EPs: 7-inch

CORAL 10-20 55

LPs: 10/12-inch

IMPERIAL....................15-25 59

Members: Jerry Meacham; Dick Burr; Bob Porter; Corky Lindgren.

Also see McGUIRE SISTERS / Lancers / Dorothy Collins / Teresa Brewer

LANDIS, Jerry *P&R '63*

(Paul Simon)

Singles: 7-inch

AMY (875 "Lone Teen Ranger")........25-35 62
CANADIAN AMERICAN (130 "I'm Lonely")....................25-50 61
MGM (12822 "Anna Belle") 25-50 59
WARWICK (552 "Just a Boy")...........25-50 60
WARWICK (588 "Just a Boy")...........25-50 60
WARWICK (619 "Play Me a Sad Song")....................40-60 61

Also see SIMON, Paul

LANDS, Liz

Singles: 7-inch

GORDY (7026 "What He Lived For")....................20-25 63
ONE-DERFUL 5-10 67

LANDS, Liz / Martin Luther King

Singles: 7-inch

GORDY (7023 "We Shall Overcome")....................15-25 63

Also see KING, Rev. Martin Luther, Jr.

LANDS, Liz, & Temptations

Singles: 7-inch

GORDY (7030 "Keep Me") 25-50 64

Also see LANDS, Liz
Also see TEMPTATIONS

LANE, Mickey Lee *P&R '64*

Singles: 7-inch

MALA....................5-8 68
SWAN....................5-10 64-66

LANE, Robin, & Chartbusters *P&R '80*

Singles: 7-inch

W.B. 3-5 80-81

Picture Sleeves

W.B. 3-5 80

LPs: 10/12-inch

W.B. 5-8 80-81

Members: Robin Lane; Leroy Radcliffe; Asa Brebner; Scott Baerenwald; Tim Jackson.

LANE BROTHERS *P&R '57*

Singles: 78 rpm

RCA....................5-15 57

Singles: 7-inch

FXL 3-4 81
LEADER 5-10 60
RCA (6810 "Marianne")..................10-20 57
RCA (6900 "Uh-uh Honey")...............20-30 57
RCA (7220 "Boppin' in the Sack").....20-30 58
RCA (7304 "Little Brother")..............20-30 58

Members: Pete Lane; Arthur Lane; Frank Lane.

LANE BROTHERS / Julius La Rosa

EPs: 7-inch

RCA....................10-20 57
(Promotional issue only.)

Also see LANE BROTHERS
Also see LA ROSA, Julius

LANG, k.d. *LP '88*

(k.d. lang & the Reclines)

Singles: 7-inch

SIRE 3-4 88-91
W.B. 3-4 90s

Picture Sleeves

SIRE 3-4

LPs: 10/12-inch

SIRE 5-8 88-90
W.B. 8-10 90s

Also see DION
Also see ORBISON, Roy, & K.D. Lang

LANIER & CO. *P&R/R&B '82*

Singles: 7-inch

LARC 3-4 82-83

LPs: 10/12-inch

LARC 5-8 83

Member: Farris Lanier Jr.

LANIN, Lester, & His Orch. *LP '57*

Singles: 78 rpm

EPIC....................3-5 56-57

Singles: 7-inch

EPIC....................4-8 56-62

EPs: 7-inch

EPIC....................4-8 56-58

LPs: 10/12-inch

EPIC....................5-15 56-62
PHILIPS 5-10 65

LANOIS, Daniel *LP '90*

LPs: 10/12-inch

W.B./OPAL 5-8 89

LANSON, Snooky *P&R '48*

(With the Ray Noble Orchestra)

Singles: 78 rpm

DECCA 3-6 52
DOT 3-6 55-56
LONDON....................3-6 49-51
MERCURY....................4-8 48
REPUBLIC....................3-6 53

Singles: 7-inch

DECCA 5-10 52
DOT 5-10 55-56
LONDON....................5-10 50-51
REPUBLIC....................5-10 53
STARDAY....................3-6 68

LPs: 10/12-inch

CAMDEN (200 series) 10-20 55
DOT 10-15 60
STARDAY....................5-10 68

LANZ, David *LP '88*

(With Paul Speer)

LPs: 10/12-inch

NARADA....................5-8 88

LANZA, Mario *P&R '50*

Singles: 78 rpm

RCA 3-5 50-57

Singles: 7-inch

RCA (0400 series) 3-5 71
RCA (3200 thru 8500 series) 5-10 51-59
RCA (1300 series) 4-6 50

Picture Sleeves

RCA (3300 "The Loveliest Night of the Year")....................15-25 51
RCA (4209 "Song of India") 15-25 51
RCA 5-8 50s
(For generic, die-cut paper sleeves with artist photo. Not for any specific release.)

EPs: 7-inch

RCA (Except 1837)....................8-15 53-61
RCA (1837 "The Student Prince").....15-25 54
(Soundtrack.)

LPs: 10/12-inch

CAMDEN (Except 400 series) 5-15 63
CAMDEN (400 series) 10-20 57
(With "CAL" prefix. Monaural.)
CAMDEN (400 series) 8-15 63
(With "CAS" prefix. Stereo.)
RCA (75 "Toast of New Orleans").....45-60 51
(Soundtrack. (10-inch LP.)
RCA (86 thru 1181)....................20-30 51-53
RCA (1750 "A Legendary Performer")..5-8 76
RCA (1837 "The Student Prince").....35-45 54
(Soundtrack.)
RCA (1860 thru 2090)....................15-25 54-57
(Black label.)
RCA (1860 thru 2090)....................6-12 68
(Orange label.)
RCA (2211 "Seven Hills of Rome")....................20-30 58
(Soundtrack tunes on side one, other Mario Lanza songs on side two.)
RCA (2331 thru 2333) 15-25 59-61
(Black label.)
RCA (2331 thru 2333) 6-12 68
(Orange label.)
RCA (2338 "For the First Time")....................20-30 59
(Soundtrack.)
RCA (2339 thru 2790) 10-20 60-64
(Black or Red Seal label.)
RCA (2339 thru 2790) 6-12 68
(Orange or Red Seal label.)
RCA (2800 series)....................4-8 78
RCA (2900 thru 3200)....................8-15 68-71
RCA (4158 "The Mario Lanza Collection")....................35-45 81
(Boxed, five-disc set.)
RCA/TELEHOUSE....................5-10 74
(Mail order offer.)

LARKIN, Billy *LP '66*

(With the Delegates)

Singles: 78 rpm

MELODY 20-30 56

Singles: 7-inch

BRYAN 3-5 75
CASINO....................3-5 76
MELODY (103 "Rock-it, Davy Crockett")....................50-75 56
MERCURY 3-5 78-79
SUNBIRD 3-5 80-81
WORLD PACIFIC....................4-8 66

LPs: 10/12-inch

AURA....................15-25 65-66
BRYAN 5-10 75
WORLD PACIFIC....................10-20 65-69

LARKS *R&B '51*

Singles: 78 rpm

APOLLO (427 "Eyesight to the Blind")....................100-200 51
APOLLO (429 "Little Side Car") 100-200 51
APOLLO (430 "Ooh . . . It Feels So Good")....................100-200 51
APOLLO (435 "My Lost Love")......100-200 51
APOLLO (437 "Darlin' ")...............100-200 52
APOLLO (475 "Honey from the Bee")....................50-100 55
APOLLO (1177 "My Heart Cries for You")....................100-200 51
APOLLO (1180 "Hopefully Yours") 100-200 51
APOLLO (1184 "My Reverie").......150-300 51
APOLLO (1189 "Shadrack")..........100-200 52
APOLLO (1190 "Stolen Love")......100-200 52
APOLLO (1194 "Hold Me")...........100-200 52
LLOYDS (108 "Margie")...............100-200 54
LLOYDS (110 "If It's a Crime") 100-200 54
LLOYDS (112 "No Other Girl") 100-200 54
LLOYDS (114 "Forget It") 100-200 54

Singles: 7-inch

APOLLO (429 "Little Side Car") 500-750 51
APOLLO (430 "Ooh, It Feels So Good")....................500-750 51
APOLLO (435 "My Lost Love")......500-750 51
APOLLO (437 "Darlin' ")...............500-750 52
APOLLO (475 "Honey from the Bee")....................250-350 55
APOLLO (1180 "Hopefully Yours")....................500-750 51
APOLLO (1184 "My Reverie")...1000-2000 51
(Black vinyl)
APOLLO (1184 "My Reverie")...3000-5000 51
(Colored vinyl.)
APOLLO (1189 "Shadrack")..........500-750 52
APOLLO (1190 "Stolen Love")......500-750 52
(Black vinyl)
APOLLO (1190 "Stolen Love") .2000-4000 52
(Colored vinyl)
APOLLO (1194 "Hold Me")...........500-750 52
LLOYDS (108 "Margie")...............500-750 54
LLOYDS (110 "If It's a Crime") 400-600 54
LLOYDS (112 "No Other Girl") 400-600 54
LLOYDS (114 "Forget It") 300-500 54

Members: Gene Mumford; Allen Bunn; Ray Barnes; Thermon Ruth; Dave McNeil; Hadie Rowe; Orville Brooks; David Bowers; Isaiah Bing; Glen Burgess.
Also see FIVE LARKS

LARKS *P&R/R&B '61*

Singles: 7-inch

CROSS FIRE (74-50 "Fabulous Cars & Diamond Rings") ... 15-25 62
GUYDEN (2098 "I Want Her to Love Me") ... 8-12 62
GUYDEN (2103 "Fabulous Cars & Diamond Rings") ... 8-12 62
JETT (3001 "Love Me True") ... 75-125 65
SHERYL (334 "It's Unbelievable") ... 20-30 61
SHERYL (338 "There Is a Girl") ... 20-30 61
STACY ... 5-10 63
VIOLET (1051 "I Want Her to Love Me") ... 15-25 63

LPs: 10/12-inch

SHERYL ("It's Unbelievable") ... 100-200 62
(Selection number not known.)

LARKS *P&R '64*
(Don Julian & the Larks)

Singles: 7-inch

JERK ... 4-8 65
MONEY ... 4-8 64-71
NASCO ... 3-5 72

LPs: 10/12-inch

AMAZON (1009 "Greatest Hits") ... 45-55 63
MONEY ... 15-20 65-67
Also see MASON, Barbara, & Larks

LA ROSA, Julius *P&R '53*

Singles: 78 rpm

CADENCE ... 3-6 53-55

Singles: 7-inch

ABC ... 4-6 67
BARNABY ... 3-5 70
CADENCE (1200 series) ... 5-10 53-55
CADENCE (1400 series) ... 4-8 63-64
KAPP ... 4-8 60-62
MGM ... 4-6 66
MGM CELEBRITY SCENE (CS5-5 "Julius LaRosa") ... 10-20 66
(Boxed set of five singles with bio insert and title strips.)
METROMEDIA ... 3-5 70
RCA (0900 series) ... 3-5 73
RCA (6000 & 7000 series) ... 5-10 56-58
ROULETTE ... 4-8 59

EPs: 7-inch

CADENCE ... 5-15 54-58
RCA (EPA-841 "Julius LaRosa") ... 5-10 56
RCA (EPB-1299 "Julius LaRosa") ... 15-25 56

LPs: 10/12-inch

CADENCE (1007 "Julie's Best") ... 20-30 55
FORUM ... 10-15 60
KAPP ... 10-15 61
MGM ... 10-15 66-67
METROMEDIA ... 5-10 71
RCA (1299 "Julius LaRosa") ... 20-30 56
ROULETTE ... 10-20 59
Also see LANE BROTHERS / Julius La Rosa

LA ROSA, Julius, & Bob Crewe Generation

Singles: 7-inch

CREWE ... 3-6 69
Also see CREWE, Bob
Also see LA ROSA, Julius

LARRICE *D&D '84*

Singles: 12-inch

STREETWISE ... 4-6 84

LARRY & JOHNNY

Singles: 7-inch

JOLA (1000 "Beatle Time") ... 10-15 64
Members: Larry Williams; Johnny "Guitar" Watson.
Also see WILLIAMS, Larry, & Johnny Watson

LARRY LEE: see LEE, Larry

LARSEN, Neil *LP '79*

Singles: 7-inch

A&M ... 3-5 79
W.B. ... 3-4 83

LPs: 10/12-inch

A&M ... 5-8 79
HORIZON ... 8-10 78-79
W.B. ... 5-8 83
Also see LARSEN - FEITEN BAND

LARSEN - FEITEN BAND *P&R/LP '80*

Singles: 7-inch

W.B. ... 3-5 80

LPs: 10/12-inch

W.B. ... 5-8 80
Members: Neil Larsen; Buzz Feiten.
Also see LARSEN, Neil
Also see MR. MISTER

LARSON, Nicolette *P&R/LP '78*

Singles: 7-inch

MCA ... 3-4 85-86
W.B. ... 3-5 78-82

Picture Sleeves

W.B. ... 3-5 80

LPs: 10/12-inch

MCA ... 5-8 86
W.B. ... 5-8 78-82
Session: Michael McDonald. Steve Wariner.
Also see DOOBIE BROTHERS & Nicolette Larson
Also see NITTY GRITTY DIRT BAND
Also see WARINER, Steve
Also see WINCHESTER, Jesse
Also see YOUNG, Neil

LA RUE, D.C. *P&R/LP '76*

Singles: 12-inch

CASABLANCA ... 4-6 79-80
PYRAMID ... 4-8 78-79

Singles: 7-inch

CASABLANCA ... 3-5 79-80
PYRAMID ... 4-6 76-79

LPs: 10/12-inch

CASABLANCA ... 5-8 79-80
PYRAMID ... 5-10 76-79
Also see CHRISTIE, Lou

LA SALLE, Denise *P&R/R&B '71*

Singles: 7-inch

ABC ... 3-5 77-79
CHESS ... 4-8 68
MCA ... 3-5 79-80
MALACO ... 3-4 81-85
TARPEN ... 4-8 67
WESTBOUND ... 3-5 71-75

LPs: 10/12-inch

ABC ... 8-10 77-78
MCA ... 5-8 80
MALACO ... 5-8 81-85
WESTBOUND ... 8-10 72-75

LASLEY, David *P&R/R&B '82*

Singles: 12-inch

EMI AMERICA ... 4-6 84

Singles: 7-inch

EMI AMERICA ... 3-4 82-84

LASSIES *P&R '56*

Singles: 78 rpm

DECCA ... 5-10 56

Singles: 7-inch

DECCA ... 8-12 56

LAST, James *P&R/LP '72*
(James Last Band)

Singles: 7-inch

POLYDOR ... 3-5 71-82

LPs: 10/12-inch

POLYDOR ... 5-10 72-81

LAST POETS *LP '70*

Singles: 7-inch

DOUGLAS ... 3-5 71

LPs: 10/12-inch

BLUE THUMB ... 8-12 72-73
DOUGLAS ... 10-15 70-71

LAST WORD *P&R '67*
(Last Words)

Singles: 7-inch

ATCO ... 4-8 67-68
BOOM ... 4-8 66
DOWNEY ... 5-10 65

LPs: 10/12-inch

ATCO ... 10-20 68

LATEEF, Yusef *LP '69*
(Yusef Lateef Quintet)

Singles: 7-inch

ATLANTIC ... 3-5 68-70
IMPULSE ... 3-6 64
NEW JAZZ ... 4-8 60
PRESTIGE ... 3-6 63-69

LPs: 10/12-inch

ATLANTIC ... 8-15 68-76
CTI ... 5-8 77-79
CADET ... 10-15 69
CHARLIE PARKER ... 20-30 62
EVEREST ... 5-10 74
IMPULSE (56 thru 9125) ... 10-20 63-66
IMPULSE (9200 & 9300 series) ... 5-10 73-78
MILESTONE ... 8-12 73
MOODSVILLE ... 25-35 61
NEW JAZZ ... 25-40 59-61
PRESTIGE (7122 "The Sounds of Yusef Lateef") ... 50-100 57
(Yellow label.)
PRESTIGE (7400 thru 7800 series) .. 10-20 66-71
PRESTIGE (24000 series) ... 8-15 72-74
RIVERSIDE (300 series) ... 20-30 60
(Monaural.)
RIVERSIDE (3000 series) ... 10-20 68
RIVERSIDE (9300 series) ... 25-35 60
(Stereo.)
SAVOY (2200 series) ... 8-12 76-79
SAVOY (12000 series) ... 25-50 56-58
SAVOY (13000 series) ... 25-50 58
TRIP ... 5-10 73
VERVE (8217 "Before Dawn") ... 50-100 57
(Reads "Verve Records, Inc." at bottom of label.)
VERVE (8217 "Before Dawn") ... 25-35 60s
(Reads "MGM Records - a Division of Metro-Goldwyn-Mayer, Inc." at bottom of label.)

LATIMORE, Benny *R&B '73*
(Latimore)

Singles: 7-inch

ATLANTIC ... 4-8 69
DADE ... 5-10 67-68
GLADES ... 3-6 73-79
HIT ... 4-6 60s
MALACO ... 3-4 83-86

LPs: 10/12-inch

GLADES ... 8-10 73-78
MALACO ... 5-8 83-86

LATTISAW, Stacy *R&B '79*

Singles: 7-inch

COTILLION ... 3-5 79-84
MOTOWN ... 3-4 86-88

Picture Sleeves

MOTOWN ... 3-4 86

LPs: 10/12-inch

COTILLION ... 5-8 79-84
MOTOWN ... 5-8 86-88
Also see KING DREAM CHORUS & Holiday Crew

LATTISAW, Stacy, & Johnny Gill *R&B/D&D/LP '84*

Singles: 7-inch

COTILLION ... 3-5 84-85

LPs: 10/12-inch

COTILLION ... 5-8 84
Also see GILL, Johnny
Also see LATTISAW, Stacy

LAUPER, Cyndi *P&R/LP '83*

Singles: 12-inch

PORTRAIT ... 4-6 83-87

Singles: 7-inch

EPIC ... 3-4 88-89
PORTRAIT ... 3-4 83-88

Picture Sleeves
EPIC 3-5 88
PORTRAIT 3-4 83-87
LPs: 10/12-inch
PORTRAIT (Except 39610) 5-8 83-86
PORTRAIT (39610 "She's So Unusual") 20-25 83
(Picture disc.)
Also see BLUE ANGEL
Also see HOOTERS
Also see U.S.A. for AFRICA

LAURA & JOHNNY R&B '69
Singles: 7-inch
SILVER FOX 4-6 69

LAURA LEE: see LEE, Laura

LAURAN, Niki D&D '83
Singles: 12-inch
WAVE 4-6 83

LAUREN, Rod P&R '59
Singles: 7-inch
CHANCELLOR 5-10 62
RCA 8-12 59-62
Picture Sleeves
RCA 10-15 59-60
LPs: 10/12-inch
RCA (LPM-2176 "I'm Rod Lauren") ... 20-40 61
(Monaural.)
RCA (LSP-2176 "I'm Rod Lauren") ... 30-50 61
(Stereo.)
Also see COOKE, Sam / Rod Lauren / Neil Sedaka / Browns

LAURENCE, Paul R&B '85
Singles: 12-inch
CAPITOL 4-6 86
Singles: 7-inch
CAPITOL 3-4 85-86
LPs: 10/12-inch
CAPITOL 5-8 86
Also see JACKSON, Freddie
Also see THOMAS, Lillo

LAURIE, Annie R&B '49
Singles: 78 rpm
DELUXE 5-15 47-57
REGAL 5-10 49
OKEH 5-10 55
SAVOY 5-10 56
Singles: 7-inch
DELUXE 10-20 57-60
DOVE 4-6 68
GUSTO 3-5 78
OKEH 10-15 55
RITZ 4-8 62
SAVOY 10-15 56
LPs: 10/12-inch
AUDIO LAB (1510 "It Hurts to Be in Love") 100-150 58

LAURIE, Linda P&R '59
Singles: 7-inch
ANDIE 5-10 60
GLORY 5-10 59
KEETCH 4-8 64
RECONA 4-8 63
RUST 4-8 60-63

LAURIE SISTERS P&R '55
Singles: 78 rpm
MERCURY 4-6 54-55
VIK 4-6 56
Singles: 7-inch
MGM 5-10 59-60
MERCURY 5-10 54-55
PORT 4-8 63
VIK 5-10 56
LPs: 10/12-inch
CAMDEN (CAL-545 "Hits of the Great Girl Groups") 15-25 60
(Monaural.)
CAMDEN (CAS-545 "Hits of the Great Girl Groups") 25-35 60
(Stereo.)

LAVERNE & SHIRLEY P&R '76
Singles: 7-inch
ATLANTIC 3-6 76-77
LPs: 10/12-inch
ATLANTIC 8-10 76
Members: Penny Marshall; Cindy Williams.

LAVETTE, Betty R&B '62
(Betty Lavett; Bettye LaVette)
Singles: 7-inch
ATCO 3-5 72-73
ATLANTIC 8-12 62-63
BIG WHEEL 4-8 66
CALLA 5-10 65
EPIC 3-5 75
KAREN 4-8 68-69
LUPINE (123 "Witch Craft in the Air") 20-30 64
LUPINE (1021 "Witch Craft in the Air") 10-15 64
MOTOWN 3-5 81-82
SSS INT'L 3-5 71
SILVER FOX 4-6 69-70
TCA 3-5 71
WEST END 4-8 78
LPs: 10/12-inch
MOTOWN 5-8 81

LAWRENCE, Eddie P&R '56
Singles: 78 rpm
CORAL 3-5 56-57
Singles: 7-inch
CORAL 4-8 56-63
EPIC 4-6 65
SHASTA 4-8 60
SIGNATURE 4-8 60
Picture Sleeves
CORAL 5-10 56
EPIC 4-8 65
LPs: 10/12-inch
CORAL 15-25 55-62
EPIC 8-15 65
SIGNATURE 10-20 59

LAWRENCE, Steve P&R '52
Singles: 78 rpm
CORAL 5-15 55-57
KING 5-10 52-53
Singles: 7-inch
ABC 3-5 73
ABC-PAR 6-12 58-60
CALENDAR 4-8 67-68
COLUMBIA (Black vinyl) 5-10 62-68
COLUMBIA (42865 "Walking Proud") 15-25 63
(Colored vinyl. Promotional issue only.)
CORAL 10-20 55-59
KING (1200 series) 10-20 53
KING (5000 series) 4-8 60-64
KING (15000 series) 10-20 52-53
MGM 3-5 71-73
RCA 3-6 69-70
ROULETTE 3-5 73
STAGE 2 .... 3-4 84
20TH FOX 3-5 75-77
U.A. (200 & 300 series) 5-10 60-61
U.A. (900 thru 1100 series) 3-5 76-78
W.B. 3-5 78
Picture Sleeves
COLUMBIA 5-10 62-63
STAGE 2 .... 3-4 84
U.A. 10-15 60-61
EPs: 7-inch
COLUMBIA 5-10 64-69
(Juke box issues only.)
CORAL 5-10 60
(Juke box issues only.)
KING 10-20 53
RCA 4-8 70
LPs: 10/12-inch
ABC-PAR 20-30 57-60
APPLAUSE 5-10 81
COLUMBIA 10-25 63-68
COLUMBIA RECORD CLUB 8-15 75
CORAL (57050 "About That Girl") 20-40 56
CORAL (57182 "Songs By Steve Lawrence") 20-30 57
CORAL (57204 "Here's Steve Lawrence") 20-30 57
CORAL (57268 "All About Love") 20-30 58
(Monaural.)
CORAL (57434 "Songs Everybody Knows") 12-20 62
(Monaural.)
CORAL (757268 "All About Love") 20-40 58
(Stereo.)
CORAL (757434 "Songs Everybody Knows") 15-25 62
(Stereo.)
GALA 5-10 77
GUEST STAR 5-10 64
HARMONY 6-12 68-71
KING (593 "Steve Lawrence") 25-35 58
MGM 5-10 71
RCA 6-12 69-70
SESAC 10-20 59
SPINORAMA 8-15 63
U.A. 10-20 61-64
VERSATILE 5-8 77
VOCALION 5-12 66-69

LAWRENCE, Steve / Tennessee Ernie Ford
LPs: 10/12-inch
CAMAY 15-25 60
Also see FORD, Tennessee Ernie

LAWRENCE, Steve, & Eydie Gorme
(Steve & Eydie) P&R '63
Singles: 78 rpm
CORAL 5-15 55
Singles: 7-inch
CALENDAR 4-6 68
COLUMBIA 4-8 62-67
CORAL 10-20 55
MGM 3-5 72-73
RCA 3-5 68-69
EPs: 7-inch
ABC 10-15 60
(Juke box issues only.)
ADVERTISING COUNCIL (5071 "Celebrity Spots") 15-30
(Promotional issue, with other artists.)
COLUMBIA 5-10 64-69
(Juke box issues only.)
CORAL 10-20 58
LPs: 10/12-inch
ABC 5-10 73-76
ABC/LONGINES ("Romantic Treasury") 30-45 67
(Boxed, six-disc set.)
ABC-PAR 15-25 59-64
CBS 10-15 63
CALENDAR 8-15 68
COLUMBIA 10-20 63-67
CORAL (57336 "Steve and Eydie") ... 15-25 60
ENCORE 5-8 84
HARMONY 5-10 64-71
MCA 5-10
MGM 5-10 72-73
MATI-MOR (8003 "It's Us Again") 10-15
(Promotional issue made for Silvikrin Shampoo.)
PICKWICK 5-10 70s
RCA 6-12 69-72
STAGE 2 .... 5-10 78-84
U.A. 10-20 61-62
VOCALION 5-12 67
Also see GORME, Eydie
Also see OSMONDS, Steve Lawrence & Eydie Gorme

LAWRENCE, Steve / Trini Lopez
LPs: 10/12-inch
DIPLOMAT 10-15 65
Also see LAWRENCE, Steve
Also see LOPEZ, Trini

LAWRENCE, Vicki P&R/C&W/LP '73
Singles: 7-inch
BELL 3-5 73-74
ELF 4-6 69
FLASHBACK 3-5 74

PRIVATE STOCK 3-5 75-76
U.A. 3-5 71

LPs: 10/12-inch

BELL 8-12 73
WINDMILL 5-10 79

LAWS, Debra P&R/R&B/LP '81

Singles: 7-inch

ELEKTRA 3-5 80-81

LPs: 10/12-inch

ELEKTRA 5-8 81

LAWS, Eloise P&R/R&B/LP '78

Singles: 7-inch

ABC 3-5 77-78
CAPITOL 3-4 82
COLUMBIA 4-6 68-70
INVICTUS 3-5 75-77
LIBERTY 3-5 80-81
MUSIC MERCHANT 3-5 72-73

Picture Sleeves

LIBERTY 3-5 80

LPs: 10/12-inch

ABC 8-10 77-78
CAPITOL 5-8 82
INVICTUS 5-10 76
LIBERTY 5-8 80

LAWS, Hubert R&B/LP '73

Singles: 7-inch

ATLANTIC 4-6 65
CTI 4-6 70-75
COLUMBIA 3-5 78

LPs: 10/12-inch

ATLANTIC 8-18 66-81
CTI 8-15 70-77
COLUMBIA 5-10 76-80

LAWS, Hubert, & Earl Klugh LP '80

LPs: 10/12-inch

COLUMBIA 5-10 80

Also see KLUGH, Earl
Also see LAWS, Hubert

LAWS, Ronnie R&B/LP '75
(With Pressure)

Singles: 7-inch

BLUE NOTE 3-5 75-77
CAPITOL 3-4 83-84
LIBERTY 3-5 80-81
U.A. 3-5 75-80

LPs: 10/12-inch

BLUE NOTE 6-12 75-77
CAPITOL 5-8 83
LIBERTY 5-10 81
U.A. 5-10 75-80

Also see EARTH, WIND, & FIRE
Also see PRESSURE

LAYNA, Magda D&D '83

Singles: 12-inch

MEGATONE 4-6 83

LAYNE, Joy P&R '57

Singles: 78 rpm

MERCURY 5-10 57

Singles: 7-inch

LUCKY FOUR 4-8 61
MERCURY 5-10 57

LAZY RACER P&R '79

Singles: 7-inch

A&M 3-5 79-80

LPs: 10/12-inch

A&M 5-10 79-80

LEACH, Billy P&R '57

Singles: 78 rpm

BALLY 5-10 57

Singles: 7-inch

BALLY 5-10 57
BREMNER 4-8 56

LEADON, Bernie LP '77
(With the Michael Georgiades Band)

Singles: 7-inch

ASYLUM 3-5 77

LPs: 10/12-inch

ASYLUM 8-10 77

Also see EAGLES

LEAGUE UNLIMITED ORCH. LP '82

Singles: 7-inch

A&M 3-4 82

LPs: 10/12-inch

A&M 5-8 82

Also see HUMAN LEAGUE

LEAPY LEE C&W/P&R '68

Singles: 7-inch

CADET 4-6 69
DECCA 4-8 68-71
MAM 3-5 72
MCA 3-5 75

Picture Sleeves

MCA 3-5 75

LPs: 10/12-inch

DECCA 10-20 68-70

LEATHERWOLF LP '88

LPs: 10/12-inch

ISLAND 5-8 88-89

LEAVES P&R/LP '66

Singles: 7-inch

CAPITOL (5799 "Lemon Princess") 8-12 66
MIRA (202 "Too Many People") 10-20 65
MIRA (207 "Hey Joe, Where You Gonna Go") 10-20 65
MIRA (213 "You Better Move On") 5-10 66
MIRA (222 "Hey Joe"/"Funny Little World") 5-10 66
MIRA (222 "Hey Joe"/"Girl from the East") 5-10 66
MIRA (227 "Too Many People") 5-8 66
MIRA (231 "Get Out of My Life Woman") 5-10 66
MIRA (234 "You Better Move On") 5-10 66
PANDA (1003 "Hey Joe") 8-12 82
(Colored vinyl on one side, picture on flip. Leaf-shaped disc.)

LPs: 10/12-inch

CAPITOL (T-2638 "All the Good That's Happening") 25-50 67
(Monaural.)
CAPITOL (ST-2638 "All the Good That's Happening") 30-60 67
(Stereo.)
MIRA (LP-3005 "Hey Joe") 25-35 66
(Monaural.)
MIRA (LPS-3005 "Hey Joe") 30-40 66
(Stereo.)

Members: John Beck; Bob Arlin; Jim Pons; Tom Ray; Bill Rheinhart; Robert Reiner; Jim Kern.
Also see MERRY-GO-ROUND
Also see MOTHERS of INVENTION
Also see TURTLES

LEAVILLE, Otis R&B '65
(Otis Leavill)

Singles: 7-inch

BLUE ROCK 8-12 65
BRUNSWICK 5-10 67
COLUMBIA 8-12 66
DAKAR 4-8 69-70
LIMELIGHT (3020 "I'm Amazed") 10-20 64
LIMELIGHT (3037 "Jane Girl") 10-20 64
LUCKY (1004 "Got a Right to Cry") 25-40 64
SMASH 4-8 68

LEAVY, Calvin R&B '70

Singles: 7-inch

BLUE FOX 3-5 70

LE BLANC, Lenny P&R '77

Singles: 7-inch

BIG TREE 3-6 76-77
CAPITOL 3-5 81

LPs: 10/12-inch

BIG TREE 8-12 76-77
CAPITOL 5-10 81

LE BLANC & CARR LP '78

Singles: 7-inch

BIG TREE 3-5 77-78

LPs: 10/12-inch

ATLANTIC (003 "Live from the Atlantic Studios") 8-12 78
(Promotional issue only.)
BIG TREE 8-10 77

Members: Lenny LeBlanc; Pete Carr.
Also see LE BLANC, Lenny

LED ZEPPELIN P&R/LP '69

Singles: 7-inch

ATLANTIC (2613 "Good Times, Bad Times") 10-15 69
ATLANTIC (2690 "Whole Lotta Love") 5-8 69
(Edited version [3:12].)
ATLANTIC (2777 "The Immigrant Song"/"Hey Hey, What Can I Do") 15-25 70
(Has "Do What Thou Wilt Shall Be the Whole of the Law" etched in the vinyl trail-off.)
ATLANTIC (2777 "The Immigrant Song"/"Hey Hey, What Can I Do") 10-15 70
(Does not have "Do What Thou Wilt Shall Be the Whole of the Law" etched in the vinyl trail-off.)
ATLANTIC (2849 "Black Dog") 5-10 71
ATLANTIC (2865 "Rock & Roll") 5-10 72
ATLANTIC (2970 "Over the Hills and Far Away") 5-10 73
ATLANTIC (2986 "D'yer Mak'er") 5-10 73
ATLANTIC (13116 "Whole Lotta Love") 4-6 70s
ATLANTIC (13131 "The Immigrant Song") 4-6 70s
ATLANTIC (13129 "Black Dog") 4-6 70s
ATLANTIC (13130 "Rock & Roll") 4-6 70s
Note: Atlantic 13000 numbers are "Oldies Series" reissues.
SWAN SONG (70102 "Trampled Under Foot") 4-6 75
SWAN SONG (70110 "Candy Store Rock") 4-6 76
SWAN SONG (71003 "Fool in the Rain") 4-6 76

Picture Sleeves

ATLANTIC (175 "Stairway to Heaven") 50-75 72
(Promotional issue only.)

Promotional Singles

ATLANTIC (157 "Gallows Pole") 50-75 71
ATLANTIC (175 "Stairway to Heaven") 50-75 72
ATLANTIC (269 "Stairway to Heaven") 20-30 77
ATLANTIC (1019 "Dazed and Confused") 75-100 69
(With picture sleeve.)
ATLANTIC (2613 "Good Times Bad Times") 25-35 69
(Black and white label.)
ATLANTIC (2613 "Good Times Bad Times") 20-30 69
(Red and white label.)
ATLANTIC (2690 "Whole Lotta Love"/"Living Loving Maid") 15-25 69
ATLANTIC (2690 "Whole Lotta Love" [5:33] / Whole Lotta Love" [3:12]) 25-35 69
ATLANTIC (2777 "The Immigrant Song"/"The Immigrant Song") 15-25 70
ATLANTIC (2777 "The Immigrant Song"/ Blank) 15-25 70
(Single-sided.)
ATLANTIC (2849 "Black Dog") 15-20 71
ATLANTIC (2865 "Rock & Roll") 15-20 72
ATLANTIC (2970 "Over the Hills and Far Away") 10-20 73
ATLANTIC (2986 "D'yer Mak'er") 10-20 73
SWAN SONG (70102 "Trampled Under Foot") 10-15 75
SWAN SONG (70110 "Candy Store Rock") 10-15 76
SWAN SONG (71003 "Fool in the Rain") 10-15 76
(Blue label. Side one runs 6:08; side two is edited [3:20].)
SWAN SONG (71003 "Fool in the Rain") 8-12 76
(White label. Both sides run 6:08.)

EPs: 7-inch

ATLANTIC (7-7208 "Led Zeppelin") 50-75 71
(Juke box issue only.)
ATLANTIC (7-7255 "Houses of the Holy") 50-75 73
(Juke box issue only.)

LPs: 10/12-inch

ATLANTIC (7201 "Led Zeppelin III") .. 10-15 70
ATLANTIC (7208 "Led Zeppelin IV") 10-15 71
(Their fourth LP though no title is actually shown on cover.)
ATLANTIC (7255 "Houses of the Holy") 15-20 73
(With "Led Zeppelin paper band around cover.)
ATLANTIC (7255 "Houses of the Holy") 10-15 73
(Without "Led Zeppelin paper band around cover.)
ATLANTIC (8216 "Led Zeppelin") ... 50-100 69
(Pink and brown label.)
ATLANTIC (8216 "Led Zeppelin") 10-20 69
(Red and green label.)
ATLANTIC (8236 "Led Zeppelin II") .. 10-15 69
ATLANTIC (19126 "Led Zeppelin") 5-10 80s
ATLANTIC (19127 "Led Zeppelin II") .. 5-10 80s
ATLANTIC (19128 "Led Zeppelin III") 5-10 80s
ATLANTIC (19129 "Led Zeppelin IV") 5-10 80s
ATLANTIC (19130 "Houses of the Holy") 5-10 80s
ATLANTIC (82144 "Led Zeppelin") ... 50-75
(Boxed, six-disc set. Includes 36-page booklet.)
ATLANTIC MUSIC SERVICE 10-15 69
(Record club issue.)
MFSL (065 "Led Zeppelin II") 25-50 82
SWAN SONG (2-200 "Physical Graffiti") 10-15 75
SWAN SONG (2-201 "The Song Remains the Same") 10-15 76
(Embossed print on cover. With bound-in eight-page booklet. Soundtrack.)
SWAN SONG (2-201 "The Song Remains the Same") 8-12 76
(Standard, not-embossed, cover.)
SWAN SONG (8416 "Presence") 8-12 76
SWAN SONG (16002 "In Through the Out Door") 8-12 79
SWAN SONG (90051 "Coda") 8-10 82

Promotional LPs

ATLANTIC (7201 "Led Zeppelin III") 100-150 70
(White label. Monaural.)
ATLANTIC (7201 "Led Zeppelin III") 100-150 70
(White label. Stereo.)
ATLANTIC (7208 "Led Zeppelin IV") 100-150 71
(White label. No title actually shown on cover; however, it was their fourth LP.)
ATLANTIC (7225 "Houses of the Holy") 100-150 73
(White label. Monaural.)
ATLANTIC (7225 "Houses of the Holy") 100-150 73
(White label. Stereo.)
ATLANTIC (8216 "Led Zeppelin") 100-150 69
(White label.)
ATLANTIC (8236 "Led Zeppelin II") 100-150 69
(White label.)
SWAN SONG (200 "Physical Graffiti") 15-20 75
(With "FT" suffix.)
SWAN SONG (2-201 "The Song Remains the Same") 15-20 76
(With "MO" suffix.)
SWAN SONG (8416 "Presence") 10-20 76
(With "MO" suffix.)
SWAN SONG (16002 "In Through the Out Door") 10-15 79
(With "MO" suffix.)
SWAN SONG (90051 "Coda") 10-12 82
(With designate promo stamping on back cover.)
Members: Robert Plant; Jimmy Page; John Paul Jones; John Bonham.
Also see DENNY, Sandy
Also see HARPER, Roy
Also see JONES, John Paul
Also see PAGE, Jimmy
Also see PLANT, Robert

LED ZEPPELIN / King Curtis

Singles: 7-inch

ATLANTIC/ATCO (2690 / 6779 "Whole Lotta Love") 40-50 71
(Promotional issue only. Atlantic label on Zep side; Atco label on flip, King Curtis' version of same song.)
Also see KING CURTIS
Also see LED ZEPPELIN

LEDERNACKEN D&D '84

Singles: 12-inch

4TH & BROADWAY 4-6 84

LEE, Alvin LP '75

(Alvin Lee & Company; with Ten Years Later)

Singles: 7-inch

COLUMBIA 3-5 74
RSO 3-5 79

LPs: 10/12-inch

ATLANTIC 5-8 80-81
COLUMBIA 10-12 73-75
LONDON 8-10 78
RSO 10-12 77-79
21 RECORDS 5-8 86
Also see TEN YEARS AFTER

LEE, Alvin, & Mylon LeFevre LP '74

Singles: 7-inch

COLUMBIA 3-5 74

LPs: 10/12-inch

COLUMBIA 10-12 73
Also see LEE, Alvin
Also see LE FEVRE, Mylon

LEE, Bobby R&B '66

Singles: 7-inch

A-B-S (106 "Miss Mary") 150-200
CONFEDERATE 3-5
DECCA 5-10 60-61
FALEW 5-10 64
GOLD COAST INT'L 4-8 60s
MUSICOR 4-6 68-69
PORT 4-8 67
RAMCO 4-8 67
SAGE 5-10 60s
SUE 4-8 66
VISTONE 4-8 60s

LPs: 10/12-inch

LITTLE RICHIE 8-12 76
Session: Lloyd Green; Charlie McCoy; Pig Robbins; Bob Moore; Buddy Spicher; Buddy Harmon; Kelso Hersten; Billy Stanford; Nashville Edition.
Also see McCOY, Charlie
Also see MOORE, Bob

LEE, Brenda

(Brenda Lee Jones)

Singles: 78 rpm

APOLLO 10-20 56

Singles: 7-inch

APOLLO (490 "I Ain't Gonna Give Nobody None") 15-25 56
(Listed primarily to distinguish this singer from the following Brenda Lee.)
Also see JONES, Brenda

LEE, Brenda P&R/C&W '57

(With the Jordanaires; with Holladays)

Singles: 78 rpm

DECCA 20-50 56-58

Singles: 7-inch

DECCA (30050 "Jambalaya") 20-30 56
DECCA (30107 "Christy Christmas") 15-25 56
DECCA (30198 "One Step at a Time") 15-20 57
DECCA (30333 "Dynamite") 15-20 57
DECCA (30411 "One Teenager to Another") 10-20 57
DECCA (30535 "Rock-A-Bye Baby Blues") 10-20 57
DECCA (30673 "Ring-A My Phone") 20-30 58
DECCA (30776 "Rockin' Around the Christmas Tree") 10-15 58
DECCA (30806 "Bill Bailey") 10-15 59
DECCA (30967 "Sweet Nothin's") 8-12 59
(Price range of 30050 through 30967 is for black, pink or green label originals. Pink and green were promotional only. Decca multi-color labels in that series are $4 to $8 reissues.)
DECCA (31093 thru 32330) 5-10 60-68
DECCA (32428 thru 32975) 4-6 69-72
DECCA (34330 "Interview") 10-20 72
(Promotional issue only.)
DECCA (88215 "I'm Gonna Lasso Santa Claus") 20-30 56
(Decca "Children's Series.")
ELEKTRA 3-5 78
MCA 3-5 73-86

Picture Sleeves

W.B. 3-4 91
DECCA (30776 "Rockin' Around the Christmas Tree") 15-25 59
DECCA (30967 "Sweet Nothin's") 25-35 59
DECCA (31093 thru 32428) 5-15 60-69
DECCA (34000 series) 5-10 62
(Compact 33 stereo.)
DECCA (88215 "I'm Gonna Lasso Santa Claus") 30-40 56
(For either 45 or 78 rpm single sleeve.)

EPs: 7-inch

DECCA 10-20 60-65

LPs: 10/12-inch

CORAL 5-10 73
DECCA (4039 thru 4104) 20-35 60-61
(Monaural.)
DECCA (4176 thru 4755) 15-30 61-66
(Monaural.)
DECCA (4757 "10 Golden Years") 15-25 66
(Gatefold cover. Monaural.)
DECCA (4757 "10 Golden Years") 10-15 60s
(Standard cover. Monaural.)
DECCA (4825 thru 4955) 10-20 66-68
(Monaural.)
DECCA (8873 "Grandma, What Great Songs You Sang") 30-40 59
(Monaural.)
DECCA (74039 thru 74104) 25-40 60-61
(Stereo.)
DECCA (74176 thru 74755) 20-35 61-66
(Stereo.)
DECCA (74757 "10 Golden Years") .. 20-30 66
(Gatefold cover. Stereo.)
DECCA (74757 "10 Golden Years") .. 10-15 60s
(Standard cover. Stereo.)
DECCA (74825 thru 75232) 10-20 66-70
(Stereo.)
DECCA (78873 "Grandma, What Great Songs You Sang") 35-45 59
(Stereo.)
MCA (Except 700 series) 8-10 73-86
MCA (700 series) 5-8
PICKWICK 5-10 70s
TEE-VEE 5-10 78
VOCALION 10-15 67-70
WARWICK (5083 "Little Miss Dynamite") 5-10 80
(TV mail order offer.)
Session: Anita Kerr; Bob Moore; Boots Randolph; Jordanaires; James "Buzz" Cason.
Also see KERR, Anita
Also see MOORE, Bob
Also see NELSON, Willie, & Brenda Lee
Also see RANDOLPH, Boots

LEE, Brenda / Carl Dobkins, Jr.

EPs: 7-inch

DECCA (38169 "Datesetters, U.S.A.") 15-25 60
(Celanese Special Products issue.)
Also see DOBKINS, Carl, Jr.

LEE, Brenda / Bill Haley & Comets / Kalin Twins / Four Aces

EPs: 7-inch

DECCA (7-2661 "Top Teen Hits") 15-25 59
(Stereo.)
Also see FOUR ACES

Also see HALEY, Bill
Also see KALIN TWINS

LEE, Brenda / Tennessee Ernie Ford

LPs: 10/12-inch

DECCA (9226 "Brenda Lee/Tennessee Ernie Ford Show for Christmas Seals")............20-30
(Promotional issue only.)
Also see FORD, Tennessee Ernie

LEE, Brenda, & Pete Fountain LP '68

Singles: 7-inch

DECCA..4-6 68

EPs: 7-inch

DECCA (734528 "Brenda & Pete") 5-10 68
(Juke box issue.)

LPs: 10/12-inch

DECCA..10-15 68
PICKWICK..5-10 70s
Also see FOUNTAIN, Pete

LEE, Brenda, & Oak Ridge Boys

Singles: 7-inch

MCA..3-5 82
Also see OAK RIDGE BOYS

LEE, Curtis P&R '61

Singles: 7-inch

ABC..3-5 74
DUNES (801 "California GL-903")..... 10-20 60
DUNES (1001 "Pretty Little Angel Eyes")......................................25-35 60
DUNES (2001 "Special Love") 10-20 60
DUNES (2003 "Pledge of Love")....... 10-20 61
DUNES (2007 "Pretty Little Angel Eyes")......................................10-20 61
DUNES (2008 "Under the Moon of Love") 10-20 61
DUNES (2010 "Let's Take a Ride")... 10-20 61
DUNES (2012 "Just Another Fool")... 10-20 62
DUNES (2015 "The Wobble") 10-20 62
DUNES (2017 "Afraid")................... 10-20 62
DUNES (2020 "Lonely Weekends") .. 10-20 63
DUNES (2021 "Pickin' Up the Pieces of My Heart") 10-20 63
DUNES (2023 "I'm Sorry")............... 10-20 63
HOT (7 "Gotta Have You") 25-35 60
MCA..3-4
MIRA (240 "Sweet Baby").................. 10-20 67
ROJAC (114 "In My Bag") 5-10 67
SABRA (517 "Let's Take a Ride") 15-25 61
WARRIOR (1555 "With All My Heart")..20-30 59

Picture Sleeves

DUNES (2003 "Pledge of Love")....... 20-30 61
Also see HALOS

LEE, Dick P&R '61

(With the Big Action Sound)

Singles: 78 rpm

ESSEX...4-8 54
VIK...4-8 56
"X"...4-8 55

Singles: 7-inch

ABC...4-6 67
ACTION 3-6
BLUE BELL 4-8 61
CAPITOL..4-6 68
CENTAUR..5-8 59
DOT..4-8 66
ESSEX..5-10 54
FELSTED 5-8 60
KAPP..4-6 69
MGM..5-10 59
METRO..4-8 65
ROULETTE 4-8 62-63
20TH FOX 4-8 65
VIK...5-10 56
"X"...5-10 55

Picture Sleeves

FELSTED 8-12 60

LEE, Dickey P&R/R&B/LP '62

(With the Collegiates; Dickie Lee)

Singles: 78 rpm

SUN (280 "Good Lovin'") 15-25 57
SUN (297 "Dreamy Nights") 20-30 57
TAMPA (131 "Dream Boy") 15-25 57

Singles: 7-inch

ABC..3-5 73
ATCO 4-8 68
DIAMOND 4-8 69
DICKIE LEE STORY.......................... 15-20 77
(No label name or number used. Promotional issue only.)
DOT 10-15 60
ERIC..3-5 70s
HALL 5-10 64
MERCURY..3-5 79-82
OLDIES 45..4-6 65
RCA 3-5 70-78
RENDEZVOUS (188 "Stay True Baby")...15-25 62
SMASH 5-10 62-64
SUN (280 "Good Lovin'")................. 15-25 57
SUN (297 "Dreamy Nights")............. 20-30 57
TCF 4-8 65
TCF HALL 5-10 64-65
TAMPA (131 "Dream Boy")............... 15-25 57
TRACIE 4-8 67

LPs: 10/12-inch

RCA 6-12 71-76
MERCURY...5-8 79-80
SMASH 20-30 62
TCF HALL 15-20 65

LEE, Dickey, & Kathy Burdick C&W '81

Singles: 7-inch

MERCURY...3-4 81-82
Also see LEE, Dickey

LEE, Jackie P&R '59

Singles: 7-inch

SWAN 8-12 59

LEE, Jackie P&R/R&B '65

(Earl Nelson)

Singles: 7-inch

ABC.. 10-20 68
FAYETTE 5-10 64
KEYMAN 5-10 67-68
MIRWOOD..5-10 65-66
UNI 3-6 70

LPs: 10/12-inch

MIRWOOD....................................... 15-25 66
Also see BOB & EARL

LEE, Jackie, & Dolores Hall

Singles: 7-inch

MIRWOOD...4-8 66
Also see LEE, Jackie

LEE, Jimmy, & Artis R&B '52

Singles: 78 rpm

MODERN 10-20 52

Singles: 7-inch

MODERN (885 "Let's Talk It Over").. 25-35 52

LEE, John (John Lee Henley/Hooker): see JOHN LEE

LEE, Johnny C&W '75

Singles: 7-inch

ABC/DOT..3-5 75
ASTRO..3-5 80
ASYLUM 3-5 80-82
CURB..3-4 89
EPIC...3-5 81
FULL MOON/W.B. 3-4 80-86
GRT 3-5 76-78

Picture Sleeves

ASYLUM 3-5 80

LPs: 10/12-inch

ACCORD 5-8 83
ASYLUM 5-10 80-81
FULL MOON/W.B. 5-8 80-86
GRT 8-10 77
JMS..8-12
PLANTATION 5-10 81
Session: Deborah Allen; Michael Murphey; Charlie Daniels.
Also see DANIELS, Charlie
Also see GILLEY, Mickey, & Johnny Lee
Also see MURPHEY, Michael
Also see NELSON, Willie / Johnny Lee / Mickey Gilley

LEE, Johnny, & Lane Brody C&W '84

Singles: 7-inch

W.B. 3-4 84-86

LEE, Johnny / Eagles

Singles: 7-inch

ASYLUM..3-5 80-81

Picture Sleeves

ASYLUM..3-5 80
Also see EAGLES

LEE, Johnny, Michael Martin Murphey, & Charlie Daniels

(Johnny Lee & Friends) C&W '82

Singles: 7-inch

FULL MOON...3-4 82
Also see DANIELS, Charlie
Also see LEE, Johnny
Also see MURPHEY, Michael

LEE, Julia R&B '46

(With Her Boy Friends; with Her Scat Cats)

Singles: 78 rpm

CAPITOL 10-20 46-52

Singles: 7-inch

CAPITOL (Except 2203)................... 10-25 49-52
CAPITOL (2203 "Last Call for Alcohol") 25-35 52

EPs: 7-inch

CAPITOL (EBF-228 "Party Time") 50-75 50

LPs: 10/12-inch

CAPITOL (H-228 "Party Time").......75-100 50
(10-inch LP.)
CAPITOL (T-228 "Party Time") 50-75 55
Members: Julia Lee; Baby Lovett; Tommy Douglas; Jim Daddy Walker; Clint Weaver.

LEE, Laura LP '72

Singles: 7-inch

ARIOLA AMERICA..............................3-5 76
ARLEN (732 "What's Done Is Done")...15-25 63
CHESS 8-15 67-69
COTILLION..5-8 69
HOT WAX..3-6 71-73
INVICTUS...4-8 74
RIC TIC...10-20 66

LPs: 10/12-inch

CHESS 10-20 72
HOT WAX..8-12 72-73
INVICTUS...8-12 74

LEE, Leapy: see LEAPY LEE

LEE, Leon R&B '74

Singles: 7-inch

CROSSOVER 3-5 74

LEE, Michele P&R '68

Singles: 7-inch

ABC-PAR 4-8 62-63
COLUMBIA...4-8 65-69

LPs: 10/12-inch

COLUMBIA...10-20 66-68

LEE, Nickie R&B '68

Singles: 7-inch

DADE...4-8 67
MALA..10-15 68-69

LEE, Peggy P&R '45

(With Benny Goodman's Orchestra)

Singles: 78 rpm

CAPITOL 5-15 41-58
OKEH 5-15 41-42

Singles: 7-inch

A&M..3-5 75
ATLANTIC 3-5 74
CAPITOL (801 thru 2000 series) 8-12 49-51
CAPITOL (2100 thru 3400 series).........3-6 68-72
CAPITOL (3800 thru 5900 series).........4-8 58-67
CAPITOL (90000 series) 4-8
COLUMBIA...3-5 76
DECCA (25000 series)..........................4-6 64
DECCA (28000 & 29000 series) 4-8 52-58
DECCA (30000 series)..........................4-8 58-59

EPs: 7-inch

CAPITOL (Except 100 series).......... 10-20 57-59

CAPITOL (100 series)........................20-40 52
COLUMBIA.......................................20-40 50-51
DECCA...15-30 52-55

LPs: 10/12-inch

A&M...5-8 75
ATLANTIC 5-8 74
CAPITOL (183 "A Natural Woman") ...8-12 69
CAPITOL (H-155 "Rendezvous with Peggy")..50-75 52
(10-inch LP.)
CAPITOL (T-155 "Rendezvous with Peggy")..25-50 55
CAPITOL (H-204 "My Best to You")..50-75 52
(10-inch LP.)
CAPITOL (377 thru 810)....................5-10 69-71
CAPITOL (864 "The Man I Love").....20-40 56
CAPITOL (979 "Jump for Joy")..........20-40 57
CAPITOL (T-1049 thru T-1969)..........15-25 58-63
(Monaural.)
CAPITOL (ST-1049 thru ST-1969)....20-30 58-63
(Stereo.)
CAPITOL (T-2096 thru T-2887).........10-20 64-68
(Monaural.)
CAPITOL (ST-2096 thru ST-2887).....10-20 64-68
CAPITOL (6600 series)......................5-10 70
CAPITOL (11000 series)....................5-10 72-79
CAPITOL (16000 series).....................4-8 80
COLUMBIA (6033 "Benny Goodman & Peggy Lee")..40-60 50
(10-inch LP.)
DRG..5-8 79
DECCA (DXB-164 "Best of Peggy Lee")..15-25 60
(Monaural.)
DECCA (DXSB7-164 "Best of Peggy Lee")..10-20 66
(Stereo.)
DECCA (DL-4000 series).................10-15 64
(Monaural.)
DECCA (DL7-4000 series)...............15-20 64
(Stereo.)
DECCA (5482 "Black Coffee").........50-75 53
(10-inch LP.)
DECCA (5539 "Songs in an Intimate Style")..50-75 53
(10-inch LPs.)
DECCA (8411 "Dream Street").........30-50 56
DECCA (8358 "Black Coffee")..........30-50 57
DECCA (8591 "Sea Shells")..............30-50 58
DECCA (8816 "Miss Wonderful")......20-40 59
EVEREST...5-8 74
GLENDALE...4-8 82
HARMONY (7000 series).................15-25 58
HARMONY (30000 series)..................5-10 70
HORIZON (1004 "Best of Peggy Lee")..25-35 62
MERCURY...5-8 77
VOCALION..6-12 66-70

Also see CROSBY, Bing, & Peggy Lee
Also see FITZGERALD, Ella, & Peggy Lee
Also see GOODMAN, Benny, Orchestra
Also see JENKINS, Gordon, & His Orchestra

LEE, Peggy, & Dean Martin

Singles: 78 rpm

CAPITOL (15349 "You Was")...........20-30 49

Also see MARTIN, Dean

LEE, Peggy, & George Shearing

Singles: 7-inch

CAPITOL...4-8 59

LPs: 10/12-inch

CAPITOL (1219 "Beauty and the Beat")..20-30 59
(Capitol logo on left side of label.)
CAPITOL (1219 "Beauty and the Beat")..10-20 62
(Capitol logo at the top of label.)

LEE, Peggy, & Mel Torme

Singles: 78 rpm

CAPITOL...5-10 49

Singles: 7-inch

CAPITOL...10-15 49

Also see LEE, Peggy
Also see TORME, Mel

LEE, Roberta — P&R '51

Singles: 78 rpm

DECCA 4-6 51-54
TEMPO 4-8 50-51
"X" 4-6 54

Singles: 7-inch

DECCA 5-10 51-54
TEMPO 5-10 50-51
TOWER 4-6 68
"X" 5-10 54

LEE, Toney — D&D '83

Singles: 12-inch

RADAR 4-6 83

Singles: 7-inch

CRITIQUE..3-4 85

LEE & PAUL — P&R '59

Singles: 7-inch

COLUMBIA 5-10 59-65

Members: Lee Pockriss; Paul Vance.
Also see VANCE, Paul

LEFEVRE, Raymond, & Orch. — P&R '58

Singles: 7-inch

ATLANTIC..4-6 61
4 CORNERS...4-6 67-68
JAMIE..4-6 60
KAPP...3-8 58-66
MERCURY..4-8 60
VERVE...4-6 62

LPs: 10/12-inch

ATLANTIC...8-15 61
BUDDAH..5-10 71-72
4 CORNERS.......................................5-10 67-68
KAPP...8-15 59-66
MONUMENT..6-12 67

LEFT BANKE — P&R '66

Singles: 7-inch

CON AMERICA......................................5-8 78
SMASH (Except 2243)........................5-10 66-69
SMASH (2243 "Myrah") 30-40 69

Picture Sleeves

SMASH (Except 2243)......................10-20 67
SMASH (2243 "Myrah") 30-40 69

LPs: 10/12-inch

RHINO..5-8 85
SMASH (27088 "Walk Away Renee")..20-30 67
(Monaural.)
SMASH (67088 "Walk Away Renee")..25-35 67
(Stereo.)
SMASH (67113 "Left Banke Too")....25-35 69
MERCURY...5-10 81

Members: Michael Brown; George Cameron; Tom Finn; Steve Martin; Rick Brand; Jeff Winfield; Tom Feher.
Also see STORIES

LEGACY — R&B '82

Singles: 7-inch

BRUNSWICK...3-5 82
PRIVATE I...3-4 85

LEGENDARY MASKED SURFERS

Singles: 7-inch

U.A. (270 "Summer Means Fun") 10-15 73
(Tan label. This track, previously included on the Jan & Dean LPs *The Little Old Lady from Pasadena* and *Popsicle* was mistakenly used for this single.)
U.A. (270 "Summer Means Fun") 10-15 73
(White label, promotional issue. Same incorrect track as noted above.)
U.A. (270 "Summer Means Fun") 100-125 73
(Tan label, promotional issue. Has the intended, new version with added vocal backing, not available elsewhere. Can be identified by playing, or visually by the following letters etched in the vinyl trail-off: Side 1 "BJ/TM/DT." Side 2 "GG/ILY/DOT.")
U.A. (270 "Summer Means Fun") 100-125 73
(White label, promotional issue. Has correct version as described above.)
U.A. (670 "Gonna Hustle You").........10-20 75
(Reissued in 1977.)
U.A. (50958 "Gonna Hustle You").....10-20 72

Picture Sleeves

U.A. (270 "Summer Means Fun")......20-30 73
(Add $5.00 if accompanied by explanatory note from Dean Torrence.)

Members: Jan Berry; Dean Torrece; Brian Wilson; Bruce Johnston; Terry Melcher; Leon Russell; Glen Campbell; Larry Knechtel.
Also see CAMPBELL, Glen
Also see JAN & DEAN
Also see RUSSELL, Leon
Also see WILSON, Brian

LEGRAND, Michel, & Orch. — LP '55

Singles: 7-inch

A&M...3-4 83
BELL...3-5 71-72
COLUMBIA..4-8 55-59
DECCA...3-6 68
FLASHBACK...3-5 73
MCA..3-5 73-76
MGM...3-6 67-68
PHILIPS...4-6 63-66
RCA...3-5 75
20TH FOX 3-5 77
U.A. 3-5 70
W.B. 3-6 68-76

Picture Sleeves

MGM...8-15 67

EPs: 7-inch

COLUMBIA...5-10 56-59

LPs: 10/12-inch

BELL..5-10 72-74
COLUMBIA..10-20 55-71
GRYPHON 5-8 75-79
HARMONY 5-10 66-74
KORY 4-8 77
MCA..8-15 73-76
MERCURY 8-15 65
PABLO...4-8 83
PHILIPS...8-15 62-64
SPRINGBOARD....................................4-8 77
20TH FOX 5-10 77
U.A. 6-12 69
VERVE 8-15 68-72
W.B. 6-12 71-76

Also see HORNE, Lena, & Michel Legrand
Also see VAUGHAN, Sarah

You'll find many more listings by this artist in *The Official Price Guide to Movie/TV Soundtracks and Original Cast Albums*, containing over 8,000 listings.

LEHRER, Tom — LP '65

Singles: 7-inch

REPRISE...3-6 69

EPs: 7-inch

LEHRER (1 "Songs By Tom Lehrer")..50-100 52
(Double EP, gatefold cover.)

LPs: 10/12-inch

LEHRER (101 "Songs By Tom Lehrer")..50-100 52
(10-inch LP.)
LEHRER (102 "More Songs By Tom Lehrer")..30-50 59
LEHRER (202 "An Evening Wasted with Tom Lehrer")..30-50 59
REPRISE...10-20 65-66

LE JETE — D&D '83

Singles: 12-inch

MEGATONE...4-6 83

LEKAKIS, Paul — P&R '87

Singles: 7-inch

ZYX..3-4 87

LEMMONS, Billy — P&R '77

Singles: 7-inch

ARIOLA AMERICA..................................3-5 77

LEMON PIPERS — P&R '67

Singles: 7-inch

BUDDAH 4-8 67-69
CAROL 8-12

ERIC 3-5 78

Picture Sleeves

BUDDAH 5-10 68

LPs: 10/12–inch

BUDDAH 12-20 68

Members: Ivan Browne; Bill Bartlett; Paul Lenka; Bill Albaugh; Steve Walmsley; Reg Nave.

Also see 1910 FRUITGUM COMPANY / Lemon Pipers

Also see RAM JAM

LENNON, John *P&R/LP '69*

(John & Yoko; Plastic Ono Band; with Plastic Ono Nuclear Band; with Flux Fiddlers)

Singles: 12–inch

CAPITOL (9585/6 "Imagine"/"Come Together") 25-35 86
(Promotional issue only.)
CAPITOL (9894 "Happy Xmas")....150-200 86
(Promotional issue only. Black label.)
CAPITOL (9894 "Happy Xmas")........40-50 86
(Promotional issue only. Silver label.)
CAPITOL (9917 "Rock & Roll People") 50-60 86
(Promotional issue only.)
CAPITOL (9929 "Happy Xmas")........35-45 86
(Promotional issue only.)
CAPITOL (79453 "Stand by Me") 30-40 88
(Promotional issue only.)
GEFFEN (919 "Starting Over")..........60-75 80
(Promotional issue only.)
GEFFEN (1079 "Happy Xmas") 25-30 82
(Price range includes special sleeve. Promotional issue only.)
POLYDOR (250 "Nobody Told Me") 25-30 83

Singles: 7–inch

AMERICOM (435 "Give Peace a Chance") 500-750 69
(Plastic "Pocket Disc" soundsheet.)
APPLE (1809 "Give Peace a Chance") 4-6 69
APPLE (1813 "Cold Turkey") 4-6 69
APPLE (1818 "Instant Karma") 15-30 70
(With Capitol logo.)
APPLE (1818 "Instant Karma") 5-10 70
(No Capitol logo.)
APPLE (1827 "Mother")......................8-12 70
(No "Mono" print on label.)
APPLE (1827 "Mother")....................30-40 70
(With "Mono" on label.)
APPLE (1830 "Power to the People") 8-12 71
APPLE (1840 "Imagine") 8-12 71
APPLE (1842 "Happy Xmas") 10-15 71
(Label pictures John & Yoko.)
APPLE (1842 "Happy Xmas") 5-10 71
(Standard Apple label.)
APPLE (1848 "Woman Is the Nigger of the World") 5-8 72
(With Elephant's Memory.)
APPLE (1868 "Mind Games") 4-6 73
APPLE (1874 "Whatever Gets You Through the Night") 4-6 74
APPLE (1878 "#9 Dream") 5-8 74
APPLE (1881 "Stand by Me")...............5-8 75
CAPITOL (Except 1842 & 1878) 10-15 76
(Orange labels.)
CAPITOL (1842 "Happy Xmas")........40-50 76
CAPITOL (1878 "#9 Dream") 30-40 76
CAPITOL 5-10 78-88
(Purple or black labels.)
CAPITOL (6244 "Stand by Me") 40-50 86
(Blue "Starline" series label.)
CAPITOL (17644 "Happy Xmas")..........3-4 94
(Colored vinyl, 30th Anniversary juke box issue. Mistakenly has a slash following title: "Happy Xmas (War Is Over)/".)
CAPITOL (17644 "Happy Xmas") 3-5 95
(Colored vinyl, 30th Anniversary juke box issue. Erroneous slash removed from title.)
CAPITOL (17783 "Give Peace a Chance") 75-100 94
CAPITOL (57849 "Imagine") 30-50 92
COLLECTABLES (4307 "Nobody Told Me") 15-20 92
GEFFEN (0408 "Starting Over") 3-5 81
(Cream color label. Logo has narrow print.)
GEFFEN (0408 "Starting Over") 20-30 81
(Cream color label. Logo has bold print.)
GEFFEN (0408 "Starting Over") 15-30 80
(Black label.)
GEFFEN (0415 "Watching the Wheels") 3-5 81
(Cream color label. Logo has narrow print.)
GEFFEN (0415 "Watching the Wheels") 30-40 82
(Cream color label. Logo has bold print.)
GEFFEN (0415 "Watching the Wheels") 20-30 86
(Black label without bar code symbol.)
GEFFEN (0415 "Watching the Wheels") 5-10 88
(Black label with bar code symbol.)
GEFFEN (29855 "Happy Xmas") 3-5 82
GEFFEN (49604 "Starting Over") 3-5 80
GEFFEN (49644 "Woman") 3-5 80
GEFFEN (49695 "Watching the Wheels") 3-4 81
ORANGE PEEL (70078 "Interview") 15-20 81
(John is interviewed by David Peel. Picture disc.)
POLYDOR 4-8 84-86

Promotional Singles

APPLE (1809 "Give Peace a Chance") 8-12 69
APPLE (1813 "Cold Turkey") 20-25 69
APPLE (1818 "Instant Karma") 150-200 70
APPLE (1827 "Mother") 25-35 70
APPLE (1830 "Power to the People") 15-25 71
APPLE (1840 "Imagine") 10-15 71
APPLE (1848 "Woman Is the Nigger of the World") 12-15 72
APPLE (1868 "Mind Games") 40-50 73
APPLE (1874 "Whatever Gets You Through the Night") 35-45 74
APPLE (1878 "#9 Dream") 40-50 74
APPLE (1878 "What You Got") 75-100 74
(Two separate promo singles have the same selection number [1878]. On commercial issues these tracks were back to back.)
APPLE (1881 "Stand by Me") 40-50 75
APPLE (1883 "Ain't That a Shame") 150-200 75
APPLE (1883 "Slippin' and Sliddin') 150-200 75
(Two separate promo singles are numbered 1883.)
APPLE (47663/4 "Happy Xmas").. 600-750 71
(White label with black print.)
CAPITOL (44230 "Jealous Guy")...... 10-15 88
CAPITOL (57849 "Imagine") 30-50 92
COTILLION (104/5 "John Lennon on Ronnie Hawkins") 30-35 70
(John Lennon promotes a 1970 Ronnie Hawkins Cotillion release.)
EVA-TONE ("John Lennon Radio Play") 400-600 69
(Soundsheet only. Originally included with a boxed set issue of *Aspen* Magazine. Price for complete set would be double that of just the Lennon disc.)
EVA-TONE (101075 "The Rock Generation") 30-40 76
(Issued with the book *The Rock Generation* Has a brief Lennon interview. Price for book with disc would be double that of just the disc.)
GEFFEN (29855 "Happy Xmas") 10-15 82
GEFFEN (49604 "Starting Over") 15-20 80
GEFFEN (49644 "Woman") 15-20 80
GEFFEN (49695 "Watching the Wheels") 15-20 81
KYA ("KYA 1969 Peace Talk") 150-200 69
(Radio KYA's Tom Campbell and Bill Holley's telephone interview with John Lennon.)
POLYDOR 10-15 84-86
QUAKER 10-15 86
(Picture disc soundsheet, issued with Quaker Granola Dipps. See "Great Moments in Rock N Roll" in Picture Disc Chapter for other titles.)
QUAYE/TRIDENT (3419 "Rock-N-Roll") 400-500 75
(Contains a one minute radio spot for the "Rock 'N' Roll" LP. For radio stations only.)
WHAT'S IT ALL ABOUT 15-20 70s
(Public service disc for radio play.)

Picture Sleeves

APPLE (1809 "Give Peace a Chance") 10-15 69
APPLE (1813 "Cold Turkey") 50-75 69
APPLE (1818 "Instant Karma") 10-15 70
APPLE (1827 "Mother") 100-125 70
APPLE (1830 "Power to the People") 20-30 71
APPLE (1842 "Happy Xmas") 10-20 71
APPLE (1848 "Woman Is the Nigger of the World") 15-25 72
APPLE (1868 "Mind Games") 10-15 73
CAPITOL (44230 "Jealous Guy") 3-5 88
GEFFEN (29855 "Happy Xmas") 3-5 82
GEFFEN (49604 "Starting Over")..........3-4 80
GEFFEN (49644 "Woman") 3-4 80
GEFFEN (49695 "Watching the Wheels") 3-4 81
POLYDOR 3-5 84

LPs: 10/12–inch

ADAM VIII LTD. (8018 "Great Rock & Roll Hits—Roots") 750-1000 75
APPLE (3361 "Wedding Album") .. 125-150 69
(Price range is for complete boxed set with all inserts.)
APPLE (3362 "Live Peace in Toronto") 30-40 69
(With Capitol logo. Has 16-page photo calendar, valued separately at $20 to $40.)
APPLE (3362 "Live Peace in Toronto") 10-20 70
(No Capitol logo. Has 16-page photo calendar, valued separately at $20 to $40.)
APPLE (3372 "John Lennon, Plastic Ono Band") 15-20 70
APPLE (3379 "Imagine") 15-25 71
(Includes bonus poster and photo card.)
APPLE (3392 "Sometime in New York City") 20-30 72
APPLE (3414 "Mind Games") 10-20 73
APPLE (3416 "Walls & Bridges") 10-20 74
(Includes booklet.)
APPLE (3419 "Rock 'N' Roll") 10-20 75
APPLE (3421 "Shaved Fish")............10-20 75
APPLE/TETRAGRAMMATON (5001 "Two Virgins") 125-150 68
(With brown paper outer sleeve.)
APPLE/TETRAGRAMMATON (5001 "Two Virgins") 75-100 68
(Without paper outer sleeve.)
APPLE/TETRAGRAMMATON (5001 "Two Virgins") 10-15 85
(Reissue, with brown paper outer sleeve that does NOT cover entire jacket.)
CAPITOL (3362 "Live Peace in Toronto") 10-15 82
(Purple label.)
CAPITOL (3362 "Live Peace in Toronto") 50-60 83
(Black label.)
CAPITOL (3372 "John Lennon, Plastic Ono Band") 10-20 78
(Purple label with "Mfd. by Capitol, etc." print, or black label.)
CAPITOL (3372 "John Lennon, Plastic Ono Band") 20-30 78
(Purple label with "Manufactured. by Capitol, etc." print.)
CAPITOL (3379 "Imagine") 5-10 78
(Purple label with "Mfd. by Capitol, etc." print.)
CAPITOL (3379 "Imagine") 20-30 86
(Black or purple label with "Manufactured by Capitol, etc." print.)
CAPITOL (3392 "Sometime in New York City") 20-30 72
CAPITOL (3414 "Mind Games")........35-45 78

CAPITOL (3416 "Walls & Bridges") .. 15-30 78
(Purple or black label.)
CAPITOL (3419 "Rock 'N' Roll")...... 25-35 75
CAPITOL (3421 "Shaved Fish") 8-12 78
(Purple label. Without Capitol logo on back cover.)
CAPITOL (3421 "Shaved Fish") 25-40 78
(Purple or black label. With Capitol logo on back cover.)
CAPITOL (16068 "Mind Games") 8-12 78
CAPITOL (16069 "Rock 'N' Roll") 8-12 78
CAPITOL (12451 "Live in New York City") 10-15 86
CAPITOL (12533 "Menlove Ave.") 10-15 86
CAPITOL (91425 "Double Fantasy") 15-25 89
GEFFEN (2001 "Double Fantasy") 10-15 80
(Cream color label. Logo has narrow print.)
GEFFEN (2001 "Double Fantasy") 40-50 80
(Cream color label with bold logo print.)
GEFFEN (2001 "Double Fantasy") 25-50 86
(Black label or purple label.)
GEFFEN (2023 "John Lennon Collection") 15-20 82
MFSL (153 "Imagine") 40-50 85
(Half-speed mastered.)
NAUTILUS (47 "Double Fantasy") 50-60 82
(Half-speed mastered.)
POLYDOR (Except colored vinyl) 10-20 84
POLYDOR (817160 "Milk and Honey") 100-150 84
(Colored vinyl.)
SILHOUETTE (10014 "Reflections and Poetry") 15-25 84
ZAPPLE (3357 "Life with the Lions") 20-25 69

Promotional LPs

APPLE (3392 "Sometime In New York City") 700-900 72
GEFFEN (2023 "John Lennon Collection") 35-45 82
(Quiex II "Limited Edition Pressing.")
NAUTILUS (47 "Double Fantasy") 50-60 82
(Issued in promotional white cover with blue print. Commercial disc.)
POLYDOR (817 238-1 "Heart Play") 20-30 83
(Includes program notes and copy of a letter from Yoko on her stationary.)
SILHOUETTE (10014 "Reflections and Poetry") 60-75 84
U.A. (671010 "How I Won the War") 200-250 66
(Promotional issue only with radio advertisements.)
Also see BEATLES
Also see ELEPHANT'S MEMORY
Also see HAWKINS, Ronnie
Also see JOHN, Elton / John Lennon
Also see ONO, Yoko
Also see PEEL, David, & Lower East Side / John Lennon & Yoko Ono

LENNON, Julian — P&R/LP '84

Singles: 12-inch

ATLANTIC 5-8 85

Singles: 7-inch

ATLANTIC 3-5 84-89

Picture Sleeves

ATLANTIC 3-5 84-89

LPs: 10/12-inch

ATLANTIC 5-10 84-89

LENNON, Julian, & Stevie Wonder

Singles: 7-inch

CAPITOL 3-5 80s

Picture Sleeves

CAPITOL 3-5 80s
Also see LENNON, Julian
Also see WONDER, Stevie

LENNON SISTERS — P&R '56

(With Lawrence Welk)

Singles: 78 rpm

BRUNSWICK 4-6 57
CORAL 4-6 56

Singles: 7-inch

BRUNSWICK 5-10 57-59
CORAL 5-10 56
DOT 4-8 58-67
MERCURY 3-6 68

EPs: 7-inch

BRUNSWICK 5-10 57

LPs: 10/12-inch

BRUNSWICK 10-25 57
DOT 5-15 59-67
HAMILTON 5-12 64
MERCURY 8-12 68-69
RANWOOD 4-8 68-81
VOCALION 5-10 69-70
WING 5-10 69
Members: Kathy Lennon; Peggy Lennon; Janet Lennon; Dianne Lennon.
Also see WELK, Lawrence

LENNOX, Annie, & Al Green — P&R '88

Singles: 7-inch

A&M 3-4 88

Picture Sleeves

A&M 3-4 88
Also see EURYTHMICS
Also see GREEN, Al

LENNY & STORKS: see WELCH, Lenny

LENOIR, J.B. — R&B '55

(J.B. Lenore; J.B. Lenor; with His African Hunch Rhythm)

Singles: 78 rpm

CHESS (1449 "My Baby Told Me") ... 25-50 51
CHESS (1463 "Deep in Debt Blues") 25-50 51
J.O.B. (112 "People Are Meddlin' in Our Affairs") 25-50 52
PARROT 25-50 54-55

Singles: 7-inch

CHECKER (844 "Let Me Die with the One I Love") 20-30 56
CHECKER (856 "Don't Touch My Head") 20-30 56
CHECKER (874 "Five Years") 15-25 57
CHECKER (901 "Don't Talk to Your Son") 15-25 58
J.O.B. (1012 "The Mojo") 75-100 52
J.O.B. (1102 "Play a Little While") .. 75-100 52
PARROT (Except 802) 75-100 54-55
PARROT (802 "Eisenhower Blues") 75-100 54
PARROT (802 "Tax Paying Blues") 75-125 54
(Black vinyl.)
PARROT (802 "Tax Paying Blues") 300-350 54
(Colored vinyl. *Eisenhower Blues* was retitled *Tax Paying Blues* and was issued using the same selection number. They are slightly different recordings.)
PARROT (809 "Man Watch Your Woman") 75-100 54
PARROT (814 "Mama, Your Daughter Is Going to Miss Me") 75-100 55
PARROT (821 "Fine Girls") 75-100 55
SHAD (5012 "Back Door") 15-25 59
U.S.A. 10-15 63
VEE JAY 10-15 60

LPs: 10/12-inch

CHESS (1410 "Natural Man") 30-40 63
POLYDOR 10-15 70
Also see WELLS, Junior

LEONETTI, Tommy — P&R '55

Singles: 78 rpm

CAPITOL 4-8 54-56
VIK 5-10 57

Singles: 7-inch

ATLANTIC 5-8 60
CAPITOL 5-10 54-56
COLUMBIA 4-6 67-73
DECCA 4-6 68-69
EPIC 3-5 74
RCA 3-8 59-77
20TH FOX 3-5 77
VIK 5-10 57

Picture Sleeves

COLUMBIA 4-8 68

LPs: 10/12-inch

CAMDEN 10-20 59
RCA 10-20 64-67

LE PAMPLEMOUSSE — P&R/R&B '77

Singles: 12-inch

A.V.I. 4-8 78-85

Singles: 7-inch

A.V.I. 3-5 77-85

LPs: 10/12-inch

A.V.I. 5-8 78-85

LEPPARD, Def: see DEF LEPPARD

LE 'ROI BROTHERS — LP '87

EPs: 7-inch

AMAZING 8-10 81
DEMON 4-8 84

LPs: 10/12-inch

JUNGLE 8-10 83
PROFILE 5-8 85-87

LE ROUX — P&R/LP '78

(Louisiana's LeRoux)

Singles: 7-inch

CAPITOL 3-6 78
NEW ORLEANS LADY 5-10
RCA 3-5 82-83

LPs: 10/12-inch

CAPITOL 5-8 78-81
NEW ORLEANS LADY 20-30
RCA 5-8 82

LES COMPAGNONS DE LA CHANSON — P&R '52

Singles: 78 rpm

COLUMBIA 3-6 52

Singles: 7-inch

CAPITOL 4-6 59-60
COLUMBIA 5-8 52

LESEAR, Anne — R&B '84

Singles: 7-inch

H.C.R.C. 3-5 84

LESTER, Bobby

Singles: 7-inch

CHECKER 5-10 59
COLUMBIA 3-5 70

LPs: 10/12-inch

COLUMBIA 10-15 70

LESTER, Bobby, & Moonglows

Singles: 7-inch

CHESS 5-8 62

LPs: 10/12-inch

CHESS (1471 "Best of Bobby Lester and the Moonglows") 30-40 62
Also see MOONGLOWS

LESTER, Bobby, & Moonlighters

Singles: 78 rpm

CHECKER (806 "So All Alone") 20-30 54

Singles: 7-inch

CHECKER (806 "So All Alone") 50-75 54
(Checkerboard top label.)
CHECKER (806 "So All Alone") 10-20 58
(Vertical logo.)

LESTER, Ketty — P&R/R&B/LP '62

Singles: 7-inch

COLLECTABLES 3-4 80s
ERA 5-10 62-63
EVEREST 4-8 62
PETE 4-6 68-69
RCA 4-6 64
TOWER 4-6 65-66

LPs: 10/12-inch

AVI 5-8 80
ERA (EL-108 "Love Letters") 25-35 62
(Monaural.)
ERA (ES-108 "Love Letters") 30-40 62
(Stereo.)
MEGA 5-8 85
PETE 10-15 69
RCA 10-20 64-65
SHEFFIELD 8-10 77
TOWER 10-15 66

Also see EVERETT, Betty, & Ketty Lester

LET'S ACTIVE
LP '84

LPs: 10/12-inch

I.R.S. 5-8 84-86

LETTERMEN
P&R '61

Singles: 7-inch

ALPHA-OMEGA 3-5 78-88
APPLAUSE 3-4 83
CAPITOL 3-8 61-76
W.B. 5-8 60

Picture Sleeves

CAPITOL 5-10 61-71

LPs: 10/12-inch

ALPHA-OMEGA 5-15 77-88
APPLAUSE 5-8 82
CANDELITE 5-10 70s
CAPITOL (138 thru 836 except 577) ... 5-15 68-71
CAPITOL (577 "The Lettermen") 10-20 62-68
(Boxed three-disc set.)
CAPITOL (1669 thru 2934) 10-20 62-68
(With "T" or "ST" prefix.)
CAPITOL (2500 & 2700 series) 5-8 80s
(With "SM" prefix.)
CAPITOL (11000 series) 5-10 71-75
CAPITOL (16000 series) 4-8 80-83
CAPITOL (90000 series) 10-20
LONGINES (220 "Time for Us") 15-30
(Boxed, five-disc boxed set.)
LONGINES (220 "From the Lettermen, with Love") 5-8 72
(Bonus LP, issued with the above box set.)
PICKWICK (577 "The Lettermen") 10-15 70
(Three-disc set.)
PICKWICK (3000 series) 5-10 70-77

Members: Tony Butala; James Pike; Bob Engemann; Gary Pike; Donny Pike; Chad Nichols; Don Campo.

Also see CAMPBELL, Glen / Lettermen / Ella Fitzgerald / Sandler & Young
Also see PETER & GORDON / Lettermen
Also see SONNY & CHER / Bill Medley / Lettermen / Blendells

LEVEL 42
D&D '84

Singles: 12-inch

A&M 4-6 84

Singles: 7-inch

A&M 3-4 84
POLYDOR 3-4 82-88

Picture Sleeves

POLYDOR 3-4 86-87

LPs: 10/12-inch

A&M 5-8 84
POLYDOR 5-10 82-88

Members: Mark King; Mike Lindup; Phil Gould; Boon Gould; Krys Mach.

LEVERT
R&B '85

Singles: 7-inch

ATLANTIC 3-4 86-88
TEMPRE 3-5 85

LPs: 10/12-inch

ATLANTIC 5-8 86-90

Members: Sean Levert; Gerald Levert; Marc Gordon.

LEVINE, Hank
P&R '61

(With the Minature Men)

Singles: 7-inch

ABC-PAR 4-8 61
DOLTON 4-8 62-63
TOPS 4-8 60

Also see CONNORS, Carol
Also see MINIATURE MEN

LEVON & HAWKS

(Featuring Levon Helm)

Singles: 7-inch

ATCO 10-20 65-68

Also see BAND
Also see HELM, Levon
Also see HAWKINS, Ronnie

LEVY, Marcy

Singles: 7-inch

EPIC 3-5 82

LPs: 10/12-inch

EPIC 8-15 82

Also see CLAPTON, Eric

LEVY, Marcy, & Robin Gibb

Singles: 7-inch

RSO 3-4 80

Picture Sleeves

RSO 3-5 80

Also see GIBB, Robin
Also see LEVY, Marcy

LEWIS, Barbara
P&R/R&B '63

Singles: 7-inch

ATLANTIC 5-10 62-67
ENTERPRISE 3-5 70-71
KAREN (313 "My Heart Went Do Dat Da") 15-25 61
REPRISE 3-5 73

LPs: 10/12-inch

ATLANTIC (8086 thru 8173) 20-35 63-68
ATLANTIC (8286 "Best of Barbara Lewis") 10-15 71
COLLECTABLES 6-8 88
ENTERPRISE 10-12 70
SOLID SMOKE 8-10 70s

Also see DELLS

LEWIS, Bobby
P&R/R&B '61

(With Dave Hamilton's Peppers)

Singles: 78 rpm

SPOTLIGHT 10-15 56

Singles: 7-inch

ABC-PAR 4-8 64
BELTONE 10-15 61-62
ERIC 3-4 70s
LANA 3-6 60s
MERCURY (71245 "Mumbles Blues") 10-20 57
PHILIPS (40519 "Soul Seekin'") 10-20 68
ROULETTE 8-12 59
SPOTLIGHT (394 "Mumbles Blues") 20-40 56
SPOTLIGHT (397 "Solid As a Rock") 50-100 57

LPs: 10/12-inch

BELTONE (4000 "Tossin' and Turnin' ") 50-100 61

LEWIS, Gary, & Playboys
P&R '65

Singles: 7-inch

LIBERTY (Except 56144) 4-8 64-69
LIBERTY (56144 "I Saw Elvis Presley Last Night") 10-15 69

Picture Sleeves

LIBERTY 5-10 65-67

EPs: 7-inch

LIBERTY (227 "Doin' the Flake") 10-20 65
(Liberty/Kellogg's Premium Record. Issued with paper sleeve.)

LPs: 10/12-inch

GUSTO 5-8 72
LIBERTY (Except 10000 series) 15-30 65-69
LIBERTY (10000 series) 5-8 81
SUNSET 12-15 69
U.A. (Except 1000 series) 8-10 75
U.A. (1000 series) 5-8 81

LEWIS, Huey, & News
P&R/LP '82

Singles: 12-inch

CHRYSALIS (Except 8V8-42795) 4-8 84-89
CHRYSALIS (8V8-42795 "The Heart of Rock & Roll") 8-12 84
(Picture disc.)

Singles: 7-inch

CHRYSALIS 3-5 80-89

Promotional Singles

CHRYSALIS (2589 "Do You Believe in Love") 8-12 80
(Colored vinyl. With Valentine card. Promotional issue only.)
CHRYSALIS (43065 "Hip to Be Square") 10-15 85
(Four disc set, each of a different color vinyl.)

Picture Sleeves

CHRYSALIS 3-5 82-89

LPs: 10/12-inch

CHRYSALIS 5-8 80-89
MFSL 15-20 85

Members: Huey Lewis; Bill Gibson; Mario Cipollina; Sean Hopper; Chris Hayes; Johnny Colla.

Also see EDMUNDS, Dave
Also see U.S.A. for AFRICA

LEWIS, J.D.
R&B '89

Singles: 7-inch

SING ME 3-4 89

LEWIS, J.G.
R&B '76

Singles: 7-inch

IX CHAINS 4-6 76

LEWIS, Jerry
P&R/LP '56

Singles: 78 rpm

CAPITOL 4-8 50-53
DECCA 4-8 56-57

Singles: 7-inch

CAPITOL 5-10 50-53
DECCA 5-10 56-62
DOT 4-8 60
LIBERTY 4-8 63

EPs: 7-inch

CAPITOL 6-12 56
DECCA 6-10 56

LPs: 10/12-inch

CAPITOL 10-15 64
DECCA 15-25 56
DOT 10-15 60
VOCALION 8-12 66

Also see MARTIN, Dean, & Jerry Lewis

LEWIS, Jerry Lee
P&R/C&W/R&B '57

(With "His Pumping Piano")

Singles: 78 rpm

SUN 25-75 56-58

Singles: 7-inch

AMERICA SMASH 3-5 86
BUDDAH 3-6 71
ELEKTRA 3-5 79-82
MCA 3-5 82-83
MERCURY 3-6 70-82
POLYDOR 3-4 89
SCR (386 "Get Out Your Big Roll, Daddy") 3-5 85
(Colored vinyl.)
SSS/SUN 3-5 69-84
(Includes numbers below 100 and over 1000.)
SMASH (1857 thru 2122) 5-10 63-67
SMASH (2146 thru 2257) 4-8 68-70
SUN (169/213 "Whole Lotta Shakin' Going On"/"Great Balls of Fire") 5-10 94
(Colored vinyl. Promotional issue only.)
SUN (259 "Crazy Arms") 20-30 56
SUN (267 thru 296) 15-25 56-58
SUN (300 series) 10-20 58-65

Picture Sleeves

POLYDOR 3-4 89
SUN (281 "Great Balls of Fire") 25-50 57
SUN (296 "High School Confidential") 25-50 57

EPs: 7-inch

MERCURY (6 "Special Radio Cuts from *Would You Take Another Chance on Me*") . 15-25 71
(Promotional issues only.)
MERCURY (14 "Special Radio Cuts from *The Killer Rocks On*") 15-25 72
(Promotional issues only.)
SCR 10-15 86
SSS/SUN (108 "Golden Cream of the Country") 15-25 69
(Juke box issue only.)
SSS/SUN (114 "A Taste of Country") 15-25 69
(Juke box issue only.)
SMASH (2 "Jerry Lee Lewis") 20-25 64
SMASH (28 "Open-End Interview") ... 30-40 64
(Promotional issue only.)
SUN (107 "Great Ball of Fire") 75-125 57
(Issued with a paper sleeve.)
SUN (108 "Jerry Lee Lewis") 50-100 57
(Blue cover. First track listed is *Don't Be Cruel.*)

SUN (109 "Jerry Lee Lewis")..........50-100 58
(Yellow cover. First track listed is *Ubangi Stomp*.)
SUN (110 "Jerry Lee Lewis")..........50-100 58
(Red cover. First track listed is *High School Confidential*.)

LPs: 10/12-inch

ACCORD....................................5-8 81-82
AURA.......................................5-8 82
BUCKBOARD..............................8-10 75
ELEKTRA..................................5-10 79-82
EVEREST..................................8-12 75
HILLTOP.................................10-12 72
KOALA......................................8-15 79
MCA..5-8 82-84
MERCURY (SRM1 series)................8-15 72-78
MERCURY (SRM2-803 "Session")...15-20 73
MERCURY (3 "Southern Roots")......20-35 73
MERCURY (61318 "In Loving Memories")..............................30-40 71
MERCURY (61323 "There Must Be More to Love Than This")..............................8-12 71
MERCURY (61343 "Touching Home")....................................15-20 71
(Cover is mostly an artist's drawing with a small photo of Lewis on the right side.)
MERCURY (61343 "Touching Home")....................................12-15 71
(Cover pictures Lewis standing in front of a brick wall.)
MERCURY (61346 "Would You Take Another Chance on Me")..........................8-12 71
MERCURY (61366 "Who's Gonna Play This Old Piano")...8-12 72
OUT of TOWN DIST..........................5-8 82
PICKWICK.................................10-12 70-74
POLYDOR (839516 "Great Ball of Fire")..5-8 89
(Includes tracks by other artists.)
POLYSTAR..................................8-10
POWER PAK...............................8-10 74
RHINO (255 "Original Sun Greatest Hits")......................................10-15 83
(Picture disc.)
SCR..5-10 85
SSS/SUN...................................5-10 69-84
SEARS.....................................10-15
SMASH (690 "Jerry Lee Lewis Radio Special")......................................40-50 73
(Promotional issue only.)
SMASH (7001 "Golden Rock Hits").......5-8 82
SMASH (27040 "Golden Hits of Jerry Lee Lewis")....................................20-30 64
(Monaural.)
SMASH (27056 "Greatest Live Show on Earth")...15-20 64
(Monaural.)
SMASH (27063 "Return of Rock").....20-25 65
(Monaural.)
SMASH (27071 "Country Songs for City Folks")..15-20 65
(Monaural.)
SMASH (27079 "Memphis Beat")......20-25 65
(Monaural.)
SMASH (27086 "By Request")..........15-20 66
(Monaural.)
SMASH (27097 "Soul My Way")........20-25 67
(Monaural.)
SMASH (67040 "Golden Hits of Jerry Lee Lewis")....................................25-35 64
(Stereo.)
SMASH (67040 "Golden Rock Hits of Jerry Lee Lewis")....................................20-30 60s
(Reissue.)
SMASH (67056 "Greatest Live Show on Earth")...20-25 64
(Stereo.)
SMASH (67063 "Return of Rock").....25-30 65
(Stereo.)
SMASH (67071 "Country Songs for City Folks")..20-25 65
(Stereo.)
SMASH (67071 "All Country")...........10-15 69
(Stereo. Reissue.)
SMASH (67079 "Memphis Beat")......25-30 65
(Stereo.)
SMASH (67086 "By Request")..........20-25 66
(Stereo.)
SMASH (67097 "Soul My Way").......25-30 67
(Stereo.)
SMASH (67104 thru 67131)...............8-15 68-70
SUN (1230 "Jerry Lee Lewis").......75-125 58
SUN (1265 "Jerry Lee's Greatest") 75-125 62
SUNNYVALE...............................8-10 77
TRIP...8-10 74
WING (125 "The Legend of Jerry Lee Lewis")......................................20-30 69
WING (12000 series)....................12-15 66-67
(Monaural.)
WING (16000 series)....................15-20 66-67
(Stereo.)
Also see CLANTON, Jimmy / Frankie Ford / Jerry Lee Lewis / Patsy Cline
Also see HAWK
Also see KING, Ben E.
Also see McDOWELL, Ronnie, & Jerry Lee Lewis
Also see NELSON, Willie / Jerry Lee Lewis / Carl Perkins / David Allan Coe

LEWIS, Jerry Lee / Curly Bridges / Frank Motley

LPs: 10/12-inch

DESIGN....................................10-15 63

LEWIS, Jerry Lee / Johnny Cash

LPs: 10/12-inch

SSS/SUN...................................8-10 71
Also see CASH, Johnny
Also see CASH, Johnny / Jerry Lee Lewis / Jeanie C. Riley
Also see PERKINS, Carl, Jerry Lee Lewis, Roy Orbison & Johnny Cash

LEWIS, Jerry Lee, & Friends C&W '79

Singles: 7-inch

SSS/SUN (1139 "Save the Last Dance for Me")..4-6 78
(Colored vinyl.)
SSS/SUN (1141 "Cold, Cold Heart")....4-6 79

LPs: 10/12-inch

SSS/SUN (1011 "Duets")..................8-12 78
(Colored vinyl.)
SSS/SUN (1011 "Duets")..................8-12 78
(Black vinyl, even though cover indicates "Special Gold Vinyl." RCA Record Club issue.)
Members: Jerry Lee Lewis; Jimmy Ellis; Charlie Rich.
Also see RICH, Charlie

LEWIS, Jerry Lee & Linda Gail Lewis C&W '69

Singles: 7-inch

SMASH.......................................3-6 69-70
SUN..5-10 63

LPs: 10/12-inch

SMASH.....................................15-25 69

LEWIS, Jerry Lee / Roger Miller / Roy Orbison

LPs: 10/12-inch

PICKWICK..................................8-10 70s
Also see MILLER, Roger
Also see ORBISON, Roy

LEWIS, Jerry Lee, Carl Perkins & Charlie Rich

LPs: 10/12-inch

SSS/SUN (1018 "Trio +")..................8-10 78
(With Jimmy Ellis.)
Also see ELLIS, Jimmy
Also see LEWIS, Jerry Lee, & Friends
Also see PERKINS, Carl

LEWIS, Jerry Lee / Charlie Rich / Johnny Cash

LPs: 10/12-inch

POWER PAK...............................8-10 80s
Also see CASH, Johnny, Carl Perkins & Jerry Lee Lewis
Also see LEWIS, Jerry Lee

LEWIS, Jimmy R&B '75

(With the L.A. Street Band)

Singles: 7-inch

HOTLANTA...................................3-5 75
MCA..3-4 84

LPs: 10/12-inch

HOTLANTA..................................5-10 74

LEWIS, Lenny, & His Orch. R&B '46

Singles: 78 rpm

QUEEN.......................................4-8 46

LEWIS, Linda R&B '75

Singles: 7-inch

ARISTA......................................3-5 75-78
REPRISE....................................3-5 73

LPs: 10/12-inch

REPRISE....................................8-10 74

LEWIS, Monica, & Ames Bros. P/R '48

Singles: 78 rpm

SIGNATURE................................5-10 48
Also see AMES BROTHERS

LEWIS, Ramsey LP '62

(Ramsey Lewis Trio; Ramsey Lewis & Co.)

Singles: 12-inch

COLUMBIA..................................4-6 79-85

Singles: 7-inch

ABC..3-5 74
ARGO..4-8 58-65
CADET.......................................3-6 65-72
CHESS.......................................3-5 73
COLUMBIA..................................3-5 72-87
EMARCY.....................................4-8 59

EPs: 7-inch

ARGO (687 "Sound of Christmas")...15-25 61

LPs: 10/12-inch

ARGO (611 "Gentleman of Swing")..40-60 58
ARGO (627 "Gentleman of Jazz").....40-60 58
ARGO (642 "Ramsey Lewis Trio with Len Winchester")..............................30-50 59
ARGO (645 "An Hour with the Ramsey Lewis Trio")..25-50 59
ARGO (665 "Stretching Out")...........25-50 60
ARGO (680 "From the Soil")............25-50 61
ARGO (687 "Sound of Christmas")...25-50 61
ARGO (693 "Sound of Spring").........25-35 62
ARGO (700 series)........................20-40 62-65
CADET.......................................10-20 65-72
COLUMBIA..................................6-12 72-85
EMARCY (36150 "Down to Earth")...25-45 59
(Monaural.)
EMARCY (80029 "Down to Earth")...35-60 59
(Stereo.)
TRIP..5-8 75
Members: Ramsey Lewis; Eldee Young; Red Holt; Cleveland Eaton; Maurice White.
Also see DUSHON, Jean, & Ramsey Lewis Trio
Also see EARTH, WIND & FIRE with Ramsey Lewis
Also see YOUNG HOLT UNLIMITED

LEWIS, Ramsey, & Nancy Wilson LP '84

LPs: 10/12-inch

COLUMBIA..................................5-10 84
Also see LEWIS, Ramsey
Also see WILSON, Nancy

LEWIS, Shirley P&R '89

Singles: 7-inch

VENDETTA..................................3-4 89

LEWIS, Smiley R&B '52

Singles: 78 rpm

COLONY (106 "Sad Life")................50-75 52
COLONY (110 "Where Were You")..50-75 52
DELUXE (3099 "Turn Your Volume On, Baby")......................................50-75 47
IMPERIAL..................................15-40 50-57

Singles: 7-inch

DOT..5-8 64
IMPERIAL (5124 "My Baby Was Right")......................................75-125 52
IMPERIAL (5194 "The Bells Are Ringing")..................................50-100 52
IMPERIAL (5208 "Gumbo Blues")...50-100 52
IMPERIAL (5224 "Gypsy Blues")......50-100 54
IMPERIAL (5234 "Play Girl").........50-100 53
(Black vinyl.)
IMPERIAL (5234 "Play Girl").........150-200 53
(Colored vinyl.)

IMPERIAL (5241 "Caldonia's Party") 50-100 53
IMPERIAL (5252 "Little Fernandez") 50-100 53
IMPERIAL (5268 "Down the Road") 50-100 54
IMPERIAL (5279 "I Love You for Sentimental Reasons") 50-100 54
IMPERIAL (5296 "Can't Stop Loving You") 50-100 54
IMPERIAL (5316 "Too Many Drivers") 50-100 54
IMPERIAL (5325 "Jailbird") 50-100 54
IMPERIAL (5349 "Real Gone Lover") 50-100 55
IMPERIAL (5356 "I Hear You Knocking") 50-75 55
IMPERIAL (5372 "Queen of Hearts") 50-75 55
IMPERIAL (5380 "One Night") 50-75 56
IMPERIAL (5389 "She's Got Me Hook, Line and Sinker") 50-75 56
IMPERIAL (5404 "Down Yonder We Go Ballin' ") 50-75 56
IMPERIAL (5418 "Shame, Shame, Shame") 50-75 56
IMPERIAL (5431 thru 5820) 15-30 57-62
KNIGHT 10-15 59
LOMA 5-10 65
OKEH 5-10 62

LPs: 10/12-inch

IMPERIAL (9141 "I Hear You Knocking") 150-200 61
Also see BARTHOLOMEW, Dave

LEWIS, Webster — R&B/LP '80

(With the Post-Pop Space Rock Be-Bop Gospel Tabernacle Orchestra & Chorus; with Love Unlimited Orchestra)

Singles: 12-inch

EPIC 4-8 77
UNLIMITED GOLD 4-6 81

Singles: 7-inch

EPIC 3-5 77-81
UNLIMITED GOLD 3-5 81

LPs: 10/12-inch

EPIC 5-10 78-80
UNLIMITED GOLD 5-10 81

LEWIS & CLARKE — P&R '67

(Lewis & Clarke Expedition)

Singles: 7-inch

CHARTMAKER 4-8 66
COLGEMS (1006 "I Feel Good") 5-10 67
COLGEMS (1011 "Destination Unknown") 8-12 67
COLGEMS (1022 "Why Need Pretend") 8-12 68
COLGEMS (1028 "Daddy's Plastic Child") 8-12 68

Picture Sleeves

COLGEMS (1006 "I Feel Good") 8-12 67

LPs: 10/12-inch

COLGEMS (105 "Lewis & Clarke Expedition") 20-35 67
Members: Travis Lewis; Boomer Clarke (Castleman); John London. Session: Jim Pewter; Michael Murphey.
Also see CASTLEMAN, Boomer
Also see MURPHEY, Michael

LEWIS CONNECTION

LP: 10/12-inch

("The Lewis Connection") 300-400 79
(No label name nor selection number used. Prince plays guitar and sings backup on *Got to Be Something Here.*)
Member: Sonny Thompson. Session: Prince.
Also see PRINCE

LIA, Orsa — P&R '79

Singles: 7-inch

INFINITY 3-5 79
RCA 4-6 68

LIBERACE — P&R '52

Singles: 78 rpm

ADVANCE 5-8 55
COLUMBIA 3-6 52-57
DECCA 3-6 52

Singles: 7-inch

A.V.I. 3-5 76-77
COLUMBIA (39000 thru 41000 series) 5-10 52-58
COLUMBIA (48000 series) 3-6
CORAL 4-6 59-61
DECCA (28000 series) 5-10 52
DOT 4-6 64-67
MGM 3-5 73
W.B. 3-5 71

Picture Sleeves

COLUMBIA 10-15 54

EPs: 7-inch

COLUMBIA 5-15 52-56
DECCA 10-20 52

LPs: 10/12-inch

ABC 5-8 74
A.V.I. 5-8 73-79
BROOKVILLE 8-15
COLUMBIA (589 "Christmas") 30-45 54
COLUMBIA (600 "At the Hollywood Bowl") 30-45 55
COLUMBIA (645 "Hollywood Bowl Encore") 35-45 55
COLUMBIA (661 "By Candlelight") 25-45 55
COLUMBIA (800 "Sincerely Yours") 25-45 56
COLUMBIA (896 "At Home") 20-40 56
COLUMBIA (1000 thru 1200 series) 15-25 57-58
COLUMBIA (2516 "Piano Reverie") 50-75 56
(10-inch LP.)
COLUMBIA (2592 "Kiddin' on the Keys") 50-75 56
(10-inch LP.)
COLUMBIA (6217 "At the Piano") 50-100 52
(10-inch LP.)
COLUMBIA (6239 "Evening with Liberace") 50-100 53
(10-inch LP.)
COLUMBIA (6269 "Concertos for You") 50-100 53
(10-inch LP.)
COLUMBIA (6283 "Dream of Olwen") 50-100 54
(10-inch LP.)
COLUMBIA (6327 "Liberace Plays Chopin") 50-100 54
(10-inch LP.)
COLUMBIA (9800 series) 5-10 69
CORAL 8-15 59-64
DECCA 5-10 72
DOT 8-15 63-68
FORWARD 5-10 69
HARMONY 8-15 59-70
HAMILTON 5-10 65
MISTLETOE 5-8 74
PARAMOUNT 5-10 73-74
TRIP 4-8 76
VOCALION 5-10 68
W.B. 5-10 71
Also see PRESLEY, Elvis

LIEBERMAN, Lori — LP '73

Singles: 7-inch

CAPITOL 3-5 72-75
MILLENIUM 3-5 78

LPs: 10/12-inch

CAPITOL 8-12 72-74

LIFESTYLE — R&B '77

Singles: 7-inch

MCA 3-5 77

LPs: 10/12-inch

MCA 8-10 77

LIGGETT, Otis — D&D '83

Singles: 12-inch

EMERGENCY 4-6 83

Singles: 7-inch

EMERGENCY 3-5 83

LIGGINS, Jimmy — R&B '48

(With His 3-D Music)

Singles: 78 rpm

ALADDIN 15-25 54
SPECIALTY 15-25 47-54

Singles: 7-inch

ALADDIN (3250 "I Ain't Drunk") 25-50 54
ALADDIN (3251 "No More Alcohol") 25-50 54
DUPLEX 4-6
SPECIALTY (434 "Brown Skin Baby") 25-50 49
SPECIALTY (470 "Drunk") 20-40 53
(Black vinyl.)
SPECIALTY (470 "Drunk") 50-100 53
(Colored vinyl.)
SPECIALTY (484 "Going Away") 25-50 54

LIGGINS, Joe — P&R/R&B '45

(With His Honeydrippers)

Singles: 78 rpm

DOT 8-15 51-56
EXCLUSIVE 15-25 45-48
SMASH 10-20 54
SPECIALTY 10-20 49-54

Singles: 7-inch

ALADDIN (3368 "Justina") 15-25 56
DOT (1031 "The Honey Dripper") 15-25 56
DOT (1032 "I've Got a Right to Cry") 15-25 56
DOT (1033 "Tanya") 15-25 56
MERCURY (70440 "Yeah, Yeah, Yeah") 20-30 54
SPECIALTY (338 "The Honey Dripper") 20-40 49
SPECIALTY (379 "Little Joe's Boogie") 20-40 51
SPECIALTY (392 "Frankie Lee") 20-40 51
SPECIALTY (402 "Whiskey, Gin and Wine") 20-40 52
SPECIALTY (409 "Louisiana Woman") 20-40 52
SPECIALTY (413 "So Alone") 20-40 52
SPECIALTY (426 "Boogie Woogie Lou") 20-40 52
SPECIALTY (430 "Tanya") 20-40 52
SPECIALTY (441 "Goin' Back to New Orleans") 20-40 52
SPECIALTY (453 "Freight Train Blues") 20-40 53
SPECIALTY (465 "Farewell Blues") 20-40 53
SPECIALTY (474 "Everyone's Down on Me") 20-40 53
SPECIALTY (529 "Whiskey, Women and Loaded Dice") 25-50 54

LPs: 10/12-inch

BLUES SPECTOR 15-25
Also see MILTON, Roy / Joe Liggins

LIGHT, Enoch, & His Orch. — P&R '37

(Terry Snyder & All-Stars; Command All-Stars; with Light Brigade; with Brass Menagerie)

Singles: 78 rpm

VOCALION 4-6 37

Singles: 7-inch

COMMAND 4-6 61

LPs: 10/12-inch

COMMAND 8-20 59-72
GRAND AWARD 10-15 59
PROJECT 5-10 67-71
REALISTIC 5-10
WALDORF (185 "Melody of Love") 35-55 54
(10-inch LP. Cover pictures Tina Louise, although she is not heard on the disc.)
WALDORF (193 "Moments to Remember") 35-55 54
(10-inch LP. Cover pictures Tina Louise, although she is not heard on the disc.)
WALDORF (1214 "Moments to Remember") 25-50 57
(Cover pictures Jayne Mansfield, although she is not heard on the disc.)
WALDORF (1232 "Melody of Love") 20-40 57

(10–inch LP. Cover pictures Tina Louise, although she is not heard on the disc.)
WALDORF (1329 "Moments to Remember") 20-40 58
(Cover pictures Tina Louise, although she is not heard on the disc.)
Members: Enoch Light; Terry Snyder; Charles Magnante; Dick Hyman; Jack Lesberg; Teddy Sommer; Bob Haggart; Tony Mattola; Willie Rodriguez; Moe Wechsler; Urbie Green; Bobby Byrne; Pee Wee Erwin; Artie Marotti; Dominic Cortese; Ezelie Watson; Russ Banzer; Stanley Webb; Milt Yaner; Leonard Calderon; George Dessinger; Bernie Kaufman.

LIGHTFOOT, Gordon — LP '69
(Gord Lightfoot)

Singles: 7–inch
ABC-PAR 10-20 62
CHATEAU 5-10 65
REPRISE 3-5 70-77
U.A. 3-8 65-69
W.B. (Except 5621) 3-5 78-86
W.B. (5621 "For Lovin' Me") 5-10 65

Picture Sleeves
U.A. (50152 "The Way I Feel") 5-10 67
W.B. 3-4 86

LPs: 10/12–inch
AME ("Early Lightfoot") 75-100
(Number not known.)
K-TEL 5-8
LIBERTY 5-8 80
MFSL (018 "Sundown") 25-50 78
PICKWICK 5-8 79
REPRISE (Except 93228) 5-12 70-76
REPRISE (93228 "Sit Down Young Stranger") 10-20 70
U.A. (Except 3400 & 6400 series) 5-10 69-74
U.A. (3400 series) 10-15 66-69
(Monaural.)
U.A. (6400 series) 10-20 66-69
(Stereo.)
W.B. 5-8 78-86

LIGHTHOUSE — LP '70

Singles: 7–inch
EVOLUTION 3-5 71-72
POLYDOR 4-6 73-74
RCA 3-4 69-70

LPs: 10/12–inch
EVOLUTION 10-15 71-72
JANUS 8-10 76
POLYDOR 8-12 73-74
RCA 10-15 69-70

LIGHTNIN' SLIM — R&B '59
(Otis Hicks)

Singles: 78 rpm
ACE (505 "Bad Feeling Blues") 50-75 54
EXCELLO 10-20 55-57
FEATURE (3006 "Rock Me, Mama") 50-75 54
FEATURE (3008 "I Can't Live Happy") 10-25 54
FEATURE (3012 "Bugger Bugger Boy") 10-25 54

Singles: 7–inch
ACE (505 "Bad Feeling Blues") 75-125 54
EXCELLO (2000 series) 20-30 55-56
EXCELLO (2100 series) 10-20 57-61
EXCELLO (2200 & 2300 series) 4-8 62-72
FEATURE (3006 "Rock Me, Mama") 100-200 54
FEATURE (3008 "I Can't Live Happy") 25-50 54
FEATURE (3012 "Bugger Bugger Boy") 25-50 54

LPs: 10/12–inch
EXCELLO (8000 "Rooster Blues") 30-50 60
EXCELLO (8004 "Bell Ringer") 15-25 65
EXCELLO (8018 "High and Low Down") 10-15 71
EXCELLO (8023 "London Gumbo") 10-15 72

LIGHTNING SEEDS — LP '90

LPs: 10/12–inch
MCA 5-8 90

LIMAHL — P&R/D&D/LP '85
(Chris Hamill)

Singles: 12–inch
EMI AMERICA 4-6 85-86

Singles: 7–inch
EMI AMERICA 3-4 85-86

Picture Sleeves
EMI AMERICA 3-4 85-86

LPs: 10/12–inch
EMI AMERICA 5-8 85-86
Also see KAJAGOOGOO

LIME — D&D '83

Singles: 12–inch
PRISM 4-6 83
TSR 4-6 85

Singles: 7–inch
PRISM 3-5 83

LPs: 10/12–inch
PRISM 5-8 83

LIMELITERS — P&R/LP '61

Singles: 7–inch
ELEKTRA 5-10 60-61
RCA 5-10 61-64
W.B. 4-8 68

Picture Sleeves
RCA 8-12 61-63

EPs: 7–inch
RCA ("Introducing . . .") 10-15 61
(Promotional issue only. Introduces 11 new RCA acts with about 30 seconds of music by: Limeliters, Cables; Toni Harper; Gary Judis; Cleo Jons; Baker Knight; Langan Sisters; Barry Martin; Penny & Jean; Gordon Terry; Universals.)

LPs: 10/12–inch
CAMDEN 5-10 74
ELEKTRA 15-25 60-61
LEGACY 8-10 70
PICKWICK 5-8 72
RCA (Except 2336) 10-25 61-68
RCA (2336 "Pure Gold") 5-8 77
STAX 6-10 74
W.B. 8-15 68
Members: Glen Yarbrough; Lou Gottlieb; Alex Hassilev; Ernie Sheldon.
Also see ANN-MARGRET
Also see YARBROUGH, Glen

LIMIT — R&B '82

Singles: 12–inch
PORTRAIT 4-6 84

Singles: 7–inch
ARISTA 3-5 82
PORTRAIT 3-4 84
Also see GUTHRIE, Gwen

LIMITED WARRANTY — P&R '86

Singles: 7–inch
ATCO 3-4 86

Picture Sleeves
ATCO 3-4 86

LPs: 10/12–inch
ATCO 5-8 86

LIMMIE & FAMILY COOKIN' — P&R '72

Singles: 7–inch
AVCO 3-6 72

LIND, Bob — P&R/LP '66

Singles: 7–inch
CAPITOL 3-5 71
VERVE/FOLKWAYS 4-6 66
WORLD PACIFIC 4-8 65-66

LPs: 10/12–inch
CAPITOL 10-15 71
VERVE/FOLKWAYS 10-20 66
WORLD PACIFIC 10-20 66

LINDEN, Kathy — P&R '58
(With Joe Leahy's Orchestra)

Singles: 7–inch
CAPITOL 4-8 62-63
FELSTED 5-15 58-59
MONUMENT 5-10 60-61
NATIONAL 4-8 60s
RECORD PROD. CORP 4-8 61

Picture Sleeves
FELSTED 10-20 58-59
MONUMENT 4-8 60-61

EPs: 7–inch
FELSTED (35001 "Hits") 35-45 58

LPs: 10/12–inch
FELSTED (7501 "That Certain Boy") 40-60 59

LINDISFARNE — P&R '72

Singles: 7–inch
ATCO 3-5 78
ELEKTRA 3-5 72-73

LPs: 10/12–inch
ATCO 8-12 78
ELEKTRA 10-15 71-74

LINDLEY, David — LP '81
(With El Rayo)

Singles: 7–inch
ASYLUM 3-5 81

LPs: 10/12–inch
ASYLUM 5-10 81
ELEKTRA 5-8 88
Also see BROWNE, Jackson

LINDSAY, Mark — P&R '69

Singles: 7–inch
COLUMBIA 3-6 69-75
GREEDY 3-6 76
W.B. 3-6 77

LPs: 10/12–inch
COLUMBIA 10-15 70-71
Also see REVERE, Paul, & Raiders
Also see UNKNOWNS

LINEAR — P&R/LP '90

LPs: 10/12–inch
ATLANTIC 5-8 90

LINER — P&R '79

Singles: 7–inch
ATCO 3-5 79

LPs: 10/12–inch
ATCO 5-10 79

LINK - EDDY COMBO — R&B '61

Singles: 7–inch
REPRISE 8-12 61

Singles: 12–inch
Members: Al Garcia; Fred Mendoza; Vince Bumatay; Art Rodriguez.

LINKLETTER, Art — LP '66

Singles: 7–inch
CAPITOL 3-5 69

EPs: 7–inch
COLUMBIA 5-10 56
WORD 3-5 69

LPs: 10/12–inch
CAPITOL 8-15 61
COLUMBIA 15-25 56
HARMONY 8-15 59
20TH FOX 8-15 63-66
WORD 5-10 68

LINX — R&B/LP '81

Singles: 7–inch
CHRYSALIS 3-4 81

Picture Sleeves
CHRYSALIS 3-4 81

LPs: 10/12–inch
CHRYSALIS 5-8 81
Members: David Grant; Peter Martin.
Also see GRANT, David

LIONS & GHOSTS — LP '87

LPs: 10/12–inch
EMI AMERICA 5-8 87

LIPPS, INC. — P&R/R&B/LP '80

Singles: 7–inch
CASABLANCA 3-5 79-83

LPs: 10/12–inch
CASABLANCA 5-8 79-81

LIQUID GOLD *P&R '79*

Singles: 12-inch

CRITIQUE 4-6 83
PARACHUTE 4-8 79

Singles: 7-inch

CRITIQUE 3-4 83
PARACHUTE 3-5 79

LPs: 10/12-inch

PARACHUTE 5-10 79

LIQUID LIQUID *D&D '83*

Singles: 12-inch

99 RECORDS 4-6 83

LIQUID SMOKE *P&R '70*

Singles: 7-inch

AVCO EMBASSY 4-8 70

LPs: 10/12-inch

AVCO EMBASSY (33005 "Liquid Smoke") 20-30 70
Member: Sandy Dantaleo.

LISA *D&D '83*

Singles: 12-inch

MOBY DICK 4-6 83-84

LISA LISA *P&R/R&B/D&D/LP '85*
(With Cult Jam & Full Force)

Singles: 12-inch

COLUMBIA 4-6 85-86

Singles: 7-inch

COLUMBIA 3-4 85-89

Picture Sleeves

COLUMBIA 3-4 87-88

LPs: 10/12-inch

COLUMBIA 5-8 84-89
Member: Lisa Velez.
Also see FULL FORCE
Also see KING DREAM CHORUS & Holiday Crew

LITES, Shirley *D&D '83*

Singles: 12-inch

WEST END 4-6 83

LITTLE, Rich *LP '82*

Singles: 7-inch

BOARDWALK 3-4 82
MERCURY 3-5 71

LPs: 10/12-inch

BOARDWALK 5-8 82
CAEDMON 5-10 72
KARR 8-15 68
MERCURY 8-10 71
PIZZA HUT ("Pizza Hut '73") 15-20 73
(Souvenir of an annual company meeting. Promotional issue only. No selection number used.)

LITTLE AMERICA *LP '87*

LPs: 10/12-inch

GEFFEN 5-8 87

LITTLE ANTHONY & IMPERIALS
(Anthony & Imperials; Imperials) *P&R/R&B '58*

Singles: 7-inch

APOLLO (755 "The Fires Burn No More") 15-20 61
AVCO 4-6 74-75
DCP 5-10 64-66
END (1027 "Tears on My Pillow") 15-25 58
(First issued as by the Imperials.)
END (1036 "So Much") 15-25 58
END (1038 "The Diary") 15-25 58
END (1039 "When You Wish Upon a Star") 10-20 58
END (1047 "A Prayer and a Juke box") 10-20 59
END (1053 "I'm Alright") 10-20 59
END (1060 "Shimmy Shimmy Ko-Ko Bop") 10-20 59
END (1067 "My Empty Room") 10-20 60
END (1074 "Only Sympathy") 10-20 60
END (1080 "Limbo") 10-20 60
END (1083 "Formula of Love") 10-20 60
END (1086 "Please Say You Want Me") 10-20 61
END (1091 "Traveling Stranger") 10-20 61
END (1104 "A Lovely Way to Spend an Evening") 10-20 61
JANUS 4-6 71-72
MCA 3-4 80
OLD HIT 3-4
PCM 3-4 83
PURE GOLD 3-5 76
ROULETTE 5-10 61-63
U.A. 4-6 69-70
VEEP 5-10 66-68

Picture Sleeves

DCP 10-20 65
VEEP 10-20 66

EPs: 7-inch

END (203 "Little Anthony and the Imperials") 50-100 58
END (204 "We Are the Imperials Featuring Little Anthony") 50-100 59

LPs: 10/12-inch

ACCORD 5-10 83
AVCO 8-10 74
DCP 20-40 64-66
EMUS 5-10 79
END (303 "We Are the Imperials Featuring Little Anthony") 75-125 59
END (311 "Shades of the '40s") 50-100 60
FORUM CIRCLE 10-15
LIBERTY 5-8 81
ROULETTE 20-30 65
SUNSET 10-15 70
U.A. (Except 1000 series) 10-15 69-74
U.A. (1000 series) 5-8 80
VEEP 15-20 66-68
Members: Anthony Gourdine; Clarence Collins; Sam Strain; Tracy Lord; Ernie Wright; Gloucester Rogers.
Also see IMPERIALS
Also see LITTLE ANTHONY
Also see O'JAYS

LITTLE ANTHONY & IMPERIALS / Platters

LPs: 10/12-inch

EXACT 5-10 80
Also see LITTLE ANTHONY & IMPERIALS
Also see PLATTERS

LITTLE BEAVER *R&B '72*
(Willie Hale)

Singles: 7-inch

CAT 3-5 72-76
PHIL-LA of SOUL 4-8 67
Also see BIRDLEGS & PAULINE
Also see WRIGHT, Betty

LITTLE BILL & BLUENOTES *P&R '59*
(With the Adventurers & Shalimars; Little Bill)

Singles: 7-inch

BOLO (725 "Little Angel") 20-30 62
DOLTON (4 "I Love an Angel") 15-25 59
TOPAZ (1303 "Sweet Cucumber") 25-50 60
TOPAZ (1305 "Louie Louie") 50-75 61

LPs: 10/12-inch

CAMELOT (102 "The Fiesta Club Presents Little Bill & the Blue Notes") 100-200 60
Members: Bill Engelhart; Frank Dutra; Tom Giving; Buck Ormsby; Lassie Aanes; Buck England; Tom Morgan.

LITTLE BOOKER
(James Booker)

Singles: 78 rpm

IMPERIAL 25-45 54

Singles: 7-inch

ACE 10-20 58
IMPERIAL (5293 "Thinkin' 'Bout My Baby") 50-75 54
Also see BOOKER, James

LITTLE CAESAR *R&B '52*

Singles: 78 rpm

BIG TOWN 15-25 53
RPM 15-25 53
RECORDED in HOLLYWOOD 15-25 53

Singles: 7-inch

BIG TOWN (106 "Big Eyes") 25-50 53
BIG TOWN (110 "What Kind of Fool Is He") 25-50 53
RPM (393 "Chains of Love Have Disappeared") 25-50 53
RECORDED in HOLLYWOOD (234 "The River") 25-50 53
RECORDED in HOLLYWOOD (235 "Goodbye Baby") 25-50 53
RECORDED in HOLLYWOOD (236 "Talking to Myself") 25-50 53
RECORDED in HOLLYWOOD (237 "Atomic Love") 25-50 53
Also see WILSON, Jimmy / Thrillers / Little Caesar

LITTLE CAESAR & CONSULS *P&R '65*

Singles: 7-inch

MALA 8-12 65

LITTLE CAESAR & ROMANS
(Caesar & the Romans) *P&R/R&B '61*

Singles: 7-inch

DEL-FI (4158 "Those Oldies But Goodies") 10-20 61
DEL-FI (4164 "Hully Gully Again") 10-20 61
DEL-FI (4166 "Memories of Those Oldies But Goodies") 25-50 61
DEL-FI (4170 "Ten Commandments of Love") 20-40 61
DEL-FI (4176 "Popeye One More Time") 10-20 62
HI-NOTE (194 "What's Wrong with You") 5-10

LPs: 10/12-inch

DEL-FI (1218 "Memories of Those Oldies But Goodies") 50-75 61
Members: David "Little Caesar" Johnson; Larry Sanders; Johnny Simmons; Carl Burnett.
Also see BLUE JAYS / Little Caesar & Romans

LITTLE CAESAR & ROMANS / Ron Holden

Singles: 7-inch

TRIP 3-5 70s
Also see HOLDEN, Ron
Also see LITTLE CAESAR & ROMANS

LITTLE DIPPERS *P&R '60*
(Anita Kerr Singers)

Singles: 7-inch

DOT 5-10 64
UNIVERSITY 8-12 59-60
Also see KERR, Anita

LITTLE ESTHER *R&B '50*
(Esther Phillips; Little Esther Phillips; with Earle Warren Orchestra; with Johnny Otis Orchestra)

Singles: 78 rpm

DECCA 15-25 54
FEDERAL 25-50 51
SAVOY 10-20 56

Singles: 7-inch

ATLANTIC 8-15 64-67
DECCA (28804 "Talkin' All Out of My Head") 25-50 54
DECCA (48305 "Stop Cryin'") 25-50 54
DECCA (48314 "He's a No Good Man") 50-75 54
FEDERAL (12023 "I'm a Bad Girl") 75-125 51
FEDERAL (12042 "Crying and Sighing") 75-125 51
FEDERAL (12055 "Crying Blues") 75-125 52
FEDERAL (12063 "Summertime") 75-125 52
FEDERAL (12065 "Better Beware") 75-125 52
FEDERAL (12078 "Aged and Mellow") 75-125 52
FEDERAL (12090 "Ramblin' Blues") 75-125 52
FEDERAL (12126 "Hound Dog") 75-125 53
FEDERAL (12142 "Cherry Wine") 75-125 53
GUSTO 3-5
KUDU 4-6 72-76
LENOX 10-15 62-63
MERCURY 3-5 77-79

ROULETTE 4-6 69
SAVOY (1100 series) 20-30 56
SAVOY (1500 series) 10-20 58-59
WARWICK 10-20 60-61
WINNING 3-5 83

LPs: 10/12-inch

ATLANTIC (1500 & 1600 series) 8-12 70-76
ATLANTIC (8100 series) 20-30 65-66
KING (622 "Memory Lane") 1000-2000 59
KUDU 8-12 72-76
LENOX (227 "Release Me") 30-50 62
MERCURY 5-10 78-81
YORKSHIRE 8-12

Also see ADAMS, Faye / Little Esther / Shirley & Lee
Also see PHILLIPS, Esther, & Joe Beck

LITTLE ESTHER & DOMINOES
(With the Earle Warren Orchestra)

Singles: 78 rpm

FEDERAL 100-200 51

Singles: 7-inch

FEDERAL (12036 "Heart to Heart") 300-400 51

Also see LITTLE ESTHER with the Earle Warren Orchestra (With the Dominoes)
Also see LITTLE ESTHER & Clyde McPhatter

LITTLE ESTHER & BIG AL DOWNING

Singles: 7-inch

LENOX 10-15 63

Also see DOWNING, Al

LITTLE ESTHER & JUNIOR WITH JOHNNY OTIS ORCHESTRA / Johnny Otis Orchestra with Vocaleers

Singles: 78 rpm

SAVOY (824 "Get Together Blues") . 20-30 51

Also see VOCALEERS

LITTLE ESTHER & LITTLE WILLIE LITTLEFIELD

Singles: 78 rpm

FEDERAL 40-60 52

Singles: 7-inch

FEDERAL (12108 "Last Laugh Blues") 75-125 52
FEDERAL (12115 "Turn the Lamps Down Low") 75-125 52

Also see LITTLEFIELD, Little Willie

LITTLE ESTHER & CLYDE MCPHATTER

Singles: 7-inch

FEDERAL (12344 "Heart to Heart") .. 40-60 58

Also see LITTLE ESTHER & DOMINOES
Also see McPHATTER, Clyde

LITTLE ESTHER & BOBBY NUNN

Singles: 78 rpm

FEDERAL 50-100 52-53

Singles: 7-inch

FEDERAL (12100 "Saturday Night Daddy") 250-450 52
FEDERAL (12122 "You Took My Love Too Fast") 250-450 53

Also see NUNN, Bobby

LITTLE ESTHER & MEL WALKER
(With the Johnny Otis Orchestra)

Singles: 78 rpm

FEDERAL 15-25 52
SAVOY 15-25 50

Singles: 7-inch

FEDERAL (12055 "Ring-A-Ding Doo") 100-150 52
SAVOY (735 "Mistrustin' Blues") ... 100-150 50
SAVOY (759 "Deceivin' Blues") 100-150 50

Also see OTIS, Johnny

LITTLE ESTHER & EARLE WARREN ORCHESTRA
(With the Dominoes)

Singles: 78 rpm

FEDERAL (12016 "The Deacon Moves In") 150-250 51
FEDERAL (12036 "Heart") 100-200 51

Singles: 7-inch

FEDERAL (12016 "The Deacon Moves In") 400-600 51
FEDERAL (12036 "Heart") 350-500 51

Also see DOMINOES
Also see LITTLE ESTHER & DOMINOES

LITTLE EVA — P&R/R&B/LP '62

Singles: 7-inch

ABC 3-5 74
AMY 4-8 65-66
BELL 3-5 72
DIMENSION 5-10 62-65
MCA 3-4 80
SPRING 3-5 70
VERVE 4-8 66

Picture Sleeves

DIMENSION (1035 "Makin' with the Magilla") 20-30 64

LPs: 10/12-inch

DIMENSION (DLP-6000 "L-L-L-L-Locomotion") 35-55 62
(Monaural.)
DIMENSION (DLPS-6000 "L-L-L-L-Locomotion") 50-75 62
(Stereo.)

Also see COOKIES / Little Eva / Carole King
Also see IRWIN, Big Dee
Also see KING, Ben E.

LITTLE FEAT — LP '74

Singles: 7-inch

W.B. 3-6 70-78

LPs: 10/12-inch

MFSL (013 "Waiting for Columbus") 75-125 78
NAUTILUS (24 "Time Loves a Hero") 20-25 70s
(Half-speed mastered.)
W.B. (984 "Hoy Hoy") 15-20 81
(Promotional issue only.)
W.B. (1890 thru 2884) 8-15 70-76
W.B. (3015 thru 3538) 6-12 77-81
W.B. (25000 & 26000 series) 5-8 88-90

Members: Lowell George; Ken Gradney; Richard Hayward; Sam Clayton; Fred Tackett; Paul Barrere; Bill Payne; Roy Estrada.

Also see BRAMLETT, Bonnie
Also see CARTER, Valerie
Also see COODER, Ry
Also see GEORGE, Lowell
Also see HARRIS, Emmylou
Also see MOTHERS of INVENTION
Also see TOWER of POWER
Also see ZEVON

LITTLE JO ANN — P&R '62

Singles: 7-inch

KAPP 8-12 62

LITTLE JOE & MORROCOS

Singles: 7-inch

BUMBLE BEE 15-20 58

Member: Joe Cook.

Also see LITTLE JOE & THRILLERS

LITTLE JOE & THRILLERS — P&R '57
(Little Joe; Little Joe the Thriller)

Singles: 78 rpm

EPIC 15-25 57
OKEH 15-25 56-57

Singles: 7-inch

ENJOY 4-8 64
EPIC (7088 "Peanuts") 15-25 57
(Canadian. Has same number as on Okeh)
EPIC (9292 "It's Too Bad We Had to Say Goodbye") 10-15 58
(Canadian.)
MGM 3-5 70-73
OKEH (7075 "This I Know") 15-25 56
OKEH (7088 "Peanuts") 15-25 57
(Purple label.)
OKEH (7088 "Peanuts") 10-15 57
(Yellow label.)
OKEH (7094 "Echoes Keep Calling Me") 10-20 57
(Yellow label.)
OKEH (7099 "What Happened to Your Halo") 15-25 57
OKEH (7116 thru 7140) 10-15 59-61
PEANUT 5-10
REPRISE 5-8 63
ROSE 5-8 63
TWENTIETH CENTURY (1214 "For Sentimental Reasons") 25-35 61

EPs: 7-inch

EPIC (7198 "Little Joe and the Thrillers") 75-125 58

Members: Joe Cook; Richard Frazier; Farris Hill; Don Burnett; Harry Pascle.

Also see LITTLE JOE & MORROCOS

LITTLE JOE BLUE — R&B '66

Singles: 7-inch

CHECKER 4-8 66
MOVIN' 4-8 66

LITTLE JOEY & FLIPS — P&R '62
(Joey Hall)

Singles: 7-inch

JOY 8-10 62

Also see DRIFTERS / Little Joey & Flips

LITTLE JUNIOR'S BLUE FLAMES
(Junior Parker) — R&B '53

Singles: 78 rpm

SUN 50-100 53

Singles: 7-inch

SUN (187 "Feelin' Good") 100-200 53
SUN (192 "Love My Baby") 100-200 53

Also see PARKER, Little Junior

LITTLE MAC & BOSS SOUNDS — R&B '65

Singles: 7-inch

ATLANTIC 4-8 65

Member: Ann Mason.

LITTLE MILTON — R&B '62
(Milton Campbell)

Singles: 78 rpm

METEOR 50-100 57
SUN (194 "Beggin' My Baby") 50-100 53
SUN (200 "If You Love Me") 75-125 54
SUN (220 "Homesick for My Baby") 100-150 55

Singles: 7-inch

BOBBIN (101 "I'm a Lonely Man") 20-30 58
BOBBIN (108 "Long Distance Operator") 20-30 59
BOBBIN (112 "Strange Dreams") 20-30 59
BOBBIN (117 "Hold Me Tight") 20-30 59
BOBBIN (120 "Dead Love") 20-30 60
BOBBIN (125 "Hey Love") 20-30 61
BOBBIN (128 "Cross My Heart") 20-30 61
CHECKER (0124 thru 0252) 4-6 72-76
CHECKER (977 thru 1239) 5-15 61-71
CHESS 3-6 73-76
EAR 3-5 80
GLADES 3-5 76-78
GOLDEN 3-5 80
MCA 3-5 83
MALACO 3-4 84-86
METEOR (5040 "Love at First Sight") 100-200 57
METEOR (5045 "Let My Baby Be") 100-200 57
MIER 3-5 78
STAX 3-6 71-83
SUN (194 "Beggin' My Baby") 200-300 53
SUN (200 "If You Love Me") 250-350 54
SUN (220 "Homesick for My Baby") 300-500 55

LPs: 10/12-inch

CHECKER (2995 "We're Gonna Make It") 20-30 65
CHECKER (3002 "Big Blues") 20-30 66
CHECKER (3011 "Grits Ain't Groceries") 15-20 69
CHECKER (3012 "If Walls Could Talk") 15-20 70
CHESS 10-15 72-76
GLADES 8-10 76-77

GOLDEN 5-10 80
MCA 5-8 83
MALACO 5-8 84-92
STAX 6-12 73-81
Also see CAMPBELL, Little Milton
Also see MANN, Herbie

LITTLE MILTON & ALBERT KING

LPs: 10/12-inch

STAX 5-10 79
Also see KING, Albert

LITTLE MILTON & JACKIE ROSS

Singles: 7-inch

EAR 3-5 80

LPs: 10/12-inch

EAR 5-10 81
Also see LITTLE MILTON
Also see ROSS, Jackie

LITTLE RICHARD P&R '56

Singles: 78 rpm

PEACOCK 25-50 53
RCA (4392 "Taxi Blues") 50-100 51
RCA (4582 "Get Rich Quick") 50-100 52
RCA (4772 "Ain't Nothing Happenin'") 50-75 52
RCA (5025 "Please Have Mercy on Me") 50-75 52
SPECIALTY 20-40 56-57

Singles: 7-inch

ABC 3-5 73
ATLANTIC 5-10 63
BELL 3-5 73
BRUNSWICK 5-10 68
CORAL 5-10 63
END (1057 "Save Me Lord") 10-15 59
END (1058 "Milky White Way") 10-15 59
GREEN MOUNTAIN 3-5 73
KENT 3-5 73
MCA 3-4 86
MANTICORE 3-5 75
MERCURY 5-10 61
MODERN 15-25 57-58
(Black label.)
MODERN 5-10 66-67
(Red or white label.)
OKEH 5-10 66-69
PEACOCK (1658 "Little Richard's Boogie") 50-75 53
PEACOCK (1673 "Maybe I'm Right") 50-75 54
RCA (4392 "Taxi Blues") 200-300 51
(Turqoise label.)
RCA (4582 "Get Rich Quick") 200-300 52
(Turqoise label.)
RCA (4772 "Ain't Nothing Happenin'") 100-200 52
(Black label.)
RCA (5025 "Please Have Mercy on Me") 100-200 52
(Black label.)
REPRISE 3-6 70-72
SPECIALTY (561 thru 664) 20-30 56-59
SPECIALTY (670 thru 699) 10-20 59-64
SPECIALTY (SPBX series) 15-20 85
(Boxed sets of six colored vinyl 45s.)
TRIP 3-5 71
VEE JAY 5-10 64
W.B. 3-5 87

Picture Sleeves

MCA 3-4 86
MODERN (1018 "Holy Mackeral") 25-35 57
OKEH (7251 "Poor Dog") 10-15 66
SPECIALTY (606 "Jenny Jenny") 20-40 57
SPECIALTY (611 "Keep a Knockin'") 20-40 57
SPECIALTY (624 "Good Golly Miss Molly") 20-40 58
SPECIALTY (633 "Ooh! My Soul") 20-40 58
SPECIALTY (736 "All Around the World") 4-6 85

EPs: 7-inch

CAMDEN (416 "Little Richard") 150-200 56
CAMDEN (446 "Little Richard Rocks") 100-150 56
KAMA SUTRA (17 "Little Richard") .. 10-20 70
SPECIALTY (400 "Here's Little Richard") 40-60 56
SPECIALTY (401 "Here's Little Richard") 40-60 56
SPECIALTY (402 "Here's Little Richard") 40-60 56
SPECIALTY (403 "Little Richard") 40-60 57
SPECIALTY (404 "Little Richard") 40-60 57
SPECIALTY (405 "Little Richard") 40-60 57

LPs: 10/12-inch

ACCORD 5-10 81
AUDIO ENCORES 20-25 80
BUDDAH 10-12 69
CAMDEN (420 "Little Richard") 150-200 56
CAMDEN (2430 "Every Hour") 20-30 70
CORAL 20-30 63
CROWN 15-25 63
CUSTOM 10-12 60s
EPIC 10-12 71
EVEREST 5-8 82
EXACT 5-10 80-81
EXODUS 5-10
51 WEST 5-8 80s
GRT 5-8 77
GOLD DISC 10-15
GUEST STAR 10-15 64
KAMA SUTRA 10-12 70
MERCURY 20-30 61
MODERN 10-20 66
OKEH 10-20 67
PICKWICK 10-15 72
REPRISE 10-15 70-72
ROULETTE 10-15 68
SCEPTER 10-15
SPECIALTY (100 "Here's Little Richard") 300-500 57
(Reissued as Specialty 2100.)
SPECIALTY (2100 "Here's Little Richard") 50-100 57
(Label indicates "Natural Sound.")
SPECIALTY (2100 "Here's Little Richard") 25-50 60s
(Label indicates "Stereo Natural Sound.")
SPECIALTY (2103 "Little Richard") 50-100 57
SPECIALTY (2104 "The Fabulous Little Richard") 50-100 58
SPECIALTY (2111 "Biggest Hits") 20-30 63
SPECIALTY (2113 "Grooviest 17 Original Hits") 10-15 68
SPECIALTY (2154 "The Essential Little Richard") 8-12 84
SPIN-O-RAMA 10-15 60s
SUMMIT 10-15
TRIP 10-15 71-78
20TH FOX 15-25 63
UNITED 8-10 70s
U.A. 8-10 75
UPFRONT 8-10 77
VEE JAY 15-25 64-65
VEE JAY/DYNASTY 10-12
W.B. 5-8 87
WING 10-20 64

Session: Lee Allen.

Notes: Many Specialty reissues exist, some of which are very similar in appearance to '50s originals. Any with a zip code on covers are obviously post-1963 reissues. Discs from the '50s are heavier than reissues. Many reissues have a raised vinyl ridge around the record's outer edge—originals do not. Any on colored, or semi-transparent vinyl are reissues. Some reissues do have an identifying copyright date.

Also see ALLEN, Lee
Also see BAILEY, Philip, & Little Richard
Also see BEACH BOYS & Little Richard
Also see CANNED HEAT
Also see CHARLES, Ray / Little Richard / Sam Cooke
Also see COOKE, Sam / Lloyd Price / Larry Williams / Little Richard
Also see DUCES of RHYTHM & Tempo Toppers
Also see HENDRIX, Jimi, & Little Richard
Also see McPHATTER, Clyde / Little Richard / Jerry Butler
Also see UPSETTERS Featuring Little Richard

LITTLE RICHARD / John Cougar Mellancamp

Singles: 7-inch

ELEKTRA 3-5 88

Picture Sleeves

ELEKTRA 4-6 88
Also see MELLENCAMP, John Cougar

LITTLE RICHARD / Arthur Crudup / Red Callendar Sextet

LPs: 10/12-inch

CAMDEN (371 "Little Richard, Arthur Crudup & Red Callendar Sextet") 75-125 56
Also see CRUDUP, Arthur

LITTLE RICHARD / Sister Rosetta

LPs: 10/12-inch

GUEST STAR 10-15
Also see LITTLE RICHARD

LITTLE RIVER BAND P&R/LP '76

(LRB)

Singles: 12-inch

CAPITOL 4-6 83

Singles: 7-inch

CAPITOL 3-4 79-85
HARVEST 3-5 76-78

Picture Sleeves

CAPITOL 3-5 81-85
HARVEST 3-5 78

LPs: 10/12-inch

CAPITOL 5-8 79-85
HARVEST 5-8 75-80
MFSL 20-30 79
Member: John Farnham.
Also see FARNHAM, John
Also see SHORROCK, Glen

LITTLE SISTER P&R '70

Singles: 7-inch

STONE FLOWER 5-10 70-72

LPs: 10/12-inch

STONE FLOWER 10-15 70
Members: Vanetta Stewart; Elva Melton; Mary Rand.

LITTLE STEVEN P&R/LP '82

Singles: 7-inch

EMI AMERICA 3-5 82-84

LPs: 10/12-inch

EMI AMERICA 5-8 82-84
MANHATTAN 5-8 87
Also see BEAUVOIR, Jean
Also see SPRINGSTEEN, Bruce

LITTLE SYLVIA

Singles: 78 rpm

CAT (102 "Fine Love") 10-20 53
JUBILEE 10-20 52
SAVOY (816 "Little Boy") 15-25 51

Singles: 7-inch

CAT (102 "Fine Love") 15-25 53
JUBILEE (5093 "Drive, Daddy, Drive") 25-35 52
Also see MICKEY & SYLVIA
Also see SYLVIA

LITTLE WALTER R&B '52

(With His Jukes; with Night Caps; with Night Cats; Little Walter Trio; Little Walter J.; Marion Walter Jacobs)

Singles: 78 rpm

CHANCE (1116 "That's Allright") .. 100-150 52
CHECKER 15-25 52-57
ORA NELLE (711 "Ora Nelle Blues [That's Allright]") 50-100 47

Singles: 7-inch

CHANCE (1116 "That's Allright") .. 250-350 52
CHECKER (758 "Juke") 20-40 52
CHECKER (764 "Mean Old World") . 20-40 52
CHECKER (770 "Off the Wall") 20-40 53
(Black vinyl.)
CHECKER (770 "Off the Wall") 75-100 53
(Colored vinyl.)
CHECKER (780 "Quarter to Twelve") 15-25 53
CHECKER (786 "Lights Out") 15-25 53

CHECKER (793 "Rocker") 15-25 54
CHECKER (799 "You Better Watch Yourself") 15-25 54
(Black vinyl.)
CHECKER (799 "You Better Watch Yourself") 50-75 54
(Colored vinyl.)
CHECKER (800 series) 10-20 54-58
CHECKER (900 thru 1100 series) 8-15 58-65

LPs: 10/12-inch

CHESS (Except 1428) 10-20 69-74
CHESS (1428 "Best of Little Walter") 50-100 57
Also see ROBINSON, Freddy
Also see SUNNYLAND SLIM

LITTLEFIELD, Little Willie — R&B '48

Singles: 78 rpm

EDDIE'S (1202 "Little Willie's Boogie") 50-75 48
EDDIE'S (1205 "Chicago Bound") 50-75 48
EDDIE'S (1212 "Swanee River") 50-75 49
FEDERAL 25-50 52-57
MODERN 25-50 49-50

Singles: 7-inch

BULLS-EYE (1005 "Ruby-Ruby") 25-40 58
FEDERAL (12101 "Sticking on You, Baby") 75-125 52
FEDERAL (12110 "K.C. Loving") 75-125 52
FEDERAL (12137 "The Midnight Hour Was Shining") 75-125 53
FEDERAL (12148 "Miss K.C.'s Fine") 75-125 53
FEDERAL (12163 "Please Don't Go-o-o-o-oh") 75-125 53
FEDERAL (12174 "Falling Tears") .. 75-125 54
FEDERAL (12221 "Jim Wilson's Boogie") 50-100 55
FEDERAL (12300 series) 15-25 57-59
RHYTHM (108 "Ruby-Ruby") 200-300 56
Also see LITTLE ESTHER & Little Willie Littlefield

LITTLEFIELD, Little Willie / Goree Carter

Singles: 78 rpm

FREEDOM (1502 "Littlefield Boogie") 50-75 49
Also see LITTLEFIELD, Little Willie

LIVERPOOL FIVE — P&R '66

Singles: 7-inch

RCA 5-10 65-67

LPs: 10/12-inch

RCA (LPM-3583 "The Liverpool Five Arrive") 20-25 66
(Monaural.)
RCA (LSP-3583 "The Liverpool Five Arrive") 20-30 66
(Stereo.)
RCA (LPM-3682 "Out of Sight") 20-25 67
(Monaural.)
RCA (LSP-3682 "Out of Sight") 20-30 67
(Stereo.)
Also see ASTRONAUTS / Liverpool Five

LIVIGNI, John — P&R '75

Singles: 7-inch

RAINTREE 3-5 75

LIVING COLOUR — LP '88

Singles: 7-inch

EPIC 3-4 88-90

LPs: 10/12-inch

EPIC 5-8 88-90
Members: Corey Glover; Vernon Reid; Muzz Skillings; William Calhoun.

LIVING IN A BOX — P&R/LP '87

Singles: 12-inch

CHRYSALIS 4-6 87

Singles: 7-inch

CHRYSALIS 3-4 87

Picture Sleeves

CHRYSALIS 3-4 87

LPs: 10/12-inch

CHRYSALIS 5-8 87

LIVING STRINGS — LP '61

(With the Living Voices)

Singles: 7-inch

COMMAND 3-5 59
GRAND AWARD 3-5 59

LPs: 10/12-inch

CAMDEN 5-15 60-62
COMMAND 5-10 59
GRAND AWARD 5-10 59
RCA 5-8 78

LIZARD, King: see KING LIZARD

LIZZY BORDEN — LP '86

Soundsheets

EVATONE (1029231CS "Me Against the World") 4-6 87

LPs: 10/12-inch

ENIGMA/METAL BLADE 5-8 86-89

LLOYD, Charles, Quartet — LP '67

LPs: 10/12-inch

ATLANTIC 10-15 67
Also see HAMILTON, Chico

LLOYD, Ian — P&R '79

Singles: 7-inch

POLYDOR 3-5 76
SCOTTI BROTHERS 3-4 79

LPs: 10/12-inch

POLYDOR 5-10 76
SCOTTI BROTHERS 5-8 79
Also see STORIES

LOAF, Meat: see MEAT LOAF

LOBO — P&R/LP '71

(Roland Kent Lavole)

Singles: 7-inch

BIG TREE 3-6 71-75
ELEKTRA 3-5 80
EVERGREEN 3-4 85
FLASHBACK 3-5 73
LOBO 3-5 81-82
MCA 3-4 79
MARIANNE 3-5 77
PHILIPS 3-5
W.B. 3-5 76-78

LPs: 10/12-inch

BIG TREE 10-15 71-75
CALUMET 10-15 73
MCA 5-10 79
Also see LEE, Robin, & Lobo
Also see STAFFORD, Jim
Also see WOLFPACK

LOCKLIN, Hank — C&W '49

Singles: 78 rpm

DECCA 5-10 52
4 STAR 5-10 49-54
RCA 5-10 55-57

Singles: 7-inch

COUNTRY ARTISTS 3-4 83
DECCA (29000 series) 10-15 52
4 STAR (1500 & 1600 series) 10-15 52-54
KING (5000 series) 5-8 59
MGM 3-5 74
PLANTATION 3-5 76-77
RCA (0030 thru 0900 series) 3-5 72-74
RCA (6100 thru 7600 series) 8-15 55-59
RCA (7700 thru 9900 series) 4-8 60-71

EPs: 7-inch

RCA 8-15 58-61

LPs: 10/12-inch

ARCADE 5-8
CAMDEN 8-15 62-74
DESIGN 10-15 62
INTERNATIONAL AWARD 8-12 60s
KING (600 & 700 series) 15-25 61
MGM 5-10 75
METRO 10-15 65
PICKWICK/HILLTOP 8-15 65-68
PLANTATION 5-8 77-81
RCA (Except 1673 series) 10-20 62-71
RCA (1673 "Foreign Love") 15-25 58
SEARS 8-12 60s
STEREO SPECTRUM 5-10 60s
WRANGLER 10-15 62
Session: Jordanaires.
Also see CLINE, Patsy / Hank Locklin / Miller Brothers / Eddie Marvin
Also see SNOW, Hank / Hank Locklin / Porter Wagoner

LOCKLIN, Hank, with Danny Davis & Nashville Brass — C&W '70

Singles: 7-inch

RCA 3-6 69-70

LPs: 10/12-inch

RCA 8-10 70
Also see DAVIS, Danny
Also see LOCKLIN, Hank

LOCKSMITH — R&B '80

Singles: 7-inch

ARISTA 3-5 80

LPs: 10/12-inch

ARISTA 5-10 80

LODGE, John — LP '77

Singles: 7-inch

LONDON 3-5 77

LPs: 10/12-inch

LONDON (683 "Natural Avenue") 10-15 77
Also see HAYWARD, Justin, & John Lodge
Also see MOODY BLUES

LOFGREN, Nils — LP '75

Singles: 7-inch

A&M 3-5 75-77

LPs: 10/12-inch

A&M (Except 8362) 8-10 75-82
A&M (8362 "Authorized Bootleg") 25-30 76
(Promotional issue only.)
BACKSTREET 5-8 81
COLUMBIA 5-8 85
EPIC 8-10 76
RYKODISC 5-8 91
Also see GRIN

LOGG — R&B '81

Singles: 7-inch

SALSOUL 3-5 81

LPs: 10/12-inch

SALSOUL 5-8 81

LOGGINS, Dave — P&R/LP '74

Singles: 7-inch

EPIC 3-5 74-81
VANGUARD 4-6 72-74

LPs: 10/12-inch

CAPITOL 5-8 84
EPIC 8-10 74-81
VANGUARD 8-12 72
Also see MURRAY, Anne, & Dave Loggins

LOGGINS, Kenny — P&R/LP '77

Singles: 12-inch

COLUMBIA 4-8 81-86

Singles: 7-inch

COLUMBIA 3-5 77-88

Picture Sleeves

COLUMBIA 3-4 83-88

LPs: 10/12-inch

COLUMBIA (Except 45387) 6-12 72-88
COLUMBIA (45387 "Nightwatch") 10-15 81
(Half-speed mastered.)
Also see U.S.A. for AFRICA

LOGGINS, Kenny, & Stevie Nicks

Singles: 7-inch

COLUMBIA 3-5 78
Also see NICKS, Stevie

LOGGINS, Kenny, & Steve Perry

Singles: 7-inch

COLUMBIA 3-5 82

Picture Sleeves

COLUMBIA 3-5 82
Also see LOGGINS, Kenny
Also see PERRY, Steve

LOGGINS & MESSINA — P&R/LP '72

Singles: 7-inch

COLUMBIA 3-5 72-76
LOS ANGELES KINGS/COLUMBIA (10444 "Angry Eyes") 3-5 76

(Promotional issue for "Columbia/Kings Record Night" at the L.A. Forum.)

Picture Sleeves

LOS ANGELES KINGS/COLUMBIA (10444 "Angry Eyes")....3-5 76
(Promotional issue for "Columbia/Kings Record Night" at the L.A. Forum.)

LPs: 10/12-inch

COLUMBIA (30000 series)....8-10 72-82
COLUMBIA (44000 series)....10-15 82
(Half-speed mastered.)
DIRECT-DISK (16606 "Full Sail")....15-25 82
(Half-speed mastered.)
Members: Kenny Loggins; Jim Messina.
Session: Larry Sims; Vince Denham; Merle Bregante; Jon Clarke; Don Roberts; Steve Forman.
Also see LOGGINS, Kenny
Also see MESSINA, Jim

LOGGINS & MESSINA / David Bromberg

LPs: 10/12-inch

COLUMBIA....8-15 72
(Promotional only.)
Also see BROMBERG, David
Also see LOGGINS & MESSINA

LOLITA P&R '60

Singles: 7-inch

4 CORNERS....4-6 65
KAPP....5-8 60-61

Picture Sleeves

KAPP....10-15 61

LPs: 10/12-inch

KAPP....15-25 61

LOMAX, Jackie LP '69

Singles: 7-inch

APPLE (1802 "Sour Milk Sea")....10-20 68
APPLE (1807 "New Day")....10-15 69
APPLE (1819 "How the Web Was Woven")....4-8 70
CAPITOL....3-5 77
EPIC....4-8 68
W.B. 3-5 71-73

Promotional Singles

APPLE (1802 "Sour Milk Sea")....20-30 68

Picture Sleeves

APPLE (1819 "How the Web Was Woven")....5-10 70

LPs: 10/12-inch

APPLE (3354 "Is This What You Want")....12-20 69
CAPITOL....5-10 76-77
W.B. 8-12 71-72
Also see BADGER
Also see CLAPTON, Eric
Also see McCARTNEY, Paul
Also see STARR, Ringo

LOMBARDO, Guy P&R '27

(With the His Royal Canadians)

Singles: 78 rpm

BRUNSWICK....4-8 32-34
COLUMBIA....4-8 27-31
DECCA....3-8 34-57
VICTOR....3-6 36-38

Singles: 7-inch

CAPITOL....3-6 59-67
DECCA....3-8 50-73

EPs: 7-inch

CAMDEN....5-10
CAPITOL....5-10 56-59
DECCA....5-10 50-59
RCA....5-10 60

LPs: 10/12-inch

CAMDEN....10-30 54-65
CAPITOL (Except 739 thru 1598)....5-15 61-81
CAPITOL (739 thru 1598)....10-25 56-61
DECCA....10-30 50-67
LONDON....5-8 73
MCA....5-8 75
RCA....5-8 72-77
SUFFOLK....5-8
VOCALION....5-10 66-68
Also see ARMSTRONG, Louis, & Guy Lombardo
Also see SMITH, Kate

LONDON, Julie P&R '55

(With Barney Kessel, Roy Leatherwood & Felix Slatkin's Orchestra; with Russ Garcia & His Orchestra; with Bobby Troup's Quintet)

Singles: 78 rpm

LIBERTY....5-10 55-57

Singles: 7-inch

BETHLEHEM....5-10 59
LIBERTY....5-15 55-68

Picture Sleeves

LIBERTY (55269 "Time for Lovers")....10-15 61

EPs: 7-inch

BETHLEHEM (133 "Julie London")....10-20 59
LIBERTY (1001 "Cry Me a River")....10-20 56
LIBERTY (1-2-3 3006 "Julie Is Her Name")....10-20 56
(Price is for any of three volumes.)
LIBERTY (1-2-3 3012 "Lonely Girl")....10-20 56
(Price is for any of three volumes.)
LIBERTY (1-2-3 3060 "Make Love to Me")....10-20 57
(Price is for any of three volumes.)
LIBERTY (1-2-3 9002 "Calendar Girl")....10-20 56
(Price is for any of three volumes.)

LPs: 10/12-inch

GUEST STAR....5-10 64
LIBERTY (3006 "Julie Is Her Name")....35-50 56
(Monaural.)
LIBERTY (3012 "Lonely Girl")....35-50 56
(Monaural.)
LIBERTY (3043 "About the Blues")....20-40 57
(Monaural.)
LIBERTY (3060 "Make Love to Me")....20-40 57
(Monaural.)
LIBERTY (3096 "Julie Swings")....20-40 58
(Monaural.)
LIBERTY (3100 "Julie Is Her Name, Vol. 2")....20-40 58
(Monaural.)
LIBERTY (3105 "London By Night")....15-30 59
(Monaural.)
LIBERTY (3119 "Swing Me an Old Song")....15-30 59
(Monaural.)
LIBERTY (3130 "Your Number Please")....15-30 59
(Monaural.)
LIBERTY (3152 "Julie at Home")....15-30 60
(Monaural.)
LIBERTY (3164 "Around Midnight")....15-30 60
(Monaural.)
LIBERTY (3171 "Send for Me")....15-30 61
(Monaural.)
LIBERTY (3192 "Whatever Julie Wants")....15-30 61
(Monaural.)
LIBERTY (3203 "Sophisticated Lady")....15-25 62
(Monaural.)
LIBERTY (3231 "Love Letters")....15-25 62
(Monaural.)
LIBERTY (3249 "Love on the Rocks")....15-25 62
(Monaural.)
LIBERTY (3278 "Latin in a Satin Mood")....15-25 63
(Monaural.)
LIBERTY (3291 "Golden Hits")....15-25 63
(Monaural.)
LIBERTY (3300 "End of the World")....15-25 63
(Monaural.)
LIBERTY (3324 "Wonderful World of Julie London")....15-25 63
(Monaural.)
LIBERTY (3342 "Julie London")....15-25 64
(Monaural.)
LIBERTY (3375 "Julie London in Person at the Americana")....15-25 64
(Monaural.)
LIBERTY (3392 "Our Fair Lady")....15-25 65
(Monaural.)
LIBERTY (3416 "Feeling Good")....15-25 65
(Monaural.)
LIBERTY (3478 "For the Night People")....15-25 66
(Monaural.)
LIBERTY (3493 "Nice Girls Don't Stay for Breakfast)....15-25 67
(Monaural.)
LIBERTY (3514 "With Body and Soul")....15-25 67
(Monaural.)
LIBERTY (5501 "Best of Julie")....20-30 62
(Monaural.)
LIBERTY (6601 "Best of Julie")....25-35 62
(Stereo.)
LIBERTY (7012 "About the Blues")....50-75 57
(Stereo.)
LIBERTY (7027 "Julie Is Her Name")....75-100 60
(Stereo. Colored vinyl.)
LIBERTY (7029 "Lonely Girl")....20-35 60
(Stereo.)
LIBERTY (7060 "Make Love to Me")....20-35 60
(Stereo.)
LIBERTY (7100 "Julie Is Her Name, Vol. 2")....20-35 59
(Stereo.)
LIBERTY (7105 "London By Night")....20-35 59
(Stereo.)
LIBERTY (7119 "Swing Me an Old Song")....20-35 59
(Stereo.)
LIBERTY (7130 "Your Number Please")....20-35 59
(Stereo.)
LIBERTY (7152 "Julie at Home")....20-35 60
(Stereo.)
LIBERTY (7164 "Around Midnight")....20-35 60
(Stereo.)
LIBERTY (7171 "Send for Me")....20-35 61
(Stereo.)
LIBERTY (7192 "Whatever Julie Wants")....20-35 61
(Stereo.)
LIBERTY (7203 "Sophisticated Lady")....20-30 62
(Stereo.)
LIBERTY (7231 "Love Letters")....20-30 62
(Stereo.)
LIBERTY (7249 "Love on the Rocks")....20-30 62
(Stereo.)
LIBERTY (7278 "Latin in a Satin Mood")....20-30 63
(Stereo.)
LIBERTY (7291 "Golden Hits")....20-30 63
(Stereo.)
LIBERTY (7300 "End of the World")....20-30 63
(Stereo.)
LIBERTY (7324 "Wonderful World of Julie London")....20-30 63
(Stereo.)
LIBERTY (7342 "Julie London")....20-30 64
(Stereo.)
LIBERTY (7375 "Julie London in Person at the Americana")....20-30 64
(Stereo.)
LIBERTY (7392 "Our Fair Lady")....20-30 65
(Stereo.)
LIBERTY (7416 "Feeling Good")....20-30 65
(Stereo.)
LIBERTY (7478 "For the Night People")....20-30 66
(Stereo.)

LIBERTY (7493 "Nice Girls Don't Stay for Breakfast") 15-25 67
(Stereo.)
LIBERTY (7514 "With Body and Soul") 15-25 67
(Stereo.)
LIBERTY (7546 "Easy Does It") 15-20 68
LIBERTY (7609 "Yummy, Yummy, Yummy") 15-20 69
LIBERTY (9002 "Calendar Girl") 40-60 56
SUNSET 8-15 66-68
U.A. (437 "Very Best of Julie London") 5-10 75
Session: Barney Kessel; Ray Leatherwood; Bobby Troup; Buddy Collette; Howard Roberts; Bob Enevoldsen; Don Heath.
Also see CONNOR, Chris / Julie London / Carmen McRae

LONDON, Julie, & Bud Shank Quintet

LPs: 10/12-inch

LIBERTY (3434 "All Through the Night") 10-20 66
(Monaural.)
LIBERTY (7434 "All Through the Night") 15-25 66
(Stereo.)
Also see LONDON, Julie
Also see SHANK, Bud

LONDON, Laurie — P&R/R&B '58

Singles: 7-inch

CAPITOL 8-10 58-59
ROULETTE 5-10 59

EPs: 7-inch

CAPITOL (10182 "Laurie London") 20-30 58
CAPITOL (10191 "Laurie London") 20-30 58

LPs: 10/12-inch

CAPITOL (1016 "Laurie London") 30-50 58

LONDON QUIREBOYS — LP '90

LPs: 10/12-inch

CAPITOL 5-8 90

LONDON SYMPHONY ORCH. — LP '79

(With Ian Anderson)

Singles: 7-inch

RCA (14262 "Elegy") 3-4 86

LPs: 10/12-inch

RCA (4000 series) 5-8 83
RCA (7067 "A Classic Case") 8-10 86
RSO 5-8 79

LONE JUSTICE — P&R/LP '85

Singles: 7-inch

GEFFEN 3-4 85-87

LPs: 10/12-inch

GEFFEN 5-8 85-86
Member: Tony Gilkyson.
Also see X

LONG, Shorty — P&R/R&B '66

Singles: 78 rpm

RCA 20-50 56

Singles: 7-inch

RCA (6572 "Vacation Rock") 40-60 56
RCA (6873 "You Don't Have to Be a Baby to Cry") 25-50 57
SOUL 8-15 64-68
TRI-PHI (1006 "I'll Be There") 25-35 62
TRI-PHI (1015 "Too Smart") 25-35 62
TRI-PHI (1021 "Going My Way") 25-35 62
VALLEY (108 "I Got Nine Little Kisses") 50-100

LPs: 10/12-inch

SOUL (709 "Here Comes the Judge") 10-20 68
SOUL (719 "The Prime") 10-15 69

LONG, Tom

(Gene Autry)

Singles: 78 rpm

Sunrise (33070 "I'll Be Thinking Of You Little Girl") 25-75
Also see AUTRY, Gene

LONGET, Claudine — P&R '66

Singles: 7-inch

A&M 3-6 66-70
BARNABY 3-5 70-73

LPs: 10/12-inch

A&M 5-12 67-69
BARNABY 5-10 70-72

LONGHAIR, Professor: see PROFESSOR LONGHAIR

LONGMIRE, Wilbert — R&B '80

Singles: 7-inch

TAPPAN ZEE 3-5 79-80
WORLD PACIFIC 4-6

LPs: 10/12-inch

TAPPAN ZEE 5-8 79-80

LOOKING GLASS — P&R/LP '72

Singles: 7-inch

EPIC 3-5 72-74

LPs: 10/12-inch

EPIC 10-12 72-73
Members: Elliot Lurie; Carolyn Davis; Jeff Grob; Barbara Massey; P. Sweval; Larry Gonsky.

LOOSE CHANGE — R&B '80

Singles: 7-inch

CASABLANCA 3-5 79-80

LPs: 10/12-inch

CASABLANCA 5-10 79

LOOSE ENDS — P&R/R&B/D&D/LP '85

Singles: 12-inch

MCA 4-6 85-86

Singles: 7-inch

MCA 3-4 85-90

Picture Sleeves

MCA 3-4 85

LPs: 10/12-inch

MCA 5-8 85-90

LOOSE JOINTS — D&D '84

Singles: 12-inch

4TH & BROADWAY 4-6 84

Singles: 7-inch

4TH & BROADWAY 3-4 84

LOPEZ, Denise — P&R/LP '88

LPs: 10/12-inch

A&M 5-8 88

LOPEZ, Trini — P&R/R&B/LP '63

Singles: 12-inch

ROULETTE 5-8 77

Singles: 7-inch

CAPITOL 3-5 71-72
D.R.A. 5-10 61
GRIFFIN 3-5 73-75
KING (5173 "Nola") 10-15 59
KING (5187 "Rock On") 15-25 59
KING (5198 "Here Comes Sally") 10-15 59
KING (5234 thru 5487) 8-15 59-61
KING (5800 series) 5-10 63-64
KING (6000 series) 4-8 65-66
MARIANNE 3-5 77
PRIVATE STOCK 3-5 75
REPRISE 4-8 63-71
ROULETTE 3-5 77
UNITED MODERN 4-8 64
VOLK (101 "The Right to Rock") 15-25 58

Picture Sleeves

REPRISE 5-10 62-66

EPs: 7-inch

COLUMBIA/W.B. (124178 "Trini Lopez Sings His Greatest Hits") 10-15 67
(Special products issue for Coca-Cola/Fresca.)
KING (483 "Teenage Idol") 15-25 63
REPRISE 8-12 63-68

LPs: 10/12-inch

CAPITOL 5-10 72
CROWN 6-12 65
EXACT 5-8 81
GRIFFIN 8-10 72
HARMONY 8-10 70
KING (863 "Teenage Love Songs") 20-30 63
KING (877 "More of Trini Lopez") 20-30 63
REPRISE 10-20 63-69
ROULETTE 5-8 78
SILVER EAGLE 5-10 82
WEA LATINA 5-8 91
Also see LAWRENCE, Steve / Trini Lopez
Also see RIVERS, Johnny / Trini Lopez

LOPEZ, Trini / Scott Gregory

LPs: 10/12-inch

GUEST STAR (1499 "Trini Lopez / Scott Gregory [Bill Haley]") 30-50 64
Also see HALEY, Bill

LOPEZ, Trini, & Ventures & Nancy Ames

LPs: 10/12-inch

REPIRSE (6361 "The Trini Lopez Show") 10-15 70
Also see AMES, Nancy
Also see LOPEZ, Trini
Also see VENTURES

LOR, Denise — P&R '54

Singles: 78 rpm

LIBERTY 3-5 56
MAJAR 4-6 54
MERCURY 3-5 55

Singles: 7-inch

LIBERTY 4-8 56
MAJAR 5-10 54
MERCURY 4-8 55

EPs: 7-inch

MERCURY 5-10 55

LORAIN, A'Me — P&R '90

Singles: 7-inch

RCA 3-4 90

Picture Sleeves

RCA 3-4 90

LORBER, Jeff — LP '79

(Jeff Lorber Fusion; with Audrey Wheeler; with Karyn White)

Singles: 12-inch

ARISTA 4-6 85

Singles: 7-inch

ARISTA 3-5 79-85
INNER CITY 3-5 78
W.B. 3-4 86

Picture Sleeves

W.B. 3-4 86

LPs: 10/12-inch

ARISTA 5-8 79-85
INNER CITY 5-10 78
W.B. 5-8 86
Members: Kenny Gorelick; Karyn White; Michael Jeffries.
Also see KENNY G.
Also see UNLIMITED TOUCH
Also see WHITE, Karyn

LORD, C.M. — R&B '82

Singles: 12-inch

MONTAGE 4-6 82-84
WAVE 4-6 83

Singles: 7-inch

CAPITOL 3-5 76
MONTAGE 3-4 82-84

LPs: 10/12-inch

CAPITOL 8-10 76
MONTAGE 5-8 84

LORD ROCKINGHAM'S XI — P&R '58

Singles: 7-inch

LONDON 5-10 58

LORD SUTCH — LP '70

(With His Heavy Friends)

LPs: 10/12-inch

COTILLION (9015 "Lord Sutch & His Heavy Friends") 20-30 70
COTILLION (9049 "Hands of Jack the Ripper") 15-25 72
Member: Daniel Edwards.
Also see BECK, Jeff
Also see BLACKMORE, Ritchie
Also see HOPKINS, Nicky
Also see MOON, Keith

Also see PAGE, Jimmy

LORDS OF THE NEW CHURCH *LP '85*

Singles: 12-inch

I.R.S. 4-6 83

Singles: 7-inch

I.R.S. 3-4 82-85

LPs: 10/12-inch

I.R.S. 5-8 82-85

Member: Stiv Bators.

Also see BATORS, Stiv

LORELEIS *P&R '55*

Singles: 78 rpm

BALLY 5-15 57
DOT 5-10 54
SPOTLIGHT 5-10 55

Singles: 7-inch

BALLY 5-15 57
BRUNSWICK 3-5 64
DOT 5-12 54
SPOTLIGHT 5-15 55

LOREN, Bryan *R&B '84*

Singles: 12-inch

PHILLY WORLD 4-6 83-84

Singles: 7-inch

PHILLY WORLD 3-4 83

LORETTA LYNN: see LYNN, Loretta

LORING, Gloria *LP '86*

Singles: 7-inch

ATLANTIC 3-4 86
MGM 3-5 72

LPs: 10/12-inch

ATLANTIC 5-8 86

LORING, Gloria, & Carl Anderson *P&R '86*

Singles: 7-inch

CARRERE 3-4 86

Picture Sleeves

CARRERE 3-4 86

LPs: 10/12-inch

EPIC 5-8 85

Also see ANDERSON, Carl

LOS ADMIRADORES *LP '60*

LPs: 10/12-inch

COMMAND 8-15 60

LOS BRAVOS *P&R/LP '66*

Singles: 7-inch

LONDON 3-4 70s
PARROT 4-8 68
PRESS 4-8 66-68

LPs: 10/12-inch

PARROT (71021 "Bring a Little Lovin'") 20-30 68
PRESS (83003 "Black Is Black") 30-40 66

Member: Mike Kennedy.

Also see DRIFTERS / Lesley Gore / Roy Orbison / Los Bravos

Also see KENNEDY, Mike

LOS INDIOS TABAJARAS *P&R/LP '63*

Singles: 7-inch

RCA 4-6 63-64

LPs: 10/12-inch

RCA (LPM-1788 "Sweet and Savage") 20-30 58
(Monaural.)
RCA (LSP-1788 "Sweet and Savage") 30-50 58
(Stereo.)
RCA (2800 thru 3505) 10-20 63-66

Members: Natalicio; Antenor Moreyra Lima (aka Musaperi & Herundy).

LOS LOBOS *LP '84*

Singles: 12-inch

SLASH 5-8 86
(Promotional issue only.)

Singles: 7-inch

LOS LOBOS 5-10 81
SLASH 3-4 83-90

Picture Sleeves

SLASH 3-4 85-87

LPs: 10/12-inch

SLASH 5-8 83-90

Member: David Hidalgo.

LOS POP-TOPS: see POP-TOPS

LOST GENERATION *P&R/R&B '70*

Singles: 7-inch

BRUNSWICK 3-5 70-71
INNOVATION 3-5 74

LPs: 10/12-inch

BRUNSWICK 10-12 70

Members: Lowrell Simon; Fred Lowrell; Larry Brownlee.

Also see C.O.D.s

Also see MYSTIQUE

LOU, Bonnie: see BONNIE LOU

LOUDERMILK, John D. *P&R '61*

Singles: 7-inch

COLUMBIA 5-10 58-60
MUSIC IS MEDICINE 3-5 78-79
RCA 4-8 61-69
W.B. 3-5 71

Picture Sleeves

COLUMBIA (41165 "Yearbook") 10-20 58
RCA (8101 "Road Hog") 5-10 62

LPs: 10/12-inch

MUSIC IS MEDICINE 5-8 78
RCA 15-25 61-69
W.B. 8-12 71

Also see DEE, Johnny

Also see SNEEZER, Ebe, & Epidemics

LOUDNESS *LP '85*

LPs: 10/12-inch

ATCO 5-8 85-87

LOUIE LOUIE *P&R/LP '90*
(Louie Cordero)

Singles: 7-inch

WTG 3-4 90

LPs: 10/12-inch

WTG 5-8 90

LOUISIANA'S LE ROUX: see LE ROUX

LOVE *P&R/LP '66*

Singles: 7-inch

BLUE THUMB 4-6 69-70
ELEKTRA (45603 "My Little Red Book") 5-8 66
ELEKTRA (45605 "7 & 7 Is") 5-8 66
ELEKTRA (45608 "Stephanie Knows Who") 10-20 66
ELEKTRA (45608 "She Comes in Colors") 5-8 67
(Same number and flip used again.)
ELEKTRA (45613 "Que Vida") 15-25 67
ELEKTRA (45629 thru 45700) 5-10 68-70
RSO 4-6 74-75

LPs: 10/12-inch

BLUE THUMB (8822 "False Start") .. 20-30 70
BLUE THUMB (9000 "Out Here") 15-25 69
ELEKTRA (4001 "Love") 25-40 66
(Monaural.)
ELEKTRA (4005 "Da Capo") 25-40 66
(Monaural.)
ELEKTRA (4013 "Forever Changes") 25-40 67
(Monaural.)
ELEKTRA (74001 "Love") 25-35 66
(Stereo.)
ELEKTRA (74005 "Da Capo") 25-35 67
(Stereo.)
ELEKTRA (74013 "Forever Changes") 20-30 67
(Stereo.)
ELEKTRA (74049 "Four Sail") 20-30 69
(Stereo.)
ELEKTRA (74058 "Revisited") 20-30 70
(Gatefold cover.)
ELEKTRA (74058 "Revisited") 5-8 81
(Standard cover.)
MCA 5-8 82
RSO 8-10 74
RHINO (251 "Love Live") 8-10 82
RHINO (800 "Best of Love") 5-8 80

Members: Arthur Lee; John Echols; John Fleckenstein; Don Conka; Ken Forssi; Al Pfisterer; Michael Stuart; Tjay Contrelli; Bryan Maclean; Gary Rowles.

LOVE, Candace *R&B '69*

Singles: 7-inch

AQUARIUS 4-8 68

LOVE, Darlene *P&R '63*

Singles: 12-inch

RHINO (855 "Live at Hop Singh's") 8-10 85

Singles: 7-inch

COLUMBIA 3-5 88
ELEKTRA (79647 "River Deep, Mountain High") 3-5 85
(Promotional issue only.)
PHILLES (111 "The Boy I'm Gonna Marry"/"My Heart Beat a Little Bit Faster") 12-18 63
PHILLES (111 "The Boy I'm Gonna Marry"/"Playing for Keeps") 8-12 63
PHILLES (114 "Wait Till My Bobby Gets Home") 10-15 63
PHILLES (117 "A Fine, Fine Boy") 8-15 63
PHILLES (119 "Christmas, Baby Please Come Home") 15-25 63
PHILLES (123 "He's a Quiet Guy") 30-50 64
PHILLES (125 "Christmas, Baby Please Come Home") 15-25 64
REPRISE 4-8 66
RHINO 5-8 86
W.B./SPECTOR 3-6 74-77

Picture Sleeves

COLUMBIA 3-5 88
ELEKTRA (79647 "River Deep, Mountain High") 3-5 85
(Promotional issue only.)

LPs: 10/12-inch

COLUMBIA (40605 "Paint Another Picture") 8-12 88

Also see BLOSSOMS

Also see BOB B. SOXX & Blue Jeans

Also see CRYSTALS

Also see RONETTES / Crystals / Darlene Love / Bob B. Soxx & Blue Jeans

LOVE, Darlene / Annie Golden

Singles: 7-inch

ELEKTRA 3-5 85

Picture Sleeves

ELEKTRA 3-5 85

LOVE, Darlene / Ronettes

Singles: 7-inch

CHRYSALIS (3202 "Phil Spector's Christmas Mix") 3-5 87

Picture Sleeves

CHRYSALIS (3202 "Phil Spector's Christmas Mix") 3-5 87

Also see LOVE, Darlene

Also see RONETTES

LOVE, Johnny
(With the Way Singers)

Singles: 7-inch

MERCURY 10-15 59-60
STARTIME (5001 "Chills and Fever") 25-35 60
TEE PEE (295 "Consolation") 15-20

Also see LOVE, Ronnie

LOVE, Le Juan *R&B '88*

Singles: 7-inch

LUKE SKY 3-4 88

LOVE, Mike

Singles: 7-inch

BOARDWALK 3-5 81

LPs: 10/12-inch

BOARDWALK 8-10 81

Also see ASSOCIATION / Bobby Vee / Mike Love / Mary MacGregor

Also see BEACH BOYS

Also see CELEBRATION

Also see MIKE & DEAN

Also see WILSON, Brian, & Mike Love

LOVE, Mike / Dean Torrence: see MIKE & DEAN

LOVE, Monie LP '90
LPs: 10/12-inch
W.B. 5-8 90

LOVE, Ronnie P&R/R&B '61
Singles: 7-inch
ALMERIA (4001 "Nothing to It") 15-25
D TOWN (1027 "Judy") 75-125 64
D TOWN (1047 "Judy") 30-50 65
DOT 5-10 60-61
STARTIME (5003 "Shakin' and a Breakin' ") 20-30 61
Also see LOVE, Johnny

LOVE, Rudy, & Love Family R&B '76
Singles: 7-inch
CALLA 3-5 76
LPs: 10/12-inch
CALLA 5-10 76

LOVE, Vikki: see NUANCE

LOVE & KISSES LP '77
Singles: 7-inch
CASABLANCA 3-5 77-79
LPs: 10/12-inch
CASABLANCA 8-10 77-79

LOVE & MONEY P&R/LP '89
Singles: 7-inch
MERCURY 3-4 89
Picture Sleeves
MERCURY 3-4 89
LPs: 10/12-inch
MERCURY 5-8 89
Member: Stuart Kerr.
Also see TEXAS

LOVE & ROCKETS LP '86
Singles: 7-inch
BIG TIME 3-4 86
RCA 3-4 89
Picture Sleeves
RCA 3-4 89
LPs: 10/12-inch
BEGGARS BANQUET 5-8 89
BIG TIME 5-8 86-87
Members: David Jor; Kevin Haskins; Daniel Ash.
Also see BAUHAUS

LOVE BUG STARSKI D&D '83
Singles: 12-inch
ATLANTIC 3-4 85
FEVER 4-6 83

LOVE CHILD'S AFRO CUBAN BLUES BAND P&R/R&B/LP '75
(Love Child's Latin Soul Afro Blues Band)
Singles: 7-inch
A&M 3-6 69
ROULETTE 3-5 75
LPs: 10/12-inch
ROULETTE 5-10 75

LOVE CLUB D&D '83
Singles: 12-inch
WEST END 4-6 83

LOVE COMMITTEE R&B '76
Singles: 7-inch
ARIOLA AMERICA 3-5 75-76
GOLD MIND 3-5 77-78
Also see ETHICS

LOVE GENERATION P&R '67
Singles: 7-inch
IMPERIAL 4-8 67-68
LPs: 10/12-inch
IMPERIAL 12-15 67
U.A. 8-10 77
Also see CLIMAX

LOVE / HATE LP '90
LPs: 10/12-inch
COLUMBIA 5-8 90

LOVE NOTES R&B '57
Singles: 7-inch
HOLIDAY (2605 "United") 30-50 57
(Glossy label stock.)
HOLIDAY (2605 "United") 10-15
(Flat label stock.)
HOLIDAY (2607 "If I Could Make You Mine") 20-30 57

LOVE PATROL R&B '85
Singles: 7-inch
4TH & BROADWAY 3-4 85

LOVE, PEACE & HAPPINESS R&B '72
Singles: 7-inch
RCA 3-5 71-72
LPs: 10/12-inch
RCA 8-10 71
Members: Ann Bogan; Leslie Wilson; Melvin Wilson.
Also see NEW BIRTH

LOVE UNLIMITED P&R/R&B/LP '72
(Love Unlimited Orchestra)
Singles: 7-inch
CASABLANCA 3-5 70s
MCA 3-4
20TH FOX 3-5 73-77
UNI 3-5 72
UNLIMITED GOLD 3-5 77-84
LPs: 10/12-inch
20TH FOX 8-10 74-76
UNI 5-10 72
UNLIMITED GOLD 5-8 77-84
Member: Kenny Gorelick.
Also see KENNY G.
Also see WHITE, Barry

LOVELITES R&B '69
Singles: 7-inch
ATCO 4-8 69
BANDERA 8-10 67
LOCK 4-8 69
LOVELITE 3-6 70-71
20TH FOX 3-6 73
UNI 3-6 69-70
LPs: 10/12-inch
UNI 10-15 70

LOVELY, Ike R&B '73
Singles: 7-inch
WAND 3-5 73

LOVERBOY P&R/LP '81
Singles: 7-inch
COLUMBIA 3-4 81-87
Picture Sleeves
COLUMBIA 3-5 81-87
LPs: 10/12-inch
COLUMBIA (Except 169961) 5-10 80-89
COLUMBIA (169961 "Loverboy") 10-15 82
Members: Mike Reno; Matthew Frenette; Paul Dean; Doug Johnson; Scott Smith.
Also see RENO, Mike, & Ann Wilson

LOVERDE D&D '83
Singles: 12-inch
MOBY DICK 4-6 83

LOVERS P&R/R&B '57
Singles: 78 rpm
DECCA 15-25 56
Singles: 7-inch
ALADDIN (3419 "Tell Me") 20-30 58
DECCA (29862 "Don't Touch Me") 20-30 56
IMPERIAL (5845 "Darling It's Wonderful") 10-20 62
IMPERIAL (5960 "Let's Elope") 10-20 63
KELLER (101 "Strange As It Seems") 100-200 61
LAMP (2005 "Darling It's Wonderful") 25-50 58
LAMP (2013 "Let's Elope") 25-50 58
LAMP (2018 "Tell Me") 25-50 58
POST (10007 "Darling It's Wonderful") 10-15 63
Member: Tarheel Slim.

LOVERS P&R '77
Singles: 7-inch
MARLIN 3-5 77

LOVESMITH R&B '83
(Michael Lovesmith)
Singles: 7-inch
MOTOWN 3-4 81-85
LPs: 10/12-inch
MOTOWN 5-8 81

LOVETTE, Eddie P&R '69
Singles: 7-inch
STEADY 4-8 69
LPs: 10/12-inch
STEADY 8-10 70

LOVICH, Lene LP '79
Singles: 7-inch
STIFF 3-5 79-83
LPs: 10/12-inch
STIFF 5-8 79-83

LOVIN' SPOONFUL P&R/LP '65
Singles: 7-inch
ERIC 3-4 78
KAMA SUTRA 3-8 65-72
Picture Sleeves
KAMA SUTRA 5-10 65-67
EPs: 7-inch
KAMA SUTRA (1 "Nashville Cats") 10-15 67
(Promotional issue only.)
LPs: 10/12-inch
AZZURRA (5801 "Anthology") 5-10 83
BACK-TRAC 5-8 85
BUDDAH 8-10 73
51 WEST 5-8 80s
GRT 8-15 76
GUSTO 5-8 80s
KAMA SUTRA (750 "24 Karat Hits") 10-15 68
KAMA SUTRA (2000 series) 8-15 70-76
KAMA SUTRA (8050 thru 8054) 15-25 65-66
KAMA SUTRA (8056 "Best of the Lovin' Spoonful") 15-25 67
(Add $10 to $20 if accompanied by four color photos.)
KAMA SUTRA (8058 thru 8073) 15-25 67-69
KAMA SUTRA (91102 "Best of the Lovin' Spoonful") 8-10
Members: John Sebastian; Zalman Yanovsky; Joe Butler; Steve Boone; Jerry Yester.
Also see SEBASTIAN, John

LOW, Gary D&D '83
Singles: 12-inch
QUALITY 4-6 83

LOWE, Bernie P&R '58
(Bernie Lowe Orchestra)
Singles: 7-inch
CAMEO 4-8 58-63
LPs: 10/12-inch
CAMEO 15-25 62-63

LOWE, Jim P&R '53
Singles: 78 rpm
DOT 5-15 55-57
MERCURY 4-8 53-54
Singles: 7-inch
BUDDAH 4-6 68
DECCA 4-8 60-61
DOT (15300 thru 16200 series) 5-10 55-60
DOT (16600 series) 4-8 64
MERCURY 5-10 53-54
20TH FOX 4-8 63
U.A. 4-6 67
EPs: 7-inch
DOT 10-20 57
MERCURY 10-20 57
LPs: 10/12-inch
DOT (3051 "The Green Door") 25-35 57
DOT (3114 "Wicked Women") 25-35 58
DOT (3681 "The Green Door") 10-20 66
(Monaural.)
DOT (25681 "The Green Door") 10-20 66
(Stereo.)

KATS KARAVAN (100 "Old Favorites") 50-100 50s
MERCURY (20246 "Door of Fame") 25-35 57

LOWE, Nick *LP '78*
(With Rockpile; with His Cowboy Outfit)
Singles: 7-inch
COLUMBIA 3-5 78-86
LPs: 10/12-inch
COLUMBIA 5-10 78-86
REPRISE 5-8 90
Also see NICK & ELVIS

LOWE, Nick, & Dave Edmunds
Singles: 7-inch
COLUMBIA 3-5 81
EPs: 7-inch
COLUMBIA (1219 "Nick Lowe & Dave Edmunds Sing the Everly Brothers") 5-10 80
(Promotional issue only.)
Also see EDMUNDS, Dave
Also see LOWE, Nick
Also see ROCKPILE

LOWRELL *R&B '78*
Singles: 7-inch
AVI 3-5 78-80

LOZ NETTO: see NETTO, Loz

L'TRIMM *P&R/LP '88*
Singles: 7-inch
ATLANTIC 3-4 88
LPs: 10/12-inch
ATLANTIC 5-8 88

LUBOFF, Norman, Choir *LP '55*
Singles: 78 rpm
COLUMBIA 3-5 54-59
Singles: 7-inch
COLUMBIA 3-6 54-59
EPs: 7-inch
COLUMBIA 4-8 54-59
LPs: 10/12-inch
COLUMBIA 5-15 54-60
HARMONY 5-10 61
RCA 5-10 61-62

LUCAS, Buddy *R&B '52*
(With His Band of Tomorrow; with Wigglers; with Studio "B" Orchestra)
Singles: 78 rpm
BELL 10-15 57
GROOVE 10-15 54
JUBILEE 10-15 51-52
RCA 10-15 53
Singles: 7-inch
BELL 10-20 57
CAPRICE 5-10 63
CARLTON 10-15 59
GONE 10-15 58
GROOVE 15-25 54
JUBILEE 15-25 51-52
LAWN 4-8 64
PIONEER 4-8
RCA 15-25 53
TRU SOUND 5-10 62
VIM 8-12 59-60
LPs: 10/12-inch
CAMDEN 10-15 67
U.A. 10-20 66
Also see GONE ALL STARS

LUCAS, Carrie *P&R/R&B/LP '77*
(Carrie)
Singles: 12-inch
CONSTELLATION 4-6 84-85
Singles: 7-inch
CONSTELLATION 3-4 84-85
SOLAR 3-5 79-82
SOUL TRAIN 3-5 77
LPs: 10/12-inch
CONSTELLATION 5-8 85
SOLAR 5-10 79-82
SOUL TRAIN 8-10 77

LUCAS, Carrie, & Whispers *R&B '85*
Singles: 7-inch
CONSTELLATION 3-4 85
Also see LUCAS, Carrie
Also see WHISPERS

LUCAS, Frank *P&R/R&B '77*
("The Good Thing Man")
Singles: 7-inch
ICA 3-5 77-78

LUCAS, Matt *P&R '63*
Singles: 7-inch
DOT 4-8 63-64
KAREN (2524 "Baby You Better Go") 50-75
RENE 10-15 63
SMASH 4-8 63

LUGEE & LIONS
Singles: 7-inch
ROBBEE (112 "The Jury") 50-75 61
Members: Lou Christie; Kay Chick; Amy Sacco; Bill Faveck.
Also see CHRISTIE, Lou
Also see CLASSICS

LUGO, Danny, & Destinations *D&D '84*
Singles: 12-inch
C&M 4-6 84

LUKE, Robin *P&R/R&B '58*
Singles: 7-inch
BERTRAM INT'L (206 "Susie Darlin'") 20-40 58
BERTRAM INT'L (208 thru 212) 15-25 58-59
DOT 5-10 58-61
Picture Sleeves
BERTRAM INT'L (206 "Susie Darlin'") 40-60 58
DOT (16096 "Everlovin' ") 10-20 60
EPs: 7-inch
DOT (1092 "Susie Darlin' ") 50-75 60

LUKE, Robin, & Roberta Shore
Singles: 7-inch
DOT 4-8 62
Also see LUKE, Robin

LUKE the Drifter: see WILLIAMS, Hank

LUKE the Drifter Jr.: see WILLIAMS, Hank, Jr.

LULU *P&R '64*
(With the Luvers; with Dixie Flyers)
Singles: 7-inch
ALFA 3-5 79-82
ATCO 3-6 69-72
CHELSEA 3-5 73-75
EPIC 4-8 67-68
PARROT (9000 series) 5-10 64-65
PARROT (40000 series) 4-8 67
ROCKET 3-5 78
Picture Sleeves
ALFA (7006 "I Could Never Miss You More") 4-6 81
(Pictures Lulu without headband.)
ALFA (7006 "I Could Never Miss You More") 3-5 81
(Pictures Lulu wearing headband.)
ALFA (7011 "If I Were You") 3-4 81
EPIC 4-8 67-68
LPs: 10/12-inch
ALFA 5-10 81
ATCO 10-12 70-72
CAPRICORN 8-10 74
CHELSEA 10-12 73-77
EPIC 10-15 67-70
HARMONY 10-12 70
PARROT (61016 "From Lulu with Love") 50-100 67
(Monaural.)
PARROT (71016 "From Lulu with Love") 50-100 67
(Stereo.)
PICKWICK 8-10 73
ROCKET 5-8 78
Also see CLARK, Dave, Five / Lulu
Also see MOORE, Jackie

LUMAN, Bob *C&W/P&R/R&B '60*
Singles: 78 rpm
IMPERIAL 20-50 57
Singles: 7-inch
CAPITOL 10-20 58
EPIC 3-5 68-77
HICKORY (1200 series) 4-8 63-64
HICKORY (1300 thru 1500 series) 3-5 65-70
IMPERIAL (5705 "Red Cadillac and a Black Mustache") 10-20 60
(Black label. Reissue of 8311.)
IMPERIAL (8311 "Red Cadillac and a Black Mustache") 35-55 57
(Maroon label.)
IMPERIAL (8313 "Red Hot") 40-60 57
(Maroon label.)
IMPERIAL (8313 "Red Hot") 30-40 59
(Black label.)
IMPERIAL (8315 "Make Up Your Mind Baby") 20-30 57
(Maroon label.)
IMPERIAL (8315 "Make Up Your Mind Baby") 10-15 59
(Black label.)
POLYDOR 3-5 77-78
W.B. 5-15 59-62
Picture Sleeves
W.B. 15-25 60-62
EPs: 7-inch
HICKORY (124-006 "Selections from Livin' Lovin' Sounds") 10-20 65
(Promotional "Six-Pac" issue only.)
ROLLIN' ROCK (34 "Bob Luman") 5-8 80s
W.B. (1396 "Let's Think About Livin' ") 50-75 60
W.B. (5506 "Bob Luman") 50-75 60
(Promotional issue only.)
LPs: 10/12-inch
EPIC 8-15 68-77
HARMONY 10-15 72
HICKORY (124 "Livin' Lovin' Sounds") 15-25 65
HICKORY (4000 series) 8-12 74
POLYDOR 8-12 78
W.B. (W-1396 "Let's Think About Livin' ") 30-40 60
(Monaural.)
W.B. (WS-1396 "Let's Think About Livin' ") 40-60 60
(Stereo.)

LUMAN, Bob, & Sue Thompson
Singles: 7-inch
HICKORY 4-8 63
Also see LUMAN, Bob
Also see THOMPSON, Sue

LUNAR FUNK *P&R/R&B '72*
Singles: 7-inch
BELL 3-5 72

LUNCEFORD, Jimmie, Orch. *P&R '34*
Singles: 78 rpm
DECCA 4-8 33-52
MAJESTIC 4-6 46
EPs: 7-inch
DECCA 10-15 50s
Also see DELTA RHYTHM BOYS

LUND, Art, & His Orchestra *P&R '47*
Singles: 78 rpm
CORAL 3-5 52-57
MGM 3-6 47-55
Singles: 7-inch
CORAL 4-8 52-58
MGM 5-10 50-55
U.A. 3-6 65
EPs: 7-inch
MGM 5-10 54-55
LPs: 10/12-inch
MGM 10-20 55

LUNDBERG, Victor *P&R '67*
Singles: 7-inch
LIBERTY 4-6 67
LPs: 10/12-inch
LIBERTY 10-15 68

LUNDY, Pat R&B '73
(Pat Lundi)
Singles: 7-inch
COLUMBIA....4-6 67-68
DELUXE....4-6 69
HEIDI....4-8 65
LEOPARD....3-5
PYRAMID....3-5 76
RCA....3-5 73
TOTO....4-8 62
VIGOR....3-5 75
LPs: 10/12-inch
COLUMBIA....10-15 68
PYRAMID....5-8 76

LUNDY, Pat, & Bobby Harris
Singles: 7-inch
HEIDI....4-8 65
Also see HARRIS, Bobby
Also see LUNDY, Pat

LUSHUS DAIM & PRETTY VAIN R&B '85
Singles: 7-inch
MOTOWN....3-4 85
LPs: 10/12-inch
MOTOWN....5-8 85

LUTCHER, Joe R&B '48
(With His Society Cats)
Singles: 78 rpm
CAPITOL....5-10 48
MODERN....5-10 49
SPECIALTY....5-10 48-51
Singles: 7-inch
SPECIALTY (303 "Rockin' Boogie") . 50-75 51

LUTCHER, Nellie P&R/R&B '47
(With Her "Rhythm")
Singles: 78 rpm
CAPITOL....5-10 47-50
Singles: 7-inch
CAPITOL....8-15 50
EPs: 7-inch
CAPITOL (232 "Real Gone")....20-40 50
LIBERTY....5-10 56
LPs: 10/12-inch
CAPITOL (H-232 "Real Gone")....35-55 50
(10-inch LP.)
CAPITOL (T-232 "Real Gone")....20-30 55
EPIC (1108 "Whee! Nellie")....25-35 55
LIBERTY (3014 "Our New Nellie")....20-30 56

LUTCHER, Nellie, & Nat "King" Cole R&B '50
Singles: 78 rpm
CAPITOL....5-10 50
Singles: 7-inch
CAPITOL....8-12 50
Also see COLE, Nat "King"
Also see LUTCHER, Nellie

LUTHER R&B '76
(Luther Vandross)
Singles: 7-inch
COTILLION....3-5 76-77
LPs: 10/12-inch
COTILLION....8-10 77
Also see VANDROSS, Luther

LY-DELLS P&R '61
(With Frank Slay & His Orchestra)
Singles: 7-inch
MASTER (111 "Genie of the Lamp")....100-150 61
MASTER (251 "Wizard of Love")....50-75 61
ROULETTE (4493 "Karen")....20-30 63
SCA (18001 "Book of Songs")....25-50 62
SOUTHERN SOUND (122 "Hide and Seek")....25-35 65
LPs: 10/12-inch
CLIFTON....8-12
Also see SLAY, Frank, & His Orchestra

LYLE, Bobby R&B '78
Singles: 7-inch
CAPITOL....3-5 78

LYMAN, Arthur LP '58
(Arthur Lyman Group)
Singles: 7-inch
GNP....3-5 64-75
HI FI....4-6 59-69
ORBIT....4-8
LPs: 10/12-inch
GNP....8-15 63-75
HI FI....10-20 58-69
OLYMPIC....5-8 79

LYME & CYBELLE P&R '66
Singles: 7-inch
WHITE WHALE....5-10 66-67
Also see ZEVON, Warren

LYMON, Frankie P&R/R&B '56
(With the Teenagers)
Singles: 78 rpm
GEE (1002 "Why Do Fools Fall in Love")....30-60 55
(Red label, gold print.)
GEE (1002 "Why Do Fools Fall in Love")....15-25 55
(Red label, black print.)
GEE (1012 thru 1039)....20-30 56-57
ROULETTE....15-25 57
Singles: 7-inch
ABC....3-4 73
BIG KAT....5-10 68
COLUMBIA (43094 "Somewhere")....8-12 64
GEE (1002 "Why Do Fools Fall in Love")....400-600 55
(Colored vinyl.)
GEE (1002 "Why Do Fools Fall in Love")....75-125 55
(Red label, gold print.)
GEE (1002 "Why Do Fools Fall in Love")....20-40 55
(Red label, black print.)
GEE (1012 "I Want You to Be My Girl")....20-40 56
GEE (1018 "I Promise to Remember")....20-40 56
GEE (1022 "The ABCs of Love")....20-40 56
GEE (1032 "Paper Castles")....15-25 57
GEE (1035 "Love Is a Clown")....15-25 57
GEE (1036 "Out in the Cold Again")....15-25 57
GEE (1039 "Goody Goody")....25-50 57
(Credits "Frankie Lymon & the Teenagers.")
GEE (1039 "Goody Goody")....15-25 59
(Does not mention the Teenagers.)
GEE (1052 "Goody Good Girl")....15-25 59
MURRAY HILL....3-5 80s
RAMA (34 "I Want You to Be My Girl")....5-10 64
(Golden Goodies Series.)
ROULETTE (4026 "So Goes My Love")....15-25 57
ROULETTE (4068 "Portable on My Shoulder")....15-25 58
ROULETTE (4093 "Melinda")....15-25 58
ROULETTE (4128 "No Matter What You've Done")....10-20 59
ROULETTE (4150 "Before I Fall Asleep")....10-20 59
ROULETTE (4257 "Little Bitty Pretty One")....10-20 60
ROULETTE (4283 "Buzz Buzz Buzz")....10-20 60
ROULETTE (4310 "Silhouettes")....10-20 60
ROULETTE (4348 "So Young")....10-20 61
ROULETTE (4391 "I Put the Bomp")....10-20 61
TCF (11 "To Each His Own")....8-12 64
Picture Sleeves
BIG KAT (7008 "I Want You to Be My Girl")....5-10 68
EPs: 7-inch
GEE (601 "The Teenagers Go Rockin'")....75-125 56
GEE (601 "The Teenagers Go Romantic")....75-125 56
ROULETTE (304 "Frankie Lymon at the London Palladium")....50-75 58
LPs: 10/12-inch
ACCORD....5-10 82
GEE (701 "The Teenagers Featuring Frankie Lymon")....200-300 57
(Red or white label.)
GEE (701 "The Teenagers Featuring Frankie Lymon")....50-100 61
(Gray label.)
MURRAY HILL (148 "Frankie Lymon and the Teenagers")....50-75 80s
(Boxed, five-LP set, with booklet and bonus single.)
ROULETTE (25013 "Frankie Lymon at the London Palladium")....50-100 58
ROULETTE (25036 "Rock & Roll")....50-100 58
ROULETTE (25250 "Frankie Lymon's Greatest")....25-50 64
Members: Frankie Lymon; Herman Santiago; Sherman Garnes; Jim Merchant; Joe Negroni.
Also see TEENAGERS

LYNCH, Ray LP '89
LPs: 10/12-inch
MUSIC WEST....5-10 89

LYNCH MOB LP '90
LPs: 10/12-inch
ELEKTRA....5-8 90

LYNDELL, Linda R&B '68
Singles: 7-inch
VOLT....4-8 68

LYNN, Barbara P&R/R&B '62
Singles: 7-inch
ATLANTIC....3-5 67-72
COLLECTABLES....3-4 80s
JAMIE....4-8 62-65
TRIBE....4-8 66-67
LPs: 10/12-inch
ATLANTIC....10-20 68
JAMIE....20-30 62-64

LYNN, Barbara, & Lee Maye
Singles: 7-inch
JAMIE....4-8 65
Also see LYNN, Barbara

LYNN, Cheryl P&R/R&B/LP '78
Singles: 12-inch
COLUMBIA....4-6 78-85
Singles: 7-inch
COLUMBIA....3-5 78-85
MANHATTAN....3-4 87
PRIVATE I....3-4 85
LPs: 10/12-inch
COLUMBIA....5-10 78-84

LYNN, Cheryl, & Luther Vandross R&B '82
Singles: 7-inch
COLUMBIA....3-5 82
Also see LYNN, Cheryl
Also see VANDROSS, Luther

LYNN, Donna P&R '64
Singles: 7-inch
CAPITOL (Except 5127)....4-8 63-65
CAPITOL (5127 "My Boyfriend Got a Beatle Haircut")....15-20 64
EPIC....4-8 63
PALMER (5016 "Don't You Dare")....15-25 67
LPs: 10/12-inch
CAPITOL....15-25 64

LYNN, Ginie R&B '78
Singles: 7-inch
ABC....3-5 78

LYNN, Jeff: see LYNNE, Jeff

LYNN, Loretta LP '67
(With the Coal Miners)
Singles: 7-inch
DECCA (31384 thru 31966)....5-10 62-66
DECCA (32045 thru 32851)....4-8 66-71
DECCA (32900 "Here in Topeka")....10-15 71
DECCA (32900 "One's on the Way")....3-6 71
DECCA (32974 thru 33039)....3-6 72

MCA....................3-5 73-86
ZERO (107 "I'm a Honky Tonk Girl")....................50-75 60
ZERO (110 "New Rainbow")....................60-100 61
ZERO (112 "The Darkest Day")....................60-100 61

Picture Sleeves

DECCA (31000 series)....................8-12 66
DECCA (32000 series)....................4-6 70
MCA....................3-5 78

EPs: 7-inch

DECCA....................10-20 64-65

LPs: 10/12-inch

CORAL....................5-8 73
COUNTRY MUSIC MAGAZINE....................15-20 76
(Mail-order LP sold by *Country Music* magazine.)
DECCA (DL-4457 "Loretta Lynn Sings")....................40-60 63
(Monaural.)
DECCA (DL7-4457 "Loretta Lynn Sings")....................45-65 63
(Stereo.)
DECCA (DL-4541 "Before I'm Over You")....................30-40 65
(Monaural.)
DECCA (DL7-4541 "Before I'm Over You")....................35-45 65
(Stereo.)
DECCA (DL-4620 "Songs from My Heart")....................30-40 65
(Monaural.)
DECCA (DL7-4620 "Songs from My Heart")....................35-45 65
(Stereo.)
DECCA (DL-4665 "Blue Kentucky Girl")....................15-25 65
(Monaural.)
DECCA (DL7-4665 "Blue Kentucky Girl")....................20-30 65
(Stereo.)
DECCA (DL-4655 "Hymns")....................15-25 65
(Monaural.)
DECCA (DL7-4655 "Hymns")....................20-30 65
(Stereo.)
DECCA (DL-4744 "I Like 'Em Country")....................15-25 66
(Monaural.)
DECCA (DL-4744 "I Like 'Em Country")....................15-25 66
(Monaural.)
DECCA (DL7-4744 "I Like 'Em Country")....................15-25 66
(Stereo.)
DECCA (DL7-4783 "You Ain't Woman Enough")....................15-25 66
(Monaural.)
DECCA (DL7-4783 "You Ain't Woman Enough")....................15-25 66
(Stereo.)
DECCA (DL7-4817 "A Country Christmas")....................15-25 66
(Monaural.)
DECCA (DL7-4817 "A Country Christmas")....................15-25 66
(Stereo.)
DECCA (DL-4842 "Don't Come Home a Drinkin' ")....................15-25 67
(Monaural.)
DECCA (DL7-4842 "Don't Come Home a Drinkin' ")....................15-25 67
(Stereo.)
DECCA (DL-4928 "Who Says God Is Dead")....................15-25 67
(Monaural.)
DECCA (DL7-4928 "Who Says God Is Dead")....................15-25 67
(Stereo.)
DECCA (DL-4930 "Singin' with Feeling")....................15-25 67
(Monaural.)
DECCA (DL7-4930 "Singin' with Feeling")....................15-25 67
(Stereo.)
DECCA (DL-4997 "Fist City")....................15-25 68
(Monaural.)
DECCA (DL7-4997 "Fist City")....................10-20 68
(Stereo.)
DECCA (75000 "Greatest Hits")....................12-25 68
DECCA (75113 "Woman of the World/To Make a Man")....................25-35 69
DECCA (75198 "Loretta Lynn Writes 'Em and Sings 'Em")....................12-25 70
DECCA (75163 "Wings Upon Your Horns")....................12-25 70
DECCA (75253 "Coal Miner's Daughter")....................10-20 71
DECCA (75282 "I Want to Be Free") 12-25 71
DECCA (75310 "You're Looking at Country")....................12-25 71
DECCA (75334 "One's on the Way")....................12-25 72
DECCA (75351 "God Bless America Again")....................12-25 72
DECCA (75381 "Here I Am Again")..12-25 72
DECCA (75084 "Your Squaw Is on the Warpath")....................25-35 69
(Has the track, *Barney*.)
DECCA (75084 "Your Squaw Is on the Warpath")....................15-20 69
(Without *Barney*.)
L.L....................20-25 76
MCA....................5-10 73-86
TEE VEE....................8-12 78
TROLLEY CAR....................8-10 81
VOCALION....................8-15 68-72

Promotional LPs

MCA (1934 "Loretta Lynn's Greatest Hits")....................30-40 74
(Cover shows title as simply *Loretta Lynn*.)
MCA (35013 "Allis-Chalmers Presents Loretta Lynn")....................30-40 78
MCA (35018 "Crisco Presents Loretta Lynn's Country Classics")....................30-40 79

Session: Bob Hempker; Chuck Flynn; Ken Riley; Dave Thornhill; Gene Dunlap; Don Ballenger; Jordanaires.

Also see BEATLES / Loretta Lynn
Also see PIERCE, Webb / Loretta Lynn
Also see STARR, Kenny
Also see TUBB, Ernest, & Loretta Lynn
Also see TWITTY, Conway, & Loretta Lynn
Also see WILBURN BROTHERS

LYNN, Loretta, & Conway Twitty — C&W/P&R '71

Singles: 7-inch

CRLX (7211281"Seasons Greetings")....................50-100 80s
(Picture disc. Promotional issue only.)
DECCA....................4-6 71-72
MCA....................3-5 73-81

LPs: 10/12-inch

DECCA....................8-15 71-72
MCA....................5-10 73-84
TVP....................8-12 76

Also see LYNN, Loretta
Also see TWITTY, Conway

LYNN, Loretta / Tammy Wynette

LPs: 10/12-inch

RADIANT....................5-8 81

Also see LYNN, Loretta
Also see WYNETTE, Tammy

LYNN, Vera — P&R '48

Singles: 78 rpm

LONDON....................3-5 51-57

Singles: 7-inch

ARCO....................4-6 67
DJM....................4-6 69
LONDON....................5-10 51-64
U.A.....................4-6 67

EPs: 7-inch

LONDON....................10-20 52-56

LPs: 10/12-inch

LONDON....................15-30 52-64
MGM....................8-12 61
U.A.....................5-10 67

LYNNE, Gloria — P&R/R&B/LP '61

Singles: 7-inch

CANYON....................3-5 70
EVEREST....................4-8 59-66
FONTANA....................4-6 64-69
HI FI....................4-6 66
IMPULSE....................3-5 76
MERCURY....................3-5 72
SEECO....................4-8 61

LPs: 10/12-inch

CANYON....................5-10 70
DESIGN....................10-15 62
EVEREST (300 series)....................5-10 75
EVEREST (1000 series)....................20-30 58-65
(Stereo.)
EVEREST (5000 series)....................15-25 58-65
(Monaural.)
FONTANA....................10-20 64-69
HI FI....................10-15 66
IMPULSE....................5-10 76
MERCURY....................8-12 69-72
PAUL WINLEY....................5-10 74
SUNSET....................8-15 66-67
UPFRONT....................5-10 72

LYNNE, Gloria / Nina Simone / Billie Holiday

LPs: 10/12-inch

ALMOR....................10-15

Also see HOLIDAY, Billie
Also see SIMONE, Nina

LYNNE, Jeff — P&R '84

(Jeff Lynn)

Singles: 12-inch

JET....................5-8 77

Singles: 7-inch

JET....................3-5 77
REPRISE....................5-8 90
TWIN-SPIN....................10-15 65
VIRGIN....................3-4 84

Also see ELECTRIC LIGHT ORCHESTRA
Also see MOVE
Also see TRAVELING WILBURYS

LYNYRD SKYNYRD — LP '73

Singles: 7-inch

ATNIA (129 "Need All My Friends")....................4-8 78
MCA (Except 1966)....................3-6 74-78
MCA (1966 "Gimmie Back My Bullets")....................8-12 77
(Promotional concert souvenir issue.)

EPs: 7-inch

MCA....................10-15 76
(Promotional issue only.)

LPs: 10/12-inch

MCA (2000 & 3000 series, except 3029)....................8-10 75-78
MCA (3029 "Street Survivors")....................30-40 77
(Front cover pictures the group surrounded by flames.)
MCA (3029 "Street Survivors")....................8-10 77
(Pictures the group without flames.)
MCA (5000 series)....................5-8 79-82
MCA (6000 series)....................10-15 76-81
MCA (8011 "Live at the Fox")....................10-15 76
MCA (8027 "Southern by the Grace of God")....................8-12 88
MCA (10000 series)....................10-15 79-81
MCA (37000 series)....................5-8 79-82
MCA (42000 series)....................5-8 87
MCA/SOUNDS of the SOUTH (300 & 400 series)....................8-15 73-74

Promotional LPs

MCA (1946 "Special Advance Preview *Live* Album")....................25-35 76
MCA (2170 "Gimmie Back My Bullets")....................25-35 76
(White label. Concert souvenir copy.)

Members: Ronnie Van Zant; Gary Rossington; Allen Collins; Steve Gaines; Cassie Gaines; Ed King; Rick Medlocke; Greg Walker; Leon Wildeson; Billy Powell; Artimus Pyle; Bob Burns.

Also see ALIAS
Also see BLACKFOOT
Also see ROSSINGTON - COLLINS BAND
Also see STRAWBERRY ALARM CLOCK

LYTLE, Johnny *P&R/LP '66*

(Johnny Lytle Quintet; J Trio)

Singles: 7–inch

PACIFIC JAZZ	4-6	68
RIVERSIDE	4-8	63
SOLID STATE	4-6	68
TUBA	5-10	65-66

EPs: 7–inch

NEOPHON	10-15	

LPs: 10/12–inch

JAZZLAND	15-25	60-62
MILESTONE	5-10	72
MUSE	5-8	78-81
PACIFIC JAZZ	8-15	67
RIVERSIDE	10-20	63-68
SOLID STATE	8-15	67-69
TUBA	10-15	66

LYTLE, Johnny, & Ray Barretto

LPs: 10/12–inch

JAZZLAND	15-25	62

Also see BARRETTO, Ray
Also see LYTLE, Johnny

DUNES
RECORDS
Record No.
DU-1001
Time: 2:41
A4KM-0914
S-P-R-Music
Corp.
BMI
PRETTY LITTLE ANGEL EYES
(Lee-Boyce)
CURTIS LEE
Prod. by Phil Spector

SPECIAL PROMOTION SIX-PAC
33⅓—7″—COMPACT
SELECTIONS FROM
BOB LUMAN'S
"LIVIN,' LOVIN' SOUNDS"
HICKORY LPM 124
HSP-124-006

JOHN LENNON
SINGS THE GREAT ROCK & ROLL HITS
ROOTS

THE GREAT BALL of FIRE
Jerry Lee Lewis
MEAN WOMAN BLUES
I'M FEELIN' SORRY
WHOLE LOT OF SHAKIN' GOIN' ON
TURN AROUND

DONNA LOREN
JUST A LITTLE GIRL
BLOWING OUT THE CANDLES
Capitol

TRINI LOPEZ
reprise 0336
LEMON TREE · PRETTY EYES
Arranged and Produced by Don Costa

Julie London
LRP 3105
LIBERTY
London
by night

Columbia/ Los Angeles KINGS
Record
Night
Featuring
Loggins & Messina
ANGRY EYES
from the LP
"THE BEST OF FRIENDS"
PC 34388
DEMONSTRATION
NOT FOR SALE
3-10444

M P&R/LP '79
(Robin Scott)
Singles: 12-inch
SIRE 8-10 79
Singles: 7-inch
SIRE 3-5 79-81
Picture Sleeves
SIRE 3-5 79
LPs: 10/12-inch
SIRE 8-10 79-82

M., Boney: see BONEY M

M/A/R/R/S P&R/R&B '87
Singles: 7-inch
4TH & BROADWAY....3-4 87-88
Picture Sleeves
4TH & BROADWAY....3-4 87

M.C. CHILL R&B '86
Singles: 12-inch
FEVER....4-6 86

M.C. HAMMER: see HAMMER, M.C.

M.C. SHAN R&B '87
(Featuring T.J. Swan)
Singles: 7-inch
COLD CHILL 3-4 87

MC-5 P&R/LP '69
(Motor City 5)
Singles: 7-inch
A^2 (333 "Looking At You")....50-75 68
(Reportedly 500 made.)
AMG (1001 "I Can Only Give You Everything"/ "One of the Guys")....35-55 67
AMG (1001 "I Can Only Give You Everything"/"I Just Don't Know")....15-25 69
ATLANTIC (2678 "Tonight")....4-8 69
ATLANTIC (2724 "Shakin' Street")....4-8 70
ELEKTRA (MC5-1 "Kick Out the Jams")....50-75 68
(Promotional issue only. Given away at a 1968 New York concert.)
ELEKTRA (45648 "Kick Out the Jams")....5-10 69
Picture Sleeves
A^2 (333 "Looking at You")....100-125 68
(Reportedly 500 made.)
LPs: 10/12-inch
ALIVE/TOTAL ENERGY ("Looking at You")....5-10 95
(10-inch LP. Selection number not known.)
ALIVE/TOTAL ENERGY (0005 "Power Trip")....5-10 94
(10-inch LP.)
ALIVE/TOTAL ENERGY (0008 "Ice Pick Slim")....5-10 95
(10-inch LP.)
ALIVE/TOTAL ENERGY (0051 Alive")....5-10 95
(10-inch LP.)
ALIVE/TOTAL ENERGY (2010 "American Ruse")....5-10 95
(10-inch LP.)
ATLANTIC (8247 "Back in the USA")....25-50 70
ATLANTIC (8285 "High Time")....25-50 71
ELEKTRA (74042 "Kick Out the Jams")....30-35 69
(Title track has X-rated intro. Back cover has Sinclair liner notes and Grimshaw artwork.)
ELEKTRA (74042 "Kick Out the Jams")....12-18 69
(Title track has censored intro. Back cover has neither Sinclair liner notes nor Grimshaw art.)
ELEKTRA (74042 "Kick Out the Jams")....5-8 91
(Title track has censored intro. Back cover has Grimshaw art but no Sinclair liner notes.)
Members: Rob Tyner; Robert Derminer; Fred "Sonic" Smith; Michael Davis; Wayne Kramer; Sigrid Dobat; Dennis Thompson.

MFSB LP '73
(Mothers, Fathers, Sisters, Brothers)
Singles: 7-inch
PHILADELPHIA INT'L....3-5 74-78
TSOP 3-5 81
LPs: 10/12-inch
PHILADELPHIA INT'L....8-10 73-78
TSOP 5-8 80
Members: Norman Harris; Ronnie Baker; Bobby Eli; Bobby Martin; Earl Young; Don Renaldo; Albert Barone; Charles Apollonia; Angelo Petrella; Diana Barnett; Davis Barnett; Romeo Distefano; Rudy Maliazia; Christine Reeves; Joe Donofrio; Leno Zachery; Joe DeAngelis; Danny Ellions; Scott Temple; Milton Phibbs; Frederich Jainer; Fred Linge; Ricci Genovese; Edward Casceralle; Rocco Bene; Robert Hartzell; Karl Chambers; Roland Chambers; Dexter Wansel; Ron Harding; Terri Wells; James Smith; Evon Solot; Larry McKenna; Clifford Rudd; Miguel Fuentes; Evette Benton; John Usry; Dennis Harris; Don Renaldo; Marc Rubin; Derek Graves; Lenny Pakula; John Faith; Alphonso Carey; Billy Johnson; Steve Green; Leon Huff; Carleton Kent; Quinton Joseph; Carla Benson; Bob Malach; David Cruse; Steve Gold; Barbara Ingram; Joel Bryant.
Also see B-H-Y
Also see DE VAUGN, William
Also see ELECTRIC INDIAN
Also see ELI'S SECOND COMING
Also see HUFF, Leon
Also see JAMES BOYS
Also see MUSIC MAKERS
Also see NOBLES, Cliff
Also see PEOPLE'S CHOICE
Also see PHILADELPHIA INTERNATIONAL ALL STARS
Also see TRAMMPS
Also see WANSEL, Dexter
Also see WELLS, Terri

MFSB & THREE DEGREES P&R '74
Singles: 7-inch
PHILADELPHIA INT'L....3-5 74
Also see MFSB
Also see THREE DEGREES

M+M: see MARTHA & MUFFINS

M.O.D. LP '87
LPs: 10/12-inch
CAROLINE....5-8 88
MEGAFORCE....5-8 87-89

MABLEY, Moms LP '61
Singles: 7-inch
MERCURY....3-5 69-71
EPs: 7-inch
CHESS....5-10 63
LPs: 10/12-inch
CHESS....15-25 61-64
MERCURY....10-20 64-70

MABLEY, Moms, & Pigmeat Markham
LPs: 10/12-inch
CHESS....10-20 64-71
Also see MABLEY, Moms
Also see MARKHAM, Pigmeat

MABON, Willie R&B '52
(With His Combo)
Singles: 78 rpm
CHESS....10-20 52-56
FEDERAL 15-25 57
PARROT....50-100 53
Singles: 7-inch
CHESS (1531 "I Don't Know")....100-200 53
(Colored vinyl.)
CHESS (1531 "I Don't Know")....40-60 53
(Black vinyl.)
CHESS (1538 "I'm Mad") 40-60 53
CHESS (1548 "You're a Fool")....40-60 53
CHESS (1554 "I Got to Go")....40-60 53
CHESS (1564 "Would You, Baby")....40-60 54
CHESS (1580 "Poison Ivy")....40-60 54
CHESS (1608 "The Seventh Son")....30-50 55
CHESS (1627 "Knock on Wood")....30-50 56
DELTA (3004 "Light Up Your Lamp")....5-10
FEDERAL (12306 "Light Up Your Lamp")....15-25 57
FORMAL....4-6 62
MAD (1298 "I Gotta Go Now")....10-20 60
MAD (1300 "I Don't Know")....10-20 60
PARROT (1050 "I Don't Know")....150-250 53
U.S.A. 5-10 63-65
LPs: 10/12-inch
CHESS (1439 "Willie Mabon")....75-125 59

MAC, Fleetwood: see FLEETWOOD MAC

MAC BAND R&B/LP '88
(Featuring the McCampbell Brothers)
Singles: 7-inch
MCA....3-4 88
LPs: 10/12-inch
MCA....5-8 88

MacALPINE, Tony LP '87
LPs: 10/12-inch
SQUAWK 5-8 87

MacARTHUR, James P&R '63
Singles: 7-inch
SCEPTER 4-8 62-63
TRIODEX....5-10 61

MacDONALD, Jeanette, & Nelson Eddy LP '59
EPs: 7-inch
RCA (Except 220)....4-8 61
RCA (220 "Rose Marie")....10-20 52
LPs: 10/12-inch
RCA (16 "Rose Marie")....40-50 52
RCA (526 "Rose Marie")....10-20 66
RCA (1000 series) 5-10 75
RCA (1700 series)....10-20 59
RCA (2400 series) 5-8 77
RCA (3900 series) 5-8 81

MacDONALD, Ralph R&B/LP '77
Singles: 12-inch
POLYDOR....4-6 84-85
Singles: 7-inch
MARLIN 3-5 76-79
POLYDOR....3-4 84-85
LPs: 10/12-inch
MARLIN....6-10 76-79
POLYDOR....5-8 84-85

MacDONALD, Ralph, & Bill Withers P&R '84
Singles: 7-inch
POLYDOR....3-4 84
Also see MacDONALD, Ralph
Also see WITHERS, Bill

MACEO & MACKS R&B '70
Singles: 7-inch
PEOPLE....3-6 73-74
LPs: 10/12-inch
PEOPLE....8-12 74
Member: Maceo Parker.
Also see PARLIAMENT

MacGREGOR, Byron P&R/C&W '74
Singles: 7-inch
CAPITOL 3-5 75
WESTBOUND....3-5 74
LPs: 10/12-inch
WESTBOUND....5-10 74

MacGREGOR, Mary — P&R '76

Singles: 7-inch

ARIOLA 3-5 78
ARIOLA AMERICA 3-5 76-77
RSO 3-5 79-80

LPs: 10/12-inch

ARIOLA AMERICA 8-10 77

Also see ASSOCIATION / Bobby Vee / Mike Love / Mary MacGregor

MACHINATIONS — D&D '83

Singles: 12-inch

A&M 4-6 83

Singles: 7-inch

A&M 3-5 83

LPs: 10/12-inch

A&M 5-8 83

MACHINE — R&B '79

Singles: 7-inch

RCA 3-5 79-80

LPs: 10/12-inch

RCA 5-10 80

MACHO — LP '78

Singles: 7-inch

PRELUDE 3-5 78

LPs: 10/12-inch

PRELUDE 5-10 78

MACK, Lonnie — P&R/R&B/LP '63

(With Pismo)

Singles: 7-inch

ABC 3-5 73
A.M.G. 3-6
BARRY 3-5
CAPITOL 3-5 77
COLLECTABLES 3-4 80s
ELEKTRA 3-5 71
FRATERNITY 5-10 63-68
ROULETTE 3-5 75

LPs: 10/12-inch

ALLIGATOR 5-8 85-86
CAPITOL 8-10 77
ELEKTRA 10-20 69-71
FRATERNITY (SF-1014 "Wham of That Memphis Man") 25-35 63
(Monaural.)
FRATERNITY (SSF-1014 "Wham of That Memphis Man") 35-55 63
(Stereo.)
TRIP 8-10 75

Members: Lonnie Mack; Jim Keltner; Tim Drummond.

MACK, Lonnie, & Rusty York

LPs: 10/12-inch

QCA 10-15 73

Also see MACK, Lonnie
Also see YORK, Rusty

MACK, Warner — C&W/P&R '57

Singles: 78 rpm

DECCA 5-15 57

Singles: 7-inch

DECCA (30301 thru 31684) 5-15 57-64
DECCA (31774 thru 33045) 3-6 65-73
KAPP 5-10 61-62
LOST GOLD 3-5 93
MCA 3-5 73-76
PAGEBOY 3-5 77-81
SCARLET 5-10 60
TOP RANK 5-10 60

EPs: 7-inch

DECCA 5-10 65

LPs: 10/12-inch

CORAL 5-10 73
DECCA 8-18 65-70
KAPP 12-25 61-66
PAGEBOY 5-10
SAPPHIRE 5-10

Session: Jordanaires.
Also see DEAN, Jimmy / David Houston / Warner Mack / Autry Inman

MacKENZIE, Gisele — P&R '52

Singles: 78 rpm

CAPITOL 3-5 51-54
VIK 3-5 56
"X" 3-5 55

Singles: 7-inch

CAPITOL 5-10 51-54
EVEREST 4-8 60
MERCURY 4-8 63
VIK 5-10 56
"X" 5-10 55

Picture Sleeves

VIK 5-10 56
"X" 5-10 55

EPs: 7-inch

CAPITOL 5-10 53-69
VIK 5-10 56

LPs: 10/12-inch

CAMDEN 10-20 59
EVEREST 10-20 60
GLENDALE 5-8 78
MERCURY 10-20 63
RCA 10-20 59
SUNSET 8-12 67
VIK 15-25 56

MacRAE, Gordon — P&R '47

Singles: 78 rpm

CAPITOL 3-5 47-57

Singles: 7-inch

CAPITOL 4-8 50-68

EPs: 7-inch

CAPITOL 5-10 54-57
ROYALE 5-10

LPs: 10/12-inch

CAPITOL 10-25 54-69
RONDO-LETTE 15-30

Also see DESMOND, Johnny / John Gary / Gordon MacRae
Also see MARTIN, Dean / Bob Eberly / Gordon MacRae

MacRAE, Gordon, & Jo Stafford — P&R '48

Singles: 78 rpm

CAPITOL 4-8 48-50

Singles: 7-inch

CAPITOL 4-8 62

LPs: 10/12-inch

CAPITOL (1600 & 1900 series) 10-20 62-63
CAPITOL (11000 series) 4-8 79

Also see BRYANT, Anita / Jo Stafford & Gordon MacRae
Also see MacRAE, Gordon
Also see STAFFORD, Jo

MAD LADS — P&R/R&B '65

Singles: 7-inch

MARK-FI (1934 "Why") 20-40 62
CAPITOL 5-10 64
STAX 10-20 64
VOLT (100 series) 5-15 65-68
VOLT (4000 series) 3-8 69-73

LPs: 10/12-inch

COLLECTABLES 6-8 86
VOLT (400 series) 15-25 66
VOLT (6000 series) 10-15 69-73

Members: Julius Green; John Williams; Robert Phillips; Sam Nelson; Cliff Billops Jr.; William Brown.
Also see OLLIE & NIGHTINGALES

MAD RIVER — LP '69

Singles: 7-inch

CAPITOL 5-10 68-69

EPs: 7-inch

WEE (10021 "Mad River") 25-50 68

LPs: 10/12-inch

CAPITOL (185 "Paradise Bar and Grill") 25-35 69
CAPITOL (2985 "Mad River") 25-35 68

Members: David Robinson; Tom Manning; Lawrence Hammond; Rick Bochner; Greg Dewey; Ron Wilson.

MADAGASCAR — R&B '81

Singles: 7-inch

ARISTA 3-5 81-82

Members: John Barnes; Marva King.

MADAME X — R&B/LP '87

Singles: 7-inch

ATLANTIC 3-4 87
LORIMAR 3-4 88

LPs: 10/12-inch

ATLANTIC 5-8 87

MADDOX, Johnny — P&R '52

(With the Rhythmasters)

Singles: 78 rpm

DOT 3-8 50-57

Singles: 7-inch

ABC 3-5 74
DOT 5-15 50-63

EPs: 7-inch

DOT 5-10 52-56

LPs: 10/12-inch

DOT (Except 102) 10-25 55-67
DOT (102 "Authentic Ragtime") 20-30 52
(10-inch LP.)
HAMILTON 10-15 64
PARAMOUNT 5-10 74

MADE IN U.S.A. — R&B '77

Singles: 7-inch

DE-LITE 3-5 77

MADHOUSE — R&B/LP '87

Singles: 7-inch

PAISLEY PARK 3-4 87

Picture Sleeves

PAISLEY PARK 3-4 87

LPs: 10/12-inch

PAISLEY PARK 5-8 87

Also see PRINCE

MADIGAN, Betty — P&R '54

Singles: 78 rpm

CORAL 3-6 57
JAY DEE 3-6 54
MGM (11000 series) 3-6 53-56

Singles: 7-inch

CORAL 4-8 57-59
JAY DEE 5-10 54
MGM (11000 series) 5-10 53-56
MGM (13000 series) 4-6 66-67
20TH FOX 4-6 64
U.A. 4-8 60-61

EPs: 7-inch

JAY DEE 5-10 54
MGM 5-10 57

LPs: 10/12-inch

CORAL 10-20 62
MGM 10-20 57-69

MADNESS — LP '80

Singles: 12-inch

GEFFEN 4-6 83
STIFF 8-12
(Promotional only.)

Singles: 7-inch

GEFFEN 3-4 83-84
SIRE 3-5 80-81

Picture Sleeves

GEFFEN 3-4 83-84

LPs: 10/12-inch

GEFFEN 5-8 83-84
SIRE 5-8 80-81

MADONNA — P&R/R&B/D&D/LP '83

Singles: 12-inch

MAVERICK (6074 "Fever") 15-20 92
(Two colored vinyl discs. Promotional issue only.)
MAVERICK (40585 "Erotica") 4-8 92
SIRE (20212 "Borderline") 5-10 84
SIRE (20239 "Like a Virgin") 5-10 84
SIRE (20304 "Material Girl") 5-10 85
SIRE (20335 "Angel") 5-10 85
SIRE (20369 "Dress You Up") 5-10 85
SIRE (20461 "Live to Tell") 5-10 86
SIRE (20597 "Open Your Heart") 5-10 87
SIRE (20633 "La Isla Bonita") 5-10 87
SIRE (20762 "Causing a Commotion") 5-10 87
SIRE (21170 "Like a Prayer") 5-10 89
SIRE (21225 "Express Yourself") 5-10 89
SIRE (21427 "Keep It Together") 5-10 90

SIRE (21513 "Vogue")........................5-10 90
SIRE (21820 "Justify My Love")...........5-10 91
SIRE (21813 "Rescue Me")..................5-10 91
SIRE (23867 "Holiday") 5-10 83
SIRE (26553 "True Blue")...................5-10 86
SIRE (29715 "Physical Attraction")......5-10 83

Singles: 7-inch

GEFFEN..3-5 85
SIRE (Black vinyl)...............................3-6 83-92
SIRE (28591 "True Blue")....................5-8 86
(Colored vinyl.)

Picture Sleeves

GEFFEN..3-5 85
SIRE (Except 29354)..........................3-8 83-90
SIRE (29354 "Borderline")..................5-10 84
(Poster sleeve.)

LPs: 10/12-inch

Sire (PRO-A7311 "Bedtime Stories")..45-55 ??
(Double colored vinyl LP set. Promotional issue only.)
SIRE (23867 "Madonna") 5-8 83
SIRE (25157 "Like a Virgin") 5-8 83
(Black vinyl.)
SIRE (1-25157 "Like a Virgin") 75-125 83
(Colored vinyl. Promotional issue only.)
SIRE (25442 "True Blue")....................5-8 86
SIRE (25611 "Who's That Girl") 5-8 87
SIRE (25535 "You Can Dance")............5-8 87
SIRE (25844 "Like a Prayer")..............5-8 89
SIRE (26209 "I'm Breathless") 5-8 90
Also see BERLIN / Madonna

MADURA LP '71

LPs: 10/12-inch

COLUMBIA.......................................10-15 71-73

MAESTRO, Johnny P&R '61
(With the Crests; with Coeds; Johnny Mastro)

Singles: 7-inch

APT (25075 "She's All Mine Alone") . 15-25 65
BUDDAH 5-10 71-72
CAMEO 10-20 63-64
COED (545 "Model Girl")...................15-25 61
COED (549 "What a Surprise") 15-25 61
COED (552 "Mr Happiness")..............15-25 61
COED (557 "I.O.U.")..........................25-35 61
COED (562 "Besame Baby")...........75-100 61
COLLECTABLES 3-4 80s
PARKWAY (118 "Is It You") 10-20 67
PARKWAY (987 "Heartburn") 10-15 66
PARKWAY (987 "Heartburn") 30-40 66
(Single sided disc. Promotional issue only.)
SCEPTER (12112 "I'm Stepping Out of the Picture")..50-100 65
U.A. (474 "Before I Loved Her") 20-30 62

LPs: 10/12-inch

BUDDAH (5091 "The Johnny Maestro Story")..25-35 71
(Price includes inserts.)
HARVEY (1000 "Biggest Hits") 10-20 81
(Colored vinyl.)
Also see BROOKLYN BRIDGE
Also see CRESTS
Also see MASTERS, Johnny

MAESTRO, Johnny, & Tymes

Singles: 7-inch

POPULAR REQUEST...........................3-6
Also see MAESTRO, Johnny
Also see TYMES

MAGAZINE 60 P&R '86

Singles: 7-inch

BAJA..3-4 86

MAGGARD, Cledus C&W/P&R '75
(With the Citizen's Band)

Singles: 7-inch

MERCURY 3-5 75-79

LPs: 10/12-inch

MERCURY 6-12 76

MAGIC LADY P&R '82

Singles: 12-inch

A&M...4-6 82

Singles: 7-inch

A&M...3-4 82

MOTOWN 3-4 88

LPs: 10/12-inch

A&M 5-8 82
ARISTA..5-8 80
MOTOWN 5-8 88
Members: Linda Stokes; Jackie Ball; Kimberly Ball; Jackie Steele.

MAGIC LANTERNS P&R '68

Singles: 7-inch

ATLANTIC...5-10 68-70
BIG TREE 3-5 71
CHARISMA 3-5 72
EPIC..4-8 66

Picture Sleeves

EPIC (10062 "Excuse Me Baby")...... 10-15 66

LPs: 10/12-inch

ATLANTIC..12-15 69
Members: Jim Bilsbury; Bev Beveridge; Mike "Ozzy" Osborne; Peter Garner; Harry Paul Ward; Albert Hammond.

MAGIC MUSHROOMS P&R '66

Singles: 7-inch

A&M (815 "Never More").................... 8-12 66
EAST COAST (1001 "Let the Rain Be Me").. 8-12 68
PHILIPS (40483 "Look in My Face") ... 8-12 67
Members: Chris Gaylord; Michael Allen.

MAGIC ORGAN LP '72
(Jerry Smith)

Singles: 7-inch

RANWOOD.. 3-5 72-77

LPs: 10/12-inch

RANWOOD... 4-8 72-83
SUNNYVALE 4-6 79
Also see SMITH, Jerry

MAGIC TOUCH P&R '71

Singles: 7-inch

BLACK FASHION 3-5 71

MAGISTRATES P&R '68

Singles: 7-inch

MGM 4-8 68-69
Member: Jean Hillary.
Also see DOVELLS

MAGNIFICENT MEN P&R/LP '67

Singles: 7-inch

CAPITOL... 4-8 66-68
MERCURY... 3-6 69

LPs: 10/12-inch

CAPITOL... 10-20 67-68
MERCURY... 8-12 70
Members: Dave Bupp; Buddy King; Tom Pane; Bob Angelucci; Terry Crousore; Tommy Hoover; Jimmy Seville; Billy Richter.

MAGNIFICENTS R&B '56

Singles: 78 rpm

VEE JAY 25-50 56-58

Singles: 7-inch

CHECKER (1016 "Do You Mind")....... 5-10 62
COLLECTABLES.................................. 3-4 80s
KANSOMA (03 "Do You Mind") 5-10 62
VEE JAY (183 "Up on the Mountain").. 30-60 56
VEE JAY (208 "Caddy Bo") 40-75 56
VEE JAY (235 "Off the Mountain").... 30-60 57
VEE JAY (281 "Don't Leave Me") 50-75 58
VEE JAY (367 "Up on the Mountain").. 10-15 60
Also see EL DORADOS

MAGNUM FORCE R&B '85

Singles: 7-inch

PAULA 3-4 85

LPs: 10/12-inch

WIZARD... 5-8 78

MaGOO, Mr: see BACKUS, Jim

MAHAL, TAJ: see TAJ MAHAL

MAHARIS, George P&R/LP '62

Singles: 7-inch

EPIC.. 4-6 62-66

Picture Sleeves

EPIC 4-6 62-64

LPs: 10/12-inch

EPIC 10-15 62-66

MAHOGANY D&D '83

Singles: 12-inch

WEST END 4-6 82

Singles: 7-inch

WEST END 3-4 82

MAHOGANY RUSH LP '74

Singles: 7-inch

COLUMBIA...3-5 76-82
20TH FOX 3-5 74-75

LPs: 10/12-inch

COLUMBIA...8-12 76-82
20TH FOX 10-12 73-75
Member: Frank Marino.
Also see MARINO, Frank, & Mahogany Rush

MAHONEY, Skip, & Casuals R&B '74

Singles: 7-inch

ABET 4-8 76-77
D.C. INT'L 4-6 74
Members: Skip Mahoney; Tracy Reid; Julius Jerome; Elwood Morgan.
Also see SKIP & CASUALS

MAI TAI R&B '85

Singles: 12-inch

MERCURY 4-6 87

Singles: 7-inch

CRITIQUE 3-4 85-86
MERCURY 3-4 87

Picture Sleeves

CRITIQUE 3-4 86

LPs: 10/12-inch

MERCURY 5-8 87
Members: Carol DeWindt; Jettie Well; Mildred Douglas.

MAIN ATTRACTION R&B '86

Singles: 7-inch

RCA..3-4 86

LPs: 10/12-inch

RCA..5-8 86

MAIN INGREDIENT P&R/R&B/LP '70
(Featuring Cuba Gooding)

Singles: 7-inch

RCA..3-5 69-81
ZAKIA 3-4 86

Picture Sleeves

RCA..3-6 70-81

LPs: 10/12-inch

COLLECTABLES 5-8 88
RCA..8-12 70-81
Members: Cuba Gooding; Don McPherson; Luther Simmons; Tony Sylvester.
Also see GOODING, Cuba
Also see POETS

MAINSTREETERS R&B '73

Singles: 7-inch

EVENT 3-5 73

MAJESTY R&B '85

Singles: 7-inch

GOLDEN BOY......................................3-4 85

MAJOR LANCE: see LANCE, Major

MAJORS P&R/R&B '62

Singles: 7-inch

IMPERIAL..8-15 62-64

LPs: 10/12-inch

IMPERIAL (9222 "Meet the Majors")..25-35 63
(Monaural.)
IMPERIAL (12222 "Meet the Majors")..25-35 63
(Stereo.)
Members: Ricky Cordo; Eugene Glass; Idella Morris; Frank Troutt; Ronald Gathers.

MAKEBA, Miriam LP '63

Singles: 7-inch

KAPP 4-8 62

MERCURY 4-6 66
RCA 4-8 64
REPRISE 4-6 67-68

LPs: 10/12-inch

KAPP 10-20 62
MERCURY 10-15 66
PETERS INT'L 5-8 81
RCA 10-20 60-68
REPRISE 10-15 67

Also see BELAFONTE, Harry, & Miriam Makeba
Also see MANHATTAN BROTHERS & Miriam Makeba

MAKEM, Tommy: see CLANCY BROTHERS & Tommy Makem

MALCOLM X — R&B '84

Singles: 7-inch

TOMMY BOY 3-4 83-84

LPs: 10/12-inch

DOUGLAS 8-15 68-71

MALICE — LP '87

LPs: 10/12-inch

ATLANTIC 5-8 87
ENIGMA 5-8

MALMKVIST, Siw — P&R '64

(With Umberto Marcato)

Singles: 7-inch

JUBILEE 4-6 64
KAPP 4-8 61

MALMSTEEN, Yngwie J. — LP '85

(Yngwie J. Malmsteen's Rising Force)

LPs: 10/12-inch

MERCURY 5-8 86
POLYDOR 5-8 85-88

Also see ALCATRAZZ
Also see DIO, Ronnie
Also see HEAR 'N AID

MALO — P&R/LP '72

Singles: 7-inch

TRAQ 3-5 81
W.B. 3-5 72-73

LPs: 10/12-inch

W.B. 8-12 72-74

Also see AZTECA
Also see SANTANA, Jorge

MALTBY, Richard, & Orch. — P&R '54

Singles: 78 rpm

VIK 3-5 56
"X" 3-5 54-55

Singles: 7-inch

COLUMBIA 4-8 59
ROULETTE 4-8 60-61
VIK 5-10 56
"X" 5-10 54-55

Picture Sleeves

VIK 10-15 56

EPs: 7-inch

COLUMBIA 5-10 59
VIK 5-10 56
"X" 8-15 54-55

LPs: 10/12-inch

CAMDEN 10-20 60-62
COLUMBIA 10-20 59
HARMONY 10-20 61
ROULETTE 10-20 60-62
VIK (1051 "Hue-Fi Moods") 20-30 56
VIK (1068 "Manhattan Bandstand") 20-30 56
"X" (1038 "Make Mine Maltby") 20-30 56

MAMA CASS: see ELLIOT, Cass

MAMA'S BOYS — LP '84

Singles: 7-inch

JIVE 3-4 84-87

LPs: 10/12-inch

JIVE 5-8 84-87

MAMAS & PAPAS — P&R/LP '66

Singles: 7-inch

ABC 3-5 70
DUNHILL 4-8 65-72
MCA 3-5 80-82

Picture Sleeves

DUNHILL (4020 "California Dreamin'") 50-100 65
(Promotional issue only.)
DUNHILL (4083 "Creeque Alley") 25-35 67
(Promotional issue only.)
DUNHILL (4113 "Dancing Bear") 4-8 67

EPs: 7-inch

ABC 8-15 71
(Promotional issues only.)
DUNHILL 15-20 65

LPs: 10/12-inch

ABC 6-10 76
DUNHILL 10-20 66-73
MCA 5-8 80-82
PICKWICK 6-10 72

Members: John Phillips "Mama" Cass Elliot; Denny Doherty; Michelle Phillips.
Also see ELLIOT, Cass
Also see McGUIRE, Barry
Also see PHILLIPS, John

MAMAS & PAPAS / Association / Fifth Dimension

LPs: 10/12-inch

TEE VEE/W.B. SPECIAL PRODUCTIONS 10-20 79

Also see ASSOCIATION
Also see FIFTH DIMENSION

MAMAS & PAPAS / Barry McGuire

EPs: 7-inch

DUNHILL (50005 "This Precious Time") 10-15 66

Also see MAMAS & PAPAS
Also see McGUIRE, Barry

MAN PARRISH: see PARRISH, Man

MANASSAS — LP '72

LPs: 10/12-inch

ATLANTIC 8-12 72-73

Also see STILLS, Stephen

MANCHA, Steve — R&B '66

(Clyde Wilson)

Singles: 7-inch

GROOVESVILLE (1001 "You're Still in My Heart") 10-20 65
GROOVESVILLE (1002 "I Don't Want to Lose You") 8-12 66
GROOVESVILLE (1004 "Friday Night") 50-75 66
GROOVESVILLE (1005 "Don't Make Me a Story Teller") 8-12 67
GROOVESVILLE (1007 "Sweet Baby") 10-20 67
WHEELSVILLE (102 "Did My Baby Call") 50-100 65

Also see BARNES, J.J., & Steve Mancha
Also see 100 PROOF Aged in Soul

MANCHESTER, Melissa — LP '73

Singles: 12-inch

ARISTA 4-6 82
CASABLANCA 4-6 84
MCA 4-6 85

Singles: 7-inch

ARISTA 3-5 75-84
BELL 3-5 74
CASABLANCA 3-4 84
MB 4-8 67
MCA 3-4 85

LPs: 10/12-inch

ARISTA 8-10 75-83
BELL 10-12 73-74
CASABLANCA 5-8 84
MCA 5-8 79-85
MFSL 25-50 79

Also see NATIONAL LAMPOON

MANCHESTER, Melissa, & Peabo Bryson — P&R '81

Singles: 7-inch

ARISTA 3-5 81

Also see BRYSON, Peabo
Also see MANCHESTER, Melissa

MANCHILD — R&B/LP '77

Singles: 7-inch

CHI-SOUND 3-5 77

LPs: 10/12-inch

CHI-SOUND 8-10 77

Members: Kenny Edmonds; Robert Parson; Chuck Bush; Daryl Simmons; Reggie Griffin.
Also see DEELE
Also see GRIFFIN, Reggie, & Technofunk
Also see REDD HOTT

MANCINI, Henry — LP '59

(Henry Mancini's Orchestra & Chorus)

Singles: 7-inch

LIBERTY (1400 series) 3-4 82
LIBERTY (55000 series) 4-8 58-59
RCA (Except 8184) 3-8 59-85
RCA (8184 "Banzai Pipeline") 5-10 63
U.A. 3-4 78
W.B. 3-4 79-83

Picture Sleeves

RCA (Except 8184) 5-12 59-77
RCA (8184 "Banzai Pipeline") 10-15 63
W.B. 3-5 79

EPs: 7-inch

RCA 5-15 60-62

LPs: 10/12-inch

AVCO EMBASSY 10-20 70
CAMDEN 5-15 66-74
LIBERTY (3000 series) 15-25 57-59
LIBERTY (51000 series) 4-8 82
MCA 6-12 75-76
PARAMOUNT 10-15 70
RCA (0013 thru 0098) 5-10 72-73
RCA (0270 "Country Gentleman") 5-8 74
RCA (0672 thru 1928) 5-10 74-76
RCA (1956 "Music from Peter Gunn") 15-25 59
RCA (2040 "More Music from Peter Gunn") 15-25 59
RCA (2101 "Mancini Touch") 15-25 59
RCA (2147 "Blues and the Beat") 15-25 60
RCA (2198 "Music from Mr. Lucky") 15-25 60
RCA (2360 "Mr. Lucky Goes Latin") 15-25 61
RCA (2362 "Just You and Me Together Love") 4-8 77
RCA (2258 "Combo") 15-20 62
RCA (2600 series) 10-20 63-64
RCA (2800 & 2900 series) 8-15 64-65
RCA (3000 series) 4-8 78
RCA (3356 "The Latin Sound of Henry Mancini") 10-20 65
RCA (3347 "Best of Henry Mancini, Volume 3") 5-8 79
RCA (3500 series) 6-12 66
RCA (3612 "Merry Mancini Christmas") 10-15 66
RCA (3667 "Pure Gold") 4-8 80
RCA (3668 "Mancini Country") 4-8 80
RCA (3694 thru 3713) 10-20 66-67
RCA (3756 "Warm Shade of Ivory") 4-8 80
RCA (3822 "Best of Henry Mancini") 4-8 80
RCA (3877 "Music of Hawaii") 4-8 81
RCA (3887 "Encore") 8-15 67
RCA (3943 "Mancini Sound") 4-8 68
RCA (3954 "Country Gentleman") 4-8 67
RCA (3997 thru 4689) 5-15 68-72
RCA (5000 series) 4-8 85
RCA (6000 series) 8-15 66-72
SUNSET 5-10 66
U.A. 10-12 70
W.B. 10-20 59-73

You'll find many more listings by this artist in *The Official Price Guide to Movie/TV Soundtracks and Original Cast Albums,* containing over 8,000 listings.

Also see ANN-MARGRET
Also see HIRT, Al / Henry Mancini / Perez Prado
Also see MATHIS, Johnny, & Henry Mancini
Also see PRIDE, Charley

MANCINI, Henry, & Doc Severinsen — LP '73

LPs: 10/12-inch

RCA 5-8 72-80

Also see MANCINI, Henry
Also see SEVERINSEN, Doc

MANDEL, Harvey *LP '69*

Singles: 7-inch

PHILIPS....4-8 68

LPs: 10/12-inch

JANUS....8-12 70-74
OVATION....10-15 71
PHILIPS....10-15 68-69
Also see CANNED HEAT

MANDELL, Howie *LP '86*

LPs: 10/12-inch

W.B. 5-8 86

MANDELL, Mike *R&B '81*

Singles: 7-inch

VANGUARD....3-5 81

MANDRE *R&B/LP '77*
(Andre Lewis)

Singles: 7-inch

MOTOWN....3-5 77-79

LPs: 10/12-inch

MOTOWN....5-10 77-79
Also see MAXAYN

MANDRELL, Barbara *C&W '69*

Singles: 7-inch

ABC....3-5 78-79
ABC/DOT....3-6 75-78
COLUMBIA....4-8 69-75
EMI....3-4 87-88
KFC (003 "Sweet Weekend Encounter")....8-12 79
(Coincides with "National Winners Kentucky Fried Chicken Song Writing Contest." Promotional issue only.)
MCA (Black vinyl)....3-5 79-86
MCA (8950 "3 Out of 3 Ain't Bad")....40-60 79
(Picture disc. Promotional issue only.)
MCA (52737 "Fast Lanes and Country Roads")....15-20 85
(Colored vinyl. Promotional issue only.)
MCA (52802 "When You Get to the Heart")....15-20 86
(Colored vinyl. Promotional issue only.)
MOSRITE (190 "Queen for a Day")...30-50 66

Picture Sleeves

MCA....3-5 79-85

LPs: 10/12-inch

ABC....8-10 78-79
ABC/DOT....8-12 76-77
COLUMBIA....6-15 71-81
COLUMBIA SPECIAL PRODUCTS....5-8 82
EMI....5-8 88
MCA....5-10 79-86
SONGBIRD....5-8 82
Session: Deborah Allen; Janie Fricke; Waylon Jennings; Charlie McCoy; Randy Wright.
Also see HOUSTON, David, & Barbara Mandrell
Also see JENNINGS, Waylon
Also see McCOY, Charlie

MANDRELL, Barbara, & Lee Greenwood *C&W/LP '84*

Singles: 7-inch

MCA....3-4 84

LPs: 10/12-inch

MCA....5-8 84
Also see GREENWOOD, Lee

MANDRELL, Barbara, & Oak Ridge Boys *C&W '86*

Singles: 7-inch

MCA....3-4 86
Also see MANDRELL, Barbara
Also see OAK RIDGE BOYS

MANDRILL *P&R/LP '71*

Singles: 7-inch

ARISTA....3-5 77-80
LIBERTY....3-4 83
MONTAGE....3-4 82
POLYDOR....3-5 71-74
U.A. 3-5 75-76

LPs: 10/12-inch

ARISTA....8-10 77-80
LIBERTY....5-8 83
POLYDOR....10-12 71-75
U.A. 8-10 75
Also see MASSER, Michael, & Mandrill
Also see SURFACE

MANFRED MANN: see MANN, Manfred

MANGANO, Silvana *P&R '53*

Singles: 78 rpm

MGM....3-6 53

Singles: 7-inch

MGM....5-10 53

MANGIONE, Chuck *P&R/LP '71*
(Chuck Mangione Quintet; Gap & Chuck Mangione)

Singles: 7-inch

A&M....3-5 75-80
COLUMBIA....3-4 82-84
MERCURY....3-5 71-77

Picture Sleeves

A&M....3-5 78-80

LPs: 10/12-inch

A&M....5-10 75-81
COLUMBIA....5-8 82-84
JAZZLAND (84 "Recuerdo")....40-50 62
JAZZLAND (984 "Recuerdo")....45-60 62
(Stereo.)
MFSL....25-50 82
MERCURY....6-12 71-78
MILESTONE....5-8 77
RIVERSIDE (371 "Jazz Brothers")....40-50 61

MANHATTAN BROTHERS & MIRIAM MAKEBA *P&R '56*

Singles: 78 rpm

LONDON....3-6 56

Singles: 7-inch

LONDON....5-10 56
Also see MAKEBA, Miriam

MANHATTAN TRANSFER *P&R/LP '75*

Singles: 7-inch

ATLANTIC....3-5 75-88
STOOP SOUNDS (102 "Gloria")....75-125 96
(Limited edition of only a few dozen made.)

Picture Sleeves

ATLANTIC....3-5 83-88

LPs: 10/12-inch

ATLANTIC....8-10 75-87
COLLECTABLES....6-8 88
MFSL (022 "Live")....35-50 78
MFSL (199 "Extensions")....20-25 90s
Members: Tim Hauser; Alan Paul; Gary Chester; Garnett Brown; Ken Buttrey; Cheryl Bentyne; Janis Siegel; Don Roberts.
Also see PISTILLI, Gene, & Manhattan Transfer

MANHATTANS *P&R/R&B '65*

Singles: 12-inch

COLUMBIA....4-6 84-85

Singles: 7-inch

AVANTI (1601 "What Should I Do")..15-25 63
CAPITOL (4591 "I Ain't Down Yet")..10-20 62
CAPITOL (4730 "Sing all the Day")..10-20 62
CARNIVAL (504 "For the Very First Time")....10-20 64
CARNIVAL (506 "Call Somebody Please")....30-50 64
(Identification number is "CA-1010." Credits "A Joe Evans Production.")
CARNIVAL (506 "Call Somebody Please")....25-45 64
(Identification number is "CA-1010x. Credits "A Joe Evans-Bob McGhee Production.")
CARNIVAL (507 thru 542)....5-15 65-69
COLUMBIA....3-6 73-87
DELUXE....4-8 69-73

Picture Sleeves

COLUMBIA....3-4 85

LPs: 10/12-inch

CARNIVAL (201 "Dedicated to You")....100-150 66
CARNIVAL (202 "For You and Yours")....100-150 66
COLUMBIA....8-12 73-85
DELUXE....10-15 70-72
SOLID SMOKE....5-8 81
Members: George Smith; Ken Kelly; Sonny Bivens; Winfred Scott; Richard Taylor; Gerald Alston; Regina Bell.

MANILOW, Barry *P&R/LP '74*

Singles: 12-inch

ARISTA (Black vinyl)....3-5 74-90
ARISTA (ASPD 1 "One Voice")....25-35 83
(Profile-shaped picture disc, made for Fox Photo. Promotional issue only.)
BELL....3-5 73-74
FLASHBACK....3-4 76
RCA....3-4 86

Promotional Singles

ARISTA (11 "It's Just Another New Year's Eve")....4-8 77
ARISTA (9318 "Paradise Cafe")....3-5 84
(Clear vinyl.)

Picture Sleeves

ARISTA (Except 11)....3-5 78-88
ARISTA (11 "It's Just Another New Year's Eve")....4-8 77
(Promotional issue only.)
ARISTA (9318 "Paradise Cafe")....3-5 84

LPs: 10/12-inch

ARISTA (Except A2L-8601)....5-10 74-90
ARISTA (A2L-8601 "Greatest Hits") 10-20 78
(Two picture discs.)
BELL (1129 "Barry Manilow")....15-25 74
BELL (1314 "Barry Manilow II")....10-15
MFSL (097 "I"....25-35 82
RCA....5-8 86
Also see LADY FLASH

MANILOW, Barry / Atlanta Rhythm Section

Singles: 7-inch

WHAT'S IT ALL ABOUT....3-5 79
Also see ATLANTA RHYTHM SECTION

MANILOW, Barry / Firefall

Singles: 7-inch

WHAT'S IT ALL ABOUT....3-5 79
Also see FIREFALL

MANILOW, Barry / Kid Creole & Coconuts *P&R '88*

Singles: 7-inch

ARISTA....3-4 88
Also see KID CREOLE & COCONUTS
Also see MANILOW, Barry

MANN, Barry *P&R '61*

Singles: 7-inch

ABC....3-5 73
ABC-PAR....10-20 60-62
ARISTA....3-5 76
CAPITOL....4-8 66-68
CASABLANCA....3-4 80
COLPIX....5-10 63
JDS....15-25 59
MCA....3-4 80s
NEW DESIGN....3-5 71-72
RCA....3-5 74-76
RED BIRD....8-12 64
ROULETTE....3-5 70s
SCEPTER....3-5 70
U.A. 3-5 77-78
W.B. 3-5 79

LPs: 10/12-inch

ABC-PAR (ABC-399 "Who Put the Bomp in the Bomp Bomp Bomp")....50-80 62
(Monaural.)
ABC-PAR (ABCS-399 "Who Put the Bomp in the Bomp Bomp Bomp")....75-100 62
(Stereo.)
CASABLANCA....5-8 80
NEW DESIGN....10-12 71
RCA (0860 "Survivor")....8-12 75
RCA (1162 "Interview")....12-15 75
(Promotional issue only.)

U.A. 8-10 77
Also see HALOS

MANN, Bobby
(Bobby Bloom)
Singles: 7-inch
KAMA SUTRA 5-10 66
Also see BLOOM, Bobby

MANN, Carl P&R/R&B '59
Singles: 7-inch
ABC/DOT 3-5 76
JAXON (502 "Gonna Rock and Roll Tonight") 200-300 57
PHILLIPS INT'L 10-20 59-61
SUN 3-5 70s
LPs: 10/12-inch
GRT/SUNNYVALE 6-10 77
PHILLIPS INT'L (1960 "Like Mann") 400-500 60

MANN, Charles R&B '73
Singles: 7-inch
ABC 3-5 73
LANOR (529 "Hey Little Girl") 5-15
LANOR (540 "Dreams to Remember") 5-15
LANOR (543 "Red Red Wine") 5-15
Note: Confusion reigns here. We've seen these Lanor titles sold for from $4 to $20 for NM. Plus, there are others we haven't listed. Opinions vary widely for years of release. Finally, are Lanor & ABC by the same Mann?)

MANN, Gloria P&R '55
(With the Carter Rays; with Don Costa's Orchestra)
Singles: 78 rpm
ABC-PAR 5-10 57
DECCA 3-6 56
DERBY 4-8 56
JUBILEE 4-8 54
SLS 10-15 54
SOUND 5-10 54-55
Singles: 7-inch
ABC-PAR 5-10 57
DECCA 5-10 56
DERBY 5-10 56
JUBILEE 8-12 54
SLS (102 "Goodnight Sweetheart") ... 30-40 54
SOUND 10-20 54-55
Also see COSTA, Don, Orchestra

MANN, Herbie LP '62
Singles: 12-inch
ATLANTIC 4-6 83
Singles: 7-inch
A&M 3-5 68
ATLANTIC 3-8 60-83
BETHLEHEM 4-8 59-62
COLUMBIA 3-5 70
EMBRYO 3-5 71
PRESTIGE 4-6 66
Picture Sleeves
ATLANTIC 3-5 79
LPs: 10/12-inch
A&M 8-12 68
ATLANTIC (300 series) 8-12 72
ATLANTIC (1300 & 1400 series) 10-20 60-66
ATLANTIC (1500 thru 1600 series) 8-12 69-76
ATLANTIC (8000 series) 8-15 67
ATLANTIC (18000 & 19000 series) 5-10 77-83
BETHLEHEM (24 "Flamingo") 50-100 55
BETHLEHEM (40 "Herbie Mann") ... 50-100 56
BETHLEHEM (63 "Love and the Weather") 50-100 56
BETHLEHEM (1018 "East Coast Jazz") 75-100 54
(10-inch LPs.)
BETHLEHEM (6001 "The Bethlehem Years") 5-8 76
BETHLEHEM (6067 "The Epitome of Jazz") 25-35 63
COLUMBIA 8-18 65-81
EMBRYO 8-12 70-71
EPIC (3395 "Salute to the Flute") 60-80 57
EPIC (3499 "Herbie Mann") 50-70 58
FINNADAR 5-10 76
INTERLUDE 20-35 59
JAZZLAND (5 "Californians") 35-55 60
MILESTONE 8-12 73
MODE (114 "Flute Fraternity") 40-60 57
NEW JAZZ (8211 "Just Wailin'") 50-60 58
PREMIER 20-30 63
PRESTIGE (7101 "Flute Souffle") ... 75-100 57
PRESTIGE (7124 "Flute Flight") 75-100 57
PRESTIGE (7136 "Mann in the Morning") 75-100 58
PRESTIGE (7432 "Best of Herbie Mann") 20-30 65
RIVERSIDE (03 "Blues for Tomorrow") 5-8 82
RIVERSIDE (234 "Sultry Serenade") 50-75 57
RIVERSIDE (245 "Great Ideas") 50-75 57
RIVERSIDE (3000 series) 8-12 69
ROULETTE 10-15 67
SAVOY (1100 series) 5-8 76
SAVOY (12107 "Mann Alone") 30-40 57
SAVOY (12108 "Yardbird Suite") 35-50 57
SOLID STATE 8-12 68
SURREY 10-15 65
U.A. (4000 & 5000 series) 20-40 59
U.A. (5300 series) 8-10 72
U.A. (14000 & 15000 series) 20-40 62-63
VSP 8-15 66
VERVE 20-40 57-61
(Reads "Verve Records, Inc." at bottom of label.)
VERVE 15-25 63
(Reads "MGM Records - A Division of Metro-Goldwyn-Mayer, Inc." at bottom of label.)
VERVE 5-10 69-73
(Reads "Manufactured By MGM Record Corp.," or mentions either Polydor or Polygram at bottom of label.)
Session: King Curtis; Little Milton.
Also see AYERS, Roy
Also see KING CURTIS
Also see LITTLE MILTON
Also see JONES, Tamiko, & Herbie Mann

MANN, Herbie, & Cissy Houston R&B '76
Singles: 7-inch
ATLANTIC 3-5 76
Also see HOUSTON, Cissy

MANN, Herbie / Maynard Ferguson
LPs: 10/12-inch
ROULETTE 8-12 71
Also see FERGUSON, Herbie
Also see MANN, Herbie

MANN, Johnny, Singers LP '63
Singles: 7-inch
DECCA 3-5 66
EPIC 3-5 72
EUREKA 4-8 60
LIBERTY 4-6 62-68
LPs: 10/12-inch
EPIC 5-10 72
LIBERTY 10-20 59-69
LIGHT 5-10 76
SUNSET 5-10 66-70
U.A. 6-12 71-72
Also see McDANIELS, Gene
Also see ZENTNER, Si

MANN, Manfred P&R/LP '64
(Manfred Mann's Earth Band)
Singles: 7-inch
ARISTA 3-4 84-85
ASCOT (Except 2157 & 2165) 6-12 64-68
ASCOT (2157 "Do Wah Diddy Diddy") 4-8 64
ASCOT (2165 "Sha La La") 4-8 64
MERCURY 3-6 66-69
POLYDOR 3-5 71-74
PRESTIGE 8-10 64
U.A. 4-8 66
W.B. 3-5 76-81
Picture Sleeves
ASCOT 10-20 64-65
MERCURY 8-15 68
W.B. 3-5 76
EPs: 7-inch
U.A. (10030 "Manfred Mann") 10-20 64
(Promotional issue only. Not issued with cover.)
LPs: 10/12-inch
ARISTA 5-8 83
ASCOT (13015 "Manfred Mann") 25-35 64
(Monaural.)
ASCOT (13018 "Five Faces of Manfred Mann") 25-35 65
(Monaural.)
ASCOT (13024 "Mann Made") 25-35 66
(Monaural.)
ASCOT (16015 "Manfred Mann") 35-45 64
(Stereo.)
ASCOT (16018 "Five Faces of Manfred Mann") 35-45 65
(Stereo.)
ASCOT (16024 "Mann Made") 35-45 66
(Stereo.)
CAPITOL 5-8 80
EMI AMERICA 10-12 77
JANUS 12-15 74
MERCURY 15-20 68
POLYDOR 10-15 70-74
U.A. 20-35 66-68
W.B. 5-8 74-81
Members: Manfred Mann; Mike D'Abo; Paul Jones; Tom McGuinnes; Mick Rogers; Mick Vickers; Chris Slade; Colin Pattenden; Mike Hugg; Steve York; Mick Rogers.
Also see BELL, Madeline
Also see FIRM
Also see McGUINNESS FLINT
Also see THOMPSON, Chris, & Night

MANNA, Charlie LP '61
Singles: 7-inch
DECCA 4-6 61
JUBILEE 4-6 65
Picture Sleeves
DECCA 4-8 61
LPs: 10/12-inch
DECCA 10-20 61-62
VERVE 10-15 66

MANNHEIM STEAMROLLER LP '84
LPs: 10/12-inch
AMERICAN GRAMAPHONE 5-8 75-90
Also see WILLIAMS, Mason, & Mannheim Steamroller

MANONE, Wingy, & Orch. P&R '35
Singles: 78 rpm
BLUEBIRD 3-8 36-38
COLUMBIA 3-5 54
DECCA 4-8 57
VOCALION 3-8
Singles: 7-inch
COLUMBIA 5-10 54
DECCA 8-12 57
IMPERIAL 4-6 62
KEM 4-6 61
EPs: 7-inch
COLUMBIA 5-10 54
VIK 5-10 56
LPs: 10/12-inch
IMPERIAL 8-15 62
MCA 5-10 83
PRESTIGE 5-10 70
RCA 5-10 69
SAVOY 5-10 73
STORYVILLE 5-10 83
VIK 10-20 56

MANTOVANI P&R '35
(Mantovani & His Orchestra)
Singles: 78 rpm
COLUMBIA 3-8 36
LONDON (Except 1761) 3-5 51-65
LONDON (1761 "Let Me Be Loved") 4-6 57
Singles: 7-inch
LONDON (Except 1761) 3-8 51-65
LONDON (1761 "Let Me Be Loved") 4-8 57
Picture Sleeves
LONDON (Except 1761) 4-8 57-65
LONDON (1761 "Let Me Be Loved") 30-45 57
(*Let Me Be Loved* is the main theme from the

film, *The James Dean Story.* Sleeve pictures Dean.)

EPs: 7-inch

LONDON 4-8 51-59

LPs: 10/12-inch

BAINBRIDGE 5-10 82
LONDON 8-18 51-72

Also see PRESLEY, Elvis
Also see WHITFIELD, David

MANTRA *R&B '81*

Singles: 7-inch

CASABLANCA 3-4 81

LPs: 10/12-inch

CASABLANCA 5-10 81

MANTRONIX *D&D '85*

(With Wondress)

Singles: 12-inch

SLEEPING BAG 4-6 85

Singles: 7-inch

SLEEPING BAG 3-4 85

LPs: 10/12-inch

CAPITOL 5-8 88-90
SLEEPING BAG 5-8 86

MANU DIBANGO: see DIBANGO, Manu

MANZANERA, Phil *LP '79*

(Phil Manzanera Quiet Sun; with 801; Manzanera)

Singles: 12-inch

EDITIONS E.G. 5-8 82

Singles: 7-inch

POLYDOR 3-5 78

LPs: 10/12-inch

ANTILLES 8-10
ATCO 8-10
EDITIONS E.G. 5-8 82
POLYDOR 8-10 78

Also see NICO
Also see ROXY MUSIC

MANZAREK, Ray *LP '75*

Singles: 7-inch

MERCURY 4-6 73-74

LPs: 10/12-inch

A&M 5-10 84
MERCURY 8-12 74-75

Also see DOORS

MARA, Tommy *P&R '58*

Singles: 78 rpm

MGM 4-6 55

Singles: 7-inch

B&F 5-10 60
FELSTED 5-10 58-59
MGM 5-10 55

MARATHONS *P&R/R&B '61*

Singles: 7-inch

ARGO (5389 "Peanut Butter") 5-10 61
ARVEE (5027 "Peanut Butter") 10-12 61
(Other Arvee releases by the Marathons are by a different group. See the following section.)
CHESS (1790 "Peanut Butter") 5-10 61
PLAZA 5-10 62

EPs: 7-inch

MARK '56 ("Laura Scudder's Magic Record") 4-8 69
(Laura Scudder's potato chip mail-order, coupon giveaway item. Has three tracks, including *Peanut Butter,* imbedded in a single band on each side. When needle begins tracking, it's unknown which song will play. Price includes paper picture sleeve.)

LPs: 10/12-inch

ARVEE (428 "Peanut Butter") 50-75 61

Members: James Johnson; Carl Fisher; Dick Owens; Dave Govan; Don Bradley.
Also see JAYHAWKS
Also see VIBRATIONS

MARATHONS

Singles: 7-inch

ARVEE (Except 5027) 5-10 61-62
(Arvee 5027 is by a different group and is listed in the preceeding section.)

MARCELS *P&R/R&B '61*

(With the Stu Phillips Orchestra; Marcelles)

Singles: 7-inch

COLPIX (186 "Blue Moon") 15-25 61
COLPIX (186 "Blue Moon") 20-30 61
(Mistakenly credits "Marcelles." Canadian.)
COLPIX (196 "Summertime") 10-20 61
COLPIX (606 "You Are My Sunshine") 10-20 61
COLPIX (612 "Heartaches") 15-25 61
COLPIX (617 "Merry Twistmas") 15-25 61
COLPIX (621 "My Melancholy Baby") 100-200 62
(Promotional issue only.)
COLPIX (624 "My Melancholy Baby") 15-25 62
COLPIX (629 "Footprints in the Sand") 25-50 62
COLPIX (651 "Friendly Loan") 25-35 62
COLPIX (665 "Alright, Okay, You Win") 15-25 62
COLPIX (683 "That Old Black Magic") 10-20 63
COLPIX (687 "I Want to Be the Leader") 20-30 63
COLPIX (694 "One Last Kiss") 50-75 63
888 (101 "Lonely Boy") 10-15 63
ERIC 3-4 70s
KYRA ("Comes Love") 100-150 64
(No selection number used.)
MONOGRAM (113 "Over the Rainbow") 10-20 75
(Colored vinyl.)
MONOGRAM (115 "Two People in the World") 5-8 75
QUEEN BEE (47001 "In the Still of the Night") 10-15 73
SIR RENDER (005 "A Fallen Tear") 5-8
(Colored vinyl.)
ST. CLAIR 5-10 75

Picture Sleeves

COLPIX (186 "Blue Moon") 30-50 61
COLPIX (612 "Heartaches") 30-50 61
COLPIX (624 "Merry Twistmas") 40-60 61

LPs: 10/12-inch

COLPIX (416 "Blue Moon") 75-125 61
(Gold label.)
COLPIX (416 "Blue Moon") 30-50 63
(Blue label.)
CRYSTAL BALL 8-10
EMUS 8-10 79
MURRAY HILL 8-10

Members: Cornelius Harp; Fred Johnson; Ron Mundy; Gene Bricker; Richard Knauss; Walt Maddox; Al Johnson.

MARCH, Little Peggy *P&R/R&B/LP '63*

(Peggy March)

Singles: 7-inch

OLDE WORLD 3-5 75
RCA 4-8 62-71

Picture Sleeves

RCA 10-20 63

EPs: 7-inch

RCA 15-25 63

LPs: 10/12-inch

RCA (Except 2732) 15-20 65-68
RCA (LPM-2732 "I Will Follow Him") 50-60 63
(Monaural.)
RCA (LSP-2732 "I Will Follow Him") 75-100 63
(Stereo.)

MARCH, Little Peggy, & Bennie Thomas

LPs: 10/12-inch

RCA 15-20 65

MARCH, Peggy, & Gary Marshal

Singles: 7-inch

RCA 4-8 66

Also see MARCH, Little Peggy

MARCHAN, Bobby *P&R/R&B '60*

(With the Tick Tocks; with Clowns; Bobby Marchon)

Singles: 78 rpm

ACE 10-20 56
ALADDIN 10-20 53
DOT 10-20 54
FIRE (1022 "There's Something on Your Mind") 300-400 60
GALE 10-20 57

Singles: 7-inch

ABC 3-5 73
ACE (523 "Chickie Wah Wah") 20-30 56
ACE (557 "Rockin' Behind the Iron Curtain") 15-25 59
ACE (3000 series) 4-8 74-75
ALADDIN (3189 "Just a Little Walk") 30-40 53
BOBBY ROBINSON 3-6 73
CAMEO 5-10 66-67
DIAL 4-10 64-74
DOT (1203 "Just a Little Ol' Wine") ... 20-30 54
FIRE 10-20 59-62
FLASHBACK 3-5 65
GALE 20-30 57
GAMBLE 5-10 68
MERCURY 3-5 77
RIVER CITY 10-20
SANSU 5-10 60s
SPHERE SOUND 5-10 65
VOLT 8-12 63

LPs: 10/12-inch

COLLECTABLES 5-8 88
SPHERE SOUND (7004 "There's Something on Your Mind") 30-50 64

Also see SMITH, Huey

MARCY JO & EDDIE RAMBEAU

Singles: 7-inch

ROBBEE 5-10 62
SWAN 10-20 63

Also see MARCY JOE
Also see RAMBEAU, Eddie

MARCY JOE *P&R '61*

(Marcy Jo)

Singles: 7-inch

ROBBEE 5-10 61
SWAN 8-12 62

Also see CHRISTIE, Lou

MARDIS, Bobby *R&B '86*

Singles: 12-inch

PROFILE 4-6 86

Singles: 7-inch

PROFILE 3-4 86

MARDONES, Benny *P&R/LP '80*

Singles: 7-inch

POLYDOR 3-5 80-89
PRIVATE STOCK 3-5 78

EPs: 7-inch

PRIVATE STOCK (1000 "Thank God for Girls") 5-8 78
(Colored vinyl. Promotional issue only.)

LPs: 10/12-inch

POLYDOR 5-10 80
PRIVATE STOCK 5-10 78

MARESCA, Ernie *P&R/R&B '62*

Singles: 7-inch

LAURIE 5-10 66
RUST 8-12 64
SEVILLE 8-12 60-65

LPs: 10/12-inch

LAURIE (4006 "Original Songs of Ernie Maresca") 10-15 78
SEVILLE (77001 "Shout! Shout! [Knock Yourself Out])" 30-60 62
(Monaural.)
SEVILLE (87001 "Shout! Shout! [Knock Yourself Out])" 40-80 62
(Stereo.)

MARGRET, Ann: see ANN-MARGRET

MARIACHI BRASS (Featuring Chet Baker) LP '66

LPs: 10/12-inch

WORLD PACIFIC.... 8-12 66

MARIE, Diane D&D '83

Singles: 12-inch

PRELUDE.... 4-6 83

MARIE, Teena R&B/LP '79

Singles: 12-inch

EPIC.... 4-6 83-85

Singles: 7-inch

EPIC.... 3-4 83-88
GORDY.... 3-5 79-81
MOTOWN.... 3-4

Picture Sleeves

EPIC.... 3-4 84-88

LPs: 10/12-inch

EPIC.... 5-8 83-90
GORDY.... 5-10 79-81
Also see KING DREAM CHORUS & Holiday Crew

MARIE: see OSMOND, Marie

MARIE & REX P&R '59

Singles: 7-inch

CARLTON (502 "I Can't Sit Down").... 10-15 59
Members: Marie Knight; Rex Garvin.
Also see KNIGHT, Marie

MARIGOLDS R&B '55

Singles: 78 rpm

EXCELLO.... 10-20 55

Singles: 7-inch

EXCELLO (2057 "Rollin' Stone").... 20-40 55
EXCELLO (2061 "Two Strangers").... 20-40 55
EXCELLO (2078 "Foolish Me").... 20-40 56
EXCELLO (2091 "It's You, Darling, It's You").... 20-40 56
Members: Johnny Bragg; Henry Jones; Hal Hebb; Willie Wilson.

MARILLION LP '83

Singles: 7-inch

CAPITOL.... 3-4 83-87

Picture Sleeves

CAPITOL.... 3-4 85

LPs: 10/12-inch

CAPITOL.... 5-8 83-87
Members: Fish; Steve Hogarth; Steve Rothany; Mark Kelly; Pete Trewavas; Ian Mosely.
Also see GTR

MARIMBA CHIAPAS P&R '56

Singles: 78 rpm

CAPITOL.... 3-6 56

Singles: 7-inch

CAPITOL.... 5-8 56

MARINERS P&R '50

Singles: 78 rpm

CADENCE.... 4-8 55-56
COLUMBIA.... 4-8 50-55

Singles: 7-inch

CADENCE.... 5-15 55-56
COLUMBIA.... 5-15 50-55
TIARA.... 5-10 58

EPs: 7-inch

COLUMBIA.... 5-10 51-55

LPs: 10/12-inch

CADENCE (1008 "Spirituals").... 30-40 56
(10-inch LP.)
COLUMBIA.... 15-25 51-55
EPIC.... 10-20 59
HARMONY.... 10-20 59
Also see GODFREY, Arthur

MARINO, Frank LP '77
(With Mahogany Rush)

Singles: 7-inch

COLUMBIA.... 3-5 77-81

LPs: 10/12-inch

COLUMBIA.... 5-10 77-81
Also see MAHAGONY RUSH

MARK - ALMOND BAND LP '71

Singles: 7-inch

ABC.... 3-5 75
BLUE THUMB.... 3-5 72
COLUMBIA.... 3-5 72-73

LPs: 10/12-inch

A&M.... 8-10 78
ABC.... 8-10 76
BLUE THUMB.... 8-12 70-73
COLUMBIA.... 8-10 72-73
MCA.... 5-8
PACIFIC ARTS.... 8-10 81
Members: Jon Mark; Johnny Almond.
Also see ALMOND, Marc

MARK II P&R '60

Singles: 7-inch

WYE.... 5-10 60-61
Member: Winston Cogswell.

MARK IV P&R '58

Singles: 7-inch

COSMIC.... 10-15 58
MERCURY (71000 series).... 5-10 59

MARK IV R&B '72

Singles: 7-inch

MERCURY (73000 series).... 3-5 72-73

LPs: 10/12-inch

MERCURY.... 10-12 73
Members: James Ponder; Larry Jones.

MARKETTS P&R '62
(Mar-Kets)

Singles: 7-inch

LIBERTY.... 8-12 62
MERCURY.... 3-5 73
UNI.... 4-6 69
UNION.... 15-20 61-62
W.B. (Except 5391).... 4-8 63-66
W.B. (5391 "Outer Limits").... 5-10 63
W.B. (5391 "Out of Limits").... 4-8 63
(Note title change.)
WORLD PACIFIC.... 4-8 67

LPs: 10/12-inch

DORE.... 5-8 82
LIBERTY (3226 "Surfer's Stomp").... 25-30 62
(Monaural.)
LIBERTY (3226 "Surfing Scene").... 20-25 62
(Monaural. Reissue.)
LIBERTY (7226 "Surfer's Stomp").... 30-35 62
(Stereo.)
LIBERTY (7226 "Surfing Scene").... 25-30 62
(Stereo. Reissue.)
MERCURY.... 10-15 73
PHONORAMA.... 5-8 84
SEMINOLE (501 M*A*S*H Theme").... 3-5 76
W.B. (W-1509 "Take to Wheels").... 20-25 63
(Monaural.)
W.B. (WS-1509 "Take to Wheels").. 25-30 63
(Stereo.)
W.B. (W-1537 "Out of Limits").... 20-25 64
(Monaural.)
W.B. (WS-1537 "Out of Limits").... 25-30 64
(Stereo.)
W.B. (W-1642 "Batman Theme").... 20-30 66
(Monaural.)
W.B. (WS-1642 "Batman Theme").... 25-30 66
(Stereo.)
WORLD PACIFIC (1870 "Sun Power").... 15-25 67
Members: Ben Benay; Mike Henderson; Ray Pohlman; Tommy Tedesco; Bill Pittman; Gene Pello; Tom Hensley; Richard Hobaica.

MAR-KEYS P&R/R&B '61

Singles: 7-inch

SATELITE (107 "Last Night").... 10-15 61
STAX.... 4-8 61-66

LPs: 10/12-inch

ATLANTIC.... 20-25 61-62
STAX.... 10-20 66-71
Members: Donald Dunn; Steve Cropper; Don Nix; Charles Axton; Wayne Jackson; Smoochie Smith; Terry Johnson; Andrew Love; Joe Arnold.
Also see PACKERS

MAR-KEYS / Booker T. & MGs LP '67

LPs: 10/12-inch

STAX (720 "Back to Back").... 12-18 67
Also see BOOKER T. & MGs
Also see MAR-KEYS

MARKHAM, Pigmeat P&R/R&B/LP '68

Singles: 7-inch

ABC.... 3-5 74
CHESS.... 4-8 64-70
WIG.... 6-12

EPs: 7-inch

CHESS (5128 "Pigmeat Markham – *The Trial* Excerpts").... 10-15 61

LPs: 10/12-inch

CHESS.... 10-20 61-69
JEWEL.... 5-10 72-73
Also see MABLEY, Moms, & Pigmeat Markham

MARKS, Guy P&R '68

Singles: 7-inch

ABC.... 4-6 68
ARIOLA AMERICA.... 3-5 76
RADNOR.... 3-5 70

LPs: 10/12-inch

ABC.... 10-20 66-68

MARLEY, Bob, & Wailers LP '75
(Wailers)

Singles: 7-inch

COTILLION.... 3-5 81
ISLAND.... 3-5 76-84
SHELTER.... 3-5 71
TUFF GONG.... 4-6 74

Picture Sleeves

ISLAND.... 3-4 83

LPs: 10/12-inch

AUDIO FIDELITY (350 "Bob Marley").... 10-15 83
(Picture disc.)
CALLA (1200 series).... 10-15 76
CALLA (34000 series).... 8-10 77
COTILLION.... 5-8 81
ISLAND (11 "Babylon By Bus").... 10-12 78
ISLAND (9000 series, except 9329).... 8-12 75-80
ISLAND (9329 "Catch a Fire").... 15-25 75
(Shaped cover.)
ISLAND (9329 "Catch a Fire").... 8-10 75
(Standard cover.)
ISLAND (90000 series).... 5-8 83-86
MFSL (221 "Exodus").... 20-25 94
MFSL (236 "Catch a Fire").... 20-25 95
Also see MELODY MAKERS
Also see TOSH, Peter

MARLEY, Ziggy, & Melody Makers: see MELODY MAKERS

MARLEY MARL LP '88

LPs: 10/12-inch

COLD CHILL.... 5-8 88

MARLO, Micki P&R '57

Singles: 78 rpm

ABC-PAR (Except 9841).... 5-10 57
ABC-PAR (9841 "What You've Done to Me").... 10-20 57
(With "Vocal assist by Paul Anka.")
ABC-PAR (9841 "What You've Done to Me").... 5-10 57
(Has the singer humming the lines done by Paul Anka on first pressing.)
CAPITOL.... 4-8 54-56

Singles: 7-inch

ABC-PAR (Except 9841).... 5-10 57
ABC-PAR (9841 "What You've Done to Me").... 10-20 57
(With "Vocal assist by Paul Anka.")
ABC-PAR (9841 "What You've Done to Me").... 5-10 57
(Has the singer humming the lines done by Paul Anka on first pressing.)
CAPITOL.... 5-10 54-56

LPs: 10/12-inch

ABC-PAR.... 15-25 60

Also see ANKA, Paul

MARLOWE, Marion P&R '54
(With Frank Parker)
Singles: 78 rpm
CADENCE....4-6 55-56
COLUMBIA....4-6 53-54
Singles: 7-inch
CADENCE....5-10 55-56
COLUMBIA....5-10 53-54
EPs: 7-inch
COLUMBIA....6-12 53-55
LPs: 10/12-inch
BARNABY....5-8 76
COLUMBIA....20-35 53-55
HARMONY....10-15 60

MARMALADE P&R/LP '70
Singles: 7-inch
ARIOLA AMERICA....3-5 76
EMI....3-5 74
EPIC....4-8 67-69
LONDON....3-6 70-72
LPs: 10/12-inch
EPIC....10-15 70
G&P....8-10 81
LONDON....10-15 70
Members: Dean Ford; Junior Campbell.
Also see BLUE

MARRINER, Neville LP '84
LPs: 10/12-inch
FANTASY....5-8 84

MARS, Mitzi R&B '53
Singles: 78 rpm
CHECKER (773 "I'm Glad")....15-25 53
Singles: 7-inch
CHECKER (773 "I'm Glad")....20-40 53

MARS BONFIRE: see BONFIRE, Mars

MARSALIS, Branford LP '84
(Branford Marsalis Quartet Featuring Terence Blanchard)
LPs: 10/12-inch
COLUMBIA....5-8 84-90

MARSALIS, Wynton LP '82
LPs: 10/12-inch
COLUMBIA....5-8 82-91
WHO'S WHO in JAZZ....5-8 83

MARSH, Little Toni D&D '83
Singles: 12-inch
PRISM....4-6 83

MARSHALL - HAIN P&R '78
Singles: 7-inch
HARVEST....3-5 78
LPs: 10/12-inch
HARVEST....5-8 78
Members: Julian Marshall; Kit Hain.
Also see EYE to EYE

MARSHALL TUCKER BAND LP '73
Singles: 7-inch
CAPRICORN....3-5 73-78
MERCURY....3-4 87-88
W.B.....3-5 79-83
Picture Sleeves
W.B.....3-5 79
LPs: 10/12-inch
CAPRICORN....8-12 73-78
MERCURY....5-10 87
W.B.....5-10 79-83
Members: Doug Gray; Tom Caldwell; Troy Caldwell; Franklin Wilkie; Jack Eubanks; Paul Riddle.

MARTERIE, Ralph, & Orch. P&R '51
Singles: 78 rpm
MERCURY....3-5 50-57
Singles: 7-inch
MERCURY....4-8 50-60
U.A.....3-6 61-62
EPs: 7-inch
MERCURY....5-10 50-59
LPs: 10/12-inch
MERCURY....8-18 50-60
U.A.....5-10 61-62
WING....5-10 56-60

MARTHA & MUFFINS LP '80
(M+M)
Singles: 12-inch
RCA....4-6 83-84
Singles: 7-inch
DINDISC/VIRGIN....3-5 80
RCA....3-4 83-84
LPs: 10/12-inch
CURRENT....5-8 84
RCA....5-8 83
VIRGIN....5-8 80

MARTHA & VANDELLAS
(Martha Reeves & the Vandellas) P&R/R&B/LP '63
Singles: 7-inch
GORDY (7011 "I'll Have to Let Him Go")....15-25 62
GORDY (7014 "Come and Get These Memories")....10-20 62
GORDY (7022 thru 7062)....6-12 63-67
(Black vinyl.)
GORDY (7062 "Love Bug Leave My Heart Alone")....8-15 67
(Colored vinyl. Promotional issue only.)
GORDY (7067 thru 7127)....4-8 67-72
(Black vinyl.)
GORDY (7113 "In and Out of My Life")....8-15 71
(Colored vinyl. Promotional issue only.)
MOTOWN....3-4
MOTOWN/TOPPS (7 "Dancing in the Street")....50-75 67
(Topps Chewing Gum promotional item. Single-sided, cardboard flexi, picture disc. Issued with generic paper sleeve.)
MOTOWN/TOPPS (14 "Heat Wave")....50-75 67
(Topps Chewing Gum promotional item. Single-sided, cardboard flexi, picture disc. Issued with generic paper sleeve.)
TAMLA/MOTOWN....4-8
Picture Sleeves
GORDY (7033 "Dancing in the Street")....20-30 64
EPs: 7-inch
GORDY (60920 "Watchout")....15-25 67
MOTOWN (2009 "Martha & the Vandellas")....15-25
MOTOWN (2017 "Hittin'")....15-25
LPs: 10/12-inch
ERA....5-10 79
GORDY (902 "Come and Get These Memories")....100-125 63
(Monaural.)
GORDY (S-902 "Come and Get These Memories")....100-150 63
(Stereo.)
GORDY (907 "Heat Wave")....50-75 63
(Monaural.)
GORDY (S-907 "Heat Wave")....60-80 63
(Stereo.)
GORDY (915 "Dance Party")....50-75 65
(Monaural.)
GORDY (S-915 "Dance Party")....60-80 65
(Stereo.)
GORDY (917 "Greatest Hits")....20-30 66
GORDY (920 "Watchout")....20-30 67
GORDY (925 "Live")....15-25 66
GORDY (926 thru 958)....15-20 68-72
MOTOWN (Except 100 & 200 series)....12-15 74
MOTOWN (100 & 200 series)....5-8 81-82
Members: Martha Reeves; Rosalind Ashford; Annette Beard; Betty Kelly; Lois Reeves; Sandra Tilley.
Also see BROWN, James / Martha & Vandellas
Also see DEL-PHIS
Also see GAYE, Marvin
Also see HONDELLS / Del Shannon / Martha & Vandellas
Also see HOOKER, John Lee
Also see REEVES, Martha
Also see VELLS
Also see VELVELETTES

MARTIKA P&R '88
(Martika Marrero)
Singles: 7-inch
COLUMBIA....3-4 88-91
Picture Sleeves
COLUMBIA....3-4 88
LPs: 10/12-inch
COLUMBIA....5-8 89

MARTIN, Bobbi P&R '64
Singles: 7-inch
BUDDAH....3-5 71-72
CORAL....4-8 61-67
GREEN MENU....3-5 75
MGM....3-5 73
MAYPOLE....5-10 60
U.A.....4-6 68-70
Picture Sleeves
CORAL....4-8 65
EPs: 7-inch
CORAL....5-10 65
LPs: 10/12-inch
BUDDAH....5-10 71
CORAL....10-20 65
SUNSET....5-10 71
U.A.....8-12 68-70
VOCALION....5-10 70

MARTIN, Dean P&R '49
Singles: 78 rpm
APOLLO (1088 "Oh Marie")....100-150 47
APOLLO (1116 "Santa Lucia")....100-150 48
CAPITOL (545 thru 2001)....15-25 49-52
CAPITOL (2037 "Hey, Brother, Pour the Wine")....20-30 54
(Seven-inch 78 rpm. Promotional issue only.)
CAPITOL (2071 thru 3841)....10-20 52-57
CAPITOL (15000 series)....20-40 48-49
DIAMOND (2035 "Which Way Did My Heart Go")....100-150 46
DIAMOND (2036 "I Got the Sun in the Morning")....100-150 46
EMBASSY (124 "One Foot in Heaven")....500-1000 49
Singles: 7-inch
CAPITOL (401 "Dean Martin Sings")....75-100 53
(Boxed, four-disc set.)
CAPITOL (247 "Silver Bells")....10-15 66
(Promotional issue only.)
CAPITOL (691 thru 981)....15-25 49-50
CAPITOL (987 "Sleep Warm")....50-100 59
(Promotional issue only.)
CAPITOL (1002 thru 1458)....10-20 50-51
CAPITOL (1609 "I Met a Girl")....50-100 60
(Promotional issue only.)
CAPITOL (1703 thru 3238)....10-15 51-55
CAPITOL (3295 thru 4570)....8-12 55-61
CAPITOL (6000 series)....4-6 64
CAPITOL (44153 "That's Amore")....3-4 88
MCA (52662 "L.A. Is My Home")....15-25 85
REPRISE (190 thru 193)....4-8 64
(Compact 33 singles. Promotional issues only.)
REPRISE (200 "Sophia")....150-200 65
(Promotional issue only.)
REPRISE (0252 thru 1178)....3-6 64-73
REPRISE (20,000 series)....4-8 62-63
REPRISE (40,000 series)....10-15 62
(Stereo 33 singles.)
TEXAS DESERT CIRCUS WEEK (2160 "It's 1200 Miles from Texas to Palm Springs")....50-100 58
(Single-sided promotional disc. Made especially for play in Palm Springs, promoting a circus. Incorrect title is shown on label—should read *It's 1200 Miles from Palm Springs to Texas.*)
W.B. (29584 "My First Country Song")..3-4 83
(With Conway Twitty.)
W.B. (29480 "Drinking Champagne")....3-4 83
Picture Sleeves
CAPITOL (987 "Sleep Warm")....100-200 59

CAPITOL (1609 "I Met a Girl")......... 50-100 60
(Promotional issue only. Sleeve reads: "From the Soundtrack of the Motion Picture *Bells are Ringing.*")
CAPITOL (4028 "Volare")................. 15-25 58
CAPITOL (4222 "On an Evening in Roma").. 15-25 59
REPRISE (20,116 "Who's Got the Action") 15-20 62

EPs: 7-inch

CAPITOL (EAP-401 "Dean Martin Sings") 25-50 53
(Price is for either of two volumes.)
CAPITOL (EBF-401 "Dean Martin Sings")..75-125 53
(Double EP boxed set.)
CAPITOL (481 "Sunny Italy")............ 25-50 53
CAPITOL (576 "Swingin' Down Yonder")... 20-40 59
(Price is for any of three volumes.)
CAPITOL (701 "Memories Are Made of This")... 25-50 55
CAPITOL (702 "Artists & Models").... 25-50 55
CAPITOL (806 "Hollywood Or Bust")... 25-50 57
CAPITOL (840 "Ten Thousand Bedrooms")...................................... 25-50 57
CAPITOL (849 "Pretty Baby")............. 20-40 58
(Price is for any of three volumes.)
CAPITOL (939 "Return to Me")......... 20-40 58
CAPITOL (1027 "Volare")................. 20-40 58
CAPITOL (1285 "Winter Romance") 20-40 59
(Price is for any of three volumes.)
CAPITOL (1580 "Dean Martin")......... 20-30 61
(Compact Double 33.)
CAPITOL (EAP-1659 "Dino - Italian Love Songs") 15-25 61
CAPITOL (SU-1659 "Dino - Italian Love Songs") 15-25 61
(Juke box issue.)
CAPITOL (DU-2601 "The Best of Dean Martin") 15-25 61
(Juke box issue.)
CAPITOL (9123 "Dean Martin")......... 25-50 54
18 TOP HITS (27 "Dean Martin") 20-40 54-55
(Price for either 45 and 78 rpm EPs.)
LLOYDS (705 "Dean Martin")............ 25-50 54
(Mail-order offer.)
REPRISE... 10-20 62-73
(Juke box 33 compact issues.)

LPs: 10/12-inch

CAPITOL (100 series)........................ 8-15 69
CAPITOL (300 series)........................ 8-15 69
CAPITOL (H-401 "Dean Martin Sings") 50-100 53
(10-inch LP.)
CAPITOL (T-401 "Dean Martin Sings") 25-50 55
(Red cover.)
CAPITOL (TT-401 "Dean Martin Sings") 10-20 59
(Pink cover.)
CAPITOL (523 "Return to Me"/"You're Nobody Till Somebody Loves You") 8-12 70
CAPITOL (576 "Swingin' Down Yonder")... 30-40 55
CAPITOL (849 thru 2601)................. 15-30 57-66
(With "T" or "ST" prefix.)
CAPITOL (849 thru 2601).................. 8-15 63-65
(With "DT" prefix.)
CAPITOL (2815 "Dean Martin Deluxe Set")... 15-25 67
(Boxed, three-disc set.)
CAPITOL (2941 "Favorites") 8-12 68
COSMIC (450 "Dean Martin")........... 15-20
LONGINES (5234 "Memories Are Made of This") 25-50 73
(Boxed, five-disc set. Includes booklet.)
LONGINES (5235 "That's Amore")...... 8-15 73
PAIR 6-10 83
PICKWICK.. 6-12 70s
REPRISE.. 8-18 63-78
S.M.I. 10-20
SEARS 15-25 60s
TALKING BOOK (58007 "Look: December 26, 1967") 15-25 67
(Reading of a Dean interview/story in *Look.* Produced by the American Foundation for the Blind. Plays at 16 2/3 rpm.)
TEE VEE... 10-20 78
TOWER (5006 "The Lush Years").... 20-30 65
TOWER (5018 "Relaxin' ")............... 20-30 66
TOWER (5036 "Happy in Love") 20-30 66
TOWER (5059 "Like Never Before") 20-30 67
WALDORF (27 "Dean Martin Sings")... 50-75 53
(10-inch LP.)
W.B. 5-8 83

Promotional LPs

("Dean Martin Testimonial Dinner") 200-300 59
(Presented by the Friars Club, and sold as a "Collectors Item" for $25 at the dinner. Three LPs in triple pocket jacket. No label name nor selection number used. With guest appearances by Jimmy Durante, Joey Bishop, Tony Martin, George Burns, Dinah Shore, Mort Sahl, Judy Garland; Sammy Cahn, Danny Thomas, Sammy Davis Jr., Bob Hope, Frank Sinatra and others.)
REPRISE (246 "Dean Martin Radio Sampler") 35-50 66
Also see BURNS, George
Also see DURANTE, Jimmy
Also see GARLAND, Judy
Also see GILKYSON, Terry
Also see GOLDDIGGERS
Also see HOPE, Bob
Also see LEE, Peggy, & Dean Martin
Also see MARTIN, Tony
Also see SAHL, Mort
Also see SHORE, Dinah
Also see SINATRA, Frank, Sammy Davis Jr. & Dean Martin
Also see SINATRA, Nancy
Also see THOMAS, Danny
Also see TWITTY, Conway

MARTIN, Dean / Glen Campbell

LPs: 10/12-inch

ZENITH/CAPITOL.............................. 10-20 72
(Issued with paper cover. Special products.)
Also see CAMPBELL, Glen

MARTIN, Dean / Jeff Clark / Arlene James

EPs: 45/78 rpm

POPULAR (1035 "Oh Marie")........... 10-15 54
(78 rpm. Not issued with special cover.)
VICTORY (1031 "Walking My Baby Back Home") 10-15 54
(78 rpm. Not issued with special cover.)
POPULAR (1035 "Oh Marie")........... 10-20 54
(45 rpm. Not issued with special cover.)
VICTORY (1031 "Walking My Baby Back Home") 20-40 54
(45 rpm. Colored vinyl. Not issued with special cover.)

MARTIN, Dean, & Nat "King" Cole

Singles: 78 rpm

CAPITOL.. 4-6 54

Singles: 7-inch

CAPITOL.. 5-10 54
Also see COLE, Nat "King"

MARTIN, Dean / Bob Eberly / Gordon MacRae

LPs: 10/12-inch

BRIGADE (131 "Dino, Gordon & Bob Sing")... 15-25 50s
Also see DORSEY, Jimmy, Orchestra & Chorus
Also see MacRAE, Gordon

MARTIN, Dean / Jane Froman

Singles: 78 rpm

CAPITOL.. 4-6 53

Singles: 7-inch

CAPITOL (20030 "Who's Your Little Who Zis")... 8-15 53
(Promotional issue only.)
Also see FROMAN, Jane

MARTIN, Dean / Jackie Gleason

LPs: 10/12-inch

CAPITOL SPECIAL MARKETS 8-10
Also see GLEASON, Jackie

MARTIN, Dean / Rock Hudson

Singles: 7-inch

NATIONAL FEATURES (2785 "Showdown") 20-30 73
(Interviews with *Showdown* film stars. Promotional issue only. Includes script.)

MARTIN, Dean / Red Ingle & Natural Seven

Singles: 78 rpm

CAPITOL (726 "Vieni Su")................. 8-15 49
(Promotional issue only.)

MARTIN, Dean, & Jerry Lewis

P&R '48

Singles: 78 rpm

CAPITOL (15000 series) 5-10 48
NATIONAL MASK & PUPPET CORP. ("Puppet Show") 10-20 50s
(Promotional issue only.)

EPs: 7-inch

CAPITOL (533 "Living It Up")........ 100-150 54
CAPITOL (752 "Pardners")........... 100-150 56

LPs: 10/12-inch

MEMORABILIA (714 "Dean Martin & Jerry Lewis: First Show") 10-15 74
RADIOLA (1102 "Dean Martin & Jerry Lewis on the Radio") 10-15
Also see LEWIS, Jerry

MARTIN, Dean / Nicolini Lucchesi

LPs: 10/12-inch

AUDITION (5936 "Dean Martin Sings, Niccolini Lucchesi Plays") 25-50 56

MARTIN, Dean / Johnny Mathis / St. James Pop Orchestra

EPs: 7-inch

JIMMY McHUGH (400 "Music by Jimmy McHugh")... 10-15 81
(Promotional issue only.)
Also see MATHIS, Johnny

MARTIN, Dean, & Ricky Nelson

Singles: 7-inch

W.B. (2262 "My Rifle, My Pony and Me") 400-500 59
(Promotional issue only.)
Also see NELSON, Rick

MARTIN, Dean, & Nuggets

Singles: 78 rpm

CAPITOL... 5-10 55

Singles: 7-inch

CAPITOL (3468 "I'm Gonna Steal You Away")... 10-20 55

MARTIN, Dean, & Helen O'Connell

Singles: 78 rpm

CAPITOL 4-6 51

Singles: 7-inch

CAPITOL 5-10 51
Also see O'CONNELL, Helen

MARTIN, Dean / Patti Page

LPs: 10/12-inch

DECCA (79224 "Christmas Seals for 1962").. 30-40 62
(Public service program for TB. Dean's show on one side, Patti's on flip.)
DECCA (79235 "Christmas Seals for 1962") 20-30 62
(Public service program for TB. Dean's and Patti's shows on one side, flip has Si Zenter and Vaughn Monroe.)
Also see MONROE, Vaughn
Also see PAGE, Patti
Also see ZENTER, Si

MARTIN, Dean, & Line Renaud

Singles: 78 rpm

CAPITOL.. 4-6 55

Singles: 7-inch
CAPITOL 5-10 55

MARTIN, Dean / Nelson Riddle
EPs: 7-inch
CAPITOL (1063 "Rio Bravo") 250-350 59
(Promotional only. Has special paper sleeve.)
Also see RIDDLE, Nelson

MARTIN, Dean, & Margaret Whiting
Singles: 78 rpm
CAPITOL 4-6 50
Singles: 7-inch
CAPITOL 5-10 50
Also see MARTIN, Dean
Also see WHITING, Margaret

MARTIN, Derek — P&R/R&B '65
Singles: 7-inch
BUTTERCUP 5-10
CRACKERJACK 8-12 63
ROULETTE 5-10 65
SUE 10-20 66
VOLT 4-8 68

MARTIN, Eric — LP '83
(Eric Martin Band)
Singles: 7-inch
CAPITOL 3-4 85
ELEKTRA 3-4 83
Picture Sleeves
CAPTIOL 3-4 85
LPs: 10/12-inch
ELEKTRA 5-8 83
Also see MR. BIG

MARTIN, Freddy, & Orchestra — P&R '33
Singles: 78 rpm
BLUEBIRD 3-6 38-42
BRUNSWICK 3-6 33-36
RCA 3-5 46-56
VICTOR 3-6 42-45
Singles: 7-inch
CAPITOL 4-6 63
DECCA 4-6 67-68
KAPP 4-6 61
RCA 5-8 50-56
EPs: 7-inch
CAMDEN 5-10 54-56
RCA 5-10 50-54
LPs: 10/12-inch
CAMDEN 10-20 54-56
CAPITOL 5-15 59-79
DECCA 5-10 67
KAPP 5-15 61-66
MCA 4-8 73-75
RCA 8-20 51-72
Also see GRIFFIN, Merv

MARTIN, George, & Orch. — P&R/LP '64
Singles: 7-inch
U.A. (745 "Ringo's Theme") 15-20 64
U.A. (750 "A Hard Day's Night") 75-125 64
U.A. (800 series) 4-8 65
U.A. (50148 "Love in the Open Air") . 20-25 67
Picture Sleeves
U.A. (745 "Ringo's Theme") 75-100 64
U.A. (750 "A Hard Day's Night") 1000-1200 64
Promotional Singles
U.A. (745 "Ringo's Theme") 20-30 64
(White label.)
LPs: 10/12-inch
U.A. (3377 "Off the Beatle Track") 30-40 64
(Monaural.)
U.A. (3383 "A Hard Day's Night") 20-30 64
(Monaural.)
U.A. (3420 "George Martin") 15-25 65
(Monaural.)
U.A. (3448 "Help") 20-30 65
(Monaural.)
U.A. (3539 "The Beatle Girls") 25-35 66
(Monaural.)
Note: Promotional copies of 3383, 3448 & 3539 can be worth twice the above price ranges. We have yet to verify promo copies of the stereo versions, though, if any exist, at least the same increase would apply.
U.A. (6377 "Off the Beatle Track") 30-40 64
(Stereo.)
U.A. (6383 "A Hard Day's Night") 20-30 64
(Stereo.)
U.A. (6420 "George Martin") 15-25 65
(Stereo.)
U.A. (6448 "Help") 20-30 65
(Stereo.)
U.A. (6539 "The Beatle Girls") 25-35 66
(Stereo.)
U.A. (6647 "London by George") 10-15 68
(Stereo.)
Also see BEATLES
Also see GERRY & PACEMAKERS

MARTIN, Janis — P&R '56
Singles: 78 rpm
RCA (Except 6652) 8-15 56-57
RCA (6652 "My Boy Elvis") 10-20 56
Singles: 7-inch
BIG DUTCH 3-5 77
PALETTE (5071 "Teen Street") 5-10 61
RCA (6400 & 6500 series) 15-25 56
RCA (6652 "My Boy Elvis") 25-35 56
RCA (6700 thru 7300 series) 10-20 56-58
Promotional Singles
BIG DUTCH 4-6 77
PALETTE (5071 "Teen Street") 10-20 61
RCA (6400 & 6500 series) 20-40 56
RCA (6652 "My Boy Elvis") 35-45 56
RCA (6700 thru 7300 series) 20-40 56-58
EPs: 7-inch
RCA (4093 "Just Squeeze Me") 75-100 58

MARTIN, Janis / Otto Bash
EPs: 7-inch
RCA (38 "Dealer's Prevue") 50-75 56
(Promotional issue only.)

MARTIN, Janis / Hank Snow
EPs: 7-inch
RCA (76 "Love Me to Pieces") 25-50 56
(Promotional issue only.)
Also see MARTIN, Janis
Also see SNOW, Hank

MARTIN, Kenny — R&B '58
Singles: 7-inch
BIG TOP (3053 "Lovin' Man") 10-20 60
FEDERAL (12310 "I'm the Jivin' Mr. Lee") 50-75 57
FEDERAL (12330 "I'm Sorry") 25-50 58
FEDERAL (12350 "Now I Know") 25-50 59
FEDERAL (12354 "My Wish") 15-25 59
FEDERAL (12362 "Ask Me") 100-200 59
FEDERAL (12379 "Last Words of the Jivin' Mr. Lee") 15-25 60
PJ 5-10 66

MARTIN, Marilyn — P&R/LP '86
Singles: 7-inch
ATLANTIC 3-4 86-88
Picture Sleeves
ATLANTIC 3-4 86-88
LPs: 10/12-inch
ATLANTIC 5-8 86-88
Also see COLLINS, Phil, & Marilyn Martin

MARTIN, Moon — P&R/LP '79
(John Martin)
Singles: 7-inch
CAPITOL 3-5 78-79
LPs: 10/12-inch
CAPITOL 5-10 78-82
Member: Jude Cole.
Also see COLE, Jude

MARTIN, Nancy — R&B '82
Singles: 7-inch
ATLANTIC 3-4 82

MARTIN, Paul — R&B '65
Singles: 7-inch
ASCOT 8-12 65
IMPEX 5-10 66

MARTIN, Ray, Orchestra — LP '61
Singles: 7-inch
RCA 3-6 61-62
U.A. 4-8 58
Picture Sleeves
RCA 4-8 61
U.A. 5-10 58
LPs: 10/12-inch
CAMDEN 5-10 67-70
LONDON 8-12 63
MONUMENT 5-10 67
RCA 10-15 61

MARTIN, Steve — P&R/LP '77
(With Toot Uncommons)
Singles: 7-inch
W.B. 3-5 77-79
Picture Sleeves
W.B. 3-5 77-78
LPs: 10/12-inch
W.B. 5-10 77-81

MARTIN, Tony — P&R '38
Singles: 78 rpm
BRUNSWICK 4-8 38
DECCA 3-6 39-42
MERCURY 3-6 46-50s
RCA 3-6 47-57
Singles: 7-inch
CHART 3-5 70
DOT 4-6 61-66
DUNHILL 3-6 67
MERCURY 5-10 50s
MOTOWN 5-10 64-66
NAN 4-6 64
PARK AVENUE 4-6 63
RCA 5-10 50-60
EPs: 7-inch
DECCA 5-10 51-56
MERCURY 5-10 54-56
RCA 5-10 51-57
LPs: 10/12-inch
CAMDEN 10-20 59-60
CHART 5-10 70
CHARTER 10-15 63
CORAL 5-8 73
DECCA 15-25 51-56
DOT 10-15 61-62
MERCURY 10-20 54-61
RCA 15-25 51-60
20TH FOX 10-15 64
WING 10-15 59-60
Also see MARTIN, Dean
Also see SHORE, Dinah, Tony Martin, Betty Hutton & Phil Harris

MARTIN, Trade — P&R '62
Singles: 7-inch
COED (Except 594) 8-15 62-64
COED (594 "Joanne") 30-50 64
GEE 10-15 59
RCA 4-8 66-67
ROULETTE 5-10 60
STALLION 4-6
TOOT 4-6 68
LPs: 10/12-inch
BUDDAH 10-15 72

MARTIN, Vince — P&R '56
(With the Tarriers; with Fred Neil)
Singles: 78 rpm
GLORY 5-10 56
Singles: 7-inch
ABC-PAR 5-10 59
GLORY 10-15 56
ELEKTRA 4-8 64
LPs: 10/12-inch
CAPITOL 5-10 73
ELEKTRA 10-20 64
Also see TARRIERS

MARTINDALE, Wink — P&R/C&W '59
Singles: 7-inch
ABC/DOT 3-5 76
DOT 5-10 58-66
RANWOOD 3-5 73
Picture Sleeves
DOT 10-20 59-60
LPs: 10/12-inch
DOT 15-25 59-66

HAMILTON 10-20 64

MARTINDALE, Wink, & Robin Ward

Singles: 7–inch

DOT 4-8 63-64

LPs: 10/12–inch

DOT 15-25 64

Also see MARTINDALE, Wink
Also see WARD, Robin

MARTINE, Layng P&R '71

(Layng Martine Jr.)

Singles: 7–inch

BARNABY 3-5 71
DATE 5-10 66
GENERAL INT'L 4-8 66
PLAYBOY 3-5 76

Also see MORRISON, Professor

MARTINEZ, Nancy P&R '86

Singles: 12–inch

ATLANTIC 4-6 86

Singles: 7–inch

ATLANTIC 3-4 86-87

LPs: 10/12–inch

ATLANTIC 5-8 86

MARTINO, Al P&R '52

Singles: 78 rpm

BBS 5-10 52
CAPITOL 3-5 52-57

Singles: 7–inch

BBS (101 "Here in My Heart") 10-15 52
(Black vinyl.)
BBS (101 "Here in My Heart") 15-25 52
(Colored vinyl.)
CAPITOL (Except F-2122 thru F-4593) 3-8 62-81
CAPITOL (F-2122 thru F-4593) 5-15 52-61
JUBILEE (6000 series) 10-15 53
(Colored vinyl.)
MAZE (7025 "There's No Tomorrow") 5-10 62
20TH FOX 5-10 59-64

Picture Sleeves

CAPITOL 5-10 63-66
MAZE (7025 "There's No Tomorrow") 8-12 62

EPs: 7–inch

CAPITOL 10-15 63-64
(Juke box issues & Compact 33s.)

LPs: 10/12–inch

CAPITOL 5-20 62-80
GUEST STAR 5-10 64
MOVIETONE 5-10 67
SPRINGBOARD 5-8 78
20TH FOX 10-20 59-65

MARVELETTES P&R/R&B '61

Singles: 7–inch

MOTOWN 3-4
MOTOWN/TOPPS (12 "Please Mr. Postman") 50-75 67
(Topps Chewing Gum promotional item. Single-sided, cardboard flexi, picture disc. Issued with generic paper sleeve.)
TAMLA (54046 thru 54088) 6-12 61-63
TAMLA (54091 "He's a Good Guy [Yes He Is]") 6-12 64
(With subtitle.)
TAMLA (54091 "Yes He Is") 40-60 64
(No subtitle. Single-sided. Promotional issue only.)
TAMLA (54097 thru 54198) 5-10 64-71
(Black vinyl.)
TAMLA 8-12 69
(Colored vinyl. Promotional issues only.)

Picture Sleeves

TAMLA (54046 "Please Mr. Postman") 20-30 61
TAMLA (54054 "Twistin' Postman") ..20-30 62
TAMLA (54097 "You're My Remedy") 15-25 64

EPs: 7–inch

MOTOWN (2003 "Marvelettes") 15-25 60s
TAMLA (60253 "Greatest Hits") 15-25 66
TAMLA (60274 "Marvelettes") 15-25 67

LPs: 10/12–inch

MOTOWN (Except 100 series) 10-15 75
MOTOWN (100 series) 5-8 82
TAMLA (228 "Please Mr. Postman") 150-250 61
TAMLA (229 "Marvelettes Sing Smash Hits of '62") 500-750 62
TAMLA (229 The Marvelettes Sing") 50-100 62
(Reissue with shorter title)
TAMLA (231 "Playboy") 50-100 62
TAMLA (237 "Marvelous Marveletes") 50-100 63
TAMLA (243 "On Stage") 50-75 63
TAMLA (253 "Greatest Hits") 15-20 66
TAMLA (274 "The Marvelettes") 15-20 67
TAMLA (286 thru 305) 10-20 68-70

Members: Gladys Horton; Kathy Anderson; Georgeanna Tillman; Wanda Young; Juanita Cowart; Ann Bogan.

Also see THEM / Marvelettes

MARVELETTES / Mary Wells / Miracles / Marvin Gaye

Singles: 7–inch

TAMLA/MOTOWN ("Album Excerpts") 30-40 63
(Though from Tamla/Motown, no label name is shown, nor is there a title. Promotional issue only.)

Also see GAYE, Marvin
Also see MARVELETTES
Also see MIRACLES
Also see WELLS, Mary

MARVELOWS P&R/R&B '65

(Mighty Marvelows)

Singles: 7–inch

ABC 4-8 66-69
ABC-PAR 8-10 64-66

LPs: 10/12–inch

ABC 15-20 68

Members: Melvin Mason; Frank Paden; Johnny Paden; Jesse Smith; Sonny Stevenson; Andrew Thomas.

MARVIN & JOHNNY R&B '53

Singles: 78 rpm

ALADDIN 10-20 56
MODERN 15-30 54-56
RAYS 10-20 54
SPECIALTY 15-25 53-55

Singles: 7–inch

ALADDIN 15-25 56
ERIC 3-4 70s
FELSTED 4-8 63
FIREFLY 10-15 60
JAMIE 5-10 61
KENT (303 "Cherry Pie") 10-20 58
LIBERTY 3-5 80
MODERN 20-40 54-56
RAYS 15-25 54
SPECIALTY (Except 479) 25-50 53-55
SPECIALTY (479 "Baby Doll") 35-50 53
(Black vinyl.)
SPECIALTY (479 "Baby Doll") 50-80 53
(Colored vinyl.)
SWINGIN 8-12 61

LPs: 10/12–inch

CROWN (5381 "Marvin & Johnny") .. 35-55 63

Members: Marvin Phillips; Johnny Dean.

Also see ISLEY BROTHERS / Marvin & Johnny
Also see JESSE & MARVIN

MARX, Groucho LP '72

Singles: 78 rpm

DECCA 4-8 51
YOUNG PEOPLE'S RECORDS 3-6 54

Singles: 7–inch

A&M 3-5 73
DECCA 10-20 51
YOUNG PEOPLE'S RECORDS 5-10 54

LPs: 10/12–inch

A&M (3515 "An Evening with Groucho") 5-10 72
A&M (PR-3515 "An Evening with Groucho") 15-20 78
(Picture disc. Includes booklet. Limited numbered edition.)
DECCA (5405 "Horray for Captain Spaulding") 100-150
(10–inch LP.)

Also see KAYE, Danny, Jimmy Durante, Jane Wyman & Groucho Marx
Also see MARX BROTHERS

MARX, Richard P&R/LP '87

Singles: 7–inch

EMI 3-4 88-90
EMI/MANHATTAN 3-4 88
MANHATTAN 3-4 87

Picture Sleeves

EMI 3-4 89
EMI/MANHATTAN 3-4 88
MANHATTAN 3-4 87

LPs: 10/12–inch

CAPITOL 5-8 91-92
EMI 5-8 89
EMI/MANHATTAN 5-8 88
MANHATTAN 5-10 87

Also see SCHMIT, Timothy B.
Also see WAYBILL, Fee

MARX BROTHERS LP '69

LPs: 10/12–inch

DECCA (9169 "Marx Brothers") 8-12 69
(With Gary Owens.)

Also see MARX, Groucho

MARY JANE GIRLS R&B/D&D/LP '83

Singles: 12–inch

GORDY 4-6 83-85
MOTOWN 4-6 85-87

Singles: 7–inch

GORDY 3-4 83-87
MOTOWN 3-4 85-87

Picture Sleeves

GORDY 3-4 85
MOTOWN 3-4 86

LPs: 10/12–inch

GORDY 5-8 83-87

Members: Joane "Jo Jo" McDuffie; Candice "Candy" Ghant; Kim "Maxi" Wuletich; Yvette "Corvette" Marine.

MAS, Carolyn P&R/LP '79

Singles: 7–inch

MERCURY 3-5 79

LPs: 10/12–inch

MERCURY 5-10 79

MASCARA D&D '84

Singles: 12–inch

OH MY 4-6 84

MASEKELA, Hugh P&R/LP '67

(With the Union of South Africa)

Singles: 12–inch

JIVE AFRIKA 4-6 84

Singles: 7–inch

BLUE THUMB 3-5 74
CASABLANCA 3-5 75-77
CHISA 3-6 67-71
JIVE AFRIKA 3-4 84
MGM 3-6 66-68
MERCURY 3-8 63-68
UNI 3-6 67-69

LPs: 10/12–inch

BLUE THUMB 5-10 72-74
CASABLANCA 5-10 75-77
CHISA 8-15 67-71
IMPULSE 5-10 78
MGM 8-15 66-68
MERCURY 8-18 63-67
UNI 8-12 67-69
UPFRONT 5-8 77
VERVE 8-15 68
WING 6-12 68

Also see ALPERT, Herb, & Hugh Masekela

MASHMAKHAN P&R '70

Singles: 7–inch

EPIC 3-6 70
JAMIE 4-8 69

LPs: 10/12-inch
EPIC 10-12 70-71
Members: Puerre Senecal; Jerry Mercer; Ray Blake; Brian Edwards.
Also see APRIL WINE

MASKED MARAUDERS LP '70
Singles: 7-inch
DEITY 5-8 69
LPs: 10/12-inch
DEITY (6378 "Masked Marauders") .. 15-20 69

MASKMAN & AGENTS R&B '68
Singles: 7-inch
DYNAMO 4-8 68-69
GAMMA 4-8 68
HITBOUND 3-5
LOOP 10-15 72
MUSICOR 3-5 70
VIGOR (707 "Stand Up") 5-10
LPs: 10/12-inch
DYNAMO 10-15 69
MUSICOR 10-15 70
Members: Harmon Bethea; Paul Williams; John Hood; Ty Gray.
Also see BETHEA, Harmon

MASON R&B '87
Singles: 7-inch
ELEKTRA 3-4 87

MASON, Barbara P&R/R&B/LP '65
(With the Futures)
Singles: 12-inch
WEST END 4-8 83-84
Singles: 7-inch
ARCTIC 4-8 64-68
BUDDAH 3-5 71-75
CHARGER 4-8 65
NATIONAL GENERAL 3-5 70
PHONORAMA 3-5 84
PRELUDE 3-5 78
WMOT 3-5 80-81
WEST END 3-5 83-84
LPs: 10/12-inch
ARCTIC 15-25 65-68
BUDDAH 8-12 72-75
GNC 10-15 70
NATIONAL GENERAL 10-15 70
PHONORAMA 5-8 84
PRELUDE 8-10 78
WMOT 8-10 81
W.B. 8-12 77
WIND 8-10 81
Also see FUTURES
Also see HIGGINS, Monk

MASON, Barbara, & Larks
Singles: 7-inch
CRUSADER (114 "Dedicated to You") 8-12 64
Also see LARKS

MASON, Barbara, & Bunny Sigler
Singles: 7-inch
W.B. 3-5 77
Also see MASON, Barbara
Also see SIGLER, Bunny

MASON, Bonnie Jo
(Cher)
Singles: 7-inch
ANNETTE (1000 "Ringo, I Love You") 500-1000 64
Also see CHER

MASON, Dave P&R/LP '70
Singles: 7-inch
ABC 3-5 74
BLUE THUMB 3-5 70-78
COLUMBIA 3-5 73-81
MARBLE 3-4 83
LPs: 10/12-inch
ABC 8-10 75
BLUE THUMB (19 "Alone Together") 10-12 70
(Black vinyl.)
BLUE THUMB (19 "Alone Together") 20-25 70
(Colored vinyl.)
BLUE THUMB (34 thru 54) 10-15 72-73
BLUE THUMB (800 series) 8-10 75
BLUE THUMB (6000 series) 8-10 74-78
COLUMBIA (Black vinyl) 8-10 73-81
COLUMBIA (Colored vinyl) 10-15 73-81
(Promotional issue only.)
ISLAND 5-8 83
Also see MERRYWEATHER, Neil
Also see TRAFFIC

MASON, Dave, & Cass Elliot LP '71
Singles: 7-inch
DUNHILL 3-4 70-71
LPs: 10/12-inch
BLUE THUMB 12-15 71
Also see ELLIOT, Cass
Also see MASON, Dave

MASON, Harvey R&B '76
Singles: 7-inch
ARISTA 3-5 76-81
LPs: 10/12-inch
ARISTA 5-10 78-81

MASON, Jackie LP '62
Singles: 7-inch
VERVE 3-6 62
EPs: 7-inch
VERVE (5076 "The Greatest Comedian in the World, Only Nobody Knows It") 5-10 62
(Promotional issue only.)
LPs: 10/12-inch
VERVE 8-18 62-64
W.B. 5-8 87

MASON, Nick LP '81
(Nick Mason's Fictitious Sports)
Singles: 12-inch
COLUMBIA 4-6 85
Singles: 7-inch
COLUMBIA 3-5 81-85
LPs: 10/12-inch
COLUMBIA 5-8 81-85
Also see PINK FLOYD

MASON, Nick, & Rick Fenn LP '85
Singles: 7-inch
COLUMBIA 3-4 85
LPs: 10/12-inch
COLUMBIA 5-8 85
Also see MASON, Nick

MASON, Vaughan P&R/R&B '80
(With the Crew)
Singles: 12-inch
BRUNSWICK 4-6 80-81
LPs: 10/12-inch
BRUNSWICK 5-8 80
Also see AM-FM

MASON, Vaughan, & Butch Dayo R&B '81
Singles: 12-inch
SALSOUL 4-6 83
Singles: 7-inch
SALSOUL 3-4 82-83
LPs: 10/12-inch
SALSOUL 5-8 83
Also see MASON, Vaughan

MASON DIXON DANCE BAND R&B '79
Singles: 7-inch
ALEXANDER STREET 3-5 79

MASON PROFFIT LP '71
Singles: 7-inch
AMPEX 3-5 71
HAPPY TIGER 4-6 70
LPs: 10/12-inch
AMPEX 8-10 71
HAPPY TIGER 8-12 70-71
W.B. 8-10 72-73
Members: John Talbot; Terry Talbot.

MASQUERADERS P&R/R&B '68
Singles: 7-inch
ABC 3-5 75-76
AMERICAN GROUP 3-5 69
BANG 3-4 80
BELL 4-8 68
HI 3-5 75
HOT BUTTERED SOUL 3-5 75-76
MK (101 "Man's Temptation") 10-15 60s
STAIRWAY 10-20 60s
TOWER 4-8 66
WAND (1168 "Let's Face Facts") 15-25 67
WAND (1172 "Sweet Lovin' Woman") 25-35 67
LPs: 10/12-inch
ABC 8-10 75
Members: Lee Hatim; Robert Wrightsil; David Sanders; Harold Thomas; Sam Hutchins.
Also see LARKS / Masqueraders

MASS PRODUCTION P&R/R&B/LP '77
Singles: 7-inch
COTILLION 3-5 76-83
LPs: 10/12-inch
COTILLION 5-8 76-83
Members: Larry Marshall; Tiny Kelly; Ricardo Williams; Greg McCoy; James Drumgole; Lecoy Bryant; Kevin Douglas; Tyrone Williams; Emmanuel Redding; Samuel Williams.

MASSER, Michael, & Mandrill R&B '77
Singles: 7-inch
ARISTA 3-5 77
Picture Sleeves
ARISTA 3-5 77
Also see MANDRILL

MASSEY, Wayne P&R '80
Singles: 7-inch
MCA 3-4 83
MERCURY 3-4 89
POLYDOR 3-5 80

MASSIAH, Maurice D&D '83
Singles: 12-inch
RFC/QUALITY 4-6 83

MASTER OF CEREMONY Featuring Don Barron R&B '87
Singles: 7-inch
4TH & BROADWAY 3-4 87-88
LPs: 10/12-inch
4TH & BROADWAY 3-4 88

MASTERDON COMMITTEE R&B '86
Singles: 12-inch
PROFILE 4-6 86-87
Singles: 7-inch
PROFILE 3-4 86-87
LPs: 10/12-inch
PROFILE 5-8 86

MASTERPIECE R&B '80
Singles: 7-inch
WHITFIELD 3-5 80
LPs: 10/12-inch
WHITFIELD 5-10 80

MASTERS, Johnny
(Johnny Maestro)
Singles: 7-inch
COED (527 "Say It Isn't So") 15-20 60
Also see MAESTRO, Johnny

MASTERS, Sammy P&R '60
Singles: 78 rpm
DECCA 8-12 57
4 STAR 25-50 57
Singles: 7-inch
DECCA 8-12 57
DOT 5-10 60-66
4 STAR (1695 "Pink Cadillac") 30-50 57
4 STAR (1697 "Whop-T-Bop") 30-50 57
GALAHAD 4-8 62-72
KAPP 4-8 64
LODE 5-10 60-61
TJB BRANDES 5-10

W.B. 5-10 60
EPs: 7-inch
4 STAR (26 "Sammy Masters") 50-75 57
(Promotional issue only. Not issued with cover.)

MATERIAL ISSUE LP '91
LPs: 10/12-inch
MERCURY 5-8 91

MATHEWS, Tobin P&R '60
(Tobin Mathews & Co.; Tobin Matthews)
Singles: 7-inch
CHIEF 8-12 60-61
COLUMBIA 4-8 63
U.S.A. (718 "Think It Over") 10-20 61

MATHIEU, Mireille LP '69
LPs: 10/12-inch
CAPITOL 8-12 69

MATHIS, Johnny P&R/R&B/LP '57
(With Ray Conniff)
Singles: 78 rpm
COLUMBIA 15-30 57-58
Singles: 7-inch
AURAVISION (6726 "Starbright") 8-12 64
(Cardboard flexi-disc, one of six by six different artists. Columbia Record Club "Enrollment Premium." Set came in a special paper sleeve.)
COLUMBIA (Except 40000 series) 3-5 74-85
COLUMBIA (40784 thru 42916) 5-15 58-63
COLUMBIA (44266 thru 46048) 3-8 67-74
MERCURY 4-8 63-66
Picture Sleeves
COLUMBIA (40993 "Chances Are") .. 10-20 57
COLUMBIA (41060 thru 42799) 5-10 58-63
MERCURY 4-8 63-66
EPs: 7-inch
COLUMBIA (Except 8800 series) 10-20 57-59
COLUMBIA (8871 thru 8873) 15-25 56
LPs: 10/12-inch
COLUMBIA (Except 887) 5-15 57-87
COLUMBIA (887 "Johnny Mathis") 35-50 56
COLUMBIA HOUSE (6030 "Johnny Mathis") 15-25 73
(Boxed 6-disc set. Record club offer.)
COLUMBIA SPECIAL PRODUCTS 5-8
CONCERT 8-12
(TV mail-order offer.)
HARMONY 5-10
MFSL (171 "Heavenly") 20-30 85
MERCURY 8-15 64-67
Also see CONNIFF, Ray
Also see FAITH, Percy, Orchestra / Johnny Mathis
Also see KNIGHT, Gladys, & Johnny Mathis
Also see NELSON, Willie / Nat "King" Cole / Johnny Mathis / Shirley Bassey

MATHIS, Johnny, & Henry Mancini LP '87
LPs: 10/12-inch
COLUMBIA 5-8 87
Also see MANCINI, Henry

MATHIS, Johnny, & Dionne Warwick P&R '82
Singles: 7-inch
ARISTA 3-5 82
Also see WARWICK, Dionne

MATHIS, Johnny, & Deniece Williams P&R/R&B/LP '78
Singles: 7-inch
COLUMBIA 3-5 78-84
LPs: 10/12-inch
COLUMBIA (35435 "That's What Friends Are For") 15-25 78
(Picture disc. Promotional issue only.)
COLUMBIA (35435 "That's What Friends Are For") 5-10 78
(Standard vinyl disc.)
Also see MATHIS, Johnny
Also see WILLIAMS, Deniece

MATHIS, Kathy R&B '87
Singles: 7-inch
TABU 3-4 87

MATLOCK, Ronn R&B '79
Singles: 7-inch
COTILLION 3-5 79

MATTHEWS, David LP '77
LPs: 10/12-inch
CTI 5-10 77
Also see WASHINGTON, Grover, Jr.

MATTHEWS, Ian LP '72
Singles: 7-inch
DECCA 3-5 70-71
COLUMBIA 3-5 76-77
ELEKTRA 3-5 73
MUSHROOM 3-5 78-79
VERTIGO 3-5 71-72
LPs: 10/12-inch
CAPITOL 8-10 71
COLUMBIA 8-10 77
DECCA 8-12 71
ELEKTRA 8-10 73-74
MUSHROOM (Except 5012) 8-10 78
MUSHROOM (5012 "Stealin' Home") 10-20 78
(Picture disc. Promotional issue only.)
MUSHROOM (5012 "Stealin' Home") 8-10 78
(Standard vinyl disc.)
VERTIGO 10-12 71-72
Also see FAIRPORT CONVENTION
Also see HI FI Featuring David Surkamp & Ian Matthews
Also see MATTHEWS' SOUTHERN COMFORT

MATTHEWS, Milt R&B '78
Singles: 7-inch
H&L 3-5 78

MATTHEWS, Tobin: see MATHEWS, Tobin

MATTHEWS' SOUTHERN COMFORT
(Featuring Ian Matthews) P&R/LP '71
Singles: 7-inch
DECCA 3-5 71
LPs: 10/12-inch
DECCA 10-15 70-71
MCA 5-10 78
Also see MATTHEWS, Ian
Also see SOUTHERN COMFORT

MATYS BROTHERS P&R '63
Singles: 78 rpm
CORAL (61941 "Crazy Street") 20-40 57
ESSEX 3-6 54
Singles: 7-inch
BEE-BEE 5-10
CORAL (61941 "Crazy Street") 25-50 57
ESSEX 5-10 54
SELECT 5-10 62
SOUND 5-10

MAUDS P&R '68
Singles: 7-inch
DUNWICH 5-10 67
MERCURY 4-8 67-69
RCA 3-6 70
LPs: 10/12-inch
MERCURY 15-25 67

MAURIAT, Paul LP '67
Singles: 7-inch
PHILIPS 3-5 67-71
Picture Sleeves
PHILIPS 3-5 68
LPs: 10/12-inch
PHILIPS 8-18 67-71

MAURICE & RADIANTS: see RADIANTS

MAX Q LP '89
LPs: 10/12-inch
ATLANTIC 5-8 89

MAXAYN R&B '73
Singles: 7-inch
CAPRICORN 3-5 72-74
LPs: 10/12-inch
CAPRICORN 8-10 72-74
Members: Maxayn Lewis; Andre Lewis; Emilio Thomas; Marlo Henderson.
Also see IKETTES
Also see MANDRE

MAXIM TRIO R&B '49
(Maxin Trio)
Singles: 78 rpm
DOWNBEAT (171 "Confession Blues") 40-60 49
Members: Ray Charles; G.D. McGhee; Milton Garred.
Also see CHARLES, Ray

MAXWELL, Diane P&R '59
Singles: 7-inch
CAPITOL 4-8 61
CHALLENGE 5-10 59
LPs: 10/12-inch
CHALLENGE (607 "Almost Seventeen") 30-40 59
(Monaural.)
CHALLENGE (2501 "Almost Seventeen") 40-60 59
(Stereo.)
Also see FULLER, Jerry, & Diane Maxwell

MAXWELL, Robert P&R/LP '64
(Bobby Maxwell)
Singles: 78 rpm
MGM 3-5 57
MERCURY 3-5 52
TEMPO 3-5 51-52
Singles: 7-inch
DECCA 3-5 64
MGM 4-6 57
MERCURY 5-10 52
TEMPO 5-10 51-52
EPs: 7-inch
MGM 4-8 57
MERCURY 5-10 52
TEMPO 5-10 51-52
LPs: 10/12-inch
COMMAND 5-10 60s
DECCA 5-10 64
MGM 10-15 57
TEMPO 10-20 52

MAY, Billy, & His Orchestra P&R '52
Singles: 78 rpm
CAPITOL 3-5 50-56
Singles: 7-inch
CAPITOL 5-10 50-56
EPs: 7-inch
CAPITOL 5-10 50-56
LPs: 10/12-inch
CAPITOL 8-18 50-56

MAY, Brian LP '83
(Brian May & Friends)
Singles: 7-inch
CAPITOL 3-4 83
LPs: 10/12-inch
CAPITOL 5-8 83
Also see QUEEN
Also see REO SPEEDWAGON
Also see VAN HALEN

MAYALL, John LP '68
(With the Blues Breakers Featuring Eric Clapton)
Singles: 7-inch
ABC 3-5 76
IMMEDIATE 4-8 67
LONDON 5-10 66-68
POLYDOR 3-8 69-74
LPs: 10/12-inch
ABC 8-12 76-78
BLUE THUMB 8-12 74
DJM 8-12 79
ISLAND 5-8 90
LONDON 10-15 67-78
MCA 5-8
MFSL (183 "Bluesbreakers Featuring Eric Clapton") 25-35 85
MFSL (246 "Blues Alone") 20-25 95
POLYDOR 10-12 69-74
Also see BRUCE, Jack

Also see CLAPTON, Eric
Also see FLEETWOOD MAC
Also see HARTLEY, Keef, Band
Also see TAYLOR, Mick

MAYANA D&D '83

Singles: 12-inch

ATLANTIC ... 4-6 83

Singles: 7-inch

ATLANTIC ... 3-4 83

MAYER, Nathaniel P&R/R&B '62
(With the Fabulous Twilights; with Fortune Braves)

Singles: 7-inch

FORTUNE (449 "Village of Love") ... 10-15 62
FORTUNE (487 "Hurting Love") ... 15-25 62
FORTUNE (500 series) ... 10-20 62-69
U.A. ... 5-10 62

LPs: 10/12-inch

FORTUNE (8014 "Goin' Back to the Village of Love") ... 40-50 64

MAYFIELD, Curtis P&R/R&B/LP '70

Singles: 7-inch

ARISTA ... 3-4 89
BOARDWALK ... 3-5 81-82
CRC ... 3-4 85
CURTOM ... 3-5 70-80
RSO ... 3-5 80

Picture Sleeves

ARISTA ... 3-4 89
CURTOM ... 3-5 71-78

LPs: 10/12-inch

ABC ... 10-20 73
BOARDWALK ... 5-10 81-82
CURTOM ... 8-12 70-78
RSO ... 5-10 79-80
Also see IMPRESSIONS
Also see REED, Jimmy

MAYFIELD, Curtis, & Linda Clifford R&B '79

Singles: 7-inch

CURTOM ... 3-5 79-80

LPs: 10/12-inch

RSO ... 5-10 80
Also see CLIFFORD, Linda
Also see MAYFIELD, Curtis

MAYFIELD, Percy P&R/R&B '50

Singles: 78 rpm

CHESS (1599 "Double Dealing") ... 25-50 55
KING (4480 "Two Years of Torture") 15-25 51
RECORDED in HOLLYWOOD ("Two Years of Torture") ... 25-35 51
(First issue. Selection number not known.)
SPECIALTY ... 10-30 50-57

Singles: 7-inch

ATLANTIC ... 3-5 74
BRUNSWICK ... 5-10 68
CHESS (1599 "Double Dealing") ... 50-100 55
IMPERIAL (5577 "One Love") ... 15-25 59
KING (4480 "Two Years of Torture") ... 50-100 51
RCA ... 4-6 70
SPECIALTY (375 "Please Send Me Someone to Love") ... 40-60 50
SPECIALTY (390 "Lost Love") ... 40-60 51
SPECIALTY (400 "Nightless Lover") ... 40-60 51
SPECIALTY (408 "My Blues") ... 40-60 51
SPECIALTY (416 "Cry Baby") ... 40-60 52
SPECIALTY (425 "Big Question") ... 40-60 52
SPECIALTY (432 "Louisiana") ... 40-60 52
SPECIALTY (439 "My Heart") ... 40-60 53
SPECIALTY (451 "I Dare You, Baby") ... 40-60 54
SPECIALTY (460 "Lonely One") ... 40-60 54
(Black vinyl.)
SPECIALTY (460 "Lonely One") ... 100-200 54
(Colored vinyl.)
SPECIALTY (473 "How Deep Is the Well") ... 40-60 54
(Black vinyl.)
SPECIALTY (473 "How Deep Is the Well") ... 100-200 54
(Colored vinyl.)
SPECIALTY (485 "I Need You So Bad") ... 40-60 54
SPECIALTY (499 "You Don't Exist No More ... 40-60 55
SPECIALTY (537 "You Were Lyin' to Me") ... 25-50 55
SPECIALTY (607 "Please Believe Me") ... 20-30 57
SPECIALTY (690 "What Must I Do") 15-25 60
TANGERINE ... 5-15 62-67

LPs: 10/12-inch

BRUNSWICK ... 10-20 69
RCA ... 10-15 70-71
SPECIALTY ... 8-12 70
TANGERINE ... 15-25 66-67

MAZARATI R&B/LP '86

Singles: 12-inch

PAISLEY PARK ... 4-6 86

Singles: 7-inch

PAISLEY PARK ... 3-4 86

LPs: 10/12-inch

PAISLEY PARK ... 5-8 86
Member: Casey Terry; Brown Mark.
Also see BROWNMARK

MAZE P&R/R&B/LP '77
(Featuring Frankie Beverly)

Singles: 12-inch

CAPITOL ... 4-6 84

Singles: 7-inch

CAPITOL ... 3-5 77-86

Picture Sleeves

CAPITOL ... 3-5 81-85

LPs: 10/12-inch

CAPITOL ... 5-10 78-86
W.B. ... 5-8 89

MBULU, Letta R&B/LP '77

Singles: 7-inch

A&M ... 3-5 77

LPs: 10/12-inch

A&M ... 5-10 77

McANALLY, Mac P&R '77

Singles: 7-inch

ARIOLA ... 3-5 78
ARIOLA AMERICA ... 3-5 77
MCA ... 3-4 92
W.B. ... 3-4 90

LPs: 10/12-inch

ARIOLA AMERICA ... 5-10 78

McBRIDE & RIDE LP '91

Singles: 7-inch

MCA ... 3-4 91-92

LPs: 10/12-inch

MCA ... 5-8 91-92
Members: Terry McBride; Billy Thomas; Ray Herndon; Kenny Vaughn; Keith Edwards.

McCALL, Al R&B '83

Singles: 7-inch

PROFILE ... 3-4 83

McCALL, C.W. C&W/P&R '74

Singles: 7-inch

MGM ... 3-5 74-75
POLYDOR ... 3-5 76-79

LPs: 10/12-inch

MGM ... 5-10 75
POLYDOR ... 5-8 76-79

McCALL, Cash R&B '66

Singles: 7-inch

CHECKER ... 4-8 67
COLUMBIA ... 3-5 76-77
EXECUTIVE ... 4-6 60s
M-PAC ... 4-8 64
PAULA ... 3-5 75
RONN ... 3-5 75
THOMAS ... 4-8 66

McCALL, Toussaint P&R/R&B '67

Singles: 7-inch

COLLECTABLES ... 3-4 80s
RONN ... 4-8 67-68

LPs: 10/12-inch

RONN ... 10-12 67
Also see NEVILLE, Aaron / Toussaint McCall

McCALLUM, David LP '66

Singles: 7-inch

CAPITOL ... 4-8 66

Picture Sleeves

CAPITOL ... 5-10 66

LPs: 10/12-inch

CAPITOL ... 10-15 66

McCANN, Les LP '69

Singles: 7-inch

ATLANTIC ... 3-5 69-75
LIMELIGHT ... 4-6 65
PACIFIC JAZZ ... 4-8 60-65
WORLD PACIFIC ... 3-6 60s

LPs: 10/12-inch

ATLANTIC ... 5-10 69-75
LIMELIGHT ... 10-20 65
PACIFIC JAZZ ... 15-25 60-65
Also see FLACK, Roberta
Also see HOLMES, Richard "Groove," & Les McCann
Also see JAZZ CRUSADERS
Also see RAWLS, Lou, & Les McCann Ltd.

McCANN, Les, & Eddie Harris LP '69

Singles: 7-inch

ATLANTIC ... 3-5 69-70

LPs: 10/12-inch

ATLANTIC ... 5-10 69-71
Also see HARRIS, Eddie
Also see McCANN, Les

McCANN, Peter P&R/LP '77

Singles: 7-inch

COLUMBIA ... 3-5 79
20TH FOX ... 3-5 77

LPs: 10/12-inch

20TH FOX ... 8-10 77

McCARTNEY, Paul LP '70
(Wings; with Wings; with Linda McCartney)

Singles: 12-inch

CAPITOL (15212 "Spies Like Us") ... 10-20 85
CAPITOL (15235 "Press") ... 8-12 86
CAPITOL (15499 "Oul Est Le Soleil") ... 8-12 89
COLUMBIA (03019 "Take It Away") ... 8-12 82
COLUMBIA (05077 "No More Lonely Nights") ... 8-12 84
("Playout version.")
COLUMBIA (05077 "No More Lonely Nights") ... 20-30 84
("Special Dance Mix.")
COLUMBIA (10940 "Goodnight Tonight") ... 70-90 79
COLUMBIA (39927 "No More Lonely Nights") ... 15-20 84
(Picture disc.)

Promotional 12-inch Singles

CAPITOL (8574 "Maybe I'm Amazed") ... 60-80 77
CAPITOL (9556 "Spies Like Us") ... 20-30 85
CAPITOL (9763 "Press") ... 15-20 86
CAPITOL (9797 "Angry") ... 20-25 86
CAPITOL (9861 "Stranglehold") ... 20-25 86
CAPITOL (9928 "Pretty Little Head") ... 40-50 86
COLUMBIA (775 "Coming Up") ... 50-60 80
(Red label.)
COLUMBIA (775 "Coming Up") ... 40-50 80
(White label.)
COLUMBIA (1940 "No More Lonely Nights") ... 15-20 84
COLUMBIA (10940 "Goodnight Tonight") ... 15-25 79

Singles: 7-inch

APPLE (1829 "Another Day") ... 8-12 71
APPLE (1839 "Uncle Albert Admiral Halsey") ... 10-20 71
(With sliced apple on flip side.)
APPLE (1839 "Uncle Albert Admiral Halsey") ... 40-50 71
(With unsliced apple on flip side.)

APPLE (1847 "Give Ireland Back to the Irish")....................10-20 72
APPLE (1851 "Mary Had a Little Lamb")....................8-10 72
APPLE (1857 "Hi Hi Hi")....................8-10 72
APPLE (1861 "My Love")....................5-8 73
APPLE (1863 "Live and Let Die")..........5-8 73
APPLE (1869 "Helen Wheels")............5-8 73
APPLE (1871 "Jet"/"Mamunia").....100-125 74
(Label has 2:49 on A-side.)
APPLE (1871 "Jet"/"Mamunia")............8-10 74
(Label has 4:08 on A-side.)
APPLE (1871 "Jet"/"Let Me Roll It") 5-8 74
APPLE (1873 "Band on the Run").........5-8 74
APPLE (1875 "Junior's Farm")............5-8 74
CAPITOL (1829 "Another Day")........10-15 76
CAPITOL (1839 "Uncle Albert Admiral Halsey")....................10-15 76
CAPITOL (1847 "Give Ireland Back to the Irish")....................15-20 76
CAPITOL (1851 "Mary Had a Little Lamb")....................10-15 76
CAPITOL (1857 "Hi Hi Hi")..............10-15 76
CAPITOL (1861 "My Love")..............15-20 76
CAPITOL (1863 "Live and Let Die")..10-15 76
CAPITOL (1869 "Helen Wheels").....10-15 76
CAPITOL (1871 "Jet")....................10-15 76
CAPITOL (1873 "Band on the Run") 10-15 76
CAPITOL (1875 "Junior's Farm")......10-15 76
CAPITOL (4091 "Listen to What the Man Said")....................3-5 75
CAPITOL (4145 "Letting Go")..............3-5 75
CAPITOL (4175 "Venus & Mars Rock Show")....................3-5 75
CAPITOL (4256 "Silly Love Songs")......3-5 76
(Capitol custom label.)
CAPITOL (4256 "Silly Love Songs")......5-8 76
(Black label.)
CAPITOL (4293 "Let 'Em In")..............3-5 76
(Capitol custom label.)
CAPITOL (4293 "Let 'Em In")..............5-8 76
(Black label.)
CAPITOL (4385 Maybe I'm Amazed")...3-5 77
(Capitol custom label.)
CAPITOL (4385 Maybe I'm Amazed")....................15-20 77
(Black label.)
CAPITOL (4504 "Mull of Kintyre") 100-125 77
CAPITOL (4559 "With a Little Luck")....3-5 78
CAPITOL (4594 "I've Had Enough")......3-5 78
CAPITOL (4625 "London Town").........3-5 78
CAPITOL (5537 "Spies Like Us")..........5-8 85
CAPITOL (5597 "Press")....................3-5 86
CAPITOL (5636 "Stranglehold")...........3-5 86
CAPITOL (5672 "Only Love Remains")....................3-5 87
CAPITOL (17318 "Off the Ground")......4-6 94
CAPITOL (17318 "Off the Ground")......4-6 93
(Black vinyl or colored vinyl.)
CAPITOL (17319 "Biker Like an Icon")....................4-6 93
(Black vinyl.)
CAPITOL (17319 "Biker Like an Icon")....................3-4 93
(Colored vinyl.)
CAPITOL (17489 "C'mon People")........4-6 94
(Colored vinyl.)
CAPITOL (17643 "Wonderful Christmastime")....................4-6 94
(Colored vinyl.)
CAPITOL (44637 "My Brave Face")....5-10 89
CAPITOL (56785 "Biker Like an Icon")....................4-6 93
COLUMBIA (02171 "Silly Love Songs")....................15-25 81
COLUMBIA (03018 "Take It Away")......3-4 82
COLUMBIA (03235 "Tug of War").......8-10 82
COLUMBIA (04127 "Wonderful Christmastime")....................20-30 83
COLUMBIA (04296 "So Bad")..............3-4 83
COLUMBIA (04581 "No More Lonely Nights")....................3-4 84
COLUMBIA (10939 "Goodnight Tonight")....................3-4 79
COLUMBIA (11020 "Getting Closer")....4-6 79
COLUMBIA (11070 "Arrow Through Me")....................4-6 79
COLUMBIA (11162 "Wonderful Christmastime")....................5-10 79
COLUMBIA (11263 "Coming Up")........3-4 80
(Listed here as a single even though there are two tracks on the B-side.)
COLUMBIA (11335 "Waterfalls")..........4-6 80
COLUMBIA (33000 series)...............5-10 80
(Red label, "Hall of Fame" series.)
COLUMBIA (33000 series)..............25-35 85
(Gray label, "Hall of Fame" series.)

Picture Sleeves

APPLE (1847 "Give Ireland Back to the Irish")....................20-30 72
APPLE (1851 "Mary Had a Little Lamb")....................25-35 72
("Little Woman Love" printed under photo, on reverse side of sleeve.)
APPLE (1851 "Mary Had a Little Lamb")....................15-25 72
("Little Woman Love" not printed under photo, on reverse side of sleeve.)
CAPITOL (4091 "Listen to What the Man Said")....................8-12 75
CAPITOL (4504 "Mull of Kintyre").......8-12 77
CAPITOL (5537 "Spies Like Us")..........3-5 85
CAPITOL (5597 "Press")....................3-5 86
CAPITOL (5636 "Stranglehold")...........3-5 86
CAPITOL (5672 "Only Love Remains")....................3-5 87
CAPITOL (44637 "My Brave Face")......3-5 89
COLUMBIA (03018 "Take It Away")......5-8 82
(Reads "Not for Sale" on back side. Promotional issue only.)
COLUMBIA (03018 "Take It Away")......3-4 82
COLUMBIA (04296 "So Bad")..............3-5 83
COLUMBIA (04296 "So Bad")............5-10 83
(Reads "Not for Sale" on back side. Promotional issue only.)
COLUMBIA (04581 "No More Lonely Nights")....................4-6 84
(Title has white print.)
COLUMBIA (04581 "No More Lonely Nights")....................20-30 84
(Title has gray print.)
COLUMBIA (11020 "Getting Closer")....................20-30 79
COLUMBIA (11162 "Wonderful Christmastime")....................10-15 79
COLUMBIA (11263 "Coming Up").........4-6 80
COLUMBIA (11335 "Waterfalls")......15-20 80

Promotional Singles

APPLE (1829 "Another Day")...........60-75 71
APPLE (1839 "Uncle Albert Admiral Halsey")....................60-75 71
APPLE (1851 "Mary Had a Little Lamb")....................300-350 72
APPLE (1861 "My Love")..............150-200 73
APPLE (1871 "Jet")....................40-50 74
APPLE (1873 "Band on the Run")....25-35 74
APPLE (1875 "Junior's Farm")..........40-50 74
APPLE (1875 "Sally G")..................60-80 74
APPLE (6786 "Helen Wheels").........40-50 73
APPLE (6787 "Country Dreamer")....................300-350 73
CAPITOL (4145 "Letting Go")...........25-30 75
CAPITOL (4175 "Venus & Mars Rock Show")....................25-30 75
CAPITOL (4256 "Silly Love Songs.")....................20-25 76
CAPITOL (4293 "Let 'Em In")............20-25 76
CAPITOL (4594 "I've Had Enough") 20-25 78
(Add $20 if accompanied by special promotional flyer.)
CAPITOL (4625 "London Town")......20-30 78
CAPITOL (5597 "Press")..................10-15 86
CAPITOL (5636 "Stranglehold")........10-15 86
CAPITOL (5672 "Only Love Remains")....................10-15 87
CAPITOL (8138 "Listen to What the Man Said")....................20-30 75
CAPITOL (8570/1 "Maybe I'm Amazed")....................20-30 77
CAPITOL (8746/7 "Mull of Kintyre")....................20-30 77
CAPITOL (8812 "With a Little Luck")....................20-25 78
CAPITOL (9765 "Press")..............200-250 86
CAPITOL (9952 "Spies Like Us")......15-20 85
CAPITOL (44367 "My Brave Face")..10-15 89
CAPITOL (79700 "This One").......300-350 89
COLUMBIA (1204 "Coming Up")...........5-8 80
(Single-sided disc.)
COLUMBIA (03018 "Take It Away")....8-10 82
COLUMBIA (03235 "Tug of War").....15-20 82
COLUMBIA (04296 "So Bad")...........10-15 83
COLUMBIA (04581 "No More Lonely Nights")....................8-10 84
COLUMBIA (10939 "Goodnight Tonight")....................10-15 79
COLUMBIA (11020 "Getting Closer")....................10-15 79
COLUMBIA (11070 "Arrow Through Me")....................10-15 79
COLUMBIA (11162 "Wonderful Christmastime")....................10-15 79
COLUMBIA (11263 "Coming Up").....10-15 80
COLUMBIA (11335 "Waterfalls").......10-15 80
MIRAMAX (4202 "Rock Show").....500-600 75
(Contains three radio spots. Issued to radio stations only.)

LPs: 10/12-inch

APPLE (3363 "McCartney")..............60-75 70
(Label with Capitol logo shows Paul's full name beneath LP title.)
APPLE (3363 "McCartney")..............20-30 70
(Label shows Paul's full name beneath LP title. No Capitol logo.)
APPLE (3363 "McCartney")..............20-25 70
(Label doesn't show Paul's name beneath LP title.)
APPLE (3375 "Ram")......................40-50 71
(With Capitol logo.)
APPLE (3375 "Ram")......................20-30 71
(No Capitol logo. No "All Rights Reserved, etc." perimeter print.)
APPLE (3375 "Ram")....................75-100 75
(With "All Rights Reserved, etc." perimeter print.)
APPLE (3386 "Wild Life")................10-15 71
APPLE (3409 "Red Rose Speedway")....................15-20 73
APPLE (3415 "Band on the Run").....15-20 73
(Price includes bonus poster.)
CAPITOL (3363 "McCartney")...........15-25 70s
CAPITOL (3375 "Ram")..................20-30 70s
CAPITOL (3386 "Wildlife")...............20-30 70s
CAPITOL (3409 "Red Rose Speedway")....................20-30 70s
CAPITOL (3415 "Band on the Run")....................20-30 76
(Price includes bonus poster.)
CAPITOL (11419 "Venus & Mars")....10-15 75
(Price includes bonus posters and stickers.)
CAPITOL (11525 "Wings at the Speed of Sound")....................8-10 76
CAPITOL (11593 "Wings Over America")....................15-25 76
CAPITOL (11777 "London Town")....10-15 78
(Price includes bonus poster.)
CAPITOL (11901 "Band on the Run")....................40-50 78
(Picture disc.)
CAPITOL (11905 "Wings Greatest") 10-15 78
(Price includes bonus poster.)
CAPITOL (12475 "Press to Play").......8-12 87
CAPITOL (48287 "All the Best!").......10-20 87
CAPITOL (91653 "Flowers in the Dirt")....................10-20 89
CAPITOL (94778 "Tripping the Live Fantastic")....................50-60 90
CAPITOL (595379 "Tripping the Live Fantastic: Highlights")....................10-15 90
COLUMBIA (36057 "Back to the Egg")....................5-10 79
(Photo label.)
COLUMBIA (36057 "Back to the Egg")....................30-40 84
(Red label.)

COLUMBIA (36478 "McCartney")...... 15-20 80
COLUMBIA (36479 "Ram") 15-20 80
COLUMBIA (36480 "Wild Life")......... 15-20 80
COLUMBIA (36481 "Red Rose Speedway")....................................... 15-20 80
COLUMBIA (JC-36482 "Band on the Run").. 10-15 80
(Photo label.)
COLUMBIA (36482 "Band on the Run").. 30-40 80
(Red label. With "JC" or "PC" prefix.)
COLUMBIA (HC-36482 "Band on the Run").. 60-70 80
(Red label. Half-speed mastered.)
COLUMBIA (FC-36511 "McCartney II") 10-15 80
(Issued with bonus single [1204] *Coming Up*, which represents $5 to $8 of the price range. Photo label.)
COLUMBIA (FC-36511 "McCartney II") 15-25 80
(Red label.)
COLUMBIA (PC-36511 "McCartney II") 75-100 80
(Red label.)
COLUMBIA (36801 "Venus & Mars") 10-20 80
(Price includes bonus posters.)
COLUMBIA (36987 "The McCartney Interview") 8-12 80
COLUMBIA (37409 "Wings at the Speed of Sound") 15-20 81
COLUMBIA (TC-37462 "Tug of War") 5-10 82
(With Stevie Wonder on *Ebony and Ivory*)
COLUMBIA (PC-37462 "Tug of War") 20-30 84
(Photo label.)
COLUMBIA (PC-37462 "Tug of War") 75-100 84
(Red label.)
COLUMBIA (37990 "Wings Over America") 40-50 82
COLUMBIA (39149 "Pipes of Peace") 8-12 83
(With Michael Jackson on *Say Say Say*)
COLUMBIA (39613 "Give My Regards to Broad Street") 10-15 84
COLUMBIA (46482 "Band on the Run") 10-15 80
(Half-speed mastered.)
LIBERTY (50100 Live and Let Die") 5-8 84
(With McCartney on title track only.)
LONDON (76007 "Family Way") 80-90 67
(Soundtrack. Monaural.)
LONDON (82007 "Family Way") 90-120 67
(Soundtrack. Stereo.)
U.A. (100 "Live and Let Die") 15-20 73
(Copies with cut corners are valued at about one-half of the above price range. McCartney is heard on title track only.)

Promotional LPs

APPLE (3375 "Ram") 3000-3500 71
(Monaural.)
APPLE (6210 "Brung to Ewe By") 350-450 71
CAPITOL (2955 "Band on the Run Radio Interview") 1000-1200 73
CAPITOL (11525 "Wings at the Speed of Sound") 200-250 76
COLUMBIA (821 "The McCartney Interview") 30-40 80
COLUMBIA (36057 "Back to the Egg") 25-35 79
COLUMBIA (36511 "McCartney II")... 20-30 80
W.B. ("The Family Way") 350-450 67
(10-inch LP. Ad spots for radio stations.)
Also see BEATLES
Also see BRASS RING
Also see COUNTRY HAMS
Also see GREASE BAND
Also see LOMAX, Jackie
Also see NEWMAN, Thunderclap
Also see PERKINS, Carl
Also see SUZY & Red Stripes

McCARTNEY, Paul, & Michael Jackson — P&R/R&B '82

Singles: 12-inch

COLUMBIA (1758 "Say Say Say").... 10-15 83
COLUMBIA (04169 "Say Say Say").... 5-10 83

Promotional 12-inch Singles

COLUMBIA (04169 "Say Say Say").. 12-18 83

Singles: 7-inch

COLUMBIA (04168 "Say Say Say")...... 3-4 83
EPIC (03288 "The Girl Is Mine") 3-4 82
EPIC (03372 "The Girl Is Mine") 8-12 82
(Single-sided pressing with small, LP size, hole.)

Picture Sleeves

COLUMBIA (04168 "Say Say Say")...... 3-4 83

Promotional Picture Sleeves

COLUMBIA (04168 "Say Say Say").... 5-10 83
EPIC (03288 "The Girl Is Mine") 5-10 82

Promotional Singles

COLUMBIA (04168 "Say Say Say").... 8-12 83
EPIC (03288 "The Girl Is Mine") 8-12 82
(Identification number shown as 169138.)
EPIC (03288 "The Girl Is Mine") 20-30 82
(Identification number shown as 169202. Reads "New Edited Version.")
Also see JACKSON, Michael

McCARTNEY, Paul / Rochestra / Who / Rockpile

Singles: 12-inch

ATLANTIC (388 "Every Night")..... 150-250 81
(Promotional issue only.)
Also see ROCKPILE
Also see WHO

McCARTNEY, Paul, & Stevie Wonder — P&R/R&B '82

Singles: 12-inch

COLUMBIA (02878 "Ebony & Ivory").. 8-12 82

Promotional 12-inch Singles

COLUMBIA (1444 "Ebony & Ivory") 20-30 82

Singles: 7-inch

COLUMBIA (02860 "Ebony & Ivory") 20-30 82
COLUMBIA (02860 "Ebony & Ivory").... 3-4 82
(Ampersand [&] in title is replaced by "and.")

Promotional Singles

COLUMBIA (02860 "Ebony & Ivory") 15-25 82

Picture Sleeves

COLUMBIA (02860 "Ebony & Ivory").. 8-10 82

Promotional Picture Sleeves

COLUMBIA (02860 "Ebony & Ivory").. 5-10 82
Also see McCARTNEY, Paul
Also see WONDER, Stevie

McCLAIN, Alton, & Destiny — P&R/R&B/LP '79

Singles: 7-inch

POLYDOR 3-5 79-81

LPs: 10/12-inch

POLYDOR 5-10 79-81
Also see ALTON & JOHNNY

McCLAIN, Janice — R&B '80

Singles: 12-inch

MCA 4-6 86

Singles: 7-inch

MCA 3-4 86
RFC 3-4 80

LPs: 10/12-inch

MCA 5-8 86

McCLARY, Thomas — R&B '84

Singles: 7-inch

MOTOWN 3-4 84-85

LPs: 10/12-inch

MOTOWN 5-8 85
Also see COMMODORES

McCLINTON, Delbert — LP '79

Singles: 7-inch

ABC 3-5 75-77
BOBILL (101 "I Know She Knows") 8-10 67
BROWNFIELD 8-12 65
CAPITOL 3-5 80-81
CAPRICORN 3-5 78
JUBILEE (9012 "I Know She Knows") 8-12 65
LE CAM (717 "Hey Baby") 3-5 79
LE CAM (1220 "Mr. Pitiful") 3-5 79
LONDON (9544 "Angel Eyes") 15-25 62
PARAMOUNT (0016 "Fannie Mae").... 5-10 69
SOFT (1041 "100 Pounds of Honey") ... 4-6 70

LPs: 10/12-inch

ABC 10-20 75-77
ACCORD 8-12 81
CAPITOL 8-12 80-81
CAPRICORN 10-15 78-79
INTERMEDIA 5-10 84
MCA 5-10 81
POLYDOR 10-20 79
Also see DELBERT & GLEN

McCLINTON, O.B. — C&W '72

(With Peggy Jo Adams)

Singles: 7-inch

ENTERPRISE 3-5 72-75
EPIC 3-5 78-87
MERCURY 3-5 76
MOON SHINE 3-4 84
SUNBIRD 3-5 80

LPs: 10/12-inch

ENTERPRISE 8-10 72-74

McCLURE, Bobby — P&R/R&B '66

Singles: 7-inch

CHECKER 4-8 66-67
Also see BASS, Fontella, & Bobby McClure

McCOLLUM, Hazel: see EL DORADOS

McCONNELL, C. Lynda — D&D '84

Singles: 12-inch

ATLANTIC 4-6 84

Singles: 7-inch

ATLANTIC 3-4 84

McCOO, Marilyn — R&B '83

Singles: 7-inch

RCA 3-4 83

LPs: 10/12-inch

RCA 5-8 83

McCOO, Marilyn, & Billy Davis Jr. — P&R/R&B/LP '76

Singles: 12-inch

COLUMBIA 4-6 79

Singles: 7-inch

ABC 3-5 76-78
COLUMBIA 3-5 78

LPs: 10/12-inch

ABC 8-10 76-77
COLUMBIA 5-10 78
Also see FIFTH DIMENSION
Also see McCOO, Marilyn

McCORMICK, Gayle — P&R/LP '71

Singles: 7-inch

DECCA 3-5 72
DUNHILL 3-5 71-72
MCA 3-5 73

LPs: 10/12-inch

DECCA 10-12 72
DUNHILL 10-12 71
FANTASY 8-10 74
Also see SMITH

McCOY, Charlie — P&R '61

Singles: 7-inch

CADENCE 4-8 61-62
MONUMENT 3-6 68-83

EPs: 7-inch

MONUMENT (0001 "Charlie McCoy") 5-10
(Promotional issue only.)

LPs: 10/12-inch

EPIC 5-8 82
MONUMENT 5-10 69-78
Session: Barefoot Jerry.
Also see AREA CODE 615
Also see DYLAN, Bob
Also see LEE, Bobby
Also see McDOWELL, Ronnie
Also see TUBB, Ernest

McCOY, Freddie P&R '67

Singles: 7-inch

PRESTIGE 4-6 67

McCOY, Van R&B '74

(With the Soul City Symphony; Van McCoy Strings)

Singles: 12-inch

MCA 4-8 79

Singles: 7-inch

AMHERST 3-5 70s
AVCO 3-5 74-75
CGC 3-5 70
COLUMBIA 4-8 65-66
EPIC 3-6 69
H&L 3-5 76
LIBERTY 4-8 62
MCA 3-5 78-79
ROCK 'N (101 "Mr. D.J.") 10-20 61
ROCK 'N (1012 "Girls Are Sentimental") 10-15 61
SHARE 3-5 69
SILVER BLUE 3-5 73

LPs: 10/12-inch

AVCO 8-10 74-75
BUDDAH 8-10 72-75
COLUMBIA 12-18 66
H&L 8-10 76
MCA 8-10 77-79

McCOYS P&R/LP '65

Singles: 7-inch

BANG 5-10 65-67
MERCURY 8-15 68
SOLID GOLD 3-4 73

LPs: 10/12-inch

BANG (212 "Hang on Sloopy") 25-35 65
(Monaural.)
BANG (S-212 "Hang on Sloopy") 35-45 65
(Stereo.)
BANG (213 "You Make Me Feel So Good") 25-35 66
(Monaural.)
BANG (S-213 "You Make Me Feel So Good") 35-45 66
(Stereo.)
MERCURY (61163 "Infinite McCoys") 20-25 68
MERCURY (61207 "Human Ball") 20-25 69
Also see DERRINGER, Rick
Also see STRANGELOVES

McCRACKLIN, Jimmy P&R/R&B '58

(With His Blues Blasters; Jimmie McCracklin)

Singles: 78 rpm

ALADDIN 20-30 51
CAVATONE 25-50 47
COURTNEY 25-50 45
DOWN TOWN 20-30 48
EXCELSIOR 25-50 45
GLOBE 25-50 45
HOLLYWOOD 15-25 55
IRMA 15-30 56-57
MODERN 20-30 49
PEACOCK 15-25 52-54
RPM 20-30 50
SWING TIME 15-25 51-52
TRILON 25-50 49

Singles: 7-inch

ART-TONE 5-10 61-62
CHECKER 10-20 58
CHESS 5-10 62
GEDINSON'S 4-8 61
HI (2023 "Things I Meant to Say") 10-20 60
HOLLYWOOD (1054 "It's All Right") 25-35 55
IMPERIAL 4-8 62-67
IRMA (102 "You're the One") 15-25 56
IRMA (103 "Take a Chance") 15-25 56
IRMA (107 "I'm the One") 15-25 57
IRMA (109 "Love for You") 15-25 57
KENT 4-8 62
LIBERTY 3-5 70
MERCURY 8-12 59-61
MINIT 4-8 67-70
MODERN (926 "Blues Blasters Boogie") 20-30 54
MODERN (934 "Darlin' Share Your Love") 20-30 54
MODERN (951 "Forgive Me Baby") 20-30 54
MODERN (967 "Gonna Tell Your Mother") 20-30 55
OAK CITY 4-6
PEACOCK (1605 "She's Gone") 30-40 52
PEACOCK (1615 "Share and Share Alike") 30-40 53
PEACOCK (1634 "The End") 30-40 53
PEACOCK (1639 "The Cheater") 30-40 53
PEACOCK (1683 "The Swinging Thing") 10-20 58
PREMIUM (101 "You're the One") 15-20
SWING TIME (291 "House Rockin' Blues") 15-25 51

LPs: 10/12-inch

CHESS (1464 "Jimmy McCracklin Sings") 40-60 62
CROWN 15-20 61
IMPERIAL 20-35 63-66
MINIT 12-18 67-69
STAX 8-12 72-81
Also see BROWN, Charles, & Jimmy McCracklin

McCRACKLIN, Jimmy / T-Bone Walker / Charles Brown

LPs: 10/12-inch

IMPERIAL (9257 "Best of the Blues, Vol. 1") 15-25 64
Also see BROWN, Charles
Also see WALKER, T-Bone

McCRAE, George P&R/R&B/LP '74

Singles: 7-inch

GOLD MOUNTAIN 3-4 84
SOUL CITY 4-8
T.K. 4-6 74-79

LPs: 10/12-inch

CAT 8-10 76
GOLD MOUNTAIN 5-8 84
TK 8-10 74-77

McCRAE, George & Gwen P&R/R&B '75

Singles: 7-inch

CAT 3-5 76
Also see GEORGE & GWEN
Also see McCRAE, George
Also see McCRAE, Gwen

McCRAE, Gwen R&B '70

Singles: 7-inch

ATLANTIC 3-4 81-83
BLACK JACK 3-4 84
CAT 3-5 74-75

LPs: 10/12-inch

ATLANTIC 5-8 81-83
CAT 8-10 74-76
Also see McCRAE, George & Gwen

McCRARYS P&R/R&B/LP '78

Singles: 7-inch

CAPITOL 3-4 80-82
PORTRAIT 3-5 78-79

LPs: 10/12-inch

CAPITOL 5-8 80
PORTRAIT 5-10 78
Members: Sam McCrary; Linda McCrary; Al McCrary; Charity McCrary.

McCREE, Earl-Jean: see EARL-JEAN

McCULLOUGH, Ian LP '89

LPs: 10/12-inch

SIRE 5-8 89

McCULLOUGH, Ullanda R&B '81

Singles: 7-inch

ATLANTIC 3-5 81

McCURN, George P&R '63

Singles: 7-inch

A&M 4-8 63-64
LIBERTY 4-8 62
REPRISE 4-6 66

LPs: 10/12-inch

A&M 15-25 63

McDANIEL, Donna P&R '77

Singles: 7-inch

MIDLAND INT'L 3-5 77

McDANIELS, Gene P&R/R&B '61

(Eugene McDaniels)

Singles: 7-inch

COLUMBIA 4-8 66-67
LIBERTY 5-15 60-65
MGM 3-5 73
ODE '70 .... 3-5 75

EPs: 7-inch

LIBERTY 10-20 60s

LPs: 10/12-inch

ATLANTIC 10-15 70-71
LIBERTY 15-25 60-67
ODE '70 .... 8-12 75
SUNSET 10-15 66
U.A. 8-12 75
Also see MANN, Johnny, Singers

McDEVITT, Charles, Skiffle Group

(Featuring Nancy Wiskey) P&R '57

Singles: 7-inch

CHIC 5-10 57
KAPP 5-8 58
ORIOLE 5-10 57

McDONALD, Country Joe P&R '75

Singles: 7-inch

FANTASY 3-5 75-79
VANGUARD 3-6 71-74

LPs: 10/12-inch

FANTASY 5-10 75-79
MFSL 25-50 81
PICCADILLY 10-15 78
VANGUARD 8-12 69-76
Also see COUNTRY JOE & FISH

McDONALD, Kathi LP '74

Singles: 7-inch

CAPITOL 3-6 74

LPs: 10/12-inch

CAPITOL 10-20 74
Also see BALDRY, Long John, & Kathi McDonald
Also see BIG BROTHER & Holding Company

McDONALD, Michael P&R/R&B/LP '82

Singles: 7-inch

MCA 3-4 86
W.B. 3-4 82-85

Picture Sleeves

MCA 3-4 86
W.B. 3-4 82-85

LPs: 10/12-inch

MCA 5-8 86
MFSL (149 "If That's What It Takes") 20-30 85
REPRISE 5-8 90
W.B. 5-8 82-85
Also see CROSS, Christopher
Also see DAL BELLO, Lisa
Also see DOOBIE BROTHERS
Also see HOLLAND, Amy
Also see LABELLE, Patti, & Michael McDonald
Also see MEMPHIS HORNS
Also see PACK, David
Also see STEELY DAN
Also see WINANS
Also see WOOD, Lauren

McDONALD, Michael, & James Ingram P&R/R&B '83

Singles: 7-inch

QWEST 3-4 83
Also see INGRAM, James
Also see McDONALD, Michael

McDOWELL, Carrie R&B '87

Singles: 7-inch

MOTOWN 3-4 87

McDOWELL, Ronnie P&R/C&W '77

Singles: 7-inch

EPIC 3-5 79-85
GRT 3-5 77
MCA/CURB 3-4 86
SCORPION (Except 0533) 3-6 77-79
SCORPION (0533 "Only the Lonely") 4-8 77

LPs: 10/12-inch
DICK CLARK (79 "Elvis") 8-12 79
(TV soundtrack.)
EPIC 5-10 79-85
MCA/CURB 5-8 86
SCORPION (0010 "Live at the Fox") 10-15 78
SCORPION (8021 "The King Is Gone") 10-15 77
(Includes copy of front page of newspaper with news that 'The King' is gone.)
SCORPION (8028 "I Love You, I Love You, I Love You") 10-15 78
STRAWBERRY 8-10 70s
Session: Jordanaires; Conway Twitty; Kathy Westmoreland; Charlie McCoy; David Briggs; Chip Young; Dale Sellers; Bobby Ogden; Mike Leech.
Also see McCOY, Charlie
Also see TWITTY, Conway

McDOWELL, Ronnie, & Jerry Lee Lewis
C&W '89

Singles: 7-inch
CURB 3-5 88
Also see LEWIS, Jerry Lee
Also see McDOWELL, Ronnie

McDUFF, Brother Jack
LP '63

Singles: 7-inch
ATLANTIC 4-6 67
CADET 3-6 68
BLUE NOTE 3-6 69
PRESTIGE 4-8 62
LPs: 10/12-inch
BLUE NOTE 8-12 69
PRESTIGE (7000 series) 25-50 60-64
(Yellow label.)
PRESTIGE (7000 series) 15-25 64-65
(Blue label.)
Also see BENSON, George

McDUFF, Brother Jack, & Gene Ammons

LPs: 10/12-inch
PRESTIGE 30-50 61
(Yellow label.)
Also see AMMONS, Gene

McDUFF, Brother Jack, & Willis Jackson
LP '66

LPs: 10/12-inch
PRESTIGE 15-25 66
Also see JACKSON, Willis
Also see McDUFF, Brother Jack

McENTIRE, Reba
C&W '76

Singles: 7-inch
MCA 3-5 84-92
MERCURY 5-15 76-83
Picture Sleeves
MCA 3-5
LPs: 10/12-inch
MCA 5-8 84-90
MERCURY (1177 "Reba McEntire") 50-100 77
MERCURY (4047 "Unlimited") 15-25 82
MERCURY (5002 "Reba McEntire") . 25-50 77
MERCURY (5017 "Out of a Dream") 25-50 79
MERCURY (5029 "Feel the Fire") 20-30 80
MERCURY (6003 "Heart to Heart") ... 20-30 81
MERCURY (57062 thru 76157) 10-15 81-82
MERCURY (812781 "Behind the Scene") 10-15 83
Session: Chris Austin; Pake McEntire.

McEUEN, John
C&W '85

Singles: 7-inch
W.B. 3-4 85

McFADDEN, Bob
P&R '59

(With Dor)

Singles: 7-inch
BRUNSWICK 10-15 59
CORAL 8-12 60
U.S. RUBBER CO. ("Noah's Ark and What's a Nauga?") 5-10
(Promotional only issue. Square cardboard picture disc. Made for U.S. Naugahyde & Naugaweave Co.)
Picture Sleeves
BRUNSWICK (55140 "The Mummy") 15-25 59
LPs: 10/12-inch
BRUNSWICK (54056 "Songs Our Mummy Taught Us") 75-125 59
(Monaural.)
BRUNSWICK (7-54056 "Songs Our Mummy Taught Us") 100-150 59
(Stereo.)
Members: Bob McFadden; Rod McKuen.
Also see McKUEN, Rod

McFADDEN & WHITEHEAD
P&R/R&B/LP '79

Singles: 12-inch
PHILADELPHIA INT'L 4-8 79
SUTRA 4-6
Singles: 7-inch
CAPITOL 3-4 82-83
PHILADELPHIA INT'L 3-5 79
SUTRA 3-4
TSOP 3-4 80
LPs: 10/12-inch
CAPITOL 5-8 83
PHILADELPHIA INT'L 5-8 79
TSOP 5-8 80
Members: Gene McFadden; John Whitehead.
Also see WHITEHEAD, John

McFARLAND, Gary
LP '69

Singles: 7-inch
SKYE 4-8 69
LPs: 10/12-inch
SKYE 10-15 69

McFERRIN, Bobby
LP '87

Singles: 7-inch
EMI 3-4 88-90
Picture Sleeves
EMI 3-4 88
LPs: 10/12-inch
BLUE NOTE 5-10 87
EMI 5-8 88-90

McGEE, Parker
P&R '77

Singles: 7-inch
BIG TREE 3-5 77
LPs: 10/12-inch
BIG TREE 5-10 76

McGHEE, Brownie
R&B '48

(With His Jook Block Busters; with His Sugar Men)

Singles: 78 rpm
ALERT 10-15 46-47
DERBY 10-20 52
DISC 10-20 47
DOT 50-75 53
ENCORE 10-20 53
HARLEM 20-30 52
JAX 50-75 52
LONDON 10-20 51
PAR 10-20 52
RED ROBIN 50-75 52-53
SAVOY 10-20 44-57
SITTIN' in WITH 10-20 48
Singles: 7-inch
DOT (1184 "Cheatin' and Lying") 150-200 53
HARLEM (2323 "Christina") 30-40 52
HARLEM (2329 "Bluebird") 30-40 52
JACKSON (2304 "Mean Old Frisco") 100-125 52
(Colored vinyl.)
JAX (304 "I Feel So Good") 75-100 52
(Colored vinyl.)
JAX (307 "Meet You in the Morning") 75-100 52
(Colored vinyl.)
JAX (310 "Stranger's Blues") 75-100 52
(Colored vinyl.)
JAX (312 "I'm 10,000 Years Old") ... 75-100 52
(Colored vinyl.)
JAX (322 "New Bad Blood") 75-100 52
(Colored vinyl.)
RED ROBIN (111 "Don't Dog Your Woman") 100-200 53
SAVOY (800 series) 15-25 51-52
SAVOY (1100 thru 1500 series) 8-18 55-59
LPs: 10/12-inch
FOLKWAYS (Except 20, 30 & 2000 series) 8-10
FOLKWAYS (20, 30 & 2000 series) .. 20-40 54-55
STORYVILLE 5-8
VANGUARD 8-12 60s
Session: Sonny Terry; Mickey Baker.
Also see DUPREE, Champion Jack

McGHEE, Brownie, & Sonny Terry
LP '73

Singles: 78 rpm
SAVOY 10-20 44-48
Singles: 7-inch
PRESTIGE BLUESVILLE 5-10 60-62
LPs: 10/12-inch
A&M 8-10 73
BLUESWAY 10-12 69-73
EVEREST 10-12 69
FANTASY (3000 series) 15-25 61-62
(Black vinyl.)
FANTASY (3000 series) 25-50 61-62
(Colored vinyl.)
FANTASY (8000 series) 15-20 62
(Black vinyl.)
FANTASY (8000 series) 25-40 62
(Colored vinyl.)
FANTASY (24000 series) 8-10 72-81
FOLKWAYS (2000 & 3000 series) 15-30 55-61
FOLKWAYS (31000 series) 8-10
FONTANA 10-15 69
MFSL (233 "Sonny & Browny") 20-25 94
MAINSTREAM (6000 series) 15-20 65
MAINSTREAM (300 series) 8-10 71
MUSE 5-8 81
OLYMPIC 8-10 73
PRESTIGE (1000 series) 25-30 60
PRESTIGE (7000 series) 8-10 69-70
PRESTIGE BLUESVILLE 20-40 60-62
PRESTIGE FOLKLORE 12-15
ROULETTE 25-35 59
SAVOY (1100 series) 5-8 84
SAVOY (12000 series) 8-10 73
SAVOY (14000 series) 25-30 58
SHARP (2003 "Down Home Blues") 25-50 59
SMASH 15-20 65
VERVE 20-25 61
VERVE/FOLKWAYS 15-20 65
WORLD PACIFIC 25-30 60
Also see BROONZY, Big Bill
Also see HOPKINS, Lightnin' / Brownie McGhee & Sonny Terry
Also see McGHEE, Brownie
Also see TERRY, Sonny
Also see WILLIS, Ralph

McGHEE, Stick
P&R/R&B '49

(With His Buddies; with Ramblers; Sticks McGhee)

Singles: 78 rpm
ATLANTIC 20-40 49-52
DECCA (48104 "Drinkin' Wine Spo-Dee-O-Dee") 15-25 47
ESSEX 10-15 52
HARLEM (1018 "Blues Mixture") 15-25 47
KING 20-30 53-55
LONDON 25-75 51
SAVOY 10-15 55
Singles: 7-inch
ATLANTIC (955 "Wee Wee Hours") 50-75 52
ATLANTIC (991 "New Found Love") 40-60 52
ATLANTIC CLASSICS (873 "Drinkin' Wine Spo-Dee-O-Dee") 10-20 71
("Classics Revisited" reissue series. Original Atlantic 45s of this number—from 1949—do not exist.)

GUSTO ... 3-4
HERALD ... 5-10 60
KING (4610 "Little Things We Used to Do") ... 50-75 53
KING (4628 "Blues in My Heart") ... 50-75 53
KING (4672 "Dealin' from the Bottom") ... 50-75 53
KING (4700 "I'm Doin' All the Time") ... 50-75 53
KING (4783 "Double Crossin' Liquor") ... 50-100 55
KING (4800 "Get Your Mind Out of the Gutter") ... 50-75 55
LONDON (978 "You Gotta Have Something on the Ball") ... 100-200 51
SAVOY ... 15-25 55

McGHEE, Sticks / John Lee Hooker

LPs: 10/12-inch

AUDIO LAB (1520 "Highway of Blues") ... 100-125 59

Also see DUPREE, Champion Jack
Also see HOOKER, John Lee
Also see McGHEE, Stick

McGILL, Rollee — *R&B '55*

(With the Rhythm Rockers; Rollie McGill)

Singles: 78 rpm

MERCURY ... 10-15 55-56
PINEY ... 15-25 55

Singles: 7-inch

LANDA (702 "Come Home") ... 8-10 64
MERCURY (70582 "There Goes That Train") ... 15-25 55
MERCURY (70652 "Rhythm Rockin' Blues") ... 15-25 55
MERCURY (70725 "There's Madness in My Heart") ... 15-25 55
MERCURY (70807 "Oncoming Train") ... 15-25 56
MERCURY (70914 "Come on In") ... 15-25 56
PINEY (104 "There Goes That Train") ... 40-60 55
(First issue.)

McGILPIN, Bob — *P&R '78*

Singles: 7-inch

BUTTERFLY ... 3-5 77-78

LPs: 10/12-inch

BUTTERFLY (Black vinyl) ... 5-10 78-79
BUTTERFLY (Colored vinyl) ... 12-18 78
CASABLANCA ... 5-8 80

McGOVERN, Maureen — *P&R/LP '73*

Singles: 7-inch

CASABLANCA ... 3-5 70s
EPIC ... 3-5 78
MAIDEN VOYAGE ... 3-5 70s
20TH FOX ... 3-5 73-75
W.B. ... 3-5 79-80
WOODEN NICKEL ... 3-5 73

LPs: 10/12-inch

20TH FOX ... 8-12 73-75
W.B. ... 5-10 79

McGRIFF, Jimmy — *P&R/R&B/LP '62*

(Jimmy McGriff Trio)

Singles: 7-inch

BLUE NOTE ... 3-5 71
CAPITOL ... 3-5 70-71
COLLECTABLES ... 3-4 80s
GROOVE MERCHANT ... 3-5 75
JELL (100 series) ... 5-10 62
JELL (500 series) ... 4-8 65
LRC ... 3-5 78
MILESTONE ... 3-4 83
SOLID STATE ... 4-6 66-70
SUE ... 5-10 62-64
U.A. ... 3-5 71-78

EPs: 7-inch

SOLID STATE ... 8-12 66

LPs: 10/12-inch

BLUE NOTE ... 8-12 70-71
COLLECTABLES ... 6-8 88
51 WEST ... 5-8 80s
GROOVE MERCHANT ... 8-12 71-76
LRC ... 8-10 77-78
MILESTONE ... 5-8 81-83
SOLID STATE ... 10-15 66-70
SOUL SUGAR ... 10-12 70
SUE ... 20-30 62-65
U.A. ... 8-12 71
VEEP ... 10-15 68

Also see HOLMES, Richard "Groove"
Also see PARKER, Little Junior, & Jimmy McGriff

McGUFFEY LANE — *P&R '81*

Singles: 7-inch

ATCO ... 3-4 81-82
ATLANTIC AMERICA ... 3-4 84

LPs: 10/12-inch

ATCO ... 5-10 82

Members: Robert McNelley; Steve Douglass.

McGUINN, Roger — *LP '73*

Singles: 7-inch

COLUMBIA ... 3-5 73-77

LPs: 10/12-inch

ARISTA ... 5-8 90
COLUMBIA (Except "Airplay Anthology") ... 8-12 73-77
COLUMBIA ("Airplay Anthology") ... 20-30 77
(Promotional issue only.)

Members: Jim (Roger) McGuinn; Chris Hillman; Gene Clark.
Also see HILLMAN, Chris
Also see McGUINN, Roger
Also see MITCHELL, Chad, Trio

McGUINN, CLARK & HILLMAN

(Roger McGuinn & Chris Hillman featuring Gene Clark) — *P&R/LP '79*

Singles: 7-inch

CAPITOL ... 3-5 79

LPs: 10/12-inch

CAPITOL ... 5-8 79-82

Members: Roger McGuinn; Gene Clark; Chris Hillman.
Also see BYRDS
Also see HILLMAN, Chris, & Roger McGuinn

McGUIRE, Barry — *P&R/LP '65*

(With the Horizon Singers)

Singles: 7-inch

ABC ... 3-5 70
DUNHILL ... 4-8 65-66
HORIZON ... 4-8 63
ODE '70 ... 3-5 70
MCA ... 3-5
MIRA ... 4-6 66
MOSAIC ... 4-8 61-62
MYRRH ... 3-5 73
ROULETTE ... 3-5

Picture Sleeves

DUNHILL ... 5-10 65

LPs: 10/12-inch

BIRDWING ... 5-8 80
DUNHILL ... 20-30 65
HORIZON ... 15-25 63
MYRRH ... 5-8 73-75
ODE '70 ... 8-10 70
SPARROW ... 5-8 79
SURREY ... 12-15 65

Also see MAMAS & PAPAS
Also see NEW CHRISTY MINSTRELS

McGUIRE, Barry, & Barry Kane

Singles: 7-inch

HORIZON ... 4-8 62

LPs: 10/12-inch

HORIZON ... 15-25 62
SURREY ... 12-18 66

McGUIRE, Phyllis — *P&R '64*

Singles: 7-inch

REPRISE ... 4-6 64-65
ORPHEUM ... 4-6 68

LPs: 10/12-inch

ABC-PAR ... 10-20 66

Also see McGUIRE SISTERS

McGUIRE SISTERS — *P&R '54*

(With Lawrence Welk's Orchestra)

Singles: 78 rpm

CORAL ... 4-8 54-58

Singles: 7-inch

ABC-PAR ... 4-6 66
CORAL (Except 61000 & 98000 series) ... 4-8 58-65
CORAL (61000 series) ... 5-10 54-58
CORAL (98000 series) ... 10-15 60
(Stereo.)
MCA ... 3-4 70s
REPRISE ... 4-6 63-65

Picture Sleeves

CORAL ... 5-15 56-61

EPs: 7-inch

CORAL ... 10-15 55-60

LPs: 10/12-inch

ABC-PAR ... 10-20 66
CORAL (6 "Best of the McGuire Sisters") ... 15-25 65
CORAL (56123 "By Request") ... 25-50 55
CORAL (57000 series) ... 15-25 56-65
MCA ... 5-8 78
VOCALION ... 10-20 60-67

Members: Phyllis McGuire; Dorothy McGuire; Christine McGuire.
Also see DESMOND, Johnny, Eileen Barton & McGuire Sisters
Also see McGUIRE, Phyllis
Also see WELK, Lawrence, & His Orchestra

McGUIRE SISTERS / Lancers / Dorothy Collins / Teresa Brewer

EPs: 7-inch

CORAL (98015 "Christmas Alphabet") ... 15-25 50s
(Promotional issue only.)

Also see BREWER, Teresa
Also see COLLINS, Dorothy
Also see LANCERS
Also see McGUIRE SISTERS

McIAN, Peter — *P&R '80*

Singles: 7-inch

COLUMBIA/ARC ... 3-5 80

LPs: 10/12-inch

COLUMBIA/ARC ... 5-8 80

McKEE, Lonette — *R&B '74*

Singles: 7-inch

SUSSEX ... 3-5 74
W.B. ... 3-5 79

McKEE, Maria — *LP '89*

Singles: 7-inch

GEFFEN ... 3-4 89

LPs: 10/12-inch

GEFFEN ... 5-8 89

McKENDREE SPRING — *LP '70*

Singles: 7-inch

DECCA ... 3-6 69-72
MCA ... 3-5 73
PYE ... 3-5 76

LPs: 10/12-inch

DECCA ... 10-15 69-72
MCA ... 8-10 73
PYE ... 8-10 75-76

McKENZIE, Bob & Doug — *P&R/LP '82*

Singles: 7-inch

MERCURY ... 3-5 82

Picture Sleeves

MERCURY ... 3-5 82

LPs: 10/12-inch

MERCURY ... 5-10 81

Session: Geddy Lee.
Also see RUSH

McKENZIE, Scott — *P&R/LP '67*

(McKenzie's Musicians)

Singles: 7-inch

CAPITOL ... 4-8 65-67
EPIC ... 3-6 67-72
ODE (Except 103) ... 4-8 67-71
ODE (103 "San Francisco [Wear Some Flowers in Your Hair]") ... 8-10 67
ODE (103 "San Francisco [Be Sure to Wear Flowers in Your Hair]") ... 4-8 67
(Note slight change in title.)

LPs: 10/12-inch
ODE (44000 series)....15-25 67
ODE (34000 series)....8-10 77
ODE (77000 series)....10-15 70

McKUEN, Rod P&R '62
(With the Keytones; with Horizon Singers)
Singles: 7-inch
A&M....4-8 63
BUDDAH....3-5 73-74
DECCA....5-10 59
HORIZON....4-8 63
JUBILEE....4-8 62
KAPP....4-8 61
LIBERTY....8-12 56
RCA....4-8 66-67
SPIRAL....4-8 61-62
STANYAN....3-5 74
VISTA....3-5 71
W.B. 3-6 68-72
Picture Sleeves
VISTA....3-5 71
W.B. 3-5 71
LPs: 10/12-inch
DECCA (4900 series)....10-15 68
DECCA (8800 series)....20-30 59
DECCA (75000 series)....10-12 69
CAPITOL....15-20 64
HARMONY....8-10 71
HI FI....20-30 58-59
EPIC (600 & 3800 series)....15-20 62
EPIC (26000 series)....10-12 68
EVEREST....10-12 68
HORIZON....15-25 63
IN....15-20 64
JUBILEE....20-25 62
KAPP (1200 & 3200 series)....15-25 61
KAPP (1500 & 3500 series)....10-20 67
LIBERTY (Except 3011)....10-15 67
LIBERTY (3011 "Songs for a Lazy Afternoon")....25-40 56
PICKWICK....5-10 70s
RCA....10-20 65-69
STANYAN....10-15 66-72
SUNSET....8-10 70
TRADITION....10-12 68
VISTA....8 10 71
W.B. 8-15 67-76
Also see McFADDEN, Bob
Also see SAN SEBASTIAN STRINGS

McLACHLAN, Sarah LP '89
LPs: 10/12-inch
ARISTA....5-8 89

McLAGAN, Ian LP '80
Singles: 7-inch
MERCURY....3-5 79
LPs: 10/12-inch
MERCURY....5-10 79
Also see FACES
Also see SMALL FACES

McLAIN, Tommy P&R '66
Singles: 7-inch
COLLECTABLES....3-4 80s
JIN (Except 197)....4-8 66-69
JIN (197 "Sweet Dreams")....5-10 66
MSL....4-8 66
STARFLIGHT....3-5 79
Also see FENDER, Freddy, & Tommy McLain

McLAREN, Malcom D&D '83
(With the World's Famous Supreme Band; with World's Famous Supreme Team)
Singles: 12-inch
ISLAND....4-6 82-85
Singles: 7-inch
ISLAND....3-4 82-85
LPs: 10/12-inch
ISLAND....5-8 83-85
Also see WORLD'S FAMOUS SUPREME TEAM

McLAUGHLIN, John LP '72
(Mahavishnu Orchestra & John McLaughlin; Mahavishnu John McLaughlin; with One Truth Band)
LPs: 10/12-inch
COLUMBIA....5-10 72-83
DOUGLAS....8-12 72
POLYDOR....8-15 69-72
W.B. 5-8 81
Also see SANTANA, Carlos, & Mahavishnu John McLaughlin

McLAUGHLIN, Pat LP '88
LPs: 10/12-inch
CAPITOL....5-8 88

McLAURIN, Bette P&R '52
(With the Four Fellows; with Striders; Betty McLaurin)
Singles: 78 rpm
CENTRAL....10-15 54
CORAL....10-15 53
DERBY (700 series)....10-15 50-52
DERBY (804 "My Heart Belongs to Only You")....20-40 52
GLORY....10-15 55
JUBILEE....10-15 55
Singles: 7-inch
ALMONT (309 "You're the Greatest")....50-100 58
CAPITOL (4320 "Remember")....15-25 59
CENTRAL (1004 "It's Easy to Remember")....20-30 54
CORAL (61129 "If You Believed in Me")....15-25 53
DERBY (790 "I May Hate Myself in the Morning")....20-30 51
DERBY (804 "My Heart Belongs to Only You")....50-75 52
GLORY (233 "Grow Old Along with Me")....25-50 55
GLORY (237 "Just Come a Little Bit Closer")....25-50 55
GLORY (241 "I'm Past Sixteen")....25-50 55
JUBILEE (5139 "Please Don't Leave Me")....15-25 55
JUBILEE (5155 "Ever So Lonely")....15-25 55
JUBILEE (5179 "How Can I")....15-25 55
O GEE (100 "The Masquerade Is Over")....15-25 59
PULSE....5-10 65
Also see FOUR FELLOWS

McLEAN, Don P&R/LP '71
Singles: 7-inch
ARISTA....3-5 78
CAPITOL....3-4 87-88
EMI AMERICA (Except 9100)....3-4 87
EMI AMERICA (9100 "American Pie")..4-8 92
(Full length [8:30] version.)
LIBERTY....3-5
MEDIARTS....3-6 70
MILLENNIUM....3-5 81-83
RCA....3-4 83
U.A. 3-5 71-75
Picture Sleeves
U.A. 3-5 71-73
LPs: 10/12-inch
ARISTA (4149 "Prime Time")....5-10 77
(Black vinyl.)
ARISTA (4149 "Prime Time")....10-15 77
(Colored vinyl. Promotional issue only.)
CASABLANCA....8-10 79
LIBERTY....5-8 82-83
MEDIARTS (41-4 "Tapestry")....8-12 70
MILLENNIUM....5-8 81
U.A. 10-12 71-74
Promotional LPs
RCA ("Special Radio Series")....10-15 81

McLEAN, Penny P&R/R&B '76
Singles: 7-inch
ATCO....3-5 75-76
Also see SILVER CONVENTION

McLEAN, Phil P&R '61
Singles: 7-inch
VERSATILE....4-8 61-62

McLOLLIE, Oscar
(With the Honey Jumpers; Oscar Lollie)
Singles: 78 rpm
CLASS....5-10 57
MERCURY....5-10 51-56
MODERN....10-20 52-55
WING....10-15 56
Singles: 7-inch
CLASS....6-12 57-59
MERCURY (70000 series)....10-15 56
MODERN (902 "Honey Jump")....30-40 52
MODERN (915 "Be Cool, My Heart") 25-35 52
MODERN (920 "Falling in Love with You")....25-35 54
MODERN (928 "Mama Don't Like")...20-30 54
MODERN (932 "Hot Banana")....20-30 54
MODERN (940 "Love Me Tonight")...20-30 54
MODERN (943 "Dig That Crazy Santa Claus")....20-30 54
MODERN (950 "Hey Lolly Lolly")....20-30 55
MODERN (955 "Eternal Love")....20-30 55
MODERN (970 "Convicted")....20-30 55
RENDEZVOUS....5-10 61
WING....10-15 56
LPs: 10/12-inch
CROWN (5016 "Oscar McLollie & His Honey Jumpers")....150-200 56

McLOLLIE, Oscar, & Jeanette Baker P&R '58
Singles: 7-inch
CLASS (228 "Hey Girl - Hey Boy")....10-15 58

McLOLLIE, Oscar, & Nancy Lamarr
Singles: 7-inch
SAHARA....5-10 63
Also see McLOLLIE, Oscar

McLYTE LP '89
LPs: 10/12-inch
FIRST PRIORITY....5-8 89

McMAHON, Gerard P&R '83
Singles: 7-inch
FULL MOON....3-4 83
LPs: 10/12-inch
FULL MOON....5-8 83

McMURTRY, James LP '89
LPs: 10/12-inch
COLUMBIA....5-8 89

McNALLY, Larry John P&R '81
Singles: 7-inch
ARC....3-4 81

McNAMARA, Robin P&R '70
Singles: 7-inch
STEED....3-5 69-71
LPs: 10/12-inch
STEED....10-15 70

McNEELY, Big Jay R&B '49
(With His Blue Jays; with Little Sonny Warner)
Singles: 78 rpm
ALADDIN....20-30 49-54
BAYOU....20-30 53
FEDERAL....10-20 52-54
EXCLUSIVE....15-25 46
IMPERIAL....10-20 51-52
SAVOY....10-20 48-54
VEE JAY....10-20 55-56
Singles: 7-inch
ALADDIN (3242 "Real Crazy Cool") 15-25 54
BAYOU (014 "Hometown Jamboree")....40-60 53
BAYOU (018 "Catastrophe")....40-60 53
FEDERAL (12102 "The Goof")....20-30 52
FEDERAL (12111 "Earthquake")....20-30 52
FEDERAL (12141 "Nervous, Man Nervous")....20-30 53
FEDERAL (12151 "3-D")....20-30 53
FEDERAL (12168 "Mule Walk")....20-30 54

FEDERAL (12179 "Hot Cinders")......20-30 54
FEDERAL (12186 "Let's Work")........20-30 54
FEDERAL (12191 "Beachcomber")...20-30 54
IMPERIAL (5219 "Deacon's Express")......................................25-35 53
SAVOY (1143 "Deacon's Hop").........15-25 54
SWINGIN'.......................................10-15 59-61
VEE JAY (142 "Big Jay's Hop").........25-35 55
VEE JAY (212 "Jay's Rock") 25-35 56
W.B. 4-8 63

EPs: 7–inch

FEDERAL (246 "Go! Go! Go! with Big Jay McNeely") 100-200 53
FEDERAL (301 Big Jay McNeely, Vol. 2")......................................100-150 54
FEDERAL (332 Wild Man of the Saxophone") 100-150 54
FEDERAL (373 Just Crazy") 75-100 55

LPs: 10/12–inch

COLLECTABLES 5-8 88
FEDERAL (96 "Big Jay McNeely") 600-800 54
(10–inch LP.)
FEDERAL (530 "Big Jay in 3-D")...250-350 57
KING (650 "Big Jay in 3-D") 50-75 59
SAVOY (15045 "Rhythm & Blues Concert")......................................250-350 55
(10–inch LP.)
W.B. (W-1523 "Big Jay McNeely") 25-35 63
(Monaural.)
W.B. (WS-1523 "Big Jay McNeely") .30-40 63
(Stereo.)
Also see OTIS, Johnny

McNEELY, Big Jay / Paul Williams

Singles: 78 rpm

SAVOY 10-15 49-55

Singles: 7–inch

SAVOY (1100 series) 15-25 55
Also see McNEELY, Big Jay
Also see WILLIAMS, Paul

McNEIR, Ronnie R&B '75

Singles: 7–inch

CAPITOL 3-4 84
DETO (2878 "Sitting in My Class") 75-125
PRODIGAL..3-5 75

LPs: 10/12–inch

CAPITOL 5-8 84

McNICHOL, Kristy & Jimmy P&R/LP '78

Singles: 7–inch

RCA..3-5 78

Picture Sleeves

RCA..3-5 78

LPs: 10/12–inch

RCA...5-10 78

M'COOL, Shamus P&R '81

Singles: 7–inch

PERSPECTIVE 3-4 81

McPHATTER, Clyde P&R/R&B '56

Singles: 78 rpm

ATLANTIC (1081 thru 1185).............20-30 56-57
ATLANTIC (1199 "A Lover's Question")..40-60 58

Singles: 7–inch

AMY 5-15 65-67
ATLANTIC (1000 series) 15-25 56-58
ATLANTIC (2000 series) 10-20 58-60
DECCA..4-8 70
DERAM..4-8 68-69
MGM (12000 series)..........................10-15 59-60
(Monaural.)
MGM (50134 "Let's Try Again") 20-40 60
(Stereo.)
MERCURY 6-12 60-65

EPs: 7–inch

ATLANTIC (584 "Clyde McPhatter") .50-75 58
ATLANTIC (605 "Rock with Clyde McPhatter")....................................50-75 58
ATLANTIC (618 "Clyde McPhatter") .50-75 59
MERCURY ("Golden Blues Hits") 10-15 62
(Has paper sleeve. Number not known. Promotional issue only.)

LPs: 10/12–inch

ALLEGIANCE 5-8 80s
ATLANTIC (8024 "Love Ballads") 100-150 59
(Black label.)
ATLANTIC (8024 "Love Ballads")..... 25-50 59
(Red label.)
ATLANTIC (8031 "Clyde") 50-100 59
ATLANTIC (8077 "Best of Clyde McPhatter") 25-35 63
DECCA 15-25 70
MGM (E-3775 "Let's Start Over Again")... 30-40 59
(Monaural.)
MGM (SE-3775 "Let's Start Over Again")... 40-50 59
(Stereo.)
MGM (E-3866 "Greatest Hits").......... 30-40 60
(Monaural.)
MGM (SE-3866 "Greatest Hits") 40-50 60
(Stereo.)
MERCURY.. 20-35 60-64
WING 20-30 62
Session: King Curtis.
Also see BROWN, Ruth, & Clyde McPhatter
Also see DOMINOES
Also see DRIFTERS
Also see KING CURTIS
Also see LITTLE ESTHER & Clyde McPhatter

McPHATTER, Clyde / Little Richard / Jerry Butler

LPs: 10/12–inch

PICKWICK (3233 "Rhythm & Blues and Greens") 15-20 70s
Also see BUTLER, Jerry
Also see LITTLE RICHARD
Also see McPHATTER, Clyde

McPHERSON, Wyatt (Earp) P&R/R&B '61

Singles: 7–inch

SAVOY 4-8 61

McPHERSON, Wyatt "Earp," & Paul Williams

Singles: 7–inch

BATTLE 4-8 63
Also see McPHERSON, Wyatt "Earp"
Also see WILLIAMS, Paul

McRAE, Carmen P&R '56

Singles: 78 rpm

DECCA 3-6 55-57
VENUS.. 4-8 54

Singles: 7–inch

COLUMBIA 4-6 62
DECCA 5-10 55-57
KAPP 4-8 63
VENUS.. 5-10 54

Picture Sleeves

COLUMBIA 4-8 62

EPs: 7–inch

DECCA 5-10 55

LPs: 10/12–inch

BETHLEHEM (1023 "Carmen McRae") 75-125 54
(10–inch LP.)
COLUMBIA....................................... 15-25 61-65
DECCA (8100 thru 8800 series) 40-60 55-58
(Black and silver label.)
DECCA (8100 thru 8800 series) 15-25 64
(Black label with horizonal rainbow stripe.)
FOCUS 15-25 65
KAPP 20-40 58-59
MAINSTREAM.................................. 10-20 65-67
TIME.. 15-25 63
Also see CONNOR, Chris / Julie London / Carmen McRae
Also see DAVIS, Sammy, Jr., & Carmen McRae
Also see SIMONE, Nina, Chris Connor & Carmen McRae

McSHANN, Jay P&R '41

(With His Orchestra; Combo; Trio; Quartet; Sextet; Kansas City Stompers; Jazz Men)

Singles: 78 rpm

ALADDIN 10-15 50
CAPITOL.. 10-20 44-45
DECCA 10-15 41-43
DOWN BEAT 10-15 48-49
MERCURY 10-15 45-46
MODERN..10-15 50
PHILO/ALADDIN 10-20 45
PREMIER 10-15 45
SWING TIME.....................................10-15 48-52
VEE JAY 5-10 55-56

Singles: 7–inch

SWING TIME (314 "Jeromimo")........20-25 52
VEE JAY...10-20 55-56

EPs: 7–inch

DECCA (742 "Kansas City Memories") 50-100 54

LPs: 10/12–inch

CAPITOL 15-20 67
DECCA (5503 "Kansas City Memories") 250-350 54
(10–inch LP. With Charlie Parker, Al Hibbler, Walter Brown, & Paul Paul Quinichette.)
DECCA (9000 series).......................10-15 68
Also see HIBBLER, Al
Also see WITHERSPOON, Jimmy

McSHANN, Jay, With Johnny Moore's Three Blazers

Singles: 78 rpm

MODERN.......................................10-15 50
Also see MOORE, Johnny

McSHANN, Jay, & Priscilla Bowman

Singles: 78 rpm

VEE JAY...5-10 55

Singles: 7–inch

VEE JAY...10-15 55
Also see BOWMAN, Priscilla
Also see McSHANN, Jay

McSHY D LP '87

LPs: 10/12–inch

LUKE SKYWALKER 5-8 87

McVEA, Jack P&R/R&B '47

(With His All-Stars)

Singles: 78 rpm

APOLLO 10-15 45
BLACK & WHITE 10-20 45-47
EXCLUSIVE 10-15 47
COMBO 8-12 56
MELODISC 10-20 45

Singles: 7–inch

COMBO (Except 55).........................10-20 56
COMBO (55 "Let's Ride, Ride, Ride")..15-25 55
TAG 10-15 56
Also see BROWN, Clarence "Gatemouth"

McVIE, Christine LP '76

Singles: 7–inch

W.B. 3-4 84

Picture Sleeves

W.B. 3-4 84

LPs: 10/12–inch

SIRE 8-10 76
W.B. 5-8 84
Also see BURNETTE, Billy, & Christine McVie
Also see FLEETWOOD MAC
Also see NEWMAN, Randy

McWILLIAMS, Paulette R&B '77

Singles: 7–inch

FANTASY..3-5 77
Also see AMERICAN BREED
Also see RUFUS

MEAD, Sister Janet P&R '74

Singles: 7–inch

A&M..3-5 74

MEADER, Vaughn LP '62

LPs: 10/12–inch

CADENCE..10-20 62-63
KAMA-SUTRA......................................8-15 60s

MEADOWS BROTHERS R&B '77

Singles: 7–inch

KAYVETTE..3-4 87

MEAGAN D&D '84

Singles: 7-inch

NEXT PLATINUM....4-6 84

MEAN MACHINE R&B '81

Singles: 7-inch

SUGAR HILL....3-4 81

MEAT LOAF LP '77

(Marvin Lee Aday; with Ellen Foley)

Singles: 12-inch

EPIC (477 "Meat Loaf")....5-8 77
(Promotional issue only.)

Singles: 7-inch

EPIC....3-5 77-83
RCA....3-4 85
RSO....3-5 74

Picture Sleeves

RCA....3-5 85

LPs: 10/12-inch

CLEVELAND INT'L....5-8 81-83
EPIC (30000 series, except 34974 & 36007)....5-10 77-80
EPIC (34974 "Bat Out of Hell")....5-10 77
EPIC (E99-34974 "Bat Out of Hell")..20-25 77
(Picture disc. With bats on front cover.)
EPIC (E99-34974 "Bat Out of Hell")..25-35 77
(Picture disc. Without bats on front cover. Promotional issue only.)
EPIC (34974 "Bat Out of Hell")....25-35 77
(Picture disc. Canadian.)
EPIC (36007 "Dead Ringer")....25-35 81
(Picture disc. Promotional issue only.)
EPIC (40000 series)....12-15 80
(Half-speed mastered.)
Also see FOLEY, Ellen
Also see STONEY & Meat Loaf

MECO P&R/R&B/LP '77

(Meco Monardo)

Singles: 12-inch

ARISTA....4-6 83

Singles: 7-inch

ARISTA....3-4 82-83
MILLENNIUM....3-5 77-78
RSO....3-5 80

LPs: 10/12-inch

ARISTA....5-8 82-84
CASABLANCA....5-10 79-80
MILLENNIUM....5-10 77-78
RSO....5-8 80
Also see STAR WARS INTERGALACTIC DROID CHOIR & CHORALE

MEDEIROS, Glenn P&R/LP '87

Singles: 7-inch

AMHERST....3-4 87-88

Picture Sleeves

AMHERST....3-4 87-88

LPs: 10/12-inch

AMHERST....5-8 87
MCA....5-8 90
Also see PARKER, Ray, Jr.

MEDEIROS, Glenn, & Bobby Brown

Singles: 7-inch

MCA....3-4 90

Picture Sleeves

MCA....3-4 90
Also see BROWN, Bobby

MEDEIROS, Glenn, & Stylistics P&R '90

Singles: 7-inch

MCA....3-4 90
Also see MEDEIROS, Glenn
Also see STYLISTICS

MEDLEY, Bill P&R/R&B/LP '68

Singles: 7-inch

A&M....3-5 71-73
CURB....3-5 89
ELEKTRA....3-4 90
LIBERTY....3-5 81
MGM....4-8 68
PARAMOUNT....3-5 71
PLANET....3-4 82-83
RCA....3-4 83-85
REPRISE....4-8 65
SCOTTI BROTHERS....3-4 88
U.A. 3-5 78-80
VERVE....4-8 67

Picture Sleeves

SCOTTI BROTHERS....3-4 88

LPs: 10/12-inch

A&M....8-12 71-73
LIBERTY....5-10 81
MCA/CURB....5-10 88
MGM....10-20 68-70
PLANET....8-10 82
RCA....5-8 83-85
U.A. 5-10 78-85
Also see KNIGHT, Gladys, & Bill Medley
Also see RIGHTEOUS BROTHERS
Also see SONNY & CHER / Bill Medley / Lettermen / Blendells

MEDLEY, Bill, & Jennifer Warnes P&R '87

Singles: 7-inch

RCA....3-4 87

Picture Sleeves

RCA....3-4 87
Also see MEDLEY, Bill
Also see WARNES, Jennifer

MEDLIN, Joe P&R '59

Singles: 7-inch

BRUNSWICK....4-8 61
MERCURY....4-8 59-60

MEGADETH LP '86

EPs: 7-inch

MEGAFORCE....5-10 89

LPs: 10/12-inch

CAPITOL....5-8 86-90
Members: Dave Mustaine; Dave Ellefson; Gar Samuelson.

MEGATONS P&R '62

Singles: 7-inch

CHECKER....5-10 62
DODGE....10-15 62
FOREST....4-8 63
JELL....4-8 62
Member: Billy Lee Riley.
Also see RILEY, Billy Lee

MEGATRONS P&R '59

Singles: 7-inch

ACOUSTICON (101 "Velvet Waters")....30-40 59
(First issue.)
AUDICON (101 "Velvet Waters")....10-20 59
AUDICON (104 "Whispering Winds")....10-20 60
AUDICON (107 "Ranchero")....10-20 60
AUDICON (110 "By the Waters of Minnetonka")....10-20 61
LAURIE (3291 "Velvet Waters")....6-12 63
LAURIE (3310 "Detroit Sound")....6-12 65

MEISNER, Randy P&R/LP '80

Singles: 7-inch

ASYLUM....3-5 78
EPIC....3-5 80-82

LPs: 10/12-inch

ASYLUM....8-10 78
EPIC....5-10 80-82
Also see EAGLES
Also see NELSON, Rick
Also see POCO

MEL & KIM P&R/R&B '87

Singles: 7-inch

ATLANTIC....3-4 87

Picture Sleeves

ATLANTIC....3-4 87
Members: Mel Appleby; Kim Appleby.

MEL & TIM P&R/R&B '69

Singles: 7-inch

BAMBOO....4-6 69-70
COLLECTABLES....3-4 80s
ERIC....3-4 70s
STAX....3-5 72-74

LPs: 10/12-inch

BAMBOO....10-15 70
STAX....8-12 72-74
Members: Mel Harden; Tim McPherson.

MELACHRINO, George, & His Orchestra LP '55

Singles: 78 rpm

RCA....3-5 50-57

Singles: 7-inch

RCA....4-8 50-59

EPs: 7-inch

RCA....5-10 50-59

LPs: 10/12-inch

RCA....10-20 50-61

MELANIE LP '69

(With the Edwin Hawkins Singers)

Singles: 7-inch

ABC/MCA....3-5 75
AMHERST....3-4 85
ATLANTIC....3-5 77
BLANCHE....3-4 82
BUDDAH....3-8 69-73
CASABLANCA....3-5 74
COLUMBIA (44349 "God's Only Daughter")....10-15 67
COLUMBIA (44524 "Garden in the City")....8-12 68
ERIC....3-4 78
FLASHBACK....3-4 70s
GOLDIES....3-4 70s
GORDIAN....5-10 85
MIDSONG INT'L....3-5 78-79
NEIGHBORHOOD....3-5 71-75
PORTRAIT....3-4 81
RADIO ACTIVE GOLD....3-4 80s
STORK....5-10 70
(Promotional issue only.)
TOMATO....3-5 78-79
WHAT'S IT ALL ABOUT....4-6 70s
(Promotional issue only.)
WORLD UNITED....3-5 78

Picture Sleeves

BUDDAH....3-4 70-72
NEIGHBORHOOD....3-4 72-73

EPs: 7-inch

BUDDAH....5-8 70
(Juke box issue.)

LPs: 10/12-inch

ABC....8-10 75
ACCORD....5-8 81-82
AMHERST....8-10 85
ARISTA....5-10 75-77
ATLANTIC....8-10 76
BELL....8-10 71
BLANCHE....5-8 82
BUDDAH....10-15 69-77
51 WEST....5-8 79
KOALA....5-10 79
MCA/MIDSONG....5-10 77-78
NEIGHBORHOOD....8-10 71-75
PAIR....5-10 88
PICKWICK....8-10 71
TELLENHOUSE....15-25 78
TOMATO....5-10 79
Also see HAWKINS, Edwin, Singers

MELBA & KASHIF: see MOORE, Melba, & Kashif

MELLAA R&B '83

Singles: 7-inch

LARC....3-4 83

MELLE MEL & DUKE BOOTEE R&B '82

Singles: 12-inch

SUGAR HILL....4-6 82
Also see BOOTEE, Duke
Also see GRANDMASTER FLASH & Furious Five

MELLENCAMP, John Cougar

(John Cougar; Johnny Cougar; John Mellencamp) *P&R/LP '79*

Singles: 7-inch

MAIN MAN (4001 "Kid Inside")......100-125 83
(Picture disc. Has four tracks. Promotional issue only.)
MAIN MAN (4001 "Kid Inside")........75-100 83
(Picture disc. Has two tracks. Promotional issue only. Autographed.)
MAIN MAN (4001 "Kid Inside")..........60-80 83
(Picture disc. Has two tracks. Promotional issue only. Not Autographed.)

Singles: 7-inch

MERCURY 3-4 87-90
RIVA (Except 211 & 215) 3-5 79-85
RIVA (211 "Hand to Hold on To")..........3-4 82
RIVA (211 "Hand to Hold on To")......20-25 82
(Promotional only picture disc.)
RIVA (215 "Pink Houses")..................5-10 83
(Colored vinyl.)

Picture Sleeves

MERCURY 3-4 87-90
RIVA 4-8 79-86

EPs: 7-inch

GULCHER ("U.S. Male")..................50-75 75
(Selection number not known.)

LPs: 10/12-inch

MCA (2225 "Chestnut Street Incident")..........................15-20 77
MAIN MAN ("Chestnut Street Incident")..........................30-40 76
MAIN MAN (601 "Kid Inside").............5-10 83
MERCURY (Except 349)......................5-8 87-90
MERCURY (349 "Let It All Hang").....25-35 87
(Interview LP. Promotional issue only.)
MFSL (222 "Lonesome Jubilee").......20-25 94
RIVA 5-10 79-85

Members: John Cougar Mellencamp; Larry Crane; David Parman; Terrence Sala; Wayne Hall; Tom Wince; Michael Wanchic; Doc Rosser; Ken Aronoff; George Perry; Toby Myers; John Cascalle.

MELLODEERS: see MELODEERS

MELLO-KINGS

(Mellokings; Mellotones) *P&R '57*

Singles: 78 rpm

HERALD (502 "Tonite Tonite")......150-250 57
(Credits "The Mellotones.")
HERALD (502 "Tonite Tonite")........75-125 57
(Credits "The Mello-Kings.")

Singles: 7-inch

COLLECTABLES 3-4 80s
FLASHBACK......................................3-5 65
HERALD (502 "Tonite Tonite")......300-500 57
(Credits "The Mellotones.")
HERALD (502 "Tonite Tonite").........15-25 57
(Credits "The Mello-Kings." Has logo in script print inside the flag.)
HERALD (502 "Tonite Tonite").........10-15
(Credits "The Mello-Kings." Has logo in block print inside the flag.)
HERALD (507 thru 567) 10-20 57-61
LESCAY 10-15 62

EPs: 7-inch

HERALD (451 "The Fabulous Mello-Kings")..........................200-250 60

LPs: 10/12-inch

COLLECTABLES..................................6-8 84
HERALD (1013 "Tonight Tonight") 350-500 60
RELIC 5-10 80s

Members: Larry Esposita; Bob Scholl; Jerry Scholl; Eddie Quinn; Neil Areana.

MELLO-MOODS

(Mellow Moods; Mello Moods; Mellomoods; with Teacho Wiltshire & Band; with Schubert Swanston Trio) *R&B '52*

Singles: 78 rpm

PRESTIGE (799 "Call on Me")......100-200 53
PRESTIGE (856 "I'm Lost")..........100-200 53
ROBIN (104 "I Couldn't Sleep a Wink Last Night")...................................100-300 52
ROBIN (105 "Where Are You")..... 100-300 52

Singles: 7-inch

HAMILTON (143 "I'm Lost")............. 10-15
PRESTIGE (799 "Call on Me")...................................... 1000-2000 53
PRESTIGE (856 "I'm Lost") 1000-2000 53
ROBIN (104 "I Couldn't Sleep a Wink Last Night") 1000-2000 52
ROBIN (105 "Where Are You") 1000-2000 52

Members: Ray "Buddy" Wooten; Bobby Williams; Monte Owens; Bobby Baylor; Jimmy Bethea.
Also see SOLITAIRES

MELLOTONES: see MELLO-KINGS

MELLO-TONES

(With Hank Ivory's Orchestra) *P&R '57*

Singles: 78 rpm

FASCINATION.............................. 50-75 57
GEE 20-30 57

Singles: 7-inch

FASCINATION (1001 "Rosie Lee")................................... 150-250 57
GEE (1037 "Rosie Lee") 25-50 57
GEE (1040 "Ca-Sandra")................. 25-50 57

MELODEERS

(Mellodeers) *P&R '60*

Singles: 7-inch

SHELLEY (127 "The Letter") 10-20 61
SHELLEY (161 "Born to Be Mine")... 15-25 62
STUDIO (9908 "Rudolph the Red Nosed Reindeer") 10-20 60

Picture Sleeves

STUDIO (9908 "Rudolph the Red Nosed Reindeer") 20-40 60
(Sleeve credits "Mellodeers.")
STUDIO (9909 "Happy Teenage Times")...................................... 15-25 60

MELODY MAKERS

(Ziggy Marley & Melody Makers) *P&R/LP '88*

Singles: 12-inch

EMI AMERICA 4-6 84-85

Singles: 7-inch

EMI AMERICA 3-4 84-85
VIRGIN.. 3-4 88

Picture Sleeves

VIRGIN.. 3-4 88

LPs: 10/12-inch

EMI AMERICA 5-8 84-85
VIRGIN.. 5-8 88-91

Members: David "Ziggy" Marley; Steve Marley; Cedella Marley; Sharon Marley. All are the children of Bob Marley.
Also see MARLEY, Bob

MELVIN, Harold

(With the Bluenotes) *R&B '65*

Singles: 12-inch

PHILADELPHIA INT'L........................ 4-8 80
SOURCE... 4-8 79-80

Singles: 7-inch

ABC... 3-5 76-78
ARCTIC.. 5-10 67
LANDA (703 "You May Not Love Me").. 25-35 64
MCA 3-5 81
PHILADELPHIA INT'L....................... 3-5 72-79
PHIL-L.A. of SOUL.......................... 3-5 71
PHILLY WORLD 3-4 84-85
SOURCE.. 3-5 79-80

Picture Sleeves

PHILADELPHIA INT'L........................ 3-5 72-75

LPs: 10/12-inch

ABC... 8-10 77
MCA 5-8 81
PHILADELPHIA INT'L...................... 8-12 72-76
PHILLY WORLD 5-8 84-85
SOURCE... 5-10 80

Also see BLUENOTES
Also see PAIGE, Sharon
Also see PENDERGRASS, Teddy

MELVINS: see NIRVANA / The Melvins

MEMPHIS HORNS

R&B '76

Singles: 7-inch

COTILLION..4-6 69
RCA 3-5 76-78

LPs: 10/12-inch

RCA 5-10 77-78

Members: Wayne Jackson; Andrew Love; Jimmy Brown; Andy Love; Floyd Newman; Don Chandler; Charlie Freeman; Tommy McClure; Sammy Creason.
Also see CRAY, Robert, Band, with the Memphis Horns
Also see McDONALD, Michael
Also see MOORE, Jackie
Also see POINTER SISTERS

MEMPHIS SLIM

(With His House Rockers; Peter Chatman) *R&B '48*

Singles: 78 rpm

BLUEBIRD...25-50 40-41
CHESS 20-40 52
FEDERAL..20-40 49-50
HY-TONE 20-40 46
MASTER...20-40 48-49
KING...20-40 49
MELODY LANE 20-40 46
MERCURY 10-20 51-52
MIRACLE..20-40 47-49
MONEY 15-25 54
OLD SWINGMASTER.........................20-40 48
PEACOCK...20-40 49
PREMIUM..20-30 50-52
UNITED 15-25 52-54

Singles: 7-inch

JOSIE 4-8 67
KING (6300 series)............................3-5 70
MERCURY 20-40 51-52
MONEY 20-40 54
PEACOCK (1600 series)....................20-40 52
STRAND..10-20 61
UNITED (Black vinyl).........................25-50 52-54
UNITED (156 "The Comeback")......50-100 53
(Colored vinyl.)
UNITED (166 "Call Before You Go Home")..50-100 53
(Colored vinyl.)
UNITED (176 "Sassy Mae") 50-100 54
(Colored vinyl.)
VEE JAY..10-15 58-60

LPs: 10/12-inch

BATTLE (6118 "Alone with My Friends") 20-30 63
BARNABY 8-12 72
BLACK LION 8-10 74
BUDDAH 10-20 69
CANDID (8024 "Memphis Slim U.S.A.")...35-45 62
(Monaural.)
CANDID (9024 "Memphis Slim U.S.A.")...40-50 62
(Stereo.)
CHESS (1455 "Memphis Slim") 50-75 61
CHESS (1510 "Real Folk Blues")......20-35 66
EVEREST..10-15 68-74
FANTASY..10-12 72
FOLKWAYS 8-10 74
GNP..8-12 74
JAZZMAN 5-8 82
JEWEL 8-12 71
KING (885 "Memphis Slim") 40-60 64
KING (1082 "Messin' Around with the Blues") 10-15 70
MUSE 6-12 81
PEARL..5-10 78
PRESTIGE BLUESVILLE..................20-40 61-64
SCEPTER (535 "Self-Portrait") 15-25 66
SPIN-O-RAMA...................................10-15 60s
STORYVILLE 5-8 84
STRAND (1046 "World's Foremost Blues Singer")...25-40 61
TRIP 8-10 70s
U.A. (3137 "Broken Soul Blues").......30-40 61
(Monaural.)
U.A. (6137 "Broken Soul Blues").......40-50 61
(Stereo.)

VEE JAY (1012 "At the Gate of Horn") 60-80 59
W.B. 10-15 71-72
Also see DIXON, Willie, & Memphis Slim
Also see HOOKER, John Lee
Also see HUNTER, Ivory Joe / Memphis Slim
Also see WILLIAMSON, Sonny Boy

MEMPHIS SLIM & LOWELL FULSOM

LPs: 10/12-inch

INNER CITY 5-8
Also see FULSON, Lowell

MEMPHIS SLIM & CURTIS JONES

LPs: 10/12-inch

CANDID (8023 "Tribute to Big Bill Broonzy") 35-45 61
(Monaural.)
CANDID (9023 "Tribute to Big Bill Broonzy") 40-50 62
(Stereo.)

MEMPHIS SLIM & MATT MURPHY

LPs: 10/12-inch

ANTONE'S 5-10 87

MEMPHIS SLIM & ROOSEVELT SYKES

LPs: 10/12-inch

OLYMPIC 8-12 75
Also see SYKES, Roosevelt

MEMPHIS SLIM & VAGABONDS / Reverend Bounce

Singles: 78 rpm

PREMIUM 15-25 50
Also see MEMPHIS SLIM

MEN at WORK — P&R/LP '82

Singles: 12-inch

COLUMBIA 4-6 82-83

Singles: 7-inch

COLUMBIA 3-4 82-85

Picture Sleeves

COLUMBIA (Except 1633) 3-4 83-85
COLUMBIA (1633 "Overkill") 5-10 83
(Promotional issue only.)

LPs: 10/12-inch

COLUMBIA (1650 "Cargo World Premier Weekend") 10-15 83
(Promotional issue only.)
COLUMBIA (37978 "Business As Usual") 5-10 82
(With "ARC" or "FC" prefix.)
COLUMBIA (PAL-37978 "Business As Usual") 35-45 83
(Picture disc. Promotional issue only.)
COLUMBIA (38167 "Business As Usual") 5-8 82
COLUMBIA (38660 "Cargo") 5-8 83
COLUMBIA (40078 "Two Hearts") 5-8 85
COLUMBIA (47978 "Business As Usual") 10-15 85
(Half-speed mastered.)
COLUMBIA (48660 "Cargo") 10-15 85
Members: Colin Hay; Ron Strykert; Jerry Speiser; John Rees; Greg Ham.
Also see HAY, Colin James

MEN WITHOUT HATS — P&R/D&D/LP '83

Singles: 12-inch

BACKSTREET 4-6 83
MCA 4-6 83-84

Singles: 7-inch

BACKSTREET 3-4 83
MCA 3-4 83-84
MERCURY 3-4 87

Picture Sleeves

BACKSTREET 3-4 83
MCA 3-4 83
MERCURY 3-4 87

LPs: 10/12-inch

BACKSTREET 5-8 83
MCA 5-8 84
MERCURY 5-8 87

MENAGE — D&D '83

Singles: 12-inch

PROFILE 4-6 83-85

Singles: 7-inch

PROFILE 3-4 83-85

LPs: 10/12-inch

PROFILE 5-8 83

MENDES, Sergio — P&R/LP '66

(With Brasil '66; Brasil '77; Trio)

Singles: 12-inch

A&M 4-6 82

Singles: 7-inch

A&M (807 thru 1257) 3-6 66-71
A&M (1279 thru 2700 series) 3-5 71-85
ATLANTIC 4-6 67-68
BELL 3-5 73
ELEKTRA 3-5 75-80

Picture Sleeves

A&M 3-6 68-69

LPs: 10/12-inch

A&M (Except 4100 series) 5-12 69-84
A&M (4100 series) 10-15 66-69
ATLANTIC 15-25 65-68
BELL 8-10 73-74
CAPITOL (T-2294 "In a Brazilian Bag") 40-50 65
(Monaural.)
CAPITOL (ST-2294 "In a Brazilian Bag") 50-60 65
(Stereo.)
ELEKTRA 8-10 75-79
EVEREST 8-10 74
MFSL 15-25 84
PHILIPS 10-12 68
TOWER (T-5052 "In a Brazilian Bag") 30-40 65
(Monaural.)
TOWER (ST-5052 "In a Brazilian Bag") 40-50 65
(Stereo.)
Also see ADDERLEY, Julian "Cannonball," & Sergio Mendes
Also see HALL, Lani

MENUDO — R&B/LP '84

Singles: 7-inch

RCA 3-4 84-85

LPs: 10/12-inch

RCA 5-8 84-85
Also see KING DREAM CHORUS & Holiday Crew

MERC & MONK — R&B '85

Singles: 7-inch

MANHATTAN 3-5 85
Members: Eric Mercury; Thelonious Monk.
Also see MERCURY, Eric
Also see MONK, Thelonious

MERCER, Johnny — P&R '38

Singles: 78 rpm

CAPITOL 4-8 42-52
DECCA 4-8 38

Singles: 7-inch

CAPITOL 5-10 50-52

EPs: 7-inch

CAPITOL (210 "Music of Kern") 10-20 50

LPs: 10/12-inch

CAPITOL (210 "Music of Kern") 40-50 50
(10-inch LP.)
CAPITOL (214 "Mercer Sings") 40-50 50
(10-inch LP.)
CAPITOL (907 "Ac-Cent-Tchu-Ate the Positive") 25-40 57
JUPITER (1001 "Just for Fun") 25-45 56
Also see CROSBY, Bing, & Johnny Mercer
Also see DARIN, Bobby, & Johnny Mercer

MERCURY, Eric

LPs: 10/12-inch

AVCO EMBASSY 10-15 69
CAPITOL 5-10 81
ENTERPRISE 8-12 72-73
SACK (1 "Lonely Girl") 300-500
Also see FLACK, Roberta, & Eric Mercury
Also see MERC & MONK

MERCURY, Freddie — P&R/D&D '84

Singles: 12-inch

COLUMBIA 4-6 84

Singles: 7-inch

COLUMBIA 3-5 84-85
EMI (6151 "Great Pretender") 30-40 87
(Antique radio-shaped picture disc.)

Picture Sleeves

COLUMBIA 4-8 84-85

LPs: 10/12-inch

COLUMBIA 5-8 85
Also see QUEEN

MERCURY, Freddie / Giorgio Moroder

Singles: 12-inch

COLUMBIA 4-6 84
Also see MERCURY, Freddie
Also see MORODER, Giorgio

MERCY — P&R/LP '69

Singles: 7-inch

SUNDI 4-8 69
W.B. 4-8 69

LPs: 10/12-inch

SUNDI 15-20 68
W.B. 10-15 69
Members: James Marvell; Ronnie Coudill; Roger Fuentes; Buddy Good; Debbie Lewis; Brenda McNish.

MERCY DEE — R&B '49

(Mercy Dee Walton)

Singles: 78 rpm

BAYOU 25-50 50
COLONY 20-40 50
FLAIR 15-25 55
IMPERIAL 20-40 50
RHYTHM 50-75 54
SPECIALTY 15-25 53
SPIRE 20-40 49

Singles: 7-inch

BAYOU (013 "Danger Zone") 75-125 50
FLAIR (1073 "Romp & Stomp Blues") 40-60 55
RHYTHM (1774 "Trailing My Baby") 150-200 54
SPECIALTY (Except 466) 20-40 53-54
SPECIALTY (466 "Rent Man Blues") 20-40 53
(Black vinyl.)
SPECIALTY (466 "Rent Man Blues") 75-125 53
(Colored vinyl.)

LPs: 10/12-inch

ARHOOLIE 15-25 61

MERGE — R&B '82

Singles: 7-inch

RCA 3-4 87

MERMAIDS: see MURMAIDS

MERMAN, Ethel — P&R '32

Singles: 78 rpm

BRUNSWICK 4-8 33-35
DECCA 4-6 46-54
VICTOR 4-10 32-43

EPs: 7-inch

DECCA (2277 "Memories") 15-25 55

LPs: 10/12-inch

DECCA (153 "Autobiography") 25-35 58
DECCA (5053 "Songs She Made Famous") 40-60 49
(10-inch LP.)
DECCA (9028 "Memories") 30-45 55
VIK (1004 "On Stage") 25-35 55
You'll find many more listings by this artist in *The Official Price Guide to Movie/TV Soundtracks and Original Cast Albums,* containing over 8,000 listings.

MERMAN, Ethel, Dick Haymes — P&R '51

Singles: 78 rpm

DECCA 3-5 51

Singles: 7-inch

DECCA 5-10 51

Also see HAYMES, Dick
Also see MERMAN, Ethel

MERRY-GO-ROUND P&R/LP '67

Singles: 7-inch

A&M 5-10 67-69

LPs: 10/12-inch

A&M (4132 "Merry-Go-Round") 20-30 67
RHINO 5-8 85

Members: Emitt Rhodes; Joel Larson; Gary Kato; Bill Reinhart.
Also see GRASS ROOTS
Also see LEAVES
Also see RHODES, Emitt

MERRYWEATHER: see MERRYWEATHER, Neil

MERRYWEATHER, Neil LP '69
(With Friends; Merryweather)

Singles: 7-inch

CAPITOL 3-6 69

LPs: 10/12-inch

CAPITOL 10-20 69
MERCURY 10-15 74-75

Also see MASON, Dave
Also see MILLER, Steve

MERRYWEATHER, Neil, & John Richardson

LPs: 10/12-inch

KENT 10-15 72

MERRYWEATHER & CAREY

LPs: 10/12-inch

RCA 8-12 71

Members: Neil Merryweather; Lynn Carey.
Also see MERRYWEATHER, Neil

MESA P&R '77

Singles: 7-inch

ARIOLA AMERICA 3-5 77

MES'AY R&B '87

Singles: 7-inch

SUPERSTAR I. 3-4 87

MESSENGERS P&R '71

Singles: 7-inch

BEAM 5-10 64
ERA 4-8 65
HOME MADE (01 "Right On") 15-25 69
MGM 4-8 64-65
RARE EARTH 3-6 71
SOUL 4-8 67
U.S.A. (866 "Midnight Hour"/"Up Till News") 8-12 67
U.S.A. (866 "Midnight Hour"/"Hard Hard Year") 8-12 67
(Note different flip.)

LPs: 10/12-inch

RARE EARTH (509 "Messengers") 8-12 69
(With standard cover.)
RARE EARTH (509 "Messengers") ... 20-25 69
(With rounded-top cover. Promotional issue.)

Members: Greg Jennings [Jeresek]; Jesse Roe; Peter Barans; Jeff Taylor; Augie Jurishica; Rob Leslie; Michael Morgan; Mike Demling; John Hoier; Bob Cavallo.

MESSINA, Jim LP '79
(With the Jesters; Jimmy Messina)

Singles: 7-inch

AUDIO FIDELITY 15-25 64
COLUMBIA 3-5 79-80
VIV 10-15
W.B. 3-5 81-83

LPs: 10/12-inch

AUDIO FIDELITY (7037 "The Dragsters") 45-55 64
COLUMBIA 5-8 79
THIMBLE 10-12 73
W.B. 5-8 81-83

Also see BUFFALO SPRINGFIELD
Also see LOGGINS & MESSINA
Also see POCO
Also see YOUNG, Neil, & Jim Messina

METAL CHURCH LP '86

LPs: 10/12-inch

ELEKTRA 5-8 86-89

METALLICA LP '84

Singles: 7-inch

ELEKTRA (Except 69357) 3-4 88-89
ELEKTRA (69357 "Eye of the Beholder") 5-10 88

Picture Sleeves

ELEKTRA (Except 69357) 3-5 88-89
ELEKTRA (69357 "Eye of the Beholder") 10-15 88

LPs: 10/12-inch

ELEKTRA (Except 60757) 5-10 84-89
ELEKTRA (60757 "Garage Days Revisited") 25-50 87
ENIGMA 5-10 84
MEGAFORCE 12-25 84-86

Members: James Hetfield; Kirk Hammett; Lars Ulrich; Cliff Burton; Jason Newsted.

METERS P&R/R&B/LP '69

Singles: 7-inch

JOSIE 3-6 69-71
REPRISE 3-5 74-76
SANSU 4-6
W.B. 3-5 77

LPs: 10/12-inch

ISLAND 8-10 75
JOSIE 10-12 69-70
REPRISE 8-10 72-75
VIRGO 8-10 75
W.B. 8-10 77

Also see NEVILLE BROTHERS

METHENY, Pat LP '78
(With Lyle Mays)

Singles: 7-inch

ECM 3-4 79-84

LPs: 10/12-inch

ECM 5-10 76-84
EMI AMERICA 5-8 85
GEFFEN 5-8 87-90
W.B. 5-8 83

Also see BOWIE, David, & Pat Metheny Group

MIAMI R&B '74

Singles: 7-inch

DRIVE 3-5 74-76

LPs: 10/12-inch

DRIVE 5-10 76

Member: Robert Moore.

MIAMI DISCO BAND R&B '79

Singles: 7-inch

SALSOUL 3-5 79

Member: Beverly Barkley.

MIAMI SOUND MACHINE
(Gloria Estefan & Miami Sound Machine)
P&R/R&B/D&D/LP '85

Singles: 12-inch

EPIC 4-6 84-88

Singles: 7-inch

EPIC 3-4 84-88

Picture Sleeves

EPIC 3-4 85-88

LPs: 10/12-inch

EPIC 5-8 84-88

Members: Marcos Avila; Kiki Garcia; Gloria Estefan; Emilio Estefan Jr.
Also see ESTEFAN, Gloria

MICHAEL, George P&R '86

Singles: 12-inch

COLUMBIA 4-6 86-87

Singles: 7-inch

COLUMBIA 3-4 86-90

Picture Sleeves

COLUMBIA 3-4 86-89

LPs: 10/12-inch

COLUMBIA 5-8 86-90

Also see ESTUS, Deon, & George Michael
Also see FRANKLIN, Aretha, & George Michael
Also see JOHN, Elton
Also see WHAM!

MICHAELS, Lee LP '69

Singles: 7-inch

A&M 4-6 67-71
COLUMBIA 3-5 73

Picture Sleeves

A&M 4-6 70-71

LPs: 10/12-inch

A&M (Except 3158 & 4140) 10-15 67-73
A&M (3158 "Lee Michaels") 5-8 82
A&M (4140 "Carnival of Life") 15-25 67
COLUMBIA 10-12 73-75

Promotional LPs

COLUMBIA ("In Hawaii") 35-45 75

MICHELE LEE: see LEE, Michele

MICKEY & SYLVIA R&B '56

Singles: 78 rpm

GROOVE (175 "Love Is Strange") 10-20 56
RAINBOW 10-20 55
VIK 10-20 57

Singles: 7-inch

ALL PLATINUM 3-6 69
GROOVE (175 "Love Is Strange") 15-25 56
KING (6006 "Love Is Strange") 4-8 65
RCA (47-7774 "Sweeter As the Day Goes By") 8-12 60
RCA (61-7774 "Sweeter As the Day Goes By") 15-25 60
(Stereo.)
RCA (47-7811 "What Would I Do") ... 10-15 60
RCA (61-7811 "What Would I Do") ... 20-40 60
(Stereo.)
RCA (37-7877 "Love Lesson") 20-40 61
(Compact 33 Single.)
RCA (47-7877 "Love Lesson") 8-12 61
RCA (8517 "Let's Shake Some More") 8-12 65
RAINBOW (316 "I'm So Glad") 20-30 55
RAINBOW (318 "Rise Sally Rise") 15-25 55
STANG 4-8 69
VIK (0267 "There Ought to Be a Law") 10-15 57
VIK (0280 "Love Will Make You Fail in School") 10-15 57
VIK (0324 "Bewildered") 10-15 58
WILLOW (23000 "Baby, You're So Fine" 10-15 61
WILLOW (23002 "Darling") 10-15 61
WILLOW (23004 "Since I Fell for You") 10-15 62
WILLOW (23006 "Love Is Strange") 10-20 61

EPs: 7-inch

GROOVE (18 "Love Is Strange") 50-100 57
VIK (262 "Mickey & Sylvia") 40-60 57

LPs: 10/12-inch

CAMDEN (863 "Love Is Strange") 35-50 65
RCA 15-20 73
VIK (1102 "New Sounds") 100-200 57

Members: Mickey Baker; Sylvia Vanderpool.
Also see LITTLE SYLVIA
Also see SYLVIA

MICO WAVE R&B '87

Singles: 7-inch

COLUMBIA 3-4 87-88

MIDLER, Bette P&R/LP '72

Singles: 7-inch

ATLANTIC 3-5 72-90

Picture Sleeves

ATLANTIC 3-5 72-89

LPs: 10/12-inch

ATLANTIC 5-10 72-90

Also see REDD, Sharon, Ula Hedwig & Charlotte Crossley
Also see U.S.A. for AFRICA

MIDNIGHT OIL LP '84

Singles: 12-inch

COLUMBIA 4-6 84

Singles: 7-inch

COLUMBIA 3-4 82-89

Picture Sleeves

COLUMBIA 3-5 82-88

LPs: 10/12-inch

COLUMBIA (Black vinyl) 5-8 84-90

COLUMBIA (45398 "Blue Sky Mining")....10-12 90
(Colored vinyl.)

MIDNIGHT STAR R&B '80

Singles: 12-inch

SOLAR....4-6 82-86

Singles: 7-inch

SOLAR....3-4 80-88

Picture Sleeves

SOLAR....3-4 86

LPs: 10/12-inch

SOLAR....5-8 82-88

Members: Cino-Vincent Calloway; Reggie Calloway.

Also see CALLOWAY

MIDNIGHT STRING QUARTET LP '66

LPs: 10/12-inch

VIVA....5-10 66-68

MIDNIGHTERS R&B '54

Singles: 78 rpm

FEDERAL....25-75 54-57

Singles: 7-inch

FEDERAL (12169 "Work with Me Annie")....50-100 54
(Silver top label.)
FEDERAL (12169 "Work with Me Annie")....25-50 55
(Green label.)
FEDERAL (12177 "Give It Up")....50-75 54
FEDERAL (12185 "Sexy Ways")....50-75 54
FEDERAL (12195 "Annie Had a Baby")....50-75 54
FEDERAL (12200 "Annie's Aunt Fannie")....50-75 54
FEDERAL (12202 "Tell Them")....50-75 54
FEDERAL (12205 "Moonrise")....50-75 54
FEDERAL (12210 "Ashamed of Myself")....50-75 55
FEDERAL (12220 "Switchie, Witchie, Titchie")....50-75 55
FEDERAL (12224 "Henry's Got Flat Feet")....50-75 55
FEDERAL (12227 "It's Love Baby")....50-75 55
FEDERAL (12230 "Give It Up")....10-20 55
FEDERAL (12240 "That House on the Hill")....50-75 55
FEDERAL (12243 "Don't Change Your Pretty Ways")....50-75 55
FEDERAL (12251 "Partners for Life")....50-75 56
FEDERAL (12260 "Rock Granny Roll")....50-75 56
FEDERAL (12270 "Tore Up Over You")....30-60 56
FEDERAL (12285 "Come on and Get It")....30-60 56
FEDERAL (12288 "Let Me Hold Your Hand")....30-60 56
FEDERAL (12293 "In the Doorway Crying")....30-60 57
FEDERAL (12299 "Oh So Happy")....25-50 57
FEDERAL (12305 "Let 'Em Roll")....25-50 57
FEDERAL (12317 "Stay By My Side")....25-50 58
FEDERAL (12339 "Baby Please")....25-50 58

Members: Henry Booth; Hank Ballard; Sonny Woods; Charles Sutton; Lawson Smith; Alonzo Tucker.

Also see BALLARD, Hank, & Midnighters
Also see JOHN, Little Willie / 5 Royales / Earl (Connelly) King / Midnighters
Also see ROYALS

MIDNIGHTERS, Thee: see THEE MIDNIGHTERS

MIDWAY R&B/D&D '84

Singles: 12-inch

PERSONAL....4-6 84

Singles: 7-inch

PERSONAL....3-4 84

MIGHTY CLOUDS OF JOY R&B/LP '74

Singles: 12-inch

EPIC....4-6 79

Singles: 7-inch

ABC....3-5 76-77
DUNHILL....3-5 74-75
EPIC....3-5 79-80
MYRRH....3-4 82
PEACOCK....3-6 61-73

LPs: 10/12-inch

ABC....5-8 75-76
DUNHILL....5-8 74
EPIC....5-8 79
MYRRH....5-8 81-83
PEACOCK....5-10 65-73
PRIORITY....5-8 82

Member: Bunker Hill.

Also see HILL, Bunker.
Also see ROGER

MIGHTY FIRE R&B '80

Singles: 7-inch

ELEKTRA....3-4 81-82
ZEPHYR....3-5 80

LPs: 10/12-inch

ELEKTRA....5-8 81-82

MIGHTY FLEA R&B '68

Singles: 7-inch

ELDO....4-8 67

MIGHTY HANNIBAL R&B '66

(James T. Shaw)

Singles: 7-inch

DECCA....4-8 65
JOSIE....4-8 66-67
LOMA....4-8 68
SHURFINE....4-8 66

Also see HANNIBAL

MIGHTY LEMON DROPS LP '90

LPs: 10/12-inch

SIRE....5-10 86-90

Members: Paul Marsh; David Newton; Tony Linehan; Keith Rowley.

MIGHTY MARVELOWS: see MARVELOWS

MIGHTY POPE R&B '77

Singles: 7-inch

PRIVATE STOCK....3-5 77

MIKE & DEAN

(Mike Love & Dean Torrence)

Singles: 7-inch

BUDWEISER (8246 "Budweiser Fight Song/Be True to Your Bud")....35-45 83
(Add $8 to $12 if accompanied by two Mike & Dean posters and a story insert. Promotional issue only.)
HITBOUND....10-20 82
PREMORE (23/24 "Da Doo Ron Ron"/"Baby Talk")....20-30 83

Picture Sleeves

PREMORE (23/24 "Da Doo Ron Ron"/"Baby Talk")....20-30 83

LPs: 10/12-inch

PREMORE (983 "Rock'n Roll Again")....30-50 83
(Also has tracks by the Association, Rip Chords, and Paul Revere & the Raiders.)
PREMORE (3009 "Rock'n Roll City")....30-50 83
(Also has tracks by other artists.)

Members: Mike Love; Dean Torrence.

Also see ASSOCIATION
Also see JAN & DEAN
Also see LOVE, Mike
Also see REVERE, Paul, & Raiders
Also see RIPCHORDS

MIKE + MECHANICS P&R/LP '85

Singles: 7-inch

ATLANTIC....3-4 85-89

Picture Sleeves

ATLANTIC....3-4 85-89

LPs: 10/12-inch

ATLANTIC....5-8 85-90

Members: Mike Rutherford; Paul Carrack; Paul Young; Peter Van Hooke; Adrian Lee.

Also see CARRACK, Paul
Also see RUTHERFORD, Mike
Also see SAD CAFE
Also see YOUNG, Paul

MIKKI R&B '82

Singles: 7-inch

EMERALD INT'L....3-4 82-83
POP ART....3-4 84

MILBURN, Amos R&B '48

(With the Aladdin Chickenshackers)

Singles: 78 rpm

ALADDIN....10-40 45-56

Singles: 7-inch

ALADDIN (3014 "Chicken Shack Boogie")....75-125 50
ALADDIN (3018 "Bewildered")....50-100 50
ALADDIN (3068 "Bad Bad Whiskey")....50-75 50
ALADDIN (3080 "Let's Rock Awhile")....50-75 51
ALADDIN (3090 "Everybody Clap Hands")....50-75 51
ALADDIN (3093 "Ain't Nothing Shaking")....50-75 51
ALADDIN (3105 "Boogie Woogie")....50-75 51
ALADDIN (3124 "Drinkin' and Thinkin' ")....40-60 52
ALADDIN (3125 "Flying Home")....40-60 52
ALADDIN (3133 "Roll Mr. Jelly")....40-60 52
ALADDIN (3150 "Greyhound")....40-60 52
ALADDIN (3159 "Rock, Rock, Rock")....40-60 52
ALADDIN (3164 "Let Me Go Home, Whiskey")....30-50 53
ALADDIN (3168 "Please, Mr. Johnson")....30-50 53
ALADDIN (3197 "One Scotch, One Bourbon, One Beer")....30-50 53
ALADDIN (3218 "Good Good Whiskey")....25-45 53
ALADDIN (3226 "Rocky Mountain")....25-45 54
ALADDIN (3240 "Milk & Water")....25-45 54
ALADDIN (3248 "Glory of Love")....25-45 54
ALADDIN (3253 "Vicious Vicious Vodka")....25-45 54
ALADDIN (3269 "One Two Three Everybody")....25-45 54
ALADDIN (3293 "My Happiness Depends on You")....25-45 55
ALADDIN (3306 "House Party")....25-45 55
ALADDIN (3320 "I Need Someone ")....20-40 56
ALADDIN (3332 "Chicken Shack")....20-40 56
IMPERIAL....5-10 62
KING (5000 series)....5-10 60-61
KING (6000 series)....4-8 67
MOTOWN (1038 "My Baby Gave Me Another Chance")....15-25 63
MOTOWN (1046 "My Daily Prayer")....15-25 63

LPs: 10/12-inch

ALADDIN (704 "Rockin' the Boogie")....500-750 55
(Black vinyl. 10-inch LP.)
ALADDIN (704 "Rockin' the Boogie")....2000-3000 55
(Colored vinyl. 10-inch LP.)
ALADDIN (810 "Rockin' the Boogie")....200-300 56
IMPERIAL (9176 "Million Sellers")....50-75 62
MOSAIC (155 "Complete Aladdin Recordings of Amos Milburn")....140-150 90s
(Boxed 10-disc audiophile set. 3500 made.)
MOTOWN (608 "The Blues Boss")....500-750 63
SCORE (4012 "Let's Have a Party")....100-200 57

Also see BROWN, Charles, & Amos Milburn

MILBURN, Amos / Wynonie Harris / Velma Nelson / Crown Prince Waterford

LPs: 10/12-inch

ALADDIN (703 "Party After Hours")....500-1000 56
(Black vinyl. 10-inch LP.)
ALADDIN (703 "Party After Hours")....2000-3000 56
(Colored vinyl. 10-inch LP.)
Also see HARRIS, Wynonie
Also see MILBURN, Amos

MILES, Buddy P&R/LP '69
(Buddy Miles Express; with Freedom Express)

Singles: 7-inch

CASABLANCA....3-5 75-76
COLUMBIA....3-5 73-74
MERCURY....3-6 68-72

Picture Sleeves

MERCURY....3-6

LPs: 10/12-inch

CASABLANCA....8-10 75
COLUMBIA....8-12 73-74
MERCURY....10-15 68-72
Also see CALIFORNIA RAISINS
Also see ELECTRIC FLAG
Also see FIDELITYS
Also see HENDRIX, Jimi
Also see SANTANA, Carlos, & Buddy Miles

MILES, Garry P&R '60
(With the Statues; Gary Miles; Buzz Cason)

Singles: 7-inch

LIBERTY (54000 series)....5-8 68
LIBERTY (55000 series)....10-15 60-64

Picture Sleeves

LIBERTY (55261 "Look for a Star")...10-20 60

EPs: 7-inch

LIBERTY (1005 "Look for a Star")....50-75 60
Also see STATUES

MILES, John P&R/LP '76

Singles: 12-inch

LONDON....5-8 77-80

Singles: 7-inch

ARISTA....3-5 78
LONDON....3-5 76-77
WEA....3-4 85

LPs: 10/12-inch

ARISTA....5-10 78
LONDON....5-10 76-80
VALENTINO....5-8 85
WEA....5-8 85
Also see PARSONS, Alan, Project

MILES, Lenny P&R '60

Singles: 7-inch

GROOVE....5-10 62
RCA....5-10 62
SCEPTER....8-12 61

MILKWOOD

LPs: 10/12-inch

PARAMOUNT (6046 "How's the Weather")....25-35 73
Also see CARS

MILLER, Chuck P&R '55

Singles: 78 rpm

MERCURY....5-15 55-58

Singles: 7-inch

MERCURY....10-15 55-58

LPs: 10/12-inch

MERCURY (20195 "After Hours")....40-60 56
(10-inch LP.)

MILLER, Clint P&R '58

Singles: 7-inch

ABC-PAR (9878 "Bertha Lou")....15-25 58
BIG TOP....5-10 59
HEADLINE....5-10 60-61
LENOX....4-8 62

MILLER, Frankie P&R/LP '77

Singles: 7-inch

CAPITOL....3-4 82
CHRYSALIS....3-5 75-79

Picture Sleeves

CAPITOL....3-4 82

LPs: 10/12-inch

CAPITOL....5-10 82
CHRYSALIS....8-12 73-80

MILLER, Glenn, & His Orch. P&R '35
(New Glenn Miller Orchestra with Ray McKinley; with Buddy DeFranco)

Singles: 78 rpm

BLUEBIRD....5-10 38-44
BRUNSWICK....5-10 37-38
COLUMBIA....5-10 35
DECCA....15-25 37
RCA....4-8 47-58
VICTOR....5-10 42-46

Singles: 7-inch

EPIC....3-6 65-69
RCA....3-10 50-67

EPs: 7-inch

EPIC....5-15 54-56
RCA (Except 6700 series)....5-15 50-61
RCA (6700 "Anthology Limited Edition, Vol. 1")....25-50 56
RCA (6701 "Anthology Limited Edition, Vol. 2")....25-50 56
RCA (6702 "Army Air Force Band")..20-30 56

LPs: 10/12-inch

BRIGHT ORANGE....5-8 73
CAMDEN....5-10 63-74
COLUMBIA....5-8 82
EPIC (1000 & 3000 series)....20-40 54-56
EPIC (16000 series)....12-25 60
EPIC (24000 & 26000 series)....10-20 65-66
EVEREST (Except 4004)....5-8 82
EVEREST (4004 "Glenn Miller")....20-30 82
(Boxed, five-disc set.)
GREAT AMERICAN....5-10 77
HARMONY....5-10 70
KORY....5-8 77
MOVIETONE....8-15 67
RCA (16 thru 30)....25-50 56
(10-inch LPs.)
RCA (0600 thru 3800 series)....5-10 74-81
(With "ANL," "AYL" or "CPL" prefix.)
RCA (LPT-3000 series)....25-50 52-54
(10-inch LP.)
RCA (1000 thru 1500 series)....20-40 54-57
(Black label.)
RCA (1100 thru 1500 series)....5-10 68-69
(Orange label.)
RCA (1600 thru 3900 series)....10-25 58-68
(Black label. With "LPM" or "LSP" prefix.)
RCA (1900 thru 4100 series)....5-10 68-69
(Orange or gold label.)
RCA (5000 series)....5-10 75-80
RCA (6000 series)....5-15 69-73
RCA (6100 series)....15-30 59-63
RCA (6700 "Anthology–Limited Edition, Vol. 1")....75-100 56
(Five-LP set with booklet and special gold or silver case.)
RCA (6700 "Anthology–Limited Edition, Vol. 1")....50-75 62
(Reissue, has '60s RCA labels.)
RCA (6701 "Anthology–Limited Edition, Vol. 2")....75-100 56
(Five-LP set with booklet and special gold or silver case.)
RCA (6701 "Anthology–Limited Edition, Vol. 2")....50-75 62
(Reissue, has '60s RCA labels.)
RCA (6702 "Army Air Force Band")..50-75 56
SPRINGBOARD....4-8 77
20TH FOX (100 series)....20-30 59
20TH FOX (900 series)....5-10 73
20TH FOX (3000 series)....15-25 59
20TH FOX (3100 series)....10-15 65
20TH FOX (4100 series)....10-15 65
20TH FOX (72000 series)....6-12 73

MILLER, Jody P&R '64

Singles: 7-inch

CAPITOL....5-10 63-70
EPIC....3-6 70-79

Picture Sleeves

CAPITOL....5-10 65

LPs: 10/12-inch

CAPITOL (1913 "Wednesday's Child Is Full of Woe")....15-25 63
CAPITOL (2349 thru 2996)....10-20 65-69
CAPITOL (11000 series)....5-10 73
EPIC....5-10 70-77
PICKWICK/HILLTOP....10-15 66
SEARS....8-12

MILLER, Jody, & Johnny Paycheck C&W '72

EPIC....3-5 72
Also see MILLER, Jody
Also see PAYCHECK, Johnny

MILLER, Marcus R&B '83

Singles: 12-inch

W.B.....4-6 83-84

Singles: 7-inch

W.B.....3-4 83-84

MILLER, Mrs. Elva P&R/LP '66
(Mrs. Miller)

Singles: 7-inch

AMARET....4-8 69-70
CAPITOL....5-10 66

LPs: 10/12-inch

AMARET....10-20 69
CAPITOL....20-35 66-67

MILLER, Mitch P&R '50
(Mitch Miller's Orchestra & Chorus; Mitch Miller & Sing-Along Gang)

Singles: 78 rpm

COLUMBIA....3-6 50-57

Singles: 7-inch

("Christmas Carol Medley")....5-8 50s
(Rectangular picture disc. Three other Christmas titles were made. Same value for each. No label name or selection numbers used.)
COLUMBIA....4-10 50-65
DECCA....3-6 65-66
DIAMOND....3-6 68
GOLD-MOR....3-5 73
U.A.....3-6 68

Picture Sleeves

COLUMBIA....5-8 59-63

EPs: 7-inch

COLUMBIA....5-10 55-61

LPs: 10/12-inch

ATLANTIC....5-8 70
COLUMBIA (Except 2780/6380)....5-20 56-82
COLUMBIA (2780 "Major Dundee")..35-45 65
(Soundtrack. Monaural.)
COLUMBIA (6380 "Major Dundee")..45-55 65
(Soundtrack. Stereo.)
DECCA....5-12 66
HARMONY....5-12 65-71
Also see LAINE, Frankie
Also see SANDPIPERS with Mitch Miller & Orchestra / Mitch Miller & Orchestra

MILLER, Ned C&W/P&R '62

Singles: 78 rpm

DOT (Except 15601)....8-12 57
DOT (15601 "From a Jack to a King")....15-25 57

Singles: 7-inch

CAPITOL (2000 series)....3-6 68
CAPITOL (4600 series)....5-8 61
CAPITOL (5400 thru 5800 series)....3-8 65-67
DOT (Except 15601)....8-12 57
DOT (15601 "From a Jack to a King")....15-25 57
FABOR....4-8 62-65
JACKPOT....8-12 59
REPUBLIC....4-6 69-70

LPs: 10/12-inch

CAPITOL....10-15 65-67
FABOR (1001 "From a Jack to a King")....15-25 63
(Black vinyl.)
FABOR (1001 "From a Jack to a King")....50-75 63
(Colored vinyl.)

PLANTATION....5-8 81
REPUBLIC....8-10 70

MILLER, Red, Trio — R&B '48

Singles: 78 rpm

BULLET....15-25 48
SWING BEAT....10-20 49

Singles: 7-inch

PRIZE (801 "Mary Jo")....20-30 50s

MILLER, Roger — C&W '60

Singles: 7-inch

BUENA VISTA....3-5 70
COLUMBIA....3-5 73-74
DECCA....5-10 59
ELEKTRA....3-4 81
MCA....3-4 85-86
MERCURY....3-5 70-72
MUSICOR (1102 "You're Forgettin' Me")....4-8 65
RCA (7000 series)....8-15 60-63
RCA (8000 series)....4-6 62-65
SMASH....3-8 64-76
STARDAY (356 "You're Forgettin' Me")....10-15 58
STARDAY (718 "Playboy")....4-8 65
STARDAY (7029 "Under Your Spell Again")....4-8 65
20TH CENTURY....3-5 79
WINDSONG....3-5 77

Picture Sleeves

BUENA VISTA....4-6 70
SMASH....5-10 64-68

LPs: 10/12-inch

CAMDEN....8-10 64-65
COLUMBIA....5-10 73
EVEREST....5-8 75
HILLTOP....8-12 60s
MCA....5-8 86
MERCURY....5-10 72
NASHVILLE....8-12
PICKWICK....5-10 70s
SMASH (Except 7000 series)....10-20 64-70
SMASH (7000 series)....5-8 82
STARDAY....10-20 65
20TH FOX....5-8 79
WINDSONG....5-8 77
WING....6-12 69

Also see LEWIS, Jerry Lee / Roger Miller / Roy Orbison
Also see NELSON, Willie, & Roger Miller
Also see TUBB, Justin / Roger Miller
Also see YOUNG, Donny, & Roger Miller

MILLER, Roger, & Willie Nelson (With Ray Price) — C&W '82

Singles: 7-inch

COLUMBIA....3-5 82

LPs: 10/12-inch

COLUMBIA....5-8 82

Also see MILLER, Roger
Also see NELSON, Willie
Also see PRICE, Ray

MILLER, Steve (Steve Miller Band) — P&R/LP '68

Singles: 12-inch

CAPITOL (Except 9992)....4-8 81-85
CAPITOL (9992 "I Wanna Be Loved")....5-10 86
(Colored vinyl. Promotional issue only.)

Singles: 7-inch

CAPITOL (2156 "Sittin' in Circles")....5-10 68
CAPITOL (2287 "Living in the USA")..5-10 68
CAPITOL (2447 thru 3344)....4-8 69-72
CAPITOL (3732 thru 4496)....3-5 73-77
CAPITOL (5000 series)....3-4 81-87
CAPITOL (44000 series)....3-4 88

Picture Sleeves

CAPITOL (2156 "Sittin' In Circles")....8-12 67
CAPITOL....3-4 80-88

LPs: 10/12-inch

CAPITOL (184 thru 748)....10-15 69-71
CAPITOL (2900 series)....15-20 68
CAPITOL (11000 thru 16000)....5-10 72-86
CAPITOL (11872 "Greatest Hits")....20-30 78
(Colored vinyl. Promotional issue only.)
CAPITOL (11903 "Book of Dreams") 15-20 78
(Picture disc.)
CAPITOL (48000 series)....5-8 88
MFSL (021 "Fly Like an Eagle")....50-75 78
MERCURY....5-10 81

Also see BERRY, Chuck
Also see DAVIS, Tim
Also see GOLDBERG - MILLER BLUES BAND
Also see MERRYWEATHER, Neil
Also see SCAGGS, Boz

MILLER, Steve, Band / Band / Quicksilver Messenger Service

LPs: 10/12-inch

CAPITOL (288 "Steve Miller Band / The Band /Quicksilver Messenger Service")....35-45 69
(Three-disc set, with one by each group.)

Also see BAND
Also see MILLER, Steve
Also see QUICKSILVER

MILLI VANILLI — P&R/LP '89

Singles: 7-inch

ARISTA....3-4 89-90

Picture Sleeves

ARISTA....3-4 89

LPs: 10/12-inch

ARISTA....5-8 89-90

Members: Rob Pilatus; Fabrice Morvan.

MILLINDER, Lucky, & His Orchestra — P&R/R&B '42

Singles: 78 rpm

DECCA....5-15 41-48
KING....10-30 51-57
RCA....10-20 49-51

Singles: 7-inch

KING (4449 "Chew Tobacco Rag")....25-45 51
KING (4453 "I'm Waiting for You")....25-45 51
KING (4476 "The Grape Vine")....25-45 51
KING (4496 "The Right Kind of Lovin'")....25-45 51
(Black vinyl.)
KING (4496 "The Right Kind of Lovin'")....50-100 51
(Colored vinyl.)
KING (4545 "When I Have You")....50-75 52
KING (4557 "Lord Knows I Tried")....50-75 52
KING (4571 "Please Be Careful")....50-75 52
KING (4803 "Goody Good Love")....15-25 55
KING (5200 series)....5-10 59
RCA (0054 "D Natural Blues")....30-50 51
(Colored vinyl.)
TODD....5-10 59
WARWICK....5-10 60

EPs: 7-inch

KING (268 "Lucky Millinder")....25-50 54
KING (336 "Lucky Millinder, Vol. 2") 25-50 54

Also see HARRIS, Wynonie
Also see STIDHAM, Arbee

MILLINDER, Lucky, & Admirals

Singles: 78 rpm

KING (4792 "It's a Sad Sad Feeling")....15-20 55

Singles: 7-inch

KING (4792 "It's a Sad Sad Feeling")....40-60 55

Also see MILLINDER, Lucky

MILLIONS LIKE US — P&R/LP '87

Singles: 7-inch

VIRGIN....3-4 87

Picture Sleeves

VIRGIN....3-4 87

LPs: 10/12-inch

VIRGIN....5-8 87

MILLS, Frank — P&R '72

Singles: 7-inch

POLYDOR....3-4 78-79
SUNFLOWER....3-4 72

LPs: 10/12-inch

CAPITOL....5-8 85
POLYDOR....5-8 79

Also see BELLS

MILLS, Gary — P&R '60

Singles: 7-inch

IMPERIAL....8-12 60
LONDON....5-10 62
TOP RANK....8-12 60

MILLS, Hayley — P&R '61

Singles: 7-inch

BUENA VISTA....5-10 61-62
MAINSTREAM....4-8 66

Picture Sleeves

BUENA VISTA....10-20 61-62

EPs: 7-inch

DISNEYLAND....15-25 60

LPs: 10/12-inch

BUENA VISTA (3311 "Let's Get Together")....20-25 62
(Monaural.)
BUENA VISTA (STER-3311 "Let's Get Together")....25-35 62
(Stereo.)
MAINSTREAM (6090 "Gypsy Girl")....15-25 66
(Soundtrack.)

Also see ANNETTE / Hayley Mills

MILLS, Hayley, & Jimmie Bean

EPs: 7-inch

DISNEYLAND....15-25 60

MILLS, Hayley, & Maurice Chevalier

Singles: 7-inch

BUENA VISTA....5-8 62

Also see MILLS, Hayley

MILLS, Hayley, & Eddie Hodges

Singles: 7-inch

BUENA VISTA....5-8 63

Picture Sleeves

BUENA VISTA....10-15 64

Also see HODGES, Eddie

MILLS, Hayley, & Burl Ives (With Eddie Hodges & Deborah Walley)

Singles: 7-inch

BUENA VISTA (4023 "Summer Magic")....5-8 63
(Alcoa Wrap promotional issue.)

Picture Sleeves

BUENA VISTA (4023 "Summer Magic")....10-15 63
(Alcoa Wrap promotional issue.)

EPs: 7-inch

ALCOA WRAP (701 "Music from *Summer Magic*")....15-25 63
(Promotional issue only.)

Also see IVES, Burl
Also see MILLS, Hayley

MILLS, Stephanie — P&R/R&B/LP '79

Singles: 12-inch

CASABLANCA....4-6 82-85
MCA....4-6 85-86
20TH FOX....4-8 79-81

Singles: 7-inch

ABC....3-5 74
CASABLANCA....3-4 82-86
MCA....3-4 85-89
MOTOWN....3-5 75
PARAMOUNT....3-5 74
20TH FOX....3-5 79-81

Picture Sleeves

MCA....3-4 87
20TH FOX....3-5 80

LPs: 10/12-inch

ABC....8-10 75
CASABLANCA....5-8 82-85
MCA....5-8 86-89
MOTOWN (800 series)....8-10 75
MOTOWN (6000 series)....5-8 82
20TH FOX....5-10 79-81

Also see KING DREAM CHORUS & Holiday Crew

MILLS, Stephanie, & Teddy Pendergrass — P&R/R&B '81

Singles: 7-inch

20TH FOX....3-5 81

Also see MILLS, Stephanie
Also see PENDERGRASS, Teddy

MILLS, Yvonne: see SENSATIONS

MILLS BROTHERS — P&R '31

Singles: 78 rpm

BANNER 5-10 34
BRUNSWICK 5-10 31-47
CONQUEROR 5-10
DECCA (100 thru 4300 series) 5-10 34-42
DECCA (11000 thru 24000 series) 5-10 42-57

Singles: 7-inch

ABC 3-5 74
DECCA 8-15 50-61
DOT (15000 series) 5-10 58-59
DOT (16000 series) 4-6 60s
DOT (17000 series) 3-6 68-69
MCA 3-5 73-74
PARAMOUNT 3-5 71-72
RANWOOD 3-5 73-76

EPs: 7-inch

DECCA 5-15 50-63
DOT 5-10 58-59

LPs: 10/12-inch

ABC 5-8 74
DECCA (100 series) 10-15 66
DECCA (4000 series) 10-20 61-67
DECCA (5000 series) 20-50 49-55
(10-inch LPs.)
DECCA (7000 series) 20-30 55
DECCA (8000 series) 15-30 55-59
DECCA (75000 series) 5-10 70
DOT 5-20 58-70
EVEREST 5-10 75-77
GNP 5-8 73
MCA 5-10 73
MFP/MCA 5-8 82
PARAMOUNT 5-10 72-74
PICKWICK 5-10 70s
RANWOOD 5-10 74-81
SONGBIRD 6-12 74
VOCALION 5-10 66-69

Members: Herb Mills; Harry Mills; Donald Mills; John Mills.
Also see CROSBY, Bing, & Mills Brothers
Also see FITZGERALD, Ella, & Mills Brothers

MILLS BROTHERS & LOUIS ARMSTRONG — P&R '37

Singles: 78 rpm

DECCA 5-15 40

Singles: 7-inch

DECCA 4-6 61

Also see ARMSTRONG, Louis

MILLS BROTHERS & COUNT BASIE

LPs: 10/12-inch

ABC 5-8 74
DOT 8-12 68

Also see BASIE, Count
Also see MILLS BROTHERS

MILSAP, Ronnie — R&B '65

Singles: 7-inch

BOBLO 3-5 77
CAPITOL 3-4 90s
CHIPS 5-10 70
FESTIVAL 3-5 77
RCA (Black vinyl) 3-5 74-92
RCA (Colored vinyl) 5-10 74-89
(Promotional only.)
SCEPTER 10-20 65-69
W.B. (5405 "It Went to Your Head") 5-10 63
W.B. (8000 series) 3-5 75-76

Picture Sleeves

RCA 3-5 79-85

LPs: 10/12-inch

BUCKBOARD 8-10 76
CRAZY CAJUN 8-10 75
51 WEST 5-8 80s
HSRD 8-10 82
RCA 5-10 74-92
TIME-LIFE 5-10 81
TRIP 8-10 76
W.B. 8-10 71-75

Also see PRESLEY, Elvis

MILSAP, Ronnie, & Mike Reid — C&W '88

Singles: 7-inch

RCA 3-4 88

MILSAP, Ronnie, & Kenny Rogers — C&W '87

Singles: 7-inch

RCA 3-4 87

Also see MILSAP, Ronnie
Also see ROGERS, Kenny

MILTON, Roy — P&R/R&B '46

(With His Solid Senders; Roy Milton Sextet)

Singles: 78 rpm

DOOTONE 20-30 55-56
DELUXE 15-25 50s
HAMP-TONE 20-40 45
JUKE BOX 20-40 46
KING 10-15 56-57
ROY MILTON (111 "Groovin' with Joe") 20-40 46
ROY MILTON (207 "Them There Eyes") 20-40 46
SPECIALTY 15-25 47-55

Singles: 7-inch

CENCO 10-15 61
DOOTONE (363 "I Cant' Go On") 25-50 55
DOOTONE (369 "You Got Me Reeling and Rocking") 25-50 55
DOOTONE (377 "I Want to Go Home") 25-50 55
DOOTONE (398 "Baby, I'm Gone") 25-50 56
KING (4900 & 5000 series) 10-20 56-58
KING (5600 series) 5-10 62
SPECIALTY (414 "Short, Sweet and Snappy") 20-40 50
SPECIALTY (429 "So Tired") 40-60 51
SPECIALTY (436 "Flying Saucer") 30-50 52
SPECIALTY (438 "Night and Day") 30-50 52
SPECIALTY (446 "Believe Me Baby") 50-75 52
SPECIALTY (458 "Some Day") 30-50 53
(Black vinyl.)
SPECIALTY (458 "Some Day") 75-125 53
(Colored vinyl.)
SPECIALTY (464 "Let Me Give You All My Love") 30-50 54
(Black vinyl.)
SPECIALTY (464 "Let Me Give You All My Love") 75-125 54
(Colored vinyl.)
SPECIALTY (480 thru 545) 20-30 54-55
SPECIALTY (700 series) 4-6 69
WARWICK (662 "So Tired") 10-15 60

LPs: 10/12-inch

KENT (554 "Great Roy Milton") 40-60 63

Also see HOWARD, Camille, Trio
Also see HUMES, Helen

MILTON, Roy, & Mickey Champion

Singles: 78 rpm

DOOTONE 20-30 55

Singles: 7-inch

DOOTONE (378 "Bam a Lam") 25-50 55

MILTON, Roy / Joe Liggins

Singles: 78 rpm

SPECIALTY 10-20 53

Singles: 7-inch

SPECIALTY 20-25 53

Also see LIGGINS, Joe
Also see MILTON, Roy

MIMMS, Garnet — P&R/R&B/LP '63

(With the Enchanters; with Trucking Co.)

Singles: 7-inch

ARISTA 3-5 77
GSF 3-6 72
LIBERTY 3-4 81
U.A. 8-15 63-66
VEEP 4-8 66
VERVE 5-10 68-70

Picture Sleeves

U.A. 5-10 63

LPs: 10/12-inch

ARISTA (4153 "Garnett Mimms Has It All") 8-12 78
GUEST STAR (1907 "Garnet Mimms") 20-25 64
U.A. (3305 "Cry Baby") 25-40 63
(Monaural.)
U.A. (3396 "As Long As I Have You") 25-40 64
(Monaural.)
U.A. (3498 "I'll Take Good Care of You") 35-50 66
(Monaural.)
U.A. (6305 "Cry Baby") 35-50 63
(Stereo.)
U.A. (6396 "As Long As I Have You") 35-50 64
(Stereo.)
U.A. (6498 "I'll Take Good Care of You") 35-50 66
(Stereo.)

Members: Garnet Mimms; Samuel Bell; Charles Boyer; Zola Pearnell.
Also see ENCHANTERS

MIMMS, Garnet / Maurice Monk

LPs: 10/12-inch

GRAND PRIX (424 "Garnett Mimms & Maurice Monk") 15-20 63

Also see MIMMS, Garnet

MINA — P&R '61

(With Her Orchestra "I Solitari")

Singles: 7-inch

CHIRP 4-8
TIME 4-8 61

MINDBENDERS — P&R/LP '66

Singles: 7-inch

FONTANA 5-10 65-67

LPs: 10/12-inch

FONTANA (27554 "A Groovy Kind of Love") 30-40 66
(Monaural. With *Ashes to Ashes*)
FONTANA (27554 "A Groovy Kind of Love") 20-30 66
(Monaural. Without *Ashes to Ashes*)
FONTANA (67554 "A Groovy Kind of Love") 30-40 66
(Stereo. With *Ashes to Ashes*)
FONTANA (67554 "A Groovy Kind of Love") 20-30 66
(Stereo. Without *Ashes to Ashes*)

Members: Eric Stewart; Bob Lang; Ric Rothwell.
Also see FONTANA, Wayne, & Mindbenders

MINEO, Sal — P&R '57

Singles: 78 rpm

EPIC 15-25 57

Singles: 7-inch

DECCA 4-8 64
EPIC 10-20 57-59
FONTANA 4-8 65

Picture Sleeves

EPIC 15-25 57-59

EPs: 7-inch

EPIC (7187 "Sal Mineo") 20-30 57
EPIC (7194/7195 "Sal") 20-30 58
(Price is for either volume.)
EPIC (7194 "Sal") 20-30 58
EPIC (7204 "Souvenirs of Summertime") 20-30 58

LPs: 10/12-inch

EPIC (3405 "Sal") 50-100 58

MINIATURE MEN — P&R '62

Singles: 7-inch

DOLTON 5-10 62

Also see LEVINE, Hank

MINISTRY — D&D/LP '83

Singles: 12-inch

ARISTA 4-6 83
SIRE 4-6 86
WAX TRAX 4-6 85

Singles: 7-inch

ARISTA ... 3-4 83
SIRE ... 3-4 86-89
WAX TRAX ... 3-4 85

LPs: 10/12-inch

ARISTA ... 5-8 83
SIRE ... 5-8 86-89

MINK DE VILLE
LP '77

Singles: 7-inch

ATLANTIC ... 3-4 81-84
CAPITOL ... 3-5 77-78

LPs: 10/12-inch

ATLANTIC ... 5-8 81-83
CAPITOL ... 5-8 77-82

MINNEAPOLIS GENIUS 94 EAST
R&B '86

Singles: 7-inch

HOT PINK ... 3-4 86

MINNELLI, Liza
LP '64

Singles: 7-inch

A&M ... 3-6 68-71
ABC ... 3-5 73
CADENCE ... 5-10 63
CAPITOL (4900 thru 5700 series) ... 5-10 63-65
COLUMBIA ... 3-5 72-75
U.A. ... 3-5 77

LPs: 10/12-inch

A&M ... 10-15 68-73
ABC (752 "Cabaret") ... 10-15 72
(Soundtrack. With Joel Grey.)
ARISTA (4069 "Lucky Lady") ... 8-10 76
(Soundtrack.)
CADENCE (4012 "Best Foot Forward") ... 30-40 63
(Monaural. Original cast.)
CADENCE (24012 "Best Foot Forward") ... 40-60 63
(Stereo. Original cast.)
CAPITOL (T-2100 and T-2400 series) ... 10-20 64-66
(Monaural.)
CAPITOL (ST-2100 and ST-2400 series) ... 15-25 64-66
(Stereo.)
CAPITOL (2200 series) ... 5-8 78
CAPITOL (11000 series) ... 5-10 72-78
COLUMBIA ... 8-15 72-77
DRG (6101 "The Act") ... 8-10 78
EPIC ... 5-8 89
MCA (752 "Cabaret") ... 5-8
(Soundtrack. With Joel Grey.)
STET ... 8-10
TELARC ... 10-12 87
Also see GARLAND, Judy, & Liza Minnelli

MINOGUE, Kylie
P&R/LP '88

Singles: 7-inch

GEFFEN ... 3-4 88

Picture Sleeves

GEFFEN ... 3-4 88

LPs: 10/12-inch

GEFFEN ... 5-8 88

MINOR DETAIL
P&R/LP '83

Singles: 7-inch

POLYDOR ... 3-4 83-84

Picture Sleeves

POLYDOR ... 3-4 83

LPs: 10/12-inch

POLYDOR ... 5-8 83
Members: John Hughes; Willie Hughes.

MINTS: see COPELAND, Ken / Mints

MINTZ, Junier
(Frank Zappa)

Singles: 7-inch

REPRISE/STRAIGHT (1027 "Tears Began to Fall") ... 20-30 71
Also see ZAPPA, Frank

MIRABAI
LP '75

LPs: 10/12-inch

ATLANTIC ... 5-10 75

MIRACLES
P&R '59

(Smokey Robinson & Miracles; featuring Bill Smokey Robinson; featuring Billy Griffin)

Singles: 12-inch

COLUMBIA ... 4-6 77

Singles: 7-inch

CHESS (119 "Bad Girl") ... 3-5 84
CHESS (1734 "Bad Girl") ... 25-50 59
(Black label.)
CHESS (1734 "Bad Girl") ... 10-20 59
(Blue label.)
CHESS (1768 "All I Want") ... 25-35 60
COLUMBIA ... 3-5 77-78
END (1016 "Got a Job") ... 45-55 58
END (1029 "Money") ... 40-50 58
(No mention of Roulette Records.)
END (1029 "Money") ... 30-40 58
(Has "A Division of Roulette Records Inc".)
END (1084 "Money") ... 10-15 61
MOTOWN (G1 "Bad Girl") ... 500-1000 59
MOTOWN (400 & 500 series) ... 3-5 80s
MOTOWN (2207 "Bad Girl") ... 400-450 59
MOTOWN/TOPPS (11 "Shop Around") ... 50-75 67
(Topps Chewing Gum promotional item. Single-sided, cardboard flexi, picture disc. Issued with generic paper sleeve.)
ROULETTE ... 3-5 70s
STANDARD GROOVE (13090 "I Care About Detroit") ... 150-200 68
(Tamla logo at top, Artist credit at bottom. Promotional issue only.)
STANDARD GROOVE (13090 "I Care About Detroit") ... 100-150 68
(Artist credit at top. Promotional issue only.)
TAMLA (009 "The Christmas Song") ... 100-200 63
(Promotional issue only.)
TAMLA (54028 "The Feeling Is So Fine"/"You Can Depend on Me") ... 300-400 60
(With common version of *You Can Depend on Me.*)
TAMLA (54028 "The Feeling Is So Fine"/"You Can Depend on Me") ... 400-500 60
(With alternate take of *You Can Depend on Me,* Can be identified by the letter "A" following the identification number in the trail-off.)
TAMLA (54028 "Way Over There"/"Depend on Me") ... 100-150 60
(With alternate take of *Way Over There,* not available elsewhere.)
TAMLA (54028 "Way Over There"/"Depend on Me") ... 25-50 60
(With the hit version of *Way Over There,* the same as is heard on their Tamla LPs.)
TAMLA (54034 "Shop Around") ... 100-125 60
(Horizontal lines across top half of label. Has an alternate take of *Shop Around.* Has either "H55518 A-2" or "45-L1 37003" etched in the trail-off.)
TAMLA (54034 "Shop Around") ... 35-50 60
(No horizontal lines and Tamla globe logo at top. Has an alternate take of *Shop Around.* Etched in trail-off is "H55518 A-2.")
TAMLA (54034 "Shop Around") ... 10-20 60
(Has the hit version of *Shop Around.* Etched in trail-off is "L1" or "ARP L-1.")
TAMLA (54036 "Ain't It Baby") ... 50-75 61
TAMLA (54044 "Mighty Good Lovin'") ... 25-50 61
TAMLA (54048 "You Gotta Pay Some Dues") ... 50-100 61
(Note title variation.)
TAMLA (54048 "Everybody's Gotta Pay Some Dues") ... 25-50 61
TAMLA (54053 "What's So Good About Goodbye") ... 15-25 62
(Black vinyl.)
TAMLA (54053 "What's So Good About Goodbye") ... 20-30 62
(Colored vinyl. Promotional issue only.)
TAMLA (54059 "I'll Try Something New") ... 10-20 62
TAMLA (54069 "Way Over There") ... 10-20 62
TAMLA (54073 thru 54184) ... 5-10 62-69
TAMLA (54189 "Point It Out") ... 4-8 69
(Black vinyl.)
TAMLA (54189 "Point It Out") ... 15-20 69
(Colored vinyl. Promotional issue only.)
TAMLA (54194 thru 54268) ... 3-5 70-76

Picture Sleeves

TAMLA (54044 "Mighty Good Lovin'") ... 75-125 61
TAMLA (54048 "Everybody's Gotta Pay Some Dues") ... 50-75 61
TAMLA (54059 "I'll Try Something New") ... 40-60 62
TAMLA (54098 "I Like It Like That") .. 15-25 62
TAMLA (54127 thru 54194) ... 10-20 65-70

EPs: 7-inch

TAMLA ("Greatest Hits from the Beginning") ... 25-35 66
(Selection number not known.)
TAMLA (60267 "Going to a Go Go") 15-25 66

LPs: 10/12-inch

COLUMBIA ... 8-10 77-78
IMPERIAL HOUSE ... 8-12 79
MOTOWN (Except 793 & 8238) ... 5-10 82-84
MOTOWN (793 "Anthology") ... 12-18 74
MOTOWN (8238 "Greatest Hits from the Beginning") ... 8-12
NATURAL RESOURCES ... 5-10 78
TAMLA (220 "Hi! We're the Miracles") ... 150-250 61
(White label.)
TAMLA (220 "Hi! We're the Miracles") ... 200-300 61
(Yellow label with globes.)
TAMLA (223 "Cookin' with the Miracles") ... 150-250 61
(White label.)
TAMLA (223 "Cookin' with the Miracles") ... 200-300 62
(Yellow label with globes.)
TAMLA (230 "I'll Try Something New") ... 100-150 62
TAMLA (236 "Christmas with the Miracles") ... 150-200 62
TAMLA (238 "The Fabulous Miracles") ... 150-200 63
TAMLA (238 "You Really Got a Hold on Me") ... 75-125 63
(Reissue with new title.)
TAMLA (241 "On Stage") ... 50-100 63
TAMLA (245 "Mickey's Monkey") ... 50-75 63
(Monaural.)
TAMLA (245 "Mickey's Monkey") ... 75-125 63
(Stereo.)
TAMLA (254 "Greatest Hits from the Beginning") ... 25-35 63
(Monaural.)
TAMLA (254 "Greatest Hits from the Beginning") ... 35-45 63
(Stereo.)
TAMLA (267 "Going to a Go Go") ... 40-50 65
(Tamla globe label.)
TAMLA (271 thru 297) ... 15-30 66-70
TAMLA (301 thru 344) ... 10-20 71-76
Members: William "Smokey" Robinson; Pete Moore; Bobby Rogers; Ron White; Claudette Rogers; Billy Griffin; Marv Tarplin.
Also see GRIFFIN, Billy
Also see MARVELETTES / Mary Wells / Miracles / Marvin Gaye
Also see ROBINSON, Smokey
Also see RON & BILL

MIRAN, Wayne, & Rush Release
R&B '75

Singles: 7-inch

ROULETTE ... 3-5 75

MIRANDA, Carmen
P&R '41

(With the Bando Da Lua)

Singles: 78 rpm

DECCA ... 5-15 39-53
MGM ... 10-20

Picture Sleeves

DECCA ... 20-30 39

EPs: 7–inch
DECCA (2066 "Carmen Miranda") 15-25 53

MIRANDA, Carmen, & Andrews Sisters P&R '50
(With Vic Shoen & His Orchestra)
Singles: 78 rpm
DECCA 4-8 50
Also see ANDREWS SISTERS
Also see MIRANDA, Carmen

MIRETTES P&R/R&B '68
Singles: 7–inch
MIRWOOD 4-8 66
REVUE 4-8 67-69
UNI 3-6 69
LPs: 10/12–inch
REVUE 12-18 68
UNI 10-15 69
Members: Vanetta Fields; Jessie Smith; Robbie Montgomery.
Also see IKETTES

MISS ABRAMS: see ABRAMS, Miss

MISS THANG R&B '86
Singles: 12–inch
TOMMY BOY 4-6 86

MISS TONI FISHER: see FISHER, Miss Toni

MISSING PERSONS P&R/LP '82
Singles: 12–inch
CAPITOL 4-6 82-86
Singles: 7–inch
CAPITOL 3-4 82-86
Picture Sleeves
CAPITOL 3-5 82-84
EPs: 7–inch
KOMOS 5-8 80
LPs: 10/12–inch
CAPITOL 5-8 82-86
Members: Dale Bozzio; Terry Bozzio; Warren Cuccurullo.
Also see DURAN DURAN
Also see MOTHERS of INVENTION

MISSION R&B '74
Singles: 7–inch
PARAMOUNT 3-5 74

MISSION R&B '87
Singles: 7–inch
COLUMBIA 3-4 87-88
Member: Wayne Hussey.
Also see DEAD OR ALIVE
Also see MISSION

MISSION U.K. LP '87
LPs: 10/12–inch
MERCURY 5-8 87-90

MISSOURI LP '79
Singles: 7–inch
PANAMA 3-5 78
POLYDOR 3-5 79
LPs: 10/12–inch
PANAMA 8-12 77
POLYDOR 5-10 79

MR. BIG P&R '77
Singles: 7–inch
ARISTA 3-4 77
ATLANTIC 3-4 91
LPs: 10/12–inch
ARISTA 5-10 76
ATLANTIC 5-8 89
Members: Eric Martin.
Also see MARTIN, Eric

MR. GOON BONES & MR. FORD P&R '49
Singles: 78 rpm
CRYSTALETTE 4-8 49-56
Singles: 7–inch
CRYSTALETTE 5-10 56
DOT 4-8 59

MR. MISTER P&R/LP '84
Singles: 7–inch
RCA 3-4 84-87
Picture Sleeves
RCA 3-4 85-87
LPs: 10/12–inch
RCA 5-8 84-87
Members: Richard Page; Pat Mastelotto; Steve Farris; Steve George; Buzz Feiten.
Also see LARSEN - FEITEN BAND
Also see PAGES

MR. T. R&B '84
(Lawrence Tero)
Singles: 12–inch
COLUMBIA (9C9-39911 "Mr. T's Commandments") 8-12 84
(Picture disc.)
Singles: 7–inch
COLUMBIA 3-4 84
MCA 3-4 84
Picture Sleeves
COLUMBIA 3-4 84
LPs: 10/12–inch
COLUMBIA 5-8 84
MCA 5-8 84

MR. TWELVE STRING
(Glen Campbell)
Singles: 7–inch
WORLD PACIFIC 5-10 65
Also see CAMPBELL, Glen

MISTRESS P&R/LP '79
Singles: 7–inch
RSO 3-5 79
LPs: 10/12–inch
RSO 5-10 79

MITCHELL, Billy R&B '69
(Billy Mitchell Group)
Singles: 78 rpm
ATLANTIC 50-100 51-52
Singles: 7–inch
ATLANTIC (933 "My Love, My Desire") 150-200 51
CALLA 5-10 69
JUBILEE 5-10 61
RON 5-10 61-62
U.A. 5-10 60
WARWICK 5-10 59
Also see CLOVERS

MITCHELL, Bobby R&B '56
(With the Toppers)
Singles: 78 rpm
IMPERIAL 25-50 53-57
Singles: 7–inch
IMPERIAL (5236 "I'm Cryin'") 250-500 53
IMPERIAL (5250 "One Friday Morning") 250-500 53
IMPERIAL (5270 "Baby's Gone") 75-125 54
IMPERIAL (5282 "Angel Child") 75-125 54
IMPERIAL (5295 "The Wedding Bells Are Ringing") 100-200 54
IMPERIAL (5309 "I'm a Young Man") 75-125 54
IMPERIAL (5326 "I Wish I Knew") 50-75 55
IMPERIAL (5346 "I Cried") 25-50 55
IMPERIAL (5378 "Try Rock & Roll") 15-25 56
IMPERIAL (5412 "You're My Angel") 15-25 56
IMPERIAL (5378 "No No No") 15-25 57
IMPERIAL (5392 "I Try So Hard") 15-25 57
IMPERIAL (5412 "I've Got My Fingers Crossed") 15-25 57
IMPERIAL (5440 "You Always Hurt the One You Love") 15-25 57
IMPERIAL (5475 "I'm Gonna Be a Wheel Someday") 15-25 57
IMPERIAL (5511 "I Love to Hold You") 15-25 58
IMPERIAL (5558 "Hearts of Fire") 15-25 58
IMPERIAL (5923 "I Don't Want to Be a Wheel No More") 10-20 63
RON (337 "Send Me Your Picture") .. 10-20 61
RON (342 "There's Only One of You") 10-20 61

SHOW-BIZ 10-20 59

MITCHELL, Chad
Singles: 7–inch
AMY 3-6 68-69
W.B. 4-8 66-67
LPs: 10/12–inch
BELL 10-15 69
W.B. 10-20 66-67

MITCHELL, Chad, Trio P&R/LP '62
Singles: 7–inch
COLPIX 5-10 59-61
KAPP 5-10 61-63
MAY 4-8 62
MERCURY 4-8 63-64
Picture Sleeves
KAPP 10-15 61
MERCURY 8-12 63-65
LPs: 10/12–inch
COLPIX 20-30 60
KAPP 15-25 61-64
MERCURY 15-20 63-64
Members: Chad Mitchell; Joe Frazier; Mike Kobluk; Jim [Roger] McGuinn.
Also see McGUINN, Roger
Also see MITCHELL, Chad
Also see MITCHELL TRIO

MITCHELL, Chad, Trio, & Gatemen
LPs: 10/12–inch
COLPIX 20-25 64
Also see MITCHELL, Chad, Trio

MITCHELL, Freddie, & Orch. R&B '49
(With Rip Harrigan)
Singles: 78 rpm
ABC-PAR 3-5 57
BRUNSWICK 4-6 53
CORAL 4-6 53
DERBY 4-8 49-52
MERCURY 4-6 52
Singles: 7–inch
ABC-PAR 4-8 57-61
BRUNSWICK 5-10 53
CORAL 5-10 53
DERBY 5-15 49-52
MERCURY 5-10 52
ROCK 'N' ROLL 5-8
LPs: 10/12–inch
ALLEGRO/ROYAL (1600 "That Boogie Beat") 20-30 50s
TRIP 10-15 60s
"X" (1030 "Boogie Bash") 40-60 56
Session: King Curtis.
Also see KING CURTIS

MITCHELL, Guy P&R '50
(Al Cernick)
Singles: 78 rpm
COLUMBIA 5-15 50-57
KING (15125 "Cabaret") 10-15 51
Singles: 7–inch
CHALICE (711 "My Angel"/"Bit of Love") 15-25 63
CHALICE (711 "My Angel"/"Mr. Hobo") 15-25 63
(Note different flip.)
CHALICE (712 "Take Your Time") 15-25 63
CHALICE (713 "Your Imagination") 15-25 63
COLLECTABLES 3-4 80s
COLUMBIA 10-20 50-61
ERIC 3-4 83
GMI 4-6 74
JOY 4-8 62-63
KING (15125 "Cabaret") 20-30 51
(Previously issued as by Al Grant, Al Cernick's pseudonym before using Guy Mitchell.)
REPRISE 4-6 66
STARDAY 4-6 67-69
Picture Sleeves
COLUMBIA (40769 "Singing the Blues") 15-20 56
COLUMBIA (40820 "Knee Deep in the Blues") 15-20 57
COLUMBIA (40877 "Rock-A-Billy") ... 10-20 57

COLUMBIA (41476 "Heartaches By the Number") 10-15 60
COLUMBIA (41853 "Sunshine Guitar") 10-15 60
COLUMBIA (42231 "Soft Rain") 10-15 61

EPs: 7-inch

COLUMBIA 10-15 54-57

LPs: 10/12-inch

COLUMBIA (1211 "Guy in Love") 15-25 58
(Monaural.)
COLUMBIA (1226 "Greatest Hits") 15-25 59
COLUMBIA (1552 "Sunshine Guitar") 15-25 60
(Monaural.)
COLUMBIA (6231 "Open Spaces") 25-50 53
(10-inch LP.)
COLUMBIA (8011 "Guy in Love") 20-30 58
(Stereo.)
COLUMBIA (8352 "Sunshine Guitar") 20-30 60
(Stereo.)
KING (644 "Sincerely Yours") 150-250 59
(Mitchell pictured but not identified on cover. Includes tracks recorded as Al Grant.)
NASHVILLE 5-10 70
STARDAY 10-15 68-69

Also see CAVALLARO, Carmen, Featuring Al Cernick
Also see CLOONEY, Rosemary, & Guy Mitchell
Also see GRANT, Al

MITCHELL, Guy, & Mindy Carson

Singles: 78 rpm

COLUMBIA 5-10 52-53

Singles: 7-inch

COLUMBIA 8-12 52-53

Also see CARSON, Mindy

MITCHELL, Guy / Eileen Rodgers

EPs: 7-inch

COLUMBIA 10-15 56

Also see RODGERS, Eileen
Also see MITCHELL, Guy

MITCHELL, Joni — LP '68

Singles: 7-inch

ASYLUM 3-5 72-80
ELEKTRA 3-5 75
GEFFEN 3-4 82-91
REPRISE 3-6 68-72

Picture Sleeves

GEFFEN 3-4 82-85

LPs: 10/12-inch

ASYLUM 8-10 72-80
GEFFEN 5-8 82-91
REPRISE 10-20 68-71

MITCHELL, Joni, & L.A. Express

LPs: 10/12-inch

ASYLUM (202 "Miles of Aisles") 20-30 74

Also see L.A. EXPRESS
Also see MITCHELL, Joni

MITCHELL, Kim — P&R/LP '85

Singles: 7-inch

BRONZE 3-4 85

LPs: 10/12-inch

BRONZE 5-8 85

MITCHELL, McKinley — R&B '62

Singles: 7-inch

BLACK BEAUTY 3-5
BOXER 10-15 59
CHIMNEYVILLE 3-5 77-78
MALACO 3-6
ONE-DERFUL 5-10 62-65
RETTAS 4-8
SOUTHERN BISCUIT 8-12
SANDMAN 5-10
SPOONFUL 10-15
TODDLIN' TOWN 4-8 69

MITCHELL, Philip — R&B '75

(Prince Philip Mitchell)

Singles: 7-inch

ATLANTIC 3-5 78-79
EVENT 3-5 75
HI (Except 2240) 5-10 72-73
HI (2240 "Oh How I Love You") 10-15 73
ICHIBAN 3-4 86

MITCHELL, Rubin — LP '67

Singles: 7-inch

CAPITOL 3-6 67-68

Picture Sleeves

CAPITOL 4-8 67

LPs: 10/12-inch

CAPITOL 10-15 67

MITCHELL, Willie — P&R/R&B '64

(With the Four Kings, "Vocal D. Bryant"; Willie Mitchell Orchestra; "Vocal by Billy Taylor")

Singles: 7-inch

HI 4-8 62-69
HOME of the BLUES 5-10 60-61
MOTOWN 3-5
SKIPPER (1001 "Wasting My Time") 15-25
STOMPER TIME (1160 "Walking At Your Will") 500-1000 58

Picture Sleeves

HI 5-10 68

EPs: 7-inch

HI (72 "Willie Mitchell") 10-15 60s
HI (32026 "It's Dance Time") 10-15 60s
(Stereo. Juke box issue only.)

LPs: 10/12-inch

BEARSVILLE 5-8 81
HI (12010 thru 12042) 10-20 63-68
(Monaural.)
HI (32010 thru 32058) 10-25 63-71
(Stereo.)
HI (8000 series) 5-8 77
MOTOWN 8-10 82

MITCHELL TRIO — LP '64

Singles: 7-inch

MERCURY 4-8 65-66
REPRISE 4-8 67

Picture Sleeves

MERCURY 5-10 63-66

LPs: 10/12-inch

MERCURY (20944 "Slightly Irreverent Mitchell Trio") 15-20 64
(Monaural.)
MERCURY (20992 "Typical American Boys") 15-20 65
(Monaural.)
MERCURY (21049 "That's the Way It's Gonna Be") 15-20 65
(Monaural.)
MERCURY (21067 "Violets of Dawn") 15-20 65
(Monaural.)
MERCURY (60944 "Slightly Irreverent Mitchell Trio") 20-25 64
(Stereo.)
MERCURY (60992 "Typical American Boys") 20-25 65
MERCURY (61049 "That's the Way It's Gonna Be") 20-25 65
(Stereo.)
MERCURY (21067 "Violets of Dawn") 20-25 65
(Stereo.)
REPRISE (6354 "Alive") 15-20 67

Members: Chad Mitchell; Joe Frazier; Mike Kobluk; John Denver; David Boise; Michael Johnson.
Also see DENVER, John
Also see JOHNSON, Michael
Also see MITCHELL, Chad, Trio

MITCHUM, Robert — P&R '58

(With the Calypso Band)

Singles: 78 rpm

CAPITOL 5-15 57-58

Singles: 7-inch

CAPITOL (Except 3986) 5-10 57
CAPITOL (3986 "The Ballad of Thunder Road") 8-12 58
(Purple label.)
CAPITOL (3986 "The Ballad of Thunder Road") 4-8 62
(Orange/yellow label.)
CAPITOL STARLINE 4-8 60s
MONUMENT 4-6 67

EPs: 7-inch

CAPITOL (853 "Calypso Is Like So") 15-25 57
(Price is for any of three volumes.)

LPs: 10/12-inch

CAPITOL (853 "Calypso Is Like So") 25-50 57
MONUMENT (8086 "That Man") 15-20 67
(Monaural.)
MONUMENT (18086 "That Man") 20-25 67
(Stereo.)

MIXTURES — P&R '71

Singles: 7-inch

SIRE 3-5 71

MOB — P&R '71

Singles: 7-inch

COLOSSUS 3-5 71-72
MGM 4-6 72
MERCURY 4-8 68
PRIVATE STOCK 3-5 76-77

Picture Sleeves

COLOSSUS 3-6 71-72

LPs: 10/12-inch

COLOSSUS 10-15 71
MGM (4839 "The Mob") 10-15 72
PRIVATE STOCK 8-12 75

Members: Art Herrera; Al Herrera; James Holvay; Gary Beiser.

MOBY GRAPE — P&R/LP '67

Singles: 7-inch

SAN FRANCISCO SOUND 100-125 84
(Set of six picture discs.)

Singles: 7-inch

COLUMBIA 6-12 67-69

Picture Sleeves

COLUMBIA 20-25 67

LPs: 10/12-inch

COLUMBIA (2698 "Moby Grape") 35-45 67
(Monaural. Cover pictures Don Stevenson's middle finger over washboard. Price includes bonus poster, which represents about $5 to $10 of the value.)
COLUMBIA (2698 "Moby Grape") 10-20 67
(Monaural. Cover pictures Don Stevenson's hand closed. Price includes bonus poster.)
COLUMBIA (9498 "Moby Grape") 40-50 67
(Stereo. Cover pictures Don Stevenson's middle finger over washboard. Price includes bonus poster, which represents about $5 to $10 of the value.)
COLUMBIA (9498 "Moby Grape") 10-20 67
(Stereo. Cover pictures Don Stevenson's hand closed. Price includes bonus poster.)
COLUMBIA (9613 "Wow") 10-15 68
COLUMBIA (9696 "Moby Grape '69") 10-15 69
COLUMBIA (9912 "Truly Fine Citizen") 10-15 69
COLUMBIA (31098 "Great Grape") 10-15 72
ESCAPE (A1A "Live Grape") 8-10 78
HARMONY (30393 "Omaha") 10-12 71
REPRISE (6460 "20 Granite Creek") 10-12 71
SAN FRANCISCO SOUND 10-15 83
(Black vinyl.)
SAN FRANCISCO SOUND (04830 "Moby Grape '84") 20-25 83
(Picture disc.)

Promotional LPs

COLUMBIA (MGS-1 "Grape Jam") 15-25 68
(With Mike Bloomfield and Al Kooper.)
ESCAPE (95018 "Live Grape") 15-25 78
(Colored vinyl.)

Members: Don Stevenson; Jerry Miller; Peter Lewis; Skip Spence; Jeff Blackburn.
Also see BLOOMFIELD, Mike, & Al Kooper
Also see FRANKLIN, Aretha / Union Gap /Blood, Sweat & Tears / Moby Grape
Also see FRANTICS

MOCEDADES — P&R/LP '74

Singles: 7-inch

TARA 3-5 74

LPs: 10/12-inch
TARA 5-10 74

MODEL 500 — D&D '85
Singles: 12-inch
METROPLEX 4-6 85

MODELS — P&R/LP '86
Singles: 12-inch
GEFFEN 4-6 86
Singles: 7-inch
GEFFEN 3-4 86
Picture Sleeves
GEFFEN 3-4 86
LPs: 10/12-inch
GEFFEN 5-8 86
WINDSONG 5-8 80

MODERN ENGLISH — P&R/D&D/LP '83
Singles: 12-inch
SIRE 4-6 82-86
Singles: 7-inch
4AD 3-5 80-84
4AD/SIRE 3-4 83-86
LIMP ("Drowning Man") 5-8 79
(Selection number not known.)
SIRE 3-4 86
LPs: 10/12-inch
4AD/SIRE 5-10 83-84
SIRE 5-8 86
TVT 5-8 90

MODERN ROCKETRY — D&D '83
Singles: 12-inch
MEGATONE 4-6 83

MODERNAIRES — P&R '45
(With Paula Kelly)
Singles: 78 rpm
COLUMBIA 3-6 45-50
CORAL 3-5 51-56
Singles: 7-inch
CAPITOL 3-6 69
COLUMBIA (38000 series) 5-10 50
CORAL 5-10 51-56
MERCURY 4-8 59
U.A. 4-6 62
EPs: 7-inch
CORAL 5-10 51-55
LPs: 10/12-inch
COLUMBIA 10-25 50-66
CORAL 15-25 51-55
LIBERTY 5-10 84
MERCURY 8-12 60
ROSS 5-10 79
U.A. 10-20 61-62
WING 10-15 62
Members: Paula Kelly; John Drake; Allan Copeland; Francis Scott; Hal Dickenson.

MODUGNO, Domenico — P&R/R&B/LP '58
Singles: 7-inch
DECCA 5-15 58-64
MCA 3-5 78
MGM 4-6 66
RCA 4-6 68-72
U.A. INT'L 4-6 67
EPs: 7-inch
DECCA 10-15 58
LPs: 10/12-inch
DECCA 15-25 58-61
RCA 10-15 66
U.A. INT'L 8-12 67

MODULATIONS — R&B '74
Singles: 7-inch
BUDDAH 3-5 74-75
LP: 10/12-inch
BUDDAH 8-12 74

MOE & JOE: see STAMPLEY, Joe

MOJO MEN — P&R '65
(Mojo)
Singles: 7-inch
AUTUMN 8-12 65-66
GRT 4-8 69
REPRISE 5-10 66-68
LPs: 10/12-inch
GRT (10003 "Mojo Magic") 15-20 69
Members: Dennis DeCarr; Paul Curcio; Jim Alaimo; Don Metchick.

MOLLY HATCHET — LP '78
Singles: 7-inch
EPIC 3-5 79-86
Picture Sleeves
EPIC 3-5 79
EPs: 7-inch
CSP ("Molly Hatchet") 4-8 81
(Promotional issue only. Made for Nestle's candy.)
LPs: 10/12-inch
EPIC (Except picture discs and 40137) 5-10 78-87
EPIC (694 "Flirtin' with Disaster") 40-50 79
(Picture disc. Has die-cut cover. Promotional issue only.)
EPIC (884 "Beatin the Odds") 30-40 80
(Picture disc. Promotional issue only. 1350 made.)
EPIC (1320 "Take No Prisoners") 20-25 81
(Picture disc. Promotional issue only.)
EPIC (35347 "Molly Hatchet") 40-50 78
(Picture disc. Promotional issue only.)
EPIC (36110 "Flirtin' with Disaster") 50-60 79
(Picture disc. Promotional issue only. 450 made.)
EPIC (40137 "Double Trouble Live") 10-15 79
EPIC (40137 "Double Trouble Live") 15-25 79
(White label. Promotional issue only.)
Members: Danny Joe Brown; Jimmy Farrar.
Also see BROWN, Danny Joe

MOM & DADS — LP '71
Singles: 7-inch
GNP 3-5 71-80
LPs: 10/12-inch
GNP 5-10 71-87
Members: Harold Hendren; Doris Crow; Les Welch; Quentin Ratliff.

MOMENT OF TRUTH — R&B '74
Singles: 7-inch
ROULETTE 3-5 75
Members: Bill Jones; Michael Garrison; Norris Harris.
Also see CHAIN REACTION
Also see CHOCOLATE SYRUP

MOMENTS — P&R '63
Singles: 7-inch
ERA 5-10 63-64
HIT 5-10 63
WORLD ARTISTS 4-8 64
Also see SHACKLEFORDS

MOMENTS — P&R/R&B '68
Singles: 7-inch
STANG 3-6 68-78
SUGAR HILL 3-4 80-81
LPs: 10/12-inch
STANG 8-12 70-78
VICTORY 5-8 82
Also see O'JAYS / Moments
Also see RAY, GOODMAN & BROWN
Also see SYLVIA & MOMENTS

MOMENTS & WHATNAUTS — R&B '74
Singles: 7-inch
STANG 3-5 74
Also see MOMENTS
Also see WHATNAUTS

MONAE, Tia — D&D '84
Singles: 12-inch
FIRST TAKE 4-6 84

MONARCHS — P&R '64
Singles: 7-inch
MONUMENT 4-6 60s
SOUND STAGE 7 .... 8-12 64

MONDAY, Julie — P&R '66
Singles: 7-inch
RAINBOW 4-8 66
SSS INT'L 3-6 68

MONDAY AFTER — R&B '76
Singles: 7-inch
BUDDAH 3-5 76

MONDO ROCK — P&R '87
Singles: 7-inch
ATLANTIC 3-4 82
COLUMBIA 3-4 85-87
LPs: 10/12-inch
ATLANTIC 5-8 82
COLUMBIA 5-8 85

MONET — R&B '87
Singles: 7-inch
LIGOSA 3-4 87

MONET & NOLAN THOMAS — R&B '87
Singles: 7-inch
LIGOSA 3-4 87
Also see MONET
Also see THOMAS, Nolan

MONEY, Eddie — P&R/LP '78
Singles: 12-inch
COLUMBIA 4-6 84
Singles: 7-inch
CBS (165196 "Maybe I'm a Fool") 20-30 79
(Picture disc. Promotional issue only.)
COLUMBIA 3-5 78-89
POLYDOR 3-4 85
Picture Sleeves
COLUMBIA 3-5 82-88
LPs: 10/12-inch
COLUMBIA 6-9 77-89
POLYDOR 5-8 85

MONEY, Eddie, & Zane Buzby
Singles: 7-inch
COLUMBIA 3-5 79

MONEY, Eddie, & Valerie Carter — P&R '80
Singles: 7-inch
COLUMBIA 3-5 80
Also see CARTER, Valerie

MONEY, Eddie, & Ronnie Spector
Singles: 7-inch
COLUMBIA 3-5 86
Also see MONEY, Eddie
Also see SPECTOR, Ronnie

MONGO SANTAMARIA: see SANTAMARIA, Mongo

MONITORS — P&R/R&B '66
Singles: 7-inch
BUDDAH 3-5 72
MOTOWN 3-5
SOUL (35049 "Step By Step") 8-15 68
V.I.P. (25028 thru 25046) 10-20 65-68
V.I.P. (25049 "Step By Step") 20-40 68
LPs: 10/12-inch
SOUL (714 "Greetings") 50-75 69

MONK, T.S. — R&B '80
(Thelonious Monk Jr.)
Singles: 7-inch
MIRAGE 3-4 80-82
LPs: 10/12-inch
MIRAGE 5-8 81-82

MONK, Thelonious — LP '63
Singles: 7-inch
COLUMBIA 3-8 63-69
PRESTIGE 3-8 60-69
EPs: 7-inch
PRESTIGE 20-40 52
LPs: 10/12-inch
BLACK LION 5-10 74
BLUE NOTE (100 thru 500 series) 6-12 73-76
BLUE NOTE (1510 "Genius of Modern Music, Vol. 1") 50-75 56

(Label has Lexington Ave. street address for Blue Note Records.)
BLUE NOTE (1510 "Genius of Modern Music, Vol. 1") 40-50 58
(Label reads, "Blue Note Records Inc. New York, U.S.A.")
BLUE NOTE (1510 "Genius of Modern Music, Vol. 1") 15-25 60s
(Label reads "Blue Note Records - a Division of Liberty Records Inc.")
BLUE NOTE (1511 "Genius of Modern Music, Vol. 2") 50-75 56
(Label has Lexington Ave. street address for Blue Note Records.)
BLUE NOTE (1511 "Genius of Modern Music, Vol. 2") 40-50 58
(Label reads, "Blue Note Records Inc. New York, U.S.A.")
BLUE NOTE (1511 "Genius of Modern Music, Vol. 2") 15-25 60s
(Label reads "Blue Note Records - a Division of Liberty Records Inc.")
BLUE NOTE (5002 "Theolonious Monk") 200-300 52
(10–inch LP.)
BLUE NOTE (5009 "Theolonious Monk") 200-300 52
(10–inch LP.)
COLUMBIA (1900 thru 2600 series) . 12-25 63-67
(Monaural.)
COLUMBIA (8700 thru 9800 series) . 15-30 63-69
(Stereo.)
COLUMBIA (32000 thru 38000 series)..5-15 74-83
EVEREST..5-10 78
MILESTONE..5-15 75-84
PAUSA..5-10 83
PRESTIGE (142 "Thelonious Monk Trio")..100-200 52
(10–inch LP.)
PRESTIGE (180 "Thelonious Monk with Frank Foster")..100-200 54
(10–inch LP.)
PRESTIGE (189 "Thelonious Monk with Art Blakey")..100-200 54
(10–inch LP.)
PRESTIGE (7053 thru 7245)............30-60 56-62
(Yellow labels.)
PRESTIGE (7000 thru 7600 series).. 15-25 65-69
(Blue labels.)
PRESTIGE (24000 series)..................8-12 72
RIVERSIDE (12-201 thru 12-323).....30-60 55-60
RIVERSIDE (400 series)..................15-30 62-67
RIVERSIDE (1100 series)..................25-50 58-60
RIVERSIDE (3000 series)..................10-20 68-69
RIVERSIDE (9400 series)..................15-30 62-63
TOMATO..5-10 78
TRIP..5-10 73
Also see COLTRANE, John, & Thelonious Monk
Also see DAVIS, Miles, & Thelonious Monk
Also see MERC & MONK
Also see MULLIGAN, Gerry, & Thelonious Monk

MONK, Thelonious, & Sonny Rollins

EPs: 7–inch

PRESTIGE..20-40 52

LPs: 10/12–inch

PRESTIGE (166 "Thelonious Monk & Sonny Rollins")..150-250 52
(10–inch LP.)
PRESTIGE (200 series)..................50-75 57-58
PRESTIGE (7000 series)..................50-75 57-59
PRESTIGE (1100 series)..................40-60 58

MONKEES *P&R/LP '66*

Singles: 12–inch

ARISTA..8-12 86
(Promotional issue only.)

Singles: 7–inch

ARISTA (0201 "Daydream Believer")....4-8 76
ARISTA (9000 series)..........................3-6 76-86
COLGEMS (Except picture discs).......5-10 66-70
COLGEMS..15-30 67
(Cardboard 5½-inch picture disc cutouts from cereal boxes. Four different graphic designs were used. Each lists four tracks, but only plays one. Song on any given disc is indicated by a number stamped into label area. A total of four different songs with four different pictures totals 16 variations.)
COLLECTABLES (0904300717 "18 Great Singles, Vol. 1")..30-40 94
(Colored vinyl.)
FLASHBACK..3-5 73
RHINO (Except 74411)..........................3-5 87
RHINO (74411 "Every Step of the Way")..15-20 87
(Picture disc.)

Picture Sleeves

ARISTA..3-5 86
COLGEMS (1000 series)..................10-20 66-68
COLGEMS (5000 series)..................15-25 69-70
RHINO..3-5 87

EPs: 7–inch

COLGEMS (Cardboard discs) 5-10 67
(Single-sided, four track discs, originally attached to cereal boxes. Not issued with covers, although discs were illustrated.)
COLGEMS (101 "The Monkees")..... 50-75 66
(Stereo 33 compact. Juke box issue.)
COLGEMS (102 "More of the Monkees")..50-75 67
(Stereo 33 compact. Juke box issue.)

LPs: 10/12–inch

ARISTA (4000 series)..........................8-12 76
ARISTA (8000 series)..........................5-8 86
BELL (6081 "Refocus")..........................20-30 73
COLGEMS (COM-101 "The Monkees")..20-30 66
(Monaural. With *Papa Gene's Blues.*)
COLGEMS (COS-101 "The Monkees")..30-40 66
(Stereo. With *Papa Gene's Blues.*)
COLGEMS (COM-101 "The Monkees")..15-25 66
(Monaural. Without *Papa Gene's Blues.*)
COLGEMS (COS-101 "The Monkees")..20-30 66
(Stereo. Without *Papa Gene's Blues.*)
COLGEMS (COM-102 "More of the Monkees")..15-25 67
(Monaural.)
COLGEMS (COS-102 "More of the Monkees")..20-30 67
(Stereo.)
COLGEMS (COM-103 "Headquarters")..15-25 67
(Monaural.)
COLGEMS (COS-103 "Headquarters")..20-30 67
(Stereo.)
COLGEMS (COM-104 "Pisces, Aquarius, Capricorn and Jones")..........................15-25 67
(Monaural.)
COLGEMS (COS-104 "Pisces, Aquarius, Capricorn and Jones")..........................20-30 67
(Stereo.)
COLGEMS (COM-109 "The Birds, The Bees, and the Monkees")..50-75 68
(Monaural.)
COLGEMS (COS-109 "The Birds, The Bees, and the Monkees")..20-30 68
(Stereo.)
COLGEMS (113 "Instant Replay").... 25-35 69
COLGEMS (115 "The Monkees Greatest Hits")..30-50 69
COLGEMS (117 "The Monkees Present")..50-75 69
COLGEMS (119 "Changes")........... 75-100 70
COLGEMS (329 "Golden Hits").... 100-125 71
(RCA Special Products issue.)
COLGEMS (1001 "A Barrel Full of Monkees")..50-75 71
COLGEMS (5008 "Head")..................35-45 68
LAURIE HOUSE..20-30 73
(Mail-order offer.)
PAIR (0188 "The Monkees")............15-25 82
RCA (329 "Golden Hits")..................50-75 72
RCA (7000 series)..8-10
RHINO (Except 701)..........................5-10 82-87
RHINO (701 "Monkee Business")..... 15-20 82
(Picture disc.)
SILHOUETTE (10012 "Tails of the Monkees")..10-15 83
(Picture disc.)
Members: Michael Nesmith; Davy Jones; Micky Dolenz; Peter Tork.
Also see DOLENZ, Micky
Also see DOLENZ, JONES & TORK
Also see JONES, Davy
Also see NESMITH, Michael

MONOTONES *P&R/R&B '58*

Singles: 78 rpm

ARGO (5290 "Book of Love")............25-50 58

Singles: 7–inch

ARGO (Except 5339)..........................15-25 58-59
ARGO (5339 "Tell It to the Judge") ...20-30 59
CHESS..3-5 73
COLLECTABLES..3-4 80s
ERIC..3-4 70s
HICKORY..5-10 64-65
HULL (735 "Reading the Book of Love")..50-60 60
HULL (743 "Daddy's Home But Momma's Gone")..15-20 61
MASCOT (124 "Book of Love").....250-500 57
ROULETTE..3-5 73

LPs: 10/12–inch

MURRAY HILL..5-8
Members: Warren Davis; Frank Smith; John Raynes; George Malone; Charles Patrick; James Patrick.

MONRO, Matt *P&R/LP '61*

Singles: 7–inch

CAPITOL..3-6 66-72
LIBERTY..3-8 62-66
U.A. 3-5 74
WARWICK..4-8 61

LPs: 10/12–inch

CAPITOL..8-15 67-70
LIBERTY..10-20 62-66
LONDON (1611 "Blue and Sentimental")..20-30 57
WARWICK (2045 "My Kind of Girl") . 15-25 61
Also see BARRY, John

MONROE, Marilyn *P&R '54*

Singles: 78 rpm

RCA (5745 "River of No Return").... 50-100 54
(Has picture of Marilyn on label. Promotional issue only.)
RCA (6033 "Heat Wave")..................10-20 55
RCA/SIMON HOUSE (5745 "River of No Return")..100-200 54
(Has "Who Is She?" label. Promotional issue only.)
U.A. (161 "I Wanna Be Loved By You")..25-50 59

Singles: 7–inch

RCA (5745 "River of No Return").... 50-100 54
(Has picture of Marilyn on label. Promotional issue only.)
RCA (6033 "Heat Wave")..................15-25 55
20TH FOX (311 "River of No Return")..10-15 62
U.A. (161 "I Wanna Be Loved By You")..10-15 59

Picture Sleeves

RCA (5745 "River of No Return")..50-100 54
RCA (6033 "Heat Wave")................50-100 55
20TH FOX (311 "River of No Return")..50-75 62

EPs: 7–inch

MGM (208 "Gentlemen Prefer Blondes")..25-50 53
(Soundtrack. With Jane Russell.)
RCA (593 "There's No Business Like Show Business")..30-40 55
U.A. (1005 "Some Like It Hot")..........25-35 59
(With "This Is Hot!" publicity insert for the film.)
U.A. (1005 "Some Like It Hot")..........15-25 59
(Without film publicity insert.)

LPs: 10/12–inch

ASCOT (13500 "Some Like It Hot") .. 20-30 64
(Monaural. Soundtrack.)

ASCOT (16500 "Some Like It Hot") .. 30-40 64
(Stereo. Soundtrack. Also has selections from other films.)
AUDIO FIDELITY (50005 "The Ten") ... 25-35 84
(Picture disc.)
COLUMBIA (1527 "Let's Make Love") ... 30-50 60
(Monaural. Soundtrack.)
COLUMBIA (8327 "Let's Make Love") ... 40-60 60
(Stereo. Soundtrack.)
COLUMBIA/CSP (8327 "Let's Make Love") ... 8-12
(Soundtrack. With Yves Montand and Frankie Vaughan.)
MGM (208 "Gentlemen Prefer Blondes") ... 75-100 53
(10-inch LP.)
MGM (3231 "Gentlemen Prefer Blondes") ... 40-60 55
(Soundtrack. With Jane Russell. One side has music from *Till the Clouds Roll By.*)
MOVIETONE (72016 "Unforgettable") ... 15-25 67
SANDY HOOK (Except 2013) ... 5-10 79
SANDY HOOK (2013 "Rare Recordings 1948-'62") ... 30-40 84
STET ... 8-10
20TH FOX (5000 "Marilyn") ... 75-125 62
(With bonus photo of Marilyn nude.)
20TH FOX (5000 "Marilyn") ... 50-75 62
(Without bonus photo.)
U.A. (272 "Some Like It Hot") ... 8-12 74
(Soundtrack.)
U.A. (4030 "Some Like It Hot") ... 35-55 59
(Monaural. Soundtrack.)
U.A. (5030 "Some Like It Hot") ... 50-75 59
(Stereo. Soundtrack.)

MONROE, Michael — LP '89

LPs: 10/12-inch

MERCURY ... 5-8 89

MONROE, Vaughn — P&R '40

Singles: 78 rpm

BLUEBIRD ... 5-10 40-42
RCA ... 3-8 47-58
VICTOR ... 4-8 42-47

Singles: 7-inch

DOT ... 3-6 62-63
JUBILEE ... 4-6 61
MGM ... 4-6 60
RCA ... 5-8 50-59
ROD ... 3-5 68
U.A. ... 4-6 60

Picture Sleeves

RCA ... 10-15 57

EPs: 7-inch

CAMDEN ... 5-10 56
RCA ... 5-10 50-56

LPs: 10/12-inch

CAMDEN ... 15-25 56
DOT ... 10-20 62-64
HAMILTON ... 10-20 65
KAPP ... 10-20 65
RCA (11 thru 3066) ... 20-40 50-53
(10-inch LPs.)
RCA (1400 thru 1700 series) ... 15-25 56-58
(12-inch LPs.)
RCA (1100 series) ... 5-10 75
RCA (3800 series) ... 10-15 67
RCA (6000 series) ... 5-10 72
Also see MARTIN, Dean / Patti Page
Also see PRESLEY, Elvis / Vaughn Monroe / Gogi Grant / Robert Shaw

MONROES — P&R/LP '82

Singles: 7-inch

ALFA ... 3-5 82

LPs: 10/12-inch

ALFA (15015 "The Monroes") ... 5-10 82

MONTANA ORCHESTRA — LP '81

LPs: 10/12-inch

MJS ... 5-8 81

MONTANA SEXTET — D&D '83

Singles: 12-inch

PHILLY SOUND ... 4-6 83

MONTANAS — P&R '68

Singles: 7-inch

INDEPENDENCE ... 5-10 67-69
W.B. ... 4-8 66-68

MONTCLAIRS — R&B '72

Singles: 7-inch

PAULA ... 3-6 71-74

LPs: 10/12-inch

PAULA ... 8-12 72
Members: Phil Perry; Kevin Samlin; George McLellan; David Frye; Scotty Williams.

MONTE, Lou — P&R '54

Singles: 78 rpm

RCA (Except 6704) ... 3-5 53-56
RCA (6704 "Elvis Presley for President") ... 10-20 56

Singles: 7-inch

GWP ... 3-5 71-72
JAMIE ... 3-5 72
RCA (5382 thru 6600 series) ... 10-20 53-56
RCA (6700 thru 7600 series, except 6704) ... 5-15 56-60
RCA (6704 "Elvis Presley for President") ... 20-30 56
RCA (8700 thru 9000 series) ... 5-10 65-67
RAGALIA ... 3-6 69
REPRISE ... 5-10 62-65
ROULETTE ... 5-10 60-61

Picture Sleeves

REPRISE ... 8-12 62-63

EPs: 7-inch

RCA (Except 18) ... 10-20 57-59
RCA (18 "Elvis Presley for President") ... 25-35 56
(Promotional issue only. Not issued with cover.)

LPs: 10/12-inch

CAMDEN ... 15-20 58
DESIGN ... 10-15
HARMONY ... 10-15 68
RCA (1600 thru 1900 series) ... 20-35 57-59
RCA (3000 series) ... 10-20 66-67
ROULETTE ... 15-25 60
REPRISE ... 15-25 61-65
Also see PRESLEY, Elvis / Martha Carson / Lou Monte / Herb Jeffries

MONTENEGRO, Hugo — LP '66

(With Orchestra & Chorus)

Singles: 7-inch

RCA ... 3-5 64-75
TIME ... 4-6 61-63
20TH FOX ... 5-8 59

LPs: 10/12-inch

CAMDEN ... 10-20 62
GWP ... 5-10 70
MAINSTREAM ... 10-15 67-68
MOVIETONE ... 8-12 67
PICKWICK ... 5-10 70s
RCA (0025 thru 2300 series) ... 5-10 72-77
RCA (LOC-1113 "Hurry Sundown") .. 35-40 67
(Monaural. Soundtrack.)
RCA (LSO-1113 "Hurry Sundown") .. 40-50 67
(Stereo. Soundtrack.)
RCA (2900 series) ... 10-15 64
RCA (LPM-3475 "Man from U.N.C.L.E.") ... 25-35 65
(Monaural. Soundtrack.)
RCA (LSP-3475 "Man from U.N.C.L.E.") ... 30-40 65
(Stereo. Soundtrack.)
RCA (LPM-3574 "Man from U.N.C.L.E., Volume 2") ... 30-40 66
(Monaural. Soundtrack.)
RCA (LSP-3574 "Man from U.N.C.L.E., Volume 2") ... 35-45 66
(Stereo. Soundtrack.)
RCA (3500 thru 4600 series) ... 5-15 66-71
RCA (6000 series) ... 5-10 71
TIME ... 8-15 60-64
20TH FOX ... 5-15 59-68
Also see HIRT, Al, & Hugo Montenegro

MONTEZ, Chris — P&R/R&B '62

Singles: 7-inch

A&M ... 4-6 65-68
COLLECTABLES ... 3-4 80s
ERA ... 3-5 72
ERIC ... 3-4 70s
JAMIE ... 3-5 73
MONOGRAM ... 5-10 62-64
PARAMOUNT ... 3-5 71-73

LPs: 10/12-inch

A&M ... 10-20 66-67
MONOGRAM (100 "Let's Dance") ... 45-65 63
Members: Joel Hill; Carol Kaye; Julius Wechter; Pete Jolly; Tom Tedesco; Hal Blaine.
Also see BAJA MARIMBA BAND
Also see JOLLY, Pete

MONTGOMERY, Melba — C&W '63

Singles: 7-inch

CAPITOL ... 3-5 69-76
COMPASS ... 3-4 86
ELEKTRA ... 3-5 73-75
KARI ... 3-5 80
MUSICOR ... 3-6 66-69
U.A. (500 thru 900 series) ... 4-8 63-66
U.A. (1000 & 1100 series) ... 3-5 77

Picture Sleeves

MUSICOR ... 4-8 66

LPs: 10/12-inch

CAPITOL ... 8-12 69-75
ELEKTRA ... 5-10 73-75
MUSICOR ... 10-20 66-68
UNART ... 8-12 67
U.A. (Except 600 series) ... 10-20 64
U.A. (600 series) ... 5-10 78
Also see JONES, George, Gene Pitney & Melba Montgomery
Also see JONES, George, & Melba Montgomery
Also see PITNEY, Gene, & Melba Montgomery
Also see WEST, Dottie / Melba Montgomery

MONTGOMERY, Tammy — P&R '63

(Tana Montgomery; Tammi Terrell)

Singles: 7-inch

CHECKER (1072 "If I Would Marry You") ... 25-35 64
(Maroon label.)
CHECKER (1072 "If I Would Marry You") ... 15-25 64
(Multi-color label.)
SCEPTER (1224 "If You See Bill") ... 30-50 61
TRY ME (28001 "I Cried") ... 20-30 63
WAND (123 "Voice of Experience") .. 20-30 62
Also see TERRELL, Tammi

MONTGOMERY, Tana: see MONTGOMERY, Tammy

MONTGOMERY, Wes — LP '65

(Wes Montgomery Quartet)

Singles: 7-inch

A&M ... 3-5 67-70
PACIFIC JAZZ ... 4-8 60
RIVERSIDE ... 4-8 61-64
VERVE ... 4-6 65-68

EPs: 7-inch

A&M (126 "Greatest Hits") ... 5-10 70
(Juke box issue only.)
A&M (3001 "A Day in the Life") ... 5-10 67
(Juke box issue only.)

LPs: 10/12-inch

A&M ... 10-15 67-70
ACCORD ... 5-8 82
BLUE NOTE ... 6-12 75
MFSL (508 "Bumpin'") ... 15-20
MGM ... 10-15 70
MILESTONE ... 8-15 73-83
PACIFIC JAZZ (5 "Montgomeryland") ... 35-45 60
PACIFIC JAZZ (10000 & 20000 series) ... 10-20 66-68
RIVERSIDE (034 thru 089) ... 5-8 82-83
RIVERSIDE (300 & 400 series) ... 15-30 59-67
RIVERSIDE (3000 series) ... 10-15 68-69

VERVE 10-20 65-72
(Reads "MGM Records - A Division of Metro-Goldwyn-Mayer, Inc." at bottom of label.)
VERVE 5-10 73-84
(Reads "Manufactured By MGM Record Corp.," or mentions either Polydor or Polygram at bottom of label.)
Also see SMITH, Jimmy, & Wes Montgomery

MONTRE-EL, Jackie — R&B '68

Singles: 7-inch

ABC 5-10 68

MONTROSE — LP '74

Singles: 7-inch

W.B. 3-5 74-77

LPs: 10/12-inch

ENIGMA 5-8 87
W.B. 8-12 73-78
Members: Ronnie Montrose; Sammy Hagar.
Also see HAGAR, Sammy

MONTROSE, Ronnie — LP '78

Singles: 7-inch

W.B. 3-5 78

LPs: 10/12-inch

W.B. 5-10 78
Also see GAMMA
Also see MONTROSE
Also see WINTER, Edgar

MONTY PYTHON — LP '75

Singles: 7-inch

ARISTA 4-6 80

LPs: 10/12-inch

ARISTA (4039 "Matching Tie and Handkerchief") 10-20 75
ARISTA (4050 "Album of the Soundtrack of the Trailer of the Film of *Monty Python and the Holy Grail*") 10-20 75
ARISTA (4073 "Monty Python Live! At the City Center") 10-20 76
ARISTA (9536 "Monty Python's Contractual Obligation Album") 10-20 80
CHARISMA/BUDDAH (1049 "Another Monty Python Record") 15-25 72
CHARISMA/BUDDAH (1063 "Monty Python's Previous Record") 15-25 72
MCA (6121 "Meaning of Life") 8-12 83
W.B. (3396 "Life of Brian") 10-15 79
PYE (12116 "Monty Python's Flying Circus") 15-20 75
Members: John Cleese; Graham Chapman; Eric Idle; Michael Palin; Terry Jones; Terry Gilliam.
Also see RUTLES

MONYAKA — D&D '83

Singles: 12-inch

EASY STREET 4-6 83

MOODY BLUES — P&R '65

Singles: 7-inch

DERAM 4-8 68-72
LONDON (200 series) 3-5 78
LONDON (1005 "This Is My House") .. 8-12 67
LONDON (9726 "Go Now") 5-10 65
LONDON (9764 "From the Bottom of My Heart") 10-15 65
LONDON (9799 "Ev'ry Day") 10-15 65
LONDON (9810 "Stop") 10-15 66
LONDON (20000 series) 8-12 66
POLYDOR (Black vinyl) 3-4 86-88
POLYDOR (7078 "The Other Side of Life") 4-6 86
(Colored vinyl.)
THRESHOLD (600 series) 3-4 81-85
THRESHOLD (67000 series) 3-6 70-72

Picture Sleeves

POLYDOR (7078 "The Other Side of Life") 4-6 86
POLYDOR (870990 "No More Lies") 3-4 88
POLYDOR (883906 "Your Wildest Dreams") 3-4 86
POLYDOR (885201 "The Other Side of Life") 3-4 86
POLYDOR (887600 "I Know You're Out There Somewhere") 3-4 88
THRESHOLD (602 "The Voice") 3-4 81
THRESHOLD (604 "Sitting at the Wheel") 3-4 81
THRESHOLD (67006 "The Story in Your Eyes") 3-5 71

LPs: 10/12-inch

DERAM (16012 "Days of Future Passed") 30-40 68
(Monaural.)
DERAM (18012 "Days of Future Passed") 10-20 68
(Stereo.)
DERAM (18017 "In Search of the Lost Chord") 10-20 68
(Gatefold cover.)
DERAM (18017 "In Search of the Lost Chord") 5-10
(Standard cover.)
DERAM (18025 "On the Threshold of a Dream") 10-20 69
(Gatefold cover.)
DERAM (18025 "On the Threshold of a Dream") 5-10 69
(Standard cover.)
DERAM (18051 "In the Beginning") .. 10-20 69
DERAM (820006 "Days of Future Passed") 5-10
LONDON (428 "Go Now") 20-25 65
(Stereo.)
LONDON (690/1 "Caught Live") 10-20 77
LONDON (708 "Octave") 8-10 78
(Black vinyl.)
LONDON (708 "Octave") 20-25 78
(Colored vinyl. Promotional issue only.)
LONDON (3428 "Go Now") 25-45 65
(Monaural.)
MFSL (042 "Days of Future Past") 50-70 80
MFSL (151 "Seventh Sojourn") 50-70 85
MFSL (215 "On the Threshold of a Dream") 20-25 94
MFSL (232 "Every Good Boy Deserves Favour") 20-25 95
POLYDOR (835765 "Sur la Mer") 5-10 88
POLYDOR (849433 "Keys of the Kingdom") 5-10 91
THRESHOLD (1 "To Our Children's Children's Children") 8-12 69
(Gatefold cover.)
THRESHOLD (1 "To Our Children's Children's Children") 5-10
(Standard cover.)
THRESHOLD (3 "A Question of Balance") 8-12 70
(Gatefold cover.)
THRESHOLD (3 "A Question of Balance") 5-10
(Standard cover.)
THRESHOLD (5 "Every Good Boy Deserves Favor") 8-10 71
(Gatefold cover.)
THRESHOLD (7 "Seventh Sojourn") .. 8-10 72
(Gatefold cover.)
THRESHOLD (12/13 "This Is the Moody Blues") 10-12 70
THRESHOLD (2901 "Long Distance Voyager") 5-10 81
(Gatefold cover.)
THRESHOLD (2902 "The Present") ... 5-10 83
THRESHOLD (820155 "Voices in the Sky") 5-10 85
THRESHOLD (820517 "Prelude") 5-10 86
THRESHOLD (829179 "Other Side of Life") 5-10 86
THRESHOLD (840659 "Greatest Hits") 5-10 89
Members: Michael Pinder; Ray Thomas; Graeme Edge; Brian Hines (a.k.a. Denny Laine); Clint Warwick; John Lodge; Justin Hayward; Patrick Moraz; Rod Clarke.
Also see EDGE, Graeme
Also see HAYWARD, Justin, & John Lodge
Also see LODGE, John
Also see MORAZ, Patrick
Also see PINDER, Michael
Also see THOMAS, Ray

MOOG MACHINE — LP '69

LPs: 10/12-inch

COLUMBIA 5-10 69

MOON, Keith — LP '75

Singles: 7-inch

MCA (40316 "Don't Worry Baby") 20-30
(Promotional issue.)
TRACK 3-5 75

LPs: 10/12-inch

MCA 8-10 75
Also see NELSON, Rick
Also see WHO

MOONEY, Art, & His Orch. — P&R '48

Singles: 78 rpm

MGM 3-5 48-57
VOGUE (Except R711 & R713) 25-40 46-48
(Picture discs.)
VOGUE (R711 "Seems Like Old Time"/"Warsaw Concerto") 300-400 46
(Picture disc.)
VOGUE (R711/R713 "Seems Like Old Time"/"I've Been Working on the Railroad") 60-80 46
(Picture disc.)
VOGUE (R713 "I've Been Working on the Railroad"/"You're Nobody 'Til Somebody Loves You") 350-450 46
(Picture disc.)
VOGUE (R713/R732 "I've Been Working on the Railroad"/"I Don't Know Why") 60-80 46
(Picture disc.)
VOGUE (R-713-2/R-732-13 "I've Been Working on the Railroad"/"I Don't Know Why") ... 60-80 46
(Picture disc.)
VOGUE (R730 "Piper's Junction") 70-80 46
(Picture disc.)
VOGUE (R732 "In the Moonmist") 60-80 46
(Picture disc.)
VOGUE (R732-13/R732 "In the Moonmist") 70-90 46
(Picture disc.)

Singles: 7-inch

DECCA 3-6 61-62
KAPP 3-6 64-65
MGM (Except 12312) 4-8 50-64
MGM (12312 "Rebel Without a Cause"/"East of Eden") 10-15 56
RIVERSIDE 3-5 62

Picture Sleeves

MGM (12312 "Rebel Without a Cause"/"East of Eden") 20-40 56
(Billed as a "Tribute to James Dean.")

EPs: 7-inch

MGM (Except 1342) 5-10 55-56
MGM (1342 "Music from Movies Starring James Dean") 30-40 55-56

LPs: 10/12-inch

DECCA 10-15 62
DIPLOMAT 6-12 60s
KAPP 10-15 64
MGM 15-25 55-61
RCA 8-12 67
SPINORAMA 8-12 62
Also see AMES BROTHERS
Also see GORDON, Barry

MOONEY, Art / Frankie Carle

LPs: 10/12-inch

CORONET 5-10 60s
Also see MOONEY, Art, & His Orch.

MOONGLOWS — R&B '54

Singles: 78 rpm

CHAMPAGNE (7500 "I Just Can't Tell No Lie") 200-300 52
(Reportedly 2,500 made.)
CHANCE 1147 "Baby Please") 50-100 53
CHANCE (1150 "Just a Lonely Christmas") 50-100 53
CHANCE (1152 "Secret Love") 50-100 54
CHANCE (1156 "I Was Wrong") 50-100 54
CHANCE (1161 "219 Train") 50-100 54
CHESS (1500 & 1600 series) 20-50 54-57

Singles: 7-inch

BIG P 4-6 71

CHAMPAGNE (7500 "I Just Can't Tell No Lie") 1000-1500 52
(Reportedly 1,500 made.)
CHANCE (1147 "Baby Please") 1500-2000 53
(Colored vinyl.)
CHANCE (1150 "Just a Lonely Christmas") 1500-2000 53
(Colored vinyl.)
CHANCE (1152 "Secret Love") ... 750-1000 54
(Blue and silver label.)
CHANCE (1152 "Secret Love") 500-700 54
(Yellow and black label.)
CHANCE (1156 "I Was Wrong") . 750-1000 54
(Yellow and black label.)
CHANCE (1156 "I Was Wrong") ... 400-600 55
(White and black label.)
CHANCE (1161 "219 Train") 800-1200 54
(White and black label.)
CHESS (1581 "Sincerely") 40-60 54
(Silver top label with chess pieces.)
CHESS (1581 "Sincerely") 5-10 60s
(Blue label.)
CHESS (1589 "Most of All") 40-60 54
(Silver top label with chess pieces.)
CHESS (1589 "Most of All") 5-10 60s
(Blue label.)
CHESS (1598 "Foolish Me") 40-60 55
(Silver top label with chess pieces.)
CHESS (1598 "Foolish Me") 5-10 60s
(Blue label.)
CHESS (1605 "Starlite") 40-60 55
(Silver top label with chess pieces.)
CHESS (1605 "Starlite") 5-10 60s
(Blue label.)
CHESS (1611 In My Diary") 30-50 55
(Silver top label with chess pieces.)
CHESS (1611 In My Diary") 5-10 60s
(Blue label.)
CHESS (1619 "We Go Together") 30-50 56
(Silver top label with chess pieces.)
CHESS (1619 "We Go Together") 5-10 60s
(Blue label.)
CHESS (1629 "See Saw") 25-50 56
(Silver top label with chess pieces.)
CHESS (1629 "See Saw") 5-10 60s
(Blue label.)
CHESS (1646 "Over and Over Again") 25-50 56
(Silver top label with chess pieces.)
CHESS (1646 "Over and Over Again") 5-10 60s
(Blue label.)
CHESS (1651 "I'm Afraid the Masquerade Is Over") 25-50 56
(Silver top label with chess pieces.)
CHESS (1651 "I'm Afraid the Masquerade Is Over") 5-10 60s
(Blue label.)
CHESS (1661 "Please Send Me Someone to Love") 25-50 57
(Silver top label with chess pieces.)
CHESS (1661 "Please Send Me Someone to Love") 5-10 60s
(Blue label.)
CHESS (1669 "The Beating of My Heart") 25-50 57
CHESS (1681 "Too Late") 15-25 58
CHESS (1689 "Soda Pop") 15-25 58
CHESS (1701 "This Love") 15-25 58
CHESS (1717 "I'll Never Stop Wanting You") 15-25 58
CHESS (1770 "Junior") 10-20 60
CHESS (1781 "Mama") 15-25 61
CRIMSON (1003 "My Imagination") .. 15-20 64
LANA 3-6 64
RCA 3-6 72
TIMES SQUARE 10-15 64
VEE JAY 8-12 61

EPs: 7-inch

CHESS (5122 "Look! It's the Moonglows") 150-250 59
CHESS (5123 "Look! It's the Moonglows, Vol. 2") 100-200 59

LPs: 10/12-inch

CHESS (701 "The Moonglows") 10-15 76
CHESS (1471 "Best of Bobby Lester & the Moonglows") 10-15 70s
CHESS (1430 "Look, It's the Moonglows") 200-300 59
CHESS (8403 "Current Sides") 5-10 83
CONSTELLATION (2 "Collectors Showcase") 20-30 64
LOST-NITE 8-12 81
RCA 10-15 72
SUGARHILL/MCA 5-10 84

Members: Harvey Fuqua; Bobby Lester; Alex Graves; Prentiss Barnes; Marvin Gaye; Reese Palmer; James Knowland; Chester Simmons; George Thorpe; Dock Green; Berle Ashton.
Also see DIDDLEY, Bo
Also see DRIFTERS
Also see FLAMINGOS / Moonglows
Also see GAYE, Marvin
Also see HARVEY & MOONGLOWS
Also see LESTER, Bobby

MOONLION — P&R '76

Singles: 7-inch

P.I.P. 3-5 76

MOORE, Bill — R&B '48

Singles: 78 rpm

SAVOY 15-25 48
Also see WILLIAMS, Paul

MOORE, Bob — P&R/R&B/LP '61

Singles: 7-inch

HICKORY 4-6 65-68
MONUMENT 4-8 59-64

Picture Sleeves

MONUMENT 4-8 62-63

LPs: 10/12-inch

HICKORY 10-15 66
MONUMENT 10-20 61-67
Also see ATKINS, Chet
Also see DRAGON, Paul
Also see LEE, Bobby
Also see LEE, Brenda
Also see NELSON, Willie
Also see PRESLEY, Elvis

MOORE, Bobby — P&R/R&B '66

(With the Rhythm Aces)

Singles: 12-inch

SCEPTER (12417 "Try to Hold On") 5-8 75
(Promotional issue only.)

Singles: 7-inch

CHECKER 4-8 66-68

LPs: 10/12-inch

CHECKER (3000 "Searching for My Love") 20-25 66

MOORE, Bobby — P&R/R&B '75

Singles: 7-inch

SCEPTER 3-5 75-76

MOORE, Dorothy — R&B '73

(Dorothy Moore)

Singles: 12-inch

STREETKING 4-6 84

Singles: 7-inch

GSF 3-5 73
HANDSHAKE 3-4 82
MALACO 3-5 76-80
STREETKING 3-4 84

LPs: 10/12-inch

MALACO 5-8 76-78
Also see CHEE-CHEE & PEPPY
Also see POPPIES

MOORE, Dorothy, & Eddie Floyd — R&B '77

Singles: 7-inch

MALACO 3-5 77
Also see FLOYD, Eddie
Also see MOORE, Dorothy

MOORE, Gary — LP '83

(Gary Moore Band)

Singles: 7-inch

JET 3-5 79
MIRAGE 3-4 83-86
VIRGIN 3-4 87-89

LPs: 10/12-inch

CHARISMA 5-8 90
JET 5-10 78
MIRAGE 5-8 83-86
PETERS INT'L (9004 "Grinding Stone") 12-15 73
(Red label.)
PETERS INT'L (9004 "Grinding Stone") 10-12 73
(Orange label.)
VIRGIN 5-8 87-89
Also see THIN LIZZY

MOORE, Jackie — P&R/R&B '70

(With the Memphis Horns; with Dixie Flyers)

Singles: 12-inch

COLUMBIA 4-8 79-84

Singles: 7-inch

ATLANTIC 3-5 70-73
CATAWBA 3-4 83
COLUMBIA 3-5 79-84
KAYVETTE 3-5 75-81
SHOUT 4-8 68

LPs: 10/12-inch

COLUMBIA 5-10 79
Also see LULU
Also see MEMPHIS HORNS

MOORE, Johnny — R&B '46

(With the Blazers; with Three Blazers; with New Blazers; with Twigs; Johnny Moore's Orchestra with Mal Hogan & Twigs)

Singles: 78 rpm

ALADDIN 20-50 45-48
BLAZE 10-20 54
EXCLUSIVE 20-40 46-48
HOLLYWOOD 10-20 55-56
MODERN 10-20 48-50
MODERN MUSIC 10-20 45-46
PHILO 10-20 46
RCA 15-25 50
SWING TIME 10-20 51

Singles: 7-inch

ALADDIN (112 "Drifting Blues") 100-150 51
BLAZE (101 "Miss Mosey") 25-50 54
BLAZE (108 "Pretty Please") 25-50 54
BRUNSWICK 4-6 71
HOLLYWOOD (1031 "Why Johnny Why") 25-50 55
HOLLYWOOD (1045 "Christmas Eve Baby") 25-50 55
HOLLYWOOD (1056 "I Send My Love") 25-50 56
MODERN (800 & 900 series) 20-30 53
RCA (0009 "This Is One Time Baby") 50-100 50
(Colored vinyl.)
RCA (0018 "Bop-A-Bye Baby") 50-100 50
(Colored vinyl.)
RCA (0026 "Walkin' Blues") 50-100 50
(Colored vinyl.)
RCA (0031 "Shuffle Shuck") 50-100 50
(Colored vinyl.)
RCA (0043 "So Long") 50-100 50
(Colored vinyl.)
RCA (0073 "Misery Blues") 50-100 50
(Colored vinyl.)
RCA (0086 "Rain-Check") 50-100 50
(Colored vinyl.)
RCA (0095 "Jumping Jack") 50-100 50
(Colored vinyl.)
RENDEZVOUS (115 "Bullfrog") 10-15 60

Members: Johnny Moore; Charles Brown; Eddie Williams.
Also see BROWN, Charles
Also see DIXON, Floyd, & Johnny Moore's Three Blazers
Also see McSHANN, Jay, & Johnny Moore's Three Blazers

MOORE, Johnny, & Linda Hayes

Singles: 7-inch

HOLLYWOOD (1031 "Why, Johnny [Ace] Why 30-50 55
Also see HAYES, Linda
Also see MOORE, Johnny

MOORE, Lee *R&B '79*

Singles: 7-inch

SOURCE 3-5 79

MOORE, Melba *LP '71*

Singles: 12-inch

CAPITOL 4-6 83-86
EPIC 4-8 79-80

Singles: 7-inch

BUDDAH 3-5 75-78
CAPITOL 3-4 82-87
EMI AMERICA 3-4 81-82
EPIC 3-5 78-80
MERCURY 3-6 69-72
MUSICOR 4-8 66

Picture Sleeves

BUDDAH 3-5 76

LPs: 10/12-inch

ACCORD 5-10 81
BUDDAH 8-10 75-79
CAPITOL 5-8 83-86
EMI AMERICA 5-10 81
EPIC 5-10 78-80
MERCURY 10-15 70-72
Also see THOMAS, Lillo, & Melba Moore

MOORE, Melba, & Freddie Jackson *R&B '88*

Singles: 7-inch

CAPITOL 3-4 86-88
Also see JACKSON, Freddie

MOORE, Melba, & Kashif *R&B '86*
(Melba & Kashif)

Singles: 7-inch

CAPITOL 3-4 86
Also see KASHIF
Also see MOORE, Melba

MOORE, Tim *P&R '73*

Singles: 7-inch

ASYLUM 3-5 74-79
DUNHILL 3-5 73

Picture Sleeves

ASYLUM 3-5 75

LPs: 10/12-inch

ASYLUM 5-10 74-75
SMALL (0601 "Second Avenue") 10-15 74

MOORE, Vinnie *LP '88*

LPs: 10/12-inch

SQUAWK 5-8 88

MORALES, Michael *P&R/LP '89*

Singles: 7-inch

WING 3-4 89

Picture Sleeves

WING 3-4 89

LPs: 10/12-inch

WING 5-8 89

MORAZ, Patrick *LP '76*

LPs: 10/12-inch

ATLANTIC 8-12 76
CHRISIMA 5-8 78
IMPORT 8-10 77
PASSPORT 5-8
Also see MOODY BLUES
Also see YES

MORGAN, Denroy *R&B '81*

Singles: 12-inch

BECKET 4-6 81-82

Singles: 7-inch

BECKET 3-5 81

MORGAN, Jane *P&R/LP '57*
(With the Troubadors)

Singles: 78 rpm

KAPP 3-8 54-57

Singles: 7-inch

ABC 4-6 67-68
EPIC 4-6 65-68
COLPIX 4-8 63-65
KAPP 5-10 54-62
RCA 3-6 69-70

EPs: 7-inch

KAPP 5-10 55-59

Picture Sleeves

COLPIX 5-10 63
ELEKTRA 3-4 82
EPIC 4-8 65
KAPP 5-12 57-59

LPs: 10/12-inch

ABC 5-10 68
COLPIX 10-20 63-66
EPIC 10-15 65-67
KAPP 10-20 56-63
MCA 5-10 73
RCA (Except 1160) 8-12 69-70
RCA (1160 "Marry Me, Marry Me") 10-15 69
(Soundtrack.)
HARMONY 5-8 70
Also see WILLIAMS, Roger, & Jane Morgan

MORGAN, Jaye P. *P&R '53*

Singles: 78 rpm

DECCA 3-6 54-55
DERBY 3-6 53
RCA 3-6 54-56

Singles: 7-inch

ABC-PAR 4-6 65
BEVERLY HILLS 3-5 69-72
DECCA 5-10 54-55
DERBY 5-10 53
GIGOLO 3-5
MGM 4-8 59-63
RCA 5-10 54-56

EPs: 7-inch

DECCA 10-20 55
DERBY 10-20 53

LPs: 10/12-inch

BAINBRIDGE 5-10 82
BEVERLY HILLS 5-8 70
MGM 15-25 59-61
RCA (1155 "Jaye P. Morgan") 20-30 55
ROYALE (18122 "Jaye P. Morgan") 20-30 55
(10-inch LP. Side 2 has uncredited instrumentals.)
Also see ARNOLD, Eddy, & Jaye P. Morgan
Also see COMO, Perry, & Jaye P. Morgan
Also see PRESLEY, Elvis / Jaye P. Morgan

MORGAN, Lee *P&R/R&B/LP '64*

Singles: 7-inch

BLUE NOTE 4-6 64-69
BUZZ 3-5 79-80
VEE JAY 4-8 60

LPs: 10/12-inch

BLUE NOTE (200 series) 8-12 74
BLUE NOTE (900 & 1000 series) 5-10 79-81
BLUE NOTE (1500 series) 50-75 56-58
(Label gives New York street address for Blue Note Records.)
BLUE NOTE (1500 series) 25-50 58
(Label reads: "Blue Note Records Inc. - New York, USA.")
BLUE NOTE (1500 series) 15-25 66
(Label shows Blue Note Records as a division of either Liberty or United Artists.)
BLUE NOTE (4000 series) 30-40 61
(Label gives New York street address for Blue Note Records.)
BLUE NOTE (4000 series) 15-25 62
(Label reads: "Blue Note Records Inc. - New York, USA.")
BLUE NOTE (4000 series) 10-20 66
(Label shows Blue Note Records as a division of either Liberty or United Artists.)
BLUE NOTE (4100 thru 4200 series) 15-25 63
(Label reads: "Blue Note Records Inc. - New York, USA.")
BLUE NOTE (4100 thru 4200 series) 10-20 66-67
(Label shows Blue Note Records as a division of either Liberty or United Artists.)
BLUE NOTE (84000 series) 30-40 61
(Label gives New York street address for Blue Note Records.)
BLUE NOTE (84000 series) 20-30 62
(Label reads: "Blue Note Records Inc. - New York, USA.")
BLUE NOTE (84000 series) 10-20 66
(Label shows Blue Note Records as a division of either Liberty or United Artists.)
BLUE NOTE (84100 thru 84200 series) 15-30 63-69
(Label reads: "Blue Note Records Inc. - New York, USA.")
BLUE NOTE (84100 thru 84300 series) 10-20 66-70
(Label shows Blue Note Records as a division of either Liberty or United Artists.)
BLUE NOTE (89000 series) 10-15 71
GNP 6-12 73
JAZZLAND 15-25 62
MCA 5-8 74
PACIFIC JAZZ 5-8 81
PRESTIGE 5-8 81
SAVOY (12091 "Introducing Lee Morgan") 50-75 56
SUNSET 5-10 69
TRADITION 8-15 68
TRIP 6-10 73
VEE JAY 25-50 60-65

MORGAN, Lorrie *C&W '79*

Singles: 7-inch

ABC/HICKORY 3-6 79
MCA 3-5 79
RCA 3-4 88-91

LPs: 10/12-inch

RCA 5-8 88-90

MORGAN, Lorrie & George *C&W '79*

Singles: 7-inch

FOUR STAR 3-5 79
Also see MORGAN, Lorrie

MORGAN, Meli'sa *R&B '85*

Singles: 12-inch

CAPITOL 4-6 86

Singles: 7-inch

CAPITOL 3-4 86-88

Picture Sleeves

CAPITOL 3-4 86

LPs: 10/12-inch

CAPITOL 5-8 86-87
Also see KASHIF & Meli'sa Morgan

MORGAN, Russ, & His Orch. *P&R '35*

Singles: 78 rpm

BRUNSWICK 4-6 36-38
COLUMBIA 4-6 35
DECCA 3-5 38-56

Singles: 7-inch

DECCA 5-10 50-56
EVEREST 4-6 61
VEE JAY 4-6 64-65

EPs: 7-inch

DECCA 5-10 51-56
EPIC 5-10 53

LPs: 10/12-inch

CAPITOL 10-15 62
CIRCLE 5-10 81
DECCA 10-30 51-67
EVEREST 10-15 60-63
GNP 5-10 73
MCA 5-10 73
PICKWICK 5-10 65
SUNSET 8-12 66
VEE JAY 10-15 65

MORGAN BROTHERS *P&R '59*

Singles: 7-inch

MGM 4-8 58-60
RCA 5-10 55

MORISETTE, Johnnie *P&R/R&B '62*

Singles: 7-inch

BAYTONE (116 "Run") 10-20
CHECKER 8-12
SAR 10-15 60-63

MORLEY, Cozy P&R '57

Singles: 78 rpm

ABC-PAR 10-20 57

Singles: 7-inch

ABC-PAR 10-20 57

MORMON TABERNACLE CHOIR P&R/LP '59

Singles: 7-inch

COLUMBIA..3-5 59

Picture Sleeves

COLUMBIA..4-8 59

LPs: 10/12-inch

COLUMBIA..5-10 59-76
RCA..5-10 60

MORNING MIST P&R '71

Singles: 7-inch

EVENT 3-5 71
Members: Terry Cashman; Tommy West.
Also see CASHMAN & WEST

MORNING, NOON & NIGHT R&B '77

Singles: 7-inch

ROADSHOW..3-5 77

LPs: 10/12-inch

ROADSHOW..8-10 77

MORODER, Giorgio P&R '72
(Giorgio)

Singles: 12-inch

COLUMBIA..4-6 84
MCA..4-6 84

Singles: 7-inch

BACKSTREET 3-4
CASABLANCA..3-5 79-80
COLUMBIA..3-4 84
DUNHILL..3-5 72
EMI AMERICA..3-4 84
MCA..3-4 84
POLYDOR..3-5 80
VIRGIN 3-4

Picture Sleeves

COLUMBIA..3-4 84

LPs: 10/12-inch

CASABLANCA..5-10 77-79
DUNHILL..10-12 72
POLYDOR..5-10 80
Also see MERCURY, Freddie / Giorgio Moroder
Also see SUMMER, Donna

MORODER, Giorgio, & Phil Oakey D&D '84

Singles: 12-inch

VIRGIN 4-6 84
Also see HUMAN LEAGUE
Also see MORODER, Giorgio

MORRIS, David, Jr. R&B '76

Singles: 7-inch

BUDDAH 3-5 76
PHILIPS..4-8 68

MORRIS, Gary C&W '80

Singles: 7-inch

UNIVERSAL..3-4 89
W.B. 3-5 80-88

LPs: 10/12-inch

W.B. 5-8 82-88
Also see ANDERSON, Lynn, & Gary Morris
Also see GAYLE, Crystal, & Gary Morris

MORRIS, Joe, & His Orch. R&B '53
(With Laurie Tate; Mr. Stringbean; Al Savage; Joe Morris Blues Calvalcade)

Singles: 78 rpm

ATLANTIC (Except 950, 954 & 974)..10-20 47-57
ATLANTIC (950 "Verna Lee") 20-30 51
ATLANTIC (954 "Someday You'll Be Sorry")..20-30 52
ATLANTIC (974 "Bald Headed Woman")..20-30 52
DECCA..10-15 49-50
HERALD..10-20 53-54
MANOR 10-15 46-47

Singles: 7-inch

ATLANTIC (933 "Pack Up All Your Bags")..100-150 51
(Vocal by Billy Mitchell.)
ATLANTIC (950 "Verna Lee")....... 100-150 51
(Vocal by Billy Mitchell.)
ATLANTIC (954 "Someday You'll Be Sorry") 50-100 52
(Vocal by Billy Mitchell.)
ATLANTIC (974 "Bald Headed Woman") 50-100 52
(Vocal by Billy Mitchell.)
ATLANTIC (1100 series)................. 10-20 57
HERALD (Except 420)...................... 15-30 53-54
HERALD (420 "Travelin' Man")......... 20-30 54
(Black vinyl.)
HERALD (420 "Travelin' Man")......... 40-60 54
(Colored vinyl.)
Also see ADAMS, Faye

MORRIS, Joe, & His Orch.
(Featuring Billy Mitchell)

Singles: 78 rpm

ATLANTIC..10-20 51-52

Singles: 7-inch

ATLANTIC..20-40 51-52
Also see MITCHELL, Billy

MORRIS, Joe, & His Orch. R&B '50
(Featuring Laurie Tate)

Singles: 78 rpm

ATLANTIC (914 "Anytime, Any Place, Anywhere")..25-50 50
ATLANTIC (923 "Don't Take Your Love Away from Me")..25-50 50
Also see TATE, Laurie

MORRIS, Marlowe, Quintet P&R '62

Singles: 7-inch

COLUMBIA 4-8 62

MORRISON, Dorothy P&R '69

Singles: 7-inch

BUDDAH..3-5 70
ELEKTRA..4-6 69

LPs: 10/12-inch

BUDDAH..10-15 70
Also see HAWKINS, Edwin, Singers

MORRISON, Junie D&D '84

Singles: 12-inch

ISLAND 4-6 84

Singles: 7-inch

ISLAND 3-4 84
Also see JUNIE

MORRISON, Professor P&R '68
(Professor Morrison's Lollipop)

Singles: 7-inch

WHITE WHALE 5-10 68-69

MORRISON, Van P&R/LP '67

Singles: 7-inch

BANG..4-8 67-68
MERCURY 3-4 85-90
SOLID GOLD 3-4 73
W.B. 3-5 70-83

LPs: 10/12-inch

BANG (BLP-218 "Blowin' Your Mind")..20-25 67
(Monaural.)
BANG (BLPS-218 "Blowin' Your Mind")..25-30 67
(Stereo. White label. Has 45 rpm version of *Brown-Eyed Girl*, with "makin' love in the green grass behind the stadium" lyrics.)
BANG (BLPS-218 "Blowin' Your Mind")..25-30 67
(Stereo. White label. Has edited *Brown-Eyed Girl*, with "laughin' and a runnin' behind the stadium" lyrics.)
BANG (BLPS-218 "Blowin' Your Mind")..10-15 70
(Yellow label.)
BANG (400 "T.B. Sheets")............... 10-15 74
LONDON..10-15 74
MERCURY..5-10 85-90
W.B. 8-15 68-83
Also see THEM

MORRISON, Van, & Chieftains LP '88

LPs: 10/12-inch

MERCURY 5-8 88
Also see CHIEFTAINS
Also see MORRISON, Van

MORRISSEY LP '88

LPs: 10/12-inch

SIRE..5-8 88-91

MORROW, Buddy, & Orch. P&R '51

Singles: 78 rpm

MERCURY 3-5 54-57
RCA..3-5 50-57

Singles: 7-inch

EPIC..4-6 64
MERCURY 4-8 54-62
RCA..5-10 50-59
U.A. 4-8 68
WING..4-8 55-56

EPs: 7-inch

MERCURY 5-15 54-61
RCA..5-15 52-61

LPs: 10/12-inch

EPIC (Except 24095 & 26095) 5-15 64-65
EPIC (24095 "Big Band Beatlemania")..15-25 64
(Monaural.)
EPIC (26095 "Big Band Beatlemania")..20-30 64
(Stereo.)
MERCURY 15-30 54-62
RCA (2000 & 2100 series)................10-20 59-60
RCA (2200 & series)........................8-15 60
RCA (3100 & 3200 series)...............25-50 52-54
(10-inch LPs.)
U.A. 5-10 68
WING..10-20 56

MORSE, Ella Mae P&R/R&B '43
(With Freddie Slack; with Big Dave & His Orchestra)

Singles: 78 rpm

CAPITOL 5-15 43-57

Singles: 7-inch

CAPITOL (1600 thru 3400 series).......5-10 50-57

EPs: 7-inch

CAPITOL..10-20 54-57

LPs: 10/12-inch

CAPITOL (H-513 "Barrelhouse Boogie, and the Blues")..75-125 54
(10-inch LP.)
CAPITOL (T-513 "Barrelhouse Boogie, and the Blues") 50-75 55
CAPITOL (898 "Morse Code")...........50-75 57
CAPITOL (1802 "Hits")......................30-45 62

MORSE, Steve, Band LP '84

LPs: 10/12-inch

MCA..5-8 89
MUSICIAN/ELEKTRA 5-8 84
Also see DIXIE DREGS
Also see KANSAS

MOSBY, Johnny & Jonie C&W '63

Singles: 7-inch

CAPITOL..3-6 67-73
CHALLENGE..5-10 60
COLUMBIA..4-8 62-66
STARDAY 4-6 65
TOPPA 5-8 61

Picture Sleeves

CAPITOL 3-5 70

LPs: 10/12-inch

CAPITOL..8-12 68-71
COLUMBIA..10-15 65
HARMONY 5-10 70

MOSS, Bill R&B '69
(With Celestials)

Singles: 7-inch

BELL..3-5 69
BILESSE..4-6

MOST, Donny P&R '76

Singles: 7-inch

U.A. 3-5 76-77
VENTURE 3-5 78

Picture Sleeves

U.A. 3-5 76

LPs: 10/12-inch

U.A. 8-12 76

MOTELS LP '79

Singles: 7-inch

CAPITOL 3-6 79-85

Picture Sleeves

CAPITOL 3-5 82-85

LPs: 10/12-inch

CAPITOL 5-10 79-85

Members: Martha Davis; Martin Jourard; Jeff Jourard; Brian Glascock; Tim McGovern; Mike Goodroe.

Also see DAVIS, Martha

MOTHER EARTH LP '69

Singles: 7-inch

MERCURY 4-8 68-69
REPRISE 3-5 71
U.A. 5-10 68

LPs: 10/12-inch

MERCURY 10-20 69-70
REPRISE 10-15 71

Members: Tracy Nelson; John Andrews; Bob Arthur; George Rains. Session: Boz Scaggs.

Also see NELSON, Tracy
Also see SCAGGS, Boz

MOTHER'S FINEST P&R/LP '76

Singles: 12-inch

EPIC 4-8 77-79

Singles: 7-inch

EPIC 3-5 76-79

LPs: 10/12-inch

ATLANTIC 5-10 81
EPIC 5-10 76-79
RCA 8-12 72

Members: Glenn Murdock; Joyce Kennedy; Gary Moore; Jerry Seay; Barry Borden; Michael Keek.

Also see KENNEDY, Joyce

MOTHERLODE P&R/LP '69

Singles: 7-inch

BUDDAH 4-6 69

EPs: 7-inch

BUDDAH (11 "When I Die") 8-12 69

LPs: 10/12-inch

BUDDAH 10-15 69-72

MOTHERS OF INVENTION LP '67

(Mothers)

Singles: 7-inch

BIZARRE/REPRISE 10-15 70
DISCREET 6-10 73
VERVE (Except 10418) 15-25 66-68
VERVE (10418 "How Could I Be Such a Fool") 50-75 66

Promotional Singles

BIZARRE/REPRISE 12-25 70
DISCREET 8-10 73
VERVE (Except 10418) 20-30 66-68
VERVE (10418 "How Could I Be Such a Fool") 60-80 66

EPs: 7-inch

REPRISE (332 "Uncle Meat") 35-45 69
(Promotional issue only.)

LPs: 10/12-inch

BIZARRE (2024 "Uncle Meat") 35-45 69
(Blue label. With 12-page booklet.)
BIZARRE (2024 "Uncle Meat") 20-30 69
(Blue label. Without booklet.)
BIZARRE (2024 "Uncle Meat") 10-15 70s
(Brown label.)
BIZARRE (2028 "Weasles Ripped My Flesh") 20-30 70
(Blue label.)
BIZARRE (2028 "Weasles Ripped My Flesh") 5-10 70s
(Brown label.)
BIZARRE (2042 "The Mothers Live/Fillmore East") 20-30 71
(Blue label.)
BIZARRE (2042 "The Mothers Live/Fillmore East") 5-10 70s
(Brown label.)
BIZARRE (2075 "Just Another Band from L.A.") 20-30 72
(Blue label.)
BIZARRE (2093 "Grand Wazoo") 20-30 72
(Blue label.)
BIZARRE (2093 "Grand Wazoo") 5-10 70s
(Brown label.)
BIZARRE (6370 "Burnt Weeny Sandwich") 30-40 69
(Blue label. With folder of bonus photos.)
BIZARRE (6370 "Burnt Weeny Sandwich") 15-25 69
(Blue label. Without folder of photos.)
BIZARRE (6370 "Burnt Weeny Sandwich") 5-10 70s
(Brown label.)
DISCREET (2149 "Over-Nite Sensation") 15-25 73
DISCREET (MS4-2149 "Over-Nite Sensation") 30-40 73
(Quadrophonic.)
MGM (112 "Mothers of Invention") 30-40 70
MGM (4754 "Worst of the Mothers") 25-35 71
REPRISE 8-12 73-74
(Reissues of Bizarre catalog.)
VERVE (5005 "Freak Out!") 75-125 66
(Monaural. With mail-order "Freak Out - Hot Spots" map/poster offer printed on inside of cover.)
VERVE (5005 "Freak Out!") 50-100 67
(Monaural. Without mail-order map/poster offer printed on inside of cover.)
VERVE (V6-5005 "Freak Out!") 50-100 66
(Stereo. With mail-order "Freak Out - Hot Spots" map/poster offer printed on inside of cover.)
VERVE (V6-5005 "Freak Out!") 40-80 67
(Stereo. Without mail-order map/poster offer printed on inside of cover.)
VERVE (5013 "Absolutely Free") 60-80 67
(Monaural. Includes Libretto or Freak Map.)
VERVE (5013 "Absolutely Free") 50-75 67
(Monaural. Without Libretto or Freak Map.)
VERVE (V6-5013 "Absolutely Free") 50-75 67
(Stereo. Includes Libretto or Freak Map.)
VERVE (V6-5013 "Absolutely Free") 40-50 67
(Stereo. Without Libretto or Freak Map.)
VERVE (5045 "We're Only in It for the Money") 50-75 67
(Monaural. With "Only Money" insert.)
VERVE (5045 "We're Only in It for the Money") 30-50 67
(Monaural. Without "Only Money" insert.)
VERVE (V6-5045 "We're Only in It for the Money") 50-75 67
(Stereo. With "Only Money" insert.)
VERVE (V6-5045 "We're Only in It for the Money") 30-50 67
(Stereo. Without "Only Money" insert.)
VERVE (5068 "Mothermania") 20-40 69
VERVE (5074 "XXXX of the Mothers") 20-25 69

Notes: Price range of Verve LPs is for commercial copies on the blue & black labels as well as white MGM/Verve labels. Several reissues came out in the early '80s that are nearly identical to originals, except their cover stock is glossier than are '60s issues. Among the reissues we have verified are: *Freak Out, We're Only in It for the Money,* and *Absolutely Free.*)

W.B. 8-10 77

Promotional LPs

BIZARRE (2024 "Uncle Meat") 40-60 69
BIZARRE (2028 "Weasles Ripped My Flesh") 35-45 70
BIZARRE (2042 "The Mothers Live/Fillmore East") 35-45 71
BIZARRE (2075 "Just Another Band from L.A.") 30-40 72
BIZARRE (2093 "Grand Wazoo") 30-40 72
BIZARRE (6370 "Burnt Weeny Sandwich") 30-30 69
VERVE (5005 "Freak Out!") 100-200 66
VERVE (5013 "Absolutely Free") 75-125 67
VERVE (5045 "We're Only in It for the Money") 75-125 67
VERVE (5068 "Mothermania") 50-100 69
VERVE (5074 "XXXX of the Mothers") 50-100 69

Members: Frank Zappa; Jimmy Carl Black; Roy Estrada; Ray Collins; Elliot Ingber; Jim Pons; Lowell George.

Also see CAPTAIN BEEFHEART
Also see DUKE, George
Also see FLO & EDDIE
Also see GAMBLERS
Also see GEORGE, Lowell
Also see LEAVES
Also see MISSING PERSONS
Also see PRESTON, Billy
Also see RUBEN & JETS
Also see ZAPPA, Frank

MOTIVATION R&B '83

Singles: 7-inch

DE-LITE 3-4 83

MOTLEY CRUE LP '83

Singles: 7-inch

ELEKTRA 3-4 83-88

Picture Sleeves

ELEKTRA 3-4 84-89

LPs: 10/12-inch

ELEKTRA 5-10 82-89
LEATHÜR ("Too Fast for Love") 50-75 81
(Black lettering on cover.)
LEATHÜR ("Too Fast for Love") 25-50 81
(White lettering on cover.)
WEA/ELEKTRA (60395 "Helter Skelter") 10-15 84
(Picture disc. Price includes poster.)

Member: Vince Neil; Nikki Sixx; Mick Mars; Tommy Lee; John Corabi.

MOTORHEAD LP '82

Singles: 7-inch

MERCURY 3-4 80-83

LPs: 10/12-inch

EMI AMERICA 5-8 85
GWR/PROFILE 5-8 86-87
MERCURY 5-8 80-83

Members: Ian "Lemmy" Kilmister; Phil Campbell; Pete Gill; Mick "Wurzel" Burston.

Also see GLITTER BAND
Also see HAWKWIND
Also see SAXON

MOTORS P&R/LP '80

Singles: 7-inch

VIRGIN 3-5 77-80

Picture Sleeves

VIRGIN 3-5 80

LPs: 10/12-inch

VIRGIN 8-10 77-80

Also see TCHAIKOVSKY, Bram

MOTT LP '75

Singles: 7-inch

COLUMBIA 3-5 75-76

LPs: 10/12-inch

COLUMBIA 5-10 75-76

Also see MOTT the HOOPLE

MOTT THE HOOPLE LP '70

Singles: 7-inch

ATLANTIC 4-6 70
COLUMBIA 3-5 72-74

LPs: 10/12-inch

ATLANTIC 12-18 70-74
COLUMBIA 10-15 72-75

Member: Ian Hunter.

Also see BRITISH LIONS
Also see HUNTER, Ian
Also see MOTT

MOTTOLA, Tony LP '62

LPs: 10/12-inch

COMMAND ... 10-15 62-65
PROJECT 3 ... 5-10 67-70

MOULD, Bob LP '89

LPs: 10/12-inch

VIRGIN ... 5-8 88-90

MOUNTAIN P&R/LP '70

Singles: 7-inch

WINDFALL ... 3-6 69-71

LPs: 10/12-inch

COLUMBIA ... 10-15 73-74
SCOTTI BROTHERS ... 5-8 85
WINDFALL ... 10-15 69-72

Members: Leslie West; Corky Laing; Steve Knight; Felix Pappalardi; David Perry.
Also see WEST, Leslie

MOUSKOURI, Nana LP '91

Singles: 7-inch

BELL ... 3-5 72-74
FONTANA ... 4-8 62-71
MERCURY ... 5-8 60
PRESIDENT ... 5-8 61
RIVERSIDE ... 4-8 62

LPs: 10/12-inch

BELL ... 5-10 73
FONTANA ... 10-20 62-69
PHILIPS ... 5-8 91

Also see BELAFONTE, Harry, & Nana Mouskouri
Also see HAYWARD, Justin

MOUTH & MacNEAL P&R/LP '72

Singles: 7-inch

PHILIPS ... 3-5 72

Picture Sleeves

PHILIPS ... 3-5 72

LPs: 10/12-inch

PHILIPS ... 10-12 72-73

Members: Will Duyn; Maggie MacNeal.

MOUZON, Alphonse R&B/LP '82

(With Carol Dennis; Alphonze Mouzon)

Singles: 12-inch

PRIVATE I ... 4-6 84

Singles: 7-inch

BLUE NOTE ... 3-5 73-74
HIGHRISE ... 3-4 82
PRIVATE I ... 3-4 84

LPs: 10/12-inch

BLUE NOTE ... 5-10 73-76
HIGHRISE ... 5-8 82
PAUSA ... 5-8 81
PRIVATE I ... 5-8 84

Also see MOUZON'S ELECTRIC BAND

MOUZON, Alphonse, & Larry Coryell

LPs: 10/12-inch

ATLANTIC ... 5-10 77

Also see CORYELL, Larry
Also see MOUZON, Alphonse

MOUZON'S ELECTRIC BAND

Singles: 12-inch

VANGUARD ... 4-6 83

Singles: 7-inch

VANGUARD ... 3-4 83

Also see MOUZON, Alphonse

MOVE P&R '72

Singles: 7-inch

A&M ... 5-10 67-69
CAPITOL ... 10-15 70
DERAM ... 5-10 67
MGM ... 8-10 71
U.A. ... 4-8 72-73

EPs: 7-inch

A&M ("Something Else") ... 75-125 68
(May have been released only in the U.K. If issued in the U.S., may have been a promo only. Verification needed. Selection number also needs to be verified from actual EP.)

LPs: 10/12-inch

A&M (3181 "Shazam") ... 5-8 82
A&M (3625 "Best of the Move") ... 15-25 74
A&M (4259 "Shazam") ... 20-25 69
CAPITOL ... 15-25 71
PICKWICK ... 10-15 70s
U.A. ... 10-15 73

Members: Jeff Lynne; Roy Wood; Bev Bevan; Denny Cordell; Richard Tandy; Carl Wayne; Rick Price; Trevor Burton; Ace Kefford.
Also see LYNNE, Jeff
Also see WOOD, Roy

MOVIES R&B '86

Singles: 7-inch

A&M ... 3-5 76
ARISTA ... 3-5 76-77

LPs: 10/12-inch

A&M ... 8-10 76
ARISTA ... 8-10 76

MOVING PICTURES P&R/LP '82

Singles: 7-inch

GEFFEN ... 3-4 89
NETWORK ... 3-5 82

Picture Sleeves

NETWORK ... 3-5 82

LPs: 10/12-inch

NETWORK ... 5-8 82

Members: Alex Smith; Garry Frost.
Also see 1927

MOYET, Alison P&R/D&D/LP '85

Singles: 12-inch

COLUMBIA ... 4-6 85

Singles: 7-inch

COLUMBIA ... 3-4 85

Picture Sleeves

COLUMBIA ... 3-4 85

LPs: 10/12-inch

COLUMBIA ... 5-8 85-87

Also see YAZ

MOZART, Mickey, Quintet P&R '59

Singles: 7-inch

ROULETTE ... 5-10 59-61

MR: see MISTER

MRS. MILLER: see MILLER, Mrs.

MTUME R&B '78

Singles: 12-inch

EPIC ... 4-8 79-86

Singles: 7-inch

EPIC ... 3-5 78-87

LPs: 10/12-inch

EPIC ... 5-8 78-86

Members: James Mtume; Tawatha Agee.

MUDDY WATERS: see WATERS, Muddy

MUGWUMPS

(Mugwump Establishment)

Singles: 7-inch

SIDEWALK (900 "Bald Headed Woman") ... 10-20 66
W.B. ... 5-10 64-67

LPs: 10/12-inch

W.B. (W-1697 "Mugwumps") ... 15-25 67
(Monaural.)
W.B. (WS-1697 "Mugwumps") ... 20-30 67
(Stereo.)

Members: Cass Elliot; Denny Doherty; James Hendricks; John Sebastain; Zal Yanovsky.
Also see ELLIOT, Cass
Also see SEBASTAIN, John

MUHAMMAD, Idris P&R/R&B/LP '77

Singles: 12-inch

FANTASY ... 4-6 83

Singles: 7-inch

FANTASY ... 3-5 80-83
KUDU ... 3-5 77-78
PRESTIGE ... 3-5 72

LPs: 10/12-inch

FANTASY ... 5-8 83
KUDU ... 8-10 76-77
PRESTIGE ... 8-10 72

MULDAUR, Maria LP '73

Singles: 7-inch

REPRISE ... 3-5 73-76
W.B. ... 3-5 78-79

LPs: 10/12-inch

MYRRH ... 5-8 82
REPRISE ... 8-12 73-76
TAKOMA ... 5-8 80
W.B. ... 5-10 78-79

MULL, Martin P&R '73

(Martin Mull Orchestra)

Singles: 7-inch

ABC ... 3-5 77
CAPRICORN ... 3-5 72-77
ELEKTRA ... 3-5 79

LPs: 10/12-inch

ABC ... 8-10 77-78
CAPRICORN ... 8-12 73
ELEKTRA ... 5-10 79
MCA ... 5-8 80s

MULLICAN, Moon P&R '47

(With the Showboys)

Singles: 78 rpm

KING ... 15-25 46-56

Singles: 7-inch

CORAL 62042 "Moon's Rock") ... 20-30 58
DECCA (30962 "Cush Cush Ky-Yay") ... 10-20 59
HALL (1923 "I'll Pour the Wine") ... 10-20 60s
KING (830 "I'll Sail My Ship Alone") .. 25-40 49
KING (1000 series) ... 20-35 52-54
KING (4000 series) ... 15-25 55-56
KING (5000 series) ... 8-15 59-60
STARDAY ... 5-10 60-61

EPs: 7-inch

KING (214 "King of the Hillbilly Piano Players") ... 20-30 50s
KING (227 "Piano Solos") ... 15-25 50s
KING (314 "Moon Mullican") ... 15-25 50s
STARDAY (154 "Moon Mullican") ... 20-30 60

LPs: 10/12-inch

AUDIO LAB ... 50-75
CORAL (57235 "Moon Over Mullican") ... 150-250 58
KAPP ... 20-30 69
KING (555 "All-Time Greatest Hits") ... 50-100 57
KING (628 "16 Favorite Tunes") ... 50-75 59
KING (681 "Many Moods") ... 50-75 60
KING (937 "24 Favorite Tunes") ... 40-60 65
NASHVILLE ... 10-20 70
PHONORAMA ... 5-8 83
PICKWICK/HILLTOP ... 10-15 66
SPUR (3005 "Moon Mullican Sings & Plays") ... 100-150
STARDAY ... 20-40 67
STERLING (601 "I'll Sail My Ship Alone") ... 50-75 50s
WESTERN ... 5-8

Also see KERR, Anita

MULLICAN, Moon / Cowboy Copas / Red Sovine

LPs: 10/12-inch

DIPLOMAT ... 5-10 60s

Also see COPAS, Cowboy
Also see SOVINE, Red

MULLICAN, Moon / Cotton Thompson

Singles: 78 rpm

KING ... 10-20 48

Also see MULLICAN, Moon
Also see THOMPSON, Cotton

MULLIGAN, Gerry LP '59

(Gerry Mulligan Quartet; Jazz Combo)

Singles: 7-inch

PACIFIC JAZZ ... 4-6 61
PHILIPS ... 4-6 64
VERVE ... 4-8 60

EPs: 7-inch

CAPITOL ... 30-45 53
COLUMBIA ... 10-20 59
EMARCY ... 10-20 56
PACIFIC JAZZ ... 25-50 53-57
PRESTIGE (1317 "Gerry Mulligan Blows") ... 50-100 52

PRESTIGE (1318 "Gerry Mulligan Blows") 50-100 52
U.A. 10-20 58

LPs: 10/12-inch

A&M 8-12 72
ABC-PAR (225 "Jazz Concerto") 75-125 58
BLUE NOTE 5-8 81
CTI 8-12 75
CAPITOL (H-439 "Gerry Mulligan") 150-250 53
(10-inch LP.)
CAPITOL (691 "Modern Sounds") 100-150 56
(One side is by Shorty Rogers.)
CAPITOL (2000 series) 20-40 63
CAPITOL (11000 series) 8-12 72
CHIAROSCURO 5-10 77
COLUMBIA (1307 thru 1932) 20-45 59-63
(Monaural.)
COLUMBIA (8116 thru 8732) 25-50 59-63
(Stereo.)
COLUMBIA (34000 series) 5-10 77
CROWN 10-20 63-64
DRG 5-8 80
EMARCY (1000 series) 5-8 81
EMARCY (36056 "Gerry Mulligan Sextet") 100-150 56
EMARCY (36101 "Mainstream") 100-150 57
GRP 5-8 83
GENE NORMAN (3 "Gerry Mulligan Quartet") 150-250 52
(10-inch LP.)
GENE NORMAN (26 "Gerry Mulligan/Chet Baker/Buddy DeFranco") 50-100 57
GENE NORMAN (56 "Gerry Mulligan/Chet Baker/Buddy DeFranco") 20-40 61
INNER CITY 5-8 80
KIMBERLY 20-30 63
LIMELIGHT (82000 series) 12-25 65-66
(Monaural.)
LIMELIGHT (86000 series) 15-30 65-66
(Stereo.)
MERCURY (20453 "Profile") 40-60 59
ODYSSEY 10-20 68
PACIFIC JAZZ (1 "Gerry Mulligan Quartet") 200-300 53
(10-inch LP.)
PACIFIC JAZZ (2 "Gerry Mulligan Quartet") 200-300 53
(10-inch LP.)
PACIFIC JAZZ (5 "Gerry Mulligan") 200-300 53
(10-inch LP.)
PACIFIC JAZZ (10 "Gerry Mulligan") 150-250 54
(10-inch LP.)
PACIFIC JAZZ (1201 "California Concert") 100-150 55
PACIFIC JAZZ (1207 "Original Quartet") 100-150 55
PACIFIC JAZZ (1210 "Paris Concert") 100-150 56
PACIFIC JAZZ (1228 "Mulligan at Storyville") 100-150 57
PACIFIC JAZZ (1237 "Songbook") 100-150 57
PACIFIC JAZZ (1241 "Reunion") 100-150 57
PACIFIC JAZZ (10000 & 20000 series) 10-20 66
PAUSA 5-10 76
PHILIPS 10-20 63-64
PRESTIGE (003 "Mulligan Plays Mulligan") 5-8 82
PRESTIGE (120 "Gerry Mulligan Blows") 200-300 52
(10-inch LP.)
PRESTIGE (141 "Mulligan Too Blows") 200-300 53
(10-inch LP.)
PRESTIGE (7006 "Gerry Plays Mulligan") 75-100 56
(Yellow label.)
PRESTIGE (7251 "Historically Speaking") 30-40 63
(Yellow label.)
SUNSET 10-15 66
TRIP 6-12 75-76
U.A. (4006 "I Want to Live") 30-40 58
(Monaural.)
U.A. (4006 "I Want to Live") 40-50 58
(Stereo.)
V.S.P. 10-20 66
VERVE 25-50 58-60
(Reads "Verve Records, Inc." at bottom of label.)
VERVE 10-25 61-72
(Reads "MGM Records - A Division Of Metro-Goldwyn-Mayer, Inc." at bottom of label.)
VERVE 5-12 73-84
(Reads "Manufactured By MGM Record Corp.," or mentions either Polydor or Polygram at bottom of label.)
WHO'S WHO in JAZZ 5-8 78
WING 10-20 67
WORLD PACIFIC (1241 "Reunion") 50-100 58
WORLD PACIFIC (1253 "Annie Ross Sings with Mulligan") 50-100 59

Also see BRUBECK, Dave, & Gerry Mulligan
Also see GETZ, Stan, & Gerry Mulligan

MULLIGAN, Gerry, & Paul Desmond

(Gerry Mulligan / Paul Desmond)

LPs: 10/12-inch

FANTASY (220 "Gerry Mulligan/Paul Desmond") 100-150 56
(Colored vinyl.)
RCA (2642 "Two of a Mind") 40-60 62
VERVE (8246 "Gerry Mulligan/Paul Desmond") 50-100 58
(Reads "Verve Records, Inc." at bottom of label.)
VERVE (8246 "Gerry Mulligan/ Paul Desmond") 25-50 62
(Reads "MGM Records - A Division Of Metro-Goldwyn-Mayer, Inc." at bottom of label.)

Also see DESMOND, Paul

MULLIGAN, Gerry, & Johnny Hodges

LPs: 10/12-inch

VERVE 30-40 60
(Reads "Verve Records, Inc." at bottom of label.)
VERVE 15-25 62
(Reads "MGM Records - A Division of Metro-Goldwyn-Mayer, Inc." at bottom of label.)

Also see HODGES, Johnny

MULLIGAN, Gerry, & Thelonious Monk

LPs: 10/12-inch

MILESTONE 8-12 82
RIVERSIDE (247 "Mulligan Meets Monk") 50-100 57
RIVERSIDE (1106 "Mulligan Meets Monk") 40-60 58

Also see MONK, Thelonious

MULLIGAN, Gerry, & Oscar Peterson

LPs: 10/12-inch

VERVE (8235 "Gerry & Oscar at Newport") 50-100 57
VERVE (8559 "Gerry & Oscar at Newport") 30-40 63
(Monaural.)
VERVE (68559 "Gerry & Oscar at Newport") 30-40 63
(Stereo.)

Also see MULLIGAN, Gerry
Also see PETERSON, Oscar

MUNDY, Nick — R&B '84

Singles: 7-inch

COLUMBIA 3-4 84

MUNGO JERRY — P&R/LP '70

Singles: 7-inch

BELL 3-5 71-73
FLASHBACK 3-5 73
JANUS 3-5 70-71
PYE 3-5 72-75

LPs: 10/12-inch

JANUS 10-15 70

MUNICH MACHINE — LP '78

Singles: 7-inch

CASABLANCA 3-5 78

LPs: 10/12-inch

CASABLANCA 5-10 78

MURAD, Jerry: see HARMONICATS

MURDOCK, Lydia — R&B '83

Singles: 12-inch

TEEN 4-6 83

Singles: 7-inch

TEEN 3-4 83

MURDOCK, Shirley — R&B '86

Singles: 12-inch

ELEKTRA 4-6 86

Singles: 7-inch

ELEKTRA 3-4 86-88

LPs: 10/12-inch

ELEKTRA 5-8 87-88

Also see ZAPP

MURE, Billy — P&R '59

(With the Wild-Cats; with Trumpeteers; with 7 Karats)

Singles: 78 rpm

RCA 5-10 57-58

Singles: 7-inch

COLPIX 5-8 61
DANCO 4-8 65
EVEREST 5-10 60
MGM 4-8 60-66
PARIS 5-10 60
RCA 5-15 57-58
RIVERSIDE 4-8 63
SRG 5-8 61
SPLASH 8-12 58
STRAND 5-8 61

EPs: 7-inch

RCA 10-15 58

LPs: 10/12-inch

EVEREST 15-20 60-61
KAPP 15-20 61
MGM 15-20 59-66
RCA 25-30 57-58
STRAND 15-20 61
SUNSET 10-12 67
U.A. (3031 "Bandstand Record Hop") 30-40 59

Also see DE MARCO, Ralph
Also see EMOTIONS
Also see TRUMPETEERS
Also see WILD-CATS

MURE, Billy & Benny

Singles: 7-inch

MGM 4-8 64

Also see MURE, Billy

MURMAIDS — P&R '63

(Mermaids)

Singles: 7-inch

CHATTAHOOCHEE (628 "Popsicles and Icicles") 5-10 63
(Exists with three different flips: *Huntington, Flats, Comedy and Tragedy* and *Blue Dress.* We have yet to learn of a difference in value for any of the three releases.)
CHATTAHOOCHEE (636 "Heartbreak Ahead") 5-10 64
CHATTAHOOCHEE (650 "Wild and Wonderful") 5-10 65
CHATTAHOOCHEE (711 "Go Away") 5-10 67
LIBERTY (56078 "Paper Sun") 4-8 68

LPs: 10/12-inch

CHATTAHOOCHEE 8-10 81

LPs: 10/12-inch

CHATTAHOOCHEE 8-10 81

Members: Cathy Fischer; Terry Fischer; Sally Gordon.

MURPHEY, Michael — P&R/LP '72

(Michael Martin Murphey; with Ryan Murphey)

Singles: 7-inch

A&M 3-5 72
CAPITOL 3-5 74

EMI AMERICA 3-4 84-85
EPIC 3-5 74-79
LIBERTY 3-4 82-84
W.B. 3-4 86-91

Picture Sleeves

A&M 3-5 72
EPIC 3-5 74

LPs: 10/12-inch

A&M 8-10 72-73
EMI AMERICA 5-8 84-85
EPIC 8-12 74-78
LIBERTY 5-8 82-83
W.B. 5-8 86-91

Also see DENVER, John
Also see LEE, Johnny, Michael Martin Murphey, & Charlie Daniels
Also see LEWIS & CLARKE

MURPHEY, Michael Martin, & Holly Dunn C&W '87

Singles: 7-inch

W.B. 3-4 87

MURPHEY, Michael, & Katy Moffatt C&W '81

Singles: 7-inch

EPIC 3-5 81

Also see MURPHEY, Michael

MURPHY, Eddie R&B/LP '82

Singles: 12-inch

COLUMBIA 4-6 83-85

Singles: 7-inch

COLUMBIA 3-4 83-86

Picture Sleeves

COLUMBIA 3-4 83-85

LPs: 10/12-inch

COLUMBIA (Except picture discs) 5-8 82-86
COLUMBIA (1763 "Comedian") 10-15 83
(Picture disc. Promotional issue only.)
COLUMBIA (9C9-39151 "Comedian") 10-15 83
(Picture disc.)

MURPHY, Peter LP '88

LPs: 10/12-inch

BEGGAR'S BANQUET 5-8 88-90

MURPHY, Rose R&B '48

(With the Selah Jubilee Quartette; Rose Murphy Trio)

Singles: 78 rpm

DECCA 5-10 55
MAJESTIC 5-10 48

Singles: 7-inch

DECCA (29000 series) 8-12 55
DECCA (32000 series) 4-8 66
REGINA 4-8 63

LPs: 10/12-inch

MUSE 5-8
ROYALE (1835 "Rose Murphy") 30-40 52
(10-inch LP.)
VERVE 20-30 57

Also see BAILEY, Pearl / Rose Murphy / Ivie Anderson

MURPHY, Rose, & Slam Stewart

Singles: 7-inch

DECCA 3-5 61

LPs: 10/12-inch

U.A. 15-25 63

Also see MURPHY, Rose

MURPHY, Walter P&R/R&B/LP '76

(With the Big Apple Band)

Singles: 12-inch

PRIVATE STOCK 4-8 77

Singles: 7-inch

MCA 3-4 82
PRIVATE STOCK 3-5 76-77

Picture Sleeves

MCA 3-4 82

LPs: 10/12-inch

MCA 5-8 82
PRIVATE STOCK 5-10 76-77

MURPHY'S R&B '82

Singles: 7-inch

GRT (130 "Dancin'") 4-6 77

THUNDERBIRD (514 "Great Pretender") 10-20 60s
VENTURE 3-5 82

MURRAY, Anne C&W/P&R/LP '70

(With Doug Mallory)

Singles: 7-inch

ARC 5-10 69
(Canadian.)
CAPITOL 3-5 70-86

Picture Sleeves

CAPITOL 3-4 79-86

LPs: 10/12-inch

ARC (782 "What About Me") 10-20 69
(Canadian.)
AURA 5-8 83
CAPITOL (Except "Let's Keep It That Way" picture disc) 5-10 70-87
CAPITOL ("Let's Keep It That Way") 50-100 78
(Picture disc. Promotional issue only. One of a four-artist, four-LP set. 250 made.)
SESAME ST. 5-10 79

Also see CAMPBELL, Glen, & Anne Murray
Also see CAMPBELL, Glen / Anne Murray / Kenny Rogers / Crystal Gayle
Also see WINCHESTER, Jesse

MURRAY, Anne, & Dave Loggins C&W '84

Singles: 7-inch

CAPITOL 3-4 84

Also see LOGGINS, Dave

MURRAY, Anne, & Kenny Rogers C&W '89

Singles: 7-inch

CAPITOL 3-4 89

Also see MURRAY, Anne
Also see ROGERS, Kenny

MURRAY, Mickey P&R/R&B '67

Singles: 7-inch

SSS INT'L 4-8 67-68

LPs: 10/12-inch

FEDERAL 8-12 71
SSS INT'L 10-15 67

MURRAY, Mickey & Clarence

Singles: 7-inch

SSS INT'L 4-8 68

Also see MURRAY, Mickey

MUSCLE SHOALS HORNS R&B/LP '76

Singles: 7-inch

ARIOLA AMERICA 3-5 77
BANG 3-5 76
MONUMENT 3-4 83

LPs: 10/12-inch

ARIOLA AMERICA 8-12 77
BANG 10-15 76
MONUMENT 8-12 83

MUSIC EXPLOSION P&R/LP '67

Singles: 7-inch

ATTACK (1404 "Little Black Egg") 10-20 66
LAURIE 5-10 67-69

LPs: 10/12-inch

LAURIE 20-30 67

Members: Jamie Lyons; Don Atkins; Bob Avery; Rick Nesta; Butch Stahl.
Also see BLOOM, Bobby
Also see KASENETZ-KATZ SINGING ORCHESTRAL CIRCUS

MUSIC MACHINE P&R '66

Singles: 7-inch

BELL 5-10 69
ORIGINAL SOUND 5-10 66-67
W.B. 5-10 68

Picture Sleeves

ORIGINAL SOUND (82 "Hey Joe") 15-25 67
(Has die-cut center hole on both sides.)

LPs: 10/12-inch

ORIGINAL SOUND (5015 "Turn on the Music Machine") 20-30 66
(Monaural.)
ORIGINAL SOUND (8875 "Turn on the Music Machine") 75-100 66
(Stereo.)

Members: Sean Bonniwell; Mark Landon; Keith Olsen; Ron Edgar; Doug Rhodes.

MUSIC MACHINE / Bubble Puppy

Singles: 7-inch

ORIGINAL SOUND 3-4 85

Also see BUBBLE PUPPY
Also see MUSIC MACHINE

MUSIC MAKERS P&R '67

Singles: 7-inch

GAMBLE 4-8 67-68

LPs: 10/12-inch

GAMBLE 12-18 68

Also see MFSB

MUSICAL YOUTH P&R/R&B '82

Singles: 12-inch

MCA 4-6 82-84

Singles: 7-inch

MCA 3-4 82-84

Picture Sleeves

MCA 3-4 82-84

LPs: 10/12-inch

MCA 5-8 82-84

MUSIQUE P&R/R&B/LP '78

Singles: 12-inch

PRELUDE 5-10 78

Singles: 7-inch

PRELUDE 3-5 78-79

LPs: 10/12-inch

PRELUDE 5-10 78

MUSTANGS P&R '64

Singles: 7-inch

KEETCH 5-10 64
PROVIDENCE 8-12 63-64
SURE SHOT 5-10 64

LPs: 10/12-inch

PROVIDENCE (1 "Dartel Stomp") 35-45 64

MYERS, Alicia R&B '82

Singles: 12-inch

MCA 4-6 81-85

Singles: 7-inch

MCA 3-4 81-85

LPs: 10/12-inch

MCA 5-8 84

MYLES, Alannah P&R/LP '90

Singles: 7-inch

ATLANTIC 3-4 89

LPs: 10/12-inch

ATLANTIC 5-8 89

MYLES, Billy P&R '57

Singles: 78 rpm

EMBER 15-25 57-58

Singles: 7-inch

COLLECTABLES 3-4 80s
EMBER (1026 "The Joker") 15-25 57
EMBER (1040 "Piece of Your Love") 10-20 58
EMBER (1046 "I'm Gonna Walk") 10-20 58
KING (5395 "Dance Little Girl") 8-12 60

MYRICK, Gary LP '83

(With the Figures)

Singles: 7-inch

EPIC 3-4 83-84

LPs: 10/12-inch

EPIC 5-8 83-84

MYSTIC MERLIN R&B '81

Singles: 7-inch

CAPITOL 3-5 80-82

LPs: 10/12-inch

CAPITOL 5-10 80-82

Members: Clyde Bullard; Jerry Anderson; Barry Strutt; Sly Randolph; Keith Gonzales; Freddie Jackson.
Also see JACKSON, Freddie

MYSTIC MOODS ORCHESTRA LP '66

Singles: 7-inch

PHILIPS....................4-6 66-70
SOUNDBIRD....................3-5 75-78
W.B. 3-5 72-73

LPs: 10/12-inch

BAINBRIDGE....................5-10 72
MFSL (001 "Emotions")....................25-50 78
MFSL (002 "Cosmic Force")....................25-50 78
MFSL (003 "Stormy Weekend")....................25-50 78
PHILIPS....................8-12 66-70
SOUNDBIRD....................5-10 75-78
W.B. 5-10 72-73

MYSTICS P&R '59

Singles: 7-inch

AMBIENT SOUND....................3-5 82
COLLECTABLES....................3-4 80s
LAURIE (3028 "Hushabye")....................10-20 59
LAURIE (3028S "Hushabye")....................30-40 59
(Stereo.)
LAURIE (3038 "Don't Take the Stars")....................10-20 59
LAURIE (3047 thru 3086)....................10-20 59
LAURIE (3104 "Sunday Kind of Love")....................15-25 61

LPs: 10/12-inch

AMBIENT SOUND....................5-8 82
COLLECTABLES....................6-8 87

Members: Phil Cracolici; Albee Cracolici; Bob Ferrante; George Galfo.

MYSTICS / Passions

LPs: 10/12-inch

LAURIE....................5-10 79

Also see MYSTICS
Also see PASSIONS

MYSTIQUE R&B '77

Singles: 7-inch

CURTOM....................3-5 77

LPs: 10/12-inch

CURTOM....................5-10 77

Members: Ralph Johnson; Fred Lowrell; Larry Brownlee; Charles Fowler; Fred Simon.

Also see C.O.D.s
Also see IMPRESSIONS

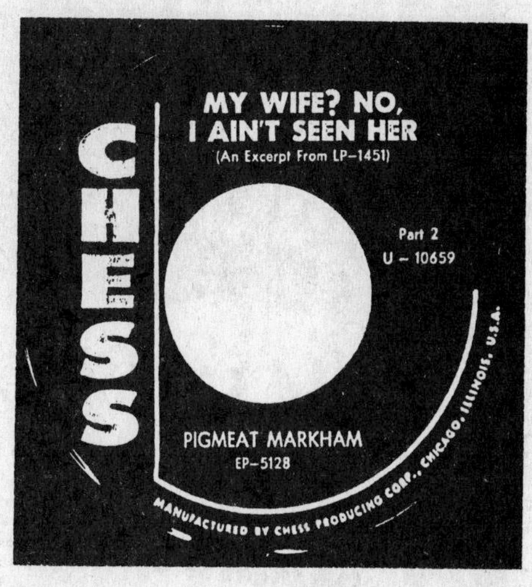

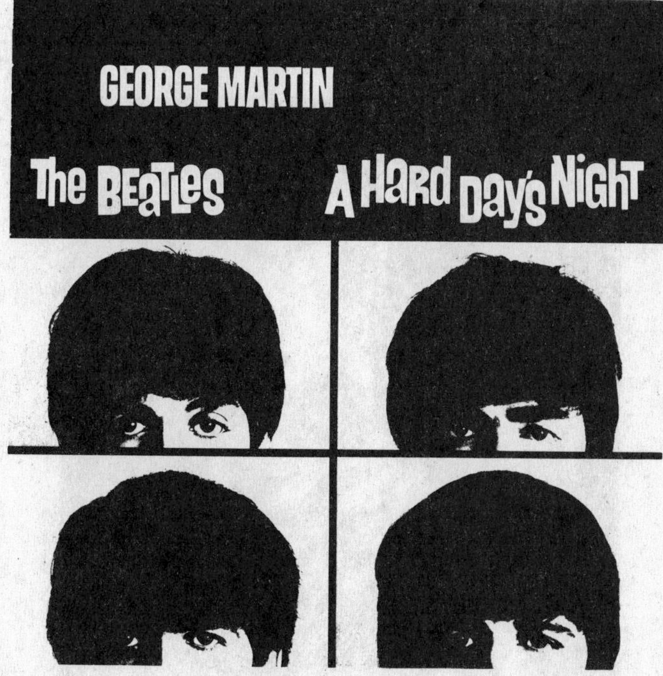

EAP 1-9123
Capitol
HIGH FIDELITY RECORDING
Dean Martin
With chorus and orchestra conducted by DICK STABILE
Let Me Go, Lover
MAMBO ITALIANO
The Naughty Lady of Shady Lane
That's All I Want From You

CLYDE
Mc PHATTER'S
GREATEST
HITS

TONIGHT-TONIGHT
the Mellokings
Herald
2Y 8105

The McGuire Sisters
CORAL
HIGH FIDELITY
LIVIN' DANGEROUSLY
LOVERS LULLABYE

HAYLEY MILLS sings "LET'S GET TOGETHER"
from
"The PARENT TRAP"
....also "Cobbler, Cobbler"

Borderline

N.C.C.U. R&B '77

Singles: 12-inch

U.A. ... 4-8 77

Singles: 7-inch

U.A. ... 3-5 77

LPs: 10/12-inch

U.A. ... 5-10 77

NRBQ LP '69
(New Rhythm & Blues Quintet)

Singles: 7-inch

BEARSVILLE ... 3-5 83
BUDDAH ... 3-5 74
COLUMBIA ... 4-8 69
KAMA SUTRA ... 4-6 73
MERCURY ... 4-6 78
RED ROOSTER ... 3-6 77
ROUNDER ... 3-5 80-83
VIRGIN ... 3-5 89-90

Picture Sleeves

RED ROOSTER ... 3-5 77
ROUNDER ... 3-5 80

EPs: 7-inch

ROUNDER ... 5-10 82

LPs: 10/12-inch

ANNUIT COEPTIS ... 10-15 76
BEARSVILLE ... 5-8 83
KAMA SUTRA ... 10-15 72-73
MERCURY ... 8-12 78
COLUMBIA ... 10-15 69
RED ROOSTER ... 8-10 77-83
ROUNDER ... 5-10 79-80
VIRGIN ... 5-8 89

Members: Frank Gadler; Terry Adams; G.T. Stanley; Jody St. Nicholas; Steve Ferguson; Don Adams; Al Anderson; Tom Staley; Joey Spampinato; Tommy Ardolino.
Also see DAVIS, Skeeter, & NRBQ
Also see PERKINS, Carl, & NRBQ

NV D&D '83

Singles: 12-inch

SIRE ... 4-6 83-84

Singles: 7-inch

SIRE ... 3-4 83-84

N.W.A. LP '89
(Niggas with Attitude)

LPs: 10/12-inch

N.W.A. ... 5-8 89-90

NABORS, Jim LP '66
(Jimmy Nabors)

Singles: 7-inch

COLUMBIA ... 3-6 65-74
RANWOOD ... 3-4 77
ROULETTE ... 8-12 58

LPs: 10/12-inch

COLUMBIA ... 5-15 65-75
HARMONY ... 5-10 71
RANWOOD ... 4-8 76-82

Also see STREISAND, Barbra / Doris Day / Jim Nabors / Andre Kostelanetz

NAILS LP '86

Singles: 7-inch

RCA ... 3-4 86

LPs: 10/12-inch

RCA ... 5-8 86

NAIROBI & AWESOME FOURSOME R&B '82

Singles: 7-inch

STREETWISE ... 3-4 82

NAJEE R&B/LP '87

Singles: 7-inch

EMI ... 3-4 87-90

LPs: 10/12-inch

EMI ... 5-8 87-90

Also see THOMAS, Vaneese

NAKED EYES P&R/D&D/LP '83

Singles: 12-inch

EMI AMERICA ... 4-6 83-84

Singles: 7-inch

EMI AMERICA ... 3-4 83-84

Picture Sleeves

EMI AMERICA ... 3-4 83-84

LPs: 10/12-inch

EMI AMERICA ... 5-8 83-84

Members: Pete Byrne; Rob Fisher.
Also see CLIMIE FISHER

NAPOLEON XIV P&R '66
(Jerry Samuels)

Singles: 7-inch

ERIC ... 3-5 76
W.B. (5800 series) ... 5-10 66
W.B. (7700 series) ... 4-6 73

LPs: 10/12-inch

RHINO ... 5-8 80s
W.B. (W-1661 "They're Coming to Take Me Away") ... 50-60 66
(Monaural.)
W.B. (W-1661 "They're Coming to Take Me Away") ... 75-100 66
(White label. Promotional issue only.)
W.B. (WS-1661 "They're Coming to Take Me Away") ... 75-100 66
(Stereo.)

NASH, Graham P&R/LP '71

Singles: 7-inch

ATLANTIC (2000 series) ... 3-5 71-73
ATLANTIC (89000 series) ... 3-4 86
CAPITOL ... 3-5 79-80

Picture Sleeves

ATLANTIC ... 3-4 86
CAPITOL ... 3-5 79

LPs: 10/12-inch

ATLANTIC (7000 series) ... 8-12 71-73
ATLANTIC (81000 series) ... 5-8 86
CAPITOL ... 8-10 80

Also see CROSBY, David, & Graham Nash
Also see CROSBY, STILLS & NASH
Also see HOLLIES
Also see YOUNG, Neil, & Graham Nash

NASH, Johnny P&R '57

Singles: 12-inch

EPIC ... 4-8 79

Singles: 7-inch

ABC-PAR ... 8-18 57-61
ARGO ... 5-10 64-65
ATLANTIC ... 4-8 66
BABYLON ... 4-8 69
CADET ... 10-20 66
EPIC ... 3-6 72-80
GROOVE (18 "Helpless") ... 5-10 63
GROOVE (21 "Deep in the Heart of Harlem") ... 20-40 63
GROOVE (26 "It's No Good for Me") .. 5-10 63
GROOVE (30 "I'm Leaving") ... 5-10 64
JAD ... 4-8 68-70
JANUS ... 3-6 70
JODA ... 5-10 65-66
MGM ... 4-8 66-67
W.B. ... 5-10 62-63

Picture Sleeves

ABC-PAR ... 10-20 59-60
GROOVE ... 8-12 63-64

EPs: 7-inch

ABC-PAR ... 10-20 58-61

LPs: 10/12-inch

ABC-PAR ... 20-30 58-61
ARGO ... 15-20 64
CADET ... 10-15 73
EPIC ... 10-15 72-74
JAD ... 12-25 68-69

Also see ANKA, Paul, George Hamilton IV & Johnny Nash

NASH, Johnny, & Kim Weston

Singles: 7-inch

BABYLON ... 4-6 69

Also see NASH, Johnny
Also see WESTON, Kim

NASHVILLE BRASS: see DAVIS, Danny

NASHVILLE TEENS P&R '64

Singles: 7-inch

LONDON ... 5-10 64-65
MGM ... 5-10 65-67
U.A. ... 3-5 72

LPs: 10/12-inch

LONDON (407 "Tobacco Road") ... 40-50 64
(Stereo.)
LONDON (3407 "Tobacco Road") ... 50-60 64
(Monaural.)

Members: Arthur Sharp; John Allen; Roger Groom; Ray Phillips; Barry Jenkins.

NATASHA D&D '83

Singles: 12-inch

EMERGENCY ... 4-6 83

NATIONAL LAMPOON P&R/LP '72

Singles: 7-inch

BLUE THUMB ... 4-6 72-73
EPIC (193 "Have a Kung-Fu Christmas") ... 3-4 75
(Promotional issue only.)
LABEL 21 ... 3-5 78-80

Picture Sleeves

EPIC (193 "Have a Kung-Fu Christmas") ... 4-6 75
(Promotional issue only.)
LABEL 21 ... 3-5 78-80

EPs: 7-inch

EPIC (1095 "A History of the Beatles") ... 10-15 75
(Promotional issue only.)

LPs: 10/12-inch

BANANA ... 10-15 72-74
BLUE THUMB ... 10-15 72-74
EPIC ... 8-12 75-76
IMPORT ... 8-10 77
LABEL 21 (Except PIC-2001) ... 5-8 78-80
LABEL 21 (PIC-2001 "That's Not Funny, That's Sick") ... 10-15 80
(Picture disc.)
NATIONAL LAMPOON ... 15-20 74
PASSPORT ... 5-8 82
VISA ... 5-8 78

Members: John Belushi; Chevy Chase; Melissa Manchester; Tony Hendra; Jim Payne; John Lopresti.
Also see BELUSHI, John
Also see MANCHESTER, Melissa

NATIVE R&B '84

Singles: 7-inch

JAMAICA ... 3-4 84

NATURAL FOUR R&B '69

Singles: 7-inch

ABC (11205 "Why Should We Stop Now") ... 4-6 69
ABC (11236 "Same Thing in Mind") ... 5-10 69
ABC (11253 "Hurt") ... 15-25 70
BOOLA BOOLA (2382 "Hurt") ... 20-30
CHESS ... 5-10 72
CURTOM ... 3-6 73-76
PATH ... 8-12

LPs: 10/12-inch

CURTOM ... 8-12 74-75

Members: Chris James; Steve Striplin; Del Mos Whitley; Darryl Canady.

NATURALS R&B '72

Singles: 7-inch

CALLA ... 3-5 71
MOTOWN ... 3-5 72

NATURE ZONE R&B '76

Singles: 7-inch

LONDON ... 3-5 76

NATURE'S DIVINE *P&R/R&B/LP '79*

Singles: 7-inch

INFINITY ... 3-5 79

LPs: 10/12-inch

INFINITY ... 5-10 79

NATURE'S GIFT *R&B '74*

Singles: 7-inch

ABC ... 3-5 74

NAUGHTON, David *P&R '79*

Singles: 7-inch

RSO ... 3-5 78-79

Picture Sleeves

RSO ... 3-5 79

NAYLOR, Jerry *P&R '70*

Singles: 7-inch

COLUMBIA ... 3-6 68-71
HITSVILLE ... 3-5 76
MC/CURB ... 3-5 78
MGM ... 3-6 71-72
MELODYLAND ... 3-5 74-75
OAK ... 3-5 80
PACIFIC CHALLENGER ... 3-5 82
SKLYA ... 10-15 61-62
SMASH ... 5-10 65
TOWER ... 5-15 65-68
W.B./CURB ... 3-5 79
WEST ... 3-4 86
Session: Davie Allan.
Also see ALLAN, Davie
Also see CRICKETS
Also see HONDELLS

NAYLOR, Jerry, & Kelli Warren *C&W '79*

Singles: 7-inch

JEREMIAH ... 3-5 79
Also see NAYLOR, Jerry

NAYOBE *D&D '85*

Singles: 12-inch

FEVER ... 4-6 85-86

Singles: 7-inch

FEVER ... 3-4 85-86

NAZARETH *LP '73*

Singles: 7-inch

A&M ... 3-5 73-80
MCA ... 3-4 83-84
W.B. ... 3-8 71

Picture Sleeves

A&M ... 3-5 75-80

LPs: 10/12-inch

A&M ... 5-10 73-82
MCA ... 5-8 83-84
W.B. ... 8-12 72
Members: Dan McCafferty; Pete Agnew; Darrell Sweet; Manny Charlton.

NAZTY *R&B '76*

Singles: 7-inch

MANKIND ... 3-5 76

LPs: 10/12-inch

MANKIND ... 5-10 76

NAZZ

Singles: 7-inch

VERY RECORD (001 "Lay Down and Die, Goodbye") ... 750-1000 67
Members: Vince "Alice Cooper" Furnier; M. Bruce; G. Buxton; D. Dunaway; T. Speer.
Also see COOPER, Alice

NAZZ *LP '68*

Singles: 7-inch

S.G.C. (001 "Hello It's Me") ... 10-20 68
(Light yellow label. Periods after letters. No horizontal lines.)
SGC (001 "Hello It's Me") ... 8-12 69
(Dark yellow label. No periods in logo. With horizontal lines.)
SGC (001 "Hello It's Me") ... 4-8 70
(Green label with yellow top.)
SGC (006 "Not Wrong Long") ... 8-10 69
SGC (009 "Some People") ... 8-10 69

Picture Sleeves

S.G.C. (001 "Hello It's Me") ... 30-40 68

Promotional Singles

SGC (001 "Hello It's Me") ... 10-20 68
SGC (006 "Not Wrong Long") ... 10-15 69
SGC (009 "Some People") ... 10-15 69
SGC (009 "Kicks") ... 15-25 70

LPs: 10/12-inch

SGC (5001 "Nazz") ... 30-50 68
SGC (5002 "Nazz-Nazz") ... 40-60 69
(Black vinyl.)
SGC (5002 "Nazz-Nazz") ... 50-100 69
(Colored vinyl. Pink and orange label. SGC logo is blue. Identification number is 691531.)
SGC (5002 "Nazz-Nazz") ... 50-100 69
(Colored vinyl. White label. Promotional issue only.)
SGC (5002 "Nazz-Nazz") ... 75-100 69
(Colored vinyl. Mail-order edition. Red and orange label. SGC logo is purple. Identification number is 691531-MO.)
SGC (5004 "Nazz III") ... 30-50 71
(Black vinyl.)
SGC (5004 "Nazz III") ... 40-50 81
(Picture disc.)
Members: Todd Rundgren; Robert Antoni; Carson Van Osten; Tom Petersson; Rick Nielson.
Also see CHEAP TRICK
Also see RUNDGREN, Todd

N'COLE *R&B '78*

Singles: 7-inch

MILLENNIUM ... 3-5 78

NDUGU & CHOCOLATE JAM CO. *R&B '80*

Singles: 7-inch

EPIC ... 3-5 80

NEELY, Sam *P&R/LP '72*

Singles: 7-inch

A&M ... 3-5 74-75
CAPITOL ... 3-5 72-73
ELEKTRA ... 3-5 77
MCA ... 3-4 83-84

LPs: 10/12-inch

A&M ... 8-10 74
CAPITOL ... 8-12 72-73

NEIGHBORHOOD *P&R '70*

Singles: 7-inch

ACTA (813 "Maintain") ... 5-10 68
BIG TREE ... 4-8 70
BULLET (102269 "Why Can't You See") ... 15-25 69

LPs: 10/12-inch

BIG TREE ... 10-15 70

NEIL & JACK

Singles: 7-inch

DUEL (508 "You Are My Love at Last") ... 100-200 62
DUEL (517 "I'm Afraid") ... 100-200 62
Members: Neil Diamond; Jack Parker.
Also see DIAMOND, Neil

NEIL & Shocking Pinks see YOUNG, Neil

NEKTAR *LP '74*

Singles: 7-inch

PASSPORT ... 3-5 74-75

LPs: 10/12-inch

PASSPORT ... 8-12 74-76
POLYDOR ... 8-10 77
VISA ... 8-10 78

NELSON *P&R/LP '90*

Singles: 7-inch

DGC ... 3-4 90

LPs: 10/12-inch

DGC ... 5-8 90
Members: Gunnar Nelson; Matthew Nelson.

NELSON, Jimmy *R&B '51*
(With the Brer Rabbit Trio)

Singles: 78 rpm

CHESS ... 15-25 53
OLLIET (100 "Baby Chile") ... 60-80 48
RPM ... 10-20 53

Singles: 7-inch

ALL BOY ... 5-10 62
CHESS (1587 "Free and Easy Mind") ... 25-50 53
CHESS (1800 series) ... 8-12 63
RPM (325 "T-99 Blues") ... 100-200 53
RPM (353 "Big Eyed, Brown Eyed Girl of Mine") ... 100-200 53
RPM (389 "Second Hand Fool") ... 50-75 53
RPM (385 "Meet Me with Your Black Dress On") ... 25-50 53
RPM (389 "Second Hand Fool") ... 25-50 53
RPM (397 "Mean Poor Girl") ... 25-50 53
Also see TURNER, Joe / Jimmy Nelson

NELSON, Karen, & Billy T. *P&R '77*

Singles: 7-inch

AMHERST ... 8-10 77
Members: Karen Nelson; Billy Tragesser.

NELSON, Phyllis *R&B/D&D '85*

Singles: 12-inch

CARRERE ... 4-6 85-86

Singles: 7-inch

CARRERE ... 3-4 85-86

Picture Sleeves

CARRERE ... 3-4 86

LPs: 10/12-inch

CARRERE ... 5-8 86

NELSON, Rick *P&R/R&B/LP '57*
(With the Stone Canyon Band; with Jordanaires; Ricky Nelson)

Singles: 12-inch

CAPITOL ... 5-10 82

Singles: 78 rpm

IMPERIAL ... 40-100 57-58
VERVE ... 40-60 57

Singles: 7-inch

DECCA ... 4-8 63-72
CAPITOL ... 4-8 82
EPIC ... 3-5 77-86
IMPERIAL (5463 "Be-Bop Baby") ... 30-40 57
(Maroon label.)
IMPERIAL (5463 "Be-Bop Baby") ... 10-20 58
(Black label.)
IMPERIAL (5483 "Stood Up") ... 25-35 57
(Maroon label.)
IMPERIAL (5483 "Stood Up") ... 10-20 58
(Black label.)
IMPERIAL (5503 "Believe What You Say") ... 15-25 58
IMPERIAL (5528 "Poor Little Fool") ... 15-25 58
IMPERIAL (5545 "Lonesome Town") 15-25 58
(Black vinyl.)
IMPERIAL (5545 "Lonesome Town") ... 150-200 58
(Colored vinyl.)
IMPERIAL (5565 "It's Late") ... 15-25 59
IMPERIAL (5595 "Just a Little Too Much") ... 10-20 59
IMPERIAL (5614 "Mighty Good") ... 10-20 59
IMPERIAL (5663 "Young Emotions") 10-20 60
IMPERIAL (5685 "I'm Not Afraid") ... 10-20 60
IMPERIAL (5707 "You Are the Only One") ... 10-20 60
IMPERIAL (5741 "Travelin' Man") ... 10-15 61
(Black vinyl.)
IMPERIAL (5741 "Travelin' Man") 150-200 61
(Colored vinyl. Promotional issue only.)
IMPERIAL (5770 thru 5935) ... 10-15 61-63
IMPERIAL (5958 "Long Vacation") ... 8-12 63
(Black vinyl.)
IMPERIAL (5958 "Long Vacation") . 50-100 63
(Colored vinyl.)
IMPERIAL (5985 "Time After Time") 10-12 63
IMPERIAL (66000 series) ... 8-15 63-64
LIBERTY ... 3-4 80s
MCA ... 3-5 73-86
VERVE (10047 "A Teenager's Romance") ... 25-35 57
VERVE (10070 "You're My One and Only Love") ... 25-35 57
(Flip side is a Barney Kessell instrumental.)

Picture Sleeves

DECCA..8-18 63-70
EPIC..3-5 86
IMPERIAL (5483 "Stood Up")............20-30 57
IMPERIAL (5503 "Believe What You Say")..20-30 58
IMPERIAL (5545 "Lonesome Town") 15-25 58
IMPERIAL (5565 "It's Late") 15-25 59
IMPERIAL (5595 "Just a Little Too Much")..15-25 59
IMPERIAL (5614 "Mighty Good").......15-25 59
IMPERIAL (5663 "Young Emotions") 15-20 60
IMPERIAL (5685 "I'm Not Afraid") 15-20 60
IMPERIAL (5707 "You Are the Only One") 15-20 60
IMPERIAL (5741 "Travelin' Man") 10-20 61
IMPERIAL (5770 thru 5935) 10-20 61-63
MCA..3-5 86

EPs: 7-inch

DECCA (2760 "One Boy Too Late") . 25-50 63
DECCA (4419 "For Your Sweet Love") 25-50 63
(Juke box issue.)
DECCA (4460 "Best Always") 25-50 65
(Juke box issue.)
IMPERIAL (153/154/155 "Ricky")......35-55 58
(Price is for any of three volumes.)
IMPERIAL (157/158 "Ricky Nelson"). 35-55 58
(Price is for either of two volumes.)
IMPERIAL (159/160/161 "Ricky Sings Again")..35-55 58
(Price is for any of three volumes.)
IMPERIAL (162/163/164 "Songs By Ricky") 35-55 59
(Price is for any of three volumes.)
IMPERIAL (165 "Ricky Sings Spirituals") 50-75 60
VERVE (5048 "Ricky") 75-100 57
(Has one track by Barney Kessell.)

LPs: 10/12-inch

CAPITOL..5-8 81
DECCA (DL-4419 "For Your Sweet Love") 25-50 63
(Monaural.)
DECCA (DL7-4419 "For Your Sweet Love") 25-50 63
(Stereo.)
DECCA (DL-4479 "For You") 25-50 63
(Monaural.)
DECCA (DL7-4479 "For You") 25-50 63
(Stereo.)
DECCA (DL-4559 "The Very Thought of You")...25-50 64
(Monaural.)
DECCA (DL7-4559 "The Very Thought of You")...25-50 64
(Stereo.)
DECCA (DL-4608 "Spotlight on Rick") 25-50 64
(Monaural.)
DECCA (DL7-4608 "Spotlight on Rick") 25-50 64
(Stereo.)
DECCA (DL-4660 "Best Always")......25-50 65
(Monaural.)
DECCA (DL7-4660 "Best Always")....25-50 65
(Stereo.)
DECCA (DL-4678 "Love and Kisses")..25-50 65
(Monaural.)
DECCA (DL7-4678 "Love and Kisses")..25-50 65
(Stereo.)
DECCA (DL-4779 "Bright Lights and Country Music")..25-50 66
(Monaural.)
DECCA (DL7-4779 "Bright Lights and Country Music")..25-50 66
(Stereo.)
DECCA (DL-4827 "Country Fever") .. 25-50 67
(Monaural.)
DECCA (DL7-4827 "Country Fever") 25-50 67
(Stereo.)
DECCA (DL-4944 "Another Side of Rick")...25-50 67
(Monaural.)
DECCA (DL7-4944 "Another Side of Rick")...25-50 67
(Stereo.)
DECCA (75014 "Perspective")..........15-25 68
DECCA (75162 "In Concert")............15-25 70
DECCA (75236 "Rick Sings Nelson")...15-25 70
DECCA (75297 "Rudy the Fifth") 15-25 71
DECCA (75391 "Garden Party") 15-25 72
EPIC..8-15 77-86
EPIC/NU-DISK...................................10-15 81
IMPERIAL (9048 "Ricky")..................50-80 57
("Imperial" across top of label.)
IMPERIAL (9048 "Ricky")..................15-25 64
("IR-Imperial" logo on left.)
IMPERIAL (9050 "Ricky Nelson") 45-65 58
("Imperial" across top of label.)
IMPERIAL (9050 "Ricky Nelson") 15-25 64
("IR-Imperial" logo on left.)
IMPERIAL (9061 "Ricky Sings Again")..25-50 59
(Monaural.)
IMPERIAL (9082 "Songs By Ricky") 25-50 59
(Monaural.)
IMPERIAL (9122 "More Songs By Ricky")..25-50 60
(Monaural.)
IMPERIAL (9152 "Rick Is 21")..........20-40 61
(Monaural.)
IMPERIAL (9167 "Album Seven").....20-40 62
(Monaural.)
IMPERIAL (9218 "Best Sellers") 20-40 63
(Monaural.)
IMPERIAL (9223 "It's Up to You")..... 20-40 63
(Monaural.)
IMPERIAL (9232 "Million Sellers By Rick Nelson")..20-40 63
(Monaural.)
IMPERIAL (9244 "Long Vacation") ... 20-40 63
(Monaural.)
IMPERIAL (9251 "Rick Nelson Sings for You") 20-40 63
(Monaural.)
IMPERIAL (12059 "More Songs By Ricky")..40-60 60
(Stereo. Black vinyl.)
IMPERIAL (12059 "More Songs By Ricky")..300-400 60
(Stereo. Colored vinyl.)
IMPERIAL (12090 "Ricky Sings Again")..20-30 64
(Stereo.)
IMPERIAL (12071 "Rick Is 21").........20-40 61
(Stereo.)
IMPERIAL (12082 "Album Seven")... 20-40 62
(Stereo.)
IMPERIAL (12218 "Best Sellers")..... 20-40 63
(Stereo.)
IMPERIAL (12223 "It's Up to You")... 20-40 63
(Stereo.)
IMPERIAL (12232 "Million Sellers By Rick Nelson")..20-40 64
(Stereo.)
IMPERIAL (12244 "Long Vacation") 20-40 63
(Stereo.)
IMPERIAL (12251 "Rick Nelson Sings for You") 20-40 64
(Stereo.)
LIBERTY 5-10 81-83
MCA (Except 1517).........................10-15 73-74
MCA (1517 "The Decca Years") 5-10 82
MCA/SILVER EAGLE 5-10 86
RHINO (Except 259) 5-10 85
RHINO (259 "Greatest Hits") 8-12 85
(Picture disc.)
SESSIONS (1003 "Ricky Nelson Story") 15-30 79
(Three-disc, mail-order offer.)
SESSIONS (1003 "Ricky Nelson Story") 15-25 79
(Three-disc, mail-order offer.)
SUNSET 10-20 66-68
TIME-LIFE 10-15 86
U.A. (330 "Very Best of Rick Nelson")..10-15 75
U.A. (1004 "Ricky")..............................5-10 80
U.A. (9960 "Legendary Masters")......15-25 71
Session: James Burton; Joe Osborn; Jordanaires; Jerry Fuller; Randy Meisner; Al Kemp; Steve Duncan.
Also see APPLETREE THEATRE CO.
Also see DILLARDS
Also see FULLER, Jerry
Also see GRAPPELLI, Stephane, & Barney Kessel
Also see KESSEL, Barney / Grant Green / Oscar Moore / Mundell Lowe
Also see MARTIN, Dean, & Ricky Nelson
Also see MEISNER, Randy
Also see MOON, Keith
Also see RIVERS, Johnny / Ricky Nelson / Randy Sparks

NELSON, Rick, & Jack Lemmon

Singles: 7-inch

THEATRE PROMOTION RECORD (760 "Do You Know What It Means to Miss New Orleans")..150-200 60
(Promotional issue, made for theatre play.)

NELSON, Rick / Joannie Sommers / Dona Jean Young

LPs: 10/12-inch

DECCA (DL-4836 "On the Flip Side")..20-30 66
(Monaural.)
DECCA (DL7-4836 "On the Flip Side")..25-35 66
(Stereo.)
Also see NELSON, Rick
Also see SOMMERS, Joannie

NELSON, Sandy — P&R/R&B '59

Singles: 7-inch

COLLECTABLES 3-4 80s
ERA 3-5 72
IMPERIAL...4-8 61-69
LIBERTY...3-4 80s
ORIGINAL SOUND 10-15 59
U.A. 3-5 74
VEEBLETRONICS 3-5 81

EPs: 7-inch

IMPERIAL...10-20 65
(Stereo juke box "Little LPs.")

LPs: 10/12-inch

IMPERIAL (Except 9105 & 12044).... 10-25 61-69
IMPERIAL (9105 "Teen Beat") 20-30 60
(Monaural.)
IMPERIAL (12044 "Teen Beat") 20-30 60
(Stereo.)
LIBERTY..5-10 82-83
SKYCLAD..5-8 89
SUNSET 10-20 66-70
U.A. 8-12 75
Also see ALLEN, Richie
Also see GAMBLERS
Also see TEDDY BEARS

NELSON, Tracy — LP '74

Singles: 7-inch

ATLANTIC 3-5 75
CAPITOL 3-5 77
MCA...3-5 75
MERCURY 5-10 69

LPs: 10/12-inch

ADELPHI...5-10 83
ATLANTIC 8-12 75
AUDIO DIRECTIONS...........................5-10 82
COLUMBIA...10-12 72
FLYING FISH..5-10 75-81
MCA..8-10 76-81
PRESTIGE (7303 "Deep Are the Roots")..15-20 65
PRESTIGE (7726 "Deep Are the Roots")..8-12 69
REPRISE...10-12 72
Also see MOTHER EARTH
Also see NELSON, Willie & Tracy

NELSON, Tyka — R&B '88

Singles: 7-inch

COOLTEMPO..3-4 88

NELSON, Willie C&W '62
(Willy Nelson)

Singles: 78 rpm

SARG (260 "A Storm Has Just Begun")......100-200 55

Singles: 7-inch

AMERICAN GOLD......3-5 76
ATLANTIC......3-5 73-75
BETTY......10-15 64
BELLAIRE (107 "Night Life")......15-25 63
(Black vinyl.)
BELLAIRE (107 "Night Life")......40-50 63
(Colored vinyl.)
BELLAIRE (5000 series)......3-5 76
CAPITOL......3-5 78
COLUMBIA......3-5 75-91
D (1084 "Man With the Blues")......15-25 59
D (1131 "What a Way to Live")......15-25 60
DOUBLE BARREL......4-8
LIBERTY (55155 "No Dough")......15-25 58
LIBERTY (55386 "Mr. Record Man")......10-15 61
LIBERTY (55439 thru 55638)......5-10 62-64
LIBERTY (56000 series)......4-6 69
LONE STAR......3-5 78
MONUMENT (800 series)......4-6 64
RCA (0100 thru 0800 series)......3-5 69-72
RCA (8500 thru 9900 series)......4-8 65-71
RCA (10000 thru 12000 series)......3-5 75-81
SARG (260 "A Storm Has Just Begun")......200-300 55
SONGBIRD......3-5 80
U.A. (641 "Night Life")......5-10 63
U.A. (700 thru 1200 series)......3-5 76-78
WILLIE NELSON (628 "No Place for Me")......150-250 57
(Reportedly 3,000 made.)

Picture Sleeves

COLUMBIA......3-5 84
RCA (12000 series)......3-5 81

LPs: 10/12-inch

ACCORD......5-8 82-83
ALLEGIANCE......5-8 83
ATLANTIC......8-12 73-76
AUDIO FIDELITY (213 "Willie Nelson")......10-15
(Picture disc.)
AURA......5-8 82-83
BACK-TRAC......5-8
CBS (Except PAL-35305)......5-8 78-83
CBS (PAL-35305 "Stardust")......25-45 78
CAMDEN......8-12 70-74
CASINO......8-10 84
COLUMBIA (30000 series, except 38250 and picture discs)......5-15 75-91
COLUMBIA (38250 "Willie Nelson")......100-150 83
(Boxed, 10-disc boxed set. Includes bonus picture disc, which is priced separately below.)
COLUMBIA (38250 [38258/59] "Always on My Mind")......50-75 83
(Picture disc. Boxed set bonus issue.)
COLUMBIA (35305 "Stardust")......25-35 78
(Picture disc.)
COLUMBIA (39943 "Always on My Mind")......10-20 83
(Picture disc.)
COLUMBIA (40000 series, except "HC," half-speed mastered series)......5-10 85-90
COLUMBIA (HC-40000 series)......20-35 82-83
(Half-speed mastered.)
DELTA......5-8 82
EXACT......5-8 83
HBO (171010 "Willie Nelson and Family")......15-25 83
(Picture disc. Promotional issue only.)
H.S.R.D.......8-10 84
HEARTLAND......10-15 87
HOT SCHATZ......5-10 84
LIBERTY (3239 "And Then I Wrote")......25-35 62
(Monaural.)
LIBERTY (7239 "And Then I Wrote")......30-40 62
(Stereo.)
LIBERTY (10000 series)......5-10 80s
LONE STAR......8-12 78
MCA......5-10 80
MASTERS......5-10
OUT of TOWN DIST.......5-10
PICKWICK......5-10 74-76
PICKWICK/CAMDEN......5-10 70s
PLANTATION......5-10 82
POTOMAC......10-15 82
PREMORE......5-10
RCA (1100 thru 3200 series)......5-10 75-79
RCA (LPM-3400 thru LPM-3900 series)......10-20 65-68
(Monaural.)
RCA (LSP-3400 thru LSP-4700 series)......10-25 65-72
(Stereo.)
RCA (3600 thru 4800 series)......4-8 80-83
(With "AYL1" prefix.)
RCA (7158 "Willie")......5-8 85
RCA/CANDELITE......8-10 80
SHOTGUN......10-20 77
SOLID GOLD......5-10
SONGBIRD......5-10 80
SUNSET......10-20 66
TAKOMA......5-8 83
TIME-LIFE (16000 series)......15-25 83
(Three-disc set.)
U.A. 8-12 73-78

Session: Paul Buskirk; Herb Remington; Bob White; Clyde Brewer; Dick Shannon; Pete Wade; Ray Edenton; Jimmy Day; Hargus "Pig" Robbins; Bob Moore; Willie Ackerman; Billy Strange; Glen Campbell; Leon Russell; Red Callender; Muddy Berry; Harold Bradley; David Briggs; Anita Kerr Singers; Ernie Freeman; Cal Smith; Jerry Reed; Buddy Emmons; Velma Smith; Johnny Bush; Chet Atkins; Bill Pursell; Roy Huskey; Buddy Harman; Buddy Spicher; Doug Sahm; Larry Gatlin.

Also see ATKINS, Chet
Also see CAMPBELL, Glen
Also see CHARLES, Ray, & Willie Nelson
Also see COCHRAN, Hank, & Willie Nelson
Also see COE, David Allan, & Willie Nelson
Also see DARRELL, Johnny / George Jones / Willie Nelson
Also see DAVIS, Danny, Willie Nelson, & Nashville Brass
Also see EDDY, Duane
Also see FREEMAN, Ernie
Also see GATLIN, Larry
Also see HAGGARD, Merle, & Willie Nelson
Also see HARRIS, Emmylou
Also see IGLESIAS, Julio, & Willie Nelson
Also see JENNINGS, Waylon
Also see JENNINGS, Waylon, & Willie Nelson
Also see KERR, Anita
Also see KRISTOFFERSON, Kris, Willie Nelson, Dolly Parton, & Brenda Lee
Also see LEE, Brenda, & Willie Nelson
Also see MILLER, Roger, & Willie Nelson
Also see MOORE, Bob
Also see PARTON, Dolly, & Willie Nelson
Also see PRICE, Ray, & Willie Nelson
Also see PURSELL, Bill
Also see REED, Jerry
Also see SAHM, Doug
Also see SMITH, Cal
Also see SMITH, Sammi
Also see STRANGE, Billy
Also see TUBB, Ernest

NELSON, Willie / Nat "King" Cole / Johnny Mathis / Shirley Bassey

EPs: 7-inch

JIMMY McHUGH (300 "Three Guys and a Gal")......8-12 81
(Promotional issue only. Includes Jimmy McHugh bio insert)
Also see BASSEY, Shirley
Also see COLE, Nat "King"
Also see MATHIS, Johnny

NELSON, Willie, & Shirley Collie C&W '62

Singles: 7-inch

LIBERTY......5-10 62

NELSON, Willie, & Kris Kristofferson C&W/LP '84

LPs: 10/12-inch

COLUMBIA......5-8 84
Also see KRISTOFFERSON, Kris

NELSON, Willie, & Brenda Lee C&W '83

Singles: 7-inch

MONUMENT......3-5 83
Also see LEE, Brenda

NELSON, Willie, & Johnny Lee

LPs: 10/12-inch

QUICKSILVER......5-8 84

NELSON, Willie / Johnny Lee / Mickey Gilley

LPs: 10/12-inch

PLANTATION......5-8 82
Also see GILLEY, Mickey
Also see LEE, Johnny

NELSON, Willie / Jerry Lee Lewis / Carl Perkins / David Allan Coe

LPs: 10/12-inch

PLANTATION......5-10 75
Also see COE, David Allan
Also see LEWIS, Jerry Lee
Also see PERKINS, Carl

NELSON, Willie & Tracy C&W '74

Singles: 7-inch

ATLANTIC......3-5 74
Also see NELSON, Tracy

NELSON, Willie, & Webb Pierce C&W '82

Singles: 7-inch

COLUMBIA......3-4 82

LPs: 10/12-inch

COLUMBIA......5-8 82
Also see PIERCE, Webb

NELSON, Willie, & Ray Price C&W/LP '80

Singles: 7-inch

COLUMBIA......3-4 80

LPs: 10/12-inch

COLUMBIA......5-8 80
Also see PRICE, Ray

NELSON, Willie, & Leon Russell C&W '79

Singles: 7-inch

COLUMBIA......3-5 79

LPs: 10/12-inch

COLUMBIA......5-10 79
Also see RUSSELL, Leon

NELSON, Willie, & Hank Wilson C&W '84

Singles: 7-inch

PARADISE......3-4 84

NELSON, Willie / Faron Young

LPs: 10/12-inch

COLUMBIA......5-10
ROMULUS......5-10
Also see NELSON, Willie
Also see YOUNG, Faron

NENA P&R/D&D '83

Singles: 12-inch

EPIC......4-6 83-84

Singles: 7-inch

EPIC......3-4 83-84

LPs: 10/12-inch

EPIC......5-8 84

NEON PHILHARMONIC P&R '69

Singles: 7-inch

MCA......3-5 76
TRX......3-5 72
W.B. 4-6 69-71

LPs: 10/12-inch

W.B. 10-15 69

NERO, Peter — LP '61
(With Boston Pops Orchestra)

Singles: 7-inch

ARIOLA AMERICA 3-5 76
ARISTA 3-5 75
COLUMBIA 3-5 69-73
RCA 3-6 61-68

Picture Sleeves

RCA 3-5 62-63

LPs: 10/12-inch

ARISTA 5-10 75
CAMDEN 5-10 67-73
COLUMBIA 5-10 69-75
CONCORD JAZZ 5-8 78
HARMONY 5-10 71
PREMIER 10-15 63
RCA 5-15 61-76

Also see ANN-MARGRET
Also see BOSTON POPS ORCHESTRA
Also see CRAMER, Floyd / Peter Nero / Frankie Carle

NERVOUS NORVUS — P&R '56
(With Red Blanchard; Jimmy Drake)

Singles: 12-inch

BIG BEAT (12 "Transfusion") 10-15 85
(Includes picture cover.)

Singles: 78 rpm

DOT 10-25 56-57

Singles: 7-inch

DOT (15000 series) 10-20 56
(Maroon label.)
DOT (15000 series) 8-12 57
(Black label.)
DOT (16000 series) 4-8 65
EMBEE 10-15 59

Also see BLANCHARD, Red
Also see FOUR JOKERS

NESMITH, Michael — P&R/LP '70
(With the First National Band; with Second National Band)

Singles: 7-inch

EDAN (1001 "Just a Little Love") 50-75 65
ISLAND 5-8 77
OMNIBUS 15-25 63
PACIFIC ARTS 8-10 75-79
RCA 10-20 70-75

Picture Sleeves

RCA (0453 "Nevada Fighter") 15-25 71

LPs: 10/12-inch

PACIFIC ARTS ("Conversation with Michael Nesmith – Music Radio Special") 25-35 78
(Promotional issue only.)
PACIFIC ARTS (101 "The Prison") 25-50 78
(Boxed edition. With booklet.)
PACIFIC ARTS (101 "The Prison") 10-20 78
(Standard LP. With booklet.)
PACIFIC ARTS (106 thru 130) 10-20 78-79
RCA 20-30 70-75
RHINO 8-10 89

Also see BLESSING, Michael
Also see MONKEES
Also see WICHITA TRAIN WHISTLE

NETTO, Loz — P&R '83

Singles: 7-inch

21 .... 3-4 83

Picture Sleeves

21 .... 3-4 83

LPs: 10/12-inch

21 .... 5-8 82

Also see SNIFF 'N the TEARS

NEVIL, Robbie — P&R/R&B/LP '86

Singles: 12-inch

MANHATTAN 4-6 86

Singles: 7-inch

EMI 3-4 88
MANHATTAN 3-4 86-87

Picture Sleeves

EMI 3-4 88
MANHATTAN 3-4 86-87

LPs: 10/12-inch

EMI 5-8 88
MANHATTAN 5-8 86

NEVILLE, Aaron — R&B '60
(Arron Neville)

Singles: 7-inch

AIRECORDS (333 I've Done It Again") 15-25 63
BELL 4-8 68-69
HEAD 3-5
MERCURY 3-5 72-73
MINIT 10-20 60-63
PAR-LO 4-8 66-67
POLYDOR 3-5 77
SAFARI 4-8 67
WHO DAT? 4-6

LPs: 10/12-inch

COLLECTABLES 6-8 88
MINIT (40007 "Like It 'Tis") 15-25 67
(Monaural.)
MINIT (40007 "Like It 'Tis") 15-25 67
(Stereo.)
PAR-LO (1 "Tell It Like It Is") 20-30 67
(Monaural.)
PAR-LO (1 "Tell It Like It Is") 25-35 67
(Stereo.)

Also see NEVILLE BROTHERS
Also see RONSTADT, Linda, & Aaron Neville

NEVILLE, Aaron / Toussaint McCall

Singles: 7-inch

TRIP 3-5 70s

Also see McCALL, Toussaint
Also see NEVILLE, Aaron

NEVILLE, Ivan — LP '88

Singles: 7-inch

POLYDOR 3-4 88-89

LPs: 10/12-inch

POLYDOR 5-8 88

NEVILLE BROTHERS — LP '81

Singles: 7-inch

A&M 3-5 81-90
CAPITOL 3-6 78

LPs: 10/12-inch

A&M 5-10 81-90
BLACK TOP 5-10 86
CAPITOL (11865 "Neville Brothers") 20-30 78
EMI AMERICA 5-8 87
RHINO 5-8 87
SPINDLE TOP 5-8 87

Members: Aaron Neville; Art Neville; Charles Neville; Cyril Neville.
Also see METERS
Also see NEVILLE, Aaron

NEW BIRTH — P&R/R&B/LP '71

Singles: 7-inch

ARIOLA AMERICA 3-5 79
BUDDAH 3-5 75
RCA 3-5 71-75
W.B. 3-5 76-78

LPs: 10/12-inch

ARIOLA AMERICA 5-10 79
BUDDAH 8-12 75
COLLECTABLES 5-10 88
RCA (Except APD1-0285 & LSP-4000 series) 5-10 73-82
RCA (APD1-0285 "It's Been a Long Time") 15-25 74
(Quadrophonic.)
RCA (LSP-4000 series) 10-15 70-72
W.B. 8-12 76-77

Members: Harvey Fuqua; Tony Churchill; Alan Frye; Robert Jackson; Joe Porter; Leslie Wilson; Mel Wilson; Londee Loren; Bobby Downs; Ann Bogan; Austin Lander; James Baker; Leroy Taylor; Robin Russell; Ben Boytel; Roger Voice; James Hall.
Also see LOVE, PEACE & HAPPINESS
Also see NITE-LITERS

NEW CACTUS BAND — LP '73

Singles: 7-inch

ATCO 3-6 73

LPs: 10/12-inch

ATCO 8-12 73

Members: Mike Pinera; Duane Hitchings; Manuel Bertematti; Roland Robinson; Jerry Norris.
Also see CACTUS

NEW CENSATION — R&B '74

Singles: 7-inch

PRIDE 3-5 74-75

LPs: 10/12-inch

PRIDE 8-12 74

NEW CHOICE — R&B '87

Singles: 7-inch

RCA 3-4 87

NEW CHRISTY MINSTRELS — P&R/LP '62

Singles: 7-inch

COLUMBIA (42000 series) 4-8 62-63
COLUMBIA (43000 & 44000 series) 4-6 64-69
GREGAR 3-5 70-72
W.B. 3-5 79

Promotional Singles

COLUMBIA (Colored vinyl) 5-10 63-65

Picture Sleeves

COLUMBIA 4-8 62

LPs: 10/12-inch

COLUMBIA (1800 thru 2500 series) 10-20 62-66
(Monaural.)
COLUMBIA (8600 thru 9300 series) 10-30 62-66
(Stereo.)
COLUMBIA (9600 & 9700 series) 10-15 68
GREGAR 8-12 70
HARMONY 8-12 68-72

Members: Randy Sparks; Barry McGuire; Kenny Rogers; Mike Settle; Thelma Lou Camacho; Terry Williams; Mickey Jones; Jackie Miller; Gayle Caldwell; Gene Clark; Larry Ramos; Rex Kramer.
Also see ASSOCIATION
Also see CLARK, Dave, Five / New Christy Minstrels / Bobby Vinton / Jerry Vale
Also see CLARK, Gene
Also see FIRST EDITION
Also see McGUIRE, Barry
Also see SPARKS, Randy

NEW COLONY SIX — P&R '66

Singles: 7-inch

CENTAUR 4-8 66
MCA 3-6 74
MERCURY ("Attacking a Straw Man") 10-20 69
(Promotional issue only. Number not known.)
MERCURY (72737 thru 73004) 4-8 67-70
MERCURY (73063 "People and Me") 8-15 70
MERCURY (73093 "Close Your Eyes Little Girl") 8-15 70
SENTAR 10-20 66-67
SUNLIGHT 3-5 71-72
TWILIGHT 3-5 73

Picture Sleeves

MERCURY 4-8 67-68

LPs: 10/12-inch

MERCURY 20-30 68-69
SENTAR (101 "Breakthrough") 150-250 66
SENTAR (3001 "Colonization") 50-75 67

Members: Ronnie Rice; Ray Graffia; Craig Kemp; Jerry Kollenberg; Pat McBride; Chick James; Billy Herman; Chuck Lobes; Wally Kemp.

NEW EDITION — P&R/R&B/D&D/LP '83

Singles: 12-inch

MCA 4-6 84-86
STREETWISE 4-6 83

Singles: 7-inch

MCA (Black vinyl) 3-4 84-89
MCA (Colored vinyl) 4-6 85
STREETWISE 5-8 83

Picture Sleeves

MCA 3-5 84-89

LPs: 10/12-inch

MCA 5-8 84-89
STREETWISE 5-8 83

Members: Johnny Gill; Bobby Brown; Ricky Bell; Michael Bivins; Ronnie DeVoe.
Also see BELL BIV DeVOE

Also see GILL, Johnny
Also see KING DREAM CHORUS & Holiday Crew

NEW ENGLAND P&R/LP '79

Singles: 7-inch

ELEKTRA......3-5 80-81
INFINITY (100103 "Don't Ever Want to Lose You")......3-5 79
(Black vinyl.)
INFINITY (100103 "Don't Ever Want to Lose You")......10-15 79
(Picture disc.)

LPs: 10/12-inch

ELEKTRA......5-10 80-81
INFINITY......5-10 79

NEW ENGLAND CONSERVATORY RAGTIME ENSEMBLE LP '73

Singles: 7-inch

ANGEL......3-4 80

LPs: 10/12-inch

ANGEL......5-8 73
GOLDEN CREST......5-10 75

NEW ESTABLISHMENT P&R '69

Singles: 7-inch

COLGEMS......5-8 69
MERCURY......4-8 67

NEW GUYS ON THE BLOCK R&B '83

Singles: 7-inch

SUGAR HILL......3-4 83

NEW HOPE P&R '70

Singles: 7-inch

JAMIE......4-8 69-71

LPs: 10/12-inch

JAMIE (3034 "The New Hope")......20-30 69
Members: Kit Stewart; Carl Von Hausman; John Bradley; Ron Shane.

NEW HORIZONS R&B '83

Singles: 7-inch

COLUMBIA......3-4 83

LPs: 10/12-inch

COLUMBIA......5-8 83
Members: Mark Thomas; Art Thomas; Varges Thomas.

NEW JERSEY MASS CHOIR R&B/D&D '85

Singles: 12-inch

SAVOY......4-6 85
Also see FOREIGNER

NEW KIDS ON THE BLOCK R&B '86

Singles: 12-inch

COLUMBIA......4-6 86

Singles: 7-inch

COLUMBIA......3-4 86-90

Picture Sleeves

COLUMBIA......3-4 88

LPs: 10/12-inch

COLUMBIA......5-8 86-90
Members: Jordan Knight; Jon Knight; Joe McIntyre; Danny Wood; Donny Wahlberg.
Also see PAGE, Tommy

NEW KINGSTON TRIO

Singles: 7-inch

CAPITOL......3-6 71
Also see KINGSTON TRIO

NEW MARKETTS R&B '76
(Danny Welton & New Marketts)

Singles: 7-inch

CALLIOPE......3-6 77
FARR......3-6 76-77
SEMINOLE......3-6 76

LPs: 10/12-inch

CALLIOPE......8-12 77
Also see MARKETTS

NEW ORDER R&B/D&D '83

Singles: 12-inch

FACTUS......4-6 83
QWEST......4-6 85
STREETWISE......4-6 83

Singles: 7-inch

QWEST......3-4 85-89
STREETWISE......3-4 83

Picture Sleeves

QWEST......3-4 87-89

LPs: 10/12-inch

QWEST (Except 25621)......5-8 85-89
QWEST (25621 "Substance")......8-12 87
Members: Bernard Sumner; Peter Hook; Gillian Gilbert; Stephen Morris.
Also see ELECTRONIC
Also see JOY DIVISION

NEW RIDERS OF PURPLE SAGE LP '71

Singles: 7-inch

COLUMBIA......3-5 71-74
MCA......3-5 76-77

LPs: 10/12-inch

A&M......5-8 81
BUDDAH......8-12 75
COLUMBIA......10-15 71-75
MCA......8-10 76-77
RELIX (Except 2025)......5-8 86-87
RELIX (2025 "Vintage")......5-8 87
(Black vinyl.)
RELIX (2025 "Vintage")......30-50 87
(Picture disc.)
Members: Skip Battin; David Turbert. Also, assorted Grateful Dead members guested on Columbia and Relix issues.
Also see GRATEFUL DEAD
Also see KINGFISH

NEW ROTARY CONNECTION

LPs: 10/12-inch

CHESS......8-12 71
Also see ROTARY CONNECTION

NEW SEEKERS P&R '70

Singles: 7-inch

ELEKTRA......3-5 70-72
MGM/VERVE......3-5 72-73

Picture Sleeves

MGM/VERVE......3-5 72-73

EPs: 7-inch

COCA-COLA......5-10 69
(Promotional issue only.)

LPs: 10/12-inch

ELEKTRA......10-12 71-72
MGM/VERVE......8-10 73
Member: Keith Potger.
Also see SEEKERS

NEW VAUDEVILLE BAND P&R/LP '66

Singles: 7-inch

FONTANA......3-6 66-68

LPs: 10/12-inch

FONTANA......10-15 67

NEW VENTURES: see VENTURES

NEW YORK CITI PEECH BOYS R&B/D&D '83

Singles: 12-inch

GARAGE......4-6 83-84
ISLAND......4-6 83-84

Singles: 7-inch

ISLAND......3-4 83-84

LPs: 10/12-inch

ISLAND......5-8 84
Also see PEECH BOYS

NEW YORK CITY P&R/R&B/LP '73

Singles: 7-inch

CHELSEA......3-5 73-75

LPs: 10/12-inch

CHELSEA......10-15 73-77
Also see CADILLACS
Also see FIVE SATINS

NEW YORK COMMUNITY CHOIR R&B '77

Singles: 7-inch

RCA......3-5 77

NEW YORK DOLLS LP '73

Singles: 7-inch

MERCURY......3-5 73-76

Picture Sleeves

MERCURY......4-8 73

LPs: 10/12-inch

MERCURY (675 "New York Dolls")......20-25 73
MERCURY (1001 "Too Much, Too Soon")......15-20 74
REACH OUT INT'L......5-10 81
Members: David Johansen; Jerry Nolan; Arthur Kane; Johnny Thudners; Sylvain Sylvain.
Also see JOHANSEN, David
Also see SYLVAIN SYLVAIN
Also see W.A.S.P.

NEW YORKERS P&R '61

Singles: 7-inch

WALL (547 "Miss Fine")......15-25 61
WALL (548 "Tears in My Eyes")......15-25 61
Members: Fred Parris; Richard Freeman; Wesley Forbes; Louis Peebles; Silvester Hopkins.
Also see FIVE SATINS

NEW YOUNG HEARTS R&B '70

Singles: 7-inch

SOULTOWN......10-20
ZEA......3-5 70

NEWBEATS P&R/LP '64

Singles: 7-inch

ABC......3-5 74
HICKORY......4-8 64-72
PLAYBOY......3-5 74

EPs: 7-inch

HICKORY (120-005 "Bread and Butter")......20-30 65
(Compact 33. Promotional issue only.)

LPs: 10/12-inch

HICKORY (LP-120 "Bread and Butter")......25-45 65
(Monaural.)
HICKORY (LPS-120 "Bread and Butter")......75-125 65
(Stereo.)
HICKORY (LP-122 "Big Beat Sound")......25-45 65
(Monaural.)
HICKORY (LPS-122 "Big Beat Sound")......50-75 65
(Stereo.)
HICKORY (LP-128 "Run Baby Run")......25-45 65
(Monaural.)
HICKORY (LPS-128 "Run Baby Run")......50-75 65
(Stereo.)
Members: Larry Henley; Dean Mathis; Mark Mathis.
Also see DEAN & MARC

NEWBERRY, Booker, III R&B/D&D '83

Singles: 12-inch

BOARDWALK......4-6 83

Singles: 7-inch

BOARDWALK......3-4 83
OMNI......3-4 86

NEWBURY, Mickey P&R/LP '71

Singles: 7-inch

ABC/HICKORY......3-5 77-79
AIRBORNE......3-4 88
ELEKTRA......3-5 71-73
HICKORY (1312 thru 1463)......4-8 65-67
HICKORY (1600 series)......3-4 80
MCA......3-5 79
MERCURY......3-6 69-70
RCA......3-6 68-70

Picture Sleeves

RCA......3-6 68

LPs: 10/12-inch

ABC/HICKORY......5-10 77-79
MCA......5-8 79
ELEKTRA......8-10 71-75

MERCURY (4024 "After All These Years") 5-8 81
MERCURY (61236 "Looks Like Rain") 10-12 69
RCA 8-12 68-72

NEWCITY ROCKERS P&R '87

Singles: 7-inch

CRITIQUE 3-4 87

Picture Sleeves

CRITIQUE 3-4 87

NEWCLEUS R&B '83

Singles: 12-inch

SUNNYVIEW 4-6 83-86

Singles: 7-inch

SUNNYVIEW 3-4 83-86

LPs: 10/12-inch

SUNNYVIEW 5-8 84-86

NEWCOMERS P&R/R&B '71

Singles: 7-inch

STAX 3-5 71
TRUTH 3-5 74-75
VOLT 4-8 69
Members: Terry Bartlett; Bert Brown; William Sumlin.
Also see BAR-KAYS
Also see KWICK

NEWHART, Bob LP '60

LPs: 10/12-inch

HARMONY 10-15 69
W.B. (1300 thru 1500 series) 20-30 60-65
W.B. (1600 thru 1700 series) 15-25 66-67

NEWLEY, Anthony P&R '60

Singles: 7-inch

KAPP 4-6 69
LONDON 4-8 58-63
MGM 3-5 71-74
RCA 4-8 66-67
U.A. 3-5 76-77
W.B. 4-6 68

LPs: 10/12-inch

BELL 8-10 71
LONDON 10-20 62-66
MGM 8-12 71-73
RCA 10-20 64-69
U.A. 5-10 77

NEWMAN, Jimmy C&W '54

(Jimmy C. Newman; with Cajun Country)

Singles: 78 rpm

DOT 5-15 54-57

Singles: 7-inch

DECCA 3-8 60-71
DOT (Except 15766) 5-15 54-57
DOT (15766 "Carry On") 50-75 58
LA LOUISANNE 4-6 73
MGM 5-10 58-60
MONUMENT 3-5 72
PLANTATION 3-5 76-80
SHANNON 3-5 73

EPs: 7-inch

DECCA 5-10 64

LPs: 10/12-inch

CROWN 8-12 60s
DECCA 10-25 62-70
DELTA 5-8 82
DOT (3000 series) 30-40 60s
DOT (25000 series) 20-25 60s
LA LOUISANNE 5-10 73
MGM 25-35 59-62
PICKWICK/HILLTOP 8-12
PLANTATION 5-10 77-81
SWALLOW 5-8

NEWMAN, Jimmy C., Danny Davis & Nashville Brass

Singles: 7-inch

RCA 3-4 80
Also see DAVIS, Danny
Also see NEWMAN, Jimmy C.

NEWMAN, Randy LP '71

Singles: 78 rpm

REPRISE (0284 "I Think It's Gonna Rain Today") 8-10 78
(Promotional issue only.)

Singles: 7-inch

CHELSEA 3-5 74
DOT 4-8 62
REPRISE (Except 0771) 3-6 68-88
REPRISE (0771 "Last Night I Had a Dream") 10-20 68
W.B. 3-5 77-85

Picture Sleeves

REPRISE 3-4 88
W.B. 3-5 78

LPs: 10/12-inch

EPIC (147 "Peyton Place") 20-30 65
(TV Soundtrack.)
REPRISE (Except 6286) 5-10 70-88
REPRISE (6286 "Randy Newman") 15-20 68
(Cover pictures Randy in sweater and coat.)
REPRISE (6286 "Randy Newman") 10-15 68
(Cover picture is a close-up of Randy.)
W.B. 5-10 77-85
Also see BISHOP, Stephen
Also see EAGLES
Also see McVIE, Christine
Also see RONSTADT, Linda
Also see SEGER, Bob

NEWMAN, Randy, & Paul Simon / Randy Newman P&R '83

Singles: 7-inch

W.B. 3-5 83

Picture Sleeves

W.B. 3-5 83
Also see NEWMAN, Randy
Also see SIMON, Paul

NEWMAN, Ted P&R '57

Singles: 78 rpm

REV 20-30 57

Singles: 7-inch

RCA 10-15 58
REV 10-20 57

NEWMAN, Thunderclap P&R '69

Singles: 7-inch

MCA 3-4 80s
TRACK (2000 series) 4-8 69-70
TRACK (60000 series) 3-5 75

LPs: 10/12-inch

ATLANTIC/TRACK 10-20 70
MCA/TRACK 5-10 73
Members: Andy Newman; Jimmy McCulloch; Speedy Keen.
Also see McCARTNEY, Paul

NEWSOM, Chubby R&B '49

(With Her Hip Shakers; with Lee Allen)

Singles: 78 rpm

DELUXE 15-25 49
MILTONE 15-25 49

Singles: 7-inch

WINLEY (216 "Toodle Luddle Baby") 25-40 57
Also see ALLEN, Lee
Also see GAYTEN, Paul

NEWSOME, Bobby R&B '72

Singles: 7-inch

SPRING 3-5 72

NEWSOME, Frankie R&B '69

Singles: 7-inch

GWP 4-6 69

NEWTON, Juice P&R '78

Singles: 7-inch

CAPITOL 3-5 78-84
RCA 3-4 84-89

Picture Sleeves

CAPITOL 3-5 81-83
RCA 3-4 84

LPs: 10/12-inch

CAPITOL 5-10 78-84
RCA 5-8 84-87
Also see RABBITT, Eddie, & Juice Newton

NEWTON, Juice, & Silver Spur C&W '76

Singles: 7-inch

CAPITOL 3-5 77
RCA 3-5 75-76

LPs: 10/12-inch

CAPITOL (11000 series) 8-10 77
CAPITOL (16000 series) 5-8 81
RCA (1000 series) 8-12 75
RCA (4000 series) 5-8 81
Also see NEWTON, Juice

NEWTON, Wayne P&R/LP '63

Singles: 7-inch

ARIES II 3-5 79-80
CAPITOL (Except 5338) 4-8 63-71
CAPITOL (5338 "Comin' on Too Strong") 10-20 64
(With Bruce Johnston & Terry Melcher.)
CHALLENGE 4-8 64
CHELSEA 3-5 72-76
GEORGE (7777 "Little White Cloud That Cried") 10-15 62
MGM 3-6 68
20TH FOX 3-5 78
W.B. 3-5 70-77

Picture Sleeves

CAPITOL 4-8 65-66

LPs: 10/12-inch

AIRES II 5-8 79-80
CAMDEN 5-10 74
CAPITOL (573 "Wayne Newton") 15-25 70
(Three-LP set.)
CAPITOL (T-1973 thru T-2847) 10-20 63-68
(Monaural.)
CAPITOL (ST-1973 thru ST-2847) 15-25 63-68
(Stereo.)
CAPITOL (SM-2300 series) 5-8 75
CAPITOL (SPC-3400 series) 5-8
CAPITOL (11000 series) 5-8 79
CAPITOL (16000 series) 5-8 80
CHELSEA 10-15 72-75
MGM 6-12 68-72
MUSICOR 5-8 79
SILVER EAGLE 8-10
20TH FOX 5-8 78
Also see BRUCE & TERRY

NEWTON, Wayne, & Tammy Wynette C&W '89

Singles: 7-inch

CURB 3-4 89
Also see NEWTON, Wayne
Also see WYNETTE, Tammy

NEWTON BROTHERS

(Featuring Wayne)

Singles: 7-inch

CAPITOL (4236 "The Real Thing") 60-80 59
GEORGE (7778 "Little Juke box") 15-20 61
GEORGE (7780 "I Still Love You") 10-15 61
LAMA (7794 "I Was Born When You Kissed Me") 25-50 63
Members: Wayne Newton; Jerry Newton.
Also see NEWTON RASCALS

NEWTON RASCALS

Singles: 7-inch

RANGER (401 "If the Easter Bunny Knew the Fun He'd Have on Xmas") 15-25 58
(Issued with a paper insert picturing 12-year-old Wayne and 14-year-old Jerry as "The Rascals in Rhythm." Value of insert is about the same as for disc.)
Members: Wayne Newton; Jerry Newton.
Also see NEWTON, Wayne
Also see NEWTON BROTHERS

NEWTON-JOHN, Olivia P&R/LP '71

Singles: 12-inch

MCA (Except 1150) 4-6 81-84
MCA (1150 "Twist of Fate") 5-10 83
(Promotional issue only.)

Singles: 7-inch

GEFFEN 3-4 89
KIRSHNER (5005 "Goin' Back") 10-15 70

MCA (Except 40043) 3-5 73-88
MCA (40043 "Take Me Home Country Roads") 5-10 73
RSO 3-5 78
UNI (55281 "If Not for You") 5-10 71
UNI (55304 "Banks of the Ohio") 4-8 71
UNI (55317 "What Is Life") 4-8 72
UNI (55348 "Just a Little Too Much") .. 8-12 72

Promotional Singles

MCA (1810 "Deeper Than the Night") 30-40 79
(Picture disc. Promotional issue only.)
WHAT'S IT ALL ABOUT 25-50 74

Picture Sleeves

MCA (Except 40418) 3-5 75-88
MCA (40418 "Please Mr. Please") 6-10 75

EPs: 7-inch

MCA 12-15 73
(Promotional issues only.)

LPs: 10/12-inch

GEFFEN 5-8 89
MCA (389 "Let Me Be There") 10-12 73
MCA (411 "If You Love Me, Let Me Know") 12-15 74
(With *I Love You, I Honestly Love You.* Note longer title.)
MCA (411 "If You Love Me, Let Me Know") 8-10 74
(With *I Honestly Love You.* Note shorter title.)
MCA (2000 & 3000 series) 8-10 75-78
MCA (5000 & 6000 series) 5-8 80-83
MCA (37000 series) 5-8 80-83
MFSL (040 "Totally Hot") 25-50 80
UNI (73117 "If Not for You") 50-75 71
(Cover depicts a field scene.)
UNI (73117 "If Not for You") 20-30 71
(Field scene removed from cover.)
Also see DENVER, John, & Olivia Newton-John
Also see FOSTER, David, & Olivia Newton-John
Also see TOMORROW
Also see WILSON, Carl

NEWTON-JOHN, Olivia, & Electric Light Orchestra — P&R/LP '80

Singles: 7-inch

MCA (41285 "Xanadu") 3-5 80

Picture Sleeves

MCA (41285 "Xanadu") 3-5 80

LPs: 10/12-inch

MCA (6100 "Xanadu") 8-10 80
MCA (10384 "Xanadu") 750-1000 80
(Picture disc. Promotional issue only. Also has Cliff Richard, Gene Kelly, and the Tubes.)
Also see ELECTRIC LIGHT ORCHESTRA
Also see RICHARD, Cliff
Also see TUBES

NEWTON-JOHN, Olivia, & Andy Gibb — P&R '80

Singles: 12-inch

POLYDOR (104 "Rest Your Love on Me") 10-15 79

Singles: 7-inch

RSO 3-5 80
Also see GIBB, Andy

NEWTON-JOHN, Olivia, & Cliff Richard — P&R '80

Singles: 7-inch

MCA (51007 "Suddenly") 4-6 80
(Custom MCA/Xanadu label. Has artist credit at top, title at bottom.)
MCA (51007 "Suddenly") 3-5 80
(Standard MCA label. Has artist credit at bottom, title at top.)

Picture Sleeves

MCA (51007 "Suddenly") 3-5 80
Also see RICHARD, Cliff

NEWTON-JOHN, Olivia, & John Travolta — P&R '78

Singles: 7-inch

RSO 3-5 78

Picture Sleeves

RSO 3-5 78
Also see NEWTON-JOHN, Olivia
Also see TRAVOLTA, John

NEXT MOVEMENT — R&B '84

Singles: 7-inch

NUANCE 3-4 84

NICE — LP '70

Singles: 7-inch

IMMEDIATE 4-8 68
MERCURY 3-5 70-71

LPs: 10/12-inch

CHARISMA 8-12
COLUMBIA 8-12
IMMEDIATE 10-15 68-71
MERCURY 10-12 70-72
SIRE 10-12 75
Members: Keith Emerson; Lee Jackson; Brian Davison; Joe Harriot; Davy O'List.
Also see EMERSON, Keith, & Nice

NICHOLAS, Paul — P&R '77

Singles: 7-inch

COLUMBIA 3-5 74
RSO 3-5 76-78

LPs: 10/12-inch

RSO 5-10 77

NICHOLS, Mike, & Elaine May — LP '59

Singles: 7-inch

MERCURY 3-6

LPs: 10/12-inch

MERCURY 15-30 59-72

NICK & ELVIS

Singles: 12-inch

COLUMBIA 4-8 84
Members: Nick Lowe; Elvis Costello.
Also see COSTELLO, Elvis
Also see LOWE, Nick

NICKIE LEE: see LEE, Nickie

NICKS, Stevie — LP '81

Singles: 12-inch

MODERN 4-8 81-86

Singles: 7-inch

MODERN 3-5 81-89

Picture Sleeves

MODERN 3-5 82-89

LPs: 10/12-inch

MFSL (121 "Bella Donna") 25-35 84
MODERN 5-10 81-89
Also see BUCKINGHAM NICKS
Also see EGAN, Walter
Also see FLEETWOOD MAC
Also see LOGGINS, Kenny, & Stevie Nicks
Also see STEWART, John
Also see STEWART, Sandy

NICKS, Stevie, & Don Henley — P&R '81

Singles: 7-inch

MODERN 3-5 81
Also see HENLEY, Don

NICKS, Stevie, & Tom Petty & Heartbreakers — P&R '81

Singles: 7-inch

MODERN 3-5 81-86
Also see PETTY, Tom, & Heartbreakers

NICOLE — R&B '85

Singles: 12-inch

PORTRAIT 4-6 85-86

Singles: 7-inch

EPIC 3-4 88
PORTRAIT 3-4 85-86

LPs: 10/12-inch

PORTRAIT 5-8 86

NIELSEN - PEARSON — P&R '80

Singles: 7-inch

CAPITOL 3-5 80-83
EPIC 3-5 78

LPs: 10/12-inch

CAPITOL 5-10 80-81
EPIC 5-10 78
Members: Reid Nielsen; Mark Pearson.

NIGHT — P&R/LP '79

Singles: 7-inch

PLANET 3-5 79-81

Picture Sleeves

PLANET 3-5 80-81

LPs: 10/12-inch

PLANET 5-10 79-80
Members: Chris Thompson; Nicky Hopkins; Derek Austin; Bill Payne; Michael McDonald; Vince Melamed; Steve Porcaro; James Johnson.

NIGHT RANGER — LP '82

Singles: 7-inch

BOARDWALK 3-4 83
MCA/CAMEL 3-4 83-88

Picture Sleeves

MCA/CAMEL 3-4 84-88

LPs: 10/12-inch

BOARDWALK 5-10 82
MCA/CAMEL 5-10 83-88
Member: Jack Blades.
Also see DAMN YANKEES

NIGHTCRAWLERS — P&R '67

Singles: 7-inch

KAPP (110 "Little Black Egg") 8-12 67
KAPP (709 "Little Black Egg") 5-10 65
KAPP (746 "Basket of Flowers") 5-10 66
KAPP (826 "My Butterfly") 8-12 67
LEE (101 "Cry") 20-30 64
LEE (1012 "Little Black Egg") 10-20 65
MARLIN (1904 "Basket of Flowers") 10-15 66
SCOTT (28 "I Don't Remember") 8-12 66

LPs: 10/12-inch

KAPP (1520 "Little Black Egg") 25-40 67
(Monaural.)
KAPP (3520 "Little Black Egg") 30-50 67
(Stereo.)
Members: Chuck Conlon; Rob Rouse; Sylvan Wells; Tom Ruger; Pete Thomason.

NIGHTHAWK — R&B '82

Singles: 7-inch

QUALITY 3-5 82

NIGHTHAWK, Robert — R&B '49

(With His Nighthawks Band; Nighthawks; Robert McCollum)

Singles: 78 rpm

ARISTOCRAT (413 "Six Three O") ... 50-75 48
ARISTOCRAT (2301 "Black Angel Blues") 50-75 48
CHESS (1484 "My Sweet Lovin' Woman") 50-75 48
STATES 50-75 53
UNITED (102 "Kansas City Blues") ... 50-75 51
UNITED (105 "Feel So Sad") 50-75 51

Singles: 7-inch

STATES (131 "The Moon Is Rising") 200-300 53

LPs: 10/12-inch

ROUNDER 5-8
Also see TAYLOR, Hound Dog / Robert Nighthawk / John Littlejohn / Earl Hooker
Also see TAYLOR, Koko

NIGHTHAWKS — LP '80

LPs: 10/12-inch

ADELPHI 6-12 76-82
ALADDIN (101 "Rock & Roll") 50-75 75
CHESAPEAKE (Black vinyl) 5-10 83
CHESAPEAKE (Colored vinyl) 10-15 83
VARRICK 5-10 83
MERCURY 5-10 80
Members: Mark Wenner; Jim Thackery.

NIGHTINGALE, Maxine — P&R/R&B/LP '76

Singles: 7-inch

A&M 3-5 81
HIGHRISE 3-5 82
RCA 3-5 80
U.A. 3-5 76
WINDSONG 3-5 79

Picture Sleeves

WINDSONG 3-5 79

LPs: 10/12-inch

HIGHRISE 5-10 82
U.A. 5-10 76-79
WINDSONG 5-10 80

NIGHTINGALE, Maxine, & Jimmy Ruffin R&B '82

Singles: 7-inch

HIGHRISE 3-5 82
Also see NIGHTINGALE, Maxine
Also see RUFFIN, Jimmy

NIGHTINGALE, Ollie R&B '71

Singles: 7-inch

MEMPHIS 3-5 71
PATHFINDER 3-5 78
PRIDE 3-5 72-73

LPs: 10/12-inch

PRIDE 8-12 73

NILE, Willie LP '80

Singles: 7-inch

ARISTA 3-5 80-81

LPs: 10/12-inch

ARISTA 5-10 80-81

NILSSON, Harry P&R/LP '69
(With the New Salvation Singers; Nilsson)

Singles: 7-inch

POLYDOR 3-4 85
RCA 3-6 67-77
TOWER (100 series) 5-8 64-65
TOWER (500 series) 4-6 69

Picture Sleeves

RCA 3-6 74-77

EPs: 7-inch

RCA (248 "Excerpts from *The Point*) ... 8-10 71
(Promotional issue only.)

LPs: 10/12-inch

51 WEST 5-8 80s
MUSICOR 8-10 77
PICKWICK 5-10 70s
POLYDOR 5-8 85
RCA (0097 thru 0817, except "APD1" series) 8-12 73-75
RCA ("APD1" series) 10-20 74-75
(Quadrophonic.)
RCA (1003 "The Point") 10-12 71
(With Davy Jones and Mickey Dolenz.)
RCA (1031 thru 3811) 5-10 76-80
RCA (3874 "Pandemonium Shadow Show") 15-20 67
RCA (3956 "Aerial Ballet") 10-20 68
RCA (4197 thru 4717) 8-12 69-72
RAPPLE 8-12 74
SPRINGBOARD 5-10 78
TOWER (5095 "Spotlight") 10-15 69

Promotional LPs

RCA (567 "Scatalogue") 30-40 60s
RCA ("Pandemonium Shadow Show – Boxed Set") 50-75 67
(Includes photos and inserts.)
Also see BO PETE
Also see CHER & NILSSON
Also see DOLENZ, Mickey
Also see FOTO-FI FOUR
Also see JONES, Davy
Also see STARR, Ringo, & Harry Nilsson

NIMOY, Leonard LP '67

Singles: 7-inch

DOT 8-12 67-69

LPs: 10/12-inch

CAEDMON 10-15 70s
DOT 25-50 67-69
JRT ("The Mysterious Golem") 20-40 82
PARAMOUNT 20-40 74
PICKWICK 15-25 60s
SEARS 15-25 60s

NINE INCH NAILS LP '90

LPs: 10/12-inch

TVT 5-8 90

9TH CREATION R&B '77

Singles: 7-inch

HILLTAK 3-5 79-80
PRELUDE 3-5 77

LPs: 10/12-inch

PRELUDE 8-10 77
RITE TRACK 10-12

9.9 P&R/R&B/D&D/LP '85

Singles: 12-inch

RCA 4-6 85-86

Singles: 7-inch

RCA 3-4 85-86

LPs: 10/12-inch

RCA 5-10 85

999 LP '80

Singles: 7-inch

POLYDOR 3-5 81

LPs: 10/12-inch

PVC 5-10 79
POLYDOR 5-10 80-81

1910 FRUITGUM CO. P&R/LP '68

Singles: 7-inch

ATTACK 4-8 70
BUDDAH 4-8 67-69
SUPER K 4-8 70

LPs: 10/12-inch

BUDDAH 15-25 68-70
Also see KASENETZ - KATZ SINGING ORCHESTRAL CIRCUS

1910 FRUITGUM COMPANY / Lemon Pipers

LPs: 10/12-inch

BUDDAH 15-20 68-70
Also see LEMON PIPERS
Also see 1910 FRUITGUM COMPANY

1927 P&R '89

Singles: 7-inch

ATLANTIC 3-4 89

Picture Sleeves

ATLANTIC 3-4 89

LPs: 10/12-inch

ATLANTIC 5-8 89
Members: Garry Frost; Eric Weideman; Bill Frost; Charles Cole.
Also see MOVING PICTURES

NINO & EBB TIDES P&R '61
(Nino & Ebb-Tides)

Singles: 7-inch

MADISON (162 "Those Oldies But Goodies") 25-50 61
MADISON (166 "Juke Box Saturday Night") 20-40 61
MALA (480 "Linda Lou") 15-25 64
MARCO (105 "Someday") 50-100 61
MR. PEACOCK (102 "Wished I Was Home") 15-25 61
MR. PEACOCK (117 "Lovin' Time") . 15-25 62
MR. PEEKE (123 "Tonight") 15-25 63
RECORTE (405 "Puppy Love") 25-50 58
RECORTE (408 "The Real Meaning of Christmas") 100-125 58
RECORTE (409 "I'm Confessin'") 25-50 58
RECORTE (413 "I Love Girls") 25-50 58
Member: Nino Aiello.

NINO & EBB TIDES / Miss Frankie Nolan

Singles: 7-inch

MADISON (151 "A Week from Sunday") 10-20 61
Also see NINO & Ebb Tides

NIRVANA LP '91

Singles: 7-inch

GEFFEN 3-4 91
SUB POP (23 "Love Buzz") 50-100 88
(1000 made.)

EPs: 7-inch

TUPELO (8 "Blew") 20-30 89

LPs: 10/12-inch

SUB POP (34 "Bleach") 35-50 89
(Colored vinyl.)
SUB POP (34 "Bleach") 15-25 89
(Black vinyl. Includes poster.)
SUB POP (73 "Sliver") 15-25 90
(Colored vinyl.)
DGC 10-15 91
DGC/SUB POP (24607 "In Utero") 20-30 93
(Clear vinyl, limited edition.)
MCA (24727 "Unplugged") 8-10 90s
MFSL (258 "Nevermind") 20-25 96
SUB POP 10-15 92
Members: Kurt Cobain; Krist "Chris" Novoselic; Jason Everman; Chad Channing; Dave Grohl; Dave Foster.

NIRVANA / The Fluid

Singles: 7-inch

SUB POP (97 "Molly's Lips") 10-20 91
(Black vinyl. 3,500 made.)
SUB POP (97 "Molly's Lips") 10-20 91
(Colored vinyl. 4,000 made.)

Picture Sleeves

SUB POP (97 "Molly's Lips") 10-20 91

NIRVANA / The Melvins

Singles: 7-inch

COMMUNION (23 "Here She Comes Now") 10-15 91
(Black vinyl.)
COMMUNION (23 "Here She Comes Now") 10-15 91
(Colored vinyl.)
Also see NIRVANA

NITEFLYTE P&R/R&B '79

Singles: 7-inch

ARIOLA AMERICA 3-5 79-81

LPs: 10/12-inch

ARIOLA AMERICA 5-10 79-81
Also see JOHNSON, Howard

NITE-LITERS P&R/R&B/LP '71

Singles: 7-inch

RCA 3-5 71-72

LPs: 10/12-inch

RCA 8-12 71-72
Members: Harvey Fuqua; Tony Churchill; Austin Lander; James Baker; Robert Jackson; Leroy Taylor; Robin Russell; Ben Boytel; Roger Voice; James Hall.
Also see NEW BIRTH

NITRO LP '89

LPs: 10/12-inch

RHINO 5-8 89

NITTY GRITTY DIRT BAND P&R/LP '67
(Dirt Band)

Singles: 78 rpm

LIBERTY (2889 "Mr. Bojangles") 20-30 70
(Promotional issue only.)
U.A. (69 "All the Good Times") 20-30 71
(Promotional issue only. Includes script and booklet.)

Singles: 7-inch

LIBERTY (1000 series) 3-5 81-84
LIBERTY (50000 series) 4-8 67-70
U.A. 3-5 71-80
W.B. 3-4 84-86

Picture Sleeves

LIBERTY (1000 series) 3-5 81-84
LIBERTY (50000 series) 8-12 67
U.A. 3-5 71-80

EPs: 7-inch

LIBERTY (37 "Special Radio Interview") 10-15 70
(Promotional issue only. Has paper cover.)
U.A. (69 "All the Good Times") 20-30 71
(Promotional issue only. Includes script and booklet.)

LPs: 10/12-inch

LIBERTY (1100 series) 5-10 81
LIBERTY (3501 "Nitty Gritty Dirt Band") 15-20 67
(Monaural.)
LIBERTY (7501 "Nitty Gritty Dirt Band") 15-25 67
(Stereo.)
LIBERTY (7501 thru 7611) 10-20 67-69
LIBERTY (7642 "Uncle Charlie") ... 100-125 70
(Gatefold promotional edition. Includes two bonus singles, photos and booklet.)

LIBERTY (LST-7642 "Uncle Charlie") 10-20 70
LIBERTY (LATO-7642 "Uncle Charlie") 5-8
LIBERTY (51146 "Let's Go") 5-8 83
U.A. (117 "Interview") 15-25 75
(Promotional issue only.)
U.A. (UA-LA184 "Stars and Stripes Forever") 10-20 74
U.A. (LWB-184 "Stars and Stripes Forever") 8-10
U.A. (469 "Dream") 8-12 75
U.A. (469 "Dream - Programmers Guide") 15-25 75
(Promotional issue only.)
U.A. (UA-LA670 "Dirt, Silver and Gold") 15-20 76
U.A. (LKCL-670 "Dirt, Silver and Gold") 10-12
U.A.(854 thru 1042) 5-10 78-80
U.A. (5500 series) 8-12 71
U.A. (9801 "Will the Circle Be Unbroken") 30-40 72
(Three-disc set.)
UNIVERSAL (12500 "Will the Circle Be Unbroken, Vol. 2") 10-15 89
W.B. 5-10 84-86
Session: Nicolette Larson; Al Garth; Merle Bregante.
Also see DENVER, John, & Nitty Gritty Dirt Band
Also see LARSON, Nicolette
Also see SKAGGS, Ricky

NITTY GRITTY DIRT BAND & ROY ACUFF — C&W '71

Singles: 7-inch

U.A. 3-5 71

NITTY GRITTY DIRT BAND, ROSANNE CASH & JOHN HIATT — C&W '90

Singles: 7-inch

MCA 3-4 90
Also see CASH, Rosanne

NITTY GRITTY DIRT BAND & JIMMY MARTIN — C&W '73

Singles: 7-inch

U.A. 3-5 73

NITTY GRITTY DIRT BAND & LINDA RONSTADT

Singles: 7-inch

U.A. 3-5 79
Also see NITTY GRITTY DIRT BAND
Also see RONSTADT, Linda

NITZINGER — LP '72

(John Nitzinger)

Singles: 7-inch

CAPITOL 4-6 72-73
20TH FOX 3-5 76

LPs: 10/12-inch

CAPITOL 10-15 72-73
20TH FOX 8-10 76
Members: John Nitzinger; Bugs Henderson.

NITZSCHE, Jack — P&R '63

Singles: 7-inch

FANTASY 3-5 76
MCA 3-5 78
REPRISE 4-8 63-65

Picture Sleeves

REPRISE (20,202 "Lonely Surfer") ... 15-25 63

LPs: 10/12-inch

MCA 8-10 78
REPRISE (2000 series) 8-12 73
REPRISE (6100 series) 15-25 63-64
REPRISE (6200 series) 10-20 66
Also see ALLEY CATS

NIVENS, Pamela — R&B '83

Singles: 7-inch

SUN VALLEY 3-5 83

NIX, Don — P&R/LP '71

Singles: 7-inch

CREAM 3-5 76
ELEKTRA 3-5 71

LPs: 10/12-inch

CREAM 5-10 79
ELEKTRA 8-12 71
ENTERPRISE 8-10 73

NIXON, Mojo, & Skid Roper — LP '87

Singles: 7-inch

ENIGMA 3-5 87-89

LPs: 10/12-inch

ENIGMA 5-8 87-89

NOBLE, Nick — P&R '55

Singles: 78 rpm

MERCURY 5-15 56-57
WING 5-10 55-56

Singles: 7-inch

CAPITOL 3-5 73
CHESS 5-10 63-64
CHURCHILL 3-5 77-80
COLUMBIA 4-6 69
CORAL 8-12 59-66
DATE 4-6 67-68
EPIC 3-5 77
FRATERNITY 10-20 58
GONE (5039 "School Day Crush") ... 20-30 58
LIBERTY 4-8 62-63
MERCURY 10-20 56-57
TMS 3-5 79
20TH FOX 4-8 65
WING 10-15 55-56

LPs: 10/12-inch

COLUMBIA 8-12 69
LIBERTY 10-15 63
WING 15-25 60

NOBLES, Cliff — P&R/R&B/LP '68

(Cliff Nobels & Co.)

Singles: 7-inch

ATLANTIC 4-8 66-67
PHIL L.A. of SOUL 4-6 68-69
JAMIE 3-5 72
ROULETTE 3-5 73

LPs: 10/12-inch

MOON SHOT 15-25
PHIL L.A. of SOUL 10-20 68
Also see MFSB

NOCERA — R&B '86

Singles: 7-inch

SLEEPING BAG 3-4 86-87

NOEL — P&R '87

(Noel Pagan)

Singles: 7-inch

4TH & BROADWAY 3-4 87-88
VIRGIN 3-4 79

Picture Sleeves

4TH & BROADWAY 3-4 87-88
VIRGIN 3-4 79

LPs: 10/12-inch

4TH & BROADWAY 5-8 88

NOGUEZ, Jacky, & His Orch. — P&R '59

Singles: 7-inch

JAMIE 4-8 59-60

Picture Sleeves

JAMIE 8-10 60

LPs: 10/12-inch

JAMIE 10-20 60

NOLAN: see PORTER, Nolan

NOLAN, Kenny — P&R '76

Singles: 7-inch

CASABLANCA 3-5 79-80
DOT 4-8 68
FORWARD 4-8 69
HIGHLAND 4-8 68
LION 3-5 72
MGM 3-5 71
POLYDOR 3-5 78
20TH FOX 3-5 76-77

LPs: 10/12-inch

CASABLANCA 5-10 79
MCA 5-10 82
POLYDOR 5-10 78
20TH FOX 5-10 77

NORMA — D&D '83

(Norma Lewis)

Singles: 12-inch

ERC 4-6 83

NORMA JEAN — R&B/LP '78

(Norma Jean Wright)

Singles: 12-inch

BEARSVILLE (Black vinyl.) 4-8 79-80
BEARSVILLE (Colored vinyl.) 10-15 79-80

Singles: 7-inch

BEARSVILLE 3-5 78-80

LPs: 10/12-inch

BEARSVILLE 5-10 78
Also see CHIC

NORMAN, Jimmy — P&R/R&B '62

(With the Hollywood Teeners; with Viceroys)

Singles: 7-inch

DOT 10-20 59
FUN 10-15 60
GOOD SOUND 10-20 61
JOSIE 5-10 68
LITTLE STAR 5-10 62-63
MERCURY (72658 "It's Beautiful") 5-10 67
MERCURY (72727 "I'm Leaving") 20-30 67
MUN RAB (102 "Thank Him") 10-20 59
POLO 5-10 64
RAY STAR 8-15 61-62
SAMAR 4-8 66

LPs: 10/12-inch

BADCAT 5-10
Also see BARNUM, H.B.
Also see CHARGERS
Also see COASTERS

NORMAN, Jimmy, & Dorothy Berry

Singles: 7-inch

LITTLE STAR 8-12 62
Also see BERRY, Dorothy

NORMAN, Jimmy / Willie "The Moon Man" Echols

Singles: 7-inch

GOOD SOUND 5-10 61

NORMAN, Jimmy, & O'Jays

Singles: 7-inch

LITTLE STAR 5-10 63
Also see NORMAN, Jimmy
Also see O'JAYS

NORTH, Freddie — P&R/R&B '71

Singles: 7-inch

A-BET 5-10 67-69
CAPITOL 8-12 62
RIC (119 "The Hurt") 20-30 64
MANKIND 3-6 71-76
PHILLIPS INT'L 10-20 61

LPs: 10/12-inch

A-BET 10-15
MANKIND 8-12 71-75
PHONORAMA 5-8

NORTHCOTT, Tom — P&R '68

Singles: 7-inch

UNI 3-5 71
W.B. 4-8 67-69

LPs: 10/12-inch

UNI 8-12 71

NORTHERN LIGHT — P&R '75

Singles: 7-inch

COLUMBIA 3-5 75
GLACIER 3-5 75-77

NORVUS, Nervous: see NERVOUS NORVUS

NORWOOD — R&B '87

Singles: 7-inch

MAGNOLIA 3-4 87

NORWOOD, Dorothy — R&B '73
(With the Norwood Singers)
Singles: 7-inch
GRC....3-5 72-75
JEWEL....3-5 78
SAVOY....4-8 63-69
LPs: 10/12-inch
JEWEL....5-10 78
SAVOY....8-18 63-83

NOTATIONS — R&B '70
Singles: 7-inch
C.R.A....3-5 73
GEMIGO....3-5 75-76
MERCURY....3-5 77
SUE....4-8 69
TAD....5-8 68
TWINIGHT....3-5 70
LPs: 10/12-inch
GEMIGO....8-12 76
Members: Clifford Curry; Bobby Thomas; Lasalle Matthews; Jimmy Stroud; Walter Jones.
Also see CURRY, Clifford

NOVA, Aldo — P&R/LP '82
Singles: 12-inch
PORTRAIT....5-8 82
(Black vinyl.)
PORTRAIT (1427 "Fantasy")....15-20 82
(Picture disc. Promotional issue only.)
Singles: 7-inch
PORTRAIT....3-4 82
Picture Sleeves
PORTRAIT....3-4 82
LPs: 10/12-inch
PORTRAIT....5-10 82-83

NOVAS — P&R '65
Singles: 7-inch
MEAN MOUNTAIN (942 "The Crusher")....4-8
(Canadian.)
PARROT (45005 "Crusher")....30-50 64
TWIN TOWN (713 "Novas Coaster")....25-35 65

NOVELLE, Jay — D&D '84
Singles: 12-inch
EMERGENCY....4-6 84

NOVO COMBO — LP '81
Singles: 7-inch
POLYDOR....3-5 82
LPs: 10/12-inch
POLYDOR....5-10 81-82
Member: Mike Shrieve.
Also see SANTANA

NU ROMANCE CREW — R&B '87
Singles: 7-inch
EMI AMERICA....3-4 87

NU SHOOZ — P&R/R&B/LP '86
Singles: 7-inch
ATLANTIC....3-4 86-88
Picture Sleeves
ATLANTIC....3-4 86-88
LPs: 10/12-inch
ATLANTIC....5-8 86-88
Members: Valerie Day; John Smith.

NU TORNADOS — P&R '58
Singles: 7-inch
CARLTON....5-15 58-59
FELSTED....5-10 59

NUANCE — R&B/D&D '84
(Featuring Vikki Love)
Singles: 12-inch
4TH & BROADWAY....4-6 84-85
Singles: 7-inch
4TH & BROADWAY....3-4 84-85

NUCLEAR ASSULT — LP '88
LPs: 10/12-inch
I.R.S....5-8 88
IN-EFFECT....5-8 89
UNDER ONE FLAG (21 "Survive")....15-20 88
(Picture disc.)

NUCLEAR VALDEZ — LP '90
LPs: 10/12-inch
EPIC....5-8 90

NUGENT, Ted — LP '75
(With the Amboy Dukes; with Brian Howe)
Singles: 7-inch
ATLANTIC....3-5 84-88
DISCREET....3-5 74
EPIC....3-5 76-80
Picture Sleeves
ATLANTIC....3-5 84
LPs: 10/12-inch
ATLANTIC....5-10 82-88
DISCREET....8-10 74
EPIC (Except 607)....8-15 75-81
EPIC (607 "State of Shock")....25-50 79
(Picture disc.)
MAINSTREAM (10-01 "Ted Nugent and the Amboy Dukes")....5-10 82
MAINSTREAM (421 "Ted Nugent and the Amboy Dukes")....8-12
POLYDOR (4035 "Survival of the Fittest")....10-20 71
Also see AMBOY DUKES
Also see BAD COMPANY
Also see DAMN YANKEES
Also see HEAR 'N AID

NUGGETS — R&B '79
Singles: 7-inch
MERCURY....3-4 79
LPs: 10/12-inch
MERCURY....5-10 79

NUMAN, Gary — LP '79
(With the Tubeway Army)
Singles: 7-inch
ATCO....3-5 79-81
LPs: 10/12-inch
ATCO....5-10 79-81

NUMONICS — R&B '84
Singles: 7-inch
HODISK....4-8 84

NUNN, Bobby — R&B/LP '82
(Bobby Nunn Jr.)
Singles: 7-inch
MOTOWN....3-4 82-84
LPs: 10/12-inch
MOTOWN....5-10 82-84

NURSERY SCHOOL — D&D '83
Singles: 12-inch
EPIC....4-6 83

NUTMEGS — R&B '55
Singles: 78 rpm
HERALD....25-50 55-57
Singles: 7-inch
COLLECTABLES....3-4 80s
FLASHBACK....4-8 65
HERALD (452 "Story Untold")....25-50 55
HERALD (459 "Ship of Love")....25-50 55
HERALD (466 "Whispering Sorrows")....25-50 55
HERALD (475 "Key to the Kingdom")....50-75 56
HERALD (492 "A Love So True")....20-40 56
HERALD (538 "My Story")....25-35 59
HERALD (574 "Rip Van Winkle")....10-20 62
LANA....4-8 64
RELIC....4-8
TEL (1014 "A Dream of Love")....100-200 60
TIMES SQUARE (6 "Let Me Tell You")....50-75 63
(Colored vinyl.)
TIMES SQUARE (14 "The Way Love Should Be")....25-50 63
TIMES SQUARE (27 "Down in Mexico")....20-30 64
TIMES SQUARE (103 "You're Crying")....20-30 64
EPs: 7-inch
HERALD (452 "The Nutmegs")....150-250 60
LPs: 10/12-inch
COLLECTABLES....5-10 84
LOST NITE....8-10
RELIC....8-12 70s
Members: Leroy Griffin; Jimmy Tyson; Leroy McNeil; James "Sonny" Griffin; Bill Emery; Ed Martin; Sonny Washburn; Harold Jones.
Also see LYRES
Also see RAJAHS

NUTMEGS / Admirations
Singles: 7-inch
TIMES SQUARE (19 "Down to Earth")....25-50 64

NUTMEGS / Volumes
Singles: 7-inch
TIMES SQUARE (22 "Why Must We Go to School")....50-100 63
Also see NUTMEGS
Also see VOLUMES

NUTTY SQUIRRELS — P&R/R&B '59
Singles: 7-inch
COLUMBIA....5-10 60
HANOVER....5-10 59-60
RCA....4-8 64
Picture Sleeves
COLUMBIA....10-15 60
HANOVER....10-15 59
EPs: 7-inch
HANOVER (301 "Nutty Squirrels")....15-25 60
LPs: 10/12-inch
COLUMBIA....20-25 61
HANOVER (8014 "Nutty Squirrels")..25-35 60
MGM....15-25 64

NYLONS
(Rumblers)
Singles: 7-inch
DOWNEY (109 "Maid-in-Japan")....10-20 63
Also see RUMBLERS

NYLONS — LP '86
Singles: 7-inch
OPEN AIR....3-5 82-87
Picture Sleeves
OPEN AIR....3-5 87
LPs: 10/12-inch
OPEN AIR....5-10 85-87
WINDHAM HILL....5-8 89
Members: Claude Morrison; Marc Connors; Paul Cooper; Arnold Robinson.

NYRO, Laura — LP '68
Singles: 7-inch
COLUMBIA....3-6 68-71
VERVE/FOLKWAYS....4-8 66-67
VERVE/FORECAST....4-6 68-69
Picture Sleeves
COLUMBIA....4-8 68
LPs: 10/12-inch
COLUMBIA....5-15 68-84
VERVE/FOLKWAYS....10-20 67
VERVE/FORECAST....10-15 69
Also see LABELLE, Patti

NYTRO — R&B '77
Singles: 12-inch
WHITFIELD....4-8 79
Singles: 7-inch
WHITFIELD....3-5 76-79
LPs: 10/12-inch
WHITFIELD....5-10 77-79

O ROMEO D&D '83
Singles: 12-inch
BOB CAT ... 4-6 83
OH MY ... 4-6 84
Members: Lorilee Svedberg; Dora Suppes; Terry Weinberg.

O.M.D. see ORCHESTRAL MANOEUVERS in the DARK

OAK P&R '79
Singles: 7-inch
MERCURY ... 3-5 79-80
Also see PINETTE, Rick, & Oak

OAK RIDGE BOYS C&W '76
(Oak Ridge Quartet; Oaks)
Singles: 7-inch
ABC ... 3-5 78-79
ABC/DOT ... 3-5 77
CADENCE ... 6-12 59
COLUMBIA ... 3-5 73-79
HEARTWARMING ... 3-5 71
IMPACT ... 3-5 71
MCA ... 3-5 79-90
(Black vinyl.)
MCA (51247 "Sail Away") ... 25-50 79
(Picture disc. Promotional issue only. Made for Western Merchandiser's 11th Annual Convention.)
RCA ... 3-4 90-91
W.B. ... 3-8 63
Picture Sleeves
MCA ... 3-5
LPs: 10/12-inch
ABC ... 5-10 78-79
ABC/DOT ... 8-10 77
ACCORD ... 5-10 81-82
CADENCE (3019 "The Oak Ridge Quartet") ... 35-55 58
CANAAN ... 8-15 66
COLUMBIA ... 5-10 74-83
EXACT ... 5-10 83
51 WEST ... 5-8
HEARTWARMING ... 5-8 71-74
INTERMEDIA ... 5-8
MCA ... 5-10 80-86
NASHVILLE ... 8-10 70
OUT of TOWN DIST. ... 5-10 82
PHONORAMA ... 5-8 83
PICKWICK ... 5-8 70s
POWER PAK ... 5-10 70s
PRIORITY ... 5-10 82
SKYLITE ... 10-20 64-66
STARDAY ... 10-20 65
U.A. ... 10-20 66
VISTA ... 5-8
W.B. ... 10-20 63
Members: William Lee Golden; Duane Allen; Rich Sterban; Joe Bonsall; Steve Sanders; Willie Wynn.
Also see CASH, Johnny, Carter Family & Oak Ridge Boys
Also see FOWLER, Wally
Also see JONES, George
Also see LEE, Brenda, & Oak Ridge Boys
Also see MANDRELL, Barbara, & Oak Ridge Boys

OAKEY, Philip: see MORODER, Giorgio, & Philip Oakey

OAKTOWN'S 3-5-7 LP '89
LPs: 10/12-inch
CAPITOL ... 5-8 89
Also see HAMMER, M.C.

OAS, Holly D&D '84
Singles: 12-inch
DND ... 4-6 84

O'BANION, John P&R/LP '81
Singles: 7-inch
ELEKTRA ... 3-5 81
LPs: 10/12-inch
ELEKTRA ... 5-10 81

O'BRYAN P&R/R&B/LP '82
(O'Bryan Burnette)
Singles: 12-inch
CAPITOL ... 4-6 82-86
Singles: 7-inch
CAPITOL ... 3-4 82-87
LPs: 10/12-inch
CAPITOL ... 5-8 82-86

OCASEK, Ric P&R/D&D/LP '83
Singles: 12-inch
GEFFEN ... 4-6 83
Singles: 7-inch
GEFFEN ... 3-4 83-86
Picture Sleeves
GEFFEN ... 3-4 83-86
LPs: 10/12-inch
GEFFEN ... 5-8 83-86
Also see CARS

OCEAN P&R/LP '71
Singles: 7-inch
KAMA SUTRA ... 3-5 71-72
LPs: 10/12-inch
KAMA SUTRA ... 8-12 71-72
Members: Janice Morgan; Greg Brown; David Tamblyn; Charles Slater.

OCEAN, Billy P&R/R&B '76
Singles: 12-inch
EPIC ... 4-8 80-82
JIVE ... 4-6 84-86
Singles: 7-inch
ARIOLA AMERICA ... 3-5 76
EPIC ... 3-5 77-82
JIVE ... 3-4 84-89
Picture Sleeves
JIVE ... 3-4 84-89
LPs: 10/12-inch
EPIC ... 5-10 81-82
JIVE ... 5-8 84-89

OCEAN BLUE LP '90
LPs: 10/12-inch
SIRE ... 5-8 90

OCHS, Phil LP '66
(With the Pan African Ngembo Rumba Band)
Singles: 7-inch
A&M ... 5-10 67-73
SPARKLE (9966 "Bwatue") ... 3-5 91
(Canadian. 1,000 numbered copies made.)
Picture Sleeves
SPARKLE (9966 "Bwatue") ... 3-5 91
(Canadian. 1,000 numbered copies made.)
LPs: 10/12-inch
A&M ... 10-20 67-76
ELEKTRA ... 15-25 64-66

O'CONNELL, Helen P&R '51
Singles: 78 rpm
CAPITOL ... 3-5 51-54
KAPP ... 3-5 55
VIK ... 3-5 57
Singles: 7-inch
CAMEO ... 4-6 63
CAPITOL ... 5-10 51-54
KAPP ... 5-8 55
VIK ... 5-8 57
EPs: 7-inch
CAPITOL ... 8-12 54
VIK ... 8-12 57
LPs: 10/12-inch
CAMDEN ... 10-20 59-62
CAMEO ... 10-15 63
LONGINES ... 5-10 70s
MARK '56 ... 5-10 77
RCA ... 5-10 72
VIK (1093 "Helen O'Connell") ... 25-35 57
W.B. ... 10-20 61
Also see MARTIN, Dean, & Helen O'Connell

O'CONNER, Carroll LP '72
LPs: 10/12-inch
A&M ... 8-12 72
AUDIO FIDELITY ... 5-10 76
CAL STATE (6280 "Carnival of the Animals") ... 10-20 65

O'CONNER, Carroll, & Jean Stapleton P&R '71
(With Rob Reiner, Sally Struthers and Mike Evans)
Singles: 7-inch
ATLANTIC ... 3-5 71
Picture Sleeves
ATLANTIC ... 3-5 71
LPs: 10/12-inch
ATLANTIC ... 8-10 71
Also see O'CONNER, Carroll

O'CONNOR, Sinead LP '88
Singles: 7-inch
CHRYSALIS ... 3-4 86
ENSIGN ... 3-4 90
LPs: 10/12-inch
CHRYSALIS ... 5-8 86
ENSIGN ... 5-8 90
Members: Sinead O'Connor; Andy Rourke; Mike Joyce.
Also see SMITHS

O'DAY, Alan P&R/LP '77
Singles: 7-inch
PACIFIC ... 3-5 77-85
VIVA ... 3-5 71
LPs: 10/12-inch
PACIFIC ... 5-10 77

O'DAY, Anita P&R '47
Singles: 78 rpm
CLEF ... 5-10 53
CORAL ... 5-10 52
LONDON ... 5-10 51
SIGNATURE ... 5-10 47
MERCURY ... 5-10 52-53
VERVE ... 5-10 56-57
Singles: 7-inch
CLEF ... 5-15 53
CLOVER ... 4-6 66
COLUMBIA ... 3-5 76
CORAL ... 5-15 52
EMILY ... 3-5 79
LONDON ... 5-15 51
MERCURY ... 5-15 52-53
VERVE ... 5-15 56-62
EPs: 7-inch
CLEF ... 25-50 53
NORGRAN ... 20-40 54
LPs: 10/12-inch
ADVANCE (8 "Specials") ... 150-200 51
(10-inch LP.)
AMERICAN RECORDING SOCIETY (426 "For Oscar") ... 50-75 57
CLEF (130 "Anita O'Day") ... 100-150 53
COLUMBIA ... 8-10 74
CORAL (56073 "Singin' and Swingin'") ... 100-150 53
DOBRE ... 5-10 78
EMILY ... 5-10 79-82
FLYING DUTCHMAN ... 5-10 74
GNP ... 5-10 79
MPS ... 5-10 73
NORGRAN (30 "Anita O'Day") ... 75-100 54
(10-inch LP.)
NORGRAN (1049 "Anita O'Day Sings Jazz") ... 50-75 55
NORGRAN (1057 "An Evening with Anita O'Day") ... 50-75 56
PAUSA ... 5-10 81
SIGNATURE ... 5-10 75
VERVE (2000 series) ... 30-60 56
(Has "Verve Records Inc." at bottom of label.)

VERVE (2100 series) 25-50 58-61
(Has "Verve Records Inc." at bottom of label.)
VERVE (6000 series) 25-50 59-60
(Has "Verve Records Inc." at bottom of label.)
VERVE (8200 thru 8500 series)........15-30 59-64
(Has "Verve Records Inc." at bottom of label.)
VERVE (2000 series) 30-60 56
(Has "Verve Records Inc." at bottom of label.)
VERVE 12-25 61-72
(Has "MGM Records - A Division Of Metro-Goldwyn-Mayer, Inc." at bottom of label.)
VERVE 5-10 79-82
(Has "Manufactured By MGM Record Corp." or mentions either Polydor or Polygram at bottom of label.)

O'DAY, Anita, & Cal Tjader

LPs: 10/12-inch

VERVE 15-25 62
(Has "MGM Records - A Division Of Metro-Goldwyn-Mayer, Inc." at bottom of label.)
Also see O'DAY, Anita
Also see TJADER, Cal

ODDS & ENDS R&B '70

Singles: 7-inch

TODAY 4-6 71-72

O'DELL, Brooks P&R/R&B '63

Singles: 7-inch

BELL (618 "Slow Motion") 10-20 65
GOLD (214 "Watch Your Step")..........5-10 63

O'DELL, Kenny P&R '67

Singles: 7-inch

ABC 3-5 73
CAPRICORN 3-5 73-79
KAPP 3-5 72
MAR-KAY 5-10 65
VEGAS 4-8 67-68
WHITE WHALE 4-6 69

LPs: 10/12-inch

CAPRICORN 5-10 74-78
VEGAS 15-25 68

ODETTA LP '63

(Odetta & Larry; Odetta Holmes)

Singles: 7-inch

DUNHILL 4-6 69
POLYDOR 3-5 70
RCA 4-8 63
RIVERSIDE 4-8 62
VANGUARD 5-10 59
VERVE/FOLKWAYS 4-6 66
VERVE/FORECAST 4-6 68

EPs: 7-inch

FANTASY (4017/4018 "Odetta & Larry") 15-20 54
(Price is for either of two volumes.)

LPs: 10/12-inch

EVEREST 5-10 73
FANTASY (15 "Odetta & Larry")........40-60 54
(10-inch LP.)
FANTASY (3252 "Odetta") 35-50 58
(Colored vinyl.)
POLYDOR 5-10 70
RCA 10-25 62-66
RIVERSIDE (400 series) 15-25 62
RIVERSIDE (3000 series) 10-20 68
RIVERSIDE (9400 series) 20-30 62
TRADITION (1010 "Odetta Sings Ballads and Blues") 25-35 57
TRADITION (1025 "At the Gate of Horn") 20-30 58
TRADITION (1052 "Best of Odetta") 10-15 67
(Monaural.)
TRADITION (2052 "Best of Odetta") 10-20 67
(Stereo.)
U.A. 5-10 76
VANGUARD 10-20 59-67
VERVE/FOLKWAYS 10-15 67

ODYSSEY P&R/R&B/LP '77

Singles: 12-inch

RCA 4-8 77-82

Singles: 7-inch

MOWEST 3-5 72
RCA 3-5 77-82

LPs: 10/12-inch

MOWEST 10-12 72
RCA 8-10 77-82
Members: Lillian Lopez; Louise Lopez.

OFARIM, Esther & Abraham P&R '68

(Esther Ofarim; with Abi Ofarim)

Singles: 7-inch

PHILIPS 4-6 64-68

LPs: 10/12-inch

CAPITOL 5-10 68
PHILIPS 5-15 63-70

OFF BROADWAY USA P&R/LP '80

Singles: 7-inch

ATLANTIC 3-5 80

LPs: 10/12-inch

ATLANTIC 5-10 80

OFFITT, Lillian P&R/R&B '57

Singles: 78 rpm

EXCELLO 10-20 57

Singles: 7-inch

CHIEF (7012 "The Man Won't Work") 20-30 60
EXCELLO 10-20 57

OH ROMEO: see O ROMEO

O'HENRY, Lenny P&R/R&B '64

(With Short Stories)

Singles: 7-inch

ABC-PAR 10-15 61
ATCO 5-10 64-67
SMASH 5-10 63

OHIO EXPRESS P&R '67

(Ohio Ltd.)

Singles: 7-inch

ATTACK 3-6 70
BUDDAH 4-6 68-73
CAMEO 5-8 67
ERIC 3-5 78
SUPER K 4-6 69-70

LPs: 10/12-inch

BUDDAH 10-20 68-70
CAMEO (20,000 "Beg, Borrow and Steal") 20-30 68
Also see KASENETZ-KATZ SINGING ORCHESTRAL CIRCUS
Also see RARE BREED
Also see REUNION
Also see 10CC

OHIO LTD: see OHIO EXPRESS

OHIO PLAYERS R&B '68

Singles: 7-inch

AIR CITY 3-4 84
ARISTA 3-5 79
BOARDWALK 3-5 81
CAPITOL 4-6 69
COMPASS 4-8 68
MERCURY 3-5 74-78
TRC 4-6 70
TANGERINE 4-8 67
TRACK 3-4 88
WESTBOUND 3-5 71-76

LPs: 10/12-inch

ACCORD 5-10 81
ARISTA 5-10 79
BOARDWALK 5-10 81
CAPITOL (192 "Observations in Time") 10-20 69
CAPITOL (11291 "Ohio Players") 8-12 74
MERCURY 8-12 74-78
SPRINGBOARD 8-10 70s
TRIP 8-10 72
U.A. 8-10 75
WESTBOUND 8-12 72-75
Members: Joe Harris; Marshall Jones; Clarence Satchell; Jimmy Williams; Marvin Pierce; Billy Beck; Ralph Middlebrook; Leroy Bonner.
Also see JUNIE

OINGO BOINGO LP '80

Singles: 12-inch

A&M 4-8 81
MCA 4-6 85-86

Singles: 7-inch

A&M 3-5 81-83
MCA 3-4 85-86

Picture Sleeves

MCA 3-4 85-86

LPs: 10/12-inch

A&M 5-10 81-89
I.R.S. 5-10 80
MCA 5-8 85-90
Members: Danny Elfman; Steve Bartek; John Hernandez; Dale Turner; Kerry Hatch; Richard Gibbs.
Also see ELFMAN, Danny

O'JAYS P&R/R&B '63

Singles: 12-inch

PHILADELPHIA INT'L 4-8 83

Singles: 7-inch

ALL PLATINUM 3-5 74
APOLLO (759 "Miracles") 20-30 61
ASTROSCOPE 3-6 74
BELL 3-6 67-73
EPIC 3-4 83
IMPERIAL (5942 "How Does It Feel") 10-15 63
IMPERIAL (5976 "Lonely Drifter")........5-10 63
IMPERIAL (66007 thru 66131) 5-10 64-65
IMPERIAL (66145 "I'll Never Let You Go") 30-50 65
IMPERIAL (66162 "I'll Never Forget You") 25-35 66
IMPERIAL (66177 thru 66200) 5-10 66
LIBERTY 3-5 81
LITTLE STAR (124 "How Does It Feel") 15-25 63
LITTLE STAR (125 "Dream Girl")......15-25 63
LITTLE STAR (1401 "Just to Be with You") 15-25 63
MANHATTAN 3-4 89-90
MINIT 5-10 67
NEPTUNE 4-6 69-70
PHILADELPHIA INT'L 3-6 72-87
SARU 3-6 71
TSOP 3-5 80-81

LPs: 10/12-inch

BELL (6014 "Back on Top") 10-20 68
BELL (6082 "The O'Jays") 8-12 73
EMI 5-8 89-90
EPIC 5-8 83
IMPERIAL (9290 "Coming Through") 30-35 65
(Monaural.)
IMPERIAL (12290 "Coming Through") 35-40 65
(Stereo.)
KORY 8-10 77
MINIT (24008 "Soul Sounds") 20-30 67
(Stereo.)
MINIT (40008 "Soul Sounds") 15-25 67
(Monaural.)
PHILADELPHIA INT'L 5-10 72-86
SUNSET 10-15 68
TSOP 5-10 80
TRIP 8-10 73
U.A. 8-12 72
Members: Bob Massey; Eddie LeVert; Walt Williams; Bill Powell; Bill Isles; Sam Strain.
Also see LITTLE ANTHONY & IMPERIALS
Also see NORMAN, Jimmy, & O'Jays
Also see PHILADELPHIA INTERNATIONAL ALL STARS

O'JAYS / Moments

LPs: 10/12-inch

STANG 8-12 74
Also see MOMENTS
Also see O'JAYS

O'KAYSIONS P&R/R&B/LP '68

Singles: 7-inch

ABC 5-8 68
COTILLION 3-5 70

NORTH STATE (1001 "Girl Watcher")....20-30 68
ROULETTE....3-5 70s
SPARTON (1676 "Girl Watcher")....5-8 68
(Canadian.)

Picture Sleeves

NORTH STATE (1001 "Girl Watcher")....25-45 68

EPs: 7-inch

ABC (664 "Girl Watcher")....15-25 68
(Juke box issue.)

LPs: 10/12-inch

ABC (664 "Girl Watcher")....15-25 68
Members: Donnie Weaver; Jim Spidel; Jim Hennant; Ron Turner; Bruce Joyner.

O'KEEFE, Danny — P&R/C&W/LP '72

Singles: 7-inch

ATLANTIC....3-5 75
JERDEN....4-8 66
SIGNPOST....3-5 72
W.B. 3-5 77-78

Picture Sleeves

W.B. 3-5 77-78

LPs: 10/12-inch

ATLANTIC....8-12 73-75
COTILLION....10-15 70
FIRST AMERICAN....8-10 70s
PANORAMA (105 "Introducing Danny O'Keefe")....20-30 66
SIGNPOST....10-12 72
W.B. 5-10 77-79

OLA & JANGLERS — P&R '69

Singles: 7-inch

GNP....4-8 68-69
LONDON....4-8 67

LPs: 10/12-inch

GNP....15-20 69
Member: Ola Hakansson.

OLD AND IN THE WAY — LP '75

LPs: 10/12-inch

ROUND (103 "Old and in the Way")....20-25 75
SUGAR HILL....5-8 85
Members: Peter Rowan; Jerry Garcia; Vassar Clements; David Grisman.
Also see GARCIA, Jerry
Also see ROWANS

OLD AND IN THE WAY / Keith & Donna / Robert Hunter / Phil Lesh & Ned Lagin

Singles: 7-inch

ROUND (02 & 03 "Sampler for Dead Heads")....40-60 75
(Promotional, fan club two-disc set. Price also includes a letter from Anton Round, a letter about members of the Grateful Dead, several miniature LP covers, and a mailer advertising posters.)
ROUND (02 & 03 "Sampler for Dead Heads")....20-30 75
(Price is for both discs, without inserts. Divide in half for either one of the two records.)
Also see GRATEFUL DEAD
Also see OLD and in the WAY

OLDFIELD, Mike — LP '73
(With Sally Oldfield)

Singles: 7-inch

EPIC....3-5 81-82
VIRGIN....3-5 73-82

Picture Sleeves

VIRGIN....3-6 74

EPs: 7-inch

VIRGIN (199 "Tubular Bells")....5-10 74
(Promotional issue only.)

LPs: 10/12-inch

EPIC (44116)....5-10 81-82
EPIC (44116 "Tubular Bells")....20-40 73
(Half-speed mastered.)
VIRGIN (Except 2001)....5-15 73-88
VIRGIN (2001 "Tubular Bells")....10-12 73
(Picture disc.)
Also see SALLYANGIE

OLIVER — P&R/LP '69
(Bill Oliver Swofford)

Singles: 7-inch

CREWE....3-5 69-70
JUBILEE....4-6 69
LIBERTY....3-5
PARAMOUNT....3-5 73
PEOPLE SONG....3-5 82
U.A. 3-5 70-71

Picture Sleeves

CREWE....4-6 69

LPs: 10/12-inch

CREWE....10-15 69-70
U.A. 8-12 71

OLIVER, David — R&B/LP '78

Singles: 7-inch

MERCURY....3-5 78-80

LPs: 10/12-inch

MERCURY....5-10 78-79

OLIVOR, Jane — P&R/LP '77

Singles: 7-inch

COLUMBIA....3-5 77-85

LPs: 10/12-inch

COLUMBIA....5-10 77-85

OLLIE & JERRY — P&R/R&B/D&D '84

Singles: 12-inch

POLYDOR....4-6 84-85

Singles: 7-inch

POLYDOR....3-4 84-85
Members: Ollie Brown; Jerry Knight.
Also see KNIGHT, Jerry

OLLIE & NIGHTINGALES — P&R/R&B '68

Singles: 7-inch

STAX....4-8 68

LPs: 10/12-inch

STAX....10-15 69
Also see MAD LADS

OLSON, Rocky — P&R '59

Singles: 7-inch

CHESS....10-15 59

OLSSON, Nigel — P&R '75

Singles: 7-inch

BANG....3-5 78-79
COLUMBIA....3-5 78
ROCKET....3-5 75
UNI....3-5 71-72

LPs: 10/12-inch

BANG....5-10 79-80
COLUMBIA....5-10 78
ROCKET....8-12 73-75
UNI....8-12 71
Also see JOHN, Elton

OLYMPIC RUNNERS — R&B '74

Singles: 7-inch

LONDON....3-5 74-77
POLYDOR....3-5 79

LPs: 10/12-inch

LONDON....8-10 74-77
POLYDOR....5-10 79
Members: Pete Wingfield; DeLisle Harper; George Chandler; Joe Jammer. Glen LeFleur.
Also see WINGFIELD, Pete

OLYMPICS — P&R/R&B '58

Singles: 78 rpm

DEMON....25-50 58

Singles: 7-inch

ABC....3-5 73
ARVEE (562 "Hully Gully")....10-20 59
ARVEE (595 "Big Boy Pete")....10-20 60
ARVEE (5006 "Shimmy Like Kate")....10-20 60
ARVEE (5020 "Dance By the Light of the Moon")....10-20 61
ARVEE (5023 "Little Pedro")....10-20 61
ARVEE (5031 "Stay Where You Are")....30-50 61
ARVEE (5044 "The Stomp")....10-15 61
ARVEE (5051 "Twist")....10-15 62
ARVEE (5056 "The Scotch")....10-15 62
ARVEE (5073 "What'd I Say")....10-15 63
ARVEE (6501 "Big Boy Pete '65")....10-15 63
COLLECTABLES....3-4 80s
DEMON (1508 "Western Movies")....15-25 58
DEMON (1512 "Dance with the Teacher")....15-25 58
DEMON (1514 "Your Love")....15-25 59
DUO DISC....5-10 64
ERIC....3-5 70s
JUBILEE....5-10 69
LIBERTY....5-10 63
LOMA....5-10 65
MGM....3-5 73
MIRWOOD....5-10 66-67
PARKWAY....5-10 68
TITAN (1718 "The Chicken")....15-25 61
TRI DISC....8-15 62-63
W.B. 3-5 70
ZEE (101 "The Slop")....15-25 58
ZEE (103 "Western Movies")....20-30 58

EPs: 7-inch

ARVEE (423 "Doin' the Hully Gully")....50-100 60

LPs: 10/12-inch

ARVEE (423 "Doin' the Hully Gully")....100-200 60
ARVEE (424 "Dance by the Light of the Moon")....100-125 61
ARVEE (429 "Party Time")....100-125 61
EVEREST....5-10 81
MIRWOOD (M-7003 "Something Old, Something New")....20-30 66
(Monaural.)
MIRWOOD (MS-7003 "Something Old, Something New")....25-35 66
(Stereo.)
POST....8-10 70s
RHINO....5-8 80s
TRI-DISC (1001 "Do the Bounce")....40-60 63
Members: Walter Ward; Eddie Lewis; Melvin King; Charles Figer; Julius McMichaels.
Also see PARAGONS
Also see REYNOLDS, Jody / Olympics

O'MALLEY, Lenore — P&R '80

Singles: 7-inch

POLYDOR....3-5 80

OMAR & HOWLERS — LP '87

Singles: 7-inch

COLUMBIA ("Border Girl")....8-12 87
(Picture disc. Promotional issue only. No selection number used.)

LPs: 10/12-inch

COLUMBIA....5-8 87

100 PROOF Aged in Soul — P&R/R&B '69

Singles: 7-inch

HOT WAX....3-6 69-72

LPs: 10/12-inch

HOT WAX....10-15 70-73
Members: Steve Mancha; Joe Stubbs; Eddie Anderson.
Also see MANCHA, Steve

101 STRINGS — LP '59

Singles: 7-inch

SOMERSET....3-5 59

LPs: 10/12-inch

ALSHIRE....5-10 60s
SOMERSET....5-10 59-61
STEREO FIDELITY....5-10 59-61

ONE ON ONE — R&B '84

Singles: 7-inch

KEE WEE....3-4 84

ONE 2 MANY — P&R '89

Singles: 7-inch

A&M....3-4 89

Picture Sleeves

A&M....3-4 89

ONE TO ONE — P&R '86

Singles: 7-inch

W.B. 3-4 86

Picture Sleeves

W.B. 3-4 86

LPs: 10/12-inch

W.B. 5-8 86

Members: Louise Reny; Leslie Howe.

ONE WAY LP '79
(Featuring Al Hudson)
Singles: 12-inch
MCA....4-6 82-86
Singles: 7-inch
MCA....3-5 79-87
LPs: 10/12-inch
MCA....5-10 79-86
Also see HUDSON, Al

O'NEAL, Alexander R&B/D&D/LP '85
Singles: 12-inch
TABU....4-6 85-86
Singles: 7-inch
TABU....3-4 85-90
Picture Sleeves
TABU....3-4 85-88
LPs: 10/12-inch
TABU....5-8 85-90

O'NEAL, Alexander, & Cherrelle R&B '86
Singles: 7-inch
TABU....3-4 86-88
Also see CHERRELLE
Also see O'NEAL, Alexander

ONO, Yoko LP '71
(With the Plastic Ono Band)
Singles: 12-inch
POLYDOR....5-10 85-86
Singles: 7-inch
APPLE....4-8 71-73
GEFFEN....3-5 81
POLYDOR....3-5 82-86
Promotional Singles
APPLE (OYB-1 "Open Your Box")....600-800 70
APPLE (1853 "Now Or Never")....25-30 72
APPLE (1867 "Woman Power")....20-25 73
GEFFEN....5-8 81
POLYDOR....4-6 82-86
Picture Sleeves
APPLE (1853 "Now Or Never")....8-12 72
GEFFEN....3-4 81
LPs: 10/12-inch
APPLE....15-20 71-73
GEFFEN....5-10 81
POLYDOR....5-10 82-86
Promotional LPs
GEFFEN (934 "Walking on Thin Ice")....20-25 81
GEFFEN (975 "No No No")....25-30 81
Also see LENNON, John

OPUS P&R/LP '86
Singles: 7-inch
POLYDOR....3-4 86
LPs: 10/12-inch
POLYDOR....5-8 86

OPUS SEVEN R&B '79
Singles: 7-inch
SOURCE....3-5 79
LPs: 10/12-inch
SOURCE....5-10 79

OPUS 10 R&B '85
Singles: 7-inch
PANDISC....3-4 85

ORBISON, Roy P&R '56
(With the Teen Kings; with Candy Men; with Roses; with Friends)
Singles: 78 rpm
QUALITY....20-40 56
SUN....40-80 56-57
Singles: 12-inch
VIRGIN (2667 "She's a Mystery to Me")....10-15 89
(Includes cover.)
Singles: 7-inch
ASYLUM....3-5 78-79
COLLECTABLES....3-4 85
MGM....4-8 65-73
MGM CELEBRITY SCENE (CSN9-5 "Roy Orbison")....50-75 66
(Boxed set of five singles with bio insert and juke box title strips.)
MERCURY....4-8 74
MONUMENT (409 "Paper Boy")....20-30 59
MONUMENT (412 "Uptown")....15-25 59
MONUMENT (421 thru 467)....10-20 60-62
MONUMENT (800 & 900 series)....8-15 63-66
MONUMENT (500 series)....5-8 63
MONUMENT (8600 series)....3-5 76
MONUMENT (8900 series)....3-5 72
MONUMENT (45000 series)....3-5 76-77
QUALITY (1499 "Ooby Dooby")....50-100 56
QUALITY (1559 "Rockhouse")....50-100 56
RCA (7381 "Sweet and Innocent")....20-30 58
RCA (7447 "Jolie")....20-30 59
SSS/SUN....3-5 70s
SUN (242 "Ooby Dooby")....20-40 56
SUN (251 "Rockhouse")....20-40 56
SUN (265 "Sweet and Easy to Love")....20-40 56
SUN (284 "Chicken Hearted")....20-40 58
SUN (353 "Sweet and Easy to Love")....8-10 61
(Yellow label.)
SUN (353 "Sweet and Easy to Love")....10-15 61
(White label. Promotional issue only.)
VIRGIN....3-5 87-89
Picture Sleeves
MGM....8-15 65-67
MONUMENT (400 series)....15-25 60-62
MONUMENT (800 series)....10-20 63-64
VIRGIN....3-6 89
EPs: 7-inch
MGM (4379 "Classic Roy Orbison")..30-50 66
(Juke box issue only.)
MONUMENT (2 "Crying")....20-30 62
(Compact 33, "Special Promotional Six-Pac." Not issued with special cover.)
MONUMENT (3 "Roy Orbison")....20-30 62
(Compact 33, "Special Promotional Six-Pac." Not issued with special cover.)
STARS INC. (101 "Roy Orbison and the Teen Kings")....300-400 59
(Promotional issue, distributed to fan club members.)
LPs: 10/12-inch
ACCORD....5-8 81
ASYLUM....5-8 78-79
BUCKBOARD....8-10
CANDLELITE MUSIC....10-15 70s
DESIGN....10-15 60s
MGM (E-4308 thru E-4514)....15-20 65-67
(Monaural.)
MGM (SE-4308 thru SE-4514)....20-30 65-67
(Stereo.)
MGM (4636 thru 4934)....10-20 69-73
MGM/CAPITOL (90454 "There Is Only One Roy Orbison")....10-20 65
(Label reads "Mfd. by Capitol Records." Record club issue.)
MERCURY....8-12 75
MONUMENT (4002 "Lonely and Blue")....100-150 61
(Monaural.)
MONUMENT (4007 "Crying"....40-60 62
(Monaural.)
MONUMENT (4009 "Greatest Hits") 30-40 62
(Monaural.)
MONUMENT (6600 series)....8-10
MONUMENT (7600 "Regeneration")..8-10 76
MONUMENT (8000 "Greatest Hits") 25-30 63
(Monaural.)
MONUMENT (8003 "In Dreams")....30-40 63
(Monaural.)
MONUMENT (8023 "Early Orbison") 30-40 64
(Monaural.)
MONUMENT (8024 "More Greatest Hits")....20-25 64
(Monaural.)
MONUMENT (8035 "Orbisongs")....25-30 65
(Monaural.)
MONUMENT (8045 "Very Best")....30-40 66
(Blue cover. Monaural.)
MONUMENT (8045 "Very Best")....20-30 66
(Purple cover. Monaural.)
MONUMENT (14002 "Lonely and Blue")....125-200 61
(Stereo.)
MONUMENT (14007 "Crying")....50-75 62
(Stereo.)
MONUMENT (14009 "Greatest Hits")....40-50 62
(Stereo.)
MONUMENT (18000 "Greatest Hits")....35-40 63
(Stereo.)
MONUMENT (18003 "In Dreams")....40-50 63
(Stereo.)
MONUMENT (18024 "More Greatest Hits")....25-30 64
(Stereo.)
MONUMENT (18035 "Orbisongs")....35-40 65
(Stereo.)
MONUMENT (18023 "Early Orbison")....30-40 64
(Stereo.)
MONUMENT (18045 "Very Best")....30-40 66
(Blue cover. Stereo.)
MONUMENT (18045 "Very Best")....20-30 66
(Purple cover. Stereo.)
MONUMENT (31484 "All-Time Greatest Hits")....8-12 82
MONUMENT (38384 "All-Time Greatest Hits")....6-10 82
RHINO....5-8 88
SPECTRUM....15-20 60s
SSS/SUN....5-10 69
SUN (1260 "Rock House")....200-300 61
SUNNYVALE....8-10 77
TIME-LIFE....10-15 86
TRIP....8-10 74
VIRGIN....6-12 87-89
Session: Bobby Goldsboro; Bruce Springsteen.
Also see CANDYMEN
Also see DRIFTERS / Lesley Gore / Roy Orbison / Los Bravos
Also see GOLDSBORO, Bobby
Also see HIGGINS, Bertie, & Roy Orbison
Also see JAN & DEAN / Roy Orbison / 4 Seasons / Shirelles
Also see LEWIS, Jerry Lee / Roger Miller / Roy Orbison
Also see PERKINS, Carl, Jerry Lee Lewis, Roy Orbison & Johnny Cash
Also see SPRINGSTEEN, Bruce
Also see TEEN KINGS
Also see TRAVELING WILBURYS

ORBISON, Roy / Bobby Bare / Joey Powers
LPs: 10/12-inch
CAMDEN....15-25 64
Also see BARE, Bobby
Also see POWERS, Joey

ORBISON, Roy, & Emmylou Harris / Craig Hundley C&W/P&R '80
Singles: 7-inch
W.B....3-5 80
Also see HARRIS, Emmylou

ORBISON, Roy, & k.d. Lang C&W '87
Singles: 7-inch
VIRGIN....3-4 87
Also see LANG, k.d.
Also see ORBISON, Roy

ORBIT R&B '82
(Featuring Carol Hall)
Singles: 12-inch
QUALITY/RFC....4-6 82-84
Singles: 7-inch
QUALITY/RFC....3-4 82-84

ORCHESTRAL MANOEUVERS IN THE DARK LP '82
(OMD)
Singles: 12-inch
A&M....4-6 84-86

Singles: 7-inch

A&M..........3-4 84-88
EPIC..........3-5 82-83

Picture Sleeves

A&M..........3-4 85-88

LPs: 10/12-inch

A&M..........5-8 84-88
EPIC..........5-10 82-83

ORIGINAL ANIMALS: see ANIMALS

ORIGINAL CADILLACS

Singles: 7-inch

JOSIE (821 "Hurry Home")..........20-30 57
Members: Earl Carroll; Earl Wade; Charles Brooks; Bobby Phillips; Junior Glanton; Roland Martinez.
Also see CADILLACS

ORIGINAL CASTE P&R '69

(Featuring Dixie Lee Innes)

Singles: 7-inch

DOT..........4-8 68
T-A..........4-8 69-70

Picture Sleeves

T-A..........4-8 69

LPs: 10/12-inch

T-A..........10-20 70

ORIGINAL CASUALS P&R/R&B '58

(Featuring Gary Mears)

Singles: 7-inch

BACK BEAT (503 "So Tough")..........10-20 58
BACK BEAT (510 "Ju-Judy")..........10-20 58
BACK BEAT (514 "Three Kisses Past Midnight")..........15-25 57

EPs: 7-inch

BACK BEAT (40 "Three Kisses Past Midnight")..........50-100 58
Members: Gary Mears; Paul Kearney; Jay Adams.

ORIGINAL CONCEPT R&B '86

Singles: 7-inch

DEF JAM..........3-4 86

ORIGINAL GROUP

(Monarchs)

Singles: 7-inch

SMASH (2219 "Look Homeward Angel")..........4-6 69

Picture Sleeves

SMASH (2219 "Look Homeward Angel")..........10-12 69
Also see MONARCHS

ORIGINAL CRESTS: see CRESTS

ORIGINAL LAST POETS LP '71

LPs: 10/12-inch

JUGGERNAUT..........10-15 71

ORIGINAL RED CAPS: see GIBSON, Steve

ORIGINALS P&R/R&B '69

Singles: 7-inch

FANTASY..........3-5 78
MOTOWN (1 "Young Train")..........100-200 73
(Promotional issue only.)
MOTOWN (1300 series)..........4-6 75
PHASE II..........3-5 81
SOUL (35029 thru 35061)..........6-12 67-69
SOUL (35066 thru 35119)..........4-8 69-76
(Black vinyl.)
SOUL (Colored vinyl)..........8-15
(Promotional issue only.)

LPs: 10/12-inch

FANTASY..........5-10 78-79
MOTOWN..........5-10 74-80
SOUL (716 "Baby I'm for Real")..........20-40 69
SOUL (724 "Portrait")..........15-20 70
SOUL (729 "Naturally Together")..........15-20 70
SOUL (734 thru 746)..........8-15 73-76
Members: Ty Hunter; Henry Dixon; Joe Stubbs; Walt Gaines; C.P. Spencer; Freddie Gorman.
Also see HUNTER, Ty

ORIGINALS & JERMAINE JACKSON

Singles: 12-inch

MOTOWN..........4-8 76
Also see JACKSON, Jermaine
Also see ORIGINALS

ORIOLES P&R/R&B '48

(With the Sid Bass Orchestra; Sonny Til & Orioles; Sonny Til's Orioles)

Singles: 78 rpm

IT'S a NATURAL (5000 "It's Too Soon to Know")..........50-150 48
JUBILEE (5000 "It's too Soon to Know")..........25-75 48
JUBILEE (5001 "Dare to Dream")..........25-75 48
JUBILEE (5001 "Lonely Christmas")..........25-75 48
JUBILEE (5002 "Please Give My Heart a Break")..........25-75 49
JUBILEE (5005 "Tell Me So")..........25-75 49
JUBILEE (5008 "I Challenge Your Kiss")..........25-75 49
JUBILEE (5009 "A Kiss and a Rose")..........25-75 49
JUBILEE (5016 "So Much")..........25-75 49
JUBILEE (5017 "What Are You Doing New Year's Eve")..........25-75 49
JUBILEE (5018 "Would You Still Be the One in My Heart")..........25-75 50
JUBILEE (5025 "At Night")..........25-75 50
JUBILEE (5026 "Moonlight")..........25-75 50
JUBILEE (5028 "You're Gone")..........25-75 50
JUBILEE (5031 "I'd Rather Have You Under the Moon")..........20-60 50
JUBILEE (5037 "I Need You So")..........20-60 50
JUBILEE (5040 "I Cross My Fingers")..........20-60 50
JUBILEE (5045 "Oh Holy Night")..........20-60 50
JUBILEE (5051 "I Miss You So")..........20-60 51
JUBILEE (5057 "Would I Love You")..........20-60 51
JUBILEE (5061 "I'm Just a Fool in Love")..........20-60 51
At least 10 of the above 78 rpm singles were reissued around 1951 on 45s. It's likely that others in the 5001-5061 series appeared on early '50s Jubilee 45s, but those listed below are the only ones we can verify.
JUBILEE (5061 thru 5231)..........15-45 51-56
VEE JAY..........15-35 56-57

Singles: 7-inch

ABNER (1016 "Sugar Girl")..........25-50 58
CHARLIE PARKER..........8-15 62-63
COLLECTABLES..........3-4 80s
JUBILEE (5000 "It's Too Soon to Know")..........3000-5000 51
JUBILEE (5005 "Tell Me So")..........2000-3000 51
JUBILEE (5016 "So Much")..........1000-2000 51
JUBILEE (5017 "What Are You Doing New Year's Eve")..........500-1000 51
JUBILEE (5025 "At Night")..........500-1000 51
JUBILEE (5040 "I Cross My Fingers")..........500-750 51
JUBILEE (5045 "Oh Holy Night")..........500-750 51
JUBILEE (5051 "I Miss You So")..........500-750 51
(Black vinyl.)
JUBILEE (5051 "I Miss You So")..........1000-2000 51
(Colored vinyl.)
JUBILEE (5055 "Pal of Mine")..........400-600 51
JUBILEE (5061 "I'm Just a Fool in Love")..........400-600 51
JUBILEE (5065 "Baby, Please Don't Go")..........400-500 51
(Black vinyl.)
JUBILEE (5065 "Baby, Please Don't Go")..........1000-2000 51
(Colored vinyl.)
JUBILEE (5071 "When You're Not Around")..........300-500 51
JUBILEE (5074 "Trust in Me")..........400-600 52
JUBILEE (5082 "It's Over Because We're Through")..........400-600 52
JUBILEE (5084 "Barfly")..........250-450 52
JUBILEE (5092 "Don't Cry Baby")..........250-450 52
(Black vinyl.)
JUBILEE (5092 "Don't Cry Baby")..........1000-1500 52
(Colored vinyl.)
JUBILEE (5102 "You Belong to Me")..........250-450 52
JUBILEE (5107 "I Miss You So")..........200-400 53
(Reissued in 1963, using the same catalog number, but credited to Sonny Til & Orioles. Black vinyl.)
JUBILEE (5107 "I Miss You So")..........1000-1500 53
(Colored vinyl.)
JUBILEE (5108 "Teardrops on My Pillow")..........200-300 53
(Black vinyl.)
JUBILEE (5108 "Teardrops on My Pillow")..........1000-1500 53
(Colored vinyl.)
JUBILEE (5115 "Bad Little Girl")..........200-300 53
JUBILEE (5120 "I Cover the Waterfront")..........200-300 53
(Black vinyl.)
JUBILEE (5120 "I Cover the Waterfront")..........1000-1500 53
(Colored vinyl.)
JUBILEE (5122 "Crying in the Chapel")..........50-75 53
JUBILEE (5127 "In the Mission of St. Augustine")..........50-75 53
JUBILEE (5134 "There's No One But You")..........50-75 54
JUBILEE (5137 "Secret Love")..........50-75 54
JUBILEE (5143 "Maybe You'll Be There")..........50-100 54
JUBILEE (5154 "In the Chapel in the Moonlight")..........50-75 54
JUBILEE (5161 "If You Believe")..........50-75 54
JUBILEE (5172 "Runaround")..........50-75 54
JUBILEE (5177 "I Love You Mostly")..........25-50 55
JUBILEE (5189 "I Need You Baby")..........25-50 55
JUBILEE (5221 "Please Sing My Blues Tonight")..........25-50 55
JUBILEE (5231 "Angel")..........30-60 56
JUBILEE (5363 "Tell Me So")..........10-20 59
JUBILEE (5384 "First of Summer")..........10-20 60
JUBILEE (5383 "Come On Home")..........10-20 60
JUBILEE (5394 "Night and Day")..........50-75 60
JUBILEE (6001 "Crying in the Chapel")..........10-15 59
ROULETTE..........3-5 70s
(Jubilee 5066 and 5076 are credited to Sonny Til.)
VEE JAY (196 "Happy Till the Letter")..........25-50 56
VEE JAY (228 "For All We Know")..........25-50 56
VEE JAY (244 "Sugar Girl")..........25-50 57
VIRGO..........3-5 70s

Picture Sleeves

JUBILEE (5017 "What Are You Doing New Year's Eve")..........300-500 54
(Sleeve for 78 rpm.)
JUBILEE (5017 "What Are You Doing New Year's Eve")..........400-600 54
(Sleeve for 45 rpm.)
JUBILEE (5045 "Oh Holy Night")..........400-600 54
(Both Jubilee sleeves were issued in late 1954 and sold with 1954 pressings, actually second pressings of both. These were blue script Jubilee labels with the line under the logo.)
LANA..........3-6 63

EPs: 7-inch

JUBILEE (5000 "The Orioles Sing")..........1000-2000 53

LPs: 10/12-inch

BIG A RECORDS (2001 "Greatest All Time Hits")..........20-30 69
CHARLIE PARKER (816 "Modern Sounds")..........50
100..........62
COLLECTABLES..........5-10 84
MURRAY HILL..........30-40 80s
(Boxed, five-disc set. Number not known.)

MURRAY HILL (61277 "The Orioles Featuring Sonny Til") 30-40 80s
(Boxed, five-disc set.)
ROULETTE 5-10
Members: Sonny Til; Alex Sharp; George Nelson; John Reed; Tom Gaither; Charles Harris; Greg Carroll; Billy Adams; Jerry Holman; Al Russell; Jerry Rodriguez; Bill Taylor.
Also see CADILLACS / Orioles
Also see TIL, Sonny

ORION THE HUNTER P&R/LP '84

Singles: 7-inch

PORTRAIT 3-5 84-85

LPs: 10/12-inch

PORTRAIT (39239 "Orion the Hunter") 20-40 84
Member: Barry Goudreau.
Also see BOSTON

ORLANDO, Tony

Singles: 7-inch

MILO (101 "Ding Dong") 30-50 59
(Listed primarily to distinguish this singer from the following Tony Orlando.)
Also see SIMON, Paul

ORLANDO, Tony P&R '61

Singles: 12-inch

CASABLANCA 5-10 79

Singles: 7-inch

ATCO 4-8 65
CAMEO 4-8 67
CASABLANCA 3-5 79-80
EPIC (9000 series) 5-10 61-64

Promotional Singles

EPIC (55299 "Happy Times Are Here to Stay") 8-12 61

LPs: 10/12-inch

EPIC (611 "Bless You") 35-40 61
(Stereo.)
EPIC (3808 "Bless You") 35-40 61
(Monaural.)
EPIC (33785 "Before Dawn") 10-12 75
CASABLANCA 5-10 79-80

Picture Sleeves

EPIC 8-10 61-62
Also see WIND

ORLANDO, Tony, & Dawn P&R/LP '70

Singles: 7-inch

ARISTA 3-5 75
BELL 3-5 71-74
ELEKTRA 3-5 75-78

LPs: 10/12-inch

ARISTA 8-10 75-76
ASYLUM 8-10 75
BELL (6000 series) 10-12 70-71
BELL (1000 series) 8-10 73-75
ELEKTRA 8-10 75-78
KORY 8-10 74-77
Also see DAWN
Also see ORLANDO, Tony

ORLEANS P&R/LP '75

Singles: 7-inch

ABC 3-5 73
ASYLUM 3-5 75-77
INFINITY 3-5 79
MCA 3-4 86

LPs: 10/12-inch

ABC 10-12 73-78
ASYLUM 8-10 75-76
INFINITY 5-10 79
RADIO 5-8 82
Member: John Hall.
Also see HALL, John

ORLONS P&R/R&B/LP '62

Singles: 7-inch

ABC 4-8 67
ABKCO 3-5
CALLA (113 "Spinnin' Top") 8-12 66
CAMEO (198 "I'll Be True") 30-50 61
CAMEO (211 "Mr. Twenty-One") 30-50 62
CAMEO (218 thru 372) 8-15 62-65
CAMEO (384 "Envy") 30-40 65

Picture Sleeves

CAMEO 5-10 62-64

LPs: 10/12-inch

CAMEO (1020 "Wah Watusi") 30-60 62
CAMEO (1033 "All the Hits") 25-50 62
CAMEO (1041 "South Street") 25-50 63
CAMEO (1054 "Not Me") 25-50 63
CAMEO (1061 "Biggest Hits") 25-50 63
CAMEO (1073 "Memory Lane") 25-50 63
Members: Shirley Brickley; Rosetta Hightower; Steve Caldwell; Marlena Davis.
Also see ZIP & ZIPPERS

ORLONS / Dovells

LPs: 10/12-inch

CAMEO (1067 "Golden Hits") 25-50 63
Also see DOVELLS
Also see ORLONS

ORPHEUS LP '68

Singles: 7-inch

MGM 4-6 68-69

Picture Sleeves

MGM 4-6 69

LPs: 10/12-inch

BELL 10-12 71
MGM 10-15 68-69

ORR, Benjamin P&R/LP '86

Singles: 7-inch

ELEKTRA 3-4 86

Picture Sleeves

ELEKTRA 3-4 86

LPs: 10/12-inch

ELEKTRA 5-8 86
Also see CARS

ORRALL, Robert Ellis P&R/LP '83

(With Carlene Carter)

Singles: 7-inch

RCA 3-5 81-91

LPs: 10/12-inch

RCA 5-10 81-91
Also see CARTER, Carlene

OSBORNE, Jeffrey P&R/R&B/LP '82

Singles: 12-inch

A&M 4-6 82-86

Singles: 7-inch

A&M 3-5 82-88
ARISTA 3-4 90

Picture Sleeves

A&M 3-5 82-88

LPs: 10/12-inch

A&M 5-10 82-88
ARISTA 5-8 90
Also see KENNEDY, Joyce, & Jeffrey Osborne
Also see L.T.D.
Also see WARWICK, Dionne, & Jeffrey Osborne

OSBORNE & GILES R&B '85

Singles: 7-inch

RED LABEL 3-4 85

LPs: 10/12-inch

RED LABEL 5-8 85
Members: Billy Osborne; Attala Giles.

OSBOURNE, Ozzy LP '81

Singles: 7-inch

EPIC (37640 "Mr. Crowley Live") 30-40 82
(Picture disc.)
JETT (6400 "Mr. Crowley Live") 20-30 81
(Picture disc. Promotional issue only.)
JET (7670 "Diary of a Madman") 30-40 81
(Picture disc. Promotional issue only.)
JET (7670 "Diary of a Madman") 45-55 81
(Picture disc. Promotional issue only. Has KMET logo on one side.)

Singles: 7-inch

CBS ASSOCIATED 3-4 83-86
JET 3-5 82

Picture Sleeves

CBS ASSOCIATED 3-4 86
JET 3-5 82

LPs: 10/12-inch

CBS ASSOCIATED (Black vinyl) 5-8 83-90
CBS ASSOCIATED (40543 "Ultimate Live Ozzy") 25-35 86
(Picture disc. Promotional issue only.)
JET (Black vinyl) 5-10 81-82
JET (1327 "Diary of a Madman") 45-50 81
(Promotional only picture disc.)
Also see BLACK SABBATH
Also see FORD, Lita, & Ozzy Osbourne
Also see QUIET RIOT

OSBOURNE, Ozzy, & Randy Rhoads LP '87

LPs: 10/12-inch

CBS ASSOC 5-8 87

OSIBISA LP '71

Singles: 7-inch

DECCA 3-5 72
ISLAND 3-5 76-77
MCA 3-4
W.B. 3-5 73-74

LPs: 10/12-inch

BUDDAH 8-10 73
DECCA 10-12 71-72
ISLAND 8-10 77
MCA 5-8
W.B. 8-10 73-74

OSIRIS R&B '79

Singles: 7-inch

INFINITY 3-5 79
W.B. 3-5 79

LPs: 10/12-inch

INFINITY 5-10 79
W.B. 5-10 79
Members: Osiris Marsh.

OSKAR, Lee P&R/R&B/LP '76

Singles: 7-inch

ELEKTRA 3-5 78-81
U.A. 3-5 76

LPs: 10/12-inch

ELEKTRA 5-10 78-79
U.A. 8-10 76
Also see WAR

OSMOND, Donny P&R/LP '71

Singles: 7-inch

CAPITOL 3-4 89
MGM 3-5 71-75
POLYDOR 3-5 76-78

Picture Sleeves

CAPITOL 3-4 89
MGM 3-5 71-75

LPs: 10/12-inch

CAPITOL 5-8 89-90
MGM 8-10 71-74
POLYDOR 5-10 76-77
Also see OSMONDS

OSMOND, Donny & Marie P&R/LP '74

Singles: 7-inch

MGM 3-5 74-75
POLYDOR 3-5 76-78

LPs: 10/12-inch

MGM 8-10 74-75
POLYDOR 5-10 76-78
Also see D&M
Also see OSMOND, Donny
Also see OSMOND, Marie

OSMOND, Jimmy P&R/LP '72

(Little Jimmy Osmond)

Singles: 7-inch

MGM 3-5 70-75
MERCURY 3-5 78

LPs: 10/12-inch

MGM 8-10 72
Also see OSMONDS

OSMOND, Marie C&W/P&R/LP '73

(Marie)

Singles: 7-inch

CURB 3-4 90
CURB/CAPITOL 3-5 85-89
ELEKTRA/CURB 3-5 82-84
MGM 3-5 73-75
POLYDOR 3-5 76-78

RCA/CURB 3-5 84

Picture Sleeves

MGM 3-5 73-75
POLYDOR 3-5 77
RCA 3-5 84

LPs: 10/12-inch

CURB/CAPITOL 5-8 85-88
MGM 8-12 73-75
POLYDOR 5-8 77

Also see OSMOND, Donny & Marie
Also see OSMONDS

OSMOND, Marie, & Paul Davis
C&W '86

Singles: 7-inch

CAPITOL 3-4 86-88

Also see DAVIS, Paul

OSMOND, Marie, & Osmond Brothers

LPs: 10/12-inch

UNITED (12924 "Our Best to You") 5-10 85
(Special products promotional issue, made for Case International.)

Also see OSMONDS

OSMOND, Marie, & Dan Seals
C&W '85

Singles: 7-inch

CURB/CAPITOL 3-4 85

Also see OSMOND, Marie
Also see SEALS, Dan

OSMONDS
P&R/R&B/LP '71

(Osmond Brothers)

Singles: 7-inch

BARNABY 4-6 68-69
CURB/EMI 3-4 85-86
EMI AMERICA 3-4 85-86
ELEKTRA/CURB 3-5 82-83
MGM (13126 thru 14159) 4-6 63-70
MGM (14193 thru 14831) 3-5 70-75
MERCURY 3-5 79
POLYDOR 3-5 76-77
UNI (55015 "I Can't Stop") 4-8 67
UNI (55276 "I Can't Stop") 3-5 71
W.B./CURB 3-5 83-85

Picture Sleeves

MGM 3-5 73-74

LPs: 10/12-inch

EMI AMERICA 5-8 86
ELEKTRA 5-10 82
MGM (7 "Preview – the Osmond Brothers") 15-20 70s
(Promotional issue only.)
MGM (4100 & 4200 series) 25-35 63-65
MGM (4724 thru 5012) 8-12 70-75
MERCURY 5-10 79
METRO 10-20 65
POLYDOR 5-10 76-77
W.B./CURB 5-8 83-85

Members: Donny Osmond; Alan Osmond; Merrill Osmond; Wayne Osmond; Jimmy Osmond; Marie Osmond.

Also see CURB, Mike
Also see OSMOND, Donny
Also see OSMOND, Jimmy
Also see OSMOND, Marie

OSMONDS, Steve Lawrence & Eydie Gorme
P&R '72

Singles: 7-inch

MGM 3-5 72

Also see LAWRENCE, Steve, & Eydie Gorme
Also see OSMONDS

O'SULLIVAN, Gilbert
P&R/LP '72

Singles: 7-inch

EPIC 3-5 77-81
MAM 3-8 71-76

Picture Sleeves

MAM 3-5 72

LPs: 10/12-inch

EPIC 5-10 81
MAM 10-15 72-73

OTHER ONES
P&R/LP '87

Singles: 7-inch

VIRGIN 3-4 87

Picture Sleeves

VIRGIN 3-4 87

LPs: 10/12-inch

VIRGIN 5-8 87

Members: Alf Klimek; Johnny Klimek; Steven Gottwald; Andreas Schwartz-Ruszczynski.

OTIS, Johnny
R&B '50

(Johnny Otis Show; Quintette; with Peacocks; with Debbie Lindsay; with Barbara Morrison)

Singles: 78 rpm

CAPITOL 10-25 57
DIG 10-25 55-57
EXCELSIOR 15-25 45-47
MERCURY 10-25 51-53
PEACOCK (Except 1625) 10-25 52
PEACOCK (1625 "Young Girl") 20-40 52
REGENT 10-25 50-51
SAVOY 10-20 50-54

Singles: 7-inch

CAPITOL (3799-3802 "The Johnny Otis Show") 400-600 57
(Four discs with special four-pocket cover.)
CAPITOL (3799 thru 3802) 15-25 57
(Price for four records without cover.)
CAPITOL (3852 "Good Golly") 15-25 57
CAPITOL (3966 "Willie and the Hand Jive"/ "Ring-A-Ling") 15-25 58
CAPITOL (3966 "Willie and the Hand Jive"/ "Willie and the Hand Jive") 20-40 58
(Blue label. Promotional issue only.)
CAPITOL (4060 "Crazy Country Hop") 15-25 58
CAPITOL (4168 "Castin' My Spell") 15-25 59
(Monaural.)
CAPITOL (S-4168 "Castin' My Spell") 25-50 59
(Stereo.)
CAPITOL (4226 thru 4326) 10-20 59-60
DIG (119 "Let the Sunshine in My Life") 25-50 56
DIG (122 "Midnight Creeper") 25-50 56
DIG (131 "Tough Enough") 25-50 57
DIG (132 "My Eyes Are Full of Tears") 25-50 57
DIG (134 "Wa-Wa") 25-50 57
DIG (139 "The Night Is Young") 25-50 57
ELDO (105 "The New Bo Diddley") 10-20 60
ELDO (153 "Long Distance") 5-10 67
EPIC 3-5 70
HAWK SOUND 3-5 75
IT WILL STAND 3-5 82
JAZZ WORLD 3-5 78
KENT 4-6 69
KING 8-12 61-63
MERCURY (8263 "Oopy Doo") 50-75 51
MERCURY (8273 "Goomp Blues") 50-75 51
MERCURY (8289 "Call Operator 210") 50-75 52
MERCURY (8295 "Gypsy Blues") 50-75 52
MERCURY (70038 "Why Don't You Believe Me") 50-75 52
MERCURY (70050 "The Love Bug Boogie") 30-50 52
OKEH 4-6 69
PEACOCK (1625 "Young Girl") 50-75 52
PEACOCK (1636 "Shake It") 25-50 52
PEACOCK (1648 "Sittin' Here Drinkin'") 25-50 52
PEACOCK (1675 "Butterball") 25-50 52
RED HOT 15-25
REGENT (1036 "Hangover Blues") 20-40 51
SAVOY 20-40 50-54

EPs: 7-inch

CAPITOL (940 "Johnny Otis Show") 75-100 58
CAPITOL (1134 "Johnny Otis") 50-75 59
RITZ-EE (5214 Blackouts of 1959) 40-60 59
(Has one Otis track, *Backstage at the Blackouts*. Promotional issue only. Not issued with cover.)

LPs: 10/12-inch

ALLIGATOR (4726 "The New Johnny Otis Show") 5-10 82
BLUES SPECTRUM 10-15
CAPITOL (940 "Johnny Otis Show") 150-250 58
DIG (104 "Rock & Roll Hit Parade") 500-750 57
(Gold cover. Counterfeits of Dig 104 exist, some of which have a yellow cover. Others have a gold cover. Regardless, the discs of originals are noticeably thicker than is used on the fakes.)
EPIC 10-15 70-71
JAZZ WORLD 5-10 78
KENT 10-20 70
RED HOT 5-10
SAVOY 5-10 78-80

Referenced below are some of the artists who performed with the Johnny Otis Show, or with whom he or his orchestra appears.

Also see ACE, Johnny
Also see ADAMS, Marie
Also see ALLEN, Tony
Also see FREEMAN, Ernie
Also see JACQUET, Illinois
Also see McNEELY, Big Jay
Also see RUSHING, Jimmy
Also see WATSON, Johnny

OTIS, Johnny, & Preston Love

Singles: 7-inch

KENT 3-5 70

Also see OTIS, Shuggie, & Preston Love

OTIS, Johnny, Orchestra, with Little Esther & Mel Walker
R&B '50

Singles: 78 rpm

REGENT 20-40 51
SAVOY 20-40 50-51

Singles: 7-inch

REGENT (1036 "I Dream") 50-75 51
SAVOY (750 "Cupid's Boogie") 50-75 50
SAVOY (775 "Love Will Break Your Heart") 50-75 51

Also see LITTLE ESTHER & Mel Walker

OTIS, Johnny, Quintette, with Little Esther & Robins
R&B '50

Singles: 78 rpm

SAVOY 40-60 50

Singles: 7-inch

SAVOY (731 "Double Crossing Blues") 75-100 50

Also see LITTLE ESTHER
Also see OTIS, Johnny
Also see ROBINS

OTIS, Shuggie
LP '70

Singles: 7-inch

EPIC 3-5 70-75

LPs: 10/12-inch

EPIC 10-15 70-75

Also see KOOPER, Al, & Shuggie Otis

OTIS, Shuggie, & Preston Love

Singles: 7-inch

KENT 3-5 70

Also see OTIS, Johnny, & Preston Love
Also see OTIS, Shuggie

OTIS & CARLA
P&R/R&B/LP '67

Singles: 7-inch

ATCO 4-6 69
STAX 5-10 67-68

LPs: 10/12-inch

STAX 10-20 67

Members: Otis Redding; Carla Thomas.

Also see REDDING, Otis
Also see THOMAS, Carla

OUTFIELD
LP '85

Singles: 7-inch

COLUMBIA 3-4 85-87

Picture Sleeves

COLUMBIA 3-4 86-87

LPs: 10/12-inch

COLUMBIA 5-8 85-87

Members: Tony Lewis; Alan Jackman; John Spinks.

OUTLAWS LP '76

Singles: 7-inch

ARISTA....3-5 75-83

LPs: 10/12-inch

ARISTA....5-10 75-83
DIRECT DISC (16617 "Outlaws")....15-25 80s
(Half-speed mastered.)
PASHA....5-8 86
PEAR....8-12 84
Members: Hughie Thomasson; Henry Paul; David Dix; Billy Jones; Fred Salem; Rick Cua; David Dix; Harvey Dalton Arnold; Frank O'Keefe; Monte Yoho; Chuck Glass; Steve Grisham.
Also see PAUL, Henry, Band

OUTPUT R&B '84

Singles: 12-inch

CBS ASSOCIATED....4-6 83

Singles: 7-inch

CBS ASSOCIATED....3-5 83
TUFF CITY....3-4 84

OUTSIDERS P&R/LP '66

Singles: 7-inch

BELL....4-6 70
CAPITOL....5-10 66-68
KAPP....4-6 70

Picture Sleeves

CAPITOL....8-12 66-67

LPs: 10/12-inch

CAPITOL....20-30 66-67
Members: Sonny Geraci; Bill Bruno; Tom King; Rickey Baker; Merdin Madsen.
Also see CLIMAX

OVATIONS P&R/R&B '65
(Ovation)

Singles: 7-inch

CHESS....3-5 75
GOLDWAX....8-12 64-69
MGM....4-6 73
SOUNDS of MEMPHIS....4-6 72-73

LPs: 10/12-inch

MGM....10-15 73
SOUNDS of MEMPHIS....10-20 72
Members: George Jackson; Louis Williams; Bill Davis; Rochester Neal; Quincy Billops Jr.
Also see JACKSON, George

OVERBEA, Danny R&B '53

Singles: 78 rpm

CHECKER....25-50 53-55

Singles: 7-inch

APEX (7751 "Don't Laugh At Me")....10-20 59
CHECKER (774 "40 Cups of Coffee")....50-100 53
(Black vinyl.)
CHECKER (774 "40 Cups of Coffee")....150-200 53
(Colored vinyl.)
CHECKER (768 "Train Train Train")....75-125 53
CHECKER (784 "Sorrento")....75-125 54
CHECKER (788 "Stomp and Whistle")....75-125 54
CHECKER (796 "Roamin' Man")....75-125 54
CHECKER (808 "A Toast to Lovers")....75-125 55
CHECKER (816 "Hey, Pancho")....50-100 55
FEDERAL (12434 "Book of Tears")..10-20 61
SHEP (101 "Like Crazy")....10-20 60

OVERKILL LP '87

LPs: 10/12-inch

MEGAFORCE....5-8 87-89

OVERLANDERS P&R '64

Singles: 7-inch

HICKORY....10-15 64-66
MERCURY....5-10 63

OVERTON, C.B. R&B '78

Singles: 7-inch

SHOCK....3-5 78

OWEN-B P&R '70

Singles: 7-inch

JANUS....3-5 70

LPs: 10/12-inch

MUS-I-COL (101209 "Owen-B")....40-60 70

OWEN, Reg, & His Orch. P&R '58

Singles: 7-inch

PALETTE....4-6 58-62

EPs: 7-inch

RCA....5-10 50s

LPs: 10/12-inch

PALETTE....15-25 59-60

OWENS, Buck C&W '59
(With the Buckaroos)

Singles: 78 rpm

CAPITOL....25-50 57

Singles: 7-inch

CAPITOL (2000 thru 4000 series)....3-8 67-75
(Orange label.)
CAPITOL (3824 "Come Back")....15-25 57
(Purple label.)
CAPITOL (3957 "Sweet Thing")....15-25 58
(Purple label.)
CAPITOL (4000 series)....8-15 59-63
(Purple or orange/yellow label.)
CAPITOL (5000 series)....3-6 63-67
CHESTERFIELD (44223 "Leavin' Dirty Tracks")....15-25 60s
HILLTOP (6027 "Hot Dog")....25-50 60s
NEW STAR (6418 "Hot Dog")....100-150 58
PEP (105 "Down on the Corner of Love")....25-50 56
PEP (106 "Right After the Dance")...25-50 56
PEP (109 "There Goes My Love")....25-50 57
STARDAY (588 "Down on the Corner of Love")....10-20 61
STARDAY (5000 series)....4-8 64
W.B. (Except 8316)....3-6 76-80
W.B. (8316 "World Famous Holiday Inn")....5-10 77
W.B. (8316 "World Famous Paradise Inn")....3-5 77
(Note title change.)

Picture Sleeves

CAPITOL....10-25 66-69

EPs: 7-inch

CAPITOL....15-30 61-65

LPs: 10/12-inch

BUCKBOARD....5-10
CAPITOL (131 thru 550 series)....10-20 69-70
CAPITOL (574 "Buck Owens")....20-30 70
(Three-disc set.)
CAPITOL (628 thru 860)....10-15 70-72
CAPITOL (T-1482 thru T-1989)....30-40 61-63
(Monaural.)
CAPITOL (ST-1482 thru ST-1989)...35-50 61-63
(Stereo.)
CAPITOL (DT-1400 series)....10-20 69
CAPITOL (2100 thru 2700 series)....12-25 64-67
CAPITOL (2800 thru 2900 series)....10-20 68
CAPITOL (2980 "Buck Owens Minute Masters")....30-40 66
(Promotional issue only.)
CAPITOL (11000 series)....5-8 72-78
COUNTRY FIDELITY....?? 83
GUEST STAR....8-12 60s
HALL of MUSIC....8-12
LA BREA (8017 "Buck Owens")...100-200 61
OUT of TOWN DIST....5-8 82
PICKWICK/HILLTOP....5-10 78
SPRINGBOARD....5-10
STARDAY (172 "Fabulous Country Music Sound of Buck Owens")....15-25 62
STARDAY (300 series)....15-20 64-65
STARDAY (400 series)....10-15 75
STARPAK....5-8 79
SUNRISE MEDIA....?? 81
TIME-LIFE....5-10 82
TRIP....5-8 76
W.B. 5-10 76-77
Also see JONES, Corky
Also see JONES, George / Buck Owens / David Houston / Tommy Hill.
Also see YOAKAM, Dwight, & Buck Owens

OWENS, Buck, & Buddy Alan
(Buck & Buddy; with the Buckaroos) C&W '68

Singles: 7-inch

CAPITOL....4-6 68

OWENS, Buck / Tennessee Ernie Ford

LPs: 10/12-inch

CAPITOL (6720 "Music Hall")....8-12
Also see FORD, Tennessee Ernie

OWENS, Buck, & Emmylou Harris

Singles: 7-inch

W.B. 3-4 79
Also see HARRIS, Emmylou

OWENS, Buck, & Rose Maddox C&W '63

Singles: 7-inch

CAPITOL....5-8 63

OWENS, Buck, & Susan Raye C&W/LP '70

Singles: 7-inch

CAPITOL....3-5 70-73

LPs: 10/12-inch

CAPITOL....5-10 70-73
Also see RAYE, Susan

OWENS, Buck, & Ringo Starr C&W '89

Singles: 7-inch

CAPITOL (79805 "Gonna Have Love")....5-8 89
(Commercial issue.)
CAPITOL (79805 "Gonna Have Love")....8-10 89
(Promotional issue.)
Also see STARR, Ringo

OWENS, Buck / Faron Young / Ferlin Husky

LPs: 10/12-inch

PICKWICK/HILLTOP....8-12 65
Also see HUSKY, Ferlin
Also see OWENS, Buck
Also see YOUNG, Faron

OWENS, Donnie P&R '58
(Donny Owens)

Singles: 7-inch

ARA....4-8
GUYDEN....10-15 58-59
TREY....5-10 60
Also see EDDY, Duane

OWENS, Gwen R&B '69

Singles: 7-inch

BIG TREE....3-5 79
JOSIE....4-6 69

OWENS, Tony R&B '71

Singles: 7-inch

COTILLION....4-6 71
SOUL SOUND....10-20

OXO P&R/LP '83

Singles: 7-inch

GEFFEN....3-4 83

LPs: 10/12-inch

GEFFEN....5-8 83
Also see FOXY

OZARK MOUNTAIN DAREDEVILS P&R/LP '74

Singles: 7-inch

A&M....3-5 74-78
COLUMBIA....3-5 80

Picture Sleeves

A&M....3-5 75-76

LPs: 10/12-inch

A&M....8-12 73-78
COLUMBIA....5-10 80

OZO P&R '76

Singles: 7-inch

DJM....3-5 76

LPs: 10/12–inch

DJM 5-10 76

OZONE *R&B '80*

Singles: 7–inch

MOTOWN 3-5 80-83

LPs: 10/12–inch

MOTOWN 5-10 80-83

Members: Jimmy Stewart; Charles Glenn; Benny Wallace; Thomas Bumpass; Ray Woodward; William White; Greg Hargrove; Paul Hines.

OZUNA, Sunny: see SUNGLOWS

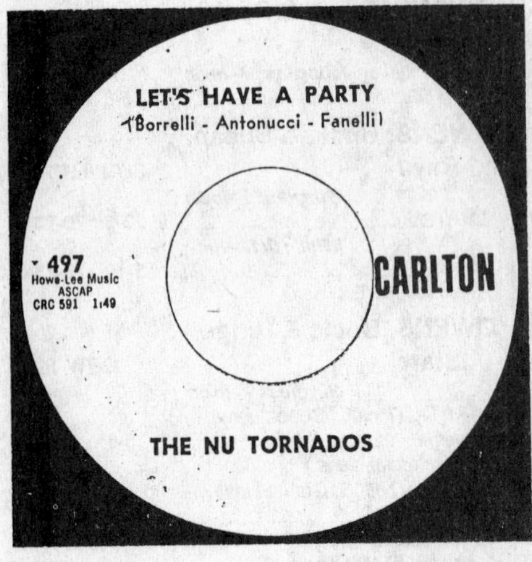

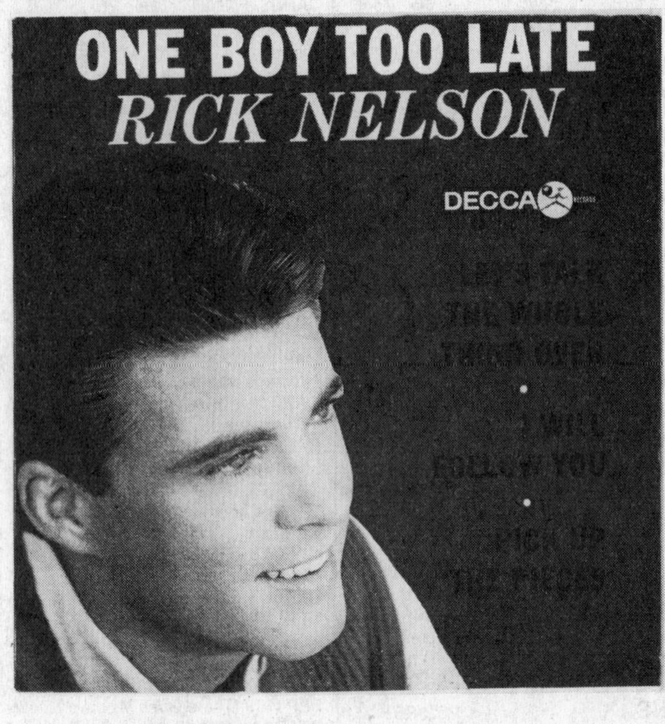

P.F.M. LP '73
(Premiata Forneria Marconi)

Singles: 7-inch
ASYLUM....3-5 76-77
MANTICORE....3-5 73-75
LPs: 10/12-inch
ASYLUM....5-10 76-77
MANTICORE....8-12 73-74
PETERS INT'L....5-10 76

P CREW R&B '83
Singles: 7-inch
PRELUDE....3-4 83

P. FUNK ALL-STARS R&B '82
Singles: 12-inch
UNCLE JAM....4-6 84
Singles: 7-inch
CBS ASSOCIATED....3-4 83
HUMP....3-5 82
UNCLE JAM....3-4 84
LPs: 10/12-inch
CBS ASSOCIATED....5-8 84
UNCLE JAM....5-8 84

PG&E: see PACIFIC GAS & ELECTRIC

PABLO CRUISE LP '75
Singles: 7-inch
A&M....3-5 75-84
Picture Sleeves
A&M....3-5 77-84
LPs: 10/12-inch
A&M....5-10 75-84
MFSL (029 "A Place in the Sun")....25-35 79
(Half-speed mastered.)
NAUTILUS....10-20 81
Members: Dave Jenkins; Steven Price; Cory Lerios; Bud Cockrell.
Also see IT'S a BEAUTIFUL DAY

PACIFIC GAS & ELECTRIC LP '69
(PG&E; Pacific Gas & Electric Blues Band)

Singles: 7-inch
BRIGHT ORANGE....5-10 68
COLUMBIA....3-6 69-72
POWER....5-10 69
LPs: 10/12-inch
ABC....8-10 70s
BRIGHT ORANGE (701 "Get It On") 40-80 68
COLUMBIA....8-12 69-73
KENT (547 "Get It On")....10-20 68
POWER....10-15 69
Members: Charlie Allen; Frank Cook; Brent Block; Tom Marshall; Glenn Schwartz.
Also see SEEGER, Pete, & Pacific Gas & Electric

PACK, David P&R '86
Singles: 7-inch
W.B. 3-4 86
LPs: 10/12-inch
W.B. 5-8 86
Also see AMBROSIA
Also see McDONALD, Michael
Also see PARSONS, Alan, Project
Also see TREFETHEN

PACKERS P&R/R&B '65
Singles: 7-inch
HBR....4-8 66
IMPERIAL....4-6 69
PURE SOUL MUSIC....4-8 65
SOUL BABY....4-8 60s
TAG LTD.....4-8 67
TANGERINE....4-8 68
LPs: 10/12-inch
IMPERIAL....10-15 68
PURE SOUL MUSIC....15-20 66
Member: Charles Axton.
Also see MAR-KEYS

PAGAN, Bruni R&B '79
Singles: 7-inch
ELEKTRA....3-5 79

PAGAN, Ralfi R&B '71
Singles: 7-inch
FANIA....3-5 71
Also see SYLVIA & Ralfi Pagan

PAGE, Gene LP '75
Singles: 7-inch
ARISTA....3-5 78-80
ATLANTIC....3-5 74-75
LPs: 10/12-inch
ARISTA....5-10 78-80
ATLANTIC....8-12 74-75

PAGE, Jimmy LP '82
Singles: 7-inch
GEFFEN....3-4 88
Picture Sleeves
GEFFEN....4-6 88
(Promotional issue only.)
LPs: 10/12-inch
GEFFEN....5-8 88
SWAN SONG....5-10 82
Also see CARTOONE
Also see CLAPTON, Eric, Jeff Beck & Jimmy Page
Also see FIRM
Also see HERMAN'S HERMITS
Also see HONEYDRIPPERS
Also see LED ZEPPELIN
Also see LORD SUTCH
Also see STEWART, Al
Also see WILLIE & Poor Boys
Also see YARDBIRDS

PAGE, Jimmy, & Robert Plant
LPs: 10/12-inch
W.B. (62706 "No Quarter")....10-15 94
Also see PLANT, Robert

PAGE, Jimmy, and Sonny Boy Williamson
LPs: 10/12-inch
SPRINGBOARD....10-20 72
Also see WILLIAMSON, Sonny Boy, & Yardbirds

PAGE, Patti
(With Al Clauser & the Oklahomans)

Singles: 78 rpm
OKLA (66 "My Sweet Papa")....5-10 40s
(Listed primarily to distinguish this singer from the following Patti Page.)

PAGE, Patti P&R '48
(With the George Barnes Trio; with Jack Rael Quartet/Orchestra)

Singles: 78 rpm
MERCURY (A-95 thru A-1025)....5-15 50-52
(Boxed set of singles.)
MERCURY (505 "Confess")....5-10 50
MERCURY (5061 thru 5899)....5-10 47-52
MERCURY (70025 thru 71101)....5-10 52-57
MERCURY (71177 thru 71331)....10-20 57-58
PLAYCRAFT....5-10 53-55
Singles: 7-inch
AVCO....3-5 74-75
COLUMBIA....4-6 62-70
EPIC....3-5 73-74
LANGWORTH....10-20 49
(Eight-inch, 33 rpm transcriptions.)
MERCURY (A-95 thru A-1025)....10-20 50-52
(Boxed set of singles.)
MERCURY (505 "Confess")....10-15 50
MERCURY (5344 thru 5899)....10-15 50-52
MERCURY (7000 series)....5-15 61
(Compact 33 stereo.)
MERCURY (10000 series)....5-10 58-60
(Stereo.)
MERCURY (30000 series)....5-10 58
MERCURY (70025 thru 72123)....5-15 52-62
MERCURY (73000 series)....3-5 70-72
PLANTATION....3-5 81-83
(Black vinyl.)
PLANTATION....4-8 81-83
(Colored vinyl.)
PLAYCRAFT....5-10 53-55
Picture Sleeves
MERCURY....10-20 54-63
EPs: 7-inch
MERCURY....8-18 52-61
PLAYCRAFT....5-10 59
LPs: 10/12-inch
ACCORD....5-10 82
AHED....5-8 76
BRYLEN....5-8 82
CANDLELITE....8-12 73
COLUMBIA (Except "CL" & "CS" series)....8-15 70-77
COLUMBIA (CL-2049 thru 2761)....10-20 63-68
(Monaural.)
COLUMBIA (CS-8849 thru 9999)....15-25 63-69
(Stereo.)
EMARCY (2-100 "The East Side – The West Side")....50-80 58
(Two LPs.)
EMARCY (36074 "In the Land of Hi Fi")....40-60 56
(No Mercury logo on cover or label.)
EMARCY (36074 "In the Land of Hi Fi")....30-40 58
(Mercury logo on cover and label.)
EMARCY (80000 "In the Land of Hi Fi")....35-45 58
(Stereo.)
EMARCY (36116 "West Side")....20-30 58
(Monaural.)
EMARCY (36136 "East Side")....20-30 58
(Monaural.)
EMARCY (60113 "East Side")....20-30 59
(Stereo.)
EMARCY (60114 "West Side")....20-30 59
(Stereo.)
EVEREST....5-8 83
EXACT....5-8 80
51 WEST....5-8 79
GOOD MUSIC....5-8 85
HARMONY....5-10 69-70
HARTLAND....5-8 86
HINDSIGHT....5-8 86
IMPACT....5-8 79
MERCURY (100 series)....8-12 69
MERCURY (20076 thru 20226)....20-40 55-56
MERCURY (20318 thru 20952)....15-30 57-64
(Monaural.)
MERCURY (25059 thru 25210)....20-40 50-54
(10-inch LPs.)
MERCURY (60049 thru 60011)....20-40 57-58
(Stereo.)
MERCURY (60025 thru 60952)....20-35 58-64
(Stereo.)
MERCURY (61344 "I'd Rather Be Sorry")....10-20 71
PAIR....5-8 87
PICKWICK....5-8 72
PILLSBURY (001 "Big Records")....15-25 57
(Special products issue made for Pillsbury.)
PLANTATION....5-10 81-82
PLAYCRAFT (1300 "Patti Page")....15-25 58
SUFFOLK....5-8 88
WING (2-100 series)....5-12 72
WING (12121 thru 12174)....10-20 58-59
(Monaural.)
WING (12250 thru 12295)....5-12 65
(Monaural.)
WING (16000 series)....5-15 61-68
(Stereo.)
Also see MARTIN, Dean / Patti Page

PAGE, Patti, & Rex Allen
Singles: 78 rpm
MERCURY....5-10 50
EPs: 7-inch
MERCURY....5-15 53
Also see ALLEN, Rex

PAGE, Patti, & Vic Damone

Singles: 78 rpm

MERCURY 5-10 48

Also see DAMONE, Vic

PAGE, Patti, & Rusty Draper

EPs: 7-inch

MERCURY 5-15 53
PLAYCRAFT 5-10 59

Also see DRAPER, Rusty

PAGE, Patti, & Tom T. Hall C&W '72

Singles: 7-inch

MERCURY 3-5 72

Also see HALL, Tom T.
Also see PAGE, Patti

PAGE, Tommy P&R/LP '89

Singles: 7-inch

SIRE 3-4 89-90

Picture Sleeves

SIRE 3-4 89

LPs: 10/12-inch

SIRE 5-8 89-90

Also see NEW KIDS on the BLOCK

PAGES P&R '79

Singles: 7-inch

CAPITOL 3-5 81
EPIC 3-5 79-80

LPs: 10/12-inch

CAPITOL 5-10 81
EPIC 5-10 78-79

Members: Richard Page; Steve George; Russell Battelene; Jerry Manfredi; Peter Leinheiser.

Also see MR. MISTER

PAIGE, Kevin P&R/LP '89

Singles: 7-inch

CHRYSALIS 3-4 89

Picture Sleeves

CHRYSALIS 3-4 89

LPs: 10/12-inch

CHRYSALIS 5-8 89

PAIGE, Sharon P&R '75

(With Harold Melvin & the Bluenotes)

Singles: 7-inch

PHILADELPHIA INT'L 3-5 75
SOURCE 3-5 80

Also see MELVIN, Harold

PAINTER P&R '73

Singles: 7-inch

ELEKTRA 3-5 73

LPs: 10/12-inch

ELEKTRA 8-12 73

PAJAMA PARTY P&R '89

Singles: 7-inch

ATLANTIC 3-4 89

LPs: 10/12-inch

ATLANTIC 5-8 89

PALLAS, Laura D&D '84

Singles: 12-inch

TVI 4-6 84

PALM BEACH BAND BOYS LP '67

Singles: 7-inch

RCA 3-6 66-67

LPs: 10/12-inch

RCA 5-10 66-67

PALMER, Gladys R&B '47

Singles: 78 rpm

MIRACLE 10-20 47

PALMER, Robert LP '75

Singles: 12-inch

ISLAND 4-6 83-86

Singles: 7-inch

EMI/MANHATTAN 3-4 88
ISLAND 3-5 75-86

Picture Sleeves

EMI/MANHATTAN 3-4 88
ISLAND 3-5 83-88

LPs: 10/12-inch

EMI 5-8 88-90
ISLAND (Except 819) 5-10 75-86
ISLAND (819 "Secrets") 35-40 79
(Picture disc. Promotional issue only.)

Also see BOWN, Alan
Also see POWER STATION

PAMPLEMOUSSE, LE: see LE PAMPLEMOUSSE

PANIC BUTTON R&B '69

Singles: 7-inch

CHALOM 4-8 68
GAMBLE 4-6 69

PAONE, Nicola P&R '59

Singles: 7-inch

ABC-PAR 3-6 59
CADENCE 3-6 59

EPs: 7-inch

CADENCE 5-10 59

LPs: 10/12-inch

ABC-PAR 10-20 59-60
ROULETTE 10-15 65

PAPER LACE P&R/LP '74

Singles: 7-inch

BANG 3-5 72
MERCURY 3-5 74-75

LPs: 10/12-inch

MERCURY 8-10 74

PARACHUTE CLUB D&D '83

Singles: 12-inch

RCA 4-6 83

Singles: 7-inch

RCA 3-4 83

LPs: 10/12-inch

RCA 5-8 83

PARADE P&R '67

Singles: 7-inch

A&M 4-8 67-69

Members: Jerry Riopelle; Murray MacLeod; Smokey Roberds.

Also see RIOPELLE, Jerry

PARADISE EXPRESS P&R '79

Singles: 12-inch

FANTASY 4-8 78-81

Singles: 7-inch

FANTASY 3-5 78-81

LPs: 10/12-inch

FANTASY 5-10 78

PARADONS P&R/R&B '60

(With the Rockets Combo)

Singles: 7-inch

COLLECTABLES 3-4 80s
ERA 3-5 72
MILESTONE (2003 "Diamonds and Pearls") 15-20 60
(Maroon label.)
MILESTONE (2003 "Diamonds and Pearls") 10-15 60
(Red label.)
MILESTONE (2003 "Diamonds and Pearls") 5-10 60
(Green label.)
MILESTONE (2005 "Bells Ring") 15-20 60
MILESTONE (2015 "I Had a Dream") 25-35 62
TUFFEST (102 "Never Again") 75-125 61
W.B. (5186 "Take All of Me") 10-15 61

Members: Bill Myers; Chuck Weldon; Wes Tyler; Bill Powers.

PARAGONS P&R '61

("Featuring Mack Starr")

Singles: 7-inch

ABC 3-5 73
BUDDAH 3-5 75
COLLECTABLES 3-4 80s
LOST-NITE 4-8
MUSIC CLEF (3001 "Time After Time") 15-25 63
MUSICRAFT (1102 "Wedding Bells") 20-30 60
(Maroon label.)
MUSICRAFT (1102 "Wedding Bells") 15-25 60
(Red label.)
TAP (500 "If") 40-60 61
TAP (503 "Begin the Beguine") 25-50 61
TAP (504 "If You Love Me") 25-50 61
TIMES SQUARE (9 "So You Will Know") 15-25 63
VIRGO 3-5 72-73
WINLEY (215 "Florence") 50-100 57
(Has "Winley" in 3/8-inch letters.)
WINLEY (215 "Florence") 50-75 61
(Has "Winley" in 1/4-inch, sans serif letters.)
WINLEY (215 "Florence") 20-30 61
(Has "Winley" in 1/4-inch, serif letters.)
WINLEY (215 "Florence") 10-20 61
(Has "Winley" in 5/8-inch letters.)
WINLEY (220 "Let's Start All Over Again") 50-100 57
(Has "Winley" in 3/8-inch letters.)
WINLEY (220 "Let's Start All Over Again") 20-30 61
(Has "Winley" in 1/4-inch letters.)
WINLEY (223 "Two Hearts Are Better Than One") 50-100 58
(Has title in all upper case letters.)
WINLEY (223 "Two Hearts Are Better Than One") 20-30 61
(Has title in upper and lower case letters.)
WINLEY (227 "Twilight"/"The Wows of Love") 1000-1500 58
(Note spelling error on "Vows.")
WINLEY (227 "Twilight"/"The Vows of Love") 20-30 61
(Title error corrected.)
WINLEY (228 "So You Will Know") 25-50 59
(Has "Winley" in 3/8-inch letters.)
WINLEY (228 "So You Will Know") 20-30 61
(Has "Winley" in 1/4-inch letters.)
WINLEY (236 "Darling, I Love You") 25-50 59
WINLEY (240 "So You Will Know") 20-30 60
WINLEY (250 "Just a Memorie") 100-200 61
(Note spelling error on "Memory.")
WINLEY (250 "Just a Memory") 20-30 61
(Title error corrected.")

LPs: 10/12-inch

COLLECTABLES 6-8 86
LOST-NITE 8-12 81
RARE BIRD (8002 "Simply the Paragons") 35-50

Members: Julius McMichaels; Mack Starr; Al Brown; Don Travis; Ben Frazier; Bill Witt; Rick Jackson. Session: Dave "Baby" Cortez.

Also see CORTEZ, Dave "Baby"
Also see HARPTONES / Paragons
Also see JESTERS / Paragons
Also see OLYMPICS

PARAMOR, Norrie, & His Orch. LP '56

Singles: 78 rpm

ESSEX 3-6 53

Singles: 7-inch

ESSEX 5-10 53

EPs: 7-inch

CAPITOL 8-15 56

LPs: 10/12-inch

CAPITOL 10-25 55-66
ESSEX 10-20 54
HAYNES & BARRA 5-10 79

PARAMOURS

Singles: 7-inch

MOONGLOW (214 "There She Goes") 25-50 62
(Black vinyl.)
MOONGLOW (214 "There She Goes") 50-100 62
(Colored vinyl.)
SMASH (1701 "That's the Way We Love") 10-20 61
SMASH (1718 "Cutie Cutie") 10-20 61

Members: Bill Medley; Bobby Hatfield.
Also see RIGHTEOUS BROTHERS

PARIS LP '76

Singles: 7-inch

CAPITOL 3-5 76

LPs: 10/12-inch

CAPITOL 8-12 76

Members: Bob Welch; Glen Cornick; Bernie Marsden; Thom Mooney.
Also see WELCH, Bob

PARIS LP '90

LPs: 10/12-inch

TOMMY BOY 5-8 90

PARIS, Mica P&R/LP '89

Singles: 7-inch

ISLAND 3-4 89

Picture Sleeves

ISLAND 3-4 89

LPs: 10/12-inch

ISLAND 5-8 89

PARIS SISTERS P&R '61

Singles: 78 rpm

CAVALIER 10-15
DECCA 10-15 54-56
IMPERIAL 10-15 57-58

Singles: 7-inch

ABC 3-5 73
CAPITOL 4-8 68
CAVALIER (828 "Bully, Bully Man") 15-25 53
CAVALIER (829 "Christmas in My Home Town") 15-25 53
COLLECTABLES 3-4 80s
DECCA (29000 series) 15-25 54-56
DECCA (30554 "Don't Tell Anybody") 10-20 58
ERIC 3-4 70s
GNP 5-8 68
GREGMARK (2 "Be My Boy") 15-25 61
GREGMARK (6 "I Love How You Love Me") 15-25 61
GREGMARK (10 "He Knows I Love Him Too Much") 15-25 61
GREGMARK (12 "Let Me Be the One") 15-25 62
GREGMARK (13 "Yes I Love You") .. 15-25 62
IMPERIAL (5465 "Old Enough to Cry") 10-20 57
IMPERIAL (5487 "Someday") 10-20 58
MGM 5-10 64
MERCURY 5-10 64-65
REPRISE 5-10 66-67

Picture Sleeves

MGM 10-20 64
MERCURY 8-10 64

LPs: 10/12-inch

REPRISE (R-6259 "Everything Under the Sun") 15-20 67
(Monaural.)
REPRISE (RS-6259 "Everything Under the Sun") 20-25 67
(Stereo.)
SIDEWALK 12-18
UNIFILMS 10-15

Members: Priscilla Paris; Sherrell Paris; Albeth Paris. Session: Davie Allan.
Also see ALLAN, Davie

PARKAYS P&R '61

Singles: 7-inch

ABC-PAR 5-10 61
FONTANA 4-8 65

PARKER, Bobby P&R '61

Singles: 7-inch

AMANDA (1001 "Foolish Love") 50-75 60
V-TONE (223 "Watch Your Step") 10-15 61

PARKER, Fess P&R '55
(With Buddy Ebsen)

Singles: 78 rpm

COLUMBIA 4-8 55
DISNEYLAND 5-10 57

Singles: 7-inch

BUENA VISTA 4-8 63
CASCADE 5-10 59
COLUMBIA 8-12 55
DISNEYLAND 5-10 57
GUSTO 4-8 63
RCA 4-8 64-69

Picture Sleeves

BUENA VISTA 5-10 63
DISNEYLAND 10-20 57
RCA 4-8 64

EPs: 7-inch

COLUMBIA (2031 "Indian Fighter") .. 20-25 55
COLUMBIA (2032 "Davy Crockett Goes to Congress") 20-25 55
COLUMBIA (2033 "At the Alamo") 20-25 55

LPs: 10/12-inch

COLUMBIA (666 "Davy Crockett") ... 50-75 55
DISNEYLAND (1200 series) 10-20 64-65
DISNEYLAND (1300 series) 5-10 70
DISNEYLAND (1900 series) 10-20 63
DISNEYLAND (3007 "Yarns and Songs") 25-35 55
DISNEYLAND (3900 series) 10-20 64
HARMONY 10-20 60
RCA 10-20 64

PARKER, Fess, & Buddy Ebsen / Gene Autry

Singles: 7-inch

COLUMBIA/CHRYSLER (3 "Story of Davy Crockett") 5-10 55
(Promotional issue, made by Columbia for Chrysler. Plays at 16 2/3 rpm.)

Picture Sleeves

COLUMBIA/CHRYSLER (3 "Story of Davy Crockett") 10-15 55
(Promotional issue, made by Columbia for Chrysler.)
Also see AUTRY, Gene
Also see PARKER, Fess

PARKER, Graham P&R/LP '77
(With Rumour; with Shot)

Singles: 7-inch

ARISTA 3-5 79-83
ELEKTRA 3-4 85
MERCURY 3-5 76-77

Picture Sleeves

ARISTA 3-5 80-83
ELEKTRA 3-4 85
MERCURY 3-5 77

EPs: 7-inch

MERCURY (74000 "Hold Back the Night") 5-8 77
(Colored vinyl.)

LPs: 10/12-inch

ARISTA 5-10 78-83
ELEKTRA 5-8 85
MERCURY 5-10 77-78
RCA 5-8 88-89

Promotional LPs

ARISTA (41 "Mercury Poisoning") 25-35 78
ARISTA (63 "Live Sparks") 25-35 79
Also see RUMOUR
Also see SPRINGSTEEN, Bruce

PARKER, Junior: see PARKER, Little Junior

PARKER, Little Junior R&B '57
(With His Blue Flames; with Blue Blowers; with Bill Johnson's Blue Flames; Junior Parker)

Singles: 78 rpm

DUKE 15-30 54-57
MODERN (864 "Bad Women, Bad Whiskey") 25-50 52

Singles: 7-inch

ABC 3-5 73
BLUE ROCK 4-6 68-69
CAPITOL 3-6 70-71
DUKE (120 "Dirty Friend Blues") 25-50 54
DUKE (127 "Pretty Baby Blues") 25-50 54
DUKE (137 "Backtrackin' ") 25-50 55
DUKE (147 "Driving Me") 20-40 55
DUKE (157 "Mother-in-Law Blues") ... 20-40 56
DUKE (164 "My Dolly Bee") 20-40 56
DUKE (168 "Pretty Baby") 15-25 57
DUKE (177 "Peaches") 15-25 57
DUKE (184 "Wondering") 15-25 58
DUKE (193 "Barefoot Rock") 15-25 58
DUKE (300 series) 8-15 59-66
DUKE (400 series) 5-8 67
GM 4-8
MCA 3-4
MERCURY 4-8 66-68
MINIT 4-8 69

LPs: 10/12-inch

ABC 8-10 76
BLUE ROCK 10-15 69
BLUESWAY 8-12 73
CAPITOL 10-15 70
DUKE (76 "Driving Wheel") 60-100 62
(Cover pictures a Cadillac.)
DUKE (76 "Driving Wheel") 35-55 62
(Cover pictures a Wagon Wheel.)
DUKE (83 "Best of Junior Parker") 8-12 74
GROOVE MERCHANT 10-15
MCA 5-8
MERCURY 12-20 67
MINIT 10-15 69
Also see BLAND, Bobby / Little Junior Parker
Also see LITTLE JUNIOR'S BLUE FLAMES

PARKER, Little Junior, & Jimmy McGriff

LPs: 10/12-inch

CAPITOL 10-15 71
U.A. 10-15 71
Also see McGRIFF, Jimmy
Also see PARKER, Little Junior

PARKER, Paul D&D '83

Singles: 12-inch

MEGATONE 4-6 83

PARKER, Ray, Jr. P&R/LP '80
(With Raydio; with Helen Terry)

Singles: 12-inch

ARISTA 4-6 84-85

Singles: 7-inch

ARISTA (Except 1035) 3-5 80-85
ARISTA (1035 "Christmas Time Is Here") 3-5 82
(Promotional issue only.)
ATLANTIC 3-4 86
FLASHBACK 3-4 82
GEFFEN 3-4 87

Picture Sleeves

ARISTA (Except 1035) 3-4 80-85
ARISTA (1035 "Christmas Time Is Here") 3-5 82
(Promotional issue only.)
ATLANTIC 3-4 86
GEFFEN 3-4 87

LPs: 10/12-inch

ARISTA 5-8 80-85
GEFFEN 5-8 87

Members: J.D. Nicholas; Arnell Carmichael; Jack Ashford; Ollie Brown.
Also see MEDEIROS, Glenn
Also see RAYDIO

PARKER, Ray, Jr., & Natalie Cole R&B '87

Singles: 7-inch

GEFFEN 3-4 87
Also see COLE, Natalie
Also see PARKER, Ray, Jr.

PARKER, Robert P&R/R&B '66

Singles: 7-inch

HEAD 3-5 72
IMPERIAL (5842 "Mash Potatoes All Night Long") 10-15 62
ISLAND 3-5 75-76
NOLA 4-8 66-67
RON 5-10 59-60
SILVER FOX 4-6 69

LPs: 10/12-inch

NOLA (1001 "Barefootin' ") 20-30 66
(Monaural.)

NOLA (S-1001 "Barefootin'") 30-40 66
(Stereo.)
Also see BO, Eddie

PARKER, Winfield R&B '71

Singles: 7-inch

ARCTIC 4-6 69
GSP 3-5 72
RU-JAC (24 "Fallen Star") 4-8 68
SPRING 3-5 71

PARKING METER D&D '84

Singles: 12-inch

ATLANTIC 4-6 84

Singles: 7-inch

ATLANTIC 3-5 84

PARKS, Michael LP '69

Singles: 7-inch

MGM 3-5 70

LPs: 10/12-inch

MGM 10-15 69-70
VERVE 8-12 71

PARLET R&B '78

("Parlet Featuring Jeanette Washington")

Singles: 7-inch

CASABLANCA 3-5 78-80

LPs: 10/12-inch

CASABLANCA 5-10 79
Members: Mahalia Franklin; Shirley Hayden.

PARLIAMENT R&B '71

(Parliament Thang)

Singles: 12-inch

CASABLANCA 5-10 78

Singles: 7-inch

CASABLANCA 3-6 74-81
INVICTUS 5-10 70-71
SOULTOWN 3-5

Picture Sleeves

CASABLANCA (950 "Aqua Boogie") 4-6 79

LPs: 10/12-inch

CASABLANCA (Except NBPIX-7125) 8-12 74-80
CASABLANCA (NBPIX-7125 "Motor Booty Affair") 10-15 79
(Picture disc.)
INVICTUS (7302 "Osmium") 50-75 70
Members: George Clinton; Raymond Davis; Calvin Simon; Clarence Haskins; Grady Thomas; Glen Collins; Pedro Bell; Mahalia Franklin; Shirley Hayden; Debbie Wright; Lynn Marby; William "Bootsy" Collins; Dawn Silva; Ron Banks; Larry Demps; Junie Morrison; Donny Sterling; Fred Wesley; Gary Shider; Eddie Hazell; Michael Brecker; Randy Brecker; Peter Chase; Jerome Bailey; Tiki Fulwood; Grady Thomas; Michael Hampton; Willie Nelson; Maceo Parker; Gary Cooper; Cordell Mosson.
Also see BOOTSY'S RUBBER BAND
Also see BRIDES of FUNKENSTEIN
Also see MACEO & MACKS
Also see PARLIAMENTS
Also see WORRELL, Bernie

PARLIAMENTS P&R/R&B '67

Singles: 7-inch

ATCO (6675 "A New Day Begins") 8-12 69
GOLDEN WORLD (46 "Heart Trouble") 25-50 67
REVILOT (207 "Testify") 10-20 67
REVILOT (211 "All Your Goodies Are Gone") 10-20 67
REVILOT (214 "The Goose") 10-20 68
REVILOT (217 "Sentimental Lady") ..10-20 68
Members: George Clinton; Ray Davis; Calvin Simon; Clarence Haskins; Grady Thomas; Bernie Worrell; Bootsy Collins; Frank Waddy; Maceo Parker; Fred Wesley.
Also see CLINTON, George, Band
Also see FUNKADELIC
Also see PARLIAMENT

PARR, John P&R/LP '84

Singles: 12-inch

ATLANTIC 4-6 86

Singles: 7-inch

ATLANTIC 3-4 84-86

Picture Sleeves

ATLANTIC 3-4 85-86

LPs: 10/12-inch

ATLANTIC 5-8 84-86

PARRIS, Fred P&R '82

(With the Satins; with "Scarlets Originally the Five Satins"; with Passionettes; with Black Satin; with Restless Hearts; Fred Paris)

Singles: 7-inch

ATCO 5-10 66
BIRTH 4-8
BUDDAH 3-5 75
CANDLELITE 5-10 63
CHECKER 5-10 65
ELEKTRA (47411 "Memories of Days Gone By") 5-10 82
GREEN SEA 5-10 66
KLIK (7905 "She's Gone") 75-125 58
MAMA SADIE (1001 "In the Still of the Night") 5-10 67
RCA (9232 "It's Okay to Cry") 5-10 67
(A Freddie Paris also recorded for RCA at this time. Note slightly different spelling.)

LPs: 10/12-inch

BUDDAH 30-50 75
ELEKTRA 10-15 82
Also see FIVE SATINS

PARRISH, Dean P&R '66

(Dean Parish)

Singles: 7-inch

BOOM 10-20 66
LAURIE 5-10 67
MUSICOR 5-10 65

PARRISH, Man R&B '83

Singles: 7-inch

IMPORTE 3-4 83
SUGAR SCOOP 3-4 85

LPs: 10/12-inch

IMPORTE 5-8 83

PARSONS, Alan, Project P&R/LP '76

(Alan Parsons)

Singles: 12-inch

ARISTA (66 "Damned If I Do") 5-10 79
(Promotional issue only.)
ARISTA (9348 "Days Are Numbers") 4-8 85
(Promotional issue only.)

Singles: 7-inch

ARISTA 3-5 77-89
20TH FOX 3-5 76

Picture Sleeves

ARISTA 3-5 84-87

LPs: 10/12-inch

ARISTA (111 "No Gambler") 15-20 80
ARISTA (68 "Complete Audio Guide") 50-75 82
(Boxed, five-disc set.)
ARISTA (140 "Complete Audio Guide") 75-100 82
(Boxed, eight-disc set.)
ARISTA (4000 series) 5-10 78
(Black vinyl.)
ARISTA (4180 Pyramid") 15-20 78
(Colored vinyl. Promotional issue only.)
ARISTA (7002 I Robot") 5-10 77
ARISTA (8000 series, except 8263) 5-8 83-89
ARISTA (8263 "Vulture Culture") 5-8 85
ARISTA (PD-8263 "Vulture Culture") 30-40 85
(Picture disc. Promotional issue only.)
ARISTA (9000 series) 5-10 79-82
MERCURY (832 820 "Tales of Mystery and Imagination") 8-12 87
(Remastered limited edition with booklet.)
MFSL (084 "I Robot") 30-50 82
MFSL (UHQR 084 "I Robot") 75-100 82
(Boxed set.)
MFSL (175 "Best of the Alan Parsons Project") 25-35 85
MFSL (204 "Tales of Mystery and Imagination") 20-25 94
20TH FOX (508 "Tales of Mystery and Imagination") 15-25 76
(Includes eight-page booklet.)
20TH FOX (508 "Tales of Mystery and Imagination") 8-12 76
20TH FOX (539 "Tales of Mystery and Imagination") 5-10 77
Members: Alan Parsons; David Paton; Stuart Tosh; Eric Woolfson; Lenny Zakatek; Ian Bairnson; B.J. Cole; Stuart Elliott; Colin Blunstone; Allan Clarke; Andrew Powell; John Miles; Gary Brooker; Christopher Rainbow; Duncan Mackay; Richard Cottle; Laurie Cottle; Geoff Barradale.
Also see AMBROSIA
Also see BROWN, Arthur
Also see CLARKE, Alan
Also see HOLLIES
Also see MILES, John
Also see PACK, David
Also see PILOT
Also see POWELL, Andrew
Also see VITAMIN Z

PARSONS, Bill P&R '58

(Bobby Bare)

Singles: 7-inch

ABC 3-5 73
COLLECTABLES 3-4 80s
FRATERNITY (835 "The All American Boy") 10-20 58
(Fraternity 838, by the real Bill Parsons—not Bobby Bare—is listed in the following section.)
Also see BARE, Bobby

PARSONS, Bill

Singles: 7-inch

FRATERNITY (838 "Educated Rock & Roll") 10-15 59
(Fraternity 835, credited to Bill Parsons [Bobby Bare], is listed in the preceding section.)
STARDAY (526 "Hot Rod Volkswagen") 25-35 60
STARDAY (544 "A-Waitin'") 5-10 61

PARSONS, Gram LP '74

(With the Fallen Angels)

Singles: 7-inch

REPRISE 3-5 73
SIERRA 3-5 79

EPs: 7-inch

SIERRA 8-10 82
(Promotional issue only.)

LPs: 10/12-inch

REPRISE 8-12 73
SHILOH 10-15 73
SIERRA 5-10 79-82
Also see BYRDS
Also see FLYING BURRITO BROTHERS
Also see HARRIS, Emmylou

PARTLAND BROTHERS P&R/LP '87

Singles: 7-inch

MANHATTAN 3-4 87

Picture Sleeves

MANHATTAN 3-4 87

LPs: 10/12-inch

MANHATTAN 5-8 87

PARTNERS IN KRYME P&R '90

Singles: 7-inch

SBK 3-4 90

PARTON, Dolly C&W '67

Singles: 12-inch

RCA (Black vinyl) 4-8 78-83
RCA (Colored vinyl) 8-12 78

Singles: 7-inch

COLUMBIA 3-4 90s
GOLDBAND (1086 "Puppy Love") 20-40 59
MERCURY (71982 "It's Sure Gonna Hurt") 15-25 62
MONUMENT (800 thru 1000 series) ... 5-10 65-68
RCA (0132 thru 0950) 3-6 69-76
RCA (5000 series) 3-4 86
RCA (9500 thru 9900 series) 4-6 68-71
RCA (10031 thru 11240) 3-5 74-78

RCA (11296 "Heartbreaker")..............5-10 78
(Label mistakenly reads: "From the *Sure Thing* album.)
RCA (11296 "Heartbreaker")................3-5 78
(Label reads: "From the *Heartbreaker* album.)
RCA (11420 thru 14297) 3-5 78-86
RCA GOLD STANDARD...........................3-4 80

Promotional Singles

RCA (Colored vinyl).............................4-8 77-85

Picture Sleeves

RCA...3-8 69-85

LPs: 10/12-inch

ALSHIRE..8-12 69-71
CAMDEN..5-10 72-78
COLUMBIA..5-8 87
MONUMENT (7600 series) 5-10 78
MONUMENT (8085 "Hello, I'm Dolly") 15-20 67
MONUMENT (18000 series) 12-20 67
MONUMENT (18100 series) 8-15 70
MONUMENT (31000 series) 8-15 72
MONUMENT (33000 series) 8-10 75
RCA (812 "HBO Presents")................15-20 83
(Picture disc. Promotional issue only.)
RCA (0033 thru 5000 series)................5-12 73-87
(With "AFL1," "AHL1," "APD1," "APL1," or "AYL1" prefix.)
RCA (2314 "Personal Music Dialogue") 10-20 77
(Interview. Promotional issue only.)
RCA (CPL1-3413 "Great Balls of Fire") 15-20 79
(Picture disc. Promotional issue only.)
RCA (LPM-3949 "Just Because I'm a Woman")...15-25 68
(Monaural.)
RCA (LSP-3949 "Just Because I'm a Woman")...15-20 68
(Stereo.)
RCA (LSP-4188 "My Blue Ridge Mountain Boy") 15-20 69
RCA (LSP-4099 "In the Good Old Days") 15-20 69
RCA (LSP-4288 "Fairest of Them All") 10-20 70
RCA (LSP-4387 "A Real Live Dolly") 20-30 70
RCA (LSP-4398 "Golden Streets of Glory")...30-50 71
RCA (4422 "Greatest Hits")...............25-50 82
(Without *Islands in the Stream*)
RCA (4422 "Greatest Hits")...................5-8 82
(With *Islands in the Stream*.)
RCA (LSP-4449 "Best of Dolly Parton")...10-20 70
RCA (LSP-4507 "Joshua")................10-20 71
RCA (LSP-4603 "Coat of Many Colors")...10-20 71
RCA (LSP-4686 "Touch Your Woman")..10-20 72
RCA (LSP-4752 "Dolly Parton Sings [Porter Wagoner]")...10-20 72
RCA ("HBO Presents Dolly")..............15-25 83
(Picture disc. Promotional issue only.)
SOMERSET 10-20 63-68
STEREO-FIDELITY..............................10-20 63-68
TIME-LIFE 5-8 81

Session: Jordanaires; Ricky Skaggs; Porter Wagoner.
Also see HARRIS, Emmylou
Also see KRISTOFFERSON, Kris, Willie Nelson, Dolly Parton, & Brenda Lee
Also see ROGERS, Kenny, & Dolly Parton
Also see SKAGGS, Ricky
Also see WAGONER, Porter, & Dolly Parton

PARTON, Dolly / George Jones

LPs: 10/12-inch

STARDAY (429 "Dolly Parton and George Jones")...30-40 68
Also see JONES, George

PARTON, Dolly, & Ricky Van Shelton C&W '91

Singles: 7-inch

COLUMBIA...3-4 91
Also see VAN SHELTON, Ricky

PARTON, Dolly, & Willie Nelson C&W '82

Singles: 7-inch

MONUMENT...3-4 82
Also see NELSON, Willie

PARTON, Dolly, Linda Ronstadt, & Emmylou Harris

LP '87

LPs: 10/12-inch

W.B. 5-8 87
Also see HARRIS, Emmylou
Also see RONSTADT, Linda

PARTON, Dolly, & Ricky Van Shelton C&W '91

Singles: 7-inch

RCA 3-4 91
Also see SHELTON, Ricky Van

PARTON, Dolly / Kitty Wells

LPs: 10/12-inch

EXACT...5-8 80
Also see PARTON, Dolly
Also see WELLS, Kitty

PARTRIDGE FAMILY P&R/LP '70

("Starring Shirley Jones," "Featuring David Cassidy")

Singles: 7-inch

BELL 3-5 70-73
FLASHBACK...3-4 70s

Picture Sleeves

BELL 3-5 70-71

LPs: 10/12-inch

BELL 10-25 70-74
Also see CASSIDY, David

PARTY LP '90

LPs: 10/12-inch

HOLLYWOOD 5-8 90

PASADENAS LP '89

Singles: 7-inch

COLUMBIA 3-4 89

LPs: 10/12-inch

COLUMBIA 5-8 89

PASSIONS P&R '59

Singles: 7-inch

ABC-PAR (10436 "The Empty Seat") 20-30 63
AUDICON (102 "Just to Be with You") 20-40 59
AUDICON (105 "I Only Want You") .. 20-40 59
AUDICON (106 "Gloria").................... 20-40 60
AUDICON (108 "Beautiful Dreamer")..20-40 60
AUDICON (112 "Made for Lovers")... 20-40 61
COLLECTABLES......................................3-4 80s
CRYSTAL BALL.......................................4-8 90
DIAMOND (146 "16 Candles")......... 30-50 63
DORE (505 "Tango of Love")........... 15-25 58
JASON SCOTT...4-8
JUBILEE (5406 "Lonely Road") 10-15 61
LAURIE..3-5 70s
OCTAVIA (8005 "Aphrodite")........ 500-750 62

LPs: 10/12-inch

CLIFTON..5-10

Members: Jim Gallagher; Tony Armato; Al Galione; Vince Acerno; Louis Rotondo.
Also see MYSTICS / Passions

PASSPORT LP '75

Singles: 7-inch

ATCO 3-5 76
ATLANTIC...3-5 78

LPs: 10/12-inch

ATCO..8-12 74-77
ATLANTIC...5-10 78-82
REPRISE...8-12 72

PASTEL SIX P&R '62

Singles: 7-inch

CHATTAHOOCHEE 5-10 65
DOWNEY (101 "Twitchin'") 10-20 62
DOWNEY (101 "Open House at the Cinder")..10-20 62
DOWNEY (102 "Brahm's Nightmare")..10-20 62
ERA 3-5 72
ZEN (102 "Cinnamon Cinder") 15-25 62
ZENITH (105 "A Sing-Along Song").. 10-20 63

LPs: 10/12-inch

ZEN (1001 "Cinnamon Cinder") 50-100 62
Member: Sonny Patterson.

PASTELS P&R/R&B '58

Singles: 78 rpm

ARGO (5287 "Been So Long")...........25-35 58

Singles: 7-inch

ARGO (5287 "Been So Long")..........15-20 58
ARGO (5297 "You Don't Love Me Anymore")..15-25 58
ARGO (5314 "So Far Away") 10-20 58
CADET 3-5 70s
CHESS 3-5 73
MASCOT (123 "Been So Long") ... 150-250 57

Members: Big Dee Irwin; Richard Travis; Tony Thomas; J.B. Wellington.
Also see IRWIN, Big Dee

PASTORIUS, Jaco LP '81

LPs: 10/12-inch

W.B. 5-8 81-83
Also see WEATHER REPORT

PAT & SATELLITES P&R '59

Singles: 7-inch

ATCO...8-12 59

Members: Pat Otts; King Curtis; Wayne Lips.
Also see KING CURTIS

PATE, Johnny P&R/R&B '58

(Johnny Pate Trio)

Singles: 78 rpm

FEDERAL..5-10 57
GIG 5-10 56

Singles: 7-inch

ARGO 4-6 64
FEDERAL...5-10 57-59
GIG 10-15 56

LPs: 10/12-inch

GIG 40-50 56
KING (561 "Jazz Goes Ivy League") 30-50 58
(Monaural.)
KING (KSD-561 "Jazz Goes Ivy League")......................................50-75 59
(Stereo.)
KING (584 "Swingin' Flute")..............30-50 58
KING (611 "A Date with Johnny Pate")...30-50 58
SALEM 25-35 58
STEPHENY (4002 "Johnny Pate at the Blue Note")...45-55 57

PATIENCE R&B '80

Singles: 7-inch

COLUMBIA...3-5 80

PATIENCE & PRUDENCE P&R '56

Singles: 78 rpm

LIBERTY...10-15 56-57

Singles: 7-inch

CHATTAHOOCHEE.....................................5-8 64-65
LIBERTY...10-20 56-57
U.A. 3-5 70s

Picture Sleeves

LIBERTY (55084 "You Tattletale")... 20-30 57
Also see CLIFFORD, Mike, with Patience & Prudence

PATRICK, Keith R&B '86

Singles: 7-inch

OMNI 3-4 86

PATRIS D&D '85

Singles: 12-inch

EMERGENCY 4-6 85

PATTERSON, Bobby R&B '69

(With the Mustangs)

Singles: 7-inch

ABNAK 4-8 65-66
ALL PLATINUM..3-5 77

GRANITE............3-5 76
JETSTAR............4-8 66-69
(Black vinyl.)
JETSTAR (111 "Funky No More").......8-12 68
(Colored vinyl. Promotional issue only.)
PAULA............6-12 72-73
PROUD............5-10

PATTERSON, Kellee *P&R/R&B '77*

Singles: 7-inch
SHADYBROOK............3-5 75-77
LPs: 10/12-inch
SHADYBROOK............5-10 76-79
Shadybrook may also be shown as Shady Brook (two words).

PATTI & EMBLEMS: see PATTY & EMBLEMS

PATTON, Robbie *P&R/LP '81*

Singles: 7-inch
ATLANTIC............3-4 83-85
BACKSTREET............3-5 79
LIBERTY............3-5 81
LPs: 10/12-inch
ATLANTIC............5-8 85
LIBERTY............5-10 81

PATTY & EMBLEMS *P&R/R&B '64*

(Patti & Emblems)
Singles: 7-inch
COLLECTABLES............3-4 80s
CONGRESS............10-20 66
HERALD............10-20 64
KAPP............10-20 66-68
LOST-NITE............3-5
SPHERE SOUND............10-20 64

PAUL, Billy *LP '70*

Singles: 12-inch
PHILADELPHIA INT'L............4-8 79
Singles: 7-inch
FINCH............8-12 60
JUBILEE (5081 "That's Why I Dream")............10-20 52
JUBILEE (5086 "You Didn't Know")............10-20 52
NEPTUNE............3-6 70
PHILADELPHIA INT'L............3-5 71-81
LPs: 10/12-inch
GAMBLE............10-20 67
NEPTUNE............10-15 70
PHILADELPHIA INT'L............5-10 71-80
Also see PHILADELPHIA INTERNATIONAL ALL STARS

PAUL, Bunny *P&R '53*

Singles: 78 rpm
BRUNSWICK............8-12 57
CAPITOL............8-12 55
DOT............8-12 53
GORDY............12-15 63
POINT............10-20 56
Singles: 7-inch
BRUNSWICK............10-20 57
CAPITOL............10-20 55
DOT............10-20 53
GORDY (7017 "I'm Hooked")............15-25 63
POINT (5 "Sweet Talk")............25-50 56
ROULETTE (4186 "Such a Night")....10-20 59

PAUL, Bunny, & Harptones

(Bunny Paul)
Singles: 78 rpm
ESSEX (352 "Such a Night")............20-30 54
ESSEX (352 "Lovey Dovey")............20-30 54
ESSEX (364 "I'll Never Tell")............30-50 54
Singles: 7-inch
ESSEX (352 "Such a Night")..........50-100 54
ESSEX (352 "Lovey Dovey")..........50-100 54
ESSEX (364 "I'll Never Tell").........100-200 54
Also see HALEY, Bill
Also see HARPTONES
Also see PAUL, Bunny

PAUL, Henry, Band *LP '79*

Singles: 7-inch
ATLANTIC............3-5 79-81
LPs: 10/12-inch
ATLANTIC............5-10 79-81
Also see OUTLAWS

PAUL, Les *P&R '48*

(Les Paul Trio)
Singles: 78 rpm
CAPITOL............5-10 50-53
DECCA............5-10 54
Singles: 7-inch
CAPITOL............5-15 50-53
DECCA............5-15 54
EPs: 7-inch
DECCA............10-20 50-53
LPs: 10/12-inch
CAPITOL (200 series)............5-10 77
CAPITOL (16000 series)............5-8
DECCA (5018 "Hawaiian Paradise")............50-100 49
(10-inch LP.)
DECCA (5376 "Galloping Guitars")... 50-75 52
(10-inch LP.)
DECCA (8589 "More of Les")..........30-50 57
GLENDALE............5-8 78
LONDON............6-12 68-79
VOCALION............6-12 68
Also see ANDREWS SISTERS
Also see ATKINS, Chet, & Les Paul

PAUL, Les, & Mary Ford *P&R '50*

(Mary Ford with Les Paul; Mary Ford)
Singles: 78 rpm
CAPITOL............5-15 50-57
Singles: 7-inch
CALENDAR............3-5
CAPITOL............5-15 50-57
COLUMBIA............4-10 58-64
Picture Sleeves
COLUMBIA............4-8 58-64
EPs: 7-inch
CAPITOL............10-20 50-57
LPs: 10/12-inch
CAPITOL (SM-200 series)............5-8 78
CAPITOL (H-226 thru H-577)..........25-50 50-55
(10-inch LPs.)
CAPITOL (T-226 thru T-802)..........20-40 55-57
CAPITOL (T-1400 & T-1500 series) 15-25 60-61
(Monaural.)
CAPITOL (ST-1400 & ST-1500 series)............20-30 60-61
(Stereo.)
CAPITOL (11000 series)............5-10 74
COLUMBIA............10-20 61-63
HARMONY............8-12 61-65
Also see PAUL, Les

PAUL, Pope: see POPE PAUL

PAUL & PAULA *P&R/R&B '62*

Singles: 7-inch
LE CAM (300 series)............3-5 74-82
LE CAM (99 "Beginning of Love").......8-12 63
PHILIPS (40000 series)............4-8 62-66
PHILIPS (44000 series)............3-5 70s
SOFT (106 "Hey Paula '69")............8-12 69
UNI............4-8 68
U.A.............3-5 70
Picture Sleeves
PHILIPS............8-12 63-64
LPs: 10/12-inch
PHILIPS (200078 "For Young Lovers")............25-40 63
(Monaural.)
PHILIPS (200089 "We Go Together")............25-40 63
(Monaural.)
PHILIPS (200101 "Holiday for Teens")............25-40 63
(Monaural.)
PHILIPS (600078 "For Young Lovers")............25-50 63
(Stereo.)
PHILIPS (600089 "We Go Together")............25-50 63
(Stereo.)
PHILIPS (600101 "Holiday for Teens")............25-50 63
(Stereo.)
Members: Ray Hildebrand; Jill Jackson.
Also see CHANNEL, Bruce / Paul & Paula
Also see JACKSON, Jill
Also see JILL & RAY
Also see RON-DELS

PAULETTE SISTERS *P&R '55*

Singles: 78 rpm
CAPITOL............4-8 55
Singles: 7-inch
CAPITOL............5-10 55
CONTEMPO............4-8 63
DECCA............4-6 60s
RIBBON............4-8 60
20TH FOX............4-8 61

PAULSEN, Pat *LP '68*

Singles: 7-inch
MERCURY (105 "Open End Interview")............5-10 68
(Promotional issue only.)
LPs: 10/12-inch
MERCURY............8-15 68-70

PAUPERS *LP '67*

Singles: 7-inch
VERVE ("If I Called You By Some Name")............20-30 66
(Canadian. Selection number not known.)
VERVE/FOLKWAYS............8-15 66-67
VERVE/FORECAST............5-10 67-68
Picture Sleeves
VERVE/FOLKWAYS............10-20 67
LPs: 10/12-inch
VERVE/FORECAST............15-25 67-68

PAVLOV'S DOG *LP '75*

Singles: 7-inch
COLUMBIA............3-5 76
LPs: 10/12-inch
ABC............10-15 75
COLUMBIA............8-12 75-76
Members: David Surkamp; Mike Abebe; Murray Krugman; Sandy Pearlman; Mike Safron; Richard Stockton; David Hamilton; Doug Rayburn; Steve Scorfina; Bill Bruford.
Also see YES

PAVONE, Rita *P&R/LP '64*

Singles: 7-inch
RCA............4-8 63-66
Picture Sleeves
RCA............4-8 64-65
LPs: 10/12-inch
RCA............10-20 64-67

PAVAROTTI, Luciano *LP '79*

Singles: 7-inch
LONDON............3-4 79-84
LPs: 10/12-inch
LONDON............5-8 76-84

PAXTON, Tom *LP '69*

Singles: 7-inch
ASYLUM............3-5 70
ELEKTRA............4-8 69
REPRISE............3-5 71
LPs: 10/12-inch
ANCHOR............8-12
ELEKTRA............10-15 64-71
FLYING FISH............5-8
PRIVATE STOCK............8-10 75
REPRISE............10-15 71-73

PAYCHECK, Johnny *C&W '65*

(With Charnissa)
Singles: 7-inch
ABC............3-5 74
AMI............3-5 84-85
CERTRON............4-6 70
CUTLASS............3-5 72
DAMASCUS............3-4 89
DESPERADO............3-4 88
EPIC............3-5 71-82
HILLTOP............8-15 64-66

LITTLE DARLIN' (008 thru 0072) 5-10 66-69
LITTLE DARLIN' (7000 series)............3-5 78-79
MERCURY 3-5 86-87

LPs: 10/12-inch

ACCORD 5-10 82
ALLEGIANCE 5-10 83
CERTRON 8-15 70
EPIC 5-10 71-83
EXCELSIOR 5-8 80
GUSTO 5-10 83
IMPERIAL 5-10 80
LAKESHORE 5-8
LITTLE DARLIN' (0571 thru 0792) 5-10 79-80
LITTLE DARLIN' (4001 "Johnny Paycheck at Carnegie Hall") 20-30 66
(Monaural.)
LITTLE DARLIN' (4001 "Johnny Paycheck in Concert")......................................10-15 66
(Repackage of *At Carnegie Hall*. Monaural.)
LITTLE DARLIN' (8001 "Johnny Paycheck at Carnegie Hall") 20-30 66
(Stereo.)
LITTLE DARLIN' (8001 "Johnny Paycheck in Concert")......................................15-20 66
(Repackage of *At Carnegie Hall*. Stereo.)
LITTLE DARLIN' (4003 thru 4006) 10-20 66-67
(Monaural.)
LITTLE DARLIN' (8003 thru 8023) 10-20 66-69
(Stereo.)
LITTLE DARLIN' (10000 series)..........8-12 79
MERCURY 5-8 86
PICKWICK/HILLTOP............................5-10 72
POWER PAK 5-8
Session: Jordanaires.
Also see HAGGARD, Merle, & Johnny Paycheck
Also see JENNINGS, Waylon / Johnny Paycheck
Also see JONES, George, & Johnny Paycheck
Also see MILLER, Jody, & Johnny Paycheck
Also see TUBB, Ernest
Also see YOUNG, Donny

PAYCHECK & HAGGARD C&W '81

Singles: 7-inch

EPIC 3-4 81
Members: Johnny Paycheck; Merle Haggard.
Also see HAGGARD, Merle
Also see PAYCHECK, Johnny

PAYNE, Cecil, Orchestra R&B '50

Singles: 78 rpm

DECCA...5-10 50

PAYNE, Freda R&B '69

Singles: 12-inch

CAPITOL 4-8 79

Singles: 7-inch

ABC 3-5 75
ABC-PAR 5-10 62-63
CAPITOL 3-5 77-78
DUNHILL 3-5 74
IMPULSE...5-10 63
INVICTUS..3-8 69-73
MGM 10-20 66
RIPETE..3-6
SUTRA 3-5 82

Picture Sleeves

CAPITOL 3-5 77-78
INVICTUS..4-8 71-73

LPs: 10/12-inch

ABC 8-10 75
CAPITOL 5-10 78-79
DUNHILL 8-10 74
IMPULSE..15-25 64
INVICTUS...10-15 70-72
MGM 10-20 66-70
U.S.A. 10-15 71

PAYNE, Scherrie D&D '84

(With Phillip Ingram)

Singles: 12-inch

MEGATONE 4-6 84

Singles: 7-inch

ALTAIR 3-5
INVICTUS..3-5 72
MOTOWN..3-5 80
SUPERSTAR INT'L................................3-5
Also see DECO
Also see GLASS HOUSE
Also see SCHERRIE & SUSAYE
Also see SUPREMES

PAYTON, Lawrence R&B '74

Singles: 7-inch

DUNHILL... 3-5 73-74
Also see FOUR TOPS

PEACHES & HERB P&R/R&B '66

Singles: 7-inch

COLUMBIA 3-5 71-74
DATE 4-6 66-70
MCA 3-5 77
MERCURY 3-5 73

Picture Sleeves

DATE 4-8 67-68

LPs: 10/12-inch

DATE 10-20 67-68
EPIC.. 8-10 79
MCA 8-10 77
Members: Francine Barker; Herb Fame.

PEACHES & HERB LP '78

Singles: 12-inch

POLYDOR 4-8 78-79

Singles: 7-inch

COLUMBIA 3-5 83
POLYDOR 3-5 78-83

LPs: 10/12-inch

POLYDOR 5-10 78-81
Members: Linda Green; Herb Fame.

PEANUT BUTTER CONSPIRACY P&R/LP '67

Singles: 7-inch

CHALLENGE... 5-8 69
COLUMBIA 8-10 67
VAULT 10-15 66

LPs: 10/12-inch

CHALLENGE (200 "For Children of All Ages").. 20-25 69
COLUMBIA (2654 "Peanut Butter Conspiracy Is Spreading") 20-25 67
(Monaural.)
COLUMBIA (2790 "The Great Conspiracy")... 20-30 68
(Monaural.)
COLUMBIA (9454 "Peanut Butter Conspiracy Is Spreading") 25-30 68
(Stereo.)
COLUMBIA (9590 "The Great Conspiracy")... 20-25 68
(Stereo.)
COLUMBIA (38000 series) 8-10 82
Members: Sandi Robison; Alan Brackett; Lance Fent; Bill Wolf; Jim Voight; John Merrill.

PEANUT BUTTER CONSPIRACY / Ashes / Chambers Brothers

LPs: 10/12-inch

VAULT (113 "West Coast Love-In").. 30-50 68
Also see CHAMBERS BROTHERS

PEARL, Leslie P&R '82

Singles: 7-inch

RCA 3-5 82

PEARL HARBOR LP '80

(With the Explosions)

Singles: 7-inch

W.B. 3-5 80-81

LPs: 10/12-inch

W.B. 5-10 80-81

PEARL JAM LP '92

Singles: 7-inch

EPIC (5610 "Angel") 4-6 94
(Promotional issue only.)

Picture Sleeves

EPIC (5610 "Angel") 5-10 94
(Promotional issue only.)

LPs: 10/12-inch

EPIC.. 5-10 92-95
Members: Eddie Vedder; Mike McCready; Jeff Ament; Stone Gossard; Dave Krusen.

PEARLETTES P&R '62

Singles: 7-inch

CRAIG 8-12 61
VEE JAY..8-10 61-62

PEARLS BEFORE SWINE LP '69

Singles: 7-inch

ESP (4554 "Morning Song").............20-30 67
ESP (4576 "I Saw the World")..........20-30 68
REPRISE (0873 "These Things Too") 5-10 69
W.B./REPRISE (0949 "Rocket Man") ... 4-8 70

LPs: 10/12-inch

ADELPHI 8-12 80
ESP (1054 "One Nation Underground") 30-50 67
ESP (1075 "Balaklava")....................20-40 68
W.B./REPRISE..................................10-20 69-71
Members: Tom Rapp; Richard Alderson; Bob Elizabeth; Warren Smith; Charlie McCoy; Lane Lender; Wayne Harley.
Also see RAPP, Tom

PEARSON, Duke LP '69

Singles: 7-inch

BLUE NOTE 4-8 60-66

LPs: 10/12-inch

ATLANTIC...10-20 66
BLUE NOTE 25-40 59-61
(Label gives New York street address for Blue Note Records.)
BLUE NOTE 20-30 63-64
(Label reads "Blue Note Records Inc. - New York, USA.")
BLUE NOTE 10-20 66-74
(Label shows Blue Note Records as a division of either Liberty or United Artists.)
PRESTIGE 10-15 70

PEARSON, Mr. Danny R&B '78

Singles: 7-inch

UNLIMITED GOLD 3-5 78

LPs: 10/12-inch

UNLIMITED GOLD 5-10 79

PEASTON, David LP '89

LPs: 10/12-inch

GEFFEN 5-8 89

PEBBLES R&B '87

Singles: 7-inch

MCA...3-4 87-90

Picture Sleeves

MCA...3-4 87-88

LPs: 10/12-inch

MCA...5-8 87-90

PEDESTRIANS / Association / Five Americans / Soulblenders

EPs: 7-inch

WLAV (6873 "Think Twice")..............10-20 60s
(Promotional issue only.)
Also see ASSOCIATION
Also see FIVE AMERICANS
Also see PEDESTRIANS
Also see SOULBLENDERS

PEDICIN, Mike P&R '56

(Michael Pedicin, Jr; Mike Pedicin Quintet)

Singles: 78 rpm

CAMEO (125 "Shake a Hand") 10-20 57
MALVERN (100 "Dickie-Doo") 15-25 57
RCA (6369 "Large, Large House") 5-10 56

Singles: 12-inch

PHILADELPHIA INT'L 4-8 79-82

Singles: 7-inch

ABC-PAR 5-10 62
APOLLO (534 "Hey Pop, Give Me the Keys") 25-35 59
CAMEO (125 "Shake a Hand") 10-20 57
FEDERAL..8-12 61
MALVERN (100 "Dickie-Doo") 15-20 57
PHILADELPHIA INT'L 3-5 79-82
RCA (6369 "Large, Large House") 10-15 56
20TH CENTURY (5019 "Is That What You Call Love") 5-10 60s

EPs: 7–inch

RCA....................15-25 56
("General Electric Flash Blub Limited Edition.")

LPs: 10/12–inch

APOLLO (484 "Musical Medicine")....50-75 59
PHILADELPHIA INT'L....................5-10 79

PEDRICK, Bobby P&R '58

(Bobby Pedrick Jr.)

Singles: 7–inch

BIG TOP....................8-12 58-60
DUEL....................5-10 62-63
MGM....................4-8 65
SHELL....................15-20 60
VERVE (10402 "Maybe")....................40-50 66
Also see JOHN, Robert

PEEBLES, Ann R&B '69

Singles: 7–inch

HI....................3-6 69-80
MOTOWN....................3-4 82

LPs: 10/12–inch

HI....................8-12 69-75
MOTOWN....................5-8 82

PEECH BOYS R&B '82

Singles: 7–inch

WEST END....................3-4 82
Also see NEW YORK CITI PEECH BOYS

PEEK, Dan P&R '79

Singles: 7–inch

LAMB & LION....................4-6 79
SONGBIRD....................3-5 79

LPs: 10/12–inch

LAMB & LION....................6-12 79
SONGBIRD....................5-10 79
Also see AMERICA

PEEK, Paul P&R '61

Singles: 7–inch

COLUMBIA....................4-8 66
FAIRLANE....................10-15 61
MERCURY....................4-8 62-63
NRC....................10-20 58-60
1-2-3....................4-6 69

PEEL, David, & Lower East Side LP '69

Singles: 7–inch

APPLE (6498 "F Is Not a Dirty Word")....................100-125 72
(Promotional issue only.)
APPLE (6545 "Hippie from New York City")....................100-125 72
(Promotional issue only.)
ORANGE....................4-6 77
ORANGE PEEL (70078PD "Interview")....................15-20 80
(Picture disc. With John Lennon.)

LPs: 10/12–inch

APPLE (3391 "The Pope Smokes Dope")....................50-75 72
ELEKTRA (74032 "Have a Marijuana")....................15-25 68
ELEKTRA (74069 "American Revolution")....................15-25 70
ORANGE....................8-12 77

PEEL, David, & Lower East Side / John Lennon & Yoko Ono

Singles: 7–inch

ORANGE (8374 "Amerika")....................3-5 90
(Promotional bonus with book purchase.)
ORANGE (789001 "Ballad of New York City")....................3-5 87

Picture Sleeves

ORANGE (8374 "Amerika")....................3-5 90
(Promotional bonus with book purchase.)
Also see LENNON, John
Also see PEEL, David, & Lower East Side

PEELS P&R '66

Singles: 7–inch

KARATE....................4-8 66

LPs: 10/12–inch

KARATE (5402 "Juanita Banana")....55-65 66
(Monaural.)
KARATE (5402 "Juanita Banana")....65-75 66
(Stereo.)

PEEPLES P&R '88

Singles: 7–inch

MERCURY....................3-4 88

Picture Sleeves

MERCURY....................3-4 88

PEEPLES, Nia R&B/LP '88

Singles: 7–inch

MERCURY....................3-4 88

LPs: 10/12–inch

MERCURY....................5-8 88

PEERCE, Jan P&R '48

Singles: 78 rpm

RCA....................3-6 48-51

Singles: 7–inch

BLUEBIRD....................4-6 60
RCA....................5-10 51
U.A.....................4-6 63

EPs: 7–inch

RCA....................5-10 51

LPs: 10/12–inch

RCA (Except 2900 series)....................10-20 51
RCA (2900 series)....................5-10 78
U.A.....................5-15 63-65
VANGUARD....................5-15 63-67

PEGGY LEE: see LEE, Peggy

PENDERGRASS, Teddy P&R/R&B/LP '77

Singles: 12–inch

PHILADELPHIA INT'L....................4-8 78-82

Singles: 7–inch

ASYLUM....................3-4 84-88
ELEKTRA....................3-4 88-90
PHILADELPHIA INT'L....................3-5 77-84

Picture Sleeves

ELEKTRA....................3-4 89

LPs: 10/12–inch

ASYLUM....................5-8 84-86
ELEKTRA....................5-8 88-90
EPIC....................5-10 83
PHILADELPHIA INT'L (30000 series, except JZ-30595)....................5-10 77-84
PHILADELPHIA INT'L (JZ-30595 "Life Is a Song")....................15-25 78
(Picture disc. Promotional issue only.)
PHILADELPHIA INT'L (40000 series)....................10-15 82
(Half-speed mastered.)
Also see MELVIN, Harold
Also see MILLS, Stephanie, & Teddy Pendergrass
Also see PHILADELPHIA INTERNATIONAL ALL STARS

PENDERGRASS, Teddy, & Whitney Houston P&R '84

Singles: 7–inch

ASYLUM....................3-4 84

Picture Sleeves

ASYLUM....................3-4 84
Also see HOUSTON, Whitney
Also see PENDERGRASS, Teddy

PENDULUM P&R '80

Singles: 7–inch

VENTURE....................3-5 80

LPs: 10/12–inch

VENTURE....................5-10 81

PENGUINS P&R/R&B '54

("Featuring Cleve Duncan"; Penquins)

Singles: 78 rpm

ATLANTIC....................10-20 57
DOOTO....................20-30 57
DOOTONE....................20-30 54-55
MERCURY....................15-25 55-57
WING....................10-20 56

Singles: 7–inch

ATLANTIC (1132 "Pledge of Love")..10-20 57
DOOTO (348 "Earth Angel")....................8-10 62
(Reissue of DooTONE 348.)
DOOTO (428 "That's How Much I Need You")....................25-30 57
DOOTO (432 "Let Me Make Up Your Mind")....................25-30 58
DOOTO (435 "Do Not Pretend")....................25-30 58
(Dootone 345 is found in the following section: PENGUINS / Dootsie Williams Orchestra.)
DOOTONE (348 "Earth Angel")......75-125 54
(Red label.)
DOOTONE (348 "Earth Angel")........40-60 54
(Maroon label.)
DOOTONE (348 "Earth Angel")........35-45 54
(Blue label.)
DOOTONE (348 "Earth Angel")........20-30 54
(Black label.)
DOOTONE (353 "Love Will Make Your Mind Go Wild")....................40-50 54
(Red label.)
DOOTONE (353 "Love Will Make Your Mind Go Wild")....................30-40 54
(Maroon label.)
DOOTONE (353 "Love Will Make Your Mind Go Wild")....................20-30 54
(Blue label.)
DOOTONE (353 "Love Will Make Your Mind Go Wild")....................15-20 54
(Black label.)
DOOTONE (362 "Kiss a Fool Goodbye")....................20-40 55
GLENVILLE....................4-6
MERCURY (70610 "Be Mine Or Be a Fool")....................20-30 55
MERCURY (70654 "It Only Happens with You")....................20-25 55
MERCURY (70703 "Devil That I See")....................20-30 55
MERCURY (70762 "Christmas Prayer")....................40-50 55
MERCURY (70799 "My Troubles Are Not at an End")....................25-35 56
(Maroon label.)
MERCURY (70799 "My Troubles Are Not at an End")....................15-20 56
(Black label.)
MERCURY (70943 "Earth Angel")....20-25 56
MERCURY (71033 "Will You Be Mine")....................15-25 57
ORIGINAL SOUND (27 "Memories of El Monte")....................30-40 63
ORIGINAL SOUND (54 "Heavenly Angel")....................15-25 65
POWER....................4-8
SUN STATE (001 "Believe Me")........25-50 62
WING (90076 "Peace of Mind")........15-25 56

Picture Sleeves

POWER....................5-10

EPs: 7–inch

DOOTO (241/243/244 "Cool, Cool Penguins")....................40-60 59
(Price is for any of three volumes.)
DOOTONE (101 "The Penguins"). 100-150 55

LPs: 10/12–inch

COLLECTABLES....................5-8 80s
DOOTO (242 "Cool, Cool Penguins")....................150-250 59
(Yellow label with red lettering. Full-color cover.)
DOOTO (242 "Cool, Cool Penguins")....................10-15 60s
(Multi-color label.)
Members: Cleve Duncan; Curtis Williams; Dexter Tisby; Bruce Tate; Randy Jones; Ted Harper; Walter Saulsberry.

PENGUINS / Dootsie Williams Orchestra

Singles: 78 rpm

DOOTONE....................25-40 54

Singles: 7–inch

DOOTONE (345 "No There Ain't No News Today")....................75-100 54

PENGUINS / Meadowlarks / Medallions / Dootones

LPs: 10/12-inch

DOOTONE (204 "Best in Rhythm & Blues") 150-250 57
(Flat maroon label.)
DOOTONE (204 "Best in Rhythm & Blues") 10-20 60s
(Glossy label.)
Note: All colored vinyl pressings of this LP are bootlegs.
Also see PENGUINS

PENN, Michael LP '89

Singles: 7-inch

RCA 3-4 89-90

Picture Sleeves

RCA 3-4 89

LPs: 10/12-inch

RCA 5-8 89

PENTAGONS P&R '61

Singles: 7-inch

DONNA (1337 "To Be Loved") 15-25 61
DONNA (1344 "For a Love That Is Mine") 15-25 61
ERIC 3-4 70s
FLEET INT'L (100 "To Be Loved") 100-150 60
JAMIE (1201 "I Wonder") 20-30 61
JAMIE (1210 "I'm in Love") 10-15 61
ORIGINAL SOUND (4560 "To Be Loved") 5-10
SPECIALTY (644 "It's Spring Again") 20-30 58
SUTTER (100 "Forever Yours") 50-100 61

PENTAGONS / Earl Phillips

Singles: 7-inch

OLDIES 45 .... 4-8 64
Also see PENTAGONS

PENTANGLE LP '68

Singles: 7-inch

REPRISE 4-8 68-69
TRANSATLANTIC 4-6

LPs: 10/12-inch

REPRISE 10-20 68-72
Members: Jacqui McShee; Bert Jansch; Danny Thompson; John Renbourn; Terry Cox.

PEOPLE P&R/LP '68

Singles: 7-inch

CAPITOL 5-10 67-69
PARAMOUNT 4-8 69-70
POLYDOR 3-5 71
ZEBRA (102 "Come Back Beatles") 5-10 78
(Includes a note suggesting the Beatles reunite.)

LPs: 10/12-inch

CAPITOL 20-30 68-69
PARAMOUNT 10-20 69-70
Members: Larry Norman; Robb Levin; Tom Tucker; John Tristao; Gene Mason; Geoff Levin.

PEOPLE'S CHOICE P&R/R&B '71

Singles: 7-inch

CASABLANCA 3-5 80
PALMER (5020 "Easy to Be True") 100-200 67
PHIL-L.A. of SOUL 4-8 71-73
PHILADELPHIA INT'L 4-8 71
PHILIPS 5-10 69
TSOP 3-5 74-77

LPs: 10/12-inch

CASABLANCA 5-10 80
DECCA 10-15 69
PHILADELPHIA INT'L 5-10 78
TSOP 8-10 75-76
Members: Roger Andrews; Guy Fiske; David Thompson; Bob Eli; Frankie Brunson.
Also see MFSB

PEPPERMINT, Danny, & Jumping Jacks P&R '61

Singles: 7-inch

CARLTON 5-10 61

LPs: 10/12-inch

CARLTON (LP-20001 "Danny Peppermint") 25-35 62
(Monaural.)
CARLTON (STLP-20001 "Danny Peppermint") 35-50 62
(Stereo.)
Member: Danny Lamego.

PEPPERMINT HARRIS R&B '50

(With the Cross Town Blues Band; Harrison Nelson)

Singles: 78 rpm

ALADDIN 20-40 51-52
CASH 50-75 54
COMBO 15-30 56
MODERN 20-40 51
MONEY 20-40 54
SITTIN' in WITH 25-50 50-51
"X" 20-40 55

Singles: 7-inch

ALADDIN (3097 "I Got Loaded") ... 100-150 51
(Black vinyl.)
ALADDIN (3097 "I Got Loaded") ... 250-500 51
(Colored vinyl.)
ALADDIN (3107 "Have Another Drink and Talk to Me") 75-125 51
ALADDIN (3108 "P. H. Blues") 75-125 51
ALADDIN (3130 "Right Back On") .. 75-125 52
ALADDIN (3141 "There's a Dead Cat on the Line") 75-125 52
ALADDIN (3154 "I Sure Do Miss My Baby") 75-125 51
ALADDIN (3177 "Wasted Love") 75-125 51
ALADDIN (3183 "Don't Leave Me All Alone") 75-125 53
ALADDIN (3206 "I Never Get Enough of You") 75-125 51
CASH (1003 "Cadillac Funeral") ... 100-150 54
(First issue.)
COMBO (114 "Love at First Sight") 50-100 56
DART (103 "Messin' Around with the Blues") 15-25 59
DUKE (319 "Ain't No Business") 15-25 60
JEWEL 5-10 65-68
LUNAR 3-5
MAISON DE SOUL 5-10
MODERN (936 "Black Cat Bone") .. 50-100 51
MONEY (214 "Cadillac Funeral") 50-100 54
SITTIN' in WITH (543 "Rainin' in My Heart") 100-125 51
"X" (0142 "I Need Your Lovin'") 100-150 55

LPs: 10/12-inch

TIME (5 "Peppermint Harris") 50-100 62
Session: Laurels.
Also see NELSON, Peppermint
Also see REED, Jimmy / Peppermint Harris

PEPPERMINT RAINBOW P&R/LP '69

Singles: 7-inch

DECCA 4-6 68-69

Picture Sleeves

DECCA 5-10 69

LPs: 10/12-inch

DECCA 15-20 69

PEPPERMINT TROLLEY CO. P&R '68

Singles: 7-inch

ACTA 8-12 67-68
VALIANT (752 "Lollipop Train") 10-15 66

LPs: 10/12-inch

ACTA (38007 "Peppermint Trolley Co.") 15-25 68

PEPPERS P&R/R&B '74

Singles: 7-inch

BIG TREE 3-5 75
EVENT 3-5 74-75

LPs: 10/12-inch

EVENT 8-12 74

PEPSI & SHIRLIE P&R '87

Singles: 7-inch

POLYDOR 3-4 87-88

Picture Sleeves

POLYDOR 3-4 87-88

LPs: 10/12-inch

POLYDOR 5-8 88
Members: Pepsi DeMacque; Shirlie Holliman.
Also see WHAM!

PERCELLS P&R '63

Singles: 7-inch

ABC-PAR 5-10 63-64

PERCY & THEM R&B '74

Singles: 7-inch

PLAYBOY 3-5 73
ROULETTE 5-8 75

PERFECT GENTLEMEN LP '90

Singles: 7-inch

COLUMBIA 3-4 90

PERICOLI, Emilio P&R '62

Singles: 7-inch

VESUVIUS 4-6 62
W.B. 4-6 62-63

Picture Sleeves

W.B. 5-10 62

LPs: 10/12-inch

W.B. 10-20 63-66
VESUVIUS 10-20 62

PERKINS, Al R&B '69

Singles: 7-inch

ATCO 4-6 69-70
HI 3-5 72
SALEM 5-10 61
U.S.A. 4-8 64-65

PERKINS, Carl C&W/P&R/R&B '56

(The "Rockin' Guitar Man"; with the C.P. Express)

Singles: 78 rpm

FLIP (501 "Movie Magg") 200-300 55
SUN (224 "Gone Gone Gone") 50-100 56
SUN (234 thru 287) 25-75 56-57

Singles: 7-inch

AMERICA/SMASH 3-5 86-87
BANTAM 4-6
COLUMBIA (3-41000 & 3-42000 series) 25-50 60-62
(Compact 33 Singles.)
COLUMBIA (4-41000 thru 4-43000 series) 10-25 58-64
COLUMBIA (4-44000 & 4-45000 series) 5-10 64-72
DECCA 5-10 63-64
DOLLIE 15-25 67
FLIP (501 "Movie Magg") 300-500 55
JET 3-5 79
MERCURY 4-6 73-77
MUSIC MILL 4-6 76
SSS/SUN 3-5 70s
SUEDE 3-5 81
SUN (224 "Gone Gone Gone") 100-150 56
SUN (234 "Blue Suede Shoes") 20-40 56
SUN (243 "Boppin' the Blues") 25-50 56
SUN (249 "Dixie Fried") 30-60 56
SUN (261 "Matchbox") 25-50 57
SUN (274 "Forever Yours") 25-45 57
SUN (287 "Glad All Over") 25-45 57
(Counterfeits exist of most early Sun releases.)
UNIVERSAL 3-4 89

Picture Sleeves

AMERICA/SMASH 3-5 86
COLUMBIA (41131 "Pink Pedal Pushers") 25-45 58
COLUMBIA (42405 "Hollywood City") 20-30 62
COLUMBIA (42514 "Hambone") 40-60 62

EPs: 7-inch

COLUMBIA (12341 "Whole Lotta Shakin'") 200-300 58
SUN (115 "Blue Suede Shoes") 100-200 58

LPs: 10/12-inch

ACCORD 5-10 82
ALBUM GLOBE 8-12
ALLEGIANCE 5-10 84
COLUMBIA (1234 "Whole Lotta Shakin'") 100-200 58
(Red label.)

COLUMBIA (1234 "Whole Lotta Shakin'") 150-250 58
(White label. Promotional issue only.)
COLUMBIA (9833 "Greatest Hits") 10-20 69
COLUMBIA (10117 "Greatest Hits") 8-10 74
DESIGN 10-20 60s
DOLLIE 10-20 67
GRT/SUNNYVALE 8-12 77
HARMONY 8-12 72
HILLTOP 5-10
JET 8-12 78
KOALA 5-10 80
MERCURY 8-12 73
PICKWICK/HILLTOP 5-10
ROUNDER 5-10 89
SSS/SUN 5-10 69-84
SUEDE 8-10 81
SUN (1225 "Dance Album") 500-750 57
SUN (1225 "Teen Beat") 200-250 61
(Repackage of *Dance Album*.)
TRIP 8-10 74
UNIVERSAL 5-10 89
TRIP 8-12 74
Also see McCARTNEY, Paul
Also see NELSON, Willie / Jerry Lee Lewis / Carl Perkins / David Allan Coe
Also see STATLER BROTHERS
Also see YOUNG, Faron / Carl Perkins / Claude King

PERKINS, Carl / Sonny Burgess

LPs: 10/12-inch

SSS/SUN 5-10

PERKINS, Carl, Jerry Lee Lewis, Roy Orbison & Johnny Cash — *LP '86*

LPs: 10/12-inch

AMERICA ("Class of '55") 20-30 86
(Mail-order edition. Has souvenir booklet and audio cassette with interviews of the singers.)
AMERICA/SMASH (830002 "Class of '55") 5-10 86
AMERICA/SMASH (830002 "Class of '55") 30-40 86
(Picture disc. Promotional issue only.)
Also see CASH, Johnny, Carl Perkins & Jerry Lee Lewis
Also see LEWIS, Jerry Lee, Carl Perkins & Charlie Rich
Also see ORBISON, Roy

PERKINS, Carl, & NRBQ

Singles: 7-inch

COLUMBIA 3-5 70

LPs: 10/12-inch

COLUMBIA 10-15 70
Also see NRBQ
Also see PERKINS, Carl

PERKINS, George — *P&R/R&B '70*

(With the Silver Stars)

Singles: 7-inch

SILVER FOX 4-8 69
SOUL POWER 3-6 72

LPs: 10/12-inch

CRYIN' in the STREETS 8-12 77

PERKINS, Joe — *P&R '63*

Singles: 7-inch

BERRY 4-8 60s
BLUFF CITY 3-6 74
MUSICOR 4-8 65
SOUND STAGE 7 .... 4-8 63

PERKINS, Tony — *P&R '57*

Singles: 78 rpm

RCA 8-12 57

Singles: 7-inch

RCA 8-12 57

Picture Sleeves

RCA 10-20 57

LPs: 10/12-inch

EPIC (3394 "Tony Perkins") 25-35 57
RCA (1679 "From My Heart") 20-30 58
RCA (LPM-1853 "On a Rainy Afternoon") 20-30 58
RCA (LSP-1853 "On a Rainy Afternoon") 30-40 58

PERKINS, Tony / James Dean

Singles: 78 rpm

RAINBO (5-21-57 "Dean & Perkins") 30-50 57
(Flexi, picture disc.)
Also see PERKINS, Tony

PERRY, Greg — *R&B '74*

Singles: 12-inch

ALFA 4-6 82

Singles: 7-inch

ALFA 3-4 82
CASABLANCA 3-5 74-75
CHESS 4-8 68
RCA 3-5 77

LPs: 10/12-inch

CASABLANCA 8-12 75

PERRY, Jeff — *R&B '75*

Singles: 7-inch

ARISTA 3-5 75-76
EPIC 3-5 77

PERRY, Joe, Project — *LP '80*

Singles: 7-inch

COLUMBIA 3-5 80-81

LPs: 10/12-inch

COLUMBIA 5-10 80-81
MCA 4-8 83
Members: Joe Perry; Ralph Morman; Ronnie Stewart; David Hull.
Also see AEROSMITH

PERRY, Linda — *R&B '73*

Singles: 7-inch

MAINSTREAM 3-5 73

PERRY, Roxy — *D&D '83*

Singles: 12-inch

PERSONAL 4-6 83

PERRY, Steve — *P&R '82*

Singles: 7-inch

COLUMBIA 3-4 84-85

Picture Sleeves

COLUMBIA 3-4 84

LPs: 10/12-inch

COLUMBIA 5-8 84-85
Also see JOURNEY
Also see LOGGINS, Kenny, & Steve Perry
Also see U.S.A. for AFRICA

PERRY & SANLIN — *R&B '80*

Singles: 7-inch

CAPITOL 3-5 80

LPs: 10/12-inch

CAPITOL 5-10 80

PERSIANS — *R&B '68*

Singles: 7-inch

ABC 4-8 68
CAPITOL 3-5 71-72
GRAPEVINE 3-5 70
GWP 3-6 69-70
Members: James Gill; Freddie Lewis; James Harlee; Jim Brown.

PERSON, Houston — *R&B '75*

Singles: 78 rpm

PRESTIGE 3-6 52

Singles: 7-inch

EASTBOUND 3-5
PRESTIGE 5-10 52
WESTBOUND 3-5 75-76

PERSUADERS — *P&R/R&B '71*

Singles: 7-inch

ATCO 4-8 71-75
CALLA 3-5 77
WIN OR LOSE 3-5 71-72

LPs: 10/12-inch

ATCO 8-12 73-74
CALLA 8-10 77
WIN OR LOSE 10-15 72
Members: Doug Scott; James Barnes; Charles Stodghill; Willie Holland; Thomas Hill; Richard Gant; Willie Coleman.

PERSUASIONS — *LP '71*

Singles: 7-inch

A&M 3-5 74-75
CAPITOL 5-10 71-72
CATAMOUNT (Black vinyl) 3-6 70s
CATAMOUNT (Colored vinyl) 10-15 70s
ELEKTRA 5-10
ERICA 10-20
KING TUT 5-10
MCA 3-5 73
PAY-4-PLAY 5-10
(Colored vinyl.)
REPRISE 10-15 70
TOWER 5-10 65-66

LPs: 10/12-inch

A&M 10-15 74
CAPITOL 15-25 71-72
CATAMOUNT 8-10 70s
ELEKTRA 10-12 77
FLYING FISH 5-10 79
MCA 8-12 73
ROUNDER 5-8 80s
STRAIGHT 25-35 70
Members: Jerry Lawson; Jimmy Hayes; Jayotis Washington; Joe Russell; Herb Rhoad.

PET SHOP BOYS — *P&R/R&B/LP '86*

Singles: 12-inch

EMI 4-6 86-87

Singles: 7-inch

EMI 3-4 86-90

Picture Sleeves

EMI 3-4 86-89

LPs: 10/12-inch

EMI (Except 90263) 5-10 86-90
EMI (90263 "Actually") 10-15 88
(With bonus 12-inch single, *Always on My Mind*)
Members: Neil Tennant; Chris Lowe.
Also see ELECTRONIC

PET SHOP BOYS & DUSTY SPRINGFIELD

Singles: 7-inch

EMI 3-4 87
Also see PET SHOP BOYS
Also see SPRINGFIELD, Dusty

PETER & GORDON — *P&R/LP '64*

Singles: 7-inch

CAPITOL 5-10 64-69

Picture Sleeves

CAPITOL 8-15 64-67

LPs: 10/12-inch

CAPITOL (T-2115 thru T-2882) 15-25 64-68
(Monaural.)
CAPITOL (ST-2115 thru ST-2882) 20-30 64-68
(Stereo.)
CAPITOL (SM-2549 "Best of Peter & Gordon") 5-10 77
CAPITOL (SN-16084 "Best of Peter & Gordon") 5-8 80
Members: Peter Asher; Gordon Waller.

PETER & GORDON / Lettermen

Singles: 7-inch

CAPITOL CREATIVE PROD. 5-10 66
(Fritos Company promotional issue.)
Also see LETTERMEN
Also see PETER & GORDON

PETER, PAUL & MARY — *P&R/LP '62*

Singles: 7-inch

"EUGENE McCARTHY for PRESIDENT" 10-20 68
(Promotional issue only. No label name used.)
W.B. (5000 series) 4-8 62-66
W.B. (7000 series) 3-6 67-70

Picture Sleeves

W.B. 4-8 62-64

EPs: 7-inch

W.B. 5-10 63-64
(Juke box issues only.)

LPs: 10/12-inch

GOLD C. 5-8 87
W.B. (1449 thru 1648) 20-30 62-66
(Gold or gray labels.)

W.B. (1700 thru 2552)........................8-15 67-70
W.B. (3000 series)..............................5-10 77-78
Members: Peter Yarrow; Paul Stookey; Mary Travers.
Also see STOOKEY, Paul
Also see TRAVERS, Mary
Also see YARROW, Peter

PETERS, Bernadette *P&R/LP '80*

Singles: 7-inch

ABC-PAR 4-8 65
COLUMBIA..4-8 67
MCA...3-5 78-81
U.A. 5-10 62

Picture Sleeves

MCA...3-5 80-81

LPs: 10/12-inch

MCA...5-10 80-81

PETERSEN, Paul *P&R '62*

Singles: 7-inch

ABC 3-5 74
COLPIX (Except 720) 5-15 62-65
COLPIX (720 "She Rides with Me")... 25-35 64
ERIC 3-4 70s
MCA...3-4
MOTOWN...10-20 67-68

Picture Sleeves

COLPIX (632 "Keep Your Love Locked")..10-20 61
COLPIX (663 "My Dad") 10-20 62

LPs: 10/12-inch

COLPIX (CP-429 "Lollipops and Roses")...25-35 62
(Monaural.)
COLPIX (SCP-429 "Lollipops and Roses")...35-45 62
(Stereo.)
COLPIX (CP-442 "My Dad") 30-40 63
(Monaural.)
COLPIX (SCP-442 "My Dad")...........35-45 63
(Stereo.)
Session: Beach Boys; Honeys; Billy Strange; Hal Blaine; Tommy Tedesco; Plas Johnson; Steve Douglas; David Gates; Richie Frost.
Also see BEACH BOYS
Also see DARREN, James / Shelly Fabares / Paul Petersen
Also see GATES, David
Also see STRANGE, Billy

PETERSEN, Paul, & Shelly Fabares

Singles: 7-inch

COLPIX (631 "What Did They Do Before Rock & Roll") 5-10 62
Also see FABARES, Shelly
Also see PETERSEN, Paul

PETERSON, Bobby *P&R '59*
(Bobby Peterson Quintet)

Singles: 7-inch

ATLANTIC 4-8 62
V-TONE..5-10 59-60

PETERSON, Lucky, Blues Band *R&B '71*

Singles: 7-inch

TODAY..3-5 71

LPs: 10/12-inch

TODAY 10-15 71

PETERSON, Oscar *LP '63*
(Oscar Peterson Trio)

Singles: 78 rpm

CLEF 4-6 53-56
MERCURY 4-8 51-52
NORGRAN..4-6 55
VERVE 4-8 57

Singles: 7-inch

CLEF 5-15 53-56
LIMELIGHT...4-8 65-66
MERCURY (8900 series) 5-15 51-52
MERCURY (72000 series) 4-8 64
MERCURY (89000 series) 5-15 52-53
NORGRAN...5-15 55
PRESTIGE 4-6 69
VERVE 5-10 57-64

EPs: 7-inch

CLEF 25-50 52-55
RCA (3006 "This Is Oscar Peterson") 75-125 51

LPs: 10/12-inch

BASF..8-12 74-76
CLEF (106 "Piano Solos")............. 100-200 52
(10-inch LP.)
CLEF (107 "At Carnegie Hall")...... 100-200 52
(10-inch LP.)
CLEF (110 "Collates")................. 100-200 52
(10-inch LP.)
CLEF (116 "Oscar Peterson Quartet").. 100-200 52
(10-inch LP.)
CLEF (119 "Oscar Peterson Plays Pretty") 100-200 52
(10-inch LP.)
CLEF (127 "Collates, No. 2") 100-150 53
(10-inch LP.)
CLEF (145 "Oscar Peterson Sings").. 100-150 54
(10-inch LP.)
CLEF (155 "Oscar Peterson Plays Pretty, No. 2") 100-150 54
(10-inch LP.)
CLEF (168 "Oscar Peterson Quartet, No. 2").. 100-150 55
(10-inch LP.)
CLEF (600 series).......................... 50-100 53-56
EMARCY.. 8-12 76
LIMELIGHT (1000 series) 5-8 82
LIMELIGHT (82000 & 86000 series) 10-20 65-67
MFSL (243 "Very Tall") 20-25 95
(Half-speed mastered.)
MGM (100 series) 8-12 70
MPS 8-12 72-76
MERCURY (20975 "Trio+One")........ 20-30 64
(Monaural.)
MERCURY (60975 "Trio+One")........ 25-35 64
(Stereo.)
METRO 10-15 65
PABLO 6-12 75-83
PAUSA... 5-10 79-81
PRESTIGE.. 8-15 69-74
RCA (3006 "This Is Oscar Peterson") 200-250 51
(10-inch LP.)
TRIP.. 5-8 75-76
VSP... 10-20 66-67
VERVE... 35-75 56-60
(Reads "Verve Records, Inc." at bottom of label.)
VERVE... 10-25 61-72
(Reads "MGM Records - A Division of Metro-Goldwyn-Mayer, Inc." at bottom of label.)
VERVE... 5-15 73-83
(Reads "Manufactured By MGM Record Corp.," or mentions either Polydor or Polygram at bottom of label.)
WING 8-12 67
Members (Oscar Peterson Trio): Ray Brown; Herb Ellis.
Also see ARMSTRONG, Louis, & Oscar Peterson
Also see BASIE, Count, & Oscar Peterson
Also see FITZGERALD, Ella, & Oscar Peterson
Also see GETZ, Stan, & Oscar Peterson
Also see HUBBARD, Freddie, & Oscar Peterson
Also see MULLIGAN, Gerry, & Oscar Peterson
Also see RIDDLE, Nelson

PETERSON, Ray *P&R '59*

Singles: 7-inch

CLOUD 9 .... 3-5 75
DECCA.. 3-5 71
DUNES 5-10 60-63
MGM 4-8 64-66
POLYDOR 3-5 70s
RCA (47-7000 series) 10-15 58-60
RCA (47-8000 series) 4-8 64
RCA (61-7578 "My Blue Angel") 15-25 60
(Stereo.)
RCA (61-7745 "Tell Laura I Love Her").. 15-25 60
(Stereo.)
RCA (61-7779 "Teenage Heartache")...15-25 60
(Stereo.)
REPRISE..4-6 69
UNI 3-5 70

Picture Sleeves

DUNES (2002 "Corrina Corrina") 8-12 60
MGM (13269 "Oh No").......................5-10 64
MGM (13336 "House Without Windows") 5-10 64
RCA (7635 "Goodnight My Love").......8-12 59

EPs: 7-inch

RCA (4367 "Tell Laura I Love Her") 40-60 60

LPs: 10/12-inch

CAMDEN...10-20 66
DECCA..8-12 71
MGM...20-30 64-65
RCA (LPM-2297 "Tell Laura I Love Her")..40-60 60
(Monaural.)
RCA (LSP-2297 "Tell Laura I Love Her")..60-80 60
(Stereo.)
UNI 10-15 70

PETITE *R&B '86*

Singles: 7-inch

YORK'S 3-4 86

PETS *P&R '58*

Singles: 78 rpm

ARWIN 10-15 58

Singles: 7-inch

ARWIN 10-15 58
Member: Seph Acre.

PETTUS, Giorge *R&B '87*

Singles: 7-inch

MCA...3-4 86-88

Picture Sleeves

MCA...3-4 86

PETTY, Norman, Trio *P&R '54*

Singles: 78 rpm

ABC-PAR 5-10 57
COLUMBIA (Except 41039) 5-10 57
COLUMBIA (41039 "Moondreams").. 50-75 57
(With Buddy Holly on guitar.)
NOR VA JAK.....................................15-20 57
"X"...4-8 54-55

Singles: 7-inch

ABC-PAR 5-10 57
COLUMBIA (Except 41039) 5-10 57
COLUMBIA (41039 "Moondreams").. 50-75 57
(With Buddy Holly on guitar.)
FELSTED 4-8 62
JARO 5-10 60
NOR VA JAK (Except 1325).............15-20 57-59
NOR VA JAK (1325 "True Love Ways")..50-75 60
NORMAN..5-10 60
"X"...5-10 54-55

EPs: 7-inch

COLUMBIA (2139 "Four Hits") 15-25 58
COLUMBIA (10921 "Moondreams")...............................50-100 58
"X" (82 "In Full Fidelity")..................15-25 55

LPs: 10/12-inch

COLUMBIA (1092 "Moondreams") .50-100 58
TOP RANK (R-639 "Petty for Your Thoughts") 20-30 60
(Monaural.)
TOP RANK (RS-639 "Petty for Your Thoughts") 30-40 60
(Stereo.)
VIK (1073 "Corsage") 30-45 57
Members: Norman Petty; Vi Petty; Jack Petty.
Also see HOLLY, Buddy

PETTY, Tom, & Heartbreakers *P&R/LP '77*

Singles: 7-inch

BACKSTREET 3-5 79-83
(Black vinyl.)

BACKSTREET (52181 "Change of Heart") 5-8 83
(Colored vinyl.)
MCA 3-4 85-90
SHELTER 3-5 77-78

Picture Sleeves

BACKSTREET 3-5 79-83
MCA 3-4 85-90
SHELTER 3-5 77-78

LPs: 10/12-inch

BACKSTREET 5-10 79-82
MCA 5-8 85-90
SHELTER 8-15 76-78

Promotional LPs

SHELTER (12677 "Official Live 'Leg") 15-25 76
SHELTER (52029 "You're Gonna Get It") 15-25 78
(Colored vinyl.)
Members: Tom Petty; Mike Campbell; Stan Lynch; Beaumont Tench; Ron Blair; Howie Epstein.
Also see DYLAN, Bob, & Heartbreakers / Michael Rubini
Also see NICKS, Stevie, with Tom Petty & Heartbreakers

PETTY, Vi: see PETTY, Norman, Trio

PHANTOM, ROCKER & SLICK — LP '85

Singles: 7-inch

EMI AMERICA 3-5 85-86

LPs: 10/12-inch

EMI AMERICA 5-10 85-86
Members: Jim Phantom; Lee Rocker; Earl Slick.
Also see SILVER CONDOR
Also see STRAY CATS

PHELPS, James — P&R/R&B '65

(With the Du-Ettes; Jimmy Phelps)

Singles: 7-inch

ARGO 4-8 65
CADET 4-8 66
FONTANA 4-8 66-67
MECCA (5 "Blue Point Drive") 15-25 60
PARAMOUNT 3-5 71-72
Also see SOUL STIRRERS

PHILADELPHIA INTERNATIONAL ALL STARS — P&R/R&B '77

Singles: 7-inch

PHILADELPHIA INT'L 3-5 77
Members: Archie Bell; the O'Jays; Billy Paul; Teddy Pendergrass; Lou Rawls; Dee Dee Sharpe.
Also see BELL, Archie
Also see MFSB
Also see O'JAYS
Also see PAUL, Billy
Also see PENDERGRASS, Teddy
Also see RAWLS, Lou
Also see SHARPE, Dee Dee

PHILADELPHIA STORY — R&B '77

Singles: 7-inch

H&L 3-5 77

PHILHARMONICS — P&R/R&B '77

Singles: 7-inch

CAPRICORN 3-5 77

LPs: 10/12-inch

CAPRICORN 5-10 77

PHILLINGANES, Greg — R&B '81

Singles: 12-inch

PLANET 4-6 85

Singles: 7-inch

PLANET 3-4 81-85

LPs: 10/12-inch

PLANET 5-8 81-85
Also see KING DREAM CHORUS & Holiday Crew

PHILLIPS, Anthony — LP '77

Singles: 7-inch

PASSPORT 3-5 77-78

LPs: 10/12-inch

PASSPORT (Except 9828) 5-10 77-78
PASSPORT (9828 "Wise After the Event") 15-20 78
(Picture disc.)
Also see GENESIS

PHILLIPS, Esther: see LITTLE ESTHER

PHILLIPS, Esther, & Joe Beck

LPs: 10/12-inch

KUDU 8-10 76
Also see BECK, Joe
Also see LITTLE ESTHER

PHILLIPS, John — P&R/C&W/LP '70

Singles: 7-inch

ATCO 3-5 74
COLUMBIA 3-5 73
DUNHILL 3-5 70

LPs: 10/12-inch

DUNHILL 10-15 70
Also see MAMAS & PAPAS

PHILLIPS, Little Esther: see LITTLE ESTHER

PHILLIPS, Phil — P&R/R&B '59

(With the Twilights)

Singles: 7-inch

CLIQUE 4-8 66
KHOURY'S (711 "Sea of Love") ... 300-500 59
LANOR (It's All Right") 15-25 59
(Selection number not known.)
MERCURY (10021 "Verdi Mae") 20-30 59
(Stereo.)
MERCURY (71000 series) 8-12 59-61
MERCURY CELEBRITY SERIES 3-5
Also see K-DOE, Ernie / Phil Phillips

PHILLIPS, Shawn — LP '72

Singles: 7-inch

A&M 3-5 70-75
ASCOT 4-8 64

LPs: 10/12-inch

A&M 8-12 70-77
RCA 5-10 78-81

PHILLIPS, Wes — R&B/D&D '84

Singles: 12-inch

QUALITY 4-6 84

Singles: 7-inch

QUALITY 3-4 84

PHILLY CREAM — P&R/R&B '79

Singles: 12-inch

WMOT 4-8 79

Singles: 7-inch

FANTASY 3-5 79
WMOT 3-5 79

LPs: 10/12-inch

WMOT 5-10 79

PHILLY DEVOTIONS — P&R/R&B '75

Singles: 7-inch

BRY-WEK (1038 "I'll Never Color You a Rainbow") 5-10 73
DON DE (127 "I Just Can't Say Goodbye") 4-8 74
COLUMBIA 3-5 75-76

PHOTOGLO, Jim — P&R/LP '80

(Photoglo)

Singles: 7-inch

CASABLANCA 3-5 83
20TH FOX 3-5 80-81

LPs: 10/12-inch

CASABLANCA 5-10 83
20TH FOX 5-10 80-81

PIAF, Edith — P&R '50

(With Theo Sarapo)

Singles: 78 rpm

CAPITOL 4-8 56-58
COLUMBIA 4-8 50-52

Singles: 7-inch

CAPITOL 5-15 56-61
CAPITOL STARLINE 4-6 60s
COLUMBIA 5-15 50-52

EPs: 7-inch

ANGEL 5-15 55-56
COLUMBIA 5-15 50-52
DECCA 5-15 54

LPs: 10/12-inch

ANGEL 25-40 55-56
CAPITOL (10210 "Piaf") 15-25 59
CAPITOL (10283 "Piaf of Paris") 10-20 61
CAPITOL (10295 "Potpourri Par Piaf") 10-20 62
CAPITOL (10348 "Piaf & Sarapo") 10-20 63
CAPITOL (16000 series) 5-10 81-82
CAPITOL STARLINE 5-10 60s
COLUMBIA (898 "La Vie En Rose") 20-40 56
COLUMBIA (6223 "Encore Parisiennes") 25-50 52
(10-inch LP.)
COLUMBIA (9500 series) 25-50 51-52
(10-inch LPs.)
COLUMBIA (37000 series) 5-10 81
DECCA (6004 "Chansons des Cafes de Paris") 25-50 54
(10-inch LP.)
DISCOS 20-30 56
PHILIPS 10-20 64-67
RCA 10-15 64
VOX (3050 "Edith Piaf Sings") 25-50 53
(10-inch LP.)
VOX (3060 "Edith Piaf Favorites") 25-50 53
(10-inch LP.)

PIANO RED — R&B '50

(Willie Perryman)

Singles: 78 rpm

CHECKER 20-40 58
GROOVE 15-30 54-57
RCA 20-50 50-57

Singles: 7-inch

CHECKER (911 "Get Up Mare") 15-25 58
GROOVE 25-50 54-57
JAX 8-12 59
RCA (0099 "Rockin' with Red") 50-75 50
(Colored vinyl.)
RCA (0106 "The Wrong YoYo") 25-50 50
RCA (0118 "Jumpin' the Boogie") 25-50 51
RCA (0130 "Baby What's Wrong") 25-50 51
RCA (4265 "Let's Have a Good Time") 25-50 51
RCA (4380 "Hey Good Lookin'") 25-50 51
RCA (4524 "Bouncin' with Red") 25-50 52
RCA (4766 "Sales Tax Boogie") 25-50 52
RCA (4957 "Voo Doopee Doo") 25-50 52
RCA (5101 "I'm Gonna Rock Some More") 20-35 52
RCA (5224 "I'm Gonna Tell Everybody") 20-35 53
RCA (5337 "Your Mouth's Got a Hole") 20-35 52
RCA (5544 "Right and Ready") 20-35 52
RCA (6000 & 7000 series) 15-25 57-58

EPs: 7-inch

GROOVE (3 "Jump Man, Jump") 40-60 56
GROOVE (10026/27/28 "Piano Red in Concert") 35-50 56
(Price is for any of three volumes.)
RCA (587 "Rockin' with Red") 50-100 54
RCA (5091 "Rockin' with Red") 40-60 59
(Black label.)
RCA (5091 "Rockin' with Red") 50-100 59
(Maroon label.)

LPs: 10/12-inch

ARHOOLIE 8-10
BLACK LION 8-10 76
GROOVE (1001 "Jump Man, Jump") 500-750 56
GROOVE (1002 "Piano Red in Concert") 150-250 56
KING 10-20 70
RCA 8-10 74
Also see DOCTOR FEELGOOD

PIANO RED / June Valli

EPs: 7-inch

RCA (92 "Dealer's Prevue") 15-25 56
(Promotional issue only.)
Also see PIANO RED
Also see VALLI, June

PICKETT, Bobby — P&R/R&B/LP '62
(Bobby [Boris] Pickett & Crypt-Kickers; Featuring Bobby Paine)

Singles: 12-inch
EASY STREET....4-8 84

Singles: 7-inch
ANTHEM....3-5
ATMOSPHERE....5-10 65
CAPITOL....5-10 63-64
EASY STREET....3-5 84
GARPAX (1 "Monster Mash")....8-12 62
GARPAX (724 "I'm Down to My Last Heartbreak")....5-10
GARPAX (44000 series)....5-10 62-64
LONDON....3-5 70s
METROMEDIA (0089 "Me and My Mummy")....4-8 68
METROMEDIA (9989 "Me and My Mummy")....3-6 73
PARROT....4-8 70-73
RCA....5-10 64
WHITE WHALE....4-8 70

Picture Sleeves
GARPAX....10-20 62-63

LPs: 10/12-inch
GARPAX (GP-67001 "Monster Mash")....30-50 62
(Monaural.)
GARPAX (SGP-67001 "Monster Mash")....50-75 62
(Stereo.)
PARROT....10-20 73

PICKETT, Wilson — P&R/R&B '63

Singles: 7-inch
ATLANTIC (2200 thru 2400 series)....6-12 64-67
ATLANTIC (2500 thru 2900 series)....4-8 68-72
ATLANTIC (8000 series)....3-4 88
BIG TREE....3-5 78
CORREC-TONE (501 "Let Me Be Your Boy")....40-60 62
CUB (9113 "Let Me Be Your Boy")....25-35 62
DOUBLE-L....8-12 63
EMI AMERICA....3-5 79-81
MOTOWN....3-4 87
RCA....3-5 73-74
ROWE/AMI....5-10 66
("Play Me" Sales Stimulator promotional issue.)
VERVE....10-20 65
WICKED....4-8 75-76

Picture Sleeves
ATLANTIC....3-4 88

EPs: 7-inch
ATLANTIC (SD-8250 "Right On")....10-15 70
(Stereo. Juke box issue only. With paper envelope-sleeve.)

LPs: 10/12-inch
ATLANTIC (Except 8100 series)....10-15 69-73
ATLANTIC (8100 series)....12-25 65-68
BIG TREE....5-10 78
BROOKVILLE....8-12 77
DOUBLE-L (DL-8300 "It's Too Late")....25-35 63
(Monaural.)
DOUBLE-L (SDL-8300 "It's Too Late")....30-40 63
(Stereo.)
EMI AMERICA....5-10 79-81
RCA....8-12 73-77
WAND....10-15 68
WICKED....8-12 76
Also see FALCONS

PICKETT, Wilson / Sam & Dave

LPs: 10/12-inch
ATLANTIC (ST-136 "Excerpts from *Hey Jude*)....15-25 69
(Promotional issue for in-store use.)
Also see PICKETT, Wilson
Also see SAM & DAVE

PICKETT & PAYNE

Singles: 7-inch
METROMEDIA (0089 "It's Not the Same Without You")....5-8 68
METROMEDIA (9989 "It's Not the Same Without You")....4-6 73
Members: Bobby Pickett; Joan Payne.
Also see PICKETT, Bobby

PICKETTYWITCH — P&R '70

Singles: 7-inch
JANUS....3-5 70
PYE....3-5 71

LPs: 10/12-inch
JANUS....8-12 70
Member: Polly Brown.
Also see BROWN, Polly

PICTURE PERFECT — R&B '87

Singles: 7-inch
ATLANTIC....3-4 87

PIECES OF A DREAM — R&B/LP '81

Singles: 12-inch
ELEKTRA....4-6 84

Singles: 7-inch
ELEKTRA....3-5 81-84
MANHATTAN....3-4 88

LPs: 10/12-inch
ELEKTRA....5-10 81-84
MANHATTAN....5-8 86

PIECES OF EIGHT — P&R '67

Singles: 7-inch
A&M....5-10 67-68
ACTION....5-10 60s
MALA....5-10 68
Also see SWINGIN' MEDALLIONS

PIED PIPERS — P&R '44
(With Paul Weston's Orchestra)

Singles: 78 rpm
CAPITOL....5-10 44-55
RCA....4-8 48

Singles: 7-inch
CAPITOL....8-12 49-55
RCA....5-10 48

EPs: 7-inch
CAPITOL....10-20 50-55

LPs: 10/12-inch
CAPITOL (H-212 "Harvest Moon")....30-50 50
(10-inch LP.)
GOLDEN TONE....5-10
Members: Jo Stafford; Chuck Lowry; Hal Hopper; Clark Yocum; June Hutton; Sue Allen.
Also see SINATRA, Frank, & Pied Pipers
Also see STAFFORD, Jo

PIERCE, Webb — C&W '52

Singles: 78 rpm
DECCA....5-15 51-52
4 STAR....10-20 51-52

Singles: 7-inch
DECCA (28091 thru 29804)....10-20 52-56
DECCA (30045 "Teenage Boogie")....25-35 56
DECCA (31000 thru 33000 series)....5-10 59-73
DECCA (46000 series)....10-20 51-52
KING....5-10 60
MCA....3-5 73-74
PLANTATION....3-5 75-77
SOUNDWAVES....3-4 83

EPs: 7-inch
DECCA....10-20 53-65

LPs: 10/12-inch
BULLDOG....5-10
CASTLE....5-10
CORAL....5-10 73
DECCA (181 "Webb Pierce Story")....15-25 64
(Includes booklet.)
DECCA (DL-4015 "Webb with a Beat")....20-30 60
(Monaural.)
DECCA (DL7-4015 "Webb with a Beat")....20-40 60
(Stereo.)
DECCA (DL-4079 thru 4964)....10-25 60-67
DECCA (DL7-4079 thru 4964)....15-30 60-67
DECCA (5536 "Wondering Boy")....40-60 53
(10-inch LP.)
DECCA (8129 "Webb Pierce")....20-40 55
DECCA (8295 "Wondering Boy")....20-40 56
DECCA (8728 "Just Imagination")....20-40 57
DECCA (DL-8889 "Bound for the Kingdom")....20-40 59
(Monaural.)
DECCA (DL7-8889 "Bound for the Kingdom")....25-50 59
(Stereo.)
DECCA (DL-8899 "Webb!")....20-30 59
(Monaural.)
DECCA (DL7-8899 "Webb!")....25-35 59
(Stereo.)
DECCA (74000 & 75000 series)....8-12 68-73
KING (648 "The One and Only Webb Pierce")....20-40 59
KOALA....5-8 80
MCA....5-12 73-78
MUSIC MASTERS....5-10
PICCADILLY....5-8 80
PICKWICK/HILLTOP....10-15 65
PLANTATION....5-8 76-77
SEARS....8-12 60s
SESAC....30-50 59
SKYLITE....5-8 77
VOCALION....5-15 66-70
Also see NELSON, Willie, & Webb Pierce
Also see SOVINE, Red, & Webb Pierce
Also see WELLS, Kitty, & Webb Pierce

PIERCE, Webb / Patsy Cline / T. Texas Tyler

LPs: 10/12-inch
DESIGN (901 "Three of a Kind")....8-12 63
Also see CLINE, Patsy

PIERCE, Webb / Loretta Lynn

LPs: 10/12-inch
PHILCO/MCA....15-25 69
Also see LYNN, Loretta

PIERCE, Webb / Wynn Stewart

LPs: 10/12-inch
DESIGN....8-12 62
Also see STEWART, Wynn

PIERCE, Webb, & Mel Tillis — C&W '63

Singles: 7-inch
DECCA....4-6 62

PIERCE, Webb, & Wilburn Brothers — C&W '54

Singles: 78 rpm
DECCA....5-10 54

Singles: 7-inch
DECCA....10-15 54
Also see PIERCE, Webb
Also see WILBURN BROTHERS

PILOT — P&R/LP '75

Singles: 7-inch
ARISTA....3-5 77
CAPITOL....3-5 77
EMI....3-5 74-76

LPs: 10/12-inch
ARISTA....8-10 77
EMI....8-10 74-76
Members: David Paton; Ian Bairnson; Stuart Tosh; William Lyall.
Also see PARSONS, Alan, Project
Also see 10CC

PILTDOWN MEN — P&R '60

Singles: 7-inch
CAPITOL....8-12 60-62
Members: Lincoln Mayorga; Bob Bain; Earl Palmer; Jack Kel.

PINDER, Michael — LP '76

LPs: 10/12-inch
THRESHOLD (18 "The Promise")....8-12 76
Also see MOODY BLUES

PINERA, Mike — P&R '80

Singles: 7-inch
CAPRICORN....3-5 78
SPECTOR....3-5 80
SRI....3-5 79

LPs: 10/12-inch
SRI....5-10 79
Also see BLUES IMAGE

Also see CACTUS
Also see IRON BUTTERFLY
Also see RAMATAM

PINETOPPERS *C&W '50*
(With the Beaver Valley Sweethearts)
Singles: 78 rpm
CORAL 4-6 50-54
DECCA 3-5 54-56
Singles: 7-inch
CORAL 8-12 50-54
DECCA 5-10 54-56
PEER SOUTHERN 4-6 67
EPs: 7-inch
CORAL 5-10 50-56
LPs: 10/12-inch
CORAL 10-20 50-56
Members: Roy Horton; Vaughn Horton. Ray Smith; Trudy Martin; Gloria Martin; John Bowers; Rusty Keefer.

PINETTE, Rick, & Oak *P&R '80*
Singles: 7-inch
MERCURY 3-5 80
LPs: 10/12-inch
MERCURY 5-10 80
Also see OAK

PINK FLOYD *LP '67*
Singles: 12-inch
COLUMBIA (1635 "Selections/Final Cut") 15-20 83
(Promotional issue only.)
COLUMBIA (2878 "On the Turning Away") 8-12 87
(Promotional issue only.)
Singles: 7-inch
CAPITOL 5-15 71-78
COLUMBIA (Black vinyl) 3-8 75-94
COLUMBIA (Colored vinyl) 5-10 87
(Promotional issue only.)
HARVEST 5-15 73-74
TOWER (333 "Arnold Layne") 35-55 67
TOWER (356 "See Emily Play") 35-55 67
TOWER (378 "The Gnome") 35-55 67
TOWER (426 "It Would be So Nice") 35-55 68
TOWER (440 "Let There Be More Light") 35-55 68
Picture Sleeves
TOWER 100-200 67
(We are not yet certain which of the Tower 45s came with sleeves.)
COLUMBIA 3-8 80-87
EPs: 7-inch
HARVEST (6746/7 "Pink Floyd, from *Dark Side of the Moon*") 75-125 73
(Promotional issue only. Issued with paper sleeve.)
LPs: 10/12-inch
CAPITOL (Except 11902) 5-8 78-83
CAPITOL (11902 "Dark Side of the Moon") 30-40 78
(Picture disc.)
COLUMBIA (Except Half-Speed Mastered, Quadraphonic, & Colored vinyl) 6-10 75-88
COLUMBIA (HC-43453 "Wish You Were Here") 25-50 80
(Half-speed mastered.)
COLUMBIA (PCQ-43453 "Wish You Were Here") 40-60 75
(Quadraphonic.)
COLUMBIA (HC-47680 "Collection of Great Dance Songs") 20-40 80s
(Half-speed mastered.)
COLUMBIA (H2C-46183 "The Wall") 150-200 80s
(Half-speed mastered.)
COLUMBIA (64200 "Division Bell") 8-12 94
(Colored vinyl.)
HARVEST (STBB-388 "Ummagumma") 25-35 69
HARVEST (SMAS-382 "Atom Heart Mother") 15-20 70
HARVEST (759 "Relics") 10-15 71
HARVEST (832 "Meddle") 10-15 71
HARVEST (11078 "Obscured By Clouds") 10-15 72
HARVEST (11163 "The Dark Side of the Moon") 8-12 73
HARVEST (11198 "More") 10-15 73
(Soundtrack.)
HARVEST (11000 series) 10-15 72-73
HARVEST (11257 "A Nice Pair") 10-15 73
HARVEST (16234 "Relics") 5-10 82
MFSL (017 "Dark Side of the Moon") 60-80 78
MFSL/UHQR (017 "Dark Side of the Moon") 100-150 78
(Boxed set.)
MFSL (190 "Meddle") 40-60 79
MFSL (202 "Atom Heart Mother") 20-25 94
(Half-speed mastered.)
TOWER (T-5093 "Piper at the Gates of Dawn") 100-125 67
(Monaural.)
TOWER (ST-5093 "Piper at the Gates of Dawn") 50-75 67
(Orange label. Stereo.)
TOWER (5093 "Piper at the Gates of Dawn") 40-50 67
(Striped label.)
TOWER (5131 "A Saucerful of Secrets") 50-100 68
(Orange label.)
TOWER (5131 "A Saucerful of Secrets") 50-100 68
(Striped label.)
TOWER (5169 "More") 25-40 69
(Soundtrack.)
Promotional LPs
CAPITOL (8116 "Tour '75") 30-50 75
COLUMBIA (1 "Animals") 75-100 77
(With inserts.)
COLUMBIA (1636 "Final Cut") 15-20 83
(Tracks not banded for airplay.)
COLUMBIA (1636 "Final Cut") 30-40 83
(Tracks are banded for easy airplay.)
COLUMBIA (33453 "Wish You Were Here") 50-75 75
COLUMBIA (34474 "Animals") 40-60 77
(Quadraphonic.)
COLUMBIA (36183 "The Wall") 50-75 79
Members: David Gilmour; Roger Waters; Rick Wright; Nick Mason; Syd Barrett.
Also see BARRETT, Syd
Also see GILMOUR, David
Also see MASON, Nick
Also see WATERS, Roger

PINK LADY *P&R '79*
Singles: 7-inch
ELEKTRA 3-5 79
Picture Sleeves
ELEKTRA 3-5 79
LPs: 10/12-inch
ELEKTRA 5-10 79
Members: Mie; Kei.

PIPEDREAM *D&D '84*
Singles: 12-inch
ZOO YORK 4-6 84

PIPER, Wardell *R&B '79*
Singles: 7-inch
MIDSONG INT'L 3-5 79-80
Also see FIRST CHOICE

PIPKINS *P&R/LP '70*
Singles: 7-inch
CAPITOL 4-8 70
LPs: 10/12-inch
CAPITOL 10-15 70
Members: Tony Burrows; Roger Greenaway
Also see ALLEY CATS
Also see BURROWS, Tony
Also see UNTOUCHABLES
Also see WHITE PLAINS

PIPS: see KNIGHT, Gladys

PIRATES
(Temptations)
Singles: 7-inch
MEL-O-DY (105 "Mind Over Matter") 50-75 62
Also see TEMPTATIONS

PISCOPO, Joe *D&D/LP '85*
Singles: 12-inch
COLUMBIA 4-6 85
Singles: 7-inch
COLUMBIA 3-5 85
Picture Sleeves
COLUMBIA 3-5 85
LPs: 10/12-inch
COLUMBIA 5-10 85

PISTILLI, Gene
Singles: 7-inch
CAPITOL 3-5 69
Also see CASHMAN, PISTILLI & WEST

PISTILLI, Gene, & Manhattan Transfer
Singles: 7-inch
CAPITOL 3-6 70-71
LPs: 10/12-inch
CAPITOL (778 "Jukin' ") 8-12 71
CAPITOL (11405 "Jukin' ") 6-10 75
CAPITOL (16223 "Jukin' ") 5-8 80
MUSIC for PLEASURE 5-10
Also see MANHATTAN TRANSFER

PISTILLI, Gene, & Michael Small
(With Sporting Club Band)
Singles: 7-inch
BUDDAH 4-6 71
Also see PISTILLI, Gene

PITMAN, Donnell *R&B '86*
(With the Chi-Lites)
Singles: 7-inch
AFTER FIVE 3-4 86
Also see CHI-LITES

PITNEY, Gene *P&R '61*
Singles: 7-inch
COLLECTABLES 3-4 80s
EPIC 3-5 77
ERIC 3-4 70s
FESTIVAL (25002 "Please Come Back Baby") 15-20 61
MUSICOR (1000 series) 8-15 60-65
MUSICOR (1100 thru 1400 series) 4-8 65-72
Picture Sleeves
MUSICOR (1000 series) 5-10 60-65
MUSICOR (1100 thru 1400 series) 5-15 66-69
EPs: 7-inch
MUSICOR (500 "Looking Through the Eyes of Love") 15-20 65
(Issued without cover. Promotional issue only.)
LPs: 10/12-inch
COLUMBIA HOUSE 10-15 75
(Columbia Record Club issue.)
EVEREST 5-8 81
KOALA 5-10 79
MUSIC DISC 10-15 69
MUSICOR (1000 series) 8-10
MUSICOR (2001 thru 2008) 20-35 62-64
(Monaural.)
MUSICOR (2015 thru 2134) 15-25 64-67
(Monaural.)
MUSICOR (3001 thru 3008) 20-40 62-64
(Stereo.)
MUSICOR (3015 thru 3134) 15-25 64-67
(Stereo.)
MUSICOR (3148 thru 3193) 10-20 67-71
MUSICOR (3200 series) 8-12 71-73
MUSICOR (5025 "This Is Gene Pitney") 15-25 68
(Columbia Record Club issue.)
MUSICOR (5600 series) 8-10 78
PHOENIX 20 6-12
RHINO 5-8 85
SPRINGBOARD 5-10 76
TRIP 5-10 76
51 WEST 5-10 79

Also see BRYAN, Billy
Also see JAMIE & JANE
Also see JONES, George, & Gene Pitney
Also see ROE, Tommy / Bobby Rydell / Gene Pitney

PITNEY, Gene, & Melba Montgomery C&W '66

Singles: 7-inch

MUSICOR....4-8 65

LPs: 10/12-inch

BUCKBOARD....8-10 76
MUSICOR....15-20 66

PITNEY, Gene / Newcastle Trio

LPs: 10/12-inch

DESIGN....8-12 60s
Also see PITNEY, Gene

PIXIES LP '89

LPs: 10/12-inch

ELEKTRA....5-8 89-90

PIXIES THREE P&R '63

Singles: 7-inch

MERCURY 8-12 63-64

Picture Sleeves

MERCURY (72130 "Birthday Party")....10-20 63
MERCURY (72208 "Cold, Cold Winter")....15-20 63
MERCURY (72288 "It's Summertime")....10-20 64

LPs: 10/12-inch

MERCURY (20912 "Party")....50-75 64
(Monaural.)
MERCURY (60912 "Party")....75-100 64
(Stereo.)
Members: Debra Swisher; Midge Bollinger; Kay McCool.

PIZANI, Frank P&R '57

Singles: 78 rpm

BALLY 5-10 57

Singles: 7-inch

AFTON 5-10 59
BALLY 5-10 57
WARWICK....5-10 59
Also see HIGHLIGHTS

PLACE, Mary Kay C&W/P&R '76
("Mary Kay Place as Loretta Haggers")

Singles: 7-inch

COLUMBIA....3-5 76-78

LPs: 10/12-inch

COLUMBIA....5-10 76-77

PLACE, Mary Kay, & Willie Nelson C&W '77

Singles: 7-inch

COLUMBIA....3-5 77
Also see NELSON, Willie
Also see PLACE, Mary Kay

PLANET P P&R/LP '83
(Planet P Project)

Singles: 7-inch

GEFFEN....3-4 83
MCA (52515 "What I See")....3-5 84
(Colored vinyl.)

Picture Sleeves

GEFFEN....3-4 83

LPs: 10/12-inch

GEFFEN....5-8 83
Member: Tony Carey.
Also see CAREY, Tony

PLANET PATROL R&B '82

Singles: 12-inch

TOMMY BOY....4-6 83-84

Singles: 7-inch

TOMMY BOY....3-4 82-84

LPs: 10/12-inch

TOMMY BOY....5-8 84

PLANT, Robert P&R/LP '82

Singles: 7-inch

ESPARANZA....5-8 85

Singles: 7-inch

ATLANTIC 3-5 83
ESPARANZA....3-4 83-89
SWAN SONG 3-5 82

Picture Sleeves

ATLANTIC....3-5 83
ESPARANZA....3-4 83-88
SWAN SONG 3-5 82

LPs: 10/12-inch

ESPARANZA (Except 2244)....5-8 83-90
ESPARANZA (2244 "Non-Stop, Go!")....30-50 88
(Interview on 2 LPs. Promotional issue only.)
SWAN SONG 5-10 82
Also see BAND of JOY
Also see HONEYDRIPPERS
Also see LED ZEPPELIN

PLASMATICS LP '81
(Featuring Wendy O. Williams)

LPs: 10/12-inch

CAPITOL....5-8 82
PVC....5-8 84
STIFF AMERICA....8-10 80-81
Also see WILLIAMS, Wendy O.

PLASTIC BERTRAND: see BERTRAND, Plastic

PLASTIC COW LP '69

Singles: 7-inch

DOT 4-6 69

LPs: 10/12-inch

DOT 10-15 69

PLASTIC ONO BAND: see LENNON, John

PLATINUM BLONDE P&R '86

Singles: 7-inch

EPIC....3-4 86-87

LPs: 10/12-inch

EPIC....5-8 86-87
Members: Mark Holmes; Ken MacLean.

PLATT, Eddie, & Orch. P&R/R&B '58

Singles: 78 rpm

ABC-PAR....5-10 58

Singles: 7-inch

ABC-PAR....10-20 58
GONE 10-20 58

PLATTERS P&R/R&B '55
(Featuring Tony Williams)

Singles: 78 rpm

FEDERAL (12153 "Give Thanks")....50-75 53
FEDERAL (12164 "I Need You All the Time")....50-75 54
FEDERAL (12181 "Roses of Picardy")....25-50 54
FEDERAL (12188 thru 12204)....25-50 54-55
FEDERAL (12244 "Only You")....25-50 55
FEDERAL (12250 "Tell the World")....10-20 55
FEDERAL (12271 "I Need You All the Time")....10-20 56
MERCURY (Except 71289)....10-20 55-58
MERCURY (71289 "Twilight Time")....50-100 58

Singles: 7-inch

ANTLER....3-5 82
COLLECTABLES....3-4
FEDERAL (12153 "Give Thanks") 150-250 53
FEDERAL (12164 "I Need You All the Time")....200-300 54
FEDERAL (12181 "Roses of Picardy")....150-250 54
FEDERAL (12188 "Tell The World")....150-250 54
FEDERAL (12198 "Voo-Vee-Ah-Bee")....150-250 54
FEDERAL (12204 "Take Me Back")....150-250 54
FEDERAL (12244 "Only You")....200-300 55
FEDERAL (12250 "Tell The World")....100-150 55
FEDERAL (12271 "I Need You All the Time")....50-100 56
GUSTO 3-4 80s
MERCURY (10001 "Smoke Gets in Your Eyes")....25-50 58
(Stereo.)
MERCURY (10018 "Where")....25-50 59
(Stereo.)
MERCURY (10038 "Red Sails in the Sunset")....25-50 60
(Stereo.)
MERCURY (70633 "Only You")....25-50 55
(Pink label.)
MERCURY (70633 "Only You")....15-25 55
(Black label.)
MERCURY (70753 "The Great Pretender")....20-30 55
(Maroon label.)
MERCURY (70753 "The Great Pretender")....10-20 56
(Black label.)
MERCURY (70819 "The Magic Touch")....20-30 56
(Maroon label.)
MERCURY (70819 "The Magic Touch")....10-20 56
(Black label.)
MERCURY (70893 "My Prayer")....20-30 56
(Maroon label.)
MERCURY (70893 "My Prayer")....10-20 56
(Black label.)
MERCURY (70948 "You'll Never Never Know")....15-25 56
MERCURY (71011 "One in a Million")....15-25 56
MERCURY (71032 "I'm Sorry")....20-30 56
(Maroon label.)
MERCURY (71032 "I'm Sorry")....10-20 56
(Black label.)
MERCURY (71093 "My Dream")....20-30 56
(Maroon label.)
MERCURY (71093 "My Dream")....10-20 56
(Black label.)
MERCURY (71184 thru 71904)....10-20 57-61
MERCURY (71921 thru 72359)....8-15 62-64
MERCURY (30,000 series)....5-8 60s
(Celebrity Series reissues.)
MUSICOR....5-10 66-71
OWL....3-5 73
POWER....5-10 60s

Picture Sleeves

MERCURY 15-25 60-64

EPs: 7-inch

FEDERAL (378 The Platters Sing for Only You")....300-400 56
KING (378 "The Platters")....100-200 56
KING (651 "The Platters")....100-200 56
(All copies of **Federal** 651 are bootlegs. Originals are only on King.)
MERCURY 25-50 56-61

LPs: 10/12-inch

CANDLELITE ("The Platters")....30-40 70s
(Boxed, four-disc set.)
EVEREST....5-10 81
FEDERAL (549 "The Platters")....500-1000 57
51 WEST....5-10 80s
GUEST STAR 10-15 60s
KING (651 "The Platters")....200-400 59
KING (5002 "10 Hits")....8-12 59
MERCURY (4000 series)....5-8 82
MERCURY (8000 series)....5-8
MERCURY (20146 "The Platters")....50-100 56
MERCURY (20216 "The Platters, Vol. 2")....50-100 56
MERCURY (20298 "The Flying Platters")....50-75 57
MERCURY (20410 thru 20983)....15-30 59-65
(Monaural.)
MERCURY (60043 thru 60983)....20-50 59-65
(Stereo.)
MUSIC DISC 10-12 69
MUSICO (1002 "Only You")....8-10 70
MUSICOR (2000 & 3000 series)....15-20 66-69
MUSICOR (4600 series)....10-15 77
PICKWICK....8-10 70s
RHINO....8-12 80s
SPRINGBOARD....8-10 76

TRIP 8-10 76
WING 12-25 62-67

Members: Tony Williams; David Lynch; Herb Reed; Linda Hayes: Sandra Dawn; Nate Nelson; Sonny Turner; Zola Taylor; Paul Robi; Alex Hodge.

Also see HAYES, Linda, & Platters
Also see LITTLE ANTHONY & IMPERIALS / Platters
Also see PLATTERS '65
Also see WILLIAMS, Tony

PLATTERS / Exotic Guitars

LPs: 10/12-inch

GUEST STAR 10-15 64

PLATTERS / Inez & Charlie Foxx / Jive Five / Tommy Hunt

LPs: 10/12-inch

MUSICOR 10-20 67

Also see FOXX, Inez
Also see HUNT, Tommy
Also see JIVE FIVE

PLATTERS '65

Singles: 7-inch

ENTREE 4-8 65

Also see PLATTERS

PLAYBOYS P&R '58

Singles: 7-inch

CAMEO (142 "Over the Weekend") .. 15-25 58
MARTINIQUE (101 "Over the Weekend") 25-50 58
MARTINIQUE (400 "Please Forgive Me") 25-50 59

PLAYER P&R/R&B/LP '77

Singles: 7-inch

CASABLANCA 3-5 80
RCA 3-5 82
RSO 3-5 77-78

LPs: 10/12-inch

CASABLANCA 5-10 80
RCA 5-10 81
RSO 5-10 77-78

Member: J.C. Crowley.

PLAYERS R&B '66

Singles: 7-inch

MINIT 4-8 66-67

LPs: 10/12-inch

MINIT 10-20 68

PLAYERS ASSOCIATION R&B '80

Singles: 12-inch

VANGUARD 4-8 79-80

Singles: 7-inch

VANGUARD 3-5 77-80

LPs: 10/12-inch

VANGUARD 5-10 77-80

PLAYMATES P&R '58

Singles: 78 rpm

ROULETTE 15-25 57-58

Singles: 7-inch

ABC-PAR 5-10 63-64
BELL 3-5 71
COLPIX 5-10 64-65
CONGRESS 5-10 65
ROULETTE 10-25 57-63

LPs: 10/12-inch

FORUM 15-25 60
ROULETTE 20-40 57-61

Members: Donny Conn; Morey Carr; Chic Hetti.

PLEASURE R&B/LP '76

Singles: 12-inch

FANTASY 4-8 76-80

Singles: 7-inch

FANTASY 3-5 76-80
RCA 3-4 82-83

LPs: 10/12-inch

FANTASY 5-10 76-80
RCA 5-8 82

Members: Sherman Davis; Nate McClain; Marlon McClain; Michael Hepburn; Donald Hepburn; Bruce Carter; Bruce Smith; Dennis Springer.

PLEASURE, King: see KING PLEASURE

PLEASURE & BEAST D&D '84

Singles: 12-inch

AIRWAVE 4-6 84

PLEDGES

Singles: 78 rpm

REV (3517 "Betty Jean") 10-20 57

Singles: 7-inch

REV (3517 "Betty Jean") 10-20 57

Members: Gary Paxton; Clyde Batton.

Also see SKIP & FLIP

PLEIS, Jack, & His Orchestra P&R '56

Singles: 7-inch

ATCO 4-6 65
COLUMBIA 4-6 61
DECCA 5-10 53-60
LONDON 5-10 50-51
RANWOOD 3-5 76

EPs: 7-inch

DECCA 5-10 55-57

LPs: 10/12-inch

CAMEO 10-20 63
COLUMBIA 10-15 61
DECCA 10-20 55-57
RANWOOD 5-8 76

PLEIS, Jack, & Owen Bradley

EPs: 7-inch

DECCA (2593 "Bandstand Hop") 10-15 58

LPs: 10/12-inch

DECCA (8724 "Bandstand Hop") 20-30 58

Also see BRADLEY, Owen
Also see PLEIS, Jack, & His Orchestra

PLIMSOULS LP '81

Singles: 12-inch

BEAT (1001 "Zero Hour") 15-25 80
BOMP 5-8 80

Singles: 7-inch

BOMP 3-5 80
GEFFEN 3-4 83
SHAKY CITY 3-5

Picture Sleeves

BOMP 3-5 80
GEFFEN 3-4 83
SHAKY CITY 3-5

LPs: 10/12-inch

GEFFEN 5-8 83
PLANET 5-10 81

PLUSH R&B '82

Singles: 7-inch

RCA 3-5 82

LPs: 10/12-inch

RCA 5-10 82

P-NUT GALLERY P&R '71

(Circa '58 & Peanut Gallery)

Singles: 7-inch

BUDDAH 3-5 71

POCKETS R&B/LP '77

Singles: 7-inch

ARC 4-6 79
COLUMBIA 4-6 77-78

LPs: 10/12-inch

ARC 5-10 79
COLUMBIA 5-10 77-78

Members: Al McKinney; Larry Jacobs; Gary Grainger; Kevin Barnes; Charles Williams; George Gray; Irving Madison; Jacob Sheffer.

POCO LP '69

Singles: 7-inch

ABC 3-5 75-79
ATLANTIC 3-4 82-84
EPIC 3-6 69-75
MCA 3-5 79-82
RCA 3-4 89

Picture Sleeves

EPIC 3-6 70-72
MCA 3-5 80
RCA 3-4 89

LPs: 10/12-inch

ABC 8-12 75-78
ATLANTIC 5-8 82-84
EPIC (26460 "Pickin' Up the Pieces") 10-15 69
EPIC (26522 "Poco") 10-15 70
EPIC (30209 "Deliverin'") 8-12 71
EPIC (EQ-30209 "Deliverin'") 15-25 71
(Quadrophonic.)
EPIC (30753 "From the Inside") 5-10 71
EPIC (31601 "A Good Feelin' to Know") 5-10 72
EPIC (32354 "Crazy Eyes") 5-10 73
EPIC (EQ-32354 "Crazy Eyes") 10-15 73
(Quadrophonic.)
EPIC (32895 "Seven") 5-10 74
EPIC (33192 "Cantamos") 5-10 74
(Quadrophonic.)
EPIC (PEQ-33192 "Cantamos") 10-15 74
EPIC (33537 thru 36210) 5-10 75-81
MCA 5-10 80-82
MFSL (020 "Legend") 25-50 78
RCA 5-8 89

Members: Richie Furay; Jim Messina; Rusty Young; Timothy Schmit; Paul Cotton.

Also see BUFFALO SPRINGFIELD
Also see EAGLES
Also see FURRAY, Richie
Also see ILLINOIS SPEED PRESS
Also see MEISNER, Randy
Also see MESSINA, Jim
Also see SCHMIT, Timothy B.

POETS

(James Brown & His Band)

Singles: 7-inch

TRY ME (28006 "Devil's Den") 10-15 63

Also see BROWN, James

POETS P&R/R&B '66

Singles: 7-inch

CHAIRMAN (4408 "Number One") 8-12 63
J-2 (1302 "Wrapped Around Your Finger") 75-125
SYMBOL (214 "She Blew a Good Thing") 8-12 66
SYMBOL (216 "So Young") 8-12 66
VEEP (1286 "The Hustler") 10-20 68

POGUES LP '88

LPs: 10/12-inch

ISLAND 5-8 88-90

POINDEXTER, Buster, & His Banshees of Blue P&R '87

Singles: 7-inch

RCA 3-4 87

Picture Sleeves

RCA 3-4 87

LPs: 10/12-inch

RCA 5-8 87

Members: David Johansen.

Also see JOHANSEN, David

POINT BLANK LP '76

Singles: 7-inch

ARISTA 3-6 76-77
MCA 3-5 79-81

LPs: 10/12-inch

ARISTA 5-10 76-77
MCA 5-8 79-82

Members: Bubba Keith; John O'Daniel.

POINTER, Anita R&B '87

Singles: 7-inch

RCA 3-4 87-88

Also see POINTER SISTERS

POINTER, Bonnie P&R/R&B/LP '78

Singles: 12-inch

MOTOWN 4-8 78-81
PRIVATE I 4-6 84-85

Singles: 7-inch

MOTOWN (Except 1451) 3-5 78-81
MOTOWN (1451 "Free Me from My Freedom") 3-4 78
(Black vinyl.)
MOTOWN (1451 "Free Me from My Freedom") 4-8 78

(Colored vinyl.)
PRIVATE I ... 3-4 84-85

Picture Sleeves

MOTOWN (1451 "Free Me from My Freedom") ... 3-5 78

LPs: 10/12-inch

MOTOWN ... 5-10 78-79
PRIVATE I ... 5-8 84
Also see POINTER SISTERS

POINTER, June — R&B '83

Singles: 12-inch

PLANET ... 4-6 83-84

Singles: 7-inch

PLANET ... 3-4 83-84

LPs: 10/12-inch

PLANET ... 5-8 83

POINTER, Noel — LP '77

Singles: 12-inch

U.A. ... 4-6 77

Singles: 7-inch

BLUE NOTE ... 3-5 77
LIBERTY ... 3-5 81
U.A. ... 3-5 78-80

LPs: 10/12-inch

BLUE NOTE ... 5-10 77
LIBERTY ... 5-8 81
U.A. ... 5-8 78-80

POINTER SISTERS — P&R/R&B/LP '73

Singles: 12-inch

PLANET ... 4-8 78-85
RCA ... 4-6 85-86

Singles: 7-inch

ABC ... 3-6 75-78
ATLANTIC (2845 "Don't Try to Take the Fifth") ... 10-20 72
ATLANTIC (2893 "Destination, No More Heartaches") ... 10-20 72
BLUE THUMB ... 3-6 73-78
MCA ... 3-4 87
PLANET ... 3-5 78-85
RCA ... 3-4 85-88

Picture Sleeves

MCA ... 3-4 87
PLANET ... 3-5 78-85
RCA ... 3-4 85-86

LPs: 10/12-inch

BLUE THUMB ... 8-12 73-77
MCA ... 5-10 81
PLANET ... 5-10 78-84
RCA ... 5-8 85-88
Members: Bonnie Pointer; Anita Pointer; Ruth Pointer; June Pointer.
Also see MEMPHIS HORNS
Also see POINTER, Anita, & Earl Thomas Conley
Also see POINTER, Bonnie
Also see POINTER, June

POISON — R&B '75

Singles: 12-inch

ROULETTE ... 4-8 76

Singles: 7-inch

ROULETTE ... 3-5 75-76

LPs: 10/12-inch

ROULETTE ... 5-10 76

POISON — LP '86

Singles: 7-inch

CAPITOL ... 3-4 87
ENIGMA ... 3-4 86-88

Picture Sleeves

CAPITOL ... 3-4 87
ENIGMA ... 3-4 87-88

LPs: 10/12-inch

CAPITOL ... 5-8 86-90
ENIGMA ... 5-8 86-88
Members: Bret Michaels; Rikki Rocket; C.C. DeVille; Bobby Dall; Richie Kotzen; Blues Saraceno.

POLE, Keith — R&B '85

Singles: 7-inch

SUPERTRONICS ... 3-4 85

POLICE — P&R/LP '79

Singles: 12-inch

A&M (4401 "Don't Stand So Close to Me") ... 200-250 81
(Picture disc. Promotional issue only. 25 made.)
A&M (17122 "Message in a Bottle") ... 5-8 79
(Promotional issue only.)

Singles: 7-inch

A&M (Except 25000, and picture discs) ... 3-5 79-84
A&M (25000 "De Do Do Do, De Da Da Da") ... 10-20 80
(Spanish/Japanese language version.)
A&M ("Roxanne") ... 250-500 79
(Rose-shaped picture disc. Production pressing.)
A&M (2096 "Roxanne") ... 35-40 79
(Badge-shaped picture disc. Promotional issue only. Includes custom folder.)
A&M (4401 "Don't Stand So Close to Me") ... 25-30 81
(Star-shaped picture disc.)
A&M (4401 "Don't Stand So Close to Me") ... 30-35 81
(Star-shaped picture disc. Promotional issue only. Identified by promo sticker on cover.)
SIRE ... 3-4 86

Picture Sleeves

A&M (Except 25000) ... 3-5 80-86
A&M (25000 "De Do Do Do, De Da Da Da") ... 4-6 80

LPs: 10/12-inch

A&M (Except 3713 & 3735) ... 5-15 79-86
A&M (3713 "Reggatta de Blanc") ... 10-20 79
(Two 10-inch LPs. Includes poster. Promotional issue only.)
A&M (3735 "Synchronicity") ... 75-100 83
(Black and white cover.)
A&M (3735 "Synchronicity") ... 40-50 83
(Gold, gray and brown cover.)
NAUTILUS (40 "Ghost in the Machine") ... 40-50 80s
NAUTILUS (19 Zenyata Mondata") ... 25-35 81
Members: Gordon "Sting" Sumner; Andy Summers; Stewart Copeland.
Also see COPELAND, Stewart
Also see FRIPP, Robert, & Andy Summers
Also see STING

POLITICIANS — R&B '72

Singles: 7-inch

HOT WAX ... 3-5 72

LPs: 10/12-inch

HOT WAX ... 8-12 72
Members: McKinley Jackson.

POLNAREFF, Michel — P&R/LP '76

Singles: 12-inch

ATLANTIC ... 4-8 76

Singles: 7-inch

ATLANTIC ... 3-5 76
4 CORNERS (141 "Time Will Tell") ... 8-12 67
KAPP ... 4-8 65-66

LPs: 10/12-inch

ATLANTIC ... 8-10 75
4 CORNERS ... 10-15 67

PONDEROSA TWINS + ONE — P&R/R&B '71

Singles: 7-inch

ASTROSCOPE ... 3-5 72
HOROSCOPE ... 3-5 71

LPs: 10/12-inch

HOROSCOPE ... 8-12 71
Members: Alfred Pelham; Alvin Pelham; Keith Gardner; Kirk Gardner; Ricky Spencer.

PONI-TAILS — P&R/R&B '58

Singles: 78 rpm

ABC-PAR ... 20-40 57
MARC ... 10-20 57
POINT ... 10-20 57

Singles: 7-inch

ABC ... 3-5 73
ABC-PAR ... 10-20 57-60
MCA ... 3-4
MARC ... 10-20 57
POINT ... 10-20 57
Members: Toni Cistone; LaVern Novak; Pat McCabe.
Also see ELEGANTS / Poni-Tails

PONSAR, Serge — D&D '83

Singles: 12-inch

W.B. ... 4-6 83

Singles: 7-inch

W.B. ... 3-4 83

PONTY, Jean-Luc — LP '75

Singles: 7-inch

ATLANTIC ... 3-5 76-85

LPs: 10/12-inch

ATLANTIC ... 5-10 75-85
BLUE NOTE ... 5-10 76-81
MPS ... 5-10 72-73
PACIFIC JAZZ ... 8-18 68-78
PAUSA ... 5-10 80
PRESTIGE ... 8-15 70
WORLD PACIFIC ... 15-25 69

POOLE, Brian — P&R '64

(With the Tremeloes)

Singles: 7-inch

DATE ... 5-10 66
LONDON ... 5-10 63
MONUMENT ... 5-10 64-65

LPs: 10/12-inch

AUDIO FIDELITY ... 15-25 66-67
Also see TREMELOES

POOR RIGHTEOUS TEACHERS — LP '90

LPs: 10/12-inch

PROFILE ... 5-8 90

POP, Iggy — LP '73

(Iggy & Stooges)

Singles: 12-inch

A&M ... 4-8 86

Singles: 7-inch

A&M ... 3-4 86
RCA ... 3-5 77
SIAMESE ... 3-6 77

Picture Sleeves

A&M ... 3-4 86

EPs: 7-inch

BOMP ... 5-10 78

LPs: 10/12-inch

A&M ... 5-8 86
ANIMAL ... 5-10 82
ARISTA ... 8-12 79-81
BOMP (1018 "Kill City") ... 10-15 78
(Black vinyl.)
BOMP (1018 "Kill City") ... 20-30 78
(Colored vinyl.)
COLUMBIA ... 10-20 73
ENIGMA ... 5-8 84
IMPORT ... 8-10 77
INVASION ... 8-10 83
RCA ... 5-10 77-78
VIRGIN ... 5-8 90
Also see BOWIE, David / Iggy Pop
Also see STOOGES

POP, Iggy, & James Williamson

EPs: 7-inch

BOMP ... 5-10 78

LPs: 10/12-inch

BOMP ... 5-10 78
Also see POP, Iggy

POP TOPS — P&R/R&B '68

(Los Pop Tops)

Singles: 7-inch

ABC ... 3-5 71
CALLA ... 4-8 68

POPE JOHN XXIII — LP '63

LPs: 10/12-inch

MERCURY ... 5-10 63

POPE JOHN PAUL II — LP '79

LPs: 10/12-inch

BETHLEHEM ... 5-8 79
INFINITY ... 5-8 79
VOX CHRISTIANA ... 5-8 79

POPPIES P&R '66

Singles: 7-inch

EPIC (9893 "Lullaby of Love")..............4-8 66
EPIC (10019 "He's Ready")...................4-8 66
EPIC (10059 "Do It with Soul")..............5-10 66
EPIC (10086 "There's a Pain in My Heart")..............................10-20 66
TUFF (372 "Johnny Don't Cry")..........10-15 63

Picture Sleeves

EPIC (10019 "He's Ready")...................5-10 66

LPs: 10/12-inch

EPIC (24200 "Lullaby of Love")..........20-30 66
(Monaural.)
EPIC (26200 "Lullaby of Love")..........25-35 66
(Stereo.)
Members: Dorothy Moore; Rosemary Taylor; Pet McCune.
Also see MOORE, Dorothy

POPPY FAMILY P&R/LP '70
(Featuring Susan Jacks)

Singles: 7-inch

LONDON..3-5 70-72

LPs: 10/12-inch

LONDON..10-15 70-71
Members: Susan Jacks; Terry Jacks.
Also see JACKS, Susan
Also see JACKS, Terry

PORTER, David R&B/LP '70

Singles: 7-inch

ENTERPRISE.......................................3-5 70-72
STAX..10-15 64

LPs: 10/12-inch

ENTERPRISE.......................................8-12 70-72
Also see HAYES, Isaac, & David Porter

PORTER, Nolan P&R/R&B '71
(N.F. Porter; Nolan)

Singles: 7-inch

ABC..3-5 73
LIZARD...3-5 71

LPs: 10/12-inch

LIZARD...8-12 71

PORTNOY, Gary P&R '83

Singles: 7-inch

APPLAUSE..3-4 83
EARTHTONE..3-4 84

Picture Sleeves

EARTHTONE..3-5 84

POSEY, Sandy P&R/LP '66

Singles: 7-inch

AUDIOGRAPH......................................3-4 83
COLUMBIA..3-5 71-73
MGM...4-6 66-67
MONUMENT...3-5 76
POLYDOR..3-4 83
W.B. 3-5 76-79

Picture Sleeves

MGM...4-8 66-67

LPs: 10/12-inch

COLUMBIA..5-10 72
51 WEST...5-8 83
GUSTO..5-8 80s
MGM...8-15 66-70

POSEY, Sandy / Skeeter Davis

LPs: 10/12-inch

GUSTO..5-8
Also see DAVIS, Skeeter
Also see POSEY, Sandy

POST, Mike P&R/LP '75
(Mike Post Coalition)

Singles: 7-inch

BELL...3-5 71
ELEKTRA...3-4 81-82
EPIC...3-5 77
MGM...3-5 75
MUSIC FACTORY.................................4-6 68
POLYDOR..3-4 87
REPRISE...4-6 65-66
W.B. 3-6 69

Picture Sleeves

ELEKTRA...3-5 81-82

LPs: 10/12-inch

ELEKTRA...5-8 82
RCA..5-8 83
MGM...5-10 75
POLYDOR..5-8 87
W.B. 8-12 69

POTLIQUOR P&R/LP '72

Singles: 7-inch

CAPITOL...3-5 79
JANUS..3-5 72

LPs: 10/12-inch

CAPITOL...5-10 79
JANUS..10-15 70-73

POURCEL, Franck P&R/R&B '59
(Franck Pourcel's French Fiddles)

Singles: 7-inch

BLUE..3-5 69
CAPITOL...4-8 59-64
IMPERIAL..3-6 66-68
PARAMOUNT.......................................3-5 71-73

EPs: 7-inch

CAPITOL...5-10 59

LPs: 10/12-inch

ATCO..5-10 69
CAPITOL...5-20 56-79
IMPERIAL..5-15 66-68
PARAMOUNT.......................................5-8 70-73
WESTMINSTER.....................................10-25 54-55

POUSETTE-DART BAND LP '77

Singles: 7-inch

CAPITOL...3-5 76-79

LPs: 10/12-inch

CAPITOL...5-10 76-80
Member: Jon Pousette-Dart.

POWELL, Adam Clayton LP '67

LPs: 10/12-inch

JUBILEE..10-15 67

POWELL, Bobby P&R/R&B '65

Singles: 7-inch

EXCELLO..5-10 73
JEWEL..5-10 67
WHIT..5-10 65-71

LPs: 10/12-inch

EXCELLO..10-15 73

POWELL, Cozy P&R '74

Singles: 7-inch

CHRYSALIS...3-5 74
Also see BECK, Jeff
Also see BEDLAM
Also see EMERSON, LAKE & POWELL

POWELL, Jane P&R '56

Singles: 78 rpm

MGM...4-6 51
VERVE..4-6 56

Singles: 7-inch

RANWOOD..3-5 68
MGM...5-10 51
VERVE..4-8 56

LPs: 10/12-inch

COLUMBIA..15-30 55-57
LION...10-20 59
MGM...20-40 55
VERVE..20-35 56
Also see ASTAIRE, Fred, & Jane Powell

POWER STATION P&R/D&D/LP '85

Singles: 12-inch

CAPITOL...4-6 85

Singles: 7-inch

CAPITOL...3-4 85

Picture Sleeves

CAPITOL...3-4 85

LPs: 10/12-inch

CAPITOL...5-8 85
Members: Andy Taylor; John Taylor; Robert Palmer; Tommy Thompson.
Also see DURAN DURAN
Also see PALMER, Robert
Also see TAYLOR, Andy
Also see TAYLOR, John

POWERS, Joey P&R '63
(Joey Powers' Flower)

Singles: 7-inch

AMY...5-10 63-67
MGM...5-10 65
RCA (8000 series)................................4-8 62
RCA (9700 series)................................3-6 69

LPs: 10/12-inch

AMY...15-25 64
Also see ORBISON, Roy / Bobby Bare / Joey Powers

POWERS, Tom P&R '77

Singles: 7-inch

BIG TREE..3-5 77

POWERSOURCE P&R '87

Singles: 7-inch

POWERVISION.....................................3-4 87

POZO - SECO SINGERS P&R/LP '66
(Susan Taylor & the Pozo Seco Singers; Pozo Seco; Pozo-Seco Singers Featuring Don Williams)

Singles: 7-inch

CERTRON..3-5 70
COLUMBIA..4-8 65-70
EDMARK (10017 "Down the Road I Go"/ "Time")..10-20 65

LPs: 10/12-inch

CERTRON..10-15 70
COLUMBIA..10-20 66-68
EXCELSIOR...5-10
Members: Don Williams; Susan Taylor; Lofton Kline.
Also see WILLIAMS, Don

PRADO, Perez, & His Orch. P&R '53

Singles: 78 rpm

RCA..4-6 50-58

Singles: 7-inch

RCA..5-15 50-64
U.A. 3-6 64

Picture Sleeves

RCA..8-10 59

EPs: 7-inch

BELL (2 "Perez Prado")........................5-10
RCA..8-15 54-61

LPs: 10/12-inch

CAMDEN...10-15 60
RCA..5-10 76
(With "ANL1" prefix.)
RCA..10-30 54-72
(With "LPM," "LSP" or "VPS" prefix.)
SPIN-O-RAMA.....................................8-12 62
SPRINGBOARD....................................5-10 77
U.A. 10-15 65-68
Also see CLOONEY, Rosemary, & Perez Prado
Also see HIRT, Al / Henry Mancini / Perez Prado

PRATT, Andy P&R/LP '73

Singles: 7-inch

COLUMBIA..3-5 73
NEMPEROR...3-5 76-77

LPs: 10/12-inch

COLUMBIA..8-12 73
NEMPEROR...5-10 76-79
POLYDOR..10-15 70
Also see SPRINGSTEEN, Bruce / Andy Pratt

PRATT - McCLAIN P&R/LP '76

Singles: 7-inch

REPRISE...3-5 76-77

LPs: 10/12-inch

DUNHILL...8-12 73
REPRISE...8-10 76
Members: Truett Pratt; Jerry McClain.

PRECISIONS P&R/R&B '67

Singles: 7-inch

ATCO..4-8 69
D-TOWN (1033 "My Lover Come Back")..75-125 65
D-TOWN (1055 "Mexican Love Song")..10-20 65
DREW (1001 "Such Misery")..................15-25 66
DREW (1003 "If This Is Love")..............10-20 66
HEN-MAR..3-5 73

PREFAB SPROUT LP '85

Singles: 7-inch

EPIC 5-8 85

LPs: 10/12-inch

EPIC 10-15 85

PRELUDE P&R '74

Singles: 7-inch

ISLAND 3-5 74
PYE 3-5 75

LPs: 10/12-inch

ISLAND 8-10 74
PYE 8-10 75

PRELUDES FIVE P&R '61
(Preludes)

Singles: 7-inch

PIK (231 "Don't You Know") 15-20 61

PREMIATA FORNERIA MARCONI: see P.F.M.

PREMIERS P&R '64

Singles: 7-inch

FARO 6-12 64-67
FINE 4-8 60s
LEO 5-10 64
W.B. 4-8 64

LPs: 10/12-inch

RAMPART ("Farmer John") 25-35 64
(Number not known.)
W.B. (1565 "Farmer John") 15-25 64

PRENTISS, Lee D&D '83

Singles: 12-inch

MSB 4-6 83

PREPARATIONS R&B '68

Singles: 7-inch

HEART and SOUL 4-8 68

PRESIDENTS P&R/R&B '70

Singles: 7-inch

DELUXE 4-8 69
HOLLYWOOD 4-8 68
SUSSEX 3-6 70-71

LPs: 10/12-inch

SUSSEX 15-25 70
Members: Tony Boyd; Archie Powell; Bill Shorter.

PRESLEY, Elvis C&W '55
(With Scotty & Bill; with Jordanaires; with Imperials; with J.D. Sumner & Stamps; with Mello Men; with Amigos; with Jubilee Four & Carol Lombard Trio)

Singles: 78 rpm
(Commercial and Promotional)

RCA (6357 "Mystery Train") 100-150 55
RCA (6380 "That's All Right") 100-150 55
RCA (6381 "Good Rockin' Tonight") 100-150 55
RCA (6382 "Milkcow Blues Boogie") 100-150 55
RCA (6383 "Baby, Let's Play House") 100-150 55
RCA (6420 "Heartbreak Hotel") 75-100 56
(Black label.)
RCA (6420 "Heartbreak Hotel") 400-500 56
(White label. Promotional issue only. Opinions vary as to authenticity.)
RCA (6540 "I Want You, I Need You, I Love You") 75-100 56
(Black label.)
RCA (6540 "I Want You, I Need You, I Love You") 400-500 56
(White label. Promotional issue only. Opinions vary as to authenticity.)
RCA (6604 "Don't Be Cruel") 75-100 56
(Black label.)
RCA (6604 "Don't Be Cruel") 400-500 56
(White label. Promotional issue only. Opinions vary as to authenticity.)
RCA (6636 "Blue Suede Shoes") 75-100 56
(Black label.)
RCA (6637 "I Got a Woman") 75-100 56
(Black label.)
RCA (6638 "I'm Gonna Sit Right Down and Cry") 75-100 56
(Black label.)
RCA (6639 "Tryin' to Get to You") 75-100 56
(Black label.)
RCA (6640 "Blue Moon") 75-100 56
(Black label.)
RCA (6641 "Money Honey") 75-100 56
(Black label.)
RCA (6642 "Lawdy Miss Clawdy") 75-100 56
(Black label.)
RCA (6643 "Love Me Tender") 50-75 56
(Black label.)
RCA (6643 "Love Me Tender") 400-500 56
(White label. Promotional issue only. Opinions vary as to authenticity.)
RCA (6800 "Too Much") 75-125 57
(Black label.)
RCA (6800 "Too Much") 400-500 57
(White label. Promotional issue only. Opinions vary as to authenticity.)
RCA (6870 "All Shook Up") 75-125 57
(Black label.)
RCA (6870 "All Shook Up") 400-500 57
(White label. Promotional issue only. Opinions vary as to authenticity.)
RCA (7000 "Teddy Bear") 75-125 57
(Black label.)
RCA (7000 "Teddy Bear") 400-500 57
(White label. Promotional issue only. Opinions vary as to authenticity.)
RCA (7035 "Jailhouse Rock") 100-150 57
(Black label.)
RCA (7035 "Jailhouse Rock") 400-500 57
(White label. Promotional issue only. Opinions vary as to authenticity.)
RCA (7150 "Don't") 100-150 58
RCA (7240 "Wear My Ring Around Your Neck") 100-150 58
RCA (7280 "Hard Headed Woman") 100-200 58
RCA (7410 "One Night") 400-500 58
ROYAL ("Elvis Presley Show") 150-250 56
(Single-sided disc, issued to radio stations to promote Elvis in concert. Includes an excerpt of *Heartbreak Hotel.*)
SUN (209 "That's All Right") 600-1200 54
SUN (210 "Good Rockin' Tonight") 500-1000 54
SUN (215 "Milkcow Blues Boogie") 600-1200 55
SUN (217 "Baby Let's Play House") 500-1000 55
SUN (223 "Mystery Train") 500-1000 55

Notes: All Elvis RCA and Sun 78s were simultaneously issued on 45 rpm singles. For 78 rpm plastic soundsheets and flexi-discs, see a separate section that follows. RCA and Sun 78s can be found with many label variations. Sun promotional singles were marked with the word "sample" rubber stamped on the label. White label promotional 78s are still listed; however, their authenticity has been challenged by some experts.

Singles: 7-inch
(Commercial)

COLLECTABLES (Black vinyl) 3-5 86-87
COLLECTABLES (Gold vinyl) 3-5 92
RCA (0088 "Raised on Rock") 4-6 73
RCA (0130 "How Great Thou Art") 15-20 69
RCA (0196 "Take Good Care of Her") 4-6 74
RCA (0280 "If You Talk in Your Sleep") 8-12 74
(Has title on one line.)
RCA (0280 "If You Talk in Your Sleep") 4-6 74
(Two lines are used for title.)
RCA (0572 "Merry Christmas Baby") 12-15 71
RCA (0619 "Until It's Time for You to Go") 4-6 72
RCA (0651 "He Touched Me") 100-150 72
(Has the *He Touched Me* side pressed at about 35 rpm instead of 45. These copies—the result of a production error—were commercial issues. Flip, *Bosom of Abraham,* plays at 45 rpm.)
RCA (0651 "He Touched Me") 4-6 72
RCA (0672 "An American Trilogy") 15-20 72
RCA (0769 "Burning Love") 4-6 72
(Orange label.)
RCA (0769 "Burning Love") 100-125 72
(Gray label.)
RCA (0815 "Separate Ways") 4-6 71
RCA (0910 "Fool") 4-6 73
RCA (1017 "It's Only Love") 4-6 71
RCA (2458 "My Boy"/"Loving Arms") 500-750 74
(Produced in the U.S. for European distribution.)
RCA (6357 "Mystery Train") 30-40 55
RCA (6380 "That's All Right") 30-40 55
RCA (6381 "Good Rockin' Tonight") 30-40 55
RCA (6382 "Milkcow Blues Boogie") . 30-40 55
RCA (6383 "Baby Let's Play House") 30-40 55
RCA (6420 "Heartbreak Hotel") 20-30 56
RCA (6540 "I Want You, I Need You, I Love You") 20-30 56
RCA (6604 "Don't Be Cruel") 20-30 56
RCA (6636 "Blue Suede Shoes") 30-40 56
RCA (6637 "I Got a Woman") 30-40 56
RCA (6638 "I'm Gonna Sit Right Down and Cry") 30-40 56
RCA (6639 "Tryin' to Get to You") 30-40 56
RCA (6640 "Blue Moon") 30-40 56
RCA (6641 "Money Honey") 30-40 56
RCA (6642 "Lawdy Miss Clawdy") 30-40 56
(Dog is pictured on label.)
RCA (6642 "Lawdy Miss Clawdy"). 150-200 56
(Dog is not shown on label.)
RCA (6643 "Love Me Tender") 20-30 56
RCA (6800 "Too Much") 20-30 57
(Dog is pictured on label.)
RCA (6800 "Too Much") 200-300 57
(Dog is not shown on label.)
RCA (6870 "All Shook Up") 20-30 57
RCA (7000 "Teddy Bear") 20-30 57
RCA (7035 "Jailhouse Rock") 20-30 57
(Black label, black vinyl.)
RCA (7035 "Jailhouse Rock") 750-1000 57
(Gold label, gold vinyl.)

Note: All RCA singles from 6357 through 7035 can be found on various black labels, both with or without a horizontal silver line.

RCA (7150 "Don't") 12-15 58
RCA (7240 "Wear My Ring Around Your Neck") 12-15 58
RCA (7280 "Hard Headed Woman") 12-15 58
RCA (7410 "One Night") 12-15 58
RCA (7506 "I Need Your Love Tonight") 12-15 59
RCA (7600 "A Big Hunk O' Love") 12-15 59
RCA (47-7740 "Stuck on You") 8-10 60
RCA (61-7740 "Stuck on You") 350-450 60
(Living Stereo.)
RCA (47-7777 "It's Now Or Never") 500-750 60
(Pressed without the piano track.)
RCA (47-7777 "It's Now Or Never") 8-10 60
RCA (61-7777 "It's Now Or Never") 400-600 60
(Living Stereo.)
RCA (47-7810 "Are You Lonesome To-night") 8-10 60
RCA (61-7810 "Are You Lonesome To-night") 400-600 60
(Living Stereo.)
RCA (37-7850 "Surrender") 500-700 61
(Compact 33 Single.)
RCA (47-7850 "Surrender") 8-10 61
RCA (61-7850 "Surrender") 600-800 61
(Living Stereo.)
RCA (68-7850 "Surrender") 1000-1500 61
(Stereo Compact 33 Single.)
RCA (37-7880 "I Feel So Bad") 1000-1500 61
(Compact 33 Single.)
RCA (47-7880 "I Feel So Bad") 8-10 61

RCA (37-7908 "His Latest Flame") 4000-6000 61
(Compact 33 Single.)
RCA (47-7908 "His Latest Flame")......8-10 61
RCA (37-7968 "Can't Help Falling in Love") 5000-8000 61
(Compact 33 Single.)
RCA (47-7968 "Can't Help Falling in Love") 8-10 61
RCA (37-7992 "Good Luck Charm") 8000-12000 62
(Compact 33 Single.)
RCA (47-7992 "Good Luck Charm") ... 8-10 62
RCA (8041 "She's Not You") 8-10 62
RCA (8100 "Return to Sender")....8-10 62
RCA (8134 "One Broken Heart for Sale") 8-10 63
RCA (8188 "Devil in Disguise") 75-100 63
(Flip side title is incorrectly shown as *Please Don't Drag That String ALONG.*)
RCA (8188 "Devil in Disguise") 6-10 63
(Flip side title correctly shown as *Please Don't Drag That String AROUND.*)
RCA (8243 "Bossa Nova Baby") 6-10 63
RCA (8307 "Kissin' Cousins")....6-10 64
RCA (8360 "Viva Las Vegas")....6-10 64
RCA (8400 "Such a Night") 6-10 64
RCA (8440 "Ask Me") 6-10 64
RCA (8500 "Do the Clam")....6-10 65
RCA (8585 "Easy Question")....6-10 65
RCA (8657 "I'm Yours")....6-10 65
RCA (8740 "Tell Me Why")....6-10 65
RCA (8780 "Frankie and Johnny") 6-10 66
RCA (8870 "Love Letters") 6-10 66
RCA (8941 "Spinout")....6-10 66
RCA (8950 "If Everyday Was Like Christmas") 6-10 66
RCA (9056 "Indescribably Blue")....6-10 67
RCA (9115 "Long Legged Girl") 6-10 67
RCA (9287 "There's Always Me")....6-10 67
RCA (9341 "Big Boss Man")....6-10 67
RCA (9425 "Guitar Man") 6-10 68
RCA (9465 "U.S. Male") 6-10 68
RCA (9547 "Your Time Hasn't Come Yet Baby") 6-10 68
RCA (9600 "You'll Never Walk Alone") 6-10 68
RCA (9610 "Almost in Love") 6-10 68
Note: Commercial issues of all RCA singles from 6357 through 9600 are on black labels.
RCA (9670 "If I Can Dream")....4-6 68
RCA (9731 "Memories") 4-6 69
RCA (9741 "In the Ghetto") 4-6 69
RCA (9747 "Clean Up Your Own Back Yard")....4-6 69
RCA (9764 "Suspicious Minds")....4-6 69
RCA (9768 "Don't Cry Daddy")....4-6 69
RCA (9791 "Kentucky Rain")....4-6 70
RCA (9835 "The Wonder of You")....4-6 70
RCA (9873 "I've Lost You") 4-6 70
RCA (9916 "You Don't Have to Say You Love Me") 4-6 70
RCA (9960 "I Really Don't Want to Know") 4-6 70
RCA (9980 "Rags to Riches") 4-6 71
RCA (9985 "Life") 4-6 71
RCA (9998 "I'm Leavin'") 4-6 71
Note: RCA numbers in the 10000 to 14000 series with a "GB" prefix are Gold Standards and are listed in a separate Gold Standard Singles section.
RCA (10074 "Promised Land")....4-6 74
(Orange label.)
RCA (10074 "Promised Land")....20-30 74
(Gray label.)
RCA (10191 "My Boy") 4-6 75
(Orange label.)
RCA (10191 "My Boy") 8-12 75
(Tan or brown label.)
RCA (10278 "T-r-o-u-b-l-e")....4-6 75
(Orange label.)
RCA (10278 "T-r-o-u-b-l-e")....8-10 75
(Tan label.)
RCA (10278 "T-r-o-u-b-l-e")....75-100 75
(Gray label.)
RCA (10401 "Bringing It Back").... 150-200 75
(Orange label.)
RCA (10401 "Bringing It Back") 4-6 75
(Tan label.)
RCA (10601 "For the Heart") 4-6 76
(Tan label.)
RCA (10601 "For the Heart") 90-100 76
(Black label.)
RCA (10857 "Moody Blue").... 3-5 76
(Black vinyl. Colored vinyl 45s of *Moody Blue*, were experimental and are listed in the Promotional Singles section that follows.)
RCA (10998 "Way Down").... 3-5 77
RCA (11099 thru 11113).... 3-4 77
(Discs in this series were originally packaged in either 11301 and/or 11340, both of which are boxed sets of singles with sleeves.)
RCA (11165 "My Way").... 3-5 77
(Flip side shown as *America.*)
RCA (11165 "My Way").... 15-20 77
(Fith flip side shown as *America the Beautiful.*)
RCA (11212 " Unchained Melody")...... 3-5 78
RCA (11301 "15 Golden Records") .. 45-55 77
(Boxed set of 15 Elvis singles with picture sleeves.)
RCA (11320 "Teddy Bear").... 3-5 78
RCA (11340 "20 Golden Hits").... 65-75 77
(Boxed set of 10 Elvis singles with picture sleeves.)
RCA (11533 "Are You Sincere") 3-5 79
RCA (11679 "I Got a Feelin' in My Body").... 12-18 79
(With production and backing credits shown on label.)
RCA (11679 ("I Got a Feelin' in My Body").... 3-5 79
(With backing credits removed, leaving only production credits.)
RCA (12158 "Guitar Man").... 3-5 81
RCA (12205 "Lovin' Arms").... 3-5 81
RCA (13058 "You'll Never Walk Alone").... 3-5 82
RCA (13351 "The Elvis Medley") 3-5 82
RCA (13500 "I Was the One") 3-5 83
RCA (13547 "Little Sister").... 3-5 83
RCA (13875 "Baby, Let's Play House") 30-40 84
(Colored vinyl.)
RCA (13885 thru 13890).... 3-4 84
(Discs in this series were originally packaged in 13897, *Golden Singles, Vol. I.* May include juke box title strips.)
RCA (13891 thru 13896).... 3-4 84
(Discs in this series were originally packaged in 13898, *Golden Singles, Vol. II.* May include juke box title strips.)
RCA (13897 "Golden Singles, Vol. I").... 15-25 84
(Package of six colored vinyl singles with sleeves.)
RCA (13898 "Golden Singles, Vol. II").... 15-25 84
(Package of six colored vinyl singles with sleeves.)
RCA (13929 "Blue Suede Shoes").... 10-15 84
(Colored vinyl. Incorrectly shows *Blue Suede Shoes* as stereo and *Promised Land* as mono.)
RCA (13929 "Blue Suede Shoes")...... 8-12 84
(Colored vinyl. Correctly shows *Blue Suede Shoes* as mono and *Promised Land* as stereo.)
RCA (14090 "Always on My Mind")..... 8-12 85
(Colored vinyl.)
RCA (14237 "Merry Christmas Baby").... 10-15 85
(Black vinyl.)
RCA (14237 "Merry Christmas Baby").... 10-15 85
(Colored vinyl.)
RCA (62402 "Don't Be Cruel") 10-15 92
(Colored vinyl.)
RCA (62403 "Blue Christmas")......... 10-15 92
(Colored vinyl.)
RCA (62449 "Heartbreak Hotel") 10-15 92
(Colored vinyl.)
Note: RCA numbers in the 10000-14000 series with a "GB" prefix are Gold Standard Series and are listed in a separate Gold Standard Singles section. Regular series issues are in the preceding section.
SUN (209 "That's All Right")...... 1000-2000 54
SUN (210 "Good Rockin' Tonight") 800-1200 54
SUN (215 "Milkcow Blue Boogie")....1000-2000 55
SUN (217 "Baby Let's Play House")....800-1200 55
SUN (223 "Mystery Train") 800-1200 55
TRIBUTE (501 "A Tribute to Elvis Presley")....50-100 56
(Has Elvis plus guest appearances by Edward R. Murrow, Steve Allen, Ed Sullivan, Danny Kaye, Jimmy Durante, Gabriel Heater, Sid Ceaser, Liberace, Mantovani, Jack Benny, Gene Vincent, Gloria DeHaven, Nat King Cole, Nelson Eddy, and Jane Russell.)
Note: Plastic soundsheets or flexi-discs are listed in a separate section that follows.

Picture Sleeves (Commercial and Promotional)

LAUREL (41 623 "Treat Me Nice")....5000-10000 57
(Pictures Elvis but credits Vince Everett. Black and white sleeve made as a prop for the *Jailhouse Rock* film. The printed sheets have no reverse side, but are applied to a randomly selected EP. No Laurel records of this title exist. Unlike 41 624 and 41 625, there is no question about the authenticity of this sleeve.)
LAUREL (41 624 "Jailhouse Rock")....75-100 57
LAUREL (41 625 "Young and Beautiful")....75-100 57
(Above two picture Elvis but credit Vince Everett. Black-and-white, cardboard, EP-like cover. May have been made as a film prop. While many researchers question the authenticity—and therefore the date of production—of these, these prices have been paid. No Laurel records of these titles exist.).
PECA ("Could I Fall in Love").... 4000-8000 66
(Pictures Elvis but credits Guy Lambert with George and His G-Men. A full color sleeve made as a prop for the *Double Trouble* film. No Peca records of this title exist.)
RCA (76 "Don't"/"Wear My Ring Around Your Neck")....1000-1500 60
(Promotional issue only.)
RCA (0088 "Raised on Rock") 8-12 73
RCA (118 "King of the Whole Wide World")....150-200 62
(Promotional issue only.)
RCA (0130 "How Great Thou Art")....100-150 69
RCA (162 "How Great Thou Art")....150-200 67
(Promotional issue only.)
RCA (0196 " Take Good Care of Her")....8-12 74
RCA (0280 "If You Talk in Your Sleep")....8-12 74
RCA (0572 "Merry Christmas Baby")....20-30 71
RCA (0619 "Until It's Time for You to Go") 8-12 71
RCA (0651 "He Touched Me") 50-75 71
RCA (0672 "An American Trilogy") ... 15-25 72
RCA (0769 "Burning Love")....8-12 72
RCA (0815 "Separate Ways") 8-12 71
RCA (0910 "Fool")....8-12 73
RCA (1017 "It's Only Love") 8-12 71
RCA (6357 "Mystery Train") 1000-2000 55
(Cartoon "This Is His Life" series. Previously thought to have come with *I Want You, I Need You, I Love You*, but recent evidence points to it being *Mystery Train.* Promotional issue only.)
RCA (6604 "Don't Be Cruel")....65-75 55
(Shows *Don't Be Cruel* c/w *Hound Dog.*)
RCA (6604 "Hound Dog")....55-65 56
(Shows *Hound Dog* c/w *Don't Be Cruel.*)

RCA (6643 "Love Me Tender")...... 100-150 56
(Black and white sleeve.)
RCA (6643 "Love Me Tender")......... 60-75 56
(Black and green sleeve.)
RCA (6643 "Love Me Tender")......... 35-45 56
(Black and dark pink sleeve.)
RCA (6643 "Love Me Tender")......... 30-40 56
(Black and light pink sleeve.)
RCA (6800 "Too Much")................... 50-75 57
RCA (6870 "All Shook Up").............. 50-75 57
RCA (7000 "Teddy Bear") 40-60 57
RCA (7035 "Jailhouse Rock") 40-60 57
(Sleeve only.)
RCA/MGM "Jailhouse Rock")...... 750-1000 57
(MGM *Jailhouse Rock* film preview invitation ticket. A promotional item for the media, the ticket came wrapped around a commercial single and sleeve. Deduct about 50% if ticket stub is detached. Counterfeits exist.)
RCA (7150 "Don't")......................... 40-50 58
RCA (7240 "Wear My Ring Around Your Neck").. 40-50 58
RCA (7280 "Hard Headed Woman"). 35-45 58
RCA (7410 "One Night")................... 35-45 58
RCA (7506 "I Need Your Love Tonight") 300-500 59
(Has advertising for the *Elvis Sails* EP on reverse.)
RCA (7506 "I Need Your Love Tonight") 25-35 59
(Has a listing of Elvis EPs and 45s on reverse.)
RCA (7600 "A Big Hunk O' Love") 25-35 59
RCA (7740 "Stuck on You") 15-25 60
RCA (7777 "It's Now Or Never")........ 15-25 60
RCA (7810 "Are You Lonesome To-night") 15-25 60
RCA (37-7850 "Surrender").......... 600-800 61
(Compact 33 Single sleeve. Copies without some ring wear are very scarce.)
RCA (47-7850 "Surrender").............. 15-20 61
RCA (37-7880 "I Feel So Bad"). 1000-1500 61
(Compact 33 Single sleeve.)
RCA (47-7880 "I Feel So Bad")......... 15-25 61
RCA (37-7908 "His Latest Flame") 4000-6000 61
(Compact 33 Single sleeve.)
RCA (47-7908 "His Latest Flame").... 15-25 61
RCA (37-7968 "Can't Help Falling in Love") 5000-8000 61
(Compact 33 Single sleeve.)
RCA (47-7968 "Can't Help Falling in Love") 15-20 61
RCA (37-7992 "Good Luck Charm") 8000-12000 62
(Compact 33 Single sleeve.)
RCA (47-7992 "Good Luck Charm") 15-20 62
RCA (8041 "She's Not You") 15-20 62
RCA (8100 "Return to Sender")......... 15-20 62
RCA (8134 "One Broken Heart for Sale") 15-20 63
RCA (8188 "Devil in Disguise") 15-20 63
RCA (8243 "Bossa Nova Baby") 15-20 63
RCA (8307 "Kissin' Cousins")............ 15-20 64
RCA (8360 "Viva Las Vegas")........... 15-20 64
RCA (8400 "Such a Night") 15-20 64
RCA (8440 "Ask Me")........................ 15-20 64
RCA (8500 "Do the Clam")............... 15-20 65
RCA (8585 "Easy Question")............ 15-20 65
RCA (8657 "I'm Yours")................... 15-20 65
RCA (8740 "Tell Me Why")............... 15-20 65
RCA (8780 "Frankie & Johnny") 15-20 66
RCA (8870 "Love Letters") 15-20 66
RCA (8941 "Spinout")....................... 15-20 66
RCA (8950 "If Everyday Was Like Christmas") 15-20 66
RCA (9056 "Indescribably Blue")....... 15-20 67
RCA (9115 "Long Legged Girl") 15-20 67
RCA (9287 "There's Always Me")...... 15-20 67
RCA (9341 "Big Boss Man")............. 15-20 67
RCA (9425 "Guitar Man") 10-20 68
RCA (9465 "U.S. Male") 10-20 68
RCA (9547 "Your Time Hasn't Come Yet Baby") 10-20 68
RCA (9600 "You'll Never Walk Alone") 50-75 68
RCA (9610 "Almost in Love")........... 10-15 68
RCA (9670 "If I Can Dream") 10-15 68
RCA (9731 "Memories").................... 10-15 69
RCA (9741 "In the Ghetto").............. 10-15 69
RCA (9747 "Clean Up Your Own Back Yard") 10-15 69
RCA (9764 "Suspicious Minds") 8-12 69
RCA (9768 "Don't Cry Daddy") 8-12 69
RCA (9791 "Kentucky Rain")............... 8-12 70
RCA (9835 "The Wonder of You")..... 8-12 70
RCA (9873 "I've Lost You")................ 8-12 70
RCA (9916 "You Don't Have to Say You Love Me").. 8-12 70
RCA (9960 "I Really Don't Want to Know")... 8-12 70
RCA (9980 "Where Did They Go Lord").. 8-15 71
RCA (9985 "Life")............................ 20-30 71
RCA (9998 "I'm Leavin' ")................... 8-15 71
RCA (10074 "Promised Land").......... 8-10 74
RCA (10191 "My Boy")...................... 8-10 75
RCA (10278 "T-r-o-u-b-l-e")............... 8-10 75
RCA (10401 "Bringing It Back") 8-12 75
RCA (10601 "For the Heart") 8-10 76
RCA (10857 "Moody Blue")................ 6-10 76
RCA (10998 "Way Down")................. 6-10 77
RCA (11099 thru 11113)..................... 3-4 77
(Sleeves in this series were originally packaged in either RCA 11301 and/or 11340, both boxed sets of singles with sleeves.)
RCA (11165 "My Way")..................... 6-10 77
(Flip side title shown as *America*.)
RCA (11165 "My Way")..................... 15-25 77
(Flip side title shown as *America the Beautiful*)
RCA (11212 "Softly, As I Leave You") 5-10 78
RCA (11320 "Teddy Bear")................ 5-10 78
RCA (11533 "Are You Sincere") 5-10 79
RCA (11679 "I Got a Feelin' in My Body").. 5-10 79
RCA (12158 "Guitar Man").................. 5-10 81
RCA (13058 "You'll Never Walk Alone").. 5-10 82
RCA (13302 "The Impossible Dream") 75-100 82
(Promotional issue only.)
RCA (13351 "The Elvis Medley") 5-10 82
RCA (13500 "I Was the One") 5-10 83
RCA (13547 "Little Sister")................. 5-10 83
RCA (13875 "Baby, Let's Play House") 20-40 84
RCA (13885 thru 13896)..................... 3-4 84
(Sleeves in this series were originally packaged in RCA 13897 and 13898, *Golden Singles.*)
RCA (13929 "Blue Suede Shoes")...... 5-10 84
RCA (14090 "Always on My Mind")...... 5-10 85
RCA (14237 "Merry Christmas Baby")... 8-12 85

Notes: There may be slight price differences between "Coming Soon" and "Ask For" variations, with "Ask For" sleeves rarer overall. Likewise for variations in colors and paper stock used. Often, the difference is simply which one is needed to complete a run. Regardless, sleeve variations within the price range given do not require separate listings. If the value varies beyond the given range, a separate listing will be added. Sleeves for the RCA "447" Gold Standard Series are listed in a separate section following the Gold Standard Singles. A slight premium—perhaps $3 to $5—may be placed on RCA's "Living Stereo" paper sleeves. These were used for many different RCA stereo singles and were not exclusively an Elvis item.

Gold Standard Singles with "447" prefix (Commercial)

RCA (0600 thru 0639)...................... 15-25 59-64
(Black label, dog on top.)
RCA (0600 thru 0639)........................ 8-12 65-66
(Black label, dog on side.)
RCA (0600 thru 0639)..................... 50-75 68-69
(Orange label.)
RCA (0600 thru 0639)........................ 5-10 70-74
(Red label.)
RCA (0600 thru 0639) 4-6 77
(Black label, dog near top.)
RCA (0640 thru 0642) 20-25 64
(Black label, dog on top.)
RCA (0640 thru 0642) 8-12 65-66
(Black label, dog on side.)
RCA (0640 thru 0642) 50-75 68-69
(Orange label.)
RCA (0640 thru 0642) 5-10 70-74
(Red label.)
RCA (0643 "Crying in the Chapel") 6-10 65
(Black label, dog on side.)
RCA (0643 "Crying in the Chapel") 5-8 70s
(Red label.)
RCA (0643 "Crying in the Chapel") 4-6 77
(Black label, dog near top.)
RCA (0644 thru 0646) 25-35 65
(Black label, dog on top.)
RCA (0644 thru 0646) 8-12 65
(Black label, dog on side.)
RCA (0644 thru 0646) 50-75 68-69
(Orange label.)
RCA (0644 thru 0646) 5-10 70-74
(Red label.)
RCA (0644 thru 0646) 4-6 77
(Black label, dog near top.)
RCA (0647 thru 0650) 8-12 65
(Black label, dog on side.)
RCA (0647 thru 0650) 5-10 70-74
(Red label.)
RCA (0647 thru 0650) 4-6 77
(Black label, dog near top.)
RCA (0651 & 0652)......................... 10-15 66
(Black label, dog on side.)
RCA (0651 & 0652)........................... 5-10 70s
(Red label.)
RCA (0653 thru 0658) 8-12 66-68
(Black label, dog on side.)
RCA (0653 thru 0658) 5-10 70-74
(Red label.)
RCA (0653 thru 0658) 4-6 77
(Black label, dog near top.)
RCA (0659 "Indescribably Blue")....... 10-15 70
(Red label.)
RCA (0660 "Long Legged Girl") 40-60 70
(Red label.)
RCA (0661 "Judy") 10-20 70
(Red label.)
RCA (0662 "Big Boss Man")............. 10-15 70
(Red label.)
RCA (0663 thru 0685) 5-10 70-73
(Red label.)
RCA (0663 thru 0685) 4-6 77
(Black label, dog near top.)
RCA (0720 "Blue Christmas") 10-20 64
(Black label, dog on top.)

Gold Standard Singles with "GB" prefix (Commercial)

RCA (10156 thru 10489)...................... 5-10 75-76
(Red label.)
RCA (10156 thru 10489) 4-6 77
(Black label, dog near top.)
RCA (11326 thru 13275) 4-6 77
(Black label, dog near top.)
Gold Standard *promotional* singles are in numerical sequence in the section for Promotional Singles.

Gold Standard Picture Sleeves

RCA (0601 "That's All Right")........ 100-200 64
RCA (0602 "Good Rockin' Tonight") 100-200 64
RCA (0605 "Heartbreak Hotel")..... 100-200 64
RCA (0608 "Don't Be Cruel")......... 100-200 64
RCA (0618 "All Shook Up")........... 100-200 64
RCA (0639 "Kiss Me Quick").......... 20-25 64
RCA (0643 "Crying in the Chapel") ... 15-20 65
RCA (0647 "Blue Christmas") 20-25 65
(Pictures Elvis on a Christmas card among wrapped gifts.)
RCA (0647 "Blue Christmas") 8-10 77
(Pictures Elvis in a circle among colored ornaments.)
RCA (0650 "Puppet on a String") 20-25 65
RCA (0651 "Joshua Fit the Battle") ... 50-75 66

RCA (0652 "Milky White Way")........50-75 66
RCA (0651 & 0652 "Special Easter Programming Kit")...750-1000 66
(Picture sleeve-mailer. Contained both 1966 Easter singles, *Joshua Fit the Battle* and *Milky White Way* in their sleeves and an Easter greeting card from Elvis. Price is for the complete kit.)
RCA (0651 & 0652 "Special Easter Programming Kit")...750-850 66
(Picture sleeve-mailer only.)
RCA (0720 "Blue Christmas") 30-35 64

Promotional Singles

CREATIVE RADIO ("Elvis 10th Anniversary"/ "The Elvis Hour")..................................15-20 87
(Demonstration disc, promoting the syndicated 10th anniversary radio special.)
CREATIVE RADIO ("Memories of Elvis"/ "The Elvis Hour")..................................15-20 87
(Demonstration disc, promoting the syndicated 10th anniversary radio special.)
For *Elvis 50th Birthday Special*, see PRESLEY, Elvis / Buddy Holly.
For *The Elvis Hour*, see PRESLEY, Elvis / Gary Owens.
CREATIVE RADIO ("Nearer My God to Thee")..5-10 89
(Promotional souvenir only. Issued as a bonus single with the LP, *Between Takes with Elvis.*)
CREATIVE RADIO ("Mystery Train") ..5-10 92
(Single-sided demonstration disc, taken from the syndicated 15th anniversary radio special.)
PARAMOUNT PICTURES ("Easy Come, Easy Go")..................................200-400 67
(Issued only to select theatres, designed for lobby play.)
PARAMOUNT PICTURES (1800 "Blue Hawaii") 300-500 61
(Single-sided pressing. Issued only to select theatres, designed for lobby play. Has excerpts of songs from the film.)
PARAMOUNT PICTURES (2017 "Girls! Girls! Girls!")......................................500-750 64
(Issued only to select theatres, designed for lobby play.)
PARAMOUNT PICTURES (2413 "Roustabout")..........................2000-4000 64
(Issued only to select theatres, designed for lobby play. Track is an alternate take.)
RCA (15 "Old Shep")....................600-800 56
RCA (76 "Don't"/"Wear My Ring Around Your Neck")......................................600-800 60
(Issued with special sleeve, listed in the Picture Sleeves section.)
RCA (0088 "Raised on Rock") 8-10 73
(Yellow label.)
RCA (118 "King of the Whole Wide World")......................................175-225 62
(Issued with a special sleeve, which is listed in the Picture Sleeves section. Includes dee jay insert.)
RCA (0130 "How Great Thou Art")....35-50 69
(Yellow label.)
RCA (139 "Roustabout")..............200-250 64
RCA (162 "How Great Thou Art")..150-200 67
(Issued with a special sleeve, listed in the Picture Sleeves section.)
RCA (0196 "Take Good Care of Her")..8-10 74
(Yellow label.)
RCA (0280 "If You Talk in Your Sleep")..8-10 74
(Yellow label.)
RCA (0517 "Little Sister")..............100-125 83
(12-inch single.)
RCA (0572 "Merry Christmas Baby"). 12-15 71
(Yellow label.)
RCA (0601 "That's All Right")..........50-100 64
(White label.)
RCA (0602 "Good Rockin' Tonight")....................................50-100 64
(White label.)
RCA (0605 "Heartbreak Hotel").......50-100 64
(White label.)
RCA (0608 "Don't Be Cruel")..........50-100 64
(White label.)
RCA (0618 "All Shook Up")..........50-100 64
(White label.)
RCA (0619 "Until It's Time for You to Go")..10-12 72
(Yellow label.)
RCA (0639 "Kiss Me Quick")..........20-25 64
(White label.)
RCA (0643 "Crying in the Chapel")... 15-20 65
(White label.)
RCA (0647 "Blue Christmas")..........25-30 65
(White label.)
RCA (0650 "Puppet on a String")......25-30 65
(White label.)
RCA (0651 "Joshua Fit the Battle")..50-100 66
(White label.)
RCA (0652 "Milky White Way").......50-100 66
(White label. See Gold Standard Picture Sleeves section for special mailing sleeve used with 0651 & 0652.)
RCA (0651 "He Touched Me")..........50-75 72
(Yellow label.)
RCA (0672 "An American Trilogy")... 12-15 72
(Yellow label.)
RCA (0720 "Blue Christmas")..........25-30 64
(White label.)
RCA (0769 "Burning Love")...............8-10 72
(Yellow label.)
RCA (0808 "Blue Christmas")... 2000-3000 57
RCA (0815 "Separate Ways")............8-10 72
(Yellow label.)
RCA (0910 "Fool")...........................8-10 73
(Yellow label.)
RCA (6357 "Mystery Train")..........200-300 55
(White "Record Prevue" label.)
RCA (8360 "Viva Las Vegas")..........20-25 64
(White label.)
RCA (8400 "Such a Night")....... 4000-5000 64
(White label.)
RCA (8440 "Ask Me")......................20-30 64
(White label.)
RCA (8500 "Do the Clam")..............20-25 65
(White label.)
RCA (8585 "It Feels So Right").........20-25 65
(White label.)
RCA (8657 "I'm Yours")...................20-25 65
(White label.)
RCA (8740 "Tell Me Why")..............20-25 65
(White label.)
RCA (8780 "Frankie & Johnny") 20-25 66
(White label.)
RCA (8870 "Love Letters")...............20-25 66
(White label.)
RCA (8941 "Spinout")......................20-25 66
(White label.)
RCA (8950 "If Everyday Was Like Christmas")...20-35 66
(White label.)
RCA (9056 "Indescribably Blue")......20-25 67
(White label.)
RCA (9115 "Long Legged Girl").......20-25 67
(White label.)
RCA (9287 "There's Always Me").....20-25 67
(White label.)
RCA (9341 "Big Boss Man")............20-25 67
(White label.)
RCA (9425 "Guitar Man")................15-20 68
(Yellow label.)
RCA (9465 "U.S. Male")...................15-20 68
(Yellow label.)
RCA (9547 "Your Time Hasn't Come Yet Baby")...15-20 68
(Yellow label.)
RCA (9600 "You'll Never Walk Alone")...15-20 68
(Yellow label.)
RCA (9610 "Almost in Love")............10-15 68
(Yellow label.)
RCA (9670 "If I Can Dream")............10-15 68
(Yellow label.)
RCA (9731 "Memories")....................10-15 69
(Yellow label.)
RCA (9741 "In the Ghetto")..............10-15 69
(Yellow label.)
RCA (9747 "Clean Up Your Own Back Yard")...10-15 69
(Yellow label.)
RCA (9764 "Suspicious Minds")........10-15 69
(Yellow label.)
RCA (9768 "Don't Cry Daddy")..........10-15 69
(Yellow label.)
RCA (9791 "Kentucky Rain")............10-15 70
(Yellow label.)
RCA (9835 "The Wonder of You")..... 10-15 70
(Yellow label.)
RCA (9873 "I've Lost You") 10-15 70
(Yellow label.)
RCA (9916 "You Don't Have to Say You Love Me")...10-15 70
(Yellow label.)
RCA (9960 "I Really Don't Want to Know")...10-15 70
(Yellow label.)
RCA (9980 "Where Did They Go Lord")...10-15 71
(Yellow label.)
RCA (9985 "Life")............................10-15 71
(Yellow label.)
RCA (9998 "I'm Leavin'")..................10-15 71
(Yellow label.)
RCA (10074 "Promised Land")...........8-10 74
(Yellow label.)
RCA (10191 "My Boy").......................8-10 75
(Yellow label.)
RCA (10278 "T-r-o-u-b-l-e")...............8-10 75
(Yellow label.)
RCA (10401 "Bringing It Back")..........8-10 75
(Yellow label.)
RCA (10601 "Hurt")............................8-10 76
(Yellow label.)
RCA (10857 "Moody Blue")..................6-10 76
(Yellow label. Black vinyl.)
RCA (10857 "Moody Blue").........900-1000 76
(Experimental colored vinyl pressings. Not intended for distribution.)
RCA (10951 "Let Me Be There")...100-125 77
RCA (10998 "Way Down")............125-150 77
(White label.)
RCA (10998 "Way Down")..................6-10 77
(Yellow label.)
RCA (11165 "My Way")........................6-10 77
(Yellow label.)
RCA (11212 "Unchained Melody")......6-10 78
(Yellow label.)
RCA (11320 "Teddy Bear")..................6-10 78
(Yellow label.)
RCA (11533 "Are You Sincere")..........6-10 79
(Yellow label.)
RCA (11679 "I Got a Feelin' in My Body")...6-10 79
(Yellow label.)
RCA (12158 "Guitar Man")..................6-10 81
(Yellow label. Black vinyl.)
RCA (12158 "Guitar Man")...........200-300 81
(Yellow label. Colored vinyl.)
RCA (12205 "Lovin' Arms")..................6-10 81
(Yellow label. Black vinyl.)
RCA (12205 "Lovin' Arms")..........200-300 81
(Yellow label. Colored vinyl.)
RCA (13058 "You'll Never Walk Alone")...6-10 82
(Yellow label.)
RCA (13302 "The Impossible Dream")...75-100 82
RCA (13351 "Elvis Medley")...............6-10 82
(Yellow label. Black vinyl.)
RCA (13351 "Elvis Medley")..........200-300 82
(Gold label. Colored vinyl.)
RCA (13500 "I Was the One").............6-10 83
(Yellow label. Black vinyl.)
RCA (13500 "I Was the One").......200-300 83
(Yellow label. Colored vinyl.)
RCA (13547 "Little Sister")..................6-10 83
(Yellow label. Black vinyl.)
RCA (13547 "Little Sister")...........200-300 83
(Blue label. Colored vinyl.)

RCA (13875 "Baby, Let's Play House")....................................150-250 84
(Gold label. Colored vinyl.)
RCA (13929 "Blue Suede Shoes) 6-10 84
(Gold label. Colored vinyl.)
RCA (14090 "Always on My Mind") 6-10 85
(Gold label. Colored vinyl.)
RCA (14237 "Merry Christmas Baby")...6-10 85
Note: Elvis 50th Anniversary singles—RCA 13875 through 14237—used the same gold label for both commercial and promotional issues. Promo singles have "Not For Sale" printed on the label.
RCA (4-834-115 "I'll Be Back") .4000-6000 66
(White label. Single-sided disc. Reads "For Special Academy Consideration Only." Made for submission to the Academy of Motion Picture Arts and Sciences.)
ROYAL CARIBBEAN CRUISE LINES (12690 "Follow That Dream - Take 2") 10-20 90
(Souvenir disc for Elvis cruise passengers.)
UNITED STATES AIR FORCE (125 "It's Now Or Never"): see PRESLEY, Elvis / Jaye P. Morgan.
UNITED STATES AIR FORCE (159 "Surrender"): see PRESLEY, Elvis / Lawrence Welk.
WHAT'S IT ALL ABOUT (78 "Life"): see PRESLEY, Elvis / Helen Reddy
WHAT'S IT ALL ABOUT (1840 "Elvis Presley")..70-75 80
WHAT'S IT ALL ABOUT (3025 "Elvis Presley") 50-60 82
Note: Plastic soundsheets and flexi-discs are listed in a separate section that follows. Promotional 78s are included with Singles: 78 rpm, at the beginning of the Presley section.

Plastic Soundsheets/Flexi-discs

EVA-TONE (38713 "Elvis Speaks! The Truth About Me")......................................30-40
(Eva-Tone number is not on label but is etched in the trail-off.)
EVA-TONE (52578 "The King Is Dead Long Live the King")......................................90-100 78
EVA-TONE (831942 "50,000,000 Elvis Fans Weren't Wrong!")...................................5-10 83
EVA-TONE (726771 "The Elvis Presley Story")...5-10 77
EVA-TONE (1037710 "Elvis Live")....30-40 78
(Price for magazine, titled *Collector's Issue*, with bound-in soundsheet.)
EVA-TONE (1037710 "Elvis Live")....15-20 78
(Price for soundsheet only.)
EVA-TONE (1227785 "Thompson Vocal Eliminator") 15-20 78
(Has segments of songs by three artists including Elvis.)
EVA-TONE (10287733 "Elvis: Six Hour Special") 15-20 77
EVA-TONE/RCA ("Love Me Tender")...25-35 74
(Price for April 1974 issue of *Teen Magazine* with bound-in soundsheet.)
EVA-TONE/RCA ("Love Me Tender")...15-25 74
(Price for soundsheet only.)
LYNCHBURG AUDIO ("The Truth About Me") 125-150 56
(Lynchburg Audio number is not on label but is etched in the trail-off.)
RAINBO ("Elvis Speaks, in Person")....................................300-325 56
(Price for magazine, *Elvis Answers Back*, with 78rpm flexi-disc still attached to front cover.)
RAINBO ("Elvis Speaks, in Person")....................................100-125 56
(Price for flexi-disc only.)
RAINBO ("The Truth About Me")...300-325 56
(Price for magazine, *Elvis Answers Back*, with 78rpm paper flexi-disc still attached to front cover.)
RAINBO ("The Truth About Me")....100-125 56
(Price for flexi-disc only.)
Note: All soundsheets and flexi-discs were used for some type of promotional purpose.

EPs: 7-inch (Commercial and Promotional)

RCA (22 "Elvis Presley")........... 1000-1500 56
(May have "Elvis" in either light or dark pink letters on front cover. Two-EP bonus promotional item. Discs are numbered 9121 & 9122.)
RCA (23 "Elvis Presley").......... 3500-5000 56
(Three-EP bonus promotional item. Includes "How to Use and Enjoy Your RCA Victor Elvis Presley Autograph Automatic 45 Victrola Portable Phonograph," which represents $75 to $100 of the value. Discs are numbered 9123, 9124 & 9125.)
RCA (128 "Elvis by Request").......... 60-80 61
RCA (747 "Elvis Presley")............ 200-250 56
(Black label, without dog.)
RCA (747 "Elvis Presley").............. 75-100 56
(Black label, dog on top. Has song title strip across the top of front cover.)
RCA (747 "Elvis Presley")................ 50-70 65
(Black label, dog on side.)
RCA (747 "Elvis Presley")............ 100-200 69
(Orange label.)
RCA (747 "Blue Suede Shoes").... 600-750 56
(Temporary paper sleeve for 1956 issue of EPA-747. Price is for sleeve only.)
RCA (821 "Heartbreak Hotel")...... 200-250 56
(Black label, without dog.)
RCA (821 "Heartbreak Hotel")........ 75-100 56
(Black label, dog on top. Has song title strip across the top of front cover.)
RCA (821 "Heartbreak Hotel")......... 50-70 65
(Black label, dog on side.)
RCA (821 "Heartbreak Hotel")...... 100-200 69
(Orange label.)
RCA (830 "Elvis Presley").............. 75-100 56
(Black label, dog on top. Has song title strip across the top of front cover.)
RCA (830 "Elvis Presley")............ 200-250 56
(Black label, without dog.)
RCA (830 "Elvis Presley")................ 50-70 65
(Black label, dog on side.)
RCA (830 "Elvis Presley")............ 100-200 69
(Orange label.)
RCA (940 "The Real Elvis")........... 75-100 56
(Black label, dog on top. Has song title strip across the top of front cover.)
RCA (940 "The Real Elvis")......... 200-250 56
(Black label, without dog. Reissued as Gold Standard 5120.)
RCA (965 "Any Way You Want Me").. 75-100 56
(Black label, dog on top. Has song title strip across the top of front cover.)
RCA (965 "Any Way You Want Me").. 200-250 56
(Black label, without dog.)
RCA (965 "Any Way You Want Me").. 50-70 65
(Black label, dog on side.)
RCA (965 "Any Way You Want Me")... 100-200 69
(Orange label.)
RCA (992 "Elvis, Vol. 1")............... 75-100 56
(Black label, dog on top. Has song title strip across the top of front cover.)
RCA (992 "Elvis, Vol. 1")............. 200-250 56
(Black label, without dog.)
RCA (992 "Elvis, Vol. 1").................. 50-70 65
(Black label, dog on side.)
RCA (992 "Elvis, Vol. 1")............. 100-200 69
(Orange label.)
RCA (993 "Elvis, Vol. 2")................ 75-100 56
(Black label, dog on top. Has song title strip across the top of front cover.)
RCA (993 "Elvis, Vol. 2")............. 200-250 56
(Black label, without dog.)
RCA (993 "Elvis, Vol. 2").................. 50-70 65
(Black label, dog on side.)
RCA (993 "Elvis, Vol. 2")............. 100-200 69
(Orange label.)
RCA (994 "Strictly Elvis")............. 75-100 56
(Black label, dog on top. Has song title strip across the top of front cover.)
RCA (994 "Strictly Elvis")..............200-250 56
(Black label, without dog.)
RCA (994 "Strictly Elvis")...................50-70 65
(Black label, dog on side.)
RCA (994 "Strictly Elvis")..............100-200 69
(Orange label.)
RCA (1254 "Elvis Presley") 500-600 56
(Black label, without dog. Two EP set.)
RCA (1254 "Elvis Presley") 300-400 56
(Black label, dog on top. Two EP set.)
RCA (1254 "Most Talked-About New Personality")..............................3500-5000 56
(Two EPs, also numbered 0793 & 0794, in a single pocket paper sleeve. Promotional issue only. Includes a copy of *Dee-Jay Digest*, which represents $50 to $75 of the value.)
RCA (1254 "Most Talked-About New Personality")..................................500-750 56
(Price for the two EPs without the sleeve. Either disc would be worth about half the amount shown for both. Discs, numbered 0793 & 0794, are untitled. Promotional issue only.)
RCA (1-1515 "Loving You, Vol. 1") .75-100 57
(Black label, dog on top. Has song title strip across the top of front cover.)
RCA (1-1515 "Loving You, Vol. 1")....50-70 65
(Black label, dog on side.)
RCA (1-1515 "Loving You, Vol. 1")...100-200 69
(Orange label.)
RCA (2-1515 "Loving You, Vol. 2")...75-100 57
(Black label, dog on top. Has song title strip across the top of front cover.)
RCA (2-1515 "Loving You, Vol. 2")....50-70 65
(Black label, dog on side.)
RCA (2-1515 "Loving You, Vol. 2")...100-200 69
(Orange label.)
RCA (2006 "Aloha from Hawaii").......60-75 74
(Includes sheet of 10 title strips. Made for juke box operators only.)
RCA (4006 "Love Me Tender")......200-250 56
(Black label, without dog. Has song title strip across the top of front cover.)
RCA (4006 "Love Me Tender")........75-100 56
(Black label, dog on top. Has song title strip across the top of front cover.)
RCA (4006 "Love Me Tender")..........50-70 65
(Black label, dog on side.)
RCA (4006 "Love Me Tender")......100-200 69
(Orange label.)
RCA (4041 "Just for You")............200-250 57
(Black label, without dog. Has EP title strip across the top of front cover.)
RCA (4041 "Just for You")..............75-100 57
(Black label, dog on top. Has EP title strip across the top of front cover.)
RCA (4041 "Just for You")................50-70 65
(Black label, dog on side.)
RCA (4041 "Just for You")............100-200 69
(Orange label.)
RCA (4054 "Peace in the Valley")...75-100 57
(Black label, dog on top. Has EP title strip across the top of front cover. Reissued as Gold Standard 5121.)
RCA (4108 "Elvis Sings Christmas Songs")..75-100 57
(Black label, dog on top. Has EP title strip across the top of front cover.)
RCA (4108 "Elvis Sings Christmas Songs")..50-70 65
(Black label, dog on side.)
RCA (4108 "Elvis Sings Christmas Songs")...100-200 69
(Orange label.)
RCA (4114 "Jailhouse Rock") 65-85 57
(Black label, dog on top.)
RCA (4114 "Jailhouse Rock") 50-70 65
(Black label, dog on side.)
RCA (4114 "Jailhouse Rock") 100-200 69
(Orange label.)
RCA (4319 "King Creole")..............75-100 58
(Reissued as Gold Standard 5122.)

RCA (4321 "King Creole, Vol. 2")......65-85 58
(Black label, dog on top.)
RCA (4321 "King Creole, Vol. 2")......50-70 65
(Black label, dog on side.)
RCA (4321 "King Creole, Vol. 2") .100-200 69
(Orange label.)
RCA (4325 "Elvis Sails") 75-100 58
(Reissued as Gold Standard 5157.)
RCA (4340 "Christmas with Elvis") .75-100 58
(Black label, dog on top.)
RCA (4340 "Christmas with Elvis")....50-70 65
(Black label, dog on side.)
RCA (4340 "Christmas with Elvis")..100-200 69
(Orange label.)
RCA (4368 "Follow That Dream") 70-90 62
(Black label, dog on top. Playing times are incorrectly listed for three of the four tracks: *Follow That Dream* shown as 1:35, should be 1:38; *Angel* shown as 2:35, should be 2:40; and *I'm Not the Marrying Kind* shown as 1:49, should be 2:00.)
RCA (4368 "Follow That Dream") 50-70 62
(Black label, dog on top. All playing times are correctly shown.)
RCA (4368 "Follow That Dream") ...75-100 62
(Promotional issue only. Marked "Not For Sale.")
RCA (4368 "Follow That Dream") 120-160 62
(Special paper sleeve, issued to radio stations and juke box operators. Promotional issue only. Price is for sleeve only.)
RCA (4368 "Follow That Dream") 50-70 65
(Black label, dog on side.)
RCA (4368 "Follow That Dream") 100-200 69
(Orange label.)
RCA (4371 "Kid Galahad") 60-80 62
(Black label, dog on top.)
RCA (4371 "Kid Galahad") 50-70 65
(Black label, dog on side.)
RCA (4371 "Kid Galahad") 100-200 69
(Orange label.)
RCA (4382 "Viva Las Vegas")..........65-85 64
(Black label, dog on top.)
RCA (4382 "Viva Las Vegas")..........50-70 65
(Black label, dog on side.)
RCA (4382 "Viva Las Vegas")......100-200 69
(Orange label.)
RCA (4383 "Tickle Me") 50-70 65
(Black label, dog on side.)
RCA (4383 "Tickle Me") 100-200 69
(Orange label.)
RCA (4387 "Easy Come, Easy Go") .50-70 67
(Black label, dog on side.)
RCA (4387 "Easy Come, Easy Go") 100-150 67
(White label. Promotional Issue Only.)
RCA (5088 "A Touch of Gold, Vol. I") 450-550 59
(Maroon label.)
RCA (5088 "A Touch of Gold, Vol. I") 75-100 59
(Black label, dog on top. Add $15 to $25 if accompanied by "I am a loyal Elvis fan" insert card.)
RCA (5088 "A Touch of Gold, Vol. I") 50-70 65
(Black label, dog on side.)
RCA (5088 "A Touch of Gold, Vol. I") 100-200 69
(Orange label.)
RCA (5101 "A Touch of Gold, Vol. II") 450-550 59
(Maroon label.)
RCA (5101 "A Touch of Gold, Vol. II") 75-100 59
(Black label, dog on top. Add $15 to $25 if accompanied by "I am a loyal Elvis fan" insert card.)
RCA (5101 "A Touch of Gold, Vol. II") 50-70 65
(Black label, dog on side.)
RCA (5101 "A Touch of Gold, Vol. II") 100-200 69
(Orange label.)

RCA (5120 "The Real Elvis")........ 500-750 59
(Maroon label. Reissue of 940.)
RCA (5120 "The Real Elvis")........... 55-75 59
(Black label, dog on top.)
RCA (5120 "The Real Elvis")........... 50-70 65
(Black label, dog on side.)
RCA (5120 "The Real Elvis")....... 100-200 69
(Orange label.)
RCA (5121 "Peace in the Valley")...................................... 500-750 59
(Maroon label. Reissue of 4054.)
RCA (5121 "Peace in the Valley")..... 60-80 59
(Black label, dog on top.)
RCA (5121 "Peace in the Valley")..... 50-70 65
(Black label, dog on side.)
RCA (5121 "Peace in the Valley") 100-200 69
(Orange label.)
RCA (5122 "King Creole")........ 5000-7500 59
(Maroon label. Reissue of 4319. Though we have been told of the existence of this item by one collector, it remains one of very, very few U.S. Elvis collectibles that we have not personally confirmed. Price estimate is based on offers, as we know of no sales.)
RCA (5122 "King Creole")............... 60-80 59
(Black label, dog on top.)
RCA (5122 "King Creole")............... 50-70 65
(Black label, dog on side.)
RCA (5122 "King Creole")........... 100-200 69
(Orange label.)
RCA (5141 "A Touch of Gold, Vol. 3")...................................... 425-500 60
(Maroon label.)
RCA (5141 "A Touch of Gold, Vol. 3")... 75-100 60
(Black label, dog on top.)
RCA (5141 "A Touch of Gold, Vol. 3")... 50-70 65
(Black label, dog on side.)
RCA (5141 "A Touch of Gold, Vol. 3")...................................... 100-200 69
(Orange label.)
RCA (5157 "Elvis Sails")................. 50-70 65
(Black label, dog on top. Reissue of 4325.)
RCA (5157 "Elvis Sails")................. 50-70 65
(Black label, dog on side.)
RCA (5157 "Elvis Sails")............. 100-200 69
(Orange label.)
RCA (8705 "TV Guide Presents Elvis") 1000-1500 56
(Price for disc only. Insert sheets are priced separately below. No sleeve or special cover exists for this disc. Promotional issue only.)
RCA (8705 "TV Guide Presents Elvis")....................................... 50-100 56
(Price for "Elvis Exclusively" gray insert.)
RCA (8705 "TV Guide Presents Elvis")...................................... 100-200 56
(Price for *Elvis Exclusively* pink insert, with suggested continuity.)
RCA (9089 "SPD-15 Elvis EP").... 400-500 56
(Black label. Just the Elvis disc from SPD-15.)
RCA (9089 "SPD-15 Elvis EP").... 400-500 56
(Gray label. The Elvis disc from SPD-15. Gray label pressings were for juke box operators.)
RCA (9113 "SPD-19 Elvis EP").... 300-400 56
(The Elvis disc from SPD-19, *The Sound of Leadership*.)
RCA (9141 "SPD-26 Elvis EP").... 200-250 56
(Black label. The Elvis disc from SPD-15, *Great Country/Western Hits*.)
RCA (64476 "Heartbreak Hotel")......... 4-8 96
(Issued with paper sleeve.)

Notes: Unless listed and priced separately, all EP values include both disc and cover with approximately half of the total attached to each. Some of the rarer pieces that are often traded individually (disc or sleeve), as well as those sleeves that have an exceptionally higher value than their disc, are listed separately in this section. All EPs in the 5000 series are Gold Standard Series issues although none are identified as such on the labels, only on the covers. Remember, if you don't find the EP in this section it may contain two, three or four artists, and will be listed following the Presley LP section.

LPs: 10/12–inch
(Commercial and Promotional)

ABC RADIO (1003 "Elvis Memories") 475-575 78
(Three-LP boxed set. Add $25 to $50 if accompanied by a 16-page programmer's booklet and four pages of additional information. Issued only to radio stations. Add $40 to $50 if accompanied by a 7–inch reel tape, with spots and promotional announcements. Highlights of this program were issued on Michelob 810.)
ASSOCIATED BROADCASTERS (1001 "Legend of a King") 125-150 80
(White label. Advance pressing.)
ASSOCIATED BROADCASTERS (1001 "Legend of a King") 25-30 80
(Picture disc. First pressings are numbered from 3000 through 6000. Number appears under "Side One" on the disc itself. Cover is standard, die-cut, picture disc cover. Has several spelling errors on back cover, including "idle" for idol and "Jordinaires" instead of Jordanaires.)
ASSOCIATED BROADCASTERS (1001 "Legend of a King") 20-25 80
(Picture disc. Second pressings are numbered from 6001 through 9000. Most of the spelling errors were corrected on this cover.)
ASSOCIATED BROADCASTERS (1001 "Legend of a King") 15-20 80
(Picture disc. Third pressings are numbered from 00001 through 02999 and 09001 through 15000. Cover errors have all been corrected.)
ASSOCIATED BROADCASTERS (1001 "Legend of a King") 10-12 84
(Picture disc. Fourth pressings are also numbered from 3000 through 6000, but were packaged in a clear plastic sleeve instead of a conventional cover.)
ASSOCIATED BROADCASTERS (1001 "Legend of a King") 8-10 85
(Picture disc. Discs are not numbered. Packaged in a plastic sleeve.)
ASSOCIATED BROADCASTERS ("Legend of a King") 200-250 85
(Three hour, three-LP set. Not boxed. Price includes six pages of cue sheets. Available to radio stations only.)
ASSOCIATED BROADCASTERS ("Legend of a King") 300-350 85
(Same as above, but packaged in a specially printed box.)
ASSOCIATED BROADCASTERS ("Legend of a King") 300-350 86
(Three-LP boxed set, same as above except time on segment 1-B is increased from 14:25 to 15:15 in order to include a Johnny Bernero interview.)
ASSOCIATED PRESS (1977 "The World in Sound")..80-100 78
(News highlights of 1977, including coverage of Elvis' death.)
BOXCAR ("Having Fun with Elvis on Stage")..100-125 74
(No selection number used. Sold in conjunction with Elvis' concert appearances. Reissued as RCA CPM1-0818.)
CAEDMON (1572 "On the Record") .60-80 78
(Various news items and artists featured.)
CAMDEN (2304 "Flaming Star") 15-20 69
(First issued as RCA PRS-279, reissued in 1975 as Pickwick 2304.)
CAMDEN (2408 "Let's Be Friends")..15-20 70
(Reissued in 1975 as Pickwick 2408.)
CAMDEN (2428 "Elvis' Christmas Album")..15-20 70
(Eight songs on this LP were first issued on RCA LOC-1035. Reissued in 1975 as Pickwick 2428.)
CAMDEN (2440 "Almost in Love").... 25-30 70
(With *Stay Away Joe*.)
CAMDEN (2440 "Almost in Love").... 15-20 73
(*Stay Away* replaces *Stay Away Joe*. Reissued in 1975 as Pickwick 2440.)

CAMDEN (2472 "You'll Never Walk Alone") 15-20 71
(Reissued in 1975 as Pickwick 2472.)
CAMDEN (2518 "C'mon Everybody") 15-20 71
(Reissued in 1975 as Pickwick 2518.)
CAMDEN (2533 "I Got Lucky") 15-20 71
(Reissued in 1975 as Pickwick 2533.)
CAMDEN (2567 "Elvis Sings Hits from His Movies") 15-20 72
(Reissued in 1975 as Pickwick 2567.)
CAMDEN (2595 "Burning Love") 20-30 72
(Add $25 to $35 if accompanied by the bonus 8" x 10" Elvis photo. Reissued in 1975 as Pickwick 2595.)
CAMDEN (2611 "Separate Ways") ... 15-20 73
(Reissued in 1975 as Pickwick 2611.)
COUNTRY SESSIONS U.S.A. (126 "A Tribute to Elvis") 225-250 83
(Price includes cue sheets. Promotional issue only.)
CREATIVE RADIO ("Elvis Remembered") 100-125 78
(Three discs. Price includes six insert pages. Advance copies of this set, which was not issued with a special cover or package, were with plain white, handwritten, labels. These copies may be valued at $150 to $250. Promotional issue only.)
CREATIVE RADIO ("Elvis, the Country Side") 75-85 84
(Two discs. Promotional issue only.)
CREATIVE RADIO ("Elvis 50th Anniversary") 250-275 85
(Six-disc set. Price includes seven pages of programming instructions and cues. Packaged in a plain, unprinted box. Promotional issue only.)
CREATIVE RADIO ("Elvis 10th Anniversary") 150-175 87
(Six-disc set. Price includes eight pages of programming instructions and cues. Packaged in a custom printed box. Promotional issue only.)
CREATIVE RADIO ("Christmas with Elvis") 25-30 87
(Promotional issue only. Not issued with special cover.)
CREATIVE RADIO ("Birthday Tribute To Elvis") 25-30 88
(Promotional issue only. Not issued with special cover.)
CREATIVE RADIO ("The Elvis Hour") 10-12 86-88
(Price is for any of the weekly discs in this series. The first 52 discs in the series have been selling as a set for $450 to $475. Promotional issues only.)
CREATIVE RADIO ("Demo of 10 Creative Radio Programs") 25-30 90s
(Includes segments of *The Elvis Hour, 10th Anniversary Special* and *Memories of Elvis*, along with portions of other shows by other artists. Promotional issue only.)
CREATIVE RADIO (E1 "Elvis Exclusive Interview") 175-200 88
(Price for *complete* 1956 Little Rock concert copies. Only the first 100 copies were pressed with the full concert. The only way to visually identify these is to check the disc. On the full concert pressings, the grooves take up nearly the entire disc.)
CREATIVE RADIO (E1 "Elvis Exclusive Interview") 20-30 88
(Has edited concert songs. On this pressing the grooves occupy only about two-thirds of the disc.)
CREATIVE RADIO ("Between Takes with Elvis") 150-250 89
(Three-disc set. Promotional issue only. Though not packaged inside covers—shrink wrapped at the factory—each LP set came with the bonus single, *Nearer My God to Thee/You Gave Me a Molehill.*)
Note: On any of the above listings, Creative Radio may be shown as Creative Radio Shows or Creative Radio Network.)
DRAKE-CHENAULT ("Elvis: a Three Hour Special") 300-350 77
(Boxed, three-disc set. Includes three pages of cue sheets.)
EMR ENTERPRISES (8 "The Age of Rock") 100-125 69
(Various artists. Promotional issue only.)
EARTH NEWS ("August 29, 1977") 325-375 77
(Promotional issue only. Price includes one-page letter.)
ELEKTRA (60107 "Diner") 10-20 82
(Soundtrack.)
FRANKLIN MINT (4 "The Official Grammy Award Winners") 150-200 85
(Boxed set of four colored vinyl discs. One in a series of 14 boxed sets, but only this one (titled *The Great Singers*) has Elvis. Includes booklet.)
GOLDEN EDITIONS LIMITED (1 "The First Year") 8-15 79
(Print in upper corners on front cover is in white. Label is black. Add $5 to $8 if accompanied by a 12-page booklet and one-page copy of the 1954 Elvis/Scotty Moore contract.)
GOLDEN EDITIONS LIMITED (101 "The First Year") 15-25 79
(Print in upper corners on front cover is in gold. Label is white. Add $5 to $8 if accompanied by a 12-page booklet and one-page copy of the 1954 Elvis/Scotty Moore contract. Most of the material on this LP was previously issued on HALW 00001.)
GREAT NORTHWEST (4005 "The Elvis Tapes") 10-15 77
(Repackaged on Starday 995.)
GREAT NORTHWEST (4006 "The King Speaks") 8-10 77
(This press conference was first issued as Green Valley 2001.)
GREEN VALLEY (2001 "Elvis 1961 Press Conference") 30-50 77
(Cover is thin, soft stock and does not have black bar on spine. Label does not show selection number.)
GREEN VALLEY (2001 "Elvis 1961 Press Conference") 12-15 77
(Cover is standard stock and has black bar on spine. Label has the selection number. Repackaged as one half of Green Valley 2001/2003. It was later repackaged as Great Northwest 4006.)
GREEN VALLEY (2001/2003 "Elvis Speaks to You") 25-30 78
(GV-2001 was first issued as a single LP.)
HALW (00001 "The First Years") 25-30 78
(Repackaged in 1979 on Golden Editions 1.)
INTERNATIONAL HOTEL PRESENTS ELVIS 1969 .... 1000-1500 69
(Custom gift box prepared by Col. Parker and RCA for International Hotel guests. Originally contained: RCA LPM-4088 & LSP-4155, three 8" x 10" Elvis photos, RCA Elvis catalog, calendar and a nine-page letter. Price is for complete set but box itself represents 90-95% of value.)
INTERNATIONAL HOTEL PRESENTS ELVIS 1970 .... 1000-1500 70
(Custom gift box prepared by Col. Parker and RCA for International Hotel guests. Originally contained: RCA LSP-6020 & 45-9791, one 8" x 10" Elvis photo, photo album, RCA Elvis catalog, calendar, menu and letter. Price is for complete set but box itself represents 90-95% of value.)
K-TEL (9900 "Elvis Love Songs") 15-20 81
LOUISIANA HAYRIDE (3061 "The Beginning Years") 300-400 84
(White label advance pressing from RCA, Indianapolis, where this LP was manufactured.)
LOUISIANA HAYRIDE (3061 "The Beginning Years") 15-25 84
(Price includes 20-page *D.J. Fontana Remembers Elvis* booklet, a four sheet copy of Elvis' Hayride contract and a 10" x 10" *Presleyana, Second Edition* flyer, all of which represent about $5 to $10 of the value. Selections from this LP are also on the Music Works 3601 & 3602.)
MFSL (059 "From Elvis in Memphis") 30-50 82
(First issued as RCA LSP-4155.)
MARCH of DIMES (0653 "Discs for Dimes") 1400-1600 56
(Various artists, 16–inch disc. Promotional issue only. Includes 16 pages of notes.)
MARCH of DIMES (0657 "Disc Jockey Interviews") 1400-1600 56
(Various artists, 16–inch disc. Promotional issue only. Includes scripts and notes.)
MARVENCO (101 "1954-1955, The Beginning") 10-15 88
(Has material perviously issued on Golden Editions 101.)
MEDIA ENTERTAINMENT ("The King's Gold") 50-75 85
(Three reel-to-reel tapes, issued only to radio stations. Price includes cue sheets. Not known to exist on disc.)
MICHELOB (810 "Highlights of Elvis Memories") 175-200 78
(A Michelob in-house promotional issue only.) *Elvis Memories* was first issued on ABC Radio 1003.
MUSIC WORKS (3601 "The First Live Recordings") 8-10 84
(First issued on Louisiana Hayride 3061.)
MUSIC WORKS (3602 "Hillbilly Cat") 8-10 84
(First issued on Louisiana Hayride 3061.)
OAK (1003 "Vintage 1955") 70-100 91
PAIR (1010 "Double Dynamite") 20-25 82
(First issued as Pickwick 5001.)
PAIR (1037 "Remembering Elvis") 20-25 83
PICKWICK (2304 "Flaming Star") 8-10 75
(First issued as RCA PRS-279.)
PICKWICK (2408 "Let's Be Friends") 8-10 75
(Black vinyl. First issued as Camden 2408.)
PICKWICK (2408 "Let's Be Friends") 500-600 70s
(Colored vinyl. Experimental pressing only. There is no colored vinyl commercial or promotional edition of this issue.)
PICKWICK (2428 "Elvis' Christmas Album") 8-10 75
(First issued as Camden 2428.)
PICKWICK (2428 "Elvis' Christmas Album") 15-25 86
(Has RCA Special Products on label and cover.)
PICKWICK (2440 "Almost in Love") 8-10 75
(First issued as Camden 2440.)
PICKWICK (2472 "You'll Never Walk Alone") 8-10 75
(First issued as Camden 2472.)
PICKWICK (2518 "C'mon Everybody") 8-10 75
(First issued as Camden 2518.)
PICKWICK (2533 "I Got Lucky") 8-10 75
(First issued as Camden 2533.)
PICKWICK (2567 "Elvis Sings Hits from His Movies") 8-10 75
(First issued as Camden 2567.)
PICKWICK (2595 "Burning Love") 8-10 75
(First issued as Camden 2595.)
PICKWICK (2611 "Separate Ways") ... 8-10 75
(First issued as Camden 2611.)
PICKWICK (5001 "Double Dynamite") 25-30 75
(Repackaged in 1982 as Pair 1010.)
PICKWICK (7007 "Frankie & Johnny") 10-15 75
(First issued as RCA 3553.)
PICKWICK (7064 "Mahalo from Elvis") 15-20 78
PREMORE (589 "Early Elvis") 5-10 89
(Mail-order album from the Solo Cup Company.)
RCA (EPC-1 "Special Christmas Program" Reel Tape) 300-325 67
(Price includes programming inserts, which represent $25-35 of the value. Never issued commercially on disc, all 10–inch red vinyl LPs of this material are bootlegs.)

RCA (TB-1 "Collectors Edition")....100-150 76
(Boxed, five-disc set.)
RCA (010 "Elvis! His Greatest Hits")..400-450 79
(White box edition. Boxed, eight-disc set, sold mail-order by *Reader's Digest*.)
RCA (010 "His Greatest Hits")..........40-60 83
(Yellow box edition. Boxed, seven-disc set, sold mail-order by *Reader's Digest*. See RCA 181 for the bonus LP offered with this set.)
RCA RBA-040: see READER'S DIGEST 040
RCA (0056 "Elvis") 40-50 73
(Mustard color label. Cover shows "Brookville Records" in upper right. A mail-order LP offer.)
RCA (0056 "Elvis") 20-25 73
(Blue label. Cover doesn't show "Brookville Records." Mail-order LP offer. Repackaged in 1978 and titled *Elvis Commemorative Album*.)
RCA (0056 "Elvis Commemorative Album")..75-80 78
(Price includes a "Registered Certificate of Ownership." A mail-order LP offer. First titled *Elvis*, using the same selection number.)
RCA (072 "Great Hits of 1956-57")....10-20 87
(Offered as a bonus LP from *Reader's Digest*, with the purchase of one of their non-Elvis boxed sets.)
RCA (0168 "Elvis in Hollywood").......35-45 76
(Add $10 to $15 is accompanied by a 20-page photo booklet.)
RCA (181 "Elvis Sings Inspirational Favorites") 15-20 83
(Special Products, Reader's Digest mail-order bonus LP for buyers of the 1983 edition of RCA 010. Price includes 24-page Reader's Digest Music catalog.)
RCA (191 "Elvis, the Legend Lives On") 40-45 86
(Boxed, seven-disc set, sold mail-order by Reader's Digest. Includes booklet.)
RCA (242 "Elvis Sings Country Favorites") 20-30 84
(Bonus LP from Reader's Digest, given with the purchase of their seven-disc boxed set, *The Great Country Entertainers*, which has no Elvis tracks.)
RCA (0263 "Elvis Presley Story")......30-40 77
(Special Products five-disc boxed set. A Candelite Music mail-order offer.)
RCA (0264 "Songs of Inspiration")....10-15 77
(Special Products issue. A Candelite Music mail-order bonus LP for buyers of RCA 0263.)
RCA (279 "Singer Presents Elvis")....70-80 68
(Reissued in 1969 as Camden 2304 and in 1975 as Pickwick 2304.)
RCA (0283 "Elvis, Including Fool")....50-60 73
RCA (0341 "Legendary Performer, Vol. 1")..20-25 74
(With die-cut cover. Add $5 to $10 if accompanied by *The Early Years* booklet.)
RCA (0341 "Legendary Performer, Vol. 1")..5-10 83
(With standard cover—not die-cut.)
RCA (0341 "Legendary Performer, Vol. 1")..................................800-1000 78
(Picture discs of the 0341 material but with pictures from any of about six different LP covers pressed on the disc. RCA in-house, experimental items.)
RCA (0347 "Memories of Elvis") 35-45 78
(Special Products five-disc boxed set. A Candelite Music mail-order offer. Add $8 to $10 if accompanied by a 16-page booklet and an Elvis print. Not all sets were issued with the print and booklet.)
RCA (0348 "Greatest Show on Earth")..10-12 78
(Special Products issue. A Candelite Music mail-order bonus LP for buyers of RCA 0347.)
RCA (0388 "Raised on Rock") 15-20 73
(Orange label.)
RCA (0388 "Raised on Rock") 8-10 77
(Black label.)
RCA (0401 RCA Radio Victrola Division Spots").....................................800-1200 56
(Single-sided disc with four 50-second radio commercials for RCA's Victrolas, as well as for the SPD-22 and SPD-23 EPs that were offered as a bonus. Elvis is the announcer on all of the spots, which include excerpts of some of his songs. Issued only to radio stations scheduling the spots.)
RCA (0412 "The Legendary Recordings")................................... 30-40 79
(Special Products six-disc boxed set. A Candelite Music mail-order offer.)
RCA (0413 "Greatest Moments in Music") 10-15 80
(Special Products issue. A Candelite Music mail-order bonus LP for buyers of RCA 0412.)
RCA (0437 "Rock 'N Roll Forever") 10-15 81
(Candelite Music mail-order LP offer.)
RCA (461 "Special Palm Sunday Programming")............................ 500-600 67
(Add $75 to $100 if accompanied by a programming packet. Promotional issue only.)
RCA (0461 "The Legendary Magic") 10-15 80
(Candelite Music mail-order LP offer.)
RCA (CPL1-0475 "Good Times") 15-20 74
VICTOR (AFL1-0475 "Good Times").. 8-10 77
RCA (571 " Elvis As Recorded at Madison Square Garden")................................. 250-300 72
(Two-disc, double pocket issue. Promotional issue only. Commercially issued as RCA LSP-4776.)
RCA (APD1-0606 "On Stage in Memphis").................................. 120-130 74
(Quadradisc. Orange label.)
RCA (CPL1-0606 "On Stage in Memphis").. 15-18 74
(Orange label.)
RCA (DJL1-0606 "On Stage in Memphis")................................... 250-275 74
(Banded edition. Promotional issue only.)
RCA (CPL1-0606 "On Stage in Memphis").. 10-15 76
(Tan label.)
RCA (CPL1-0606 "On Stage in Memphis")... 8-10 77
(Black label.)
RCA (AFL1-0606 "On Stage in Memphis")... 8-10 77
RCA (0632 "The Elvis Presley Collection").................................... 50-60 84
(Special Products three-disc boxed set, produced for Candlelite Music. Includes booklet. A mail-order LP offer.)
RCA (DPL1-0647 "Elvis Country").... 30-40 84
(Special Products issue for ERA Records.)
RCA (DPK1-0679 "Savage Young Elvis")... 5-10 84
(Cassette tape of a package that was never available on LP. Price is for tape still attached to 12" x 12" photo card.)
RCA (0704 "Elvis, HBO Special")..... 25-35 84
(Includes color poster. Special Products issue for HBO cable TV subscribers. This material was first issued as RCA LPM-4088.)
RCA (0710 "50 Years-50 Hits")......... 20-25 85
(Three-disc set. Offered by TV mail-order and through the RCA Record Club.)
RCA (0728 "Elvis, His Songs of Faith and Inspiration")................................. 15-20 86
(Two-disc, mail-order offer.)
RCA (CPM1-0818 "Having Fun with Elvis on Stage") 15-20 74
(Orange label.)
RCA (CPM1-0818 "Having Fun with Elvis on Stage") 10-15 76
(Tan label.)
RCA (AFM1-0818 "Having Fun with Elvis on Stage") 8-10 77
(First issued on Boxcar without a selection number.)
RCA (0835 "Elvis Presley Interview Record") 75-100 84
(Promotional issue only.)
RCA (APL1-0873 "Promised Land") 20-25 75
(Orange label.)
RCA (APL1-0873 "Promised Land") . 10-15 76
(Tan label.)
RCA (AFL1-0873 "Promised Land")....8-10 77
RCA (APD1-0873 "Promised Land") 100-125 75
(Quadradisc. Orange label.)
RCA (APD1-0873 "Promised Land") 40-50 77
(Quadradisc. Black label.)
RCA (ANL1-0971 "Pure Gold") 15-18 75
(Orange label.)
RCA (ANL1-0971 "Pure Gold") 10-15 76
(Yellow label.)
RCA (ANL1-0971 "Pure Gold") 8-10 77
(Black label.)
Reissued in 1980 as AYL1-3732.
RCA (1001 "The Sun Collection")..... 20-25 75
(Label does not have "Starcall" on it. Back cover pictures other LPs.)
RCA (1001 "The Sun Collection") 15-20 75
(Label has "Starcall" on it. Back cover with liner notes. This English import was distributed throughout the U.S. It was repackaged in 1976 as RCA 1675.)
RCA (LOC-1035 "Elvis' Christmas Album")..............................10000-20000 57
(Experimental, one-of-a-kind pressing.)
RCA (LOC-1035 "Elvis' Christmas Album")..500-550 57
(Black vinyl. With gold foil, gift-giving sticker.)
RCA (LOC-1035 "Elvis' Christmas Album")..375-475 57
(Black vinyl. Without gold foil, gift-giving sticker. Repackaged in 1958 as RCA 1951, in 1970 as Camden 2428 and in 1985 as RCA 5486. May be found with either gold or silver print on the spine.)
RCA (APL1-1039 "Today")...............20-25 75
(Orange label.)
RCA (APL1-1039 "Today")...............10-15 76
(Tan label.)
RCA (AFL1-1039 "Today") 8-10 77
RCA (APD1-1039 "Today") 100-125 75
(Quadradisc. Orange label.)
RCA (APD1-1039 "Today") 40-50 77
(Quadradisc. Black label.)
RCA (LPM-1254 "Elvis Presley")...100-125 56
(Monaural. Black label, "Long Play" at bottom. Cover has selection number in upper right corner.)
RCA (LPM-1254 "Elvis Presley")...... 50-75 63
(Black label, "Mono" at bottom. Cover has selection number on left.)
RCA (LPM-1254 "Elvis Presley")...... 25-50 64
(Black label, "Monaural" at bottom. Cover has selection number on left.)
RCA (LSP-1254e "Elvis Presley") 150-200 62
(Stereo. Black label, all print on label is silver.)
RCA (LSP-1254e "Elvis Presley") 25-50 64
(Black label, RCA logo is white, other label print is silver.)
RCA (LSP-1254e "Elvis Presley") 20-30 68
(Orange label.)
RCA (LSP-1254e "Elvis Presley") 10-20 76
(Tan label.)
RCA (AFL1-1254e "Elvis Presley")...... 8-15 77
(Digitally remastered in 1984 on RCA 5198.)
RCA (ANL1-1319 "His Hand in Mine")..10-15 76
(First issued as LPM/LSP-2328.)
RCA (1349 "Legendary Performer, Vol. 2")..50-65 76
(Does not have the false starts and outtakes on *Such a Night* and *Cane and a High Starched Collar*. Mistakenly has only the complete take of both songs. Add $5 to $10 if accompanied by *The Early Years Continued* booklet.)
RCA (1349 "Legendary Performer, Vol. 2")..20-25 76
(With die-cut cover. Add $5 to $10 if accompanied by *The Early Years Continued* booklet.)

RCA (1349 "Legendary Performer, Vol. 2") 5-10 83
(With standard cover—not die-cut.)
RCA (LPM-1382 "Elvis") 750-1000 56
(Monaural. Black label, "Long Play" at bottom. Cover has selection number in upper right corner. Has an otherwise unreleased [on vinyl] alternate take of *Old Shep*. These usually have either a "15S," "17S" or "19S" following the identification number stamped in the vinyl trail-off.)
RCA (LPM-1382 "Elvis") 200-250 56
(Black label, selections numbered as "Band 1" through "Band 6.")
RCA (LPM-1382 "Elvis") 100-125 56
(Black label, "Long Play" at bottom. Cover has selection number in upper right corner.)
RCA (LPM-1382 "Elvis") 45-55 63
(Black label, "Mono" at bottom. Cover has selection number on left.)
RCA (LPM-1382 "Elvis") 25-30 64
(Black label, "Monaural" at bottom. Cover has selection number on left.)
RCA (LSP-1382e "Elvis") 75-85 62
(Stereo. Black label, all print on label is silver.)
RCA (LSP-1382e "Elvis") 25-30 64
(Black label, RCA logo is white, other print on label is silver.)
RCA (LSP-1382e "Elvis") 10-20 68
(Orange label.)
RCA (LSP-1382e "Elvis") 10-15 76
(Tan label.)
RCA (AFL1-1382e "Elvis") 8-10 77
(Digitally remastered in 1984 on RCA 5199.)
RCA (APL1-1506 "From Elvis Presley Boulevard") 12-15 76
RCA (AFL1-1506 "From Elvis Presley Boulevard") 8-10 77
RCA (LPM-1515 "Loving You") 100-125 57
(Monaural. Black label, "Long Play" at bottom. Cover has selection number in upper right corner.)
RCA (LPM-1515 "Loving You") 45-55 63
(Black label, "Mono" at bottom. Cover has selection number on left.)
RCA (LPM-1515 "Loving You") 4000-5000
(Picture disc, but with the cover of a European *G.I. Blues* album being the picture imbeded in the vinyl. Experimental disc—only one copy made. Has just five *Loving You* tracks, the others being randomly selected instrumentals)
RCA (LPM-1515 "Loving You") 25-30 64
(Black label, "Monaural" at bottom. Cover has selection number on left.)
RCA (LSP-1515e "Loving You") 75-85 62
(Stereo. Black label, all print on label is silver.)
RCA (LSP-1515e "Loving You") 25-30 64
(Black label, RCA logo is white, other label print is silver.)
RCA (LSP-1515e "Loving You") 10-20 68
(Orange label.)
RCA (LSP-1515e "Loving You") 10-15 76
(Tan label.)
RCA (AFL1-1515e "Loving You") 5-10 77
RCA (APM1-1675 "The Sun Sessions") 12-15 76
RCA (AFM1-1675 "The Sun Sessions") 8-10 77
(First issued as RCA HY-1001 and was reissued in 1981 as RCA AYM1-3893.)
RCA (LPM-1707 "Elvis' Golden Records") 100-125 58
(Monaural. Black label, "Long Play" at bottom. Cover has selection number in upper right corner and LP title in light blue letters.)
RCA (LPM-1707 "Elvis' Golden Records") 45-55 63
(Black label, "Mono" at bottom. Cover has selection number on left and LP title in white letters.)
RCA (LPM-1707 "Elvis' Golden Records") 25-30 64
(Black label, "Monaural" at bottom. Cover has selection number on left.)
RCA (LSP-1707e "Elvis' Golden Records") 75-85 62
(Stereo. Black label, all print on label is silver.)
RCA (LSP-1707e "Elvis' Golden Records") 25-30 64
(Black label, RCA logo is white, other label print is silver.)
RCA (LSP-1707e "Elvis' Golden Records") 10-20 68
(Orange label.)
RCA (LSP-1707e "Elvis' Golden Records") 10-15 76
(Tan label.)
RCA (AFL1-1707e "Elvis' Golden Records") 8-10 77
RCA (AQL1-1707e "Elvis' Golden Records") 5-10 79
(Digitally remastered in 1984 on RCA 5196.)
RCA (LPM-1884 "King Creole") 100-125 58
(Monaural. Black label, "Long Play" at bottom. Cover has selection number in upper right corner. Add $75 to $100 if accompanied by an 8" x 10" black and white bonus photo of Elvis in uniform.)
RCA (LPM-1884 "King Creole") 45-55 63
(Black label, "Mono" at bottom. Cover has selection number on left.)
RCA (LPM-1884 "King Creole") 25-30 64
(Black label, "Monaural" at bottom. Cover has selection number on left.)
RCA (LSP-1884e "King Creole") 75-85 62
(Stereo. Black label, all print on label is silver.)
RCA (LSP-1884e "King Creole") 25-30 62
(Black label, RCA logo is white, other label print is silver.)
RCA (LSP-1884e "King Creole") 10-20 68
(Orange label.)
RCA (LSP-1884e "King Creole") 10-15 76
(Tan label.)
RCA (AFL1-1884e "King Creole") 8-10 77
(Reissued in 1980 as RCA AYL1-3733.)
RCA (ANL1-1936 "Wonderful World of Christmas") 5-10 77
(First issued as RCA LSP-4579.)
RCA (LPM-1951 "Elvis' Christmas Album") 90-100 58
(Monaural. Black label, "Long Play" at bottom. Cover has selection number in upper right corner.)
RCA (LPM-1951 "Elvis' Christmas Album") 45-55 63
(Black label, "Mono" at bottom. Cover has selection number on left.)
RCA (LPM-1951 "Elvis' Christmas Album") 25-30 64
(Black label, "Monaural" at bottom. Cover has selection number on left.)
RCA (LSP-1951e "Elvis' Christmas Album") 25-30 64
(Stereo. Black label, RCA logo is white, other label print is silver.)
RCA (LSP-1951e "Elvis' Christmas Album") 20-25 68
(Orange label. Repackage of RCA LOC-1035. It was repackaged in 1970 as Camden 2428 and again in 1985 as RCA AFM1-5486.)
RCA (1981 "Felton Jarvis Talks About Elvis") 200-250 81
(Price includes three script sheets. Add $25 to $50 if accompanied by silver and black *Guitar Man* engraved Elvis belt buckle.)
RCA (LPM-1990 "For LP Fans Only") 100-125 59
(Monaural. Black label, "Long Play" at bottom. Cover has selection number in upper right corner.)
RCA (LPM-1990 "For LP Fans Only") 45-55 63
(Black label, "Mono" at bottom. Cover has selection number on left.)
RCA (LPM-1990 "For LP Fans Only") 200-225 65
(Black label, "Monaural" at bottom. Cover has same Elvis photo on front and back.)
RCA (LPM-1990 "For LP Fans Only") 25-30 65
(Black label, "Monaural" at bottom. Cover has selection number on left.)
RCA (LSP-1990 "For LP Fans Only") 200-225 65
(Black label. Cover has same Elvis photo on front and back.)
RCA (LSP-1990e "For LP Fans Only") 25-30 65
(Stereo. Black label, RCA logo is white, other label print is silver.)
RCA (LSP-1990e "For LP Fans Only") 10-20 68
(Orange label.)
RCA (LSP-1990e "For LP Fans Only") 10-15 76
(Tan label.)
RCA (AFL1-1990e "For LP Fans Only") 8-10 77
RCA (LPM-2011 "A Date with Elvis") 400-600 59
(Monaural. Black label, "Long Play" at bottom. Has gatefold cover and 1960 calendar. With "New Golden Age of Sound" wrap-around banner.)
RCA (LPM-2011 "A Date with Elvis") 150-175 59
(Black label, "Long Play" at bottom. Has gatefold cover and 1960 calendar, but *does not* have "New Golden Age of Sound" banner.)
RCA (LPM-2011 "A Date with Elvis") 45-55 65
(Black label, "Mono" at bottom. Cover has selection number on left.)
RCA (LPM-2011 "A Date with Elvis") 25-30 65
(Black label, "Monaural" at bottom. Cover has selection number on left.)
RCA (LSP-2011e "A Date with Elvis") 25-30 65
(Stereo. Black label, RCA logo is white, other label print is silver.)
RCA (LSP-2011e "A Date with Elvis") 10-20 68
(Orange label.)
RCA (LSP-2011e "A Date with Elvis") 10-15 76
(Tan label.)
RCA (AFL1-2011e "A Date with Elvis") 8-10 77
RCA (LPM-2075 "Elvis' Golden Records, Vol. 2") 100-125 59
(Monaural. Black label, "Long Play" at bottom. Cover has selection number in upper right corner.)
RCA (LPM-2075 "Elvis' Golden Records, Vol. 2") 45-55 63
(Black label, "Mono" at bottom. Cover has selection number on left.)
RCA (LPM-2075 "Elvis' Golden Records, Vol. 2") 25-30 64
(Black label, "Monaural" at bottom. Cover has selection number on left.)
RCA (LSP-2075e "Elvis' Golden Records, Vol. 2") 75-85 62
(Stereo. Black label, all print on label is silver.)
RCA (LSP-2075e "Elvis' Golden Records, Vol. 2") 25-30 64
(Black label, RCA logo is white, other label print is silver.)
RCA (LSP-2075e "Elvis' Golden Records, Vol. 2") 10-20 68
(Orange label.)
RCA (LSP-2075e "Elvis' Golden Records, Vol. 2") 10-15 76
(Tan label.)
RCA (AFL1-2075e "Elvis' Golden Records, Vol. 2") 8-10 77
(May also be shown as *50,000,000 Elvis Presley Fans Can't Be Wrong*. Digitally remastered in 1984 on RCA 5197.)
RCA (2227 "Great Performances") ... 10-20 90
RCA (LPM-2231 "Elvis Is Back") ... 100-150 60
(Monaural. Black label, "Long Play" at bottom. No song titles printed on cover. May have a yellow sticker on cover showing song titles.)

RCA (LPM-2231 "Elvis Is Back")....... 45-55 63
(Black label, "Mono" at bottom. Cover has selection number on left.)
RCA (LPM-2231 "Elvis Is Back")....... 25-30 64
(Black label, "Monaural" at bottom. Cover has selection number on left.)
RCA (LSP-2231 "Elvis Is Back") ... 120-160 60
(Stereo. Black label, "Living Stereo" at bottom. No song titles printed on cover. May have a yellow sticker on cover showing song titles.)
RCA (LSP-2231 "Elvis Is Back") 25-30 64
(Black label, RCA logo is white, other label print is silver.)
RCA (LSP-2231 "Elvis Is Back") 10-20 68
(Orange label.)
RCA (LSP-2231 "Elvis Is Back") 10-15 76
(Tan label.)
RCA (AFL1-2231 "Elvis Is Back")........ 8-10 77
RCA (LPM-2256 "G.I. Blues")........ 100-125 60
(Monaural. Black label, "Long Play" at bottom. Add $15 to $25 if accompanied by "Elvis Is Back" inner sleeve. Add $100 to $150 if cover has a heart-shaped announcement for *Wooden Heart.)*
RCA (LPM-2256 "G.I. Blues")............ 45-55 63
(Black label, "Mono" at bottom.)
RCA (LPM-2256 "G.I. Blues")............ 25-30 64
(Black label, "Monaural" at bottom.)
RCA (LSP-2256 "G.I. Blues")........ 100-125 60
(Stereo. Black label, "Living Stereo" at bottom. Add $15 to $25 if accompanied by "Elvis Is Back" inner sleeve. Add $100 to $150 if cover has a heart-shaped announcement for *Wooden Heart.)*
RCA (LSP-2256 "G.I. Blues")............ 25-30 64
(Black label, RCA logo is white, other label print is silver.)
RCA (LSP-2256 "G.I. Blues")............ 10-20 68
(Orange label.)
RCA (LSP-2256 "G.I. Blues")............ 10-15 76
(Tan label.)
RCA (AFL1-2256 "G.I. Blues") 8-10 77
(Reissued in 1980 as RCA AYL1-3735.)
Note: For *G.I. Blues* picture disc, see *Loving You* (RCA LPM-1515).
RCA (APL1-2274 "Welcome to My World")... 10-15 77
RCA (AFL1-2274 "Welcome to My World")... 8-10 77
RCA (AQL1-2274 "Welcome to My World")... 5-10 79
RCA (LPM-2328 "His Hand in Mine").. 75-100 60
(Monaural. Black label, "Long Play" at bottom.)
RCA (LPM-2328 "His Hand in Mine")... 40-50 63
(Black label, "Mono" at bottom.)
RCA (LPM-2328 "His Hand in Mine")... 25-30 64
(Black label, "Monaural" at bottom.)
RCA (LSP-2328 "His Hand in Mine").. 100-125 60
(Stereo. Black label, "Living Stereo" at bottom.)
RCA (LSP-2328 "His Hand in Mine") 25-30 64
(Black label, RCA logo is white, other label print is silver.)
RCA (LSP-2328 "His Hand in Mine") 10-20 68
(Orange label.)
RCA (LSP-2328 "His Hand in Mine") 10-15 76
(Tan label.)
(Repackaged in 1976 as RCA ANL1-1319 and in 1981 as RCA AYM1-3935.)
RCA (2347 "Elvis-Greatest Hits, Volume One") 10-15 81
(Has embossed letters on front cover.)
RCA (2347 "Elvis-Greatest Hits, Volume One") 5-10 83
(Standard cover print—not embossed.)
RCA (LPM-2370 "Something for Everybody") 75-100 61
(Monaural. Black label, "Long Play" at bottom. Back cover promotes Compact 33s.)
RCA (LPM-2370 "Something for Everybody") 40-50 63
(Black label, "Mono" at bottom.)
RCA (LPM-2370 "Something for Everybody") 25-30 64
(Black label, "Monaural" at bottom.)
RCA (LSP-2370 "Something for Everybody") 125-150 61
(Stereo. Black label, "Living Stereo" at bottom. Back cover promotes Compact 33s.)
RCA (LSP-2370 "Something for Everybody") 25-30 64
(Black label, RCA logo is white, other label print is silver.)
RCA (LSP-2370 "Something for Everybody") 10-20 68
(Orange label.)
RCA (LSP-2370 "Something for Everybody") 10-15 76
(Tan label.)
RCA (AFL1-2370 "Something for Everybody") 8-10 77
(Reissued in 1981 as RCA AYM1-4116.)
RCA (LPM-2426 "Blue Hawaii")........ 75-90 61
(Monaural. Black label, "Long Play" at bottom.)
RCA (LPM-2426 "Blue Hawaii")........ 40-50 63
(Black label, "Mono" at bottom.)
RCA (LPM-2426 "Blue Hawaii")........ 25-30 64
(Black label, "Monaural" at bottom.)
RCA (LSP-2426 "Blue Hawaii")....... 90-100 61
(Stereo. Black label, "Living Stereo" at bottom.)
RCA (LSP-2426 "Blue Hawaii") 25-30 64
(Black label, RCA logo is white, other label print is silver.)
RCA (LSP-2426 "Blue Hawaii") 10-20 68
(Orange label.)
RCA (LSP-2426 "Blue Hawaii") 10-15 76
(Tan label.)
RCA (AFL1-2426 "Blue Hawaii")......... 8-10 77
(Reissued in 1981 as RCA AYL1-3683.)
RCA (AFL1-2428 "Moody Blue")................................ 1000-1200 77
(Colored vinyl—any color *other than blue or black*. Experimental production discs for RCA in-house use only.)
RCA (AFL1-2428 "Moody Blue")....... 10-12 77
(Blue vinyl.)
RCA (AFL1-2428 "Moody Blue")... 125-150 77
(Black vinyl.)
RCA (AQL1-2428 "Moody Blue") 8-10 79
RCA (LPM-2523 "Pot Luck")............ 75-90 62
(Monaural. Black label, "Long Play" at bottom.)
RCA (LPM-2523 "Pot Luck")............ 40-50 63
(Black label, "Mono" at bottom.)
RCA (LPM-2523 "Pot Luck")............ 25-30 64
(Black label, "Monaural" at bottom.)
RCA (LSP-2523 "Pot Luck") 90-100 62
(Stereo. Black label, "Living Stereo" at bottom.)
RCA (LSP-2523 "Pot Luck") 25-30 64
(Black label, RCA logo is white, other label print is silver.)
RCA (LSP-2523 "Pot Luck") 10-20 68
(Orange label.)
RCA (LSP-2523 "Pot Luck") 10-15 76
(Tan label.)
RCA (AFL1-2523 "Pot Luck")............. 8-10 77
RCA (APL1-2558 "Harum Scarum") 8-10 77
(First issued as RCA LPM/LSP-3468. Reissued in 1980 as RCA AYL1-3734.)
RCA (APL1-2560 "Spinout") 8-10 77
(First issued as RCA LPM/LSP-3702. Reissued in 1980 as RCA AYL1-3684.)
RCA (APL1-2564 "Double Trouble")... 8-10 77
(First issued as RCA LPM/LSP-3787.)
RCA (APL1-2565 "Clambake") 8-10 77
(First issued as RCA LPM/LSP-3893.)
RCA (APL1-2568 "It Happened at the World's Fair") 8-10 77
(First issued as RCA LPM/LSP-2697.)
RCA (APL2-2587 "Elvis in Concert") 15-20 77
RCA (CPL2-2587 "Elvis in Concert") 12-15 82
RCA (LPM-2621 "Girls! Girls! Girls!") 75-90 62
(Monaural. Black label, "Long Play" at bottom.)
RCA (LPM-2621 "Girls! Girls! Girls!") 40-50 63
(Black label, "Mono" at bottom.)
RCA (LPM-2621 "Girls! Girls! Girls!").. 25-30 64
(Black label, "Monaural" at bottom.)
RCA (LSP-2621 "Girls! Girls! Girls!")... 90-100 62
(Stereo. Black label, "Living Stereo" at bottom.)
RCA (LSP-2621 "Girls! Girls! Girls!").. 25-30 64
(Black label, RCA logo is white, other label print is silver.)
RCA (LSP-2621 "Girls! Girls! Girls!") 10-20 68
(Orange label.)
RCA (LSP-2621 "Girls! Girls! Girls!") 10-15 76
(Tan label.)
RCA (AFL1-2621 "Girls! Girls! Girls!")... 8-10 77
RCA (CPD2-2642 "Aloha from Hawaii") 15-20 75
(Orange label.)
RCA (CPD2-2642 "Aloha from Hawaii") 10-12 77
(Black label. First issued as RCA VPSX-6089.)
RCA (LPM-2697 "It Happened at the World's Fair") 75-90 63
(Monaural. Black label, "Long Play" at bottom. Add $100 to $125 if accompanied by an 8" x 10" bonus color photo.)
RCA (LPM-2697 "It Happened at the World's Fair") 40-50 63
(Black label, "Mono" at bottom.)
RCA (LPM-2697 "It Happened at the World's Fair") 25-30 64
(Black label, "Monaural" at bottom.)
RCA (LSP-2697 "It Happened at the World's Fair") 90-110 63
(Stereo. Black label, "Living Stereo" at bottom. Add $100 to $125 if accompanied by an 8" x 10" bonus color photo.)
RCA (LSP-2697 "It Happened at the World's Fair") 25-30 64
(Black label, RCA logo is white, other label print is silver. Reissued in 1977 as RCA APL1-2568.)
RCA (LPM-2756 "Fun in Acapulco") .60-70 63
(Monaural. Black label, "Mono" at bottom.)
RCA (LPM-2756 "Fun in Acapulco") .25-30 64
(Black label, "Monaural" at bottom.)
RCA (LSP-2756 "Fun in Acapulco")..60-70 63
(Stereo. Black label, all print on label is silver.)
RCA (LSP-2756 "Fun in Acapulco")..25-30 64
(Black label, RCA logo is white, other label print is silver.)
RCA (LSP-2756 "Fun in Acapulco")..10-20 68
(Orange label.)
RCA (LSP-2756 "Fun in Acapulco")..10-15 76
(Tan label.)
RCA (AFL1-2756 "Fun in Acapulco")..8-10 77
RCA (LPM-2765 "Elvis' Golden Records, Vol. 3") 90-100 63
(Monaural. Black label, "Mono" at bottom.)
RCA (LPM-2765 "Elvis' Golden Records, Vol. 3") 25-30 64
(Black label, "Monaural" at bottom.)
RCA (LSP-2765 "Elvis' Golden Records, Vol. 3") 90-100 63
(Stereo. Black label, all print on label is silver.)
RCA (LSP-2765 "Elvis' Golden Records, Vol. 3") 25-30 64
(Black label, RCA logo is white, other label print is silver.)
RCA (LSP-2765 "Elvis' Golden Records, Vol. 3") 10-20 68
(Orange label.)
RCA (LSP-2765 "Elvis' Golden Records, Vol. 3") 10-15 76
(Tan label.)
RCA (AFL1-2765 "Elvis' Golden Records, Vol. 3") 8-10 77
RCA (AFL1-2772 "He Walks Beside Me") 8-10 77
RCA (LPM-2894 "Kissin' Cousins") 100-200 64
(Monaural. Black label, "Mono" at bottom. *Does not* picture film cast in lower right corner photo on cover.)

RCA (LPM-2894 "Kissin' Cousins")...60-70 64
(Black label, "Mono" at bottom. Pictures film cast in lower right corner photo on cover.)
RCA (LPM-2894 "Kissin' Cousins")...25-30 64
(Black label, "Monaural" at bottom.)
RCA (LSP-2894 "Kissin' Cousins")................................ 100-150 64
(Stereo. Black label, all print on label is silver. *Does not* picture film cast in lower right corner photo on cover.)
RCA (LSP-2894 "Kissin' Cousins") ... 60-70 64
(Black label, all print on label is silver. Pictures film cast in lower right corner photo on cover.)
RCA (LSP-2894 "Kissin' Cousins") ... 25-30 64
(Black label, RCA logo is white, other label print is silver.)
RCA (LSP-2894 "Kissin' Cousins") ... 10-20 68
(Orange label.)
RCA (LSP-2894 "Kissin' Cousins") ... 10-15 76
(Tan label.)
RCA (LSP-2894 "Kissin' Cousins")............................... 1000-1200 77
(Blue vinyl. Experimental pressing only.)
RCA (AFL1-2894 "Kissin' Cousins").... 8-10 77
(Reissued in 1981 as RCA AYM1-4115.)
RCA (CPL1-2901 "Elvis Sings for Children")...................................... 8-10 78
(Includes "Special Memories" greeting card.)
RCA (LPM-2999 "Roustabout").........60-70 64
(Monaural. Black label, "Mono" at bottom.)
RCA (LPM-2999 "Roustabout")........25-30 65
(Black label, "Monaural" at bottom.)
RCA (LSP-2999 "Roustabout") 500-600 64
(Stereo. Black label. All print on label—including RCA logo—is silver.)
RCA (LSP-2999 "Roustabout") 25-30 64
(Black label, RCA logo is white, other label print is silver.)
RCA (LSP-2999 "Roustabout") 10-20 68
(Orange label.)
RCA (LSP-2999 "Roustabout") 10-15 76
(Tan label.)
RCA (AFL1-2999 "Roustabout")..........8-10 77
RCA (3078 "Legendary Performer, Vol. 3")... 15-20 78
(Picture disc. Add $5 to $10 if accompanied by *Yesterdays* booklet. May be found with the actual disc pressed on either blue or black vinyl. Also issued on standard black vinyl as 3082.)
RCA (3082 "Legendary Performer, Vol. 3")... 8-12 78
(Add $5 to $10 if accompanied by *Yesterdays* booklet. Also issued on a picture disc, as RCA 3078.)
RCA (3279 "Our Memories of Elvis") ..8-10 79
RCA (LPM-3338 "Girl Happy") 40-50 65
(Monaural.)
RCA (LSP-3338 "Girl Happy")..........40-50 65
(Stereo. Black label.)
RCA (LSP-3338 "Girl Happy").......... 10-20 68
(Orange label.)
RCA (LSP-3338 "Girl Happy").......... 10-15 76
(Tan label.)
RCA (AFL1-3338 "Girl Happy") 8-10 77
RCA (3448 "Our Memories of Elvis Vol. 2")... 8-10 79
(A sampling of these tracks is on RCA 3455, *Pure Elvis*.)
RCA (LPM-3450 "Elvis for Everyone")....................................... 40-50 65
(Monaural.)
RCA (LSP-3450 "Elvis for Everyone")....................................... 40-50 65
(Stereo. Black label.)
RCA (LSP-3450 "Elvis for Everyone")....................................... 10-20 68
(Orange label.)
RCA (LSP-3450 "Elvis for Everyone")....................................... 10-15 76
(Tan label.)
RCA (AFL1-3450 "Elvis for Everyone")....................................... 8-10 77
Reissued in 1982 as RCA AYL1-4232.
RCA (3455 "Pure Elvis")...............275-325 79
(Cover reads "Pure Elvis," but label shows "Our Memories of Elvis - Vol. 2." Promotional issue only.)
RCA (LPM-3468 "Harum Scarum")... 35-50 65
(Monaural. Add $60 to $85 if accompanied by bonus 12" x 12" photo.)
RCA (LSP-3468 "Harum Scarum") ... 35-50 65
(Stereo. Add $60 to $85 if accompanied by bonus 12" x 12" photo. Reissued in 1977 as RCA APL1-2558 and in 1980 as RCA AYL1-3734.)
RCA (LPM-3553 "Frankie & Johnny") 35-50 66
(Monaural. Add $60 to $85 if accompanied by bonus 12" x 12" print.)
RCA (LSP-3553 "Frankie & Johnny") 35-50 66
(Stereo. Add $60 to $85 if accompanied by bonus 12" x 12" print. Reissued in 1977 as RCA APL1-2559. A repackage appeared in 1976 on Pickwick 7007.)
RCA (LPM-3643 "Paradise Hawaiian Style")... 35-45 66
(Monaural.)
RCA (LSP-3643 "Paradise Hawaiian Style")... 35-45 66
(Stereo. Black label.)
RCA (LSP-3643 "Paradise Hawaiian Style")... 10-20 68
(Orange label.)
RCA (LSP-3643 "Paradise Hawaiian Style")... 10-15 76
(Tan label.)
RCA (AFL1-3643 "Paradise Hawaiian Style")... 8-10 77
RCA (AYL1-3683 "Blue Hawaii") 5-10 80
(First issued as RCA LPM/LSP-2426.)
RCA (AYL1-3684 "Spinout") 5-10 80
(First issued as RCA LPM/LSP-3702, reissued in 1977 as RCA APL1-2560.)
RCA (CPL8-3699 "Elvis Aron Presley")..................................... 80-100 80
(Boxed, eight-disc set. Add $5 to $10 if accompanied by 20-page booklet.)
RCA (CPL8-3699 "Elvis Aron Presley")..................................... 450-500 80
(REVIEWER SERIES edition. Silver sticker on back also identifies the Reviewer Series copy as "NS-3699." Add $5 to $10 if accompanied by 20-page booklet.)
RCA (CPK8-3699 "Elvis Aron Presley")..................................... 80-100 80
(Boxed, four-cassette tape set. Add $10 to $20 if accompanied by 20-page booklet and eight 12" x 12" Elvis photos.)
RCA (CPS8-3699 "Elvis Aron Presley")..................................... 100-125 80
(Boxed, four 8-track tape set. Add $10 to $20 if accompanied by 20-page booklet and eight 12" x 12" Elvis photos. *Excerpts* of songs in this set appeared on RCA 3729. *Selections* from this LP are on RCA 3781.)
RCA (LPM-3702 "Spinout")............. 35-50 66
(Monaural. Add $60 to $85 if accompanied by bonus 12" x 12" photo.)
RCA (LSP-3702 "Spinout") 35-50 66
(Stereo. Add $60 to $85 if accompanied by bonus 12 " x 12" photo. Reissued in 1977 as APL1-2560.)
RCA (3729 "Elvis Aron Presley Excerpts")................................... 100-125 80
(Has 37 excerpts from RCA 3699. Promotional issue only.)
RCA (AYL1-3732 "Pure Gold") 5-10 80
(First issued as RCA ANL1-0971.)
RCA (AYL1-3733 "King Creole")........ 5-10 80
(First issued as RCA LSP-1884.)
RCA (AYL1-3734 "Harum Scarum") ... 5-10 80
(First issued as RCA LPM/LSP-3468.)
RCA (AYL1-3735 "G.I. Blues")........... 5-10 80
(First issued as RCA LPM/LSP-2256.)
RCA (LPM-3758 "How Great Thou Art") 40-50 67
(Monaural.)
RCA (LSP-3758 "How Great Thou Art") 35-45 67
(Stereo. Black label.)
RCA (LSP-3758 "How Great Thou Art").. 10-20 68
(Orange label.)
RCA (LSP-3758 "How Great Thou Art").. 10-15 76
(Tan label.)
RCA (AFL1-3758 "How Great Thou Art").. 8-10 77
RCA (3781 "Elvis Aron Presley Selections")................................ 100-125 80
(Has 12 selections from RCA 3699. Promotional issue only.)
RCA (LPM-3787 "Double Trouble")... 40-50 67
(Monaural. Front cover reads "Special Bonus Full Color Photo." Add $25 to $35 if accompanied by bonus 7" x 9" photo.)
RCA (LPM-3787 "Double Trouble")... 30-40 68
("Special Bonus Full Color Photo" is replaced by "Trouble Double.")
RCA (LSP-3787 "Double Trouble") ... 40-50 67
(Stereo. Front cover reads "Special Bonus Full Color Photo." Add $25 to $35 if accompanied by bonus 7" x 9" photo. Black label.)
RCA (LSP-3787 "Double Trouble") ... 30-40 68
("Special Bonus Full Color Photo" is replaced by "Trouble Double.")
RCA (LSP-3787 "Double Trouble") ... 10-20 68
(Orange label.)
RCA (LSP-3787 "Double Trouble") ... 10-15 76
(Tan label.)
(Reissued in 1977 as RCA APL1-2564.)
RCA (AYL1-3892 "Elvis in Person") 5-10 81
(First issued as RCA LSP-4428.)
RCA (LPM-3893 "Clambake") 175-200 67
(Monaural. Add $30 to $50 if accompanied by bonus 12" x 12" photo. Reissued in 1977 as RCA APL1-2565.)
RCA (LSP-3893 "Clambake")........... 30-50 67
(Stereo. Add $30 to $50 if accompanied by bonus 12" x 12" photo. Reissued in 1977 as RCA APL1-2565.)
RCA (AYM1-3893 "Sun Sessions")..... 5-10 81
(First issued as RCA APM1-1675.)
RCA (AYM1-3894 "Elvis TV Special") 5-10 81
(First issued RCA LPM-4088.)
RCA (3917 "Guitar Man") 8-12 81
(Includes a "This Is Elvis" flyer. Producer Felton Jarvis talks about Elvis as well as the making of this LP [RCA 1981].)
RCA (LPM-3921 "Elvis' Gold Records, Vol. 4") 1000-2000 68
(Monaural.)
RCA (LSP-3921 "Elvis' Gold Records, Vol. 4")... 60-90 68
(Stereo. Black label.)
RCA (LSP-3921 "Elvis' Gold Records, Vol. 4")... 10-20 68
(Orange label.)
RCA (LSP-3921 "Elvis' Gold Records, Vol. 4")... 10-15 76
(Tan label.)
RCA (AFL1-3921 "Elvis' Gold Records, Vol. 4")... 8-10 77
RCA (AYM1-3935 "His Hand in Mine")... 5-10 81
(First issued as RCA LPM/LSP-2328.)
RCA (AYL1-3956 "That's The Way It Is").. 5-10 81
First issued as RCA LSP-4460.
RCA (LPM-3989 "Speedway")... 1000-2000 68
(Monaural. Add $25 to $50 if accompanied by bonus 8" x 10" photo.)
RCA (LSP-3989 "Speedway") 35-45 68
(Stereo. Black label. Add $25 to $50 if accompanied by bonus 8" x 10" photo.)
RCA (LSP-3989 "Speedway") 10-20 68
(Orange label.)
RCA (LSP-3989 "Speedway") 10-15 76
(Tan label.)
RCA (AFL1-3989 "Speedway") 8-10 77
RCA (4031 "This Is Elvis").............. 10-15 80
RCA (LPM-4088 "Elvis TV Special") 15-20 68
(Orange label. Rigid disc.)

RCA (LPM-4088 "Elvis TV Special") 10-15 72
(Orange label. Flexible disc.)
RCA (LPM-4088 "Elvis TV Special") 10-15 76
(Tan label.)
RCA (AFM1-4088 "Elvis TV Special") 8-10 77
(Reissued in 1981 as RCA AYM1-3894. Repackaged for HBO as RCA 0704.)
RCA (AYL1-4114 "That's The Way It Is")... 5-10 81
(First issued as RCA LSP-4445.)
RCA (AYM1-4115 "Kissin' Cousins")... 5-10 81
(First issued as RCA LPM/LSP-2894.)
RCA (AYM1-4116 "Something for Everybody") 5-10 81
(First issued as RCA LPM/LSP-2370.)
RCA (LSP-4155 "From Elvis in Memphis")....................................... 20-25 69
(Orange label. Rigid disc. Add $30 to $40 if accompanied by 8" x 10" Elvis photo.)
RCA (LSP-4155 "From Elvis in Memphis")....................................... 10-15 72
(Orange label. Flexible disc.)
RCA (LSP-4155 "From Elvis in Memphis")....................................... 10-15 69
(Tan label.)
RCA (AFL1-4155 "From Elvis in Memphis").. 8-10 77
(A half-speed mastered issue of this LP was released in 1982 as MFSL 059.)
RCA (AYL1-4232 "Elvis for Everyone") 5-10 82
(First issued as RCA LPM/LSP-3450.)
RCA (LSP-4362 "On Stage")............ 15-20 70
(Orange label. Rigid disc.)
RCA (LSP-4362 "On Stage")............ 10-15 72
(Orange label. Flexible disc.)
RCA (LSP-4362 "On Stage")............ 10-15 76
(Tan label.)
RCA (AFL1-4362 "On Stage")........... 10-12 77
RCA (AQL1-4362 "On Stage") 5-10 83
RCA (4395 "Memories of Christmas").. 8-10 82
RCA (LSP-4428 "Elvis in Person").... 15-20 70
(Orange label.)
RCA (LSP-4428 "Elvis in Person").... 10-15 76
(Tan label.)
RCA (AFL1-4428 "Elvis in Person") 8-10 77
(First released as half of RCA LSP-6020, then reissued in 1981 as RCA AYL1-3892.)
RCA (LSP-4429 "Elvis Back in Memphis").. 15-20 70
(Orange label.)
RCA (LSP-4429 "Elvis Back in Memphis").. 10-15 76
(Tan label.)
RCA (AFL1-4429 "Elvis Back in Memphis").. 8-10 77
(First issued as half of RCA LSP-6020.)
RCA (LSP-4445 "That's the Way It Is")... 15-20 70
(Orange label.)
RCA (LSP-4445 "That's the Way It Is")... 10-15 76
(Tan label.)
RCA (LSP-4445 "That's the Way It Is")... 8-10 77
(Black label.)
RCA (AFL1-4445 "That's the Way It Is")... 8-10 77
(Reissued in 1981 as RCA AYL1-4114.)
RCA (LSP-4460 "Elvis Country")....... 15-20 71
(Orange label. Add $10 to $15 if accompanied by 7" x 9" Elvis photo.)
RCA (LSP-4460 "Elvis Country")....... 10-15 76
(Tan label.)
RCA (AFL1-4460 "Elvis Country") 8-10 77
(Reissued in 1981 as RCA AYL1-3956.)
RCA (LSP-4530 "Love Letters") 35-45 71
(Orange label. Full title, *Love Letters From Elvis*, on TWO lines on front cover.)
RCA (LSP-4530 "Love Letters") 20-35 71
(Orange label. Full title, *Love Letters From Elvis*, on THREE lines on front cover.)

RCA (LSP-4530 "Love Letters")........ 10-15 76
(Tan label.)
RCA (AFL1-4530 "Love Letters")........ 8-10 77
(Reissued in 1981 as RCA AYL1-3956.)
RCA (AHL1-4530 "Elvis Medley") 8-10 82
RCA (LSP-4579 "Wonderful World of Christmas") 20-25 71
(Orange label. Add $4 to $8 if accompanied by a 5" x 7" Elvis postcard. Reissued in 1977 as RCA ANL1-1936.)
RCA (LSP-4671 "Elvis Now")........... 50-60 72
(Has white titles/times sticker on front cover. Promotional issue only.)
RCA (LSP-4671 "Elvis Now")........... 15-18 72
(Orange label.)
RCA (LSP-4671 "Elvis Now")........... 10-15 76
(Tan label.)
RCA (AFL1-4671 "Elvis Now")........... 8-10 77
RCA (LSP-4690 "He Touched Me").. 50-60 72
(Has white titles/times sticker on front cover. Promotional issue only.)
RCA (LSP-4690 "He Touched Me").. 15-18 72
(Orange label.)
RCA (LSP-4690 "He Touched Me").. 10-15 76
(Tan label.)
RCA (AFL1-4690 "He Touched Me") .. 8-10 77
RCA (4678 "I Was the One") 8-10 83
RCA (LSP-4776 " Elvis As Recorded at Madison Square Garden") 50-60 72
(Orange label. Has white programming stickers applied to front cover. Promotional issue only. For double disc promotional, see RCA 571.)
RCA (LSP-4776 " Elvis As Recorded at Madison Square Garden") 15-20 72
(Orange label.)
RCA (LSP-4776 " Elvis As Recorded at Madison Square Garden") 10-15 76
(Tan label.)
RCA (AQL1-4776 " Elvis As Recorded at Madison Square Garden") 8-10 77
RCA (4809 "A Country Christmas, Vol. 2").. 8-10 83
RCA (4848 "Legendary Performer, Vol. 4").. 8-10 83
(Price includes a 12-page *Memories of the King* booklet.)
RCA (4941 "Elvis' Gold Records, Vol. 5").. 5-10 84
RCA (5172 "Golden Celebration") 40-50 84
(Boxed, six-disc set. Price includes custom inner sleeves and an envelope containing an 8" x 10" Elvis photo and a 50th Anniversary flyer.)
RCA (5172 "Golden Celebration") 15-20 84
(Special "Advance Cassette" boxed set sampler.)
RCA (5182 "Rocker")......................... 5-10 84
RCA (5196 "Elvis' Golden Records") .. 5-10 84
(Digitally remastered, quality mono pressing. Price includes gold "The Definitive Rock Classic" banner. First issued as RCA LPM-1707.)
RCA (5197 "Elvis' Gold Records, Vol. 2").. 5-10 84
(Digitally remastered, quality mono pressing. Price includes gold "The Definitive Rock Classic" banner. First issued as RCA LPM-2075.)
RCA (5198 "Elvis Presley")................ 5-10 84
(Digitally remastered, quality mono pressing. Price includes gold "The Definitive Rock Classic" banner. First issued as RCA LPM-1254.)
RCA (5199 "Elvis")............................ 5-10 84
(Digitally remastered, quality mono pressing. Price includes gold "The Definitive Rock Classic" banner. First issued as RCA LPM-1382.)
RCA (5353 "Valentine Gift for You") ... 8-10 85
(Colored vinyl.)
RCA (5353 "Valentine Gift for You") ... 5-10 85
(Black vinyl.)
RCA (5418 "Reconsider Baby") 5-10 85
RCA (5430 "Always on My Mind")....... 5-10 85
RCA (5486 "Elvis' Christmas Album") 5-10 85
(Colored vinyl.)
RCA (5486 "Elvis' Christmas Album") 20-40 85
(Black vinyl. Thus far, all black vinyl copies discovered were packaged with stickers reading "pressed on green vinyl.")
RCA (5600 "Return of the Rocker")..... 5-10 86
RCA (5697 "Special Christmas Programming")........................... 800-1000 67
(Promotional issue only.)
RCA (LSP-6020 "From Memphis to Vegas") 30-40 69
(Orange label. Incorrectly shows writers of *Words* as Tommy Boyce & Bobby Hart. Also shows writer of *Suspicious Minds* as Frances Zambon. Add $20 to $40 if accompanied by two 8" x 10" black and white Elvis photos.)
RCA (LSP-6020 "From Memphis to Vegas") 20-30 69
(Orange label. Correctly shows writers of *Words* as Barry, Robin & Maurice Gibb, and writer of *Suspicious Minds* as Mark James. Add $20 to $40 if accompanied by two 8" x 10" Elvis photos.)
RCA (LSP-6020 "From Memphis to Vegas") 15-20 76
(Tan label.)
RCA (LSP-6020 "From Memphis to Vegas") 10-15 77
(Black label. Each of the two LPs in this set was reissued individually, *Elvis in Person at the International Hotel* as LSP-4428 and *Elvis Back in Memphis* as LSP-4429, both in 1970.)
RCA (VPSX-6089 "Aloha from Hawaii") 3000-5000 73
(Has "Chicken of the Sea" sticker on cover. Quadradisc and contents stickers also are on cover. Includes programming insert card. Promotional in-house issue by the Van Camps Company.)
RCA (VPSX-6089 "Aloha from Hawaii") 1000-2000 73
(Has white titles/times sticker on front cover. Promotional issue only.)
RCA (VPSX-6089 "Aloha from Hawaii") 75-100 73
(Has Quadradisc and contents stickers on cover. Red/orange label.)
RCA (VPSX-6089 "Aloha from Hawaii") 25-30 74
(Has Quadradisc/RCA logo in lower right corner of front cover. Titles are printed on back cover. Orange label.)
RCA (VPSX-6089 "Aloha from Hawaii") 25-30 76
(Tan label. Issued through the RCA Record Club as RCA 213736 and later (1977) as RCA CPD2-2642.)
RCA (6221 "Memphis Record")......... 10-15 87
(Includes a bonus color 15" x 22" poster and *Elvis Talks* LP flyer.)
RCA (6313 "Elvis Talks!") 10-15 87
(Mail-order offer.)
RCA (6382 "Number One Hits").......... 8-10 87
(Includes a bonus color 15" x 22" poster and *Elvis Talks* LP flyer.)
RCA (6383 "Top Ten Hits") 10-12 87
(Includes a bonus color 15" x 22" poster and *Elvis Talks* LP flyer.)
RCA (LPM-6401 "Worldwide 50 Gold Hits, Vol. 1") 60-75 70
(Orange label. Boxed, four-disc set. Add $30 to $40 if accompanied by a 16-page Elvis photo booklet.)
RCA (LPM-6401 "Worldwide 50 Gold Hits, Vol. 1") 30-40 76
(Tan label.)
RCA (LPM-6401 "Worldwide 50 Gold Hits, Vol. 1") 20-25 77
(Black label. Two of the LPs in this set were repackaged for the RCA Record Club in 1974 as RCA 213690. The other two came out in 1978 as RCA 214657.)
RCA (LPM-6402 "Worldwide 50 Gold Hits, Vol. 2") 60-75 71
(Orange label. Boxed, four-disc set. Add $25 to $50 if accompanied by an Elvis print, and an envelope with piece of material.)

RCA (LPM-6402 "Worldwide 50 Gold Hits, Vol. 2") 30-40 76
(Tan label. With bonus items shown as included.)
RCA (LPM-6402 "Worldwide 50 Gold Hits, Vol. 2") 25-35 76
(Tan label. No bonus items shown as being included.)
RCA (LPM-6402 "Worldwide 50 Gold Hits, Vol. 2") 20-25 77
(Black label. Two of the LPs in this set were repackaged for the RCA Record Club in 1978 as RCA 214567.)
RCA (6414 "The Complete Sun Sessions")...................................10-15 87
(Includes a bonus color 15" x 22" poster and *Elvis Talks* LP flyer.)
RCA (6738 "Essential Elvis")..............5-10 88
RCA (6985 "The Alternate Aloha")......5-10 88
RCA (7031 "Elvis Forever")..............25-35 74
(TV mail-order offer.)
RCA (7065 "Canadian Tribute") 10-12 78
(Price includes photo inner-sleeve. Canadian issues of this LP had the same number but are clearly marked on back cover as Canadian.)
RCA (8468 "Elvis in Nashville")..........5-10 88
RCA (9586 "Elvis Gospel")..................5-10 89
RCA (9589 "Stereo '57, Essential Elvis, Vol. 2") 5-10 89
RCA (213690 "Worldwide Gold Award Hits, Parts 1&2")..75-100 74
(Orange label. RCA Record Club issue only.)
RCA (213690 "Worldwide Gold Award Hits, Parts 1&2")..25-30 76
(Tan label. RCA Record Club issue only.)
RCA (213690 "Worldwide Gold Award Hits, Parts 1&2")..12-15 77
(Black label. RCA Record Club issue only. The two discs in this set were first issued as half of RCA LPM-6401.)
RCA (213736 "Aloha from Hawaii")... 45-55 73
(Orange label.)
RCA (213736 "Aloha from Hawaii")... 18-20 76
(Tan label.)
RCA (214657 "Worldwide Gold Award Hits, Parts 3&4")..12-15 78
(RCA Record Club issue only. The two discs in this set were first issued as half of RCA LPM-6401.)
RCA (233299 "Country Classics")..... 20-25 80
(RCA Record Club issue only.)
RCA (234340 "From Elvis with Love") 20-25 78
(RCA Record Club issue only.)
RCA (244047 "Legendary Concert Performances")..............................20-25 78
(RCA Record Club issue only.)
RCA (244069 "Country Memories")... 20-25 78
(RCA Record Club issue only.)
SILHOUETTE (10001/10002 "Personally Elvis")..20-25 79
STARDAY (995 "Interviews with Elvis")..30-50 78
(Previously issued on Great Northwest 4005.)
SUN (1001 "The Sun Years")...........75-80 77
(Light yellow label, "Memphis" at bottom. Light yellow cover with light brown printing.)
SUN (1001 "The Sun Years")............15-20 77
(Darker yellow label, four target circles. Dark yellow cover with dark brown printing.)
SUN (1001 "The Sun Years")...........20-25 77
(White cover with brown printing.)
TM ("The Presley Years").............100-200 81
(12-LP boxed syndicated radio show. Includes script and cue sheets.)
TIME-LIFE (106 "Elvis Presley: 1954-1961") 15-20 86
(Boxed, three-disc set. Part of the *Rock 'N' Roll Era* series of sets available from Time-Life by mail-order. Includes brochure.)
TIME-LIFE (126 "Elvis the King") 20-30 89
(Boxed, two-disc set.)
UNITED STATIONS ("Elvis Presley Birthday Tribute")......................................125-150 89
(Four hour radio show. Includes four pages of cue sheets. Promotional issue only.)
WATERMARK ("The Elvis Presley Story, 1975")..800-900 75
(13-disc set. White label, pink letters. Includes a 48-page operations manual. Promotional issue only. Not issued with a special cover or package.)
WATERMARK ("The Elvis Presley Story, 1977")..700-800 77
(13-disc set. White label, pink letters. Includes a 48-page operations manual, which represents about $100 of the value. Promotional issue only. Not issued with a special cover or package.)
WESTWOOD ONE ("A Golden Celebration") 200-250 84
(Boxed, three-disc set. Price includes instructions and cue sheets, which represent $5-10 of the value. Issued to radio stations only.)
WORLD of ELVIS PRESLEY 50-100 83
(One hour weekly radio show, numbered as program 1 through program 30. The show ceased operation after 30 programs. Each disc was accompanied by a single cue sheet. Price is for any one of the discs, although program #3 is by far the rarest of them all.)
Session: Chet Atkins; Bill Black; Hal Blaine; Blossoms; David Briggs; James Burton; Floyd Cramer; D.J. Fontana; Glen Hardin; Jordanaires; Jerry Kennedy; Anita Kerr; Ronnie Milsap; Bob Moore; Scotty Moore; Larry Muhoberac; Shaun Neilsen; Boots Randolph; Jerry Reed; J.D. Sumner & Stamps; Sweet Inspirations; Kathy Westmoreland; John Wilkinson; Bobby Wood.

Also see ALLEN, Steve
Also see ATKINS, Chet
Also see AUDREY
Also see BLACK, Bill
Also see BLOSSOMS
Also see COLE, Nat "King"
Also see CRAMER, Floyd
Also see CRICKETS
Also see DONNER, Ral
Also see DURANTE, Jimmy
Also see HARRIS, Emmylou
Also see KENNEDY, Jerry
Also see KERR, Anita
Also see LIBERACE
Also see MANTOVANI
Also see MILSAP, Ronnie
Also see MOORE, Bob
Also see RANDOLPH, Boots
Also see REED, Jerry
Also see SINATRA, Nancy
Also see SWEET INSPIRATIONS
Also see VINCENT, Gene

- Various artists compilations are not included in this guide.
- Prefix letters or numbers are used on some LP listings in order to more quickly identify the variations available.
- A few items that have no label name are listed by title, such as the International Hotel boxed sets.
- Beginning in 1961, many Elvis LPs had a separate sticker, promoting such things as certain songs or bonus photos. When not listed separately in this edition, a premium of 10%-20% could be placed on LPs with these original stickers.
- LPs with a sticker applied over the selection number, showing a new number, are valued approximately the same as those without the sticker.
- Some albums were pressed with the "Dog Near Top" label using the older LSP prefix, prior to being switched to the AFL1 series. These are not listed separately since there seems to be no consequential price difference between the two.
- If you don't find a record in the preceding sections, it may contain two, three or four artists, and is listed in a section that follows.
- As imposing as our Elvis Presley section here may seem, it is but a drop in the bucket. For a far more comprehensive study of Elvis collectibles — records and compact discs (including various artists compilations) plus memorabilia — get Jerry Osborne's *Official Price Guide to Elvis Presley Records and Memorabilia.*

PRESLEY, Elvis / Beatles

Singles: 7-inch

OSBORNE ENTERPRISES ("The 1967 Elvis Medley")..4-8 88
(Flip side is titled *The #1 Hits Medley, 1956-69.* Includes insert. 1000 made.)
OSBORNE ENTERPRISES ("The 1967 Elvis Medley")..8-12 89
(Flip side is titled *The #1 Hits Medley, 1956-70.* 100 made.)

LPs: 10/12-inch

UNITED DISTRIBUTORS (2382 "Lightning Strikes Twice")..25-50 81
(Promotional issue only. Has five songs by each artist.)

Also see BEATLES

PRESLEY, Elvis / Martha Carson / Lou Monte / Herb Jeffries

EPs: 7-inch

RCA (2 "Dealer's Prevue") 900-1200 57
(Issued with paper envelope/sleeve. Promotional issue only.)

Also see MONTE, Lou

PRESLEY, Elvis / Jean Chapel

EPs: 7-inch

RCA (7 "Love Me Tender")............150-200 56
(Not issued with a special sleeve or cover. Promotional issue only.)

PRESLEY, Elvis / Buddy Holly

Singles: 7-inch

CREATIVE RADIO ("Elvis 50th Birthday Special") 10-20 85
(Demonstration disc. A promotional issue.)

Also see HOLLY, Buddy

PRESLEY, Elvis / Fear

LPs: 10/12-inch

DISCONET (309 "The Original Elvis Presley Medley"/"Fear Medley") 25-50 80
(Promotional issue only.)

PRESLEY, Elvis / David Keith

Singles: 7-inch

RCA (8760 "Heartbreak Hotel").......50-100 88
(White label. Promotional issue only.)
RCA (8760 "Heartbreak Hotel")............4-6 88
(Red label. Printing on both sides of label.)
RCA (8760 "Heartbreak Hotel")............4-8 88
(Red label. Printing on Elvis side only.)
RCA (8760 "Heartbreak Hotel")............4-8 88
(Red label. Printing on David Keith side only.)

Picture Sleeves

POPULAR LIBRARY/FAWCETT ("Heartbreak Hotel")..300-400 88
(Produced by the publisher of the book, which inspired the screenplay. Promotional issue only.)
RCA (8760 "Heartbreak Hotel").......50-100
(Pictures, but doesn't identify, RCA's Butch Waugh. Promotional issue only.)
RCA (8760 "Heartbreak Hotel")............4-8 88
(Pictures Elvis and others in a Cadillac.)

PRESLEY, Elvis / Vaughn Monroe / Gogi Grant / Robert Shaw

EPs: 7-inch

RCA (3736 "Pop Transcribed 30 Sec. Spot")..500-600 58
(Not issued with a special sleeve or cover. Promotional issue only.)

Also see GRANT, Gogi
Also see MONROE, Vaughn

PRESLEY, Elvis / Jaye P. Morgan

Singles: 7-inch

UNITED STATES AIR FORCE (125 "It's Now Or Never")..300-400 61
(Add $30 to $50 if accompanied by printed, cardboard mailing box. Issued only to radio stations.)

EPs: 7–inch

RCA (992 & 689 "Elvis/Jaye P. Morgan")............7500-10000 56
(Two-EP set, with 992 by Presley and 689 by Jaye P. Morgan coupled together in a promotional double-pocket package. Since the discs were standard pressings, nearly all of the value is represented by the custom EP cover.)
Also see MORGAN, Jaye P.

PRESLEY, Elvis / Gary Owens

Singles: 7–inch

CREATIVE RADIO ("Elvis Hour")......20-30 86
(Demonstration disc. A promotional issue.)

PRESLEY, Elvis / Helen Reddy

Singles: 7–inch

WHAT'S IT ALL ABOUT (78 "Life")..45-55 77
(Issued only to radio stations.)
Also see REDDY, Helen

PRESLEY, Elvis / Dinah Shore

EPs: 7–inch

RCA (56 "Too Much")...................150-200 57
(Not issued with a special sleeve or cover. Promotional issue only.)
Also see SHORE, Dinah

PRESLEY, Elvis / Frank Sinatra / Nat King Cole

EPs: 7–inch

CREATIVE RADIO ("Elvis Remembered")................................40-45 79
(Promotional demonstration disc.)
Also see COLE, Nat "King"
Also see SINATRA, Frank

PRESLEY, Elvis / Hank Snow / Eddy Arnold / Jim Reeves

EPs: 7–inch

RCA (12 "Old Shep")......................4000-6000 56
(Issued with a paper, "WOHO Featuring RCA Victor" sleeve. Deduct $3,000 to $5,000 if sleeve is missing. Promotional only.)
Also see ARNOLD, Eddy
Also see REEVES, Jim
Also see SNOW, Hank

PRESLEY, Elvis / Lawrence Welk

Singles: 7–inch

UNITED STATES AIR FORCE (159 "Surrender")................................300-400 61
(Add $30 to $50 if accompanied by printed, cardboard mailing box. Issued only to radio stations.)
Also see WELK, Lawrence

PRESLEY, Elvis / Hank Williams

LPs: 10/12–inch

SUNRISE MEDIA (3011 "History of Country Music")..10-20 81
(Has four songs by each artist.)
Also see PRESLEY, Elvis
Also see WILLIAMS, Hank

PRESLEY, Elvis
(Michael Conley)

Singles: 7–inch

ELVIS CLASSIC (5478 "Tell Me Pretty Baby")...4-8 78
(Despite being labeled as a 1954 recording by Elvis Presley, this track is simply a 1978 recording by Michael Conley, performing in an Elvis style. It is listed separately to eliminate confusion.)

Picture Sleeves

ELVIS CLASSIC (5478 "Tell Me Pretty Baby")..8-10 78
(Sleeve pictures an artist's sketch of Elvis Presley.)

PRESSURE R&B '80

Singles: 7–inch

LAX...3-5 79-80
MCA...3-5 80

LPs: 10/12–inch

LAX...5-10 79
Also see LAWS, Ronnie

PRESSURE DROP R&B '82

Singles: 12–inch

TOMMY BOY...4-6 82

Singles: 7–inch

TOMMY BOY...3-5 82

PRESTON, Billy LP '65

Singles: 12–inch

MEGATONE...4-6 84
MONTAGE...4-6 84

Singles: 7–inch

APPLE/AMERICOM (1808/433 "That's the Way God Planned It")........................300-400 69
(Four–inch flexi, "pocket disc.")
APPLE...6-12 69-72
APPLE (1808/6555 "That's the Way God Planned It")...50-60 69
CAPITOL...4-8 66-69
CONTRACT...8-12 61
DERBY...8-12 63
MOTOWN...3-5 79-82
VEE JAY...5-10 65

Picture Sleeves

A&M...4-8 72-75
APPLE (1808 "That's the Way God Planned It")...5-10 69
APPLE (1817 "All That I've Got")...... 10-15 70

LPs: 10/12–inch

A&M...8-12 71-82
APPLE (3359 "That's the Way God Planned It")...40-50 69
(With portrait cover photo.)
APPLE (3359 "That's the Way God Planned It")...15-25 69
(Full figure cover photo.)
APPLE (3370 "Encouraging Words") 10-20 70
BUDDAH...10-15 69
CAPITOL (T-2532 "Wildest Organ") 10-15 66
CAPITOL (ST-2532 "Wildest Organ")...10-20 66
CAPITOL (SM-2532 "Wildest Organ").. 5-8 75
DERBY (701 "16-Year-Old Soul")..... 50-75 63
EXODUS...15-20 65
GNP...10-15 73
MOTOWN...5-10 79-82
MYRRH...5-10 78
PEACOCK...8-12 73
PICKWICK...5-8 70s
SPRINGBOARD...5-10 78
TRIP...8-12 73
VEE JAY...15-25 65-66
Also see BEATLES
Also see MOTHERS of INVENTION
Also see VANDROSS, Luther

PRESTON, Billy, & Syreeta R&B '80

Singles: 7–inch

MOTOWN...3-5 79-81
TAMLA...3-5 80

LPs: 10/12–inch

MOTOWN...5-10 79-81
Also see PRESTON, Billy
Also see SYREETA

PRESTON, Jimmy R&B '49

Singles: 78 rpm

DERBY...10-20 50
GOTHAM...15-25 49-50

PRESTON, Johnny P&R '59

Singles: 7–inch

ABC...3-6 68-73
HALL/HALL WAY...4-8 64-66
IMPERIAL...4-8 63
MERCURY (10027 "Cradle of Love")...15-25 60
(Stereo [reprocessed].)
MERCURY (10036 "Feel So Fine") .. 20-30 60
(Stereo.)
MERCURY (71000 series)................ 8-12 59-62
(Monaural.)
TCF...4-8 65

Picture Sleeves

MERCURY...10-15 60-62

EPs: 7–inch

MERCURY (3397 "Johnny Preston")...30-50 60

LPs: 10/12–inch

MERCURY (20592 "Running Bear") 50-70 60
(Monaural.)
MERCURY (20609 "Come Rock with Me")...50-70 60
(Monaural.)
MERCURY (60250 "Running Bear")...60-90 60
(Stereo. Black label)
MERCURY (60250 "Running Bear")...8-12 81
(Chicago "Skyline" label)
MERCURY (60609 "Come Rock with Me")...60-90 60
(Stereo.)
WING (12246 "Running Bear")..........20-30 63
(Monaural.)
WING (16246 "Running Bear")..........25-35 63
(Stereo.)

PRESTON, Mike P&R '58

Singles: 7–inch

LONDON...5-8 58-63

PRESTON, Terry
(Ferlin Husky)

Singles: 78 rpm

CAPITOL...8-15 52-53

Singles: 7–inch

CAPITOL...10-20 52-53
Also see HUSKY, Ferlin

PRETENDERS P&R/LP '80

Singles: 12–inch

SIRE...4-6 84

Singles: 7–inch

SIRE...3-5 79-90

Picture Sleeves

SIRE...3-5 80-87

LPs: 10/12–inch

NAUTILUS (38 "Pretenders")...........25-35 80s
SIRE...5-10 80-90
Members: Chrissie Hynde; Robbie MacIntosh; Pete Farndon; Martin Chambers; Malcomb Foster.
Also see UB40

PRETENDERS / Maurice Simon

Singles: 7–inch

CARNIVAL...4-8

PRETTY BOY
(Don Covay; with Johnny Fuller's Band)

Singles: 78 rpm

ATLANTIC...50-75 57
BIG...50-75 57
RHYTHM (1768 "I'm Bad")...............30-50 54

Singles: 7–inch

ATLANTIC (1147 "Bip Bop Bip")....... 50-75 57
BIG (617 "Switchin' in the Kitchen") .. 50-75 57
Session: King Curtis.
Also see COVAY, Don
Also see KING CURTIS

PRETTY BOY FLOYD LP '90

LPs: 10/12–inch

MCA...5-8 90

PRETTY MAIDS LP '87

LPs: 10/12–inch

EPIC...5-10 87

PRETTY POISON R&B/D&D '84

Singles: 12–inch

MONTAGE...4-6 84
SVENGALI...4-6 84

Singles: 7–inch

MONTAGE...3-4 84
SVENGALI...3-4 84
VIRGIN...3-4 87-88

Picture Sleeves

VIRGIN...3-4 87-88

LPs: 10/12–inch

VIRGIN...5-10 88

PRETTY THINGS LP '75

Singles: 7–inch

FONTANA...5-10 64-66

LAURIE....4-8 68
SWAN SONG....3-5 75-76

LPs: 10/12-inch

FONTANA (27544 "Pretty Things")...35-55 66
(Monaural.)
FONTANA (67544 "Pretty Things")...35-55 66
(Stereo.)
MOTOWN....10-15 76
RARE EARTH (506 "S.F. Sorrow")..15-25 69
(With standard square cover.)
RARE EARTH (506 "S.F. Sorrow")..20-40 69
(With rounded-top cover. Promotional issue.)
RARE EARTH (515 "Parachute")......15-20 70
RARE EARTH (549 "Rare Earth").......8-12 76
(Reissue of material from 506 & 515.)
SIRE....8-10 76
SWAN SONG....8-10 75-76
W.B.....8-10 73-80
Also see GREEN, Jack

PRETTY TONY — R&B '84

(Tony Butler)

Singles: 7-inch

MUSIC....3-4 84

PREVIN, Andre — P&R/LP '59

(With the David Rose Orchestra)

Singles: 78 rpm

MODERN....3-5 51

Singles: 7-inch

COLUMBIA....3-6 60-64
DECCA....3-6 61
MGM....4-8 59
MODERN....10-20 51
RCA (214 "Andre Previn")....10-20 49
(Boxed, three-disc set.)
RCA (9000 series)....3-5 67

EPs: 7-inch

MGM....5-10 59

LPs: 10/12-inch

ALLEGIANCE....5-8 84
ANGEL....5-8 80-81
CAMDEN....5-10 64
COLUMBIA....10-20 60-65
CONTEMPORARY....15-30 57-60
CORONET....5-10 60s
DECCA (4000 series)....8-15 61-63
(Decca LP numbers in this series preceded by a "7" or a "DL-7" are stereo issues.)
DECCA (8000 series)....20-40 55-56
EVEREST....5-10 70
GUEST STAR....5-15 60s
HARMONY....5-10 67
MFSL....20-40 82
MGM....10-15 59-64
METRO JAZZ....10-20 59
MONARCH (203 "All Star Jazz").......60-80 54
(10-inch LP.)
MONARCH (204 "Andre Previn Plays Duke")....60-80 54
(10-inch LP.)
ODYSSEY....8-12 68
RCA (1000 series)....5-10 75
(With an "ARL1" prefix.)
RCA (1000 series)....20-45 54
(With an "LPM" prefix.)
RCA (1356 "Three Little Words")......40-60 56
RCA (2900 series)....6-12 67
RCA (3002 ("Andre Previn Plays Harry Warren")....75-100 51
(10-inch LP.)
RCA (3400 thru 3800 series)....10-20 65-67
U.A. (5200 series)....5-10 71
VERVE....15-25 63

You'll find many more listings by this artist in *The Official Price Guide to Movie/TV Soundtracks and Original Cast Albums,* containing over 8,000 listings.

Also see ANDREWS, Julie, & Andre Previn / Vic Damone / Jack Jones / Marian Anderson
Also see ASTAIRE, Fred, & Red Skelton / Helen Kane
Also see CARROLL, Diahann, & Andre Previn
Also see DAY, Doris, & Andre Previn
Also see ROSE, David
Also see SHORE, Dinah, & Andre Previn

PREYER, Ron — R&B '78

Singles: 7-inch

SHOCK....3-5 78

PRICE, Alan — P&R '66

(Alan Price Set)

Singles: 7-inch

COTILLION....4-8 69
EPIC....3-4 84
JET....3-5 77-79
PARROT....5-10 66-68
W.B.....3-5 72

LPs: 10/12-inch

ACCORD....5-10 82
JET....8-12 77-80
PARROT....15-25 68
TOWNHOUSE....5-10 81
W.B.....8-12 73
Also see ANIMALS
Also see FAME & PRICE

PRICE, Lloyd — R&B '52

(Lloyd Price Orchestra; with the Dukes)

Singles: 78 rpm

ABC-PAR....10-20 57
KRC (587 "Just Because")....30-40 57
SPECIALTY....10-15 55-56

Singles: 7-inch

ABC....3-6 67-73
ABC-PAR (Monaural)....10-20 57-60
ABC-PAR (S-9972 "Stagger Lee")....20-40 59
(Stereo.)
ABC-PAR (S-9997 "Where Were You")....20-30 59
(Stereo.)
COLLECTABLES....3-4 80s
DOUBLE-L....5-10 63-66
GSF....3-5 72-73
JAD....4-8 68
KRC (Except 587)....10-20 57-59
KRC (587 "Just Because")....40-50 57
LPG....3-5 76
LUDIX....5-10 63
MCA....3-4 70s
MONUMENT....4-8 64-65
PARAMOUNT....3-5 72
REPRISE....4-8 66
ROULETTE....3-5 70s
SCEPTER....3-5 71
SPECIALTY (SPBX series)....15-20 86
(Boxed sets of six colored vinyl 45s.)
SPECIALTY (428 "Lawdy, Miss Clawdy")....30-40 52
(Black vinyl.)
SPECIALTY (428 "Lawdy, Miss Clawdy")....50-100 52
(Colored vinyl.)
SPECIALTY (440 "Ooh Ooh Ooh")... 30-40 52
SPECIALTY (452 "Ain't It a Shame")....30-40 53
(Black vinyl.)
SPECIALTY (452 "Ain't It a Shame")....50-75 53
(Colored vinyl.)
SPECIALTY (457 "What's the Matter Now")....30-40 53
(Black vinyl.)
SPECIALTY (457 "What's the Matter Now")....50-75 53
(Colored vinyl.)
SPECIALTY (463 "Where You At")... 30-40 53
(Black vinyl.)
SPECIALTY (463 "Where You At")... 50-75 53
(Colored vinyl.)
SPECIALTY (471 "I Wish Your Picture Was You")....30-40 54
SPECIALTY (483 "Let Me Come Home, Baby")....30-40 54
(Black vinyl.)
SPECIALTY (483 "Let Me Come Home, Baby")....50-75 54
(Colored vinyl.)
SPECIALTY (494 "Walkin' the Track")....30-40 54
SPECIALTY (535 "Oo Ee Baby")...... 15-25 55
SPECIALTY (540 "Trying to Find Someone to Love")....15-25 55
SPECIALTY (571 "Woe Ho Ho")....... 15-25 56
SPECIALTY (578 "Country Boy Rock")....15-25 56
SPECIALTY (582 "Forgive Me Clawdy")....15-25 56
SPECIALTY (602 "Baby Please Come Home")....15-25 57
SPECIALTY (661 "Lawdy, Miss Clawdy")....10-15 59
TURNTABLE....4-6 69

Picture Sleeves

DOUBLE-L (729 "Billie Baby")........... 10-15 64

EPs: 7-inch

ABC-PAR (277 "The Exciting Lloyd Price")....25-45 59
ABC-PAR (315 "Mr. Personality Sings the Blues")....25-45 60
ABC-PAR (324 "Four Songs from Mr. Personality's Big 15 Hits")....25-45 60

LPs: 10/12-inch

ABC....8-10 72-76
ABC-PAR (ABC-277 "The Exciting Lloyd Price")....25-45 59
(Monaural.)
ABC-PAR (ABCS-277 "The Exciting Lloyd Price")....30-50 59
(Stereo.)
ABC-PAR (ABC-297 "Mr. Personality")....25-45 59
(Monaural.)
ABC-PAR (ABCS-297 "Mr. Personality")....30-50 59
(Stereo.)
ABC-PAR (ABC-315 "Mr. Personality Sings the Blues")....25-45 60
(Monaural.)
ABC-PAR (ABCS-315 "Mr. Personality Sings the Blues")....30-50 60
(Stereo.)
ABC-PAR (ABC-324 "Mr. Personality's Big 15")....25-45 60
(Monaural.)
ABC-PAR (ABCS-324 "Mr. Personality's Big 15")....30-50 60
ABC-PAR (ABC-346 "The Fantastic Lloyd Price")....25-45 60
(Monaural.)
ABC-PAR (ABCS-346 "The Fantastic Lloyd Price")....30-50 60
(Stereo.)
ABC-PAR (ABC-366 "Lloyd Price Sings the Million Sellers")....25-45 61
(Monaural.)
ABC-PAR (ABCS-366 "Lloyd Price Sings the Million Sellers")....25-45 61
(Stereo.)
ABC-PAR (ABC-382 "Cookin'")........25-45 61
(Monaural.)
ABC-PAR (ABCS-382 "Cookin'")......30-50 61
(Stereo.)
ABC-PAR (ABCX-763 "16 Greatest Hits")....10-15 72
DOUBLE-L....20-30 63
GRAND PRIX....10-15 60s
GUEST STAR....10-15 64
JAD....10-15 69
MCA....5-10 82
MONUMENT....10-20 65
OLDE WORLD....8-10 78
PICKWICK....10-15 67
SPECIALTY (2105 "Lloyd Price")......40-50 59
TRIP....8-10 76
TURNTABLE....10-15 69
UPFRONT....8-12 70s
Also see COOKE, Sam / Lloyd Price / Larry Williams / Little Richard
Also see DOMINO, Fats

PRICE, Priscilla — R&B '73

Singles: 7-inch

BASF....3-5 73

PRICE, Ray C&W '52
(With the Cherokee Cowboys)
Singles: 78 rpm
BULLET (701 "Jealous Lies").........75-125 52
COLUMBIA...5-15 52-57
Singles: 7-inch
ABC 3-5 75
ABC/DOT 3-5 75-77
COLUMBIA (10000 series)...................3-4 74-77
COLUMBIA (20000 & 21000 series) 10-20 52-56
COLUMBIA (40000 thru 43000 series)..5-15 57-66
COLUMBIA (44000 thru 45000 series) 3-6 67-73
COLUMBIA HALL of FAME..................3-4
GOLDIES 45.......................................3-4
DIMENSION 3-4 81-82
MONUMENT 3-5 78-79
MYRRH 3-4 74-75
STEP ONE 3-4 85-86
W.B. 3-4 82-83
WORD 3-4 78
Picture Sleeves
COLUMBIA...4-6 67
EPs: 7-inch
COLUMBIA (1700 thru 2800 series) .15-25 53-57
COLUMBIA (8556 "Ray Price") 10-20 50s
COLUMBIA (10000 thru 14000 series)..10-20 57-60
(White label. Promotional issue only.)
LPs: 10/12-inch
ABC/DOT 6-12 75-77
ARTCO...20-40
(Titel and selection number not known.)
CBS 5-10
COLUMBIA (28 "The World of Ray Price")...8-12 70
COLUMBIA (157 "The Same Old Me") 10-15 66
(Record club exclusive.)
COLUMBIA (1015 "Heart Songs").....30-40 57
COLUMBIA (1148 "Talk to Your Heart") 25-35 58
COLUMBIA (1400 thru 2600 series) .10-25 60-67
(Monaural)
COLUMBIA (8200 thru 9400 series, except 9422)...15-30 60-67
(Stereo)
COLUMBIA (9422 "Heart Songs").....25-35 67
(Stereo.)
COLUMBIA (9700 thru 9900 series)....8-12 68-70
COLUMBIA (10000 series)..................5-10 73-79
COLUMBIA (30000 thru 37000 series)...5-10 70-81
COLUMBIA SPECIAL PRODUCTS....5-10
COLUMBIA STAR SERIES................5-15
DIMENSION 5-8 81
51 WEST..5-8 84
HARMONY 8-15 66-71
MONUMENT 5-10 79
MYRRH 5-8 74
PAIR 8-10 82
RADIANT..5-8 81
SEASHELL..5-10
STEP ONE 5-10 86
SUNRISE MEDIA 5-8 81
VIVA 5-10
W.B. 5-8 83
WORD 5-8 77
Session:Johnny Bush; Willie Nelson; Johnny Gimble.
Also see ANDERSON, Lynn / Ray Price
Also see MILLER, Roger, & Willie Nelson
Also see NELSON, Willie, & Ray Price
Also see ROBBINS, Marty / Johnny Cash / Ray Price

PRICE, Ray / Lefty Frizzell / Carl Smith
LPs: 10/12-inch
COLUMBIA (1257 "Greatest Western Hits")..20-30 59
(Monaural.)
COLUMBIA (8776 "Greatest Western Hits") 15-25 63
(Stereo.)
Also see FRIZZELL, Lefty
Also see SMITH, Carl

PRICE, Ray / Johnny Horton / Carl Smith / George Morgan
EPs: 7-inch
COLUMBIA (2157 "4 Big Hits")......... 20-25 60
Also see HORTON, Johnny
Also see SMITH, Carl

PRIDE, Charley C&W '66
(With the Pridesmen; with Henry Mancini; Country Charley Pride)
Singles: 7-inch
RCA (0073 thru 0942 series) 4-8 69-73
RCA (8700 & 8800 series)................. 5-10 66
RCA (9000 thru 9996)......................... 4-8 66-71
RCA (10030 thru 11655)...................... 3-6 74-79
RCA 11736 "Dallas Cowboys")............ 3-5 79
(Black label.)
RCA 11736 "Dallas Cowboys")........... 8-12 79
(Gray and blue label. Special Dallas Cowboys Edition.)
RCA (11751 thru 14296)...................... 3-5 79-86
RCA GOLD STANDARD 3-5
16TH AVE... 3-4 87-89
Picture Sleeves
RCA 4-6 71-74
EPs: 7-inch
RCA 5-10 60s
(Juke box issues.)
LPs: 10/12-inch
CAMDEN 5-10 72
RCA (Except LPM/LSP 3700 thru 4800 series)... 5-10 74-86
RCA (3700 thru 4800 series) 10-20 66-73
(With "LPM" or "LSP" prefix.)
RCA SPECIAL PRODUCTS (0208 "Charley's Favorites").. 8-12
READER'S DIGEST/RCA ("Charley Pride") 30-40
(Boxed 6-LP set with booklet. Mail order offer.)
TELEHOUSE 5-10
Also see ANDERSON, Lynn / Charley Pride
Also see DAVE & SUGAR
Also see MANCINI, Henry

PRIEST, Maxi P&R/LP '88
Singles: 7-inch
VIRGIN.. 3-4 88
Picture Sleeves
VIRGIN.. 3-4 88
LPs: 10/12-inch
CHARISMA.. 5-8 90
VIRGIN.. 5-8 88

PRIMA, Louis P&R '35
Singles: 78 rpm
BRUNSWICK...................................... 5-10 35
COLUMBIA 4-6 52-53
DECCA 4-8 54
HIT.. 5-10 44-45
MAJESTIC 4-8 45
MERCURY... 4-8 50
RCA 4-8 47
ROBIN HOOD...................................... 4-8 50
SAVOY.. 4-8 53
VOCALION 5-10 37
Singles: 7-inch
ABC... 3-6 68-74
BUENA VISTA..................................... 3-6 66-74
CAPITOL... 4-8 62
COLUMBIA 5-10 52-53
DECCA 5-10 54
DOT 4-8 59-62
HBR 4-6 66
KAMA SUTRA...................................... 4-6 66
MERCURY.. 5-10 50
PRIMA... 4-8 63-64
ROBIN HOOD...................................... 5-10 50
SAVOY.. 5-10 53
U.A. 3-6 67
EPs: 7-inch
CAPITOL... 5-15 56
JUBILEE 5-15 55
VARSITY... 5-15 54
LPs: 10/12-inch
BUENA VISTA 8-18 65-74
CAPITOL..10-20 56-62
DE-LITE...5-10 68
DOT 10-15 60
HBR 5-12 66
HAMILTON 5-10 65
MERCURY (25142 "For the People")..30-40 53
(10-inch LP.)
PRIMA 5-8 72-76
RONDO/RONDOLETTE 10-20 59
U.A. 5-10 67

PRIMA, Louis, & Keely Smith
(With Sam Butera & the Witnesses) P&R/R&B/LP '58
Singles: 78 rpm
ROBIN HOOD 5-10 50
Singles: 7-inch
CAPITOL 4-8 58-59
DOT 4-8 59-61
Picture Sleeves
CAPITOL (4063 "That Old Black Magic")...5-10 58
(Sleeve has a die-cut center hole)
DOT 5-10 59
EPs: 7-inch
CAPITOL 8-12 58
DOT (103 "The Frantic '40s") 10-20 60
(Promotional issue, made for the Desert Inn as a giveaway.)
DOT (1093 "Louis & Keely") 5-10 60
LPs: 10/12-inch
CAPITOL (With "SM" prefix.).................5-8 75
CAPITOL (With "T" or "ST" prefix.) ...20-35 58-61
COLUMBIA (1206 "Breaking It Up")...20-30 58
CORONET 10-15 60s
DESIGN..10-15 60s
DOT...15-25 59-60
Also see SMITH, Keely

PRIMA, Louis, & Keely Smith / Louis Prima & Sam Butera
Singles: 7-inch
CAPITOL (719 "Album Highlights")... 10-15 57
(Promotional issue only.)
Also see PRIMA, Louis
Also see PRIMA, Louis, & Keely Smith

PRIMATIVES LP '88
LPs: 10/12-inch
RCA...5-8 88-89

PRIME TIME R&B '84
Singles: 7-inch
TOTAL EXP...3-4 84

PRIMETTES
(Supremes)
Singles: 7-inch
LUPINE (120 "Tears of Sorrow")...200-300 64
(Lu-pine [hyphenated] 120 is also a Joe Stubbs single.)
Also see SUPREMES

PRINCE ♀ P&R/R&B/LP '78
(With the Revolution; "Artist Formerly Known As Prince")
Singles: 12-inch
BELLMARK (71003 "Beautiful Experience") 15-20
(Includes 10" x 10" booklet.)
HOT PINK (3223 "Just Another Sucker")...20-25 86
(Promotional issue only.)
PAISLEY PARK (1082 "Let's Pretend We're Married") 30-50 84
(Promotional issue only. With title sleeve.)
PAISLEY PARK (2300 "America") 15-20 85
(Promotional issue only. With title sleeve.)
PAISLEY PARK (2313 "Raspberry Beret")...15-20 85
(Promotional issue only. With title sleeve.)
PAISLEY PARK (2331 "Pop Life") 15-20 85
(Promotional issue only. With title sleeve.)
PAISLEY PARK (2448 "Kiss" [Edit]).... 8-12 86
(Promotional issue only.)

PAISLEY PARK (2458 "Kiss" [Extended]) 8-12 86
(Promotional issue only.)
PAISLEY PARK (2476 "Mountains") ... 8-10 86
(Promotional issue only.)
PAISLEY PARK (2687 "Sign O' the Times") 8-10 87
(Promotional issue only.)
PAISLEY PARK (2758 "If I Was Your Girlfriend") 8-10 87
(Promotional issue only.)
PAISLEY PARK (2770 "I Could Never Take the Place of Your Man") 8-10 87
(Promotional issue only.)
PAISLEY PARK (2771 "U Got the Look") 8-10 87
(Promotional issue only.)
PAISLEY PARK (3704 "Scandalous Sex Suite") 8-10 89
PAISLEY PARK (4345 "Thieves in the Temple") 10-15 90
(Promotional issue only. With picture cover.)
PAISLEY PARK (4515 "New Power Generation") 8-10 90
(Promotional issue only.)
PAISLEY PARK (4578 "New Power Generation" [Remix]) 8-10 90
(Promotional issue only.)
PAISLEY PARK (4977 "Gett Off") 10-15 91
(Promotional issue only.)
PAISLEY PARK (4977 "Gett Off") 250-300 91
(Special birthday issue, with artwork by Prince. Promotional issue only.)
PAISLEY PARK (5141 "Insatiable") .. 15-25 91
(Promotional issue only. With picture cover.)
PAISLEY PARK (5148 "Diamonds & Pearls") 8-12 91
(Promotional issue only.)
PAISLEY PARK (5298 "Money Don't Matter") 15-25 91
(Promotional issue only. With picture cover.)
PAISLEY PARK (5570 "Sexy M-F") .. 10-15 91
(Promotional issue only.)
PAISLEY PARK (5770 "My Name Is Prince") 15-25 92
(Promotional issue only. With picture cover.)
PAISLEY PARK (20170 "Let's Pretend We're Married") 5-10 84
(With picture cover.)
PAISLEY PARK (20355 "Raspberry Beret") 5-8 85
(With picture cover.)
PAISLEY PARK (20357 "Pop Life") 5-8 85
(With picture cover.)
PAISLEY PARK (20389 "America") 5-8 85
(With picture cover.)
PAISLEY PARK (20516 "Anotherloverholenyo-head") 5-8 85
(With picture cover.)
PAISLEY PARK (20728 "I Could Never Take the Place of Your Man") 8-10 87
(With picture cover.)
PAISLEY PARK (20930 "Alphabet St.") 5-8 88
(With picture cover.)
PAISLEY PARK (21074 "I Wish U Heaven") 5-8 88
(With picture cover.)
PAISLEY PARK (21422 "Scandalous Sex Suite") 5-8 89
(With picture cover.)
PAISLEY PARK (21598 "Thieves in the Temple") 5-8 90
(With picture cover.)
PAISLEY PARK (21783 "New Power Generation") 4-6 90
(With picture cover.)
PAISLEY PARK (40138 "Gett Off") 4-6 91
(With picture cover.)
PAISLEY PARK (40197 "Cream") 4-6 88
(With picture cover.)
PAISLEY PARK (41833 "Space") 4-6 94
(With picture cover.)

W.B. (741 "Just As Long As We're Together") 75-100 78
(Promotional issue only.)
W.B. (832 "I Wanna Be Your Lover") 50-75 79
(Promotional issue only.)
W.B. (848 "Why You Wanna Treat Me So Bad") 75-100 80
(Promotional issue only.)
W.B. (870 "Still Waiting") 75-100 79
(Promotional issue only.)
W.B. (904 "Uptown") 40-60 80
(Promotional issue only.)
W.B. (915 "Head") 50-75 80
(Promotional issue only. Single-sided.)
W.B. (916 "When You Were Mine") .. 50-75 80
(Promotional issue only.)
W.B. (937 "Head") 50-75 80
(Promotional issue only. Double-sided.)
W.B. (980 "Controversy") 30-50 81
(Promotional issue only. With title sleeve.)
W.B. (1004 "Let's Work") 50-75 81
(Promotional issue only.)
W.B. (1035 "Do Me Baby") 50-75 81
(Promotional issue only.)
W.B. (1070 "1999") 30-50 82
(Promotional issue only. With title sleeve.)
W.B. (1082 "Let's Pretend We're Married") 30-50 84
(Promotional issue only. With title sleeve.)
W.B. (2001 "Little Red Corvette") 30-50 83
(Promotional issue only. With title sleeve.)
W.B. (2080 "Delirious") 30-50 83
(Promotional issue only. With title sleeve.)
W.B. (2042 "1999") 30-50 82
(Promotional issue only. With title sleeve.)
W.B. (2139 "When Doves Cry") 15-25 84
(Black vinyl. Promotional issue only. With title sleeve.)
W.B. (2139 "When Doves Cry") 20-30 84
(Colored vinyl. Promotional issue only. With title sleeve.)
W.B. (2173 "Let's Go Crazy" [Edit]) .. 15-25 84
(Promotional issue only. With title sleeve.)
W.B. (2182 "Let's Go Crazy" [Dance Mix]) 15-25 84
(Promotional issue only. With title sleeve.)
W.B. (2192 "Purple Rain") 20-30 84
(Colored vinyl. Promotional issue only. With title sleeve.)
W.B. (2233 "I Would Die 4 U") 15-25 84
(Promotional issue only.)
W.B. (2263 "Take Me with U") 15-20 85
(Promotional issue only. With title sleeve.)
W.B. (3579 "Batdance") 5-8 89
(Promotional issue only.)
W.B. (3702 "Batdance") 8-12 89
(Promotional issue only.)
W.B. (3705 "Partyman") 8-12 89
(Promotional issue only.)
W.B. (20228 "When Doves Cry") 8-10 84
(With picture cover.)
W.B. (20246 "Let's Go Crazy") 5-8 84
(With picture cover.)
W.B. (20267 "Purple Rain") 5-8 85
(With picture cover.)
W.B. (20291 "I Would Die 4 U") 25-35 84
W.B. (21257 "Batdance") 4-6 89

Note: Designate promotional copies – as indicated by a gold sticker – of any 12-inch singles *not* listed separately, are roughly in the same price as commercial issues. Also, some may have picture covers or title sleeves, even though not shown here as with them.

Singles: 7-inch

PAISLEY PARK 4-8 85-93
W.B. (8619 "Soft and Wet") 15-25 78
W.B. (8713 "Just As Long As We're Together") 10-20 78
W.B. (20129 "Little Red Corvette") ... 20-25 83
(Picture disc.)
W.B. (22757 "Arms of Orion") 4-6 89
W.B. (22814 "Partyman") 3-6 89
W.B. (22824 "Scandalous") 3-6 89
W.B. (22924 "Batdance") 3-6 89
W.B. (29079 "Take Me with U") 4-6 85
W.B. (29121 "I Would Die 4 U") 4-6 84
W.B. (29174 "Purple Rain") 4-6 84
(Black vinyl.)
W.B. (29174 "Purple Rain") 8-10 84
(Colored vinyl.)
W.B. (29216 "Let's Go Crazy") 4-6 84
W.B. (29286 "When Doves Cry") 4-6 84
(Black vinyl.)
W.B. (29286 "When Doves Cry") 5-10 84
(Colored vinyl.)
W.B. (29503 "Delirious") 4-6 83
W.B. (29548 "Let's Pretend We're Married") 4-6 84
W.B. (29746 "Little Red Corvette") 5-10 83
(Black vinyl.)
W.B. (29746 "Little Red Corvette") 10-15 83
(Picture disc.)
W.B. (29896 "1999") 10-15 82
W.B. (49050 "I Wanna Be Your Lover") 10-20 79
W.B. (49178 "Why You Wanna Treat Me So Bad") 10-15 80
W.B. (49226 "Still Waiting") 20-30 80
W.B. (49559 "Uptown") 10-15 80
W.B. (49638 "Dirty Mind") 10-15 81
W.B. (49808 "Controversy") 10-15 81
W.B. (50002 "Let's Work") 10-15 81
W.B. BACK to BACK HITS 3-4

Promotional Singles

PAISLEY PARK (Except 2939 & 29052) 4-8 85-93
PAISLEY PARK (2939 "Hot Thing") .. 15-25 87
PAISLEY PARK (29052 "Paisley Park") 15-25 85
W.B. (8619 "Soft and Wet") 15-25 78
W.B. (8713 "Just As Long As We're Together") 10-20 78
W.B. (22757 "Arms of Orion") 4-6 89
W.B. (22814 "Partyman") 3-6 89
W.B. (22824 "Scandalous") 3-6 89
W.B. (22924 "Batdance") 3-6 89
W.B. (29079 "Take Me with U") 4-6 85
W.B. (29121 "I Would Die 4 U") 4-6 84
W.B. (29174 "Purple Rain") 4-6 84
(Black vinyl.)
W.B. (29174 "Purple Rain") 8-12 84
(Colored vinyl.)
W.B. (29216 "Let's Go Crazy") 4-6 84
W.B. (29286 "When Doves Cry") 4-8 84
(Black vinyl.)
W.B. (29286 "When Doves Cry") 8-10 84
(Colored vinyl.)
W.B. (29503 "Delirious") 4-6 83
W.B. (29548 "Let's Pretend We're Married") 4-8 84
W.B. (29746 "Little Red Corvette") 5-10 83
W.B. (29896 "1999") 10-15 82
W.B. (49050 "I Wanna Be Your Lover") 10-20 79
W.B. (49178 "Why You Wanna Treat Me So Bad") 10-15 80
W.B. (49226 "Still Waiting") 15-25 80
W.B. (49559 "Uptown") 10-15 80
W.B. (49638 "Dirty Mind") 10-15 81
W.B. (49808 "Controversy") 10-15 81

Picture Sleeves

PAISLEY PARK 4-8 85-89
W.B. (22757 "Arms of Orion") 4-6 89
W.B. (22814 "Partyman") 3-6 89
W.B. (22824 "Scandalous") 3-6 89
W.B. (22924 "Batdance") 3-6 89
W.B. (29079 "Take Me with U") 4-6 85
W.B. (29121 "I Would Die 4 U") 4-6 84
W.B. (29174 "Purple Rain") 4-6 84
W.B. (29216 "Let's Go Crazy") 4-6 84
W.B. (29286 "When Doves Cry") 4-6 84
W.B. (29503 "Delirious") 15-25 83
(Poster sleeve.)
W.B. (29548 "Let's Pretend We're Married") 4-8 84
W.B. (29896 "1999"/"1999") 15-20 82
(Promotional issue only.)
W.B. (29896 "1999"/"How Come U Don't Call Me Anymore") 10-15 82

W.B. (49178 "Why You Wanna Treat Me So Bad") 15-25 80
W.B. (49559 "Uptown") 10-15 80

LPs: 10/12-inch

HOT PINK (3223 "Minneapolis Genuis 94 East") 10-15 85
PAISLEY PARK (726 "Interruptus Collectus") 8-12 93
(Two discs.)
PAISLEY PARK (25286 "Around the World in a Day") 5-10 85
PAISLEY PARK (25395 "Parade") 5-10 86
PAISLEY PARK (25577 "Sign O' the Times") 8-12 87
(Two discs.)
PAISLEY PARK (25720 "Lovesexy") 5-8 88
(Tracks not banded.)
PAISLEY PARK (25720 "Lovesexy") 10-15 88
(Tracks are banded for easy selection.)
PAISLEY PARK (27493 "Graffiti Bridge") 5-10 88
W.B. (2896 "Yulesville") 40-60 78
(Colored vinyl. Promotional issue only.)
W.B. (3150 "For You") 10-15 78
W.B. (3328 "Winter Warnerland") 30-50 79
(Two colored vinyl discs; one red, one green. Promotional issue only.)
W.B. (3366 "Prince") 10-15 79
W.B. (3478 "Dirty Mind") 5-10 80
W.B. (3601 "Controversy") 10-15 81
(Includes poster.)
W.B. (3601 "Controversy") 5-10 81
(Without poster.)
W.B. (23720 "1999") 10-15 82
(Two discs.)
W.B. (25110 "Purple Rain") 8-10 84
(Black vinyl. Includes poster.)
W.B. (25110 "Purple Rain") 10-15 84
(Colored vinyl. Includes poster.)
W.B. (25110 "Purple Rain") 25-35 84
(Colored vinyl. Includes poster. With gold sticker. Promotional issue only.)
W.B. (25677 "Black Album") 3000-4000 87
W.B. (25936 "Batman") 5-10 89

Note: Designate promotional copies – as indicated by a gold sticker – of any albums *not* listed separately, are in the $10 to $20 range.

Session: Lisa Coleman; Levi Seacer; Tony M.; Tommy Barbarella; Kirk Johnson; Damon Dickson; Sonny Thompson; Michael B.; Rosie Gaines; Dez Dickerson.

Also see BROWNMARK
Also see CYMONE, Andre
Also see LEWIS CONNECTION
Also see MADHOUSE
Also see SHEILA E.

PRINCE & SHEENA EASTON — P&R '87

Singles: 7-inch

PAISLEY PARK (28289 "U Got the Look") 4-6 87
W.B. 3-4 89

Picture Sleeves

PAISLEY PARK (28289 "U Got the Look") 4-6 87
W.B. 3-5 89

Also see EASTON, Sheena
Also see PRINCE

PRINCE BUSTER — P&R/R&B '67

(With the Sea Busters; Buster Campbell)

Singles: 7-inch

AMY 5-10 64
ATLANTIC 5-10 64
PHILIPS 4-8 67
RCA 4-8 67
STELLAR 5-10 64

LPs: 10/12-inch

RCA 10-20 67

PRINCE HAROLD — R&B '66

Singles: 7-inch

MERCURY 4-8 66
SPRING 4-8 67
VERVE 4-8 67

PRINCE LA LA — R&B '61

Singles: 7-inch

AFO 5-10 61-62

PRINCESS — R&B/D&D '85

Singles: 12-inch

NEXT PLATINUM 4-6 85-86
POLYDOR 4-6 86

Singles: 7-inch

POLYDOR 3-4 86-87

PRINCIPLE, Jamie — D&D '85

Singles: 12-inch

PERSONA 4-6 85

PRINE, John — LP '72

Singles: 7-inch

ASYLUM 3-5 78
ATLANTIC 3-5 71-75
OH BOY (Colored vinyl) 3-5 81-86

LPs: 10/12-inch

ASYLUM 5-10 78-80
ATLANTIC 8-12 71-76
OH BOY 5-8 84-86

PRINE, John / Daryl Hall & John Oates / Barnaby Bye / Delbert & Glen

EPs: 7-inch

ATLANTIC (195 "Something for Nothing") 5-8 73

Also see DELBERT & GLEN
Also see HALL, Daryl, & John Oates
Also see PRINE, John

PRISM — P&R/LP '77

Singles: 7-inch

ARIOLA AMERICA 3-5 77-79
CAPITOL 3-5 82

Picture Sleeves

CAPITOL 3-5 82

LPs: 10/12-inch

ARIOLA AMERICA (Except 50034) 10-15 77-79
ARIOLA AMERICA (50034 "Live Tonite") 15-25 78
(Promotional issue only.)
CAPITOL 5-10 80-82

PRISTER, Jerome "Secret Weapon" — R&B '88

Singles: 7-inch

TUFF CITY 3-4 88

PROBY, P.J. — P&R '64

(James Smith)

Singles: 7-inch

IMPERIAL 5-10 64
LIBERTY 8-15 61-68
LONDON 5-10 64
SURFSIDE 8-12 65

Picture Sleeves

LIBERTY 10-20 67

LPs: 10/12-inch

LIBERTY 15-30 65-68

Also see FOCUS & P.J. Proby

PROCESS & DOO RAGS — R&B '85

Singles: 7-inch

COLUMBIA 3-4 85-87

PROCLAIMERS — LP '89

Singles: 7-inch

CHRYSALIS 3-4 89
EMI 3-5 94

LPs: 10/12-inch

CHRYSALIS 5-8 89

PROCOL HARUM — P&R/R&B/LP '67

Singles: 7-inch

A&M 4-8 67-72
CHRYSALIS 3-6 73-77
DERAM 5-10 67

Picture Sleeves

A&M 4-8 72-73
CHRYSALIS 4-8 73

LPs: 10/12-inch

A&M (Except 4294 & 8053) 8-12 68-73
A&M (4294 "Broken Barricades") 12-15 71
(With die-cut gatefold cover.)
A&M (4294 "Broken Barricades") 10-12 72
(With standard cover.)
A&M (8053 "Procol Harum Lives") 30-40 70s
(Promotional issue only.)
CHRYSALIS 8-10 73-77
DERAM (16008 "Procol Harum") 50-75 67
(Monaural. With bonus poster, which represents $15 to $20 of the value.)
DERAM (18008 "Procol Harum") 50-75 67
(Stereo. Includes bonus poster which represents $15 to $20 of the value.)

Members: Gary Brooker; Bobby Harrison; Matthew Fisher; Dave Knights; Ray Royer; Robin Trower; Diz Derrick.

Also see BROOKER, Gary
Also see TROWER, Robin

PRODUCERS — P&R/LP '81

Singles: 7-inch

PORTRAIT 3-5 81-82

LPs: 10/12-inch

PORTRAIT 5-10 81-82

PROFESSOR FUNK & HIS EIGHTH STREET FUNK BAND — R&B '73

Singles: 7-inch

ROXBURY 3-5 73

PROFESSOR GRIFF & LAST ASIATIC DISCIPLES — LP '90

LPs: 10/12-inch

SKYYWALKER 5-8 90

PROFESSOR LONGHAIR

(With the Clippers; with His Blues Scholars; with His Shuffling Hungarians; with His New Orleans Boys)

Singles: 78 rpm

ATLANTIC (897 "Mardi Gras in New Orleans") 75-125 50
ATLANTIC (906 "Walk Your Blues Away") 75-125 50
STAR TALENT (808 "Mardi Gras in New Orleans") 150-200 49
STAR TALENT (809 "She Ain't Got No Hair") 150-200 49

Singles: 7-inch

ATLANTIC (1020 "In the Night") 100-150 53
EBB (106 "Misery") 50-100 57
EBB (101 "Cry Pretty Baby") 50-100 57
EBB (121 "Looka No Hair") 50-100 57
RIP (155 "I Believe I'm Gonna Leave") 30-40 62
RON (326 "Cuttin' Out") 10-15 58
(Yellow label.)
RON (329 "Goin' to the Mardi Gras") 10-15 59
(Yellow label.)
RON (Red label) 5-10
WATCH (1900 series) 8-12 65
WATCH (6000 series) 15-20 63

EPs: 7-inch

MERCURY 75-100
(1970s promotional EP, issued without special cover. Has two Professor Longhair tracks and two by other artists.)

LPs: 10/12-inch

ALLIGATOR 5-8 80
ATLANTIC 10-15 72-82
HARVEST 8-12 78
J.S.P. 8-12
NIGHTHAWK 5-10 82
MARDI GRAS 8-12

Also see BOYD, Robert
Also see BYRD, Roy

PROFESSOR MORRISON: see MORRISON, Professor

PROFILES — R&B '68

Singles: 7-inch

BAMBOO 4-8 69
DUO 4-8 68

PROJECT FUTURE R&B '83

Singles: 12-inch

CAPITOL 4-6 83

Singles: 7-inch

CAPITOL 3-4 83

PROPHECY R&B '75

Singles: 7-inch

AIRBORNE 3-5 70s
ALL PLATINUM 3-5 74
MAINSTREAM 3-5 75

Picture Sleeves

AIRBORNE 3-5 70s

Member: Nick Rozakis.

PROPHET LP '88

LPs: 10/12-inch

MEGAFORCE 5-8 88

PROPHETS, Thee: see THEE PROPHETS

PROTHEROE, Brian P&R '75

Singles: 7-inch

CHRYSALIS 3-5 75

LPs: 10/12-inch

CHRYSALIS 8-12 75-76

PROVINE, Dorothy LP '61

Singles: 7-inch

W.B. 3-6 61

LPs: 10/12-inch

W.B. 15-25 60-61

PROVINE, Dorothy, & Joe "Fingers" Carr

LPs: 10/12-inch

W.B. 15-25 60-62

Also see CARR, Joe "Fingers"
Also see PROVINE, Dorothy

PRUETT, Jeanne C&W '71
(Jean Pruett)

Singles: 7-inch

AUDIOGRAPH 3-4 83
DECCA 3-6 68-72
IBC 3-5 79-80
MCA 3-5 73-77
MSR 3-4 87
MERCURY 3-5 78
PAID 3-4 81
RCA 4-6 63-64

LPs: 10/12-inch

ALLEGIANCE 5-8 84
AUDIOGRAPH 5-8 83
DECCA 8-12 72
IBC 5-10 79
MCA 5-10 73-75
OUT of TOWN DIST 5-10 82

PRUETT, Jeanne, & Marty Robbins C&W '83

Singles: 7-inch

AUDIOGRAPH 3-4 83

Also see PRUETT, Jeanne
Also see ROBBINS, Marty

PRYOR, Richard LP '74

Singles: 7-inch

LAFF 3-5 80
W.B. 4-6 76-79

LPs: 10/12-inch

DOVE 10-15 68
LAFF 5-10 71-81
PARTEE 5-10 74
REPRISE 6-12 68-77
TIGER LILY 5-10 77
W.B. 5-10 76-85

PRYSOCK, Arthur R&B '52

Singles: 78 rpm

DECCA 4-8 52-54
MERCURY 4-8 54-55
PEACOCK 5-10 57

Singles: 7-inch

BETHLEHEM 3-5 72
DECCA (25000 series) 4-8 65
DECCA (27000 thru 29000 series) 5-10 52-54
DECCA (31000 series) 4-8 64-65
GUSTO 3-5 79
KING 3-6 69-71
MCA 3-5 78
MGM 3-5 70
MERCURY 5-10 54-55
OLD TOWN (100 series) 3-5 73-76
OLD TOWN (1000 series) 4-8 59-60
(Light blue label.)
OLD TOWN (1000 series) 3-5 76-77
(Dark blue or black label.)
OLD TOWN (1100 series) 4-6 61-66
PEACOCK 5-10 57
VERVE 3-6 66-69

EPs: 7-inch

OLD TOWN (9 "Double Header") 8-10 65

LPs: 10/12-inch

DECCA 15-20 64-65
KING 8-12 69-71
MCA 5-10 78
OLD TOWN (100 series) 20-30 60-62
OLD TOWN (2000 series) 15-25 62-65
OLD TOWN (12000 series) 5-10 73-77
POLYDOR 5-10 77
VERVE 10-20 66-69

Also see ECKSTINE, Billy / Arthur Prysock
Also see JOHNSON, Buddy

PRYSOCK, Arthur, & Count Basie LP '66

Singles: 7-inch

VERVE 3-6 66

LPs: 10/12-inch

VERVE 15-20 66

Also see BASIE, Count

PRYSOCK, Arthur / Leroy Bivins

LPs: 10/12-inch

GUEST STAR 5-10 64

Also see PRYSOCK, Arthur

PSEUDO ECHO P&R/LP '87

Singles: 7-inch

RCA 3-4 87

LPs: 10/12-inch

RCA 5-8 87

PSYCHEDELIC FURS LP '80

Singles: 12-inch

COLUMBIA 4-6 84-86

Singles: 7-inch

A&M 3-4 86
COLUMBIA 3-5 80-89

Picture Sleeves

A&M 3-4 86
COLUMBIA 3-5 80-87

LPs: 10/12-inch

COLUMBIA 5-10 80-89

Members: Tim Butler; Richard Butler; John Ashton; Mars Williams; Paul Garisto; Marty Williamson.

PUBLIC ENEMY R&B/LP '88

Singles: 7-inch

DEF JAM 3-4 88-90

LPs: 10/12-inch

DEF JAM 5-8 88-90

PUBLIC IMAGE LTD. LP '80

Singles: 12-inch

VIRGIN 4-6 87

LPs: 10/12-inch

ELEKTRA 5-8 86
ISLAND 8-10 80
VIRGIN 5-8 87-89
W.B. 8-10 81

Also see SEX PISTOLS

PUCKETT, Gary P&R '67
(With the Union Gap; Union Gap Featuring Gary Puckett)

Singles: 7-inch

COLUMBIA 4-8 67-72
COLUMBIA HALL of FAME 3-4 70s
GUSTO 3-4 81-83

Picture Sleeves

COLUMBIA 5-10 67-70

LPs: 10/12-inch

BACK-TRAC 5-8 85
CSP 8-10 72
COLUMBIA (Except 10171) 10-20 68-71
COLUMBIA (10171 "Young Girl") 5-10
COLUMBIA HOUSE (6272/3 "Fillin' the Gap") 20-30 75
(Three-discs; one double and one single LP set.)
51 WEST 5-10 82
GUSTO 5-8 83
HARMONY 8-12 72

Members: Gary Puckett; Paul Wheatbread; Gary Withem; Kerry Chater; Dwight Bement.
Also see FRANKLIN, Aretha / Union Gap / Blood, Sweat & Tears / Moby Grape

PULLINS, Leroy C&W/P&R '66

Singles: 7-inch

KAPP 4-8 66

LPs: 10/12-inch

KAPP (3488 "I'm a Nut") 20-30 66
KAPP (3557 "Funny Bones and Hearts") 15-25 68

PULSE R&B '82

Singles: 7-inch

SILVER CLOUD 3-5 82

PUMPKIN & PROFILE ALL-STARS R&B '84

Singles: 12-inch

PROFILE 4-6 84

Singles: 7-inch

PROFILE 3-4 84

Also see FRESH 3 MCs

PUPPETS D&D '84

Singles: 12-inch

QUALITY/RFC 4-6 84

Singles: 7-inch

QUALITY/RFC 3-4 84

PURDIE, Pretty P&R/R&B '67
(Bernard Purdie)

Singles: 7-inch

COLUMBIA 4-6 69
DATE 4-8 67-68

LPs: 10/12-inch

DATE 10-20 67
FLYING DUTCHMAN 8-12 73
PRESTIGE 8-12 71

PURE ENERGY R&B '80

Singles: 12-inch

PRISM 4-6 80-84

Singles: 7-inch

PRISM 3-5 80-84

PURE LOVE & PLEASURE LP '70

Singles: 7-inch

DUNHILL 3-5 70

LPs: 10/12-inch

DUNHILL 10-15 70

PURE PRAIRIE LEAGUE P&R/LP '75

Singles: 7-inch

RCA 3-5 72-79
CASABLANCA 3-5 80-81
EPIC 3-5 77

LPs: 10/12-inch

CASABLANCA 5-10 80-81
RCA 6-12 72-80

Members/Session: John Call; George Powell; Billy Hinds; David Sanborn; Mick Ronson; Michael O'Connor; Johnny Gimble; Don Felder; Vince Gill; Chet Atkins; Larry Goshorn.
Also see AMERICAN FLYER
Also see ATKINS, Chet
Also see FELDER, Don
Also see GILL, Vince
Also see RONSON, Mick
Also see SANBORN, David

PURIFY, James & Bobby P&R/R&B '66

Singles: 7-inch

BELL 4-8 66-69
CASABLANCA 3-5 74-75
MERCURY 3-5 76-77
SPHERE SOUND 4-8 66

LPs: 10/12-inch

BELL....10-20 66-67
MERCURY....8-12 77
Members: James Purify; Bobby Dickey.

PURIM, Flora LP '75

LPs: 10/12-inch

MILESTONE....5-10 74-77
W.B.....5-10 77-78
Also see HART, Mickey, Airto & Flora Purim

PURPLE REIGN P&R '75

Singles: 7-inch

GO-RILLA....4-8 75
HILLSIDE (1006 "Wish You Didn't Have to Go")....15-25
PRIVATE STOCK....3-5 75

PURSELL, Bill P&R/R&B/LP '63

Singles: 7-inch

COLUMBIA....3-6 62-66
DOT....3-5 69
EPIC....3-5 67
SPAR....10-15 60s

LPs: 10/12-inch

COLUMBIA....8-15 63-65
Also see NELSON, Willie
Also see ROBBINS, Marty

PURSUIT OF HAPPINESS LP '88

LPs: 10/12-inch

CHRYSALIS....5-8 88

PUSHE' D&D '84

Singles: 12-inch

PARTYTYME....4-6 84

PYRAMIDS P&R/LP '64

Singles: 7-inch

BEST (1 "Pyramid's Stomp")....15-25 63
BEST (102 "Penetration")....20-30 63
BEST (13001 "Pyramid's Stomp")....8-12 63
BEST (13002 "Penetration")....8-12 63
CEDWICKE (13005 "Midnight Run")....20-30 64
CEDWICKE (13006 "Contact")....20-30 64
SUNDAZED....5-10 90s
(Colored vinyl.)

Picture Sleeves

BEST (13002 "Penetration")....20-30 63

LPs: 10/12-inch

BEST (16501 "Penetration")....75-125 64
(Monaural.)
BEST (36501 "Penetration")....100-200 64
(Stereo.)
WHAT....5-8 83

PYTHON LEE JACKSON P&R/LP '72
(With Rod Stewart)

Singles: 7-inch

EUROGRAM (5001 "In a Broken Dream")....10-15
GNP....4-6 72
Also see SMALL FACES
Also see STEWART, Rod

Q P&R/LP '77

Singles: 7-inch

EPIC....3-5 77

Picture Sleeves

EPIC....3-5 77

LPs: 10/12-inch

EPIC....8-10 77
Members: Robert Peckman; Don Garvin.
Also see JAGGERZ

Q FEEL P&R '89

Singles: 7-inch

JIVE (1220 "Dancing in Heaven")....3-4 89
JIVE (2001 "Dancing in Heaven")....4-8 83

Picture Sleeves

JIVE (1220 "Dancing in Heaven")....3-4 89

QUADRANT SIX R&B/D&D '83

Singles: 12-inch

ATLANTIC....4-6 83

Singles: 7-inch

ATLANTIC....3-4 83

QUAITE, Christine P&R '64

Singles: 7-inch

WORLD ARTISTS....5-8 64

QUAKER CITY BOYS P&R '58

Singles: 7-inch

SWAN....8-15 58-59

QUALLS, Sidney Joe R&B '74
(Sidney Qualls)

Singles: 7-inch

DAKAR....3-5 74

QUANDO QUANDO D&D '83

Singles: 12-inch

FACTORY....4-6 83

QUARTER NOTES P&R '59
(Quarter-Notes)

Singles: 78 rpm

DOT (15685 "Like You Bug Me")....15-25 57

Singles: 7-inch

BISON (757 "Frantic Flip")....15-20 60
DOT (15685 "Like You Bug Me")....20-30 57
GLENN (2550 "The Shock")....10-20 62
(First issued as *Guitar Bass Boogie*, by Gary Vallet. Has sound effects added.)
GUYDEN (2083 "Pretty Pretty Eyes")....10-15 63
IMPERIAL (5647 "Frantic Flip")....10-15 60
LITTLE STAR (112 "Baby")....1000-2000 62
RCA (7327 "Punkanilla")....10-20 58
WIZZ (715 "Record Hop Blues")....15-25 '59

QUARTERFLASH P&R/LP '81

Singles: 12-inch

GEFFEN....4-6 81-82

Singles: 7-inch

GEFFEN....3-5 81-85
W.B.....3-5 82

Picture Sleeves

GEFFEN....3-5 82-85

LPs: 10/12-inch

GEFFEN....5-10 81-85
Also see SEAFOOD MAMA

QUARTERMAN, Joe R&B '72
(With Free Soul)

Singles: 7-inch

GSF....3-5 72-74
MERCURY....3-5 74

QUARTZ R&B '78

Singles: 7-inch

COLUMBIA....3-5 72-73
RCA....3-5 77-78

LPs: 10/12-inch

COLUMBIA....8-10 73
RCA....5-10 77-78

QUATEMAN, Bill P&R '73

Singles: 7-inch

COLUMBIA....3-5 72-73
RCA....3-5 77-78

LPs: 10/12-inch

COLUMBIA....8-10 73
RCA....5-10 77-78

QUATRO, Suzi P&R/LP '74
(Susie Quatro)

Singles: 7-inch

ARISTA....3-5 75
BELL....3-5 73-74
BIG TREE....3-5 76
DREAMLAND....3-5 80-81
RAK....5-10 72-74
RSO....3-5 79

Picture Sleeves

DREAMLAND....3-5 80

LPs: 10/12-inch

ARISTA....8-10 75
BELL....10-12 74
DREAMLAND....5-10 80
RSO....5-10 79

QUATRO, Suzi, & Chris Norman P&R '79

Singles: 7-inch

RSO....3-5 79
Also see QUATRO, Suzi
Also see SMOKIE

QUAZAR R&B/LP '78

Singles: 7-inch

ARISTA....3-5 78

LPs: 10/12-inch

ARISTA....5-10 78

QUEEN LP '73

Singles: 12-inch

CAPITOL....4-8 84-86
ELEKTRA (11401 "Fat Bottom Girls and Bicycle Race")....12-18
(Promotional issue.)

Singles: 7-inch

CAPITOL....3-5 84-89
ELEKTRA....3-6 74-82
HOLLYWOOD....3-4 92

Picture Sleeves

CAPITOL....3-5 84-89
ELEKTRA (Except 45478)....4-8 77-82
ELEKTRA (45478 "It's Late")....10-20 78

LPs: 10/12-inch

CAPITOL....5-10 84-89
ELEKTRA (Except 5064)....6-12 73-82
ELEKTRA (5064 "Queen")....10-15 73
(With gold foil title stamped on cover.)
ELEKTRA (5064 "Queen")....5-10 73
(With title printed on cover.)
ELEKTRA (5064 "Queen")....20-30 73
(Quadrophonic.)
MFSL (067 "A Night at the Opera")....35-50 82
MFSL (211 "The Game")....20-25 94
WARNER SPECIAL PRODUCTS....5-10 84

Promotional LPs

ELEKTRA (1026 "Sheer Heart Attack")....10-15 74
ELEKTRA (75082 "Queen II")....40-50 74
Members: Freddie Mercury; John Deacon; Brian May; Roger Taylor.
Also see MAY, Brian
Also see MERCURY, Freddie
Also see SMILE
Also see TAYLOR, Roger

QUEEN & DAVID BOWIE P&R '81

Singles: 7-inch

ELEKTRA....3-5 81

Picture Sleeves

ELEKTRA....3-5 81
Also see BOWIE, David
Also see QUEEN

QUEEN LATIFAH LP '89

LPs: 10/12-inch

TOMMY BOY....5-8 89

QUEENSRYCHE LP '83

Singles: 7-inch

EMI....3-4 83-86

LPs: 10/12-inch

CAPITOL (30711 "Promised Land")....8-10 90s
EMI (Except 01435)....5-8 83-90
EMI (01436 "Operation Mind Crime")....20-25 88
EMI (SPRO-01436 "Operation Mind Crime")....70-80 88
(Promotional only picture disc. 500 made.)
EMI (04194 "Speak the Word")....10-20 88
(Promotional only interview.)
EMI (19006 "Queensryche")....20-30
(Promotional issue only. Issued in metal film can with photo.)
Members: Geoff Tate; Chris DeGarmo; Michael Wilton; Eddie Jackson; Scott Rokenfield.

? & MYSTERIANS *P&R/LP '66*
(Question Mark & the Mysterians)
Singles: 7-inch
ABKCO ... 3-4 80s
CAMEO ... 4-8 66-67
CAPITOL ... 5-10 68
CHICORY (410 "Talk Is Cheap") ... 10-20 67
LUV ... 4-6 73
MILLION SELLER ... 3-4
PA-GO-GO (102 "96 Tears") ... 75-125 66
PEACOCK ("Time Is on My Side") ... 8-12
(Selection number not known.)
SUPER K ... 4-8 69
TANGERINE (392 "Ain't It a Shame") ... 5-10
LPs: 10/12-inch
CAMEO (2004 "96 Tears") ... 50-100 66
CAMEO (2006 "Action") ... 50-100 67
Members: Rudy Martinez; Robert Martinez; Frank Rodriguez; Larry Borjas; Bob Balderamma; Frank Lugo.

QUICK *R&B '81*
Singles: 12-inch
EPIC ... 4-6 82
PAVILLION ... 4-6 81
Singles: 7-inch
EPIC (37000 series) ... 3-5 82
PAVILLION ... 3-5 81
LPs: 10/12-inch
EPIC ... 5-10 82

QUICKEST WAY OUT *R&B '75*
Singles: 7-inch
W.B. ... 3-5 75-76

QUICKSILVER *LP '68*
(Quicksilver Messinger Service)
Singles: 7-inch
CAPITOL ... 4-8 68-76
LPs: 10/12-inch
CAPITOL (120 "Happy Trails") ... 20-30 69
CAPITOL (288 "Quicksilver Messenger Service") ... 30-50 69
CAPITOL (391 thru 819) ... 10-25 69-71
CAPITOL (2904 "Quicksilver Messenger Service") ... 20-30 68
CAPITOL (11000 series) ... 10-15 72-75
CAPITOL (16000 series) ... 5-10 80
Members: John Cipolina; Dave Freiberg.
Also see COPPERHEAD
Also see HOPKINS, Nicky
Also see JEFFERSON AIRPLANE
Also see MILLER, Steve / Band / Quicksilver Messinger Service

QUIET ELEGANCE *R&B '73*
Singles: 7-inch
HI ... 3-5 72-77
Members: Frankie Gearing; Mildred Vaney; Lois Reeves.
Also see GLORIES

QUIET RIOT *P&R/LP '83*
Singles: 12-inch
PASHA ... 4-6 83-85
Singles: 7-inch
CBS ... 3-4 83
PASHA ... 3-4 83-86
Picture Sleeves
CBS ... 3-4 83
PASHA ... 3-4 83-86
LPs: 10/12-inch
MOONSTONE ... 5-10 93
PASHA (Except 8Z8-39203) ... 5-10 83-88
PASHA (8Z8-39203 "Metal Health") ... 8-12 83
(Picture disc.)
RHINO ... 5-8 93
Members: Kevin DuBrow; Rudy Sarzo; Frankie Banali; Randy Rhoads; Chuck Wright; Paul Shortino; Sean McNabb; Kenny Hillery; Carlos Cavazo.
Also see HEAR 'N AID
Also see OSBOURNE, Ozzy

QUINELLA *R&B '81*
Singles: 7-inch
BECKET ... 3-5 81

QUINN, Carmel *LP '55*
Singles: 78 rpm
COLUMBIA ... 3-5 55-56
Singles: 7-inch
COLUMBIA ... 5-10 55-56
DOT ... 4-6 64
HEADLINE ... 4-8 59-62
EPs: 7-inch
COLUMBIA ... 8-12 55
LPs: 10/12-inch
CAMDEN ... 10-15 65
COLUMBIA ... 15-25 55-56
DOT ... 10-15 65
HEADLINE ... 10-20 59-62
Also see GODFREY, Arthur /Carmel Quinn / Frank Parker / Janette Davis

QUIN-TONES *P&R/R&B '58*
Singles: 7-inch
COLLECTABLES ... 3-4 80s
HUNT (321 "Down the Aisle of Love") ... 20-30 58
HUNT (322 "What Am I to Do") ... 25-50 58
RED TOP (108 "Down the Aisle of Love") ... 50-75 58
(Blue label)
RED TOP (108 "Down the Aisle of Love") ... 20-30 59
(Red label)
RED TOP (116 "Oh Heavenly Father") ... 50-75 59
Members: Roberta Haymon; Phylis Carr; Carolyn Holmes; Ronnie Scott; Jeannie Crist; Ken Sexton.

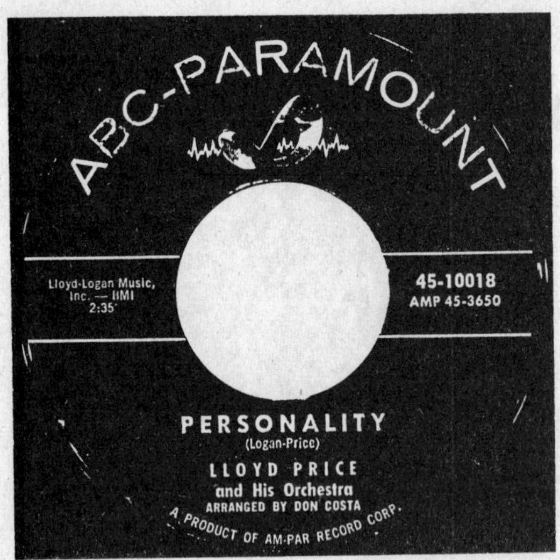

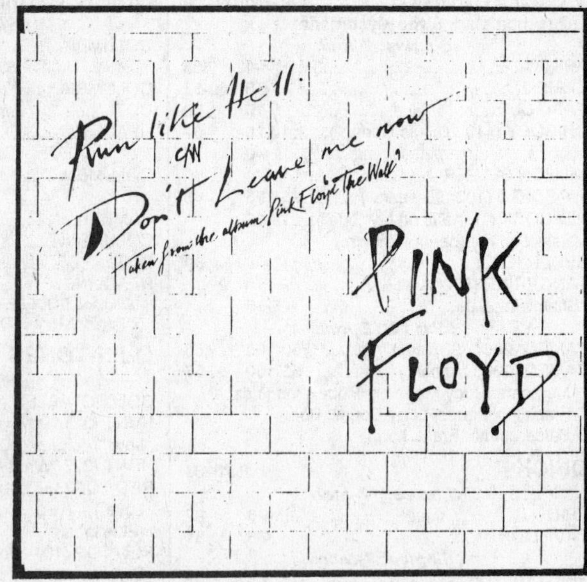

CUSTOM HIGH FIDELITY
Mercury
EP-1-3341
THE FLYING PLATTERS
HEAVEN ON EARTH
REMEMBER WHEN
I'M SORRY
GLORY OF LOVE
Printed in U.S.A.

RCR — P&R/R&B '80
Singles: 7-inch
RADIO 3-5 80
Members: Donna Rhodes; Charles Chalmers; Sandy Rhodes.

R.E.M. — P&R '83
Singles: 7-inch
EVA-TONE (105900 "Dark Globe") 5-10 90
(Promotional issue, *Sassy* magazine insert. Add $3 to $5 if accompanied by the appropriate issue of *Sassy*.)
HIBTONE (Radio Free Europe") 50-75 81
I.R.S. 3-8 82-87
MCA 3-5 85
W.B. 3-6 88-93
Picture Sleeves
I.R.S. 4-8 82-88
W.B. 3-4 89
EPs: 7-inch
I.R.S. 5-10 82
LPs: 10/12-inch
I.R.S. 5-10 82-88
MFSL (231 "Murmur") 20-25 94
(Half-speed mastered.)
W.B. 5-8 88-93
Members: J. Michael Stipe; Bill Berry; Peter Buck; Mike Mills.
Also see HINDU LOVE GODS

REO SPEEDWAGON — LP '74
Singles: 7-inch
EPIC (Except 10000 & 11000 series) 3-5 75-90
EPIC (10000 & 11000 series) 3-5 72-74
Picture Sleeves
EPIC 3-5 80-88
EPs: 7-inch
CSP 4-8 81
(Nestles candy promotional issue.)
LPs: 10/12-inch
EPIC (Except 40000 series) 6-12 71-90
EPIC (40000 series) 12-15 81-82
(Half-speed mastered.)
Promotional LPs
EPIC (643 "Nine Lives") 15-20 80s
EPIC (36844 "Hi Infidelity") 50-75 81
(Picture disc, made for Western Merchanders. All copies mistakenly have music by unknown artists. 100 made.)
Members: Kevin Cronin; Neal Doughty; Al Gratzer; Bruce Hall; Terry Luttrell.
Also see MAY, Brian

R.J.'S LATEST ARRIVAL — R&B '81
(Ralph James)
Singles: 7-inch
ARIOLA AMERICA 3-5 79
ATLANTIC 3-4 85
BUDDAH 3-5 81
LARC 3-4 83
EMI MANHATTAN 3-4 88
MANHATTAN 3-4 87
QUALITY/RFC 3-4
SUTRA 3-5 81
ZOO YORK 3-5 82
LPs: 10/12-inch
ARIOLA AMERICA 5-10 79
ATLANTIC 5-8 85

RABBITT, Eddie — C&W '74
Singles: 7-inch
DATE 4-8 68
ELEKTRA (Except 378) 3-5 74-83
ELEKTRA (378 "Song of Ireland") 5-10 78
(Colored vinyl—green of course. With green insert. Promotional issue only.)
RCA 3-4 85-89
20TH FOX 5-10 64
UNIVERSAL 3-4 89
W.B. 3-5 83-85
Picture Sleeves
ELEKTRA 3-5 81
LPs: 10/12-inch
ELEKTRA 5-10 75-82
RCA 5-8 86
W.B. 5-8 84-85

RABBITT, Eddie, & Crystal Gayle — C&W/P&R '82
Singles: 7-inch
ELEKTRA 3-5 82
Also see GAYLE, Crystal

RABBITT, Eddie, & Juice Newton — C&W '86
Singles: 7-inch
RCA 3-4 86
Also see NEWTON, Juice
Also see RABBITT, Eddie

RABIN, Trevor — LP '78
Singles: 7-inch
CHRYSALIS 3-5 78-80
LPs: 10/12-inch
CHRYSALIS 5-10 78-80
ELEKTRA 5-8 89

RACE — R&B '83
Singles: 7-inch
OCEAN FRONT 3-4 83

RACING CARS — LP '77
Singles: 7-inch
CHRYSALIS 3-5 77-78
LPs: 10/12-inch
CHRYSALIS 5-10 77-78

RADIANCE — R&B/D&D '85
(With Andrea Stone)
Singles: 12-inch
ARE 'N BE 4-6 83
Singles: 7-inch
W.B. 3-4 85

RADIANTS — P&R '62
(Maurice McAlister & Radiants; Maurice & Radiants)
Singles: 7-inch
CHESS 5-10 62-69
ERIC 3-4 70s
TWINIGHT 3-5 71
Members: Maurice McAlister; Wallace Sampson; Jerome Brooks; Elzie Butler; Green McLauren; Frank McCollum; Leonard Caston, Jr; James Jameson; Mitchell Bullock; Victor Caston.
Also see McALISTER, Maurice

RADIATORS — LP '87
Singles: 7-inch
EPIC 3-4 87-89
LPs: 10/12-inch
EPIC 5-8 87-89
Members: Dave Malone; Frank Bua; Reggie Scanlan; Ed Volker; Camile Baudoin; Glenn Sears.

RADICE, Mark — R&B '76
Singles: 7-inch
U.A. 3-5 76
LPs: 10/12-inch
ROADSHOW 8-12 77

RADNER, Gilda — LP '79
Singles: 7-inch
W.B. 3-5 79-80
LPs: 10/12-inch
W.B. 5-10 79

RAE, Fonda — R&B '82
(Fonda Raye)
Singles: 12-inch
POSSE 4-6 83
VANGUARD 4-6 82
Singles: 7-inch
VANGUARD 3-4 82
Also see WISH

RAE, Robbie — D&D '83
Singles: 12-inch
QUALITY 4-6 83
Singles: 7-inch
QUALITY 3-4 83

RAELETTES — P&R/R&B '67
(Raeletts; Raelets)
Singles: 7-inch
TRC 3-5 70
TANGERINE 3-6 67-73
LPs: 10/12-inch
TRC 8-12 71-72
TANGERINE 8-12 72
Members: Clydie King; Mable John.
Also see CHARLES, Ray
Also see JOHN, Mable
Also see KING, Clydie
Also see TURNER, Ike & Tina

RAES — P&R '78
Singles: 7-inch
A&M 3-5 78
LPs: 10/12-inch
A&M 5-10 79
Members: Robbie Rae; Cherrill Rae.

RAFFERTY, Gerry — P&R/LP '78
Singles: 12-inch
U.A. (171 "Baker Street") 5-10 78
Singles: 7-inch
BLUE THUMB 3-5 72
LIBERTY 3-4 82
SIGNPOST 3-5 72
U.A. 3-5 77-80
Picture Sleeves
U.A. 3-5 77-78
LPs: 10/12-inch
BLUE THUMB 8-10 73-78
LIBERTY 5-8 82
MFSL 25-50 81
U.A. 8-10 78-80
VISA 5-10 78
Also see STEALERS WHEEL

RAG DOLLS — P&R '64
Singles: 7-inch
MALA 8-12 65
Member: Jean Thomas.

RAG DOLLS / Caliente Combo
Singles: 7-inch
PARKWAY 5-10 64
Also see RAG DOLLS

RAGING SLAB — LP '89
LPs: 10/12-inch
RCA 5-8 89

RAIDERS & Paul Revere: see REVERE, Paul, & Raiders

RAIL — LP '84
Singles: 7-inch
EMI AMERICA 3-4 84
LPs: 10/12-inch
DYNASTY 5-10 80
EMI AMERICA 5-8 84
PASSPORT 5-8 83

RAINBOW — LP '77
Singles: 12-inch
MERCURY (195 "Stone Cold") 5-10 82
(Colored vinyl.)
Singles: 7-inch
MERCURY 3-4 82-83
POLYDOR 3-5 79
Picture Sleeves
MERCURY 3-4 82-83

LPs: 10/12-inch
MERCURY 5-10 82-86
OYSTER 8-12 77
POLYDOR 5-10 78-81
Members: Ritchie Blackmore; Roger Glover; Cozy Powell; Ronnie James Dio; Joe Turner; Tony Carey.
Also see ALCATRAZZ
Also see BLACKMORE'S RAINBOW
Also see CAREY, Tony
Also see GLOVER, Roger

RAINDROPS P&R/R&B '63
Singles: 7-inch
JUBILEE 10-20 63-65
VIRGO 3-5 73
LPs: 10/12-inch
JUBILEE (J-5023 "Raindrops") 30-50 63
(Monaural.)
JUBILEE (SJ-5023 "Raindrops") 50-75 63
(Stereo.)
MURRAY HILL 5-8 80s
Members: Jeff Barry; Ellie Greenwich. (The third person pictured on the Roulette LP cover, Ellie's sister, Laura, is not heard on their records.)
Also see GREENWICH, Ellie

RAINES, Rita P&R '56
Singles: 78 rpm
DEED 5-10 56
JAMIE 5-10 57
Singles: 7-inch
DEED 8-12 56
JAMIE 8-12 57

RAINEY, Big Memphis Ma: see MARAINEY, Big Memphis

RAINEY, Ma P&R '25
(Gertrude Rainey)
Singles: 78 rpm
PARAMOUNT (12000 series) 100-200 24-38
LPs: 10/12-inch
BIOGRAPH 8-12 67-69
MILESTONE 8-12 67-74

RAINMAKERS LP '86
Singles: 7-inch
ERA 5-10 65

RAINWATER, Marvin C&W/P&R '57
Singles: 78 rpm
CORAL 5-10 56
MGM (Except 12240 & 12370) 5-15 55-57
MGM (12240 "Hot and Cold") 10-15 56
MGM (12370 "Get off the Stool") 10-15 56
Singles: 7-inch
BRAVE 4-6 63-67
CORAL 8-12 56
HILLTOP 5-10 70s
MGM (12000 & 12100 series) 10-20 55
MGM (12240 "Hot and Cold") 30-40 56
MGM (12313 "Why Did You Have to Go and Love Me") 10-20 56
MGM (12370 "Get off the Stool") 30-40 56
MGM (12412 thru 12938) 5-10 57-60
NU TRAYL 3-5 76
U.A. 4-6 65-66
W.B. 3-5 69-70
WARWICK 5-10 61
EPs: 7-inch
MGM (1464/1465/1466 "Songs By Marvin Rainwater") 15-25 57
(Price is for any of three volumes.)
LPs: 10/12-inch
CROWN 5-10 60s
GUEST STAR 5-10
MARK IV 8-12
MGM (3534 "Songs by Marvin Rainwater") 50-100 57
MGM (3721 "With a Heart With a Beat") 50-100 58
MGM (4046 "Gonna Find Me a Bluebird") 50-100 62
MOUNT VERNON 8-10
SPINORAMA 8-10 60s
Also see DEAN, Jimmy / Marvin Rainwater
Also see FRANCIS, Connie, & Marvin Rainwater

RAINY DAZE P&R '67
Singles: 7-inch
CHICORY (404 "That Acapulco Gold") 10-15 67
UNI 5-10 67
WHITE WHALE 5-10 68
LPs: 10/12-inch
UNI (73002 "That Acapulco Gold") ... 15-25 67
Members: Tim Gilbert; Bob Heckendorf; Mac Ferris; Kip Gilbert; Sam Fuller.

RAIZY DAZE / King Toke
Singles: 7-inch
I.P. (100 "That Acapulco Gold") 25-35 66
Also see RAINY DAZE

RAITT, Bonnie LP '72
Singles: 7-inch
CAPITOL 3-4 89-91
W.B. 3-4 72-86
Picture Sleeves
W.B. 4-8 72-79
LPs: 10/12-inch
CAPITOL 5-8 89-91
W.B. 6-12 71-86
Also see MULDAUR, Geoff, & Bonnie Raitt

RAITT, Bonnie / Gilley's "Urban Cowboy" Band
Singles: 7-inch
FULL MOON/ASYLUM 3-5 80
Picture Sleeves
FULL MOON/ASYLUM 3-5 80
Also see RAITT, Bonnie

RAJAHS
(Nutmegs)
Singles: 7-inch
KLIK (7805 "I Fell in Love") 250-350 57
Also see NUTMEGS

RAKE R&B '83
Singles: 7-inch
PROFILE 3-4 83

RALKE, Don P&R '59
("Big Sound of Don Ralke")
Singles: 78 rpm
CROWN 3-6 55
Singles: 7-inch
CROWN 5-15 55
DRUM BOY 4-6 66
REAL 5-15 56
W.B. 5-10 59-64
LPs: 10/12-inch
CROWN 10-20 55
W.B. 10-20 59-60
Also see BYRNES, Edward
Also see JAN & ARNIE

RALPH, Sheryl Lee D&D '84
Singles: 12-inch
NYM 4-6 84-85
Singles: 7-inch
NYM 3-4 84-85
Also see HARNEY, Ben, & Sheryl Lee Ralph

RAM JAM P&R/LP '77
Singles: 12-inch
EPIC 5-10 77
Singles: 7-inch
EPIC 3-5 77-78
LPs: 10/12-inch
EPIC 8-12 77-78
Also see LEMON PIPERS
Also see WILSON, Dennis / Ram Jam / Joan Baez

RAMA D&D '84
Singles: 12-inch
SUGARSCOOP 4-6 84

RAMATAM LP '72
Singles: 7-inch
ATLANTIC 3-5 72-73
LPs: 10/12-inch
ATLANTIC 10-15 72-73
Also see PINERA, Mike

RAMBEAU, Eddie P&R/LP '65
Singles: 7-inch
BELL 3-5 69
DYNA VOICE 4-8 65-66
SWAN 4-8 61-62
20TH FOX 4-8 64
VIRGO 3-4 73
LPs: 10/12-inch
DYNO VOICE 15-25 65
Also see MARCY JO & Eddie Rambeau

RAMBLERS P&R '60
Singles: 7-inch
ADDIT (1257 "Rambling") 10-20 60
Members: Chuck Kenney; Michael Burke; Michael Anthony; Kip Martin.

RAMBLERS P&R '64
Singles: 7-inch
ALMONT (311 "Father Sebastian") ... 15-25 64
ALMONT (313 "School Girl") 15-25 64
ALMONT (315 "Silly Little Boy") 15-25 64
SIDEWINDERS 10-20 64
Members: John Herbert; Sal Nastasi.

RAMIN, Sid, & Orchestra LP '63
LPs: 10/12-inch
RCA 8-12 63

RAMISTELLA, Johnny
(Johnny Rivers)
Singles: 7-inch
SUEDE (1401 "Little Girl") 100-200 58
Also see RIVERS, Johnny

RAMONES LP '76
Singles: 7-inch
RSO 3-6 81
SIRE 5-10 76-80
Picture Sleeves
SIRE 8-12 77-79
EPs: 7-inch
SIRE (805 "Rock 'N' Roll High School") 12-18 79
(Promotional issue only.)
LPs: 10/12-inch
SIRE (Except 6063 & 7528) 5-8 76-89
SIRE (6063 "Road to Ruin") 10-20 78
(Black vinyl.)
SIRE (6063 "Road to Ruin") 25-35 78
(Yellow vinyl.)
SIRE (7528 "Leave Home") 15-25 77
(Has *Carbona Not Glue*, which is not on reissues.)

RAMRODS P&R '61
Singles: 7-inch
AMY (813 "Riders in the Sky") 15-25 60
AMY (817 "Take Me Back to My Boots & Saddle") 10-20 61
AMY (846 "War Cry") 10-20 61
BARCLAY (13127 "War Party") 8-12 60s
QUALITY (1256 "Riders in the Sky") 8-12 60
QUEEN (24014 "Slee-Zee") 8-12 62
Members: Vincent Bell; Eugene Morrow; Richard Lane; Claire Lane.
Also see BELL, Vincent

RAMRODS R&B '72
Singles: 7-inch
R&H (1001 "Night Ride") 15-25 63
RAMPAGE (1000 "Soultrain") 4-6 72
Member: King Curtis.
Also see KING CURTIS

RANDAZZO, Teddy P&R '58
(With All 6)
Singles: 7-inch
ABC-PAR 4-8 59-62
COLPIX 4-8 62-63
DCP 4-8 64-66
MGM 4-8 66
VERVE/FOLKWAYS 4-8 67
VIK 5-10 58
LPs: 10/12-inch
ABC-PAR 20-30 61-62
MGM 15-20 66

VIK (1121 "I'm Confessing") 30-50 58
Also see CHUCKLES
Also see THREE CHUCKLES

RAN-DELLS P&R/R&B '63

Singles: 7-inch

RSVP (1104 "Beyond the Stars") 10-15 64
CHAIRMAN (4403 "Martian Hop") 10-15 63
CHAIRMAN (4407 "Come on and Love Me Too") 10-15 63

Picture Sleeves

CHAIRMAN (4403 "Martian Hop") 30-40 63
Members: Steve Rappaport; John Sprit.

RANDOLPH, Boots P&R/R&B/LP '63
(Homer Randolph)

Singles: 7-inch

LOGO 4-8
MONUMENT 3-8 61-83
PAJ (7041 "Yakety Sax") 4-8
PALO ALTO 3-4
RCA (37-7835 "Big Daddy") 10-20 60
(Compact 33 Single.)
RCA (47-7000 series) 5-10 59-61

Picture Sleeves

MONUMENT 8-12 64

EPs: 7-inch

MONUMENT (361 "Boots & Stockings") 5-10 69
(Promotional issue only.)
MONUMENT (514 "More Yakety Sax") 5-10 60s
(Promotional issue only.)
RCA (7835 "Big Daddy") 10-20
(Compact 33.)

LPs: 10/12-inch

CAMDEN 10-20 64
GUEST STAR 5-10 64
MONUMENT (Except 8000 & 18000 series) 6-12 71-82
MONUMENT (8000 & 18000 series) 10-20 63-71
PALO ALTO 5-8
RCA (LPM-2165 "Yakety Sax") 15-25 60
(Monaural.)
RCA (LSP-2165 "Yakety Sax") 25-35 60
(Stereo.)
TEXIZE (1 "Nashville Sound") 10-15 68
(Promotional issue only.)
Also see ANN-MARGRET
Also see ATKINS, Chet, Floyd Cramer & Boots Randolph
Also see FRANCIS, Connie
Also see HALEY, Bill / Boots Randolph
Also see HIRT, Al, & Boots Randolph
Also see KNIGHTSBRIDGE STRINGS
Also see LEE, Brenda
Also see PRESLEY, Elvis
Also see RANDOLPH, Randy
Also see TILLOTSON, Johnny
Also see VELVETS

RANDOLPH, Randy
(Homer Randolph)

Singles: 7-inch

RCA 8-15 58-59
Also see RANDOLPH, Boots

RANDY & RAINBOWS P&R/R&B '63

Singles: 7-inch

B.T. PUPPY 5-8 67
CRYSTAL BALL 4-8 77
LAURIE 3-5 70s
MIKE 5-10 66
RUST (Except 5059) 8-12 63-64
RUST (5059 "Denise") 20-25 63
(Blue label.)
RUST (5059 "Denise") 5-10 63
(Rust and white label.)

LPs: 10/12-inch

AMBIENT SOUND 8-10 82
AMBIENT SOUND/ROUNDER 8-10 84
MAGIC CARPET 8-10
Members: Dominick "Randy" Safuto; Frank Safuto; Mike Zero; Sal Zero; Ken Arcipowski.

RANK & FILE LP '83

Singles: 7-inch

SLASH 3-4 83-84

LPs: 10/12-inch

SLASH 5-8 83-84
Also see SEATRAIN

RANKIN, Billy P&R/LP '84

Singles: 7-inch

A&M 3-4 84

LPs: 10/12-inch

A&M 5-8 84

RANKIN, Kenny LP '72
(Ken Rankin)

Singles: 7-inch

ABC-PAR 6-12 61
COLUMBIA 4-8 63-65
DECCA 10-15 58-60
LITTLE DAVID 3-5 73-77
MERCURY 4-6 68-69

Picture Sleeves

COLUMBIA 8-12 63
MERCURY 5-8 68

LPs: 10/12-inch

ATLANTIC 5-10 80
LITTLE DAVID 8-10 72-77
MERCURY 10-15 67-69

RANKING ROGER LP '88

LPs: 10/12-inch

I.R.S. 5-8 88

RAPPIN' DUKE R&B '86

Singles: 12-inch

TOMMY BOY 4-6 86

RARE BIRD LP '70

Singles: 7-inch

ABC 3-5 72
POLYDOR 3-5 73-74
PROBE 3-5 70

LPs: 10/12-inch

ABC 8-10 72
POLYDOR 8-10 73-74
PROBE 10-12 70

RARE BREED

Singles: 7-inch

ATTACK (1401 "Beg, Borrow and Steal") 20-25 66
(Reissued, with a different flip side, and shown as by the Ohio Express.)
ATTACK (1403 "Come and Take a Ride in My Boat") 10-20 66
Also see OHIO EXPRESS

RARE EARTH LP '69

Singles: 7-inch

MOTOWN 3-5 81
PRODIGAL 3-4 78
RARE EARTH (Black vinyl) 3-6 69-76
RARE EARTH (Colored vinyl) 4-8 72
(Promotional issue only.)
VERVE 4-8 68

Picture Sleeves

RARE EARTH 4-6 71-73

LPs: 10/12-inch

MOTOWN 5-8 81
PRODIGAL 5-8 77-78
RARE EARTH (Except 507) 8-12 70-76
RARE EARTH (507 "Get Ready") 8-12 69
(With standard, square cover.)
RARE EARTH (507 "Get Ready") 30-40 69
(With rounded-top cover. Promotional issue.)
VERVE 10-20 68
Members: Peter Hoorelbeke; Gil Bridges; Ray Monette; Pete Rivera; Mark Olson; Michael Urso; Edward Guzman; John Persh; Ken James.

RARE ESSENCE R&B '82

Singles: 12-inch

FANTASY 4-8 82

Singles: 7-inch

ATCO 3-4 90

RASCALS P&R '65
(Young Rascals)

Singles: 7-inch

ATLANTIC (Except 2428) 4-8 65-70
ATLANTIC (2428 "Groovin' [in Italian]") 10-20 67
(Backed with *Groovin'* in Spanish.)
ATLANTIC OLDIES 3-4 70s
COLUMBIA 3-5 71-72

Picture Sleeves

ATLANTIC 5-10 66-70

EPs: 7-inch

ATLANTIC (190 "Time Peace") 10-15 68
(Promotional issue only.)

LPs: 10/12-inch

ATLANTIC (137 "Freedom Suite") 20-30 69
(Promotional issue only.)
ATLANTIC (901 "Freedom Suite") 20-30 69
(Without cut corner or BB holes.)
ATLANTIC (901 "Freedom Suite") 10-20 69
(With cut corner or BB holes.)
ATLANTIC (8123 thru 8148) 15-25 66-67
ATLANTIC (8169 thru 8276) 10-15 68-71
COLUMBIA 8-12 71-72
PAIR 8-10 86
RHINO 5-8 87
W.F.O. (1000 "The Rascals") 8-12 72
Members: Felix Cavaliere; Ed Brigati; Dino Danelli; Gene Cornish; David Brigati.
Also see BULLDOG
Also see CAVALIERE, Felix
Also see DEE, Joey
Also see FOTOMAKER
Also see SWEET INSPIRATIONS

(YOUNG) RASCALS / Buggs / Four Seasons / Johnny Rivers

LPs: 10/12-inch

CORONET (283 "The Young Rascals") 20-30 66
Also see 4 SEASONS
Also see RIVERS, Johnny

(YOUNG) RASCALS / Isley Brothers

LPs: 10/12-inch

DESIGN (253 "Young Rascals and the Isley Brothers") 15-25 60s
Also see ISLEY BROTHERS
Also see RASCALS

RASPBERRIES P&R/LP '72

Singles: 7-inch

CAPITOL 4-8 72-74

Picture Sleeves

CAPITOL 6-10 73

LPs: 10/12-inch

CAPITOL (11036 thru 11329) 20-30 72-74
CAPITOL (11524 "Raspberries' Best") 8-12 76
CAPITOL (16095 "Raspberries' Best") 5-10 80
Members: Eric Carmen; Wally Bryson; Jim Bonfanti; John Aleksic; Dave Smalley.
Also see CHOIR
Also see FOTOMAKER

RATCHELL LP '72

Singles: 7-inch

DECCA 3-5 72

LPs: 10/12-inch

DECCA 10-15 71-72

RATIONALS P&R '66

Singles: 7-inch

A^2 (101 "Look What You've Done") 15-25 65
A^2 (103 "Feelin' Lost") 10-20 66
A^2 (103/4 "Feelin' Lost"/"Leavin' Here") 20-30 66
(Promotional issue only.)
A^2 (104 "Leavin' Here") 10-20 66
A^2 (105 "Leavin' Here") 10-20 67
A^2 (106 "Leavin' Here") 10-20 68
A^2 (107 "I Need You") 10-20 68
CAMEO (455 "Hold on Baby") 10-15 66-67
CAPITOL (2124 "I Need You") 8-12 68
CREWE 5-8 69
DANBY'S (125850 "Turn On") 30-40 66
(Promotional issue made for Danby's clothier.)
GENESIS (1 "Guitar Army") 5-8 69

LPs: 10/12-inch

ALIVE/TOTAL ENERGY 5-10 95
(10-inch LP.)
CREWE (1334 "Rationals") 25-35 69
Also see SRC / Rationals

RATT P&R/LP '84

Singles: 7-inch

ATLANTIC 3-4 84-89
TIME COAST 3-5 83-84

Picture Sleeves

ATLANTIC 3-4 84-88

LPs: 10/12-inch

ATLANTIC 5-8 84-90
TIME COAST 5-10 83-84
Members: Stephen Pearcy; Warren D. Martin; Robbin Crosby; Juan Crocier; Bobby Blotzer.

RATTLES P&R '70

Singles: 7-inch

LONDON 3-5
MERCURY 5-10 66
PROBE 4-6 70

LPs: 10/12-inch

MERCURY (21127 "Greatest Hits") .. 30-40 67
(Monaural.)
MERCURY (61127 "Greatest Hits") .. 40-60 67
(Stereo.)
Also see SEARCHERS / Rattles

RAVAN, Genya P&R/LP '78

Singles: 7-inch

COLUMBIA 3-5 71-72
DE LITE 3-5 75
DUNHILL 3-8 73
20TH FOX 3-5 78-79

LPs: 10/12-inch

COLUMBIA 8-12 72
DUNHILL 8-15 73
20TH FOX 5-10 78-79
Also see TEN WHEEL DRIVE

RAVEN LP '85

Singles: 7-inch

RAMPART 3-5

LPs: 10/12-inch

ATLANTIC 5-8 85-86

RAVEN, Marcia D&D '83

Singles: 12-inch

PROFILE 4-6 83

Singles: 7-inch

PROFILE 3-5 83

RAVENS P&R '47

("Featuring Jimmy Ricks")

Singles: 78 rpm

ARGO 50-75 56-57
CHECKER 15-25 57
COLUMBIA 200-400 50-51
HUB (3032 "Out of a Dream") 50-100 46
HUB (3033 "Bye Bye Baby Blues") . 50-100 46
KING 50-100 48-49
JUBILEE 15-25 55-56
MERCURY 25-50 51-55
OKEH (6825 "Whiffenpoof Song") 200-300 51
OKEH (6843 "That Old Gang of Mine") 200-300 51
OKEH (6888 "Mam'selle") 100-150 52
NATIONAL 200-300 47-51
RENDITION (5001 "Write Me a Letter") 50-100 51

Singles: 7-inch

ARGO (5255 "Kneel and Pray") 50-75 56
ARGO (5261 "A Simple Prayer") 75-125 56
(Rigid disc.)
ARGO (5261 "A Simple Prayer") 50-75 56
(Flexible disc.)
ARGO (5276 "That'll Be the Day") 30-50 57
ARGO (5284 "Here Is My Heart") 30-50 57
CHECKER (871 "That'll Be the Day") 15-25 57
COLUMBIA (1-903 "Time Takes Care of Everything") 1000-2000 50
(Compact 33 Single.)
COLUMBIA (6-903 "Time Takes Care of Everything") 1000-2000 50
COLUMBIA (1-925 "I'm So Crazy for Love") 1000-2000 50
(Compact 33 Single.)
COLUMBIA (6-925 "My Baby's Gone") 1000-2000 50
COLUMBIA (39112 "You Don't Have to Drop a Heart to Break It") 1000-2000 51
COLUMBIA (39194 "You're Always in My Dreams") 1000-2000 51
COLUMBIA (39408 "You Foolish Thing") 1000-2000 51
JUBILEE (5184 "Bye Bye Baby Blues") 25-50 55
JUBILEE (5203 "Green Eyes") 25-50 55
JUBILEE (5217 "On Chapel Hill") 25-50 55
JUBILEE (5237 "I'll Always Be in Love with You") 25-50 55
MEDIA ("Sixty Minute Man") 3-5 93
(Colored vinyl.)
MERCURY (5764 "There's No Use Pretending") 150-250 51
MERCURY (5800 "Begin the Beguine") 100-200 52
MERCURY (5853 "Why Did You Leave") 100-200 52
MERCURY (8291 "Write Me One Sweet Letter") 100-150 52
MERCURY (8296 "Too Soon") 100-150 52
MERCURY (70060 "Don't Mention My Name") 100-200 52
MERCURY (70119 "Come a Little Bit Closer") 100-150 53
MERCURY (70213 "Who'll Be the Fool") 100-150 53
MERCURY (70240 "Without a Song") 100-150 53
MERCURY (70307 "September Song") 100-150 54
MERCURY (70330 "Lonesome Road") 100-150 54
MERCURY (70413 "Love Is No Dream") 200-300 54
(Pink label.)
MERCURY (70413 "Love Is No Dream") 100-150 54
(Black label.)
MERCURY (70505 "White Christmas") 200-300 54
(Pink label.)
MERCURY (70505 "White Christmas") 75-125 54
(Black label.)
MERCURY (70554 "Write Me a Letter") 200-300 55
(Pink label.)
MERCURY (70554 "Write Me a Letter") 75-125 55
(Black label.)
NATIONAL (9111 "Count Every Star") 2000-3000 50
OKEH (6825 "Whiffenpoof Song") 1000-2000 51
OKEH (6843 "That Old Gang of Mine") 1000-2000 51
OKEH (6888 "Mam'selle") 400-600 52
SAVOY (1540 "White Christmas") 20-30 58
TOP RANK (2003 "Into the Shadows") 15-25 59
TOP RANK (2016 "Solitude") 15-25 59
VIRGO 3-5 72

Picture Sleeves

MEDIA ("Sixty Minute Man") 3-4 93

EPs: 7-inch

KING (310 "The Ravens Featuring Jimmy Ricks") 500-750 54
RENDITION (104 "Ol' Man River") 500-750 52

LPs: 10/12-inch

HARLEM HITPARADE 10-20 75
REGENT (6062 "Write Me a Letter") 100-150 57
(Green label.)
REGENT (6062 "Write Me a Letter") 50-100 50s
(Red label.)
SAVOY 10-15 78
Members: Warren Suttles; Ollie Jones; Joe Van Loan; Jimmy Ricks; Leonard Puzey; Maithe Marshall; Joe Medlin; Louis Heyward; James Stewart; Louis Frazier; Tom Evans; James Van Loan; David Bowers; Paul Van Loan; Rich Cannon; Bob Kornegay; Willis Sanders; Willie Ray.
Also see CUES

RAVENS & DINAH WASHINGTON

Singles: 78 rpm

MERCURY 20-40 51

Singles: 7-inch

MERCURY (8257 "Hey Good Lookin'") 50-75 51
Also see WASHINGTON, Dinah

RAVENS / Three Clouds

Singles: 78 rpm

KING 25-50 48-49
Also see RAVENS

RAW SILK R&B '82

Singles: 12-inch

WEST END 4-6 83

Singles: 7-inch

WEST END 3-5 82-83

RAWLS, Lou LP '63

Singles: 12-inch

PHILADELPHIA INT'L 4-8 79

Singles: 7-inch

ARISTA 3-5 75
BELL 3-5 74
CANDIX 5-10 60-61
CAPITOL 3-8 61-70
EPIC 3-4 82-85
GAMBLE 3-4 87
MGM 3-5 71-73
PHILADELPHIA INT'L 3-5 76-81
SHAR-DEE 8-12 60

Picture Sleeves

CAPITOL 4-8 67

EPs: 7-inch

CAPITOL 5-10 60s
(Includes Juke box issues and 33 Compacts.)

LPs: 10/12-inch

ALLEGIANCE 5-8 84
BELL 8-10 74
CAPITOL (Except 1700 thru 2900 series) 5-12 69-77
CAPITOL (1700 thru 2900 series) 12-25 63-68
EPIC 5-8 82-83
MGM 8-10 71-73
PHILADELPHIA INT'L 5-10 76-80
PICKWICK 5-10 69
POLYDOR 8-10 76
Also see COOKE, Sam
Also see PHILADELPHIA INTERNATIONAL ALL STARS
Also see VEGA, Tata

RAWLS, Lou, & Les McCann Ltd.

Singles: 7-inch

CAPITOL 4-6 62

LPs: 10/12-inch

CAPITOL 5-8 75

With "SM" prefix.)
CAPITOL 20-30 62
(With "T" or "ST" prefix.)
Also see McCANN, Les
Also see RAWLS, Lou

RAY, Baby: see BABY RAY

RAY, Diane P&R '63

Singles: 7-inch

MERCURY 4-8 63-64

Picture Sleeves

MERCURY 10-15 63

LPs: 10/12-inch

MERCURY 20-30 64

RAY, Don P&R/LP '78

Singles: 7-inch

POLYDOR 3-5 78

LPs: 10/12-inch

POLYDOR....5-10 78

RAY, Harry R&B '82

Singles: 7-inch

SUGAR HILL....3-4 82-83

LPs: 10/12-inch

SUGAR HILL....5-8 83

Also see RAY, GOODMAN & BROWN

RAY, James P&R '61

(With the Hutch Davie Orchestra)

Singles: 7-inch

CAPRICE....10-20 61-62
CONGRESS....10-20 63-64
DYNAMIC....10-20 62

LPs: 10/12-inch

CAPRICE (LP-1002 "James Ray")....40-60 62
(Monaural.)
CAPRICE (SLP-1002 "James Ray")....75-100 62
(Stereo.)

Also see DAVIE, Hutch
Also see GRANT, Janie

RAY, Johnnie P&R '51

(With the Four Lads)

Singles: 78 rpm

COLUMBIA....5-10 52-58
OKEH....8-12 52

Singles: 7-inch

CADENCE....5-10 60
COLUMBIA....8-15 52-60
DECCA....4-6 63-64
GROOVE....4-6 64
LIBERTY....4-8 62
OKEH (6809 "Wiskey and Gin")....15-25 51
OKEH (6840 "Cry")....10-20 51
OKEH RHYTHM & BLUES (6840 "Cry")....15-25 51
U.A.....4-8 61

Picture Sleeves

COLUMBIA....10-20 57

EPs: 7-inch

COLUMBIA....10-20 52-59
EPIC....10-20 52-54

LPs: 10/12-inch

COLUMBIA (961 "Big Beat")....30-50 57
COLUMBIA (1093 thru 1227)....20-40 57-59
COLUMBIA (1385 "On the Trail")....15-25 59
(Monaural.)
COLUMBIA (2510 "I Cry for You")....30-50 56
(10 Inch LP.)
COLUMBIA (6199 "Johnnie Ray")....35-55 51
(10 Inch LP.)
COLUMBIA (8180 "On the Trail")....20-30 59
(Stereo.)
EPIC (1120 "Johnnie Ray")....30-50 55
(10-inch LP.)
HARMONY....5-10 71
SUNSET....10-15 66

Also see DAY, Doris, & Johnnie Ray
Also see FOUR LADS

RAY, Johnnie, & Timi Yuro

Singles: 7-inch

LIBERTY....5-8 61

Also see RAY, Johnnie
Also see YURO, Timi

RAY, Link: see WRAY, Link

RAY, Ricardo P&R '68

Singles: 7-inch

ALEGRE....4-6 68

RAY & BOB P&R '62

Singles: 7-inch

LEDO....8-10 62

Members: Ray Swayne; Bob Appleberry.

RAY, GOODMAN & BROWN R&B '79

Singles: 7-inch

EMI AMERICA....3-4 87
PANORAMIC....3-4 84
POLYDOR....3-5 80-81

LPs: 10/12-inch

POLYDOR....5-10 80-81

Members: Harry Ray; Al Goodman; Bill Brown.

Also see MOMENTS
Also see RAY, Harry

RAYBURN, Margie P&R '57

Singles: 78 rpm

ALMA....4-8 54
LIBERTY....5-10 56-57
S&G....4-8 54

Singles: 7-inch

ALMA....5-10 54
CAPITOL....4-6 65
CHALLENGE....4-8 61
DOT....4-8 62-66
LIBERTY....5-10 56-62
S&G....5-10 54

Picture Sleeves

LIBERTY....10-15 57

LPs: 10/12-inch

LIBERTY (3126 "Margie")....20-25 59
(Monaural.)
LIBERTY (7126 "Margie")....25-35 59
(Stereo.)

RAYDIO R&B '77

(Featuring Ray Parker Jr.)

Singles: 7-inch

ARISTA....3-5 78-79

Picture Sleeves

ARISTA....3-5 78-79

LPs: 10/12-inch

ARISTA....5-10 78-79

Also see KNIGHT, Jerry
Also see PARKER, Ray, Jr.

RAYE, Colin C&W/LP '91

Singles: 7-inch

EPIC....3-4 91-92

LPs: 10/12-inch

EPIC....5-8 91

RAYE, Fonda: see RAE, Fonda

RAYE, Susan C&W/LP '70

Singles: 7-inch

CAPITOL....3-6 69-76
U.A.....3-5 76-77
WESTEXAS....3-4 85-86

Picture Sleeves

CAPITOL....3-5 71

LPs: 10/12-inch

CAPITOL....10-20 70-76
U.A.....5-10 77

Also see OWENS, Buck, & Susan Raye

RAY-O-VACS R&B '49

Singles: 78 rpm

ATCO....10-20 57
COLEMAN....8-12 49
DECCA....5-10 50-53
JOSIE....10-15 54
JUBILEE....10-15 52
KAISER....10-15 56

Singles: 7-inch

ATCO....10-20 57
DECCA....10-20 50-53
JOSIE....15-25 54
JUBILEE....15-22 52
KAISER....15-25 56
SHARP....15-25 60

Members: Lester Harris; Herb Milliner.

RAYS P&R/R&B '57

Singles: 78 rpm

CAMEO (117 "Silhouettes")....20-40 57
CAMEO (128 "Triangle")....20-40 58
CHESS....10-30 55-57
XYZ (100 "My Steady Girl")....15-25 57
XYZ (102 "Silhouettes")....30-50 57

Singles: 7-inch

ABKCO....3-4 80s
ARGO....3-5
CAMEO (117 "Silhouettes")....10-20 57
CAMEO (128 "Triangle")....15-25 58
CAMEO (133 "Rags to Riches")....15-25 58
CHESS (1613 "Tippity Top")....15-20 55
CHESS (1678 "Second Fiddle")....15-25 57
PERRI (1004 "Are You Happy Now")....15-25 62
(With Frankie Valli.)
XYZ (100 "My Steady Girl")....35-45 57
XYZ (102 "Silhouettes")....75-125 57
(Gray label.)
XYZ (102 "Silhouettes")....30-50 57
(Blue label.)
XYZ (106 "Souvenirs of Summertime")....30-40 58
XYZ (600 "Why Do You Look the Other Way")....30-40 59
XYZ (605 "Mediterranean Moon")....25-30 59
XYZ (607 "Magic Moon")....25-30 60
(Blue label.)
XYZ (607 "Magic Moon")....10-15 60
(Red label.)
XYZ (608 "Old Devil Moon")....10-15 60
XYZ (2001 "Souvenirs of Summertime")....25-35 58
(First issued in 1958 on XYZ 106.)

EPs: 7-inch

CHESS (5120 "The Rays")....150-250 58

Members: Harold "Hal" Miller; Walter Ford; David Jones; Harry James.

RAYS R&B '88

Singles: 7-inch

EMI MANHATTAN....3-4 87

RAZOR'S EDGE P&R '66

Singles: 7-inch

POW....10-15 66-67
POWER (4932 "Get Yourself Together")....15-25 67

Members: Bill Ande; Tom Condra; Dave Hieronymous; Jim Tolliver.

RAZZY: see BAILEY, Razzy

REA, Chris P&R/LP '78

Singles: 7-inch

COLUMBIA....3-5 82
GEFFEN....3-4 89-90
MOTOWN....3-4 87
RCA....3-4 84
U.A.....3-5 78-79

Picture Sleeves

GEFFEN....3-4 89
MOTOWN....3-4 87
U.A.....3-5 78

LPs: 10/12-inch

COLUMBIA....5-8 80-82
GEFFEN....5-8 89-90
RCA....5-8 84
U.A.....5-8 78

Also see WILLIE & Poor Boys

READ, John Dawson P&R '75

Singles: 7-inch

CHRYSALIS....3-5 75

LPs: 10/12-inch

CHRYSALIS....5-10 75-76

READY FOR THE WORLD R&B '84

Singles: 12-inch

MCA....4-6 84-86

Singles: 7-inch

BLUE LAKE....4-6 84
MCA....3-4 84-87

Picture Sleeves

MCA....3-4 85-86

LPs: 10/12-inch

MCA....5-8 86-88

REAL LIFE P&R '83

Singles: 12-inch

CURB/MCA....4-6 83-86

Singles: 7-inch

CURB/MCA....3-4 83-86

Picture Sleeves

CURB/MCA....3-4 84

LPs: 10/12-inch

CURB/MCA....5-8 83-89

REAL ROXANNE R&B '85

(With Hitman Howie Tee)

Singles: 12-inch

SELECT....4-6 85-86

REAL THING P&R/R&B '76

Singles: 12-inch

BELIEVE in a DREAM....4-6 81
EPIC....4-8 79

Singles: 7-inch

BELIEVE in a DREAM....3-5 81
EPIC....3-5 79
U.A....3-5 76-77
WHIZ....4-6 69

LPs: 10/12-inch

U.A....5-10 76

REAL TO REEL R&B/D&D '84

Singles: 12-inch

ARISTA....4-6 83-84

Singles: 7-inch

ARISTA....3-4 83-84

LPs: 10/12-inch

ARISTA....5-8 83

REAVES, Paulette R&B '77

Singles: 7-inch

BLUE CANDLE....3-5 77-78

REBELS P&R '62

Singles: 7-inch

MAR-LEE (0094 "Wild Weekend")....20-40 60
QUALITY (1024 "Wild Weekend")....25-50 60
(Canadian.)
Also see BUFFALO REBELS
Also see ROCKIN' REBELS

REBENNACK, Mac
(With the Soul Orchestra)

Singles: 7-inch

AFO (309 "The Point")....15-25 62
ACE (611 "Good Times")....15-25 61
REX (1008 "Storm Warning")....30-50 59
Also see ANDERSON, Elton
Also see DR. JOHN

RECORD, Eugene R&B '77

Singles: 12-inch

W.B....4-8 79

Singles: 7-inch

W.B....3-5 77-79

LPs: 10/12-inch

W.B....5-10 77-79
Also see CHI-LITES

RECORDS P&R/LP '79

Singles: 7-inch

VIRGIN....3-5 79-81

Picture Sleeves

VIRGIN....3-5 79-81

EPs: 7-inch

VIRGIN....3-6 79
(Issued as a bonus with Virgin LP 13130, *The Records*.)

LPs: 10/12-inch

VIRGIN....8-10 79-82

RED COATS with STEVE ALAIMO: see ALAIMO, Steve

RED FLAG LP '89

LPs: 10/12-inch

ENIGMA....5-8 89

RED HOT CHILI PEPPERS LP '87

Singles: 12-inch

EMI AMERICA....4-6 85

Singles: 7-inch

EMI AMERICA....3-4 84-85
EMI RECORDS GROUP....4-6
("For Juke boxes Only!" series.)
W.B....3-4 91

LPs: 10/12-inch

CAPITOL (29665 "Out in L.A.")....8-10 90s
EMI AMERICA....5-8 84-85
EMI MANHATTAN....5-8 87
W.B. (Except 5170)....5-8 91
W.B. (5170 "Blood Sugar Sex Magic")....15-25 91
(Double LP "Radio Ready" [censored] issue. Promotional issue only.)
Members: Anthony Kiedis; Jack Irons; Hillel Slovak; Mike Balzary; John Frusciante; Chad Smith.

RED RIDER P&R/LP '80

Singles: 7-inch

CAPITOL....3-5 80-86

Picture Sleeves

CAPITOL....3-5 80-84

LPs: 10/12-inch

CAPITOL....5-10 80-86
Members: Tom Cochrane; Rob Baker; Peter Boynton; Ken Greer; Jeff Jones.
Also see COCHRANE, Tom

RED RIVER DAVE P&R '60
(Dave McEnery)

Singles: 7-inch

COPYRIGHT....4-8 61
SAVOY....4-8 60-65

EPs: 7-inch

VARSITY....5-10

LPs: 10/12-inch

BLUEBONNET....8-12 60s
CONTINENTAL....10-20 62
PLACE....10-15 60s
SUTTON....5-10

RED ROCKERS P&R/D&D/LP '83

Singles: 12-inch

COLUMBIA....4-6 83-85

Singles: 7-inch

COLUMBIA....3-4 83-85

LPs: 10/12-inch

COLUMBIA....5-8 83

RED 7 LP '85

Singles: 7-inch

MCA....3-4 87

Picture Sleeves

MCA....3-4 87

LPs: 10/12-inch

MCA....5-8 85-87

RED SIREN LP '89

LPs: 10/12-inch

MERCURY....5-8 89

REDBONE P&R/LP '70

Singles: 7-inch

EPIC....3-5 71-74
RCA....3-5 78

LPs: 10/12-inch

ACCORD....5-10 82
EPIC....8-15 70-75
RCA....5-10 77
Members: Pat Vegas; Lolly Vegas.

REDBONE, Leon LP '76

Singles: 78 rpm

W.B....5-10 78
(Promotional only.)

Singles: 7-inch

EMERALD CITY....3-8 81
W.B....5-12 77-78

LPs: 10/12-inch

ACCORD....10-15 82
EMERALD CITY....10-15 81
W.B....15-30 77-78

REDD R&B '87

Singles: 7-inch

RCA....3-4 87

REDD, Sharon R&B '81

Singles: 12-inch

PRELUDE....4-6 81-83

Singles: 7-inch

COLUMBIA....3-5 78
PRELUDE....3-5 81-83
VEEP....4-8 67

LPs: 10/12-inch

COLUMBIA....5-10 78
PRELUDE....5-8 82

REDD, Sharon, Ula Hedwig & Charlotte Crossley

Singles: 7-inch

COLUMBIA....3-5 77-78
Also see MIDLER, Bette
Also see REDD, Sharon

REDD HOT R&B '81
(Redd Hott)

Singles: 7-inch

VENTURE....3-5 81-82
Members: Kevin "Flash" Ferrell; Robert Parson; Daryl Simmons; Greg Russell; De Morris Smith.
Also see MANCHILD

REDDING, Gene P&R/R&B '74

Singles: 7-inch

HAVEN....3-5 74

REDDING, Otis P&R/R&B '63
(With the Pinetoppers; with Pinetones; with Shooters)

Singles: 7-inch

ATCO....5-8 68-71
BETHLEHEM (3083 "Shout Bamalama")....10-15 64
CONFEDERATE (135 "Shout Bamalama")....20-40 62
FINER ARTS (2016 "She's All Right")....30-50 61
(Previously issued as by the Shooters.)
KING (6149 "Shout Bamalama")....5-10 68
ORBIT (135 "Shout Bamalama")....50-75 61
STONE (209 "You Left the Water Running")....4-8 76
VOLT (103 thru 121)....10-20 62-64
VOLT (124 thru 163)....10-15 65-68

EPs: 7-inch

VOLT....20-30 66

LPs: 10/12-inch

ATCO (33-161 "Pain in My Heart")....50-70 64
(Monaural.)
ATCO (SD-33-161 "Pain in My Heart")....60-80 64
(Stereo.)
ATCO (200 series)....10-15 68-69
ATCO (300 series)....8-12 70
ATCO (801 "Best of Otis Redding")..10-20 72
(Currently available with same selection number.)
ATLANTIC....5-10 82
VOLT (Except 411)....20-35 65-68
VOLT (411 "Soul Ballads")....35-55 65
(Monaural.)
VOLT (411 "Soul Ballads")....40-60 65
(Stereo.)
Members: Steve Cropper; Booker T. Jones; Isaac Hayes; Donald "Duck" Dunn; Lewis Steinberg; Al Jackson Jr. Session: Wayne Cochran; Johnny Jenkins; William Bell; Tommie Lee Williams; Veltones; Drapels.
Also see BAR-KAYS
Also see BOOKER T. & MGs
Also see COCHRAN, Wayne
Also see HAYES, Isaac
Also see SHOOTERS

REDDING, Otis / Little Joe Curtis

LPs: 10/12-inch

ALSHIRE....8-12 68
SOMERSET....8-12 68

REDDING, Otis / Jimi Hendrix LP '70

LPs: 10/12-inch

REPRISE (2029 "Otis Redding/The Jimi Hendrix Experience")....10-15 70
REPRISE (93371 "Otis Redding/The Jimi Hendrix Experience")....15-20 70
(Same as 2029, but with different front cover. Disc reads "Music from the Monterey Pop Soundtrack.")
Also see HENDRIX, Jimi

REDDING, Otis / Carla Thomas / Sam & Dave / Eddie Floyd

LPs: 10/12-inch

STAX (722 "Stax/Volt Revue, Vol. 2") 15-25 67

Also see FLOYD, Eddie
Also see OTIS & CARLA
Also see REDDING, Otis
Also see SAM & DAVE
Also see THOMAS, Carla

REDDINGS P&R/R&B/LP '80

Singles: 12-inch

BELIEVE in a DREAM 4-8 83

Singles: 7-inch

BELIEVE in a DREAM 3-5 80-83
POLYDOR 3-4 85-88

LPs: 10/12-inch

BELIEVE in a DREAM 5-10 80-83
POLYDOR 5-8 85

Members: Otis Redding III; Dexter Redding; Mark Locket.

REDDS & BOYS R&B '85

Singles: 7-inch

4TH & BROADWAY 3-5 85

REDDY, Helen P&R/LP '71

Singles: 12-inch

CAPITOL 4-6 79

Singles: 7-inch

CAPITOL 3-5 71-81
FONTANA 3-6 68
MCA 3-5 81-83

LPs: 10/12-inch

CAPITOL 5-10 71-81
MCA 5-8 81-83

Also see PRESLEY, Elvis / Helen Reddy

REDEYE P&R/LP '70

Singles: 7-inch

PENTAGRAM 3-5 70-71

LPs: 10/12-inch

PENTAGRAM 10-15 70-71

Members: Doug "Red" Mark; David Hodkins; Bobby Bereman; Bill Kman.
Also see SUNSHINE COMPANY

REDJACKS P&R '58

Singles: 7-inch

APT (25006 "Big Brown Eyes") 20-30 58
OKLAHOMA (5005 "Big Brown Eyes") 75-125 58

REDNOW, Eivets P&R '68
(Stevie Wonder)

Singles: 7-inch

GORDY (7076 "Alfie") 10-20 68

LPs: 10/12-inch

GORDY (932 "Eivets Rednow") 25-35 68

Also see WONDER, Stevie

REDWAY, Michael P&R '73
(Mike Redway)

Singles: 7-inch

LONDON 4-8 64
PHILIPS 3-5 73

REED, Clarence: see REID, Clarence

REED, Dan, Network P&R/LP '88

Singles: 7-inch

MERCURY 3-4 88-89

Picture Sleeves

MERCURY 3-4 88

LPs: 10/12-inch

MERCURY 5-8 88-89

REED, Dean P&R '59

Singles: 7-inch

CAPITOL 8-12 59-61
IMPERIAL 5-10 61

REED, Denny P&R '60

Singles: 7-inch

ASPIRE 3-5 77
DOT 5-10 62

MCI (1024 "A Teenager Feels It Too") 20-30 60
(First issue.)
TREY (3007 "A Teenager Feels It Too") 10-20 60
TREY (3014 "Lonely Little Bluebird") 10-15 61
TOWER 4-8 65
U.A. 5-10 61

REED, Jerry P&R '62
(With the Hully Girlies; with Seidina; with Friends)

Singles: 78 rpm

CAPITOL 5-15 55-56

Singles: 7-inch

CAPITOL 10-20 55-56
COLUMBIA 5-10 61-63
NRC 5-10 59
RCA (Except 8500 thru 9700) 3-5 69-85
RCA (8500 thru 9700) 4-8 65-69

Picture Sleeves

COLUMBIA 8-10 61
RCA 3-4 72-85

LPs: 10/12-inch

CAMDEN 5-10 72-74
HARMONY 8-12 71
PICKWICK/HILLTOP 5-10
RCA (Except "LPM" & "LSP" series) 5-10 73-83
RCA ("LPM" & "LSP" series) 8-18 67-73

Also see HART, Freddie / Sammi Smith / Jerry Reed
Also see JENNINGS, Waylon, & Jerry Reed
Also see JUSTIS, Bill / Jerry Reed
Also see NELSON, Willie
Also see PRESLEY, Elvis

REED, Jerry, & Chet Atkins

LPs: 10/12-inch

RCA 10-20 72

Also see ATKINS, Chet
Also see REED, Jerry

REED, Jimmy R&B '55

Singles: 78 rpm

CHANCE (1142 "High and Lonesome") 75-125 53
VEE JAY 20-40 53-58

Singles: 7-inch

ABC 3-5 73
ABC-PAR 4-8 66
BLUESWAY 3-6 67
CANYON 3-6 70
CHANCE (1142 "High and Lonesome") 300-400 53
(Reissue of Vee Jay 100.)
COLLECTABLES 3-4 80s
EXODUS 4-8 66
MAGIC 8-12
OLDIES 45 .... 4-6 64
RRG 4-8
TRIP 3-5 70s
VEE JAY (100 "High and Lonesome") 125-175 53
(Black vinyl.)
VEE JAY (100 "High and Lonesome") 250-350 53
(Colored vinyl.)
VEE JAY (105 "I Found My Baby") 100-150 53
(Black vinyl.)
VEE JAY (105 "I Found My Baby") 200-300 53
(Colored vinyl.)
VEE JAY (119 "You Don't Have to Go") 30-40 54
(Black vinyl.)
VEE JAY (119 "You Don't Have to Go") 200-300 54
(Colored vinyl.)
VEE JAY (132 "Pretty Thing") 20-35 55
VEE JAY (153 "She Don't Want Me No More") 25-30 55
VEE JAY (168 thru 248) 10-20 56-57
VEE JAY (253 thru 298) 8-15 57-58
VEE JAY (304 thru 709) 5-10 59-65
VEE JAY (1050 "Just Jimmy Reed") 15-25 62
(Stereo. Juke box issue only.)

LPs: 10/12-inch

ANTILLES 10-20
BLUES on BLUES 8-10
BLUESWAY 10-30 67-73
BUDDAH 10-15 69
EVEREST 5-10 69
EXODUS 10-15 66
GNP 8-10 74
KENT 8-12 69-71
RRG 10-20
ROKER 5-10
SUNSET 10-15 68
TRADITION 8-12
TRIP 8-15 71-78
UPFRONT 8-12
VEE JAY (1004 "I'm Jimmy Reed") 75-125 58
(Maroon label.)
VEE JAY (1004 "I'm Jimmy Reed") 50-75 59
(Black label.)
VEE JAY (1008 "Rockin' with Reed") 60-100 59
(Maroon label.)
VEE JAY (1008 "Rockin' with Reed") 40-60 59
(Black label.)
VEE JAY (1022 "Found Love") 25-50 60
VEE JAY (1025 "Now Appearing") 25-50 60
VEE JAY (1035 "At Carnegie Hall") .. 25-40 61
VEE JAY (1039 thru 1095) 20-40 62-64
VEE JAY (8501 "The Legend, the Man") 20-30 65
VERSATILE 8-10 78

Also see DIXON, Willie
Also see MAYFIELD, Curtis
Also see UPCHURCH, Phil

REED, Jimmy / Peppermint Harris

EPs: 7-inch

LUNAR (2009 "Tells It Like It Is") 5-10 81

Also see PEPPPERMINT HARRIS
Also see REED, Jimmy

REED, Lou LP '72
(With the Velvet Underground)

Singles: 12-inch

RCA 4-8 84

Singles: 7-inch

ARISTA 3-5 76
RCA 3-5 73-86

LPs: 10/12-inch

ARISTA 5-10 76-80
PRIDE 8-12 73
RCA ("AFL1" series) 5-10 80-83
RCA ("ANL1" series) 5-10 77
RCA ("APL1" series) 6-12 73-77
RCA ("AYL1" series) 5-8 80-83
RCA ("CPL1" series) 8-12 74
RCA ("LSP" series) 8-12 72
SIRE 5-8 89-90

Also see DION
Also see VELVET UNDERGROUND

REED, Lou, & John Cale LP '90

LPs: 10/12-inch

SIRE 5-8 90

Also see CALE, John
Also see REED, Lou

REED, Vivian R&B '68

Singles: 7-inch

ATCO 3-5 73
EPIC 4-8 68-69
U.A. 3-5 78-79

LPs: 10/12-inch

EPIC 10-15 69
U.A. 5-10 78

REESE, Della P&R '57
(With the Meditation Singers)

Singles: 78 rpm

JUBILEE 10-20 57

Singles: 7-inch

ABC 3-6 67-73
ABC-PAR 4-6 65-66
AVCO EMBASSY 3-6 69-72
CHI-SOUND 3-5 77
JUBILEE (5000 series) 10-15 57-59
(Monaural.)

JUBILEE (9007 "Stormy Weather")... 15-25 58
(Stereo.)
LMI.......3-5 73
RCA.......8-12 59-64
VIRGO.......3-5 72

Picture Sleeves

AVCO EMBASSY.......4-8 69-72
RCA.......10-15 60-63

EPs: 7-inch

RCA.......10-20 61

LPs: 10/12-inch

ABC.......5-10 76
ABC-PAR.......15-20 65-67
APPLAUSE.......5-8 83
DESIGN.......5-10
JUBILEE (1000 & 5000 series).......20-30 57-63
JUBILEE (6000 series).......10-15 69
LMI.......5-10 73
PICKWICK.......5-8 78
RCA (2000 thru 4600 series).......10-25 60-72
SUNSET.......5-10 71
Also see ANN-MARGRET / Kitty Kalen / Della Reese

REEVES, Del C&W '61
(With the Goodtime Charlies)

Singles: 7-inch

CHART.......3-5 70
COLUMBIA.......4-6 64
DECCA.......4-8 61-62
KOALA.......3-5 80-82
LAS VEGAS.......10-15 59
PEACH.......10-15 60
PLAYBACK.......3-4 86
REPRISE.......4-8 63
U.A. 3-6 66-78

Picture Sleeves

KOALA.......3-4 80
U.A. 3-6 67

LPs: 10/12-inch

KOALA.......5-8 79-80
STARDAY.......5-8
SUNSET.......5-10 69-70
U.A. (200 thru 600 series).......5-10 73-76
U.A. (3000 & 6000 series).......10-20 65-71

REEVES, Del, & Penny DeHaven C&W '72

Singles: 7-inch

U.A. 3-5 72

REEVES, Del, & Bobby Goldsboro C&W '68

Singles: 7-inch

U.A. 3-6 65-71

LPs: 10/12-inch

U.A. 10-20 68
Also see GOLDSBORO, Bobby

REEVES, Del / Red Sovine

LPs: 10/12-inch

EXACT.......5-8 80
Also see SOVINE, Red

REEVES, Del, & Billie Jo Spears C&W '76

Singles: 7-inch

U.A. 3-5 76

LPs: 10/12-inch

LIBERTY.......5-8 82
U.A. 5-10 76
Also see REEVES, Del

REEVES, Dianne R&B/LP '88

Singles: 7-inch

BLUE NOTE.......3-4 87

LPs: 10/12-inch

BLUE NOTE.......5-8 88
EMI.......5-8 90

REEVES, Jim C&W '53
(With His Circle O Ranch Boys)

Singles: 78 rpm

ABBOTT (Black plastic).......15-25 53-55
ABBOTT (Colored plastic).......25-50 53-55
MACY'S (115 "Teardrops of Regret").......150-250 50
MACY'S (132 "Never Been So Blue").......150-250 51
RCA.......10-20 55-57

Singles: 7-inch

ABBOTT (100 series, except 116).... 10-25 53-55
(Black vinyl.)
ABBOTT (115 "Wagon Load of Love").......15-25 53
(Black vinyl.)
ABBOTT (115 "Wagon Load of Love").......35-50 53
(Colored vinyl.)
ABBOTT (116 "Mexican Joe").......15-25 53
(Black vinyl.)
ABBOTT (116 "Mexican Joe").......35-50 53
(Colored vinyl.)
ABBOTT (137 "Butterfly Love").......15-25 53
(Black vinyl.)
ABBOTT (137 "Butterfly Love").......35-50 53
(Colored vinyl.)
ABBOTT (143 "El Rancho Del Rio") 15-25 53
(Black vinyl.)
ABBOTT (143 "El Rancho Del Rio") 35-50 53
(Colored vinyl.)
ABBOTT (148 "Bimbo").......15-25 53
(Black vinyl.)
ABBOTT (148 "Bimbo").......35-50 53
(Colored vinyl.)
ABBOTT (160 thru 186).......10-20 54-55
ABBOTT (3000 series).......10-20 55
ABBOTT (4000 series).......4-8
RCA (0135 thru 0963).......3-8 69-74
RCA (6200 thru 7557).......10-20 55-59
RCA (7643 "He'll Have to Go").......5-10 59
RCA (7643 "He'll Have to Go")..... 150-250 59
(Single-sided. Promotional issue only.)
RCA (7756 thru 9969).......4-10 60-71
RCA (10133 thru 13693).......3-6 75-84

Picture Sleeves

RCA (Except 8252).......8-15 60-65
RCA (8252 "Señor Santa Claus")..... 15-20 63

EPs: 7-inch

RCA (Except 1256).......25-50 56-61
RCA (1256 "Singing Down the Lane").......50-100 56
(Double EP set.)

LPs: 10/12-inch

ABBOTT (5001 "Jim Reeves Sings").......800-1200 56
CMF (008 "Live at the Opry").......5-10
CAMDEN (Except 583 thru 686).......5-15 64-73
CAMDEN (583 thru 686).......10-20 60-63
CANDLELIGHT ("Jim Reeves").......15-25 83
(Boxed five-disc set. Selection number not known.)
GUEST STAR.......10-15 64
HISTORY of COUNTRY MUSIC.......6-10 72
PAIR.......6-12 82
PICKWICK.......5-10 72
PICKWICK/HILLTOP.......5-10 74
RCA (0039 thru 5044).......5-10 73-84
(With "AHL," "ANL," "APL," "AYL" or "CPL" prefix.)
RCA (0126 "The Jim Reeves Collection").......10-15 75
(Special Products issue, Two LPs.)
RCA (0246 "Take My Hand, Precious Lord").......10-15
(Special Products issue. Two LPs.)
RCA (0587 "Golden Collection").......30-35
(Special Products issue, five-disc set.)
RCA (LPM-1256 "Singing Down the Lane").......100-200 56
RCA (LPM-1410 "Bimbo").......40-60 57
RCA (LPM-1576 "Jim Reeves").......30-50 57
RCA (LPM-1685 "Girls I Have Known").......25-50 58
RCA (LPM-1950 "God Be with You").......20-40 58
(Monaural.)
RCA (LSP-1950 "God Be with You").......20-40 58
(Stereo.)
RCA (LPM-2001 thru LPM-2339)...... 15-25 59-61
(Monaural.)
RCA (LSP-2001 thru LSP-2339).......20-30 59-61
(Stereo.)
RCA (LPM-2487 thru LPM-3903).......10-20 62-67
RCA (LSP-2487 thru LSP-3903).......10-25 62-67
RCA (LPM-3987 "A Touch of Sadness").......25-35 68
(Monaural.)
RCA (LSP-3987 "A Touch of Sadness").......10-15 68
(Stereo.)
RCA (LSP-4062 thru LSP-4749).......8-15 68-72
RADIANT.......5-10
READER'S DIGEST/RCA (210 "Unforgettable Jim Reeves").......25-35 76
(Boxed, six-disc set.)
TAMPA/RCA SPECIAL PRODUCTS (0126 "Jim Reeves").......8-10 75
Also see CRAMER, Floyd
Also see KERR, Anita
Also see PRESLEY, Elvis / Hank Snow / Eddy Arnold / Hank Snow

REEVES, Jim, & Deborah Allen C&W '79

Singles: 7-inch

RCA.......3-5 79-80

REEVES, Jim, & Patsy Cline C&W '81
(Patsy Cline & Jim Reeves)

Singles: 7-inch

MCA.......3-5 82
RCA.......3-5 81

LPs: 10/12-inch

MCA.......5-10 82
RCA.......5-10 81
Also see CLINE, Patsy

REEVES, Jim / Alvadean Coker

Singles: 78 rpm

ABBOTT.......10-20 54

Singles: 7-inch

ABBOTT.......15-25 54

REEVES, Jim / Hugi & Lugi Chorus

Singles: 7-inch

U.S.A.F. (89 "In a Mansion Stands My Love").......20-30 60s
(Promotional issue only.)

REEVES, Jim, & Dottie West

Singles: 7-inch

RCA.......4-6 64
Also see REEVES, Jim
Also see WEST, Dottie

REEVES, Martha P&R/R&B '74

Singles: 12-inch

FANTASY.......4-8 78-79

Singles: 7-inch

ARISTA.......3-5 75-77
FANTASY.......3-4 78-80
MCA.......3-4 74-75

LPs: 10/12-inch

ARISTA.......8-10 76
FANTASY.......5-8 78-80
MCA.......8-12 74
PHONORAMA.......5-8
Also see MARTHA & VANDELLAS

REFLECTIONS P&R '64

Singles: 7-inch

ABC-PAR (10794 "Like Adam and Eve").......15-25 66
ABC-PAR (10822 "You're Gonna Find Out You Need Me").......20-30 66
ERIC.......3-4 70s
FLAX.......4-8
GOLDEN WORLD.......10-15 64-65
KAY•KO (1003 "Helpless").......100-150 63
MALONE.......10-15 60s
TIGRE (602 "In the Still of the Night").......20-30 62

LPs: 10/12-inch

GOLDEN WORLD (300 "[Just Like] Romeo & Juliet").......50-75 64
Members: Tony Micale; John Dean; Phil Castrodale; Dan Bennie; Ray Steinberg.

REFLECTIONS P&R/R&B '75

Singles: 7-inch

CAPITOL (4078 "3 Steps from True Love") 10-15 75
CAPITOL (4137 "Love On Delivery") 10-15 75
CAPITOL (4222 "Day After Day") 5-10 76
CAPITOL (4358 "Gift Wrap My Love") 5-10 76

Members: Herman Edwards; Josh Pridgen; Edmund "Butch" Simmons; John Simmons.

RE-FLEX P&R/D&D/LP '83

Singles: 12-inch

CAPITOL 4-6 83-84

Singles: 7-inch

CAPITOL 3-4 83-84

Picture Sleeves

CAPITOL 3-4 83-84

LPs: 10/12-inch

CAPITOL 5-8 83

REGAL DEWY R&B '77

Singles: 12-inch

MILLENNIUM 8-10 77

Singles: 7-inch

MILLENNIUM 3-5 77

REGAN, Bob, & Lucille Starr C&W '70

Singles: 7-inch

DOT 3-5 69

LP: 10/12-inch

A&M 8-12

REGAN, Joan P&R '53

Singles: 78 rpm

LONDON 3-5 53-55

Singles: 7-inch

COLUMBIA 4-6 66
LONDON 5-10 53-55

Picture Sleeves

COLUMBIA 4-8 66

REGENTS P&R/R&B '61

Singles: 7-inch

ABC 3-5 73
COUSINS (1002 "Barbara Ann") 200-250 61
GEE (1065 "Barbara Ann") 15-25 61
GEE (1071 "Runaround") 20-25 61
GEE (1073 "Don't Be a Fool") 15-25 61
GEE (1075 "Lonesome Boy") 15-25 62
ROULETTE 3-5 70s

LPs: 10/12-inch

CAPITOL (KAO-2153 "Live at the AM-PM Discotheque") 35-45 64
(Monaural.)
CAPITOL (SKAO-2153 "Live at the AM-PM Discotheque") 45-55 64
(Stereo.)
EMUS 5-10 79
GEE (GLP-706 ("Barbara Ann") 75-100 61
(Monaural.)
GEE (SGLP-706 ("Barbara Ann") 100-125 61
(Stereo.)
MURRAY HILL 5-8 85

Members: Guy Villari; Sal Cuomo; Chuck Fassert; Don Jacobucci; Tony Gravagna.

REGINA P&R/R&B/LP '86
(Regina Richards)

Singles: 7-inch

ATLANTIC 3-4 86-88

Picture Sleeves

ATLANTIC 3-4 86-88

LPs: 10/12-inch

ATLANTIC 5-8 86

REID, Clarence P&R/R&B '69
(With the Delmiras; Clarence Reed)

Singles: 7-inch

ALSTON 4-8 68-74
DEEP CITY 10-20 60s
DIAL 8-12 64
PHIL-L.A. of SOUL 5-10 67
REID (2744 "I Refuse to Give Up") 20-30 60s
SELMA 10-20 63
TAY-STER 5-10 67
WAND (1106 "Somebody Will") 10-20 65
WAND (1121 "I'm Your Yes Man") 20-30 65

LPs: 10/12-inch

ATCO (307 "Dancin' with Nobody But You Babe") 15-25 69

REID, Terry LP '68

Singles: 7-inch

ATLANTIC 3-5 73
CAPITOL 3-5 78
EPIC 4-6 69

LPs: 10/12-inch

ATLANTIC 8-12 73
CAPITOL 5-10 78
EPIC 10-15 68-69

REILLY, Mike P&R '71

Singles: 7-inch

PARAMOUNT 3-5 70-71

REINER, Carl, & Mel Brooks LP '73

LPs: 10/12-inch

CAPITOL (1600 series) 15-25 61
CAPITOL (2900 series) 10-15 68
W.B. (2741 "2000 & Thirteen") 5-10 73
W.B. (2744 "2000 Years with Carl Reiner & Mel Brooks") 15-25 73
(Three-disc set.)
WORLD PACIFIC (1401 "2000 Years with Carl Reiner & Mel Brooks") 25-35 60

REIRRUC, Det: see DET REIRRUC

REISMAN, Joe, & His Orch. P&R '56

Singles: 78 rpm

RCA 4-8 55-57

Singles: 7-inch

LANDA 5-10 61
RCA 10-20 55-59
ROULETTE 5-10 59-60

EPs: 7-inch

RCA 5-10 56

LPs: 10/12-inch

CAMDEN 5-10 72
RCA 15-30 56
ROULETTE 10-20 59-60

Also see DE CASTRO SISTERS
Also see VALLI, June

REJOICE P&R '68

Singles: 7-inch

DUNHILL 4-6 68-69

LPs: 10/12-inch

DUNHILL 10-15 69

Members: Tom Brown; Nancy Brown.

REMBRANDTS LP '91

LPs: 10/12-inch

ATCO 5-8 90

RENAISSANCE LP '73

Singles: 7-inch

I.R.S. 3-4 82
SIRE (Except 1022) 3-5 76-78
SIRE (1022 "Northern Lights") 12-18 78
(Picture disc. Promotional issue only.)

LPs: 10/12-inch

CAPITOL 8-12 72-78
ELEKTRA (74068 "Renaissance") 15-25 69
I.R.S. 5-8 81-83
MFSL (099 "Scheherazade and Other Stories") 25-40 82
SIRE 8-10 74-79
SINGCORD 8-10 76-77
SOVEREIGN 8-12 73

Members: John Tout; Mike Dunford; Jim McCarty; Annie Haslam; Keith Relf; Jon Camp; Terry Sullivan; Louis Cennamo; Jane Relf.

Also see ARMAGEDDON
Also see HASLAM, Annie
Also see RELF, Keith

RENAISSANCE LP '71

Singles: 7-inch

RANWOOD 3-5 71

LPs: 10/12-inch

RANWOOD 5-10 70

RENARD, Jacques, & Orch. P&R '30

Singles: 78 rpm

BRUNSWICK 3-8 30-45

RENAY, Diane P&R/LP '64

Singles: 7-inch

ATCO 5-10 62-63
D MAN (101 "Can't Help Lovin' ") 15-25
DICE (8018 "Navy Blue") 15-20 87
ERIC 3-4 70s
FONTANA 8-15 69
MGM (13335 "I Had a Dream") 10-20 64
NEW VOICE 5-10 65
REX (293 "Maybe") 15-25
20TH FOX 8-15 64
U.A. (50048 "Please Gypsy") 10-15 66

LPs: 10/12-inch

20TH FOX (TF-3133 "Navy Blue") 25-40 64
(Monaural.)
20TH FOX (TFS-3133 "Navy Blue") 30-50 64
(Stereo.)

RENDER, Rudy R&B '49

Singles: 78 rpm

LONDON 4-6 49-51

Singles: 7-inch

DOT 4-8 60-61
EDISON INT'L 4-8 59
LONDON 5-10 51

RENE, Delia R&B '81

Singles: 7-inch

AIRWAVE 3-5 81

RENE, Googie R&B '60

Singles: 78 rpm

CLASS 8-15 57-58

Singles: 7-inch

CLASS 5-15 57-66
KAPP 4-6 62
NEW BAG 4-6 67
REED 5-10 60
RENDEZVOUS 8-12 60

Picture Sleeves

RENDEZVOUS 10-20 60

LPs: 10/12-inch

CLASS 15-30 59-63

RENÉ, Henri, & His Orch. P&R '40

Singles: 78 rpm

RCA 3-5 48-56
STANDARD 3-5 52-53
VICTOR 3-6 40-47

Singles: 7-inch

DECCA 3-6 62
IMPERIAL 4-8 59
RCA 4-8 51-56
STANDARD 4-8 52-53

Picture Sleeves

RCA 5-10 55

EPs: 7-inch

CAMDEN 5-10 54-57
RCA 5-10 53-56

LPs: 10/12-inch

CAMDEN 10-20 54-57
KAPP 5-10 67
RCA (Except 1046 & 3000 series) 10-20 56-61
RCA (1046 "Music for Bachelors") 25-50 54
(Cover pictures Jayne Mansfield, although she is not heard on the disc.)
RCA (3000 series) 15-25 53
(10-inch LPs.)

Also see BELL SISTERS

RENE & ANGELA R&B '80

Singles: 12-inch

MERCURY 4-6 85-86

Singles: 7-inch

CAPITOL 3-5 80-83
MERCURY 3-4 85-86

Picture Sleeves

MERCURY 3-4 85-86

LPs: 10/12-inch

CAPITOL 5-10 80-83
MERCURY 5-8 85-86

RENE & RAY *P&R '62*

Singles: 7-inch

DONNA (1360 "Queen of My Heart") 10-15 62
DONNA (1368 "Too Late") 10-15 62

RENE & RENE *P&R '64*

Singles: 7-inch

ABC 3-5 73
ABC-PAR 4-8 65
ARU 4-8 64
CERTRON 3-5 71
COBRA 4-8 65
COLUMBIA 4-8 64
EPIC 3-6 69
FALCON 4-8 68
JOX 8-10 64-66
WHITE WHALE 3-6 68-69

Picture Sleeves

COLUMBIA 8-12 64

LPs: 10/12-inch

CERTRON 8-10 70
EPIC 10-15 69
WHITE WHALE 10-15 68
Members: Rene Ornelas; J. Ramirez.

RENFRO, Anthony *R&B '76*
(Anthony C. Renfro Orchestra)

Singles: 7-inch

RENFRO (43 "Gloria's Theme") 3-5 76
RENFRO (122 "This Is Our Moment of Love") 25-50

RENO, Mike, & Ann Wilson *P&R '84*

Singles: 7-inch

COLUMBIA 3-4 84

Picture Sleeves

COLUMBIA 3-4 84
Also see LOVERBOY
Also see WILSON, Ann

RENRUT, Icky
(Ike Turner)

Singles: 7-inch

STEVENS (104 "Jack Rabbit") 25-35 59
STEVENS (107 "Hey - Hey") 25-35 59
Also see TURNER, Ike

REO, Diamond: see DIAMOND REO

REPARATA *P&R '65*
(With the Delrons; Mary Aiese)

Singles: 7-inch

BIG TREE 4-6 71
KAPP 5-10 69-70
LAURIE 4-6 72
MALA 5-10 67-68
NORTH AMERICAN MUSIC 4-6 74
POLYDOR 4-6 75
RCA 10-15 65-67
WORLD ARTISTS 5-10 64-65

LPs: 10/12-inch

AVCO EMBASSY 10-20 70
WORLD ARTISTS (3006 "Whenever a Teenager Cries") 40-60 65
Members: Mary Aiese; Sheila Reillie; Carol Drobnicki; Nanette Licari; Lorraine Mazzola; Cookie Sirico.

REPLACEMENTS *LP '86*

Singles: 7-inch

SIRE 3-5 85-90
TWIN TONE 3-5 82-84

Picture Sleeves

SIRE 3-5 89

LPs: 10/12-inch

SIRE 5-10 85-90
TWIN/TONE 5-10 84

Promotional LPs

SIRE ("Interview with Paul Westerberg") 20-25 85
Members: Paul Westerberg; Tom Stinson; Chris Mars.

RESTIVO, Johnny *P&R '59*

Singles: 7-inch

EPIC (9537 "My Reputation") 10-15 62
RCA (47-7559 "The Shape I'm In") ... 10-15 59
(Monaural.)
RCA (61-7559 "The Shape I'm In") ... 25-50 59
(Stereo.)
RCA (7601 "Dear Someone") 10-15 59
RCA (7636 "Come Closer") 10-15 59
RCA (7697 "High School Play") 10-15 60
RCA (7758 "I Can't Take It") 10-15 60
RCA (7818 "Two Crazy Kids") 10-15 60
20TH FOX (260 "Sweet Lovin' ") 10-15 61
20TH FOX (279 "Doctor Love") 10-15 61

Picture Sleeves

RCA (7559 "The Shape I'm In") 20-30 59
RCA (7601 "Dear Someone") 15-25 59
20TH FOX (279 "Doctor Love") 15-25 61

LPs: 10/12-inch

RCA (LPM-2149 "Oh Johnny") 40-60 59
(Monaural.)
RCA (LSP-2149 "Oh Johnny") 50-100 59
(Stereo.)
Session: King Curtis.
Also see KING CURTIS

RESTLESS HEART *C&W '85*

Singles: 7-inch

RCA (Except 28487) 3-4 85-91
RCA (28487 "Why Does It Have to Be") 10-15 87
(Picture disc. Promotional issue only.)

Picture Sleeves

RCA 3-4

LPs: 10/12-inch

RCA 5-8 85-91

RETURN TO FOREVER *LP '73*

Singles: 7-inch

COLUMBIA 3-5 77-79
POLYDOR 3-5 75

LPs: 10/12-inch

COLUMBIA 5-10 76-79
ECM 8-10 75
POLYDOR 8-12 73-75
Members: Chick Corea; Lenny White; Stanley Clarke; Al DiMeola.
Also see CLARKE, Stanely
Also see COREA, Chick
Also see DI MEOLA, Al
Also see WHITE, Lenny

REUNION *P&R '74*

Singles: 7-inch

MR. G. 4-8 68
RCA 3-5 74-75
Also see OHIO EXPRESS

REVELATION *P&R/R&B '76*

Singles: 7-inch

COMBINE 4-8 67
HANDSHAKE 3-5 80-82
MERCURY 3-5 70
MUSIC FACTORY 4-8 68
RCA 3-5 79
RSO 3-5 76

LPs: 10/12-inch

HANDSHAKE 5-10 82
MERCURY 8-12 70
RCA 5-10 79

REVELS *P&R/R&B '59*

Singles: 7-inch

NORGOLDE (103 "Dead Mans' Stroll") 30-50 59
NORGOLDE (103 "Midnight Stroll") .. 10-15 59
NORGOLDE (104 "Foo Man Choo") 10-20 59

REVENGE *LP '90*

LPs: 10/12-inch

CAPITOL 5-8 90

REVERBERI *LP '76*

Singles: 7-inch

U.A. 3-5 77

LPs: 10/12-inch

U.A. 5-10 76

REVERE, Paul, & Raiders *P&R '61*
(Raiders; "Featuring Mark Lindsay")

Singles: 7-inch

("The Judge") 15-25 69
(Promotional 33 rpm for Pontiac GTO. No label name or selection number used.)
APEX (106 "Beatnik Sticks") 50-100 60
(First issue.)
COLUMBIA (10126 "Gonna Have a Good Time") 3-5 75
COLUMBIA (42814 thru 42373) 8-15 63-65
COLUMBIA (43375 "Steppin' Out") 4-8 65
(Black vinyl, whether commercial or promo.)
COLUMBIA (43375 "Steppin' Out") ... 15-25 65
(Colored vinyl. Promotional issue only.)
COLUMBIA (43461 "Just Like Me") 4-8 65
(Black vinyl, whether commercial or promo.)
COLUMBIA (43461 "Just Like Me") ... 15-25 65
(Colored vinyl. Promotional issue only.)
COLUMBIA (43556 "Kicks") 4-8 66
(Black vinyl, whether commercial or promo.)
COLUMBIA (43556 "Kicks") 15-25 66
(Colored vinyl. Promotional issue only.)
COLUMBIA (43678 "Hungry") 4-8 66
(Black vinyl, whether commercial or promo.)
COLUMBIA (43678 "Hungry") 15-25 66
(Colored vinyl. Promotional issue only.)
COLUMBIA (43810 "The Great Airplane Strike") 4-8 66
(Black vinyl, whether commercial or promo.)
COLUMBIA (43810 "The Great Airplane Strike") 15-25 66
(Colored vinyl. Promotional issue only.)
COLUMBIA (43907 "Good Thing") 4-8 67
(Black vinyl, whether commercial or promo.)
COLUMBIA (43907 "Good Thing") 15-25 67
(Colored vinyl. Promotional issue only.)
COLUMBIA (44018 thru 45898) 3-6 68-74
COLUMBIA (105499 "SS 396"/"Corvair Baby") 8-12 66
(Promotional issue only.)
DRIVE 3-5 76
GARDENA (106 "Beatnik Sticks") 20-30 60
GARDENA (115 "Paul Revere's Ride") 20-30 61
GARDENA (116 "Like Long Hair") ... 20-30 61
GARDENA (118 "Like, Charleston") . 15-25 61
GARDENA (123 "All Night Long") 15-25 62
GARDENA (127 "Like, Bluegrass") ... 15-25 62
GARDENA (131 "Shake It Up") 15-25 62
GARDENA (137 "Tall Cool One") 15-25 62
JERDEN (807 "So Fine") 15-25 63
RAIDER AMERICA 5-10 82
SANDE (101 "Louie Louie") 25-35 63
TEEN SCOOP ("Interview") 15-25 60s
(Square cardboard picture disc. Included in magazine.)
20TH FOX 3-5 76

Picture Sleeves

COLUMBIA 8-15 66-69

EPs: 7-inch

JERDEN (JRLS-7004 "In the Beginning") 35-45 66
(Juke box issue only. Includes title strips.)

LPs: 10/12-inch

BACK-TRAC 5-8 85
COLUMBIA (12 "Two Great Selling LPs") 15-20 69
COLUMBIA (462 "Greatest Hits") 20-25 67
COLUMBIA (2307 thru 2721) 20-30 65-67
(Monaural.)
COLUMBIA (2755 "Christmas Present and Past") 40-60 67
(Monaural.)
COLUMBIA (2805 "Goin' to Memphis") 20-30 68
(Monaural.)
COLUMBIA (9107 thru 9521) 25-40 65-67
(Stereo.)
COLUMBIA (9555 "Christmas Present and Past") 40-60 67
(Stereo.)
COLUMBIA (9605 "Goin' to Memphis") 20-25 68
(Stereo.)

COLUMBIA (9665 thru 9964) 10-20 68-70
COLUMBIA (30000 series)................. 8-15 71-76
COLUMBIA SPECIAL PROD. (141714 "The Judge") 150-200 69
(Promotional issue only.)
HARMONY 10-15 70-72
GARDENA (1000 "Like Long Hair").................................. 250-300 61
JERDEN (7004 "In the Beginning") 75-125 66
PICKWICK.................................. 10-15 70s
RAIDER.................................... 10-15 82
SANDE (1001 "Paul Revere and the Raiders")................................ 250-300 63
SEARS 40-50
(Special Products Sears promotional issue.)
Members: Mark Lindsay; Freddy Weller; Paul Revere; Keith Allison; Joe Correro Jr; Carl Driggs; Omar Martinez; Doug Heath; Ron Foos; Danny Krause; Mike Smith; Drake Levin; Philip Volk; Mike Holiday.
Also see BROTHERHOOD
Also see CYRKLE / Paul Revere & Raiders
Also see LINDSAY, Mark
Also see MIKE & DEAN
Also see WELLER, Freddy

REX, T.: see T REX

REYNOLDS, Burt C&W/P&R '80

Singles: 7-inch

MCA.. 3-5 80
MERCURY 3-5 73-74

Picture Sleeves

MCA.. 3-5 80

LPs: 10/12-inch

MERCURY 8-12 73

REYNOLDS, Debbie P&R '57

Singles: 78 rpm

CORAL 5-10 57
MGM.. 4-8 55-57

Singles: 7-inch

ABC 3-5 74
ABC-PAR 4-8 65
BEVERLY HILLS........................ 3-5 72
CORAL 5-10 57-58
DOT... 4-8 59-63
JANUS....................................... 3-5 70
MCA.. 3-4 80s
MGM (11000 & 12000 series)............ 5-10 55-59
MGM (13000 series)...................... 4-8 63-66
PARAMOUNT 3-5 73

Picture Sleeves

DOT... 5-10 60
MGM.. 8-15 58-66

EPs: 7-inch

CORAL 10-20 58
MGM.. 10-20 55

LPs: 10/12-inch

DOT (Except 25295)....................... 15-20 59-63
DOT (25295 "Am I That Easy to Forget")................................. 15-25 60
(Black vinyl.)
DOT (25295 "Am I That Easy to Forget")................................. 50-75 60
(Colored vinyl.)
MGM.. 15-25 60-66
METRO...................................... 10-15 65
Also see CARPENTER, Carleton, & Debbie Reynolds
Also see FISHER, Eddie, & Debbie Reynolds

REYNOLDS, Jeannie R&B '75

Singles: 7-inch

CASABLANCA 3-5 75

REYNOLDS, Jody P&R/R&B '58

Singles: 78 rpm

DEMON (1507 "Endless Sleep")....... 25-50 58

Singles: 7-inch

ABC 3-5 73
BRENT 4-8 63
COLLECTABLES 3-4 80s
DEMON 10-20 58-59
PULSAR 3-6 69
SMASH...................................... 4-8 63
TITAN 4-8 66

LPs: 10/12-inch

TRU-GEMS 8-10 78

Also see CASEY, Al
Also see CLARK, Sanford

REYNOLDS, Jody, & Bobbie Gentry

Singles: 7-inch

TITAN.. 4-8 67
Also see GENTRY, Bobbie

REYNOLDS, Jody / Olympics

Singles: 7-inch

DEMON 10-20 58
LIBERTY 4-8 63
TITAN.. 4-8 62

Picture Sleeves

DEMON (1801 "Endless Sleep")....... 15-25 58
Also see OLYMPICS

REYNOLDS, Jody, & Storms

Singles: 7-inch

INDIGO (127 "Thunder")................. 15-25 61
Also see CASEY, Al
Also see REYNOLDS, Jody

REYNOLDS, L.J. R&B '71
(With Chocolate Syrup)

Singles: 12-inch

CAPITOL.................................... 4-6 82

Singles: 7-inch

CAPITOL.................................... 3-5 81-82
FANTASY 3-4 85-87
LAW-TON 3-5 71-72
MAINSTREAM 4-6 69
MERCURY.................................. 3-4 84

LPs: 10/12-inch

CAPITOL.................................... 5-10 81-82
MERCURY.................................. 5-8 84
Also see CHOCOLATE SYRUP
Also see DRAMATICS

REYNOLDS, Lawrence P&R '69

Singles: 7-inch

COLUMBIA 3-5 72
W.B. 3-6 69-70

LPs: 10/12-inch

W.B. 8-12 69

RHEIMS, Robert LP '59
(Robert Rheims Carrolers)

Singles: 7-inch

RHEIMS 3-5 59

EPs: 7-inch

RHEIMS 4-8 59

LPs: 10/12-inch

MISTLETOE............................... 5-8 75
RHEIMS 5-15 58-63
U.A. 5-8 72-74

RHINOCEROS LP '68

Singles: 7-inch

ELEKTRA................................... 4-6 69-70

LPs: 10/12-inch

ELEKTRA................................... 10-20 68-70
Members: Alan Gerber; Billy Mundi; Michael Fonfara; John Finley; Danny Weis; Jerry Penrod; Peter Hodgson.
Also see EARTH OPERA

RHODES, Emitt LP '70

Singles: 7-inch

DUNHILL.................................... 3-5 70-73

LPs: 10/12-inch

A&M... 10-15 70
DUNHILL.................................... 8-12 70-73
Also see MERRY-GO-ROUND

RHODES, Todd R&B '48

Singles: 78 rpm

KING 10-15 48-54
MODERN 10-15 49
SENSATION (Except 6)................. 10-20 47-49
SENSATION (6 "Blues for the Red Boy")...................................... 25-35 47
VITACOUSTIC............................ 10-20 47

Singles: 7-inch

KING (4469 "Gin Gin Gin") 50-75 51
KING (4486 "Good Man")............... 30-50 51
KING (4509 "Your Daddy's Doggin' Around") 30-50 51
(Black vinyl.)
KING (4509 "Your Daddy's Doggin' Around").................................. 60-80 51
(Colored vinyl.)
KING (4528 "Rocket 69")............... 60-80 52
KING (4556 thru 4601) 15-25 52-53
(Lavern Baker is the vocalist on one side of each of the four King issues in the 4556-4601 series)
KING (4648 thru 4775) 10-20 53-54

EPs: 7-inch

KING... 30-40 52-54

LPs: 10/12-inch

KING (88 "Todd Rhodes Plays the Hits")..................................... 75-100 53
KING (658 "Dance Music")............. 35-55 60
Also see BAKER, Lavern
Also see BARTHOLOMEW, Dave

RHYTHM R&B '76

Singles: 7-inch

POLYDOR.................................. 3-5 76

RHYTHM CORPS LP '88

LPs: 10/12-inch

PASHA 5-8 88

RHYTHM HERITAGE P&R/R&B '75

Singles: 12-inch

ABC 4-8 78

Singles: 7-inch

ABC 3-5 75-78

LPs: 10/12-inch

ABC 5-10 76-77
Members: Steve Barri; Mike Omartian; Luther Waters.

RHYTHM MAKERS R&B '76

Singles: 7-inch

VIGOR....................................... 3-5 76

LPs: 10/12-inch

VIGOR....................................... 8-10 76

RHYZE R&B '80

Singles: 7-inch

SAM.. 3-5 80
20TH FOX 3-5 81

LPs: 10/12-inch

20TH FOX 5-10 81

RIBBONS P&R '63

Singles: 7-inch

ERA 3-5 72
MARSH..................................... 10-15 63
PARKWAY 5-10 64

RIBEIRO, Alfonso R&B '85

Singles: 7-inch

PRISM 3-4 85

RICE, Mack R&B '65
(Sir Mack Rice)

Singles: 7-inch

ATCO... 3-6 69
BLUE ROCK................................ 4-8 65
CAPITOL 15-20
LUPINE...................................... 4-8 63-64
MAX DAY................................... 5-10
MERCURY (72541 "It's All Right") 20-30 66
STAX 3-6 67-78
TRUTH 3-6 78
Also see FALCONS
Also see OLLIE & NIGHTINGALES

RICE, Sir Mack: see RICE, Mack

RICH, Buddy LP '66
(Buddy Rich Band)

Singles: 78 rpm

CLEF 4-8 54
NORGRAN.................................. 4-8 55-56

Singles: 7-inch

ARGO.. 4-8 61
CLEF 5-10 54
EVEREST................................... 3-5 71
GROOVE MERCHANT 3-5 74
MCA.. 3-4 81
NORGRAN.................................. 5-10 55-56
PACIFIC JAZZ............................. 3-6 66-67
RCA.. 3-5 76

EPs: 7–inch

NORGRAN 20-40 54-56

LPs: 10/12–inch

ARGO (676 "Playtime") 35-45 61
CLEF (684 "Gene Krupa & Buddy Rich") 100-150 56
EMARCY 10-20 65-76
GREAT AMERICAN 5-8 78
GROOVE MERCHANT 5-10 74-75
GRYPHON 5-10 79
LIBERTY 8-12 70
MCA 5-8 81
MERCURY (126 "Buddy Rich Story") 10-20 69
MERCURY (20448 "Rich vs. Roach") 50-75 59
(Monaural.)
MERCURY (20451 "Richcraft") 50-75 60
(Monaural.)
MERCURY (20461 "The Voice Is Rich") 40-60 60
(Monaural.)
MERCURY (60133 "Rich vs. Roach") 60-85 59
(Stereo.)
MERCURY (60136 "Richcraft") 60-85 60
(Stereo.)
MERCURY (60144 "The Voice Is Rich") 45-65 60
(Stereo.)
NORGRAN (26 "Swingin'") 75-125 54
NORGRAN (1031 "Sing and Swing") 60-80 55
NORGRAN (1038 "Buddy Rich and Sweets Edison") 60-80 55
NORGRAN (1052 "Swingin'") 60-80 55
NORGRAN (1078 "Wailin'") 50-75 56
NORGRAN (1086 "One for Basie") ... 50-75 56
PACIFIC JAZZ (Except 10000 series) 8-18 66-70
PACIFIC JAZZ (10000 series) 5-8 81
PAUSA 5-8 80s
RCA 8-12 72-77
ROOST 10-20 66
TRIP 8-10 76
VSP 10-15 67
VERVE (2009 "Buddy Rich Sings Johnny Mercer") 50-75 57
VERVE (8129 "Buddy Rich and Sweets Edison") 50-75 57
VERVE (8142 "Swingin'") 50-75 57
VERVE (8168 "Wailin'") 50-75 57
VERVE (8176 "One for Basie") 50-75 57
VERVE (8285 "In Miami") 50-75 58
VERVE (8425 "Blue Caravan") 30-40 62
VERVE (8471 "Burnin' Beat") 30-40 62
(Monaural.)
VERVE (8484 "Drum Battle: Gene Krupa & Buddy Rich") 25-40 62
VERVE (68471 "Burnin' Beat") 35-45 62
(Stereo.)
VERVE (68778 "Super Rich") 10-15 69
VERVE (68824 "Monster") 10-15 73
WHO'S WHO in JAZZ 5-10 78
WING 8-12 69
WORLD PACIFIC 10-15 68
Also see DAVIS, Sammy, Jr., & Buddy Rich
Also see TORME, Mel

RICH, Buddy, & Max Roach

LPs: 10/12–inch

MERCURY 5-10 81
Also see RICH, Buddy

RICH, Charlie — P&R '60

Singles: 7–inch

COLUMBIA 3-4 82
EPIC 3-5 70-81
ELEKTRA 3-5 78-81
GROOVE 4-8 63-64
HI 4-8 66-67
MERCURY 3-5 73-74
MONUMENT 3-5
PHILLIPS INT'L 15-25 59-63
RCA (Except 8000 series) 3-5 74-77
RCA (8000 series) 4-8 64-65
SSS/SUN 3-5 70s
SMASH 4-8 65-66
U.A. 3-5 78-80

Picture Sleeves

GROOVE (0020 "She Loved Everybody But Me") 10-20 63
EPIC (AE7-1065) 3-6 73
(Promotional bonus only. Title not known.)
MONUMENT 4-6

EPs: 7–inch

EPIC (1099 "Silver Linings") 8-12 76
(Promotional issue only.)

LPs: 10/12–inch

BUCKBOARD 8-10 70s
CAMDEN 8-10 70-74
CELEBRITY INT'L 5-8 91
EPIC (Except 139) 6-12 68-78
EPIC (139 "Everything You Wanted to Hear by Charlie Rich") 15-20 76
(Promotional issue only.)
ELEKTRA 5-10 80
51 WEST 5-10
GROOVE (G-1000 "Charlie Rich") 15-25 64
(Monaural.)
GROOVE (GS-1000 "Charlie Rich") 20-30 64
(Stereo.)
HARMONY 8-10 73
HI (Except 32037) 8-10 74-77
HI (32037 "Charlie Rich") 15-25 67
HILLTOP 8-10 70s
MERCURY 10-15 74
PHILLIPS INT'L (1970 "Lonely Weekends") 500-750 60
PHONORAMA 5-8 83
PICKWICK 5-10 70s
POWER PAK 8-10 74-75
RCA (Except 3000 series) 8-10 73-77
RCA (3000 series) 15-25 65-66
SSS/SUN 5-10 69-79
SMASH 15-25 65-66
SUNNYVALE 5-10 77
TIME-LIFE 5-10 81
TRIP 8-10 74
U.A. 5-10 78-79
WING 15-25 69
Session: Jordanaires; David Wills; Anita Kerr Singers.
Also see CASH, Johnny
Also see KERR, Anita
Also see LEWIS, Jerry Lee, Carl Perkins & Charlie Rich
Also see SHERIDAN, Bobby
Also see TUBB, Ernest

RICH, Charlie, & Janie Fricke — C&W '78

Singles: 7–inch

EPIC 3-5 78
Also see RICH, Charlie

RICHARD, Cliff — P&R '59

(With the Drifters; with Shadows)

Singles: 12–inch

EMI AMERICA 4-8 83

Singles: 7–inch

ABC-PAR 10-15 59-61
BIG TOP 4-8 62
CAPITOL 10-15 59
DOT 4-8 62
EMI AMERICA 3-5 79-84
EPIC 4-8 63-67
MONUMENT 3-5 70-72
ROCKET 3-5 76-79
SIRE 3-5 73
STRIPED HORSE 3-4 87
UNI 5-10 68-69
W.B. 4-6 69

Picture Sleeves

EMI AMERICA 3-5 80-81
EPIC 8-15 63-66
STRIPED HORSE 3-4 87

LPs: 10/12–inch

ABC-PAR (ABC-321 "Cliff Sings") 30-40 60
(Monaural.)
ABC-PAR (ABCS-321 "Cliff Sings").. 40-60 60
(Stereo.)
ABC-PAR (ABC-391 "Listen to Cliff") 25-35 61
(Monaural.)
ABC-PAR (ABCS-391 "Listen to Cliff") 35-45 61
(Stereo.)
EMI AMERICA 5-10 79-83
EPIC 15-25 63-65
ROCKET 5-10 76-78
Also see NEWTON-JOHN, Olivia, & Electric Light Orchestra
Also see NEWTON-JOHN, Olivia, & Cliff Richard

RICHARD, Little: see LITTLE RICHARD

RICHARD & YOUNG LIONS — P&R '66

Singles: 7–inch

PHILIPS 4-8 66-67

Picture Sleeves

PHILIPS 10-20 66
Member: Richard Bloodworth.

RICHARDS, Diane — R&B '83

Singles: 7–inch

ZOO YORK 3-4 83

RICHARDS, Keith — LP '88

Singles: 7–inch

ROLLING STONES (316 "Before They Make Me Run") 5-10 78
ROLLING STONES (39311 "Run Rudolph, Run") 4-6 79
VIRGIN (99287 "Take It So Hard") 3-4 88

Picture Sleeves

ROLLING STONES (316 "Before They Make Me Run") 10-15 78
VIRGIN (99287 "Take It So Hard") 4-6 88
(Promotional issue only.)
ROLLING STONES (316 "Before They Make Me Run") 10-15 78

LPs: 10/12–inch

VIRGIN 5-8 88
Also see ROLLING STONES

RICHARDS, Turley — P&R '70

(Richard Turley)

Singles: 7–inch

ATLANTIC 3-5 80
COLUMBIA 4-8 66-67
EPIC 3-5 76-78
KAPP 4-8 68
MGM 4-8 64
20TH FOX 4-8 65
W.B. 3-5 70

Picture Sleeves

COLUMBIA 4-8 66

LPs: 10/12–inch

ATLANTIC 5-10 80
EPIC 5-10 76
20TH FOX 10-20 65
W.B. 10-15 70-71

RICHARDSON, Jape

(With His Japettes)

Singles: 78 rpm

MERCURY 10-20 57

Singles: 7–inch

MERCURY (71219 "Beggar to a King") 20-40 57
MERCURY (71312 "Teenage Moon") 25-50 58
Also see BIG BOPPER

RICHIE, Lionel — P&R/R&B/LP '82

Singles: 12–inch

MOTOWN (Except 139) 4-8 83-86
MOTOWN (139 "Hello") 8-12 84
(Picture disc. Promotional issue only.)

Singles: 7–inch

MOTOWN 3-4 82-92

Picture Sleeves

MOTOWN 3-4 83-87

LPs: 10/12–inch

MOTOWN 5-8 82-86
Also see COMMODORES
Also see ROSS, Diana, & Lionel Ritchie
Also see U.S.A. for AFRICA

RICHIE, Lionel, & Alabama — C&W '86

Singles: 12-inch

MOTOWN (195 "Special Motown Service to Country Radio") ... 8-12 86
(Promotional issue only.)

Singles: 7-inch

MOTOWN ... 3-4 86

Also see ALABAMA
Also see RICHIE, Lionel

RICHIE'S ROOM 222 GANG — R&B '71

Singles: 7-inch

SCEPTER ... 3-5 71

RICHMOND EXTENSION — R&B '74

Singles: 7-inch

SILVER BLUE ... 3-5 74

RICK & Cast of Idoits: see DEES, Rick

RICK & KEENS — P&R '61

Singles: 7-inch

AUSTIN (303 "Peanuts") ... 35-50 61
JAMIE (1219 "Your Turn to Cry") ... 10-15 62
LE CAM (721 "Peanuts") ... 25-35 61
LE CAM (133 "Darla") ... 15-25 61
SMASH (1705 "Peanuts") ... 10-15 61
TOLLIE (9016 "Darla") ... 10-15 64
TROY ... 20-30 63

RICKLES, Don — LP '68

LPs: 10/12-inch

W.B. ... 8-12 68-69

RIDDLE, Nelson, & His Orch. — P&R '54

Singles: 78 rpm

CAPITOL ... 3-5 53-57

Singles: 7-inch

CAPITOL ... 4-10 53-62
EPIC ... 3-6 67
LIBERTY ... 3-6 67
REPRISE ... 3-6 63-66
20TH FOX ... 3-6 66
VERVE ... 5-8 59

Picture Sleeves

CAPITOL ... 5-10 60
EPIC ... 4-8 67

EPs: 7-inch

CAPITOL ... 8-15 55-59
VERVE ... 6-12 59

LPs: 10/12-inch

ALSHIRE ... 5-10 70-71
AVON ... 5-8 70
CAPITOL ... 5-20 55-78
DAYBREAK ... 5-8 73
HARMONY ... 5-10 69
LIBERTY ... 5-10 67
MPS ... 5-10 73
PICKWICK ... 5-10 65
REPRISE ... 5-15 63-65
SOLID STATE ... 5-10 67
SUNSET ... 5-10 68
U.A. ... 5-10 68
VERVE ... 5-15 59

You'll find many more listings by this artist in *The Official Price Guide to Movie/TV Soundtracks and Original Cast Albums,* containing over 8,000 listings.

Also see FITZGERALD, Ella
Also see MARTIN, Dean / Nelson Riddle
Also see PETERSON, Oscar
Also see RONSTADT, Linda

RIDGELEY, Andrew — LP '90

LPs: 10/12-inch

COLUMBIA ... 5-8 90

Also see WHAM!

RIDGWAY, Stan — LP '86

Singles: 7-inch

I.R.S. ... 3-4 86

LPs: 10/12-inch

I.R.S. ... 5-8 86

Also see WALL of VOODOO

RIGHT CHOICE — R&B '88

Singles: 7-inch

MOTOWN ... 3-4 88

RIGHT KIND — R&B '68

Singles: 7-inch

GALAXY ... 4-8 68

RIGHTEOUS BROTHERS — P&R '63

Singles: 7-inch

HAVEN ... 3-5 74-76
MGM ... 3-5 78-79
MGM CELEBRITY SCENE (8 "Righteous Brothers") ... 35-45 66
(Boxed set of five singles with bio insert and juke box title strips.)
MGM GOLDEN CIRCLE ... 3-4
MOONGLOW ... 5-10 63-66
PHILLES (Except 130) ... 5-10 64-66
PHILLES (130 "Ebb Tide") ... 1000-1500 65
(Custom label. Has Phil Spector's picture on the label. Promotional issue only.)
PHILLES (130 "Ebb Tide") ... 5-10 65
(No picture on label.)
POLYDOR ... 3-5
VERVE ... 4-8 65-70
VERVE SOUNDS of FAME ... 3-4 70s

Picture Sleeves

PHILLES ... 8-12 65-66
VERVE ... 5-10 66-67

EPs: 7-inch

MOONGLOW (71004 "Best of the Righteous Brothers") ... 10-15 66
(Juke box issue.)

LPs: 10/12-inch

HAVEN ... 10-15 74-75
MGM ... 10-15 70-73
MOONGLOW (1001 "Right Now") ... 20-30 63
MOONGLOW (1002 "Some Blue Eyed Soul") ... 20-30 64
MOONGLOW (1003 "This Is New") .. 20-30 65
MOONGLOW (1004 "Best of the Righteous Brothers) ... 20-30 66
PHILLES (4007 "You've Lost That Lovin' Feeling) ... 25-45 64
PHILLES (4008 "Just Once in My Life") ... 25-45 65
PHILLES (4009 "Back to Back") ... 25-45 65
RHINO ... 8-12 89
VERVE (5001 "Soul & Inspiration") ... 15-20 66
VERVE (5004 "Go Ahead and Cry") 15-20 66
VERVE (5010 "Sayin' Something") ... 15-20 67
VERVE (5020 "Greatest Hits") ... 15-20 67
VERVE (5031 "Souled Out") ... 15-20 66
VERVE (5058 "One for the Road") ... 15-20 68
VERVE (5076 "Re-Birth") ... 15-20 69
(With Jimmy Walker instead of Bill Medley.)

Members: Bill Medley; Bobby Hatfield.
Also see HATFIELD, Bobby
Also see MEDLEY, Bill
Also see PARAMOURS

RILEY, Billy Lee — P&R '72

(With His Little Green Men)

Singles: 78 rpm

SUN ... 25-75 56-57

Singles: 7-inch

ATLANTIC ... 3-6 68
BRUNSWICK (55085 "Rockin' on the Moon") ... 150-250 58
ENTRANCE ... 3-5 72
GNP ... 4-8 66
HIP ... 4-8 68
HOME of the BLUES (233 "Flip, Flop and Fly") ... 20-30 61
MERCURY ... 5-10 64-65
MOJO ... 4-8 67
SUN (245 "Rock with Me Baby") ... 50-75 56
SUN (260 "Flying Saucers Rock & Roll") ... 50-75 57
SUN (277 "Red Hot") ... 25-50 57
SUN (289 "Wouldn't You Know") ... 10-20 58
SUN (313 "No Name Girl") ... 10-20 58
SUN (322 "Got the Water Boiling") ... 50-75 59
SSS/SUN ... 4-6 69-70

LPs: 10/12-inch

CROWN ... 15-20 63
GNP ... 15-20 66
MERCURY ... 15-20 64-65
MOJO ... 15-20 79

Also see MEGATONS

RILEY, Cheryl Pepsii — P&R/LP '88

Singles: 7-inch

COLUMBIA ... 3-4 88

Singles: 7-inch

COLUMBIA ... 3-4 88

Picture Sleeves

COLUMBIA ... 3-4 88

LPs: 10/12-inch

COLUMBIA ... 5-8 88

RILEY, Jeannie C. — C&W/P&R/LP '68

(With the Red River Symphony)

Singles: 7-inch

CAPITOL ... 3-6 69
CROSS COUNTRY ... 3-4 79
GARPAX ... 3-4 80
GOD'S COUNTRY ... 3-5 75
MCA ... 3-4 82
MGM ... 3-5 71-74
MERCURY ... 3-5 74
PLANTATION (Black vinyl) ... 3-4 68-72
PLANTATION (Colored vinyl) ... 4-8 68-72
W.B. ... 3-5 76

Picture Sleeves

PLANTATION ... 4-8 68-72

EPs: 7-inch

PLANTATION ... 5-10 68

LPs: 10/12-inch

ALBUM GLOBE ... 5-8 80s
CAPITOL ... 8-12 69
CROSS COUNTRY ... 5-10 79
HSRD/PLEASANT SOUNDS ... 5-8 82
HEARTWARMING ... 4-8 79
LITTLE DARLIN' ... 10-15 68
MGM ... 10-20 72-74
OUT of TOWN DIST ... 5-8 82
PICKWICK ... 5-10 70s
PLANTATION ... 5-12 68-82
POWER PAK ... 5-8 80s
SONGBIRD ... 4-8 81-83
TRIP ... 8-12 74

Also see CASH, Johnny / Jerry Lee Lewis / Jeanie C. Riley
Also see CASH, Johnny / Jeanie C. Riley

RIMSHOTS — R&B '72

Singles: 7-inch

A-1 (4000 "Soul Train") ... 4-8 72
A-1 (4002 "Save That Thing") ... 8-12 72
ASTROSCOPE ... 3-5 74
HAPPY HEARTS ... 3-5
STANG ... 3-5 76-77

LPs: 10/12-inch

STANG ... 5-10 76

RINGS — P&R/LP '81

Singles: 7-inch

MCA ... 3-5 81

LPs: 10/12-inch

MCA ... 5-10 81

RINKY DINKS — P&R/R&B '58

(Featuring Bobby Darin)

Singles: 7-inch

ATCO (6121 "Early in the Morning") . 25-50 58
(Previously issued as by the Ding Dongs. Later issued as by "Bobby Darin & the Rinky Dinks.")

Also see DARIN, Bobby
Also see DING DONGS

RIOS, Augie — P&R '58

(With the Notations)

Singles: 7-inch

MGM ... 4-8 60-64
METRO ... 5-10 58-59
SHELLEY ... 10-20 63-64

RIOS, Miguel — LP '70

Singles: 7-inch

A&M ... 3-5 70

Picture Sleeves

A&M ... 3-5 70

LPs: 10/12-inch

A&M ... 10-15 70

RIOS, Waldo de los — P&R/LP '71

LPs: 10/12-inch

U.A. .... 5-10 — 71

RIOT — LP '81

Singles: 7-inch

MOTOWN .... 3-5 — 74

LPs: 10/12-inch

CBS .... 5-8 — 88
CAPITOL .... 5-8 — 80-82
ELEKTRA .... 5-8 — 81-82
FIRE-SIGN (87001 "Rock City") .... 15-25 — 78
MOTOWN .... 8-10 — 74
QUALITY/RFC .... 5-8 — 84

RIP CHORDS — P&R '63

Singles: 7-inch

COLUMBIA (42687 "Here I Stand") ... 10-15 — 63
COLUMBIA (42812 "Gone") .... 10-15 — 63
(Black vinyl.)
COLUMBIA (42812 "Gone") .... 20-30 — 63
(Colored vinyl. Promotional issue only.)
COLUMBIA (42921 "Hey Little Cobra") .... 10-15 — 63
(Black vinyl.)
COLUMBIA (42921 "Hey Little Cobra") .... 20-30 — 63
(Colored vinyl. Promotional issue only.)
COLUMBIA (43035 "Three Window Coupe") .... 10-15 — 64
(Black vinyl.)
COLUMBIA (43035 "Three Window Coupe") .... 20-30 — 64
(Colored vinyl. Promotional issue only.)
COLUMBIA (43093 "One-Piece, Topless Bathing Suit") .... 10-15 — 64
COLUMBIA (43221 "Don't Be Scared") .... 10-15 — 64
COLUMBIA (3-42000 series) .... 10-20 — 63
(Compact 33 singles.)

Picture Sleeves

COLUMBIA (42687 "Here I Stand") ... 15-25 — 63
(Promotional issue only.)
COLUMBIA (42812 "Gone") .... 15-25 — 63

LPs: 10/12-inch

COLUMBIA (2151 "Hey Little Cobra") .... 25-35 — 64
(Monaural.)
COLUMBIA (2216 "Three Window Coupe") .... 30-40 — 64
(Monaural.)
COLUMBIA (8951 "Hey Little Cobra") .... 25-35 — 64
(Stereo.)
COLUMBIA (9016 "Three Window Coupe") .... 30-40 — 64
(Stereo.)
Members: Bruce Johnston; Terry Melcher; Phil Stewart; Ernie Bringas; Steve Barri; Phil Sloan; Glen Campbell; Hal Blaine; Tommy Tedesco.
Also see BRUCE & TERRY
Also see CAMPBELL, Glen
Also see FANTASTIC BAGGYS
Also see MIKE & DEAN

RIPERTON, Minnie — LP '74

Singles: 12-inch

EPIC .... 4-8 — 77

Singles: 7-inch

CAPITOL .... 3-5 — 79-81
EPIC .... 3-5 — 74-77
GRT .... 3-5 — 72
JANUS .... 3-5 — 75-76

LPs: 10/12-inch

ACCORD .... 5-8 — 82
CAPITOL .... 5-10 — 79-81
EPIC .... 10-12 — 74-77
51 WEST .... 5-8 — 80s
GRT .... 10-15 — 70
JANUS .... 8-12 — 74
Also see DAVIS, Andrea
Also see JONES, Quincy
Also see ROTARY CONNECTION

RIPPINGTONS Featuring Russ Freeman — LP '88

LPs: 10/12-inch

GRP .... 5-8 — 89
PASSPORT .... 5-8 — 88
Member: Steve Reid.

RIPPLE — P&R/R&B '73

Singles: 7-inch

GRC .... 3-5 — 73-75
SALSOUL .... 3-5 — 77-78

LPs: 10/12-inch

GRC .... 8-10 — 74
SALSOUL .... 5-8 — 77

RIPPLES & WAVES Plus Michael (Jackson Five)

Singles: 7-inch

STEELTOWN (688 "Let Me Carry Your School Books") .... 25-50 — 69
(Mono. "Steeltown" is in all upper case letters on label.)
STEELTOWN (688 "Let Me Carry Your School Books") .... 50-75 — 69
(Stereo. "Steeltown" is in upper and lower case letters.)
Also see JACKSONS

RITCHARD, Cyril — LP '61

LPs: 10/12-inch

RIVERSIDE .... 8-15 — 61-62

RITCHIE FAMILY — P&R/R&B/LP '75

Singles: 12-inch

MARLIN .... 4-8 — 76
RCA .... 4-6 — 82

Singles: 7-inch

CASABLANCA .... 3-5 — 79-80
MARLIN .... 3-5 — 76-78
RCA .... 3-4 — 82-83
20TH FOX .... 3-5 — 75

LPs: 10/12-inch

CASABLANCA .... 5-10 — 79-80
MARLIN .... 5-10 — 76-78
RCA .... 5-8 — 82
20TH FOX .... 5-10 — 75

RITENOUR, Lee — LP '77

Singles: 7-inch

ELEKTRA .... 3-4 — 81-82
EPIC .... 3-5 — 76-80

Picture Sleeves

ELEKTRA .... 3-4 — 81

LPs: 10/12-inch

ELEKTRA .... 5-8 — 78-84
EPIC .... 5-10 — 76-80
GRP .... 5-8 — 85
JVC .... 5-10 — 78
MFSL (147 "Captain Fingers") .... 20-30 — 85
MUSICIAN .... 5-8 — 82
Also see ANGELO
Also see FOURPLAY
Also see GRUSIN, Dave, & Lee Ritenour

RITTER, Tex — C&W/P&R '44
(With the Texans; with Plainsmen)

Singles: 78 rpm

CAPITOL .... 5-10 — 44-57
CHAMPION .... 10-20 — 30s
CONQUEROR .... 10-20 — 30s
DECCA .... 5-10 — 30s-41
U.A. ("High Noon Ballad – Do Not Forsake Me") .... 20-40 — 52
(Single-sided disc. Promotional issue only.)

Singles: 7-inch

CAPITOL (1100 thru 3900 series) .... 5-10 — 50-58
(Purple labels.)
CAPITOL (2000 thru 4000 series) .... 3-6 — 68-76
(Orange labels.)
CAPITOL (4000 thru 5900 series) .... 4-8 — 58-67
CAPITOL (10485 "High Noon") .... 15-25 — 52
(Single-sided disc. Promotional issue only.)

Picture Sleeves

CAPITOL .... 4-8 — 68

EPs: 7-inch

CAPITOL (Except 431) .... 10-20 — 59-60
CAPITOL (431 "Tex Ritter Sings") .... 20-40 — 53

LPs: 10/12-inch

ALBUM GLOBE .... 5-8 — 80s
BUCKBOARD .... 5-8 — 80s
CAPITOL (213 thru 467) .... 8-12 — 69-71
CAPITOL (971 "Songs from the Western Screen") .... 25-40 — 58
CAPITOL (1100 "Psalms") .... 20-30 — 59
CAPITOL (T-1292 "Blood on the Saddle") .... 15-25 — 60
(Monaural.)
CAPITOL (ST-1292 "Blood on the Saddle") .... 15-30 — 60
(Stereo.)
CAPITOL (SM-1292 "Blood on the Saddle") .... 5-10 — 78
CAPITOL (1623 thru 2800) .... 10-20 — 61-68
CAPITOL (W-1562 "The Lincoln Hymns") .... 25-30 — 61
(Monaural.)
CAPITOL (SW-1562 "The Lincoln Hymns") .... 30-35 — 61
(Stereo.)
CAPITOL (4004 "Cowboy Favorites") .... 50-75 — 53
(10-inch LP.)
CORONET .... 8-12 — 60s
HILLTOP .... 10-15 — 60s
LA BREA (8036 "Jamboree") .... 30-40 — 62
PICKWICK/HILLTOP .... 6-12 — 66-68
PREMIER 5-10
SHASTA .... 8-12 — 60s
SPIN-O-RAMA .... 8-12 — 60s
Session: Rio Grande River Boys.
Also see KENTON, Stan, & Tex Ritter

RIVERA, Hector — R&B '66

Singles: 7-inch

BARRY .... 5-10 — 66

LPs: 10/12-inch

EPIC .... 10-20 — 61
WING .... 10-20 — 60

RIVERS, Joan — LP '93

LPs: 10/12-inch

BUDDAH .... 5-10 — 69
GEFFEN .... 5-8 — 83
W.B. .... 10-15 — 65

RIVERS, Johnny — P&R/LP '64
(Johnny Ramistella)

Singles: 7-inch

ATLANTIC .... 3-5 — 74
BIG TREE .... 3-5 — 77-78
CAPITOL .... 4-8 — 62-64
CHANCELLOR .... 8-12 — 61-62
CORAL .... 5-10 — 64
CUB (9047 "Everyday") .... 10-20 — 59
CUB (9058 "Answer Me My Love") .... 10-15 — 60
DEE DEE .... 10-15 — 59
EPIC .... 3-5 — 75-76
ERA .... 5-10 — 61
GONE (5026 "Baby Come Back") .... 20-30 — 58
GUYDEN (2003 "Hole in the Ground") .... 10-15 — 58
GUYDEN (2110 "Hole in the Ground") .. 4-8 — 64
IMPERIAL .... 4-8 — 64-70
MGM .... 5-8 — 64
RSO .... 3-5 — 80
RIVERAIRE (1001 "Don't Bug Me Baby") .... 10-20 — 59
ROULETTE (4565 "Baby Come Back") .... 8-12 — 64
ROWE/AMI .... 5-10 — 66
("Play Me" Sales Stimulator promotional issue.)
SOUL CITY (Except 008) .... 3-5 — 76-77
SOUL CITY (008 "Slow Dancing") .... 4-8 — 77
U.A. (Except 700 series) .... 3-5 — 71-73
U.A. (700 series) .... 4-8 — 64

Picture Sleeves

IMPERIAL .... 5-10 — 64-69
U.A. .... 3-5 — 71

LPs: 10/12-inch

ATLANTIC .... 8-10 — 74
BIG TREE .... 8-10 — 77

CAPITOL (T-2161 "Sensational Johnny Rivers")....35-50 64
(Monaural.)
CAPITOL (ST-2161 "Sensational Johnny Rivers")....50-75 64
(Stereo.)
CUSTOM....8-12 60s
EPIC....8-10 75
GUEST STAR....10-15 64
IMPERIAL....10-20 64-70
KOALA....5-10 79
LIBERTY....5-8 82
MCA....5-8 85
PICKWICK....8-10 70s
PRIORITY....5-8 83
RSO....5-10 80
SEARS (417 "Mr. Teenage")....20-30 60s
(Special Products issue, made for sale in Sears stores)
SOUL CITY....8-10 77
SUNSET....8-12 67-69
U.A. (Except UAL, UAS & UXS series)....5-10 73-75
U.A. (UAL-3386 "Go Johnny, Go")....20-25 64
(Monaural.)
U.A. (UAS-6386 "Go Johnny, Go")....20-30 64
(Stereo.)
U.A. (UAS-5532 "Homegrown")....10-15 71
U.A. (UAS-5650 "L.A. Reggae")....10-15 72
U.A. (UXS-93 "Johnny Rivers")....12-15 72
UNART....10-20 67
Also see JONES, Tom / Freddie & Dreamers / Johnny Rivers
Also see RAMISTELLA, Johnny
Also see WILSON, Brian

RIVERS, Johnny / Steve Alaimo

LPs: 10/12-inch

CUSTOM....8-12 60s
Also see ALAIMO, Steve

RIVERS, Johnny / Jerry Cole

LPs: 10/12-inch

CROWN....10-20 64
Also see COLE, Jerry

RIVERS, Johnny / 4 Seasons / Jerry Butler / Jimmy Soul

LPs: 10/12-inch

GLADWYNNE (2004 "Shindig Hullabaloo Spectacular")....10-20 65
Also see BUTLER, Jerry
Also see 4 SEASONS
Also see SOUL, Jimmy

RIVERS, Johnny / Trini Lopez

LPs: 10/12-inch

CUSTOM....8-12 60s
Also see LOPEZ, Trini

RIVERS, Johnny / Ricky Nelson / Randy Sparks

LPs: 10/12-inch

MGM (E-4256 "Johnny Rivers, Ricky Nelson, Randy Sparks")....20-25 64
(Monaural.)
MGM (SE-4256 "Johnny Rivers, Ricky Nelson, Randy Sparks")....20-30 64
(Stereo.)
Also see NELSON, Ricky
Also see RASCALS / Buggs / Four Seasons / Johnny Rivers
Also see SIMON, Paul
Also see SPARKS, Randy

RIVERS, Johnny / Tremonts / Luke Gordon / Charlie Francis

LPs: 10/12-inch

CORONET (246 "Swingin' Shindig") 10-20 64
PREMIER (P-9037 "Swingin' Shindig")....10-20 64
(Monaural.)
PREMIER (PS-9037 "Swingin' Shindig")....15-25 64
(Stereo.)
Also see RIVERS, Johnny

RIVIERAS — P&R '58

Singles: 7-inch

COED (503 "Count Every Star")....20-30 58
COED (508 "Moonlight Serenade")..20-30 58
COED (513 "Our Love")....15-25 59
COED (522 "Since I Made You Cry") 15-25 59
COED (529 "Moonlight Cocktails")...15-25 60
COED (538 "My Friend")....10-20 60
COED (542 "Easy to Remember")....10-20 60
COED (561 "Eldorado")....10-20 61
COED (592 "Moonlight Cocktails")....5-10 64
COLLECTABLES....3-4 80s
ERIC....3-4 70s
HOUSE of SOUNDS....4-8 60s
LOST-NITE....4-8 70s

LPs: 10/12-inch

POST....10-15 70s
Members: Ronald Cook; Homer Dunn; Andy Jones; Charles Allen.
Also see DUPREES / RIVIERAS

RIVIERAS — P&R/LP '64

Singles: 7-inch

DELTA (3211 "California Sun")....5-10 63
(Canadian.)
LANA....3-6 60s
RIVIERA (1401 "California Sun"/"H.B. Goose Step")....5-10 63
RIVIERA (1401 "California Sun"/"Played On")....15-25 63
(1,000 made. Note different flip.)
RIVIERA (1402 "Little Donna")....8-10 64
RIVIERA (1403 "Rockin' Robin")....8-10 64
RIVIERA (1405 "Rip It Up"/"Whole Lotta Shakin'")....8-10 64
RIVIERA (1405 "Whole Lotta Shakin"/ "Lakeview Lane")....10-15 64
(Has a different take of *Lakeview Lane* than found on 1406.)
RIVIERA (1406 "Let's Go to Hawaii"/"Lakeview Lane")....8-10 65
RIVIERA (1407 "Somebody New")....8-10 65
(Credited to Rivieras, but actually by Bobby Whiteside.)
RIVIERA (1409 "Bug Juice")....10-15 65

LPs: 10/12-inch

RIVIERA (701 "Campus Party")....50-100 64
USA (102 "Let's Have a Party")....50-100 64
Members: Marty Fortson; Paul Dennert; Otto Nuss; Doug Gean; Joe Pennell.

RIVINGTONS — P&R '62

Singles: 7-inch

A.R.E. AMERICAN (100 "All That Glitters")....15-25 64
BATON MASTER....5-10 67
COLUMBIA....5-10 66
J.D....3-5 76
LADERA....3-5
LIBERTY (55427 "Papa Oom Mow Mow")....10-20 62
LIBERTY (55513 "Kickapoo Joy Juice")....10-20 62
LIBERTY (55528 "Mama Oom Mow Mow")....10-20 62
LIBERTY (55553 "The Bird's the Word")....10-20 63
LIBERTY (55585 "The Shaky Bird").10-20 63
LIBERTY (55610 "Cherry")....20-40 63
LIBERTY (55671 "Fairy Tales")....10-20 64
QUAN....5-10 67
RCA....5-10 69
REPRISE....5-10 64
VEE JAY....5-10 64-65
WAND....3-5 73

Picture Sleeves

LIBERTY (55553 "The Bird's the Word")....15-25 63

LPs: 10/12-inch

LIBERTY (3282 "Doin' the Bird")....50-60 63
(Monaural.)
LIBERTY (7282 "Doin' the Bird")....50-75 63
(Stereo.)
LIBERTY (10184 "Papa-Oom-Mow-Mow")....5-10 82
Members: Carl White; Al Frazier; Sonny Harris; Turner Wilson; Darryl White.

RIX, Jerry — R&B '77

Singles: 7-inch

A.V.I....3-5 77

ROACHFORD — P&R/LP '89

Singles: 7-inch

EPIC....3-4 89

ROAD — LP '70

Singles: 7-inch

GOODTIME....4-6
KAMA SUTRA....4-6 68-71
RADIOACTIVE GOLD....3-5

LPs: 10/12-inch

KAMA SUTRA....10-15 69-71
Members: Jerry Hudson; Phil Hudson; Joseph Hesse; Jim Hesse; Ralph Parker; Nick Distefano; Don Jakubowski.

ROAD APPLES — P&R '75

Singles: 7-inch

MUMS....3-5 75
POLYDOR....3-5 75

ROB BASE & D.J. EZ-Rock

(Rob Base) — P&R/R&B/LP '88

Singles: 7-inch

PROFILE....3-4 88-89

Picture Sleeves

PROFILE....3-4 89

LPs: 10/12-inch

PROFILE....5-8 88

ROBBINS, Marty — C&W '52

(With the Ray Conniff Orchestra & Chorus)

Singles: 78 rpm

COLUMBIA (20965 thru 21324)....15-25 52-54
COLUMBIA (21351 thru 21545)....20-30 54
COLUMBIA (21352 thru 21414)....10-20 54-55
COLUMBIA (40000 thru 41000 series)....20-50 56-58

Singles: 7-inch

COLUMBIA (02000 & 03000 series)....3-4 81-83
COLUMBIA (10305 thru 11425)....3-5 76-81
COLUMBIA (20965 thru 21324)....20-30 52-54
COLUMBIA (21351 "That's All Right")....30-50 54
COLUMBIA (21352 thru 21414)....15-25 54-55
COLUMBIA (21446 "Maybellene")....30-50 55
COLUMBIA (21461 "Pretty Mama")...30-50 55
COLUMBIA (21477 "Tennessee Toddy")....30-50 56
COLUMBIA (21508 "Singing the Blues")....15-25 56
COLUMBIA (21545 "Singing the Blues")....10-20 56
COLUMBIA (30589 "Big Iron")....20-40 60
(Compact 33 stereo.)
COLUMBIA (31749 "Little Rich Girl") 20-40 62
(Compact 33 stereo.)
COLUMBIA (31751 "Kinda Halfway Feel")....20-40 62
(Compact 33 stereo.)
COLUMBIA (33013 "El Paso")....20-40 61
(Compact 33 stereo.)
COLUMBIA (40679 "Long Tall Sally")....30-50 56
COLUMBIA (40706 "Respectfully Miss Brooks")....30-50 56
COLUMBIA (40815 thru 41408)....8-15 57-59
COLUMBIA (41511 thru 43770)....4-8 59-66
COLUMBIA (43845 thru 45775)....3-6 67-73
DECCA....4-6 72
MCA....3-5 73-75

Picture Sleeves

COLUMBIA (40815 thru 41408)....10-30 57-59
COLUMBIA (41511 thru 43770)....5-15 59-66

EPs: 7-inch

COLUMBIA (1785 "Marty Robbins") 20-40 56
COLUMBIA (2116 "Singing the Blues")....20-40 56
COLUMBIA (2134 "A White Sport Coat")....20-30 57
COLUMBIA (2153 "Marty Robbins") 15-25 56

COLUMBIA (2808 "Marty Robbins") 20-30 57
COLUMBIA (2814 "Marty Robbins") 10-20 58
COLUMBIA (9761/9762/9763 "The Song of Robbins")........10-20 57
(Price is for any of three volumes.)
COLUMBIA (10000 thru 14000 series)........10-20 57-60

LPs: 10/12-inch

ARTCO (110 "Best of Marty Robbins")........40-50 73
(Covers shows 110 but label has 644.)
CBS (19738 "Cause I Love You")........5-10 84
CANDLELITE........8-12 77
COLUMBIA (15 "Marty's Country")....10-15 69
COLUMBIA (31 "Open-End Columbia Artists Interviews")........35-50 60s
(Promotional issue only.)
COLUMBIA (32 "Columbia Artists Interviews with Frank Jones")........50-75
(Includes 42-page booklet. Promotional issue only.)
COLUMBIA (237 "Saddle Tramp")....25-35 66
(Columbia Record Club issue.)
COLUMBIA (445 "Bend in the River")........35-45 68
(Columbia Record Club issue.)
COLUMBIA (890 "Marty Robbins Gold")........8-10 75
COLUMBIA (976 "The Song of Robbins")........25-45 57
COLUMBIA (1087 "Song of the Islands")........25-45 57
COLUMBIA (1189 "Marty Robbins") 25-45 58
COLUMBIA (1256 "Return of the Gunfighter")........15-20 69
(Columbia "Country Star" series.)
COLUMBIA (1325 "Marty's Greatest Hits")........15-25 59
COLUMBIA (1349 "Gunfighter Ballads and Trail Songs")........15-25 59
COLUMBIA (1481 "More Gunfighter Ballads and Trail Songs")........15-25 60
COLUMBIA (1599 "Marty's Greatest Hits")........15-20 69
(Columbia "Country Star" series issue.)
COLUMBIA (1635 "More Greatest Hits")........15-25 61
COLUMBIA (1666 "Just a Little Sentimental")........15-25 61
COLUMBIA (1801 "Marty After Midnight")........40-50 62
COLUMBIA (1855 "Portrait of Marty")........25-35 62
(With bonus portrait of Marty.)
COLUMBIA (1855 "Portrait of Marty")........15-25 62
(Without bonus portrait of Marty.)
COLUMBIA (1918 "Devil Woman")...15-20 62
COLUMBIA (2016 "The Heart of Marty Robbins")........80-100 69
(Columbia "Country Star" series issue.)
COLUMBIA (2040 "Hawaii's Calling Me")........20-30 62
COLUMBIA (2072 "Return of the Gunfighter")........15-20 63
COLUMBIA (2167 "Island Woman") .25-35 64
COLUMBIA (2220 "R.F.D.")........25-35 64
COLUMBIA (2304 "Turn the Lights Down Low")........20-40 65
COLUMBIA (2448 "What God Has Done")........15-20 65
COLUMBIA (2527 "The Drifter")........10-20 66
COLUMBIA (2563 "What God Has Done")........15-20 69
(Columbia "Country Star" series issue.)
COLUMBIA (2601 "Rock'n Roll'n Robbins")........500-750 56
(10-inch LP.)
COLUMBIA (2645 "My Kind of Country")........15-20 67
COLUMBIA (2725 "Tonight Carmen")........10-20 67
COLUMBIA (2735 "Christmas with Marty Robbins")........20-30 67
COLUMBIA (2762 "More Gunfighter Ballads and Trail Songs")........15-20 69
(Columbia "Country Star" series issue.)
COLUMBIA (2817 "By The Time I Get to Phoenix")........20-30 68
COLUMBIA (3557 "The Drifter")........15-20 69
(Columbia "Country Star" series issue.)
COLUMBIA (3867 "My Kind of Country")........15-20 69
(Columbia "Country Star" series issue.)
COLUMBIA (5489 "Tonight Carmen")........15-20 69
(Columbia "Country Star" series issue.)
COLUMBIA (5498 "Christmas with Marty Robbins")........15-20 69
(Columbia "Country Star" series issue.)
COLUMBIA (5812 "Marty")........20-40 72
(Five-LP set. Columbia Special Products issue.)
COLUMBIA (6994 "I Walk Alone")....15-20 69
(Columbia "Country Star" series issue.)
COLUMBIA (CS-8158 "Gunfighter Ballads and Trail Songs")........15-25 59
COLUMBIA (PC-8158 "Gunfighter Ballads and Trail Songs")........5-10
COLUMBIA (CS-8272 "More Gunfighter Ballads and Trail Songs")........15-25 60
COLUMBIA (PC-8272 "More Gunfighter Ballads and Trail Songs")........5-10
COLUMBIA (CS-8435 "More Greatest Hits")........15-20 61
COLUMBIA (PC-8435 "More Greatest Hits")........5-10
COLUMBIA (8466 "Just a Little Sentimental")........15-25 61
COLUMBIA (8601 "Marty After Midnight")........25-35 62
COLUMBIA (8655 "Portrait of Marty")........25-35 62
(With bonus portrait of Marty.)
COLUMBIA (8655 "Portrait of Marty")........15-25 62
(Without bonus portrait.)
COLUMBIA (8718 "Devil Woman")... 15-20 62
COLUMBIA (8840 "Hawaii's Calling Me")........20-30 62
COLUMBIA (8872 "Return of the Gunfighter")........15-20 63
COLUMBIA (8976 "Island Woman") 35-40 64
COLUMBIA (CS-9020 "R.F.D.")........25-35 64
COLUMBIA (CSRP-9020 "R.F.D.")....8-10
(Columbia Special Products issue.)
COLUMBIA (9104 "Turn the Lights Down Low")........20-40 65
COLUMBIA (CS-9248 "What God Has Done")........15-20 65
COLUMBIA (ACS-9248 "What God Has Done")........5-10
(Columbia Special Products issue.)
COLUMBIA (9327 "The Drifter")........10-20 66
COLUMBIA (9421 "The Song of Robbins")........30-40 67
COLUMBIA (9445 "My Kind of Country")........15-25 67
COLUMBIA (9525 "Tonight Carmen")........10-20 67
COLUMBIA (9535 "Christmas with Marty Robbins")........10-20 67
COLUMBIA (9617 "By the Time I Get to Phoenix")........8-12 68
COLUMBIA (9725 "I Walk Alone")........8-15 68
COLUMBIA (9811 "It's a Sin")........20-30 69
COLUMBIA (9978 "My Woman, My Woman, My Wife")........8-12 70
COLUMBIA (10022 thru 10579)........8-10 73-75
(Columbia's Limited Edition series. All Have an "LE" prefix.)
COLUMBIA (10980 "Christmas with Marty Robbins")........15-20 70
(Columbia Special Products issue.)
COLUMBIA (11221 "By the Time I Get to Phoenix")........5-10 80s
(Columbia Special Products issue.)
COLUMBIA (11222 "Marty's Greatest Hits")........5-10 75
COLUMBIA (11311 "By the Time I Get to Phoenix")........5-10 70
(Columbia Special Products issue.)
COLUMBIA (11513 "By the Time I Get to Phoenix")........15-20 71
(Columbia Special Products issue.)
COLUMBIA (12416 "Marty Robbins' Own Favorites")........12-15 74
(Special Products issue for Vaseline Hair Tonic.)
COLUMBIA (13358 "Christmas with Marty Robbins")........5-10 72
(Columbia Special Products issue.)
COLUMBIA (14035 "Legendary Music Man")........8-12 77
(Columbia Special Products issue.)
COLUMBIA (14613 "Best of Marty Robbins")........5-10 78
(Columbia Special Products issue.)
COLUMBIA (15594 "Number One Cowboy")........5-10 81
(Columbia Special Products issue.)
COLUMBIA (15812 "Marty Robbins' Best")........5-10 82
(Columbia Special Products issue.)
COLUMBIA (16561 "Reflections")........5-10 82
(Columbia Special Products issue.)
COLUMBIA (16578 "Classics")........15-20 83
(Three-LP set. Columbia Special Products issue.)
COLUMBIA (16914 "Country Classics")........5-10 83
(Columbia Special Products issue.)
COLUMBIA (17120 "Sincerely")........5-10 83
(Columbia Special Products issue.)
COLUMBIA (17136 "Forever Yours")..5-10 83
(Columbia Special Products issue.)
COLUMBIA (17137 "That Country Feeling")........5-10 83
(Columbia Special Products issue.)
COLUMBIA (17138 "Banquet of Songs")........5-10 83
(Columbia Special Products issue.)
COLUMBIA (17159 "The Great Marty Robbins")........5-10 83
(Columbia Special Products issue.)
COLUMBIA (17206 "The Legendary Marty Robbins")........5-10 83
(Columbia Special Products issue.)
COLUMBIA (17209 "Country Cowboy")........5-10 83
(Columbia Special Products issue.)
COLUMBIA (17367 "Song of the Islands")........5-10 83
(Columbia Special Products issue.)
COLUMBIA (17730 "Great Love Songs")........5-10 80s
(Columbia Special Products issue.)
COLUMBIA (30000 thru 40000 series)........5-12 70-86
DECCA........8-12 72
GUSTO/COLUMBIA........8-10 81
HARMONY (Except 31258)........8-15 69-72
HARMONY (31258 "Song of the Islands")........20-25 72
K-TEL........8-10 77
MCA........6-12 73-74
ORBIT........8-10 84
PICKWICK........5-10 70s
READER'S DIGEST (054 "Greatest Hits")........20-30 83
(Boxed, five-disc set.)
SUNRISE MEDIA........5-10 81
TIME-LIFE........5-10 81
WORD........5-10

Session: Ray Conniff Singers; Jordanaires; David Briggs; Bobby Braddock; Grady Martin; Bob Bishop; Bill Pursell; Buddy Spicher; Arlene Harden; Bobby Sykes.

Also see CONNIFF, Ray
Also see PRUETT, Jeanne, & Marty Robbins
Also see PURSELL, Bill
Also see SMITH, Carl / Lefty Frizzell / Marty Robbins
Also see TUBB, Ernest

ROBBINS, Marty / Johnny Cash / Ray Price

LPs: 10/12-inch

COLUMBIA 8-10 70

Also see CASH, Johnny

Also see PRICE, Ray

ROBBINS, Rockie R&B '79

Singles: 7-inch

A&M 3-5 79-81

MCA 3-4 85

Picture Sleeves

A&M 3-5 80

LPs: 10/12-inch

A&M 5-10 80-81

MCA 5-8 85

ROBBS LP '68

Singles: 7-inch

ABC 4-6 70

ATLANTIC 5-10 68

DUNHILL 4-8 69-70

MERCURY 5-10 66-67

Picture Sleeves

ABC 4-8 70

MERCURY 8-12 67

EPs: 7-inch

WRIT 10-15 66

LPs: 10/12-inch

MERCURY (21130 "Robbs") 20-25 67
(Monaural.)

MERCURY (61130 "Robbs") 20-30 67
(Stereo.)

ROBE R&B '87

Singles: 7-inch

2000 AD 3-4 87

ROBERT & JOHNNY P&R/R&B '58

Singles: 78 rpm

OLD TOWN 15-25 56-57

Singles: 7-inch

ATLANTIC OLDIES SERIES 3-5 70s

COLLECTABLES 3-4 80s

OLD TOWN 12-25 56-62

SUE (792 "A Perfect Wife") 15-20 62

Members: Robert Carr; Johnny Mitchell.

ROBERT & JOHNNY / Fiestas

Singles: 7-inch

ATCO 3-5 80s

Also see FIESTAS

Also see ROBERT & JOHNNY

ROBERTA LEE: see LEE, Roberta

ROBERTINO LP '62

Singles: 7-inch

KAPP 4-6 61

LPs: 10/12-inch

KAPP 10-20 61-62

ROBERTS, Austin P&R '72

Singles: 7-inch

ARISTA 3-5 78

CHELSEA 3-5 72-75

COLLECTABLES 3-4 80s

GUSTO 3-4 80s

PHILIPS 4-6 68-71

PRIVATE STOCK 3-5 75-76

LPs: 10/12-inch

CHELSEA 8-12 72-73

PRIVATE STOCK 6-10 75

ROBERTS, John P&R/R&B '67

Singles: 7-inch

DUKE 4-8 67-69

ROBERTS, Lea R&B '69

Singles: 7-inch

MINIT 4-8 69

U.A. 3-5 74-75

ROBERTSON, Don P&R '56

Singles: 78 rpm

CAPITOL 3-5 56-57

Singles: 7-inch

CAPITOL 4-8 56-59

MONUMENT 3-5 66-76

RCA 3-8 61-68

LPs: 10/12-inch

RCA 10-15 65

ROBERTSON, Robbie LP '87

GEFFEN 3-4 87

Picture Sleeves

GEFFEN 3-4 87

LPs: 10/12-inch

GEFFEN 5-8 87

Also see BAND

ROBEY P&R/D&D '85

Singles: 12-inch

SILVER BLUE 4-6 84-85

Singles: 7-inch

SILVER BLUE 3-5 84-85

ROBIC, Ivo P&R '59

Singles: 7-inch

LAURIE 4-8 59-60

PHILIPS 3-6 62

ROBIN
(Robin Ward)

Singles: 7-inch

DOT (16519 "Top 40 Blues") 5-10 63

Also see WARD, Robin

ROBIN, Cock: see COCK ROBIN

ROBIN, Tina P&R '61

Singles: 78 rpm

CORAL 5-10 57

Singles: 7-inch

CORAL 5-10 57-59

MERCURY 4-8 61-63

ROBINS R&B '50
(Robbins)

Singles: 78 rpm

ALADDIN (3031 "Don't Like the Way You're Doing") 200-300 49

ATCO 25-50 55

CROWN 50-75 54

RCA 50-75 53

RECORDED in HOLLYWOOD (112 "Bayou Baby Blues") 150-250 51

RECORDED in HOLLYWOOD (121 "Falling Star") 150-250 51

SAVOY (726 "If It's So Baby") 50-75 50

SAVOY (732 "Turkey Hop") 50-75 50

SAVOY (738 "Our Romance Is Gone") 50-75 50

SAVOY (752 "There's Rain in My Eyes") 50-75 50

SAVOY (762 "I'm Through") 50-75 50

SCORE (4010 "Around About Midnight") 50-75 49

SPARK 30-50 54-55

WHIPPET 30-50 56-57

Singles: 7-inch

ARVEE (5001 "Just Like That") 15-25 60

ARVEE (5013 "Oh No!") 15-25 60

ATCO (6059 "Smokey Joe's Cafe") 30-50 55

CROWN (106 "I Made a Vow") 150-250 54

CROWN (120 "Key to My Heart") 150-250 54

GONE (5101 "Baby Love") 15-25 61

KNIGHT (2001 "Quarter to Twelve") 25-50 58

KNIGHT (2008 "It's Never Too Late") 50-75 58

RCA (5175 "A Fool Such As I") 300-500 53

RCA (5271 "All Night Baby") 200-400 53

RCA (5434 "How Would You Know") 200-400 53

RCA (5486 "My Baby Done Told Me") 200-300 53

RCA (5489 "Ten Days in Jail") 100-200 53

RCA (5564 "Don't Stop Now") 100-200 53

SPARK (103 "Riot in Cell Block No. 9") 200-300 54

SPARK (107 "Framed") 200-300 54

SPARK (110 "If Teardrops Were Kisses") 200-300 55

SPARK (113 "One Kiss") 200-300 55

SPARK (116 "I Must Be Dreaming") 100-200 55

SPARK (122 "Smokey Joe's Cafe") 200-300 55

WHIPPET (100 "Cherry Lips") 75-100 56

WHIPPET (200 "Cherry Lips") 50-75 56

WHIPPET (201 "Hurt Me") 50-75 56

WHIPPET (203 "Since I First Met You") 50-75 56

WHIPPET (206 "A Fool in Love") 50-75 57

WHIPPET (208 "Every Night") 50-75 57

WHIPPET (211 "In My Dreams") 50-75 57

WHIPPET (212 "You Wanted Fun") 50-75 58

LPs: 10/12-inch

GNP 5-10 75

WHIPPET (703 "Rock 'N' Roll with the Robins") 500-750 58

Members: Ty Terrell; Bobby Nunn; Carl Gardner; Bill Richards; Grady Chapman; H.B. Barnum; Roy Richards; Richard Berry.

Also see BARNUM, H.B.

Also see COASTERS

Also see NUNN, Bobby

Also see OTIS, Johnny, Quintette, with Little Esther & Robins

ROBINS / Mel Walker & Bluenotes

Singles: 78 rpm

REGENT (1016 "I'm Not Falling in Love with You") 25-35 50

Also see ROBINS

ROBINS, Jimmy R&B '67
(James Robbins)

Singles: 7-inch

FEDERAL 4-8 63

JERHART 4-8 67

KENT 4-8 68

ROBINSON, Alvin P&R/R&B '64

Singles: 7-inch

ATCO 4-8 68

BLUE CAT 5-10 65

JOE JONES 4-8 66

RED BIRD 5-10 64

TIGER 4-8 64

ROBINSON, Bert R&B '87

Singles: 7-inch

CAPITOL 3-4 87

Also see BLU, Peggi, & Bert Robinson

ROBINSON, Dutch R&B '84

Singles: 7-inch

CBS ASSOCIATED 3-4 84-85

ROBINSON, Ed R&B '70

Singles: 7-inch

COTILLION 3-5 70

ROBINSON, Fat Man R&B '49

Singles: 78 rpm

MOTIF 10-20 49

ROBINSON, Floyd P&R/R&B '59

Singles: 7-inch

DOT 4-8 61-62

GROOVE 4-8 64

JAMIE 4-8 61

RCA 8-12 59-60

U.A. 5-10 63-66

EPs: 7-inch

RCA (4350 "Makin' Love") 50-75 59

LPs: 10/12-inch

RCA (LPM-2162 "Floyd Robinson") 30-60 60
(Monaural.)

RCA (LSP-2162 "Floyd Robinson") 50-100 60
(Stereo.)

ROBINSON, Freddy P&R/R&B/LP '70

Singles: 7-inch

CHECKER 10-15 66

LIBERTY 3-5 70

LIMELIGHT 10-15 58

MERCURY 10-15 58

PACIFIC JAZZ 3-5 69-70

QUEEN 8-12 61

WORLD PACIFIC 3-5 70

LPs: 10/12-inch

ENTERPRISE 8-12 71

PACIFIC JAZZ 10-15 69-70

Also see LITTLE WALTER
Also see HOWLING WOLF

ROBINSON, J.P. *R&B '69*

Singles: 7-inch

ALSTON 3-6 68-69

ROBINSON, Jackie *R&B '76*

Singles: 7-inch

ARIOLA AMERICAN 3-5 76

ROBINSON, James *R&B '87*

Singles: 7-inch

TABU 3-4 87

ROBINSON, Roscoe *P&R/R&B '66*

(Rosco Robinson)

Singles: 7-inch

ATLANTIC 3-5 69
FAME 3-5 70
PAULA 3-5 70s
SOUND STAGE 7 .... 4-8 67-69
TUFF 4-6 70s
WAND 4-8 66-67

ROBINSON, Smokey *P&R/R&B/LP '73*

(William Robinson)

Singles: 7-inch

TAMLA 3-5 73-86
MOTOWN 3-4 87-88

Picture Sleeves

MOTOWN 3-4 87

LPs: 10/12-inch

MOTOWN 5-10 82-90
TAMLA 5-12 73-86
Also see JAMES, Rick, & Smokey Robinson
Also see KENNY G. & Smokey Robinson
Also see MIRACLES
Also see ROSS, Diana, Stevie Wonder, Marvin Gaye & Smokey Robinson
Also see TEMPTATIONS
Also see U.S.A. for AFRICA
Also see VANITY / Smokey Robinson

ROBINSON, Smokey, & Barbara Mitchell *P&R/R&B '83*

Singles: 7-inch

TAMLA 3-5 83
Also see HIGH INERGY
Also see ROBINSON, Smokey

ROBINSON, Stan *P&R '59*

Singles: 7-inch

AMY 5-10 60-61
MONUMENT 5-10 59
TOTSY (601 "Start to Jump") 75-100

ROBINSON, Sugar "Chile *R&B '49*

Singles: 78 rpm

CAPITOL 20-30 49-50

Singles: 7-inch

CAPITOL (1259 "Christmas Boogie") 50-75 50

LPs: 10/12-inch

CAPITOL (589 "Boogie Woogie") ... 75-125 55

ROBINSON, Sugar "Chile" / Harry Belafonte

Singles: 78 rpm

CAPITOL (70037 "Numbers Boogie") 25-45 49
(Promotional issue only.)
Also see BELAFONTE, Harry
Also see ROBINSON, Sugar "Chile"

ROBINSON, Tom, Band *LP '78*

Singles: 7-inch

HARVEST 3-5 78-79
I.R.S. 3-5 80

LPs: 10/12-inch

HARVEST 5-10 78-79
I.R.S. 5-8 80

ROBINSON, Vicki Sue *P&R/R&B/LP '76*

Singles: 12-inch

PROFILE 8-12 83-84

Singles: 7-inch

PROFILE 3-4 83-84
RCA 3-5 76-77

LPs: 10/12-inch

PROFILE 5-8 83
RCA 5-10 76-81

ROBINSON, Wanda *LP '71*

LPs: 10/12-inch

PERCEPTION 5-10 71

ROBOTNICK, Alexander *R&B '85*

Singles: 7-inch

SIRE 3-5 85

ROCCA, John *R&B/D&D '84*

Singles: 12-inch

STREETWISE 4-6 84

Singles: 7-inch

STREETWISE 3-4 84
Also see FREEEZ

ROCHELL & CANDLES *P&R/R&B '61*

Singles: 7-inch

CHALLENGE (9158 "Each Night") ... 40-50 62
CHALLENGE (9191 "Let's Run Away and Get Married") 15-25 62
COLLECTABLES 3-4 80s
SWINGIN' (623 "Once Upon a Time") 10-20 60
SWINGIN' (634 "So Far Away") 10-20 61
SWINGIN' (640 "Peg O' My Heart") .. 10-20 61
SWINGIN' (652 "Long Time Ago") 10-20 62
Members: Rochell Henderson; Johnny Wyatt; T. C. Henderson; Mel Sasso.

ROCHELLE *D&D '85*

Singles: 12-inch

W.B. 4-6 85

Singles: 7-inch

W.B. 3-4 85

ROCHES *LP '79*

LPs: 10/12-inch

W.B. 5-10 79-82
Members: Maggie Roche; Terre Roche; Suzzy Roche.

ROCK & HYDE *P&R/LP '87*

Singles: 7-inch

CAPITOL 3-4 87

Picture Sleeves

CAPITOL 3-4 87

LPs: 10/12-inch

CAPITOL 5-8 87

ROCK FLOWERS *P&R '72*

Singles: 7-inch

WHEEL 4-8 71-73

LPs: 10/12-inch

WHEEL 10-15 71-72

ROCK MASTER SCOTT & DYNAMIC THREE *R&B '84*

Singles: 12-inch

REALITY 4-6 84-85

Singles: 7-inch

REALITY 3-4 84-85

ROCK SQUAD *D&D '85*

Singles: 12-inch

TOMMY BOY 4-6 85

ROCK STEADY CREW *D&D '84*

Singles: 12-inch

ATLANTIC 4-6 83-84

Singles: 7-inch

ATLANTIC 3-4 83-84

ROCK-A-TEENS *P&R '59*

Singles: 7-inch

APEX (76591 "Woo-Hoo") 10-20 59
(Canadian.)
DORAN (3515 "Woo-Hoo") 40-60 59
ROULETTE (4192 "Woo-Hoo") 10-20 59
ROULETTE (4217 "Doggone It Baby") 15-20 60

LPs: 10/12-inch

MURRAY HILL 5-10 80s
ROULETTE (R-25109 "Woo-Hoo") 75-100 60
(Monaural.)
ROULETTE (SR-25109 "Woo-Hoo") 100-125 60
(Stereo.)

ROCKER'S REVENGE *R&B '82*

Singles: 12-inch

STREETWISE 4-6 83-84

Singles: 7-inch

STREETWISE 3-5 82-84

ROCKET *R&B/D&D '83*

Singles: 12-inch 33/45

QUALITY/RFC 4-6 83

LPs: 10/12-inch

QUALITY/RFC 5-8 83

ROCKETS *P&R/LP '79*

Singles: 7-inch

RSO 3-5 79
TORTOISE INT'L 3-5 77-78

LPs: 10/12-inch

ELEKTRA 5-10 81
RSO 5-10 79-80
TORTOISE INT'L 8-12 77
Members: Jim McCarty; Dennis Robbins.
Also see DETROIT
Also see RYDER, Mitch

ROCKIN' R's *P&R '59*

Singles: 7-inch

STEPHENY (1842 "Walking You to School") 15-25 60
TEMPUS (1507 "Heat") 15-20 59
TEMPUS (7541 "The Beat") 20-30 59
VEE JAY (334 "I'm Still in Love with You") 10-20 60
VEE JAY (346 "Hum Bug") 10-20 60
Also see VOLZ, Ron, & Rockin' R's

ROCKIN' REBELS *P&R '62*

Singles: 7-inch

ABC 3-5 73
ERIC 3-4 70s
ITZY (8 "Wild Weekend") 15-25 60s
REO 10-20 62-63
(Canadian.)
STORK (3 "Bongo Blue Beat") 10-15 64
SWAN (4125 "Wild Weekend") 8-12 62
SWAN (4140 "Rockin' Crickets") 10-15 63
(Previously issued as by the Hot Toddys.)
SWAN (4150 "Another Wild Weekend") 8-12 63
SWAN (4161 "Monday Morning") 8-12 63
SWAN (4248 "Wild Weekend") 5-10 66
(Thought not credited, the flip of 4248, *Donkey Twine*, is by Kathy Lynn & Playboys.)

LPs: 10/12-inch

SWAN (509 "Wild Weekend") 50-100 63
Members: Tom Gorman; Paul Balon; Mickey Kipler; Jim Kipler.
Also see BUFFALO REBELS
Also see HOT-TODDYS
Also see REBELS

ROCKIN' SIDNEY: see ROCKIN' SYDNEY

ROCKIN' SYDNEY *LP '85*

(With His All Stars; Rockin' Sidney)

Singles: 7-inch

AVENUE 5-10 60s
EPIC 3-5 84-85
JIN 8-12 59-63
MAISON DE SOUL (1024 "My Toot Toot") 3-5 85

LPs: 10/12-inch

EPIC 5-10 85
Member: Sidney Sidiem.

ROCKINGHAM, David, Trio *P&R '63*

Singles: 7-inch

DEE DEE 8-12 63
JOSIE 4-8 63-64

ROCKPILE *P&R/LP '80*

Singles: 7-inch

COLUMBIA 3-5 80

EPs: 7-inch

COLUMBIA (1219 "Nick Lowe and Dave Edmunds") 3-5 80

(Bonus EP, issued with the LP *Seconds of Pleasure*.)

LPs: 10/12-inch

COLUMBIA (36886 "Seconds of Pleasure") 5-10 80

(Includes the bonus EP, 1219, *Nick Lowe & Dave Edmunds.*)

Members: Nick Lowe; Dave Edmunds; Terry Williams; Billy Bremmer.

Also see CARTER, Carlene

Also see LOWE, Nick, & Dave Edmunds

Also see McCARTNEY, Paul / Rochestra / Who / Rockpile

ROCKWELL P&R/R&B/D&D/LP '84

Singles: 12-inch

MOTOWN 4-6 84-86

Singles: 7-inch

MOTOWN 3-4 84-86

LPs: 10/12-inch

MOTOWN 5-8 84-86

Also see JACKSON, Michael

ROCKY FELLERS P&R '63

Singles: 7-inch

DONNA 5-10 63
PARKWAY 5-10 62
SCEPTER 8-15 62-63
W.B. 4-8 64-65

Picture Sleeves

SCEPTER (1254 "Like the Big Guys Do") 10-15 63

LPs: 10/12-inch

SCEPTER (SP-512 "Killer Joe") 25-35 63
(Monaural.)
SCEPTER (SPS-512 "Killer Joe") 30-40 63
(Stereo.)

Members: Eddie; Albert; Tony; Junior; Pop.

ROD R&B '80

Singles: 7-inch

PRELUDE 3-5 80

RODGERS, Eileen P&R '56

Singles: 78 rpm

COLUMBIA 3-6 56-57

Singles: 7-inch

COLUMBIA 5-10 56-60
KAPP 4-6 61

EPs: 7-inch

COLUMBIA 5-10 58

LPs: 10/12-inch

COLUMBIA 15-25 58

Also see MITCHELL, Guy / Eileen Rodgers

RODGERS, Jimmie

("With Michele") P&R/C&W/R&B/LP '57

Singles: 78 rpm

ROULETTE 10-30 57

Singles: 7-inch

A&M 3-6 67-70
ABC 3-5 73
DOT 4-8 62-67
EPIC 3-5 71-72
RCA 3-5 73-75
ROULETTE (Monaural) 5-10 57-61
ROULETTE (SSR-4158 "Ring-a-Ling-a-Lario") 10-20 59
(Stereo.)
ROULETTE (SSR-4218 "T.L.C.") 10-20 60
(Stereo.)
ROULETTE (SSR-8001 "Bo Diddley") 15-25 59
(Stereo.)
ROULETTE (SSR-8007 "Froggy Went A-Courtin'") 10-20 59
(Stereo.)
SCRIMSHAW 3-5 78

Picture Sleeves

DOT 4-8 62-64
ROULETTE 10-15 58-61

EPs: 7-inch

ROULETTE 10-20 57-60

LPs: 10/12-inch

A&M 8-15 67-70
DOT 10-20 62-67
FORUM 10-20 60
HAMILTON 10-20 64-65
RCA 8-12 73-75
ROULETTE (25020 thru 25057) 20-30 57-59
ROULETTE (R-25071 thru R-25199) 10-20 59-63
(Monaural.)
ROULETTE (SR-25071 thru SR-25199) 15-25 59-63
(Stereo.)
ROULETTE (42000 series) 5-10
SCRIMSHAW 5-10 78

RODGERS, Nile P&R/R&B/D&D '85

Singles: 12-inch

W.B. 4-6 85

Singles: 7-inch

W.B. 3-4 85

LPs: 10/12-inch

MIRAGE 5-10 84
W.B. 5-8 85

Also see CHIC

Also see HONEYDRIPPERS

RODGERS, Paul LP '83

Singles: 7-inch

ATLANTIC 3-5 83

Picture Sleeves

ATLANTIC 3-5 83

LPs: 10/12-inch

ATLANTIC 5-10 83

Also see BAD COMPANY

Also see FIRM

Also see FREE

RODNEY-O - JOE COOLEY LP '89

LPs: 10/12-inch

ATLANTIC 5-8 90
EGYPT 5-8 89

RODRIGUEZ, Johnny C&W '72

Singles: 7-inch

CAPITOL 3-4 87-89
COLUMBIA 3-5 80
EPIC 3-5 79-86
MERCURY 3-6 72-79

Picture Sleeves

MERCURY 3-5 77

LPs: 10/12-inch

EPIC 5-10 80-84
K-TEL 5-10 77
MERCURY 5-12 73-79

Session: Waylon Jennings.

Also see HALL, Tom T.

Also see JENNINGS, Waylon

RODRIGUEZ, Johnny, & Charly McClain C&W '79

Singles: 7-inch

EPIC 3-5 79

Also see RODRIGUEZ, Johnny

RODWAY P&R '82

(Steve Rodway)

Singles: 7-inch

MILLENNIUM 3-5 82

LPs: 10/12-inch

MILLENNIUM 5-10 82

ROE, Tommy P&R/R&B/LP '62

(With the Satins; with Flamingos; with Roemans)

Singles: 7-inch

ABC 4-8 66-71
ABC-PAR 5-10 62-66
AERTAUN (1108 "Wendy") 5-8 60s
CURB/MCA 3-5 85-86
JUDD (1018 "Caveman") 15-25 60
JUDD (1022 "Sheila") 25-45 62
MCA 3-4 70s
MGM/SOUTH 3-5 72-73
MARK IV (001 "Caveman") 25-50 60
MERCURY 3-5 86-87
MONUMENT 3-5 72-77
ROULETTE 3-5 70s
TRUMPET (1401 "Caveman") 50-75 60
W.B./CURB 3-5 78-80

Picture Sleeves

ABC 4-8 66-70
ABC-PAR (10362 "Susie Darlin'") 8-12 62

LPs: 10/12-inch

ABC (594 thru 762) 10-15 67-72
ABC-PAR (ABC-423 thru ABC-574) 20-35 62-66
(Monaural.)
ABC-PAR (ABCS-423 thru ABCS-575) 25-40 62-66
(Stereo.)
ACCORD 5-10 82
GUSTO 5-10 80s
MCA 5-10 82
MONUMENT 8-12 76-77

ROE, Tommy / Bobby Rydell / Gene Pitney

LP: 10/12-inch

INT'L AWARD 10-15 60s

Also see PITNEY, Gene

ROE, Tommy / Bobby Rydell / Ray Stevens

LPs: 10/12-inch

DESIGN (178 "Young Lovers") 15-25 63

Also see RYDELL, Bobby

Also see STEVENS, Ray

ROE, Tommy / Al Tornello

LPs: 10/12-inch

DIPLOMAT 10-20 60s

ROE, Tommy / Bobby Lee Trammell

LPs: 10/12-inch

CROWN 15-20 63

Also see ROE, Tommy

Also see TRAMMELL, Bobby Lee

ROGER P&R/R&B/LP '81

(Featuring Shirley Murdock; with Mighty Clouds of Joy; Roger Troutman)

Singles: 7-inch

REPRISE 3-4 87-88
W.B. 3-5 81-85

Picture Sleeves

REPRISE 3-4 87

LPs: 10/12-inch

REPRISE 5-8 87
W.B. 5-10 81-84

Also see MIGHTY CLOUDS of JOY

Also see SCRITTI POLITTI & ROGER

Also see ZAPP

ROGERS, D.J. P&R/R&B/LP '76

Singles: 12-inch

COLUMBIA 4-8 79

Singles: 7-inch

ARC 3-5 79-80
COLUMBIA 3-5 78-80
RCA 3-5 75-76

LPs: 10/12-inch

COLUMBIA 5-10 78-80
RCA 5-10 76-77
SHELTER 5-10 77

Also see RUSHEN, Patrice, & D.J. Rogers

ROGERS, Dann P&R '79

Singles: 7-inch

IA 3-5 79
MCA 3-4 87

LPs: 10/12-inch

IA 8-10 79

Also see CUMMINGS, Burton

Also see DELANEY & BONNIE

ROGERS, Eric, & His Orch. LP '61

LPs: 10/12-inch

LONDON/PHASE 4 .... 5-15 61-66

ROGERS, Jimmy R&B '57

(With His Trio; with His Rocking Four)

Singles: 78 rpm

CHESS 25-50 50-57

Singles: 7-inch

CHESS (1506 "I Used to Have a Woman") 50-100 52
CHESS (1519 "The Last Time") 50-100 52
CHESS (1543 "Left Me with a Broken Heart") 50-75 53
CHESS (1574 "Chicago Bound") 50-75 54
CHESS (1616 "You're the One") 40-60 55

CHESS (1643 "If It Ain't Me") 40-60 56
CHESS (1659 "One Kiss") 40-60 57
CHESS (1721 "My Last Meal")..........20-30 59

LPs: 10/12-inch

CHESS 8-12
Also see SUNNYLAND SLIM
Also see WATERS, Muddy
Also see WILLIAMSON, Sonny Boy

ROGERS, Jimmy, & Freddy King

LPs: 10/12-inch

SHELTER....................................8-10 73
Also see KING, Freddy
Also see ROGERS, Jimmy

ROGERS, Julie P&R '64

Singles: 7-inch

MEGA...3-5 72
MERCURY 4-8 64-66

Picture Sleeves

MERCURY 5-10 65

LPs: 10/12-inch

MEGA...5-10 72
MERCURY 15-25 65

ROGERS, Kenny C&W '75

(Kenneth Rogers; with Linda Davis)

Singles: 7-inch

CARLTON (454 "That Crazy Feeling") 25-50 58
CARLTON (468 "For You Alone") 25-50 58
EVA-TONE/READER'S DIGEST ("His Greatest Hits") 10-15 83
(Single-sided, square, cardboard soundsheet. Promotional issue only.)
JOLLY ROGERS 3-5 73-74
KEN-LEE (102 "Jole Blon") 50-100 50s
LIBERTY.......................................3-4 80-86
MERCURY 5-10 66
RCA..3-4 84-89
REPRISE.......................................3-4 89-91
U.A. 3-5 76-80

Picture Sleeves

LIBERTY.......................................3-4 80-83
RCA..3-4 84-86
U.A. 3-5 79-80

LPs: 10/12-inch

BREAKAWAY 5-8 84
JOLLY ROGERS (5001 "Backroads")..............................100-200 75
(Promotional picture disc.)
LIBERTY (Except 8344) 5-10 80-85
LIBERTY (8344 "HBO Presents Kenny Rogers Greatest Hits") 15-20 83
(Promotional only picture disc.)
MFSL (044 "The Gambler")..............25-35 80
MFSL (049 "Greatest Hits") 25-35 80
MASTERS 5-10
PICKWICK.....................................5-10 79
QSP 5-10 84
RCA..5-8 84-87
REPRISE.......................................5-8 89
U.A. (Except 934) 5-8 76-80
U.A. (934 "The Gambler")..................5-10 78
(Black vinyl.)
U.A. (934 "The Gambler")...............50-100 78
(Picture disc. Promotional issue only. One of a four-artist, four-LP set.)
Also see CAMPBELL, Glen / Anne Murray / Kenny Rogers / Crystal Gayle
Also see MILSAP, Ronnie, & Kenny Rogers
Also see MURRAY, Anne, & Kenny Rogers
Also see U.S.A. for AFRICA

ROGERS, Kenny, & Kim Carnes C&W/P&R '80

Singles: 7-inch

U.A. 3-5 80

Picture Sleeves

U.A. 3-5 80
Also see CARNES, Kim

ROGERS, Kenny, Kim Carnes & James Ingram C&W/P&R/R&B '84

Singles: 7-inch

RCA..3-4 84

Picture Sleeves

RCA 3-4 84
Also see INGRAM, James
Also see ROGERS, Kenny, & Kim Carnes

ROGERS, Kenny, & Holly Dunn C&W '90

Singles: 7-inch

REPRISE 3-4 90

ROGERS, Kenny, & Sheena Easton C&W/P&R '83

Singles: 7-inch

LIBERTY.......................................3-4 83

Picture Sleeves

LIBERTY.......................................3-4 83

LPs: 10/12-inch

LIBERTY.......................................5-10 84
Also see EASTON, Sheena

ROGERS, Kenny, & Dolly Parton P&R '83

Singles: 7-inch

RCA 3-4 83-85
REPRISE 3-4 90

Picture Sleeves

RCA 3-4 83
Also see PARTON, Dolly

ROGERS, Kenny, & Nickie Ryder C&W '86

Singles: 7-inch

RCA 3-4 86

ROGERS, Kenny, & First Edition P&R/C&W/LP '69

Singles: 7-inch

JOLLY ROGERS 3-5 72-73
REPRISE 4-8 68-72

LPs: 10/12-inch

JOLLY ROGERS 8-12 72-73
REPRISE 10-25 69-72
Members: Kenny Rogers; Mike Settle; Terry Williams; Mickey Jones; Kin Vassey; Mary Arnold.
Also see FIRST EDITION

ROGERS, Kenny, & Dottie West C&W '78

Singles: 7-inch

LIBERTY.......................................3-5 81-84
U.A. 3-5 78-79

LPs: 10/12-inch

U.A. 5-10 78-80

LPs: 10/12-inch

Also see ROGERS, Kenny
Also see WEST, Dottie

ROGERS, Lee R&B '65

Singles: 7-inch

D-TOWN (1029 "Sad Affair")............ 10-20 64
D-TOWN (1035 "I Want You to Have Everything")................................ 10-20 64
D-TOWN (1050 "Boss Love") 10-20 64
NSTANT..3-5 72
LOADSTONE..................................3-5 72
MAH'S (9 "Walk On By")..................15-25 60s
PLATINUM SOUND...........................3-5 79
PREMIUM STUFF (4 "Jack the Playboy") 15-25 67
WHEELSVILLE 15-25 66

ROGERS, Roy P&R '38

(With Dale Evans; with Sons of the Pioneers)

Singles: 78 rpm

DECCA 10-20 40-44
GOLDEN.......................................4-6 50s
RCA..5-15 50-57
VICTOR 8-15 45-48
VOCALION 20-30 38

Singles: 7-inch

CAPITOL.......................................3-5 70-71
GOLDEN.......................................5-8 50s
MCA 3-5 80
NEW DISC.....................................8-12 56
RCA (Except 215) 5-15 51-52
RCA (215 "Souvenir Album") 20-40 49
(Boxed set of three colored vinyl 45s.)
20TH FOX 3-5 74-75

Picture Sleeves

GOLDEN 5-8 50s

EPs: 7-inch

BLUEBIRD.....................................10-20 50s
RCA (Except 3041)..........................12-25 50-57
RCA (3041 "Souvenir Album") 25-50 52

LPs: 10/12-inch

BLUEBIRD.....................................15-25 59
CAMDEN.......................................10-20 60-75
CAPITOL.......................................10-30 62-72
GHOST TOWN 10-20
GOLDEN.......................................15-30 62
NOSTALGIA MERCHANT 8-10
PICKWICK.....................................5-10 70s
RADIOLA......................................8-10
RCA (1439 "Sweet Hour of Prayer")..20-30 57
RCA (3041 "Souvenir Album") 40-60 52
(10-inch LP.)
RCA (3168 "Hymns of Faith")............30-50 54
(10-inch LP.)
20TH FOX 5-10 75
WORD..4-8 73-77
Also see SONS of the PIONEERS

ROGERS, Roy, & Clint Black C&W '91

Singles: 7-inch

RCA..3-4 91
Also see BLACK, Clint

ROGERS, Roy, with Spade Cooley's Buckle Busters

Singles: 78 rpm

CORAL (8004 "Square Dances") 15-25 50
(Boxed, three-disc set.)

Singles: 7-inch

CORAL (8004 "Square Dances") 25-50 50
(Boxed, three-disc set.)
Also see ROGERS, Roy

ROGERS, Timmie P&R '57

(Timmie "Oh Yeah" Rogers; with Excelsior Hep Cats; with Stomp Russell Trio; Timmy Rogers; Super Soul Brother Alias Clark Dark.)

Singles: 78 rpm

CAMEO 10-25 57-58
CAPITOL.......................................5-10 53
EXCELSIOR...................................10-20 45
MAJESTIC.....................................10-20 46
MERCURY 10-20 54
REGIS 10-20 45
VARSITY 10-20 50s

Singles: 7-inch

CADET 3-5 71
CAMEO 5-10 57-58
CAPITOL.......................................5-10 53
EPIC 4-8 65-66
MERCURY (70451 "If I Give My Heart to You")...20-30 54
PARKWAY 5-10 60
PARTEE.......................................3-5 73
PHILIPS.......................................4-8 62
SIGNATURE 5-10 60

LPs: 10/12-inch

EPIC 15-20 65
PARTEE.......................................10-15 73
PHILIPS.......................................15-20 63

ROLLE, Ralph D&D '85

Singles: 12-inch

STREETWISE.................................4-6 85

Singles: 7-inch

STREETWISE.................................3-4 85

ROLLERS P&R/R&B '61

Singles: 7-inch

LIBERTY (55303 "Got My Eye on You")...10-15 61
LIBERTY (55320 "The Continental Walk") 10-15 61
LIBERTY (55357 "The Bounce") 10-15 61
Member: Al Wilson; Eddie Wilson; Don Sampson; Willie Willingham.
Also see WILSON, Al

ROLLIN, Dana — P&R '66

Singles: 7-inch

TOWER....4-8 67

ROLLING STONES — P&R/LP '64

Singles: 12-inch

ATCO (4616 "Miss You")....10-20 79
ROLLING STONES (70 "Hot Stuff")....50-100 76
(Promotional issue only.)
ROLLING STONES (119 "Miss You")....25-50 78
(Promotional issue only.)
ROLLING STONES (253 "If I Was a Dancer")....25-50 79
(Promotional issue only.)
ROLLING STONES (367 "Emotional Rescue")....20-40 80
(Promotional issue only.)
ROLLING STONES (397 "Start Me Up")....20-40 81
(Promotional issue only. Price includes special cover.)
ROLLING STONES (574 "She Was Hot")....20-40 84
(Promotional issue only.)
ROLLING STONES (685 "Undercover of the Night")....25-40 83
(White label. Promotional issue only.)
ROLLING STONES (685 "Undercover of the Night")....20-40 83
(Yellow label. Promotional issue only.)
ROLLING STONES (692 "Too Much Blood")....20-40 85
(Promotional issue only. Price includes special cover.)
ROLLING STONES (2275 "Harlem Shuffle")....10-15 86
(Price includes special cover.)
ROLLING STONES (2275 "Harlem Shuffle")....10-20 86
(Promotional issue only. Price includes special cover.)
ROLLING STONES (2340 "One Hit")....10-15 86
(Price includes color cover.)
ROLLING STONES (2340 "One Hit")....20-30 86
(Price includes black and white cover. Promotional issue only.)
ROLLING STONES (4609 "Miss You")....10-15 78
(Price includes special cover.)
ROLLING STONES (4616 "Miss You"/"Hot Stuff")....15-25 78
ROLLING STONES (96902 "Too Much Blood")....10-15 85
(Price includes special cover.)
ROLLING STONES (96978 "Undercover of the Night")....10-15 83
(Price includes special cover.)

Singles: 7-inch

ABKCO (4701 "I Don't Know Why")....5-10 75
ABKCO (4702 "Out of Time")....5-10 75
COLUMBIA....3-5 90-91
LONDON (901 thru 910)....4-8 66-69
LONDON (9641 "Stoned")....2000-4000 64
LONDON (9657 "Not Fade Away")....10-15 64
(Purple and white label.)
LONDON (9657 "Not Fade Away")....5-10 65
(Blue and white swirl label.)
LONDON (9682 "Tell Me")....10-15 64
(Purple and white label.)
LONDON (9682 "Tell Me")....5-10 65
(Blue and white swirl label.)
LONDON (9687 "It's All Over Now") 10-15 64
(Purple and white label.)
LONDON (9687 "It's All Over Now")....5-10 65
(Blue and white swirl label.)
LONDON (9708 "Time Is on My Side")....10-15 64
(Purple and white label.)
LONDON (9708 "Time Is on My Side")....25-50 64
(Purple label with silver print. Canadian.)
LONDON (9708 "Time Is on My Side")....5-10 65
(Blue and white swirl label.)
LONDON (9725 "Heart of Stone")....10-15 65
(Purple and white label.)
LONDON (9725 "Heart of Stone")....25-50 65
(Purple label with silver print. Canadian.)
LONDON (9725 "Heart of Stone")....4-6 65
(Blue and white swirl label.)
LONDON (9741 "The Last Time")....5-10 65
(Purple and white label.)
LONDON (9741 "The Last Time")....4-6 65
(Blue and white swirl label.)
LONDON (9766 "Satisfaction")....5-10 65
LONDON (9766 "Satisfaction")....25-50 65
(Purple label with silver print. Canadian.)
LONDON (9792 "Get Off of My Cloud")....5-10 65
LONDON (9808 "As Tears Go By")....5-10 65
LONDON (9823 "19th Nervous Breakdown")....5-10 66
ROLLING STONES (Except 99724)....3-5 71-86
ROLLING STONES (99724 "Miss You"/"Too Tough")....10-15 78
VIRGIN (38448 "Love Is Strong")....3-4 94
WMEE 97FM (001 "The Stones on 97")....4-8

Note: The three Canadian purple label with silver print issues are the only ones we have confirmed so far with that label – the same as used by London in the '50s and early '60s. If any other early Stones singles came on this label, we would like to know of them.

Promotional Singles

ABKCO (4701 "I Don't Know Why")....8-12 75
ABKCO (4702 "Out of Time")....8-12 75
COLUMBIA....5-10 90
LONDON (901 thru 910)....20-30 66-69
LONDON (9641 "Stoned")....1000-2000 64
LONDON (9657 "Not Fade Away") 50-100 64
LONDON (9682 "Tell Me")....25-50 64
LONDON (9687 "It's All Over Now") 25-50 64
LONDON (9708 "Time Is on My Side")....25-50 64
LONDON (9725 "Heart of Stone")....25-50 65
LONDON (9741 "The Last Time")....25-50 65
LONDON (9766 "Satisfaction")....15-25 65
LONDON (9792 "Get Off of My Cloud")....15-25 65
LONDON (9808 "As Tears Go By")..15-25 65
LONDON (9823 "19th Nervous Breakdown")....15-25 66
ROLLING STONES (228 "Time Waits for No One")....15-25 76
ROLLING STONES (316 "Before They Make Me Run")....15-25 78
ROLLING STONES (05000 series)....5-15 86
ROLLING STONES (19000 thru 21301, except 19307)....5-15 71-82
ROLLING STONES (19307 "Miss You"/Far Away Eyes")....5-15 78
ROLLING STONES (19307 "Far Away Eyes"/ Far Away Eyes")....50-100 78
ROLLING STONES (90000 series, except 99724)....5-10 82-85
ROLLING STONES (99724 "Miss You"/"Miss You")....15-25 78

Picture Sleeves

LONDON (901 "Paint It Black")....15-25 66
LONDON (902 "Mother's Little Helper")....15-25 66
LONDON (903 "Have You Seen Your Mother Baby, Standing in the Shadows")....15-25 66
LONDON (904 "Ruby Tuesday")....15-25 67
LONDON (905 "Dandelion")....100-150 67
LONDON (906 "She's a Rainbow")...15-25 67
LONDON (908 "Jumpin' Jack Flash")....10-20 68
LONDON (909 "Street Fighting Man")....5000-10000 68
(Thus far, 12 copies are known to exist.)
LONDON (910 "Honky Tonk Women")....10-20 69
LONDON (9657 "Not Fade Away")....150-250 64
LONDON (9682 "Tell Me")....75-125 64
LONDON (9687 "It's All Over Now")....50-100 64
LONDON (9708 "Time Is on My Side")....50-100 64
LONDON (9725 "Heart of Stone").400-600 65
LONDON (9741 "The Last Time")....25-50 65
LONDON (9766 "Satisfaction")....50-100 65
LONDON (9792 "Get Off of My Cloud")....25-35 65
LONDON (9808 "As Tears Go By")...25-35 65
LONDON (9823 "19th Nervous Breakdown")....25-45 66
ROLLING STONES (Except 228, 316 and 19309)....3-6 78-86
ROLLING STONES (228 "Time Waits for No One")....15-25 76
(Promotional issue only.)
ROLLING STONES (316 "Before They Make Me Run")....15-25 78
(Promotional issue only.)
ROLLING STONES (19309 "Beast of Burden")....1000-2000 78
ROLLING STONES....3-6 71-81
(For generic, die-cut paper sleeves with Rolling Stones tongue logo. Not for any specific release.)
VIRGIN (38448 "Love Is Strong")....3-4 94

EPs: 7-inch

ATLANTIC (900 "Exile on Main Street")....50-75 72
(Juke box issue only.)
ATLANTIC (5901 "Goats Head Soup")....50-75 73
(Juke box issue only.)
LONDON (34 "Rolling Stones Now")....100-200 64
(Juke box issue only.)
LONDON (37 "Out of Our Heads")....100-200 64
(Juke box issue only.)
LONDON (43 "December's Children")....100-200 64
(Juke box issue only.)
LONDON (54 "Their Satanic Majesties Request")....150-250 64
(Juke box issue only.)
ROLLING STONES (287 "The Rolling Stones")....50-100 77
(Promotional issue only.)

LPs: 10/12-inch

ABKCO (0268 "Greatest Hits")....20-25 70s
(TV mail-order offer.)
ABKCO (1077 "30 Greatest Hits")....20-25 77
(Canadian.)
ABKCO (1089 "Greatest Hits, Vol. II")....20-25 77
ABKCO (1218 "Singles Collection")..15-25 89
(Four-LP set.)
CAPITOL (61755 "Voodoo Lounge") 10-15 90s
CAPITOL (7527 "Stripped")....10-15 90s
CRAWDADDY ("Rolling Stones Tour Special")....150-200 76
(Promotional issue to college radio stations only.)
D.I.R. (312 "King Biscuit Flower Hour")....150-200 80
(Promotional issue only.)
D.I.R. (325 "King Biscuit Flower Hour")....150-200 80
(Promotional issue only.)
INS RADIO (1003 "It's Here Luv")...75-125 65
LONDON (1 "Big Hits")....15-25 66
(Monaural.)
LONDON (RSD1 "The Promotional Album")....800-1000
LONDON (2 "Their Satanic Majesties Request")....75-125 67
(Monaural. Has 3-D cover.)
LONDON (2 "Their Satanic Majesties Request")....20-30 67
(Stereo. Has 3-D cover.)
LONDON (2 "Their Satanic Majesties Request")....10-15 70
(Stereo. With standard cover.)

LONDON (3 "Through the Past Darkly") 8-10 69
LONDON (4 "Let It Bleed") 10-20 69
(With bonus poster.)
LONDON (4 "Let It Bleed") 8-10 69
(Without poster.)
LONDON (5 "Get Your Ya-Yas Out") .. 8-10 70
LONDON (375 "Rolling Stones") 30-50 64
(Stereo. Add $75 to $100 if accompanied by a 12" x 12" bonus, color photo. Cover has printed note about photo at lower left. With "Full Frequency Range Recording" label.)
LONDON (375 "Rolling Stones") 8-10 65
(No mention of photo on cover. Does not have "Full Frequency Range Recording" on label.)
LONDON (402 "12 x 5") 30-50 64
(Stereo. With "Full Frequency Range Recording" label.)
LONDON (402 "12 x 5") 8-10 65
(Does not have "Full Frequency Range Recording" on label.)
LONDON (420 "Rolling Stones Now") 30-50 65
(Stereo. With "Full Frequency Range Recording" label.)
LONDON (420 "Rolling Stones Now") 8-10 65
(Does not have "Full Frequency Range Recording" on label.)
LONDON (429 "Out of Our Heads") .. 30-50 65
(Stereo. With "Full Frequency Range Recording" label.)
LONDON (429 "Out of Our Heads") 8-10 65
(Does not have "Full Frequency Range Recording" on label.)
LONDON (451 "December's Children") 30-50 65
(Stereo. With "Full Frequency Range Recording" label.)
LONDON (451 "December's Children") 8-10 65
(Does not have "Full Frequency Range Recording" on label.)
LONDON (476 "Aftermath") 8-10 66
(Stereo.)
LONDON (493 "Got Live If You Want It") 8-10 66
(Stereo.)
LONDON (499 "Between the Buttons") 8-10 67
(Stereo.)
LONDON (509 "Flowers") 8-10 67
(Stereo.)
LONDON (539 "Beggars Banquet") 8-12 68
(All songs are shown as written by Jagger & Richard.)
LONDON (539 "Beggars Banquet") 8-10 60s
(*Prodigal Son* is shown as written by Rev. Wilkins.)
LONDON (606/7 "Hot Rocks") 10-12 71
LONDON (626/7 "More Hot Rocks") 10-12 72
LONDON (3375 "The Rolling Stones") 75-100 64
(Monaural. With "Full Frequency Range Recording" label. Add $75 to $100 if accompanied by a 12" x 12" bonus, color photo. Cover has printed note about photo at lower left.)
LONDON (3375 "The Rolling Stones") 30-40 65
(Does not have "Full Frequency Range Recording" on label.)
LONDON (3375 "The Rolling Stones") 400-600 64
(White label, monaural. Promotional issue only.)
LONDON (3402 "12 x 5") 50-75 64
(Monaural. With "Full Frequency Range Recording" label.)
LONDON (3402 "12 x 5") 30-40 65
(Does not have "Full Frequency Range Recording" on label.)
LONDON (3420 "Rolling Stones Now") 50-75 65
(Monaural. With "Full Frequency Range Recording" label.)
LONDON (3420 "Rolling Stones Now") 30-40 65
(Does not have "Full Frequency Range Recording" on label.)
LONDON (3429 "Out of Our Heads") 50-75 65
(Monaural. With "Full Frequency Range Recording" label.)
LONDON (3429 "Out of Our Heads") 30-40 65
(Does not have "Full Frequency Range Recording" on label.)
LONDON (3451 "December's Children") 50-75 65
(Monaural. With "Full Frequency Range Recording" label.)
LONDON (3451 "December's Children") 30-40 65
(Does not have "Full Frequency Range Recording" on label.)
LONDON (3476 "Aftermath") 20-30 66
(Monaural.)
LONDON (3493 "Got Live If You Want It") 20-30 66
(Monaural.)
LONDON (3499 "Between the Buttons") 20-30 67
(Monaural.)
LONDON (3509 "Flowers") 20-30 67
(Monaural.)
LONDON (9134 "Big Hits, High Tide & Green Grass") 1000-1500 69
(Test picture disc. Some have photo of the group Ten Years After on one side. All have music from *Thru the Past Darkly.*)
LONDON/ABKCO (66671 "Hot Rocks") 15-18 96
LONDON/ABKCO (62671 "Fazed Cookies") 15-18 96
LONDON/ABKCO (70,000 series) 10-15 96
LONDON/ABKCO (80,000 series) 10-15 96
MFSL (1 "Rolling Stones") 250-300 85
(11-LP boxed set, includes booklet, postcard and alignment tool.)
MFSL (060 "Sticky Fingers") 30-50 82
MFSL (087 "Some Girls") 30-50 82
MUTUAL BROADCASTING SYSTEM ("Rolling Stones: Past and Present") 800-1200 84
(Boxed, 12-disc set, issued only to radio stations. Price includes programming sheets.)
ROLLING STONES (2900 "Exile on Main St.") 10-15 72
(Add $3 to $5 if accompanied by sheet of 12 bonus postcards.)
ROLLING STONES (9001 "Love You Live") 10-15 77
ROLLING STONES (16015 "Emotional Rescue") 5-10 80
ROLLING STONES (16028 "Sucking in the Seventies") 5-10 81
ROLLING STONES (16052 "Tattoo You") 5-10 81
ROLLING STONES (39108 "Some Girls") 10-15 78
(With all girls' faces shown.)
ROLLING STONES (39108 "Some Girls") 5-10 78
(Not all girls' faces shown. Cover is "Under Construction.")
ROLLING STONES (39113 "Still Life") 5-10 82
ROLLING STONES (39114 "Still Life") 40-50 82
(Picture disc.)
ROLLING STONES (40250 "Dirty Work") 5-10 86
ROLLING STONES (45333 "Steel Wheels") 5-10 89
ROLLING STONES (47456 "Flashpoint") 8-10 91
ROLLING STONES (59100 "Sticky Fingers") 8-10 71
(Yellow label.)
ROLLING STONES (59100 "Sticky Fingers") 150-250 71
(White label. Promotional issue only.)
ROLLING STONES (59101 "Goats Head Soup") 8-10 73
ROLLING STONES (79101 "It's Only Rock & Roll") 8-10 74
ROLLING STONES (79102 "Made in the Shade") 8-10 75
ROLLING STONES (79104 "Black and Blue") 8-10 76
ROLLING STONES (90120 "Undercover") 5-10 83
ROLLING STONES (90176 "Rewind") 5-10 84
SILHOUETTE (10005 "Precious Moments") 10-15 81
(Picture disc. Is this title correct?)
VIRGIN 8-10 94

Members: Mick Jagger; Keith Richards; Bill Wyman; Brian Jones; Charlie Watts; Mick Taylor; Ron Wood.

Also see BEACH BOYS
Also see FAITHFUL, Marianne
Also see HOPKINS, Nicky
Also see JAGGER, Mick
Also see JONES, Brian
Also see RICHARDS, Keith
Also see ROCKET 88
Also see TAYLOR, Mick
Also see WILLIE & Poor Boys
Also see WOOD, Ron
Also see WYMAN, Bill

ROMAN, Dick P&R '62

Singles: 78 rpm

ABC-PAR 4-8 56
DOUBLE AA 4-6 55-56

Singles: 7-inch

ABC-PAR 5-10 56
CHARLIE PARKER 4-8 62
CORAL 4-6 60s
DOUBLE AA 5-10 55-56
EPIC 4-8 59-61
FORD 4-8 60s
HARMON 5-10 62-63
MGM 4-6 60s
PRESIDENT 4-6 60s
SEVILLE 4-6 60s
SMASH 4-8 63

LPs: 10/12-inch

HARMON 15-25 62

ROMAN, Lyn R&B '86

Singles: 7-inch

DOT 4-6 68
ICHIBAN 3-4 86

ROMAN HOLLIDAY P&R/LP '83

Singles: 12-inch

JIVE 4-6 83

Singles: 7-inch

JIVE 3-4 83-85

LPs: 10/12-inch

JIVE 5-10 83

ROMANS (With Little Caesar): see LITTLE CAESAR & ROMANS

ROMANTICS P&R/LP '80

Singles: 12-inch

NEMPEROR 4-8 83-85

Singles: 7-inch

BOMP 4-6 78
NEMPEROR 3-5 80-85
SPIDER 8-12 77

Picture Sleeves

BOMP 4-6 78
NEMPEROR 3-5 80-85

EPs: 7-inch

BOMP 5-8 78

LPs: 10/12-inch

NEMPEROR 5-10 80-85

ROMEO R&B '87

Singles: 7-inch

TRIPLE 3-4 87

ROMEO & JULIET P&R '69
("Dialogue from film soundtrack")
Singles: 7-inch
CAPITOL....3-6 69

ROMEO VOID LP '82
Singles: 12-inch
COLUMBIA....4-6 82-84
415 (007 "Never Say Yes")....5-10 81
Singles: 7-inch
COLUMBIA....3-4 82-84
LPs: 10/12-inch
COLUMBIA....5-8 82-84
415....8-12 82
Members: Debora Iyall; Peter Woods; Benjamin Bossi; Larry Carter; Frank Zincavage.

ROMEO'S DAUGHTER P&R/LP '88
Singles: 7-inch
JIVE....3-4 88
Picture Sleeves
JIVE....3-4 88
LPs: 10/12-inch
JIVE....5-8 88

ROMEOS P&R/R&B '67
Singles: 7-inch
MARK II....4-8 67
LPs: 10/12-inch
MARK II....15-20 67
Members: Kenny Gamble; Thom Bell; Roland Chambers; Winnie Walford; Karl Chambers; Leon Huff.
Also see HUFF, Leon

RON & D.C. CREW P&R '87
Singles: 7-inch
PROFILE....3-4 87

RON C LP '90
LPs: 10/12-inch
PROFILE....5-8 90

RONALD & RUBY P&R '58
Singles: 7-inch
RCA....8-12 58
Members: Lee Morris; Beverly Ross.

RONDELS P&R '61
Singles: 7-inch
AMY....8-12 61-62
NOTE....8-12 61

RON-DELS P&R '65
Singles: 7-inch

RON-DELS P&R '65
(Rondels; Ron-Dells)
Singles: 7-inch
ARLEN (723 "Slow Down")....15-25 63
BILLIE FRAN (101 "Matilda")....15-25 60s
BROWNFIELD (2 "Hey Baby '66")....10-15 66
BROWNFIELD (13 "100 Pounds of Honey")....10-15 66
BROWNFIELD (16 "Just When You Think You're Somebody")....10-20 65
BROWNFIELD (18 "If You Really Want Me to, I'll Go")....10-20 65
BROWNFIELD (23 "Lost My Love Today")....10-20 65
BROWNFIELD (33 "Cryin' Over You")....10-15 66
BROWNFIELD (303 "I Know She Knows")....10-20 64
BROWNFIELD (1037 "You Made Me Cry")....8-12 67
CHARAY (75 "100 Pounds of Honey")..4-6
DOT (17323 "Matilda")....4-6 70
LE CAM (130 "Matilda")....25-35 63
(First issue.)
LE CAM (130 "Matilda")....3-6 73
SHAH (980 "I Ain't Never")....15-25 63
SHALIMAR (104 "Matilda")....15-25 63
SMASH (1986 "If You Really Want Me to, I'll Go")....8-12 65
SMASH (2002 "She's My Girl")....8-12 65
SMASH (2014 "Lose Your Money")....8-12 65
Members: Delbert McClinton; Billy Sanders; Jerry Foster; Jimmy Rodgers; Ronnie Kelly; Mike Clark; Darrell Norris; Carl Tanner; Ray Torres. Session: Ray Hildebrand; Bruce Channel.
Also see CHANNEL, Bruce
Also see McCLINTON, Delbert
Also see PAUL & PAULA

RONDO, Don P&R '56
Singles: 78 rpm
DECCA....3-5 55
JUBILEE....5-10 56-57
Singles: 7-inch
ATLANTIC....4-8 63
CARLTON....4-8 60-61
DECCA....5-10 55
JUBILEE....5-10 56-66
ROULETTE....4-8 59-60
TRIP....3-5
TUBA....4-6 65
U.A....4-6 66-67
VIRGO....3-5 72
LPs: 10/12-inch
JUBILEE....10-20 57-58
VOCALION....5-10 70

RONETTES P&R/R&B '63
(Ronnettes; "Featuring Veronica")
Singles: 7-inch
A&M....5-10 69
BUDDAH....5-10 73-74
COLPIX (646 "I'm Gonna Quit While I'm Ahead")....40-60 62
MAY (114 "Silhouettes")....30-40 63
MAY (138 "The Memory")....30-40 63
PAVILLION....3-5 82
PHILLES....10-15 63-66
Promotional Singles
A&M....8-12 69
BUDDAH....10-15 73-74
COLPIX (646 "I'm Gonna Quit While I'm Ahead")....30-40 62
MAY (114 "Silhouettes")....30-40 63
MAY (138 "The Memory")....30-40 63
PAVILLION....4-8 82
PHILLES....10-20 63-66
Picture Sleeves
PHILLES (123 "Walking in the Rain")....25-35 64
PHILLES (126 "Born to Be Together")....25-35 65
PHILLES (128 "Is This What I Get for Loving You")....30-40 65
LPs: 10/12-inch
COLPIX (486 "The Ronettes, Featuring Veronica")....50-100 65
(Blue label. Monaural.)
COLPIX (486 "The Ronettes, Featuring Veronica")....75-150 65
(Gold label. Monaural.)
COLPIX (486 "The Ronettes, Featuring Veronica")....60-75 65
(Blue label. Stereo.)
COLPIX (486 "The Ronettes, Featuring Veronica")....100-200 65
(Gold label. Stereo.)
COLPIX (486 "The Ronettes, Featuring Veronica")....75-100 65
(White label. Promotional issue only.)
PHILLES (4006 "Presenting the Fabulous Ronettes")....100-125 64
(Blue label. Monaural.)
PHILLES (4006 "Presenting the Fabulous Ronettes")....75-150 64
(Yellow label. Monaural.)
PHILLES (4006 "Presenting the Fabulous Ronettes")....200-300 64
(Yellow label with red print. Stereo.)
PHILLES (4006 "Presenting the Fabulous Ronettes")....200-250 64
(Yellow label with black print. Stereo issue through Capitol Record Club.)
MURRAY HILL....5-10 86
Members: Veronica Bennett-Spector; Estelle Bennett; Nedra Talley-Ross.
Also see DEE, Joey
Also see LOVE, Darlene / Ronettes
Also see RONNIE & RELATIVES
Also see SPECTOR, Ronnie

RONETTES / Crystals / Darlene Love
Singles: 7-inch
PAVILLION (1354 "Phil Spector's Christmas Medley")....3-5 81
(Promotional issue only.)

RONETTES / Crystals / Darlene Love / Bob B. Soxx & Blue Jeans
EPs: 7-inch
PHILLES ("Christmas EP")....20-40 63
LPs: 10/12-inch
APPLE (3400 "Phil Spector's Christmas Album")....10-12 72
PASSPORT (3604 "Phil Spector's Christmas Album")....5-8 85
PAVILLION....5-10 81
PHILLES (4005 "A Christmas Gift for You")....50-100 63
(Blue label.)
PHILLES (4005 "A Christmas Gift for You")....40-60 63
(Yellow and red label.)
W.B./SPECTOR....8-12
(Phil Spector is heard speaking on this LP. The Apple and Passport LPs are reissues of the Philles album.)
Also see BOB B. SOXX & Blue Jeans
Also see CRYSTALS
Also see HARVEY, Phil
Also see LOVE, Darlene
Also see RONETTES

RONNIE & HI-LITES P&R '62
Singles: 7-inch
ABC-PAR (10685 "High School Romance")....10-20 65
COLLECTABLES....3-4 80s
ERIC....3-4 70s
JOY (260 "I Wish That We Were Married")....15-25 62
JOY (265 "Send My Love")....15-25 62
RAVEN (8000 "Valerie")....10-15 63
(Black label.)
RAVEN (8000 "Valerie")....15-25 63
(White label. Promotional issue only.)
WIN (250 "A Slow Dance")....15-25 63
WIN (251 "The Fact of the Matter")...15-25 63
WIN (252 "High School Romance")..20-30 63

RONNIE & RELATIVES
(Ronettes)
Singles: 7-inch
COLPIX (601 "I Want a Boy")....50-100 61
MAY (111 "My Guiding Angel")....100-150 62
Also see RONETTES

RONNY & DAYTONAS P&R/LP '64
Singles: 7-inch
BARRY (3272 "G.T.O.")....5-10 64
(Canadian.)
MALA....6-12 64-66
RCA....5-10 66-68
SHOW-BIZ....8-12 68
Picture Sleeves
RCA (8896 "Dianne, Dianne")....15-25 66
LPs: 10/12-inch
MALA (4001 "G.T.O.")....50-100 64
MALA (4002 "Sandy")....20-35 66
(Monaural.)
MALA (4002-S "Sandy")....75-100 66
(Stereo.)
Members: Ronny Dayton; John "Bucky" Wilkin; Buzz Cason.

RONSON, Mick LP '74
LPs: 10/12-inch
RCA....8-12 74
Also see HUNTER, Ian, & Mick Ronson
Also see PURE PRAIRIE LEAGUE

RONSTADT, Linda P&R '68
(With the Stone Poneys; with Nelson Riddle Orchestra)
Singles: 7-inch
ASYLUM....3-5 73-85
CAPITOL (2004 "Different Drum")....5-10 67
CAPITOL (2110 "Up to My Neck in High Muddy Water")....10-15 68
CAPITOL (2195 "Some of Shelly's Blues")....5-10 68
CAPITOL (2438 "Dolphins")....5-10 69
CAPITOL (2767 "Lovesick Blues")....4-8 70
CAPITOL (2846 thru 4050)....3-6 70-75
CAPITOL (5838 "All the Beautiful Things")....8-12 67
CAPITOL (5910 "Evergreen")....5-10 67
ELEKTRA....3-5 75-78
SIDEWALK (937 "So Fine")....75-100 66
Picture Sleeves
ASYLUM....3-5 78-82
CAPITOL (2110 "Up to My Neck in High Muddy Water")....15-25 68
LPs: 10/12-inch
ASYLUM (Except 401 & 60489)....5-10 73-86
ASYLUM (401 "Living in the USA")....10-15 78
(Picture disc.)
ASYLUM (60489 " 'Round Midnight")....10-15 86
CAPITOL (208 thru 635)....10-15 69-72
CAPITOL (2000 series)....12-18 68
CAPITOL (11000 series)....8-12 74-77
CAPITOL (16000 series)....5-10 80
ELEKTRA....5-10 80-87
MFSL (158 "What's New")....20-30 85
NAUTILUS (26 "Simple Dreams")....15-25 81
PICKWICK....8-10 70s
Session: Davie Allan; Nelson Riddle.
Also see ALLAN, Davie
Also see AXTON, Hoyt
Also see CASH, Johnny / Roy Clark / Linda Ronstadt
Also see CHRISTMAS SPIRIT
Also see EAGLES
Also see GLASS, Phillip
Also see NEWMAN, Randy
Also see NITTY GRITTY DIRT BAND & Linda Ronstadt
Also see PARTON, Dolly, Linda Ronstadt, & Emmylou Harris
Also see RIDDLE, Nelson
Also see STONE PONEYS

RONSTADT, Linda, & Emmylou Harris
Singles: 7-inch
ASYLUM....3-5 75
Also see HARRIS, Emmylou

RONSTADT, Linda, & James Ingram P&R '86
Singles: 7-inch
MCA....3-4 86
Picture Sleeves
MCA....3-4 86
Also see INGRAM, James

RONSTADT, Linda, & Aaron Neville LP '89
LPs: 10/12-inch
ELEKTRA....5-8 89
Also see NEVILLE, Aaron

RONSTADT, Linda, & J.D. Souther C&W '82
Singles: 7-inch
ASYLUM....3-4 82
Also see RONSTADT, Linda
Also see SOUTHER, J.D.

ROOFTOP SINGERS
P&R/C&W/R&B/LP '63
Singles: 7-inch
ATCO....4-6 67
VANGUARD....4-8 62-65
Picture Sleeves
VANGUARD....5-10 63
LPs: 10/12-inch
VANGUARD....10-20 63-65
Members: Erik Darling; Lynne Taylor; Bill Svanoe.
Also see TARRIERS

ROOMATES P&R '61
Singles: 7-inch
ADDIT (2211 "Making Believe")....10-20 60
BAN (691 "A Place Called Love")....3-5 85
CAMEO (233 "A Sunday Kind of Love")....15-25 62
CANADIAN AMERICAN (166 "My Heart")....15-25 64
COLLECTABLES....3-4 80s
PHILIPS (40105 "Gee")....10-20 63
PHILIPS (40153 "The Nearness of You")....20-25 63
PHILIPS (40153 "The Nearness of You")....15-20 64
PROMO (2211 "Making Believe")....10-15 64
VALMOR (8 "Glory of Love")....10-15 61
VALMOR (10 "Band of Gold")....10-15 61
VALMOR (13 "My Foolish Heart")....10-20 61
LPs: 10/12-inch
RELIC....5-10 80s
Also see CATHY JEAN & ROOMATES

ROS, Edmundo, & His Orch. P&R '58
Singles: 78 rpm
LONDON....3-5 51-57
Singles: 7-inch
LONDON....4-8 51-63
EPs: 7-inch
CORAL....5-10 54
LONDON....5-10 52-59
LPs: 10/12-inch
CORAL....8-15 54
LONDON....5-15 52-78

ROSCOE & MABLE R&B '77
Singles: 7-inch
CHOCOLATE CITY....3-5 77

ROSE, Andy P&R '58
(With the Thorns)
Singles: 7-inch
AAMCO....10-20 58
CORAL....5-10 59-62
EMBER....4-8 64
GOLDEN CREST....4-8 64

ROSE, Biff LP '69
Singles: 7-inch
BUDDAH....3-5 71
TETRAGRAMMATON....3-5 68-70
LPs: 10/12-inch
BUDDAH....8-12 71
TETRAGRAMMATON....10-15 68-69
U.A.....8-12 73

ROSE, David, & His Orch. P&R '43
Singles: 78 rpm
MGM....3-5 50-57
VICTOR....4-6 43-44
Singles: 7-inch
CAPITOL....3-6 66-69
MGM....3-8 50-67
Picture Sleeves
MGM....4-8 56-62
EPs: 7-inch
KAPP....5-10 59
MGM....5-10 51-58
ROYALE....5-10 50s
LPs: 10/12-inch
CAPITOL....8-15 66-69
DINO....5-10 72
KAPP....10-20 59-61
LION....10-20 59
MCA....5-8 83
MGM....5-20 51-70
METRO....5-15 65-66
SPIN-O-RAMA....5-10 60s
Also see PREVIN, Andre

ROSE BROTHERS R&B '86
Singles: 12-inch
MUSCLE SHOALS....4-6 86
Singles: 7-inch
MUSCLE SHOALS....3-4 86-88
LPs: 10/12-inch
MUSCLE SHOALS....5-8 86
Members: Bob Rose; Larry Rose; Kenny Rose; Greg Rose.

ROSE COLORED GLASS P&R '71
Singles: 7-inch
BANG....3-5 71

ROSE GARDEN P&R '67
Singles: 7-inch
ATCO....5-10 67-68
LPs: 10/12-inch
ATCO (255 "Rose Garden")....15-25 68
Members: Diana DiRose; James Groshong; John Noreen; Bill Fleming; Bruce Boudin.

ROSE ROYCE P&R/R&B/LP '76
Singles: 12-inch
MONTAGE....4-8 84
Singles: 7-inch
C&R....3-4 84
MCA....3-5 76-77
OMNI....3-4 86-87
WHITFIELD....3-5 77-82
LPs: 10/12-inch
EPIC....5-8 82
MCA....5-10 76
WHITFIELD....5-10 77-81

ROSE TATOO LP '80
Singles: 7-inch
MIRAGE....3-5 80-82
LPs: 10/12-inch
MIRAGE....5-10 80-82

ROSELLI, Jimmy LP '65
Singles: 7-inch
RIC....4-8 65
U.A.....4-6 65-69
LPs: 10/12-inch
RIC....10-15 65
U.A.....5-12 65-72

ROSIE P&R '60
(With the Originals; Rosie "Formerly with the Originals")
Singles: 7-inch
ABC....3-5 73
HIGHLAND....10-20 60-61
BRUNSWICK....10-20 61
LPs: 10/12-inch
BRUNSWICK (54102 "Lonley Blue Nights")....40-60 61
(Monaural.)
BRUNSWICK (754102 "Lonley Blue Nights")....50-80 61
(Stereo.)

ROSS, Charlie P&R '75
Singles: 7-inch
BIG TREE....3-5 75-76
TOWN HOUSE....3-4 82-83

ROSS, Diana P&R/R&B/LP '70
Singles: 12-inch
MOTOWN....5-10 78-80
Singles: 7-inch
MOTOWN....3-6 70-81
(Black vinyl.)
RCA....3-5 81-87
MOTOWN....5-10 70-81
(Colored vinyl. Promotional issue only.)
Picture Sleeves
MOTOWN....3-6 70-80
RCA....3-5 82-87
EPs: 7-inch
MOTOWN (7588 "Sneak Preview from Lady Sings the Blues")....8-12 72
(Promotional issue only.)
LPs: 10/12-inch
DORAL (104 "Diana Ross")....150-200 60s
(Promotional mail-order issue, from Doral cigarettes.)
KORY....8-10 77
MOTOWN (100 series)....5-10 81-83
MOTOWN (711 thru 907)....8-12 70-78

MOTOWN (923 "The Boss") 5-10 79
(Black vinyl.)
MOTOWN (923 "The Boss") 10-20 79
(Colored vinyl. Promotional issue only.)
MOTOWN (951 thru 960) 6-12 81
MOTOWN (5000 series) 5-15 83
MOTOWN (6000 series) 6-12 83-89
(Black vinyl.)
MOTOWN (6381 "Remixes") 10-12 90s
(Colored vinyl. Promotional issue only.)
PARAMOUNT (181/182 "Lady Sings the Blues") 35-50 72
(An "MRA Multiple Record Album, serving the requirements of both radio and TV stations," this LP has a 15-minute interview with Diana Ross. Includes scripts. Promotional issue only.)
RCA 5-10 81-87
Also see DENVER, John / Diana Ross
Also see GAYE, Marvin, & Diana Ross
Also see IGLESIAS, Julio, & Diana Ross
Also see SUPREMES
Also see TEMPTATIONS
Also see U.S.A. for AFRICA

ROSS, Diana, & Bill Cosby / Diana Ross & Jackson Five

EPs: 7-inch

MOTOWN 5-10 70
Also see COSBY, Bill
Also see JACKSONS

ROSS, Diana, & Michael Jackson — P&R/R&B '78

Singles: 7-inch

MCA 3-5 78

Picture Sleeves

MCA 3-5 78
Also see JACKSON, Michael

ROSS, Diana, & Lionel Richie — P&R/R&B '81

Singles: 7-inch

MOTOWN 3-5 81
POLYGRAM ("Dreaming of You") 10-15 81
(Promotional issue only. No number given.)
Also see RICHIE, Lionel

ROSS, Diana, Stevie Wonder, Marvin Gaye, Smokey Robinson — P&R/R&B '79

Singles: 7-inch

MOTOWN (1455 "Pops, We Love You") 3-5 79
(Black vinyl.)
MOTOWN (1455 "Pops, We Love You") 5-10 79
(Heart shaped disc. Red vinyl.)
MOTOWN (1455 "Pops, We Love You") 10-20 79
(Green vinyl. Promotional issue only.)

LPs: 10/12-inch

MOTOWN 5-10 79
Also see DIAMOND, Neil / Diana Ross & Supremes
Also see GAYE, Marvin
Also see ROBINSON, Smokey
Also see ROSS, Diana
Also see WONDER, Stevie

ROSS, Jack — P&R '62

Singles: 7-inch

DOT 4-8 61-63
ROMAL 5-10 61

LPs: 10/12-inch

DOT (3429 "Cinderella") 15-25 62

ROSS, Jackie — P&R/R&B '64

(Jacki Ross)

Singles: 7-inch

BRUNSWICK 4-8 67-68
CAPITOL 3-5 76
CHESS 4-8 64
FOUNTAIN 4-6 69
GSF 3-5 72-73
MERCURY 3-5 70-71
SAR (129 "Hard Times") 5-10 62
SCEPTER 3-5 72

LPs: 10/12-inch

CHESS (1489 "Full Bloom") 15-25 64
Also see LITTLE MILTON & Jackie Ross

ROSS, Jimmy — R&B '81

Singles: 7-inch

RFC 3-5 81

ROSS, Spencer — P&R '60

(Robert Mersey)

Singles: 7-inch

BIGTOP 5-10 60
COLUMBIA 8-12 59-60

LPs: 10/12-inch

COLUMBIA 15-25 60

ROSSINGTON - COLLINS BAND — P&R/LP '80

(Rossington Band)

Singles: 7-inch

MCA 3-5 80-88

LPs: 10/12-inch

MCA 5-10 80-88
Members: Gary Rossington; Al Collins.
Also see LYNYRD SKYNYRD

ROTA, Nino — P&R '72

Singles: 7-inch

PARAMOUNT 3-5 72
U.A. 3-5 72

ROTARY CONNECTION — LP '68

Singles: 7-inch

CADET CONCEPT 4-8 68-70

LPs: 10/12-inch

CADET CONCEPT 15-25 68-70
Members: Minnie Riperton; Sidney Barnes.
Also see RIPPERTON, Minnie

ROTH, David Lee — P&R/LP '85

Singles: 7-inch

W.B. 3-4 85-90

Picture Sleeves

W.B. 3-4 85-88

LPs: 10/12-inch

W.B. 5-10 85-90
Also see BEACH BOYS
Also see VAN HALEN

ROUGH DIAMOND — LP '77

Singles: 7-inch

ISLAND 3-5 77

LPs: 10/12-inch

ISLAND 8-10 77
Members: Byron Britton; Geoff Britton.
Also see URIAH HEEP

ROUGH TRADE — P&R '82

Singles: 7-inch

BOARDWALK 3-5 82

LPs: 10/12-inch

UMBRELLA 10-15 77

ROUND ROBIN — P&R '64

Singles: 7-inch

CAPITOL 4-8 67
DOMAIN 5-10 63-65
SHOT 4-8 66

LPs: 10/12-inch

CHALLENGE (620 "Land of 1000 Dances") 15-25 65
DOMAIN (101 "Greatest Dance Hits Slauson Style") 25-35 64

ROUND ROBINS / Joe Cenna

Singles: 7-inch

BELL 4-8 60s

ROUNDTREE — R&B '78

Singles: 12-inch

ISLAND 4-8 78

Singles: 7-inch

ISLAND 3-5 78
Members: Diva Gray; Bernard Edwards; Luther Vandross; David Lasley.
Also see CHIC
Also see GRAY, Diva, & Oyster
Also see VANDROSS, Luther

ROUNDTREE, Richard — R&B '76

Singles: 7-inch

ARTISTS of AMERICA 3-5 76
MGM 3-5 73
VERVE 3-5 72-73

LPs: 10/12-inch

MGM 8-12 72

ROUSSOS, Demis — P&R/LP '78

Singles: 7-inch

BIG TREE 3-5 74-75
MGM 3-5 73
MERCURY 3-5 76-78

Picture Sleeves

MERCURY 3-5 78

LPs: 10/12-inch

BIG TREE 8-12 74-75
MGM 10-15 72
MERCURY 5-10 76-78

ROUTERS — P&R '62

Singles: 7-inch

W.B. 8-12 62-64

LPs: 10/12-inch

MERCURY 10-15 73
W.B. (1490 "Let's Go") 20-30 63
W.B. (1524 "1963's Great Instrumental Hits") 20-30 63
W.B. (1559 "Charge!") 20-30 64
W.B. (1595 "Chuck Berry Songbook") 20-30 65
Members: Joe Saraceno; Rene Hall; Mike Gordon. Ed Kay.

ROVER BOYS — P&R '56

Singles: 78 rpm

ABC-PAR 5-10 56
CORAL 5-10 54
VIK 10-15 56-57

Singles: 7-inch

ABC 3-5 73
ABC-PAR 10-20 56
CORAL 10-20 54
DECCA 5-10 63
RCA 8-12 58-59
U.A. 5-10 61
VIK 10-20 56-57
Member: Billy Albert.

ROVERS — C&W '81

(Irish Rovers)

Singles: 7-inch

EPIC 3-5 81

LPs: 10/12-inch

CLEVELAND INT'L 5-10 81-82
Also see IRISH ROVERS

ROWANS — P&R '76

Singles: 7-inch

ASYLUM 3-5 75-76
COLUMBIA 3-5 72-73

LPs: 10/12-inch

ASYLUM 8-10 75-77
COLUMBIA 10-15 72
Members: Peter Rowan; Chris Rowan; Lorin Rowan.
Also see EARTH OPERA
Also see GARCIA, Jerry
Also see OLD and in the WAY

ROWLES, John — P&R/LP '71

Singles: 7-inch

KAPP 3-6 68-71
UNI 3-6 68

LPs: 10/12-inch

KAPP 10-15 69-71
MCA 5-8

ROXANNE — P&R '88

Singles: 7-inch

SCOTTI BROS 3-4 88
Members: Jamie Brown; John Butler; Dave Landry; Joe Infante.

ROXANNE WITH UTFO — D&D '85

Singles: 12-inch

SELECT 4-6 85

Singles: 7-inch

SELECT 3-4 85

Also see UTFO

ROXETTE P&R/LP '89

Singles: 12-inch

CAPITOL (15018 "Hartland") 5-10 84

Singles: 7-inch

EMI (Except 04409) 3-4 89

EMI (04409 "Listen to Your Heart") 3-6 89

(Promotional issue only. Commercial single release on cassette only.)

LPs: 10/12-inch

EMI 5-8 89-91

ROXY MUSIC LP '73

Singles: 7-inch

W.B. (2033 "Avalon") 5-8 82

Singles: 7-inch

ATCO 3-6 75-80

REPRISE 4-8 72

W.B. (Except 7779) 3-5 82-83

W.B. (7779 "Do the Strand") 4-8 73

Promotional Singles

ATCO 5-10 75-80

W.B. 3-5 82-83

Picture Sleeves

W.B. 3-5 82-83

LPs: 10/12-inch

ATCO (Except 106 & 8114) 8-15 74-83

ATCO (106 "Country Life") 20-35 75

(Cover pictures two women in their underwear.)

ATCO (106 "Country Life") 8-15 75

(The two women are not pictured on cover.)

ATCO (38114 "Manifesto") 25-30 75

(Picture disc. Promotional issue only.)

ATLANTIC 8-10 74

REPRISE (2114 "Roxy Music") 15-25 72

W.B. (Except 2696) 5-10 82-83

W.B. (2696 "For Your Pleasure") 15-25 73

Member: Bryan Ferry.

Also see CARRACK, Paul

Also see ENO, Brian

Also see FERRY, Bryan, & Roxy Music

Also see MANZANERA, Phil

ROY, Barbara D&D '84

Singles: 12-inch

ASCOT 4-6 84

Singles: 7-inch

RCA 3-4 86

Also see ECSTASY, PASSION & PAIN

ROY C. R&B '65

(Roy Charles Hammond)

Singles: 7-inch

ALAGA 3-5 71

BLACK HAWK 4-8 65-66

MERCURY 3-5 73-77

SHOUT 4-6 66

UPTOWN 4-6 66

LPs: 10/12-inch

MERCURY 8-12 77

Also see GENIES

ROY - SARAH & TRAITS

Singles: 7-inch

LORI (9551 "You'll Never Make Me Blue") 10-20 60s

(Same song as *Treat Me Right,* the title track of Roy Head's Scepter LP.)

Member: Roy Head.

Also see HEAD, Roy

ROYAL, Billy Joe P&R/LP '65

Singles: 7-inch

ALL WOOD 5-10 62

ATLANTIC (2300 series) 4-8 66

ATLANTIC (87000 thru 89000 series) 3-4 85-91

ATLANTIC AMERICA 3-5 85-89

COLUMBIA (43305 "Down in the Boondocks") 4-8 65

(Black vinyl.)

COLUMBIA (43305 "Down in the Boondocks") 10-20 65

(Colored vinyl. Promotional issue only.)

COLUMBIA (43390 "I Knew You When") 4-8 65

(Black vinyl.)

COLUMBIA (43390 "I Knew You When") 10-20 65

(Colored vinyl. Promotional issue only.)

COLUMBIA (43465 thru 45620) 4-8 65-72

FAIRLANE 8-12 61-62

KAT FAMILY 3-5 81

MGM/SOUTH 3-5 73

MERCURY 3-5 80

PLAYER'S 5-10 65

PRIVATE STOCK 3-5 78

SCEPTER 3-5 76

TOLLIE 5-10 64

Picture Sleeves

ATLANTIC AMERICA 3-6 80s

TOLLIE 8-12 64

LPs: 10/12-inch

ATLANTIC AMERICA 5-10 86-89

BACK-TRAC 5-8 85

BRYLEN 5-10

COLUMBIA (Except 45063) 15-25 65-69

COLUMBIA (45063 "Greatest Hits") 5-8 89

51 WEST 5-10 83

KAT FAMILY 5-10 81

MERCURY 5-10 80

Also see FARGO, Donna, & Billy Joe Royal

Also see SOUTH, Joe / Billy Joe Royal

ROYAL GUARDSMEN P&R '66

Singles: 7-inch

LAURIE 4-8 66-69

Picture Sleeves

LAURIE 5-10 67

LPs: 10/12-inch

AUDIO FIDELITY (1913 "Snoopy's Christmas") 10-15 83

(Picture disc.)

LAURIE 10-20 67-68

Members: Chris Nunley; Barry Winslow; Bill Balough; Tom Richards.

ROYAL HARMONY QUARTET R&B '42

Singles: 78 rpm

KEYNOTE 5-10 42

Members: Julius Ginyard; Ted Brooks; Bill Johnson; John Jennings; George McFadden.

ROYAL HOUSE R&B '88

Singles: 7-inch

IDLERS WAR 3-4 88

ROYAL JOKERS P&R '55

Singles: 78 rpm

ATCO 10-20 55-56

HI-Q 15-25 57

Singles: 7-inch

ATCO (6052 "You Tickle Me Baby") 25-35 55

ATCO (6062 "Don't Leave Me, Fanny") 20-30 55

ATCO (6077 "She's Mine, All Mine") 25-35 55

FORTUNE (560 "You Tickle Me Baby") 15-20 63

FORTUNE (840 "Sweet Little Angel") 20-25 57

HI-Q (5004 "September in the Rain") 25-30 57

ROYAL PHILHARMONIC ORCH.

(Conducted by Louis Clark) P&R/LP '81

Singles: 7-inch

RCA 3-4 81-83

LPs: 10/12-inch

RCA 5-8 81-83

ROYAL SCOTS DRAGOON GUARDS P&R/LP '72

Singles: 7-inch

RCA 3-5 72

LPs: 10/12-inch

RCA 5-10 72

ROYAL SONS QUINTET

(Five Royales)

Singles: 78 rpm

APOLLO (253 "Bedside of a Neighbor") 100-200 52

APOLLO (266 "Come Over Here") 50-100 52

Members: Johnny Tanner; Lowman Pauling; Clarence Pauling; William Samuels; Otto Jeffries; Clarence Pauling.

Also see FIVE ROYALES

ROYAL TEENS P&R/R&B '58

("Joey Villa & Royal Teens")

Singles: 78 rpm

ABC-PAR 15-25 57-58

POWER (215 "Short Shorts") 50-100 57

Singles: 7-inch

ABC 3-5 73

ABC-PAR (9882 "Short Shorts") 10-20 57

ABC-PAR (9918 "Big Name Button") 10-20 58

ABC-PAR (9945 "Hangin' Around") 10-20 58

ABC-PAR (9955 "My Kind of Dream") 10-20 58

ALLNEW (1415 "Royal Twist") 10-15 62

ASTRA 10-15 60

CAPITOL 12-25 59-60

JUBILEE (5418 "Royal Twist") 5-10 62

MCA 3-4 80s

MIGHTY (111 "Leotards") 15-25 58

MIGHTY (112 "Cave Man") 20-30 59

MIGHTY (200 "My Memories of You") 20-30 58

MUSICOR 5-8 69-70

POWER (113 "Mad Gass") 10-20 59

POWER (215 "Short Shorts") 75-100 57

SPARTON (534 "Short Shorts") 25-50 58

(Canadian. Runs 2:39. That's 27 seconds longer than ABC-Paramount single, which fades out at 2:12.)

SWAN (4200 "I'll Love You") 50-75 65

(Previously issued on Bluejay as by the Bluetones.)

TCF 5-10 65

LPs: 10/12-inch

DEMAND 10-15

MUSICOR 10-15 70

TRU-GEMS 8-10 74

Members: Bob Gaudio; Al Kooper; Buddy Randell; Joey Villa; Billy Crandall; Tom Austin; Tony Grochowski.

Also see 4 SEASONS

Also see KOOPER, Al

ROYALCASH R&B '83

Singles: 12-inch

SUTRA 4-6 83

Singles: 7-inch

SUTRA 3-5 83

ROYALETTES P&R/R&B '65

Singles: 7-inch

CHANCELLOR 8-12 62-63

MGM 8-12 64-66

ROULETTE 5-10 67

W.B. 5-10 64

LPs: 10/12-inch

MGM 15-25 65-66

Members: Anita Ross; Sheila Ross; Terry Jones; Ronnie Brown.

ROYALS R&B '53

Singles: 78 rpm

FEDERAL (12064 "Every Beat of My Heart") 100-200 52

FEDERAL (12077 "Starting from Tonight") 100-200 52

FEDERAL (12088 "Moonrise") 100-200 52

FEDERAL (12098 "A Love in My Heart") 50-100 52

FEDERAL (12113 "Are You Forgetting") 50-100 52

FEDERAL (12121 "The Shrine of St. Cecilia") 50-100 53

FEDERAL (12133 "Get It") 40-60 53
FEDERAL (12150 "Hey Miss Fine") .. 40-60 53
FEDERAL (12160 "That's It") 40-60 54
FEDERAL (12169 "Work with Me Annie") 40-60 54

Singles: 7-inch

FEDERAL (12064 "Every Beat of My Heart") 500-750 52
(Black vinyl.)
FEDERAL (12064 "Every Beat of My Heart") 2500-3500 52
(Colored vinyl.)
FEDERAL (12077 "Starting from Tonight") 1000-2000 52
FEDERAL (12088 "Moonrise") 1000-2000 52
FEDERAL (12098 "A Love in My Heart") 750-1000 52
FEDERAL (12113 "Are You Forgetting") 500-1000 52
FEDERAL (12121 "The Shrine of St. Cecilia") 500-1000 53
FEDERAL (12133 "Get It") 200-300 53
FEDERAL (12150 "Hey Miss Fine") 150-250 53
FEDERAL (12160 "That's It") 150-250 54
FEDERAL (12169 "Work with Me Annie") 150-250 54
FEDERAL (12177 "Give It Up") 150-250 54
(White label. Test pressing only. Commercial copies credit: "The Midnighters, Formally Known as the Royals.")
GUSTO 3-5 80s

Note: Federal titles reissued as by the Midnighters are in the Midnighters' section.
Members: Henry Booth; Hank Ballard; Charles Sutton; Lawson Smith; Alonzo Tucker; Sonny Woods.
Also see BALLARD, Hank
Also see MIDNIGHTERS

ROYALTONES P&R '58

Singles: 7-inch

ABC 3-5 73
GOLDISC 10-15 60-61
JANUS GOLD 3-5
JUBILEE (Blue label) 10-15 58-59
JUBILEE (Black label) 5-10 62
MALA 5-10 63-64
PENTHOUSE (777 "Clip Clop") 25-35 59
PORT (70037 "Poor Boy") 8-12 64
ROULETTE 3-5 71
TWIRL 5-8 62
VIRGO 3-5 72

RUBBER BAND LP '69

Singles: 7-inch

GRT 4-6 69

LPs: 10/12-inch

GRT 10-15 69

RUBBER RODEO P&R '84

Singles: 7-inch

MERCURY 3-5 84-85

LPs: 10/12-inch

MERCURY 5-10 85

RUBEN & JETS
(Mothers of Invention)

Singles: 7-inch

VERVE (10632 "Any Way the Wind Blows") 20-30 68
VERVE (10632 "Deseri") 20-30 68

LPs: 10/12-inch

VERVE (5055 "Crusin' with Ruben and the Jets") 30-40 68
(Issued with three paper inserts, any of which can add $15 to $25 to the value.)
Also see MOTHERS of INVENTION

RUBETTES P&R '74

Singles: 7-inch

MCA 3-5 76
POLYDOR 3-5 74-75

LPs: 10/12-inch

MCA 6-10 76

RUBICON P&R/LP '78

Singles: 7-inch

20TH FOX 3-5 78-79

LPs: 10/12-inch

20TH FOX 5-10 78-79
Also see SLY & Family Stone

RUBINOOS P&R '77

Singles: 12-inch

W.B. 4-8 80-83

Singles: 7-inch

BESERKLEY 3-5 77-79
W.B. 3-4 84

Picture Sleeves

BESERKLEY 3-5 77-79

LPs: 10/12-inch

BESERKLEY 5-10 77-79
Also see KIHN, Greg, Band / Earthquake / Modern Lovers / Rubinoos
Member: Jon Rubin.

RUBY & PARTY GANG R&B '71

Singles: 7-inch

GAMBLE 3-5 72
LAW-TON 3-5 71

RUBY & ROMANTICS P&R/R&B/LP '63

Singles: 7-inch

A&M 4-6 69
ABC 4-8 67-68
KAPP 5-10 62-67
MCA 3-4 70s

Picture Sleeves

KAPP 5-10 63-64

LPs: 10/12-inch

ABC 10-20 68
KAPP 15-25 63-67
MCA 5-10 80s
PICKWICK 8-10 70s
Members: Ruby Nash; Edward Roberts; Ronald Mosley; Leroy Fann; George Lee.

RUE R&B '87

Singles: 7-inch

ASIANA 3-4 87

RUFFIN, David P&R/R&B/LP '69

Singles: 7-inch

ANNA (1127 "I'm in Love") 35-55 60
CHECK MATE (1003 "You Can Get What I Got") 30-50 61
CHECK MATE (1010 "Mr. Bus Driver") 30-50 61
MOTOWN 3-6 69-76
W.B. 3-5 79-80

LPs: 10/12-inch

MOTOWN (100 & 200 series) 5-10 82
MOTOWN (600 series) 10-15 69
MOTOWN (700 & 800 series) 8-10 73-76
W.B. 8-10 77-80
Also see BUSH, Little David
Also see HALL, Daryl, John Oates, David Ruffin & Eddie Kendrick
Also see TEMPTATIONS
Also see VOICE MASTERS

RUFFIN, David, & Eddie Kendricks R&B '87

Singles: 7-inch

RCA 3-4 87-88
Also see KENDRICKS, Eddie

RUFFIN, David & Jimmy P&R/R&B '70
(Ruffin Brothers)

Singles: 7-inch

SOUL 3-6 70

LPs: 10/12-inch

MOTOWN 5-10 80
SOUL (728 "My Brother's Keeper") ... 10-20 70
Also see RUFFIN, David
Also see RUFFIN, Jimmy

RUFFIN, Jimmy P&R/R&B '66

Singles: 12-inch

EPIC 4-8 77

Singles: 7-inch

EPIC 3-4 77
MIRACLE (1 "Heart") 50-100 61
MOTOWN 3-5
RSO 3-5 80
SOUL (Except 35002 & 35022) 8-15 65-71
SOUL (35002 "Since I've Lost You") 15-25 64
SOUL (35022 "What Becomes of the Broken Hearted") 5-10 66
(Black vinyl.)
SOUL (35022 "What Becomes of the Broken Hearted") 15-25 66
(Colored vinyl. Promotional issue only.)

EPs: 7-inch

SOUL (69704 "Top Ten") 15-25 66

LPs: 10/12-inch

RSO 5-8 80
SOUL (704 "Sings Top Ten") 20-30 66
SOUL (708 "Ruff 'N' Ready") 20-30 67
SOUL (727 "Groove Governor") 15-25 70
Also see NIGHTINGALE, Maxine, & Jimmy Ruffin
Also see RUFFIN, David & Jimmy

RUFFNER, Mason LP '87

LPs: 10/12-inch

CBS ASSOC 5-8 87

RUFUS R&B/LP '73
("Featuring Chaka Khan")

Singles: 12-inch

W.B. 4-6 83-84

Singles: 7-inch

ABC 3-5 74-78
ATLANTIC 3-5 74
BEARSVILLE 3-5 75
EPIC 3-5 70-71
MCA (Except picture discs) 3-5 79-81
MCA (9162 "Party 'Til You're Broke") 20-25 81
(Dollar-shaped picture disc. Promotional issue only. Includes picture cover.)
MCA (9288 "Do You Love What You Feel") 15-25 81
(Strawberry-shaped picture disc. Promotional issue only. Includes strawberry scented picture cover. 1000 made.)
W.B. 3-4 83-84

LPs: 10/12-inch

ABC (Except picture discs) 8-10 73-78
ABC (AA-1049 "Street Player") 25-30 78
(Picture disc. Promotional issue only.)
ABC (AA-1098 "Numbers") 20-25 79
(Picture disc. Promotional issue only. 100 made.)
COMMAND 8-10 74-75
MCA 5-10 79-82
W.B. 5-8 83
W.B. (23679 "Stompin' at the Savoy") 8-12
Members: Paulette McWilliams; Chaka Khan.
Also see AMERICAN BREED
Also see KHAN, Chaka
Also see McWILLIAMS, Paulette

RUFUS & CARLA

Singles: 7-inch

SATELLITE 10-20 60
STAX 5-10 64-65
Members: Rufus Thomas; Carla Thomas.
Also see THOMAS, Carla
Also see THOMAS, Rufus

RUGBYS P&R '69

Singles: 7-inch

AMAZON (Except 1) 5-10 69-70
AMAZON (1 "You, I") 5-8 69
(Black vinyl.)
AMAZON (1 "You, I") 10-15 69
(Colored vinyl. Promotional issue only.)
SMASH 5-10 65
TOP DOG (2315 "Endlessly") 10-15 66

LPs: 10/12-inch

AMAZON (1000 "Hot Cargo") 15-20 70
Members: Steve McNicol; Jim McNicol; Chris Hubbs; Ed Vernon; Mike Morner; Glen Howerton.

RUMBLERS P&R '63

Singles: 7-inch

DOT 5-10 63-64

DOWNEY 10-20 63-65
HIGHLAND (1026 "Intersection") 20-30 62
LPs: 10/12-inch
DOT (3509 "Boss") 20-25 63
(Monaural.)
DOT (25509 "Boss") 25-30 63
(Stereo.)
DOWNEY (DLP-1001 "Boss") 40-60 63
(Monaural.)
DOWNEY (DLPS-1001 "Boss") 50-75 63
(Stereo.)
Members: Adrian Lloyd; Johnny Kirkland; Bob Jones; Wayne Matteson; Mike Kelishes; Greg Crowner.

RUMOUR — LP '77

Singles: 7-inch
ARISTA 3-5 79
MERCURY 3-5 78
LPs: 10/12-inch
ARISTA 5-10 79
MERCURY 8-10 77
Also see PARKER, Graham
Also see SCHWARTZ, Brinsley

RUN - D.M.C. — R&B '83

Singles: 12-inch
PROFILE 4-6 83-86
QUALITY/RFC 4-6 83
Singles: 7-inch
PROFILE (Black vinyl) 3-4 83-90
PROFILE (Colored vinyl) 4-8 89
Picture Sleeves
PROFILE 3-4 86-88
LPs: 10/12-inch
PROFILE 5-8 84-90
Members: "Run" Joe Simmons; Daryll McDaniels; Jason Mizell.
Also see AEROSMITH
Also see KING DREAM CHORUS & Holiday Crew
Also see KRUSH GROVE ALL STARS

RUNAWAYS — LP '76

Singles: 7-inch
MERCURY 5-10 76-77
LPs: 10/12-inch
MERCURY (1090 "Runaways") 15-25 76-77
MERCURY (1126 "Queens of Noise") 15-25 77
MERCURY (3705 "Waiting for the Night") 15-25 77
RHINO (250 "Little Lost Girls") 5-10 82
RHINO (250 "Little Lost Girls") 25-30 82
(Picture disc.)
Members: Joan Jett; Cherie Currie; Lita Ford; Sandy West; Vicki Blue.
Also see FORD, Lita
Also see JETT, Joan

RUNDGREN, Todd — LP '71

(Todd Rundgren's Utopia)
Singles: 7-inch
BEARSVILLE (Except 0003) 3-5 77-83
BEARSVILLE (0003 "I Saw the Light") 5-10 72
(Black vinyl.)
BEARSVILLE (0003 "I Saw the Light") 10-15 72
(Colored vinyl.)
LPs: 10/12-inch
BEARSVILLE (524 "Todd Rundgren Radio Show") 40-50 70s
(Promotional issue only.)
BEARSVILLE (597 "Radio Interview") 120-130 81
(Promotional issue only.)
BEARSVILLE (788 "Todd Rundgren Radio Sampler") 25-40 79
(Promotional issue only.)
BEARSVILLE (2066 "Something/ Anything") 10-12 72
BEARSVILLE (2066 "Something/ Anything") 150-200 72
(Colored vinyl. Price includes lyrics insert.
BEARSVILLE (2133 "A Wizard/A True Star") 5-10 73
BEARSVILLE (3522 "Healing") 8-10 81
(Price includes the bonus single, *Time Heals*.)
BEARSVILLE (6952 "Todd") 12-15 74
(Price includes bonus poster.)
BEARSVILLE (6957 "Initiation") 8-10 75
BEARSVILLE (6961 "Another Live") 10-12 75
BEARSVILLE (6963 "Faithful") 8-10 76
BEARSVILLE (6965 "Ra") 10-12 77
BEARSVILLE (6970 "Oops, Wrong Planet") 10-12 77
BEARSVILLE (6981 "Hermit of Mink Hollow") 5-8 78
BEARSVILLE (6986 "Back to the Bars") 8-10 78
BEARSVILLE (23732 "Ever Popular Tortured Artist Effect") 5-8 83
Also see NAZZ
Also see RUNT
Also see TYLER, Bonnie
Also see UTOPIA

RUNNER — LP '79

Singles: 7-inch
ISLAND 3-5 79
LPs: 10/12-inch
ISLAND 5-10 79
Members: Steve Gould; Mickie Feat; David Dowle; Allan Merrill.

RUNT — P&R '70

(Featuring Todd Rundgren)
Singles: 7-inch
AMPEX 5-10 70
BEARSVILLE 4-8 71
LPs: 10/12-inch
AMPEX (10105 "Runt") 100-150 70
(With *Say No More* and a full-length version of *Baby Let's Swing*.)
AMPEX (10105 "Runt") 50-100 70
(Does not have *Say No More*. Has *Baby Let's Swing* as part of a medley.)
AMPEX (10116 "The Ballad of Todd Rundgren") 50-100 71
W.B. 5-8 85-91
Also see RUNDGREN, Todd

RUSH — LP '74

Singles: 7-inch
MERCURY 3-5 75-87
Picture Sleeves
MERCURY 3-5 81-85
EPs: 7-inch
MERCURY 5-10 80
LPs: 10/12-inch
ATLANTIC 5-8 89
MERCURY (1000 thru 4000 series, except 1300) 5-8 74-82
MERCURY (1300 "Hemispheres") 35-45 78
(Picture disc.)
MERCURY (7000 series) 8-12 76-81
MERCURY (9000 series) 10-15 76-81
MERCURY (800000 series) 5-8 84-88
Members: Geddy Lee; Neil Peart; Alex Lifeson.
Also see McKENZIE, Bob & Doug

RUSH, Bobby — R&B '71

Singles: 7-inch
ABC 3-6 68
CHECKER 4-8 67
GALAXY 48 71
ICHIBAN 3-4 93
JEWEL 4-8 60s-73
PHILADELPHIA INT'L 3-5 79
SALEM 8-12 69
SEDGRICK 8-12
TOP 3-5 70s
LPs: 10/12-inch
PHILADELPHIA INT'L 5-10 79

RUSH, Jennifer — P&R '86

Singles: 7-inch
EPIC 3-4 86
LPs: 10/12-inch
EPIC 5-8 86-87

RUSH, Jennifer, & Elton John — P&R '87

Singles: 7-inch
EPIC 3-4 87
Also see JOHN, Elton

RUSH, Merrilee — P&R/LP '68

(With the Turnabouts)
Singles: 7-inch
AGP 3-6 69-70
BELL 4-8 68
GTP 4-8 68
MERRILIN 10-15 65-66
RU-RO 8-12 67
SCEPTER 3-5 71
SPHERE SOUND 3-5
U.A. 3-5 77-78
LPs: 10/12-inch
BELL 10-20 68
LIBERTY 5-8 82
U.A. 8-10 77

RUSH, Otis — R&B '56

Singles: 78 rpm
COBRA 10-20 56-57
Singles: 7-inch
BLUES TOWN 15-25
CHESS 5-10 60
COBRA 15-30 56-59
COTILLION 4-6 69
DUKE 5-10 62
LPs: 10/12-inch
BLUE HORIZON 10-15 68-70
BULLFROG 8-10 77
COTILLION 10-15 69
DELMARK 10-20 75-79
Also see KING, Albert, & Otis Rush

RUSH, Tom — LP '66

Singles: 7-inch
COLUMBIA 3-5 72-74
ELEKTRA 4-6 66-70
PRESTIGE 4-8 64
LPs: 10/12-inch
COLUMBIA 6-12 70-76
ELEKTRA 8-15 65-70
FANTASY 5-10 72
LY CORNU 15-20
PRESTIGE 10-20 64-68

RUSHEN, Patrice — LP '77

Singles: 12-inch
ELEKTRA 4-8 79-84
Singles: 7-inch
ARISTA 3-4 87
ELEKTRA 3-5 80-84
PRESTIGE 3-5 76
Picture Sleeves
ELEKTRA 3-5 80-82
LPs: 10/12-inch
ARISTA 5-8 87
ELEKTRA 5-10 78-84
PRESTIGE 5-10 75-80

RUSHEN, Patrice, & D.J. Rogers — R&B '80

Singles: 7-inch
ELEKTRA 3-5 80
Also see ROGERS, D.J.
Also see RUSHEN, Patrice

RUSS, Lonnie — P&R '62

(Lonn Russ)
Singles: 7-inch
4J (501 "My Wife Can't Cook") 10-15 62
KERWOOD 8-12

RUSSELL, Bobby — C&W/P&R '68

(With the Beagles; with Tennessee Three; with Sadie Russell)
Singles: 7-inch
COLUMBIA 3-5 73-74
D 5-10 60
ELF 4-6 68-69
FELSTED 5-10 59
FILLY-COLT 3-5 78
IMAGE 4-8 61
MONUMENT 4-8 65-66

NATIONAL GENERAL 3-5 70
PRIVATE STOCK 3-5 75
RISING SONS 3-5 67
SPAR 10-15 64
U.A. 3-5 71-72
VISTA 3-6 69

LPs: 10/12-inch

BELL 8-12 69
ELF 10-15 68
U.A. 8-10 71

RUSSELL, Brenda *P&R/R&B/LP '79*
(With Joe Esposito)

Singles: 7-inch

A&M 3-4 79-88
HORIZON 3-5 79

Picture Sleeves

A&M 3-4 88

LPs: 10/12-inch

A&M 5-8 79-88
HORIZON 5-8 79
Also see ESPOSITO, Joe "Bean"

RUSSELL, Lee
(Leon Russell)

Singles: 7-inch

BATON 10-15 59
ROULETTE 10-20 58
Also see RUSSELL, Leon

RUSSELL, Leon *LP '70*
(With the Shelter People; with New Grass Revival)

Singles: 7-inch

A&M (700 series) 4-8 64
A&M (1200 series) 3-5 71
ABC 3-5 78
COLUMBIA 3-5 70s
DOT 4-8 65
MCA 3-4
PARADISE 3-5 76-81
SHELTER 3-5 70-76

Picture Sleeves

PARADISE 3-5 78-84
SHELTER 3-5 74

LPs: 10/12-inch

MCA 5-10 79
OLYMPIC 8-12 73
PARADISE 5-10 78-81
SHELTER (1000 & 2000 series) 10-20 70-75
SHELTER (8000 series, except 8917) 10-15 71-73
SHELTER (8917 "Leon Live") 12-20 73
SHELTER (52000 series) 8-10 76
Also see CLAPTON, Eric
Also see COCKER, Joe
Also see DAVID & LEE
Also see HARRISON, George
Also see JAN & DEAN
Also see KING, Freddie
Also see LEGENDARY MASKED SURFERS
Also see NELSON, Willie, & Leon Russell
Also see RUSSELL, Lee

RUSSELL, Leon & Mary *P&R '76*

Singles: 7-inch

PARADISE 3-5 76-77

LPs: 10/12-inch

PARADISE 8-10 76-77
Also see RUSSELL, Leon

RUSSELL, Luis *R&B '46*

Singles: 78 rpm

APOLLO 10-20 46-48

RUSSELL, Sam *R&B '73*

Singles: 7-inch

PLAYBOY 3-5 73

RUSSO, Charlie *P&R '63*

Singles: 7-inch

DIAMOND 4-8 63
LAURIE 4-6 67
PART 4-8 64

RUSTIX *LP '69*

Singles: 7-inch

RARE EARTH 4-8 69

LPs: 10/12-inch

RARE EARTH (508 "Bedlam") 8-12 69
(Standard cover.)
RARE EARTH (508 "Bedlam") 20-40 69
(Rounded-top cover. Promotional issue.)

RUTH, Babe: see BABE RUTH

RUTHERFORD, Mike *LP '80*

Singles: 7-inch

ATLANTIC 3-4 83

LPs: 10/12-inch

ATLANTIC 5-8 83
PASSPORT 5-10 80
Also see GENESIS
Also see MIKE + the MECHANICS

RUTLES *LP '78*

Singles: 12-inch

W.B. (723 "The Rutles") 15-20 78
(Colored vinyl. Promotional issue only.)

Singles: 7-inch

PASSPORT 3-5 70s
W.B. 3-5 78

LPs: 10/12-inch

W.B. (3151 "Meet the Rutles") 10-15 78
(Add $4 to $6 if accompanied by bonus booklet.)
Members: Neil Innes; Rick Fataar; Eric Idle; John Hasley.
Also see BONZO DOG BAND
Also see FLAME
Also see MONTY PYTHON

RYAN, Barry *P&R '68*

Singles: 7-inch

MGM 4-8 68
POLYDOR 3-6 70
PRIDE 3-5 71

RYAN, Charlie *C&W/P&R '60*
(With the Timberline Riders; with Livingston Brothers)

Singles: 78 rpm

SOUVENIR (101 "Hot Rod Lincoln") 10-20 55

Singles: 7-inch

4 STAR 8-15 60-63
SOUVENIR (101 "Hot Rod Lincoln") 20-40 55

Picture Sleeves

4 STAR (1745 "Side Car Cycle") 10-20 60

LPs: 10/12-inch

KING (751 "Hot Rod") 40-60 61

RYDELL, Bobby *P&R/R&B '59*

Singles: 7-inch

ABKCO 3-4 70s
CAMEO ("Steel Pier") 15-20 60s
(No selection number used. Single-sided, promotional issue from the Steel Pier in Atlantic City.)
CAMEO (160 "Please Don't Be Mad") 25-50 59
CAMEO (164 "All I Want Is You") 10-20 59
CAMEO (167 thru 186) 5-15 59-61
CAMEO (190 thru 361) 4-8 61-65
CAMEO (1070 "Forget Him"/"A Message from Bobby") 10-15 63
(Packaged as a bonus single with *Top Hits of 1963*.)
CAPITOL 4-8 64-66
P.I.P. 3-5 76
PERCEPTION 3-5 74
RCA 3-5 70
REPRISE 4-6 68
TIME 5-8 59
VEKO (731 "Fatty Fatty") 25-50 58
VENISE (201 "Fatty Fatty") 15-25 62

Picture Sleeves

CAMEO 8-15 59-64
CAPITOL 5-10 64

EPs: 7-inch

CAPITOL 10-20 65

LPs: 10/12-inch

CAMEO (1006 "We Got Love") 50-80 59
CAMEO (1007 "Bobby Sings, Bobby Swings") 25-35 60
CAMEO (1009 "Bobby's Biggest Hits") 40-50 61
(Gatefold cover. With 12" x 12" photo insert.)
CAMEO (1009 "Bobby's Biggest Hits") 30-35 61
(Gatefold cover. Without 12" x 12" photo.)
CAMEO (1009 "Bobby's Biggest Hits") 15-25 62
(Standard cover. Some copies with 1009 on the cover may have Cameo 1008 on the disc.)
CAMEO (1010 "Bobby Rydell Salutes the Great Ones") 20-30 61
CAMEO (1011 "Rydell at the Copa") 20-30 61
(Monaural.)
CAMEO (SC-1011 "Rydell at the Copa") 25-35 61
(Stereo.)
CAMEO (1019 "All the Hits") 20-30 62
CAMEO (1028 "Bobby's Biggest Hits, Vol. 2") 25-35 62
CAMEO (1040 "All the Hits, Vol. 2") 20-30 62
(Monaural.)
CAMEO (SC-1040 "All the Hits, Vol. 2") 25-35 62
(Stereo.)
CAMEO (1043 "Bye Bye Birdie") 25-30 63
(Monaural.)
CAMEO (SC-1043 "Bye Bye Birdie") 30-35 63
(Stereo.)
CAMEO (1055 "Wild [Wood] Days") 20-30 63
(Monaural.)
CAMEO (1070 "Top Hits of 1963 Sung by Robby Rydell") 25-35 63
(Monaural. With bonus single *Forget Him/A Message from Bobby*.)
CAMEO (1070 "Top Hits of 1963 Sung by Robby Rydell") 15-25 63
(Monaural. Without bonus single.)
CAMEO (SC-1070 "Top Hits of 1963 Sung by Robby Rydell") 30-40 63
(Stereo. With bonus single *Forget Him/A Message from Bobby*.)
CAMEO (SC-1070 "Top Hits of 1963 Sung by Robby Rydell") 20-30 63
(Stereo. Without bonus single.)
CAMEO (1080 "Forget Him") 20-30 64
CAMEO (2001 "18 Golden Hits") 20-30 60s
CAMEO (4017 "An Era Reborn") 20-30 64
(Monaural.)
CAMEO (SC-4017 "An Era Reborn") 25-35 64
(Stereo.)
CAPITOL (2281 "Somebody Loves You") 15-25 65
DESIGN 10-20 60s
P.I.P. 8-12 76
SPINORAMA 10-20 60s
STRAND (1120 "Bobby Rydell Sings") 35-45 60
Also see CHECKER, Chubby, & Bobby Rydell
Also see CHRISTIE, Lou / Len Barry & Dovells / Bobby Rydell / Tokens
Also see ROE, Tommy / Bobby Rydell / Gene Pitney
Also see ROE, Tommy / Bobby Rydell / Ray Stevens

RYDELL, Bobby / Barry Norman / Steve Garrick

LPs: 10/12-inch

VENISE (7035 "Twistin'") 15-20 62
Also see RYDELL, Bobby

RYDER, John & Anne *P&R '69*

Singles: 7-inch

DECCA 4-6 69

LPs: 10/12-inch

DECCA 10-15 70

RYDER, Mitch *P&R '65*
(With the Detroit Wheels)

Singles: 7-inch

ABC 3-5 73
AVCO EMBASSY 3-6 70
DOT 4-6 69
DYNO VOICE 4-8 67-68
ERIC 3-4
NEW VOICE (Except 820) 4-8 65-68

NEW VOICE (820 "Sock It to Me-Baby") 5-10 67
(With "Feels like a punch" lyrics.)
NEW VOICE (820 "Sock It to Me-Baby") 4-6 67
(With "Hits me like a punch" lyrics.)
RIVA 3-4 83
VIRGO 3-4 73

Picture Sleeves

NEW VOICE 4-8 67

LPs: 10/12-inch

CREWE 12-15
DOT 12-15 69
DYNO VOICE 10-20 67
NEW VOICE 20-30 66-68
RIVA 5-8 83
ROULETTE 5-10
SEEDS & STEMS 5-10 78-80
VIRGO 8-10 73

Members: Mitch Ryder; Joe Kubert; Jim McCallister; Jim McCarty; Johnny Badanjek.
Also see DETROIT
Also see ROCKETS

RYLES, John Wesley *C&W/P&R '68*
(John Wesley Ryles I)

Singles: 7-inch

ABC 3-5 78-79
ABC/DOT 3-5 77
COLUMBIA 4-6 68-70
GRT 3-5 70
MCA 3-5 79-83
MUSIC MILL 3-5 75-76
PLANTATION 3-5 71-73
PRIMERO 3-5 82-83
RCA 3-5 74
16TH AVE. 3-4 84
W.B. 3-4 87-88

LPs: 10/12-inch

ABC 5-10 78
ABC/DOT 8-10 77
COLUMBIA 10-15 69
MCA 5-10 79-83
PLANTATION 5-10 77

RYSER, Jimmy *P&R '90*

Singles: 7-inch

ARISTA 3-4 90

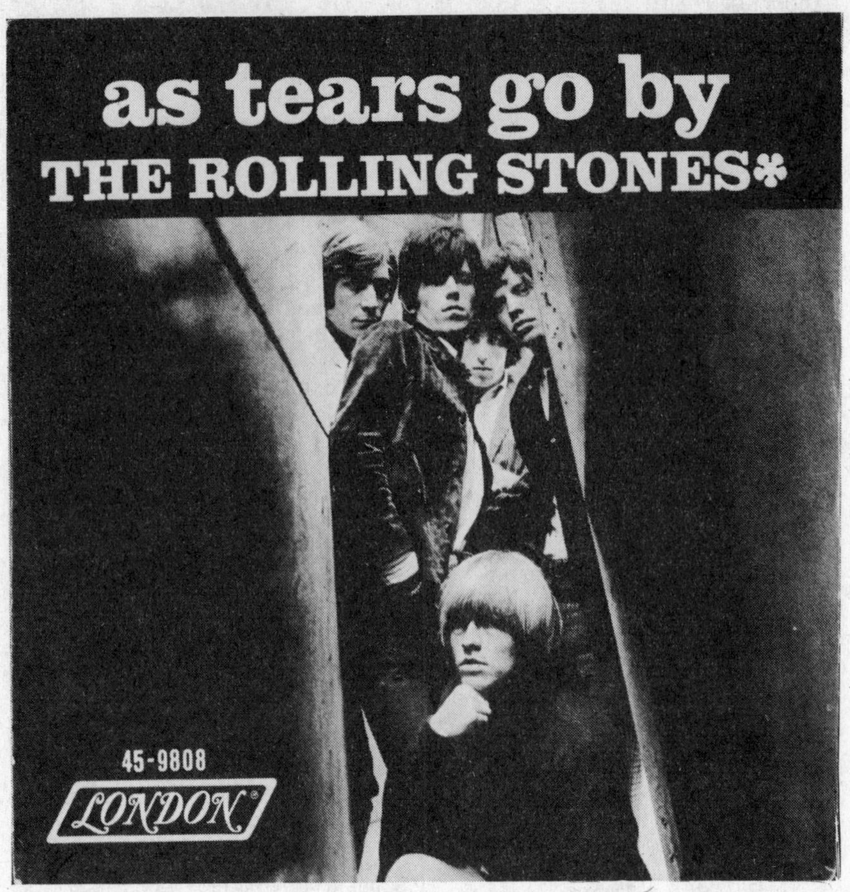

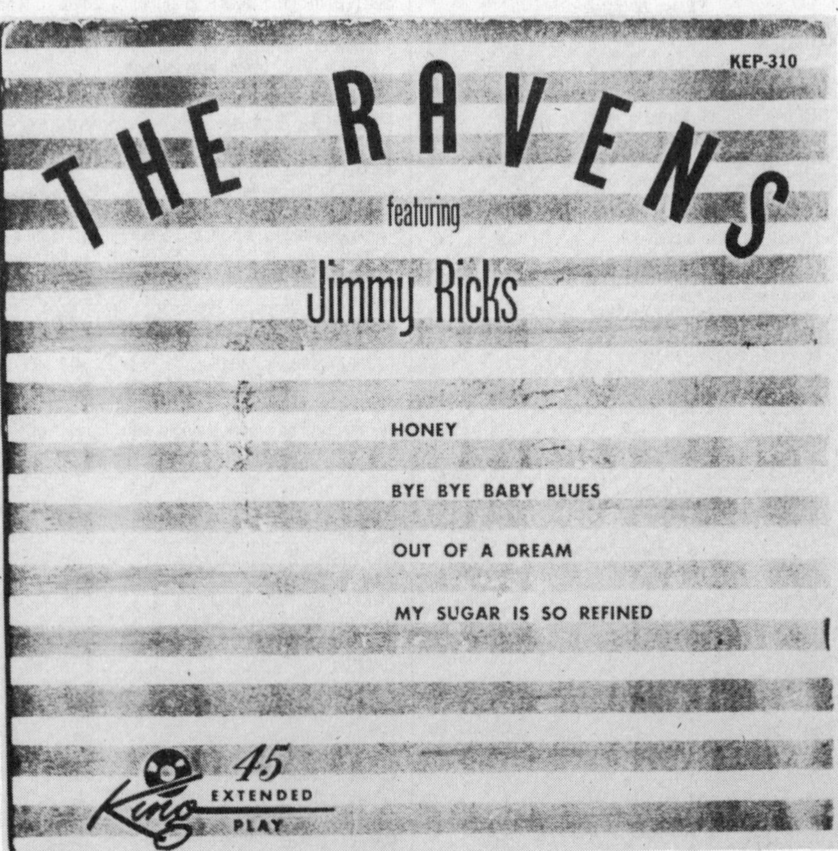

S.O.S. BAND — P&R/LP '80

Singles: 12-inch

TABU ... 4-6 80-89

Singles: 7-inch

TABU ... 3-5 80-89

Picture Sleeves

TABU ... 3-5 84-86

LPs: 10/12-inch

TABU ... 5-10 80-89

Member: Mary Davis; Willie Killebrew; Billy Ellis; Jason Bryant; John Simpson; Bruno Speight; James Earl Jones III; Jerome Thomas; Abdul Raoof; Pennye Ford.

SRC — LP '68

(Scott Richard Case)

Singles: 7-inch

A^2 (301 "I'm So Glad") ... 10-20 67
BIG CASINO ... 4-8 71
CAPITOL ... 5-10 68-69

LPs: 10/12-inch

CAPITOL (134 "Milestones") ... 30-40 69
CAPITOL (273 "Travelers Tale") ... 15-25 69
CAPITOL (2991 "SRC") ... 40-60 68

Members: Scott Richardson; Steve Lyman; Glen Quackenbush; Gary Quackenbush; Robin Dale.

SRC / Rationals

Singles: 7-inch

A^2 (402 "Get the Picture") ... 10-20 67

Also see SRC

S.S.O. — P&R '76

Singles: 7-inch

SHADY BROOK ... 3-5 75-76

S.S.Q. — D&D '84

Singles: 12-inch

ENIGMA ... 4-6 84

Singles: 7-inch

EMI ... 3-4 84
ENIGMA ... 3-4 84

LPs: 10/12-inch

EMI ... 5-8 84
ENIGMA ... 5-8 84

Also see ST. JAMES, Jon
Also see STACEY Q

SAAD, Sue, & Next — LP '80

Singles: 7-inch

PLANET ... 3-5 80

LPs: 10/12-inch

PLANET ... 5-10 80

SACCO

(Lou Christie)

Singles: 12-inch

LIFESONG (81775 "People Theme") .. 8-10 78

Singles: 7-inch

LIFESONG (81775 "People Theme") ... 30-50 78

Also see CHRISTIE, Lou

SACRED REICH — LP '90

LPs: 10/12-inch

ENIGMA ... 5-8 90
METAL BLADE (73411 "Surf Nicaragua") ... 10-15 89
(Picture disc.)

SAD CAFE — P&R/LP '79

Singles: 7-inch

A&M ... 3-5 78-79
SWAN SONG ... 3-5 81

Picture Sleeves

SWAN SONG ... 3-5 81

LPs: 10/12-inch

A&M ... 5-10 78-79
ATLANTIC ... 5-8 85
SWAN SONG ... 5-10 81

Members: Paul Young; Doreen Chanter; Irene Chanter; John Stimpson; Vic Emerson; Ian Wilson; Ashley Mulford; Lenni Zaksen.

Also see MIKE + the MECHANICS
Also see YOUNG, Paul

SADANE, Marc — R&B '81

(Sadane)

Singles: 7-inch

W.B. ... 3-5 81-82

Picture Sleeves

W.B. ... 3-5 81

LPs: 10/12-inch

W.B. ... 5-10 81

SADE — R&B/D&D '84

Singles: 12-inch

PORTRAIT ... 4-6 84-86

Singles: 7-inch

EPIC ... 3-4 88
PORTRAIT ... 3-4 84-86

Picture Sleeves

EPIC ... 3-4 88
PORTRAIT ... 3-4 84-86

LPs: 10/12-inch

EPIC ... 5-8 88
PORTRAIT ... 5-8 85-86

SADLER, Barry — P&R/C&W/LP '66

(S/SGT. Barry Sadler)

Singles: 7-inch

GAS ... 3-5 78
RCA ... 4-6 66-67

Picture Sleeves

RCA ... 5-10 66-67

LPs: 10/12-inch

RCA ... 10-20 66-67
VETERAN ... 8-12 74

Also see ANN-MARGRET

SAFARIS — P&R '60

(With Phantom's Band)

Singles: 7-inch

DEE JAY (203 "My Image of a Girl") ... 3-5 89
ELDO (101 "Image of a Girl") ... 15-25 60
ELDO (105 "Girl With a Story in Her Eyes") ... 15-25 60
ELDO (110 "Shadows") ... 15-25 60
ELDO (113 "Garden of Love") ... 15-25 60
OLD HIT ... 3-5

Members: Jimmy Stephens; Sheldon Breier; Marv Rosenberg.

SA-FIRE — P&R/LP '88

Singles: 7-inch

CUTTING ... 3-4 88-89
MERCURY ... 3-4 89

Picture Sleeves

CUTTING ... 3-4 88-89
MERCURY ... 3-4 89

LPs: 10/12-inch

CUTTING ... 5-8 88

SAGA — P&R/LP '82

Singles: 7-inch

ATLANTIC ... 3-4 87
POLYDOR ... 3-5 79
PORTRAIT ... 3-4 82-85

Picture Sleeves

ATLANTIC ... 3-4 87
PORTRAIT ... 3-4 83

LPs: 10/12-inch

ATLANTIC ... 5-8 87
POLYDOR ... 5-10 79
PORTRAIT ... 5-10 82-85

SAGER, Carole Bayer — P&R '77

(Carole Bayer)

Singles: 7-inch

BOARDWALK ... 3-5 81
ELEKTRA ... 3-5 77-78
METROMEDIA ... 3-5 72

Picture Sleeves

BOARDWALK ... 3-5 81

LPs: 10/12-inch

BOARDWALK ... 5-10 81
ELEKTRA ... 5-10 77-78

SAGITTARIUS — P&R '67

Singles: 7-inch

COLUMBIA ... 5-10 67-69
TOGETHER ... 5-10 68-69

LPs: 10/12-inch

BACK-TRAC ... 5-10 85
COLUMBIA (9644 "Present Tense") 20-30 68
TOGETHER (1002 "Blue Marble") ... 25-35 69

Members: Gary Usher; Glen Campbell; Bruce Johnston; Terry Melcher; Curt Boetcher; Mike Fennelly; Lee Mallory; Ron Edgar.

Also see BRUCE & TERRY
Also see CAMPBELL, Glen

SAHL, Mort — LP '60

Singles: 7-inch

GNP ... 3-5 73
REPRISE ... 3-6 61
VERVE ... 4-8 60

LPs: 10/12-inch

GNP ... 5-10 73
MERCURY ... 8-12 67
REPRISE ... 10-20 61
VERVE ... 10-20 59-64

Also see MARTIN, Dean

SAHM, Doug — LP '73

(With the Mex Trip; with Texas Tornados)

Singles: 7-inch

ABC/DOT ... 4-6 76
ATLANTIC ... 5-10 73
CASABLANCA (0828 "Roll with the Punches") ... 10-20 75
CHRYSALIS ... 3-5 81
COBRA (116 "Just a Moment") ... 40-50 61
CRAZY CAJUN ... 3-5 74
HARLEM (107 "Why, Why, Why") ... 20-35 60
HARLEM (108 "Baby, Tell Me") ... 20-30 60
(Black vinyl.)
HARLEM (108 "Baby, Tell Me") ... 40-60 60
(Colored vinyl. Promotional issue only.)
HARLEM (116 "Just a Moment") ... 40-50 61
PERSONALITY (260 "Baby, What's on Your Mind") ... 30-50 59
PLAYBOY ... 3-5 76
RENNER (212 "Big Hat") ... 20-30 61
(Black vinyl.)
RENNER (212 "Big Hat") ... 50-75 61
(Colored vinyl. Promotional issue only.)
RENNER (215 "Baby, What's on Your Mind") ... 20-30 61
(Black vinyl.)
RENNER (215 "Baby, What's on Your Mind") ... 50-75 61
(Colored vinyl.
(Promotional issue only.)
RENNER (226 "Just Because") ... 20-30 62
RENNER (232 "Cry") ... 20-30 63
RENNER (240 "Lucky Me") ... 20-30 63
RENNER (247 "Mr. Kool") ... 20-30 64
SATIN (100 "Crazy Daisy") ... 30-50 59
SOFT (1031 "Cry") ... 20-30 65
SWINGIN' (625 "Why Oh Why") ... 15-25 60
TEXAS RECORD (108 "Henrietta") .. 10-20 76
W.B. ... 3-5 74
WARRIOR (507 "Crazy Daisy") ... 40-60 58

Picture Sleeves

CHRYSALIS ... 3-5 81

LPs: 10/12-inch

ANTONE'S ... 5-8 88
ATLANTIC ... 8-12 73
HARLEM ... 8-10 79
MERCURY ... 10-20 73
TAKOMA ... 5-10 80
W.B. ... 10-20 74

Also see BROMBERG, David
Also see DR. JOHN
Also see DYLAN, Bob
Also see FENDER, Freddy, & Sir Douglas
Also see LITTLE DOUG
Also see NELSON, Willie

Also see SALDAÑA, Sir Doug
Also see SIR DOUGLAS QUINTET

SAHM, Doug, & Augie Meyers

Singles: 7-inch

TEARDROP ... 3-4 83

Picture Sleeves

TEARDROP ... 3-5 83

Also see SAHM, Doug

SAILCAT P&R/LP '72

Singles: 7-inch

ELEKTRA ... 3-5 72-73

LPs: 10/12-inch

ELEKTRA ... 10-15 72

Members: Johnny Wyker; Court Pickett.

SAIN, Oliver R&B '75

Singles: 7-inch

ABET ... 3-5 71-77
BOBBIN ... 4-8 62
HCRC ... 3-5 82
VANESSA ... 5-10

LPs: 10/12-inch

ABET (400 series) ... 8-12 71-73
ABET (8700 series) ... 5-10 77

ST. JAMES, Jon R&B '84

Singles: 12-inch

EMI AMERICA ... 4-6 84

Singles: 7-inch

EMI AMERICA ... 3-4 84

LPs: 10/12-inch

EMI AMERICA ... 5-10 84

Also see SSQ

ST. PAUL R&B '87
(Paul Peterson)

Singles: 7-inch

ATLANTIC ... 3-4 87
MCA ... 3-4 87

Picture Sleeves

ATLANTIC ... 3-4 87
MCA ... 3-4 87

Also see FAMILY
Also see TIME

ST. PETERS, Crispian P&R '66

Singles: 7-inch

JAMIE ... 4-8 66-68

LPs: 10/12-inch

JAMIE (3027 "The Pied Piper") ... 20-30 66

ST. ROMAIN, Kirby P&R '63

Singles: 7-inch

DIMENSION ... 5-10 63
IMCO ... 4-8 64
INETTE ... 5-10 63-64
KARSONG ... 5-10 63
TEARDROP ... 5-10 64

SAINT TROPEZ LP '77

Singles: 12-inch

BUTTERFLY (Except 3100) ... 4-8 77-79
BUTTERFLY (3100 "Belle De Jour"). 15-25 79
(Picture disc. Promotional issue only. 1000 made.)
DESTINY ... 4-6 82-83

Singles: 7-inch

BUTTERFLY ... 3-5 77-79
DESTINY ... 3-4 82-83

LPs: 10/12-inch

BUTTERFLY (Black vinyl) ... 5-10 77-79
BUTTERFLY (Colored vinyl) ... 10-15 77-79
DESTINY ... 5-10 82

SAINTE-MARIE, Buffy LP '66

Singles: 7-inch

ABC ... 3-5 76
MCA ... 3-5 74-75
VANGUARD ... 3-8 65-72

LPs: 10/12-inch

ABC ... 5-10 76
MCA ... 5-10 74-75
VANGUARD ... 8-15 64-74

SAKAMOTO, Kyu P&R/R&B/LP '63

Singles: 7-inch

CAPITOL ... 4-6 63-64
EMI ... 3-4 75

LPs: 10/12-inch

CAPITOL ... 10-20 63

SALES, Soupy P&R/LP '65

Singles: 7-inch

ABC-PAR ... 5-10 65
CAPITOL ... 5-10 66
MOTOWN (1141 "Muck-Arty Park") . 15-25 69
REPRISE ... 5-10 62
WIZDOM ... 3-5

Picture Sleeves

CAPITOL ... 10-15 66

LPs: 10/12-inch

ABC-PAR ... 15-25 64-65
MOTOWN (686 "A Bag of Soup") ... 25-35 69
REPRISE ... 20-30 61-62

SALSOUL ORCHESTRA
(Featuring Cognac) P&R/R&B/LP '75

Singles: 12-inch

SALSOUL ... 4-6 78-83

Singles: 7-inch

SALSOUL ... 3-5 75-83

LPs: 10/12-inch

SALSOUL ... 5-10 75-83

Member: Jocelyn Brown.
Also see BROWN, Jocelyn
Also see CHARO
Also see HOLLOWAY, Loleatta

SALT-N-PEPA P&R/R&B/LP '87

Singles: 7-inch

NEXT PLATEAU ... 3-4 87-90

LPs: 10/12-inch

NEXT PLATEAU ... 5-8 87-90

SALTY DOG LP '90

LPs: 10/12-inch

GEFFEN ... 5-8 90

SALVAGE P&R '71

Singles: 7-inch

ODAX ... 3-5 71

SALVO, Sammy P&R '58

Singles: 78 rpm

RCA ... 10-20 57

Singles: 7-inch

DOT ... 10-15 60
HICKORY ... 5-10 61-63
IMPERIAL ... 5-10 59-60
MARK V ... 10-20 58
RCA ... 10-20 57-59

SAM, Butch, & Station Band R&B '85

Singles: 7-inch

PRIVATE I ... 3-4 85

SAM & BILL P&R/R&B '65

Singles: 7-inch

DECCA ... 4-8 67
JODA ... 4-8 65-66

Members: Sam Gary; Bill Johnson.

SAM & DAVE P&R/R&B/LP '66

Singles: 7-inch

ATLANTIC ... 3-8 68-71
ROULETTE ... 5-10 62-66
STAX ... 5-10 65-68
U.A. ... 3-5 74-75

LPs: 10/12-inch

ATLANTIC (8205 "I Thank You") ... 15-20 68
ATLANTIC (8218 "Best of Sam & Dave") ... 8-12 69
GUSTO ... 5-10
ROULETTE (25323 "Sam & Dave") 15-25 66
STAX (708 "Hold On, I'm Coming") .. 20-30 66
STAX (712 "Double Dynamite") ... 20-30 66
STAX (725 "Soul Men") ... 20-30 67
U.A. ... 8-12 74-75

Members: Sam Moore; Dave Prater.
Also see MOORE, Sam
Also see PICKETT, Wilson / Sam & Dave
Also see REDDING, Otis / Carla Thomas / Sam & Dave / Eddie Floyd
Also see STARS on 45 (Featuring Sam & Dave)

SAM THE SHAM & PHARAOHS
(Sam the Sham Revue; Sam; Sam Samudio) P&R/R&B/LP '65

Singles: 7-inch

DINGO (001 "Haunted House") ... 20-30 64
FRETONE (048 "The Wookie") ... 3-5 77
MGM (13000 series, except 13972) 5-10 64-69
MGM (13972 "I Couldn't Spell !!*@!") ... 10-15 69
MGM (14000 series) ... 3-5 73
POLYDOR ... 3-4 80s
TUPELO (2982 "Betty & Dupree") ... 35-55 63
WARRIOR ... 20-30 60s
XL (905 "Signifyin' Monkey") ... 15-25 64
XL (906 "Wooly Bully") ... 30-50 65

Picture Sleeves

MGM ... 8-12 65-67

LPs: 10/12-inch

MGM ... 15-25 65-68

Also see SAMUDIO, Sam

SAMI JO: see COLE, Sami Jo

SAMPLE, Joe LP '78

Singles: 7-inch

ABC ... 3-5 78-79
MCA ... 3-4 80-83

LPs: 10/12-inch

ABC ... 5-10 78-79
MCA ... 5-8 81-83
MFSL ... 25-50 78
W.B. ... 5-8 89

Also see CRUSADERS

SAMUELS, Bill
(With the Cats 'N' Jammer Three; Cats 'N' Jammers) R&B '46

Singles: 78 rpm

MERCURY ... 20-50 46-48

Singles: 7-inch

MERCURY (70205 "I Cover the Waterfront") ... 50-75 53
SOMA ... 8-10 61

SAN FRANCISCO SYMPHONY ORCHESTRA LP '73

LPs: 10/12-inch

DG ... 8-12 73

SAN REMO GOLDEN STRINGS P&R '65

Singles: 7-inch

GORDY ... 10-20 67
RIC-TIC ... 8-15 65-66

LPs: 10/12-inch

GORDY (923 "Hungry for Love") ... 25-35 67
GORDY (928 "Swing") ... 15-25 68
RIC-TIC (901 "Hungry for Love") ... 30-60 66

SAN SEBASTIAN STRINGS LP '67
(With the San Sebastian Strings)

Singles: 7-inch

W.B. ... 3-6 67-73

LPs: 10/12-inch

W.B. (Except 2754) ... 8-15 67-75
W.B. (2754 "Spring, Summer, Winter, Autumn") ... 15-20 73
(Four-disc set.)

Also see McKUEN, Rod

SANBORN, David R&B/LP '76

Singles: 12-inch

W.B. ... 4-8 81-85

Singles: 7-inch

REPRISE ... 3-4 88
W.B. ... 3-5 76-87

LPs: 10/12-inch

REPRISE ... 5-8 88
W.B. ... 5-10 76-87

Also see JAMES, Bob, & David Sanborn
Also see PURE PRAIRIE LEAGUE

SANDALS LP '67

Singles: 7-inch

WORLD PACIFIC (415 "Theme from *Endless Summer*) ... 10-15 64
WORLD PACIFIC (421 "Always") ... 15-25 64

WORLD PACIFIC (77000 series)........8-12 65-67

LPs: 10/12-inch

WORLD PACIFIC (WP-1832 "Endless Summer")........................20-25 66
(Monaural. Soundtrack)

WORLD PACIFIC (ST-1832 "Endless Summer")........................25-30 66
(Stereo. Soundtrack)

Members: John Blakely; Danny Brawner; John Gibson; Gaston Georis; Walter Georis.

Also see SANDELLS

SANDELLS

Singles: 7-inch

AURA (4501 "School's Out!")............10-15 65
WORLD PACIFIC (405 "Out Front") .10-15 64

LPs: 10/12-inch

WORLD PACIFIC (WP-1818 "Scramblers")........................25-35 64
(Monaural.)

WORLD PACIFIC (ST-1818 "Scramblers")........................35-45 64
(Stereo.)

WORLD PACIFIC (1818 "Scramblers")........................50-75 64
(Colored vinyl.)

Also see SANDALS

SANDERS, Felicia — P&R '55

Singles: 78 rpm

COLUMBIA........................3-5 52-57

Singles: 7-inch

COLUMBIA........................5-10 52-57
DECCA........................4-8 59-61
MGM........................4-8 65
TIME........................4-8 60

EPs: 7-inch

COLUMBIA........................8-12 55-56

LPs: 10/12-inch

COLUMBIA........................15-25 55-57
DECCA........................15-20 58
SPECIAL EDITIONS........................5-10 67
TIME........................10-15 60-64

Also see FAITH, Percy
Also see VALE, Jerry, Peggy King & Felicia Sanders

SANDERS, Pharoah — LP '69

Singles: 7-inch

ARISTA........................3-5 78

LPs: 10/12-inch

ARISTA........................5-10 78
IMPULSE........................10-15 69-74
INDIA NAVIGATION........................5-10 77
NOVUS........................5-10 81
THERESA........................5-12 80-81
TRIP........................8-12 71

Also see COLTRANE, Alice, & Pharoah Sanders

SANDLER, Tony, & Ralph Young — LP '66
(Sandler & Young)

Singles: 7-inch

CAPITOL........................3-6 66-70

LPs: 10/12-inch

A.V.I........................5-10 79
CAPITOL........................5-15 66-78

Also see CAMPBELL, Glen / Lettermen / Ella Fitzgerald / Sandler & Young

SANDPEBBLES — P&R/R&B '67

Singles: 7-inch

ABC........................3-5 73
CALLA........................5-10 67-69

Members: Calvin White; Lonzine Wright; Andrea Bolden.

Also see C & SHELLS

SANDPIPERS — P&R/LP '66

Singles: 7-inch

A&M........................3-6 66-72
KISMET........................15-25 66
TRU-GLOW-TOWN........................5-10 66

EPs: 7-inch

THREE on ONE........................5-10

LPs: 10/12-inch

A&M........................8-15 66-73

SANDS, Evie — P&R '69

Singles: 7-inch

ABC-PAR........................4-8 63-64
A&M........................3-6 68-70
BLUE CAT........................5-10 65
CAMEO........................4-6 66-68
GOLD........................4-8 64
HAVEN........................3-5 75-76
RCA........................3-5 79

LPs: 10/12-inch

A&M........................10-15 69
HAVEN........................8-10 74
RCA........................5-10 79

SANDS, Jodie — P&R '57

Singles: 78 rpm

BERNLO........................8-12 57
CHANCELLOR........................5-10 57
TEEN........................5-10 55

Singles: 7-inch

ABC........................3-5 74
ABC-PAR........................4-8 62-63
BERNLO........................8-12 57
CHANCELLOR........................5-10 57-59
PARIS........................5-10 60-61
SIGNATURE........................5-10 59
TEEN........................10-20 55
THOR........................8-12 59

SANDS, Tommy — P&R/R&B/LP '57
(With the Raiders)

Singles: 78 rpm

CAPITOL........................10-25 57
RCA........................8-12 54-56

Singles: 7-inch

ABC-PAR........................4-8 63-64
CAPITOL (3639 thru 4082)........................10-15 57-58
CAPITOL (4160 thru 4580)........................5-10 59-61
IMPERIAL........................4-8 66-67
LIBERTY........................4-8 65
RCA........................10-20 54-56
SUPERSCOPE........................3-6 69

Picture Sleeves

CAPITOL........................10-20 58-59

EPs: 7-inch

CAPITOL (1-2-3 848 "Sing Boy Sing")........................15-25 57
(Price is for any of three volumes.)

CAPITOL (898 "Teen-Age Crush")... 20-30 57

CAPITOL (1-2-3 929 "Sing Boy Sing")........................15-25 58
(Price is for any of three volumes.)

CAPITOL (1123 "This Thing Called Love")........................15-20 59

LPs: 10/12-inch

BRUNSWICK........................8-10 78
CAPITOL (848 "Steady Date")..........35-50 57
CAPITOL (929 "Sing Boy Sing").......35-50 58
CAPITOL (1081 "Sands Storm").......30-50 58

CAPITOL (T-1123 "This Thing Called Love")........................30-40 59
(Monaural.)

CAPITOL (ST-1123 "This Thing Called Love")........................35-45 59
(Stereo.)

CAPITOL (T-1239 "When I'm Thinking of You")........................30-40 59
(Monaural.)

CAPITOL (ST-1239 "When I'm Thinking of You")........................35-45 59
(Stereo.)

CAPITOL (T-1364 "Sands at the Storm")........................30-40 60
(Monaural.)

CAPITOL (ST-1364 "Sands at the Sands")........................35-45 60
(Stereo.)

CAPITOL (T-1426 "Dream with Me")........................30-40 60
(Monaural.)

CAPITOL (ST-1426 "Dream with Me")........................35-45 60
(Stereo.)

Also see ANNETTE & Tommy Sands
Also see VINCENT, Gene / Tommy Sands / Sonny James / Ferlin Husky

SANDS OF TIME
(Tokens)

Singles: 7-inch

KIRSHNER........................4-8 76

Also see TOKENS

SANFORD - TOWNSEND BAND — P&R/LP '77

Singles: 7-inch

W.B.........................3-5 77-79

LPs: 10/12-inch

W.B.........................5-10 78-79

Members: Ed Sanford; John Townsend.

SANG, Samantha — P&R '77

Singles: 7-inch

ATCO........................4-6 69
PRIVATE STOCK........................3-5 77-78
U.A.........................3-5 79

LPs: 10/12-inch

PRIVATE STOCK........................5-10 77-78
U.A.........................5-10 79

Also see BEE GEES

SANS, Billie — P&R '71

Singles: 7-inch

INVICTUS........................3-5 71

SANTA ESMERALDA — P&R/LP '77

Singles: 12-inch

CASABLANCA........................4-8 77-78

Singles: 7-inch

CASABLANCA........................3-5 77-78

LPs: 10/12-inch

CASABLANCA........................5-10 77-80

Member: Leroy Gomez.

SANTAMARIA, Mongo
(With His Afro-Latin Group) — P&R/R&B/LP '63

Singles: 12-inch

TAPPAN ZEE........................4-8 79

Singles: 7-inch

ATLANTIC........................3-6 69-72
BATTLE........................4-8 63
COLLECTABLES........................3-4 80s
COLUMBIA........................4-6 64-69
FANTASY........................4-8 61-62
RIVERSIDE........................4-8 62-66
TAPPAN ZEE........................3-5 79
TRIP........................3-6
VAYA........................3-5 73

LPs: 10/12-inch

ATLANTIC........................8-12 70
BATTLE........................15-25 63
COLUMBIA........................5-15 65-79
FANTASY........................10-25 59-62
MILESTONE........................6-12 73-76
PRESTIGE........................6-12 72
RIVERSIDE........................10-20 62-66
VAYA........................6-12 73-74

SANTANA — P&R/LP '69
(Carlos Santana)

Singles: 12-inch

COLUMBIA........................4-6 85

Singles: 7-inch

COLUMBIA........................3-5 69-90

Picture Sleeves

COLUMBIA........................3-5 70-85

LPs: 10/12-inch

COLUMBIA (Except quad and half-speed mastered)........................5-12 69-90

COLUMBIA (CQ-30130 "Abraxas")... 10-15 75
(Quadraphonic.)

COLUMBIA (CQ-32900 "Illuminations")........................10-15 74
(Quadraphonic.)

COLUMBIA (HC-40130 "Abraxas") ... 40-60 81
(Half-speed mastered.)

Members: Devadip Carlos Santana; Armando Peraza; Graham Lear; David Margen; Richard Baker; Alex Ligertwood; Orestes Vilato; Raul Rekow.

Also see AZTECA
Also see BOOKER T. & MGs
Also see COLTRANE, Alice, & Carlos Santana
Also see ESCOVEDO, Coke

Also see FABULOUS THUNDERBIRDS
Also see FRANKLIN, Aretha
Also see HAGAR, SCHON, AARONSON, SHRIEVE
Also see HANCOCK, Herbie
Also see NOVO COMBO

SANTANA, Carlos, & Mahavishnu John McLaughlin LP '73

LPs: 10/12-inch

COLUMBIA (32034 "Love, Devotion, Surrender")....5-10 73

Also see McLAUGHLIN, John

SANTANA, Carlos, & Buddy Miles P&R/LP '72

Singles: 7-inch

COLUMBIA....3-5 72

LPs: 10/12-inch

COLUMBIA....6-12 72

Also see MILES, Buddy
Also see SANTANA

SANTANA, Jorge R&B '79

Singles: 7-inch

TOMATO....3-5 78-79

LPs: 10/12-inch

TOMATO....5-10 78

Also see MALO

SANTIAGO R&B '76

Singles: 7-inch

AMHERST....3-5 76

SANTO & JOHNNY P&R/R&B '59

Singles: 7-inch

CANADIAN AMERICAN....5-12 59-66
ERIC....3-4 70s
IMPERIAL....4-8 67-68
PAUSA....3-5 76
U.A....4-8 66

Picture Sleeves

CANADIAN AMERICAN....8-15 60-65

LPs: 10/12-inch

CANADIAN AMERICAN....20-40 59-64
IMPERIAL....10-20 67-69

Members: Santo Farina; Johnny Farina.

SANTOS, Larry P&R '76

Singles: 7-inch

ATLANTIC (2250 "Someday")....10-20 64
CASABLANCA....3-5 76-77
EVOLUTION....5-15 69-71

LPs: 10/12-inch

CASABLANCA....8-10 77
EVOLUTION....10-20 69

Also see 4 SEASONS

SAPPHIRES P&R/R&B '64

Singles: 7-inch

ABC....3-5 73
ABC-PAR....5-15 64-66
COLLECTABLES....3-4 80s
ERIC....3-4 70s
ITZY (5 "Who Do You Love")....20-30 63
SWAN....8-10 63-64

LPs: 10/12-inch

SWAN (513 "Who Do You Love")....40-60 64

Members: Carol Jackson; George Gainer; Joe Livingston.

SARAYA P&R/LP '89

Singles: 7-inch

POLYDOR....3-4 89

Picture Sleeves

POLYDOR....3-4 89

LPs: 10/12-inch

POLYDOR....5-8 89

SARDUCCI, Father Guido LP '80

Singles: 7-inch

A&M....3-5 74
W.B....3-4 80

LPs: 10/12-inch

W.B....5-10 80

SARIDIS, Saverio P&R '62

Singles: 7-inch

U.A....3-6 66
W.B....4-8 61-62

Picture Sleeves

W.B....4-8 61

LPs: 10/12-inch

W.B....10-20 62

SARSTEDT, Peter P&R '69

Singles: 7-inch

SIRE....3-5 78
U.A....3-5 72
WORLD PACIFIC....4-6 69

LPs: 10/12-inch

U.A....8-12 71
WORLD PACIFIC....10-15 69

SASS R&B '77

Singles: 7-inch

20TH FOX....3-5 77

SATELLITE, Billy: see BILLY SATELLITE

SATISFACTIONS P&R/R&B '70

Singles: 7-inch

LIONEL (3201 "This Bitter Earth")....8-12 70
LIONEL (3205 "One Light, Two Lights")....10-15 71

Members: James Isom; Earl Jones; Lorenzo Hines; Fletcher Lee.

SATRIANI, Joe LP '87

Singles: 12-inch

RELATIVITY (8193 "Always with Me")..4-8 87
(Clear vinyl. Promotional issue only.)

LPs: 10/12-inch

RELATIVITY (8110 "Not of This Earth")....10-15 88
(Colored vinyl.)

SATTERFIELD, Esther LP '76

Singles: 7-inch

A&M....3-5 76

LPs: 10/12-inch

A&M....5-10 76

SATURDAY NIGHT BAND R&B/LP '78

Singles: 7-inch

PRELUDE....3-5 78

LPs: 10/12-inch

PRELUDE....5-10 78

SAULSBERRY, Rodney R&B '84

Singles: 7-inch

ALLEGIANCE....3-4 84-85
RYAN....3-4 88

SAUNDERS, Merl LP '73
(Merle Saunders & Heavy Turbulence)

Singles: 7-inch

FANTASY....4-8 64-69
GALAXY....3-5 71

LPs: 10/12-inch

FANTASY....10-20 68-73

Session: Tom Fogerty.
Also see GARCIA, Jerry

SAVAGE GRACE LP '70

Singles: 7-inch

REPRISE....3-5 70-71

LPs: 10/12-inch

REPRISE....10-15 70-71

SAVALAS, Telly LP '75

Singles: 7-inch

MCA....3-5 74-75

LPs: 10/12-inch

AUDIO FIDELITY....5-10 75
MCA....5-10 74-76

SAVATAGE LP '86

Singles: 7-inch

ATLANTIC....3-4 86-90

LPs: 10/12-inch

ATLANTIC....5-8 86-90

SAVOY, Ronnie P&R '61

Singles: 7-inch

CANDELO....5-10 59
EPIC....4-8 63-64
GONE....5-10 59
MGM....10-20 60-61
PHILIPS....4-8 62-63
TUFF (416 "Pitfall")....20-30 65
WINGATE (001 "Loving You")....10-20 65

SAVOY BROWN P&R/LP '69
(Savoy Brown Blues Band)

Singles: 7-inch

LONDON....3-5 74-75
PARROT....3-6 69-73
TOWN HOUSE....3-5 81

LPs: 10/12-inch

LONDON (600 & 700 series)....8-10 74-77
LONDON (50000 "Best of Savoy Brown")....5-8 77
PARROT....10-15 68-73
TOWN HOUSE (Except 7562)....8-12 81
TOWN HOUSE (7562 "Prime Cuts") 10-15 81
(Promotional issue only.)

Also see FOGHAT

SAWYER, Ray P&R/C&W '76

Singles: 7-inch

CAPITOL....3-5 76-79
SANDY (1030 "Rockin' Satellite")....20-30 60
SANDY (1037 "I'm Gonna Leave")....10-20 61

LPs: 10/12-inch

CAPITOL....8-10 76

Also see DR. HOOK

SAWYER BROWN C&W '84

Singles: 7-inch

CAPITOL....3-5 84-90

LPs: 10/12-inch

CAPITOL....5-10 85-90

Members: Mark Miller; Bob Randall; Jim Scholten; Gregg Hubbard; Joe Smyth.

SAWYER BROWN & "CAT" JOE BONSALL C&W '86

Singles: 7-inch

CAPITOL....3-4 86

Also see SAWYER BROWN

SAXON LP '83

Singles: 7-inch

CARRERE....3-5 83-84

LPs: 10/12-inch

CAPITOL....5-10 83-87

Also see MOTORHEAD

SAYER, Leo P&R/LP '75

Singles: 7-inch

W.B....3-5 73-84

LPs: 10/12-inch

W.B....6-10 75-84

SCAFFOLD P&R '68

Singles: 7-inch

BELL....4-8 68
W.B....3-5 74

LPs: 10/12-inch

BELL (6018 "Thank U Very Much")....25-30 68

Members: Mike McGear; Roger McGough; John Gorman; Mike Vickers; Lol Creme; Andy Roberts; Zoot Money.
Also see GODLEY, Kevin, & Lol Creme

SCAGGS, Boz P&R/LP '71

Singles: 7-inch

ATLANTIC....4-8 69
COLUMBIA....3-8 71-88
FULL MOON....3-5 81

Picture Sleeves

COLUMBIA....3-6 76-88

EPs: 7-inch

COLUMBIA....5-10 76

LPs: 10/12-inch

ATLANTIC (8239 "Boz Scaggs")....8-12 69
ATLANTIC (19166 "Boz Scaggs")....5-8 78
COLUMBIA (Except 40000 series)....6-10 71-80
COLUMBIA (40463 "Other Roads")....5-8 88
COLUMBIA (43920 "Silk Degrees")..15-20 80
(Half-speed mastered.)

Promotional LPs

COLUMBIA (A2S-71 "Boz Scaggs KSAN Live Concert")....200-300 74
(Promotional issue only. Two-LP set.)

COLUMBIA (203 "The Boz Scaggs Sampler") 10-20 76
Also see MILLER, Steve
Also see MOTHER EARTH

SCALES, Harvey — P&R/R&B '67
(With the Seven Sounds)

Singles: 7-inch

KASHGOLD 3-4 90

Singles: 7-inch

CADET CONCEPT 4-8 71
CASABLANCA 3-5 79
CHESS 3-5 69-70
CUCA 5-10 63-67
EARTHTONE 3-4 86-91
KASHGOLD 3-4 90
MAGIC TOUCH 3-8 67-76
MERCURY 3-6 69
STAX 3-5 72

LPs: 10/12-inch

CASABLANCA 8-10 78-79
Members: Rudy Jacobs; Rollo Armstead; Ben Petrey; Monnie Smith; Al Vance; Vic Pitts; Roy Scott; Billy Stonewall; Melvin Taylor.

SCANDAL — P&R '82
(Featuring Patty Smyth)

Singles: 12-inch

COLUMBIA 4-6 82-85

Singles: 7-inch

COLUMBIA 3-5 82-85

Picture Sleeves

COLUMBIA 3-5 83-85

EPs: 7-inch

COLUMBIA (8C8-39905 "Warrior") 10-15 82
(Picture disc.)

LPs: 10/12-inch

COLUMBIA 5-10 82-85

SCARBURY, Joey — P&R '71

Singles: 7-inch

BELL 3-5 71-73
BIG TREE 3-5 73
COLUMBIA 3-5 77-79
ELEKTRA 3-5 81
LIONEL 3-5 71
PLAYBOY 3-5 74
RCA 3-4 84
REENA 4-6 68

Picture Sleeves

ELEKTRA 3-5 81

LPs: 10/12-inch

ELEKTRA 5-10 81

SCARLET & BLACK — LP '88

Singles: 7-inch

VIRGIN 3-4 88

Picture Sleeves

VIRGIN 3-4 88

LPs: 10/12-inch

VIRGIN 5-8 88
Members: Robin Hild; Sue West.

SCATTERBRAIN — LP '90

LPs: 10/12-inch

IN-EFFECT 5-8 90

SCHAFER, Kermit — LP '58

Singles: 78 rpm

JUBILEE 5-10 56

Singles: 7-inch

JUBILEE (5258 "Rock Around the Blooper") 10-15 56

LPs: 10/12-inch

AUDIO FIDELITY 8-12 69
JUBILEE 10-20 58-63
KAPP 8-12 68-70
KING 10-15 64
MCA 5-10 74-77
Kermit Schafer has also released numerous comedy albums of "Bloopers," which we have not attempted to list. Their value is minimal, usually under $10.

SCHENKER, Michael, Group — LP '80

Singles: 7-inch

CHRYSALIS 3-5 80-83

LPs: 10/12-inch

CHRYSALIS 5-10 80-83
Also see ALCATRAZZ
Also see McAULEY SCHENKER GROUP
Also see UFO

SCHIFRIN, Lalo — LP '62

Singles: 12-inch

CTI 5-10 76
TABU 4-8 78-79

Singles: 7-inch

A&M 3-5 75
CTI 3-5 76-77
DOT 3-5 67
MCA 3-5 77-83
MGM 4-6 63-70
PABLO 3-5 77
PARAMOUNT 4-6 69
TABU 3-5 78-79
TETRAGRAMMATON 4-6 69
20TH FOX 3-5 74-75
U.A. 3-5 70
VERVE 4-6 63-71
W.B. 3-6 68-69

LPs: 10/12-inch

AUDIO FIDELITY 5-15 62-68
CTI 5-10 76-77
COLPIX 10-20 64
DOT (25852 "There's a Whole Lalo Schifrin Goin' On") 10-15 68
MCA (5000 series) 5-10 81
MGM 5-15 63-70
ROULETTE 10-15 62
TABU 5-10 79
TICO 10-20 60
VERVE (Except 8624) 10-20 63-69
You'll find many more listings by this artist in *The Official Price Guide to Movie/TV Soundtracks and Original Cast Albums,* containing over 8,000 listings.

SCHILLING, Nina — D&D '84

Singles: 12-inch

MOBY DICK 4-6 84

SCHILLING, Peter — P&R/D&D/LP '83

Singles: 12-inch

ELEKTRA 4-6 83

Singles: 7-inch

ELEKTRA 3-4 83-89

Picture Sleeves

ELEKTRA 3-4 89

LPs: 10/12-inch

ELEKTRA 5-10 83

SCHMIT, Timothy B. — P&R '82

Singles: 7-inch

FULL MOON 3-5 82
MCA 3-4 87

Picture Sleeves

FULL MOON 3-5 82
MCA 3-4 87

LPs: 10/12-inch

ASYLUM 5-10 84
MCA 5-8 87
Also see EAGLES
Also see MARX, Richard
Also see POCO

SCHNEIDER, Fred, & Shake Society — D&D '84

Singles: 12-inch

W.B. 4-6 84

Singles: 7-inch

W.B. 3-4 84

SCHNEIDER, John — C&W/P&R/LP '81

Singles: 7-inch

MCA 3-4 84-87
SCOTTI BROS 3-5 81-83

Picture Sleeves

MCA 3-4 84-87
SCOTTI BROS 3-5 81-83

LPs: 10/12-inch

MCA 5-8 84-87
SCOTTI BROS 5-10 81-83

SCHNEIDER, John, & Jill Michaels

Singles: 7-inch

SCOTTI BROS 3-4 83
Session: Waylon Jennings.
Also see JENNINGS, Waylon
Also see SCHNEIDER, John

SCHON, Neal, & Jan Hammer — LP '81

LPs: 10/12-inch

COLUMBIA 5-10 81-83
Also see HAGAR, SCHON, AARONSON, SHRIEVE
Also see HAMMER, Jan
Also see JOURNEY

SCHOOLBOYS — P&R/R&B '57

Singles: 78 rpm

OKEH 15-30 56-57

Singles: 7-inch

JUANITA (103 "Angel of Love") 75-100 58
OKEH (7076 "Please Say You Want Me") 25-35 56
(Purple label.)
OKEH (7076 "Please Say You Want Me") 10-20 57
(Yellow label.)
OKEH (7085 "Mary") 25-35 57
OKEH (7090 "Carol") 15-25 57
(Purple label.)
OKEH (7090 "Carol") 25-35 57
(White label. Promotional issue only.)
OKEH (7090 "Carol") 10-20 57
(Yellow label.)
Members: Les Martin; Jim Edwards; Roger Hayes; Jim McKay; Renaldo Gamble.

EPs: 7-inch

MAGIC CARPET 5-10
Also see CADILLACS

SCHOOLEY D — LP '88

LPs: 10/12-inch

JIVE 5-8 88

SCHORY, Dick — LP '59
(Dick Schory's Percussion Pops Orchestra)

LPs: 10/12-inch

RCA 5-15 59-63

SCHUMANN, Walter — P&R '53
(Voices of Walter Schumann)

Singles: 78 rpm

CAPITOL 3-5 52
RCA 3-5 53-56

Singles: 7-inch

CAPITOL 4-6 52
RCA 4-6 53-56

EPs: 7-inch

CAPITOL 5-10 52
RCA 5-10 53-56

LPs: 10/12-inch

CAPITOL 5-15 52
RCA 5-15 53-56

SCHUUR, Diane — LP '88
(With Jose Feliciano)

Singles: 7-inch

GRP (3016 "American Wedding Song") 3-4 85
(With insert.)

LPs: 10/12-inch

GRP 5-8 88-90
Also see FELICIANO, Jose

SCHWARTZ, Eddie — P&R '81

Singles: 7-inch

ATCO 3-5 81-82

LPs: 10/12-inch

ATCO 5-10 82

SCORPIONS — LP '79

Singles: 7-inch

MERCURY 3-4 79-91
RCA 3-5 74-80

Picture Sleeves

MERCURY 3-4 84-88

LPs: 10/12-inch

MERCURY 5-8 79-90
RCA 5-10 74-84

Members: Klaus Meine; Francis Bucholz; Matt Jabs; Herman Rarebell; Uli Roth; Rudolf Schenker.

SCOTT, Billy P&R '58

Singles: 78 rpm

CAMEO 10-20 57

Singles: 7-inch

CAMEO 10-20 57-58
EVEREST 5-10 59

SCOTT, Bobby P&R '56

Singles: 78 rpm

ABC-PAR 5-10 56

Singles: 7-inch

ABC 3-5 73
ABC-PAR 10-15 56

SCOTT, Christopher LP '69

(Sir Christopher Scott)

LPs: 10/12-inch

DECCA 5-10 69-70
MCA 5-10 73

SCOTT, Freddie P&R/R&B '63

(Freddy Scott)

Singles: 7-inch

ABC 3-5 74
COLPIX 5-10 63-64
COLUMBIA 5-15 64-65
ELEPHANT V LTD. 4-6
ERIC 3-5 68
J&S (1761 "Turn Lamps Down Low") 15-25 56
JOY 8-12 61-63
MARLIN 4-8 66
P.I.P. 3-5 72
PROBE 3-5 70
SHOUT 4-8 66-71
SOLID GOLD 3-5 73
VANGUARD 3-5 71

LPs: 10/12-inch

COLPIX (Gold label) 30-40 64
COLPIX (Blue label) 15-25 65
COLUMBIA 10-20 64-67
PROBE 10-15 70
SHOUT 10-20 67

Also see CHIMES

SCOTT, Gloria R&B '74

Singles: 7-inch

CASABLANCA 3-5 74-75

SCOTT, Jack P&R/R&B '58

(With the Chantones)

Singles: 78 rpm

ABC-PAR 50-100 57

Singles: 7-inch

ABC (10843 "Before the Bird Flies") ... 5-10 66
ABC-PAR (9818 "Baby, She's Gone") 50-75 57
(Black label.)
ABC-PAR (9818 "Baby, She's Gone") 40-60 57
(White label. Promotional issue only.)
ABC-PAR (9860 "Two Timin' Woman") 50-75 57
(Black label.)
ABC-PAR (9860 "Two Timin' Woman") 40-60 57
(White label. Promotional issue only.)
CAPITOL 15-25 61-63
CARLTON (462 "My True Love") 15-25 58
CARLTON (483 "With Your Love") ... 15-25 58
CARLTON (493 "Goodbye Baby") 15-25 58
CARLTON (504 "I Never Felt Like This") 10-20 59
(Beige label.)
CARLTON (504 "I Never Felt Like This") 25-35 59
(Red label. Promotional issue only.)
CARLTON (514 "The Way I Walk") .. 10-20 59
CARLTON (519 "There Comes a Time") 10-20 59
(Monaural.)
CARLTON (ST-519 "There Comes a Time") 25-50 59
(Stereo.)
COLLECTABLES 3-4 80s
DOT 3-5 73
ERIC 3-4 70s
GRT 3-5 70
GROOVE (0027 "There's Trouble Brewin'") 10-15 63
GROOVE (0031 "I Knew You First") ... 5-10 64
GROOVE (0037 "Wiggle on Out") 10-15 64
GROOVE (0042 "Thou Shalt Not Steal") 10-15 64
GROOVE (0049 "Flakey John") 10-15 64
GUARANTEED (209 "What Am I Living For") 10-20 60
GUARANTEED (211 "Go Wild Little Sadie") 15-25 60
JUBILEE 5-10 67
RCA 5-10 65
TOP RANK (2028 "What in the World's Come Over You") 10-20 60
TOP RANK (2041 "Burning Bridges") 10-20 60
(Monaural.)
TOP RANK (2041 "Burning Bridges") 25-50 60
(Stereo.)
TOP RANK (2055 "It Only Happened Yesterday") 10-20 60
TOP RANK (2075 "Patsy") 10-20 60
TOP RANK (2093 "Is There Something on Your Mind") 10-20 60

Picture Sleeves

CAPITOL 20-30 61-62
CARLTON 20-30 58-59
TOP RANK 20-30 60-61

EPs: 7-inch

CARLTON (1070 "Jack Scott") 50-100 58
CARLTON (1071 "Presenting Jack Scott") 50-100 58
CARLTON (1072 "Jack Scott Sings") 50-100 59
TOP RANK (1001 "Jack Scott") 50-100 60

LPs: 10/12-inch

CAPITOL (2035 "Burning Bridges") 100-125 64
CAPITOL (8-2035 "Burning Bridges") 100-125 64
(Capitol Record Club issue.)
CARLTON (LP-107 "Jack Scott") 100-150 58
(Monaural.)
CARLTON (STLP-12 107 "Jack Scott") 150-200 58
(Stereo.)
CARLTON (LP-122 "What Am I Living For") 100-200 60
(Monaural.)
CARLTON (STLP-12 122 "What Am I Living For") 200-300 60
(Stereo.)
JADE 10-15
PONIE 8-10 74-77
SESAC (4201 "Soul Stirring") 75-100 59
TOP RANK (348 "The Spirit Moves Me") 75-125 60
TOP RANK (319 "I Remember Hank Williams") 75-125 60
(Monaural.)
TOP RANK (619 "I Remember Hank Williams") 100-150 60
(Stereo.)
TOP RANK (326 "What in the World's Come Over You") 75-125 61
(Monaural.)
TOP RANK (626 "What in the World's Come Over You") 100-150 61
(Stereo.)

SCOTT, Judy P&R '57

Singles: 78 rpm

DECCA 5-10 57

Singles: 7-inch

CAPITOL 4-8 60
DECCA 5-10 57-59
EMBER 4-8 64
TOP RANK 4-8 59

SCOTT, Linda P&R/R&B '61

Singles: 7-inch

CANADIAN AMERICAN 10-20 61-62
CONGRESS 8-15 62-64
ERIC 3-4 70s
KAPP 5-10 64-66
RCA 4-8 68

EPs: 7-inch

CONGRESS (1005 "Starlight Starbright") 25-35 62
CONGRESS (3001 "Linda Scott") 25-35 62
(Promotional issue only. Issued with picture insert, but not with cover.)

LPs: 10/12-inch

CANADIAN AMERICAN (CALP-1005 "Starlight Starbright") 35-45 61
(Monaural.)
CANADIAN AMERICAN (SCALP-1005 "Starlight Starbright") 40-50 61
(Stereo.)
CANADIAN AMERICAN (CALP-1007 "Great Scott") 35-45 62
(Monaural.)
CANADIAN AMERICAN (SCALP-1007 "Great Scott") 40-50 62
(Stereo.)
CONGRESS (3001 "Linda") 25-35 62
KAPP (3424 "Hey Look at Me Now"). 25-35 65

SCOTT, Mabel R&B '48

Singles: 78 rpm

BRUNSWICK 5-10 52
CORAL 5-10 51-52
EXCELSIOR 8-12 47-48
EXCLUSIVE 8-12 48
FESTIVAL 5-10 55
HOLLYWOOD 5-10 54
HUB 10-15 46
KING 5-10 50-51
PARROT 15-25 53

Singles: 7-inch

BRUNSWICK (84001 "Wailin' Daddy") 15-25 52
CORAL 15-25 51-52
FESTIVAL 15-25 55
HOLLYWOOD 15-25 54
PARROT (780 "Mr. Fine") 20-30 53
(Black vinyl.)
PARROT (780 "Mr. Fine") 50-75 53
(Colored vinyl.)
PARROT (794 "Fool Burro") 20-30 53

Also see BROWN, Charles

SCOTT, Marilyn P&R '77

Singles: 7-inch

BIG TREE 3-5 77
MERCURY 3-4 83-85

LPs: 10/12-inch

ATCO 5-10 79
MERCURY 5-8 83

SCOTT, Millie R&B '86

(Mildred Scott)

Singles: 7-inch

4TH & BROADWAY 3-4 86-87

SCOTT, Neal P&R '61

(With the Concords; Neil Scott; Neil Bogart)

Singles: 7-inch

CAMEO 5-10 67
CLOWN 10-15 60
COMET 10-15 62
HERALD 10-15 63
PORTRAIT 8-12 61-62

Also see BECK, BOGART & APPICE

SCOTT, Peggy, & Jo Jo Benson P&R/R&B '68

Singles: 7-inch

SSS INT'L 4-8 68-69
SUN 3-5 70s

LPs: 10/12-inch

AVI 5-10 84
SSS INT'L 10-15 69

SCOTT, Rena *R&B '79*

Singles: 7-inch

BUDDAH 3-5 79
EPIC 3-5 72-74
SEDONA 3-4 88

SCOTT, Tom *R&B/LP '74*
(With the L.A. Express; with California Dreamers)

Singles: 12-inch

SIRE 4-6 83

Singles: 7-inch

A&M 3-5 72
ATLANTIC 3-5 83
COLUMBIA 3-5 79
IMPULSE 4-6 68
ODE 3-5 74-79
SIRE 3-4 83

LPs: 10/12-inch

COLUMBIA 5-10 78-81
EPIC/ODE 5-8 84
IMPULSE 20-30 68
ODE 8-10 74-77
MUSICIAN 5-10 82
RCA 5-10 81
Also see CLAYTON, Merry
Also see HARRISON, George
Also see L.A. EXPRESS

SCOTT-HERON, Gil *R&B '78*
(With Pretty Purdie & Playboys)

Singles: 7-inch

ARISTA 3-5 75-84
FLYING DUTCHMAN 3-5 71-74

LPs: 10/12-inch

ARISTA 6-12 75-84
FLYING DUTCHMAN (100 thru 0600 series) 8-15 71-74
FLYING DUTCHMAN (3800 series) 5-8 80

SCOTT-HERON, Gil, & Brian Jackson *P&R/LP '75*

Singles: 7-inch

ARISTA 3-5 75-80

LPs: 10/12-inch

ARISTA 6-12 75-80
STRATA-EAST 8-15 74
Also see SCOTT-HERON, Gil

SCREAMIN' BLUE MESSIAHS *LP '88*

LPs: 10/12-inch

ELEKTRA 5-8 87

SCRITTI POLITTI *D&D '84*

Singles: 12-inch

W.B. 4-6 84-86

Singles: 7-inch

W.B. 3-4 84-88

Picture Sleeves

W.B. 3-4 85-88

LPs: 10/12-inch

W.B. 5-8 84-86

SCRITTI POLITTI & ROGER *P&R '88*

Singles: 7-inch

W.B. 3-4 88

Picture Sleeves

W.B. 3-4 88
Also see ROGER
Also see SCRITTI POLITTI

SCRUFFY THE CAT *LP '88*

Singles: 12-inch

RELATIVITY 4-6 87

LPs: 10/12-inch

RELATIVITY 5-8 88

SCRUGGS, Earl *C&W '70*
(Earl Scruggs Revue)

Singles: 7-inch

COLUMBIA 3-5 70-83

LPs: 10/12-inch

COLUMBIA 5-10 73-83
Also see FLATT, Lester, & Earl Scruggs
Also see HALL, Tom T., & Earl Scruggs
Also see SKAGGS, Ricky

SCRUGGS, Faye: see ADAMS, Faye

SEA, Johnny *C&W '59*
(Johnny Seay)

Singles: 7-inch

CAPITOL 4-8 61
COLUMBIA 3-5 67-69
NRC 5-10 59-60
PHILIPS 4-6 64-65
VIKING 3-5 70-71
W.B. 4-6 66-67

Picture Sleeves

COLUMBIA 3-5 68

LPs: 10/12-inch

GUEST STAR 8-12 66
PHILIPS 10-15 64-65
PICKWICK/HILLTOP 8-12 65
W.B. 10-20 66

SEA HAGS *LP '89*

LPs: 10/12-inch

CHRYSALIS 5-8 89

SEA LEVEL *LP '77*

Singles: 7-inch

ARISTA 3-5 80
CAPRICORN 3-5 77-79

LPs: 10/12-inch

ARISTA 5-10 80
CAPRICORN 5-10 77-80
Also see ALLMAN BROTHERS BAND

SEAFOOD MAMA
(Quarterflash)

Singles: 7-inch

WHITEFIRE ("Harden My Heart") 15-25 80
(No label number given.)

Picture Sleeves

WHITEFIRE ("Harden My Heart") 30-40 80
Also see QUARTERFLASH

SEAL *P&R '91*
(Sealhenry Samuel)

Singles: 7-inch

SIRE 3-4 91

SEALS, Dan *P&R '80*
(England Dan Seals)

Singles: 7-inch

ATLANTIC 3-5 80-82
CAPITOL 3-4 87-90
EMI AMERICA 3-4 84-87
LIBERTY 3-4 83-84

LPs: 10/12-inch

ATLANTIC 5-10 80-82
EMI AMERICA 5-8 84-87
LIBERTY 5-8 83
Also see ENGLAND DAN & John Ford Coley

SEALS, Dan, & Marie Osmond

Singles: 7-inch

CAPITOL 3-4 85
Also see OSMOND, Marie
Also see SEALS, Dan

SEALS, Jimmy

Singles: 7-inch

CARLTON (470 "Sneaky Pete") 20-30 58
CHALLENGE 10-20 62-65
WINSTON 10-20 58
Also see SEALS & CROFTS

SEALS & CROFTS *LP '70*

Singles: 7-inch

T.A. 4-6 69-71
W.B. 3-5 71-80

Picture Sleeves

W.B. 3-5 77

LPs: 10/12-inch

T.A. 20-25 69-70
W.B. (Except 2809) 6-12 71-80
W.B. (2809 "Seals & Crofts I & II") 10-12 74
Members: Jimmy Seals; Dash Crofts.
Session: Louie Shelton; Jack Lenz; Ed Green; Wilton Felder; Jim Horn.
Also see CHAMPS
Also see SEALS, Jimmy
Also see TUCKER, Tanya

SEARCHERS *P&R/LP '64*

Singles: 7-inch

ERIC 3-4
KAPP 5-10 64-67
LIBERTY (55646 "Sugar & Spice") 8-12 63
LIBERTY (55689 "Sugar & Spice") 5-10 63
MERCURY 5-10 63
RCA 4-6 71-72
SIRE 3-5 80-81
SOUND CLASSICS 3-5

Picture Sleeves

KAPP (577 "Needles and Pins") 10-20 64
KAPP (609 "Some Day We're Gonna Love Again") 10-20 64

LPs: 10/12-inch

KAPP 20-30 64-66
MERCURY (20914 "Hear! Hear!") 25-35 64
(Monaural. Red label.)
MERCURY (20914 "Hear! Hear!") 40-60 64
(White label. Promotional issue only.)
MERCURY (60914 "Hear! Hear!") 25-35 64
(Stereo. Red label.)
MERCURY (60914 "Hear! Hear!") 40-60 64
(White label. Promotional issue only.)
PYE 10-12 76
RHINO 5-8 85
SIRE 8-10 80-81

SEARCHERS / Rattles

LPs: 10/12-inch

MERCURY (20994 "The Searchers Meet the Rattles") 35-45 65
(Monaural. Red label.)
MERCURY (20994 "The Searchers Meet the Rattles") 50-75 65
(White label. Promotional issue only.)
MERCURY (60994 "The Searchers Meet the Rattles") 35-45 65
(Stereo. Red label.)
MERCURY (60994 "The Searchers Meet the Rattles") 50-75 65
(White label. Promotional issue only.)
Also see SEARCHERS

SEASE, Marvin *LP '87*

LPs: 10/12-inch

LONDON 5-8 87

SEATRAIN *LP '69*

Singles: 7-inch

A&M 4-8 68
CAPITOL 3-6 71-72
W.B. 3-5 73

LPs: 10/12-inch

A&M 10-15 69
CAPITOL (800 series) 8-12 71
CAPITOL (16000 series) 5-10 80
W.B. 8-10 73
Also see BLUES PROJECT
Also see RANK & FILE

SEAWIND *LP '77*

Singles: 7-inch

A&M 3-5 80-82
CTI 3-5 77-78
HORIZON 3-5 79

LPs: 10/12-inch

A&M 5-10 80-82
CTI 5-10 77-78
HORIZON 5-10 79

SEBASTIAN, John *P&R '69*

Singles: 7-inch

KAMA SUTRA 4-6 68-70
MGM 4-6 68-70
REPRISE 3-5 70-77

Picture Sleeves

KAMA SUTRA 4-8 69

LPs: 10/12-inch

KAMA SUTRA 10-15 70
MGM 10-15 69-70
REPRISE 8-12 70-76
Also see LOVIN' SPOONFUL
Also see MUGWUMPS
Also see SIMPSONS

SECO, Pozo, Singers: see POZO SECO SINGERS

SECOND VERSE R&B '74
Singles: 7-inch
IX CHAINS.....3-5 74

SECRET TIES P&R '86
Singles: 7-inch
NIGHT WAVE.....3-4 86

SECRET WEAPON R&B '82
Singles: 7-inch
PRELUDE.....3-5 82-83

SECRETS P&R '63
Singles: 7-inch
DCP.....5-10 65
OMEN.....5-10 66
PHILIPS.....8-12 63-64
Picture Sleeves
PHILIPS.....10-20 64
Members: Jackie Allen; Pat Miller; Karen Gray; Carol Raymont.

SEDAKA, Neil P&R '58
(With the Marvels)
Singles: 12-inch
CURB.....4-8
ELEKTRA.....4-8 70s
Singles: 7-inch
CURB.....3-5
DECCA (30520 "Laura Lee").....50-75 57
(We have yet to confirm U.S. 78 rpms of this, or any of Neil's singles, though they may exist – especially the Decca and first RCAs.)
ELEKTRA.....3-5 77-80
GUYDEN (2004 "Ring-a-Rockin'").....35-50 58
KIRSHNER.....3-5 72-80
LEGION (133 "Ring-a-Rockin'").....50-75 58
MCA.....3-5 75-84
MGM.....3-5 73
RCA (96 "Special DJ Spots").....2-50 60
(Promotional issue only.)
RCA (7408 "The Diary").....10-20 58
(Black label.)
RCA (7408 "The Diary").....25-40 58
(White, photo label. Promotional issue only.)
RCA (7473 "I Go Ape").....15-25 59
RCA (47-7595 "Oh Carol").....10-15 59
(Monaural.)
RCA (61-7595 "Oh Carol").....25-50 59
(Stereo.)
RCA (47-7709 "Stairway to Heaven").....10-15 60
(Monaural.)
RCA (61-7709 "Stairway to Heaven").....25-50 60
(Stereo.)
RCA (47-7781 "Run Sampson Run").....10-15 60
(Monaural.)
RCA (61-7781 "Run Sampson Run").....25-50 60
(Stereo.)
RCA (37-7829 "Calendar Girl").....25-50 60
(Compact 33 Single.)
RCA (47-7829 "Calendar Girl").....10-15 60
(Monaural.)
RCA (61-7829 "Calendar Girl").....25-50 60
(Stereo.)
RCA (37-7874 "Little Devil").....25-50 61
(Compact 33 Single.)
RCA (47-7874 "Little Devil").....10-15 61
RCA (37-7922 "Sweet Little You").....15-25 61
(Compact 33 Single.)
RCA (47-7922 "Sweet Little You").....10-15 61
RCA (37-7957 "Happy Birthday Sweet Sixteen").....25-50 61
(Compact 33 Single.)
RCA (47-7957 "Happy Birthday Sweet Sixteen").....10-15 61
RCA (37-8007 "King of Clowns").....25-50 62
(Compact 33 Single.)
RCA (47-8007 "King of Clowns").....10-15 62
RCA (37-8007 "King of Clowns").....25-50 62
(Compact 33 Single.)
RCA (8046 thru 9004).....8-15 62-66
RCA GOLD STANDARD.....3-6 60s-89
RSO.....3-4
ROCKET.....3-5 74-76
S.G.C......5-8 68-69
Picture Sleeves
RCA.....10-20 60-65
RSO.....3-4
EPs: 7-inch
RCA (105 "Neil's Best").....15-25 61
(Compact 33 Double.)
RCA (135 "Little Devil").....15-25 61
(Compact 33 Double.)
RCA (4334 "I Go Ape").....30-40 59
RCA (4353 "Oh Carol").....25-35 59
LPs: 10/12-inch
ACCORD.....5-10 81
CAMDEN.....8-12 60s
CROWN.....10-20 60s
CURB.....5-10
ELEKTRA.....5-10 77-81
51 WEST.....5-8 80s
GUEST STAR.....10-20 60s
INTERMEDIA.....5-8 85
KIRSHNER.....10-15 71-72
MCA.....5-10 84
ORBIT (17196 "Bravo!").....5-10 83
PICKWICK.....10-15 70s
POLYDOR.....5-10
RCA (AFL1 & APL1 series).....8-10 75-78
RCA (ANL1 series).....5-10 75-79
RCA (VPL1 series).....8-12 76
RCA (LPM-2035 "Neil Sedaka").....35-45 59
(Monaural.)
RCA (2035 "Neil Sedaka").....50-100 59
(Stereo.)
RCA (LPM-2317 thru LPM-2627).....20-30 61-62
(Monaural.)
RCA (LSP-2317 thru LSP-2627).....25-35 61-62
(Stereo.)
RCA (10181 "Smile").....15-20 66
ROCKET.....8-10 74-77
Session: King Curtis.
Also see ANKA, Paul / Sam Cooke / Neil Sedaka
Also see COOKE, Sam / Rod Lauren / Neil Sedaka / Browns
Also see JOHN, Elton
Also see KING CURTIS
Also see SIMON, Paul
Also see 10CC
Also see WILLOWS

SEDAKA, Neil & Dara P&R '80
Singles: 7-inch
ELEKTRA.....3-5 80
MCA.....3-4 84

SEDAKA, Neil, & Tokens
LPs: 10/12-inch
GUEST STAR.....10-20 60s
VERNON.....10-15 60s

SEDAKA, Neil, & Tokens / Coins
LPs: 10/12-inch
CROWN (366 "Neil Sedaka").....10-20 63

SEDAKA, Neil, & Tokens / Angels / Jimmy Gilmer & Fireballs
LPs: 10/12-inch
ALMOR (105 "Teen Bandstand").....15-25 60s
Also see ANGELS
Also see GILMER, Jimmy
Also see SEDAKA, Neil
Also see TOKENS

SEDUCTION P&R/LP '89
Singles: 7-inch
VENDETTA.....3-4 89-90
LPs: 10/12-inch
A&M.....5-8 89
VENDETTA.....5-8 90
Members: April; Michelle; Idalis.

SEEDS P&R '66
(Featuring Sky Saxon)
Singles: 7-inch
GNP (354 "Can't Seem to Make You Mine"/"Daisy Mae").....5-10 65
GNP (354 "Can't Seem to Make You Mine"/"I Tell Myself").....4-8 67
GNP (364 "Your Pushing Too Hard"/"Out of the Question").....8-12 65
(Reissued on 372 as *Pushing too Hard*, with a different flip, *Try to Understand*.)
GNP (370 "The Other Place").....5-10 65
GNP (372 thru 422).....4-8 66-69
MGM.....8-12 69-70
Picture Sleeves
GNP (354 "Can't Seem to Make You Mine"/"I Tell Myself").....10-20 67
GNP (383 "Mr. Farmer").....10-20 67
GNP (394 "A Thousand Shadows").....10-20 67
LPs: 10/12-inch
GNP (2023 thru 2043).....20-30 66-67
(All Seeds LPs, except 2043, *Raw and Alive*, were reissued with original selection numbers. First issue, red label, 1960s LPs have the logo, "GNP/Crescendo," on a horizontal line. Reissues have the label name in a circular manner on the label.)
GNP (2100 series).....5-10 77
Also see FULLER, Bobby / Seeds

SEEGER, Pete LP '63
Singles: 7-inch
COLUMBIA.....4-6 63-67
FOLKWAYS.....5-10 59
PIONEER.....4-8 60
LPs: 10/12-inch
ARAVEL.....10-20 63-64
ARCHIVE of FOLK MUSIC.....10-15 65
BROADSIDE.....10-20 63
CAPITOL.....10-20 64-67
COLUMBIA.....10-20 63-72
DISC.....10-20 64
FOLKWAYS.....8-20 59-75
(Black vinyl.)
FOLKWAYS (7610 "Animal Folk Songs").....25-35
(Colored vinyl.)
HARMONY.....5-10 68-70
ODYSSEY.....8-12 68
OLYMPIC.....5-10 73
PHILIPS.....10-20 63
STINSON (57 "Pete Seeger Concert").....20-30 54
(10-inch LP.)
STINSON (90 "Pete").....5-10 70
TRADITION.....5-10 73
VANGUARD.....6-12 78
VERVE/FOLKWAYS.....10-20 65
VOX.....5-10 72
W.B......5-10 79
Also see ALMANAC SINGERS
Also see BROONZY, Big Bill, & Pete Seeger
Also see SEEGERS
Also see WEAVERS

SEEGER, Pete, & Arlo Guthrie LP '75
LPs: 10/12-inch
REPRISE.....8-12 75
W.B......5-10 81
Also see GUTHRIE, Arlo

SEEGER, Pete, with Pacific Gas & Electric
LPs: 10/12-inch
COLUMBIA (3540 "Tell Me That You Love Me, Junie Moon").....10-15 70
(Soundtrack.)
Also see PACIFIC GAS & ELECTRIC

SEEGERS
LPs: 10/12-inch
PRESTIGE.....10-20 65
Members: Pete Seeger; Peggy Seeger; Mike Seeger; Barbara Seeger; Penny Seeger.
Also see SEEGER, Pete

SEEKERS P&R/LP '65

Singles: 7-inch

ATMOS....5-8 65
CAPITOL....5-10 65-68
MARVEL....5-8 65

Picture Sleeves

CAPITOL....5-10 65

LPs: 10/12-inch

CAPITOL (100 series)....8-12 69
CAPITOL (2000 series)....10-20 65-67
CAPITOL (16000 series)....5-10 80
MARVEL....15-20 65

Members: Judy Durham; Keith Potger.
Also see JAMES, Sonny / Seekers
Also see NEW SEEKERS

SEELY, Jeannie C&W/P&R '66

Singles: 7-inch

CHALLENGE....4-6 64-65
COLUMBIA....3-5 77-78
DECCA....3-5 69-73
MCA....3-5 73-75
MONUMENT....3-5 66-68

LPs: 10/12-inch

DECCA....6-12 69-70
HARMONY....5-10 72
MCA....5-8 73
MONUMENT....6-12 66-77

Also see GREENE, Jack, & Jeannie Seely

SEGAL, George LP '67

(With the Imperial Jazzband)

Singles: 7-inch

FLYING DUTCHMAN....3-5 74
PHILIPS....4-6 67

LPs: 10/12-inch

PHILIPS....10-20 67
SIGNATURE....5-10 74

SEGER, Bob P&R '68

(With the Last Heard; with Silver Bullet Band; Bob Seger System)

Singles: 7-inch

CAPITOL (8433 "Travelin' Man")....10-15 75
(Promotional issue.)

Singles: 7-inch

ABKCO....3-6 72-75
CAMEO (438 "East Side Story")....15-25 66
CAMEO (444 "Sock It to Me Santa")....20-30 66
CAMEO (465 "Persecution Smith")....15-25 66
CAMEO (473 "Vagrant Winter")....15-25 66
CAMEO (494 "Heavy Music")....10-20 67
CAPITOL (Except 2000 series)....3-5 71-86
CAPITOL (2000 series)....4-8 68-70
HIDEOUT (1013 "East Side Story")....25-50 66
HIDEOUT (1014 "Persecution Smith")....25-50 66
HIDEOUT (1232 "Heavy Music")....50-100 66
(Single-sided.)
MCA....3-4 87
PALLADIUM....3-6 71-74
REPRISE....3-6 72

Promotional Singles

CAPITOL (Colored vinyl)....4-8 78
CAPITOL (9878 "Shame on the Moon")....3-6 82
(Edited version [4:22], not the promo that runs 4:55.)

Picture Sleeves

CAPITOL (Except 4951)....3-6 78-86
CAPITOL (4951 "Horizontal Bop")....30-50 80
MCA....3-4 87

LPs: 10/12-inch

CAPITOL (ST-172 "Ramblin' Gamblin' Man")....15-25 69
CAPITOL (SM-172 "Ramblin' Gamblin' Man")....8-10 75
CAPITOL (ST-236 "Noah")....50-70 69
CAPITOL (SKAO-499 "Mongrel")....15-25 70
CAPITOL (SM-499 "Mongrel")....8-10 75
CAPITOL (ST-731 "Brand New Morning")....30-50 71
CAPITOL (8433 "Live Bullet, Consensus Cuts")....20-30 75
(Promotional issue only.)
CAPITOL (11000 series, except 11557 & 11904)....6-12 75-78
CAPITOL (ST-11557 "Night Moves")....5-10 78
CAPITOL (ST-11557 "Night Moves")....25-35 78
(Picture disc. Promotional issue only. 800 made.)
CAPITOL (SW-11904 "Stranger in Town")....5-10 78
CAPITOL (SEAX-11904 "Stranger in Town")....15-20 79
(Picture disc.)
CAPITOL (12000 series)....6-10 80-86
CAPITOL (16000 series)....5-8 80
CAPITOL (30334 "Greatest Hits")....10-15 90s
CAPITOL (91124 "Fire Inside")....8-10 91
INNER VIEW ("Demonstration Record: Bob Seger")....15-25 76
(Promotional issue only.)
MFSL (034 "Night Moves")....35-50 79
MFSL (127 "Against the Wind")....25-30 85
PALLADIUM (1006 "Smokin' O.P.'s")....15-25 72
PALLADIUM (2126 "Back in '72")....50-75 73
REPRISE....10-15 72-74

Also see BEACH BUMS
Also see BROWNSVILLE STATION
Also see NEWMAN, Randy

SELECTOR LP '80

Singles: 7-inch

CHRYSALIS....3-5 79-81

LPs: 10/12-inch

CHRYSALIS....5-10 79-81

SELENA

Singles: 7-inch

EMI LATIN....3-4 95
FREDDIE (451 "No Puedo Estar Sin Ti")....50-100 79
(Reports indicate approximately 100 made.)
Members: Selena Quintanilla; Abraham Quintanilla; A.B. Quintanilla; Suzette Quintanilla; Rena Dearman; Rodney Pyeatt.

SELF, Ronnie P&R '58

ABC-PAR....25-50 56
COLUMBIA....15-25 57

Singles: 7-inch

ABC-PAR (9714 "Pretty Bad Blues")....75-100 56
ABC-PAR (9768 "Sweet Love")....50-75 56
AMY....5-10 68
COLUMBIA (40989 "Ain't I'm a Dog")....25-35 57
COLUMBIA (41101 "Bop-A-Lena")....25-35 58
COLUMBIA (41166 "Big Blon Baby")....25-35 58
COLUMBIA (41241 "Petrified")....75-125 58
DECCA (30958 "Big Town")....15-25 59
DECCA (31131 "I've Been There")....10-20 60
DECCA (31351 "Instant Man")....10-20 62
DECCA (31431 "Oh Me, Oh My")....10-20 62
KAPP....5-10 63

EPs: 7-inch

COLUMBIA (2149 "Ain't I'm a Dog")....175-200 57

SELLARS, Marilyn C&W/P&R '74

Singles: 7-inch

MEGA....3-5 74-77
ZODIAC....3-5 76-77

LPs: 10/12-inch

MEGA....5-10 74-77
ZODIAC....5-10 77

SEMBELLO, Michael P&R/D&D/LP '83

Singles: 12-inch

CASABLANCA....4-6 83
W.B.....4-6 83-84

Singles: 7-inch

A&M....3-4 86
CASABLANCA....3-5 83
GEFFEN....3-4 85
W.B.....3-5 83-84

LPs: 10/12-inch

A&M....5-8 86
MCA....5-8 85
W.B.....5-10 83

SEMBELLO, Michael / Basil Poledouris

Singles: 7-inch

W.B.....3-4 82

Picture Sleeves

W.B.....3-4 82

Also see SEMBELLO, Michael

SENATOR BOBBY P&R '67

Singles: 7-inch

RCA....4-8 67-68

Also see HARDLY WORTHIT PLAYERS

SENATOR McKINLEY: see HARDLY WORTHIT PLAYERS

SENAY, Eddy R&B '72

Singles: 7-inch

SUSSEX....3-5 72-73

LPs: 10/12-inch

SUSSEX....8-12 72

SEÑOR SOUL R&B '69

Singles: 7-inch

DOUBLE SHOT....4-8 67-68
WHIZ....3-6 69-70

LPs: 10/12-inch

DOUBLE SHOT....10-15 68-69

SENSATIONS R&B '56

(Yvonne Baker & Sensations)

Singles: 78 rpm

ATCO....15-25 55

P&R '95 *Singles: 7-inch*

ARGO (5391 "Music Music Music")....10-20 61
ARGO (5405 "Let Me In")....10-20 62
ARGO (5412 "That's My Desire")....10-20 62
ARGO (5420 "Party Across the Hall")....10-20 62
ATCO (6056 "Yes Sir, That's My Baby")....25-50 55
ATCO (6067 "Please Mr. Disc Jockey")....25-50 56
ATCO (6075 "My Heart Cries for You")....25-50 56
ATCO (6083 "Such a Love")....25-50 57
ATCO (6090 "My Debut to Love")....25-50 57
ATCO (6115 "Romance in the Dark")....25-50 58
CHESS....3-5 73
JUNIOR (1002 "We Were Meant to Be")....15-25 62
JUNIOR (1005 "You Made a Fool Out of Me")....15-25 63
JUNIOR (1006 "Baby")....15-25 63
JUNIOR (1010 "I Can't Change")....10-20 63
JUNIOR (1021 "We Were Meant to Be")....8-12 64
TOLLIE (9009 "You Made a Fool Out of Me")....10-15 64

LPs: 10/12-inch

ARGO (4022 "Let Me In")....150-250 63

SEQUENCE R&B '80

Singles: 7-inch

SUGAR HILL....3-5 80-82

LPs: 10/12-inch

SUGAR HILL....5-10 81

SEQUINS R&B '70

Singles: 7-inch

GOLD STAR....3-5 70

Members: Linda Jackson; Ronnie Gonzalez; Dottie Hayes.

SERENDIPITY SINGERS P&R/LP '64

Singles: 7-inch

PHILIPS....4-8 64-66
U.A.....3-5 67-69

Picture Sleeves

PHILIPS....4-8 64-66

LPs: 10/12-inch

PHILIPS....10-20 64-65
WING....8-12 68

SERGE! R&B '83

Singles: 7-inch

W.B. 3-5 83

SERIOUS INTENTION D&D '84

Singles: 12-inch

EASY STREET........ 4-6 84

SESAME STREET KIDS: see ERNIE

SETZER, Brian LP '86

Singles: 7-inch

EMI 3-4 86-88

LPs: 10/12-inch

EMI 5-8 86-88

Also see STRAY CATS

SEVELLE, Taja P&R/R&B '87

Singles: 7-inch

PAISLEY PARK........ 3-4 87
REPRISE........ 3-4 87-88

Picture Sleeves

REPRISE........ 3-4 87

707 P&R '80

Singles: 7-inch

BOARDWALK 3-5 82
CASABLANCA 3-5 80

LPs: 10/12-inch

BOARDWALK........ 5-10 82
CASABLANCA 5-10 80

SEVEN DWARFS P&R '38

Singles: 78 rpm

VICTOR (25735 "Heigh-Ho")........ 10-20 38

SEVEN SECONDS LP '89

LPs: 10/12-inch

RESTLESS........ 5-8 89

7TH WONDER R&B '73

(Seventh Wonder)

Singles: 12-inch

CASABLANCA 4-6 80
PARACHUTE 4-8 79

Singles: 7-inch

ABET 3-5 73
CASABLANCA 3-5 80
CHOCOLATE CITY........ 3-5 80
PARACHUTE 3-5 78-79

LPs: 10/12-inch

CHOCOLATE CITY........ 5-10 80
PARACHUTE 5-10 78-79

Members: Allen Williams; Wilbert Cox; Deborah Matthews; William Butler; Lloyd Obie; Julius Chislom; Jerome Thorton; Marvin Patton; Johnnie Hammon.

SEVERINSEN, Doc, Orchestra LP '66

(With the Dodge City Boys; Tonight Show Band with Doc Severinsen)

Singles: 7-inch

COMMAND........ 3-5 65-70
EPIC 4-6 59-76
FRONTLINE 3-4 80
RCA........ 3-4 72-73

Picture Sleeves

COMMAND........ 3-5 70

LPs: 10/12-inch

ABC 5-10 71-73
AMHERST........ 5-8 86
COMMAND........ 5-15 61-73
EPIC 5-8 76-81
EVEREST........ 5-8 78
JUNO........ 5-10 70-79
MCA........ 4-8 82
RCA........ 5-10 71

Also see MANCINI, Henry, & Doc Severinsen

SEVILLE, David P&R '56

(Ross Bagdasarian)

Singles: 78 rpm

LIBERTY........ 5-15 56-57

Singles: 7-inch

LIBERTY........ 8-15 56-61

Picture Sleeves

LIBERTY (55079 "Gotta Get to Your House")........ 10-20 57

EPs: 7-inch

LIBERTY (1003 "Witch Doctor") 35-50 57
(Issued with paper sleeve.)

LPs: 10/12-inch

LIBERTY (3073 "The Music of David Seville") 50-75 57
LIBERTY (3092 "Witch Doctor") 50-75 58

Also see ALFI & HARRY
Also see CHIPMUNKS

SEVILLES P&R '61

Singles: 7-inch

CAL-GOLD (172 "Don't You Know I Care") 10-20 62
GALAXY........ 10-15 63-64
J.C. (116 "Charlena")........ 20-30 60
J.C. (118 "Louella")........ 20-25 61
J.C. (120 "Fat Sally")........ 10-15 61

SEX PISTOLS LP '77

Singles: 7-inch

W.B. (8516 "Submission") 3-6 78

Picture Sleeves

W.B. (8516 "Submission") 3-6 78

LPs: 10/12-inch

W.B. (3147 "Never Mind the Bollocks, Here's the Sex Pistols")........ 15-20 77
(With cover sticker which reads: "Includes Submission.")
W.B. (3147 "Never Mind the Bollocks, Here's the Sex Pistols")........ 10-15 77
(Without "Submission" cover sticker.)
W.B. (72256 "Swindle Continues") 8-10 90s
W.B. (72511 "Live at Chelmsford Prison")........ 8-10 90s

Also see PUBLIC IMAGE LTD.
Also see SIOUXSIE & BANSHEES

S-EXPRESS P&R '88

Singles: 7-inch

CAPITOL........ 3-4 88

Picture Sleeves

CAPITOL........ 3-4 88

SEXTON, Ann R&B '73

Singles: 7-inch

DASH 3-5 77
IMPEL 5-10
MONUMENT........ 3-5 77
SEVENTY-SEVEN........ 5-10 72-74
SOUND STAGE........ 3-5 77

SEXTON, Charlie P&R/LP '85

Singles: 7-inch

MCA 3-4 85-89

Picture Sleeves

MCA 3-4 85-89

LPs: 10/12-inch

MCA 5-8 86-89

Also see ELY, Joe

SEXTON, Charlie, & Ron Wood

LPs: 10/12-inch

MCA 5-8 84

Also see SEXTON, Charlie
Also see WOOD, Ron

SEYMOUR, Phil P&R/LP '81

Singles: 7-inch

BOARDWALK........ 3-5 81

LPs: 10/12-inch

BOARDWALK........ 5-10 81

Also see TEXTONES
Also see TWILLEY, Dwight, Band

SHA NA NA LP '69

Singles: 7-inch

KAMA SUTRA........ 3-5 70-75
SUTRA........ 3-5 74

Picture Sleeves

KAMA SUTRA........ 3-5 71

LPs: 10/12-inch

ACCORD 5-10 81-83
BUDDAH........ 5-10 77
CSP........ 8-12 78
EMUS........ 5-10 78
K-TEL........ 5-10 81
KAMA SUTRA........ 10-15 69-76
NASHVILLE 5-10 80

Members: Lennie Baker; Jon "Bowzer" Bauman; Johnny Contardo; Denny Green; Henry Gross; Jocko Marcellino; Danny McBride; Scott Powell; David-Allan "Chico" Ryan; "Screamin' Scott Simon; Donny York.

Also see GROSS, Henry
Also see TRAVOLTA, John / Sha Na Na

SHACK R&B '71

Singles: 7-inch

VOLT 5-10 71

SHACKLEFORDS P&R '63

Singles: 7-inch

CAPITOL........ 4-6 66
LHI........ 4-6 67-68
MERCURY 5-10 63

LPs: 10/12-inch

CAPITOL........ 10-20 66
MERCURY 15-25 63

Members: Lee Hazlewood; Marty Cooper; Al Stone; Garcia Nitzsche.

Also see HAZLEWOOD, Lee
Also see MOMENTS

SHADES OF BLUE P&R/R&B '66

Singles: 7-inch

COLLECTABLES 3-4 80s
IMPACT........ 8-15 66-67
SHADES........ 5-10 68

LPs: 10/12-inch

IMPACT (101 "Happiness Is") 30-50 66
(Monaural.)
IMPACT (101 "Happiness Is") 50-75 66
(Stereo.)

Member: George Shuput.

SHADES OF LOVE R&B '82

Singles: 7-inch

VENTURE 3-5 82

SHADOW R&B '79

Singles: 7-inch

ELEKTRA........ 3-5 79-81

LPs: 10/12-inch

ELEKTRA........ 5-10 79-81

Members: Jimmy Williams; Billy Beck; Chet Willis.

SHADOWFAX LP '83

Singles: 7-inch

WINDHAM HILL 3-5 82

LPs: 10/12-inch

CAPITOL........ 5-8 88
PASSPORT........ 8-10 76
WINDHAM HILL 5-8 82-86

SHADOWS R&B '50

Singles: 78 rpm

LEE (200 "I've Been a Fool")........ 15-25 49
LEE (202 "I'd Rather Be Wrong Than Blue") 15-25 50
LEE (207 "Don't Blame My Dreams") 15-25 50

Members: Jasper Edwards; Ray Reed; Sam McClure; Scott King; Bobby Buster.

SHADOWS OF KNIGHT P&R/LP '66

Singles: 7-inch

ATCO........ 8-12 69
COLUMBIA/AURAVISION ("Shadows of Knight Sing Potato Chip") 50-75 66
(Square 5-inch cardboard picture disc. Included in boxes of Fairmont Potato Chips.)
DUNWICH (116 "Gloria") 10-20 66
(Label makes no reference to distribution by Atco.)
DUNWICH (116 "Gloria") 5-10 66
(Label reads "Distributed by Atco.")
DUNWICH (122 thru 167) 10-20 66-67
SUPER K........ 5-10 69
TEAM........ 5-10 68

Picture Sleeves

DUNWICH (122 "Oh Yeah")........ 15-20 66
DUNWICH (128 "Bad Little Woman")........ 20-30 66

LPs: 10/12-inch

DUNWICH (666 "Gloria") 50-100 66
DUNWICH (667 "Back Door Men") 50-100 66

SUNDAZED.......5-10 90s
SUPER K (6002 "The Shadows of Knight").......15-25 69

SHAFTO, Bobby P&R '64

Singles: 7-inch

RUST.......5-8 64-65

SHAKATAK D&D '84

Singles: 12-inch

POLYDOR.......4-6 82-84

Singles: 7-inch

POLYDOR.......3-4 82-84

LPs: 10/12-inch

POLYDOR.......5-8 82

SHAKIN' STEVENS: see STEVENS, Shakin'

SHALAMAR P&R/R&B/LP '77

Singles: 12-inch

COLUMBIA.......4-6 84-85
SOLAR.......4-6 79-85

Singles: 7-inch

COLUMBIA.......3-4 84-85
ELEKTRA.......3-4 85
MCA.......3-4 84
SOLAR.......3-5 78-87
SOUL TRAIN.......3-5 77

Picture Sleeves

COLUMBIA.......3-4 84
SOLAR.......3-5 83

LPs: 10/12-inch

SOLAR.......5-10 78-85
SOUL TRAIN.......5-10 77
Members: Howard Hewett; Jody Watley; Jeffrey Daniel; Gerald Brown; Delisa Davis; Micki Free; Sidney Justin.
Also see HEWETT, Howard
Also see WATLEY, Jody

SHANA P&R '89
(Shana Petrone)

Singles: 7-inch

VISION.......3-4 89

LPs: 10/12-inch

VISION.......5-8 89

SHANGO P&R '69

Singles: 12-inch

CELLULOID.......4-8 83

Singles: 7-inch

A&M.......4-6 69
CELLULOID.......3-4 83
GNP.......3-6 69

LPs: 10/12-inch

A&M.......10-15 69
DUNHILL.......8-12 70
Also see BAMBAATAA, Afrika

SHANGRI-LAS P&R/R&B '64
(Shangra-Las)

Singles: 7-inch

COLLECTABLES.......3-4 80s
ERIC.......3-5 70s
LANA.......3-6 60s
MERCURY.......4-8 66-67
RED BIRD.......5-10 64-66
SSS INT'L.......3-5 80s
SCEPTER.......10-15 65
SMASH.......10-20 63
SPOKANE.......10-20 64
TRIP.......3-4 70s

LPs: 10/12-inch

BACK-TRAC.......5-10 85
COLLECTABLES (5011 "At Their Best").......5-10 82
(Black vinyl.)
COLLECTABLES (5011 "At Their Best").......10-15 82
(Picture disc.)
MERCURY (21099 "Golden Hits of the Shangri-las").......20-30 66
(Monaural.)
MERCURY (21099 "Golden Hits").....50-75 66
(Shown as monaural but plays in true stereo.)
MERCURY (61099 "Golden Hits").....25-35 66
(Stereo.)
POST.......10-12
RED BIRD (101 "Leader of the Pack").......30-50 65
RED BIRD (104 "Shangri-Las '65").......50-100 65
RED BIRD (104 "I Can Never Go Home Anymore").......50-85 65
Members: Mary Weiss; Marge Ganser; Mary Ann Ganser.

SHANK, Bud P&R/LP '66

Singles: 78 rpm

GOOD TIME JAZZ.......4-6 54

Singles: 7-inch

GOOD TIME JAZZ.......5-10 54
PACIFIC JAZZ.......3-8 61-70
WORLD PACIFIC.......3-6 64-68

EPs: 7-inch

NOCTURNE (3/4 "The Bud Shank Quintet").......50-75 53
(Price is for either volume.)
PACIFIC JAZZ.......20-30 54-58

LPs: 10/12-inch

CONCORD JAZZ.......5-8 76
CROWN.......10-20 63
KIMBERLY.......10-20 63
NOCTURNE (2 "The Bud Shank Quintet").......150-200 53
(10-inch LP.)
PACIFIC JAZZ (14 "Bud Shank with Three Trombones").......75-125 54
(10-inch LP.)
PACIFIC JAZZ (20 "Bud Shank & Bob Brookmeyer").......75-125 55
(10-inch LP.)
PACIFIC JAZZ (4 thru 89).......15-25 60-65
(12-inch LPs.)
PACIFIC JAZZ (404 "Jazz Swings Broadway").......40-60 57
PACIFIC JAZZ (411 "The Swing's to TV").......40-60 57
PACIFIC JAZZ (1205 "Bud Shank & Shorty Rogers").......40-60 55
PACIFIC JAZZ (1213 "Strings and Trombones").......40-60 56
PACIFIC JAZZ (1215 "The Bud Shank Quartet").......40-60 56
PACIFIC JAZZ (1219 "Jazz at Cal-Tech").......40-60 56
PACIFIC JAZZ (1226 "Flute 'N Oboe").......40-60 57
PACIFIC JAZZ (1230 "The Bud Shank Quartet").......40-60 57
PACIFIC JAZZ (10000 & 20000 series).......5-15 66-81
SUNSET.......8-12 66
WORLD PACIFIC (1000 thru 1200 series).......20-40 58-60
WORLD PACIFIC (1400 series).......15-30 61-63
WORLD PACIFIC (1800 series).......15-20 64-67
WORLD PACIFIC (21000 series).......10-20 66-68
Also see FOLKSWINGERS
Also see LONDON, Julie, & Bud Shank Quintet

SHANKAR, Ravi LP '67
(With Yehudi Menuhin)

Singles: 7-inch

APPLE (1838 "Joi Bangla").......5-10 71
DARK HORSE.......3-5 75
PACIFIC.......4-8 60s
WORLD PACIFIC.......4-8 59-68

Picture Sleeves

APPLE (1838 "Joi Bangla").......20-25 71

LPs: 10/12-inch

ANGEL.......10-20 67
APPLE (3384 "Raga").......12-18 71
APPLE (3396 "In Concert 1972").......40-50 73
CAPITOL.......10-20 67-72
COLUMBIA.......10-20 66-68
DARK HORSE.......8-12 74-76
FANTASY.......5-10 73
PRESTIGE.......10-20 68
SPARK.......5-10 73
WORLD PACIFIC.......10-20 59-69
Also see BEATLES
Also see HARRISON, George

SHANNON P&R '69
(Marty Wilde)

Singles: 7-inch

EPIC/MAGNET.......3-5 75
HERITAGE.......4-6 69
Also see WILDE, Marty

SHANNON P&R/R&B/D&D '83
(Brenda Shannon Greene)

Singles: 12-inch

EMERGENCY.......4-6 83-84
MIRAGE.......4-6 84-85

Singles: 7-inch

ATLANTIC.......3-4 86
EMERGENCY.......3-5 83-84
MIRAGE.......3-5 84-85

Picture Sleeves

MIRAGE.......3-5 84-85

LPs: 10/12-inch

MIRAGE.......5-10 84-85

SHANNON, Del P&R/R&B '61

Singles: 7-inch

AMY.......4-8 64-65
BERLEE.......5-10 63-64
BIG TOP.......10-20 61-63
COLLECTABLES.......3-4 80s
DUNHILL.......4-8 69
ERIC.......3-5 70s
ISLAND.......3-5 75
LANA.......3-6 60s
LIBERTY.......5-10 66-68
NETWORK.......4-6 81-82
TERRIFIC.......3-5
TRIP.......3-6
TWIRL.......4-6 60s
W.B.......3-5 85

Picture Sleeves

LIBERTY.......8-12 68

LPs: 10/12-inch

AMY (8003 "Handy Man").......30-50 64
(Monaural.)
AMY (S-8003 "Handy Man").......40-60 64
(Stereo.)
AMY (8004 "Del Shannon Sings Hank Williams").......30-50 65
(Monaural.)
AMY (S-8004 "Del Shannon Sings Hank Williams").......40-60 65
(Stereo.)
AMY (8006 "1,661 Seconds").......30-50 65
(Monaural.)
AMY (S-8006 "1,661 Seconds").......40-60 65
(Stereo.)
BIG TOP (1303 "Runaway").......100-200 61
(Monaural.)
BIG TOP (1303 "Runaway").......400-600 61
(Stereo.)
BIG TOP (1308 "Little Town Flirt").....40-60 63
BUG.......5-10 85
DOT (3834 "Best of Del Shannon")...25-45 67
(Monaural.)
DOT (25834 "Best of Del Shannon").25-45 67
(Stereo.)
LIBERTY.......20-30 66-68
NETWORK/ELEKTRA.......8-10 81
PHOENIX 20.......8-10 80
PICKWICK.......8-10 70s
POST.......10-15
SIRE.......10-15 75
SUNSET.......10-15 70
U.A.......10-15 73
Also see HONDELLS / Del Shannon / Martha & Vandellas

SHANNON, Jackie
(Jackie Shannon & Cajuns; Jackie DeShannon)

Singles: 7-inch

DOT (15928 "Just Another Lie").......15-20 59
FRATERNITY (836 "Just Another Lie").......10-15 59
P.J. (101 "Trouble").......30-40 59
SAGE (290 "Just Another Lie").......20-30 59
SAND (330 "Trouble").......20-30 59
Also see DE SHANNON, Jackie

SHANTE, Roxanne R&B/D&D '85

Singles: 12-inch

POP ART....4-6 85

Singles: 7-inch

POP ART....3-4 85

LPs: 10/12-inch

POP ART....5-8 85

Also see JAMES, Rick, & Roxanne Shante

SHANTELLE R&B '85

Singles: 7-inch

PANDISC....4-6 85

SHAPIRO, Helen P&R '61

Singles: 7-inch

CAPITOL....8-10 61-62
EPIC....4-8 62-63
JANUS....3-5 70
MUSICOR....4-6 65
TOWER....4-6 67

Picture Sleeves

EPIC....4-8 62

LPs: 10/12-inch

EPIC....10-20 63

SHA-RAE, Billy R&B '71
(Sha-Rae)

Singles: 7-inch

BAY-UKE....5-10 61-62
HOUR GLASS....3-5
LAURIE....3-5
SPECTRUM....4-6 71

Also see HEBB, Bobby / Billy Sha-Rae

SHARKEY, Feargal P&R/LP '86

Singles: 12-inch

A&M/VIRGIN....4-6 86

Singles: 7-inch

A&M/VIRGIN....3-4 86-88

Picture Sleeves

A&M/VIRGIN....3-4 86-88

LPs: 10/12-inch

A&M/VIRGIN....5-8 86

Also see UNDERTONES

SHARKS LP '73

Singles: 7-inch

MCA....3-5 73-74

LPs: 10/12-inch

MCA....8-12 73-74

SHARP, Dee Dee P&R/R&B/LP '62
(Dee Dee Sharp Gamble)

Singles: 7-inch

ABKCO....3-5 83-84
ATCO....4-8 66-68
CAMEO....5-10 62-66
FAIRMOUNT....5-10 66
GAMBLE (219 "You're Gonna Miss Me")....8-12 68
PHILADELPHIA INT'L....3-5 77-81
TSOP....3-5 76

Picture Sleeves

CAMEO....5-10 62-65

LPs: 10/12-inch

CAMEO (C-1018 "It's Mashed Potato Time")....20-30 62
CAMEO (C-1022 "Songs of Faith")...20-30 62
(Monaural.)
CAMEO (SC-1022 "Songs of Faith") 30-40 62
(Stereo.)
CAMEO (C-1032 "All the Hits")....20-30 62
(Monaural.)
CAMEO (SC-1032 "All the Hits")....20-30 62
(Stereo.)
CAMEO (C-1050 "Do the Bird")....20-30 62
(Monaural.)
CAMEO (SC-1050 "Do the Bird")....20-30 62
(Stereo.)
CAMEO (C-1062 "Biggest Hits")....20-30 63
(Monaural.)
CAMEO (SC-1062 "Biggest Hits")....20-30 63
(Stereo.)
CAMEO (C-1074 "Down Memory Lane")....20-30 63
(Monaural.)
CAMEO (SC-1074 "Down Memory Lane")....20-30 63
(Stereo.)
CAMEO (C-2002 "18 Golden Hits")..20-30 60s
(Monaural.)
CAMEO (SC-2002 "18 Golden Hits")....20-30 60s
(Stereo.)
PHILADELPHIA INT'L....8-10 75-81

Also see CHECKER, Chubby, & Dee Dee Sharp
Also see KING, Ben E., & Dee Dee Sharp
Also see PHILADELPHIA INTERNATIONAL ALL STARS

SHARPE, Mike P&R '67

Singles: 7-inch

LIBERTY....4-8 66-69

LPs: 10/12-inch

LIBERTY....10-20 67-69

Also see CLASSICS IV

SHARPE, Ray P&R/R&B '59
(With the Blues Whalers; with Soul Set)

Singles: 7-inch

A&M....3-5 71
ATCO....4-8 66
DOT....5-10 59
FLYING HIGH....3-5
GAREX....5-10 63
GREGMARK....5-10 62
HAMILTON....8-12 59
JAMIE (Except 1128)....5-10 58-60
JAMIE (1128 "Linda Lu"/"Monkey's Uncle")....10-15 59
JAMIE (1128 "Linda Lu"/"Red Sails In the Sunset")....5-10 59
LHI....4-6 60s
MONUMENT....4-8 65
PARK AVE....4-8 60s
SOCK & SOUL....4-8 60s
TREY....5-10 61

LPs: 10/12-inch

AWARD (711 "Welcome Back")....25-50
FLYING HIGH....5-10

Session: Duane Eddy; Al Casey; Jim Horn; King Curtis.
Also see CASEY, Al
Also see EDDY, Duane
Also see KING CURTIS

SHARPEES P&R '66

Singles: 7-inch

ONE-DERFUL....5-10 65-66

Members: Herbert Reeves; Vernon Guy; Stacy Johnson.

SHARPLES, Bob P&R '56
(Bob Sharples' Living Strings)

Singles: 78 rpm

LONDON....3-5 56-57

Singles: 7-inch

LONDON....4-6 56-61

LPs: 10/12-inch

CAMDEN....5-10 60
LONDON....5-15 61-64
METRO....5-10 65

SHAW, Georgie P&R '54

Singles: 78 rpm

DECCA (Except 28937)....3-6 53-56
DECCA (28937 "Honeycomb")....5-10 54

Singles: 7-inch

DECCA (Except 28937)....5-10 53-56
DECCA (28937 "Honeycomb")....10-15 54
METRO....5-10 58

EPs: 7-inch

DECCA....5-10 56

LPs: 10/12-inch

DECCA....10-20 53-56

Also see KALLEN, Kitty, & Georgie Shaw

SHAW, Marlena P&R/R&B '67

Singles: 12-inch

COLUMBIA....4-8 79
SOUTH BAY....4-6 83

Singles: 7-inch

BLUE NOTE....3-5 72-76
CADET....4-6 66-69
COLUMBIA....3-5 77-79
SOUTH BAY....3-5 83

Picture Sleeves

CADET....4-8 67

LPs: 10/12-inch

BLUE NOTE....8-12 72-75
CADET....10-15 68-69
COLUMBIA....5-10 77-79

SHAW, Robert, Chorale LP '57

Singles: 78 rpm

RCA....3-5 50-58

Singles: 7-inch

RCA....4-8 50-62

EPs: 7-inch

RCA....5-10 54-56

LPs: 10/12-inch

ALMANAC....5-10 66
CAMDEN....5-10 64
RCA....5-15 50-70
VICTROLA....4-8 70

SHAW, Roland, Orchestra LP '65

Singles: 78 rpm

LONDON....3-5 56-57

Singles: 7-inch

LONDON....3-6 56-67

LPs: 10/12-inch

LONDON....5-10 64-78

SHAW, Sandie P&R '64

Singles: 7-inch

MERCURY....4-8 64
RCA....3-6 68-70
REPRISE....4-8 64-67

LPs: 10/12-inch

REPRISE....15-20 65-66

SHAW, Timmy P&R/R&B '64

Singles: 7-inch

JAMIE....5-15 61-62
SCEPTER....4-6 73
WAND....5-10 63-64

SHAW, Tommy P&R/LP '84

Singles: 7-inch

A&M....3-4 84-85
ATLANTIC....3-4 88

Picture Sleeves

A&M....3-4 84-85
ATLANTIC....3-4 88

LPs: 10/12-inch

A&M....5-8 84-85

Also see STYX

SHAWN, Damon R&B '72

Singles: 7-inch

WESTBOUND....3-5 73

SH-BOOMS
(Chords)

Singles: 78 rpm

CAT....10-20 55
VIK....15-25 57

Singles: 7-inch

ATCO (6213 "Sh-Boom")....8-12 61
ATLANTIC (2074 "Blue Moon")....10-20 60
CAT (117 "Could It Be")....25-35 55
VIK (0295 "I Don't Want to Set the World on Fire")....15-25 57

Also see CHORDS

SHEAR, Jules D&D '84

Singles: 12-inch

EMI AMERICA....4-6 84-85

Singles: 7-inch

EMI AMERICA....3-4 84-85

Picture Sleeves

EMI AMERICA....3-4 85

LPs: 10/12-inch

EMI AMERICA....5-8 83

Also see JULES & Polar Bears

SHEARING, George, Quintet LP '56

Singles: 78 rpm

CAPITOL....3-5 55-57
MGM....3-6 50-56

Singles: 7-inch

CAPITOL 4-8 55-67
LONDON 3-6 63
MGM 6-12 50-56
SHEBA 3-5 71

EPs: 7-inch

CAPITOL 5-15 55-60
MGM 5-15 51-55

LPs: 10/12-inch

ARCHIVE of FOLK MUSIC 6-12 68
BASF 5-10 73
CAPITOL (Except 648 thru 1628) 5-20 62-77
CAPITOL (648 thru 1628) 20-40 55-61
CONCORD JAZZ 5-8 80-82
CORONET 5-10 60s
DISCOVERY (3002 "George Shearing Quintet") 30-50 50
(10-inch LP.)
EVEREST 5-10 69
LION 10-20 59
MGM (90 "A Touch of Genius") 20-40 51
(10-inch LP.)
MGM (155 "I Hear Music") 20-40 52
(10-inch LP.)
MGM (226 "When Lights Are Low") ... 20-40 53
(10-inch LP.)
MGM (252 "An Evening with George Shearing") 20-40 55
(10-inch LP.)
MGM (100 series) 5-10 70
MGM (3000 series) 15-25 55-60
MGM (4000 series) 10-20 62-63
MPS 5-10 74-75
METRO 10-15 65
MOSAIC (157 "Complete Capitol Live Recordings") 90-100 90s
(Boxed, seven-disc audiophile set. 7500 made.)
PAUSA 5-8 79-82
PICKWICK 5-8
SAVOY (12093 "Midnight on Cloud 69") 15-25 57
SAVOY (15003 "Piano Solo") 30-50 51
(10-inch LP.)
SHEBA 5-10 71-76
VSP 10-15 66-67
Also see COLE, Cozy
Also see COLE, Nat "King," & George Shearing
Also see COLE, Natalie
Also see LEE, Peggy, & George Shearing

SHEARING, George & Montgomery Brothers

Singles: 7-inch

JAZZLAND 3-6 62

LPs: 10/12-inch

JAZZLAND (55 "George Shearing & Montgomery Brothers) 25- 40 61
(Cover pictures Shearing with the three brothers.)
JAZZLAND (55 "George Shearing & Montgomery Brothers) 15- 25 62
(Cover pictures a woman.)
RIVERSIDE 5-10 82
Also see MONTGOMERY BROTHERS
Also see SHEARING, George, Quintet
Also see WILSON, Nancy, & George Shearing

SHEEN, Bobby — R&B '75

Singles: 7-inch

CAPITOL 10-20 66-69
CHELSEA 3-5 75
DIMENSION 8-12 65
LIBERTY 5-10 62
W.B. 10-15 72
Also see ALLEY CATS
Also see BOB B. SOXX & Blue Jeans

SHEEP — P&R '66

Singles: 7-inch

BOOM (6000 "Hide & Seek") 10-20 66
Also see STRANGELOVES

SHEILA — R&B '80

(Sheila B. Devotion; Anny Chancel)

Singles: 7-inch

CARRERE 3-5 80-81
CASABLANCA 3-5 78

Picture Sleeves

CARRERE 3-5 80-81

Promotional Singles

CARRERE (37675 "Little Darlin'") 4-6 81
(Price includes special sleeve.)

LPs: 10/12-inch

CARRERE 5-10 80
CASABLANCA 5-10 78

SHEILA E. — P&R/R&B/D&D/LP '84

(Sheila Escovedo)

Singles: 12-inch

W.B. 4-6 84-85

Singles: 7-inch

PAISLEY PARK 3-4 85-87
W.B. 3-4 84-85

Picture Sleeves

PAISLEY PARK 3-4 85-87
W.B. 3-4 84

LPs: 10/12-inch

PAISLEY PARK 5-10 85-87
W.B. 5-10 84-91
Also see KRUSH GROOVE ALL-STARS
Also see PRINCE

SHELLEY, Pete — P&R '74

(Peter Shelley)

Singles: 12-inch

ARISTA 4-6 82-83

Singles: 7-inch

ARISTA 3-4 82-83
BELL 3-5 74

LPs: 10/12-inch

ARISTA 5-8 82-83
Also see BUZZCOCKS

SHELLS — P&R '60

Singles: 78 rpm

CANDLELITE (436 "Baby Oh Baby") 10-15 72
(Colored vinyl.)

Singles: 7-inch

ABC 3-5 75
BOARDWALK 3-5 75
COLLECTABLES 3-4 80s
END (1022 "Pretty Little Girl") 50-100 58
END (1050 "Whispering Winds") 25-40 59
GONE (5103 "Pretty Little Girl") 10-20 61
JOHNSON (099 "My Cherie") 4-8 72
JOHNSON (104 "Baby Oh Baby"/"Angel Eyes") 25-50 57
(Has selection number [104] centered between the horizontal lines on the right side of label.)
JOHNSON (104 "Baby Oh Baby"/"What's in an Angel Eyes") 8-12 60
(Has two parallel lines with one thinner than the other. These lines are both the same thickness on the '57 issue. MOST 1957 issues have the shorter flip side title, but ALL 1960 issues have the longer title.)
JOHNSON (106 "Pleading No More") 150-250 58
JOHNSON (107 "Explain It to Me") ... 20-30 61
JOHNSON (109 "Better Forget Him") 20-30 61
JOHNSON (110 "In the Dim of the Dark") 20-30 61
JOHNSON (112 "Sweetest One") 20-30 61
JOHNSON (119 "Deep in My Heart") 25-50 62
JOHNSON (120 "A Toast on Your Birthday") 20-25 62
JOHNSON (127 "On My Honor") 30-40 63
JOHNSON (332 "Explain It to Me") ... 15-25 61
JOSIE (912 "Deep in My Heart") 15-25 63
ROULETTE (4156 "She Wasn't Meant for Me") 15-25 59
SELSOM 10-15 65
SNOWFLAKE (1959 "If You Were Gone from Me"/"Misty") 10-20 64
(Blank, orange labels.)
SOUNDS from the SUBWAY 4-6 77
(Colored vinyl.)

LPs: 10/12-inch

CANDLELITE 10-15 70s
COLECTABLES 5-8 80s
GRECO 5-8
JUBILEE 10-20
SNOWFLAKE (1000 "Acappella Session with the Shells") 25-35
Members: Nathaniel Bouknight; Shade Alston; Bobby Nurse; Danny Small; Gus Geter; Roy Jones.
Also see DUBS / Shells
Also see FIVE SATINS / Youngtones / Youngsters / Shells

SHELTO, Steve — D&D '83

Singles: 12-inch

SAM 4-6 83

SHELTON, Anne — P&R '49

Singles: 78 rpm

COLUMBIA 4-6 56

Singles: 7-inch

COLUMBIA 5-10 56
EPIC 4-8 59

SHELTON, Ricky Van — C&W '86

Singles: 7-inch

COLUMBIA 3-4 86-92

LPs: 10/12-inch

COLUMBIA 5-8 87-91
Also see JOEL, Billy / Ricky Van Shelton
Also see PARTON, Dolly, & Ricky Van Shelton

SHELTON, Roscoe — R&B '65

Singles: 7-inch

BATTLE 4-8 62-63
EXCELLO 5-10 59-61
SIMS 4-8 64-65
SOUND STAGE 7 .... 4-8 65-68

LPs: 10/12-inch

EXCELLO (8002 "Roscoe Shelton") 40-50 61
SOUND STAGE 7 .... 15-20 66

SHEP & LIMELITES — P&R/R&B '61

(Featuring James Sheppard)

Singles: 7-inch

ABC 3-5 73
HULL (Except 770) 15-20 61-65
HULL (770 "A Party for Two") 20-30 65
ROULETTE 3-5 73

LPs: 10/12-inch

HULL (1001 "Our Anniversary") 300-400 62
ROULETTE (25350 "Our Anniversary") 35-45 67
Also see HEARTBEATS
Also see HEARTBEATS / Shep & Limelites

SHEPARD, Jean — C&W/P&R '53

Singles: 78 rpm

CAPITOL 4-8 53-57

Singles: 7-inch

CAPITOL 5-10 53-61
(Purple labels.)
CAPITOL 3-8 61-72
(Orange, orange/yellow, or red labels.)
MERCURY 3-5 72
SCORPION 3-4 78
U.A. 3-5 73-77

EPs: 7-inch

CAPITOL 5-10 56-61

LPs: 10/12-inch

CAPITOL (100 thru 800 series) 10-20 69-71
CAPITOL (700 thru 1200 series) 15-25 56-59
(With a "T" prefix.)
CAPITOL (1500 thru 2900 series) 10-15 61-68
CAPITOL (11000 series) 5-10 72-79
FIRST GENERATION 5-10 81
MERCURY 5-10 71
PICKWICK/HILLTOP 5-12 67-68
POWER PAK 5-8 75-80s
U.A. 5-10 73-76
Session: Justin Tubb; Red Sovine.
Also see SOVINE, Red

SHEPARD, Jean, & Ferlin Huskey — C&W/P&R '53

Singles: 78 rpm

CAPITOL 3-5 53

Singles: 7-inch

CAPITOL 4-8 53

Also see HUSKY, Ferlin

SHEPARD, Jean, & Ray Pillow *C&W '66*

Singles: 7-inch

CAPITOL....4-6 66

Also see SHEPARD, Jean

SHEPARD SISTERS: see SHEPHERD SISTERS

SHEPHERD SISTERS *P&R '57*

(Sheppard Sisters; Shepard Sisters; Shephard Sisters)

Singles: 78 rpm

LANCE....5-10 57
MELBA....5-10 56
MERCURY....5-10 57

Singles: 7-inch

ABC....3-5 73
ATLANTIC....5-10 63
COLLECTABLES....3-4 80s
LANCE....5-10 57
MGM....4-8 59
MELBA....10-15 56
MERCURY....5-10 57
20TH FOX....4-8 64
U.A....5-10 61
WARWICK....5-10 59-60
YORK....4-8 65

EPs: 7-inch

MERCURY (3369 "The Sheppard Sisters")....20-30 57

Members: Mary Lou Shepherd; Judy Shepherd; Martha Shepherd; Gayle Shepherd.

SHEPPARD, T.G. *C&W '74*

Singles: 7-inch

COLUMBIA....3-4 85
HITSVILLE....3-5 76
MELODYLAND....3-5 74-75
W.B....3-4 77-85

LPs: 10/12-inch

COLUMBIA....5-8 85
CURB....5-8 84
HITSVILLE....5-10 76
MELODYLAND....8-10 75-76
W.B....5-8 78-83

Also see COLLINS, Judy, & T.G. Sheppard

SHEPPARD, T.G., & Karen Brooks *C&W '82*

Singles: 7-inch

W.B....3-4 82

SHEPPARD, T.G., & Clint Eastwood *C&W/P&R '84*

Singles: 7-inch

W.B....3-4 84

Also see SHEPPARD, T.G.

SHEPPARD SISTERS: see SHEPHERD SISTERS

SHERBET *P&R '76*

(Sherbs)

Singles: 7-inch

ATCO....3-5 81
MCA....3-5 76-77

LPs: 10/12-inch

ATCO....5-10 80-82
MCA....5-10 76-77

SHERBS: see SHERBET

SHERIDAN, Bobby

(Charlie Rich)

Singles: 7-inch

SUN (354 "Sad News")....10-20 61

Also see RICH, Charlie

SHERIDAN, Tony & Beat Brothers: see BEATLES

SHERIFF *P&R '83*

Singles: 7-inch

CAPITOL....3-5 83

Picture Sleeves

CAPITOL....3-5 83

LPs: 10/12-inch

CAPITOL....5-8 83
OBSERVATORY....6-10 79

Members: Wolf Hassel; Arnold Lanni; Fred Curci; Steve DeMarchi.

Also see FROZEN GHOST

SHERMAN, Allan *LP '62*

(With Friends; with Boston Pops Orchestra)

Singles: 7-inch

RCA....4-6 68
W.B....5-10 63-66

Picture Sleeves

W.B....8-15 63-64

LPs: 10/12-inch

JUBILEE....10-20 62
RCA (Except 310)....10-15 64
RCA (310 "Alan Sherman & You")....20-30 64

(Promotional issue only. Includes 25-page script, letter from Allan and a comments postcard.)

RHINO....5-8 85-86
W.B....15-25 62-65

Also see BOSTON POPS ORCHESTRA

SHERMAN, Bobby *P&R/LP '69*

Singles: 7-inch

CAMEO (403 "Happiness Is")....4-8 66
CAMEO (403 "Happiness Is")....8-12 66

(Single-sided. Promotional issue only.)

CONDOR....4-8 69
DECCA....5-10 64-65
DOT....4-8 63
EPIC....4-8 67
GRT....3-5 76
JANUS....3-5 75
METROMEDIA....3-5 69-73
PARKWAY....5-10 65
STARCREST....5-10 62

Picture Sleeves

DECCA....8-12 65
METROMEDIA....3-5 69-72

EPs: 7-inch

METROMEDIA ("Bobby Sherman")....4-8 70

(Flexi-disc.)

LPs: 10/12-inch

METROMEDIA....5-10 69-73

SHERMAN, Joe, & His Orchestra

(With the Arena Brass) *P&R '63*

Singles: 78 rpm

KAPP....3-5 56-57

Singles: 7-inch

EPIC....3-5 65-66
KAPP....4-6 56-61
WORLD ARTISTS....3-6 63-65

LPs: 10/12-inch

COLUMBIA....5-10 68
EPIC....5-10 66
RCA....5-10 67
WORLD ARTISTS....5-12 63-64

Also see VIDELS

SHERRICK *R&B '87*

Singles: 7-inch

W.B....3-4 87

SHERRYS *P&R/R&B '62*

Singles: 7-inch

GUYDEN....8-12 62-63
MERCURY....5-10 64
ROBERTS....5-10 60s

LPs: 10/12-inch

GUYDEN (503 "At the Hop")....75-125 62

SHERWOOD, Roberta *P&R '56*

Singles: 78 rpm

DECCA....3-5 56-57

Singles: 7-inch

DECCA....4-8 56-64
DUNHILL....3-6 68
HAPPY TIGER....3-6 69
HARMON....3-6 62-63
KING....3-5 71-72
MCA....3-5 73
OLEN....4-6 65

EPs: 7-inch

DECCA....5-10 56-59

LPs: 10/12-inch

ABC-PAR....5-15 63-64
DECCA....8-18 56-65
HARMONY....5-15 63
KING....5-8 70
VOCALION....5-10 66-68

SHIELDS *P&R/R&B '58*

Singles: 7-inch

DOT (136 "You Cheated")....5-10 66

(Black vinyl.)

DOT (136 "You Cheated")....20-30 66

(Colored vinyl. Promotional issue only.)

DOT (15805 "You Cheated")....20-30 58
DOT (15856 "I'm Sorry Now")....30-40 58
DOT (15940 "Play the Game Fair")....20-30 59
FALCON (100 "The Girl Around the Corner")....50-75 60
TENDER (513 "You Cheated")....50-75 58

(Label does NOT read "Dist. By Dot.")

TENDER (513 "You Cheated")....20-40 58

(Label reads "Dist. By Dot.")

TENDER (518 "I'm Sorry Now")....30-50 59
TENDER (521 "Play the Game Fair")....30-50 59
TENDER (567 "You Cheated")....10-15
TRANSCONTINENTAL (1013 "The Girl Around the Corner")....100-200 60

(First issue.)

LPs: 10/12-inch

BRYLEN....5-10

Members: Frankie Ervin; Charles Wright; Nathaniel Wilson; Jesse Belvin; Johnny "Guitar" Watson; Mel Williams.

Also see BELVIN, Jesse
Also see WATSON, Johnny
Also see WRIGHT, Charles

SHINDIGS

(Bobby Fuller Four)

Singles: 7-inch

MUSTANG....10-15 65

Also see FULLER, Bobby

SHINDOGS *P&R '66*

Singles: 7-inch

VIVA....4-8 66
W.B....4-8 65

Members: Delaney Bramlet; Bonnie Bramlett.

Also see DELANEY & BONNIE

SHINEHEAD *LP '88*

LPs: 10/12-inch

ELEKTRA....5-8 88-90

SHIRLEE MAY

(Shirley Ellis)

Singles: 7-inch

MERCURY (71969 "Lonely Birthday")....8-12 62

Also see ELLIS, Shirley

SHIRELLES *P&R '58*

Singles: 7-inch

COLLECTABLES....3-4 80s
BLUE ROCK....4-8 68
DECCA....10-20 58-61
ERIC....3-4 70s
GUSTO....3-4
RCA....5-10 71-73
SCEPTER (1203 "Dedicated to the One I Love")....15-25 59

(White label.)

SCEPTER (1203 "Dedicated to the One I Love")....10-15 59

(Red label.)

SCEPTER (1205 thru 1208)....15-20 59-60

(White label.)

SCEPTER (1205 thru 1208)....10-15 59-60

(Red label.)

SCEPTER (1211 "Tomorrow")....20-25 60
SCEPTER (1211 "Will You Love Me Tomorrow")....10-15 60

(Note longer title.)

SCEPTER (1217 thru 1292)....5-10 61-64
SCEPTER (12000 series)....4-8 65-67

TIARA (6112 "I Met Him On a Sunday") 100-125 57
U.A. 3-5 70-71

Picture Sleeves

SCEPTER 10-20 63

LPs: 10/12-inch

BACK-TRAC 5-10 85
EVEREST 5-10 81
GUSTO 5-10 80s
PHOENIX 5-10 81
PRICEWISE 15-25 60s
RCA 10-15 71-72
RHINO 5-8 85
SCEPTER (SRM-501 "Tonight's the Night") 60-80 61
(Monaural.)
SCEPTER (S-501 "Tonight's the Night") 75-100 61
(Stereo.)
SCEPTER (502 thru 562) 25-40 61-67
SCEPTER (599 "Remember When") 15-20 72
SPRINGBOARD 8-10 72
U.A. 10-15 71-75

Members: Shirley Jackson-Alston; Beverly Lee; Doris Coley-Jackson; Addie "Micki" Harris-McFadden.
Also see JAN & DEAN / Roy Orbison / 4 Seasons / Shirelles
Also see KING, Carole
Also see SHIRLEY & SHIRELLES

SHIRELLES & KING CURTIS

LPs: 10/12-inch

SCEPTER (505 "A Twist Party") 25-35 62
SCEPTER (569 "Eternally Soul") 25-35 68

Also see KING CURTIS
Also see SHIRELLES

SHIRLEY, Donald — LP '55

(Don Shirley Trio)

Singles: 7-inch

BARNABY 3-4 76
CADENCE 4-8 60-64
COLUMBIA 3-6 68-69

EPs: 7-inch

CADENCE 8-15 56-59

LPs: 10/12-inch

ATLANTIC 5-12 72
AUDIO FIDELITY 10-25 59
CADENCE 20-40 55-63
COLUMBIA 10-15 65-69

SHIRLEY & CO. — P&R/R&B/LP '75

Singles: 7-inch

VIBRATION 3-5 75-76

LPs: 10/12-inch

VIBRATION 8-10 75

Members: Shirley Goodman; Kenny Jeremiah.
Also see SHIRLEY & LEE
Also see SOUL SURVIVORS

SHIRLEY & LEE — P&R '52

Singles: 78 rpm

ALADDIN 10-30 52-57

Singles: 7-inch

ABC 3-4 73
ALADDIN (3153 "I'm Gone") 50-75 52
ALADDIN (3173 "Baby") 50-100
ALADDIN (3192 "Shirley's Back") 30-50 53
ALADDIN (3205 "Two Happy People") 25-40 53
ALADDIN (3222 "Why Did I") 25-40 53
ALADDIN (3244 "Confessin'") 25-40 54
ALADDIN (3258 "Comin' Over") 25-40 54
ALADDIN (3289 "Feel So Good") 15-25 55
ALADDIN (3302 "Lee's Dream") 15-25 55
ALADDIN (3313 "That's What I'll Do") 20-30 55
ALADDIN (3325 "Let the Good Times Roll") 10-20 56
ALADDIN (3338 "I Feel Good") 10-20 56
ALADDIN (3362 "When I Saw You") 10-20 57
ALADDIN (3369 "I Want to Dance") 10-20 57
ALADDIN (3380 "Rock All Night") 10-20 57
ALADDIN (3390 "Rockin' with the Clock") 10-20 57
ALADDIN (3405 "I'll Thrill You") 10-20 57
ALADDIN (3418 "Everybody's Rockin'") 10-20 58
ALADDIN (3432 "All I Want to Do Is Cry") 10-20 58
ALADDIN (3455 "True Love") 10-20 59
IMPERIAL 5-10 62-63
LIBERTY 3-4 80s
U.A. 3-5 73
WARWICK 5-10 60-61

LPs: 10/12-inch

ALADDIN (807 "Let the Good Times Roll") 300-400 56
IMPERIAL (9179 "Let the Good Times Roll") 50-75 62
SCORE (4023 "Let the Good Times Roll") 100-150 57
U.A. 20-25 73-74
WARWICK (2028 "Let the Good Times Roll") 75-100 61

Members: Shirley Goodman; Leonard Lee.
Also see ADAMS, Faye / Little Esther / Shirley & Lee
Also see KING, Ben E.
Also see SHIRLEY & COMPANY

SHIRLEY & SQUIRRELY — C&W/P&R '76

Singles: 7-inch

GRT 3-5 76

LPs: 10/12-inch

GRT 5-10 76

Also see SHIRLEY, SQUIRRELY & MELVIN

SHIRLEY & SHIRELLES

(Featuring Shirley Alston)

Singles: 7-inch

BELL 8-12 69

Also see SHIRELLES

SHIRLEY, SQUIRRELY & MELVIN

Singles: 7-inch

EXCELSIOR 3-4 81

Picture Sleeves

EXCELSIOR 3-5 81

LPs: 10/12-inch

EXCELSIOR 5-10 81

Also see SHIRLEY & SQUIRRELY

SHOCK — R&B '81

Singles: 12-inch

FANTASY 4-6 81-83

Singles: 7-inch

FANTASY 3-4 81-83
NEBULA 3-5 79

LPs: 10/12-inch

FANTASY 5-10 81-82

SHOCKED, Michelle — P&R/LP '88

Singles: 7-inch

MERCURY 3-4 88-89

Picture Sleeves

MERCURY 3-4 88

LPs: 10/12-inch

MERCURY 5-8 88-89

SHOCKING BLUE — P&R '69

Singles: 7-inch

BUDDAH 3-5 71
COLOSSUS 3-6 69-71
MGM 3-5 72-73

Picture Sleeves

COLOSSUS 4-6 69-70

LPs: 10/12-inch

COLOSSUS 10-20 70

Members: Robby Van Leevwen; Mariska Veres; Klassje Van Der Wal; Cornelis Van Der Beck.

SHOES — P&R/LP '79

Singles: 7-inch

BOMP 3-5 78
ELEKTRA 3-5 79

Picture Sleeves

BOMP 3-5 78
ELEKTRA 3-5 79

EPs: 7-inch

BOMP 5-10 78

LPs: 10/12-inch

BLACK VINYL 8-12 70s
ELEKTRA 5-10 77-82
PVC 5-10 78

Members: John Murphy; Jeff Murphy; Gary Klebe; Skip Meyer.

SHONDELL, Troy — P&R '61

(Troy Shondel; Troy Shundell; Gary Shelton)

Singles: 7-inch

AVM 3-4 88
BRITE STAR 3-5 73-74
COLLECTABLES 3-4 80s
COMMERCIAL 3-5 78
DECCA 4-8 64
EVEREST 4-8 62-64
GAYE (2010 "This Time") 20-25 61
GOLDCREAST (161 "This Time") 15-20 61
(Note misspelled label name.)
GOLDCREST (161 "This Time") 10-15 61
LIBERTY 5-10 61-62
LUCKY 3-5 75
MASTER 10-15 60s
RIC 4-8 65
STAR-FOX 3-5 79
SUNSHINE 3-5 76
TRX 4-8 67-69
TELESONIC 3-5 80-81
3 RIVERS 4-8 60s
WRITERS & ARTISTS (001 "This Time") 25-35 61

LPs: 10/12-inch

EVEREST (1206 "Many Sides") 25-35 63
STAR-FOX 5-10 79
SUNSET 10-15 67

SHONDELLS

(Featuring Tommy James)

Singles: 7-inch

RED FOX (110 "Hanky Panky") 15-25 66
SELSOM (102 "Why Do Fools Fall in Love") 10-20 65
SNAP (101 "Pretty Little Red Bird") 25-45 63
SNAP (102 "Hanky Panky") 50-75 63
(No mention of distribution by Red Fox.)
SNAP (102 "Hanky Panky") 20-25 65
(Reads, "Distributed by Red Fox Records.")

Also see JAMES, Tommy

SHO-NUFF — R&B '78

Singles: 12-inch

MALACO 4-6 81-84

Singles: 7-inch

MALACO 3-4 81-84
STAX 3-5 78-79

LPs: 10/12-inch

STAX 5-10 78

SHOOTING STAR — P&R/LP '80

Singles: 7-inch

EPIC 3-4 82
GEFFEN 3-4 85
VIRGIN 3-5 80

Picture Sleeves

GEFFEN 3-4 85
VIRGIN 3-5 80

LPs: 10/12-inch

ENIGMA 5-8 89
EPIC 5-8 81-83
VIRGIN 5-10 80-82

Members: Gary West; Van McLain; Ron Verlin; Keith Mitchell; Charles Waltz; Bob Guffy; Steve Thomas.

SHORE, Dinah — P&R '40

(With Dick Todd; with Woody Herman)

Singles: 78 rpm

BLUEBIRD 5-10 40-42
COLUMBIA 4-8 46
RCA 3-6 50-57
VICTOR 4-8 40-46

Singles: 7-inch

CAPITOL 4-8 60-62
CAPITOL CUSTOM (3793 "Purex Presents Dinah Shore") 5-10 61
(Single-sided promotional issue, made for Purex.)
DECCA 3-5 69

MERCURY 3-5 74
PROJECT 3............ 3-6 67-68
RCA............ 8-15 50-57

Picture Sleeves

CAPITOL CUSTOM (3793 "The Purex Dinah Shore Special")............ 5-10 61
(Promotional issue, made for Purex.)
RCA............ 10-20 53

EPs: 7-inch

CAMDEN............ 5-10 56
CAPITOL............ 4-8 59
CAPITOL CUSTOM ("Season's Greetings: Dinah Shore")............ 5-10 50s
COLUMBIA............ 4-8 59
RCA............ 5-15 51-57

LPs: 10/12-inch

BAINBRIDGE............ 5-8 82
CAMDEN............ 5-10 59-60
CAPITOL (1200 series)............ 10-20 59-60
CAPITOL (1354 "Dinah Sings Some Blues with Red Norvo")............ 20-30 60
CAPITOL (1600 & 1700 series)............ 10-20 62
COLUMBIA (6000 series)............ 20-40 50-51
(10-inch LPs.)
COLUMBIA (34000 series)............ 5-10 77
DECCA............ 5-10 69
HARMONY............ 5-10 59-60
NABISCO (001 "Nabisco Invitational")............ 30-40 83
(Picture disc. Promotional issue only.)
PROJECT 3............ 5-10 68
RCA (11 "Tangos")............ 25-35 51
RCA (1100 & 1200 series)............ 20-30 55-56
RCA (3000 series)............ 20-30 53-54
(10-inch LPs.)
REPRISE............ 10-15 65
S&H GREEN STAMPS (1 "Dinah")............ 10-20 62
(TV show preview LP. Promotional issue only.)
Also see CUGAT, Xavier, & Dinah Shore
Also see KINGSTON TRIO / Dinah Shore
Also see MARTIN, Dean

SHORE, Dinah, & Tony Martin

Singles: 78 rpm

RCA............ 5-10 51

Singles: 7-inch

RCA............ 10-15 51

SHORE, Dinah, Tony Martin, Betty Hutton & Phil Harris

Singles: 78 rpm

RCA............ 5-10 51

Singles: 7-inch

RCA............ 10-15 51
Also see HARRIS, Phil
Also see HUTTON, Betty
Also see MARTIN, Tony

SHORE, Dinah, & Andre Previn

LPs: 10/12-inch

CAPITOL............ 15-25 60
Also see PREVIN, Andre
Also see SHORE, Dinah

SHORR, Mickey, & Cutups — P&R '62

Singles: 7-inch

TUBA............ 5-10 62

SHORROCK, Glenn — P&R '83

Singles: 7-inch

CAPITOL............ 3-4 83

Picture Sleeves

CAPITOL............ 3-5 83
Also see LITTLE RIVER BAND

SHORT, Bobby — LP '72

LPs: 10/12-inch

ATLANTIC............ 10-25 59-72

SHORTER, Wayne — LP '75

LPs: 10/12-inch

BLUE NOTE............ 20-30 62
(Label reads "Blue Note Records Inc. - New York, USA.")
BLUE NOTE............ 15-20 66
(Label shows Blue Note Records as a division of either Liberty or United Artists.)

COLUMBIA............ 5-10 75
VEE JAY (Maroon label)............ 30-40 60
VEE JAY (Black label)............ 20-30 61-62
Also see WEATHER REPORT

SHOT IN THE DARK — P&R '81

Singles: 7-inch

RSO............ 3-5 81

LPs: 10/12-inch

RSO............ 5-10 81
Members: Peter White; Bryan Savage; Krysia Kristianne; Robin Lamble; Adam Yurman.
Also see STEWART, Al

SHOTGUN — R&B '77

Singles: 12-inch

MONTAGE............ 4-6 82

Singles: 7-inch

ABC............ 3-5 77-79
MCA............ 3-5 80
MONTAGE............ 3-5 82

LPs: 10/12-inch

ABC............ 5-10 77-79
MCA............ 5-10 79-80
MONTAGE............ 5-10 82
Members: Tyrone Steels; Richard Sebastion; Greg Ingram; Billy Talbert; Ernest Latimore; Larry Austin.
Also see SUN, Joe, & Shotgun

SHOTGUN MESSIAH — LP '89

LPs: 10/12-inch

RELATIVITY............ 5-8 89

SHOW STOPPERS — P&R '68
(Showstoppers)

Singles: 7-inch

AMBER............ 5-10 63
COLLECTABLES............ 3-4 80s
COLUMBIA............ 10-15 66-67
HERITAGE............ 4-6 68
SHOWTIME............ 4-8 67

LPs: 10/12-inch

COLLECTABLES............ 5-10

SHOWDOWN — R&B '77

Singles: 7-inch

HONEY BEE............ 3-5 77

LPs: 10/12-inch

HONEY BEE............ 5-10 77

SHOWMEN — P&R '61

Singles: 7-inch

AIRECORDS............ 10-20
AMY............ 5-10 68
BB (4015 "In Paradise")............ 10-15 67
IMPERIAL (66033 "It Will Stand")............ 8-12 64
IMPERIAL (66071 "Country Fool")............ 8-12 64
JOKERS THREE (100 "A Little Bit of Your Love")............ 50-75
LIBERTY............ 4-8 70-81
MINIT (632 "It Will Stand")............ 20-40 61
(Orange label.)
MINIT (632 "It Will Stand")............ 15-25 61
(Black label.)
MINIT (643 "The Wrong Girl")............ 20-40 62
MINIT (647 "Comin' Home")............ 15-25 62
MINIT (654 "True Fine Mama")............ 15-25 62
MINIT (662 "39-21-46")............ 15-25 63
SWAN (4213 "In Paradise")............ 15-25 65
SWAN (4241 "Please Try to Understand")............ 15-25 65
Member: General Johnson.
Also see JOHNSON, General
Also see THOMAS, Irma / Ernie K-Doe / Showmen / Benny Spellman.

SHRIEKBACK — D&D/LP '83

Singles: 12-inch

ARISTA............ 4-6 84
W.B.............. 4-6 83

Singles: 7-inch

W.B.............. 3-4 83

LPs: 10/12-inch

ISLAND............ 5-8 87-88
W.B.............. 5-8 83
Members: Barry Andrews; David Allen.
Also see GANG of FOUR

Also see XTC

SHUNDEL, Troy: see SHONDELL, Troy

SHY — LP '87

Singles: 7-inch

RCA............ 3-4 87

LPs: 10/12-inch

RCA............ 5-8 87

SIBERRY, Jane — LP '86

Singles: 7-inch

OPEN AIR............ 3-4 86

LPs: 10/12-inch

OPEN AIR............ 5-8 86

SIDE EFFECT — R&B '76

Singles: 12-inch

FANTASY............ 4-6 78-81

Singles: 7-inch

ELEKTRA............ 3-4 80-82
FANTASY............ 3-5 75-81

LPs: 10/12-inch

ELEKTRA............ 5-8 80-82
FANTASY............ 5-8 75-81
Members: Miki Howard; Augie Johnson; Louis Patton; Sylvia Nabors; Gregory Matta; Helen Lowe; Sylvia St. James.
Also see HOWARD, Miki
Also see L.A. BOPPERS

SIDE OF THE ROAD GANG — C&W '76

Singles: 7-inch

CAPITOL............ 3-5 76

LPs: 10/12-inch

CAPITOL............ 8-10 76

SIDEKICKS — P&R '66

Singles: 7-inch

RCA............ 4-8 66-67

LPs: 10/12-inch

RCA............ 10-20 66

SIDEWINDERS — LP '89

LPs: 10/12-inch

MAMMOUTH............ 5-8 89

SIFFRE, Labi — R&B '87

Singles: 7-inch

CHINA............ 3-4 87

SIGLER, Bunny — P&R/R&B '67
(Mr. Emotions)

Singles: 12-inch

SALSOUL............ 4-6 80

Singles: 7-inch

BEE (1114 "Laddy Daddy")............ 10-20 59
(Bee 1114 is also the number of a Don Ellis release.)
CRAIG............ 10-15 61
DECCA............ 10-25 65-67
GOLD MINE............ 3-6 78-79
NEPTUNE............ 5-10 60s
PARKWAY............ 5-10 67-69
PHILADELPHIA INT'L............ 5-15 71-76
SALSOUL............ 3-5 80

LPs: 10/12-inch

GOLD MIND............ 5-10 78-79
PARKWAY............ 10-20 67
SALSOUL............ 5-10 80
Also see HOLLOWAY, Loleatta, & Bunny Sigler
Also see MASON, Barbara, & Bunny Sigler

SIGUE SIGUE SPUTNIK — LP '86

Singles: 12-inch

MANHATTAN............ 4-6 86

Singles: 7-inch

MANHATTAN............ 3-4 86

LPs: 10/12-inch

MANHATTAN............ 5-10 86
Member: Tony James.
Also see GENERATION X

SILAS, Alfie — R&B '82
(Alfie)

Singles: 7-inch

MOTOWN............ 3-4 84-86
RCA............ 3-4 82-84

LPs: 10/12-inch

MOTOWN.......................................5-8 85
RCA...5-8 82-84
Also see KING, Bobby

SILENCERS P&R '80

Singles: 7-inch

PRECISION...................................3-5 80

LPs: 10/12-inch

PRECISION...................................5-10 80-81
Member: Frank Czuri.
Also see DIAMOND REO

SILENCERS P&R/LP '87

Singles: 7-inch

RCA...3-4 87

LPs: 10/12-inch

RCA...5-8 87-90

SILENT UNDERDOG R&B '85

Singles: 12-inch

PROFILE......................................4-6 85

SILHOUETTES P&R/R&B '58
(With Dave McRae Orchestra)

Singles: 78 rpm

EMBER.......................................50-75 57
JUNIOR......................................50-100 57

Singles: 7-inch

ABC...3-5 73
ACE (552 "I Sold My Heart to the Junkman")......................12-15 58
COLLECTABLES.............................3-4 80s
EMBER (1029 "Get a Job")..............15-25 57
(Red label.)
EMBER (1029 "Get a Job")..............10-15 60
Black label.)
EMBER (1032 "Headin' for the Poorhouse")..............................15-25 58
EMBER (1037 "Bing Bong")...........50-100 58
(Glossy red label.)
EMBER (1037 "Bing Bong")............15-25 58
(Flat red label.)
FLASHBACK..................................4-8 65
GOODWAY (101 "Not Me Baby") 100-200 68
GRAND (142 "Wish I Could Be There")..150-250 61
IMPERIAL (5899 "The Push")..........10-15 62
JUNIOR (391 "Get a Job")............250-500 57
(Brown label.)
JUNIOR (391 "Get a Job")............200-300 57
(Blue label.)
JUNIOR (396 "I Sold My Heart to the Junkman")..................................75-125 58
JUNIOR (400 "Evelyn")............1000-2000 59
JUNIOR (993 "Your Love")..............50-75 63

LPs: 10/12-inch

GOODWAY (100 "Get a Job").......100-150 68
Also see HORTON, Bill, & Silhouettes
Also see KING, Ben E.

SILICON TEENS

LPs: 10/12-inch

SIRE...5-10 80

SILK LP '69

Singles: 7-inch

ABC...5-10 69
DECCA...4-6 71

LPs: 10/12-inch

ABC (694 "Smooth As Raw Silk").....15-25 69
Members: Michael Stanley Gee; Chris Jones; Randy Sabo; Courtney Johns.
Also see KING, Ben E.

SILK LP '69

Singles: 7-inch

ABC...5-10 69
DECCA...4-6 71

LPs: 10/12-inch

ABC (694 "Smooth As Raw Silk")...15-25 69
Members: Michael Stanley Gee; Chris Jones; Randy Sabo; Courtney Johns.
Also see STANLEY, Michael, Band

SILK R&B '77

Singles: 12-inch

PHILADELPHIA INT'L.......................4-8 79-80

Singles: 7-inch

PHILADELPHIA INT'L.......................3-5 79-80
PRELUDE......................................3-5 77
PYE...3-5 76

LPs: 10/12-inch

ARISTA...5-10 77
PHILADELPHIA INT'L.......................5-10 79
Member: Debra Henry.
Also see BUTLER, Jerry, & Debra Henry

SILK, J.M. D&D '85

Singles: 12-inch

D.J. INT'L.....................................4-6 85

SILKIE P&R '65

Singles: 7-inch

FONTANA......................................4-8 65-66

LPs: 10/12-inch

FONTANA (27548 "You've Got to Hide Your Love Away")..............................20-30 65
(Monaural.)
FONTANA (67548 "You've Got to Hide Your Love Away")..............................25-35 65
(Stereo.)
Also see BEATLES

SILOS LP '90

LPs: 10/12-inch

RCA...5-8 90

SILVA-TONES P&R '57

Singles: 78 rpm

ARGO...20-30 57
MONARCH.....................................25-50 57

Singles: 7-inch

ARGO (5281 "That's All I Want from You")..20-30 57
(Silver and black label with "ship" logo.)
ARGO (5281 "Chi-Wa-Wa, That's All I Want from You")..15-25 57
(Black label, silver print. No "ship" logo. Note title variation.)
MONARCH (615 "That's All I Want from You")..30-50 57
(Yellow label.)
MONARCH (615 "That's All I Want from You")..20-30 57
(Black label.)

SILVER P&R/LP '76

Singles: 7-inch

ARISTA...3-5 76-77

LPs: 10/12-inch

ARISTA...8-10 76
Members: John Batdorf; Brent Mydland.
Also see GRATEFUL DEAD

SILVER, Horace, Quintet LP '65

Singles: 78 rpm

BLUE NOTE...................................4-8 54-57

Singles: 7-inch

BLUE NOTE (300 thru 1000 series).....3-5 73-77
BLUE NOTE (1600 & 1700 series).....5-10 54-61
BLUE NOTE (1800 & 1900 series).......4-8 61-69

LPs: 10/12-inch

BLUE NOTE (1518 "Horace Silver Quintet")......................................50-75 56
(Label gives New York street address for Blue Note Records.)
BLUE NOTE (1518 "Horace Silver Quintet")......................................25-50
(Label gives New York street address for Blue Note Records.)
BLUE NOTE (1520 "New Faces")......50-75 56
(Label gives New York street address for Blue Note Records.)
BLUE NOTE (1520 "New Faces")......25-50
(Label reads "Blue Note Records Inc. - New York, U.S.A.")
BLUE NOTE (1562 "Stylings")..........50-75 57
(Label gives New York street address for Blue Note Records.)
BLUE NOTE (1562 "Stylings")..........25-50
(Label reads "Blue Note Records Inc. - New York, U.S.A.")
BLUE NOTE (1562 "Stylings")..........15-25
(Label shows Blue Note Records as a division of Liberty.)
BLUE NOTE (1589 "Further Explorations")..............................50-75 58
(Label gives New York street address for Blue Note Records.)
BLUE NOTE (1589 "Further Explorations")..............................25-50
(Label reads "Blue Note Records Inc. - New York, U.S.A.")
BLUE NOTE (1589 "Further Explorations")..............................15-25
(Label shows Blue Note Records as a division of Liberty.)
BLUE NOTE (4000 series)..............30-50 59-60
(Label gives New York street address for Blue Note Records.)
BLUE NOTE (4000 series)..............20-30 59-65
(Label reads "Blue Note Records Inc. - New York, U.S.A.")
BLUE NOTE (4000 series)..............15-20 66-68
(Label shows Blue Note Records as a division of either
BLUE NOTE (5018 "New Faces") 100-150 53
(10-inch LP.)
BLUE NOTE (5034 "Horace Silver Trio")..100-150 54
(10-inch LP.)
BLUE NOTE (5058 "Horace Silver Quintet")....................................100-150 55
(10-inch LP.)
BLUE NOTE (5062 "Horace Silver Quintet")....................................100-150 55
(10-inch LP.)
BLUE NOTE (84000 series).............30-40 59-60
(Label gives New York street address for Blue Note Records.)
BLUE NOTE (84000 series).............20-30 59-65
(Label reads "Blue Note Records Inc. - New York, U.S.A.")
BLUE NOTE (84000 series).............10-20 66-80
(Label shows Blue Note Records as a division of either
EPIC (3326 "Silver's Blue")............75-125 57
EPIC (16006 "Silver's Blue")...........60-80 58
Also see STITT, Sonny, Kai Winding & Horace Silver

SILVER, Horace, Quintet, & Stanley Turrentine

LPs: 10/12-inch

BLUE NOTE...................................10-15 68
Also see SILVER, Horace, Quintet
Also see TURRENTINE, Stanley

SILVER APPLES LP '68

Singles: 7-inch

KAPP...4-8 68-69

LPs: 10/12-inch

KAPP...10-15 68-69

SILVER CONDOR P&R/LP '81

Singles: 7-inch

COLUMBIA.....................................3-4 81

Picture Sleeves

COLUMBIA.....................................3-5 81

LPs: 10/12-inch

COLUMBIA.....................................5-10 81
Members: Joe Cerisano; Earl Slick; John Corey; Claude Pepper; Jay Davis.
Also see PHANTOM, ROCKER & SLICK

SILVER CONVENTION P&R/R&B/LP '75

Singles: 7-inch

MIDLAND INT'L...............................3-5 75-77
MIDSONG INT'L...............................3-5 77-78

Picture Sleeves

MIDLAND INT'L...............................3-5 76

LPs: 10/12-inch

MIDLAND INT'L...............................5-10 75-77
MIDSONG INT'L...............................5-10 77
Member: Penny McLean.
Also see McLEAN, Penny

SILVER PLATINUM R&B '80

Singles: 7-inch

SRI...3-5 81

SPECTOR ... 3-5 81
LPs: 10/12-inch
SPECTOR ... 5-10 81

SILVER, PLATINUM & GOLD R&B '75
Singles: 7-inch
FARR ... 3-5 76-77
W.B. ... 3-5 74-75
LPs: 10/12-inch
NEPTUNE ... 5-10 82

SILVERADO P&R '81
Singles: 7-inch
PAVILLION ... 3-5 81
RCA ... 3-5 77
LPs: 10/12-inch
PAVILLION ... 5-10 81
RCA ... 5-10 77

SILVERSPOON, Dooley P&R/R&B '75
Singles: 7-inch
COTTON ... 3-5 74-75

SILVERSTEIN, Shel LP '73
Singles: 7-inch
COLUMBIA ... 3-6 71-75
ELEKTRA ... 8-12 60
RCA ... 4-6 69-70
LPs: 10/12-inch
ATLANTIC (8072 "Inside Folk Songs") ... 20-30 63
(Monaural.)
ATLANTIC (SD-8072 "Inside Folk Songs") ... 25-35 63
(Stereo.)
ATLANTIC (8200 series) ... 10-15 70
CBS (39611 "Where the Sidewalk Ends") ... 8-12 84
(Picture disc.)
CADET ... 15-25 65-66
COLUMBIA ... 5-12 72-84
CRESTVIEW ... 15-25 63
ELEKTRA (176 "Hairy Jazz") ... 30-40 59
(Monaural.)
ELEKTRA (7-176 "Hairy Jazz") ... 40-50 59
(Stereo.)
FLYING FISH ... 5-8 80
JANUS ... 8-12 73
PARACHUTE (Except 20512) ... 5-10 78
PARACHUTE (20512 "Selected Cuts from *Songs and Stories*") ... 15-20 78
(Promotional issue only.)
RCA ... 10-15 69

SILVETTI P&R/R&B '77
Singles: 7-inch
SALSOUL ... 3-5 77
LPs: 10/12-inch
SALSOUL ... 5-10 77

SIMEONE, Harry, Chorale P&R '58
Singles: 7-inch
COLUMBIA ... 3-5 66-67
KAPP ... 3-5 64-68
MERCURY ... 3-5 62-64
MISTLETOE ... 3-4 74
20TH FOX ... 3-5 58-79
Picture Sleeves
MERCURY ... 4-6 62
20TH FOX ... 4-8 58-63
Promotional Picture Sleeve
20TH FOX (121 "Little Drummer Boy") ... 5-10 58
(This "Prepare to Be Enchanted" sleeve was sent only to radio stations.)
LPs: 10/12-inch
DECCA ... 5-15 62-64
DIPLOMAT ... 5-10 60s
KAPP ... 5-10 65
MERCURY ... 5-15 63-64
MISTLETOE ... 4-8 73
MOVIETONE ... 5-10 67
20TH FOX ... 5-15 58-79
WING ... 5-10 69

SIMMONS, Chandra R&B '87
Singles: 7-inch
FRESH ... 3-4 87

SIMMONS, Gene P&R/LP '64
(Jumpin' Gene Simmons; Morris Gene Simmons)
Singles: 7-inch
AGP ... 5-10 60s
CHECKER (948 "Goin' Back to Memphis") ... 15-25 60
EPIC ... 3-5 70
DELTUNE ... 3-5 77-78
HI ... 8-15 61-67
HURSHEY ... 3-5 73
MALA ... 5-10 68
SANDY ... 8-12 60s
SUN (299 "Drinkin' Wine") ... 25-50 58
TUPELO (2981 "Little Rag Doll") .. 100-200 60s
LPs: 10/12-inch
HI (2018 "Jumpin' Gene Simmons") 20-40 64
(Monaural.)
HI (32018 "Jumpin' Gene Simmons") ... 25-50 64
(Stereo.)
(Stereo.)

SIMMONS, Gene P&R/LP '78
Singles: 7-inch
CASABLANCA ... 3-4 78-79
LPs: 10/12-inch
CASABLANCA (7120 "Gene Simmons") ... 12-20 78
(With poster order form.)
CASABLANCA (7120 "Gene Simmons") ... 8-12 78
(Without poster order form.)
CASABLANCA (PIX-7120 "Gene Simmons") ... 40-50 79
(Picture disc.)
Also see KISS

SIMMONS, Patrick P&R/R&B/D&D/LP '83
Singles: 12-inch
ELEKTRA ... 4-8 83
Singles: 7-inch
ELEKTRA ... 3-5 83
LPs: 10/12-inch
ELEKTRA ... 5-10 83
Also see DOOBIE BROTHERS
Also see EAGLES

SIMMONS, Simtec R&B '75
(With the Mechanical Monster; with Band)
Singles: 7-inch
INNOVATION ... 3-5 75
MAURCI (105 "Tea Pot") ... 4-8 60s

SIMMONS, Simtec, & Wylie Dixon
Singles: 7-inch
TODDLIN' TOWN ... 4-8 69
Also see SIMMONS, Simtec
Also see SIMTEC & WYLIE

SIMMS, John & Arthur R&B '80
Singles: 7-inch
CASABLANCA ... 3-5 80
LPs: 10/12-inch
CASABLANCA ... 5-10 80

SIMMS TWINS: see SIMS TWINS

SIMON, Carly P&R/LP '71
Singles: 7-inch
ARISTA ... 3-4 86-90
COLUMBIA ... 3-5 73
ELEKTRA ... 3-5 71-79
EPIC ... 3-4 85-86
MIRAGE ... 3-5 82
W.B. ... 3-5 80-83
Picture Sleeves
ARISTA (Except 9525) ... 3-5 86-89
ARISTA (9525 "Coming Around Again") ... 4-8 86
(Pictures Meryl Streep and Jack Nicholson.)
ARISTA (9525 "Coming Around Again") ... 3-5 86
(Pictures Carly Simon.)
ELEKTRA ... 3-5 75-79
W.B. ... 3-5 80-83
LPs: 10/12-inch
ARISTA ... 5-8 86-90
ELEKTRA ... 5-10 71-79
EPIC ... 5-8 85-86
W.B. ... 5-10 80-83
Also see JAGGER, Mick
Also see SIMON SISTERS

SIMON, Carly, & James Taylor P&R '74
Singles: 7-inch
ELEKTRA ... 3-5 74-78
Also see SIMON, Carly
Also see TAYLOR, James

SIMON, Joe R&B '65
(With the Checkmates; with Mainstreeters)
Singles: 7-inch
COMPLEAT ... 3-5 70s
DOT ... 4-8 64
GEE BEE (077 "Say") ... 15-25
HUSH ... 10-15 60-62
IRRAL ... 4-8 63
MONUMENT ... 3-5 70-72
POSSE ... 3-5 81-82
SOUND STAGE 7 ... 3-6 66-72
SPRING ... 3-5 69-75
VEE JAY ... 4-8 64-65
Picture Sleeves
GEE BEE (077 "Say") ... 15-20
SPRING ... 3-5 71-73
LPs: 10/12-inch
BUDDAH ... 10-15 69
POSSE ... 5-8 81-82
SOUND STAGE 7 ... 8-15 67-75
SPRING ... 8-12 71-78

SIMON, Paul P&R/LP '72
(With Urubamba; with Los Incas)
Singles: 7-inch
W.B. (2503 "You Can Call Me Al") ... 4-8 86
(Promotional issue.)
W.B. (2652 "Boy in the Bubble") ... 4-8 86
(Promotional issue.)
Singles: 7-inch
COLUMBIA ... 3-5 72-77
W.B. ... 3-4 80-90
Picture Sleeves
COLUMBIA ... 3-8 73-77
W.B. ... 3-5 80-87
LPs: 10/12-inch
COLUMBIA (Except C5X & 43000 series) ... 6-12 72-77
COLUMBIA (C5X-37581 "Paul Simon's Collected Works") ... 30-40 81
(Boxed, five-disc set.)
COLUMBIA (43000 series) ... 15-20 81
(Half-speed mastered.)
W.B. (140 ""Interview Show") ... 20-30 86
(Promotional issue only. Two LPs with interview and *Graceland* songs.)
W.B. (3472 "One-Trick Pony") ... 5-10 80
W.B. (23942 thru 26098) ... 5-10 80-90
Also see BOOKER T. & MGs
Also see CYRKLE
Also see DION
Also see DIXIE HUMMINGBIRDS
Also see 4 SEASONS
Also see FRANKLIN, Aretha
Also see GARFUNKEL, Art, James Taylor & Paul Simon
Also see GLASS, Philip
Also see KANE, Paul
Also see LANDIS, Jerry
Also see NEWMAN, Randy, & Paul Simon
Also see ORLANDO, Tony
Also see RIVERS, Johnny
Also see SEDAKA, Neil
Also see SIMON & GARFUNKEL
Also see TAYLOR, True
Also see TICO & TRIUMPHS
Also see U.S.A. for AFRICA
Also see VALERY, Dana
Also see YES

SIMON, Paul, & Phoebe Snow
(With the Jessy Dixon Singers) *P&R '75*
Singles: 7-inch
COLUMBIA....................................3-5 75
Also see SNOW, Phoebe

SIMON & GARFUNKEL *P&R '65*
Singles: 7-inch
ABC-PAR (10788 "This Is My Story") 10-15 66
COLUMBIA (10000 series)...................3-5 75
COLUMBIA (11000 series)...................5-8 66
COLUMBIA (33000 series)...................3-6 60s
COLUMBIA (43396 "The Sounds of Silence")..................................4-8 65
COLUMBIA (43396 "The Sounds of Silence")..................................30-40 65
(Colored vinyl. Promotional issue only.)
COLUMBIA (43511 "Homeward Bound")......................................4-8 66
COLUMBIA (43511 "Homeward Bound")......................................30-40 66
(Colored vinyl. Promotional issue only.)
COLUMBIA (43617 "I Am a Rock").......4-8 66
COLUMBIA (43617 "I Am a Rock")...30-40 66
(Colored vinyl. Promotional issue only.)
COLUMBIA (43728 thru 45663)...........4-8 66-75
TEEN SCOOP/Columbia ("Exclusive Interview")..............................20-35 65
(Square cardboard picture disc issued in premier issue of *Teen Scoop* magazine. Includes magazine with disc intact.)
TEEN SCOOP/Columbia ("Exclusive Interview")..............................10-20 65
(Square cardboard picture disc issued in premier issue of *Teen Scoop* magazine. No selection number used.)
TEEN SCOOP (789 "Visits with Simon & Garfunkel")...............................10-20 66
(*Teen Scoop* magazine bonus soundsheet.)
W.B. 3-5 82
Picture Sleeves
COLUMBIA....................................5-10 66-75
EPs: 7-inch
COLUMBIA....................................10-20 68-69
(Juke box issues only.)
LPs: 10/12-inch
COLUMBIA (CL-2249 "Wednesday Morning 3 A.M.")......................................10-20 64
(Monaural.)
COLUMBIA (CL-2469 "Sounds of Silence")......................................10-20 66
(Monaural.)
COLUMBIA (CL-2563 "Parsley, Sage Rosemary and Thyme")...............................10-20 66
(Monaural.)
COLUMBIA (KCL-2729 "Bookends") 15-25 68
(Monaural. Includes poster.)
COLUMBIA (OS-3180 "The Graduate")...................................12-15 68
(Soundtrack.)
COLUMBIA (3654 "Concert in Central Park")...8-12 82
COLUMBIA (CS-9049 "Wednesday Morning 3 A.M.")......................................10-15 64
(Stereo.)
COLUMBIA (PC-9049 "Wednesday Morning 3 A.M.")......................................5-10
COLUMBIA (CS-9269 "Sounds of Silence")......................................10-15 66
(Stereo.)
COLUMBIA (CS-9363 "Parsley, Sage Rosemary and Thyme")...............................10-15 66
(Stereo.)
COLUMBIA (PC-9363 "Parsley, Sage Rosemary and Thyme")...............................5-10
COLUMBIA (KCS-9529 "Bookends") 10-15 68
(Stereo. Includes poster.)
COLUMBIA (PC-9529 "Bookends") 5-10
COLUMBIA (9914 "Bridge Over Troubled Water")......................................10-15 70
COLUMBIA (30995 "Bridge Over Troubled Water")......................................10-20 71
(Quadrophonic.)
COLUMBIA (31350 "Greatest Hits")....5-10 72
COLUMBIA (37587 "Simon & Garfunkel's Collected Works")..........................30-40 81
(Boxed, five-disc set.)
COLUMBIA (41350 "Greatest Hits") 10-15 81
(Half-speed mastered.)
COLUMBIA (49914 "Bridge Over Troubled Water")......................................40-60 80
(Half-speed mastered.)
MFSL (173 "Bridge over Troubled Water")......................................20-30 85
OFFSHORE..................................10-15
PICKWICK (3059 "Hit Sound of Simon & Garfunkel")...............................50-75 66
SEARS (435 "Simon & Garfunkel") .. 20-30
W.B. 5-8 82
Members: Paul Simon; Art Garfunkel.
Also see GARFUNKEL, Art
Also see SIMON, Paul
Also see TOM & JERRY

SIMON SAID *R&B '75*
Singles: 7-inch
ATCO..3-5 75-76
ROULETTE....................................3-5 75

SIMON SISTERS *P&R '64*
Singles: 7-inch
COLUMBIA (02600 series)..................3-4 82
COLUMBIA (45000 series)..................3-5 73
KAPP...4-8 64-65
LPs: 10/12-inch
COLUMBIA (21525 "Lobster Quadrille")....................................10-15 69
COLUMBIA (21539 "Simon Sisters Sing for Children")..........................10-12 73
COLUMBIA (24506 "Lobster Quadrille")....................................15-20 69
(Special childrens' book edition.)
COLUMBIA (37000 series)..................5-10 82
KAPP...15-25 64
W.B. 5-10 80
Members: Carly Simon; Lucy Simon.
Also see DOOBIE BROTHERS / Kate Taylor & Simon-Taylor Family
Also see SIMON, Carly

SIMONE, Nina *P&R/R&B '59*
Singles: 7-inch
BETHLEHEM...................................3-8 59-70
CTI...3-5 78
COLPIX..4-8 59-63
PHILIPS...4-6 64-66
RCA..3-6 67-71
TRIP..3-4 72
EPs: 7-inch
BETHLEHEM...................................5-10 59
LPs: 10/12-inch
ACCORD..5-10 80
BETHLEHEM...................................20-30 59
CTI...5-10 78-79
COLPIX..15-30 59-66
PHILIPS...10-20 64-69
QUINTESSENCE..............................5-10 80
RCA..8-15 67-76
STROUD..5-10 73
TRIP..5-10 72-77
UPFRONT......................................5-10 72
VERSATILE....................................5-10 78
Also see LYNNE, Gloria / Nina Simone / Billie Holiday

SIMONE, Nina, Chris Connor & Carmen McRae
LPs: 10/12-inch
BETHLEHEM...................................20-30 60
Also see CONNOR, Chris
Also see McRAE, Carmen
Also see SIMONE, Nina

SIMPLE MINDS *LP '83*
Singles: 12-inch
A&M..4-6 82-86
Singles: 7-inch
A&M..3-4 82-86
Picture Sleeves
A&M..3-5 84-86
LPs: 10/12-inch
A&M..5-10 82-91
PVC...8-10 79
DIPLOMAT.....................................5-10 60s
Members: John Giblin; Charles Burchill; Jim Kerr; Michael MacNeil; Mel Gaynor.

SIMPLY RED *D&D '85*
Singles: 12-inch
ELEKTRA..4-6 85-86
Singles: 7-inch
ELEKTRA..3-4 85-89
Picture Sleeves
ELEKTRA..3-4 86-89
LPs: 10/12-inch
ELEKTRA..5-8 85-89
Member: Mick Hucknall.

SIMPSON, Paul *D&D '83*
(Paul Simpson Connection)
Singles: 12-inch
EASY STREET.................................4-6 85
STREETWISE..................................4-6 83
Singles: 7-inch
STREETWISE..................................3-4 83

SIMPSON, Valerie *LP '71*
Singles: 7-inch
TAMLA...3-5 71-72
LPs: 10/12-inch
TAMLA...8-10 71-77
Also see ASHFORD & SIMPSON

SIMPSONS *LP '90*
Singles: 7-inch
GEFFEN...3-4 91
LPs: 10/12-inch
GEFFEN (24308 "Sing the Blues")........5-8 90
Members: Dan Castellaneta; Julie Kavner; Nancy Cartwright; Yeardley Smith; Matt Groening. With guests: Harry Shearer; Ron Taylor; Harry Shearer; Buster Poindexter; Joe Walsh; B.B. King; John Sebastian; D.J. Jazzy Jeff; Andrew Gold; Dr. John.
Also see D.J. JAZZY JEFF & Fresh Prince
Also see DR. JOHN
Also see GOLD, Andrew
Also see KING, B.B.
Also see SEBASTAIN, John
Also see WALSH, Joe

SIMS TWINS *P&R/R&B '61*
(Simms Twins)
Singles: 7-inch
ABKCO...3-5 70s
CROSSOVER..................................3-5 74
KENT...3-5 71
PARKWAY......................................4-8 68
SAR...5-10 61-62
SPECIALTY....................................3-5 70s
Members: Bobby Sims; Kenneth Sims.

SIMTEC & WYLIE
Singles: 7-inch
MISTER CHAND...............................3-6 70-72
SHAMA..4-8 69-70
LPs: 10/12-inch
MISTER CHAND...............................8-12 71-72
Members: Simtec Simmons; Wylie Dixon.
Also see SIMMONS, Simtec, & Wylie Dixon

SINATRA, Frank *P&R '42*
(With Harry James & His Orchestra; with Axel Stordahl & His Orchestra; Tommy Dorsey Orchestra Featuring Frank Sinatra)
Singles: 78 rpm
BLUEBIRD (10726 "East of the Sun")...30-50 42
BLUEBIRD (10771 "Whispering").....30-50 42
BLUEBIRD (11463 "Night & Day")....30-50 42
BLUEBIRD (11515 "The Song Is You")...30-50 42
BRUNSWICK (8443 "From the Bottom of My Heart")....................................400-600 39
(Credited to Harry James & His Orchestra.)
CAPITOL (1699 thru 3900)................5-10 53-58
COLUMBIA (5492 "Soliloquy")..........15-25 46
(12-inch disc. At least one source says this selection number is 7492. We don't yet know who's right.)
COLUMBIA (35209 thru 41133).........5-15 39-58

COLUMBIA (50003 thru 50079) 4-8 50s
COLUMBIA (55037 "Ol Man River") . 15-25 44
(12–inch disc.)
RCA (1522 thru 3500) 4-8 43-49
RCA (13247 "Oh Look at Me Now") .. 40-60 82
(Single-sided. Promotional issue only. 1000 numbered copies made.)
RCA (36396 "Without a Song") 15-25 42
(12–inch disc.)
VICTOR (26500 thru 27974) 4-8 40-43
(Some in this series may be shown as "RCA Victor.")

Albums: 78 rpm

COLUMBIA (112 "The Voice of Frank Sinatra")..25-50 46
(Four discs.)
COLUMBIA (117 "All Time Favorites by Harry James")...25-50 46
(Four discs. *Ciribiribin* is by Sinatra.)
COLUMBIA (117 "All Time Favorites by Harry James")..15-25 46
(Four discs. *Ciribiribin* is by Harry James.)
COLUMBIA (124 "Songs By Sinatra")..25-50 47
(Four discs.)
COLUMBIA (167 "Christmas Songs by Sinatra")..25-50 48
(Four discs.)
COLUMBIA (185 "Frankly Sentimental") 25-50 49
(Four discs.)
COLUMBIA (197 "Dedicated to You")...25-50 50
(Four discs.)
COLUMBIA (218 "Sing and Dance with Frank Sinatra")..25-50 50
(Four discs.)
COLUMBIA (455 "Young at Heart")... 25-50 51
(Four discs.)
COLUMBIA (637 "Frank Sinatra Conducts the Music of Alec Wilder") 100-150 46
(Three 12–inch Masterworks discs.)
RCA (80 "Getting Sentimental") 20-40 40
(Four discs.)
RCA (150 "Starmaker") 20-40 41
(Four discs.)
RCA (163 "All Time Hits")..................20-40 42
(Four discs.)
RCA (247 "And the Band Sang Too") 20-40 43
(Three discs.)

Singles: 12–inch

QUEST (2216 "Mack the Knife") 10-20 84
(Promotional issue only.)
REPRISE (674 "Night & Day")........... 50-75 77
(Promotional issue only. Only 647 made.)
REPRISE (865 "New York, New York")...25-50 80
(Promotional issue only.)

Singles: 7–inch

CAPITOL ("No One Ever Tells You")...35-45 56
(No selection number used. Promotional issue only. Add $4 to $6 if accompanied by Capitol "Rush" paper sleeve.)
CAPITOL (596 "All the Way")........250-350 58
(Promotional issue only. 101 made.)
CAPITOL (1069 "Come Dance with Me") 50-75 59
(Five singles in a paper sleeve. For juke box use. With "XE" prefix.)
CAPITOL (1417 "Nice 'N' Easy ")...... 50-75 60
(Five singles in a paper sleeve. For juke box use. With "XE" prefix.)
CAPITOL (1491 "Sinatra's Swingin' Session") 50-75 61
(Five singles in a paper sleeve. For juke box use. With "XE" prefix.)
CAPITOL (1594 "Come Swing with Me") 50-75 62
(Five singles in a paper sleeve. For juke box use. With "XE" prefix.)
CAPITOL (1676 "Point of No Return") 50-75 63
(Five singles in a paper sleeve. For juke box use. With "XE" prefix.)
CAPITOL (1699 "I've Got the World on a String") 20-30 51
CAPITOL (1729 "Sinatra Sings of Love and Things").. 50-75 60s
(Five singles in a paper sleeve. For juke box use. With "XE" prefix.)
CAPITOL (1707/8 "Mistletoe & Holly")... 75-100 60
(Promotional issue for Christmas Seals.)
CAPITOL (2450 "Lean Baby")........... 15-25 53
CAPITOL (2505 thru 4070)............... 10-20 53-58
CAPITOL (4103 "To Love and Be Loved").. 8-12 58
CAPITOL (4103 "To Love and Be Loved")..................................... 150-250 58
(White label. Promotional issue only.)
CAPITOL (4155 "French Foreign Legion") 8-12 59
CAPITOL (4214 "High Hopes")........... 8-12 59
(Purple label.)
CAPITOL (4214 "High Hopes")....... 50-100 60
(Red label. Promotional issue only.)
CAPITOL (4284 thru 4815)................. 6-12 59-62
CAPITOL (6019 thru 6195).................. 4-6 62
(Starline reissue series.)
COLUMBIA (112 "The Voice of Frank Sinatra") 50-75 46
(Four discs.)
COLUMBIA (167 "Christmas Songs by Sinatra") 50-75 48
(Four discs.)
COLUMBIA (197 "Dedicated to You") 50-75 50
(Four discs.)
COLUMBIA (218 "Sing and Dance with Frank Sinatra") 50-75 50
(Four discs.)
COLUMBIA (673 "If I Ever Love Again")... 40-60 67
(Promotional issue only.)
COLUMBIA (1-106 thru 1-936) 40-60 48-51
(Microgroove 33 singles.)
COLUMBIA (6-718 thru 6-936) 15-25 50-51
(45 rpm.)
COLUMBIA (3842 "I Guess I'll Have to Dream the Rest") 40-60 71
(Promotional issue only.)
COLUMBIA (12194 "All Or Nothing at All")... 30-40 55
(Promotional issue only.)
COLUMBIA (33000 series) 3-8 60s
(Hall of Fame series. With "13" prefix.)
COLUMBIA (33011 thru 39213)........ 40-60 50s
(Microgroove 33 singles. With "3" prefix.)
COLUMBIA (36814 thru 41133)........ 15-30 50-58
(45 rpm. With "4" prefix.)
COLUMBIA (50003 thru 50079)........ 10-15 55-59
(Hall of Fame series. With "4" prefix.)
COLUMBIA (116427 "White Christmas") 40-60 63
(Promotional issue only.)
"HIGH HOPES with JACK KENNEDY"/"Jack Kennedy All the Way" 150-250 60
(Presidential campaign promotional issue only. No label name or artist shown. Reportedly 1,000 made.)
RCA (15 "Getting Sentimental")........ 35-50 50
(Boxed, four-disc set.)
RCA (20 "All Time Hits").................. 35-50 51
(Boxed, four-disc set.)
RCA GOLD STANDARD SERIES........ 4-8 60-70
(With "447" prefix.)
REPRISE ("A Special Message to You from Frank Sinatra") 750-1000 61
(Single-sided. Made as a Reprise sales and promotional tool. No selection number used. Two different pressings exist.)
REPRISE (45 "Frank Sinatra reads from Gunga Din") 300-600 66
(Promotional issue only.)
REPRISE (PRO-162 thru 406).......... 25-50 63-69
(White label, promotional issues only.)
REPRISE (0243 thru 0380)................. 5-10 63-65
REPRISE (396 "Radio Spot for *Watertown*") 15-25 70
(Promotional issue only.)
REPRISE (0398 thru 1386).................. 3-8 65-77
REPRISE (20001 thru 20151) 4-8 61-63
REPRISE (20157 "California") 150-250 77
(Promotional issue only. Reportedly 1000 made.)
REPRISE (20184 "Come Blow Your Horn") 4-8 63
REPRISE (20184 "Come Blow Your Horn") 50-75 63
(White label. Promotional issue only.)
REPRISE (20209 thru 20235) 4-8 63
REPRISE (28000 & 29000 series) 3-4 82
REPRISE (40001 thru 40050) 8-10 60s
(33 rpm. Juke box issues.)
REPRISE (40063 thru 40092) 4-8
(33 rpm. Juke box issues.)
REPRISE (49000 series)........................ 3-5 80-83
REPRISE/CAL NEVADA LODGE (101 "Ring-A-Ding-Ding") 50-75 63
(Promo souvenir, available from the lodge.)

Picture Sleeves

CAPITOL (596 "All the Way")........ 250-350 58
(Promotional issue only. 101 made.)
CAPITOL (4103 "To Love and Be Loved") 250-350 58
(Promotional issue only.)
CAPITOL (4214 "High Hopes") 250-350 60
(Promotional issue only.)
REPRISE (0429 "It Was a Very Good Year").. 10-20 65
REPRISE (0531 "That's Life") 10-20 66
REPRISE (20010 "Granada")............ 10-20 61
REPRISE (20063 "Everybody's Twistin' ")... 10-20 62
REPRISE (20157 "California") 300-400 77
(Promotional issue only. Reportedly 1000 made.)
REPRISE (20184 "Come Blow Your Horn") 100-150 63
(Promotional issue only.)
REPRISE (29903-7 "To Love a Child").. 8-12 82
(Dedicated to Mrs. Nancy Reagan. With the Reprise Children's Chorus featuring Nikka Costa. Promotional issue only.)
REPRISE (49233 "New York, New York")... 3-5 80
REPRISE/CAL NEVADA LODGE (101 "Ring-A-Ding-Ding") 100-150 63
(Promo souvenir, available from the lodge.)
SINATRA.. 3-4 75

EPs: 7–inch

CAPITOL (3 "Vocal Standards").......... 5-15 60s
(33 rpm.)
CAPITOL (100 "Special 1981 Birthday Tribute") 75-125 81
(33 rpm. Promotional issue only. Includes "Thank You" insert.)
CAPITOL (280 "Disc Jockey Interview Record for the film *High Society*") 125-175 56
(Promotional issue only.)
CAPITOL 426: see SINATRA, Frank / Roger Wagner / Hollywood Bowl Symphony
CAPITOL (434 "Selections from *Pal Joey*.) 125-175 57
(Promotional issue only.)
CAPITOL (488 thru 1594)................. 8-18 53-62
(Single-disc EPs, with "EAP" prefix.)
CAPITOL (488 thru 855)............... 12-25 53-57
(Two-disc EPs, with "EBF" prefix.)
CAPITOL (SU-581 "In the Wee Small Hours").. 5-15 60s
(33 rpm.)
CAPITOL (DU-653 "Songs for Swingin' Lovers") 5-15 60s
(33 rpm.)
CAPITOL (DU-768 "This Is Sinatra")... 5-15 60s
(33 rpm.)
CAPITOL (SU-920 "Come Fly with Me")... 5-15 60s
(33 rpm.)
CAPITOL (1549 "Selections from *Can-Can*")...................................... 300-500 60
(Promotional issue only.)

CAPITOL (1762 "The Great Years")....5-15 60s
(33 rpm.)
Capitol (1864 "Come Swing with Capitol - New Albums for August 1961")...............30-50 61
(Promotional issue only.)
CAPITOL (11583 "Frank Sinatra") 10-15 60s
(33 rpm.)
COLUMBIA (112 thru 455) 40-60 50-54
(Two-disc EPs.)
COLUMBIA (1524 thru 2641) 10-25 50-59
(Single-disc EPs.)
COLUMBIA (7431 thru 9533) 10-20 55-57
(Single-disc EPs.)
COLUMBIA (10321/10322 "Christmas Dreaming")................................10-15 57
(Price is for either of two volumes.)
COLUMBIA (28595 "Nancy")..............75-100 58
(Promotional issue, made for B.T. Babbit and attached to their soap boxes. With custom cover.)
RCA (102 "Tommy Dorsey Originals")....................................10-20 60
(Compact 33 Double.)
RCA (3005 "This Is Tommy Dorsey")..25-50 50
(Two-discs.)
RCA (3028 "Getting Sentimental") 25-50 50
(Two-discs.)
RCA (3030 "All Time Hits")...............25-50 51
(Two-discs.)
RCA (3063 "Fabulous Frankie") 25-50 52
(Two-discs.)
RCA (5007 thru 5147) 12-25 58-60
RCA (6038 "This Is Tommy Dorsey")..10-15 60s
(Juke box issue only.)
REPRISE..10-15 62-74
(Juke box issues.)

LPs: 10/12–inch

CAMDEN (650 thru 800) 5-15 61-73
CAMDEN (9027 I'm Getting Sentimental Over You")..8-12 72
CAPITOL ("Radio/TV Sampler")....200-250 58
(Number unknown. Yellow label. Promotional issue only.)
CAPITOL (200 & 300 series, except LS-308)...8-15 69
CAPITOL (LS-308 "Sinatra: The Works")..75-125 71
(Boxed, 10-disc set. Includes booklet. Add $75 to $100 if accompanied by the bonus LP, *Sinatra Like Never Before*.")
CAPITOL (H-488 thru H-581)...........30-50 54-55
(10–inch LPs.)
CAPITOL (488 thru 1164, except 735)..20-30 54-59
(With "T" or "W" prefix.)
CAPITOL (W-735 "Frank Sinatra Conducts Tone Poems of Color") 75-100 56
CAPITOL (581 thru 1676)..................5-15 61-78
(With "DT," "DW," "SM," "STBB," "SW," or "W" prefix.)
CAPITOL (T-1221 thru T-1676).........10-20 59-62
(Monaural.)
CAPITOL (ST-1221 thru ST-1676).... 10-20 59-62
(Stereo.)
CAPITOL (PRO-1624 "The Best of Sinatra")..75-100 61
(Promotional issue only. Issued with paper sleeve.)
CAPITOL (1729 "Love & Things")..... 10-20 62
CAPITOL (1762 "Sinatra: The Great Years")..20-30 62
(Three-disc set.)
CAPITOL (1825 thru 2700)...............15-30 62-68
(With "T" or "W" prefix. Monaural.)
CAPITOL (1825 thru 2700)...............10-20 62-68
(With "DT" or "DW" prefix. Reprocessed stereo.)
CAPITOL (2814 "Deluxe Set")..........40-60 67
(Boxed, six-disc set.)
CAPITOL (2974 "Frank Sinatra Minute Masters")...................................100-150 65
CAPITOL (7630 "The Sinatra Touch") 50-75 68
(Boxed, six-disc set. Includes booklet.)
CAPITOL (11000 & 12000 series).......5-10 74-80
CAPITOL (16000 series)...................... 5-8 80-82
CAPITOL (89611 "Duets") 8-10 90s
CAPITOL (90000 thru 94000 series) 20-40 64-74
(Capitol Record Club issues.)
COLUMBIA (6 "The Frank Sinatra Story") 15-25 58
COLUMBIA (S3L-42 "Essential Frank Sinatra") 20-30 67
(Boxed, three LP set. Monaural.)
COLUMBIA (S3S-42 "Essential Frank Sinatra") 20-30 67
(Boxed, three-disc set. Stereo.)
COLUMBIA (S3S-842 "Essential Frank Sinatra") 10-20
(Boxed, three-disc set. Reissue.)
COLUMBIA (606 "Frankie")................ 25-40 55
(Cover pictures Sinatra wearing a hat and alone.)
COLUMBIA (606 "Frankie") 15-25 50s
(Cover pictures Sinatra not wearing a hat and with two other people.)
COLUMBIA (743 "The Voice of Sinatra") 25-35 55
COLUMBIA (902 "That Old Feeling")... 20-30 56
COLUMBIA (842 "Essential Frank Sinatra") 30-50 67
(Three-disc set. Includes booklet.)
COLUMBIA (953 "Adventures of the Heart").. 15-25 57
COLUMBIA (1032 "Christmas Dreaming").. 15-25 57
COLUMBIA (1130 thru 1359)........... 20-40 58-59
COLUMBIA (1448 "Reflections") 30-60 60
COLUMBIA (CL-2474 "Greatest Hits: The Early Years, Vol. 1") 10-15 66
(Monaural.)
COLUMBIA (2521 "Get Happy") 25-40 55
(10–inch LP.)
COLUMBIA (2539 "I've Got a Crush on You") 25-40 55
(10–inch LP.)
COLUMBIA (2542 "Christmas with Frank Sinatra") 25-40 55
(10–inch LP.)
COLUMBIA (CL-2572 "Greatest Hits: The Early Years, Vol. 2") 10-15 66
(Monaural.)
COLUMBIA (2475 "The Voice, Sampler") 10-15 86
(Samples tracks from C6X-40343.)
COLUMBIA (CL-2739 thru 2913)...... 10-15 66-69
(Monaural.)
COLUMBIA (4271 "Frank Sinatra Conducts the Music of Alec Wilder")................ 125-175 50
(Green Masterworks label.)
COLUMBIA (6001 "The Voice of Sinatra") 75-100 48
(10–inch LP.)
COLUMBIA (6059 "Frankly Sentimental")................................. 50-75 49
(10–inch LP.)
COLUMBIA (6087 "Songs By Sinatra, Vol. 1") 50-75 50
(10–inch LP.)
COLUMBIA (6096 "Dedicated to You") 50-75 50
(10–inch LP.)
COLUMBIA (6143 "Sing and Dance with Frank Sinatra") 50-75 50
(10–inch LP.)
COLUMBIA (6290 "I've Got a Crush on You") 50-75 52
(10–inch LP.)
COLUMBIA (6339 "Young at Heart").. 50-75 54
(10–inch LP.)
COLUMBIA (CS-9274 "Greatest Hits: The Early Years, Vol. 1") 8-15 66
(Stereo.)
COLUMBIA (CS-9372 "Greatest Hits: The Early Years, Vol. 2") 8-15 66
(Stereo.)
COLUMBIA (CS-9539 thru 9541)........ 8-15 66-67
(Stereo.)
COLUMBIA (10000 series).................5-10 73
COLUMBIA (30000 thru 45000 series, except 31358 & 40343).....................5-12 73-87
COLUMBIA (31358 "In the Beginning") 8-12 72
(Two-disc set.)
COLUMBIA (40343 "The Voice").......30-50 86
(Boxed, six-disc set.)
EARTH NEWS 50-100 80
(Radio show on disc. Includes cue sheet/script.)
HARMONY 10-20 66-71
KATWHISKER ("Frank Sinatra: Biography in Song")...................................750-1000 75
(Boxed, eight-disc set. Includes cue sheets. Promotional issue only. Reportedly only 25 made.)
MFSL (1 "Frank Sinatra") 350-500 85
(Boxed, 16-disc set. Includes booklet and alignment tool. Numbered edition of 25,000 made.)
MFSL (086 "Nice 'N' Easy")..............25-30 82
MFSL (130 "Swing Easy") 25-30 85
MFSL (131 "In the Wee Small Hours").......................................25-30 85
MFSL (132 "Close to You") 25-30 85
MFSL (133 "A Swingin Affair")..........25-30 85
MFSL (134 "Where You Are") 25-30 85
MFSL (2-135 "A Jolly Christmas").....30-40 85
MFSL (136 "Come Fly with Me") 25-30 85
MFSL (137 "Only the Lonely") 25-30 85
MFSL (138 "Come Dance with Me") 25-30 85
MFSL (139 "Look at Your Heart")......25-30 85
MFSL (140 "No One Cares") 25-30 85
MFSL (141 "Sinatra's Swingin").........25-30 85
MFSL (142 "All the Way")..................25-30 85
MFSL (143 "Come Swing with Me") ..25-30 85
MFSL (145 "Sinatra Swings")............25-30 85
MFSL (146 "Songs for Swingin' Lovers") 25-30 85
NARWOOD ("U.S. Army Reserve Presents William B. & Company") 150-200 76
(Two-LP, public service radio show. Has Sinatra interview. Promotional issue only.)
ODYSSEY 10-20 68
PICKWICK...5-10 70s
RCA (10 "Getting Sentimental") 35-50 50
(10–inch LP.)
RCA (15 "All Time Hits")...................35-50 51
(10–inch LP.)
RCA (017 "I'll See You in My Dreams")...8-12 70s
RCA (050 "What'll I Do") 5-8
RCA (474 "The Radio Years")............5-10 74
RCA (0497 "What'll I Do") 8-10 74
RCA (583 "This Love of Mine")............8-12
RCA (1569 "Frankie & Tommy") 20-40 57
RCA (1586 "Frank Sinatra with the Tommy Dorsey Orchestra") 5-8 75
RCA (1632 "We Three")...................20-40 57
RCA (3005 "This Is Tommy Dorsey")...25-50 50
(10–inch LP.)
RCA (3063 "Fabulous Frankie")........25-50 52
(10–inch LP.)
RCA (4334 "The Dorsey/Sinatra Sessions, Vols. 1 & 2") 8-10 82
RCA (4335 "The Dorsey/Sinatra Sessions, Vols. 3 & 4") 8-10 82
RCA (4336 "The Dorsey/Sinatra Sessions, Vols. 5 & 6") 8-10 82
RCA (6003 "The Sentimental Gentleman")...................................20-40 53
(10–inch LP.)
RCA (4700 series) 5-8 83
RCA/PAIR...5-10 84
REPRISE (R-1001 thru R-1010)........ 10-15 61-63
(Monaural.)
REPRISE (R9-1001 thru R9-1010).... 10-20 61-63
(Stereo.)
REPRISE (F-1001 thru F-1010) 5-10 60s
(Monaural reissues.)
REPRISE (FS-1001 thru FS-1010)......8-12 60s
(Stereo reissues.)
REPRISE (1011 thru 1015) 8-12 64-65

REPRISE (1016 "A Man and His Music, Part II")....................................300-400 66
(Promotional issue, made for Budweiser Beer distributors. About 1,000 made.)
REPRISE (FS4-1029 thru FS4-2207)....................................15-25 70s
(Quadrophonic.)
REPRISE (1018 thru 1034)................8-15 66-72
REPRISE (2013 thru 2022)................20-40 62-64
REPRISE (2155 thru 2275)................5-15 73-78
REPRISE (2300 "Trilogy")................15-25 80
(Three-disc set.)
REPRISE (2305 "She Shot Me Down")....................................5-8 81
REPRISE (5230 "Songbook, Vol. 1")....................................25-35 71
REPRISE (5267 "Songbook, Vol. 2")....................................50-100 72
(Two-disc set.)
REPRISE (6000 series)....................15-25 61-72
SINATRA....................................5-10 75
Also see ALI, Muhammad, & Frank Sinatra
Also see ANTHONY, Ray
Also see BLOCH, Ray, & Orchestra
Also see CROSBY, Bing / Grace Kelly / Frank Sinatra / Celeste Holm
Also see CROSBY, Bing, & Frank Sinatra
Also see DAY, Doris & Frank Sinatra
Also see DORSEY, Tommy, Orchestra
Also see JAMES, Harry
Also see KINGSTON TRIO / Frank Sinatra
Also see PRESLEY, Elvis / Frank Sinatra / Nat King Cole
Also see VINCENT, Gene / Frank Sinatra / Sonny James / Ron Goodwin
Also see ZENTNER, Si

SINATRA, Frank, & Charioteers

Singles: 78 rpm

COLUMBIA....................................5-15 45
Also see CHARIOTEERS

SINATRA, Frank, & Count Basie — LP '63

EPs: 7-inch

REPRISE (1012 "It Might As Well Be Swing")....................................8-12 63
(Promotional issue only.)

LPs: 10/12-inch

REPRISE....................................10-20 63-66
Also see BASIE, Count

SINATRA, Frank / Nat King Cole

EPs: 7-inch

CAPITOL (500 "Witchcraft")................35-55 58
(Promotional issue only.)
Also see COLE, Nat King

SINATRA, Frank, Bing Crosby & Russ Columbo

Singles: 7-inch

RCA (5 "Immortal Performances")....................................50-75 50
(Boxed three disc set, one by each artist. Includes bio/booklet.)

LPs: 10/12-inch

RCA (5 "Immortal Performances")....................................50-75 50
(10-inch LP.)

SINATRA, Frank, Bing Crosby & Dean Martin

Singles: 7-inch

REPRISE (20,217 "The Oldest Established [Permanent Floating Crap Game in New York])....................................15-25 62

Picture Sleeves

REPRISE (20,217 "The Oldest Established [Permanent Floating Crap Game in New York])....................................100-125 62

SINATRA, Frank, Bing Crosby, & Fred Waring

LPs: 10/12-inch

REPRISE....................................10-15 64
Also see CROSBY, Bing
Also see CROSBY, Bing, & Grace Kelly / Bing Crosby & Frank Sinatra
Also see WARING, Fred

SINATRA, Frank, Sammy Davis Jr. & Dean Martin — P&R '62

(Frankie, Dino & Sammy)

Singles: 7-inch

REPRISE (20,128 "Me and My Shadow"/"Sam's Song")....................................4-6 62

Picture Sleeves

REPRISE (20,128 "Me and My Shadow"/"Sam's Song")....................................10-15 62

LPs: 10/12-inch

LATIMER (247-17 "Summit Meeting at the 500, Atlantic City, N.J.")....................250-350 64
(Private issue only, by the 500 Club. Three different paste-on covers exist for this LP.)

SINATRA, Frank, & Duke Ellington — LP '68

Singles: 7-inch

REPRISE....................................3-5 68

LPs: 10/12-inch

REPRISE....................................8-15 68
Also see ELLINGTON, Duke

SINATRA, Frank, & Antonio Carlos Jobim — LP '67

LPs: 10/12-inch

REPRISE....................................8-15 67-71
Also see JOBIM, Antonio Carlos

SINATRA, Frank / Jonah Jones

Singles: 7-inch

CAPITOL (4214 "High Hopes").......50-100 60
(Promotional issue only.)

Picture Sleeves

CAPITOL (4214 "High Hopes").....300-400 60
(Promotional issue only.)

SINATRA, Frank, with Quincy Jones & His Orchestra — LP '84

Singles: 12-inch

QWEST (2216 "Mack the Knife")......25-50 84

Singles: 7-inch

QWEST....................................3-5 84

LPs: 10/12-inch

QWEST....................................5-10 84
Also see JONES, Quincy

SINATRA, Frank, Dean Martin, Sammy Davis Jr., & Bing Crosby

LPs: 10/12-inch

REPRISE (5031 "Summit").........500-1000 64
(British issue only.)
Also see CROSBY, Bing
Also see DAVIS, Sammy, Jr.
Also see MARTIN, Dean

SINATRA, Frank, & Pied Pipers

Singles: 78 rpm

RCA....................................4-8 41
Also see PIED PIPERS

SINATRA, Frank, & Keely Smith — P&R '58

Singles: 78 rpm

CAPITOL (3952 "Nothing in Common")....................................15-25 58
(This is the last commercially-issued Sinatra 78 rpm.)

Singles: 7-inch

CAPITOL (3952 "Nothing in Common")....................................5-10 58
Also see SMITH, Keely

SINATRA, Frank / Roger Wagner Chorale / Hollywood Bowl Symphony

EPs: 7-inch

CAPITOL (426 "Christmas Around the World")....................................75-100 57
(Promotional issue only.)

SINATRA, Frank & Nancy — P&R '67

(Sinatra Family)

Singles: 7-inch

REPRISE....................................3-6 66-71

LPs: 10/12-inch

REPRISE....................................8-15 69
Members: Sinatra Family included Frank Sinatra, Frank Jr., Nancy and Tina.
Also see SINATRA, Nancy

SINATRA, Nancy — P&R '65

Singles: 7-inch

ELEKTRA....................................3-5 80
PRIVATE STOCK....................................3-5 75-77
RCA....................................3-5 72-73
REPRISE....................................3-6 61-71

Picture Sleeves

REPRISE....................................4-8 62-67

EPs: 7-inch

REPRISE....................................10-12 66
(Juke box issue only.)

LPs: 10/12-inch

RCA....................................8-10 72
REPRISE....................................15-30 66-72
Also see BARRY, John
Also see MARTIN, Dean
Also see PRESLEY, Elvis
Also see SINATRA, Frank & Nancy

SINATRA, Nancy, & Lee Hazlewood — P&R/LP '68

Singles: 7-inch

PRIVATE STOCK....................................3-5 76
RCA....................................3-5 72
REPRISE....................................4-8 67-68

LPs: 10/12-inch

RCA....................................8-10 72
REPRISE....................................10-15 68
Also see HAZLEWOOD, Lee
Also see SINATRA, Nancy

SINCLAIR, Gordon — P&R '74

Singles: 7-inch

AVCO....................................3-5 74

SINFIELD, Pete — LP '73

Singles: 7-inch

MANTICORE....................................3-5 73

LPs: 10/12-inch

MANTICORE....................................8-10 73

SINGING BELLES — P&R '60

Singles: 7-inch

MADISON....................................8-10 60

SINGING DOGS — P&R '55

(Don Charles Presents the Singing Dogs)

Singles: 78 rpm

RCA....................................3-5 55

Singles: 7-inch

RCA....................................3-6 55-72

Picture Sleeves

RCA (6344 "Oh! Susanna")..............10-20 55
RCA (6432 "Hot Dog Rock & Roll") ..10-20 56

SINGING NUN — P&R/LP '63

(Janine Deckers)

Singles: 7-inch

PHILIPS....................................3-5 63-64

Picture Sleeves

PHILIPS....................................4-8 63-64

LPs: 10/12-inch

PHILIPS....................................5-15 63-69

SINGLE BULLET THEORY — P&R '83

Singles: 7-inch

NEMPEROR....................................3-4 83

Picture Sleeves

NEMPEROR....................................3-4 83

LPs: 10/12-inch

NEMPEROR....................................5-8 83

SINITTA — P&R '89

Singles: 7-inch

ATLANTIC....................................3-4 88-89
OMNI....................................3-4 87

Picture Sleeves

ATLANTIC....................................3-4 88-89

SINNAMON — D&D '83

Singles: 12-inch

BECKET....................................4-6 82-83
JIVE....................................4-6 84

Singles: 7-inch
BECKET........3-4 82-83

SIOUXSIE & BANSHEES LP '84
Singles: 12-inch
GEFFEN........4-6 84-86
PVC........4-8 80-82
Singles: 7-inch
GEFFEN........3-4 84-88
PVC........3-5 80-82
POLYDOR........3-5 79
Picture Sleeves
GEFFEN........3-4 88
LPs: 10/12-inch
GEFFEN........5-8 84-90
PVC........5-10 80-82
POLYDOR........8-10 79
Also see SEX PISTOLS

SIR CHAUNCEY P&R '60
(Ernie Freeman)
Singles: 7-inch
PATTERN........10-15 60
W.B. 4-8 60
Also see FREEMAN, Ernie

SIR DOUGLAS QUINTET P&R '65
(Sir Douglas Band)
Singles: 7-inch
ATLANTIC........4-8 73
CASABLANCA (0828 "Roll with the Punches")........5-15 75
MERCURY........3-5 71
PACEMAKER (260 "Sugar Bee")......15-20 64
PHILIPS........3-5 70-71
SMASH........4-8 68-70
TRIBE........5-10 65
(No Indian on label.)
TRIBE........4-8 65-67
(Label pictures Indian.)
Picture Sleeves
PHILIPS........3-5 70-71
LPs: 10/12-inch
ACCORD........5-10 82
ATLANTIC........10-15 73
MERCURY........10-15 72
PHILIPS........15-25 70-71
SMASH........15-25 68-70
TAKOMA........5-10 80-83
TRIBE (47001 "Best of Sir Douglas Quintet")........40-60 66
Members: Doug Sahm; Augie Meyers; Jack Barber; Leon Baetty; John Perez; Frank Morin; Jim Stallings.
Also see CASCADES / Sir Douglas Quintet
Also see SAHM, Doug

SIR LORD BALTIMORE LP '71
Singles: 7-inch
MERCURY........3-5 70-71
LPs: 10/12-inch
MERCURY........8-12 70-71

SIR MIX-A-LOT P&R/LP '88
Singles: 7-inch
NASTYMIX........3-4 88-90
Picture Sleeves
NASTYMIX........3-4 88
LPs: 10/12-inch
NASTYMIX........5-8 88-90

SIRENNE, Gianni D&D '84
Singles: 12-inch
ATLANTIC........4-6 84
Singles: 7-inch
ATLANTIC........3-4 84

SISTER SLEDGE P&R '75
Singles: 12-inch
ATLANTIC........4-6 85
COTILLION........4-8 79-83
Singles: 7-inch
ATCO........3-5 73-75
ATLANTIC........3-4 85
COTILLION........3-5 76-83
Picture Sleeves
ATLANTIC........3-4 85
LPs: 10/12-inch
ATCO........8-10 75
ATLANTIC........5-8 85
COTILLION........5-10 76-83

SISTERS OF MERCY LP '88
Singles: 12-inch
ELEKTRA........4-8 83-87
LPs: 10/12-inch
ELEKTRA........5-8 88-90
Members: Wayne Hussey; Andrew Eldritch; Doktor Avalanche; Patricia Morrison.
Also see DEAD OR ALIVE
Also see MISSION

SIX TEENS P&R '56
("Featuring 13-Year-Old Trudy Williams"; "Featuring Trudy & Louise")
Singles: 78 rpm
FLIP (315 thru 326)........15-25 56-57
FLIP (329 "My Secret")........25-50 58
Singles: 7-inch
FLIP (315 "A Casual Look")........15-25 56
FLIP (317 "Send Me Flowers")........15-25 56
FLIP (320 "My Special Guy")........15-25 56
FLIP (322 "Arrow of Love")........15-25 56
FLIP (326 "My Surprise")........15-25 57
FLIP (329 "My Secret")........15-25 58
FLIP (333 "Danny")........15-25 58
FLIP (338 "Baby-O")........15-25 58
FLIP (346 "Why Do I Go to School") 20-30 59
FLIP (350 "So Happy")........15-25 60
FLIP (351 "A Little Prayer")........15-25 60
Members: Trudy Williams; Louise Williams; Ed Wells; Beverly Pecot; Kenneth Sinclair; Darryl Lewis.

SIX TEENS / Brenda & Tabulations
Singles: 7-inch
COBRA........3-5
Also see BRENDA & TABULATIONS

SIX TEENS / Donald Woods / Richard Berry
LPs: 10/12-inch
FLIP (1001 "12 Flip Hits")........100-125 59
Also see WOODS, Donald

SKA KINGS P&R '64
Singles: 7-inch
ATLANTIC........4-8 64

SKAGGS, Ricky C&W '80
(With Tony Rice; with Sharon White)
Singles: 7-inch
EPIC........3-5 81-90
ROUNDER........3-6 80
SUGAR HILL (3700 series)........3-6 80
SUGAR HILL (04000 series)........3-5 83-84
LPs: 10/12-inch
EPIC........5-10 81-86
REBEL (1550 "That's It")........10-15 75
ROUNDER........5-10 82
SUGAR HILL........5-10 79-80
WEL DUN........10-15 78
Also see CASH, Rosanne
Also see NITTY GRITTY DIRT BAND
Also see PARTON, Dolly
Also see SCRUGGS, Earl

SKAGGS, Ricky, & Keith Whitley
LPs: 10/12-inch
REBEL........10-15 71-72
Also see SKAGGS, Ricky

SKELLERN, Peter P&R '72
Singles: 7-inch
LONDON........3-5 72
PRIVATE STOCK........3-5 75
LPs: 10/12-inch
LONDON........5-10 76

SKELTON, Red P&R '69
Singles: 78 rpm
MGM........4-6 56
Singles: 7-inch
CBS/AURAVISION ("Pledge of Allegiance")........10-15 69
(Promotional 5-inch cardboard picture disc. Made for Burger King.)
COLUMBIA........4-6 69
MGM........5-10 56
LPs: 10/12-inch
LIBERTY........10-15 65-66
Also see ASTAIRE, Fred, & Red Skelton / Helen Kane

SKHY, A.B: see A.B. SKHY

SKID ROW P&R/LP '89
Singles: 7-inch
ATLANTIC........3-4 89
EPIC........3-5 71
Picture Sleeves
ATLANTIC........3-4 89
LPs: 10/12-inch
ATLANTIC........5-8 89-91
EPIC........10-15 71

SKIP & CASUALS R&B '74
Singles: 7-inch
D.C. INT'L........3-5 74
Members: Skip Mahoney; Tracy Reid; Julius Jerome; Elwood Morgan.
Also see MAHONEY, Skip, & Casuals

SKIP & FLIP P&R '59
Singles: 7-inch
BRENT........10-20 59-62
COLLECTABLES........3-4 80s
ERIC........3-4 70s
TIME........8-12 61
Members: Clyde "Skip" Battin; Gary Paxton.
Also see GARY & CLYDE
Also see PLEDGES

SKIPWORTH & TURNER D&D '85
Singles: 12-inch
4TH & BROADWAY........4-6 85
W.B. 4-6 86
Singles: 7-inch
4TH & BROADWAY........3-4 85
W.B. 3-4 86
LPs: 10/12-inch
W.B. 5-8 86
Members: Rodney Skipworth; Philip Turner.

SKO: see SCHUYLER, KNOBLOCH & OVERSTREET

SKOOL BOYZ R&B '81
Singles: 12-inch
COLUMBIA........4-6 84-85
Singles: 7-inch
COLUMBIA........3-4 84-85
DESTINY........3-5 81-82
LPs: 10/12-inch
DESTINY........5-10 81
Members: Stan Sheppard; Bill Sheppard; Chauncy Matthews.
Also see TRIPLE "S" CONNECTION

SKRATCH D&D '85
Singles: 12-inch
PASSION........4-6 85

SKY LP '70
Singles: 7-inch
RCA........3-5 71-72
LPs: 10/12-inch
RCA........10-12 70-71

SKY LP '80
Singles: 7-inch
ARISTA........3-5 81
LPs: 10/12-inch
ARISTA........8-10 80
Member: Doug Fieger.
Also see KNACK

SKYLARK P&R/LP '73
Singles: 7-inch
CAPITOL........3-5 72-73
Picture Sleeves
CAPITOL........3-5 73
LPs: 10/12-inch
CAPITOL........8-10 72-74

Members: Donny Gerrard; Carl Graves; B.J. Cook; David Foster; Duris Maxwell; Norm McPherson; Steven Pugsley.
Also see GERRARD, Donny
Also see GRAVES, Carl

SKYLINERS P&R '59
(Jimmy Beaumont & Skyliners; with Lenny Martin Orchestra.)
Singles: 12-inch
TORTOISE INT'L (11345 "Love Bug")....8-10 76
(Promotional issue only.)
Singles: 7-inch
ATCO (6270 "Since I Fell for You")...25-35 63
CALICO (103 "Since I Don't Have You")....20-30 59
CALICO (106 "This I Swear")....20-30 59
CALICO (109 "It Happened Today")..20-30 59
CALICO (114 "How Much")....15-25 60
CALICO (117 "Pennies from Heaven")....15-25 60
CALICO (120 "Believe Me")....15-25 60
CAMEO (215 "Three Coins in the Fountain")....15-25 62
CAPITOL (3979 "I Could Have Loved You")....15-25 75
CLASSIC ARTISTS....3-5 90
COAST....5-8
COLPIX (188 "I'll Close My Eyes")....20-30 61
COLPIX (613 "Close Your Eyes")....20-30 61
JUBILEE....8-12 65-66
ORIGINAL SOUND (35 thru 37)....5-10 63
ORIGINAL SOUND (4500 series)....3-4 84
TORTOISE INT'L....4-8 77
VIRGO....3-5 73
VISCOUNT (104 "Comes Love")....15-25 62
LPs: 10/12-inch
CALICO (3000 "Skyliners")....150-250 59
KAMA SUTRA (2026 "Once Upon a Time")....15-25 71
ORIGINAL SOUND (5010 "Since I Don't Have You")....15-25 63
(Monaural.)
ORIGINAL SOUND (8873 "Since I Don't Have You")....20-30 64
(Stereo.)
ORIGINAL SOUND (8873 "Greatest Hits")....5-10 87
(Reissued using same number, but with 20 tracks.)
RELIC....5-10
TORTOISE INT'L....8-10 78
Members: Jimmy Beaumont; Janet Vogel; Wally Lester; Jack Taylor; Joe Verscharen.
Also see BEAUMONT, Jimmy

SKYLINERS / Preston Epps
Singles: 7-inch
OLDIES 45....3-5 60s
Also see EPPS, Preston

SKYLINERS / Wade Flemons
Singles: 7-inch
OLDIES 45....3-5 60s
Also see FLEMONS, Wade
Also see SKYLINERS

SKYNYRD, Lynyrd: see LYNYRD SKYNYRD

SKYY LP '79
Singles: 12-inch
CAPITOL....4-6 86
SALSOUL....4-8 79-85
Singles: 7-inch
CAPITOL....3-4 86
SALSOUL....3-5 79-85
Picture Sleeves
CAPITOL....3-4 86
LPs: 10/12-inch
ATLANTIC....5-8 89
CAPITOL....5-8 86
SALSOUL....5-10 79-83
Members: Denise Dunning; Bonnie Dunning; Delores Dunning; Solomon Roberts; Anibal Sierra; Larry Greenberg; Tommy McConnell; Gerald LaBou.

SLACK, Freddie: see MORSE, Ella Mae

SLADE P&R/LP '72
Singles: 7-inch
CBS ASSOCIATED....3-4 84-85
COTILLION....3-5 71-72
POLYDOR....3-5 72-73
REPRISE....3-5 73
W.B. 3-5 73-76
LPs: 10/12-inch
CBS ASSOCIATED....5-8 84-85
COTILLION....10-15 70
POLYDOR....8-10 72-73
REPRISE....10-12 73
W.B. 8-10 74-76

SLADES P&R '58
Singles: 7-inch
DOMINO (500 "You Cheated")....35-45 58
(Add $50 to $75 if accompanied by photo/bio insert.)
DOMINO (800 "You Gambled")....25-35 58
DOMINO (901 "Just You")....20-30 59
DOMINO (906 "It's Your Turn")....25-35 61
DOMINO (1000 "You Must Try")....20-30 61
LIBERTY (55118 "You Mean Everything to Me")....15-25 58
Picture Sleeves
DOMINO (901 "Just You")....40-60 59
Member: Don Burch.
Also see SPADES

SLATKIN, Felix, Orchestra P&R '60
Singles: 7-inch
LIBERTY....5-10 60-62
LPs: 10/12-inch
ANGEL....5-10 72
CAPITOL....10-15 59
LIBERTY....10-15 60-64
SUNSET....5-10 66-68
U.A. 5-10 71

SLAUGHTER P&R/LP '90
Singles: 7-inch
CHRYSALIS....3-4 90
LPs: 10/12-inch
BITE BACK....5-10 80
CHRYSALIS....5-8 90
DJM....5-10 80
Members: Mark Slaughter; Dana Strum; Mike Ross; Eddie Garrity; Howard; Bates; Phil Rowland.
Also see VINCENT, Vinnie, Invasion

SLAVE P&R/LP '77
(Slave-Arrington)
Singles: 12-inch
COTILLION....4-6 83
Singles: 7-inch
COTILLION....3-5 77-84
ICHIBAN....3-4 86-87
LPs: 10/12-inch
COTILLION....5-10 77-84
ICHIBAN....5-8 86
Members: Steve Arrington; Floyd Miller; Steve Washington; Charles Bradley; Tom Lockett, Jr.; Mark Adams; Mark Hicks; Danny Webster; Orion Wilhoite; Tim Dozier; Starleana Young.
Also see ARRINGTON, Steve
Also see AURRA
Also see DEJA

SLAY, Frank, & His Orchestra P&R '61
Singles: 7-inch
SCA....4-8 63
SWAN....8-10 61
Also see ANDREWS, Lee
Also see CANNON, Freddy
Also see LY-DELLS

SLAY RIDERS
(Frank Slay & Orchestra)
Singles: 7-inch
ATCO....5-10 63
Also see SLAY, Frank, & His Orchestra

SLAYER LP '86
Singles: 7-inch
METAL BLADE....3-4 85
LPs: 10/12-inch
DEF AMERICAN....5-8 90
DEF JAM....5-8 86-88
ENIGMA (72015 "Live Undead")....15-25 85
(Picture disc.)
ENIGMA/METAL BLADE....5-8 85
W.B. (45522 "Divine Intervention")....8-10 90s

SLEDGE, Percy P&R/LP '66
Singles: 7-inch
ATLANTIC....4-8 66-72
CAPRICORN....3-6 74-76
MONUMENT....3-5 83
RIPETE....3-4 89
EPs: 7-inch
ATLANTIC (8180 "Take Time to Know Her")....20-30 68
LPs: 10/12-inch
ATLANTIC....10-20 66-69
CAPRICORN....8-10 74-75
MONUMENT....5-10 83
Also see JACKSON, Chuck / Percy Sledge

SLEDGE, Sister: see SISTER SLEDGE

SLEEPY KING: see KING, Sleepy

SLEEZE BEEZ LP '90
LPs: 10/12-inch
ATLANTIC....5-8 90

SLICK, Grace LP '68
(With the Great Society)
Singles: 7-inch
GRUNT....4-6 72-74
RCA....3-5 80-81
Picture Sleeves
RCA....3-5 80
LPs: 10/12-inch
COLUMBIA (CS-9624 "Conspicuous Only")....20-30 68
COLUMBIA (PC-9624 "Conspicuous Only")....5-10
COLUMBIA (CS-9702 "How It Was") 15-20 68
COLUMBIA (30459 "Collector's Item")....10-15 71
GRUNT....8-12 74
HARMONY....10-15 71
RCA....5-10 80-83
Promotional LPs
RCA ("*Dreams* Interview")....25-30 80
RCA (3922 "*Wrecking Ball* Interview")....20-30 81
RCA (3923 "Special Radio Series")..10-15 81
RCA (13708 "Interview LP")....5-10 80s
Also see CROSBY, David
Also see GREAT!! SOCIETY!!
Also see JEFFERSON AIRPLANE
Also see KANTNER, Paul, & Grace Slick

SLICK RICK LP '89
LPs: 10/12-inch
DEF JAM....5-8 88

SLIM, Guitar: see GUITAR SLIM

SLIM, Tarheel: see TARHEEL SLIM

SLIM & ANN: see TARHEEL SLIM & Little Ann

SLIM HARPO: see HARPO, Slim

SLINGSHOT D&D '83
Singles: 12-inch
QUALITY/RFC....4-6 83
Singles: 7-inch
QUALITY/RFC....3-4 83

SLOAN, P.F. P&R '65

(Phil Sloan; Phillip "Flip" Sloan)

Singles: 7-inch

ATCO....4-6 69
DUNHILL....4-8 65-67
MART (802 "She's My Girl")....50-75 60
MUMS....3-5 72

Picture Sleeves

DUNHILL (4064 "Sunflower")....5-8 67

LPs: 10/12-inch

ATCO....10-15 68
DUNHILL....10-20 65-66
MUMS....8-10 72
RHINO....5-8 86

Also see FANTASTIC BAGGYS
Also see GRASS ROOTS
Also see SLOAN, Flip

SLY

(Sly Stone; Sly Stewart)

Singles: 7-inch

AUTUMN (14 "Buttermilk")....10-15 65
AUTUMN (26 "Temptation Walk")....10-15 65

Also see SLY & FAMILY STONE
Also see STEWART, Sly
Also see STONE, Sly

SLY & FAMILY STONE P&R/LP '68

Singles: 12-inch

EPIC....4-8 79

Singles: 7-inch

EPIC....3-6 67-75
W.B....3-5 79-85

Picture Sleeves

EPIC....3-6 68-70

EPs: 7-inch

EPIC....15-20 60s
(Juke box only.)

LPs: 10/12-inch

EPIC (264 "Everything You Always Wanted to Hear")....10-20 76
(Promotional issue only.)
EPIC (26000 series)....10-15 67-69
EPIC (KE-30325 "Greatest Hits")....8-12 70
EPIC (PE-30325 "Greatest Hits")....5-10 70s
EPIC (EQ-30325 "Greatest Hits")....25-50 73
(Quadrophonic. Has some true stereo tracks that were rechanneled on earlier issues.)
EPIC (30335 thru 37071)....5-10 70-81
W.B....5-10 79-83

Members: Sylvester "Sly Stone" Stewart; Rose Stone; Larry Graham; Fred Stone; Gregg Errico; Jerry Martini.

Also see BANKS, Rose
Also see GRAHAM, Larry
Also see RUBICON
Also see SLY
Also see STEWART, Sly
Also see STEWART BROTHERS
Also see STONE, Sly

SLY FOX P&R '85

Singles: 12-inch

CAPITOL....4-6 85-86

Singles: 7-inch

CAPITOL....3-4 85-86

Picture Sleeves

CAPITOL....3-4 86

LPs: 10/12-inch

CAPITOL....5-8 86

Members: Mike Camacho; Gary Cooper.

SMALL, Millie P&R/LP '64

("The Blue Beat Girl")

Singles: 7-inch

ATCO....5-10 65
ATLANTIC....5-10 64
BRIT....5-10 65
SMASH....4-8 64

LPs: 10/12-inch

SMASH....15-25 64

SMALL FACES P&R '67

Singles: 7-inch

IMMEDIATE....5-10 67-68
PRESS....8-12 65-68
RCA....8-12 66
W.B....4-8 70-75

Picture Sleeves

IMMEDIATE (5003 "Tin Soldier")....10-20 68
W.B....5-10 73

LPs: 10/12-inch

ABKCO....8-12 73
ACCORD....5-10 82
ATLANTIC....8-10 77-78
COMPLEAT....5-8 86
IMMEDIATE (002 "There Are But Four Small Faces")....20-30 68
IMMEDIATE (008 "Ogden's Nut Gone Flake")....20-30 68
IMMEDIATE (4225 "Ogden's Nut Gone Flake")....10-15 73
MGM....10-15 74
PRIDE....10-15 72-73
SIRE....10-15
W.B....10-15 70

Members: Steve Marriott; Ronnie Lane; Kenny Jones; Ian McLagen.

Also see FACES
Also see HUMBLE PIE
Also see McLAGAN, Ian
Also see PYTHON LEE JACKSON
Also see WHO

SMITH P&R/LP '69

Singles: 7-inch

DUNHILL....4-6 69-70
GOLDIES....3-5 73
ROULETTE....3-5 70s

Picture Sleeves

DUNHILL....4-8 69

LPs: 10/12-inch

DUNHILL....10-15 69-70

Member: Gayle McCormick.

Also see McCORMICK, Gayle

SMITH, Arthur C&W/P&R '48

(Arthur "Guitar Boogie" Smith; with Crossroads Quartet)

Singles: 78 rpm

MGM....5-10 48-57
SUPER DISC (1004 "Guitar Boogie")....20-30 48

Singles: 7-inch

MGM (10229 thru 12791)....5-15 49-60
STARDAY....4-8 63

EPs: 7-inch

DOT (600 "Original Guitar Boogie")....8-12 64
(Stereo. Juke box issue only.)
MGM....10-20 51-56

LPs: 10/12-inch

ABC-PAR....15-25 63
DOT....10-15 64-66
FOLKWAYS....10-15 64
HAMILTON....10-15 64
MGM (236 "Foolish Questions")....25-35 54
(10-inch LP.)
MGM (533 "Fingers on Fire")....25-35 51
(10-inch LP.)
MGM (3301 "Specials")....25-35 56
MONUMENT....6-12 70-75
NASHVILLE....8-12 68
STARDAY (186 thru 415)....10-30 62-68

Also see HAMILTON, George, IV / Arthur Smith

SMITH, Bessie P&R '23

Singles: 78 rpm

COLUMBIA (3000 & 4000 series)....25-50 23
COLUMBIA (13000 & 14000 series)....25-50 23-33
OKEH (8000 series)....20-30 31

Singles: 7-inch

OKEH (6893 "Gimmie a Pig Foot")....20-30 52

LPs: 10/12-inch

COLUMBIA....10-15 70-72

SMITH, Betty P&R '58

(Betty Smith Group)

Singles: 7-inch

ECHO (584 "Oh Yeah")....20-30
LONDON....5-10 58

SMITH, Bro P&R '76

Singles: 7-inch

BIG TREE....3-5 76

Picture Sleeves

BIG TREE....3-5 76

SMITH, Carl C&W '51

(With the Tunesmiths)

Singles: 78 rpm

COLUMBIA....5-10 51-57

Singles: 7-inch

ABC/HICKORY....3-5 76-78
COLUMBIA (20000 & 21000 series)....8-15 51-56
COLUMBIA (40823 thru 42858)....4-10 57-63
COLUMBIA (42949 thru 45923)....3-8 64-73
HICKORY....3-5 74-76

Picture Sleeves

COLUMBIA....5-10 59

EPs: 7-inch

COLUMBIA (2801 thru 10223)....8-15 57-58
COLUMBIA (10964 "Taste of Country")....5-10 72
(Juke box issue.)
COLUMBIA (11721)....8-15 58

LPs: 10/12-inch

ABC/HICKORY....10-15 77-78
COLUMBIA (31 "Anniversary Album")....8-12 70
COLUMBIA (DS-341 thru DS-517)....5-15
(Record club issues.)
COLUMBIA (900 thru 1100 series)....25-50 57-58
COLUMBIA (1500 thru 2600 series)....10-20 60-69
COLUMBIA (2579 "Carl Smith")....50-75 56
(10-inch LP.)
COLUMBIA (8300 thru 9800 series)....10-20 60-72
COLUMBIA (9023 "Sentimental Songs")....50-75 54
(10-inch LP.)
COLUMBIA (9026 "Softly and Tenderly")....50-75 54
(10-inch LP.)
COLUMBIA (10000 series)....5-10 73
COLUMBIA (30000 series)....10-20 70-84
COLUMBIA SPECIAL PRODUCTS (8000 series)....10-15
COUNTRY CLASSICS....5-10
GUSTO....5-8 80
HICKORY....5-10 75
HARMONY....5-15 64-72
LAKE SHORE....5-10

Session: Lewis Pruitt.

Also see PRICE, Ray / Lefty Frizzell / Carl Smith
Also see PRICE, Ray / Johnny Horton / Carl Smith / George Morgan

SMITH, Carl / Lefty Frizzell / Marty Robbins

LPs: 10/12-inch

COLUMBIA (2544 "Carl, Lefty & Marty")....150-250 56
(10-inch LP.)

Also see FRIZZELL, Lefty
Also see ROBBINS, Marty
Also see SMITH, Carl

SMITH, Connie C&W '64

Singles: 7-inch

COLUMBIA....3-5 73-77
EPIC....3-4 85
MONUMENT....3-5 77-83
RCA....3-8 64-74

Picture Sleeves

RCA....4-6 67

LPs: 10/12-inch

CAMDEN....5-10 67-72
COLUMBIA....5-10 73-77
MONUMENT....5-8 77-78
RCA (0100 thru 1200 series)....5-10 73-75
RCA (3300 thru 4800 series)....8-15 65-73

SMITH, Connie, & Nat Stuckey C&W '70

Singles: 7-inch

RCA....3-5 70

Also see SMITH, Connie

SMITH, Frankie P&R/LP '81

Singles: 12-inch

WMOT....4-6 81

Singles: 7–inch

WMOT 3-5 81

LPs: 10/12–inch

WMOT 5-10 81

SMITH, Hank

(George Jones; with Nashville Playboys; Hank Smith / Bud Roman & Topppers / "Scat" Benny / Sue Richards / Bob Sandy)

Singles: 78 rpm

GILMAR 30-40 50s

EPs: 7–inch

HOLLYWOOD HIT CLUB (280 "Heartbreak Hotel") 30-50 56
TOPS (280 "Heartbreak Hotel") 30-40 56
Also see JONES, George

SMITH, Huey — P&R '57

(With His Band; with Clowns; with Pitter Pats; Huey "Piano" Smith)

Singles: 78 rpm

ACE 10-25 56-58
SAVOY 20-30 54

Singles: 7–inch

ABC 3-5 73
ACE (521 thru 571) 10-15 56-59
ACE (584 thru 672) 5-10 60-65
COLLECTABLES 3-4 80s
CONSTELLATION 4-8 63
COTILLION 3-5 72
IMPERIAL 5-10 61
INSTANT 4-8 68-69
OLDIES 45 .... 4-6 64
SAVOY (1113 "You Made Me Cry") .. 40-60 54
VIN 5-10 60

EPs: 7–inch

ACE (104 "Having Fun") 50-75 59

LPs: 10/12–inch

ACE (1004 "Having Fun") 75-125 59
ACE (1015 "For Dancing") 50-100 61
ACE (1027 "'Twas the Night Before Christmas") 50-100 62
ACE (2021 "Rock & Roll Revival") 25-35 74
GRAND PRIX 10-20 60s
Session: Lee Allen.
Also see ALLEN, Lee
Also see CHIMES / Huey "Piano" Smith
Also see FORD, Frankie
Also see KING, Earl
Also see MARCHAN, Bobby

SMITH, Hurricane — P&R '72

Singles: 7–inch

CAPITOL 3-5 72-73
EMI 3-5 74

LPs: 10/12–inch

CAPITOL 8-10 72

SMITH, Jerry — C&W/P&R/LP '69

(With His Pianos)

Singles: 7–inch

ABC 3-5 69
AD 4-8 59-61
CHART 4-6 67
DECCA 3-5 70-72
RANWOOD 3-5 73-78
RICE 4-6 67
SOUND STAGE 7 .... 4-8 65

LPs: 10/12–inch

ABC 5-10 69
DECCA 5-10 70-72
RANWOOD 5-8 73-75
Also see DIXIEBELLES
Also see MAGIC ORGAN

SMITH, Jimmie

(Gene Autry)

Singles: 78 rpm

TIMELY TUNES (1554 "I'm a Truthful Fellow") 25-75
TIMELY TUNES (1555 "I'm Blue and Lonesome") 25-75
TIMELY TUNES (1556 "Bear Cat Mama from Horner Corner") 25-75
TIMELY TUNES (1557 "She's a Hum Dinger") 25-75
Also see AUTRY, Gene

SMITH, Jimmy — P&R/LP '62

Singles: 7–inch

BLUE NOTE 4-8 56-63
MGM 3-4 78
MERCURY 3-4 77
PRIDE 3-5 74
VERVE 3-6 62-73

LPs: 10/12–inch

BLUE NOTE 40-80 56-60
(Label gives New York street address for Blue Note Records.)
BLUE NOTE 20-30 61-63
(Label reads "Blue Note Records Inc. - New York, USA.")
BLUE NOTE 10-20 66-73
(Label shows Blue Note Records as a division of either Liberty or United Artists.)
COBBLESTONE 6-12 72
ELEKTRA 5-10 82-83
GUEST STAR 8-12 64
INNER CITY 5-10 81
MGM 8-12 70
MERCURY 5-10 77-78
METRO 8-15 67
MOJO 5-10 75
PRIDE 5-10 74
SUNSET 5-10 70
VERVE 10-25 63-72
(Reads "MGM Records - A Division of Metro-Goldwyn-Mayer, Inc." at bottom of label.)
VERVE 5-10 73-84
(Reads "Manufactured By MGM Record Corp.," or mentions either Polydor or Polygram at bottom of label.)
Also see BURRELL, Kenny, & Jimmy Smith

SMITH, Jimmy, & Wes Montgomery — LP '67

LPs: 10/12–inch

VERVE 10-20 66-69
Also see MONTGOMERY, Wes
Also see SMITH, Jimmy

SMITH, Kate — P&R '27

(With Guy Lombardo's Orchestra)

Singles: 78 rpm

COLUMBIA 3-6 27-46
VICTOR 3-6 38-42
MGM 3-5 48

Singles: 7–inch

ATLANTIC 3-5 74
CRICKET 4-8
MGM 3-4 78
RCA 3-5 63-68
TOPS 4-6 60

Picture Sleeves

RCA 4-8 63-64

EPs: 7–inch

MGM 4-8 52-57
RCA 4-8 59

LPs: 10/12–inch

CAMDEN 4-8 70-73
CAPITOL 5-15 54-57
COLUMBIA (6000 series) 10-20 50
(10–inch LPs.)
HARMONY 5-12 57
KAPP 5-15 58
LION 5-12 57-60
MGM 5-15 52-66
METRO 5-10 67
RCA 5-15 63-80
RONDO 5-10 60s
TOPS 5-10
Also see LOMBARDO, Guy

SMITH, Keely — LP '58

Singles: 78 rpm

CAPITOL 3-8 56-58

Singles: 7–inch

ATLANTIC 4-6 67
CAPITOL 5-15 56-58
DOLTON 3-5 64
DOT 5-10 59-62
RCA 3-6 66-71
REPRISE 4-8 63-66

Picture Sleeves

DOT 8-12 60

EPs: 7–inch

CAPITOL 10-15 58-59
DOT 8-12 60

LPs: 10/12–inch

CAPITOL 10-25 58-75
DOT 10-15 59-62
HARMONY 5-10 69
REPRISE 8-15 63-65
Also see PRIMA, Louis, & Keely Smith
Also see SINATRA, Frank, & Keely Smith

SMITH, Lonnie — LP '70

Singles: 7–inch

BLUE NOTE 3-6 69-70
GROOVE MERCHANT 3-5 75
LRC 3-5 78-79

LPs: 10/12–inch

BLUE NOTE 8-15 68-70
COLUMBIA 10-15 67
GROOVE MERCHANT 5-10 75-76
KUDU 5-10 71
LRC 5-10 78

SMITH, Lonnie Liston — LP '75

(With the Cosmic Echoes)

Singles: 12–inch

COLUMBIA 4-8 79

Singles: 7–inch

COLUMBIA 3-5 78-80
DOCTOR JAZZ 3-4 83
FLYING DUTCHMAN 3-5 75-76
RCA 3-5 77

LPs: 10/12–inch

COLUMBIA 5-10 78-79
DOCTOR JAZZ 5-8 83
FLYING DUTCHMAN 6-12 73-76
RCA 5-10 76-77

SMITH, O.C. — P&R/LP '68

(Ocie Smith)

Singles: 78 rpm

CADENCE 5-10 56-57
MGM 5-10 56

Singles: 7–inch

BIG TOP 4-8 60
BROADWAY 10-20
CADENCE 8-12 56-57
CARIBOU 3-5 76-77
CITATION 8-12 59
COLUMBIA 3-8 66-74
FAMILY 3-5 80
GORDY 3-5 82
MGM 10-15 56
MOTOWN 3-5 82
RENDEZVOUS 3-4 86-87
SHADYBROOK 3-4 78
SOUL WEST 3-5 72
SOUTH BAY 3-4 82

Picture Sleeves

COLUMBIA 4-8 69

LPs: 10/12–inch

CARIBOU 5-10 79
COLUMBIA 8-12 67-74
HARMONY 8-10 71
MGM 8-10 72
MOTOWN 5-10 82
SOUTH BAY 5-8 82

SMITH, Patti — LP '75

(Patti Smith Group)

Singles: 7–inch

ARISTA 3-5 76-79
MER (601 "Hey Joe") 50-75 74
SIRE 3-6 74-77

Picture Sleeves

ARISTA 4-8 78-79

LPs: 10/12–inch

ARISTA 6-12 75-88
Members: Patti Smith; Ivan Kral; Jay Dee Daugherty; Lenny Kaye; Allen Lanier; Richard Sohl; Andy Paley.

SMITH, Ray — P&R '60

Singles: 7–inch

ABC 3-5 73

CELEBRITY CIRCLE 5-10 64
CINNAMON 3-5 73-74
COLLECTABLES 3-4 80s
CORONA 3-5 75-77
DIAMOND 4-8 65
HEART (250 "Gone Baby Gone") . 150-200 50s
INFINITY 5-10 61
JUDD 10-20 59-61
NATIONAL 10-20
SMASH 4-8 62
SSS INT'L 3-5 70s
SSS/SUN 3-5 70s
SUN (298 "Right Behind You Baby") . 20-30 58
SUN (308 "Why Why Why") 15-25 59
SUN (319 thru 375) 10-20 59-62
TOLLIE 8-10 64
VEE JAY 5-10 64
W.B. 5-10 63
WIX 3-5 78

LPs: 10/12-inch

BOOT 5-10 78
JUDD (701 "Travelin' with Ray") 200-300 60
T (56062 "Best of Ray Smith") 20-30
WIX 10-15

Also see DONNER, Ral / Ray Smith / Bobby Dale

SMITH, Ray / Pat Cupp

LPs: 10/12-inch

CROWN 15-25 63

Also see SMITH, Ray

SMITH, Rex — P&R/LP '79

Singles: 7-inch

COLUMBIA 3-5 76-81

Picture Sleeves

COLUMBIA 3-5 79-80

LPs: 10/12-inch

COLUMBIA 5-10 76-81

SMITH, Rex, & Rachel Sweet

Singles: 7-inch

COLUMBIA 3-5 81

Picture Sleeves

COLUMBIA 3-5 81

Also see SMITH, Rex
Also see SWEET, Rachel

SMITH, Richard Jon — D&D '83

Singles: 12-inch

JIVE 4-6 83

Singles: 7-inch

JIVE 3-4 83

LPs: 10/12-inch

JIVE 5-8 83

SMITH, Roger — P&R '59

Singles: 7-inch

JEROME 4-8 61
W.B. 5-10 59

Picture Sleeves

W.B. 10-15 59

LPs: 10/12-inch

W.B. (1305 "Beach Romance") 30-40 59

SMITH, Sammi — C&W '68

Singles: 7-inch

COLUMBIA 3-8 67-69
CYCLONE 3-5 79
ELEKTRA 3-5 75-78
MEGA 3-5 70-76
SOUND FACTORY 3-4 80-82
STEP ONE 3-4 86
TRIP 3-4 74
ZODIAC 3-4 76

Picture Sleeves

MEGA 3-5 70

LPs: 10/12-inch

BARNABY 5-10
BUCKBOARD 5-10 70s
CYCLONE 5-8 79
ELEKTRA 5-10 76-78
HARMONY 5-10 71
MEGA 5-10 70-75
PICKWICK 5-10 70s
SOUND FACTORY 3-4 80-82
STEP ONE 3-4 85-86
TRIP 5-8 74
U.A. 5-10 75
ZODIAC 5-8 76

Also see HART, Freddie / Sammi Smith / Jerry Reed
Also see NELSON, Willie
Also see STEVENS, Even, & Sammi Smith

SMITH, Somethin,' & Redheads — P&R '55

Singles: 78 rpm

EPIC 4-8 54-57

Singles: 7-inch

EPIC 5-10 54-59
MGM 4-6 61

Picture Sleeves

EPIC 10-15 58

EPs: 7-inch

EPIC 10-20 59

LPs: 10/12-inch

EPIC 15-25 59
MGM 10-20 61

SMITH, Tab — P&R '51

(With His Band; with His Orchestra; with Robie Kirk & the Ruppert-Aires)

Singles: 78 rpm

ARCO 5-10 48
ATLANTIC 10-15 52
CHESS 5-10 52
DECCA 5-10 44
EBONY 5-10 46
HARLEM 5-10 46
HUB 5-10 45-46
KING 5-10 46
MANOR 5-10 44-48
QUEEN 5-10 46
REGIS 5-10 44
SOUTHERN 5-10 46
20TH CENTURY 5-10 45
UNITED 5-15 51-57

Singles: 7-inch

ARGO 10-20 58-59
ATLANTIC (961 "Echo Blues") 15-25 52
B&F 10-15 61
CHECKER 10-15 59
CHESS 20-40 52
EBONY (1008 "Romance Time") 50-100 58
KING (4000 series) 20-40 52
KING (5000 series) 10-15 60-61
UNITED (Black vinyl) 15-25 51-57
UNITED (Colored vinyl) 25-50 51

EPs: 7-inch

KING 10-20 54

LPs: 10/12-inch

CHECKER (2971 "Keeping Tab") 25-50 59
(Black vinyl.)
CHECKER (2971 "Keeping Tab") ... 50-100 59
(Colored vinyl. Promotional issue only.)
UNITED (001 "Music Styled by Tab Smith") 75-125 52
UNITED (003 "Red Hot and Cool Blue Moods") 50-100 53

SMITH, Verdelle — P&R '66

Singles: 7-inch

CAPITOL 4-8 66-67
COLUMBIA 4-8 65
JANUS 3-5 75

Picture Sleeves

COLUMBIA 4-8 65

LPs: 10/12-inch

CAPITOL 15-25 66
JANUS 8-10 75

SMITH, Warren — P&R '57

Singles: 78 rpm

QUALITY 50-100 56
(Canadian.)
SUN 50-100 56-57

Singles: 7-inch

LIBERTY 4-8 60-64
MERCURY 4-6 68
QUALITY (1558 "Ubangi Stomp") 40-60 56
(Canadian.)
SUN (239 "Rock 'N' Roll Ruby") 50-100 56
SUN (250 "Ubangi Stomp") 40-60 56
SUN (268 thru 314) 15-25 57-59
SSS/SUN 3-5 80
W.B. 10-20 59

LPs: 10/12-inch

LIBERTY (3199 "First Country Collection") 35-45 61
(Monaural.)
LIBERTY (7199 "First Country Collection") 40-60 61
(Stereo.)

SMITH, Warren, & Shirley Collie — C&W '61

Singles: 7-inch

LIBERTY 5-10 61

Also see SMITH, Warren

SMITH, Whistling Jack — P&R '67

Singles: 7-inch

DERAM 4-6 67-69

LPs: 10/12-inch

DERAM 10-15 67

SMITHEREENS — LP '86

Singles: 7-inch

CAPITOL/ENIGMA 3-4 88
ENIGMA 3-5 85-86

Picture Sleeves

CAPITOL/ENIGMA 3-4 88
ENIGMA 3-5 85-86

LPs: 10/12-inch

CAPITOL/ENIGMA 5-8 88-89
ENIGMA 5-10 85-89

Members: Pat Dinizio; Jim Babjak; Dennis Diken; Mike Mesaros.

SMITHS — LP '84

Singles: 12-inch

SIRE 4-6 84-86

Singles: 7-inch

SIRE 3-4 84-88

LPs: 10/12-inch

SIRE 5-8 84-88

Members: Andy Rourke; Mike Joyce.
Also see O'CONNOR, Sinead

SMOKE RING — P&R '69

Singles: 7-inch

BUDDAH 4-8 69
CERTRON 3-5 70
MALA 5-10 67

SMOKESTACK LIGHTNIN' — LP '69

Singles: 7-inch

BELL 4-6 68-70
WHITE WHALE 4-6 67

LPs: 10/12-inch

BELL 10-15 69

SMOKIE — P&R '75

(Smokey)

Singles: 7-inch

MCA 3-5 75
RSO 3-5 76-79

LPs: 10/12-inch

MCA 8-10 75
RSO 5-10 76-79

Members: Chris Norman; Terry Utley; Peter Spencer.
Also see QUATRO, Suzi, & Chris Norman

SMOTHERS, Dick

Singles: 7-inch

MERCURY (72717 "Saturday Night at the World") 10-20 67

Picture Sleeves

MERCURY (72717 "Saturday Night at the World") 15-25 67

Also see SMOTHERS BROTHERS

SMOTHERS BROTHERS — LP '62

Singles: 7-inch

MERCURY 5-10 62-65
SMOTHERS INCORPORATED ("The Christmas Bunny") 25-35 69
(No selection number used. Promotional issue only.)

Picture Sleeves

MERCURY (72483 "Three Song") 8-12 64

MERCURY (72519 "The Toy Song")... 8-12 65
SMOTHERS INCORPORATED ("The Christmas Bunny") ... 25-50 69
(Promotional issue only.)

EPs: 7–inch

MERCURY (104 "Comedy Hour") ... 10-15 68
(Promotional issue only.)
MERCURY (628 "Two Sides") ... 10-20 62

LPs: 10/12–inch

MERCURY (20 "Best of the Smothers Brothers") ... 25-35 64
(Promotional issue only.)
MERCURY (25 "Brothers Smothers Month") ... 25-35 64
(Promotional issue only. Open-end interview.)
MERCURY (20000 series, except 20904) ... 10-20 61-68
(Monaural.)
MERCURY (20904 "It Must Have Been Something I Said") ... 15-20 64
(Commercial issue.)
MERCURY (20904 "It Must Have Been Something I Said") ... 20-30 60s
(White label. Promotional issue. Has some different material than on commercial copies.)
MERCURY (60000 series) ... 12-25 61-68
(Stereo.)
Members: Dick Smothers; Tom Smothers.
Also see SMOTHERS, Dick
Also see TOM & DICK
Also see WILLIAMS, Mason / Smothers Brothers

SMYTH, Patty — P&R/LP '87

Singles: 7–inch

COLUMBIA ... 3-4 87

Picture Sleeves

COLUMBIA ... 3-4 87

LPs: 10/12–inch

COLUMBIA ... 5-8 87
Also see DION

SNAIL — P&R/LP '78

Singles: 7–inch

CREAM ... 3-5 78-79

LPs: 10/12–inch

CREAM ... 5-10 78-79

SNAP! — LP '90

Singles: 7–inch

ARISTA ... 3-4 90

LPs: 10/12–inch

ARISTA ... 5-8 90

SNEAKER — P&R/LP '81

Singles: 7–inch

HANDSHAKE ... 3-4 81-82

Picture Sleeves

HANDSHAKE ... 3-4 81

LPs: 10/12–inch

HANDSHAKE ... 5-10 81

SNEEZER, Ebe, & Epidemics

(Featuring John D. Loudermilk)

Singles: 7–inch

COLONIAL ... 10-15 57
Also see LOUDERMILK, John D.

SNIFF 'N' THE TEARS — P&R/LP '79

Singles: 7–inch

ATLANTIC ... 3-5 79-80
MCA ... 3-5 81

LPs: 10/12–inch

ATCO ... 5-10 79
ATLANTIC ... 5-10 79-80
MCA ... 5-10 81
Members: Paul Roberts; Mick Dyche; Luigi Salvoni; Alan Fealdman; Chris Birkin; Noz Netto.
Also see NETTO, Loz

SNOW, Hank — C&W '49

(The Singing Ranger & His Rainbow Ranch Boys; with Kelly Foxton)

Singles: 78 rpm

BLUEBIRD ... 15-30 40s
RCA ... 5-10 49-57

Singles: 7–inch

RCA (0100 & 0900 series) ... 3-5 69-74
(Orange labels.)
RCA (0300 & 0400 series) ... 8-12 50-51
(Green or gray labels.)
RCA (4346 thru 7748) ... 5-10 52-60
RCA (7803 thru 9907) ... 3-6 61-70
RCA (10000 & 11000 series) ... 3-5 74-80

Picture Sleeves

RCA ... 4-8 63

EPs: 7–inch

RCA (295 thru 1113) ... 12-25 54-56
RCA (1156 "Old Doc Brown") ... 35-45 55
RCA (1200 series) ... 20-30 55
RCA (1400 series) ... 15-25 57
RCA (3000 series) ... 30-50 52-54
RCA (4000 series) ... 15-20 58
RCA (5000 series) ... 12-25 58-60

LPs: 10/12–inch

CAMDEN ... 8-15 59-74
DETOUR ... 5-10
HANK SNOW SCHOOL of MUSIC (1149/50 "The Guitar") ... 250-300 58
(Special issue from the Hank Snow School of Music. Includes guitar instruction booklet.)
PICKWICK ... 5-10 75-76
RCA (0134 "Living Legend") ... 100-125 78
(RCA Special Products issue.)
RCA (0162 thru 0908) ... 5-10 73-75
RCA (1004 "I'm Movin' On") ... 15-20 82
(RCA Special Products issue.)
RCA (1052 thru 3511) ... 5-10 75-79
(With ""AHL1, "ANL1" or APL1" prefix.)
RCA (1113 "Just Keep-A-Movin' ") ... 25-35 55
(With "LPM" prefix.)
RCA (1156 "Old Doc Brown") ... 150-175 55
RCA (1233 thru 1861) ... 25-45 55-58
RCA (2043 thru 4708) ... 10-25 60-72
RCA (3026 "Country Classics") ... 50-75 52
(10–inch LP.)
RCA (3070 "Hank Snow Sings") ... 50-75 52
(10–inch LP.)
RCA (3131 "Hank Snow Salutes Jimmie Rodgers") ... 50-75 53
(10–inch LP.)
RCA (3192 "Tennessee Jamboree") ... 50-75 53
(10–inch LP.)
RCA (3220 "Country Western Caravan") ... 50-75 54
(10–inch LP.)
RCA (3267 "Country Guitar") ... 50-75 53
(10–inch LP.)
RCA (3000 & 3100 series) ... 40-60 52-54
(10–inch LPs.)
RCA (6014 "This Is My Story") ... 20-30 66
RCA SPECIAL PRODUCTS/KRAFT FOODS ... 10-20 64-67
(TV mail-order offer.)
RCA SPECIAL PRODUCTS/TEE VEE ... 10-15 74-78
READER'S DIGEST (216 "I'm Movin' On") ... 125-150
(Six-LP boxed set.)
Session: Jordanaires; Anita Kerr Singers; Jimmy Snow.
Also see KERR, Anita
Also see MARTIN, Janis / Hank Snow
Also see PRESLEY, Elvis / Hank Snow / Eddy Arnold / Hank Snow

SNOW, Hank, & Chet Atkins

Singles: 78 rpm

RCA ... 4-8 55

Singles: 7–inch

RCA (5900 series) ... 5-10 55

LPs: 10/12–inch

RCA (2952 "Reminiscing") ... 20-30 64
RCA (4254 "By Special Request") ... 20-30 70
Also see ATKINS, Chet

SNOW, Hank, & Anita Carter

(Anita Carter & Hank Snow; with the Rainbow Ranch Boys) — C&W '51

Singles: 78 rpm

RCA ... 4-8 51-56

Singles: 7–inch

RCA ... 8-12 51-56

LPs: 10/12–inch

RCA (2580 "Together Again") ... 15-25 62

SNOW, Hank / Hank Locklin / Porter Wagoner

LPs: 10/12–inch

RCA (2723 "Three Country Gentlemen") ... 15-25 63
Also see LOCKLIN, Hank
Also see SNOW, Hank
Also see WAGONER, Porter

SNOW, Phoebe — LP '74

Singles: 7–inch

COLUMBIA ... 3-5 76-78
MIRAGE ... 3-5 81
SHELTER ... 3-5 74-75

LPs: 10/12–inch

COLUMBIA ... 5-10 76-81
ELEKTRA ... 5-8 89
MCA ... 5-10 79
MIRAGE ... 5-10 81
SHELTER ... 8-10 74
Also see GOODMAN, Steve, & Phoebe Snow
Also see JEFFREYS, Garland, & Phoebe Snow
Also see SIMON, Paul, & Phoebe Snow

SNUFF — C&W '82

Singles: 7–inch

ELEKTRA ... 3-4 82
W.B./CURB ... 3-4 83
Member: Jim Bowling.

SNYDER, Terry, & All-Stars: see LIGHT, Enoch

SO — P&R/LP '88

Singles: 7–inch

EMI ... 3-4 88

Picture Sleeves

EMI ... 3-4 88

LPs: 10/12–inch

EMI ... 5-8 88

SOBER, Errol — P&R '79

Singles: 7–inch

ABC ... 3-5 74
ABNAK ... 3-5 70
BELL ... 3-5 72
CAPITOL ... 3-5 76
NUMBER ONE ... 3-4 79

SOCCIO, Gino — P&R/LP '79

Singles: 12–inch

ATLANTIC ... 4-6 80-84
W.B./RFC ... 4-6 79-80

Singles: 7–inch

ATLANTIC ... 3-5 80-84
W.B./RFC ... 3-5 79-82

LPs: 10/12–inch

ATLANTIC ... 5-10 80-84
W.B./RFC ... 5-10 79-80

SOCIAL DISTORATION — LP '90

LPs: 10/12–inch

EPIC ... 5-8 90
RCA (43500 "Mommy's Little Monster") ... 8-10 90s
RCA (43501 "Prison Bound") ... 8-10 90s
RCA (43502 "Mainliner") ... 8-10 90s

SOFFICI, Piero — P&R '61

Singles: 7–inch

JUBILEE ... 4-8 61
KIP ... 4-8 61

SOFT CELL — P&R/LP '82

Singles: 12–inch

SIRE ... 4-6 82

Singles: 7–inch

SIRE ... 3-5 82

Picture Sleeves

SIRE ... 3-5 82

LPs: 10/12–inch

ACCORD ... 5-10 82
SIRE ... 5-10 82-83
Members: Marc Almond; David Ball.

Also see ALMOND, Marc

SOFT MACHINE LP '68

Singles: 7-inch

PROBE....4-6 69

LPs: 10/12-inch

ACCORD....5-10 82
COLUMBIA....8-12 70-73
COMMAND....12-18 73
PROBE (4500 "Soft Machine")....20-30 68
(With movable parts cover.)
PROBE (4500 "Soft Machine")....15-20 69
(With standard cover.)
PROBE (4505 "Soft Machine, Vol. 2")....15-25 69
RECKLESS....5-10 88

SOHO P&R/LP '90

Singles: 7-inch

ATCO....3-4 90

LPs: 10/12-inch

ATCO....5-8 90

SOLARIS R&B '80

Singles: 7-inch

DANA....3-5 80

LPs: 10/12-inch

DANA....5-10 80

SOLO D&D '84

Singles: 12-inch

NEXT PLATINUM....4-6 84

SOME, Belouis P&R '85

Singles: 12-inch

CAPITOL....4-6 85

Singles: 7-inch

CAPITOL....3-4 85

Picture Sleeves

CAPITOL....3-4 85

LPs: 10/12-inch

CAPITOL....5-10 85

SOMERVILLE, Jimmy LP '90

LPs: 10/12-inch

LONDON....5-8 90
Also see BRONSKI BEAT
Also see COMMUNARDS

SOMMER, Bert P&R '70

Singles: 7-inch

BUDDAH....3-5 71
CAPITOL....3-5 77-78
ELEUTHERA....3-5 70

LPs: 10/12-inch

BUDDAH....8-12 71
CAPITOL....8-10 77
ELEUTHERA....10-15 70

SOMMERS, Joanie P&R '60

Singles: 7-inch

ABC....3-5 78
CAPITOL....4-6 67
COLUMBIA....4-8 66
HAPPY TIGER....3-5 70
W.B. (107 "Sommers' Hot, Sommers' Here")....10-15 60
(Promotional issue only.)
W.B. (5000 series)....4-8 60-65
W.B. (7000 series)....3-5 68

LPs: 10/12-inch

COLUMBIA....10-20 66
DISCOVERY....5-10 83
W.B.....15-25 59-62
Also see BYRNES, Edd "Kookie," with Joanie Sommers & Mary Kaye Trio
Also see NELSON, Rick / Joanie Sommers / Dona Jean Young

SOMMERS, Joanie, & Laurindo Almeida

LPs: 10/12-inch

W.B.....15-25 64
Also see ALMEIDA, Laurindo
Also see SOMMERS, Joanie

SOMMERS, Ronny
(Sonny Bono)

Singles: 7-inch

SWAMI (1001 "Don't Shake My Tree")....10-20 61
Also see SONNY

SONIC YOUTH LP '90

LPs: 10/12-inch

DGC....5-8 90
ENIGMA....5-10 80s
HOMESTEAD....5-10 80s
SST....5-10 80s
Members: Thurston Moore; Kim Gordon; Lee Ranaldo; Steve Shelley.

SONNY P&R '65
(Sonny Bono)

Singles: 7-inch

ATCO....4-8 65-67
HIGHLAND....5-10 63
MCA....3-5 72-74
SPECIALTY....3-8 65-72

LPs: 10/12-inch

ATCO....12-20 67
Also see CHRISTY, Don
Also see SOMMERS, Ronny
Also see SONNY & CHER

SONNY & CHER P&R/LP '65

Singles: 7-inch

ATCO....4-8 65-70
KAPP....3-6 71-72
MCA....3-5 73-74
REPRISE....5-10 64-65
VAULT (916 "The Letter")....10-15 65
W.B.....3-5 77

Picture Sleeves

VAULT (916 "The Letter")....10-15 65

EPs: 7-inch

ATCO....8-12 65
(Juke box issues only.)
REPRISE....15-25 65

LPs: 10/12-inch

ATCO....12-20 65-72
KAPP....10-15 71-72
MCA....8-12 73-74
TVP....8-10 77
Members: Salvatore Bono; Cher LaPiere; Cher Bono.
Also see CAESAR & CLEO
Also see CHER
Also see HALE & HUSHABYES
Also see SONNY

SONNY & CHER / Bill Medley / Lettermen / Blendells

LPs: 10/12-inch

REPRISE (6177 "Baby Don't Go")....25-35 65
(Shown as by "Sonny & Cher and Friends.")
Also see BLENDELLS
Also see LETTERMEN
Also see MEDLEY, Bill
Also see SONNY & CHER

SONS OF CHAMPLIN LP '69
(Sons)

Singles: 7-inch

ARIOLA AMERICA....4-6 75-77
CAPITOL....4-8 69-70
COLUMBIA....4-6 73
GOLDMINE....8-12
VERVE....5-10 67

LPs: 10/12-inch

ARIOLA AMERICA....8-10 75-77
CAPITOL (200 "Loosen Up Naturally")....20-30 69
CAPITOL (332 "Sons Minus Seeds and Stems")....15-20 69
MILL VALLEY ("Sons Minus Seeds and Stems")....20-30 94
(Reportedly 1000 made.)
SONS of CHAMPLIN ("Sons Minus Seeds and Stems")....300-400 69
(Reportedly 100 made.)
COLUMBIA....10-15 73
Members: Bill Champlin; Geoff Palmer; Bill Bowen; Al Strong; Jim Myers; Tim Caine.

SONS OF THE PIONEERS P&R '34

Singles: 78 rpm

DECCA....5-10 34-44
RCA....4-8 45-56

Singles: 7-inch

BLUEBIRD (105 "Sugarfoot")....5-10 58
CORAL....5-10 54
DECCA (29000 series)....5-10 56
RCA (0100 thru 0400 series)....5-10 50-51
(Black vinyl.)
RCA (0100 thru 0400 series)....10-20 50-51
(Colored vinyl.)
RCA (2000 thru 6000 series)....5-10 50-56
RCA (8000 series)....4-6 60s

Picture Sleeves

BLUEBIRD (105 "Sugarfoot")....10-20 58

EPs: 7-inch

RCA (103 "Tumbling Tumbleweeds")....8-15 61
RCA (168 "Cowboy Classics")....25-40 52
(Boxed set of three colored discs.)
RCA (400 thru 1400 series)....5-15 55-57
RCA (3000 series)....15-25 52-53
RCA (4000 series)....8-12 58
RCA (5000 series)....5-10 59

LPs: 10/12-inch

AMERICAN FOLK MUSIC....6-12 81
CAMDEN....8-18 58-73
COLUMBIA....5-8 82
GRANITE....6-10 76
HARMONY....10-15 64
J.E.M.F....8-10
LONG....10-15
MCA....4-8 83
PICKWICK....5-10 75
RCA (1092 "Cool Water")....5-10 76
RCA (1130 thru 2957, except 1431)....20-40 55-64
(With "LPM" or "LSP" prefix.)
RCA (1431 "How Great Thou Art")....30-40 57
RCA (2332 thru 2808)....5-10 77-78
RCA (3032 "Cowboy Classics")....30-50 52
(10-inch LP.)
RCA (3095 "Cowboy Hymns and Spirtuals")....30-50 52
(10-inch LP.)
RCA (3162 "Western Classics")....30-50 53
(10-inch LP.)
RCA (3351 thru 4119)....10-20 65-68
(With "LPM" or "LSP" prefix.)
RCA (3468 "Best of the Sons of the Pioneers")....5-10 79
RCA (4000 series)....4-8 81
VOCALION....8-12 64
Members: Roy Rogers; Tim Spencer; Bob Nolan; Ken Curtis; Hugh Farr; Karl Farr; Lloyd Perrymen; Shug Fisher; Tommy Doss; Pat Brady.
Also see ALLEN, Rex, Jr., & Sons of the Pioneers
Also see ROGERS, Roy

SOPWITH CAMEL P&R '66

Singles: 7-inch

KAMA SUTRA....4-8 66-67
REPRISE....3-5 73

Picture Sleeves

KAMA SUTRA....4-8 67

LPs: 10/12-inch

KAMA SUTRA....15-20 67-73
REPRISE....15-20 73
Member: Peter Kraemer.

SOUL: see S.O.U.L.

SOUL, David P&R/LP '77

Singles: 7-inch

MGM....4-6 66-67
PARAMOUNT....3-5 70
PRIVATE STOCK....3-5 77

LPs: 10/12-inch

PRIVATE STOCK....8-10 77

SOUL, Jimmy P&R '62
(With the Chants)

Singles: 7-inch

S.P.Q.R.....5-10 62-65

20TH FOX 4-8 63
Picture Sleeves
S.P.Q.R. 10-15 62-63
LPs: 10/12-inch
S.P.Q.R. (16001 "If You Wanna Be Happy") 40-60 63
Also see BENTON, Brook / Chuck Jackson / Jimmy Soul
Also see RIVERS, Johnny / 4 Seasons / Jerry Butler / Jimmy Soul

SOUL, Jimmy / Belmonts
LPs: 10/12-inch
SPINORAMA 20-25 63
Also see BELMONTS
Also see SOUL, Jimmy

SOUL ASYLUM LP '92
LPs: 10/12-inch
EPIC 8-10 90s
TWIN/TONE 8-10 88
W.B. 8-10 90s
Members: Dan Murphy; Grant Young; Dave Pirner; Karl Mueller.

SOUL BROTHERS SIX P&R '67
Singles: 7-inch
ATLANTIC 8-15 67-69
GRT 4-6 76
(Canadian.)
LYDELL 5-10 66
PHIL-L.A. of SOUL 4-6 72-74
Members: John Ellison; Sam Armstrong; Charles Armstrong; Von Elle Benjamin; Lester Peleman; Moses Armstrong.

SOUL CHILDREN P&R/LP '69
Singles: 12-inch
STAX 4-8 78-79
Singles: 7-inch
EPIC 3-5 75-76
STAX 3-8 69-74
LPs: 10/12-inch
EPIC 8-10 76
STAX 8-12 69-79
Members: Anita Louis; Shelbra Bennett; John Colbert; Norman West.

SOUL CLAN P&R '68
Singles: 7-inch
ATLANTIC (2530 "Soul Meeting") 8-12 68
Picture Sleeves
ATLANTIC (2530 "Soul Meeting") 10-15 68
LPs: 10/12-inch
ATCO ("Soul Meeting") 15-25 68
(Selection number not known.)
Members: Solomon Burke; Arthur Conley; Don Covay; Ben E. King; Joe Tex.
Also see BURKE, Solomon
Also see CONLEY, Arthur
Also see COVAY, Don
Also see KING, Ben E.
Also see TEX, Joe

SOUL SISTERS P&R '64
Singles: 7-inch
GUYDEN 5-10 62
KAYO 5-10 63
SUE 5-10 64-65
VEEP 5-10 68
LPs: 10/12-inch
SUE (1022 "I Can't Stand It") 25-35 64

SOUL SURVIVORS P&R/LP '67
Singles: 7-inch
ATCO 4-8 68-69
CRIMSON 4-8 67-68
DECCA 4-8 67
PHILADELPHIA INT'L 3-5 76
TSOP 3-5 74-75
LPs: 10/12-inch
ATCO (277 "Take Another Look") 15-20 69
CRIMSON (502 "When the Whistle Blows") 20-25 67
TSOP 8-10 75
Members: Richard Ingui; Charles Ingui; Kenny Jeremiah; Chuck Trois; Paul Venturini.
Also see SHIRLEY & COMPANY

SOUL TRAIN GANG P&R '75
Singles: 7-inch
SOUL TRAIN 3-5 75-77
LPs: 10/12-inch
SOUL TRAIN 8-10 76

SOUL II SOUL P&R/LP '89
Singles: 7-inch
VIRGIN 3-4 89
Picture Sleeves
VIRGIN 3-4 89
LPs: 10/12-inch
VIRGIN 5-8 89-90

SOULFUL STRINGS LP '67
Singles: 7-inch
CADET 3-6 66-73
LPs: 10/12-inch
CADET 5-10 67-73

SOUNDGARDEN LP '90
Singles: 7-inch
A&M (17933 "Hands All Over") 4-6 89
(Promotional issue only.)
EPs: 7-inch
("Screaming Life") 5-8 87
(Colored vinyl.)
LPs: 10/12-inch
A&M 5-8 89
SST (911 "Flower") 10-15 89
(Colored vinyl.)
Members: Chris Cornell; Hiro Yamamoto; Matthew Cameron; Kim Thayil.

SOUNDS OF SUNSHINE P&R/LP '71
Singles: 7-inch
P.I.P. 3-5 76
RANWOOD 3-5 71-73
LPs: 10/12-inch
P.I.P. 5-10 76
RANWOOD 5-10 71-72

SOUNDS ORCHESTRAL P&R/LP '65
Singles: 7-inch
JANUS 4-8 60s
PARKWAY 4-8 62-66
LPs: 10/12-inch
PARKWAY 10-15 62-67

SOUP DRAGONS LP '90
LPs: 10/12-inch
BIG LIFE 5-8 90
POLYDOR (522732 "Hydrophonic") 5-10 90s
SIRE 5-10 87

SOUTH, Joe P&R '58
(With the Believers)
Singles: 7-inch
A&M 4-8 68
ALL WOOD 8-12 62
APT 5-10 65
CAPITOL 3-8 67-75
COLUMBIA 8-12 67
FAIRLANE 8-12 61-62
ISLAND 3-5 75
MGM 5-10 63-64
NRC (Except 002) 10-15 58-60
NRC (002 "I'm Snowed") 30-40 58
LPs: 10/12-inch
ACCORD 5-10 81
CAPITOL 8-15 68-72
ISLAND 8-12 75
MINE 8-12 70

SOUTH, Joe / Dells
LPs: 10/12-inch
APPLE (3377 "Come Together") 15-25 71
Also see DELLS

SOUTH, Joe / Billy Joe Royal
LPs: 10/12-inch
NASHVILLE (2092 "You're the Reason") 5-10 70s
Also see ROYAL, Billy Joe
Also see SOUTH, Joe

SOUTH SHORE COMMISSION P&R '75
Singles: 7-inch
WAND 3-5 75-76

SOUTHCOTE P&R '74
Singles: 7-inch
BUDDAH 3-6 74

SOUTHER, J.D. LP '76
(John David Souther)
Singles: 7-inch
ASYLUM 3-5 74-76
COLUMBIA 3-5 79
W.B. 3-4 85
LPs: 10/12-inch
ASYLUM 8-10 72-76
COLUMBIA 5-10 79
W.B. 5-8 85
Also see JOHN DAVID & CINDERS
Also see RONSTADT, Linda, & J.D. Souther
Also see TAYLOR, James, & J.D. Souther
Also see TILLOTSON, Johnny, & J.D. Souther

SOUTHER - HILLMAN - FURAY BAND P&R/LP '74
Singles: 7-inch
ASYLUM 3-5 74-75
LPs: 10/12-inch
ASYLUM 8-10 74-75
Members: J. D. Souther; Chris Hillman; Richie Furay.
Also see FURAY, Richie
Also see HILLMAN, Chris
Also see SOUTHER, J.D.

SOUTHERN, Jeri P&R '51
Singles: 78 rpm
DECCA 4-8 51-58
Singles: 7-inch
CAPITOL 4-8 59
DECCA 5-10 51-58
ROULETTE 5-10 57-59
EPs: 7-inch
DECCA 5-10 55-56
LPs: 10/12-inch
CAPITOL 10-20 59
DECCA 15-25 55-58
ROULETTE 10-20 57-59

SOUTHERN COMFORT LP '71
Singles: 7-inch
CAPITOL 3-5 71-72
COTILLION 4-6 69
LPs: 10/12-inch
BRYLEN 5-8
CAPITOL 10-12 71
COLUMBIA 10-12 70
SIRE 12-15 69
Also see MATTHEWS' SOUTHERN COMFORT

SOUTHSIDE JOHNNY & ASBURY JUKES LP '76
(With the Jukes; Jukes; Southside Johnny)
Singles: 7-inch
ATLANTIC 3-4 86
EPIC 3-5 77-78
MERCURY 3-5 79
MIRAGE 3-4 83-84
Picture Sleeves
ATLANTIC 3-4 86
LPs: 10/12-inch
ATLANTIC 5-8 86
CYPRESS 5-8 88
EPIC 8-10 76-79
MERCURY 5-10 79-81
MIRAGE 5-8 83-84
Also see FIVE SATINS

SOUTHSIDE MOVEMENT P&R '73
Singles: 7-inch
20TH FOX 3-5 74-75
WAND 3-5 73
LPs: 10/12-inch
20TH FOX 5-10 75
WAND 8-10 73
Also see SIMTEC & WYLIE

SOUTHWEST F.O.B. P&R '68

Singles: 7-inch

GPC....4-8 68
HIP....5-10 68-69

LPs: 10/12-inch

HIP (7001 "Smell of Incense")....25-35 69

Members: Dan Seals; John Ford Coley; Shane Keister.

Also see ENGLAND DAN & John Ford Coley

SOVINE, Red C&W '55
(With the Girls)

Singles: 78 rpm

DECCA (Except 30239)....5-10 54-57
DECCA (30239 "Juke Joint Johnny") 10-15 57
MGM....5-10 50-53

Singles: 7-inch

CHART....3-5 71-75
DECCA (Except 30239)....5-10 54-66
DECCA (30239 "Juke Joint Johnny") 20-30 57
GUSTO....3-5 77-80
MGM....8-15 50-53
RCA....4-8 62
RIC....4-6 64-65
STARDAY (Except 500 thru 800 series)....3-5 70-78
STARDAY (500 thru 800 series)....4-8 60-70

EPs: 7-inch

MGM....10-20 57

LPs: 10/12-inch

CMI....5-10 77
CHART....5-10 72-74
DECCA (4400 series)....15-25 64
DECCA (4700 series)....10-20 66
GUSTO/STARDAY....5-10 78
LAKE SHORE....8-12
MGM (3465 "Red Sovine")....30-40 57
METRO....10-15 67
NASHVILLE....6-12 70
POWER PAK....5-10 80s
RIC....10-15 65
SOMERSET....8-12 63
STARDAY (Except 100 series)....10-20 65-76
STARDAY (100 series)....15-25 61-62
STEREO FIDELITY....8-12 63
VOCALION....8-12 68

Also see FELTS, Narvel / Red Sovine / Mel Tillis
Also see MULLICAN, Moon / Cowboy Copas / Red Sovine
Also see REEVES, Del / Red Sovine
Also see SHEPARD, Jean

SOVINE, Red, & Goldie Hill C&W '55

Singles: 78 rpm

DECCA....4-8 55

Singles: 7-inch

DECCA....5-10 55

SOVINE, Red, & Webb Pierce C&W '56

Singles: 78 rpm

DECCA....4-8 56

Singles: 7-inch

DECCA....8-12 56

Also see PIERCE, Webb
Also see SOVINE, Red

SOXX, Bob B.: see BOB B. SOXX & Blue Jeans

SPACE P&R '79

Singles: 12-inch

CASABLANCA....4-6 79-80

Singles: 7-inch

CASABLANCA....3-5 79-80
U.A....3-5 77

LPs: 10/12-inch

CASABLANCA....5-10 78-79
U.A....8-10 77

Also see BELL, Madeline

SPACEMEN P&R '59
(Space Men)

Singles: 7-inch

ALTON....5-10 59-60
FELSTED....5-10 59
JAMECO....4-8 65
JUBILEE....5-10 59
MARKEY....4-8 62

LPs: 10/12-inch

ROULETTE....15-25 64-66

SPADES
(Slades)

Singles: 7-inch

LIBERTY (55118 "You Mean Everything to Me")....50-75 58

Also see SLADES

SPADES
(Thirteenth Floor Elevators)

Singles: 7-inch

ZERO (10001 "I Need a Girl")....100-200 65
ZERO (10002 "You're Gonna Miss Me")....200-300 65
(A different recording than later issued by the 13th Floor Elevators.)

Also see THIRTEENTH FLOOR ELEVATORS

SPANDAU BALLET P&R/D&D/LP '83

Singles: 12-inch

CHRYSALIS....4-6 84-85

Singles: 7-inch

CHRYSALIS....3-4 83-85

Picture Sleeves

CHRYSALIS....3-5 83-85

LPs: 10/12-inch

CHRYSALIS....5-8 83-85
MFSL (152 "True")....20-30 85

Also see BAND AID

SPANIELS P&R '57
(Spanials)

Singles: 78 rpm

CHANCE (1141 "Baby It's You")....50-100 53
VEE JAY (101 "Baby, It's You")....100-200 53
VEE JAY (103 "Bells Ring Out")....50-100 53
VEE JAY (107 "Goodnite Sweetheart, Goodnite")....75-100 53
(Black vinyl. Mistakenly credits the "Spanials.")
VEE JAY (107 "Goodnite Sweetheart, Goodnite")....50-75 53
(Black vinyl. Properly credits the "Spaniels.")
VEE JAY (116 thru 200 series)....25-75 54-58

Singles: 7-inch

BUDDAH....4-8 69
CALLA....3-5 70
CANTERBURY....3-4 74
CHANCE (1141 "Baby It's You")....250-350 53
(Black vinyl.)
CHANCE (1141 "Baby It's You")....400-600 53
(Colored vinyl.)
COLLECTABLES....3-4 80s
ERIC....3-4 70s
LOST-NITE....3-5
NEPTUNE....3-5
NORTH AMERICAN....3-5 70
OWL....3-5 73
TRIP....3-5
VEE JAY (101 "Baby It's You")....400-600 53
(Black vinyl. Maroon label.)
VEE JAY (101 "Baby It's You") 3000-5000 53
(Colored vinyl.)
VEE JAY (101 "Baby It's You")....20-30 61
(Black label.)
VEE JAY (103 "Bells Ring Out")....100-200 53
(Black vinyl.)
VEE JAY (103 "Bells Ring Out")....500-750 53
(Colored vinyl.)
VEE JAY (107 "Goodnite Sweetheart, Goodnite")....125-200 53
(Mistakenly credits the "Spanials.")
VEE JAY (107 "Goodnite Sweetheart, Goodnite")....100-150 53
(Properly credits the "Spaniels.")
VEE JAY (107 "Goodnite Sweetheart, Goodnite")....300-500 53
(Red vinyl. No "Trade Mark Reg." on label.)
VEE JAY (107 "Goodnite Sweetheart, Goodnite")....8-12 93
(Red vinyl, Vee Jay commemorative issue. Has "Trade Mark Reg." on label.)
VEE JAY (116 "Play It Cool")....50-75 54
(Black vinyl.)
VEE JAY (116 "Play It Cool")....500-750 54
(Colored vinyl.)
VEE JAY (131 "Do-Wah")....40-60 55
(Black vinyl.)
VEE JAY (154 "You Painted Pictures")....40-50 55
VEE JAY (154 "Painted Picture")....30-40 55
(Mistakenly credits the "Spanials.")
VEE JAY (178 "False Love")....75-100 56
VEE JAY (189 "Dear Heart")....75-100 56
VEE JAY (202 "Since I Fell for You")....75-100 56
VEE JAY (229 thru 328)....30-45 56-58
VEE JAY (342 "People Will Say We're in Love")....50-75 59
VEE JAY (350 "I Know")....20-25 60

Picture Sleeves

VEE JAY (107 "Goodnite Sweetheart, Goodnite")....2-4 93
(Commemorative issue with this title although no specific artist or titles are shown.)

LPs: 10/12-inch

LOST-NITE (19 "The Spaniels")....8-12 81
LOST-NITE (137 "The Spaniels")....15-20 70s
VEE JAY (1002 "Goodnite, It's Time to Go")....200-300 59
(Maroon label.)
VEE JAY (1002 "Goodnite, It's Time to Go")....75-100 61
(Black label.)
VEE JAY (1024 "Spaniels")....200-250 60
UPFRONT....10-20

Members: Pookie Hudson; Jerry Gregory; Ernest Warren; Willie Jackson; Opal Courtney; James Cochran; Carl Rainge; Don Porter; Andy Magruder; Bill Carey.

Also see HUDSON, Pookie

SPANKY & OUR GANG P&R/LP '67

Singles: 7-inch

EPIC....3-5 75-76
MERCURY....4-8 67-69

Picture Sleeves

MERCURY....4-8 67-68

EPs: 7-inch

MERCURY (90 "Like to Get to Know You")....10-20 67
(Promotional issue only. Issued with paper sleeve.)

LPs: 10/12-inch

EPIC....8-10 75
MERCURY....10-20 67-71
RHINO....5-8 86

Members: Elaine "Spanky" McFarlane; Lefty Baker; Malcolm Hale; Nigel Pickering; John Seiter.

SPARKLETONES, with Joe Bennett: see BENNETT, Joe, & Sparkletones

SPARKS LP '74

Singles: 12-inch

ATLANTIC....4-6 84

Singles: 7-inch

ATLANTIC....3-4 82-84
BEARSVILLE....3-5 72
COLUMBIA....3-5 78
ELEKTRA....3-5 79
FINE ARTS....3-4 88
ISLAND....3-5 73-76
RCA....3-5 81

Picture Sleeves

ATLANTIC....3-4 82-83

LPs: 10/12-inch

ATLANTIC....5-10 82-84
BEARSVILLE....12-15 72-73
COLUMBIA (Black vinyl)....8-10 77
COLUMBIA (Colored vinyl)....12-15 77
ELEKTRA....8-10 79
ISLAND....8-10 74-76
RCA....5-10 81

Members: Ron Mael; Russell Mael.

SPARKS & JANE WIEDLIN P&R '83

Singles: 12-inch

ATLANTIC....4-6 83

Singles: 7-inch

ATLANTIC....3-4 83

Picture Sleeves

ATLANTIC 3-4 83
Also see SPARKS
Also see WIEDLIN, Jane

SPARKY D D&D '85

Singles: 12-inch

NIA 4-6 85

SPARQUE D&D '84

Singles: 12-inch

WEST END 4-6 84

SPARROW, Johnny R&B '50

(With His Bows & Arrows)

Singles: 78 rpm

GOTHAM 10-15 53-54
MIRAGE 10-15 50

Singles: 7-inch

GOTHAM (7282 "Sparrow in the Barrel") 15-25 53
GOTHAM (7292 "Paradise Rock") 20-30 54
(Colored vinyl.)

SPATS P&R '64

Singles: 7-inch

ABC-PAR 5-10 64-66
ENITH 10-20 64
JANO 10-20 67

LPs: 10/12-inch

ABC-PAR 20-25 65
Member: Dick Johnson.

SPEARS, Billie Jo C&W '68

Singles: 7-inch

CAPITOL 3-5 68-71
LIBERTY 3-4 81
PARLIAMENT 3-4 84
U.A. (Except 50000 series) 3-5 74-80
U.A. (50000 series) 3-6 66-67

LPs: 10/12-inch

CAPITOL 5-15 68-79
KOALA 5-10 80s
LIBERTY 5-8 81
PICKWICK/HILLTOP 5-8 70s
U.A. 5-10 75-80
Also see BUTLER, Larry, & Friends
Also see REEVES, Del, & Billie Jo Spears

SPECIAL AKA D&D '84

Singles: 12-inch

CHRYSALIS 4-6 84

Singles: 7-inch

CHRYSALIS 3-4 84

LPs: 10/12-inch

CHRYSALIS 5-8 84
Also see SPECIALS

SPECIAL DELIVERY R&B '76

(Featuring Terry Huff)

Singles: 7-inch

MAINSTREAM 3-5 75-76
SHIELD 3-5 77-78
Also see BRUNSON, Tyrone "Tystick"
Also see HUFF, Terry

SPECIAL ED LP '89

LPs: 10/12-inch

PROFILE 5-8 89-90

SPECIALS LP '80

Singles: 12-inch

CHRYSALIS 4-6 81

Singles: 7-inch

CHRYSALIS 3-5 79-80

Picture Sleeves

CHRYSALIS 3-5 79

LPs: 10/12-inch

CHRYSALIS 5-10 80
Also see FUN BOY THREE
Also see SPECIAL AKA

SPECTOR, Phil

Singles: 7-inch

PHILLES ("Thanks for Giving Me the Right Time") 150-250 63
(Promotional issue only.)
Also see HARVEY, Phil
Also see SPECTORS THREE

SPECTOR, Ronnie P&R '71

(With the Ronettes; with E Street Band)

Singles: 12-inch

EPIC/CLEVELAND INT'L (350 "Say Goodbye to Hollywood") 8-12 77
(Promotional issue only.)

Singles: 7-inch

ALSTON 5-8 78
APPLE 5-10 70-71
BUDDAH 4-6 74
EPIC/CLEVELAND INT'L (50374 "Say Goodbye to Hollywood") 5-10 77
COLUMBIA 3-4 87
POLISH 3-5 80
TOM CAT (Black vinyl) 3-5 75-76
TOM CAT (Colored vinyl) 5-8 75
(Promotional issues only.)
W.B./SPECTOR 3-5 76

Picture Sleeves

APPLE 8-10 71
COLUMBIA 3-5 87
EPIC/CLEVELAND INT'L (50374 "Say Goodbye to Hollywood") 20-25 77

LPs: 10/12-inch

POLISH 8-12 80
Also see MONEY, Eddie, & Ronnie Spector
Also see RONETTES
Also see SPRINGSTEEN, Bruce
Also see VERONICA

SPECTORS THREE

Singles: 7-inch

TREY 10-20 59-60
Member: Phil Spector.
Also see SPECTOR, Phil
Also see TEDDY BEARS

SPEEDO & CADILLACS

(Cadillacs)

Singles: 7-inch

JOSIE (876 "It's Love") 20-25 60
Also see CADILLACS

SPEEDO & IMPALAS

(Impalas)

Singles: 7-inch

CUB (9066 "All Alone") 15-25 60
Also see IMPALAS

SPEEDO & PEARLS

Singles: 7-inch

JOSIE (865 "Who Ya Gonna Kiss") .. 10-20 59
Also see CADILLACS
Also see SPEEDO & CADILLACS

SPELLBINDERS P&R '65

Singles: 7-inch

COLUMBIA 4-8 65-66
DATE 4-8 67
MIRAMAR 4-8 60s

LPs: 10/12-inch

COLUMBIA 10-20 66
Members: Bob Shivers; Jimmy Wright; Ben Grant; McArthur Munford; Elouise Pennington.

SPELLBOUND P&R '78

Singles: 7-inch

EMI AMERICA 3-5 78

LPs: 10/12-inch

EMI AMERICA 5-10 78

SPELLMAN, Benny P&R '62

Singles: 7-inch

ACE 10-15 61
ALON 4-8 66
ATLANTIC 4-8 65
MINIT 10-15 62
SANSU 4-8 67
WATCH 4-8 64
Also see K-DOE, Ernie
Also see THOMAS, Irma / Ernie K-Doe / Showmen / Benny Spellman

SPENCE, Judson P&R/LP '88

Singles: 7-inch

ATLANTIC 3-4 88

Picture Sleeves

ATLANTIC 3-4 88

LPs: 10/12-inch

ATLANTIC 5-8 88

SPENCER, Sonny P&R '59

Singles: 7-inch

MEMO (17984 "Gilee") 10-20 59
MUSIC HALL (24002 "Hold My Hand") 20-30
ONDA (111 "Bessie Lou") 15-25

SPENCER, Tracie P&R/LP '88

Singles: 7-inch

CAPITOL 3-4 88-91

Picture Sleeves

CAPITOL 3-4 88-89

LPs: 10/12-inch

CAPITOL 5-8 88-91

SPENCER & SPENCER P&R '59

Singles: 7-inch

ARGO (5331 "Russian Bandstand") . 10-20 59
GONE (5053 "Stagger Lawrence") 15-25 59
Members: Dickie Goodman; Mickey Shorr.
Also see GOODMAN, Dickie
Also see SHORR, Mickey, & Cutups

SPERRY, Steve P&R '77

Singles: 7-inch

CUCA (1008 "Our Summer Love") 15-25 60
MERCURY 3-5 77

SPHEERIS, Jimmie LP '75

Singles: 7-inch

COLUMBIA 3-5 72
EPIC 3-5 75

LPs: 10/12-inch

EPIC 8-10 75

SPIDER P&R/LP '80

Singles: 7-inch

DREAMLAND 3-5 80-81

Picture Sleeves

DREAMLAND 3-5 80

LPs: 10/12-inch

DREAMLAND 5-10 80-81
Member: Holly Knight.
Also see KNIGHT, Holly

SPIDERS R&B '54

Singles: 78 rpm

IMPERIAL 25-75 54-57

Singles: 7-inch

IMPERIAL (5265 "I Didn't Want to Do It") 75-125 53
IMPERIAL (5280 "Tears Began to Flow") 75-125 54
IMPERIAL (5291 "I'm Searching") ... 75-125 54
IMPERIAL (5305 "Real Thing") 75-125 54
IMPERIAL (5318 "She Keeps Me Wondering") 50-100 54
IMPERIAL (5331 "That's Enough") . 50-100 55
IMPERIAL (5344 "Am I the One") 50-100 55
IMPERIAL (5354 "Bells in My Heart") 75-100 55
(Red label.)
IMPERIAL (5354 "Bells in My Heart") 25-50 57
(Black label.)
IMPERIAL (5366 "Is It True") 100-150 55
(Blue label.)
IMPERIAL (5366 "Is It True") 25-50 55
(Red label.)
IMPERIAL (5376 "Don't Pity Me") 20-30 56
IMPERIAL (5393 "Dear Mary") 20-30 56
IMPERIAL (5405 "Goodbye") 20-30 56
IMPERIAL (5423 "Honey Bee") 20-30 56
IMPERIAL (5618 "I Didn't Want to Do It") 20-30 59
IMPERIAL (5714 "You're the One") ... 15-25 60
IMPERIAL (5739 "Witchcraft") 15-25 61
OWL 3-5 73

LPs: 10/12-inch

IMPERIAL (9142 "I Didn't Want to Do It") 250-500 61
Member: Chuck Carbo.

SPIDERS

Singles: 7-inch

MASCOT (112 "Why Don't You Love Me") 750-1000 65
SANTA CRUZ (003 "Don't Blow Your Mind") 350-400 66
Members: Vince "Alice Cooper" Furnier; John Speer; Glen Buxton; Dennis Dunaway; Mike Bruce.
Also see COOPER, Alice

SPIDERS FROM MARS — LP '76

Singles: 7-inch

PYE 3-5 76

LPs: 10/12-inch

PYE 8-10 76
Also see BOWIE, David

SPIN — P&R '76

Singles: 7-inch

ARIOLA AMERICA 3-5 76

LPs: 10/12-inch

ARIOLA AMERICA 8-10 76

SPINAL TAP — LP '84

Singles: 7-inch

ENIGMA (1144 "Christmas with the Devil") 8-12 84
(Picture disc.)
POLYDOR 3-4 84

Picture Sleeves

ENIGMA (1143 "Christmas with the Devil") 3-5 84

LPs: 10/12-inch

MCA (10514 "Break Like the Wind") 10-12 92
(Picture disc.)
POLYDOR 5-8 84
Also see CREDIBILITY GAP
Also see HEAR 'N AID

SPINDRIFTS

(Featuring Freddy Cannon; with the Downbeats)

Singles: 7-inch

ABC-PAR (9904 "Cha Cha Doo") 25-35 58
HOT ("Cha Cha Doo") 50-100 58
(Selection number not known.)
Also see CANNON, Freddy

SPINNERS — P&R '61

(Spinners / Harvey)

Singles: 7-inch

ATLANTIC 3-6 72-85
MOTOWN (1067 thru 1136) 8-15 64-68
MOTOWN (1155 "In My Diary") ... 500-1000 69
MOTOWN (1235 "Bad Bad Weather") .. 4-6 73
TRI-PHI (1001 "That's What Girls Are Made For") 10-20 61
TRI-PHI (1004 "Love") 15-20 61
TRI-PHI (1007 "What Did She Use"). 15-20 62
TRI-PHI (1010 "She Loves Me So") .. 15-20 62
TRI-PHI (1013 "I've Been Hurt") 15-20 62
V.I.P. (25050 "In My Diary") 10-20 70
V.I.P. (25057 "It's a Shame") 3-5 70
V.I.P. (25060 "We'll Have It Made") 4-6 71

LPs: 10/12-inch

ATLANTIC 6-10 73-84
MOTOWN (Except 639) 5-10 73-82
MOTOWN (639 "Original Spinners") 20-40 67
PICKWICK 8-10 76
V.I.P. (405 "Second Time Around") ... 20-40 70
Members: Bobby Smith; Henry Fambrough; Pervis Jackson; Bill Henderson; G.C. Cameron; Philippe Wynne; Reese Palmer; Jim Knowland; Ed Edwards; Chester Simmons.
Also see ABBA / Spinners / Firefall / England Dan & John Ford Coley
Also see CAMERON, G.C.
Also see WARWICK, Dionne, & Spinners
Also see WYNNE, Philippe

SPIRAL STARECASE — P&R/LP '69

Singles: 7-inch

COLUMBIA 4-6 69-70

LPs: 10/12-inch

COLUMBIA (9852 "More Today Than Yesterday") 15-20 69
COLUMBIA (10172 "More Today Than Yesterday") 8-12
Members: Pat Upton; Dick Lopes; Vinny Parello; Bob Raymond; Harvey Kaplan.

SPIRIT — LP '68

Singles: 12-inch

MERCURY 4-6 84

Singles: 7-inch

EPIC 3-6 70-74
MERCURY 3-5 75-76
ODE 4-8 68-70
POTATO 3-5 78
RHINO 3-4 81

Picture Sleeves

EPIC 4-8 74
POTATO 3-4 78

LPs: 10/12-inch

EPIC 8-12 70-73
MERCURY (Except 818514) 10-15 75-77
MERCURY (818514 "Spirit of '84") 5-8 84
ODE (44003 "Spirit") 20-25 68
(Monaural.)
ODE (44004 "Spirit") 15-20 68
(Stereo.)
ODE (44014 "The Family That Plays Together") 10-20 68
ODE (44016 "Clear") 10-15 69
POTATO 10-15
RHINO 5-8 81
Members: Jay Ferguson; Randy California; Mark Andes; Ed Cassidy; John Locke; John Arliss.
Also see FERGUSON, Jay
Also see FIREFALL
Also see HEART
Also see YELLOW BALLOON

SPLINTER — P&R/LP '74

Singles: 7-inch

DARK HORSE 3-6 74-77

LPs: 10/12-inch

DARK HORSE 8-10 74-77
Members: Bill Elliott; Bob Purvis.
Also see HARRISON, George

SPLIT ENZ — P&R/LP '80

Singles: 7-inch

A&M (Except 2339 & AMS-8128) 3-5 80-84
A&M (2339 "One Step Ahead") 4-6 82
("Laser Etched Single.")
A&M (AMS-8128 "Shark Attack") 75-100 82
(Laser etched, shaped picture disc. Promotional issue only.)

Picture Sleeves

A&M 3-5 80-82

EPs: 7-inch

A&M (4848 "I Don't Want to Dance") 15-25 81
(Picture disc. Promotional issue only.)

LPs: 10/12-inch

A&M 5-10 80-84
CHRYSALIS 8-10 77
Members: Tim Finn; Neil Finn.
Also see CROWDED HOUSE
Also see FINN, Tim

SPOKESMEN — P&R '65

Singles: 7-inch

DECCA 4-8 65-66
WINCHESTER 4-8 67

LPs: 10/12-inch

DECCA 25-30 65
Members: Johnny Madara; David White.

SPOOKY TOOTH — LP '69

(Gary Wright's Spooky Tooth)

Singles: 7-inch

A&M 4-6 69
MALA 5-10 68
ISLAND 3-5 72

LPs: 10/12-inch

A&M 10-15 69-73
ACCORD 5-10 82
BELL 15-20 68
ISLAND 8-10 73-74
Members: Gary Wright; Mike Harrison; Luther Grosvenor.
Also see BOXER
Also see GROSVENOR, Luther
Also see HARRISON, Mike
Also see WRIGHT, Gary

SPORTS — P&R/LP '79

Singles: 7-inch

ARISTA 3-5 79

Picture Sleeves

ARISTA 3-5 79

LPs: 10/12-inch

ARISTA 5-10 79-80

SPRINGFIELD, Dusty — P&R/LP '64

Singles: 7-inch

ATLANTIC 3-6 68-71
CASABLANCA 3-5 82
DUNHILL 3-5 73
PHILIPS 4-8 63-68
20TH FOX 3-5 80
U.A. 3-5 77-79

Picture Sleeves

PHILIPS 5-10 64-67
ATLANTIC 4-6 68

LPs: 10/12-inch

ATLANTIC 10-15 69-70
CASABLANCA 5-8 82
DUNHILL 8-10 73
PHILIPS 12-20 64-67
U.A. 5-10 78-79
WING 10-15 68
Also see HONDELLS / Dusty Springfield
Also see PET SHOP BOYS & Dusty Springfield
Also see SPRINGFIELDS

SPRINGFIELD, Rick — P&R/LP '72

Singles: 12-inch

RCA 4-6 83-84

Singles: 7-inch

CAPITOL 3-6 72-73
CHELSEA 3-5 76-77
COLUMBIA 3-5 74
MERCURY 3-4 84-85
RCA 3-5 81-85

Picture Sleeves

CAPITOL 4-8 72
MERCURY 3-5 84
RCA 3-5 81-88

LPs: 10/12-inch

CAPITOL (11000 series) 15-20 72-73
CAPITOL (16000 series) 5-10 81
CHELSEA 8-12 76
COLUMBIA (KC-32000 series) 10-15 73
COLUMBIA (PC-32000 series) 5-8
MERCURY 5-8 84
RCA 5-10 80-88

SPRINGFIELD, Rick, & Randy Crawford — P&R '84

Singles: 7-inch

RCA 3-5 84

Picture Sleeves

RCA 3-5 84
Also see CRAWFORD, Randy
Also see SPRINGFIELD, Rick

SPRINGFIELDS — C&W/P&R '62

Singles: 7-inch

PHILIPS 4-6 62-63

LPs: 10/12-inch

PHILIPS 15-25 62-63
Members: Dusty Springfield; Tom Springfield; Tim Field.
Also see SPRINGFIELD, Dusty

SPRINGSTEEN, Bruce — P&R/LP '75

(With the E Street Band)

Singles: 12-inch

COLUMBIA (1329 "Santa Claus Is Comin' to Town") 30-40 81
(White label. Promotional issue only.)
COLUMBIA (2007 "I'm on Fire") 20-25 85
(Red label. Black and white cover. Promotional issue only.)
COLUMBIA (2082 "Glory Days") 20-25 85
(Red label. Black and white cover. Promotional issue only.)

COLUMBIA (2174 "I'm Goin' Down"). 20-25 85
(Red label. Black and white cover. Promotional issue only.)
COLUMBIA (2233 "My Hometown").. 20-25 85
(Red label. Black and white cover. Promotional issue only.)
COLUMBIA (2543 "Bruce Springsteen & E Street Band Live, 1975-85")..................... 20-25 86
(Eight track sampler. Promotional issue only.)
COLUMBIA (05028 "Dancing in the Dark")... 5-8 84
COLUMBIA (05028 "Dancing in the Dark")... 20-30 84
(With black and white cover. Promotional issue only.)
COLUMBIA (05028 "Dancing in the Dark")... 15-25 84
(Promotional issue with color cover and gold promo stamp.)
COLUMBIA (05087 "Cover Me") 5-8 84
COLUMBIA (05147 "Born in the USA")... 4-6 84
COLUMBIA (05147 "Born in the USA")... 15-20 84
(White label. Promotional issue only.)
COLUMBIA (44445 "Chimes of Freedom").. 5-8 88

Singles: 7-inch

COLUMBIA (03243 "Hungry Heart")...... 3-5 84
COLUMBIA (04463 "Dancing in the Dark")... 3-5 84
COLUMBIA (04561 "Cover Me") 3-5 84
COLUMBIA (04680 "Born in the USA")... 3-5 84
COLUMBIA (04772 "I'm on Fire") 3-5 85
COLUMBIA (04924 "Glory Days") 3-5 85
COLUMBIA (05606 "I'm Goin' Down") 3-5 85
COLUMBIA (05728 "My Hometown").... 3-5 85
COLUMBIA (06432 "War") 3-4 86
COLUMBIA (06657 "Fire") 3-4 87
COLUMBIA (07595 "Brilliant Disguise") 3-4 87
COLUMBIA (07663 "Tunnel of Love")... 3-4 87
COLUMBIA (07726 "One Step Up")...... 3-4 88
COLUMBIA (08400 series) 3-4 88
(Columbia Hall of Fame series.)
COLUMBIA (10209 "Born to Run").... 10-15 75
COLUMBIA (10274 "Tenth Avenue Freeze-Out") 8-12 75
COLUMBIA (10763 "Prove It All Night") 8-12 78
COLUMBIA (10801 "Badlands") 3-6 78
COLUMBIA (11391 "Hungry Heart")...... 3-4 80
COLUMBIA (11431 "Fade Away"/"To Be True").. 15-25 81
COLUMBIA (11431 "Fade Away"/"Be True")... 3-4 81
COLUMBIA (33323 "Born to Run")...... 8-10 76
(Red label. Columbia Hall of Fame series.)
COLUMBIA (33323 "Born to Run")........ 3-4 84
(Gray label. Columbia Hall of Fame series.)
COLUMBIA (45805 "Blinded By the Light") 150-250 73
COLUMBIA (45864 "Spirit in the Night")... 300-500 73

Promotional Singles: 7-inch

COLUMBIA (1329 "Santa Claus Is Comin' to Town") 10-15 81
COLUMBIA (2557 "War") 10-15 86
(Has 1:55 spoken intro on one side.)
COLUMBIA (04463 "Dancing in the Dark")... 8-10 84
COLUMBIA (04561 "Cover Me") 6-10 84
COLUMBIA (04680 "Born in the USA")... 6-10 84
COLUMBIA (04772 "I'm on Fire") 6-10 85
COLUMBIA (04924 "Glory Days") 6-10 85
COLUMBIA (05606 "I'm Goin' Down"). 6-10 85
COLUMBIA (05728 "My Hometown").. 6-10 85
COLUMBIA (06432 "War") 5-8 86
COLUMBIA (07595 "Brilliant Disguise") 5-8 87
COLUMBIA (07663 "Tunnel of Love")... 5-8 87
COLUMBIA (07726 "One Step Up")...... 5-8 88
COLUMBIA (10209 "Born to Run")... 30-35 75
(With large letters on label.)
COLUMBIA (10209 "Born to Run")... 20-25 75
(With small letters on label.)
COLUMBIA (10274 "Tenth Avenue Freeze-Out").................................. 15-20 75
COLUMBIA (10763 "Prove It All Night") 15-20 78
COLUMBIA (10801 "Badlands") 15-20 78
COLUMBIA (11391 "Hungry Heart") 15-20 80
COLUMBIA (11431 "Fade Away") 10-15 81
COLUMBIA (45805 "Blinded By the Light")... 45-55 73
COLUMBIA (45864 "Spirit in the Night") 35-45 73

Picture Sleeves

COLUMBIA (1329 "Santa Claus Is Comin' to Town") 15-20 81
(Promotional issue only.)
COLUMBIA (2557 "War") 10-15 86
(Sleeve for spoken intro promo.)
COLUMBIA (04463 "Dancing in the Dark") 5-10 84
COLUMBIA (04561 "Cover Me") 5-10 84
COLUMBIA (04680 "Born in the USA") 5-10 84
COLUMBIA (04772 "I'm on Fire") 5-10 85
COLUMBIA (04924 "Glory Days") 5-10 85
COLUMBIA (05606 "I'm Goin' Down")... 5-10 85
COLUMBIA (05728 "My Hometown") . 5-10 85
COLUMBIA (06432 "War") 4-8 86
COLUMBIA (07595 "Brilliant Disguise") 4-8 87
COLUMBIA (07663 "Tunnel of Love") .. 4-8 87
COLUMBIA (07726 "One Step Up") 4-8 88
COLUMBIA (11391 "Hungry Heart") 4-8 80
COLUMBIA (11431 "Fade Away") 4-8 81
COLUMBIA (45805 "Blinded By the Light") 300-500 73

LPs: 10/12-inch

COLUMBIA (KC-31903 "Greetings from Asbury Park") 15-20 73
COLUMBIA (PC-31903 "Greetings from Asbury Park") 8-12 75
COLUMBIA (JC-31903 "Greetings from Asbury Park") 5-8 78
COLUMBIA (KC-32432 "The Wild Innocent and the E Street Shuffle") 15-18 73
COLUMBIA (PC-32432 "The Wild Innocent and the E Street Shuffle") 10-15 73
COLUMBIA (JC-32432 "The Wild Innocent and the E Street Shuffle") 5-8 78
COLUMBIA (PC-33795 "Born to Run") 25-30 75
(Credits show Jon Landau as "John.")
COLUMBIA (PC-33795 "Born to Run") 15-20 75
(Has "Jon" correction strip applied to cover.)
COLUMBIA (PC-33795 "Born to Run") 8-12 75
(Has "Jon" correction printed on cover.)
COLUMBIA (JC-33795 "Born to Run") . 5-8 78
COLUMBIA (JC-35318 "Darkness on the Edge of Town") 5-8 78
COLUMBIA (36854 "The River") 10-15 80
COLUMBIA (38358 "Nebraska") 5-8 82
COLUMBIA (38653 "Born in the USA") 5-8 84
COLUMBIA (40558 "Bruce Springsteen & E Street Band Live, 1975-85") 30-40 86
(Includes 36-page booklet.)
COLUMBIA (40999 "Tunnel of Love") .. 5-8 87
COLUMBIA (HC-43795 "Born to Run") 25-35 80
(Half-speed mastered.)
COLUMBIA (HC-45318 "Darkness on the Edge of Town") 40-60 81
(Half-speed mastered.)
COLUMBIA (67060 "Greatest Hits") 10-15 95
COLUMBIA (67484 "The Ghost of Tom Joad") 8-10 96

Promotional LPs

COLUMBIA (978 "As Requested Around the World") 30-40 81
COLUMBIA (1957 "Born in the USA") 20-30 84
COLUMBIA (31903 "Greetings from Asbury Park") 35-45 73
(White label.)
COLUMBIA (32432 "The Wild Innocent and the E Street Shuffle") 35-45 73
(White label.)
COLUMBIA (33795 "Born to Run") 750-1000 75
(With "script" title cover.)
COLUMBIA (33795 "Born to Run").... 40-50 75
(White label.)
COLUMBIA (JC-35318 "Darkness on the Edge of Town") 30-40 78
(White label.)
COLUMBIA (PAL-35318 "Darkness on the Edge of Town") 100-150 78
(Picture disc. 200 made. Add $15 to $25 if lyric sheet is included.)
COLUMBIA (36854 "The River") 25-35 80
(White label.)
COLUMBIA (38358 "Nebraska") 15-25 82
(White label.)
COLUMBIA (38653 "Born in the USA") 15-20 84
(White label.)

Also see BONDS, Gary "U.S.".
Also see CLEMONS, Clarence
Also see LITTLE STEVEN
Also see ORBISON, Roy
Also see PARKER, Graham
Also see SPECTOR, Ronnie
Also see THOMPSON, Robbin, Band
Also see U.S.A. for AFRICA

SPRINGSTEEN, Bruce / Jackson Browne

Singles: 12-inch

ASYLUM (11442 "Medley") 40-50 70
(45 rpm. Has plain sleeve with info sticker.)

Also see BROWNE, Jackson

SPRINGSTEEN, Bruce / Andy Pratt

Singles: 7-inch

COLUMBIA/PLAYBACK (AS-45 "Blinded By the Light") 75-100 73
(Add $40 to $50 if accompanied by booklet.)

Picture Sleeves

COLUMBIA/PLAYBACK (AS-45 "Blinded By the Light") 5-10 73

Also see PRATT, Andy

SPRINGSTEEN, Bruce / Loudon Wainwright III / Taj Mahal / Albert Hammond

Singles: 7-inch

COLUMBIA/PLAYBACK (AS-52 "The Circus Song [Recorded Live]") 75-100 73
(Add $40 to $50 if accompanied by booklet.)

Picture Sleeves

COLUMBIA/PLAYBACK (AS-52 "The Circus Song") 5-10 73

Also see HAMMOND, Albert
Also see TAJ MAHAL
Also see WAINWRIGHT, Loudon, III

SPRINGSTEEN, Bruce / Johnny Winter / Hollies

Singles: 7-inch

COLUMBIA/PLAYBACK (AS-66 "Rosalita") 75-100 73
(Add $40 to $50 if accompanied by booklet.)

Picture Sleeves

COLUMBIA/PLAYBACK (AS-66 "Rosalita") 5-10 73

Also see HOLLIES
Also see SPRINGSTEEN, Bruce
Also see WINTER, Johnny

SPRINGWELL — P&R '71

Singles: 7-inch

PARROT 3-5 71

SPYRO GYRA — P&R/LP '78

Singles: 7-inch

AMHERST 3-5 78
INFINITY 3-5 79

MCA....................3-5 80-85

Picture Sleeves

INFINITY....................3-5 79

EPs: 7-inch

INFINITY (1011 "Live Spyro Gyra")..... 5-10 79
(Promotional issue only. With insert. Not issued with cover.)

LPs: 10/12-inch

AMHERST....................5-10 78
GRP....................5-8 90-91
INFINITY....................5-10 79
MCA (5000 series)....................5-10 80-86
MCA (6000 series)....................8-10 84-89
MCA (9004 "Morning Dance")....................40-60 79
(Picture disc. Promotional issue only.)
MCA (42000 series)....................5-8 87
Members: Chet Catallo; Jay Beckenstein.

SPYS — P&R/LP '82

Singles: 7-inch

EMI AMERICA....................3-5 82

LPs: 10/12-inch

EMI AMERICA....................5-10 82
Also see FOREIGNER

SQUEEZE — LP '80
(U.K. Squeeze)

Singles: 7-inch

A&M....................3-5 79-87

Picture Sleeves

A&M....................3-5 80-87

LPs: 10/12-inch

A&M (Except 3413 & 4687)....................5-10 79-89
A&M (3413 "Squeeze")....................10-20 72
A&M (4687 "U.K. Squeeze")....................10-15 78
I.R.S. 5-8 90
Members: Chris Difford; Glenn Tilbrook; Jools Holland; Gilson Lavis; Keith Wilkinson; Andy Metcalfe.
Also see CARRACK, Paul
Also see DIFFORD & TILBROOK
Also see HOLLAND, Jools, & Millionaires

SQUIER, Billy — LP '80

Singles: 7-inch

CAPITOL (Except 79694)....................3-5 80-88
CAPITOL (79694 "Don't You Love Me")....................5-10 89
(Promotional issue only. Commercial single release on cassette only.)

Picture Sleeves

CAPITOL....................3-5 80-86

LPs: 10/12-inch

CAPITOL....................5-10 80-91

SQUIRE, Chris — LP '76

Singles: 7-inch

ATLANTIC....................3-5 76

LPs: 10/12-inch

ATLANTIC....................8-10 76
Also see YES

STABILIZERS — P&R '87

Singles: 7-inch

COLUMBIA....................3-4 87

Picture Sleeves

COLUMBIA....................3-4 87

STACEY Q — P&R/LP '86
(Stacey Swain)

Singles: 12-inch

ATLANTIC....................4-6 86-87

Singles: 7-inch

ATLANTIC....................3-4 86-88
ON the SPOT....................3-4 87

Picture Sleeves

ATLANTIC....................3-4 86-88

LPs: 10/12-inch

ATLANTIC....................5-8 86-88
Also see SSQ

STACKHOUSE, Ruby
(Ruby Andrews)

Singles: 7-inch

KELLMAC....................4-8 65
Also see ANDREWS, Ruby

STACKRIDGE — LP '74

Singles: 7-inch

DECCA....................3-5 71-72
MCA....................3-5 73
ROCKET....................3-5 76
SIRE....................3-5 74-75

LPs: 10/12-inch

DECCA....................10-12 71
MCA....................8-10 73
ROCKET....................5-10 76
SIRE....................8-10 74-75
Members: Andrew Davis; Jim Warren; Mutter Slater.
Also see KORGIS

STACY, Clyde — P&R '57
(With the Nitecaps)

Singles: 7-inch

ARGYLE....................8-12 59
BULLSEYE (Except 1008)....................10-15 58
BULLSEYE (1008 "Sure Do Love You Baby")....................35-50 58
CANDLELIGHT (1015 "Hoy Hoy")....................30-40 57
G&H....................10-20 58
LEN....................15-25 61

STAFFORD, Jim — P&R '73

Singles: 7-inch

COLUMBIA....................3-4 84
ELEKTRA....................3-5 80-81
ISLAND....................3-5 74
MGM....................3-5 73-75
POLYDOR....................3-5 75-78
TOWN HOUSE....................3-5 82
W.B. 3-5 76-80

LPs: 10/12-inch

MGM....................8-10 74-75
POLYDOR....................5-10 76
Also see LOBO

STAFFORD, Jo — P&R '44

Singles: 78 rpm

CAPITOL....................3-8 43-50
COLUMBIA....................3-5 50-57
COLUMBIA/SNOWY BLEACH (22270 "St. Louis Blues")....................10-15 50s
(Promotional issue for Snowy Bleach and Glass Wax. No actual label name shown. Seven-inch 78 rpm.)

Singles: 7-inch

COLPIX....................4-6 62
COLUMBIA....................5-10 50-60
DECCA....................4-6 68
DOT....................4-6 65
REPRISE....................4-6 63

EPs: 7-inch

CAPITOL....................5-15 50-57
COLUMBIA....................5-15 50-59

LPs: 10/12-inch

BAINBRIDGE....................5-8 82
CAPITOL (H-75 thru H-435)....................20-40 50-53
(10-inch LPs.)
CAPITOL (T-197 thru T-435)....................15-25 55
CAPITOL (T-1653 thru T-2166)....................10-20 62-64
(Monaural.)
CAPITOL (ST-1653 thru ST-2166)....................12-25 62-64
(Stereo.)
CAPITOL (9014 "Songs of Faith")....................20-30 54
(10-inch LP.)
CAPITOL (11000 series)....................5-8 79
COLUMBIA (584 thru 1339)....................15-25 54-59
(Monaural.)
COLUMBIA (1561 "Jo Plus Jazz")....................30-50 60
(Monaural.)
COLUMBIA (2500 series)....................15-30 55
(10-inch LPs.)
COLUMBIA (6000 series)....................20-35 50-54
(10-inch LPs.)
COLUMBIA (8080 "I'll Be Seeing You")....................20-30 59
(Stereo.)
COLUMBIA (8139 "Ballad of the Blues")....................20-30 59
(Stereo.)
COLUMBIA (8361 "Jo Plus Jazz")....................40-60 60
(Stereo.)
COLUMBIA/SNOWY BLEACH (22500 "I Only Have Eyes for You")....................15-25 50s
(Promotional issue for Snowy Bleach. No actual label name shown.)
DECCA....................10-15 68
DOT....................10-15 66
TRIBUTE....................5-10 71
VOCALION....................8-12 68-69
Also see EDWARDS, Jonathan & Darlene
Also see INGLE, Red, & Natural Seven
Also see LAINE, Frankie, & Jo Stafford
Also see MacRAE, Gordon, & Jo Stafford
Also see MERCER, Johnny, Jo Stafford & Pied Pipers
Also see PIED PIPERS
Also see WESTON, Paul

STAFFORD, Terry — P&R/LP '64

Singles: 7-inch

ATLANTIC....................3-5 73-74
CASINO....................3-5 77
COLLECTABLES....................3-4 80s
CRUSADER....................5-10 64
ERIC....................3-5 70s
FIRSTLINE....................3-5 81
LANA....................3-6 60s
MGM....................3-5 71
MELODYLAND....................3-5 75
MERCURY....................4-8 66
PLAYER....................3-4 89
SIDEWALK....................4-8 66-67
TERRIFIC....................3-5
W.B. 3-6 69

LPs: 10/12-inch

ATLANTIC....................8-12 73
CRUSADER (1001 "Suspicion")....................20-25 64
(Monaural)
CRUSADER (1001 "Suspicion")....................25-35 64
(Stereo)
Session: Davie Allan.
Also see ALLAN, Davie

STAGE DOLLS — P&R/LP '89

Singles: 7-inch

CHRYSALIS....................3-4 89

LPs: 10/12-inch

CHRYSALIS....................5-8 89

STALLION — P&R/LP '77

Singles: 7-inch

CASABLANCA....................3-5 77-78

LPs: 10/12-inch

CASABLANCA....................5-10 77-78

STALLONE, Frank — P&R '80

Singles: 12-inch

RSO....................4-6 83

Singles: 7-inch

POLYDOR....................3-4 84-85
SCOTTI BROS....................3-5 80

Picture Sleeves

POLYDOR....................3-4 84

LPs: 10/12-inch

POLYDOR....................5-8 84

STAMPEDERS — P&R/LP '71

Singles: 7-inch

BELL....................3-5 71
CAPITOL....................3-5 73
FLASHBACK....................3-4 74
MGM....................4-8 68
QUALITY....................3-5 76

LPs: 10/12-inch

BELL....................10-15 71
CAPITOL....................8-12 73-74
PRIVATE STOCK/QUALITY....................8-10 76

STAMPLEY, Joe — C&W '71

Singles: 7-inch

ABC....................3-5 77
ABC/DOT....................3-5 75-76
CHESS (1798 "Creation of Love")....................10-20 63
DOT....................3-6 70-74
EPIC....................3-5 75-86
EVERGREEN....................3-4 88-89
IMPERIAL....................10-15 59
PARAMOUNT....................3-6 70
PAULA....................3-5 74

LPs: 10/12-inch

ABC 5-10 77
ABC/DOT 8-12 74-76
ACCORD 5-10 82
DOT 8-12 73
EPIC 5-10 75-85
PHONORAMA 5-10 70s
Also see UNIQUES

STANDELLS — P&R/LP '66

Singles: 7-inch

COLLECTABLES 3-4 80s
LIBERTY 10-20 64
MGM 10-20 65
SUNSET 10-20 66
TOWER 10-20 66-68
VEE JAY 10-20 65

Picture Sleeves

TOWER 15-20 67
VEE JAY 15-25 65

LPs: 10/12-inch

LIBERTY (3384 "In Person at P.J.'s") 40-50 64
(Monaural.)
LIBERTY (7384 "In Person at P.J.'s") 50-60 64
(Stereo.)
RHINO 5-8
SUNSET (1136 "Live and Out of Sight") 15-25 66
(Monaural.)
SUNSET (5136 "Live and Out of Sight") 20-30 66
(Stereo.)
TOWER (T-5027 "Dirty Water") 40-50 66
(Monaural.)
TOWER (ST-5027 "Dirty Water") 50-60 66
(Stereo.)
TOWER (T-5044 "Why Pick on Me") 40-50 66
(Monaural.)
TOWER (ST-5044 "Why Pick on Me") 50-60 66
(Stereo.)
TOWER (T-5049 "Hot Ones") 40-50 66
(Monaural.)
TOWER (ST-5049 "Hot Ones") 50-60 66
(Stereo.)
TOWER (T-5098 "Try It") 40-50 66
TOWER (ST-5098 "Try It") 50-60 66
Members: Dick Dodd; Larry Tamblyn; Gary Lane; Tony Valentino; Dave Burke.

STANDLEY, Johnny — P&R '52

Singles: 78 rpm

CAPITOL 4-8 52-56

Singles: 7-inch

CAPITOL 8-15 52-56
MAGNOLIA (1003 "Rock & Roll Must Go") 40-60 60

EPs: 7-inch

CAPITOL (697 "It's in the Book") 25-45 52

STANKY BROWN GROUP — LP '76
(Stanky Brown)

Singles: 7-inch

SIRE 3-5 76-78

LPs: 10/12-inch

SIRE 8-10 76-78

STANLEY, Michael, Band — LP '75

Singles: 7-inch

ARISTA 3-5 78-79
EMI AMERICA 3-5 80-83
EPIC 3-5 77
TUMBLEWEED 3-5 72-73

LPs: 10/12-inch

ARISTA 5-8 78-79
EMI AMERICA 5-8 80-83
EPIC 8-10 75-76
MCA 10-12 73
TUMBLEWEED 8-12 73
Also see CIRCUS
Also see SILK

STANLEY, Pamala — D&D '83

Singles: 12-inch

KOMANDER 4-6 83
MIRAGE 4-6 84-85
TSR 4-6 84

Singles: 7-inch

EMI AMERICA 3-5 79
MIRAGE 3-4 84-85

LPs: 10/12-inch

EMI AMERICA 5-10 79

STANLEY, Paul — P&R/LP '78

Singles: 7-inch

CASABLANCA 3-5 78

LPs: 10/12-inch

CASABLANCA (7123 "Paul Stanley") 12-20 78
(With poster order form.)
CASABLANCA (7123 "Paul Stanley") 8-12 78
(Without poster order form.)
CASABLANCA (PIX-7123 "Paul Stanley") 40-50 79
(Picture disc.)
Also see KISS

STANSFIELD, Lisa — P&R/LP '90

Singles: 7-inch

ARISTA 3-4 90

Picture Sleeves

ARISTA 3-4 90

LPs: 10/12-inch

ARISTA 5-8 90

STAPLE SINGERS — P&R '67
(The Staples)

Singles: 78 rpm

UNITED 50-100 54

Singles: 7-inch

ABC 3-5 73
CURTOM 3-5 75-77
EPIC 3-6 64-71
PRIVATE I 3-4 84-86
RIVERSIDE 4-6 62-63
SHARP 4-8 60
STAX 3-6 68-74
20TH FOX 3-5 81
UNITED (165 "It Rained, Children") 200-300 54
VEE JAY 4-8 59-62
W.B. 3-5 76-80

LPs: 10/12-inch

BUDDAH 5-10 69
CREED 5-10 73
CURTOM 5-10 76
EPIC 8-12 65-71
EVEREST 8-12 68-69
FANTASY 5-10 73
51 WEST 5-8 80s
GOSPEL 5-15 59
HARMONY 5-10 72
MILESTONE 5-10 75
PRIVATE I 5-8 84-86
RIVERSIDE 10-15 62-65
STAX 5-10 68-81
20TH FOX 5-10 81
TRIP 5-10 71-77
VEE JAY 10-15 59-63
W.B. 5-10 76-78
Members: Mavis Staples; Roebuck Staples; Cleo Staples; Yvonne Staples.
Also see STAPLES, Mavis

STAPLES, Mavis — P&R/LP '70

Singles: 7-inch

CURTOM 3-5 77
PHONO 3-4 84
VOLT 3-5 70-72
W.B. 3-4 79-86

LPs: 10/12-inch

VOLT 8-12 69-70
W.B. 5-10 79-86
Also see BELL, William, & Mavis Staples
Also see FLOYD, Eddie, & Mavis Staples
Also see STAPLE SINGERS

STAPLETON, Cyril, & His Orchestra — P&R '56

Singles: 78 rpm

LONDON 3-5 51-63
MGM 3-5 55-56

Singles: 7-inch

DECCA 3-6 67
LONDON 4-8 51-63
MGM 4-8 55-56
STAGE 3-6 62

EPs: 7-inch

LONDON 4-8 55-57
MGM 4-8 55-56

LPs: 10/12-inch

IMPERIAL 5-10 61
LONDON 5-15 55-59
MGM 5-15 55-56
RICHMOND 5-15 59-61

STAR WARS INTERGALACTIC DROID CHOIR & CHORALE — P&R '80

Singles: 7-inch

RSO 3-5 80

Picture Sleeves

RSO 3-5 80
Also see MECO

STARBUCK — P&R/LP '76

Singles: 7-inch

A.V.I. 3-4 84
ATCO 3-5 73
ELEKTRA 3-5 71
PRIVATE STOCK 3-5 76-77
U.A. 3-5 78-79

LPs: 10/12-inch

PHONORAMA 5-10 70s
PRIVATE STOCK 8-10 76
U.A. 8-10 78
Members: Bruce Blackman; James Cobb; Ken Crysler; Sloan Hayes; Dave Shaver; Bo Wagner.
Also see ETERNITY'S CHILDREN
Also see KORONA

STARCASTLE — LP '76

Singles: 7-inch

EPIC 3-5 76-78

LPs: 10/12-inch

EPIC (Except PAL-34935) 5-10 76-79
EPIC (PAL-34935 "Citadel") 50-75 79
(Picture disc. Promotional issue only.)

STARCHER, Buddy — C&W '49

Singles: 78 rpm

4 STAR 4-8 49-50s

Singles: 7-inch

BOONE 3-6 66
DECCA 3-6 66
4 STAR 5-10 50s
HEARTWARMING 3-5 67
STARDAY 4-8 59-66

EPs: 7-inch

4 STAR 5-10 50s
STARDAY 5-10 61

LPs: 10/12-inch

BLUEBONNET 10-20
DECCA 10-20 66
HEARTWARMING 5-10 68
STARDAY 10-20 62-66

STARGARD — P&R/LP '78

Singles: 12-inch

W.B. 4-8 79-81

Singles: 7-inch

MCA 3-5 77-78
W.B. 3-5 79-81

LPs: 10/12-inch

MCA 5-10 78-82
W.B. 5-10 79-81
Members: Debra Anderson; Janice Williams; Rochelle Runnells.

STARGAZE — D&D '83

Singles: 12-inch

T.N.T. 4-8 83

STARK & McBRIEN — *P&R '75*

Singles: 7-inch

RCA ... 3-5 74-76

LPs: 10/12-inch

RCA (1065 "Big Star") ... 8-10 75
Members: Fred Stark; Rod McBrien.

STARLAND VOCAL BAND — *P&R/C&W/LP '76*

Singles: 7-inch

WINDSONG ... 3-5 76-80

LPs: 10/12-inch

WINDSONG ... 8-10 76-80
Members: Bill Danoff; Taffy Danoff.

STARLETS

Singles: 7-inch

ASTRO (202 "P.S. I Love You") ... 20-30 60
ASTRO (204 "Romeo and Juliet") ... 15-20 60
Also see ANGELS

STARLETS — *P&R '61*

Singles: 7-inch

LUTE (5909 "I'm So Young") ... 15-25 60
PAM (1003 "Better Tell Him No") ... 10-20 61
PAM (1004 "My Last Cry") ... 10-20 61
Members: Maxine Edwards; Bernice Williams; Liz Walker.
Also see BLUE BELLES

STARLITES

Singles: 7-inch

FLASHBACK ... 5-10 65
FURY (1034 "Valerie") ... 50-75 60
FURY (1045 "Silver Lining") ... 25-50 60
SPHERE SOUND (705 "Seven Day Fool") ... 25-50 65
Also see JACKIE & STARLITES

STARPOINT — *LP '81*

Singles: 12-inch

BOARDWALK ... 4-6 83
CHOCOLATE CITY ... 4-8 80-82
ELEKTRA ... 4-6 83-85

Singles: 7-inch

BOARDWALK ... 3-4 83
CHOCOLATE CITY ... 3-5 80-82
ELEKTRA ... 3-4 83-87

Picture Sleeves

ELEKTRA ... 3-4 85-87

LPs: 10/12-inch

CHOCOLATE CITY ... 5-10 80-82
ELEKTRA ... 5-8 83-87
Members: George Phillips; Greg Phillips; Ernest Phillips; Orlando Phillips; Renee Diggs; Kayode Adeyemo.
Also see DAWSON, Cliff, & Renee Diggs

STARR, Brenda K. — *D&D '85*

Singles: 12-inch

MIRAGE ... 4-6 85

Singles: 7-inch

MCA ... 3-4 87-88
MIRAGE ... 3-4 85

Picture Sleeves

MCA ... 3-4 87-88

LPs: 10/12-inch

MCA ... 5-8 88

STARR, Edwin — *P&R '65*

Singles: 12-inch

20TH FOX ... 4-8 77-80

Singles: 7-inch

CASABLANCA ... 3-4 84
GRANITE ... 3-5 75-76
GORDY (Black vinyl) ... 3-8 67-71
GORDY (Colored vinyl) ... 10-15 69-70
(Promotional issues only.)
MONTAGE ... 3-4 82
MOTOWN ... 3-5 73-74
RIC-TIC (103 "Agent Double-O Soul") ... 10-15 65
RIC-TIC (107 "Back Street") ... 10-15 65
RIC-TIC (109 "Stop Her on Sight [S.O.S.]") ... 10-15 66
RIC-TIC (109X "Scott's on Swingers [S.O.S.]") ... 40-50 66
(Promotional issue only.)
RIC-TIC (114 "Headline News") ... 10-15 66
RIC-TIC (118 "It's My Turn Now") ... 10-15 66
RIC-TIC (120 "You're My Mellow") ... 25-50 67
SOUL ... 3-5 72-73
20TH FOX ... 3-5 77-84

LPs: 10/12-inch

GORDY (931 "Soul Masters") ... 15-25 68
GORDY (940 "25 Miles") ... 15-25 69
GORDY (948 "War & Peace") ... 10-20 70
GORDY (956 "Involved") ... 10-15 71
GRANITE ... 8-10 75
MOTOWN ... 8-10 73-82
20TH FOX ... 8-10 77-81

STARR, Edwin, & Blinky

Singles: 7-inch

GORDY ... 4-8 69

LPs: 10/12-inch

GORDY (945 "Just We Two") ... 10-20 69
Also see BLINKY
Also see STARR, Edwin

STARR, Kay — *P&R '48*

(With the Crystalette All Stars)

Singles: 78 rpm

CAPITOL ... 5-10 48-57
CRYSTALETTE ... 10-15 50
JEWEL (1000 "I Ain't Gonna Cry") ... 20-40 45
MODERN ... 15-25 49
RCA ... 4-8 55-57

Singles: 7-inch

ABC ... 3-5 67-68
CAPITOL (811 thru 2887) ... 10-20 50-54
CAPITOL (4000 & 5000 series) ... 5-15 58-64
CRYSTALETTE (632 "Where Or When") ... 15-25 50
(Black vinyl.)
CRYSTALETTE (632 "Where Or When") ... 20-40 50
(Colored vinyl.)
DOT ... 4-6 68
GNP ... 3-5 74-75
HAPPY TIGER ... 3-5 70
RCA (0100 series) ... 3-5 73
RCA (6000 & 7000 series) ... 5-15 55-59

Picture Sleeves

CAPITOL ... 8-12 62

EPs: 7-inch

CAPITOL ... 10-20 50-61
RCA ... 10-15 55-58

LPs: 10/12-inch

ABC ... 5-15 68
ALLEGRO ... 5-10
CAMDEN ... 10-20 60-61
CAPITOL (With "DT" or "SM" prefix) ... 5-15 63-75
(Reissue series including reprocessed stereo.)
CAPITOL (H-211 "Songs By Kay Starr") ... 50-100 50
(10-inch LP.)
CAPITOL (T-211 "Songs By Kay Starr") ... 30-40 55
CAPITOL (H-363 "Kay Starr Style") .. 50-75 53
(10-inch LP.)
CAPITOL (T-363 "Kay Starr Style") ... 30-40 55
CAPITOL (H-415 "The Hits of Kay Starr") ... 50-75 53
(10-inch LP.)
CAPITOL (T-415 "The Hits of Kay Starr") ... 30-40 55
(10-inch LP.)
CAPITOL (T-580 "In a Blue Mood") .. 30-40 55
CAPITOL (1254 thru 1681) ... 25-40 59-62
(With "T" or "ST" prefix.)
CAPITOL (1795 thru 2100 series) ... 15-30 62-64
(With "T" or "ST" prefix.)
CAPITOL (11000 series) ... 5-10 74-79
CORONET ... 10-20 63
CRYSTALETTE (4500 "Kay Starr Sings") ... 50-100 52
(10-inch LP.)
GNP ... 5-10 74-75
GALAXY ... 5-10
LIBERTY (3280 "Swingin' with the Starr") ... 15-25 63
LIBERTY (9001 "Swingin' with the Starr") ... 35-45 56
RCA (1100 thru 1700 series) ... 15-25 55-57
RONDO-LETTE (3 "Them There Eyes") ... 20-30 58
SUNSET ... 8-12 60s
Also see WILLIAMS, Tex

STARR, Kay, & Count Basie

LPs: 10/12-inch

MCA ... 5-8 83
PARAMOUNT ... 10-15 69
Also see BASIE, Count

STARR, Kay, & Tennessee Ernie Ford

Singles: 78 rpm

CAPITOL ... 4-8 50-56

Singles: 7-inch

CAPITOL ... 10-20 50-56

EPs: 7-inch

CAPITOL ... 5-15 56
Also see FORD, Tennessee Ernie

STARR, Kay / Erroll Garner

LPs: 10/12-inch

CROWN ... 15-30 57
MODERN (1203 "Singin' & Swingin'") ... 40-60 56
Also see GARNER, Erroll
Also see STARR, Kay

STARR, Kenny — *C&W '73*

Singles: 7-inch

MCA ... 3-5 73-78
SRO ... 3-5 82
S.S. TITANIC ... 3-4 81

LPs: 10/12-inch

MCA ... 5-10 75
SRO ... 5-10 82
Also see LYNN, Loretta

STARR, Lucille — *P&R '64*

Singles: 7-inch

A&M ... 4-8 66
ALMO ... 4-8 64-65
EPIC ... 4-6 67-69

LPs: 10/12-inch

A&M ... 20-30 66
EPIC ... 20-30 69

STARR, Randy — *P&R '57*

Singles: 78 rpm

DALE ... 8-12 57

Singles: 7-inch

DALE ... 8-12 57-59
MAYFLOWER ... 5-10 59
Also see ISLANDERS

STARR, Randy, & Frank Metis

LPs: 10/12-inch

MAYFLOWER ... 15-25 59
Also see STARR, Randy

STARR, Ringo — *P&R/LP '70*

Singles: 12-inch

ATLANTIC (93 "Drowning in the Sea of Love") ... 15-20 77
(Promotional issue only.)

Singles: 7-inch

APPLE (1831 "It Don't Come Easy") ... 4-8 71
APPLE (1849 "Back Off Boogaloo") 40-60 72
(With a blue apple on the label.)
APPLE (1849 "Back Off Boogaloo") ... 4-6 73
(With a green apple on the label.)
APPLE (1865 "Photograph") ... 3-5 73
APPLE (1870 "You're Sixteen") ... 5-8 73
(With standard apple label.)
APPLE (1870 "You're Sixteen") ... 4-6 73
(With 5-point star label.)
APPLE (1872 "Oh My My") ... 4-6 74
APPLE (1876 "Only You") ... 4-6 74
APPLE (1880 "No No Song") ... 4-6 75
APPLE (1882 "It's All Down to Goodnight Vienna") ... 4-6 75

APPLE (2969 "Beaucoups of Blues")....4-8 70
ATLANTIC (3361 "Dose of Rock 'N' Roll")....10-20 76
ATLANTIC (3371 "Hey Baby")....10-20 76
ATLANTIC (3412 "Drowning in the Sea of Love")....75-100 77
ATLANTIC (3429 "Wings")....8-12 77
BOARDWALK (130 "Wrack My Brain")....3-5 81
BOARDWALK (134 "Private Property")....3-5 82
CAPITOL (Orange label)....4-8 75
CAPITOL (Purple label)....3-5 78
CAPITOL (Black label)....3-4 83
PORTRAIT (70015 "Lipstick Traces")....5-10 78
PORTRAIT (70018 "Heart on My Sleeve")....4-8 78

Picture Sleeves

APPLE (1826 "Beaucoups of Blues")....25-35 70
(Selection number 2969 mistakenly shown as Apple 1826.)
APPLE (1831 "It Don't Come Easy") 10-15 71
APPLE (1849 "Back Off Boogaloo") . 10-15 72
APPLE (1865 "Photograph")....8-12 73
APPLE (1870 "You're Sixteen")....8-12 73
APPLE (1876 "Only You")....5-10 74
APPLE (1882 "It's All Down to Goodnight Vienna")....8-10 75
APPLE (2969 "Beaucoups of Blues")....12-18 70
(Selection number correctly shown.)
BOARDWALK (130 "Wrack My Brain")....3-5 81

Promotional Singles

APPLE (1831 "It Don't Come Easy") 15-20 71
APPLE (1849 "Back Off Boogaloo") . 35-45 72
(White label.)
APPLE (1865 "Photograph")....20-30 73
APPLE (1870 "You're Sixteen")....20-30 73
APPLE (1872 "Oh My My")....20-30 74
APPLE (1876 "Only You")....20-30 74
APPLE (1880 "No No Song")....20-30 75
APPLE (1882 "It's All Down to Goodnight Vienna")....20-30 75
APPLE (1882 "Oo-Wee")....25-30 75
ATLANTIC (3361 "Dose of Rock 'N' Roll")....20-30 76
(White label.)
ATLANTIC (3361 "Dose of Rock 'N' Roll")....10-15 76
(Blue label.)
ATLANTIC (3371 "Hey Baby")....20-30 76
(White label.)
ATLANTIC (3371 "Hey Baby")....10-15 76
(Red-white and blue labels.)
ATLANTIC (3371 "Hey Baby")....25-35 76
(Single-sided disc.)
ATLANTIC (3412 "Drowning in the Sea of Love")....10-20 77
ATLANTIC (3429 "Wings")....20-25 77
(White label.)
ATLANTIC (3429 "Wings")....10-12 77
(Red-white and blue labels.)
BOARDWALK (130 "Wrack My Brain")....8-12 81
BOARDWALK (134 "Private Property")....8-12 82
PORTRAIT (70015 "Lipstick Traces")....8-12 78
PORTRAIT (70018 "Heart on My Sleeve")....8-12 78

LPs: 10/12-inch

APPLE (3365 "Sentimental Journey")....10-15 70
APPLE (3368 "Beaucoups of Blues")....10-15 70
APPLE (3417 "Goodnight Vienna")....10-15 75
APPLE (3422 "Blast from Your Past")....10-15 75
APPLE (3413 "Ringo")....15-20 73
(Includes a 20-page booklet.)
APPLE (3413 "Ringo")....10-15 73
(With 4:05 version of *Six O'Clock*.)
ATLANTIC (18193 "Ringo's Rotogravure")....8-12 76
ATLANTIC (19108 "Ringo the 4th")....8-12 77
BOARDWALK (33246 "Stop and Smell the Roses")....8-10 81
CAPITOL....5-12 80-81
PORTRAIT (35378 "Bad Boy")....8-10 78

Promotional LPs

APPLE (3413 "Ringo")....100-125 73
(With 5:26 version of *Six O'Clock*. Some copies list the track at 5:26 though it actually runs only 4:05.)
ATLANTIC (18193 "Ringo's Rotogravure")....10-20 76
(With programming sticker on front cover.)
ATLANTIC (19108 "Ringo the 4th").. 10-20 77
(With programming sticker on front cover.)
PORTRAIT (35378 "Bad Boy")....25-30 78
(Labels reads "Advance Promotion.")
PORTRAIT (35378 "Bad Boy")....15-20 78
(Labels reads "Demonstration, Not For Sale.")
Also see BEATLES
Also see CLAPTON, Eric
Also see FRAMPTON, Peter
Also see JOHN, Elton
Also see LOMAX, Jackie
Also see NILSSON
Also see OWENS, Buck, & Ringo Starr

STARS ON — *P&R/LP '81*

(Stars on 45; Stars on Long Play)

Singles: 12-inch

RADIO....5-8 81-82

Singles: 7-inch

RADIO....3-5 81-82
21....3-4 83

LPs: 10/12-inch

RADIO....5-10 81-82
21....5-8 83

STARS ON 45 FEATURING SAM & DAVE

Singles: 7-inch

21 (99636 "Sam & Dave Medley")....3-5 85

STARS ON 45 FEATURING NEW SAM & DAVE REVUE

Singles: 7-inch

21 (99636 "Sam & Dave Medley")....3-5 85
Also see SAM & DAVE
Also see STARS ON
Also see STARS on 45 Featuring Sam & Dave

STARSHINE — *D&D '83*

Singles: 12-inch

PRELUDE....4-6 83

Singles: 7-inch

PRELUDE....3-4 83

STARSHIP — *P&R/LP '85*

(Jefferson Starship)

Singles: 7-inch

GRUNT....3-4 85-87
RCA....3-4 89

Picture Sleeves

RCA....3-5 89

LPs: 10/12-inch

GRUNT....5-8 85-87
Also see JEFFERSON STARSHIP

STARZ — *P&R/LP '76*

Singles: 7-inch

CAPITOL....3-5 76-79
(Black vinyl.)
CAPITOL (4399 "Cherry Baby")....5-10 77
(Colored vinyl.)

Picture Sleeves

CAPITOL....3-5 76-79

LPs: 10/12-inch

CAPITOL....8-10 76-78
(Black vinyl.)
CAPITOL (11617 "Violation")....15-20 77
(Colored vinyl.)
VIOLATION....5-8 83
Member: Richie Ranno; Joe Dube; Brendan Harkin.

STATE OF GRACE — *D&D '83*

Singles: 12-inch

PROFILE....4-6 83

Singles: 7-inch

PROFILE....3-4 83

STATLER BROTHERS — *C&W/P&R '65*

Singles: 7-inch

COLUMBIA....4-6 64-69
MERCURY....3-6 70-90

Picture Sleeves

MERCURY....3-4

LPs: 10/12-inch

CBS....5-10 82-85
COLUMBIA (CL-2000 series)....15-25 66-67
(Monaural.)
COLUMBIA (CS-9000 series)....12-25 66-69
(Stereo.)
COLUMBIA (PC-9000 series)....5-8 80s
COLUMBIA (31000 series)....8-10 70s
51 WEST....5-8 80s
HARMONY....6-12 71-73
MERCURY....5-10 71-90
PRIORITY....5-8 82
REALM....5-10
TIME-LIFE....5-8 81
Members: Harold Reid; Don Reid; Lew DeWitt; Phil Balsley; Jimmy Fortune.
Session: Carl Perkins; Ernest Tubb.
Also see CASH, Johnny
Also see PERKINS, Carl
Also see TUBB, Ernest

STATON, Candi — *P&R '69*

Singles: 7-inch

FAME....3-6 69-73
L.A.....3-4 81
SUGAR HILL....3-4 82
UNITY (711 "Now That You Have the Upper Hand")....75-125
W.B.....3-5 74-80

LPs: 10/12-inch

FAME....8-12 70-72
SUGAR HILL....5-8 82
W.B.....8-10 74-80
Also see SOURCE, & Candi Staton

STATON, Dakota — *LP '58*

Singles: 78 rpm

CAPITOL....4-8 55-63

Singles: 7-inch

CAPITOL....4-8 55-63
GROOVE MERCHANT....3-5 72

EPs: 7-inch

CAPITOL....5-15 58-60

LPs: 10/12-inch

CAPITOL (800 thru 1600 series)....20-40 58-63
HALF MOON....5-8 83
LONDON....10-15 67
U.A.....10-20 63-64
VERVE....8-12 71

STATUES — *P&R '60*

Singles: 7-inch

LIBERTY (55245 "Blue Velvet")....15-25 60
LIBERTY (55279 "Dream Girl")....15-25 60
LIBERTY (55292 "White Christmas")....10-20 60
LIBERTY (55363 "Love at First Sight")....10-20 61
Members: James "Buzz" Cason (a.k.a. Garry Miles); Richard Williams; Hugh Jarrett.
Also see MILES, Garry

STATUS QUO — *P&R '68*

Singles: 7-inch

A&M....3-5 73-74
CADET/CONCEPT....4-8 68-69
CAPITOL....3-5 75-77
JANUS....3-5 72
PYE....3-5 75
RIVA....3-5 80

LPs: 10/12-inch

A&M....8-10 73-74
CADET CONCEPT....10-15 68
CAPITOL....8-10 74-79
JANUS....10-12 71

PYE 10-12 72
Also see BAND AID

STATUS VI D&D '83

Singles: 12-inch

RADAR 4-6 83

STEADY B LP '87

LPs: 10/12-inch

JIVE 5-8 87-88

STEALERS WHEEL P&R/LP '73

Singles: 7-inch

A&M 3-5 73-78

Picture Sleeves

A&M 3-5 73

LPs: 10/12-inch

A&M 6-12 73-78
PICKWICK 5-8 80
Members: Gerry Rafferty; Joe Egan.
Also see RAFFERTY, Gerry

STEALIN' HORSES LP '88

Singles: 7-inch

ARISTA 3-4 88

LPs: 10/12-inch

ARISTA 5-8 88

STEAM P&R '69

Singles: 7-inch

FONTANA 3-6 69
MERCURY 3-5 70-76

Picture Sleeves

MERCURY (30160 "Na Na Hey Hey Kiss Him Goodbye") 10-15 76
(Promotional Chicago White Sox sleeve.)

LPs: 10/12-inch

MERCURY 12-18 69

STEEL BREEZE LP '82

Singles: 7-inch

RCA 3-4 82-83

LPs: 10/12-inch

RCA 5-8 82

STEEL PULSE LP '82

Singles: 7-inch

ELEKTRA 3-4 82-84

LPs: 10/12-inch

ELEKTRA 5-8 82-84
MCA 5-8 88
MANGO 5-8 80

STEELE, Ben, & His Bare Hands D&D '83

Singles: 12-inch

VANITY 4-6 83

STEELE, Maureen P&R '85

Singles: 7-inch

MOTOWN 3-4 85

Picture Sleeves

MOTOWN 3-4 85

STEELERS P&R '69

Singles: 7-inch

DATE 4-8 69
EPIC 3-6 71
Members: Leonard Truss; Wes Wells; Wales Walace; Alonzo Wells; George Wells.

STEELEYE SPAN LP '75

Singles: 7-inch

CHRYSALIS 3-5 72-78

LPs: 10/12-inch

BIG TREE 12-15 71
CHRYSALIS 8-12 72-78
MFSL (027 "All Around My Hat") 30-50 79
TAKOMA 8-10 81

STEELY DAN P&R/LP '72

Singles: 7-inch

ABC 3-5 72-78
MCA 3-5 78-81

EPs: 7-inch

ABC 5-10 73-77
(Juke box issues only.)

LPs: 10/12-inch

ABC 6-10 72-78
COMMAND 8-10 74
MCA 5-10 79-82
MFSL (007 "Katy Lied") 25-50 79
MFSL (033 "Aja") 40-60 79
Members: Donald Fagen; Walter Becker; Jim Hodder; Jeff Baxter. Session: Bernard Purdie; Chuck Rainey; Victor Feldman; Larry Carlton; Tom Scott.
Also see FAGEN, Donald
Also see McDONALD, Michael
Also see ULTIMATE SPINACH

STEIN, Lou P&R '57

Singles: 78 rpm

BRUNSWICK 3-5 52-53
EPIC 3-5 55-56
JUBILEE 3-5 54
MERCURY 3-5 55-58
RKO UNIQUE 3-5 57

Singles: 7-inch

BRUNSWICK 4-6 52-53
EPIC 4-6 55-56
JUBILEE 4-6 54
MERCURY 4-6 55-58
MURBO 3-5 69
RKO UNIQUE 4-6 57

EPs: 7-inch

EPIC 4-8 55-56
JUBILEE 4-8 54

LPs: 10/12-inch

CHIAROSCURO 4-8 76-81
CORAL 5-15 53
EPIC 5-15 55-56
EVEREST 5-12 60
JUBILEE 5-15 54
MERCURY 5-15 55-60
MUSICOR 5-10 67-68
OLD TOWN 5-15 61
WING 5-10 62
WORLD JAZZ 4-8 81
Also see COLLINS, Al "Jazzbo," & Lou Stein

STEINBERG, David LP '71

Singles: 7-inch

COLUMBIA 3-5 74

LPs: 10/12-inch

COLUMBIA 5-10 74-75
ELEKTRA 5-10 70
UNI 8-15 68

STEINMAN, Jim P&R/LP '81

Singles: 7-inch

EPIC/CLEVELAND INT'L 3-6 81

Picture Sleeves

EPIC/CLEVELAND INT'L 4-8 81

LPs: 10/12-inch

EPIC/CLEVELAND INT'L 5-10 81

STEPHENSON, Van P&R '81

Singles: 7-inch

HANDSHAKE 3-5 81
MCA 3-4 84

Picture Sleeves

MCA 3-4 84

LPs: 10/12-inch

HANDSHAKE 5-10 81
MCA 5-8 84

STEPPENWOLF P&R/LP '68

Singles: 7-inch

ABC 3-5 70
DUNHILL 4-8 67-71
IMMEDIATE 4-8 67
MCA 3-4 80s
MUMS 3-5 74-75
ROULETTE 3-5 70s

Picture Sleeves

DUNHILL 4-8 71
MUMS 3-5 74

EPs: 7-inch

DUNHILL 5-10 68
(Juke box issues only.)

LPs: 10/12-inch

ABC 8-12 75-76
ALLEGIANCE 5-8
DUNHILL (Except 50053) 10-20 68-73
DUNHILL (50053 "At Your Birthday Party") 20-30 69
EPIC 8-12 75-76
MCA 5-10 79
MUMS 8-10 74
Members: John Kay; Goldy McJohn; Michael Monarch; Jerry Edmonton; Nick St. Nicholas.
Also see HARD TIMES
Also see KAY, John
Also see T.I.M.E.

STEREO FUN INC. D&D '83

Singles: 12-inch

MOBY DICK 4-6 83

STEREOS

Singles: 7-inch

MINK (22 "Memory Lane") 40-50 59
(*Memory Lane* was reissued later in 1959, showing the group as the Tams. the same track was again issued in 1963, shown as by the Tams and then by the Hippies.)
Also see HIPPIES / Reggie Harrison
Also see TAMS

STEREOS P&R '61

Singles: 7-inch

CADET (5577 "Stereo Freeze") 5-8 67
CADET (5626 "I Can't Stop These Tears") 5-8 67
COLLECTABLES 3-5 86
CUB (Except 9106) 10-20 61
CUB (9106 "Do You Love Me") 10-15 62
(Black vinyl.)
CUB (9106 "Do You Love Me") 25-35 62
(Black vinyl.)
GIBRALTAR (105 "Love for You") 20-25 59
(Dark blue label.)
GIBRALTAR (105 "Love for You") 10-15 59
(Light blue label.)
WORLD ARTISTS (1012 "Good News") 10-15 63
Members: Bruce Robinson; Ronnie Collins; Sam Profit; George Otis; Nathaniel Hicks.

STEVE & EYDIE: see LAWRENCE, Steve, & Eydie Gorme

STEVENS, April P&R '51
(April)

Singles: 78 rpm

RCA 5-10 51-52
SOCIETY (10 "Don't Do It") 10-15 50

Singles: 7-inch

A&M 3-5 72
ATCO 4-6 65
CONTRACT 4-8 61
IMPERIAL 4-8 59-65
KING 4-6 64
MGM 4-6 67
RCA 8-12 51-52
SOCIETY (10 "Don't Do It") 15-25 50
VERVE 3-5 71

EPs: 7-inch

KING 10-20 54

LPs: 10/12-inch

IMPERIAL 15-20 61-64
LIBERTY 5-8 83
Also see APRIL
Also see TEMPO, Nino, & April Stevens

STEVENS, April / Marg Phelan

LPs: 10/12-inch

AUDIO LAB 15-20 59
Also see STEVENS, April

STEVENS, Cat P&R/LP '71

Singles: 12-inch

A&M 5-8 77

Singles: 7-inch

A&M 3-5 70-79
DERAM 4-6 66-72

Picture Sleeves

A&M 3-5 71-78

EPs: 7-inch

A&M 8-10 70
(Juke box issue only.)

LPs: 10/12-inch

A&M....5-10 69-84
DERAM....10-15 67-72
LONDON....5-10 78
MFSL (035 "Tea for the Tillerman")...60-80 79
MFSL (UHQR 035 "Tea for the Tillerman")....80-100 79
(Boxed set.)
MFSL (244 "Teaser & the Firecat")...20-25 95
MFSL (254 "Izitso")....20-25 96

STEVENS, Connie — P&R '60

Singles: 7-inch

BELL....4-8 70-72
MGM....10-15 68
PARAMOUNT ("Why Can't He Care for Me")....35-50 58
(Promotional issue only. No actual label name or number is shown, but this may have been distributed by Paramount to promote the film, *Rock-A-Bye Baby*, in which Connie starred.)
W.B. (Except 5092)....5-10 59-66
W.B. (5092 "Apollo")....10-20 59

Picture Sleeves

W.B. (5159 "Too Young to Go Steady")....15-25 60

LPs: 10/12-inch

HARMONY....10-20 69
W.B. (1208 "Conchetta")....40-50 58
W.B. (1335 thru 1460)....20-40 59-62
Also see BYRNES, Edward

STEVENS, Dodie — P&R '59

Singles: 7-inch

CRYSTALETTE (724 "Pink Shoe Laces")....10-20 59
CRYSTALETTE (728 "Yes-Sir-ee")...10-20 59
DOLTON....5-10 63
DOT....8-15 59-62
IMPERIAL....5-10 63

Picture Sleeves

CRYSTALETTE (724 "Pink Shoe Laces")....30-50 59

LPs: 10/12-inch

DOT....20-40 60-61
Session: Billy Vaughn Orchestra.
Also see VAUGHN, Billy, Orchestra

STEVENS, Ray — P&R '61
(With the Merry Melody Singers)

Singles: 7-inch

BARNABY....3-5 70-76
CAPITOL....8-12 58-59
MCA (Except 53661)....3-4 85-89
MCA (53661 "I Saw Elvis in a UFO")...5-10 89
MERCURY (66 "Butch Barbarian")....10-15 64
(Promotional issue only.)
MERCURY (71000 & 72000 series)....5-10 61-68
MERCURY (810000 series)....3-5 83
MONUMENT....4-8 65-69
NRC....10-20 59-60
PREP....10-20 57
PRIORITY....3-4 80s
RCA....3-5 81-82
W.B./AHAB....3-5 76-79

Picture Sleeves

BARNABY....4-6 70
MCA....3-5 86
MERCURY....10-20 61-64
W.B./AHAB....3-5 79

EPs: 7-inch

MERCURY (85 "Ray Stevens")....10-20 62
(Promotional issue only. Not issued with cover.)

LPs: 10/12-inch

BARNABY....8-10 70-78
MCA....5-8 85-89
MERCURY (20732 "1,837 Seconds of Humor")....50-75 62
MERCURY (20732 "Ahab the Arab")....20-25 62
(Reissue of *1,837 Seconds of Humor*.)
MERCURY (20828 "This Is Ray Stevens")....20-30 63
MERCURY (60732 "1,837 Seconds of Humor")....60-80 62
MERCURY (60732 "Ahab the Arab")....25-35 62
(Reissue of *1,837 Seconds of Humor*.)
MERCURY (60828 "This Is Ray Stevens")....25-35 63
MERCURY (61272 "The Best of Ray Stevens")....10-15 70
MERCURY (810000 series)....5-8 83
MONUMENT....10-15 66-69
PICKWICK....5-10
PRIORITY....5-8 82
RCA....5-10 80-82
W.B.....5-10 76-79
WING....10-15 68
Session: Minnie Pearl; Jerry Clower.
Also see ARCHIES
Also see 4 SEASONS / Ray Stevens
Also see HENHOUSE FIVE PLUS TOO
Also see MINNIE PEARL
Also see ROE, Tommy / Bobby Rydell / Ray Stevens
Also see VELVETS

STEVENS, Ray / Hal Winters

LPs: 10/12-inch

CROWN....12-18 63
Also see STEVENS, Ray

STEVENS, Shakin' — P&R '84

Singles: 7-inch

EPIC....3-5 81-84
EPIC/NU-DISKS....3-5 81-84

LPs: 10/12-inch

EPIC....5-10 81-84

STEVENS, Steve — LP '89
(Steve Stevens' Atomic Playboys)

LPs: 10/12-inch

W.B.....5-8 89

STEVENSON, B.W. — P&R/LP '73

Singles: 7-inch

MCA....3-5 80
PRIVATE STOCK....3-5 78
RCA....3-5 73
W.B.....3-5 77-78

LPs: 10/12-inch

MCA....5-10 80
RCA....5-10 72-77
W.B.....5-10 77

STEVIE B — P&R/LP '88

Singles: 7-inch

LMR....3-4 87-90

LPs: 10/12-inch

LMR....5-8 87
Also see JAYA

STEWART, Al — LP '74

Singles: 7-inch

ARISTA....3-5 78-82
ENIGMA....3-4 88
JANUS....3-5 74-77

Picture Sleeves

JANUS....3-5 74

LPs: 10/12-inch

ARISTA (Except 40)....5-10 78-81
ARISTA (40 "Live Radio Concert")...25-35 80
(Promotional issue only.)
ENIGMA....5-8 88
EPIC....20-25 70
JANUS....10-15 74-77
MFSL (009 "Year of the Cat")....40-60 78
MFSL (082 "Time Passages")....25-35 82
Also see PAGE, Jimmy

STEWART, Amii — P&R/LP '79

Singles: 12-inch

ARIOLA (Black vinyl)....4-8 79
ARIOLA (7736 "Knock on Wood"/"When You Are Beautiful")....8-12 79
(Picture disc.)
ARIOLA (7736 "Knock on Wood"/"Knock on Wood")....15-25 79
(Picture disc.)
ARIOLA (7736 "Knock on Wood"/"Light My Fire")....20-30 79
(Picture disc. Promotional issue only.)
EMERGENCY....4-6 85

Singles: 7-inch

ARIOLA....3-5 79
EMERGENCY....3-4 85

LPs: 10/12-inch

ARIOLA AMERICA....5-10 79
HANDSHAKE....5-8 81

STEWART, Amii, & Johnny Bristol — P&R '80

Singles: 7-inch

HANDSHAKE....3-5 80
Also see BRISTOL, Johnny
Also see STEWART, Amii

STEWART, Andy — P&R '61

Singles: 7-inch

CAPITOL....4-6 62
EPIC....4-6 64
WARWICK....4-8 61

LPs: 10/12-inch

CAPITOL....5-15 62-72
EPIC....5-15 64-68
GREEN LINNET....4-8 83
WARWICK....15-25 61

STEWART, Baron — P&R '75

Singles: 7-inch

U.A.....3-5 75

LPs: 10/12-inch

U.A.....8-10 75

STEWART, Billy — P&R '62
(With the Marquees)

Singles: 78 rpm

ARGO (5256 "Billy's Blues")....10-15 56
CHESS (1625 "Billy's Blues")....15-25 56
OKEH (7095 "Baby, You're My Only Love")....150-200 57

Singles: 7-inch

ARGO (5256 "Billy's Blues")....20-40 56
CHESS (Except 1625)....5-15 62-73
CHESS (1625 "Billy's Blues")....40-60 56
(Reissued three months later on Argo.)
ERIC....3-4 70s
OKEH (7095 "Baby, You're My Only Love")....150-200 57
U.A.....8-12 61

LPs: 10/12-inch

CADET....8-10 74
CHESS (1496 "I Do Love You")....100-125 65
(Red cover. Black label.)
CHESS (1496 "I Do Love You")....50-100 65
(Blue cover. Blue label.)
CHESS (1499 "Unbelievable")....20-40 65
CHESS (1513 "Billy Stewart Teaches Old Standards New Tricks")....15-25 67
CHESS (1547 "Billy Stewart Remembered")....10-15 70
CHESS (50059 "Cross My Heart")....10-15
Also see STEWART, Billy

STEWART, Bobby — D&D '83

Singles: 12-inch

SOS....5-8 82
W.B.....4-6 83

Singles: 7-inch

SOS....3-5 86

STEWART, Dave, & Barbara Gaskin — P&R '81

Singles: 7-inch

PLATINUM....3-5 81

STEWART, Danny
(Danny [Sly] Stewart)

Singles: 7-inch

LUKE (1008 "Long Time Alone")...500-750 61
(Reissued as by Sylvester Stewart.)
PHILLIPS INT'L (3561 "I'll Change My Ways")....20-30 60
Also see STEWART, Danny
Also see STEWART, Sly

STEWART, Gary — C&W '73
(With the Nashville Edition; with Dean Dillon)

Singles: 7-inch

CORY (101 "Walk On Boy")....10-20 64

DECCA 3-5 71
HIGHTONE 3-4 88-89
KAPP 3-6 68-70
MCA 3-5 75
RCA 3-5 73-83
RED ASH 3-4 84

Picture Sleeves

RCA 3-5 82

LPs: 10/12-inch

MCA 4-8 75
RCA 5-10 75-83
Also see CROWELL, Rodney
Also see HARRIS, Emmylou

STEWART, Jermaine — P&R/LP '85

Singles: 12-inch

ARISTA 4-6 84-86

Singles: 7-inch

ARISTA 3-4 84-88

Picture Sleeves

ARISTA 3-4 86-88

LPs: 10/12-inch

ARISTA 5-8 85-88
Also see CULTURE CLUB

STEWART, John — P&R/LP '69

Singles: 7-inch

ALLEGIANCE 3-4
CAPITOL 4-6 69
RCA 3-5 73-75
RSO 3-5 77-80
W.B. 3-5 71

Picture Sleeves

RCA 3-5 70s

LPs: 10/12-inch

ALLEGIANCE 5-8 80s
CAPITOL 10-15 69-70
RCA 5-10 73-75
RSO 5-10 77-80
SHIP 5-8 87
W.B. 8-12 71
Also see BUCKINGHAM, Lindsey
Also see KINGSTON TRIO
Also see NICKS, Stevie

STEWART, John, & Buffy Ford

LPs: 10/12-inch

CAPITOL 10-15 68

STEWART, John, & Nick Reynolds

LPs: 10/12-inch

TAKOMA 5-10
Also see KINGSTON TRIO
Also see STEWART, John

STEWART, Rod — LP '69

(With Faces)

Singles: 12-inch

W.B. 5-10 78-82

Singles: 7-inch

GEFFEN 3-4 87
GNP 3-5 73
MERCURY 4-8 70-76
POLYDOR 3-4 92
PRESS (8722 "Good Morning Little Schoolgirl") 15-25 65
PRIVATE STOCK 3-5 76
W.B. 3-4 75-93

Picture Sleeves

GEFFEN 3-4 87
MERCURY 5-15 72-73
POLYDOR 3-4 92
W.B. 3-5 78-93

LPs: 10/12-inch

ACCORD 5-8 81
MERCURY (Except 61000 series) 8-12 71-76
MERCURY (61000 series) 10-20 69-70
MFSL (054 "Blondes Have More Fun") 25-50 81
PRIVATE STOCK 8-10 77
SPRINGBOARD 8-12 72
TRIP 8-10 77
W.B. (Except BSP-3276) 5-10 75-88
W.B. (BSP-3276 "Blondes Have More Fun") 10-15 79
(Picture disc.)
Also see BECK, Jeff, & Rod Stewart
Also see FACES
Also see PYTHON LEE JACKSON

STEWART, Rod, & Ronald Isley — P&R '90

Singles: 7-inch

W.B. 3-4 90
Also see ISLEY, Ron
Also see STEWART, Rod

STEWART, Sandy — P&R '53

Singles: 78 rpm

EPIC 3-6 54
OKEH 3-6 53
20TH CENTURY 3-6 54
"X" 3-6 55

Singles: 7-inch

ATCO 4-8 59
COLPIX 4-8 62-63
DCP 3-6 64
EAST WEST 4-8 58
EPIC 5-10 54
OKEH 5-10 53
20TH CENTURY 5-10 54
U.A. 4-8 60-61
"X" 5-10 55

Picture Sleeves

COLPIX 5-10 62

LPs: 10/12-inch

COLPIX (441 "My Coloring Book") 15-20 63

STEWART, Sandy / Dave Garroway

Singles: 7-inch

DICK CHARLES ("May You Always") 8-12 63
(Promotional issue only. No selection number used.)

STEWART, Sly

Singles: 7-inch

AUTUMN (3 "I Just Learned to Swim") 10-20 64
Also see SLY
Also see SLY & FAMILY STONE
Also see STEWART BROTHERS
Also see STONE, Sly

STEWART, Sylvester

Singles: 7-inch

G&P (901 "Long Time Alone") 250-350 61
(First issued as by Danny [Sly] Stewart.)
Also see STEWART, Danny
Also see STEWART, Sly

STEWART, Wynn — C&W '56

(With the Tourists)

Singles: 78 rpm

CAPITOL 5-10 56-57

Singles: 7-inch

ATLANTIC 3-4 74
CAPITOL (2000 series) 3-5 67-71
CAPITOL (3000 series) 8-15 56-57
CAPITOL (5000 series) 4-8 62-67
CHALLENGE 5-10 59-64
4 STAR 3-4 80
JACKPOT 10-15 59
PLAYBOY 3-5 75-76
PRETTY WORLD 3-4 85
RCA 3-5 72-73
WINS 3-5 78-79

Picture Sleeves

CAPITOL 4-8 67-69

LPs: 10/12-inch

CAPITOL 10-20 67-75
PICKWICK/HILLTOP 5-12 67
PLAYBOY 5-10 76
STARDAY 8-12 68
WRANGLER (1006 "Wynn Stewart") 15-25 62
Member: Bobby Austin.
Also see PIERCE, Webb / Wynn Stewart

STEWART, Wynn, & Jan Howard — C&W '60

Singles: 7-inch

CHALLENGE 5-10 60

STEWART BROTHERS

Singles: 7-inch

ENSIGN (4032 "The Rat") 75-125 59
KEEN (82113 "Sleep on the Porch") 15-25 60

Picture Sleeves

KEEN (82113 "Sleep on the Porch") 25-50 60
Member: Syl Stewart; Danny Stewart.
Also see STEWART, Sly

STILLS, Stephen — P&R/LP '70

(With Manassas; with Michael Finnigan)

Singles: 7-inch

ATLANTIC 3-5 70-84
COLUMBIA 3-5 75-78

Picture Sleeves

ATLANTIC 3-5 71-84

EPs: 7-inch

ATLANTIC (77206 "Stephen Stills Two") 6-12 71

LPs: 10/12-inch

ATLANTIC 5-10 70-84
COLUMBIA (Except PCQ-33575) 5-10 75-78
COLUMBIA (PCQ-33575 "Stills") 10-15 75
(Quadrophonic.)
Also see AU GO-GO SINGERS
Also see BLOOMFIELD, Mike, Al Kooper & Steve Stills
Also see BUFFALO SPRINGFIELD
Also see CROSBY, STILLS & NASH
Also see JEFFERSON AIRPLANE
Also see MANASSAS
Also see STILLS - YOUNG BAND

STILLS - YOUNG BAND — LP '76

Singles: 7-inch

REPRISE 3-5 77

LPs: 10/12-inch

REPRISE 5-10 76
Members: Stephen Stills; Neil Young.
Also see STILLS, Stephen
Also see YOUNG, Neil

STILLWATER — P&R '77

Singles: 7-inch

CAPRICORN 3-5 77-78

LPs: 10/12-inch

CAPRICORN 5-10 78-79
Member: Jimmy Hall.

STING — P&R/D&D/LP '85

(Gordon Sumner)

Singles: 12-inch

A&M 4-6 85-87

Singles: 7-inch

A&M 3-4 85-90
ABC 3-5 78

Picture Sleeves

A&M 3-4 85-88

LPs: 10/12-inch

A&M 5-8 85-90
ABC 5-10 78
Also see BAND AID
Also see POLICE

STITES, Gary — P&R '59

Singles: 7-inch

CARLTON 10-15 59-60
EPIC 4-8 66
MADISON 10-15 60-61
MR. PEEKE 8-12 62

LPs: 10/12-inch

CARLTON (STLP-120 "Lonely for You") 40-50 60
(Monaural.)
CARLTON (STLP-120 "Lonely for You") 50-75 60
(Stereo.)

STITES, Gary, & Sammi Smith

Singles: 7-inch

JEANNIE 3-6
Also see SMITH, Sammi
Also see STITES, Gary

STITT, Sonny — LP '67

Singles: 78 rpm

PRESTIGE 5-10 50s
ROYAL ROOST 5-10 54

Singles: 7-inch

ARGO 5-10 58-65
ATLANTIC 4-6 63
CADET 3-5 74

CATALYST....3-5 77
ENTERPRISE....3-5 69
IMPULSE....4-8 64
PRESTIGE....5-10 63-69
ROULETTE....4-6 65-67
ROYAL ROOST....5-10 54
WINGATE....8-15 65-66
WORLD PACIFIC....4-6 63

EPs: 7–inch

PRESTIGE....10-25 53

LPs: 10/12–inch

ARGO....20-50 58-65
ATLANTIC....15-30 62-64
CADET....10-25 65-74
CATALYST....5-10 76-77
CHESS....8-12 76
COLPIX....10-20 66
EVEREST....5-8 82
FLYING DUTCHMAN....5-10 75-76
IMPULSE....15-25 63-64
JAMAL....8-12 71
JAZZLAND....20-40 62
JAZZTONE (1231 "Early Modern")....50-75 56
JAZZTONE (1263 "Early Modern")....40-60 57
MUSE....5-10 73-82
PACIFIC JAZZ....20-30 63
PAULA....5-10 74
PRESTIGE (060 "Kaleidoscope")....5-10 83
PRESTIGE (103 "Sonny Stitt Plays")....100-200 51
(10–inch LP.)
PRESTIGE (111 "Mr. Saxophone")....100-200 51
(10–inch LP.)
PRESTIGE (126 "Favorites")....100-200 52
(10–inch LP.)
PRESTIGE (148 "Favorites")....100-200 53
(10–inch LP.)
PRESTIGE (7000 series)....25-75 56-64
(Yellow label.)
PRESTIGE (7000 series)....10-25 65-70
(Blue labels.)
PRESTIGE (10000 series)....8-12 71-74
PRESTIGE (20000 series)....8-15 74
ROOST (418 "At the Hi Hat")....150-250 52
(10–inch LP.)
ROOST (1200 series)....30-50 56
ROOST (2200 series)....15-35 57-66
ROULETTE....10-25 65-70
SAVOY (9006 "Be-Bop")....100-200 53
(10–inch LP.)
SOLID STATE....10-15 69
TRIP....8-12 73
UPFRONT....5-10 77
VERVE....40-80 57-59
(Reads "Verve Records, Inc." at bottom of label.)
VERVE....12-25 62-72
(Reads "MGM Records - A Division Of Metro-Goldwyn-Mayer, Inc." at bottom of label.)
VERVE....5-10 73-84
(Reads "Manufactured By MGM Record Corp." or mentions either Polydor or Polygram at bottom of label.)

STITT, Sonny, & Kai Winding

LPs: 10/12–inch

JAZZTONE (1231 "Early Modern")....70-100 56
JAZZTONE (1263 "Early Modern")....50-75 57

STITT, Sonny, Kai Winding & Horace Silver

LPs: 10/12–inch

ROOST (415 "From the Pen of Johnny Richards")....150-250 52
(10–inch LP.)
Also see AMMONS, Gene, & Sonny Stitt
Also see SILVER, Horace
Also see STITT, Sonny
Also see WINDING, Kai

STOKES, Simon — P&R '69

(With the Nighthawks; Simon T. Stokes)

Singles: 7–inch

CASABLANCA....3-5 74
ELEKTRA....4-8 69-70
IN SOUND....5-10 68
U.A. 3-5 77

LPs: 10/12–inch

MGM....10-15 70
SPINDIZZY....8-12 73
U.A. 5-10 77

STOLOFF, Morris — P&R '56

(Morris Stoloff Conducts the Columbia Studio Orchestra)

Singles: 78 rpm

DECCA....3-5 56
MERCURY....3-5 54

Singles: 7–inch

COLPIX....4-8 59
DECCA....5-10 56
MERCURY....5-10 54
REPRISE....3-6 65

LPs: 10/12–inch

DECCA....5-15 56
W.B. (1416 "Fanny")....25-35 61
(Soundtrack.)

STOMPERS — P&R '62

Singles: 7–inch

LANDA....10-20 61-62
MERCURY (72111 "Frump")....8-12 63
Members: Bobby Pickett; Leonard Capizzi; Bill Capizzi; Ron Deltorto; Lou Toscano; Don Squire.
Also see PICKETT, Bobby

STOMPERS — P&R '83

Singles: 7–inch

BOARDWALK....3-5 83
MERCURY (880000 series)....3-4 84

LPs: 10/12–inch

MERCURY....5-8 84
Members: Sal Baglio; Mark Cuccinello; David Friedman; Stephan Gilligan.

STOMPERS / Dick Dale

LPs: 10/12–inch

CLOISTER (6301 "Sounds of the Silver Surf")....50-75 63
Also see DALE, Dick

STONE, Cliffie, & His Orch. — C&W '47

(With His Barn Dance Band; Cliffie Stone Singers)

Singles: 78 rpm

CAPITOL (Except 2910)....3-6 47-57
CAPITOL (2910 "Blue Moon of Kentucky")....4-8 54

Singles: 7–inch

CAPITOL (Except 2910)....4-10 50-69
CAPITOL (2910 "Blue Moon of Kentucky")....10-20 54
TOWER....3-6 67

LPs: 10/12–inch

CAPITOL (100 thru 300 series)....5-10 68-69
CAPITOL (1000 thru 1600 series)....20-40 58-62
CAPITOL (2100 series)....10-20 64
TOWER....10-15 67

STONE, Doug — LP '90

LPs: 10/12–inch

EPIC....5-8 90

STONE, Kirby, Four — P&R/LP '58

(Kirby Stone Quartet)

Singles: 78 rpm

COLUMBIA....4-8 57

Singles: 7–inch

COLUMBIA....5-15 57-65
MGM....4-8 67
W.B. 4-8 63-64

LPs: 10/12–inch

CADENCE....10-15
COLUMBIA....10-20 58-62
CORONET....8-12 60s
GOLDEN TONE....8-12
RONDO....8-12 60s
W.B. 10-15 63-64
Members: Kirby Stone; Edward Hall; Michael Gardner; Larry Foster.
Also see FOUR FRESHMEN / Kirby Stone Four / University Four

STONE, Sly — LP '75

(Sylvester "Sly Stone" Stewart)

Singles: 12–inch

EPIC....4-8 80

Singles: 7–inch

EPIC....3-5 75-79

LPs: 10/12–inch

EPIC....5-10 79
Also see JOHNSON, Jesse, & Sly Stone
Also see SLY & Family Stone
Also see STEWART, Sly

STONE FURY — LP '84

Singles: 7–inch

MCA....3-4 84

LPs: 10/12–inch

MCA....5-8 84

STONE PONEYS — P&R/LP '67

(Featuring Linda Ronstadt)

Singles: 7–inch

CAPITOL....5-10 67

Picture Sleeves

CAPITOL....5-10 67

LPs: 10/12–inch

CAPITOL (2600 & 2700 series)....15-25 67
Also see RONSTADT, Linda

STONE ROSES — LP '90

LPs: 10/12–inch

SILVERTONE....5-8 90

STONEBOLT — P&R '78

Singles: 7–inch

PARACHUTE....3-5 78-79
RCA....3-5 80

LPs: 10/12–inch

PARACHUTE....5-10 78
RCA....5-10 80

STONEY & MEAT LOAF — P&R '71

Singles: 7–inch

RARE EARTH....3-5 71

LPs: 10/12–inch

PRODIGAL....5-10 78
RARE EARTH....10-15 71
Also see MEAT LOAF

STOOGES — LP '69

(Featuring Iggy Pop)

Singles: 7–inch

ELEKTRA....5-10 69-70

LPs: 10/12–inch

BOMP (114 "Jesus Loves the Stooges")....8-12 78
(10–inch LP. With 3-D cover and 3-D glasses.)
ELEKTRA....15-25 69-70
Also see POP, Iggy

STOOKEY, Paul — P&R/LP '71

Singles: 7–inch

ERIC....3-5 70s
W.B. 3-5 71-72

LPs: 10/12–inch

NEWPAX....5-8
W.B. 10-15 71
Also see PETER, PAUL & MARY

STOREY SISTERS — P&R '58

Singles: 7–inch

BATON....10-20 58
CAMEO....10-20 58
MERCURY....10-15 59
Members: Lillian Storey; Ann Storey.

STORIES — P&R/LP '72

Singles: 7–inch

ERIC....3-5 70s
KAMA SUTRA (Except 545)....3-5 72-74
KAMA SUTRA (545 "I'm Coming Home")....5-8 72
(Cardboard cover.)
RADIOACTIVE GOLD....3-5 74

LPs: 10/12–inch

KAMA SUTRA....8-12 72-73
Members: Michael Brown; Ian Lloyd; Bryan Madey; Steve Love.

Also see BROWN, Michael
Also see LLOYD, Ian

STORM, Billy P&R '59
(With the Valiants)
Singles: 7-inch
ATLANTIC....10-15 60-61
BARBARY COAST (1001 "The Way to My Heart")....100-200 58
BUENA VISTA....8-12 63
COLUMBIA....10-20 59
EARLY BIRD (1001 "This Is the Nite")..4-6 95
(Colored vinyl.)
EARLY BIRD (1003 "Please Wait My Love")....4-6 95
(Colored vinyl.)
ENSIGN (4035 "We Knew")....15-25 59
GREGMARK....10-15 61
HBR (474 "Please Don't Mention Her Name")....10-15 66
INFINITY....10-15 62-63
LOMA....8-12 64-65
ODE....5-10 69
Picture Sleeves
HBR (474 "Please Don't Mention Her Name")....15-20 66
LPs: 10/12-inch
BUENA VISTA (3315 "Billy Storm")..25-50 63
FAMOUS (504 "This Is the Night")....20-30 69
Also see VALIANTS

STORM, Gale P&R '55
(With Billy Vaughn's Orchestra)
Singles: 78 rpm
DOT....5-15 55-56
Singles: 7-inch
CONFIDEO....5-10
DOT (Maroon label)....12-25 55-56
DOT (Black label)....5-10 57-60
DOT (Orange label)....3-6 60s
Picture Sleeves
DOT....10-20 58
EPs: 7-inch
DOT....15-25 55-56
LPs: 10/12-inch
DOT....25-35 56-59
HAMILTON....10-15 66
MCA....5-10 82
Also see VAUGHN, Billy, Orchestra

STORM, Warren P&R '58
Singles: 7-inch
NASCO (6015 "Prisoner's Song")....20-30 58
NASCO (6025 "Troubles Troubles")..25-45 59
Singles: 7-inch
ATCO....4-8 68
DOT (16272 "Gotta Go Back to School")....10-15 61
KINGFISH....4-8
NASCO (6015 "Prisoner's Song")....15-25 58
NASCO (6025 "Troubles Troubles")....15-25 59
NASCO (6028 "I've Got My Heart in My Hand")....15-25 59
ROCKO (512 "Oh Oh Baby")....15-20 59
SINCERE (102 "Love Me Cherry")....20-40 57
SINCERE (107 "Honky Tonk Song")....20-40 58
SOUTH STAR....3-4 83
STARFLITE....3-5 79
ZYNN....10-20
Also see SHONDELLS / Rod Bernard / Warren Storm / Skip Stewart

STOTT, Lally P&R '71
Singles: 7-inch
PHILIPS....3-5 71

STRAIT, George C&W '81
Singles: 7-inch
D....15-25 76
MCA....3-5 81-91
LPs: 10/12-inch
MCA....5-10 81-91

STRANGE, Billy P&R/LP '64
(With the Telstars; with Transients)
Singles: 78 rpm
CAPITOL....5-10 54-55
DECCA....5-10 55
Singles: 7-inch
BUENA VISTA....4-8 62-63
CAPITOL....5-15 54-55
COLISEUM....4-8 63
DECCA....5-15 55
GNP....4-8 64-65
LIBERTY....4-8 61-62
TOWER....4-6 69
LPs: 10/12-inch
COLISEUM....10-20 62
GNP....5-15 63-75
HORIZON....10-15 63
SUNSET....8-10 68
SURREY....10-15 65
TRADITION....8-12 68
Also see CAMPBELL, Glen, & Billy Strange
Also see NELSON, Willie
Also see PETERSEN, Paul

STRANGELOVES P&R/LP '65
Singles: 7-inch
BANG....5-10 65-67
SIRE....4-8 68
SWAN....8-10 64
LPs: 10/12-inch
BANG (BLP-211 "I Want Candy")....35-45 65
(Monaural.)
BANG (BLPS-211 "I Want Candy")..45-65 65
(Stereo.)
Members: Bob Feldman; Jerry Goldstein; Richie Gottehrer.
Also see McCOYS

STRANGERS P&R '59
Singles: 7-inch
TITAN (1701 "Caterpillar Crawl")....10-20 59
TITAN (1702 "Hill Stomp")....10-20 59
TITAN (1704 "Boogie Man")....10-20 60
TITAN (1711 "Navajo")....10-20 60
Member: Joel Hill.
Member: Joel Hill.

STRANGLERS LP '87
Singles: 12-inch
EPIC....4-6 83
Singles: 7-inch
A&M....3-5 77
EPs: 7-inch
A&M (1973 "Something Better Change")....10-15 77
LPs: 10/12-inch
A&M (Black vinyl)....5-10 77-78
A&M (Colored vinyl)....10-15 78
(Promotional only.)
EPIC....5-8 83-87
I.R.S....5-10 80
STIFF....5-10 81

STRAWBERRY ALARM CLOCK P&R/LP '67
Singles: 7-inch
ALL AMERICAN (373 "Incense and Peppermints")....40-60 67
MCA....3-4 73-80s
UNI (Except 55218)....5-15 67-70
UNI (55218 "California Day")....10-20 70
LPs: 10/12-inch
BACK-TRAC....5-10 85
UNI (73014 "Incense and Peppermints")....20-40 67
UNI (73025 "Wake Up, It's Tomorrow")....20-40 67
UNI (73035 "The World in a Seashell")....20-40 68
UNI (73054 "Good Morning Starshine")....20-40 69
UNI (73074 "The Best of the Strawberry Alarm Clock")....20-40 70
VOCALION (73915 "Changes")....15-20 71
Members: George Munford; Randy Seol; Ed King; Lee Freeman; George Bunnel; Gary Loverto; Mark Weitz; Jimmy Pitman; Gene Gunnels.
Also see LYNYRD SKYNYRD
Also see SIXPENCE
Also see WHO / Strawberry Alarm Clock

STRAWBS LP '72
Singles: 7-inch
A&M....4-8 68-75
ARISTA....3-5 78
OYSTER....3-5 76-77
LPs: 10/12-inch
A&M....8-15 71-78
ARISTA....5-10 78
OYSTER....8-10 76-77
Also see DENNY, Sandy, & Strawbs
Also see WAKEMAN, Rick

STRAY CATS P&R/LP '82
(With 14 Karat Soul)
Singles: 7-inch
EMI AMERICA (8122 "Stray Cat Strut")....4-6 82
EMI AMERICA (8132 "Rock This Town")....4-6 82
EMI AMERICA (8168 "Sexy + 17")....4-6 83
EMI AMERICA (8169-1/2 'Sexy + 17' & 'Cruisin' ")....5-10 83
(Two singles in gatefold cover.)
EMI AMERICA (8185 "I Won't Stand In Your Way")....5-10 83
EMI AMERICA (8194 "Look at That Cadillac")....4-6 84
Picture Sleeves
EMI AMERICA....4-6 82-84
EPs: 7-inch
EMI AMERICA....5-10 83
LPs: 10/12-inch
EMI (91401 "Blast Off")....5-10 89
EMI AMERICA (17070 "Built for Speed")....5-10 82
EMI AMERICA (17102 "Rant'n Rave with the Stray Cats")....5-10 83
EMI AMERICA (17226 "Rock Therapy")....5-10 86
Members: Brian Setzer; Lee Rocker; Slim Jim Phantom; Brian McDonald; Gary Barnacle; Lee Allen.
Also see ALLEN, Lee
Also see PHANTOM, ROCKER & SLICK
Also see SETZER, Brian

STREEK P&R '81
Singles: 7-inch
COLUMBIA....3-5 81
LPs: 10/12-inch
COLUMBIA....5-10 81

STREET, Janey P&R/LP '84
Singles: 7-inch
ARISTA....3-4 84
Picture Sleeves
ARISTA....3-4 84
LPs: 10/12-inch
ARISTA....5-8 84-85

STREET PEOPLE P&R '70
Singles: 7-inch
MUSICOR....4-8 69-70
VIGOR....3-5 75-77
LPs: 10/12-inch
MUSICOR....15-20 70
PICKWICK....8-10 72
Also see HOLMES, Rupert

STREETS P&R/LP '83
(Nightstreets)
Singles: 7-inch
ATLANTIC....3-4 83-84
EPIC....3-5 79-80
LPs: 10/12-inch
ATLANTIC....5-8 83-84
EPIC....5-10 79
Member: Steve Walsh; Rick Taylor; Rick Taylor; Joyce Hawthorne.
Also see KANSAS

STREISAND, Barbra LP '63

Singles: 12-inch

COLUMBIA (White label) 15-25 79-85
(Promotional issues only.)
COLUMBIA (39909 "Emotion").......... 20-30 85
(Picture disc.)
COLUMBIA (99-1791 "The Way He Makes Me Feel") 30-40 85
(Picture disc. Promotional issue only.)

Singles: 7-inch

ARISTA (123 "More Than You Know").. 4-6 75
COLUMBIA (02065 thru 05680) 3-5 83-85
COLUMBIA (10450 thru 11364) 3-6 76-80
COLUMBIA (3-42648 "My Coloring Book") 20-30 62
(Compact 33 Single.)
COLUMBIA (4-42648 "My Coloring Book") 8-12 62
COLUMBIA (42631 "Happy Days Are Here Again") 5-10 63
COLUMBIA (42965 thru 43469) 4-6 64-65
COLUMBIA (43518 thru 46024) 3-5 66-74
COLUMBIA (80826 "All I Ask of You") .. 4-8 88

Promotional Singles

COLUMBIA (02065 thru 05680) 4-8 83-85
COLUMBIA (10450 thru 11364) 4-8 76-80
COLUMBIA (4-42648 "My Coloring Book") 20-30 62
COLUMBIA (42631 "Happy Days Are Here Again") 15-25 63
COLUMBIA (42965 thru 43469) 10-20 64-65
(Black vinyl.)
COLUMBIA (42965 "People")........... 40-60 64
(Colored vinyl.)
COLUMBIA (43518 thru 46024) 6-12 66-74
COLUMBIA (79581 "People – Special Open-End Interview") 15-25 64
(Promotional issue only. Compact 33.)
COLUMBIA (80826 "All I Ask of You") 5-10 88

Picture Sleeves

COLUMBIA (Except 43896 & 79581) 3-5 73-85
COLUMBIA (43896 "Ave Maria")........... 4-8 66
COLUMBIA (79581 "People – Special Open-End Interview") 15-25 64
(Promotional issue only.)

EPs: 7-inch

CAPITOL (2636 "Complete Solo Tracks from the Capitol Original Broadway Cast Album *Funny Girl*") 15-25 64

LPs: 10/12-inch

ARISTA.. 8-10 75
CAPITOL (2059 "Funny Girl")............ 10-20 64
COLUMBIA (1779 "The Legend of Barbra Streisand") 35-45 83
(Promotional, one-hour interview program.)
COLUMBIA (CL-2007 thru 2682) 15-25 63-67
(Monaural. Black vinyl.)
COLUMBIA (2054 "The Second Barbra Streisand Album") 100-200 63
(Colored vinyl. Promotional issue only.)
COLUMBIA (2478 "Color Me Barbra") 100-200 66
(Colored vinyl. Promotional issue only.)
COLUMBIA (3220 "Funny Girl") 10-15 68
COLUMBIA (CS-8807 thru 9557) 15-25 63-68
(Stereo. Black vinyl.)
COLUMBIA (8854 "The Second Barbra Streisand Album") 100-200 63
(Colored vinyl. Promotional issue only.)
COLUMBIA (9278 "Color Me Barbra") 100-200 66
(Colored vinyl. Promotional issue only.)
COLUMBIA (9710 thru 9968) 10-15 68-70
COLUMBIA (PC-8000 & PC-9000 series) 5-8
COLUMBIA (JC-9000 series) 5-8
COLUMBIA (30086 thru 39480) 5-15 70-84
With "FC," "JC," "KC," or "PC" prefix.)
COLUMBIA (30378 thru 33815) 10-20 71-75
(Quadrophonic. With "PCQ" prefix.)
COLUMBIA (40092 thru 45369) 5-10 85-89
COLUMBIA (42801 thru 47678) 15-30 82
(Half-speed mastered. With "HC" prefix.)
20TH FOX 10-15 69

Also see ARLEN, Harold, with "Friend"
Also see BLOOD, SWEAT & TEARS

STREISAND, Barbra, & Kim Carnes P&R '84

Singles: 7-inch

COLUMBIA 3-4 84
Also see CARNES, Kim

STREISAND, Barbra / Marilyn Cooper

Singles: 7-inch

COLUMBIA 5-10
(Promotional issue only.)

STREISAND, Barbra / Doris Day / Jim Nabors / Andre Kostelanetz

LPs: 10/12-inch

COLUMBIA (1075 "Season's Greetings from Barbra Streisand & Friends") 15-25
(Special products issue for Maxwell House Coffee Co.)
Also see DAY, Doris
Also see KOSTELANETZ, Andre, & His Orchestra
Also see NABORS, Jim

STREISAND, Barbra, & Neil Diamond P&R '78

Singles: 7-inch

COLUMBIA 3-5 78
Also see DIAMOND, Neil

STREISAND, Barbra, & Barry Gibb P&R '80

Singles: 7-inch

COLUMBIA 3-4 80-81
Also see GIBB, Barry

STREISAND, Barbra, & Don Johnson P&R '88

Singles: 7-inch

COLUMBIA 3-4 88

Picture Sleeves

COLUMBIA 3-4 88

STREISAND, Barbra, & Donna Summer P&R '79

Singles: 12-inch

COLUMBIA/CASABLANCA.............. 8-10 79
(Promotional issue only. With special cover.)

Singles: 7-inch

COLUMBIA 3-5 79

Picture Sleeves

COLUMBIA 3-5 79
Also see STREISAND, Barbra
Also see SUMMER, Donna

STRIKERS LP '81

Singles: 7-inch

PRELUDE... 3-5 81

LPs: 10/12-inch

PRELUDE... 5-10 81

STRING-A-LONGS P&R '61

Singles: 7-inch

ATCO (6694 "Popi")......................... 10-15 69
(Reportedly recorded by the Fireballs but credited to the String-A-Longs.)
DOT 5-10 62-65
WARWICK (603 "Wheels"/"Tell the World") 10-15 60
WARWICK (603 "Wheels"/"Am I Asking Too Much") 8-10 61
WARWICK (606 "Tell the World") 10-15 61
WARWICK (625 thru 675) 8-12 61-62

LPs: 10/12-inch

ATCO (241 "World Wide Hits")......... 15-25 68
(Reportedly recorded by the Fireballs but credited to the String-A-Longs.)
DOT 15-25 62-66
WARWICK (W-2036 "Pick-A-Hit").... 40-50 61
(Monaural.)
WARWICK (WST-2036 "Pick-A-Hit") 50-75 61
(Stereo.)

Members: Keith McCormick; Jimmy Torres; Don Allen; Aubrey Lee de Cordova; Richard Stephens.
Also see FIREBALLS

STROLLERS P&R '61

Singles: 7-inch

CARLTON (546 "There's No One But You") 15-25 61

STRONG, Barrett P&R '60
(With the Rayber Voices)

Singles: 78 rpm

ANNA (1111 "Money").................. 100-200 60

Singles: 7-inch

ANNA (1111 "Money")...................... 15-25 60
ANNA (1116 "Yes No, Maybe So").... 15-25 60
ATCO (6225 "Seven Sins") 25-35 62
CAPITOL 3-5 75
EPIC 3-5 73
MOTOWN.. 3-4
TAMLA (54022 "Let's Rock")...... 800-1200 60
TAMLA (54027 "Money") 35-55 60
(Horizontal lines on label.)
TAMLA (54027 "Money") 15-25 60
(Tamla globe logo on label.)
TAMLA (54029 "Yes No, Maybe So") 30-50 60
TAMLA (54033 "Whirlwind")............ 30-50 60
TAMLA (54035 "Money and Me") 30-50 61
TAMLA (54043 "Misery") 30-50 61
TOLLIE (9023 "I Better Run") 15-25 64

Picture Sleeves

EPIC 3-5 73

LPs: 10/12-inch

CAPITOL 8-10 74
Also see HOLLAND, Eddie

STRUNK, Jud C&W/P&R/LP '73
(With the Coplin Kitchen Band)

Singles: 7-inch

CAPITOL 3-5 74
COBURT 3-5 71
COLUMBIA.. 3-5 70
MCA.. 3-5 77
MGM.. 3-5 72-73
MELODYLAND...................................... 3-5 75-76

LPs: 10/12-inch

COLUMBIA.. 6-12 70
HARMONY 5-10 73
MCA.. 5-10 77
MGM.. 5-10 71-73

STRYPER LP '85

Singles: 7-inch

ENIGMA (Except 1135) 3-4 84-89
ENIGMA (1135 "Reason for the Season") 5-10 84
(Picture disc.)

Picture Sleeves

ENIGMA 3-4 87-88

LPs: 10/12-inch

ENIGMA (Except 73277) 5-8 84-90
ENIGMA (73277 "Stryper") 10-20 86
(Picture disc.)
Members: Michael Sweet; Oz Fox; Tim Gaines; Robert Sweet.

STUDENTS R&B '61

Singles: 78 rpm

CHECKER (902 "I'm So Young") 50-75 58

Singles: 7-inch

ARGO (5386 "I'm So Young") 15-25 61
BRASS RING 4-6 71
CADET 5-10 65
CHECKER (902 "I'm So Young") 20-30 58
CHECKER (1004 "My Vow to You") . 15-25 61
CHESS 3-5 73
COLLECTABLES 3-4 80s
NOTE (10012 "I'm So Young")...... 200-300 58
NOTE (10019 "My Vow to You")...... 200-300 58
Members: Leroy King; Emerson "Rocky" Brown; Rich Havens.

STUFF LP '76

Singles: 7-inch

W.B. 3-5 76-80

LPs: 10/12-inch
W.B. 5-10 76-80

STYLE COUNCIL LP '83
Singles: 7-inch
GEFFEN 3-4 84-85
POLYDOR 3-4 83-88
Picture Sleeves
GEFFEN 3-4 84
LPs: 10/12-inch
GEFFEN 5-8 84-85
POLYDOR 5-8 83-88
Also see BAND AID
Also see JAM

STYLERS P&R '56
(Dick Thomas & Stylers)
Singles: 78 rpm
GOLDEN CREST 15-25 57
JUBILEE 10-15 55-57
Singles: 7-inch
GOLDEN CREST (1181 "You Tell Me") 15-25 57
GOLDEN CREST (1291 "Kiss and Run Lover") 15-25 57
GOLDEN CREST (1292 "Sweetheart of All My Dreams") 15-25 58
GORDY (7018 "Going Steady Anniversary") 25-35 63
JUBILEE 12-25 54-57

STYLISTICS P&R/LP '71
Singles: 7-inch
AMHERST 3-4 85
AVCO 3-6 70-76
H&L 3-5 76-79
MERCURY 3-5 79
PHILADELPHIA INT'L 3-5 82
SEBRING (8370 "You're a Big Girl Now") 15-25 70
STREETWISE 3-4 84-86
TSOP 3-4 80-84
Picture Sleeves
AVCO 3-5 76
LPs: 10/12-inch
AVCO 5-10 71-75
H&L 5-10 76-79
MERCURY 5-10 78-79
PHILADELPHIA INT'L 5-10 82
STREETWISE 5-8 84-86
TSOP 5-10 80-81
Members: Russell Tompkins, Jr.; Airrion Love; Herb Murrell; James Dunn; James Smith.
Also see MEDEIROS, Glenn, & Stylistics

STYX P&R '72
Singles: 7-inch
A&M 3-5 76-84
PARAMOUNT 3-5 71-72
RCA 3-5 76
WOODEN NICKEL 3-5 72-78
Picture Sleeves
A&M 3-5 77-84
LPs: 10/12-inch
A&M (Except 4604 & PR-4724) 5-10 75-84
A&M (4604 "Crystal Ball") 20-30 76
A&M (PR-4724 "Pieces of Eight") 10-15 79
(Picture disc.)
MFSL (026 "Grand Illusion") 25-50 79
NAUTILUS (27 "Cornerstone") 20-30 81
RCA 5-10 72-82
WOODEN NICKEL 8-10 72-77
Promotional LPs
A&M (8431 "Styx Radio Special") 15-25 77
(Two-disc set.)
A&M (17053 "Styx Radio Special") 35-40 78
(Three-disc set.)
A&M (17222 "Radio Sampler") 10-20 83
JIM LADD HOSTS (26-5 "Innerview") 8-12 76
ROLLING STONE (82-46 "Continuous History of Rock & Roll") 10-15 81
Members: Dennis De Young; James Young; Tommy Shaw; John Panozzo; Chuck Panozzo.
Also see DE YOUNG, Dennis
Also see SHAW, Tommy

SUAVE P&R/LP '88
Singles: 7-inch
CAPITOL 3-4 88
Picture Sleeves
CAPITOL 3-4 88
LPs: 10/12-inch
CAPITOL 5-8 88

SUBJECT D&D '85
Singles: 12-inch
POW WOW WOW 4-6 85

SUGAR BEARS P&R '72
Singles: 7-inch
BIG TREE 4-6 72
LPs: 10/12-inch
BIG TREE 10-20 71
Members: Michael McGinnis; Kim Carnes; Baker Knight; Mike Settle; Mitch Murray.
Also see CARNES, Kim

SUGAR CUBES LP '88
Singles: 12-inch
ELEKTRA 4-6 88
Singles: 7-inch
ELEKTRA 3-4 88-89
Picture Sleeves
ELEKTRA 3-4 88-89
LPs: 10/12-inch
ELEKTRA 5-10 88-89
Members: Björk Gudmundsdottir; Bragi Olafsson; Einar Örn; Margret Ornolfsdottir; Sigtryggur Baldursson; Thor Eldon.

SUGARHILL GANG P&R '79
Singles: 12-inch
SUGAR HILL (Except 542) 5-10 80-85
SUGAR HILL (542 "Rapper's Delight") 20-30 79
Singles: 7-inch
SUGAR HILL 3-5 79-85
LPs: 10/12-inch
SUGAR HILL 5-10 80-85
Also see FURIOUS FIVE & Sugarhill Gang

SUGARLOAF P&R/LP '70
(With Jerry Corbetta)
Singles: 7-inch
BRUT 3-5 73-74
CLARIDGE 3-5 74-76
LIBERTY 3-5 70-71
U.A. 3-5 71
Picture Sleeves
BRUT 4-6 73-74
LIBERTY 4-6 71
LPs: 10/12-inch
BRUT 8-10 73
CLARIDGE 8-10 75
LIBERTY 10-15 70-71
Members: Jerry Corbetta; Bob Webber.
Also see CORBETTA, Jerry

SUICIDAL TENDENCIES LP '87
Singles: 7-inch
FRONTIER 3-4 84
LPs: 10/12-inch
CAROL 5-8 87
EPIC 5-8 88-90
JANA 8-10 86
Members: Mike Muir; Rocky George; Mike Clark; R.J. Herrera; Bob Heathcote; Robert Trujillo.

SULTON, Kasim LP '82
Singles: 7-inch
EMI AMERICA 3-5 82
LPs: 10/12-inch
EMI AMERICA 5-10 82

SUMMER, Donna P&R/LP '75
Singles: 12-inch
CASABLANCA 5-8 78-80
GEFFEN 4-8 80-87
MERCURY 4-8 83
OASIS 5-10 75-76
Singles: 7-inch
ATLANTIC 3-4 89
CASABLANCA 3-5 75-80
GEFFEN 3-4 80-87
MERCURY 3-4 83
OASIS 3-6 75-76
Picture Sleeves
ATLANTIC 3-4 89
GEFFEN 3-5 80-87
MERCURY 3-4 83
OASIS 3-6 76
LPs: 10/12-inch
ATLANTIC 5-8 89
CASABLANCA (Except NBPIX-7119 & 20110) 5-10 75-80
CASABLANCA (NBPIX-7119 "The Best of Live and More") 10-15 78
(Picture disc.)
CASABLANCA (20110 "Once Upon a Time") 12-15 77
(Promotional issue only.)
GEFFEN 5-10 80-87
MERCURY 5-10 83
OASIS 6-12 75-76
Also see BROOKLYN DREAMS
Also see MORODER, Giorgio
Also see STREISAND, Barbra, & Donna Summer

SUMMER, Henry Lee LP '88
Singles: 7-inch
CBS ASSOCIATED 3-4 88-89
Picture Sleeves
CBS ASSOCIATED 3-4 88
LPs: 10/12-inch
CBS ASSOCIATED 5-8 88-89

SUMMERS, Andy, & Robert Fripp: see FRIPP, Robert, & Andy Summers

SUMMERS, Bill LP '81
(With Summers Heat)
Singles: 12-inch
MCA 4-6 81-84
Singles: 7-inch
MCA 3-5 81-84
PRESTIGE 3-5 77-80
LPs: 10/12-inch
MCA 5-10 81
Also see HANCOCK, Herbie

SUN P&R '76
Singles: 7-inch
AIR CITY 3-4 84
CAPITOL 3-5 76-82
Picture Sleeves
CAPITOL 3-5 76-82
LPs: 10/12-inch
CAPITOL 5-10 77-82
Members: Nikki Buzz; Randy Fredrix; Clyde Isom; Tim Hollans.

SUN, Joe C&W '78
Singles: 7-inch
A.M.I. 3-4 84-85
ELEKTRA 3-4 82-83
OVATION 3-5 78-80
LPs: 10/12-inch
ELEKTRA 5-8 82-83
OVATION 5-10 78-80

SUN, Joe, & Shotgun C&W '82
Singles: 7-inch
ELEKTRA 3-4 82

SUNDAYS LP '90
LPs: 10/12-inch
DGC 5-8 90

SUNDOWN COMPANY P&R '76
Singles: 7-inch
POLYDOR 3-5 76

SUNGLOWS P&R/LP '63
(Sunny & Sunglows; Sunny & Sunliners; Sunny Ozuna & Sunliners)
Singles: 7-inch
BLACK WHALE 5-10
DISCO GRANDE (1021 "Peanuts") .. 15-20 65
KEY LOC 4-8 66
LONDON 5-10
OKEH 5-10 61

RPR....4-6 69
SUNGLOW....6-12 62-66
TEAR DROP....4-8 63-64

LPs: 10/12-inch

KEY LOC....10-20 66
SIESTA (101 "Original Peanuts")....20-30 65
SUNGLOW (103 "Peanuts")....25-35 65
TEAR DROP (2000 "Talk to Me")....30-50 63

SUNNY & SUNGLOWS or SUNLINERS: see SUNGLOWS

SUNNYSIDERS *P&R '55*

Singles: 78 rpm

KAPP....4-6 55-57
MARQUEE....4-6 55-56

Singles: 7-inch

KAPP....5-10 55-60
MARQUEE....5-10 55-56
NRC....4-8 60
ZENITH....4-8 60

EPs: 7-inch

KAPP....5-10 56

LPs: 10/12-inch

KAPP....10-20 56

SUNRAYS *P&R '65*

Singles: 7-inch

TOWER....8-12 64-67
W.B. 8-12 62

Picture Sleeves

TOWER (340 "Loaded with Love")....15-25 67

LPs: 10/12-inch

TOWER (5017 "Andrea")....50-100 66
Members: Rick Henn; Bryon Case; Vince Hozier; Ed Medora; Marty DiGiovanni.
Also see ALLAN, Davie / Eternity's Children / Main Attraction / Sunrays

SUNSHINE BAND: see KC & Sunshine Band

SUNSHINE COMPANY *P&R/LP '67*

Singles: 7-inch

IMPERIAL....4-8 67-68

LPs: 10/12-inch

IMPERIAL....10-20 67-68
Members: Doug "Red" Mark; Maury Manseau; Larry Sims; Merle Bregante; Mary Nance.
Also see REDEYE

SUPER NATURE *D&D '85*

Singles: 12-inch

POP ART....4-6 85

SUPER SONICS: see SUPER-SONICS

SUPERBS *P&R '64*

Singles: 7-inch

ALTEEN (3004 "You Don't Care")....10-20
COLLECTABLES....3-4 80s
DT (107 "In and Out of Love")....10-20 60s
DORE....15-30 64-67
HERITAGE (103 "Rainbow of Love") 25-35 61

SUPERSAX *LP '73*

LP: 10/12-inch

CAPITOL....5-10 73-74
MFSL (511 "Play Bird")....20-30 80s

SUPER-SONICS *P&R '53*

(With Third Dimension Sound)

Singles: 78 rpm

RAINBOW....10-20 53

Singles: 7-inch

RAINBOW (214 "New Guitar Boogie Shuffle")....10-25 53
(Black vinyl.)
RAINBOW (214 "New Guitar Boogie Shuffle")....25-35 53
(Colored vinyl.)
RAINBOW (214 "Guitar Boogie Shuffle")....15-25 55
(Note title change.)

SUPERTRAMP *LP '74*

Singles: 12-inch

A&M....4-6 82-85

Singles: 7-inch

A&M....3-5 71-85

Picture Sleeves

A&M....3-5 77-85

LPs: 10/12-inch

A&M (Except 3730 & 17236)....8-12 70-87
A&M (3730 "Breakfast in America")....400-600 79
(Picture disc. Promotional issue only.)
A&M (17236 "Supersampler")....10-15 83
(Promotional issue only.)
MFSL (005 "Crime of the Century")..50-70 78
MFSL/UHQR (005 "Crime of the Century")....75-125 78
(Boxed set.)
MFSL (045 "Breakfast in America")....40-60 80
Members: Rick Davies; Roger Hodgson; Doug Thomson; Bob Benberg; John Helliwell.
Also see HODGSON, Roger

SUPREMES *P&R '62*

(Diana Ross & Supremes)

Singles: 12-inch

MOTOWN....8-10 79-81

Singles: 7-inch

AMERICAN INT'L PICTURES ("Dr. Goldfoot and the Bikini Machine")....30-40 66
(Single-sided disc, used to promote the film of the same name.)
GEORGE ALEXANDER INC. (1079 "The Only Time I'm Happy")....30-40 65
(Special premium record. Has a Supremes interview on the flip.)
COLGEMS ("Snatches from the Soundtrack: *The Happening*")....50-100 67
(No selection number used. Promotional issue only.)
EEOC ("Things Are Changing")....50-100 65
(Equal Employment Opportunity Center promotional issue.)
MOTOWN (400 series)....3-4
MOTOWN (1008 "I Want a Guy")....500-1000 61
MOTOWN (1027 "Your Heart Belongs to Me")....15-25 62
MOTOWN (1034 "Let Me Go the Right Way")....35-50 62
MOTOWN (1040 "My Heart Can't Take It No More")....25-45 63
MOTOWN (1044 "A Breath Taking, First Sight Soul Shaking, One Night Love Making, Next Day Heart Breaking Guy")....50-75 63
(Promotional issue only.)
MOTOWN (1044 "A Breath Taking Guy")....15-25 63
(Reissue, with much shorter title.)
MOTOWN (1051 "When the Lovelight Starts Shining Through His Eyes")....10-15 63
MOTOWN (1054 "Run Run Run")....15-25 64
MOTOWN (1060 thru 1080)....10-15 64-65
MOTOWN (1083 "I Hear a Symphony")....5-10 65
(Black vinyl.)
MOTOWN (1083 "I Hear a Symphony")....20-30 65
(Colored vinyl. Promotional issue only.)
MOTOWN (1085 "Children's Christmas Song")....15-25 65
(Colored vinyl. Promotional issue only.)
MOTOWN (1089 thru 1156)....5-10 66-69
MOTOWN (1488 "Medley of Hits")....3-5 80
MOTOWN (1523 "Medley of Hits")....3-5 81
MOTOWN/TOPPS (1 "Baby Love")..50-75 67
MOTOWN/TOPPS (2 "Stop in the Name of Love")....50-75 67
MOTOWN/TOPPS (3 "Where Did Our Love Go")....50-75 67
MOTOWN/TOPPS (15 "Come See About Me")....50-75 67
MOTOWN/TOPPS (16 "My World Is Empty Without You")....50-75 67
(Motown 1 through 16 are Topps Chewing Gum promotional, single-sided, cardboard, flexi, picture discs. Issued with generic sleeves.)
TAMLA (54038 "I Want a Guy")....75-125 61
TAMLA (54045 "Buttered Popcorn")....50-100 61

Picture Sleeves

EEOC ("Things Are Changing")....50-100 65
(Equal Employment Opportunity Center promotional issue.)
MOTOWN (1027 "Your Heart Belongs to Me")....50-100 62
MOTOWN (1060 "Where Did Our Love Go")....20-40 64
MOTOWN (1066 "Baby Love")....20-40 64
MOTOWN (1074 "Stop in the Name of Love")....20-40 64
MOTOWN (1075 "Back in My Arms Again")....20-40 65
MOTOWN (1080 "Nothing But Heartaches")....20-40 65
MOTOWN (1097 "You Can't Hurry Love")....15-25 66
MOTOWN (1101 "You Keep Me Hanging On")....15-25 66

EPs: 7-inch

MOTOWN (60621 "Where Did Our Love Go")....25-50 64
MOTOWN (60623 "A Little Bit of Liverpool")....25-50 64
MOTOWN (60627 "More Hits")....25-50 65
MOTOWN (60649 "A Go Go")....20-40 66

LPs: 10/12-inch

MOTOWN (100 & 200 series)....5-10 80-82
MOTOWN (606 "Meet the Supremes")....400-600 63
(Front cover pictures each member sitting on a chair.)
MOTOWN (606 "Meet the Supremes")....50-75 63
(Front cover pictures the head of each group member.)
MOTOWN (621 "Where Did Our Love Go")....20-40 64
MOTOWN (623 "A Little Bit of Loverpool")....20-30 64
MOTOWN (625 "Country Western and Pop")....20-30 65
MOTOWN (627 "More Hits")....15-25 65
MOTOWN (629 "We Remember Sam Cooke")....20-30 65
MOTOWN (636 "At the Copa")....20-30 65
MOTOWN (638 "Merry Christmas")..25-35 65
MOTOWN (643 thru 708)....15-25 66-70
MOTOWN (737 "Touch")....10-20 70s
MOTOWN (794 "Anthology")....15-20 74
(Three-disc set. Includes 12-page booklet.)
MOTOWN (900 series)....5-10 75
MOTOWN (5000 series, except 5381)....5-12 83-84
MOTOWN (5381 "25th Anniversary")....15-20 86
(Three-LP set. Includes 12-page booklet.)
NATURAL RESOURCES....5-10 78
Members: Diana Ross; Mary Wilson; Florence Ballard; Cindy Birdsong.
Also see DIAMOND, Neil / Diana Ross & Supremes
Also see PRIMETTES
Also see ROSS, Diana
Also see WILSON, Mary

SUPREMES & FOUR TOPS *P&R '70*

Singles: 7-inch

MOTOWN (400 series)....3-4
MOTOWN (1100 series)....4-8 70-71

EPs: 7-inch

MOTOWN (717 "Magnificent Seven")....5-15 70
(Juke box issue.)

LPs: 10/12-inch

MOTOWN (100 series)....5-10 82
MOTOWN (700 series)....10-15 70-71
Also see FOUR TOPS

SUPREMES & TEMPTATIONS *P&R/LP '68*

Singles: 7-inch

MOTOWN (400 series)....3-4
MOTOWN (1100 series)....4-8 68-69

Picture Sleeves
MOTOWN (1137 "I'm Gonna Make You Love Me")..10-20 68
LPs: 10/12-inch
MOTOWN (100 series)........................5-10 82
MOTOWN (600 series)........................10-15 68-69
Also see SUPREMES
Also see TEMPTATIONS

SUPREMES P&R/LP '70

Singles: 7-inch
MOTOWN (400 series)........................3-4
MOTOWN (1162 thru 1415)..................4-8 70-77
(Black vinyl.)
MOTOWN (1172 "Stoned Love")......10-15 70
(Colored vinyl. Promotional issue only.)
LPs: 10/12-inch
MOTOWN (102 "Touch")..................15-20 71
(Open-end interview LP. Price includes script. Promotional issue only.)
MOTOWN (702 thru 904)...................6-12 70-78
Members: Jean Terrell; Mary Wilson; Cindy Birdsong.
Also see PAYNE, Scherrie
Also see TERRELL, Jean

SURFACE P&R/LP '87

Singles: 12-inch
COLUMBIA..4-6 86
SALSOUL...4-6 83
Singles: 7-inch
COLUMBIA..3-4 86-90
SALSOUL...3-4 83
LPs: 10/12-inch
COLUMBIA..5-8 86-90
Members: Bernard Jackson; David Townsend; Dave Conley.
Also see MANDRILL

SURFARIS P&R/LP '63

Singles: 7-inch
ABC...3-4 74
CHANCELLOR.......................................5-8 63
DFS (11 "Wipe Out")..................500-1000 63
DECCA...5-10 63-66
DOT (Except 144 & 16479)................5-10 65-67
DOT (144 "Wipe Out")........................4-6 66
(Black vinyl.)
DOT (144 "Wipe Out").......................25-30 66
(Colored vinyl. Promotional issue only.)
DOT (16479 "Wipe Out")......................4-8 63
KOINKIDINK (101 "Scatter Shield")......3-5 82
MCA...3-5 73
PRINCESS (50 "Wipe Out")...............25-50 63
(Short version, same as Dot issue. Has "RE-1" etched in the vinyl trail-off.)
PRINCESS (50 "Wipe Out")..............50-75 63
(Long version. Does not have "RE-1" etched in the vinyl trail-off.)
REGANO...5-10 63
UNIVERSAL (965 "Wipe Out")..........20-40 63
Picture Sleeves
KOINKIDINK (101 "Scatter Shield")......3-5 82
EPs: 7-inch
DECCA (2765 "Wipe Out")................20-40 63
LPs: 10/12-inch
DECCA...25-45 63-65
DOT (3535 "Wipe Out")....................30-45 63
(Front cover reads "The Original Hit Version, Wipe Out.")
DOT (3535 "Wipe Out")....................25-35 63
(Front cover reads "Wipe Out and Surfer Joe and Other Popular selections By Other Instrumental Groups." The Surfaris are heard only on *Wipe Out* and *Surfer Joe*. Remaining tracks are by the Challengers.)
DIPLOMAT..15-25 60s
PICKWICK..10-15 78
SUNDAZED...5-10 90s
Members: Ron Wilson; Jim Fuller; Jim Pash; Pat Connolly; Bob Berryhill; Ken Forssi. Session: Richie Podolor; Chuck Girard; Gary Usher.
Also see DALE, Dick / Surfaris / Fireballs
Also see SURFARIS / Challengers

SURFARIS
(Original Surfaris)

Singles: 7-inch
CHANCELLOR (1143 "Midnight Surf")...10-20 63
DEL-FI (4219 "Surfari")......................10-20 63
FELSTED (Except 8688)...................10-15 64
FELSTED (8688 "Psyche-Out")........10-20 64
REGANO (201 "Surfin' 63")..............15-20 63
(First issued as *Steppin' Out*, credited to the Customs.)
SURFARI (301 "Gum Dipped Slicks")..20-30 64
LPs: 10/12-inch
DIPLOMAT..15-25 63
Members: Larry Weed; Doug Weisman; Mike Biondo; Jim Tran; Chuck Vehle.
Also see DALE, Dick / Surfaris / Surf Kings (Beach Boys)

SURFARIS / Biscaynes

Singles: 7-inch
NORTHRIDGE (1001 "Moment of Truth")..15-25 63
REPRISE (20180 "Moment of Truth")..10-15 63
Also see SURFARIS (Original Surfaris)

SURFARIS / Challengers

Singles: 7-inch
DOT...5-10 65
Also see SURFARIS

SURVIVOR P&R/LP '80

Singles: 12-inch
SCOTTI BROS....................................4-6 79-86
Singles: 7-inch
CASABLANCA......................................3-4 84
SCOTTI BROS....................................3-5 80-88
Picture Sleeves
SCOTTI BROS....................................3-5 82-87
LPs: 10/12-inch
SCOTTI BROS (Except 362)..............5-10 79-88
SCOTTI BROS (362 "Rebel Girl")....10-12 80
(Promotional issue only.)
Members: Dave Bickler; Jim Peterik; Frank Sullivan; Dennis Johnson; Gary Smith; Jim Jameson.
Also see COBRA
Also see PETERIK, Jim

SURVIVORS

Singles: 7-inch
CAPITOL (5102 "Pamela Jean")... 150-200 64
Members: Brian Wilson; Dave Nowlen; Bob Norberg; Rich Peterson.
Also see BEACH BOYS
Also see BOB & SHERRY

SUSAN LP '79

Singles: 7-inch
RCA...3-5 79
SCEPTER...3-5 70
LPs: 10/12-inch
RCA...5-10 79

SUTCH, Screaming Lord: see LORD SUTCH

SUTHERLAND BROTHERS
(With Quiver) P&R/LP '73

Singles: 7-inch
COLUMBIA..3-5 75-79
ISLAND...3-5 72-73
LPs: 10/12-inch
COLUMBIA..6-10 75-76
ISLAND...6-10 72-74
Members: Gavin Sutherland; Ian Sutherland.

SUTTON, Glenn C&W/P&R '79

Singles: 7-inch
ABC...3-5 73
EPIC..4-6 67
MGM..4-8 64-65
MERCURY..3-5 78-86
LPs: 10/12-inch
MERCURY..5-10 79
Also see KELLUM, Murray / Glenn Sutton

SUZY & RED STRIPES P&R '77
(Linda McCartney & Wings)

Singles: 12-inch
CAPITOL (15244 "Seaside Woman")...10-20 86
EPIC (361 "Seaside Woman")..........20-30 77
(Promotional issue only.)
Singles: 7-inch
CAPITOL (5608 "Seaside Woman").....3-6 86
(Remixed version.)
EPIC (50403 "Seaside Woman")..........4-8 77
Promotional Singles
CAPITOL (5608 "Seaside Woman") 10-15 86
EPIC (50403 "Seaside Woman")......30-40 77
(Colored vinyl.)
EPIC (50403 "Seaside Woman")......35-45 77
(Black vinyl. White label, states "Advance Promotion")
EPIC (50403 "Seaside Woman")......40-50 77
(Black vinyl. White label, no mention of "Advance Promotion")
Also see McCARTNEY, Paul

SWALLOWS R&B '51

Singles: 78 rpm
AFTER HOURS (104 "My Baby") 100-200 54
KING (4458 "Will You Be Mine")... 100-200 51
KING (4466 "Since You've Been Away")......................................150-250 51
KING (4501 "Eternally")..............100-200 51
KING (4515 "Tell Me Why")...........150-250 51
KING (4525 "Beside You")..............50-100 52
KING (4533 "I Only Have Eyes for You")..50-100 52
KING (4579 "Where Do I Go from Here")..50-100 52
KING (4612 "Laugh")......................50-100 53
KING (4632 "Nobody's Lovin' Me") .50-100 53
KING (4656 "Trust Me")..................50-100 53
KING (4676 "I'll Be Waiting")...........50-100 53
Singles: 7-inch
AFTER HOURS (104 "My Baby")..800-1200 54
GUSTO...3-5 80s
KING (4458 "Will You Be Mine")..................................1000-1500 51
KING (4501 "Eternally")..............800-1200 51
(Black vinyl.)
KING (4501 "Eternally")............2000-3000 51
(Colored vinyl.)
KING (4515 "Tell Me Why").........800-1200 51
KING (4525 "Beside You")...........500-750 52
KING (4533 "I Only Have Eyes for You")..500-1000 52
KING (4579 "Where Do I Go from Here")..500-1000 52
KING (4612 "Laugh")..................500-1000 53
KING (4632 "Nobody's Lovin' Me")..400-600 53
KING (4656 "Trust Me")................400-600 53
KING (4676 "I'll Be Waiting").........400-600 53
Members: Junior Denby; Ed Rich; Earl Hurley; Fred Johnson; Norris Mack; Dee Bailey; Buddy Bailey; Irving Turner; Al France; Cal Kollette.

SWALLOWS P&R '58

Singles: 7-inch
FEDERAL (12319 "Angel Baby").......50-75 58
FEDERAL (12328 "We Want to Rock")..40-60 58
FEDERAL (12329 "Beside You")......50-75 58
FEDERAL (1233 "Itchy Twitchy Feeling")...50-75 58

SWAN, Billy C&W/P&R/LP '74

Singles: 7-inch
A&M..3-5 78-79
COLUMBIA..3-5 76-77
EPIC..3-4 81-83
MGM..5-10 68
MERCURY..3-4 86-87
MONUMENT...4-6 66-76
RISING SONS......................................4-6 67
LPs: 10/12-inch
A&M..5-10 78

COLUMBIA/MONUMENT....................5-10 77
EPIC....................5-10 81
MONUMENT....................5-10 74-78

SWANN, Bettye P&R '67

Singles: 7-inch

A-BET....................3-6 72-74
ATLANTIC....................3-6 72-76
BIG TREE....................3-5 70s
CAPITOL....................4-8 68-70
FAME....................3-5 71
MONEY....................5-10 65-67

Picture Sleeves

CAPITOL....................4-8 69

LPs: 10/12-inch

A-BET....................8-10 72
ATLANTIC....................8-10 72-75
CAPITOL....................10-12 69
MONEY....................10-20 67

Also see DEES, Sam, & Bettye Swann

SWANS P&R '64

Singles: 7-inch

CAMEO (302 "The Boy with the Beatle Hair")....................25-35 64
SWAN (4151 "He's Mine")....................10-15 63

Also see ALICE WONDER LAND

SWANSON, Brad, & His Whispering Organ Sound LP '69

LPs: 10/12-inch

THUNDERBIRD....................5-10 69

SWAYZE, Patrick P&R '87
(Featuring Wendy Fraser)

Singles: 7-inch

RCA....................3-4 87

Picture Sleeves

RCA....................3-5 87

SWAYZE, Patrick, & Wendy Fraser / Maurice Williams & Zodiacs

Singles: 7-inch

RCA....................3-5 88

Also see SWAYZE, Patrick
Also see WILLIAMS, Maurice

SWEAT, Keith P&R/LP '88
(With Jacci McGhee)

Singles: 7-inch

ELEKTRA....................3-4 87
VINTERTAINMENT....................3-4 88-90

Picture Sleeves

VINTERTAINMENT....................3-4 88

LPs: 10/12-inch

VINTERTAINMENT....................5-8 88-90

Also see ENTOUCH

SWEAT BAND LP '80

Singles: 7-inch

UNCLE JAM....................3-5 80

LPs: 10/12-inch

UNCLE JAM....................5-10 80

Also see BOOTSY'S RUBBER BAND

SWEATHOG P&R '71

Singles: 7-inch

COLUMBIA....................3-5 71

LPs: 10/12-inch

COLUMBIA....................8-10 71-72

SWEENY TODD P&R '76

Singles: 7-inch

LONDON....................4-8 76

LPs: 10/12-inch

LONDON (694 "If Wishes Were Horses")....................20-25 77

Members: Nick Gilder; James McCulloch; Bryan Guy Adams.
Also see ADAMS, Bryan
Also see GILDER, Nick

SWEET P&R '71

Singles: 7-inch

BELL....................3-5 71-74
CAPITOL....................3-5 75-79
PARAMOUNT....................5-10 71

LPs: 10/12-inch

BELL....................10-20 73
CAPITOL (Except 16000 series)....................8-10 75-79
CAPITOL (16000 series)....................5-8 80-82
KORY....................8-10 77

Promotional LPs

CAPITOL (8849 "Short & Sweet")....................20-30 78
CAPITOL (11129 "Cut Above the Rest")....................45-55 79
(Boxed set, containing the LP, 8-track and cassette issues of *Cut Above the Rest*, plus a group photo and biography.)

Members: Brian Connolly; Steve Priest; Andy Scott; Mick Tucker.

SWEET, Matthew LP '92

LPs: 10/12-inch

ZOO/BMG (1 "Girlfriend")....................8-10 91
(Colored vinyl. Promotional issue only.)

SWEET, Rachel C&W '76

Singles: 12-inch

STIFF/COLUMBIA....................10-15 79
(Promotional issue only.)

Singles: 7-inch

COLUMBIA....................3-5 81-83
DERRICK....................3-5 76-78
PREMIER....................3-5 74
STIFF/COLUMBIA....................3-5 79-80

LPs: 10/12-inch

ARC....................5-10 81
COLUMBIA....................5-10 81-82
STIFF/COLUMBIA....................5-10 79-80

Also see SMITH, Rex, & Rachel Sweet

SWEET DREAMS P&R '74

Singles: 7-inch

ABC....................3-5 74

Member: Polly Brown.
Also see BROWN, Polly

SWEET F.A. LP '90

LPs: 10/12-inch

MCA....................5-8 90

SWEET G. D&D '83

Singles: 12-inch

FEVER....................4-6 83

SWEET INSPIRATIONS P&R '67

Singles: 12-inch

RSO....................4-8 79

Singles: 7-inch

ATLANTIC....................3-8 67-71
CARIBOU....................3-5 77
RSO....................3-5 79
STAX....................3-5 73-74

LPs: 10/12-inch

ATLANTIC....................10-12 68-70
RSO....................5-10 79
STAX....................8-10 73

Members: Cissy Houston; Sylvia Shemwell; Myrna Smith; Estelle Brown.
Also see FRANKLIN, Aretha
Also see HOUSTON, Cissy
Also see PRESLEY, Elvis
Also see RASCALS

SWEET SENSATION P&R/LP '75

Singles: 7-inch

PYE....................3-5 74-75

LPs: 10/12-inch

PYE....................5-10 75

SWEET SENSATION P&R '87

Singles: 7-inch

ATCO....................3-4 88-90
NEXT PLATEAU....................3-4 86-87

Picture Sleeves

ATCO....................3-4 88-89

LPs: 10/12-inch

ATCO....................5-8 88-90

SWEET TEE LP '89

Singles: 7-inch

PROFILE....................3-4 88

LPs: 10/12-inch

PROFILE....................5-8 88

SWEET THUNDER LP '78

Singles: 7-inch

FANTASY....................3-5 78-79
WMOT....................3-5 79

LPs: 10/12-inch

WMOT....................5-10 78

SWEETWATER LP '69

Singles: 7-inch

REPRISE....................3-6 68-71

LPs: 10/12-inch

REPRISE....................10-15 68-71

SWING OUT SISTER P&R/LP '87

Singles: 7-inch

FONTANA....................3-4 89
MERCURY....................3-4 87

Picture Sleeves

FONTANA....................3-4 89
MERCURY....................3-4 87

LPs: 10/12-inch

FONTANA....................5-8 89
MERCURY....................5-8 87

Members: Andy Connell; Corrine Drewery; Martin Jackson.

SWINGIN' MEDALLIONS P&R/LP '66

Singles: 7-inch

CAPITOL....................4-8 68
COLLECTABLES....................3-4 80s
DOT....................5-10 65
4 SALE (002 "Double Shot")....................20-30 66
1-2-3....................3-5 70
SMASH....................4-8 66-67

LPs: 10/12-inch

SMASH (27083 "Double Shot")....................25-35 66
(Monaural.)
SMASH (67083 "Double Shot")....................25-35 66
(Stereo.)

SWINGING BLUE JEANS P&R/LP '64

Singles: 7-inch

CAPITOL (72152 "Good Golly Miss Molly")....................5-10 64
(Canadian.)
IMPERIAL....................5-10 64-67

LPs: 10/12-inch

IMPERIAL (9261 "Hippy Hippy Shake")....................50-75 64
(Monaural.)
IMPERIAL (12261 "Hippy Hippy Shake")....................30-50 64
(Stereo.)
LIBERTY....................5-10 82

Members: Ray Ennis; Ralph Ellis; Les Braid; Norman Kuhlke.

SWINGLE SINGERS LP '63

LPs: 10/12-inch

COLUMBIA....................4-6 76
PHILIPS....................5-10 63-72

SWITCH P&R/LP '78

Singles: 7-inch

GORDY (Black vinyl)....................3-4 78-82
GORDY (Colored vinyl)....................4-8 78-82
(Promotional issues only.)
TOTAL EXPERIENCE....................3-4 82-84

LPs: 10/12-inch

GORDY....................5-10 78-81
TOTAL EXPERIENCE....................5-8 82-84

Members: Philip Ingram; Bobby DeBarge; Tommy DeBarge; Greg Williams; Jody Sims; Eddie Fluellen.
Also see DE BARGE
Also see DECO

SWOFFORD, Bill Oliver: see OLIVER

SYBIL P&R/LP '89

Singles: 7-inch

NEXT PLATEAU....................3-4 87-89

LPs: 10/12-inch

NEXT PLATEAU....................5-8 87-89

SYKES, Keith LP '80

Singles: 7-inch

BACKSTREET....................3-5 80

LPs: 10/12-inch
BACKSTREET 5-10 80
MIDLAND INT'L 8-10 77
VANGUARD 10-12 70-71

SYLVAIN SYLVAIN LP '80

Singles: 7-inch
RCA 3-5 79
LPs: 10/12-inch
RCA 5-10 79
Also see NEW YORK DOLLS

SYLVERS P&R '72

Singles: 12-inch
CASABLANCA 4-8 79
GEFFEN 4-6 84-85
SOLAR 4-6 81-82
Singles: 7-inch
CAPITOL 3-5 75-78
CASABLANCA 3-5 78-79
GEFFEN 3-4 84-85
MGM 3-5 72-74
PRIDE 3-5 72-73
SOLAR 3-4 81-82
VERVE 3-5 71
Picture Sleeves
GEFFEN 3-4 84-85
PRIDE 3-5 72-73
LPs: 10/12-inch
CAPITOL 5-10 75-78
CASABLANCA 5-10 78-79
CONCEPT 5-10 81
GEFFEN 5-8 84
MGM 8-10 72-74
PRIDE 8-10 72-73
SOLAR 5-10 81
Members: Foster Sylvers; Edmund Sylvers; Pay Sylvers; Angie Sylvers.
Also see SYLVERS, Foster

SYLVERS, Foster P&R/LP '73

Singles: 7-inch
MGM 3-5 73
PRIDE 3-5 73
LPs: 10/12-inch
MGM 6-10 74
PRIDE 8-10 73
Also see SYLVERS

SYLVESTER P&R/LP '78

(Sylvester James)
Singles: 12-inch
FANTASY 4-8 78-79
MEGATONE 4-6 83-86
Singles: 7-inch
FANTASY (Black vinyl) 3-5 78-79
FANTASY (Colored vinyl) 4-8 78-79
(Promotional issues only.)
HONEY 3-5 80-81
MEGATONE 3-4 83-86
W.B. 3-4 87
LPs: 10/12-inch
FANTASY 5-10 78-81
HONEY 5-10 80-81
MEGATONE 5-8 83-86
W.B. 5-8 87

SYLVIA P&R/LP '73

(Sylvia Vanderpool; Sylvia Robinson)
Singles: 12-inch
SUGARHILL 4-6 82
VIBRATION 4-8 77
Singles: 7-inch
ALL PLATINUM 3-5 74
STANG 3-5 70
SUGARHILL 3-5 81
VIBRATION 3-5 73-78
LPs: 10/12-inch
SUGARHILL 5-10 81
VIBRATION 6-10 73-78
Also see LITTLE SYLVIA
Also see MICKEY & SYLVIA
Also see SYLVIA & MOMENTS
Also see SYLVIA & Ralfi Pagan
Also see TURNER, Ike & Tina

SYLVIA & RALFI PAGAN R&B '73

Singles: 7-inch
VIBRATION 3-5 73
Also see PAGAN, Ralfi
Also see SYLVIA

SYLVIA C&W '79

(Sylvia Kirby Allen)
Singles: 7-inch
RCA 3-5 79-87
RCA GOLD STANDARD 3-4 81
Picture Sleeves
RCA 3-4 81-86
LPs: 10/12-inch
RCA 5-10 81-86
Also see GALWAY, James, & Sylvia

SYLVIA & MICHAEL JOHNSON C&W '85

Singles: 7-inch
RCA 3-4 86
Also see JOHNSON, Michael
Also see SYLVIA (Sylvia Kirby Allen)

SYLVIA, Margo, & Tune Weavers: see TUNE WEAVERS

SYLVIA & MOMENTS P&R/R&B '74

Singles: 7-inch
ALL PLATINUM 3-5 74
Also see MOMENTS

SYMBA R&B '80

Singles: 7-inch
VENTURE 3-5 80

SYMBOL 8 R&B '77

Singles: 7-inch
SHOCK 3-5 77-78

SYMBOLIC THREE R&B '85

(Featuring D.J. Dr. Shock)
Singles: 7-inch
REALITY 3-4 85

SYMS, Sylvia P&R '56

Singles: 78 rpm
ATLANTIC 3-6 52-53
DECCA 3-6 56-57
Singles: 7-inch
ATLANTIC 5-10 52-53
COLUMBIA 4-8 59-65
DECCA 4-10 56-64
PRESTIGE 4-6 67
RORI 4-6 62
EPs: 7-inch
ATLANTIC 5-15 56
DECCA 5-15 55
LPs: 10/12-inch
A&M 5-10 78
ATLANTIC (137 "Songs By Sylvia Syms") 50-100 53
(10-inch LP.)
ATLANTIC (1243 "Songs By Sylvia Syms") 20-40 56
(Has Atlantic logo at top of label.)
ATLANTIC (1243 "Songs By Sylvia Syms") 15-25 60
(Has Atlantic logo on side of label.)
ATLANTIC (18000 series) 5-10 76
COLUMBIA 20-30 60
DECCA (8188 "Sylvia Sings") 35-45 55
DECCA (8639 "Song of Love") 30-40 58
KAPP 15-25 61
MOVIETONE 10-15 67
PRESTIGE 15-25 65-67
REPRISE 5-10 82
20TH FOX 10-20 64
VERSION (103 "After Dark") 40-50 54
(10-inch LP.)

SYNCH P&R '86

(Jimmy Harnen & Synch)
Singles: 7-inch
COLUMBIA (05788 "Where Are You Now") 3-4 86
MICKI (001 "Where Are You Now") 10-15
WTG (68625 "Where Are You Now") 3-4 89
Member: Jimmy Harnen.

SYNDICATE OF SOUND P&R/LP '66

Singles: 7-inch
BELL 4-8 66-67
BUDDAH 3-5 70
CAPITOL 3-6 69
DEL-FI (4304 "Prepare for Love") 10-20 65
HUSH (228 "Little Girl") 20-30 66
SCARLET (5-3 "Prepare for Love") 15-25 65
LPs: 10/12-inch
BELL (LP-6001 "Little Girl") 25-35 66
(Monaural.)
BELL (SLP-6001 "Little Girl") 30-45 66
(Stereo.)
PERFORMANCE 5-8 88
Members: Jim Sawyers; Bob Gonzalez; John Sharkey; Don Baskin; John Duckworth; Larry Roy; Carl Scott; Barrie Thompson; Dennis Tracy.

SYNERGY LP '75

Singles: 7-inch
PASSPORT 3-5 76
LPs: 10/12-inch
PASSPORT (Black vinyl) 5-10 75-84
PASSPORT (Clear vinyl) 8-12 78

SYREETA LP '72

(Syreeta Wright)
Singles: 7-inch
MOTOWN 3-5 74-80
MOWEST 3-5 72
TAMLA 3-5 80-83
LPs: 10/12-inch
MOTOWN 5-10 74-81
MOWEST 8-12 72
TAMLA 5-10 77-81
Also see JENNIFER / Syretta
Also see PRESTON, Billy, & Syreeta
Also see WRIGHT, Rita

SYSTEM P&R/R&B/D&D/LP '83

Singles: 12-inch
MIRAGE 4-6 83-86
Singles: 7-inch
ATCO 3-4 88
ATLANTIC 3-4 87
MIRAGE 3-4 83-86
Picture Sleeves
ATCO 3-4 88
ATLANTIC 3-4 87
LPs: 10/12-inch
ATLANTIC 5-8 87
MIRAGE 5-10 83-86

SZABO, Gabor LP '67

Singles: 7-inch
BLUE THUMB 3-5 70
BUDDAH 3-5 70
CTI 3-5 73
IMPULSE 3-5 66-68
MERCURY 3-5 76-77
REPRISE 3-5 73
SKYE 3-6 68-70
LPs: 10/12-inch
BLUE THUMB 8-12 70
BUDDAH 8-12 70
CTI 8-12 73-74
IMPULSE 10-20 66-70
MCA 5-8 82
MERCURY 5-10 76
SALVATION 5-10 75
SKYE 8-12 68-70
Also see HORNE, Lena, & Gabor Szabo
Also see WOMACK, Bobby

ATLANTIC

Together For The First Time!
THE SOUL CLAN
SOLOMON BURKE • ARTHUR CONLEY • DON COVAY • BEN E. KING • JOE TEX
"SOUL MEETING"
c/w "THAT'S HOW IT FEELS"
Atlantic 2530

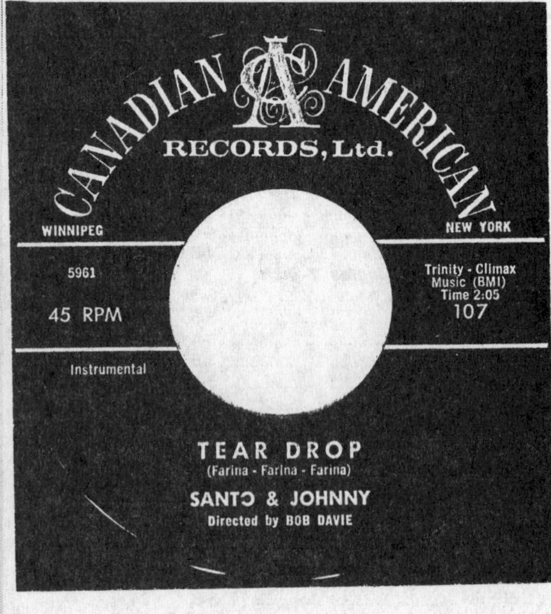
CANADIAN AMERICAN
RECORDS, Ltd.
WINNIPEG
NEW YORK
5961
45 RPM
Instrumental
Trinity - Climax
Music (BMI)
Time 2:05
107
TEAR DROP
(Farina - Farina - Farina)
SANTO & JOHNNY
Directed by BOB DAVIE

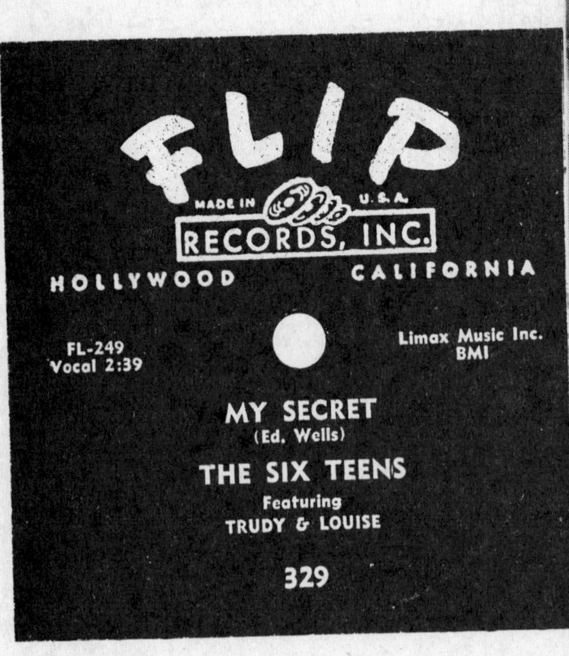
FLIP
MADE IN U.S.A.
RECORDS, INC.
HOLLYWOOD CALIFORNIA
FL-249
Vocal 2:39
Limax Music Inc.
BMI
MY SECRET
(Ed. Wells)
THE SIX TEENS
Featuring
TRUDY & LOUISE
329

Carly
Simon
Coming
Around
Again

T-BONES P&R '65

Singles: 7-inch

LIBERTY ... 5-10 64-66

EPs: 7-inch

LIBERTY ... 8-12 65
(Juke box issues only.)

LPs: 10/12-inch

LIBERTY ... 15-25 64-66
SUNSET ... 10-20 66

Members: Dan Hamilton; Gene Pello; Joe Frank Carollo; Tom Reynolds; Judd Hamilton; Richard Torres; George Dee.
Also see HAMILTON, JOE FRANK & REYNOLDS

T-CONNECTION P&R/R&B/LP '77

Singles: 12-inch

CAPITOL ... 4-6 81-84

Singles: 7-inch

CAPITOL ... 3-5 81-84
DASH ... 3-5 77-79

LPs: 10/12-inch

CAPITOL ... 5-10 81-84
DASH ... 5-10 77-79

Members: Theophilus T. Coakley; David Mackey; Anthony Flowers; Kirkwood Coakley.

T. REX P&R/LP '71
(Tyrannosaurus Rex)

Singles: 7-inch

A&M ... 5-10 68
BLUE THUMB ... 4-8 71-72
CASABLANCA ... 3-5 75
REPRISE ... 3-6 71-74

LPs: 10/12-inch

A&M (3000 series) ... 10-15 72
A&M (4000 series) ... 15-20 68
BLUE THUMB (7 "Unicorn") ... 10-20 71
BLUE THUMB (18 "Beard of Stars") 10-20 72
(Add $5 to $10 if accompanied by the bonus single *Ride a White Swan.*)
CASABLANCA ... 8-10 74
REPRISE ... 8-12 71-73

Members: Marc Bolan; Steve Peregrine Took; Mickey Finn; Bill Legend; Dino Dines; Steve Currie; Jack Green; Gloria Jones.
Also see BOLAN, Marc
Also see GREEN, Jack

T.F.O. R&B '80

Singles: 7-inch

VENTURE ... 3-5 80-81

THP ORCHESTRA R&B/LP '78

Singles: 7-inch

ATLANTIC ... 3-5 79
BUTTERFLY (Black vinyl) ... 3-4 77-78
BUTTERFLY (Colored vinyl) ... 3-5 77-78

LPs: 10/12-inch

ATLANTIC ... 5-8 79
BUTTERFLY ... 8-10 77

TKA P&R/R&B '86
(Total Knowledge in Action)

Singles: 12-inch

TOMMY BOY ... 4-6 86

Singles: 7-inch

TOMMY BOY ... 3-4 86-88

LPs: 10/12-inch

TOMMY BOY ... 5-8 86-88

TKO LP '79

Singles: 7-inch

INFINITY ... 3-5 79

LPs: 10/12-inch

INFINITY ... 5-10 79

T.K.O.'s R&B '66

Singles: 7-inch

TEN STAR ... 4-8 65-67

T.M.G. P&R '79

Singles: 7-inch

ATCO ... 3-5 79

LPs: 10/12-inch

ATCO ... 5-10 79

TMP BAND R&B '86

Singles: 7-inch

CRITIQUE ... 3-4 86

TNT LP '87

LPs: 10/12-inch

MERCURY ... 5-8 84-89

TNT BAND R&B '69

Singles: 7-inch

COTIQUE ... 3-5 69

TSOL LP '87
(True Sounds of Liberty)

LPs: 10/12-inch

ENIGMA ... 5-8 87

T.S.U. TORONADOS P&R/R&B '69
(Tornados)

Singles: 7-inch

ATLANTIC ... 4-6 68-69
OVIDE ... 5-10
VOLT ... 3-5 69-70

TTF R&B '80
(Today, Tomorrow, Forever)

Singles: 7-inch

CURTOM ... 3-5 80
GOLD COAST ... 3-5 81
RSO ... 3-5 80

LPs: 10/12-inch

GOLD COAST ... 5-10 81

T.Z. D&D '83

Singles: 12-inch

STREET SOUND ... 4-6 83

TA MARA & SEEN P&R/R&B/D&D '85

Singles: 12-inch

A&M ... 4-6 85-86

Singles: 7-inch

A&M (Black vinyl) ... 3-4 85-88
A&M (4402 "Blueberry Gossip") ... 8-12 88
(Lips-shaped picture disc.)

Picture Sleeves

A&M ... 3-4 85

LPs: 10/12-inch

A&M ... 5-8 85

TA'BOO D&D '84

Singles: 12-inch

ACME ... 4-6 84

TACO P&R/D&D/LP '83
(Taco Ockerse)

Singles: 12-inch

RCA ... 4-6 83-84

Singles: 7-inch

RCA ... 3-4 83-84

LPs: 10/12-inch

RCA ... 5-8 83-84

TAJ MAHAL LP '69

Singles: 7-inch

COLUMBIA (10000 series) ... 3-5 75
COLUMBIA (44000 series) ... 4-8 67-69
COLUMBIA (45000 series) ... 3-6 69-74

Picture Sleeves

COLUMBIA ... 4-8 67

LPs: 10/12-inch

COLUMBIA ... 6-12 68-81
W.B. ... 5-10 77

Also see SPRINGSTEEN, Bruce / Albert Hammond / Loudon Wainwright III / Taj Mahal

TAKA BOOM: see BOOM, Taka

TAKANAKA R&B '86

Singles: 7-inch

AMHERST ... 3-4 86

TAKE 6 LP '89

LPs: 10/12-inch

REPRISE ... 5-8 89-90

TALK TALK P&R/LP '82

Singles: 12-inch

EMI AMERICA ... 4-8 82-86

Singles: 7-inch

EMI AMERICA ... 3-5 82-86

Picture Sleeves

EMI AMERICA ... 3-5 84-86

LPs: 10/12-inch

EMI AMERICA ... 5-10 82-86

TALKING HEADS LP '77

Singles: 12-inch

SIRE ... 4-8 79-86

Singles: 7-inch

SIRE ... 3-5 77-88

Picture Sleeves

SIRE ... 3-5 78-86

LPs: 10/12-inch

SIRE (Except 23771) ... 5-10 77-88
SIRE (23771 "Speaking in Tongues") ... 20-30 83
(Promotional issue only.)
W.B. (104 "Live on Tour") ... 25-45 79
(Promotional issue only.)

Members: David Byrne; Jerry Harrison; Tina Weymouth; Brian Eno; Robert Fripp; Chris Frantz.
Also see BYRNE, David
Also see MODERN LOVERS
Also see TOM TOM CLUB

TAMI SHOW P&R '88

Singles: 7-inch

CHRYSALIS ... 3-4 88

Picture Sleeves

CHRYSALIS ... 3-4 88

TAMPA RED P&R '36
(Hudson Whittaker)

Singles: 78 rpm

BLUEBIRD ... 15-30 44-45
RCA ... 10-20 45-54

Singles: 7-inch

RCA (47-4000 & 47-5000 series) ... 25-45 51-54
RCA (50-0000 series) ... 50-100 49-51

LPs: 10/12-inch

BLUEBIRD ... 10-15 75
BLUES CLASSICS ... 5-10
PRESTIGE BLUESVILLE ... 20-35 61-62
YAZOO ... 10-15

Also see BIG MACEO

TAMS

Singles: 7-inch

MINK (22 "Memory Lane") ... 20-30 59
(*Memory Lane* was first issued in 1959, showing the group as the Stereos. The same track was reissued in 1963, shown first as by the Tams and then by the Hippies.)
PARKWAY (863 "Memory Lane") ... 10-15 63

Also see HIPPIES / Reggie Harrison
Also see STEREOS

TAMS P&R/R&B '62

Singles: 7-inch

ABC ... 3-6 68-73
ABC-PAR ... 5-10 63-64
APT/ABC ... 3-5 72
ARLEN (711 "Disillusioned") ... 10-20 62
ARLEN (717 "Deep Inside Me") ... 10-20 62
ARLEN (720 "You'll Never Know") ... 10-20 62
ARLEN (729 "Find Another Love") ... 10-20 62
CAPITOL ... 3-6 71
COLLECTABLES ... 3-4 80s
COMPLEAT ... 3-5 83
DAISY ... 5-10 60s
DUNHILL ... 3-5 71
GENERAL AMERICAN (714 "Find Another Love") ... 10-15 62
GUSTO ... 3-5 80

HERITAGE (101 "Vacation Time") 150-250 61
1-2-3 .... 3-5 70
KING 5-10 65
MCA 3-4 80s
RIPETE 3-5 82
ROULETTE 3-4 70s
SOUTH 3-5 73
SWAN (4055 "Sorry") 30-40 60
WONDER 3-5 82

LPs: 10/12-inch

ABC 10-15 67-69
ABC-PAR 20-30 64
BRYLEN 5-10 84
CAPITOL 5-10 79
COMPLEAT 5-8 83
1-2-3 .... 8-10 70
SOUNDS SOUTH 8-10 77

Members: Joe Pope; Charles Pope; Robert Lee Smith; Horace Key; Floyd Ashton; Albert Cottle.

TANEGA, Norma P&R '66

Singles: 7-inch

ABC 3-5 73
ERIC 3-4 70s
NEW VOICE 4-8 66-67
VIRGO 3-4 73

LPs: 10/12-inch

NEW VOICE 15-20 66

TANGERINE DREAM LP '74

Singles: 7-inch

EMI AMERICA 3-4 84
VIRGIN 3-5 75-77

LPs: 10/12-inch

EMI AMERICA 5-8 84
ELEKTRA 5-10 81
MCA 5-10 77-86
VIRGIN 8-12 74-77

Members: Peter Baumann; Chris Franks; Ed Froese.
Also see BAUMANN, Peter

TANGERINE DREAM / Jon Anderson / Bryan Ferry

LPs: 10/12-inch

MCA (6165 "Legend") 8-10 86
(Soundtrack.)
Also see ANDERSON, Jon
Also see FERRY, Bryan
Also see TANGERINE DREAM

TANGIER P&R/LP '89

Singles: 7-inch

ATCO 3-4 89-90

Picture Sleeves

ATCO 3-4 89

LPs: 10/12-inch

ATCO 5-8 89-90

TANNER, Gary P&R '78

Singles: 7-inch

20TH FOX 3-5 78

TANNER, Marc, Band P&R/LP '79

Singles: 7-inch

ELEKTRA 3-5 79
PRIVATE I 3-4 80s

LPs: 10/12-inch

ELEKTRA 5-10 78-80
PRIVATE I 5-10 80s

TANTRUM LP '80

Singles: 7-inch

OVATION 3-5 79

LPs: 10/12-inch

OVATION 5-10 79

TARHEEL SLIM
(Alden Bunn)

Singles: 78 rpm

FIRE 50-100 59

Singles: 7-inch

FIRE 15-25 59-60
FURY 20-30 59

TARHEEL SLIM & LITTLE ANN
(Slim & Ann; Slim & Little Ann; Tarheel Slim & Lil' Annie) R&B '59

Singles: 78 rpm

FIRE 50-100 59

Singles: 7-inch

ATCO 5-10 63
FIRE 15-25 59-62
PORT 4-8 65

Also see TARHEEL SLIM

TARNEY - SPENCER BAND P&R/LP '78

Singles: 7-inch

A&M 3-5 78-81
PRIVATE STOCK 3-5 76

LPs: 10/12-inch

A&M 5-10 78-79

Members: Alan Tarney; Trevor Spencer.

TARRIERS P&R '56

Singles: 78 rpm

GLORY 8-12 56

Singles: 7-inch

DECCA 4-8 63-64
GLORY 10-15 56
U.A. 5-10 59

LPs: 10/12-inch

ATLANTIC 15-25 60
DECCA 10-20 62-64
GLORY (1200 "The Tarriers") 40-60 57
KAPP 10-20 63
U.A. 15-25 59

Members: Erik Darling; Alan Arkin; Bob Carey.
Also see MARTIN, Vince
Also see ROOFTOP SINGERS
Also see WEISSBERG, Eric

TASSELS P&R '59

Singles: 7-inch

AMY (946 "To a Soldier Boy") 8-12 66
MADISON (117 "To a Soldier Boy") .. 15-25 59
MADISON (121 "To a Young Lover") 10-20 59

TASTE LP '69

Singles: 7-inch

ATCO 3-5 69-70

LPs: 10/12-inch

ATCO 10-15 69-70

Member: Rory Gallagher.
Also see GALLAGHER, Rory

TASTE OF HONEY P&R/R&B/LP '78

Singles: 12-inch

CAPITOL (Except 9572) 4-8 78-79
CAPITOL (9572 "Sukiyaki") 8-10 80
(Fan shaped disc. Promotional issue only.)
MCA 4-6 84

Singles: 7-inch

CAPITOL 3-5 78-82
MCA 3-4 84

Picture Sleeves

CAPITOL 3-5 78-82

LPs: 10/12-inch

CAPITOL 5-10 78-82

Members: Janice Marie Johnson; Hazel Payne.
Also see FELDER, Wilton
Also see JOHNSON, Janice Marie

TATE, Howard P&R/R&B '66

Singles: 7-inch

ATLANTIC 3-6 71-72
EPIC 3-5 74
TURNTABLE 5-10 69-70
UTOPIA (510 "Half a Man") 15-25 66
VERVE 4-8 66-68

LPs: 10/12-inch

ATLANTIC 10-20 71
TURNTABLE 8-10 70
VERVE 10-20 67-68

Also see DOGGETT, Bill

TATE, Laurie
(With Joe Morris Blues Cavalcade)

Singles: 78 rpm

ATLANTIC 25-35 52

Singles: 7-inch

ATLANTIC (965 "Rock Me Daddy") ... 50-75 52

Also see MORRIS, Joe, & His Orchestra

TATE, Tommy R&B '72

Singles: 7-inch

ABC-PAR (10626 "What's the Matter") 15-25 65
JACKSON SOUND 8-10 70
KOKO 3-6 72-76
OKEH 8-12 66

TAVARES P&R/R&B '73

Singles: 12-inch

CAPITOL 4-8 77-79
RCA 4-6 82-84

Singles: 7-inch

CAPITOL 3-5 73-80
RCA 3-4 82-84

LPs: 10/12-inch

CAPITOL 8-10 73-81
RCA 5-10 82-83

TAWATHA R&B '87

Singles: 7-inch

EPIC 3-4 87

TAXXI LP '82

Singles: 7-inch

FANTASY 3-5 82

LPs: 10/12-inch

FANTASY (9617 "States of Emergency") 20-30 82
MCA 10-15 85

TAYLOR, Alex LP '71

Singles: 7-inch

BANG 3-5 78-79
CAPRICORN 3-5 71
DUNHILL 3-5 74

LPs: 10/12-inch

CAPRICORN 8-10 71
DUNHILL 8-10 74

TAYLOR, Andy P&R '86

Singles: 12-inch

ATLANTIC 4-6 86

Singles: 7-inch

ATLANTIC 3-4 86
MCA 3-4 86-87

Picture Sleeves

ATLANTIC 3-4 86
MCA 3-4 86

LPs: 10/12-inch

MCA 5-8 87

Also see DURAN DURAN
Also see POWER STATION

TAYLOR, Austin P&R '60

Singles: 7-inch

LAURIE 5-10 60-61

Also see TAYLOR, Ted

TAYLOR, B.E., Group P&R '84

Singles: 12-inch

EPIC 4-6 84

Singles: 7-inch

EPIC 3-4 84-86
MCA 3-5 83-84

Picture Sleeves

EPIC 3-4 86

LPs: 10/12-inch

MCA 5-10 82

Members: B.E. Taylor; Dave Kerr; Rick Withowski; Joe Macre; Joe D'Amico.
Also see CRACK the SKY

TAYLOR, Bobby P&R/R&B '68
(With the Vancouvers)

Singles: 7-inch

BUDDAH 4-6 72
GORDY (Black vinyl, except 7088) ... 10-20 68-69
GORDY (7088 "Oh I've Been Blessed") 300-400 69
GORDY (Colored vinyl) 10-20 68
(Promotional issue only.)
HOUR 10-15
INTEGRA (103 "This Is My Woman") 50-75 68

MOWEST 5-10
PLAYBOY 3-6 75
SUNFLOWER (126 "There Are Roses Somewhere in This World") 15-25 72
TOMMY 3-6 73
V.I.P. (Black vinyl, except 25053) 5-10 69-70
V.I.P. (25053 "Oh I've Been Blessed") 10-20 69
V.I.P. (Colored vinyl.) 10-20 70
(Promotional issue only.)

LPs: 10/12-inch

GORDY (930 "Bobby Taylor & the Vancouvers") 40-60 68
GORDY (942 "Taylor Made Soul") 40-60 69
Members: Bobby Taylor; Wes Henderson; Eddie Patterson; Robbie King; Ted Lewis; Tommy Chong.
Also see CHEECH & CHONG

TAYLOR, Debbie — R&B '68

Singles: 7-inch

ARISTA 3-5 75-76
DECCA 4-6 68
GWP 4-6 69
POLYDOR 3-5 74
TODAY 3-5 72

LPs: 10/12-inch

TODAY 6-10 72

TAYLOR, Felice — P&R/R&B '67

Singles: 7-inch

KENT 4-6 68
MUSTANG 4-8 67

TAYLOR, Gary — R&B '88

Singles: 7-inch

VIRGIN 3-4 88

TAYLOR, Gloria — P&R/R&B '69

Singles: 7-inch

COLUMBIA 3-5 74
GLO-WHIZ 4-6 69
KING SOUL (493 "Poor Unfortunate Me") 15-25 68
SILVER FOX 4-6 69

TAYLOR, James — P&R/LP '70

(With the Original Flying Machine)

Singles: 7-inch

APPLE (1805 "Carolina in My Mind"/"Taking It In") 200-300 69
APPLE (1805 "Carolina in My Mind"/ "Something's Wrong") 5-10 70
(Note different flip.)
APPLE (PRO-1805 "Carolina on My Mind) 25-35 70
(Note title variance. Promotional issue only.)
APPLE (4675 "More Apples, Radio Co-Op Ads") 150-200 69
(Single-sided disc. Promotional issue only.)
CAPITOL 3-5 76
COLUMBIA 3-5 77-88
EUPHORIA 3-5 71
W.B. 3-5 70-76

Picture Sleeves

COLUMBIA 3-4 81-88

LPs: 10/12-inch

APPLE 20-30 69-70
COLUMBIA 5-10 77-88
EUPHORIA 12-15 71
SPRINGBOARD 5-10 70s
TRIP 8-10 73
W.B. 8-10 70-77
Also see DOOBIE BROTHERS, James Hall & James Taylor
Also see DOOBIE BROTHERS / Kate Taylor & Simon-Taylor Family
Also see FLYING MACHINE
Also see GARFUNKEL, Art, James Taylor & Paul Simon
Also see HALL, James, & James Taylor
Also see KING DREAM CHORUS & HOLIDAY CREW
Also see KORTCHMAR, Danny
Also see SIMON, Carly, & James Taylor

TAYLOR, James, & J.D. Souther — P&R '81

Singles: 7-inch

COLUMBIA 3-5 81
Also see SOUTHER, J.D.
Also see TAYLOR, James

TAYLOR, John — P&R '86

(With Jonathan Elias)

Singles: 12-inch

CAPITOL 4-6 86

Singles: 7-inch

CAPITOL 3-4 86

LPs: 10/12-inch

CAPITOL 5-8 86
Also see DURAN DURAN
Also see POWER STATION

TAYLOR, Johnnie — P&R/R&B '63

(Johnny Taylor; the "Soul Philosopher")

Singles: 7-inch

BEVERLY GLEN 3-5 82
COLUMBIA 3-5 76-80
DERBY 4-8 63-64
MALACO 3-4 83-87
RCA 3-5 77
SAR (Except 131) 5-10 61-65
SAR (131 "Never Never") 15-25 61
STAX 3-6 66-77

LPs: 10/12-inch

BEVERLY GLEN 5-10 82
COLUMBIA 6-10 76-81
MALACO 5-8 83-86
RCA 8-10 77
STAX 6-10 67-83

TAYLOR, Johnnie, & Carla Thomas

Singles: 7-inch

STAX 4-6 69
Also see TAYLOR, Johnnie
Also see THOMAS, Carla

TAYLOR, Kate — LP '71

Singles: 7-inch

COLUMBIA 3-5 77-79
COTILLION 3-5 71

LPs: 10/12-inch

COLUMBIA 5-10 78-79
COTILLION 5-10 71
Also see DOOBIE BROTHERS / Kate Taylor & Simon-Taylor Family

TAYLOR, Koko — P&R/R&B '66

(Cocoa Taylor; Ko Ko Taylor)

Singles: 7-inch

CHECKER 4-8 66-68
U.S.A. 5-10 63
YAMBO 4-6 60s

LPs: 10/12-inch

ALLIGATOR 5-10 76-89
CHESS 10-12 69-72
Session: Willie Dixon.
Also see DIXON, Willie

TAYLOR, Little Johnny — P&R/R&B/LP '63

Singles: 7-inch

GALAXY 5-10 63-66
RONN 3-6 71-79

LPs: 10/12-inch

BEVERLY GLEN 5-8 87
GALAXY 15-25 63
RONN 5-10 72-79

TAYLOR, Little Johnny, & Ted Taylor

LPs: 10/12-inch

RONN 5-10 73
Also see TAYLOR, Little Johnny
Also see TAYLOR, Ted

TAYLOR, Livingston — LP '70

Singles: 7-inch

CAPRICORN 3-5 70-73
EPIC 3-5 78-80

LPs: 10/12-inch

ATCO 8-12 70
CAPRICORN 5-10 71-79
EPIC 5-10 78
Also see DOOBIE BROTHERS / Kate Taylor & Simon-Taylor Family

TAYLOR, Livingston, & Leah Kunkel — C&W '88

Singles: 7-inch

CRITIQUE 3-4 88
Also see KUNKEL, Leah
Also see TAYLOR, Livingston

TAYLOR, Mick — LP '79

Singles: 7-inch

COLUMBIA 3-5 79

LPs: 10/12-inch

COLUMBIA 5-10 79
Also see MAYALL, John
Also see ROLLING STONES

TAYLOR, R. Dean — P&R '70

Singles: 7-inch

AUDIO MASTER (1 "At the High School Dance") 100-150 60
BARRY (3023 "At the High School Dance") 75-125 60
(Canadian.)
FARR 3-5 76
JANE 3-5 77
MALA (444 "I'll Remember") 25-50 62
MOTOWN 3-5
RAGAMUFFIN 3-5 79
RARE EARTH (Black vinyl) 3-5 70-72
RARE EARTH (Colored vinyl) 5-10 70-71
STRUMMER 3-4 83
20TH FOX 3-5 81
V.I.P. 10-20 65-68

Picture Sleeves

RARE EARTH 3-5 71

LPs: 10/12-inch

RARE EARTH 10-15 70

TAYLOR, Roger — LP '81

Singles: 7-inch

CAPITOL 3-4 84
ELEKTRA 3-5 81

LPs: 10/12-inch

CAPITOL 5-8 84
ELEKTRA 5-10 81
Also see ARCADIA
Also see QUEEN

TAYLOR, Ted — P&R/R&B '65

(With the Bob Reed Orchestra; Ted Taylor Combo)

Singles: 7-inch

ALARM 3-6 76
APT 4-8 62
ATCO 4-8 65-66
DADE 4-8 63
DUKE 8-12 59
EBB (132 "Keep Walkin' On") 10-15 58
EPIC 4-8 66
GOLD EAGLE 10-15 61
JEWEL 4-8 66-67
MELATONE (1003 "I'm Leaving You") 5-10 60s
OKEH 4-8 62-65
RONN 4-6 67-72
SONCRAFT 8-12 61
TOP RANK 10-15 60-61
WARWICK 10-15 61
WATTS 5-8

LPs: 10/12-inch

OKEH 15-25 63-66
MCA 5-10 78
RONN 5-10 69-72
Also see CADETS
Also see TAYLOR, Austin
Also see TAYLOR, Little Johnny & Ted Taylor

TAYLOR, True

(Paul Simon)

Singles: 7-inch

BIG (614 "Teenage Fool") 20-40 58
Also see SIMON, Paul

TCHAIKOVSKY, Bram — P&R/LP '79

Singles: 7-inch

ARISTA 3-5 81

POLYDOR....3-5 79

LPs: 10/12-inch

ARISTA....5-10 81
POLYDOR....5-10 79-80
Also see MOTORS

TEAGARDEN, Jack
(With the Five Keys)

LPs: 10/12-inch

CAPITOL (820 "Swing Low, Sweet Spirtual")....150-250 54
Also see FIVE KEYS

TEARDROP EXPLODES LP '81

Singles: 7-inch

MERCURY....3-5 81-82

LPs: 10/12-inch

MERCURY....5-10 81-82
Member: Julian Cope.
Also see COPE, Julian

TEARS for FEARS P&R/LP '83

Singles: 12-inch

MERCURY....4-6 83-86

Singles: 7-inch

FONTANA....3-4 89
MERCURY....3-4 83-86

Picture Sleeves

FONTANA....3-4 89
MERCURY....3-4 85-86

LPs: 10/12-inch

FONTANA....5-8 89
MERCURY....5-8 83-86
SELECT ONE....12-18

TEASE R&B '86

Singles: 12-inch

EPIC....4-6 86
RCA....4-6 83

Singles: 7-inch

EPIC....3-4 86-88
RCA....3-4 83

LPs: 10/12-inch

EPIC....5-8 86
RCA....5-8 83

TECHNIQUE D&D '83

Singles: 12-inch

ARIAL....4-6 83

TECHNIQUES P&R '57

Singles: 78 rpm

ROULETTE....10-15 57

Singles: 7-inch

ROULETTE....10-15 57-58
STARS....15-25 57

TECHNOTRONIC P&R/LP '89
(Featuring Felly)

Singles: 7-inch

SBK....3-4 89-90

Picture Sleeves

SBK....3-4 89

LPs: 10/12-inch

SBK....5-8 89-90

TEDDY & TWILIGHTS P&R '62

Singles: 7-inch

SWAN....10-20 62

TEDDY BEARS P&R/R&B '58

Singles: 7-inch

COLLECTABLES....3-4 80s
DORE (503 "To Know Him Is to Love Him")....15-25 58
DORE (520 "Wonderful Loveable You")....15-25 59
IMPERIAL (5562 "Oh Why")....10-20 58
IMPERIAL (5581 "You Said Goodbye")....10-20 59
IMPERIAL (5594 "Don't Go Away")...10-20 59

LPs: 10/12-inch

IMPERIAL (9067 "The Teddy Bears Sing")....200-300 59
(Monaural.)
IMPERIAL (12010 "The Teddy Bears Sing")....400-600 59
(Stereo.)
Members: Phil Spector; Annette Kleinbard; Marshall Leib.
Also see CONNORS, Carol
Also see HARVEY, Phil
Also see NELSON, Sandy

TEE, Willie P&R/R&B '65
(Wilson Turbinton)

Singles: 7-inch

A.F.O....10-15 62
ATLANTIC (2273 "Teasin' You")....8-10 65
CAPITOL....4-8 68-70
CINDERELLA (1202 "Foolish Girl")..20-30
GATOR (509 "First Taste of Love")..10-20
GATOR (701 "She Really Did Surprise Me")....20-30 71
GATOR (8001 "Get Up")....10-20
HOT LINE....4-8
NOLA (708 "Teasin' You")....30-40 64
NOLA (737 "Please Don't Go")....100-200 65
U.A.....3-5 76

LPs: 10/12-inch

CAPITOL....10-15 69
U.A.....5-10 76

TEE SET P&R/LP '70

Singles: 7-inch

COLLECTABLES....3-4 80s
COLOSSUS....3-5 70-71

Picture Sleeves

COLOSSUS....3-5 70

LPs: 10/12-inch

COLOSSUS....10-15 70

TEEGARDEN & VAN WINKLE P&R '70

Singles: 7-inch

ATCO....4-8 68
PLUMM (68102 "God, Love & Rock & Roll")....8-12 70
WESTBOUND....3-8 69-72

Picture Sleeves

WESTBOUND....3-5 70

LPs: 10/12-inch

ATCO....10-15 68
WESTBOUND....8-12 69-72
Members: David Teegarden; Skip Knape.

TEEN DREAM R&B '87
(With Valentino)

Singles: 7-inch

W.B.....3-4 87-88

TEEN KINGS

Singles: 78 rpm

JE-WEL (101 "Ooby Dooby")....200-300 56

Singles: 7-inch

JE-WEL (101 "Ooby Dooby")....500-600 56
(May read "Vocal Roy Oribson," instead of "Orbison," on some labels. Beware since some counterfeits exist that are difficult to identify. Consult an expert if in doubt.)
Members: Roy Orbison; Johnny "Peanuts" Wilson; Billy Par Ellis; James Monroe; Jack Kennelly.
Also see ORBISON, Roy
Also see ROGERS, Weldon

TEEN QUEENS P&R/R&B '56

Singles: 78 rpm

RPM....10-20 56-57

Singles: 7-inch

ANTLER....5-10 60-61
COLLECTABLES....3-4 80s
KENT....4-8 61
RCA....5-10 58
RPM....10-20 56-57

Picture Sleeves

ANTLER....10-20 60

LPs: 10/12-inch

CROWN (5022 "Eddie My Love")....50-100 56
CROWN (5373 "Teen Queens")....20-30 63
UNITED....8-12
Members: Rose Collins; Betty Collins.

TEENA MARIE: see MARIE, Teena

TEENAGERS

Singles: 78 rpm

GEE (1046 "Flip-Flop")....15-25 57

Singles: 7-inch

END (1071 "Crying")....30-40 60
END (1076 "Can You Tell Me")....20-30 60
GEE (1046 "Flip-Flop")....15-25 57
ROULETTE (4086 "Broken Heart")...35-50 58
Members: Billy Lobrano; Herman Santiago; Sherman Garnes; Jim Merchant; Joe Negroni.
Also see LYMON, Frankie

TEMPER R&B/D&D '84

Singles: 12-inch

MCA....4-6 84

Singles: 7-inch

MCA....3-4 84
Member: Anthony Malloy.
Also see ANTHONY & CAMP

TEMPO, Nino P&R '73
(With 5th Ave. Sax)

Singles: 7-inch

A&M....3-5 73-74
RCA....5-10 59-60
TOWER....4-6 67
U.A.....5-10 60

LPs: 10/12-inch

A&M....8-10 74
ATCO....10-15 66
Also see ARCHIES

TEMPO, Nino, & April Stevens P&R '62

Singles: 7-inch

A&M....3-5 72-75
ABC....3-5 73
ATCO....4-8 62-66
BELL....3-6 69
CHELSEA....3-5 76
MARINA....3-5 72
WHITE WHALE....4-6 66-68

LPs: 10/12-inch

ATCO....10-15 63-66
CAMDEN....10-15 64
WHITE WHALE....10-15 69
Also see STEVENS, April
Also see TEMPO, Nino

TEMPO TOPPERS
(Featuring Little Richard)

Singles: 78 rpm

PEACOCK....20-40 53-54

Singles: 7-inch

PEACOCK (1616 "A Fool at the Wheel")....50-75 53
PEACOCK (1628 "Always")....40-60 54
Members: Richard Penniman; Jimmy Swan; Barry Gilmore; Bill Brooks.
Also see DUCES of RHYTHM & Tempo Toppers
Also see LITTLE RICHARD

TEMPOS P&R '59

Singles: 78 rpm

KAPP....10-20 57

Singles: 7-inch

CLIMAX (102 "See You in September")....10-15 59
CLIMAX (105 "Crossroads of Love") 10-15 59
KAPP (178 "Kingdom of Love")....10-20 57
KAPP (199 "Prettiest Girl in School") 10-20 57
KAPP (213 "I Got a Job")....10-20 58
PARIS (550 "Look Homeward Angel")....10-15 59
ROULETTE....3-5 70s

TEMPREES P&R '72

Singles: 7-inch

EPIC....3-5 76
STAX....3-4 84
WE PRODUCE....3-4 72-74

LPs: 10/12-inch

STAX....5-8 84
WE PRODUCE....5-10 72-74
Members: Del Juan Calvin; Jasper Phillips; Harold Scott.

TEMPTATIONS P&R '60

Singles: 7-inch

GOLDISC (3001 "Barbara")............. 15-25 60
(Black label.)
GOLDISC (3001 "Barbara")............. 10-15 60
(Multi-color label.)
GOLDISC (3007 "Fickle Little Girl")... 15-25 60
ROULETTE 3-5 71

TEMPTATIONS R&B '62

Singles: 7-inch

ATLANTIC...3-5 77-78
GORDY (1631 thru 1933)....................3-4 82-88
GORDY (7001 "Dream Come True") 25-30 62
GORDY (7010 "Paradise")..............20-25 62
GORDY (7015 "I Want a Love I Can See").. 15-20 63
GORDY (7020 "Farewell My Love") .. 15-20 63
GORDY (7028 thru 7074)..................8-15 64-68
GORDY (7081 thru 7213)...................3-8 68-81
MIRACLE (5 "Oh Mother of Mine") 50-100 61
MIRACLE (12 "Check Yourself") 40-60 62
MOTOWN...3-4 84-87
MOTOWN/TOPPS (4 "My Girl")........50-75 67
MOTOWN/TOPPS (13 "The Way You Do the Things You Do") 50-75 67
(Topps Chewing Gum promotional item. Single-sided, cardboard flexi, picture disc. Issued with generic paper sleeve.)

Picture Sleeves

GORDY (7038 "My Girl") 25-50 65
GORDY (7055 "Beauty Is Only Skin Deep")..10-20 66
GORDY (7099 "Ball of Confusion")... 10-20 70

EPs: 7-inch

GORDY (60914 "Tempting Temptations") 15-25 65
GORDY (60918 "Getting Ready") 15-25 66
GORDY (60919 "Greatest Hits") 15-25 66
MOTOWN (2004 "Temptations")....... 15-25 60s
MOTOWN (2010 "It's the Temptations") 15-25

LPs: 10/12-inch

ATLANTIC..5-10 77-78
GORDY (911 "Meet the Temptations") 20-30 64
GORDY (S-911 "Meet the Temptations") 25-35 64
GORDY (912 "The Temptations Sing Smokey")......................................15-25 65
GORDY (914 "The Tempting Temptations") 15-25 65
GORDY (918 "Gettin' Ready")........... 15-25 66
GORDY (919 Greatest Hits)............. 15-20 66
GORDY (921 "Live")......................... 15-25 67
GORDY (922 "With a Lot O' Soul")... 15-25 67
GORDY (924 "In a Mellow Mood") 15-25 67
GORDY (927 "Wish It Would Rain") 15-25 68
GORDY (933 thru 1006)....................8-18 69-80
GORDY (6000 series) 5-8 82-86
KORY 8-10 77
MOTOWN (100 & 200 series) 5-10 81-82
MOTOWN (782 "Anthology")............. 15-20 73
(Three-disc set. Includes 12-page color booklet.)
MOTOWN (998 "Give Love at Christmas")...................................... 12-18 80
(Promotional issue only.)
MOTOWN (5389 "25th Anniversary") 10-15 86
(Includes eight-page color booklet.)
MOTOWN (6246 "Together Again")...... 5-8 87
NATURAL RESOURCES....................5-10 78
Members: David Ruffin; Eddie Kendricks; Melvin Franklin; Otis Williams; Paul Williams; Damon Harris; Dennis Edwards.
Also see DISTANTS
Also see FOUR TOPS / Temptations
Also see KENDRICKS, Eddie
Also see LANDS, Liz, & Temptations
Also see PIRATES
Also see ROBINSON, Smokey
Also see ROSS, Diana
Also see RUFFIN, David
Also see SUPREMES & TEMPTATIONS

TEMPTATIONS & FOUR TOPS

LPs: 10/12-inch

MOTOWN (134 "Battle of the Champions") 10-20
(Promotional issue only.)
SILVER EAGLE (1052 "T N T")........ 10-15 87
(Three-disc set.)
Also see FOUR TOPS

TEMPTATIONS & RICK JAMES R&B '82

Singles: 12-inch

GORDY.. 4-6 82

Singles: 7-inch

GORDY.. 3-4 82
Also see JAMES, Rick

TEMPTATIONS / Stevie Wonder

LPs: 10/12-inch

GORDY/TAMLA/MOTOWN (100 "The Sky's the Limit") 15-25 71
(Promotional issue only.)
Also see TEMPTATIONS
Also see WONDER, Stevie

10CC P&R '73

Singles: 7-inch

MERCURY.. 3-5 75-77
POLYDOR 3-5 78
UK.. 3-5 72-74

Picture Sleeves

MERCURY.. 5-8 75-77

LPs: 10/12-inch

MERCURY...................................... 10-15 75-77
POLYDOR 5-8 78-79
UK.. 10-15 73-75
W.B. 8-10 80
Members: Kevin Godley; Lol Creme; Graham Gouldman; Eric Stewart; Paul Burgess; Rick Fenn; Tony O'Malley; Stuart Tosh.
Also see GODLEY, Kevin, & Lol Creme
Also see GOULDMAN, Graham
Also see HOTLEGS
Also see KASENETZ-KATZ SINGING ORCHESTRAL CIRCUS
Also see KOKOMO
Also see OHIO EXPRESS
Also see PILOT
Also see SEDAKA, Neil
Also see WAX

10 SPEED R&B '84

Singles: 12-inch

QUALITY/RFC................................. 4-6 83

Singles: 7-inch

QUALITY/RFC 3-5 83

10,000 MANIACS LP '87

Singles: 7-inch

ELEKTRA.. 3-4 87-89

Picture Sleeves

ELEKTRA.. 3-5 88-89

LPs: 10/12-inch

ELEKTRA.. 5-10 87-90
MARK (20247 "Human Conflict No. 5")................................. 100-150 82
MARK (20389 "Secrets of the I Ching") 75-100 83
(Includes lyrics/print insert.)
Members: Natalie Merchant; Robert Buck; Dennis Drew; Steven Gustafson; John Lombardo; Robert Wachter; Jerome Augustyniak.

TEN WHEEL DRIVE P&R/LP '70
(With Genya Ravan)

Singles: 7-inch

CAPITOL... 3-5 73
POLYDOR 4-6 69-71

LPs: 10/12-inch

CAPITOL... 8-10 73
POLYDOR 10-12 69-71
Member: Genya Ravan.
Also see RAVAN, Genya
Also see ZAGER, Michael, Band

TEN YEARS AFTER LP '68

Singles: 7-inch

COLUMBIA 3-5 71-73
DERAM..4-6 68-70

Picture Sleeves

DERAM..4-6 68

LPs: 10/12-inch

CHRYSALIS 5-10 83-89
COLUMBIA..8-12 71-76
DERAM...8-12 68-75
LONDON 5-10 77
Member: Alvin Lee.
Also see LEE, Alvin

TENDER SLIM P&R '60

Singles: 7-inch

GREY CLIFF 5-10 59
HERALD 4-8 62

TENNESSEE ERNIE: see FORD, "Tennessee" Ernie

TENNILLE, Toni LP '84

Singles: 7-inch

MIRAGE 3-5 84

LPs: 10/12-inch

GAIA 5-8 87
MIRAGE...5-8 84
Also see CAPTAIN & TENNILLE

TEPPER, Robert P&R/LP '86

Singles: 7-inch

SCOTTI BROTHERS 3-4 85-86

Picture Sleeves

SCOTTI BROTHERS 3-4 86

LPs: 10/12-inch

SCOTTI BROTHERS 5-8 85-86

TERRELL, Jean R&B '78

Singles: 7-inch

A&M...3-5 78

LPs: 10/12-inch

A&M...8-10 78
Also see SUPREMES

TERRELL, Tammi P&R/R&B '66

Singles: 7-inch

MOTOWN...4-8 65-69

LPs: 10/12-inch

MOTOWN (200 series)......................5-10 82
MOTOWN (652 "Irresistible") 40-60 66
Also see GAYE, Marvin, & Tammi Terrell
Also see JACKSON, Chuck, & Tammi Terrell
Also see MONTGOMERY, Tammy

TERRY, Sonny
(Sonny "Hootin'" Terry & His Night Owls; with His Buckshot Five)

Singles: 78 rpm

ASCH..15-25 45
CAPITOL 15-40 47-50
GOTHAM...15-25 51
GRAMERCY......................................15-25 52
GROOVE...15-25 54-55
HARLEM...15-25 52
JACKSON 25-50 52
JAX...15-25 50s
JOSIE 15-25 56
OLD TOWN.......................................15-25 56
RCA 25-50 53
RED ROBIN.......................................25-50 53
SAVOY 15-25 48
SOLO 15-25 49

Singles: 7-inch

CAPITOL (931 "Telephone Blues")... 50-75 50
CHESS (1860 "Dangerous Woman")..10-15 63
CHOICE...5-10 61
GOTHAM (517 "Baby, Let's Have Some Fun")..20-30 51
GOTHAM (518 "Harmonica Rumbo")..20-30 51
GRAMERCY (1004 "Hootin' Blues") . 25-35 52
(Black vinyl.)
GRAMERCY (1004 "Hootin' Blues") . 50-75 52
(Colored vinyl.)
GROOVE...15-25 54-55
HARLEM (2327 "Dangerous Woman")..40-50 52

JACKSON (2302 "That Woman Is Killing Me") 50-100 52
(Colored vinyl.)
JAX (305 "I Don't Worry") 200-300 50s
(Colored vinyl.)
JOSIE 10-20 56
OLD TOWN 10-20 56
RCA (5492 "Hootin' & Jumpin' ") 50-75 53
RCA (5577 "Sonny Is Drinkin' ") 50-75 53
RED ROBIN (110 "Harmonica Hop")..75-125 53

LPs: 10/12-inch

ARCHIVE of FOLK MUSIC...............15-25 65
EVEREST.......................................5-10 70s
PRESTIGE BLUESVILLE...................20-30 61-63
WASHINGTON (702 "Talkin' About the Blues") 25-35 61
Session: Mickey Baker; Brownie McGhee.
Also see BAGBY, Doc
Also see HOPKINS, Lightnin,' & Sonny Terry
Also see McGHEE, Brownie, & Sonny Terry

TERRY, Tony — P&R/R&B '87

Singles: 7-inch

EPIC 3-4 87-90

Picture Sleeves

EPIC 3-4 88

LPs: 10/12-inch

EPIC 5-8 87-91

TESLA — P&R/LP '87

Singles: 7-inch

GEFFEN..3-4 87-90

Picture Sleeves

GEFFEN..3-4 87

LPs: 10/12-inch

GEFFEN..5-8 87-90
Members: Jeff Keith; Brian Wheat; Frank Hannon; Tommy Skeoch; Troy Luccketta.

TESTAMENT — LP '88

LPs: 10/12-inch

MEGAFORCE 5-8 88-90

TEX, Joe — P&R '64

(With the Class Mates; with Vibrators)

Singles: 78 rpm

KING 20-50 55-57

Singles: 12-inch

EPIC 4-8 77

Singles: 7-inch

ACE (544 "Cut It Out")......................40-60 58
ACE (549 "Blessed Are These Tears")......................................40-60 58
ACE (550 "Mother's Advice")............50-75 58
ACE (673 "Boys Will Be Boys").........15-25 60
ANNA (1119 "All I Could Do Was Cry")..15-25 60
ANNA (1124 "I'll Never Break Your Heart")..15-25 60
ANNA (1128 "Ain't I a Mess") 15-25 61
ATLANTIC 3-5 72
CHECKER......................................10-15 63
DIAL (1000 series)...........................3-6 71-76
DIAL (2800 series)...........................3-5 78
DIAL (3000 series)...........................5-10 61-64
DIAL (4000 series)...........................4-8 64-69
EPIC 3-5 77-79
HANDSHAKE...................................3-5 81
JALYNNE 5-10 61
KING (4840 "Come in This House")..40-60 55
KING (4884 "My Biggest Mistake")....25-50 56
KING (4980 "Pneumonia")................25-50 56
KING (4911 "She's Mine") 25-50 65
KING (5064 "Ain't Nobody's Business").......................................25-50 57
KING (5981 "Come in This House")....5-10 65

LPs: 10/12-inch

ACCORD.......................................5-10 82
ATLANTIC 10-15 65-72
CHECKER......................................20-30 64
DIAL...8-10 72-79
EPIC 5-10 77-78
KING 15-25 65
LONDON 5-10 79
PARROT 15-25 65
PRIDE...8-10 73

Members: Mike Appell; Rod Bristow.
Also see SOUL CLAN

TEXANS — P&R '61

Singles: 7-inch

GOTHIC (001 "Rockin' Johnny Home") 15-25 61
INFINITY (001 "Green Grass of Texas") 20-30 61
VEE JAY (658 "Green Grass of Texas") 8-12 65
Members: Dorsey Burnette; Johnny Burnette.
Also see BURNETTE, Johnny & Dorsey

TEXAS "GUITAR" SLIM

(Johnny Winter)

Singles: 7-inch

JIN (174 "Broke and Lonely")........... 30-50 62
(This same number was used for *Something's Wrong*, by Rockin' Sidney.)
MOON-LITE 75-100 60
Also see GUITAR SLIM
Also see WINTER, Johnny

TEXAS SLIM

(John Lee Hooker)

Singles: 78 rpm

KING (Except 4377)......................... 50-75 48-49
KING (4377 "Moaning Blues")......... 75-125 50
Also see HOOKER, John Lee

TEXTONES — LP '84

Singles: 7-inch

GOLD MOUNTAIN............................. 3-4 84
I.R.S./FAULTY PRODUCTS.............. 3-5 80

LPs: 10/12-inch

GOLD MOUNTAIN............................. 5-8 84
Members: Carla Olson; Mark Cuff; Kathy Valentine; David Provost; George Callins; Phil Seymour; Tom Morgan; Joe Read.
Also see CLARK, Gene, & Carla Olson
Also see DREAM SYNDICATE
Also see GO-GOs
Also see SEYMOUR, Phil

THE, The — D&D '83

Singles: 12-inch

EPIC... 4-6 84-89
SIRE... 4-6 83-84

Singles: 7-inch

EPIC... 3-4 83-85

LPs: 10/12-inch

EPIC... 5-8 84-89

THEE MIDNITERS — P&R '65

Singles: 7-inch

CHATTAHOOCHEE (666 "Land of 1000 Dances")............................. 8-12 65
CHATTAHOOCHEE (674 "Sad Girl") 8-12 65
CHATTAHOOCHEE (675 "Sad Girl") 8-12 65
CHATTAHOOCHEE (684 "Whitter Boulevard").. 8-12 65
CHATTAHOOCHEE (693 "I Need Someone") 8-12 65
CHATTAHOOCHEE (694 "It's Not Unusual")... 8-12 66
CHATTAHOOCHEE (706 "Are You Angry") 8-12 66
UNI... 5-10 69
WHITTIER (200 "Sad Girl") 15-25 60s
WHITTIER (201 "That's All").............. 15-25 60s
WHITTIER (202 "I Need Someone") 15-25 60s
WHITTIER (500 thru 509)................ 10-20 66-67
WHITTIER (511 "You're Gonna Make Me Cry")...................................... 100-200 68
WHITTIER (674 "Sad Girl") 5-10 68

LPs: 10/12-inch

CHATTAHOOCHEE (C-1001 "Thee Midniters") 20-30 65
(Monaural.)
CHATTAHOOCHEE (CS-1001 "Thee Midniters") 25-45 65
(Stereo.)
RHINO... 5-8 83
WHITTIER (5000 "Special Delivery") 15-25 66
WHITTIER (5001 "Unlimited") 15-25 66
WHITTIER (5002 "Giants")...............15-25 67

THEE PROPHETS — P&R/LP '69

Singles: 7-inch

KAPP..4-8 68-70
TEE PEE 5-10 67

LPs: 10/12-inch

KAPP..15-20 69
Members: Brian Lake; Jim Anderson; Dave Leslie; Chris Michaels; Mark Sandusky; Tony Gazzana; Joe Kopecky; Jerry George; Jose Salazar; Dave Maciolek; Lee Johnson.

THEM — P&R/LP '65

(Featuring Van Morrison)

Singles: 7-inch

HAPPY TIGER 4-6 69-70
LOMA 5-8 66
LONDON 3-4 70s
PARROT (Except 365) 5-10 64-66
PARROT (365 "Gloria")......................10-15 65
(Copies with later copyright dates are reissues. Later released on Parrot 9727.)
RUFF...8-10 67
SULLY 15-20 60s
TOWER..4-8 67-69

LPs: 10/12-inch

HAPPY TIGER (1004 "Them")...........20-30 69
HAPPY TIGER (1012 "In Reality") 20-30 71
LONDON 5-10 77
PARROT (61005 "Them") 50-100 65
(Cover does not highlight *Gloria*.)
(Monaural.)
PARROT (61005 "Them") 30-35 65
(Cover highlights *Gloria*.)
(Monaural.)
PARROT (61008 "Them Again").......25-30 66
(Monaural.)
PARROT (71005 "Them")................50-100 65
(Cover does not highlight *Gloria*.)
(Stereo.)
PARROT (71005 "Them") 40-50 65
(Cover highlights *Gloria*.)
(Stereo.)
PARROT (71008 "Them Again").......40-50 66
(Stereo.)
PARROT (71053 "Them Featuring Van Morrison")................................10-15 72
TOWER (5104 "Now and Them") 25-35 68
TOWER (5116 "Time Out")...............25-35 68
Members: Van Morrison; Billy Harrison; Alan Henderson; Peter Bardens; J. McAuley; John Stark.
Also see BARDENS, Peter
Also see BELFAST GYPSIES
Also see MORRISON, Van

THEM / Marvelettes

Singles: 7-inch

A&M (1201 "Baby, Please Don't Go")....3-4 88

Picture Sleeves

A&M (1201 "Baby, Please Don't Go")....3-4 88
Also see MARVELETTES
Also see THEM

THEO VANESS — LP '79

Singles: 7-inch

PRELUDE 3-5 79

LPs: 10/12-inch

PRELUDE 5-10 79

THEODORE, Mike, Orchestra — LP '77

Singles: 7-inch

WESTBOUND...................................3-5 77-79

LPs: 10/12-inch

WESTBOUND...................................5-10 77-79

THERESA — R&B '87

Singles: 7-inch

RCA...3-4 87-88
Members: Theresa King; Victor Porter.

THEY MIGHT BE GIANTS — LP '88

LPs: 10/12-inch

BAR NONE......................................5-8 88
ELEKTRA..5-8 90

THIN LIZZY
P&R/LP '76

Singles: 12-inch

W.B. 4-8 78
(Promotional only.)

Singles: 7-inch

LONDON 3-5 73
MERCURY 3-5 76-77
VERTIGO 3-5 75
W.B. 3-5 78-79

Picture Sleeves

VERTIGO 3-5 75

LPs: 10/12-inch

LONDON (500 & 600 series) 10-15 71
LONDON (20000 series) 8-12 72
LONDON (50000 series) 5-10 77
MERCURY 8-12 76-77
VERTIGO 10-12 74-75
W.B. 5-10 78-84
Members: Philip Lynott; Gary Moore; Brian Robertson.
Also see MOORE, Gary

THINK
P&R '71

Singles: 7-inch

BIG TREE 3-5 74
LAURIE 3-5 71

LPs: 10/12-inch

LAURIE 8-10 72
Member: Lou Stallman.

THIRD BASS
LP '89

LPs: 10/12-inch

DEF JAM 5-8 89-91

THIRD POWER
LP '70

Singles: 7-inch

BARON (626 "Snow") 10-20 68
VANGUARD 4-8 70

LPs: 10/12-inch

VANGUARD (6554 "Believe") 15-20 70
Members: Jim Craig; Drew Abbott.

THIRD RAIL
P&R '67

Singles: 7-inch

CAMEO 4-8 66
EPIC 3-6 67-69

LPs: 10/12-inch

EPIC 20-30 67
Member: Joey Levine; Kris Resnik; Art Resnik.

THIRD WORLD
LP '78

Singles: 12-inch

COLUMBIA 4-6 81-85
ISLAND 4-8 78-80

Singles: 7-inch

ABRAXAS 3-5 76
COLUMBIA 3-5 81-85
ISLAND 3-5 79

LPs: 10/12-inch

COLUMBIA 5-8 81-85
ISLAND 5-10 76-80
MERCURY 5-8 89
Member: Stevie Wonder.
Also see WONDER, Stevie

THIRTEENTH FLOOR ELEVATORS
P&R '66

Singles: 7-inch

CONTACT (5269 "You're Gonna Miss Me") 50-75 66
(First issue of *You're Gonna Miss Me.*)
HBR (492 "You're Gonna Miss Me") 50-75 66
(Third issue of *You're Gonna Miss Me.*)
INTERNATIONAL ARTISTS (107 "You're Gonna Miss Me") 10-20 66
(Second issue of *You're Gonna Miss Me.* May be found with: a) two tone light blue label; b) solid dark blue label [which exists with both "IA" and "AI" at top]; c) green and yellow label; d) white label, promotional issue. We have yet to learn of a noteworthy price difference between these.)
INTERNATIONAL ARTISTS (111 through 130) 10-20 66-68

LPs: 10/12-inch

INTERNATIONAL ARTISTS (1 "Psychedelic Sounds") 75-100 67
(Does NOT have "Masterfonics" stamped in the vinyl trail-off.)
INTERNATIONAL ARTISTS (5 "Easter Everywhere") 40-60 67
(Does NOT have "Masterfonics" stamped in the vinyl trail-off.)
INTERNATIONAL ARTISTS (8 "Live") 40-60 68
(Does NOT have "Masterfonics" stamped in the vinyl trail-off.)
INTERNATIONAL ARTISTS (9 "Bull of the Woods") 40-60 68
(Does NOT have "Masterfonics" stamped in the vinyl trail-off.)
INTERNATIONAL ARTISTS 10-20 79
(Reissues. With "Masterfonics" stamped in the vinyl trail-off.)
INTERNATIONAL ARTISTS (White Label) 150-225 67-68
(Promotional issues only.)
TEXAS ARCHIVE 8-10 85
Members: Roky Erickson; Tommy Hall; Stacy Sutherland; John Ike Walton; Benny Thurman.
Also see ERICKSON, Roky
Also see SPADES

.38 SPECIAL
LP '77

(Thirty Eight Special)

Singles: 7-inch

A&M 3-5 77-88
CAPITOL 3-5 84

Picture Sleeves

A&M 3-5 80-83

LPs: 10/12-inch

A&M 5-10 77-88
CAPITOL 5-8 84
Member: Dave Van Zandt.

THOMAS, B.J.
P&R '66

(With the Triumphs)

Singles: 7-inch

ABC 3-5 75
BRAGG (103 "Billy & Sue") 10-20 66
CLEVELAND INT'L 3-4 83-84
COLLECTABLES 3-4 80s
COLUMBIA 3-4 83-86
HICKORY 6-12 66
JOED (119 "Keep It Up") 10-15 65
LORI (9547 "Hey Judy") 8-10 64
LORI (9561 "For Your Precious Love") 8-10 64
MCA 3-5 77-82
MYRRH 3-4 77-81
PACEMAKER (227 "I'm So Lonesome I Could Cry") 10-15 64
PACEMAKER (231 "M-a-m-a") 10-15 65
PACEMAKER (234 "Bring Back the Time") 10-15 65
PACEMAKER (239 "Tomorrow Never Comes") 10-15 66
PACEMAKER (247 "Plain Jane") 10-15 66
PACEMAKER (253 "Baby Cried") 10-15 66
PACEMAKER (256 "I Can't Help It") 10-15 66
PARAMOUNT 3-5 73-74
SCEPTER (12100 series) 4-8 66-67
SCEPTER (12200 thru 12364) 3-6 68-72
SCEPTER (21000 series) 3-5 73-74
VALERIE 4-8 60s
W.B. (5491 "Billy & Sue") 15-20 64

Picture Sleeves

MCA 3-5 79

LPs: 10/12-inch

ABC 5-10 74-77
ACCORD 5-10 81-82
BUCKBOARD 5-10
CLEVELAND INT'L 5-10 83
COLUMBIA 5-8 86
DORAL 15-25 60s
(Promotional mail-order issue, from Doral cigarettes.)
EXACT 5-10 80
EXCELSIOR 5-10 80
EVEREST 5-10 81
51 WEST 5-10 79
HICKORY (133 "Very Best") 20-30 66
MCA 5-10 77-82
MCA/SONGBIRD 5-10 80
MYRRH 5-8 78-83
PACEMAKER (3001 "B.J. Thomas and the Triumphs") 40-50 66
PARAMOUNT 5-10 73-74
PHOENIX 20 .... 5-10 81
PICKWICK 5-8 78
PRIORITY 5-8 83
SCEPTER (535 thru 561) 10-20 66-67
SCEPTER (586 thru 597) 8-12 70-71
SCEPTER (5101 "Billy Joe Thomas") 8-12 72
SCEPTER (5108 "Country") 8-12 72
SCEPTER (5112 "Greatest All-Time Hits") 10-15 73
SPRINGBOARD 5-10 73-79
STARDAY 5-10 77
TRIP 5-10 76
U.A. 5-10 74
Also see CHARLES, Ray, & B.J. Thomas
Also see EDDY, Duane

THOMAS, B.J. / Smiley Lewis

Singles: 7-inch

OLDIES 45 3-5
Also see LEWIS, Smiley
Also see THOMAS, B.J.

THOMAS, Carla
P&R/R&B '61

Singles: 7-inch

ATLANTIC 4-8 60-65
SATELLITE (104 "Gee Whiz, Look at His Eyes") 40-60 60
STAX 3-8 65-72

Picture Sleeves

STAX 4-8 66

EPs: 7-inch

STAX 10-15 66
(Juke box issues only.)

LPs: 10/12-inch

ATLANTIC (8057 "Gee Whiz") 20-30 61
ATLANTIC (8232 "Best of Carla Thomas") 10-15 69
STAX 10-15 66-71
Also see BELL, William, & Carla Thomas
Also see OTIS & CARLA
Also see REDDING, Otis / Carla Thomas / Sam & Dave / Eddie Floyd
Also see RUFUS & CARLA
Also see TAYLOR, Johnnie, & Carla Thomas

THOMAS, David Clayton: see CLAYTON-THOMAS, David

THOMAS, Evelyn
P&R/R&B/D&D '84

Singles: 12-inch

TSR 4-6 84

Singles: 7-inch

CASABLANCA 3-5 78
TSR 3-5 84
VANGUARD 3-5 85

LPs: 10/12-inch

A.V.I. 5-10 79
CASABLANCA 5-10 78

THOMAS, Gene
P&R '61

Singles: 7-inch

HICKORY 3-5 71
TRX 4-8 69
U.A. 6-12 61-65
VENUS (1439 "Sometime") 20-30 61
VENUS (1441 "Lamp of Love") 10-20 62
VENUS (1444 "Down the Road") 50-75 62
Also see GENE & DEBBE

THOMAS, Ian
P&R '73

Singles: 7-inch

ATLANTIC 3-5 78
CHRYSALIS 3-5 75
JANUS 3-5 73-74
MERCURY 3-4 84

LPs: 10/12-inch

ATLANTIC 5-10 78
JANUS 8-10 73-74
MERCURY 5-8 84

THOMAS, Irma R&B '60

Singles: 78 rpm

RON (328 "Set Me Free") 50-75 59

Singles: 7-inch

BANDY 5-8 60s
BUMPA 10-20
CANYON 3-5 70
CHECKER 5-10
CHESS 4-6 68
COTILLION 3-5 71-72
FUNGUS 3-5 73
IMPERIAL 5-10 64-66
MAISON DE SOUL 4-6
MINIT 8-12 61-63
RCS 3-5 79-81
ROKER 4-8 71
RON (328 "Set Me Free") 10-20 59
RON (330 "Good Man") 10-20 59
ROUNDER 3-4 84

LPs: 10/12-inch

FUNGUS 8-10 73
IMPERIAL (266 "Wish Someone Would Care") 20-30 64
IMPERIAL (302 "Take a Look") 15-20 66
RCS 5-10 80
Also see BROWN, Maxine / Irma Thomas

THOMAS, Irma / Ernie K-Doe / Showmen / Benny Spellman

LPs: 10/12-inch

MINIT (0004 "New Orleans, Home of the Blues, Vol. 2") 20-30 64
Also see K-DOE, Ernie
Also see SHOWMEN
Also see SPELLMAN, Benny

THOMAS, Jamo, & Party Brothers P&R '66

Singles: 7-inch

CHESS 4-8 66
DECCA 4-8 68
SOUND STAGE 7 4-8 67
THOMAS 4-8 66

Picture Sleeves

THOMAS 4-8 66

THOMAS, Joe R&B '49
(Joe Thomas Orchestra)

Singles: 78 rpm

KING 10-20 49-51
MERCURY 10-20 51

Singles: 7-inch

KING (4299 "Page Boy Shuffle") 15-25 49
KING (4460 "Jumpin' Joe") 15-25 51
KING (4474 "You're Just My Kind") 15-25 51
MERCURY (8268 "Everybody Loves My Baby") 15-25 51
PLAYBACK ("Page Boy Shuffle") 15-25
(Selection number not known.)

THOMAS, Joe R&B '76

Singles: 7-inch

GROOVE MERCHANT 3-5 76
LRC 3-5 77-79
SUE 4-8 64

LPs: 10/12-inch

LRC 5-10 77-78
TODAY 6-12 72

THOMAS, Jon P&R/R&B '60
(John Thomas)

Singles: 78 rpm

CHECKER 10-20 55
MERCURY 15-25 57

Singles: 7-inch

ABC-PAR 8-12 60-61
CHECKER (809 "Rib Tips") 15-25 55
JUNIOR 5-10 64
MERCURY (71078 "Hard Head") 15-25 57
NOTE (1001 "Rib Tips") 8-12 60s
VEEP 5-15 67-68

LPs: 10/12-inch

ABC-PAR (351 "Heartbreak") 20-30 60
(Monaural.)
ABC-PAR (S-351 "Heartbreak") 30-40 60
(Stereo.)

WING 10-20 63

THOMAS, Leone R&B '76

Singles: 7-inch

DON 3-5 76

THOMAS, Lillo R&B '83

Singles: 12-inch

CAPITOL 4-6 83-85

Singles: 7-inch

CAPITOL 3-4 83-87

LPs: 10/12-inch

CAPITOL 5-8 83-85
Also see LAURENCE, Paul

THOMAS, Lillo, & Melba Moore R&B '84

Singles: 7-inch

CAPITOL 3-5 84
Also see MOORE, Melba
Also see THOMAS, Lillo

THOMAS, Nolan R&B/D&D '84

Singles: 12-inch

EMERGENCY 4-6 84-85

Singles: 7-inch

MIRAGE 3-5 84-85
Also see MONET & Nolan Thomas

THOMAS, Pat P&R '62

Singles: 7-inch

MGM 3-5 62-63
VERVE 3-5 62-64

Picture Sleeves

MGM 3-6 62

LPs: 10/12-inch

MGM 10-20 62-64
STRAND 10-20 61

THOMAS, Philip-Michael R&B '85

Singles: 7-inch

ATLANTIC 3-5 85

THOMAS, Ray LP '75

Singles: 7-inch

THRESHOLD 3-5 75-76

LPs: 10/12-inch

THRESHOLD (16 "From Mighty Oaks") 10-15 75
(Gatefold cover.)
THRESHOLD (17 "Hopes, Wishes and Dreams") 10-15 76
THRESHOLD (102 "Ray Thomas Discusses *From Mighty Oaks*") 15-25 75
(Promotional issue only.)
Also see MOODY BLUES

THOMAS, Rufus R&B '53
(Rufus "Bearcat" Thomas; Rufus Thomas Jr.)

Singles: 12-inch

A.V.I. 4-8 78

Singles: 78 rpm

CHESS (1466 "Night Walkin' Blues") 15-25 52
CHESS (1492 "No More Doggin' Around") 15-25 52
CHESS (1517 "Juanita") 15-25 52
STAR TALENT (807 "I'm So Worried") 20-30 50
SUN (181 "Bear Cat [Answer to Hound Dog]") 75-125 53
(With subtitle.)
SUN (181 "Bear Cat") 50-75 53
(Without subtitle.)
SUN (188 "Tiger Man") 50-100 53

Singles: 7-inch

A.V.I. 3-5 77-78
ARTISTS of AMERICA 3-5 76
HI 3-5 78
METEOR (5039 "I'm Steady Holdin' On") 100-150 56
STAX (100 & 200 series) 4-8 62-68
STAX (0010 thru 0236) 3-6 68-75
SUN (181 "Bear Cat [Answer to Hound Dog]") 100-200 53
(With subtitle.)
SUN (181 "Bear Cat") 75-125 53
(Without subtitle.)

SUN (188 "Tiger Man") 100-150 53

LPs: 10/12-inch

A.V.I. 5-10 77-78
ARTISTS of AMERICA 8-10 76
GUSTO 5-10 80
STAX (Except 704) 6-15 70-79
STAX (704 "Walking the Dog") 15-20 63
Also see RUFUS & CARLA

THOMAS, Tasha R&B '78

Singles: 7-inch

ATLANTIC 3-5 78-79
ROULETTE 4-8 69

THOMAS, Timmy P&R/R&B '72

Singles: 12-inch

GOLD MOUNTAIN 4-6 84
SPECTOR 4-6 83

Singles: 7-inch

GLADES 3-5 72-77
GOLD MOUNTAIN 3-4 84-85
GOLDWAX 4-8 67
MARLIN 3-5 80-81
SPECTOR 3-4 83
TM 3-5 78

LPs: 10/12-inch

GLADES 8-10 72-76
GOLD MOUNTAIN 5-8 84

THOMAS, Vaneese R&B '87

Singles: 7-inch

GEFFEN 3-4 87
Also see NAJEE

THOMPSON, Chris, & Night P&R '79

Singles: 7-inch

PLANET 3-5 79
Also see MANN, Manfred
Also see NIGHT
Also see WARNES, Jennifer, & Chris Thompson

THOMPSON, Hank C&W '48
(With the Brazos Valley Boys)

Singles: 78 rpm

BLUE BONNET 25-50 47
(Title and selection number not known.)
CAPITOL 10-25 47-57
GLOBE (124 "Whoa Sailor") 100-200 46

Singles: 7-inch

ABC 3-5 75-79
ABC/DOT 3-5 74-77
CAPITOL (1000 thru 3000 series) 5-15 50-58
CAPITOL (4000 & 5000 series) 4-8 58-66
CHURCHILL 3-4 81-83
DOT 3-5 68-74
MCA 3-4 79-80
W.B. 4-6 66-67

Picture Sleeves

CAPITOL (4649 "Lost John") 5-10 61

EPs: 7-inch

CAPITOL 10-20 53-59

LPs: 10/12-inch

ABC 5-8 78
ABC/DOT 5-10 74-77
CAPITOL (H-418 "Songs of the Brazos Valley") 60-80 53
(10-inch LP.)
CAPITOL (T-418 "Songs of the Brazos Valley") 50-75 55
(Green label.)
CAPITOL (T-618 "North of the Rio Grande") 40-60 55
(Green label.)
CAPITOL (T-729 "New Recordings") 30-50 55
CAPITOL (T-826 "Hank!") 30-40 57
CAPITOL (T-975 "Dance Ranch") 30-40 58
CAPITOL (T-1111 thru 2154) 15-25 59-64
(Monaural.)
CAPITOL (ST-1111 through 2154) 15-30 59-64
(Stereo.)
CAPITOL (SM-2000 series) 5-8 75
CAPITOL (T-2274 thru 2800) 10-20 65-67
(Monaural.)
CAPITOL (ST-2274 through 2826) 10-25 65-67
(Stereo.)

CAPITOL (H-9111 "Favorites")........50-100 52
(10-inch LP.)
CAPITOL (11000 series)......................5-8 79
CHURCHILL..5-8 84
DOT...5-15 68-74
GUSTO...5-8 80
MCA/DOT...5-8
PICKWICK/HILLTOP...........................5-15 67-68
PROVINCIA..5-8
SEARS (135 "How Many Teardrops Will It Take")..10-15 60s
STEP ONE...5-8 87
TOWER..8-15 68
WACO (101 "Hank Thompson Sings and Plays Bob Wills")..................................30-50
Session: Buddy Cagle.

THOMPSON, Hank, & Merle Travis
(With the Brazos Valley Boys) *C&W '55*

Singles: 78 rpm

CAPITOL..5-10 55

Singles: 7-inch

CAPITOL..8-12 55
Also see THOMPSON, Hank

THOMPSON, Kay
P&R '56

Singles: 78 rpm

CADENCE...3-5 56
MGM..3-5 54-55

Singles: 7-inch

CADENCE...4-8 56
MGM..4-8 54-55

Picture Sleeves

CADENCE...5-10 56

THOMPSON, Richard
LP '83

Singles: 7-inch

HANNIBAL..3-4 83
POLYDOR...3-4 85-86
REPRISE...3-5 72

LPs: 10/12-inch

CAPITOL..5-8 88
HANNIBAL..5-8 83
POLYDOR...5-8 85-86
REPRISE...8-10 72
Also see FAIRPORT CONVENTION

THOMPSON, Richard & Linda

Singles: 7-inch

CHRYSALIS..3-5 78
ISLAND...3-5 74-75

LPs: 10/12-inch

CHRYSALIS..5-10 78
ISLAND...5-10 74-75
Also see THOMPSON, Richard

THOMPSON, Robbin, Band
P&R/LP '80

Singles: 7-inch

COLPAR..4-6
NEMPEROR...3-5 76-77
OVATION..3-5 80
RICHMOND...3-5
SHORT PUMP.......................................3-4 80s

LPs: 10/12-inch

NEMPEROR...5-10 76
OVATION..5-10 80
RICHMOND...10-15
Also see SPRINGSTEEN, Bruce

THOMPSON, Roy
R&B '67

Singles: 7-inch

OKEH...4-8 66-67

THOMPSON, Sonny
P&R/R&B '48

Singles: 78 rpm

CHART..10-15 56
KING..5-15 50-57
MIRACLE...10-15 48

Singles: 7-inch

CHART..15-25 56
KING (4400 thru 5300 series).............5-15 51-60
KNIGHT..5-10 61

EPs: 7-inch

KING..20-40 52-54

LPs: 10/12-inch

KING (568 "Moody Blues")..............75-100 58
KING (655 "Mellow Blues")...............50-75 59
Also see KING, Freddie / Lulu / Sonny Thompson
Also see REED, Lulu

THOMPSON, Sue
P&R '61

Singles: 78 rpm

DECCA..5-10 55
MERCURY...5-10 51-54

Singles: 7-inch

DECCA..10-15 55
GUSTO...3-4 80s
HICKORY (Except 1100 & 1200 series)..4-8 66-76
HICKORY (1100 & 1200 series).........5-10 61-65
MERCURY...10-20 51-54

Picture Sleeves

HICKORY..5-8 64

LPs: 10/12-inch

HICKORY (Except 104 through 121)..8-15 69-74
HICKORY (104 thru 121)..................15-25 62-65
WING...10-15 66
Also see GIBSON, Don, & Sue Thompson
Also see LUMAN, Bob, & Sue Thompson

THOMPSON TWINS
R&B/LP '82

Singles: 12-inch

ARISTA...4-6 83-86

Singles: 7-inch

ARISTA...3-4 82-87
W.B. 3-4 89

Picture Sleeves

ARISTA...3-5 83-87
W.B. 3-4 89

LPs: 10/12-inch

ARISTA...5-10 82-87
Members: Tom Bailey; Alannah Currie; Joe Leeway; Chris Bell.
Also see GENE LOVES JEZEBEL

THOMSON, Ali
P&R/LP '80

Singles: 7-inch

A&M..3-5 80-81

Picture Sleeves

A&M..3-5 80

LPs: 10/12-inch

A&M..5-10 80

THORNE, David
(David Throne) *P&R '62*

Singles: 7-inch

ADMIRAL..4-8 64-65
CHOICE..5-10 60
RIVERSIDE..4-8 62
SAVOY..5-10 59

THORNTON, Big Mama: see THORNTON, Willie Mae

THORNTON, Fonzi
R&B '83

Singles: 12-inch

RCA...4-6 83

Singles: 7-inch

RCA...3-4 83

LPs: 10/12-inch

RCA...5-8 83

THORNTON, Willie Mae
(Big Mama Thornton) *R&B '53*

Singles: 78 rpm

PEACOCK...15-30 52-57

Singles: 7-inch

ABC..3-5 73
ARHOOLIE..4-6 68
BAY TONE..10-15 61
CAROLYN..5-10
GALAXY..4-8 66
KENT..4-8 65
MERCURY...3-6 69
PEACOCK (Maroon label)................35-50 52
PEACOCK (Red label).......................25-35 53-55
PEACOCK (White label)...................10-20 56-57
(White label numbers below 1676 are reissues, which Peacock continued carrying in their catalog through the '70s.)
ST. CAROLYN..4-6
SOTOPLAY..5-10 65

LPs: 10/12-inch

ARHOOLIE..10-15 66-67
BACK BEAT..20-25 70
MERCURY...10-15 69-70
PENTAGRAM...12-25 71
ROULETTE..10-15 70
VANGUARD...8-10 74-75

THOROGOOD, George
(With the Destroyers) *LP '78*

Singles: 12-inch

EMI (Black vinyl)..................................4-6 83-85
EMI (9293 "Rock & Roll Christmas")...5-10 83
(Colored vinyl. Promotional issue only.)

Singles: 7-inch

EMI (Except 17517)..............................3-5 82-94
EMI (17517 "Get a Haircut")................5-10 94
(White label, black vinyl. Reads: "For Juke boxes Only!")
EMI (17517 "Get a Haircut")...............10-15 94
(White label, colored vinyl. Reads: "For Juke boxes Only!")
MCA..3-5 79
ROUNDER...3-5 78-80

LPs: 10/12-inch

EMI..5-8 82-91
MCA..5-10 79
ROUNDER...6-12 77-80

THORPE, Billy
P&R/LP '79

Singles: 7-inch

CAPRICORN..3-5 79
POLYDOR...3-5 79
PASHA (Except "Retail Teaser")...........3-4 85
PASHA ("Retail Teaser")......................4-8 85

LPs: 10/12-inch

CAPRICORN..15-20 79
ELEKTRA..5-8 80
PASHA..8-12 82-85
POLYDOR...5-8 79

THOSE FOUR ELDORADOS
(El Dorados)

Singles: 7-inch

ACADEMY (8138 "A Lonely Boy").250-500 58
Members: Juel Jones; Louis Bradley; Marvin Smith; James Maddox.
Also see EL DORADOS

3
LP '88

Singles: 7-inch

GEFFEN...3-4 88

LPs: 10/12-inch

GEFFEN...5-8 88
Members: Keith Emerson; Carl Palmer.
Also see EMERSON, LAKE & PALMER

THREE CHUCKLES
(Featuring Teddy Randazzo) *P&R '54*

Singles: 78 rpm

BOULEVARD (100 "Runaround").....20-25 53
VIK..5-10 56
"X"..8-12 54-56

Singles: 7-inch

BOULEVARD (100 "Runaround")...50-100 53
CLOUD (507 "Runaround")................5-10 66
VIK (0186 "Anyway").........................10-15 56
VIK (0194 "And the Angels Sing").....10-15 56
VIK (0216 "Gypsy in My Soul")..........10-15 56
VIK (0232 "Midnight Till Dawn").........10-20 56
VIK (0244 "Won't You Give Me a Chance")...10-20 56
"X" (0066 "Runaround")....................15-20 54
"X" (0095 "Foolishly").......................15-20 55
"X" (0134 "So Long").........................15-20 55
"X" (0150 "Realize")..........................15-20 55
"X" (0162 "Times Two, I Love You").15-20 55
"X" (0186 "Anyway")..........................15-20 55
"X" (0194 "And the Angels Sing")......15-20 56
"X" (0216 "Gypsy in My Soul")...........15-20 56

EPs: 7-inch

RCA (192/193/194 "Three Chuckles")...15-25 55
(Price is for any of three volumes.)
VIK (4 "Three Chuckles")..................20-40 57
(Promotional issue only. Not issued with cover.)

LPs: 10/12-inch

VIK (1067 "Three Chuckles")........100-150 55
Members: Teddy Randazzo; Phil Benti; Tom Romano; Russ Gilberto.
Also see CHUCKLES

Also see RANDAZZO, Teddy

THREE DEGREES P&R '65

Singles: 7-inch

ARIOLA AMERICA....3-5 78-80
EPIC....3-5 76
ICHIBAN....3-4 89
METROMEDIA....4-6 69
NEPTUNE....3-5 70
PHILADELPHIA INT'L....3-5 73-76
ROULETTE....3-5 70-73
SWAN....6-12 64-66
W.B.....4-8 68

LPs: 10/12-inch

ARIOLA AMERICA....5-10 78-81
EPIC....8-10 77
PHILADELPHIA INT'L....8-10 74-76
ROULETTE....10-20 70-75
Also see MFSB & Three Degrees

THREE DOG NIGHT P&R/LP '69
(3 Dog Night)

Singles: 7-inch

ABC....3-5 70-76
DUNHILL (Except 4168)....3-6 69-75
DUNHILL (4168 "Nobody")....5-8 68
PASSPORT....3-4 83

Picture Sleeves

DUNHILL (Except 4168)....3-5 70
DUNHILL (4168 "Nobody")....20-30 68
(Promotional issue only.)

EPs: 7-inch

DUNHILL (PRO-50158 "Cyan")....8-12 73
(Promotional only issue.)

LPs: 10/12-inch

ABC....8-12 75-76
COMMAND ("CQD" series)....15-25 74-75
(Quadraphonic.)
DUNHILL (50048 thru 50068)....10-15 68-69
DUNHILL (50078 "It Ain't Easy")....50-100 70
(Cover pictures nude people.)
DUNHILL (50078 "It Ain't Easy")....10-12 70
(Cover doesn't show nudes.)
DUNHILL (50088 thru 50158)....10-15 70-73
DUNHILL (50168 "Hard Labor")....15-20 74
(With baby delivery cover.)
DUNHILL (50168 "Hard Labor")....10-12 74
(With Band-Aid cover.)
DUNHILL (50178 "Joy to the World")..8-10 74
K-TEL....5-10
MCA....5-8 82
PASSPORT....5-8 83
PICKWICK....5-8 79
Members: Danny Hutton; Cory Wells; Chuck Negron; Mike Allsup; Jimmy Greenspoon; Joe Schermie; Floyd Sneed.
Also see HUTTON, Danny
Also see WELLS, Cory

THREE FLAMES P&R/R&B '47

Singles: 78 rpm

COLUMBIA....15-25 47-51
GOTHAM....15-25 46
HARMONY....10-20 49
MGM....10-20 50

LPs: 10/12-inch

MERCURY (20239 "At the Bon Soir")....25-50 57
Member: Tiger Haynes; Rill Pollard; Roy Testamark.
Also see BARNES, Mae

3 FRIENDS P&R '61
(Three Friends)

Singles: 7-inch

CAL-GOLD (169 "Blue Ribbon Baby")....100-150 61
IMPERIAL (5763 "Dedicated to the Songs I Love")....20-30 61
IMPERIAL (5773 "Go on to School") 10-20 61

THREE Gs P&R '58

Singles: 7-inch

COLUMBIA....5-10 58-61

THREE GRACES

Singles: 7-inch

GOLDEN CREST....5-10 59-60

THREE GRACES / Wailers

EPs: 7-inch

GOLDEN CREST (88601/2 "Four Songs on 45 rpm")....75-125 60
(With paper sleeve-mailer. Both sides have label pictures.)
Also see WAILERS

THREE MAN ISLAND P&R '88

Singles: 7-inch

CHRYSALIS....3-4 88

Picture Sleeves

CHRYSALIS....3-4 88

LPs: 10/12-inch

CHRYSALIS....5-8 88

THREE MILLION R&B/D&D '83

Singles: 12-inch

COTILLION....4-6 84-84

Singles: 7-inch

COTILLION....3-5 83-84

THREE O'CLOCK LP '85

Singles: 7-inch

I.R.S.....3-4 85

LPs: 10/12-inch

I.R.S.....5-8 85

3 OUNCES OF LOVE R&B '78

Singles: 7-inch

MOTOWN....3-5 78

LPs: 10/12-inch

MOTOWN....5-10 78
Members: Elaine Alexander; Ann Alexander; Regina Alexander.

THREE PLAYMATES P&R '58

Singles: 7-inch

SAVOY....8-12 58

THREE SUNS P&R '44
(With Larry Green)

Singles: 78 rpm

HIT....3-6 44
MAJESTIC....3-6 46
RCA....3-5 47-57

Singles: 7-inch

RCA....4-8 50-64

EPs: 7-inch

RCA....5-10 50-61
ROYALE....5-10 50s
VARSITY....5-10 52

LPs: 10/12-inch

CAMDEN....5-15 60-64
MUSICOR....5-10 66
RCA....5-20 50-76
RONDO....5-15 59
ROYALE....10-15 50s
VARSITY....10-20 50-52
Members: Al Nevins; Marty Nevins; Art Dunn.

THREE SUNS, Rosalie Allen & Elton Britt C&W '50

Singles: 78 rpm

RCA....5-10 50

THREE TIMES DOPE LP '89

LPs: 10/12-inch

ARISTA....5-8 89

THRILLS LP '81

Singles: 7-inch

G&P....3-5 80-81

LPs: 10/12-inch

G&P....5-10 80-81

THUNDER, Johnny P&R '62

Singles: 7-inch

ABC....3-5 74
CALLA....4-6 69
DIAMOND....4-8 62-68
EPIC....5-10 59
U.A.....3-5 70

Picture Sleeves

DIAMOND....8-12 63

LPs: 10/12-inch

DIAMOND (D-5001 "Loop De Loop")....25-35 63
(Monaural.)
DIAMOND (SD-5001 "Loop De Loop")....35-45 63
(Stereo.)
REAL RECORDS....10-15
Also see ARCHIES / Johnny Thunder

THUNDER, Johnny, & Ruby Winters P&R/R&B '67

Singles: 7-inch

DIAMOND....4-8 67-68
Also see THUNDER, Johnny
Also see WINTERS, Ruby

THUNDER, Margo R&B '74

Singles: 7-inch

HAVEN....3-5 74

THUNDERCLAP NEWMAN: see NEWMAN, Thunderclap

THUNDERFLASH R&B '83

Singles: 7-inch

JAMPOWER....3-5 83

THUNDERKLOUD, Billy, & Chieftones C&W/P&R '75

Singles: 7-inch

CLAREMONT....5-10
POLYDOR....3-5 76-78
SCEPTER....8-12 68
STABLE....3-5 75
SUPERIOR....3-5 74
20TH FOX....3-5 74-75
YOUNGSTOWN....8-12 68

LPs: 10/12-inch

SUPERIOR....8-12 74
20TH FOX....6-12 74-75
Members: Jack Wolf; Barry Littlestar; Richard Grayowl.

THURSTON, Bobby R&B '80

Singles: 7-inch

PRELUDE....3-5 80

TIA P&R '87

Singles: 7-inch

RCA....3-4 87

Picture Sleeves

RCA....3-4 87

TIBBS, Andrew R&B '49
(With the Dozier Boys)

Singles: 78 rpm

ARISTOCRAT....15-25 47-49
PEACOCK....10-20 52

Singles: 7-inch

M-PAC....4-8 66
PEACOCK (1597 "Mother's Letter")..25-35 52
Also see TIBBS BROTHERS

TICO & TRIUMPHS P&R '62
(Featuring Paul Simon)

Singles: 7-inch

AMY (835 "Motorcycle")....15-25 62
AMY (845 "Wild Flower")....15-25 62
AMY (860 "Cry Little Boy")....15-25 62
AMY (876 "Cards of Love")....30-40 62
MADISON (169 "Motorcycle")....20-30 61
Also see SIMON, Paul

TICTOC D&D '84

Singles: 12-inch

RCA....4-6 84

Singles: 7-inch

RCA....3-4 84

LPs: 10/12-inch

RCA....5-8 84

TIERRA P&R/R&B/LP '80

Singles: 7-inch

ASI....3-5 80
BOARDWALK....3-5 80-82

SALSOUL...3-5 81
MCA...3-5 79
TODY...3-5

LPs: 10/12-inch

ASI...5-10 80
BOARDWALK...5-10 80
SALSOUL...5-10 81

Members: Salas Brothers.
Also see EL CHICANO

TIFFANY P&R/LP '87
(Tiffany Darwisch)

Singles: 7-inch

MCA...3-4 87-89

Picture Sleeves

MCA...3-4 87-89

LPs: 10/12-inch

MCA...5-8 87-88

TIGGI CLAY P&R '84

Singles: 7-inch

MOROCCO (1716 "Flashes")...3-5 84
(Black vinyl.)
MOROCCO (1716 "Flashes")...4-6 84
(Colored vinyl. Promotional issue only.)

LPs: 10/12-inch

MOROCCO...5-10 84

Members: Romeo McCall; Fizzy Quick; Billy Peaches.

TIGHT FIT P&R '81

Singles: 12-inch

ARISTA...4-6 81
JIVE...4-6 81

Singles: 7-inch

ARISTA...3-5 81
JIVE...3-5 81

TIJUANA BRASS: see ALPERT, Herb

TIKARAM, Tanita LP '89

Singles: 7-inch

REPRISE...3-4 89

Picture Sleeves

REPRISE...3-4 89

TIL, Sonny
(With Buddy Lucas Orchestra)

Singles: 78 rpm

JUBILEE...50-75 52-53

Singles: 7-inch

JUBILEE (5066 "For All We Know")...150-200 52
(Black vinyl.)
JUBILEE (5066 "For All We Know")...400-600 52
(Colored vinyl.)
JUBILEE (5076 "Proud of You")...150-200 52
JUBILEE (5118 "Congratulations to Someone")...100-200 53
RCA...4-8 69-72
ROULETTE (4079 "Shy")...15-25 58

LPs: 10/12-inch

DOBRE...5-10 78
RCA...10-20 70-71

Also see McGRIFF, Edna, & Sonny Til
Also see ORIOLES

'TIL TUESDAY P&R/LP '85

Singles: 7-inch

EPIC...3-4 85-89

Picture Sleeves

EPIC...3-4 89

Members: Aimee Mann; Michael Hausman; Robert Holmes; Joey Pesce.

TILLMAN, Bertha P&R '62

Singles: 7-inch

BRENT (7029 "Oh My Angel")...15-20 62
BRENT (7032 "I Wish")...20-30 62

TILLOTSON, Johnny P&R '58

Singles: 7-inch

AMOS...3-5 69-70
BARNABY...3-5 76
BUDDAH...3-5 71-73
CADENCE (1300 series)...5-10 58-61
CADENCE (1400 series)...4-8 61-63
COLUMBIA...3-5 73-75
ERIC...3-4 70s
MGM...4-8 63-68
REWARD...3-4 82-84
U.A....3-5 76-77

Picture Sleeves

CADENCE...10-15 60
MGM...5-8 63-66

EPs: 7-inch

CADENCE (114 "Dreamy Eyes")...25-35 60
CADENCE (33-1 "This Is Johnny Tillotson")...15-25 61
("Cadence Little LP." With cardboard insert in clear cover.)
CADENCE (33-2 "Music By Johnny Tillotson")...15-25 61
("Cadence Little LP." With cardboard insert in clear cover.)

LPs: 10/12-inch

ACCORD...5-10 82
AMOS...10-15 69
BACK-TRAC...5-8 85
BARNABY...8-10 77
BUCKBOARD...5-10 80s
BUDDAH...10-15 72
CADENCE...25-40 61-63
EVEREST...5-8 82
METRO...10-15 66
MGM...12-20 64-71
ROWE/AMI...5-8 66
("Play Me" Sales Stimulator promotional issue.)
U.A....8-10 77

Session: Boots Randolph.
Also see IVAN / Johnny Tillotson
Also see RANDOLPH, Boots

TILLOTSON, Johnny / J.D. Souther

Singles: 7-inch

BUDDAH...3-5 71

Also see SOUTHER, J.D.
Also see TILLOTSON, Johnny

TIM TAM & TURN-ONS P&R '66

Singles: 7-inch

PALMER (5002 "Wait a Minute")...8-12 66
PALMER (5003 "Cheryl Ann")...20-30 66
PALMER (5006 "Kimberly")...20-30 66
PALMER (5014 "Don't Say Hi")...5-10 67

TIMBUK 3 P&R/LP '86

Singles: 7-inch

I.R.S....3-4 86-88

LPs: 10/12-inch

I.R.S....5-8 86-88

TIME R&B/LP '81

Singles: 12-inch

W.B....4-6 82-84

Singles: 7-inch

W.B....3-5 81-84

LPs: 10/12-inch

PAISLEY PARK...5-8 90
W.B....5-8 81-84

Members: Morris Day; Jesse Johnson; Jimmy Jam; Monte Moir; Jellybean Johnson; Stacy Adams; Terry Lewis; Paul Peterson.
Also see DAY, Morris
Also see JOHNSON, Jesse
Also see ST. PAUL
Also see VANITY 6

TIME BANDITS D&D '85

Singles: 12-inch

COLUMBIA...4-6 85

TIME ZONE D&D '84

Singles: 12-inch

CELLULOID...4-6 84

TIMELORDS P&R '88

Singles: 7-inch

TVT...3-4 88

Singles: 7-inch

TVT...3-4 88

TIMES TWO P&R/LP '88

Singles: 7-inch

REPRISE...3-4 88

Picture Sleeves

REPRISE...3-4 88

LPs: 10/12-inch

REPRISE...5-8 88

TIMETONES P&R '61

Singles: 7-inch

ATCO (6201 "I've Got a Feeling")...15-25 61
TIMES SQUARE (26 "Sunday Kind of Love")...15-20 64
TIMES SQUARE (34 "House Where Lovers Dream")...30-40 64
TIMES SQUARE (421 "Here in My Heart")...20-30 61
TIMES SQUARE (421 "In My Heart") 10-20 61
(Note shortened title.)

Member: Slim Rose.

TIMEX SOCIAL CLUB P&R/R&B '86

Singles: 12-inch

DANYA...4-6 86
JAY...4-6 86

Singles: 7-inch

DANYA...3-4 86-87
JAY...3-4 86

TIMMY T. LP '91

LPs: 10/12-inch

QUALITY...5-8 90

TIN MACHINE LP '89

LPs: 10/12-inch

EMI...5-8 89

TIN TIN P&R/LP '71

Singles: 12-inch

SIRE...4-6 81-83

Singles: 7-inch

ATCO...3-5 71

LPs: 10/12-inch

ATCO...10-15 70-71

Members: Steve Kipner; Steve Groves.

TINA & DADDY: see JONES, George

TINA B. D&D '84

Singles: 12-inch

ATLANTIC...4-6 82-84
ELEKTRA...4-6 83-84

Singles: 7-inch

ATLANTIC...3-4 82
ELEKTRA...3-4 83

LPs: 10/12-inch

ATLANTIC...5-8 82
ELEKTRA...5-8 83

TINDLEY, George R&B '69
(With the Modern Red Caps; George Tinley)

Singles: 7-inch

DOO-WOP...4-8
EMBER...10-20 60
HERALD...10-20 61
ROWAX...8-12 63
PARKWAY...5-10 62
SMASH...5-10 62
WAND...4-6 69-70

TINLEY, George: see TINDLEY, George

TINY TIM P&R/LP '68
(Herbert Khaury)

Singles: 7-inch

BLUE CAT (127 "Little Girl")...8-12 65
CLOUDS...3-5 79
NLT...3-4 88
REPRISE...3-6 68-71
SCEPTER...3-5 72
VIC TIM...3-5 71

LPs: 10/12-inch

BOUQUET...10-12
REPRISE...10-20 68

TINY TIM & MISS VICKI

Singles: 7-inch

REPRISE...3-6 71

TINY TIM / Michelle Ramos / Bruce Haack

LPs: 10/12-inch

RA-JO INT'L 5-8 86

Also see TINY TIM

TJADER, Cal LP '63

Singles: 78 rpm

FANTASY 3-5 54-57
SAVOY 3-5 53-54

Singles: 7-inch

FANTASY 3-8 54-71
SAVOY 4-8 53-54
SKYE 3-5 68
VERVE 3-6 61-66

EPs: 7-inch

FANTASY (Black vinyl) 10-25 54-55
FANTASY (Colored vinyl) 20-40 54-55
SAVOY 10-20 54

LPs: 10/12-inch

BUDDAH 8-12 70
CLASSIC JAZZ 5-8 80
CONCORD JAZZ 5-8 80-82
FANTASY (3-9 "Cal Tjader Trio") 75-125 54
(10-inch LP.)
FANTASY (3-17 "Ritmo Caliente") 75-125 54
(10-inch LP.)
FANTASY (3200 series) 25-75 54-60
(Numbers may be shown as 3-200. Double price range for colored vinyl pressings.)
FANTASY (3300 series) 25-35 60-65
FANTASY (8000 & 8100 series, except 8030) 35-45 58-61
FANTASY (8030 "Tjader Goes Latin) 75-125 59
(Colored vinyl.)
FANTASY (8300 series) 20-30 65
FANTASY (8400 series) 8-15 71-72
FANTASY (9000 series) 6-12 72-77
GALAXY 5-10 78-79
METRO 10-15 67
PRESTIGE 5-10 73
SAVOY (9036 "Cal Tjader Quartet") 75-125 54
(10-inch LP.)
SAVOY (12054 "Vib-Rations") 50-100 56
SAVOY (12000 series) 20-40 56
SKYE 8-12 68-69
VERVE 10-30 61-69
(Reads "MGM Records - A Division of Metro-Goldwyn-Mayer, Inc." at bottom of label.)
VERVE 5-12 73-84
(Reads "Manufactured By MGM Record Corp.," or mentions either Polydor or Polygram at bottom of label.)

Also see BRUBECK, Dave, Quartet
Also see O'DAY, Anita, & Cal Tjader

TJADER, Cal, & Stan Getz

LPs: 10/12-inch

FANTASY (3266 "Cal Tjader and Stan Getz") 35-45 58
FANTASY (3300 series) 15-25 65
FANTASY (8005 "Cal Tjader and Stan Getz") 45-55 58
FANTASY (8300 series) 15-25 65

Also see GETZ, Stan
Also see TJADER, Cal

TOBY BEAU P&R/LP '78

Singles: 7-inch

RCA 3-5 78-80

LPs: 10/12-inch

RCA (Except 2994) 5-10 78-81
RCA (2994 "Three You Missed, One You Didn't") 10-15 78
(Promotional issue only.)

TODAY LP '89

LPs: 10/12-inch

MOTOWN 5-8 89-90

TODAY'S PEOPLE P&R '73

Singles: 7-inch

20TH FOX 3-5 73

TODD, Art & Dotty P&R/R&B '58

Singles: 78 rpm

DIAMOND 5-10 56

Singles: 7-inch

CAPITOL 5-8 62
COLLECTABLES 3-4 80s
DAKAR 5-8 63
DART 5-10 59-67
DECCA 5-10 61
DIAMOND 10-20 56
DOT 4-8 66
ERA 8-12 58-59
M.O.L. 4-8 68
SIGNET 4-8 65

LPs: 10/12-inch

BEVERLY HILLS 8-10 73
DART 15-25 60
DOT 10-20 66
REPRISE 10-20 65

TODD, Nick P&R '57

Singles: 78 rpm

DOT 10-20 57

Singles: 7-inch

DOT 10-20 57-60

TOKENS P&R '61

Singles: 12-inch

DOWNTOWN (103 "The Lion Sleeps Tonight") 8-12 88
(Issued with cover.)

Singles: 78 rpm

MELBA (104 "While I Dream") 30-50 56

Singles: 7-inch

ABC 3-5 73
ATCO 3-5 74
B.T. PUPPY 4-8 64-69
BELL 3-5 72
BUDDAH 4-6 69-70
COLLECTABLES 3-4 84
LAURIE 10-15 63
MELBA (104 "While I Dream") 30-50 56
RCA (37-7896 "When I Go to Sleep at Night") 20-30 61
(Compact 33 Single.)
RCA (37-7925 "Sincerely") 20-30 61
(Compact 33 Single.)
RCA (37-7954 "The Lion Sleeps Tonight") 20-30 61
(Compact 33 Single.)
RCA (37-7991 "B'Wa Nina") 20-30 62
(Compact 33 Single.)
RCA (37-8018 "The Riddle") 20-30 62
(Compact 33 Single.)
RCA (47-7896 thru 47-8148) 8-12 61-65
RCA (447-0702 "The Lion Sleeps Tonight") 4-6 60s
(Gold Standard Series.)
RCA (8749 "Re-Doo-Wopp") 3-4 88
RADIO ACTIVE GOLD 3-4
W.B. 4-8 67-69
WARWICK 10-15 61

Picture Sleeves

B.T. PUPPY (591 "Greatest Moments in a Girl's Life") 10-15 66
RCA (7896 "When I Go to Sleep at Night") 10-20 61
RCA (7991 "B'Wa Nina") 10-20 62
(Orange sleeve. No mention of *The Lion Sleeps Tonight* LP.)
RCA (7991 "B'Wa Nina") 8-12 62
(Orange and white sleeve. Plugs *The Lion Sleeps Tonight* LP.)
RCA (8018 "The Riddle") 10-20 62
RCA (8052 "La Bomba") 10-15 62
RCA (8089 "I'll Do My Crying Tomorrow") 10-20 62
RCA (8114 "A Bird Flies Out of Sight") 10-20 63
RCA (8148 "Tonight I Met an Angel") 10-20 63
RCA (8210 "Hear the Bells") 10-15 63
W.B. (5900 "Portrait of My Love") 5-10 67

LPs: 10/12-inch

B.T. PUPPY 15-25 66-78
BUDDAH (5059 "Both Sides Now") 15-20 70
DOWNTOWN 5-8 88
RCA (LPM-2514 "The Lion Sleeps Tonight") 30-50 61
(Monaural.)
RCA (LSP-2514 "The Lion Sleeps Tonight") 50-75 61
(Stereo.)
RCA (LPM-2631 "We The Tokens Sing Folk") 20-40 62
(Monaural.)
RCA (LSP-2631 "We The Tokens Sing Folk") 25-50 62
(Stereo.)
RCA (LPM-2886 "Wheels") 20-40 64
(Monaural.)
RCA (LSP-2886 "Wheels") 25-50 64
(Stereo.)
RCA (LPM-3685 "The Tokens Again") 20-40 66
(Monaural.)
RCA (LSP-3685 "The Tokens Again") 20-40 66
(Stereo.)
RCA (8534 "Re-Doo-Wopp") 5-8 88
W.B. (1685 "It's a Happening World") 15-25 67

Members: Jay Siegel; Mitchell Margo; Philip Margo; Henry Medress.

Also see CHRISTIE, Lou / Len Barry & Dovells / Bobby Rydell / Tokens
Also see CROSS COUNTRY
Also see FOUR WINDS
Also see KEITH
Also see SEDAKA, Neil
Also see SANDS of TIME

TOKENS / Happenings LP '67

LPs: 10/12-inch

B.T. PUPPY 15-25 67

Also see HAPPENINGS
Also see TOKENS

TOLBERT, Israel "Popper Stopper" P&R/R&B '70

Singles: 7-inch

WARREN 3-5 70-71

LPs: 10/12-inch

WARREN 10-15 71

TOM & JERRIO P&R/R&B '65

Singles: 7-inch

ABC-PAR 4-8 65

Members: Eddie Thomas; Jerry Murray.

Also see JERRYO

TOM & JERRY P&R '57

Singles: 78 rpm

BIG 25-75 57-58

Singles: 7-inch

ABC-PAR (10363 "Surrender, Please Surrender") 15-25 62
ABC-PAR (10788 "This Is My Story") 10-15 66
BIG (613 "Hey, Schoolgirl") 20-30 57
BIG (616 "Two Teenagers") 20-30 58
BIG (618 "Don't Say Goodbye") 20-30 58
EMBER (1094 "I'm Lonesome") 25-35 59
HUNT (319 "Don't Say Goodbye") 20-25 58
KING (5167 "Hey, Schoolgirl") 35-45 58

Members: Paul Simon; Art Garfunkel.

Also see SIMON & GARFUNKEL

TOM & JERRY / Ronnie Lawrence

Singles: 7-inch

BELL (120 "Baby Talk") 20-30 60

Also see TOM & JERRY

TOM TOM CLUB LP '81

Singles: 12-inch

SIRE 4-8 81-83

Singles: 7-inch

SIRE 3-5 81-89

LPs: 10/12-inch

SIRE 5-10 81-89

Members: Chris Frantz; Tina Weymouth.

Also see TALKING HEADS

TOMLIN, Lily LP '71

Singles: 7-inch

POLYDOR....3-5 73-75

LPs: 10/12-inch

ARISTA....5-10 77
POLYDOR....5-10 71-75

TOMMY TUTONE P&R/LP '80

Singles: 7-inch

COLUMBIA....3-5 80-83

LPs: 10/12-inch

COLUMBIA (Except 1461)....5-10 80-83
COLUMBIA (1461 "Alive and Almost Dangerous")....10-15 82
(Promotional issue only.)

TOMORROW'S EDITION R&B '82

Singles: 7-inch

ATLANTIC....3-5 82
GANG....3-5 75

TOMORROW'S PROMISE R&B '73

Singles: 7-inch

CAPITOL....4-8 73-74
MERCURY....3-5 75

TOMPALL & GLASER BROTHERS
(Tompall & Glasers; Tompall Glaser) P&R '69

Singles: 7-inch

DECCA....5-10 59-65
ELEKTRA....3-5 80-82
MGM....3-8 66-71
RICH (1004 "Yakety-Yak")....15-25 61
ROBBINS (1006 "I Want You")....50-75 57

LPs: 10/12-inch

DECCA (DL-4041 "This Land")....35-45 60
(Monaural.)
DECCA (DL7-4041 "This Land")....40-60 60
(Stereo.)
ELEKTRA....5-10 81
MGM....10-20 67-75
U.A. (3540 "Ballad of *Namu the Killer Whale* and Others")....25-35 66
(Monaural.)
U.A. (6540 "Ballad of *Namu the Killer Whale* and Others")....30-40 66
(Stereo.)
VOCALION (3807 "Country Folk")....8-12 67
Members: Tompall Glaser; Jim Glaser; Chuck Glaser.
Also see GLASER, Tompall

TOMS, Gary P&R/R&B/LP '75
(Gary Toms' Empire)

Singles: 12-inch

MCA....4-8 77

Singles: 7-inch

MCA....3-5 77
MERCURY....3-5 78
P.I.P....3-5 75-76

LPs: 10/12-inch

MCA....5-10 77
MERCURY....5-10 78
P.I.P....5-10 75

TONE LOC P&R '88

Singles: 7-inch

DELICIOUS....3-4 89

Picture Sleeves

DELICIOUS....3-4 89

LPs: 10/12-inch

DELICIOUS....5-8 89

TONES R&B '83

Singles: 7-inch

CRIMINAL....3-5 83

TONEY, Oscar, Jr. P&R/R&B/LP '67

Singles: 7-inch

BELL....5-10 67-69
CAPRICORN....10-20 71-72
KING....8-12 64

LPs: 10/12-inch

BELL....10-20 67

TONEY LEE: see LEE, Toney

TONY & CAROL R&B '72

Singles: 7-inch

KING....4-6 70
ROULETTE....3-5 72
Members: Tony Issac; Carol McLean.

TONY & JOE P&R '58

Singles: 7-inch

DORE....4-8 61-62
ERA....5-10 58
FLYTE....5-10 59
GARDENA....5-10 60
Members: Tony Savonne; Joe Saraceno.
Also see BEACH BOYS / Tony & Joe

TONY, BOB & JIMMY

Singles: 7-inch

CAPITOL....4-8 62
Members: Tony Butala; Bob Engemann; Jim Pike.
Also see LETTERMEN

TONY! TONI! TONE! P&R/R&B/LP '88

Singles: 7-inch

WING....3-4 88-90

Picture Sleeves

WING....3-4 88

TOO SHORT LP '89

LPs: 10/12-inch

DANGEROUS....5-8 89
JIVE....5-8 90

TOOTS & MAYTALS LP '75

Singles: 12-inch

MANGO....4-6 82

Singles: 7-inch

MANGO....3-5 76-82

LPs: 10/12-inch

ISLAND....5-10 75
MANGO....5-10 76-82
Members: Toots Hibbert; Nathaniel Mathias; Releigh Gordon; Paul Douglas; Jackie Jackson; Winston Wright.
Also see WINWOOD, Steve

TOP SHELF R&B '70

Singles: 7-inch

LO LO....4-6 69-70
SOUND TOWN....3-5 80

TORA TORA LP '89

LPs: 10/12-inch

A&M....5-8 89

TORCH D&D '83

Singles: 12-inch

PACIFIC....4-6 83

TORCH SONG D&D '84

Singles: 12-inch

I.R.S....4-6 83-84

Singles: 7-inch

I.R.S....3-4 83-84

LPs: 10/12-inch

I.R.S....5-8 83

TORME, Mel P&R '45
(With the Meltones)

Singles: 78 rpm

BETHLEHEM....4-10 56-57
CAPITOL (1000 & 2000 series)....4-8 50-53

Singles: 7-inch

ATLANTIC....4-6 62-64
BETHLEHEM....5-10 56-58
CAPITOL (1000 & 2000 series)....5-10 50-53
(Purple labels.)
CAPITOL (2000 series)....3-6 69-70
(Orange labels.)
COLUMBIA....3-6 64-67
CORAL....5-10 53-56
LIBERTY....3-6 68
VERVE....4-8 59-61

EPs: 7-inch

CAPITOL....5-15 50
P.R.I. (9 "The Touch of Your Lips")....5-10

LPs: 10/12-inch

ATLANTIC (8000 series)....12-25 62-64
ATLANTIC (18000 series)....5-10 75
ATLANTIC (80000 series)....5-8 83
BETHLEHEM (34 "It's a Blue World")....25-50 55
BETHLEHEM (52 "Mel Torme")....25-50 56
BETHLEHEM (4000 series)....10-20 65
BETHLEHEM (6000 series)....20-40 58-60
(Maroon labels.)
BETHLEHEM (6000 series)....5-10 77-78
(Gray labels.)
CAPITOL (200 "California Suite")....50-100 50
(10-inch LP.)
CAPITOL (300 & 400 series)....8-12 69-70
COLUMBIA (2000 series)....10-20 64-66
(Monaural.)
COLUMBIA (9000 series)....10-20 64-66
(Stereo.)
CONCORD JAZZ....5-8 82
CORAL (57012 "At the Crescendo")....50-100 54
CORAL (57044 "Musical Sounds")....50-100 54
EVEREST....5-10 76
GLENDALE....5-8 78-79
GRYPHON....5-8 79
LIBERTY....8-15 68
MGM (552 "Songs By Mel Torme")....50-100 52
(10-inch LP.)
MAYFAIR....25-35 58
METRO....10-20 65
MUSICRAFT....5-8 83
STRAND....12-25 60
VERVE....20-35 58-60
(Reads "Verve Records, Inc." at bottom of label.)
VERVE....10-20 61-72
(Reads "MGM Records - A Division of Metro-Goldwyn-Mayer, Inc." at bottom of label.)
VERVE....5-10 73-84
(Reads "Manufactured By MGM Record Corp.," or mentions either Polydor or Polygram at bottom of label.)
VOCALION....5-10 70
Also see CROSBY, Bing, & Mel Torme
Also see LEE, Peggy, & Mel Torme
Also see WHITING, Margaret

TORNADER R&B '77

Singles: 7-inch

POLYDOR....3-5 77

TORNADOES P&R/R&B '62

Singles: 7-inch

LONDON....4-8 62-63
TOWER....4-8 65

LPs: 10/12-inch

LONDON....25-35 62-63
Members: Heinz Burt; Alan Caddy; Clem Cattini; George Bellamy.

TOROK, Mitchell C&W/P&R '53
(With the Louisiana Hayride Band; with Matches; with Ramona Redd)

Singles: 78 rpm

ABBOTT....10-20 53-54
DECCA....5-15 57-58
FBC (102 "Nacogdoches County Line")....15-25 48
FBC (115 "Piney Woods Boogie")....15-25 49

Singles: 7-inch

ABBOTT....12-25 53-54
CALICO....3-5
CAPITOL....4-8 62-63
DECCA....5-10 57-59
GUYDEN....5-10 59-60
INETTE....4-8 63
MERCURY....4-8 61
RCA....4-8 65
REPRISE....4-6 66-67

Picture Sleeves

GUYDEN....10-20 59-60

LPs: 10/12-inch

CALICO....10-15
GUYDEN (502 "Caribbean")....25-45 60
(Monaural.)
GUYDEN (ST-502 "Caribbean")....50-75 60
(Stereo.)
REPRISE....10-15 66

TORONTO LP '80

Singles: 7-inch

NETWORK 3-5 82
SOLID GOLD 3-5

LPs: 10/12-inch

A&M 5-10 80-81
NETWORK 5-10 82
SOLID GOLD 5-10

TORRANCE, George P&R/R&B '68
(With the Naturals; with Dippers)

Singles: 7-inch

DUO DISC 4-8 66
EPIC 5-10 61
KING 5-10 60
SHOUT 4-6 68

TORRANCE, Richard LP '75
(With Eureka)

Singles: 7-inch

CAPITOL 3-5 77-79
SHELTER 3-5 75

LPs: 10/12-inch

CAPITOL 5-10 77
SHELTER 5-10 74-75

TOSH, Peter LP '76

Singles: 12-inch

EMI AMERICA 4-6 83

Singles: 7-inch

COLUMBIA 3-5 76-77
EMI AMERICA 3-5 81-84
ROLLING STONES 3-5 78-79

Picture Sleeves

ROLLINS STONES 3-6 78

EPs: 7-inch

COLUMBIA 4-8 76
(Promotional issue only.)

LPs: 10/12-inch

COLUMBIA 5-10 76-77
EMI AMERICA 5-8 81-84
ROLLING STONES 5-10 79

TOSH, Peter, & Mick Jagger

Singles: 7-inch

ROLLING STONES (19308 "Don't Look Back") 4-6 78
(With "Rolling Stones" at top of label.)
ROLLING STONES (19308 "Don't Look Back") 3-5 78
(Without "Rolling Stones" at top of label.)

Promotional Singles

ROLLING STONES (130 "Don't Look Back") 10-20 78
ROLLING STONES (7500 "Don't Look Back") 5-10 78

LPs: 10/12-inch

ROLLING STONES 5-10 78
Also see JAGGER, Mick
Also see MARLEY, Bob, & Wailers

TOTAL COELO P&R/D&D '83

Singles: 12-inch

CHRYSALIS 4-6 83

Singles: 7-inch

CHRYSALIS 3-4 83

Picture Sleeves

CHRYSALIS 3-5 83

TOTAL CONTRAST R&B/D&D '85

Singles: 12-inch

LONDON 4-6 85-86

Singles: 7-inch

LONDON 3-4 85-88

LPs: 10/12-inch

LONDON 5-8 86

TOTO P&R/LP '78
(With the Vienna Symphony Orchestra; with Jean-Michel Byron)

Singles: 12-inch

COLUMBIA 4-8 79-85

Singles: 10-inch

COLUMBIA (168065 "Gift with the Golden Gun"/"Goodbye Elenore") 5-10 81
(Two-discs, songs from *Turn Back.*)

Picture Disc Singles

COLUMBIA (6784 "Hold the Line") ... 15-25 78
(Picture disc. Has same picture on both sides. Includes card insert autographed by band member.)
COLUMBIA (ZSS-165008 "Hold the Line") 10-15 78
(Licorice Pizza logo picture disc.)
COLUMBIA (ZSS-165008 "Hold the Line") 15-20 78
(KRBE logo picture disc.)
COLUMBIA (ZSS-165009 "Hold the Line") 15-20 78
(Roxy Invitation picture disc.)
COLUMBIA (ZSS-165009 "Hold the Line") 15-20 78
(Licorice Pizza or Wherehouse logo picture disc.)
COLUMBIA (165 792 "Georgy Porgy") 25-30 79
(Octagon picture disc. Promotional issue only.)
COLUMBIA (166 516/17 "Hydra") ... 80-100 79
(Square picture disc. Promotional issue only. 100 made. Includes folder. Some have KORL Channel 65 logo.)
COLUMBIA (166 518/19 "St. George and the Dragon") 80-100 80
(Square picture disc. Promotional issue only.)
COLUMBIA (169-156/109 "Africa"/"We Made It") 15-20 82
(Africa-shaped picture disc. Promotional issue only.)
COLUMBIA (169-156/157 "Africa"/"Good for You") 15-20 82
(Africa-shaped picture disc. Promotional issue only.)
COLUMBIA (8C8-38685 "Africa"/"Rosanna") 15-20 82
(Africa-shaped picture disc.)

Singles: 7-inch

COLUMBIA 3-5 78-88

Picture Sleeves

COLUMBIA 3-6 82-88

LPs: 10/12-inch

COLUMBIA (30000 series) 5-10 78-86
(Black viny—no picture discs.)
COLUMBIA (9C9-39911 "Isolation") 12-18 84
(Picture disc.)
COLUMBIA (PJC-35317 "Toto") 25-35 79
(Picture disc. Same value for promotional issue. Add $10 if with die-cut cover.)
COLUMBIA (37928 "Toto IV") 20-30 82
(Picture disc. Promotional issue only.)
COLUMBIA (37928 "Toto IV") 25-35 82
(Picture disc. Promotional issue only with *Strawberries*, with WBCN logo.)
COLUMBIA (37928 "Toto IV") 30-40 82
(Picture disc. Promotional issue only, with "Turtles Annual Getaway" logo.)
COLUMBIA (PD-36813 "Turn Back") 35-45 79
(Picture disc. Promotional issue only. Includes calendar insert. 400 made.)
COLUMBIA (47728 "Toto IV") 10-15 83
(Half-speed mastered.)
MFLS (250 "Toto IV") 15-25
POLYDOR 5-8 84
Members: Steve Porcaro; David Paich; Steve Lukather; David Hungate; Jeffrey Porcaro; Bobby Kimball.
Also see FAR CORPORATION
Also see VOICES of AMERICA / U.S.A. for Africa

TOUCH R&B '77

Singles: 7-inch

ATCO 3-5 80-81
BRUNSWICK 3-5 77
COLISEUM 4-6 69
LECASVER 5-8 69
PUBLIC (103 "No Shame") 5-10 60s

LPs: 10/12-inch

ATCO 5-10 80
COLISEUM (51004 "20/20 Sound") .. 15-20 68
Members: Don Gallucci; Jeff Hawks; Joe Newman; Bruce Hauser; John Bordonaro.
Also see DON & GOODTIMES

TOUCH R&B '87

Singles: 7-inch

SUPERTRONICS 3-4 87
Member: Eric McCaine.
Also see ENTOUCH

TOUCH OF CLASS R&B '75

Singles: 12-inch

NEXT PLATINUM 4-6 84

Singles: 7-inch

ATLANTIC 3-5 82
MIDLAND INT'L 3-5 75-77
ROADSHOW 3-5 79-84

LPs: 10/12-inch

MIDLAND INT'L 5-10 76
ROADSHOW 5-10 79

TOUPS, Wayne LP '89
(With Zydecajun)

LPs: 10/12-inch

MERCURY 5-8 89

TOURISTS P&R '80

Singles: 7-inch

EPIC 3-5 80

LPs: 10/12-inch

EPIC 5-10 81
Members: Annie Lennox; David Stewart; Ed Chin; Pete Coombes; Jim Toomey.
Also see EURYTHMICS

TOWER OF POWER LP '71

Singles: 7-inch

COLUMBIA 3-5 76-78
SAN FRANCISCO 4-8 64-73
W.B. 4-8 72-75

EPs: 7-inch

SAN FRANCISCO (7-204 "East Bay Grease") 15-25 71
(Promotional issue only.)

LPs: 10/12-inch

COLUMBIA 5-10 76-79
SAN FRANCISCO (204 "East Bay Grease") 10-20 71
W.B. 8-15 72-76
Members: Greg Adams; Mic Gillette; Steve Kupka; Emilio Castillo; Lenny Pickett; Chester Thompson; Francis Prestia; Edward McGhee; Rufus Miller; Lenny Williams.
Also see LITTLE FEAT
Also see WILLIAMS, Lenny

TOWNES, Carol Lynn P&R/R&B/D&D '84

Singles: 12-inch

POLYDOR 4-6 84-85

Singles: 7-inch

POLYDOR 3-4 84-85

LPs: 10/12-inch

POLYDOR 5-8 84

TOWNS, Eddie R&B '86
(ET)

Singles: 12-inch

TOTAL EXPERIENCE 4-6 86

Singles: 7-inch

TOTAL EXPERIENCE 3-4 86

LPs: 10/12-inch

TOTAL EXPERIENCE 5-8 86

TOWNSEND, Ed P&R/R&B '58

Singles: 7-inch

ALADDIN (3373 "Love Never Dies") 10-15 57
CAPITOL 8-15 58-59
CHALLENGE 5-10 61-62
DYNASTY 5-10 60
GLO-TOWN 4-8 66
LIBERTY 5-10 62-63
MGM 5-10 67
MAXX 10-20 64
POLYDOR 3-6 70
W.B. 5-10 60-61

EPs: 7-inch

CAPITOL (985 "New in Town") 20-40 58
(Promotional issue only.)
CAPITOL (1091 "Ed Townsend") 20-40 58

LPs: 10/12-inch

CAPITOL (1140 "New in Town") 25-50 59

CAPITOL (1214 "Glad to Be Here")....20-40 59
CURTOM....8-12 76

TOWNSHEND, Pete — LP '72

Singles: 7-inch

ATCO....3-5 80-85

Picture Sleeves

ATCO....3-5 85

LPs: 10/12-inch

ATCO....5-10 80-87
ATLANTIC....5-8 89
DECCA/TRACK....10-12 72
Also see WHO

TOWNSHEND, Pete, & Ronnie Lane — LP '77

Singles: 7-inch

MCA....3-5 77-78

LPs: 10/12-inch

MCA....8-10 77
Also see CLAPTON, Eric
Also see ENTWISTLE, John
Also see LANE, Ronnie
Also see TOWNSHEND, Pete
Also see WOOD, Ron, & Ronnie Lane

TOWNSHEND, Simon — LP '83

Singles: 12-inch

POLYDOR (357 "Moving Target")....5-10 85
(Clear vinyl. Promotional issue only.)

Singles: 7-inch

21....3-4 83

LPs: 10/12-inch

21....5-8 83

TOY DOLLS — P&R '62

Singles: 7-inch

ERA....5-10 62

TOY MATINEE — LP '91

LPs: 10/12-inch

REPRISE....5-8 90

TOYS — P&R/R&B '65

Singles: 7-inch

ABC....3-5 73
DYNO VOICE....4-8 65-66
ERIC....3-4 70s
GUSTO....3-4 80s
MUSICOR....4-8 68
PHILIPS....4-8 67
VIRGO....3-5 72

LPs: 10/12-inch

DYNO VOICE (9002 "A Lover's Concerto"/"Attack")....25-35 66
(Monaural.)
DYNO VOICE (9002-S "A Lover's Concerto"/"Attack")....20-30 66
(Stereo.)
SECTET....5-10 81
Members: Barbara Harris; June Montiero; Barbara Parritt.

T'PAU — P&R/LP '87

Singles: 7-inch

VIRGIN....3-4 87

Picture Sleeves

VIRGIN....3-4 87

LPs: 10/12-inch

VIRGIN....5-8 87

TRACY, Jeanie — D&D '84

(Jeanne Tracy)

Singles: 12-inch

MEGATONE....4-6 84-85

Singles: 7-inch

FANTASY....3-5 83
SMOGSVILLE....4-8 67

TRADE WINDS — P&R '65

Singles: 7-inch

ERIC....3-5 70s
KAMA SUTRA (212 "Mind Excursion")....15-20 66
KAMA SUTRA (218 "Catch Me in the Meadow")....10-15 66
KAMA SUTRA (234 "Mind Excursion")....8-12 67
RED BIRD (020 "New York's a Lonely Town")....8-12 65
RED BIRD (028 "The Girl from Greenwich Village")....10-20 65
RED BIRD (033 "Summertime Girl")....40-60 65

LPs: 10/12-inch

KAMA SUTRA....25-35 67
Members: Pete Anders; Vinnie Poncia.

TRAFFIC — P&R '67

(Traffic Etc.)

Singles: 7-inch

ASYLUM....3-5 74
ISLAND....3-5 72-73
U.A....5-10 67-72

Picture Sleeves

U.A....8-10 67

LPs: 10/12-inch

ASYLUM....10-15 74
ISLAND (Except 9000 series)....5-8 83
ISLAND (9000 series)....10-15 71-75
MFSL (209 "The Low Spark of High Heeled Boys")....20-30 94
(Half-speed mastered.)
U.A....10-20 68-75
Members: Jim Capaldi; Dave Mason; Steve Winwood; Chris Wood.
Also see CAPALDI, Jim
Also see MASON, Dave
Also see WINWOOD, Steve

TRAITS — P&R '66

Singles: 7-inch

ASCOT....15-25 62
PACEMAKER....10-15 67
RENNER (221 "Linda Lou")....10-15 62
RENNER (229 "Got My Mojo Working")....10-15 62
(Black vinyl.)
RENNER (229 "Got My Mojo Working")....20-30 62
(Colored vinyl. Promotional issue only.)
SCEPTER....3-5 66
TNT....10-15 59-60
UNIVERSAL....10-15 66

LPs: 10/12-inch

TNT (101 "Roy Head and the Traits")....100-150 65
Member: Roy Head.
Also see HEAD, Roy

TRAMAINE — R&B/D&D '85

(Tramaine Hawkins)

Singles: 12-inch

A&M....4-6 85-86

Singles: 7-inch

A&M....3-4 85-87

LPs: 10/12-inch

A&M....5-8 86

TRAMMPS — P&R/R&B '72

Singles: 7-inch

ATLANTIC....3-5 75-80
BUDDAH....3-5 72-76
ERIC....3-5 78
GOLDEN FLEECE....3-5 73-75

Picture Sleeves

ATLANTIC....3-5 77

LPs: 10/12-inch

ATLANTIC....5-10 76-80
BUDDAH....5-10 75
GOLDEN FLEECE....5-10 75
PHILADELPHIA INT'L....5-10 77
Also see B-H-Y
Also see MFSB

TRAMPS — R&B '83

Singles: 7-inch

VENTURE....3-5 83

TRANSVISION VAMP — P&R/LP '88

Singles: 7-inch

UNI....3-4 88

Picture Sleeves

UNI....3-4 88

LPs: 10/12-inch

UNI....5-8 88

TRANS-X — P&R '86

Singles: 12-inch

ATCO....4-6 86
MIRAGE....4-6 86

Singles: 7-inch

ATCO....3-4 86

TRAPEZE — LP '74

Singles: 7-inch

PAID....3-5 81
THRESHOLD....4-8 72
W.B....3-5 74-75

LPs: 10/12-inch

PAID....5-10 81
POLYDOR ("Medusa")....50-100 71
(Number not known.)
SHARK....8-10
THRESHOLD (2 "Trapeze")....25-50 71
THRESHOLD (4 "Medusa")....75-100 71
THRESHOLD (8 "You Are the Music, We're Just the Band")....25-50 72
THRESHOLD (11 "Final Swing")....25-50 72
W.B....8-10 74-75
Also see DEEP PURPLE

TRASH CAN SINATRAS — LP '91

LPs: 10/12-inch

LONDON....5-8 91

TRASHMEN — P&R '63

Singles: 7-inch

APEX (Except 76925)....15-25 63-65
APEX (76925 "New Generation")....25-35 64
ARGO (5516 "Bird '65")....50-75 65
BEAR....10-20 66
ERA....3-5 72
ERIC....3-4 70s
GARRETT....10-20 63-64
LANA....3-6 60s
METROBEAT....12-18 68
SOMA....4-8
TRIBE (8315 "Same Lines")....25-35 66

Picture Sleeves

GARRETT (4012 "Whoa Dad")....60-80 64
GARRETT (4013 "Real Live Doll")....100-125 64

LPs: 10/12-inch

SOMA/GARRETT (GA-200 "Surfin' Bird")....50-75 64
(Monaural.)
SOMA/GARRETT (GAS-200 "Surfin' Bird")....100-150 64
(Stereo.)
SUNDAZED....5-10 90s
Members: Tony Andreason; Bob Reed; Dal Winslow; Steve Wahrer; Gary Nielsen.

TRASHMEN / Castaways

Singles: 7-inch

SOMA....4-6 60s
Also see TRASHMEN

TRAVELING WILBURYS — P&R/LP '88

Singles: 7-inch

WILBURY (27732 "Handle with Care")....4-8 88
(Commercial issue.)
WILBURY (27732 "Handle with Care")....10-20 88
(Promotional issue.)
WILBURY (27637 "End of the Line")....10-15 88
(Commercial issue.)
WILBURY (27637 "End of the Line")....10-20 88
(Promotional issue.)

Picture Sleeves

WILBURY (27732 "Handle with Care")....4-8 88
WILBURY (27637 "End of the Line")....10-20 88

LPs: 10/12-inch

WILBURY....8-15 88-90

Members: George Harrison; Bob Dylan; Roy Orbison; Tom Petty; Jeff Lynne.
Also see DYLAN, Bob
Also see HARRISON, George
Also see LYNNE, Jeff
Also see ORBISON, Roy
Also see PETTY, Tom, & Heartbreakers

TRAVERS, Mary *P&R/LP '71*
Singles: 7-inch
CHRYSALIS 3-5 78-79
W.B. 3-5 71-73
LPs: 10/12-inch
CHRYSALIS 5-10 78
W.B. 6-12 71-74
Also see DENVER, John
Also see PETER, PAUL & MARY

TRAVERS, Pat *LP '77*
(Pat Travers Band; Black Pearl)
Singles: 7-inch
POLYDOR....3-5 77-80
LPs: 10/12-inch
POLYDOR....5-10 76-84

TRAVIS, McKinley *P&R/R&B '70*
Singles: 7-inch
PRIDE....3-5 70

TRAVIS, Merle *C&W/P&R '46*
Singles: 78 rpm
CAPITOL 5-10 46-57
Singles: 7-inch
CAPITOL (1100 thru 3100 series)....5-15 50-55
CAPITOL (5600 series) 4-6 66
EPs: 7-inch
CAPITOL 10-20 56-57
LPs: 10/12-inch
CMH 8-15 79-81
CAPITOL (T-650 "Guitar")....50-80 56
CAPITOL (SM-650 "Guitar")....5-10 75
CAPITOL (891 "Back Home") 50-60 57
CAPITOL (1391 "Walkin' the Strings")....50-60 60
CAPITOL (1664 "Travis") 30-40 62
CAPITOL (1956 "Songs of the Coal Mine")....50-60 57
CAPITOL (T/ST-2662 "Best of Merle Travis") 15-25 67
CAPITOL (SM-2662 "Best of Merle Travis") 5-10 75
CAPITOL (2938 "Strictly Guitar")....20-30 69
PICKWICK/HILLTOP....10-15 66
PREMIER ....??
SHASTA....10-15
SPIN-O-RAMA....8-12 60s
Sessions: Renfro Valley Pioneers.
Also see THOMPSON, Hank, & Merle Travis

TRAVIS, Merle, & Johnny Bond
LPs: 10/12-inch
CAPITOL (249 "Great Songs of the Delmore Brothers")....25-50 69
Also see BOND, Johnny

TRAVIS, Randy *C&W '85*
(Randy Traywick)
Singles: 7-inch
W.B. 3-4 85-91
LPs: 10/12-inch
W.B. 5-8 85-91
Also see TRAYWICK, Randy
Also see WYNETTE, Tammy, & Randy Travis

TRAVIS, Randy, & George Jones *C&W '90*
Singles: 7-inch
W.B. 3-4 90

TRAVIS & BOB *P&R/R&B '59*
Singles: 7-inch
BARREL 10-15 59
(Canadian.)
BIG TOP 5-10 60
MERCURY 5-10 61
SANDY (1017 "Tell Him No") 10-15 59
(No "Distributed By Dot" on label.)
SANDY (1017 "Tell Him No" 5-10 59
(Has "Distributed By Dot" on label)
SANDY (1019 thru 1029)....8-12 59
Members: Travis Pritchett; Bob Weaver.

TRAVOLTA, Joey *P&R '78*
Singles: 7-inch
CASABLANCA....3-5 78-79
MILLENIUM....3-5 78
Picture Sleeves
MILLENNIUM 3-5 78
LPs: 10/12-inch
CASABLANCA....5-10 78-79
MILLENNIUM....5-10 78

TRAVOLTA, John *P&R/LP '76*
Singles: 7-inch
MIDLAND INT'L 3-5 76-80
RCA 3-5 77
RSO 3-5 78-79
Picture Sleeves
MIDLAND INT'L (Except 10623)....3-5 76-80
MIDLAND INT'L (10623 "Let Her In")....4-8 76
RCA 3-5 77
RSO 3-5 78-79
LPs: 10/12-inch
MIDLAND INT'L 5-10 76-77
MIDSONG INT'L 5-10 78
Also see NEWTON-JOHN, Olivia, & John Travolta

TRAVOLTA, John / Sha Na Na
Singles: 7-inch
RSO 3-5 78
Also see SHA NA NA
Also see TRAVOLTA, John

TRAYWICK, Randy *C&W '79*
Singles: 7-inch
PAULA (429 "Dreamin'")....8-12 78
PAULA (431 "She's My Woman")....5-10 78
Also see TRAVIS, Randy

TREASURES *R&B '76*
Singles: 7-inch
EPIC....3-5 77
MERCURY....3-5 76
LPs: 10/12-inch
EPIC....5-10 77

TREAT HER RIGHT *LP '88*
LPs: 10/12-inch
RCA 5-8 88

TREE SWINGERS *P&R '60*
Singles: 7-inch
BIG TOP (3058 "Only Forever")....5-10 60
GUYDEN (2036 "Kookie Little Paradise")....8-12 60
Members: Art Polhemus; Terry Byrnes.

TREMELOES *P&R/LP '67*
Singles: 7-inch
DJM....3-5 74-75
EPIC....4-8 66-70
Picture Sleeves
EPIC....4-8 67
LPs: 10/12-inch
DJM....8-10 74
EPIC....15-25 67-68
Also see POOLE, Brian

TREMELOES / Hollies
Singles: 7-inch
EPIC (10184 "Silence is Golden"/ "Carrie-Anne")....10-20 67
(Colored vinyl. Promotional issue only.)
Also see HOLLIES
Also see TREMELOES

TRENIERS *R&B '51*
Singles: 78 rpm
BRUNSWICK....10-20 57-58
EPIC....5-15 54-56
LONDON....10-15 50
OKEH....10-15 51-55
VIK 8-12 56
Singles: 7-inch
BRUNSWICK....10-20 57-58
DOM....4-8 68
DOT 8-12 58-59
EPIC 10-20 54-56
OKEH 15-30 51-55
VIK....10-20 56
EPs: 7-inch
EPIC (7014 "Go Go Go")....35-50 56
EPIC (7103 "On TV")....35-50 56
EPIC (7014 "Go Go Go")....35-50 57
LPs: 10/12-inch
DOT (3257 "Souvenir Album") 50-75 60
EPIC (3125 "On TV")....100-150 56
Members: Milt Trenier; Cliff Trenier; Claude Trenier.

TRIBE *R&B '73*
Singles: 7-inch
ABC 3-5 73-74
C & CT....3-5 71
LPs: 10/12-inch
ABC 5-10 73-74
FARR....5-10 77
PICKWICK....10-15 75

TRIBE CALLED QUEST *LP '90*
LPs: 10/12-inch
JIVE 5-8 90

TRINERE *R&B '85*
Singles: 7-inch
JAM PACKED 3-4 85-87
LPs: 10/12-inch
JAM PACKED 5-8 86

TRINERE / FREESTYLE / DEBBIE DEB *LP '89*
(Trinere & Friends)
LPs: 10/12-inch
PANDISC....5-8 89
Also see DEBBIE DEB
Also see FREESTYLE
Also see TRINERE

TRIO+ : see LEWIS, Jerry Lee, Carl Perkins & Charlie Rich

TRIPLE "S" CONNECTION *R&B '80*
Singles: 12-inch
20TH FOX 4-6 79-80
Singles: 7-inch
20TH FOX 3-5 79-80
LPs: 10/12-inch
20TH FOX 5-10 79
Also see LIVIN' PROOF
Also see SKOOL BOYZ

TRITT, Travis *C&W '89*
Singles: 7-inch
W.B. 3-4 89-91

TRITT, Travis, & Marty Stuart *C&W '91*
Singles: 7-inch
W.B. 3-4 91
Also see STUART, Marty
Also see TRITT, Travis

TRIUMPH *P&R/LP '79*
Singles: 7-inch
MCA (Black vinyl)....3-4 85-86
MCA (Colored vinyl)....3-5 85-86
RCA....3-5 78-84
Picture Sleeves
MCA....3-4 85-86
RCA....3-5 79
LPs: 10/12-inch
MCA....5-8 85-87
RCA....5-10 78-84
Members: Mike Levine; Gil Moore; Rik Emmett.

TRIUMVIRAT *LP '74*
Singles: 7-inch
CAPITOL 3-5 79
LPs: 10/12-inch
CAPITOL 5-10 74-80
HARVEST 10-12 74

TROGGS P&R/LP '66

Singles: 7-inch

ATCO (6415 "Wild Thing"/"With a Girl Like You") 10-15 66
(Writer credited is "Presley.")
ATCO (6415 "Wild Thing"/"With a Girl Like You") 5-10 66
(Writer credited is "Taylor.")
ATCO (6415 "I Want You") 5-10 66
(Same number used twice.)
ATCO (6444 "I Can't Control Myself") 5-10 66
BELL 3-5 73
FONTANA 4-8 66-69
PAGE ONE 3-6 69-70
PRIVATE STOCK 3-5 77
PYE 3-5 75-76

LPs: 10/12-inch

ATCO (33-193 "Wild Thing") 35-45 66
(Monaural.)
ATCO (SD-33-193 "Wild Thing") 25-35 66
(Stereo.)
FONTANA (27556 "The Troggs") 25-35 66
(Monaural.)
FONTANA (67556 "The Troggs") 20-30 66
(Stereo.)
FONTANA (67576 "Love Is All Around") 20-30 68
LIBERTY (3472 "You're Gonna Hear from Me") 25-35 66
(Monaural.)
LIBERTY (7472 "You're Gonna Hear from Me") 25-35 66
(Stereo.)
MKC 8-10 80
PRIVATE STOCK 10-15 76
PYE 10-15 75
RHINO 5-8 84
SIRE 10-15 76

TROGGS / Brook Benton

Singles: 7-inch

MILLER BEER (621 "Radio Spots") 5-10 60s

Picture Sleeves

MILLER BEER (621 "Radio Spots") 10-15 60s
Also see BENTON, Brook
Also see TROGGS

TROLLS P&R '66

Singles: 7-inch

ABC 5-10 66-67
U.S.A. 10-20 68

TROOP R&B/LP '88

Singles: 7-inch

ATLANTIC 3-4 88-90

LPs: 10/12-inch

ATLANTIC 5-8 88-90

TROOPER P&R/LP '78

Singles: 7-inch

LEGEND 3-5 75-77
MCA 3-5 77-78

LPs: 10/12-inch

LEGEND 8-10 75-76
MCA 5-10 78-80
RCA 5-8 82

TROPEA LP '76
(John Tropea)

Singles: 7-inch

MARLIN 3-5 76-77

LPs: 10/12-inch

MARLIN 8-10 76-77
Also see DEODATO

TROUBADOURS DU ROI BAUDOUIN LP '69

LPs: 10/12-inch

PHILIPS 5-10 63-69

TROUBLE R&B '80

Singles: 7-inch

AL & KIDD 3-5 80
U.A. 3-5 77

LPs: 10/12-inch

U.A. 8-10 77

TROUBLE FUNK R&B/LP '82

Singles: 12-inch

ISLAND 4-6 85-86
SUGAR HILL 4-6 82

Singles: 7-inch

D.E.T.T. 3-4 83
ISLAND 3-4 85-86
TF 3-5 80

LPs: 10/12-inch

ISLAND 5-8 86
SUGAR HILL 5-8 82

TROUTMAN, Tony R&B '75

Singles: 7-inch

GRAM-O-PHONE 3-5 75
T. MAIN 3-4 82-83

TROWER, Robin LP '73

Singles: 12-inch

GNP (2 "No Time") 5-8 87
(Promotional issue only.)

Singles: 7-inch

CHRYSALIS 3-5 72-78

LPs: 10/12-inch

ATLANTIC 5-8 88
CHRYSALIS 5-12 73-82
GNP 5-8 83-87
PASSPORT 5-10 85
Also see BRUCE, Jack, & Robin Trower
Also see PROCOL HARUM

TROY, Benny R&B '75
(With Maze)

Singles: 7-inch

DE-LITE 3-5 75
20TH FOX 3-5

TROY, Doris P&R/R&B '63

Singles: 7-inch

APPLE 5-10 70
ATLANTIC 5-10 63-65
CALLA (114 "Heartaches") 10-20 66
CAPITOL 5-10 67
MIDLAND INT'L 3-6 76

LPs: 10/12-inch

APPLE (3371 "Doris Troy") 15-20 70
ATLANTIC (8088 "Just One Look") 20-30 64

TROYER, Eric P&R '80

Singles: 7-inch

CHRYSALIS 3-5 80

LPs: 10/12-inch

CHRYSALIS 5-10 80

TRUE, Andrea P&R/R&B/LP '76
(Andrea True Connection)

Singles: 7-inch

BUDDAH 3-5 76-78
ERIC 3-5 78

Picture Sleeves

BUDDAH 4-8 76

LPs: 10/12-inch

BUDDAH 5-10 76-78

TRUE LOVE R&B '87

Singles: 7-inch

CRITIQUE 3-4 87

TRUMPETEERS R&B '48

Singles: 78 rpm

KING 10-15 50
SCORE 10-25 48

LPs: 10/12-inch

GRAND 25-40
SCORE (4021 "Milky White Way") 100-150 56

TRUMPETEERS P&R '59

Singles: 7-inch

SPLASH 8-10 59
Member: Billy Mure.
Also see MURE, Billy

TRUSSELL R&B '80

Singles: 7-inch

ELEKTRA 3-5 80

LPs: 10/12-inch

ELEKTRA 5-10 80

TRUTH R&B '74

Singles: 7-inch

ROULETTE 3-5 74-75
SOC 3-5

LPs: 10/12-inch

PARAGON 5-10 78
ROULETTE 5-10 75

TRUTH R&B '80

Singles: 7-inch

DEVAKI 3-5 80-81

TRUTH P&R/LP '87

Singles: 7-inch

I.R.S. 3-4 87

Picture Sleeves

I.R.S. 3-4 87

LPs: 10/12-inch

I.R.S. 5-8 87

TRYTHALL, Gil LP '70

Singles: 7-inch

ATHENA 3-6 69-70

LPs: 10/12-inch

ATHENA 5-10 69-70
PANDORA 5-8 81

TUBB, Ernest P&R '41
(With the Texas Troubadours; with "Friends")

Singles: 78 rpm

BLUEBIRD (6693 "The Passing of Jimmie Rodgers") 200-400 30s
BLUEBIRD (7000 "T.B. Is Whipping Me") 100-200 30s
BLUEBIRD (8899 "Married Man Blues") 100-150 30s
BLUEBIRD (8966 "Right Train to Heaven") 100-150 30s
DECCA 10-20 40-57

Singles: 7-inch

CACHET 3-5 79
DECCA (28067 thru 30872) 5-10 52-59
DECCA (30952 thru 33014) 3-8 59-72
DECCA (46000 series) 5-15 50-52
1ST GENERATION 3-5 77
MCA 3-5 73
RHINO (74415 "Walking the Floor Over You") 3-5 91
(Gold vinyl.)
RHINO (74415 "Walking the Floor Over You") 4-6 91
(Blue vinyl.)
RHINO (74415 "Walking the Floor Over You") 8-12 91
(Black vinyl.)

Picture Sleeves

RHINO (74415 "Walking the Floor Over You") 4-6 91

LPs: 10/12-inch

ACM 8-12
CACHET 8-12 79
CASTLE 5-10
CORAL 5-10 73
DECCA (159 "Ernest Tubb Story") 25-45 58
(Monaural. Includes booklet.)
DECCA (7-159 "Ernest Tubb Story") 30-60 58
(Stereo. Includes booklet.)
DECCA (5301 "Ernest Tubb Favorites") 50-75 51
(10-inch LP.)
DECCA (5334 "Old Rugged Cross-Favorite Sacred Songs") 40-60 51
(10-inch LP.)
DECCA (5497 "Sing a Song of Christmas") 40-60 54
(10-inch LP.)
DECCA (8291 "Ernest Tubb Favorites") 40-60 56
DECCA (8553 "Daddy of 'Em All") 35-55 56
DECCA (8834 "The Importance of Being Ernest") 35-55 59
FIRST GENERATION (001 "Living Legend") 8-12 77
FIRST GENERATION (0002 "The Legend and the Legacy") 75-125 79

(Back cover mentions "Ernest Tubb's Record Shop," "Gray Line Tours" and "Grand Ole Opry Tickets.")
FIRST GENERATION (0002 "The Legend and the Legacy")..60-80 79
(No mention on back cover of "Ernest Tubb's Record Shop," "Gray Line Tours" or "Grand Ole Opry Tickets.")
FIRST GENERATION (0002............10-20 79
MCA..5-12 73-84
PICKWICK.......................................5-10 70s
PICKWICK/HILLTOP...........................8-12
RADIOLA..5-10 83
RHINO (70902 "Live")........................5-10 91
ROUNDER.......................................5-10 82
TV (1033 "The Legend and the Legacy")..40-50 79
(TV mail order offer.)
VOCALION.....................................10-15 66-69
Session: Cal Smith; Jack Greene; Willie Nelson; Merle Haggard; Chet Atkins; Charlie Daniels; Jordanaires; Waylon Jennings; Vern Gosdin; Johnny Paycheck; Loretta Lynn; Marty Robbins; Wilburn Brothers; George Jones; Johnny Cash; Ferlin Husky/Simon Crum; Charlie Rich; Conway Twitty; Justin Tubb; Charlie McCoy; Jerry Kennedy; Grady Martin; Billy Grammer; Billy Byrd; Buddy Emmons; Pete Mitchell; Pete Drake; Kitty Wells; Webb Pierce; Patsy Cline.
Also see ANDREWS SISTERS & Ernest Tubb
Also see ATKINS, Chet
Also see CASH, Johnny
Also see CLINE, Patsy
Also see DANIELS, Charlie
Also see DRAKE, Pete
Also see FOLEY, Red, & Ernest Tubb
Also see GRAMMER, Billy
Also see GREENE, Jack
Also see HAGGARD, Merle
Also see HUSKY, Ferlin
Also see JENNINGS, Waylon
Also see JONES, George
Also see McCOY, Charlie
Also see NELSON, Willie
Also see PAYCHECK, Johnny
Also see RICH, Charlie
Also see ROBBINS, Marty
Also see SMITH, Cal
Also see STATLER BROTHERS
Also see TWITTY, Conway
Also see WELLS, Kitty

TUBB, Ernest, & Loretta Lynn — *C&W '69*

Singles: 7-inch

DECCA..3-6 69

LPs: 10/12-inch

DECCA..15-25 65-69
MCA...8-12 73
Also see LYNN, Loretta

TUBB, Ernest, & Justin Tubb

EPs: 7-inch

DECCA (2422 "Jimmie Rodgers Favorites")......................................15-25 57

TUBB, Ernest, & Wilburn Brothers — *C&W '58*

Singles: 7-inch

DECCA..5-10 58
Also see TUBB, Ernest
Also see WILBURN BROTHERS

TUBES — *LP '75*

Singles: 12-inch

CAPITOL..4-6 83

Singles: 7-inch

A&M..3-5 75-79
CAPITOL...3-4 81-85

Picture Sleeves

A&M..4-6 75
CAPITOL...3-5 81-85

LPs: 10/12-inch

A&M..5-10 75-81
CAPITOL...5-8 81-85
Members: Fee Waybill; Roger Steen.
Also see NEWTON-JOHN, Olivia, & Electric Light Orchestra
Also see WAYBILL, Fee

TUCK & PATTI — *LP '89*

LPs: 10/12-inch

WINDHAM HILL................................5-8 88-90

TUCKER, Junior — *R&B '83*

Singles: 7-inch

GEFFEN...3-4 83

LPs: 10/12-inch

GEFFEN...5-8 83

TUCKER, Louise — *P&R/LP '83*

Singles: 7-inch

ARISTA..3-4 83

LPs: 10/12-inch

ARISTA..5-8 83

TUCKER, Marshall: see MARSHALL TUCKER BAND

TUCKER, Tanya — *C&W/P&R '72*

Singles: 7-inch

ARISTA..3-5 82-84
CAPITOL...3-4 85-88
COLUMBIA......................................3-5 72-77
MCA...3-5 75-81

Picture Sleeves

COLUMBIA......................................3-6 72-75
MCA...3-5 75-81

LPs: 10/12-inch

ARISTA..5-8 82-84
CAPITOL...5-8 86
COLUMBIA ("KC" series)..................5-10 72-75
COLUMBIA ("PC" series)...................5-8 77
MCA...5-10 75-81
Sessions: John Prine; Jimmy Seals; Dash Crofts.
Also see AXTON, Hoyt
Also see CAMPBELL, Glen, & Tanya Tucker
Also see HARRIS, Emmylou
Also see SEALS & CROFTS

TUCKER, Tanya, & T. Graham Brown — *C&W '90*

Singles: 7-inch

CAPITOL...3-4 90

TUCKER, Tanya, & Glen Campbell — *C&W '80*

(Glen Campbell & Tanya Tucker)

Singles: 7-inch

CAPITOL...3-4 81
Also see CAMPBELL, Glen

TUCKER, Tanya, Paul Davis & Paul Overstreet — *C&W '87*

Singles: 7-inch

CAPITOL...3-4 87
Also see DAVIS, Paul
Also see TUCKER, Tanya

TUCKER, Tommy — *P&R/R&B '64*

Singles: 7-inch

CHECKER.......................................4-8 64-67
FESTIVAL..4-8 66
HI..5-10 59-60
RCA (47-7838 "Return of the Teenage Queen")..5-10 61
RCA (37-7838 "Return of the Teenage Queen")..10-20 61
(Compact 33 Single.)
RCA (68-7838 "Return of the Teenage Queen")..15-25 61
(Stereo Compact 33 Single.)
SUNBEAM.......................................5-10 59
XL..4-8 66

LPs: 10/12-inch

CHECKER (2990 "Hi-Heel Sneakers")......................................15-25 64

TUFANO & GIAMMARESE — *P&R '73*

Singles: 7-inch

ODE...3-5 73-76

LPs: 10/12-inch

EPIC/ODE..8-10 76-77
ODE...10-15 73-74
Members: Dennis Tufano; Carl Giammarese.
Also see BUCKINGHAMS

TUFF DARTS — *LP '78*

Singles: 7-inch

SIRE...3-5 78

Picture Sleeves

SIRE...3-6 78

LPs: 10/12-inch

SIRE...5-10 78

TULL, Jethro: see JETHRO TULL

TUNE ROCKERS — *P&R '58*

Singles: 7-inch

PET (804 "No Stoppin' This Boppin'")......................................20-30 58
U.A. (139 "Green Mosquito")..............15-25 58

TUNE WEAVERS — *P&R/R&B '57*

(Margo Sylvia & Tune Weavers)

Singles: 78 rpm

CASA GRANDE.................................20-50 57
CHECKER.......................................15-25 57

Singles: 7-inch

CASA GRANDE (101 "Little Boy")....20-25 59
CASA GRANDE (3038 "My Congratulations Baby")..20-25 60
CASA GRANDE (4037 "Happy, Happy Birthday Baby")..35-50 57
CASA GRANDE (4038 "I Remember Dear")..20-25 57
CASA GRANDE (4040 "There Stands My Love")..20-30 58
CHECKER (872 "Happy, Happy Birthday Baby")..15-20 57
(Checkerboard top label. Can be found with either of two flips: *Ol Man River* or *Yo Yo Walk*.)
CHECKER (872 "Happy, Happy Birthday Baby")..5-8 58
(No Checkerboard at top.)
CHECKER (1007 "Congratulations on Your Wedding")..15-20 62
CHESS..3-5 73
CLASSIC ARTISTS...........................3-5 88-89
COLLECTABLES...............................3-4 80s
ERIC...3-4 70s

LPs: 10/12-inch

CASA GRANDE.................................10-15 73
Members: Margo Sylvia; Charlotte Davis; Gil Lopez; John Sylvia.

TUNETOPPERS: see BROWN, Al, & His Tunetoppers

TUNNELL, Jimi — *D&D '84*

Singles: 12-inch

MCA...4-6 84

Singles: 7-inch

MCA...3-4 84

TURBANS — *P&R/R&B '55*

Singles: 78 rpm

HERALD..20-40 55-57
MONEY...50-75 55

Singles: 7-inch

ABC..3-5 73
COLLECTABLES...............................3-4 80s
FLASHBACK....................................4-8 65
HERALD (458 "When You Dance")..50-75 55
(Script print/flag logo.)
HERALD (458 "When You Dance")..15-25 57
(Block print logo.)
HERALD (469 "Sister Sookey").........25-50 55
HERALD (478 "I'm Nobody's")..........25-50 56
HERALD (486 "All of My Love")........25-50 56
HERALD (495 "Valley of Love")........25-50 57
HERALD (510 "Congratulations")......25-50 57
(Script print/flag logo.)
HERALD (510 "Congratulations")......15-25 57
(Block print logo.)
HERALD (510 "Congratulations")......25-35 57
(Single sided. Promotional issue only.)
HI-OLDIES......................................3-4 80s
IMPERIAL (5807 "Six Questions").....25-50 61
IMPERIAL (5828 "This Is My Story") 15-25 62
IMPERIAL (5847 "I Wonder")............10-20 62
MONEY (209 "No, No Cherry")......100-200 55
PARKWAY (820 "When You Dance")..15-25 61

RED TOP (115 "I Promise You Love") 25-50 59
ROULETTE (4281 "Diamonds and Pearls") 10-20 60
ROULETTE (4326 "I'm Not Your Fool Anymore") 10-20 61

LPs: 10/12-inch

COLLECTABLES 5-8 84
LOST-NITE 8-12 81
RELIC 10-15 70s

Members: Al Banks; Matt Platt; Andrew Jones; Charles Williams.

TURNER, Dwight

Singles: 7-inch

CHATOK (1001 "You're Alone") 50-75 60s

Also see TURNER, Spyder

TURNER, Ike

(With the Kings of Rhythm; with His Orchestra)

Singles: 78 rpm

CHESS (1459 "Heartbroken and Worried") 20-40 51
FEDERAL (12297 "Do You Mean It") 20-30 57
FEDERAL (12304 "Rock-A-Bucket") 25-75 57
FLAIR 20-40 52
RPM (356 "You're Driving Me Insane") 25-50 52

Singles: 7-inch

ARTISTIC 8-10 59
COBRA 8-10 59
FEDERAL (12297 "Do You Mean It") 50-75 57
FEDERAL (12304 "Rock-A-Bucket") 20-40 57
FLAIR (1040 "Cubano Jump") 40-60 52
FLAIR (1059 "Cuban Getaway") 40-60 52
KING 10-15 61
LIBERTY 3-5 70
RPM (356 "You're Driving Me Insane") 50-75 52
SUE (100 series) 4-8 66
SUE (700 series) 8-12 59
U.A. 3-5 71-74

LPs: 10/12-inch

CROWN 20-25 63
POMPEII 10-15 69
U.A. 6-12 72-73

Also see BLAND, Bobby, & Ike Turner
Also see BRENSTON, Jackie
Also see RENRUT, Icky

TURNER, Ike & Bonnie

Singles: 78 rpm

RPM (362 "Looking for a Baby") 15-25 52

Singles: 7-inch

RPM (362 "Looking for a Baby") 25-50 52

TURNER, Ike & Tina — *P&R/R&B '60*

(With the Ikettes; with Home Grown Funk)

Singles: 7-inch

A&M 4-6 69
BLUE THUMB 3-5 69-71
CENCO 4-8 60s
COLLECTABLES 3-4 80s
FANTASY 3-5 80
INNIS 3-6 68-71
KENT (400 series) 4-8 64
KENT (4500 series) 3-5 70
LIBERTY 3-5 70-71
LOMA 4-8 65
MINIT 3-6 69-70
MODERN 4-8 65
PHILLES 8-15 66
POMPEII 3-6 68-70
SONJA 4-8 63-64
SUE (100 series) 4-8 65-66
SUE (700 series) 5-10 60-63
TRC 3-5 71
TANGERINE 4-8 66
U.A. 3-5 71-75
W.B. 4-8 64

Picture Sleeves

MINIT 5-8 69
POMPEII 5-8 69
W.B. (5433 "A Fool for a Fool") 10-20 64

LPs: 10/12-inch

A&M (3179 "River Deep, Mountain High") 5-10 82
A&M (4178 "River Deep, Mountain High") 10-20 69
ABC 8-10 70s
ACCORD 5-10 81
BLUE THUMB 8-12 69-73
CAPITOL (500 series) 5-10 75
(With "SM" prefix.)
CAPITOL (500 series) 10-15 69
(With "ST" prefix.)
CENCO 15-20 60s
COLLECTABLES 5-8 88
FANTASY 5-10 80
HARMONY (11000 series) 10-12 69
HARMONY (30000 series) 8-10 71
KENT 15-25 61-64
LIBERTY (7000 series) 10-12 70
LIBERTY (51000 series) 5-8 85
LOMA 10-20 66
MINIT 10-15 69
PHILLES (4011 "River Deep, Mountain High") 10000-15000 66
(Covers for a U.S. pressing on Philles are not known to exist. British pressings [London/ Philles SHU-8298] do exist with covers.)
PICKWICK 5-10 70s
POMPEII 10-15 68-69
SUE (2001 "The Sound of Ike & Tina Turner") 100-200 61
SUE (2003 "Dance with Ike & Tina Turner's Kings of Rhythm") 100-200 62
(Instrumentals by Ike & Tina Turner's band.)
SUE (2004 "Dynamite") 250-350 63
SUE (2005 "Don't Play Me Cheap") 100-200 63
SUE (2007 "It's Gonna Work Out Fine") 100-200 63
SUE (1038 "Greatest Hits") 35-45 65
SUNSET 8-12 69-70
UNART 5-10 70s
U.A. 8-12 71-78
UNITED SUPERIOR 8-10
W.B. 10-20 65-69

Also see BLAND, Bobby, & Ike Turner
Also see IKETTES
Also see RAELETTES
Also see SYLVIA
Also see TURNER, Ike
Also see TURNER, Tina

TURNER, Jesse Lee — *P&R '59*

Singles: 7-inch

CARLTON 5-10 59
FRATERNITY 5-10 59
GNP (184 "All You Gotta Do") 4-8 62
GNP (188 "Shotgun Boogie") 40-60 62
IMPERIAL 5-10 60
SUDDEN 4-6
TOP RANK 5-10 60

Picture Sleeves

CARLTON 10-15 59
FRATERNITY (855 "Teenage Misery") 35-50 59

TURNER, Joe — *R&B '46*

(With His Blues Kings; with Pete Johnson & His Orchestra; with Van "Piano Man" Walls & His Orchestra; Big Joe Turner)

Singles: 78 rpm

ALADDIN (3013 "Morning Glory") 50-100 49
ALADDIN (3070 "Back Breaking Baby") 50-100 50
ATLANTIC 10-30 51-57
BAYOU 10-20 53
COLONY 10-20 52
CORAL (65000 series) 10-20 48
DECCA 10-20 41-56
DOOTONE (305 "I Love Ya, I Love Ya, I Love Ya") 50-100 51
DOWN BEAT 10-20 48
EXCELSIOR 10-20 49
FIDELITY 10-20 51-52
FREEDOM 10-20 50
IMPERIAL 10-20 50
MGM 10-20 48-50
NATIONAL 10-20 46-51
RPM 25-50 51
SWING BEAT 10-20 49
VOCALION 15-25 39

Singles: 7-inch

ATLANTIC (939 "Chains of Love") 50-100 51
ATLANTIC (949 "Bump Miss Susie") 50-75 51
ATLANTIC (960 "Sweet Sixteen") 50-75 52
ATLANTIC (970 "Don't You Cry") 50-75 52
ATLANTIC (982 "Still in Love") 40-60 52
ATLANTIC (1001 "Honey Hush") 20-30 53
ATLANTIC (1016 "TV Mama") 30-40 53
ATLANTIC (1026 thru 1184) 15-30 54-58
ATLANTIC (2000 series) 8-15 59-60
BAYOU (015 "The Blues Jumped a Rabbit") 100-200 53
BLUESTIME (45001 "Two Loves Have I") 25-50
BLUESWAY 4-8 67
CORAL (62000 series) 5-8 64
DECCA (29000 series) 15-25 55-56
KENT 3-6 69-71
RPM (345 "Ridin' Blues") 100-150 51
RONN 4-6 69

EPs: 7-inch

ATLANTIC (536 "Joe Turner Sings") 50-75 55
ATLANTIC (565 "Joe Turner") 50-75 56
ATLANTIC (586 "Joe Turner") 50-75 56
ATLANTIC (606 "Rock with Joe Turner") 50-75 56
EMARCY (6132 "Joe Turner and Pete Johnson") 50-75 56

LPs: 10/12-inch

ARHOOLIE 15-25 62
ATCO 8-12 71
ATLANTIC (1234 "Boss of the Blues") 100-150 58
ATLANTIC (1332 "Big Joe Rides Again") 50-75 60
ATLANTIC (8005 "Joe Turner") 100-200 57
(Black label.)
ATLANTIC (8005 "Joe Turner") 50-100 59
(Red label.)
ATLANTIC (8023 "Rockin' the Blues") 100-150 58
(Black label.)
ATLANTIC (8023 "Rockin' the Blues") 50-75 59
(Red label.)
ATLANTIC (8033 "Big Joe Is Here") 100-150 59
(Black label.)
ATLANTIC (8033 "Big Joe Is Here") 50-75 59
(Red label.)
ATLANTIC (8081 "Best of Joe Turner") 30-50 63
ATLANTIC (8812 "Boss of the Blues") 5-10 81
BIG TOWN 5-10 78
BLUES SPECTRUM 10-12
BLUESTIME (9002 "The Real Boss of the Blues") 20-30 60s
BLUESWAY 8-12 67-73
CHIARDSCURO 8-10 76
CLASSIC JAZZ 5-10 79
EMARCY (36014 "Joe Turner with Pete Johnson") 100-200 56
INTERMEDIA 5-8 83-84
KENT 8-12 70s
LMI 8-10 74
MCA 5-10 80
PABLO 5-10 76-83
SAVOY (14012 "Blues Can Make You Happy") 100-150 58
SAVOY (14106 "Carless Love") 50-75 64
SAVOY (2223 "Big Joe Is Here") 5-10 77
UNITED 8-10

Session: King Curtis.
Also see FLENNOY TRIO & JOE TURNER

Also see JOHNSON, Pete
Also see KING CURTIS

TURNER, Joe / Jimmy Nelson

LPs: 10/12-inch

CROWN 15-25 62

TURNER, Joe, & Roomful of Blues

LPs: 10/12-inch

MUSE (5293 "Blues Train") 5-10 83
Also see TURNER, Joe

TURNER, Joe Lynn LP '85

LPs: 10/12-inch

ELEKTRA 5-8 85

TURNER, Ruby LP '90
(Featuring Jonathan Butler)

Singles: 7-inch

JIVE 3-4 86-90

LPs: 10/12-inch

JIVE 5-8 86-90
Also see BUTLER, Jonathan

TURNER, Sammy P&R/R&B '59
(With the Twisters)

Singles: 7-inch

BIG TOP (3007 & 3016) 5-10 59
BIG TOP (3029 "Always") 5-10 59
(Monaural.)
BIG TOP (3029 "Always") 15-25 59
(Stereo.)
BIG TOP (3032 thru 3070) 5-10 60-61
BIG TOP (3089 "Falling") 10-15 61
ERIC 3-4 70s
MILLENNIUM 3-4 78
MOTOWN 10-20 64
PACIFIC (3016 "Lavender Blue") 25-35 59
PACIFIC (3029 "Always") 20-30 59
20TH FOX 4-8 65
VERVE (10465 "A Child Is Born") 12-25 66

LPs: 10/12-inch

BIG TOP (1301 "Lavender Blue Moods") 25-40 60
(Monaural.)
BIG TOP (ST-1301 "Lavender Blue Moods") 35-50 60
(Stereo.)
Session: King Curtis.
Also see KING CURTIS

TURNER, Sammy / Ivory Joe Hunter

Singles: 7-inch

GOLD SOUL 3-5
Also see HUNTER, Ivory Joe
Also see TURNER, Sammy

TURNER, Spyder P&R/R&B '66
(Dwight Turner)

Singles: 7-inch

KWANZA 3-5 73
MGM 5-15 66-71
POLYDOR 3-4 84
WHITFIELD 3-5 78-79

LPs: 10/12-inch

MGM 15-20 67
WHITFIELD 5-10 78-79
Also see BRISTOL, Johnny, & Spyder Turner
Also see TURNER, Dwight

TURNER, Tina R&B/LP '75

Singles: 12-inch

CAPITOL 4-6 84-87

Singles: 7-inch

CAPITOL 3-4 84-89
POMPEII 4-8 68
U.A. 3-5 75-78
WAGNER 3-5 79

Picture Sleeves

CAPITOL 3-5 84-89

LPs: 10/12-inch

AUDIO FIDELITY (100 "Tina Turner") 25-35 84
(Picture disc.)
CAPITOL 5-8 84-89
FANTASY 5-10
SPRINGBOARD 8-10 72
U.A. (Except 200) 8-10 75-78
U.A. (200 "Tina Turner Turns the Country On") 10-15 67
WAGNER 5-8 79
Also see ADAMS, Bryan, & Tina Turner
Also see BASS, Fontella, & Tina Turner
Also see BOWIE, David
Also see CLAPTON, Eric, & Tina Turner
Also see JOHN, Elton / Tina Turner
Also see TURNER, Ike & Tina
Also see U.S.A. for AFRICA

TURNER, Titus P&R/R&B '59

Singles: 78 rpm

ATLANTIC 15-25 57
OKEH 10-15 52-54

Singles: 7-inch

ATCO 4-8 64
ATLANTIC 10-15 57
COLUMBIA 4-8 63
ENJOY 4-8 62-63
GLOVER (Except 202) 5-10 59-60
GLOVER (202 "When the Sergeant Comes Marching Home") 10-20 60
GUARANTEED 4-8 61-62
JAMIE 4-8 61
JOSIE 4-6 68-69
KING (Monaural) 8-15 57-61
KING (5213 "Fall Guy") 15-25 59
(Stereo.)
MURBO 4-8 65
OKEH (6844 thru 7038) 15-25 52-54
OKEH (7200 series) 4-8 66
PHILIPS 4-8 67
WING 10-15 55

LPs: 10/12-inch

JAMIE 25-35 61
Session: Mickey Baker.

TURRENTINE, Stanley LP '67

Singles: 7-inch

BLUE NOTE 3-8 61-69
CTI 3-5 72
ELEKTRA 3-4 79-81
FANTASY 3-5 74-78
IMPULSE 3-5 67

LPs: 10/12-inch

BAINBRIDGE 5-8 81
BLUE NOTE 25-50 60-61
(Label gives New York street address for Blue Note Records.)
BLUE NOTE 15-30 62-65
(Label reads "Blue Note Records Inc. - New York, U.S.A.")
BLUE NOTE 8-18 65-85
(Label shows Blue Note Records as a division of either Liberty or United Artists.)
CTI 8-12 71-75
ELEKTRA 5-8 79-81
FPM 5-8 75
FANTASY 8-12 74-78
IMPULSE 8-15 67-78
MAINSTREAM 15-25 65
PRESTIGE 6-12 70-71
SUNSET 8-12 69
TIME 25-50 62-63
UPFRONT 6-12 72
Also see BYRD, Donald
Also see FULSON, Lowell
Also see GILBERTO, Astrud, & Stanley Turrentine
Also see HUBBARD, Freddie, & Stanley Turrentine
Also see SILVER, Horace, Quintet, & Stanley Turrentine

TURTLES P&R/LP '65

Singles: 7-inch

BUCCANEER (3002 "Happy Together") 5-10
COLLECTABLES 3-4 80s
LOST-NITE 3-5
WHITE WHALE 5-15 65-70

Picture Sleeves

WHITE WHALE 10-15 67-69

EPs: 7-inch

RHINO (RNPD-901 "Turtles 1968") 8-10 83
(Picture disc.)

LPs: 10/12-inch

RHINO 5-8 82-86
SIRE 10-15 74
TRIP 5-10 70s
WHITE WHALE 15-30 65-71
Members: Howard Kaylan; Mark Volman; Don Murray; Chuck Portz; Al Nichol; Jim Tucker; John Barbata; John Seiter; Jim Pons; Chip Douglas.
Also see CHRISTMAS SPIRIT
Also see KAYLAN, Howard, & Marc Volman
Also see LEAVES

TUTONE, Tommy: see TOMMY TUTONE

TUXEDO JUNCTION P&R/LP '78

Singles: 12-inch

BUTTERFLY 4-8 78-80

Singles: 7-inch

BUTTERFLY (Black vinyl) 3-5 78-80
BUTTERFLY (Colored vinyl) 4-6 78

LPs: 10/12-inch

BUTTERFLY (Black vinyl) 5-10 77-79
BUTTERFLY (Colored vinyl) 10-12 77
(Promotional issues only.)

TWENNYNINE R&B/LP '79
(Featuring Lenny White)

Singles: 7-inch

ELEKTRA 3-5 79-81

LPs: 10/12-inch

ELEKTRA 5-10 79-81
Also see WHITE, Lenny

21ST CENTURY P&R/R&B '75

Singles: 7-inch

RCA 3-5 75
Members: Fred Williams; Tyrone Moores; Alphonso Smith; Piere Johnson; Alonzo Martin.

24 - 7 SPYZ LP '89

LPs: 10/12-inch

IN-EFFECT 5-8 89-90

TWILIGHT 22 P&R/R&B/D&D '83

Singles: 12-inch

VANGUARD 4-6 83-84

Singles: 7-inch

VANGUARD 3-4 83-84

LPs: 10/12-inch

VANGUARD 5-8 84

TWILLEY, Dwight P&R '75
(Dwight Twilley Band)

Singles: 7-inch

ARISTA 3-5 77-79
EMI AMERICA 3-4 82-84
SHELTER 3-5 75-76

Picture Sleeves

EMI AMERICA 3-4 84
SHELTER 3-5 75-76

LPs: 10/12-inch

ARISTA 5-10 77-79
EMI AMERICA 5-8 82-84
SHELTER 5-10 75-76
Also see SEYMOUR, Phil

TWIN IMAGE R&B '85

Singles: 12-inch

CAPITOL 4-6 84-85

Singles: 7-inch

CAPITOL 3-4 84-85

LPs: 10/12-inch

CAPITOL 5-8 84

TWIN HYPE LP '89

LPs: 10/12-inch

PROFILE 5-8 89

TWINS D&D '83

Singles: 12-inch

QUALITY/RFC 4-6 83

TWISTED SISTER LP '83

Singles: 7-inch

ATLANTIC 3-4 83-87

Picture Sleeves

ATLANTIC 3-4 84-87

LPs: 10/12-inch

ATLANTIC 5-8 83-87

Members: Dee Snider; Jay Jay French; A.J. Pero; Eddie Ojeda; Mark Mendoza.

TWITTY, Conway *P&R '57*

Singles: 78 rpm

MERCURY 25-75 57

Singles: 7-inch

ABC-PAR (10507 "Go on and Cry") .. 10-15 63
ABC-PAR (10550 "My Baby Left Me") 15-25 64
CONWAY TWITTY FAN CLUB ("It's Only Make Believe") 10-15
(Promotional, fan club issue only.)
DECCA 3-8 65-72
ELEKTRA 3-4 82-83
MCA 3-5 73-90s
MGM (500 series) 3-5 78
MGM (12000 & 13000 series) 5-15 58-62
MGM (14000 series) 3-5 71-72
MGM (50000 series) 20-40 58-59
(Stereo.)
MGM GOLDEN CIRCLE 3-5
MERCURY 20-40 57-58
MUSIGRAM 3-6
(Flexi-disc.)
POLYDOR 3-4 80s
W.B. 3-4 83-86

Picture Sleeves

ELEKTRA 3-5 82
MGM 10-20 58-62

EPs: 7-inch

DECCA (34437 "Look Into My Teardrops") 10-20 66
(Juke box issue.)
MGM (1623 "It's Only Make Believe") 30-50 58
MGM (1640/1641/1642 "Conway Twitty Sings") 20-30 59
(Price is for any of three volumes.)
MGM (1678/1679/1680 "Saturday Night with Conway Twitty") 20-30 59
(Price is for any of three volumes.)
MGM (1701 "Lonely Blue Boy") 20-30 60

LPs: 10/12-inch

ACCORD 5-10 82
ALLEGIANCE 5-8 84
CT (1001 "Solid Gold") 8-12
CANDLELITE ("Living Legend") 30-50 70s
(No selection number used.)
CONWAY TWITTY/MCA (1002 "Conway Twitty") 8-10
CORAL 5-8 73
CUTLASS 40-50 72
(Title and selection number not known.)
DECCA 8-18 66-72
DEMAND 8-12 72
ELEKTRA 5-8 82-83
MCA 5-15 73-85
MGM (110 "Conway Twitty") 15-20 70
MGM (3744 "Conway Twitty Sings") 50-100 59
MGM (E-3786 "Saturday Night with Conway Twitty") 50-75 59
(Monaural.)
MGM (SE-3786 "Saturday Night with Conway Twitty") 75-100 59
(Stereo.)
MGM (E-3818 "Lonely Blue Boy") 50-75 60
(Monaural.)
MGM (SE-3818 "Lonely Blue Boy") 75-100 60
(Stereo.)
MGM (E-3849 "Conway Twitty's Greatest Hits") 50-75 60
(Monaural. Black label. With gatefold cover and poster.)
MGM (SE-3849 "Conway Twitty's Greatest Hits") 75-100 60
(Stereo. With gatefold cover and poster.)
MGM (3849 "Conway Twitty's Greatest Hits") 15-20 68
(Blue and yellow label. With standard cover.)
MGM (E-3907 "The Rock and Roll Story") 50-75 61
(Monaural.)
MGM (SE-3907 "The Rock and Roll Story") 75-100 61
(Stereo.)
MGM (E-3943 "The Conway Twitty Touch") 30-40 61
(Monaural.)
MGM (SE-3943 "The Conway Twitty Touch") 35-50 61
(Stereo.)
MGM (E-4019 thru E-4217) 20-40 62-64
(Monaural.)
MGM (SE-4019 thru SE-4217) 25-50 62-64
(Stereo.)
MGM (4650 thru 4884) 10-20 69-73
METRO 15-25 65
OPRYLAND (12636 "Conway Twitty, Then and Now") 75-100
(Six-disc set. Promotional issue only.)
PICKWICK 10-15 72
SUNRISE MEDIA 5-10 81
TEE VEE 5-10 78
TROLLY CAR 5-10
TWITTY BIRD (1001 "Solid Gold") ... 10-12 82
(Two-discs.)
W.B. 5-10 83-86

Session: Fred Carter Jr.; Anthony Armstrong Jones; Joni Lee.
Also see LYNN, Loretta, & Conway Twitty
Also see MARTIN, Dean
Also see McDOWELL, Ronnie
Also see TUBB, Ernest

2 LIVE CREW *LP '87*
(Luke Featuring 2 Live Crew)

Singles: 12-inch

LUKE SKYWALKER 4-8 88-89

Singles: 7-inch

LUKE SKYWALKER 3-4 88-89

LPs: 10/12-inch

LUKE SKYWALKER 5-8 87-90

2 OF CLUBS *P&R '67*

Singles: 7-inch

FRATERNITY 5-10 66-67

TWO SISTERS *D&D '83*

Singles: 12-inch

SUGARSCOOP 4-6 83

TWO TONS O' FUN *R&B/LP '80*
(Two Tons)

Singles: 12-inch

FANTASY 4-6 80

Singles: 7-inch

FANTASY 3-5 80
HONEY 3-5 80-81

LPs: 10/12-inch

FANTASY 5-8 80
HONEY 5-8 80

Members: Martha Wash; Izora Armstead.
Also see WEATHER GIRLS

TYCOON *P&R/LP '79*

Singles: 7-inch

ARISTA 3-5 79

LPs: 10/12-inch

ARISTA 5-10 78-81

TYLER, Bonnie *P&R/C&W/LP '78*

Singles: 7-inch

CHRYSALIS 3-5 77
COLUMBIA 3-4 83-86
RCA 3-5 78-79

Picture Sleeves

COLUMBIA 3-4 83-86
RCA 3-5 78

LPs: 10/12-inch

CHRYSALIS 8-12 77
COLUMBIA 5-8 83-86
RCA 5-10 78-81

Also see RUNDGREN, Todd

TYLER, Frankie
(Frankie Valli)

Singles: 7-inch

OKEH (7103 "I Go Ape") 50-75 58

Promotional Singles

OKEH (7103 "I Go Ape") 40-60 58

Also see VALLI, Frankie

TYMES *P&R/R&B/LP '63*

Singles: 7-inch

ABKCO 3-5 74
COLUMBIA 5-10 68-70
MGM 10-20 66
PARKWAY (Except 871) 5-10 63-64
PARKWAY (871 "So in Love") 10-20 63
PARKWAY (871 "So Much in Love") .. 5-10 63
RCA 3-6 74-77
WINCHESTER 5-10 67

Picture Sleeves

PARKWAY 10-20 63-64

LPs: 10/12-inch

ABKCO (4228 "Best of the Tymes") 8-10 74
COLUMBIA (9778 "People") 10-15 69
PARKWAY (7032 "So Much in Love") 40-60 63
(Covers has silhouette drawing of couple walking, with group's picture over the drawing.
PARKWAY (7032 "So Much in Love") 20-40 63
(Cover pictures only the group, checking the "time" on their watches.)
PARKWAY (7038 "Sound of the Wonderful Tymes") 20-40 63
PARKWAY (7039 "Somewhere") 20-40 64
RCA (0727 "Trustmaker") 8-12 74
RCA (1835 "Turning Point") 8-10 77
WYNCOTE 10-20 60s

Members: George Williams Jr; Donald Banks; Al Berry; Norman Burnett; George Hilliard.
Also see MAESTRO, Johnny, & Tymes

TYNER, McCoy *LP '75*
(McCoy Tyner Trio)

Singles: 7-inch

COLUMBIA 3-4 82
IMPULSE 4-8 65

LPs: 10/12-inch

BLUE NOTE 8-15 66-76
COLUMBIA 5-8 82
FPM 5-10 75
IMPULSE 10-30 62-78
MCA 5-10 81
MILESTONE 5-12 72-82
PAUSA 5-8 82

TYRANNOSAURUS REX: see T. REX

TYZIK *R&B/D&D/LP '84*
(Jeff Tyzik)

Singles: 12-inch

POLYDOR 4-6 84

Singles: 7-inch

CAPITOL 3-4 82
POLYDOR 3-4 84

LPs: 10/12-inch

CAPITOL 5-8 82
POLYDOR 5-8 84

UB40 *LP '83*
(With Chrissie Hynde)

Singles: 12-inch

A&M 4-6 83-86

Singles: 7-inch

A&M 3-4 83-88

Picture Sleeves

A&M 3-4 85

LPs: 10/12-inch

A&M 5-8 83-88
VIRGIN 5-8 89

Also see PRETENDERS

UFO LP '75

Singles: 7–inch

CHRYSALIS (Black vinyl)....................3-5 73-86
CHRYSALIS (2157 "Too Hot to Handle")....................3-6 77
(Colored vinyl.)

Picture Sleeves

CHRYSALIS (2157 "Too Hot to Handle")....................3-5 77

LPs: 10/12–inch

CHRYSALIS....................5-12 74-86
RARE EARTH....................10-15 71
Also see SCHENKER, Michael, Group

U.K. LP '78

Singles: 7–inch

POLYDOR....................3-5 78-79

LPs: 10/12–inch

POLYDOR....................5-10 78-79
Members: John Wetton; Eddie Jobson; Terry Bozzio; Bill Bruford; Allan Holdsworth.

U.K. SQUEEZE: see SQUEEZE

U-KREW LP '90

LPs: 10/12–inch

ENIGMA....................5-8 90

U.S. 1 P&R '75

Singles: 7–inch

PRIVATE STOCK....................3-5 75

U.S.A.- EUROPEAN CONNECTION LP '78

Singles: 7–inch

MARLIN....................3-5 78-79

LPs: 10/12–inch

MARLIN....................5-10 78-79

USA for AFRICA / Quincy Jones
(United Support of Artists for Africa)
P&R/R&B/D&D/C&W/LP '85

Singles: 12–inch

COLUMBIA....................4-6 85

Singles: 7–inch

COLUMBIA....................3-4 85

Picture Sleeves

COLUMBIA....................3-4 85

LPs: 10/12–inch

COLUMBIA....................5-8 85
Members: Dan Aykroyd; Kim Carnes; Ray Charles; Bob Dylan; Daryl Hall; James Ingram; Michael Jackson; Jean-Michael Jarre; Al Jarreau; Waylon Jennings; Billy Joel; Quincy Jones; Cyndi Lauper; Huey Lewis; Kenny Loggins; Bette Midler; Steve Perry; Lionel Richie; Smokey Robinson; Kenny Rogers; Diana Ross; Paul Simon; Bruce Springsteen; Tina Turner; Dionne Warwick; Stevie Wonder.
Also see CARNES, Kim
Also see CHARLES, Ray
Also see DYLAN, Bob
Also see HALL, Daryl
Also see INGRAM, Jámes
Also see JACKSON, Michael
Also see JARRE, Jean-Michael
Also see JARREAU, Al
Also see JENNINGS, Waylon
Also see JOEL, Billy
Also see JONES, Quincy
Also see LAUPER, Cyndi
Also see LEWIS, Huey, & News
Also see LOGGINS, Kenny
Also see MIDLER, Bette
Also see PERRY, Steve
Also see RICHIE, Lionel
Also see ROBINSON, Smokey
Also see ROGERS, Kenny
Also see ROSS, Diana
Also see SIMON, Paul
Also see SPRINGSTEEN, Bruce
Also see TURNER, Tina
Also see VOICES of AMERICA / U.S.A. for AFRICA
Also see WARWICK, Dionne
Also see WONDER, Stevie

UTFO P&R/R&B/D&D/LP '85

Singles: 12–inch

SELECT....................4-6 85-86

Singles: 7–inch

SELECT....................3-4 85-89

LPs: 10/12–inch

SELECT....................5-8 85-89
Also see ROXANNE with UTFO

U2 LP '81

Singles: 12–inch

ISLAND....................4-6 83

Singles: 7–inch

ISLAND....................3-5 81-93

Picture Sleeves

ISLAND....................3-8 81-93

EPs: 7–inch

ISLAND (99385 "Joshua Tree")....................5-10 87

LPs: 10/12–inch

ISLAND (Except 314-510347)....................5-10 81-91
ISLAND (314-510347 "Achtung Baby")....................15-20 91
(With "naked" cover.)
ISLAND (314-510347 "Achtung Baby")....................5-10 91
(Without "naked" cover.")
MFSL (207 "The Unforgettable Fire")....................20-25 94
POLYDOR....................8-10 90s
Members: Paul "Bono Vox" Hewson; David "The Edge" Evan; Adam Clayton; Larry Mullen.
Also see BAND AID

U2 & B.B. KING P&R '89

Singles: 12–inch

ISLAND....................4-6 89

Singles: 7–inch

ISLAND....................3-4 89

Picture Sleeves

ISLAND....................3-4 89
Also see KING, B.B.
Also see U2

UBIQUITY LP '78

Singles: 7–inch

ELEKTRA....................3-5 78

LPs: 10/12–inch

ELEKTRA....................5-10 78
Also see AYERS, Roy

UGGAMS, Leslie P&R '59

Singles: 7–inch

ATLANTIC....................5-15 65-70
COLUMBIA....................5-10 59-64
GORDY....................3-5 76
MGM....................5-15 54-55
SONDAY....................3-5 71

EPs: 7–inch

MGM....................5-10 54

LPs: 10/12–inch

ATLANTIC....................5-15 66-69
COLUMBIA....................15-30 59-63
MOTOWN....................5-10 75
SONDAY....................5-10 72

ULLANDA R&B '79

Singles: 7–inch

OCEAN....................3-5 79

ULLMAN, Tracey P&R/LP '84

Singles: 7–inch

MCA....................3-5 84-85

Picture Sleeves

MCA....................3-5 84-85

LPs: 10/12–inch

MCA....................5-10 84

ULTIMATE P&R/LP '79

Singles: 7–inch

CASABLANCA....................3-5 78-80

LPs: 10/12–inch

CASABLANCA....................5-10 78-80

ULTIMATE SPINACH LP '68

Singles: 7–inch

MGM....................5-10 68-69

LPs: 10/12–inch

MGM (4518 "Ultimate Spinach")....................20-30 68
MGM (4570 "Behold and See")....................20-30 68
MGM (4600 "Ultimate Spinach")....................15-25 69
Members: Barbara Hudson; Ian Bruce Douglas; Richard Nese; Jeff Baxter; Ted Myers; Tony Scheuren; Mike Levine; Russ Levine.
Also see STEELY DAN

ULTRAVOX LP '80

Singles: 12–inch

CHRYSALIS....................4-6 83

Singles: 7–inch

ANTILLES....................3-5 78-80
CHRYSALIS....................3-4 80-84
ISLAND....................8-10 77

LPs: 10/12–inch

ANTILLES....................5-10 78-80
CHRYSALIS....................5-8 80-84
ISLAND....................8-10 77
Also see BAND AID

UMILANI, Piero P&R '69
(Sweden Heaven & Hell Soundtrack)

Singles: 7–inch

ARIEL....................3-5 69

LPs: 10/12–inch

ARIEL....................8-12 69

UNCLE DOG P&R '73

Singles: 7–inch

MCA....................3-5 73

LPs: 10/12–inch

MCA....................5-10 73

UNCLE LOUIE R&B '79

Singles: 7–inch

MARLIN....................3-5 79

LPs: 10/12–inch

MARLIN....................5-10 78

UNDERGROUND SUNSHINE P&R/LP '69

Singles: 7–inch

EARTH....................8-12 69
INTREPID....................5-10 69-70

LPs: 10/12–inch

INTERPID....................15-25 69
Members: Rex Rhode; Jane Little Whirry; Bert Hohl; Frank Kohl; Chris Connors; Dave Wayne; Mike Hollihan.

UNDERTONES LP '80

Singles: 7–inch

CAPITOL....................3-4 84
HARVEST....................3-5 81
SIRE....................3-5 80

LPs: 10/12–inch

CAPITOL....................5-8 84
HARVEST....................5-10 81
SIRE....................5-10 80
Member: Feargal Sharkey.
Also see SHARKEY, Feargal

UNDERWOOD, Veronica R&B '85

Singles: 7–inch

PHILLY WORLD....................3-4 85

UNDERWORLD P&R/LP '88

Singles: 7–inch

SIRE....................3-4 88-89

Picture Sleeves

SIRE....................3-4 88-89

LPs: 10/12–inch

SIRE....................5-8 88

UNDISPUTED TRUTH P&R/R&B/LP '71

Singles: 12–inch

WHITFIELD....................4-8 77-79

Singles: 7–inch

GORDY (Black vinyl)....................3-5 71-75
GORDY (Colored vinyl)....................5-8 71-72
MOTOWN....................3-4
WHITFIELD....................3-5 76-79

LPs: 10/12–inch

GORDY....................10-20 71-75
WHITFIELD....................5-10 77-79

Members: Joe Harris; Brenda Evans; Billie Calvin; Carl Smalls; Tyrone Berkley; Tyrone Douglas; Virginia McDonald; Calvin Stevens; Melvin Stuart; Marcy Thomas; Hershel Kennedy; Taka Boom.
Also see BOOM, Taka
Also see DRAMATICS

UNFORGIVEN LP '86

LPs: 10/12-inch

ELEKTRA 5-8 86

UNICORN LP '74

Singles: 7-inch

CAPITOL 3-5 74-77

LPs: 10/12-inch

CAPITOL 8-10 74-77

UNIFICS P&R/R&B '68

Singles: 7-inch

FOUNTAIN 3-5 71
KAPP 4-8 68-69
MCA 3-4 73

Picture Sleeves

KAPP 4-8 68-69

LPs: 10/12-inch

KAPP 10-15 68
Members: Al Johnson; Michael Ward; Greg Cook; Harold Worthington; Tom Fauntleroy; Marvin Brown.

UNION GAP: see PUCKET, Gary

UNIPOP P&R '82

Singles: 7-inch

KAT FAMILY 3-4 82

LPs: 10/12-inch

KAT FAMILY 5-8 82

UNIQUE R&B/D&D '83

Singles: 12-inch

PRELUDE 4-6 83

Singles: 7-inch

PRELUDE 3-4 83

UNIQUES P&R '65

Singles: 7-inch

PARAMOUNT 3-5 70-72
PAULA 4-8 65-70

LPs: 10/12-inch

PAULA 12-25 66-70
Members: Joe Stampley; Bobby Stampley; Jim Woodfield; Mike Love; Ray Mills; Bobby Sims; Ronnie Weiss.
Also see MOUSE
Also see STAMPLEY, Joe

UNIT 4+2 P&R '65

Singles: 7-inch

LONDON 4-8 65-66

LPs: 10/12-inch

LONDON (427 "Unit 4+2") 25-35 65
(Monaural.)
LONDON (3427 "Unit 4+2") 25-40 65
(Stereo.)
Member: Russ Ballard.
Also see BALLARD, Russ

UNITED STATES AIR FORCE BAND LP '63

LPs: 10/12-inch

RCA 5-10 63

UNITED STATES MARINE BAND LP '63

LPs: 10/12-inch

RCA 5-10 63

UNITED STATES NAVY BAND LP '63

LPs: 10/12-inch

RCA 5-10 63

UNITED STATES OF AMERICA LP '68

LPs: 10/12-inch

COLUMBIA (9619 "United States of America") 20-30 68
(With stenciled title brown wrapper.)
COLUMBIA (9619 "United States of America") 10-20 68
(Without wrapper.)
Members: Dorothy Moskowitz; Joseph Byrd; Gordon Marron; Rand Forbes; Craig Woodson.

UNITS D&D '83

Singles: 12-inch

EPIC 4-6 83-84
UPROAR 4-6 83

Singles: 7-inch

EPIC 3-4 84

LPs: 10/12-inch

EPIC 5-8 84

UNIVERSAL ROBOT BAND P&R/R&B '77

Singles: 7-inch

RED GREG 3-6 77

LPs: 10/12-inch

RED GREG 5-10 77
Also see KLEEER

UNKNOWNS P&R '66

Singles: 7-inch

MARLIN (16008 "Tighter") 10-15 67
PARROT (307 "Melody for an Unknown Girl") 8-12 66
Members: Keith Allison; Mark Lindsay; Steve Alaimo
Also see ALAIMO, Steve.
Also see ALLISON, Keith
Also see LINDSAY, Mark

UNLIMITED TOUCH R&B/LP '81

Singles: 12-inch

PRELUDE 4-6 81-84

Singles: 7-inch

PRELUDE 3-5 81-84

LPs: 10/12-inch

PRELUDE 5-10 81-84
Also see LORBER, Jeff

UNTOUCHABLES LP '89

LPs: 10/12-inch

ENIGMA 5-8
RESTLESS 5-8 89

UP WITH PEOPLE LP '66

LPs: 10/12-inch

PACE 5-10 64-70

UPBEATS P&R '58

Singles: 7-inch

JOY 10-12 58-59
PREP 10-15 57-58
SWAN 10-15 58

UPCHURCH, Phil P&R '61
(Phil Upchurch Combo)

Singles: 7-inch

BOYD (329 "You Can't Sit Down") 10-15 61
(No mention of U.A. distribution on label.)
BOYD (329 "You Can't Sit Down") 8-10 61
(Indicates distribution by United Artists.)
BOYD (1026 "You Can't Sit Down") 4-8 66
GOLDEN FLEECE 3-5 74
MARLIN 3-4 79
U.A. 5-10 61-62

LPs: 10/12-inch

BLUE THUMB 8-10 73
BOYD (B-398 "You Can't Sit Down") 20-25 61
(Monaural.)
BOYD (BS-398 "You Can't Sit Down") 25-30 61
(Stereo.)
CADET 8-10 69
MILESTONE 5-8
U.A. 15-20 61-62
Also see CLARK, Dee
Also see REED, Jimmy

UPCHURCH, Phil, & Tennyson Stephens

LPs: 10/12-inch

KUDU 8-10 75
Also see STEPHENS, Tennyson
Also see UPCHURCH, Phil

UPFRONT D&D '83

Singles: 12-inch

SILVER CLOUD 4-6 83

UPSETTERS FEATURING LITTLE RICHARD

Singles: 7-inch

LITTLE STAR 10-20 62
Also see LITTLE RICHARD

UPTOWN P&R '86

Singles: 12-inch

SILVER SCREEN 4-6 83

Singles: 7-inch

OAK LAWN 3-4 86

URBAN DANCE SQUA LP '90

LPs: 10/12-inch

ARISTA 5-8 90

URE, Midge P&R/LP '89

Singles: 7-inch

CHRYSALIS 3-4 89

LPs: 10/12-inch

CHRYSALIS 5-8 89

URGENT P&R '85

Singles: 7-inch

MANHATTAN 3-4 85

Picture Sleeves

MANHATTAN 3-4 85

URIAH HEEP LP '70

Singles: 7-inch

CHRYSALIS 3-5 78
MERCURY 3-5 70-83
W.B. 3-5 73-78

Picture Sleeves

MERCURY 3-5 70-82

EPs: 7-inch

W.B. 8-12 73
(Juke box issue only.)

LPs: 10/12-inch

CHRYSALIS 5-10 78-79
MERCURY 5-10 70-83
W.B. 5-10 73-81
Also see HENSLEY, Ken
Also see ROUGH DIAMOND

UTOPIA LP '77

Singles: 7-inch

BEARSVILLE 3-5 76-80
NETWORK 3-4 82
PASSPORT 3-4 84-85

LPs: 10/12-inch

BEARSVILLE 5-12 77-82
NETWORK 8-10 82
PASSPORT 5-8 84-85
Members: Todd Rundgren; Willie Wilcox; Roger Powell; Kasim Sulton.
Also see CASSIDY, Shaun, & Todd Rundgren's Utopia
Also see RUNDGREN, Todd

V.S.O.P. LP '77
(Very Special One-time Performance)

LPs: 10/12-inch

COLUMBIA 5-10 77
Members: Herbie Hancock; Wayne Shorter; Freddie Hubbard; Tony Williams.

VACELS P&R '65

Singles: 7-inch

KAMA SUTRA 4-8 65

VAIN LP '89

LPs: 10/12-inch

ISLAND 5-8 89

VALADIERS P&R '61

Singles: 7-inch

GORDY (7003 "While I'm Away") 25-50 62
GORDY (7013 "I Found a Girl") 25-50 63
MIRACLE (6 "Greetings") 50-75 61
MIRACLE (6 "Greetings [This Is Uncle Sam]") 25-50 61
(Note longer title.)
Member: Paul Kelly.

VALE, Jerry P&R '53

Singles: 78 rpm

COLUMBIA 3-5 51-57

Singles: 7-inch

BUDDAH 3-5 78
COLUMBIA 3-10 51-74

Picture Sleeves

COLUMBIA 5-10 64-65

EPs: 7-inch

COLUMBIA 5-15 56-59

LPs: 10/12-inch

COLUMBIA 5-20 58-75
HARMONY 5-10 69-74
Also see CLARK, Dave, Five / New Christy Minstrels / Bobby Vinton / Jerry Vale

VALE, Jerry, Peggy King & Felicia Sanders

LPs: 10/12-inch

COLUMBIA 10-20 56
Also see KING, Peggy
Also see SANDERS, Felicia
Also see VALE, Jerry

VALENS, Ritchie P&R/R&B '58

Singles: 12-inch

DEL-FI (1287 "La Bamba") 15-25 87

Singles: 7-inch

ABC 3-5 74
DEL-FI (1287 "La Bamba '87") 3-4 87
DEL-FI (4106 "C'mon Let's Go") 15-25 58
DEL-FI (4110 "Donna") 15-25 58
(Solid green label with black print.)
DEL-FI (4110 "Donna") 10-15 58
(Has rows of circles on label.)
DEL-FI (4110 "Donna") 5-10 61
(Black label with sawtooth circle.)
DEL-FI (4111 "Fast Freight") 10-20 59
(First issued as by Arvee Allens.)
DEL-FI (4114 "That's My Little Suzie") 10-20 59
DEL-FI (4117 "Little Girl") 10-20 59
(Del-Fi "Limited Valens Memorial Series.")
DEL-FI (4128 "Stay Beside Me") 10-20 60
DEL-FI (4133 "Paddiwack") 10-20 60
ERIC 3-5 70s
GOODIES 3-5
KASEY (7040 "Donna") 5-10
LANA 3-6 60s
LOST-NITE 4-8

Picture Sleeves

DEL-FI (4114 "That's My Little Suzie") 25-50 59
DEL-FI (4117 "Little Girl") 20-40 59
(With explanatory "Concerning This Record" insert.)
DEL-FI (4117 "Little Girl") 15-25 59
(Without insert.)
DEL-FI (4128 "Stay Beside Me") 15-25 60
KASEY (7040 "Donna") 5-10

EPs: 7-inch

DEL-FI (1 "Ritchie Valens") 50-75 59
(Promotional issue only.)
DEL-FI (101 "Ritchie Valens") 50-75 59
DEL-FI (111 "Ritchie Valens Sings") 50-75 59

LPs: 10/12-inch

DEL-FI (1201 "Ritchie Valens") 75-125 59
(Back cover shows *That's My Little Suzie* as "I Got a Gal Named Sue.")
DEL-FI (1201 "Ritchie Valens") 60-80 59
(Back cover properly shows *That's My Little Suzie.*)
DEL-FI (1206 "Ritchie") 60-80 59
DEL-FI (1214 "Ritchie Valens in Concert") 100-200 61
DEL-FI (1225 "Greatest Hits") 40-60 63
DEL-FI (1247 "Greatest Hits, Vol. 2") 40-60 65
GUEST STAR 15-25 64
MGM 10-15 70
RHINO (Except 2798) 5-8 81-87
RHINO (2798 "History of Ritchie Valens") 20-25 81
Also see ALLENS, Arvee

VALENS, Ritchie / Jerry Kole

LPs: 10/12-inch

CROWN (5336 "Ritchie Valens & Jerry Kole") 20-30 63

VALENTE, Caterina P&R '55

Singles: 78 rpm

DECCA 3-5 54-57

Singles: 7-inch

DECCA 5-10 54-59
LONDON 3-6 60-68
RCA 4-8 59
TELEFUNKEN 4-8 59

EPs: 7-inch

DECCA 5-10 55

LPs: 10/12-inch

DECCA 5-15 55-64
LONDON 5-15 59-72
RCA 5-15 60-61

VALENTI, John P&R/R&B '76

Singles: 7-inch

ARIOLA AMERICA 3-5 76-77

VALENTIN, Dave R&B/LP '80

Singles: 7-inch

GRP 3-5 80-81

LPs: 10/12-inch

GRP 5-10 80-81

VALENTINE, Lezli R&B '68

Singles: 7-inch

ALL PLATINUM 3-6 68

VALENTINE BROTHERS R&B '82

Singles: 12-inch

SOURCE 4-6 78

Singles: 7-inch

A&M 3-4 84
BRIDGE 3-4 82
SOURCE 3-5 79

LPs: 10/12-inch

A&M 5-8 84
BRIDGE 5-8 82
SOURCE 5-10 79
Members: John Valentine; Billy Valentine.

VALENTINO, Danny P&R '60

Singles: 7-inch

CONTRAST 5-10 67
MGM 10-20 59-60

VALENTINO, Mark P&R '62

Singles: 7-inch

SWAN 5-10 62-63
(Shown as "Mark Valentinon" on some labels.)

LPs: 10/12-inch

SWAN (508 "Mark Valentino") 30-50 63

VALENTINOS P&R/R&B '62

Singles: 7-inch

ABKCO 3-5 70s
ASTRA 5-10 60s
CHESS 5-10 66
CLEAN 5-10 73
JUBILEE 5-10 68-69
SAR 10-20 62-64
Members: Bobby Womack; Curtis Womack.
Also see WOMACK, Bobby
Also see WOMACK BROTHERS

VALENTION, Mark: see VALENTINO, Mark

VALERIE & NICK

Singles: 7-inch

GLOVER (3000 "Lonely Town") 10-15 64
Members: Valerie Simpson; Nick Ashford.
Also see ASHFORD & SIMPSON

VALERY, Dana P&R '76

Singles: 7-inch

ABC 5-10 68-69
COLUMBIA (44004 "Having You Around") 15-25 67
LIBERTY 4-6 70
PHANTOM 3-6 75
SCOTTI BROS 3-6 79

Picture Sleeves

PHANTOM 3-5 75

LPs: 10/12-inch

BRUNSWICK 5-10
PHANTOM 5-10 75
Also see SIMON, Paul

VALIANTS P&R '57

(With the Bumps Blackwell Orchestra; Featuring Billy Storm)

Singles: 78 rpm

KEEN 20-40 57

Singles: 7-inch

ANDEX (4026 "Please Wait My Love") 100-125 58
(First issue.)
KEEN (4008 "Temptation of My Heart") 25-50 58
KEEN (4026 "Please Wait My Love") 40-60 58
KEEN (34004 "This Is the Night") 20-40 57
KEEN (34007 "Lover Lover") 20-40 58
KEEN (82120 "This Is the Night") 10-20 60
SHAR-DEE (703 "Dear Cindy") 75-125 59
(Reads: "Made in U.S.A." at bottom. No mention of distribution by London.)
SHAR-DEE (703 "Dear Cindy") 25-50 59
(Reads "Distributed by London Records, Inc." at bottom)
Also see STORM, Billy

VALINO, Joe P&R '56

Singles: 78 rpm

U.A. 8-12 57
VIK 5-10 56

Singles: 7-inch

BANDBOX 5-10 61
CLEARVIEW 5-10
CROSLEY 5-10 59-60
DEBUT 4-6 67-68
RCA 8-12 59
U.A. 10-15 57-58
VIK 10-20 56

Picture Sleeves

U.A. (101 "Legend of the Lost") 20-30 57

LPs: 10/12-inch

DEBUT 8-12 67

VALJEAN P&R/LP '62

(Valjean Johns)

Singles: 7-inch

CARLTON 4-8 62-63

Picture Sleeves

CARLTON 5-10 62

LPs: 10/12-inch

CARLTON 15-25 62-63

VALLEY, Frankie: see VALLI, Frankie

VALLI, Frankie P&R '66

(With the Travelers; Frankie Valle; Frankie Vally; with Romans)

Singles: 10/12-inch

MOTOWN 15-20 73
PRIVATE STOCK 10-15 77

Singles: 78 rpm

MERCURY 50-75 54

Singles: 7-inch

CINDY 75-100 59
COLLECTABLES 3-4 80s

CORONA (1234 "My Mother's Eyes") ... 300-500 53
DECCA (30994 "Please Take a Chance") ... 75-100 59
MCA/CURB ... 3-5 80
MERCURY (70381 "Forgive and Forget") ... 100-125 54
(Maroon label.)
MERCURY (70381 "Forgive and Forget") ... 50-75 54
(Black label.)
MOTOWN ... 8-12 73
MOWEST ... 5-10 72
PHILIPS (40407 thru 45098, except 40500) ... 4-8 66-70
PHILIPS (40500 "Donnybrook") ... 20-40 67
PHILIPS (40661 & 40680) ... 10-12 69-70
PRIVATE STOCK ... 3-5 74-78
RSO ... 3-5 78
SEASONS ... 3-5
SMASH ... 5-10 65-66
W.B./CURB ... 3-5 78-80

Promotional Singles

BOB CREWE PRESENTS (1 "The Girl I'll Never Know") ... 25-35 69
DECCA (30994 "Please Take a Chance") ... 50-75 59
MERCURY (70381 "Forgive and Forget") ... 50-75 54
MOWEST (5025 "The Night") ... 12-15 71
PHILIPS ... 8-12 66-70
PRIVATE STOCK ... 8-10 74-78
SMASH ... 8-12 65-66

Picture Sleeves

PHILIPS ... 8-15 66-69

LPs: 10/12-inch

MCA ... 5-10 79-80
MOTOWN (100 series) ... 5-8 81
MOTOWN (800 series) ... 8-12 75
PHILIPS (200247 "Solo") ... 30-40 67
(Monaural.)
PHILIPS (600000 series) ... 20-25 67-68
(Stereo.)
PRIVATE STOCK ... 8-10 75-78
W.B. ... 8-10 78

Also see BEACH BOYS with Frankie Valli & 4 Seasons
Also see FOUR LOVERS
Also see 4 SEASONS
Also see TYLER, Frankie

VALLI, Frankie, & Chris Forde — P&R '80

Singles: 7-inch

MCA ... 3-5 80

VALLI, Frankie, & Cheryl Ladd

Singles: 7-inch

CAPITOL ... 3-5 82

Also see LADD, Cheryl
Also see VALLI, Frankie

VALLI, June — P&R '52

(With Joe Reisman's Orchestra)

Singles: 78 rpm

RCA ... 3-5 52-56

Singles: 7-inch

ABC-PAR ... 4-6 63
DCP ... 4-6 64
MERCURY ... 4-8 58-61
RCA ... 5-10 52-56
U.A. ... 4-6 62

Picture Sleeves

MERCURY ... 4-8 61

EPs: 7-inch

RCA ... 5-10 55-56

LPs: 10/12-inch

AUDIO FIDELITY ... 5-10 69
MERCURY ... 8-15 60
RCA ... 12-25 55-56

Also see PIANO RED / June Valli
Also see ZABACH, Florian

VALLIE, Frankie: see VALLI, Frankie

VALUMES

(Valume's; Volumes)

Singles: 7-inch

CHEX (1000 "I Love You") ... 200-300 62

Also see VOLUMES

VAN & TITUS — R&B '68

Singles: 7-inch

ELF ... 4-8 68

VANCE, Paul — P&R '66

Singles: 7-inch

ROULETTE ... 4-8 62
SCEPTER ... 4-8 66

LPs: 10/12-inch

SCEPTER ... 10-20 66

Also see LEE & PAUL

VANDENBERG — P&R/LP '83

(Adrian Vandenberg)

Singles: 7-inch

ATCO ... 3-4 83-84

LPs: 10/12-inch

ATCO ... 5-8 83-84

VANDERPOOL, Sylvia: see LITTLE SYLVIA

VANDROSS, Luther — R&B '76

Singles: 12-inch

EPIC ... 4-6 82-85

Singles: 7-inch

COTILLION ... 3-5 76
EPIC ... 3-5 81-90

Picture Sleeves

EPIC ... 3-4 85-87

LPs: 10/12-inch

EPIC ... 5-10 81-90

Also see BOWIE, David
Also see CHANGE
Also see LUTHER
Also see LYNN, Cheryl, & Luther Vandross
Also see PRESTON, Billy
Also see ROUNDTREE
Also see WARWICK, Dionne, & Luther Vandross

VANDROSS, Luther, & Gregory Hines — P&R/R&B '87

Singles: 7-inch

EPIC ... 3-4 87

Also see HINES, Gregory

VAN DYKE, Leroy — P&R '56

Singles: 78 rpm

DOT (Except 15698) ... 4-8 56-57
DOT (15698 "Leather Jacket") ... 20-40 57

Singles: 7-inch

ABC ... 3-5 74-75
ABC/DOT ... 3-5 75-77
DECCA ... 3-5 70-72
DOT (Except 15698) ... 5-15 56-57
DOT (15698 "Leather Jacket") ... 50-75 57
KAPP ... 4-6 68-70
MCA ... 3-5 73
MERCURY ... 4-8 61-64
PLANTATION ... 3-5 78
SUN ... 3-5 79
W.B. ... 4-6 65-67

Picture Sleeves

MERCURY ... 5-8 64

LPs: 10/12-inch

DECCA ... 8-10 72
DOT ... 20-30 60s
HARMONY ... 8-12 69
KAPP ... 8-15 68-69
MCA ... 5-10 73
MERCURY ... 12-25 62-64
MOUNTAIN DEW ... 5-10
PLANTATION ... 5-10 77-79
SUN ... 5-8 74
W.B. ... 10-15 65-66
WING ... 8-15 65-66

VAN DYKES — P&R '61

Singles: 7-inch

DELUXE (6193 "Bells Are Ringing") ... 10-15 61
DONNA (1333 "Gift of Love") ... 20-30 60
FELSTED (8565 "Once Upon a Dream") ... 15-20 59
KING (5158 "Bells Are Ringing") ... 30-40 58
(Blue label.)
KING (5158 "Bells Are Ringing") ... 10-15 60s
(Yellow label.)
SPRING (1113 "Gift of Love") ... 75-125 59

Also see TEMPTATIONS

VAN DYKES — P&R/R&B '66

Singles: 7-inch

HUE (6501 "No Man Is an Island") ... 15-25 65
MALA (520 "No Man Is an Island") ... 5-8 65
MALA (530 "What Will I Do") ... 5-10 66
MALA (539 "Never Let Me Go") ... 5-10 66
MALA (549 "You're Shakin' Me Up") ... 5-10 66
MALA (566 "A Sunday Kind of Love") 5-10 66
MALA (584 "Tears of Joy") ... 20-30 67

LPs: 10/12-inch

BELL (6004 "Tellin' It Like It Is") ... 15-25 67

Members: Ron Tandy; Wenzon Mosley; Jimmy May.

VANGELIS — P&R/LP '81

Singles: 7-inch

POLYDOR ... 3-4 81
RCA ... 3-5 78

Picture Sleeves

POLYDOR ... 3-5 81

LPs: 10/12-inch

POLYDOR ... 5-10 81-86
RCA ... 5-10 78-82

Also see JON & VANGELIS

VANGUARDS — R&B '69

Singles: 7-inch

LAMP (80 "It's Too Late for Love") ... 5-10 70
LAMP (81 "Girl Go Away") ... 5-10 70
WHIZ ... 5-10 69

VAN HALEN — P&R/LP '78

Singles: 12-inch

W.B. ... 4-6 83-84
(Commercial issues.)
W.B. ... 6-12 83-84
(Promotionall issues.)

Singles: 7-inch

PALM TREE ... 4-8
W.B. ... 3-5 78-90

Promotional Singles

W.B. ... 5-10 78-90

Picture Sleeves

W.B. (Except 8556 & 8823) ... 3-8 79-88
W.B. (8556 "Running with the Devil") ... 20-30 78
W.B. (8823 "Dance the Night Away") .. 8-12 79

LPs: 10/12-inch

W.B. ... 5-10 78-90
W.B./LOONEY TUNES (705 "Van Halen") ... 10-20 78
(Colored vinyl. Promotional issue only.)

Members: David Lee Roth; Edward Van Halen; Alex Van Halen; Michael Anthony; Sammy Hagar.

Also see HAGAR, Sammy
Also see MAY, Brian
Also see ROTH, David Lee
Also see VAN HALEN, Edward

VAN HALEN, Edward

LPs: 10/12-inch

MCA ... 5-8 86

Also see JACKSON, Michael
Also see VAN HALEN

VANILLA FUDGE — P&R/LP '67

Singles: 7-inch

ATCO ... 4-8 67-70

LPs: 10/12-inch

ATCO (200 & 300 series) ... 15-20 67-69
ATCO (90000 series) ... 5-10 82

Members: Mark Stein; Tim Bogert; Vinnie Martell; Carmine Appice.

Also see BECK, BOGERT & APPICE
Also see PIGEONS

VANILLA ICE — LP '90

LPs: 10/12-inch

SKB ... 5-8 90

VANILLI, Milli: see MILLI VANILLI

VANITY *P&R/R&B/D&D/LP '84*
(Denise Matthews)

Singles: 12-inch
MOTOWN....4-6 84-86
Singles: 7-inch
MOTOWN....3-4 84-86
Picture Sleeves
MOTOWN....3-4 84-86
LPs: 10/12-inch
MOTOWN....5-8 84-86
Members: Denise Matthews; Brenda Bennett; Susan Moonsie.
Also see VANITY 6

VANITY / Smokey Robinson
LPs: 10/12-inch
MOTOWN (179 "Superstar Interviews")....10-15 84
(Promotional issue only.)
Also see ROBINSON, Smokey
Also see VANITY

VANITY FARE *P&R '69*
Singles: 7-inch
BRENT....4-8 67
DJM....3-5 75
PAGE ONE....3-6 68-70
SOMA....8-12 68
20TH FOX....3-5 73
LPs: 10/12-inch
PAGE ONE....10-15 70

VANITY 6 *R&B/LP '82*
Singles: 12-inch
W.B. 4-6 82-83
Singles: 7-inch
W.B. 3-4 82-83
LPs: 10/12-inch
W.B. 5-8 82
Member: Denise Matthews.
Also see APOLLONIA 6
Also see TIME
Also see VANITY

VANN, Teddy *P&R '61*
Singles: 7-inch
CAPITOL....3-6 67
COLUMBIA....4-8 61
END....5-10 59
JUBILEE....4-8 62
ROULETTE....4-8 60
TRIPLE-X....5-10 60

VANNELLI, Gino *P&R/LP '74*
Singles: 12-inch
HME....4-6 85
Singles: 7-inch
A&M....3-5 74-79
ARISTA....3-5 81-82
CBS ASSOCIATES....3-4 85-87
HME....3-4 85
Picture Sleeves
A&M....3-5 76-79
ARISTA....3-5 81-82
CBS ASSOCIATES....3-4 85-87
HME....3-4 85
LPs: 10/12-inch
A&M (3600 series)....5-10 74
A&M (3700 series)....5-8 81
A&M (4000 series)....8-10 74-78
ARISTA....5-10 81-82
CBS ASSOCIATES....5-8 87
HME....5-10 85
MFSL (041 "Powerful People")....25-35 80
NAUTILUS....15-20 81
(Half-speed mastered.)

VAN SHELTON, Ricky: see SHELTON, Ricky Van

VAN TIEGHEM, David *D&D '84*
Singles: 12-inch
W.B. 4-6 84
Singles: 7-inch
W.B. 3-4 84
LPs: 10/12-inch
W.B. 5-8 84

VANWARMER, Randy *C&W/P&R/LP '79*
Singles: 7-inch
BEARSVILLE....3-5 79
16TH AVE. 3-4 88
LPs: 10/12-inch
BEARSVILLE....5-10 79-83

VAN ZANT, Johnny, Band *LP '80*
(Van-Zant)
Singles: 7-inch
POLYDOR....3-5 80-82
LPs: 10/12-inch
ATLANTIC....5-8 90
GEFFEN....5-8 85
POLYDOR....5-10 80-82

VAPORS *P&R/LP '80*
Singles: 7-inch
LIBERTY....3-5 81
U.A. 3-5 80
LPs: 10/12-inch
LIBERTY....5-10 81
U.A. 5-10 80

VASEL, Marianne, & Erich Storz *P&R '58*
Singles: 7-inch
MERCURY....4-8 58
LPs: 10/12-inch
DANA....10-20 59

VAUGHAN, Frankie *P&R '58*
Singles: 7-inch
COLUMBIA....4-8 59-60
EPIC....4-8 58
PHILIPS....3-6 62-66
LPs: 10/12-inch
COLUMBIA....10-20 60
PHILIPS....10-15 62

VAUGHAN, Sarah *P&R '47*
Singles: 78 rpm
COLUMBIA....3-6 49-53
CONTINENTAL....5-10 45
MGM (Except 71)....3-6 50-51
MGM (71 "Sarah Vaughan Sings")....40-60 51
(Boxed, four-disc set.)
MERCURY....3-6 53-57
MUSICRAFT....4-8 47-48
Singles: 7-inch
ATLANTIC....3-5 81
COLUMBIA (38000 & 39000 series)....5-10 51-53
MGM (10000 & 30000 series)....5-10 50-51
MAINSTREAM....3-5 71-74
MERCURY (70000 series)....4-8 53-66
ROULETTE....4-6 60-64
W.B. 3-5 81
Picture Sleeves
MERCURY....4-8 65
EPs: 7-inch
ATLANTIC (527 "Sarah Vaughan Sings")....30-40 55
COLUMBIA....10-20 50-56
EMARCY....10-20 54-56
MGM....10-20 52-55
MERCURY....8-15 53-59
REMINGTON....5-10
ROYALE....5-10 50s
LPs: 10/12-inch
ALLEGRO....5-10
ATLANTIC....5-8 81
COLUMBIA (660 "After Hours")....35-45 55
COLUMBIA (745 "Sarah in Hi-Fi")....35-45 55
COLUMBIA (914 "Linger Awhile")....25-35 57
COLUMBIA (6133 "Sarah Vaughan")....50-100 50
(10-inch LP.)
COLUMBIA (37000 series)....5-8 82
CONCORD....15-25 56
CORONET....8-10 60s
EMARCY (400 series)....8-12 77
EMARCY (1000 series)....5-10 81
EMARCY (26005 "Images")....50-75 54
(10-inch LP.)
EMARCY (36000 series)....30-40 54-57
EVEREST....5-10 70-76
FORUM....8-12
GALAXY....8-12
GUEST STAR....8-12
HARMONY....5-15 59-69
MGM (165 "Tenderly")....50-100 51
(10-inch LPs.)
MGM (544 "Sarah Vaughan Sings")....50-100 54
(10-inch LP.)
MGM (3274 "My Kinda Love")....50-75 55
MAINSTREAM....6-12 71-75
MERCURY (100 "Great Songs")....25-35 57
MERCURY (101 "Gershwin Songs")....25-35 57
MERCURY (1000 series)....5-8 82
MERCURY (20000 series)....15-30 58-64
MERCURY (21000 series)....10-20 65-67
(Monaural.)
MERCURY (25188 "Divine Sarah")....60-80 53
(10-inch LP)
MERCURY (60000 series)....15-25 59-64
MERCURY (61000 series)....10-25 65-67
(Stereo.)
METRO....8-15 65
MUSICRAFT....5-8 83-84
PABLO....5-10 78-82
PALACE....5-10
REMINGTON (1024 "Hot Jazz")....50-100 53
(10-inch LP.)
RIVERSIDE (2511 "Sarah Vaughan Sings")....40-60 55
RONDO....20-40 59
RONDOLETTE....20-40 59
ROULETTE (100 series)....8-15 71
ROULETTE (52000 series, except 52082)....10-25 60-67
(Black vinyl.)
ROULETTE (52082 "You're Mine")....15-25 62
(Black vinyl.)
ROULETTE (52082 "You're Mine")....35-55 62
(Colored vinyl.)
SCEPTER....5-10 74
SPIN-O-RAMA....8-12 60s
SUTTON....5-10 70s
TRIP....5-10 74-76
WING....5-15 63-68
Also see BASIE, Count, & Sarah Vaughan
Also see DIAMONDS / Georgia Gibbs / Sarah Vaughan / Florian Zabach
Also see ECKSTINE, Billy, & Sarah Vaughan
Also see LEGRAND, Michel
Also see WASHINGTON, Dinah, & Sarah Vaughan

VAUGHAN, Sarah, & Quincy Jones
LPs: 10/12-inch
MERCURY....15-25 59
Also see JONES, Quincy
Also see VAUGHAN, Sarah

VAUGHAN, Stevie Ray *LP '83*
(With Double Trouble)
Singles: 7-inch
COLUMBIA....3-4 87
EPIC....3-4 85
LPs: 10/12-inch
COLUMBIA....5-8 87
EPIC (Except 8E8-39609)....5-10 84-89
EPIC (8E8-39609 "Couldn't Stand the Weather")....70-80 84
(Picture disc.)
Members: Stevie Ray Vaughan; Tommy Shannon; Chris Layton; Reese Wynans.

VAUGHAN, Stevie Ray, & Dick Dale
Singles: 7-inch
COLUMBIA (07340 "Pipeline")....3-4 87
Picture Sleeves
COLUMBIA (07340 "Pipeline")....3-5 87
Also see DALE, Dick

VAUGHAN BROTHERS *P&R/LP '90*
Singles: 7-inch
EPIC....3-4 89
LPs: 10/12-inch
EPIC....5-8 89

Members: Stevie Ray Vaughan; Jimmie Vaughan.
Also see FABULOUS THUNDERBIRDS
Also see VAUGHAN, Stevie Ray

VAUGHN, Billy, Orchestra P&R '54
(With the Billy Vaughn Singers)
Singles: 78 rpm
DOT 3-5 54-57
Singles: 7-inch
ABC 3-4 74
DOT 3-8 54-70
PARAMOUNT 3-4 70-72
Picture Sleeves
DOT 3-8 58-67
EPs: 7-inch
DOT 4-8 55-59
LPs: 10/12-inch
ABC 5-8 74
DOT 5-15 55-70
HAMILTON 5-10 65-66
MCA 5-8 83
MISTLETOE 4-8 76
MUSICOR 4-8 77
PARAMOUNT 5-8 70-74
PICKWICK 5-8 68
RANWOOD 4-8 83
Also see BRENNAN, Walter
Also see HILLTOPPERS
Also see STEVENS, Dodie
Also see STORM, Gale

VAUGHN, Denny P&R '56
Singles: 78 rpm
KAPP 3-6 56
Singles: 7-inch
KAPP 5-10 56

VEE, Bobby P&R '59
(With the Shadows; with Eligibles; with Strangers; with Johnny Mann Singers; Robert Thomas Velline)
Singles: 7-inch
COGNITO 3-5 81
LIBERTY (3331 "How Many Tears") . 20-25 61
(Stereo Compact 33 Single.)
LIBERTY (55208 "Suzie Baby") 10-20 59
LIBERTY (55234 thru 55325) 5-8 60-61
LIBERTY (55331 thru 56208) 3-6 61-70
SHADYBROOK 3-5 75-77
SOMA (1110 "Susie Baby") 40-60 59
U.A. 3-5 71-78
Picture Sleeves
LIBERTY 5-10 60-68
EPs: 7-inch
LIBERTY 25-35 60-62
U.A. 10-12 72
LPs: 10/12-inch
LIBERTY (3165 thru 3534) 20-30 60-67
(Monaural.)
LIBERTY (7165 thru 7534) 20-40 60-67
(Stereo.)
LIBERTY (7554 thru 7612) 10-20 68-69
LIBERTY (1000 series) 5-8 80
LIBERTY (10000 series) 5-8 84
SUNSET 10-15 66-67
U.A. (25-G2 "Legendary Masters") 250-350 73
(Includes bound-in booklet. Withdrawn before release, with only two or three copies surviving.)
U.A. (332 "Very Best") 8-10 73
U.A. (1008 "Golden Greats") 5-8 80
Members (Shadows): Bill Velline; Bob Korum; Jim Stillman; Dick Dunkirk; Ken Harvey.
Session: Johnny Mann Singers.
Also see ASSOCIATION / Bobby Vee / Mike Love / Mary MacGregor
Also see DE SHANNON, Jackie / Bobby Vee / Eddie Hodges

VEE, Bobby / Johnny Burnette / Ventures / Fleetwoods
LPs: 10/12-inch
LIBERTY (5503 "Teensville") 20-30 61
Also see BURNETTE, Johnny
Also see FLEETWOODS

VEE, Bobby, & Crickets LP '62
Singles: 7-inch
LIBERTY 4-8 62
Picture Sleeves
LIBERTY 10-15 60-63
LPs: 10/12-inch
LIBERTY 20-25 62
Also see CRICKETS

VEE, Bobby / Diamonds / Drifters
Singles: 7-inch
MINDSCAPE ("Mindscape and Rock 'n' Roll Are Here to Stay") 5-10 84
(Soundsheet. Promotional issue only.)
Also see DIAMONDS
Also see DRIFTERS

VEE, Bobby, & Ventures LP '63
LPs: 10/12-inch
LIBERTY 20-25 63
Also see VEE, Bobby
Also see VENTURES

VEGA, Suzanne LP '85
Singles: 7-inch
A&M 3-4 85-90
Picture Sleeves
A&M 3-4 87
LPs: 10/12-inch
A&M 5-8 85-90
Also see DNA Featuring Suzanne Vega
Also see GLASS, Philip

VEGA, Tata R&B '76
Singles: 12-inch
TAMLA 4-8 79
Singles: 7-inch
TAMLA 3-5 76-80
LPs: 10/12-inch
TAMLA 5-10 76-80
Also see EARTHQUIRE
Also see RAWLS, Lou

VEGA BROTHERS C&W '86
Singles: 7-inch
MCA 3-4 86
Members: Robert Vega; Ray Vega.

VEGAS, Lolly
Singles: 7-inch
AUDIO INTERNATIONAL (202 "It's Love") 25-35 61
Also see VEGAS, Pat, & Lolly

VEGAS, Pat
Singles: 7-inch
UNITY 10-20
Also see VEGAS, Pat, & Lolly

VEGAS, Pat, & Lolly
Singles: 7-inch
APOGEE 5-10 64
MERCURY 4-8 66
REPRISE 4-8 63
LPs: 10/12-inch
MERCURY 25-35 66
Also see REDBONE
Also see VEGAS, Lolly
Also see VEGAS, Pat

VEJTABLES P&R '65
Singles: 7-inch
AUTUMN 5-10 65-66
UPTOWN 4-8 67

VELAIRES P&R '61
Singles: 7-inch
BRENT 5-10 60s
HI-MAR 4-8 65
JAMIE (1198 "Roll Over Beethoven"/ "Brazil") 10-20 61
(First issued as by the Flairs.)
JAMIE (1198 "Roll Over Beethoven"/"Frankie & Johnny") 10-20 61
JAMIE (1203 "Dream") 10-15 61
JAMIE (1211 "Ubangi Stomp") 10-15 61
JAMIE (1223 "Memory Tree") 10-15 62
MERCURY 5-10 69
PALMS (730 "Summertime Blues") .. 30-60 61
RAMCO 5-10 60s

VELEZ, Martha LP '76
Singles: 7-inch
MCA 3-4 80
POLYDOR 3-5 73
SIRE 3-5 69-76
LPs: 10/12-inch
SIRE (6040 "American Heartbeat") 8-10 76
SIRE (7000 series) 8-10 74-76
SIRE (97000 series) 10-12 69

VELLINE, Robert Thomas: see VEE, Bobby

VELLS
(Vandellas)
Singles: 7-inch
MEL-O-DY (103 "There He Is") 25-50 62
Also see DEL-PHIS
Also see MARTHA & VANDELLAS

VELOURS P&R '57
(With Sammy Lowe Orchestra)
Singles: 78 rpm
ONYX 50-100 56-57
Singles: 7-inch
CUB (9001 "Can I Walk You Home") 20-30 58
CUB (9014 "I'll Never Smile Again") 20-30 58
CUB (9029 "Blue Velvet") 15-25 59
END (1090 "Lover Come Back") 15-25 61
GOLDISC (3012 "Sweet Sixteen") 25-35 60
GONE (5092 "Can I Come Over Tonight") 10-15 60
ONYX (501 "My Love Come Back") 100-200 56
ONYX (508 "Romeo") 400-600 57
ONYX (512 "Can I Come Over Tonight") 100-200 57
ONYX (515 "This Could Be the Night") 75-125 57
ONYX (520 "Can I Walk You Home") 75-125 58
(Black & orange label.)
ONYX (520 "Can I Walk You Home") 50-100 58
(Green label.)
ORBIT (9001 "Can I Walk You Home") 50-75 58
(Green label.)
ORBIT (9001 "Can I Walk You Home") 30-50 58
(Red label.)
RELIC (504 "Can I Come Over Tonight") 10-15 64
RELIC (516 "This Could Be the Night") 10-15 64
ROULETTE 3-5 70s
STUDIO (9902 "I Promise") 25-50 59
Members: Jerome Ramos; Pete Winston; John Pearson; Don Heywoode; John Cheatdom; Charles Moffett; Keith Williams; Troyce Key.
Also see FANTASTICS

VELS D&D '84
Singles: 12-inch
MERCURY 4-6 84-85
Singles: 7-inch
MERCURY 3-4 84-85
LPs: 10/12-inch
MERCURY 5-8 84

VELVELETTES P&R/R&B '64
Singles: 7-inch
I.P.G. (1002 "There He Goes") 4-8 63
SOUL 10-20 66
V.I.P. (Except 25021) 10-25 64-65
V.I.P. (25021 "Bird in the Hand") ... 100-200 66
Members: Carolyn Gill, Sandra Tilley; Betty Kelly.
Also see MARTHA & VANDELLAS

VELVET, Jimmy P&R '63
(Jimmy Velvet Five; James Velvet; Jimmy Tennant)
Singles: 7-inch
ABC-PAR 10-20 63-64

BELL....4-8 67
CAMEO (464 "Take Me Tonight")....15-25 67
CORREC-TONE (502 "When I Needed You")....50-100 62
CUB....5-10 61-62
DIVISION....10-20 61
MUSIC CITY....4-6 70
PHILIPS....10-20 65
ROYAL AMERICAN....4-6 68-69
SUNDI....3-6 71
TOLLIE....5-10 64
U.A. 10-20 68
VELVET (201 "You're Mine")....50-75 61
VELVET TONE....10-20 64-68

EPs: 7-inch

VELVET TONE (201 "Golden Hits")....15-25 60s

LPs: 10/12-inch

MUSIC CITY....8-12 70
U.A. (6653 "A Touch of Velvet")....15-25 68
VELVET TONE (501 "A Touch of Velvet")....20-30 68
WITCH....5-10 62
(Bi, Blue, and Teardrop releases credited to Jimmy Velvet, are actually by Jimmy Velvit, a different person.)

VELVET UNDERGROUND LP '68

Singles: 12-inch

POLYGRAM....5-10 85

Singles: 7-inch

ASPEN ("Loop")....20-40 66
(Single-sided soundsheet. Promotional issue only.)
COTILLION (44107 "Who Loves the Sun")....20-40 71
INDEX ("Interview")....30-50 67
(Single-sided picture disc soundsheet. Promotional issue only.)
MGM (14057 "What Goes On")....25-50 69
VERVE (10560 "White Light/White Heat")....25-50 68

LPs: 10/12-inch

COTILLION (9034 "Loaded")....15-20 70
COTILLION (9500 "Live")....15-20 70
MGM (131 "Velvet Underground")....8-10 71
MGM (4950 " Archetypes")....10-15 69-74
MERCURY (7504 "Velvet Underground")....12-15 72
PRIDE....10-15 73
VERVE (5046 "White Light/"White Heat")....30-40 67
VERVE (800000 series)....5-10 84-85
Members: Lou Reed; John Cale; Sterling Morrison; Maureen Tucker; Doug Yule.
Also see AMERICAN FLYER
Also see CALE, John
Also see REED, Lou

VELVET UNDERGROUND & NICO LP '67

Singles: 7-inch

VERVE (10427 "All Tomorrow's Parties")....25-50 66
(Blue label.)
VERVE (10427 "All Tomorrow's Parties")....50-75 66
(White label. Promotional issue only.)
VERVE (10466 "Sunday Morning")....25-50 66

Picture Sleeves

VERVE (10427 "All Tomorrow's Parties")....100-150 66
(Promotional issue only.)

LPs: 10/12-inch

VERVE (5008 "Velvet Underground & Nico")....100-200 67
(Monaural. With banana sticker on front cover. Back cover pictures an upside-down torso of a man behind the photo of Andy Warhol. Thus far, all copies meeting this description have been mono.)
VERVE (5008 "Velvet Underground & Nico")....50-75 67
(Stereo. With adhesive banana sticker on front cover. If a stereo copy with the upside-down male torso photo behind Andy Warhol exists, its value would approximately double.)
VERVE (5008 "Velvet Underground & Nico")....50-100 67
(With banana sticker on front cover. Back cover has a sticker above the photo of the group on stage, which reads: "The Velvet Underground & Nico.")
VERVE (5008 "Velvet Underground & Nico")....30-60 60s
(With adhesive banana sticker on front cover. Does not picture the upside-down male torso.)
VERVE (5008 "Velvet Underground & Nico")....25-35 67
(No banana sticker on front cover.)
VERVE (800000 series)....5-10 84
Also see NICO
Also see VELVET UNDERGROUND

VELVETS P&R '61

("Featuring Virgil Johnson")

Singles: 7-inch

MONUMENT (435 "That Lucky Old Sun")....20-30 61
MONUMENT (441 "Tonight")....20-30 61
MONUMENT (448 "Laugh")....20-30 61
MONUMENT (458 "The Love Express")....15-25 62
MONUMENT (464 "The Lights Go on, the Lights Go Off")....15-25 62
MONUMENT (810 "Crying in the Chapel")....10-20 64
MONUMENT (810 "Crying in the Chapel")....10-20 64
MONUMENT (961 "If")....10-15 66
PLAID (101 "Everybody Knows")....10-20 59
20TH FOX (165 "Happy Days Are Here Again")....20-30 59
Members: Virgil Johnson; Will Soloman; Mark Prince; Bob Thursby; Clarence Rigby; Jerry Sharell; Steve Novosel.

VENETIANS P&R '87

Singles: 7-inch

CHRYSALIS....3-4 87

VENTURES P&R/R&B/LP '60

Singles: 12-inch

TRIDEX (1245 "Surfin' and Spyin'")....5-8 81
(Vocals by Charlotte Caffey and Jane Weidlin.)

Singles: 7-inch

BLUE HORIZON (100 "Real McCoy")....40-60 59
BLUE HORIZON (101 "Walk Don't Run")....40-60 60
DOLTON (25 "Walk—Don't Run"/ "Home")....10-20 60
DOLTON (25-X "Walk—Don't Run"/"The McCoy")....8-12 60
DOLTON (28 thru 327)....5-10 60-66
LIBERTY....3-8 66-70
TRIDEX....3-5 81
U.A. 3-6 70-78

Picture Sleeves

DOLTON....5-15 60-66
TRIDEX....3-5 81

EPs: 7-inch

DOLTON....20-25 60

LPs: 10/12-inch

AWARD....8-12 84
DOLTON (2003 "Walk Don't Run")....25-35 60
(Light blue label. Monaural.)
DOLTON (2003 "Walk Don't Run")....15-25 61
(Dark blue label. Monaural.)
DOLTON (2004 thru 2050)....20-25 61-67
(Monaural.)
DOLTON (8003 "Walk Don't Run")....30-40 60
(Light blue label. Stereo.)
DOLTON (8003 "Walk Don't Run")....20-30 61
(Dark blue label. Stereo.)
DOLTON (8004 thru 8050)....20-30 61-67
(Stereo.)
DOLTON (16500 series)....25-35 60s
DOLTON (17000 series)....15-20 65-66
LIBERTY (2000 & 8000 series)....10-20 67-70
LIBERTY (10000 series)....5-10 81-84
LIBERTY (35000 series)....10-15 70
SUNSET....10-15 66-71
TRIDEX....5-10 81-83
U.A. 10-15 71-77
Members: Don Wilson; Bob Bogle; Mel Taylor; Nokie Edwards; Jerry McGee; Skip Moore; Howie Johnson.
Also see LOPEZ, Trini, with the Ventures & Nancy Ames
Also see MARKSMEN
Also see VEE, Bobby, & Ventures

VENUS, Vic P&R '69

Singles: 7-inch

BUDDAH....4-8 69

VERA, Billy P&R '67

(With the Contrasts; with Beaters; with Blue Eyed Soul)

Singles: 7-inch

ATLANTIC....4-6 68-69
FLAVOR....10-15 64
MACOLA....3-4 87
MIDSONG....3-5 75-76
ORANGE....4-8 73
RHINO....3-4 86-87
RUST....10-20 62

Picture Sleeves

RHINO....3-4 86

LPs: 10/12-inch

ATLANTIC....10-15 68
CAPITOL....5-8 88
MACOLA....5-8 87
MIDSONG INT'L....8-12 77
RHINO....5-8 86
Also see BILLY & BEATERS

VERA, Billy & Judy Clay P&R/R&B '67

Singles: 7-inch

ATLANTIC....4-8 67-68

LPs: 10/12-inch

ATLANTIC....10-15 68
Also see CLAY, Judy

VERA LYNN: see LYNN, Vera

VERLAINE, Tom LP '81

Singles: 7-inch

ELEKTRA....3-5 80
W.B. 3-5 81-84

LPs: 10/12-inch

ELEKTRA....5-10 80
W.B. 5-10 81-84

VERNE, Larry P&R/R&B '60

Singles: 7-inch

COLLECTABLES....3-4 80s
ERA....5-8 60-64

Picture Sleeves

ERA....10-15 60

LPs: 10/12-inch

ERA (104 "Mister Larry Verne")....25-35 60

VERONICA

(Veronica "Ronnie" Spector)

Singles: 7-inch

PHIL SPECTOR (1 "So Young")....25-50 64
PHIL SPECTOR (2 "Why Don't They Let Us Fall in Love")....40-60 64
Also see NITZSCHE, Jack
Also see SPECTOR, Ronnie

VIA AFRIKA D&D '84

Singles: 12-inch

EMI AMERICA....4-6 84

Singles: 7-inch

EMI AMERICA....3-4 84

LPs: 10/12-inch

EMI AMERICA....5-8 84

VIBRATIONS P&R/R&B '61

Singles: 7-inch

ABC....3-5 74
AMY....5-10
ARGO....5-10
ATLANTIC (2204 "Between Hello and Goodbye")....8-12 63
ATLANTIC (2221 "My Girl Sloopy")....10-20 64
BET (0001 "So Blue")....75-125 60

CHECKER (Except 954 & 987)........ 10-15 60-63
CHECKER (954 "So Blue")............ 25-50 60
CHECKER (987 "All My Love Belongs to You")............ 25-50 61
CHESS............ 3-6 74
EPIC............ 10-20 68
MANDALA............ 3-5 72
NEPTUNE............ 4-8 69-70
NORTH BAY (307 "Sneakin' ")............ 5-10
OKEH............ 10-15 64-68

LPs: 10/12-inch

CHECKER (2978 "Watusi")............ 50-75 61
MANDALA............ 10-15 72
OKEH............ 25-35 65-69

Also see JAYHAWKS
Also see MARATHONS

VIBES

("Vocal By Ronnie Franklin")

Singles: 7-inch

PERSPECTIVE (5858 "Pretty Baby")............ 50-100 58

Member: David Gates as Ronnie Franklin.
Also see GATES, Ronnie

VICIOUS BASE Featuring D.J. Magic Mike — LP '91

LPs: 10/12-inch

CHEETAH............ 5-8 91

Also see D.J. Magic Mike

VICKY D — R&B '82

Singles: 7-inch

SAM............ 3-4 82

VICTORY — LP '89

LPs: 10/12-inch

RHINO............ 5-8 89

VIDAL, Maria — P&R/D&D '84

Singles: 12-inch

EMI AMERICA............ 4-6 84

Singles: 7-inch

EMI AMERICA............ 3-4 84

Picture Sleeves

EMI AMERICA............ 3-4 84

Also see CHILD, Desmond, & Rouge

VIDEEO — R&B '82

Singles: 7-inch

H.C.R.C............ 3-5 82

VIDELS — P&R '60

(With Joe Sherman & His Orchestra; with Frank Spino & His Orchestra; Vi-Dels; Videls')

Singles: 7-inch

COLLECTABLES............ 3-4 80s
DUSTY DISC............ 5-8
JDS (5004 "Mister Lonely")............ 30-40 60
(Gray label. Reads: "Distributed by United Telefilm Records.")
JDS (5004 "Mister Lonely")............ 15-25 60
(Multi-color label. No mention of distribution by United Telefilm.)
JDS (5005 "She's Not Coming Home")............ 30-40 60
(Gray label. Reads: "Distributed by United Telefilm Records.")
JDS (5005 "She's Not Coming Home")............ 20-30 60
(Yellow label. Reads: "Distributed by United Telefilm Records.")
JDS (5005 "She's Not Coming Home")............ 10-20 60
(Multi-color label. No mention of distribution by United Telefilm.)
KAPP (361 "Streets of Love")............ 15-25 61
KAPP (405 "A Letter from Ann")............ 25-35 61
MEDIEVAL (203 "Be My Girl")............ 15-25 59
MUSICNOTE (117 "We Belong Together")............ 20-30 63
RHODY (2000 "Be My Girl")............ 50-75 59
(First issue.)
TIC-TAC-TOE (5005 "Now That Summer Is Here")............ 75-125 62

LPs: 10/12-inch

MAGIC CARPET (1005 "A Letter from the Videls")............ 8-10

Members: Pete Anders; Vinnie Poncia.
Also see SHERMAN, Joe, & His Orchestra

VIGRASS & OSBORNE — P&R '72

Singles: 7-inch

EPIC............ 3-5 74
UNI............ 3-5 72

LPs: 10/12-inch

EPIC............ 8-10 74
UNI............ 8-15 71

Members: Paul Vigrass; Gary Osborne.

VILLAGE FUGS see FUGS

VILLAGE PEOPLE — LP '77

Singles: 12-inch

CASABLANCA............ 4-8 78-79

Singles: 7-inch

CASABLANCA............ 3-5 78-79
RCA............ 3-5 81

Picture Sleeves

CASABLANCA............ 3-5 78-79
RCA............ 3-5 81

LPs: 10/12-inch

CASABLANCA (Except NBPIX – picture disc – series)............ 5-10 77-80
CASABLANCA (NBPIX series)............ 15-25 78
(Picture discs.)
RCA............ 5-10 81

Members: Victor Willis; Alexander Briley; Felipe Rose; Randy Jones; David Hodo; Glenn Hughes.

VILLAGE SOUL CHOIR — P&R/R&B '70

Singles: 7-inch

ABBOTT............ 3-5 69-70

VILLAGE STOMPERS — P&R/R&B/LP '63

Singles: 7-inch

EPIC............ 4-8 63-67

Picture Sleeves

EPIC............ 5-10 63-65

LPs: 10/12-inch

EPIC............ 10-20 63-67

Also see VINTON, Bobby, & Village Stompers

VINCENT, Gene — P&R/R&B/C&W/LP '56

(With His Blue Caps)

Singles: 78 rpm

CAPITOL............ 50-75 56-57

Promotional Singles: 78 rpm

CAPITOL............ 75-100 56-57
(White or yellow labels.)

Singles: 7-inch

CAPITOL (3450 thru 4665)............ 20-40 56-61
CAPITOL STAR LINE............ 4-8
CHALLENGE............ 15-20 66-67
FOREVER............ 10-20 69-70
KAMA SUTRA............ 8-12 70-73
PLAYGROUND (100 "Story of the Rockers")............ 150-175 68

Picture Sleeves

CAPITOL (4237 "Right Now")............ 800-1000 60

Promotional Singles: 7-inch

CAPITOL............ 50-100 56-61
(White or yellow labels.)

EPs: 7-inch

CAPITOL (438 "Dance to the Bop")............ 150-200 57
(Promotional issue only. Not issued with cover.)
CAPITOL (764 "Bluejean Bop")............ 75-125 57
(Price is for any of three volumes.)
CAPITOL (811 "Gene Vincent & His Blue Caps")............ 75-125 57
(Price is for any of three volumes.)
CAPITOL (970 "Gene Vincent Rocks & Bluecaps Roll")............ 75-125 58
(Price is for any of three volumes.)
CAPITOL (985 "Hot Rod Gang")............ 350-400 58
(Green label. Soundtrack.)
CAPITOL (985 "Hot Rod Gang")............ 400-450 58
(White label. Promotional issue.)
CAPITOL (1059 "Record Date")............ 75-125 58
(Price is for any of three volumes.)

LPs: 10/12-inch

CAPITOL (DKAO-380 "Gene Vincent's Greatest")............ 15-25 69
CAPITOL (SM-380 "Gene Vincent's Greatest")............ 5-10 78
CAPITOL (764 "Bluejean Bop")............ 200-300 56
CAPITOL (811 "Gene Vincent & His Blue Caps")............ 200-300 57
CAPITOL (970 "Gene Vincent Rocks")............ 200-300 58
CAPITOL (1059 "Gene Vincent Record Date")............ 200-300 58
CAPITOL (1207 "Sounds Like Gene Vincent")............ 200-300 59
CAPITOL (1342 "Crazy Times")............ 150-250 60
CAPITOL (11000 series)............ 8-12 74
CAPITOL (16000 series)............ 5-10 81
COLUMBIA HOUSE (516208 "Gene Vincent's Greatest")............ 8-12
DANDELION............ 10-20 70
KAMA SUTRA............ 10-20 70-71
ROLLIN' ROCK............ 5-10 80-81

Also see CHAMPS
Also see FACENDA, Tommy
Also see PRESLEY, Elvis

VINCENT, Gene / Tommy Sands / Sonny James / Ferlin Husky

LPs: 10/12-inch

CAPITOL (1009 "Teen Age Rock") 50-100 58

Also see HUSKY, Ferlin
Also see SANDS, Tommy

VINCENT, Gene / Frank Sinatra / Sonny James / Ron Goodwin

EPs: 7-inch

CAPITOL (437 "Special Hit Pressing")............ 75-100 57
(Promotional issue only. Not issued with cover.)

Also see GOODWIN, Ron
Also see JAMES, Sonny
Also see SINATRA, Frank

VINCENT, Gene / Super-Phonics

Singles: 7-inch

MEAN MOUNTAIN (1425 "Interview with Gene Vincent")............ 5-10

Also see VINCENT, Gene

VINCENT, Vinnie, Invasion — LP '86

Singles: 7-inch

CHRYSALIS............ 3-4 86-88

LPs: 10/12-inch

CHRYSALIS............ 5-8 86-88

Members: Dana Strum.
Also see KISS
Also see SLAUGHTER

VINSON, Eddie — R&B '47

(Eddie "Cleanhead" Vinson)

Singles: 78 rpm

KING............ 15-25 50-52
MERCURY............ 10-25 46-55

Singles: 7-inch

BETHLEHEM (11097 "Cherry Red")............ 8-12 61
BLUESWAY............ 4-8 67
KING (4563 "Good Bread Alley")............ 30-50 52
KING (4582 "Lonesome Train")............ 30-50 52
MERCURY (70334 "Old Man Boogie")............ 50-100 54
MERCURY (70525 "Anxious Heart")............ 50-75 54
MERCURY (70621 "Anxious Heart")............ 50-75 55
RIVERSIDE............ 5-10 62

LPs: 10/12-inch

AAMCO (312 "Eddie "Cleanhead" Vinson Sings")............ 25-35
BETHLEHEM (5005 "Eddie "Cleanhead" Vinson Sings")............ 50-75 57
BETHLEHEM (6000 series)............ 5-10 78
BLUES TIME............ 10-15 69
BLUESWAY (6007 "Cherry Red")............ 10-20 67
DELMARK............ 5-10 80
KING (634 "Eddie Vinson")............ 40-60 60
KING (1087 "Cherry Red")............ 10-15 69
MUSE............ 5-10 78-83

REGGIES 5-10 81
RIVERSIDE (3502 "Backdoor Blues") 30-40 62
Also see BROWN, Roy
Also see HARRIS, Wynonie / Roy Brown / Eddie Vinson
Also see WITHERSPOON, Jimmy / Eddie Vinson

VINSON, Eddie "Cleanhead," & Roomful of Blues

LPs: 10/12-inch

MUSE 5-10 82
Also see VINSON, Eddie

VINTON, Bobby *P&R/R&B/LP '62*

(Bobby Vinton Orchestra)

Singles: 7-inch

ABC 3-5 74-77
ALPINE 10-15 59
AURAVISION (6722 "Rain, Rain Go Away") 8-12 64
(Cardboard flexi-disc, one of six by six different artists. Columbia Record Club "Enrollment Premium." Set came in a special paper sleeve.)
CURB 3-4 88-89
ELEKTRA 3-5 78
EPIC (9000 series) 4-8 60-66
(Black vinyl.)
EPIC (9000 series) 8-10 64
(Colored vinyl.)
EPIC (10000 series) 3-6 66-75
EPIC MEMORY LANE 3-5 87
LARC 3-4 83
MELODY 10-15 59
TAPESTRY 3-5 79-82

Picture Sleeves

EPIC 3-8 62-72
TAPESTRY 3-5 80

EPs: 7-inch

EPIC 6-12 63-65
(Juke box issues.)

LPs: 10/12-inch

ABC 8-10 74-77
CSP 5-10 80s
COLUMBIA 8-10 73
EPIC (500 series) 20-25 60
EPIC (3000 series) 15-20 60
EPIC (20000 series) 8-15 62-70
(Black vinyl.)
EPIC (20468 "Blue on Blue") 20-40 63
(Colored vinyl. Promotional issue only.)
EPIC (30000 series) 5-10 72-79
HARMONY 5-10 70
TAPESTRY 5-10 80
Also see CLARK, Dave, Five / New Christy Minstrels / Bobby Vinton / Jerry Vale

VINTON, Bobby / Chuck & Johnny

Singles: 7-inch

DIAMOND (121 "I Love You the Way You Are") 5-8 62

VINTON, Bobby, & Village Stompers

LPs: 10/12-inch

EPIC 10-20 66
Also see VILLAGE STOMPERS
Also see VINTON, Bobby

VIN-ZEE *R&B '81*

Singles: 7-inch

EMERGENCY 3-5 81

VIO-LENCE *LP '88*

LPs: 10/12-inch

MECHANIC 5-8 88

VIOLENT FEMMES *LP '86*

Singles: 7-inch

SLASH 3-4 83-90

LPs: 10/12-inch

SLASH 5-8 83-91
Members: Gordon Gano; Brian Ritchie; Victor DeLorenzo.

VIRTUE, Frank

(Frank Virtue Combo; Frank Virtuoso)

Singles: 78 rpm

ARCADE 5-10 55

Singles: 7-inch

ARCADE 10-15 55
JOY 5-10 63

LPs: 10/12-inch

FAYETTE 25-35 64
Also see VIRTUES
Also see VIRTUOSO, Frank

VIRTUES *P&R/R&B '59*

(With the Virtues; Frank Virtuoso & Virtues; Frank Virtuoso & His Quintet)

Singles: 7-inch

ABC 3-5 73
ABC-PAR 5-10 59
ARCADE 8-12 50s
B.V.D. 5-10
FAYETTE 4-8 64
HIGHLAND 10-15 60
HUNT (Monaural) 5-10 59
HUNT (Stereo) 15-25 59
RHYTHM 8-12 50s
SURE (500 series) 8-12 59
SURE (1700 series) 4-8 62
VIRNON 5-10 60
VIRTUE 5-10 66-69
WYNNE 5-10 60

LPs: 10/12-inch

STRAND 20-25 60
WYNNE 25-30 60

VIRTUOSO, Frank

Singles: 7-inch

LIBERTY (55706 "Move On") 10-20 64
REFRESHMENT (1 "Mountaineer Mashed Potatoes") 25-50 60s
RHYTHM (13 "Rollin' & Rockin' ") 20-30
TONE-CRAFT (206 "San Antonio Rose") 10-20
TONE-CRAFT (207 "Rollin' and Rockin' ") 50-75
Also see VIRTUE, Frank
Also see VIRTUES

VISAGE *LP '81*

Singles: 12-inch

POLYDOR 4-6 80-82

Singles: 7-inch

POLYDOR 3-5 81

LPs: 10/12-inch

POLYDOR 5-10 80-82

VISCOUNTS *P&R '59*

(Vicounts)

Singles: 7-inch

AMY 5-10 65-66
CORAL 4-8 66-67
MADISON 10-15 59-61
MR. PEACOCK 8-12 61
MR. PEEKE 5-10 63
REO (8435 "Harlem Nocturne") 10-15 59
(Canadian.)

LPs: 10/12-inch

AMY (8008 "Harlem Nocturne") 20-30 65
MADISON (1001 "Viscounts") 50-75 60
Members: Bobby Spievak; Joe Spievak; Harry Haller; Larry Vecchio; Clark Smith.

VISUAL *R&B/D&D '83*

Singles: 12-inch

PRELUDE 4-6 83-84

Singles: 7-inch

PRELUDE 3-4 83-84

VITALE, Joe *LP '81*

Singles: 7-inch

ASYLUM 3-5 81-82
ATLANTIC 3-5 74

LPs: 10/12-inch

ASYLUM 5-10 81
ATLANTIC 5-10 74
Also see EAGLES
Also see WALSH, Joe

VITAMIN E *R&B '77*

Singles: 7-inch

BUDDAH 3-5 77

VITAMIN Z *P&R/D&D/LP '85*

Singles: 12-inch

GEFFEN 4-6 85

Singles: 7-inch

GEFFEN 3-4 85

Picture Sleeves

GEFFEN 3-4 85

LPs: 10/12-inch

GEFFEN 5-8 85
Member: Geoff Barradale.
Also see PARSONS, Alan, Project

VITO & SALUTATIONS *P&R '63*

Singles: 7-inch

APT (25079 "Walkin'") 25-35 65
BOOM (60020 "Bring Back Yesterday") 15-25 66
CRYSTAL BALL 4-8 78
HERALD (583 "Unchained Melody") 15-25 63
HERALD (586 "Extraordinary Girl") ... 20-30 63
KRAM (1202 "Your Way") 50-100 62
(First issue. Reissue is on "Kran.")
KRAN (125 "Your Way") 25-30 62
(At least one source shows this number as 5002.)
RAYNA (5009 "Gloria") 25-40 62
RED BOY (1001 "So Wonderful") 15-25 66
RED BOY (5009 "Gloria") 15-25 66
REGINA (1320 "Get a Job") 15-25 64
RUST (5106 "Can I Depend on You") 15-25 66
SANDBAG (103 "So Wonderful") 10-20 68
WELLS (1008 "Can I Depend on You") 20-40 64
(Black vinyl.)
WELLS (1008 "Can I Depend on You") 40-60 64
(Colored vinyl.)

LPs: 10/12-inch

KAPE (1002 "Greatest Hits") 10-15 73
RED BOY (200 "Greatest Hits") 20-30 81
Members: Vito Balsamo; Shelly Buchansky; Randy Silverman; Len Citrin; Frank Fox.

VIXEN *P&R/LP '88*

Singles: 7-inch

EMI 3-4 88-90

Picture Sleeves

EMI 3-4 88-89

LPs: 10/12-inch

EMI 5-8 88-90
Members: Janet Gardner; Share Pedersen; Jan Kuehnemund; Roxy Petrucci.

VOCALEERS *R&B '53*

("Vocaleers and Joe Duncan"; "with Rhythm Accompaniment")

Singles: 78 rpm

RED ROBIN 25-75 52

Singles: 7-inch

OLD TOWN (1089 "This Is the Night") 15-25 60
OLDIES 45 .... 4-6 65
PARADISE (113 "Have You Ever Loved Someone") 50-75 59
RED ROBIN (113 "Be True") 300-400 52
RED ROBIN (114 "Is It a Dream") 200-300 52
RED ROBIN (119 "I Walk Alone") 300-400 53
RED ROBIN (125 "Will You Be True") 300-400 54
RED ROBIN (132 "Angel Face") ... 300-400 54
TWISTIME (11 "A Golden Tear") 15-25 62
VEST (832 "Hear My Plea") 150-225 60

LPs: 10/12-inch

RELIC (5084 "Is It a Dream") 5-10 92
Members: Joe Duncan; Curtis Dunham; Ted Williams; Mel Walton; Bill Walker; Lamarr Cooper; Joe Powell; Richard Blandon; Leo Fuller; Curtis Blandon; Caesar Williams.
Also see LITTLE ESTHER & Junior with the Johnny Otis Orchestra / Johnny Otis Orchestra with the Vocaleers

VOCALEERS / Mango Jones

Singles: 7-inch

OLDIES 45 .... 4-6 65
Also see VOCALEERS

VOGUES P&R '65

Singles: 7-inch

ABC..3-5 73
ABC-PAR....................................4-8 65
ASTRA (1030 "You're the One")..........4-6 73
(Black vinyl.)
ASTRA (1030 "You're the One")..........5-8 73
(Colored vinyl.)
BELL..3-5 71
BLUE STAR (229 "You're the One") 10-20 65
CO & CE....................................4-8 65-67
COLLECTABLES............................3-4 80s
ERA...3-5 70s
GOLDIES 45................................3-5 73
GUSTO......................................3-4 81
MGM..4-8 67
MAINSTREAM..............................3-5 72
REPRISE (Except 0663)..................3-6 68-71
REPRISE (0663 "Just What I've Been Looking For")..........5-10 68
REVUE......................................4-8 68
ROCK'N MANIA............................3-4
SSS INT'L..................................3-4 77
SUN...3-5 77-79
20TH FOX..................................3-5 73-74

LPs: 10/12-inch

CSP...5-8 82
CO & CE..................................25-35 65-66
51 WEST...................................5-10 80s
PICKWICK.................................8-10 71
PLANTATION (43 "Golden Hits")..........5-8 81
REPRISE..................................10-15 68-70
RHINO......................................5-8 88
SSS INT'L (34 "Greatest Hits")..........5-10 77
SEARS.....................................15-20 60s

Members: Bob Bush; Bill Burkette; Hugh Geyer; Chuck Blasko; Don Miller. SSS Int'l/Plantation/51 West/CSP line-up: Charly Tichenor; Dick Stevens; Kelly Goad; Bill Packard; Bill Davidson.

VOICE MASTERS R&B '70

Singles: 7-inch

ANNA (101 "Hope and Pray")..........50-100 59
ANNA (102 "Needed")....................50-100 59
BAMBOO....................................8-15 68-70
FRISCO (15235 "In Love in Vain")..75-125 60
(Identification number shown since no selection number is used.)

Members: Ty Hunter; C.P. Spencer; Lamont Dozier; David Ruffin; Freddie Gorman.
Also see DOZIER, Lamont
Also see HUNTER, Ty
Also see ORIGINALS
Also see RUFFIN, David

VOICES OF AMERICA / U.S.A. for Africa P&R '86

Singles: 7-inch

EMI AMERICA..............................3-4 86

Picture Sleeves

EMI AMERICA..............................3-4 86
Also see TOTO
Also see U.S.A. for AFRICA

VOICES OF EAST HARLEM LP '70

Singles: 7-inch

ELEKTRA...................................3-5 70-72
JUST SUNSHINE...........................3-5 73-74

LPs: 10/12-inch

ELEKTRA...................................8-10 70
JUST SUNSHINE...........................5-10 73-74

VOIVOD LP '89

LPs: 10/12-inch

MECHANIC.................................5-8 89

VOLCANOS R&B '65

Singles: 7-inch

ARCTIC.....................................4-8 65-67
VIRTUE.....................................3-5 70
Member: Gene Faith.
Also see FAITH, Gene
Also see MFSB

VOLLENWEIDER, Andreas LP '84

Singles: 12-inch

CBS/COLUMBIA...........................4-6 86

Singles: 7-inch

CBS/COLUMBIA...........................3-4 86

LPs: 10/12-inch

CBS/COLUMBIA...........................5-8 84-89

VOLTAGE BROTHERS R&B '86

Singles: 12-inch

MTM..4-6 86

Singles: 7-inch

LIFESONG..................................3-4 78
MTM..3-4 86

LPs: 10/12-inch

LIFESONG..................................5-8 78
MTM..5-8 86

VOLUMES P&R '62

Singles: 7-inch

ABC...3-5 73
AMERICAN ARTS (6 "Gotta Give Her Love")...........20-30 64
AMERICAN ARTS (I Just Can't Help Myself")...........20-30 65
CHEX (1002 "I Love You")...............25-50 62
(First issued crediting the "Valume's.")
CHEX (1005 "The Bell")..................25-50 62
MPACT (1017 "That Same Old Feeling")...........25-50 66
INFERNO...................................10-20 67-68
JUBILEE (5446 "Sandra")................20-30 63
JUBILEE (5454 "Our Song")..............15-25 63
OLD TOWN (1154 "Why")..................10-20 64
TWIRL (2016 "I Got Love")..............25-50 61
VIRGO......................................3-5 73

LPs: 10/12-inch

RELIC......................................5-10 85
Also see NUTMEGS / Volumes
Also see VALUMES

VOLZ, Ron, & Rockin' R's

Singles: 7-inch

TEMPUS (1515 "I'm Still in Love with You")...........75-125 59
Also see ROCKIN' R's

VONTASTICS P&R/R&B '66

Singles: 7-inch

CHESS......................................4-8 67
ST. LAWRENCE............................4-8 65-66
SATELLITE (2002 "I'll Never Say Goodbye")...........25-35 65
Also see FANTASTIC VONTASTICS

VOUDOURIS, Roger P&R/LP '79

Singles: 7-inch

W.B...3-5 78-79

LPs: 10/12-inch

W.B...5-10 78

VOXPOPPERS P&R/R&B '58

Singles: 7-inch

AMP 3 (1004 "Wishing for Your Love")...........30-40 58
MERCURY (71282 "Wishing for Your Love")...........10-20 58
MERCURY (71315 "Pony Tail")........10-15 58
POPLAR (107 "Come Back Little Girl")...........15-25 58
POPLAR (112 "Come Back Little Girl")...........15-25 58
(Each of the Poplar discs has a different flip.)
VERSAILLES (200 "A Blessing After All")...........20-40 59

EPs: 7-inch

MERCURY (3391 "Voxpoppers")....75-125 58

VOYAGE R&B/LP '78

Singles: 7-inch

ATLANTIC..................................3-5 82
MARLIN.....................................3-5 78-79

LPs: 10/12-inch

ATLANTIC..................................5-8 82
MARLIN.....................................5-10 78

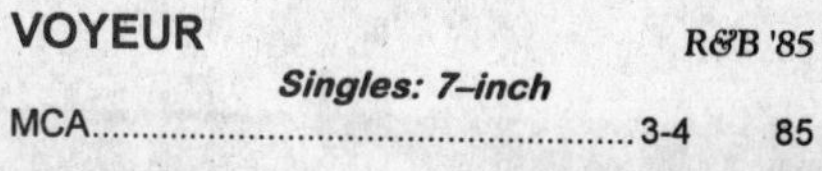

VOYEUR R&B '85

Singles: 7-inch

MCA..3-4 85

1220 CLUB
Souvenier Copy
45 RPM
MY HEART CRYS
KNIGHT RIDERS
Featuring
BILLY VERA
MCR STUDIOS
Stamford, Conn.

RON
R 118
Ron Pub. Co.
2:16
SET ME FREE
(D. Labostrie)
IRMA THOMAS
328
DIVISION OF RIC RECORDS INC. NEW ORLEANS

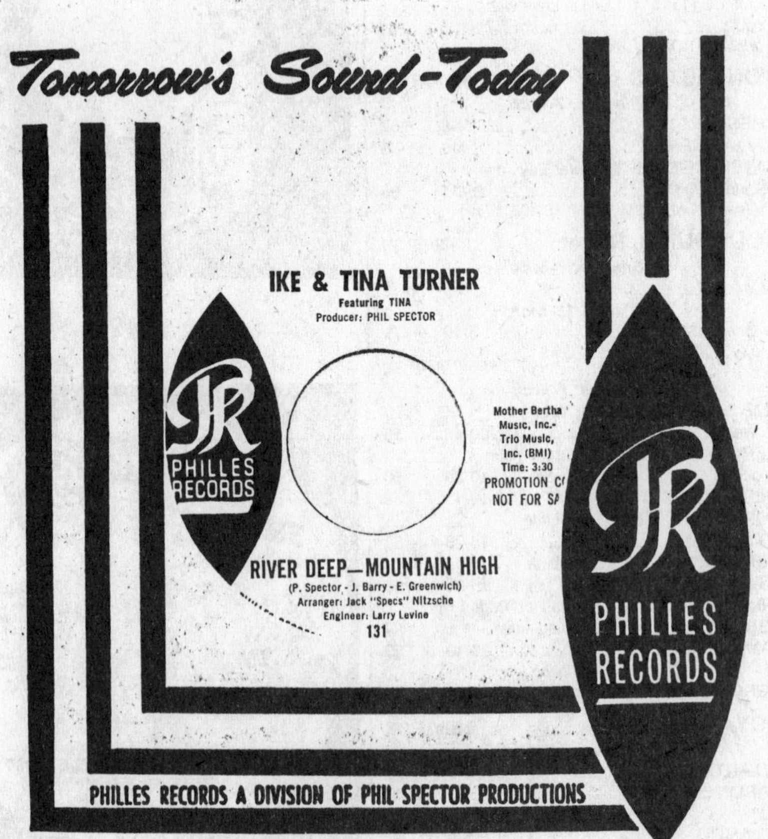
Tomorrow's Sound-Today
IKE & TINA TURNER
Featuring TINA
Producer: PHIL SPECTOR
PHILLES RECORDS
Mother Bertha Music, Inc.-
Trio Music, Inc. (BMI)
Time: 3:30
RIVER DEEP—MOUNTAIN HIGH
(P. Spector - J. Barry - E. Greenwich)
Arranger: Jack "Specs" Nitzsche
Engineer: Larry Levine
131
PHILLES RECORDS
PHILLES RECORDS A DIVISION OF PHIL SPECTOR PRODUCTIONS

THE LAST DRAG
GUITAR STROLL
THE VOXPOPPERS

JOHN TRAVOLTA
LET HER IN

W.A.G.B. *P&R '82*

Singles: 7-inch

STREET SOUNDS....3-4 82

W.A.S.P. *LP '84*

Singles: 7-inch

CAPITOL....3-4 84-89

Picture Sleeves

CAPITOL....3-4 84-87

LPs: 10/12-inch

CAPITOL....5-8 84-89

Members: Blackie Lawless; Randy Piper; Chris Holmes; Steve Riley.

Also see L.A. GUNS

Also see NEW YORK DOLLS

WA WA NEE *P&R/LP '87*

Singles: 7-inch

EPIC....3-4 87-88

Singles: 7-inch

EPIC....3-4 87

Picture Sleeves

EPIC....3-4 87

LPs: 10/12-inch

EPIC....5-8 87

WACKERS *P&R '72*

Singles: 7-inch

BOMP....3-5 75

ELEKTRA....3-5 71-73

LPs: 10/12-inch

ELEKTRA....5-10 71-72

Member: Spence Earnshaw.

WADE, Adam *P&R '60*

(With George Paxton, His Orchestra and the Bel-Aire Singers)

Singles: 7-inch

COED....8-12 59-61

EPIC....4-8 62-66

KIRSHNER....3-5 77

REMEMBER....4-6 69

W.B. 4-6 67-68

Picture Sleeves

COED....5-10 60-61

EPIC....4-8 62-63

EPs: 7-inch

COED (102 "Adam Wade")....10-20 60

(Promotional issue only.)

LPs: 10/12-inch

COED....20-25 60

EPIC....15-20 62

KIRSHNER....5-10 77

WADSWORTH MANSION *P&R '70*

Singles: 7-inch

SUSSEX....3-5 70

LPs: 10/12-inch

SUSSEX....10-20 71

(Mistakenly shown as "Wadsworth Manison" on some issues.)

WAGNER, Jack *P&R/LP '84*

Singles: 7-inch

QWEST....3-4 84-87

Picture Sleeves

QWEST....3-4 84-87

LPs: 10/12-inch

QWEST....5-8 84-87

WAGONER, Porter *C&W '54*

Singles: 78 rpm

RCA....5-10 53-57

Singles: 7-inch

RCA (0013 thru 1007)....3-6 69-74

RCA (5086 thru 7638)....5-15 53-59

RCA (7708 thru 9979)....3-8 60-71

RCA (10124 thru 11998)....3-5 74-79

W.B. 3-4 82-83

EPs: 7-inch

RCA....8-15 56

LPs: 10/12-inch

ACCORD....5-8 82

CAMDEN....5-15 63-73

COUNTRY FIDELITY....5-8 82

H.S.R.D. (782 "Natural Wonder")....15-25 81

MCA/DOT....5-8 86

MUSIC MASTERS....5-10

PICKWICK....5-10 75-77

RCA (Except 1300 through 2900 series)....5-15 66-79

RCA (1358 "A Satisfied Mind")....30-40 56

RCA (LPM-2447 thru LPM-2960)....10-20 62-65

(Monaural.)

RCA (LSP-2447 thru LSP-2960)....15-25 62-65

(Stereo.)

TUDOR....5-8 84

W.B. 5-8 83

Also see SNOW, Hank / Hank Locklin / Porter Wagoner

WAGONER, Porter, & Skeeter Davis

LPs: 10/12-inch

RCA....10-20 62

Also see DAVIS, Skeeter

WAGONER, Porter, & Dolly Parton *C&W '67*

Singles: 7-inch

RCA....3-6 67-80

LPs: 10/12-inch

RCA (Except 3926 thru 4841)....5-10 74-80

RCA (LPM-3926 "Just Between You and Me")....30-40 68

(Monaural.)

RCA (LSP-3926 thru LSP-4841)....10-20 68-73

(Stereo.)

Also see PARTON, Dolly

Also see WAGONER, Porter

WAIKIKIS *P&R '64*

Singles: 7-inch

KAPP....3-6 64-68

PALETTE....3-6 62-63

LPs: 10/12-inch

BOOT....5-8 78

KAPP....8-15 64-69

MCA....5-8 80s

WAILERS *P&R/R&B '59*

Singles: 7-inch

BELL....4-8 67

ETIQUETTE....5-15 63-66

GOLDEN CREST....10-20 59

(Label pictures the group.)

GOLDEN CREST....5-10 60-64

(No group picture on label.)

IMPERIAL....5-10 64

U.A. 4-8 67

VIVA....4-6 67

LPs: 10/12-inch

BELL (6016 "Walk Thru the People")....10-15 68

ETIQUETTE (1 "The Fabulous Wailers at the Castle")....75-100 66

ETIQUETTE (022 "The Wailers and Company")....40-60 66

ETIQUETTE (023 "Wailers Wailers Everywhere")....75-100 66

ETIQUETTE (026 "Out of Our Tree")....40-60 60s

(Reissues of Etiquette LPs have a 1980s date on back cover.)

ETIQUETTE (1100 series)....5-8 86

ETIQUETTE (22296/97 "The Wailers and Their Greatest Hits")....10-20 79

(Two discs. Includes a note from Etiquette's Roger Hart.)

GOLDEN CREST (3075 "The Fabulous Wailers")....100-150 60

(Color cover photo.)

GOLDEN CREST (3075 "The Fabulous Wailers")....40-60 60

(Black and white cover.)

GOLDEN CREST (3075 "The Wailers Wail")....25-35 60s

IMPERIAL....15-20 64

U.A. (3557 "Outburst!")....25-35 67

(Monaural.)

U.A. (6557 "Outburst!")....35-45 67

(Stereo.)

Members: Kent Morrill; Robin Roberts; Gail Harris; Mark Marush; Rich Dangel; John "Buck" Ormsby; Mike Burk; Neil Anderson; Ron Gardner; Dave Roland.

Also see THREE GRACES / Wailers

WAINWRIGHT, Loudon, III *P&R/LP '73*

Singles: 7-inch

ARISTA....3-5 76-78

COLUMBIA....3-5 73

LPs: 10/12-inch

ARISTA....5-10 76-78

ATLANTIC....10-15 70-71

COLUMBIA ("KC" series)....10-15 72-73

COLUMBIA ("PC" series)....5-10 75

ROUNDER....5-10 80-83

Also see SPRINGSTEEN, Bruce / Albert Hammond / Loudon Wainwright, III / Taj Mahal

WAITE, John *LP '82*

Singles: 12-inch

EMI AMERICA....4-6 84

Singles: 7-inch

CHRYSALIS....3-4 82-85

EMI AMERICA....3-4 84-87

Picture Sleeves

CHRYSALIS....3-4 85

EMI AMERICA....3-5 84-87

LPs: 10/12-inch

CHRYSALIS....5-8 82

EMI AMERICA....5-8 84-87

Also see BABYS

WAITRESSES *P&R/LP '82*

Singles: 7-inch

ANTILLES....3-5 80

POLYDOR....3-4 82

LPs: 10/12-inch

POLYDOR....5-8 82-83

WAITS, Tom *LP '75*

Singles: 7-inch

ASYLUM....3-5 74

ELEKTRA....3-4 83

ISLAND....3-4 83-88

LPs: 10/12-inch

ASYLUM....5-10 73-80

ELEKTRA....5-8 83

ISLAND....5-8 83-88

Also see GAYLE, Crystal, & Tom Waits

WAKELY, Jimmy *P&R '43*

(With Les Baxter Chorus; with Velma Williams)

Singles: 78 rpm

CAPITOL....3-6 48-52

CORAL....3-6 53-55

DECCA....4-8 43-57

JIMMY WAKELY SOUVENIR....5-10 50s

Singles: 7-inch

ARTCO....3-5 74

CAPITOL (1300 thru 2100 series)....5-10 50-52

CORAL....4-8 53-55

DECCA....3-8 55-70

DOT....3-6 66

SHASTA (100 series)....3-6 58-67

SHASTA (200 series)....3-4 71

Picture Sleeves

SHASTA....5-10 58

EPs: 7-inch

CAPITOL....10-20 50-53

CORAL....10-15 54

DECCA....8-12 58

LPs: 10/12-inch

ALBUM GLOBE....5-10 81

CAPITOL (4008 "Songs of the West")....25-50 50
(10–inch LP.)
CAPITOL (9004 "Christmas on the Range")....20-40 53
(10–inch LP.)
CORAL....4-8 73
DANNY....8-10
DECCA (8400 thru 8600 series)....20-35 56-57
DECCA (75000 thru 78000 series)....8-18 67-70
DOT....10-15 66
MCA....4-8 80s
MCR....10-15 74
SHASTA....5-15 58-75
TOPS....10-15
VOCALION....5-10 68-70
Also see CHANDLER, Karen, & Jimmy Wakely
Also see WHITING, Margaret, & Jimmy Wakely

WAKELIN, Johnny, & Kinshasa Band P&R '75
Singles: 7–inch
PYE....3-5 75

WAKEMAN, Rick LP '73
(With the London Symphony Orchestra & English Chamber Choir; with English Rock Ensemble)
Singles: 7–inch
A&M....3-5 73
LPs: 10/12–inch
A&M (3000 series)....5-10 74
A&M (4000 series)....5-12 73-77
A&M (QU-5000 series)....10-20 74
(Quadraphonic.)
A&M (6000 series)....10-15 79
MFSL (230 "Journey to the Centre of the Earth")....20-25 94
Also see DALTREY, Roger, & Rick Wakeman
Also see STRAWBS
Also see YES

WALDEN, Narada Michael R&B '77
(Narada)
Singles: 12–inch
ATLANTIC....4-6 82-83
NARADA (17254 "Narada Sampler")....5-8 86
(Promotional issue only.)
W.B....4-6 85
Singles: 7–inch
ATLANTIC....3-5 77-83
REPRISE....3-4 88
W.B....3-4 85
Picture Sleeves
NARADA (17254 "Narada Sampler")..5-10 86
(Promotional issue only.)
LPs: 10/12–inch
ATLANTIC....5-10 79-83

WALDEN, Narada Michael, & Patti Austin R&B '85
Singles: 7–inch
W.B....3-4 85
Also see AUSTIN, Patti

WALDMAN, Wendy P&R '78
Singles: 7–inch
EPIC....3-4 82-83
W.B....3-5 77-78
LPs: 10/12–inch
EPIC....5-8 82-83
W.B....5-10 78

WALDO R&B '82
Singles: 7–inch
COLUMBIA....3-5 82
LPs: 10/12–inch
COLUMBIA....5-10 82

WALKER, Billy C&W '54
Singles: 78 rpm
COLUMBIA....4-8 54-56
Singles: 7–inch
CAPRICE....3-4 79-80
CASINO....3-5 77
COLUMBIA (21000 series)....6-12 54-56
COLUMBIA (33000 series)....4-6 60s
COLUMBIA (40000 series)....5-10 56-60
COLUMBIA (42000 & 43000 series)....4-8 61-65
DIMENSION....3-4 83
MCA....3-5 77
MGM....3-5 70-74
MRC....3-4 77-78
MONUMENT....3-6 66-70
PAID....3-4 80
RCA....3-5 75-76
SCORPION....3-4 78
TALL TEXAN....3-4 85-88
Picture Sleeves
COLUMBIA....4-8 63-67
LPs: 10/12–inch
COLUMBIA....10-20 63-69
GUSTO....5-8 80s
H.S.R.D....5-10 84
HARMONY....8-15 64-70
MGM....6-12 70-74
MONUMENT....8-18 66-72
RCA....5-10 75-76

WALKER, Billy, & Barbara Fairchild C&W '80
Singles: 7–inch
PAID....3-5 81
LPs: 10/12–inch
PAID....5-10 81
Also see FAIRCHILD, Barbara

WALKER, Billy, & Brenda Kaye Perry C&W '77
Singles: 7–inch
MRC....3-5 77
Also see WALKER, Billy

WALKER, Bobbi R&B '80
Singles: 7–inch
CASABLANCA....3-5 80

WALKER, Boots P&R '67
Singles: 7–inch
PROVIDENCE....4-6 66
RUST....4-8 67-68

WALKER, David T. R&B '69
Singles: 7–inch
ODE....3-5 73-76
REVUE....4-6 68-69
ZEA....4-6 70
LPs: 10/12–inch
ODE....8-10 74-76
REVUE....10-15 68-69

WALKER, Gloria P&R/R&B '68
(With the Chevelles)
Singles: 7–inch
FEDERAL....5-10 72
FLAMING ARROW....4-8 68-69
PEOPLE....3-5

WALKER, Jerry Jeff P&R '68
Singles: 7–inch
ATCO....3-6 68-70
MCA....3-5 73-80
SOUTH COAST....3-4 81
TRIED & TRUE....3-4 89
LPs: 10/12–inch
ATCO (Except 297)....15-20 68-70
ATCO (297 "Five Years Gone")....30-50 69
DECCA....10-12 72
ELEKTRA....8-10 70s
MCA....5-10 73-80
SOUTH COAST....5-10 81
VANGUARD....10-12 69

WALKER, Jimmy LP '75
Singles: 7–inch
BUDDAH....3-5 75
LPs: 10/12–inch
BUDDAH....8-10 75

WALKER, Junior P&R/R&B/LP '65
(With the All Stars; with All the Stars; Junior Walker All Stars; Jr. Walker)
Singles: 12–inch
WHITFIELD....4-8 79
Singles: 7–inch
HARVEY....10-20 62-64
MOTOWN....3-4 83
SOUL (Except 35003)....5-12 65-76
(Black vinyl.)
SOUL (35003 "Monkey Jump")....10-15 64
SOUL (Colored vinyl)....8-12 70-72
(Promotional issues only.)
WHITFIELD....3-5 79
Picture Sleeves
SOUL....4-8 65-66
EPs: 7–inch
SOUL (69701 "Shotgun")....15-25 66
SOUL (69702 "Soul Sessions")....15-25 66
SOUL (69703 "Road Runner")....15-25 66
LPs: 10/12–inch
MOTOWN (Except 700 series)....5-10 80-83
MOTOWN (700 series)....8-12 74
SOUL (701 "Shotgun")....20-30 66
SOUL (702 "Soul Sessions")....20-30 66
SOUL (703 "Road Runner")....20-30 66
SOUL (705 "Live")....20-30 66
SOUL (710 "Home Cookin'")....15-20 69
SOUL (718 "Greatest Hits")....10-20 69
SOUL (718 "Greatest Hits")....10-20 69
SOUL (721 "What Does It Take")....10-20 69
SOUL (725 thru 750)....5-15 70-78
SOUL (35073 "Jr. Walker")....15-25 60s
(Colored vinyl. Promotional issue only.)
WHITFIELD....8-10 79
Members: Autry Dewalt II (Jr. Walker); Willie Woods; Vic Thomas; James Graves.
Also see FOREIGNER

WALKER, T-Bone P&R '47
("With His Guitar")
Singles: 78 rpm
ATLANTIC....10-20 55
BLACK & WHITE....15-25 46-48
COMET....15-25 48-49
CAPITOL....15-25 45-50
IMPERIAL....15-25 50-57
MERCURY....15-25 46
POST....15-25 55
RHUMBOOGIE....15-25 45-46
Singles: 7–inch
ATLANTIC (1065 Papa Ain't Salty")..30-40 55
ATLANTIC (1074 "Why Not")....30-40 55
BLUESWAY....4-8 67
CAPITOL (799 "On Your Way Blues")....50-100 49
CAPITOL (944 "Too Much Trouble Blues")....50-100 50
IMPERIAL (5202 "Street Walkin' Woman")....40-60 52
IMPERIAL (5216 "Blue Mood")....35-50 53
IMPERIAL (5228 "Railroad Station Blues")....25-50 53
IMPERIAL (5239 "Party Girl")....35-50 53
IMPERIAL (5247 "Everytime")....35-50 53
IMPERIAL (5261 "I'm About to Lose My Mind")....35-50 53
IMPERIAL (5264 "Pony Tail")....35-50 54
IMPERIAL (5274 "Vida Lee")....35-50 54
IMPERIAL (5284 "Bye Bye Baby")....35-50 54
IMPERIAL (5299 "Teenage Baby")....35-50 54
IMPERIAL (5311 "Love Is a Gamble")....20-40 55
IMPERIAL (5330 "I'll Understand")....20-40 55
IMPERIAL (5384 "Welcome Blues")..20-40 56
IMPERIAL (5695 thru 5962)....10-20 60-63
JET STREAM....5-10 66
MODERN....5-10 65
POST (2002 "I Get So Weary")....25-50 55
EPs: 7–inch
CAPITOL (370 "Classics in Jazz")....75-125 53
LPs: 10/12–inch
ATLANTIC (8020 "T-Bone Blues")..75-100 59
(Black label.)
ATLANTIC (8020 "T-Bone Blues")....50-75 60
(Red label.)
ATLANTIC (8256 "T-Bone Blues")....10-15 70
BLUE NOTE....8-12
BLUESTIME....8-12 73
BLUESWAY....10-15 67-73

BRUNSWICK 10-15 68
CAPITOL (H-370 "Classics in Jazz") 250-350 53
(10–inch LP.)
CAPITOL (T-370 "Classics in Jazz") 150-250 56
CAPITOL (1958 "Great Blues Vocals and Guitar") 40-60 63
DELMARK 8-10
FLYING DUTCHMAN/BLUESTIME .. 10-15 69
HOMECOOKING 8-12
IMPERIAL (9098 "T-Bone Walker Sings the Blues") 50-75 59
IMPERIAL (9116 "Singing the Blues") 50-75 60
IMPERIAL (9146 "I Get So Weary") .. 50-75 61
POLYDOR 10-15 70-73
REPRISE 10-15 73
WET SOUL 10-20 67

Also see GLENN, Lloyd
Also see McCRACKLIN, Jimmy / T-Bone Walker / Charles Brown
Also see WITHERSPOON, Jimmy
Also see X-RAYS

WALKER BROTHERS — P&R '65

Singles: 7–inch

SMASH 4-8 64-66

Picture Sleeves

SMASH 5-10 65-66

LPs: 10/12–inch

SMASH 20-25 66-67

Members: Scott Engel; John Maus; Gary Leeds.

WALL OF VOODOO — LP '81

Singles: 12–inch

I.R.S. 4-6 83

Singles: 7–inch

I.R.S. 3-5 81-83

Picture Sleeves

I.R.S. 3-5 83

LPs: 10/12–inch

I.R.S. 5-10 81-83

Member: Stan Ridgway.
Also see COPELAND, Stewart, & Stan Ridgway
Also see RIDGWAY, Stan

WALLACE, Jerry — P&R '54

(With the Jewels; with Jay Rand Orchestra & Chorus)

Singles: 78 rpm

ALLIED 5-15 51-54
ALPHA 4-8
CHALLENGE 10-20 57
CLASS 5-10 53
MERCURY 5-10 55-56
TOPS 5-10 53
VOGUE 5-10 52
WING 5-10 56

Singles: 7–inch

ALLIED 10-15 54
BMA 3-5 77-78
CHALLENGE (1000 series) 10-15 57
CHALLENGE (9100 series) 4-8 61-63
CHALLENGE (59000 through 59098) 10-20 58-60
CHALLENGE (59200 series) 4-8 63-65
CLASS 8-12 53
DECCA 3-5 71-72
DOOR KNOB 3-5 79-80
ERIC 3-4 70s
4-STAR 3-5 78-79
GLENOLDEN 3-6 68
GUSTO 3-4 80s
LIBERTY 3-5 67-70
MCA 3-4 73-74
MGM 3-5 75-76
MERCURY (70000 series) 5-10 55-56
MERCURY (72000 series) 4-8 64-66
SUNSET 5-10
TOPS 8-12 53
U.A. 3-5 72-75
VOGUE 10-15 52
WING 8-12 56

Picture Sleeves

CHALLENGE (59013 thru 59098) 8-12 58-60
CHALLENGE (59200 series) 4-8 63-65

EPs: 7–inch

CHALLENGE 15-25 60

LPs: 10/12–inch

BMA 8-10 77
CHALLENGE (606 "Just Jerry") 30-35 59
CHALLENGE (612 "There She Goes") 20-25 61
CHALLENGE (616 "Shutters and Boards") 15-25 63
CHALLENGE (619 "In the Misty Moonlight") 15-25 64
CHALLENGE (2002 "Greatest Hits") 10-15 69
DECCA 8-12 71-72
4-STAR 5-8 83
LIBERTY 10-12 68
MCA 8-10 73-74
MGM 8-10 75
MERCURY 10-20 66
PICKWICK 5-10 70s
U.A. 8-12 72-75
WING 10-12 68

Also see BARE, Bobby / Donna Fargo / Jerry Wallace

WALLACE, Jerry / Soul Surfers

Singles: 7–inch

CHALLENGE 4-8 64

Also see WALLACE, Jerry

WALLACE BROTHERS — P&R '64

Singles: 7–inch

JEWEL 4-6 68-69
SIMS 4-8 63-67

LPs: 10/12–inch

SIMS 15-20 65

Members: Johnny Wallace; Ervin Wallace.

WALLIS, Ruth — P&R '53

(With the Deluxe Rhumba Band)

Singles: 78 rpm

DE-LUXE 5-10 47
KING 5-10 52-53
MONARCH 5-10 53-54
WALLIS ORIGINAL 5-10 55-57

Singles: 7–inch

DE-LUXE 10-20 51
KING 10-20 52-53
MONARCH 10-15 53-54
WALLIS ORIGINAL 10-20 55-57

EPs: 7–inch

KING (215/216/217 "House Party") 15-25 52
(Price is for any of three volumes.)

LPs: 10/12–inch

KING (6 "Rhumba Party") 75-100 52
(10–inch LP.)
KING (9 "House Party") 75-100 52
(10–inch LP.)
KING (507 "House Party") 50-100 56
WALLIS ORIGINAL (2 "Ruth Wallis") 20-30 57

WALSH, Joe — LP '72

Singles: 7–inch

ABC 3-5 75-78
ASYLUM 3-5 78-81
DUNHILL 3-5 73-75
FULL MOON 3-5 80-83
MCA 3-5 79

Picture Sleeves

FULL MOON 3-5 80-83

LPs: 10/12–inch

ABC 5-10 76-78
ASYLUM 5-10 78-81
COMMAND 8-12 74-75
DUNHILL 8-10 72-74
MCA 5-10 79
W.B. 5-8 83-87

Also see EAGLES
Also see JAMES GANG
Also see SIMPSONS
Also see VITALE, Joe

WALSH, Steve — LP '80

Singles: 7–inch

KIRSHNER 3-5 80

LPs: 10/12–inch

KIRSHNER 5-10 80

Also see KANSAS

WAMMACK, Travis — P&R '64

Singles: 7–inch

ARA 5-10 64-65
ATLANTIC 4-8 66
CAPRICORN 3-5 75
CONGRESS 4-6
FAME 3-5 72-73
FRATERNITY (103 "Rock & Roll Blues") 50-100 58

LPs: 10/12–inch

CAPRICORN 5-10 75
FAME 8-12 72
PHONORAMA 5-10

WANDERERS — P&R '61

(With the Sammy Lowe Orchestra)

Singles: 78 rpm

ONYX (518 "Thinking of You") 30-50 57
SAVOY (1109 "We Could Find Happiness") 50-100 53

Singles: 7–inch

CUB (9003 "Teenage Quarrel") 15-25 58
CUB (9019 "Collecting Hearts") 25-35 58
CUB (9023 "Please") 15-25 58
CUB (9035 "I'm Not Ashamed") 15-25 59
CUB (9054 "I Walked Through a Forest") 15-25 59
CUB (9075 "I Need You More") 15-25 60
CUB (9089 "For Your Love") 15-25 61
CUB (9094 "I'll Never Smile Again") 15-25 61
CUB (9099 "She Wears My Ring") 20-40 61
CUB (9109 "As Time Goes By") 15-25 62
MGM (13082 "As Time Goes By") 10-15 62
ONYX (518 "Thinking of You") 30-50 57
ORBIT (9003 "A Teenage Quarrel") .. 50-75 58
(Green label.)
ORBIT (9003 "A Teenage Quarrel") .. 30-50 58
(Red label.)
SAVOY (1109 "We Could Find Happiness") 200-300 53
U.A. (570 "After He Breaks Your Heart") 10-15 62
U.A. (648 "I'll Know") 15-25 62

Members: Ray Pollard; Bob Yarborough; Sheppard Grant; Frank Joyner.

WANDERLEY, Walter — P&R/LP '66

Singles: 7–inch

A&M 3-5 69
GNP 3-4 81
TOWER 3-6 66-67
VERVE 3-6 66-68
WORLD PACIFIC 3-6 66

LPs: 10/12–inch

A&M 5-10 69
CAPITOL 10-15 63
GNP 5-8 81
PHILIPS 8-12 67
TOWER 8-15 66-67
VERVE 8-15 66-68
WORLD PACIFIC 8-15 66-67

Also see GILBERTO, Astrud

WANG CHUNG — P&R/D&D/LP '84

(Huang Chung)

Singles: 12–inch

GEFFEN 4-6 84

Singles: 7–inch

GEFFEN 3-4 84-89

Picture Sleeves

GEFFEN 3-4 84-89

LPs: 10/12–inch

ARISTA 5-8 83
GEFFEN 5-8 84-89

WANSEL, Dexter — R&B '76

Singles: 12–inch

PHILADELPHIA INT'L 4-8 79

Singles: 7–inch

PHILADELPHIA INT'L 3-5 76-79

LPs: 10/12–inch

PHILADELPHIA INT'L 5-10 76-79

Also see MFSB

WAR — P&R '70

Singles: 12-inch

MCA....4-8 78-79

Singles: 7-inch

BLUE NOTE....3-5 77
COCO PLUM....3-4 85
LAX....3-5 81
MCA....3-5 77-82
PRIORITY....3-4 87
RCA....3-5 82-83
U.A....3-6 71-78
WAR....3-5 77

Picture Sleeves

MCA....3-5 77
U.A. 3-5 71-75

EPs: 7-inch

U.A. (92 "The World Is a Ghetto")....10-15 72
(Promotional issue only. With paper cover.)

LPs: 10/12-inch

ABC....8-10 76
BLUE NOTE....8-10 76
MCA....8-10 77-82
PRIORITY....5-10 87
RCA....5-10 82-83
U.A. (Except 103)....8-10 71-78
U.A. (103 "Radio Free War")....15-20 74
(Colored vinyl. Promotional issue only.)

Members: Howard Scott; Lonnie Jordan; Dee Allen; B.B. Dickerson; Lee Oskar; Charles Miller; Harold Brown.

Also see AALON
Also see BURDON, Eric, & War
Also see JORDAN, Lonnie
Also see OSKAR, Lee

WARD, Anita — P&R/R&B/LP '79

Singles: 12-inch

T.K. DISCO (124 "Ring My Bell")....4-8 79

Singles: 7-inch

JUANA....3-5 79

LPs: 10/12-inch

JUANA....5-10 79

WARD, Billy, & Dominoes — R&B '51

Singles: 78 rpm

DECCA....10-30 56-57
FEDERAL....40-100 52
KING (Except 1281)....10-30 53-57
KING (1281 "Christmas in Heaven") 20-40 53
LIBERTY....20-30 57

Singles: 7-inch

ABC-PAR (10128 "You're Mine")....20-30 60
ABC-PAR (10156 "You")....20-30 60
DECCA (29933 "St. Theresa of the Roses")....25-50 56
DECCA (30043 "Will You Remember")....25-50 56
DECCA (30149 "Evermore")....25-50 56
DECCA (30199 "Rock, Plymouth Rock")....25-50 56
DECCA (30420 "To Each His Own")....25-50 57
DECCA (30514 "September Song")....25-50 57
FEDERAL (12105 "I'd Be Satisfied")....200-300 52
FEDERAL (12106 "Yours Forever")....200-300 52
FEDERAL (12114 "Pedal Pushin' Papa")....200-300 52
FEDERAL (12129 "These Foolish Things")....300-500 53
(Gold top label.)
FEDERAL (12129 "These Foolish Things")....100-200 53
(Silver top label.)
FEDERAL (12129 "These Foolish Things")....25-50 50s
(Green label.)
FEDERAL (12139 "Where Now, Little Heart")....150-250 53
FEDERAL (12162 "My Baby's 3-D")....150-250 53
FEDERAL (12178 "Tootsie Roll")....150-250 54
FEDERAL (12184 "Handwriting on the Wall")....200-300 54
FEDERAL (12193 "Above Jacob's Ladder")....75-125 54
FEDERAL (12209 "Can't Do Sixty No More")....150-250 55
FEDERAL (12218 "Cave Man")....75-125 55
FEDERAL (12263 "Bobby Sox Baby")....75-125 57
FEDERAL (12301 "St. Louis Blues")....75-125 57
GUSTO....3-5 80s
JUBILEE (5163 "Come to Me, Baby")....40-60 54
JUBILEE (5213 "Sweethearts on Parade")....40-60 55
KING (1280 "Rags to Riches")....100-150 53
KING (1281 "Christmas in Heaven")....200-300 53
KING (1342 "A Little Lie")....100-150 54
KING (1364 "Three Coins in the Fountain")....75-125 55
KING (1368 "Little Things Mean a Lot")....50-100 55
KING (1492 "Learnin' the Blues")....50-100 55
KING (1502 "Over the Rainbow")....50-100 55
KING (5322 "Have Mercy Baby")....20-30 60
KING (5463 "Lay It on the Line")....20-30 61
KING (6002 "This Love of Mine")....15-25 65
KING (6016 "Oh Holy Night")....15-25 65
LIBERTY (55071 "Stardust")....20-30 57
LIBERTY (55099 "Deep Purple")....20-30 57
LIBERTY (55111 "My Proudest Possession")....15-25 57
LIBERTY (55126 "Solitude")....15-25 58
LIBERTY (55136 "Jenny Lee")....15-25 58
LIBERTY (55181 "Please Don't Say No")....15-25 58
RO-ZAN (10001 "My Fair Weather Friend")....25-35 62
UNDERGROUND (6736 "Star Dust")... 4-6

Picture Sleeves

LIBERTY (55071 "Stardust")....50-75 57

EPs: 7-inch

DECCA (2549 "Billy Ward & His Dominoes")....100-200 58
FEDERAL (212 "Billy Ward & His Dominoes, Vol. 1")....200-300 55
(Silver top label.)
FEDERAL (262 "Billy Ward & His Dominoes, Vol. 2")....200-300 55
(Silver top label.)
FEDERAL (269 "Billy Ward & His Dominoes, Vol. 3")....200-300 55
(Silver top label.)
FEDERAL (212 "Billy Ward & His Dominoes, Vol. 1")....100-150 57
(Green label.)
FEDERAL (262 "Billy Ward & His Dominoes, Vol. 2")....100-150 57
(Green label.)
FEDERAL (269 "Billy Ward & His Dominoes, Vol. 3")....100-150 57
(Green label.)
LIBERTY (1/2/3-3083 "Yours Forever")....50-100 59
(Price is for any of three volumes.)

LPs: 10/12-inch

DECCA (8621 "Billy Ward & His Dominoes")....300-500 58
FEDERAL (94 "Billy Ward & His Dominoes")....7500-10000 54
(10-inch LP.)
FEDERAL (548 "Billy Ward & His Dominoes")....1000-1500 57
FEDERAL (559 "Clyde McPhatter with Billy Ward & His Dominoes")....1000-1500 57
KING (548 "Billy Ward & His Dominoes")....300-500 58
KING (559 "Clyde McPhatter with Billy Ward & His Dominoes")....200-400 61
KING (733 "Billy Ward & His Dominoes Featuring Clyde McPhatter & Jackie Wilson")....200-300 61
KING (952 "24 Songs")....25-50 66
KING/GUSTO....5-10
LIBERTY (3056 "Sea of Glass")....100-150 58
LIBERTY (3083 "Yours Forever")....100-150 59
LIBERTY (3113 "Pagan Love Song")....100-150 59
(Monaural.)
LIBERTY (7113 "Pagan Love Song")....200-400 59
(Stereo.)

Members: Clyde McPhatter; Jackie Wilson; Billy Ward; Gene Mumford; Milton Merle; Milton Grayson; William Lamont; Cliff Givens.

Also see DOMINOES
Also see WILSON, Jackie

WARD, Dale — P&R '63

Singles: 7-inch

BIG WAY....4-8 60s
BOYD....5-10 62-65
DOT (16000 series)....5-10 63-65
DOT (17000 series)....3-5 71-72
MONUMENT....4-6 66-69
PARAMOUNT....4-6 69-70

Picture Sleeves

BOYD....10-20 62

Also see WARD, Robin

WARD, Joe — P&R '55

Singles: 78 rpm

KING....5-10 55-56

Singles: 7-inch

KING....10-20 55-56

WARD, Robin — P&R/R&B '63

Singles: 7-inch

DOT....4-8 63-64
SONGS UNLIMITED....4-8 63

Picture Sleeves

SONGS UNLIMITED....5-10 63

LPs: 10/12-inch

DOT (3555 "Wonderful Summer")....25-35 63
(Monaural.)
DOT (25555 "Wonderful Summer")....35-45 63
(Stereo.)

Also see BOONE, Pat
Also see MARTINDALE, Wink, & Robin Ward
Also see ROBIN
Also see WARD, Dale

WARD, Little Sammy

(With Alley Kats & Kitty - Sax Kari Orchestra)

Singles: 7-inch

P-C (103 "Begging for Love")....1000-2000

Also see WARD, Singin' Sammy

WARD, Singin' Sammy — R&B '61

Singles: 7-inch

SOUL (35004 "You've Got to Change")....20-30 64
TAMLA (54030 "What Makes You Love Him")....50-100 61
(With horizontal lines.)
TAMLA (54030 "What Makes You Love Him")....20-40 61
(With Tamla globe logo.)
TAMLA (54049 "What Makes You Love Him")....20-40 62
TAMLA (54057 "Everybody Knew It")....30-40 62
TAMLA (54071 "Part Time Love")....25-35 62

Also see WARD, Little Sammy

WARE, Leon — R&B '79

Singles: 7-inch

ELEKTRA....3-5 81
FABULOUS....3-5 79
U.A. 3-5 72

LPs: 10/12-inch

FABULOUS....5-10 79
GORDY....5-10 76
U.A. 8-12 72

WARING, Fred — P&R '23

(With the Pennsylvanians)

Singles: 78 rpm

CAPITOL....3-5 57-58
DECCA....3-6 50-57

Singles: 7-inch

CAPITOL....3-6 57-59

DECCA....3-8 50-68
REPRISE....3-6 64

EPs: 7-inch

CAPITOL....4-8 57-58
DECCA....5-10 50-59
SHAWNEE PRESS ("Excerpts from the Fred Waring Band Book")....10-15 50s
(Includes 18-page "Band Book." Promotional issue only.)

LPs: 10/12-inch

CAPITOL....5-15 57-69
DECCA....5-20 50-68
HARMONY....5-10 69
MCA....5-8 77
MEGA....5-8 71
REPRISE....5-15 64-65
RCA....5-10 68
Also see SINATRA, Frank, Bing Crosby, & Fred Waring

WARNER MACK: see MACK, Warner

WARNES, Jennifer P&R/C&W/LP '77
(Jennifer Warren)

Singles: 12-inch

20TH FOX ("It Goes Like It Goes")....4-8 79
(Shown as by Jennifer Warnes. No selection number used.)
20TH FOX (379 "It Goes Like It Goes")....8-10 79
(Shown as by Jennifer Warren.)

Singles: 7-inch

ARISTA....3-4 77-82
CYPRESS....3-4 87
PARROT....3-6 68
W.B. 3-5 83

LPs: 10/12-inch

ARISTA....5-10 76-82
CYPRESS....5-8 87
REPRISE....5-10 72
Also see COCKER, Joe, & Jennifer Warnes
Also see JENNIFER
Also see MEDLEY, Bill, & Jennifer Warnes

WARNES, Jennifer, & Chris Thompson P&R '83

Singles: 7-inch

CASABLANCA....3-4 83
Also see THOMPSON, Chris, & Night

WARP 9 R&B '82

Singles: 12-inch

PRISM....4-6 83-84

Singles: 7-inch

PRISM....3-4 82-84

WARRANT P&R/LP '89

Singles: 7-inch

COLUMBIA....3-4 89-90

LPs: 10/12-inch

COLUMBIA....5-8 89-90

WARREN, Jennifer: see WARNES, Jennifer

WARREN, Rusty LP '60

Singles: 7-inch

JUBILEE....5-10 60

EPs: 7-inch

JUBILEE....10-15 62

LPs: 10/12-inch

GNP....5-12 74-77
JUBILEE....10-20 60-68

WARRIOR, Jade: see JADE WARRIOR

WARWICK, Dee Dee P&R/R&B '65
(With the Dixie Flyers)

Singles: 7-inch

ATCO....4-6 70-71
BLUE ROCK....5-10 65
HURT....5-10 66
JUBILEE....5-10 63
MERCURY....4-8 66-69
PRIVATE STOCK....3-6 75
SUTRA....3-5
TIGER....10-20 64

LPs: 10/12-inch

ATCO....8-12 70

HERITAGE SOUND....5-8 83
MERCURY....10-15 67-69

WARWICK, Dionne P&R '62
(Dionne Warwicke)

Singles: 12-inch

ARISTA....4-6 84

Singles: 7-inch

ARISTA....3-4 79-90
COLLECTABLES....3-4 80s
ERIC....3-4 70s
FOREVER....3-4 80s
MUSICOR....3-5 77
SCEPTER (1200 series)....4-8 62-65
SCEPTER (12000 series)....3-5 65-71
W.B. 3-5 72-78

Picture Sleeves

SCEPTER....3-5 63-71

LPs: 10/12-inch

ARISTA....5-8 79-90
CIRCA....5-8
EVEREST....5-8 81
51 WEST....5-8 80s
MFSL....25-50 82
MUSICOR....5-10 77
PHOENIX....5-8 81
PICKWICK....5-10 70s
RHINO....5-8 80s
SCEPTER (Except 200)....10-15 64-72
SCEPTER (200 "March Is Dionne Warwick Month")....20-25 67
(Promotional issue only.)
SCEPTER/COLUMBIA (5139/40 "Dionne")....15-25 67
(Record club issue.)
U.A. 8-10 74
TRIP....8-10 76
W.B. 8-10 72-77
Also see CAMPBELL, Glen / Dionne Warwick / Burt Bacharach
Also see DIONNE & FRIENDS
Also see DIONNE & KASHIF
Also see GIBB, Barry
Also see HAYES, Isaac, & Dionne Warwick
Also see MATHIS, Johnny, & Dionne Warwick
Also see U.S.A. for AFRICA
Also see WONDER, Stevie / Dionne Warwick

WARWICK, Dionne, & Howard Hewett R&B '88

Singles: 7-inch

ARISTA....3-4 88

WARWICK, Dionne, & Glenn Jones R&B '85

Singles: 7-inch

ARISTA....3-4 85
Also see JONES, Glenn

WARWICK, Dionne, & Jeffrey Osborne P&R/R&B '87

Singles: 7-inch

ARISTA....3-4 87

Picture Sleeves

ARISTA....3-4 87
Also see OSBORNE, Jeffrey

WARWICK, Dionne, & Spinners P&R/R&B '74

Singles: 7-inch

ATLANTIC....3-5 74

Picture Sleeves

ATLANTIC....3-5 74
Also see SPINNERS

WARWICK, Dionne, & Luther Vandross P&R/R&B '83

Singles: 7-inch

ARISTA....3-4 83

Picture Sleeves

ARISTA....3-4 83
Also see VANDROSS, Luther
Also see WARWICK, Dionne

WAS (NOT WAS) R&B '82

Singles: 12-inch

ISLAND....4-6 82

Singles: 7-inch

CHRYSALIS....3-4 88-90
GEFFEN....3-4 83
ISLAND....3-5 81-82
ZE....3-4 82

Picture Sleeves

CHRYSALIS....3-4 88-90

LPs: 10/12-inch

CHRYSALIS....5-8 88-90
GEFFEN....5-8 83
ISLAND....5-8 81
Members: Don Fagenson; David Weiss.

WASHINGTON, Baby R&B '59
(Jeanette "Baby" Washington; Justine Washington)

Singles: 7-inch

ABC-PAR (10223 "My Time to Cry") 15-25 61
A.V.I. 3-5 78
CHECKER (918 "I Hate to See You Go")....15-25 59
CHESS....4-6 70
COLLECTABLES....3-4 80s
COTILLION....4-6 69-70
J&S (1604 "There Must Be a Reason")....25-50 57
J&S (1632 "I Hate to See You Go")...20-30 58
J&S (1656 "Every Day")....25-50 61
MASTER FIVE....4-6 73-75
NEPTUNE....10-20 60-61
SIXTH AVENUE....3-5 76
SUE....5-15 62-67
VEEP....4-8 67

LPs: 10/12-inch

A.V.I. 5-10 78
COLLECTABLES....5-8 87-88
SUE....20-35 63-65
TRIP....8-10 71
UNART....10-20 67
VEEP....10-15 68
Also see HEARTS

WASHINGTON, Baby, & Don Gardner R&B '73

Singles: 7-inch

MASTER FIVE....3-5 73-74

LPs: 10/12-inch

MASTER FIVE....8-10 74
Also see WASHINGTON, Baby

WASHINGTON, Deborah R&B '78

Singles: 7-inch

ARIOLA....3-5 78

LPs: 10/12-inch

ARIOLA....5-10 78

WASHINGTON, Dinah R&B '48

Singles: 78 rpm

APOLLO....10-25 45-47
KEYNOTE....20-40 44
MERCURY....5-15 46-57

Singles: 7-inch

MERCURY (5000 series)....15-25 50-52
MERCURY (7200 series)....10-15 62
(Compact 33 singles.)
MERCURY (8100 & 8200 series)....15-25 50-52
MERCURY (10008 "What a Difference a Day Makes")....10-20 59
(Stereo.)
MERCURY (70046 thru 70968)....10-20 52-56
MERCURY (71000 & 72000 series)....5-15 57-63
MERCURY CELEBRITY SERIES....4-6 60s
ROULETTE....4-8 62-63

Picture Sleeves

MERCURY....8-12 61-62

EPs: 7-inch

EMARCY....15-25 54-56
MERCURY (3000 thru 3200 series)..15-25 51-57
MERCURY (3300 series)....10-15 60
MERCURY (4000 series)....10-15 61

LPs: 10/12-inch

EMARCY (400 series)....8-12 76
EMARCY (26032 "After Hours")....50-100 54
(10-inch LP.)

EMARCY (36011 "For Those in Love") 50-75 55
EMARCY (36028 "After Hours") 50-75 55
EMARCY (36065 "Dinah") 50-75 56
EMARCY (36073 "In the Land of Hi-Fi") 50-75 56
EMARCY (36119 "Dinah Sings Fats Waller") 50-75 57
EMARCY (36130 "Dinah Sings Bessie Smith") 50-75 58
EVEREST 8-10 75
MERCURY (103 "This Is My Story") . 20-30 63
MERCURY (121 "Original Queen of Soul") 12-15 69
MERCURY (603 "This Is My Story") . 20-30 63
MERCURY (20100 & 20200 series) .. 40-60 55-58
MERCURY (20400 thru 20900 series) 20-30 59-63
(Monaural.)
MERCURY (21100 series) 10-20 67
MERCURY (25060 "Dinah Washington") 50-100 50
(10–inch LP.)
MERCURY (25138 "Dynamic Dinah") 50-100 51
(10–inch LP.)
MERCURY (25140 "Blazing Ballads") 50-100 51
(10–inch LP.)
MERCURY (25138 "Dynamic Dinah") 50-100 51
(10–inch LP.)
MERCURY (60100 thru 60900 series) 20-40 59-63
(Stereo.)
MERCURY (61100 series) 10-15 67
PICKWICK 5-10
ROSETTA 5-8 84
ROULETTE (100 series) 10-12 71-72
ROULETTE (25000 series) 15-30 62-65
TRIP 8-10 73-78
WING 15-30 59-64
Also see BENTON, Brook, & Dinah Washington
Also see HAMPTON, Lionel & Dinah Washington
Also see JONES, Quincy
Also see RAVENS & Dinah Washington

WASHINGTON, Dinah / Ink Spots

EPs: 7–inch

WALDORF 10-20 55
Also see INK SPOTS

WASHINGTON, Dinah / Joe Williams / Sarah Vaughan

LPs: 10/12–inch

ROULETTE 15-25 64
Also see VAUGHAN, Sarah
Also see WASHINGTON, Dinah
Also see WILLIAMS, Joe

WASHINGTON, Donna — R&B '81

Singles: 7–inch

CAPITOL 3-5 81

LPs: 10/12–inch

CAPITOL 5-10 81

WASHINGTON, Ella — P&R/R&B '69

Singles: 7–inch

ATLANTIC 4-8 67
SOUND STAGE 4-6 67-69

LPs: 10/12–inch

SOUND STAGE 10-15 69

WASHINGTON, Grover, Jr. — R&B/LP '72

Singles: 7–inch

COLUMBIA 3-4 87
ELEKTRA 3-4 79-84
KUDU 3-5 71-78
MOTOWN 3-4 78-83

Picture Sleeves

ELEKTRA 3-5 80-82

LPs: 10/12–inch

COLUMBIA 5-8 87
ELEKTRA 5-10 79-84
KUDO 8-12 71-77
MOTOWN 5-10 78-83
Also see COSBY, Bill
Also see LABELLE, Patti, & Grover Washington Jr.
Also see MATTHEWS, David
Also see WITHERS, Bill

WASHINGTON, Jeanette: see WASHINGTON, Baby

WASHINGTON, Jerry — R&B '73

Singles: 7–inch

EXCELLO 4-8 73-74

WASHINGTON, Justine: see WASHINGTON, Baby

WATANABE, Sadao, & Roberta Flack — R&B '84

Singles: 7–inch

ELEKTRA 3-4 84
Also see FLACK, Roberta

WATERBOYS — LP '88

Singles: 7–inch

ISLAND 3-4 83

LPs: 10/12–inch

CHRYSALIS 5-8 88-90
ISLAND 5-10 83

WATERFRONT — P&R/LP '89

Singles: 7–inch

POLYDOR 3-4 89

Picture Sleeves

POLYDOR 3-4 89

LPs: 10/12–inch

POLYDOR 5-8 89

WATERFRONT HOME — D&D '83

Singles: 12–inch

BOBCAT 4-6 83

WATERS, Ethel — P&R '21

Singles: 78 rpm

BLACK SWAN 10-20 21-23
BRUNSWICK 10-15 33-34
COLUMBIA 10-15 25-33
CONTINENTAL 4-8 46-47
DECCA 8-12 34-38

EPs: 7–inch

CHANCEL 10-20 50s
MERCURY 15-25 55

LPs: 10/12–inch

BIOGRAPH 8-10 70
COLUMBIA 8-12 68-72
CONTINENTAL 15-25 61
JAY (3010 "Sings Her Best") 20-40 57
MERCURY (20051 "Favorites") 30-50 54
REMINGTON ("Shades of Blue") 50-75 50
(10–inch LP.)
WORD 10-15 62
"X" (1009 "Ethel Waters") 25-50 55

WATERS, Freddie — R&B '77

Singles: 7–inch

KARI 3-5 81
OCTOBER 3-5 77

WATERS, Muddy — R&B '48

Singles: 78 rpm

ARISTOCRAT (406 "Sneakin' and Cryin'") 25-50 50
ARISTOCRAT (412 "Rollin' and Tumblin'") 25-50 50
ARISTOCRAT (1302 "Gypsy Woman") 25-50 48
ARISTOCRAT (1305 "I Can't Be Satisfied") 25-50 48
ARISTOCRAT (1306 "Train Fare Home") 25-50 48
ARISTOCRAT (1307 "You're Gonna Miss Me") 25-50 49
ARISTOCRAT (1310 "Streamline Woman") 25-50 49
ARISTOCRAT (1311 "Little Geneva") 25-50 49
CHESS 20-40 50-55

Singles: 7–inch

CHESS (1509 "Country Boy") 50-100 52
CHESS (1514 "Looking for My Baby") 50-100 52
CHESS (1526 "Standing Around Crying") 50-100 52
CHESS (1537 "She's All Right") 50-75 53
CHESS (1542 "Who's Gonna Be Your Sweet Man") 50-75 52
CHESS (1550 "Blow, Wind, Blow") ... 40-60 53
CHESS (1560 "I'm Your Hootchie Coochie Man") 40-60 53
CHESS (1571 "Just Make Love to Me") 40-60 54
CHESS (1579 "I'm Ready") 40-60 54
CHESS (1585 "I'm a Natural Born Lover") 25-50 54
CHESS (1596 "I Want to Be Loved") 25-50 55
CHESS (1600 series) 20-40 55-59
CHESS (1700 series) 15-25 59-61
CHESS (1800 & 1900 series) 8-15 62-66
CHESS (2000 series) 4-8 67-73

LPs: 10/12–inch

BLUE SKY 6-12 77-81
CADET CONCEPT 10-15 68-69
CHESS (127 "Fathers and Sons") 15-20 69
CHESS (1427 "The Best of Muddy Waters") 50-100 57
CHESS (1444 "Muddy Waters Sings Big Bill") 40-60 60
CHESS (1449 "Muddy Waters at Newport") 20-30 64
CHESS (1483 "Folk Singer") 15-25 64
CHESS (1500 series) 10-20 66-71
CHESS (9000 series) 5-10
CHESS (50012 thru 50023) 6-12 72-73
CHESS (50033 "Fathers & Sons") 10-15 75
CHESS (60006 "McKinley Morganfield") 10-12 71
CHESS (60013 thru 60035) 8-15 72-75
DOUGLAS 10-15 68
MFSL (201 "Folk Singer") 20-25 94
(Half-speed mastered.)
TESTAMENT 10-12 60s
Also see COTTON, James
Also see FOSTER, Leroy, & Muddy Waters
Also see ROGERS, Jimmy
Also see WILLIAMSON, Sonny Boy
Also see WINTER, Johnny

WATERS, Muddy, & Howlin' Wolf

LPs: 10/12–inch

CHESS 10-15 74
Also see DIDDLEY, Bo, Howlin' Wolf & Muddy Waters
Also see HOWLIN' WOLF
Also see WATERS, Muddy

WATERS, Roger — LP '84

(With Madeline Bell, Katie Kissoon, Eric Clapton & Doreen Chanter; with Bleeding Heart Band)

Singles: 12–inch

COLUMBIA 4-6 84

Singles: 7–inch

COLUMBIA 3-4 84

LPs: 10/12–inch

COLUMBIA 5-10 84-87
Also see BELL, Madeline
Also see CLAPTON, Eric
Also see KISSOON, Mac & Katie
Also see PINK FLOYD

WATKINS, Tip — R&B '77

Singles: 7–inch

H&L 3-5 77

WATLEY, Jody — P&R/R&B/LP '87

(With Eric B. & Rakim)

Singles: 7–inch

MCA 3-4 87-90

Picture Sleeves

MCA 3-4 87-89

LPs: 10/12–inch

MCA 5-8 87-89
Also see CYMONE, Andre
Also see SHALAMAR

WATSON, Anthony — R&B '85

Singles: 7–inch

SRO 3-4 85

LPs: 10/12-inch
SRO 5-10 85

WATSON, Doc C&W '73
(With Merle Watson)
Singles: 7-inch
POPPY 3-5 72-74
U.A. 3-5 73-79
LPs: 10/12-inch
FLYING FISH 5-8 81
FOLKWAYS 10-20 63-69
LIBERTY 5-8 83
POPPY 6-12 72
U.A. 8-15 75-76
VANGUARD 8-18 64-77
VERVE/FOLKWAYS 10-15 66
Also see ATKINS, Chet, & Doc Watson
Also see FLATT, Lester, Earl Scruggs & Doc Watson

WATSON, Johnny R&B '55
(Johnny Guitar Watson; Young John Watson; Johnny Watson Trio)
Singles: 78 rpm
FEDERAL 40-60 53-54
KEEN 20-30 57
RPM 25-40 55-56
Singles: 7-inch
ALL STAR (7167 "Darling of My Dreams") 25-35 58
ARVEE (5016 "Untouchable") 20-30 60
CACTUS (118 "Let's Rock") 75-125 59
CLASS (246 "One More Kiss") 15-25 59
DJM 3-6 77
ESCORT 5-10
FANTASY 3-6 73-75
FEDERAL (12120 "Highway 60") .. 100-200 53
FEDERAL (12131 "Motor Head Baby") 100-200 53
FEDERAL (12143 "I Got Eyes") 100-200 53
FEDERAL (12157 "What's Going On") 100-200 53
FEDERAL (12175 "Half Pint of Whiskey") 100-200 54
FEDERAL (12183 "Gettin' Drunk") 100-200 54
GOTH (101 "Falling in Love") 75-125 60
HIGHLAND 10-20 60s
KEEN (4005 "Gangster of Love") 30-50 57
KEEN (4023 "Deana Baby") 30-50 57
KENT 8-12 60
KING (5536 "Embraceable You") 10-20 61
KING (5579 "Broke & Lonely") 10-20 61
KING (5607 "Nearness of You") 10-20 62
KING (5666 "Sweet Lovin' Mama") 10-20 62
KING (5716 "Cold Cold Heart") 10-20 62
KING (5774 "Gangster of Love") 10-20 63
KING (5833 "I Say I Love You") 10-20 64
OKEH 5-15 66-67
RPM (423 "Hot Little Mama") 50-75 55
RPM (431 "Too Tired") 50-75 55
RPM (436 "Those Lonely, Lonely Nights") 50-75 55
RPM (447 "Oh, Baby") 50-75 55
RPM (455 "Three Hours Past Midnight") 50-75 55
RPM (471 "She Moves Me") 50-75 55
VALLEY VUE 3-4 84
LPs: 10/12-inch
A&M 5-10 81
BIG TOWN 8-10 77
CADET 10-15 67
CHESS (1490 "Blues/Soul") 30-50 64
DJM 5-10 76-81
FANTASY 5-10 73-81
KING (857 "Johnny Guitar Watson") 50-75 63
OKEH 10-15 67
MCA 5-10 81
Also see BLAND, Bobby / Johnny Guitar Watson
Also see OTIS, Johnny
Also see SHIELDS
Also see WATSONIAN INSTITUTE
Also see WILLIAMS, Larry, & Johnny Watson

WATSON, Paula R&B '48
Singles: 78 rpm
MONOGRAM 5-10 49
SUPREME 5-10 48-49

WATSON, Young John: see WATSON, Johnny

WATSONIAN INSTITUTE LP '78
Singles: 7-inch
DJM 3-5 78
LPs: 10/12-inch
DJM 5-10 78
Also see WATSON, Johnny

WATTS, Ernie LP '82
Singles: 7-inch
QWEST 3-4 82
LPs: 10/12-inch
QWEST 5-10 82

WATTS, Noble P&R '57
(Noble "Thin Man" Watts & His Rhythm Sparks; Noble Watts Quintet; with Paul "Hucklebuck" Williams)
Singles: 78 rpm
BATON (246 "Easy Going") 12-25 57
BATON (249 "The Slop") 12-25 57
BATON (249 "Hard Times") 10-15 57
(Note title change.)
DELUXE 10-15 54
VEE JAY 10-15 56
Singles: 7-inch
BATON (246 "Easy Going") 12-25 57
BATON (249 "The Slop") 12-25 57
BATON (249 "Hard Times") 10-15 57
(Note title change.)
BATON (251 thru 266) 8-15 57-59
BRUNSWICK 4-8 68
CLAMIKE 5-10 63-64
CUB 8-10 60
DELUXE (6066 "Mashing Potatoes") 15-20 54
DELUXE 8-12 54
ENJOY 5-10 63
JELL ("Florida Shake") 5-10 62
(No selection number used.)
SIR 5-10 60
VEE JAY (268 "South Shore Drive") ... 8-15 56
Also see WILLIAMS, Paul

WATTS, Noble, & June Bateman
Singles: 7-inch
ENJOY 4-8 63
Also see WATTS, Noble

WATTS 103rd ST. RHYTHM BAND
(Featuring Charles Wright) P&R/R&B '67
Singles: 7-inch
KEYMEN 4-8 67
W.B. 4-8 68-71
LPs: 10/12-inch
W.B. 10-15 68-71
Also see WRIGHT, Charles

WAX R&B '81
Singles: 12-inch
RCA 4-6 86
Singles: 7-inch
RCA 3-4 81-86
LPs: 10/12-inch
COTILLION 5-10 80
RCA 5-8 81-86
Members: Graham Gouldman; Andrew Gold.
Also see GOLD, Andrew
Also see 10CC

WAYBILL, Fee LP '84
Singles: 7-inch
CAPITOL 3-4 84
LPs: 10/12-inch
CAPITOL 5-8 84
Also see MARX, Richard
Also see TUBES

WAYLON & WILLIE: see JENNINGS, Waylon, & Willie Nelson

WAYNE, James R&B '51
(With the Kidds; James Waynes; Wee Willie Wayne)
Singles: 78 rpm
ALADDIN 10-20 54
IMPERIAL 15-30 51-57
MILLION 15-25 54
PEACOCK 15-25 57
SITTIN' in WITH (573 "Gypsy Blues") 20-40 50
SITTIN' in WITH (588 "Love Me Blues") 20-40 51
SITTIN' in WITH (607 "Junco Partner") 20-40 51
SITTIN' in WITH (622 "Please Baby Please") 20-40 52
SITTIN' in WITH (639 "Money Blues") 20-40 52
Singles: 7-inch
ANGELTONE (540 "This Little Letter") 10-20 60
ALADDIN (3234 "Cryin' in Vain") 40-60 54
IMPERIAL (5258 I'm in Love with You") 40-60 53
IMPERIAL (5355 "Travelin' Mood") ... 40-60 55
IMPERIAL (5368 "Good News") 40-60 55
IMPERIAL (5696 "Hard to Handle") ... 20-30 60
IMPERIAL (5725 "Travelin' Mood") ... 15-25 61
IMPERIAL (5737 "Woman") 15-25 61
MILLION (2009 "Junco's Return") 40-60 54
PEACOCK (1672 "Yes I Do") 25-35 57
LPs: 10/12-inch
IMPERIAL (9144 "Travelin' Mood") 200-300 61
Also see CHARLES, Ray / Arbee Stidham / Li'l Son Jackson / James Wayne

WAYNE, John LP '73
Singles: 7-inch
CASABLANCA 3-4 79
RCA 3-5 73
LPs: 10/12-inch
RCA (3000 series) 5-10 79-81
RCA (4828 "America") 15-25 73

WAYNE, Scotty
(Baldemar Huerta)
Singles: 7-inch
TALENT SCOUT (1008 "Only One") 20-30 62
Also see FENDER, Freddy

WAYNE, Thomas P&R/R&B '59
(With the DeLons)
Singles: 7-inch
CAPEHART 4-8 61
CHALET 3-5 69
COLLECTABLES 3-4 80s
ERIC 3-4 70s
FERNWOOD (Except 106) 10-20 59-60
FERNWOOD (106 "You're the One That Done It") 50-75 58
MERCURY (71287 "You're the One That Done It") 30-50 58
MERCURY (71454 "You're the One That Done It") 20-30 59
OLDIES 45 .... 4-6 64
PHILLIPS INT'L 5-10 62
RACER 4-8 65
SANTO 5-10 62

WAYNE, Wee Willie: see WAYNE, James

WAYNES, James: see WAYNE, James

WAYSTED LP '87
LPs: 10/12-inch
CAPITOL 5-8 87

WE FIVE P&R/LP '65
Singles: 7-inch
A&M 4-8 65-69
MGM 3-5 73
VAULT 4-8 67
VERVE 3-5 68-73
LPs: 10/12-inch
A&M 15-20 65-69
A.V.I. 5-10 77
VAULT 10-15 70
Members: Mike Stewart; Pete Fullerton; Beverly Bivens; Bob Jones; Jerry Burgan.

WE THE PEOPLE
R&B '72

Singles: 7-inch

DAVEL....4-8 75
IMPERIAL....4-8 69
LION....3-6 72-74
MAP CITY....4-8 69
REENA....4-8 68
VERVE....4-6 71

LPs: 10/12-inch

CENTURY ADVENT (5262 "We the People")....10-15 73

Members: Terri Gonzalez; Robert Taylor; Shabi Weems; Billy McKeechun.

WEAPONS OF PEACE
R&B '76

Singles: 7-inch

PLAYBOY....3-5 76-77

Picture Sleeves

PLAYBOY....3-5 76

LPs: 10/12-inch

PLAYBOY....5-10 77

Members: Finis Henderson; David Johnson; Lonell Dantzler; Bill Leathers; Randy Hardy.

Also see HENDERSON, Finis

WEATHER GIRLS
R&B '82

Singles: 12-inch

COLUMBIA....4-6 83-85

Singles: 7-inch

COLUMBIA....3-4 83-85

LPs: 10/12-inch

COLUMBIA....5-10 84

Member: Martha Wash.

Also see BLACK BOX

Also see TWO TONS O' FUN

WEATHER REPORT
LP '71

Singles: 7-inch

COLUMBIA....3-5 73-84

LPs: 10/12-inch

ARC/COLUMBIA....5-10 78-82
COLUMBIA....5-10 71-86

Also see PASTORIUS, Jaco

Also see SHORTER, Wayne

WEATHERLY, Jim
P&R/LP '74

Singles: 7-inch

ABC....3-5 76-77
BUDDAH....3-5 74-75
ELEKTRA....3-5 79-80
ERIC....3-5 78
RCA....3-5 72-74
20TH FOX....4-8 65

Picture Sleeves

BUDDAH....3-5 74

LPs: 10/12-inch

ABC....5-10 77
BUDDAH....5-10 74-75
RCA....8-12 72

WEATHERS, Carl
R&B '81

Singles: 7-inch

MIRAGE....3-5 81

WEATHERS, Oscar
R&B '70

Singles: 7-inch

BLUE CANDLE....3-5 73
TOP & BOTTOM....3-6 69-72

WEAVER, Dennis
LP '72

(With the Good Time People)

Singles: 7-inch

CASCADE....5-10 59
CENTURY CITY....3-6 69
EVA....4-8 63
IM'PRESS....3-5 72
OVATION....3-5 75
W.B....4-8 63

LPs: 10/12-inch

IM'PRESS....8-10 72
OVATION....5-10 75

WEAVERS
P&R '50

(With Gordon Jenkins' Orchestra)

Singles: 78 rpm

DECCA....4-8 50-57

Singles: 7-inch

DECCA (27000 thru 29000 series)....10-20 50-55
DECCA (31000 series)....4-8 62
MCA....3-5 73
NSD....3-5 82
VANGUARD....4-8 60-62

EPs: 7-inch

DECCA....10-25 51-52

LPs: 10/12-inch

DECCA (173 "Best of the Weavers")....10-20 65
(Monaural.)
DECCA (7173 "Best of the Weavers")....10-20 65
(Stereo.)
DECCA (5285 "Folk Songs")....25-50 51
(10-inch LP.)
DECCA (5373 "Merry Christmas")....20-40 52
(10-inch LP.)
DECCA (8893 "Best of the Weavers")....15-25 59
DECCA (74277 "Weavers Gold")....10-15 70
VANGUARD (15-16 "Greatest Hits")....12-18 71
VANGUARD (2000 series)....15-25 59-63
VANGUARD (3000 thru 6000 series)....8-15 67-70
VANGUARD (9000 series)....15-35 56-63
VANGUARD (9100 series)....12-25 65

Members: Pete Seeger; Lee Hays; Fred Hellerman; Ronnie Gilbert.

Also see ALMANAC SINGERS

Also see JENKINS, Gordon, & His Orchestra

Also see SEEGER, Pete

WEAVERS & TERRY GILKYSON

Singles: 7-inch

DECCA....4-8 51

Singles: 7-inch

DECCA....8-10 51

Also see GILKYSON, Terry

Also see WEAVERS

WEBB, Jack
LP '55

(With Jazz Combo; with Billy May's Orchestra)

Singles: 7-inch

W.B. (5003 "You'd Never Know the Old Place Now")....5-10 58

EPs: 7-inch

RCA (0342/3 "Christmas Story")....15-25 50s
RCA (1126 "Pete Kelly's Blues")....20-35 55
RCA (3199 "Christmas Story")....50-100 53

LPs: 10/12-inch

RCA (1126 "Pete Kelly's Blues")....30-50 55
RCA (2053 "Pete Kelly's Blues")....20-30 59
RCA (3199 "Christmas Story")....75-125 53
(10-inch LP.)
W.B. (B-1207 "You're My Girl")....30-50 58
(Monaural.)
W.B. (BS-1207 "You're My Girl")....50-100 58
(Stereo.)
W.B. (B-1217 "Pete Kelly Lets His Hair Down")....30-50 58
(Monaural.)
W.B. (BS-1217 "Pete Kelly Lets His Hair Down")....50-100 58
(Stereo.)

Members: Jack Webb; Matty Matlock; Dick Cathcart; Nick Fatool; Elmer "Moe" Schneider; George Van Eps; Ray Sherman; Jud DeNaut.

WEBB, Lance
R&B '84

Singles: 7-inch

BEANTOWN....3-5 84

WEBB, Paula
P&R '75

Singles: 7-inch

WESTBOUND....3-5 75

WEBBER, Andrew Lloyd
LP '91

Singles: 7-inch

MCA....3-5 78

LPs: 10/12-inch

MCA....5-10 91

WEBER, Joan
P&R '54

Singles: 78 rpm

COLUMBIA....3-5 54-56

Singles: 7-inch

COLUMBIA....5-10 54-56
CROSLEY....4-6 63
MAPLE....4-6 61

EPs: 7-inch

COLUMBIA....5-10 55

WEBS
R&B '67

Singles: 7-inch

GUYDEN (2090 "Question")....15-25 63
MGM....5-10 66
POPSIDE....8-15 67-68
VERVE....5-10 68

WEDNESDAY
P&R '73

Singles: 7-inch

BUDDAH....3-5 75
CELEBRATION....3-5 76
SKY....3-5 76
SUSSEX....3-5 73-74

LPs: 10/12-inch

SUSSEX....8-10 74

WEE GEE
R&B '78

Singles: 7-inch

COTILLION....3-5 80
JUNEY....3-5 78

WEEKS & CO.
R&B '81

Singles: 12-inch

SALSOUL....4-6 83

Singles: 7-inch

CHEZ RO....3-5 81
SALSOUL....3-4 83

LPs: 10/12-inch

SALSOUL....5-8 83

Member: Richie Weeks.

WEIR, Bob
LP '72

Singles: 7-inch

ARISTA (315 "Bombs Away")....4-6 77
ARISTA (336 "I'll Be Doggone")....10-15 77
(Promotional issue only.)
W.B....8-12 72

LPs: 10/12-inch

ARISTA....5-10 78
W.B. (2627 "Ace")....25-30 72

Also see BOBBY & MIDNITES

Also see GRATEFUL DEAD

Also see KINGFISH

WEIR, Frank, Orchestra
P&R '54

Singles: 78 rpm

CAPITOL....3-5 56
COLUMBIA....3-5 57
LONDON....3-5 54-57

Singles: 7-inch

CAPITOL....4-8 56
COLUMBIA....4-8 57
LONDON....4-8 54-63

EPs: 7-inch

LONDON....5-10 54-55

LPs: 10/12-inch

COLUMBIA....10-20 57
LONDON....10-20 54

WEISBERG, Tim
LP '73

Singles: 7-inch

A&M....3-5 71-79
MCA....3-5 79
U.A....3-5 77-80

LPs: 10/12-inch

A&M....5-10 73-79
MCA....5-10 79-80
NAUTILUS....10-15 80
U.A....5-10 77-78

Also see FOGELBERG, Dan, & Tim Weisberg

WEISSBERG, Eric
P&R/C&W/LP '73

(With Steve Mandell; with Deliverance; with Marshall Brickman)

Singles: 7-inch

EPIC....3-5 75
W.B....3-5 72-73

LPs: 10/12-inch

ELEKTRA....15-25 63
W.B....5-10 73

Also see TARRIERS

WELCH, Bob — P&R/LP '77

Singles: 7-inch
CAPITOL 3-5 77-81
RCA 3-4 81-83

Picture Sleeves
CAPITOL 3-5 78-81

LPs: 10/12-inch
CAPITOL (Except 16000 series) 8-10 77-80
CAPITOL (16000 series) 5-8 80-82
RCA 5-10 81-83

Promotional LPs
CAPITOL (11663 "French Kiss") 15-25 79
(Picture disc.)
Also see FLEETWOOD MAC
Also see PARIS

WELCH, Lenny — P&R/R&B '60
(Lenny & the Storks)

Singles: 7-inch
ATCO 3-5 72
BARNABY 3-5 76
BIG TREE 3-5 78-83
CADENCE (Except 1399 & 1422) 8-15 59-64
CADENCE (1399 "Boogie Cha Cha") 15-25 60
CADENCE (1422 "Congratulations Baby") 15-25 62
COLUMBIA 4-8 67
COMMONWEALTH UNITED 4-6 69
DECCA 5-10 59
JASON SCOTT 4-8
KAPP 5-15 65-67
MAINSTREAM 3-5 73-74
MERCURY 4-8 68
ROULETTE 3-6 71

LPs: 10/12-inch
CADENCE 15-25 64
COLUMBIA 10-20 65
KAPP 10-20 66-67

WELK, Lawrence, & His Orchestra — P&R '38

Singles: 78 rpm
CORAL 3-5 50-57
DECCA 3-6 42-45
MERCURY 3-5 50-55
OKEH 3-6 41
VOCALION 3-8 38-39

Singles: 7-inch
CORAL 3-8 50-66
DOT 3-8 59-67
MERCURY 3-8 50-55
RANWOOD 3-8 68-77

EPs: 7-inch
CORAL 4-8 50-58
DOT 4-8 59-60
MERCURY 4-8 50-55

LPs: 10/12-inch
CORAL 5-15 50-65
DECCA 5-10 72
DOT 5-15 59-67
HAMILTON 4-8 64-66
HARMONY 4-8 68-70
MCA 4-8 74-76
PICKWICK 4-8
RANWOOD 4-8 68-85
SUNNYVALE 4-6 79
TRADITION 4-8 75
VOCALION 4-8 59-70
WING 4-8 60-62
Also see FOLEY, Red
Also see HODGES, Johnny, & Lawrence Welk
Also see HUDSON, Emperor Bob, & Lawrence Welk
Also see LENNON SISTERS
Also see McGUIRE SISTERS
Also see PRESLEY, Elvis / Lawrence Welk

WELL RED — R&B '87

Singles: 7-inch
VIRGIN 3-4 87

WELLER, Freddy — C&W/LP '69

Singles: 7-inch
ABC/DOT 3-5 75
APT 4-8 65
COLUMBIA 3-6 69-80
DORE 5-10 61

LPs: 10/12-inch
ABC/DOT 5-10 75
COLUMBIA 5-12 69-80
EPIC 8-12 74
51 WEST 5-8 80s
Also see REVERE, Paul, & Raiders

WELLES, Orson — LP '70

LPs: 10/12-inch
MEDIARTS 8-12 70
Also see CROSBY, Bing, and Orson Welles

WELLS, Brandi — R&B '81

Singles: 7-inch
WMOT 3-5 81-82

WELLS, Jean — R&B '67

Singles: 7-inch
ABC-PAR 5-10 65
CALLA 5-10 67-68
QUAKER TOWN 4-8
T.E.C. 3-5 79
VOLARE 4-8 69

WELLS, Junior — R&B '60
(With His Eagle Rockers; Junior Wells' Chicago Blues Band)

Singles: 78 rpm
STATES 25-50 52-53

Singles: 7-inch
BLUE ROCK 8-12 68-69
BRIGHT STAR 8-12 66-67
CHIEF 10-25 57-62
MEL 10-15
PROFILE 10-20 59-60
SHAD 8-12 59
STATES (122 "Cut That Out") 100-200 52
(Colored vinyl.)
STATES (134 "Hodo Man") 100-200 53
(Colored vinyl.)
STATES (139 "Lawdy Lawdy") 100-200 53
(Colored vinyl.)
STATES (143 "So All Alone") 150-250 53
(Colored vinyl.)
U.S.A. 5-10 63-64
VANGUARD 5-10 67

LPs: 10/12-inch
BLUE ROCK 10-20 68
DELMARK 10-20 66-69
VANGUARD 12-25 66-68
Also see COTTON, James, Carey Bell, Junior Wells & Billy Branch
Also see DIXON, Willie
Also see LENOIR, J.B.
Also see WATERS, Muddy

WELLS, Junior, & Buddy Guy

LPs: 10/12-inch
ATCO 8-12 72
BLIND PIG 5-8 82
INTERMEDIA 5-8
Also see WELLS, Junior

WELLS, Kitty — C&W/P&R '52

Singles: 78 rpm
DECCA 4-10 52-57
RCA 6-12 50

Singles: 7-inch
CAPRICORN 3-5 74-76
DECCA (28000 & 29000 series) 5-15 52-56
DECCA (30000 thru 32000 series) 3-10 56-71
MCA 3-4 73
RCA (0333 "Make Up Your Mind") 15-25 50
(Colored vinyl.)
RUBOCA 3-5 79-80

Picture Sleeves
DECCA 4-6 69

EPs: 7-inch
DECCA 5-15 55-65

LPs: 10/12-inch
BULLDOG 5-10
CAPRICORN 5-10 74
CORAL/MCA 5-8 84
DECCA (174 "Kitty Wells Story") 15-25 63
(Monaural. Includes booklet.)
DECCA (7-174 "Kitty Wells Story") 20-30 63
(Stereo. Includes booklet.)
DECCA (4075 thru 4929) 10-25 61-67
(Monaural.)
DECCA (7-4075 thru 7-4929) 15-30 61-67
(Stereo.)
DECCA (7-4961 thru 7-5350) 10-15 68-72
(Stereo.)
DECCA (8293 "Country Hit Parade") 35-45 56
(Monaural.)
DECCA (7-8293 "Country Hit Parade") 15-25 68
(Stereo.)
DECCA (8552 "Winner of Your Heart") 35-45 56
DECCA (7-8552 "Winner of Your Heart") 10-15 65
DECCA (8732 "Lonely Street") 30-40 58
(Monaural.)
DECCA (7-8732 "Lonely Street") 10-15 65
(Stereo.)
DECCA (8858 "Dust on the Bible") 25-35 59
(Monaural.)
DECCA (7-8858 "Dust on the Bible") 10-15 68
(Stereo.)
DECCA (8888 "After Dark") 30-40 59
(Monaural.)
DECCA (7-8888 "After Dark") 10-15 68
(Stereo.)
DECCA (8979 "Kitty's Choice") 25-35 59
(Monaural.)
DECCA (7-8979 "Kitty's Choice") 30-40 59
(Stereo.)
EXACT 5-10 80
GOLDEN COUNTRY 5-10
IMPERIAL HOUSE 5-10 80
KOALA 5-10 79
MCA 4-8 73-83
MISTLETOE 5-8 80s
PICKWICK/HILLTOP 5-10 70s
ROUNDER 5-8 82
RUBOCA 8-12 79
SUFFOLK MARKETING 5-10 80
VOCALION 8-15 66-69
Also see ACUFF, Roy, & Kitty Wells
Also see PARTON, Dolly / Kitty Wells
Also see PIERCE, Webb, & Kitty Wells
Also see TUBB, Ernest

WELLS, Kitty / Bill Anderson

LPs: 10/12-inch
MCA (734584 "Collector's Album") 8-12
Also see ANDERSON, Bill

WELLS, Kitty, & Roy Drusky — C&W '60

Singles: 7-inch
DECCA 4-8 60

LPs: 10/12-inch
PLAYBACK 5-10
Also see DRUSKY, Roy

WELLS, Kitty, & Red Foley — C&W '54

Singles: 78 rpm
DECCA 4-10 54-56

Singles: 7-inch
DECCA (29000 series) 5-15 54-56
DECCA (32000 series) 3-6 67-69

EPs: 7-inch
DECCA 8-12 59

LPs: 10/12-inch
DECCA 12-25 61-67
Also see FOLEY, Red

WELLS, Kitty / Bill Phillips / Bobby Wright / Johnny Wright

LP: 10/12-inch
DECCA (74831 "The Kitty Wells Show") 10-20 66

WELLS, Kitty, & Webb Pierce — C&W '57

Singles: 78 rpm
DECCA 5-10 57

Singles: 7-inch
DECCA 5-10 57-64

EPs: 7-inch
DECCA 10-15 59
Also see PIERCE, Webb

WELLS, Kitty, & Johnny Wright *C&W '68*

Singles: 7-inch

DECCA....3-6 68

Also see WELLS, Kitty

WELLS, Mary *R&B '60*

Singles: 12-inch

EPIC....4-8 82

Singles: 7-inch

ATCO....10-20 66-67
EPIC....3-4 82
JUBILEE....5-15 68-71
MOTOWN (1003 "Bye Bye Baby")....15-25 60
(Pink label.)
MOTOWN (1011 "I Don't Want to Take a Chance")....10-20 61
(Pink label.)
MOTOWN (1011 "I Don't Want to Take a Chance")....8-12 61
(Blue label.)
MOTOWN (1016 thru 1056)....10-20 62-64
MOTOWN (1061 "When I'm Gone")....100-200 65
MOTOWN (1065 "I'll Be Available")..15-25 65
REPRISE....5-10 71-74
20TH FOX....10-20 64-66

Picture Sleeves

MOTOWN (1003 "Bye Bye Baby")....50-75 61
MOTOWN (1011 "I Don't Want to Take a Chance")....25-50 61
MOTOWN (1024 "The One Who Really Loves You")....20-40 62
MOTOWN (1032 "You Beat Me to the Punch")....20-30 62
20TH FOX (590 "He's a Lover")....5-10 65

EPs: 7-inch

MOTOWN (60616 "Greatest Hits")....25-50 64

LPs: 10/12-inch

ALLEGIANCE....5-10 84
ATCO....15-20 66
EPIC....5-10 81
51 WEST....5-8 83
JUBILEE....10-20 68
MOTOWN (100 & 200 series)....5-10 82
MOTOWN (600 "Mary Wells")....100-125 61
(White label with blue print.)
MOTOWN (605 "The One Who Really Loves You")....75-125 62
MOTOWN (607 "Two Lovers")....50-100 63
MOTOWN (611 "On Stage")....40-60 64
MOTOWN (616 "Greatest Hits")....25-35 64
MOTOWN (617 "My Guy")....40-60 64
MOTOWN (653 "Vintage Stock")....40-60 66
MOVIETONE....15-20 66
POWER PAK....5-8
20TH FOX....20-30 65

Also see GAYE, Marvin, & Mary Wells
Also see MARVELETTES / Mary Wells / Miracles / Marvin Gaye

WELLS, Terri *R&B/D&D '84*

Singles: 12-inch

PHILLY WORLD....4-6 84

Singles: 7-inch

PHILLY WORLD....3-4 84

Also see MFSB

WENDY & LISA *P&R/LP '87*

Singles: 7-inch

COLUMBIA....3-4 87-89

Picture Sleeves

COLUMBIA....3-4 87

LPs: 10/12-inch

COLUMBIA....5-8 87-89

WERNER, David *LP '79*

Singles: 7-inch

EPIC....3-5 79
RCA....3-5 74-76

LPs: 10/12-inch

EPIC....5-10 79
RCA....5-10 75

WERNER, Max *P&R '81*

Singles: 7-inch

RADIO....3-5 81

Also see KAYAK

WESLEY, Fred *R&B '73*

(With the Horny Horns; with J.B.s)

Singles: 7-inch

ATLANTIC....3-5 77
PEOPLE....4-6 72-74
RSO....3-5 80

LPs: 10/12-inch

ATLANTIC....8-10 77

Also see BROWN, James, Band
Also see FRED & New J.B.s
Also see J.B.s

WEST, Belinda *R&B '80*

Singles: 7-inch

PANORAMA....3-5 80

WEST, Dr: see DR. WEST

WEST, Dottie *C&W '63*

(With Dale West)

Singles: 7-inch

ATLANTIC....4-8 62
LIBERTY....3-4 80-83
PERMIAN....3-4 84-85
RCA (Except 8000 series)....3-6 66-81
RCA (8000 series)....4-8 63-66
STARDAY (500 series)....4-8 60-61
STARDAY (700 series)....3-6 65
U.A.....3-4 76-80

Picture Sleeves

LIBERTY....3-5 80-81

LPs: 10/12-inch

CAMDEN....5-10 71-73
COLUMBIA....5-10 80
GUSTO....5-8 82
LIBERTY....5-8 81-82
NASHVILLE....8-12 70s
PERMIAN....5-8 85
PICKWICK....5-10 75
POWER PAK....5-10 70s
RCA....8-18 65-75
STARDAY....10-20 64-65
U.A.....5-10 73-80

Session: Jordanaires.
Also see DEAN, Jimmy, & Dottie West
Also see REEVES, Jim, & Dottie West
Also see ROGERS, Kenny, & Dottie West

WEST, Dottie, & Don Gibson *C&W '70*

Singles: 7-inch

RCA....3-5 69-70

LPs: 10/12-inch

RCA....8-12 69

Also see GIBSON, Don

WEST, Dottie / Melba Montgomery

LPs: 10/12-inch

STARDAY....10-20 65

Also see MONTGOMERY, Melba
Also see WEST, Dottie

WEST, Leslie *LP '69*

(Leslie West Band)

Singles: 7-inch

PHANTOM....3-5 75-76

LPs: 10/12-inch

PHANTOM....8-10 75-76
WINDFALL....10-15 69

Also see JAGGER, Mick
Also see MOUNTAIN
Also see WEST, BRUCE & LAING

WEST, Mae *P&R '33*

(With Somebody's Chyldren)

Singles: 78 rpm

BRUNSWICK....10-30 33

Singles: 7-inch

MGM (14491 "Great Balls of Fire")....4-8 73
PLAZA....5-10 62
TOWER....5-10 66
20TH FOX (6718 "Hard to Handle")..15-30 70

EPs: 7-inch

DECCA (838 "Fabulous Mae West") 50-75 55
(Three-disc set.)

LPs: 10/12-inch

DAGONET....10-15 66
DECCA (9016 "Fabulous Mae West")....40-60 55
DECCA (79016 "Fabulous Mae West")....10-15 70
MGM (4869 "Great Balls of Fire")....10-20 72
TOWER....15-25 66

Also see FIELDS, W.C.

WEST, BRUCE & LAING *LP '72*

Singles: 7-inch

COLUMBIA....3-5 73

LPs: 10/12-inch

COLUMBIA....8-10 74
COLUMBIA/WINDFALL....8-12 72-74

Members: Leslie West; Jack Bruce; Corky Laing.
Also see BRUCE, Jack
Also see LAING, Corky
Also see MOUNTAIN
Also see WEST, Leslie

WEST COAST CREW *R&B '86*

Singles: 7-inch

KMA....3-4 86

WEST COAST RAP ALL STARS *LP '90*

LPs: 10/12-inch

W.B.....5-8 90

WEST STREET MOB *P&R/R&B '81*

Singles: 12-inch

SUGAR HILL....4-6 81-83

Singles: 7-inch

SUGAR HILL....3-4 81-83

LPs: 10/12-inch

SUGAR HILL....5-10 82

Members: Reggie Griffin.
Also see GRIFFIN, Reggie, & Technofunk

WESTON, Kim *P&R/R&B '63*

Singles: 7-inch

BANYAN TREE....3-5
ENTERPRISE....3-5 74
GORDY....10-20 65-66
MGM....10-20 67-68
MIKIM....3-5 71-72
PEOPLE....5-15 69-70
PRIDE....3-5 70
TAMLA....15-25 63-65
VOLT....10-15 71

Picture Sleeves

MGM....4-8 67

EPs: 7-inch

MOTOWN (2005 "Kim Weston")....15-25
MOTOWN (2015 "Rock Me a Little While")....15-25

LPs: 10/12-inch

ENTERPRISE....8-12 74
MGM....15-25 67-68
VOLT....10-15 71

Also see GAYE, Marvin, & Kim Weston
Also see NASH, Johnny, & Kim Weston

WESTON, Paul, Orchestra *LP '55*

Singles: 78 rpm

CAPITOL....3-5 45-57
COLUMBIA....3-4 50-56

Singles: 7-inch

CAPITOL....4-8 57-60
COLUMBIA....4-8 50-56

EPs: 7-inch

COLUMBIA....5-10 50-56

LPs: 10/12-inch

CAPITOL....5-15 57-61
COLUMBIA....5-15 50-56
CORINTHIAN....4-8 78
HARMONY....4-8 72

Also see EDWARDS, Jonathan & Darlene
Also see STAFFORD, Jo

WET WET WET *P&R/LP '88*

Singles: 7-inch

UNI....3-4 88

Picture Sleeves

UNI....3-4 88

LPs: 10/12-inch

UNI....5-8 88

WET WILLIE — LP '73

Singles: 7-inch

CAPRICORN ... 3-5 ... 74-78
EPIC ... 3-5 ... 77-79

LPs: 10/12-inch

CAPRICORN ... 5-10 ... 71-78
EPIC ... 5-10 ... 78-79

Member: Jimmy Hall.
Also see HALL, Jimmy

WHALUM, Kirk — LP '88

LPs: 10/12-inch

COLUMBIA ... 5-8 ... 88

WHAM! — P&R/D&D/LP '83

(Wham! U.K.; Featuring George Michael)

Singles: 12-inch

COLUMBIA ... 4-6 ... 82-86

Singles: 7-inch

COLUMBIA ... 3-4 ... 83-86

Picture Sleeves

COLUMBIA ... 3-5 ... 82-86

LPs: 10/12-inch

COLUMBIA (Except 40062) ... 5-8 ... 83-86
COLUMBIA (40062 "Make It Big") ... 15-20 ... 84
(Picture disc.)

Members: George Michael; Andrew Ridgely.
Also see MICHAEL, George
Also see PEPSI & SHIRLIE
Also see RIDGELEY, Andrew

WHAT IS THIS — P&R/LP '85

Singles: 7-inch

MCA ... 3-4 ... 85

LPs: 10/12-inch

MCA ... 5-8 ... 85

WHATNAUTS — R&B '70

(With the Whatnaut Band)

Singles: 7-inch

A&I ... 3-5 ... 70
DIAL ... 3-5
GSF ... 3-5 ... 73
HARLEM INT'L ... 3-4 ... 82
STANG ... 3-5 ... 71

LPs: 10/12-inch

STANG ... 10-20 ... 70-71

Members: Billy Herndon; Garrett Jones; Gerald Pinkney.
Also see MOMENTS & WHATNAUTS

WHEELER, Billy Edd — C&W '64

(With Rashell Richmond; with Joan Sommer; with Shelly Mann)

Singles: 7-inch

CAPITOL ... 3-5 ... 75-76
KAPP ... 4-8 ... 63-68
NSD ... 3-4 ... 80-81
RCA ... 3-5 ... 70-73
RADIO CINEMA ... 3-5 ... 79
U.A. ... 3-6 ... 69

Picture Sleeves

KAPP ... 4-8 ... 67

LPs: 10/12-inch

AVALANCHE ... 8-10 ... 73
FLYING FISH ... 5-10 ... 79
KAPP ... 10-20 ... 64-68
MONITOR ... 15-25 ... 61-62
RCA ... 8-10 ... 71
U.A. ... 8-15 ... 69

WHEELER, Caron — LP '90

LPs: 10/12-inch

EMI ... 5-8 ... 90

Also see COSTELLO, Elvis

WHEN IN ROME — P&R/LP '88

Singles: 7-inch

VIRGIN ... 3-4 ... 88-89

Picture Sleeves

VIRGIN ... 3-4 ... 88-89

LPs: 10/12-inch

VIRGIN ... 5-8 ... 88

WHIRLWIND — P&R/R&B '76

Singles: 12-inch

ROULETTE ... 4-8 ... 77

Singles: 7-inch

ROULETTE ... 3-5 ... 76

WHISPERS — R&B '69

Singles: 12-inch

SOLAR ... 4-6 ... 80-84

Singles: 7-inch

COLLECTABLES ... 3-4 ... 80s
DORE ... 10-20 ... 65-66
FONTANA ... 10-20 ... 66
JANUS ... 3-6 ... 70-75
SOLAR ... 3-5 ... 79-88
SOUL CLOCK ... 4-8 ... 69-70
SOUL TRAIN ... 3-6 ... 75-77

LPs: 10/12-inch

ACCORD ... 5-10 ... 81
ALLEGIANCE ... 5-8 ... 84
CAPITOL ... 5-8 ... 90
DORE ... 5-10 ... 80
JANUS ... 8-10 ... 72-75
SOLAR ... 5-10 ... 78-87
SOUL TRAIN ... 5-10 ... 76-77

Members: Walter Scott; Wallace Scott; Nicholas Caldwell; Marcus Hudson; Leaveil DeGree.
Also see LUCAS, Carrie, & Whispers

WHISTLE — R&B '86

Singles: 12-inch

SELECT ... 4-6 ... 86

Singles: 7-inch

SELECT ... 3-4 ... 86-89

LPs: 10/12-inch

SELECT ... 5-8 ... 86-88

WHITCOMB, Ian — P&R/LP '65

(With Bluesville; with Somebody's Chyldren)

Singles: 7-inch

JERDEN ... 5-10 ... 64-65
TOWER ... 4-8 ... 65-68
U.A. ... 3-5 ... 73

Picture Sleeves

TOWER ... 4-8 ... 66

LPs: 10/12-inch

FIRST AMERICAN ... 5-10 ... 78-82
SIERRA ... 5-10 ... 80
TOWER ... 15-20 ... 65-68
U.A. ... 8-10 ... 72

WHITE, Artie "Blues Boy" — R&B '77

Singles: 7-inch

ALTEE ... 3-5 ... 77
RONN ... 3-5 ... 70s

WHITE, Barry — P&R/R&B/LP '73

(With Love Unlimited & Love Unlimited Orchestra; with Glodean)

Singles: 12-inch

20TH FOX ... 4-8 ... 73-78
UNLIMITED GOLD ... 4-6 ... 83

Singles: 7-inch

A&M ... 3-4 ... 87
BRONCO ... 5-10 ... 67
CASABLANCA ... 3-5 ... 70s
20TH FOX ... 3-6 ... 73-78
UNLIMITED GOLD ... 3-4 ... 79-83

LPs: 10/12-inch

A&M ... 5-8 ... 87
SUPREMACY ... 10-15 ... 74
20TH FOX (Except 1) ... 5-10 ... 73-81
20TH FOX (1 "Barry White Radio Special") ... 10-20 ... 70s
(Promotional issue only.)
UNLIMITED GOLD ... 5-10 ... 79-82

Also see BOB & EARL
Also see JONES, Quincy, James Ingram, Al B. Sure, El DeBarge & Barry White
Also see LOVE UNLIMITED

WHITE, Barry, & Atlantics / Atlantics

Singles: 7-inch

FARO ... 5-10 ... 63

Also see WHITE, Barry

WHITE, Beverly — R&B '43

Singles: 78 rpm

BEACON ... 5-10 ... 43
DAVIS ... 5-10 ... 46

Singles: 7-inch

PHILIPS ... 4-8 ... 62

WHITE, Danny — P&R '77

Singles: 7-inch

ABC-PAR ... 4-8 ... 64
ATLAS ... 4-8 ... 66
DECCA ... 4-8 ... 66-67
DOT ... 4-8 ... 61
FRISCO ... 10-20 ... 62
KING (5122 "That's My Doll") ... 20-30 ... 58
ROCKY COAST ... 3-5 ... 77
SSS INT'L ... 3-6 ... 69

WHITE, Danny, & Linda Nail — C&W '83

Singles: 7-inch

GRAND PRIX ... 3-4 ... 83

WHITE, John — R&B '87

Singles: 7-inch

GEFFEN ... 3-4 ... 87

WHITE, Karyn — P&R '86

Singles: 7-inch

W.B. ... 3-4 ... 86-89

Picture Sleeves

W.B. ... 3-4 ... 86-89

LPs: 10/12-inch

W.B. ... 5-8 ... 88

Also see LORBER, Jeff

WHITE, Kitty — P&R '55

Singles: 78 rpm

DECCA ... 3-5 ... 51
MERCURY ... 3-5 ... 55-56

Singles: 7-inch

CLOVER ... 3-6 ... 66
DECCA ... 5-10 ... 51
DOT ... 4-8 ... 60
GNP ... 4-8 ... 59
MERCURY ... 4-8 ... 55-56

EPs: 7-inch

EMARCY ... 5-15 ... 54
PACIFIC JAZZ ... 8-15 ... 54

LPs: 10/12-inch

EMARCY ... 30-40 ... 54
CLOVER ... 6-12 ... 66
MERCURY ... 20-30 ... 55
PACIFIC JAZZ ... 30-40 ... 54-55

WHITE, Lenny — LP '76

Singles: 7-inch

ELEKTRA ... 3-5 ... 78-83
NEMPEROR ... 3-5 ... 76

LPs: 10/12-inch

ELEKTRA ... 5-8 ... 78-83
NEMPEROR ... 8-10 ... 75-77

Also see RETURN to FOREVER
Also see TWENNYNINE

WHITE, Maurice — P&R/R&B/D&D/LP '85

Singles: 12-inch

COLUMBIA ... 4-6 ... 86

Singles: 7-inch

COLUMBIA ... 3-4 ... 85-86
ELEKTRA ... 3-5 ... 78
GOLD ... 8-12 ... 59
PRIDE ... 10-20 ... 60

Picture Sleeves

COLUMBIA ... 3-4 ... 85-86

LPs: 10/12-inch

COLUMBIA ... 5-8 ... 85-86

WHITE, Tony Joe — P&R/LP '69

(With the Mojos; with Waylon Jennings)

Singles: 7-inch

ARISTA ... 3-5 ... 79
CASABLANCA ... 3-5 ... 80
COLUMBIA ... 3-4 ... 83-85
J-BECK ... 5-8
MONUMENT ... 4-8 ... 67-70
20TH FOX ... 3-5 ... 76

LPs: 10/12-inch

CASABLANCA ... 5-10 ... 80
COLUMBIA ... 5-8 ... 83
MONUMENT ... 8-15 ... 69-70
20TH FOX ... 5-10 ... 77
W.B. ... 8-10 ... 71-73

Session: Waylon Jennings.
Also see JENNINGS, Waylon

WHITE LION LP '87

Singles: 7-inch

ATLANTIC ... 3-4 87-90

Picture Sleeves

ATLANTIC ... 3-4 87-89

LPs: 10/12-inch

ATLANTIC ... 5-8 87-90
GRAND SLAM ... 5-8 88

Members: Mike Tramp; Greg D'Angelo; Jim Lomenzo; Vito Bratta.
Also see ANTHRAX

WHITE PLAINS P&R/LP '70

Singles: 7-inch

DERAM ... 3-6 70-73
LONDON ... 3-5 70s

LPs: 10/12-inch

DERAM ... 10-15 70

Members: Tony Burrows; Ricky Wolff; Roger Greenaway; Robin Box; Robin Shaw; Pete Nelson; Roger Hills.
Also see BURROWS, Tony
Also see PIPKINS

WHITE WOLF LP '85

Singles: 7-inch

RCA ... 3-4 85-86

LPs: 10/12-inch

RCA ... 5-8 85-86

WHITEHEAD, Charles R&B '75
(With the Swamp Dogg Band)

Singles: 7-inch

ISLAND ... 3-5 75

LPs: 10/12-inch

FUNGUS ... 10-15
WIZARD ... 5-10 78

WHITEHEAD, John R&B '88

Singles: 7-inch

MERCURY ... 3-4 88

Also see McFADDEN & WHITEHEAD

WHITEHEAD, Kenny & Johnny R&B '86

Singles: 12-inch

PHILADELPHIA INT'L ... 4-6 86

Singles: 7-inch

PHILADELPHIA INT'L ... 3-4 86

LPs: 10/12-inch

PHILADELPHIA INT'L ... 5-8 86

Also see KENNY & JOHNNY

WHITEMAN, Paul, Orchestra P&R '20

Singles: 78 rpm

CAPITOL ... 3-5 42-43
COLUMBIA ... 3-6 28-32
CORAL ... 3-5 50-56
DECCA ... 3-5 38-39
VICTOR (Black Plastic) ... 3-8 20-36
VICTOR (39000 "Night with Paul Whiteman at the Biltmore") ... 300-400 30s
(Picture disc.)

Singles: 7-inch

CORAL ... 3-6 50-56
WORLD'S FAIR (82083/84 "Conducts Rhapsody 21") ... 20-25 62
(Picture disc. Souvenir from Seattle World's Fair.)

EPs: 7-inch

CORAL ... 4-8 50-56

LPs: 10/12-inch

CAPITOL ... 5-10 62
CORAL ... 5-15 50-56
GRAND AWARD ... 5-15 56-59
RCA (Black vinyl) ... 4-8 68-69
RCA (67-2000 "Night with Paul Whiteman at the Biltmore") ... 400-600 30s
(Picture disc.)
WESTMINSTER ... 4-8 74

WHITESNAKE P&R/LP '80

Singles: 12-inch

GEFFEN ... 4-6 86

Singles: 7-inch

GEFFEN ... 3-4 82-89
MIRAGE ... 3-5 80
U.A. ... 3-5 79

Picture Sleeves

GEFFEN ... 3-4 87-88
MIRAGE ... 3-5 80

LPs: 10/12-inch

GEFFEN ... 5-8 82-89
MIRAGE ... 5-10 80-81
U.A. ... 5-10 79

Members: David Coverdale; Jon Lord; Aynsley Dunbar; John Sykes; Neil Murray; Tommy Aldridge; Rudy Sarzo; Vivian Campbell; Adrian Vandenberg; Steve Vai.
Also see COVERDALE, David
Also see DEEP PURPLE
Also see DUNBAR, Aynsley
Also see LORD, Jon

WHITFIELD, David P&R '54

Singles: 78 rpm

LONDON ... 3-5 53-57

Singles: 7-inch

LONDON ... 3-8 53-63

EPs: 7-inch

LONDON ... 4-8 54

LPs: 10/12-inch

LONDON ... 5-15 54-66

Also see MANTOVANI

WHITING, Margaret P&R '46

Singles: 78 rpm

CAPITOL ... 3-8 46-56
DOT ... 3-8 57

Singles: 7-inch

CAPITOL ... 5-10 50-56
DOT ... 5-8 57-59
LONDON ... 3-6 66-70
VERVE ... 4-6 60

EPs: 7-inch

CAPITOL ... 5-10 50-56

LPs: 10/12-inch

CAPITOL ... 12-25 50-56
DOT ... 8-18 57-67
HAMILTON ... 5-15 59-65
LONDON ... 5-15 67-68
VERVE ... 10-20 60

Also see MARTIN, Dean, & Margaret Whiting
Also see TORME, Mel

WHITING, Margaret, & Jimmy Wakely C&W '49

Singles: 78 rpm

CAPITOL ... 3-8 49-51

Singles: 7-inch

CAPITOL ... 5-10 49-51

EPs: 7-inch

CAPITOL ... 8-15 53

LPs: 10/12-inch

PICKWICK ... 8-12 67

Also see WHITING, Margaret
Also see WAKELY, Jimmy

WHITLOCK, Bobby LP '72

Singles: 7-inch

DUNHILL ... 3-5 72

LPs: 10/12-inch

CAPRICORN ... 8-10 76
DUNHILL ... 10-12 72

Also see BELL, Maggie, & Bobby Whitlock
Also see DELANEY & BONNIE
Also see DEREK & DOMINOES

WHITMAN, Slim C&W/P&R '52

Singles: 78 rpm

IMPERIAL ... 5-15 52-57

Singles: 7-inch

CLEVELAND INT'L ... 3-4 80-82
EPIC ... 3-4 84
IMPERIAL (5000 series) ... 5-10 61-63
IMPERIAL (8000 thru 8200 series) ... 10-25 52-58
IMPERIAL (8300 series) ... 8-12 59-60
IMPERIAL (50000 series) ... 3-5 70-71
IMPERIAL (65000 & 66000 series) ... 3-8 61-69
U.A. ... 3-8 70-77

EPs: 7-inch

IMPERIAL ... 30-50 54-65
RCA (3217 "Slim Whitman Sings and Yodels") ... 100-150 54

LPs: 10/12-inch

CAMDEN ... 8-12 66
CLEVELAND INT'L (Except AS-99875) ... 5-10 80-81
CLEVELAND INT'L (AS-99875 "Songs I Love to Sing") ... 30-35 80
(Picture disc. Promotional issue only. Reportedly 1,600 made.)
EPIC ... 5-8 84
IMPERIAL (3004 "America's Favorite Folk Artist") ... 400-600 54
(10-inch LP. Colored vinyl.)
IMPERIAL (9000 series) ... 35-50 56-60
(Maroon or black label with "Imperial" at top.)
IMPERIAL (9000 series) ... 8-15 66
(Black label with "Imperial" on left side.)
IMPERIAL (9100 series) ... 20-40 60-62
(Black label with "Imperial" at top.)
IMPERIAL (9100 series) ... 8-15 66
(Black label with "Imperial" on left side.)
IMPERIAL (9200 & 9300 series) ... 15-25 63-67
IMPERIAL (12100 series) ... 20-30 62
(Black label with "Imperial" at top.)
IMPERIAL (12100 series) ... 8-15 66
(Black label with "Imperial" on left side.)
IMPERIAL (12200 & 12300 series) ... 12-25 65-68
IMPERIAL (12400 series) ... 8-12 68-69
LIBERTY ... 5-10 80-82
PICKWICK ... 5-10 70s
RCA (3217 "Slim Whitman Sings and Yodels") ... 250-350 54
RCA (3700 series) ... 5-8 80
SUFFOLK MARKETING ... 8-12 79-82
SUNSET ... 8-12 66-70
U.A. ... 6-12 70-80

Also see WILLIAMS, Hank / Slim Whitman

WHITNEY, Marva P&R/R&B '69

Singles: 7-inch

EXCELLO (2328 "Don't Let Our Love Fade Away") ... 5-10 73
FEDERAL ... 5-10
KING ... 5-10 67-69
T-NECK ... 4-6 70

LPs: 10/12-inch

KING ... 10-15 69

Session: Ellis Taylor.

WHITTAKER, Roger P&R/LP '75

Singles: 7-inch

MAIN STREET ... 3-4 83-84
RCA ... 3-5 70-86

Picture Sleeves

RCA ... 3-5 80

LPs: 10/12-inch

MAIN STREET ... 5-8 84
RCA ... 5-12 70-86

WHIZ KID R&B '85

Singles: 7-inch

TOMMY BOY ... 3-4 85

WHO P&R '65

Singles: 7-inch

ATCO (6409 "Substitute") ... 20-30 66
ATCO (6509 "Substitute") ... 10-15 67
DECCA (31725 "I Can't Explain") ... 15-20 64
DECCA (31801 "Anyway Anyhow Anywhere") ... 15-25 65
DECCA (31877 "My Generation") ... 15-25 65
DECCA (31988 "The Kids Are Alright") ... 15-25 66
DECCA (32058 "I'm a Boy") ... 15-25 66
DECCA (32114 "Happy Jack") ... 8-12 67
DECCA (32156 "Pictures of Lily") ... 8-12 67
DECCA (32206 "I Can See for Miles") ... 5-10 67
DECCA (32288 "Call Me Lightning") ... 8-12 68
DECCA (32362 "Magic Bus") ... 5-10 68
DECCA (32465 "Pinball Wizard") ... 4-8 69
DECCA (32519 "I'm Free") ... 4-8 69
DECCA (32670 "The Seeker") ... 5-10 70
DECCA (32708 "Summertime Blues") ... 5-10 70
DECCA (32729 "See Me, Feel Me") ... 5-10 70

DECCA (32737 "Young Man Blues") 50-75 70
DECCA (32846 "Won't Get Fooled Again") 5-10 71
DECCA (32888 "Behind Blue Eyes") .. 5-10 71
DECCA (32983 "Join Together") 5-10 72
DECCA (33041 "The Relay") 5-10 72
LIFE 20-30
MCA 3-5 74-79
POLYDOR 3-5 75-79
TRACK 4-8 72-74
W.B. 3-5 81-83

Picture Sleeves

DECCA (32114 "Happy Jack") 10-20 67
DECCA (32465 "Pinball Wizard") 8-12 69
DECCA (32729 "See Me, Feel Me") 8-12 70
DECCA (32737 "Young Man Blues") 75-125 70
POLYDOR 4-6 75-79
W.B. 3-5 81-83

Promotional Singles

ATCO (6409 "Substitute") 25-35 66
ATCO (6509 "Substitute") 10-20 67
DECCA (31725 "I Can't Explain") 20-25 64
DECCA (31801 "Anyway Anyhow Anywhere") 20-30 65
DECCA (31877 "My Generation") 20-30 65
DECCA (31988 "The Kids Are Alright") 20-30 66
DECCA (32058 "I'm a Boy") 20-30 66
DECCA (32114 "Happy Jack") 10-20 67
DECCA (32156 "Pictures of Lily") 10-20 67
DECCA (32206 "I Can See for Miles") 10-15 67
DECCA (32288 "Call Me Lightning") 10-15 68
DECCA (32362 "Magic Bus") 8-12 68
DECCA (32465 "Pinball Wizard") 5-10 69
DECCA (32519 "I'm Free") 5-10 69
DECCA (32670 "The Seeker") 10-15 70
DECCA (32708 "Summertime Blues") 10-15 70
DECCA (32729 "See Me, Feel Me") 8-12 70
DECCA (32737 "Young Man Blues") 50-75 70
DECCA (32846 "Won't Get Fooled Again") 8-12 71
DECCA (32888 "Behind Blue Eyes") .. 8-12 71
DECCA (32983 "Join Together") 8-12 72
DECCA (33041 "The Relay") 8-12 72
DECCA (34444 "Happy Jack") 20-30 67
DECCA ("Excerpts from *Tommy*") 25-35 69
(Boxed set for radio programming. Includes inserts. No number used.)
LIFE 20-30
MCA (Except 8559) 5-10 74-79
MCA (8559 "Long Live Rock") 90-120 79
(Picture disc. Has National Record Mart or NARM logo on back. Promotional issue only.)
MCA (8559 "Long Live Rock") 70-90 79
(Picture disc. With any logo other than NARM's on back.)
POLYDOR 5-10 75-79
TRACK 5-10 72-74
W.B. 4-8 81-83

LPs: 10/12-inch

DDL/MCA (16610 "Who Are You") 40-50 78
(Half-speed mastered.)
DWJ ("Musical Biography") 30-50 78
(Promotional issue only. Not issued with cover.)
DECCA (DL-4664 "My Generation") . 50-75 66
(Monaural.)
DECCA (DL-4664 "My Generation") 75-100 66
(White label. Promotional issue only.)
DECCA (DL7-4664 "My Generation") 40-60 66
(Stereo.)
DECCA (DL-4892 "Happy Jack") 50-75 67
(Monaural.)
DECCA (DL-4892 "Happy Jack") 75-100 67
(White label. Promotional issue only.)
DECCA (DL7-4892 "Happy Jack") 40-60 67
(Stereo.)
DECCA (DL-4950 "The Who Sell Out") 30-40 67
(Monaural.)
DECCA (DL-4950 "The Who Sell Out") 50-75 67
(White label. Promotional issue only.)
DECCA (DL7-4950 "The Who Sell Out") 20-30 67
(Stereo.)
DECCA (DL-5064 "Magic Bus") 50-75 68
(Monaural. White label. Promotional issue only.)
DECCA (DL7-5064 "Magic Bus") 25-30 68
DECCA (DXW-7205 "Excerpts from Tommy") 100-150 69
(Monaural. White label. Promotional issue only. Includes 12-page booklet.)
DECCA (DXSW-7205 "Tommy") 25-35 69
(Stereo. Includes 12-page booklet.)
DECCA (79175 "Live at Leeds") 50-75 70
(White label. Promotional issue only.)
DECCA (79175 "Live at Leeds") 20-30 70
(Includes insert pages.)
DECCA (79182 "Who's Next") 15-20 71
DECCA (79184 "Meaty Beaty Big and Bouncy") 15-20 71
MCA (1496 "Who's Greatest Hits") 5-10 83
MCA (1578 "Meaty Beaty Big and Bouncy") 5-10 80
MCA (1987 "Who Are You") 15-25 78
MCA (2000 series) 15-25 74
MCA (2161 "Who by Numbers") 8-10 75
MCA (3050 "Who Are You") 8-10 78
(Black vinyl.)
MCA (3050 "Who Are You") 15-20 78
(Colored vinyl.)
MCA (4067 "Happy Jack"/"The Who Sell Out") 15-25 74
MCA (4068 "My Generation"/"Magic Bus") 15-25 74
MCA (5000 series) 5-8 83-85
MCA (6000 series) 10-12 74
MCA (6895 "Quadrophenia") 8-10 80
(Does not have booklet.)
MCA (8000 series) 10-12 84
MCA (10004 "Quadrophenia") 10-12 81
MCA (10005 "Tommy") 10-12 77
MCA (11005 "The Kids Are Alright") 10-20 79
(Price includes 18-page booklet.)
MCA (12001 "Hooligans") 10-12 81
MCA (14950 "Who Are You") 12-15 79
(Picture disc.)
MCA (19501 "Join Together") 8-12 90
MCA (37000 series) 5-8 79
MFSL (115 "Face Dances") 20-30 84
TRACK/MCA (2126 "Odds & Sods") 10-20 74
(Includes insert.)
TRACK/MCA (4000 series) 10-12 74
TRACK/MCA (10004 "Quadrophenia") 15-20 73
(Includes 44-page booklet.)
W.B. 5-10 81-82
Members: Roger Daltrey; Pete Townshend; John Entwistle; Keith Moon; Kenny Jones.
Also see DALTREY, Roger
Also see ENTWISTLE, John
Also see HIGH NUMBERS
Also see McCARTNEY, Paul / Rochestra / Who / Rockpile
Also see MOON, Keith
Also see SMALL FACES
Also see TOWNSHEND, Pete

WHO / Strawberry Alarm Clock

LPs: 10/12-inch

DECCA (734586 "The Who/Strawberry Alarm Clock") 50-75 69
(Philco-Ford Special Products promotional issue.)
Also see STRAWBERRY ALARM CLOCK
Also see WHO

WHODINI — R&B '82

Singles: 12-inch

JIVE 4-6 82-86

Singles: 7-inch

JIVE 3-4 82-87

LPs: 10/12-inch

JIVE 5-8 84-87
Members: Jalil Hutchins; John Fletcher; Drew Carter.
Also see JACKSON, Millie
Also see KING DREAM CHORUS & HOLIDAY CREW

WHODINI & MILLIE JACKSON

Singles: 7-inch

JIVE 3-4 87
Also see JACKSON, Millie
Also see WHODINI

WHOLE DARN FAMILY — R&B '76

Singles: 7-inch

SOUL INT'L 3-5 76-77

LPs: 10/12-inch

SOUL INT'L 8-10 76

WICHITA TRAIN WHISTLE — LP '68

Singles: 7-inch

DOT 5-8 68

LPs: 10/12-inch

DOT 15-20 68
PACIFIC ARTS 8-10 78
Member: Michael Nesmith.
Also see NESMITH, Michael

WIDE BOY AWAKE — D&D '83

Singles: 12-inch

RCA 4-6 83

Singles: 7-inch

RCA 3-5 83

LPs: 10/12-inch

RCA 5-10 83

WIDOWMAKER — LP '77

Singles: 7-inch

JET 3-5 76-77

LPs: 10/12-inch

U.A. 8-10 76-77
Members: John Butler; Aerial Bender.
Also see GROSVENOR, Luther
Also see LOVE AFFAIR

WIEDLIN, Jane — P&R '83

Singles: 7-inch

EMI 3-4 88
I.R.S. 3-4 85

Picture Sleeves

EMI 3-4 88
I.R.S. 3-4 85-88

LPs: 10/12-inch

EMI 5-8 88
I.R.S. 5-8 85
Also see GO-GOs
Also see SPARKS & Jane Wiedlin

WIER, Rusty — P&R/LP '75

Singles: 7-inch

ABC 3-5 74
BLACK HAT 3-4 87
COLUMBIA 3-5 76
COMPLEAT 3-4 83-84
LONGHORN 4-8 65
20TH FOX 3-5 75-76

LPs: 10/12-inch

ABC 8-12 74
COLUMBIA 8-10 76
20TH FOX 8-10 75

WIGGINS, Spencer — R&B '70

Singles: 7-inch

FAME 4-8 69-70
GOLDWAX 5-10 66-69

WILBURN BROTHERS — C&W '55

Singles: 78 rpm

DECCA 5-15 54-57

Singles: 7-inch

DECCA (29190 thru 30428) 8-15 54-57
DECCA (30591 "Oo Bop Sha Boom") 15-25 58
DECCA (30686 thru 33027) 3-8 58-72
MCA 3-5 73

EPs: 7-inch

DECCA 5-15 57-62

LPs: 10/12-inch

CORAL 5-8 80s
DECCA (4142 thru 4615) 10-20 61-65

DECCA (4721 "Wilburn Brothers Show") 50-75 66
(With Loretta Lynn, Ernest Tubb & Harold Morrison.)
DECCA (4817 thru 5291) 8-15 67-71
DECCA (8774 "Side By Side") 30-40 58
(Monaural.)
DECCA (78774 "Side By Side") 50-75 58
(Stereo.)
DECCA (8959 "Livin' in God's Country") 20-30 59
(Monaural.)
DECCA (78959 "Livin' in God's Country") 30-40 59
(Stereo.)
DESIGN 8-12 60s
FIRST GENERATION 5-10
KING (746 "The Wonderful Wilburn Brothers") 25-35 61
PHONORAMA 5-10
STETSON 5-10
VOCALION 5-15 62-70
WORD 5-8
Members: Teddy Wilburn; Doyle Wilburn.
Session: Anita Kerr Singers.
Also see KERR, Anita
Also see LYNN, Loretta
Also see PIERCE, Webb, & Wilburn Brothers
Also see TUBB, Ernest, & Wilburn Brothers

WILCOX, Eddie, Orchestra — R&B '52
(Featuring Sunny Gale)
Singles: 78 rpm
DERBY 5-10 52
Singles: 7-inch
DERBY 10-20 52
(Colored vinyl.)
Also see GALE, Sunny

WILCOX, Harlow — C&W/P&R '69
(With the Oakies)
Singles: 7-inch
IMPEL (002 "Groovy Grubworm") 15-25 68
PLANTATION 4-8 69-70
SSS INT'L 3-5 70s
Picture Sleeves
PLANTATION 4-6 69
LPs: 10/12-inch
PLANTATION 5-10 70-71

WILD, Jack — P&R '70
Singles: 7-inch
BUDDAH 3-5 71
CAPITOL 3-5 70
Picture Sleeves
CAPITOL 3-5 70

WILD BLUE — P&R '86
Singles: 12-inch
CHRYSALIS 4-6 86
Singles: 7-inch
CHRYSALIS 3-4 86
Picture Sleeves
CHRYSALIS 3-4 86
LPs: 10/12-inch
CHRYSALIS 5-8 86

WILD CATS: see WILD-CATS

WILD CHERRY — P&R/R&B/LP '76
Singles: 12-inch
EPIC 4-8 76-79
Singles: 7-inch
A&M 3-5 75
BROWN BAG 3-5 72-73
EPIC/SWEET CITY 3-5 76-79
LPs: 10/12-inch
EPIC/SWEET CITY 5-10 76-79
Members: Robert Parissi; Allen Wentz; Ronald Beitle; Bryan Bassett.

WILD MAGNOLIAS — R&B '74
Singles: 7-inch
POLYDOR 3-5 74
LPs: 10/12-inch
POLYDOR 8-10 74

WILD MAN STEVE — LP '69
(Steve Gallon)
LPs: 10/12-inch
RAW 5-12 69-70

WILD ONES — LP '65
Singles: 7-inch
MAINLINE 4-8 65
MALA 4-8 67
U.A. 4-8 65-66
LPs: 10/12-inch
U.A. 15-20 65

WILD TURKEY — LP '72
Singles: 7-inch
CHRYSALIS 3-5 72-73
REPRISE 3-5 72
LPs: 10/12-inch
CHRYSALIS 8-10 72-73
REPRISE 8-12 72
Also see JETHRO TULL

WILD-CATS — P&R '59
Singles: 7-inch
U.A. (1154 "Gazachstahagen"/"Billy's Cha Cha") 15-25 58
(Monaural.)
U.A. (1154 "Gazachstahagen"/ "?????????????? ?????????????????????????") 20-30 59
(Monaural. Flip side, a novelty, has no credits — only lots of question marks on label.)
U.A. (169 "King Size Guitar") 10-20 59
U.A. (1154 "Gazachstahagen") 20-30 58
(Stereo [reprocessed].)
LPs: 10/12-inch
U.A. (3031 "Bandstand Record Hop") 35-45 59

WILDE, Danny — LP '88
LPs: 10/12-inch
GEFFEN 5-8 88
ISLAND 5-8 86

WILDE, Eugene — R&B '84
Singles: 12-inch
PHILLY WORLD 4-6 84-86
Singles: 7-inch
MCA 3-4 86
PHILLY WORLD 3-4 84-86
Picture Sleeves
PHILLY WORLD 3-4 85
LPs: 10/12-inch
PHILLY WORLD 5-8 84-86

WILDE, Kim — P&R/LP '82
Singles: 12-inch
MCA 4-6 85
Singles: 7-inch
EMI AMERICA 3-5 82
MCA 3-4 85-88
Picture Sleeves
EMI AMERICA 3-5 82
MCA 3-4 85-88
LPs: 10/12-inch
EMI AMERICA 5-10 82
MCA 5-8 85-88

WILDE, Marty — P&R '60
Singles: 7-inch
BELL 3-5 74
EPIC 5-10 58-60
LPs: 10/12-inch
EPIC (575 "Wilde About Marty") 30-40 60
(Stereo.)
EPIC (3686 "Bad Boy") 30-40 60
EPIC (3711 "Wilde About Marty") 25-35 60
(Monaural.)
Also see SHANNON

WILDER, Matthew — P&R/R&B '83
Singles: 12-inch
PRIVATE I 4-6 83-85
Singles: 7-inch
PRIVATE I 3-4 83-85
Picture Sleeves
PRIVATE I 3-4 84
LPs: 10/12-inch
PRIVATE I 5-8 83-85

WILDFIRE — P&R '77
Singles: 7-inch
CASABLANCA 3-5 77

WILDWEEDS — P&R '67
Singles: 7-inch
CADET 4-8 67-68
CADET CONCEPT 4-8 68
VANGUARD 3-5 71
LPs: 10/12-inch
VANGUARD 10-15 70

WILDWOODS
Singles: 7-inch
CAPRICE (101 "When the Swallows Come Back to Capistrano") 75-125 59
MAY (106 "Here Comes Big Ed") 10-20 61
Members: Fred Parris; Johnny Seastrand; Johnny Fisko; Jerry Greenberg.
Also see FIVE SATINS
Also see FIVE SATINS / Gerry Granahan & Five Satins

WILEY, Ed — R&B '50
(With Teddy Reynolds & King Tut)
Singles: 78 rpm
ATLANTIC 15-25 51
SITTIN' in WITH 15-25 50
Singles: 7-inch
ATLANTIC (959 "So Glad I'm Free") 100-150 51
SITTIN' in WITH (545 "Cry, Cry Baby") 100-200 50
Members: Teddy Reynolds; King Tut.

WILEY, Michelle — R&B '77
Singles: 7-inch
20TH FOX 3-5 77

WILL & THE KILL — LP '88
LPs: 10/12-inch
MCA 5-8 88

WILL POWERS — D&D '83
Singles: 12-inch
ISLAND 8-10 83

WILL TO POWER — P&R/R&B '87
Singles: 7-inch
EPIC 3-4 87-90
LPs: 10/12-inch
EPIC 5-8 87-90

WILLESDEN–DODGERS — D&D '84
Singles: 12-inch
JIVE 4-6 83-84
Singles: 7-inch
JIVE 3-4 83-84

WILLIAMS, Andre — R&B '57
(With the Don Juans; with Five Dollars; with Diablos; Andre "Bacon Fat" Williams & Inspirations; Andre "Mr. Rhythm" Williams)
Singles: 78 rpm
EPIC 10-20 57
FORTUNE 10-30 55-57
Singles: 7-inch
AVIN (103 "Rib Tips") 5-10 66
CHECKER 6-12 68-69
EPIC (9196 "Just Because of a Kiss") 10-20 57
FORTUNE (824 thru 856) 20-50 55-60
RIC TIC 10-20 60s
RONALD (1001 "Please Give Me a Chance") 50-100 50s
MIRACLE (4 "Rosa Lee") 300-500 60
SPORT 10-20 67
WINGATE 6-12 66
LPs: 10/12-inch
FORTUNE 5-8 86

WILLIAMS, Andre, & Gino Parks
Singles: 7-inch
FORTUNE (839 "Don't Touch") 35-55 57
FORTUNE (851 "Movin'") 25-50 60
Also see WILLIAMS, Andre

WILLIAMS, Andy P&R '56

Singles: 12-inch

COLUMBIA....4-6 79

Singles: 78 rpm

CADENCE....5-10 56-57

Singles: 7-inch

AURAVISION (6727 "Tammy")....5-10 64
(Cardboard flexi-disc, one of six by six different artists. Columbia Record Club "Enrollment Premium." Set came in a special paper sleeve.)
CADENCE....5-15 56-64
COLUMBIA....3-8 61-79

Picture Sleeves

CADENCE....10-20 59
COLUMBIA....3-5 61-76

EPs: 7-inch

CADENCE....10-15 57-59
COLUMBIA....5-10 62-66
(Juke box issues only.)
COLUMBIA/KFC (679 "Taste of Honey")....5-10 60s
(Promotional issue, made for Kentucky Fried Chicken.)
COLUMBIA SPECIAL PRODUCTS....4-6 60s

LPs: 10/12-inch

CADENCE....20-30 58-62
COLUMBIA....5-15 62-77
COLUMBIA SPECIAL PRODUCTS....5-10

WILLIAMS, Andy & David P&R '74

Singles: 7-inch

BARNABY....3-5 74-75
KAPP....3-5 72-73

LPs: 10/12-inch

KAPP....5-10 72

WILLIAMS, Anson P&R '77

Singles: 7-inch

CHELSEA....3-5 77

Picture Sleeves

CHELSEA....3-5 77

WILLIAMS, Beau R&B '84

Singles: 7-inch

CAPITOL....3-4 84-87

WILLIAMS, Billy P&R '47
(Billy Williams Quartet)

Singles: 7-inch

CORAL....5-10 54-57
RCA....5-10 47

Singles: 7-inch

CORAL (61212 thru 62069)....20-40 54-59
CORAL (62101 Red Hot Love")....25-50 59
CORAL (62140 thru 65500 series)....10-20 59-64
MCA....3-5 70s
MGM (10000 & 11000 series)....15-25 50-52
MGM (12000 series)....10-15 57
MERCURY....10-20 52-54

EPs: 7-inch

CORAL....15-25 57
MGM....15-25 57
MERCURY....15-25 53-55

LPs: 10/12-inch

CORAL (57184 "Billy Williams")....35-45 57
CORAL (57251 "Half Sweet Half Beat")....30-40 59
CORAL (57343 "The Billy Williams Revue")....30-40 60
MGM (3400 "The Billy Williams Quartet")....35-45 57
MERCURY (20317 "Oh Yeah!")....35-45 58
WING (12131 "Vote for Billy Williams")....30-40 59
Members: Billy Williams; Claude Riddick; John Ball; Eugene Dixon.
Also see CHARIOTEERS

WILLIAMS, Bobby R&B '76
(Bobby Williams Group)

Singles: 7-inch

CAPITOL....5-10 68
ROCK 'N' ROLL....3-6 76
SURE SHOT (5003 "Try Love")....10-20 64
SURE SHOT (5005 "Keep on Loving Me")....10-20 65
SURE SHOT (5013 "When You Play")....10-20 65
SURE SHOT (5025 "Try It Again")....10-20 66
SURE SHOT (5031 "I'll Hate Myself Tomorrow")....25-50 67

WILLIAMS, Bobby Earl R&B '74

Singles: 7-inch

IV CHAINS....3-5 74

WILLIAMS, Carol R&B '76

Singles: 12-inch

VANGUARD....4-6 83

Singles: 7-inch

SALSOUL....3-5 76

WILLIAMS, Christopher P&R '89

Singles: 7-inch

GEFFEN....3-4 89

Picture Sleeves

GEFFEN....3-4 89

WILLIAMS, Cootie R&B/C&W '44
(With Eddie "Cleanhead" Vinson)

Singles: 78 rpm

CAPITOL....10-20 46
DERBY....15-30 51
HIT....15-30 44-45

Singles: 7-inch

DERBY (756 "Shotgun Boogie")....50-100 51
RCA (6899 "Rinky Dink")....15-25 57

LPs: 10/12-inch

MOODSVILLE (27 "Solid Trumpet")....20-30 62
(Monaural.)
MOODSVILLE (27-SD "Solid Trumpet")....25-35 62
(Stereo.)
RCA (1718 "In Hi-Fi")....40-60 58
WARWICK (2027 "Do Nothing Till You Hear from Me")....40-60 59

WILLIAMS, Cootie, & Wini Brown

LPs: 10/12-inch

JARO (5001 "Around Midnight")....40-60 60
Also see BROWN, Wini
Also see VINSON, Eddie
Also see WILLIAMS, Cootie

WILLIAMS, Danny P&R/R&B/LP '64

Singles: 7-inch

PILOT....4-8 62
U.A.....4-8 61-66

LPs: 10/12-inch

U.A.....15-25 63-66

WILLIAMS, Darnell R&B '83

Singles: 7-inch

MY DISC....3-4 83

WILLIAMS, David R&B '84

Singles: 7-inch

OCEAN FRONT....3-5 84

WILLIAMS, Dee, Sextet R&B '49

Singles: 78 rpm

SAVOY....15-25 49

WILLIAMS, Deniece P&R/R&B '76

Singles: 12-inch

ARC....3-5 79-82
COLUMBIA....3-5 76-88
TODDLIN' TOWN....4-8 60s

Picture Sleeves

COLUMBIA....3-5 84-88

LPs: 10/12-inch

ARC (Except 1432)....5-10 79-82
ARC (1432 "Niecy")....20-25 82
(Picture disc. Promotional issue only.)
COLUMBIA....5-10 76-88
Also see MATHIS, Johnny, & Deniece Williams
Also see WONDER, Stevie

WILLIAMS, Diana C&W/P&R '76

Singles: 7-inch

CAPITOL....3-5 76
LITTLE GEM....3-5 77

WILLIAMS, Don C&W '72

Singles: 7-inch

ABC....3-5 75-78
ABC/DOT....3-5 74-77
CAPITOL....3-4 86
DOT....3-5 74
JMI....3-5 72-74
MCA (Except 1763)....3-4 79-85
MCA (1763 "Special Message from Don Williams for Your Radio Station")....4-8 82
(Promotional issue only.)

LPs: 10/12-inch

ABC (Except 28 & 44)....5-10 77-78
ABC (28 "Don Williams")....10-15 77
(Promotional issue only.)
MCA (44 "Expressions")....15-20 78
(Picture disc. Promotional issue only.)
ABC/DOT....8-10 74-77
CAPITOL....5-8 86
JMI....15-20 73-74
K-TEL....5-8 78
MCA (Except 44)....5-10 75-85
MCA (44 "Expressions")....15-20 78
(Picture disc.)
Also see HARRIS, Emmylou, & Don Williams
Also see POZO SECO SINGERS

WILLIAMS, Eddie R&B '49
(With His Brown Buddies)

Singles: 78 rpm

CRYSTAL....10-20 50
DISCOVERY....10-20 50
SELECTIVE....10-20 50
SUPREME....10-20 49
SWING TIME....10-20 49
Also see DIXON, Floyd

WILLIAMS, Esther R&B '76

Singles: 7-inch

FRIENDS & CO.....3-5 76-78

WILLIAMS, Hank C&W '47
(With the Drifting Cowboys; Hank Williams as "Luke the Drifter;" with Audrey Williams)

Singles: 78 rpm

MGM....10-25 47-55
STERLING (201 "Calling You")....200-400 47
STERLING (204 "Wealth Won't Save Your Soul")....150-300 47
STERLING (208 "I Don't Care")....150-250 47
STERLING (210 "Pan American")....150-250 47

Singles: 7-inch

MGM (100 series)....5-8 60s
MGM (10000 & 11000 series)....10-20 50-55
MGM (12000 series)....5-15 55-59
MGM (13000 series)....3-6 64-67

EPs: 7-inch

ARHOOLIE....4-6 83
(Not issued with cover.)
MGM (100 & 200 series)....25-50 52-54
MGM (1000 thru 1600 series)....15-30 55-60

LPs: 10/12-inch

ACM....5-10 83
BLAINE HOUSE....15-20 72
BOLL WEEVIL....8-12 76
CMF....5-10
CANDLELITE ("Golden Dream of Hank Williams")....15-20 70s
(Boxed, three-disc set.)
CANDLELITE ("1951-52: Golden Dream of Hank Williams")....8-12 76
COLUMBIA (5616 "Hank Williams Treasury")....35-45 60s
(Boxed, four-disc set. Columbia House Record Club issue.)
GOLDEN COUNTRY....5-8 82
JAMBALAYA....5-10
MGM (2 "36 of Hank Williams' Greatest Hits")....80-100 57
(Three discs.)
MGM (4 "36 More of Hank Williams' Greatest Hits")....80-100 58
(Three discs.)
MGM (107 "Hank Williams Sings")....50-100 51
(10-inch LP.)

MGM (168 "Moanin' the Blues") 50-100 52
(10-inch LP.)
MGM (202 "Memorial Album")........ 50-100 53
(10-inch LP.)
MGM (203 "Hank Williams As Luke the Drifter") 50-100 53
(10-inch LP.)
MGM (240-2 "24 Karat Hits, Hank Williams")... 15-20 68
MGM (242 "Honky Tonkin")............ 50-100 54
(10-inch LP.)
MGM (243 "I Saw the Light") 50-100 55
(10-inch LP.)
MGM (291 "Ramblin' Man") 50-100 54
(10-inch LP.)
MGM (912 "Hank Williams . . . Reflections By Those Who Loved Him") 100-200 75
(Boxed, three-disc set. Promotional issue only. Includes guest speakers: Roy Acuff, Little Jimmy Dickens, Lefty Frizzell, Pee Wee King, George Morgan, Bill Monroe, Minnie Pearl, Wesley Rose, Ernest Tubb, Grant Turner, Audrey Williams, Faron Young, and Hank Williams Jr.)
MGM (1000 series)............................ 8-10 76
(Special Products issue.)
MGM (3219 "Ramblin' Man") 50-75 55
(Blue "sketch" cover.)
MGM (3219 "Ramblin' Man") 25-45
(Yellow "suit" cover.)
MGM (3330 "Moanin' the Blues".... 100-150 56
(Yellow label.)
MGM (E-3200 thru 3900 series) 25-50 55-61
(Monaural. Through 3733, first issues have a yellow label.)
MGM (SE-3200 thru 3900 series)...... 10-20 63-70
(Reprocessed stereo. Through 3733, first issues have a yellow label.)
MGM (4000 thru 4700 series, except 4267).. 10-20 63-71
MGM (4267 "The Hank Williams Story").. 50-75 66
(Boxed, four-disc set.)
MGM (4900 thru 5400 series)............ 5-10 75-77
METRO.. 10-15 65-67
POLYDOR.. 5-15 83-84
SUNRISE MEDIA 8-10 81
TIME-LIFE (Except LCW-01)................ 5-8 81-82
TIME-LIFE (LCW-01 "Hank Williams")...................................... 10-15 81
(Boxed, three-disc set.)
Also see PRESLEY, Elvis / Hank Williams

WILLIAMS, Hank / Roy Acuff

LPs: 10/12-inch

LAMB & LION 8-12
(Three discs. Two by Hank Williams, one by Roy Acuff.)
Also see ACUFF, Roy

WILLIAMS, Hank / Slim Whitman

LPs: 10/12-inch

SUNRISE MEDIA 8-10 81
Also see WHITMAN, Slim

WILLIAMS, Hank, & Hank Williams Jr. LP '65

(Hank Williams / Hank Williams Jr.; Hank Williams Jr. & Hank Williams Sr.)

Singles: 7-inch

W.B. 3-4 89

LPs: 10/12-inch

COLUMBIA HOUSE ("Hank's Place") 5-10 81
(One side by each artist. Bonus LP with boxed set below. Selection number not known.)
COLUMBIA HOUSE "Hank Williams / Hank Williams Jr.)....................................... 20-25 81
(Boxed, five-disc record club set. Selection number not known.)
MGM (4200 series)........................... 15-25 65
MGM (4300 thru 4900 series)............ 10-15 66-74
Also see WILLIAMS, Hank
Also see WILLIAMS, Hank, Jr.

WILLIAMS, Hank, Jr. C&W/P&R '64

(With the Cheatin' Hearts; with Mike Curb Congregation; Luke the Drifter Jr.)

Singles: 7-inch

CONSOL.. 10-20
(Promotional issue from Consolidation Coal.)
ELEKTRA/CURB 3-4 79-82
MGM (13000 series) 4-8 64-68
MGM (14000 series) 3-5 68-76
MGM GOLDEN CIRCLE........................ 3-5 70s
W.B./CURB (Except 8000 series)......... 3-4 82-88
W.B./CURB (8000 series).................... 3-4 77-78

Picture Sleeves

MGM (13000 series) 5-10 64-68

LPs: 10/12-inch

CURB.. 5-8 83-84
ELEKTRA.. 5-8 79-83
MGM (Except 5009) 10-20 64-76
MGM (5009 "Hank Williams Jr. and Friends")...................................... 25-50 75
POLYDOR 5-8
W.B. (Except 2092)........................... 5-10 77-87
W.B. (2092 "Interview")...................... 8-12 83
(Promotional issue only.)
W.B./CURB 5-8 85-91
Also see BOCEPHUS
Also see CASH, Johnny, & Hank Williams Jr.
Also see CHARLES, Ray, & Hank Williams Jr.
Also see CURB, Mike
Also see FRANCIS, Connie, & Hank Williams Jr.
Also see JENNINGS, Waylon, & Hank Williams Jr.
Also see JONES, George
Also see KERSHAW, Doug, & Hank Williams Jr.
Also see KILGORE, Merle
Also see WILLIAMS, Hank, & Hank Williams Jr.

WILLIAMS, Hank, Jr., & Lois Johnson C&W '72

Singles: 7-inch

MGM 3-5 72
Also see WILLIAMS, Hank, Jr.

WILLIAMS, James "D-Train" R&B '86

Singles: 12-inch

COLUMBIA.. 4-6 86

Singles: 7-inch

COLUMBIA 3-4 86-88

LPs: 10/12-inch

COLUMBIA.. 5-8 86
Also see "D" TRAIN

WILLIAMS, Jeanette R&B '69

Singles: 7-inch

BACK BEAT...................................... 10-20 66-69

WILLIAMS, Joe R&B '52

(Joseph Goreed)

Singles: 78 rpm

BLUE LAKE 50-75 54
CHECKER 15-25 52
ROULETTE.. 5-10 57
SAVOY... 10-15 55
TRUMPET... 20-30 52

Singles: 7-inch

BLUE LAKE (102 "Tired of Moving") 150-300 54
CHECKER (762 "Every Day I Have the Blues")... 25-50 52
RCA 4-8 62-66
ROULETTE.. 5-10 57-62
SAVOY... 10-20 55
SOLID STATE.................................... 4-8 66
TEMPONIC 3-6 72

EPs: 7-inch

RCA (2762 "At Newport '63") 8-12 63

LPs: 10/12-inch

RCA 10-15 63-65
REGENT (6002 "Everyday") 35-45 56
ROULETTE.. 15-30 58-64
SOLID STATE.................................... 10-15 66
Also see BASIE, Count
Also see WASHINGTON, Dinah / Joe Williams / Sarah Vaughan

WILLIAMS, John, Orchestra P&R '75

Singles: 7-inch

ARISTA.. 3-4 77-80
COLUMBIA....................................... 3-4 83
MCA.. 3-4 74-76
RCA... 3-4 79
20TH FOX 3-4 77-78
W.B. 3-4 79

Picture Sleeves

ARISTA... 3-4 77
20TH FOX 3-4 77-78
W.B. 3-4 79

LPs: 10/12-inch

CAPITOL... 5-10 71
COLUMBIA (31091 "Changes") 5-10 71
COLUMBIA (37000 series).................. 5-8 81
DISCOVERY 4-8 84
RCA.. 5-8 77
You'll find many more listings by this artist in *The Official Price Guide to Movie/TV Soundtracks and Original Cast Albums,* containing over 8,000 listings.
Also see BOSTON POPS ORCHESTRA

WILLIAMS, Johnny

(John Lee Hooker)

Singles: 78 rpm

GOTHAM (509 "Questionnaire Blues") 15-25 52
GOTHAM (513 "Little Boy Blue")....... 15-25 53
PRIZE (704 "Miss Rosie Mae") 75-125 49
STAFF (710 "Wandering Blues") 50-75 50
STAFF (718 "Prison Bound") 50-75 50
SWING TIME.................................... 15-25 50
Also see HOOKER, John Lee

WILLIAMS, Johnny R&B/C&W '72

Singles: 7-inch

BASHIE 3-5 70
CUB.. 4-6 68
EPIC 3-5 72
PHILADELPHIA INT'L 3-5 73

WILLIAMS, L.C. R&B '49

(With Conney's Combo)

Singles: 78 rpm

BAYOU 10-20 53
FREEDOM.. 10-20 49-50
GOLD STAR...................................... 10-20 48
IMPERIAL... 8-15 52
JAX.. 10-20 52
MERCURY 8-15 52
SITTIN' in WITH 10-20 52

Singles: 7-inch

BAYOU (008 "My Darkest Hours") 40-60 53

WILLIAMS, Larry P&R/R&B '57

Singles: 7-inch

SPECIALTY...................................... 15-35 57-58

Singles: 7-inch

CHESS 8-15 59-60
MERCURY 4-8 63
OKEH 4-8 66-67
SMASH.. 4-8 66
SPECIALTY (SPBX series) 12-15 85
(Boxed set of six colored vinyl discs.)
SPECIALTY (597 thru 658)................ 12-25 57-59
SPECIALTY (665 thru 682)................ 10-20 59-60
VEE JAY.. 10-20 57
VENTURE 4-6 68

Picture Sleeves

SPECIALTY (626 "Slow Down")........ 25-50 58

LPs: 10/12-inch

OKEH (12123 "Greatest Hits") 10-15 67
SPECIALTY (2109 "Here's Larry Williams").................................... 50-75 59
SPECIALTY (2109 "Here's Larry Williams").................................... 8-10 86
(Has '80s information and copyright date on back cover.)
SPECIALTY (2158 "Unreleased Larry Williams")..................................... 8-10 86
SPECIALTY (2162 "Hocus Pocus") 8-10 86
Session: Art Neville; Rene Hall; Earl Palmer; Plas Johnson; Jewell Grant; Ted Brinson; Alvin Tyler; Roy Montrell.

Also see COOKE, Sam / Lloyd Price / Larry Williams / Little Richard
Also see NEVILLE, Art

WILLIAMS, Larry, & Johnny Watson P&R/R&B '67

Singles: 7-inch

BELL (813 "I Could Love You Baby")..5-10 69
OKEH (7274 "A Quitter Never Wins")....10-20 67
OKEH (7281 "Too Late")....10-20 67
OKEH (7300 "Nobody")....15-25 67
(With Kaleidoscope.)

LPs: 10/12-inch

OKEH (14122 "Two for the Price of One")....10-20 67
Also see KALEIDOSCOPE
Also see LARRY & JOHNNY
Also see WATSON, Johnny
Also see WILLIAMS, Larry

WILLIAMS, Lawton C&W '61
(With the Anita Kerr Singers)

Singles: 7-inch

D....5-10 60
LE BILL....5-10
MERCURY....4-8 61
RCA (7000 series)....5-10 58
RCA (8000 series)....4-6 64
Also see KERR, Anita

WILLIAMS, Lee R&B '67
(With the Moonrays; with Cymbals; Lee "Shot" Williams)

Singles: 7-inch

BLACK CIRCLE....4-8
CARNIVAL....5-10 66-69
FEDERAL....8-12 63-64
GAMMA (101 "Love Now, Pay Later")....25-35
KING (5409 "I'm So in Love")....50-100 60
RAPDA....4-8
SHAMA....5-10 69
TCHULA....4-6
TRUE....10-20
U.A.....4-8

WILLIAMS, Lenny R&B '75

Singles: 12-inch

ABC....4-6 78
ROCSHIRE....4-6 83-84

Singles: 7-inch

ABC....3-5 77-78
ATCO....3-5 72
GALAXY....5-10
KNOBHILL....3-4 86
MCA....3-5 79-81
MOTOWN....3-4 75
ROCSHIRE....3-4 83-84

LPs: 10/12-inch

ABC....8-10 77-78
MCA....5-8 79-81
MOTOWN....8-10 75
ROCSHIRE....5-8 83-84
W.B.....8-12 74
Also see KENNY G. & Lenny Williams
Also see TOWER of POWER

WILLIAMS, Linda R&B '79

Singles: 7-inch

ARISTA....3-5 79

WILLIAMS, Mason P&R/LP '68

Singles: 7-inch

W.B.....3-6 68-71

LPs: 10/12-inch

EVEREST....6-12 69
FLYING FISH....5-10 78
VEE JAY....10-20 64
W.B.....6-12 68-71

WILLIAMS, Mason, & Mannheim Steamroller LP '87

LPs: 10/12-inch

AMERICAN G.....5-8 87

WILLIAMS, Mason / Smothers Brothers

EPs: 7-inch

W.B./7 ARTS (283 "Scope Box")....20-40 70
(Promotional issue only.)
Also see SMOTHERS BROTHERS
Also see WILLIAMS, Mason

WILLIAMS, Maurice P&R/R&B '60
(With the Zodiacs; with Inspirations)

Singles: 7-inch

ATLANTIC....3-5 70
CANDI (1031 "Never Leave You Again")....30-40 63
COLE (100 "Golly Gee")....25-35 59
COLE (101 "Lover, Where Are You")....20-30 59
COLLECTABLES....3-4 80s
ERIC....3-5 70s
FLASHBACK....4-8 65
HERALD....10-20 60-62
OWL....3-5 73
SEA HORN....5-10 64
SELWYN (5121 "College Girl")....25-50 59
SPHERE SOUND....5-10 65
VEE JAY....5-10 65
VEEP....5-10 69

LPs: 10/12-inch

COLLECTABLES....6-8 84
HERALD (1014 "Stay")....50-100 61
LOST-NITE....5-10 80s
RELIC....10-15
SNYDER....25-30
SPHERE SOUND....15-20 66
Also see GLADIOLAS
Also see SWAYZE, Patrick, & Wendy Fraser / Maurice Williams & Zodiacs

WILLIAMS, Mike P&R/R&B '66

Singles: 7-inch

ATLANTIC....3-6 65-66
KING....3-6 66
Also see TEMPESTS

WILLIAMS, Otis C&W '71
(With the Midnight Cowboys)

Singles: 7-inch

STOP (388 "I Wanna Go Country")....4-6 71

LPs: 10/12-inch

STOP (1022 "Otis Williams & the Midnight Cowboys")....10-15 71
Note: These are country music releases. Solo R&B Deluxe releases credited either to "Otis Williams," or "Otis Williams & His New Group," are in the "Charms" section.
Also see CHARMS

WILLIAMS, Patrick R&B '83

Singles: 7-inch

PCM....3-4 83

WILLIAMS, Paul R&B '48
(With His Orchestra)

Singles: 78 rpm

CAPITOL....5-10 55
CLEF....5-10 52
GROOVE....5-10 54
JAX....5-10 54
JOSIE....5-10 56
MERCURY....5-10
RAMA....20-30 55
SAVOY....5-10 48-57

Singles: 7-inch

ASCOT....3-5 62
CAPITOL....8-12 55
GROOVE (0014 "Women Are the Root of All Evil")....15-25 54
("Vocal refrain by Jimmy Brown.")
JAX (313 "Thin Man")....25-35 54
(Colored vinyl.)
JOSIE....8-12 56
RAMA (167 "Ring-A-Ling")....50-75 55
(Vocalist, though not credited, is believed to be Little Willie John.)
SAVOY....6-15 51-59
SEVEN ARTS....5-10 61
VEE JAY....8-12 57
Also see JOHN, Little Willie
Also see McNEELY, Big Jay / Paul Williams
Also see McPHERSON, Wyatt "Earp," & Paul Williams
Also see WATTS, Noble

WILLIAMS, Paul LP '71

Singles: 7-inch

A&M....3-4 72-77
PAID....3-4 81
PORTRAIT....3-4 79
REPRISE....3-4 70

LPs: 10/12-inch

A&M....6-10 71-77
PAID....5-8 81
PORTRAIT....5-8 79
REPRISE....8-12 70

WILLIAMS, Robin LP '79

Singles: 12-inch

CASABLANCA....4-8 79

Singles: 7-inch

BOARDWALK....3-5 80

Picture Sleeves

BOARDWALK....3-5 80

LPs: 10/12-inch

CASABLANCA....5-10 79-83

WILLIAMS, Roger P&R '55

Singles: 78 rpm

KAPP....3-5 55-57

Singles: 7-inch

KAPP....3-8 55-72
MCA....3-4 73-78
W.B.....3-4 80

Picture Sleeves

KAPP....4-10 55-66

EPs: 7-inch

KAPP....4-8 55-58

LPs: 10/12-inch

KAPP....5-15 55-72
MCA....4-8 73-83
VOCALION....4-8 71

WILLIAMS, Roger, & Jane Morgan

Singles: 78 rpm

KAPP....3-5 56

Singles: 7-inch

KAPP....5-10 56
Also see MORGAN, Jane
Also see WILLIAMS, Roger

WILLIAMS, Roxie: see SLAUGHTER, Chuck / Roxie Williams

WILLIAMS, Sonny Boy R&B '43

Singles: 78 rpm

DECCA....15-25 43

WILLIAMS, Tex C&W '46
(With His Western Caravan; with Spade Cooley; with California Express)

Singles: 78 rpm

CAPITOL....4-8 46-51
COLUMBIA....4-8 46
DECCA....4-8 53-55

Singles: 7-inch

BOONE....4-6 65-68
CAPITOL....5-10 51-60
DECCA....5-10 53-55
DOT....4-6 66
GRANITE....3-5 74
LIBERTY....4-8 63-65
MONUMENT....3-5 70-72
SHASTA....4-8 60-61

EPs: 7-inch

CAMDEN....8-12 58
CAPITOL....10-15 56-57
DECCA....10-15 55

LPs: 10/12-inch

BOONE....10-15 66
CAMDEN (363 "Tex Williams' Best")....20-40 58
CAPITOL (1463 "Smoke! Smoke! Smoke!")....20-40 60
DECCA (4295 "Country Music Time")....15-25 62
DECCA (5565 "Dance-O-Rama")....40-60 55
(10-inch LP.)

GARU ... 5-10 81
GRANITE ... 6-12 74
IMPERIAL ... 10-15 66
LIBERTY ... 15-25 63
MONUMENT ... 8-12 71
SHASTA ... 8-12
SUNSET ... 10-15 66
Also see STARR, Kay

WILLIAMS, Tony

Singles: 7-inch

MERCURY ... 10-20 57-59
PHILIPS ... 4-8 62-63
REPRISE ... 5-10 61-62

LPs: 10/12-inch

MERCURY ... 20-30 59
PHILIPS ... 15-25 62
REPRISE ... 20-25 61
Also see PLATTERS

WILLIAMS, Tony — LP '79

LPs: 10/12-inch

COLUMBIA ... 5-10 79

WILLIAMS, Trudy, & Six Teens: see SIX TEENS

WILLIAMS, Vanessa — P&R/R&B/LP '88

Singles: 7-inch

WING ... 3-4 88-89

Picture Sleeves

WING ... 3-4 88-89

LPs: 10/12-inch

WING ... 5-8 88

WILLIAMS, Vesta — R&B '86

(Vesta)

Singles: 12-inch

A&M ... 4-6 86

Singles: 7-inch

A&M ... 3-4 86-89

LPs: 10/12-inch

A&M ... 5-8 86-89

WILLIAMS, Wilson — R&B '78

Singles: 7-inch

ABC ... 3-5 78

WILLIAMSON, Sonny Boy — R&B '47

(John Lee Williamson)

Singles: 78 rpm

BLUEBIRD ... 20-30 45
RCA ... 20-30 46-49

Singles: 7-inch

RCA (0005 "Little Girl") ... 50-100 49
RCA (0030 "Southern Dream") ... 50-100 49

WILLIAMSON, Sonny Boy — R&B '55

(Aleck "Rice" Miller; Aleck Ford)

Singles: 78 rpm

ACE ... 20-40 55
CHECKER ... 10-25 55-57
TRUMPET ... 20-40 51-54

Singles: 7-inch

ACE (511 "Boppin' with Sonny") ... 50-100 55
CHECKER (800 series) ... 15-25 55-58
CHECKER (900 series) ... 10-15 58-62
CHECKER (1000 & 1100 series) ... 5-10 62-66
TRUMPET (100 series) ... 40-75 51-52
TRUMPET (200 series) ... 30-50 53-54

LPs: 10/12-inch

ARHOOLIE ... 8-12
BLUES CLASSICS ... 15-20 64
CHESS (206 "Sonny Boy Williamson") ... 15-25 76
CHESS (417 "One Way Out") ... 15-20
CHESS (1400 series) ... 30-50 60
CHESS (1500 series) ... 10-20 66-69
CHESS (9000 series) ... 5-10
CHESS (50027 "This Is My Story") ... 15-25 72
STORYVILLE ... 5-8 80
Also see DIXON, Willie
Also see MEMPHIS SLIM
Also see PAGE, Jimmy, & Sonny Boy Williamson
Also see ROGERS, Jimmy
Also see WATERS, Muddy
Also see YARDBIRDS

WILLIAMSON, Sonny Boy, & Big Joe Williams

LPs: 10/12-inch

BLUES CLASSICS ... 5-8
Also see WILLIAMSON, Sonny Boy (Aleck "Rice" Miller)

WILLIAMSON, Sonny Boy

Singles: 7-inch

RAM (2501 "Pretty Li'l Thing") ... 25-35 61

WILLIE, Wet: see WET WILLIE

WILLIE & POOR BOYS — LP '85

Singles: 7-inch

PASSPORT (7928 "Baby Please Don't Go") ... 3-5 85
PASSPORT (7929 "These Arms of Mine") ... 3-5 85

Picture Sleeves

PASSPORT (7928 "Baby Please Don't Go") ... 4-6 85
PASSPORT (7929 "These Arms of Mine") ... 4-6 85

LPs: 10/12-inch

PASSPORT (6047 "Willie & Poor Boys") ... 5-10 85
Members: Andy Fairweather-Low; Mickey Gee; Kenny Jones; Jimmy Page; Chris Rea; Paul Rodgers; Geraint Watkins; Charlie Watts; Bill Wyman.
Also see FAIRWEATHER-LOW, Andy
Also see FREE
Also see PAGE, Jimmy
Also see REA, Chris
Also see ROLLING STONES

WILLIS, Bruce — P&R/R&B/LP '87

Singles: 7-inch

MOTOWN ... 3-4 87

Picture Sleeves

MOTOWN ... 3-4 87

LPs: 10/12-inch

MOTOWN ... 5-8 87

WILLIS, Chuck — R&B '52

(With the Royals; with Sandmen)

Singles: 78 rpm

ATLANTIC ... 10-30 56-57
COLUMBIA ... 15-25 51
OKEH ... 10-25 53-56

Singles: 7-inch

ATLANTIC (1000 & 2000 series) ... 10-25 56-59
COLUMBIA (30238 "Can't You See") ... 25-50 51
OKEH (6810 "I Tried") ... 25-40 51
OKEH (6841 "Let's Jump Tonight") ... 25-40 51
OKEH (6873 "Loud Mouth Lucy") ... 25-35 52
OKEH (6905 "My Story") ... 25-35 52
OKEH (6930 "Wrong Way to Catch a Fish") ... 25-35 52
OKEH (6952 "Going to the River") ... 25-35 53
OKEH (6985 "Don't Deceive Me") ... 25-35 53
OKEH (7004 "My Baby's Coming Home") ... 25-35 53
OKEH (7015 "What's Your Name") ... 25-35 53
OKEH (7029 "I Feel So Bad") ... 25-40 54
OKEH (7041 "Change My Mind") ... 25-35 54
OKEH (7048 "Give and Take") ... 25-35 54
OKEH (7051 "Lawdy Miss Mary") ... 25-35 55
OKEH (7055 "I Can Tell") ... 20-30 55
OKEH (7062 "Search My Heart") ... 20-30 55
OKEH (7067 "Come on Home") ... 20-30 56
REGINALD ... 10-15

EPs: 7-inch

ATLANTIC (591 "Chuck Willis") ... 50-75 57
ATLANTIC (609 "Rock with Chuck Willis") ... 50-75 58
ATLANTIC (612 "What Am I Living For") ... 50-75 58
EPIC (7070 "Sings the Blues") ... 50-75 56

LPs: 10/12-inch

ATCO ... 10-12 71
ATLANTIC (8018 "King of the Stroll") ... 50-100 58
(Black label.)
ATLANTIC (8018 "King of the Stroll") ... 25-50 59
(Red label.)
ATLANTIC (8079 "I Remember Chuck Willis") ... 50-100 63
COLUMBIA ... 5-8 80
EPIC (3425 "Chuck Willis Wails the Blues") ... 100-200 58
EPIC (3728 "A Tribute to Chuck Willis") ... 100-200 58

WILLIS, M-D-L-T — R&B '74

Singles: 7-inch

IVORY TOWER ... 3-4 74
Members: Maxine Willis; Diane Willis; Lavern Willis; Tina Willis.

WILLIS, Timmy — R&B '68

Singles: 7-inch

JUBILEE ... 4-6 69
SIDRA ("I'm Wondering") ... 5-10 67
(Number not known.)
VEEP ... 4-6 68

WILL-O-BEES — P&R '68

Singles: 7-inch

DATE ... 3-5 67
SGC ... 3-5 68-69

WILLOWS — P&R/R&B '56

Singles: 78 rpm

CLUB (1014 "This Is the End") ... 15-25 56
MELBA (102 "Church Bells Are Ringing") ... 50-75 56
MELBA (102 "Church Bells May Ring) ... 25-35 56
MELBA (106 "Do You Love Me) ... 15-25 56
MELBA (115 "Little Darlin' ") ... 50-75 57

Singles: 7-inch

ABC ... 3-5 73
CLUB (1014 "This Is the End") ... 75-100 56
(Orange label.)
CLUB (1014 "This Is the End") ... 35-45 56
(Blue label.)
COLLECTABLES ... 3-4
MELBA (102 "Church Bells Are Ringing") ... 150-250 56
MELBA (102 "Church Bells May Ring) ... 50-100 56
(Note slight title change.)
MELBA (106 "Do You Love Me) ... 50-100 56
(Black label.)
MELBA (106 "Do You Love Me) ... 25-50 56
(Red label.)
MELBA (115 "Little Darlin' ") ... 50-100 57
(Red label.)

LPs: 10/12-inch

ELDORADO (1000 "The Willows") ... 8-12
Members: Tony Middleton; Richard Davis; Ralph Martin; Joe Martin; John Steele; Richard Simon; Dotty Martin.
Also see SEDAKA, Neil

WILLS, Bob — P&R '39

(With His Texas Playboys; with Rusty McDonald; with Tommy Duncan)

Singles: 78 rpm

ANTONES ... 15-25
CAPITOL ... 3-5 76
COLUMBIA ... 5-10 43-48
DECCA ... 4-8 55-56
MGM ... 5-10 47-55
OKEH ... 5-10 40-45
VOCALION ... 10-20 33-39

Singles: 7-inch

DECCA ... 5-10 55-56
LIBERTY ... 4-8 60-64
LONGHORN ... 4-6 64
MGM ... 5-15 50-55

EPs: 7-inch

COLUMBIA ... 10-20 57
DECCA ... 10-20 55
MGM ... 10-20 56
RHINO (284 "Greatest Hits of Texas") ... 15-20 84
(Texas-shaped picture disc.)

LPs: 10/12-inch

ANTONES (6000 "The Texas Playboys") 100-200
(10-inch LP. Fan club issue.)
ANTONES (6010 "The Texas Playboys") 100-200
(10-inch LP. Fan club issue.)
AUDIO/VIDEO 5-8 82
CAPITOL 10-20 76
COLUMBIA (Except 9003) 6-12 73-82
COLUMBIA (9003 "Round-Up") 50-75 50
(10-inch LP.)
CORAL (20109 "Swing Along") 5-10 73
CORONET 8-12 60s
DECCA (5562 "Dance-O-Rama") 50-75 55
(10-inch LP.)
DECCA (DL-8727 "Bob Wills & His Texas Playboys") 35-55 57
(Monaural.)
DECCA (DL7-8727 "Bob Wills & His Texas Playboys") 15-25 66
(Reprocessed stereo.)
DELTA 5-10 81-83
ENCORE .... ?? 79
HARMONY (Except 7036) 10-20 63-69
HARMONY (7036 "Bob Wills Special") 15-25 57
KAPP 8-12 66-71
KALEIDOSCOPE 5-10 82-83
LARIAT (1 "The Tiffany Transcriptions") 50-75 77
LIBERTY 20-30 60-63
LONGHORN (001 "Bob Wills Keepsake Album, #1") 50-75 65
LONGHORN (007 "Bob Wills Collector's Series") 10-15
LONGHORN (011 "31st St. Blues") .. 10-15
MCA 6-12 73-80s
MGM (91 "Ranch House Favorites") 75-100 51
(10-inch LP.)
MGM (141 "Tribute to Bob Wills") 8-12 71
MGM (3352 "Ranch House Favorites") 50-75 56
MGM (4866 "History of Bob Wills") 10-15 73
MGM (5303 "24 Great Hits") 8-12 77
METRO 10-15 67
PICKWICK 5-10 70s
RHINO (284 "Greatest Hits of Texas") 8-12 85
(Texas-shaped, picture disc. Promotional issue only.)
STARDAY (375 "San Antonio Rose") 15-25 65
STARDAY (469 "Bob Wills Story") 8-12 70
SUNSET 8-12 66-69
TEXAS ROSE 5-10
TIME-LIFE 5-10 81
TIME-LIFE ("Bob Wills") 10-15 82
(Boxed 3-LP set.)
TISHOMINGO (1 "The Tiffany Transcriptions, 1945-1948") 30-50 78
U.A. 8-15 71-74
VOCALION (3735 "Swing Along") 10-20 65
VOCALION (3922 "San Antonio Rose") 10-20 71
WESTERN HERITAGE 5-10 76

WILMER & THE DUKES P&R '68

Singles: 7-inch

APHRODISIAC 3-6 69

LPs: 10/12-inch

APHRODISIAC 10-15 69
Member: Wilmer Alexander Jr.

WILSON, Al P&R/R&B '68

Singles: 7-inch

BELL 4-6 70
BELL GOLD 3-4 70s
CAROUSEL 3-5 71
PLAYBOY 3-5 76
ROADSHOW 3-4 79
ROCKY ROAD 3-6 72-75
SOUL CITY 4-8 67-69
WAND (1135 "Help Me") 15-25 66

LPs: 10/12-inch

PLAYBOY 8-10 76
ROADSHOW 5-8 79
ROCKY ROAD 8-12 73-74
SOUL CITY 10-15 69
Also see JEWELS
Also see ROLLERS

WILSON, Ann P&R '86
(With the Daybreaks)

Singles: 7-inch

CAPITOL 3-4 86
TOPAZ (1311 "Standin' Watchin' You") 50-100 67
(Reportedly 500 made.)
TOPAZ (1312 "Through Eyes and Glass") 50-100 67
(Reportedly 500 made.)

Picture Sleeves

CAPITOL 3-4 86
Also see HEART
Also see RENO, Mike, & Ann Wilson

WILSON, Ann, Robin Zander P&R '88

Singles: 7-inch

CAPITOL 3-4 88
Also see WILSON, Ann

WILSON, Art R&B '83

Singles: 7-inch

TABU 3-4 83

WILSON, Bobby R&B '73

Singles: 7-inch

BUDDAH 3-5 75
CHAIN 3-5 73
VOLT (144 "Let Me Down Slow") 5-10 66

WILSON, Brian P&R '66

Singles: 7-inch

CAPITOL (5610 "Caroline No") 15-20 66
SIRE (27694 "Melt Away") 3-5 88
SIRE (27814 "Love and Mercy") 3-5 88
SIRE (28350 "Let's Go to Heaven in My Car") 3-5 87

Promotional Singles

SIRE (27694 "Melt Away") 4-8 88
SIRE (27787 "Night Time") 4-8 88
SIRE (27814 "Love and Mercy") 4-8 88
SIRE (28350 "Let's Go to Heaven in My Car") 5-10 87

Picture Sleeves

SIRE (27787 "Night Time") 8-12 88
SIRE (27814 "Love and Mercy") 4-8 88
SIRE (28350 "Let's Go to Heaven in My Car") 4-8 87

LPs: 10/12-inch

SIRE (3248 "Brian Wilson: Words and Music") 15-20 88
SIRE (225669 "Brian Wilson") 5-10 88
Also see BEACH BOYS
Also see BERRY, Jan
Also see BLOSSOMS
Also see BOB & SHERI
Also see CAMPBELL, Glen
Also see CASTELLS
Also see CURRY, Tim
Also see DeSHANNON, Jackie
Also see HALE & HUSHABYES
Also see HONDELLS
Also see LEGENDARY MASKED SURFERS
Also see LOVE, Mike
Also see RIVERS, Johnny

WILSON, Brian, & Mike Love

Singles: 7-inch

BROTHER (1002 "Gettin' Hungry") 15-25 67
Also see LOVE, Mike
Also see WILSON, Brian

WILSON, Carl LP '81

Singles: 7-inch

CARIBOU 3-5 81-83

LPs: 10/12-inch

CARIBOU 5-10 81-82
Also see ANGEL
Also see BEACH BOYS
Also see CASSADY, David
Also see KING HARVEST
Also see NEWTON-JOHN, Olivia

WILSON, Dennis LP '77

Singles: 7-inch

CARIBOU 4-6 77

LPs: 10/12-inch

CARIBOU 10-15 77
Also see BEACH BOYS

WILSON, Dennis / Ram Jam / Joan Baez

EPs: 7-inch

COLUMBIA (1128 "Music for Every Ear") 15-25 77
(Promotional issue only.)
Also see BAEZ, Joan
Also see CUMMINGS, Burton / Cheap Trick / Crawler
Also see WILSON, Dennis
Also see RAM JAM

WILSON, Flip LP '87

Singles: 7-inch

FLIP WILSON (SK-1 "Flip Wilson") 5-10 60s
(Promotional issue only. No title or label shown.)
LITTLE DAVID 3-4 72-75

LPs: 10/12-inch

ATLANTIC 8-15 67-68
IMPERIAL 10-20 61
LITTLE DAVID 5-10 70-72
MINIT 8-15 68
SUNSET 8-10 70

WILSON, Hank LP '73
(Leon Russell)

Singles: 7-inch

SHELTER 3-4 73-74

LPs: 10/12-inch

SHELTER 8-10 73
Also see NELSON, Willie, & Hank Wilson
Also see RUSSELL, Leon

WILSON, J. Frank P&R/LP '64
(With the Cavaliers)

Singles: 7-inch

ABC 3-4 73
APRIL 3-5
CHARAY 3-5 69
COLLECTABLES 3-4 80s
ERIC 3-4 70s
JOSIE 4-8 64-65
JUBILEE (923 "Last Kiss") 5-10 64
(Blue label. Canadian, made by Quality.)
JUBILEE (923 "Last Kiss") 4-6 64
(Black label. Canadian, made by Phonodisc.)
LE CAM (500 series) 3-4 81
LE CAM (722 "Last Kiss") 15-25 64
LE CAM (1000 series) 4-8 65
LE CAM (12000 series) 3-4
SOLLY 3-5 66
TAMARA 8-15 64
VIRGO 3-4 72

LPs: 10/12-inch

DILL PICKEL 8-10 71
JOSIE (4006 "Last Kiss") 50-75 64

WILSON, Jackie P&R '57

Singles: 78 rpm

BRUNSWICK 25-50 57-58

Singles: 7-inch

BRUNSWICK (7-38000 series) 40-50 60
(Stereo compact 33 singles.)
BRUNSWICK (55024 thru 55086) 20-40 57-58
(Commercial issues.)
BRUNSWICK (55024 thru 55086) 25-45 57-58
(Promotional issues.)
BRUNSWICK (55105 thru 55165) 15-25 58-59
BRUNSWICK (55166 thru 55236) 10-20 60-62
BRUNSWICK (55238 thru 55504) 5-15 63-73
COLUMBIA 3-4 87
ERIC 3-4 83
GUSTO 3-4

Picture Sleeves

BRUNSWICK (55121 thru 55236) 8-12 59-62
BRUNSWICK (55238 thru 55467) 4-8 63-72
COLUMBIA 3-4 87

EPs: 7-inch

BRUNSWICK 20-35 59-63

LPs: 10/12-inch

BRUNSWICK (111 "Solid Gold")...... 10-15
(Brunswick Special Products, mail-order offer.)
BRUNSWICK (54045 "Lonely Teardrops")...................................50-100 59
BRUNSWICK (54042 "He's So Fine")...50-100 59
BRUNSWICK (54050 "So Much")..... 40-80 60
BRUNSWICK (54055 "Jackie Sings the Blues")..30-50 60
BRUNSWICK (54058 "My Golden Favorites")...30-40 60
BRUNSWICK (54059 "A Woman, a Lover, a Friend")...30-40 60
BRUNSWICK (54100 "You Ain't Heard Nothin' Yet")...25-30 61
BRUNSWICK (54101 "By Request"). 25-30 61
BRUNSWICK (54105 "Body and Soul")...25-30 62
BRUNSWICK (54106 "The World's Greatest Melodies")...................................25-30 62
BRUNSWICK (54108 "At the Copa")...25-30 62
BRUNSWICK (54110 thru 54130, except 54118)...20-25 63-67
BRUNSWICK (54118 "Soul Time")... 30-50 66
(Beginning with 54050, Brunswick indicated stereo LPs with a "7" preceeding the selection number. Numbers after 54130 were available as stereo issues only, and are shown here as the 75000 series.)
BRUNSWICK (754138 thru 754167). 15-25 68-71
BRUNSWICK (754185 thru 754212). 10-20 72-77
COLUMBIA...5-8 87
DISCOVERY...8-10 78
EPIC...10-12 83
TELE-HOUSE...10-15
Also see FREED, Alan
Also see WARD, Billy, & Dominoes
Also see WILSON, Sonny

WILSON, Jackie, & Lavern Baker — P&R/R&B '66

Singles: 7-inch

BRUNSWICK...3-5 65
Also see BAKER, Lavern

WILSON, Jackie, & Count Basie — P&R/R&B/LP '68

Singles: 7-inch

BRUNSWICK...3-5 68

LPs: 10/12-inch

BRUNSWICK...15-20 68
Also see BASIE, Count

WILSON, Jackie, & Chi-Lites — R&B '75

Singles: 7-inch

BRUNSWICK...3-4 75
Also see CHI-LITES

WILSON, Jackie, & Linda Hopkins — P&R '62

Singles: 7-inch

BRUNSWICK...3-5 62-65

EPs: 7-inch

BRUNSWICK...15-20 63

LPs: 10/12-inch

BRUNSWICK...25-35 68
Also see HOPKINS, Linda
Also see WILSON, Jackie

WILSON, Jimmy — R&B '53
(With His All Stars; with Blues Blasters)

Singles: 78 rpm

ALADDIN...25-50 51
BIG TOWN...20-40 53-54
CAVATONE...15-25 51
CHART...15-25 56
IRMA...15-25 55
RHYTHM...15-25 50-54
7-11...50-75 53

Singles: 7-inch

ALADDIN (3140 "Mistake in Life")... 50-100 51
ALADDIN (3241 "It's Time to Change")...50-100 52
BIG TOWN (101 "Tin Pan Alley")...... 40-60 53
BIG TOWN (103 "Call Me a Hound Dog")...40-60 53
BIG TOWN (107 "Blues at Sundown")...40-60 53
BIG TOWN (113 "Teardrops on My Pillow")...40-60 54
BIG TOWN (115 "Trouble in My House")...40-60 54
BIG TOWN (123 "I've Found Out")...40-60 54
CHART (610 "Louise")...40-60 56
CHART (629 "Send Me the Key")..... 40-60 56
DUKE...5-10 61-62
GOLDBAND...10-20 59
IRMA (107 "Blues in the Alley")......... 25-50 55
7-11 (2104 "Ethel Lee")................ 100-150 53
7-11 (2105 "Baby Don't Want Nobody But Me")...100-150 53

WILSON, Jimmy / Thrillers / Little Caesar

LPs: 10/12-inch

BIG TOWN (1001 "Big Town Sampler")...150-250 53
(Promotional issue only.)
Also see LITTLE CAESAR

WILSON, Kathy, & Kwils — D&D '83

Singles: 12-inch

COLUMBIA...4-6 83

WILSON, Mary — R&B '79

Singles: 7-inch

MOTOWN...3-4 79

LPs: 10/12-inch

MOTOWN...5-8 79
Also see SUPREMES

WILSON, Meri — P&R/R&B/C&W '77

Singles: 7-inch

BNA (8248 "Peter, the Meter Reader")...5-10 81
GRT...3-4 77

LPs: 10/12-inch

GRT...5-10 77

WILSON, Nancy — LP '62

Singles: 12-inch

CAPITOL...4-6 79

Singles: 7-inch

CAPITOL (Except 4000 & 5000 series) 3-5 68-79
CAPITOL (4000 & 5000 series)............ 3-6 59-67
(Includes both purple and orange/yellow labels.)

Picture Sleeves

CAPITOL...3-5 65

LPs: 10/12-inch

ASI...5-8 81
CAPITOL (100 thru 800 series).......... 5-12 69-71
CAPITOL (1300 thru 1700 series).... 15-30 59-62
CAPITOL (1800 thru 2900 series)...... 8-18 63-68
(With "T," "ST" or "SKAO" prefix.)
CAPITOL (1800 thru 2900 series)........ 5-8 78
(With "SM" prefix.)
CAPITOL (11000 & 12000 series)....... 5-10 74-80
CAPITOL (16000 series)...5-8 80
COLUMBIA...5-8 84
PICKWICK...5-8
Also see CAPITOL'S MYSTERY ARTIST
Also see LEWIS, Ramsey, & Nancy Wilson

WILSON, Nancy, & Julian "Cannonball" Adderley — R&B/LP '62

Singles: 7-inch

CAPITOL...3-5 62

LPs: 10/12-inch

CAPITOL (1657 "Nancy Wilson & Cannonball Adderley")...15-25 62
(With "T" or "ST" prefix.)
CAPITOL (1657 "Nancy Wilson & Cannonball Adderley")...5-8 75
(With "SM" prefix.)
CAPITOL (16000 series)...4-8 81
Also see ADDERLEY, Cannonball

WILSON, Nancy, & George Shearing

Singles: 7-inch

CAPITOL...3-5 61

LPs: 10/12-inch

CAPITOL (1524 "Swingin's Mutual") 15-25 61
(With "T" or "ST" prefix.)
CAPITOL (1524 "Swingin's Mutual")..... 5-8 75
(With "SM" prefix.)
Also see SHEARING, George
Also see WILSON, Nancy

WILSON, Nancy

Singles: 7-inch

WTG ("All for Love")...5-10 89
Also see HEART
Also see KNIGHT, Holly

WILSON, Phill — P&R '61

Singles: 7-inch

HURON...3-5 61

WILSON, Precious — R&B '86

Singles: 7-inch

JIVE...3-4 86

LPs: 10/12-inch

JIVE...5-8 86
Also see ERUPTION

WILSON, Shanice — P&R/R&B/LP '87

Singles: 7-inch

A&M...3-4 87-88

Picture Sleeves

A&M...3-4 87

LPs: 10/12-inch

A&M...5-8 87
Also see KIARA with Shanice Wilson

WILSON, Sonny
(Jackie Wilson)

Singles: 78 rpm

DEE GEE (4000 "Rainy Day Blues")...50-75 52
DEE GEE (4001 "Danny Boy")......... 50-75 52

Singles: 7-inch

DEE GEE (4000 "Rainy Day Blues")...75-125 52
DEE GEE (4001 "Danny Boy")......... 75-125 52
Also see WILSON, Jackie

WILSON, Timothy — R&B '67

Singles: 7-inch

BLUE ROCK (6 "Cross My Heart").... 10-20 69
BLUE ROCK (4090 "Cross My Heart")...10-20 69
BUDDAH...10-20 67-68
VEEP (1213 "Hey Girl, Do You Love Me")...25-50 65
VEEP (1223 "He Will Break Your Heart")...15-25 65

WILSON BROTHERS — P&R '79

Singles: 7-inch

ATCO...3-5 79
BIG TREE...3-5 78
RCA...3-5

LPs: 10/12-inch

ATCO...5-10 79
Members: Steve Wilson; Kelly Wilson.

WILSON PHILLIPS — LP '90

Singles: 7-inch

SBK...3-4 90

Picture Sleeves

SBK...3-4 90

LPs: 10/12-inch

SBK...5-10 90
Members: Wendy Wilson; Carnie Wilson; Chynna Phillips.

WILTON PLACE STREET BAND — P&R/R&B '77

Singles: 7-inch

ISLAND...3-5 77

WINAN, BeBe & CeCe — R&B '87

Singles: 12-inch

CAPITOL...4-6 87

Singles: 12-inch

CAPITOL...3-4 87

LPs: 10/12-inch

CAPITOL...5-8 87-89

WINANS R&B '85

Singles: 12-inch

QWEST....4-6 86

Singles: 7-inch

QWEST....3-4 85-86

LPs: 10/12-inch

LIGHT....4-8 75-85
QWEST....5-8 85-90

Members: Marvin Winan; Carvin Winan; Michael Winan; Ronald Winan.
Also see JACKSON, Michael
Also see McDONALD, Michael
Also see WINAN, BeBe & CeCe

WINANS & ANITA BAKER R&B '87

Singles: 7-inch

QWEST....3-4 87
Also see BAKER, Anita

WINBUSH, Angela R&B/LP '87

Singles: 7-inch

MERCURY....3-4 87-89

LPs: 10/12-inch

MERCURY....5-8 87-89

WINCHESTER, Jesse LP '72

Singles: 7-inch

AMPEX....3-4 70
BEARSVILLE....3-4 76-81

LPs: 10/12-inch

BEARSVILLE/AMPEX....15-20 70
BEARSVILLE....6-12 71-81

Promotional LPs

BEARSVILLE (692 "Live at the Bijou")....20-25 75
BEARSVILLE (693 "Live at the Bijou/Live Interview")....30-40 75
Also see HARRIS, Emmylou
Also see LARSON, Nicolette
Also see MURRAY, Anne

WIND P&R '69

Singles: 7-inch

LIFE....4-6 69

LPs: 10/12-inch

LIFE....15-20 69
Member: Tony Orlando.
Also see ORLANDO, Tony

WIND IN THE WILLOWS LP '68

Singles: 7-inch

CAPITOL (2274 "Uptown Girl")....5-10 68

LPs: 10/12-inch

CAPITOL (2956 "The Wind in the Willows")....40-75 68
Members: Deborah Harry; Paul Klein; Peter Brittain; Anton Carysforth; Steve DePhillips.
Also see HARRY, Debbie

WINDING, Kai, & His Orchestra
(With J.J. Johnson) P&R/LP '63

Singles: 7-inch

BETHLEHEM....4-8 60
COLUMBIA....5-10 56-59
IMPULSE....3-4 61
MGM....3-5 78
VERVE (Except 10258)....4-6 62-67
VERVE (10258 "Experiment in Terror")....10-15

EPs: 7-inch

COLUMBIA....5-15 58-59
SAVOY....10-20 53

LPs: 10/12-inch

A&M....8-12 68
COLUMBIA (900 thru 1300 series)....20-35 56-59
COLUMBIA (8100 series)....20-30 59
GLENDALE....5-8 76-77
IMPULSE....15-25 61
PICKWICK....5-10 65-70
ROOST (400 series)....50-100 52
(10-inch LPs.)
SAVOY (9000 series)....50-100 53
(10-inch LPs.)
VERVE....10-25 61-67
(Reads "MGM Records - a Division of Metro-Goldwyn-Mayer, Inc." at bottom of label.)
VERVE....5-10 73-84
(Reads "Manufactured By MGM Record Corp.," or mentions either Polydor or Polygram at bottom of label.)
WHO'S WHO in JAZZ....5-8 78
Also see STITT, Sonny, & Kai Winding

WINDJAMMER R&B '83

Singles: 7-inch

MCA....3-4 83-85

LPs: 10/12-inch

MCA....5-8 83

WINDSTORM R&B '80

Singles: 7-inch

POLYDOR....3-4 80

WINDY CITY R&B '80

Singles: 7-inch

CHI-SOUND....3-4 77
KELLI-ARTS....3-4 80

WINE, April: see APRIL WINE

WING & A PRAYER FIFE & DRUM CORPS P&R/R&B '75

Singles: 7-inch

WING and a PRAYER....3-4 75-77

LPs: 10/12-inch

WING and a PRAYER....5-8 76-77

WINGER LP '88

Singles: 7-inch

ATLANTIC....3-4 88-89

Picture Sleeves

ATLANTIC....3-4 89

LPs: 10/12-inch

ATLANTIC....5-8 88-90
Members: Kip Winger; Reb Beach; Rod Morgenstein; Paul Taylor.

WINGFIELD, Pete P&R/R&B/LP '75

Singles: 7-inch

ISLAND....3-4 75-77

LPs: 10/12-inch

ISLAND....5-8 75
Also see OLYMPIC RUNNERS

WINGS with Paul McCartney: see McCARTNEY, Paul

WINNERS R&B '78

Singles: 7-inch

ARIOLA-AMERICA....3-4 78

LPs: 10/12-inch

ARIOLA-AMERICA....5-8 78
ROADSHOW....5-10 78

WINSTON, George LP '84

Singles: 7-inch

WINDHAM HILL....3-4 84

LPs: 10/12-inch

TAKOMA (9016 "Piano Solos")....5-10 73
WINDHAM HILL....5-8 83-88

WINSTONS P&R/R&B/LP '69

Singles: 7-inch

METROMEDIA....3-4 69

LPs: 10/12-inch

METROMEDIA....8-12 69

WINTER, Edgar LP '70
(Edgar Winter Group; Edgar Winter's White Trash)

Singles: 12-inch

BLUE SKY....4-6 80
BODY ROCK....4-6 83

Singles: 7-inch

BLUE SKY....3-4 75-81
EPIC....3-4 70-75

LPs: 10/12-inch

BACK-TRAC....5-8 85
BLUE SKY....6-10 75-81
EPIC....10-15 70-75
Also see DERRINGER, Rick
Also see HARTMAN, Dan
Also see LA CROIX, Jerry
Also see MONTROSE, Ronnie
Also see WINTER, Johnny & Edgar

WINTER, Jimmy: see WINTER, Johnny

WINTER, Johnny LP '69
(With the Crystaliers; Jimmy Winter)

Singles: 7-inch

ATLANTIC....5-10 64
BLUE SKY....3-4 75
COLUMBIA....3-4 69-74
FROLIC (503 "Voo Doo Twist")....75-100 62
FROLIC (509 "Gangster of Love")....75-100 62
GRT....3-5 69
IMPERIAL....3-5 69
KRCO (107 "One Night of Love")....50-75 61
MGM....4-6 65
PACEMAKER....10-15 66
SONOBEAT....5-8 68
TODD....8-10 63

Picture Sleeves

SONOBEAT....50-75 68
(Some sleeves picture the Vulcan Gas Co., an Austin nightclub, and those are at the high end of the price range given. Sleeves that do not picture the club are priced at the lower end.)

LPs: 10/12-inch

ACCORD....5-8 81
ALLIGATOR....5-8 84-85
BLUE SKY....6-10 74-80
BUDDAH....10-15 69
CBS ASSOCIATED....5-8
COLUMBIA (9800 & 9900 series)....15-20 69
COLUMBIA (30000 thru 33000 series)....10-15 70-75
CRAZY CAJUN....8-10
GRT....10-15 69
IMPERIAL....15-20 69
JANUS....10-12 69-70
SONOBEAT ("Progressive Blues Experiment")....100-150 68
(Limited edition, autographed issue.)
SONOBEAT ("Progressive Blues Experiment")....75-125 68
(Limited edition, NOT autographed.)
U.A....8-10 73-74
Also see JOHNNY & JAMMERS
Also see GREAT BELIEVERS
Also see GUITAR SLIM
Also see SPRINGSTEEN, Bruce / Johnny Winter / Hollies
Also see TEXAS "GUITAR" SLIM
Also see WATERS, Muddy

WINTER, Johnny / Argent / Chambers Brothers / John Hammond

EPs: 7-inch

COLUMBIA/PLAYBACK (14 "Good Morning Little Schoolgirl")....15-25 72
Also see ARGENT
Also see CHAMBERS BROTHERS
Also see HAMMOND, John

WINTER, Johnny & Edgar LP '76

Singles: 7-inch

BLUE SKY....3-4 76
CASCADE....35-45 64

LPs: 10/12-inch

BLUE SKY (Except 242)....5-8 76
BLUE SKY (242 "Johnny & Edgar Winter Discuss *Together*")....10-20 76
(Promotional issue only.)
Also see LA CROIX, Jerry
Also see WINTER, Edgar
Also see WINTER, Johnny

WINTER, Paul LP '62
(With Winter Consort; Paul Winter Sextet)

Singles: 7-inch

A&M....3-4 69-77
COLUMBIA....3-5 62
EPIC....3-4 72-73

LPs: 10/12-inch

A&M....8-12 69-78
COLUMBIA....10-20 62-65
EPIC....8-10 72
LIVING MUSIC....5-8 83-86

WINTERHALTER, Hugo, & His Orchestra — P&R '49

Singles: 78 rpm

COLUMBIA....3-5 49-50
RCA....3-5 50-57

Singles: 7-inch

ABC-PAR....3-5 63
COLUMBIA....5-8 50
KAPP....3-5 64-65
MUSICOR....3-5 68-70
RCA....4-10 50-63

EPs: 7-inch

RCA....3-6 50-59

LPs: 10/12-inch

ABC-PAR....5-10 63
CAMDEN....4-8 69-72
KAPP....5-10 65
MUSIC DISC....4-8 69
MUSICOR....5-10 68-71
RCA....5-15 50-77
TRIP....4-8 76

Also see COMO, Perry
Also see DE CASTRO SISTERS / Hugo Winterhalter & His Orchestra
Also see HEYWOOD, Eddie

WINTERMUTE, Joann — C&W '89

Singles: 7-inch

CANYON CREEK....3-4 89
DOOR KNOB....3-4 89

WINTERS, Jonathan — LP '60

EPs: 7-inch

VERVE (5077 "Another Day, Another World")....8-10 62
(Promotional issue only.)

LPs: 10/12-inch

COLUMBIA....8-15 68-73
VERVE....15-30 59-60
(Reads "Verve Records, Inc." at bottom of label.)
VERVE....10-20 61-67
(Reads "MGM Records - a Division of Metro-Goldwyn-Mayer, Inc." at bottom of label.)
VERVE....5-10 73-84
(Reads"Manufactured By MGM Record Corp.," or mentions either Poly dor or Polygram at bottom of label.)

WINTERS, Robert, & Fall — R&B '80

Singles: 7-inch

BUDDAH....3-4 80-81
CASABLANCA....3-4 82-84

LPs: 10/12-inch

BUDDAH....5-8 80-81
CASABLANCA....5-8 82-83

WINTERS, Ruby — R&B '67

(Ruby Winter)

Singles: 7-inch

CERTRON....3-4 71
DIAMOND....3-5 66-69
MILLENNIUM....3-4 78
POLYDOR....3-4 73-75

LPs: 10/12-inch

MILLENNIUM....5-8 78

Also see THUNDER, Johnny, & Ruby Winters

WINWOOD, Steve — LP '71

Singles: 7-inch

ISLAND....3-4 77-87
U.A....4-8 71
VIRGIN....3-4 88-90

Picture Sleeves

ISLAND....3-4 80-88
VIRGIN....3-4 88-89

LPs: 10/12-inch

ISLAND....5-8 77-87
U.A. (5550 "Welcome to the Canteen")....8-12 71
U.A. (9950 "Winwood")....20-30 71
(With liner notes by Bobby Abrahms.)
U.A. (9964 "Winwood")....10-15 71
(Without liner notes.)
VIRGIN....5-8 88-90

Also see BAKER, Ginger
Also see BLIND FAITH
Also see DAVIS, Spencer
Also see McDONALD & GILES
Also see TOOTS & MAYTALS
Also see TRAFFIC
Also see YAMASHTA, Stomu

WIRE — LP '89

LPs: 10/12-inch

MUTE....5-8 89

Members: Graham Lewis; Colin Newman; Robert Gotobed.

WIRE TRAIN — LP '84

Singles: 12-inch

COLUMBIA....4-6 84

Singles: 7-inch

COLUMBIA....3-4 84

LPs: 10/12-inch

COLUMBIA....5-8 84-87
MCA....5-8 90

Members: Jeffrey Trott; Brian MacLeod; Anders Rundblad; Kevin Hunter.

WISH — R&B/D&D '84

(Featuring Fonda Rae)

Singles: 12-inch

KN....4-6 84

Singles: 7-inch

PERSONAL....3-4 84-85

Also see RAE, Fonda

WISHBONE ASH — LP '71

Singles: 7-inch

ATLANTIC....3-4 77
DECCA....3-4 71-72
MCA....3-4 73-78

Picture Sleeves

MCA....3-4 78

LPs: 10/12-inch

ATLANTIC....6-10 76
DECCA (Except 1922)....10-15 71-72
DECCA (1922 "Live from Memphis") 15-20 72
(Promotional issue only.)
FANTASY....5-8 82
I.R.S./NO SPEAK....5-8 90s
MCA....5-10 73-82

Members: Steve Upton; Andy Powel; Ted Turner; Martin Turner; Laurie Wisefield.

Also see FOGHAT

WITCH QUEEN — P&R/LP '79

Singles: 7-inch

ROADSHOW....3-4 79

LPs: 10/12-inch

ROADSHOW....5-8 79

WITHERS, Bill — P&R/R&B/LP '71

Singles: 12-inch

COLUMBIA....4-6 79

Singles: 7-inch

COLUMBIA....3-4 75-85
SUSSEX....3-4 71-75

Picture Sleeves

SUSSEX....3-4 72

LPs: 10/12-inch

COLUMBIA....5-8 75-85
SUSSEX....8-12 71-75

Also see MacDONALD, Ralph, & Bill Withers
Also see WASHINGTON, Grover, Jr.
Also see WOMACK, Bobby, & Bill Withers

WITHERSPOON, Jimmy — R&B '49

(With Groove Holmes; with Jay McShann & His Band; with Ben Webster; with Panama Francis & Savoy Sultans; with Wilbur de Paris.)

Singles: 78 rpm

CHECKER....20-30 54-55
FEDERAL....20-30 52-53
DOWN BEAT....15-25 48-49
MODERN....15-25 49-53
RCA....15-25 57
SUPREME....15-25 48-49
SWING BEAT....15-25 49
SWING TIME....15-25 51

Singles: 7-inch

ABC....3-5 71
BLUE NOTE....3-5 75
BLUESWAY....4-6 69
CAPITOL....3-5 74
CHECKER (798 "Big Daddy")....25-50 54
(Black vinyl.)
CHECKER (798 "Big Daddy")....100-200 54
(Colored vinyl.)
CHECKER (810 "Time Brings About a Change")....25-50 55
CHECKER (826 "It Ain't No Secret") 25-50 55
FEDERAL (12095 "Two Little Girls") 25-50 52
FEDERAL (12099 "Lucille")....25-50 52
FEDERAL (12107 "Corn Whiskey")..25-50 52
FEDERAL (12128 "One Fine Gal")...25-50 53
FEDERAL (12138 "Back Door Blues")....25-50 53
FEDERAL (12155 "Fast Woman, Slow Gin")....25-50 53
FEDERAL (12180 "It")....25-50 54
FEDERAL (12189 "I Done Told You So")....25-50 54
GNP....10-15 59
HI FI....10-15 60
KENT....3-5 71
KING....5-10 65
MODERN (877 "Love My Baby")....25-50 52
MODERN (895 "Baby Baby")....25-50 53
MODERN (903 "Each Slip of the Way")....20-40 53
MODERN (909 "I'll Be Right on Down")....25-50 53
PACIFIC JAZZ....10-15 62
PRESTIGE....5-10 63-65
RCA....15-25 57
REPRISE....10-15 61-64
RIP....15-25 58
VEE JAY....10-20 59
VERVE....5-10 66-67
WORLD PACIFIC....10-15 59

EPs: 7-inch

ATLANTIC (600 "New Orleans Blues")....50-100 57

LPs: 10/12-inch

ABC....8-10 70
ATLANTIC (1266 "New Orleans Blues")....100-200 57
BLUE NOTE....8-10 75
BLUESWAY....8-15 69-73
CAPITOL....8-10 74
CONSTELLATION....15-25 64
CROWN (215 "Jimmy Witherspoon Sings the Blues")....20-30 61
(Black Vinyl.)
CROWN (215 "Jimmy Witherspoon Sings the Blues")....50-100 61
(Colored Vinyl.)
FANTASY....10-12 72
HI FI (422 "Feelin' the Spirit")....25-50 59
INNER CITY....5-10 81
MCA....5-8 83
MUSE....5-8 83
OLYMPIC....8-10 73
PRESTIGE....10-20 64-69
RCA (1048 "Goin' to Kansas City Blues")....8-12 75
RCA (1639 "Goin' to Kansas City Blues")....40-60 58
REPRISE (2008 "Spoon")....25-35 61
REPRISE (6012 "Hey, Mrs. Jones") 25-35 62
REPRISE (6057 "Roots")....25-35 62
SURREY....12-15 65
UNITED....8-10
VERVE (5000 series)....12-15 66-68
VERVE (8000 series)....8-10 74
VERVE/FOLKWAYS (3011 "Blues Box")....25-30 66
WORLD PACIFIC (1267 "Singin' the Blues")....30-50 59
WORLD PACIFIC (1402 "There's Good Rockin' Tonight")....25-40 61

Also see BURDON, Eric, & Jimmy Witherspoon
Also see FREEMAN, Ernie
Also see HOLMES, Richard "Groove"
Also see McSHANN, Jay
Also see WALKER, T-Bone

WITHERSPOON, Jimmy, & Wilbur DeParis

LP: 10/12-inch

ATLANTIC 10-20

WITHERSPOON, Jimmy, & Lamplighters

Singles: 78 rpm

FEDERAL 10-20 52

Singles: 7-inch

FEDERAL (12156 "Sad Life") 25-50 52
FEDERAL (12173 "24 Sad Hours") ... 25-50 52

WITHERSPOON, Jimmy, & Quintones

Singles: 78 rpm

ATCO (6084 "My Girl Ivy") 25-35 57

Singles: 7-inch

ATCO (6084 "My Girl Ivy") 25-35 57

WITHERSPOON, Jimmy / Eddie Vinson

LPs: 10/12-inch

KING (634 "Battle of the Blues, Vol. 3") 200-300 59
Also see WITHERSPOON, Jimmy

WITT, Joachim D&D '83

Singles: 12-inch

W.E.A. INTERNATIONAL 4-6 83-84

WITTER, Jimmy, & Shadows P&R '61

Singles: 7-inch

ELVIS (900 "If You Love My Woman") 200-300 57
NEPTUNE (118 "My Kind of Woman") 50-75 61
U.A. (301 "Pretty Little Girl") 8-12 61

WOLCOTT, Charles, Orch. P&R '60

Singles: 7-inch

MGM 3-4 60

WOLF P&R/R&B '82
(Bill Wolfer)

Singles: 7-inch

CONSTELLATION 3-4 81-83

Picture Sleeves

CONSTELLATION 3-4 82

LPs: 10/12-inch

CONSTELLATION 5-8 83

WOLF, Howlin: see HOWLIN' WOLF

WOLF, Peter P&R/D&D/LP '84

Singles: 12-inch

EMI AMERICA 4-6 84-85

Singles: 7-inch

EMI AMERICA 3-4 84-87

Picture Sleeves

EMI AMERICA 3-4 84-87

LPs: 10/12-inch

EMI AMERICA 5-8 84-87
MCA 5-8 90
Also see FRANKLIN, Aretha
Also see GEILS, J., Band

WOLF, Peter, & Mick Jagger

Singles: 12-inch

EMI AMERICA 8-10 84

Singles: 7-inch

EMI AMERICA 3-4 84

LPs: 10/12-inch

EMI AMERICA 8-10 84
Also see JAGGER, Mick
Also see WOLF, Peter

WOLFMAN JACK
(Bob Smith)

Singles: 7-inch

AGC 4-8
WOODEN NICKEL 3-4 72-73

LPs: 10/12-inch

COLUMBIA 8-10 75
WOODEN NICKEL 8-10 72-73
Also see FLASH CADILLAC & CONTINENTAL KIDS
Also see GUESS WHO
Also see STAMPEDERS

WOLFMAN JACK & WOLF PACK

Singles: 7-inch

BREAD (71 "Wolfman Boogie") 25-30 65
BREAD (73 "New Orleans") 25-30 65

LPs: 10/12-inch

BREAD (0170 "Wolfman Jack and the Wolf Pack") 150-250 65

WOMACK, Bobby P&R/R&B/LP '68
(With the Brotherhood; with Peace)

Singles: 12-inch

ELEKTRA/WOMACK 4-6 83

Singles: 7-inch

ARISTA 3-5 79
ATLANTIC 5-8 67
ARISTA 3-5 79
ATLANTIC 4-8 67
BEVERLY GLEN 3-4 81-84
CHECKER 5-10 65
COLUMBIA 3-5 76-78
COLUMBIA/BROTHERHOOD 3-5 76-77
HIM 3-5
ELEKTRA/WOMACK 3-4 83
KEYMEN 3-5
LIBERTY 3-5 70
MCA 3-4 86
MINIT 4-8 67-70
SOUFFLE 3-5
U.A. 3-5 71-76

Picture Sleeves

MCA 3-4 86

EPs: 7-inch

U.A. 10-15 72
(Promotional issue only.)

LPs: 10/12-inch

ARISTA 5-8 79
BEVERLY GLEN 5-8 81-84
COLUMBIA 8-10 75-78
COLUMBIA/BROTHERHOOD 8-10 76
ELEKTRA/WOMACK 5-8 83
LIBERTY (7600 series) 8-10 70
LIBERTY (10000 series) 5-8 80s
MCA 5-8 85
MINIT 10-12 68-70
U.A. 8-10 71-76
Also see BROTHERHOOD
Also see FELDER, Wilton, & Bobby Womack
Also see SZABO, Gabor
Also see VALENTINOS
Also see WOMACK BROTHERS

WOMACK, Bobby, & Patti Labelle P&R/R&B '84

Singles: 7-inch

BEVERLY GLEN 3-4 84
Also see LABELLE, Patti
Also see WOMACK, Bobby

WOMACK, Bobby, & Bill Withers R&B '75

Singles: 7-inch

U.A. 3-4 75
Also see WITHERS, Bill

WOMACK & WOMACK R&B/D&D '84

Singles: 7-inch

ELEKTRA 3-4 84-85

LPs: 10/12-inch

ELEKTRA 5-8 84-85
Members: Linda Womack; Cecil Womack.

WOMACK BROTHERS

Singles: 7-inch

SAR (118 "Somebody's Wrong") 5-10 61
Members: Bobby Womack; Cecil Womack; Curtis Womack; Friendly Womack, Jr.; Warris Womack.
Also see VALENTINOS
Also see WOMACK, Bobby

WOMBLES P&R '74

Singles: 7-inch

COLUMBIA 3-4 74-75

LPs: 10/12-inch

COLUMBIA 8-10 74
Member: Mike Batt.

WOMENFOLK P&R/LP '64

Singles: 7-inch

RCA 3-4 64-66

LPs: 10/12-inch

RCA 10-15 63-66

WONDER, Stevie P&R/R&B/LP '63
(Little Stevie Wonder)

Singles: 12-inch

MOTOWN 4-8
TAMLA 4-8

Singles: 7-inch

MOTOWN 3-4 84-88
MOTOWN/TOPPS (8 "Fingertips Part 2") 50-75 67
MOTOWN/TOPPS (10 "Uptight") 50-75 67
(Topps Chewing Gum promotional items. Single-sided, cardboard flexi, picture discs. Issued with generic paper sleeve.)
TAMLA (1600 thru 1800 series) 3-4 82-86
TAMLA (54061 "I Call It Pretty Music") 25-35 62
TAMLA (54074 "Contract on Love") .. 25-35 63
TAMLA (54080 "Fingertips") 5-10 63
TAMLA (54086 "Workout Stevie, Workout") 5-10 63
TAMLA (54090 "Castles in the Sand") 8-12 64
TAMLA (54096 "Hey Harmonica Man") 8-12 64
TAMLA (54103 "Happy Street") 10-20 64
TAMLA (54119 thru 54139) 5-10 65-66
(Black vinyl.)
TAMLA (54139 "A Place in the Sun") 10-15 66
(Colored vinyl. Promotional issue only.)
TAMLA (54142 "Some Day at Christmas") 8-12 66
TAMLA (54147 thru 54323) 3-6 67-81
(Black vinyl.)
TAMLA (54147 thru 54323) 8-12 69-78
(Colored vinyl. Promotional issues only.)
MOTOWN 3-4 82

Picture Sleeves

MOTOWN 3-4 87
TAMLA (1639 thru 1846) 3-6 82-86
TAMLA (54061 "I Call It Pretty Music") 25-50 62
TAMLA (54080 "Fingertips") 15-25 63
TAMLA (54136 "Blowin' in the Wind") 15-25 66
TAMLA (54139 "A Place in the Sun") 15-25 66
TAMLA (54281 thru 54317) 4-8 77-80

EPs: 7-inch

MOTOWN (2006 "Stevie Wonder") ... 15-25 60s
MOTOWN (2020 "Songs in the Key of Life") 10-15 76
TAMLA (340 "Something Extra for *Songs in the Key of Life*") 5-8 76
TAMLA (60272 "Stevie Wonder") 15-25 67

LPs: 10/12-inch

MOTOWN (100 & 200 series) 5-8 82
MOTOWN (800 series) 12-15 77
MOTOWN (6000 series) 5-8 84-91
TAMLA (232 "Tribute to Uncle Ray") . 50-80 63
TAMLA (233 "The Jazz Soul of Stevie Wonder") 50-80 63
TAMLA (240 "Little Stevie Wonder") 40-50 63
TAMLA (250 "With a Song in My Heart") 35-55 64
TAMLA (255 "At the Beach") 35-55 64
TAMLA (268 thru 279) 15-20 66-67
TAMLA (281 "Someday at Christmas") 30-40 67
TAMLA (282 thru 371) 8-15 68-79
TAMLA (373 "Hotter Than July") 5-8 80
TAMLA (6000 series) 10-12 82-85

Promotional LPs

MOTOWN (PR-77 "Hotter Than July") 10-15 80
TAMLA (PR-61 "Stevie Wonder's Journey Through the Secret Life of Plants") . 10-15 79
TAMLA (PR-98/99 "Radio Programmer's Special") 15-20 80s

Also see CHARLENE & Stevie Wonder
Also see DIONNE & FRIENDS
Also see IGLESIAS, Julio, & Stevie Wonder
Also see JACKSONS
Also see JOHN, Elton
Also see KHAN, Chaka
Also see LENNON, Julian, & Stevie Wonder
Also see McCARTNEY, Paul, & Stevie Wonder
Also see REDNOW, Eivets
Also see ROSS, Diana, Stevie Wonder, Marvin Gaye & Smokey Robinson
Also see TEMPTATIONS / Stevie Wonder
Also see THIRD WORLD
Also see U.S.A. for AFRICA
Also see WILLIAMS, Deniece

WONDER, Stevie / John Denver

Singles: 7-inch

WHAT'S IT ALL ABOUT ... 4-8 80
(Public service, radio station issue.)
Also see DENVER, John

WONDER, Stevie, & Michael Jackson — P&R '88

Singles: 7-inch

MOTOWN ... 3-4 88

Picture Sleeves

MOTOWN ... 3-4 88
Also see JACKSON, Michael

WONDER, Stevie, & Clarence Paul

(Little Stevie Wonder & Clarence Paul)

Singles: 7-inch

TAMLA (54070 "Little Water Boy") ... 25-35 62
Also see PAUL, Clarence

WONDER, Stevie / Dionne Warwick — LP '84

LPs: 10/12-inch

MOTOWN ... 5-8 84
Also see WARWICK, Dionne
Also see WONDER, Stevie

WONDER BAND — P&R '79

Singles: 7-inch

ATCO ... 3-4 79

LPs: 10/12-inch

ATCO ... 5-8 79

WONDER LAND, Alice: see ALICE WONDER LAND

WONDER WHO? — P&R '67

(4 Seasons)

Singles: 7-inch

COLLECTABLES ... 3-4 80s
PHILIPS ... 3-5 65-67
VEE JAY ... 12-15 64

Picture Sleeves

PHILIPS ... 15-20 65-67
Also see 4 SEASONS

WOO, Gerry — R&B '87

Singles: 7-inch

POLYDOR ... 3-4 87-88

WOOD, Bobby — P&R '64

Singles: 7-inch

CHALLENGE ... 3-5 62
CINNAMON ... 3-4 74
COLT ... 3-5
JOY ... 5-10 63-65
LUCKY ELEVEN ... 3-4 73
MALA ... 3-5 66
MGM ... 3-4 67-69
SUN (369 "Everybody's Searchin'") ... 50-100 61

LPs: 10/12-inch

JOY (1001 "Bobby Wood") ... 20-30 64
Also see PRESLEY, Elvis

WOOD, Brenton — P&R/R&B/LP '67

Singles: 7-inch

BRENT (7052 "Good Lovin'") ... 5-10 66
BRENT (7057 "Cross the Bridge") ... 10-20 66
CREAM ... 3-4 76-78
DOUBLE SHOT ... 4-6 67-71
FIRST PRESIDENT (428 "The Kangaroo") ... 10-15 60
MR. WOOD ... 3-5 72-73
PROPHESY ... 3-4 73
WAND (145 "Mr. Schemer") ... 25-35 64
W.B. ... 3-6 75

LPs: 10/12-inch

CREAM ... 5-8 77
DOUBLE SHOT ... 10-20 67

WOOD, Del — P&R '51

Singles: 78 rpm

DECCA ... 3-4 53-54
MERCURY ... 3-4 62-64
RCA ... 3-4 55-59
REPUBLIC ... 3-4 51-54
TENNESSEE ... 3-6 51

Singles: 7-inch

CHART ... 3-4 71-72
DECCA ... 3-5 53-54
MERCURY ... 3-4 62-64
RCA ... 3-5 55-59
REPUBLIC ... 3-8 51-54
TENNESSEE ... 5-10 51

EPs: 7-inch

RCA ... 5-12 55-60
REPUBLIC ... 4-10 54-57

LPs: 10/12-inch

AMBASSADOR ... 5-10
CAMDEN ... 5-12 62-64
CHART ... 5-8 71
COLUMBIA ... 8-12 66
LAMB & LION ... 5-8
MERCURY ... 5-12 62-64
PICKWICK ... 5-8 70s
RCA ... 5-15 55-60
REPUBLIC ... 5-15 54-57
VOCALION ... 5-10 60s

WOOD, Lauren — P&R '79

Singles: 7-inch

W.B. ... 3-4 79-81

Picture Sleeves

W.B. ... 3-4 81

LPs: 10/12-inch

W.B. ... 5-8 81
Also see McDONALD, Michael

WOOD, Ron — LP '75

(Ronnie Wood)

Singles: 7-inch

COLUMBIA ... 3-5 79
W.B. ... 3-5 75-76

Promotional Singles

COLUMBIA ... 4-8 79
W.B. ... 4-8 75-76

LPs: 10/12-inch

COLUMBIA ... 5-8 79-81
W.B. ... 8-10 74-75
Also see BECK, Jeff, Ronnie Wood & Rod Stewart
Also see FACES
Also see ROLLING STONES
Also see SEXTON, Charlie, & Ron Wood

WOOD, Ron, & Ronnie Lane

(With Pete Townshend)

LPs: 10/12-inch

ATCO (126 "Mahoney's Last Stand") 10-15 76
(Soundtrack.)
Also see TOWNSHEND, Pete, & Ronnie Lane
Also see WOOD, Ron

WOOD, Roy — LP '73

(Roy Wood's Wizzard; Roy Wood Wizzo Band)

Singles: 7-inch

U.A. ... 3-4 73-76

LPs: 10/12-inch

U.A. ... 8-10 73-74
W.B. ... 5-8 79
Members: Roy Wood; Rick Price; Nick Pentelow; Mike Burney; Keith Smart; Charlie Grima; Bill Hunt; Bob Brady.
Also see ELECTRIC LIGHT ORCHESTRA
Also see MOVE

WOODBURY, Woody — LP '60

LPs: 10/12-inch

STEREODDITIES ... 10-25 59-63

WOODENTOPS — LP '86

Singles: 7-inch

COLUMBIA ... 3-4 86

LPs: 10/12-inch

COLUMBIA ... 5-8 86

WOODS, Maceo — R&B '69

(With the Christian Tabernacle Choir)

Singles: 78 rpm

VEE JAY (100 series) ... 5-10 55-56

Singles: 7-inch

ABC ... 3-4 73
VEE JAY (100 series) ... 4-8 55-56
VOLT ... 3-4 69

LPs: 10/12-inch

GOSPEL TRUTH ... 4-8 72-74
SAVOY ... 4-8 76-83
STAX ... 4-8 78
TRIP ... 4-8 73
VEE JAY ... 5-15 60-65
VOLT ... 5-12 69

WOODS, Ren — R&B '79

Singles: 7-inch

ARC ... 3-4 79
ELEKTRA ... 3-4 82

WOODS, Stevie — P&R/R&B/LP '81

Singles: 7-inch

COTILLION ... 3-4 81-83

LPs: 10/12-inch

COTILLION ... 5-8 81-82

WOODS EMPIRE — R&B '81

Singles: 12-inch

TABU ... 4-6 81

Singles: 7-inch

TABU ... 3-4 81

LPs: 10/12-inch

TABU ... 5-8 81
Members: Tommy Woods; Linda Woods; Rhonda Woods; Idris Woods; Judy Woods.

WOOLEY, Sheb — P&R '55

Singles: 78 rpm

BLUEBONNET ... 20-30 54
BULLET (603 "I Can't Live Without You") ... 25-50 45
MGM ... 5-15 48-57

Singles: 7-inch

BLUEBONNET (125 "Peepin' Thru the Keyhole") ... 30-60 54
BLUEBONNET (130 "Too Long with the Wrong Woman") ... 30-50 54
MGM (11000 series) ... 10-20 52-55
MGM (12000 series) ... 5-15 55-61
MGM (13000 series) ... 4-8 61-68
MGM (14000 series) ... 3-6 68-75
POLYDOR ... 3-4

Picture Sleeves

MGM ... 4-8 59-62

EPs: 7-inch

MGM ... 10-20 56-58

LPs: 10/12-inch

LAKESHORE (621-2-3 "Ben Colder and Sheb Wooley") ... 10-20 70s
MGM (3299 "Blue Guitar") ... 30-50 56
MGM (3904 "Days of Rawhide") ... 20-25 56
MGM (4136 thru 4026) ... 15-20 61-62
MGM (4275 thru 4615) ... 8-15 65-69
Also see COLDER, Ben

WOOLIES — P&R '67

Singles: 7-inch

DUNHILL ... 4-8 66-67
SPIRIT ... 10-15 65-66
TTP (156 "Black Crow Blues") ... 15-20 65

LPs: 10/12-inch

SPIRIT (2001 "Basic Rock") ... 20-30 71
SPIRIT (2005 "Live at Lizard's") ... 20-30 73
Members: Stormy Rice; Ron English; Jeff Baldori; Bob Baldori.

WOOLLEY, Bruce, & Camera Club — LP '80

Singles: 7-inch

COLUMBIA ... 3-4 80

Picture Sleeves
COLUMBIA....3-4 80
EPs: 7-inch
COLUMBIA (11264 "Bruce Woolley and the Camera Club")....4-8 80
(Issued with paper sleeve. Promotional issue only.)
LPs: 10/12-inch
COLUMBIA (36301 "Bruce Woolley and the Camera Club")....5-8 80

WORD OF MOUTH R&B/D&D '85
(Featuring D.J. Cheese)
Singles: 12-inch
BEAUTY & BEAST....4-6 85
PROFILE....4-6 86

WORLD D&D '84
Singles: 12-inch
ELEKTRA....4-6 83

WORLD CLASS WRECKIN CRU P&R/R&B '88
Singles: 7-inch
KRU'CUT....3-4 88

WORLD PARTY LP '86
Singles: 7-inch
CHRYSALIS....3-4 86-87
Picture Sleeves
CHRYSALIS....3-4 87
LPs: 10/12-inch
CHRYSALIS....5-8 86
ENSIGN....5-8 90

WORLD PREMIER R&B/D&D '84
Singles: 12-inch
CAPITOL....4-6 84
Singles: 7-inch
CAPITOL....3-4 84

WORLD'S FAMOUS SUPREME TEAM R&B/D&D '84
Singles: 12-inch
ISLAND....4-6 84
Singles: 7-inch
ISLAND....3-4 84
Also see McLAREN, Malcom

WORRELL, Bernie R&B '79
Singles: 7-inch
ARISTA....3-4 79
LPs: 10/12-inch
ARISTA....5-8 79
Also see McLAREN, Malcom
Also see PARLIAMENT

WORTH, Marion C&W '59
Singles: 7-inch
CHEROKEE....5-10 59
COLUMBIA....4-8 60-67
DECCA....3-6 67-70
GUYDEN....5-10 59-60
Picture Sleeves
COLUMBIA....3-5 61-62
LPs: 10/12-inch
COLUMBIA....10-20 63-64
DECCA....8-12 67

WRABIT LP '82
Singles: 7-inch
MCA....3-4 82
LPs: 10/12-inch
MCA....5-8 82

WRATHCHILD AMERICA LP '89
LPs: 10/12-inch
ATLANTIC....5-8 89

WRAY, Bill P&R '79
Singles: 7-inch
ABC....3-5 79

WRAY, Link P&R/R&B '58
(With His Ray Men; with His Wray Men; Link Ray)
Singles: 78 rpm
CADENCE....20-40 58
Singles: 7-inch
ATLAS....4-6 62
BARNABY....3-4 76
CADENCE....10-15 58
EPIC....5-8 59-61
HEAVY....3-5 68
KAY (3690 "I Sez Baby")....50-100 58
MR. G....3-5 69
NORTON....3-4 89
OKEH....3-5 67
POLYDOR....3-4 70-74
RUMBLE (1000 "Jack the Ripper")....15-25 61
SWAN (4137 "Jack the Ripper")....10-15 63
SWAN (4154 "Week End")....6-12 63
SWAN (4163 thru 4187)....5-10 63-64
SWAN (4201 "Good Rockin' Tonight")....10-15 65
SWAN (4211 thru 4232)....4-8 65
SWAN (4239 "Ace of Spades")....10-12 65
SWAN (4244 "Batman Theme")....5-8 66
SWAN (4261 "Ace of Spades")....8-10 66
SWAN (4273 thru 4282)....4-6 66-67
TRANS ATLAS (687 "Big City Stomp")....10-15 62
Picture Sleeves
EPIC....20-35 59
LPs: 10/12-inch
EPIC (3661 "Link Wray and the Wraymen")....40-50 60
NORTON....5-10 90s
POLYDOR....8-10 71-74
RECORD FACTORY....20-25 74
SWAN....50-60 63
VERMILLION....20-25 75
VISA....5-8 79-80
Also see DUDLEY, Dave / Link Wray
Also see GORDON, Robert
Also see GRAMMER, Billy / Judy Lynn / Link Wray

WRAY, Link / Red Saunders
Singles: 7-inch
OKEH (7100 series)....4-6 63
OKEH (7200 series)....3-5 67

WRAY, Lucky
(Link Wray)
Singles: 78 rpm
STARDAY (500 series)....10-20 56
STARDAY (608 "Teenage Cutie") 150-200 57
Singles: 7-inch
STARDAY (500 series)....20-30 56
STARDAY (608 "Teenage Cutie") 150-200 57
(These 500 and 600 series numbers should not be confused with a similar series from the '60s.)

WRAY, Vernon
(With Link Wray)
LPs: 10/12-inch
VERMILLION....20-25

WRAY BROTHERS
(Wray Family)
Singles: 7-inch
INFINITY....6-10 62
LAWN....6-10 63
Members: Link Wray; Doug Wray; Vernon Wray.
Also see WRAY, Link

WRECKING CREW R&B '83
Singles: 12-inch
ERECT....4-6 83
Singles: 7-inch
ERECT....3-4 83
SOUND of FLORIDA....3-4 83

WRECKX-N-EFFEC LP '90
(Wrecks-N-Effect)
LPs: 10/12-inch
MOTOWN....5-8 89

WRIGHT, Bernard R&B/LP '81
Singles: 12-inch
ARISTA....4-6 83
MANHATTAN....4-6 85
Singles: 7-inch
ARISTA....3-4 83-84
GRP....3-4 81-82
MANHATTAN....3-4 86
LPs: 10/12-inch
ARISTA....5-8 83
GRP....5-8 81
MANHATTAN....5-8 86

WRIGHT, Betty P&R/R&B '68
Singles: 12-inch
EPIC....4-6 81
JAMAICA....4-6 84-85
Singles: 7-inch
ALSTON....3-8 68-79
ATCO....3-4 83
DEEP CITY....10-20 66
EPIC....3-4 81-83
FANTASY....3-5 82
FIRST STRING....3-4 86
JAMAICA....3-4 84-85
MS. B....3-4 88
TK....3-4
LPs: 10/12-inch
ALSTON....6-10 72-79
ATCO....10-15 68
COLLECTABLES....5-8 88
EPIC....5-8 81-83
MS. B....5-8 88
Also see ALAIMO, Steve, & Betty Wright
Also see BROWN, Peter, & Betty Wright
Also see HUGH, Grayson, & Betty Wright
Also see KC & SUNSHINE BAND
Also see LITTLE BEAVER

WRIGHT, Billy R&B '49
Singles: 78 rpm
REGENT....10-20 51
SAVOY....10-20 49-52
Singles: 7-inch
CARROLLTON (801 "Have Mercy Baby")....10-20 59
SAVOY (776 "Mean Old Wine")....40-60 51
SAVOY (827 "Drinkin' and Thinkin'")....40-60 52

WRIGHT, Charles, & Watts 103rd Street Rhythm Band R&B/LP '69
Singles: 7-inch
ABC....3-4 75
DUNHILL....3-4 73-74
W.B.....3-4 70-71
LPs: 10/12-inch
ABC....6-10 75
DUNHILL....6-10 73-74
W.B.....8-12 70-72
Also see SHIELDS
Also see WATTS 103RD STREET RHYTHM BAND

WRIGHT, Dale P&R '58
(With the Rock-Its; with Wright Guys & Dons)
Singles: 7-inch
ALCAR....8-10 60
FRATERNITY....10-15 58-59
QUEEN-B....8-12

WRIGHT, Gary LP '75
(With Spooky Tooth)
Singles: 7-inch
A&M....3-4 70-72
W.B.....3-4 75-81
LPs: 10/12-inch
A&M....8-12 70-76
W.B.....5-8 75-81
Also see SPOOKY TOOTH

WRIGHT, Janet D&D '84
Singles: 12-inch
COTILLION....4-6 84

WRIGHT, O.V. P&R/R&B '65
Singles: 7-inch
ABC....3-4 75-76
BACK BEAT....3-8 65-74
GOLDWAX....5-10 64
HI....3-6 76-79
LPs: 10/12-inch
BACK BEAT....10-20 65-72
HI....5-10 78-79

WRIGHT, Priscilla P&R '55
Singles: 78 rpm
UNIQUE....4-8 55
Singles: 7-inch
20TH FOX....5-10 59
UNIQUE....5-10 55

WRIGHT, Ruben R&B '66
(Reuben Wright)
Singles: 7-inch
CAPITOL....3-5 64-67
WYNNE....3-5 60

WRIGHT, Ruby P&R '57
(With the Bello Larks; with Dick Pike; with Ruth Lyons)
Singles: 78 rpm
FRATERNITY....5-10 57
Singles: 7-inch
CANDEE (501 "Poor Butterfly")....8-12 59
CANDEE (502 "This Is Christmas")...10-20 59
COLUMBIA....4-8 60
FRATERNITY....5-10 57
KING (5192 "Three Stars")....10-15 59
KING (5208 "Goodbye, Jimmy, Goodbye")....5-10 59
(Monaural.)
KING (5208 "Goodbye, Jimmy, Goodbye")....15-20 59
(Stereo.)
KING (5225 "Don't Take Me for Granted")....5-10 59
(Monaural.)
KING (5225 "Don't Take Me for Granted")....15-20 59
(Stereo.)
KING (5261 "Sweet Night of Love")....5-10 59
KING (5297 "When You're Away")....5-10 60

WRIGHT, Steven LP '85
LPs: 10/12-inch
W.B....5-8 85

WRITERS R&B '79
Singles: 12-inch
COLUMBIA....4-6 79
Singles: 7-inch
COLUMBIA....3-4 78-79
LPs: 10/12-inch
COLUMBIA....5-8 79

WUF TICKET R&B '82
Singles: 12-inch
PRELUDE....4-6 81
Singles: 7-inch
PRELUDE....3-4 81

WYCOFF, Michael R&B '80
Singles: 12-inch
RCA....4-6 83
Singles: 7-inch
RCA....3-4 80-84
LPs: 10/12-inch
RCA....5-8 83
Also see CLAYTON, Merry

WYLIE, Richard R&B '71
(Richard "Popcorn" Wylie)
Singles: 7-inch
ABC....3-4 75
EPIC....10-20 62-63
KAREN (1542 "Rosemary, What Happened")....15-25 68
MOTOWN (1009 "Money")....30-40 61
MOTOWN (1019 "Have I the Right")....30-40 61
NORTHERN (3732 "Pretty Girl")....15-25 60s
SOUL....3-4 71
Picture Sleeves
EPIC....4-8 62
LPs: 10/12-inch
ABC....8-10 74
Also see POPCORN & MOHAWKS

WYMAN, Bill P&R '67
Singles: 12-inch
A&M (12041 "Je Suis Un Rock Star")....6-10 81
Singles: 7-inch
A&M (2367 "Je Suis Un Rock Star")....3-4 81
ROLLING STONES....4-6 74-75
Promotional Singles
A&M (2367 "Je Suis Un Rock Star")....4-6 81
A&M (12041 "Je Suis Un Rock Star")....15-20 81
(12-inch single.)
Picture Sleeves
A&M (2367 "Je Suis Un Rock Star")....3-5 81
LPs: 10/12-inch
ROLLING STONES....8-10 74-76
(Stereo.)
ROLLING STONES (QD 79100 "Monkey Grip")....15-20 74
(Quadraphonic.)

WYMAN, Bill / Rolling Stones
Singles: 7-inch
LONDON (907 "In Another Land")....4-6 67
Promotional Singles
LONDON (907 "In Another Land")....8-10 67
Picture Sleeves
LONDON (907 "In Another Land")....10-15 67
Also see ROLLING STONES
Also see WYMAN, Bill

WYND CHYMES R&B '83
Singles: 7-inch
RCA....3-4 82-83
LPs: 10/12-inch
RCA....5-8 82

WYNETTE, Tammy C&W '66
(With Ricky Skaggs; with Emmylou Harris)
Singles: 7-inch
EPIC (Except 1)....3-8 66-86
EPIC (1 "Wonders You Perform")....5-10 70
(Colored vinyl. Promotional issue only.)
Picture Sleeves
EPIC....3-4 69-76
LPs: 10/12-inch
COLUMBIA (Except "EQ" series)....5-10 72-73
COLUMBIA (EQ-30658 "We Sure Can Love Each Other")....10-15 71
(Quadraphonic.)
COLUMBIA HOUSE (5856 "Tammy Wynette")....25-35 73
(Boxed, six-disc set.)
COLUMBIA SPECIAL PRODUCTS....5-8 77-82
EPIC....5-15 68-86
HARMONY....5-10 70-71
TIME-LIFE....5-8 81
Session: Sue Richards.
Also see CASH, Johnny / Tammy Wynette
Also see HOUSTON, David, & Tammy Wynette
Also see JONES, George, & Tammy Wynette
Also see LYNN, Loretta / Tammy Wynette
Also see NEWTON, Wayne, & Tammy Wynette

WYNETTE, Tammy, & Randy Travis C&W '91
Singles: 7-inch
EPIC....3-4 91
Also see TRAVIS, Randy
Also see WYNETTE, Tammy

WYNNE, Philippe R&B '77
Singles: 12-inch
FANTASY....4-6 83
Singles: 7-inch
COTILLION....3-4 77
FANTASY....3-4 83
SUGAR HILL....3-4 83
UNCLE JAM....3-4 80
LPs: 10/12-inch
COTILLION....5-8 77
Also see DUNLAP, Gene
Also see SPINNERS

X LP '81
Singles: 7-inch
MERCURY (Black vinyl)....3-4 93
MERCURY (1036 "Country at War")....3-4 93
(Colored vinyl. Promotional issue only.)
Picture Sleeves
ELEKTRA....3-4 83
MERCURY (1036 "Country at War")....3-4 93
LPs: 10/12-inch
ELEKTRA....5-8 82-88
ROCSHIRE....5-8 83
SLASH (104 "Los Angeles")....10-20 80
SLASH (107 "Wild Gift")....10-20 81
Members: Dave Alvin; Exene Cervenka; John Doe; D.J. Bonebrake;
Tony Gilkyson.
Also see ALVIN, Dave
Also see BLASTERS
Also see DOE, John
Also see LONE JUSTICE

X, Malcolm: see MALCOLM X

X-CLAN LP '90
LPs: 10/12-inch
4TH & BROADWAY....5-8 90

XTC LP '80
Singles: 7-inch
EPIC....3-4 82
GEFFEN (Except "PRO" series)....3-4 83-89
GEFFEN ("PRO" series)....3-5 83-84
(Promotional issues only.)
RSO....3-4 81
VIRGIN....3-4 79-81
Picture Sleeves
GEFFEN....3-4 89
VIRGIN....3-4 79
LPs: 10/12-inch
EPIC....5-10 82
GEFFEN....5-8 84-89
RSO....5-10 81
VIRGIN....5-10 78-82
Members: Andy Partridge; Barry Andrews; Colin Moulding;
Terry Chambers; Dave Gregory.
Also see SHRIEKBACK

X-25 BAND R&B '82
Singles: 7-inch
H.C.R.C....3-4 82

XYZ LP '89
LPs: 10/12-inch
ENIGMA....5-8 89
Members: Anka Wolbert; Ronny Moorings; Pieter Nooten.

XAVIER R&B/LP '82
(Xavier Smith)
Singles: 12-inch
LIBERTY....4-6 82
Singles: 7-inch
LIBERTY....3-4 82
LPs: 10/12-inch
LIBERTY....5-8 82

XAVION R&B '85
Singles: 7-inch
ASYLUM....3-4 84-85
LPs: 10/12-inch
ASYLUM....5-8 84

XENA D&D '83
Singles: 12-inch
EMERGENCY....4-6 83

X-RAYS
R&B '49

Singles: 7-inch

SAVOY 10-15 48-49
Also see JACQUET, Illinois
Also see WALKER, T-Bone

XYMOX
LP '89

Singles: 12-inch

4AD 4-8 85-88
WING/POLYGRAM 5-8 89

LPs: 10/12-inch

4AD 5-10 85-87
WING/MERCURY 5-8 91
WING/POLYGRAM 5-8 89

Y & T
LP '83
(Yesterday & Today)

Singles: 7-inch

A&M 3-4 81-85

LPs: 10/12-inch

A&M 5-8 81-85
GEFFEN 5-8 87-89
LONDON 8-10 78

YACHTS
LP '79

Singles: 7-inch

POLYDOR 3-4 79

LPs: 10/12-inch

POLYDOR 5-8 79-80
RADAR 6-10

YAMASHTA, Stomu
LP '76
(With Steve Winwood & Michael Shrieve)

LPs: 10/12-inch

ARISTA 5-8 77
ISLAND 5-8 76-78
VANGUARD 8-10 71-74
Also see WINWOOD, Steve

YAMBU
R&B '75

Singles: 7-inch

MONTUNO GRINGO 3-4 75

YANKOVIC, "Weird Al"
P&R/LP '83

Singles: 12-inch

ROCK 'N' ROLL 4-6 84

Singles: 7-inch

CAPITOL 3-4 79
ROCK 'N' ROLL 3-4 83-89
SCOTTI BROS./CBS (2105 "Like a Surgeon") 30-40 85
(Picture disc. Promotional issue only.)
TK 3-4 81

Picture Sleeves

ROCK 'N' ROLL 3-4 83-89

LPs: 10/12-inch

ROCK 'N' ROLL 5-8 83-89

YANNI
LP '90

LPs: 10/12-inch

PRIVATE 5-8 90

YARBROUGH, Bob
C&W '71
(Bob Yarborough)

Singles: 7-inch

MUSIC MILL 3-5 76
SUGAR HILL 3-5 71

YARBROUGH, Glenn
LP '64

Singles: 7-inch

PRIDE 3-4 72
RCA 3-4 64-68
STAX 3-4 73-74
W.B. 3-4 68-71

Picture Sleeves

RCA 3-6 65

LPs: 10/12-inch

ELEKTRA (135 "Here We Go, Baby") 20-30 57
FIRST AMERICAN 5-8 81
IM'PRESS 8-10 71
RCA 10-20 64-69
STAX 8-10 74
TRADITION 8-15 67-70
W.B. 8-12 68-71
Also see LIMELITERS

YARBROUGH & PEOPLES
R&B/LP '80

Singles: 12-inch

TOTAL EXPERIENCE 4-6 82-86

Singles: 7-inch

MERCURY 3-4 80-81
TOTAL EXPERIENCE 3-4 82-86

LPs: 10/12-inch

MERCURY 5-8 80
TOTAL EXPERIENCE 5-8 82-86
Members: Calvin Yarbrough; Alisa Peoples.

YARDBIRDS
P&R/LP '65

Singles: 7-inch

CAPITOL (72274 "Heart Full of Soul") 20-40 65
(Canadian.)
EPIC (9709 "I Wish You Could") 15-20 64
EPIC (9790 thru 10204) 5-8 65-67
EPIC (10248 "Ten Little Indians") 10-15 67
EPIC (10303 "Goodnight Sweet Josephine") 15-20 68

Picture Sleeves

EPIC (Except 9709) 10-15 65-66
EPIC (9709 "I Wish You Could") 75-125 64
(Promotional issue only.)

LPs: 10/12-inch

ACCORD 5-8 81-83
COLUMBIA (11311 "Live Yardbirds") 25-35 72
(Columbia Special Products issue.)
COMPLEAT 8-12 86
EPIC (24167 "For Your Love") 50-100 65
(Monaural.)
EPIC (24177 "Having a Rave Up") 40-60 65
(Monaural.)
EPIC (24210 "Over Under Sideways Down") 40-60 66
(Monaural.)
EPIC (24246 "Greatest Hits") 30-40 66
(Monaural.)
EPIC (24313 "Little Games") 40-60 67
(Monaural.)
EPIC (26167 "For Your Love") 30-40 65
(Stereo.)
EPIC (26177 "Having a Rave Up") 30-40 65
(Stereo.)
EPIC (26210 "Over Under Sideways Down") 30-45 66
(Stereo.)
EPIC (26246 "Greatest Hits") 30-40 66
(Stereo.)
EPIC (26313 "Little Games") 35-50 67
(Stereo.)
EPIC (30135 "The Yardbirds Featuring Performances by Jeff Beck, Eric Clapton, Jimmy Page") 75-100 70
EPIC (30615 "Live Yardbirds") 50-75 71
EPIC (34490 "Yardbirds Favorites") 8-12 77
(Orange label.)
EPIC (34490 "Yardbirds Favorites") 5-8
(Black label.)
EPIC (34491 "Great Hits") 8-10 77
EPIC (38455 "The Yardbirds") 5-8 83
EPIC (48455 "The Yardbirds") 12-15 83
(Half-speed mastered.)
MERCURY (21271 "Eric Clapton & Yardbirds Live with Sonny Boy Williamson") 20-30 66
(Monaural.)
MERCURY (61271 "Eric Clapton & Yardbirds Live with Sonny Boy Williamson") 30-40 66
(Stereo. Red label.)
MERCURY (61271 "Eric Clapton & Yardbirds Live with Sonny Boy Williamson") 5-8
(Black label.)
RHINO (Black vinyl) 6-10 82-86
RHINO (253 "Afternoon Tea") 10-15 82
(Picture disc.)
SPRINGBOARD 8-10 72
Members: Eric Clapton; Jeff Beck; Keith Relf; Jimmy Page; Jim McCarty; Chris Dreja.
Also see ARMAGEDDON
Also see BECK, Jeff
Also see BOX of FROGS
Also see CLAPTON, Eric
Also see PAGE, Jimmy
Also see RELF, Keith
Also see RENAISSANCE
Also see WILLIAMSON, Sonny Boy

YARROW, Peter
P&R/LP '72

Singles: 7-inch

W.B. 3-4 68-75

LPs: 10/12-inch

W.B. 8-10 72-75
Also see PETER, PAUL & MARY

YAZ
P&R/R&B/LP '82
(Yazoo)

Singles: 12-inch

SIRE 4-6 82-84

Singles: 7-inch

SIRE (Except 29953) 3-4 82-84
SIRE (29953 "Situation") 4-6 82
(Credited to Yazoo.)
SIRE (29953 "Situation") 3-4 82
(Credited to Yaz.)

Picture Sleeves

SIRE 3-4 82

LPs: 10/12-inch

SIRE 5-8 82-83
Members: Alison Moyet; Vince Clarke.
Also see MOYET, Alison

YAZZ & PLASTIC POPULATION
P&R '88

Singles: 7-inch

ELEKTRA 3-4 88

Picture Sleeves

ELEKTRA 3-4 88

YELLO
D&D/LP '83

Singles: 12-inch

ELEKTRA 4-6 83-85
RALPH 5-8 81
STIFF 4-8

Singles: 7-inch

ELEKTRA 3-4 83-85
MERCURY 3-4 87-89
RALPH 3-4 81
STIFF (Picture discs) 4-8

Picture Sleeves

MERCURY 3-4 87

LPs: 10/12-inch

ELEKTRA 5-8 83-85
MERCURY 5-8 87-89
RALPH 8-10 81

YELLOW BALLOON
P&R '67

Singles: 7-inch

CANTERBURY 4-8 67-68

LPs: 10/12-inch

CANTERBURY 15-20 67
Members: Alex Valdez; Don Grady; Don Braucht; Forrest Green; Paul Cannella; Darryl Dragon.
Also see CAPTAIN & TENNILLE
Also see SPIRIT

YELLOW MAGIC ORCHESTRA
P&R/R&B/LP '80

Singles: 12-inch

A&M 4-6 80

Singles: 7-inch

A&M 3-4 80
HORIZON 3-4 80

Picture Sleeves

HORIZON 3-4 80

LPs: 10/12-inch

A&M 5-8 80-81
HORIZON 5-8 80

YELLOWJACKETS LP '83

Singles: 7-inch

MCA....3-4 86
W.B. 3-4 81-85

LPs: 10/12-inch

MCA....5-8 86
W.B. 5-8 81-85

YELLOWMAN D&D '84

Singles: 12-inch

COLUMBIA....4-6 84

Singles: 7-inch

COLUMBIA....3-4 84

LPs: 10/12-inch

COLUMBIA....5-8 84

YES P&R/LP '71

Singles: 12-inch

ATCO....4-6 83-86

Singles: 7-inch

ATCO....3-4 83-87
ATLANTIC (Black vinyl)....3-6 70-78
ATLANTIC (Colored vinyl)....4-8 70-78

Picture Sleeves

ATCO....3-4 83-87

LPs: 10/12-inch

ARISTA....5-8 91
ATCO....5-8 83-87
ATLANTIC (100 series)....10-15 73
ATLANTIC (500 series)....6-12 80
ATLANTIC (900 series)....10-15 74
ATLANTIC (7000 series)....8-12 71-72
ATLANTIC (8000 series)....10-15 69-71
ATLANTIC (16000 thru 19000 series)....5-10 74-82
MFSL (077 "Close to the Edge")....35-50 82

Promotional LPs

ATLANTIC ("Solos")....30-40 76

Members: Jon Anderson; Rick Wakeman; Steve Howe; Chris Squire; Tony Kaye; Alan White; Bill Bruford; Patrick Moraz; Geoff Downes; Trevor Horn.

Also see ANDERSON, Jon
Also see BANKS, Peter
Also see BRUFORD, Bill
Also see BUGGLES
Also see HOWE, Steve, Band
Also see KING CRIMSON
Also see MORAZ, Patrick
Also see PAVLOV'S DOG
Also see SIMON, Paul
Also see SQUIRE, Chris
Also see WAKEMAN, Rick

YIPES!! LP '79

Singles: 7-inch

MILLENNIUM....3-4 79-80

LPs: 10/12-inch

MILLENNIUM....5-8 79-80

YOAKAM, Dwight LP '86

Singles: 7-inch

OAK....15-25 86
REPRISE....3-4 86-90

LPs: 10/12-inch

OAK (2356 "Guitars, Cadillacs, Etc.")....500-750 84
REPRISE....5-8 86-90

YOAKAM, Dwight, & Buck Owens C&W '88

Singles: 7-inch

REPRISE....3-4 88

Also see OWENS, Buck
Also see YOAKAM, Dwight

YORGESSON, Yogi P&R '49
(With the Johnny Duffy Trio; Harry Stewart)

Singles: 78 rpm

CAPITOL....4-8 49-55
S&H (3009 "My Clam Digger Sweetheart")....10-20

Singles: 7-inch

CAPITOL (700 thru 3000 series)....5-10 49-55

EPs: 7-inch

CAPITOL....10-15 52-53

LPs: 10/12-inch

CAPITOL (336 "Family Album")....30-50 53
(10-inch LP.)

Also see KARI, Harry, & His Six Saki Sippers

YORK, Dave, & Beachcombers P&R '62

Singles: 7-inch

LANCELOT (6 "Beach Party")....15-25 62
P-K-M. (6700 "Beach Party")....8-12 62

Session: Glen Campbell; Gary Paxon; Steve Douglas; Jerry Reaple; Ray Polman.

Also see CAMPBELL, Glen

YORK, Rusty P&R '59
(With J.D. Jarvis)

Singles: 7-inch

CAPITOL....3-5 61
CHESS....5-8 59
GAYLORD....3-5 63
KING (5100 series)....5-8 58
KING (5500 series)....4-6 61-62
MERCURY....15-25 58
NOTE....20-30 59
P.J.....10-15 59
SAGE....10-15 60

EPs: 7-inch

BLUE GRASS....10-15 61
JEWEL....8-12 61

LPs: 10/12-inch

QUEEN CITY....10-15
RURAL RHYTHM....8-12

Also see MACK, Lonnie, & Rusty York

YOU KNOW WHO GROUP P&R '64

Singles: 7-inch

CASUAL....4-6 65
4 CORNERS....4-6 64
INT'L ALLIED....5-10 65

Picture Sleeves

INT'L ALLIED (823 "This Day Love") 10-15 65

LPs: 10/12-inch

INT'L ALLIED....15-20 65

YOUNG, Barry P&R '65

Singles: 7-inch

COLUMBIA (43584 "A Heart Without a Home")....4-8 66
DOT....5-10 65-66
EVA (102 "Come on Pretty Baby")....8-12 63
HOOKS BROTHERS....4-6 66

Picture Sleeves

COLUMBIA....4-8 66

LPs: 10/12-inch

DOT....15-25 65

YOUNG, Donny

Singles: 7-inch

DECCA (Except 31077)....10-15 61
DECCA (31077 "Shakin' the Blues") 20-25 60
MERCURY....5-10 61-62
TODD....4-8 64

Also see PAYCHECK, Johnny

YOUNG, Donny, & Roger Miller

Singles: 7-inch

DECCA (30763 "On This Mountain Top")....15-25 58

Also see MILLER, Roger
Also see YOUNG, Donny

YOUNG, Eve P&R '48
(Karen Chandler)

Singles: 78 rpm

RCA....4-8 48-49

Also see CHANDLER, Karen

YOUNG, Faron C&W '53
(With Margie Singleton; with Anita Kerr Singers; with Jordanaires)

Singles: 78 rpm

CAPITOL....5-10 53-57

Singles: 7-inch

CAPITOL (2200 thru 3900 series)....5-10 53-58
CAPITOL (4000 thru 4800 series)....4-8 58-62
MCA....3-5 79-80
MERCURY....3-6 63-78

Picture Sleeves

CAPITOL....5-10 61
MERCURY....4-8 62-68

EPs: 7-inch

CAPITOL....8-15 54-61
REPERTORY (1 "And Now")....10-15

LPs: 10/12-inch

ALBUM GLOBE....5-8 81
ALLEGIANCE....5-8 84
BULLDOG....5-10
CBS....5-8 83
CAPITOL (778 "Sweethearts Or Strangers")....30-50 57
CAPITOL (1004 "Object of My Affection")....30-50 58
CAPITOL (1096 "This Is Faron Young")....30-50 58
CAPITOL (1185 "My Garden of Prayer")....30-50 59
CAPITOL (1245 "Talk About Hits")....30-40 59
CAPITOL (1450 thru 2536)....12-25 60-66
(With "T," "DT" or "ST" prefix.)
CAPITOL (1500 series)....5-8 75
(With "SM" prefix.)
CASTLE....5-8
EXACT....5-8 80
FARON YOUNG (001 "20 Great Hits")....10-20
FARON YOUNG (003 "Family Favorites")....10-15
FARON YOUNG (004 "Faron Young Presents the Country Deputies")....10-15
FARON YOUNG (4-22-82 "Fortunes in Music")....8-15 82
IMPACT....5-10
K-TEL....5-10 77
MCA....4-8 79-83
MARY CARTER PAINTS (1000 "Faron Young Sings on Stage")....20-30
(Promotional issue only.)
MERCURY....5-15 63-77
MOUNTAIN DEW....5-10
PHONORAMA....5-8 82
PICADILLY....5-10 80
PICKWICK/HILLTOP....8-12 66-68
REALM....5-8 81
SEARS....8-12
TOWER....12-15 66-68
WING....8-12 68

Session: Don Adams; Jordanaires.

Also see ADAMS, Don
Also see ATKINS, Chet, Faron Young, & Anita Kerr Singers
Also see KERR, Anita
Also see NELSON, Willie / Faron Young
Also see OWENS, Buck / Faron Young / Ferlin Husky

YOUNG, Faron / Carl Perkins / Claude King

LPs: 10/12-inch

PICKWICK/HILLTOP....8-15 65

Also see KING, Claude
Also see PERKINS, Carl

YOUNG, Faron / Jean Shepard

EPs: 7-inch

CAPITOL CUSTOM (118-30 "Recorded Especially for Ballard Flour")....10-20
(Promotional issue, made for Ballard Flour.)

Also see SHEPARD, Jean
Also see YOUNG, Faron

YOUNG, Faron, & Margie Singleton C&W '64

Singles: 7-inch

MERCURY....4-6 64

Also see YOUNG, Faron

YOUNG, Georgie P&R '58
(With the Rockin' Bocs; George Young)

Singles: 7-inch

CAMEO....4-6 58-59
CHANCELLOR....3-5 61
COLUMBIA (42773 "Supercar")....10-20 63
FORTUNE....5-8 57
MERCURY (71259 "Can't Stop Me")....30-40 58

PACE SETTER 5-8
PARKWAY (809 "Gold Rush") 10-15 60
SWAN 4-6 60

YOUNG, Jesse Colin LP '72
(With the Youngbloods)

Singles: 7-inch

ELEKTRA 3-4 78
REPRISE 3-4 73
W.B. 3-4 70-77

LPs: 10/12-inch

CAPITOL (2000 series) 20-25 64
CAPITOL (11000 series) 8-10 74
CAPITOL (16000 series) 5-8 80
ELEKTRA 5-8 78
MERCURY (61005 "Young Blood") 20-25 65
MERCURY (61273 "Two Trips") 10-15 70
W.B. 8-10 72-77
Also see YOUNGBLOODS

YOUNG, John Paul P&R '75

Singles: 7-inch

ARIOLA AMERICA 3-4 75-76
SCOTTI BROTHERS 3-4 78

LPs: 10/12-inch

SCOTTI BROTHERS 5-8 78

YOUNG, Karen P&R/R&B '78

Singles: 7-inch

WEST END 3-4 78

YOUNG, Kathy P&R '60
(With the Innocents)

Singles: 7-inch

COLLECTABLES 3-4 80S
ERA 3-4 72
ERIC 3-4 70s
INDIGO 10-15 60-62
MONOGRAM 8-10 62
STARFIRE 3-6 79
VIRGO 3-4 72

Picture Sleeves

INDIGO 6-12 60-61

EPs: 7-inch

INDIGO (1001 ""Kathy Young") 50-75 61

LPs: 10/12-inch

INDIGO (504 "The Sound of Kathy Young") 50-100 61
STARFIRE (1000 "Our Best to You") 12-18 81
(Picture disc on one side, black vinyl on flip.)
Also see CHRIS & KATHY
Also see INNOCENTS
Also see WASHER WINDSHIELD

YOUNG, Kathy / Innocents

Singles: 7-inch

TRIP 3-5 70s
Also see INNOCENTS
Also see YOUNG, Kathy

YOUNG, Lester R&B '44

Singles: 78 rpm

ALADDIN 5-10 47
KEYNOTE 5-10 44

YOUNG, Neil LP '69
(With Crazy Horse; with Shocking Pinks; with Bluenotes)

Singles: 12-inch

GEFFEN 4-6 86

Singles: 7-inch

GEFFEN 3-4 83-86
REPRISE (0785 thru 0898) 3-5 68-70
REPRISE (0911 thru 1396) 3-5 70-79
(Black vinyl.)
REPRISE (1395 "Comes a Time") 250-300 78
(Picture disc. 200 numbered copies made. Promotional issue only.)
REPRISE (49000 series, except 49895) 3-5 79-81
REPRISE (49895 "Southern Pacific") 250-350 81
(Triangular picture disc. Promotional issue only. Green vinyl. 25 made.)
REPRISE (49895 "Southern Pacific") 250-350 81
(Auto- or train-shaped picture disc. Promotional issue only. 10 made of each shape.)
REPRISE (49895 "Southern Pacific") 15-25 81
(Triangular picture disc. Promotional issue only. With either red or black vinyl.)

Picture Sleeves

GEFFEN 3-4 83
REPRISE 3-4 78-81

EPs: 7-inch

REPRISE 10-15 72
(Juke box issue only.)

LPs: 10/12-inch

GEFFEN 5-8 83-87
MFSL (252 "Old Ways") 15-25 95
REPRISE (2000 series, except 2257 & 2296) 5-8 72-90
REPRISE (2257 "Decade") 12-15 77
REPRISE (2296 "Live Rust") 10-12 79
REPRISE (6317 "Neil Young") 50-100 68
(Front cover does NOT have Neil Young's name.)
REPRISE (6317 "Neil Young") 8-12 68
(Front cover shows Neil Young's name.)
REPRISE (6349 "Everybody Knows This Is Nowhere") 10-12 69
REPRISE (6383 "After the Gold Rush") 10-12 70
REPRISE (6480 "Journey Through the Past") 12-15 72
W.B. 6-15 72-79
Session: Waylon Jennings.
Also see BUFFALO SPRINGFIELD
Also see CRAZY HORSE
Also see CROSBY, STILLS, NASH & YOUNG
Also see HARRIS, Emmylou
Also see JENNINGS, Waylon
Also see LARSON, Nicolette
Also see STILLS - YOUNG BAND

YOUNG, Neil, & Jim Messina

Singles: 7-inch

REPRISE 3-5 70
Also see MESSINA, Jim

YOUNG, Neil, & Graham Nash P&R '72

Singles: 7-inch

REPRISE 3-4 72
Also see NASH, Graham
Also see YOUNG, Neil

YOUNG, Paul P&R '83

Singles: 12-inch

COLUMBIA 4-6 83-86

Singles: 7-inch

COLUMBIA 3-4 83-86
EPIC (Except 11116) 3-4 86
EPIC (11116 "Every Fool Has His Reasons") 4-6 74

Picture Sleeves

COLUMBIA 3-4 83-86

LPs: 10/12-inch

COLUMBIA 5-8 84-90
Also see BAND AID
Also see MIKE + the MECHANICS
Also see SAD CAFE

YOUNG, Retta R&B '75

Singles: 7-inch

ALL PLATINUM 3-4 75

YOUNG, Tommie R&B '73

Singles: 7-inch

MCA 3-5 78
SOUL POWER 3-5 73-75

LPs: 10/12-inch

MCA 5-10 78

YOUNG, Val R&B/D&D '85

Singles: 12-inch

GORDY 4-6 85-86

Singles: 7-inch

AMHERST 3-4 87
GORDY 3-4 85-86

LPs: 10/12-inch

GORDY 5-8 85-86

YOUNG, Victor P&R '31

Singles: 78 rpm

BRUNSWICK 3-5 31-34
DECCA 3-4 34-57

Singles: 7-inch

DECCA 3-4 50-57

EPs: 7-inch

DECCA 3-6 50-57

LPs: 10/12-inch

DECCA 5-15 50-59
Also see CROSBY, Bing
Also see GARLAND, Judy

YOUNG AMERICANS LP '69

LPs: 10/12-inch

ABC 5-10 69

YOUNG & RESTLESS LP '90

LPs: 10/12-inch

PANDISC 5-8 90

YOUNG HEARTS P&R/R&B '68

Singles: 7-inch

AVCO EMBASSY 3-4 70
MINIT 3-5 68-69
20TH FOX 3-4 74-75

LPs: 10/12-inch

MINIT 10-12 69

YOUNG - HOLT UNLIMITED
(Young - Holt Trio) P&R/R&B '66

Singles: 7-inch

BRUNSWICK 4-6 66-69
COTILLION 3-5 70-71
ERIC 3-4 83
PAULA 3-5 73

LPs: 10/12-inch

ATLANTIC 8-10 73
BRUNSWICK 10-20 67-69
COTILLION 8-12 70-71
PAULA 5-10 73
Members: Eldee Young; Isaac Holt; Floyd Morris.
Also see LEWIS, Ramsey

YOUNG MC P&R/LP '89

Singles: 7-inch

DELICIOUS 3-4 89-90

Picture Sleeves

DELICIOUS 3-4 89-90

LPs: 10/12-inch

DELICIOUS 5-8 89-90

YOUNG RASCALS: see RASCALS

YOUNG VANDALS R&B '70

Singles: 7-inch

T-NECK 3-5 70

YOUNGBLOOD, Lonnie R&B '72
(Lonnie Youngblood's Combo)

Singles: 7-inch

CAMEO 4-8 65
EARTH 4-8 60s
LOMA 4-8 67-68
RADIO 3-5 81
SHAKAT 3-5 74
SILVER-TONE 4-6
TURBO 3-5 71-73
VIBRATION 3-5 76

LPs: 10/12-inch

RADIO 5-8 81
TURBO 8-10 71
Also see HENDRIX, Jimi, & Lonnie Youngblood

YOUNGBLOOD, Sydney P&R/LP '90

Singles: 7-inch

ARISTA 3-4 90

LPs: 10/12-inch

ARISTA 5-8 90

YOUNGBLOODS P&R '66
(Featuring Jesse Colin Young)

Singles: 7-inch

MERCURY 5-8 66-69
RCA 4-6 66-71
W.B./RACCOON 3-4 70-72

Picture Sleeves

RCA 4-6 66

LPs: 10/12-inch

RCA (3000 series) 5-8 80
(With "ALY1" prefix.)

RCA (3000 series) 12-15 67
(With "LPM" or "LSP" prefix.)
RCA (4000 series) 10-15 69-71
(With "LPM" or "LSP" prefix.)
RCA (6000 series) 12-15 72
W.B./RACOON 10-12 70-72
Members: Jesse Colin Young; Jerry Corbit; Joe Bauer; Lowell "Banana" Levinger.
Also see BOWIE, David / Joe Cocker / Youngbloods
Also see YOUNG, Jesse Colin

YURO, Timi P&R/R&B/LP '61

Singles: 7-inch

LIBERTY (55000 series) 8-15 61-64
LIBERTY (56000 series) 4-8 68
MERCURY 5-10 64-67
PLAYBOY 3-6 75

EPs: 7-inch

LIBERTY 10-15 61
(Juke box issues only.)

LPs: 10/12-inch

COLGEMS 8-10 68
LIBERTY (Except 7500 series) 15-25 61-63
LIBERTY (7500 series) 8-10 68
MERCURY 10-15 65
SUNSET 6-12 66-70
U.A. 5-8 75-76
WING 8-10 68
Also see RAY, Johnnie, & Timi Yuro

YUTAKA P&R/R&B/LP '81

(Yukata Yokokura)

Singles: 7-inch

ALFA 3-4 81

Picture Sleeves

ALFA 3-4 81

LPs: 10/12-inch

ALFA 5-8 81
Also see AUSTIN, Patti

ZZ TOP P&R/LP '72

Singles: 12-inch

W.B. 4-6 84-86

Singles: 7-inch

LONDON 3-8 70-77
SCAT (500 "Salt Lick") 100-200
W.B. 3-4 80-90

Picture Sleeves

LONDON 3-4 75-76
W.B. 3-4 83-90

LPs: 10/12-inch

LONDON (Except 1001) 8-12 71-77
LONDON (1001 "World Wide Texas Tour") 10-20 76
(Promotional issue only.)
W.B. 5-15 79-90
Members: Bill Gibbons; Frank Beard; Dusty Hill.
Also see AMERICAN BLUES
Also see MOVING SIDEWALKS
Also see WARLOCKS

ZABACH, Florian P&R '51

Singles: 78 rpm

DECCA 3-5 51-54
MERCURY 3-5 56-57

Singles: 7-inch

CADENCE 4-8 61
DECCA 5-10 51-54
MERCURY 5-10 56-58

EPs: 7-inch

DECCA 5-10 51-54
MERCURY 5-10 56-58

LPs: 10/12-inch

DECCA 5-15 51-65
MERCURY 5-15 56-60
VOCALION 4-8 63-66
WING 4-8 63
Also see DIAMONDS / Georgia Gibbs / Sarah Vaughan / Florian Zabach
Also see VALLI, June

ZACHARIAS, Helmut P&R '56

(Helmut Zacharias' Magic Violins)

Singles: 78 rpm

DECCA 3-4 56-57

Singles: 7-inch

CAPITOL 3-4 69
DECCA 3-4 56-64

EPs: 7-inch

DECCA 3-6 56-58

LPs: 10/12-inch

CAPITOL 4-8 69
DECCA 5-15 56-61
PHILIPS 4-8 62
RCA 4-8 66

ZACHERLE, John P&R/R&B '58

(Zacherle; Zacherley; John Zacherlie "Cool Ghoul")

Singles: 78 rpm

CAMEO 25-50 58

Singles: 7-inch

ABKCO 3-4 80s
CAMEO 10-15 58
COLPIX 4-6 64
ELEKTRA 4-6 60
PARKWAY 3-5 62

LPs: 10/12-inch

CRESTVIEW 25-35 63
ELEKTRA 25-35 60
PARKWAY 25-35 62-63

ZADORA, Pia C&W '79

(With the London Symphony Orchestra)

Singles: 12-inch

MCA 4-6 83

Singles: 7-inch

CURB 3-4 83
ELEKTRA 3-4 82-83
MCA 3-4 83-84
W.B./CURB 3-4 78-80

LPs: 10/12-inch

CBS ASSOCIATED 5-8 86
ELEKTRA 5-8 82
Also see JACKSON, Jermaine, & Pia Zadora
Also see LITTLE PIA

ZADORA, Pia, & Lou Christie

Singles: 7-inch

MIDSONG (72013 "Don't Knock My Love") 15-20 80
Also see CHRISTIE, Lou
Also see ZADORA, Pia

ZAGER, Michael, Band P&R/R&B/LP '78

Singles: 12-inch

CBS ASSOCIATED 4-6 84
COLUMBIA 4-6 79-80

Singles: 7-inch

BANG 3-4 78
CBS ASSOCIATED 3-4 84
PRIVATE STOCK 3-4 78

LPs: 10/12-inch

COLUMBIA 5-8 79
PRIVATE STOCK 5-8 78
Also see TEN WHEEL DRIVE

ZAGER, Michael, Moon Band, & Peabo Bryson P&R/R&B '76

Singles: 7-inch

BANG 3-4 76
Also see BRYSON, Peabo
Also see ZAGER, Michael, Band

ZAGER & EVANS P&R/LP '69

Singles: 7-inch

RCA 3-5 69-70
TRUTH 8-12 69
VANGUARD 3-4 71

Picture Sleeves

VANGUARD 4-8 71

LPs: 10/12-inch

RCA (1000 series) 8-10 75
RCA (4000 series) 12-15 69-70
VANGUARD 10-12 71
WHITE WHALE 12-15 69
Members: Denny Zager; Rick Evans.

ZAHND, Ricky, & Blue Jeaners P&R '55

Singles: 78 rpm

COLUMBIA 4-6 55-56

Singles: 7-inch

COLUMBIA 5-10 55-56

Picture Sleeves

COLUMBIA 8-12 55-56

ZAPP P&R/R&B/LP '80

Singles: 12-inch

REPRISE (40982 "Zapp & Roger") 4-8 93

Singles: 7-inch

W.B. 3-4 80-89

LPs: 10/12-inch

W.B. 5-8 80-89
Members: Roger Troutman; Shirley Murdock; Lester Troutman; Larry Troutman; Tony Troutman.
Also see BOOTSY'S RUBBER BAND
Also see MURDOCK, Shirley
Also see ROGER

ZAPPA, Dweezil & Moon

(Dweezil)

Singles: 7-inch

BARKING PUMPKIN (03366 "My Mother Is a Space Cadet") 3-5 83

Picture Sleeves

BARKING PUMPKIN (03366 "My Mother Is a Space Cadet") 3-5 83
Also see ZAPPA, Frank & Moon

ZAPPA, Frank LP '70

(With the Mothers; Francis Vincent Zappa)

Singles: 12-inch

BARKING PUMPKIN (1114 "Goblin Girl") 20-30 79
(Picture disc. Promotional issue only.)
BARKING PUMPKIN (1115 "Baby Snakes") 40-50 82
(Picture disc.)
RHINO/DEL-FI (604 "Rare Meat") 10-20 83
(Cover has portrait of Zappa.)
RHINO/DEL-FI (604 "Rare Meat") 5-10 83
(Plain cover, no portrait of Zappa.)
ZAPPA (1001 "I Don't Want to Get Drafted") 8-10 80

Singles: 7-inch

BARKING PUMPKIN 3-4 82
BIZARRE/REPRISE (0800 series) 10-15 69-70
BIZARRE/REPRISE (0900 series) 6-10 70
DISCREET 3-5 73-74
ROTATE 3-5
U.A. 5-8 71
VERVE 8-12 66-68
W.B. 4-6 76-77
ZAPPA 3-5 79-80

Promotional Singles

DISCREET (586 "Cosmik Debris") 10-12 74

EPs: 7-inch

REPRISE (336 "Hot Rats") 35-40 72
(Promotional issue only.)
U.A. ("200 Motels") 35-40 71
(Promotional issue only.)

Picture Sleeves

ZAPPA 3-5 80

LPs: 10/12-inch

BARKING PUMPKIN (37000 series) 10-15 81
BARKING PUMPKIN (38000 series) ... 5-10 82-83
BARKING PUMPKIN (74000 series) ... 5-10 84-88
BIZARRE (2030 "Chunga's Revenge") 15-25 70
(Blue label.)
BIZARRE (2030 "Chunga's Revenge") 5-10 70s
(Brown label.)
BIZARRE (2094 "Waka Jawaka") 15-25 70
(Blue label.)
BIZARRE (2094 "Waka Jawaka") 5-10 70s
(Brown label.)

BIZARRE (6356 "Hot Rats")............. 15-25 69
(Blue label.)
BIZARRE (6356 "Hot Rats")............... 5-10 70s
(Brown label.)
DEL-FI (604 "Rare Meat")................. 35-45 83
DISCREET (DS-2175 "Apostrophe") 15-25 74
DISCREET (DS4-2175 "Apostrophe")................................. 30-40 74
(Quardophonic.)
DISCREET (DSK-2175 "Apostrophe").................................. 8-10 79
DISCREET (2202 "Roxy and Elsewhere") 20-30 74
DISCREET (2216 "One Size Fits All") 15-25 75
DISCREET (2234 "Bongo Fury")....... 15-25 75
DISCREET (2290 "Zappa in New York")... 300-400 78
(Has *Punky's Whips* and a full-length *Titties and Beer*. May have been on test pressings only.)
DISCREET (2290 "Zappa in New York").. 100-200 78
(Cover indicates *Punky's Whips* and a full-length *Titties and Beer*, though discs have neither.)
DISCREET (2290 "Zappa in New York")... 20-30 78
(Omits *Punky's Whips* and has an edited *Titties and Beer*.)
DISCREET (2291 "Studio Tan")........ 10-15 78
DISCREET (2294 "Orchestral Favorites") 10-15 79
EMI/ANGEL (38170 "Boulez Conducts Zappa") 10-15 84
REPRISE.. 8-12 72
RHINO (70907 "Beat the Boots") .. 100-175 91
(Boxed, eight-disc set. Includes button and T-shirt.)
VERVE (8741 "Lumpy Gravy") 25-30 68
U.A. 20-30 71
ZAPPA (1501 "Sheik Yerbouti") 10-20 79
ZAPPA (1502 "Joe's Garage, Acts I & III") 10-20 79
ZAPPA (1603 "Joe's Garage, Act I") 10-15 79
W.B. 5-10 76

Promotional LPs

BARKING PUMPKIN (1111 "Shut Up 'N' Play Yer Guitar") 15-20 81
(Mail-order LP offer.)
BARKING PUMPKIN (1112 "Shut Up 'N' Play Yer Guitar Some More")........................ 15-20 81
(Mail-order LP offer.)
BARKING PUMPKIN (1113 "Return of Shut Up 'N' Play Yer Guitar") 15-20 81
(Mail-order LP offer.)
BIZARRE (368 "Zapped")................. 30-40 69
(Photo collage cover with title in red. Also has tracks by Alice Cooper; Captain Beefheart & His Magic Band; Judy Henske & Jerry Yester; Tim Buckley; Wild Man Fischer; Tim Dawe; Lord Buckley; Jeff Simmons; & GTO's.
BIZARRE (368 "Zapped")................. 20-30 69
(Cover pictures only Frank Zappa. Title in black.)
BIZARRE (2030 "Chunga's Revenge").. 30-40 70
ZAPPA (78 "Sheik Yerbouti, Clean Cuts").. 20-30 79
ZAPPA (129 "Joe's Garage, Acts I, II & III") 30-40 79
Also see BABY RAY & FERNS
Also see GUY, Bob
Also see MINTZ, Junior
Also see MOTHERS of INVENTION
Also see NED & NELDA

ZAPPA, Frank & Moon

Singles: 12-inch

BARKING PUMPKIN (03069 "Valley Girl")... 5-8 82

Singles: 7-inch

BARKING PUMPKIN (02972 "Valley Girl")... 3-4 82

Picture Sleeves

BARKING PUMPKIN (02972 "Valley Girl")... 3-4 82

Promotional Singles

BARKING PUMPKIN (1490 "Valley Girl") 4-6 82
Also see ZAPPA, Dweezil & Moon
Also see ZAPPA, Frank

ZAVARONI, Lena P&R '74

Singles: 7-inch

STAX.. 3-5 74

ZEBRA P&R/LP '83

Singles: 7-inch

ATLANTIC.. 3-4 83-84

LPs: 10/12-inch

ATLANTIC.. 5-8 83-84

ZELLA, Danny P&R '59

(With the Larados & His Zell Rocks)

Singles: 7-inch

DIAL (100 "Sapphire").................. 100-150 59
FOX (10057 "Wicked Ruby") 20-30 59
RED ROCKET 15-25
SHO-BIZ.. 4-8 60s

ZENO LP '86

LPs: 10/12-inch

MANHATTAN................................... 5-8 86
Member: Zeno Roth; Michael Flexig.

ZENTNER, Si, & His Orch. P&R/LP '61

(With the Johnny Mann Singers)

Singles: 7-inch

BEL CANTO.................................... 5-10 59
LIBERTY 5-10 59-67
RCA 4-6 64-66

Picture Sleeves

LIBERTY 5-10 62

EPs: 7-inch

LIBERTY 5-10 59-67

LPs: 10/12-inch

BEL CANTO.................................. 10-20 59
LIBERTY 10-20 59-67
RCA 5-10 65-66
SUNSET 5-10 66
Also see DENNY, Martin
Also see MANN, Johnny, Singers
Also see MARTIN, Dean / Patti Page
Also see SINATRA, Frank

ZEPHYR LP '69

Singles: 7-inch

PROBE 5-8 70
W.B. 3-4 70

Promotional Singles

PROBE 10-12 70

LPs: 10/12-inch

PROBE (4510 "Zephyr") 30-40 69
RED SNEAKERS.............................. 5-10 82
W.B. 25-30 71-72
Members: Candy Givens; Tommy Bolin.
Also see BOLIN, Tommy

ZEPPELIN, Led: see LED ZEPPELIN

ZEVON, Warren LP '76

(Zevon)

Singles: 7-inch

ASYLUM 3-4 76-80
CHRYSALIS...................................... 3-4 87

Picture Sleeves

CHRYSALIS...................................... 3-4 87

LPs: 10/12-inch

ASYLUM 5-8 76-82
ELEKTRA (11386 "Werewolves of London").. 70-90 78
(Picture disc. Promotional issue only.)
IMPERIAL 10-12 70
VIRGIN... 5-8 87
Members: Richard Hayward; Kenny Gradney; Greg Beck; Karen Childs.
Also see HINDU LOVE GODS
Also see LITTLE FEAT
Also see LYME & CYBELLE

ZILL, Pat P&R '61

Singles: 7-inch

BIG C 3-5 62
ERA.. 3-5 63
INDIGO 3-5 61

SAND.. 5-8 61

ZINGARA R&B '80

Singles: 7-inch

WHEEL.. 3-4 80-81

LPs: 10/12-inch

WHEEL.. 5-8 81

ZINO D&D '84

Singles: 12-inch

PACIFIC 6 .... 4-6 84

ZODIAC MINDWARP & LOVE REACTION LP '88

LPs: 10/12-inch

VERTIGO 5-8 88

ZOMBIES P&R '64

Singles: 7-inch

DATE.. 4-8 68-69
EPIC 3-5 74
ERIC 3-4 83
LONDON 3-5
PARROT 5-10 64-66
(U.S. issues.)
PARROT (9695 "She's Not There") .. 15-25 64
(Blue label. Canadian.)
PARROT (9695 "She's Not There") 5-10 60s
(Black label. Canadian.)

Picture Sleeves

PARROT 10-20 65

LPs: 10/12-inch

BACK-TRAC...................................... 5-8 85
DATE (4013 "Odessey & Oracle")..... 20-25 68
(No promotional mention of *Time of the Season* on front cover.)
DATE (4013 "Odessey & Oracle")..... 15-20 68
(With promo for *Time of the Season* on front cover.)
EPIC 10-15 74
LONDON 10-15 69
PARROT 30-35 65
RHINO.. 5-8
Members: Colin Blunstone; Rod Argent.
Also see ARGENT

ZOOM R&B '81

Singles: 7-inch

MCA... 3-4 83
POLYDOR... 3-4 81-82

LPs: 10/12-inch

A&M.. 8-10 74
MCA.. 5-8 83
POLYDOR.. 5-8 81

ZULEMA R&B '73

(Zulema Cusseaux)

Singles: 7-inch

LE JOINT... 3-4 78-79
RCA 3-4 74-76
SUSSEX... 3-4 72-73

LPs: 10/12-inch

LE JOINT... 5-8 78
RCA 5-8 75-76
SUSSEX... 8-10 72-74
Also see FAITH, HOPE & CHARITY

ZWOL P&R '78

(Walter Zwol)

Singles: 7-inch

EMI AMERICA (Except 8905)................ 3-4 78-79
EMI AMERICA (8905 "New York City") 4-8 78
(Alternate version on white vinyl. Promotional issue only.)

LPs: 10/12-inch

EMI AMERICA.................................... 5-8 78-79

ZYDECO, Buckwheat: see BUCKWHEAT ZYDECO

BRUNSWICK
Printed in U.S.A.
EB 771045
FULL-RANGE FIDELITY
STEREC
Brunswick
RECORDS
JACKIE
WILSON
That's Why (I Love You So)
Love Is All
You Better Know It
Each Time (I Love You More)

EPIC
A PRODUCT OF CBS
NOT
FOR SALE
45 RPM
5-9300
JZSP 45486
Andval Mus.
(BMI) 2:05
RAW-HIDE
-M. Grant-F. Wray-
LINK WRAY AND
THE WRAYMEN

BRIAN
WILSON
LOVE
AND
MERCY

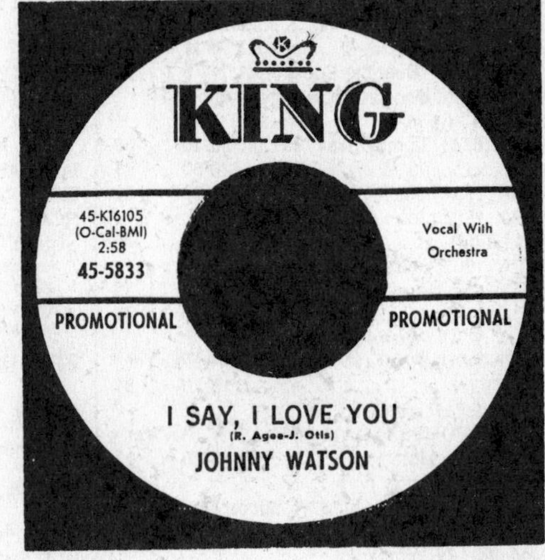
KING
45-K16105
(O-Cal-BMI)
2:58
45-5833
Vocal With
Orchestra
PROMOTIONAL
PROMOTIONAL
I SAY, I LOVE YOU
(R. Agee-J. Otis)
JOHNNY WATSON

PEANUTS
(J. Cook)
THE WONDER WHO
45
45
VJ
VEE-JAY
RECORDS
PROMOTIONAL
COPY
VJ
VEE-JAY
RECORDS
PROMOTIONAL
COPY
45
45
62-2639 — VOCAL
Cherio Music-BMI
VJ-717

BUYERS–SELLERS DIRECTORY

The pages in every Official Price Guide Buyers-Sellers Directory are packed with personal and business ads, certain to appeal to anyone with an interest in music collecting.

Most books in the Osborne series offer an outstanding opportunity to cost-effectively spread the word of your products and services to a targeted worldwide audience. An ad in the Buyers-Sellers Directory is also an excellent and inexpensive way to locate those elusive discs you've been seeking for your collection. For over 22 years, the results of advertising in the Osborne books have proven to be tremendous. We are especially proud of our high rate of repeat advertisers, one that far surpasses industry standards.

Look the ads over carefully. You might just find the dealer or contact you've been wanting to assist you in building your collection. When responding to any of our advertisers, be sure to say you saw their ad in this publication.

You can advertise in the next *Official Price Guide to Records,* or any of the other books in our series. Simply contact our office and ask for complete details. Let us do for you what we have done for many others!

Osborne Enterprises
Box 255
Port Townsend WA 98368
Phone: (360) 385-1200 — Fax: (360) 385-6572
www.olympus.net/personal/jpo — e-mail: jpo@olympus.net

BUY YOUR RECORDS AT
THE ATTIC